THE INTERNATIONAL MONETARY FUND

1945-1965

Volume I: Chronicle

THE INTERNATIONAL MONETARY FUND 1945-1965

Twenty Years of International Monetary Cooperation

VOLUME I: CHRONICLE

By
J. Keith Horsefield

INTERNATIONAL MONETARY FUND
WASHINGTON, D.C.
1969

ISBN 0-939934-05-1 (v.I)
ISBN 0-939934-08-6 (set)

Second printing, February 1972
Third printing, May 1981
Fourth printing, March 1986

CONTENTS

PART II: THE BEGINNINGS

PART III: FORGING AHEAD

APPENDICES

INDEXES

TABLES

ILLUSTRATIONS

FOREWORD

The history of the International Monetary Fund might be written in many ways and from many points of view. Its activities are so interwoven with the international economy that a full appraisal of them would require a comprehensive analysis of the world's monetary situation since 1945. More, since each member of the Fund is affected to a greater or less degree by its membership, such an appraisal would necessitate a review of the situation in each individual country as well as in the world as a whole. No such compendium is attempted here.

The purpose of this history is much more modest. It is an attempt to recount objectively what were the origins of the Fund and what its plans and activities during the first twenty years of its existence. For this purpose the focus throughout is on the Board of Executive Directors, but without neglecting the work of the Governors on the one hand and that of the staff on the other. The authors have been given full access to the Board's records and to the complete files of the Fund, and have had a free hand in describing what they found. They have also been able to study many records relating to the origins of the Fund. The result is history written from the inside. It is, however, the personal responsibility of the authors. No statement or opinion expressed here commits the Fund in any way.

The three volumes of this work have different ends in view. Volume I, *Chronicle,* begins with a description of the plans devised by Mr. White, Lord Keynes, and others, and tries to show how these were consummated at Bretton Woods. Thereafter it attempts to relate straightforwardly what the Fund did in each of the three distinct periods into which its postwar history naturally falls. The main theses are briefly recapitulated in Chapter 23. A supplementary chapter summarizes the most important developments in the period 1966–68, which is not otherwise dealt with. This *Chronicle* is the work of Mr. J. Keith Horsefield, who was for ten years a member of the Fund's staff and from 1960 to 1966 its Chief Editor.

Volume II, *Analysis,* traces separately the evolution of the Fund's policies in relation to its most important responsibilities. As an aid to understanding the environment in which these policies have been formulated and executed, the chapters in Volume II include some description of the international economy. Since many of the problems with which the Fund has been wrestling have been the subject of debate among economists, some references to these discussions are also included. No detailed attempt is made, however, to take into account the vast volume of technical literature on the topics covered.

The greater part of Volume II was written by Mrs. Margaret G. de Vries, a member of the Fund's staff from 1946 to 1959. Other contributors were Mr. Horsefield, who also edited the volume, Mr. Joseph Gold, the General Counsel of the Fund, and three former members of the Fund staff, Miss Mary H. Gumbart, Miss Gertrud Lovasy, and Mr. Emil G. Spitzer.

Volume III reproduces the most important documents related to the prehistory of the Fund, as well as pertinent documents published by the Fund between 1946 and the end of 1968.

This history is being made available to the public in the hope that it will enable those interested to understand more of the nature of the Fund's work, of its problems, and of the techniques which it has devised. Whether the Fund has succeeded or failed in its objectives it is not the purpose of this history to decide. It seeks only to provide information to enable each reader to answer that question for himself.

PIERRE-PAUL SCHWEITZER
Managing Director
International Monetary Fund

PREFACE TO VOLUME I

Part I of this *Chronicle*, comprising the first five chapters, deals with the plans and negotiations that culminated in the United Nations Monetary and Financial Conference at Bretton Woods in July 1944, and with the Conference itself. Readers whose concern is only with the Fund after it was established, and not with these preliminary stages, will nevertheless find certain passages in these chapters helpful to an understanding of the influences which were brought to bear upon the Fund in its early days—in particular the first five sections of Chapter 1 (pp. 3–16); the section headed "U.S. Views on the Keynes Plan" on pages 28–30; the section headed "The Protagonists" on pages 54–57; the final paragraphs of the discussion of "Right to Draw" on pages 75–77; and the three middle sections of Chapter 4 (pp. 81–87). A synopsis of the Articles of Agreement will be found on pages 110–13.

In Parts II, III, and IV of this volume, each chapter is concerned, in principle, with the activities of the Fund from one Annual Meeting to the next—or, as time goes on, with its work in two such twelve-month periods. This arrangement has been preferred to the alternatives of relating each chapter either to the calendar year or to the fiscal year of the Fund, because the Annual Meetings have the advantage of being occasions on which the work of the Fund is traditionally reviewed. Nevertheless, any cutoff date is necessarily artificial, since the Fund's activities are continuous. Moreover, consideration of many topics recurred on the agenda of the Executive Board over a period of years, and it would often be unhelpful to limit discussion only to that part of the total debate which took place during a single year. In many instances, therefore, the description of the Board's actions in relation to a given topic has been concentrated in one chapter out of the several to which it would be relevant chronologically.

It should also be understood that only a small selection of the work of the Fund has been dealt with here. In addition to the topics discussed, the Board's agenda contained a mass of other items. Some of these were of a routine character. Many, however, were important in themselves, though offering no fresh insights into the Fund's work. All these have perforce been neglected. The reader should therefore bear in mind that when theoretical issues were considered by the Board it was in the context of specific problems not always detailed and against the background of continuous contact between the Fund and its members.

A reader wishing to identify the areas of interest of individual Executive Directors may refer to Appendix A, which lists the countries that appointed or elected them. As an approximation to this identification, the name of each Executive Director, when first mentioned in any section of the history, is followed by the name of his country of origin in parentheses. A similar course has been followed for Alternate Executive Directors, each of whom is also linked, on the first occasion when he is mentioned, to the Executive Director who appointed him.

Grateful acknowledgment is made to the following for assistance in the preparation of this volume.

To Her Britannic Majesty's Treasury and to the Bank of England, for permission to examine their files of material bearing on the Fund for the period 1941–45, and to quote from them; to Mrs. Anne Terry White, for permission to use and to quote from the papers of Harry Dexter White, now on deposit at Princeton University Library; and to Lord Kahn for permission to quote from Lord Keynes' correspondence.

To Mr. Elting Arnold, Mr. E. M. Bernstein, Mr. Johan W. Beyen, Mr. Henry J. Bittermann, Sir George Bolton, K.C.M.G., Mr. Emilio G. Collado, Mr. Jean de Largentaye, Miss G. A. Koen, Sir Frank Lee, G.C.M.G., Mr. Ansel F. Luxford, Mr. August Maffry, Professor James Meade, Professor Raymond F. Mikesell, Mr. Redvers Opie, Lord Robbins, C.H., Mr. Leroy D. Stinebower, Mr. G. H. Tansley, Professor Jacob Viner, and Mr. George H. Willis, for information freely given in response to inquiries.

To Mr. Allan G. B. Fisher, formerly Chief Editor of the Fund, and to Mr. Lucius P. Thompson-McCausland, for continuous help, comment, and criticism of the drafts.

To present and former Executive Directors and members of the staff of the Fund, who have supplied inside information and corrected many errors.

To the Archivist of the Fund and to the Joint Bank-Fund Librarian, and their staffs, who have greatly facilitated the task of identifying and consulting the relevant documents and books.

To the author's research assistant, Mrs. Helen G. Burrows, who prepared Appendix A, purged successive drafts of inconsistencies and infelicities, and maintained a constant head of steam for the project throughout its course.

To Mrs. Jane B. Evensen, Assistant Editor of the Fund, for her masterly revision of the final text.

But the author alone is responsible for the obtusenesses and inaccuracies that still remain.

J. K. H.

ABBREVIATIONS AND DEFINITIONS

Annual Meetings, 19—	Annual Meetings of the Boards of Governors of the Fund and the Bank, in the year specified. The Meetings of the two institutions are held at the same time and in the same place, and some of the sessions are held jointly. Other sessions, however, are held separately by the Fund and the Bank. When the term Annual Meeting (in the singular) is used, the reference is to a Meeting of the Fund Governors.
Annual Report, 19—	*Annual Report of the Executive Directors for the Fiscal Year Ended April 30, 19—*
Articles of Agreement; Articles; Fund Agreement	*Articles of Agreement of the International Monetary Fund*
Atlantic City	[Site of] meeting of technicians, June 1944, preparatory to Bretton Woods Conference
Bank; World Bank	International Bank for Reconstruction and Development
BIS	Bank for International Settlements
Bretton Woods	[Site of] United Nations Monetary and Financial Conference, July 1944
Canadian Plan	*Tentative Draft Proposals of Canadian Experts for an International Exchange Union*
Consultations	Annual consultations with members by the Executive Board under Article XIV, and parallel consultations with members that have accepted the obligations of Article VIII
Drawing	Purchase from the Fund by a member of another member's currency (or other members' currencies). Amounts are always expressed in U.S. dollars.
E.B. Decision	Decision of the Executive Board. Until Meeting 630 (at the beginning of 1951), the formal

decisions and policy actions of the Executive Board were numbered *x-y*, where *x* was the number of the meeting and *y* that of the decision taken at that meeting (e.g., 2-1 was the first decision taken at Executive Board Meeting 2). Beginning with Meeting 630, the decisions were numbered consecutively; thereafter the number was *z*-(*x*), where *z* was the consecutive number of the decision and *x* that of the meeting (e.g., 7-(648) was the seventh policy decision taken since Meeting 630, and was taken at Meeting 648). From January 1, 1952, the number of the decision has been followed by the last two figures of the year and the number of the meeting in that year in parentheses (e.g., Decision No. 102-(52/11) was the 102nd decision since Meeting 630, and was taken at the eleventh meeting in 1952).

ECA — Economic Cooperation Administration (U.S.)

ECE — Economic Commission for Europe (UN)

ECOSOC — Economic and Social Council (UN)

EEC — European Economic Community

EPU — European Payments Union

ERP — European Recovery Program (U.S.)

FAO — Food and Agriculture Organization (UN)

French Plan — *Suggestions Regarding International Monetary Relations*

GAB — General Arrangements to Borrow

GATT — General Agreement on Tariffs and Trade

Group of Ten — The countries associated in the General Arrangements to Borrow, viz., Belgium, Canada, France, Germany, Italy, Japan, the Netherlands, Sweden, the United Kingdom, the United States

IFNS — *International Financial News Survey*

IFS — *International Financial Statistics*

ILO — International Labor Office

ITO — International Trade Organization

Joint Statement	*Joint Statement by Experts on the Establishment of an International Monetary Fund*
Key-Currency Plan	Professor John H. Williams' proposals
Keynes Plan	Proposals for an International Clearing Union
OECD	Organization for Economic Cooperation and Development
OEEC	Organization for European Economic Cooperation
Princeton papers	Harry Dexter White papers deposited at Princeton University
Proceedings	*Proceedings and Documents of the United Nations Monetary and Financial Conference, Bretton Woods, New Hampshire, July 1–22, 1944,* 2 vols. (Washington, 1948).
Resolution	Resolution of the Board of Governors of the Fund. Resolutions at the Annual Meetings of Governors are referred to by the number of the Annual Meeting followed by a dash and the number of the resolution. Resolutions passed at the Inaugural Meeting (Savannah, March 1946) are listed as IM-1, etc., those at the First Annual Meeting (Washington, September 1946) as 1-1, and so on. Resolutions passed by Governors between Annual Meetings are given the number of the next succeeding Annual Meeting.
Savannah	[Site of] Inaugural Meeting of Governors
Selected Decisions	*Selected Decisions of the Executive Directors and Selected Documents,* 3rd issue, January 1965
Selected Documents	*Selected Documents, Board of Governors Inaugural Meeting, Savannah, Ga., March 8 to 18, 1946* (compare *Summary Proceedings* below)
Summary Proceedings, 19—	*Summary Proceedings of the . . . Annual Meeting of the Board of Governors* (issued after each Annual Meeting). In early years *Summary Proceedings* were really summaries, but latterly most speeches made at the Annual Meetings have been printed in full. In these printed reports Governors are named, but in the records maintained in the Fund's files they are

	not, being referred to as "Governor" whether they were in fact Governors, Alternate Governors, or Temporary Alternate Governors. Unless, therefore, the speaker can be identified in other ways, it has been necessary, in those parts of this *Chronicle* that are drawn from unpublished reports, to cite only "Governor for . . . ".
TAB	Technical Assistance Board (UN)
UN	United Nations
UNCTAD	United Nations Conference on Trade and Development
White Plan	Proposals for an International Stabilization Fund
World Bank; Bank	International Bank for Reconstruction and Development

PART I

Prehistory

CHAPTER

1

The Keynes and White Plans (1941-42)

IT IS DIFFICULT even for those familiar with the International Monetary Fund as a working organization to realize what a remarkable achievement its creation was. It came into being as a result of a supreme act of faith—the decision to surrender to an untried and imperfectly visualized international body the supervision of one of the most cherished attributes of national sovereignty, the right to change the rate of exchange. That this surrender was hedged round with safeguards is not surprising; that it was made at all, and was accompanied by vesting in the same body an appreciable fraction of the members' international reserves, can be explained only by the coincidence of the hour and the men.

The men primarily concerned were two: Harry Dexter White and John Maynard Keynes (later Baron Keynes of Tilton). White joined the staff of the U.S. Treasury in 1934, becoming an Assistant Director in the Division of Research and Statistics in 1936, Director of the Division of Monetary Research on March 25, 1938, Assistant to the Secretary on August 30, 1941, and Assistant Secretary on January 3, 1945. He resigned on May 1, 1946 to take up the post of U.S. Executive Director of the Fund. He relinquished this position with effect from June 1, 1947, and died a little over a year later, on August 16, 1948. Keynes combined a brilliant and multifaceted career with the position, from July 1940 until his death on April 21, 1946, of Honorary Advisor to the British Treasury. Both men, in the proposals that they put forward, were animated by a belief that the economic distresses of the interwar years could be avoided after the end of World War II only by international cooperation on a previously untried scale.

Their proposals were drafted in 1941 and 1942, negotiated in 1943, and adopted at an international conference in 1944. To understand how, in the midst of World War II, it was possible to focus the attention of the major powers on postwar monetary reconstruction, we must recall briefly how complete had been the collapse of the international financial mechanism upon which, until 1931, the world had relied.

BACKGROUND

During the 1920's, the leading industrial nations had concentrated their efforts on restoring the gold standard, shattered by World War I. But the exchange rates established, particularly that of sterling, took insufficient account of the divergences of prices and costs since 1914. The precarious equilibrium that resulted was undermined by the onset of the Great Depression in the United States in 1930 and by the departure of the United Kingdom from the gold standard in 1931.

The ensuing decade saw the greatest collapse of commodity prices and shrinkage of world trade that the modern world has ever known. Between 1929 and 1932 the world price index, measured in gold values, fell by 47.5 per cent. During the same three years the gold value of world trade fell by 63 per cent. The decline was, as always, felt most acutely by the less developed countries: the price index of raw and partly manufactured goods fell by 56 per cent. Even for industrial countries, the fall in the gold value of manufactured products by 37.5 per cent was more than sufficient to create major problems. No country could avoid almost overwhelming deflationary pressures and nearly every major country began to seek ways of defending itself against undercutting of its prices from abroad—some by exchange depreciation, some by introducing flexible exchange rates or multiple rates, some by direct controls over imports and other international transactions. Sooner or later, the currencies of practically all countries were effectively devalued. But all these arrangements concerned individual countries only; the London Monetary and Economic Conference in 1933 showed only the diversity of national interests, and there was no international cooperation in monetary matters until 1936. Even the Tripartite Agreement then negotiated was not much more than a token move toward a new international system. It did little to offset the division of the major currencies between those based on gold and those related to sterling.

The most extreme example of individualism in currency arrangements was afforded by Germany. Under the guidance of Dr. Schacht,[1] exchange control and import licensing were progressively intensified with a view to limiting imports to what could be afforded. Discrimination in imports admitted was accompanied by a moratorium on payments in foreign exchange of interest and dividends.

[1] Dr. Hjalmar Schacht was President of the Reichsbank from 1933 to 1939 and Minister of Economics of Germany from 1934 to 1937.

In addition, a number of bilateral agreements were negotiated, especially with countries in southeastern Europe and Latin America, through which increased imports were exchanged for increased exports. For some of these agreements Germany fixed rates of exchange for the mark below the official rate, thus obtaining the benefits of devaluation without actually devaluing. The system as a whole constituted a regime which was as far as possible removed from the multilateralism and automatism of the theoretical gold standard. Dislike of it was part of the common ground on which the United States and the United Kingdom stood in their subsequent approach to international monetary arrangements.

This, then, was the situation which had developed when World War II began: an international economic community where "beggar-my-neighbor" policies were the rule, and where the best-intentioned attempts to restore order to the financial system were endangered by the desperate attempts of weaker countries to hold their own in the face of cutthroat competition. It was a situation which challenged most notably the economists of those countries that might expect to lead the postwar world. This book is the record of one of the ways in which that challenge was met.

❖ ❖ ❖

Despite the generality of the situation just described, its characteristics in the United States differed materially from those in the United Kingdom, and the differences were reflected in the main purposes of the schemes which Keynes and White prepared. White was prompted by a vivid appreciation—heightened indeed by personal experience—of the Great Depression. The change in the current of U.S. economic life from 1929 to 1932 had indeed been catastrophic. Industrial production in these three years had fallen by 47 per cent and the national income by 52 per cent. By March 1933, there were at least 14 million unemployed. The depression had stemmed primarily from domestic developments and, in particular, from the speculative fever of the period 1928–29. It had, however, been accentuated by the difficulties of export industries, and particularly of U.S. agriculture, confronted with the progressive devaluation of competitors' currencies as the depression took its course. The United States had not suffered from an overvalued currency and the U.S. Treasury foresaw no need to repeat the devaluation of the dollar effected in 1933. At the same time, it disliked and distrusted the fragmentation of the international monetary scene into currency areas—the sterling area being a particular bugbear—and the proliferation of multiple currency practices and the like.

Hence, for White, the prime need for the postwar years was a mechanism which would ensure the stability of currencies and avoid the recurrence of competitive devaluations and of the restrictions on payments which other countries had built up after 1933 against the competitive power of U.S. exports.

In the U.S. scene, such a plan had to be so framed as to be acceptable to a Congress of isolationist tendencies and conservative financial outlook, which was still concerned about the use made by President Roosevelt in 1933 of the authority given to him to change the gold content of the dollar.

For the United Kingdom, on the other hand, the political problem was simpler. If a plan could be "sold" to the Treasury and, with its help, to the Cabinet, its acceptance by Parliament could safely be expected. In two other respects, also, British conditions imposed fewer constraints than were felt in Washington: one was the absence of a written constitution; the other was the greater extent to which the older financial institutions (especially the gold standard) had been discredited while their antithesis, the Schachtian regime, had become a bogey to be feared. Both in and out of Parliament memories were long; they reached back to 1921, when, after a short boom in the immediate postwar years, British industry had suffered a slump from which it had never fully recovered—at least, until rearmament in 1938–39. In 1921 more than 2,400,000 persons were unemployed—some 22 per cent of those available for work. After settling at about half that figure from 1923 to 1929, the total again exceeded two million from 1930 to 1935. The effects of the world-wide slump were accentuated for the United Kingdom by the restoration in 1925 of the pre-1914 exchange rate, which (as Keynes thought at the time) overvalued the pound.

There was in both countries a widespread fear that the end of World War II would be followed by a slump, as had the end of World War I. But when considering how to avoid such a recurrence, it had to be borne in mind that for the United Kingdom, unlike the United States, exports were of overwhelming importance: British industry was export oriented to a degree far greater than that of the United States. The lesson which Keynes drew from these considerations was similar to White's in stressing the importance of international trade, but differed in that, for Keynes, the right to correct an overvaluation of the currency was an essential part of any postwar plan. While, therefore, White drew up his proposals in terms of a stabilization fund, Keynes' proposals for an international clearing mechanism were coupled with specific proposals for countries to adjust their exchange rates as and when required to encourage exports and maintain a steady expansion in the economy. These factors need to be borne in mind when considering the details of the plans which were developed.

PRECEDENTS

Anyone attempting in 1941 or 1942 to sketch out a plan for an international monetary agreement would naturally turn, in the first place, to the Tripartite Agreement signed on September 25, 1936. This arose from the decision of the

French Government to devalue the franc. By it, the Governments of France, the United Kingdom, and the United States accepted the need for the French devaluation and undertook to take steps to minimize the resulting disturbance to international transactions. The Agreement specifically provided for consultations for this purpose between the three Governments, but took no steps to create formal institutional machinery.

In addition to the metropolitan governments concerned, the Agreement extended to the whole of the sterling bloc and of the French franc area. On September 26 the Belgian Government adhered to it, and some two months later the participants were joined by Switzerland and the Netherlands.

In pursuance of the Agreement, the Secretary of the U.S. Treasury announced on October 13 that, subject to revocation at 24 hours' notice, he would sell gold for immediate export to, or earmark it for the account of, the exchange equalization funds of those countries willing to reciprocate, provided that the gold which these latter countries offered was made available at such rates and upon such terms and conditions as the Secretary deemed advantageous to the public interest. The United Kingdom and France were named on October 13 as complying with this condition. On November 24, the offer was extended to Treasuries and fiscal agencies in countries willing to reciprocate, and Belgium, the Netherlands, and Switzerland were added to those participating.[2] This arrangement assured the monetary authorities of the countries adhering to the Tripartite Agreement of obtaining gold in settlement for balances of any other participant's currency which they acquired on their own markets.

About the same time, the Bank for International Settlements, which had inherited a long tradition of informal inter-central-bank cooperation, put into operation a plan of its own for facilitating international payments for commercial transactions. It offered to central banks facilities for granting one another reciprocal credits in their own currencies or in gold, thus enabling each to provide credits for its exporters without incurring exchange risks.[3]

In July 1937 the United States entered into the first of a series of stabilization arrangements with Brazil, under which the United States agreed to sell gold to Brazil up to a total of $60 million. It also undertook to make dollar exchange available to the Government of Brazil, under conditions which would safeguard the interests of both countries, for the purpose of promoting exchange equilibrium.[4] Similar arrangements were negotiated with other Latin American

---

[2] *Report of the Secretary of the U.S. Treasury, Fiscal Year 1937*, pp. 258–62.

[3] Roger Auboin, *The Bank for International Settlements, 1930–1955*, Princeton University, Essays in International Finance, No. 22 (Princeton, 1955), p. 12. Bank for International Settlements, *Eighth Annual Report* (Basle, 1938), p. 109.

[4] *Report of the Secretary of the U.S. Treasury, Fiscal Year 1938*, p. 268.

countries—for example, with Mexico in November 1941 for $40 million.[5] At the Treasury, White was directly responsible for administering these agreements.

Although the United Kingdom had felt it necessary to establish a few bilateral clearings in defense of its own interests with countries that had been particularly affected by the Schachtian controls, it had no liking for monetary agreements of that kind in peacetime. After the outbreak of World War II, however, somewhat similar arrangements were negotiated with France in December 1939 and with Belgium and the Netherlands in June 1940 as a part of economic mobilization. Each party to these agreements undertook to accumulate balances of the other's currency in unlimited amounts, and not to seek settlement in gold. The principal purpose of the agreements was to conserve gold for purchases from the United States, which had at that time to be made in cash. Currency accumulated under the terms of the agreements could be used only for purchases in the country issuing it, or in its currency area. Necessary elements in these arrangements were undertakings to fix the rate of exchange between the currencies of the two countries concerned, to carry out all transactions at that rate, and not to change the rate without consultation.

Certain common features of the agreements referred to above will be obvious. In the first place, they provided for the exchange of value for value, and not for the extension of a loan. Secondly, they temporarily shifted responsibility for settling a deficit in a country's balance of payments from the debtor to the creditor. By this means, they enabled the debtor to avoid, at least for the time being, an exchange rate adjustment or the imposition of restrictions that might have been harmful to international trade. Both the U.S. stabilization agreements and the British monetary agreements effected this by exchanging currencies between creditor and debtor, thereby making it possible to limit the settlement to bilateral balances. The Tripartite Agreement, however, provided for an exchange of currency for gold, and thus implicitly permitted a multilateral settlement.

The third feature which the agreements had in common was the stabilization, albeit temporary, of the exchange rate between the two countries concerned. This was coupled with provisions for the adjustment of the exchange rate by agreement between the countries. The Tripartite Agreement provided, in effect, that 24 hours' notice should be given of a wish to change the exchange rate, so that transactions currently in hand between the two countries' central banks could be completed without exchange loss.[6]

---

[5] *Report of the Secretary of the U.S. Treasury, Fiscal Year 1942*, p. 291. A draft of this agreement, dated August 25, 1941, is reproduced in U.S. Congress, Senate, Committee on the Judiciary, *Interlocking Subversion in Government Departments* (Hearings Before the Internal Security Subcommittee), 84th Cong., 1st sess., 1955, pp. 2344–46.

[6] League of Nations, *International Currency Experience: Lessons of the Inter-War Period* (Geneva, 1944), p. 147.

In a report, dated January 26, 1938, which he was invited to make by the Governments of the United Kingdom and France, Mr. Paul van Zeeland of Belgium suggested the revision and extension of the Tripartite Agreement to help to meet the threat to international trade posed by monetary disturbances. He proposed that those countries willing to cooperate should (1) define the reciprocal parities of their currencies, and pledge themselves to keep variations in exchange rates within certain limits for a long enough period—six months to a year—to free current *commercial* operations from risk; (2) agree upon an adjustment of external debts; and (3) provide those countries which were free of exchange restrictions with credit facilities—for example, by an agreed extension of the method of reciprocal credits instituted by the Bank for International Settlements and described above.[7]

It may be added that, early in 1938, the Austrian Government suggested that the abolition of exchange control "would be facilitated if several countries were to undertake it simultaneously, and if the risks of the transition period could be guarded against by means of an international equalisation fund." [8]

That the Tripartite Agreement would be in White's mind when he started to think about an international plan is made additionally probable by the fact that he had recommended such an arrangement in 1935. In March of that year, he sent to his superior in the U.S. Treasury a report entitled "Recovery Program: The International Monetary Aspect." [9] In this he discussed the subject of international disequilibrium (which continued to preoccupy him for the rest of his life), and reviewed the appropriateness of the exchange rates of the United Kingdom, France, and Japan. He suggested that "the United States, through diplomatic channels, ascertain whether or not England and France are willing to enter upon an agreement or understanding covering a year or two. This informal agreement should specify as a minimum no change in the relationship . . . sterling = $4.65, yen = 28¢, and franc = 5.60¢. . . . The inescapable conclusion is that at least agreement on the essential points should be arrived at informally and secretly." [10] The informality was necessary because "a new alignment of exchange rates may be called for and the readjustment would take place more easily if the agreement provided for that contingency, or if we were not bound by any formal agreement but were merely acting co-operatively toward a tentatively agreed upon goal of stabilization." [11] That "stabilization" was the last word in this report may also be thought significant.

---

[7] Mr. van Zeeland's report was published by the British Government as Cmd. 5648, pp. 14–17 (translated at pp. 38–41).

[8] League of Nations, *Report on Exchange Controls* (Geneva, 1938), p. 45.

[9] Harry Dexter White's papers deposited at the Princeton University Library (hereafter cited as "Princeton papers"), Box 1, File 6.

[10] *Ibid.*, pp. 45, 47.

[11] *Ibid.*, p. 58.

The importance attached to the Tripartite Agreement in the countries concerned was made abundantly clear in official statements. A typical example, and one directly relevant to the present purpose, is the following quotation from the *Report of the Secretary of the U.S. Treasury, Fiscal Year 1940:*

> In the years before the outbreak of war . . . the accord proved that cooperation among stabilization funds can have definite value. The stabilization funds, working together, can iron out short-term fluctuations and prevent speculative drives from producing erratic exchange movements. The funds can also, in cooperation, facilitate orderly readjustment of a currency to a lower level and prevent explosive movements from carrying exchange rates below the level deliberately sought.[12]

Nevertheless, the effectiveness of such agreements—even of the Tripartite Agreement—was limited. In a memorandum on the future of gold, written early in 1940, White expressed the view that the arrangements between the United Kingdom and France could not be expected to work in peacetime conditions.[13] Similarly, an early draft of his plan for a stabilization fund adduced the argument that the provisions for changing exchange rates in the Tripartite Agreement had "worked only tolerably well."[14] The Agreement's limitations were partly due to its restricted scope: even at its widest, it included the originators of little more than 50 per cent of international trade. But these limitations were also partly a consequence of relying on the individual creditor to finance the deficits of its debtors—an arrangement that threatened to break down if one country accumulated credits to an extent greater or more prolonged than was within its reasonable capacity to carry. Hence, in both the United Kingdom and the United States, the conviction arose that any more permanent arrangement must provide for the international financing of future deficits.

ORIGINS OF THE WHITE PLAN

On February 7, 1940, an Inter-American Financial and Economic Advisory Committee, created in the previous year by the Meeting of the Ministers of Foreign Affairs of the American Republics at Panama, adopted a resolution recommending to the Governments of the American Republics the establishment of an Inter-American Bank.[15] The committee simultaneously submitted to the Governments drafts of a convention, a charter, and by-laws for the bank. In preparing these, the committee had been assisted by a group of experts from the

---

[12] *Report of the Secretary of the U.S. Treasury, Fiscal Year 1940*, p. 137.

[13] A draft, undated but referable on internal evidence to the first half of 1940, was reproduced in the Hearings Before the Internal Security Subcommittee cited above (note 5), pp. 2664–92; reference is to p. 2686.

[14] Draft dated April 1942 (reproduced below, Vol. III, p. 66); see also p. 21 of this chapter.

[15] *Federal Reserve Bulletin*, Vol. 26 (1940), pp. 517-25.

U.S. Departments of State and Treasury, the Board of Governors of the Federal Reserve System, and the Federal Loan Agency. Of this group, White was a member.

The powers of the bank, as set out in Section 5B of the draft by-laws, were those needed for the conduct of normal commercial and investment banking functions. Its purposes, set out in Section 5A, included, in addition to these functions, the following:

> (2) Assist in stabilizing the currencies of American Republics; encourage general direct exchanges of the currencies of American Republics; encourage the maintenance of adequate monetary reserves; promote the use and distribution of gold and silver; and facilitate monetary equilibrium.
>
> (3) Function as a clearing house for, and in other ways facilitate, the transfer of international payments.
>
> (8) Engage in research and contribute expert advice on problems of public finance, exchange, banking, and money as they relate specifically to the problems of American Republics.

The bank was to have a capital of $100 million to be contributed in graduated numbers of $1,000 shares by the American Republics, the scale of participation being decided "in relation to the dollar value of the total foreign trade of each" during 1938. Each participating Government was to have 20 votes, plus one for each share held in excess of 20. For certain purposes a four-fifths majority vote was required.

The administration of the bank was to be vested in a board of directors, composed of one director and one alternate appointed by each participating country. The board might appoint an executive committee.

The U.S. Government signed the convention establishing the bank on May 10, 1940. It was not, however, ratified by Congress, and no further progress was made with the plan for an Inter-American Bank until 1960.

With the exception of the three purposes detailed above, the bank bore little resemblance to the International Monetary Fund. A number of incidental features mentioned above, however, recur in White's drafts for the Fund, and they clearly formed part of the background against which these drafts were evolved.

It appears from the evidence of associates that White began to give thought to the possibility of a comprehensive international agreement in the monetary field not later than the early part of 1941. His ideas envisaged both an organization to stabilize exchange rates and the means of providing the long-term capital that would be needed after the war. There is reason to believe that the first half of this plan had taken shape in his mind by the summer of

1941, and that the second part was drafted during a visit that he paid to Cuba in October of that year.[16]

An opportunity to present his ideas for an agreement was offered in December 1941. At 2:00 A.M. on December 14, Mr. Henry Morgenthau, Jr., Secretary of the U.S. Treasury, asked White to prepare a plan for an inter-allied stabilization fund to be used (1) during the war to give monetary aid to the allies and to hamper the enemy, (2) as a basis for postwar international monetary arrangements, and (3) to provide for a postwar "international currency." [17] No doubt the changed circumstances resulting from the attack on Pearl Harbor on December 7 had turned the Secretary's mind to these problems, but there was also imminent the Third Meeting of Ministers of Foreign Affairs of the American Republics, to be held in Rio de Janeiro in the second half of January 1942.

White's response to this invitation was to produce, before the end of December, a "Suggested Program for Inter-Allied Monetary and Bank Action." [18] The objectives of this program were stated as follows:

> (1) To provide the means, the instrument, and the procedure to stabilize foreign exchange rates and strengthen the monetary systems of the Allied countries.
>
> (2) To establish an agency with means and powers adequate to provide the capital necessary:
>
> (a) to aid in the economic reconstruction of the Allied countries;
>
> (b) to facilitate a rapid and smooth transition from a war-time economy to a peace-time economy in the Allied countries;
>
> (c) to supply short-term capital necessary to increase the volume of foreign trade—where such capital is not available at reasonable rates from private sources.

Two organizations were visualized:

> The task of supplying Allied countries with necessary capital not otherwise available except on too costly terms, should be the function of an inter-allied bank created for that specific purpose; whereas the task of monetary stabilization requires a different agency. Monetary stabilization is a highly specialized function calling for a special structure, special personnel, and special organization. . . .
>
> It therefore is recommended that consideration be given to the establishment of two separate institutions:
>
> (1) An Inter-Allied Bank; and
>
> (2) An Inter-Allied Stabilization Fund.

[16] In discussion in 1950 with Mr. R. W. Oliver, Mr. Frank Coe, then Secretary of the Fund, who was a former colleague of White's, is reported to have stated that the plan for the Bank was prepared in the late summer or early autumn of 1941.—R. W. Oliver, *The Origins of the International Bank for Reconstruction and Development*, unpublished thesis, Princeton University, 1959, pp. 320–21.

[17] John Morton Blum, *From the Morgenthau Diaries: Years of War, 1941–45* (Boston, 1967), p. 228.

[18] The first surviving draft is dated December 30, 1941.

The accompanying outline of the Stabilization Fund contained almost all the features of the developed plan discussed later in this chapter.

After some revision in the Division of Monetary Research in the U.S. Treasury, the plan was shown to Mr. Sumner Welles, Under Secretary of State, in connection with the preparations for the meeting in Rio de Janeiro, which both Welles and White were to attend. Mr. Welles was impressed by the plan, and proposed to base on it a resolution for a conference to establish a stabilization fund. Secretary Morgenthau, however, felt that it was unwise to propose at the Rio meeting, without consulting the larger European powers, a scheme for so sweeping an international project. As a result, the resolution which was passed before the meeting broke up called only for a special conference of Ministers of Finance of the American Republics "for the purpose of considering the establishment of an international stabilization fund."

On his return to Washington, White continued to refine his proposals. An undated typescript, preserved among the White papers at Princeton, appears to comprise parts of several redrafts, some of which clearly preceded the preparation of a definitive typed version, dated March 1942.[19] The latter, with relatively small changes, became the first mimeographed text of the plan, dated April 1942, which is described below.

The text of these drafts shows that they were influenced to no small degree by the climate of U.S. Government policies at the time. Unlike the British system, which concentrated in the Treasury the ultimate responsibility for all aspects of international economic relations, the U.S. governmental organization limited the Treasury's sphere to purely financial matters. In other fields—trade, commodity arrangements, the Export-Import Bank, even aviation and telecommunications—responsibility lay with the State Department, which, under Secretary Cordell Hull, was evolving a foreign economic policy based on concepts of trade liberalization and on a recognition of the need for reconstruction and development finance. It was against such a background that White devised his financial institutions.

Another indication of the way in which the wind was blowing in Washington at the beginning of 1942 was afforded by the visit to London of Professor Alvin H. Hansen, the Harvard economist, who was then advising the Federal Reserve Board, and Mr. Luther Gulick, a consultant of the National Planning Board and an expert on the Tennessee Valley Authority. Their visit was sponsored by the State Department,[20] and resulted in a memorandum, the substance of which was embodied in a paper on the postwar balance of payments of the United Kingdom, presented to the War Cabinet by the Economic Section on January 31, 1942. This suggested that the Governments of the United Kingdom

[19] Both versions are in Princeton papers, Box 8, File 24.

[20] R. F. Harrod, *The Life of John Maynard Keynes* (London, 1951), p. 527.

and the United States, in pursuance of policies to promote full employment, increasing production, a rising standard of living, economic stability, and world trade, should (1) establish an International Economic Board to advise the collaborating Governments on economic policy; (2) undertake an international resources survey; and (3) establish an International Development Corporation, with stock subscribed by Governments, to make development expenditures with the proceeds of bonds guaranteed by these Governments.

Before leaving this account of the origins of the White Plan, it is right to point out that, while the inspiration and the driving force that produced it were White's own, its technical elaboration owed much to his colleagues in the Treasury. In particular, a leading part in developing the plan was played by Mr. Edward M. Bernstein, at that time a member of the Division of Monetary Research at the U.S. Treasury, and later Director of Research at the Fund. Mr. Bernstein combined high academic qualifications with exceptional lucidity of exposition, and supplied what White, for all his brilliance, lacked—technical sophistication and the power of persuasion.

ORIGINS OF THE KEYNES PLAN

In the summer of 1941, Keynes was in Washington discussing with the U.S. authorities the terms of an agreement for lend-lease. On June 12 he had sent to Lord Halifax, the British Ambassador to Washington, a proposal to deal with the problem of "consideration," which was to be the British response to the effective gift by the United States of lend-lease commodities. In his letter, Keynes had suggested that the United Kingdom would "agree . . . to make such contribution as lies in their power" to avoid encumbrances on free economic intercourse, and he had suggested that the Governments of the United Kingdom and the United States set up forthwith an Anglo-American Commission to consider how this should be done. Draft terms of reference for this commission provided that it would review the economic policies of the United States and of the British Commonwealth and recommend modifications to promote commerce between them. Subsequently, the Prime Minister decided that it was politically inadvisable to set up such a commission at that moment, but the aim of promoting Anglo-American trade remained in the forefront of the British negotiators' proposals.

On July 28, 1941, the U.S. State Department handed to Keynes a draft for "the terms and conditions upon which the United Kingdom receives defense aid from the United States of America and the benefits to be received by the United States of America in return therefor." Article VII of the draft agreement, which dealt with these terms and conditions, provided that they should be "such as not to burden commerce between the two countries but to promote mutually advantageous economic relations between them and the betterment of world-wide economic relations." The Article then went on to provide specifically against discrimination in either the United States or the United Kingdom against imports from the other country, and concluded by specifying that the terms and conditions "shall provide for the formulation of measures for the achievement of these ends." This provision was symptomatic of Secretary Hull's policy, already mentioned, of seeking to promote unencumbered international trade.

Shortly afterward, Keynes returned to London and reported to the British Government on the draft agreement, with particular reference to the avoidance of discrimination. He had warned the U.S. State Department that, unless there was a large Anglo-American effort to restore equilibrium in international trade when the war was over, the United Kingdom would be obliged to perpetuate and, indeed, intensify the measures of exchange control and bilateral payments agreements which had been developed since 1939.[21] But, although greatly concerned about the difficulty of abandoning discrimination while British resources were so depleted, he did not himself believe that bilateralism was an appropriate solution. Even before he left Washington he had turned his attention instead to what he called "elaborating a truly international plan which would avoid these difficulties," by easing the pressure on debtors and compelling creditors to lend the resources which liberal trading and monetary policies would require.

He may well have judged that the time was ripe for such a plan. The Atlantic Charter, promulgated on August 14, 1941, at a conference between Mr. Roosevelt and Mr. Churchill, further emphasized the British commitment to postwar international cooperation. Its fourth point promised that the United States and the United Kingdom

> will endeavour, with due respect for their existing obligations, to further enjoyment by all States, great or small, victor or vanquished, of access, on equal terms, to the trade and to the raw materials of the world which are needed for their economic prosperity.

And the fifth point of the Charter recorded that

> they desire to bring about the fullest collaboration between all nations in the economic field, with the object of securing for all improved labour standards, economic advancement, and social security.

There is no evidence that at this stage Keynes knew anything about White's plan. Certainly during his visit to Washington he had seen White, whom he had known since at least 1935,[22] for, late in 1941, he reported to Whitehall that "White was a constructive mind."[23] But at that point the objectives of the

---

21 *Ibid.*, p. 513.

22 See Report by White to Mr. Haas, dated June 13, 1935 (Princeton papers, Box 1, File 4).

23 Harrod, *op. cit.*, p. 507.

two men were different: White was mainly interested in stabilizing exchange rates and Keynes in devising means by which nondiscrimination could be accepted by the United Kingdom despite the imminent exhaustion of British monetary reserves. In any case, Keynes had no need to borrow ideas; he had long before adumbrated a plan somewhat similar to White's Stabilization Fund in his *Treatise on Money* (1930), where he had conceived a Supernational Bank which would act as a central bank for central banks.[24] What was needed now was to link such an institution with the control of exchange rates and to clothe it with disciplinary powers. The result was a first draft of his proposals for a Clearing Union, which was circulated inside the British Treasury on September 8, 1941. These proposals are discussed later in this chapter.

References in the U.S. press to the resolution at the meeting in Rio de Janeiro, mentioned above, were transmitted by Sir Frederick Phillips, the British Treasury representative in Washington, to London on January 23, 1942; these may have helped to stimulate interest in London in the Clearing Union proposals. It was not until July 9, 1942, however, that a copy of the White Plan was sent to London for transmission to Keynes. Sir Frederick Leith-Ross writes of this episode:

> Harry White . . . was not on close terms with Phillips, as he gave me, unasked, a copy of the American proposals for what was eventually the Bretton Woods agreement which Phillips had vainly been trying to obtain.[25]

In return, nearly at the end of August, a copy of the Clearing Union draft was handed by Sir Frederick Phillips to White for transmission to Secretary Morgenthau.

UNOFFICIAL PROPOSALS

It may be well to mention at this point that a variety of proposals for postwar international economic and monetary mechanisms began from 1941 onward to appear in the technical journals, or as pamphlets issued by interested organizations. Three of these, summarized below, were mentioned by Keynes when he was asked, in October 1942, to what he had referred when stating in the preamble to his plan that "there is also a growing measure of agreement about the general character of any solution to the problem likely to be successful."

In the issue of *Foreign Affairs* for January 1942, Mr. Herbert Feis, advisor on international economic affairs to the U.S. State Department, proposed in a personal capacity a scheme for a "Trade Stabilization Budget or Fund," by which the U.S. Government would set aside an annual sum—initially \$3–4 billion—which could be made available to designated foreign countries to enable

[24] John Maynard Keynes, *Treatise on Money* (London, 1930), Vol. II, pp. 399–402.
[25] Sir Frederick Leith-Ross, *Money Talks* (London, 1968), p. 298.

them to pay for imports of goods or services or to discharge debts. The scheme envisaged stabilized exchange rates and the abolition of exchange controls.[26]

About the same time, an article by Mr. Zygmunt Karpinski, who was attached to the Polish Government-in-Exile in London and who later was for two months an Alternate Executive Director of the Fund, was published in *The Polish Economist*.[27] This article advocated, in effect, the generalization of the procedures of the Tripartite Agreement, together with provisions for the absorption of excessive balances by triangular operations, by the sale of gold, or by changes in exchange rates.

In an address to the Economic and Business Foundation in May 1942, Professor Jacob Viner called for the creation of a workable international monetary system combining exchange stability and price-level stability. He urged the major countries to "accept a code which will prohibit resort to beggar-my-neighbor methods of escape from an impending depression," and conceived of

> a modified international gold standard, under which, to prevent world-wide inflation or deflation, and also to permit orderly adjustment when needed of the exchange-parities of particular currencies, changes in the monetary value of gold for at least the major countries would be permitted—or perhaps ordered—by an international body operating under general rules embodied in an international agreement.[28]

Keynes also cited "a good number of private memoranda." Among these were a number of proposals and counterproposals put forward by members of the governments-in-exile in London, who were kept in touch by the Treasury with the planning that was going forward. The authors of these memoranda included Mr. Johan W. Beyen [29] and Mr. Camille Gutt, both of whom were later to be associated with the Fund.

Mention may here be made also of an alternative to the internationalism of the Keynes and White Plans which attracted considerable support, particularly in banking circles, but which proved a blind alley. This was the so-called key-currency plan, expounded by Professor John H. Williams in December 1936 [30] and again in July 1943.[31] By it, the major countries would have had currencies

[26] *Foreign Affairs*, Vol. 20 (1941–42), pp. 282–92.

[27] *The Polish Economist* (London), January–June 1942, pp. 40–53.

[28] "Objectives of Post-War International Economic Reconstruction," reprinted in *American Economic Objectives*, William McKee, ed., Economic and Business Foundation (New Wilmington, Pa., 1942), pp. 161–77. The quotations are from pp. 168, 174.

[29] For Mr. Beyen's views, see his *Money in a Maelstrom* (New York, 1949), especially pp. 148–51.

[30] John H. Williams, Paper delivered to American Economic Association and American Statistical Association, December 28, 1936 (reprinted in *American Economic Review*, Vol. XXVII, No. 1, Supplement, March 1937, pp. 151–68). Partly reproduced below, Vol. III, pp. 119–23.

[31] John H. Williams, "Currency Stabilization: The Keynes and White Plans," *Foreign Affairs*, Vol. 21 (1943), pp. 645–58. Partly reproduced below, Vol. III, pp. 124–27.

linked to gold and countries of less international significance would have undertaken less rigid obligations. The links between member countries would have been similar to those in the Tripartite Agreement, but the cooperation between them would have been closer than was provided for in that Agreement and would have extended to coordination of internal policies. The essential feature of the plan was that it would have started with the U.S. dollar and sterling, and been extended only gradually to other currencies. Such a procedure was ruled out by the U.S. and British officials because of its discrimination between countries.

DETAILS OF THE KEYNES PLAN

Both the Keynes and White Plans went through a number of drafts before being made public. There is no need here to recapitulate all the formulations which were successively attempted. It will suffice, in the first place, to describe the Plans as they were at the time when the White Plan reached London. So far as the Keynes Plan is concerned, this entails giving details of the fourth draft of the Plan, which was circulated on February 11, 1942.[32]

Much of the detail of the Plan as circulated described the need for it and the merits of it. This part of the argument can largely be taken for granted and is not summarized here. What follows is basically the bare bones of the Plan together with notes on certain special features which proved to have importance in later discussions.

The title given by Keynes to the Plan was *Proposals for an International Currency (or Clearing) Union.* The alternatives in this title reflected some uncertainty in Keynes' mind as to the best name for his project. In the first draft, he conceived of an International Currency Union managing an International Clearing Bank (par. 3), and in later drafts the term Currency Union was retained as a general description for the body he envisaged.

This body was to keep banking accounts for central banks in exactly the same way as central banks in each country kept accounts for commercial banks. These accounts were to be denominated in an international currency, which, in this fourth draft, Keynes called bancor. (In the first draft, it had been tentatively called grammor.) Bancor was to be defined in terms of gold, but its value was not to be unalterable (pars. 1, 43). The Union would have power to change the value if it deemed this desirable. Member countries could obtain bancor in exchange for gold but could not obtain gold in exchange for bancor (par. 41).

Since the Currency Union was conceived primarily as a central bank for central banks to be run along the lines of the British banking system, it was provided

[32] Reproduced below, Vol. III, pp. 3–18.

that the debit balances, when they arose, should take the form of overdrafts and not of specific loans (par. 5). Unlike any ordinary banking system, however, the Union was to charge a rate of interest on both credit and debit balances (par. 17 (3)). This procedure, so far as creditors were concerned, was part of Keynes' deliberate plan to place part of the burden of balance of payments adjustments on creditor countries (par. 16). Keynes was, however, conscious that it would not do to be too hard on creditors, if only because without them the Union would be unable to help its potential debtors. The slightly ambivalent attitude which resulted from this dilemma was neatly, if somewhat rudely, summed up by Professor Dennis Robertson in a letter to Keynes on March 3, 1943. "Are we," he asked—

> Are we to love, honour, cherish and thank or
> To kick in the bottom the blokes who hold bancor? [33]

Elsewhere in the Plan, Keynes argued that credit balances would be no burden to creditors, being equivalent merely to idle reserves (par. 7). But while he wished to discourage credit balances in order to avoid the contractionary effect on international trade of large balance of payments surpluses, he also stressed the need for debit balances to be controlled (par. 17 (4)). He expressly commented that the right to an overdraft was no substitute for necessary readjustments in countries' internal economies (par. 14).

In addition to the provision for charging interest on credit and debit balances, Keynes proposed to limit the right to accumulate a debit balance in any one year to one fourth of a quota to be allotted to each country (par. 17 (4) (*a*)). This quota would be related to its foreign trade; specifically, he suggested that the quota might be equivalent to, or perhaps somewhat less than, the total of exports and imports of the member averaged over three prewar years (par. 17 (2)). The quota was to be adjusted annually to the average of three (or, after a time, five) preceding years. The interest to be charged on both debit and credit balances was quoted as 1 per cent of balances over one fourth and up to one half of the quota, and an additional 1 per cent on balances exceeding one half of the quota (par. 17 (3)). Keynes suggested, however, that member countries should be able to avoid these charges by debtors borrowing from creditors after consulting the Governing Board of the Union (par. 17 (3)).

The Plan also provided for exchange rates to be fixed in terms of bancor and not to be altered without the permission of the Governing Board; however, the Governing Board was, during the first five years after the inception of the system, to "give special consideration to appeals for adjustments in the exchange-value

---

[33] In his *Utility and All That* (London, 1952), p. 173, Professor Robertson quotes a quatrain, of which these (slightly revised) were the two concluding lines, as having been evolved and circulated by "someone" during discussions of the Clearing Union. There seems little doubt that he was himself the author.

of a national currency on the ground of unforeseen circumstances" (par. 17 (1)). At the same time, if a member had a debit balance in excess of one fourth of its quota on the average during the previous year, it was to be entitled to reduce the value of its currency by not more than 5 per cent yearly without the consent of the Governing Board (par. 17 (4) (*a*)). As balances increased in terms of quotas, so the action to be taken was more specifically provided. For example, as a condition of allowing a member state to increase its debit balance to more than half of its quota, the Governing Board was empowered to require the member to take all or any of the following measures: (1) devaluation by a specific amount, (2) imposition of control on outward capital transactions, (3) the outright surrender of a suitable proportion of the member's international reserves in reduction of the balance (par. 17 (4) (*b*)). Should the debit balance nevertheless further increase to a point where it exceeded three fourths of the quota, or was excessive in the opinion of the Governing Board, the Board could require the member to take measures to improve its position; if these failed within two years, the Governing Board might declare the member in default and cancel its drawing rights (par. 17 (4) (*c*)).

Somewhat similar provisions applied to members with credit balances exceeding one half of their quota for a year (par. 17 (5)). They would be required to discuss with the Governing Board (while, however, retaining the ultimate decision in their own hands) appropriate measures, such as (1) the expansion of domestic credit, (2) a revaluation of the currency, (3) an increase in wage rates, (4) the reduction of tariffs, etc., or (5) making international development loans.

It was mentioned above that one of the measures which might be recommended to a debtor was the control of outward capital transactions. The Plan, however, contemplated that such control would normally exist, and recommended that, if possible, all capital movements should be controlled in all countries (par. 45). The main object, on the one hand, was to control short-term speculative movements and, on the other hand, to distinguish between long-term loans by surplus countries and movements of funds out of deficiency countries lacking the means to finance them (par. 46).

The Plan, as drafted, contemplated world-wide membership of the Union. Nevertheless, it provided for a special position for the United States and the United Kingdom as founder members (par. 3). It suggested that these two should be able to outvote the remainder of the members and that the head office of the Union should be in London, with the Governing Board meeting alternately in London and in Washington (pars. 56, 57). Another aspect of the special relationship envisaged for the founder members was implicit in the provision for a period of relief and reconstruction after the war. This clearly envisaged that, despite lend-lease assistance, the United Kingdom would emerge from the war impoverished and in debt, and the United States as a major creditor (pars. 10, 61). One of the arguments put forward for the Plan, accordingly, was that it would be of particular value in this postwar period (par. 61)—the "transitional period," whose prospective length proved to be one of the issues on which it was most difficult to reach agreement. It may be inferred from the provision for changes in the members' exchange rates, cited above, that at this time Keynes was envisaging a transitional period of about five years (par. 17 (1)).

As put forward by Keynes, the Plan dealt only with the Clearing Union. It did, however, specifically contemplate a number of parallel organizations, including international bodies charged with postwar relief, rehabilitation, and reconstruction (par. 54). The Union was conceived as facilitating the work of such bodies, not only by setting up clearing accounts through which their transactions could be channeled, but also by giving them preliminary overdraft facilities—to be eventually discharged, if necessary, out of the Union's reserves or a levy on credit balances in the Union. Other international bodies which were envisaged included one with functions similar to the United Nations, another charged with the management of a Commodity Control, a Board for International Investment, and an International Economic Board, with the function of maintaining the stability of prices and controlling the trade cycle, which also might advantageously work in harmony with the Clearing Union.

The Plan quite specifically contemplated some surrender of member countries' sovereign rights, although it argued that the surrender was no greater than that required in a commercial treaty (par. 50). A greater readiness to accept supernational arrangements was, however, stipulated as a prerequisite for the postwar world (par. 51).

DETAILS OF THE WHITE PLAN

The White Plan as circulated in April 1942 was entitled *Preliminary Draft Proposal for a United Nations Stabilization Fund and a Bank for Reconstruction and Development of the United and Associated Nations.* It therefore covered what became both the International Monetary Fund and the International Bank for Reconstruction and Development. Only the part of the draft dealing with the Fund is discussed here.[34] The objectives which the Plan had in view were conveniently summarized in the first section, and the order in which these were stated has some significance. The purposes read as follows (par. I and pp. 46–48):

1. To stabilize foreign exchange rates of the United Nations.
2. To encourage the flow of productive capital among the United Nations.
3. To liberate blocked balances.

[34] The memorandum comprises an outline in the form of a series of numbered paragraphs, reproduced in Vol. III below on pp. 41–45, followed by a detailed commentary, partly reproduced on pp. 46–82. The parenthetical references in the discussion here are to the numbered paragraphs and/or to the pages in Volume III where the commentary is to be found.

4. To help correct the maldistribution of gold among the United Nations.
5. To facilitate the settlement and servicing of international debts—both public and private.
6. To shorten the periods of disturbing disequilibrium in the international accounts of member countries and help stabilize price levels.
7. To reduce the necessity and use of foreign exchange controls.
8. To eliminate multiple currency practices and bilateral clearing arrangements.
9. To promote sound note issuing and credit policies and practices among the United Nations.
10. To reduce barriers to foreign trade.
11. To promote more efficient and less expensive clearings of international exchange transactions.

Unlike the Clearing Union, the White Plan was a contributory one, with subscriptions totaling "at least $5 billion" (par. IV.1 and p. 73). No provisions were made in the outline of the Plan for the size of individual countries' contributions, but in the commentary a somewhat complicated formula was suggested, based on proportions of gold holdings, gold production, national income, foreign trade, population, foreign investments, and foreign debts (p. 74). The effect of this formula would have been to require contributions, inter alia, as follows: from the United States, $3,196 million; from the British Commonwealth, $1,055 million ($635 million from the United Kingdom); from the U.S.S.R., $164 million; from the Netherlands and colonies, $157 million; and from Brazil, $50 million. Fifty per cent of the country's contribution was to be paid up, consisting of 25 per cent in interest-bearing government securities (on which the interest and principal were to be payable in "gold or its equivalent") plus a minimum of 12½ per cent in gold and a maximum of 12½ per cent in the member's own currency (par. IV.2).

Any member might purchase from the Fund the currency of any other member on three conditions, viz.: (1) The currency demanded from the Fund was required to meet an adverse balance of payments vis-à-vis the country issuing the currency. (2) After the purchase, the total in the Fund of the currency of the country making the purchase should not exceed the total of the gold, currency, and government securities contributed by that member. (3) The relevant rate of exchange would be determined by the Fund (par. II.2 and pp. 49–50).

Provision was made for a member country to purchase a larger amount from the Fund than specified in the previous paragraph, provided that the member could secure 80 per cent of the members' votes, and provided (1) that the Fund had reason to believe that it could dispose of its excess holdings of the purchasing member's currency within a reasonable time, (2) that those holdings were matched by actual, or prospective, gold holdings of the member, or, as a further alternative, (3) that the member undertook measures recommended by the Fund to correct its balance of payments (par. II.3 and pp. 52–54). For such an additional purchase, the Fund would stipulate a time limit within which it should be repaid (p. 52).

Detailed provisions were made for the governments of member countries to sell to the Fund blocked foreign balances acquired from their nationals, within limits to be set by the Fund. Among the conditions to be imposed were that the country selling the blocked balances and the country in which the balances were held should each agree to purchase 40 per cent of them from the Fund at the rate of not less than 2 per cent a year, beginning after three years (par. II.4 and pp. 54–59). The former would do so either in the currency that it had received from the Fund or in its own currency, at the Fund's option. The country in which the balances were originally held would pay the Fund either in gold or in New International Units, later called Unitas (p. 87) to be issued by the Bank for Reconstruction and Development (p. 81). The remaining 20 per cent would be sold by the Fund as soon as the 80 per cent thus underwritten had been repurchased. A service charge of 1 per cent of the balances, payable in local currency, would be made against each country, and possibly also an annual charge of 1 per cent on the balances actually held by the Fund (par. II.4.g and p. 56).

As noted above, the Fund could determine the rates at which it would exchange one member's currency for another's. When doing so, it was to aim at stability in exchange relationships (par. II.5 and p. 60). Changes in the rates were to be made only "when essential to correction of a fundamental disequilibrium"—a term which was to give rise to prolonged but unsuccessful attempts at definition—and only with the consent of 80 per cent of members' votes. A similar majority was required for several other activities by the Fund, including (1) the retention of nonmember countries' currencies beyond 60 days (par. II.8); (2) the borrowing of any currency (par. II.9 and p. 60); (3) investing any currency it held in short-term securities—commercial or government (par. II.10); (4) selling the obligations of a member country (par. II.11); and (5) selling any currency for the purpose of adjustment of a foreign debt (par. II.12 and p. 61). For purposes of (3) and (4) above, the approving votes had to include that of the country whose securities were involved. By a 75 per cent majority, the Fund could permit any member to borrow its own currency from the Fund for a year or less, up to three fourths of the Fund's holdings of that currency. The member would pay only 1 per cent per annum interest to the Fund and thus might find borrowing from the Fund cheaper than borrowing in its own market (par. II.13 and p. 60).

Eligibility to participate in the Fund was offered to all members of the United and Associated Nations, provided, however, that they agreed (1) to abandon within a year all restrictions and controls over foreign exchange transactions with member countries, except with the approval of the Fund (par. III.1 and pp. 63–64);

(2) to alter their exchange rates only with the consent of the Fund, except for a narrow range to be fixed by the Fund and permitted to all member currencies (par. III.2 and pp. 64–66); (3) not to accept or permit deposits or investments from another member country without the consent of that country, and to make available to the government of any member at its request all property in the form of deposits, investments, and securities of the nationals of that member country (par. III.3 and pp. 66–67); (4) not to enter upon any bilateral clearing arrangements (par. III.4) nor to establish any "geographically preferential exchange rates" (p. 67); (5) not to adopt any monetary or general price measure or policy, the effect of which, in the opinion of a majority of the members' votes, would bring about, sooner or later, a serious disequilibrium in the balance of payments, providing that 80 per cent of the votes of the Fund members disapproved the adoption of such a measure (par. III.5 and pp. 68–69); (6) to embark upon a gradual reduction of trade barriers (par. III.6 and p. 69); (7) not to permit any defaults on foreign obligations of the government, central bank, or government agency without the approval of the Fund (par. III.7 and p. 71); and (8) not to subsidize, directly or indirectly, exports to member countries without the consent of the Fund (par. III.8 and pp. 71–72).

The Fund was to be managed by a Board of Directors. Each member would appoint one Director, and the Board would elect a Chairman and a small operating committee (par. V.1, 2 and pp. 75–76), whose members would devote their full time to the Fund's work. It was suggested that the Fund might need branch offices on each continent, and that it would require to be served by a large and highly skilled technical staff (pp. 48, 52, 76). It was contemplated that there would be regular consultations between the Fund and its members, although whether these would be conducted by a committee of Directors or by the staff was not made clear (p. 69). Provision was made for an executive committee to examine requests for changes in exchange rates, since the obvious need for secrecy would preclude the open discussions of such requests (p. 65). To keep the Board informed, the staff would need to watch, inter alia, quarterly balance of payments figures for each member (p. 59).

Each member of the Board would have 100 votes, plus 1 vote for the equivalent of every million dollars subscribed in gold or currency to the Fund by his government (par. V.3 and pp. 76–77). It was calculated that this would give the United States 25.32 per cent of the total votes, Latin America 34.47 per cent, the British Empire 17.56 per cent, other European countries and their colonies 15.91 per cent, the U.S.S.R. 2.85 per cent, and China 2.26 per cent (p. 75). The President of the Bank for Reconstruction and Development, who was to be a member of the Board of the Fund, would have 100 votes, or 1.63 per cent of the total (par. V.6 and pp. 75, 77). When considering proposed changes in exchange rates, however, each country would have 1 vote only (p. 66). Finally, the profits were to be distributed in the currency of each member, after 50 per cent of the net profits earned had been placed to reserve until the reserves equaled 10 per cent of the Fund's assets (par. IX).

❖ ❖ ❖

On May 16, 1942, Secretary Morgenthau sent a copy of the preamble to the White Plan to President Roosevelt, with a memorandum calling attention to the political capital to be made from the Stabilization Fund as a Free World answer to the "New Orders" being imposed by the Axis powers on Europe and Asia. He recalled that Resolution XV of the Rio meeting proposed an international conference to consider the establishment of a stabilization plan. In preparation for such a conference, he suggested that an Interdepartmental Committee should be set up to work with the Treasury on the White Plan. He enclosed a draft invitation to the conference, an agenda and timetable for it, and a list of Finance Ministers who might be invited.[35]

On the same day the President replied asking for a continuance of the studies in progress, in conjunction with the State Department, the Board of Economic Warfare, and the Export-Import Bank of Washington. He suggested that Secretary Morgenthau should mention the matter of a conference to him again when the studies had been completed and the opinion had been obtained of the Secretary of State (Hull) and the Under Secretary of State (Welles). An Interdepartmental Committee was duly constituted, and met for the first time on May 25. It set up a technical subcommittee, chaired by White, which met on May 28 and at frequent intervals thereafter.

The later evolution of both the White Plan and the Keynes Plan is described in the next chapter.

---

[35] Morgenthau papers, Hyde Park, N.Y. The original of the memorandum is undated, but there is a dated carbon copy in Princeton papers, File 24 (not in a box).

CHAPTER

2

Reshaping the Plans (1942-43)

WHEN THE STABILIZATION FUND proposals reached London in July 1942, Keynes was on the whole very favorably impressed with them. He found them somewhat diffuse and in need of some tightening up, but he thought it "striking and encouraging that the general objects" of the White Plan were the same as those which he had been pursuing. In particular, he pointed out that the concessions of national sovereignty recommended were the same as, or greater than, in the Keynes Plan, and that the White Plan's attitude toward laissez faire and the regulation of foreign trade did not differ materially from that of the United Kingdom. The proposals that members should refuse to accept investments from abroad except with the permission of the investing country, and should make all such investments available to the government of the investing country on reasonable terms, were welcomed as likely to solve the problem of the control of capital movements. Keynes also commented most favorably on the proposal to absorb the blocked balances into the Fund, pointing out that the liquid resources which this proposal would make available would be greater than those offered through the normal operations of the Fund.

On the other hand, he felt that the White Plan would be helpful only to countries that had a gold reserve already, and helpful to them in proportion to the amount of this reserve.[1] "To him that hath. . . ." Further, he noted that there was no provision for altering the volume of international currency in accordance with need; it would remain mainly dependent on the volume of gold mining and the policy of those countries that already had large gold reserves. Keynes also thought that the proposals for subscriptions and voting foreshadowed some curious results: the minor Latin American countries would be able to outvote the United States, while the United States could outvote the British Empire, the Netherlands Empire, Russia, and China, all added together.

---

[1] John Morton Blum, *From the Morgenthau Diaries: Years of War, 1941–45* (Boston, 1967), p. 236.

THE KEYNES PLAN REVISED

As a result of his reflections on these matters, Keynes produced, in August 1942, a fifth draft of the Clearing Union proposals. Most of the changes introduced were drafting. However, as a preamble, Keynes set out eight requisites for a successful international currency plan, which, it will be seen, specifically reflect some of the deficiencies which he had diagnosed in the Stabilization Fund proposal. What was required was, in summary:

(1) a generally acceptable international currency for international clearing, making blocked balances and bilateral clearings unnecessary;

(2) an orderly and agreed method of determining exchange rates;

(3) a quantum of international currency not dependent on gold production or gold reserve policies, but capable of deliberate expansion and contraction;

(4) a stabilizing mechanism to bring pressure to bear on a country in balance of payments disequilibrium;

(5) an agreed plan to start off each country after the war with appropriately large reserves;

(6) a method of employing unused balance of payments surpluses in the interests of international planning and relief and economic health;

(7) a central technical institution to aid and support other international economic institutions; and

(8) reassurance to a troubled world that any country conducting its affairs with due prudence would not be made anxious, by causes not of its own making, about its balance of payments, thus making unnecessary the methods of restriction and discrimination hitherto employed in self-protection.

In this fifth draft, Keynes suggested that the Fund should have executive offices not only in London but also in New York, with its Board of Managers meeting alternately[2] in London and Washington. He proposed that the Board of Managers should consist of about 12 persons. The major States (including the founder-States) should each appoint a member of the Board, while the other members would be appointed by groups of minor States. Each member of the Board would cast votes proportionate to the quotas of those who had appointed him. He also introduced a discussion of the relationship of the Clearing Union to commercial policy—a subject which was beginning to attract the attention of the British Cabinet because of the stipulations in Clause VII of the Lend-Lease Agreement, as eventually signed on February 23, 1942, calling for "agreed action

[2] The word used was "alternatively," but in the fourth and sixth drafts the word was "alternately," and it seems likely that this was intended in the fifth draft also.

by the United States of America and the United Kingdom . . . directed to . . . the elimination of all forms of discriminatory treatment in international commerce, and to the reduction of tariffs and other trade barriers. . . ."

U.S. VIEWS ON THE KEYNES PLAN

It was, of course, this fifth draft of the Keynes Plan which was brought to the United States late in August 1942 and handed to U.S. Secretary of the Treasury Morgenthau. It was given very careful consideration by the Treasury and by the Interdepartmental Committee that had been set up in May 1942 to consider the White Plan. There emerged from these reviews two documents—a detailed comparison of the provisions of the Stabilization Fund and the Clearing Union and a series of questions to Keynes on details of the latter.

The detailed comparison made it clear that the two plans had many common features. Nevertheless, some provisions in the Stabilization Fund were not paralleled in the Clearing Union, and some Clearing Union proposals were not matched in the Stabilization Fund; there were also important differences of treatment of common topics in the two plans. As a starting point for the process of assimilation which occupied most of the next two years, it may be worth examining in a little detail what these various points were.

The Stabilization Fund alone provided for the following elements: a contributed capital, a definite termination of bilateral clearing, the absorption of blocked balances, a qualified veto by the Fund on national monetary policies, provisions for the distribution of profits, and a requirement that members would provide the Fund with periodic reports and information.

On the other hand, the Clearing Union alone provided for furnishing to each member an immediate addition to its monetary reserves (in the form, of course, of the right to an overdraft), specific provision for a transitional period during which some of the ultimate provisions of the plan would be suspended, and a proposal for the location of the organization.

The following points were probably the most important ones on which different provisions were made in the two plans:

(1) The Stabilization Fund proposed that the Fund should operate in what later was to be called "a mixed bag" of currencies—that is, in the currencies of its member countries. The Clearing Union, on the other hand, would operate in bancor, an international currency which it would create ad hoc.

(2) The Stabilization Fund proposed, as an objective, to help to correct the maldistribution of gold, but the Clearing Union proposed to relegate gold to a secondary position in the international monetary mechanism.

(3) The Stabilization Fund proposed that exchange rates should be fixed by the Fund and changed only with the consent of 80 per cent of the voting power.

The Clearing Union envisaged exchange rates being agreed between the Union and its members and provided for special consideration to be given to changes proposed in a transitional period. Further, there were to be automatic devaluations should debit balances exceed certain limits.

(4) The extent to which international clearing would be effected by the two organizations differed to some extent. The Stabilization Fund (although its provisions were not entirely clear) appeared to visualize daily clearing between central banks, but the Clearing Union specifically contemplated that the Union would clear residual balances only after normal transactions between central banks had been completed.

(5) There were considerable differences between the rights to use the Fund, on the one hand, and the Union, on the other, and in the penalties which the two organizations could impose on debtors or creditors. These differences have been elaborated in the previous chapter.

(6) The Stabilization Fund contemplated the abolition of exchange control, except when approved by the Fund. The Clearing Union, on the other hand, offered no objection to exchange controls and specifically advocated the control by member countries of capital movements.

(7) There were some differences, although partly in terminology, between the procedures for management envisaged by the two plans. The Stabilization Fund proposed a Governing Board comprised of one representative of each member, delegating some functions to an executive committee in permanent session. The Clearing Union visualized a Board of Managers representing all members, but designed to ensure that the management was permanently entrusted to the founder-States (United States, United Kingdom, and perhaps U.S.S.R.).

(8) The Stabilization Fund proposed a formula for voting which was deliberately intended as a compromise between a system under which each member would have one vote and a system under which voting power would be weighted in proportion to the contributions made by members. These contributions, in turn, would be based on a formula taking account of seven factors collectively indicative of the country's economic strength and, to a minor degree, of its international trade. In the Clearing Union, on the other hand, votes would be proportionate to members' quotas, which would be based on their international trade alone. But it was also suggested that the effective voting power should inhere permanently, or at least for five years, in the founder-States.

The questions which were put as a result of the deliberations of the Interdepartmental Committee may be roughly grouped into two sections.

The first four questions were concerned purely with clarification of the meaning of the Clearing Union proposals. They included the following inquiries: (1) Would the transactions of the Union be effected at par or at exchange rates varying within the gold points? (2) What was the exact role envisaged for bancor? (3) What was the membership envisaged for countries in the British Commonwealth? (4) Would not the special position allotted to founder-States conflict with the object of securing international collaboration?

More significant than the foregoing was a second group of questions, which indicated causes of concern to the U.S. committee. Perhaps the most important of these sought information about the total of quotas which the Clearing Union envisaged, about the potential liability of the United States within this total, and about the rights of creditors—who, it was pointed out, might well find themselves with a minority of votes. Other questions sought to ascertain how the Clearing Union proposals could prevent members from exhausting too soon the quotas allotted to them; and how, under the Union plan, it would be possible to contract the total of credit created should inflationary conditions make this desirable.

Of all the considerations which were adumbrated in the two documents summarized above, three appeared to the Interdepartmental Committee to be of overwhelming importance, and in each of these three it was felt that the Stabilization Fund had superior attractiveness for the United States. The first of these was the need to limit the liability of the United States as potentially the largest creditor in the postwar world. Secondly, and allied to the first, was the need to ensure that, in any organization that was set up, the main creditors would have sufficient power to prevent their being outvoted on major issues by the collective votes of debtor countries. The third issue was that of acceptability to Congress, and here it was felt that the Stabilization Fund, based as it was on concepts already familiar in the U.S. political scene, would be far more likely to secure congressional approval than the Clearing Union, which introduced the unfamiliar concepts of a new international currency and of overdrafts.

ACTIVITY IN WASHINGTON

In October 1942 White visited London for discussions with Keynes and others in the British Treasury. On his return to Washington, he reported to the Interdepartmental Committee that Keynes had urged three main points: (1) quotas should be proportionate to the volume of trade; (2) while it would be preferable to avoid the use of gold, it might be necessary to provide for its use because of widespread popular feeling; and (3) the United Kingdom and the United States ought to agree on a plan before any other country was approached. White said that he had explained why the United States favored quotas related to the assets made available to the Fund, but that he had agreed that the contribution in gold could be scaled to the availability of gold in member countries.

Shortly after his return, White received a copy of a new draft of the Keynes Plan, dated November 9, 1942. Thereafter, the Stabilization Fund proposals were intensively examined and redrafted. A draft dated November 25, 1942 was redrafted three times in December and three times in January 1943. Some evidence of the priorities accorded by White at this time to the different features of his plan may be found in a paper on "Postwar Currency Stabilization" that he delivered to the American Economic Association on January 7, 1943.[3] This listed four tasks for an international monetary agency, three of them related to exchange rates and the fourth to loans for reconstruction.

At the beginning of February 1943, the third January draft was transmitted by the State Department to the British Treasury and, on March 4, it was sent to the representatives of 37 countries with an invitation to an informal conference to discuss the proposals.[4] On March 17, Secretary Morgenthau told the President that the Keynes Plan was shortly to be published, and suggested that the White Plan should also be released to the press. On April 1, the President decided against this, but on April 5 the London *Financial News* contained a full summary of the White Plan, and as a result the decision not to publish it was rescinded. On the same day Secretary Morgenthau communicated to the U.S. Congress a slightly revised version of the plan, which was published in Washington on April 7 and in London shortly afterward. On April 7 a White Paper containing Keynes' *Proposals for an International Clearing Union* was published in London.[5]

The White Plan was further revised and new versions were produced on May 8, June 15, June 26, and July 10, 1943,[6] following discussions with a number of different countries. A summary of the final version was issued on August 19.

In May, the representatives in Washington of 46 countries were invited to discuss the White Plan and to answer a questionnaire calling for comment on it. For the purpose of these discussions an extensive document, setting out replies to a number of questions which had been raised, was produced and circulated. On June 1, the formula for the calculation of quotas in the form which was eventually used at Bretton Woods was produced in the U.S. Treasury and a few days later this was sent to the United Kingdom. From June 15 to June 17 informal group discussions took place in Washington, being attended by representatives of 18 countries: Australia, Belgium, Brazil, Canada, China, Czechoslovakia, Ecuador, Egypt, France, Luxembourg, the Netherlands, Norway, Paraguay, the Philippines, Poland, the United Kingdom, the U.S.S.R., and Venezuela. On June 22–24 there were further meetings with the United Kingdom alone. Subsequently, Professor Dennis Robertson, a wartime recruit

[3] *American Economic Review*, Vol. XXXIII (1943), Supplement, pp. 382–87.

[4] *Report of the Secretary of the U.S. Treasury, Fiscal Year 1943*, p. 349.

[5] Cmd. 6437. Both plans were reproduced in the *Federal Reserve Bulletin*, Vol. 29 (1943), pp. 501–21, and this version of the Keynes Plan is reproduced below, Vol. III, pp. 19–36.

[6] The last of these is reproduced below, Vol. III, pp. 83–96.

to the British Treasury, who was at that time attached to the British Embassy in Washington, had discussions with representatives of the U.S. Treasury and the Federal Reserve Board to clarify some outstanding points.

These official activities did not, of course, take place in an intellectual vacuum. The publication in April 1943 of the two sets of proposals was noted in almost every serious journal in the English-speaking world, and in a host of speeches and pamphlets.[7] Most commentators contented themselves with summarizing the two plans, but, in those articles that attempted to draw conclusions, it is possible to detect something approaching polarization: the British journals tended to criticize the White Plan and the U.S. journals to decry the Keynes Plan. This was, of course, natural to the extent that the two plans reflected the needs and aspirations of the two countries that had produced them. But this negative response was not necessarily accompanied by wholehearted support for the plan emanating from the writer's own side of the Atlantic. More support was forthcoming in the United Kingdom than in the United States, where the "key currency" plan rivaled both the Stabilization Fund and the Clearing Union for attention and where (for this and other reasons) writers were prepared to find serious faults in both plans. On the other hand, it is difficult to discover, in all the technical comments that were poured out in 1943, any British writer who preferred the White to the Keynes Plan, or any American one who thought better of the Clearing Union than of the Stabilization Fund.

* * *

Before going further with an analysis of the two competing plans, we may pause to examine the outcome of the activities noted above. This will involve anticipating to some extent changes in the White Plan not yet detailed, since these were introduced while the consultations with other countries were proceeding. However, the alternative of describing the revisions of the plan first would have the disadvantage of examining these revisions in advance of describing the suggestions which may have influenced the framers of the Stabilization Fund to effect them. Accordingly, the next section of this chapter summarizes the suggestions made by the representatives of the countries (other than the United Kingdom) consulted by the U.S. Treasury in 1943. The three following sections survey three alternative plans put forward. We shall then return to a consideration of the redrafting of the White and Keynes Plans, leading to the form which they eventually assumed in the summer of that year.

From September 15 to October 9, 1943, a definitive series of meetings between a group of U.S. officials and a British delegation was held in Washington. These

[7] *Bretton Woods Agreements: A Bibliography, April 1943–December 1945*, Board of Governors of the Federal Reserve System (Washington, 1946), lists 162 articles, etc., on the Fund and Bank published in the last nine months of 1943.

meetings and the Joint Statement of Experts, a first draft of which was prepared at them, are discussed in Chapter 3.

CHANGES PROPOSED IN THE PLANS

Not all the countries consulted by U.S. officials during 1943 proposed specific changes in the draft Stabilization Fund, and in many instances the same suggestion was put forward by more than one country. It seems therefore convenient to summarize these suggestions by subject rather than by country of origin. This is the more appropriate in that changes introduced in the Stabilization Fund as a result of the discussions were presumably the consequence of the cumulative pressure of the several opinions expressed rather than being a response to criticisms uttered by any one country's representative. In what follows, the recommendations listed are attributed to the country whose representative propounded them, but this is of course done only for the sake of convenience; the recommendations made did not necessarily represent the considered view of the government of the country mentioned. We shall discuss the main subjects in descending order of the number of countries which expressed views about them.

Quotas, contributions, and votes

A larger total than the $5 billion proposed in the Stabilization Fund plan was recommended by Poland ($15 billion), by Belgium, Canada, France, and Norway ($10–12 billion), and by Australia (no figure mentioned). On the other hand, Bolivia, Czechoslovakia, and the Philippines thought that $5 billion would suffice. Australia and Norway asked for larger shares, requesting respectively 5 per cent and 1 per cent of the total, while Panama, representing that the Fund would be of no service to it, asked that its quota should be purely nominal. Australia, Belgium, Bolivia, Brazil, Chile, Czechoslovakia, France, the Netherlands, Norway, and Poland suggested changes in the formula, mostly designed to include elements favorable to the country making the suggestion. Australia and the Netherlands suggested that the quota used as a basis for drawings and votes should be different from that used for calculating contributions.

As regards the composition of contributions, Belgium, Bolivia, Czechoslovakia, France, and Norway thought that the proportion of gold was too high, and the Philippines suggested that no country should be required to contribute gold to an extent greater than 20 per cent of its own gold and dollar balances. Bolivia and Cuba thought that part of the quota should be paid in silver. Brazil and France objected to part of the subscription being in the form of negotiable securities. Canada suggested that 85 per cent of the quota should be paid in the member's own currency. Finally, Belgium, Bolivia, Haiti, and Norway proposed that at least part of a country's contribution should be includable in the country's own reserves.

On the subject of voting rights, Australia, Belgium, and Norway objected to the provision giving the United States an effective veto, and the Netherlands thought that the requirement that certain decisions would have to be supported by 80 per cent of the members' votes would introduce an undue rigidity into the system. Brazil suggested that a member's votes should be related to its population or trade, and China that they should take account of the sacrifices endured by the member during the war. Cuba and Mexico preferred that decisions should be taken by a majority of the number of members, although Mexico was prepared to agree that, except where the "dignity" of a member was involved, one half of the total votes should be weighted according to quotas. Norway put forward three variations on the weighting formula included in the Stabilization Fund draft. Bolivia and Norway objected to a proposal, copied from the Keynes Plan, to augment the voting strength of creditor countries and reduce that of debtor countries.

Exchange rates

The establishment of initial exchange rates was widely regarded as likely to be difficult. Belgium, Bolivia, Canada, France, Norway, and the Philippines thought that it would be necessary for the initial exchange rate to be negotiated, and several of these countries assumed that the first step would be for the United States and the United Kingdom to agree on the dollar-sterling rate. Czechoslovakia and Mexico suggested that a technical appraisal of the appropriateness of any suggested rate would be essential. Brazil, Chile, and Mexico pointed out that the proposal in the Stabilization Fund plan to fix the initial rate at the level prevailing on July 1, 1943 would be inappropriate to the conditions in these countries. Greece and Norway thought that any initial exchange rate should be provisional; Norway wished the period allowed after joining the Fund for the establishment of the exchange rate to be six months, instead of the three months proposed.

Australia, Canada, Mexico, the Netherlands, Norway, and the Philippines criticized the provision for changes in the exchange rate. Australia thought that a conservative management would be likely to resist a request by a member country for authority to devalue. The Netherlands and Norway thought that for a limited period after joining—Norway suggested two years—a country should be free to alter its exchange rate if it needed to do so, and Canada and Norway would have preferred a provision for an automatic devaluation if a country got into difficulties. The Philippines drew attention to the problem of re-establishing a stable rate in an occupied country and thought that it would be necessary to allow a wider margin of fluctuation than the plan proposed.

Finally, El Salvador and Panama both objected to the Fund having power to impose a devaluation.

Drawings and repurchases

The limitation on the quantum of drawings was criticized by Bolivia, Brazil, Canada, and Norway. Canada (as subsequently in its own plan) suggested permissible drawings of 50 per cent of quota per annum, the maximum amount that could be drawn being equal to 200 per cent of quota. Australia, Czechoslovakia, France, Greece, Haiti, and Paraguay also objected to the requirement that countries with adequate reserves should pay in gold for 50 per cent of amounts drawn. The "policing" of drawings was criticized by Belgium, El Salvador, Norway, and the Philippines. All four countries disliked the Fund's power to impose obligations as a condition of drawings, and the Philippines proposed that the Fund's power should be limited to making a report. Panama thought that the charges proposed to be levied were exorbitant.

On the other hand, Canada, the Netherlands, and South Africa suggested that the Stabilization Fund should exert greater pressure on debtors; the Netherlands thought that there should be a specific prohibition on the use of amounts drawn from the Fund for certain types of international expenditure. South Africa thought that a member should be required to exhaust its reserves before coming to the Fund.

The provisions for using accretions to members' reserves to repurchase drawings from the Fund were disliked by Bolivia and France. Norway thought that they should not apply if the accretions were less than $50 a head of the population, and the Philippines commented that, because of their monetary legislation, the requirement would involve them in a budgetary problem.

Scarce currency

A variety of points was raised about the provision for exerting pressure on creditor countries. Belgium, Bolivia, Brazil, France, Greece, Norway, and the Philippines all put forward proposals for this purpose, most of which concentrated on reducing tariffs and stimulating foreign investment. Australia also thought that greater pressure ought to be exerted on creditors, and Greece argued that the Stabilization Fund showed too much consideration for a country whose currency was becoming scarce. Proposals to increase the ability of the Fund to avoid the development of scarcity were made by Canada, the Netherlands, and Paraguay. Belgium proposed that, when a currency did become scarce, it should be allocated in the first place to countries that had not drawn more than 25 per cent of their quota.

Administrative proposals

A number of countries suggested additional provisions in the area which may be broadly described as administration. Norway advocated that, as in the Clearing Union plan, the Executive Offices of the Fund should be located in London and New York, and proposed that the Fund should have extraterritoriality. Replying to a question by the U.S. officials as to the matters which should be delegated to the Executive Committee, Norway thought that these should be limited to those needing only a simple majority for decision. Bolivia, France, and the Philippines favored a broader delegation of authority. South Africa suggested that Executive Directors should be paid by the Fund, and not by the members appointing them, in order to strengthen their independence. Mexico drew attention to the need for a highly qualified staff, and Norway recommended that at least one member of the staff should be drawn from each member country. Finally, Belgium put forward a detailed proposal for the liquidation of the Fund, should this become necessary.

Other proposals

In addition to the foregoing, a considerable number of minor aspects of the Stabilization Fund were criticized. Belgium and Poland wished to be satisfied that the provision for dealing with blocked balances would cover the debts owed to them by Germany. Norway wished the Fund to have powers to borrow, in order to ensure that its resources would be adequate to cover blocked balances. Bolivia thought that the charges proposed to be made for handling such balances were too large.

Little was said in the discussions about unitas, the proposed international currency. Mexico, however, did propose that part of the metallic backing for unitas should be silver, and Norway suggested that a unitas should be worth $2 (not $10) and that it should be called bancor because the word unitas was pronounced differently in different countries. Norway also deprecated the acceptance of deposits in unitas, on the ground that the Fund was not a bank.

Bolivia, France, Greece, the Netherlands, and the Philippines thought that the Stabilization Fund should have specific provisions for regulating relations between members and nonmembers. Belgium wished to exclude the Belgian-Luxembourg Economic Union from the scope of the Fund's prohibition of bilateral arrangements. Belgium and Panama considered it impossible to provide the information about foreign investments for which the Fund called, and Norway suggested that the objectives of the Fund should be set out more elaborately than had been done in the draft. Finally, the Netherlands submitted two lengthy memoranda arguing against the international basis for the Fund and in favor of the key-currency approach advocated by Professor Williams (see Chapter 1 above).

THE FRENCH PLAN

In the early spring of 1943, two French economists, Mr. André Istel and Mr. Hervé Alphand, put forward an alternative to the Keynes and White Plans.[8] This proposal closely resembled that in the van Zeeland report of 1938.[9] It consisted essentially of seven points. The first four of them—covering agreements on exchange rates and an undertaking to exchange currencies, within fixed limits, with other member countries—corresponded closely to the obligations of the Tripartite Agreement, which would be extended to all countries willing to participate. The other three points were as follows: each participating country would deposit approved collateral to cover an agreed proportion of the amount of its currency held by other members; each would sterilize the inflow of foreign exchange during periods of inflation; and some method of international consultation should be set up, preferably (but not necessarily) in the form of a permanent organization—a "Monetary Stabilization Office" or, in a version of the plan published in the *New York Times*, an "International Clearing Office."

The defects of any such plan for a less than comprehensive scheme were exposed in a speech by Professor Robertson on August 26, 1943.[10] His main criticisms, which applied also to the key-currency plan of Professor Williams, were that it was impracticable to leave to chance the linking of European currencies to an Anglo-American system; that Europe could in any case make important contributions to the new order if fully integrated into it; and that it was politically unwise to appear, in any scheme put forward, to impose Anglo-American leadership. Similar criticisms had been made by White in discussions with the Netherlands representatives on April 23, 1943, and in a meeting at the Federal Reserve Board on August 11, 1943.

THE CANADIAN PLAN

Following the discussions between Canadian officials and U.S. officials in May 1943, the former concluded that it would be better to produce a Canadian draft plan. This was in form to resemble the Stabilization Fund plan, but would embody those features of the Clearing Union proposals that Canada thought should be incorporated. Keynes was somewhat doubtful of the desirability of injecting another plan into the discussions, but on further consideration the Canadian officials decided that offering a third plan would be the best way to

[8] The English version is reproduced below, Vol. III, pp. 97–102. The French version was published by the Bank for International Settlements as H.S. 99. The *New York Times* version appeared on May 9, 1943. See also Williams, "Currency Stabilization: The Keynes and White Plans," note 11 (reproduced below, Vol. III, p. 126).

[9] See Chapter 1 above.

[10] D. H. Robertson, "The Post-War Monetary Plans," *Economic Journal*, Vol. LIII (1943), pp. 352–60.

work toward what they regarded as a necessary compromise. A draft plan was thereupon prepared in Ottawa and sent to Keynes on June 3. A slightly revised version was given a limited distribution in Ottawa on June 9 and subsequently printed and made generally available.[11] The principal novelties in this plan, some of which, it will be seen below, were incorporated in later versions of the Stabilization Fund, were as follows:

(1) The organization was called "International Exchange Union," the word "Union" being used to distinguish the institution from the resources which it administered.[12]

(2) The aggregate of quotas was fixed at $8 billion and the Union would have power to require countries to lend, in addition, up to 50 per cent of their quotas (Sections II.1, II.2).

(3) It was proposed that the whole of countries' quotas should be paid up at the outset, at least 15 per cent in gold and the remainder in local currency. There were to be no interest-bearing securities (Section II.1 (*b*)).

(4) The initial fixing of an exchange rate was to require the country's consent. In appropriate circumstances, a debtor member might devalue by 5 per cent without obtaining the Union's approval (Sections IV.1, IV.2).

(5) The resources of the Union could be used to meet "an adverse balance on current account" not limited to the currency of an individual country with which an adverse balance was experienced (Section V.1 (*a*)).

(6) Drawings might amount to 50 per cent of quota a year, within a total of drawings equivalent to 200 per cent of quota, but were not to be available to a member whose monetary reserves exceeded its quota (Section V.1 (*a*) to (*c*)).

(7) Drawings in excess of the limits in paragraph (6) might be allowed by a special vote of the Governing Board. For this purpose, and for the purpose of voting on changes in quotas, the voting strength of creditors would be augmented and that of debtors diminished in relation to their normal entitlement (Sections V.1 (*c*) and IX.3). (Keynes had suggested the former but not the latter application of this provision.)

In other respects, the Canadian Plan strongly resembled the Stabilization Fund proposals, including, though in a much shortened form, provisions for dealing with abnormal wartime balances, and containing also very similar provisions for a scarce currency. In the draft sent to Keynes, the international currency unit was entitled "monad," but in the published version it was given no name other than "Unit" (Section III.1).

In principle the Canadian proposal remained on the table for consideration during the negotiations described in the next chapter, but it appears that, in

[11] Reproduced below, Vol. III, pp. 103–18.
[12] Footnote to Table of Contents.

practice, the modification of the Stabilization Fund proposals described below, together with the pressure exerted by the British delegation in support of the Clearing Union proposals, made it unnecessary to discuss the Canadian Plan separately.

THE FEDERAL RESERVE BOARD PLAN

The staff of the Board of Governors of the Federal Reserve System had been following the discussions about the Keynes and White Plans with close attention. As early as December 1942 they took occasion to urge the need to limit the U.S. contribution to $2–2.5 billion. In the spring of 1943, ideas had begun to crystallize at the Board for an improved version of the White Plan, and on June 1 such a plan was submitted to, and given the tentative approval of, the Board of Governors. On the next day, it was discussed at one of the meetings of the Interdepartmental Committee. A few days later, some features of the plan were modified. The following are the principal features of the modified plan.

(1) The aggregate contributions of the Fund (excluding Germany, Italy, and Japan) should be $14 billion.

(2) Each country's quota should equal one third of its foreign trade, on average, for the years 1936–38, subject to some adjustment for abnormal conditions in individual countries. On this basis, the U.S. contribution would be $2 billion.

(3) All contributions were to be made in gold, up to a limit equivalent to one half or three fourths of each country's gold holdings. This should bring some $7 billion of gold into the Fund.

(4) All countries were to be allowed to buy gold only from the Fund, and to sell gold only to the Fund, which would be obliged to buy all gold offered to it (subject to limits which it might set for newly mined gold).

(5) Each member had the right to purchase foreign exchange equal in amount to its original contribution, plus the value of all gold sold by it to the Fund.

(6) Each member should have one vote for each $1 million contributed to the Fund, plus one vote for each $1 million of its currency made available to other members.

(7) A debtor country might devalue its currency by 5 per cent when its deficit was equal to one fourth of its quota, and by a further 5 per cent when its deficit reached one half of its quota. It might be required by the Fund to devalue if its deficit exceeded one half of its quota.

(8) A creditor country might appreciate its currency by 5 per cent when its credit balance reached one fourth of its quota, and by a further 5 per cent when its credit balance reached one half of its quota.

(9) In addition to the power to require a devaluation, mentioned above, the Fund might require countries to control capital movements. It might also *recommend* the following:

(*a*) To debtors: control of excessive internal expansion; technological and management steps to reduce costs; control of wage increases causing income inflation; and imposition of exchange control on current account;

(*b*) To creditors: measures of internal expansion; appreciation of their currencies when such expansion threatened to become an inflation; international lending; tariff reductions; and increases in wage rates.

(10) The machinery of the Fund should start to operate at once, but the initial exchange rates set should be treated as experimental for a period of two to four years. During that period, exchange control would be permitted, but the Fund would advise countries on measures which would enable them to dispense with controls.

The two features of this plan to which most importance was attached were the obligation to buy and sell gold only through the Fund and the provision for augmenting the votes of creditor countries. The former was expected to induce all wealthy countries to join the Fund, and therefore to ensure that the Fund obtained an adequate stock of gold; the latter was intended to add rapidly to the influence exerted by creditor countries, and thus ensure that the Fund recommended measures that would effectively maintain stability in international monetary affairs.

However, the U.S. Treasury refused to consider the first of these proposals, or to allow it to be discussed at the meetings with 18 countries which were about to begin; the Treasury view was that such a monopoly of gold dealings would ruinously impair the prestige of gold. Lacking such an inducement to join the Fund, the Federal Reserve Board officials were unable to persuade the representatives of the 18 countries that their gold contributions should be stepped up as the Federal Reserve Plan required. The plan was therefore discarded, the Board's officials being nonetheless gratified that the revision of the White Plan dated June 15 proposed to increase members' gold contributions by relating them to the proportion which their gold reserves bore to their quotas, and that the Canadian Plan included a scheme of weighted voting, which, though less swift-acting than their own, was a step in the right direction.

EVOLUTION OF THE WHITE PLAN

We now return to a consideration of the evolution of the Stabilization Fund. It is apparent from a comparison of the successive drafts that the changes made by the Interdepartmental Committee were partly designed to introduce features which had proved attractive in the several rival plans, and partly to give effect to the suggestions by other countries consulted, which were summarized above. It will be convenient to consider the redrafts by subject rather than chronologically. The following six groups of changes were the most important which can be distilled from the successive drafts.[13]

Unitas

The April 1942 draft of the Stabilization Fund had no provision for an international currency such as the bancor underlying the Clearing Union. The accompanying draft proposals for an International Bank contained a lengthy argument to the effect that such a currency would be unhelpful, except as a money of account for notes issued by the Bank itself (Vol. III below, pp. 78–82). The November draft provided that the Stabilization Fund could "fix the gold equivalent of any international monetary unit which may be established." In the next draft (December 11), a separate section was introduced under the title "Monetary Unit of the Fund," citing this as the "unitas," consisting of 137 1/7 grams of fine gold (equivalent to $10). The accounts of the Fund and the value of the currency of each member country were to be expressed in unitas. In the January, April, and May 1943 drafts, provision was made for deposits to be made in unitas. These were to be transferable and redeemable in gold or in the currency of any member country.

The significance of unitas in the Stabilization Fund was a source of some perplexity to the United Kingdom. After a number of discussions with U.S. officials, Sir Frederick Phillips cabled to London in May 1943 that it was merely a measuring rod except in the clause providing for deposits of gold; there it became "a warehouse receipt for gold." Perhaps as a result of this clarification, or of the criticism by Norway, the clause in question subsequently disappeared, being replaced in the June 26 and July 10 versions by a requirement (Sec. III, par. 2) that countries must not buy gold at a price above par, nor sell it at a price below par.

Some insight into the reasons why U.S. officials were anxious to limit the role of unitas was given in a discussion between Professor Robertson and a representative of the Federal Reserve Board in July. It appeared that the U.S. officials had discussed whether bancor, if used, could be sterilized by government purchases, along the lines on which the British Exchange Equalization Account worked. They had concluded that there would be public opposition to such use of government funds, and that accumulations of bancor would have to be absorbed into the Federal Reserve system, with, as they feared, explosive effects.

[13] The final version of the Stabilization Fund is reproduced below, Vol. III, pp. 83–96.

CONTRIBUTIONS

The outline of the proposed Articles in the April 1942 draft did not mention any formula to be used to calculate contributions, although a reference to one was made in the accompanying commentary. The first mention in the Articles came in the December 24 draft, where it appeared in a quite general phrase. Although by June 1, 1943, the U.S. Treasury had evolved the formula subsequently used, this was not incorporated in any of the drafts. Instead, these continued to quote a much simplified version, which by July 1943 became "e.g., a country's holdings of gold and free foreign exchange, the magnitude and the fluctuations of its balance of international payments, its national income, etc." (Sec. II, par. 4).

The provision that the member's initial contribution should be 50 per cent of its subscription was maintained in all drafts through May 1943. This initial contribution consisted normally of 12½ per cent in gold, 25 per cent in its government's interest-bearing securities, and the remaining 12½ per cent in the member's currency. If the member wished, it might contribute a larger proportion in gold, thus increasing its drawing rights. However, as noted earlier, White had agreed with Keynes in November 1942 that the gold contribution to be made by members might be reduced where appropriate. In the November draft this agreement was reflected in a provision that a country having less than $100 million of gold might pay 5 per cent (instead of 12½ per cent) of its subscription in gold, and a country having more than $100 million and less than $300 million of gold might pay 7½ per cent (instead of 12½ per cent) of its subscription in gold. With some later redrafting, this provision was retained until May 1943. From December 24 the subscription was called the member's quota.

The provision for the payment of the second half of the quota was as follows:

> The member countries . . . may be called upon to make further provision toward meeting their quotas pro rata at such times, in such amounts, and in such form as the Board of Directors of the Fund may determine, provided that the proportion of gold called for shall not exceed [one fourth], and provided that a four-fifths vote of the Board shall be required for subsequent calls to meet quotas.[14]

From June 1943 onward it was stipulated that the member's initial contribution was to be equal to its quota, and a somewhat complicated provision related the size of its gold contribution (up to a maximum of 50 per cent of quota) to the proportion which its gold reserves bore to its quota. The remainder of the quota was to be contributed in the member's own currency or (up to a maximum of 50 per cent of quota) in its interest-bearing securities.

No provision was made in the early drafts of the plan for changes in members' quotas, but in the December 16, 1942 draft it was provided that such

[14] April 1943 draft.

changes would require the support of 80 per cent of members' votes. In the draft of June 15, 1943, arrangements for the periodic review of quotas were included, and the stipulation as to 80 per cent of votes was attached to changes in the formula. Finally, in July 1943, it was provided that no member's quota could be increased without its consent (Sec. II, par. 7).

Throughout the whole period, the estimated aggregate of quotas was "at least $5 billion," of which the United States was expected to contribute $2–2½ billion, a sum related to the resources of the U.S. Government's Stabilization Fund, which consisted chiefly of the profit—about $2 billion—derived from the increase in the price of gold in 1934. The concern of U.S. officials that the obligations of the United States should not exceed that amount stemmed partly from the belief (later proved unfounded) that the resources of the U.S. Stabilization Fund could be subscribed to the International Stabilization Fund without fresh authority from the Congress, and partly from the belief of the U.S. monetary authorities that something like such a sum could be made available without unmanageable inflationary effects, whereas any substantially larger sum might produce such effects. It should be noted, however, that while the text of the plan continued to quote "at least $5 billion," a calculation of the effect of the proposed formula, handed to the British officials in Washington on June 13, 1943, showed a total of $10,064 million, the U.S. share being $2,929 million, that of the United Kingdom and colonies $1,275 million, and that of the U.S.S.R. $763 million.

Responding to a suggestion by the representatives of several countries, a paragraph was inserted in the July 1943 draft (Sec. II, par. 3 (*a*) (iv)) authorizing a member to include in its legal reserves the equivalent of its gold contribution to the Fund, less its net drawings.

Drawing rights

It will be recalled that, in the April 1942 draft of the Stabilization Fund, the country's right to purchase currencies from the Fund was limited by a provision that, after a purchase, the Fund's holdings of the drawing country's currency should not exceed its total contribution. Apparently as a result of White's discussions with Keynes, this provision was liberalized in December, although the Fund was permitted to require collateral against large drawings. Subsequently, the limits were progressively tightened until May, after which (presumably in response to protests from the other countries consulted) they were again relaxed. The final version (July 10, 1943) permitted the Fund's holdings of the member's currency to rise to 150 per cent of its quota in the first year and to 200 per cent in the second and subsequent years. Since the member's initial currency subscription was a minimum of 50 per cent of its quota, and might be more if its gold holdings were small, drawings were limited to a maximum of

100 per cent of quota in the first year and 150 per cent thereafter. The Fund was, however, authorized to restrict purchases by a member that was, in the judgment of the Fund, exhausting its quota more rapidly than was justified (Sec. V, par 2 (*d*)). On the other hand, drawings beyond the figures mentioned might be permitted on certain conditions, which included the deposit of collateral and the adoption of appropriate measures of reform by the member concerned.

In the draft of December 24, an explicit provision was introduced, recognizing a member's right to purchase currencies from the Fund "to the amount of its quota," subject to the "scarce currency" provisions noted below. However, by April 1943 this had become a recognition of such a right "only to the extent of its quota," and in the June 26 and July 10 drafts it was replaced by a mere statement that the member's right was limited by the "scarce currency" provisions (July, Sec. V, par. 5). Moreover, in the June 15 and subsequent drafts, the member's rights were further curtailed by a requirement that if its reserves exceeded 50 per cent of its quota, it should pay for half the currency bought from the Fund in gold or foreign exchange acceptable to the Fund (July 10 draft, Sec. V, par. 2 (*a*)).

The December 11, 1942 draft introduced for the first time a provision for a charge of 1 per cent per annum, payable in gold, on the excess of the Fund's holdings over the country's quota.

No provisions similar to the repurchase requirements, which later played so large a part in the Fund, emerged in this period. The only approach to these was a paragraph introduced in the December 16 and subsequent drafts by which each member country agreed that it would "offer to sell to the Fund for its local currency or for foreign currencies which it needs all foreign exchange and gold it acquires in excess of the amount it possessed when joining the Fund." In order to effectuate this, members would agree to discourage the unnecessary accumulation of foreign balances by their nationals. This obligation was modified in June so as to require the payment of one half of any increase in reserves, and in July so as to apply only if the member's reserves exceeded 25 per cent of its quota (July draft, Sec. V, par. 6). The Fund was free to accept or reject any foreign exchange offered to it. It was also provided in the second January draft and subsequently that the Fund might resell to a member country upon the latter's request any excess of the Fund's holdings of a member's currency above its quota (July draft, Sec. V, par. 7).

Scarce currency

When reporting to the Interdepartmental Committee on December 1, 1942, White had called attention to a paragraph in the November draft which would "make it easier for the Fund to use its assets to acquire needed foreign exchange." This, he said, warranted the relaxation of limits on drawings mentioned above.

The paragraph in question enabled the Fund to reinforce its holdings of a currency that it needed after such holdings dropped below 15 per cent of the member's quota and after the Fund had expended on purchases of the currency (1) as much gold as the country had originally contributed, and (2) the 25 per cent of its quota contributed by the country in interest-bearing obligations. Thereafter, the Fund had "the authority and the duty to render a report to the country" analyzing the causes of the reduction in its holdings, forecasting the balance of payments of the country, and setting out recommendations designed to increase the Fund's holdings. This report was to be made public and members were to agree that their governments would give immediate and careful attention to the Fund's recommendations. In May 1943, the criterion of 15 per cent was supplemented by requiring the prescribed action to be taken if the Fund's holdings became "excessively small in relation to prospective acquisitions and needs for that currency," and in the June 26 and July 10 drafts the latter became the sole determinant (Sec. V, par. 4).

A curious feature of the provision described in the preceding paragraph was that (until June 1943) it was to operate "when the Fund's holdings of any particular currency drop below 15 per cent of the quota of that country," although (also until June) the member's initial contribution of its own currency was normally limited to 12½ per cent of its quota. The seemingly most likely explanation, that "currency" included the equivalent of the securities which a member contributed, does not seem to tally with the implication that holdings could drop below 15 per cent before "the Fund has used for additional purchases of that currency [the gold and securities contributed]." Possibly in drafting this provision it was assumed that, before it was used, members would have completed the subscription of the whole of their quota, although, as noted above, the provision for the payment of the balance was somewhat restrictive.

In the December 16 draft, the foregoing arrangements were reinforced by the "scarce currency" clause. This provided that, when it appeared to the Fund that its holdings of a particular currency were likely to be exhausted, the Board of Directors should propose a method for the equitable distribution of the Fund's holdings of that currency. It was to make every effort to increase the supply of the scarce currency by acquiring it from member countries, and the rights of members to purchase this currency were to be limited by a rationing arrangement. Apart from drafting changes, these provisions remained unaltered through July 1943 (Sec. V, par. 5). The British reaction to these proposals is described below.

The origin of the scarce currency clause is somewhat mysterious. It was not mentioned at any contemporary meeting of which the record has been preserved. Specifically, it was not among the points made by White in an exposé of the draft dated December 16, 1942, at a meeting of the official committee held by

Secretary Morgenthau on the previous day. However, the climate of opinion in U.S. official circles at that time seems to have been such that the scarce currency provisions may have emerged as a natural precaution against a future scarcity of dollars. One indication of this is that a *jeu d'esprit* among U.S. officials produced the spelling "$carce ¢urrency." More seriously, the Department of Commerce's study *The United States in the World Economy*, which was at that time in draft, includes several passages like the following:

> It would be tragic indeed if the United States . . . were to permit another abrupt fall in the supply of dollars to disturb the recreated international trading and financial mechanism, whether willfully through increased trade restrictions, carelessly through the misbehavior of foreign investment, or involuntarily through the improper functioning of the domestic economy.[15]

In a discussion with Australian representatives on May 15, 1943, the U.S. officials explained that they did not expect rationing ever to be necessary as, in their opinion, such a situation would indicate that the Fund had failed to achieve its objectives.

Exchange rates

The original conception of the Stabilization Fund was that exchange rates would be fixed by the Fund (April 1942 draft, par. II.2.c.).[16] To this, the November draft added a provision limiting changes in exchange rates to those essential to correct a fundamental disequilibrium, and requiring the consent of 80 per cent of members' votes. As late as May 1943, the conception was still that the Fund would fix and alter exchange rates, as was stated in Question 11 of "Replies to Questions on the International Stabilization Fund," dated May 1943. However, in the June 15 draft, this proposal was substantially modified. Initial exchange rates were to be based on those prevailing seven months before the Fund came into operation, subject to the Fund having power to call for a reconsideration of this rate if it was "clearly inappropriate," and subject to special provisions for countries occupied by the enemy. Changes were to be "considered" only to correct a fundamental disequilibrium and would require the concurrence of 75 per cent of members' votes; special consideration was again given to countries occupied by the enemy.

In the June 26 and July 10 drafts, the provisions for initial rates were loosened; they were to be based on the value of the currency on July 1, 1943, subject to adjustment by consultation between the member country and the Fund if this rate was judged "clearly inappropriate" by either party (Sec. IV, par. 2 (*a*)). Provisions for changing rates were left substantially unaltered from the June 15 text, except that during the first three years of the Fund's operation changes

[15] Hal B. Lary and associates, *The United States in the World Economy*, U.S. Bureau of Foreign and Domestic Commerce, Economic Series, No. 23 (Washington, 1943), p. 25.

[16] Below, Vol. III, pp. 42, 60.

might be made "at the special request" of the member with the approval of a majority of votes (Sec. IV, par. 5 (*a*)). Also, any member might change its exchange rate by not more than 10 per cent after consulting the Fund on the advisability of this action (Sec. IV, par. 5 (*b*)). This last was a concession to the British view that greater elasticity in changing exchange rates was necessary. The philosophy behind the changes in June and July was spelled out in the September 15, 1943 edition of *Questions and Answers on the International Stabilization Fund:* "The Fund proposal recognizes the special interest of a country in its own exchange rate and provides that a change in the exchange value of a currency shall require the approval of the country concerned" (Question 17).[17]

Management

The provision in the April 1942 draft for an operating committee was dropped in the November draft, but reinstated in the December 11 draft in the form of an Executive Committee of not less than 11 members. The Executive Committee was to be continuously available at the head office of the Fund and to exercise authority delegated to it by the Board of Directors (i.e., the governing body comprising a representative of each member country). Each member of the Executive Committee was to have an alternate to act in his absence. The Board was to appoint a Managing Director and one or more Assistant Managing Directors. The Board was to hold an annual meeting and such other meetings as might prove desirable.

The provisions for voting were amended in the December 11 and later drafts to limit the votes of any one member to 25 per cent (after May, 20 per cent) of the total (July 10 draft, Sec. VI, par. 2). In the June 26 and July 10 drafts, arrangements were introduced to weight the votes of creditor countries more heavily, and those of debtor countries less heavily, than their basic voting entitlements when deciding requests for drawings. Also, when voting to suspend or restore membership, each country could cast only a single vote (Sec. VI, par. 3).

❖ ❖ ❖

Except for the points mentioned above, the provisions of the April 1942 text continued largely unchanged, drafting alterations excepted. A preliminary paragraph detailing the purposes of the Fund, similar to that which had introduced the April 1942 draft, reappeared in January 1943—although the words used were less expansive than in the previous year—and an explanatory preamble

[17] For the final version (June 10, 1944) of the U.S. commentary, entitled *Questions and Answers on the International Monetary Fund,* see below, Vol. III, pp. 136–82. Question 17 is on pp. 155–57.

was added in the June 26 and July 10 drafts. The somewhat elaborate provisions dealing with blocked balances continued to be included. In the second January and the April and May drafts, however, the word "blocked" was temporarily replaced by the words "abnormal war." This was a British suggestion, prompted by a fear that the use of the word "blocked" might encourage countries to restrict balances in order to qualify them for funding. In June and subsequently, the text reverted to "blocked balances."

The only other noteworthy changes related to the duties of member countries. That of avoiding defaults on external obligations was transferred, in and after the December 11, 1942 draft, to the plan for an International Bank. At the same time the requirement that export subsidies should be discarded was deleted from the text. In the next draft the obligation to remove trade barriers was similarly dropped. The reason for these two omissions appears to have been that planning for trade liberalization was a matter for the State Department and not for the Treasury.

* * *

Out of the flux of changes described above, certain minimum requirements for U.S. participation gradually crystallized. In the view of the Interdepartmental Committee, four stipulations would have to be accepted if congressional approval for any monetary plan was to be obtained. These conditions, as expounded by White to members of the staff of the British Embassy in Washington at a meeting on June 23, 1943, were as follows: (1) the United Kingdom must not alter its exchange rate until after the Fund had begun operations (later interpreted as requiring the exchange rate for sterling to be fixed at $4=£1); (2) the commitment of the United States must be limited to $3 billion as a maximum, and it might have to be limited to $2 billion; (3) the Fund must be based on initial subscriptions from its members and not on the principle of bank overdrafts; and (4) the United States must be able to veto any proposal to change the value of the dollar or of unitas.

EVOLUTION OF THE KEYNES PLAN

In contrast to the extensive redrafting of the Stabilization Fund which took place between April 1942 and July 1943, only minor changes were made in the Keynes Plan from the draft (the fifth) which had been sent to Secretary Morgenthau in August 1942. Most of these changes emerged from consultations with representatives of Australia, Canada, India, New Zealand, and South Africa in London on October 26–29, 1942. At this conference, Keynes expounded the Clearing Union proposals, which he explained as having been designed to meet the four difficulties confronting any plan to tackle postwar problems:

(1) What was to be the source of the capital required? The Clearing Union short-circuited this by not requiring any.

(2) How were credit facilities to be shared out? The Clearing Union related them to the value of foreign trade in a recent period; it was not obvious that other, more complex, criteria would give better results.

(3) What was to be the "self-righting" element in the scheme? This was the most difficult problem; creditors needed to be disciplined, but, in order to attract them into the scheme, the pressures that might be exerted could only be slight.

(4) What was the code of good conduct proposed and how far would national sovereignty have to be surrendered? The Clearing Union proposed a somewhat far-reaching code of conduct, including eschewing bilateral currency arrangements and competitive depreciations, but did not involve any great surrender of sovereignty since no country could be forced to join the Union.

At the same conference, Sir Frederick Phillips reported that his discussions with U.S. officials had revealed fears that the open-ended obligation to provide credit, involved in the Clearing Union, might have an inflationary effect in the United States, with adverse results on the dollar. The conferees considered whether this problem might be met by limiting to the equivalent of the creditor's quota the amount of bancor which a creditor must accept, but feared that this might lead to a lack of confidence in bancor as the creditor approached the point at which bancor would no longer be acceptable. Another possibility considered was to require the Union, at the request of a creditor, to pay off the excess balance in gold or in the currencies of debtors in proportion to the debtors' debit balances. Neither of these proposals, however, was adopted.

The minor changes actually made in the next draft of the Clearing Union (dated November 9, 1942) presumably reflected Keynes' discussion with White, who had returned to Washington by November 3. But these changes were also clearly directed to the problems discussed at the conference with the Dominions. They included a separate section on the liabilities which the plan should place on creditor countries, leading to the conclusion that these liabilities lay entirely within the countries' own control. Several minor changes strengthened the Union's ability to deal with an inflationary situation, including powers (1) to limit charges on creditors and increase them on debtors; (2) to require collateral on drawings exceeding 50 per cent of quota; (3) to declare a country in default if it failed to take action to reduce a debit balance which was "increasing at an excessive rate"; and (4) to reduce quotas if an inflation threatened.

On receiving the January 1943 draft of the White Plan, Keynes made a detailed comparison between his plan and White's. He suggested that "from a practical point of view the most important questions under the Stabilization Fund are the nature of the provisions for exchange control, the adequacy of the quotas, and the workability of the proposed solution for dealing with scarce currencies."

A tabulated analysis of the main features of the two schemes, which he included in his survey, shows that in his mind the important advantages of the Clearing Union were its expansionist bias and its ability to bring pressure to bear on creditors. It shows also that he expected conditions in the postwar world to require the universal use of exchange controls.

Keynes concluded that, when it was decided which of the alternative provisions in the two schemes were preferable, the framework of either scheme could be used to set out the result. Later, he commented that the Stabilization Fund scheme "represents a big advance, and if it turns out that it is the sort of set-up which appeals to people, it will not be too difficult to make something of it. . . . The main point at the present stage is that America should get itself committed to some scheme." In May he was reported to be planning to prepare a version of the Stabilization Fund which he thought would be reasonably satisfactory.

Keynes had some difficulty in knowing whether the scarce currency clause in the Stabilization Fund proposal could be taken seriously. His first idea was that rationing of this kind would be unworkable, but in a letter dated April 12, 1943 to a correspondent who had called attention to the clause, he said, "It is of course absolutely essential to the logic of the scheme. For under the American plan clearly a currency can become scarce, and some answer must be produced to the question what one then does about it. . . . If it really is a proposal to limit and ration American exports, it is, of course, of the highest significance." But he wondered whether the full meaning of the proposal had been appreciated in the United States. It is perhaps noteworthy that Mrs. Joan Robinson, who had close intellectual links with Keynes, called attention in the summer of 1943 to an inconsistency between the provisions of the "scarce currency" clause and the emphasis elsewhere in the White Plan on the removal of restrictions and discrimination.[18]

Meanwhile Keynes' Plan, which had been reprinted unchanged in February 1943, underwent further (and final) redrafting in preparation for its publication as a White Paper in April.[19] Two features of the earlier drafts disappeared, viz., the concept of founder-States with special privileges, and the emphasis on members' unimpaired rights to trade restrictions, export subsid[illegible] etc. The former was replaced by a provision that members' quotas governed their responsibility for management as well as their access to the Union's resources; the latter by a demonstration that the Union was not incompatible with the retention of

[18] Joan Robinson, "The International Currency Plans," *Economic Journal*, Vol. LIII (1943), p. 167. See also below, pp. 58–59.

[19] Reproduced below, Vol. III, pp. 19–36. Professor Dennis Robertson stated on August 26, 1943 that the Keynes Plan was still being revised, but that no new version had been published (*Economic Journal*, Vol. LIII (1943), pp. 352–53). I have been unable to trace any draft of a revision subsequent to the printed version in April 1943.

exchange control. Two additional provisions were that members not directly represented on the Governing Board might appoint permanent delegates to watch their interests, and that the Union's resources might not be used for long-term or medium-term loans.

After the publication of the two plans in April, Keynes continued to study the Stabilization Fund proposals, analyzing them in memoranda dated April 16 and 27 and June 22, 1943, and comparing them with the Clearing Union in a speech in the House of Lords on May 18, 1943.[20] When the July draft of the Stabilization Fund became available, he produced further memoranda, dated July 19 and 26, which were the basis for an official submission to Ministers, seeking instructions for the delegation which was to visit Washington in September.

The principal conclusions which Keynes reached may be summarized as follows:

(1) The main feature of the Clearing Union was that it provided for multilateral clearing, and it was a defect of the Stabilization Fund that it failed to do so.

(2) Postwar conditions would make it necessary to provide countries with international reserves; however, it was possible that the quantum suggested in the Clearing Union—equal to 75 per cent of prewar exports plus imports—was too large and should be somewhat scaled down.

(3) Another essential was to combine penalties for improvidence by debtor countries with discouragement of hoarding reserves by creditors.

(4) An international currency, such as bancor or unitas, was essential.

(5) It was not timely to provide for the absorption of blocked balances by the Union or the Fund.

He would also have wished to see the "overdraft" principle of the Clearing Union maintained, but, after Sir Frederick Phillips had explained that this was completely unacceptable to American opinion, he abandoned this.

Of these conclusions, the Chancellor of the Exchequer, speaking in the House of Commons on May 12,[21] had stressed in particular the fourth, but emphasized that, because unitas was exchangeable for gold and vice versa, its introduction would constitute a nearer return to the gold standard than would the introduction of bancor, which was obtainable for gold but for which gold could not be obtained.

The stress laid by the Chancellor and by Keynes on the need for an international currency may be traced to fears that the possession by the Stabilization

[20] *Hansard,* House of Lords, 5th Series, Vol. CXXVII, Cols. 527–37.

[21] *Hansard,* House of Commons, 5th Series, Vol. 389, Cols. 645–62.

Fund of supplies of countries' currencies would lead to its dealing in these currencies in exchange markets. Keynes commented that

> it is true that it [the Stabilization Fund] would only deal with Central Banks and not with the public. But it would exercise its discretion whether or not to accept or to supply particular currencies. It would purchase only those currencies which it decided (on no clear criterion) to be "in good standing" and (also on no clear criterion) the sale of which "is required to meet an adverse balance of payments predominantly on current account"; and it would ration scarce currencies. . . . Such a system could be so worked as seriously to jeopardise the international position of sterling.

The phrases quoted by Keynes in this comment were taken from the July 10, 1943 draft of the Stabilization Fund, Sec. V, pars. 1 and 2. The expression "in good standing" appeared in that draft for the first time, but must have been under consideration in Washington considerably earlier, because on May 17, 1943, British Treasury officials there, having inquired into its meaning, cabled to London that it signified the currency of a country "e.g., which had not drawn as much as 25 per cent of its quota." In the same cablegram the use of the word "predominantly," first inserted in the draft dated May 8, 1943, was explained as a concession to the Canadian view that it would not be practicable to limit drawing rights to adverse balances on current account, as had been proposed in the earlier drafts.

The decision not to accept the American proposal to absorb blocked balances into the Fund appears to have been reached at quite a late stage. Keynes pointed out that the Stabilization Fund proposals, although they purported to throw half the responsibility for paying off the balances in annual installments onto the country owning the balances, did not in fact do so. The United Kingdom would, in effect, have to foot the bill for this half as well as for its own half of the annual payments, since the sterling repurchased by the owning country would be *free* sterling in its hands, which it could immediately change for some other currency. Moreover, the disproportion between the blocked balances and the quotas under the Stabilization Fund, which at first he had welcomed as largely expanding the resources to be made available, came later to trouble him. He was afraid that the effect would be to increase the risk that the Fund would run short of scarce currencies. Nevertheless, in his view, the scheme provided a means whereby the sterling balances could be funded on easy terms, and in his memorandum of June 22, 1943, he commented that "something of this kind seems to me an indispensable feature of the Stabilization Fund."

Official British opinion, however, viewed the matter differently, and at the Treasury Sir Wilfrid Eady preferred to "consider the problem of the abnormal war balances separately and in a different context." Consequently the delegation to Washington in September 1943 was instructed "to go slow until we know more precisely what the financial conditions of the postwar period would be."

By June 1944, Keynes and Sir Wilfrid were jointly expressing the view that "it was essential for the United Kingdom that this problem should not be within the jurisdiction of an international body, but should remain for discussion and settlement between the United Kingdom and [the creditors]." They gave the significant reason that otherwise "convertibility of sterling might be indefinitely delayed." As will be seen in Chapter 5 below, this was the line adopted by the British delegation at Bretton Woods. What had apparently happened was that the British Government had come to the conclusion that there would have to be a "Grand Assize" after the war, in which war debts would be pooled, and in the course of which the blocked balances would be scaled down,[22] as was in fact provided for in the Anglo-American Financial Agreement in 1945.

Looking at the U.S. proposals as a whole, the British officials concluded, and advised Ministers, that the four stipulations made in June 1943 (see above) should be accepted, together with the proposals in the White Plan for quotas and voting power. On the British side, the minimum requirements for which the delegation must press should be as follows:

1. The Fund must not buy or sell currencies, but only transfer unitas in its books.
2. The initial subscription must include a small proportion of gold and the remainder in securities negotiable only in the event of default, withdrawal, or liquidation.
3. The size of the Fund must be adequate (e.g., $10 billion).
4. Member countries must not be deprived of reasonable facility to alter their exchange rates if they thought this necessary.

The directive to the delegation, in addition to covering these points, also provided that:

5. The aim should be to agree with the U.S. officials on a clear statement of principles, which should be remitted to Ministers for consideration before being given to a drafting committee.
6. The blocked balances should be excluded from the scheme.

Such were the terms of reference with which Keynes and his colleagues sailed for Washington early in September 1943.

[22] See E. F. Penrose, *Economic Planning for the Peace* (Princeton and London, 1953), p. 55.

CHAPTER

3

The Joint Statement (1943-44)

ON SEPTEMBER 13, 1943, Keynes had a conversation with Secretary Morgenthau about the Anglo-American talks on the White and Keynes Plans, then about to begin. Keynes said that he expected that these talks would lead quickly to the appointment of a committee, to be selected from among all the United Nations, to draft an agreed plan. However, the Chancellor of the Exchequer had promised to permit Parliament to debate the question before any proposal for the Fund took final form. Keynes therefore hoped that the United States would agree to some statement of general principles for Parliament to use as a basis for debate.[1]

From September 15 through October 9, 1943, nine meetings on the plans were held in Washington between a U.S. group, headed by White, and a British delegation, headed by Keynes. These meetings formed part of a wider series, covering also proposals for postwar international investment, commodity policy, and commercial policy, all arising from Clause VII of the Lend-Lease Agreement. Those on the monetary plans, described below, took as their starting point the July 10, 1943 draft of the Stabilization Fund (and the summary version of it, dated August 19), the published version of the Clearing Union, and the Canadian Plan. The outcome of the meetings was the first draft of what became the Joint Statement by Experts on the Establishment of an International Monetary Fund. This title for the Fund was not, however, adopted until the end of January 1944, being suggested by London in a cablegram on January 22, 1944 and accepted by White some time between then and January 29 (the date of the tenth draft of the Joint Statement, prepared by the United States).

THE PROTAGONISTS

Each of the two groups of officials represented several different organizations. On the U.S. side these included the Treasury, the Department of State, the Board of Governors of the Federal Reserve System, the Department of Commerce, the

[1] John Morton Blum, *From the Morgenthau Diaries: Years of War, 1941–45* (Boston, 1967), p. 243.

Office of Economic Warfare, the Reconstruction Finance Corporation, and the White House. The British delegation represented the Treasury, the Bank of England, the Board of Trade, and the Economic Section of the War Cabinet Secretariat. The officials participating on both sides of the table were highly qualified to discuss the issues that arose, and many of them had long been steeped in just these issues. Yet there is no doubt that White and Keynes dominated the discussion, which indeed was for much of the time a dialogue between them.

What sort of men were these, who could monopolize negotiations of such high technical quality? How did they regard each other? The meetings in Washington in the autumn of 1943 constituted their first prolonged confrontation. It is important for an understanding of these negotiations, and of others that followed over the ensuing two and a half years, to appreciate the characters of the two principals.

Keynes has been fortunate in his biographer. From the pages of Harrod's *Life* [2] he emerges as the natural aristocrat, who could charm his hearers with his courtesy and understanding and yet could wield a rapier wit. Of his intellectual abilities, no further evidence is needed than the revolution in economic thought engendered by his *General Theory*,[3] which has altered government policies throughout the world. He was equally zestful and equally effective as lecturer, as conversationalist, as governmental advisor, and as patron of the arts. However, he was not an ideal negotiator: at times he "did not wholly appreciate political difficulties in Washington";[4] his approach to purely administrative problems was often too broad and general to satisfy Civil Service responsibilities on either side of the Atlantic; and he was disposed on occasion to disregard instructions with which he disagreed. He could be impatient, stubborn, and blind to the pain caused by his frequently impish, and sometimes intolerant, comments. Yet the final impression made on all who knew him was that he stood head and shoulders above most of his contemporaries. In 1943 he was 60 years of age.

White could in many ways have scarcely been a greater contrast. Nine years younger than Keynes, and without corresponding initial advantages, he was aggressive, domineering, and ambitious; the descriptions of those who worked with him tend to ring the changes on the word "difficult," but all pay tribute to his immense driving power.[5] His intellect was powerful; his ideas imaginative, but not flexible. He was no theorist, but essentially a pragmatist. In argument he wielded not the rapier but the bludgeon. He tended to exploit to the full a

---

[2] R. F. Harrod, *The Life of John Maynard Keynes* (London, 1951).

[3] John Maynard Keynes, *The General Theory of Employment, Interest, and Money* (London and New York, 1936).

[4] E. F. Penrose, *Economic Planning for the Peace* (Princeton and London, 1953), p. 43, note.

[5] Blum, *op cit.*, p. 90. See also Harrod, *op. cit.*, p. 557.

position of strength—such as that which he occupied during the International Monetary Fund negotiations by reason of Secretary Morgenthau's reliance on him and because the financial help of the United States would clearly be essential in the postwar world. But he could be considerate, even genial, and on occasions showed extreme patience with those less conversant than himself with the subject under discussion. Above all, he expected no one to work harder than he did himself, and these qualities enabled him to inspire and dominate for a decade a team of U.S. advisors of high caliber and intellectual achievement.

The relationship between the two men was a curious combination of respect and exasperation.[6] As already noted, they had met in 1935, when White consulted Keynes (among many others) about a possible monetary agreement. On later occasions, Keynes was often infuriated by White's truculence and intransigence, and by the diffuseness of his memoranda; but he came increasingly to recognize the strength of White's intellect. White had a grudging though genuine admiration for Keynes' ability, but he never entirely got over an antipathy to Keynes' intellectual brilliance and his wit. On at least one occasion, a duel between the two momentarily degenerated into open hostility; later, their mutual respect blossomed and they fraternized with every appearance of enjoyment.

Both men were continuously aware of the problem of converting their ideas into legislative action. Keynes sought from an early stage so to frame his plan as to justify it to the British Parliament and public; his successive drafts were consciously written to persuade, and, while he was inclined to be scornful of the intellectual quality of those who opposed his proposals, he spared no effort to build up a convincing case, using to the full his effective literary style and his oratorical opportunities. White's private attitude toward Congress showed a marked irreverence for its quirks,[7] but he was equally alive to the need to satisfy the congressional legislative conscience. Because the effective way of doing this was by question and answer in congressional hearings, the successive drafts of his plan show much more effort devoted to remedying possible defects in its structure than to expounding the proposals with literary skill.[8]

Two anecdotes may serve to illustrate some of the difficulties that arose between the principals in the Washington talks and also the more genial rela-

---

[6] Richard N. Gardner, *Sterling-Dollar Diplomacy* (Oxford, 1956), pp. 111–12. Blum, *op cit.*, p. 243.

[7] "Imaginary Hearings on Gold Before the Senate Committee on Banking and Currency" (May 1937), and "Imaginary Hearings Before the Special Senatorial Committee on Silver" (February 1939), in Princeton papers, Box 2, Files 7 and 8. Both were written by White for Secretary Morgenthau. A quotation from the 1939 document (p. 19) will give its flavor: "SENATOR SHIPSTEAD: If the gentleman from Utah would spend less time with Greek mythology and more with current monetary history, I suspect he would think that silver had less the aroma of nobility than of pork. As I read the history of our silver program, Senator, it smells to heaven. . . ."

[8] Jacob Viner, "Two Plans for International Monetary Stabilization," *Yale Review*, Vol. 33 (1943–44), pp. 77–107. The reference is to p. 83.

tions established between other members of the two groups. On one occasion, in a moment of exasperation at receiving a long U.S. draft which purported to meet the British points but was in fact a mere restatement of the U.S. position, Keynes exclaimed, "This is intolerable. It is the Talmud all over again. We had better simply break off negotiations." White, replying in kind, said, "We will try to produce something Your Highness *can* understand." On that note the discussion was adjourned, but it was smoothly resumed later in the day, on production of a revised U.S. document. On another occasion, Keynes was moved to complain of the somewhat tortuous language necessary to express the operations of the Stabilization Fund in a "mixed bag" of currencies, compared with the simplicity of operations in bancor. "I prefer not to speak in Cherokee," he said, "when I can use good Christian English." A day or two later, Mr. Edward M. Bernstein, who was White's deputy at the discussions, was dining with two of the British delegation. He took the opportunity to embroider on Keynes' remark a tale of two Indian tribes, the Choctaws and the Cherokees, who had joined in invoking the Great Spirit for assistance in a common disaster. After each had spoken, the Choctaw leader commended the respectful language in which the other tribe had made its appeal, but commented that it seemed strange that the Great Spirit should be expected to understand an appeal made in Cherokee. The story was received by the British officials with delighted approval.

AGREEMENTS AND DISAGREEMENTS

The discussions in Washington in September–October 1943 covered some fourteen points on which there was a difference of view between the United States and the United Kingdom. The significance of these points varied quite widely, a few reflecting a fundamental cleavage of outlook in the two countries, but more arising only from opposing ideas about the appropriate technical methods of achieving agreed aims.

In fact, agreement was reached at the meetings on only half a dozen of these topics, and the continuing differences between the U.S. and British views on the remainder were reflected at the end of the meetings in alternative drafts for what was to become the Joint Statement by Experts. As will be seen in later sections of this chapter, all but one of these unresolved issues were settled by discussions between U.S. and British officials before the major international conferences in June and July 1944, from which emerged the Articles of Agreement of the International Monetary Fund. The remaining one continued to be a subject of dispute between the two countries even after the Fund had started operations.

The questions which were settled in Washington in September–October 1943 are summarized in the following paragraphs.

Form of statement to be produced

Although the discussions were nominally based both on the Stabilization Fund and on the Clearing Union, it rapidly became the practice to cite paragraphs from the Stabilization Fund proposals. As was noted in the previous chapter, Keynes had realized months earlier that the major objectives of the Clearing Union could equally be achieved under the form of the Stabilization Fund and, as the meetings now under discussion progressed, it became clear to him and to the rest of the British delegation that the eventual draft would have to be in Stabilization Fund terms. As a result, Keynes gave notice at a meeting on October 6 that he would produce a draft for an agreed statement cast in the form of proposals for a stabilization fund, though reserving—a point noted more in detail below—the problem of the role to be played by unitas. On the following day he produced the draft, which was then revised three times by the U.S. officials. Their third version formed the basis for a final meeting on October 9, when the differences of view of the two groups were clarified. From that meeting emerged a fifth draft—this time prepared by the British—giving alternative paragraphs for the matters still in dispute.

Size of quotas

The second point on which agreement was reached was the aggregate of quotas. The Stabilization Fund draft still showed a total of $5 billion. Keynes suggested contributed quotas totaling $8 billion and borrowing quotas totaling $12 billion (as in the Canadian Plan), but he recognized the force of a U.S. argument that a total of borrowing rights in excess of contributions would be incompatible with the U.S. need to limit its commitments to $2-3 billion. As soon, therefore, as White stated that the United States was thinking in terms of an aggregate of $8.5 billion for the countries forming the United and Associated Nations (equivalent to an estimated $10 billion for the world as a whole), Keynes accepted this proposal.

Rationing

In July 1943, Professor Kyriakos Varvaressos, the Greek envoy in Washington, had sent to White a memorandum appraising the Stabilization Fund proposals, in which he emphasized their weakness in relation to persistent creditors. He pointed out that the scarce currency proposals prescribed only action by the Fund; they said nothing about the responsibilities of the member whose currency was declared scarce, nor about the duties of others toward that member. A copy of this memorandum reached Keynes at the end of July, and he appears to have been impressed by it. When the proposals for dealing with a scarce currency were considered on September 29 and October 4, he argued that the apportionment of a currency by the Fund must release all members from their obligations in regard to that currency. In particular, no member should be obliged to continue to draw on its gold reserve in order to settle balances with the member whose currency was scarce. After discussion, it was agreed that the declaration that a currency was scarce would operate to permit all other members temporarily to introduce exchange restrictions against the member concerned. The Canadians had been unsuccessful in persuading U.S. officials to agree to this, and Keynes later telephoned to Professor Varvaressos, congratulating him on the acceptance of his criticism.

Changes in value of unitas

The original U.S. proposal had been that a change in the gold value of unitas would require 85 per cent of members' votes, thus of course giving the United States a veto. This proposal lost its importance with the decline in the significance of unitas, and the U.S. officials made no difficulty about an alternative provision, substituted by Keynes, that a change in the value of unitas would require an 80 per cent vote or a majority vote which included every member whose votes exceeded 10 per cent of the total. This equally achieved the U.S. objective.

Withdrawal

The right of the Fund to require a member to give notice of its wish to withdraw was linked in the early part of the discussion with the member's ability to change its exchange rate, inasmuch as withdrawal was regarded as its remedy for a refusal by the Fund to allow a devaluation. As the discussion proceeded, however, it became clear that it was not practicable to tie an unwilling member to the Fund, and it was agreed that a member should be permitted to withdraw without restriction.

Currencies to be drawn

The April 1943 and earlier drafts of the Stabilization Fund provided that the Fund might sell to member A the currency of member B only if A had a debit in its balance of payments with B. As Keynes observed, this meant that the Stabilization Fund failed to provide for multilateral clearing. In June 1943, Professor Dennis Robertson had pointed out in discussion with U.S. officials that it was possible for A to require the currency of B to settle a balance of payments debit with C, even though its balance of payments with B was favorable. As noted in the previous chapter, this had been met in July by amending the relevant clause to read "to meet an adverse balance of payments predominantly on current account with any member country" (July 10 draft, Sec. V, par. 2 (*a*)). However, in the same draft, a different qualification was introduced: the currency offered to the Fund had to be "in good standing" to be acceptable by the Fund (Sec. V, par. 1). This was criticized by both British and

U.S. officials at the meeting on September 17, and did not reappear in the Joint Statement.

CONVERGENCE OF VIEWS

The version of the Joint Statement which emerged at the close of the Washington discussions in September–October 1943 formed the basis for a series of redrafts. The sixth draft was sent by White to Keynes on November 19, 1943. On December 18, Keynes sent to Washington two drafts, the seventh in terms of unitas (the last in which unitas was mentioned) and the eighth without unitas. During January and February 1944, the Statement was redrafted three times in Washington. A final text was produced on April 4, 1944, and published.[9] In the course of these revisions, agreement was reached on seven points of difference between the views of the two countries: four in December 1943, two in February 1944, and one in April 1944. A brief outline of these problems follows.

Gold subscriptions

The British delegation had come to Washington with the intention of pressing for a gold subscription not exceeding 12½ per cent of the quota. This represented not only British views about the need to conserve London's gold reserves but also the feelings of other European countries who had been sounded out on the matter and felt even more strongly that in the postwar period they must have an adequate gold reserve in their own hands. However, it became clear that the U.S. counterproposal of a gold subscription equivalent to 25 per cent of quota or 10 per cent of gold reserves (whichever was the smaller) would have very much the same effect so far as the United Kingdom was concerned, and this proposal was accepted in December.

Sterilization of contributions

Another point which the British representatives pressed was that the contributions made by member countries to the Fund, whether in gold or in securities, should be "pledged," i.e., should not be at the free disposition of the Fund for purposes of dealing. Partly, this was a reflection of the mistrust felt in London at the prospect of the Fund dealing in markets, a subject which is discussed in more detail below. Keynes also argued, however, (1) that members would wish to know that the gold which they subscribed to the Fund could be recovered, for example, in liquidation, and (2) that it was undesirable that a country's securities should be available for sale or for use as collateral in another country. On the first point, the U.S. delegation argued that the Fund must have gold at its disposal, not only to strengthen it but also to enable it to obtain

[9] Reproduced below, Vol. III, pp. 131–35.

members' currencies when needed. On the second point, agreement was reached on substituting holdings of nonnegotiable, noninterest-bearing government obligations for holdings of securities. On further reflection, the United Kingdom agreed in December to accept the U.S. view about the need for the Fund to be able to use its gold.

Changes in exchange rates

It will be recalled that, from the beginning, the United Kingdom had been anxious to ensure that the rules of the Fund should not preclude its changing its exchange rate in circumstances of such difficulty as arose in 1931. The British officials were content with the latest U.S. proposal for determining initial exchange rates, but they thought that the U.S. draft went too far in removing a member's sovereign right to change its rate, and did not provide for appropriate machinery for discussing in the necessary secrecy proposals to make such a change. Keynes, therefore, submitted to the meeting a four-part proposal, as follows: (1) Members would agree not to propose changes in their exchange rate except to deal with fundamental disequilibrium. (2) The Fund should not withhold approval of any changes which did not in total exceed 10 per cent in each ten years. (3) When considering other proposed changes, the Fund should take into account costs of production, balances of payments, and reserves. It should not take notice of a country's social or political policies. (4) If it was impossible for a member to take the time to obtain the prior approval of the Fund, a member might change its rate by not more than 10 per cent after consulting the Chairman and seek the Fund's approval later. If this approval was refused by a majority vote, the member might either cancel the change or withdraw from the Fund.

This proposal was put forward at a meeting on September 15. The first part was accepted without difficulty, but the others were questioned. U.S. officials disliked the apparent precision of the criteria in the third part of the proposal and there was a general discussion on whether it would be possible to devise an objective test by which the appropriateness of a devaluation might be calculated. Sections of British opinion favored the substitution of such a test for the discretion of the Fund, particularly in the Fund's early years, when it would not yet have gained adequate experience. Keynes was, however, opposed to the idea, and the conclusion reached in the discussion was that an objective test would be impracticable. A fortnight later, when the subject recurred, a new point arose: might a member devalue its currency vis-à-vis a scarce currency? The U.S. answer was that the member might ration the use of the scarce currency, and it was, consequently, unnecessary to devalue against it.

On October 4, the U.S. delegation put forward a counterproposal to deal with the situation discussed in the second and fourth of Keynes' original ideas. This was that a member should have the right once to change its rate by an amount not exceeding 10 per cent, and a further right to require the Fund to decide within 48 hours on a proposal to change the rate by not more than a further 10 per cent. White suggested, however, that, if the Fund refused permission for this further change, the member would have to give six months' notice of its wish to withdraw.

Keynes then asked whether it would not suffice for the member to consult the Fund rather than obtain its approval? But the U.S. answer was that their proposal already represented a large concession compared with the original conception of the Stabilization Fund—a concession perhaps greater than U.S. public opinion would accept—and Keynes' counterproposal would irretrievably weaken the Fund. As mentioned above, the proposal to require six months' notice of withdrawal was subsequently abandoned. At a later meeting, Keynes proposed again that the right to change the exchange rate unilaterally by 10 per cent should be renewed every ten years. At first, White was inclined to accept this, but on the following day decided it was not feasible. The final draft, therefore, showed two alternative proposals for changes in exchange rates—one transcribing the U.S. proposal of October 4 and the other, Keynes' counterproposal for a right renewable each decade. On further consideration, however, the United Kingdom decided in December not to press the latter point.

Gold payment for drawings

In the June 15 draft of the Stabilization Fund, a requirement had been inserted to the effect that a member holding gold and free foreign exchange to an amount greater than half its quota should pay for one half of any exchange bought from the Fund with gold or acceptable foreign exchange. At the meeting on October 4, Keynes suggested that the provision should operate only if the member's reserves were twice as large as its quota. The U.S. group decided to offer to increase the minimum size of the member's reserves from 50 per cent of its quota to 100 per cent of its quota. In the fifth draft of the Joint Statement, which was agreed with alternative provisions, the U.S. suggestion was included, the British version being altogether silent on the requirement. In December, however, the United Kingdom decided to accept the U.S. proposal. In the printed version, the requirement was expressed in terms of holdings of gold and gold-convertible exchange; if these exceeded the member's quota, the member was required to pay in gold for one half of any drawing (Clause III. 7 *(b)*).

Drawings for capital purposes

Throughout the Washington meetings the two parties were agreed that the Fund should not be used for long-term investment purposes, although the formulations suggested were somewhat dissimilar. After some clarifying discussions, the difference of view was narrowed to the supervision to be exercised by the Fund over the member. The U.S. version in the fifth draft stated that the provision excluding use for capital purposes was "not intended to interfere with transactions which do not involve a substantial requirement of foreign exchange, or transactions required in trade, banking, and other business." The British version, after stating that the Fund might ask a member to exercise controls over capital movements, continued that the provisions of the draft Statement were "not intended to prevent the use of the Fund for capital transactions of reasonable amount *approved by the member country's control as being required* in the ordinary course of trade, banking and other business, or for the expansion of exports" [italics supplied]. A final proviso stated that it was not intended to prevent capital movements met out of a member country's own resources. This comparatively narrow issue was debated in discussions between U.S. and British officials for a considerable period; but it was eventually settled in January by accepting the U.S. version, with the addition of the final British proviso qualified by the words "provided such capital movements are in accordance with the purposes of the Fund."

Repurchase provisions

The draft of the Stabilization Fund which was discussed at the meetings in Washington provided that a member must offer to sell to the Fund one half of any increase in its reserves, provided that these reserves were larger than one fourth of its quota in the Fund.[10] At the beginning of the meetings, Keynes made a counterproposal that the member should be obliged to pay over the increase in its reserves, provided that these reserves exceeded its quota and provided that it had drawn on the Fund during the preceding year. The U.S. officials agreed to this formulation, provided that the reserves were defined as covering gold and free foreign exchange. But Keynes insisted that the reserves should be counted only to the extent that they included gold and gold-convertible currency. The draft of the Joint Statement which emerged from the meetings included alternative formulations. That for the United Kingdom provided that if at the end of the Fund's financial year a member's holdings of gold and gold-convertible exchange had increased, the rules of the Fund might require the member to employ the whole or part of the increase to repurchase from the Fund any excess of the Fund's holdings of its currency above the member's quota. The U.S. version obliged the member to pay over half the increase in its reserves, provided that these reserves were adequate and that the Fund's holdings exceeded the member's quota.

Subsequently, the U.S. officials had second thoughts and, on November 19, they proposed that the obligation should apply if the Fund's holdings of a member's currency were not less than one half of that member's quota. In a

---

[10] Draft dated July 10, 1943, Sec. V, par. 6; below, Vol. III, p. 91.

revision of the draft Joint Statement sent to White in December, Keynes repeated the British view that the obligation should apply only if the member's reserves were greater than its quota, if the Fund's holdings were not less than its quota, and if the reserves were defined in the same way as elsewhere in the draft, i.e., net of liabilities. Thus defined, the United Kingdom's net reserves were almost certain to be less than its quota, unless and until its currency liabilities were reduced. (A plan to fund these formed part of the Anglo-American Financial Agreement, but was never brought to fruition.)

On January 7, 1944, White sent to Keynes a revised proposal, limiting the obligation to cases where reserves were not less than the quota and the Fund's holdings not less than 75 per cent of quota. He resisted the concept of net reserves, but was prepared to accept the term "gold-convertible" currency. In discussion with British representatives in Washington in February, this text was agreed, although correspondence about its exact significance continued for some time longer. It may, however, be pointed out that British officials subsequently discovered that no currency in the world could, in the strict sense, be called "gold-convertible," and by the time of the Bretton Woods Conference the corresponding concept had become "convertible" currency, a term specially defined in the Articles themselves, as discussed below.

Monetization of unitas

One apparently fundamental difference between the two countries' officials concerned the proposed international currency, called by Keynes "bancor" and by White "unitas." It has been seen above that for Keynes this would have been a true medium of exchange, in which loans would have been made by the Clearing Union, but that for White it was no more than a standard of value, which could be discarded without impairing in any way the working of the Stabilization Fund.

At the outset of the discussions in Washington, Keynes put forward a memorandum in which he sought to imbue unitas with the qualities which he had proposed for bancor. His motives for this proposal were complex; they included (1) concern that the Fund should be "passive," in the sense that it should not deal in exchange markets, (2) the consideration that a contribution made in gold by a central bank to the Fund would seem to involve a loss of reserves to that bank, (3) the advantage that the holder of unitas could utilize the credit anywhere rather than having a claim against an individual country, and (4) a belief that the structure of the Fund could be more simply and understandably stated in terms of unitas than of a "mixed bag" of currencies. The first and second of these motives were implied in the instructions that the delegation had received. While these instructions were based on a memorandum that Keynes himself had written, he cited in it views other than his own which were strongly held in London.

Keynes' proposal was resisted by the U.S. officials, who suggested that the British, "unable to secure the redistribution of real gold, proposed to create a substitute out of thin air." They agreed, however, that the Fund should be "passive" in the sense indicated above, and that this position should be indicated by requiring the Fund to act only on the initiative of the member. (A consequence of this agreement was the omission from the Joint Statement of the provision in the White Plan empowering the Fund, inter alia, to buy, sell, and hold gold, currencies, etc.) On Keynes' second point, they argued that the remedy was for the central bank to amend its bookkeeping procedures; the real effect of the transactions between the Fund and the central bank would be the same whether unitas was used or not. While not admitting the third and fourth points, they countered that the effect of Keynes' proposal would be the same as that of the Clearing Union itself, namely, to expand the U.S. commitment beyond its contribution.

It appears that by the end of the Washington meetings Keynes had been persuaded—as indeed other British officials had earlier been persuaded—that the difference between the formulation of the Fund with and without unitas was not of fundamental importance. Nevertheless, official opinion in London continued to be concerned at the dangers of entrusting the Fund with members' currencies, and when putting forward the British proposals at the end of the Washington meetings in a form not based on unitas, Keynes expressly stated that this was done to meet the convenience of the U.S. Treasury and in no way committed the British representatives to accept that form. Early in January 1944 the British Embassy in Washington made a fresh attempt to persuade White to accept a version in terms of unitas, but without success; White was convinced that it would be impracticable to approach Congress with a proposal which would be tantamount to a surrender of sovereignty by measuring the value of the dollar not in gold but in terms of an international currency over which the United States would not have control.[11]

The issue remained open throughout February and March, the difficulties for the British officials being that it was regarded as so fundamental a point that Ministers would have to decide it; that it was not thought possible to put it to Ministers except in the context of an over-all review of the problems arising under Clause VII of the Lend-Lease Agreement; and that in the spring of 1944 the war was creating such pressures upon Ministers that no time could be found for such a comprehensive review. However, the U.S. Government became

[11] According to Blum (*op. cit.*, p. 247), "the British opposed any reference to White's Unitas, because they were defined in terms of grains of gold." This indicates a misunderstanding. It was the United States that opposed the use of unitas. See H. D. White, *Some Notes on the Articles of Agreement of the International Monetary Fund*, May 1946 (Princeton papers, Box 10, File 27), p. 28. The British objection was to the definition of currencies exclusively in terms of gold.

increasingly desirous of publishing the Joint Statement, which clearly could not be done until the matter of unitas had been settled, and in mid-April the decision was reached in London that the non-unitas version of the Joint Statement could be accepted.[12]

It was not, however, without considerable misgivings that Ministers so decided. Despite the agreements reached between Keynes and White, certain features of the Joint Statement continued to cause concern in London; in particular, the consideration that, while the Fund was theoretically to be passive, the provisions of the Statement in its non-unitas form did not effectively preclude the Fund from dealing in sterling in a way which could be disadvantageous to the sterling area. It was also feared that the proposal to fix the gold value of sterling and to limit the United Kingdom's right to change this value might seriously restrict the country's freedom of action in certain eventualities, and that the obligations of convertibility, applied to sterling balances, would be unmanageable.

Before agreeing to support the Joint Statement, therefore, the British authorities instructed Mr. Redvers Opie, who was then Financial Advisor to the British Ambassador in Washington, to send to White a letter setting out the understandings on which the United Kingdom was willing to proceed. There were three of these, all amounting to emphasizing that the commitments embodied in the Joint Statement would not apply to the transitional period. The first understanding was that the Fund was designed for operation in the long term, and would need to be supplemented by other organizations to provide for reconstruction and development; the second, that it should begin to operate by stages, deferring the use of the quotas until it had gained experience; and the third, that the United Kingdom would not commit itself to accept the Fund until it saw how the difficulties of the transitional period were to be met.

On these understandings the Joint Statement was published in Washington on April 21 and in London on the following day.

How far did Keynes feel able to support the Joint Statement in its final form? It would seem from his speech in the House of Lords on May 23, 1944 that he had no hesitation in backing it wholeheartedly.[13] He commended it then as being in some important respects a considerable improvement on both the White Plan and his own Clearing Union. He saw in it five major advantages: the transitional period; the prospect subsequently of benefiting from the general obligation of convertibility; the addition to reserves afforded by the quotas; the scarce currency clause; and the permanent institution to be set up. He called attention also to members' right to control capital movements, and to the fact that the Fund would have the duty to approve changes in exchange rates that

[12] Explanatory Notes prefixed to the British print of the Joint Statement, pars. 1 and 2; below, Vol. III, pp. 128–29.

[13] *Hansard*, House of Lords, 5th Series, Vol. CXXXI, Cols. 838–49.

were required to make these rates conform to the needs of domestic policies. In this last respect, he said, "these proposals are the exact opposite of the gold standard."

We have no similar means of discovering White's personal feelings about the Joint Statement, but the official U.S. view may be learnt from Secretary Morgenthau's speech to a group of congressional committees on April 21, 1944, and from a press release issued by the Department of State on the following day. In both these pronouncements the Joint Statement was warmly commended, but the features of it picked out for comment were not those on which Keynes laid stress. On the one hand, both Secretary Morgenthau and the Secretary of State emphasized, and indeed somewhat exaggerated, the collaborative aspects of the plan. "Under the leadership of the Treasury Department," the State Department's press release stated, "technicians of this and 30 other countries have worked out a set of basic principles with which all these technicians are in substantial agreement."[14] On the other hand, both Secretaries urged that the prospect of achieving stability of the exchanges was the most significant promise of the new plan. "Through international cooperation now," Mr. Morgenthau said to the members of Congress, "we can assure a stable and orderly pattern of postwar exchange rates."[15]

Neither Keynes nor the Secretaries made reference to the one remaining issue left open by the publication of the Joint Statement: the degree of conditionality to be attached to drawings from the Fund. This problem, which remained an issue even after the Fund had started operations, proved to be of such major importance for the Fund's work that it is necessary to study its evolution in detail. The following is an attempt to elucidate the position reached in June 1944.

RIGHT TO DRAW

It will be recalled that both the Clearing Union and the Stabilization Fund proposals provided for a quantitative limit on drawings. In the December 1941 draft of the Clearing Union, this limit was put at 25 per cent of quota per annum; above 50 per cent of quota, the permission of the governing body was needed; and there was a top limit of 100 per cent of quota. In the Stabilization Fund proposals, the limits for permissible drawings varied from draft to draft; by the date of the meetings in Washington (September–October 1943), they had settled at maxima of 100 per cent of quota in the first year and a further 50 per cent of quota thereafter. The Canadian Plan provided for drawings not exceeding 50 per cent of quota annually, with a maximum of 200 per cent of quota. All parties therefore agreed on the need for a quantitative limit. They also

[14] *Department of State Bulletin*, Vol. X (1944), p. 371.

[15] *Federal Reserve Bulletin*, Vol. 30 (1944), p. 437.

agreed that the right to draw should be modified appropriately if a currency was declared scarce. There was, however, a major difference of view between U.S. and British officials about the extent to which access to the Fund's resources, within these limits, needed the permission of the governing body.

On October 26, 1942, Keynes, commenting on the Clearing Union Plan at the meeting with representatives of the Dominions, had said that "it was obviously necessary that some limitation should be placed on the right of individual countries to obtain credits," but made no reference to any limitation other than quantitative. Several months afterwards, the Chancellor of the Exchequer, speaking in the House of Commons, referred only in quantitative terms to the need to apply pressure to debtors.[16] Keynes, in his speech in the House of Lords a week later, touched only briefly on the subject. He said that his plan "provides in such case for consultation and advice. . . . There remains in the background . . . the severe penalty of depriving the improvident country of any further facilities." [17] By this time, however, the views of the U.S. officials, discussed below, were becoming known, and more positive expressions of distrust in any restriction other than quantitative began to appear. The Australian representatives who discussed the Stabilization Fund proposals in Washington in May 1943 neatly summed up their view by claiming that "member nations are to give up vital sovereignty in exchange for rights, not privileges." British officials took the same line. For example, Professor Robertson, in a speech on August 26, 1943 at a conference in Chicago (at which White was present), said:

> The Clearing Union Plan contains provisions—if they are not thought stiff enough they can be stiffened up—for limiting the size of the cushion which any country can obtain. But having obtained its cushion, great or small, every country, under the Plan as it stands, can use it with complete confidence—there is no question of its cheque being returned to it as non-acceptable.[18]

This quotation fairly reflects the attitude with which the British delegation entered on the Washington discussions. As early as the second meeting, Keynes argued that, if drawings were to be policed from the start, no country would have any certainty as to its position. He thought that there should be no policing until a country's drawings were equivalent to its quota.

We may turn now to consider the attitude on the U.S. side. The first mimeographed draft of the Stabilization Fund (April 1942) contained two long paragraphs (below, Vol. III, pp. 49–50), of which the gist was that the Fund was to judge whether a member's transactions were "illegitimate," so as to deprive it of access to the Fund's resources. A year later, in discussions with the Australians, White stressed that some countries might attempt to use the

16 *Hansard*, House of Commons, 5th Series, Vol. 389, Col. 657 (May 12, 1943).

17 *Hansard*, House of Lords, 5th Series, Vol. CXXVII, Col. 530 (May 18, 1943).

18 D. H. Robertson, "The Post-War Monetary Plans," *Economic Journal*, Vol. LIII (1943), p. 358.

resources provided by the Fund as a source of long-term capital, and it would be necessary to prevent such misuse of the Fund's resources. The point was driven home with the comment that some individual countries might not be fully capable of appreciating their own long-term interests. In August 1943, at a meeting at the Federal Reserve Board in Washington, White said that there was no intention to continue to provide exchange to countries attempting to maintain an unbalanced position. When, therefore, the problem arose in the second meeting between the United States and the United Kingdom in Washington, White stated that the United States wished the Fund to exercise control over drawings from the very beginning. He added that this should not be difficult to administer since, for the most part, policing would consist merely of watching the situation.

He gave a number of examples of the kind of criteria for such supervision which he had in mind. The Fund's facilities should not be used to finance either a flight of capital or the issue of foreign loans by a country which could not afford to undertake foreign lending. Again, the Fund would be justified in intervening where a country was using its quota for rearmament. On the other hand, it would not be justified in the case of an unbalanced budget. In general, the Fund would intervene only in extreme cases of violation of qualitative rules, and would bear the burden of proof.

At the third meeting of the two groups, at which White was not present, Mr. Bernstein proposed that the Fund might make a firm commitment to supply a limited amount of foreign exchange within a given period (say, six months), to be renewed at the Fund's discretion halfway through the period. The Fund should have discretion to refuse to renew the commitment if its resources were being abused.[19] Mr. Bernstein has since described the proposal as permitting the Fund to enter into stand-by agreements with its members.[20] The suggestion was rejected by Keynes on two grounds. He thought that it would induce members to use up their recourse to the Fund as rapidly as possible in case it might not be renewed.[21] And he argued that Mr. Bernstein's proposal seemed to cut at the root of the confidence which it was the real function of reserves to give.[22] Sympathy with the latter view was expressed by other members of the U.S. delegation, who thought that no great country would submit to the sort of scrutiny which Mr. Bernstein had suggested, and that this was the reason for relying on arithmetical limitations to drawings.[23]

---

19 British minutes of meeting on September 24, 1943. The U.S. minutes do not mention the Fund's discretionary power, nor that it should renew the commitment halfway through the period.

20 *Washington Post*, June 5, 1968, p. D-9.

21 U.S. minutes of meeting; the British minutes do not mention this reason.

22 British minutes of meeting; the U.S. minutes do not mention this reason.

23 British minutes of meeting. These statements are not reported in the U.S. minutes.

The subject was taken up again at a meeting on October 4. The British and U.S. minutes of this meeting do not differ substantially, except in one respect noted below; however, the British version is here used in order to make clear what the British delegation thought the U.S. offer was. Keynes said that the United Kingdom had accepted the limitation of drawing rights to 25 per cent of the quota a year. He had also agreed that if members broke the rules, they should be denied facilities, and that the Fund should have discretion to refuse a drawing if the member had exhausted two thirds of its maximum drawing rights. He thought, however, that this should be the full extent of the Fund's power to intervene. (The reference to two thirds appears to relate to Keynes' original proposal that quotas for borrowing purposes should be 50 per cent greater than contributions.)

The minutes then record White as replying that the U.S. group considered the Fund's facilities were a privilege, not a right, and the misbehavior of the member should therefore entail withdrawal of the privilege. Nevertheless, he (White) appreciated the British point, that confidence in the availability of the Fund's resources was an essential condition of the proper functioning of the scheme. He said that the U.S. group therefore proposed that (1) all members should be free unconditionally to obtain currencies from the Fund up to the extent of their gold subscriptions; (2) thereafter, until the Fund's holdings of their currencies equaled 150 per cent of their quotas, the Fund should have the right to refuse to accept more than a further 25 per cent of their quotas (over a 12 months' notice period); (3) when the Fund's holdings of their currencies exceeded 150 per cent of quotas, the notice period would be reduced to 6 months and the further currency acceptable to the Fund would be reduced to 12½ per cent of the quotas. He added that the grounds for a curtailment of drawings would be an unwise use of the Fund's resources, e.g., a use far in excess of a country's seasonal need. In the U.S. note of this meeting the word "seasonal" does not occur. White is there quoted as stating the grounds for giving notice to a member, so as to limit its drawing rights, to be "firstly, the rate at which a country uses the resources of the Fund, and secondly, using the Fund's resources in a manner that clearly has the effect of preventing or unduly delaying the establishment of a sound balance in its international accounts." This latter formula reappeared in a U.S. draft of the relevant clause in the Joint Statement, as will be seen below.

To this exposition Keynes replied that he thought that there was only a remote chance that his authorities would accept White's proposal; major countries would not tolerate an inquisition of that kind. Some sympathy for this view was again expressed by members of the U.S. group, and White said he would revise the proposals. He did not, however, have an opportunity to do so until after the first draft of the Joint Statement had been prepared by Keynes. In this draft, the fourth general purpose of the Fund is stated to be "to give confidence to member countries by the provision of actual and potential support." The only limitations on drawing rights proposed were quantitative, viz., 25 per cent of quota per annum until the Fund's holdings reached 200 per cent of quota. Keynes, however, added a parenthetical clause, reading: "It is for consideration whether a member shall be required to conform to any other appropriate conditions for the use of the Fund."

The counterproposal by the U.S. group, embodying White's promised redraft, limited the Fund's holdings of a member's currency to 125 per cent of quota during the first year, 150 per cent during the second, 175 per cent during the third, and 200 per cent thereafter. Since the gold subscription proposed by the U.S. draft was not to exceed 25 per cent of quota, this counterproposal was tantamount to fixing a maximum drawing in the first year equal to 50 per cent of quota. The U.S. draft then went on to provide, following White's comment on October 4, that a currency offered in exchange for a drawing would be accepted by the Fund "if the Fund has not previously given notice that a member country is making use of the Fund's resources at an unwarranted rate or in a manner that clearly has the effect of preventing or unduly delaying the establishment of a sound balance in its international accounts." The general purpose corresponding to that quoted above from the British draft was expressed as "to facilitate the correction of maladjustments by the provision of actual and potential support to member countries."

These drafts were considered at meetings on October 8 and 9, as a result of which an agreed final text, giving alternative versions, was prepared. Both were concerned to define the "acceptability" of a currency, i.e., the extent to which the Fund would accept a member's currency in exchange for others that the member wished to draw. The relevant provisions were as follows:

<table>
<tr><td></td><td>(ii) A currency is acceptable:</td></tr>
<tr><td>U.S. Statement</td><td>(a) If at the time the currency is tendered to the Fund the member country represents that the currency demanded is presently needed for making payments in that currency which are consistent with the purposes of the Fund.</td></tr>
<tr><td></td><td>(b) If the Fund's total holdings of the currency of the member country have not increased by more than 25 per cent of the quota during the previous twelve months, and if they do not exceed 200 per cent of the quota; and</td></tr>
<tr><td>U.S. Statement</td><td>(c) If the Fund has not previously given notice of 6 months to a year which has expired that a member country is making use of the Fund's resources in a manner that clearly has the effect of preventing or unduly delaying the establishment of a sound balance in its international accounts.</td></tr>
<tr><td>U.K.</td><td>[Add to the above] The Fund will not give notice if its holdings of the member currency do not exceed 166 per cent of its quota.</td></tr>
</table>

Of these clauses, (b) was acceptable to both the United States and the United Kingdom, but (a) and (c) were U.S. formulations, of which the latter was acceptable to Keynes only if the proviso was added.

The importance of this difference of view was of course fully recognized. Keynes included it in a summary of "reserved passages of importance," which he sent to London by cablegram on October 14, as a question "whether Fund should be given powers in extreme cases to discipline a country's use of Fund's facilities before it has exhausted two thirds of such facilities." The other outstanding differences, discussed above, were noted in the same cablegram, to which Keynes appended a comment as follows: "Americans have made large concessions to our views. In our opinion most of remaining differences can be resolved without excessive difficulty or our giving away what we consider essential." In a letter to Professor Viner, written four days later, Keynes elaborated on the issue of the freedom to borrow unconditionally from the Fund. He wrote:

> This is one of the matters on which we have not yet reached final accommodation. Our view has been very strongly that if countries are to be given sufficient confidence they must be able to rely in all normal circumstances on drawing a substantial part of their quota without policing or facing unforeseen obstacles. Indeed, we have been inclined to think, on second thoughts, that the Clearing Union may have been too strict on this, though this was actually balanced under the Clearing Union by the much greater size of the quotas. If the Clearing Union provisions were applied to the lower quotas now contemplated, we gravely doubt whether those concerned, particularly some of the smaller countries, would feel adequate confidence. . . . I am sure that it would be very unwise to try to make an untried institution too grandmotherly.

It should be noted particularly that in the clause quoted above, the first condition for a currency being acceptable to the Fund is that the member "*represents* [italics supplied] that the currency demanded is presently needed for making payments. . . ." This has sometimes been interpreted as implying that the Fund would automatically accept such a representation. It would appear, however, from the terms of Keynes' cablegram, and of his letter to Professor Viner, that he did not so understand it. Certainly the U.S. delegation did not: at a meeting of the U.S. technical group at Atlantic City on June 25, 1944, when the meaning of the words "the member represents that" was discussed, White remarked that it should be possible for the Fund to say that a country was mistaken in saying that its reason for requesting exchange from the Fund was consistent with the purposes of the Fund.

On December 18, 1943, Keynes accepted the U.S. draft of the clause, subject only to "wider and less specific definition of the criterion on which the Fund is entitled to act." Accompanying this was a new draft of the Joint Statement, prepared by the United Kingdom, in which the provisions were again completely redrafted without affecting their sense. They now became par. 4 (2). Briefly summarized, they authorized a member to draw from the Fund, provided (*a*) that it represented that it had a need consistent with the purposes of the Fund; (*b*) that the currency asked for had not been declared scarce; (*c*) that the Fund's holdings of the currency offered had not increased by more than 25 per cent during the previous 12 months, and were not over 200 per cent of quota; (*d*) that the Fund had not "previously given appropriate notice that the member is suspended from making further use of the Fund's resources on the ground that it is making use of them in a manner contrary to the purposes and policy" of the Fund.

The only question raised on drawing rights, when this draft was discussed in Washington between U.S. and British officials, concerned the provision for half-payment in gold where a member's own holdings were as large as the quota—a matter discussed above (page 62). This may have been partly due to the fact that the British draft of December provided for the first time a text covering the "Transitional Arrangements," for which previously only a *pro memoria* note had been inserted. Subsequent discussions in Washington tended to concentrate on this new section, and on an argument about the definition of "net official holdings."

Meanwhile, pressure was building up from the U.S. side for a decision on the question whether the United Kingdom would abandon its insistence on the use of unitas (see above, page 66). In consequence, Sir David Waley of the British Treasury, who was then in Washington, prepared on January 17, 1944 a submission to Ministers recommending the acceptance of the Joint Statement. In the course of this, he commented as follows on the question of drawing rights:

> We lose part of our freedom to alter the exchange rate and thus to some extent our internal policy for maintaining maximum production and full employment may be prejudiced by our obligations under the scheme. In return we, *so long as the Fund thinks we are behaving reasonably*, [italics supplied] obtain a credit in dollars or other needed currencies, until these currencies become "scarce." Thus we cannot count for certain on any precise amount of facilities and have given up part of our birthright for a mess of potage [*sic*] which is likely to disappear from the menu just when our appetite is keenest.
>
> But, despite these inevitable limitations, the Stabilization Fund scheme is surely far better than no scheme at all. . . . The Stabilization Fund scheme provides Member States with considerable reserves and thus does a good deal, at any rate, to facilitate a policy of expansion when that policy is needed to avoid a slump.

Some apparent conflict between the sense of the first and second paragraphs quoted above does not eliminate one's impression that for Sir David, at any rate, access to the Fund's resources was regarded as conditional on the Fund's approval. Mr. Opie, who handled the negotiations with White after Sir David returned to London later in January, has confirmed this view, and has stated that he himself had no doubt that the United States would insist on their proposal to "police" drawings.

This situation makes it the more surprising that, on January 26, 1944, Keynes drafted for Ministers a report on the Currency Plans, in which he wrote, inter alia:

> The American representatives had set out in their Stabilization Fund with quite a different conception of the functions of the new institution. In their eyes it should have wide discretionary and policing powers and should exercise something of the same measure of grandmotherly influence and control over the Central Banks of the member countries, that these Central Banks in turn are accustomed to exercise over the other banks within their own countries. This was a rather one-sided conception, for it would only have applied in practice to member countries making use of the Fund's facilities for assistance, whereas the Americans conceived that they themselves would be strong enough never to apply for such aid. Thus the Fund would have powers of supervision over the others which would never apply in the case of the United States.
>
> In the course of discussion, however, the American representatives were persuaded of the inacceptability of such a scheme of things, of the undesirability of starting off by giving so much authority to an untried institution, and of the importance of giving the member countries as much certainty as possible about what they had to expect from the new institution and about the amount of facilities which would be at their full disposal. In the final draft, therefore, all the matters at issue, except one, have been in the end settled to our satisfaction.

The outstanding matter was the use of unitas, which was later disposed of as mentioned above.

Keynes evidently felt, however, that the provision for the transitional period embodied in the Joint Statement meant that the problem was not an immediate one. He explained this to the representatives of the Dominions and India at a conference in London on March 15, 1944:

> It was essential that the Fund should not be waterlogged at the start by having to meet abnormal short-term needs with resources which would be inadequate, simultaneously for that purpose and for the long-term functions of the Scheme. It was a question for further examination with other countries whether the Scheme should further define the conditions in which access to the facilities of the Fund was postponed. For example, it might be held that so long as a country was not accepting the obligations of multilateral convertibility . . . it should not draw upon its quota. . . .
>
> The point had not been fully discussed with the Americans, who might be thinking of the free use of quotas from the outset. Personally he thought this would be a mistake. . . . It did not seem expedient to press the point with the Americans at this stage, especially as the views of other countries on such a matter would have to be considered.

In the event, the only step apparently taken vis-à-vis the U.S. officials was to embody a reference to the postponement of drawings in the letter sent by

Mr. Opie to White, on instructions from London, immediately before the publication of the Joint Statement. And the only change actually introduced in the relevant clause was to stipulate that the limit of 25 per cent per annum should not begin to apply until the Fund's holdings of the member's currency, if below 75 per cent of quota, had been raised to 75 per cent.

Finally, the Explanatory Notes prefaced to the British print of the Joint Statement by Experts commented on the relevant clause (which by now had become III.2) as follows:

> The proposals of the *Clearing Union*, to prevent a country . . . from drawing on the *Fund* too freely in conditions in which its own resources are adequate without drawing on the *Fund*, are worked out more fully in clauses III (2) and (7) but without difference of intention.[24]

(Clause III. 7 was the final version of the provision for half-payment in gold for drawings, discussed above.)

Meanwhile, the U.S. Treasury had been holding meetings with a delegation from the U.S.S.R., and the question of drawing rights had arisen several times in these meetings. The quantitative limits were questioned at meetings on January 3, January 11, and February 3, 1944, and at the second of these meetings the Soviet delegate asked whether the provision for notice to a member misusing the Fund's resources meant that a member could be refused access to these resources before it had exhausted its annual 25 per cent. White replied that this was so, but said that he thought the occasions on which it would be necessary to make use of this power would be rare. He added that this clause had been the subject of extended discussion.

The Soviet delegation again raised the question on March 13, apropos the sanctions that the Fund might exercise against a member that disregarded recommendations for action made by the Fund where the member was pursuing policies that the Fund considered would have undesirable international consequences. The U.S. officials pointed to the relevant paragraph, but emphasized that "there would have to be a clear case of a country's making excessive use of the Fund's resources before such conditions would be imposed."

❖ ❖ ❖

Any attempt to sum up from these indications the participants' beliefs in this matter of drawing rights, as they stood in June 1944, must be a hazardous one. It is necessary to try to reconstruct the states of mind of the principal participants. It seems safe to say that the U.S. view was that the Fund should have the right to prevent a country from drawing if it concluded that the member's policies were internationally harmful, although this right was unlikely

[24] Below, Vol. III, p. 130.

to be often invoked. This was primarily a U.S. Treasury view, and, as noted above, some hesitation about accepting it was originally shown by at least one other Department, but by the end of October 1943 it had become the agreed U.S. position.

The British view, on the other hand, seems to have remained a divided one. Officials who had been most closely in contact with the U.S. Treasury appear to have been prepared to accept that some such measure of supervision as the United States contemplated was a necessary price to pay for U.S. support of the Fund. But Keynes still hankered after a provision which would leave the Fund no discretion to reject a drawing within the agreed quantitative limits, i.e., for a provision—to take effect, at any rate, after the transitional period had ended—embodying what later became known as the "automaticity" of drawing rights. This idiosyncracy may well find an explanation in his personal qualities. In the first place, the right to draw without challenge had been a keystone of the British position, and Keynes may well have wished, as any negotiator might, not to let White "get away with it." Secondly, as has been suggested above, Keynes apparently failed to appreciate the importance that the U.S. group attached to arrangements that would satisfy congressional requirements of accountability. This may have hampered him from realizing the U.S. officials' need to satisfy Congress that the Fund could prevent an irresponsible drain on the supply of dollars with which it would have to operate, even though he specifically reported this motive for their proposals. Thirdly, Keynes' own instincts strongly favored the view, widely held in London, that the management of sterling could not be entrusted to an international body. After all, the Fund visualized by the Joint Statement would be under entirely different auspices from the Clearing Union, which was to have been under Anglo-American management, with its head office in London.

Some surprise may be felt that Keynes, feeling as he did, made no effort to secure a further amendment of the Joint Statement in this respect, before it was published in April 1944. A possible explanation is that the terms of the Joint Statement contained paragraphs acceptable both to the United Kingdom (Clauses III.2 (*a*) and III.2 (*c*), which concentrated on the right of the member to draw) and to the United States (Clause III.2 (*d*), which dealt with the right of the Fund to question a drawing), and that Keynes did not choose to press matters to a conclusion that might have been unfavorable to him.[25]

One other consideration remained in the background, although Keynes had given expression to it at the meeting in Washington on September 17. He then said that

> such discretionary rights as might be accorded to the Fund should be framed to distinguish between the case of a developed country managing its affairs prudently,

[25] See the second quotation from Keynes on p. 74.

so as to avoid recourse to the Fund, and that of an irresponsible small country anxious to exploit a new source of borrowing.

It may well have been the case, as the British delegation to Washington suspected, that underlying the position of the U.S. officials there was an even sharper dichotomy, stemming from the conviction that the United States, alone among potential member countries, would never be likely to draw from the Fund.[26]

On this ambiguous note we must leave the question. It will, however, arise again in the next two chapters, where we review the meetings at Atlantic City and Bretton Woods in which the Joint Statement by Experts was transformed into the Articles of Agreement of the International Monetary Fund.

DISCUSSIONS WITH U.S.S.R.

Before we finish with the period during which the Joint Statement was being redrafted, we should record the results of the discussions between U.S. officials and a delegation from the U.S.S.R. to which a brief reference was made in the preceding section. A Soviet official had participated in the meetings held with various countries in June 1943 (of which the outcome was summarized in Chapter 2, pages 33–36) but without elucidating the view of the U.S.S.R. on the Stabilization Fund proposals. From January 3 through May 10, 1944, however, a series of meetings took place in Washington between a formal Soviet delegation and members of the U.S. Interdepartmental Committee.[27] The first nine of these meetings, between January 3 and March 14, were concerned with the Fund; the later meetings with the International Bank for Reconstruction and Development.

The greater part of the meetings about the Fund were devoted to explaining to the delegation from the U.S.S.R. the origin and significance of various provisions of the Stabilization Fund and the Joint Statement. Toward the end of this series of meetings, however, the Soviet officials leveled a number of criticisms at the whole plan for the Fund, criticisms which are the more important as they may indicate the kind of consideration which moved the U.S.S.R. not to join the Bretton Woods organizations.

The Soviet delegation urged that gold contributions should be limited to 15 per cent of quota for all members, and that for occupied countries (including the U.S.S.R.) this proportion should be cut to 7½ per cent; that members should not be required to pay for 50 per cent of any drawings in gold, and that newly mined gold should be ignored in calculating a member's gold resources; that it

---

[26] See the first quotation from Keynes on p. 74.

[27] On these and subsequent discussions see Raymond F. Mikesell, "Negotiating at Bretton Woods, 1944," in *Negotiating with the Russians*, Raymond Dennett and Joseph E. Johnson, eds. (Boston, World Peace Foundation, 1951), pp. 101–16.

should not be obliged to "give consideration to the views of the Fund on any existing or proposed monetary or economic policy . . .,"[28] nor to provide any more information than was mutually agreed between it and the Fund; that the exchange rate of the ruble should not be controlled by the Fund (since the rate did not affect the competitive position of other countries); and that rubles made available in drawings should be used only to make purchases from the U.S.S.R.

It is perhaps desirable to put on record here that the U.S. officials accepted that the economic strength of the U.S.S.R. was inadequately reflected in a quota calculated according to the accepted formula, even though, in the absence of information about Soviet gold stocks, it was not possible to determine quite what that quota would have been. In the calculations made in the U.S. Treasury in June 1943, the quota of the U.S.S.R. was put at $763 million. However, in discussion with the Soviet delegation on March 13, 1944, White said that the U.S.S.R. could be assured of 10 per cent of the total of quotas, and somewhat less than 10 per cent of the total of votes. On the next day, he undertook that the U.S. delegation at the prospective international conference would support an increase of one third in the Soviet quota, and the quota negotiated at Bretton Woods was $1,200 million.

[28] Quoted from the July 10, 1943 draft of the Stabilization Fund proposals, Sec. VII, par. 6; below, Vol. III, p. 96.

CHAPTER

4

Atlantic City

(June 1944)

BY EARLY IN APRIL 1944 it appeared to Secretary Morgenthau that the time had come when interested countries should be invited to a formal conference on monetary cooperation. The President agreed, and on May 25, 1944 the Secretary of State dispatched invitations to 44 governments (including the French Committee of National Liberation) to send representatives to a conference at Bretton Woods, New Hampshire, beginning on July 1, 1944, "for the purpose of formulating definite proposals for an International Monetary Fund and possibly a Bank for Reconstruction and Development." At the same time, the Danish Minister to Washington, whose country could not formally participate since it had no government-in-exile, was invited to attend in a personal capacity.

THE SETTING

In addition to the full-scale conference at Bretton Woods, a limited group of countries was invited to send representatives to a preliminary drafting conference at Atlantic City in the second half of June. U.S. officials arrived there on June 15, 1944, and were joined four days later by about 30 technical experts representing 13 other countries. On June 23, 19 delegates arrived from Europe, having been delayed by "regulations imposed by the highest military authorities." D-day was June 6. Among those delegates were technicians from 3 countries that were not represented in the original group of 30 experts. When formal proceedings began on Saturday, June 24, therefore, 16 countries besides the United States were represented—Australia, Belgium, Brazil, Canada, Chile,

China, Cuba, Czechoslovakia, France, Greece, India, Mexico, the Netherlands, Norway, the U.S.S.R., and the United Kingdom.[1]

This drafting group was organized into four committees, as follows: Purposes, Policies, and Subscriptions; Operations of the Fund; Organization and Management; and Establishment of the Fund. Among them, they covered 21 topics that were expected to represent the agenda for the full conference at Bretton Woods. White's plan was that these committees should report daily to meetings of the full drafting group. They were provided with copies of the Joint Statement, and of amendments proposed by the U.S. officials partly based on a new draft prepared by Treasury lawyers. To these were added a series of alternative suggestions put forward by the representatives of the 16 countries, including several submitted by the British delegation from London as a result of four meetings with representatives of Belgium, China, Czechoslovakia, Greece, India, the Netherlands, Norway, and Poland, who had crossed the Atlantic on the same ship as the British group. (Poland was not, however, represented at Atlantic City.) Thus the conference was faced with a highly involved documentation.

Over the ensuing weekend, the secretariat prepared a combined draft in which the Joint Statement was reproduced in conjunction with the various amendments that had been proposed. This new draft was further added to over the next few days. It had been intended that the consolidated document should be reviewed, clause by clause, by the whole conference, of which White was elected chairman; any matters that proved too intricate for settlement in that way were to be referred to ad hoc subcommittees after sufficient discussion to make the sense of the conference clear. This was an ambitious program for a five-day meeting, especially as the last two days of it were to be devoted to the proposals for the International Bank. It is not therefore surprising that all that could be accomplished was to review some of the more important amendments, without attempting to reach a decision on them, and to remit almost all to the Bretton Woods Conference.

However, it had not been U.S. policy to offer a *fait accompli* at Bretton Woods, although White had hoped that before leaving Atlantic City he and Keynes would be able to reach agreement on many, at least, of the major issues, so as to achieve thereafter a common U.S.-U.K. front.[2] As will be seen, this hope was only partially realized, although on a number of important matters an agreed amendment was in fact put forward jointly by the two delegations at Bretton Woods. As none of the actual amendments were voted on at Atlantic City, and most of them reappeared, more or less unchanged, at Bretton Woods, it is unnecessary here to discuss the exact wording of the proposals.

[1] See J. P. Young, "Developing Plans for an International Monetary Fund and a World Bank," *Department of State Bulletin*, Vol. XXIII (1950), p. 786.

[2] John Morton Blum, *From the Morgenthau Diaries: Years of War, 1941–45* (Boston, 1967), p. 253.

FOREWARNINGS OF CONTROVERSY

On June 23, before the arrival of the delegations from London, White prepared a memorandum for Secretary Morgenthau which surveyed the criticisms of the Joint Statement that had been made by the original group of 30 experts. Their arguments, many of which have been referred to in the two preceding chapters, may be summarized as follows:

Quotas and votes

A number of countries—in particular, Australia, China, India, the U.S.S.R., and the United Kingdom—had expressed dissatisfaction with the proposals for quotas and votes. White recalled that the U.S. view was that quotas should not exceed $8.5 billion in all, that the U.S. quota should be $2.5–2.75 billion, that the quota for the United Kingdom and colonies should not exceed $1.3 billion, and that the quotas for the British Empire as a whole should be less than that of the United States. The proposal which had been put forward by the United States and Canada for voting strengths to be adjusted for decisions on drawings—adding to the votes of creditors and deducting from those of debtors—was expected to be troublesome. Australia, Belgium, and Mexico had sought to impose a limit of 20 per cent of total votes for any one member, as had been done in the final draft of the Stabilization Fund. The U.S.S.R. wanted a formula which would increase its votes at least to 10 per cent of the total, and decrease its contribution. Finally, the United Kingdom was suggesting a special method of voting in the Executive Committee, by which the United States would have 25 per cent of the total votes, the United Kingdom 20 per cent, the U.S.S.R. 15 per cent, China and France 10 per cent each, and four elected members, representing among them all other members, 5 per cent each.

Gold

The U.S.S.R. and others were seeking a reduction in the gold subscription from occupied countries. The U.S.S.R. wished to except newly mined gold from the obligation in the Joint Statement to use gold to repurchase currency. On the first of these points, White reminded the Secretary that, since a country's possible drawings would vary inversely with the Fund's holdings of its currency, the substitution of rubles for gold in the contribution of the U.S.S.R. would lessen its drawing rights. The United Kingdom was also raising questions about the gold contribution, seeking to reduce its obligation by offsetting liabilities expressed in gold against its gold assets.

Exchange rates

Several countries, especially some occupied by the enemy, were seeking to increase the flexibility provided in the Joint Statement for exchange rates and, in particular, to ensure that initial exchange rates should be provisional only. The U.S.S.R. had raised a somewhat novel point, arguing that, because the exchange rate of the ruble had no international significance, it should be free to change this rate without the approval of the Fund.

Pressure on creditors

Several countries, in particular Australia, were seeking to include provisions for bringing pressure to bear on creditors of the Fund as well as on debtors. This request was likely to be sharpened as a result of the U.S. proposals to impose a graduated scale of charges upon debtors, and White thought it probable that an attempt would be made to apply these charges to creditors also. He added that Canada believed that if the proposed charges were applied to countries that were indebted to the Fund, then penalties should also be applied to creditors. White was unable to see how the Fund could effectively penalize creditors.

Silver

Mexico, with the support of Bolivia, was pressing for silver to be joined with gold as a basis for Fund quotas and contributions.

VIEWS INTRODUCED BY UNITED KINGDOM

The arrival of the delegations from across the Atlantic showed that White had correctly assessed the nature of the most important issues to be thrashed out. He had not, however, foreshadowed all the problems that would be raised, nor was he, it would appear, entirely prepared for the intensity with which the newly arriving delegations would argue for the positions that they supported. What these positions were can best be seen by summarizing a memorandum submitted by the British delegation on its arrival at Atlantic City. This memorandum covered the views of all the delegations that had traveled from London. The most significant of the topics which it discussed were as follows:

Exchange rates

The British delegates thought it extremely important that members should be free to pursue desired domestic policies, even though these might have an effect on exchange rates; the delegation sought a more forthright statement of this independence in the Articles than had been included in the Joint Statement.

At a preliminary meeting to brief the delegation, the Chancellor of the Exchequer had intimated that

> the delegation should press for an overriding proviso reserving to a country, in case of necessity, the exercise of its sovereign rights over the parity of its exchange

in consultation with the Fund, subject to the right of the Fund at its discretion to suspend the member from continued use of the Fund's facilities if the Fund disagreed with the exchange policy proposed.

The British delegation from Washington had already attempted to meet this instruction by introducing an amendment which stipulated, inter alia, that "Nothing in the above provisions shall affect the right of members to modify their exchange rates as they may consider necessary or advisable." To this, as will be seen below, the U.S. delegation took strong exception, and after the arrival of the London contingent the British delegation withdrew the offending clause, but only after Keynes had said that he "hoped to be able to prepare a redraft which would be of help to the U.S. authorities in securing acceptance for the plan in America, whilst enabling the Chancellor to meet Parliamentary criticism." The problem had not been solved when the delegations left Atlantic City.

On a subsidiary issue, the British delegation suggested that if a member could not accept the ruling of the Fund about its exchange rate, the best remedy was not necessarily its enforced withdrawal from the Fund. This would mean that it would escape its obligations to the Fund; besides, the difficulty might prove to be only temporary. The United Kingdom therefore proposed to substitute suspension for enforced withdrawal in such circumstances, and put forward a new draft for the relevant section of the Joint Statement.

Gold-convertible exchange

It has been mentioned above that, in the British view, no currency could be strictly considered "gold-convertible." The delegates therefore proposed to substitute "convertible," to be defined in the Articles. In the same context, they wished to define "holdings" of currencies as the net holdings of official institutions. Thirdly, they criticized the requirement in the Joint Statement (Clause III.7 (*b*)) that a member with adequate reserves should pay for half its drawings in gold, pointing out that this could always be evaded by the member's drawing twice as much as it really needed. The delegates therefore proposed dropping this requirement, and concentrating on requiring the member to repurchase its currency if its position improved after the drawing.

Convertibility of currency

The British delegates saw a danger in the phrasing of the requirement in the Joint Statement (Clause III.5), that a member should buy any of its own currency held by another member with gold or that member's currency; this phrasing might be held to require the conversion of balances acquired in the distant past, whereas they thought it should be limited to amounts currently acquired, or at any rate needed for making current payments. A redraft was suggested to cover this point.

SANCTIONS

The British delegates suggested that stronger measures than those contemplated in the Joint Statement might need to be taken against a member that refused to abandon exchange restrictions when the Fund considered that it could do so. A draft Article providing in such circumstances for suspension of the member, or its forced withdrawal, was submitted.

TRANSITIONAL PERIOD

The British delegates were concerned about the reference to three years in Clause X.3 of the Joint Statement, which provided that after that lapse of time a member maintaining exchange restrictions should consult the Fund about their retention. It was feared that this might be taken to imply that the transitional period would last only three years, whereas the British delegation wished to emphasize that its duration was uncertain. Supporting the latter view, Keynes said that because of international, even more than domestic, developments it might well be impossible after three years for the United Kingdom to abandon exchange controls; he added that the Chancellor had assured Parliament that the United Kingdom retained its freedom in this regard. The delegation proposed that five years should be substituted for three years as the period after which members must consult the Fund about the retention of exchange restrictions; and that the duration of the transitional period itself should be left indefinite. However, the U.S. view that the transitional period should have a certain and reasonably proximate end remained unchanged, and the discussion was continued at Bretton Woods.

These proposals by the United Kingdom suggested to White that there was some rough sailing ahead. In a further memorandum to Secretary Morgenthau, dated June 25, he reported on them, and commented as follows:

> 1. The British want to increase the flexibility and ease of alterations of exchange rates. We think we should not budge one bit.
>
> 2. They are advocating changes in the direction of making the resort to the resources of the Fund much more automatic and a matter of right as compared with our view that the resort to the resources of the Fund is always conditional upon the taking of measures for correcting the situation and always in a sense that they are implicit or explicit of the Fund [*sic*].
>
> 3. They strenuously object to what we call "deterrent charges" on those who utilize the Fund. These deterrent charges are in effect interest rates which increase progressively with the amount purchased from the Fund by any one country and likewise increase the longer the period before which they are repurchased. . . . We regard this as an important feature in our proposal and it looks as though the American delegation will be in for a nasty fight on this matter at the conference.
>
> 4. The British are going to back the small countries in their demands for larger quotas, particularly Australia, and are going also to back India's demand that it be accorded an equivalent position with that of China.

5. There also appears on the horizon a technical fight on what constitutes gold holdings and offsets and a large number of other technical points of complex though minor character. We hope that most of these minor and technical points will be ironed out before the conference so that the delegates will be free to handle the larger issues.

White's unwillingness to "budge one bit" led to trouble. One member of the British delegation reported the next day that "White . . . refused to accept any change whatsoever in the exchange and convertibility clauses. . . . He . . . tried hard to persuade us to abandon the idea of an indeterminate transitional period. Keynes has threatened to walk out if he is pressed . . . on this matter." The report of the U.S. delegation on the same meeting is less dramatic, but makes it clear that strong views were expressed. It records that Keynes was asked if "the British recognized that in joining the Fund they were accepting some obligation to modify their domestic policy in the light of its international effects on stability"; he replied that they did—but at their own discretion. "He finally seemed to admit," the minutes went on, "that it might be helpful to have an obligation to the Fund to back up those who were working for some modification of domestic policy, providing the Fund did not issue orders on some specific phase of domestic policy such as wages."

PROBLEMS AHEAD

It was not only the United Kingdom, of course, that found difficulty in some of the proposals brought forward at Atlantic City. Other countries also were seriously concerned about some of the implications of the proposals in the Joint Statement and the amendments to it proposed by the U.S. delegation. Some of these preoccupations have already been exposed in the previous sections of this chapter. Dealing with the remainder in the order of the Articles of Agreement to which they related (which is not necessarily their relative order of importance to the protesting delegations), we may summarize the views expressed as follows:

Purposes

The Indian delegation offered two amendments to the statement of the purposes of the Fund. One urged that these should specifically include assisting in the fuller utilization of the resources of economically underdeveloped countries, and the other sought to reinstate the settlement of blocked balances, described as "abnormal indebtedness arising out of the war."

Drawings

Pursuing the criticisms of the limitations on drawings mentioned in Chapter 2, Australia and France put forward plans for a more generous scale than that contemplated in the Joint Statement, which was equivalent to 25 per cent of the quota per annum, with a top limit to the Fund's holdings of 200 per cent of quota. Australia suggested that the amount permitted annually should be the equivalent of one third of the quota, and France a (cumulative) rate such that the Fund's holdings of the country's currency might reach 125 per cent of quota in the first year, 150 per cent in the second year, and 175 per cent in the third year; 200 per cent would remain as the maximum.

A preliminary discussion of the provisions for the repurchase of currencies from the Fund led to a proposal by Belgium that the Fund's right to require half of any increase in a member's monetary reserves to be used for that purpose should be limited to half the amount of any increase over the member's reserves as they stood at the moment when it joined the Fund.

Charges

As White had foreseen, the U.S. proposal for a graduated scale of charges, rising with the proportion of the quota that had been drawn and with the length of time for which the drawing was outstanding, met with general resistance by those delegations—naturally the majority at Atlantic City—who looked to the Fund as a potential source of assistance in expected postwar difficulties.

Capital movements

The Canadian delegation proposed a new clause applying to a country of whose currency the Fund had held less than 75 per cent of quota for six months. In order more quickly to adjust its balance of payments, such a country should be permitted to draw from the Fund "for any purpose, including capital transfers."

Management

The British delegation had come prepared to concede that the management of the Fund would have important issues to decide, including par values, the waiver of conditions for drawings, the exercise of judgment to ensure that the Fund's resources were not being used to meet an outflow of capital, the rationing of scarce currencies, and the special relations with members during the transitional period. Nevertheless, they did not consider that the regular work of the Fund would call for frequent decisions on matters of policy—certainly not to the extent of requiring the Directors to be continuously in residence. Nor, indeed, did they conceive that a large and high-powered management would be necessary. "So far as practicable," the delegation's submission continued, "we want to aim at a governing structure doing a technical job and developing a sense of corporate responsibility to all the members, and not the need to guard the interests of particular countries."

This view they supported in the Committee on Organization and Management set up by the conference to consider how to constitute the controlling bodies of the Fund. The committee, of which a British delegate was chairman, represented also China, Mexico, the Netherlands, the U.S.S.R., and the United States. It agreed on a two-tier organization and on the appointment of a Governor by each member country. It agreed also on the minimum functions of the Governors. As regards the Executive Directors, the committee reported agreement on the appointment of (say) five by the five member countries having the largest quotas, and on the election biennially of (say) six others. It also accepted that Directors should be paid by the Fund. There, however, agreement ended.

The United States believed that the Executive Directors would have a full-time duty, and should therefore be permanently available at the headquarters of the Fund. The Chinese delegate agreed with this view, at any rate as regards the first five years of the Fund's work. But the British delegate, with some support from the other members of the committee, strongly resisted this proposal, repeating the arguments set forth above. The controversy was unresolved when the Atlantic City conference ended.

Location of Fund

A U.S. amendment provided for the headquarters of the Fund to be located in the member country having the largest quota. The British delegation, on the other hand, had hoped that it might be situated in Europe: preferably in London, but failing that, perhaps in Amsterdam. This had been the expressed wish of the Chancellor of the Exchequer. In fact, it had become clear to the delegation, soon after their arrival in New York, that the United States assumed that both the Fund and the Bank would be in Washington. Nevertheless, as their instructions required, the British delegation continued to press for a location elsewhere, and the struggle was resumed at Bretton Woods.

TASK LEFT FOR BRETTON WOODS

The total number of amendments put forward at Atlantic City—disregarding proposals by the U.S. delegation (based on the work of the U.S. Treasury lawyers) that did not materially alter the sense of the Joint Statement—was about seventy. Not all of these were as controversial as those referred to in the preceding pages. Some were formal, such as proposals by the United States to define the powers of the Fund, to confer upon it immunity from legal process, and to exempt it and its employees from taxation. Others put forward variations in wording in clauses that did not raise important questions of principle—for example, in the provisions for selecting and guaranteeing the performance of the duties of the depositories for the Fund's gold. Nevertheless, as the delegates moved on from Atlantic City to Bretton Woods, they realized that a great deal of work had yet to be done to produce an agreed basis for the Fund that all wished to see created.

The transformation of the documents resulting from the Atlantic City conference into the basic material for the next stage was undertaken by two legal members of the U.S. delegation in the course of June 30, as their train pursued its way from New Jersey to New Hampshire. Keynes had wished to discard many of the minor amendments that had been offered, and to present to the delegates at Bretton Woods a streamlined initial text, closely based on the U.S. and British drafts. He was, however, overruled, and a comprehensive draft embodying the whole of the amendments put forward was distributed at Bretton Woods soon after the delegates arrived there. This was the starting point for the final stage in the prehistory of the Fund.

CHAPTER

5

Bretton Woods (July 1944)

THE INTERNATIONAL MONETARY and Financial Conference of the United and Associated Nations was convened at the Mount Washington Hotel, Bretton Woods, New Hampshire, on July 1, 1944.[1] The location of the Conference had been a matter of some difficulty, partly owing to wartime restrictions. The Mount Washington Hotel, closed since 1942, was being prepared for reopening when taken over for the Conference, and the much-needed renovations were not wholly completed by the time the delegates began to arrive. The hotel is situated at the foot of Mount Washington, in extensive wooded grounds. These are separated from the road by a river crossed by a single bridge—a feature which readily permitted the proceedings to be safeguarded against intrusion. As it turned out, not all the 730 persons who attended—a number about three times as large as had originally been expected—could be accommodated at the Conference headquarters, and other hotels, up to five miles off, had to be utilized to house the overflow, mainly of technicians.

ORGANIZATION OF THE CONFERENCE

Originally, the Conference had been expected to last a little less than three weeks, dispersing on Wednesday, July 19. The Hot Springs Conference in 1943, from which had emerged the Interim Food and Agriculture Organization, had lasted only ten days, and it had been thought that twice this length of time would suffice for Bretton Woods. In any case, the U.S. Treasury had been anxious to terminate the Conference early enough for its results to be available before the election campaign began. The imminence of the Democratic Convention and of President Roosevelt's renomination there, due on July 20, may similarly have

[1] The Conference documentation has been reproduced in *Proceedings and Documents of United Nations Monetary and Financial Conference, Bretton Woods, New Hampshire, July 1–22, 1944* (Department of State, Washington, 1948), hereafter cited as *Proceedings*.

Mount Washington Hotel, Bretton Woods, N.H.

influenced the proposed closing date. As things turned out, however, it proved impossible to complete the task of the Conference by the nineteenth, and its termination was postponed until Saturday, July 22, the delegates leaving the hotel on the following day. As this involved the management of the hotel in postponing the arrival of numerous guests who had reserved accommodation from the twentieth, the negotiation of the extension of time was not without difficulty.

In addition to the delegates from the 44 members of the United and Associated Nations, the Conference was attended by a representative of Denmark and delegations from the International Labor Office, the United Nations Relief and Rehabilitation Administration, the Economic Section of the League of Nations, and the United Nations Interim Commission on Food and Agriculture. The official language of the Conference was English, but some difficulty was caused by the imperfect acquaintance of some delegations with this language.

Secretary Morgenthau was elected Permanent President of the Conference, and representatives of Australia, Belgium, Brazil, and the U.S.S.R. were elected Vice-Presidents. The Conference operated through three Commissions: Commission I on the Fund, chaired by White; Commission II on the Bank, chaired by Keynes; and Commission III on Other Means of International Financial Cooperation, chaired by Mr. Eduardo Suarez of Mexico.

Commission I, with which we shall here be concerned almost exclusively, had as Reporting Delegate Mr. Louis Rasminsky (Canada). It was divided into four main committees, appointed on July 4, as shown in Table 1. In addition to these main committees, a Steering Committee, of which Secretary Morgenthau was chairman, was appointed on July 3. Eight ad hoc committees were appointed to deal with special topics, three on July 8, four on July 10, and one on July 15. The Commission appointed a Drafting Committee on July 10 and a Special Committee on Unsettled Problems on July 13. The committees in turn appointed drafting subcommittees.

Table 1. Bretton Woods: Organization of Commission I

Number and Subject of Committee	Chairman	Reporting Delegate
1. Purposes, Policies, and Quotas of the Fund	Tingfu F. Tsiang (China)	Kyriakos Varvaressos (Greece)
2. Operations of the Fund	N. A. Maletin (U.S.S.R.)	Robert Mossé (France)
3. Organization and Management of the Fund	Arthur de Souza Costa (Brazil)	Ervin Hexner (Czechoslovakia)
4. Form and Status of the Fund	Manuel B. Llosa (Peru)	Wilhelm Keilhau (Norway)

Source: *Proceedings*, pp. 88–90, 405–11.

It took a little time for the Conference to begin serious work, partly because of its size and partly because of the necessary formalities connected with its inauguration. Commission I had an organizational meeting on July 3, and met to consider drafts on July 5, 10, 13, 14, 15, 18, and 19. Its main committees held a total of 26 meetings on July 4–8, 11, and 12. After July 10, attention began to be given also to the draft proposals for the Bank; Commission II met on July 11, 13, 16, 19, 20, and 21; its committees were also active. Delegations were thus overwhelmingly busy, and those with few members faced competing claims on their manpower. The creation of ad hoc committees enabled difficult problems to receive special attention, and the main committees in such instances could work on the basis of recommendations made to them by the ad hoc committees. Issues that Commission I could not resolve were passed to the Special Committee on Unsettled Problems, whose suggestions were generally formulated in precise language by the Drafting Committee chaired by Mr. Rasminsky, before coming back to the Commission. The Special Committee and the Drafting Committee met at times when neither the Commissions nor the regular committees were sitting, and consequently tended to operate into the small hours of the morning. It was the intensive pressure to which this procedure subjected the Special Committee on Unsettled Problems that eventually forced the prolongation of the Conference.

How overwhelming the task before the Conference proved to be was graphically described by Keynes. "It is as though," he wrote, ". . . one had to accomplish the preliminary work of many interdepartmental and Cabinet committees, the job of the . . . draftsmen, and the passage . . . of two intricate legislative measures of large dimensions, all this carried on in committees and commissions numbering anything up to 200 persons in rooms with bad acoustics, shouting through microphones, many of those present . . . with an imperfect knowledge of English, each wanting to get something on the record which would look well in the press down at home, and . . . the Russians only understanding what was afoot with the utmost difficulty. . . . We have all of us worked every minute of our waking hours . . . all of us . . . are all in." [2]

The initial documentation provided for the delegates included the composite draft which had been prepared, as mentioned at the end of Chapter 4, from the discussions at Atlantic City. To this draft numerous other amendments were offered at Bretton Woods itself. In all, the documents issued at the Conference numbered over 500 and in their English version alone fill some 1,200 printed pages. It is clearly impossible here to cover with any degree of completeness the contents of material as extensive as this. All that can be done is to touch upon a few of the major controversies, with particular reference to those whose origin

---

[2] John Morton Blum, *From the Morgenthau Diaries: Years of War, 1941–45* (Boston, 1967), p. 273.

was studied in the preceding chapters. Provisions in the Articles on which there was no disagreement in principle at Bretton Woods will here be unnoticed. Moreover, no attempt will be made to expound the precise significance of phrases which it was found necessary to interpret at later stages of the Fund's history; this can more intelligibly be done in the context of the particular problems to which they were relevant. What follows is, therefore, only an introduction to the study of the Fund's charter.

FROM ARGUMENTS TO ARTICLES

The major controversies that emerged at Bretton Woods, insofar as they are reflected in the formal minutes and in such informal records as are available, are summarized in the remainder of this chapter. It is clear, however, that many—probably the great majority—of the controversies that emerged were dealt with in informal negotiations. To a large extent, these took place within the drafting committees, but, as at all such conferences, the representatives of the two countries most concerned often thrashed out their differences bilaterally. This was particularly true of negotiations between the representatives of the United States and the U.S.S.R.[3]

No official minutes have survived except for a few, mostly formal, records preserved in the *Proceedings.* It has sometimes been possible to supplement these minutes by reference to unofficial verbatim reports, but the incomplete and provisional nature of these reports makes them of uncertain value. It follows that what can now be reconstructed is at best an imperfect picture of the intensive three weeks in which the Articles of Agreement of the International Monetary Fund took shape. Nevertheless, it is believed that the greater part of the most important issues found their way into, or were at least hinted at in, the printed *Proceedings*, and that the following notes on the various Articles will therefore provide an adequate clue to the conditions under which the Fund was founded and started work.[4]

Article I. Purposes

The two points which the representative of India made at Atlantic City were discussed again at Bretton Woods. India had proposed an amendment to Article I (ii) which would have required the Fund "to assist in the fuller utilisation of the resources of economically underdeveloped countries." [5] The proposal was supported by Ecuador, but was opposed by South Africa and the United Kingdom, mainly on the ground that the development of underdeveloped countries was a matter for the Bank rather than for the Fund. India attempted

---

[3] *Ibid.*, pp. 260–65.

[4] The Articles of Agreement are reproduced below, Vol. III, pp. 185–214.

[5] Alternative C, *Proceedings*, p. 23.

to meet this criticism by proposing a revised version of Article I (ii) which would have called for "the development of the resources and productive power of all member countries, with due regard to the needs of economically backward countries." [6] This, however, met with similar criticisms, and eventually Commission I agreed to the present wording, which concludes with the phrase "the development of the productive resources of all members as primary objectives of economic policy." This was generally accepted, but the Australian delegation entered a reservation to Article I as a whole, to the effect that the Article placed

> too little emphasis on the promotion and maintenance of high levels of employment, and too much emphasis on the promotion of exchange stability and on shortening the duration and lessening the degree of disequilibrium in international balances of payments.[7]

India's second proposal at Atlantic City, calling for the settlement of "abnormal indebtedness arising out of the war," [8] was supported by Egypt, which put forward a similar amendment covering "foreign credit balances accumulated during the war." [9] When arguing for these amendments, which were prompted by their very large sterling balances, both India and Egypt referred to the precarious economic position of their countries and the impact on them of the strains of war. Speakers opposing the amendments were generally sympathetic toward these pleas, but thought that the problem of war balances was too large a one for the Fund to tackle. The United States also drew attention to the possibility envisaged in Article VI, Section 1 (*b*) (i), which permits the use of the Fund's resources to finance "capital transactions of reasonable amount. . . ." In an attempt to meet the argument that the Fund could not undertake so large a task as the settlement of war balances, India submitted a further amendment asking only for "the multilateral settlement of a reasonable portion of the foreign credit balances," [10] but this was similarly opposed by the British and French delegations, and was rejected.[11]

Article III. Quotas and Subscriptions

The determination of the quotas of individual members was entrusted at the Conference to an ad hoc Committee on Quotas, representing Belgium, Brazil, Canada, China, Cuba, Czechoslovakia, Egypt, France, India, Mexico, New Zealand, Norway, the U.S.S.R., the United Kingdom, and the United States. This committee was chaired by Mr. Fred M. Vinson, Vice-Chairman of the U.S. delegation. It has left no record of the basis of its work, except for a statement

[6] Alternative I (Document 162), *Proceedings*, p. 184.
[7] *Proceedings*, p. 1088.
[8] Alternative G, *Proceedings*, p. 24. See also above, p. 85.
[9] Alternative H, *Proceedings*, p. 122.
[10] Alternative K, *Proceedings*, p. 278.
[11] *Proceedings*, p. 433.

in its report that "the Mexican Delegation agreed to relinquish $10 million of its quota in favor of $5 million each for Colombia and Chile." [12] It seems, however, that its starting point was the formula evolved by the U.S. Treasury in June 1943.[13] This formula was as follows:

> 90 per cent of the total of
> 2 per cent of national income, 1940,
> *plus* 5 per cent of gold and dollar balances on July 1, 1943,
> *plus* 10 per cent of maximum variation of exports, 1934–38,
> *plus* 10 per cent of average imports, 1934–38,
>
> increased for each country in the same ratio as average exports, 1934–38, bore to national income.

The author of the formula was Professor Raymond Mikesell, then in the U.S. Treasury. White had stipulated to him that the formula should use data for international trade and exchange reserves, and that it should yield a quota of about $2.5 billion for the United States, about half this for the United Kingdom, and such figures for the U.S.S.R. and China as should assure them third and fourth places, respectively, in the list of quotas. In order to achieve this result, Mr. Mikesell introduced also data for national income. These last had usually to be approximated, and their uncertainty afforded opportunities for making minor adjustments to the suggested quotas when these did not conform to political realities.

A number of calculations were made by the U.S. Treasury before the Bretton Woods Conference, to show what countries' quotas would be on the basis of this formula. Column (2) of Table 2 shows the illustrative figures circulated with the formula in June 1943. The figures in column (3) were approximations communicated to the United Kingdom some time before February 1944, and were shown by the British Treasury to the countries participating in the conference with the Dominions and India on monetary and other problems, held in London in February–March 1944.[14] This conference suggested a general increase in the smaller quotas; its detailed proposals are shown in column (4). The figures in column (5) represent calculations for the application of the formula to all the United and Associated Nations; they seem to have been those which the U.S. delegation made available at Bretton Woods. The differences between the figures in columns (3) and (5) reflect the difficulty of estimating national incomes

---

[12] *Proceedings*, p. 635.

[13] See above, p. 31. For a discussion of the formula, see Oscar L. Altman, "Quotas in the International Monetary Fund," *Staff Papers*, Vol. V (1956–57), pp. 136–41.

[14] See above, p. 74. This list was also communicated by the British Treasury to representatives of the Allied Governments-in-Exile in London on May 1–3, 1944. See Norway, Stortinget, *Om samtykke til at Norge tiltrer avtalene om det internasjonale valutafond m.v.* [Concerning approval of Norway's acceptance of the international monetary fund agreements, etc.], Supplement 3, p. 120.

Table 2. Suggested Quotas [1]
(In millions of U.S. dollars)

Member Country (1)	U.S. Calculation June 1943 (2)	U.S. Proposal Jan. 1944 (3)	British Proposal Mar. 1944 (4)	U.S. Calculation July 1944 (5)	Recommended by Committee on Quotas July 1944 (6)
Australia	149	150	300	149	200
Belgium	—	235	300	250	225
Bolivia	—	9	20	9	10
Brazil	107	100	200	107	150
Canada	278	300	300	278	300
Chile	—	36	70	37	50
China	350	600	500	350	550
Colombia	—	30	60	30	50
Costa Rica	—	4	10	3	5
Cuba	—	37	75	37	50
Czechoslovakia	—	116	230	117	125
Denmark	—	—	—	—	. . .[2]
Dominican Republic	—	—	—	—	5
Ecuador	—	5	10	5	5
Egypt	—	59	120	59	45
El Salvador	—	5	10	5	2.5
Ethiopia	—	—	—	—	6
France	—	500	500	620	450
Greece	—	41	80	41	40
Guatemala	—	7	15	7	5
Haiti	—	5	10	5	5
Honduras	—	3	5	3	2.5
Iceland	—	—	—	4	1
India and Burma	367	300	400	367	400
Iran	—	—	—	—	25
Iraq	—	—	—	—	8
Liberia	—	—	—	—	0.5
Luxembourg	—	7	15	7	10
Mexico	63	80	150	63	90
Netherlands	—	250	300	325	275
New Zealand	54	54	110	54	50
Nicaragua	—	2	5	—	2
Norway	—	65	130	66	50
Panama	—	. . .	. . .	—	0.5
Paraguay	—	3	5	2	2
Peru	—	21	40	21	25
Philippines	—	—	—	—	15
Poland	—	113	225	114	125
Union of South Africa	175	150	300	175	100
U.S.S.R.	763	900	900	763	1,200
United Kingdom and colonies	1,275	1,300	1,300	1,275	1,300
United States	2,929	2,900	2,900	2,929	2,750
Uruguay	—	23	45	22	15
Venezuela	—	25	50	25	15
Yugoslavia	—	55	110	85	60
Rest of U.A.N.[3]	3,554	—	—	—	—
Total	10,064	8,490	9,800	8,409	8,800

Sources:

Col. (2): U.S. Treasury, *A Suggested Formula for the Determination of Member Country Quotas*, June 9, 1943.

Col. (3): U.S. Treasury. Provided to United Kingdom some time before February 1944.

Col. (4): British Treasury.

Col. (5): U.S. Treasury. Provided for use of the Committee on Quotas. The figures given here have been rounded to the nearest unit.

Col. (6): *Proceedings*, p. 634.

[1] A dash (—) signifies that the country was not named in the list. Three dots (. . .) signify that the country was named in the list but that no figure was given.

[2] Quota to be determined later.

[3] United and Associated Nations.

and other relevant data for countries where the appropriate statistical work had not yet been done. Column (6) lists the quotas agreed at the Conference.

Mr. Vinson, in his speech presenting the report of the ad hoc Committee, made pointed reference to the list submitted by the delegates of the United States, which had been based on the formula. The comparison set out in Table 2, however, shows clearly that other considerations were also taken into account.

In the early years of the Fund's work, the question of the extent to which quotas were calculated according to the formula was much discussed. It appears therefore desirable here to collect such indications as are available on this issue. At a meeting between British Treasury officials and Allied experts on May 1, 1944 (i.e., before the Conference), Keynes said that neither of the formulae previously suggested had been found to fit every case, so it had been agreed to drop a specific formula at that stage. He went on to say that discussion and agreement between the United Kingdom and the United States had therefore been limited to agreeing on the U.S. quota ($3 billion), the British quota ($1.3 billion), and the aggregate ($8.5 billion for the United and Associated Nations).

When reporting to the Conference, Mr. Vinson said that the formula had "had to be discarded because a period that would be fair to one country could not be fair to other countries." Professor Mossé, a member of the French delegation to Bretton Woods, has stated that, in the end, quotas were established more or less arbitrarily by the United States in a series of deals.[15] Perhaps, however, the most authoritative description of the Committee's proceedings, even though it was not given until nearly three years later, is contained in a statement made by White at a meeting of the Executive Directors on April 24, 1947:

> . . . he wished to record for future reference his recollection of the place which the so-called "formula" had played with respect to the establishment of quotas at Bretton Woods.
>
> . . . the formula had been suggested by the United States Government to facilitate consideration of the problem and was circulated to other governments as early as 1943. As a result of discussion and comment it had been recognized that no single formula could possibly accommodate all of the considerations involved in fixing quotas for forty-four nations. Furthermore, in some cases even the factual data which the formula would reflect were either unavailable or of questionable accuracy. Hence there was general agreement that the formula could only be useful as a point of departure for discussion and negotiation.
>
> At Bretton Woods the results given by the formula were discussed among various delegations and were given to the members of the Quota Committee as a reference point for their work. The Committee undertook negotiations and reached agreement with all but a few delegations, but generally not at the amount

[15] Robert Mossé, *Le système monétaire de Bretton Woods et les grands problèmes de l'après-guerre* (Paris, 1948), p. 48. See also his *Les problèmes monétaires internationaux* (Paris, 1967), p. 270.

set in the formula. Many other considerations had to be taken into account. In a few special cases further negotiations were carried on by the Executive Committee, and again the formula was departed from. Thus in the final result it was recognized by all concerned that the formula was only one of the factors entering into consideration and could in no sense be called definitive. The only significant figures were those which had been negotiated and accepted by the participating nations.

The largest differences between the figures in column (5) and those in column (6) were in the quotas for the U.S.S.R. and China. The increase for the U.S.S.R. followed the recognition by the U.S. delegation, noted in Chapter 3, that the formula insufficiently reflected the economic importance of the U.S.S.R. That for China no doubt took into account the Chinese representatives' criticism of national income figures that ignored its large agricultural population engaged in subsistence activities. Similar considerations may well have underlain other changes in the figures.

The ad hoc Committee's report was unanimous except for reservations by China, Egypt, France, India, and New Zealand, which all felt that their quotas should be larger than those suggested.[16] When the report was presented to the Commission, a number of other countries that had been allotted what they regarded as too small quotas also protested that they needed larger ones. Australia, Ethiopia, Greece, Iran, and Yugoslavia, which had not been represented on the ad hoc Committee, joined the five countries that had already entered reservations.[17] However, Mr. Vinson, on behalf of the ad hoc Committee, stressed the extreme difficulty of the task with which it had been faced, and recommended that the proposals should be accepted as they stood. This was, in fact, done, and the figures in the final column of Table 2 are those that appear in Schedule A of the Articles of Agreement. By the time the Conference closed, the reservations of China, Egypt, Ethiopia, Greece, New Zealand, and Yugoslavia had been withdrawn, leaving only those of Australia, France, India, and Iran to be entered on the record.[18] It may here be noted that the French quota was increased in 1946 and that of Iran in 1947. The quota for India was retained unchanged after partition in 1947, and thus in effect increased per capita. For Australia, see Chapter 8 below.

It will be recalled that, during discussions in 1943 on the proportion of gold to be contributed by members, the United Kingdom and the United States had agreed upon payments equivalent to 25 per cent of the member's quota, or 10 per cent of its net official holdings of gold and U.S. dollars, whichever was the less. This provision of the Joint Statement was generally acceptable. Nevertheless, the U.S.S.R. and Czechoslovakia had put forward at Atlantic City

[16] *Proceedings*, p. 635.

[17] *Proceedings*, pp. 653, 1045.

[18] *Proceedings*, pp. 1045, 1088–90.

amendments designed to deal with the special problems of war-torn countries. That of Czechoslovakia would have enabled such a member to postpone for not more than nine months the payment of its gold contribution; [19] that of the U.S.S.R. would have permitted the member to reduce its gold payment to between 75 per cent and 50 per cent of the amount it would otherwise have had to pay.[20] The U.S. delegation, sympathizing with this latter plan, had proposed an amendment in similar terms, but omitting the figures.[21] Neither the Czechoslovak nor the Soviet amendment was favorably received at Bretton Woods, and, although the U.S.S.R. pointed to the relevant section in the July 1943 version of the Stabilization Fund in support of its view that a reduction in the gold contribution would be appropriate, the Commission decided not to accept the amendment. The U.S.S.R. entered a reservation, to the effect that their proposal should have been included in the Articles.[22] The French delegation also entered a "reservation as to the deletion of a clause in favor of enemy-occupied countries and relative to gold payments." [23]

The preoccupation of some countries, notably Bolivia and Mexico, with the monetary use of silver found expression in attempts to ensure that silver was accorded a place in the work of the Fund, as well as gold. In pursuance of this objective, Bolivia put forward an amendment to Article III, Section 3, which would have permitted that part of the quota not contributed in gold to be subscribed "in local currencies or, if a member nation so wishes, in silver and its local currency in a proportion to be agreed upon in each individual case." [24] Other amendments dealing with the use of silver were put forward in connection with Article V [25] and Article VIII,[26] and it may be convenient here to mention that the whole subject of silver was remitted for consideration to Commission III and resulted in the following statement:

> The problems confronting some nations as a result of the wide fluctuation in the value of silver were the subject of serious discussion in Commission III. Due to the shortage of time, the magnitude of the other problems on the agenda, and other limiting considerations, it was impossible to give sufficient attention to this problem at this time in order to make definite recommendations. However, it was the sense of Commission III that the subject should merit further study by the interested nations.[27]

---

[19] Alternative B, *Proceedings*, p. 25.

[20] Alternative B, *Proceedings*, p. 27. Cf. above, p. 77.

[21] Alternative C, *Proceedings*, p. 27.

[22] *Proceedings*, p. 1090.

[23] *Proceedings*, p. 1089.

[24] Alternatives C and D, *Proceedings*, p. 157.

[25] *Proceedings:* Alternative E, p. 121 (Mexico); Alternative F (Document 148), p. 158 (Belgium); Alternative B, p. 159 (Bolivia).

[26] Alternative B, *Proceedings*, pp. 156–57 (Bolivia).

[27] Resolution IV, *Proceedings*, p. 939.

One more of the issues in relation to contributions which had been raised at earlier discussions was again briefly referred to at Bretton Woods. The representative of Haiti asked in Committee 1 of Commission I why no provision was made for a member's quota to be counted as part of its reserves, as had been done (although the delegate did not say so) in the final draft of the Stabilization Fund. The U.S. delegate replied that this was a matter for local legislation and not for decision by the Fund, and the matter was dropped.

Article IV. Par Values of Currencies

Two sections of Article IV evoked substantial controversies: Section 5 (Changes in par values) and Section 7 (Uniform changes in par values). The only other provision where any appreciable controversy developed was that in Section 4 (*b*) (Obligations regarding exchange stability), where Colombia wished to include a provision permitting payment of bonuses to gold producers.[28] This was rejected by the Drafting Committee of Committee 1 and was not further pressed.

Article IV, Section 5

As regards individual changes in par values, two substantive amendments were put forward. The first was an addition to the clause which permitted a member to make a 10 per cent change in its initial par value without objection from the Fund and required the Fund to decide within 48 hours on a request for a further 10 per cent change. Mexico proposed to permit a member having less than 10 per cent of the total voting power of the Fund to substitute 20 per cent for 10 per cent in each part of this clause.[29] Australia again put forward a proposal, originally tabled at Atlantic City, that a country should be permitted to change its exchange rate to deal with "a serious and persistent deficit in the balance of payments on current account accompanied by a substantially adverse change in the terms of trade." [30]

The discussion in Committee 2 ranged over the whole subject of flexibility versus stability of exchange rates, but ultimately Commission I adopted in essentials the provisions of the Joint Statement.[31] Australia maintained its objection in the form of a reservation.[32]

In connection with the same section, the U.S.S.R., without submitting a formal amendment, proposed in the course of the discussions in Commission I that the power of the Fund to control exchange rates should not apply to an

[28] Alternative C, *Proceedings*, p. 432; cf. p. 501.
[29] Alternative B, *Proceedings*, p. 225.
[30] Alternative C, *Proceedings*, pp. 278–79.
[31] *Proceedings*, p. 628.
[32] *Proceedings*, p. 1089.

exchange rate which had no effect on international transactions.[33] This was accepted by the Commission and incorporated as Article IV, Section 5 (*e*).

Article IV, Section 7

Article IV, Section 7, provided that a uniform change in par values (i.e., a change in the world price of gold) should require the consent of a majority of the total voting power and of each member which had 10 per cent or more of the total of quotas. Mexico and Cuba put forward amendments to give smaller countries a greater say in a decision to make such a change.[34] In support of its amendment, Mexico made specific reference to its need to protect its sovereign right to control its exchange rate, a right which it felt was threatened by the provision as drafted. The Special Committee on Unsettled Problems recommended that a member might give notice within 72 hours of the Fund's action that it did not wish its par value to be changed as a result of such action. A suggestion in the Commission that 72 hours was too short a time for a country to make such an important decision was successfully scotched by a vivid description, given by Mr. Bernstein on behalf of the U.S. delegation, of the chaos that would ensue if countries' exchange rates remained uncertain for a longer period. In the outcome, the Special Committee's proposal was accepted.[35] Neither Mexico nor Cuba maintained its objection, but the French delegation entered a reservation against the veto permitted to countries which had 10 per cent or more of the total of quotas.[36]

ARTICLE V. TRANSACTIONS WITH THE FUND

The use of the Fund's resources was naturally the focus of a great deal of discussion at Bretton Woods. Four Sections in particular were extensively debated.

Article V, Section 3. Conditions governing use of the Fund's resources

Article V, Section 4. Waiver of conditions

The draft on which discussions were based provided that, on certain conditions, a country might draw from the Fund the equivalent of 25 per cent of its quota per annum up to the point at which the Fund's holdings of its currency equaled 200 per cent of its quota.[37] The relevant subsection also provided that, if the Fund's holdings of the member's currency before the drawing totaled less than 75 per cent of the quota, the member might draw, in addition to the 25 per cent of quota, the shortfall of the holdings below 75 per cent of the quota.

---

33 *Proceedings*, p. 648. Cf. above, pp. 78, 82.

34 *Proceedings:* Alternative B, p. 121 (and see pp. 128–29); Alternative C, p. 184.

35 *Proceedings*, pp. 605, 628.

36 *Proceedings*, p. 1089.

37 Joint Statement, Clause III.2 (below, Vol. III, p. 132), and Alternative A (United States and United Kingdom), *Proceedings*, pp. 28–29.

The amendments to this provision submitted at Atlantic City by the representatives of Australia and France were noted in the previous chapter. At Bretton Woods both countries urged that greater elasticity was needed, and the French delegate stressed in particular the desirability of the member being able to carry over an unused drawing right from one year to the next. Belgium submitted a further amendment which would have provided that the member might draw in any year 25 per cent of the quota, plus any shortfall in the holdings of the member's currency by the Fund below 100 per cent (instead of 75 per cent) of the quota.[38]

Committee 2 considered these proposals but decided in favor of retaining the provisions in the original draft, subject to an elaboration of the clause (now Section 4) permitting the Fund to waive any of the stipulated conditions. (This clause was of particular interest to the French delegation and was strongly defended in the Committee by Mr. Mossé.) The elaboration consisted in phrases permitting the waiver

> especially in the case of members with a record of avoiding large or continuous use of the Fund's resources. In making a waiver it [the Fund] shall take into consideration periodic or exceptional requirements of the member requesting the waiver.

At the instance of Mexico, a further qualification was added, authorizing the Fund to take into consideration a member's willingness to pledge collateral.[39] These proposals were accepted by the Commission, and the final text, which became Article V, Section 4, reflects them. However, Australia and France entered final reservations in favor of their proposals.[40]

Article V, Section 7. Repurchase by a member of its currency held by the Fund

No other part of the Articles of Agreement went through so exhaustive a process of evolution during the Conference as the provisions for repurchase by a member of the Fund's holdings of its currency. The relevant provision in the Joint Statement permitted the Fund to require a member to acquire its currency from the Fund with one half of the increase during the year of the member's holdings of gold and gold-convertible exchange, so long as this did not reduce the Fund's holdings of the country's currency below 75 per cent of its quota, or the member's holdings of gold and gold-convertible exchange below an amount equal to its quota.[41]

At Atlantic City a series of amendments had been put forward. One of these, suggested by Greece, would have specifically empowered the Fund to waive the

---

[38] Alternative F (Document 147), *Proceedings*, p. 158.

[39] *Proceedings*, pp. 487, 539.

[40] *Proceedings*, p. 1089.

[41] Joint Statement, Clause III.7 (*c*); below, Vol. III, p. 133.

repurchase obligation "if its application would reduce the facilities accorded by the Fund to that Country in a way contrary to the purposes and policies of the Fund. . . ." [42] At Bretton Woods, Belgium proposed a further amendment, which would have changed the minimum amount of the Fund's holdings of the member's currency from 75 per cent of quota to 100 per cent of quota.[43] Bolivia, as mentioned above, would have introduced silver on a par with gold and gold-convertible exchange.[44] All these proposals were reviewed in Committee 2 and in the Commission, and were remitted to a drafting committee to give effect to the principles which had emerged from the discussion.

For the use of the drafting committee the British delegation worked out an elaborate plan, which took into account a number of considerations brought out during the discussion (for example, the possibility that the increase in the member's reserves was due to a currency previously inconvertible having become convertible during the year for which the obligation was calculated). It also set out the proportions in which the member should repurchase its currency from the Fund with different types of reserves which it held.[45] With one minor amendment, this plan was adopted by the drafting committee.[46] Eventually it was found necessary to divide the provision between Article V, Section 7, and Schedule B, which set out the mechanics of repurchases in more detail, although not so as to avoid the need for much interpretation subsequently.

Article V, Section 8. Charges

The Joint Statement had made no provision for charges to be levied by the Fund, but the initial draft provided by the United States for the Bretton Woods Conference suggested that the Fund might levy a service charge, plus "charges uniform among members" payable on the amount of the Fund's holdings of the member's currency in excess of its quota.[47] The United Kingdom had submitted an alternative suggestion, providing for a charge of not more than 1 per cent per annum on the amount of currency held in excess of the quota of the drawing country, together with an additional charge on any holdings by the Fund of the member's currency in excess of 200 per cent of quota.[48]

The Commission accepted the principle, advocated by the U.S. delegation, that charges should increase both with the proportion of drawings to quota and with the time during which the Fund's holdings of the member's currency exceeded its quota. The United Kingdom suggested also that the charges as

[42] Alternative D, *Proceedings*, p. 34.
[43] Alternative E, *Proceedings*, p. 122.
[44] Alternative F (Document 148), *Proceedings*, p. 158.
[45] Alternative G, *Proceedings*, pp. 653–55.
[46] *Proceedings*, pp. 665–67.
[47] Alternative A, *Proceedings*, p. 35.
[48] Alternative B, *Proceedings*, p. 35.

adopted in the Articles might be varied with the consent of 75 per cent of the members' votes.[49] The U.S. delegation made it clear that the proposed charges were intended to deter member countries from running persistent overdrafts. The discussion was also influenced, on the one hand, by the realization that the Fund would need income to cover its expenses and, on the other, by an apprehension that charges on drawings from the Fund might inhibit members from using its resources.

Both the U.S. and the British proposals had provided that the charges be paid in gold, although the former had made an exception in favor of a member whose holdings of gold and gold-convertible exchange were less than one half of its quota, providing that such a member might pay a proportion of the charges in its own currency. Australia reserved its position, contending that the charges proposed were too high.[50]

Article VI. Capital Transfers

No great difficulty was encountered in the discussion of this Article. The Canadian delegation supported the amendment which it had submitted at Atlantic City, providing that if the Fund's holdings of a currency of a member had remained below 75 per cent of its quota for not less than six months, the member might draw from the Fund for any purpose, including capital transfers.[51] Purchases for capital transfers were not, however, to be allowed to raise the Fund's holdings of the member's currency above 75 per cent of its quota, or to reduce the Fund's holdings of the currency purchased below 75 per cent of the quota of the member whose currency was purchased. No objections were raised to the inclusion of this section, which became Article VI, Section 2.

Article VIII. General Obligations of Members

Article VIII, Section 4. Convertibility of foreign held balances

The provision in the Joint Statement requiring a member to be prepared to buy its own currency from any other member with the latter member's currency or with gold was a matter of extreme concern to the United Kingdom. It immediately brought into question the sterling balances accumulated by such countries as India during the war.

During the course of discussions at Atlantic City, a draft had been evolved which required a member to buy balances of its currency held by another member (with certain exceptions) under two conditions. The first was that the balances to be bought had been currently acquired. The second, expressed as an alternative, was that the conversion of these balances was needed by the

[49] Alternative C, *Proceedings*, pp. 442, 540. For details of charges, see below, p. 322.
[50] *Proceedings*, p. 1089.
[51] *Proceedings*, p. 29.

member who owned them to make current payments.[52] This draft was accepted by the United Kingdom as an adequate compromise between the Conference's pressing wish to extend convertibility and the need to safeguard sterling, and was adopted by the Conference.

Questioned about the significance of the conditions by the Indian delegate in Commission I, the British delegate made it clear that his understanding was that after the transitional period "currently acquired sterling will be freely convertible." This expressly excluded the conversion of balances of sterling acquired in the past unless the withdrawal of the balance was "for the purpose of buying goods or indulging in other current transactions." No such obligation to convert long-standing balances would arise if the purpose for which they were to be used was to make a transfer of them from London to some other center.

Article VIII, Section 5. Furnishing of information

The problem of the provision of information to the Fund to enable it to conduct its operations had arisen at Atlantic City and had been remitted to a Special Committee on Furnishing Information, of which Mr. A. P. Morozov (U.S.S.R.) was chairman. The report of this committee was made available to the Bretton Woods Conference.[53] In principle, the committee suggested that the Fund would need fairly extensive information on such subjects as monetary reserves; production, exports, and imports of gold; balance of payments; national income; prices; exchange rates; and exchange controls. The committee realized that some countries would be unable to supply some of the information needed and considered that an escape clause to this effect should be provided. The U.S.S.R. delegation felt that it was unable to undertake to supply certain information without specific authority from Moscow, and at one stage the Conference took a much-needed holiday for twenty-four hours while this authority was obtained. In the event, the Conference accepted the committee's view, with qualifications permitting the Fund to take into consideration the varying ability of members to furnish data and excepting data dealing with the affairs of individuals or corporations. Other data could be obtained by agreement with members. No reservation was entered to this text.

Article XII. Organization and Management

The Sections of Article XII dealing with the Executive Directors gave rise to much discussion at Bretton Woods. There was general agreement on the provisions for the Board of Governors and for the Managing Director and staff, subject to one minor point mentioned below.

---

52 Alternative A, *Proceedings*, p. 32. The penultimate word was printed "currency," but this was an error. Cf. *Proceedings*, p. 598.

53 *Proceedings*, pp. 141–43.

Article XII, Section 3. Executive Directors

Section 3 (b), dealing with the number and geographic distribution of Executive Directorships, was closely linked with the size of quotas, and at one point discussions were suspended until the size of quotas had been settled. The draft originally placed before the Conference proposed a Board of twelve members, of whom five would be nominated by the five members having the largest quotas, six would be elected biennially by other members, and one would be the General Manager of the Fund.[54] Minor changes in this arrangement were proposed by Cuba, Belgium, and India.[55] A different note was struck in an amendment by Cuba proposing a Board of fourteen, five of whom would represent the five members with the largest quotas, three the members in the economic area of the British Empire, three the members in "the economic area of the American Republics," and three the remaining members.[56] Later, Cuba modified this to a total of twelve Directors, five appointed by the five members with the largest quotas, two elected by "the American Republics" (other than the United States), and five elected by all other members.[57] Egypt then proposed a Board of twelve Directors, of whom two would represent the Latin American countries and one "the Middle East countries." Some delegations, however, thought it might be difficult to define "Middle East countries," and on the suggestion being put to the vote, it was defeated. In practice, however, the countries in the Middle East have combined to elect an Executive Director, who throughout the period covered by this volume has been Mr. Ahmed Zaki Saad (United Arab Republic).

Meanwhile, Canada had proposed an amendment to add not more than two Directors, to be appointed by members not otherwise entitled to appoint Directors, whose quotas had been used, on the average over the preceding two years, in the largest amounts in terms of gold.[58] With this amendment, which became Section 3 (*c*), the final Cuban proposal was adopted.[59] It was generally expected that Canada would presently become entitled to appoint a Director under the terms of the amendment which its delegation sponsored, and this in fact happened in 1958. Until 1968, when Italy similarly qualified, no other member did so.

Section 3 (e). The proposal to provide each Executive Director with an Alternate was accepted in principle. The discussion was to some extent a reflection of the debate on whether Executive Directors should be continuously

[54] Alternative A, *Proceedings*, p. 44.

[55] *Proceedings:* Alternative E, p. 277 (Cuba); Alternative D, p. 159 (Belgium); Alternative D, p. 222 (India).

[56] Alternative C, *Proceedings*, p. 160.

[57] Alternative J, *Proceedings*, p. 503.

[58] Alternative K, *Proceedings*, p. 544.

[59] *Proceedings*, p. 653.

functioning (see Section 3 (*g*), below). A minor controversy, however, developed over the way in which the Alternate Executive Directors should be selected. The proposal submitted by the United States did not suggest a method for selecting Alternate Executive Directors,[60] but a special subcommittee, appointed to consider all proposals relative to the Executive Directors, proposed that each Executive Director might appoint an Alternate.[61] Norway put forward an amendment to this by which the Alternates as well as the Executive Directors would be elected by the members whom the Executive Director represented.[62] The Norwegian delegation thought that it might be difficult for each member country to reach agreement with the Executive Director on the suitability of an Alternate proposed by the latter. As against this, it was argued that it was better to regard the Executive Director and his Alternate as a team of two and, in order to ensure that the team was harmonious, the Director should be able to choose his own Alternate. The latter view was accepted by the Commission and the proposal that Executive Directors should appoint Alternates adopted.

Section 3 (g). The proposal in the U.S. draft, that the Executive Directors should be in continuous session at the principal office of the Fund for at least the first three years of operations, was resisted by several delegations. The United Kingdom put forward arguments resembling those advanced at Atlantic City. The Netherlands delegation contended that it was essential that the Directors should be drawn from among the most senior officials in the member countries, and argued that this would be impossible if they had to be continuously in residence in Washington. The discussion which took place on these alternatives has not been recorded, but it would appear that the majority of the delegations accepted as a practical compromise a formula requiring the Directors to "function in continuous session" at the headquarters of the Fund, and to "meet as often as the business of the Fund may require." The problem recurred at the first meeting of the Board of Governors, and is discussed in that context in Chapter 6.

Article XII, Section 4. Managing Director and staff

The proposals of the United States and the United Kingdom for the appointment of a Managing Director and for the provision of staff were accepted after some redrafting. The only substantial point that arose was a proposal by India to stipulate that "in employing staff due regard shall be paid to the fair representation of the nationals of member countries."[63] The Special Committee on Executive Directors suggested instead that the Managing Director in appointing staff should be required to "pay due regard to the importance of selecting per-

60 *Proceedings*, p. 44.
61 *Proceedings*, p. 275.
62 Alternative C, *Proceedings*, p. 221.
63 Alternative D, *Proceedings*, p. 222.

sonnel recruited on as wide a geographical basis as is possible." [64] The latter principle was adopted. The Fund has, therefore, never been obliged to pay predominant attention to the nationality of staff members in choosing from applicants to fill vacant posts. As the Committee recommended, it has had regard to "the paramount importance of securing the highest standards of efficiency and of technical competence."

Article XIII. Offices and Depositories

Article XIII, Section 1. Location of offices

The United States proposed, as at Atlantic City, that the principal office of the Fund should be located in "the member having the largest quota." [65] The United Kingdom, which, as we have seen, had hoped that the principal office could be located in Europe, proposed as an alternative that the location of the principal office should be decided at the first meeting of the Board of Governors.[66] The object of this amendment was to ensure that voting on the proposal should take place not in the Conference, where each delegation had one vote, but at the Board of Governors, where voting would be weighted. Discussion between the British and U.S. delegations, however, revealed that the latter was convinced that Congress would not accept the proposal for the Fund unless its headquarters were in the United States. The United Kingdom accordingly withdrew its alternative and the U.S. proposal was adopted, although the British delegation entered the reservation that "the Government of the United Kingdom may later find it desirable to ask the governments to consider the general question of the location of various international bodies." [67]

Article XIV. Transitional Period

The main principles underlying Article XIV had been evolved, as has been seen in the previous chapters, during the preparation of the Joint Statement. The draft submitted to the Conference by the United States and the United Kingdom, jointly, was briefly discussed and, subject to some redrafting, accepted.[68] It distinguished between the postwar transitional period during which countries might maintain restrictions, on the one hand, and, on the other, the periods of three years from the date when the Fund should begin operations (after which the Fund was to report annually on restrictions) and of five years from that date (after which, in addition, members were to consult with the Fund on the retention of restrictions). In this way, it met the apprehensions of the United Kingdom

[64] *Proceedings*, p. 276.
[65] Alternative A, *Proceedings*, p. 51.
[66] Alternative B, *Proceedings*, p. 51.
[67] *Proceedings*, p. 825.
[68] *Proceedings*, pp. 56–57, 537–38, 607, 629.

that the length of the transitional period might be thought to be confined to three years, and instead left it undefined.

Article XV. Withdrawal from Membership

Article XV, Section 1. Right of members to withdraw

The proposal put by the United States to the Conference was that a member might withdraw from the Fund at any time on giving written notice and that the withdrawal would become effective when the notice was received.[69] To this, Australia offered an amendment to the effect that the right of withdrawal should not be prejudiced by membership of the Fund being made a condition of membership of any other international body.[70] This, of course, referred to the obligation placed upon countries joining the Bank to become members of the Fund. Supporting its amendment in Committee 4, the Australian delegation urged that the freedom to withdraw from the Fund was the country's ultimate right; the way in which it could effectively exert its sovereignty.[71] However, when Article XV was discussed in the Commission, the amendment was not pressed, and the U.S. draft was accepted.

Article XVII. Amendments

The principles that amendments to the Articles should be channeled through the Board of Governors, and should require for their acceptance the approval of members having four fifths of the aggregate votes, were set out in the draft originally submitted by the United States, which was elaborated from its proposal at Atlantic City.[72] These principles were sustained by the Conference. As finally drafted, the provision required the concurrence of three fifths of the members, having four fifths of the total votes.

Article XVIII. Interpretation

The problem facing the Conference in connection with this Article, as explained to Commission I by the reporting delegate of Committee 4, was that of

> keeping disputes concerning the interpretation of the Agreement between the Fund and any member country, within the setup of the Fund itself, but, at the same time, to secure for the member in question privileges of fair treatment.[73]

---

[69] Alternative A, *Proceedings*, p. 52.
[70] Alternative B, *Proceedings*, p. 52.
[71] *Proceedings*, p. 428.
[72] *Proceedings*, pp. 57–58.
[73] *Proceedings*, p. 428.

The problem was extensively debated in the Committee, the resulting draft being accepted by Commission I.[74]

The distinguishing feature of this Article, that interpretation of the Articles of Agreement was entrusted to the Executive Directors, with the Board of Governors as a final court of appeal, was at the time unique (except for the similar provision in the Articles of the Bank) among the charters of international organizations. Since 1944, however, it has been widely adopted.

Article XX. Final Provisions

Article XX, Section 4. Initial determination of par values

China proposed that a country which had been occupied by the enemy might postpone communicating a par value and meanwhile might use the Fund's resources after agreeing with the Fund on a provisional initial rate of exchange,[75] and Norway proposed that in such a country the initial par value might be recognized as a provisional one.[76] South Africa went further than Norway, and suggested that for a period of two years all par values should be provisional. This proposal, however, was rejected on the advice of the U.S. delegation, which pointed out that the exchange rates of at least thirty countries could be regarded as firm, so that to require all initial parities to be provisional would substantially weaken the international exchange network. The Chinese proposal was substantially adopted, and a concession was made to the Norwegian contention by permitting the period during which a par value must be communicated to the Fund, normally 90 days, to be extended for a member whose metropolitan territory had been occupied by the enemy, by agreement between the Fund and the member.

RESULTS OF THE CONFERENCE

The Final Act, embodying the Articles of Agreement of the Fund and of the Bank together with a number of resolutions that are of less direct concern to this history, was signed by representatives of all delegations on July 22, 1944. The commitment of the delegations was a qualified one. As Keynes pointed out at an Executive Plenary Session on July 20, the whole proceedings were *ad referendum*.[77] He therefore urged that the reservations made by several delegates, noted above, should not be made part of the Final Act of the Conference, but

[74] *Proceedings*, p. 629. For a discussion of the powers of interpretation conferred by this Article, see Joseph Gold, *Interpretation by the Fund*, IMF Pamphlet Series, No. 11 (Washington, 1968).

[75] Alternative A, *Proceedings*, p. 486.

[76] Alternative B, *Proceedings*, pp. 220–21. Cf. above, p. 34.

[77] *Proceedings*, pp. 1197-98.

should be retained in the minutes of Commission I. This suggestion was adopted.[78]

It can only be regarded as remarkable that there emerged from the deliberations of so large and multilingual a conference, documents as coherent and self-consistent as the Articles of Agreement of the two institutions have proved themselves to be. The Articles of Agreement of the Fund transcend in many respects the Joint Statement of Experts on which they were originally based. Nevertheless, the pressure of time took its toll. "There were ambiguities in the text," as Mr. Rasminsky said later, "some intended and others not." As he had been chairman of the Drafting Committee, his comment was clearly authoritative. Sometimes, in the telling phrase of the first Managing Director of the Fund, "voluntary misunderstandings" helped to ease the path of the drafters. But on other occasions, irreconcilable differences of view emerged and a "deliberately ambiguous text was devised."

These limitations must be borne in mind in any attempt to summarize the principal features of the Articles. Nevertheless, such an attempt must here be made, both to indicate the considerations which weighed with prospective members when, over the months following Bretton Woods, they deliberated whether to join the new institutions, and also to prepare for the discussion of the activities of the Fund, which will occupy the remainder of this volume.

For ease of exposition, the contents of the Articles may be divided into four categories—purposes, obligations, benefits, and administration.

Purposes

The importance which the Conference attached to the statement of the purposes of the Fund is clear from the final sentence of Article I, which reads: "The Fund shall be guided in all its decisions by the purposes set forth in this Article." After providing for the creation of a permanent institution, the Article sets out that a function of the Fund is

> to facilitate the expansion and balanced growth of international trade, and to contribute thereby to the promotion and maintenance of high levels of employment and real income and to the development of the productive resources of all members as primary objectives of economic policy.

There is no doubt that it was the prospect of escaping from the vicious circle of boom and slump which motivated many of the prospective members of the Fund to accept the obligations which the Articles imposed.

Obligations

Upon adherence to the Articles, each member undertook to carry out all its obligations under the Agreement. These included commitments to observe

[78] *Proceedings*, pp. 1088-91.

certain rules of good conduct in the monetary field, of which the following are some leading examples. Members undertook to collaborate with the Fund to promote exchange stability, to maintain orderly exchange arrangements with other members, and to avoid competitive exchange rate alterations. They agreed to establish, by agreement with the Fund, an initial par value; to maintain the rates for exchange transactions in their territories within specified margins of this par value; not to change the par value except to correct a fundamental disequilibrium; and not to change it without the concurrence of the Fund, except for minor adjustments totaling 10 per cent of the initial par value.

Members also undertook to make their currencies convertible as defined in the Articles. They agreed that they would not introduce or adapt restrictions on payments and transfers for current international transactions, discriminatory currency arrangements, or multiple currency practices, except with the prior approval of the Fund. Each member was given the opportunity, however, of notifying the Fund whether it was prepared to carry out these obligations in respect of convertibility at once or whether it intended to avail itself of certain transitional arrangements under which it would be subject to a less rigorous regime. The latter permitted the maintenance or adaptation of restrictions on payments and transfers for current international transactions at the discretion of the member and without the prior approval of the Fund. Members whose territories had been occupied by the enemy, but only such members, could also introduce restrictions where necessary. A member electing to avail itself of the transitional arrangements was obliged to notify the Fund as soon thereafter as it was prepared to accept all the obligations of convertibility. The Fund itself was required to report on the restrictions still in force three years after it began operations, and each year thereafter. Beginning five years after the Fund started operations, members still maintaining restrictions under the transitional arrangements were required to consult the Fund annually as to their further retention.

An additional obligation of members was to provide the resources with which the Fund would operate. Each member had to pay to the Fund a subscription equal to its quota, partly in gold and partly in its own currency. No part of the subscription could be recovered except upon withdrawal from membership and in accordance with a settlement of accounts agreed with the Fund, or upon the liquidation of the Fund.

Members also committed themselves to provide statistical and other data needed for the Fund's operations, and to be bound by the decisions of the Fund, including its interpretations of the provisions of the Articles.

Benefits

The benefits to be derived from the Agreement were of two distinct kinds, one related to Articles I and IV and the other to Article V. Whether a country joined the Fund or not, it might expect to share in the steady growth of the international economy envisaged in Article I. But in addition, members could count, under that Article and Article IV, on the active cooperation of fellow members in maintaining stable exchanges and avoiding competitive depreciation.

The benefits to be expected from Article V were more specific, viz., that the member might, when its circumstances necessitated this, draw (borrow) from the Fund for a limited period certain of the resources with which the latter had been endowed. Precisely under what conditions members might draw remained to be clarified; differences of views as to members' rights in this respect have already been described in some length in Chapter 3, and it will be necessary to return to the subject in Part II. Nevertheless, this right formed a major attraction to countries considering membership of the Fund.

Administration

Three points about the structure of the Fund, as created by the Articles, are perhaps worth making. The first is that the Fund's decisions were to be taken by a weighted system of voting, giving proportionately greater power to the members with larger quotas and, for certain decisions, slightly augmented voting power to creditor countries at the expense of debtor countries. The second point is that the Fund was to be managed in its day-to-day affairs by a Board of Executive Directors in permanent session; it was not to be controlled by a group meeting occasionally, whether in response to emergencies or on some periodic basis. This may have suggested to prospective members the hope that the Fund would be able to act in good time to forestall the difficulties which it was intended to counteract. The third point to be mentioned was the provision for interpreting the Articles. The inclusion of such a provision, like the corresponding power of the Supreme Court of the United States to rule on the constitutionality of laws, was a testimony to the realization of the Bretton Woods conferees that no constitution could successfully cope with changing circumstances for many years after it was drafted. Some degree of elasticity of this kind was particularly desirable in view of the haste with which the Articles were prepared. But it is significant that the power of interpretation was conferred upon the Fund itself.

RATIFICATION OF THE AGREEMENT

Article XX, Section 2 (*d*), provided that, as each country adhered to the Articles of Agreement, it should transmit 1/100 of 1 per cent of its quota to the U.S. Government to meet the administrative expenses of the Fund; and that if the Agreement did not come into force by December 31, 1945, these payments should be returned to the signatory governments. The condition for the entry into force of the Agreement, stated in Article XX, Section 1, was that countries having 65 per cent of the total quotas allotted at Bretton Woods should have signed it and deposited instruments of ratification. In effect, therefore, if the Conference was to eventuate in an organization, countries with quotas totaling $5,720 million would have to sign the Agreement and deposit instruments of acceptance by the end of 1945. Of this total, the United States and the United Kingdom, which could presumably be counted upon as certain members, would provide $4,050 million. The remainder had to come from other countries, which would certainly wait for a lead from the United States at any rate.

The U.S. Bretton Woods Agreements Act, which authorized acceptance of the Fund's Articles of Agreement by the United States, was approved by the President on July 31, 1945.[79] Its passage through Congress was assisted by the fact that two Senators and two members of the House of Representatives had been among the U.S. delegates to Bretton Woods, and two other Representatives among the delegation's technical advisors. Nevertheless, it encountered opposition in both houses of Congress. It is unnecessary here to detail the course of the debate, which has been effectively described by Professor Gardner.[80] However, certain features of the Act proved to have important consequences for the subsequent work of the Fund, and these must be elucidated.

The significant clauses in the U.S. Bretton Woods Agreements Act were four. Of these, the first was Section 3, which laid down, inter alia, that the Executive Directors and Alternates for the United States should be appointed by the President "by and with the advice and consent of the Senate." While such a stipulation is normal in connection with the appointment of high officials in U.S. Government service, its application to the U.S. members of the Board of the Fund seemed to confirm the trend away from the technical organization which Keynes had envisaged toward the politically influenced constitution which U.S. officials had long regarded as indispensable for an organization which was to secure the support of Congress.

The next section, following the precedent of the abortive Inter-American Bank of 1940, set up a National Advisory Council on International Monetary and Financial Problems. The members of the Council were to be the Secretary of the Treasury, the Secretary of State, the Secretary of Commerce, the Chairman of the Board of Governors of the Federal Reserve System, and the Chairman of the Board of Trustees of the Export-Import Bank of Washington.[81] To this body

[79] Public Law 171, 79th Congress, 1st Session; reproduced in International Monetary Fund, *Selected Decisions of the Executive Directors and Selected Documents*, Third Issue (Washington, January 1965), pp. 146–56.

[80] Richard N. Gardner, *Sterling-Dollar Diplomacy* (Oxford, 1956), pp. 129–43.

[81] The supervisory committee proposed in 1940 (called the Inter-American Bank Committee) was to have comprised the Secretary of State, the Secretary of the Treasury, the Chairman of the Board of Governors of the Federal Reserve System, and the Federal Loan Administrator. —U.S. Congress, Senate, Committee on Foreign Relations, *Inter-American Bank* (Hearings Before a Subcommittee . . . on Executive K), 77th Cong., 1st sess., 1941, p. 14.

was entrusted the duty of recommending to the President "general policy directives for the guidance of the representatives of the United States on the Fund and the Bank." Moreover, it was specified that whenever the Articles of Agreement required the approval, consent, or agreement of the United States to any act by the Fund, the Council was to decide whether that approval, consent, or agreement should be given or refused. Finally, the Council was to transmit reports not less frequently than semiannually on the participation of the United States in the Fund, and special reports every two years on such subjects as the extent to which the Fund had achieved the purposes for which it was established and whether its resources should be increased or decreased. The special reports were also to include "an over-all appraisal of the extent to which the operations and policies of the Fund and the Bank have served, and in the future may be expected to serve, the interests of the United States and the world in promoting sound international economic cooperation and furthering world security."

Section 5 of the Act required the Administration to seek the approval of Congress for any change in the U.S. quota in the Fund, any change in the par value of the U.S. dollar, or any amendment of the Articles of Agreement; or for making any loan to the Fund.

By Section 13.(a), the Governor and the Executive Director appointed by the United States were directed to

> obtain promptly an official interpretation by the Fund as to whether its authority to use its resources extends beyond current monetary stabilization operations to afford temporary assistance to members in connection with seasonal, cyclical, and emergency fluctuations in the balance of payments of any member for current transactions, and whether it has authority to use its resources to provide facilities for relief, reconstruction, or armaments, or to meet a large or sustained outflow of capital on the part of any member.

While some of the points covered by this section were clearly explicit in the Articles of Agreement—as, for example, the prohibition of the use of the Fund's resources to meet large or sustained outflows of capital—other phrases seemed designed to limit the activities of the Fund to short-term operations even more rigidly than the Articles themselves contemplated.

This aspect of the Act caused concern to Keynes. He did not see how it was possible to interpret the Articles strictly in conformity with the words "seasonal, cyclical, and emergency fluctuations in the balance of payments," and he felt that the interpretation for which the Act asked could only be given in somewhat more general terms. Over and above this legal point, he was apprehensive that the effect of Section 13 might be to limit the day-to-day accessibility of the Fund to its members. He feared that this might follow if the Fund had discretion to refuse the use of its resources by a member on the ground that a particular drawing was not to meet a balance of payments problem of the specific types mentioned.

Steps toward the adherence of the United Kingdom itself to the Bretton Woods Agreement had not progressed far when Keynes expressed the fears just quoted, partly because the action of the United States was awaited, but also because there was growing concern in London about the financial position of the United Kingdom after the war, which was now clearly near its end. These fears were sharply accentuated by the cessation of Lend-Lease aid on September 1, 1945. It became brutally clear to Treasury officials in London that unless some emergency aid could be provided by the United States to replace Lend-Lease, the United Kingdom could not afford to commit itself to such obligations as those in the Articles of Agreement. Until it was known what financial assistance the United States was prepared to make available, no action on the Bretton Woods Agreement was possible. Negotiations had begun in Washington in August, but were adjourned to allow the new British Government to be fully briefed. They were resumed with Keynes as the chief negotiator, on September 13.

This is not the place to detail the long and painful negotiations out of which emerged the Anglo-American Financial Agreement of 1945, with its provision of a loan of $3.75 billion on terms which, though more onerous than Keynes had optimistically hoped when he came to Washington, were far more generous than would have befitted a commercial negotiation.[82] The Financial Agreement was eventually signed in Washington on December 6, and the Bretton Woods Agreement and the Financial Agreement were presented together to the British Parliament for approval. Owing in part to the influence of one of Keynes' most eloquent speeches, the necessary legislation was passed on December 18, and signature of the Articles of Agreement by the United Kingdom therefore became possible.

A review undertaken by the U.S. Treasury on November 14, 1945 had shown that, in addition to the United States, only the Union of South Africa and Venezuela were ready to sign the Agreement, and the former was waiting for the United Kingdom to do so first. (In fact, Venezuela's signature was delayed for a year by technical difficulties.) By December 18, however, 11 countries, with quotas totaling $4,806 million, had completed the necessary legislative action, and 8 more, with quotas totaling $1,575 million, were expected to do so shortly. Arrangements were accordingly made for a formal ceremony at the Department of State on December 27, at which representatives of 29 countries, with quotas totaling $7,079.5 million, signed the Agreement, viz., Belgium, Bolivia, Brazil, Canada, China, Colombia, Costa Rica, Czechoslovakia, Ecuador, Egypt, Ethiopia, France, Greece, Guatemala, Honduras, Iceland, India, Iraq, Luxembourg, the Netherlands, Norway, Paraguay, the Philippines, Poland, the Union of South Africa, the United Kingdom, the United States, Uruguay, and Yugoslavia. On the next day, they were joined by the Dominican Republic and

[82] For a good account of the negotiations, see Gardner, *op. cit.*, pp. 188–223.

Iran, and on December 31 by Chile, Cuba, Mexico, and Peru. Thus, by the deadline implicit in Article XX, 35 countries, with quotas representing 83.22 per cent of the total, had taken at least the first step toward joining the organization. Actual members at that date numbered 30, because the deposit of the instruments of acceptance by Brazil, Costa Rica, Cuba, Poland, and Uruguay was delayed until after the turn of the year. The quotas for the 30 that had completed the formalities totaled $6,979.5 million, well in excess of the $5,720 million needed to bring the Agreement into force.

The most notable of the absentees was, of course, the U.S.S.R. No formal refusal to join the Fund was forthcoming from the Soviet Government, whose representatives merely stated to U.S. officials that Moscow needed more time to consider the terms of the Agreement.[83] The reasons why the U.S.S.R. did not proceed with membership, despite the active participation of the Soviet delegation in the Bretton Woods meetings and the amendment of drafts of several provisions of the Articles to meet Soviet views, can therefore only be guessed. Some indication of the attitude of the U.S.S.R. may be found in the difficulties raised by the Soviet delegation in discussions with the U.S. Interdepartmental Committee in the first quarter of 1944. Other reasons may be inferred from the reservations which the Soviet delegation attached to the minutes of the final meeting of Commission I at Bretton Woods,[84] although it is noteworthy that these did not include an objection to the provision of information, which had throughout seemed likely to be an obstacle. But the timing was probably also important. By the end of 1945 the European war had been over for six months and the war with Japan for four. Lend-Lease aid had been cut off, and those frictions between East and West that Churchill later described as an iron curtain had begun to assert themselves. The high tide of cooperation between the U.S.S.R. and the Atlantic powers, at least in financial affairs, had passed.

Of the other participants at Bretton Woods that had not signed the Articles of Agreement by the end of 1945, three—El Salvador, Nicaragua, and Panama—did so during the first meeting of the Governors of the Fund, held at Savannah, Georgia, in March 1946 (described in the next chapter). Denmark, whose membership had been delayed through the absence of a government during the war, joined shortly afterward, on March 30, 1946. The expansion of membership from 39 on March 30, 1946 to 103 two decades later will be recorded in detail hereafter. It may here be noted, however, that Australia deferred joining the Fund until August 5, 1947; the delay may be partly explained by the reservations entered by its delegation at Bretton Woods. Haiti's signature had to be postponed for technical reasons until September 8, 1953. Liberia did not become

[83] Raymond F. Mikesell, "Negotiating at Bretton Woods, 1944," in *Negotiating with the Russians*, Raymond Dennett and Joseph E. Johnson, eds. (Boston, World Peace Foundation, 1951), p. 114.

[84] *Proceedings*, pp. 1090–91.

a member until March 28, 1962; New Zealand, not until August 31, 1961. Venezuela's membership, as mentioned above, dates from December 30, 1946. Thus, of the 45 United and Associated Nations invited to participate in the Bretton Woods Conference, only the U.S.S.R. has so far failed to join the Fund.

With the ceremonial signing of the Agreement by the first 29 members on December 27, 1945, the Fund's prehistory ends. The story of the ensuing twenty years will occupy us throughout the rest of this volume.

PART II

The Beginnings

CHAPTER

6

Savannah (March 1946)

THE INAUGURAL MEETING of the Boards of Governors of the International Monetary Fund and the International Bank for Reconstruction and Development convened at the General Oglethorpe Hotel, Wilmington Island, Savannah, Georgia, on Friday, March 8, 1946.[1] The United States, which by Article XX, Section 3 (*a*), of the Articles of Agreement was responsible for organizing the meeting, had sent out invitations on January 28. Preparations for the meeting had begun in Washington in the previous September. On January 24, 1946 drafts of an agenda for the meeting and of by-laws for the two institutions had been distributed for comment to technicians from a dozen member countries and had been discussed with these technicians at a series of meetings at the U.S. Treasury. The draft agenda, which contemplated that the Boards should meet jointly, had been approved, and only drafting amendments had been made to most of the by-laws. It had been decided, however, that these should provide for the Fund's Annual Report to the Governors to be submitted by the Executive Directors and not, as in the original U.S. draft, by the Managing Director. This change appears to have been significant of a wish to strengthen the hands of the Board vis-à-vis the staff. A provision that Executive Directors and Alternates should be regarded as full-time officers had been opposed by the representatives of a number of countries, and dropped. However, the United States maintained its view that it was necessary for the Directors to be engaged full time, and the subject was intensively debated at the meeting.

THE GOVERNORS MEET

Those present at Savannah included Governors and Alternate Governors for the 38 countries that were already members of the Fund, or became members during the meeting; observers from Australia, Denmark, New Zealand, the

[1] No official report of the proceedings was issued, but the Temporary Secretary prepared a compilation entitled *Selected Documents, Board of Governors' Inaugural Meetings* (hereafter cited as *Selected Documents*).

LEO ROSENTHAL

Inaugural Meeting of Governors, Savannah, Ga., March 1946

U.S.S.R., and Venezuela; and a representative of the UN Economic and Social Council (ECOSOC). Haiti and Liberia had also been invited to send observers, but did not do so. Mr. Vinson, who in 1945 had succeeded Mr. Morgenthau as U.S. Secretary of the Treasury, was elected as Chairman.

The opening joint session of the meeting, on March 9, was devoted to speeches and to the adoption of provisional regulations, under which committees were appointed to deal with credentials, the agenda, and nominations to the working committees for the later business of the meeting. Mr. Vinson's remarks from the chair referred in somewhat emotional terms to the atmosphere of the Bretton Woods Conference, and to the peace-building legacy which had devolved upon the Governors. He was followed by the representatives of China, Czechoslovakia, France, and Mexico, who all spoke hopefully of the future of the Fund, though not without some references to the problems left unsolved at Bretton Woods.

The final speaker at this first session was Lord Keynes, in his capacity as Governor for the United Kingdom. What he said has been reproduced in full in his biography.[2] It was no ordinary speech: Keynes was rarely ordinary. Departing from platitudes, it evoked the assistance of the good fairies to watch over the Bretton Woods twins (whose names, he suggested in passing, should have been interchanged). But at the end a darker note intruded; he hoped that the fairy Carabosse had not been forgotten, lest coming uninvited she should curse the children. "You two brats," he visualized her saying, "shall grow up politicians; your every thought and act shall have an *arrière-pensée;* everything you determine shall not be for its own sake or on its own merits but because of something else."

The speech reflected many unspoken thoughts: Keynes had hoped that the meeting could have been arranged somewhat later than it was, and had been overruled; he had hoped that the Fund would be located in New York, if not in Europe, and had learnt that it had to be in Washington; he had hoped that White would be Managing Director of the Fund, to guide its initial steps along the technical lines which he had visualized for it, and he had learnt that this was not to be; and he feared that the determination of the U.S. delegation at Bretton Woods to insist on full-time Executive Directors meant, in Washington, full-time political control of the new organizations. Moreover, he was a sick man (he died six weeks later). This was almost his swan song; and it did not prevail. Mr. Vinson had his own ideas about the way in which the meeting must be shaped—ideas which were strongly influenced by his keen politician's sense of what Congress would be looking for, and what would conduce to congressional passage of the Anglo-American Financial Agreement, which was still pending on Capitol Hill.

---

[2] R. F. Harrod, *The Life of John Maynard Keynes* (London, 1951), pp. 631–32.

Some clash between the two men was probably inevitable. Mr. Vinson liked even less than White the elusive wit and the barbed thrusts which were characteristic of Keynes' forensic style. Mr. Vinson was a lawyer, not an economist, and was Secretary of the Treasury only as an interlude in a legal career. (He later became Chief Justice of the United States.) He believed in the Fund and the Bank; but he believed in them as political rather than as monetary organizations. He had not, of course—as his predecessor had—lived through the formative period when the Fund had emerged from the joint thinking of White, Keynes, and the multitude of other national representatives who had been consulted along the way. It was all plain sailing for him; and he saw no occasion for the British representatives to make awkward objections.

Yet there were points which the British could not concede without a fight. Official views in London retained enough hankering for Keynes' original concept of a quasi-automatic monetary mechanism, and enough fear that the sterling area might be endangered by the inept handling of a politically dominated Fund, to impel the delegation to resist the final steps toward the American plan for the Fund. Their opportunities came as the formalities were completed and the business of the meeting began.

UNCONTROVERSIAL BUSINESS

We may first dispose of those items on the agenda at Savannah which, however important for the future of the Fund, did not arouse serious controversy at the time, reserving for fuller treatment in the next section the topics which engendered real disagreement.

The formal business of the meeting went smoothly. There were joint sessions of the Boards of Governors on Saturday, March 9, and daily from the following Wednesday. On each Monday, March 11 and March 18 (the last day of the meeting), the Boards of the two institutions met to transact business that concerned them separately. In the first Fund session, the Governors elected Mr. Vinson Permanent Chairman of the Board. At later sessions, a quota of $68 million was determined for, and accepted by, Denmark, and an invitation from ECOSOC to negotiate a relationship with the Fund and Bank was referred to the Executive Directors. Temporary Secretaries of the Fund and Bank were appointed, and resolutions passed providing for interim financial arrangements.[3] The draft by-laws were reviewed by a committee and approved with minor amendments. Members were recommended to exempt from taxation the salaries and allowances paid to the Managing Director, the Executive Directors, and staff, as required by Article IX, Section 9 (*b*). The first meeting of the Executive Direc-

[3] Resolutions IM-1, IM-2, *Selected Documents*, pp. 17–18. (For the system of numbering Governors' Resolutions, see Abbreviations and Definitions: Resolution, p. xvii above).

tors was convened for "about May 1," in Washington, with the U.S. Executive Director in the chair until a Managing Director took office. (Subsequently the date was fixed for May 6.) It was decided that Executive Directors and their Alternates would take office on the date of the first Board meeting or on that of their appointment, whichever was the later. It should be added that the selection of four of the five Executive Directors to be appointed under Article XII, Section 3 (*b*) (i), was made known at Savannah: Mr. White (United States), Mr. Yee-Chun Koo (China), Mr. Pierre Mendès-France (France), and Mr. Jagannath Vishwanath Joshi (India). No appointment of the Executive Director for the United Kingdom had been made by the time the Governors dispersed.

A number of other matters that gave rise to discussion without arousing real controversy are described below.

Fiscal year

Mr. Vinson, as Governor for the United States, proposed that the fiscal year should coincide with the calendar year. This was expected to mean that future Annual Meetings of the Boards of Governors would be held in March. The Governors for a number of other countries, however, objected to this, on the ground that budget timetables made it impossible for Ministers of Finance to leave their own countries in March. It appeared that September was the most convenient month for their attendance. It was accordingly decided that the fiscal year should run from July 1 to June 30, and that the first Annual Meeting of the Governors should be held in September 1946.

Procedures Committee

At the session of the Governors on March 11, Mr. Vinson announced the appointment of a steering committee—an "Executive Committee"—of twelve members, with himself in the chair and Keynes as vice-chairman; he thought it would be as well to have such a committee "to which matters might be referred, particularly in the way of procedure." It would appear, however, that some members of this committee feared that, as conceived by the chairman, it would have formed an overriding body controlling the actions of the Executive Directors. Therefore, when the committee met two days later, it decided that a Procedures Committee, consisting of the same members, should be appointed instead, to be available for consultation by the Chairman during the interval between the Inaugural Meeting and the First Annual Meeting and to meet, if necessary, immediately before the latter. This was accepted by the Governors.

It may be added that the Procedures Committee has since been reconstituted at each Annual Meeting. It has never been consulted between Meetings, but is convened a day or two in advance of each Annual Meeting, at which time it performs the functions that might otherwise have been delegated to agenda, credentials, and steering committees.

Quota for Paraguay

The Governor for Paraguay urged that the quota for his country, fixed at $2 million at Bretton Woods, should be increased to $5 million. He was supported by the Governors for El Salvador, Honduras, and Mexico, the Governor for El Salvador urging that the Procedures Committee should consider the question promptly and make a recommendation on which the Governors could forthwith take action. The Procedures Committee, however, had already reviewed the application and decided that it would be better that the Executive Directors should consider it. The Board agreed, on the understanding that the Executive Directors would be asked to make a recommendation as soon as possible and to seek a decision from the Governors by mail or cable.

The Alternate Governor for Iran, Mr. Taghi Nassr, sought to obtain a similar instruction to the Executive Directors to consider an increase in the Iranian quota, but as no formal application for a revision had been made, this was ruled out by the Chairman.

New members

The Governors extended until December 31, 1946 the time within which countries that had been invited to Bretton Woods might accept membership of the Fund and Bank.

Applications for membership received from four countries not represented at Bretton Woods—Italy, Lebanon, Syria, and Turkey—were referred to the Executive Directors for determination of quotas and other appropriate action. The Governors for Greece and Yugoslavia raised the question whether a former enemy country which had not so far signed a Treaty of Peace—i.e., Italy—should be admitted; this question was also remitted to the Executive Directors.

Appointed Directors

The Governor for India, Sir Chintaman Deshmukh, called attention to an apparent inconsistency in the Articles concerning appointed Executive Directors. Article XII, Section 3 (*b*) (i), provided that the five members with the largest quotas should appoint one Director each; Article XII, Section 3 (*f*), provided that Directors were to continue in office until their successors were appointed or elected. But what if a new member joined the Fund with a larger quota than the previously fifth largest? The question was of particular importance to India, because it was, in the absence of the U.S.S.R., the fifth largest member; should the U.S.S.R. belatedly join the Fund, what would happen to the Indian appointee?

The problem was remitted to an ad hoc committee, which recognized that the two subsections mentioned failed to deal with the contingency to which the Indian Governor had referred, and recommended that they should be interpreted in such a way as to cover it. The interpretation suggested, which was remitted to the Executive Directors for decision, was that the subsections should mean that

> any member having one of the five largest quotas at the date of a regular election or at any date between regular elections shall be entitled to appoint an Executive Director who shall hold office until the next regular election without prejudice to the right of a subsequently admitted member to appoint a Director if it has one of the five largest quotas.

Size of Executive Board

Also at the instance of the Governor for India, the ad hoc committee mentioned above took note of the fact that the Articles did not provide for an expansion of the number of Executive Directors—initially twelve—as and when countries not invited to Bretton Woods came to join the Fund. It therefore recommended that if at any time before the second election of Executive Directors—i.e., before September 1948—there had been an accretion of such countries with votes totaling 4,000 or more, any members who had not participated in the election of the Executive Directors already installed should participate in the election of an additional Director. This recommendation was accepted by the Governors, and became Resolution IM-10.

Interpretations

It will be recalled that the U.S. Bretton Woods Agreements Act (P.L. 171) had instructed the U.S. Governor and the U.S. Executive Director to seek an interpretation of the Articles of Agreement as to the functions of the Fund. The British Government was also anxious to obtain an interpretation, but on a different point: given its pursuit of a policy of full employment, would any "steps necessary to protect a member from unemployment of a chronic or persistent character, arising from pressure on its balance of payments, . . . be measures necessary to correct a fundamental disequilibrium"? Both questions were remitted to the Executive Directors for decision.[4]

ELECTION OF EXECUTIVE DIRECTORS

A touch of comedy was introduced in the concluding meeting of the Governors of the Fund. Schedule C of the Articles of Agreement had laid down the necessarily complicated procedure for the election of five Executive Directors by the Governors of the member countries that were entitled neither to appoint

[4] Resolutions IM-5 and IM-6, *Selected Documents*, p. 19.

Directors under Article XII, Section 3 (*b*) (i), nor to vote for those to be elected by the American Republics under Article XII, Section 3 (*b*) (iv). This procedure required that no nominee could be elected who received fewer than 19 per cent of the total votes. In principle, moreover—and subject to the condition that no Governor's votes could be split—no Director was to have more than 20 per cent of the total votes. If on a first ballot fewer than five Executive Directors were elected, a second ballot was to be taken to elect the remainder. For this purpose it was necessary to decide which of the votes cast for each elected Director were to be counted toward the 19 per cent necessary to elect him. This was to be done by counting first the votes cast for him by the Governor with the largest number of votes, then the votes cast by the Governor with the next largest number of votes, and so on. The votes cast by any Governors whose votes were found in this way to be wholly unnecessary for the election of an elected Director were to be disregarded. Those participating in the second ballot were to be the Governors whose votes were thus disregarded in the first ballot, together with those who had then cast their votes for nominees not elected.

Unfortunately, in devising this procedure two points were overlooked. There was a mathematical difficulty, in that the blocks of votes to be cast by each Governor were relatively large. It was inherently improbable that the groups to elect Directors would be so formed that no four of them would cast more than 81 per cent of the votes. If the Governors forming these groups cast collectively more than 81 per cent of the total votes, the fifth Director could be elected only if it were possible to divert the votes of one or more Governors without reducing any of the groups below 19 per cent of the total; and since no country had less than 1 per cent of the total votes this might well be impracticable. The second difficulty was that most member countries would have some preference for a particular Executive Director, and the Governors concerned would not wish to see their votes diverted from that Director to another one in order to comply with the rule.

At Savannah, there were 16 member countries eligible to vote for the five Executive Directors; the total of their votes was 18,100, so that a minimum of 3,439 votes was necessary to secure election. On the first ballot, three Executive Directors were elected: Mr. Louis Rasminsky (Canada) with 4,260 votes, Mr. Gijsbert W. J. Bruins (Netherlands) with 4,250 votes, and Mr. Jan V. Mládek (Czechoslovakia) with 3,850 votes. The other two candidates, Mr. Ahmed Zaki Saad (Egypt) and Mr. Camille Gutt (Belgium), received 2,890 votes and 2,850 votes, respectively. But the only member country whose votes were wholly unnecessary to secure the election of any one of the three elected Directors was Iceland, with 260 votes, and although on a second ballot these were cast for Mr. Gutt, they were insufficient to secure the latter's election. A third ballot, with the same result, showed that an impasse had been reached. It was broken only by inventing a new rule; the Chairman suggested to the meeting that, as there were five vacancies and only five candidates, it was obvious that Messrs. Gutt and Saad should be seated, and this was unanimously agreed by the Board. A provision of this kind has been included in the rules for subsequent elections, and as an additional safeguard the spread between maximum and minimum percentages has been widened.

Meanwhile, the two Latin American Executive Directors had been successfully elected, Mr. Francisco Alves dos Santos-Filho (Brazil) receiving 4,575 votes and Mr. Rodrigo Gómez (Mexico), 4,370.

LOCATION OF THE FUND

There remain for consideration two issues which were of particular concern to the United Kingdom, and which were already acute at Bretton Woods—the location of the Fund and the functions of Executive Directors.

It was mentioned at the beginning of this chapter that Keynes was aware, even at the first session of the Meeting, that the United States had decided that the Fund must be situated in Washington. Officially, however, the subject was referred to a Committee on Site, consisting of 17 Governors. That the principal office of the Fund must be located in the United States had been settled by Article XIII, Section 1. But this did not decide the question between New York and Washington. The arguments adduced for these two cities can best be reproduced in the committee's own words.[5] For New York, they were that

> the Fund as an international institution should not be associated too closely with the capital of any nation, and the staff and officials should be in an atmosphere conducive to allegiance to the Fund. New York, in addition to being a financial and economic world center, would afford a good opportunity for cooperation with the Social and Economic Councils [*sic*] of the United Nations Organization. The selection of New York would minimize the technical difficulties of operation; transportation facilities would be better.

The reasons given for preferring Washington were that

> the Fund, as an intergovernmental institution, should be free of any possible influence from economic, financial, or commercial private interests. In recent years there has been a shift from New York to Washington of international financial policy making. The judgment of the government of the country in which the Fund is to be located should be given substantial weight. Washington, D.C., affords a better opportunity for the members to communicate with the representatives of their respective governments. In Washington the officers of the Fund would have ready access to data and material relating to the economies of many countries.

The arguments in favor of New York were urged mainly by Keynes, but he drew support from the spokesmen for France and India. On the other side, a

[5] *Selected Documents*, pp. 29–30.

strong statement by the Alternate Governor for the United States, Mr. William L. Clayton, was reinforced by comments from Canada, China, Czechoslovakia, the Dominican Republic, Mexico, and Poland. At the end of the meeting, Keynes conceded defeat. "In the light of the unyielding attitude taken up by the American representative," he said, "we are . . . prepared to accept the proposal of the United States, but I am afraid that the arguments employed have not persuaded us that a mistake is not being made." The committee accordingly recommended, *nem. con.*, that

> the principal office of the Fund shall be located within the metropolitan area of Washington, D.C., United States of America.
>
> The Executive Directors may establish and maintain agencies or branch offices at any place in the territories of other members, whenever it is necessary to do so in order to facilitate the efficient conduct of the business of the Fund.

This recommendation was accepted by the Governors on March 14.

Was a mistake made? It is not the purpose of this history to anticipate events, but it seems clear that Keynes' essential thesis—that the Fund should be a technician-managed, semiautomatic mechanism—was never in fact feasible. Concerned as it would be with politically sensitive subjects such as exchange rates and exchange restrictions, the Fund was bound to be politically controlled; and in these conditions it mattered little whether it was located in New York, like that other political body the United Nations, or in Washington. For the rest, the arguments in favor of Washington seem to have worn better than those in favor of New York. Were Keynes able now to revise his judgment, he might feel that this was a battle which had not been worth fighting.

DUTIES OF EXECUTIVE DIRECTORS

The second controversy which divided the meeting was closely related to the preceding one. It, too, had been broached at Bretton Woods. The question was whether Executive Directors should be engaged full time on Fund business, or should have functions in their home countries and devote part time only to Fund affairs. What their remuneration should be would, of course, depend on the answer to the main question. The problem was accordingly remitted to a Committee on Functions and Remuneration of the Executive Directors and Alternates. As a subcommittee of the By-Laws Committee, but otherwise unchanged, this committee also considered the question of expenses for Governors.

The committee was faced at the outset with a problem of the interpretation of the Articles of Agreement. The relevant passage was Article XII, Section 3 (*g*), which reads: "The Executive Directors shall function in continuous session at the principal office of the Fund and shall meet as often as the business of the

Fund may require." What was the meaning of the phrase "function in continuous session"? Keynes said that, at Bretton Woods, these words had been interpreted as meaning that the Executive Directors need not be permanently in Washington. He contrasted the phrase "function in continuous session" with an earlier draft which said that the Executive Directors would be in residence at the Fund's headquarters.

To elucidate this, we must recall briefly the stages through which the requirement that became Article XII, Section 3 (*g*), passed. In the first mimeographed draft of the Stabilization Fund (April 1942), the relevant passage was "members of the operating committee should devote full time to the management of the Fund." In the December 11, 1942 draft and all subsequent ones, this became "the Executive Committee shall be continuously available at the head office of the Fund." In the Clearing Union, there had been no provision of this kind at all. In the Canadian Plan, the requirement was that "meetings of the Executive Committee shall be held at least once every two months and more frequently if the Executive Committee shall so decide." In the Joint Statement, the clause dealing with management provided only for the existence of an Executive Committee and said nothing about the conditions under which it should meet. The Section clearly needed substantial elaboration, and at Atlantic City both the United States and the United Kingdom put forward drafts for this purpose. The U.S. draft provided that "the Executive Directors . . . shall be in continuous session." [6] The British draft for Atlantic City had only a marginal note, "add reference to frequency of meetings," but at Bretton Woods the British delegation proposed that "the Executive Directors shall meet not less than once every three months." [7] Shortly afterward, Cuba proposed an alternative which provided that "the Executive Committee shall meet as often as the business of the Fund may require." [8] Later, the United States and the United Kingdom jointly put forward a further redraft, which on this particular point adopted the phrase from the U.S. alternative.[9] The change from "be in continuous session" to "function in continuous session" may possibly have reflected a proposal by Norway that "the Executive Directors shall be continuously in function." [10]

No surviving draft, in fact, calls for Executive Directors to be in residence at the Fund and Keynes was probably mistaken in referring to such a draft. He may, indeed, have been thinking of the stipulation in the U.S. draft for Article XII which requires the Chairman to "reside at the Headquarters of the Fund." This failure of memory did not, however, affect the substance of his contention that "function in continuous session" did not require the continuous

[6] Alternative A, *Proceedings*, p. 44.

[7] Alternative B, *Proceedings*, p. 46.

[8] Alternative C, *Proceedings*, p. 161.

[9] Combined Alternatives A and B, *Proceedings*, p. 162.

[10] Alternative C, *Proceedings*, p. 221.

presence of the Executive Directors in Washington. This was challenged, however, by the U.S. Alternate Governor, Mr. Clayton, who suggested that "continuous session" must mean "continuous service." He thought that no one could be said to be giving continuous service to his employer unless he was on full time. The Governor for Honduras, Ambassador Julian R. Cáceres, supporting him, suggested that "continuous session" must mean "daily work, daily meetings." Keynes, on the other hand, claimed that all that "continuous session" meant was that the Directors would be available to act whenever necessary—unlike the Governors, who met only at specified intervals. He argued that the precise point at issue at Bretton Woods was whether the Executive Directors would have to be full-time officials, and that the language used was chosen in order to leave the matter open.

Much necessarily depended upon what the Executive Directors were to do, and here again there were sharply contrasting views. On the one hand, Keynes thought that the right way to run an institution such as the Fund was for the Board to "consist of individuals very high in confidence of their own Treasury or Central Bank, individuals who were spending most of their time in contact with the formation of the high financial policies of their own countries." Directors should leave the staff to deal with details that did not give rise to any point of policy. In these circumstances, he could not conceive how there would be enough work on the Board for "15 highly qualified monetary experts." He would agree that, for the first few months, the approval of exchange rates, and possibly some points on the organization of the staff, would need fairly lengthy meetings of the Board. But after that, it seemed to him, a full-time Board would be an idle Board. It was true that another function of the Board would be "the exercise of discipline, making sure that the members are kept following the principles and policies of the Fund." But this could only be done at intervals; it would be intolerable if that kind of question were raised daily on particular transactions. The daily jobs should be left to the Managing Director and a competent international staff. Along the same lines, Mr. Graham F. Towers, Alternate Governor for Canada, believed that the Board could not achieve the best results if it was engaged in a continuous study of figures or memoranda. The Executive Directors would be efficient in proportion to the contacts which they maintained, and these would be seriously restricted if they remained in Washington.

On the other hand, Mr. Clayton said that he thought Executive Directors "ought to operate in the mundane sphere of day to day operation [and] observation of the trend of policies in the countries that belong to the Fund, so that when they see something going wrong . . . they can immediately investigate. . . ." He suggested that the Managing Director might well assign special problems to individual Executive Directors to study and report on to the Board. Mr. Clayton drew attention to the requirements of Article XII, Section 3(*a*), that the Executive

Directors would be responsible for the conduct of the general operations of the Fund, and to Article XII, Section 4 (*b*), requiring the Executive Directors to direct the Managing Director in the conduct of the ordinary business of the Fund. He asked how the Executive Directors could discharge these grave responsibilities if they were absent most of the time in their own countries and had other tasks to which they were devoting their principal attention.

At this stage, the problem resolved itself into the nature of an Executive Director's main responsibility. Was this to the Fund, or to the country or countries that had appointed or elected him? Mr. Towers clearly distinguished between the allegiance owed by the Managing Director and the staff to the Fund and the obligation of the Executive Directors to look to their Governments. This distinction won general acceptance. White said that an Executive Director did not have "to be international to the exclusion of his own national interest. Quite the contrary." Indeed, as he explained, the U.S. Executive Director would be responsible to the National Advisory Council. However, while the Executive Director would continue to be a representative of his country on the Board, he would also be a representative of the Board in conveying the Fund's views to his Government.

The Governor for Greece, Professor Xenophon Zolotas, pointed out that the position of elected Directors was somewhat different from that of appointed Directors, to which he thought most of the remarks of the U.S. and British Governors had been addressed. If an elected Director continued to be a responsible official in his own country, he would not be able to retain the confidence of the other countries which had elected him, since a clash of interests might well make it impossible for him to act impartially. Keynes agreed that his observations had mainly been concerned with appointed Directors, and went on to say that he had not visualized an elected Executive Director as representing the three or four Governments that had elected him. "I had rather thought," he said, "those countries would have gone direct to the Manager of the Fund."

This last statement was linked to a point which Keynes had made earlier and which also formed part of the clash of views. He had urged that the Managing Director of the Fund should be consulted well in advance about prospective changes in exchange rates, and said that no country would be willing to confide in the Managing Director if the Executive Directors were to be made acquainted with everything that was going on. White's reply to this argument was that economic developments of the kind that Keynes had in mind could not be kept secret from experts, and that the Executive Board should so inform itself as to become aware of the difficulties in each member country almost as soon as these became clear to the Government or central bank of that country. Moreover, he asked, what could the Managing Director do if entrusted with confidences? He could not commit his Board; he could only give advice. And while this might be wise advice, it would not be what member countries wanted. The Governor for India asked how the Managing Director could be expected to keep a secret from the Executive Board that had appointed him. In reply, Keynes pointed again to the fact that the Managing Director and staff, unlike the Executive Directors, would owe allegiance only to the Fund.

The conflicting views outlined above were sharply contrasted in two memoranda, one prepared by the United Kingdom and the other by the United States. The former suggested that the Executive Directors should have discretion as to how they divided their duties with the Alternates; that "function in continuous session" meant that meetings with full power to transact business could be summoned at any time at short notice; and that "it shall be the duty of a Director and his alternate between them to devote such time and attention to the business of the Fund as the interests of the Fund may require." The United States, on the other hand, proposed that Executive Directors and Alternates "shall have no other employment and that their remuneration and procedures shall be established on the understanding that they will devote their full time and attention to the business of the Fund." However, the need for compromise was so clear that the United States subsequently revised its recommendation and proposed instead that "it shall be the duty of an Executive Director and his alternate to devote all the time and attention to the business of the Fund that its interests require, and between them to be continuously available at the principal office of the Fund."

This compromise was readily accepted by the United Kingdom and was later adopted by the Governors as part of the By-Laws.[11] It did not, however, settle the question of remuneration for Executive Directors. Keynes proposed that an Executive Director should be paid a salary sufficient to allow something for an Alternate, on the understanding that, broadly speaking, only one of the two would be in the service of the Fund at a given time. This was resisted by the U.S. delegation, which said that it was the U.S. intention to appoint four full-time men (two for the Fund and two for the Bank). White added that the terms of the compromise had been put forward only in recognition of the difficulty of finding sufficient qualified men to fill all 48 posts in the two institutions. The Governor for Mexico, Ambassador Antonio Espinosa de los Monteros, also resisted Keynes' proposal because of the difficulties this would create for elected Directors.

With this background, the problem of the amount of salaries to be paid was remitted to a subcommittee composed of representatives of the United States, the United Kingdom, Brazil, Canada, France, and Luxembourg. After considerable debate the subcommittee recommended, with Keynes abstaining, that the maximum salaries of Executive Directors should be $17,000 net of tax, and those

[11] By-Laws, Section 14 (d); below, Vol. III, p. 282.

of Alternates $11,500 net of tax. These sums were calculated to correspond, at U.S. rates of tax, to gross salaries of $25,000 and $15,000, respectively.

When the report of the subcommittee was considered by the Governors, it was accepted by everyone except Keynes, who formally dissented, on instructions from the Chancellor of the Exchequer. This was the only occasion during the meeting when a negative vote was recorded.

MANAGING DIRECTOR

Article XII, Section 4 (*a*), provides for the Executive Directors to select a Managing Director, who shall not thereafter be an Executive Director or a Governor. The Managing Director was to be Chairman of the Executive Board. The reason why the U.S. authorities did not propose White for this post appears to have been that they considered that the Bank would have to be headed by a U.S. citizen in order to win the confidence of the banking community, and that it would be impracticable to appoint U.S. citizens to head both the Bank and the Fund.

Discussions among the delegations showed that there was substantial support for the appointment of Mr. Camille Gutt, the Executive Director for Belgium, Iceland, and Luxembourg, who was a Minister of State and former Finance Minister of Belgium. Mr. Gutt was approached by Keynes on the matter and signified his willingness to serve if selected by the Executive Directors.

The report of the Committee on Functions and Remuneration recommended that the term of office of the Managing Director should be five years and his salary $30,000 net of tax. These recommendations were accepted by the Governors.

Camille Gutt, Managing Director, 1946–51

CHAPTER

7

First Steps

(May-September 1946)

THE INAUGURAL MEETING of the Governors at Savannah had paved the way, but until the Executive Directors could take office, the Fund was still *in posse* rather than *in esse*. In order that preparations might be made for Executive Directors to meet, the Governors appointed at Savannah a Temporary Secretary, Mr. Roman L. Horne, and empowered him to draw up to $200,000 from the initial contributions of 1/100 of 1 per cent of quotas which countries were required to make under Article XX, Section 2 (*d*); these contributions totaled nearly $750,000.

The task which the Temporary Secretary faced was no light one. Accommodation in Washington was exceedingly scarce and wartime shortages of equipment still severe. In the face of these, he had, within eight weeks, to create an environment in which the Directors could begin to function. With the aid of a small staff, on loan from the U.S. Treasury, temporary accommodation was found in the Washington Hotel from April 1, and was equipped for the needs of the Directors with office furniture borrowed from the U.S. Government. By May 6, when the Directors were due to meet, the Temporary Secretary's staff had increased to eight and he had provided for the newly arriving Board a dossier of some twenty-five tasks that awaited them. Among these was the provision of a permanent home for the Fund, and there the Temporary Secretary was able to report that an option had been obtained on premises at 1818 H Street, Northwest, one floor of which was to be available late in May and the rest, which was to be shared with the Bank, over the ensuing weeks.

THE EXECUTIVE BOARD

Of the twelve Executive Directors who assembled under the temporary chairmanship of Mr. White (United States) for their first meeting on May 6, nine had been at Bretton Woods. The variety of experience which the Directors brought to their tasks was formidable. The United Kingdom had appointed as its Director Mr. G. L. F. (later Sir George) Bolton, an Executive Director of the Bank of England, who was responsible there for the supervision of the sterling area arrangements. The Director appointed by China, Mr. Y. C. Koo, had been Vice-Minister of Finance. The French Director, Mr. Pierre Mendès-France, had been Financial Commissioner of the French Provisional Government in 1943–44 and Minister of the National Economy in the first postliberation Government, 1944–45. Mr. Mendès-France did not, however, attend any meetings of the Executive Board, and on July 1 he was succeeded by Mr. Jean de Largentaye, Inspecteur des Finances, who had also been a member of the French delegation at Bretton Woods and, from the first meeting of the Board, had acted as Mr. Mendès-France's Alternate. Mr. Jagannath V. Joshi, the appointed member for India, was Economic Advisor to the Reserve Bank of India.

Of the elected Directors, Mr. Gijsbert W. J. Bruins (Netherlands) had been Royal Commissioner of the Netherlands Bank; Mr. Rodrigo Gómez (Mexico) was General Manager of the Bank of Mexico; Mr. Camille Gutt (Belgium) had formerly been his country's Minister of Finance; after his appointment as Managing Director, he was succeeded by Mr. Hubert Ansiaux (Belgium), who was a Director of the National Bank of Belgium; Mr. Jan V. Mládek (Czechoslovakia) had been Chief of the Monetary and Banking Division of the Czechoslovak Ministry of Finance; Mr. Louis Rasminsky (Canada) was Alternate Chairman of the Canadian Foreign Exchange Control Board; Mr. Ahmed Zaki Saad (Egypt) was Under Secretary of State for Finance in Egypt; and Mr. Francisco A. dos Santos-Filho (Brazil) was Director of Foreign Exchange in the Bank of Brazil.[1]

Experienced as these men were, there was no doubt that it was Mr. White who was the dominant figure, by the force of his conviction of the vital role that the Fund was to play and by his willingness to act as the Board's leader in its exploration of the territory lying before it. His initial speech as Temporary Chairman set the tone for the Board's approach to its problems. He spoke of "assuming the responsibilities of our office in that spirit of humility which our difficult task and our profound obligations to the world evoke," and added, "there is much that we must explore, there is much we have to learn."

He himself was at this time striving to set down his ideas of the significance of the Articles of Agreement as they affected the Board's work.[2] His draft began with a list of the fifteen types of "judgments and decisions" which, in his view, the Executive Directors would be repeatedly called upon to make. These included such difficult tasks as the following:

---

[1] For the countries which elected these Directors, see Appendix A below, pp. 624 ff. For a note on their identification by country of origin, see above, p. xiv.

[2] *Some Notes on the Articles of Agreement of the International Monetary Fund*, pp. 1–46, 55–83, 94–106 (Princeton papers, Box 10, File 27).

> Determine currently whether each member in its economic policies and practices is promoting exchange stability, maintaining an orderly exchange arrangement with others and avoiding competitive exchange alterations.
>
> Determine when a member is using the resources of the Fund in a manner contrary to the purposes of the Fund, and, where desirable, recommend appropriate remedial steps.
>
> Determine when any of the conditions under which a member may buy currencies from the Fund may be waived, and on what terms.
>
> Determine when capital movements are not in accord with the purposes of the Fund. Advise a member when to place exchange controls over capital movements. Estimate the amount of capital transactions required for expansion of exports, or in ordinary course of trade, banking or other business.[3]

After a preliminary 20 pages devoted to Article I, Mr. White began an exposition of the remaining Articles. But 80 pages proved inadequate to set out his views even on the single Article IV (exchange rates), and he appears to have abandoned the effort to provide a complete commentary. Much of the surviving text is devoted to a lengthy examination of the requirement that a change in an exchange rate should be made only when this is essential to correct a fundamental disequilibrium.

While it would appear that this written commentary was never distributed to members of the Board, Mr. White continually stressed in oral exposition the importance and difficulty of the role of the Executive Directors in leading member countries toward the goal of monetary equilibrium. During the relatively short time that he was an Executive Director, he set the Board upon the path which it was to follow for the next few years.

Meanwhile, his position as Temporary Chairman ended after the second meeting. One of the first actions of the Board was to select Mr. Gutt as Managing Director, and after a day or two during which the terms of his contract were worked out, he assumed the chair at the third meeting of the Board on May 9. In his address of acceptance he emphasized that mutual good will and understanding, rather than the precise texts agreed at Bretton Woods and Savannah, would be of paramount importance for the Fund's success. On that note the discussions of the Board began.

IMMEDIATE TASKS

The work of the Executive Directors of the Fund, and in particular the formulation of policy, has never lacked intellectual challenge. But the tasks that now confronted the Board were especially taxing, for they were literally unprecedented. There was no past experience to guide such an international

---

[3] *Ibid.*, pp. 8–9.

EXECUTIVE DIRECTORS, 1946–47

Hubert Ansiaux
(Belgium)

George L. F. Bolton
(United Kingdom)

Gijsbert W. J. Bruins
(Netherlands)

Jean de Largentaye
(France)

EXECUTIVE DIRECTORS, 1946–47

Rodrigo Gómez
(Mexico)

Jagannath V. Joshi
(India)

Yee-Chun Koo
(China)

Jan V. Mládek
(Czechoslovakia)

EXECUTIVE DIRECTORS, 1946–47

Louis Rasminsky
(Canada)

Ahmed Zaki Saad
(Egypt)

Francisco Alves dos Santos-Filho
(Brazil)

Harry Dexter White
(United States)

body seeking to shepherd a disturbed world into monetary tranquillity. As if that were not sufficient, the world which the Board confronted was still dislocated by the effects of the war; and currency convertibility, which had been the keystone of the Articles of Agreement, was clearly unattainable in the foreseeable future. The day-to-day decisions that the Executive Directors took in the first months of the Fund, therefore, had to serve both the needs of the short term and the need to lay the foundations for a more stable world.

It must not be thought that an altruistic internationalism was instantly achieved by the Executive Directors, individually or collectively. This, indeed, would have been incompatible with their responsibilities to their governments, as clarified at Savannah. Where national interests appeared to be jeopardized, the Executive Director concerned sought ways of protecting them, limited only by the need to avoid injuring the national interests of his colleagues. The primary interest of the U.S. Director had necessarily to be to safeguard the Fund's supplies of dollars from being drained away by needy members. The British Director sought first and foremost to avert any steps by the Board that might conflict with the maintenance of the sterling area. The main concern of the Executive Director for France was to protect his country's legal rights under the Articles of Agreement, while the Directors for the less developed countries sought to obtain the maximum benefits from the Fund's resources within these legal rights. The Chinese and Indian Directors wished to protect their countries' positions as the third and fifth largest members. Yet, despite all these special interests—indeed, to some extent, because of their mutual interaction and because of the influence of the concept of the Fund on each individual's position—the Board quickly found it possible to take an international view of some of its major problems. First, however, much organizational work had to be done.

For example, rules of procedure for Board meetings had to be adopted. These were in no way unusual unless it was that they required the Chairman ordinarily to ascertain the sense of the meeting instead of taking a formal vote, although the right of any Director to require a vote was protected.[4] A substantial simplification of the Fund's problems compared with those of the United Nations was achieved by the decision that the working language of the Fund would be English and that all documents would ordinarily be written in that language.[5]

It was agreed that the Board would usually meet on the mornings of Mondays, Wednesdays, and Fridays, leaving Tuesdays and Thursdays for the meetings of the Bank Board, of which some Executive Directors were also members. This practice has since been regularly followed by the Fund Board, although at times of pressure afternoon meetings have been not uncommon, and occasionally, by arrangement with the Bank, Tuesday or Thursday morning

[4] Rules and Regulations C-10; below, Vol. III, p. 290.

[5] *Ibid.*, C-13.

has also been pre-empted. Changes in exchange rates have frequently necessitated meetings at weekends.

The second urgent problem was the provision of staff and accommodation. Recruitment was no immediate difficulty; the Temporary Secretary had been able to report at the first meeting of the Board that over 150 applications for positions had already been received, and by May 22 the number had risen to nearly 1,400. However, the organization of the staff so as best to serve the Board, the relations of the staff to the Board itself, and such issues as salary scales and the exemption of salaries from taxation, all needed the Board's attention. The structure of the staff, as evolved during the first few weeks and approved by the Board on June 21, consisted of a Research Division, an Operations Division, a Legal Division, the Secretary's Office, the Comptroller's Office, and an Administrative Services unit.[6]

In the Research Division, the Assistant Director, acting in charge, was Mr. Bernstein, who, as already mentioned, had been Mr. White's deputy at the discussions with the United Kingdom in September–October 1943 and had been intimately concerned with the Fund since then. He became the Director a year later. The Director of the Operations Division, Mr. John Lenox Fisher, had been a member of the staff of the Bank of England. The Legal Division had as General Counsel a Belgian, Mr. André van Campenhout, who was later elected to the Board as an Executive Director, and two Counsellors, one from the U.S. Treasury and the other a Brazilian. The Secretary's Office was headed by Mr. Frank Coe, also drawn from the U.S. Treasury, where he had succeeded Mr. White as Director of the Division of Monetary Research. The Temporary Secretary nominated at Savannah, Mr. Roman L. Horne, now became Assistant Secretary, and one of the nucleus staff whom he had borrowed for the weeks of preparation for the Board (Mr. Phillip Thorson, later Director of Administration) became Assistant to the Secretary. The Comptroller's Office was for the time being supervised by an Assistant Comptroller, Mr. Charles M. Powell (a Canadian), and the Administrative Services were in the charge of a Director of Materiel, who was also one of those who had assisted the Temporary Secretary between March and May. By the beginning of September, when the staff numbered about 100, from 15 countries, the "Divisions" were being styled "Departments," a nomenclature that has since been maintained.

Provision was made, at first in the Secretary's Office and later in the Office of the Managing Director, for an officer charged with maintaining external relations, now known as the Special Representative to the United Nations. His duties at first extended to liaison not only with other international organizations and with nongovernmental agencies, but also with the press and the

[6] The organization of the staff in 1946 and subsequent years is set out in Appendix B below, p. 636.

public. From 1948 to 1950 he was assisted by an Information Officer. Since the latter date public relations have been handled separately.

The office accommodation at 1818 H Street, which had been found by the Director of Materiel, was first occupied by the Board on June 10, 1946. Negotiations to rent the building were protracted, but in November 1946 it was arranged that the Bank would take a lease of the whole of it, subletting to the Fund the parts occupied by the latter. A suggestion that the Fund should rent an apartment building to house members of the staff, because of the scarcity of accommodation in Washington, was eventually abandoned in favor of the payment of settling-in allowances, similar to those provided by the United Nations. It was decided to establish a separate pension scheme for Fund employees.

A third issue which faced the Board in its early days was the problem of relations with the Bank. A committee was appointed to review with a corresponding body from the Bank the problem of liaison between the two organizations. It was recognized that there was a considerable area of common interest, but that in their day-to-day activities the two organizations would necessarily operate independently. The committee therefore recommended that liaison should be maintained at the levels of the Secretary and the Chairman. The two Secretaries would keep each other informed about matters of mutual interest and each Secretary would inform the Chairman of his Board. The two Chairmen would also keep in close touch with one another and each might invite the other Board to send a representative to meetings of the Executive Directors where he thought fit. It was recommended that each Secretary be given permission to pass over documents which might be of interest to the other. For some problems of mutual concern, joint committees composed of Directors of the two institutions were formed. Later in the year, a Joint Standing Committee evolved a procedure for an exchange of information between the Fund and the Bank about their respective operations. This also provided for the Fund to keep the Bank informed about members' economic positions. Subsequently, close working relations were built up between the staffs of the Fund and the Bank dealing with similar problems, although the frequent absence of members of both staffs from Washington has made it impossible to institutionalize these relationships.

A more difficult issue was raised by the problem of liaison with the United Nations. As was noted in the previous chapter, the President of ECOSOC had written to the Board of Governors at Savannah, inviting the Fund to enter into negotiations for relations between the two bodies, as contemplated by Articles 57 and 63 of the UN Charter. The problem took on a new form late in May when the Economic and Employment Commission of ECOSOC submitted to its parent body a report which sought to centralize in ECOSOC the responsibility for

Fund and Bank Offices, 1818 H Street, N.W., Washington, D.C. (1946)

advising on methods of promoting full employment and economic stability and also on balance of payments problems, and which suggested that Governments should be asked to prepare for ECOSOC balance of payments statements at less than yearly intervals. At the same time, the Statistical Commission of ECOSOC recommended that the United Nations should become the central agency for collecting, analyzing, publishing, standardizing, and improving all statistics serving the general purposes of international organizations. It contemplated that Specialized Agencies might collect data needed by them but that the United Nations should concern itself with the nature of the data so collected.

These recommendations appeared to the Executive Directors to be likely to hamper the Fund in obtaining information necessary for its operations in accordance with Article VIII, Section 5. The Board therefore appointed a committee to discuss with ECOSOC the nature of the Fund's concern, and asked individual Executive Directors to explain to the countries that had appointed or elected them the nature of the Fund's reservations to the proposals of the reports of the two Commissions.

Shortly afterward, ECOSOC sent a further request for the Fund to enter into negotiations leading to an agreement, and at the end of August submitted a formal agreement for this purpose to the Fund. The Board felt, however, that it was premature to bind itself by a legal document to maintain relations of any detailed kind with ECOSOC until experience had been gained in the operations of the Fund and it was possible to see what would in fact be practicable. The Managing Director was therefore asked to write to the Secretary-General of the United Nations to the effect that the Fund did not wish at that stage to enter into an agreement. This letter was dispatched on September 10. It was not until a year later that a formal agreement was signed, designating the Fund a Specialized Agency of the United Nations.[7]

In the meantime, agreement had been reached on a substantially modified version of the proposals of the Statistical Commission, which recognized the Fund's responsibility for collecting data in accordance with Article VIII, Section 5. The Fund's particular concern with balance of payments statistics was accepted, and led to its being charged with the task of continuing the annual series of balance of payments analyses that had been inaugurated by the League of Nations.

During these early months, Mr. White sent a series of memoranda to his fellow Directors. One on June 5 was concerned with the organization of the Fund's work in economic statistics. He suggested a system of "country books" (in which the information reaching the Fund about each member country should be systematically tabulated), the preparation of a weekly digest of news and cabled information, and the publication of a monthly or quarterly statistical

[7] See below, Vol. III, pp. 215–18.

bulletin. The difficulty of defining the scope of "country books," and still more the problem of keeping them up to date, made that proposal soon appear impracticable, but its intention was fulfilled by the steady accumulation in the Research Department of the kind of information which Article VIII, Section 5, had contemplated. In 1948 the books were replaced by the monthly statistical publication which Mr. White had proposed. His suggested weekly digest also came in due course to fruition, and will be noticed below. Mr. White's other memoranda were concerned with the tasks of the Board in determining initial par values for members' currencies, and are referred to in that context later in this chapter.

One other action of the Board in its earliest days should be recorded: noting with regret the death of Lord Keynes, it authorized a message from the Chairman to Lady Keynes in the following terms:

> At this moment, when we are initiating the International Monetary Fund, our thoughts naturally turn to Lord Keynes, a man who has contributed so much to the shaping of the Bretton Woods proposals.
>
> In the name and on behalf of the Executive Directors of the International Monetary Fund, I wish to extend to you our deep sympathy in your great loss. We feel that we, too, have lost a great friend and valuable adviser.

THE GOVERNORS' REQUESTS

Among the tasks which the Executive Directors had inherited from the Inaugural Meeting of the Board of Governors were requests from three countries for interpretations of the Articles of Agreement. It will be remembered that India, the United States, and the United Kingdom had sought interpretations from the Governors, and the latter had remitted the requests to the Directors.

The interpretation sought by India related to the apparent insufficiency of Article XII, Section 3 (*b*) (i), to deal with the possibility that, after the Executive Board had been constituted, another country might join the Fund and be given a quota larger than that of one of the five countries having the right to appoint an Executive Director. The Directors had no difficulty in adopting the interpretation suggested by the Governors.[8]

The interpretation asked by the United States as the result of Section 13.(a) of U.S. Public Law 171 presented no serious difficulty in principle but proved difficult to draft. It will be recalled that the interpretation covered two related topics. On the one hand, it was asked whether the Fund's authority to use its resources extended "beyond current monetary stabilization operations to afford temporary assistance to members in connection with seasonal, cyclical, and

[8] This is set out above, p. 127. See also E.B. Decision No. 2–1, May 8, 1946; below, Vol. III, p. 267. For a note on the system of numbering Executive Board Decisions, see above, p. xv.

emergency fluctuations in the balance of payments of any member for current transactions." On the other, it was asked whether the Fund had "authority to use its resources to provide facilities for relief, reconstruction, or armaments, or to meet a large or sustained outflow of capital on the part of any member." Broadly speaking, the answer to both questions was clearly in the negative. However, when a recommendation for returning a negative reply came before the Board early in September, it was pointed out that the Articles of Agreement did not envisage that the Fund would finance any particular type of import. A somewhat simplified interpretation was therefore suggested in which the answer to the second question was couched in the form of a statement that members would use the resources of the Fund to help to finance over-all deficits in their balances of payments, with the reminder that all uses of the Fund resources had to be consistent with the purposes of the Fund. This redraft was considered by the Executive Directors under some pressure of time because the First Annual Meeting of the Governors was due to convene two days later. It was felt, however, that it was unwise to make an interpretation which appeared to rely unduly on a drafting technicality, and the U.S. Executive Director was asked to consider the matter further with his legal advisors. As a result, a greatly simplified interpretation was given, as follows:

> The Executive Directors of the International Monetary Fund interpret the Articles of Agreement to mean that authority to use the resources of the Fund is limited to use in accordance with its purposes to give temporary assistance in financing balance of payments deficits on current account for monetary stabilization operations.[9]

This interpretation continued to guide the Fund for some fifteen years, but, as we shall see, it came under question in 1961 and was then clarified.

The interpretation sought by the United Kingdom of Article IV, Sections 3 and 5, presented no problem. The Board decided to adopt the terms suggested by the United Kingdom, with modifications which preserved the Fund's right to question the justification for any proposed change in an exchange rate. These the British Executive Director had no difficulty in accepting.

When the applications for membership made by Italy, Lebanon, Syria, and Turkey, remitted to the Executive Directors by the Governors, were brought before the Executive Board, it approved requests to these countries for data that would enable the Board to recommend quotas. The data were delayed, but a Committee on Membership set up in August nonetheless recommended quotas calculated by the formula underlying the figures produced at Bretton Woods, using for the purpose statistics prepared by the Research Department. On September 12 the Board accepted the recommendations of the committee and proposed to the Governors that all four countries should be admitted on these

[9] E.B. Decision No. 71-2, September 26, 1946; below, Vol. III, p. 245.

terms, reserving to the Governors, however, the question whether Italy as an ex-enemy country could be allowed to join the Fund. This question was answered in the affirmative by the Governors, and a detailed statement of terms for joining the Fund was sent to each of the four countries during October.[10]

A somewhat curious contrast with the procedure adopted to calculate quotas for new members emerged when a request from Paraguay for an increase in quota came before the Board on September 20. Mr. Rubén Benítez, the representative of Paraguay, who had been invited (in accordance with Section 19 (*a*) of the By-Laws) to state his country's case for a quota of $5 million instead of the $2 million awarded it at Bretton Woods, sought to support it by citing the formula. The Board, however, ruled that the calculations based on the formula had had no official standing at Bretton Woods and were merely used as a point of departure for negotiations. After discussion, an increase to $3.5 million was recommended to the Governors and approved by them. It took effect on January 26, 1948, when the Fund was notified that Paraguay had correspondingly increased its subscription to the World Bank.

It may conveniently be noted at this point that in June 1947 the Board decided that a change in a member's quota effected between two regular biennial elections of Executive Directors would change by the same amount the voting power of the elected Executive Director who cast the votes of that member.[11] The increase in quota for Paraguay therefore added 15 votes to the 4,575 previously cast by Mr. Santos-Filho (Brazil).

Meanwhile, France had submitted a request for a substantial increase, arguing that the quota of $450 million set at Bretton Woods should be increased by 50 per cent. This would have raised the relative position of France among the first five countries from fourth to third, and it evoked a request by China that its quota ought to be increased by 30 per cent, i.e., from $550 million to $715 million. After some debate the Board decided to recommend an increase in the quota of France, but only from $450 million to $525 million. China then withdrew its request. The increase for France was approved by the Governors.

RULES AND REGULATIONS

In his dossier of actions which the Executive Directors should take, prepared for the first meeting of the Executive Board, the Temporary Secretary had included a reminder that the Board of Governors proposed to review at their First Annual Meeting any rules and regulations adopted by the Directors.[12]

[10] Resolution 1-6, *Summary Proceedings, 1946,* pp. 49, 67–74.
[11] E.B. Decision No. 180-5, June 25, 1947; below, Vol. III, p. 268.
[12] By-Laws, Section 16; below, Vol. III, p. 283.

In order to assist the Directors in preparing rules and regulations, Mr. White distributed some "Notes to Be Used as Basis for Drafting and Discussion," which were closely based on a draft prepared in the U.S. Treasury. These "Notes" were in some directions very elaborate and, in the process of revision during the summer, the Executive Directors drastically shortened them. The "Notes" had grouped the proposed regulations under eight headings. Four of these presented no real problem to the Board, but the other four—dealing with exchange rates, the Fund's transactions, exchange controls, and ineligibility to use the Fund's resources—raised questions with which Executive Directors had considerable difficulty. Between them, these four groups of regulations, as presented in the "Notes," contained 115 paragraphs; the extent to which the Board streamlined them is clear from the fact that the corresponding provisions in the Rules and Regulations ultimately adopted numbered only seventeen.[13]

Two principal objections were raised to the U.S. Treasury draft of these four groups of regulations. One was that they spelled out in full and, indeed, unnecessary detail the action that the Fund should take at every stage in dealing with questions that arose in these fields. The other, not entirely dissimilar, point was that the "Notes" visualized detailed supervision by the Fund of the member countries with respect to each of the four areas. The revisions made by the Directors in the process of redrafting were largely directed to meeting both these objections.

Two groups of regulations in the "Notes," however, were criticized for more specific reasons. The "Notes" covering the Fund's transactions provided as follows:

> (C-8) A drawing for less than 5 per cent of a member's quota within any 30 days would be consummated within 6 business days.
>
> (C-9) A drawing for more than 5 per cent but not more than 10 per cent of the member's quota within 30 days would be consummated within 10 business days.
>
> (C-10) Drawings for larger amounts would be consummated when the Fund regarded it as desirable.

These provisions were criticized by Mr. Bolton (United Kingdom), Mr. de Largentaye (France), and Mr. Rasminsky (Canada), on two main grounds. They thought that the legality of the provisions, in the light of the terms of Article V, Section 3, was at least doubtful. In addition, there was in Mr. Bolton's view a practical objection to the procedure proposed, namely, that a central bank must be able to make its arrangements to meet obligations without doubt of its ability to pay the sum arranged on a specific date. Mr. Bolton and Mr. Rasminsky appear to have felt that the proposed progressive lengthening of the period

[13] Rules and Regulations F-1 to F-3, G-1 to G-4, H-1 to H-5, K-1 to K-5; below, Vol. III, pp. 291–94, 299–300.

within which the Fund would consummate a drawing reflected a view that the Fund should satisfy itself of the accuracy of the member's statements before meeting the member's request. Mr. Bolton suggested that this would be impracticable, since the Fund could not accumulate sufficiently up-to-date data of a member's position to justify more than a suspicion—certainly not a decision—about its bona fides.

As a result, no doubt, of criticisms similar to those just mentioned, the first Fund draft of the regulations governing drawings provided that drawings should be consummated within one business day after the receipt of the request. This, however, was subject to the member notifying the Fund five days in advance of a prospective drawing if this would amount, with other previous drawings during the preceding 30 days, to 5 per cent of its quota. Failing such notice, the Fund might postpone consummation of the transaction for five days. This proved equally objectionable, in that it still appeared to limit members' right of access to the Fund. It would seem that the wish of the drafters was to protect the Fund from sudden demands upon it which might have been embarrassing, for a fourth draft provided that drawings would be dealt with after two working days "if the Fund has in its possession in liquid form a sufficient amount of the required currency." However, the critics of these successive qualifications continued to argue that they were inconsistent with the Articles of Agreement, and the regulation presented to the Governors in September included none of them. Eventually, in February 1947, the Directors adopted an amendment providing that when a requested drawing would increase a member's purchases to more than 5 per cent of its quota during any 30 days, the Managing Director should notify each Executive Director of the fact and call a special meeting to discuss the request if he so wished or if any Executive Director so asked.[14] This, however, was no more than a stage in the long discussion of the rights of members to draw upon the Fund—rights that had already been extensively debated, as we have seen, during the evolution of the Articles of Agreement. They continued to occupy much of the time of the Executive Board until in 1952 a policy on the use of the Fund's resources was evolved. Even then the controversy was not fully ended, but it ceased from that time to be in the forefront of the Board's discussions.

The other group of draft regulations which attracted specific criticism was that dealing with exchange controls. Here again, Mr. Bolton and Mr. Rasminsky were the most articulate critics. Mr. Bolton pointed out that the draft regulations appeared to be based on a comprehensive suspicion of every form of exchange control and of all types of clearing agreements, payments agreements, and currency agreements. This attitude was unjustified, he suggested, if only because a member had a perfect right to impose exchange controls in order to manage

[14] Rules and Regulations G-5; below, Vol. III, p. 293.

capital movements; and while clearing agreements were no doubt undesirable, "it would be highly imprudent to condemn all other monetary arrangements . . . when very frequently their real purpose is to maintain exchange stability." Both Directors also saw practical difficulty in the procedure contemplated by the draft regulation, which required each member to submit to the Fund a full description of the controls on payments and transfers which it proposed to continue in effect after the Fund began its operations. Mr. Bolton doubted whether the Fund was equipped to absorb and act upon the ensuing massive inflow of laws, regulations, and instructions written in many languages. He thought that the Fund should be content for the time being to rely, for evidence that a member was transgressing the Articles of Agreement in relation to exchange restrictions, upon complaints from other members. Ultimately, but only over a period, the Fund would be able to build up a body of case law adequate to establish general rules governing members' behavior in this field. The regulations finally adopted conformed very closely to the line which Mr. Bolton had suggested.[15]

INITIAL PAR VALUES

Although the Executive Directors were in office and the organization of the Fund was starting to take shape, exchange transactions could not yet begin. The prerequisites for their commencement were set out in the Articles as follows:

> Article XX, Section 4 (*h*), provided that when members having 65 per cent of total quotas were eligible to draw from the Fund, it should begin transactions.
>
> Article XX, Section 4 (*c*), provided that, to be eligible to draw from the Fund, the member must have established, in agreement with the Fund, a par value for its currency.
>
> Article XX, Section 4 (*a*) and (*b*), therefore provided that when the Fund would shortly be ready to begin transactions, it should request members to notify their par values within thirty days. These par values would be the exchange rates actually existing on October 28, 1945 (the sixtieth day before the entry into force of the Agreement), unless members satisfied the Fund that these were inappropriate. (Article XX, Section 4 (*d*), relaxed this rule for members whose metropolitan territory had been occupied by the enemy.)

A related requirement in Article III, Section 3 (*a*), was that a member must have paid its subscription in full on or before the date when it became eligible to draw from the Fund.

Three main tasks therefore faced the Directors in the summer of 1946: to formulate principles by which to guide them in considering proposed par values,

---

[15] Rules and Regulations H-1 to H-3.

and then to apply these to the par value put forward by each member; to clarify the responsibilities of members and of the Fund for changes in exchange rates undertaken before the approved par values became effective; and to instruct members on the payment of subscriptions, which in turn involved elucidating the provisions of the Articles in relation to members' holdings of gold and U.S. dollars. The evolution of the necessary principles for these operations was largely completed before the meeting of the Governors on September 27, so that, although their application was postponed until the last quarter of 1946, it seems advisable to consider the whole problem now.

Par values—theoretical

In mid-June, Mr. White circulated to the Executive Board "Some Observations re Agreement on Initial Rates." In this, he argued that the Fund should leave it to the member country to decide what exchange rate should be reported as the initial par value. He reminded the Board that the member might claim that the rate in existence at the end of October 1945 was "unsatisfactory." The Fund, however, was limited to objecting to a rate suggested by a member on the ground that it was likely to be prejudicial either to the member proposing it or to others. The Fund's obligation was to agree to a "suitable" rate if that prevailing at the end of October 1945 was not proposed.[16]

Mr. White went on to consider what circumstances would be likely to result in exchange rates other than those at the end of October 1945 being submitted; in particular, the possible effect of devaluation of such a rate on the country proposing it needed careful thought. He believed that most monetary authorities would come to the conclusion that a devaluation was not worthwhile.

On the question of procedure, he thought it would be best not to determine par values individually, but wait until all members had submitted their rates and until the Executive Board had reached tentative agreement on them, in order that their mutual interactions could be fully considered.

The theoretical considerations which weighed with the Board were later expounded by the Managing Director in an address at Harvard University. Mr. Gutt explained that, while normally an exchange rate has two functions, to let exports flow and to limit imports, it was not possible under the conditions prevailing in 1946 for the exchange rate to perform this second function in some countries. Exchange rates could not be expected to limit imports to the proper level or to apportion them among the various goods which the economy most urgently needed. In a country in which the shortage of goods was so great that rationing was necessary, it was inconceivable that the exchange rate could be

[16] Article XX, Section 4 (*b*); below, Vol. III, p. 208.

expected to bring about an adequate limitation of the demand for imports. "For these reasons," Mr. Gutt continued, "it appeared to the Fund that for the present the one practical test that could be applied to determine the suitability of an exchange rate was whether it enables a country to export." [17]

Against this background, the Board proceeded in October to consider by what criteria it should judge the initial par values proposed to it. One member of the Board thought that the economic data available made it impossible to decide what par value would be appropriate. Most Directors, however, felt that the Articles of Agreement required the Board to determine whether a proposed rate was such that it would not cause undue recourse to the Fund's resources (Article XX, Section 4 (*b*) (ii)). But they thought that, unless the discrepancy in the proposed rate appeared to be substantial, no action by the Board would be required. They agreed at the same time that, in order to form any judgment on a proposed rate, the Board must consider pertinent economic data and other information. How far the Board would, in practice, be able to review proposed par values would, therefore, depend on the capacity of the Research Department to provide data, and on the time available to the Board to consider them.

A special problem was raised by Venezuela, which reported to the Board that it had a number of different exchange rates and that it could not see its way to dispensing with these multiple currency practices for the time being. This difficulty was discussed by the Executive Directors and by a committee of the Governors at the Annual Meeting. The Directors decided to call Venezuela's attention to the provisions of Articles VIII and XIV and to say that the member would have to submit some rate as an initial par value for consideration by the Board.

Par values—practicalities

While these theoretical issues were being thrashed out, the procedure for inviting proposals for par values was gotten under way. At their meeting on July 31, the Executive Directors were asked to request the members that had appointed or elected them to furnish the data needed to enable the Board to consider proposed par values. Drafts of a formal request to members to communicate their proposed par values, together with measures to safeguard the confidentiality of the communications, were considered by the Board between August 28 and September 9. It was not until September 12, however, that the request was dispatched to members, a difficulty having arisen at the last moment: a proposal to include in the invitation a pledge of secrecy had to be discarded because the United States "wished to be informed on proposals

[17] Camille Gutt, *The Practical Problem of Exchange Rates: An address before the Littauer School of Public Administration, Harvard University, Cambridge, Mass., February 13, 1948* (Washington, [1948]), pp. 4–5.

relating to changes in par values." By the middle of September countries had begun to communicate par values, and early in October a program for their consideration was worked out. Thereafter the Board reviewed the proposals put forward by all the member countries, beginning with the U.S. dollar, for which purpose the staff provided an appraisal of each of the par values proposed. The review occupied the Directors throughout November and the early part of December.

On December 18 the Board released a "Statement Concerning Initial Par Values," listing the par values of the currencies of 32 of the Fund's 39 members and of most of the nonmetropolitan areas of Belgium, France, the Netherlands, and the United Kingdom.[18] Discussions with two members—Brazil and Uruguay—had not been concluded. The remaining five members—China, the Dominican Republic, Greece, Poland, and Yugoslavia—had asked for more time for the determination of their initial par values. The Board commented that "this is the first time that a large number of nations have submitted their exchange rates to consideration by an international organization and thus a new phase of international monetary cooperation has begun." Pointing out that the initial par values announced were those proposed by members and were based on existing rates of exchange, the Board observed that this was not to be interpreted as a guarantee that all the rates would remain unchanged. Substantial disparities in price and wage levels existed among a number of countries and, although such disparities did not have the same significance as in normal times, some of the rates might well be found later to be incompatible with the maintenance of a balanced international payments position at a high level of economic activity.

> For practically all countries [the statement went on], exports are being limited mainly by difficulties of production or transport, and the wide gaps which exist in some countries between the cost of needed imports and the proceeds of exports would not be appreciably narrowed by changes in their currency parities. . . . Furthermore, for many countries now concerned with combating inflation there is a danger that a change in the exchange rate would aggravate the internal tendencies toward inflation.
>
> In view of all these considerations, the Fund has reached the conclusion that the proper course of action is to accept as initial par values the existing rates of exchange.

It may be noted that the par values established were the exchange rates prevailing on October 28, 1945 with two exceptions: France proposed the lower rate to which the franc had been devalued on December 26, 1945, and Canada proposed parity with the U.S. dollar, which had been achieved on July 5, 1946, instead of the rate of Can$1=US$0.90, which had been in force on October 28, 1945.

---

[18] *Annual Report, 1947*, pp. 70–71.

PREPARING FOR EXCHANGE TRANSACTIONS

Exchange rate changes

In parallel with the foregoing, the Board was facing the problems which would be created if a member wished to change its exchange rate before establishing an initial par value. One question was whether such changes needed the Fund's approval. The view of the Legal Department was that, once the invitation to submit par values had been sent out, the member must consult before changing its rate. A more difficult question, the Department thought, was whether a similar obligation existed between the time when the Executive Board was constituted as a functioning body (and could therefore be consulted by a member) and the issue of the invitation to submit par values; on the whole, the Department thought it did. These views were challenged by Mr. Rasminsky (Canada), who suggested that the obligation to consult the Fund only arose after a par value had been agreed. However, his point was not pressed and, in fact, Brazil and China, which alone wished to change their existing rates before adopting a par value, consulted the Fund on their proposals.

Arising from the consideration of these suggested par values, the question of confidentiality recurred. Taking advantage of the discussion of the relevant section of the draft Rules and Regulations, Mr. Rasminsky proposed the following draft decision:

> The Managing Director will not be held to have neglected his duty to the Board if he has informal conversations with Members on the subject of changes in par values without advising the Board of these conversations before a formal request or application is made to the Fund.

Objection was taken to this proposal, and for the first time at Board meetings there was a formal vote. Those voting for Mr. Rasminsky's proposal were Mr. Ansiaux (Belgium), Mr. Bruins (Netherlands), Mr. de Largentaye (France), Mr. Mládek (Czechoslovakia), Mr. Rasminsky, and Mr. A. P. Grafftey-Smith (United Kingdom), Alternate to Mr. Bolton. Against it were Mr. Gómez (Mexico), Mr. Koo (China), Mr. Saad (Egypt), Mr. Santos-Filho (Brazil), and Mr. White (United States). The motion was accordingly defeated by 12,125 votes. Mr. Rasminsky stated that the matter would be raised at the Annual Meeting by the Governor for Canada and, following on conversations initiated there by Mr. James L. Ilsley and Mr. Towers, there was a further discussion in the Board on October 9. At its conclusion Mr. Gutt stated that

> he would use his discretion in deciding at what time to inform the Executive Board of any confidential and informal discussions with members held in advance of any formal application or proposal to the Fund, it being understood that he would not inform any member or Executive Director of any discussion regarding possible changes in the par value of any currency without at the same time informing the Executive Board as a whole.

This was accepted as a working rule, subject to re-examination after a period.

Subscriptions

The issue by the Fund on September 12, 1946 of the invitation to members to communicate the par values of their currencies implied that the time was approaching when members would begin to subscribe the remainder of their quotas, of which, so far, only 1/100 of 1 per cent had been paid in. The relevant provisions of the Articles were as follows:

> Article III, Section 3
>
> (*b*) Each member shall pay in gold, as a minimum, the smaller of
>
> (i) twenty-five percent of its quota; or
>
> (ii) ten percent of its net official holdings of gold and United States dollars as at the date when the Fund notifies members under Article XX, Section 4 (*a*) that it will shortly be in a position to begin exchange transactions.
>
> Each member shall furnish to the Fund the data necessary to determine its net official holdings of gold and United States dollars.
>
> (*c*) Each member shall pay the balance of its quota in its own currency.

There were also provisions (Article III, Section 3 (*d*)) covering the circumstances of a member whose holdings of gold and U.S. dollars at the relevant date were not ascertainable because its territory had been occupied by the enemy.

These requirements gave rise to a number of requests for interpretation; in particular, the definition of "net official holdings" involved legal questions of some nicety. Did they include resources derived from current loans, and, if so, were the corresponding liabilities deductible? Did they include credits available but not yet drawn upon? Did they include gold pledged to a third party? These three questions were asked by Mr. Bruins. Mr. Mládek, on behalf of Poland, asked whether 10 per cent of the member's holdings of U.S. dollars could be paid in dollars instead of in gold. The Government of the Philippines inquired whether the 1/100 of 1 per cent of quota already paid could count toward the gold subscription. Some countries had problems of an even more recondite nature. The United Kingdom had offered, on December 14, 1945, to provide to Egypt the amount of gold required for the latter's gold subscription to the Fund; Mr. Saad sought to know whether this amount should be counted among Egypt's net official holdings on September 12, 1946.

To all these questions the Executive Directors returned appropriate answers. While stressing that the exact circumstances in each case would need to be considered, the Board ruled that, in principle, "net official holdings" did include resources derived from current loans, and could be reduced by the deduction of liabilities only if these carried clearly defined rights of conversion into gold or U.S. dollars. They did not include credits available but not yet drawn upon, nor pledged gold to the extent that the loan for which the gold had been hypothecated had actually been spent. As regards the gold part of the subscription, the

Board decided that, if the option of contributing 10 per cent of gold and U.S. dollars was chosen, the whole of this amount must be paid in gold, except that the 1/100 of 1 per cent advance payment could always be treated as part of the gold contribution. On Egypt's problem, the Board decided that the offer by the United Kingdom did not become effective until after September 12, 1946, and that the amount involved was therefore, at that date, part of the net official holdings of the United Kingdom.

The question whether a member's gold subscription to the Fund could be counted as part of its reserve against its note issue was raised once more, this time by Egypt. The staff suggested that there was no reason why a member country should not show the status of its subscription in whatever way was most significant for its purpose, but the Board preferred not to rule on the matter.

On the practical details of the payment of subscriptions, the nature and quality of notes (securities) to be accepted in lieu of currency were considered in some detail; it was eventually decided not to prescribe a form but to ask members to submit specimens of the notes they proposed to issue, and to verify the authority for them. Problems also arose over the depositories which were to be used for the currency subscriptions; while these would normally be the central banks of the countries concerned, there were some members that had no central banks. It was decided that such members might designate their Treasuries as depositories instead.

Date for beginning operations

Behind all the preliminary issues discussed in the preceding sections was the crucial question: when would the Fund be able to begin operations?

This problem was approached in two stages. A fortnight before the Annual Meeting the Board considered whether the number of countries that would be able to use the Fund's resources early in the new year would be such as to justify an assumption that operations should begin about January 1, 1947 as originally planned. The staff suggested that only a few member countries would then be so dependent on aid for relief or reconstruction as not to be qualified to use the Fund's resources; certainly the number was not large enough to necessitate any postponement of the crucial date. The Board, with one dissentient, decided that while the disturbed economic and political situation was likely to make initial transactions risky, this had always been realized and did not justify postponing operations.

In the light of this decision, the staff made an estimate of the Fund's possible earnings from charges over the eighteen months from January 1, 1947 to June 30, 1948. This suggested that drawings over this period might amount to $680 million, of which about one half was expected to be drawn by member countries in Western Europe other than the United Kingdom, $150 million by members in the Far East, $120 million by members in Eastern Europe, and $30 million each by members in the Middle East and Latin America. The forecast proved to be a very accurate one: actual drawings were $631 million.

An interesting commentary on this estimate was provided by Mr. Bolton (United Kingdom) in a memorandum dated October 18, 1946, in which he argued that the Bank would not be in a position for some time to make any extensive loans, and the Fund would therefore have to bear the brunt of members' requirements for assistance for the time being.

The second stage in the Board's consideration of the date for commencing operations was reached early in December, after most of the discussions of par values had been concluded and when there was a clear prospect that an announcement of these par values would be forthcoming shortly. The Board decided that some time would still be needed for perfecting arrangements within the Fund to handle members' requests to use its resources; that arrangements with the depositories to receive subscriptions would also need some time to complete; and that the Fund would need to discuss with some of its members the conditions under which they could use its resources. These considerations prompted some postponement of the effective date, and it was decided to fix March 1, 1947 as the day on which the Fund would begin operations, if by then members having 65 per cent of the total of quotas had become eligible to use the Fund's resources.

ANNUAL REPORT

Section 10 of the By-Laws adopted by the Governors at Savannah requires the Executive Directors to

> have prepared for presentation at the annual meeting of the Board of Governors an annual report in which shall be discussed the operations and policies of the Fund and which shall make recommendations to the Board of Governors on the problems confronting the Fund.

This obligation was not an easy one to fulfill in the summer of 1946, when the "operations and policies of the Fund" were being shaped from day to day and when opportunities to draft "recommendations . . . on problems confronting the Fund" were hard to come by. It is not, therefore, surprising that the Executive Directors were unable to tackle the problem of the Report until September 19, when they had before them a first draft prepared by the staff. By September 25, with the assistance of a drafting committee of Directors—Mr. de Largentaye (France), Mr. Grafftey-Smith (United Kingdom), and Mr. Rasminsky (Canada)—a final text had been agreed, and the Report was transmitted to the Governors in time for their Meeting, which began two days later.

The Report was a short one, under six thousand words in all. It was prefaced by a letter of transmittal in which Mr. Gutt stressed the spirit of cooperation shown by the Executive Directors in approaching their tasks, and justified the plans which they had made for an early start to operations: "Immobility," he urged, "is not a policy."

The Report itself was divided roughly into two halves. The first was a factual report of the state of the Fund at the end of September—including membership, Executive Directors, staff, and financial position—and of the actions taken by the Executive Board in relation to Rules and Regulations and to par values. The second half of the Report described the economic distortions that beset so much of the world; the wide spread of exchange controls; and the need to rehabilitate weak currencies. It made a reference, which experience was to prove optimistic, to the beneficial effects of the imminent convertibility of sterling. It pointed out that if the Fund was to fulfill its role in these difficult conditions, it would have to run the risk that its resources might be used for other than short-term needs. And it concluded by reminding the Governors that the Fund's scope was a limited one, the basic need of the world being for wise policies, increased production, and long-term aid for relief and reconstruction.

In this connection the Board took the opportunity to define the purposes for which exchange transactions would be permitted. This was approached by the easier course of delimiting purposes for which the use of the Fund's resources would be unsuitable. The Fund was not a relief agency, like UNRRA, and was not giving foreign exchange away.

> Nor [the Report went on] would it sell foreign exchange to a member when there is no reasonable prospect that the member will be able to repay the Fund. Members could not properly use the Fund to finance long-term reconstruction plans which involve sustained use of the Fund's resources to meet a continuing deficit in their balance of international payments. The Fund is not empowered to provide financing of that sort. The essential test of the propriety of use of the Fund's resources is . . . whether the prospective balance of payments position of the country concerned . . . will be such that its use of the Fund's resources will be of relatively short duration.[19]

This concept of temporary use was formalized in the interpretation given at the request of the U.S. Executive Director, as mentioned earlier in this chapter. Its adoption as a working rule of the Fund was perhaps the most important step which the Directors took during these early months of the Fund's work.

ANNUAL MEETING

The First Annual Meeting of the Boards of Governors of the Fund and the Bank convened on Friday, September 27, 1946, and continued through Saturday,

[19] *Annual Report, 1946,* p. 13.

October 5. To a large extent, the proceedings were formal. Committees were established to review the Rules and Regulations, the proposals for quota revisions, applications for membership, and financial matters, but their deliberations did not modify materially the recommendations which had been put to them by the Executive Directors. A request by Iran for an increase in quota was referred to the Executive Directors for advice.

A subcommittee of the Committee on Rules and Regulations, set up to consider a draft resolution submitted by the Government of Mexico, recommended its adoption as follows:

> The Fund shall gather whatever material is available and obtainable on the monetary uses of silver; the real function of silver coins; risks and uncertainties of its monetary uses; possibilities of cooperation in the use of silver for monetary purposes, et cetera. . . .

This recommendation was accepted by the Governors.

Precedents were of course being set. One of them was that the Head of State welcomed the Boards of Governors; on this occasion, the President of the United States sent a message, which was read by the Alternate Governor for the United States, Mr. Clayton.[20] Another was that the Managing Director addressed the Board of Governors of the Fund to present the Annual Report.[21] He surveyed the work which the Directors had been doing and stressed the reference in the Annual Report to the fact that the Fund would be running some risk in starting operations, although this risk was not perhaps as great as might appear at first sight. Mr. Gutt reminded the Governors that member countries had given the Fund important powers to deal with international economic problems, and he concluded by repeating that the spirit in which the Executive Directors had tackled their task was one appropriate to a truly international body.

At the closing Joint Session, it was resolved, on the recommendation of the Procedures Committee, that the Second Annual Meeting should be held in London.

---

[20] *Summary Proceedings, 1946,* p. 31.

[21] *Ibid.,* pp. 38–42.

CHAPTER

8

The First Full Year (1946-47)

CHAPTER 7 recorded some of the preoccupations of the Executive Directors during the early part of the twelve months following the First Annual Meeting of the Board of Governors. Other questions coming before the Board during this, its first full, year included some similar to those which it had already tackled. In addition, a number of new problems arose, of which some could be disposed of fairly quickly but some remained on the Board's agenda for a long time to come. In what follows, we shall deal first with minor and transitory issues, reserving for fuller discussion toward the end of the chapter those major subjects which the Board was unable wholly to dispose of before the Second Annual Meeting of the Board of Governors.

MEMBERSHIP AND BOARD

Six countries joined the Fund during the year—Venezuela on December 30, 1946; Turkey on March 11, 1947; Italy on March 27; Syria on April 10; Lebanon on April 15; and Australia on August 5. Applications for membership from Finland and Austria were also received. That from Finland was referred to the Board of Governors, which approved it in Resolution 2-2; that from Austria was received too late for attention in 1946–47 and was dealt with in 1947–48. A preliminary inquiry from New Zealand sought clarification of the compatibility of its system of exchange control with membership in the Fund, and the Governments of Siam and Pakistan made informal inquiries about membership.

In November 1946 an inquiry was sent to all members that had not yet indicated whether they were prepared to accept the obligations of Article VIII, Sections 2, 3, and 4. The inquiry showed that only five—El Salvador, Guatemala, Mexico, Panama, and the United States—were prepared to do so. All other members opted to avail themselves of the transitional arrangements in Article XIV.

There were two changes during the year in the membership of the Executive Board. Mr. White (United States) resigned on March 31, 1947, to return to private enterprise as an economic consultant. He remained an Executive Director until June 1, his departure having been postponed at the request of the Managing Director in order that he could continue to act as Chairman while Mr. Gutt was absent visiting member countries in Europe. Mr. White's departure was signalized by a formal resolution of the Executive Board, putting on record its thanks for the outstanding services he had rendered to the Fund and appointing him honorary Advisor. His death fourteen months later was the subject of resolutions of regret by the Executive Directors and by the Governors at their Third Annual Meeting.[1]

On July 1, 1947, Mr. White was succeeded by Mr. Andrew Overby, formerly Assistant Vice-President of the Federal Reserve Bank of New York, who since the previous August had served as Special Assistant to the Secretary of the Treasury in charge of international monetary and financial affairs. On May 14, the Board was enlarged from twelve to thirteen members by the addition of Mr. Guido Carli (Italy), a member of the Board of Administration and General Counsellor of the Italian Exchange Office.

Resolution IM-10 had provided that a thirteenth Executive Director should be elected when two conditions applied: (1) when one or more countries not listed in Schedule A to the Articles of Agreement had been admitted to membership; and (2) when the votes of new members (i.e., members whose votes were not included in those entitled to be cast by Executive Directors holding office at the time the additional Director was elected) amounted to 4,000. The Resolution also provided that the Director chosen should be deemed to be elected by all the members eligible to participate in the election of the thirteenth Director.

The two conditions necessary for the election were fulfilled with the admission of Italy on March 27. At that date there were four members who were not entitled to appoint Executive Directors and who had not voted for any existing Executive Director, viz., Denmark, Venezuela, Turkey, and Italy; their potential votes totaled 4,060. In the normal way, these four members would have been invited to elect, between them, an Executive Director to fill the thirteenth seat. Certain problems, however, arose.

One, which was fairly simply disposed of, was that Venezuela was a Latin American country and normally, therefore, would have been expected to vote for one of the two Latin American Directors. The Board, however, decided on April 2 that the terms of Resolution IM-10 were such as to include Venezuela among the countries entitled to vote for the thirteenth Director.

A more difficult problem arose in connection with Denmark. Denmark had joined the Fund after the initial election of Executive Directors and had, there-

[1] Resolution 3-9, *Summary Proceedings, 1948,* p. 51.

fore, not voted for any of them. It had, however, been represented on an unofficial basis by the Belgian Executive Director and strongly wished this arrangement to continue. At the First Annual Meeting the Governors had considered a request to this effect and referred it to the Executive Directors. Mr. Ernest de Selliers (Belgium), Alternate to Mr. Ansiaux, therefore pressed, on Denmark's behalf, that the Governors should be asked to amend Resolution IM-10. His first suggestion was that the amendment should permit Denmark to vote for Mr. Ansiaux. Alternatively he proposed that the Resolution be so amended as to permit Denmark to abstain from voting for the thirteenth Director. Neither course, however, commended itself to the Board, which decided that whether Denmark voted or not the thirteenth Executive Director would be entitled to cast Denmark's votes.

A third problem concerned the date when the election would be held. It was suggested that the election might be deferred until Australia, whose application was pending, could complete the formalities for membership, on the understanding that Australia could then vote for the new Director. As Australia would have 2,250 votes, compared with 2,050 votes to be cast by Italy, it was thought possible that the Director elected might be an Australian and not an Italian. Mr. Saad (Egypt) pressed the point, however, that Resolution IM-10 did not contemplate a delay after the 4,000 votes were available, and Mr. White proposed that, instead, the Governors should be invited to authorize the election of a fourteenth Executive Director at about the end of 1947 if sufficient votes were then forthcoming.

The first outcome of these discussions was the establishment of a standing committee of the Board, called the Committee on Interpretation, charged with considering and making reports and recommendations to the Executive Directors on questions of interpretation. The original members of this committee were Mr. Saad (Chairman), Mr. Bolton (United Kingdom), Mr. de Largentaye (France), Mr. Gómez (Mexico), Mr. Joshi (India), and Mr. White. Within a week the committee had presented two reports. The view of the majority of its members was that, once the two conditions laid down in Resolution IM-10 had been fulfilled, no member subsequently joining the Fund could vote for the thirteenth Executive Director. Mr. Maurice H. Parsons (United Kingdom), deputizing for Mr. Bolton, whose Alternate he was, put forward a minority report disagreeing with this conclusion.

The issues were debated over several days in the Board, and resulted in the only formal votes recorded during the year. These were taken on April 8, when a consensus in favor of proceeding at once with the election of the additional Executive Director had become clear. The first vote was on a proposal by Mr. Parsons to delay the decision by two days to allow for the outcome of certain negotiations then pending. This was rejected by 45,335 votes to

33,960. The second vote, on a proposal by Mr. Parsons to pass the problem to the Governors, was defeated by the same margin. A proposal by Mr. de Selliers, to defer a decision until the Board of the Bank (which was understood to be tentatively in favor of consulting the Governors) had made up its mind, was rejected by 45,335 votes against 30,110.

Mr. Saad then proposed that the Board should formally decide in favor of the majority view of the committee. This was approved by 45,335 votes to 25,350. Finally, Mr. Parsons said that the interpretation put forward by Mr. Saad, which the Board had approved, would be appealed to the Governors under Article XVIII (*b*). He therefore proposed that the Board should take no further action pending this appeal. This proposal was defeated by 45,335 votes to 38,210.

Subsequently the Legal Department advised the Board that Article XVIII (*b*) did not give member countries any right of appeal to the Board of Governors from a decision of the Executive Directors on questions of interpretation other than of the Articles of Agreement. However, it was open to a member, under Section 3 (b) or Section 6 (b) of the By-Laws, to request the Governors to declare by resolution that the action taken by the Executive Board in debarring certain members from voting in the election was "inconsistent with action taken by the Board of Governors" under Section 15 of the By-Laws (which limits the Governors' delegation of powers to Executive Directors). In view of this, and of the right of any Governor to raise any matter at a meeting of the Board of Governors, the Executive Directors decided that members already had available a procedure for requesting the Governors to review any decision of the Executive Board.

As a result of the decisions mentioned in the penultimate paragraph, instructions were given to the Secretary to proceed immediately with the election of a thirteenth Director. On April 10, two further proposals were made to postpone action, but were rejected without a formal vote. The election then took place. Italy, Turkey, and Venezuela voted for Mr. Carli, the only candidate nominated; Denmark abstained from voting. Mr. Carli then joined the Board as noted above. However, by arrangement between Mr. Ansiaux and Mr. Carli, the former continued to represent Denmark at the Board, although Mr. Carli cast Denmark's votes.

VIEWS ON DIRECTORS' DUTIES

As is explained below, some Executive Directors went during the year on missions to member countries. This naturally militated against their constant attendance in Washington fulfilling the duties which Mr. White (United States) had envisaged for them there. Nevertheless, the differences in attendance between individual Directors were sufficiently wide as to suggest that there was a sharp cleavage between those who reflected the U.S. concept of a full-time Executive Director devoting his whole attention to Fund affairs, and those who subscribed to the British concept of a high official in regular employment at home who would function as Executive Director only at intervals. During the twelve months October 1946 to September 1947 there were 160 meetings of the Board, including 35 in the afternoon, three on board R.M.S. *Queen Elizabeth* en route to the Annual Meetings in London, and one which was attended also by the Executive Directors of the Bank. A survey of attendances during the year shows that only three Directors were present at more than 75 per cent of the meetings, and that three attended less than 25 per cent. The last-mentioned naturally included Mr. Bolton (United Kingdom), who was present at 35 meetings. Mr. Ansiaux (Belgium) came to 17, Mr. Gómez (Mexico) to 33, and Mr. Rasminsky (Canada) to 64. Mr. Carli (Italy) attended 20 out of the 53 held after his election. These five Directors may be said to have illustrated, more or less fully, the British concept. On the other hand, the U.S. idea was fulfilled most completely by Mr. Joshi (India), who came to 134 meetings; by Mr. White and his successor, who attended 121; and by Mr. Koo (China), who also attended 121.

The difference between the concepts of the role of Executive Directors held by the United States and the United Kingdom did not extend to that of Alternate Executive Directors. At Bretton Woods both delegations had visualized that when a Director was unable to attend the Board he would be replaced by his Alternate, so that the member or members appointing or electing him would always be represented. During 1946–47 this ideal was realized virtually completely by eight of the thirteen Directors, and there were only two by whom it was achieved to a lesser extent than 90 per cent.

Two Directors, finding that their Alternates would be unable to be present when they themselves must be absent, appointed Temporary Alternates to attend the Board instead. This practice was regularized by the Governors at the Second Annual Meeting by altering the relevant Section 14 (d) of the By-Laws. The right was, however, limited to fifteen working days a year. (The Directors had suggested a limit of ten days, but the Governors thought that inadequate.) The procedure of appointing Temporary Alternate Directors has been much used over the years.

ORGANIZATIONAL DETAILS

Staff

By June 30, 1947, the staff had increased to 355, of whom 162 were men. They were nationals of 27 member countries. Of the eight most senior posts, three were held by U.S. citizens, two by Belgians, and one each by a Canadian, an Englishman, and a Frenchman. No considerable changes in organization had been introduced during the year. Mr. Bernstein, Assistant Director in charge of the Research Department, became its Director, and Mr. Powell, Assistant Comptroller, was promoted to Comptroller. Two Assistants to the Managing Director were appointed, of whom one, Mr. Oscar L. Altman, had general responsibility for administration and later became Director of Administration.

Fiscal and financial years

At the end of May the Board reconsidered the definition of the fiscal year. The prospect of repurchase obligations arising from the transactions that had by then begun made it necessary also to fix a financial year, at the end of which members' monetary reserves would have to be calculated and any repurchase obligations would become due. It was decided that, to avoid confusion, the financial and fiscal years of the Fund should in future coincide. It was also decided that the factor determining the concluding date for the fiscal year should be that it would provide adequate, but no more than adequate, time for the completion and auditing of accounts and the preparation of year-end reports before the Annual Meetings of the Governors in September. For these purposes a fiscal year ending on June 30, as fixed at Savannah, allowed too little time. It was, however, too late to alter the fiscal year 1946/47. Accordingly, the Board recommended that the first fiscal year should run from July 1, 1946 to June 30, 1947 and the second fiscal year from July 1, 1947 to April 30, 1948. The first financial year would run from March 1, 1947 to April 30, 1948. Thereafter both fiscal and financial years were to run from May 1 to April 30. The Governors agreed.

QUOTA PROBLEMS

When Australia's request for membership came before the Board on April 15, the quota suggested (as in Schedule A of the Articles of Agreement) was $200 million. Mr. Saad (Egypt) pointed out, however, that the so-called Bretton Woods formula would have yielded a quota of $134 million only. He asked whether Egypt and Iran, each of which regarded its quota as inadequate, would receive similarly generous treatment. Mr. Saad was reminded that the formula had no binding status and that the $200 million quota had been fixed at Bretton Woods. There had been no significant change in Australia's circumstances since then. The figure of $200 million for Australia was accordingly agreed, but later in the year the Directors recommended to the Board of Governors that the quota for Egypt should be increased from $45 million to $60 million and that of Iran from $25 million to $35 million, and this was done. At the request of the World Bank, both increases were made conditional upon the members' increasing correspondingly their subscriptions to the Bank.

A keen argument developed early in 1947 over the change in the quota for France, from $450 million to $525 million. The question was whether this was an adjustment of the initial quota or an increase. France had not paid its subscription when the change was effected, and, so far as the $450 million was concerned, would be required by Article III, Section 3 (*b*), to pay in gold 10 per cent of its holdings of gold and U.S. dollars, this amount being less than 25 per cent of $450 million. Would this payment also cover the gold portion of the added $75 million? The answer depended on whether or not Article III, Section 4 (*a*), dealing with increases in quotas, applied to the $75 million, since this Section required 25 per cent of increases in quotas to be paid in gold.

The matter came before the Board on September 30, 1946, in the form of a memorandum by the Legal Department arguing that Article III, Section 4 (*a*), could not be applied to increases in quotas effected before a member had paid its subscription. This was accepted by the French authorities as exempting them from any further payment in gold, but was later challenged by Mr. Saad and by Mr. B. K. Madan (India), Alternate to Mr. Joshi, who argued that 25 per cent of the increase from $450 million to $525 million, like any other increase in quota, should be paid in gold. Further legal argument developed from a reply to Mr. Madan by Mr. de Largentaye (France).

The problem was not finally disposed of until July 1950, by which time the gold and dollar holdings of France in September 1946 had been determined. After further discussion at the Committee on Interpretation and at the Board, the arguments advanced by Mr. Saad and Mr. Madan prevailed, and it was decided that Article III, Section 4 (*a*), applied to all increases in quotas.[2] However, the Board agreed that, since France had originally been led to believe that it would not apply to the change in the French quota from $450 million to $525 million, the payment of 10 per cent of the French gold and dollar holdings should be accepted as applying to the whole $525 million.

Four further problems, of a minor character, arose during the year in connection with subscriptions. It was decided that payments made under Article III, Section 3 (*b*) (ii), were provisional in the sense that if, after the payment had been made, it was found that the amount paid was incorrect, an adjustment would be called for. Secondly, the Board was advised by the Legal Department that countries that had joined the Fund remained members even if they failed to pay their subscriptions. At the time that this opinion was written (July 1947), there were ten members in this position. Thirdly, the United Kingdom sought unsuccessfully to secure a reduction in the proportion (10 per cent) of

[2] E.B. Decision No. 595-3, July 20, 1950; below, Vol. III, p. 222.

its subscription which by Rule E-2 must be made available to the Fund in currency, i.e., in the form of a bank deposit, as distinct from nonnegotiable, noninterest-bearing securities. When the question was raised again three years later, however, the Board agreed to reduce the minimum limit to 1 per cent. Fourthly, the question whether subscriptions might be shown in a member's reserves was again raised by Egypt and Guatemala, and on May 20, 1947 the Board took the following decision:

> The following principles should be observed by members in reflecting their participation in the Fund in their accounts:
>
> (1) Gold and currency subscribed to the Fund are clearly within its unrestricted ownership. They do not belong in any way to the subscriber.
>
> (2) Although the accounting practices of a member are primarily its own concern, each member should prepare its accounts in such a way that misconceptions as to the ownership of the gold and currency subscribed to the Fund would be avoided, and that if the right to purchase foreign exchange from the Fund were noted in the accounts, its conditional character should be emphasized.

PROPOSED WORLD FOOD BOARD

During the year, the Fund was invited to participate in the preparatory meetings for two other international organizations. The Preparatory Commission for one of these—the World Food Board, proposed at the Second Session of the UN Food and Agriculture Organization (FAO)—showed a disposition to expect more financial assistance from the Fund than the Articles permitted the Fund to provide. By contrast, the negotiators of the other—the proposed International Trade Organization, discussed in the next section—sought at one stage to clothe it with powers that would have duplicated those of the Fund. As will be seen, both these dangers were averted.

The World Food Board had been conceived by Sir John Boyd Orr as a means of dealing with malnutrition in the less developed parts of the world and, in particular, with famines. His conception fell into two parts: On the one hand, the Food Board would have had the responsibility for "developing and organizing production, distribution and utilization of the basic foods to provide diets on a health standard for the peoples of all countries." On the other hand, it would have had responsibility for "stabilizing agricultural prices at levels fair to the producers and consumers alike."

The Preparatory Commission was convened in Washington on October 28, 1946. It was attended on behalf of the Executive Directors by Mr. de Selliers (Belgium) and by a member of the staff. Mr. de Selliers reported periodically to the Executive Board. His first report indicated that the attitude of the major powers, especially the United States, to the project had greatly changed since it was conceived at FAO's Second Session. The main reason for this change was financial. The United States no longer wished to support the buffer stock plan, which was the main element in Sir John Boyd Orr's proposal, and the United Kingdom had stated that on balance of payments grounds it also could not provide finance for an ambitious policy.

At one stage the Preparatory Commission was reported as proposing to invite the Fund to provide resources for agricultural development. Later, however, Mr. de Selliers informed the Board that the extent to which the Fund was likely to be asked to contribute to the whole project had greatly diminished. Early in January 1947, the Commission considered a proposal for making agricultural products available at concessional prices, and the U.S. delegate to the Commission suggested that the Fund might be asked to certify the foreign exchange position of prospective recipients to enable them to qualify for international aid of this kind. He also suggested that the Fund might be invited to advise on the foreign exchange aspects of long-term programs designed to help countries with populations suffering from chronic malnutrition. The Board considered these suggestions and authorized Mr. de Selliers to say that the Fund would be willing to assist in the directions requested.

In the event, however, the final report of the Preparatory Commission suggested only that the Fund should be asked to advise on the balance of payments repercussions of sales of agricultural products at special prices, without involving the Fund in the responsibility of indicating whether a prospective recipient would or would not qualify for assistance. This request the Fund had no difficulty in accepting.

INTERNATIONAL TRADE ORGANIZATION

Both Mr. White and Lord Keynes had visualized that the organizations needed for international economic cooperation in the postwar world would include a body responsible for trade relations. This concept found expression in Resolution VII at Bretton Woods, which recommended to the participating governments that they seek to reach agreement as soon as possible on ways and means to reduce obstacles to international trade and in other ways to promote mutually advantageous international commercial relations.[3] The same Resolution urged participating governments to harmonize national policies designed to promote and maintain high levels of employment and progressively rising standards of living. Accordingly, when in 1946 the United Nations issued invitations to its member countries and, inter alia, to the Fund, they were to a Preparatory Committee for an International Conference on Trade and Employment.

---

[3] *Proceedings*, p. 941.

Initial problems

During the year with which we are now concerned, there were two meetings of this Preparatory Committee—in London from October 15 to November 20, 1946, and in Geneva from April 10 to August 25, 1947. Between these, a drafting committee met in Washington from January 20 to February 25, 1947.

When the invitation to the Conference to be held in London reached the Executive Directors of the Fund at the time of the Annual Meeting in 1946, the Directors at once realized that it would be essential to have the Fund's interests represented. They entrusted the leadership of a delegation for this purpose to Mr. George F. Luthringer (United States), Alternate to Mr. White, and members of the Research Department of the Fund were designated to accompany him.

The draft Charter for an International Trade Organization (ITO), which was placed before the Preparatory Committee by the U.S. delegation and which formed the basis for the Committee's work, covered a much wider field than that in which the Fund was interested. No attempt can be made here to examine all its provisions, nor even to follow the lengthy negotiations on those parts of the Charter which were of direct concern to the Fund. Indeed, since the two sessions of the Preparatory Committee were not conclusive, but were followed by a third at Havana in the following winter, it would not be worthwhile to detail the provisions which emerged at this stage.

Nevertheless, the general outcome must be indicated, because the Fund's interest in the whole negotiations was acute. The field of activity of the proposed Organization would, at the least, run parallel to that of the Fund. It might, indeed, be so formulated as to encroach upon the Fund's responsibilities. Alternatively, the rules of the Organization might provide for its members a means of escape from the jurisdiction of the Fund. In either case, the Fund's influence was bound to be impaired. How to prevent this formed a major preoccupation of the Executive Directors during the Preparatory Committee's sessions. They were afraid that divergent policies of the Fund and the ITO might produce confusion, in the course of which members might be inspired or permitted to introduce restrictions which would conduce to a shrinkage of world trade. Even if the policies of the two organizations were harmonized, there was a danger that countries might use the escape clauses of the ITO Charter to avoid the pressure that might otherwise be exerted on them by the Fund, especially as the sanctions available to the ITO released its members from their commitments under its Charter. The Board was concerned to assert the Fund's right under its Articles to supervise countries' use of exchange techniques, whether for the control of trade or for any other purpose.

On the instructions of the Board, Mr. Luthringer took an opportunity at an early meeting of the first session of the Preparatory Committee to state the Fund's position. He stressed the significance in the Fund Agreement of the transitional period, emphasizing that it was regarded as a step toward the complete attainment of the Fund's objectives and that, in the meantime, the restrictions which were permitted to members were under the Fund's constant scrutiny. In view of this, he suggested that proposals in the draft Charter which would restrict members' freedom under Article XIV of the Fund Agreement should be approached with caution, but that, on the other hand, the use of quantitative restrictions should be subject to similar supervision.

Looking beyond the transitional period, he emphasized that it would be essential for actions authorized by the ITO to be in harmony with actions authorized by the Fund. In this connection, he suggested that the Preparatory Committee should bear in mind that other courses open to members in difficulties might be less harmful than quantitative restrictions on trading: for example, the proper solution might be a devaluation of the currency. Moreover, the Fund's hope and aim was that, once the transitional period had been passed, countries would cease to need restrictions; their own reserves, together with their drawing rights in the Fund, should suffice to see them through periods of temporary difficulty. Hence, he thought that the Charter of the ITO should seek to limit the use of quantitative restrictions to circumstances in which other techniques had been exhausted. In these conditions, the ITO should request the Fund to make a finding as to whether the member's balance of payments and reserves warranted the imposition of the proposed restrictions. He added that the ITO should subsequently consult the Fund on the possibilities for the progressive removal of restrictions that had been authorized.

The proposal for consultation with the Fund of course presupposed common membership of the two organizations, which had indeed been prescribed in the original draft. Although the Executive Directors would have welcomed such a stipulation, the Preparatory Committee decided instead to require such of the members of ITO as were not members of the Fund to enter into a Special Exchange Agreement, by which they would assume obligations parallel to those in the Fund's Articles. The question whether it would be necessary to amend the Fund's Articles of Agreement to enable the Fund to deal with nonmembers under the terms of a Special Exchange Agreement was considered by the Legal Department and was answered in the negative.

Second session

Considerable progress was made during the first session of the Preparatory Committee toward attaining the Fund's objectives, and these were further advanced by the drafting committee, so that when the second session opened in Geneva the Fund's position in relation to the ITO had been much more clearly defined. For this second session the Fund's delegation was headed by Mr. Saad (Egypt), with whose assistance the process of clarification was carried further.

The first weeks of the new session were occupied with negotiations for tariff reductions. When discussion of the draft Charter was resumed, a number of fresh problems arose and were dealt with. One such was the question of the exchange rate to be used for the calculation of tariffs. For some countries, this involved consideration of multiple currency practices, and Mr. Saad secured insertion in the draft Charter of a provision which made it clear that such practices were the responsibility of the Fund and not of the ITO. Again, provisions in the draft Charter for the control of international investment needed modification to ensure that they would not interfere with the freedom to impose controls over capital movements which was allowed by the Fund Agreement.

As a result of his work, Mr. Saad was able to report at the end of the second session that the jurisdiction of the Fund in its own field had been fully recognized in the Charter, and that duplication of functions between the Fund and the ITO had been reduced to a minimum. The draft Charter provided for the coordination of policy between the ITO and the Fund, both on the exchange questions (which were within the jurisdiction of the Fund) and on quantitative restrictions and other trade measures (which were to be within the jurisdiction of the ITO).

The draft Charter also provided that the ITO would consult the Fund fully on all questions about monetary reserves, balances of payments, and foreign exchange arrangements, and would accept the Fund's findings on (1) facts in these fields; (2) whether members' actions were consistent with the Fund's Articles of Agreement or with Special Exchange Agreements, as the case might be; (3) what was a serious decline of monetary reserves, a low level of reserves, or a reasonable rate of increase of reserves, where members were seeking to impose restrictions for balance of payments purposes; and (4) "financial aspects of other matters."

In their Annual Report for 1947, the Executive Directors remarked that "the importance to the Fund of a successful International Trade Organization can hardly be overemphasized." [4] The activities of the Fund's delegations to the two sessions of the Preparatory Committee had helped to ensure that the Charter of the ITO would be compatible with members' existing commitments and, at the same time, had averted the weakening of the Fund's powers of control of its members, which would necessarily have resulted had the Charter been such that members could play off the ITO against the Fund.

Third session

The Fund was represented at the Havana Conference on Trade and Employment, which opened on November 21, 1947, by Messrs. Saad and Luthringer,

---

[4] *Annual Report, 1947*, p. 38.

assisted by members of the staff. Mr. Gutt also visited Havana and addressed the Conference.

Mr. Luthringer reported to the Board early in January 1948 that the provisions of the draft Charter dealing with preference and quantitative restrictions were under attack. He feared that, if this continued, the usefulness of the Charter might be seriously impaired. However, the final report by Mr. Saad on the outcome of the Conference suggested that this danger had been largely averted. The fundamental provisions of the Geneva Charter that directly concerned the Fund had been maintained at Havana. Indeed, a possible source of friction had been removed by the elimination of the provision which would have permitted the challenging of a member's actions in the exchange field, even though such actions were consistent with the Fund Agreement, on the ground that they frustrated the intent of the Charter's provisions on quantitative restrictions.

Mr. Saad emphasized that the interdependence of the roles of the Fund and the ITO made it imperative that there should be full cooperation between the two bodies, and he suggested that the Board should forthwith consider the terms of a possible agreement with the ITO for such cooperation. For this purpose, a Committee on Liaison with the ITO was formed in July; it comprised Mr. Saad (Chairman), Mr. Beyen (Netherlands), Mr. Overby (United States), Mr. Octavio Paranaguá (Brazil), Alternate to Mr. Santos-Filho, and Mr. Roland Wilson (Australia), Alternate to Mr. Stuart G. McFarlane. This committee put forward detailed proposals for cooperation with the ITO which were approved by the Board as a basis for negotiation with the Interim Commission of the ITO.

Pending action by the prospective members of the ITO, the General Agreement on Tariffs and Trade (GATT) was put into provisional application during the summer, and in September 1948 the Board approved proposals by the Chairman of the CONTRACTING PARTIES for informal cooperation between the GATT and the Fund.

It was unfortunate, and not only for the Fund, that the long and arduous negotiations that culminated at Havana failed to establish an International Trade Organization. But it was to the benefit of the Fund that the GATT, which did emerge from the negotiations, inherited the relations with the Fund which had been so carefully defined by the Preparatory Committee.

MULTIPLE CURRENCY PRACTICES

In the previous section, passing reference was made to problems connected with multiple currency practices. This was a subject which loomed large in the work of the Executive Board during 1946–47. It involved difficult questions of the Fund's jurisdiction and even more difficult problems of finding practical alternatives to existing exchange arrangements.

Early in January 1947, the Board began to consider a series of memoranda describing multiple currency practices in fourteen countries, analyzing their economic significance, and reviewing in a preliminary way the jurisdictional issues. Its first task was to decide upon its powers of action. These derived from a sentence in Article XIV, Section 4, which reads:

> The Fund may, if it deems such action necessary in exceptional circumstances, make representations to any member that conditions are favorable for the withdrawal of any particular restriction, or for the general abandonment of restrictions, inconsistent with the provisions of any other article of this Agreement.

Two questions arose. The first was whether there was any limitation on the time when these powers might be exercised. Specifically, did the Board need to wait until the end of the periods specified in the earlier part of the Section, viz., three years from the date when operations began (after which the Fund was required to report on restrictions) or five years from that date (after which the members were required to consult the Fund on any restrictions they were maintaining)? On this, the Board decided that its powers applied at any time after the entry into force of the Fund Agreement. The second question was what was meant by "in exceptional circumstances." Here it was agreed that it was for the Fund, and not for the member, to decide that "exceptional circumstances" existed. Before doing so the Fund would have to take account of the importance to the member and to other members of the particular restrictions that were being maintained, and of the bearing of these restrictions upon the purposes of the Fund.[5]

Thereupon the Board decided that its best course would be to examine the exchange arrangements in a number of member countries, preparatory to formulating policies; and it did in fact consider, during the second half of January, the practices of some thirty. Following these reviews, the Board felt it to be necessary for a number of members to whom multiple currency practices were clearly important to be visited by Executive Directors. As a result of such visits, the Board was given firsthand surveys of the situation in a number of member countries, as described later in this chapter.

On further consideration of the somewhat complex issues arising, the Board decided in May 1947 to set up an ad hoc Committee on Spreads and Multiple Currency Practices. The chairman of the Committee was Mr. Mládek (Czechoslovakia) and the other members were Mr. Bruins (Netherlands), Mr. Joshi (India), Mr. Luthringer (United States), and Mr. Raul Martínez-Ostos (Mexico), Alternate to Mr. Gómez, assisted by the Heads of the Legal, Operations, and Research Departments. This committee reported on August 5, 1947, and, following further discussion in the Board, a circular letter to members was issued on December 18, as described below.

[5] E.B. Decision No. 117-1, January 6, 1947; below, Vol. III, p. 269.

The considerations which came before the Board in connection with multiple currency practices may be brought into focus by summarizing the report of the ad hoc committee. This began by distinguishing between the different types of multiple currency practices which were in use by members of the Fund. The committee pointed out that an exchange arrangement was subject to review by the Fund if it produced an exchange rate varying by more than 1 per cent from the par value agreed with the Fund. Subject to this limitation, the committee thought that the principal types of multiple currency practices were as follows: (1) preferential buying (export) rates, including arrangements for the preferential retention of export proceeds; (2) unfavorable selling (import) rates, one type of which was a tax on foreign exchange; (3) unfavorable buying (export) rates; (4) preferential selling (import) rates; (5) an excessive spread between the effective buying rate and the effective selling rate; (6) the compulsory investment of export proceeds in government bonds; (7) free market rates; (8) the allocation of foreign exchange by auction; and (9) black market rates.

The committee pointed out that many of the countries using such arrangements found them easier to administer than licensing procedures, and less subject to corruption and discrimination; that the fiscal effects of multiple currency practices were often important for the damping down of inflation and were less harmful than quantitative restrictions, especially where an effective control of prices was impracticable; and that it was by no means easy to suggest satisfactory alternative techniques if multiple currency practices were to be abandoned. In this connection, an interim report by the committee advocated the use of tariffs as a substitute for multiple currency practices. The Board, however, decided to avoid any general pronouncement to that effect.

In its final report, the committee summarized its problem as follows:

> On the one hand, it is clear that at this time for certain countries the only practicable sort of foreign exchange restriction is multiple currency practices. Denying them use of these would be excluding them from having any sort of control. This is hardly a policy the Fund would wish to follow and as a matter of fact it cannot pursue it in the transitional period when Articles VIII and XIV permit the maintenance and adaptation of multiple currency practices.
>
> On the other hand, it is obvious that some multiple currency practices are undesirable because they have harmful effects on international trade and monetary relations. Besides, they fit rather badly into the concept of stable rates based on an agreed par value.

This quotation also indicates the dual nature of the Fund's jurisdiction in this field. Multiple currency practices are deviations from exchange rate parities and therefore in conflict with Article IV; they are also a type of exchange restriction and, accordingly, subject to Articles VIII and XIV.

The committee recommended that the Board should adopt a policy along the following lines: Multiple currency practices are justifiable when and insofar as they are restrictions necessary to preserve the equilibrium of the balance of payments. Some types are more undesirable than others. Those which constitute a serious menace to international economic relations should be attacked first. The Board should bear in mind the advantages to the countries using these practices; therefore if it decided that these practices in a particular country could not be tolerated, the whole situation in that country would need to be reviewed. Conceivably, one step might be to limit the scope of free markets where they exist and, if possible, confine them to capital transactions. A similar restriction on the use of auction methods would be helpful.

Specifically, the committee concluded that members might maintain multiple currency practices under the provisions of Article XIV, Section 2, only if such maintenance was necessary for settling their balance of payments in a manner which did not unduly encumber their access to the resources of the Fund. (The last-mentioned phrase, which was quoted from the Article cited, has not been officially interpreted, but is understood to be equivalent to "without the need for undue financial assistance from the Fund.") If the member had accepted the obligations of Article VIII, Section 3, it would be required to consult with the Fund on the progressive removal of multiple currency practices, or to obtain the Fund's approval of their continued use. As regards the introduction of new practices, the committee referred to the distinction in the Articles between members formerly occupied by the enemy (which might introduce such practices where necessary) and other members. ("Other members" might introduce new practices only under Article VIII, Section 3, which provides expressly that the member must obtain approval from the Fund.) Finally, as regards the adaptation of existing practices, the committee concluded that any adaptation needed the approval of the Fund, whether under Article XIV or under Article VIII. In this connection, the committee found that the reclassification of commodities between different exchange rates was an adaptation which required the Fund's approval.

When the committee's report came before the Executive Board, some questions were raised about the jurisdiction which the Fund exercised. Mr. de Largentaye (France) thought that the provisions of Article XIV, Section 2, controlling the use of exchange restrictions in the transitional period, took precedence over those of Article IV, Section 4, requiring members to maintain exchange rates within the permitted limits of parity. This view was, however, challenged on the ground that, as mentioned above, multiple currency practices were both exchange rates deviating from par values and exchange restrictions, and the Fund therefore had jurisdiction under both the Articles mentioned. The Board agreed with the latter view.

Mr. Martínez-Ostos pointed out that in some countries multiple currency practices could not be described as harmful. They had little effect on trade, partly because they were in essence unaggressive and partly because the trade of many countries using them was small. He also stressed the importance of multiple currency practices to some countries for purposes of monetary management. He thought that, at the least, the Fund should not issue any decision about multiple currency practices without being able to say that it was studying other types of exchange restrictions, which in his view were often more harmful. Mr. Martínez-Ostos further argued that the committee was wrong in suggesting that the multiple currency practices involving floating exchange rates were more harmful than those with fixed exchange rates; in his view, the opposite was true.

The Board, however, accepted the conclusions of the ad hoc committee, and decided that member countries should be advised of the view which the Board took about the undesirability of multiple currency practices. With Mr. de Largentaye dissenting, it approved for issue a statement which elaborated the analysis of the Fund's jurisdiction and of its attitude toward different types of exchange arrangements given in the committee's report. This statement, sent to all members on December 19, 1947, is set out in full in Volume III.[6]

GOLD PREMIUMS AND SUBSIDIES

Sales at premium prices

The problem of gold sales at premium prices, which in later years was to cause much trouble for the Board, was tentatively raised in August 1946 by an inquiry from Peru. A Bill was about to be introduced into the Peruvian Legislature that would permit the owners of gold mines there to have gold minted into special coins, which would then be sold abroad on their behalf by the central bank. It was expected that these would yield a premium over the bullion value of the gold. The Government inquired whether such sales would contravene the Articles of Agreement once a par value for the Peruvian sol had been adopted.

The Legal Department advised the Board that the obligation in Article IV, Section 2, not to buy gold at a price above par plus the prescribed margin, applied only to transactions between members, not to private sales of the kind contemplated. Mr. Martínez-Ostos (Mexico) notified the Board that Mexico had for some years been following a similar practice; he suggested that what the Peruvian miners proposed to do was not to sell gold as such, but to sell gold objects, which were not covered by Article IV, Section 2. Moreover, they were selling at a price above par, whereas Article IV, Section 2, prohibits sales below par only.

The Board reviewed the request, with the assistance of a representative of Peru, and decided that the Managing Director should write to Peru in terms including the following:

[6] E.B. Decision No. 237-2, December 18, 1947; below, Vol. III, p. 261.

> I must inform you that it is the opinion of the Executive Directors that the action proposed under the draft legislation would not, in itself, be inconsistent with any particular provision of the Fund Agreement, provided that such sales do not render more difficult full compliance by members with their obligations under the Fund Agreement, that the proceeds of gold sales are not transferred at rates of exchange differing from parity by more than the range prescribed in the Fund Agreement, and that such gold sales do not give rise to illicit foreign exchange transactions. . . .
>
> [But] the Board is of the opinion that such gold transactions, if conducted on an appreciable scale, may well in the course of time operate to help undermine exchange stability, the maintenance of which is one of the purposes of the Fund.
>
> For the reasons indicated, the Board would not wish to have its opinion regarding the legal position construed as encouragement of the proposed action.

This letter was dispatched on September 11, 1946.

In March 1947 the Fund became aware that the foregoing attempt to improve the lot of Peru's gold producers had not been a success, and learnt of a draft decree which would require the producers to sell their gold to the central bank for negotiable certificates. These certificates would entitle the holder both to an equivalent amount of foreign exchange and to an import license for the same value; it was therefore expected that they would sell within Peru at a premium. In practice, this decree was not issued, as the scheme proved impracticable; instead, producers were permitted by a decision of the Peruvian Government in April 1947 to sell their gold abroad for what it would fetch.

The Peruvian measures just mentioned were not formally submitted to the Fund but, at the end of April, similar issues were raised by a request from Colombia. The Board was asked whether Colombian miners could be permitted to sell gold abroad, or to sell it at home for industrial purposes, at more than the equivalent of $35 an ounce. This led to an intensive reconsideration by the Board of the whole problem of the sale of gold at premium prices. The arguments developed were partly legal and partly economic. The legal reasoning was based on the interpretation of Article I (iii) and Article IV, Sections 2 and 4, and involved a study of the legislative history of these Articles. The economic argument was that sales at premium prices threatened to undermine the stability of the exchange rate of the country making them, and that they also tended to siphon newly produced gold into hoards rather than into monetary reserves, an undesirable consequence.

On May 14, 1947, the Board remitted the whole problem to an ad hoc Committee on External Sales of Gold, consisting of Mr. Luthringer (United States), chairman, and Messrs. Bolton (United Kingdom), Bruins (Netherlands), de Selliers (Belgium), Gómez (Mexico), and Rasminsky (Canada), assisted by the Heads of the Legal, Operations, and Research Departments. The committee moved with speed, and a week later the Board was able to consider its report. This was to the effect that the Fund should strongly deprecate external sales of gold at premium prices, although it was unnecessary to take similar action with regard to internal sales. The committee considered that the Fund had authority under Article I and Article IV, Sections 2 and 4 (*a*), to prevent sales of gold that would undermine exchange stability. It thought that a statement setting out the Fund's position should be prepared and circulated to members, and that this statement should emphasize broad policy considerations rather than legalistic ones. Finally, the committee suggested that no answer could be given to Colombia's inquiry until the general policy had been decided.

When considering this report, Executive Directors raised a number of objections. Some thought that the Board's action should focus on the receiving country rather than on the selling country. Some held that gold should be considered a commodity like other imports. As against this, it was argued that because gold was held in monetary reserves, and was the basis for par values, it could not be regarded as an ordinary import, and transactions at premium prices could not fail to affect exchange rates. Moreover, the Fund's obligations under Article IV, Sections 2 and 4 (*a*), made it necessary for the policy enunciated to apply not only to members' fiscal agencies but also to the nationals of member countries.

Mr. Martínez-Ostos, in addition to submitting legal arguments, drew attention to some practical difficulties in the policy proposed by the committee. He pointed out that nonmembers were free, and would remain free, to make sales at premium prices, so that a prohibition of such sales by Fund members would only go part of the way toward attaining the Fund's objectives. Moreover, it seemed probable that if Fund members attempted to enforce the restrictions which the proposed policy suggested, the effect would be to enhance the premium at which gold was sold in the free markets and thereby add to the difficulties of preventing illegal transactions.

The Board was, however, satisfied that sales of gold at premium prices offered a real threat to the stability of exchange rates, and therefore approved the policy proposed by the committee. The first step toward implementing it was to decide what were to be the approved margins, above and below par value, for transactions in gold. Article IV, Section 2, had left these to be prescribed by the Fund. On June 10, 1947, the Board adopted a Rule (F-4) that these margins should be ¼ of 1 per cent plus the cost of converting and transporting the gold and any charges made by the custodian of the gold for effecting the transfer. On June 18, the statement suggested by the committee was sent to all members.[7] The operative paragraph was the following:

> A primary purpose of the Fund is world exchange stability and it is the considered opinion of the Fund that exchange stability may be undermined by continued and increasing external purchases and sales of gold at prices which directly or indirectly produce exchange transactions at depreciated rates. From

[7] *Annual Report, 1947*, p. 78; also reproduced below, Vol. III, p. 310.

> information at its disposal, the Fund believes that unless discouraged this practice is likely to become extensive, which would fundamentally disturb the exchange relationships among the members of the Fund. Moreover, these transactions involve a loss to monetary reserves, since much of the gold goes into private hoards rather than into central holdings. For these reasons, the Fund strongly deprecates international transactions in gold at premium prices and recommends that all of its members take effective action to prevent such transactions in gold with other countries or with the nationals of other countries.

Although, in the light of the Board's views, Colombia withdrew its request for a ruling on its proposal, the statement did not dispose of the general problem. In July, Mexico questioned both the legal basis for the statement and the necessity for its application to sales to nonmembers. Shortly afterwards the Peruvian Government drew attention to the extreme importance to its unsatisfactory balance of payments of the premium which its gold producers would otherwise be able to obtain.

The questions raised by these two countries were considered by the Board at several meetings in July and August, and in the course of these, three further objections were raised: that the prohibition could not apply to sales to nonmembers, since nonmembers had no par values in the light of which the gold price could be calculated; that such calculations were even more impracticable when nonmembers were relying on multiple currency practices; and that the statement should apply only to bullion and not, for example, to jewelry.

The economic argument which underlay the whole statement was felt by the Board to nullify these three objections, and no cause was found to vary the terms of the statement, although it appears that in practice the policy was not regarded as covering processed gold.

The reply to Mexico was that the legal basis for the Fund's action was to be found in Article I (iii) and Article IV, Section 4 (*a*), and that since the objective of the statement was to avoid an undesirable impact on the member's exchange rate, it necessarily applied to sales to nonmembers as well as to sales to other members. The reply to Peru was that the threat to the balance of payments which Peru envisaged from the cessation of sales at premium prices was clearly only a facet of a much larger economic problem, which it was suggested the Peruvian Governor might well discuss with Executive Directors during the forthcoming Annual Meeting.

Discussions at the Annual Meeting produced no satisfactory solution to Peru's difficulties, and the Governor for Peru asked for a mission. In order to advise the member, and to guide the mission, the Committee on External Sales of Gold was asked to consider what measures acceptable to the Fund members could be taken to encourage domestic gold production, with special reference to the problem experienced by Peru. There was some feeling in the committee, however, that these practical details were beyond its scope and that useful advice to members could only be given after consultation with, for example, gold mining experts. The committee decided on November 17 to ask the Executive Board for further guidance before continuing its work.

Subsidies to gold producers

A fresh element was introduced on the following day when, in the course of a discussion of Canada's economic problems, Mr. Rasminsky (Canada) stated to the Board that his Government proposed to offer to each gold mine in Canada a subsidy of $7 for each ounce of gold produced in excess of the output in the year ending June 30, 1947. Mr. Rasminsky explained that the reason for this proposal was that gold production in Canada was declining and the balance of payments was suffering in consequence. When, therefore, the request of the Committee on External Sales of Gold for clarification of its terms of reference came before the Board, it was asked specifically to examine and report on the Canadian plan.

The committee, which in the absence of Mr. Luthringer was now chaired by Mr. Carli (Italy), discussed the proposal at considerable length, but found it difficult to reach agreement on whether or not it was one which the Fund could approve. In the light of the committee's criticisms, the Canadian Government revised its proposal. Its new plan provided for a subsidy comprising some percentage of the amount by which the actual average production costs in each mine exceeded from time to time specified basic costs per fine ounce; it was to be payable on the amount by which gold production from that mine exceeded a specified percentage of the gold produced in a base year. New mines would be given the subsidy on the whole of their production in the first year and subsequently on terms similar to those of existing mines.

On December 5, the committee received a staff recommendation to the effect that this plan need not be objected to. However, on the day when the committee met to discuss the revised Canadian proposal, it was also presented with a recommendation by Mr. Overby (United States) that the Fund should issue a public statement, in more general terms than that made in June. Mr. Rasminsky pointed out that it was urgent to reach a decision on the Canadian proposal, because his Government was due to announce a legislative program, of which the part dealing with the gold subsidy was expected to be presented to Parliament on December 11 or 12. Accordingly, over the four days December 8 to 11, there were five meetings of the committee and three of the Board, at which both the draft statement that Mr. Overby had placed before the committee and the Canadian plan were discussed. The former was fairly extensively amended to meet the arguments of a number of Directors. In particular, objection was taken in the Board to a reference in Mr. Overby's draft to members having an obligation to consult the Fund before "modifying prevailing regulations and practices relating to external transactions in gold." It was contended that this was too sweeping an assertion, and there were even objections to a corresponding reference limited to subsidies. Eventually it was agreed to indicate that each proposal to subsidize or otherwise support the price of gold would require to be considered on its merits, rather than that the Board should attempt to formulate a general principle which would cover all possible cases. Reservations to different phases in the statement were maintained by Messrs. de Largentaye (France) and Martínez-Ostos, and by Mr. Geoffrey H. Tansley (United Kingdom), Alternate to Mr. Bolton. Subject to these, the statement was agreed by the Board on December 11.[8] The central element was contained in the following passage:

> In the view of the Fund, a subsidy in the form of a uniform payment per ounce for all or part of the gold produced would constitute an increase in price which would not be permissible if the total price paid by the member for gold were thereby to become in excess of parity plus the prescribed margin. Subsidies involving payments in another form may also, depending upon their nature, constitute an increase in price.

Applying these principles to the Canadian proposal, the Board decided as follows:

> . . . The Fund has examined the present Canadian proposal in the light of its own general statement of policy published today. The Fund has determined that in the present circumstances the proposed Canadian action is not inconsistent with the policy stated by the Fund.

Subsequent developments

In February 1948 a report was made to the Board on the developments in gold markets since June 1947. This showed that the Board's policy was being widely implemented, that there had probably been some fall in the volume of sales, and that the average price at which sales were occurring had risen. Mr. Overby said that gold producers in the United States were complaining that, while the United States enforced the Fund's policy, other producing countries did not do so. In reply it was stated that the number of countries willing to buy gold at premium prices was so great that effective control of such sales was unlikely to be practicable, and that, in any event, such sales earned badly needed dollars. Mr. Martínez-Ostos said that the Fund had made a mistake in excluding processed gold from the scope of its policy. He also suggested that the rise in the average price of gold sold in premium markets, which did not seem to reflect any appreciable diminution of sales, showed that the Fund's policy was misguided. Mr. de Largentaye expressed the opinion that the Fund would have done better to arrange for a plentiful supply of gold to be available at $35 an ounce, in order to eliminate the premium in free markets. Executive Directors generally, however, felt that any reduction in the volume of sales at premium

---

[8] E.B. Decision No. 233-2, December 11, 1947; below, Vol. III, p. 225.

prices would be beneficial. It was decided to ask member countries to supply information about changes in their laws, decrees, and administrative practices with regard to gold sales since the Fund's statement of June 18, 1947.

In March 1948 a proposal from Australia to give assistance to certain gold mines in desert areas was considered. Its aim was to enable certain marginal mines to remain in production despite rising costs, in order to avoid hardship to the dependent population in these areas. Mr. Overby said that, if the purpose of the Australian proposal had been to increase the production of gold for balance of payments purposes, he would have had to object to it. As it was, however, he was prepared to concur. The Board decided that the plan did not contravene either Article IV, Sections 2 and 4, or the policy enunciated in December 1947; it did not, therefore, object to the proposal.

A substantial section of the *Annual Report, 1948,* was devoted to explaining the Fund's policy along the lines of its statements of June and December 1947. The Report said that there was ample room for greater support of this policy and urged a more vigorous enforcement of the gold regulations in certain countries.[9]

Proposed investment

By an interesting anticipation of a later development, Mr. White suggested in October 1946 that the Board should consider the possibility of investing in U.S. Government securities that portion of the Fund's gold which would clearly not be needed for the time being. He pointed out that the Fund, at the beginning of its operations, would have substantially over a billion dollars in gold, of which probably one half would be located in New York, and suggested that something between $5 million and $12 million a year could readily be earned by investing part of it. The Legal Department advised that such an investment, as an exercise of the Fund's duty to administer properly its assets, would be permissible under the Articles, and could be arranged so as to be practically riskless. However, the Board deferred taking any action, mainly because some Directors thought that such an investment might impair confidence in the Fund.

CONTACTS WITH MEMBERS

Another precedent set by the Board's actions during this year concerned the provision of technical assistance to members. The problem first came before the Board early in December 1946, when a request was received from the Ecuadoran Ambassador to Washington for a technical mission to advise Ecuador on its banking and monetary situation, in order for appropriate reforms to be initiated.

[9] *Annual Report, 1948,* pp. 39–44.

This prompted a review by the Board of the general problem of maintaining contact with members. As it happened, the problem of technical assistance was also before the United Nations, and on the day after the Fund Board meeting the General Assembly considered a report drawing attention to the capability of the specialized agencies to provide technical assistance.

Early in January 1948 the World Bank approached the Fund in connection with a mission to Denmark, which had sought a loan. The Bank proposed to send a team to investigate the request, and wished a balance of payments expert from the Fund staff to accompany the team. This was approved. A preliminary report by the staff member, circulated to the Board on January 31, indicated that the krone was overvalued, and added to the Board's concern about keeping abreast of developments in member countries.

On February 6 it was decided that Mr. Ansiaux (Belgium) and Mr. Mahmoud Saleh El Falaki (Egypt), Alternate to Mr. Saad, should visit Denmark, Messrs. Santos-Filho (Brazil) and White (United States) should go to Bolivia and Ecuador, and Messrs. Gómez (Mexico) and White to Costa Rica and Nicaragua. The mission to Ecuador proved to be somewhat premature, the Government being less ready to discuss its problems than the Ambassador had indicated, but in May a fresh request for a mission was received, and two members of the staff were sent. Their report showed that Ecuador was attempting to deal with a difficult balance of payments problem by multiple currency practices. When this report came before the Board, the Managing Director took the opportunity to stress the importance for the Fund's prestige of taking a decision in issues of this kind. After further consideration the Board decided that it could give qualified approval to a request to establish these practices, and to some banking reforms that were also planned. Reports on the missions to the other four countries mentioned were made to the Board during February and March. At the same time, the Board was given firsthand information about conditions in Brazil, Chile, Panama, Paraguay, Peru, and Uruguay by Mr. Santos-Filho, in Guatemala by Mr. Gómez, and in Cuba by Mr. Martínez-Ostos (Mexico).

The Managing Director, accompanied by the Director of the Research Department, visited Europe in April, and reported to the Board on the conditions in Belgium, Denmark, France, Luxembourg, the Netherlands, and Norway. Mr. Koo (China) visited China and explained to the Board his country's problems. Mr. Mládek (Czechoslovakia) similarly reported on a visit to Czechoslovakia, Poland, and Yugoslavia, and Mr. Carli (Italy) on conditions in Italy. The situation in France was discussed in July on the basis of the Managing Director's report and others that had been submitted to the Board. Finally, Mr. Bolton (United Kingdom) kept the Board in touch with British developments, reporting on June 3 on the economic situation there and on the arrangements that had been made in anticipation of sterling becoming convertible on July 16, under the terms of the Anglo-American Financial Agreement. When the attempt at convertibility into dollars failed, the Board was notified of the exchange of letters between the United States and the United Kingdom, but agreed that no action by the Fund was called for.

In all this, the Board was feeling its way. There was as yet no systematic program of reviews of the position of members; their problems were tackled as they came to the Board's notice, whether on a request such as that of Ecuador or as a by-product of the Board's search for the basis of a general policy, such as the visits paid to countries employing multiple currency practices. But the Board was increasingly conscious of the need to strengthen its links with member countries, especially when—as discussed in the next section—members began to draw upon its resources. We shall see in later chapters how the requirements of Article XIV paved the way to the regular contacts with members that the Board desired.

FIRST DRAWINGS: PREPARATIONS AND POLICIES

Preliminary decisions

Preparations for the commencement of Fund operations, set for March 1, 1947, occupied the Board from time to time during the winter. One question considered was whether the Fund should postpone exchange transactions with any member, as it was entitled to do under Article XX, Section 4 (*i*), if the circumstances of the member were such that, "in the opinion of the Fund, they would lead to use of the resources of the Fund in a manner contrary to the purposes of this Agreement or prejudicial to the Fund or the members." No formal use was made of this provision, but as a by-product of the reviews of members' economic conditions and exchange arrangements mentioned in previous sections of this chapter, informal understandings were reached with ten members that they would not, for the time being, make use of the Fund's resources. The Board also took steps to preserve the power conferred by Article XX, Section 4 (*i*), deciding on February 18, 1947 that this did not lapse on the date when exchange transactions were begun.

One possible consequence of a resort to Article XX, Section 4 (*i*), was considered in January 1947. The Board was asked whether the use of this provision against any member would permit that member to postpone its subscription. The Board decided that, on the contrary, each member that had a par value would become "eligible" to draw from the Fund under the terms of Article XX, Section 4 (*c*) or (*d*), from the date when the Fund began operations. Consequently its subscription would become due on the previous day, i.e., on February 28, 1947. A member that had no par value on March 1, 1947, and so would not initially be eligible to draw under Article XX, Section 4 (*c*) or (*d*), need not pay its subscription until it agreed a par value with the Fund and so became eligible. It must then pay its subscription forthwith.

A second matter to which the Board gave attention was the question whether any currencies of nonmembers should be "specified" under Article XIX (*a*). If any such currencies had been specified, they would have formed parts of members' monetary reserves for purposes of the Articles. This might have been important in connection with the payment of subscriptions following the increases in quotas mentioned above. In the future the inclusion of the currencies of nonmember countries in members' monetary reserves might affect their payment of charges (Article V, Section 8 (*f*)) and their repurchase obligations (Article V, Section 7, and Schedule B). However, although the currencies of several nonmembers were reviewed, the Board decided that "no conditions appear to exist which require the specification of any currencies of nonmembers under Article XIX (*a*) at the present time, and no such currencies are specified."

A related question, which became of importance later on, concerned the date upon which an initial calculation of a member's monetary reserves must be made in preparation for the calculation of a repurchase obligation. The Board decided that increases and decreases in a member's monetary reserves were to be ignored if they occurred on or before the latest date when its subscription was due, and that the payment of a subscription, whether actually made before, on, or after this latest date, should not be regarded as resulting in a decrease in the member's monetary reserves.[10]

Preparations for operations were completed in February by the issue of instructions to members as to the procedure by which requests for drawings should be made. These instructions included the provision of a special code and cipher system and a test number, which had to be used when drawings were requested by cable. Each member was asked for an undertaking that the use of this system and number was equivalent to the provision of a signed commitment by the Government.

As the year went on, the Board reviewed on several occasions the method of handling requests by members to draw. The starting point was Rule G-5, which, as will be recalled, provided that if a requested drawing exceeded 5 per cent of the member's quota, the Managing Director should notify each Executive Director of the request. It followed that, if the member's request did not exceed 5 per cent of its quota, it could be dealt with by the Managing Director without prior reference to the Board, although the Managing Director or any Executive Director could bring such a request to the Board if he wished. We shall see later in this section that, in practice, this corollary was found to conflict with the Board's wish to be satisfied that members when drawing fulfilled the requirements of the Articles.

---

[10] E.B. Decision No. 124-2, January 22, 1947; below, Vol. III, p. 244.

The prime condition that members wishing to draw had to satisfy was set out in Article V, Section 3 (*a*) (i). This states that the member desiring to purchase a currency must represent that it is "presently needed for making in that currency payments which are consistent with the provisions of this Agreement." The interpretation of this sentence was the subject of a lengthy discussion in the Board on May 6, 1947. The decision (after a slight change of wording on May 29) was as follows:[11]

> The word "represents" in Article V, Section 3 (*a*) (i), means "declares." The member is presumed to have fulfilled the condition mentioned in Article V, Section 3 (*a*) (i), if it declares that the currency is presently needed for making payments in that currency which are consistent with the provisions of the Agreement. But the Fund may, for good reasons, challenge the correctness of this declaration, on the grounds that the currency is not "presently needed" or because the currency is not needed for payment "in that currency," or because the payments will not be "consistent with the provisions of this Agreement." If the Fund concludes that a particular declaration is not correct, the Fund may postpone or reject the request, or accept it subject to conditions. The phrase "presently needed" cannot be defined in terms of a formula uniformly applicable to all cases, but where there is good reason to doubt that the currency is "presently needed," the Fund will have to apply the phrase in each case in the light of all the circumstances.

Mr. de Largentaye (France) dissented. He considered that the only proper ground for questioning a member's representation was evidence that this representation was inaccurate. He could not accept the view of the generality of the Directors that the Fund's right to question the member necessarily involved interpretation of the qualitative standards mentioned in the Decision.

It will be realized that the Board's interpretation of "represents" corresponded to that indicated by Mr. White in 1944. In reaching that conclusion, the Board was effectively departing from the concept of an automatic right to draw on the Fund, which would have subjected a member's representations to inquiry only if the member sought to draw more than 25 per cent of its quota in a year, or if the Fund's holdings of the member's currency had reached 200 per cent of its quota.

Transactions policy

Even before this discussion in the Board, a first approach had been made to the Fund for a drawing. On April 21 a request was received from Ethiopia to draw $900,000. The request did not, however, conform to the procedure which had been prescribed, and was therefore not acceptable. The Board, when advised of the request, questioned whether so large an amount—it was equivalent to 15 per cent of Ethiopia's quota–could really be "presently needed"; some Directors thought it would be likely to meet Ethiopia's needs for a longer period

[11] Confirmed in 1948 as E.B. Decision No. 284-4, March 10, 1948; below, Vol. III, p. 227.

than would be consistent with the Articles. A reply was sent to Ethiopia explaining the procedure which would have to be followed for the drawing to be considered, but no further request was made until July 1948, when Ethiopia sought and obtained a drawing of $300,000.

On May 8, 1947 France drew $25 million from the Fund. As this was less than 5 per cent of the enlarged French quota, the request was dealt with by the Managing Director and staff, and notified to the Board on the day the transaction was completed. Shortly afterward, the Netherlands drew $6 million and £1.5 million; this again was less than 5 per cent of the member's quota. The transaction was mentioned to the Board by the Managing Director on May 20, in the course of an important statement made after visiting Europe in which he expounded to the Board his views on the relationship between the Fund and its members in connection with drawings. He urged that members must know how they stood. They must be able to rely upon being able to draw from the Fund, provided that the need was a temporary one and the purpose to make payments (not to increase reserves) and to deal with a deficit on current account (not capital account); provided also that they did not attempt to draw sums that they would not be able to repay, or to draw at a time when they were suffering from a fundamental disequilibrium. Further, once a member had made a drawing, it should be able to expect to go on drawing without objection by the Fund. It followed that the Fund would have to know the full situation of each of its members at any time to enable it to decide beforehand what its attitude to a desired drawing would be. Mr. Gutt also recommended that if the Board felt that an individual member should not use the Fund's resources, it should be told so informally, rather than that the Board should make use of Article V, Section 5. This Section provides for formal action by the Fund, possibly culminating in declaring a member ineligible to use its resources, "whenever the Fund is of the opinion that any member is using the resources of the Fund in a manner contrary to the purposes of the Fund. . . ." Mr. Gutt's reluctance to have recourse to this Section was not at the time shared by the Board (see the next paragraph), but it will be found in the sequel that, later on, Executive Directors came generally to be unwilling to use it.

The Managing Director's policy statement was generally accepted, but Directors made a number of comments, some of which appear to have indicated some hesitation about Rule G-5. Some stressed that the Board would have to have adequate information to permit of an effective and continuing review of members' situations. It was emphasized that the Managing Director would be expected to bring before the Board—as, indeed, he had undertaken to do—any requests raising special problems. As regards negotiations for drawings, Directors laid it down that liaison with the member should be in the hands of the Executive Director concerned, the Managing Director, and the staff; that missions to members should be sent only if approved by the Board; and that any proposal to limit members' rights to draw should come before the Board as a whole. An argument adduced for imposing such a limitation by the use of Article V, Section 5, was that this Section provided for an exchange of information between the Fund and the member which could be useful in assisting the Board to reach a decision.

Following this discussion, a letter was addressed to all members on June 7 which repeated the Board's interpretative Decision set out above and enclosed a memorandum embodying the gist of the Managing Director's observations.[12] Shortly afterward, France made a second drawing of $25 million.

Reflecting on the implications of the need to assess the situation of a member seeking to make a first drawing, the Managing Director decided on July 2 that such an application, whether or not it fell within the terms of Rule G-5, should be submitted to the Board. As a result, an application that had just been made by Mexico to draw $4.5 million (5 per cent of its quota) was put before the Board, which decided after a discussion that there was no objection to the purchase. Three weeks later, France applied for a third drawing of $25 million. The Board was notified of this and told that an opportunity would be provided shortly to review the French economic situation. This was in fact done on July 31. In the course of the discussion the Board considered the meaning of Article XIV, Section 1, which reads: "The Fund is not intended to provide facilities for relief or reconstruction or to deal with international indebtedness arising out of the war." It decided that this sentence was not meant to prevent countries which were undergoing reconstruction from using the Fund's resources.[13] Meanwhile, on July 28 the Netherlands had drawn another $12 million. The Board was told of this and raised no objection.

When Mexico applied for a further $9 million on August 8 (10 per cent of quota), its economic position was discussed at some length, and the Board agreed that the request should be granted.

Both France and Mexico informed the Board in connection with their drawings that they would be returning for fresh drawings later. Mr. Overby (United States), acting as Chairman in the absence of the Managing Director, reminded the Board of this on August 20 and said that he assumed that the receipt of such notifications did not imply advance concurrence by the Executive Board with the future requests. The Board agreed with this assumption and put the point upon record.

The last drawing effected during the year we are considering was one by the United Kingdom, which asked to purchase $60 million. As this was a first request, the Managing Director brought it before the Board. Mr. Bolton (United King-

[12] Reproduced below, Vol. III, pp. 307–309.

[13] E.B. Decision No. 196-2, July 31, 1947; below, Vol. III, p. 268.

dom) explained why the amount was needed and, in response to a question as to the prospects for repurchases, said that his Government intended to begin repurchases as soon as possible after equilibrium had been reached in June 1948. There followed some debate on the action which the Executive Board was called upon to take. On the one hand, it was urged that, since the drawing was less than 5 per cent of the British quota, the only action required of the Board was a decision not to invoke Article XX, Section 4 (*i*). Other Directors, however, urged that whatever the legal considerations might be the Executive Board was in fact approving the request which had been brought before it. In the event, the Board decided again to express no objection.

At the same meeting, on September 17, 1947, the Managing Director called the attention of the Board to a cabled request from Chile to purchase $8,887,450.18. This was slightly more than Chile's gold subscription (16 per cent of quota). The Managing Director had told the Governor for Chile that there was no connection between a member's gold subscription and its first drawing. He had advised the Governor that it would be better to request a smaller amount, and also to support the request with "a clearer indication that appropriate fiscal and monetary measures were in prospect." At a further meeting on the following day, there was some discussion about the propriety of the suggestions thus made to Chile. One comment was that there were no provisions in the Fund Agreement permitting the Fund to attach conditions to the use of its resources, such as asking a member to give prior evidence of fiscal and financial reforms. As against this, it was pointed out that, since Article V, Section 5, permitted the Fund to declare a member ineligible to use its resources, the Board could certainly exercise less extreme powers. Chile had been suffering a serious and prolonged inflation and, unless effective measures were taken, the temporariness of the disequilibrium for which Chile was asking assistance must be doubtful. The latter opinion prevailed and the decision was as follows:

> If in the near future a request is received from Chile to purchase 2.5 million U.S. dollars, and the request is accompanied by an indication that steps for internal fiscal and monetary reform are contemplated by Chile, the Executive Board would not object to consummation of the purchase by the Managing Director.

To the end of September 1947, the total amount drawn by the members that used the Fund's resources was $209,045,000, of which the equivalent of $6,045,000 was taken in sterling and the rest in U.S. dollars.

As will be seen in Chapter 9, the subsequent evolution of the Fund's policies for the use of its resources was interrupted by developments in Europe following Secretary Marshall's speech at Harvard on June 5. Already, however, there were indications that the simplicity of operation contemplated by Rule G-5 was not acceptable to the Board as a whole, and the replacement of this Rule by a satisfactory working procedure was to be a main preoccupation of the Board for several years to come.

DOLLAR SHORTAGE

In August 1947 the Board considered for the first time the significance of the "scarce currency" clauses (Article VII of the Fund Agreement). There had been considerable discussion, particularly in the British press, of the phenomenon which became known as "the dollar shortage," and the question was raised whether it was appropriate for the Fund to take action under Article VII, either to declare (Section 1) that a general scarcity of dollars was developing, or to decide (Section 3) that the demand for dollars seriously threatened the Fund's ability to supply them.

The Board had no difficulty in deciding that action to declare the dollar scarce under the terms of Section 3 of Article VII was inappropriate; the Fund's holdings of dollars were almost intact, and were most certainly adequate to deal with any demands for dollars that, within the 25 per cent rule under which the Fund was working, would be likely to be received for some time to come. Moreover, its gold holdings were untouched.

A more difficult question concerned the option open to the Fund to declare that a general scarcity of dollars was developing which would make it desirable to inform the members of this fact, and to issue a report on the causes of the scarcity and on possible ways of ending it. The Executive Directors agreed that there certainly was, at that time, an unusual need and demand for dollars. However, it was pointed out that the provisions in Article VII, Section 1, were intended to cover a situation in which a depression in a major producing country could curtail its imports to the point at which a shortage of its currency might seriously impair the flow of international trade. The present situation was quite different. The disparity between the demand for and the supply of dollars did not arise from any diminution of demand for imports by the United States or any refusal by it to extend credits. The disparity arose from a shortage of productive facilities, particularly in European countries, with which dollars could be earned. The real scarcity therefore was one of production, and not of dollars.

Following this argument, the Board decided that there was no reason for the Fund, at that time, to take action, either under Article VII, Section 1, or Article VII, Section 3. It may be added that at no subsequent time did the Board have recourse to Article VII, Section 1 or Section 3. For this there were at least two good reasons: in the first place, the Board was averse to any form of discrimination, and would not have wished to impose discrimination by the use of Article VII; in the second place, once the major currencies had become convertible, the fact that the U.S. dollar was generally used to intervene in foreign exchange markets made it doubtful whether the power to impose limitations on the freedom of operations in the scarce currency would be effective in restoring equilibrium.

ANNUAL REPORT AND ANNUAL MEETING

The *Annual Report of the Executive Directors for the Fiscal Year Ending June 30, 1947* was approved by the Board on August 6. It was a somewhat repetitive document, stressing from different angles one main theme, that world trade was seriously unbalanced, monetary reserves inadequate, and Europe's problem of financing essential imports acute. The Report was concerned to emphasize that the Fund was "intended as part of the permanent machinery of international monetary relations rather than as an emergency device to meet the special needs of the postwar years." [14]

The preparation of such a document as the Report, intended for issue some weeks, if not months, after it is drafted, is always subject to hazards when the economic environment is in flux. Seldom, however, has the problem been as acute as it was in 1947. On July 16 sterling had become transferable, as required by the terms of the Anglo-American Financial Agreement, and this was hailed by the Report as "the most significant development in the elimination of wartime exchange restrictions." [15] But on August 21 exchange restrictions were reintroduced in the United Kingdom. The Board considered whether to modify its Report to take account of this fact, but decided not to do so.

The Second Annual Meeting was held in London from September 11 to 17, 1947. By that time the Fund had been invited to participate in the discussions in Paris that were initiated in response to Secretary Marshall's invitation to Europe to cooperate, with U.S. assistance, in the task of reconstruction. Reference was made to these discussions both by the Chairman of the Meeting and by the Managing Director. The Chairman (Mr. Hugh Dalton, Chancellor of the Exchequer, United Kingdom) spoke of "the bold and generous initiative of Mr. Marshall" and suggested that "to avert an economic catastrophe . . . calls for many contributory approaches. One such approach is through the discussions in Paris. Another is through our discussions here in London." [16] Mr. Gutt also mentioned the "scope and magnitude" of the task of reconstruction, but laid emphasis rather on self-help by the European countries than on external aid. "When internal financial and monetary reform has been achieved," he said, "a major step will have been taken toward restoring the international economic position of the countries whose economies were devastated and disrupted by war." [17] Insofar as Mr. Gutt was speaking from personal experience, he no doubt had in mind the stringent monetary reform which he had himself brought about in Belgium. But his remarks also reflected the stress which the Board had increas-

---

[14] *Annual Report, 1947*, p. 2.

[15] *Ibid.*, p. 36.

[16] *Summary Proceedings, 1947*, p. 5.

[17] *Ibid.*, pp. 7, 9.

ingly been laying, in their reviews of member countries' economies, on the need to contain inflation.

The formal business of the Annual Meeting included the passing of a resolution providing for the election of a fourteenth Executive Director, to be held at such time after December 31, 1947 as the Board might determine. It was decided also to hold the Third Annual Meeting in Washington, the sites for future meetings being left for discussion on a later occasion.

A resolution on silver, passed by the Governors, urgently requested members to supply to the Fund data relating to silver and its uses, and asked the Fund to assemble and make these available to members not later than March 1, 1948. We may note here that by that date only a few members had supplied information, and that it was not until August 1948 that sufficient had come to hand to enable the staff to prepare a report, which even then was incomplete. This report was distributed in time for the Third Annual Meeting, but was not discussed there. The subject has not since been brought officially before the Fund.

Two notable speeches marked the closing session in London. In one, the Governor for Belgium, Mr. Maurice Frère, challenged the implications of the remark in the Annual Report that the Fund was not intended to meet the special needs of the postwar years. He agreed that the Bank "was not engaged in the 'stop-gap business'," but went on to say:

> On the other hand, the Fund, according to my conception, is engaged in the "stop-gap business". . . . The Fund was given its resources precisely in order to cope with temporary deficits in the balance of payments of its members. Its business is therefore to stop gaps, because if there were no gaps no Fund would be needed. This function is, of course, of very great importance in the present emergency and it lays upon the shoulders of the Managing Director and of the Executive Directors of the Fund a very heavy responsibility.

In his concluding address, Mr. Dalton returned to the theme of the needs of reconstruction, but he stressed that there was no need for discouragement:

> There are many Governors sitting round this table who, looking at their own national problems, must well feel anxiety and doubt as to how these problems can be solved in a fashion satisfactory to their own people. But I am confident—and the spirit of these meetings has reinforced my confidence—that solutions will be found. These two institutions of ours cannot by themselves do the whole job, but they can make, as has been shown even in the record of the work of the last twelve months, a most powerful contribution.

He went on to say that he hoped that next year's Chairman would

> be able to point to positive achievements of these two great international institutions, now developing their techniques and their constructive modes of action, and . . . be able to feel that he has presided over something which indeed in the eye of history and in the eye of contemporary events, has been well worth while.

The extent to which these hopes were fulfilled will become clear as we study the Fund's actions in 1947–48.

CHAPTER

9

Problems of Policy (1947-48)

A MAJOR ACTIVITY of the Board of Executive Directors during the twelve months beginning October 1947 was an attempt to formulate general policies to guide it in dealings with members. In connection with the use of the Fund's resources, a series of decisions clarified the application of the Articles of Agreement to practical issues posed by members' requests to draw on the Fund. But in some other directions there was less success. The reconstitution of the economic viability of Europe proceeded without the Fund's participation, and relations with a major member, France, were disrupted.

MEMBERS AND BOARD

Two further countries joined the Fund during the twelve months—Finland in January 1948 and Austria in August 1948—making a total of 47 members. The United Kingdom notified the Board that Burma and Ceylon were no longer territories on whose behalf it accepted the Articles of Agreement. Because of a difficulty experienced in paying its gold subscription, Honduras asked that its quota be reduced from \$2.5 million to \$0.5 million, and this was done in November 1948. In accordance with a decision of the Board of Governors at the Second Annual Meeting, the quota of India after partition remained the same as that allotted to undivided India at Bretton Woods. Preliminary inquiries as to membership were received from Afghanistan, Albania, and Bulgaria.

At the time of the Annual Meeting, 1947, there were eight members that had not yet established par values: Brazil, China, the Dominican Republic, Greece, Italy, Poland, Uruguay, and Yugoslavia. Each of these was asked to expedite the submission of a par value for the Board's approval, but only in two instances were par values established during the year: the Dominican Republic agreed with the Fund in February on an initial par value for its newly introduced peso, to be operative from April 1, and Brazil agreed in July on a rate for the cruzeiro. Provisional plans by Yugoslavia and Poland to propose par values for the dinar and the zloty were mentioned to the Board during the year. Each attracted some questioning about the viability of the proposed rate. In the event, the rate for the dinar was not established until May 1949 and no par value had been agreed for the zloty by the time Poland left the Fund in 1950.

The number of Executive Directors was increased from thirteen to fourteen with the election in February 1948 of Mr. Stuart G. McFarlane, Secretary of the Australian Treasury, by Australia, Lebanon, and Syria, the three members that had joined the Fund after Resolution IM-10 became operative and before the end of 1947. The membership of the Board was otherwise unchanged, except that Mr. Bruins (Netherlands) died on March 22, 1948. On April 16 Mr. Johan Willem Beyen (Netherlands) was elected by the Netherlands and South Africa to succeed Mr. Bruins. Two Alternate Executive Directors resigned during the year to take posts on the staff: Mr. Parsons (United Kingdom) became Director of Operations in November 1947, and Mr. Luthringer (United States) became Deputy Director of the Research Department in July 1948.

FUNCTIONS OF BOARD AND STAFF

Between July 31, 1947 and April 30, 1948, the staff increased by 49, to a total of 403, from 29 countries. The number of Departments was unchanged. The headquarters of the Fund and the Bank at 1818 H Street were outgrown during the year, and the Fund rented additional accommodation from April 1948 in the Premier Building, which then adjoined 1818 H Street on the southeast. An office in Paris was opened in July 1948, following an experimental period of ten weeks in Brussels. After six months in temporary quarters, the staff there moved in January 1949 to premises in the rue de Lille, which they shared with the Bank until 1966. Initially, the office was staffed from Washington. The first man appointed as its official head was Mr. Robert Triffin, who took charge in July 1948.

The relative functions of the Managing Director, Executive Directors, and staff were clarified in January 1948. It was laid down that the Executive Board would be responsible for formulating policies and taking decisions on major problems, and for satisfying itself that its decisions were being correctly carried out by the staff. The Managing Director and staff were charged with studying the major problems that had to be resolved by the Board, and presenting memoranda setting out the main factors which bore on these problems, together with the staff's conclusions and recommendations about them. The Managing Director and staff were also made responsible for the execution of Fund policies, including the handling of negotiations.

Two examples of the application of these principles may be cited. First, under the general heading of "consultations with members" the Board agreed that, guided by the general policies enunciated by the Board, the Managing Director and staff should take steps to become aware of members' thinking on pertinent problems, and should convey to the members the Fund's views. At the appropriate time the Managing Director and staff would indicate whether a formal proposal of measures to deal with a particular problem would be likely to meet with Board approval, and discuss with the member any alternatives that seemed preferable—without, however, committing the Board. Thereafter, the member would formally approach the Board for approval. In this connection, it may be noted that after this decision was taken members of the Executive Board ceased as a rule to head missions to members; except in special circumstances, these were left to the staff.

This change did not, however, extend to the representation of the Fund at the meetings of other international bodies. Accordingly, Mr. Saad (Egypt) continued for some years to act as head of the Fund missions to the meetings of the GATT. In 1954 the Board briefly discussed the desirability of such an arrangement. Three Directors then said that as a matter of principle they believed that the Fund should be represented by the staff, and not by an Executive Director, at meetings where controversial issues between governments were under discussion. However, two other Directors explicitly dissented from such a general principle, and it found no support among the rest of the Board. Mr. Saad made it clear that he personally would not have agreed to represent the Fund at the GATT had he been under instructions from any government. During the remainder of that meeting of the GATT, Mr. Saad continued to head the Fund mission, but in the summer of 1955 he withdrew from this and other commitments on his appointment as Governor of the National Bank of Egypt. Since then the Fund has always been represented at international meetings by members of the staff—or, on occasions, by the Managing Director or Deputy Managing Director.

A second example of delegation from the Executive Board to the staff is to be found in the handling of the assessment of net official holdings of gold and U.S. dollars, required by Article III, Section 3 (*b*), to calculate the gold subscription of the members who were not paying 25 per cent of their quota in gold. The principles to be adopted—a complicated interpretation of Article III, Section 3 (*b*) and (*d*), and of Article XIX (*b*), (*c*), and (*h*)—were worked out by a committee of Directors and accepted by the Board.[1] Their application to the circumstances of six members was undertaken by the committee but the problems arising in connection with another fifteen and with new members were left to the staff.

---

[1] E.B. Decision No. 298-3, April 14, 1948; below, Vol. III, pp. 220–21, 270–71.

PUBLICATIONS

The first public issues were made during the year of two of the Fund's periodic publications. *International Financial Statistics (IFS)* was designed to bring together "information essential for the analysis of international financial problems . . . exchange rates, gold and foreign exchange holdings, the money supply, prices, foreign trade and production." The collection of these data on a regular basis was arranged by enlisting the cooperation of member countries and of certain nonmembers, who were asked to nominate statistical correspondents to whom the Fund could look for regular cabled reports. The first issue of this publication appeared in January 1948. The subscription rate was fixed at $5 a year, and for the benefit of subscribers who did not have access to dollars, arrangements were made with the fiscal agents in most member countries to accept the equivalent amounts in local currencies and credit these to the Fund's account.

In July 1948 there appeared the first number of *International Financial News Survey (IFNS)*, a weekly digest of financial news from all over the world. This eight-page leaflet followed eighteen months of experimentation with an internal digest called *International Financial Notes*, which gradually assumed the form and size of the published issue. It was decided not to charge for *IFNS*; some difficulty had been experienced in securing permission to quote from a number of journals, and it was felt that this difficulty would have been compounded had it been proposed to make a charge. In any case a year's issues would cost only about $2, which seemed too small a sum with which to trouble the fiscal agents.

January 1948 also saw the first issue of the Fund's *Balance of Payments Manual*. This was compiled with the assistance of a group of statistical experts from a number of member countries, who visited Washington in the autumn of 1947. It combined a brief exposé of the methodology of balances of payments with detailed instructions for the completion of forms on which members were asked to report summaries of their international transactions. The *Manual* was distributed free of charge to member countries, and a certain number was also made available in response to requests from academic and other users.

In July 1949 the first of the Fund's *Balance of Payments Yearbooks* was issued. It gave comparative statistics on current and capital accounts covering 51 countries for the years 1938, 1946, and 1947 and, in some instances, preliminary figures for 1948. The data were not confined to Fund members, but covered, inter alia, Argentina, Germany, Japan, Sweden, and Switzerland. Regional statements for Europe and Latin America showed transactions with the United States and with the rest of the world, and there were tables setting out the network of trade among European countries.

Despite these publications, the work of the Fund continued to be profoundly misunderstood by commentators. The Board was from time to time disturbed by criticisms in the press which revealed this lack of understanding of the nature of the Fund's activities, and of the conditions under which they were carried out. In a review of the first two years of the Fund, made at a Board meeting on May 7, 1948, Mr. Gutt remarked:

> Looking at the whole picture, I think we failed in our duty only in one regard. We failed in our duty of publicizing, explaining the Fund, not so much in this country, where we did our best, as outside. . . . We did not explain enough to the technicians, governments, central banks, universities—we did not explain enough to the public at large.

He went on to say that there was a very good reason for this: the Fund was "very difficult to explain," it was "bristling with technicalities." But he believed that "public relations ought to play a more important part in our life, here and abroad."

That the need for such explanations remained acute cannot be doubted. Even four years later the young economists attending a Training Program at the Fund reported that in none of their countries was the Fund regarded as a true international organization; it was thought of as some sort of adjunct of the U.S. Government. Nevertheless, it was not until the 1960's that a systematic attempt was made, as described below in Chapter 21, to enlighten the public about the Fund's role. In the meantime, its effectiveness undoubtedly suffered from misconceptions that have even yet not been wholly overcome.

PROBLEM OF THE FRENCH FRANC

The French proposal

On January 19, 1948, Mr. de Largentaye (France) presented to the Board a request for approval of a modification of the exchange arrangements in France. The proposal included a reduction in the par value of the franc by about 44 per cent, together with the institution of a free market in which exporters earning U.S. dollars and other convertible currencies would sell half their receipts and in which the proceeds of all invisibles in these currencies would also be sold. On the import side, this free market was to be used for payments for nonbasic goods, authorized invisibles, and authorized capital transactions. The effect of the proposal would be that regular cross rates would be maintained, firstly between all the inconvertible currencies and secondly between all the convertible currencies. Mr. de Largentaye added that there would, however, "be only one disparate cross rate; namely, between the official rates of all currencies and the free rate[s] of the convertible currencies."

The arguments put forward in favor of the proposal were (1) that it would help to meet the dollar shortage in France by creating a premium on exports to the dollar area and a penalty on imports from that area; (2) that a fixed exchange rate capable of moving goods to convertible currency areas would unduly promote exports to Europe and discourage the substitution of European imports for dollar imports; (3) that a fixed exchange rate able to move goods to Europe would not promote the optimum of exports to the dollar area; (4) lastly, that a single fixed rate might have to be devalued again in a few months if French inflationary forces were not curbed.

The Board was greatly concerned at the French proposal, not because a devaluation of the franc was contemplated—indeed, one view was that an even greater devaluation was needed—but because of the risk to the stability of European currencies threatened by the introduction of differential exchange rates for the franc. Executive Directors foresaw a danger that similar practices might be adopted by other countries, which would destroy the agreed parities and result in an unrelated and disorderly series of rates. Further, the dollar premium in the market could be expected to reflect unfavorably on the value of other currencies and to encourage commodity arbitrage, besides giving France an unfair competitive advantage in dollar exports against any country that maintained a fixed parity with the dollar. As regards the legal position, the French authorities claimed the right to introduce the proposed multiple currency arrangement under Article XIV, Section 2 (which gives members whose territories had been occupied by the enemy authority to introduce exchange restrictions where necessary). The Board, however, felt that it had not been established that the particular proposal was *necessary;* it could not, therefore, be claimed that Article XIV, Section 2, required the Board to accept it.

Recognizing the grave difficulties which the French authorities faced, the Board made several efforts to find a compromise which might meet the requirements of the situation without creating the dangers foreseen. One suggestion was that the proposed free market should be supplied only by earnings from invisibles and capital, to the exclusion of receipts from exports of French goods. Alternatively, it was suggested that fluctuating rates should be established for all currencies, provided that steps were taken to safeguard cross rates. Neither of these suggestions was acceptable to the French authorities. Mr. Pierre-Paul Schweitzer (France), who was Alternate to Mr. de Largentaye (and who later became the Fund's fourth Managing Director), explained the French difficulties. A free market was essential because French opinion would not accept as viable a devaluation to an officially chosen rate; only one arrived at in a free market would be trusted. And the free market required for this purpose would not be adequate unless it was fed by the proceeds of exports. As regards the possibility of allowing all currencies to fluctuate in a free market within which stable cross rates would be maintained, the French could not accept a unilateral obligation to maintain stable cross rates in such conditions, and they would have to negotiate with their trading partners to share the load. Such negotiations would take a considerable time. As this proposal was in any case disliked by several Executive Directors, it was dropped.

As a last resort, the Managing Director addressed an appeal direct to the French Premier, Mr. Robert Schuman, pointing out the grave disadvantages the Board saw in the French proposal. However, Mr. Schuman's Cabinet could not see its way to depart from its proposal, and on Sunday, January 25, 1948, the new arrangements were announced in Paris. Simultaneously the Fund issued a statement in Washington explaining why it could not approve the plan.[2] This was the culmination of a week in which the Board had met thirteen times—once at ten o'clock at night—to examine the plan and to seek acceptable alternatives.

The formal decision, taken on January 25, 1948, was to the effect that the Fund did not agree that the French proposal was necessary, and that it must object to the proposed change in the par value of the franc, because this could not be considered separately from the proposed multiple currency practice and discriminatory currency arrangement, which the Fund did not approve. As an immediate consequence France became ineligible, under Article IV, Section 6, to use the Fund's resources.

It may be added that, on March 24, Mr. de Largentaye informed the Board that his Government had asked him to consult the Fund about a modification in the system, by which nonbasic imports from convertible currency countries were in future to be paid for at an exchange rate based on the average between the new official rate of the franc (about F 214=$1) and the fluctuating rate on the Paris market (then about F 306=$1). The Board observed that, while its views on the French system involving a multiple currency and discriminatory exchange arrangement remained unchanged, the proposal appeared to be a move toward unifying the various exchange rates, and as such was to be commended.

Consequences of French decisions

The implications of the French decisions took a considerable time to work out. One question that arose was whether the Fund would have been obliged to accept a devaluation of the French franc, unaccompanied by any multiple currency arrangements, if the Board had believed that the devaluation proposed was inadequate to cure the fundamental disequilibrium to which it was addressed. Mr. de Largentaye contended that the provisions of Article IV, Section 5, made it impossible for the Fund to refuse to concur in a proposed change of par value merely because it felt that the extent of the change was insufficient; in his view, the Fund could object to a proposed devaluation only if the amount proposed was excessive. He suggested that the Articles of Agreement could not have been

[2] *Annual Report, 1948*, p. 76.

intended to empower the Fund, if it felt that a member should take two steps in the right direction, to prevent that member from taking the first step in order to oblige it to take the second. Mr. de Selliers (Belgium) and Mr. Martínez-Ostos (Mexico) agreed with Mr. de Largentaye.

Mr. Overby (United States), however, thought that the Fund would be placed in a ridiculous position if it were forced to concur in a par value change when it was convinced that the devaluation was clearly inadequate. The acceptance by the Board of an inadequate change would give the Fund's cachet to arrangements which might jeopardize exchange stability for the member and endanger orderly exchange arrangements for all members, in contravention of Article I (iii) of the Fund Agreement. After further discussion, the Board decided that the Fund had authority, under Article IV, Section 5 (*c*) (ii) or (iii), to object to a change in par value proposed by a member when the extent of the proposed change, in the judgment of the Fund, was insufficient to correct a fundamental disequilibrium.[3] To this interpretation Mr. de Largentaye objected. He concurred, however, in the remainder of the Board's decision, which recognized that the extent of the change in a par value necessary to correct a fundamental disequilibrium could not be determined with precision; that, therefore, a member should be given the benefit of any reasonable doubt about the adequacy of a proposal; and that due consideration should be given to the views of the member about the political and social consequences of a change in par value greater than the one proposed.

Questions also arose on the responsibilities of France's trading partners. The view of the Board as a whole was that, even though France no longer had an approved par value, other members must respect their obligations under Article I and Article IV, Section 3. In effect, any new exchange rate established with France as a result of the French action would have to have the Fund's approval; this followed from the decision on multiple currency practices reported in Chapter 8. It was suggested, however, that it would probably be convenient for the Fund to approve any bilateral arrangements based on the new official rate for the French franc.

A further point was that any member establishing an exchange rate with France would thereby create a discriminatory currency arrangement, to which both members would be parties. Mr. Tansley (United Kingdom), who had throughout been concerned with the problem of broken cross rates, commented that any discrimination arising in these circumstances would be the responsibility only of France. The answer was that whether trade with France was invoiced in francs or in other members' currencies, exchange rates were inevitably established and, insofar as intergovernmental transactions were concerned, neither government could avoid responsibility. However, it was not necessary

[3] E.B. Decision No. 278-3, March 1, 1948; below, Vol. III, p. 227.

for the Fund to exercise all its powers and it might not wish to do so if transactions were related to an exchange rate based on the new official rate.

The doctrine enunciated in the previous paragraph provoked a contention, voiced especially by Mr. de Selliers, that it constituted an attempt to stretch the powers given to the Fund in the Articles of Agreement. Mr. de Selliers pointed out that the obligation placed on members by Article IV, Section 4 (*a*), was to *promote* exchange stability, not to establish it. Mr. Martínez-Ostos suggested (as Mr. de Largentaye had done a few weeks earlier) that in any case Article IV, Section 4, was overridden by Article XIV. These views were resisted with some acerbity by Mr. Overby, and Mr. Luthringer (United States) adduced the legislative history of Articles IV and XIV to disprove Mr. Martínez-Ostos' contention. Mr. Luthringer also reminded the Board that Article IV, Section 4 (*a*), required members to collaborate with the Fund and to maintain orderly exchange arrangements.

Discussions with Italy and Belgium

Over the next few weeks, the Board was consulted by Italy and by Belgium about the exchange aspects of their arrangements for bilateral trade with France. The discussion with Italy was the second occasion on which the Italian exchange arrangements came before the Board in 1947–48. In November 1947 Mr. Carli (Italy) had communicated details of changes being introduced by his authorities. After November 27, one half of all foreign exchange receipts was to be surrendered to the monetary authorities at a rate fixed monthly at the average of the free market rates of the previous month, instead of at the current free market rate as previously. The other half of the receipts had still to be sold at the official rate of 350 lire to the dollar. Again broken cross rates were involved, and Mr. Bolton (United Kingdom) protested that the Fund could not approve a system which allowed discrimination. The Board, however, decided to recognize that, while fluctuating exchange rates were not in accordance with the principles of the Fund, it might sometimes be necessary for members, for temporary periods, to institute extraordinary measures in an attempt to meet particular difficulties. Such measures, the Board said, would be looked upon with sympathy; and it felt sure that Italy would move as quickly as possible toward the establishment of fixed and stable exchange rates.[4]

The exchange arrangements for trade between France and Italy, first outlined to the Board on March 2, 1948, would have utilized the official rate for the franc on the one hand and the average between the nominal official rate of 350 lire to the dollar and the free rate for the lira (then about Lit 570=$1) on the other. The effect of this would have been to create a rate for the franc for use in trade with Italy equivalent to F 265=$1, compared with the new official rate

[4] *Annual Report, 1948*, pp. 63–64.

of F 214=$1. The staff put forward an alternative suggestion by which the average of the official and free rates for the franc would be equated to the free rate for the lira. This was designed to ensure that any changes in the rate would offset changes in costs in France and changes in prices in Italy. Neither plan commended itself greatly to the Board, but the consensus was in favor of the staff suggestion as this would avoid creating a new rate for the franc. The two members were asked to consider this, but while Italy would agree to it (and, indeed, said that this had been its own original plan), France was unwilling to do so because its free rate was applicable only to convertible currencies.

In the event, a new plan was put to the Board on March 12, providing for an exchange rate of Lit 2.20=F 1, subject to periodic adjustment. Mr. Giorgio Cigliana-Piazza (Italy), Alternate to Mr. Carli, proposed that the adjustment should be based on the free rates for the lira and the franc; Mr. de Largentaye wished the method of adjustment to be decided later. Mr. Tansley objected to the plan on the ground that it tended toward exchange instability in Europe. Mr. Willem Koster (Netherlands), Alternate to Mr. Bruins, also disliked it, but was prepared to agree to it as representing possibly a step in the right direction. Mr. Overby said he was prepared to agree to the rate of 2.20 since this was based on the existing relationships of the franc and the lira to the dollar. The Board decided to accept the proposed arrangement as a temporary measure, on the understanding that any adjustments in the exchange rate would be made in consultation with the Fund.

Plans for a legal free market for Belgian franc notes in Paris, paralleling an extensive black market in Brussels, were put forward in order that France might benefit from the large tourist trade between the two countries. These proposals were accepted by the Board with reservations. Mr. Overby said that they confirmed his views that a devaluation of the French franc to about F 275=$1 was needed. Other Executive Directors pointed out that the proposals would add a third exchange rate to the French system. Subsequently, the proposed free market was replaced by arrangements for the sale to Belgian tourists of checks encashable by French banks and hotels at a preferential exchange rate. Mr. Mládek (Czechoslovakia), Mr. Tansley, and Mr. Koster abstained from voting on this plan as they objected to all discriminatory arrangements. However, it was approved for a trial period of six months.

Cross rates for trade restored

A substantial modification of the French exchange system was introduced in October 1948. Mr. de Largentaye then notified the Board that the objections that had been expressed to broken cross rates, and to the consequential opportunities for commodity arbitrage, had influenced the French Government to take remedial steps, culminating in a decision to effect commercial transactions in inconvertible currencies at the middle rate between the official and free exchange rates—i.e., at the same rate as transactions in convertible currencies. Directors welcomed the decision as a step in the direction of a unitary currency, although they recognized that it would not eliminate the multiple currency practice nor reintroduce a par value for the French franc.

OTHER EXCHANGE PROBLEMS

While the French proposal described in the preceding section was the most serious exchange problem to come before the Board in 1947–48, it was by no means the only one. Proposals for unorthodox exchange arrangements by Bolivia, Chile, China, Colombia, Costa Rica, Ecuador, Greece, Iran, Mexico, Peru, Syria, and Uruguay were all considered by the Board; most of them were accepted with varying degrees of concern. Executive Directors were disturbed at the introduction of changes in exchange arrangements by two members without consulting the Board and by two others that had given the Board such short notice that adequate consideration was impossible. Particular anxiety was evinced at a tendency toward a proliferation of multiple rates, and the importance of inflation as the basic cause of exchange instability was increasingly stressed as the year progressed.

Fund policy toward exchange problems

The attitude which the Board adopted toward requests for its approval of exchange arrangements that did not conform to the principles of the Articles of Agreement was well expressed by the Managing Director in his speech presenting the Annual Report to the Governors. He said, in part:

> . . . we have always been eager to take into account the realities and the practicalities of the situation. And sometimes, recognizing these practical considerations, we have not objected, in the end, to solutions which did not constitute the immediate application of the policy we had recommended. . . .
>
> Our members are assured that in their dealings with the Fund they can expect a practical approach to their problems. They know that no attempt will be made to fit them into a standardized mold, unsuited to their economies. They realize that the way of the Fund in dealing with a member is to look at the member's situation from the member's point of view, and to provide such advice and such assistance of a practical kind as will enable it to work out its own problems. The essential duty of the Fund is to see that the measures taken by a member, first, are suitable to its problems, and, second, that they will not inflict damage on the economy of other countries.[5]

In what follows we shall review briefly the nature of the problems presented in Chile (the first of several Latin American countries to approach the Board

[5] *Summary Proceedings, 1948*, pp. 12–13.

in 1947–48). Points raised by China and Turkey will also be mentioned. The emergency in Mexico, as a result of which it abandoned its par value, is described in a later section.

Chile

In January 1948 the Board had before it the report of a mission to Chile, which pointed out the complexity and inadequacy of the exchange arrangements prevailing there. There were several different buying rates and three different selling rates for the peso, ranging from 19.37 pesos=US$1 (at which rate the copper companies bought pesos for local costs and tax purposes) to the par value of 31 pesos=$1. These rates had proved inadequate in Chile's inflationary system, and the Government proposed to transfer nearly one half of the total exchange budget to a free market, which was expected to depreciate below the par value.

The staff's inquiries had incidentally disclosed that individual miners in Chile who earned dollars by exporting could obtain special import licenses which they could sell at a premium. It was pointed out that this system of so-called *pareos*, which also applied on a small scale to exporters of wine, constituted a multiple currency practice on the export side, creating a range of exchange rates corresponding to the premiums obtained.

The members of the staff who had visited Chile thought that the proper course would be to devalue the peso to between 42 and 50 pesos=$1 and to restrain imports of luxury and nonessential goods by new excise taxes or, alternatively, by imposing penalty exchange rates involving a further devaluation of 20 per cent for luxury goods and 50 per cent for nonessential goods. When this recommendation was discussed by the Board, Executive Directors were inclined to question whether the devaluation suggested would be sufficient, since the peso appeared to be overvalued by some 100 per cent. The staff explained that, while prices corresponded to the latter figure, costs had not risen proportionately, and a devaluation to 42–50 pesos would adequately reflect the cost differential. On that understanding the Board commended the staff's proposal to Chile.

Mr. Martínez-Ostos (Mexico), however, said that the proposal for a devaluation could not be accepted at that time by the Chilean Government; a rate such as that suggested by the mission would in all probability become inadequate in a few months, necessitating a further devaluation, which would be prejudicial both to confidence in the peso and to the reputation of the Fund. Moreover, any devaluation would involve an immediate rise in prices in Chile, which would reinforce the inflation there. Mr. F. Mardones, who represented Chile at a later meeting of the Board, said that his Government hoped that after about six months it would be possible to present to the Board a plan resembling that which

Executive Directors favored; in the interim the proposed free market should accustom Chileans to a lower rate for the peso, so that it would be politically more possible to devalue the currency.

Executive Directors were troubled by several aspects of the Chilean plan. Mr. Luthringer (United States) criticized the increase in complexity of the system, and Mr. Mládek (Czechoslovakia) questioned whether the Board should approve the use of multiple currency practices as a method of adjusting parities which were unrealistic. Mr. Parsons (United Kingdom) said that for the free rate adequately to check Chile's import surplus, it would be necessary for it to apply to at least 60 per cent, and preferably 90 per cent, of imports, whereas it was expected to apply to only 40 per cent.

The Managing Director suggested that, in reaching a decision on requests to introduce or modify multiple currency practices, the Board should distinguish between countries that had customarily used such methods, as Chile had done, and countries that had not previously resorted to them, such as countries in Western Europe. The Board agreed with this view and took a decision to this effect.

In further discussion between the Board and the representative of Chile, a detailed program for the progressive simplification of the exchange system was evolved. Favored exchange rates, such as those available under the *pareos* system, would be abolished, the special export rates for mineral exports and the favored rate applicable to selected imports would both be integrated with the par value as soon as possible, and exchange for not less than 60 per cent of total imports would be provided only at the new rate. Chile also agreed to take such further steps as might be necessary to bring the budget into balance during 1948, and to remain in consultation with the Fund on the progress of its anti-inflationary measures. Finally, it undertook that the exchange program would be administered in such a way as to facilitate the attainment of the objectives of the Fund.

At the conclusion of the discussion, on January 30, 1948, the Board decided to make a public statement welcoming in general terms the Chilean program, which was expected to result by the beginning of 1949 in the bulk of Chile's foreign exchange transactions taking place within the revised system at a new rate of exchange to be established at a more realistic level.[6] However, a further review of the situation in August showed that expectations had been disappointed, and Chile's problems continued to exercise the Board.

China

Among the other countries mentioned at the beginning of this section, China presented particular difficulties. Because of the political situation and the rapid rise in prices, the official exchange rate (12,000 yuan=$1) had become ineffec-

[6] *Annual Report, 1948*, p. 73.

tive, and a fluctuating rate, controlled by the Equalization Fund Committee, was substituted on May 31, 1948. Executive Directors were informed that this rate would have to be changed at fairly frequent intervals, and that there would not always be time to consult the Board before making changes. In the circumstances, it was agreed that China should notify the Managing Director of contemplated changes in the exchange rates and exchange structure as far in advance as possible, and that the Managing Director would endeavor to reply at once on behalf of the Fund, unless he thought it necessary first to consult the Board. This procedure—which was the forerunner of one later adopted to deal with minor changes in other countries' multiple currency arrangements—remained in force until terminated, at China's suggestion, in December 1960.

Rates for notes

In the course of the year, the Fund was asked by Turkey whether the obligation in Article IV, Section 3 (i), to maintain spot exchange rates within 1 per cent of parity applied to transactions in paper money and coins. Some Executive Directors felt that the volume of such transactions was too small for deviations from parity to have any material effect on exchange rates. Nevertheless, it was agreed that, if there was no limit to the divergence from parity of rates for notes, any substantial diversion of settlements from drafts and cable transfers to transactions in notes might be prejudicial to exchange stability. The Board therefore decided that, while the limit of 1 per cent set in Article IV, Section 3 (i), did not apply, the more general requirement in Article IV, Section 3 (ii), must control exchange rates for transactions in notes and coins, and that members must not permit transactions in these media to negate the par values established with the Fund.[7]

UNENFORCEABILITY OF EXCHANGE CONTRACTS

During the discussion of the foregoing inquiry from Turkey, an Executive Director referred to Article VIII, Section 2 (*b*), which reads in part:

> Exchange contracts which involve the currency of any member and which are contrary to the exchange control regulations of that member maintained or imposed consistently with this Agreement shall be unenforceable in the territories of any member.

Two questions were asked: (1) What was meant by "unenforceable"? (2) Did the fact that the provision occurred in Article VIII mean that it was inapplicable to countries that had not accepted the obligations of Article VIII, Sections 2, 3, and 4, and were therefore governed by Article XIV (Transitional Period)? These were questions having an unusually wide application. The provisions of Article VIII, Section 2 (*b*), were beginning to come before the courts in the United Kingdom

[7] E.B. Decision No. 269-2, February 11, 1948; below, Vol. III, p. 226.

and the United States, and an authoritative statement of their meaning was needed to guide legal authorities there and elsewhere. The Section was also relevant to the negotiation of special exchange agreements under the aegis of the ITO, which was in progress in 1948.

After a full review of the legislative history of the Section, the Legal Department advised the Board on October 29, 1948 that the answer to the first question was as follows:

> The unenforceability of exchange contracts under Article VIII, Section 2 (*b*), means that the courts in members' territories must not lend their assistance to implement the obligations of such contracts. Thus, one of the consequences of this provision is that if an exchange contract comes before a court in a member's country and the contract involves the currency of another member and is contrary to exchange control regulations of that other member maintained or imposed consistently with the Fund Agreement, the court is not entitled to refuse to recognize the regulations because of its domestic public policy *(ordre public)*. . . .
>
> Since the exchange control regulations of a member will normally be maintained or imposed consistently with the Articles of Agreement, courts should assume, for the purposes of Article VIII, Section 2 (*b*), that this is the position unless the Fund has declared otherwise.

On the second question, the view of the Legal Department was that Article VIII, Section 2 (*b*), applied to all members, including those that had taken advantage of the transitional provisions of Article XIV. This view was based both on textual arguments and on practical considerations.

The Legal Department's submission was considered by the Board on three occasions. The Department had proposed that a letter should be sent to members drawing attention to the meaning of the Section, in order that the courts might be advised. Some doubts were expressed in the Board whether an interpretation such as was suggested could be formally made without a request from a member, and whether the proposed letter would not constitute an encroachment on the independence of the judiciary. These scruples were, however, overcome; the Board decided that it was free to interpret the provisions of the Articles without a formal request from a member, and that advertisement by members' governments of the significance of the Section could in no way be regarded as an attempt to instruct their courts. Accordingly, a circular letter was issued to members in June 1949 explaining the Section along the foregoing lines, and offering the Fund's assistance in connection with any problem that might arise in relation to it.[8]

Some years passed before any request was made for assistance in connection with the Section, but in 1957 the Fund was twice asked to provide official

---

[8] E.B. Decision No. 446-4, June 10, 1949; below, Vol. III, p. 256. This was reproduced as Fund Circular No. 8, March 15, 1950. For a review of legal proceedings involving the Articles, see Joseph Gold, *The Fund Agreement in the Courts* (Washington, 1962), and articles with the same title in *Staff Papers*, Vol. XI (1964), pp. 457–89, and Vol. XIV (1967), pp. 369–402.

statements that exchange restrictions in member countries were in accordance with the Articles, the certificates being needed for purposes of legal proceedings in which the validity of the exchange restrictions was being challenged. Subsequently, similar certificates were asked for on a number of different occasions.

INFLATION AND EXCHANGE RATES

In addition to dealing with the particular problems arising in the countries mentioned above, the Board undertook in 1947–48 a second general survey of the economic situation of members. A lead to this series of discussions was given by the Managing Director at the end of October 1947. It will be recalled that in May Mr. Gutt had told the Board that he believed that members should know in advance of requesting a drawing how the Fund would view such a request. He now suggested that it would be well to begin, as soon as possible, a general review of the monetary and exchange developments in each member country, in order that the Board might be apprised of the relevant facts before further requests were made to draw. In making this suggestion, he drew pointed attention to the rapidly changing economic situation, and commented that the time might well be coming when some par values would be found to be unsuitable. During the year missions were sent to Belgium, Bolivia, Chile, Colombia, Costa Rica, Ecuador, France, the Netherlands, Norway, Peru, Syria, and Uruguay, and the Managing Director reported on visits that he had paid to Europe. Between November 1947 and May 1948, the Research Department produced a long series of memoranda describing the problems of individual countries, with special reference to their foreign exchange prospects. Where these memoranda disclosed pressing difficulties, they were considered by the Board and recommendations were made.

As the year went on, the Board's attention focused increasingly on inflation, both active and latent, as a major cause of international disequilibrium. Staff studies of the factors responsible for inflation in Western Europe, and of the problems of latent inflation, were reviewed in May.[9] The Annual Report described at some length the dangers of the inflationary situations that had developed, and advocated fiscal and monetary measures of reform.[10] In all the aspects of the Fund's work—in connection with par values, with exchange restrictions, and with the use of its resources—stress was more and more laid upon the incompatibility of continued inflation with the fulfillment of members' obligations under the Fund Agreement. Unless members were prepared to help themselves, the Board appears to have felt, there was little that the Fund could do.

Closely related to this discussion in the Annual Report was a pointed reference to the importance of appropriate exchange rates. "If [a] country cannot bring

[9] These were later published in *Staff Papers*, Vol. I (1950–51), pp. 1–16 and 17–48.

[10] *Annual Report, 1948*, pp. 15–24.

its export prices to a competitive level in other ways," the Directors remarked, "it will of necessity have to adjust its exchange rates." The current tendency among Fund members, the Report found, was to maintain exchange rates rather than to depreciate them. But this was in no way to be attributed to the influence of the Fund Agreement, which

> makes it clear that the provisions for the regulation of exchange rates are not intended to impose upon the Fund the duty of perpetuating in the name of stability exchange rates which have lost touch with economic realities.[11]

At the appropriate time, therefore, and for countries that could not successfully adjust their economies by other means, "an adjustment of the exchange rate may sooner or later be necessary." However, such an adjustment could be useless if ill timed. There were indications that in some countries the exchange rate was becoming a restraining factor on exports and was adding to the difficulty of earning convertible currencies. Nevertheless, "so long as an exchange rate does not hamper a country's exports, there is little to be said in present world conditions for altering it." Reminding the reader that the Fund was not entitled to propose a change in the par value of a currency, the Report concluded that the Fund

> has an obligation to keep the exchange rate situation constantly under review, and its views may properly find expression in its informal consultations with members. When an exchange rate is no longer appropriate the Fund will, of course, give prompt and realistic consideration to a member's request for adjustment in the par value of its currency.[12]

A year later, sixteen members were to take the Fund at its word.

THE FUND AND THE ERP

It was against the background just described that the Board considered what its attitude should be to the interjection into the European scene of the generous U.S. aid stemming from Secretary Marshall's speech at Harvard.

The Fund consulted

We may first recall the stages by which the question presented itself to the Board. Secretary Marshall's speech was made on June 5, 1947. On June 17 the British Foreign Secretary, Mr. Ernest Bevin, having publicly welcomed the U.S. initiative, visited Paris to discuss with the French Foreign Minister, Mr. Georges Bidault, what steps should be taken to respond to it. Ten days later, Mr. Bevin met with Mr. Bidault and Mr. V. M. Molotov, Foreign Minister of the U.S.S.R., but on July 2 Mr. Molotov rejected the Franco-British plan for

[11] *Ibid.*, p. 21.
[12] *Ibid.*, p. 24.

setting up a pan-European organization to administer the Recovery Program. There followed the first European Economic Conference, which convened in Paris on July 12 under the chairmanship of Mr. Bevin and was attended by representatives of Austria, Belgium, Denmark, France, Greece, Iceland, Ireland, Italy, Luxembourg, the Netherlands, Norway, Portugal, Sweden, Switzerland, Turkey, and the United Kingdom. This Conference set up, on the following day, a Committee of Co-operation and four special committees, on Food and Agriculture, Fuel and Power, Iron and Steel, and Transport. It then adjourned until September 22, when it issued its first report.

So much was common knowledge. Of immediate concern to the Fund was a resolution passed by the Committee of Co-operation on July 31 dealing with measures to reduce the payments difficulties hampering intra-European trade. This resolution stated the intention of the participating countries to make their currencies convertible, for current requirements, into the currencies of other participating countries; recommended an immediate review of existing payments agreements; and asked the Executive Committee to instruct a Financial Committee to report on what practical steps were necessary to achieve these purposes. The penultimate clause of the resolution read as follows:

> The Committee of Co-operation draw attention to the important part which the International Monetary Fund should be able to play in advising countries on measures of monetary reform and the progressive liberalisation of inter-European payments arrangements.

As a result of this resolution, the chairman of the Committee of Co-operation sent an invitation to the Managing Director of the Fund to attend the meetings of the Financial Committee in Paris. Mr. Gutt reported this invitation to the Board on August 12. He was asked whether he had received any indication of the particular subjects on which he would be invited to consult the Financial Committee, and whether in the course of these consultations he would directly or indirectly commit the Fund or any of its members. Mr Gutt ascertained from Mr. Ansiaux (Belgium), in the latter's capacity as chairman of the Financial Committee, that the intention was to have exploratory conversations on various monetary measures, including the problems of interconvertibility of currencies. One such proposal was the creation of a currency pool which would complement the Fund in particular respects. Mr. Gutt then reassured the Executive Directors that the consultations in which he took part would in no way commit the Fund, and the Board accordingly agreed to his participation in them. He left for Paris on August 16, accompanied by the Director of the Research Department.

The Financial Committee reported on August 29, and on September 17 (the last day of the Fund's Annual Meeting in London) the Managing Director made a brief statement to the Board of Executive Directors on his talks with the Financial Committee. He added that the Fund had been asked to send an observer to a meeting of a technical group to pursue the committee's work; this group was to meet in London on September 22. Mr. Ansiaux thanked Mr. Gutt for his contribution to the Financial Committee's work and urged that the Fund should be represented at this further meeting, which would be concerned mainly with techniques for financial cooperation among the European nations. He said that the members of the Financial Committee had realized that the first step necessary was for each nation to put its internal financial administration in order—balance its budget, end inflationary credit policies, restrict the currency in circulation, and so on. The second step was to promote intra-European convertibility of currencies, but the precise technique to achieve this end had not been agreed, and it would be the function of the meeting of technicians in London to make appropriate recommendations for this purpose. One proposal, which had been examined in detail, would provide dollar credits to debtor countries to enable them to buy needed goods for dollars from their European creditors, who in turn would use the dollars to obtain supplies from the Western Hemisphere.

Executive Directors inquired whether the objective of this last proposal could not equally be achieved by permitting debtor countries to obtain credits, in excess of the limits in their payments agreements, by drawing on the Fund for their creditors' currencies. It was agreed that this would be possible, but some Directors felt that members would prefer to use their ability to draw on the Fund in order to obtain dollars; it was also pointed out that a service charge would be payable on Fund drawings. After further discussion of possible dangers in the Financial Committee's proposal, it was agreed that Mr. Rasminsky (Canada) and the Director of the Research Department should attend the London meetings as observers for the Fund.

The London group, which was styled the Committee on Payments Agreements, met under the chairmanship of Sir David Waley. Its report, dated September 27, 1947, referred to possible technical arrangements for setting off surpluses and deficits on a multilateral basis and said that Belgium, France, Italy, Luxembourg, and the Netherlands were prepared to participate in such arrangements. A meeting of technicians from these five countries was being held in Paris on October 15 to work out the functions of a central clearing house for this purpose. Other countries represented at the London meeting would be sending observers to Paris. The technicalities of the scheme evolved at these meetings, and of later schemes, need not be explained here. For our present purposes, it is more important that the report of the Committee on Payments Agreements stated that the Fund was being invited to send an observer to the Paris meeting; and that no Fund observer went.

The reason for the absence of a Fund observer is obscure. In a statement to the Board more than a year later, on November 12, 1948, Mr. Gutt said that it was due to "a genuine misunderstanding." So far as can be ascertained, the invitation was not acted upon because the Managing Director and the Director of the Research Department were both absent from Washington at the critical time, and had left no instructions for the Fund to be represented.

An oral exposé of the outcome of the London meeting was made to the Board by the Director of the Research Department on October 23, 1947, and its report was distributed to the Board on October 28. The only decisions taken on October 23 were that the staff should prepare a study on the question whether the Articles of Agreement would permit debtor countries to use the Fund to settle intra-European debts without reducing their ability to draw from the Fund; and that no action was required of the Fund at that juncture.

On November 7 the U.S. President's Committee on Foreign Aid (the so-called Harriman Committee) issued a report from which the following is extracted:

> The Paris report [i.e., that of the Committee of Co-operation] suggests that when the countries of Europe undertake stabilization programs they will require some dollars and gold to add to their reserves as assurance for the success of these programs. . . . it suggests a figure of 3 billion dollars . . . which seems larger than necessary. . . .
>
> The United States Congress has already appropriated and paid in to the International Monetary Fund 2.75 billion dollars, largely out of the country's gold, for the purpose of world currency stabilization. It would not appear reasonable to ask the Congress for a further appropriation for this purpose. The statutes of the International Monetary Fund appear to make its resources available in adequate amount for any country that carries through an effective stabilization program. However, if it is the opinion of the Directors of the Fund that its resources are not so available, the statutes should be revised to make them so.[13]

Evolution of European payments arrangements

An agreement on multilateral compensations between the five countries participating in the Paris discussions was signed on November 18, 1947. The first draft of this agreement had provided for the Fund to act as clearing agent, but in the absence of a Fund representative at the meeting an offer from the Bank for International Settlements to undertake this function was accepted.

In a brief discussion in the Board on December 2, the suggestion was made that it should discuss what interest, if any, the Fund had toward the five-nation multilateral clearing system recently established in Europe, and what role, if any, the Fund should play. The staff was requested to prepare a study on the system, and it was agreed that the matter would be discussed at an early meeting.

Before replies to the Board's inquiries were received from the staff, the Managing Director was notified of a further meeting, in Brussels, of the five-

[13] President's Committee on Foreign Aid, *European Recovery and American Aid* (Washington, November 7, 1947), p. 93.

nation committee, and informed the Board that he had arranged for his personal assistant, who would be in Brussels at the time for other reasons, to attend the meeting.

On December 29 the Board received three memoranda prepared by the staff. One, answering the question which the Board had asked on October 23, suggested that additional credits would be essential to enable the European clearing mechanism to work, and that the Fund could and should cooperate in providing credits. It should, however, distinguish between requests for drawings in dollars and for drawings in other currencies. Drawings in all currencies, including dollars, should be permitted freely to any member insofar as the Fund's holdings of its currency, after the transaction, would not exceed 75 per cent of its quota. On the other hand, requests to draw dollars should be scrutinized much more severely than requests to draw other currencies if the Fund's holdings of the currency of the member seeking to draw would, after the transaction, exceed 75 per cent of its quota.

A second memorandum, addressed to the question which the Board had asked on December 2, explained the clearing mechanism and pointed out that greater all-round possibilities of multilateral clearing in Europe were dependent upon an improvement in the position of the largest debtors vis-à-vis the largest creditors.

The third memorandum, by the Director of the Research Department, discussed the whole problem of European payments, and explained in detail the divergence of view between the five nations that had met in Paris and the other European countries, including the United Kingdom, which had felt unable to enter into formal arrangements for multilateral clearing. It offered no conclusions except those put forward in the two preceding papers.

On December 31 the Board was given the text of President Truman's message to Congress on December 19, which proposed the creation of the Economic Cooperation Administration, and which announced that the United States was proposing to enter into an agreement with each European country providing, inter alia, for it

> to take financial and monetary measures necessary to stabilize its currency, establish or maintain a proper rate of exchange, and generally to restore or maintain confidence in its monetary system.

On January 6, 1948, the Managing Director told the Board that he had been asked informally by the U.S. Government what his response would be if he was invited to testify at congressional committee hearings on the European Recovery Program (ERP). Executive Directors were divided on the desirability of Mr. Gutt's appearing before the committee, and eventually decided that the Board should first have an exchange of views on the implications of the ERP for the Fund. At the same meeting, Mr. Gutt said that an invitation had been received for a Fund representative to attend the next meeting of the Multilateral Clearing Union in Basle. "In view of the interest of the Fund," he said, he had asked a member of the staff to attend.

ERP AND THE FUND'S RESOURCES

Ten days later the Board began a discussion of the ERP. After reviewing the economic prospects of European countries, and the effects which U.S. aid might be expected to have on their balances of payments, the Board turned on January 21 to consider what effect the ERP would have on the use of the Fund's resources. (This discussion was fitted into the middle of the week devoted to the problem of the franc.) One argument was that this use might prejudicially affect countries' efforts to balance their international payments. It was suggested also that the amount of aid which the U.S. Congress had voted might implicitly indicate the volume of U.S. production which it thought should be shipped overseas during the Program; there should, therefore, not be any substantial provision of dollars by the Fund to increase the impact on the U.S. economy. A third consideration was that Europe's needs were primarily for relief and reconstruction, which were outside the functions of the Fund. Finally, the Board was reminded that a dollar deficit of some \$3.5 billion was forecast for Europe even in 1952, and although this would be offset by a surplus of some \$2 billion with non-dollar areas, it would seem that the prospects for repurchase in five years were not bright. (This appears to have been the first occasion on which a period of five years for repurchases was postulated.) For all these reasons, it was suggested that European members should not count on using the Fund's resources in the normal way.

On the other hand, it was agreed that in the event of a catastrophe in Europe, such as a crop failure, temporary drawings on the Fund would be fully justified. Some Directors also felt that, since the ERP would cover European needs for relief and reconstruction, limited access to the Fund's resources should be permitted for other special purposes. Some Directors also argued that the existence of programs such as the ERP could not diminish the legal rights which members had to use the Fund's resources; the existence of the Program would not justify any tightening of the evaluation of "reasonable doubt" (Article XIV, Section 5), and the burden of proof would still be on the Fund that members' representations were incorrect (Article V, Section 3 (*a*) (i)). This last point was challenged on the ground that the existence of the ERP would undoubtedly have a bearing on whether the Fund could regard as correct a representation that U.S. dollars were "presently needed for making . . . payments" consistent with the Fund Agreement.

When the discussion was resumed at a further meeting in the afternoon of the same day, Mr. Overby (United States) said that he believed that, while there might be individual circumstances in which the use of the Fund's resources would be justified, the general effect of the ERP should be to tighten the Fund's evaluation of "reasonable doubt." He added that the implications of the ERP would be particularly significant with respect to requests to draw U.S. dollars, since the Program would expand Europe's dollar supply.

On the subject of multilateral clearings, the Director of the Research Department explained why no clearings had yet been able to be effected through the mechanism set up by the five countries. He said that the Fund's observer at the Clearing Union meetings had concluded that the Fund could render valuable assistance by guaranteeing that particular countries would have reasonable access to particular foreign currencies, so that they would be less reluctant to exchange one debtor for another through the clearing system. There were, however, two main impediments to the use of the Fund in this way. One was the reluctance of European countries to diminish their power to obtain dollars from the Fund by drawing European currencies. The other was the eventual obligation, which drawing countries would incur, to repurchase in convertible currencies. The Director of the Research Department suggested, however, that the Fund should cooperate in the efforts being made to establish mechanisms for multilateral clearings. If clearings were accomplished through the use of the Fund, there would be less need for a separate organization to carry them through. The Board invited the staff to propose ways in which this might be done.

In the course of a discussion of the relationship between the Fund and the proposed Economic Cooperation Administration (ECA), Mr. Overby mentioned that his Government had always sought to avoid interfering with the authority and competence of the Fund. However, the Administrator of the ECA would probably be making a number of decisions which would be of great concern to the Fund. For instance, the U.S. Administration was facing congressional suggestions that a revision of exchange rates across the board should be a condition precedent to any European aid, and it was expected that certain devaluations would prove necessary. The Administrator would keep in close touch with the Fund on these and other matters in its field. Reference to a possible need for devaluations in Europe was also made in a letter dated February 10, 1948 from Mr. John W. Snyder, in his capacity as chairman of the U.S. National Advisory Council, to Representative J. D. Lodge, which was circulated to the Board a week later.

At this time, as is reviewed in the next section, the Board was concerned with defining its attitude to a number of points connected with the use of the Fund's resources, and the problem of the effects of the ERP did not come up again until March 18. The Board then had before it a staff memorandum suggesting that during the first year of the Program, at any rate, the Fund should supplement a member's own dollar resources only in exceptional circumstances, but should continue to provide a member with other currencies for purposes consistent with the Fund Agreement.

There was general support for the view that it would be in the interests of members that the Fund's dollar resources should not be used up prematurely. Messrs. Tansley (United Kingdom) and de Selliers (Belgium), however, believed that such a result could be properly achieved only by members' own forbearance; they considered that the Fund could not refuse members' exchange requests on the ground that there was an ERP, since any such action would in effect change the Fund Agreement. Mr. Rasminsky, on the other hand, held that the new effort being made through the ERP to meet the major disequilibrium in world payments should change the favorable presumption, which up to then the Fund had given to all members requesting drawing, to an unfavorable presumption for those members receiving ERP aid. Mr. Joshi (India) and Mr. McFarlane (Australia) supported this view, and the general feeling of the Board was in favor of the staff proposal. After a further discussion on March 30 and a postponement to allow Directors to consult their Governments, a formal decision was reached on April 5 in the following terms, Mr. Tansley alone opposing:

> Although the Fund recognizes that a general rule is not sufficient basis for all cases, the Fund must, in examining requests for the use of its resources, take into account the European Recovery Program, especially with respect to members who participate in the Program. Since the ERP is to be handled year by year, related policies on use of the Fund's resources should be developed at similar intervals. For the first year the attitude of the Fund and ERP members should be that such members should request the purchase of United States dollars from the Fund only in exceptional or unforeseen cases. The Fund and members participating in ERP should have as their objective to maintain the resources of the Fund at a safe and reasonable level during the ERP period in order that at the end of the period such members will have unencumbered access to the resources of the Fund. This objective conforms with the intention of Article XIV, Section 1, that during the transitional period members should not impair the capacity of the Fund to serve its members or impair their ability to secure help from the Fund after the transitional period.[14]

On the same day, in response to a request by Mr. de Selliers that the Board should clarify the position of the Fund respecting drawings of currencies other than U.S. dollars during the ERP period, the following view was unanimously agreed:

> During the European Recovery Program members of the Fund may wish to use the Fund's holdings of the currency of a country participating in ERP. No member has the right to veto or limit the Fund's sales of its currency to other members for use in accordance with the Fund Agreement. The Fund recognizes, however, that such sales should not have the effect of compelling a country to finance a

[14] *Annual Report, 1948*, p. 74.

> large bilateral surplus with some countries, while it has to make net drawings on its gold and convertible currency reserves for current payments. Such circumstances would fall within the meaning of the "exceptional or unforeseen cases" mentioned in the policy decision of April 5, 1948, made by the Fund concerning the use of the Fund's resources by ERP countries and would justify requests by a country to purchase foreign exchange from the Fund to make to other members current payments or payments authorized by Article VI, Section 2, but not to build up its monetary reserves. This is in fact the manner in which the Fund is intended to facilitate a system of multilateral payments.[15]

At a press conference three days later, the Managing Director was asked what effect the ERP would have upon the Fund's activities. He replied that he had no doubt that members receiving ERP aid would come less to the Fund, whose resources were their second line of reserves, which should not be exhausted save in exceptional cases. A misleading press interpretation of this statement on April 20 led Directors to make public the foregoing decisions, which had already been notified to members.

Further plans for Fund participation

On May 12, 1948 the Board discussed a plan put forward by the staff, as requested on January 21, for the participation by the Fund in the European multilateral clearing arrangements. This plan took account of the fact that the total credit rights of all European countries except Belgium exceeded the unused credit commitments of Belgium by $338 million. Belgium was most likely to be the ultimate creditor if all credit rights could be fully used. It was therefore suggested that external resources of $338 million made available to the Clearing Union would be sufficient to multilateralize the existing credit margins among Fund members. The plan was that the Fund should make this sum available in the form of drawings of Belgian francs or other European currencies, permitting Belgium (or the other countries whose currencies were drawn) to have corresponding access to the Fund for dollars should their balances of payments require it.

Discussing this plan, Executive Directors raised a number of questions about its possible effects. Would it not tend to postpone the solution of Europe's problems, rather than help to solve them? Would it not run counter to the decision restricting the use of the Fund's resources by the recipients of Marshall Aid (the first decision quoted above, which is usually referred to as the "ERP Decision")? Would the Fund be able to apply its normal tests to proposed drawings? What guarantee could there be that the Fund's commitments under the scheme would not be excessive, using up in a few months resources which should be made available over several years? One Director pointed out that the financial authorities of the five countries were at that time having talks on the

[15] *Ibid.*, p. 75.

system, and said that it would seem best to await proposals from them. The staff representative in Paris was accordingly asked to express the Fund's interest in the restoration of convertibility and a system of multilateral payments, and to report back any developments.

During a further review of the question, on June 2, Mr. Overby brought forward a number of additional objections to any plan which would require the Fund to provide dollars. He recalled that the ERP had been projected as mainly a European self-help program, to be supplemented by U.S. assistance. There was a danger that increasing the means of payment in Europe would encourage nonessential and luxury imports more than the essential trade which was desired. Conceivably, also, assistance given as suggested might be vitiated by the weight of the old balances under existing payments agreements. While, therefore, some Executive Directors felt that the aim of a multilateral payments system was directly in line with the Fund's aims, Mr. Overby suggested that the Fund should not go beyond the limits it had set for the use of its resources, and should not undertake to effect transactions automatically merely because they were within a payments system. Mr. de Selliers expressed concern at the prospect that the extension of further substantial credits by Belgium would run grave risks of producing an inflationary effect. In the event, the Board decided to limit itself to the following statement of its position, which was communicated to all Fund members participating in the ERP:

> For the information of the members consulting on intra-European payments, the Fund's position is:
>
> (a) That it hopes that an arrangement can be made for multilateralizing European payments;
>
> (b) That because of the imminent exhaustion of the credit margins under some payments agreements, it hopes that a revision and a moderate rise in the credits can be agreed for use in multilateral payments;
>
> (c) That it hopes any increase in the credit margins can be financed by the creditor countries as their further contribution to European recovery;
>
> (d) [This was substantially a repetition of the second ERP decision, set out on pages 219–20 above.]
>
> (e) That the Fund is willing to place its advice and technical facilities at the disposal of its members in connection with the formulation and administration of any multilateral payments arrangements and for other purposes related to their payments problems.

While the staff in the Paris Office continued to follow closely the evolution of the clearing arrangements, there were no further discussions of the ERP at the Board during the year with which we are now concerned. References to the subject in the Annual Report were confined to statements closely based upon the decisions which have been quoted above.[16] In the discussion of the Report at the

---

[16] *Ibid.*, pp. 10–11, 35, 48.

Annual Meeting there were brief approving references to these decisions by the Governors for China and Australia. A suggestion by Mr. Lieftinck, Governor for the Netherlands, that the Fund should consider what was the appropriate use of the local currency proceeds of ERP was answered by the Managing Director with the statement that this was primarily a problem for ECA, although it was admittedly undesirable that these proceeds should be used to finance budget deficits. The Governors for Czechoslovakia and Yugoslavia deprecated the attention devoted to ERP in the Annual Report, and the implication that Europe could not have recovered without this help. No Governor otherwise dissented from the decisions that the Board had taken.

Later developments

We may here summarize briefly what needs to be said about the subsequent relationship between the Fund and the ERP. In October 1948 Mr. Ansiaux described the negotiations then nearing completion for a new Agreement on Intra-European Payments and Compensations, covering the year 1948–49. He said that the OEEC appreciated the technical help given by the Fund staff, but did not plan to call on the Fund for any resources. However, he described three ways in which, in the future, the Fund might consider rendering financial assistance in Europe. One would be to sell the currencies of net European creditors to net debtors, a second to assist debtors to transfer existing bilateral credits with one country to another, and a third to finance expected ERP reimbursements temporarily.

This last suggestion was further discussed a month later. Mr. Gutt made a powerful plea for the Fund to take an active share in European plans, although he recognized that the Board was reluctant to become "entangled" in such arrangements. For various reasons, however, the Board was unwilling to act. Some Directors questioned whether prefinancing of expected ERP reimbursements would be a legitimate use of the Fund's resources, since this would lead to a building-up of members' reserves. Others doubted whether repurchases could be relied upon, and still others felt that Europe's needs were rather for reconstruction than for temporary financing. In the event, Mr. Overby said that he needed time to investigate the issues arising, and no decision was taken.

It was not until March 1949 that the Board again discussed ERP questions. Mr. Beyen (Netherlands) then initiated a brief discussion of a staff paper on the local currency proceeds of ERP grants. A little later the Board considered a memorandum prepared by Mr. Triffin (Paris Office), putting forward a proposal for a modification of the European payments arrangements which envisaged the possible use of the Fund's resources as an aid to multilateralizing payments in 1949–50. It was suggested that this might be forwarded to the OEEC as the Fund's contribution to the discussion, then in progress, of means to circumvent the bilateral tendency of the existing arrangements. The suggestion was not accepted by the Board, although one Executive Director said he was discouraged that the Fund was being so negative toward ERP issues. Mr. Southard (United States), who had meanwhile succeeded Mr. Overby, replied that he was anxious that the Fund should play an active role, but not to the extent of putting forward a proposal which had not been properly discussed. It was decided that the plan might be submitted to the OEEC by Mr. Triffin as his personal and technical proposal. It was not further considered by the Board.

A new initiative taken by Mr. Gutt in 1950, in connection with the European Payments Union, is described in Chapter 11 below.

INTERPRETING THE ARTICLES

The Board's decision about the implications of the ERP for members' drawings was only one of a number of important interpretations adopted during 1947–48. Other decisions authoritatively elucidated a number of passages in the Articles of Agreement which were of importance in governing members' rights of access to the Fund's resources. It is proposed to detail these decisions before discussing the drawings actually effected during the year.

In October 1947, the Board decided that several relevant phrases in Articles V and XX would have to be clarified. It had taken the first step in this direction in May 1947 by defining the word "represents" in Article V, Section 3 (*a*) (i). The next question that arose was whether the Fund, when faced with a request for a drawing, could delay action in order to prepare a report and then limit the member's use of the Fund's resources under Article V, Section 5, which enables the Fund to declare a member ineligible to use its resources if it is of the opinion that they are being misused. The staff suggested that the Fund had this power, but when the point was discussed briefly late in December, Mr. de Largentaye (France) said that he could not agree. He believed that, if action were to be taken under Article V, Section 5, the member would have had to be given notice before it made a request; once a request had been properly made, the member's right under Article V, Section 3, was unconditional. Mr. Overby (United States), on the other hand, said that he could not accept that the Fund's powers were so limited. If they were, he thought, the Fund would be seriously lacking both in protection and in sanctions. He added that, if it were in fact decided that the Fund could limit transactions only after a report had been sent under Article V, Section 5, he might propose that reports be sent forthwith to virtually all members of the Fund so that limitations could be applied if necessary.

When the discussion was resumed in mid-January, the Board had before it three memoranda advocating, inter alia, the development of general policies to guide Executive Directors in deciding upon requests to use the Fund's resources. One, by Mr. Martínez-Ostos (Mexico), made a number of wide-ranging suggestions for the future work of the Board. On the subject of the use of the Fund's resources, he suggested referring the relevant provisions of the Articles to the Committee on Interpretation.

A second memorandum, by the Managing Director, drew attention to the compromises and ambiguities which were to be found in the Articles of Agreement, as a necessary consequence of the diverse views held by those who had framed the Articles. Mr. Gutt urged that the Board itself, rather than a committee, should undertake their interpretation, and that it should be guided more by policy considerations than by legalistic reasoning. He again stressed the significance of inflation in connection with requests for drawings, and suggested that where inflationary conditions prevailed the Fund would have good reason to doubt that the payments contemplated by the member would be consistent with the Fund's purposes.

The third memorandum, by Mr. Overby, also stressed the importance of inflation. Mr. Overby proposed that four questions should be asked when a member sought to draw from the Fund: (1) Is its exchange rate increasing its balance of payments difficulties, and would an adjustment of the rate reduce them? (2) What are the prospects of the member's repurchasing? (3) Will the drawing be used for relief, reconstruction, or development? (4) Are the member's monetary or fiscal policies leading to fundamental disequilibrium?

Against the background of these memoranda, the Board during the next few weeks decided the following specific issues:

Use of Article XX, Section 4 (*i*)

This Section empowers the Fund to postpone exchange transactions with a member if the member's circumstances are such that, in the opinion of the Fund, a drawing would lead to prejudicial use of the Fund's resources. The Board formally reaffirmed a previous decision, that this power did not lapse when exchange transactions began in March 1947.[17] It also considered whether the power lapsed vis-à-vis each individual member when that member drew from the Fund. Mr. Saad (Egypt), Mr. Overby, and Mr. Luthringer (United States) argued that the Section continued in force, and that it was a more suitable sanction for the Board to use than challenging representations under Article V, Section 3. They were, however, overruled by the other members of the Board, and the decision was that the power to postpone transactions under Article XX, Section 4 (*i*), did not continue in force with respect to a member after it had drawn. Mr. Overby recorded his disagreement.

[17] E.B. Decision No. 284-2, March 10, 1948; below, Vol. III, p. 272. Cf. above, p. 187.

Use of Article V, Section 5

The second question decided was the one which had been raised in December, viz., whether the procedure of Article V, Section 5, could be initiated once a request to draw had been received from a member. The Board was advised by the Legal Department that the answer was in the affirmative. There was again a division between Executive Directors, but by a majority the Board decided that the Fund had power, under Article V, Section 5, to postpone a transaction if at the time when a request for a purchase was received the Fund was considering sending the member a report under that Section, or if it found when the request was before it that action under that Section should be considered.[18]

Executive Directors also agreed that the Fund's powers under Article V, Section 5, vis-à-vis a member that had had a previous exchange transaction enabled it to declare that the member was ineligible to use the Fund's resources further, or to limit the member's use of the Fund's resources, if in the opinion of the Fund it was using these resources in a manner contrary to the purposes of the Fund.[19]

Meaning of "provisions of this Agreement"

Article V, Section 3 (*a*) (i), stipulated that a member seeking to draw from the Fund must represent that it needed the desired currency for the purpose of making in that currency payments "which are consistent with the provisions of this Agreement." After reviewing the legislative history, the staff advised the Board that the phrase quoted was equivalent to "consistent with the purposes of the Agreement." Article V, Section 5, referred in a similar context to "the purposes of the Fund." In the staff view, therefore, the member's representation must cover both the provisions of the Articles of Agreement other than those in Article I, and the purposes of the Fund contained in Article I.

Mr. de Largentaye challenged this view, on the ground that the member could not know what the Fund's particular interpretation of the general purposes of Article I might be. He believed that a member's representation could be declared inconsistent with the provisions of the Agreement only if there was evidence of a clear breach of such express prohibitions as those in Article VI (respecting capital transactions) or in Article XIV, Section 1 (respecting relief, reconstruction, or international indebtedness arising out of the war). Mr. de Selliers (Belgium) agreed with the staff's view from a legal standpoint, but thought that, as Mr. de Largentaye had said, a member should not be asked to make a representation about "purposes" when it did not know how the Fund would interpret these. He therefore abstained. Other Executive Directors, however, agreed with the staff's view, and it was so decided.[20]

---

[18] E.B. Decision No. 286-1, March 15, 1948; below, Vol. III, p. 234.
[19] E.B. Decision No. 284-3, March 10, 1948; below, Vol. III, p. 234.
[20] E.B. Decision No. 287-3, March 17, 1948; below, Vol. III, p. 228.

MEANING OF "IS USING"

Article V, Section 5, empowered the Fund to present a report and, subject to conditions, to limit the access of a member to its resources if it "is of the opinion that any member is using the resources of the Fund in a manner contrary to the purposes of the Fund." What was meant by "is using"? Must a member have actually drawn from the Fund, so as to have the Fund's resources in its possession? One view was that membership in the Fund constituted a line of reserves for members; consequently, a member was making use of the Fund's resources merely by having access to them as reserves. Alternatively, it was suggested that "is using" must be interpreted to mean "would use"; i.e., that, if the drawing were permitted, it would be misapplied. A third view was that "is using" meant that a member had purchased exchange from the Fund, and the Fund's holdings of that member's currency were in excess of the lowest amount which the Fund had ever held of that currency, provided that the existing holdings were not less than 75 per cent of quota.

On further consideration of the problem, the Board decided that one criterion of "is using" must be that the member had purchased exchange from the Fund. As a result, the third interpretation noted in the previous paragraph was accepted, with the addition of provision for the case where the member was actually disposing of exchange purchased from the Fund.[21]

DRAWINGS AND CHARGES

AMOUNTS DRAWN

During the early months of 1947–48 members continued to draw fairly freely on the Fund, and the procedure of Rule G-5 remained unaltered. Eventually, a total of $419,420,000 U.S. dollars and 500 million Belgian francs (equivalent to $11,410,000) was drawn by eleven countries: the Board considered and expressed no objection to eighteen drawings totaling $284,810,000,[22] and nine others totaling $146,020,000 were approved without being reviewed by the Board. Chile, France, the Netherlands, and the United Kingdom, which had drawn from the Fund in 1946–47, continued to draw in the following year, and were joined by Belgium, Czechoslovakia, Denmark, Ethiopia, India, Norway, and Turkey. No member drew as much as 25 per cent of its quota during the twelve months.

The effect of the "ERP Decision" was, of course, to limit subsequent drawings by Western European countries. A drawing of $2.5 million by Norway, requested early in April, was not opposed by the Board because Norway had not

[21] E.B. Decision No. 292-3, March 30, 1948; below, Vol. III, p. 235.

[22] Strictly speaking this should be "the equivalent of $284,810,000" because it includes the U.S. dollar value of the Belgian francs. The constant repetition of the words "the equivalent of" in such instances would, however, be tedious, and they have been omitted here and in later chapters.

had notice of the decision, and one of $3.4 million by Denmark about the same time was handled along the same lines by the staff. Thereafter, however, the only drawings by countries receiving ERP aid were BF 300 million by the Netherlands (May) and BF 200 million by Norway (June and July).

The Managing Director brought the request of the Netherlands before the Board because it was the first occasion on which a drawing could give rise to a request by a country covered by the ERP to draw dollars in compensation. Mr. de Selliers (Belgium) confirmed that, if Belgium had to make net drawings on its gold and convertible currency reserves for current payments, it would consider itself entitled to draw dollars from the Fund to an equivalent total. The Board did not, however, regard this as prejudicing the Netherlands' case, which was based on the argument that its structural balance of payments deficit with Belgium could not be offset multilaterally because of the absence of convertibility among European currencies.

Nevertheless, Mr. Overby (United States) felt obliged to question the drawing because he had serious doubts whether in the existing circumstances the use of the Fund's resources by the Netherlands would be temporary. He pointed to the Netherlands' large budget deficit, to the high rate of investment, and to the consequential increase in inflationary pressures there. He detected an absence of effective policies to control the situation, and suggested that the Netherlands should be asked to consult the Fund before making a drawing. Meanwhile the situation should be studied intensively, for which a mission would be the appropriate procedure. Other Executive Directors, however, urged that, as the Netherlands had not been put on notice that the Fund would raise objections to the drawing, it should be permitted. In the event, the Board agreed that the drawing might be made. It was as a result of this discussion that the mission to the Netherlands, noted in a preceding section, was sent later in the summer.

Norway sought to draw BF 100 million in each of two consecutive months. No objection was raised to the first of these requests, but when the second was supported by the argument that July and August would be critical months for the Norwegian balance of payments, Mr. Overby expressed doubts about the propriety of the drawing and agreed to it only because Norway had not been warned not to draw. He suggested that Norway should be asked not to make further use of the Fund's resources. As a result, Norway also invited a mission from the Fund, which went to Oslo in September.

Mexico's problems

In July 1948 Mexico sought the help of the Fund and of the U.S. Stabilization Fund to deal with an emergency involving a serious loss of exchange reserves. When Mr. Gómez (Mexico) explained the situation to the Board, Mr. Overby said that it would be inappropriate for the Fund to take possible assistance from the Stabilization Fund into account when considering a request for a drawing, although the United States might base its action on what the Fund decided. He asked, however, whether the par value of the Mexican peso could be maintained, having regard to the apparent capital flight which Mexico's exchange controls were inadequate to check. Executive Directors generally felt that Mexico's intentions were sound, and recognized that circumstances made implementation of capital controls very difficult. The fact remained, however, that Article VI, Section 1, prohibited the use of the Fund's resources by a member to meet a large or sustained outflow of capital.

The legal issue raised by the reference to Article VI, Section 1, was not pursued because, when Mr. Gómez mentioned that Mexico needed $85 million, of which it sought to draw $22.5 million from the Fund and to borrow $62.5 million from the U.S. Stabilization Fund, Mr. Overby said that he had serious doubts whether the United States could provide the latter sum. Mr. Gómez then said that Mexico could not in these circumstances maintain its par value; it would have to declare a moratorium and allow the exchange rate to fluctuate until a new par value could be fixed. On the following day, July 22, after further discussion, the Board noted Mexico's decision and decided to take no action provided that a new par value was adopted by August 15. On August 13, however, Mr. Gómez informed the Board that Mexico could not adopt a new par value by the date required, although it was trying to stabilize the exchange rate. He sought the approval of the Board for a postponement of the date by which a new par value had to be fixed. There was a discussion of the possibility of approving the Mexican action, on the ground that the circumstances were not specifically envisaged by the Articles of Agreement, but most Executive Directors opposed any interpretation of the Agreement which would permit a member to change its par value by allowing its exchange rate to fluctuate.

The Board decided to note that Mexico would not communicate a new par value by the date requested, that a technical mission should go immediately to confer with the Mexican monetary authorities, and that this mission should report to the Board within a month in order that the Board might consider what action should be taken. In the meantime, Mexico's request to draw was not approved. At a further meeting, on September 23, the Board considered a report by the mission and came to the conclusion that Mexico should in its own interests put into effect without delay stronger fiscal and credit measures, so that its monetary reserves might be built up and the way established for a new par value at an early date. At this meeting, the question was raised as to Mexico's legal position, and the Board was advised that Mexico was technically in violation of Article IV, Sections 3 and 4, because exchange transactions were taking place at rates deviating by more than 1 per cent from the par value agreed with the Fund.

Charges

Two aspects of the charges to be levied by the Fund for the use of its resources came under question during the year. Article V, Section 8 (*a*), provided for a service charge of 3/4 of 1 per cent to be made on all transactions, "uniform for all members." This had come briefly under attack in February 1947, before any transactions had been effected, as being too heavy an impost. It had, however, been decided then that the deterrent effect of the charge was a desirable feature, and that in any case it would be better to await some experience before changing the standard laid down in the Articles. A year later the question arose again. A request was made on behalf of Nicaragua for a reduction of the service charge on temporary or seasonal drawings. Mr. Martínez-Ostos (Mexico) suggested that, without breaking the rule of uniformity vis-à-vis all members, special rates could be fixed for particular kinds of transactions. He was supported by Mr. de Selliers, who pointed out that, if a member needed a drawing for one month only, the service charge represented 9 per cent per annum. Executive Directors considered whether, instead of reducing the charge, arrangements could be made for a refund in the event of a quick repurchase, but the consensus was that this would not be consistent with the intention of the Articles. The Board then decided to maintain the charge at 3/4 of 1 per cent.

In addition to the service charge, the Articles provided (Article V, Section 8 (*c*)) for the levy of a charge in the nature of interest on drawings insofar as these drawings increased the Fund's holdings above 100 per cent of quota. As was noted in Chapter 5, this latter charge increased both with the length of time that the drawing was outstanding and with the proportion of the amount drawn to the member's quota. On the assumption that a member drew 25 per cent of its quota annually, the charge payable would rise to 4 per cent in the eighth year. The illustrative table provided at Bretton Woods was annotated to the effect that when this figure was reached the Fund and its member should consider ways and means by which the Fund's holdings of the member's currency could be reduced.[23]

By August 1947 the Fund's holdings of French francs had reached 104 per cent of the French quota, and the provisions of Article V, Section 8 (*c*), had therefore to be put into effect. Examination of the Section by the staff, however, showed that a considerable amount of clarification was required before charges could be calculated. The problem was brought to the notice of the Board in May 1948 and rulings were given which enabled the necessary Rules and Regulations to be worked out.[24] The procedure laid down in these Rules, a necessarily complicated one, has since been maintained unaltered, although (as will be seen later) the rates of charges were changed in 1951, 1954, 1959, and

---

[23] *Proceedings*, p. 465. The table of charges is reproduced below, p. 322.

[24] See Rules G-6, G-7, I-4, I-5, I-8; below, Vol. III, pp. 293, 294–97, 298.

1963. It may be added that by September 1948 charges had become payable not only by France but also by Denmark, India, the Netherlands, and the United Kingdom. The Fund's Statement of Income and Expenditure for the fiscal year July 1, 1947 to April 30, 1948 showed service charges received as $4,080,000 and charges under Article V, Section 8 (*c*), as $104,360.90, a total of $4,184,360.90. The Fund was not to earn as much again in any fiscal year until that ended April 30, 1954.

CHAPTER

10

Currency Adjustments (1948-49)

THERE CAN BE NO QUESTION that the outstanding feature of the year 1948–49 was the devaluation of currencies that immediately followed the 1949 Annual Meeting. But this does not of course mean that the pressure on the Board in other matters declined. In some directions, indeed, it increased. In the forty-nine weeks between the Annual Meetings, the Board met 108 times, and the problems facing it were in many respects as difficult as any that it had previously encountered. In addition, the volume of documentation coming before Executive Directors was steeply increased; during the forty-nine weeks the staff circulated to the Board some 660 memoranda, many of considerable length, in addition to the regular flows of statistical material and the weekly news digest. There was heard from some Directors and some Governors a *cri de coeur*, often repeated in later years, asking that staff memoranda should be shorter, but this proved impossible to achieve while at the same time supplying the full details which Directors and Governments needed to enable them to decide upon the issues involved. Indeed, as time went on, Governments began to find that the Fund's memoranda provided a comprehensive source of current economic data, the usefulness of which extended much beyond the Fund's immediate problems. Proposals to abbreviate the memoranda proved unacceptable on these grounds.

MEMBERS, BOARD, AND STAFF

Membership of the Fund increased to 48 during the year as a result of the accession of Thailand on May 3, 1949.

On September 30, 1948, during the Third Annual Meeting, the second election of Executive Directors was held. There were nine candidates for the nine elected directorships. Messrs. Beyen (Netherlands), Carli (Italy), McFarlane (Australia), Rasminsky (Canada), and Saad (Egypt) were re-elected. Mr.

Carlos A. D'Ascoli (Venezuela) was elected in place of Mr. Gómez (Mexico), Mr. de Selliers (Belgium) in place of Mr. Ansiaux, Mr. Paranaguá (Brazil) in place of Mr. Santos-Filho, and Mr. Bohumil Sucharda (Czechoslovakia) in place of Mr. Mládek. Messrs. de Selliers and Paranaguá had been Alternates to the Directors whom they succeeded. On his retirement from the Board, Mr. Mládek was appointed Deputy Director of the Operations Department.

Immediately after the Annual Meeting, Mr. B. K. Madan (India) was appointed Director by India; he replaced Mr. Joshi, whose Alternate he had been for the previous two years.

The newly constituted Board took office on November 1, 1948. The only change in its membership that occurred during the year was in the U.S. directorship: Mr. Overby became the first Deputy Managing Director of the Fund from February 9, 1949, and was succeeded as U.S. Executive Director by Mr. Frank A. Southard, Jr. (who was himself to become Deputy Managing Director some thirteen years later).

The functions of the Deputy Managing Director have never been clearly defined; much has depended upon the interests of those who have held the post, upon the characteristics of the Managing Director at the time, and upon the relationships between the two men. A prime objective in Mr. Overby's appointment was to relieve Mr. Gutt of administrative functions which he preferred to delegate and which Mr. Overby was well qualified to perform. In this respect the creation of the position of Deputy Managing Director was a success. From the point of view of the Fund as a whole, however, the appointment of Mr. Overby had certain drawbacks. It was shortly followed by a further stiffening of the U.S. attitude toward the use of the Fund's resources, as discussed below. At first sight, this appeared to be a development of the four criteria which Mr. Overby had enunciated to the Board in January 1948, and of the "ERP Decision," for which he had been largely instrumental in securing the Board's approval. The coincidence had the unfortunate result of strengthening a suspicion in the minds of many members—perhaps particularly European members—that the Fund's policy was being dictated by the United States.

At the end of the fiscal year, April 30, 1949, the Fund's staff numbered 421, an increase of 18 during the year. The number of nationalities represented on the staff remained at 29.

Toward the end of 1948 arrangements were made to open two further regional offices, in Cairo and Bombay. In charge of the former was Mr. A. M. El Kaissouni, then a member of the Fund's staff, who has subsequently held a number of ministerial positions in the United Arab Republic. Mr. Kaissouni went to Cairo in November 1948. The Bombay Office was opened in July 1949, the Fund's resident representative there being Mr. B. R. Shenoy, previously Director-in-Charge of the Department of Research and Statistics, Reserve Bank of India, Bombay, who was later Alternate Executive Director of the Fund for India (1951–53). Mr. Shenoy spent some months in Washington in 1948–49 before returning to Bombay to open the Fund Office there. A fourth regional office, for Latin America, was at one time planned, and Santiago was considered as a possible site; this proposal was not, however, proceeded with.

The functions of the Bombay and Cairo Offices, as laid down by the Board, were mainly to improve the supply of information to the Fund about the member countries which they covered. The regional representatives were instructed to provide a regular flow of economic and financial data; published and unpublished reports on local conditions were to be obtained and transmitted, and to be supplemented by observations on the spot. For this purpose the representatives were expected to visit regularly the countries which they were assigned to cover, and to keep in touch with technicians in those countries. Finally, they were to maintain contact with regional organizations operating in the same geographical region. This last activity had become (as we have seen) a major concern of the Paris Office, but that office was not intended to undertake the other functions allotted to the Cairo and Bombay Offices.

The appointments of Mr. Kaissouni and Mr. Shenoy encountered some criticism in the Board. During the discussion in April 1949 of the Budget for 1949/50, Mr. de Largentaye (France) and Mr. Tansley (United Kingdom) questioned the usefulness of regional offices, and suggested that they might cut across the work of the headquarters departments dealing with the same regions. Other Directors, however, spoke in favor of maintaining the offices, on the ground that the effective liaison that they provided was of assistance to the Fund. The Board as a whole felt that there had been insufficient time to judge the usefulness of the arrangements. A year later (March 1950) it decided to discontinue both the Cairo and the Bombay Offices, mainly because a staff reorganization, creating two area departments, was expected to increase the ability of the headquarters officials to maintain direct contact with members in the Middle East and Far East. The office in Cairo was accordingly closed in May 1950 and that in Bombay during the following month.

Gold depositories

Article XIII, Section 2 (*b*), provided that the Fund's gold assets might be held in depositories designated by the five members having the largest quotas and in such other designated depositories as the Fund might select. In 1948–49 the five members included China, which had designated Shanghai as its depository. On May 27, 1949, however, Shanghai was captured by the communists, and thereafter was not under the control of the Government which had accepted the Articles of Agreement. On July 21 the Board agreed, on the recommendation of the Managing Director, that Shanghai should be temporarily removed from the list of depositories. There was at that time no Fund gold stored there. China was authorized, at an opportune time, to raise the matter again. It did not do so, and the issue was resolved in 1959, when, as a result of an increase in the quota of Germany, China ceased to be one of the five members having the largest quotas.

DEVALUATION

If the structure of this chapter were to be dictated by artistic considerations, the present section should come last. As has already been suggested, the highlight of the year's work in the Fund was the series of devaluations that followed the Annual Meeting. After that, a description of the Board's other activities can only be anticlimactic. Nevertheless, there is good historical reason for placing this section where it is, for the growing belief that devaluations were necessary permeated much of the Board's thinking during the first nine months of 1949.

Formulating a Fund view

It will be recalled that the appropriateness of some European exchange rates was questioned in the United States early in 1948, and that the Fund's Annual Report for 1948 had called for devaluation—but not yet. No public reference was made to the subject at the Annual Meeting in London in September 1948, but shortly after the Board's return to Washington, Mr. Overby (United States) took the opportunity of a discussion of European payments arrangements to inquire whether the existing pattern of exchange rates there would impair the working of the system.

It is not easy to trace the stages by which some Executive Directors subsequently became convinced that further delay in adjusting exchange rates was undesirable. The subject of "European exchange rates" appeared on each issue of the Board's monthly agenda from November 1948 through March 1949 but it was not until March 28, 1949 that the Board discussed the subject. A possible need for devaluation in South Africa was considered in October 1948. But of the viability of European exchange rates nothing was said until the staff submitted in the second half of March three memoranda dealing with exchange problems in that area. These expounded the statistical position of Europe's balance of payments, and suggested that the large deficit vis-à-vis the dollar area could be reduced only by a substantial increase in European exports. The conclusion was that, if a devaluation of European currencies should prove necessary to achieve such an increase, there would be advantages in undertaking this sooner rather than later.

During the discussion of these memoranda on March 28, Mr. Southard (United States) called the Board's attention to a statement that had been made in February by the chairman of the U.S. National Advisory Council to the Senate

Foreign Relations Committee. In this, Mr. Snyder had said that the Council had come to the conclusion that "the exchange-rate question should be reviewed with a number of the European countries in the course of the next year." [1] Mr. Southard himself believed that the sweeping changes in the world price structure that had taken place since 1939 made the prewar pattern of exchange rates no longer appropriate. The rates in Western Europe and associated areas were clearly of special importance, and the time had come, he felt, for a searching examination of these rates both in the countries themselves and in the Fund. While the Fund could not expect to dictate specific rates to its members, it could not be looked upon as a practicable instrument if it remained quiet in the face of unrealistic rates. It should therefore conduct an intensive inquiry into the facts in order to reach a judgment whether the par values in Western Europe as a whole required prompt and effective review by the individual members in a manner in keeping with the Fund Agreement.

Mr. Rasminsky (Canada) supported Mr. Southard's comments on the price disparities which had developed, and was concerned lest intra-European payments arrangements might encourage intra-European trade rather than the essential exports to the Western Hemisphere. He recognized, however, that the Western Hemisphere countries themselves needed to adopt policies which would facilitate European sales in their markets.

Mr. de Selliers (Belgium) questioned whether devaluation was the appropriate remedy for Europe's difficulties, and emphasized that under the Articles of Agreement the Fund had no right of initiative in relation to changes in exchange rates; the Board's activities should therefore be restricted to informing itself of the position of each member so as to be able to act quickly if any proposals were made.

The discussion was continued at two later meetings. At the second of these, on April 6, the following decision was taken, some Executive Directors acceding with great reluctance and Mr. de Selliers dissenting:

> In the light of the changes that have occurred in world economic conditions since 1946, and of the urgency of maintaining adequate and effective progress toward international balance, the Fund is of the opinion that the Western European payments problem as a whole ought to be considered through the Fund's established methods of consultation with the members. In this connection attention would be given to the present and prospective payments position of these countries and related currency areas, to the tendency toward price distortion, and to the relation of existing exchange rates and exchange controls to the payments position and price situation.

The sense of the meeting was that the Managing Director should arrange informal consultations with Western European members as soon as possible.

[1] U.S. Congress, Senate, Committee on Foreign Relations, *Extension of European Recovery* (Hearings on S. 833, a Bill to Amend the Economic Cooperation Act of 1948), 81st Cong., 1st sess., 1949, p. 388.

Although some Executive Directors questioned the right of the Fund to initiate consultations, only Mr. de Selliers pressed his objection to the point of saying that his authorities would regard consultation with the Fund at that time as neither satisfactory nor desirable.

Mr. Gutt's discussions with European members took place without fanfare during May and the early part of June. On his return he reported at some length to the Board on what he had learnt in Austria, Belgium, Denmark, France, the Netherlands, Norway, and the United Kingdom. He had found an increased awareness of the problem of exchange rates and a readiness to canvass the possibility of exchange rate adjustment. His consultations had, however, shown that the problem of timing was regarded as acute; a devaluation of sterling was widely regarded as likely to be needed, and until that had been achieved, no other country could settle what its new rate should be. Mr. Gutt felt that this raised a real problem for the Board. How could a series of devaluations be synchronized while adhering to the procedure contemplated by the Articles and without a breach of secrecy?

After Mr. Gutt's report, the first order of business was the Annual Report. In view of the stress on secrecy, it is not surprising that the brief references to exchange adjustment in this Report did not go appreciably further than those in the Annual Report for 1948, quoted in the previous chapter.[2]

Meanwhile, informal discussions, both within and outside the Fund, were increasing in intensity. Officially, however, the subject did not come before the Board again until the end of July. Proposing then a recess during the first half of August, the Managing Director said that in a few days a paper would be distributed dealing with the way in which the Fund should approach questions of monetary adjustment. In order that the Board might be prepared for emergencies, he believed that a discussion of the paper should be undertaken immediately after the recess.

The memorandum to which the Managing Director had referred was distributed to the Board on August 4. It reviewed the relationship between prices and exchange rates as a guide to exchange policy, and discussed the theoretical conditions in which a devaluation would be a success. The tentative conclusion was that these conditions existed in Western Europe. However, as the Director of Research explained to the Board when the memorandum came before it, further studies were in progress.

Mr. Southard then suggested that an Ad Hoc Committee of the Board should be set up to analyze the problems arising out of the international payments situation and to clarify thinking on the relative merits of possible means of adjustment to meet these problems. Some Executive Directors doubted

---

[2] *Annual Report, 1949,* pp. 15, 21, 22.

whether the time was appropriate to seek such conclusions, but after discussion Mr. Southard's proposal was accepted, Mr. Tansley (United Kingdom) dissenting. The committee, under the chairmanship of Mr. Koo (China), comprised Messrs. Bolton (United Kingdom), Carli (Italy), D'Ascoli (Venezuela), de Largentaye (France), Rasminsky, Saad (Egypt), Southard, and Sucharda (Czechoslovakia). In practice, however, most of its meetings were attended by the whole Board, including the Managing Director and the Deputy Managing Director. Its agenda, also proposed by Mr. Southard, covered the role of exchange rate revision among other possible measures, basic considerations relative to exchange rate changes at that time, necessary supplementary measures, and techniques of rate changes.

The committee held 19 meetings between August 18 and September 8. During the first 13 of these the position of each Western European member country was reviewed seriatim. The remaining meetings were devoted to the consideration of an interim report. After summarizing the importance of the problem, and the effects to be expected from a devaluation on exports, on imports, on the allocation of domestic resources, and on progress toward convertibility, the report reached a general conclusion, of which the following is a condensation:

> In the opinion of the Committee it is essential that member countries in Western Europe should adopt with the shortest possible delay measures which will tend best to solve their balance of payments difficulties. . . . For its own part, the Committee is convinced that taking Western Europe as a whole, adjustments of exchange rates varying in degree but in most cases substantial, are opportune and essential, and . . . that the member countries should now review their rate structure, and should determine, in consultation with the Fund, to what extent adjustment should be made in each individual case where it is appropriate. . . .

The committee was not, however, unanimous. Mr. Sucharda thought that the Board could not properly come to the conclusion which the report reached. Mr. Bernard de Margerie (France), Alternate to Mr. de Largentaye, was prepared to accept the technical parts of the report, but thought it would be unwise for the committee to arrive at a text inviting members to change their exchange rates. Mr. Rasminsky and Mr. Tansley opposed the adoption of any formal report in which such an invitation was given.

The report with these reservations was given to the Board on September 8, but on the following day the Board decided to postpone further consideration "until an early practicable date after the Meeting of the Board of Governors."

Altering exchange rates

The *Queen Mary*, carrying many delegates to the Fourth Annual Meeting, arrived in New York on Monday, September 12. In view of this schedule, the beginning of the Meeting had been postponed until Tuesday. The Governors met in open session that day, and again on Friday, September 16. In the meantime, as an experiment, they conducted two informal Discussion Groups, one on Exchange and Monetary Policy (based on Chapters I and II of the Annual Report for 1949) and one on Exchange Restrictions and Monetary Reserves (based on Chapters I, III, and V).

The keynote of the Annual Meeting was struck by the Chairman of the Board of Governors of the Fund, Mr. Pierre Mendès-France, in his opening address on September 13. "A different and new problem" had arisen, he said:

> In certain countries, a sellers' market has been replaced by a buyers' market. . . . While gratifying, such a situation is also the cause of serious worries. . . . From an international point of view . . . the first effect of the buyers' market . . . is to increase the disequilibrium in balances of payments, causing great difficulties to certain countries. And it would be futile to hope that exchange stability and freedom of transactions would be durably restored without equilibrium in balances of payments.[3]

Introducing the Annual Report for 1949, Mr. Gutt drew attention to a warning in the Annual Report for 1946 that there was a risk that some countries might maintain rates of exchange which would prove too high when production had revived.[4] The warning had been repeated in subsequent reports, he pointed out,

> and its importance will escape no one's attention, especially if it is taken in conjunction with another primary purpose of the Fund: the ultimate establishment of a multilateral system of payments.[5]

Nevertheless, the only explicit reference in the open sessions of the Meeting to the subject that was uppermost in everyone's mind was made by Mr. Pavel Eisler, the Alternate Governor for Czechoslovakia, to whose country, as he said, much of the discussion was of no direct concern. He spoke of the widespread expectation in the press that devaluation would be on the agenda, and moved that all the sessions of the Annual Meeting should be open to the public in order that the arguments adduced on both sides should be made known. This motion was lost. In the Discussion Groups a similar discretion prevailed. Reporting to the Governors on the work of these Groups, the Managing Director said that, with one exception, those who had spoken had supported the view expressed in the Annual Report.[6] The one dissentient, who was again the representative of Czechoslovakia, had suggested that too much stress had been laid in the Report on exchange adjustment compared with other measures, such as the encouragement of interregional trade.

Behind the scenes, however, there was great activity. The British Chancellor of the Exchequer, Sir Stafford Cripps, had privately informed the Managing Director on Thursday, September 15, that the United Kingdom proposed to

[3] *Summary Proceedings, 1949,* p. 6.

[4] *Annual Report, 1946,* p. 12.

[5] *Summary Proceedings, 1949,* p. 10.

[6] *Ibid.,* p. 37.

devalue the pound. British officials also notified the Governors for the other sterling area countries, seeking to arrange for a simultaneous devaluation.

The outcome was that at the end of the dinner on Friday evening, which, as customary, closed the Meeting, the senior members of the staff who were present went off to the office, still in formal attire, and started to prepare for the expected announcements. At 12:22 A.M. on Saturday, September 17, letters proposing a devaluation arrived from the United Kingdom and South Africa; similar communications from Australia, Norway, and India were delivered before noon on that day, from Denmark and Egypt on Sunday afternoon and evening, from Finland, Iceland, Greece, France, Belgium, the Netherlands, and Canada on Monday, from Iraq on Tuesday, and from Luxembourg on Wednesday. For each of these countries the staff prepared an analysis of the economic situation, an appraisal of the effect of the proposed devaluation, and a recommendation whether it should be approved. The Board met twice on Saturday, three times on Sunday, and three times on Monday, September 19. Meanwhile, the principal members of the staff ate at the office and slept, when they could, at neighboring hotels.

As had long been apparent, the key devaluation was that of sterling; once the new rate for the pound had been set, other currencies could be adjusted to conform to it and to the dollar. Presenting the case for a devaluation from $4.03 to $2.80 (by 30.5 per cent), Mr. Bolton said that the United Kingdom had been forced to take this step by the growing loss of gold from its reserves. He foresaw no spectacular gain in dollar income; indeed, he was not sure whether the expected increase in the volume of exports would offset lower dollar prices. However, the competitiveness of British goods in non-dollar markets would be increased, at least to the extent that its commercial rivals did not devalue equally.

The Board accepted without difficulty the need for the devaluation, for which it had, of course, been fully prepared. The magnitude of the proposed change met with some comment, but after Mr. Bolton had explained it by the recent fall in exports from the sterling area and the rapid increase in the discount on the various types of "cheap sterling," Directors expressed willingness to accept the proposed rate since His Majesty's Government thought this necessary to achieve its purposes. Mr. Sucharda abstained from voting.

The letter from the United Kingdom had also proposed similar devaluations in the dependent territories, other than British Honduras. This created some difficulty for Directors representing less developed areas whose products competed with those from the British territories; however, on the understanding that the Ad Hoc Committee would later study the problems of primary producing countries, the proposal was accepted, Mr. D'Ascoli dissenting. Similar issues arose on the proposals by South Africa and Australia to devalue to the same extent as sterling. Mr. D'Ascoli abstained from supporting both countries' proposals, and Mr. Sucharda from supporting that of South Africa. The proposals from Finland and Greece, which had no par values, covered changes in their exchange rates, as did that for France. For French colonial possessions in the Pacific it was agreed that the par value might be abandoned and the CFP franc pegged to the French franc.

The proposed devaluations of the currencies of the dependent territories raised a general question of some difficulty, viz., whether a proposal by a member to devalue its metropolitan currency and the currencies of its dependent territories had to be considered as a whole or could be taken piecemeal. The relevant provision in the Articles of Agreement is Article IV, Section 9, which reads as follows:

> *Separate currencies within a member's territories.*—A member proposing a change in the par value of its currency shall be deemed, unless it declares otherwise, to be proposing a corresponding change in the par value of the separate currencies of all territories in respect of which it has accepted this Agreement under Article XX, Section 2 (*g*). It shall, however, be open to a member to declare that its proposal relates either to the metropolitan currency alone, or only to one or more specified separate currencies, or to the metropolitan currency and one or more separate currencies.

The view of the Legal Department, based on the logic, philosophy, and legislative history of the Section, was that the member's proposal must be regarded as a single whole; the Fund could not accept part of it and reject other parts. This view was supported by some Directors, but opposed by others. In particular, Mr. D'Ascoli argued that the obligation propounded by the Legal Department was impracticable, because it might conceivably make it necessary for the Fund either to accept an unjustified change in a dependent currency or to reject a justified change in the metropolitan currency. On the other hand, the Legal Department's opinion was supported by Messrs. Tansley and de Largentaye, who based their argument on the affinity between the metropolitan currency and the currencies of the dependent territories, by Mr. McFarlane (Australia), and by Mr. H. M. H. A. van der Valk (Netherlands), Alternate to Mr. Beyen, who concurred. No formal vote was taken, because Mr. Southard (who shared Mr. D'Ascoli's position) asked for the point to be deferred. However, it has not subsequently been raised.

The country which had the greatest difficulty in reaching a decision on a new par value was Belgium. It originally proposed, on the evening of September 19, to abandon the par value and allow the franc to fluctuate. Executive Directors were concerned at this plan, which might encourage other members similarly to embark on systems of fluctuating rates, thus undermining the stability of currencies which it was the main aim of the Fund to support. However, on a vote, the Board approved a proposal by Mr. Cigliana-Piazza (Italy) that the decision should be as follows:

> The Fund recognizes that the plan proposed by the Government of Belgium is an appropriate step in view of the exigencies of the situation. The Fund therefore raises no objection to the plan and takes note of the intention expressed by the Belgian Government to consult with the Fund and to propose a new parity as soon as circumstances warrant.

An alternative draft, which would not have included the words "an appropriate step," was defeated by 53,600 votes to 38,490. Two days later, however, Mr. de Selliers said that the Belgian Government, recognizing the dangers of a fluctuating rate, now proposed a devaluation from BF 1 = \$0.0228167 to BF 1 = \$0.02 (i.e., by 12.4 per cent), and this was readily accepted by the Board.

After the devaluations

The Ad Hoc Committee met again on September 28 to consider whether to review the problems in less developed areas, but decided that it was premature to do so until the effect of the announced devaluations on other currencies had become clearer. Two days later the Board took up the Ad Hoc Committee's report of September 8. A number of Directors opposed a motion to adopt the report, believing that to insist on coming to formal decisions in terms that anticipated members' proposals to change their exchange rates was unnecessary and dangerous. Such decisions, they thought, usurped the initiative reserved in the Articles of Agreement to members themselves, and ran the risk of forcing members to act against their will. Other Directors thought that the report was fully justified by the events that had intervened. Eventually the report was adopted by 50,400 votes against 38,240.

Following this vote, the Ad Hoc Committee was instructed to continue with its agenda. Beginning on October 4, it held 14 more meetings, at which it reviewed the problems of a number of less developed countries. Its conclusions were summarized in a second report, in which it suggested that exchange rate adjustments were not called for in these countries as a whole, and that where a need for them arose it might be due as much to changing conditions in the country's major markets as to balance of payments disequilibrium arising from other causes. In the committee's view, its work had demonstrated the great advantage to be derived from detailed examination of members' payments problems in advance of the need for policy decisions. This report, from which Mr. Tansley abstained, was accepted by the Board on November 28, and the committee having then finished its work, it was abolished.

The role of the Fund in the devaluations of 1949 has frequently been treated as unimportant. It is said, in effect, that the Fund was a mere rubber stamp for governmental decisions. It is true that, as the Board itself recognized, its preparations for dealing with proposals to devalue were inadequate, in that the problems of the primary producing countries had not been studied. But the

Board did not consist of internationalists detached from the countries which they represented; on the contrary, at every stage in the policy-forming process described in the previous subsection Governments were kept informed of the views and plans disclosed. Thus, even though the timing and the extent of the devaluation of sterling were not known until the last minute, all other Governments were far advanced with their preparations for similar action. Without this preparation, no such orderly adjustment of exchange rates could have been made so quickly and so smoothly. Moreover, it was important that each country's proposal had to run the gauntlet of the criticisms of other Directors. Even if, to put the Fund's role no higher, it functioned merely as a forum in which plans for devaluation could be announced, its existence must have encouraged the formulation of proposals that would prove acceptable to world opinion, rather than unilateral decisions of the kind that were taken after 1931.

DRAWINGS

There were no large drawings from the Fund during 1948–49. The total amount drawn was $88,610,000, of which India took $55,860,000, Brazil $15 million, and South Africa $10 million; small drawings by Costa Rica, Egypt, Nicaragua, and Yugoslavia made up the total. Norway also purchased US$6.1 million from the Fund with gold that it had been holding in Ottawa.

The transactions recorded in the previous paragraph were not completed without argument. The criteria which Mr. Overby (United States) had laid down in January 1948 were applied by him to question several of the drawings, and gave rise to an increasingly sharp division within the Board between those who still believed that members had automatic rights to draw and the United States.

The issue was first raised in a systematic form in October 1948, when the Board was told that the Netherlands might need to draw on the Fund both dollars to anticipate payments due from the ECA and Belgian francs to meet an expected balance of payments deficit vis-à-vis Belgium. For these purposes, the Netherlands sought the abrogation of the informal understanding which it had given that it would not draw on the Fund.

Mr. Beyen (Netherlands) contended that drawings of the kinds mentioned would be in accordance with the Articles, and said that capital needed for reconstruction would be obtained elsewhere. He recalled the Board's statement that it would not seek to know the use to be made of each parcel of exchange purchased.[7] Mr. Overby, however, questioned whether the drawings proposed would indeed be temporary, since the Netherlands' deficit appeared to be due to the needs of reconstruction and other nontemporary factors. Was it not the fact, he inquired, that the Netherlands' deficit was likely to continue beyond 1952? At any rate,

[7] *Annual Report, 1946*, p. 13.

it was up to the Netherlands to show how and when repayment could be effected in a relatively short time.

The Director of Research reminded the Board that the terms of the "ERP Decision" showed that the limitation on the use of the Fund's resources would be a quantitative one. The aim of the decision was to maintain members' access to the Fund at an adequate level in readiness for the end of ERP. This was significant because the drawings so far made by the Netherlands had been very limited, and its prospective need for Belgian francs was not more than 6 per cent of its quota. He thought that the Netherlands should be in balance well before 1955.

Mr. Ansiaux (Belgium) said that Belgium would not object to the Netherlands drawing Belgian francs. Other Executive Directors pointed out that on no previous occasion had a member been asked to demonstrate what arrangements it would be able to make to repay. The most forcible intervention was that of Mr. Bolton (United Kingdom). He deprecated what he called an "increasing number of interpretations reading into the Fund Agreement limitations which were not in the text. Because of such limitations [he said] the Fund was now of no use to its European members; it carried obligations but no benefits." The latter assertion was challenged by Mr. Overby. He said that he assumed that European members had as much interest as others in seeing that the Fund acted as a policymaker and umpire in administering rules of fair conduct in foreign exchange policies and practices. Apart from the use of its resources, the Fund had a vital role as advisor. However, in the outcome, Mr. Overby did not object to the withdrawal of the Netherlands' informal understanding, provided that it was agreed that the use of Article V, Sections 3 and 5, would not be estopped on a future occasion by the consideration that the member had not been warned.

On October 14, 1948, the staff reported on a discussion which it had had with the Governor of the Fund for Costa Rica about the possibility of the member's drawing up to $1.25 million (a fourth of its quota) on two conditions: (1) that Costa Rica should at once adopt a program to curtail its imports along the lines recommended by a Fund mission, and (2) that it committed itself unconditionally to repurchase the drawing within a year, out of the seasonal improvement in its exports. When the Board discussed this proposal, Mr. Martínez-Ostos (Mexico) pointed out that dollars to effect the repurchase would have to be earned within six months rather than a year, because the period of high export receipts would then end. This would mean that the service charge would be at the rate of 1½ per cent per annum. He and other Executive Directors asked whether the Fund could in fact stipulate special repurchase arrangements of the type suggested. Mr. Martínez-Ostos added that he thought it unfortunate that the Fund should attach special conditions to a drawing by one of its smallest members. The staff represented that, since the Fund had the power under Article XX, Section 4 *(i)*, to postpone a drawing, it must follow that it could take the less drastic course of stipulating special safeguards. They pointed out that this was the first occasion on which any member had sought to draw a full 25 per cent of its quota at one time. Since this was therefore a special case, no precedent for it existed, nor would one necessarily be created. On this understanding, the Board expressed no objection to the proposed drawing on the conditions suggested by the staff.

In October 1948 the Board had before it a staff report on South Africa's exchange position which called attention to the member's loss of reserves. Mr. Overby then gave warning that if South Africa sought to draw on the Fund he would have to ask questions about the effectiveness of the remedial measures that it was taking. Subsequently, as discussed below, South Africa introduced exchange restrictions, and these were before the Board when, in December, it came to the Fund with a request to draw $10 million. Mr. Overby said that he felt that the member needed to take more adequate steps to cope with its problems, and he proposed that the Board should require to be told what these steps were before any further drawings were made. The Board decided to communicate with South Africa along the lines of Mr. Overby's proposal, but to express no objection to the drawing of $10 million.

Also in December 1948 India drew $16,120,000; this transaction was not brought to the Board. During the first four months of 1949 four further drawings were made, all of which were considered by the Board and approved without difficulty—two by India, and one each by Brazil and Egypt.

POLICY ON DRAWINGS RECONSIDERED

In May 1949, however, the position was transformed by a memorandum from Mr. Southard (United States), who had become an Executive Director in February. This memorandum reported the outcome of a review by the U.S. authorities of the Fund's policy on the use of its resources. Mr. Southard recalled the interpretation of the Articles obtained by Mr. White in 1946,[8] and the notification sent to members in June 1947.[9] He insisted that drawings from the Fund were required to be temporary, and therefore should be subject to close scrutiny. If any doubt was raised by a proposed drawing, it should be resolved in favor of the Fund, not of the member. Specifically, a country which was rationing its dollar resources was, prima facie, in fundamental disequilibrium and therefore not entitled to draw on the Fund. He proposed that, for the future, requests for drawings should be tested against four criteria, each of which

[8] See above, pp. 148–49.

[9] See above, p. 191.

should require a determination by the Fund. These were (1) that the par value of the member was an appropriate one; (2) that its disequilibrium was temporary; (3) that the drawing was not needed for purposes of rehabilitation or development; and (4) that the member was "undertaking all steps essential to assume as soon as possible its full obligations under the Articles of Agreement of the Fund, in particular, maintenance of convertibility, avoidance of restrictions on current payments, and avoidance of discriminatory currency arrangements and multiple currency practices."

A few days after this memorandum was circulated, its provisions were put to the test by a request from Mexico to be given a contingent right to draw on the Fund. Mexico was endeavoring to establish a new par value, and needed for this purpose to be able to call on some reserves in addition to its existing gold and foreign exchange holdings. The Board decided to inform the Mexican authorities that (*a*) the Fund believed that early stabilization of the peso at a viable rate would be desirable; (*b*) on condition that Mexico put forward a proposal for a new rate to which the Fund could concur, and followed appropriate fiscal, credit, and trade policies, Mexico might draw on the Fund; and (*c*) specifically, the Fund would not object to drawings of $22.5 million within the ensuing twelve months. This decision created what in later years became known as a stand-by arrangement. Mexico established a new par value in June 1949, and in January 1950 the Board formally confirmed that its access to the Fund's resources was unimpaired. However, Mexico did not need to draw again on the Fund until 1954.

Despite Mr. Southard's concurrence in Mexico's request, his criteria were gravely disturbing. They appeared to restrict even further than the four tests laid down by Mr. Overby (while U.S. Executive Director) the members' access to the Fund's resources, and to reassert in unmistakable terms the intention to "police" drawings, which was so strongly opposed by the British delegation to Washington in 1943. Indeed, Mr. Southard's criteria may be regarded as a crucial stage in the establishment of the principle of conditionality of drawings. This principle was to prove an essential prerequisite for the development of a policy on the use of the Fund's resources which would win acceptance by those members whose currencies would be used.

It must also be recalled that, at the moment when Mr. Southard's principles were enunciated, doubts about the appropriateness of exchange rates in many parts of the world were already crystallizing. This implied that many members, including most of those with the largest quotas other than the United States, were already in fundamental disequilibrium and could not, therefore, justifiably draw on the Fund.

The implications of this last point became clear on July 15, when the Netherlands sought to draw BF 650 million. Mr. Southard said that the circumstances surrounding the request suggested that the Netherlands' use of the Fund's resources would not be temporary. He questioned the appropriateness of the exchange rate for the guilder and asked what measures were being taken to correct the apparent disequilibrium. The Netherlands' deficit with Belgium had increased each year since 1946; why, therefore, did the staff now suggest that the deficit for May and June should be covered by a drawing? The staff explanation was that, from July 1, the Netherlands would obtain fresh intra-European credits in Belgian francs, but that those which had been made available for 1948–49 were insufficient. Mr. Beyen (Netherlands) agreed with the staff on this point. At the same time, he did not think that the Board could properly refuse to consider future drawings. When the debate was resumed five days later, Mr. Beyen said that he believed Mr. Southard's view was inconsistent both with the Articles of Agreement and with the terms of the "ERP Decision." He was prepared to agree to a postponement of the Board's decision, but not beyond the end of July, since payment was already due to Belgium.

On July 29, the Board again considered the Netherlands' request. Mr. Beyen and Mr. Tansley (United Kingdom) pressed for an immediate decision in favor of the Netherlands, and were supported by Mr. de Selliers (Belgium) and Mr. de Margerie (France). These Directors urged that Rule G-3, which provided that the Fund would effectuate a drawing on the third business day after the receipt of a duly authenticated request, should be regarded as fundamental lest members should lose confidence in the Fund. The staff also advised that the Rule ought not to be used for unreasonable postponements or to secure the virtual rejection of the request. Mr. D'Ascoli (Venezuela), however, asked for a postponement because he was uncertain about the temporariness of the Netherlands' need, and Mr. Saad (Egypt) disagreed with the staff view about the use of Rule G-3.

In the event, the request was postponed in successive months until the matter ended by the Netherlands, on November 3, withdrawing its request. The fact that the guilder had been devalued by 30 per cent on September 19 no doubt influenced the Government's decision to withdraw.

A request by Yugoslavia to purchase $3 million was considered by the Board in September. Mr. Southard then said that, while he could not agree that a country having a fundamental disequilibrium could draw on the Fund to meet an added temporary disequilibrium, Yugoslavia was not in this position. It appeared, he said, that Yugoslavia was doing its best both to re-establish its export trade with Western Europe and to assume its full obligations under the Fund Agreement. Nevertheless there was some uncertainty about Yugoslavia's ability to repurchase. He took the opportunity to point out that some countries appeared to look on their reserves as essentially resources to be spent to finance imports; this raised a serious question of principle which the Board had not yet resolved. It was, however, helpful that the Yugoslav Government had expressed its intention of making all possible efforts to repay the purchase in approximately two years. Other Executive Directors agreed with the Yugoslav request, and the drawing was approved.

REPURCHASE OBLIGATIONS CLARIFIED

In preparation for calculating the repurchases due from members as at April 30, 1948, the staff made a close examination of the relevant provisions in Article V, Section 7, and Schedule B. This showed that some clarification of these provisions would be needed. The first question that arose concerned the date when repurchase obligations accrued: was this on April 30, or on the date when the request for repurchase was made, or on the date when the repurchase was effected? The problem was that Article V, Section 7 *(c)*, limited repurchases to amounts which would not (i) reduce the repurchasing member's own reserves below its quota; nor (ii) reduce the Fund's holdings of the repurchasing member's currency below 75 per cent of its quota; nor (iii) increase the Fund's holdings of the currencies being used to make the repurchase above 75 per cent of the quotas of the members whose currencies they were. If repurchase obligations were calculated as at April 30, but repurchases were not made until some later date, the effect of intervening transactions on the member's reserves or on the Fund's holdings might be that one or other of these limits might be breached when the repurchase was made.

Despite this difficulty, the staff advised the Board that the legislative history of the provision made it clear that repurchase obligations accrued at the end of the Fund's financial year. They pointed out that it was in the Fund's power, if so desired, to offset a reduction of the repurchasing member's currency below 75 per cent of its quota by purchasing that currency for gold.

When the staff's recommendation was considered by the Board, most of the Executive Directors felt that the solution proposed was the best one, if only because the repurchase obligation ought not to be determined by fortuitous delays between April 30 and the date when the obligation could be calculated. Mr. de Selliers (Belgium), however, asked that the Board should decide that, if a repurchase should reduce the Fund's holdings of the repurchasing member's currency below 75 per cent of its quota, the Fund should always restore these holdings to 75 per cent by purchasing that currency for gold. The Board was unwilling to commit the Fund in this way, and the only decision taken was that the staff's recommendation was accepted.[10]

The second point on which clarification proved to be needed arose from the requirement in Article V, Section 7 *(b)*, that the repurchase, to be made "at the

[10] E.B. Decision No. 419-1, April 11, 1949; below, Vol. III, p. 244.

end of each financial year," should have regard to fluctuations in the member's monetary reserves and in the Fund's holdings of its currency "during the year." Since the repurchase could not even be calculated until the year-end figures of all members' reserves were available, it was clear that it could not physically be made during the year to which it related. This meant that the repurchase would show up as a decrease in the member's reserves during the year after the one to which it related; this would affect the member's repurchase obligation at the ensuing April 30, and again at the April 30 following. In view of this, the staff recommended that the repurchase should be deemed to have been made in the year to which it related, and that the member's reserves and the Fund's holdings of the member's currency, as at the end of that year, should be adjusted by the amount of the repurchase. This was agreed by the Board without difficulty.[11]

The first actual repurchase was made in May 1949; Costa Rica then bought back colones equivalent to $874,000, paying for them with gold and U.S. dollars. This transaction discharged an obligation incurred under Article V, Section 7 *(b)*, as a result of the increase in Costa Rica's monetary reserves during the year ended April 30, 1948, on which date the Fund's holdings of colones were 93 per cent of Costa Rica's quota. Similar operations by Belgium in August and Nicaragua in September brought the total repurchased to $2,320,000. That by Belgium also resulted from an increase in its monetary reserves during the year ended April 30, 1948, in which period it had bought dollars from the Fund equivalent to 15 per cent of its quota. Some objections were raised by Belgium to the staff's calculation of the repurchase due, but these were overruled by the Board.[12] The repurchase by Nicaragua was a voluntary one, reversing its drawing in November 1948. This gave rise to a legal problem—whether such a repurchase must be made in gold—which will be reviewed in a later chapter.

RESTRICTION PROBLEMS

By coincidence, three other considerable policy questions which came before the Board during this year all related to the Union of South Africa. Two of these are discussed in the present section and the third in the following one.

Exchange restrictions

Early in November 1948 the Fund received from South Africa a letter stating that, in view of the urgent need to restrict imports other than from the sterling area, the South African Government had decided to limit such imports by means of exchange restrictions. Transmitting this letter to the Board, the staff advised

[11] E.B. Decision No. 447-5, June 17, 1949; below, Vol. III, p. 244.

[12] E.B. Decision No. 486-2, October 7, 1949; below, Vol. III, pp. 271, 272.

that the decision of the South African Government involved not a modification of exchange restrictions, which was permissible under Article XIV, but their introduction, which required the prior approval of the Fund under Article VIII, Section 2. When the Board considered the South African letter and the staff memorandum on November 12, Mr. McFarlane (Australia) justified the introduction of the restrictions by reference to the serious loss of reserves that South Africa had sustained, and urged that, despite South Africa's lack of consultation, the restrictions should be approved.

The need for some restrictions was, indeed, not challenged: South Africa's reserves and balance of payments were admittedly in a serious condition. As mentioned already, Mr. Overby (United States) pointed this out when South Africa drew from the Fund—which happened while the question of its exchange restrictions was still before the Board. Nevertheless, the Board's discussion of the restrictions took several weeks. This was because their imposition proved to raise several difficult questions. Early in January 1949, Mr. Henry J. Tasca (United States), Alternate to Mr. Overby, summarized them as follows: (1) Did South Africa's exchange measures constitute the introduction of restrictions? (2) If so, was such an introduction subject to Article VIII? (3) If Article VIII applied, were the restrictions appropriate to South Africa's problem?

On the first two of these questions, South Africa contended that the imposition of its restrictions amounted to an adaptation and not to an introduction. The measures were therefore covered by Article XIV, and Article VIII did not apply. The South African authorities argued that in earlier years they had imposed restrictions, and while these had latterly been removed, after the country's economic situation had improved, the power to impose them had been retained. Hence, South Africa could be said to be continuously adapting its restrictions to current conditions. Several Executive Directors were disposed to accept this view. Moreover, Mr. McFarlane pointed out that the South African Government had been advised by the Board in October to impose restrictions on imports, and nothing had been said then about the need for prior consultation.

The staff, however, pointed out that South Africa had in fact declared officially in November 1946 that it did not maintain any restrictions on making payments or transfers on current international transactions. On the facts, therefore, the staff advised that South Africa's action did amount to the introduction of restrictions. These were fully justified by South Africa's economic position, but the need for consultation should be asserted.

In the event, the cleavage of opinion in the Board on this issue necessitated a vote. This was taken in two stages. Directors first considered a motion to the effect that the Fund was not required to determine whether South Africa's action was an adaptation or an introduction, but should reply only on the substantive justification for the restrictions. This was defeated by 58,800 votes to

33,290. A second motion, to the effect that South Africa's action was deemed to be an introduction and subject to the approval of the Fund under Article VIII, Section 2 *(a)*, was passed by 62,580 votes to 25,760.

Following this decision, a letter was sent to South Africa recording the Board's consideration of the problem, stating that the Fund's approval should have been obtained, but approving the restrictions introduced and authorizing South Africa to adapt them to changing circumstances without prior consultation. (This last point was necessary because the staff had advised the Board that once the restrictions had been authorized under Article VIII they remained under Article VIII, so that the member needed the Fund's approval to adapt them.)

Mr. Tasca's third question involved the discriminatory nature of the restrictions imposed. Some Executive Directors felt that the difference between South Africa's economic position vis-à-vis sterling and vis-à-vis other currencies was not so marked as to justify the discrimination. Some also expressed reluctance to approve restrictions that included such a feature. Mr. Rasminsky (Canada) sought to obtain the Board's approval for a draft reply to South Africa which would have questioned whether the discrimination was justified.

However, the consensus of the Board was that, in assessing its prospects of improving its balance of payments, South Africa was justified in distinguishing between the sterling area and the rest of the world, if only because it might reasonably hope for a continuation of capital investment from the United Kingdom. Accordingly, the letter sent to South Africa only drew attention to the discriminatory character of the restrictions, and asked that the member keep in touch with the Fund on the matter.

Import restrictions

Four months after the above decision was taken—that is, in May 1949—South Africa sought the approval of the GATT for some new import restrictions, and the GATT inquired of the Fund whether these restrictions were justified by South Africa's balance of payments. This was the first time that the GATT had consulted the Fund since the inception of the agreement authorized by the Board in the previous September. The request for the Fund's advice raised doubts in the Board about the extent of the Fund's responsibility. Specifically, the question was raised whether the Fund should merely report facts to the GATT, or should also provide an evaluation of the facts.

Mr. Southard (United States) thought that full consultation, such as the agreement with the GATT visualized, necessarily implied an evaluation. Mr. McFarlane, however, differed. He suggested that only the GATT could decide on the implications of import restrictions for its other members; the Fund should not risk an independent opinion which might clash with that of the GATT. Once more the problem of discrimination arose. The exact nature of the South African proposals was not made clear at first, and Directors doubted whether enough data were available to conclude that discrimination was justified. It was accordingly decided to transmit to the GATT a staff study of the balance of payments of South Africa, which justified import restrictions, but to omit the last paragraph of this study, which would have advised the GATT that some discrimination was not unreasonable.

This did not, however, end the discussion on the role of the Fund. Mr. McFarlane continued to urge that the Board should be very cautious in such matters. As the representative of Australia, he said that his Government had understood when entering the Fund that the Fund would not interfere in matters of import restrictions. As against that, Mr. Saad (Egypt), who had been representing the Fund in the consultation with the GATT, pointed out that, where import restrictions were imposed for balance of payments reasons, the responsibilities of the Fund and the GATT were interlocked. No final decision on this issue was reached during the year, and the discussion was resumed in 1950, when further restrictions were submitted by South Africa to the GATT and a fresh consultation took place. The practice of the Fund, however, has been to provide not only the facts of a member's position but also an evaluation of these facts for the guidance of the GATT.[13]

PREMIUM PRICES FOR GOLD AGAIN

The problem of the price of gold continued to trouble the Board during 1948–49. It arose principally in connection with some plans put forward by South Africa, but there were also discussions of proposals by Belgium and Southern Rhodesia. These will be summarized first.

Belgium

In order to support gold mining in the Belgian Congo, the Belgian Government decided in October 1948 to permit sales of gold at premium prices in its domestic market. This amounted to legalizing the existing black market in gold. Some Executive Directors approved the plan in the expectation that it would strengthen, rather than weaken, the Belgian franc. Others, however, feared that it might undermine other currencies; they pointed out that some of the gold would inevitably leak out of the domestic market. In any case, the plan was clearly inconsistent with the Fund's wish to discourage sales of gold at a premium. This was pointed out to Belgium. Seven months later the Government modified its policy, and reserved its domestic market for gold for industrial, artistic, and scientific uses exclusively to the product of the Congolese gold mines. When this was reported to the Board, Mr. Southard (United States)

[13] See below, Vol. II, Chapter 16.

commented that it was an improvement on the original plan, though he still disliked it as he disliked all premium sales arrangements. The Board, however, expressed no objection to the proposal.

Southern Rhodesia

In May 1948 Southern Rhodesia introduced a production subsidy to gold mines, affording a minimum payment of £1 7s. 6d. an ounce for all gold produced in Southern Rhodesia, with additions up to a further £1 an ounce for gold from mines of economic value to Southern Rhodesia that otherwise would have had to close. As Southern Rhodesia was technically a nonmetropolitan area of the United Kingdom for purposes of the Fund Agreement, responsibility was assumed by Mr. Tansley (United Kingdom) in the discussion in the Board. He pointed out, however, that as far as internal policies were concerned Southern Rhodesia was a self-governing territory. Its Government had expressed regret that it had unwittingly broken the Fund's rules. It had explained, however, that the plan could not be modified until after the end of its current fiscal year (i.e., not before March 31, 1949). It had considered adopting the Canadian plan of a graduated subsidy, but considered this to be administratively unworkable.

A further report made to the Board in May 1949 showed that the plan had been modified so as to vary the subsidy according to the grade of ore processed, with the highest subsidy accruing to medium-grade ore. This avoided any flat rate increase in the price of gold, and the new arrangements were accordingly deemed not to contravene the Articles or the Fund's policy. During the discussion Mr. Southard repeated that the United States deprecated any plan which would increase the output of gold, a remark which drew from Mr. Joseph F. Parkinson (Canada), Alternate to Mr. Rasminsky, the comment that the Canadian plan had, indeed, increased the output of gold by some $10-15 million a year, but that this was negligible in relation to the improvement in Canada's balance of payments. Mr. McFarlane (Australia) said that Australian production had not, in fact, increased.

South Africa

More serious questions were raised by a proposal by South Africa to sell, at a premium, part of the output of its gold mines in the form of semiprocessed gold. When this plan first came before the Board, in September 1948, Mr. Overby (United States) suggested that the demand could not come from legitimate users of gold since these had no need to pay a premium; the United States and the United Kingdom were ready to supply all genuine needs for gold at slightly more than $35 an ounce. Mr. M. H. de Kock (Governor of the South African Reserve Bank and Alternate Governor of the Fund for South Africa), who represented South Africa at the ensuing discussion, replied that his Government had been informed that the amount made available in this way was insufficient to satisfy the demand. He added that the amount sold would be small, which led some Executive Directors to question whether the plan could materially assist the South African producers. Mr. de Kock's reply was that the Government was desirous of showing the mining companies that it was seeking to help the industry, and that South African producers felt entitled to a share in the world trade in premium gold. In the outcome, the Board decided on October 5 to inform South Africa that the Board could not approve the proposed sale unless South Africa was able to take effective measures to satisfy itself that gold sold under the plan would be used only for bona fide and customary industrial, professional, or artistic purposes.

Four months later South Africa informed the Fund that it was proposing to sell 100,000 ounces of gold to a London broker at $38.20 a fine ounce. That the final use of the gold would be in accordance with the Fund's requirements would be ensured by the standing of the buyer, who was bound by a condition of the sale to use the gold only for approved purposes. The staff, however, reminded the Board that semiprocessed gold of the type in question was obtainable in New York at between $35.20 and $36 an ounce; it seemed therefore inherently unlikely that the condition would be met. The Board agreed with this view, and a letter was sent to South Africa calling attention to the presumption created by the price quoted, and asking that if possible the contract should be postponed to enable further consultation to be held. At the same time, an announcement was made to the press explaining that the Fund had never approved any specific sale of gold at a premium price, and that it was in touch with the South African Government concerning its most recent proposal.

Discussions with the Government continued, but were somewhat exacerbated by a statement made in the South African Parliament by Mr. Havenga, Minister of Finance. Mr. Havenga said that the Government was assured of the bona fides of the London broker in question, and that the existence of an unsatisfied demand for gold at a premium price was confirmed by a proposal that had been made to South Africa to set up a factory there to process gold for shipment abroad at a price which would considerably more than cover the cost of processing. Unfortunately, his speech concluded with a passage which appeared to criticize the Fund's policy of maintaining par values, adding "the fiction that gold is worth only $35 an ounce cannot endure much longer."

The Board decided on receipt of a copy of this speech to issue a further press statement replying to it. A little later the Managing Director came to the conclusion that the time had come for him to make a personal appeal to Mr. Havenga. After consulting the Board, he wrote a letter in which he said, inter alia:

> For the past weeks South Africa and the Fund have been corresponding mostly by way of communiqués across the Oceans. I may tell you that neither the Directors on the Fund's Executive Board nor myself like it. We are not Homeric

> heroes, shouting abuse at each other in front of the armies. We are people entrusted with an important financial job, dealing with people, like you, with an important financial job. For that reason we should understand each other.

He went on to suggest that there should be high level discussions, either in South Africa or, if Mr. Havenga preferred, in Washington.

The upshot was that the Managing Director himself, accompanied by Mr. Parsons, Director of Operations, and two other members of the staff, visited South Africa at the beginning of May. After three days of conversations, which he described as "cordial," Mr. Gutt reported to the Board that the South African Government was prepared to require purchasers of semiprocessed gold to produce both an affidavit that it would be used only for approved purposes and an import license from the country in which it would eventually be sold. Mr. Gutt formed the opinion that the Government was genuinely anxious to ensure that the sales did not lead to a leakage of gold into hoards, and asked for the Board's approval of the Government's proposals.

The Executive Directors considered that the precautions offered by South Africa represented an improvement, and although they still doubted whether there was in fact a large genuine demand at the proposed premium price, they were prepared to accept the arrangements suggested. However, since Mr. Parkinson said that he expected that gold producers in other countries would ask for a similar concession, it was agreed that any announcement made of the Board's agreement should be in guarded terms. The matter ended with a report to the Board by the Director of Operations that South Africa appreciated the problems of other members, but suggested that the remedy was to maintain stricter precautions against undesired imports; South Africa still believed in the existence of a substantial legitimate demand for gold at a premium.

General policy

Meanwhile, the Fund's policy had been subjected to intensive review within the Board itself. At the request of Executive Directors, the staff put forward a series of memoranda which dealt respectively with the $35 price of gold, premium transactions in gold, and the Fund's gold policy. Their effect was to support the policies that the Board had been pursuing. When these were discussed in the Board in April 1949, however, Mr. de Largentaye (France) dissented completely. On the first point—the $35 price of gold—he contended that, because of the importance of gold for reserves, and of the hardships being experienced by gold producers, this price should be increased. In terms curiously foreshadowing arguments put forward during the discussion of international liquidity since 1963, he said:

> Thus the question before us is whether the amount of the gold reserves, which have scarcely increased since the war, will be adequate for the needs of international payments when throughout the world prices and wages in terms of

dollars have doubled and when the money supply in the internal markets has trebled.

In support of Mr. de Largentaye's recommendation, Mr. McFarlane said that South Africa had accepted the Fund's rules about gold on the assumption that the par values set would be realistic ones; but this was not the case (as was indeed demonstrated five months later).

Mr. Southard disagreed with Mr. de Largentaye; he said that an increase in the price of gold would not offset a depression, but would merely subsidize the producers or holders of gold. In the event, the Board decided to note the staff paper; there was no proposal before it for a uniform change in par values under Article IV, Section 7, and no action was therefore called for.

On the subject of external sales of gold at premium prices and the Fund's gold policy, Mr. de Largentaye thought that any action by the Fund that restricted the supply of gold and raised the premium was felt in all countries and impaired public confidence in all currencies. Mr. Carli (Italy), on the other hand, agreed with the staff. He said that increased international traffic in gold produced conditions which impaired public confidence in a currency, and added that he believed that the Fund's policy should be maintained. Mr. Southard, concurring, said that his authorities believed there was nothing to be gained by facilitating private hoarding of gold. Mr. Madan (India) added that the Fund's policy, by increasing the premium on gold for private purchases, had reduced the volume of hoarding.

Concluding the discussion, the Managing Director said that he believed that there was no desire in the Board to stiffen the Fund's gold policy. On the other hand, only one Director had expressed a wish to reverse it. He would bear this in mind on his visit to South Africa, which was then shortly due to begin.

Discussion at Annual Meeting

Shortly before the Annual Meeting of the Board of Governors, the South African Government submitted, for consideration at the Meeting, a resolution calling for a modification of the Fund policy which would permit a member to sell half its newly produced gold in free markets at such premium prices as might be ruling there.[14] The Governors remitted the resolution for consideration to a Committee on Gold, consisting of 18 Governors. It was there supported by the Governors for Australia, the Philippines, and South Africa. The Governor for the United States put forward a counterproposal remitting the South African resolution to the Executive Directors for study and appropriate action. In the course of the discussion he made a statement on the U.S. view about the price of gold, which included the following passages:

> The United States looks upon gold as a monetary metal of primary usefulness in financing international transactions and in providing necessary monetary

[14] *Summary Proceedings, 1949*, pp. 34–35, 59.

> reserves. The United States has ample reserves in the form of gold. There appears no reason why the United States should undertake a long-term commitment to pay more dollars for gold to add to its monetary reserves. To do so would be, in effect, to sell more United States goods and services in order to secure monetary reserves in excess of our need for such reserves. The supplying of these additional goods would represent a real cost to the United States.
>
> . . . There is, from the American viewpoint, no . . . justification for asking the American people to make an additional contribution to gold producing countries, more or less in perpetuity, and in unknown amounts determined by their capacity to expand their output of monetary metal.
>
> . . . I do not contemplate, and have never contemplated, any change in the gold value of the dollar.

The Governor for South Africa at first resisted the U.S. proposal to refer his country's resolution to the Executive Directors, on the ground that any study by the latter would need to extend over a much wider field than the specific proposal South Africa had put forward. An amended resolution, referring the resolution to the Executive Directors "for study of all relevant considerations and report to the Board of Governors," which was acceptable to Mr. Havenga, was accordingly substituted. This was passed by the committee and by the Governors, and became Board of Governors' Resolution No. 4-6.[15] The action taken by the Executive Directors on this resolution is considered in the next chapter. Meanwhile, of course, the economic position of South Africa's gold producers was radically improved by the devaluation of the South African pound (by 30.5 per cent) which immediately followed the Annual Meeting.

---

[15] *Ibid.*, pp. 35–36, 46–47.

CHAPTER

11

The End of the Beginning (1949-51)

IN THE FIRST MONTHS succeeding the devaluations of September 1949 the adjustments consequential on these changes were proceeding throughout the world. They had not been completed when in June 1950 the outbreak of hostilities in Korea introduced a new source of economic disturbance, of which the magnitude could not be foreseen. The effects of these events on the work of the Fund were slow to develop, and the Board was meanwhile obliged to "wait and see." Furthermore, in the early part of 1951 there was a change in the Managing Directorship. It seems best, therefore, for the present chapter to carry the chronicle of the Fund's activities through two years, from September 1949 to the Annual Meeting in 1951.

During these two years the Board held 250 meetings, 22 of which were in informal session. An increasing proportion of its time, averaging about one third, was devoted to a wide range of questions on exchange rates and exchange systems. Another third of its time, or rather less, was occupied by domestic matters, including prolonged discussions each year of the contents of the Annual Report and the Exchange Restrictions Report. For the remainder, consideration of the use of the Fund's resources and of gold each took up some 10 per cent of the Board's attention, while relations with other international bodies (mainly the GATT) absorbed rather more. In what follows, the discussion is necessarily confined to major issues; it is impossible even to refer to the innumerable minor questions that came constantly before the Board for settlement. This selectivity, which will become increasingly necessary as this history progresses, must be borne in mind if a true picture of the activities of the Fund is to be gained.

MEMBERSHIP AND BOARD

Membership

Two countries joined the Fund in 1950, Pakistan on July 11 and Ceylon on August 29. On August 31, 1951, Sweden became the fiftieth member. The quota of Pakistan was fixed at $100 million, that of Ceylon at $15 million, and that of Sweden at $100 million. Poland resigned its membership on March 14, 1950, alleging that the Fund had failed to fulfill the expectations of its founders and had become instead "a submissive instrument of the Government of the United States . . . which lately forced upon a number of member countries the devaluation of their currencies." This allegation was refuted by the Managing Director in a reply which drew attention to the work that the Board had in fact done in pursuance of the Fund's objectives.

In February 1950 Mr. Sucharda (Czechoslovakia), speaking for two of the countries (Czechoslovakia and Poland) that he represented, challenged the right of Generalissimo Chiang Kai-shek's Government to be treated as a member of the Fund. The Board considered this, but resolved that it was a matter for the Board of Governors to decide. Mr. Sucharda then announced that he would be unable to take any further part in the work of the Board. Subsequently, the Czechoslovak Government appointed Mr. Sucharda Governor of the Fund for Czechoslovakia, but stated that he would not take any part in the Annual Meeting, which was to be held in Paris.

In August 1950 Mr. Gutt received a cable from Chou En-lai claiming that the Central People's Government of the People's Republic of China was the sole legal Government representing the Chinese people, and seeking the exclusion from the Annual Meeting of the Chinese Governor, Executive Director, and Alternates. The Czechoslovak delegation to the Annual Meeting proposed a resolution to the same effect, which was supported by the Governors for India and Yugoslavia.[1] It was resisted by the Governor for China, who claimed that his Government was the only legally constituted Chinese Government, and by the Governor for the United States, who pointed out that his Government, with many others, had recognized the Chinese National Government. After the Governor for the Philippines had suggested that the Czechoslovak resolution was out of order because it dealt with a purely political issue then before the United Nations, it was put to a vote and lost by a show of hands.

A similar resolution was introduced by the Czechoslovak Governor at the Annual Meeting, 1951, but was opposed by the Governors for China, the Philippines, the United Kingdom, and the United States, and the Meeting decided to take no action on it.[2]

In July 1950 Honduras accepted the obligations of Article VIII, Sections 2, 3, and 4, the first country to do so since members made their initial determinations in November 1946.

---

[1] *Summary Proceedings, 1950*, pp. 63–72.

[2] *Summary Proceedings, 1951*, pp. 66–73.

The Board

At the beginning of 1950 Mr. Joshi (India), who had been the Executive Director appointed by India from 1946 to October 1948, returned to the Board, replacing Mr. Madan. On March 20, 1950, Mr. Koo, Executive Director appointed by China, resigned to become Deputy Treasurer of the Fund; he was succeeded in July by Mr. Beue Tann (China).

At the biennial election of Executive Directors on September 13, 1950, which took effect from November 1, Mr. Sucharda was replaced by Mr. Nenad Popovic (Yugoslavia), who was elected by Ceylon, Thailand, Turkey, and Yugoslavia. Mr. McFarlane was succeeded by Mr. Leslie Galfreid Melville (also of Australia), and Mr. D'Ascoli (Venezuela) by Mr. Martínez-Ostos (Mexico), who had been Alternate to Mr. Gómez from 1946 to 1948. Pakistan joined the group of countries which re-elected Mr. Saad (Egypt). Czechoslovakia did not vote and was consequently unrepresented thereafter on the Executive Board. Special arrangements were, however, made to keep Czechoslovakia in touch with the Board's decisions and to supply it with copies of Board documents.

In January 1950 the Board adopted a proposal by Mr. Southard (United States) that it meet from time to time in informal session to discuss policy, the purpose being to allow Directors to express their views without necessarily committing the countries that they represented. Formal minutes were therefore not circulated, though an informal record was maintained in the Secretary's Office for purposes of reference. The device proved useful at that time, and has since been frequently utilized for the purpose of preliminary discussion of a topic on which Board opinion has not yet crystallized.

Later in 1950 the Board considered the meaning of Article XII, Section 3 (*c*). This provided for the appointment of an Executive Director by "the two members, the holdings of whose currencies by the Fund have been, on the average over the preceding two years, reduced below their quotas by the largest absolute amounts in terms of gold as a common denominator." The Legal Department advised the Board that the evident intention of the drafters of the Article had been to permit the two countries whose currencies had been the most used by the Fund to appoint an Executive Director if they were not already entitled to do so. To give effect to this intention, however, it would be necessary to read the Section as if, instead of the words "below their quotas," the text had read "below 75 per cent of their quotas," since the normal holdings by the Fund of a member's currency were equivalent not to the whole quota but to 75 per cent of it.

The staff pointed out that a literal reading of the text of the Section would favor a member that had originally paid less than 25 per cent of its quota in gold. Such a member might then qualify under Article XII, Section 3 (*c*), to appoint an Executive Director even though a decrease in the Fund's holdings of its currency was due solely to the fact that the member had repurchased its currency as it was required by the Articles to do. It need not even be a "creditor" of the Fund; i.e., the Fund might hold more of its currency than 75 per cent of its quota. Other anomalies of the same kind were pointed out. In consequence, the Board, except for Mr. de Largentaye (France) and Mr. de Selliers (Belgium), agreed with the staff interpretation.[3] Mr. de Largentaye formally dissented from the decision; Mr. de Selliers contented himself with saying that he did not see how the staff interpretation could be supported in view of the clear text.

Section 18 of the By-Laws requires the Managing Director to notify all members of the names of any members qualifying for the appointment of a Director under Article XII, Section 3 (*c*), at least a month before the ensuing election. For this reason the Board decided in 1948 that the phrase "the preceding two years" must be understood to be the two years ending on July 31, 1948. In order to settle the matter permanently, the Board decided on July 28, 1950 that

> the phrase "the preceding two years" as used in Art. XII, Sec. 3 (*c*), shall be deemed to be the two-year period ending on the July 31 preceding the dates of regular biennial elections of Executive Directors. However, this decision shall be reconsidered if such regular elections are held in other months than September.[4]

It may be added that the Legal Department advised the Board that a member entitled to appoint a Director under Article XII, Section 3 (*c*), had a duty to do so, and could not opt instead to participate in the election of Directors under Section 3 (*b*) (iii) and (iv).

MANAGING DIRECTOR AND STAFF

Managing Director

The five years of Mr. Gutt's contract expired at the beginning of May 1951. The Executive Directors, concluding that it would be desirable to set an age limit for Managing Directors, decided at the beginning of March that, in future, Managing Directors should retire not later than April 30 of the year in which they reached their seventieth birthday.[5] In consequence the Board offered Mr. Gutt, who was then aged 66, an extension of three years, to April 30, 1954. Mr. Gutt, however, preferred not to accept this offer, and retired from the Fund in accordance with his contract. His last attendance at a Board meeting was on March 19, 1951.

---

[3] E.B. Decision No. 574-2, May 18, 1950; below, Vol. III, p. 268.

[4] E.B. Decision No. 597-4, July 28, 1950; below, Vol. III, p. 268.

[5] Approved by Resolution 6-4, *Summary Proceedings, 1951*, p. 54.

On April 10 Mr. Southard (United States) proposed to the Board that Mr. Ivar Rooth, of Sweden, should succeed Mr. Gutt. Mr. Rooth, who from 1929 to 1948 had been Governor of the Riksbank and since then Chairman of the Economic Research Institute of Sweden, was at that moment heading a World Bank mission to Iraq. The Board agreed to the nomination and Mr. Rooth accepted the offer, with effect from August 3, 1951.

Staff

In March 1950 the first major reorganization of the staff was undertaken. When presenting his proposals to the Board, Mr. Gutt pointed out that the Research Department was overburdened with too many different duties, that there was some overlapping between the activities of the departments, and that functional and area responsibilities were combined in them. He therefore proposed to create two area departments, which would handle relations with members. At the same time, the duties of the Operations Department would be reduced. For the future it would execute the exchange operations of the Fund, compute the data of monetary reserves of member countries, and supervise gold operations and practices. It would also be responsible for the financial, banking, and accounting functions of the Fund. In accordance with these changed responsibilities, it would be renamed the Treasurer's Department.

The Managing Director also proposed to create a new functional department, the Exchange Restrictions Department, to watch over an area of the Fund's work which was becoming of increasing importance. This department would be concerned with exchange restrictions, multiple currency systems, and related practices, and it would be responsible for relations with the GATT. The two area departments would be responsible, respectively, for member countries in Europe and North America, and for those in Latin America, the Middle East, and the Far East. The Research Department would retain the remainder of its previous functions, and the other departments and offices would continue unaltered.

These proposals were approved by the Board in March and took effect from March 20. The first Director of the Exchange Restrictions Department was Mr. Irving S. Friedman. The European and North American Department was headed by Mr. G. A. Ph. Weyer, and the Far Eastern, Middle Eastern, and Latin American Department by Mr. Luthringer. The number of departments has since increased, but the principle of the division of responsibility between the area departments and the functional departments has remained unchanged. An Office of Public Relations was also created as part of the reorganization, to handle relations with the United Nations and other international organizations. In 1952, these functions reverted to the Office of the Managing Director, where they had previously been located.

Ivar Rooth, Managing Director, 1951–56

It was while this reorganization was being discussed by the Board that Poland withdrew from membership. This raised the question of the retention on the Fund staff of the six Polish nationals then employed. Rule N-2 required the Board to authorize exceptions to the principle that persons on the staff of the Fund should be nationals of members of the Fund. The Board agreed that the six staff members in question should be retained.

At the end of April 1951 the staff totaled 456, including 16 on military leave or leave without pay, and was composed of nationals of 36 countries.

Prior to the reorganization, the responsibility for the activities of the staff vis-à-vis the Fund's members lay with two men only—the Directors of the Research Department and the Operations Department. After March 1950, however, five departments supervised these activities, and it immediately became clear that some coordinating machinery would be necessary. Mr. Gutt therefore set up a formal Staff Committee, consisting of the heads of departments, with himself in the chair. This committee was charged with considering all major items of business coming before the Fund, with reviewing staff memoranda dealing with questions of policy, with concerting the staff's advice to the Board, and with coordinating the actions of the staff in carrying out the Board's decisions.

The Staff Committee met first on March 22, 1950, and held 26 meetings in the next three months. After that it convened somewhat less frequently until the arrival of Mr. Rooth, but all policy issues, as they arose, continued to be canalized through it, as did major documents such as the Annual Report. The committee's usefulness was enhanced by the fact that junior members of the staff dealing with particular issues were able to attend sessions at which those issues were discussed. This ensured, on the one hand, that the committee was apprised of all relevant details and, on the other, that the staff members in question were fully acquainted with the reasons for the committee's recommendations.

There was at first some tendency among members of the Board to fear that the existence of the Staff Committee portended an attempt to undercut the Board's responsibilities for policymaking. And there was perhaps this much justification for the fear, that the existence of the committee permitted a fuller and more formal exploration within the staff of policy questions before these were brought to the Board, resulting in somewhat more assured presentations of the issues in Board memoranda. Nevertheless, a few weeks later, in June 1950, there occurred one of the rare occasions on which the work of the staff was criticized by a member of the Board for being insufficiently independent. As the comments then made included a redefinition of the relationship between Board and staff, the incident is worth describing.

The subject of Mr. Southard's criticisms was a memorandum describing the European payments plan then under discussion in Paris. Mr. Southard said that the staff might have taken a more forthright position, stating clearly how they thought the plan squared with the criteria which had been laid down by the Board, and what were the likely developments in the future with which the Fund would have to be concerned. He, personally, would have welcomed such a paper. He stressed that the staff was given great freedom to analyze problems as it thought best and to state completely and frankly its position on important issues confronting the Fund. It was important to the Board that the staff had this freedom and made use of it. Mr. Southard went on to say that, as Executive Directors were often bound by the views of governments, it was not to be expected that they would always accept the views of the staff. Even if they did not, however, these views would be helpful to the home governments, to whom Executive Directors would be likely to transmit them.

The reader will recall that the dichotomy between Executive Directors and staff to which Mr. Southard referred had been clearly brought out at the initial Governors' Meeting at Savannah. The future course of this history will show how far the staff has succeeded in filling the role there allotted to them.

Training Program

In April 1950 the Board approved recommendations by the Managing Director for the inauguration of a formal Training Program. For some months previously a few student trainees had been attached to the various departments to enable them to become acquainted with the Fund's work. It was expected that some of these trainees would return to their home countries better equipped to handle questions of international economic relations; others would be recruited to the Fund's own staff. Mr. Gutt now proposed that three set courses should be established: one to give broad training on matters of concern to the Fund at a junior level; a second to give specialized training, particularly in balance of payments techniques, to employees of member countries; and a third to provide a high-level course for senior officials. The Board approved the plan, and authorized financial assistance to trainees in the first two types of course. No assistance was authorized for the third type because it was felt that training of such a kind would be wholly for the benefit of the government employing the official, which should therefore pay for it. At the end of May, invitations were sent to member countries to nominate suitable persons for the courses of the first two types. The first general course, with ten trainees, began in January 1951. The first specialized course, in balance of payments techniques, began in September 1950 with five trainees, and a second, similar, course in March 1951. The Training Program continued to operate on a small scale until 1964, when it became the IMF Institute.

PUBLICATIONS

Three new publications were inaugurated in 1950. The first of these was the *Annual Report on Exchange Restrictions,* which was called for by Article XIV, Section 4. The Board discussed in November 1949 the scope of the Report and decided that, in addition to a factual survey of the restrictions in force (which was not to be limited to those under Article XIV, Section 2), the Report should include conclusions and recommendations. It should be drafted in the expectation that it would be published.

A first draft came before the Board in February 1950, and in the second half of that month the Directors devoted much attention to it. The Report as published contained a substantial discussion of the forms of exchange restrictions in use and the problems which these raised.[6] It concluded with considering how and in what way restrictions should be relaxed. Part II of the Report described in detail the nature of the restrictive systems in the sterling area, Europe, the Western Hemisphere, and the Middle and Far East, covering, in all, 42 countries.

In the following year the preparation of the Report was undertaken at a time when the effects of the Korean War on international trade were altering the character of the problem of exchange restrictions. Export controls were becoming increasingly important in determining the pattern of world trade.[7] At the same time, the Board discerned in the improving balance of payments situation of many countries an opportunity to relax exchange restrictions. It concluded that "many countries are in a position to undertake substantial removal of discrimination and relaxation of non-discriminatory restrictions and to make significant progress toward convertibility." The same point was stressed in Chapter III of the Annual Report for 1951, and at the Annual Meeting there was considerable support for the Board's arguments, although some Governors stressed the difficulties which still faced their countries.[8]

On February 27, 1950, the first number of a technical journal, entitled *Staff Papers,* was distributed. Its introduction had been advocated by Professor Dennis Robertson, who had become concerned that so many young economists had, by joining the Fund's staff, lost the opportunity to continue to write under their own names. He suggested to Mr. Bernstein that the Fund should provide an outlet for this purpose. Announcing the new venture, the Managing Director pointed out that this was the first time that the Fund had made studies undertaken by the staff available to governments and the public. The first issue contained articles on latent inflation, on the measurement of inflation, on the

---

[6] *First Annual Report on Exchange Restrictions* (March 1, 1950), pp. 3–37.

[7] *Second Annual Report on Exchange Restrictions* (April 1951), pp. 1, 14.

[8] *Summary Proceedings, 1951,* pp. 44–45.

effects of exchange depreciation, on the role of the ECA program in imports and exports, on the local currency proceeds of an import surplus, on the terms of trade in Latin America countries, and on cooperation between the Fund and the ITO. It will be recognized that all these papers were closely related to the problems that had come before the Board in the preceding year. The journal was offered for subscription at $3.50 per volume of three numbers. It had originally been intended that three numbers should be issued each year, but the supply of nonconfidential material which was of sufficiently high quality proved inadequate to furnish more than two issues a year until 1962. *Staff Papers* is at the present time probably the only fully professional publication in the economic field issued by an international organization.

A third publication begun during the year was a monthly statistical compilation, entitled *Direction of International Trade,* which gave country-by-country trade statistics. The first issue, which was distributed in September 1950, covered international trade in 1948, 1949, and the first quarter of 1950. This journal was a joint venture of the Fund, the World Bank, and the UN.

RATES FOR FUND COMMUNICATIONS

In May 1949 the cable companies operating in the United States filed with the Federal Communications Commission revised tariffs, effective from July 1, 1949, which would have required the Fund and the Bank to pay the full rates applicable to messages sent by private persons instead of the lower rates paid by the U.S. Government. Thereupon the Bank and the Fund filed a joint complaint with the Commission, alleging, inter alia, that the revised tariffs were illegal. The basis for this assertion was Article IX, Section 7, of the Articles of the Fund, and a corresponding provision in the Articles of the Bank, which required that the official communications of the Fund and the Bank should be accorded by members the same treatment as the official communications of other members.

On November 4, 1949 Mr. Southard (United States) asked the Fund Board for an elucidation of Article IX, Section 7, and the U.S. Executive Director on the Board of the Bank put the same question to that Board. Specifically, they inquired whether the Section applied to the rates charged for the official communications of the Fund; whether a member exercising regulatory powers over such rates was relieved of the obligations of the Section by reason of the fact that the communication facilities being used were privately owned or operated; and whether the member's obligation would be satisfied if the Fund's official communications could be sent only at rates which exceeded the rates accorded to the official communications of other members in comparable situations. It was agreed that a joint committee of Directors of the Fund and the Bank should be set up to consider these questions.

Ten days later this committee reported that the answer to Mr. Southard's first question was in the affirmative and to the other two questions in the negative. This report was considered by the Board in February 1950, and the doctrine expressed was officially adopted.[9] In consequence, the U.S. Government took the necessary steps to ensure that the rates charged for the telephonic and telegraphic communications of the Fund were limited to the concessional rates accorded to diplomatic missions in Washington.

QUOTAS REVIEWED

Article III, Section 2, requires the Fund at intervals of five years to review and, if appropriate, to propose an adjustment of the quotas of all members. In March 1949 the Board decided that for the purposes of this Article the first five-year period began on December 27, 1945.[10] Rule D-3 of the Fund required the Board at least one year before the time when quotas must be reviewed to appoint a committee to study the problem and prepare a written report. Accordingly, in December 1949 the Managing Director proposed to the Board that a committee should be appointed, but in view of the evident interest of all Directors in the problem, he suggested that it should be a Committee of the Whole. Mr. de Largentaye (France) objected to this on the ground that there was no precedent for such a committee in the Fund and that the Managing Director could not chair a Board committee. He said that he would not serve on such a committee, and that therefore it could not be constituted. The point was deferred for legal opinion, but the Legal Department advised the Board that a Committee of the Whole was a fully constitutional method of meeting the requirements of Rule D-3 and that it could be constituted even if one member of the Board was unwilling to participate. Mr. de Largentaye maintained his objections, but said that if the majority of the Board decided that membership of a Committee of the Whole was compulsory, he would have to abide by that decision. The Board then accepted the Managing Director's proposal.

In May 1950 Mr. Gutt appointed a staff working party to review the problem of quotas. Its report, sent to the Board on December 6, 1950, recommended that the size of the Fund's resources should be doubled to take account of the change in economic circumstances since the original quotas were fixed. However, the Managing Director, in submitting this to the Committee of the Whole, suggested that, in view of the uncertain conditions prevailing in the world at that time, it was inopportune to revise quotas. The committee agreed with Mr. Gutt, and so recommended to the Board. On March 8, 1951, the Board

[9] E.B. Decision No. 534-3, February 20, 1950; below, Vol. III, p. 266; *Annual Report, 1950*, pp. 118–19.

[10] E.B. Decision No. 408-2, March 11, 1949; below, Vol. III, p. 220.

concurred in this recommendation. The decision taken was that "under present international circumstances, it is difficult to reach a conclusion on this question at this time and [the Board] looks forward toward discussing the question further at as early a date as may be practicable." The opportunity did not, however, arise and nothing further was done about increasing quotas at this first Quinquennial Review. It is probable that the Board was strongly influenced by a conviction that the U.S. Congress would not agree to an increase in the U.S. quota, and that therefore the 80 per cent of the total voting power required by Article III, Section 2, for a revision of quotas would not be forthcoming.

ANNUAL REPORTS AND ANNUAL MEETINGS

The Annual Report for 1950 devoted much of its space to a discussion of the causes and effects of the devaluations of 1949. Shorter chapters discussed developments in exchange restrictions, in gold markets, and in the use of the Fund's resources. At the Annual Meeting, 1950, as in 1949, the discussion of the Report was divided between four Committees, dealing respectively with Exchange Policy, Exchange Restrictions, Finance and Organization, and Gold. Proceedings in the last two of these are briefly referred to in other sections of this chapter. In the Committee on Exchange Policy the most notable contribution was made by the Governor for the Netherlands, who expressed apprehension at the effects of rearmament and urged international cooperation to prevent increases in the prices of raw materials. The Governor for Czechoslovakia criticized the Report's treatment of devaluation as exaggerating its spontaneity, its importance, and its beneficial effects. He was answered by the Governor for the United States, who stressed that the devaluations had been justified, and the attention to them in the Report fully warranted.

The Committee on Exchange Restrictions heard from the Governor for the United States a warning that prolonged restrictions tended to distort trade, and that in such conditions restrictions tended to be self-perpetuating. On the other hand, the Governor for the United Kingdom pointed out that, in the situation in which his country found itself, it had no alternative but to maintain restrictions. The only other Governor to speak was the Governor for Belgium, who stressed that the first requisite to the ending of restrictions was to eliminate inflation.

The Annual Report for 1951 devoted a long first chapter to a careful analysis of the world economic situation. This was followed by briefer discussions of par values and exchange rates, of exchange restrictions, of the Fund's gold policy, of its transactions, and of organizational questions. The consequences of the Korean conflict were examined in detail, leading to the conclusion that the situation was not a stable one, and that to re-establish equilibrium it would be necessary for production outside the United States to increase and for "some readjustment" to take place between the prices of primary and industrial goods.[11]

This last conclusion was challenged by the Governor for Mexico during the discussion of the Annual Report at the Annual Meeting. He said that if "some readjustment" meant that the terms of trade of primary producing countries would have to deteriorate for world equilibrium to be established, he was unable to accept such a prospect. With this exception, however, the Governors offered little comment on the chapters dealing with world payments, par values, and gold; the committee to which these were remitted gave emphasis in its report to the problem of controlling inflation. It mentioned, however, that the Managing Director had explained that the sentence to which the Governor for Mexico had referred was not to be construed as advocating any particular terms of trade.

The other two committees set up to review the Annual Report were the scene of considerable controversy. In the Committee on Exchange Restrictions and Fund Transactions, the Governor for the United Kingdom suggested that the optimistic tone of the Annual Report in relation to the removal of restrictions was unduly influenced by the favorable experience of 1950. He indicated that the problems confronting his country in the fall of 1951 might call for a strengthening rather than a relaxation of restrictions, and said that he saw little prospect of any appreciable improvement in 1952 or 1953. Criticisms voiced in this committee on the subject of Fund transactions are reported later in this chapter.

The Committee on Finance and Organization heard from the Governor for the United Kingdom a plea that the Fund budget should be squeezed to correspond to the belt-tightening which members were undergoing as a result of rearmament. Spirited replies to this appeal were made by the Governor for Mexico and the Governor for Egypt (Mr. Saad), defending the efficiency and economy with which the Fund was run and urging the need to attract qualified staff.

It was in the third general session, rather than in committee, that the sharpest speeches were made. The Governor for Australia led off by stating that the standing of the Fund fell below members' hopes, and that one cause of this was a disregard of the rule of law by members casting a majority of votes on the Board. He repeated the statement frequently made by representatives of Australia, that members had joined the Fund after carefully weighing up the advantages of membership, and went on to say that they had accepted that there should be no right of appeal in the Fund on the assumption that the Articles would be administered "with close regard for the rights of members." His contention was that, on the contrary, the practice had developed of seizing upon the purposes of Article I and trying to derive from them obligations which

[11] *Annual Report, 1951*, p. 32.

overrode specific rights and duties in the rest of the text. Nor was the staff exempted from his animadversions. The Governor decried what he called the

> tendency of the Fund, which according to my information is constantly pressed on the Executive Board by a section of the staff, to interpret the law in such a way as to expand the functions of the Fund, and thus indirectly the influence of the staff. . . .

Mr. Saad, again in his capacity as Governor for Egypt, replied. He made two points: firstly, all questions of interpretation were the subject of the closest examination, by the Committee on Interpretation and subsequently by the Board itself; secondly, the only way to resolve differences of view in the Board was by vote, and the Articles had provided for weighted voting. The Governor for Canada supported this latter argument. However, the Governor for Australia was not satisfied; he was not, he explained, criticizing the Board for having departed from the letter of the Articles, but he thought that its actions had ignored their spirit. The Governor for South Africa spoke in similar terms.

These criticisms have been reported here not because they are characteristic of the remarks of Governors at Annual Meetings, but on the contrary because they were exceptional. In scarcely any other year's proceedings is it possible to find comparable attacks on the Board. The fact that they found little reflection in the speeches of other Governors suggests that the dissatisfaction voiced was limited to a few members who attached particular importance to the issues cited by the Governor for Australia—drawing rights and the Fund's role in the discussions in the GATT.

MULTIPLE RATES AND FLUCTUATING RATES

The restrictions that surrounded the use of foreign exchange at the end of the 1940's were of immense complexity. The ingenuity of monetary authorities had for years been directed on the one hand to shaping controls in such a way as to encourage exports, especially to hard currency countries, and on the other to blocking loopholes through which hard currencies could leak away from monetary reserves. So complex a structure of restrictions cannot be summarized in this volume; all that can be attempted in these pages is to look briefly at a few of the types of restrictions which, from time to time, were of particular concern to the Executive Board.

The subjects of exchange rates and exchange systems came before the Executive Directors in many forms. The Board's activities in connection with the devaluations in 1949 were described in the last chapter. Subsequently, many of the countries that did not devalue found it necessary to make changes in their exchange systems as a consequence of these events or of the outbreak of the Korean War. Executive Directors were thus faced with a series of problems so extensive that in the course of 1950–51 they reviewed the exchange systems of no less than 38 of the 50 members, several of them more than once. Many of these reviews involved comprehensive studies of the members' exchange structures; others were confined to examining the case for shifting some commodities from one to another of the categories in the members' multiple rate systems. Out of their experience in these reviews the Directors undertook two detailed studies of (1) the case for multiple rates as distinct from a single par value, and (2) the arguments for a fluctuating rather than a fixed exchange rate. The outcome of these two general reviews is described below; but the reader must remember that the discussions were not conducted *in vacuo*—rather, that the Board had in mind all the time the specific problems, affecting two thirds of the Fund's membership, that it had spent so much time reviewing.

Multiple rates

The starting point for the Board's discussion of multiple rates was a memorandum by the Director of Research, which was in origin a paper prepared for a meeting of the technicians of Latin American central banks late in 1949. Contending that countries were not likely to obtain with multiple rates the best pattern of consumption or the best system of taxation, the memorandum at the same time recognized that some countries were unwilling to apply to all their imports exchange rates that would appropriately discourage imports, or to apply sufficiently encouraging export rates to all their exports. In such circumstances, the memorandum suggested that it might be better to apply the appropriate rates to 50 per cent or 60 per cent of imports or exports rather than to continue to apply inappropriate rates to the country's whole trade. This memorandum was supplemented by two comprehensive studies of the multiple rate systems actually operated by Fund members.

In January 1950 the subject was taken up by the Board in three meetings in informal session. Directors and members of the staff explained the objects which multiple rates were designed to serve, and their advantages relative to other techniques, especially quantitative restrictions. The point was made that multiple rates were in general more harmful to the country using them than to its trading partners. Their attractions lay chiefly in the relative ease of their administration; they also provided a useful means of taxation. From the Fund's point of view they were less objectionable, because less discriminatory, than more direct restrictions.

In the third meeting the discussion concentrated on a model, proposed by one Executive Director for consideration, which provided for one export rate and one import rate, with a spread between them wider than the traditional 1 per cent, together with a legal free market for invisibles into which the government would feed a large proportion of export receipts. There was wide agreement in the Board that such a model would be the least objectionable of any multiple rate system. Even so, several Directors were concerned at its prospective adverse effect on international trade compared with the par value system provided for in the Fund Agreement.

No formal decision was taken as a result of the discussion briefly summarized above. However, in the Annual Reports for 1950 and 1951 there were passages which reflected the Board's general view of the problem.[12] Recognizing the reasons, other than balance of payments difficulties, which might commend multiple rates to members, the Reports concentrated on the desirability of simplifying as far as possible the complexities of the systems that were then in existence. Some progress in this direction was recorded.

The only general decision taken on multiple rates within the period with which we are now concerned resulted from the submission to the Board for approval of numerous minor changes in the coverage of categories of commodities in certain multiple rate systems. The Board decided that it was normally unnecessary for such minor variations to be approved by Executive Directors at a Board meeting. Mr. Gutt was accordingly asked to arrange to notify the Board of each such proposal as it was received, but not to put it on an agenda for the Board unless requested to do so by an Executive Director. If no such request was received within a limited period, to be set by the Managing Director, the proposal would be deemed to be approved. This "short-form" or "lapse of time" procedure was used for the first time a month later to approve some minor changes in the exchange system of Lebanon. It has since been found useful for dealing with a variety of other questions which, though in form requiring to be approved by the Board, do not justify full-scale discussion there.

Fluctuating rates

The problem of the attitude that the Fund should take toward fluctuating exchange rates had of course arisen during the devaluations in September 1949, being posed by Belgium's initial decision to abandon its par value and allow its exchange rate to "float." At that time the Legal Department had advised the Board that the Fund had no power to approve the adoption of a fluctuating rate as a transition from one agreed parity to another. The department pointed out that the provisions in Article IV, Section 5, for a shift from one par value to another reproduced almost unchanged the provisions of the Joint Statement. It was impossible to conceive that the experts at Bretton Woods had overlooked that in the 1930's the values of several important currencies were changed to new fixed amounts only after a period of fluctuation; the absence of any provision in the Articles for a period of transition must therefore be regarded as deliberate. The Legal Department also advised that the provisions of

[12] *Annual Report, 1950*, pp. 42, 54, 67; *Annual Report, 1951*, pp. 67–68.

Article XVI for a temporary suspension of some of the obligations of the Articles could not be used to release a single member from such obligations; they were intended only to deal with a situation in which it might be desirable to relax requirements for all members.

The establishment by Belgium of a new par value on September 21, 1949 meant that the issue ceased to be one of urgency for the Board. However, during the next few months there were some disturbing indications that in Europe the idea was taking hold that fluctuating rates would be a useful expedient to smooth the path toward a new equilibrium. Press comment to this effect was brought to the notice of the Board in October 1949, and in January 1950 Mr. Beyen (Netherlands) submitted a memorandum in which he emphasized the dangers of any such move. He distinguished between the proposal to allow European currencies to fluctuate and the abandonment of a fixed par value by a country like Peru. The latter might fairly be attributed to *force majeure*; the former suggested a doctrinaire attachment to freedom of currencies to fluctuate, which was directly contrary to the concepts of the Fund Agreement and threatened the achievements embodied in it.

Mr. Beyen's memorandum was written in the expectation that there would shortly be a discussion of the problem in the Board. This was, however, deferred, and the question did not arise again until the end of September 1950, when the Canadian Government decided that it could no longer hold the exchange rate from rising. Presenting the Canadian case to the Board, Mr. Rasminsky (Canada) explained that the main problem was the inflow of capital from the United States, which it was administratively impracticable to restrict and which was creating such easy money conditions in Canada as to threaten an inflation there. On the other hand, his Government feared that if it revalued the dollar, as it had done in 1946, it would, as then, lose reserves to a greater extent than could be afforded. The Government could see no alternative but to allow the exchange rate vis-à-vis the U.S. dollar to find its own level; the cross rate with sterling would, however, be maintained.

The Canadian proposal was received with concern, not only because of the importance of the Canadian dollar in world trade, but even more because it suggested some loosening of the convictions of Fund members that fixed par values were the proper basis for international transactions. Executive Directors and members of the staff suggested that, instead of freeing the exchange rate, Canada should either absorb the additions to its reserves by open market operations or should control the capital intake. Mr. Rasminsky repeated that the capital inflow could not, in the nature of things, be effectively controlled, and said that to absorb the increase in reserves by open market operations would entail the creation of debt by the Canadian Government on a scale which it was not prepared to undertake. Mr. Southard (United States), Mr. Beyen, and Mr. Leslie F. Crick (United Kingdom), Alternate to Sir George Bolton,[13] found Mr. Rasminsky's arguments persuasive, and the Board decided to announce that

> the Fund recognizes the exigencies of the situation which have led Canada to the proposed plan and takes note of the intention of the Canadian Government to remain in consultation with the Fund and to re-establish an effective par value as soon as circumstances warrant.

The terms of this decision were substantially similar to those with which the Board had accepted the temporary Belgian proposal, with the significant difference that they omitted the words "an appropriate step." [14] Mr. Southard said that he would have preferred a decision in which these words were used, but that he would concur in the view of the majority of the Directors.

An informal discussion in the Board in February 1951 showed that Executive Directors were aware both of the arguments for fluctuating rates and of the dangers of any spread of them. There was general recognition that in special circumstances it might be extremely difficult, if not impossible, for a country to adhere to a regime of fixed rates. But Directors agreed that in principle such a regime was preferable; the example of the 1930's made this clear. When, therefore, Mr. Rasminsky reported in April on the first seven months of free rates in Canada, claiming that the outcome justified the Government's decision, Directors expressed themselves satisfied that the experiment had worked out well, but relieved that the example had not spread.

The Board then resumed its informal discussions of the general problem. Mr. de Largentaye (France) contributed a lengthy argument in favor of fluctuating rates, in preference to fixed rates, as an environment beneficial to international trade. He thought that fixed rates were neither necessary nor sufficient for the maximum development of trade, and that fluctuating rates were more desirable than exchange restrictions, would eliminate "hot money," and would contribute more than fixed rates to the stabilization of prices. These views were challenged by other Executive Directors and by the staff, who held that generalized fluctuating rates would harm both international trade and price stability.

As the discussion progressed it became clear that to most Executive Directors the main condition that would justify fluctuating rates was a temporary emergency in which a member country was unable either to hold its existing par value or to propose a suitable new one. Several criteria were suggested by which the acceptability of a fluctuating rate in such circumstances might be tested, such as the absence of hardship to other members and a dangerously low level of reserves held by the member concerned. The more general view, however,

[13] Mr. Bolton had been knighted in January 1950.

[14] Cf. above, p. 241.

appeared to be that the only possible course would be for the member to satisfy the Fund that it would be necessary and tolerable for its exchange rate to fluctuate.

In the outcome, the Board decided on a statement of its views to be included in the Annual Report. This recognized that there might be occasional and exceptional cases where a member could not maintain *any* par value for a limited period of time, or where it was exceedingly reluctant to take the risks of a decision respecting a par value.[15] Even in such cases, however, a member should recognize that its actions might adversely affect other members. As regards the Fund's actions when faced with a proposal by a member to allow its exchange rate to fluctuate, the Report said that "if the Fund finds that the arguments of the member are persuasive it may say so, although it cannot give its approval to the action." The member would then be asked to remain in close consultation with the Fund respecting exchange arrangements in the interim, and with a view to the early establishment of a par value agreed with the Fund.

RESTRICTIONS FOR SECURITY REASONS

As the emergency in Korea developed, the United States decided that it would have to impose restrictions on the making of payments and transfers to Mainland China and North Korea. Explaining his Government's proposals to the Board at a Saturday afternoon meeting, Mr. Southard (United States) said that Article VIII did not explicitly provide for such exceptional circumstances, but that

> having in mind the precedent of GATT and ITO and the difficulties presented to the Fund in endeavoring to evaluate actions to which the economic and financial criteria embodied in the Articles do not apply, it was our tentative feeling that the Fund should not be expected to act on such restrictions.

Mr. Gutt commented that the proposed measures appeared to constitute a restriction and a discrimination in the terms of Article VIII, Section 3, but that he felt in the circumstances the Board would not hesitate to approve the U.S. measures. This view was supported by several Executive Directors. The Legal Department pointed out that legally the U.S. action was opposed to Article VIII, but said that the more important question was how any Fund authority should be exercised and what procedural arrangements could be made to ease the problem of consultation. Mr. Southard, in reply, urged that, while it was most undesirable in general that restrictions should be justified by pleas of emergency, a financial authority such as the Board was not a suitable forum for the evaluation of the need for restrictions on security grounds. He suggested that the Fund should merely note his Government's action and this was done.

---

[15] *Annual Report, 1951*, pp. 36–41.

The problems mentioned by the Legal Department proved extremely difficult to resolve, and it was not until August 1952 that the matter was finally disposed of. The Board then, after considerable discussion, decided that when a member proposed to impose restrictions on security grounds it should notify the Managing Director, preferably in advance; that such notification should be circulated to Executive Directors; and that unless the member heard to the contrary within thirty days it could assume that its proposals were approved.[16] The Fund would thereafter review the restrictions periodically, and reserved the right to modify or revoke, at any time, its approval or the effect of this approval on any restrictions that might have been imposed under it. In the light of this ruling, the Board decided to offer no objection to the U.S. measures described above, or to similar measures that had meanwhile been taken by Cuba.

It may be added that the procedure laid down was invoked in 1963 by the United States, which had imposed restrictions on transactions with Cuba, in 1965 by India in respect of restrictions against Pakistan, and in 1965 and 1966 by the United Kingdom and certain other countries in respect of restrictions against Rhodesia.

PROGRESS TOWARD A DRAWINGS POLICY

There were no drawings from the Fund during the calendar year 1950, and the whole amount drawn from October 1949 through September 1951 was only $76.8 million. Meanwhile $67.7 million of earlier drawings were repurchased. To some extent the absence of drawings was due to the improvement in the balances of payments of less developed countries as a result of the Korean conflict, and, of course, the decision excluding European countries from drawing dollars still applied. But many people, both inside the Fund and in member countries, were disturbed at the small extent to which drawings were being made available to assist member countries in the kind of difficulties which the Articles had envisaged. A great deal of time and thought in the Board and among the Fund staff was devoted to attempting to formulate ways in which drawings could be safely increased. The breakthrough in this respect did not come until the following year, but the discussions of 1949–51 laid the foundations on which later policies were built. In the process the concept of an "automatic" right to draw on the Fund—a term for which Mr. Gutt accepted responsibility—disappeared, being replaced by the idea of progressive conditionality.

It will be recalled that in May 1949 Mr. Southard (United States) had put forward four criteria by which the Board should judge whether a proposed drawing would meet the test of being temporary. During the next few months he

[16] E.B. Decision No. 144-(52/51), August 14, 1952; below, Vol. III, p. 257.

came to feel that these were insufficient, because the repurchase provisions of the Articles did not guarantee that drawings would be reversed within any limited time. The intention at Bretton Woods had been to ensure that, as a member recovered from the difficulties that had necessitated a drawing, it should share with the Fund the improvement in its reserves, rather than build these up to the full extent of the accretion achieved. This concept was, however, modified—as it had been in later versions of the Stabilization Fund and in the Joint Statement—by the imposition of certain limits, which eventually became those in Article V, Section 7 (*c*). As matters stood in 1951, the most important of these was Section 7 (*c*) (i), exempting from the repurchase obligation any member whose monetary reserves were below its quota. It had been foreseen in 1943 that, as a result, the obligation did not apply to the United Kingdom. Nor did it apply to any other country in the sterling area—for example, Australia—because the sterling area's convertible reserves were held in London, and Australia's reserves, being held in sterling, did not consist of a convertible currency. State trading countries, which could especially easily maintain their reserves below their quotas, could also escape from any repurchase obligations. Subsequently, as will be seen below, Section 7 (*c*) (iii) also came into play, preventing the use of both dollars and sterling in repurchases.

In these conditions, the Fund had to depend, to ensure the revolving character of its resources, upon the consultations prescribed by Article V, Section 8 (*d*). These became obligatory when the rate of charge payable by a member reached 4 per cent. There was, however, no charge (other than the service charge) payable by a member if the Fund's holdings of its currency were less than its quota, and even for larger drawings the rate of 4 per cent was not reached for periods that might be as long as seven years.

By 1952 the effect of these limitations was fully apparent. The total of drawings from the beginning of operations through April 30, 1951 exceeded $800 million, including $400 million by the United Kingdom and India. But repurchase obligations under Article V, Section 7, accruing in the five years ending April 30, 1952 amounted to only $190 million. Part of this was due from members that had not drawn on the Fund but had repurchase obligations because they had paid gold subscriptions of less than 25 per cent of their quotas. None of the $190 million was due from the sterling area. Repurchases actually made in the same period totaled no more than $80 million.

We shall first review briefly the 17 memoranda and 19 meetings in which this problem of the use of the Fund's resources was discussed between October 1949 and September 1951. The Board also dealt with some technical questions about repurchase obligations, and studied further the problem of voluntary repurchases which had arisen in November 1948. These subsidiary questions will be dealt with later.

PROPOSED POLICY

Three stages may be distinguished in the Board's search during these years for a solution to the problem posed by Mr. Southard, corresponding to three successive proposals to break the deadlock. The first of these, put forward by Mr. Southard himself in October 1949, would have required each member when drawing to enter into an undertaking to repurchase its currency from the Fund within five years. The second, put forward by the staff in May 1950 as the outcome of the studies of a staff working party, envisaged a system of preparatory screening, the results of which would be communicated to members so that they might know whether or not the Fund would agree to their drawing. The third plan, proposed by Mr. Gutt in November 1950, linked the right to draw to the presentation by the member concerned of a specific program of domestic action designed to help it to achieve the purposes of the Fund Agreement.

When pressing his argument for requiring members to undertake to repurchase drawings within five years, Mr. Southard said that this proposal was the outcome of an effort by the U.S. Government to find some way in which the Fund could prudently allow drawings. He felt that the present and prospective level of members' reserves, together with the general inconvertibility of currencies, made a fresh look at the control of drawings necessary. At Bretton Woods the Fund had been conceived as a revolving source of financial aid to its members, but conditions were worse than had then been envisaged and it was impossible to rely on the automatic repurchase provisions to ensure that the Fund's resources were duly reconstituted.

Mr. Southard's proposal was criticized for a number of different reasons. Mr. Beyen (Netherlands) pointed out that the Articles of Agreement defined (negatively) the purposes for which drawings might be made, but not their term. He contended also that the repurchase provisions were not meant to be the normal way of ensuring the temporary use of the Fund's resources. They were a corrective, to be applied when reduction of the Fund's holdings did not otherwise come about. Mr. Southard's proposal therefore cut right across the provisions of the Agreement.

In the view of the staff, the Board had no legal authority to set a term for repurchases unless this distinguished between members. If at the time of drawing it seemed inherently likely that a repurchase could be made reasonably soon, the Board had no power to impose conditions. If such repurchase could not be foreseen, the proper course was to refuse to allow the member to draw at all. After a drawing had been made, the Fund should remain continuously in consultation with the member, studying particularly any possible changes in its ability to repay. If it appeared that the member was not following appropriate policies, consideration should be given to cutting off its right to further use of the Fund's resources under Article V, Section 5, or Article XX, Section 4 (*i*).

Mr. Southard's proposal had been put forward in October 1949 and the staff comment cited above was circulated in December. Later that month the Board resumed discussion of the proposal and further criticisms were forthcoming. Some Executive Directors said that members' reactions to it would be unfortunate because, before joining the Fund, they had carefully weighed the prospective obligations and benefits and had not intended to accept such a severe condition for drawing rights. Mr. McFarlane (Australia) emphasized in this connection that Australia and South Africa claimed that they had rights under the Articles of Agreement which could not be modified by administrative decisions. Some Directors, while accepting that it was right to expect members to take the proper steps to repurchase from the Fund, thought that the best way would be to invite members to make voluntary offers to limit the duration of drawings or to provide statements of intent as to the policies they planned to pursue. Mr. Rasminsky (Canada) agreed with the concept of the revolving character of the Fund, but thought that Mr. Southard's proposal was neither appropriate nor necessary. The demand for drawings had dropped to a point at which they offered no danger to the Fund. Moreover, the proposed commitment would bind members to repurchase, even though they might be dependent on others for the power to earn dollars. He therefore supported the staff's suggestions. At this point, Mr. Gutt said that the staff was giving further thought to the whole problem and would submit some suggestions as soon as possible.

The outcome of this review by the staff was brought before the Board in May 1950 in the form of a report by a working party composed of members of the Legal, Research, and Treasurer's Departments and the Secretary's Office. In substance, the recommendations of the report were as follows: The prime requirement was to enable members to know whether they could rely upon the use of the Fund's resources in time of need. For this purpose there should be a system of prior review and assessment of the eligibility of each member, the outcome of which should be notified to the member. The essential criterion of eligibility to draw should be that the member was following policies which would restore its reserves by the end of the period of difficulty. Examples of inappropriate policies would be the maintenance of an overvalued currency and the persistence of domestic inflation. More positively, it was suggested that the Fund could recommend appropriate policies for the member to follow, the observance of which would be a prerequisite for the right to draw. It was open to the Fund in marginal cases to ask the member for an undertaking as to its policies or its plans for repurchase.

The report of the working party was debated in several meetings in the summer of 1950. Executive Directors saw considerable difficulty in the proposals. The Board was particularly concerned with the effect on members of a procedure which would divide them into white, gray, and black categories; such a categorization would, at best, be most difficult and invidious. Moreover, one Director suggested that the past record of a member as assessed in periodic reviews offered no guarantee that its policies would continue to be appropriate in the future. For these reasons, the view was expressed that the preferable course was that members should consult the Fund before drawing, and that the Fund must retain the right to challenge a proposed drawing at the time.

The Board agreed in July 1950 to adjourn its discussions until after the Annual Meeting, and no reference was made to the subject in that year's Annual Report. During the Annual Meeting, the Governor for the Netherlands urged on the Governors' Committee on Finance and Organization that the Fund should regard itself not as a bank, which might or might not lend, but as a secondary reserve, on which its members might count for assistance when needed. He suggested that opening up the Fund's resources to its members was a necessary step toward assisting them to re-establish convertibility of their currencies, and urged that explicit criteria should be promulgated, so that members might know where they were. In reply, the Governor for the United States reiterated his country's view about the need to ensure the temporariness of Fund drawings, which he distinguished in this respect from the longer-term loans made by the World Bank. Answering critics who had urged that members could not know whether they were regarded by the Fund as eligible to use its resources, the Governor said that there was in fact a simple procedure by which members could establish their position; they could inquire through their elected or appointed Executive Director.

On the same occasion the Governor for Canada, agreeing with the Governor for the Netherlands, expressed the hope that the Fund would not set such rigorous criteria as to make it almost impossible for any member to use its resources. The Governor for South Africa said that at Bretton Woods he had asked Professor Robertson the significance of the fact that Article V, Section 3, did not explicitly state that the Fund's permission was needed to enable a member to draw. Professor Robertson, he recalled, had said that the provisions for the use of the Fund's resources were intended to give members the "comfort" of knowing that they would not get into difficulty because they could not pay their foreign debts. The Governor for France remarked that the intervention of the Board was limited to a decision on the test of eligibility to draw; he believed that the criteria suggested by the United States would be very difficult to apply.

It was against this background that the discussion was resumed in the Executive Board. Perhaps the only clear-cut effect of the summer debate was a recognition, frankly stated by Mr. Beyen and implicitly accepted by most others, that "automaticity was a dead horse." It seemed clear, however, that the staff proposals would not be acceptable and the way was open for the subject to enter its third phase.

Intervening in the debate in November 1950, Mr. Gutt suggested that the intentions of Article I (v)—to give confidence to members by making the Fund's resources available to them under adequate safeguards—could be achieved by linking drawings to the engagement by members to enter upon specific actions to remedy their balance of payments difficulties. Enlarging on his proposal at a meeting in February 1951 devoted to a discussion of the role of the Fund in existing conditions, Mr. Gutt deplored the current tendency to write off the Fund as moribund. He felt, on the contrary, that there was every opportunity for the Fund to enter upon an increasingly active role, based primarily upon systematic consultations with its members. He urged upon the Board that the time had come to move away from theoretical and doctrinal issues to practical techniques. The plan which he had put forward in November seemed to him to offer just such a practical way out of the impasse in which the Fund found itself.

Mr. Gutt's proposal was in general favorably received. Mr. Southard welcomed it as a useful and practical addition to the procedures already available, but he entered a caveat that the repurchase problem would still exist in relation to members of the sterling area and to planned economies. Mr. de Largentaye (France) challenged the legal basis of the Managing Director's plan, saying that it tacitly assumed that members were ineligible unless they demonstrated to the contrary. Moreover, he thought that, practically, the plan would not work because no one could ensure that a member's policies—however well intentioned—would remain appropriate to its problems. Nevertheless, Mr. de Largentaye viewed Mr. Gutt's plan as preferable to the deadlock which had prevented use of the Fund's resources, and said that in the circumstances he would abstain from opposing it.

Other Executive Directors also had doubts about the legality of the plan but thought it offered a useful technique for enabling members to resume drawing from the Fund. Only the Hon. Arthur Maxwell Stamp (United Kingdom), who had succeeded Mr. Crick as Alternate to Sir George Bolton, withheld approval, saying that the British Government believed that the Managing Director's scheme would be prejudicial to the larger issue of the right of members to draw on the Fund. With his abstention, and that of Mr. de Largentaye, the Board decided to give effect to Mr. Gutt's proposal in terms similar to those in which Mr. Southard had welcomed it. The plan was accordingly adopted, on May 2, 1951, "as a procedure for use in appropriate cases in addition to and without prejudice to existing procedures or policies respecting the use of the resources of the Fund." A brief description of it was included in the Annual Report.[17]

At the Annual Meeting, 1951, the Board's actions were criticized by several Governors. The Governor for Australia complained that the Directors had disregarded what Australia considered to be the clear meaning of Article V,

[17] *Annual Report, 1951*, pp. 81–82.

Section 3 (*a*) (i). He said that the Annual Report had laid stress on the improvement in members' payments positions, but that the real reason why there had been only one transaction, for £10 million, during the fiscal year 1950/51, was that a majority in the Board was preventing the use of the Fund's resources except under its own conditions. The Governor for the Netherlands, recalling his comment in 1950, pointed out that in 1950/51 transactions had been even fewer than in 1949/50. He found the plan to relate the use of the Fund's resources to "practical programs of action to help achieve the purposes of the Fund Agreement" to be obscure, disappointing, and unrealistic; and he compared unfavorably the small use made of the Fund's resources with the large credits given by the members of the EPU among themselves.

Despite the doubts thus expressed by some Governors, the future was to show that progress had indeed been made in working out policies and procedures for the use of the Fund's resources. But not until the landmark decision of February 13, 1952 was the replacement of automaticity by conditionality given a form which enabled members, Executive Directors, management, and staff to collaborate in a practical manner.

REPURCHASE PROBLEMS

Several problems arose during 1949–51 in connection with the calculation of monetary reserves for the purpose of arriving at members' repurchase obligations under Article V, Section 7. In general they were due to the understandable difficulty of applying general rules to the varying circumstances and accounting systems of different members.[18] In two instances it proved necessary for a representative of the staff to visit the member country concerned in order to reach agreement on the figures, and one Director suggested the general conclusion that such visits might well be undertaken whenever serious difficulties arose in connection with repurchase obligations.

One issue of major importance which reached the Board was posed by the requirement in Article V, Section 7 (*c*) (iii), that no repurchase should be carried to a point at which the Fund's holdings of a currency exceeded 75 per cent of that member's quota. The general provisions of Schedule B set out the proportions in which a member was to contribute gold or convertible currencies when repurchasing its own currency held by the Fund. These were related to the proportions in which the member's reserves contained such currencies or in which its reserves had increased during the year. But Schedule B, paragraph 1 (*c*), modified this requirement by providing that if repurchases so effected would, inter alia, cause the Fund's holdings of a currency tendered for the purpose of repurchase to

[18] E.B. Decisions Nos. 493-3, November 4, 1949, and 510-2, December 16, 1949; below, Vol. III, pp. 272, 273.

exceed 75 per cent of the quota of the member issuing it, "the Fund shall require such repurchases to be made by the members proportionately in such manner that the limits will not be exceeded."

At first sight this imposed an obligation that the whole repurchase must somehow be effected in currencies which the Fund could accept, or in gold. However, an examination of the possible consequences of such a procedure led the Legal Department to feel that this could not have been intended. One problem was that a currency might be convertible for purposes of the Fund Agreement, but not convertible into gold. If a member's reserves consisted largely of such a currency, and that currency was not acceptable to the Fund, the member might find itself incurring an obligation to repay the Fund in gold or in some currency convertible into gold without possessing either such a currency or the means of obtaining it in exchange.

The Legal Department also pointed out that, while paragraph 1 (*c*) of Schedule B referred to requiring repurchases to be made "proportionately," it provided no guidance as to the way in which these proportions should be calculated—an omission quite unlike the precise formulation of requirements in paragraphs 1 (*a*) and 1 (*b*). Finally, it was of importance that paragraph 1 (*c*) covered not only the 75 per cent limit in Article V, Section 7 (*c*) (iii), but also the limits in Article V, Section 7 (*c*) (i) and (ii). The first of these provided that a repurchase should not bring a member's reserves below its quota, and the second that it should not reduce the Fund's holdings of the member's currency below 75 per cent of its quota. But it was clear that if either of these limits was reached the repurchase obligation must be curtailed, not redistributed; hence it was impossible to conclude that paragraph 1 (*c*) effectively insisted that somehow the repurchase obligation must be discharged in full.

The conclusion drawn by the Legal Department was that a repurchase obligation which would involve the breach of any one of the three limits set in Article V, Section 7 (*c*), must *pro tanto* disappear. When this recommendation was considered by the Board, in January 1950, several Executive Directors said that while they questioned its implications, they had no basis on which to oppose it. The decision therefore was to adopt the Legal Department's view.[19] In practice this has had profound effects upon members' repurchase obligations, especially in recent years when the Fund's holdings of U.S. dollars and of sterling have both been above 75 per cent of the U.S. and British quotas.

Voluntary repurchases

The questions raised by the voluntary repurchase offered by Nicaragua—whether such repurchases could be accepted, and if so whether they had to be made wholly in gold—were answered by the Legal Department in two memo-

[19] E.B. Decision No. 521-3, January 16, 1950; below, Vol. III, p. 273.

randa distributed in November 1949 and January 1950. The former suggested that voluntary repurchases could (but need not) be accepted at any time, within the limits set by Article V, Section 7 (*c*), provided that the member had no outstanding obligation to repurchase its currency under Article V, Section 7 (*b*). The proviso was necessary, as otherwise the member, by tendering a voluntary repurchase, might frustrate the requirements of the Article, and of Schedule B, as to the proportion in which its repurchase must be made in gold and in specified currencies. The Legal Department's second memorandum distinguished the offer of a voluntary repurchase such as that made by Nicaragua from a tender of gold to the Fund under Article V, Section 7 (*a*), which obliges the Fund, at a member's request, to sell to it for gold any excess of its currency above its quota which the Fund held. Since in the former case the acceptance by the Fund of an offer of repurchase was optional, it was unnecessary to hold that it must be made only in gold. If the Fund did not wish to accept the currencies proffered, it could refuse.

The Board decided that the problems raised by the Legal Department's memoranda should be remitted for consideration to the Committee on Interpretation. When this committee took up the matter in February 1950 Mr. de Largentaye (France) argued that voluntary repurchases in convertible currencies could not be accepted because they fell under the ban of Article V, Section 2, which provided that

> except as otherwise provided in this Agreement, operations on the account of the Fund shall be limited to transactions for the purpose of supplying a member, on the initiative of such member, with the currency of another member in exchange for gold or for the currency of the member desiring to make the purchase.

Mr. van Campenhout, General Counsel, replied that the "operations" contemplated by Article V, Section 2, could be single or complex. They could, for example, consist of a combination of a purchase of dollars from the Fund and a repurchase of the member's currency with dollars. The legislative history of the provision supported this concept, since if an "operation" were interpreted to mean only the purchase aspect of the dual transaction it would be impossible for the Fund to accept the repurchase even in gold of that part of the Fund's holdings of the member's currency which lay between 75 per cent and 100 per cent of its quota; such a transaction was not contemplated by the obligatory provision of Article V, Section 7 (*a*), and would therefore have to be treated as not "otherwise provided in this Agreement."

This argument was found by most Directors to be persuasive. Mr. Crick (United Kingdom), however, was disturbed at the possible effect on the position in the Fund of a member whose currency was used for repurchases. The Fund's holdings of that member's currency would of course be increased by the transaction (though not above 75 per cent of its quota) and to that extent its position in the Fund would be worsened without its being able to do anything about it. This could undermine the safeguards provided in Article VIII, Section 4 (*b*), and to that extent might discourage members from moving from Article XIV to Article VIII. He agreed, however, that this was not a legal point; it was one affecting the policy of the Fund toward its members. As such it was not pursued by Mr. Crick or his successors, and the staff thought it unnecessary to press for a decision until the need arose. The point disappeared when in 1962 the Board adopted a comprehensive policy on the selection of currencies to be used in repurchases.

When the report of the Interpretation Committee, which adopted the view of the Legal Department, was considered by the Board on March 8, 1951, Messrs. de Largentaye and Crick repeated the arguments mentioned above. The Board, however, decided by 76,725 votes to 9,910 to accept the committee's report. The decision as adopted made three points.[20]

(*a*) A member that had an outstanding obligation under Article V, Section 7 (*b*), and Schedule B must discharge that obligation in gold or currency as prescribed in those provisions.

(*b*) A member that did not have such an outstanding obligation might offer in voluntary repurchase, and the Fund could accept, gold or convertible currencies, subject to the limits in Article V, Section 7 (*c*) (ii) and (iii).

(*c*) It was not legally necessary for the consent to be obtained of the member whose currency was offered.

Mr. Crick proposed a rider to the effect that the member whose currency was used for a repurchase should be consulted, but this was not pressed.

Meanwhile the collection of data on monetary reserves, on which the calculations of repurchase obligations had to be based, was still running into difficulties. In July 1950 the Board revised the Rule (I-6) covering the provision of such data in such a way as to require members in future to provide the necessary figures within six months of the end of the fiscal year. However, on November 7, 1950, the staff reported to the Board that twenty members had so far failed to provide data relating to the previous April 30, and that fourteen of these had also omitted to supply the figures for earlier years. Executive Directors were asked to urge the members which they represented to supply the missing data as quickly as possible. Six months later the number of members from which information was still needed had been reduced to ten, and by the end of the period covered by this chapter the number was down to eight. The Board invited the Managing Director to convey to these members the Board's concern that the necessary data had not been provided, and to offer the services of the staff to assist in the compilation of the figures if this was causing difficulty.

[20] E.B. Decision No. 7-(648), March 8, 1951; below, Vol. III, p. 244.

TECHNICAL ASSISTANCE

During 1949 the United Nations undertook a series of discussions with eight specialized agencies, including the Fund and the Bank, on the need for more technical assistance for economic development. One outcome was the establishment of a Technical Assistance Board (TAB) under the terms of General Assembly Resolution 304 (IV) passed on November 16, 1949. This body was set up, as an agency of the United Nations, to administer special funds to finance an extended program of technical assistance. The Fund and the Bank were invited to participate as members in the work of TAB. Neither, however, felt able to do so, partly because neither needed to have access to outside funds to finance such operations, and partly because each had special responsibilities for technical assistance in its own field, entrusted to it by its Articles, which it could not properly relinquish to another body. The Fund agreed, however, to be represented by an observer at all meetings of TAB and its subsidiary bodies; to cooperate fully with TAB; and, on the principle of reciprocity, to supply its own technical assistance wherever compatible with the Articles of Agreement.

The concept of TAB held by the UN authorities was that of a centralized agency controlling and financing all kinds of technical assistance. The specialized agencies, on the other hand, tended to emphasize their special qualifications in their own fields. Accordingly, the new body took some time to settle down. The kind of problem that arose may be illustrated by two that were discussed at sessions of TAB in the early months of 1950. One concerned the responsibility for advice and assistance given by technical assistance missions; the other the relationship of the members of a joint mission to the chief of that mission.

On the first of these, the Fund's view was that advice and assistance given by the Fund's missions were the responsibility of the Fund. The other specialized agencies and the UN authorities were disposed at first to feel that the responsibility they incurred toward a country to which they gave technical assistance was limited to choosing competent experts to give the advice. However, after further discussion it became clear that several of the other agencies had come to adopt the Fund's viewpoint. The point was not formally clarified in TAB, but technical assistance practice has tended to conform to the concept put forward by the Fund. When the Fund's staff advises a member on any subject within the competence of the Fund, the Fund assumes responsibility for this advice. Since 1964, this responsibility extends also to the advice given by outside experts lent, through the agency of the Fiscal Affairs Department, to assist members in dealing with fiscal problems. Exceptionally, however, when central banking experts who are not members of the Fund's staff are made available through the agency of the Fund's Central Banking Service, the Fund does not hold itself responsible for the advice given. This is because such experts are typically engaged in an operating capacity in the service of the member seeking help, and assume personal responsibility for their actions as officials of the employing government or central bank.

On the second question—the responsibility of the members of a mission toward the head of that mission—the Fund has consistently held that members of the Fund's staff made available to participate in a joint mission remain responsible to the Fund; and, moreover, that responsibility for those parts of a joint report that deal with subjects in the Fund's sphere must be approved by the Fund. Directors felt it to be imperative that whatever advice was given to governments on monetary and banking policy should always reflect the needs of their countries' balances of payments. For most members at most times in the Fund's history this has necessitated stressing the control of inflation. The Board was concerned lest the natural urge of its members toward higher standards of living should cause them to yield to pressure to inflate rather than heed advice on how to progress steadily. It could not be sure that the need to combat this tendency would be asserted with equal force by advisors from some other organization.

On these terms joint missions have proved very difficult to arrange, and have largely been replaced by parallel missions, each of which is responsible to the organization that commissioned it. Arrangements of this kind were formalized in 1952 by an agreement between the Secretary-General of the United Nations, the Managing Director of the Fund, and the President of the World Bank.

FULL EMPLOYMENT REPORT

It was the problem developed in the preceding paragraphs which partly underlay the Board's reactions to the report of the experts appointed by the United Nations in August 1949 to recommend national and international measures to achieve full employment. The "national measures" recommended involved the expansion of demand in a way, as the experts themselves recognized, that might have inflationary consequences. Moreover, the recommendations of the experts touched on the work of the Fund in several other respects. On the one hand, they proposed that ECOSOC should convene a meeting of interested governments to devise methods of producing a new structural equilibrium in world trading relationships, to be followed up by further meetings at frequent intervals to adjust the targets set, in the light of progress made. This program was to be supervised by an Expert Advisory Committee responsible to ECOSOC—a procedure which the Board felt would unnecessarily duplicate the activities of the Fund itself. On the other hand, the experts proposed to entrust to the Fund additional resources to be made available to both members and nonmembers to counteract cyclical fluctuations in demand—a proposal which would involve the amendment of the Articles of Agreement. Broadly speaking, and subject to detailed qualifications, these resources were to be provided by surplus countries, which were to deposit with the Fund the equivalent of any shortfall in their imports not offset by a fall in their exports. The deposits would be sold by the Fund to deficit countries to the extent of the fall in the latter's exports to, less any decrease in their imports from, the surplus countries. The proceeds of the sales would be made available to the surplus countries to the extent that their monetary reserves might diminish in any subsequent period.

While Executive Directors welcomed the experts' recognition of the Fund's responsibilities in connection with balances of payments, they considered that the plan put forward had both weaknesses and dangers. On the technical side they foresaw great difficulty in determining with any promptitude the amount which a surplus country ought to contribute, and the amount to which a deficit country would be entitled. More fundamentally, the Board feared that the proposed transfer of resources would prove a palliative which would encourage deficit countries to postpone necessary adjustments in their international payments. While, therefore, at least one Director would have welcomed the plan as dealing with the possible effects of deflation in surplus countries, thus filling what he regarded as a gap in the scope of the Articles of Agreement, Executive Directors generally were disposed to deprecate the experts' ideas.

The Board accordingly decided that when the report of the experts was discussed at ECOSOC the Fund's representative should say that the Fund, while concerned at the existence of unemployment due to inadequate international demand, could not consider full employment more important than a freely operating multilateral trading system; that technically and administratively the experts' plan for additional Fund operations seemed defective; that the Fund was already free to use its resources to assist its members in temporary balance of payments difficulties, and if these resources were inadequate there were better ways of increasing them than by setting up a separate mechanism; and that insofar as the proposed scheme would involve the Fund in providing resources to perpetuate a state of international disequilibrium, this would be directly contrary to its obligations under its Articles. The Board's decision concluded by referring to the availability of the "scarce currency provisions" of Article VII, saying that the experts' plan was perhaps best considered as an alternative to these provisions, and that the latter deserved more careful study.

EUROPEAN PAYMENTS UNION

A new stage in the evolution of payments arrangements in Europe began with the issue in December 1949 of a draft working paper, prepared by the U.S. Economic Cooperation Administration (ECA).[21] This paper recommended the

[21] For the Fund's previous relations with European payments arrangements, see above, pp. 212–23.

establishment of a clearing union, the adoption of a common unit of account, the prior allocation of ECA dollars in accordance with estimated needs, and the use of ECA funds to cover the probable net outgo of dollars from the system. It also advocated the adoption of a scale of payments in gold and dollars by debtor to creditor countries, graduated in proportion to the relation of the debit balance to the country's quota in the proposed European Payments Union (EPU).

Drawing this to the attention of the Board in January 1950, Mr. Gutt stressed the vital interest of the Fund in the new arrangements proposed. He recommended that the Fund should participate in the forthcoming discussions, both in technical and in policy matters; that members should consult the Fund before adopting any new plan; and that the Fund should provide any new regional monetary organization required. In reply, Mr. de Selliers (Belgium) emphasized that the new proposals were the outcome of two years' experience, and that as the Fund had hitherto taken a negative attitude toward Europe's plans it was inappropriate now to request European Governments to suspend action pending consultation with the Fund. Another Director pointed out that, in any case, the staff memorandum which the Managing Director had presented to the Board would reach all Fund members. The Board then decided to note the views of the Managing Director and staff and to agree to their transmittal by Executive Directors to the member countries concerned. However, a month later it approved a proposal by the Deputy Managing Director, following a visit by him to Europe, that a strong staff mission should be made available to participate in the forthcoming discussions.

The subject was resumed in March, when the Board had before it draft instructions to the staff mission. Specific points in these instructions were criticized by the Board. Mr. Joshi (India) and Mr. Falaki (Egypt), for instance, objected to the staff's stress on the difficulties caused by the overabundance of sterling, although the staff continued to argue that the existence of large sterling balances was partly responsible for the United Kingdom's reluctance to dispense with bilateral arrangements in Europe. Several Executive Directors drew attention to the difficulty faced by the Board in instructing a staff mission to a series of meetings at which the Governments represented on the Board would be instructing their own delegates. Mr. Crick (United Kingdom) urged that the only guidance given to the mission should be to assist in formulating payments arrangements compatible with the Fund's objectives.

The draft instruction to the staff that they should support a system by which intra-European settlements should increasingly be made in gold and dollars was challenged by several Directors and taken to a vote. This resulted in the instruction being confirmed by 51,040 votes to 28,260. The instructions to the staff were then agreed. They were, in summary, as follows:

1. The Fund should assist in formulating satisfactory payments arrangements compatible with its purpose.
2. Regional payments arrangements should facilitate the attainment of convertibility, avoiding tendencies toward a closed monetary area.
3. While inflation threatens, the element of credit should be moderate; settlements should be increasingly in gold and dollars.
4. The Fund mission should stress that the conditions needed for convertibility were the same as those needed for the functioning of a satisfactory payments agreement.

Subsequent developments may be briefly noted. Mr. Gutt visited Paris in April and June and the Deputy Managing Director paid a second visit in May. As the negotiations progressed a note of disillusionment crept into the Board's discussions. Difficulties became increasingly apparent. Some were created by the fact that four of the members of the OEEC were not members of the Fund, and others by the unwillingness of European members to have European problems discussed in the Fund Board, where non-European members participated. The "ERP Decision" on the use of the Fund's resources, making it impossible for European members of the Fund to rely on access to drawings, was cited as precluding any plan for the association of the Fund with settlement arrangements. The fact that the Board was simultaneously examining proposals by the staff for a new policy on the use of the Fund's resources raised difficulties of a similar kind. One Executive Director questioned whether it was wise for the Fund to seek any special relations with the EPU, since the latter was so far removed from the kind of system which the Fund wanted. Eventually it was decided that the Fund representatives should not seek any special arrangements with the EPU, except to ensure that observers on behalf of the Fund might attend meetings of the EPU Management Committee.

The text of the new plan (which came into force on July 1, 1950) was circulated to the Board on August 15, and on the following day the Board held a preliminary discussion on proposals for the association of the Fund with the new body. The debate was inconclusive and was adjourned until after the 1950 Annual Meeting. Discussions were not, however, resumed and, while the Board was given regular reports from Paris on the working of the new plan, it did not again consider associating the Fund with it.

GATT: THE FUND'S ROLE

During the last quarter of 1950 the GATT held a series of consultations at Torquay. In accordance with the agreement between the GATT and the Fund, the latter was invited to advise the Contracting Parties on the justification for trade restrictions imposed for balance of payments reasons. This involved the Fund in an intensive study of the economic situation of the nine countries concerned—Australia, Ceylon, Chile, India, New Zealand, Pakistan, South Africa, Southern Rhodesia, and the United Kingdom. The delegation to Torquay was led by Mr. Saad (Egypt).

In the course of briefing the delegation the Board reached decisions on two major issues: that the economic situation on which the Fund's advice was to be given was the current one, not that at the time when the restrictions in question were imposed; and that the advice given should include not only facts but conclusions drawn from these facts. Both these decisions were taken to a vote. That the advice should include current conditions was decided by 64,090 votes against 21,000. The decision to put forward conclusions was adopted by 60,580 votes to 30,010. A third vote, formally approving the report to the GATT, was also decided by 60,580 to 30,010.

Opposition expressed by Australia in connection with these decisions was often reflected in later discussions of GATT matters in the Fund, and it may be useful to remark that its underlying purpose was to seek to expand the role of the GATT, and diminish that of the Fund, in the borderland where both had responsibilities. For this wish, two reasons may be discerned. On the one hand, voting in the GATT was on the basis of one country, one vote, so that Australia's voice was relatively larger than in the Fund, where it was outweighed by members with larger voting powers. In the second place, the Australian authorities appear to have felt that their representatives in the GATT had somewhat greater freedom of maneuver than in the Fund, both because countries' positions there were somewhat less firm and because the economic doctrines prevailing in the GATT were less strictly orthodox than those in the Fund. A recognition of Australia's interest in GATT matters led in later years to the appointment of the Australian Executive Director as chairman of the Board Committee on Relations with the GATT.

This, however, was in the future. At Torquay the actual consultations were protracted and at times acrimonious. Although the authority of the Fund as financial advisor to the GATT was not questioned, and its submission of current data accepted, the propriety of its submitting conclusions was contested with some acerbity. The U.S. and Belgian delegations at Torquay supported the position taken by the Fund, but those from Australia and the United Kingdom were dissatisfied.

The Australian view of the Fund's role in GATT consultations was that this was limited in three respects. Firstly, it was suggested, the Fund's concern was exclusively with exchange and other financial matters, and not at all with import restrictions or trade controls. In pursuance of this argument, Australia had refused to allow the Executive Secretary of the GATT to send to the Fund copies of certain documents related to trade restrictions, for which the Fund had asked in connection with its preparations for the consultations. Secondly, Australia still contended, as it had done at the Board, that the Fund's advice should be concerned only with the need for intensifying restrictions at the time that step was taken, and not with the current position at the time of the GATT discussions. Thirdly, Australia considered that the Fund's contribution to the consultations should be limited to detailed factual information, and that it should make judgments only in relation to monetary reserves, balances of payments, and foreign exchange arrangements. In a speech to the CONTRACTING PARTIES on December 9, 1950, the Australian delegate emphasized all these points and requested that the invitation to the Fund to consult on future occasions should be drafted by the CONTRACTING PARTIES. His delegation also gave notice that it would submit to the next meeting of the GATT detailed proposals for the procedure in later consultations. However, by the following August the Government judged that, because of proposals then being discussed for the establishment of a Secretariat and a Standing Committee for the GATT, it was appropriate to withdraw the request for a discussion of the procedure. Although at the Annual Meeting in September 1951 the Governor for Australia criticized the Board for transmitting "conclusions" to the GATT on matters which the GATT was called upon to decide, the point was not pressed. Since then the Fund's participation in GATT consultations, along the lines proposed by the Board, has not effectively been challenged.[22] A working party set up at Geneva in October 1951, under Australian chairmanship, to draft a procedure for consultations in and after March 1952, recommended only that a consultation with the GATT should not take place until the Fund had completed its consultation under Article XIV with the same member country, and that the Fund should make available to the CONTRACTING PARTIES the results of its consultation with the member.

PREMIUM PRICES FOR GOLD: LAST PHASE

Between October 1949 and September 1951 the Board on 30 separate occasions reviewed its policy, first enunciated in 1947, which deprecated the sale of gold at premium prices. The occasion for the first discussion was the resolution on the subject passed at the Fourth Annual Meeting, as described in the previous chapter. The final review arose from an attempt to find ways in which to implement the policy more effectively; from this there emerged the

[22] Gerard Curzon, *Multilateral Commercial Diplomacy* (London, 1965), pp. 138, 144. For a description of the working arrangements between the Fund and the GATT that have been developed since 1952, see below, Vol. II, Chapter 16.

last decision which the Board has ever taken on the general question of sales of gold at premium prices. In the course of the two years the Board came reluctantly to adopt a view which it had at first repudiated. How this came about can only be indicated in summary. Difficult questions were involved, and the arguments adduced can only be briefly surveyed; for the sake of cogency many subsidiary issues are here omitted altogether.

South African proposal

On October 12, 1949, the Board took into consideration the resolution passed by the Governors at the Fourth Annual Meeting, which transmitted to the Executive Directors "for study of all relevant considerations and report to the Board of Governors" a South African proposal that members should be free to sell half their gold output in free markets. The Board had some difficulty in deciding what were the "relevant considerations" to be borne in mind: among the topics mentioned were the price of gold, subsidies to gold production, domestic sales of gold, and the circulation of gold coins. However, the staff was asked to draft a report.

The staff report, a document of some sixty thousand words, reached the Board in February 1950. Part I contained a general description of premium gold markets, a study of the economic and legal aspects of the South African proposal, and an evaluation of Fund policy on premium gold markets. Part II reviewed the nature and scope of the principal gold markets individually, and was accompanied by extensive tabular material. The conclusions of the report may be summarized as follows: (*a*) Nearly everywhere the importation of gold at premium prices was a species of capital flight which diverted foreign exchange resources from reserves to less important uses. However, the total supply of gold to premium markets in 1948 was estimated to be only about 6½ per cent of the deficit of the rest of the world toward the United States on current account. (*b*) It was unlikely that the demand for gold for hoarding would continue at the level currently reached; the premium price had recently decreased quite sharply. (*c*) The control of exports by distinguishing fabricated gold was difficult because the cost of fabrication was relatively small. (*d*) The profit position of the gold mining industry was not unfavorable, even before the devaluations in 1949, while it seemed probable that the reduction in the premium which would follow if the South African proposal were adopted would be such as to eliminate any extra profit from that source.

Summing up, the report suggested that the facts justified the Fund's policy and offered little support for its abandonment on the ground of supposed hardship to gold producing countries. Nevertheless it had to be considered whether it was worthwhile for the Fund to continue to exert moral suasion in support of the policy. Premium markets were a symptom of a deep-rooted malady—the persistence of inflation. Until that malady was cured the symptom would persist, and policies such as the deprecation of sales in premium markets would be palliatives only. The staff recommended that the Fund policy should be modified by leaving gold exporting countries free from any restrictions other than those inherent in the obligations of Article IV, Section 2, of the Fund Agreement (which prohibits the purchase of gold above parity or its sale below parity) and in members' undertakings to cooperate in maintaining orderly exchange arrangements. It suggested that this modification should be coupled with offers to assist any member whose reserve position was threatened by gold transactions to find more effective means of preventing unauthorized sales and to enlist the cooperation of other members in helping to prevent the undesirable practices.

Presenting this report at two informal sessions of the Board in February 1950, the staff explained that its views on the desirability of preventing premium gold sales were unchanged; it suggested a change in the Fund policy only because this was being flouted, which was bad for the Fund. The Board was, however, reluctant to modify its policy in the way suggested, Mr. Crick (United Kingdom) in particular urging that free dealings in gold might jeopardize the official rate for sterling.

Resuming the discussion in April, the Board heard Mr. J. E. Holloway, Alternate Governor for the Union of South Africa, argue for the South African proposal. When signing the Articles of Agreement, South Africa had understood that Article IV, Section 2, permitted members to sell gold above parity; in any case, South Africa had only entered the premium markets after finding that other countries were doing so, and by agreement with the Fund. Mr. Holloway was unable to see that official hoarding of gold was any better than private hoarding. He urged that the Board should face the question of an increase in the price of gold.

Mr. Holloway's statement was debated at some length, but found no support except from Mr. McFarlane (Australia), although Messrs. de Largentaye (France) and de Selliers (Belgium) thought that the Fund's existing policy was legally untenable and economically unwise. Messrs. Crick, Joshi (India), Falaki (Egypt), Rasminsky (Canada), and Southard (United States) all supported the Fund's policy, which Mr. Crick thought should if anything be strengthened. At the end of the discussion the proposal made by South Africa at the Annual Meeting was defeated by 51,740 votes against 7,280.

Turning then to the staff's recommendation, the Board decided to maintain the 1947 policy by 55,290 votes against 16,530. On the price of gold, the staff's advice was that an increase was not justified. Mr. de Largentaye argued for an increase in order to avoid the onset of a depression, but Directors generally accepted the staff's view. Accordingly a brief report was sent to the Governors on April 24, advising them to reject the South African proposal and stating that the Directors saw no reason to alter the existing policy.[23] Chapter IV of the Annual Report was devoted to an exposition of the policy and to a review of recent tendencies in gold production and premium markets.[24]

The subject was discussed at the Annual Meeting, 1950, in the Governors' Committee on Gold. Views were expressed by the Governors for India and the United States supporting the Board's report, and by the Governors for France and Belgium advocating an increase in the price of gold. Mr. Havenga, Governor for South Africa, briefly addressed the committee in support of such an increase, and subsequently made a statement to the Governors as a whole in opposition to the Executive Board's views.[25]

Implementing the policy

There the matter stood until, in February 1951, the staff presented to the Board a review of premium gold markets in 1950, which showed that sales in these markets had increased very sharply in the second half of the year. The staff suggested that the volume of transactions was such as to make it desirable to take steps to make the Fund's policy more effective. Special attention was drawn to the large sales by South Africa. The Board considered this review, and after a postponement to allow governments to be consulted, reached a decision in the following terms:

> Since the amount of sales and purchases in the world markets of gold for jewelry, artistic and industrial purposes has recently been increasing at a rate indicating that at least a part of it finds its way to private hoards, contrary to the gold policy of the Fund established in June 1947, the Board considers the existing arrangements and practices of several countries, including South Africa, are no longer a satisfactory basis to implement the Fund's gold policy and directs the staff of the Fund urgently to elaborate, after consultation with the countries concerned, more effective methods than the existing ones.

This decision was made public on March 7, 1951, and was cited in the Annual Report for 1951 in connection with a discussion of developments in premium markets during the previous year.[26]

The Annual Report was approved for printing on July 12. Six days later Directors received copies of the staff's report, prepared in pursuance of the Board's directive. This recommended that, as a matter of principle, countries should permit the export and import of gold in any form only in order to satisfy

---

[23] *Annual Report, 1950,* pp. 90–94.

[24] *Ibid.,* pp. 70–74.

[25] *Summary Proceedings, 1950,* pp. 93–98.

[26] *Annual Report, 1951,* pp. 73–80.

legitimate industrial and artistic demands, or for refining, processing, or fabrication; and that except for movements of gold between monetary authorities, no country should permit the export of gold in any form to another country that had not subscribed to the principle mentioned. Subsidiary recommendations were that statistics of gold movements should be supplied to the Fund, that exporting countries should require evidence of the actual import of gold into the country to which it was directed on export, and that countries should not admit gold for safekeeping.

The Board did not have an opportunity to discuss this report before the 1951 Annual Meeting, but it was the subject of a somewhat scathing comment by the South African authorities. Remarking that "it is a common disease of bureaucracies to move on from one control to another," they condemned the proposals as administratively impracticable, as failing to command public support in many important countries, and as having no clear objective.

Immediately after the Annual Meeting the Board took up the staff's report. After considerable debate, in which the merits of the Fund's policy were again challenged, the Board tacitly accepted the criticisms put forward by South Africa, that the additional controls recommended by the staff were unworkable. The staff was accordingly invited to make further recommendations. This it did in a memorandum which briefly argued that the enforcement of the Board's policy was impracticable without the kind of detailed supervision which had been recommended. If this were thought to be administratively impossible, the staff suggested that the only alternative was for the Board to withdraw its request to members to observe the policy.

Directors showed considerable reluctance to accept proposals which seemed to be tantamount to abandoning the 1947 decision, but agreed in general with Mr. Southard that no uniform code for controlling gold sales appeared to be feasible, and that it would be necessary to leave to members the decision how to carry out the Fund's policy. Some difficulty was experienced in drafting a statement that carried general approval, but on September 28, 1951, the Board decided on a public announcement. This referred to the June 1947 decision, and stated that it was still desirable for gold to be held as far as possible in reserves. It went on, however, to intimate that, because it was impracticable to expect governments to take uniform measures to achieve the objectives of the policy, the Fund was leaving to its members the operating decisions necessary to do so.[27] This was the last occasion on which the Board considered what its policy should be in connection with sales at premium prices. By then, of course, Mr. Rooth had become Managing Director, and it is to his term of office that we shall now turn, after a brief retrospect.

[27] E.B. Decision No. 75-(705), September 28, 1951; below, Vol. III, p. 225.

A SUMMING-UP, 1946–51

Looking back over the Fund's first five years, the observer is bound to be impressed chiefly by what was not achieved. In 1951 member countries had not yet fully grasped what was needed from them if the Fund was to be an effective instrument. Multiple currency practices were still prevalent, and the attractiveness of a freely fluctuating currency seemed, if anything, to be on the increase. No solution had been found for the problem of reconciling access to the Fund's resources with the protection of those resources from premature dissipation. No working relationship had been established with the intercountry organizations arising in an economically united Europe, and the attempts to create one had shown that some at least of the countries concerned tended to rate their interests there above their interest in the Fund. Even the policy deprecating the sale of gold at premium prices, in which much effort had been invested, was shortly to prove unfeasible.

Yet it would be a mistake to assess the five years 1946–51 in these negative terms. International cooperation in economic matters was still in its infancy; that it progressed as far as it did was due in no small degree to the effectiveness of the Fund as a forum for the discussion of international problems. The concept of an international staff, owing its allegiance only to the Fund, had been realized, and this staff, ably led by the Director of Research, was gaining influence. Given that the Board was sometimes unable to take an international view where the interests of the Fund's largest members were involved, it had yet acted as an international conscience in many other matters. Given that the Board had little say in fixing the new exchange rates established in 1949, these devaluations had been brought about partly by the pressure which it had exerted, had been coordinated through its means, and had been accepted, under its auspices, without provoking retaliation.

In all this, the Managing Director played no small part. He supported the staff and encouraged its advocacy of forward-looking policies. Disappointed though he became because the Board was unready to take the lead which he wished it to assume, he continued to urge the importance of its potential role. It was with justification that on the occasion of his retirement the Directors expressed

> their appreciation of Mr. Gutt's wise conduct of the affairs of the Fund during its first five years, of his clear-sighted statesmanship in the field of international finance, and of the invaluable service he has rendered to the Fund and its members.

The emphasis which Mr. Gutt personally placed on the need to control inflation helped to set the tone of the Fund's most insistent thesis. Without the foundations which were laid under his leadership during the first five years of the Fund, the developments of its later years could never have come to fruition.

Despite the conditions which existed in 1946–51 within the Fund, and the economic circumstances in which its work had to be done, Mr. Gutt achieved much in building up the organization and the policies which the Fund needed. In particular, the Fund had been brought by 1951 to the threshold of effective policies and procedures for the use of its resources—a development which made it possible to take in 1952 the decisive remaining steps.

PART III

Forging Ahead

CHAPTER

12

New Functions (1951-52)

ARTICLE XIV of the Fund Agreement requires that five years after the Fund begins operations, and in each subsequent year, members maintaining exchange restrictions under that Article shall consult with the Fund as to the retention of these restrictions. The five-year period expired on March 1, 1952, and accordingly a major feature of Mr. Rooth's first year as Managing Director was the inauguration of the annual consultations, which today form a large part of the work of the Executive Board. Simultaneously, the achievement of an agreed basis for the use of the Fund's resources made it possible to place these more freely at the disposal of member countries if they needed such assistance to enable them to reduce their reliance on artificial restraints on the balance of payments. An important result of the new basis for drawings was to shorten the period between the time a drawing was made and the time when the member was required to consult the Fund about ways for reducing the Fund's holdings of its currency. Thus in two different ways the Board expected to maintain closer and more regular contacts with its members. The establishment of such contacts was undoubtedly the main feature of 1952 for the Fund.

MEMBERSHIP, BOARD, AND STAFF

Membership and Board

Four countries joined the Fund during the year: Burma on January 3, 1952, Japan on August 13, Germany on August 14, and Jordan on August 29. This brought the total membership to 54, and the number of votes that Directors could cast to 100,865. Deducting the votes of the appointed members, and of the two Directors elected for Latin America under Article XII, Section 3 (*b*) (iv), the number of votes to be cast by the remaining elected Directors was 35,005. The corresponding figure in 1950 had been 26,775. In accordance with the precedent set in 1947, the Board proposed, and the Governors approved, that the number of Directors to be elected, including the two by the American Republics, should be increased from nine to eleven. Both Mr. Martínez-Ostos (Mexico) and Mr. Paranaguá (Brazil) expressed concern that there should be this further increase in the number of elected Directors while the number representing Latin America remained fixed. However, they agreed to the Board's recommendation to the Governors on the understanding that in future elections there could be an increase in the number of Directors representing Latin America if the number of votes cast by these countries should be substantially expanded. The election was held on September 11, 1952 during the Annual Meeting, and is reported in the next chapter.

During the year there were two changes among the appointed Directors: Mr. W. R. Natu (India) succeeded Mr. Joshi from November 30, 1951, and Sir Edmund Hall-Patch (United Kingdom) succeeded Sir George Bolton, who resigned on May 19, 1952.

At the end of January 1952 Honduras asked that its quota, which in 1948 had been reduced at its request from $2.5 million to $0.5 million, should be restored to the original figure. Its Government explained that a complete reform of its monetary system, which had meanwhile been effected, enabled it to ask for a reversal of this temporary decrease. This was agreed by the Executive Board in March, and became effective in May after approval by the Board of Governors.

STAFF

On January 24, 1952, Mr. Overby resigned as Deputy Managing Director in order to become Assistant Secretary of the U.S. Treasury. Mr. H. Merle Cochran, long a career officer in the Foreign Service of the United States, retired from that Service and resigned as Ambassador to Indonesia to succeed Mr. Overby in March 1953. It may be noted here that Mr. Cochran concentrated more than either his predecessor or his successor on administrative and staff matters.

During his first few months as Managing Director, Mr. Rooth made considerable use of the Staff Committee set up by his predecessor. The committee met 35 times in the twelve months from September 1951 to August 1952 and about once a week in the last two months of 1952. Thereafter, however, less formal machinery largely took its place; the committee, as such, met only three times in the second half of the calendar year 1953, five times in the whole of 1954, six times in 1955, and six times in 1956. Its existence as a constitutional body ended with the termination of Mr. Rooth's tenure as Managing Director.

On April 30, 1952, the active staff numbered 426. A further ten were on leave without pay, 15 on military leave, and one on loan to another organization. Of the 43 most senior posts, 18 were held by citizens of the United States. The remainder were filled by five officers from the United Kingdom, four each from China and the Netherlands, two each from Czechoslovakia and France, and one each from Belgium, Canada, Chile, Egypt, India, Nicaragua, Pakistan, and Sweden.

Gold transactions service

In February 1952, as a result of a suggestion by Mr. Martínez-Ostos, the staff proposed to the Board that a new service should be offered to Fund members. Members seeking to buy or sell gold should be invited to notify the Fund of their wishes, and the staff should endeavor to "marry" requests for purchases and sales in any given market. For this service the staff suggested that a fee of 1/32 of 1 per cent should be charged to each partner, to cover cable costs, etc.; this was lower than the charges made for similar services elsewhere. The Board approved, and a letter was sent to all members on March 21, 1952, offering the Fund's assistance in the way suggested.[1]

In his address to the Governors at the ensuing Annual Meeting, the Managing Director was able to say that a number of such transactions had already been arranged.[2] There had in fact been 11 transactions, for $78 million. The success of the arrangements depended very much upon the use made of them, since any material delay in finding a buyer for a prospective seller of gold meant a potential loss of interest to him; it was calculated that if the delay was as much as a month, the seller would have found it more worth his while to have sold to the Federal Reserve Bank of New York, even though the Federal Reserve Bank charged a fee of ¼ of 1 per cent. The service has, however, remained in operation. During the nine fiscal years 1951/52 to 1960/61, 114 transactions for rather more than $1 billion were concluded, but the demand for the service then diminished, and between 1960/61 and 1965/66 there were only 6 further transactions, for $37 million.

INVESTMENT OF FUND'S ASSETS CONSIDERED

In only one of the first five years of the Fund's work—in fiscal year 1947/48—did its receipts exceed its expenditure. Almost the whole of its income was derived from charges on its holdings of members' currencies and securities in excess of their quotas; and drawings were smaller than had been expected. The exceptionally low level of drawings in 1949–51, on which a comment was made in the previous chapter, meant that the financial position steadily deteriorated. For the fiscal years 1949/50 and 1950/51, taken together, the Fund's

[1] E.B. Decision No. 103-(52/12), February 21, 1952; below, Vol. III, p. 274.

[2] *Summary Proceedings, 1952*, p. 20.

income was $5 million and its expenditure $8.5 million. In 1951/52 income was $3.25 million and expenditure $4.77 million. By April 30, 1952, there was a cumulative net deficit of $7.24 million—equivalent to 0.1 per cent of the balance-sheet total. This caused some anxiety in the Board, and influenced its decisions on such matters as the size of the staff and the amount of traveling that was undertaken. It was also the subject of discussion by the Finance and Organization Committee of the Governors at the Annual Meeting, 1952. The Governor for the United Kingdom criticized the steady increase in the Fund's annual expenditure, and the Governor for Iran, supporting him, suggested that too much paperwork was being done. The cumulative deficit was not, in fact, wiped out until 1957/58, and not until then did it become possible for the Fund to put aside reserves, as contemplated in Article XII, Section 6.

The possibility of investing some of the Fund's assets in order to increase its income, first mooted by Mr. White (United States) in October 1946, was revived in April 1951. The Board then discussed briefly the legal and policy implications of such an investment, and appointed a committee, under the chairmanship of Mr. Martínez-Ostos (Mexico), to review the matter thoroughly. The committee held two meetings, one in May 1951 and one in July 1952. At the first of these, two memoranda by the Legal Department were discussed. One dealt with the question whether the Fund had legal authority to invest its assets—the main difficulty being the prohibition in Article V, Section 2, against transactions other than those listed (which did not include the investment of assets). This memorandum elaborated the advice given to Mr. White in 1946, to the effect that Section 2 dealt with the basic transactions for which the Fund was established in order to serve its members, but did not cover activities of an administrative kind. The latter would include the investment of gold in order to earn an income to cover a deficit. In addition, the memorandum pointed out that under Article XII, Section 2 (*g*), the Board of Governors, and the Executive Directors to the extent authorized, had power "to adopt such rules and regulations as may be necessary or appropriate to conduct the business of the Fund." This, it was contended, would authorize administrative decisions of the kind mentioned.

However, the fact that the proposed transaction would be an administrative one meant that it would be subject to certain limitations and require the exercise of certain safeguards. These were discussed in the second memorandum. The amount of gold invested would have to be reasonably proportioned to the expenditures for which it was intended to produce income; also, the amount and duration of the investment would have to be such as not to hamper the Fund in selling currencies to its members. In practice, since the possession of gold enabled the Fund to replenish its stock of needed currencies, the terms of the investment should be such as to permit the Fund to transform back into gold at will the securities which it held. Moreover, such a transformation would have to be protected against loss, which meant that the gold value of the securities would have to be guaranteed. The fact that the Fund's deficit was being incurred mainly in dollars suggested that the securities which might most appropriately be considered were U.S. Government issues. The Legal Department advised that if the Fund invested gold in such securities the U.S. Government would be obliged to guarantee their gold value under Article IV, Section 8 (*a*), should there be any depreciation of the U.S. dollar during the term of the investment.

One main question to be resolved was whether prudent management would be better advised to retain the gold that the Fund held, at the expense of running a relatively small operating deficit, than to invest the gold in order to eliminate the deficit. Looking further ahead, the Legal Department suggested that similar management considerations at some future date might dictate investment in the securities of some other country. This might involve the invidious task of assessing the creditworthiness of a member government. A third point made was that nothing in the Articles of Agreement required the Fund to obtain the consent of the member in whose securities the investment was made; nevertheless, the size of the investment might well affect that member's money market, so that as a matter of policy it would be well to enter that market only with the approval of the government concerned. On two less important issues the Legal Department saw no difficulty. It could not be argued that an investment of the kind considered would give financial assistance to the member in whose securities it was made, since the investment was designed to benefit the Fund, and not that member. Finally, while the investment of currency held by the Fund would involve some loss to the member concerned, since it had the option of providing to the Fund noninterest-bearing securities instead of currency, no such problem arose if what was invested was the Fund's gold.

In sum, therefore, the Legal Department saw no obstacle to the investment of the Fund's gold in U.S. Government securities under proper safeguards. When its memoranda were discussed by the committee of Directors in May 1951, however, opinion was divided. Mr. Southard (United States) said that while he was inclined to agree with the Legal Department on the legal question, he was undecided on the policy issues; in any case, his Government had not yet reached a conclusion on the matter. Mr. Stamp (United Kingdom) questioned whether it would be wise for the Fund to incur an uncovered exchange risk by investing gold in order to earn a few dollars. Mr. Melville (Australia) urged that it was essential that the Fund should always be in a position to recover the gold invested. Mr. de Selliers (Belgium) took exception to the Legal Department's argument that the investment would be an administrative act, and therefore not excluded by Article V, Section 2; in Mr. de Selliers' view, this was an untenable distinction. Mr. Beyen (Netherlands) largely shared Mr. de Selliers' doubts, and neither he nor Mr. de Selliers was reassured by the General Counsel's advice that there was an implied power in the Articles of Agreement to make an investment to cover an operating deficit, provided that it was good management to do so. Several Executive Directors also had difficulty in accepting the Legal Department's view of the effect of Article IV, Section 8 (*a*). The committee was therefore unable to reach any conclusion.

Unfortunately, time proved no solvent for these difficulties, although during the next several months the chairman of the committee continued to explore the possibilities. He was unable to obtain any definite indication of the position of the U.S. Government as to an investment in dollar securities. An attempt to interest central banks in a plan to purchase from them with gold some of their holdings of securities, subject to a guarantee of the convertibility of these holdings back into gold, foundered despite an initial expression of interest by some Latin American central banks. Discussions with the World Bank showed that there was no practical opening for an investment of gold in World Bank securities. When, therefore, the committee met for a second time in July 1952, it was only to agree that it must report to the Board its inability to put forward any recommendation. This was done in August, and the committee was discharged from any further consideration of the proposal until the Board decided that it was time to take it up again. Three years were to elapse before this came about.

ANNUAL MEETING

The Seventh Annual Meeting of the Board of Governors, held in Mexico City from September 3 to 12, 1952, was marked by an unusually large number of speeches, covering a wide variety of problems, most of which are dealt with elsewhere in this Chronicle. One of the major contributions to the discussion was made by Mr. Pierre Mendès-France, the Governor for France.[3] He addressed himself to the problems of restoring convertibility, and was especially concerned to challenge an argument, adduced incidentally earlier in the day by Sir Percy Spender, Governor for Australia, that discriminatory regional arrangements were inimical to the attainment of general convertibility.[4] Mr. Mendès-France believed that, on the contrary, arrangements such as the EPU were a necessary step toward convertibility—necessary because of the danger that without these mutual links countries might revert to economic isolationism. He made it clear, however, that he looked for the "active intervention" of the Fund, and it became evident, to an extent somewhat greater than in earlier Annual Meetings, that Governors generally visualized the Fund as having

[3] *Summary Proceedings, 1952*, pp. 96–107.

[4] *Ibid.*, p. 89.

an important role in guiding its members along the path of economic stability and international cooperation. (It may be mentioned that the principal theme of Sir Percy's address was one regularly taken up at Annual Meetings by the Governors for South Africa—the need for an increase in the price of gold.) [5]

The meeting in Mexico City was also the scene of an experimental session at which Mr. (later Sir) Roy Harrod, at that time acting as a consultant to the Fund, and four regular members of the Fund's staff presented a series of papers on the world payments situation and outlook. Each paper comprised a group of charts illustrative of one facet of the general problem, together with a short commentary. Five Governors took part in a brief discussion that followed. After the meeting, the papers were reproduced in a brochure entitled *The World Payments Situation.*

It is convenient to record here that in the following year, 1953, a feature of the Annual Meeting was a similar symposium on "The Revival of Monetary Policy." Addresses by five members of the Fund's staff were followed by comments by four Governors. The addresses were reproduced in printed form and sent to all recipients of the *International Financial News Survey* (then some 14,000) as well as made available to those attending the Meetings.

The organization of the Annual Meeting, 1952 (as of all such Meetings held away from Washington) involved extensive preparatory work by a joint team from the Fund and the Bank, in conjunction with officials of the local Government. In addition to the formal sessions, with their requirement of adequate accommodation, documentation, and press services (and, more recently, simultaneous interpretation), provision had to be made for meetings of delegations among themselves, and for discussions between delegations and the staff and management of the Fund. The greater size of the Fund, the increasing activity of delegations, and the need to conduct parts of several consultations during the Meeting, all added to the complexity of the organization that had to be provided. The growing number of speakers at the formal sessions increased the problem of framing a timetable which would accommodate them all and correspond as far as possible to the times at which they wished to address their fellow Governors. All this was primarily the responsibility of the Secretary's Office, but on this occasion the Secretary himself could not be present. He was a U.S. citizen but, by an ominous foreshadowing of the troubles to be mentioned in the next chapter, the State Department had refused to give him a passport.

EXCHANGE PROBLEMS

While the consultations with member countries under Article XIV, which became mandatory in 1952, began to provide opportunities for the systematic

[5] *Ibid.*, pp. 85–94.

review by the Board of the economic position of those countries, they did not eliminate the examinations of individual members' problems that had characterized the Directors' work in earlier years. Indeed, the agendas of 19 of the 62 meetings held by the Board between the end of the 1951 Annual Meeting and the commencement of the consultations in July 1952 included the study of one or more member countries. Some of these discussions were devoted wholly to an economic review: for instance, the balance of payments of the United States was examined in October 1951 and recent developments in the U.S. economy in the following month. On something like half the occasions, however, the main purpose of the review was to decide upon the merits of an exchange arrangement submitted for the Fund's approval—this being a function of the Board which of course remained unimpaired by the consultation procedure.

The initiation of the annual consultations is discussed in the next section. Here we may look briefly at the Board's activities in connection with more general problems. It will not be necessary to consider individual cases in detail, but we may usefully summarize two full-dress studies which the Board undertook, and which had a bearing on its attitude during the consultations. One of these concerned the appropriateness of tariffs as a substitute for exchange surcharges, and the other the disadvantages of broken cross rates. It is noteworthy that in neither instance was a hard and fast decision reached. The Board decided instead that each case where these problems arose must be considered on its merits.

The Fund's interest in the possibility of substituting tariffs for exchange surcharges (i.e., fixed levies on the sale of exchange) arose from discussions between the staff and the officials of several member countries that were being urged to eliminate these surcharges. Some of these members were already considering increasing their tariffs; in others the staff felt that such increases might be the best way to free the exchange rate from the complications of surcharges. Submitting the problem to the Board, the staff suggested that the most appropriate use for tariffs as a substitute for exchange surcharges would arise where the latter were serving to protect domestic industries. Where the surcharges were expected to be temporary only, or where their long-run purpose was to restrain a demand for imports stimulated by inflation, the staff proposed that an increase in tariffs should not be recommended. In the first situation, tariffs would be likely to prolong the restriction of imports more than was necessary; in the second, the appropriate substitute for exchange surcharges was a more stringent domestic anti-inflationary policy. Perhaps the most difficult decisions would arise, the staff considered, where exchange surcharges provided the country with a significant source of revenue. Whether a tariff would then be a suitable substitute would have to depend upon the probable effects of the tariff as such; if these would be undesirable, other sources of revenue should be found. In the light of these varying considerations, the staff suggested that no general rule could be propounded.

The first reaction of several Directors when this memorandum was discussed in December 1951 was to question whether exchange surcharges were in fact undesirable. They suggested that surcharges were more flexible than tariffs and in every way to be preferred to them. However, other Directors regarded the growth of monetary devices to restrict international trade as an alarming development. The very flexibility of exchange surcharges, and the ease with which they could be unilaterally introduced, presented dangers. They thought that the Fund, as the only international organization with jurisdiction in this field, should be especially vigilant to prevent the abuses of multiple rates. There was general agreement with the staff's view that the problem was a complex one, but particular aspects of its analysis were questioned. Some Directors, for instance, suggested that even in the long run there might be a case for protective measures instead of, or as well as, domestic controls over inflationary tendencies. After further discussion the Board decided to note the analysis put forward by the staff, and to rule that each case involving the substitution of customs tariffs for exchange surcharges must be considered as it arose.

The problem of cross rates was brought before the Board in April 1952 by Mr. de Largentaye (France). At his request the staff had produced, some six months earlier, an analysis of the economics of broken cross rates, which elaborated the argument that these were undesirable because they tended to undermine the stability of the inconvertible currency involved and to encourage diversions of trade by commodity arbitrage. Moreover, a broken cross rate was equivalent to the devaluation of the weaker currency in that particular market, and this affected the competitive position of others.

Mr. de Largentaye said that he had asked for the discussion because the condemnation of broken cross rates, which had led in 1948 to the debarring of France from access to the Fund's resources, was apparently still Fund policy. He himself did not see how it would be possible for the Board during the forthcoming consultations to advise members to suppress discriminatory restrictions and at the same time to maintain orderly cross rates if the latter could be achieved only by discriminating. In his view, broken cross rates were permissible under the terms of Article XIV, Section 2, which (as he had previously argued) overrode Article IV. Mr. de Largentaye did not accept that there was any good economic reason for preferring orderly cross rates to discrimination; for one thing, broken cross rates arose naturally, while orderly cross rates required to be maintained by controls. Mr. de Selliers (Belgium) and Mr. Martínez-Ostos (Mexico), concurring, said that they did not regard orderly cross rates as an appropriate objective for the Fund.

Mr. Stamp (United Kingdom) replied that while Mr. de Largentaye's theoretical position might be sound, the practical problem for the Board was what to do about specific rates. In his view, broken cross rates were a particularly serious breach of the concepts of Bretton Woods because they involved competitive depreciation. He urged that the basic cause of broken cross rates was the dollar shortage, which was of special concern to the United Kingdom. While it was the intention of the British authorities to make sterling convertible as soon as possible, their ability to do so depended partly upon the actions of other countries. Messrs. Melville (Australia) and Natu (India) agreed generally with Mr. Stamp.

Mr. Southard (United States) found Mr. Stamp's comments disturbing. While he agreed that U.S. import policy could be improved, he believed that the convertibility of sterling could only be brought about by the adoption in the United Kingdom of the necessary hard adjustments in economic policy. As to the action to be taken in relation to a broken cross rate, he thought there was no need to reach a decision *in vacuo*. Mr. Rasminsky (Canada) shared Mr. Southard's views; he attributed inconvertibility primarily to inflation.

After an adjournment of the discussion, Mr. de Largentaye said that he did not disagree with the legal position put forward by the staff, that the Board's decision in connection with the French exchange rate in 1948 involved the proposition that a broken cross rate was a multiple currency practice. He was concerned only to make it clear that the Fund could legally approve such a practice. The representative of the Legal Department agreed that this would be possible, but pointed out that the Fund's approval must be specifically sought. The Board then accepted Mr. Southard's proposal not to attempt to decide in advance what could be done when broken cross rates came to light.

CONSULTATIONS BEGIN

Definition

In anticipation of the start of consultations with members under Article XIV, an attempt was made to decide upon the exact meaning of the phrase "restrictions on the making of payments and transfers for current international transactions" (Article VIII, Section 2 (*a*)). The need for a definition had become apparent at a meeting of the Board in April 1951, when Mr. Melville (Australia) challenged a description of the Australian system of exchange restrictions which had been prepared for inclusion in Part II of the *Second Annual Report on Exchange Restrictions*. Mr. Melville proposed an alternative form of words which implied that the restrictions described were a by-product of the Australian import restriction system. This was not acceptable to Mr. Saad (Egypt) or to some other Directors, who believed that the Australian measures involved both import restrictions and exchange restrictions. As a result, the Committee on Interpretation was asked to consider and report on the meaning of the phrase quoted above. The committee looked into the matter in June 1951, and had a further meeting in January 1952 to consider a staff memorandum on the subject.

There was no question in anyone's mind that the exchange restrictions over which the Fund had authority were those affecting the financial, as distinct from the material, aspects of transactions. Without attempting a precise definition, the staff proposed the following as part of "a set of guiding principles":

> Restrictions on the making of *payments and transfers* for current international transactions comprise governmental measures and practices (whether legislative or administrative, whether or not formally promulgated) which have the effect of limiting, in a specified way, the ability to agree on and to perform the financial settlement in connection with international current transactions. The restrictive measures on payments and transfers may involve suppression (or delay) of the transaction, or limitations as to its volume, direction or terms.
>
> Restrictions on the making of *transfers* for current international transactions include measures preventing (or limiting) the foreign payee from converting into his own currency payments received in the currency of the payor or in that of a third country.

This was followed by an analysis of the circumstances in which the specification of currencies became an exchange restriction.

As the staff memorandum explained, there were borderline cases where both exchange and import restrictions were created by a single governmental measure. Moreover, while the Fund was not authorized to require a member to do anything about its import restrictions, the Fund was entitled to concern itself with import restrictions to the extent that they affected international payments in general and the external financial positions of its members in particular. These considerations obviously bore heavily upon the issue of the Fund's responsibilities toward the GATT, and were therefore controversial. The committee saw no prospect of reaching agreement on a form of words which would dispose of this controversy, and preferred instead to leave the matter to be solved *ambulando*. The legal view, expressed in the staff memorandum, though used as guidance by the staff, has thus never been officially adopted by the Board, although it is reflected in a decision taken eight years later on the transition from Article XIV to Article VIII.[6] In practice, as the Committee on Interpretation foresaw, the absence of a detailed definition has not created any serious difficulties.

Accordingly, when the question arose—as it did during the consultations with Belgium and Colombia—whether the Board was entitled in its review to consider the whole of the country's restrictive system, or could deal only with exchange restrictions in the narrow sense, the Board discussed this issue as it concerned

[6] E.B. Decision No. 1034-(60/27), June 1, 1960; below, Vol. III, p. 260.

the individual member, and not as a general problem. Mr. Melville, who sought to limit discussion to exchange restrictions per se, urged that trade restrictions were a matter for the GATT and should not enter into the Board's consideration. Mr. Southard (United States), on the other hand—and in this he was supported by Mr. Saad—argued that the Board could not adequately examine the restrictive system of a country unless it looked at all its aspects. The Board agreed with the latter view.

Procedure

Active preparations for the consultations began in January 1952 with the approval by the Staff Committee of a draft procedure. This called for the collation of all available data on members' restrictions, supplemented by a questionnaire to be sent to each member country before consultations with it began. The data would be discussed with representatives of the country by senior staff members, as far as possible in Washington. A memorandum would then be prepared for the Board, setting out the data and recommending the course to be followed during the consultation by the Board, at which the member would be entitled to be specially represented if it so wished.

This procedure was discussed by the Board on January 24, 1952 and received general approval, although there were considerable differences in emphasis in the comments made by individual Executive Directors. For example, one Director stressed that the initiative for consultation should come from the member, not from the Fund, but others felt that consultation was necessarily a two-way process. Again, some Directors were desirous that possible legal issues—such as the power of the Fund to recommend the removal of exchange restrictions—should be settled in advance, but others believed that member countries were less concerned with their formal rights than in knowing what the procedure for the consultations was to be. One Executive Director urged that the representatives of each member with whom the staff discussions were held should be at as high a level as possible, and hence that the setting for these should be the member's own country rather than Washington. The staff replied to this that they would try to meet members' wishes, but that there were too few senior officers available to enable such discussions in general to take place outside Washington.

Questionnaires asking for details of members' restrictive systems were sent out in February, and inquiries were also made to bring up to date the staff's information about each country's economic situation.

The 51 countries that were members of the Fund at the end of January 1952 included only six that had accepted the obligations of Article VIII, Sections 2, 3, and 4, and consequently did not need to consult the Fund—El Salvador, Guatemala, Honduras, Mexico, Panama, and the United States. Canada joined this select group on March 25, 1952, and as Burma had not yet decided whether to accept Article VIII or to rely on Article XIV, there remained 43 countries with which consultations had to be arranged. By the end of August the staff had concluded discussions with 23 of these, and those with three more were in progress.

For its part, the Board received the first staff report on July 9, and had been given reports on 21 members by August 12. By the end of August, consultations with 18 of these 21 had been completed, and those with two others, on which some discussions had been held, had been reserved for further review after the Annual Meeting. Thus, in the first six months after the deadline of March 1, 1952, consultations had been effectively held with almost half the members to whom the requirements of Article XIV, Section 4, applied.

After the Annual Meeting the Board resumed work on the consultations, and eventually completed these with 35 of the 43 members mentioned above, and also with Germany, which had joined the Fund since the procedure began. The consultation with South Africa, adjourned in August 1952, was never completed, and consultations with seven other countries could not be carried through for lack of essential information. The countries concerned were Bolivia, Chile, Czechoslovakia, Egypt, Iran, Turkey, and Uruguay. These were included instead in the 1953 program and, with the exception of Czechoslovakia, for which data were still lacking, consultations were then completed with all of them.

The first consultation

It was natural that, as the year progressed, the process of consultation should raise fewer and fewer questions in the Board. It was, however, perhaps unfortunate that the very first consultation to be undertaken should raise important and difficult issues which resulted in its final disposition requiring a formal vote.

This consultation was with Belgium and Luxembourg. The Governments of the two countries had appointed Mr. de Selliers, Executive Director (Belgium), to conduct discussions with the staff on their behalf, and seven meetings for this purpose had been held in Washington. In its memorandum the staff reviewed the economic position and prospects of the two countries together with the exchange restrictions which they maintained, and recommended that the Board should decide that

> in view of the uncertainties, the Fund considers that it should not suggest to Belgium and Luxembourg the withdrawal or relaxation of these transitional arrangements at this time. However, the Fund considers that should some of these unfavorable uncertainties disappear, Belgium and Luxembourg should during the coming months re-examine their need for the present level of dollar restrictions.

The staff also recommended that the Fund should give temporary approval to the free market in EPU currencies (which it characterized as a multiple currency practice), but should urge the elimination of this free market as soon as possible. Finally, it proposed that the Fund should invite Belgium and Luxembourg to substitute alternative measures for the partial blocking of current receipts from EPU countries, which was formally a discriminatory currency arrangement.

When these recommendations came before the Board, on July 15, it immediately became clear that two schools of thought existed among Executive Directors; one would have approved the staff's recommendations as they stood, but the other felt that the retention of restrictions by Belgium and Luxembourg was not justified. The views of the latter group were first clarified by Mr. G. Neil Perry (Canada), Alternate to Mr. Rasminsky. Mr. Perry, who until April 1, 1952 had been a member of the staff of the Exchange Restrictions Department, enunciated three criteria which in his view would alone justify tolerance of the continuance of exchange restrictions in a member country. These were (1) that specific balance of payments difficulties existed; (2) that the retained restrictions were not excessive; and (3) that the restrictions were in fact temporary. He and Mr. Southard (United States) doubted whether Belgium and Luxembourg met these criteria. Commenting on the fact that the staff recommendation was based on the existence of uncertainties, these Directors urged that the retention of restrictions could be justified only by the existence of a real and imminent threat to the country's balance of payments.

On the other hand, Mr. Stamp (United Kingdom) argued that Mr. Perry's criteria were incomplete. A country might have a balance of payments that was satisfactory over-all, and yet have difficulties with its dollar balance. Moreover, a member's borrowing and debt position was also important. He stressed that the burden of proof did not rest on the member consulting.

This last point was also taken up by Mr. de Selliers, who contended that in the consultations the Fund was acting in an advisory, and not in a judicial, capacity. He repeated the argument, first heard five years earlier, that it was only if exceptional circumstances existed that the Fund could make representations under Article XIV, Section 4. However, he thought that if such representations were made, the effect was to end the transitional period for that member. Agreeing with this last suggestion, Mr. Southard said that the Fund could terminate the transitional period for an individual member and could also, if it wished, declare it to be at an end for all members. (This contention was not pursued at the time, but some years later it was taken up and the Board decided against it.)

At a second meeting, on the following day, Mr. de Selliers proposed that a further criterion should be added to Mr. Perry's list, viz., that there was no feasible alternative to the restrictions being maintained. Messrs. Stamp and Cigliana-Piazza (Italy) also spoke in support of the Belgian position. On the other hand, Messrs. Martínez-Ostos (Mexico) and Paranaguá (Brazil) pointed out that the Fund had been very strict in criticizing multiple currency practices in the countries that they represented; they thought that similar treatment should be accorded to Belgium and Luxembourg, whose techniques had the same effect as multiple currencies.

The discussion was then adjourned for a month, but when it was resumed the positions of the two main groups of Directors were found to be unchanged. Messrs. Natu (India) and van der Valk (Netherlands) concurred with Mr. Stamp in proposing that the Board's decision should invite Belgium and Luxembourg to keep the possibility of removing restrictions under consideration. Mr. Southard, however, considered this inadequate, and proposed a decision which made two points: (1) that the Fund considered a relaxation of exchange restrictions by Belgium and Luxembourg to be feasible, and accordingly requested the two Governments to reconsider the need for the existing level of restrictions; (2) that the Fund was examining the discriminatory arrangements in vogue in Europe, and would defer its conclusions on these aspects of the Belgian system until this examination had been completed. (The latter recommendation is further considered below.) On August 15 Mr. Southard called for a vote on his proposal, and it was adopted by 53,025 votes to 34,610.

It would not be useful to discuss in detail the reviews by the Board of the other consultations held during the summer of 1952. Instead, it is proposed to bring together some notes on the main policy issues which emerged, the decisions on which guided the staff in its approach to subsequent consultations.

Retention quota systems

The problem of European discriminatory arrangements, mentioned above, arose several times in the consultations. During that with Denmark it was mentioned that a "retention system" was being planned, such as was already in use in some other European countries. To explain why such a system was of serious concern to the Fund, a digression will be necessary.

Retention quota systems usually permitted traders to retain a fixed proportion of their earnings in convertible currencies, obtained from sales to the United States or to any country in the dollar area. The retained exchange, often referred to as an export bonus, could be transferable or not. In either case, it could be used to import from the dollar area commodities that could be sold profitably in the holder's country, since their supply in that country was limited by discriminatory import restrictions. Even if the retained exchange was not transferable it still saved the holder the charges and commissions levied on purchases and sales of foreign currencies and, perhaps, the need to go through administrative screening procedures to obtain import and exchange licenses. Similar in effect to export bonuses were "import rights," which were rights to import specified commodities.

These were granted to certain exporters, particularly those selling to the dollar area.

Retention quotas were widely used in "transit trade," i.e., the purchase of commodities in one foreign country and their sale in another foreign country. They made possible what were known as "switch transactions," for which the procedure was as follows: Merchants in soft currency country A bought commodities in soft currency country B, for soft currency (e.g., sterling); they sold these commodities at a discount in hard currency country C, and were permitted to use a portion of the hard currency proceeds to buy commodities grown or manufactured in C, which they then resold at a premium in any soft currency country D. The profit made on the last leg of this process normally more than offset the loss sustained earlier.

The results of transit trade for the countries involved were as follows: For country A there had been a conversion of soft currency holdings into hard currency (in respect of the hard currency earnings not used for purchases in C). For country B there had been a loss of potential hard currency exports. Country C had imported at a better price than would have been payable for direct imports from B. Country D had, at a premium, obtained dollar imports against payment in soft currency.

These and similar arrangements aroused general concern that trade and dollar earnings were being diverted. The Fund was especially concerned because the retention quota system could involve multiple currency practices and discriminatory currency arrangements, and have adverse effects on exchange stability. The economic effect of certain retention quota systems was to create open or concealed cross rates, putting a higher valuation on hard currencies than on soft currencies. Retention arrangements also involved a high degree of administrative discretion, and were subject to frequent variation.

Retention quota systems were also brought to light in the French and Austrian consultations, and it was agreed that no approval should be given to them until the Board had been able to make a general review of the European arrangements. At the Annual Meeting, 1952, the Governor for Belgium proposed that the Executive Directors should make a special study of the dollar retention quotas and other similar practices, and on September 9 the Governors passed a resolution as follows:

> That the Executive Directors of the Fund shall make a special study of the dollar retention quotas and other similar practices in member countries. In particular this study will take into account the situations which give rise to these practices, their magnitude in each country, the methods used for their application, their impact on other members of the Fund, and possible alternative measures. The study shall include such conclusions and recommendations as may be appropriate.[7]

[7] *Summary Proceedings, 1952,* pp. 169–70.

Two days later Mr. Rooth entertained at luncheon representatives of nine European countries in order to discuss how best to proceed with the study which the Governors had requested. While the speakers at this luncheon generally deprecated the retention quota arrangements, their remarks served mainly to illustrate the complexity of the problems which these arrangements presented. In addition to straightforward retention quotas and the artificial stimulation of transit trade, a number of related subjects were suggested for investigation, among them being cheap sterling, the structural shortage of dollars, the role of inflation, and the restrictive policies of the United States.

Against this background the staff, who had already supplied to the Board a highly critical study of retention quota arrangements, produced in February 1953 a full analysis and description of them. This suggested that retention quotas were very poor mechanisms for the adjustment of exchange rates, avoided fundamental corrective measures, and were of no help toward the relaxation of restrictions or the reduction of discrimination against dollar exports. Moreover, they harmed third countries, being, among other things, tantamount to the official facilitation of commodity arbitrage. The report was supported by detailed studies of the retention quota arrangements in Austria, Denmark, France, Germany, Italy, Japan, the Netherlands, and Sweden. A draft recommendation was put forward which would have required the abandonment of these practices and obligated the staff to work out with each member using them a specific program designed to eliminate them as soon as practicable.

The staff's memorandum was discussed at the Board on February 19, 1953, but had rather a mixed reception. Several speakers supported the staff's view and would have wished to see strong action taken along the lines of its recommendations. Other Directors, however, were less positive, their views ranging from a doubt whether it was possible precisely to define a retention quota arrangement, through a belief that other exchange practices might well be even less attractive, to a firm statement that retention quotas had real merits, and in any case were symptoms rather than root causes of trouble.

In the face of these conflicting views it proved difficult to agree on a decision, and the discussion was adjourned on three occasions before a compromise could be reached. The final text, approved on May 4, 1953, called upon members to work toward and achieve as soon as possible the removal of retention quotas and similar practices, and said that the Fund would consult with each member with a view to agreeing on a program for this purpose, including appropriate attention to the timing of such a program. It added that the Fund did not object to practices which were designed merely to simplify the administration of official exchange allocations.[8] The Managing Director was asked to transmit this decision with a covering letter, reflecting the diversity of views expressed by

[8] E.B. Decision No. 201-(53/29), May 4, 1953; below, Vol. III, p. 258.

Directors but calling attention to the fact that, insofar as the retention quota arrangements constituted exchange restrictions or multiple currency practices, they were covered by earlier decisions of the Fund.[9] The decision and covering letter were reproduced in the Annual Report for 1953.[10]

Retention quotas were also discussed during the Board's review of the draft Exchange Restrictions Report. One Director, who had dissented from the decision on May 4, asked on May 21 that his dissent should be recorded in the passage in the Report in which retention quotas were dealt with. This was resisted by other members of the Board, who urged that when the Board's decisions were publicized they should be expressed as the decisions of the Fund, and not of individuals. In the light of this, the Director agreed that it would suffice to record his dissent in the minutes. Subsequent research by the staff showed that only on one occasion had any indication of the support for a decision of the Board been publicized; that was in the announcement made on March 12, 1951 that the Board "by unanimous vote" had offered Mr. Gutt an extension of his contract.[11] The tradition that decisions are announced only as the decisions of the Board as a whole has been continued to the present time, although information concerning the voting line-up has leaked out to the press in a few instances.

Other policy issues

The consultations with the Dominican Republic and with Venezuela raised the question of the relationship between Article XIV and Article VIII. The Dominican Republic had no restrictions of any kind, and the staff remarked that if at a later stage the member wished to introduce restrictions, these would have to be authorized under Article VIII and not Article XIV. Some Executive Directors questioned whether in these circumstances the Dominican Republic should not be regarded as being already subject to the provisions of Article VIII. The staff, however, pointed out that the initiative in this respect lay with the country concerned, since by Article XIV, Section 3, the country was required to notify the Fund whether it was prepared to accept the obligations in question.

Venezuela had a multiple currency system for which there was no balance of payments justification. It was therefore necessary for approval to be sought under Article VIII and not under Article XIV, and the staff took the opportunity to suggest that the Board might invite Venezuela to consider accepting the obligations of Article VIII generally. Mr. Martínez-Ostos, however, reminded the Board that when Venezuela joined the Fund it was given the right to rely on Article XIV; this right could not now be abrogated without the member's con-

[9] For example, E.B. Decision No. 237-2, December 18, 1947; below, Vol. III, p. 261.

[10] *Annual Report, 1953*, pp. 80, 97–98.

[11] *Annual Report, 1951*, p. 89.

sent. The Board agreed, and decided not to make the recommendation which the staff had suggested.

Survey of results

In August 1952, during the consultation with Belgium and Luxembourg, Mr. Martínez-Ostos put forward for later consideration a draft statement, to be issued when the year's consultations had been completed, explaining why few countries had been asked to remove restrictions. Reverting to the subject in October, he pointed out that so far the Board had not made representations to any member to remove its restrictions, and he thought it unlikely that this would be done in any of the remaining consultations. It seemed to him that expectations aroused before the consultations began, by comments then made on the desirability of removing restrictions, would be disappointed by the Board's inaction. Other Directors, however, pointed out that the Articles of Agreement did not require countries to make their currencies convertible at the end of five years, but only to enter into consultations looking toward the abolition of restrictions when practicable. Hence, there was no need to apologize for the fact that the Fund had not asked any member to remove its restrictions. The staff suggested that it would be premature to make a statement at that point, since only about half of the 1952 consultations had been completed; the proper place to do so would be in the 1953 Exchange Restrictions Report.

This Report was issued in May 1953. It pointed out that much of the emphasis during the consultations had necessarily been placed on confirming the essential facts, and on ascertaining from the member countries the reasons why restrictions were maintained and the problems which they faced when seeking to eliminate restrictions.[12] Possible solutions to these problems had also been discussed. Nevertheless, the Fund had taken the opportunity to express its views, both formally at the conclusion of each consultation, and less formally during the discussions between staff and member.

These views were summarized in a couple of general paragraphs preceding a detailed study of the outcome of the consultations. Two main points emerged. On the one hand, it seemed to the Board that more could be done to eliminate restrictions if some members did not regard restrictions as a relatively easy way out of their difficulties. On the other hand, the Board recognized that even the elimination of inflation would be insufficient to enable some members with particularly acute balance of payments problems to remove their restrictions. This did not mean, however, that there was any the less need to stress the importance of monetary and fiscal policies; and also of appropriate complementary action by countries with balance of payments surpluses, especially in the field of commercial policy.

[12] *Fourth Annual Report on Exchange Restrictions* (1953), pp. 11–12.

RETROSPECT

It will be realized that a procedure as complex and extensive as that described above involved a very large amount of work, not only for the Fund's staff but for the countries being consulted. Some members of the staff participating in the preparation of the consultations reports had grave doubts about the value of some of the documentation prepared—documentation so extensive that they thought it almost impossible for the senior officers conducting the discussions with members to digest, and unlikely to be of great help to the Board. It was partly for reasons such as these that after the extreme activity in July and August the remainder of the consultations program was taken at a much slower pace. Nevertheless, voluminous documentation has continued to be a characteristic feature of all subsequent consultations. Its value to Executive Directors has been questioned, but its value to member countries has been repeatedly attested and is held to outweigh its disadvantages.

The plan to hold as many as possible of the discussions between the members and the staff in Washington naturally involved problems of representation for many countries. In the event, the discussions for 25 of the 35 completed consultations were held at the Fund's headquarters; 9 took place in the countries concerned, and one at Mexico City during the Annual Meeting. Nine of the 25 countries attending in Washington (including Belgium and Luxembourg, as noted above) appointed their Executive Director and/or his Alternate to represent them, assisted in some instances by officials from home. Nine countries were represented by members of the staff of their Washington embassies, although seven of these countries also provided supporting staff from home. Eight countries were wholly represented by officials sent ad hoc to Washington. Of the 24 persons who visited Washington for this purpose, and whose affiliation was noted in the consultations reports, 17 were drawn from central banks and 7 from ministries (all but one from Ministries of Finance).

A contrast between two extreme types of representation was shown in the discussions with the United Kingdom and with Germany. For the former, which took place in Washington, Mr. Stamp, Alternate Executive Director, was the sole British representative; for the latter, which was held in Bonn and Frankfurt, the German delegation numbered 32 persons, headed by the Minister of Economic Affairs and a member of the Direktorium of the Bank deutscher Länder. The latter type of discussion was obviously likely to be more effective, and it is this consideration which in subsequent years has motivated the Fund to arrange to hold staff discussions nearly exclusively in the country concerned.

In March 1953 the Board reviewed the consultations program for the past year and concluded that basically the system then adopted had been an appropriate one. It was thought that with reasonable flexibility the system could be adopted for the 1953 consultations as well. Significantly, however, the Board's decision also pointed out that the preparatory work done for the 1952 consultations would stand in good stead for those in 1953; and concluded that instead of repeating the basic review of members' economic positions which had underlain the 1952 review, the consultations in the ensuing year could concentrate on changes in these positions and in members' restrictive systems.

A DRAWINGS POLICY ACHIEVED

During the year September 1951 to September 1952, five countries drew a total of $87,125,000 from the Fund; there was a drawing of $37.5 million by Brazil and one of $30 million by Australia. In the same period repurchases totaled $114.6 million, including $65.5 million by Brazil and $27.35 million by the Netherlands. In addition, the Fund entered into its first stand-by arrangement, for $50 million, with Belgium. The evolution of the Fund's policies which contributed to the larger drawings will be described first; a number of other policy questions are reviewed in later subsections.

An initial step toward the reconsideration of the Fund's policy on drawings was taken in October 1951, when Mr. Rooth presented to the Board a staff proposal to alter the scale of charges. There were four main points in this proposal. (1) The charges for longer-term use of the Fund's resources would be increased. (2) The flat-rate service charge would be lowered from ¾ of 1 per cent to ½ of 1 per cent. (3) The point at which it became obligatory for the Fund and the member to discuss means of reducing the member's outstanding drawing would be lowered from that at which the charge reached 4 per cent to that at which it reached 3½ per cent (this point would be reached after three years for drawings raising the Fund's holdings to not more than 125 per cent of quota, and after progressively shorter periods for larger drawings). (4) The point at which charges ceased to be prescribed and were left to the decision of the Fund was put at 4 per cent instead of 5 per cent (although there was a limit of 4½ per cent for the first six months after that point, and one of 5 per cent for the next six months). Table 3 compares the new scale with that established at Bretton Woods.[13]

It will be seen that one effect of the changes was to reduce from a maximum of seven years to a maximum of three years the period during which the Fund's holdings of a member's currency might exceed its quota, before it became necessary for the member to consult the Fund about ways of reducing these holdings. This shortening of the time was one of the main purposes of the changes; as was noted in Chapter 11, the Fund was dependent upon the consultations prescribed by Article V, Section 8 (*d*), to ensure that its resources

[13] See above, pp. 103–104, 229.

were kept revolving, and seven years was regarded as too long a time to elapse before these consultations were held.

The Managing Director, when commending his proposals to the Board, expressed his belief that they would help to make it possible for the Fund to extend the use of its resources. He suggested that the new rates should apply only through 1952, but their application was subsequently extended and they remained in force until December 1953. The new scale was generally acceptable to the Board, although Messrs. Joshi (India), Melville (Australia), and Stamp

Table 3. Charges: Comparison of 1944 and 1951 Scales [1]

(In per cent)

Duration of Drawing	Number of Bracket and Proportion of Quota Held by Fund							
	1944 Scale [2]				1951 Scale			
	1st 100-125 %	2nd 126-150 %	3rd 151-175 %	4th 176-200 %	1st 100-125 %	2nd 125-150 %	3rd 150-175 %	4th 175-200 %
0-3 months	0	1	1½	2	0	1	1½	2
3-6 months	½	1	1½	2	0	1	1½	2
6-12 months	½	1	1½	2	1	1½	2	2½
1-1½ years	1	1½	2	2½	1½	2	2½	3
1½-2 years	1	1½	2	2½	2	2½	3	3½ [3]
2-2½ years	1½	2	2½	3	2½	3	3½ [3]	4 [4]
2½-3 years	1½	2	2½	3	3	3½ [3]	4 [4]	
3-3½ years	2	2½	3	3½	3½ [3]	4 [4]		
3½-4 years	2	2½	3	3½	4 [4]			
4-5 years	2½	3	3½	4 [3]				
5-6 years	3	3½	4 [3]	4½				
6-7 years	3½	4 [3]	4½	5 [5]				
7-8 years	4 [3]	4½	5 [5]					
8-9 years	4½	5 [5]						
9-10 years	5 [5]							

[1] These charges are in addition to the service charge (¾ per cent in 1944 and ½ per cent in 1951).

[2] As formulated at Bretton Woods (*Proceedings*, p. 464), the scale included two more columns, covering respectively 201-225 per cent of quota and 226-250 per cent of quota. In the first of these each rate was ½ per cent higher than for 176-200 per cent of quota, and in the second each rate was ½ per cent higher again, subject, however, to a maximum of 5 per cent in both columns.

[3] At this point the Fund is obligated to consult with the member on means to reduce the Fund's holdings of the member's currency.

[4] If the Fund decides to raise the interest rate, it may do so only to 4½ per cent for one semiannual period and 5 per cent for a second semiannual period. Thereafter the Fund may levy such charges as it regards appropriate.

[5] Thereafter subject to such charges as the Fund regards appropriate.

(United Kingdom), while approving the idea of increased reliance on automatic controls through the rate of interest, felt that a change in charges would be merely an academic exercise unless something specific were done to remove the tacit freeze on drawings. A change in charges requires, by Article V, Section 8 (*e*), the approval of three fourths of the total voting power. The minute recording the Board's decision on November 19, 1951, therefore, noted that it was supported unanimously by those Directors present at the meeting, casting 78,455 out of a total of 91,115 votes.

After general approval had been given to the new scale of charges, but before it had been formally adopted, the Managing Director outlined to the Board, on November 7, 1951, a series of principles which, he suggested, might further facilitate drawings. These included the following: repurchases to be normally effected within three years, and at the outside within five years; any member drawing from the Fund to be required to undertake or agree to repurchase within a specified time; consideration to be given to methods of making the automatic repurchase provisions work in those cases where they had not previously done so; special provision to be made for very short-term drawings, up to eighteen months; and special provision to be made for drawings within the "gold tranche" (i.e., drawings that would increase the Fund's holdings of the member's currency up to a sum no greater than 100 per cent of its quota). This last proposal, of course, represented a departure from the attitude to the gold tranche expressed by Mr. Gutt in his reply to Chile in September 1946.[14]

It may be mentioned here that the expression "tranche," meaning 25 per cent of the member's quota, is applied not only to that part of the Fund's holdings of the member's currency that lies between 75 per cent and 100 per cent of its quota, but to larger holdings also. Such holdings are said to lie in the "credit tranches": holdings equivalent to between 100 per cent and 125 per cent of the quota are in the first credit tranche; holdings between 125 per cent and 150 per cent in the second credit tranche; and so on. Holdings equivalent to less than 75 per cent of the quota are sometimes said to be in the "super gold tranche."

Mr. Rooth's proposals were generally welcomed by the Board, although a few reservations were expressed. Only Mr. de Largentaye (France) felt that the Managing Director's suggestions were misconceived. In his view, drawings in the gold tranche had to be considered a matter of right, and not as a special privilege. Moreover, Mr. Rooth's plans for very short-term drawings were inconsistent with the Articles of Agreement, which permitted the imposition of special conditions as to repurchase in accordance with Article V, Section 4 (Waiver of conditions) only for drawings above the limits of 25 per cent of quota a year or 200 per cent of quota in all. Mr. de Largentaye believed that where such special

[14] See above, p. 192.

circumstances did not exist, it would be very difficult for members to surrender the rights which were given to them by Article V, Section 3. In the light of these and other comments, the Managing Director appointed a new staff working party, drawn from all departments, to prepare definite recommendations.

The working party's report, circulated to the Board in January 1952, was discussed at a series of Board meetings. From these was evolved, after several trials, a procedure, agreed on February 13, of which the following is a condensation. It became known as the "Rooth Plan": [15]

Par. 2 (a). Exchange purchased from the Fund should not remain outstanding beyond the period reasonably related to the payments problem for which it was purchased from the Fund. This period "should fall within an outside range of three to five years."

Par. 2 (b). When discussing a prospective drawing with a member, the Fund would agree with the member upon appropriate arrangements to ensure the repurchase as soon as possible, within a maximum of five years from the date of drawing.

Par. 2 (c). If a member whose drawing had increased the Fund's holdings of its currency to not more than 100 per cent of its quota had not repurchased within three years, it would be asked to agree upon a schedule of repurchases to be completed within the next two years.[16]

Par. 2 (d). If unforeseen circumstances beyond a member's control should make the foregoing limits unreasonable, the Fund would consider an extension of time.

Par. 2 (e). A member seeking to draw would be expected to state that it accepted the foregoing principles.

Par. 2 (f). These principles would be an essential element in any determination by the Fund as to whether the member was using the resources of the Fund in accordance with the purposes of the Fund.

Par. 3. A member seeking to draw from the Fund an amount which would not increase the Fund's holdings of its currency beyond the amount of its quota could count on receiving the overwhelming benefit of any doubt respecting that drawing.

It will be noticed that two of the subjects mentioned by the Managing Director in November were not covered by this decision. No provision was included for making the automatic repurchase obligations more generally applicable. On

[15] E.B. Decision No. 102-(52/11), February 13, 1952; below, Vol. III, p. 228. The text embodies provisos, omitted here for the sake of clarity.

[16] This provision was necesary because no charge, other than the service charge, was made on drawings within the gold tranche, so that the schedule of charges did not indicate when consultations on nonrepayment should take place, as it did for larger drawings.

this, the working party reported that, while it was true that these obligations would not necessarily apply to the sterling area or to state-trading countries, the proposed universal requirement to undertake to repurchase within three to five years would effectively place these countries on the same footing as other members. As regards very short-term drawings, a proposed procedure involving a special agreement by the member to repurchase within the set term was put forward by the Managing Director and supported by Mr. Southard (United States). However, some other Directors expressed a fear that the special repurchase arrangements thus proposed might become the norm, replacing the more general obligation to repurchase within three to five years. As a result, the proposed special provision in the text of the decision was replaced by a reference to the possibility of such drawings in a covering memorandum by the Managing Director, which the Board approved at the same time (as par. 1 of the decision).

To all the Managing Director's other suggestions, however, the decision gave concrete form. For instance, it sharply differentiated "gold tranche" drawings from others, by stating that members seeking to make such drawings would be given the overwhelming benefit of any doubt. This formulation was first suggested by Mr. Stamp during an informal session of the Board on February 8, 1952. It did not appear in a draft decision prepared for that meeting, but was incorporated during the process of redrafting. It is a rare example of a highly significant phrase having been adopted by the Board as a result of oral interchanges, and without Executive Directors having had a written draft to consider in advance.

The most controversial element in the Board's decision was probably that in par. 2 (b), viz., the requirement that the negotiation of a drawing should include agreeing with the member on the period within which repurchase would be completed. This had been the subject of some prior discussion, apropos a request for a drawing received by the Board in December 1951. The request was one from Ethiopia, which sought to draw $500,000. Mr. de Largentaye and Mr. Melville had then commented on the fact that Ethiopia had made a voluntary offer to repurchase the amount drawn, and asked the reason for this, since no such offer was called for by the Articles of Agreement. On that occasion Mr. Southard had said that he was glad that Ethiopia had offered such an undertaking: in the absence of a general policy respecting members' obligations to repay, the undertaking would enable him to approve the drawing. (As it happened, however, Ethiopia withdrew its request and did not again draw from the Fund within the years covered by this history.)

It was natural, therefore, that when the Board was considering the report of the working party, and several Directors had expressed a dislike for the proposal to require undertakings to repurchase, Mr. Southard supported the plan. He said that in his view this did not modify the terms of the Articles of Agreement.

Experience had shown that some safeguards for the Fund's resources were required, for if there had been none up to that time, little of the Fund's convertible assets would have remained in its hands. Furthermore, it was necessary to stipulate the acceptance of such an obligation with each drawing, as few members had any detailed knowledge of the Fund's procedures and decisions or of the implications of drawings. He agreed that "the procedure was not precisely what certain countries had envisaged at Bretton Woods," but he insisted that international institutions had to be flexible to meet changed conditions. Several other Directors concurred.

The General Counsel, appealed to for advice on the legal position, said that he agreed entirely with the proposition that the Fund could not impose on drawings under Article V, Section 3, any conditions which were not included in that provision. However, the proposed decision did not have such an effect. As a whole it constituted a statement of policy by the Fund, and as such, generally speaking, could not be understood or interpreted in a manner inconsistent with the Fund Agreement. It was principally aimed at indicating what the Fund meant by the "temporary" use of its resources. If any member felt that its rights under the Agreement were being prejudiced, it was free to raise questions with the Fund, and if necessary to call for an interpretation under Article XVIII.

Dealing with an allied objection which some Directors had raised against the requirement in par. 2 (c) of the decision, that members wishing to draw must declare their agreement with the principles of the decision, the General Counsel said that he understood this to be the expression of a course of action which the Fund invited members to follow when they wished to use its resources, and not the addition of a condition to those included in Article V, Section 3 (*a*), of the Articles of Agreement. The nonfulfillment of this requirement would not of itself invalidate a member's request for a drawing. It was in the light of these assurances that Executive Directors, with Mr. de Largentaye abstaining, approved the decision summarized above, to take effect for a two-year trial period.

A corollary was added a month later, in March 1952, when Mr. Beyen (Netherlands) asked whether it could be assumed that the so-called "ERP Decision" of 1948 was superseded by the new arrangements. Mr. Southard said that while he had not sought the view of his Government on the point, he believed that because of changes in the structure of U.S. assistance to Europe the ERP decision had in effect ceased to operate, in the sense that any European country wishing to use the Fund's resources might apply to do so under the terms of the new arrangements just like any other member. The Managing Director accordingly said that he would take it for granted in his discussions with members that the "ERP Decision" no longer applied.

DRAWINGS IN INCONVERTIBLE CURRENCIES

Among the topics remitted to the working party in November was the possibility of finding means of using the Fund's holdings of currencies other than dollars. While the working party was still considering this, Sir George Bolton (United Kingdom) suggested to the Managing Director a technique by which drawings in inconvertible currencies might be made possible. The problem to be overcome was the requirement in the Articles that repurchases should be made with gold or convertible currencies; this naturally deterred members from drawing inconvertible currencies. Sir George suggested, as a solution, an arrangement between two members, A and B, by which A drew B's currency from the Fund on the understanding that at the end of an agreed period B would draw a corresponding amount of A's currency (thus restoring the position of both currencies in the Fund). A would then purchase B's holding of its (A's) currency—for which purpose, of course, A would have meanwhile to develop a balance of payments surplus vis-à-vis B.

The working party took account of this suggestion in its report. Although it had some doubts whether there was in fact much scope for such arrangements, it suggested that steps should be taken to explain to possibly interested members the procedure which had been outlined. The working party also commented that the possible disadvantages to participants of such arrangements (including the need for bilateral agreements) could theoretically be overcome by multilateralizing the transaction; but that this would certainly be much more difficult to arrange.

This part of the working party's report was separately considered by the Board at two meetings in March and May 1952. The discussion showed that there were differences of opinion among Directors both on the desirability of drawings in inconvertible currencies and on the effect of such drawings on the position of the member whose currency was drawn. On the former point some Directors would have discouraged such drawings on the ground that countries with inconvertible currencies were *ipso facto* not in a position to extend credit to others. They also questioned whether it would be practicable to expect that a bilateral balance would be reversed within a limited period, as the proposal would require. On the other hand, some Directors welcomed the plan because they thought that some countries with inconvertible currencies could, in fact, afford to extend credit, and for them to do so would be beneficial to international trade.

There being no agreement in sight, the Board decided to defer further consideration of the plan to facilitate drawings of inconvertible currencies. Subsequent examination disclosed complications that were not brought out at the discussion by the Board. Two examples may be given. (1) Under the provisions of the EPU, member countries did not accumulate balances of each other's currencies, but threw all their holdings into the monthly settlements. Thus if A, a member of EPU, drew the inconvertible currency of B, another member, it would not be able to accumulate subsequently a supply of B's currency to enable it to reverse the transaction at the end of the agreed period. It could only do so if the terms of the EPU were specially varied to enable it to accumulate a holding of B's currency. (2) What was to be the relation of drawings of inconvertible currencies to the Rooth Plan? If the Rooth Plan applied, no difficulty would be created for A, because the subsequent drawing by B would extinguish its liability to repurchase. But, other things being equal, B would be obliged to undertake to repurchase from the Fund, in gold or convertible currencies, and within three to five years, the amount of its currency which it used to buy A's currency to close the transaction. And while it would no doubt be possible in principle to exempt both drawings from the requirements of the Rooth Plan, there was the possibility that by the time B came to make its agreed reciprocal drawing, it might itself be in difficulties and having to use the Fund's resources under the Rooth Plan.

How far these various problems weighed with individual Executive Directors cannot be known, but their collective effect made it seem useless to bring the matter again before the Board. Eventually the plan was rendered nugatory by the extension of convertibility to most currencies used in international trade, but in the meantime the idea remained in limbo.

STAND-BY ARRANGEMENTS

There can be little doubt that the invention of stand-by arrangements in 1952 constituted one of the most important forward steps taken by the Fund since it began operations. The possibility of such arrangements had been foreshadowed by the Managing Director in a memorandum to the Board in January 1952, when he had said:

> At other times discussions between the member and the Fund may cover its general position, not with a view to any immediate drawing, but in order to ensure that it would be able to draw if, within a period of say 6 or 12 months, the need presented itself.[17]

It will be recalled that Mr. Bernstein had adumbrated such a suggestion in 1943.[18] In 1949 the Board in effect granted Mexico a stand-by arrangement when it decided not to object to drawings of $22.5 million within the ensuing twelve months. However, this proved to be an isolated example.

Mr. Rooth's idea was no doubt in Directors' minds when Australia came to the Fund in April for a drawing of $30 million, and the Board decided to permit

[17] E.B. Decision No. 102-(52/11), February 13, 1952, par. 1; below, Vol. III, p. 229.

[18] See above, p. 69.

the drawing to be made at any time before September 30, 1952. At a subsequent meeting this was referred to as a stand-by arrangement. However, it was in reality merely a deferment of the drawing, which in fact was made in August. It was in no sense an arrangement in the form of a line of credit, designed to give a member confidence without actually adding to the reserves in its possession. The occasion for a stand-by arrangement in the latter sense did not arise until June.

Early in that month representatives of the Belgian Government and of the National Bank of Belgium approached the Fund with a request for an assurance of the contingent use of the Fund's resources. The occasion was a settlement in the EPU which included provision for a balance of $50 million due to Belgium to be liquidated over five years. A secondary problem was that the position of the Belgian Treasury had been straitened by earlier credits granted through the EPU, while the advances that could be made to it by the National Bank had reached their ceiling. The proposal originally put to the Fund was that $50 million in addition to Belgium's gold tranche ($56 million) should be made available to be drawn within the ensuing twelve months if this should prove to be necessary. However, after negotiations in Washington, a modified request was made in terms that conformed to the conditions laid down in the Rooth Plan.

This was put forward by Mr. Frère, the Governor of the Fund for Belgium, on behalf of the Belgian Government. The proposal was that Belgium and the Fund should enter into a stand-by arrangement for six months, under which the Fund would undertake to grant requests for drawings by Belgium as long as such drawings did not increase the existing level of the Fund's holdings of Belgian francs by more than the equivalent of $50 million. Belgium and the Fund would remain in consultation, and the stand-by arrangement would be renewed for subsequent periods of six months each, provided that neither party determined that conditions had materially altered. The Government undertook that it would repurchase on July 1 of each year, beginning in 1953, the equivalent of $10 million of such additional Belgian francs as the Fund might be holding as a result of drawings under the stand-by arrangement.

Commending the proposal to the Board on June 19, 1952, the Managing Director called attention to Belgium's excellent record as a Fund member, and to the key position which its surplus vis-à-vis other European countries held in the EPU. Mr. de Selliers (Belgium) explained that his Government had agreed to the settlement in the EPU, mentioned above, only on condition that Belgium could have corresponding access to the Fund's resources if necessary.

Mr. Southard (United States) approved the proposal on the understanding that Belgium would pay a commitment fee for the facility requested. Mr. Albert Barraud (France), Alternate to Mr. de Largentaye, Mr. Melville (Australia), and Mr. Stamp (United Kingdom) supported the request, but inquired whether the

Fund had power to impose a commitment fee—an inquiry which the representative of the Legal Department answered by saying that the charges set out in the Articles of Agreement were not necessarily comprehensive. Mr. Martínez-Ostos (Mexico) also spoke in favor of the proposal, as did Mr. Beyen (Netherlands), who expressed the hope that it might bring the EPU and the Fund into closer contact. The request was then approved, the commitment fee being set at 1/4 of 1 per cent, and the staff was asked to consider a general procedure for stand-by arrangements.

It may be noted here that the stand-by arrangement with Belgium was renewed every six months until December 1954, and then extended for two and a half years to June 1957, completing the five years over which the EPU settlement had been stretched. No drawing was made under this arrangement until, almost at the end of the period, Belgium drew $50 million in April 1957.

Generalized plan

The staff's proposals for standardized stand-by arrangements came before the Board in August 1952 and produced a considerable debate. The main recommendations were that when approving a stand-by arrangement the Board should apply the same standards as it would if the member wished to draw immediately; that thereafter the member should be free to draw automatically, within the limits of the arrangement, unless it was formally declared ineligible; that the duration of the arrangements should be six to twelve months and renewable; that normally the amount of the stand-by credit should be limited to 25 per cent of quota; and that no charge should be made for the facility.

Mr. Barraud said that Mr. de Largentaye maintained his view that the Fund had no right to prevent a member from drawing unless it was declared ineligible to draw under Article V, Section 5. Nevertheless, since the practice of the Fund had developed differently, he was prepared to consider the proposals put forward. Mr. Southard said that the procedure adopted when considering a request for a stand-by arrangement should be the same as when considering a request for a drawing, and that such an arrangement should not last more than six months, since it was not practicable to foresee developments for longer ahead. Mr. Saad (Egypt) concurred in these views.

Mr. Perry (Canada) thought that the idea was premature, and that credits granted under stand-by arrangements would merely enable members to postpone necessary adjustments. He also urged that no credit should exceed 25 per cent of quota. Several Executive Directors thought that Mr. Perry's doubts were unjustified, and suggested that some quotas were so small that a credit limited to 25 per cent would be of no real assistance. Mr. Melville, supporting these Directors, said that the arrangements should be helpful to countries contemplating the removal of restrictions; he thought that the Fund should give a firm assurance of access to its resources and be willing to extend this beyond 25 per cent of quota. Mr. Natu (India) emphasized the same points.

The question whether a charge should be made was then debated. The general feeling was that there should be a charge; some Directors suggested that it should be 1/4 of 1 per cent, others less. The staff thought that if any charge was made it should not exceed 1/8 of 1 per cent, and should be credited against the charges for any drawing made under the arrangement.

Three weeks later the Board met again to consider a revised proposal put forward as a result of the meeting summarized above. The principal change from the original staff plan was that the new draft called for a specific decision by the Board for the continuation of any stand-by arrangement beyond six months (instead of six months to a year, as originally proposed), and for a charge of 1/8 of 1 per cent, to be repeated on each renewal of the arrangement.

It is significant of the doubts which the proposed arrangements engendered that in putting forward this revised proposal the Managing Director found it necessary to allay two fears: that stand-by arrangements, once granted, would be continuously renewed until every member country had one; and that the arrangements would immobilize a dangerously large proportion of the Fund's resources. In refutation he pointed out that the renewal of an arrangement would not be automatic, and that if drawings were made under an arrangement the Board's scrutiny would become progressively more severe as the amount drawn reached higher tranches of the member's quota. Moreover, any stand-by arrangement for a larger proportion of the quota than 25 per cent would require a waiver by the Board of the limitations in Article V, Section 3 (*a*) (iii). The charge would also be a deterrent.

The discussion was continued on October 1, 1952. It centered on three points: the duration of the arrangements, charges, and the criteria to be applied. On the first of these, several Directors felt that a limit of six months would considerably reduce the attractiveness of stand-by arrangements to countries that might otherwise benefit from them. However, Mr. Southard stressed the importance that the United States attached to a limit of six months, in view of the uncertainty of forecasting beyond that period, and it was agreed that the decision should specify periods of not more than six months. On the second point, a charge of 1/4 of 1 per cent per annum was adopted. On the third, a general formulation covering "the member's position, policies and prospects in the context of the Fund's objectives and purposes" was approved. With these amendments, the plan was adopted, to be effective until the end of December 1953.[19] As will be seen in Chapter 14, a new decision was then taken which modified the plan and in so doing adopted some of the suggestions which had been made during the discussions reported above.

[19] E.B. Decision No. 155-(52/57), October 1, 1952; below, Vol. III, p. 230.

Because of their importance for subsequent discussions, it will be advisable to reproduce here two paragraphs of the decision taken on October 1, 1952.

> 1. Stand-by arrangements would be limited to periods of not more than six months. They could be renewed by a new decision of the Executive Board.
>
> 5. A member having a stand-by arrangement would have the right to engage in the transactions covered by the stand-by arrangement without further review by the Fund. This right of the member could be suspended only with respect to requests received by the Fund after: (a) a formal ineligibility, or (b) a decision of the Executive Board to suspend transactions either generally (under Article XVI, Section 1 (*a*) (ii)) or in order to consider a proposal, made by an Executive Director or the Managing Director, formally to suppress or to limit the eligibility of the member.

These paragraphs were retained unaltered in 1953, except for the replacement of "would" by "will" and "could" by "can." [20]

Drawings under stand-by arrangements fall due to be repurchased within three years of the date of drawing. This obligation was not decided by the Board as a general principle, but was established as a working rule in connection with stand-by arrangements almost from their inception.[21] The rationale for a three-year period was that stand-by arrangements tended to tie up the Fund's resources for the period for which they were effective, plus the period for which the drawing was outstanding. These two periods, which might reach to four years if the stand-by were to be granted for a year and the drawing made toward the end of that time, constituted together an approximation to the three to five years within which repurchases under ordinary drawings had to be completed.

ECONOMIC STABILITY REPORT

The UN experts' report on *National and International Measures for Full Employment*, to which reference was made in Chapter 11, did not gain wide acceptance because its main proposals were regarded as impracticable. The United Nations therefore appointed a second group of experts in 1950, with the task of formulating alternative ways of reducing the international impact of recessions. In March 1951 these experts were asked to advise also how to reduce fluctuations in international markets affecting primary producing countries. The report of this second group (E/2156), entitled *Measures for International Economic Stability*, contained a number of recommendations of direct concern to the Fund, which may be summarized as follows.

(1) The Fund should be ready in recessions to grant waivers freely in order to allow members to draw from the Fund in excess of the limits of 25 per cent of quota annually and 200 per cent of quota in all (Article V, Section 3 (*a*) (iii)).

[20] E.B. Decision No. 270-(53/95), December 23, 1953; below, Vol. III, p. 231.

[21] Cf. *Annual Report, 1954*, p. 107; *Annual Report, 1958*, p. 24.

(2) The repurchase provisions should be modified so as to permit the replacement of automatic repurchases by contractual repurchases which could be modified if a recession developed.

(3) In a recession the Fund should not deny a member the use of its resources on the grounds either that repurchase might be difficult, or that the recession was a healthy adjustment, or that the member was pursuing restrictive policies.

(4) The Fund's resources should be increased to the point at which it could meet its share in the task of offsetting a decline in the supply of dollars amounting to $10 billion over two years. (It was estimated by the Fund staff that this would necessitate at least doubling the Fund's assets.)

(5) It should be made possible to repurchase drawings of inconvertible currencies in the same currency.

(6) Charges should be revised along the lines of the decision taken in November 1951.

The report was discussed at three meetings of the Board in April 1952, in order to instruct the Fund's representative at the meeting of ECOSOC at which the report was to be debated. There was considerable sympathy in the Board for the view that the Fund should make its resources and facilities available to offset a recession; as some Executive Directors pointed out, the Fund's resources had been conserved for just such an occasion. On the other hand, it was felt that these resources were too limited for the Fund to accept major responsibility for antideflationary measures, and that in any case short-term credit was not a cure for a depression. As a result, the Board decided that ECOSOC should be told that the Fund conceived itself to have three functions in relation to a recession: to make its resources available; to make it known that these resources could be drawn upon (knowledge that would itself have a stabilizing influence); and to provide a forum for the discussion of economic problems. On the other hand, it had to be pointed out that the Fund's resources were limited; and that while an increase in quotas had been under consideration for some time, it seemed as if this would be inhibited by members' difficulty in making the necessary additional gold payments, and also by the limited demand for drawings so far. The Board decided further to inform ECOSOC that the other recommendations of the experts would be studied, but that it was thought that the Fund already had sufficient flexibility to deal with problems likely to arise.

An exposé made to the Board after the ECOSOC meeting mentioned that the French and Belgian delegations to ECOSOC had taken the opportunity to criticize the inadequacy of the Fund's resources, and also to stress that these could not be treated as a part of the member countries' reserves. The French delegation had opposed the experts' report on the ground that, if the Articles were correctly interpreted, no recommendations on the use of the Fund's resources, such as those made by the experts, would be needed. The British delegation had introduced a draft resolution urging the Fund to be prepared to waive the limits in Article V, Section 3 (*a*) (iii), and not to be deterred from doing so by a fear that its resources might be exhausted. The British delegation had also suggested that the Fund should be asked to examine the adequacy of world reserves.

In the outcome, ECOSOC passed Resolution 427 (XIV) embodying a number of references to the Fund. These may be summarized as follows:

Par. 9. ECOSOC noted the experts' views that world reserves were inadequate even after allowing for access to the Fund's resources.

Par. 13. ECOSOC noted the Fund's decisions as to the use of its resources, and expressed confidence that the Fund would act with determination to assist its members in any future recession.

Par. 14. ECOSOC urged the Fund (a) to apply its rules flexibly, and to attend to the experts' suggestions in this regard; (b) to be prepared to use its resources as promptly and as fully as was consistent with the Articles.

Par. 15. ECOSOC asked the Fund to keep under continuing review the adequacy of monetary reserves, and to furnish an analysis on the subject for the meeting of ECOSOC in 1953.

When this resolution was circulated in July, the Board, which was then immersed in consultations, did not consider it necessary to take any decision on it. However, in pursuance of the request in par. 15 of the report, the staff prepared in April 1953 a draft study, some twenty thousand words in length, entitled "Adequacy of Monetary Reserves." This surveyed in detail the complexity of the concept of reserves and the varied factors entering into the determination of their adequacy. It also provided comparisons between the principal monetary reserves data for 1928, 1938, and 1951, and discussed the influences which during these years had made a given amount of reserves more (or less) adequate than previously. It concluded that in each of the regions used for the purposes of the analysis (except the United States and Canada) and in the majority of countries in each region, reserves were inadequate to maintain multilateral trade without recourse to the imposition of restrictions to safeguard the balance of payments.

This draft report was considered by the Board on four occasions. Some Executive Directors were inclined to feel that it was too controversial to be issued as a Fund document, but others argued that ECOSOC would look to the Fund for a realistic study; if this was not forthcoming, the Fund would be criticized. The staff pointed out that most of the points made in the draft were similar to statements made by the Board in past Annual Reports. As a result of the Board's review the draft was considerably altered in detail, and eventually presented its conclusions in the form of four alternative definitions of "adequacy." At the one end, (i), reserves might be considered "adequate" if they enabled a country in bad years, by recourse to intensified restrictions, to maintain its external debt payments and to purchase the goods and services necessary to avoid hardship to the population or dislocation of its economy. At the other extreme, (iv), reserves might be considered "adequate" if they permitted a country to maintain currency convertibility even through severe depressions (though not through prolonged periods of international deflation such as occurred in the 1930's) without the need to resort either to restrictions or to domestic deflation. Two intermediate definitions would have linked "adequacy" to the maintenance of currency convertibility, except in a severe depression, (ii), with, and, (iii), without, the use of restrictions. The report suggested that almost all countries, assuming the adoption of appropriate policies, would have reserves that were adequate under definition (i), many would qualify under definition (ii), some under definition (iii), and a few under definition (iv). The report, thus revised, was sent to ECOSOC in June 1953, being described as a technical analysis, not a statement of Fund policy. An updated version was printed in *Staff Papers* for October 1953.[22]

[22] *Staff Papers*, Vol. III (1953–54), pp. 181–227; reproduced below, Vol. III, pp. 311–48.

CHAPTER

13

A Troubled Year (1952-53)

THE YEAR 1952–53 was perhaps the least satisfactory one that the Fund has known. Its activities were at a low ebb, and its influence was impaired. European countries had devised their own payments arrangements without recourse to the Fund, and the less developed countries had small need of drawings because of the demand for primary products caused by the Korean War. Morale among the staff was suffering, partly from a feeling that the Fund was in a backwater, partly from the effects in Washington of Senator Joseph McCarthy's attacks, and partly from disagreements with the Board.

MEMBERSHIP AND BOARD

One further country joined the Fund in 1952–53: Haiti, on September 8, 1953. This brought the membership to 55 and the total of quotas to $8,738.5 million.

Executive Directors

The fourth biennial election of Executive Directors was held on September 11, 1952, the number to be chosen having been increased from nine to eleven, as described in Chapter 12. Six new Directors were elected: Mr. Otto Pfleiderer (Germany), by Germany and Yugoslavia; Mr. Carlo Gragnani (Italy), by Austria, Greece, Italy, and Turkey; Mr. Takeo Yumoto (Japan), by Burma, Ceylon, Japan, and Thailand; Mr. Alf Kristian Eriksen (Norway), by Denmark, Finland, Iceland, Norway, and Sweden; Mr. A.M. de Jong (Netherlands), by the Netherlands; and Mr. Enrique Delgado (Nicaragua), by Colombia, Costa Rica, Cuba, El Salvador, Guatemala, Honduras, Mexico, Nicaragua, and Venezuela. These six replaced Messrs. Beyen, Carli, Martínez-Ostos, and Popovic. Five Directors were re-elected, viz., Mr. de Selliers (Belgium), by Belgium and Luxembourg; Mr. Melville (Australia), by Australia and the Union of South Africa; Mr. Rasminsky (Canada), by Canada; Mr. Paranaguá (Brazil), by Bolivia, Brazil, Chile, the Dominican Republic, Ecuador, Panama, Paraguay, Peru, and Uruguay; and

Mr. Saad (Egypt), by Egypt, Ethiopia, Iran, Iraq, Jordan, Lebanon, Pakistan, the Philippines, and Syria. Czechoslovakia again did not vote for any Director.

The grouping of countries for purposes of the election was substantially different from that in 1950. The addition of Sweden to the membership enabled the Scandinavian countries for the first time to muster enough votes to elect an Executive Director, and the voting strength of Germany and Japan enabled them to secure the election of a Director each. The group comprising Ceylon, Thailand, Turkey, and Yugoslavia, which in 1950 had elected Mr. Popovic, now broke up. Ceylon and Thailand voted for Mr. Yumoto, as did Burma, voting for the first time. Turkey's votes went to Mr. Gragnani and those of Yugoslavia to Mr. Pfleiderer. Jordan, also voting for the first time, joined the group that re-elected Mr. Saad.

Because Mr. Delgado, successor to Mr. Martínez-Ostos (Mexico), came from Nicaragua, which had previously voted for Mr. Paranaguá, there were also some changes in the composition of the two Latin American groups; Nicaragua naturally voted for Mr. Delgado, while Ecuador and Panama, which had previously voted for Mr. Martínez-Ostos, now supported Mr. Paranaguá.

Two of the Directors mentioned above, Mr. de Jong and Mr. Pfleiderer, did not in fact come to Washington. Mr. de Jong resigned from January 1, 1953, and the Netherlands elected Mr. D. Crena de Iongh to replace him. (Mr. Crena de Iongh had been Alternate Executive Director to Mr. Bruins from May to December 1946.) Mr. Pfleiderer resigned from August 1953, and Mr. Otmar Emminger was elected in his stead by Germany and Yugoslavia. With these exceptions the new Board took office on November 1, 1952.

On February 5, 1953, Mr. Stamp resigned as Alternate Executive Director to Sir Edmund Hall-Patch and was appointed Director of the European and North American Department, in succession to Mr. Weyer.

Par values

Initial par values were agreed with Germany on January 30, 1953, with Austria on April 29 (effective from May 4), with Japan on May 11, and with Burma on August 7. The Board concurred in a change of Bolivia's par value from May 14, 1953; this was part of a comprehensive stabilization program being undertaken by Bolivia, which also provided for an official and a free market for foreign exchange.

A dispute with Czechoslovakia developed from an unauthorized change in the par value of the koruna in June 1953. This is reported in Chapter 14.

Quotas

On October 30, 1952, the Governor of the State Bank of Ethiopia transmitted a request for an increase in the quota of Ethiopia from $6 million to $12 million.

He pointed out that at Bretton Woods Ethiopia had been offered a quota of $10 million but had preferred a smaller one because its gold reserves were low. Since then its reserves had substantially increased, as had its economic transactions generally; moreover, it had entered into a union with Eritrea. The Board considered the request on November 26 and appointed a committee to review it. The committee decided that a good case had been made out by Ethiopia, and invited Mr. Saad to notify the member that the Board would be recommended to submit to the Governors for approval an increase in the quota to $12 million, provided that Ethiopia undertook to request a similar increase in its subscription to the Bank. Ethiopia did not pursue the matter and the proposed increase in its quota was dropped.

At the meeting on November 26, however, Mr. Paranaguá had suggested that before any individual quota was increased the Board should review the adequacy of quotas generally. The Managing Director said that the staff had been studying the problem and would furnish a report on it. Since the Board had decided as recently as 1951 that no general increase in quotas was required, the staff study concentrated on the possible need for relative increases. It pointed out that since 1937–38 world trade had increased approximately three times, but that there were eleven members whose trade had increased more than four times in that period. In addition, there were three members (Iceland, the Philippines, and Venezuela) whose quotas as fixed at Bretton Woods appeared to be badly out of line with the formula. The staff calculated the effect of revising these three quotas by reference to the formula and to the quotas of similar countries, and of increasing the quotas of all the countries in both groups in the ratio that their growth of trade bore to the growth of world trade. It found that these changes would call for an addition to quotas of $252 million, of which $75 million would accrue to Venezuela (which was in both groups), and $90 million to Brazil.

Submitting this report to the Board on January 29, 1953, the Managing Director pointed out that "by one possible criterion, viz., the level of members' trade in recent years, the quota structure of the Fund as a whole does not appear to be seriously distorted." For this reason and because a revision of quotas need not, and could not, be determined on statistical grounds alone, the Managing Director suggested that there was no need for the Board at that time to discuss quota revisions in general. The Board tacitly concurred in this view, and the memorandum was not in fact discussed.

Convertibility

One member country accepted the obligations of Article VIII, Sections 2, 3, and 4, during 1952–53, viz., the Dominican Republic on August 1, 1953.

Place of Annual Meetings

The Seventh Annual Meetings (1952) of the Boards of Governors of the Fund and the Bank were held in Mexico City, and the Eighth (1953) in Washington. One of the tasks of the Joint Procedures Committee each year was to recommend to the Governors the place at which the Meetings for the ensuing year should be held. In 1953 the committee had before it invitations from Egypt, Turkey, and the Netherlands, as well as the standing invitation from the United States. On the initiative of the British member of the committee, it was decided to recommend to the Governors (1) that the Ninth Annual Meetings (1954) should be held in Washington, (2) that the Tenth Annual Meetings (1955) should be held outside Washington, and (3) that the location of the latter Meetings should be decided during the Ninth Annual Meetings. The first of these three recommendations was accepted by the Governors.[1] The British representative also proposed that "in the interest of efficient working of the organization and of economy, and at the same time to preserve the international character of the two institutions, Meetings be held outside Washington every third year." While this principle was not formally endorsed by the Joint Procedures Committee or by the Governors, it has in fact been followed in all subsequent years.

LOYALTY INVESTIGATION

On several occasions during the period 1948–53 there were investigations in the United States on possible communist infiltration into the staffs of government offices and international organizations. Among persons named in these inquiries were Mr. White (U.S. Executive Director until June 1947) and Mr. Coe, Secretary of the Fund. Mr. White, who denied that he was or had been a communist, died in August 1948 while the investigations were continuing. Mr. Coe, who had also denied in 1948 that he was a communist, was summoned in November 1952 to appear before a Grand Jury, where he refused to answer questions, claiming the privilege of the Fifth Amendment to the U.S. Constitution against self-incrimination. He also refused to testify before a Subcommittee of the U.S. Senate. Shortly thereafter Mr. Rooth, after consulting Executive Directors, requested the resignation of Mr. Coe, who was succeeded by Mr. Roman L. Horne.

In 1953 the U.S. Government set up machinery for the review of the loyalty of U.S. citizens employed in international organizations. The Managing Director and Executive Directors were troubled by the proposal that U.S. citizens then on the staff of the Fund should be subject to investigation. However, it was recognized that the privileges and immunities of Article IX did not prevent the

[1] *Summary Proceedings, 1953,* pp. 88–89, 98.

investigation, and accordingly the Fund acquiesced in the investigation procedure. No representations to the Fund resulted.

STAFF REORGANIZATION

During the course of the discussion of the budget for the fiscal year 1952/53, the Board gave provisional approval for dividing the Far Eastern, Middle Eastern, and Latin American Department into two or three departments. By the spring of 1953 the Managing Director had decided that such a division was necessary without further delay. He would have been content to create one new department, making three area departments in all, but a majority of the Board preferred to go a step further and set up four such departments, as follows: Asian (consisting of the Far Eastern and South Asian Divisions); European (consisting of the British Commonwealth, Central and Eastern European, Northern European, and Western European Divisions); Middle Eastern (comprising the Middle Eastern Division); and Western Hemisphere (consisting of the Latin American (North), Latin American (South), and North American Divisions). The reorganization took effect from May 6, 1953. Mr. Hirendra Lal Dey was appointed Director of the Asian Department and Mr. Abol Hassan Ebtehaj, Director of the Middle Eastern Department. Mr. Stamp was assigned the European Department and Mr. Luthringer the Western Hemisphere Department.

On April 30, 1953, the active staff numbered 417, a decrease of 9 during the year. There were, in addition, 17 staff members on military or other forms of special leave. Altogether the staff was drawn from 38 countries.

RELATIONS WITH THE WORLD BANK

At the Seventh Annual Meeting (1952) the Committee on Finance and Organization endorsed some observations by the Governor for the United Kingdom calling for closer cooperation between the Fund and the World Bank in order to reduce the Fund's expenditures and so its deficit.[2] As a result the Managing Director of the Fund and the President of the Bank in December 1952 appointed a joint committee, consisting of a senior member of the staff of each institution, to examine the possibilities of cutting costs in this way.

The committee made a progress report in March 1953 and a final report to each Board in July. The latter listed the only three areas in which the committee thought that opportunities for economies presented themselves: (1) the collection and compilation of basic economic data which both institutions

[2] *Summary Proceedings, 1952*, p. 152.

required as background; (2) the use of technical manpower in staffing missions and carrying out research projects; and (3) certain administrative services.

It was only in the third of these categories that the committee found scope for joint operations. It recommended that consideration should be given to the undertaking by the staff of one or the other institution of certain additional administrative functions on behalf of both. A precedent had been set, the committee pointed out, by the libraries operated by the Fund on behalf of both Fund and Bank. Similar arrangements might be feasible for the procurement of supplies, transportation, translation services, messenger service, and the arrangements for the Annual Meetings. The committee warned, however, that savings could be expected only through a limited reduction in supervisory personnel; there was no overstaffing at the working level. No substantial financial savings were therefore to be expected, especially as the total cost of the activities affected was no more than $416,000 a year.

As regards the other two categories, the committee was even more cautious. It suggested that a certain amount could be saved by combining the presentation of basic data for the two institutions; for example, both the Fund and the Bank had recently completed reports on the economies of Brazil and India, and while each report was naturally orientated toward the principal interests of the institution preparing it, some slight economy could have been achieved by joint preparation of those parts of the reports that were common to both Fund and Bank. In other respects the committee found no scope in the operational functions of the two organizations for more than intensified cooperation. To achieve the latter, it suggested frequent and regular meetings between the heads of the operational departments of the Bank and their opposite numbers in the Fund, the results of these meetings being reviewed by a member of the management of each institution. Similar meetings were also recommended for the General Counsels, the Secretaries, and the heads of the Research Departments.

This report was considered by the Fund Board on July 24, 1953, and while some Executive Directors were disappointed that the possible savings disclosed were so small, it was decided to accept the findings and transmit a summary of them to the Governors at the Eighth Annual Meeting. This was done, and, with a reservation by the Governor for Belgium, the Governors' Committee on Finance and Organization accepted the report.[3] A suggestion by the Governor for the United Kingdom, that economies could be achieved by combining the duties of the Executive Directors of the Fund with those of the Executive Directors of the Bank, was not adopted; the Governors for several members who shared in the election of Executive Directors argued that their interests could not properly be looked after by a single Director serving on both Boards.

[3] *Summary Proceedings, 1953*, p. 93.

The Managing Director undertook that the inquiries suggested by the Governors' committee in 1952 would be continued and that joint services would be employed at all levels where common objectives could be attained most efficiently. In practice, the only additional joint service which has been found feasible has been an office charged with the duty of arranging for the Annual Meetings. The other functions mentioned by the staff committee—procurement, transportation, etc.—have not been combined because the requirements of the Fund and the Bank have differed or because the staff needed in each institution has been large enough to make separate units fully efficient.

Two opportunities arose during the year to practice cooperation in missions to member countries. In October 1952 the World Bank was sending a mission to Burma. With the remarks of the Governors at the Seventh Annual Meeting in mind, the Managing Director suggested to the President of the Bank, who agreed, that a Fund staff member should be attached to the mission to deal with monetary, banking, foreign exchange, fiscal, and balance of payments questions. When this was reported to the Board, Mr. Saad (Egypt) asked for an assurance that the independence of the staff member would be safeguarded, and that his views would be reflected in the mission's report. Mr. Rooth gave that assurance, adding that the report would not be published.

Nearly a year later, in September 1953, the Bank was planning a mission to Nigeria, and asked for the loan of a staff member from the Fund to cover the same subjects as had been done in the mission to Burma. The Managing Director told the Board that he proposed to make an officer available for the purpose. Mr. Southard (United States) then expressed his agreement with the proposal, but wished to be assured that each such request would be dealt with ad hoc, so as to avoid the possibility that on some future occasion a Bank mission might cover some important monetary or exchange problem in its report without this report having been reviewed by the Fund Board. Mr. Saad, supporting Mr. Southard, asked that any public report by a Bank mission of which a Fund technician was a member should make it clear that the latter's views did not necessarily represent those of the Fund. On the other hand, Messrs. Crick (United Kingdom) and Melville (Australia), welcoming the Managing Director's proposal, thought that the dangers envisaged by the other Directors were likely to be more theoretical than actual. At the conclusion of the discussion the Managing Director gave Mr. Southard the assurance for which he had asked, and said he would request the Bank to make clear in its reports the status of any Fund personnel included in missions.

We may here note that the problem of working arrangements between the Fund and the Bank arose again early in 1957, when the management of the Bank inquired about the possibility of creating formal arrangements to give it advance notice of the Fund's activities. A review of the system of liaison between the two organizations, made in connection with this approach, showed that the Bank was provided automatically with copies of all unclassified Fund documents, and on request with all other Fund papers except the minutes of the Board's discussions. These arrangements were supplemented by close working relationships between those members of the staffs of the Fund and the Bank who were concerned with the same member countries. It was pointed out to the Bank that in certain directions the Fund was under an obligation to maintain secrecy—for example, in relation to prospective requests for drawings. While, therefore, the Fund's decisions could be communicated to the Bank, it was not possible to ensure that the Bank was informed of all matters coming to the Fund Board before they appeared on the latter's agenda (copies of which were sent officially to the Bank). On consideration, it appeared to the management both of the Fund and of the Bank that these working arrangements, partly informal, were more likely to meet the needs of both organizations for knowledge of each other's activities than any more formal liaison would do. No further steps were therefore taken, nor did the problem recur in any serious form during the period covered by this Chronicle.

AUDIT PROCEDURE

Section 20 (b) of the By-Laws, as revised in 1947, requires that the external audit of the Fund's accounts be carried out annually by a committee of three or five persons, each nominated by a member of the Fund; at least one of these persons is to be nominated by one of the six members having the largest quotas. In pursuance of this procedure, the Managing Director is accustomed to propose to the Board each year the names of the members who should be invited to nominate auditors for that year.

When in February 1952 Mr. Rooth proposed that Cuba, France, and Pakistan should be invited to nominate auditors, the suggestion was made in the Board that in future years the audit should be undertaken by a firm of commercial accountants instead of by government nominees. This proposal was considered by a staff working party, who reported in favor of it. The working party pointed out that the World Bank had always employed commercial auditors; that a commercial firm would be available for consultation by the Treasurer throughout the year; that such an appointment would maintain continuity in auditing methods from year to year; that it would involve less time and effort on the part of the Fund staff to brief such a firm than a group of government nominees unfamiliar with the Fund's accounts; that language difficulties would be avoided; and that the cost of the audit might well be halved as a result.

The recommendation of the working party was discussed by the Board in December 1952—the subject having been postponed until after the Seventh

Annual Meeting—but no decision was reached. Some Executive Directors supported the working party's ideas. Others, however, preferred the existing arrangements. They reminded the Board that these had been approved by the Governors after extensive discussions. These Directors thought that continuity could be sufficiently ensured by better arrangements for the selection of auditors, and pointed out that the duties of the latter went far beyond those of normal commercial accountants and were much more closely allied to those of governmental auditors. Mr. Rooth undertook that the staff would study ways of selecting the auditors. Subsequently the Board decided to invite Cuba, Norway, and the United Kingdom to nominate auditors for 1953.

In January 1953 the Secretary-General of the United Nations wrote to the Managing Director drawing his attention to a resolution passed by the General Assembly in December 1952 inviting the specialized agencies to review their methods of audit. Bringing this to the attention of the Board in May, the Managing Director suggested two alternative methods of selecting the Audit Committee: either each member country when invited to provide the services of an auditor might be asked in principle to make him available for three consecutive years; or each audit team should include one man drawn either from Canada, the United Kingdom, or the United States, and this man should be available for two or three years. However, when the question was briefly discussed by the Board in June, neither alternative found favor, and the existing method, by which one of the three chosen members is asked to nominate an auditor for two successive years, was continued. No further attempt has been made to vary the procedure.

BALANCE OF PAYMENTS QUESTIONS

In the early part of 1953 two issues connected with balance of payments statistics came before the Board: one related to forecasts and the other to concepts of surpluses and deficits. Both arose from initiatives of the staff with which Executive Directors disagreed, and both led to temporary friction between Board and staff. The first was ended by an expression of regret by the Managing Director; the second by a reversal of the staff's decision.

Balance of payments forecasts

In 1952 the Secretary-General of the United Nations requested a wide range of countries to provide him with forecasts of their balances of payments. The Fund's staff believed that little reliance could be placed on such data if they were provided with a view to publication. It therefore suggested to the Secretary-General that, instead, data on a consistent basis should be obtained by the Fund and summaries made available to the United Nations for publication. The staff felt that this would prevent overlapping in requests by the United Nations and the Fund, since almost the entire Fund membership was already supplying balance of payments data to the Fund. It also believed that the time had come when, for planning purposes within the Fund, the current data needed to be supplemented by forecasts. Letters conveying the request for data were accordingly sent out on January 26, 1953.

However, at the meeting of the Board on February 6, several Directors criticized the request. They pointed out that, of necessity, balance of payments forecasts closely reflected policies which governments intended to follow, and were therefore highly confidential; it was not clear whether the secrecy of forecasts supplied to the Fund could be adequately guarded. In any event, their disclosure to the Fund staff could put the latter in a position of knowing more about a government's intentions than had been disclosed to its parliament or people. Moreover, balance of payments forecasts were not included in the list of data for which the Fund was entitled by Article VIII, Section 5, to ask, and care should obviously be exercised in asking for information not there scheduled. Finally, some members of the Board questioned whether the forecasts would in fact be of value to the Fund's work.

On the question of secrecy, Mr. Saad (Egypt) asked whether it was proposed to disclose the information to the Board. The Managing Director said he would wish to reserve that question for later consideration, but Mr. de Largentaye (France) claimed that to withhold the data from Executive Directors would be inconsistent with earlier decisions of the Board.

The representative of the staff pointed out that the only data asked for had been that required to carry out the resolution of ECOSOC. The other information sought had been only methodological, intended to enable the Fund to interpret the data provided. Nevertheless, at the conclusion of the discussion the Managing Director expressed his regret that the request had apparently led to misunderstandings and caused difficulties; no further steps would be taken in the matter without consulting the Directors.

Balance of payments concepts

Almost at the same time as the discussion summarized above, some Directors became critical of the concept of "compensatory official financing" which underlay the balance of payments statistics issued by the Fund. In the second *Balance of Payments Yearbook* issued by the Fund, this concept had been defined as the financing provided by the monetary authorities to cover a lack of balance in those international transactions [i.e., "autonomous" transactions] that have been undertaken for their own sake in the expectation that they will yield a profit, discharge a debt, or serve some personal need or other end quite unconnected with exchange stabilization.[4]

In support of this concept the staff presented to the Board, in February 1953, a full exposition of it, supported by illustrations of its usefulness in interpreting the balance of payments figures of the United States, the United Kingdom, Australia, Canada, and the Netherlands. The staff's memorandum explained the principles on which individual components of a country's official financing of its balance of payments were judged to be "autonomous" or "compensatory." Deprecating any attempt to show the significance of a country's balance of payments by a single statistic, the staff yet argued that "compensatory official financing" yielded the nearest approach to such a single statistic, and that its use facilitated the analysis necessary to determine the causes of the balance of payments position of each member country.

Mr. Melville (Australia) did not agree. In a forceful rejoinder, he took up the point made by the staff that compensatory official financing could measure only the deficit which the country had been able to finance, and in no sense its true deficit. For some countries receiving U.S. aid, for example, almost all compensatory official financing took the form of such aid; if the amount of the aid was reduced, so would be the figure for compensatory official financing. In that event, the country would have been obliged to stiffen its restrictions so as to keep its deficit within the limit of the U.S. aid. Hence, Mr. Melville contended, "compensatory official financing" could not be, as had been suggested in the *Balance of Payments Yearbook*, "a far more realistic measure of surplus or deficit in the balance of payments than the movement of international monetary reserves alone—or, for that matter, than other measures that are sometimes used." [5]

When the memoranda by the staff and by Mr. Melville were discussed at the Board, the criticisms of "compensatory official financing" found considerable support. A committee of Executive Directors, with Mr. Melville in the chair, was set up to discuss with the staff the whole problem of balance of payments concepts. The committee met twice during the summer, and made its report to the Board in October. At the suggestion of the committee, members of the Fund staff particularly concerned with the presentation of balances of payments had conferred after the Annual Meeting with experts from ten countries and the OEEC, to consider how best to present the data. As a result, the staff decided, with the committee's approval, to discard the concepts both of "compensatory official financing" and of "special official financing" (defined as "official

[4] *Balance of Payments Yearbook*, 1948 and Preliminary 1949, p. 21.

[5] *Balance of Payments Yearbook*, Vol. 3, 1949–50, p. 19.

grants or capital transactions intended to finance particular projects or to meet contractual obligations").[6]

The experts had also suggested that the balance of payments data issued by the Fund would be more valuable if provided earlier, which could be done if a loose-leaf form of presentation were adopted. Commending the latter proposal to the Board, the committee pointed out that it might increase costs. (It was subsequently found that the added costs would not exceed $1,400, which could be carried on the current budget.) The Board approved the committee's recommendations.

Accordingly, subsequent issues of the Yearbook have been issued initially in loose-leaf form, and have presented the data neutrally. Two types of table are included, a basic presentation showing the data in parallel columns for credit and debit items, which necessarily add to the same totals, and an analytic table designed to indicate separately the financing items. The final group of figures in the analytic table is always the reserve movements or monetary movements, perhaps preceded by a group of "extraordinary transactions" or an item of "economic aid received," but these groups can be combined in any way that the user wishes so as to give him surpluses or deficits according to his own definitions. The Fund no longer offers a single figure for surplus or deficit.

EXCHANGE TRANSACTIONS

Drawings and repurchases

Repurchases again exceeded new drawings during the twelve months from September 1952 to September 1953. Six countries drew a total of $96 million and six repurchased $101.9 million. Brazil, which drew $37.5 million and repurchased the same total, Chile, which drew $12.5 million and repurchased $5.37 million, and Finland, which drew $9.5 million and repurchased $2 million, appear on both lists. Turkey, which drew $10 million in U.S. dollars plus $4.4 million in deutsche mark and $5.6 million in sterling, was the first country for which a waiver was granted of the limit of 25 per cent of quota on drawings in any year; the $20 million drawn represented nearly 47 per cent of Turkey's quota. The Board accepted the staff's recommendation that 25 per cent of the quota was too small to be an adequate contribution to Turkey's difficulties.

The largest repurchase was a voluntary one by the Netherlands, amounting to $48.03 million, which was sufficient to restore the Fund's holdings of guilders to 75 per cent of the Netherlands' quota. The Netherlands offered to make this repurchase, in U.S. dollars, in April 1953. It was challenged by Mr. de Largentaye (France) on the ground that the obligatory repurchase which would accrue at

[6] *Balance of Payments Yearbook*, Vol. 4, 1950–51, p. 1, and Vol. 5, 1947–53, p. 2.

the end of that month would include some repurchase in gold. He did not think that the member should be allowed to anticipate the repurchase in order to avoid paying over gold. Other members of the Board, however, agreed with the staff view that the dollars were likely to be as useful to the Fund as gold would have been, and the voluntary repurchase was approved.

Secured drawings

Two abortive attempts were made during the year to find openings for an increased use of the Fund's resources; one would have permitted members to draw if they offered gold to be held as collateral security, and the other contemplated investment of the Fund's resources in short-term bonds of the World Bank.

During the course of a discussion of charges on Fund drawings, in November 1952, Mr. de Largentaye asked that the Board should make a general examination of transactions against gold collateral. A review by the Fund staff suggested that such transactions might be of some assistance to members, and proposals were put forward as to the terms on which they might be effectuated. The staff suggested that a member proposing a drawing against full gold collateral should receive the overwhelming benefit of any doubt; that such drawings should attract charges at the usual rates and should not be for more than two years; but that they should not be permitted if a member's gross holdings of gold and gold-convertible currency minus gold pledged were less than its quota. A memorandum embodying these suggestions was put to the Board in December 1952.

Three months later it appeared as if an opportunity might occur to consider a proposal for a drawing thus secured. Iran made a tentative request to draw 50 per cent of its quota of $35 million against a deposit of gold collateral. Subsequently, however, it had second thoughts, and the request was put into suspense. When this was intimated to the Board in March 1953, the Managing Director said that several Executive Directors had asked that the proposed general discussion of gold collateral drawings should be postponed until Iran's request had been disposed of. Iran's request was subsequently withdrawn, but the staff's memorandum was never discussed in the Board; informal inquiries had shown that Executive Directors were unsympathetic to its proposals. However, when in 1958 a member sought to draw against gold collateral, the terms proposed by the staff reflected the views expressed in its memorandum.

In January 1953 the World Bank approached the Fund with reference to a proposed issue of $50 million of three-year bonds outside the United States. A number of central banks had expressed interest in such an issue, but some of them would be unwilling to invest for as long as three years unless they had an opportunity to borrow against the bonds, without loss, should they need to do so. The Bank therefore suggested that, if and when a central bank needed to obtain cash against a pledge of the bonds, the Fund might offer to make its resources available, without regard to the quantitative limits imposed by Article V, Section 3 (*a*) (iii).

Commending the proposal to the Board, the staff suggested that the charges made for a drawing should not exceed the rate of interest on the bonds (expected to be 2½ per cent); that there should be no obligation to repurchase against such a drawing until the maturity of the bonds; and that the World Bank should pay a commission, which might either be a fixed sum of $100,000 a year or ⅛ of 1 per cent per annum on any bonds not pledged to the Fund. The staff noted that certain problems would arise. For example, the drawing would not add to a member's reserves, although it would restore them to the liquidity which they had had before the investment in World Bank bonds had been made. Again, further drawings by a member whose central bank had pledged some of the bonds would thereby be made more expensive, because they would relate to a higher tranche of its quota. Moreover, the existing scale of charges was valid only until June 30, 1953, and might thereafter be increased. Subsequently, however, the Bank withdrew its proposal, and the subject lapsed.

DRAWINGS BY NEW MEMBERS

At the Seventh Annual Meeting (1952) the Governor for Thailand, Prince Viwat, made an appeal for a right to draw from the Fund.[7] He succinctly described the problem of his country in the four words "no rain, no rice"; if the monsoon were to fail, Thailand would be faced immediately with balance of payments difficulties. The reason for his appeal, although he did not elaborate it, was that the Membership Resolution admitting Thailand to the Fund had specified that Thailand might not draw until thirty days after it had agreed a par value with the Fund;[8] and Thailand could not establish a par value so long as the broken cross rate between the dollar and sterling in Bangkok—which in turn reflected broken cross rates in Hong Kong and elsewhere—persisted.

The Managing Director undertook to look into the possibility of permitting Thailand to draw should it need to do so.[9] The problem proved, however, to be a complicated one, and it was not until June 1953 that the Board was able to consider it. The memorandum that the Legal Department then presented to the Board distinguished between original members (those that had been represented at Bretton Woods and had signed the Articles of Agreement in 1945 or 1946) and new members; and also between members that had been occupied by the

[7] *Summary Proceedings, 1952,* p. 65.

[8] Resolution 3-4, *Summary Proceedings, 1948,* pp. 46–48.

[9] *Summary Proceedings, 1952,* p. 124.

enemy and other members. Provision had been made, in Article XX, Section 4 (*d*) (ii), for an original member that had been occupied by the enemy to be permitted to draw, under conditions prescribed by the Fund, once the member had proposed an initial par value, even though this had not been agreed with the Fund. Such a concession could be extended to countries, such as Thailand, that were not original members, only by special provision in the Membership Resolution, and this had not been done in that for Thailand. Only the Governors, therefore, could authorize drawings by Thailand. To do so, they would have to amend the Membership Resolution.

Reviewing a month later the position of the other new members that were not freely eligible to draw from the Fund, the staff pointed out that Burma was in the same position as Thailand, but agreement was expected shortly on a par value for the kyat. (A par value was in fact agreed on August 7, 1953.) Indonesia would also be in the position of Thailand if it accepted membership under the terms of Governors' Resolution 7-9.[10] Greece would be qualified to take advantage of Article XX, Section 4 (*d*) (ii), and Italy of similar provisions in its Membership Resolution, except that there was some doubt whether Italy had effectively communicated a par value. When China proposed a par value it would be in the same position. Uruguay, however, as an original member that had not been occupied by the enemy, could not draw until a par value for the peso had been agreed. France had been declared ineligible to draw under Article IV, Section 6.

Explaining the difference between the position of Italy on the one hand and that of Burma, Thailand, and Indonesia on the other, the staff said that the Membership Resolution for Italy, passed by the Governors in 1946, had included a reference to Article XX, Section 4 (*d*).[11] It had been thought cumbersome to include such a reference in later Resolutions, and those for Burma, Thailand, and Indonesia had omitted it.

The Board considered at some length what steps to take to deal with the position disclosed. Initially Mr. Cochran, as Acting Managing Director, suggested that the Governors be invited to authorize all new members to draw, subject to conditions to be imposed by the Governors, once they had communicated par values. This would cover all the outstanding cases except Uruguay. As it happened, a mission was about to go to Uruguay, and perhaps a par value for the peso might later be established. This general solution was rejected because Directors felt it would be invidious to offer new members a privilege which some original members did not have. Mr. Eriksen (Norway) added that he did not think a new principle of that kind should be introduced at that stage in the Fund's history, and he doubted the legality of an attempt to

---

[10] *Ibid.*, pp. 171–74.

[11] Resolution 1-6, *Summary Proceedings, 1946*, pp. 49–51.

extend the privileges of Article XX, Section 4 (*d*) (ii), to members that had not been occupied by the enemy. It was accordingly decided to invite the Governors merely to amend the Membership Resolutions for Thailand and Indonesia so as to permit them to have recourse to Article XX, Section 4 (*d*) (ii). At the Eighth Annual Meeting the Governors agreed to this, and the necessary Resolutions were passed.[12]

THE FUND AND THE OEEC

Some relief from the prevailing discouragement was afforded by a meeting in Paris in June 1953 between the Managing Director and the Managing Board of the European Payments Union, which was part of the Organization for European Economic Cooperation (OEEC). The stand-by arrangement with Belgium, arranged in 1952, had shown how the Fund could be of assistance to its European members, and Mr. Rooth was able to say that the possibility of such arrangements would enable the Fund to undertake the kind of operations envisaged by the report of the Managing Board on the future of the EPU. There were, of course, limits to the usefulness of the stand-by arrangements. They could not, for instance, be offered to the EPU as such, but only to individual members, and their duration might be inadequate. On the latter point Mr. Rooth said that it would apparently be preferable to extend the arrangements from six months to a year, but that such an amendment to the Board's decision on stand-by arrangements could more easily be obtained if a specific case were presented to the Board. He doubted whether it would be possible to obtain such an amendment before the Annual Meeting.

Another difficulty was illustrated by an inquiry by Mr. Ansiaux, on behalf of the Managing Board, as to whether the Fund would be able to provide medium-term credits to replace exhausted EPU credits, thus in effect acting as an extension of the EPU. Mr. Rooth was obliged to say that this would have to be studied: the Fund's function was not to finance capital transactions, and there was a limit of three to five years on the permitted duration of drawings.

Nevertheless, the meeting with the Managing Board was a success. Plans were made for coordinating actions toward countries, such as Turkey, that were seeking assistance both from the Fund and from the OEEC. It was also agreed that the OEEC would be asked to send its documents officially to the Fund; the members of the Managing Board appreciated the fact that in one capacity or another they all had access to the Fund's documents. It was arranged that the discussion would be resumed during the Annual Meeting of the Fund, and the representatives of the EPU present on this second occasion subsequently reported

[12] Resolutions 8-4 (Indonesia) and 8-5 (Thailand), *Summary Proceedings, 1953*, pp. 96–97.

to the Managing Board that the exchange of views had been very interesting and useful. They recommended that such meetings should be held more often.

It may be added that the assumption by the OEEC of responsibilities for supervising the progress of its members toward the liberalization of trade led to closer liaison between it and the Fund. The OEEC early recognized the value of the reports made by the Fund staff in connection with consultations under Article XIV, and in 1953 the practice began of providing the OEEC staff with copies of Part II of consultation reports (i.e., the "background papers" on which the consultations are based).

In April 1956 the Deputy Managing Director attended a meeting of the OEEC at which administrative arrangements were discussed, and he subsequently reported to the Board that the OEEC staff had asked whether they could also be provided with Part I of the consultation reports (i.e., the review of the staff's discussions with the member and the draft decision suggested to the Board). This proposal was considered by the Board at the end of April and approved, subject to the right of any Executive Director to object to the transmission to the OEEC of any consultation report in which he was interested. Little use was, in fact, made of this right of objection, but it was invoked by Mr. Maurice Toussaint (Belgium) in September 1956 in relation to Part I of the consultation report on Turkey, one of the countries that had elected Mr. van Campenhout, whose Alternate he was.

STERLING PROBLEMS

Cheap sterling

During the Board's review of retention quotas, summarized in the last chapter, an ancillary topic, "cheap sterling," was the subject of a detailed review presented to the Board in July. The staff pointed out that dual prices, currencies at a discount, and commodity arbitrage all reflected attempts by traders to take advantage of the dollar shortage. The control of cheap sterling could therefore be effected only by international cooperation, and at best was unlikely to be completely successful. However, the staff was able to say that the volume of transactions in sterling at a discount had greatly shrunk since the middle of 1952, and was down to the almost negligible figure of some £50,000 a day; it did not think it necessary to suggest, therefore, that Executive Directors should take any special steps in the matter.

The subject was discussed in the Board in December 1953. The representative of the staff then stated that the conclusions reached in July appeared to be confirmed by the fact that transferable sterling was being quoted in New York at a discount of less than 2 per cent, and that the discount on bilateral sterling was nowhere greater than 3½ per cent. Executive Directors expressed satisfaction at this development, which clearly reflected the improved position of non-dollar countries vis-à-vis the dollar, together with a greater willingness to hold sterling reserves. They accepted, however, that it was impossible wholly to control the transactions which gave rise to the markets for cheap sterling, and that the only effective solution to all such problems was the restoration of convertibility.

A fluctuating rate for sterling

From 1951 onward the possibility of restoring the convertibility of sterling was a constant topic of discussion among the members of the Fund. Especially during 1951 and the early part of 1952, considerable pressure was brought to bear upon the United Kingdom by certain continental European members to introduce convertibility. This gave rise, within the United Kingdom, to a proposal which greatly exercised the Fund's staff, although it did not directly come before the Board. The proposal involved allowing the sterling exchange rate to fluctuate within wider margins than those set by the Fund, as the price for restoring the convertibility of newly arising sterling balances.

When this was first advocated within the British government machine, during the early months of 1952, it was described as being designed to "take the strain off the reserves and put it on the rate of exchange." [13] It was rejected by Ministers in June, but later in the year was revived in a modified form, being made subject to the condition that certain other European countries should make their currencies convertible on the same terms. This, however, failed to secure the support either of the European countries concerned or of the United States. Nevertheless this so-called Collective Approach remained under consideration for some time, and in the autumn of 1953 it reappeared in the shape of a proposal that the main European currencies should widen the spread for one another's currencies, and for the dollar, to a larger figure of perhaps 3 or 5 per cent on each side of the par value. The pressure for sterling convertibility subsequently relaxed, and late in 1954 the idea of a Collective Approach was abandoned.

Major considerations for the Fund in the face of such proposals were (*a*) how the Fund should react in the light of the fact that the Articles of Agreement, while placing upon the Fund the responsibility for safeguarding the international negotiation of exchange rates, make no provision for approving fluctuating rates; (*b*) to what extent the Fund could make its resources available to assist the United Kingdom to restore convertibility.

In June 1952 the Managing Director took with him to Europe a brief covering the possibility that the United Kingdom might take "the bold step" of cutting

[13] Earl of Birkenhead, *The Prof in Two Worlds* (London, 1961), p. 284.

sterling loose from parity and letting it fluctuate while making currently earned sterling convertible. The possible introduction of a fluctuating rate was, however, viewed extremely critically by the Fund staff. A number of memoranda were written on different aspects of the problem. One, produced in the Research Department in October 1952, contrasted the effects of a freely fluctuating rate with those of one allowed to move only between fixed, though wide, margins. It argued that, while a freely fluctuating rate had the advantage that the country could not exhaust its reserves, such a rate for sterling would inevitably destroy the par value system. On the other hand, while an exchange rate moving within a wider spread was not incompatible with the ideas enshrined in the Articles (where the figure of 1 per cent for the approved spread was only introduced at a late stage),[14] it allowed speculators to anticipate in which direction the exchange rate would move. The memorandum went on to argue that the United Kingdom could not win greater freedom for sterling than its main competitors could take for their own currencies, since they would certainly follow the British example.

In the autumn of 1953 the modified plan for sterling, calling for a spread widened to 3–5 per cent each side of par, was similarly criticized. Another Research Department memorandum concluded that it offered little scope for the relaxation of restrictions or an advance toward convertibility.

At the Annual Meeting, 1953, the main theme of Mr. Rooth's address introducing the Annual Report was the need to restore convertibility. He was at pains to point out that convertibility would not return of itself; strong domestic policies, combined with assurances that exports would not be restricted by other countries, were essential prerequisites. Laying stress in particular on the responsibilities of creditor countries, Mr. Rooth urged upon them positive measures to encourage the expansion of trade and investment. The subject was taken up by several Governors, who emphasized such factors as the need for adequate reserves;[15] but no reference was made to the possibility of flexible exchange rates.

In June 1954 the Board considered proposals by the staff for a procedure to deal with fluctuating currencies, and the possibility of a wider spread for sterling was one of the factors which Directors had in mind. In August 1954 the possibility that sterling might be allowed to fluctuate was regarded as sufficiently serious as to require further examination. In that month Mr. Bernstein, Director of Research, prepared for the Managing Director a restatement of the argument for and against such a step. Proving himself a true prophet, he said that he did not think that the United Kingdom would propose making sterling a fluctuating currency; however, convertibility, once achieved, would be practically irreversible, and there was a risk that the United Kingdom might resort to a fluctuating

[14] *Proceedings*, p. 604 (cf. p. 575).

[15] *Summary Proceedings, 1953*, pp. 42, 52.

rate for sterling if there was a danger that otherwise the convertibility of the currency could not be maintained.

Mr. Bernstein again pointed out that the Fund's basic problem would be to maintain international responsibility for exchange rates if sterling were allowed to fluctuate. However, he believed that if the Fund could work out arrangements with the United Kingdom for a full and frank consultation on exchange rate problems and policies, it could take the view that the real objective of the Articles of Agreement was being achieved. Because of the problem of secrecy in such matters, Mr. Bernstein suggested that the consultations might in practice have to be with the Managing Director rather than with the Board, the latter being kept informed of developments as soon as conditions permitted.

A possible rationale, or philosophy, of a fluctuating rate for sterling which might be acceptable to likely European critics of such an arrangement was visualized by Mr. Bernstein as involving two steps: (1) a statement by the United Kingdom to the Fund that it had ceased to accept responsibility for maintaining sterling within 1 per cent of parity, to which the Fund would reply that it had noted the action and recognized the importance of the step in the whole range of measures which the United Kingdom was taking to maintain the convertibility of sterling; and (2) an assurance that the Fund intended to exercise its international responsibility in the field of exchange rates for fluctuating as well as for fixed rates, so that all members might be assured that fluctuations would not be used to gain unfair advantage in competition for international trade. To this end the Fund would remain in close contact with the United Kingdom.

In the event, an informal discussion of the problems of sterling convertibility, arranged by the Managing Director during the Annual Meeting, 1954, did not touch on a fluctuating rate. After that meeting the probability of such a measure so diminished that it ceased seriously to concern the Fund staff, except for a short period in the summer of 1955, when it briefly appeared that a fluctuating rate might again be contemplated. The final dismissal of this proposal is recorded below in Chapter 15.

CHAPTER

14

A Question of Obligations

(1953-54)

A MAJOR PREOCCUPATION of the Board throughout the year 1953–54 was the dispute between the Fund and Czechoslovakia. This began with a disagreement over Czechoslovakia's right to change the par value of the koruna without consulting the Fund. It developed into a formal complaint of noncooperation, as a result of which Czechoslovakia was required to withdraw from membership at the end of 1954.

MEMBERSHIP AND BOARD

Two new members joined the Fund during the year, Indonesia on April 15, 1954, and Israel on July 12. This brought the total number of members to 57 and the total of quotas to $8,853 million.

The obligations of Article VIII, Sections 2, 3, and 4, were accepted by Haiti in December 1953 and by Cuba in March 1954, raising the number of countries that had achieved convertible currencies (in the Fund sense) to ten.

There were several changes in the membership of the Executive Board during the year. Mr. Melville resigned from October 31, 1953, and Mr. Leslie H. E. Bury (Australia), who had been his Alternate since March 1951, was elected to succeed him. Mr. Natu resigned from the end of November 1953, and the Indian Government appointed Mr. P. S. Narayan Prasad as his successor. Mr. de Selliers resigned from March 22, 1954, and Mr. Ansiaux (Belgium), who had been an Executive Director from June 1946 to October 1948, was elected to the vacancy. However, Mr. Ansiaux in turn resigned at the end of October 1954, and Mr. Jean C. Godeaux (Belgium), who had been Alternate Executive Director to Mr. de Selliers and to Mr. Ansiaux, was elected to succeed the latter. The British seat on the Board also sustained two changes: Sir Edmund Hall-Patch resigned from June 30, 1954, and was succeeded by Mr. Denis H. F. Rickett.

Mr. Rickett, however, remained only until the end of September 1954, when he was succeeded by the second Viscount Harcourt.

STAFF QUESTIONS

The geographical distribution of the senior staff has from time to time troubled some Executive Directors. One such occasion arose in October 1953, when the Managing Director proposed to replace Mr. Stamp, who had resigned as Director of the European Department, by Mr. John Melior Stevens, also an Englishman. At that time five of the eleven heads of departments were U.S. citizens, the other six being, respectively, from Belgium, China, Czechoslovakia, India, Iran, and the United Kingdom. Mr. de Largentaye (France) pointed out that no Frenchman had ever headed a department, and suggested that the post held by Mr. Stamp should be rotated between continental European countries before being again held by an Englishman. Other Executive Directors, however, demurred at interfering with the freedom of action of the Managing Director in selecting senior staff.

Mr. Rooth said that an extensive search had been made for a suitable successor to Mr. Stamp and that the Fund was fortunate to obtain Mr. Stevens' services. An opportunity did arise, however, for the appointment of another senior officer, to the position of Deputy Director of the Exchange Restrictions Department, and he was glad to be able to offer this to Mr. Gabriel Ferras, at that time Alternate to Mr. de Largentaye. Mr. Ferras accepted the position from December 14, 1953, and held it until June 1956, when he succeeded Mr. Stevens on the latter's resignation as Director of the European Department. (It may be noted that in January 1963 Mr. Ferras became the General Manager of the Bank for International Settlements, and in 1965 Mr. Stevens returned to the Fund as Executive Director for the United Kingdom.)

In April 1954 the active staff (excluding 10 on long leave) numbered 428, from 42 countries. This was an increase of 11 staff members and 4 countries during the year. Nevertheless, the geographical distribution was again questioned in the context of the budget for 1954/55. Mr. Bury (Australia), Mr. Crena de Iongh (Netherlands), and Mr. Prasad (India) spoke of the disadvantages of concentrating staff of a single nationality in any one organizational unit, and Mr. Bury especially stressed the dangers of doing so in the unit concerned with the country of origin of the staff. He suggested that, to enable the Fund to recruit more widely, a few additional senior positions should be created ad hoc. This proposal was not supported. Sir Edmund Hall-Patch (United Kingdom) thought that the staff was already too large, and that the simplification of work in connection with consultations should enable the numbers to be reduced.

On the immediate issue, Mr. Godeaux (Belgium) pointed out that if promotions were to be made from within, the large proportion of staff posts filled at the outset by U.S. citizens would eventually result in most of the senior positions being held by them. He thought that while such persons should be appropriately rewarded financially, the most senior posts should be geographically distributed. As regards professional staff generally, Mr. Saad (Egypt) proposed that it should be a rule that at least one technically qualified person should be recruited from each member country.

The basis proposed by Mr. Saad, of course, makes no allowance for the differing size of member countries. A rough adjustment can be made for this factor by comparing the proportion of staff from a given area with the proportion of total Fund quotas which that area commands. Such an analysis of the staff at September 1, 1954 shows that while the Western Hemisphere had contributed 40 per cent of the Fund's quotas, it had provided 55 per cent of the professional staff. The corresponding figures for Europe were 38 per cent and 28 per cent, and for the Far East and Middle East 18 per cent and 14 per cent.

By April 1955 the economies suggested as possible by Sir Edmund Hall-Patch had taken effect, and the active staff had been reduced by seven. It was now drawn from 40 countries, two fewer than a year before. In the budget proposals for 1955/56 presented to the Board, however, the Deputy Managing Director said that he had constantly in mind that the geographic distribution of the staff should be maintained. This provoked from Mr. Gragnani (Italy) the criticism that it must first be established. Mr. Albert Mansour (Egypt), Alternate to Mr. Saad, Mr. Prasad, and Mr. Yumoto (Japan) also suggested that the distribution could be improved. Mr. de Largentaye again called attention to the large number of U.S. citizens heading departments and divisions. Mr. Toussaint (Belgium) thought that one problem was that the salary scale was too low to attract first-class Europeans.

Mr. Cochran said that he was doing everything possible to secure the services of staff from a wider area and that only three U.S. citizens had been recruited for senior posts since he had come to the Fund. Mr. Southard (United States), while agreeing that there were, relatively speaking, too many U.S. nationals in senior posts, pointed out that fifteen professional staff members had acquired U.S. citizenship since joining the Fund staff. In the course of the discussion, Mr. Cochran mentioned that the annual turnover of staff was only 7 per cent.

A possible hindrance to recruitment was reduced in 1954 as a result of a proposal by Mr. Saad to liberalize the provisions for home leave for the staff. Until then, home leave (with paid transportation) had been granted every third year. Mr. Saad pointed out that in the United Nations home leave was granted every second year. In the World Bank the staff had the option of taking home leave every second year on condition that the Bank then paid one half only of the first-class transportation costs for wives and children, or every third year with the Bank then paying all first-class transportation costs for families. Mr. Saad recommended that the Fund should adopt either the United Nations' or the World Bank's procedures.

Replying to the Deputy Managing Director, who suggested that home leave every two years would be unduly expensive and disruptive, Mr. Saad pointed out that the total length of leave could be unaffected, except for traveling time, for which a solution could no doubt be found. On the other hand, he had received numerous complaints about the existing arrangements, and was convinced that they prevented the engagement of outstanding staff. Mr. de Largentaye agreed, saying that the provisions for home leave played a large part in the decisions of Frenchmen whether to join the Fund staff, and he believed that the three-year rule also presented serious obstacles to the retention of good men. As a result of Mr. Saad's initiative, the World Bank rule was adopted in the Fund. It remained in force until 1961, when it was modified to provide that staff taking home leave after two years would be reimbursed transportation costs for themselves and their families at second-class or economy rates, while those taking home leave after three years continued to be reimbursed for first-class fares.

CZECHOSLOVAKIA LEAVES THE FUND

On June 2, 1953, the Fund received from Czechoslovakia a cablegram announcing that the par value of the koruna had been changed from Kčs 50=$1 to Kčs 7.20=$1. The change was operative from June 1. As the Fund had not been consulted, the subject was placed on the Board's agenda and the Czechoslovak Government was invited to send a representative to a meeting on July 20 to discuss it. Czechoslovakia's action was the beginning of a series of difficulties with the member, which culminated in its being required to withdraw from the Fund at the end of 1954.

Par value

Discussions between Czechoslovak representatives and the Board, begun in July, were continued in August, September, and November. Two substantive issues emerged. One was whether the change in the par value did or did not "affect the international transactions of members of the Fund." Czechoslovakia claimed that it did not, and was therefore covered by Article IV, Section 5 (*e*), of the Articles of Agreement, which permitted such a par value to be changed by a member without the Fund's concurrence. The other question was whether, even though the Fund's concurrence was not necessary, the member was under an obligation to consult the Fund before changing such a par value.

On the first of these questions, Czechoslovakia relied on the facts that its international trade was state controlled, and not governed by price considerations; that most of this trade was carried on in foreign currencies; and that the remainder was effected on terms related to the gold value of the koruna, and therefore appropriately changed when the par value was changed. The alteration of the par value was part of a comprehensive overhaul of the Czechoslovak economic system, including a drastic reduction in the money supply and a revision of prices.

The Czechoslovak representative also contended that the words "does not affect" in Article IV, Section 5 (*e*), must mean "does not adversely affect," and as no member country had complained about being adversely affected, it must be assumed that none was. He went on to claim further that the Fund had only such rights as had been conceded to it by the states that were members; in case of doubt, therefore, the Articles must be construed so as to preserve the sovereignty of the members.

The Board, however, found on inquiry that there were some transactions in invisibles between Czechoslovakia and other countries that were affected by the change in the par value. Accordingly, the change in the par value of the koruna did not fall under Article IV, Section 5 (*e*), and Czechoslovakia was required to obtain the concurrence of the Fund. For this purpose the first step would be to provide economic data which would enable the Board to determine whether the change was necessary to correct a fundamental disequilibrium. Such data had not been forthcoming, and a formal request for it was sent to Czechoslovakia at the end of 1953.

On the question whether prior consultation was required, the Czechoslovak representative argued that Section 5 (*e*) of Article IV must be considered as standing in isolation from the rest of Section 5, and as it contained no references to consultation or to fundamental disequilibrium, neither of these was relevant. The Legal Department, however, advised the Board that the requirement to consult the Fund applied to all changes in par values, whether or not the Fund's concurrence was required. This view was adopted by the Board. However, since in any case the Board had ruled that Article IV, Section 5 (*e*), could not be invoked by Czechoslovakia, the point became one of academic interest only.

Other criticisms

Meanwhile, other causes of difficulty had arisen. Czechoslovakia failed to reply to questionnaires designed to obtain information on which Article XIV consultations could be held. It made koruna payments for charges on its drawings from the Fund in "new money," i.e., at the unauthorized par value. And it changed the total of the Fund's koruna account, so as to conform to the altered value of the koruna, without the Fund's permission. Together with the unauthorized change in the par value, these causes of complaint formed the basis of a proposal by Mr. Southard (United States) on September 4, 1953, that Czechoslovakia should be declared ineligible to use the Fund's resources. Emphasizing particularly the second and third points mentioned, Mr. Southard urged that the Board, as trustees for the Fund's assets, should move promptly.

Mr. Southard's specific proposal was that the Board should take a decision under the first sentence of Article XV, Section 2 (*a*), which reads: "If a member fails to fulfill any of its obligations under this Agreement, the Fund may declare the member ineligible to use the resources of the Fund." After other members of the Board, while sympathizing with Mr. Southard's concern, had pressed for adequate time to be given for Czechoslovakia to answer his criticisms, or to make restitution, it was arranged that a meeting with Czechoslovak representatives should be held on September 30.

This meeting was inconclusive. The Managing Director reported that Czechoslovakia had meanwhile written to the Fund reporting the correct balance in the Fund's koruna account, but had annotated this as "old money"; it had also purported to detail its payments of charges, but these had not been made in korunas that the Fund could recognize. As the Czechoslovak representatives at the meeting were not authorized to elucidate the member's actions, the Board decided to put formal inquiries to the Czechoslovak Government: What was the meaning of "old money"? Would Czechoslovakia pay charges on the basis of the agreed par value of the koruna? Would it provide information to enable the Fund to examine the change in the par value? If so, when and how? The Board decided to meet again on October 21 to consider, on the basis of the answers to these questions, whether Czechoslovakia should be declared ineligible to draw.

When October 21 came, however, the Managing Director reported that the member had asked for a delay of at least a fortnight. Mr. Southard saw no justification for this; the member had had ample notice of the Fund's criticisms. However, if a delay were to be granted, he proposed to add two new complaints: that the member had failed to provide the information called for by Article VIII, Section 5 (*a*), and that it had failed to consult the Fund as required by Article XIV, Section 4. Although Mr. Natu (India) demurred at introducing fresh complaints at that stage, the Board decided to transmit them to Czechoslovakia with an invitation to be represented at a Board meeting on November 4.

At this postponed meeting the Czechoslovak representatives attempted to subsume the four points in Mr. Southard's original complaint under a justification for the change in the par value. This, however, did not satisfy the Board, for reasons discussed in the previous subsection, and at the end of the meeting a decision was reached, by 86,665 votes to none, that Czechoslovakia was ineligible to use the Fund's resources.

This decision did not, however, dispose of Mr. Southard's two new complaints. On the first of these the Czechoslovak representatives stated that data had been provided to meet the Fund's requirements under Article VIII, Section 5 (*a*), except for those under four subsections, viz., (v), exports and imports; (vi), balance of payments; (viii), national income; and (ix), price indices. As to the last of these, the Czechoslovak representatives said that price indices had not been calculated, and so could not be provided. As to the other three, they claimed that data could not be made available to the Fund because to do so would infringe national security. The Board was unable to accept this plea, and again invited Czechoslovakia to cooperate.

WITHDRAWAL CONSIDERED

Six months passed, and on June 7, 1954, Mr. Southard called the Board's attention to the fact that Czechoslovakia was still failing to fulfill its obligations. He proposed that on or about June 30 the Board should consider with Czechoslovakia whether the Board should recommend to the Governors that the member should be required to withdraw under Article XV, Section 2 (*b*), which reads:

> If, after the expiration of a reasonable period the member persists in its failure to fulfill any of its obligations under this Agreement, or a difference between a member and the Fund under Article IV, Section 6, continues, that member may be required to withdraw from membership in the Fund by a decision of the Board of Governors carried by a majority of the governors representing a majority of the total voting power.

The proposed meeting, fixed by the Board for July 7, was postponed until July 23 at the request of Czechoslovakia. Its representative then argued first that Article XV, Section 2 (*b*), could not be invoked against a member unless Article XV, Section 2 (*a*), had previously been applied against that member as a sanction. This had not been done against Czechoslovakia; Article XV, Section 2 (*a*), had been used only as a means of settling the mutual relations between the Fund and Czechoslovakia. Secondly, the Czechoslovak representative contended that Article XV, Section 2 (*b*), could not be applied until after the expiration of a specific period set when action was taken under Article XV, Section 2 (*a*). Both these arguments were rejected by the Board on legal advice.[1] The Czechoslovak representative then declared, thirdly, that the references to nonfulfillment of obligations in Section 2 (*a*) and (*b*) of Article XV must be construed as meaning nonfulfillment without justification; Czechoslovakia was, however, justified in its refusal to supply data since these would jeopardize national security.

---

[1] E.B. Decision No. 343-(54/47), August 11, 1954, interpreted Article XV, Section 2, to cover both the points raised by Czechoslovakia on the use of Article XV, Section 2 (*b*). It is reproduced below, Vol. III, p. 269. The Board's decision was confirmed by the Governors (Resolution 9-7, *Summary Proceedings, 1954*, p. 112).

At a further meeting three days later several Executive Directors asked why the provision of information about the national income, balance of payments, and international trade would impair national security. In reply, the Czechoslovak representative referred to the decision taken by the Board when the United States had imposed exchange restrictions for security reasons.[2] That decision, he suggested, had implied that the question whether national security was involved was one to be decided by the member itself. Moreover, the representative went on, Article VIII, Section 5 (*b*), authorized members to refuse "to furnish information in such detail that the affairs of individuals or corporations are disclosed." Since international trade was conducted in Czechoslovakia by a single state body, this subsection exempted the Government from furnishing details of exports, imports, or the balance of payments.

The debate continued at four further meetings, the point at issue being narrowed down to the question whether national security was a sufficient justification for Czechoslovakia's refusal to provide data. In this connection the Board drew a distinction between its ruling on the U.S. restrictions for security reasons, where the Fund had full jurisdiction to decide whether or not the restrictions were justified, and the nonfulfillment of the obligation to provide data, without which the Fund could not exercise its jurisdiction at all. Accordingly, Czechoslovakia's refusal to provide data had to be considered in the general context of the requirements of the Articles of Agreement, and in that light it could not be justified. The Board therefore decided to recommend to the Governors that Czechoslovakia should be required to withdraw from the Fund unless by December 31, 1954 it had supplied the necessary information to comply with Article VIII, Section 5 (*a*), and to enable consultations to be held under Article XIV. No Director voted against this decision, but six abstained.

At the Annual Meeting, 1954, the Board's decisions were supported by the Committee on Finance and Organization, with the Governors for Burma, Finland, India, and Jordan abstaining, and approved by the Governors in Plenary Session on September 28, 1954, despite speeches by the Governor for Czechoslovakia both to the committee and to the Governors, in which he repeated the arguments set out above.[3] Accordingly, Czechoslovakia was given until December 31 to provide the necessary data.

On January 5, 1955, the Managing Director reported to the Board that the required information had not been received, and a letter was accordingly dispatched to Czechoslovakia intimating that its membership had lapsed on December 31. Czechoslovakia refused to accept this as an effective termination of its membership and countered with a letter dated May 4 withdrawing voluntarily

[2] See above, pp. 275–76.

[3] *Summary Proceedings, 1954*, pp. 97, 101, 143, and Resolution 9-8, p. 113.

from the Fund. Negotiations were then begun to reach a settlement of Czechoslovakia's debt to the Fund, and agreement was reached on June 10 on a schedule providing for half-yearly payments of $0.33 million. These were regularly made until the debt was extinguished in July 1961.

On January 7, 1955, the Board agreed that the five Czechoslovak members of the staff should be retained.

DRAWINGS AND REPURCHASES

Four countries purchased $175.54 million in 1953–54, of which $37.5 million was taken in U.S. dollars and the remainder in sterling. The largest drawings were made by Japan, which took £39.3 million ($110.04 million) in sterling. Repurchases were $319.54 million, of which $138.32 million were made voluntarily, the remainder being either obligatory repurchases under Article V, Section 7, of the Fund Agreement or made in pursuance of undertakings entered into when the drawings were made. The voluntary repurchases included $61.6 million by Japan.

Two stand-by arrangements were inaugurated during the year, one for six months (Mexico) and one for a year (Peru).

LIMITS ON DRAWINGS

A drawing of £10 million in sterling by Brazil in October 1953 raised two questions. One, which exercised Mr. Perry (Canada), was the propriety of a drawing intended by the member country for use to pay off large current arrears to a creditor country. Mr. Perry pointed out that such a transaction might be detrimental to the interests of other creditors, and even to the interests of the drawing country itself. The second question concerned a recommendation by the staff that "if any waiver is required under Article V, Section 4, it should be granted." The staff explained that this was necessary because under one interpretation of Article V, Section 3 (*a*) (iii), a waiver might be required, while on another interpretation it would not. Directors were reluctant to include a conditional waiver in their decision, and it was accordingly agreed that their readiness to grant a waiver should be recorded in the minutes but not communicated to the drawing member. The possibility that a waiver might be needed also arose in connection with a drawing by Japan of £22 million in sterling in December 1953, and the same solution was adopted.

The question whether a waiver was required for the drawings by Brazil and Japan was not easily settled. Article V, Section 3 (*a*) (iii), sets out some of the conditions that have to be satisfied if a member is to be able to draw from the Fund, as follows:

> The proposed purchase would not cause the Fund's holdings of the purchasing member's currency to increase by more than twenty-five percent of its quota during the period of twelve months ending on the date of the purchase nor to exceed two hundred percent of its quota, but the twenty-five percent limitation shall apply only to the extent that the Fund's holdings of the member's currency have been brought above seventy-five percent of its quota if they had been below that amount.

The staff pointed out that there seemed to be three possible interpretations of the first part of this subsection (ending at "the date of the purchase"). One would be to include on a gross basis all additions to the Fund's holdings of the member's currency during the year. A second, which might be styled a "completely net" solution, would involve comparing the Fund's holdings on the relevant date with the holdings twelve months previously. A third would involve interpreting the passage as follows:

> The proposed purchase would not cause the Fund's holdings of the purchasing member's currency to exceed by more than 25 percent of its quota the lowest level (or 75 percent of quota if the lowest level is below 75 percent) of the Fund's holdings of that member's currency attained during the period of twelve months ending on the date of the purchase. . . .

Not one of these three choices was without economic disadvantages, but in the view of the staff the third best fitted the language of the provision in a common-sense way.

The main objection to the first interpretation—that involving gross additions to the Fund's holdings—was that once a member had drawn 25 per cent of its quota during a year it could draw no more, even if it repurchased the drawing or if another member drew its currency. There was also evidence, in a gloss put out by the U.S. Treasury in 1944, that at Bretton Woods the provision had been intended to be construed as a net one.[4]

The difficulty about the second, "completely net," solution was that this would enable a member to draw more than 25 per cent in a year if the Fund's holdings of its currency twelve months earlier had been greater than they were at the date of the drawing. For example, if during the first half of 1953 the Fund's holdings of a member's currency were 90 per cent of its quota, and during the second half of the year they were reduced to 75 per cent of quota, then during the first half of 1954 the member could draw 40 per cent of its quota, raising the Fund's holdings to 115 per cent of quota, since this would be 25 per cent greater than a year previously. This was not only unreasonable, but was difficult to reconcile with the concept of a Fund that revolves for all members, or with the

[4] *Questions and Answers on the International Monetary Fund;* below, Vol. III, p. 142.

spirit of the provisions for waivers in Article V, Section 4, which could be exercised especially in favor of "members with a record of avoiding large or continuous use of the Fund's resources."

The staff recognized that the third solution had one drawback: that if member B drew member A's currency from the Fund, and member A subsequently drew a corresponding amount, member A's drawing rights would thereby be reduced by the amount of its drawing, without any allowance for the amount drawn by member B; whereas the "completely net" solution would have permitted A to draw the equivalent of B's drawing in addition to 25 per cent. The staff pointed out that this problem could be met by granting member A a waiver.

A preliminary discussion of the staff's proposal in the Board at the end of September 1953 led to its being referred to the Interpretation Committee, which discussed it four times between December 1953 and July 1955. In the committee the staff's proposal found general support, although some Directors were concerned that such an interpretation would discourage voluntary repurchases. (If a member made a voluntary repurchase of a recent drawing, it nevertheless would be unable to draw again until after twelve months from the date of the original drawing, except to the extent that the latter was less than 25 per cent of quota.) It was felt that this problem could be effectively dealt with by granting a waiver. Mr. Crick (United Kingdom), for example, was confident that the Fund would take a voluntary repurchase into account when dealing with any subsequent request for a drawing. He went on to make the significant remark that the old dispute about automaticity seemed largely to have evaporated in the light of the practical development of the Fund's policy regarding the use of its resources.

Mr. de Largentaye (France) and Mr. Godeaux (Belgium), however, disagreed with the interpretation that the staff recommended; they could find no basis in the Articles for it and believed that the correct alternative was that described above as "completely net," or, failing this, the "gross" interpretation. Mr. de Largentaye could not accept that the reference in Article V, Section 4, to "large or continuous use of the Fund's resources" had any relevance to Article V, Section 3 (*a*) (iii). In a memorandum discussed by the committee in March 1954, Mr. Godeaux suggested that the purpose of the waiver provision was to enable the Fund to place a member that had not made large or continuous use of the Fund's resources in the same position as one that had. The staff, however, suggested that the underlying principle of the interpretation should be that every member had a right to a normal yearly drawing, and that the interpretation should be consistent with the idea that members not only had a right to draw but also a duty to give credit through the Fund. If at any point of time the normal yearly amount had to be exceeded, a waiver would be required; and when deciding whether to grant a waiver, the Fund could give some additional benefit to those that had avoided large and continuous use of its resources. The staff believed that this was a correct interpretation of the compromise reached at Bretton Woods with those that had wished the Articles to provide for larger normal yearly increments, or for "carry-over" provisions such as those suggested by the French delegation.

At this point the discussion was adjourned. When it was resumed in July 1955 the committee agreed to recommend to the Board for approval the staff's proposed formulation of the meaning of the quantitative limit of 25 per cent of quota (the third alternative above). The Board adopted this as its decision on August 24, 1955.[5] Mr. van der Valk (Netherlands) and Mr. Daniel Dommel (France), Alternate to Mr. de Largentaye, dissented.

VOTING ON DRAWINGS

A troublesome question of interpretation was reviewed by the Board in November 1953. It concerned the provision for enhancing for certain purposes the voting power of member countries whose currencies had been used by the Fund, and diminishing the votes of members that had drawn on the Fund. These adjustments were to apply when it was necessary to vote on proposals either (1) under Article V, Section 4, to waive the conditions governing the use of the Fund's resources set out in Article V, Section 3; or (2) under Article V, Section 5, to limit a member's use or declare it ineligible to draw. The relevant voting provision in the Articles, as it emerged at Bretton Woods, was as follows:

> *Article XII, Section 5 (b).* Whenever voting is required under Article V, Section 4 or 5, each member shall have the number of votes to which it is entitled . . . adjusted
>
> (i) by the addition of one vote for the equivalent of each four hundred thousand United States dollars of net sales of its currency up to the date when the vote is taken, or
>
> (ii) by the subtraction of one vote for the equivalent of each four hundred thousand United States dollars of its net purchases of the currencies of other members up to the date when the vote is taken;
>
> provided, that neither net purchases nor net sales shall be deemed at any time to exceed an amount equal to the quota of the member involved.

The problem to be solved was the meaning in this Section of "net sales" and "net purchases." These phrases were not defined in the Articles, and their exact meaning was not apparent. They clearly included normal purchases and repurchases of a member's currency as a result of Fund transactions. But did they, for example, also include sales of one member's currency to another for gold

[5] E.B. Decision No. 451-(55/52), August 24, 1955; below, Vol. III, p. 228.

under Article V, Section 6, or acquisition of a member's currency for gold by the Fund under Article VII, Section 2 (ii)? Should the adjustments take account of transactions which produced changes in the Fund's holdings of members' currencies, but did not arise from purchases or repurchases by other members, such as administrative expenditures by the Fund, payments for charges or for Fund publications, or borrowings of currencies by the Fund under Article VII, Section 2 (i)? It was the view of the staff that none of these items should enter into the calculation, since the clear purpose of the adjustment was to increase the voting strength of those members whose subscriptions to the Fund had been used to give assistance to other members, and to reduce the voting strength of those members that had received assistance from the Fund.

As a result, the staff proposed the following formula:

> Subject to the proviso that neither net sales nor net purchases shall be deemed at any time to exceed an amount equal to the quota of a member:
>
> (*a*) The member shall receive, under Article XII, Section 5 (*b*) (i), additional votes for sales of its currency in exchange for the currency of other members, minus repurchases with that currency which have been made by other members and repurchases accruing in that currency but discharged in gold. Whenever this calculation results in a positive figure, upward adjustment will be made; whenever at any point of time the calculation results in a zero or negative figure, no adjustment will be made for the negative figure and the negative figure will not be carried forward for subsequent calculations.
>
> (*b*) [Parallel definition for reduced votes under Section 5 (*b*) (ii).]

The *raison d'être* for the exclusion of negative figures from the adjustment was that these could only arise as a result of the entry into the calculation of items which, it was argued, were not relevant.

Executive Directors found considerable difficulty in accepting the staff's proposal, and the staff was asked to produce a further memorandum showing practical applications of alternative interpretations. This was sent to the Board in June 1954, and put forward five possible formulas, including that originally suggested, which the staff still recommended. The other four differed from it by including one or more of the kinds of transaction which the staff, in its earlier memorandum, had argued should be excluded, or by expressing the same result in different terminology, which sounded simpler but did not correspond to the language used in the Article. The Board did not consider the matter further, but as it has never been found necessary to vote on a proposal to draw from the Fund, the absence of an affirmative decision has not been of importance.

RENEWAL OF DECISIONS ON DRAWINGS

Toward the end of 1953 the staff brought to the attention of the Board the pending expiration of decisions dealing with the procedures for drawings, stand-by arrangements, and charges. The first of these decisions, embodied in the Rooth Plan, had been adopted for a trial period of two years in February 1952. Reporting on the use made of the procedure down to November 1953, the staff said that eight members had made purchases, seven of them in the gold tranche, and that none had objected to the stated principles of repurchase. The staff proposed that the arrangements continue without a time limit. After a brief discussion, the Board agreed to this recommendation, on December 23, 1953, subject to review from time to time as circumstances warranted.[6]

On the subject of stand-by arrangements, the staff reported that since the relevant decision had been adopted on October 1, 1952, only one arrangement had been instituted (with Finland for $5 million), and the whole of the amount had been drawn. However, other members had expressed interest in possible arrangements, some as a support if they undertook convertibility, and others as a safeguard should their export prices fall. Several members had suggested lengthening the period of a stand-by arrangement to a year, or even omitting any time limit at all. The staff, however, recommended that the six-month period should not be extended as a matter of course, although in appropriate circumstances a longer period might be conceded ad hoc. The point might advantageously be covered by including in the formal decision an expression of the attitude toward exceptions to the six-month limit recorded in the minutes of the discussion in 1952.

When the Board reviewed the staff's recommendations much of the discussion turned on this issue. The slight use made of stand-by arrangements in the year since they had been introduced was explained by Messrs. Eriksen (Norway), Godeaux (Belgium), Gragnani (Italy), and Yumoto (Japan) as probably due to the inadequacy of a six-month arrangement. Sir Edmund Hall-Patch (United Kingdom) said that when the United Kingdom came to undertake convertibility again it would almost certainly need a stand-by arrangement for more than six months. Mr. Emminger (Germany) considered that most countries' problems would call for a more extended arrangement—as indeed had been suggested earlier in the year by an OEEC mission to the Fund. However, Mr. Emminger thought that the language proposed by the staff would provide adequate cover for any needed concession.

Mr. Southard (United States) maintained his objection to stand-by arrangements lasting more than six months, but said that in view of the special interest

[6] E.B. Decision No. 270-(53/95), December 23, 1953; below, Vol. III, p. 231.

of some countries in longer arrangements he was prepared to accept the inclusion in the decision of a reference to them. He suggested, however, that the clause to be added should relate the concession of a longer time period "particularly . . . [to] positive proposals for convertibility." Several Executive Directors—Messrs. Delgado (Nicaragua), Eriksen, Paranaguá (Brazil), Prasad (India), Saad (Egypt), and Yumoto—urged that the adoption of convertibility was not the only circumstance that would justify special consideration of the time limit. Mr. Delgado pointed out, for instance, that some countries with vulnerable economies, such as those in the Caribbean, might need a stand-by arrangement for more than six months to enable them to *maintain* convertibility. In deference to this, and at the suggestion of Mr. Saad, Mr. Southard agreed to substitute "for example" for "particularly" in the decision.

The outcome of the foregoing discussion was a somewhat ambivalent paragraph in the decision taken on December 23, 1953. Two sentences, repeated with a change of tense from the decision of October 1, 1952, prohibited stand-by arrangements for more than six months. The next two sentences provided that such arrangements could, in fact, be approved. The resulting paragraph read as follows:

> 1. Stand-by arrangements will be limited to periods of not more than six months. They can be renewed by a new decision of the Executive Board. If a member believes that the payments problems it anticipates (for example, in connection with positive programs for maintaining or achieving convertibility) can be adequately provided for only by a stand-by arrangement of more than six months, the Fund will give sympathetic consideration to a request for a longer stand-by arrangement in the light of the problems facing the member and the measures being taken to deal with them. With respect to stand-by arrangements for periods of more than six months, the Fund and the member might find it appropriate to reach understandings additional to those set forth in this decision.

With the exception of this paragraph, and of some changes in charges for stand-by arrangements discussed below, the decision of December 1953 substantially reenacted that of October 1952.

The more liberal attitude toward stand-by arrangements for longer than six months, evidenced by the foregoing discussion, was speedily effective. Two months later, in February 1954, a stand-by arrangement with Peru was concluded for a period of twelve months; this was subsequently extended several times for a year at a time. A six-month stand-by arrangement with Mexico initiated in April 1954 was extended in October 1954 for twelve months. No new stand-by arrangements were introduced in 1955, but of the eighteen new or renewed arrangements in 1956 and 1957, thirteen were for a year and only five for six months. Since 1957 stand-by arrangements for less than a year have been comparatively rare exceptions. The conditions attached to the arrangements with Peru and Mexico are described below.

The staff's recommendations in November 1953 also included a proposal that no charge should be levied on the part of a stand-by arrangement corresponding to the member's gold tranche. This was accepted, but there were objections to a further recommendation that charges for stand-by arrangements should not be payable in local currency if they were relatively small; this was held to be contrary to Article V, Section 8 (*f*), and was rejected. At the suggestion of Mr. Crena de Iongh (Netherlands), it was agreed that the charge for a stand-by arrangement should be credited against the service charge payable for a transaction under the stand-by arrangement (as had been proposed by the staff in August 1952). Finally, the Board agreed that, as with the Rooth Plan, the provision for stand-by arrangements, thus amended, should continue in effect without a time limit, subject to review from time to time.

CHARGES REVISED

The third of the decisions about to expire in December 1953 was that governing the scale of charges generally. This scale, which had been introduced late in 1951, was originally intended to be effective only until the end of 1952. Since then, however, it had been several times extended, on the last occasion from October 31, 1953 until the end of the year. Directors' views on it varied widely. Some felt that the charges were too high, some wished to simplify the scale, and some believed that the charges should be varied from time to time to reflect the Fund's view of the world economic situation, being raised when drawings should be discouraged and lowered when drawings could be more freely permitted. The view of the U.S. Government was that the charges imposed by the 1951 scale for drawings up to 125 per cent of quota were too low, but that some reduction was practicable in charges at the upper end of the scale. In consequence, Mr. Southard (United States) put forward a proposal for a new scale, which was the outcome of negotiations which he had conducted with other Directors for more than six months. The principal feature of this scale was the abandonment of a separate rate of charge for drawings up to 125 per cent of quota, and the application to this bracket of the charges on the 125–150 per cent bracket, with an effective initial rate of 2 per cent per annum. For the first three months there would be no charge except the service charge, which would eliminate the anomaly, inherent in the previous scale, that the effective annual rate of charge (including the service charge) on drawings was greater if these were repaid within a short time than if they remained outstanding for a year. Table 4 compares the new scale with that introduced in 1951.[7]

Several Directors still believed that the proposed charges were too high. Sir Edmund Hall-Patch (United Kingdom) argued that the current rate for short-term

[7] See above, p. 322.

loans in money markets was not a proper criterion for the Fund's charges; the latter should be such as would deter needless borrowing but would not penalize members who were obliged to draw. Mr. de Largentaye (France) thought that the new rates would be too hard on borrowers, and saw no justification for increasing the charge in the 100–125 per cent bracket; indeed, he thought that the charge should be lowered. Nevertheless, the new scale was accepted as a compromise by all Directors except Mr. de Largentaye, the affirmative votes totaling 93,865 out of 99,365. Several members of the Board remarked that if

Table 4. Charges: Comparison of 1951 and 1954 Scales [1]

(In per cent)

Duration of Drawing	Number of Bracket and Proportion of Quota Held by Fund						
	1951 Scale				1954 Scale		
	1st 100-125 %	2nd 125-150 %	3rd 150-175 %	4th 175-200 %	1st 100-150 %	2nd 150-175 %	3rd 175-200 %
0-3 months	0	1	1½	2	0	0	0
3-6 months	0	1	1½	2	2	2	2
6-12 months	1	1½	2	2½	2	2	2½
1-1½ years	1½	2	2½	3	2	2½	3
1½-2 years	2	2½	3	3½ [2]	2½	3	3½
2-2½ years	2½	3	3½ [2]	4 [3]	3	3½	4 [2,4]
2½-3 years	3	3½ [2]	4 [3]		3½	4 [2,4]	4½ [4]
3-3½ years	3½ [2]	4 [3]			4 [2,4]	4½ [4]	5 [4]
3½-4 years	4 [3]				4½ [4]	5 [4]	
4-4½ years					5 [4]		

[1] These charges are in addition to the service charge (½ per cent).

[2] At this point the Fund is obligated to consult with the member on means to reduce the Fund's holdings of the member's currency.

[3] If the Fund decides to raise the interest rate, it may do so only to 4½ per cent for one semiannual period and 5 per cent for a second semiannual period. Thereafter the Fund may levy such charges as it regards appropriate.

[4] Maximum charges; the Fund has discretion to make lower charges.

circumstances justified a definitive lowering of the charges, Executive Directors could ask for this to be done. The decision applied the new scale only until December 31, 1954 but, in the event, it was not altered until 1963.

In February 1954 the Board agreed to a staff proposal that Rule I-4 (a) should be altered so as to require a member to pay charges within thirty days of the dispatch of a cabled request for payment, instead of within ten days of the receipt of a request—the latter rule having run into difficulties when the date of receipt of a request could not be established.

CONDITIONS FOR STAND-BY ARRANGEMENTS

The year 1954 was notable for the formalization of the terms of stand-by arrangements. The contingent approval of a drawing given to Mexico in 1949 rested merely on the terms of the Board's decision. The arrangement with Belgium in 1952, usually considered the first stand-by arrangement proper, consisted in the acceptance by the Board of a letter from Belgium setting out certain undertakings. These included a statement that Belgium would draw under the arrangement only to meet a balance of payments deficit, that it would repay any drawings by annual installments, and that it would remain in consultation with the Fund while the arrangement was in force. The arrangement with Finland, also in 1952, was even less detailed: the Board merely decided to accept a request from Finland for a stand-by arrangement for six months under the terms of the decision of October 1, 1952, and the staff reported that Finland had undertaken that any purchases made under the stand-by arrangement would be repurchased within three years. For the two stand-by arrangements approved in 1954, however, a precedent was set by embodying the terms of the arrangements in formal sets of conditions.

The first of these arrangements was with Peru. Briefly summarized, its terms were as follows:

1. The conditions for the success of Peru's Stabilization Program were set out. The purpose of the stand-by arrangement, it was stated, was to provide financial assistance to Peru for the exchange operations needed to stabilize the exchange rate. "It is understood," the paragraph concluded, "that this stand-by arrangement will be used only for the purpose of supporting the Exchange Stabilization Program."

2. Currencies drawn would be used only for the support of the certificate market rate.

3. The Central Reserve Bank of Peru intended to conduct its exchange operations within a range which would promote equilibrium in the balance of payments. If it wished to alter this range it would consult the Fund.

4. The Fund and Peru would remain in close consultation while the stand-by arrangement was in effect. "Close consultation" was defined as comprising correspondence, and brief visits of Fund officials to Lima or of Peruvian officials to Washington. Peru would render reports on the progress of the Program at monthly intervals, or more frequently if asked by the Fund.

5. Peru would have the right for one year to purchase foreign exchange from the Fund subject to the limitation that the Fund's holdings of Peruvian soles must not exceed the amount held when the stand-by arrangement started plus the equivalent of $12.5 million.

6. Peru would pay charges in accordance with the Fund's decision of December 23, 1953.

7. "If the Fund should indicate that developments had occurred that would no longer justify the belief that the Exchange Stabilization Fund could be made effective, Peru would not draw further amounts under the stand-by arrangement before consulting the Fund and securing its consent." Peru would thereafter be free to approach the Fund for a drawing, but could not rely on the stand-by arrangement in support of this.

8. Subject, however, to paragraph 7, Peru's right to draw on the Fund could be suspended only in three circumstances: that it had been formally declared ineligible to draw, or that the Board had decided to suspend drawings, either generally under Article XVI, Section 1 (*a*) (ii), or specifically by Peru in order to consider a proposal by an Executive Director or the Managing Director to suppress or limit the eligibility of Peru.

9. Three years after each purchase under the arrangement, Peru would repurchase the amount drawn. Any other repurchases made in the meantime (e.g., under Article V, Section 7) were to be credited to the earliest outstanding drawing.

10. The exchange rate at which transactions under the arrangement would be carried out would be decided from time to time by the Fund.

The stand-by arrangement with the Fund was paralleled by a stabilization agreement between the United States and Peru. This provided that Peru could draw $12.5 million from the United States, but not until the permissible drawings under the stand-by arrangement with the Fund had been exhausted; the drawings from the United States were to be repaid before those from the Fund, and in any case within three years.

As Peru wished the stand-by arrangement to continue for a year, it came within the terms of the decision of December 23, 1953, that

> with respect to stand-by arrangements for periods of more than six months, the Fund and the member might find it appropriate to reach understandings additional to those set forth in this decision.

The principal additional "understandings" in this instance were contained in paragraphs 2, 3, and 7. The basis for these was a discussion in Lima in January between the Peruvian authorities and a Fund mission, at which the problem of the Peruvian exchange rate had been examined and the Central Reserve Bank's program for dealing with it explained. The most directly restrictive clause—paragraph 7—was suggested by the Peruvian authorities themselves.

When the proposed stand-by arrangement was brought before the Board on February 12, 1954, Mr. Bury (Australia), Mr. Godeaux (Belgium), and Mr. Saad (Egypt) criticized paragraph 7, expressing the view that it derogated greatly from the value of the stand-by arrangement to Peru. Sir Edmund Hall-Patch (United Kingdom), who also commented on this paragraph, suggested that the arrangement ought to be given some other name, since it did not fully meet the concept of a stand-by arrangement as set out in the Board's decision.

The Deputy Managing Director, in the chair, and Mr. Southard (United States), however, drew attention to the special circumstances of the Peruvian application, which the arrangement had been tailored to fit. The reason why paragraph 7 had been suggested by Peru was that the authorities there did not wish to incur a heavy liability in foreign currency for purposes which they thought would be unwise. Mr. Southard also pointed out that the arrangement was not designed to establish a new par value, as had been the contingent right to draw given to Mexico in 1949; Peru was seeking only to restrict the fluctuations of a free rate. He suggested that it was surely better to provide for a possible breakdown of the Stabilization Program within the terms of the stand-by arrangement than to have to rely on formal proceedings to render Peru ineligible to draw from the Fund if it became clear that the circumstances had changed.

After this preliminary discussion, the draft stand-by arrangement was sent to Peru, where it was promptly approved, enabling the Board to reach a final decision on February 17, 1954. Members of the Board who had been disturbed by paragraph 7 again expressed their concern. Mr. de Largentaye (France), referring to paragraph 9, suggested that it was not necessary to allow as long as three years for the repurchase of drawings under the arrangements; he thought that a country with a fluctuating currency should be able to rectify its balance of payments within a shorter period than three years, and so be in a position to repay the Fund sooner. In reply, Mr. Southard referred to the requirement of repayment within three years included in the U.S. arrangement with Peru, and suggested that it was advisable for the Fund's arrangement to be in similar terms. The members of the staff who had visited Peru pointed out that if there were favorable short-term developments the authorities there would be well advised to build up their reserves. However, it was still possible that Peru might be able to repurchase any drawing within three years; this was, of course, the outside limit. The Board then approved the stand-by arrangement as summarized above. The requirement that any drawings should be repurchased within three years has since been included in all stand-by arrangements. Its rationalization was noted in Chapter 12.

The second arrangement in 1954, that with Mexico, was of six months' duration only. It did not, therefore, call for special understandings, and the terms of the arrangement were correspondingly simpler. An initial clause recorded that Mexico had assured the Fund of its intention to maintain sound policies, and there then followed clauses corresponding to those in the Peruvian arrangement numbered 5, 6, 8 (with no preliminary "subject to"), and 9, and a final provision calling for Mexico to remain in close consultation—not, however, defined. These clauses became the basis for a standard form of which extensive use was made when stand-by arrangements were next approved in 1956.

TRANSACTIONS IN FLUCTUATING CURRENCIES

On March 18, 1954, the staff notified the Board that the calculation of Germany's monetary reserves at April 30, 1953 had shown that a repurchase obligation had been incurred amounting to $41,724,473.07. (Although Germany had not drawn from the Fund, its original gold subscription had been only 10 per cent of its quota, so that one half of subsequent increases in its reserves was payable toward reducing the Fund's holdings of its currency from 90 per cent to 75 per cent of its quota.) Of the amount due, $9,986.29 was payable in Canadian dollars. As the exchange rate of the Canadian dollar differed from the par value, the question arose as to the rate to be used for the purpose of discharging this obligation. On the same day, therefore, the staff submitted a memorandum dealing generally with the terms to be applied for transactions in fluctuating currencies. The memorandum proposed that such transactions should be effected at the midpoint between the highest and lowest rate quoted for U.S. dollars, for cable transfers for spot delivery, in the main financial center of the country whose currency was fluctuating, on the latest business day before the transaction was consummated. If for any reason the foregoing rate could not be used, that in the New York market was to be substituted. Where the rate was needed for a computation of liability instead of for a transaction, the rate to be used was that on the date for which the computation was made. There were provisions for alternatives if the foregoing rules could not be followed.

These proposals were discussed by the Board on a number of occasions in the second quarter of 1954. As a general principle they were acceptable to Executive Directors, although Mr. Saad (Egypt) pointed out that the rules should not be applied where multiple exchange rates existed. Mr. Prasad (India) suggested that a better course would be to amend the Articles of Agreement, but Mr. Eriksen (Norway) voiced the general view that this would not be practicable. On June 15, after a considerable amount of redrafting, the Board took a decision substantially embodying the rules that the staff had proposed, though qualified by a preamble stating that these would not be applied "when there is no practical interest for the Fund or members to do so."[8] In addition to the specific problem of the German repurchase, the decision was prompted by the expectation, current at the time, that sterling would become convertible and would be allowed to fluctuate within margins of perhaps 3 per cent either side of par.

[8] E.B. Decision No. 321-(54/32), June 15, 1954; below, Vol. III, p. 222.

ANNOUNCEMENT OF TRANSACTIONS

When the first drawings on the Fund took place in May 1947, the Managing Director stated, with the general agreement of the Board, that he did not propose to announce future drawings as they were made. In the following month the Board decided that the statement of transactions and currency holdings called for by Article XII, Section 7 (*a*), should be published quarterly with a delay of one month after the end of the quarter. Subsequently, however, Mr. Bolton (United Kingdom) asked whether the Board would agree to his Government making an immediate announcement of its first drawing, then being consummated. As the Board's policy had been intended for the protection of members, no objection was taken to this course. Other members followed suit, and in December 1947 Mr. Overby (United States) suggested that in these conditions there was no point in waiting a month before publishing the financial statement for the month ended November 30. He also proposed that future financial statements should be issued monthly as soon as possible after the end of the month in question. These proposals were approved by the Board on December 19, 1947, and for the next few years drawings were announced shortly after the end of each month.

In June 1954 a request was made by the Mexican Government that a drawing by Mexico, which had been made in April, should not be announced in the June issue of *International Financial Statistics*, as it would normally have been. The authorities feared that the announcement of a drawing by Mexico shortly after its change in par value would result in further drains on its reserves. The request was of course granted. Reporting the matter to the Board, the staff pointed out that it seemed desirable to have a standard rule to govern the publication of transactions. Mr. Delgado (Nicaragua) thought, on the contrary, that the policy should be flexible, so as to be able to reflect special circumstances, such as those in Mexico, which might make publication undesirable. At the least, Mr. Delgado asked, there should be a delay of three months before a drawing was announced.

Mr. Rickett (United Kingdom) and Mr. Bury (Australia) agreed with Mr. Delgado that the Fund should respect a member's wish for secrecy, but other Directors regarded early publication as desirable. Mr. Crena de Iongh (Netherlands) and Mr. Otto Donner (Germany), Alternate to Mr. Emminger, objected in principle to concealing the Fund's operations. Mr. Godeaux (Belgium) pointed out that transactions involving U.S. dollars were disclosed in U.S. Government figures, so that the Fund could not keep them secret. The Managing Director proposed as a compromise that the details of drawings should be published two months after the end of the month in which they were made; stand-by arrangements, however, would be announced at the time they were introduced. This plan was generally supported. No formal decision was taken, but the Fund's practice afterwards conformed to the Managing Director's proposal.

The decision to delay the announcement of transactions was criticized from time to time by the staff, mainly for the reason that Mr. Godeaux had adduced, and in June 1959 the matter was brought to a head by a request from the Bank for International Settlements to be supplied confidentially with details of drawings of European countries as soon as they were made. Almost at the same time a difficulty developed over the disclosure in *IFS* of countries' gold holdings for a later date than the date of drawings. Countries wished *IFS* to show that the decreases in their gold holdings caused by contributions payable in connection with the increase in quotas were accompanied by a corresponding improvement in their Fund position. However, the ban on publishing data of Fund transactions until the second month after they were consummated meant that the particulars of countries' "net Fund position" shown in *IFS* had to be two months out of date. They were thus frequently a month behind the record of changes in members' gold stocks.

The Managing Director inquired of the Executive Directors representing the countries that had earlier urged delay in publishing the details of transactions—the Earl of Cromer (United Kingdom) and Mr. Gómez (Mexico)—whether they would now object to publication with a delay of one month instead of two. Both consented to the change, which was accordingly suggested to the Board and adopted under the lapse of time procedure. Data on the new basis were first included in the issue of *IFS* for October 1959, published at the end of September.

CHANGES IN EXCHANGE RATES

World economic conditions in 1953–54 reflected three major factors: the continuing recovery of Europe, a slackening of activity in the United States in the second half of 1953, and a fall in the prices of primary products as output, which had expanded in response to the Korean hostilities, encountered diminished demand. The first of these factors encouraged the hope of a speedy return to convertibility; this is discussed in the next chapter. The second and third created difficulties for a number of primary producing countries and resulted in a series of changes in their exchange systems.

Devaluations

It will be convenient here to refer to a series of formal devaluations covering a longer period than the year immediately under discussion, since they had a number of common features. The series began with a devaluation by Bolivia in May 1953, the effect of which was to reduce the value of the boliviano by 68 per cent, from 1⅔ U.S. cents to 0.526316 U.S. cent. This was proposed to the Board as part of a comprehensive overhaul of Bolivia's exchange system, following missions by the United Nations and the Fund to advise the country on its problems. The size of the devaluation prompted some questions by Executive Directors. Mr. Perry (Canada) wondered whether it might not provoke retaliation, and Mr. de Largentaye (France) suggested that a considerably smaller devaluation could successfully deal with Bolivia's fundamental disequilibrium provided that wages and prices were thereafter stabilized. To the first of these objections Mr. Paranaguá (Brazil), who had been elected by Bolivia, replied that the nature of the world tin market, in which prices were beyond Bolivia's control, was such that no retaliation for the devaluation was to be expected. Answering Mr. de Largentaye, some other Directors pointed out that the devaluation could scarcely be regarded as excessive since Bolivia expected to have to maintain quantitative restrictions on imports in order to be able to hold the new rate. The devaluation was then approved, although the fact that there would still be a somewhat complex exchange system was disappointing.

In October 1953 Chile submitted a proposal to devalue the peso by 72 per cent, from 31 pesos=$1 to 110 pesos=$1. As a result of continued inflation, the exchange rate had depreciated until almost all Chile's international transactions were being conducted at the proposed new par value. Although the uncertain future of the price of copper created some questions about Chile's export prospects, the Government believed that it could hold the new rate. Mr. Southard (United States) pointed out that the Chilean proposals did not fully simplify the exchange system; there would still be a complex multiple currency system on the buying side. He hoped that plans made by the Ministry of Finance to eliminate the use of the exchange rate to tax important industries would be successful. The Board concurred in the proposed change in the par value.

In mid-April 1954 Mexico proposed to devalue the peso from 11.56 U.S. cents to 8.00 U.S. cents, a reduction by 31 per cent. Mr. Martínez-Ostos, a former Executive Director, who presented the Mexican case to the Board on this occasion, explained that decreased exports and the leveling off of net receipts from tourism had produced a balance of payments deficit for the preceding three years, and a further deficit of some $70 million was to be expected in 1954 unless radical measures were taken. Reserves had fallen by $45 million between the end of 1953 and the date of Mr. Martínez-Ostos' statement; of this sum, $25 million had been lost during the last two weeks of the period, mainly owing to a strong speculative outflow of capital. It was thought that a total capital outflow of more than $100 million might occur unless the situation was taken in hand; this would completely wipe out Mexico's free reserves.

Mr. Martínez-Ostos' presentation faced the Board with the problem of determining whether the situation in Mexico amounted to a fundamental disequilibrium, and if so whether the proposed devaluation was necessary to correct it. Executive Directors felt themselves somewhat hampered because the devaluation was proposed at short notice—for which Mr. Martínez-Ostos expressed regret—and because the usual remedy for an outflow of short-term capital (the imposition of exchange controls) was regarded as impracticable in Mexico. Some members of the Board were inclined to feel that a less severe devaluation would have been adequate if accompanied by appropriate anti-inflationary measures; others suggested that Mexico should revert to a fluctuating exchange rate, as it had done in 1948. Mr. Martínez-Ostos, however, replied that the Mexican Government had considered these and other alternatives to the proposed course. It was satisfied that nothing but the devaluation would suffice. The Board then concurred in the change in the par value. It also approved the stand-by arrangement for $50 million mentioned above, which was sought at the same time. Under this, Mexico immediately drew $22.5 million.

In June 1955 Nicaragua came to the Fund with a proposal to devalue the córdoba by 29 per cent, from C$5=US$1 to C$7=US$1. The latter rate had in fact been operative for imports since November 1950, and the Nicaraguan Government felt that the time had come to regularize the par value. Its proposals involved the use of the new par value for all imports; exports would go at a rate of C$6.60=US$1 (representing an export tax), while there would be a fluctuating free market rate for travel receipts. The Board concurred in the proposed change.

A month later, in July 1955, Pakistan sought to devalue the rupee by 30.5 per cent, from PRs 1=$0.30225 to PRs 1=$0.21. The change would restore the equality of the Pakistan rupee with the Indian rupee, which had been broken in September 1949; India had then devalued its rupee at the same time as sterling, but Pakistan—not yet a member of the Fund—had not. In July 1950 Pakistan had proposed as its par value the pre-1949 rate of PRs 1=$0.30225. At that time, objections were raised to the proposal by Mr. Joshi (India), and a decision was postponed until March 1951, when the suggested rate was accepted. The difference between the two exchange rates subsequently created considerable difficulty for both Pakistan and India, whose economies were partly complementary, but it was not until economic conditions became adverse to Pakistan that its Government felt a devaluation was inevitable. Lord Harcourt (United Kingdom) said that while the decision to devalue had no doubt been both difficult and unwelcome, it appeared to him to be a necessary and proper one. Mr. Bury (Australia) and Mr. Yumoto (Japan) took the same position. The Board concurred.

The sixth country that devalued in the series we are now considering was Paraguay. In this case the value of the currency was reduced to 10 per cent of its original level by three steps over two years and two months.

The first stage in this process, effective from January 1, 1954, reduced the par value of the guaraní from ₲ 6=$1 to ₲ 15=$1. This was admittedly not a definitive change; its main purpose was to eliminate a redundant exchange rate and align the par value with the basic rate in the multiple currency structure. Paraguay's domestic inflation, however, continued, and in August 1954 a further change in the basic rate, to ₲ 21=$1, was proposed. This was accepted by the Executive Directors with some reluctance, as it was accompanied by a further elaboration of the multiple currency arrangements, and the Board's decision expressed "the hope that future changes will result in substantial progress toward simplification of the exchange system."

Some simplification was achieved by the time that the third devaluation was proposed, in February 1956, when the par value was fixed at ₲ 60=$1, and this was welcomed by the Board, even though certain multiple currency features remained.

In three of the countries mentioned above—Mexico, Nicaragua, and Pakistan—the devaluation proved successful, and no further change in the exchange rate was necessary during the remainder of the time covered by this volume. In the other three, however, the deterioration in the exchange rate was not arrested. In Bolivia the rate was not stabilized until 1958, although the par value remained unchanged after 1953. The exchange rate for the Chilean currency has continuously depreciated, but again the par value has not been altered since 1953. In Paraguay the remaining multiple rates were consolidated in 1957 into a single effective rate, which fell to about 50 per cent of the par value before it proved possible in 1959 to stabilize it. No change in the par value of the guaraní has been proposed since 1956.

Minor changes

In 1953–54, as in previous and later years, a number of changes in exchange systems not involving a devaluation were brought to the Board's attention. A few examples will illustrate the nature of the decisions which the Board was called upon to make.

On Friday, October 9, 1953, the Board undertook the 1953 consultation with Brazil. It reached a decision which reviewed the various elements in the complicated exchange system of Brazil as described to the staff at its discussions with the Brazilian representatives in September, and concluded, among other things, that "the objective should be progressively to transfer exports and imports to the free market." On the following day, however, the Fund received from Brazil details of a new 12-point program, to go into force immediately. This involved substantial changes in the system, and provided, inter alia, for limiting the free exchange market to profits, capital transfers, and tourist expenditures on the one hand and incoming capital and other invisibles on the other. The Board met on Sunday afternoon to consider this, but the notice given being so short and details of the operation of the system being scanty, no decision was taken except to revoke the conclusion of the consultation and regard this as still open for further discussion. Two weeks later the staff was able to present details of the new proposals, and an analysis of their probable working, which enabled the Board to reach a fresh decision. This described at length the revised arrangements, regretted certain features (such as the proliferation of import rates), welcomed others (such as the simplification of the export rate structure), and commented that on still others (such as the free market) not enough information was yet available to form a judgment. There the matter rested until August 1954, when Brazil put forward proposals for further modifications, involving changes in the effective export rates for coffee and other products, and in certain import rates—proposals which, after review, the Board approved as necessary to meet a critical situation.

Fortunately, few exchange systems were as complicated or as rapidly changing as that of Brazil. A more characteristic request was one made by Thailand, in March 1954, for approval of (1) a change in the selling rate for the dollar for certain essentials, (2) a reduction from twenty to four in the number of categories of goods for which dollars or sterling could be obtained at that rate, and (3) the sale of dollars and sterling to commercial banks at free market rates. The Board welcomed the ensuing simplification of the Thai system, and particularly the consequential elimination of the broken cross rates for certain transactions. However, it also commented on the need for further anti-inflationary measures, in connection with which it said that the Fund would wish to remain in close contact with Thailand.

Other proposals were put forward by Iran (which, exceptionally, proposed to appreciate its exchange rate), Yugoslavia, Colombia, and Belgium-Luxembourg and the Netherlands.

An unusual request was made by Ecuador in December 1953. Submitting some proposed changes in its exchange law, it asked that they should be approved by the Fund even though they did not technically fall within the Fund's jurisdiction. The reason was that the exchange law, which had been written with the assistance of the Fund's staff, required that any change in it should have the approval of the Fund—the purpose, of course, being to strengthen the hands of the monetary authorities against any weakening of the law's requirements. This request placed the Board in some difficulty, particularly as the information available did not fully elucidate the prospective consequences of the proposed changes. Directors did not feel able, therefore, to give formal approval; however, they agreed that Ecuador might be informed that the Board had no objection to its proposals, and that the staff memorandum prepared for the 1953 consultation supported them.

PROCEDURE

It will be convenient to note here a discussion of the procedure for approving changes in exchange rates which the Board undertook, at the request of Mr. de Largentaye, in May 1953. The occasion for it was a proposal by Greece to unify its exchange rate at a new level of 30,000 drachmas=$1. This had been submitted to the Board at its meeting at 10:00 A.M. on April 9, and the member had asked for a decision by noon the same day. Mr. Gragnani (Italy), who had been elected by Greece, expressed his regret for the short notice, but said that both the proposed action and the secrecy with which it was carried out were of vital importance to Greece. He hoped therefore that his colleagues would find it possible to act quickly. After a brief recess the Board agreed with the Greek plan.

Recalling this incident a month later, Mr. de Largentaye said that Directors had a personal responsibility for passing upon proposals to change exchange rates, and that two or three hours' notice was not sufficient to enable them to give adequate consideration to such proposals. Mr. de Selliers (Belgium) supported him. Other Directors, however, suggested that there were bound to be occasions when emergency action was needed. A country might well fear that any delay would bring speculation and consequent losses of exchange, and it could be put to great hardships if the Board postponed action except for very important reasons. The consensus was that the Board could only decide in the actual circumstances whether particular conditions warranted emergency action, or whether some further time should be taken. When, two days later, the proposal for a change in the Bolivian exchange rate was submitted, the Board considered it briefly and then adjourned until 3:30 the same afternoon before approving it.

COMMODITY TRADE PROBLEMS

Three different aspects of the trade in primary commodities came before the Board during the year.

In July 1953 the Food and Agriculture Organization (FAO) asked the Fund for an analysis of world trade and payments with special reference to difficulties in trade in agricultural commodities, particularly between the dollar area and the rest of the world. A draft of a report on this subject was prepared by the staff and discussed by the Board in September 1953. Its main conclusions were (1) that the dollar problem, which had been acute in the early postwar years, had subsided by the latter part of 1952; however, the situation still contained a number of temporary elements, such as U.S. military expenditures abroad and trade restrictions in other countries, so that it could not be said that the problem had been eliminated; (2) that recent improvements in non-dollar supplies of foodstuffs and raw materials, coupled with persistent pressure on countries to buy their supplies in the cheapest market, had tended to end the premiums on such goods in soft currency markets, and there seemed to be no prospect that such premiums would return.

Executive Directors' comments on this draft were mainly confined to four points. Mr. Gragnani (Italy) thought that more should have been made of a possible further improvement in the dollar problem by reducing purchases of agricultural products from the dollar area. Mr. Bury (Australia) said that the study failed to stress the single most important factor, viz., U.S. tariffs on agricultural commodities. He thought that a new section should be added. Mr. Southard (United States), however, while recognizing the possible benefits to be derived from a reduction in the U.S. tariff, considered that this was already covered adequately in the staff's draft; no new section was needed. Sir Edmund Hall-Patch (United Kingdom) pointed out that the draft appeared to overlook the possibility of a fall in agricultural prices in the United States. Mr. Delgado (Nicaragua) thought that the references in the report to Latin American countries did not sufficiently distinguish between their differing situations.

A revised draft, taking account of Directors' comments, was submitted at a second meeting early in October 1953. Mr. Melville (Australia) then sought to have price supports discussed in the report, but Mr. Southard objected on the grounds that this was a difficult, complicated, and politically sensitive subject. The Board agreed, and after some further redrafting the staff study was sent to the FAO.

At the end of the year these problems again came to the fore. A group of experts appointed by the United Nations to review the subject of "Commodity Trade and Economic Development" presented a report to ECOSOC. Much of the report concerned agencies other than the Fund, but a section of it, dealing with contracyclical lending, contained the following criticisms:

> . . . The Fund is in effect a reservoir of contributed currencies [which] is at present much too small to provide more than marginal help in any major fluctuation, and the management of the Fund has been too timid in using its contents; but that is no reason why it should not be enlarged and become the main source of contra-cyclical lending. . . .
>
> . . . We therefore suggest that the Fund should declare its intention of using its resources boldly to maintain the flow of currency if a major industrial country is involved in depression; and that it should indicate its intention to seek an increase in its resources when its reserves of a currency reach a certain minimum level, and to negotiate with major member States to see how far such increases can be pledged in advance.[9]

Bringing the report to the notice of the Board, the staff suggested that an appropriate reply might be along the following lines: Two years previously the

[9] *Commodity Trade and Economic Development* (New York, UN Doc. E/2519, 1953), pars. 225, 227.

Fund had pointed out, in its comments on the experts' report on *Measures for International Economic Stability*, that short-term credit was insufficient as a cure for depressions. Since then the Fund had found wider scope for its operations, but the world economic situation and the favorable level of world trade had reduced its members' need for its assistance. The drawings of $230 million which had been made during 1953 were prompted not by world-wide depression but by adverse factors peculiar to the members concerned. The Fund was still convinced that it could make a useful contribution to mitigating the effects of a depression. Finally, it was ready if necessary to ask its members for more resources and to consider possible changes in its modes of operation to meet emergent situations.

This draft was considered by the Board in March 1954 and approved with minor amendments.

A third aspect of commodity trade problems was also touched on by the experts' report just noted, viz., the possible desirability of a commodity-based currency as a device to obtain greater stability in the world economy. A technical criticism of this proposal, submitted to the Board in January 1954, drew from Mr. de Largentaye (France) a defense of a commodity standard. He urged that the intrinsic instability of other monetary systems, and the potentially stabilizing effect of a commodity currency, lent support to the view that the latter would be a preferable international standard. Mr. de Largentaye found some support from Mr. Delgado, who had been disturbed by the implication in the staff's technical comments that stability of prices of primary products was unattainable even with a commodity currency. Stability of prices was most important to the countries that he represented.

Mr. de Largentaye sought to have his views reflected in the Fund's reply to the experts' report, but other Executive Directors resisted this on the grounds that a commodity currency was an academic concept which could have no practical application in the existing world situation. They did not feel, as Mr. de Largentaye had suggested, that it was incumbent on the Fund to reply to every suggestion which had monetary implications. The subject was therefore omitted from the reply made to ECOSOC.

CHAPTER

15

Hopes Rise and Fall (1954-56)

THE GRADUAL LIBERALIZATION of trade in Europe, encouraged by the efforts of the OEEC, had by 1954 raised hopes that convertibility might be just around the corner. But these hopes were doomed to disappointment; in 1955 a setback in the economic progress of most European countries revived the pressure for protective measures, and postponed convertibility until prosperity should return. It was in this environment of hope and disappointment that the Fund's work in 1954–55 was carried on.

During 1955–56 the Board was mainly engaged in day-to-day affairs leaving little mark on its history. Such significant decisions as were taken formed, for the most part, pendants to actions originating in 1954–55. It is convenient therefore to cover these two years, the last in Mr. Rooth's tenure of the Managing Directorship, in a single chapter.

MEMBERS, BOARD, AND STAFF

Four new members joined the Fund during the two-year period: Afghanistan on July 14, 1955, Korea on August 26, 1955, Argentina on September 20, 1956, and Viet-Nam on September 21, 1956. This raised the number of members to 60, and the aggregate of quotas to $8,931.5 million.

BOARD

The biennial election of Executive Directors, held on September 28, 1954, resulted in the re-election of Messrs. Bury (Australia), Crena de Iongh (Netherlands), Emminger (Germany), Godeaux (Belgium), Gragnani (Italy), Paranaguá (Brazil), Rasminsky (Canada), Saad (Egypt), and Yumoto (Japan). Mr. S. T.

Gunnar Åkermalm (Sweden), who had been Alternate to Mr. Eriksen since November 1952, succeeded him as Executive Director for the Scandinavian countries, and Mr. José Luna-Guerra (Mexico) succeeded Mr. Delgado, whose Alternate he had been for the previous fortnight. There were some changes in the countries electing Mr. Crena de Iongh (the addition of Yugoslavia, which had previously voted for Mr. Emminger, and of Israel, voting for the first time), Mr. Godeaux (the addition of Austria and Turkey, which had previously voted for Mr. Gragnani), and Mr. Gragnani (Indonesia, voting for the first time, replaced Austria and Turkey). Haiti, another new member, voted for Mr. Paranaguá. Czechoslovakia again did not vote in the election. At the end of November 1954 Mr. Godeaux resigned, and Mr. André van Campenhout (Belgium), who until then had been General Counsel of the Fund, was elected to succeed him. Mr. Crena de Iongh resigned ten months later, and was succeeded, from October 1, 1955, by Mr. Pieter Lieftinck (Netherlands). Viscount Harcourt's appointment as Executive Director for the United Kingdom, with effect from October 1, 1954, was noted in Chapter 14. There were no other changes in the Board between September 1954 and September 1956.

Managing Director and staff

Mr. Rooth's five-year term of office was due to expire on August 2, 1956, and early in that year he informed the Board of his intention to retire on that date. He was then aged 67. At the request of the Board, however, he agreed to remain as Managing Director until October 3, 1956, in order to cover the period of the Annual Meetings.

On September 7, 1956, the Board decided to offer the position of Managing Director to Mr. Per Jacobsson, also a native of Sweden. Mr. Jacobsson was a well-known figure in international economic affairs, having been economic advisor and head of the Monetary and Economic Department of the Bank for International Settlements since 1931, and as such responsible for the much-respected economic surveys in the Bank's Annual Reports. He assumed office as Managing Director on December 3, 1956, and remained with the Fund in that capacity until his death on May 5, 1963. At the time of his appointment he was 62 years of age.

At the end of April 1956 the active staff numbered 412 and came from 43 countries. This was a reduction of 16 staff members, but an increase of one country, since April 1954. Seven members of the staff were on extended leave. The only organizational change during the two years with which we are now dealing was that, in September 1956, the Treasurer's Department was renamed Office of the Treasurer in order to align it with the Offices of Administration and of the Secretary. At the same time, Mr. Horne, who had been Deputy Secretary since the departure of Mr. Coe, became Secretary of the Fund.

Per Jacobsson, Managing Director, 1956–63

SOME QUOTAS INCREASED

The second Quinquennial Review of Fund quotas, called for by Article III, Section 2, became due in 1955, and in accordance with Rule D-3 a committee to study the problem was set up in December 1954. Following the precedent of 1949, this was a Committee of the Whole, with the Managing Director as Chairman.

The committee had a first meeting at the end of January 1955. Some Executive Directors at once referred to the desires of the primary producing countries, especially in Latin America, for increases in their quotas. Mr. Southard (United States) said that he had no doubt that many members' quotas were now inadequate; he saw difficulty, however, in seeking agreement on some over-all increase in the Fund's resources, because these resources were already large and had remained relatively unused. Mr. Mansour (Egypt) agreed with this point, adding that if drawings were needed to support a return to convertibility, the need would be only a temporary one and would not justify locking up resources. More generally, he said, the liberalization of the use of the Fund's resources and the availability of waivers had eased the position of primary producing countries.[1]

Mr. de Largentaye (France) remarked that the ratio between quotas and drawing rights was now unimportant, as was that between quotas and subscriptions, since the only currency among the Fund's holdings which was effectively used was the U.S. dollar. What was important, however, was the relation between quotas and votes. He suggested that the Articles should be amended to remove the weighting of votes except when decisions were taken on transactions. Failing this, he proposed that the Bretton Woods formula should be reconsidered. Mr. Crena de Iongh (Netherlands) also thought that there was little need for any general change in the quota structure, and was troubled by the effect of any change on voting power.

At the same meeting, Mr. Southard announced that the U.S. Government was unwilling to add to its quota, and Lord Harcourt made a similar statement on behalf of the United Kingdom. This meant, as Mr. Bury (Australia) pointed out, that the necessary 80 per cent majority for a general increase in quotas (Article III, Section 2) would not be forthcoming. Mr. Bury suggested that in these circumstances the most practical way would be for Directors to approach member countries informally to ascertain their interest in any revision. This proposal was supported by Mr. van Campenhout (Belgium), Mr. J. H. Warren (Canada), Alternate to Mr. Rasminsky, and Mr. Yumoto (Japan). However, there was some evidence that members might not yet be ready to state their wishes in the matter. The Managing Director therefore undertook that the staff would further examine the problem and would present some statistical data that might be helpful.

[1] See below, p. 412.

The staff report, presented to the Board at the end of June 1955, started from the dual assumption that there could be no over-all increase in quotas, but that many quotas were too small, especially the smallest ones. It therefore suggested a graduated scale for revision, diminishing with the size of the quota, and ranging from 100–400 per cent for quotas not over $10 million, down to 10–20 per cent for quotas from $250 million to $525 million. The three largest quotas (those of China, the United Kingdom, and the United States) would not be altered. The result of the changes suggested by the report would have been to increase the total of quotas from $8,728 million to $10,238.4 million (i.e., by a little more than 17 per cent).

When this report was considered by the Committee of the Whole, Executive Directors were divided between approving it and preferring to repeat the decision reached in 1950—that the time was not opportune for an increase in quotas. Lord Harcourt, with the concurrence of Mr. Åkermalm (Sweden), Mr. V. G. Pendharkar (India), Alternate to Mr. Prasad, and Mr. Yumoto proposed as an alternative that the minimum quota should be $5 million, that countries with quotas up to $10 million should be allowed to double them, and that countries with quotas greater than $10 million and less than $20 million should be allowed to increase them to $20 million. This plan was deemed inadequate for the needs of Latin American countries by Mr. Jorge Sol (El Salvador), who had been Assistant Director of the Western Hemisphere Department of the Fund for nine months before becoming Alternate to Mr. Luna-Guerra in November 1954. Mr. B. B. Callaghan (Australia), Alternate to Mr. Bury, Mr. Rasminsky (Canada), and Mr. Saad (Egypt) commented that any proposal to limit increases to the smaller quotas would impair the Fund's liquidity by increasing only its supply of inconvertible currencies.

Mr. Saad also questioned whether it was appropriate for increases in quotas effected in the course of a Quinquennial Review to be made conditional upon the member's increasing correspondingly its subscription to the World Bank. This condition had been attached to individual increases in quotas in pursuance of a policy agreed with the President of the Bank. The staff accordingly consulted the President, but later reported to the Board that Mr. Black was not in favor of excluding quinquennial increases from the established policy.

At the meeting of the Committee of the Whole at which this report was made, in August 1955, it was agreed that at the forthcoming Annual Meetings Executive Directors would informally sound out the Governors of the countries that had appointed or elected them, to ascertain whether members wished to have increases in their quotas; after which formal requests could be made.

When Executive Directors reported, in December 1955, on their inquiries, it became clear that very few increases were sought except by Latin American countries. Half these countries had quotas over $20 million, and there was some reluctance in the Committee of the Whole to regard increases in such quotas as necessary. Eventually, in January 1956, the committee decided that it would propose no general increase, but would recommend that the Board look with favor upon requests for increases by members with small quotas, although the committee preferred not to set any maximum figure. The committee also agreed that 25 per cent of any increase in quota should normally be paid in gold, but rejected a proposal that the gold payment made at the time of an increase should be sufficient also to cover any amount by which the member's original gold contribution fell short of 25 per cent of its quota. On January 19, 1956 the Board formally accepted the committee's recommendations. Subsequently the increases which the Board was prepared to make were standardized under what became known as the "Southard Formula" or, more formally, the "Small Quotas Policy." Quotas below $5 million could be increased, on request, to $7.5 million, those of $5–8 million to $10 million, those of $10 million to $15 million, and those of $15 million to $20 million.

The outcome was that during the ensuing 21 months eight quotas were increased, two to $10 million and six to $7.5 million. In 1956 the Dominican Republic and Ecuador, whose original quotas had each been $5 million, obtained increases to $10 million, and Nicaragua obtained an increase from $2 million to $7.5 million. In connection with these three increases, Mr. Lieftinck (Netherlands) said that one of the countries that he represented (Israel, the Netherlands, and Yugoslavia) considered that quotas should be increased only where exceptional developments had occurred. However, in view of the wish of the Board to increase small quotas, he would not oppose the increases, but would abstain from voting. In 1957 five other increases to $7.5 million were approved—for Israel (original quota $4.5 million), Paraguay (previously $3.5 million), El Salvador and Honduras (each originally $2.5 million), and Haiti (originally $2 million). No objection was expressed to these changes.

CONDITIONS FOR TECHNICAL ASSISTANCE

Beginning with the year 1954–55 there was a considerable increase in the number of requests for technical assistance from the Fund staff. Four times during the two years the Board considered under what conditions such help should be given, and the discussions helped to clarify the relationships between members, Board, and staff.

The first of these discussions took place in February 1955. Brazil had asked for the services of Mr. Bernstein, Director of the Research Department, for three or four weeks to assist in analyzing certain aspects of its economic problems. When this request was brought before the Board, Mr. Southard (United States) said that he assumed that any report containing recommendations on policy would be submitted to the Board for approval. Staff technicians, he pointed out, could speak with authority only if they were supported by the Board. If a country asked for the private advice of a member of the staff, the latter should not be sent as a representative of the Fund but should be given leave of absence. Mr. Sol (El Salvador), on the other hand, felt that the obligation to obtain the Board's approval for recommendations by staff members would be likely to deter countries from seeking assistance that might be valuable to them. He said that the provision of technical assistance was a field in which informal contacts between the Fund staff and the members had proved very useful; he would regret losing such an important channel of the Fund's influence with its members, especially in matters connected with central bank policy. Mr. Sol suggested that, instead of requiring to clear a report, the Board might give the staff member detailed terms of reference.

Supporting Mr. Southard, Mr. Bury (Australia) said that he thought that if the Fund were to accept responsibility for a report the Board should approve it. Mr. P. J. Keogh (United Kingdom), Alternate to Lord Harcourt, suggested that the Board's decision should depend upon whether the member was seeking the advice of the Fund or of one of its experts. In the present instance Brazil had asked for the help of Mr. Bernstein personally. The Board accordingly agreed to make Mr. Bernstein available to Brazil by giving him leave of absence without pay. However, the Brazilian Government intimated in March that it would prefer that Mr. Bernstein should come as a representative of the Fund, and it was accordingly decided that his report and recommendations should be submitted to the Board. This was done orally on Mr. Bernstein's return from Brazil.

In May 1955, Executive Directors had a second opportunity to discuss the problem of the Board's responsibility for recommendations by the staff. At the request of Iran a technical mission had prepared a report on the exchange problem there, recommending, inter alia, that there should be no further appreciation of the rial. This report was presented to the Board for approval. Mr. Sol pointed out that it might be embarrassing for the Board if, after it had approved the recommendations, the member failed to carry them out. Mr. Rasminsky (Canada), supporting Mr. Sol, urged that the Board should recognize that the staff was an independent entity composed of competent international technicians, and as such should be entitled to express its views. He did not regard it as necessary that the Board, when transmitting such a report, should regard it as binding the 56 member governments.

Lord Harcourt (United Kingdom) suggested that if a member sought private advice from the Fund staff, the Managing Director should be free to arrange for a mission so composed as to be capable of reflecting the Board's views, and should then himself be responsible for ensuring that the staff's report was consistent with Fund policy. However, where, as in the present instance, the member had asked for the official views of the Fund and wished to publish the report, he believed that the Board's approval should be sought.

Mr. Southard said that he agreed with the importance of an independent staff. On the whole, he thought, the staff did act independently—as, for instance, in the preparation of reports for consultations. However, he could not accept that members should be given reports with which the Board disagreed. Mr. de Largentaye (France) took the view that even when a report dealt with purely technical matters the Board could not avoid responsibility for it. Executive Directors accordingly discussed the report of the mission to Iran. The decision taken was, in fact, in conformity with the staff's recommendations.

The problem of the Board's responsibility for a staff report arose again in May 1956, when the draft of a report by a mission to Colombia was considered. Mr. Southard commended the high quality of the report but objected to several of the recommendations in it, notably to one dealing with stamp taxes (which he thought was not a matter for the Fund), one suggesting a fluctuating exchange rate (which he thought the Fund ought not to recommend), and one covering a plan to make adjustments in the differential exchange rate for coffee (which he thought would encourage speculation). Mr. de Largentaye and Mr. Lieftinck (Netherlands) expressed similar views. Mr. Luna-Guerra (Mexico), however, said that Colombia would regard the report as wholly the responsibility of the staff, and while he agreed with Mr. Southard's first two criticisms, he did not think it necessary to revise the report. Mr. Warren (Canada) and Mr. Roy E. Heasman (United Kingdom), who had succeeded Mr. Keogh as Alternate to Lord Harcourt, pointed out that the report was a technical document, which could not be adjusted to cover all the possibly divergent views in the Board. In reply to Mr. Southard's point that the Board could not authorize the transmission of a report of which it disapproved, Mr. Warren agreed that if the Board was basically opposed to such a report, it would have to refuse to agree to its transmission. He did not, however, think that this was an appropriate course in connection with the report on Colombia; it would suffice for the member to see the minutes of the Board's discussion. Supporting him, Mr. Prasad (India) pointed out that Colombia must in any case be aware of what the staff's views were. However, the sections of the staff report dealing with the points that Mr. Southard had criticized were appropriately modified before it was transmitted.

The last occasion during these two years that problems connected with technical assistance came before the Board was on June 6, 1956, when Executive Directors were considering the request made for such assistance by Viet-Nam. (Viet-Nam was not yet a member, although a Membership Resolution for it was before the Governors.) Mr. de Largentaye sought to make it clear that the salary of the staff member sent to Saigon should be the responsibility solely of the

Vietnamese Government, whereas the Managing Director had proposed that there should be some sharing of costs. At the suggestion of Messrs. Bury, Lieftinck, and Southard, it was decided that until firm rules were established it should be left to the Managing Director to negotiate with the country seeking technical assistance the terms on which such assistance should be given.

NEW BUILDING

While the size of the Fund staff had remained much the same for several years, the staff of the World Bank had been growing. It became apparent early in the 1950's that the original home of the two organizations, 1818 H Street, had become altogether too small for them both, even with the addition of the adjoining and obsolete Premier Building, occupied by part of the Fund staff. Further accommodation outside 1818 H Street had progressively had to be found. At the beginning of 1955 the management of the Bank contemplated removing the staff bodily to a building one block to the east of 1818 H Street, and invited the management of the Fund to join in renting accommodation in the same building. However, the Fund decided instead to erect a new building, adjoining 1818 H Street on its west side, and meanwhile to vacate space in 1818 H Street for use by the Bank. The staff moved out for this purpose were housed temporarily in rented space in the Hurley-Wright Building, an old but refurbished one adjoining 1818 H Street on the east side.

The new building, which was occupied in stages between January and April 1958, was designed to house the whole of the Fund staff. Unfortunately it was no larger than was essential to do this, owing partly to the limitations of the site, and partly to budget considerations stemming from the fact that when the contract for the building was signed the Fund's balance sheet still showed a cumulative excess of expenditure over income of some $14 million. Accordingly, when the unforeseen influx of new member countries after 1959 necessitated a corresponding growth of staff, accommodation was soon outgrown, and from June 1961 until a further new building was added in 1965–66 some sections of the staff had to continue to be housed in rented offices nearby.

ANNUAL MEETINGS

In accordance with the decision taken by the Governors in Washington in 1954, the Tenth Annual Meetings were held in Istanbul, beginning on Monday, September 12, 1955. The problem of accommodation, always acute when the Annual Meetings are held away from Washington, was eased by housing the Joint Bank-Fund Secretariat in the S.S. *Adana*, moored in the harbor, and by the fact that, just before the Meetings began, two new and modern hotels had been

Fund Offices, 19th and H Streets, N.W., Washington, D.C. (1958)

opened in Istanbul in which the Governors could be accommodated. On the other hand, the smooth fulfillment of the week's program was hampered by a curfew which had had to be imposed in Istanbul as a result of anti-Greek riots in the preceding week.

The Meetings themselves were held in the University of Istanbul, and were chaired by Mr. Saad and Mr. Kaissouni, the Governors for Egypt, of, respectively, the Bank and the Fund. Much of the time was devoted to an exploration of the problems of member countries, both industrial and primary producing. There was no organized informal discussion, and the only committees of Governors set up were the Procedures Committee and the Committee on Finance and Organization, which concentrated on the Fund's accounts. Speeches were relatively few and short, the most considerable being an appeal of Mr. E. H. Louw, Governor for the Union of South Africa, for an increase in the price of gold so as to expand world reserves, and an address by Mr. R. A. Butler, Governor for the United Kingdom, stressing his Government's intention to maintain the sterling exchange rate.[2] Czechoslovakia not being represented, the controversial element, which had been so marked in the three or four previous years, was largely absent from the proceedings. Mr. W. Randolph Burgess, Temporary Alternate Governor for the United States, in his speech to the Governors, described the year then ending as one of "increasing understanding."[3] This process may well have been further advanced by the discussions held, in public and in private, at Istanbul.

For the Eleventh Annual Meetings, in 1956, the venue was again Washington. The Chairman was Mr. Antonio Carrillo Flores (Mexico). A symposium on "Methods of Monetary Analysis" was conducted at an informal meeting of Governors on Tuesday afternoon. This differed from similar functions at earlier Annual Meetings in that the contributors were members of delegations. Papers were read by Mr. M. W. Holtrop, President of the Netherlands Bank and Governor of the Fund for the Netherlands, by Mr. Paolo Baffi, Economic Advisor to the Bank of Italy, and by Mr. Ralph A. Young, Director, Division of Research and Statistics, Board of Governors of the Federal Reserve System. A general analysis of the problem and of the way it was met in 41 countries was prepared by the staff and distributed as a background for the discussion. All the contributions, including that of the staff, were subsequently printed in *Staff Papers*.[4]

Another new feature of the Annual Meetings was a conference between the Fund staff and the statistical correspondents of *International Financial Statistics*. The problems discussed were similar to those in the symposium just referred to, together with a number of other technical difficulties encountered in the prepara-

---

[2] *Summary Proceedings, 1955*, pp. 22–34, 37–43.

[3] *Ibid.*, p. 46.

[4] *Staff Papers*, Vol. V (1956–57), pp. 303–433.

tion of *International Financial Statistics*; and a draft of a revised version of the Fund's *Balance of Payments Manual*. Reporting on this conference to the Board in December, the Director of Research emphasized its value to the staff and to the effectiveness of the statistics which the Fund issued.

During the formal sessions of the 1956 Annual Meetings, stress was laid on the problems of the less developed countries. This feature, which partly reflected the growing number of such countries among the members, has since become increasingly important in Annual Meeting discussions. A particularly effective exposé of the problems of such countries was made by the Alternate Governor for Indonesia, Mr. R. Soegiarto, who urged—as has often been done since—that the Fund should take steps to reduce the instability of prices of primary products.[5]

An interesting suggestion by the Governor for Canada, Mr. Walter E. Harris, harked back to the thesis upheld by his predecessor at Savannah. Mr. Harris urged that the efficiency of the Fund would be increased if more of the Executive Directors of the Fund were "chosen from senior officials of treasuries or central banks who would continue to have operating responsibilities in their own countries." [6] Mr. Harris visualized that Alternate Executive Directors would continue to reside in Washington, but that Executive Directors would normally live in their own countries, visiting Washington only from time to time—as, indeed, had been the Canadian practice from the beginning. As might have been expected in view of the British position at Savannah, Mr. Harris' suggestion was supported by the Governor for the United Kingdom, Mr. Harold Macmillan. The Managing Director commented in his concluding remarks that the proposal had much to commend it, but pointed out (as had been done earlier by Mr. Holtrop) that Executive Directors representing more than one country might well find it better to reside in Washington.[7]

CONVERTIBILITY POSTPONED

Chapter 1 of the Annual Report for both 1954 and 1955 was entitled "The Prospects for Convertibility." In the first of these the Executive Directors remarked that

> it can be seen that significant progress toward convertibility and the removal of restrictions has been made possible both by a general improvement in economic conditions and by the general trend of opinion in regard to policy. There are indications of further favorable developments.[8]

[5] *Summary Proceedings, 1956*, pp. 88–93.

[6] *Ibid.*, p. 33. See above, p. 132.

[7] *Ibid.*, pp. 46, 61–62, 102–103.

[8] *Annual Report, 1954*, p. 10.

When presenting the 1954 Report to the Governors, the Managing Director pointed out that in 1953 slightly less than one half of the trade of the free world had been conducted in convertible currencies. "When sterling becomes convertible," he went on, "this proportion will be more than three fourths." [9]

It was indeed the problem of sterling upon which the prospects for convertibility hung. At the same Meeting, the Governor for the Netherlands (Mr. Holtrop) told the Governors that to induce as many members as possible to take the decisive step to convertibility

> looks like the last chance the Fund has got to bring about the realization of that high ideal, set forth by the founding fathers, of creating a truly multilateral system of international payments, based on fixed par values, and free from restrictions and discriminatory practices.[10]

But the inability of the United Kingdom to accept the responsibilities of formal convertibility for sterling blocked further progress. In the course of conversation with the Managing Director on the day after Mr. Holtrop's speech, Mr. R. A. Butler, Chancellor of the Exchequer, made it clear that the United Kingdom had no plans for the formal convertibility of sterling in the near future. At the most, the British proposed to achieve convertibility *de facto* and not *de jure.*

Article VIII and Article XIV

Against this somewhat discouraging background, discussions began soon after the Annual Meeting on the problems of the transition from a regime of Article XIV to a regime of Article VIII—i.e., to a regime where a preponderance of the major countries would accept the obligation to make their currencies effectively convertible.

As the staff saw it, in a review of the policy questions confronting the Board, the major problem was this: current progress toward convertibility would not mean the end of restrictions; even those countries that in the comparatively near future might make their currencies convertible would be likely to need to retain some restrictions. Which would be better for the Fund—a postponement of the assumption of Article VIII, or its acceptance by major countries under conditions which would necessitate the Fund approving the retention of substantial restrictions?

This problem, and parallel legal issues, were discussed by the Board in informal session in November 1954. Executive Directors found themselves in rather a dilemma and sought elucidation of a number of related questions. Asked by one Director whether the Fund could require a member to accept the obligations of Article VIII, the Legal Department replied that it could not specifically do so,

[9] *Summary Proceedings, 1954,* p. 14.

[10] *Ibid.,* p. 21.

although it could determine that the member did not maintain restrictions for balance of payments purposes; should such a member subsequently wish to reintroduce restrictions it would have to seek approval under Article VIII. The discussion that followed focused on the significance of the obligations assumed under Article VIII. It was adjourned to give time for consideration.

Bilateralism

In December the staff brought forward the special problem of bilateral agreements. While there would continue to be strong reasons for the Fund to oppose bilateral agreements, the staff thought that the possible advent of convertibility would make it advisable for the Board to adapt its tactics to the particular circumstances of each member, rather than maintain its disapproval in general terms. Discussing this recommendation in February 1955, the Board heard from Mr. Crena de Iongh (Netherlands) that defensive bilateral arrangements might be needed even after convertibility was attained, and from Mr. de Largentaye (France) an assertion that discrimination against a stronger currency than one's own was not only justifiable but advisable in the interests of increasing trade. These views, however, did not commend themselves to the majority of Directors, and the Board's decision, as recorded in the *Sixth Annual Report on Exchange Restrictions* (1955), was that in the forthcoming consultations the Fund would place special emphasis on the elimination of bilateral agreements.

This same Report included a catalog of measures taken by various member countries to reduce their reliance upon restrictions.[11] The unification of most nonresident sterling accounts, followed by the intervention of the British Exchange Equalization Account in the market for transferable sterling, and the liberalization of payments arrangements in other parts of the sterling area and in continental European countries, were all welcomed by the Fund as evidence of a wish by member countries to place increased reliance on the market mechanism. A long list of detailed relaxations of restrictions, including in particular a reduction in discrimination against dollar imports, showed that progress was being made almost everywhere toward the Fund's ideal. But the Report also stressed that much remained to be done:

> . . . The use of restrictive devices is still widespread. Restrictions have sometimes been intensified in order to cope with increased external imbalance resulting from internal conditions and policies. Certain countries are still faced with payments difficulties stemming from external causes. . . .

When therefore the staff put before the Board, on May 12, 1955, a proposal for a policy on bilateral arrangements, it was in guarded terms, and specifically recognized the difficulties which many members faced. Its recommendation to

[11] *Sixth Annual Report on Exchange Restrictions* (1955), pp. 4–8, 14.

members was that efforts should be made to reduce, and eventually to eliminate, reliance on bilateral arrangements. The Fund, it proposed, should urge the full cooperation of members in reducing reliance on such arrangements. This approach to the problem found the Board divided between those who praised its realism and those who wished the Fund to take a stronger line. The former view was expressed, for example, by Mr. Prasad (India), who pointed out that during the annual consultations many members had said that they needed the aid of bilateral arrangements to adjust their balances of payments; it was unreasonable to ask them to abandon these arrangements. Mr. Bury (Australia), on the other hand, found the staff memorandum disappointing in view of the opportunities afforded by the favorable world payments situation to get rid of bilateral agreements. Views such as these were exchanged during several meetings, in the course of which the policy proposed by the staff was redrafted, to emerge on June 22 in a form which said less about members' problems and more about the need to shed reliance on bilateral arrangements.[12] In this form it was communicated to members.

Approach to Article VIII

Resuming on June 8 the adjourned discussion on the transition from Article XIV to Article VIII, the Board reviewed a further memorandum by the staff. This drew attention to the fact that revised rules under the GATT, relating to quantitative restrictions and discrimination, would be brought into force when countries conducting at least 50 per cent of the aggregate trade of GATT members accepted the obligations of Article VIII. The accession of the United Kingdom to the group of Article VIII countries would increase the percentage to 48,[13] and as "further important moves have been made toward convertibility and there is the possibility of currencies being made convertible in the near future," it was desirable to decide upon the Board's policy. Should this be to encourage a wholesale transference of members to Article VIII? Such a move would involve the continuing approval of a wide range of restrictions and stultify the significance of Article VIII. Or should the Fund wait until all restrictions were ended? This seemed equally unrealistic, both by appearing to contemplate an indefinite delay, and by ignoring the practical convertibility of many currencies. The solution offered by the staff lay between these two extremes, viz., to encourage individual members to accept the responsibilities of Article VIII, provided that they imposed no restrictions on current transactions with other members and had no discrimination against imports. Any other restrictions, including multiple currency practices, would be regarded as tem-

[12] E.B. Decision No. 433-(55/42), June 22, 1955; below, Vol. III, p. 258.

[13] This percentage differs from that mentioned by the Managing Director at the Annual Meeting, 1954 (above, p. 398), mainly because the latter refers to the currency used, not to the country engaged.

porary and would require prior approval as well as annual review during consultations. Members unable to meet these criteria would remain under Article XIV. The staff explicitly recognized that no major trading country was likely to be willing to assume the obligations of Article VIII until the United Kingdom did so.

The two meetings of the Board at which this recommendation was discussed disclosed a wide spectrum of views, ranging from a wish that the Fund would decide forthwith to terminate the use of Article XIV to a reluctance to press any country to abandon this use. The discussion had been intended to be a preliminary one, but it was not resumed, because it became apparent almost at once that no widespread acceptance of Article VIII could be expected in the near future. Accordingly, in the Annual Report for 1955, work on which was proceeding during June, the Board diverted attention from formal convertibility to a pragmatic acceptance of such progress as members were able to make toward reducing restrictions:

> It may be concluded [the Directors said] from the developments of the past year or two that, should the trend of international payments continue to be favorable, this, even apart from formal moves in the direction of *de jure* convertibility, should bring about an extension of nondiscrimination, and a weakening of the structure of bilateralism, and thus a further extension of *de facto* convertibility.[14]

When presenting the Annual Report to the Governors in Istanbul, the Managing Director underlined this changed approach:

> Little by little, [he said] governments are narrowing the real differences between currencies already convertible and currencies still to be made convertible. The Fund welcomes every such move. The Fund is prepared to help countries to take such new steps toward realizing the common objectives of all the members of the Fund.[15]

But even this was further than the United Kingdom felt able to go. In his speech on the following day, Mr. Butler said:

> Obviously we have to move step by step to the goal of freedom in trade and payments, but, though we have moved only step by step, the immediate result of the relaxations of 1954 was to bring about an increase in our imports, especially from the dollar area. This gathered momentum and such imports—both total as well as from dollar sources—were very considerable in the first half of 1955.
>
> . . . The present must be a period of consolidation and strengthening on the home front before we make any further moves forward on the trade or the exchange front. . . .
>
> . . . My Government has taken no decision on the timing of the convertibility of sterling or on the nature of the exchange arrangements after that date.[16]

---

[14] *Annual Report, 1955*, p. 8.

[15] *Summary Proceedings, 1955*, p. 18.

[16] *Ibid.*, pp. 38–39.

The uncompromising attitude adopted by Mr. Butler was partly prompted by a technical difficulty connected with the British plans for the sterling exchange rate. It had been announced that, at the time when convertibility was restored, the margin between the buying and selling rates for the pound would be widened to 2 cents either side of parity. Since in 1955 sterling was under pressure, it was widely expected that if convertibility was restored, the rate would fall to the lower of these limits. To avoid this unwanted depreciation, therefore, it became necessary to assert firmly that convertibility was not being introduced, and that "all discussions and rumors about impending changes of the parity of, or margins for, sterling are unrealistic and irrelevant."

Discrimination

During the ensuing twelve months the subject of convertibility ceased to occupy the forefront of the Board's thinking, being replaced to some extent by the narrower topic of discrimination. On this, Executive Directors were supplied in September 1955 with an exhaustive survey by the staff of the discriminatory practices of Fund members. After a short introductory discussion in November, this survey formed the basis for an intensive series of Board meetings in March 1956. It was supplemented by a review of the world payments situation as it appeared to the staff in February.

The conclusion reached by the staff was that the degree of discrimination exercised by most countries against dollar imports had diminished and was diminishing, and that this was fully justified by the progress that had been made toward equilibrium in the pattern of world payments. This conclusion was received by the Board with somewhat mixed feelings. As Mr. Emminger (Germany) said in summing up the discussion on March 14, differences of opinion existed within the Board on all three of the main subjects which had emerged, viz., the special problems of primary producing countries, the effects of liberalizing dollar imports and ending discrimination, and the significance of U.S. aid as a contribution toward balance of payments equilibrium. Nevertheless, the consensus of the Board was generally in favor of the staff's views, and it was decided that these, and the points made in the discussions, should be borne in mind when drafting the Annual Report.

In consequence, abandoning the precedents of 1954 and 1955, the Board entitled Chapter 1 of the Annual Report for 1956 "The Current Perspective in International Finance," and emphasized in that and the following chapters the progress made toward relaxing restrictions and extending multilateral trade and payments. It was not until 1959 that the word "convertibility" re-entered the contents page of the Annual Report, and then it was external convertibility to which it referred, and not the acceptance of Article VIII.

REGULATING CAPITAL TRANSFERS

A difficult problem came to light in the course of discussions in the Board on the scope of Article VIII; it concerned the extent to which the authority given to members by Article VI, Section 3, overrode the obligations of Article VIII. When the subject was first discussed by the Board on April 6, 1956, the representative of the Legal Department gave a resumé of the legislative history of the provisions for the control of capital movements, and the whole question was remitted to the Committee on Interpretation for review.

As formulated by the chairman of the Committee on Interpretation, Mr. van Campenhout (Belgium), and the General Counsel, Mr. Fawcett, the issue involved the following questions:

1. What does the expression in Article VI, Section 3 "members may exercise . . . controls . . . necessary to regulate international capital movements" denote?
   (a) May members regulate capital movements for any reason they deem fit and for any purpose whatsoever, including discriminatory purposes?
   (b) Are the controls a member may exercise in order to regulate capital movements confined to domestic regulations or practices instituted by the member to restrict payments for capital transfers by residents or nonresidents and to make these measures effective, or do they include agreements or understandings with other countries for the purpose of controlling capital movements?
2. If the answers to question 1 are such that the controls within the scope of Article VI, Section 3, must be taken to include engaging in discriminatory currency arrangements, are such arrangements "authorized" under Article VIII, Section 3?
3. If a member, in regulating capital movements, engages in multiple currency practices, can these practices qualify as controls within the scope of Article VI, Section 3, and if so, are they "authorized" under Article VIII, Section 3?
4. What action, if any, can the Fund take if it appears that the member's engaging in discriminatory currency arrangements or multiple currency practices exercised as capital controls are not "necessary" to the regulation by it of capital movements or affect capital movements within the terms of Article VI, Section 3?

The General Counsel pointed out that the committee was faced by an apparent conflict between two general principles: (1) the freedom of members to exercise controls over capital movements, subject to the express limitations in Article VI, and (2) the rule in Article VIII, Section 3, against discriminatory currency arrangements and multiple currency practices. He thought it was a reasonable presumption that the only limitations imposed by the Articles of Agreement which were relevant to the control of capital movements were as follows:

Article VI, Section 1 (*a*), prohibiting the use of the Fund's resources to meet a large and sustained outflow of capital, and authorizing the Fund to request a member to control such capital movements;

Article VI, Section 1 (*b*) (ii), which requires that capital movements met out of a member's own resources shall be in accordance with the purposes of the Fund;

Article VI, Section 3, which requires that controls over capital movements shall not be exercised so as to restrict payments for current transactions, etc.;

Article IV, especially Section 4 (*b*), requiring the maintenance of par values.

In the ensuing discussion most Executive Directors accepted this analysis, although at a later stage it was decided to disregard Article IV. The general view was that Article VI, Section 3, recognized the sovereign right of members to regulate international capital movements in any way that would not restrict current payments. This appeared to permit discriminatory currency arrangements insofar as they were for the purpose of controlling capital movements. Concurring, Mr. Saad (Egypt) thought that Article VIII, Section 3, which prohibited discriminatory currency arrangements or multiple currency practices "except as authorized under this Agreement . . ." meant "except as otherwise provided for in this Agreement." He believed that Article VI, Section 3, could be construed as permitting members to control capital movements by discriminatory currency arrangements, and probably also by multiple currency practices. However, he suggested that it might be as well to await experience with some practical situations before reaching a decision on the latter point. This was accepted by the committee. Mr. Saad proposed a draft decision, which with minor changes became the committee's recommendation to the Board. The latter read as follows:

> Subject to the provisions of Article VI, Section 3 concerning payments for current transactions and undue delay in transfers of funds in settlement of commitments:
>
> (a) Members are free to adopt a policy of regulating capital movements for any reason, due regard being paid to the general purposes of the Fund and without prejudice to the provisions of Article VI, Section 1.
>
> (b) They may, for that purpose, exercise such controls as are necessary, including making such arrangements as may be reasonably needed with other countries, without approval of the Fund.

It was agreed by the committee that the phrases "for any reason" in paragraph (a) and "including making such arrangements as may be reasonably needed" in paragraph (b) both covered discriminatory currency arrangements.

The report and recommendation of the committee was adopted by the Board on July 25, 1956.[17]

[17] E.B. Decision No. 541-(56/39), July 25, 1956; below, Vol. III, p. 246.

PROBLEMS OF CHANGES IN EXCHANGE SYSTEMS

Proposals for changes in restrictive systems, including those numerous relaxations of restrictions to which reference was made above, came before the Board at frequent intervals. Some created no problems, and were welcomed, but others raised questions of procedure and even of jurisdiction. The principal procedural difficulty was lack of time to enable Directors to study the proposals put forward. Member countries, having decided upon changes in their exchange systems, wished to introduce them as quickly as possible; but where there appeared to be some element of discrimination in the proposals, Executive Directors wished to consider all the implications before approving them.

Jurisdictional issues

In March 1955 the United Kingdom decided that the Exchange Equalization Account should intervene in the transferable sterling market. The British Government formed the view that this was not a matter within the jurisdiction of the Fund, and accordingly notified the Board *post hoc*—waiting, in fact, until Lord Harcourt (United Kingdom) returned to Washington from a visit to London, in order that he might make an oral statement. Mr. Southard (United States) welcomed the announcement, but said that he believed that the Fund should have been consulted in advance; he thought that the Board's decision should include the grant of whatever approval was legally necessary. Mr. de Largentaye (France), on the other hand, agreed with the British view. Referring to his dissent from the Board's decision on multiple currency practices seven years earlier, he expressed his conviction that the Fund had no jurisdiction in such matters. Mr. Emminger (Germany), who followed in the discussion, said that the British decision was clearly one to be welcomed, and it did not seem to him necessary to stress the legal point. Other Directors agreed, and the decision was that the Board welcomed the British action; that the question of jurisdiction had been raised and would be studied, and that any necessary approval was granted. The last clause in the decision made it unnecessary to consider the matter further, whatever view was taken on the jurisdictional issue. However, after reviewing the relevant Article IV, Sections 3 and 4, the Legal Department was unable to accept the British view. Instead, it argued that official intervention at exchange rates differing by more than 1 per cent from parity constituted a multiple currency practice, for which the Board's approval should have been obtained. No formal decision has been taken on the point.

Difficulties also arose in connection with a series of changes introduced by Brazil. Between the end of December 1954 and the beginning of September 1955 the Board had nine separate discussions of proposals to amend the exchange arrangements in Brazil. Toward the end of the period Mr. Roberto Campos,

Director of the Brazilian Development Bank, came to Washington to explain to the Board Brazil's difficulties and its plans to deal with them. These involved the breaking of all links with the par value, and the adoption of a fluctuating currency. The staff reminded the Board that it was not possible for the Fund to give approval to such a system, although it could note the circumstances which had impelled the member to adopt it. Any further changes would, however, require to be agreed with the Fund. Mr. Paranaguá (Brazil) did not see why it was necessary for the Board to approve such changes, since the system itself had not secured the Fund's approval, but the staff recalled that changes in any multiple currency arrangements required the approval of the Fund. In the event, the Board decided that it could not agree to Brazil's proposals; while recognizing the exigencies of the member's situation, it believed that the real problem was inflation, which had yet to be dealt with. The Board therefore decided only to remain in touch with Brazil.

A third instance of a difference of view about jurisdiction arose in December 1955. The Belgian Government then decided to extend the scope of the free foreign exchange market to cover payments made for gold transactions in a liberalized gold market. Reporting this to the Board, Mr. Toussaint (Belgium) claimed that the approval of the Fund was not necessary because the measure had been taken by Belgium in pursuance of the Board's decision in September 1951, leaving to each member the implementation of the Board's policy on the prevention of sales of gold at premium prices. The staff, however, believed that the Belgian plan amounted to a multiple currency practice, and as such needed the Fund's approval. The Board did not think it was required to decide the issue, and instead agreed to apply "to the extent necessary" the approval given in July 1954 to proposals then made by the Belgian-Luxembourg Economic Union and the Netherlands to liberalize payments between them.

Transport insurance

On a more general plane, the Board dealt with a resolution passed by ECOSOC in April 1953 instructing the UN Secretary-General to bring to the notice of the Fund resolutions of the Council and the Transport and Communications Commission on the subject of discrimination in transport insurance "with a view to examination by the Fund of the possibility of achieving relaxation of exchange controls as applied to transport insurance."

After studying the matter, the staff put forward a draft reply to the effect that very few countries in fact used exchange controls to discriminate in transport insurance payments, but that something like a fourth of Fund members had legislation protecting their domestic insurance industries. The draft went on to say that the Fund sought in discussion with its members to secure the relaxation of restrictions of all kinds. This reply was approved by the Board in December

1954. Subsequently the Board was told that the Transport and Communications Commission was content to leave the problem of discrimination in transport insurance to the Fund and the GATT.

The Hague and Paris "Clubs"

In the course of the annual consultation with the United Kingdom on March 21, 1956, several references were made to the "Hague Club"—a loose grouping of European countries engaged in trade with Brazil—and the staff was asked to provide a study of the exchange arrangements involved. The "Club" had been formed as a result of a meeting at The Hague in May 1955 followed by bilateral negotiations between Brazil and each of the European countries involved—Belgium, Germany, Luxembourg, the Netherlands, and the United Kingdom by March 1956; other countries joined later.

The staff's report on the arrangements was discussed by the Board in May 1956. Mr. Paranaguá then described the "Club" as a system of parallel bilateral arrangements; by eliminating discrimination between participating countries, he said, it constituted an important step toward ending discrimination in Brazilian trade altogether. Lord Harcourt concurred, and added that the "Club" was open to anyone who wished to join. Executive Directors welcomed the arrangements "as a transitional step toward a fully multilateral and nondiscriminatory system of trade and accounts."

The "Paris Club," a similar organization of European countries engaged in trade with Argentina, operated in a tentative way from the summer of 1956, and was placed on a formal basis in November 1957. It was mentioned to the Board in the course of the annual consultations with the United Kingdom and with Argentina during 1957, but it was not thought necessary to take any formal decision in the matter.

Procedure

In February 1956 the staff brought to the notice of the Board difficulties that were being experienced in dealing with changes in multiple currency systems. The basic decision establishing the Board's jurisdiction was that taken in 1947, which required members as a minimum to consult the Fund before introducing a multiple currency practice, before making a change in any of the multiple rates of exchange, before reclassifying transactions subject to different rates, and before making any other type of significant change in their exchange systems.[18] The handling of such consultations had been simplified in 1951 by the adoption of the so-called lapse of time procedure. By this procedure, Executive Directors were notified of members' proposals for minor changes in exchange systems, and

[18] E.B. Decision No. 237-2, December 18, 1947; below, Vol. III, p. 261.

if no Director requested within a specified time that the matter should be put on the Board's agenda, approval was deemed to have been given at the next ensuing Board meeting. Increasing recourse had been had to this procedure in the intervening years, but the staff was still guided by the original concept that its use should be restricted to minor changes.

Experience had shown that difficulties in dealing with changes in multiple currency practices arose in several different ways. Sometimes the information provided by the member was inadequate to enable the staff to appraise the significance of the change proposed. Frequently the notice given of a proposed change was very short, or was received at a weekend, while the member wished to introduce the new arrangements immediately. In other instances no advance approval had been sought at all, and the changes had come to light only in the course of later discussions with the member. As a result of these difficulties the Fund had often had to decide on a proposal too quickly, and had sometimes approved proposals of which it felt some doubt, although not sufficient to warrant a refusal.

As a practical step the staff suggested that the lapse of time procedure should be adopted for a wider range of proposals, including all those that involved no more than a simplification of a multiple currency system, the elimination of some part of one, an extension of time for one previously approved with a time limit, steps toward unification of an exchange rate, or shifts of commodities to a broad free market. Furthermore, the staff proposed that more use should be made of the procedure of conditional approval of a change—i.e., approval for a limited time, or subject to some modification. Finally, the staff thought that it would be useful to encourage members to seek advance approval for programs of changes, possibly with an obligation to come back to the Fund if the program was altered. Indeed, it might be helpful for the Fund itself to propose to members, where appropriate, that such programs be submitted.

These various suggestions were in general favorably received by the Board. Mr. Southard made the interesting comment that he was beginning to feel that the Fund might be going too far in insisting on prior consultation in connection with all changes in multiple currency systems. This, however, was not taken up, and the Board decided only that the Managing Director should be free to decide whether a proposed change required discussion. If he did not, the lapse of time procedure would apply.

CONSULTATIONS SETTLE DOWN

The annual consultations with members under Article XIV, of which the beginning was described in Chapter 12, have in recent years come to form the backbone of the Board's work. This is so, not only because of the amount of time which the consultations occupy, but also because the staff's reports provide Executive Directors with much data about members' problems. These reports have become increasingly lengthy and complex as the staff's information has become more comprehensive. Each one is brought before the Board for discussion and decision. Each requires the consideration of the member's economic circumstances, an appraisal of the measures which it is taking to deal with its difficulties, and the review of a draft decision in which the Board's conclusions are to be communicated to the member concerned. It will be seen in Chapter 18 below that in 1961 consultations began to be held also with members that had accepted the obligations of Article VIII, but that in such consultations no decision is recorded.

For the purposes of this history, consultations present two problems, one minor and one major. The minor one is that the timetable does not fit the framework adopted for these chapters; it begins in the spring of each year and may last more than twelve months. The major problem is that the individuality of each consultation makes it impossible to generalize about their contents except in the widest terms. Equally, no single consultation can be cited as fully characteristic. The example given below is typical only in a very general way.

For the 1954 series of consultations the staff proposed a procedure designed to minimize as far as possible the work involved. The agenda were to be restricted to the main trends and major policies in the member countries consulted. Notice of the main topics to be discussed would be given to the members in advance. So far as possible, inquiries would be made by correspondence; formal meetings would be curtailed to a minimum. Where the member's situation had been recently discussed, an even simpler procedure would be followed, limited to an exchange of letters or at most to discussions with the Executive Director concerned or with the member's diplomatic representatives in Washington. Where field discussions were necessary, these would, if possible, be begun at the Annual Meetings. Not more than three staff members would visit any member country; they would deal at the same time with any other matters needing attention there, and would cover more than one country in the course of each trip.

This streamlined procedure was welcomed by the Board, and the decision taken spelt out the need to economize effort. However, a suggestion put forward by Sir Edmund Hall-Patch (United Kingdom), that a profound consultation with a member could hardly be held more often than once in two years, was not generally accepted.

In the event, the 1954 series of consultations covered 39 countries. In 15 instances the staff's inquiries were conducted in Washington, and for four of these the countries concerned nominated their Executive Directors to represent them. Twenty countries were visited by the staff; inquiries for the other four consultations were conducted by correspondence. Czechoslovakia (which had still provided no data) was again omitted. Consultations with Bolivia, Paraguay, Syria, the Union of South Africa, and Uruguay were postponed until the 1955 series.

The first of the 1954 consultations—with Australia—was begun by the Board on June 21, 1954, but at the request of two Directors a decision was then deferred, and it was not until October 20, 1954, that the Board's action was completed. The last consultation of the series—that with Burma—was undertaken on July 15, 1955. The 1955 consultations covered 32 countries. The first report, on Turkey, came before the Board on July 28, 1955 and the last, on Uruguay, occupied parts of three meetings in April and July 1956. More than a third of the Board's time in 1955–56 was devoted to consultations.

The following account of the 1954 consultation with Denmark will afford some insight into the procedure in a straightforward instance. Denmark had been visited for a week in February 1955 by a mission comprising Mr. J. M. Stevens, Director of the European Department, and two other staff members. Conversations were held with representatives of the National Bank of Denmark, the Foreign Ministry, the Ministry of Finance, the Statistical Department, the Ministry of Commerce, Industry and Shipping, and the Economic Secretariat. The mission's report ("Part I") was sent to the Board on March 30, 1955. It ran to some six thousand words and contained, as was customary, an account of the interviews that had been conducted, the staff's comments, and a draft decision. Appended was "Part II," a "background paper" of approximately twice the length of the report, which described the main features of Denmark's economy and of its restrictive system.

The draft decision submitted by the staff was in the following terms:

> 1. The Government of Denmark has consulted the Fund under Article XIV, Section 4, of the Fund Agreement concerning the further retention of its transitional arrangements.
>
> 2. Denmark's total output expanded in 1954. Investment activity increased, especially in building, and expenditure on consumption also rose. There was some rise in wages and some upward pressure on prices. Because of the higher level of internal demand and a relatively poor harvest, imports increased more than exports and the balance of payments showed a considerable deficit on goods and services. In addition, Denmark continued to reduce the remaining arrears on the Government dollar debt.
>
> 3. Denmark has pursued strict credit policies and has also introduced corrective fiscal measures. The Fund believes that these actions will be helpful in reducing the pressure on the balance of payments and that the increased emphasis recently given to fiscal policy may facilitate the introduction of a greater degree of flexibility in the application of credit policy.
>
> 4. Denmark continues to make use of discriminatory restrictions and bilateral agreements. The Fund notes the progress made by Denmark in relaxing restrictions against the dollar area. While recognizing that Denmark's external and reserve

positions require the use of restrictions, the Fund hopes that some further progress in reducing discrimination will be possible in the coming year. The Fund notes that there was in 1954 a greater use of the retention quota system; and, while the Fund does not object to the temporary retention of the system, it urges that consideration be given to its early removal.

5. In concluding the 1954 consultations, the Fund has no other comments to make on the transitional arrangements maintained by Denmark.

The report was considered by the Board on April 29, 1955, Mr. Vagn Hoelgaard, Economic Counselor of the Danish Embassy in Washington, being present by invitation. Mr. Torben Friis (Denmark), Alternate to Mr. Åkermalm, expounded the Danish view. He said that the mission's report was generally acceptable to the Danish Government, although he had two minor criticisms of the staff's conclusions. Other Executive Directors called attention to the maintenance of the retention quota system, to Denmark's bilateral agreements, to an apparent inconsistency between the views about Denmark's balance of payments expressed to the mission and those advanced in the OEEC, and to the degree of discrimination exercised against dollar imports. Mr. Friis, Mr. Hoelgaard, and members of the staff replied.

The Board then discussed the draft decision. At Mr. Friis' suggestion the last sentence of paragraph 2 was altered to read "In addition, Denmark repaid all remaining arrears on its Government dollar debt, leaving only two municipal dollar loans in arrears." Mr. Donner (Germany) criticized the second sentence of paragraph 3, and at Mr. Friis' instance the words "in due course" were inserted before "facilitate."

A number of changes were made in paragraph 4. At the suggestion of Mr. Warren (Canada), the first sentence was elaborated by substituting "including those involved in bilateral agreements" for the last three words. Mr. Southard (United States) proposed the deletion from the second sentence of the clause "While recognizing that Denmark's external and reserve positions require the use of restrictions . . ." He said that it had not been the practice in consultations to give specific approval to restrictions, since this was not required by the terms of Article XIV. His proposal was accepted by Mr. Friis on the understanding that the deletion did not imply any change in the Fund's attitude toward the restrictions. Mr. Friis asked that the first phrase in the third sentence of paragraph 4 should be altered to read "The Fund notes that during 1954 exports and imports under the retention quota system continued to expand . . ." and this was agreed.

Mr. Donner then proposed the omission from the last sentence of the words "the Fund does not object to the temporary retention of the system." He said that, as Mr. Southard had pointed out, the Board's decision should not be so worded as to approve the Government's actions. However, the staff explained that the retention quota system was a multiple currency practice, and as such required the affirmative approval of the Fund. Mr. Donner did not consider that the words quoted conferred such approval, and maintained his objection, but the Board generally agreed with the staff, and the phrase was retained. The Board then took its decision in terms of the staff draft as amended.

USE OF THE FUND'S RESOURCES

France's ineligibility ended

In October 1954 Mr. Southard (United States) proposed to the Board that France should no longer be ineligible to use the Fund's resources. He pointed out that while France still had no par value, it had long since abandoned the multiple currency practices and discriminatory currency arrangements which had led the Board in 1948 to invoke Article IV, Section 6, and declare France ineligible.[19] Mr. Southard therefore suggested that the Board should exercise the discretion to which it was entitled under that Section and remove the ineligibility. The Board agreed, and so decided on October 15, 1954.

Drawings and stand-by arrangements

The amount drawn from the Fund during the twelve months from September 1954 to September 1955 was smaller than that in any other such twelve months except 1950–51; three countries drew a total of $43.75 million. Repurchases were made by twelve countries and totaled $125.64 million. Nearly $86.5 million was repurchased voluntarily.

When seeking to draw $25 million from the Fund in December 1954, Colombia also approached the Federal Reserve Bank in New York for a similar sum. As Colombia's quota was $50 million, a drawing of $25 million required the granting of a waiver from the quantitative limitation in Article V, Section 3 (*a*) (iii). Mr. Donner (Germany) inquired why Colombia did not ask the Fund for the whole $50 million that it needed. Mr. Southard, in reply, commented that the granting of a waiver was "unusual in itself"; and that when asked to grant one the Fund would wish to know whether other resources were available to the member seeking to draw. This was possibly the last occasion on which the granting of a waiver was described as "unusual." A waiver was readily conceded to the Philippines, whose quota was $15 million, when it sought to draw $10 million in June 1955. The other drawing in 1954–55—$8.75 million by Iran in January 1955—was in the gold tranche and was approved without discussion.

Somewhat larger use was made of the Fund's resources in the following year, six countries drawing a total of $117.75 million. The largest single drawing

[19] See above, p. 202.

was made by Indonesia: $55 million in August 1956. Repurchases, however, again exceeded drawings; they amounted to $253.07 million, being made by nine countries. Of this total, $211.60 million was repurchased voluntarily, including $127.91 million by France and $62.44 million by Japan. The largest obligatory repurchase was made by Indonesia in June 1956; it amounted to $27 million.

A request by Burma to draw $15 million in February 1956 set a new precedent, being the first time that a drawing equivalent to 100 per cent of a member's quota had been sought. Mr. Lieftinck (Netherlands) suggested that the drawing should be restricted to $10 million, and that the member should be offered a stand-by arrangement for the other $5 million or, as an alternative, should be asked to provide collateral security to the extent of $5 million; this security might perhaps be sterling, or convertible reserves if available. Mr. de Largentaye (France) was attracted by Mr. Lieftinck's proposal, but the staff pointed out that if the security was in the form of sterling and it became necessary to foreclose, an awkward problem would be presented to the Fund: its holdings of sterling were equivalent to 82 per cent of the British quota, and by Article V, Section 7 (*c*) (iii), the Fund could not accept a currency of which its holdings exceeded 75 per cent of quota.

Executive Directors generally felt that as Burma had a very small quota, and as it had been obliged to repurchase $3.25 million in November 1955, the drawing of $15 million could be permitted without any special arrangements being made. It was accordingly approved.

Another precedent was set in September 1956, when the Egyptian Government drew Canadian dollars to the value of US$15 million. (Canadian dollars were chosen because at the time the U.S. dollar and the sterling balances of the Egyptian Government were being blocked by the U.S. and British authorities, respectively, in connection with the Suez Canal crisis, discussed in the next chapter.) This was the first occasion on which a member had drawn a fluctuating currency, and involved the application of the rules worked out in June 1954.[20]

A minor alteration in the wording of the Board's decisions in respect of drawings followed an intervention by Mr. de Largentaye in October 1955. The occasion was a drawing of $8.75 million by Iran, which required a waiver (because Iran's quota was $35 million and it had already drawn $8.75 million in January 1955). The formula proposed by the staff for the Board's decision was that the Board "expressed no objection" to the drawing—this wording having been regularly used up to that time. However, Mr. de Largentaye suggested that while this was appropriate for drawings under Article V, Section 3—that is, for drawings that conformed to the quantitative limitations in that Section—it was inappropriate for drawings that necessitated a waiver of these limitations. The

[20] See above, p. 376.

Board agreed with this view, and its decision accordingly "approved the request" of Iran.

The stand-by arrangement with Peru was renewed in February 1955 and again in February 1956. The only new stand-by arrangements introduced during the two years 1954–56 were one with Chile for $35 million for a year from April 1956 and one with Iran for $17.5 million for six months from May 1956.

Repurchases

A request by Turkey in March 1954 to postpone a repurchase which had become due on April 30, 1953 was resisted by Mr. de Largentaye on the ground that the Fund had no power to defer the collection of a repurchase which had become due. The staff referred to Rule I-6 (f), which reads:

> After [the member's repurchase obligation has been determined] the Managing Director shall send to the member a formal request for payment. . . . The member shall discharge the repurchase obligation within thirty days from the day on which the member receives the formal request for payment or within such other period as may be decided by the Executive Board.

In view of this, the Board agreed to the postponement requested by Turkey; Mr. de Largentaye abstained.

A year later the question arose again, on a request by Brazil to postpone the discharge of obligations which it had incurred under Article V, Section 7, at the end of April 1953 and of April 1954. It proposed that these should be met from a schedule of repurchases to which it had committed itself in October 1953, which repurchases were to begin in June 1957. Mr. de Largentaye repeated his contention that the Fund had no power to postpone a repurchase. On this occasion he also protested that the arrangement proposed by Brazil would be an abuse of Rule I-6 (f). In his view the last clause of this rule could not be considered to justify extending the obligatory period of thirty days to a period of several years. Nevertheless, in the light of the staff's exposé of Brazil's financial position, the member's proposal was adopted.

On the same occasion a question arose as to the correctness of rulings given by the Board in 1946 and 1948 on the calculation of monetary reserves; [21] specifically it was suggested that the treatment of pledged gold in monetary reserves was mistaken. The staff pointed out that the Board had taken comprehensive decisions on the calculation of monetary reserves, which had been reflected in the detailed instructions given to member countries in Fund Circular No. 9; to change the rules now would be most difficult. Supporting the staff, Mr. Bury (Australia) said that the calculation of monetary reserves under the existing rules was extremely complicated. If the rules were changed, it would be necessary to

[21] See above, pp. 158–59, 198. The principles established in 1946 were restated on April 14, 1948.

enter into lengthy explanations before the government officials concerned could adapt their procedures to the change. He advised against any alteration. The Managing Director, concurring, said that it was the staff view that the rules worked satisfactorily, and that it was not necessary to review them. This was accepted by the Board.

A possible clash between the provisions of the Articles of Agreement and the Rooth Plan was discussed in connection with a proposal in June 1956. Paraguay, when coming to the Board to draw $1.5 million, offered to use any excess of its reserves of gold and dollars above $3.5 million in any month to repurchase the outstanding balance ($0.5 million) of a drawing made in June 1952. Mr. van Campenhout (Belgium) pointed out that $3.5 million was equal to Paraguay's quota, and that by Article V, Section 7 (*c*) (i), Paraguay was not required to make a repurchase if its reserves were less than its quota. There was no such limitation in the Rooth Plan. He asked whether there was in fact any likelihood that Paraguay's reserves of gold and dollars—then about $1.7 million gross—would exceed its quota. The staff thought that there was some prospect that Paraguay would be able to make a repurchase in the second half of the year, and the proposal was approved. However, it proved necessary for Paraguay to draw a further $0.5 million from the Fund in February 1957, and the repurchase of the 1952 drawing was not effected until May 1957, by which time it had been outstanding for five years.

POLICIES ON DRAWINGS REVIEWED

Restatement of policy

In the Annual Report for 1955 the Directors restated the policy which had been evolved from the Rooth Plan. This formulation was repeated, in somewhat different terms, in the Annual Reports for 1956 and 1957, and eventually emerged, in the Annual Report for 1959, in the following definitive version:

> Members are given the overwhelming benefit of the doubt in relation to requests for transactions within the "gold tranche," i.e., the portion of the quota which can be regarded as equivalent to the gold subscription. The Fund's attitude to requests for transactions within the first credit tranche, that is, transactions that bring the Fund's holdings of a member's currency above 100 per cent but not above 125 per cent of quota, is a liberal one, provided that the member itself is also making reasonable efforts to solve its problems. Requests for transactions beyond these limits require substantial justification. They are likely to be favorably received when the drawings or stand-bys are intended to support a sound program aimed at establishing or maintaining the enduring stability of the member's currency at a realistic rate of exchange.[22]

[22] *Annual Report, 1959*, p. 22. See also *Annual Report, 1955*, pp. 84–86; *1956*, p. 120; *1957*, p. 120; *1958*, pp. 23–24.

It will be seen that by 1959 the distinction between drawings in the gold tranche and other drawings, established by the Rooth Plan, had been supplemented by a distinction between drawings in the first credit tranche and drawings in higher credit tranches. This principle of the progressive strictness of the criteria applied, as higher credit tranches are reached, was the final form assumed by the conditionality of drawing rights.

Mr. Rooth's review

In May 1956 Mr. Rooth presented to the Board a further review of the possibilities of promoting the use of the Fund's resources. He suggested that the primary object of drawings should be to help members to obtain a better distribution of imports over time, by enabling them to reduce fluctuations from year to year—without, however, adding to the aggregate volume of imports. To assist toward this end, the Fund should not hesitate on suitable occasions to permit drawings which would raise the Fund's holdings of the member's currency to 200 per cent of quota; this would help to compensate for the diminution of the proportion that quotas bore to world trade. In addition, members should be invited to draw their whole needs from the Fund instead of obtaining part of their requirements from the Fund and part from governments or private sources.

Mr. Rooth made four specific suggestions: (1) an increase in technical assistance activities might well disclose suitable occasions for a drawing; (2) members should be encouraged to consult the Managing Director at an early stage in any difficulties they encountered, in order that the possibility of a drawing to assist them might be explored; (3) the conditions attached to a drawing in the first credit tranche (i.e., one increasing the Fund's holding of the currency from 100 per cent to 125 per cent of the member's quota) should be assimilated to the conditions for a drawing in the gold tranche; and (4) drawings for very short periods should be encouraged.

Commending these proposals at a meeting of the Board in September 1956, a fortnight before he retired, the Managing Director said that in his view it was important that the Fund's policies in connection with the use of its resources should be kept frequently under review. He asked the Board whether anything could be done at that time to improve these policies.

Directors mentioned a number of reasons why countries did not draw from the Fund: some were reluctant to add to short-term debts; some felt that their international position was such that the amount they would be permitted to draw from the Fund was not large enough to meet their needs; some considered that the Fund's charges were too high; some, whose balance of payments needs were essentially long term, were hesitant about drawing from the Fund in view of the relatively short term for which drawings were made available; and, finally, soft currency drawings had to be repaid in convertible currencies.

On the specific proposals put forward by the Managing Director, divided views were expressed; none received universal support. The nearest approach to a consensus was a general feeling that there was no need to hoard the Fund's resources in readiness for a recession. Apart from that, and from a willingness to accept that an extended scale of drawings would add to the Fund's authority, Directors expressed widely diverging views—those from less developed countries, together with Lord Harcourt (United Kingdom), being disposed generally to welcome a relaxation of limitations on drawings, while those from the developed countries took the opposite view.

No decision was reached, but the Managing Director said that the staff would continue to study the problem in the light of the views expressed.

Charges

The scale of charges approved in December 1953 for an introductory period of twelve months came up for review three times during the two years 1954–56. The discussions revealed that the Board was still divided on the question whether charges should be related to currently prevailing rates of interest in important money markets. Several Directors expressed a wish to see the number of brackets (which had been reduced from four to three in 1953) reduced from three to two by combining the second and third brackets. This would have meant that there would be one range of rates for drawings that did not raise the Fund's holdings beyond 150 per cent of quota, and a second range for all other drawings. However, such a consolidation would have necessitated either increasing or decreasing some of the existing charges, and Directors were reluctant to make any changes. As a result, the scale formulated in 1953 was renewed at intervals until April 1963. The modification then introduced for subsequent drawings is discussed in a later chapter.

LIMITS TO PRICE OF GOLD

In March 1954 the British Government permitted the reopening of the London gold market on a restricted basis. Notifying this to the Board, Mr. F. J. Portsmore (United Kingdom), Alternate to Sir Edmund Hall-Patch, explained that his authorities continued to support the view that gold should as far as possible be canalized into monetary reserves. They had, however, come to the conclusion that the continued closure of the London market served no useful purpose and was damaging to the interests of the United Kingdom and the sterling area.

In October 1954 Lord Harcourt (United Kingdom) approached the Board with a request for a reconsideration of Rule F-4, which set the maximum and minimum price of gold at which it was permissible for central banks to buy and sell. These prices, which included the "prescribed margin" set under Article IV, Section 2, were ¼ of 1 per cent above and below $35 an ounce, plus certain charges, which presupposed shipment to a "normal center" for dealing. Lord Harcourt pointed out that these charges were inapplicable to transactions for local delivery on the London gold market, and said that the limits of ¼ per cent each way, which alone applied to dealings there, were too narrow; they had prevented the Bank of England from intervening in the market to stabilize the price of gold. Commending the British request to the Board, the staff proposed that the limits should be 1 per cent each side of parity for dealings in a member's normal center; for other dealings the existing rule would remain in force.

The Board discussed the problem in informal session on October 8. Sir George Bolton, who attended the session to explain the problem as it affected the United Kingdom, said that 60 per cent of the world output of gold had gone through the market since it was reopened. He explained that hitherto the Bank of England had not intervened in it, but that the volume of transactions had recently grown so large that the Bank felt that it should now be able to intervene in order to have another market through which the value of sterling would be maintained. Sir George said that he would prefer the widest possible margin, but would regard 1 per cent either side of parity as acceptable. However, he felt that to differentiate between transactions in different markets, as proposed, would introduce an element of artificiality which might even amount to a kind of multiple currency practice. His representations met with a sympathetic hearing and when the problem was discussed at a formal meeting of the Board during the following week, agreement was reached on a revised proposal put forward by the staff. This provided for members to be given the option of respecting limits either of 1 per cent on each side of parity or of ¼ of 1 per cent plus the recognized charges.

GOLD PRODUCTION SUBSIDIES

During 1954–55 there was some relaxation of the standards applied to determine whether proposed subsidies to gold producers infringed E.B. Decision No. 233-2. The *raison d'être* of that decision was the prohibition in Article IV, Section 2, against buying gold at a price above par value plus the prescribed margin. It accordingly stated that

> a subsidy in the form of a uniform payment per ounce for all or part of the gold produced would constitute an increase in price which would not be permissible if the total price paid by the member for gold were thereby to become in excess of parity plus the prescribed margin.

It will be recalled that objection had been taken in 1947 and 1948 to plans put forward by Canada and Southern Rhodesia because they would have infringed this ruling. Revised arrangements had however been approved for both countries.[23]

In October 1951 the Canadian Government announced, as a sequel to the change in the Fund's policy described in Chapter 11, that in future Canadian gold producers would be permitted to sell their output in the free market, provided that they obtained the appropriate import license. Insofar as they did so, however, they would cease to be entitled to the subsidy that the Government had been paying to unprofitable mines since 1947.

In December 1951 Mr. Harry L. Wolfson (Canada), Alternate to Mr. Rasminsky, asked the Board for approval of the continuation of the subsidy for a further two years. He said that his Government had no wish either to stimulate the output of gold or to continue the subsidy indefinitely; it was seeking a two-year extension of the Board's approval in order to give the mines an opportunity to plan ahead. Several Executive Directors expressed doubts about the wisdom of the subsidy, and Mr. de Largentaye (France) thought that the option of selling in the free market meant that the subsidy amounted more nearly to the increase in price that the Board had been resisting. However, Mr. Southard (United States) reminded the Board that it had previously approved the Canadian plan on the ground that the subsidy was related not to the price of gold but to the economic circumstances of each mine; an extension of two years, as asked, was then approved.

In June 1954 the Government of the Philippines sought approval for a system of subsidies for gold mining. It proposed to classify the mines in the Philippines into three categories, which would attract subsidies at different levels. The basis for classification would be the relationship of the profit made by each mine to whichever was the lower of (*a*) 10 per cent of its gross receipts or (*b*) a norm determined by the investment in the mine and its expected future lifetime. Commenting on this proposal, the staff pointed out that since the amount of the subsidy would be the same for all mines in each category, the plan would appear to conflict with Decision No. 233-2, inasmuch as the subsidy contemplated would amount to "a uniform payment per ounce for . . . part of the gold produced." The staff suggested, however, that in the past the application of Decision No. 233-2 had led to "fine distinctions which are difficult to defend." Since the total number of gold mines in the Philippines was small, only a very few mines would be receiving a subsidy at the same rate. If this feature was ignored, there was a substantial resemblance between the Philippine plan and those which the Board had approved; in particular, all related the subsidy given

[23] See above, pp. 183, 252.

to the presumed economic needs of the mines. The staff therefore recommended that the plan should be approved.

When the matter came before the Board on June 18, Mr. Saad (Egypt), the Executive Director elected by the Philippines, spoke in favor of the staff view. He agreed that a problem was created by the reference in Decision No. 233-2 to "part of the gold produced." Nevertheless he proposed, and the Board agreed, that the plan should be approved. It was subsequently modified on two occasions, and approved by the Board for continuance until July 1957.

On the occasion of the original discussion, Executive Directors also supported a proposal by the staff that Decision No. 233-2 should be re-examined. Subsequent review within the staff, however, showed that there seemed to be no way to revise the decision which would not conflict with Article IV, Section 2. The suggestion that it should be reconsidered was therefore dropped.

The more liberal interpretation of Decision No. 233-2 applied to the Philippine plan was also adopted when in October 1954 the Australian Government proposed a new subsidy arrangement, by which uniform amounts would be paid to small producers and variable amounts to large producers. Mr. Bury (Australia) explained that adequate records to enable the subsidy to be equitably varied for small producers did not exist; in any case, their total production amounted only to about 4 per cent of Australia's gold output. The Board accepted a recommendation by the staff that it was a fair inference that the plan was designed to adjust the subsidy to the economic needs of the producers, and approved the new arrangements as put forward. In 1956 it was agreed that the plan might be continued for three years.

A system of subsidies introduced by Colombia in June 1954 was brought to the notice of the Board in January 1955, and was then approved. This also involved uniform payments, but was limited to "small" producers, and to a maximum of 30 ounces monthly for each miner. The amount of the subsidy was restricted to a maximum of Col$20 (then about US$8) an ounce, and to an aggregate of Col$80,000 a month, so that the actual amount paid per ounce varied inversely with output.

Canada's gold subsidy plan was somewhat modified in 1955 and 1958, but as it remained substantially similar to that which had previously been approved, the Board concluded that it could be regarded as not inconsistent with Decision No. 233-2 and accordingly agreed to its continuance.

In 1959 Fiji introduced a subsidy for its sole gold producer, and Australia modified and extended its subsidies. Details of these and of subsequent small changes in subsidies are given in the relevant Annual Reports.[24]

---

[24] *Annual Report, 1959*, pp. 150–51; *1960*, p. 144; *1961*, p. 125; *1962*, pp. 163–64; *1963*, p. 181; *1964*, p. 109; *1965*, p. 103; *1966*, p. 119.

INVESTMENT OF FUND'S ASSETS

It will be recalled that in 1951–52 a committee under the chairmanship of Mr. Martínez-Ostos (Mexico) had examined the possibility of investing some of the Fund's assets in order to augment its income. The Legal Department at that time advised the Board that, given proper safeguards, the Fund had implied powers to invest its assets for such a purpose. The committee was not able to make progress, however, partly because the U.S. Government had not reached a decision on the acceptability of an investment by the Fund in its securities.

In April 1955 the idea was revived by Mr. Southard (United States). During a series of discussions in April and May, he said that, in the U.S. view, Directors were justified in seeking a modest addition to the Fund's income—possibly $2–3 million a year—as a cushion against further operating losses. The U.S. Government was probably not willing to give an explicit undertaking to sell back any gold invested in U.S. securities, but the Fund would have the protection of Article IV, Section 8, of which subsection (*a*) reads: "The gold value of the Fund's assets shall be maintained notwithstanding changes in the par or foreign exchange value of the currency of any member." He doubted whether the delegations at Bretton Woods had ever contemplated the Fund's working for a long period at a loss; if they had, he felt sure they would not have denied the Fund the opportunity to invest assets. As it was, he agreed that a power to do so could be implied.

Mr. Southard's proposal was supported by a number of Executive Directors, but opposed by others. Mr. de Largentaye (France) thought the time was inopportune; there was no decisive reason to expect an operating deficit in the fiscal year 1955/56. He disagreed with the Legal Department's arguments, believing that the proposed investment was *ultra vires* the Fund by reason of Article V, Section 2. He did not think that it could be regarded as an administrative decision permissible under Article XII, Section 2 (*g*). Moreover, in his view the countries represented at Bretton Woods had reluctantly assumed the burden of subscribing gold to the Fund, and had not intended this gold to be used for the purpose of earning an income for the Fund.

Mr. Prasad (India) and Mr. Mansour (Egypt) suggested that a preferable way of dealing with the operating deficit would be to encourage the use of the Fund's resources by lowering charges. If the Fund was operating as had been visualized at Bretton Woods, viz., as a short-term credit agency, the deficit would disappear. Lord Harcourt (United Kingdom) said that while the British Government accepted the legal argument that the Fund had the power to make investments, it doubted the wisdom of doing so at that time.

In consequence of these differences of view, the Board decided at the end of May that it would not be appropriate to bring the proposal before the Governors at the Annual Meeting.

The subject was taken up again in July 1955, when Mr. Southard renewed his advocacy of an investment. He pointed out that the Annual Report, which had received the unanimous approval of the Board, contained a statement on the prospective use of the Fund's resources which clearly implied that the Fund would continue for some time to have an operating deficit.[25] His observations impressed the Board, and several Directors said that they would bring the matter before their Governments.

The discussion was resumed at the end of December 1955. Lord Harcourt then said that the British Government was content that the investment should be made, provided that four conditions were met: (1) the investment must not seriously impair the Fund's liquidity; (2) the U.S. Treasury must recognize the Fund's right to repurchase gold on the sale or maturity of the investment; (3) the Fund must be protected against an exchange risk on the dollars acquired with the gold; and (4) the amount to be invested should be reviewed by the Board from time to time. Three days later Mr. Southard said that the U.S. Treasury would agree to sell the gold back to the Fund and would recommend to the President of the United States that the usual 1/4 of 1 per cent handling charge for the gold transactions should be waived, provided that the maximum amount to be invested was $200 million.

A draft decision giving effect to the conditions suggested by the Legal Department, Lord Harcourt, and Mr. Southard was brought before the Board in January, and adopted with minor changes.[26] In its final form this decision included formal interpretations (1) that the Articles of Agreement permitted the sale of a portion of the Fund's gold for investment in U.S. Treasury bills having not more that 93 days to run, subject to appropriate conditions and safeguards, one of which was that the amount of gold to be sold for investment "will be such as to produce an amount of income reasonably related to the deficit of the Fund"; and (2) that by Article IV, Section 8 (*a*), the United States would be required to maintain the gold value of assets acquired through the investment. The decision then went on to say that, subject to the receipt of an appropriate assurance from the United States, an amount of the Fund's gold sufficient to realize not more than $200 million should be sold and the proceeds invested in U.S. Treasury bills having not more than 93 days to run.

The necessary arrangements having been made with the U.S. Treasury and the Federal Reserve Bank of New York, the first investment of $200 million was made in March 1956, and the Fund's income for the fiscal year 1955/56 included

[25] *Annual Report, 1955,* p. 86.
[26] E.B. Decision No. 488-(56/5), January 25, 1956; below, Vol. III, p. 275.

$123,279.51 from this investment. For 1956/57 the income from the investment exceeded $4.9 million.

A RETROSPECT, 1951–56

The year 1956 saw the completion of ten years of the Fund's existence—an event marked by the publication of a booklet, *The First Ten Years of the International Monetary Fund.* This publication, which combined an explanation of the Fund's method of working with an appraisal of its influence, was the first attempt to acquaint a nonspecialist readership with the significance of the Fund's activities. Emphasis was divided between the responsibilities of member countries and the contribution which the Fund could make to solving their problems. Four sentences fairly summarize the views expressed.

> Useful as the Fund has been during the past ten years, there is good reason to expect that it can be even more useful in the future. How far this expectation will be realized must depend on the manner in which the Fund and its members utilize the greater opportunities for international monetary cooperation that are created by an expanding world economy.
>
> . . . The Fund can help its members to meet their payments problems by encouraging them to adopt suitable financial policies, by providing them with additional reserves to meet temporary payments difficulties, and by maintaining fair exchange standards which will make it possible to deal with their difficulties in a constructive way.
>
> In the last analysis, the objectives of the Fund can be achieved only through the diligent pursuit of policies that create conditions within each country conducive to the expansion and balanced growth of international trade.[27]

Very naturally, nothing was said in *The First Ten Years* about the relative contributions of Executive Directors, Managing Director, and staff to the achievements recorded. But it is now possible, looking back, to attempt an appraisal of the extent to which the progress made by the Fund in 1951–56 was due to the leadership of Mr. Rooth.

From one point of view, the Annual Meeting in 1956 was the end of an era. Shortly afterward, coincident with the arrival of Mr. Rooth's successor, the Fund undertook transactions on a relatively enormous scale. For this remarkable change the immediate cause was the Suez Canal crisis, the effect of which will be considered in the next chapter. But so dramatic a transformation of the Fund's fortunes would not have been possible without the preparations made during the slow years that preceded it. Mr. Rooth's own share in these preparations was acknowledged by the Board in the Annual Report for 1957, in the following terms:

> During Mr. Rooth's five years of service, the Fund's policies and procedures underwent notable evolution so as to adapt them to the far-reaching changes which were occurring in the world economy. His leadership was especially directed

[27] *The First Ten Years of the International Monetary Fund,* pp. 42, 47.

> toward modification and innovation in Fund policy governing use of its resources, culminating in its restatement in the Annual Report for 1955. The Executive Directors gratefully acknowledge the valuable contribution which Mr. Rooth made to the work of the Fund, and take this opportunity, on their own behalf and on behalf of the staff, of making public this recognition of his many fine qualities.[28]

The sudden surge of drawings in the latter part of 1956, which threw into relief the part that Mr. Rooth had played in preparing the Fund to assist its members in emergencies, had no parallel in other phases of the Fund's work. But the absence of drama in the day-to-day activities of the Fund was in itself something of a tribute to his leadership. The machinery for consultations, devised in 1952, was by 1956 running smoothly. An increasing number of requests for technical assistance testified to improved relationships between the Fund and its members, to which Mr. Rooth's quiet receptiveness made a characteristic contribution. As Mr. Rasminsky (Canada) later remarked:

> Mr. Rooth had a most difficult task because to him had fallen the job of holding the Fund together during a period when, owing to world circumstances, the Fund was not active. The maintenance of belief in an inactive institution was most difficult, and Mr. Rooth's devotion to his task was something for which all should be grateful.

It may be added that Mr. Rooth's sympathy with the problems of the less developed countries helped to bring these to the fore in the Fund's thinking, and to stress the responsibility of the Fund's more developed members toward others. Where Mr. Gutt had laid the foundations, Mr. Rooth began the superstructure which, under his successors, has grown into the Fund of the 1960's.

Mr. Rooth himself was conscious both of the significance of the work that had been done, in his words, to create "a framework of policies which should enable the Fund to operate with reasonable success," and of the justification for criticisms that the Fund's achievements had fallen short of its possibilities. In his closing address to the Executive Board he sought to analyze the cause of this failure, and found it in the difficult problem of the respective responsibilities of Executive Directors and the management and staff, which the Board had tried to clarify in January 1948. Mr. Rooth emphasized anew the desirability of entrusting to the management and staff of the Fund the application of its policies and the day-to-day administration of its activities. He believed that this would encourage members to consult the Fund more readily and at an earlier stage in their difficulties. As it was, the tendency for members to ask their Executive Directors first to discuss their problems with other Directors delayed consideration by the Fund, and resulted in insufficient use being made of the accumulated experience of the management and staff. It should be noted, however, that this practice was declining even toward the end of Mr. Rooth's tenure of office, and since 1956 it has changed decisively.

---

[28] *Annual Report, 1957*, p. 114.

We may conclude this study of the first ten years of the Fund's work by quoting a tribute paid to it by an erstwhile strong critic of the Bretton Woods institutions. Mr. W. Randolph Burgess, who in 1945, as president of the American Bankers Association, had strenuously campaigned against the Bretton Woods Agreements Act, was in 1957 Temporary Alternate Governor of the Fund for the United States at the Annual Meetings of the Fund and Bank. In that capacity he said:

> That the Fund could meet the challenge of the events of the past 12 months is not an accident. It is due to three main facts. The first is that the Fund established a body of principles to guide it and the members both in the devising of policies and in the use of its resources. The second is that the Fund patiently acquired experience during the quieter years of its existence. The third is that through analysis and through consultation with members, the Fund has assisted members in devising sound policies and programs of action.[29]

[29] *Summary Proceedings, 1957*, p. 57.

CHAPTER

16

Action and Reaction (1956-57)

THE YEAR 1956–57 was in some respects a turning point for the Fund. The volume of drawings effected, $1,478 million, was larger than the total of drawings in the nine and a half years from the time that the Fund's resources were first made available until the end of September 1956. In addition, new stand-by arrangements approved totaled $1,200 million—overwhelmingly more than the total of such arrangements in all previous years.

For this sudden spate of activity the principal cause was the Suez incident. The Canal was nationalized in July 1956. Three months later Egypt was attacked by France, Israel, and the United Kingdom. On November 2 the Canal was closed by the Egyptian authorities. It was not fully cleared until April 10, 1957, and the interruption of traffic interfered with earnings from invisibles, by France and the United Kingdom in particular. Although the mild winter reduced the direct losses sustained, speculation against sterling and the French franc continued throughout the year. The resulting drawings by the countries concerned are discussed below.

MEMBERSHIP AND BOARD

Four countries joined the Fund during the year—Ireland on August 8, 1957, Saudi Arabia on August 26, Sudan on September 5, and Ghana on September 20.

Executive Board

The biennial election of the Executive Directors was held on September 27, 1956, and resulted in the re-election of Messrs. Bury (Australia), Emminger (Germany), Gragnani (Italy), Lieftinck (Netherlands), Rasminsky (Canada), Saad (Egypt), and van Campenhout (Belgium). Mr. Torben Friis (Denmark) was elected in place of Mr. Åkermalm, whose Alternate he had been since November

1954, and Mr. Takeshi Watanabe (Japan) succeeded Mr. Yumoto. Viet-Nam, Afghanistan, and Korea, participating in the election for the first time, voted, respectively, for Mr. Bury, Mr. Saad, and Mr. van Campenhout.

On August 8, 1956, the Directors had recommended to the Board of Governors that if Argentina joined the Fund before the pending election, the number of Executive Directors representing Latin America should be increased from two to three. Argentina did in fact join on September 20, 1956, and three Directors were accordingly chosen. Mr. Paranaguá (Brazil) was re-elected, Mr. Jorge Sol (El Salvador) succeeded Mr. Luna-Guerra, whose Alternate he had been for the previous two years, and Mr. Rodolfo Corominas-Segura (Argentina) was elected as the third Director. Bolivia, Chile, Ecuador, Paraguay, and Uruguay, all of which had previously voted for Mr. Paranaguá, now voted for Mr. Corominas-Segura, as did Argentina. Colombia, which had previously voted for Mr. Luna-Guerra, now participated in the election of Mr. Paranaguá.

Later in the year 1956–57 there were three other changes in the Board. On February 1, 1957, Mr. Guy F. Thorold (United Kingdom) was appointed to succeed Lord Harcourt. On March 9, 1957, Mr. B. B. Callaghan (Australia) was elected to succeed Mr. Bury, whose Alternate he had been since November 1954, and on June 11, 1957, Mr. Bhaskar Namdeo Adarkar (India) was appointed to succeed Mr. Prasad.

Mr. Jacobsson assumed his responsibilities as Managing Director and Chairman of the Board on December 3, 1956. In a characteristic initial address he called the Board's attention to historical analogies for the problems facing the Fund, comparing the world situation in 1956 with that in 1848 and in 1931. He said that he had been pleased in his preliminary study of the Articles to find that they need not materially hamper the Fund in its attempts to deal with these problems, not only in the field of monetary policy but also in public finance and cost-price relationships; and he added that the time had come to inaugurate a "new tradition."

Consultations

The annual consultations with members continued to occupy a large proportion of the Board's time. Forty-five consultations were held during 1956–57. The procedure already described continued to operate, although as the year went on there was a tendency for the staff discussions with members to take place more and more often in members' capitals than in Washington. Again the opportunity was taken at each annual consultation to discuss all current problems arising in the member's economy. As a result of the knowledge of these problems which the Board was accumulating over the years, it became increasingly possible for Directors to approach proposals to draw on the Fund's resources with an extensive and, indeed, sympathetic knowledge of the difficulties with which members had been contending.

TECHNICAL ASSISTANCE

During the year more requests were received by the Fund for technical assistance to members—and, indeed, in one instance (Laos) to a nonmember. During the first few months of the year the Board was content to leave the financial arrangements, for the staff detailed for these duties, to be negotiated between the management and the countries concerned. In April 1957, however, difficulties experienced by some members of the staff detailed for such duties, and embarrassments caused them—for example, through having to rely for their salaries upon a dilatory government—led the management to feel that the time had come when the remuneration of staff members on technical assistance assignments should be paid by the Fund rather than be the subject of an arrangement with the country assisted. The proposal was submitted to the Board in June on the footing that the Fund would continue to pay the salary of the staff members detailed for technical assistance duties, and would pay also their traveling expenses, while the government would be asked to provide a subsistence allowance. On the understanding that this did not apply where a staff member was detached for service to a member country in a private capacity, Executive Directors agreed with the management's proposal. Indeed, the only serious question raised was whether the Fund should not also accept the responsibility for paying a subsistence allowance. Since 1965 it has been the practice for the Fund to pay such allowances in all instances except where the staff member is providing expert assistance at the request of a member country.

EXCHANGE TRANSACTIONS

The first of the major transactions of the year was a request by France for a one-year stand-by arrangement for $262.5 million, equivalent to one half of its quota. This arrangement was negotiated in Paris by Mr. Jacobsson himself. As explained to the Board, the difficulties faced by France were partly transitory and partly fundamental, and Directors had no hesitation in agreeing to the proposal. The effect of the closing of the Suez Canal, added to France's other difficulties, led to the progressive use of the stand-by arrangement until by June 1957 France had drawn the entire amount available. Meanwhile the United Kingdom had approached the Board for an even larger transaction: it drew $561,470,000 and was given a stand-by arrangement for $738,530,000 on December 10. The drawing raised the Fund's holdings of sterling to 125 per cent of the British quota, and the drawing and stand-by arrangement together represented 100 per cent of that quota. The United Kingdom's difficulties had been mounting since July, being due partly to an adverse change in "leads and lags" and partly to a running down of sterling balances by India to meet commitments under its development plan. In November these strains were reinforced by adverse speculative reactions to the hostilities against Egypt, and to a small extent by the loss of earnings from invisibles caused by the closing of the Canal. Reserves fell by $84 million in October 1956 and by $279 million in November. As it turned out, the stand-by arrangement was not used, although recurring difficulties led the United Kingdom to ask for its renewal in 1957 and again in 1958.

Other large drawings made during the year were $200 million by India, $125 million by Japan, and $75 million by Argentina. The Netherlands drew $68.75 million and obtained a stand-by arrangement for a similar sum, which, however, was not used and was canceled after six months. India drew a part of its total under a stand-by arrangement for $72.5 million agreed in February 1957. Belgium drew $50 million under the stand-by arrangement first granted in 1952. In all, as noted above, drawings totaled $1,478 million.

The effect of the drawings and the stand-by arrangements on the Fund's financial position was to make a large contribution toward wiping out the deficit of $14 million in the Fund's accounts which had existed at the beginning of the fiscal year. Between April 1956 and April 1957 the Fund earned almost $8.4 million in charges, in addition to nearly $5 million in income from investments, resulting in an excess of income over expenditure for the year of almost $8 million. The consequences of this development for the Fund's investment program are considered in Chapter 17.

CONDITIONS FOR STAND-BY ARRANGEMENTS DEVELOPED

By 1956–57 the terms for stand-by arrangements had begun to crystallize in a series of operative clauses which, with minor verbal changes, has remained the nub of all arrangements since that time. The first clause contained a description of the need for the stand-by arrangement, and of the measures which the member was taking to combat its difficulties. There followed clauses (*a*) specifying the total amount that might be drawn (in terms of a set increase over the Fund's existing holdings of its currency); (*b*) requiring the member to pay charges and to repay any drawing within three years; and (*c*) declaring that its right to draw was unchallengeable unless the member was formally declared ineligible or the Fund decided to suspend its right to draw, either under the general provisions of Article XVI, Section 1 (*a*) (ii), or in order to consider a proposal by an Executive Director or the Managing Director to suppress or limit its right to draw.

In addition to these general clauses, many of the stand-by arrangements included special provisions applicable only to the member concerned. For instance, the first stand-by arrangement approved in 1956 (that with Chile in March) raised some of the problems that had been faced when drafting the arrangement for Peru two years earlier. The arrangement was for a year, so that the proviso as to additional "understandings" in the decision of December 23, 1953 applied. Moreover, Chile had a fluctuating exchange rate. However, the terms prescribed did not follow the precedent set in the arrangement with Peru, by which the Fund could in effect terminate the contingent availability of its resources if it believed that developments had rendered the Peruvian Exchange Stabilization Fund ineffective. Instead, the special conditions were as follows: (1) Currencies drawn from the Fund were to be used to secure an orderly exchange market for a fluctuating peso in the free banking market. (2) Of the total drawings permissible under the stand-by arrangement—$35 million—only $12.5 million might be drawn immediately; if more was required, it might be drawn, "unless the Fund notifies Chile to the contrary," in installments of $6.25 million at intervals of thirty days.

The first of these conditions limited the use to be made of the sums drawn from the Fund. The second introduced the limitation known as "phasing," which has since been used with increasing frequency where there has been reason to believe that it would be appropriate for the member to have access only gradually to the resources made available. Another special clause required the member to remain in close consultation with the Fund. Since Chile's par value was inoperative, it was also stipulated that the Fund would fix the exchange rate at which the transactions would be consummated. Finally, the entire arrangement was stated to be "in consideration of" the policies and intentions of the member.

The stipulation in the arrangement with Peru, that drawing rights might be suspended on an appropriate indication by the Fund, was not repeated in any stand-by arrangement within the period with which we are now concerned. Toward the end of the period, however, an arrangement with Paraguay included a provision that the drawing rights conferred would not be exercised without consulting the Fund if certain ceilings were exceeded. These ceilings—on the volume of credit and on the commitment level for ordinary and for development budget expenditure—had been prescribed in the report of a Paraguayan Special Study Commission on the Exchange System.

Including the arrangements with Chile and Paraguay, eleven new stand-by arrangements were introduced during the eighteen months beginning April 1956. In four of these no special clauses were used; the members concerned were Cuba and Nicaragua (for each of which the arrangement was for six months), the Netherlands, and the United Kingdom. For France (twelve months) and Iran (six months) the only stipulation was that the Fund would fix the exchange rate for any transactions—there being no operative par value in either country. Each of the other five stand-by arrangements included a clause requiring the member to remain in consultation with the Fund. This was the only special clause in the arrangement with India. Those with Bolivia and Colombia were described as being "in view of" their policies and intentions; in addition, drawings by Bolivia were phased, while those by Colombia were restricted to specified purposes. The arrangement with Paraguay, in addition to the special limitation mentioned above, provided for restricted use of any sums drawn and for phasing; further, this arrangement, like that of Chile, was expressed to be "in consideration of" the member's policies and intentions.

These various stipulations were the subject of considerable comment in the Board. When the stand-by arrangement with Chile was proposed, in March 1956, Mr. Heasman (United Kingdom) commended the proposal to "phase" drawings, in the light of the dependence of the Chilean stabilization program on the achievement and maintenance of internal stability. Mr. Luna-Guerra (Mexico) observed that the conditions attached to the arrangement modified the irrevocable line of credit intended in the Board's decision of December 1953 into a *sui generis* contract suitable to the special circumstances of Chile. Other Directors supported the terms proposed, emphasizing also the importance of the obligation placed on Chile to maintain close consultation with the Fund.

The inclusion of somewhat similar terms in the arrangement with Bolivia later in 1956 was not questioned, but when in July 1957 the draft arrangement with Paraguay came before the Board it was discussed at some length. Mr. Sol (El Salvador) pointed out that the terms included in this arrangement gave the Fund, in effect, the right to cancel it; he suggested that they would more properly be placed in a covering letter than in the arrangement itself. However, Mr. Gustavo F. A. Storm, President of the Central Bank of Paraguay, who attended the meeting of the Board to support Paraguay's request, stated that the conditions proposed in the arrangements were acceptable to Paraguay, and Mr. Sol then withdrew his suggestion.

Mr. Thorold (United Kingdom) remarked that this was the first occasion on which a stand-by arrangement had been linked to budgetary figures. While he did not object to their inclusion, he wished to make it clear that this should not be taken as a precedent. Mr. P. J. J. Pinto (India), Alternate to Mr. Adarkar, thought that it would have been better to be less specific in the conditions imposed, but did not press the point since Paraguay had accepted the draft arrangement. Mr. Southard (United States) commented that in the light of its experience the Fund had learnt the advisability of adjusting the terms of its stand-by arrangements according to the situation of each country and the circumstances in which that situation had developed.

FURTHER DEVELOPMENTS

In the next two years the terms and conditions of the stand-by arrangements approved took somewhat further the process of evolving appropriate special conditions for members' varying circumstances. Three categories of arrangements may be distinguished. The simplest, having no special conditions at all, were those with South Africa in March 1958 and with the United Kingdom in December 1957 and December 1958. A second group, having only one or two special conditions, included the arrangement with France, which was said to be "in consideration of the policies and intentions" of the French Government as set forth in a memorandum attached to the arrangement. Others in this category were five approved for members with seasonal problems, which provided for the repurchase of any drawing within six months: El Salvador in August 1958 and September 1959, Honduras in November 1957, and Nicaragua in October 1957 and September 1958. These included the requirement that the member would remain in close consultation with the Fund, as did the arrangements with Pakistan in December 1958 and with Spain in July 1959. Both the latter, and also the first arrangement with Nicaragua, were expressed to be "in consideration of" the policies and intentions of the members' Governments.

The third group of arrangements, much the most numerous, included all, or almost all, the seven special conditions described above. The countries concerned were all in Latin America—Argentina, Bolivia, Brazil, Chile, Colombia, Haiti, Honduras (a second arrangement), Mexico, Paraguay, and Peru. One example will suffice: the arrangement with Chile approved in March 1958. Annexed to this was a copy of a letter to the Managing Director from the Minister of Finance and the President of the Central Bank of Chile, setting out Chile's problems and the steps which Chile proposed to take to deal with them. This letter included an undertaking that if certain ceilings were exceeded, viz., those on government expenditures, on the loans and investments of the Central Bank of Chile, or on the total currency issue of the Central Bank, Chile would consult with the Fund and agree with it on the terms on which further drawings would be made. The stand-by arrangement was expressed to be "in consideration of the policies and intentions set forth in the annexed letter," and the undertaking contained in it was mentioned as a qualification in the paragraph giving Chile the right to draw under the arrangement. In the same paragraph, reference was made to a right reserved by the Fund to give notice to Chile to cease drawing. The other requirements of the arrangement were that Chile would keep in close consultation with the Fund, would use any amounts drawn for the purpose of maintaining orderly exchanges for a fluctuating peso in the free banking market, and would limit drawings to a maximum of $2 million in each period of thirty days. The final paragraph stated that the Fund would fix the exchange rate at which transactions under the arrangement would be effected.

It may be noted here that the device of appending to the stand-by arrangement a letter describing the member's proposals for corrective measures had been inaugurated in connection with the stand-by arrangement with Peru in February 1958. Subsequently such a letter, known as a "letter of intent," became common form. It superseded less formal intimations of members' plans, which had previously either been set out in the staff's report recommending the stand-by arrangement, or been given orally to the Board, or both. The existence of letters of intent gave additional effect to the stipulation, henceforward included in nearly all stand-by arrangements, that they were granted "in consideration of" the policies and intentions set out in the letters. A letter of intent also provided an occasion for the member to undertake, as Chile did, to consult the Fund before drawing further, should the program described in the letter not be fulfilled. A large proportion of the stand-by arrangements introduced in and after 1958 have included letters of intent embodying such undertakings, in addition to the right reserved to the Fund in the stand-by arrangement itself to give notice that further drawings may not be made without consulting the Fund.

The right given to the Fund to give such notice was exercised on one occasion only. In September 1958 the staff informed the Board that Bolivia had found itself unable to carry out the stabilization program for the support of which the stand-by arrangement had been granted. By that time, $2 million out of the total of $3.5 million provided under the arrangement had been drawn. The staff recommended that notice should be given to Bolivia, under the terms of the arrangement, that no further drawings should be made until the Government and the Fund had agreed on terms for such further drawings. This was approved by the Board on September 17, and the staff then resumed discussions with Bolivia looking toward the preparation of a new program. New undertakings regarded by the staff as satisfactory were given in November. The Board accepted these under the lapse of time procedure, and Bolivia was notified that drawings might be resumed.

THE FUND'S RESOURCES REPLENISHED

Repurchases made during the year 1956–57 amounted to only $89 million, with the result that the Fund's holdings of U.S. dollars fell from $1,698 million in September 1956 to $1,142 million by the end of the calendar year. At the latter date, commitments under stand-by arrangements totaled $1,117 million. At the suggestion of Mr. Southard (United States), the Managing Director proposed to the Board that use should be made of the provisions of Article VII, Section 2, for the replenishment of the Fund's holdings of scarce currencies. Mr. Jacobsson recommended to the Board in January 1957 that $300 million worth of gold should be sold to the United States for dollars. Mr. Southard told the Board that the proposal was regarded favorably by the U.S. Treasury, which was experiencing particularly heavy calls for cash. The Federal Reserve Board had also expressed agreement, although it would wish to be kept informed of the sales of gold as they were made. The U.S. Treasury had agreed to recommend the waiver of the charge of 1/4 of 1 per cent usually made for transactions in gold. Other Directors who spoke on the proposal all agreed to it.

Four months later Mr. Southard suggested to the Managing Director, who proposed to the Board, a further sale of gold up to $300 million, since the Fund's holdings of dollars had meanwhile further been reduced to $977 million. Again the Board was content that the transaction should go through, although Mr. de Largentaye (France) questioned the staff's statement that the Fund's holdings of dollars might not be adequate. Replying to this, the staff pointed out that the Fund's outstanding obligations, including the commitment under the stand-by arrangement for the United Kingdom, totaled $968.9 million. Mr. Lieftinck (Netherlands), Mr. van Campenhout (Belgium), and Mr. Alan Bond Hockin (Canada), Alternate to Mr. Rasminsky, agreed that the position disclosed by the staff showed that there was a need for the sale, although Mr. Lieftinck did not think that the problem was an urgent one. The only hesitation expressed in the Board was by Mr. Prasad (India), who thought that the Fund should not continue to use the procedure of Article VII, Section 2, once the amount of gold sold to the United States exceeded the amount which the United States had originally contributed to the Fund (25 per cent of its quota). Against this, Mr. van Campenhout pointed out that the gold which the Fund was selling was its own gold, and should not be identified with that which the United States had originally contributed.

The gold was sold in installments, and the sale of the $600 million was completed shortly after this discussion.

While these transactions relieved the immediate strain on the Fund's resources to meet its commitments, increasing concern was expressed at the Annual Meeting, 1957, about the possibility that some more general increase in these resources would shortly become necessary. The Managing Director pointed out that the Fund's uncommitted holdings of U.S. and Canadian dollars had been halved during the year, and Mr. Abdul Qadir, Governor for Pakistan, reminded the Governors that almost all drawings and stand-by arrangements negotiated during 1956 and 1957 had required waivers of the quantitative limits in Article V, Section 3; this seemed to him to suggest that quotas were too small for the increased volume of international trade. In terms which were to be increasingly used by other speakers in later years, Mr. Wilfrid Baumgartner, Alternate Governor for France, asserted that a lack of international liquidity had become a basic problem for the Fund.[1]

[1] *Summary Proceedings, 1957*, pp. 21, 86–87, 149.

MULTIPLE RATES AGAIN

The Board continued during the year to deal with proposals for changes in exchange systems. Initial par values were agreed for Argentina and Israel, changes in par values (devaluations) for Iran and Finland, and minor variations for eight other countries. In addition, the Board took note of a series of minor changes in the exchange system of China, which were reported under the special arrangements agreed with that country in 1948.

Of more general significance than these individual decisions was a review of multiple currency practices undertaken by the Board in 1957. It was based on a staff study which showed that out of the 60 countries that were then members of the Fund, some 38 used multiple currency practices of one kind or another. In 15–18 countries such practices were important elements in the economy, and in 10–12 of these countries the systems could be described as complex.

The staff recalled that in the past the Board had acquiesced in the use of multiple currency practices in countries where the only feasible alternative was quantitative restrictions, or in countries where they permitted a relaxation of quantitative restrictions, or in those where multiple currency arrangements offered the only practicable way of depreciating an overvalued currency. The Board had, however, stressed the disadvantages of multiple exchange rates even in such circumstances, and the time seemed opportune for a full reconsideration of the subject, especially in view of the Fund's earlier studies of bilateralism and discrimination.

It seemed to the staff that the continuing use of multiple currency practices threatened undesirable consequences, not only for the countries retaining them but also for others; they tended to create unfair competition and a state of uncertainty which was harmful to trade. For these reasons the staff recommended that the Fund should increase its efforts to discourage multiple currency practices, and in particular intensify pressure on countries using them to simplify their practices as far as possible. The aim should be to encourage members which had hitherto relied on complex systems to adopt either a broad free market in which the exchange rate could fluctuate, or a small number of fixed exchange rates, or the parallel existence of fixed and free exchange rates for trade, with perhaps an additional free market for invisibles and capital.

The staff also proposed that the Fund should discontinue its practice of offering no objection to systems which it disliked but was reluctant to disapprove; that it should instead withhold approval in such circumstances, or give "advance approval" of proposed future steps toward a more desirable system. The staff suggested that the management should be free to decide that it was appropriate in a given instance to withhold approval, and to recommend this course to the Board.

This review came before the Board at the end of January 1957 and provoked an intensive discussion. The Executive Directors from the Latin American countries were naturally the most concerned. Mr. Paranaguá (Brazil) protested that undue stress was being placed on the disadvantages of multiple currency practices, which he regarded as less undesirable than certain of the arrangements maintained by some reserve currency countries. Moreover, he thought that the staff showed insufficient awareness of the deep-rooted causes of the use of multiple currency practices, and should have proposed suitable alternative measures—for instance, export taxes. Mr. Paranaguá urged that the Board should focus attention on certain consequences of multiple currency practices, including discrimination and export subsidization, rather than on the practices themselves.

Mr. Sol (El Salvador) pointed out the difficulty which an Executive Director representing a number of different countries experienced in obtaining instructions, and said that for this reason the views he expressed would necessarily be tentative. Since 38 member countries employed multiple currency practices, these were clearly important. However, several kinds of practices did not conflict with the Fund's objectives. For instance, Cuba imposed a 2 per cent tax on all foreign payments, Costa Rica had a dual exchange market, and Venezuela had two buying rates. None of these systems was discriminatory, and in Mr. Sol's view it was discriminatory arrangements that the Fund should most earnestly discourage—though even there he would not wish to press the Fund's views to the point of open conflict with members. Real progress was, in his view, being made in a number of countries, and the Fund should develop closer ties with these members and help them toward better systems.

Executive Directors representing developed countries were naturally more sympathetic with the viewpoint of the staff paper. Mr. Southard (United States) did not think that multiple currency practices were ever helpful, on balance, unless they were extremely simple ones. He suggested that the Board should intensify efforts toward the Fund's goal of unitary exchange rates, and should decide that countries with complex multiple currency practices could not count on obtaining continuing approval for them. In the past the Board's decisions not to object to certain practices had created an unsatisfactory situation. He thought that some systems—for example, those involving a wide spread in exchange rates—should not be tolerated any longer.

Mr. Heasman (United Kingdom) would go further; he thought that even simple multiple currency systems should be ended. Countries adopting multiple currency practices tended, in his view, to drift from one palliative to another, creating increasing complexities by doing so. He did not think that full internal stability, however desirable, was a necessary precursor to a unitary exchange rate. Agreeing with the two previous speakers, Mr. van Campenhout (Belgium) thought that it was time more progress was made toward the elimination of multiple currency practices, particularly where they were so complex that the concept of exchange parity had lost all meaning. He suggested that the Fund should not approve changes in multiple currency systems unless the member showed an intention of progressing toward a unitary rate.

Mr. Emminger (Germany) spoke in support of Mr. Southard's position, as did Mr. Warren (Canada). Mr. Emminger said that stress should be laid upon the technical, and especially upon the financial, help that the Fund could give to members seeking to free themselves from multiple currency practices, but Mr. Warren was doubtful whether the Fund should commit itself to drawings for the purpose. Mr. Watanabe (Japan) and Mr. Gragnani (Italy) concurred generally with the staff's recommendations, but felt that the Board must avoid dogmatism. Mr. Prasad (India) suggested that the staff should be invited to classify the 38 countries using multiple currency practices in terms of the progressive undesirability of their systems. He felt that this would assist the Board to make more rapid progress toward eliminating those practices hampering international trade.

Mr. de Largentaye (France) recalled that in 1947 he had protested against the Board's decision to approve or disapprove all changes in multiple currency practices, and suggested that this decision had created much trouble for the Board—trouble accentuated by the fact that advice of pending changes in these systems was very often received at short notice. Mr. Bury (Australia), on the other hand, agreed with Messrs. Southard and Emminger, and said that the countries which had elected him were particularly concerned about other countries' multiple currency arrangements that subsidized exports. Mr. Friis (Denmark), while welcoming the staff's paper, thought that the procedure proposed for "advance approval" was likely to encounter the difficulty that governments might be unable to enter into the necessary firm commitments.

The diversity of opinions expressed at the Board made the formulation of an agreed decision somewhat difficult, and a draft originally prepared by the staff was extensively reworked over the next several weeks. Particular objection was taken by Mr. Sol to a clause in the early drafts to the effect that the Fund would be reluctant to approve changes in even simple systems unless they were in the direction of further simplification, and this was later dropped. Eventually, on May 1, 1957, the Board approved a revised decision *ad referendum* to members. On June 26, the Executive Directors reported the approval of members, and the formal decision was accordingly taken.[2] After citing the experience of the previous ten years as showing the disadvantages of multiple currency practices, the Executive Board concluded that "it is necessary and feasible to make more rapid progress in simplifying complex multiple rate systems, to remove

[2] E.B. Decision No. 649-(57/33), June 26, 1957; below, Vol. III, p. 265.

those aspects of existing systems which adversely affect the interests of other members, and to avoid existing systems becoming more complex."

The decision taken, which is reported in full in Volume II of this history, included statements that the Fund would not approve complex multiple rate systems unless progress was being made toward simplifying and ultimately eliminating them; that it would press for the simplification of any systems found to be damaging to other members; that it would be ready to provide technical assistance in preparing programs to simplify exchange systems; and that where it deemed such programs to be adequate and appropriate it would give sympathetic consideration to requests for the use of its resources.

This decision was commended to the Governors by the Managing Director in both his opening and closing speeches at the Annual Meeting.[3] That it met with general support is clear from the references made to it by several speakers, including two—Mr. Santiago Sologuren (Alternate Governor for Bolivia) and Mr. Manuel Gill Morlis (Governor for Paraguay)—who had had experience of the benefits derived from terminating such systems in their own countries.[4]

ECONOMIC STUDIES

Early in the 1950's the staff, in addition to advising the Board on immediate problems, embarked upon more fundamental research. This was continued and, indeed, extended during 1956–57. To facilitate distinguishing between memoranda which were intended for specific consideration by the Board and others which were intended only for the Board's general information, a separate series of documents was created in 1956 to serve as a vehicle for papers of the second kind. During 1956–57 about fifty such papers were issued, ranging from monthly reports on the price of gold in various world markets to major studies on the instruments of monetary policy and detailed surveys of financial institutions and development plans in a dozen or so developing countries. These papers were in addition to two considerable investigations arising directly out of matters coming before the Board: one on the appropriate treatment of the national currency counterpart of drawings on the Fund, and the other on the effects of wage-price links in a prolonged inflation. Both of these, together with the most important of the more general studies, were printed in *Staff Papers*.[5]

National currency counterparts

During the Annual Meeting, 1956, several Governors had drawn attention in informal discussions to the problem of the correct handling of the national

[3] *Summary Proceedings, 1957*, pp. 20, 90.

[4] *Ibid.*, pp. 37, 82; cf. p. 74.

[5] *Staff Papers*, Vol. VI (1957–58), pp. 171–79, 323–68, and *passim*.

currencies that corresponded to sums drawn from the Fund. This was also noted by Mr. de Largentaye (France) in the course of the second meeting of the Executive Board at which approval was given for the sale of gold to replenish the Fund's holdings of dollars. Mr. de Largentaye pointed out that in certain circumstances the use of the national currencies created by drawings could be inflationary; he thought that this had not been realized at Bretton Woods.

The point had come before the Executive Board once before, in January 1950, when Mr. de Selliers (Belgium) proposed that the Fund should require members to sterilize the counterpart of drawings. The Board then decided, after a brief discussion, that the Fund had no power to take the action that Mr. de Selliers proposed.

As a result of the Governors' comments in 1956 the staff had been working on an analysis of the problem, and Mr. Cochran, Acting Chairman, suggested to the Board that discussion of Mr. de Largentaye's point should be deferred until this analysis was available. It was presented to the Board at the end of June 1957, and included a comprehensive review of the ways in which members that had drawn from the Fund had dealt with the national currencies corresponding to such drawings. The staff showed that where the foreign exchange provided by the Fund had been acquired by the member's central bank and sold to the public, the effect had been to increase the central bank's liabilities to the Fund and to reduce by an equal amount the money supply in the member country. More often, however, the foreign exchange had been acquired by the government, which had sold it to the central bank or to an exchange equalization fund for national currency. The effect on the money supply then depended upon what the government did with the currency received. Where it left this on deposit, the effect was the same as if the central bank had acquired the foreign exchange direct. If the government spent the national currency (for example, after substituting noninterest-bearing notes for it), no reduction in the money supply necessarily followed. Whether there was a reduction or not depended upon the object of the government's spending—for example, to repay a debt to the central bank or to the public, or to finance its current expenditure. The latter was clearly inconsistent with the policy needed to reduce a balance of payments deficit; the effects of debt repayment differed according to the subsequent actions of the government on the one hand and the public on the other. The general conclusion which the staff drew from the analysis, therefore, was that there was a considerable possibility that members might use the national currency counterpart of drawings from the Fund in such a way as to prolong an undesirable fiscal or monetary policy. Where this was done, the Fund should deprecate the practice.

This analysis was considered by the Board at a meeting on July 19, 1957. Most of the Executive Directors who spoke, while approving its general trend, questioned whether it was possible to lay down hard and fast rules for the proper treatment of national currency counterparts. Mr. Lieftinck (Netherlands) disagreed; in his belief, the national currency counterparts of drawings should always be sterilized so as to forestall any temptation to use them for internal financing, and to facilitate repurchases in due course. (It will be remembered that at the Annual Meeting in 1948 Mr. Lieftinck, then Governor for the Netherlands, had expressed disquiet about the local currency proceeds of aid under the European Recovery Program.[6] A similar point was made by Mr. Holtrop, Governor for the Netherlands in 1954, in the course of his address as Chairman of the Annual Meetings in that year.[7]) Mr. Lieftinck also mentioned an analogous problem, that some member countries tended to draw on the Fund to meet domestic treasury problems rather than because of balance of payments difficulties; he thought that where such a reason for a prospective drawing appeared to exist the member should be warned beforehand. Summing up the discussion, the Managing Director pointed to the importance of sterilization in the recovery of Austria in 1922, and suggested that it would have been better if France had sterilized the counterpart of Marshall Aid. He therefore favored sterilization as a policy, although he agreed that no hard and fast rule was practicable. He suggested that the memorandum should be made public, and (as noted above) it was subsequently published in *Staff Papers*.

Wage-price links in a prolonged inflation

During the course of the consultation with Chile in February 1957, several references were made to the link between wages and prices that had recently been severed there, and later in the year Mr. Bernstein produced an analysis of the relationship of such ties to a prolonged inflation. The main conclusion drawn was that a link between wages and prices was neither a cause of, nor a cure for, an inflation. Inflationary pressures arose whenever there was excessive expenditure financed by the creation of credit, and a study of the experiences of countries which had sustained inflations showed that links between wages and prices tended to develop after the inflation had taken hold. These ties were disadvantageous in that they were almost certain to increase to some extent the rigidity of the wage structure. On the other hand, if the wage base linked to prices was not too high for the productivity of the economy, the creation of such a link might give the monetary authority an opportunity to institute a comprehensive stabilization program.

This memorandum was also discussed by the Board on July 19. It was in general favorably received, although Mr. Callaghan (Australia) commented that a link between wages and prices might be established for other reasons than an

---

[6] See above, p. 222.

[7] *Summary Proceedings, 1954*, p. 26.

inflation, and there was some feeling on the part of other Directors that it was unwise to suggest, as had been done in the conclusion, that links between wages and prices might be helpful. Mr. Donner (Germany) also stressed that the analysis of the paper was relevant only to a prolonged inflation, and suggested that its conclusions should be revised to make this clearer. The staff was accordingly invited to reconsider the draft.

A revised version of the paper was put to the Board three months later, and discussed on October 30. The conclusion had been rewritten to avoid the appearance of recommending wage-price links, and the changes were generally approved by the Board. It was this revised memorandum that was printed in *Staff Papers.*

ANNUAL REPORT AND ANNUAL MEETING

The main theme of the Annual Report for 1957, which was considered by the Board at seven meetings in June and July 1957, was set on its opening page. "The Struggle for Stability," the title given to the first section of Chapter I of the Report, was studied against the background of the progress of Europe since World War II. Stress was laid on the all-pervasive need for capital, and on the inflation that had resulted where savings had failed to keep pace with the claims made for development purposes on the volume of production.[8]

Referring to the Suez crisis, the Report found it encouraging that difficult internal adjustments had been made with considerable success, and that it had proved possible, with the assistance of the Fund, to avoid a reintroduction of the restrictive practices that had been relaxed over the previous ten years. Nevertheless, the maintenance or re-establishment of internal stability continued to be an essential condition both for restoring balance of payments equilibrium and for other economic objectives. In this connection, the Report suggested that higher interest rates should be accepted as a necessary price to pay to secure the requisite volume of savings. Reference was also made to the continuing problem of unstable prices for primary products, and to the need for surplus countries to avoid applying anti-inflationary policies in such a way as to make it more difficult for other countries to adjust their positions.

At the formal sessions of the Governors' Meeting the topics touched upon in the Annual Report dominated the speeches. Almost every page of the printed volume which reproduced them contains references to inflation, to monetary and fiscal policies, to the balance of payments, to interest rates, or to prices.[9]

---

[8] *Annual Report, 1957,* pp. 1–8.

[9] *Summary Proceedings, 1957, passim.*

Pursuing a similar line of thought, the managements of the Fund and the Bank arranged for an informal panel discussion of "Current Problems of Credit and Fiscal Policy" to be held on the Wednesday afternoon during the Annual Meetings which took place in Washington from September 23 to 27. At this informal session, the speakers were Mr. William McChesney Martin, Chairman of the Board of Governors of the Federal Reserve System, Mr. H. V. R. Iengar, Governor of the Reserve Bank of India, Mr. Juan Pardo, Minister of Finance of Peru, and Sir Dennis Robertson, Professor of Political Economy in the University of Cambridge.

Mr. Martin spoke forcibly about the need to restrain inflationary tendencies in developed countries, Messrs. Iengar and Pardo about the problems of Asia and Latin America, and Sir Dennis Robertson about the role of the rate of interest and the dangers of inflated wage claims. Mr. Jacobsson summed up and added a historical background. A transcript of the speeches was subsequently printed and distributed to all member countries.[10]

It is tempting to quote extensively from all the addresses, but their contents belong rather to the economic history of the period than to the history of the Fund. One quotation, from Sir Dennis Robertson, must suffice. He referred to his association with the origins of the Fund and the Bank, and to the change that had come over the Fund in recent months.

> My thoughts inevitably go back [Sir Dennis said] to a sultry evening in Chicago 14 years ago, when it fell to my lot, as a very minor cog in the British Treasury machine, to join with an American colleague in explaining to a polite, but I think rather puzzled, gathering of Federal Reserve Bank directors how desirable it was that some kind of international monetary institution should be brought to birth before the end of the war. Our task was rendered somewhat delicate by the fact that our respective superiors were by no means yet in agreement as to what the shape and function of this unborn child should be. But in spite of that, and in spite of the heat, it was a very pleasant evening, and in due course the child was born, and turned out to be twins. One of them has always been a sturdy, steady-going fellow; the other at times perhaps has looked a bit pale and ill at ease. But today at any rate, both are in bouncing health. . . .

This was the last occasion on which such informal afternoon discussions were arranged by the Fund. Attendance at, and interest in, them proved to be too small to justify a place for them in the crowded agenda for the Annual Meetings.

[10] *Current Problems of Credit and Fiscal Policy: An Informal Discussion* (Washington, 1957).

CHAPTER

17

The Fund Enlarged

(1957-59)

THE YEAR FROM SEPTEMBER 1957 to September 1958 was, for the Fund, largely devoted to preparing for the events of the following year. The latter was notable in the Fund's annals for two major events: the achievement by fifteen European countries of external convertibility for their currencies, and the first general increase in quotas for members of the Fund. The two years from September 1957 to September 1959 will here be dealt with together.

MEMBERS AND BOARD

Five new members joined the Fund between the Twelfth Annual Meeting in September 1957 and the Fourteenth Annual Meeting in September–October 1959, both of which were held in Washington. The new members were Malaya, which joined in March 1958, Tunisia and Morocco (April 1958), and Spain and Libya (September 1958). In July 1958 Egypt and Syria joined together to form the United Arab Republic, which was recognized as a Fund member with a quota equal to the sum of those previously held by the two constituent countries. By September 1958, therefore, the Fund had 68 members, of whom nine had joined since the Sixth Biennial Election of Executive Directors in 1956. Accordingly, the Executive Board recommended, and the Governors agreed, that for the purposes of the Seventh Biennial Election in 1958 the number of Directors should be increased to eighteen.

At this election, which was held on October 9, 1958 during the Thirteenth Annual Meeting in New Delhi, eight Directors were re-elected: Messrs. Callaghan (Australia), Emminger (Germany), Gragnani (Italy), Lieftinck (Netherlands), Paranaguá (Brazil), Saad (United Arab Republic), van Campenhout (Belgium), and Watanabe (Japan). Mr. Eero Asp (Finland) was elected in place of Mr. Friis, Mr. Rodrigo Gómez (Mexico) returned to the Board in place of Mr. Sol, and Mr. Felipe Herrera (Chile) succeeded Mr. Corominas-Segura. The additional Director elected was Soemarno (Indonesia), who received the votes of Ghana, Indonesia, Libya, Malaya, Morocco, and Tunisia. Of the remaining countries participating for the first time, Spain voted for Mr. Gragnani and Saudi Arabia and the Sudan for Mr. Saad.

On the occasion of this election Canada became entitled to appoint a Director under the terms of Article XII, Section 3 (*b*) (ii) and (*c*), since the Canadian dollar was one of the two currencies of which the Fund's holdings had been, on the average of the two years ending July 31, 1958, reduced below the members' quotas by the largest absolute amounts. Canada appointed Mr. Rasminsky, who had previously served as an elected Director. In consequence of this arrangement, Ireland, which in October 1957 had asked Mr. Rasminsky to look after its interests in the Fund, did not vote in the election, but asked Mr. Rasminsky to continue to represent it. The only real effect of Article XII, Section 3 (*b*) (ii) and (*c*), therefore, was to reduce the votes that Mr. Rasminsky could cast below what they would otherwise have been.

Two further changes among the Executive Directors took place: Mr. Wilfried Guth (Germany) was elected to succeed Mr. Emminger from January 16, 1959, and the third Earl of Cromer (United Kingdom) was appointed to succeed Mr. Thorold from February 2.

STAFF

At the beginning of January 1958 Mr. Bernstein resigned as Director of the Research Department, in order to become an economic consultant. He was succeeded from June 1, 1958 by Mr. Jacques J. Polak.

At April 30, 1959, the staff numbered 437, including one on extended leave; they came from 49 countries. At any given moment, however, a substantial number of them were likely to be absent from Washington. A monthly report to the Board of staff members who had traveled outside the continental United States in the preceding month contained an average of 38 names in 1959. Partly this was due to an increasing number of requests for technical assistance, and to the fact that several member countries asked for continuous assistance for a year or longer at a time. Partly, also, it was due to the fact that the staff's inquiries in connection with consultations were almost all held, during 1957–59, in the member countries; of 38 staff reports forming the basis of consultations in 1957–58, 36 followed visits to members, and in 1958–59 all 37 consultations were preceded by staff visits to the members concerned.

A new responsibility was assumed by the staff in 1958. In August of that year the World Bank convened the first meeting of a Consortium to consider aid to India. The Fund was invited to participate in the meeting, and the management decided that the Deputy Managing Director should attend, accompanied by a member of the staff of the Asian Department. In a brief for the meeting, Mr. Cochran indicated that the Fund's attitude should be one of sympathy for India's problems. The contribution of the Fund's representatives should be to answer technical questions, especially on India's balance of payments, and to explain the Fund's past relations with India. The Consortium could not, however, be regarded as a suitable forum for the discussion of the Fund's future relations with the member country. Mr. Adarkar (India) was consulted by the management on the propriety of providing the Consortium with the terms of the stand-by arrangement with India, but no formal reference was made to the Board, either before or after the meeting of the Consortium.

Other aspects of the relationship between Board and staff are discussed later in this chapter.

TRAINING PROGRAM

Since 1951, when a systematic program began in the Fund, there has been a gradual evolution of the training offered to young men and women nominated by their countries to attend the Fund's courses. Beginning in September 1954, for example, 17 trainees attended a year's course, which comprised an initial series of lectures on the Fund's activities and policies, followed by short assignments to various Fund departments to enable the trainee to become better acquainted with the work done. These assignments were in turn followed by a course in social accounting principles, after which each trainee was assigned to a department of the Fund to prepare, under supervision, a report on some specific subject of interest to him.

A further development of the program took place in 1957. The 25 trainees who attended for the year beginning in September 1957 were offered five options, of which they were expected to select three. The five comprised a seminar on the Fund's policies and activities (which all took); courses on balance of payments methodology, on economic accounting, and on the analysis of economic accounts and reports; and individual assignments, lasting three to four months.

The inclusion in this syllabus of training in balance of payments methodology continued the tradition of such training by the Fund, which had been a primary object of the program since 1951. Emphasis was, however, tending to shift away from the balance of payments work toward a more general survey of the Fund's activities and of the reasoning and experience which underlay the advice which it was giving to its members.

In September 1959 a new program was begun, in which the trainees were divided into two groups. Both groups attended two series of lectures: one on the role and operations of the Fund in international affairs and one on the analysis of economic statistics. Those who came for specialized training in balance of payments statistics were also given instruction focused on the sources and methods appropriate to the preparation and interpretation of such statistics. Those not specializing in this way were given a course of lectures on the problems of economic growth and instability, followed by individual assignments to various departments of the Fund according to their needs and interests.

In the fiscal year 1962/63 the Training Program was converted from one session lasting nine months each year to two sessions lasting five months each. This enabled the program to accept 50 trainees during the year instead of the previous 25. The steeply increased number of applications received for the shortened courses showed that member countries were more willing to release suitable people to take the training course for five months than for nine months. Accordingly, the shorter courses were again offered in 1963/64. Subsequent developments are described in Chapter 21.

INCREASES IN QUOTAS

A major concern of the Board during the years 1957–59 was the need to increase the Fund's resources to meet potential claims upon them. The outcome was the first general increase in quotas, which became effective in September 1959.

The Governors' resolution

Ever since the report provided in 1953 to ECOSOC on "The Adequacy of Monetary Reserves," [1] the Research Department had kept in view the possible need to increase the Fund's ability to meet its members' needs. Early in 1956 the department began to make a fresh study of international liquidity, and reference to a possible need for increases in members' reserves other than in gold was made in a memorandum sent to the Board in May 1956. In May 1957 Mr. Callaghan (Australia) transmitted to the Managing Director a request from South Africa that the Fund staff should undertake a study of "the factors affecting the present state of international liquidity, including the world supply of monetary gold." Thereafter, the subject attracted increasing attention. During the Twelfth Annual Meeting, in September 1957, Mr. Jacobsson in his opening address pointed out that since 1944 prices had risen by about 40 per cent and the volume of world trade by 70 per cent. Commenting that the relationship of quotas to the Fund's needs was being kept under constant review, Mr. Jacobsson added, "It would, indeed, be a pity if the Fund's work were to be hampered

[1] See above, pp. 334–35.

by an inadequacy of liquid resources. . . ." The point was taken up in subsequent speeches by the Governors for Greece, Japan, Pakistan, and Mexico.[2]

Early in 1958 two more individual increases in quotas were approved by the Governors. Libya, for which the membership resolution passed by the Governors in September 1957 fixed a quota of $3 million, sought and obtained an increase to $5 million before it accepted membership. The Philippines, whose quota was $15 million, sought and obtained an increase to $50 million in recognition of the fact that the quota allotted to it at Bretton Woods was badly out of line with the formula. (This had been pointed out by the staff in 1953.)

Meanwhile the staff had been considering the points put forward at the Annual Meeting, and in April 1958 a working party presented to the management an interim report. This pointed out that the recession in the United States, and the related decline in raw material prices, were likely adversely to affect the balance of payments of primary producing countries. Accordingly, the Fund might expect to be faced with requests for drawings from member countries in Latin America, the sterling area, and other parts of Asia and the Middle East—requests which might be quite considerable in relation to the Fund's available resources. The working party saw no reason to anticipate that the Fund would exhaust its liquid resources by the end of 1958, unless the U.S. recession proved longer or much more severe than was expected, or unless several European countries faced unexpected difficulties. Nevertheless, the working party regarded it as desirable that the adequacy of the Fund's resources to meet prospective requirements should be kept under review.

The outcome was a report entitled *International Reserves and Liquidity*, which was published on September 16, 1958.[3] This was a staff document, produced under the personal supervision of the Managing Director. It expressly stated that it did not necessarily represent the views of Executive Directors. It argued that the adequacy of international liquidity did not depend solely, or even mainly, on the volume of reserves in relation to the volume of world trade. Rather it depended on a combination of factors: the level and distribution of country reserves, the existence of sufficient facilities for international credit and borrowing, and a sound international financial structure, including appropriate exchange rates. The report estimated existing gold and foreign exchange reserves at $52.9 billion, and suggested that under certain fairly specific and broad conditions these reserves should not be considered inadequate. However, contingencies in which greater reserves would be needed could easily be envisaged. The stability of balances of payments was very uncertain, and it was noteworthy that the Fund's aid had been sought in the crisis of 1956, in the boom of 1957, and in the recession of 1958. Hence, the Fund was likely to continue to play an

[2] *Summary Proceedings, 1957*, pp. 22, 42, 62, 86, 139.

[3] Reproduced below, Vol. III, pp. 349–420.

important role in the working of the international monetary system. Taking everything into account, the report concluded that it was doubtful whether the Fund's resources were sufficient to enable it fully to perform its duties under the Articles.

While this document was still in preparation, Mr. Southard (United States) circulated to the Board a copy of correspondence between President Eisenhower and Mr. Robert B. Anderson, Secretary of the U.S. Treasury and Governor of the Fund for the United States. In his letter the President had instructed the U.S. Governor to propose at the forthcoming Annual Meeting in New Delhi that prompt consideration be given to the advisability of a general increase in quotas. On September 12, 1958 Mr. Southard formally notified the Board that at New Delhi the U.S. Governor would introduce a resolution instructing the Executive Directors to study the question of increasing the Fund's resources.

Later in September the British Commonwealth Monetary and Financial Conference at Montreal also considered the problem of international liquidity and decided that support should be given to a proposal to increase the Fund's resources by at least 50 per cent.

The Annual Meeting began on October 6. On the following day the U.S. Governor (Mr. Anderson) proposed his resolution, which read as follows:

> RESOLVED:
>
> That the Executive Directors promptly consider the question of enlarging the resources of the Fund through increases in quotas and that, if, having regard to views expressed by Governors and considering all other aspects of the matter, they find that action to carry out such increases would be desirable, they submit an appropriate proposal to the Board of Governors for action either at a meeting of the Board or by vote without a meeting, as the Executive Directors may determine.

During the Annual Meeting, speeches were made by Governors from 28 countries in all parts of the world and only two expressed some hesitation about Mr. Anderson's resolution: the Governor for South Africa regretted that insufficient attention had been paid to the desirability of an increase in the price of gold, and the Governor for France, while feeling sure that the Fund would wisely use any increased facilities given to it, thought that an increase in these resources "might seem a controversial issue." The resolution was accordingly adopted.[4]

THE EXECUTIVE BOARD'S RECOMMENDATIONS

When the Executive Board met after the Annual Meeting in New Delhi, Mr. Southard put forward a memorandum setting out the main points with which he thought the Executive Directors should deal when acting upon the Governors' resolution. These topics, and Mr. Southard's suggestions for dealing with them, were as follows:

---

[4] *Summary Proceedings, 1958*, pp. 82–83, 143, 178.

(1) *The case for an increase in resources.* This should not be difficult to make out.

(2) *The amount of the increase.* Generally 50 per cent; if particular countries wished for larger increases, these could be considered on their merits.

(3) *Payment for increases.* All members should pay 25 per cent of the increase in their quotas in gold.

(4) *Scope of participation.* Members should be entitled to make their acceptance of increases conditional upon 80 per cent of the total of quotas being increased.

(5) *Facilitation of non-dollar drawings.* Non-dollar drawings should be facilitated by enabling members to repay drawings in the currency drawn.

(6) *Necessary legislative approval.* The report should pay heed to members' need to obtain legislative approval for increases in their quotas.

During November the Board held seven informal sessions and nine formal ones to prepare to deal with the Governors' resolution. As these progressed, the Board's opinion crystallized in favor of most of Mr. Southard's points. Some Directors felt, however, that relief might be needed by members for whom the requirement to pay 25 per cent of an increase in gold would cause hardship, and some considered that the minimum participation to render the increase effective might be less than 80 per cent. Several Executive Directors said that members whom they represented would ask for increases larger than 50 per cent. One of them pointed out that a recalculation of quotas applying the Bretton Woods formula to postwar figures would yield quotas five or six times larger than the present ones. Another Director cited the case of a member whose trade had doubled between 1953 and 1957, whereas in this period world trade in general had increased only by 30–40 per cent. The point was made that in existing conditions the gold tranche of most members provided too restricted a scope for drawings. For three members—Canada, Germany, and Japan—the Board generally was satisfied that the existing quota was irrationally small, especially as it seemed likely that the Fund would before long need larger amounts of each of their currencies for use in drawings.

The outcome of the Board's deliberations was the submission to the Governors at the end of December 1958 of a report, *Enlargement of Fund Resources Through Increases in Quotas.*[5] This report was devoted to an exposition of the need for an increase in quotas along the lines indicated above. Having discussed the conditions under which the use of the Fund's resources was permitted, the Directors expressed the view that these should not be changed as a result of the increases in quotas being recommended. At the same time, they said:

[5] Reproduced below, Vol. III, pp. 421–41.

> . . . It is in the general interest that by means of strengthening the Fund's position, together with continued observance of financial self-discipline, a sound monetary basis is created for the renewed expansion of world trade.

From this postulate the Directors concluded:

> It is therefore in the interest of all members of the Fund that the common pool constituting a secondary reserve should be adequate to meet the difficulties which may arise in the future.[6]

Considering that in the previous decade the volume of world trade had nearly doubled, that the rise in dollar prices by at least 50 per cent since 1944 had correspondingly reduced the real value of the Fund's resources, and that in recent years the large majority of the Fund's drawings and stand-by arrangements had involved waivers of the limit of 25 per cent of the member's quota per annum laid down in the Articles, the Directors "concluded that it is highly desirable to enlarge the Fund's resources through increases in quotas." They added, "An increase of 50 per cent is considered a reasonable basis at this time for quota increases to enlarge the resources of the Fund." Arguments then followed in support of special increases for Canada, Germany, and Japan, and for members with particularly small quotas. Finally the report referred to special arrangements being made to accommodate members that had difficulty in providing immediately the gold equivalent to 25 per cent of the increase awarded them; some of these might be permitted to pay by installments over five years, and others might be allowed to make special drawings to enable them to meet the commitment.

Appended to the report were three resolutions for action by the Governors. The first provided for a general increase of 50 per cent in quotas, subject (1) to acceptance by members individually, (2) to the concurrence by September 15, 1959 of members holding not less than 75 per cent of the total of quotas, and (3) to the achievement of a minimum aggregate increase in subscriptions to the World Bank, which was being sought in pursuance of a resolution to increase the Bank's capital by $10 billion. The second resolution provided that members to whom the special arrangements for increases in small quotas applied should be able to increase their quotas to 50 per cent above the provisions of that formula.[7] The report listed 24 countries which could seek increases under this resolution. The third resolution provided for increases in the quotas of Canada, Germany, and Japan.

The Directors' report left for further consideration the requests for special increases by other countries, and the Board resumed discussion of these requests early in 1959. After some discussion of the details, in the course of which several

[6] See below, Vol. III, pp. 426–27.

[7] See above, p. 391.

of the amounts requested were somewhat reduced, the Board submitted to the Governors on February 24 a fourth resolution providing for special increases for 14 countries.

The staff had provided the Board with an analysis of the problem which these increases presented. It pointed out that all quotas had become inadequate, but that some were more inadequate than others. However, the ranking of countries by size of quota established at Bretton Woods represented a compromise between various economic and noneconomic considerations. The staff thought that this compromise should not be overturned on economic grounds alone. Another important consideration was that increases granted to countries likely to draw on the Fund's resources, rather than to add to its usable resources, should not be allowed unduly to reduce the Fund's liquidity or to establish potential drawing rights which could not equitably be met. All this being said, however, the staff recognized that there was real justification for the requests made for special increases. Two main lines of reasoning were advanced. Some countries were seeking to adjust their quotas because at Bretton Woods they had not wanted as large a quota as had then been offered, or had been offered quotas which were not in line with the formula, or had received quotas based on incomplete or inaccurate data. (A special instance of the latter was that some of the quotas calculated for Bretton Woods had been based on visible exports only, in the absence of adequate data on the whole of international trade.) A second and quite separate reason why increases in quotas were being sought was that in the postwar years some countries had grown appreciably faster than others.

All four resolutions were duly adopted by the Governors, the first three on February 2, 1959 and the fourth on April 6, 1959. By September 9, 1959—six days before the deadline set—members holding over 76 per cent of the total of quotas had accepted increases under one or other of the four resolutions. The deadline was extended several times to enable other members who had experienced legislative or other difficulties to accept increases in their quotas, and the eventual outcome was that, of 68 members to whom the resolutions applied, 65 increased their quotas. Of these, 30 were given increases of more than 50 per cent—14 under the second resolution, 3 under the third resolution, and 13 under the fourth resolution. During 1960, special increases were approved for 4 other countries, which had not been covered by any of these three resolutions. The only member countries that did not accept increases in their quotas were China, Cuba, and Panama. (Cuba was offered a special increase under the fourth resolution, but did not take it up.)

Late in 1959 the Board was reminded that the Quinquennial Review of Quotas called for by Article III, Section 2, was due in 1960 and that by Rule D-3 the Board was required to appoint a committee to study the problem before the end of 1959. A Committee of the Whole was accordingly appointed and held two meetings. Not surprisingly, it recommended that no further general revision of quotas was necessary. The Executive Board took a decision approving this recommendation on December 16, 1960.

EXCHANGE TRANSACTIONS

The total drawn from the Fund during the two years commencing October 1957 was substantially less than in the phenomenal year 1956–57. It was, in fact, $545.3 million, made up of 60 drawings by 19 countries. In addition, 25 stand-by arrangements with 17 countries were commenced or renewed; many of the drawings were made under these arrangements. Repurchases, made by 25 members, totaled $707.3 million.

The largest individual drawings were two by France, for a total of $131.5 million, under a stand-by arrangement for that amount granted in January 1958.

DRAWINGS IN INCONVERTIBLE CURRENCIES

It will be remembered that one of the suggestions made by Mr. Southard (United States) for the Board's response to the Governors' resolution on the resources of the Fund was that ways should be found to expand drawings in currencies other than dollars. As Table 5 shows, drawings in such currencies had

Table 5. Drawings in Inconvertible Currencies, 1947–September 1958

(Equivalents in millions of U.S. dollars)

Dates of Drawings	Belgian Francs	Deutsche Mark	Netherlands Guilders	Sterling	Total
May 1947				6.03	6.03
May–July 1948	11.41				11.41
Jan. 1951				28.00	28.00
Aug.–Dec. 1953		4.40		157.64	162.04
Jan.–Sept. 1958		64.50	5.00	16.20	85.70
Totals	11.41	68.90	5.00	207.87	293.18

been made from time to time, but the total so drawn ($293 million) was small compared with the drawings of U.S. dollars ($2,900 million) plus Canadian dollars (equivalent to US$15 million).

The possibility that there might be substantial sales of deutsche mark in 1958 (as indeed happened) had earlier led the staff to consider whether anything could be done to facilitate the acceptance of inconvertible currencies by members drawing from the Fund. In March 1958 the Deputy General Counsel had proposed to the Managing Director that consideration should be given to the use of Article XIX (*g*), to increase the supply of convertible currencies. This paragraph reads:

> The Fund, after consultation with a member which is availing itself of the transitional arrangements under Article XIV, Section 2, may deem holdings of the currency of that member which carry specified rights of conversion into another currency or into gold to be holdings of convertible currency for the purposes of the calculation of monetary reserves.

The procedure under this paragraph was briefly referred to in a memorandum by the Legal Department sent to the Board in August 1958, and was fully examined in a further memorandum in November. The essential points of the latter were as follows: The Fund must consult a member whose currency it proposes to deem convertible, but need not obtain the member's agreement to this step. The "specified rights of conversion" mentioned in the paragraph must be specially created by statute, regulation, or agreement, etc., and attached to particular holdings. The "holdings" of the currency in question must be convertible into another currency or gold; the Fund could decide whether the nominated currency was an acceptable one. Currency deemed "convertible" under Article XIX (*g*) could be accepted by the Fund in repurchases up to the point at which the Fund's holdings of that currency reached 75 per cent of the member's quota. Because members' holdings of the currencies deemed convertible would not count as part of monetary reserves in the fiscal year in which they were so deemed, they could not give rise to an obligatory repurchase until the following fiscal year; but they could be accepted immediately in voluntary repurchases. One possible difficulty was foreseen—that too extensive use of these currencies in repurchases could bring the Fund's holdings of them up to 75 per cent of the members' quotas before they could be used in repurchases by members that had drawn inconvertible currencies. To guard against this, the Fund could either refuse to accept currencies deemed convertible when offered in voluntary repurchases, or accept them only from members that had drawn inconvertible currencies.

The August memorandum which first mentioned the foregoing procedure outlined the legal aspects of what it described as a "combined operation" to facilitate drawings and repurchases in inconvertible currencies. This was essentially an elaboration of the proposal put forward by Sir George Bolton in 1951. The memorandum set out a sequence of four notional steps; the first three of these, which alone concerned the Fund, corresponded to transactions specifically authorized by the Articles of Agreement. The memorandum showed that as a result of these four steps, the position of the Fund in relation to a drawing country and to a country whose currency was drawn would be the same as if a drawing country had repaid the Fund in an inconvertible currency. These four steps may be expressed symbolically as follows: (1) country A draws country B's currency from the Fund; (2) country B buys country A's currency from the Fund with gold; (3) the Fund buys country B's currency from it with the same gold; (4) country A and country B exchange their holdings of each other's currency. It will be seen that step (2) cancels the effect of the drawing on the Fund's holdings of A's currency, step (3) similarly cancels the effect on its holdings of B's currency, and step (4) restores the holdings by A of B's currency and by B of A's currency to what they were before the drawing.

Precisely the same final position would result if A, having drawn B's currency from the Fund, subsequently repurchased its own currency with B's currency. However, since the notional procedure involved actions by B and by the Fund, the consent of both would be necessary beforehand if it was planned to reverse a drawing in this way. Provided these consents were forthcoming, the memorandum concluded that the Fund had authority to permit a drawing member to repurchase in an inconvertible currency that it had drawn.

In some contrast to the theoretical construction just described, the Research Department, in a memorandum put to the Board in November 1958, stressed the significance of the fact that by Article V, Section 7 (*c*) (iii), no currency could be used in repurchases unless the Fund held less of that currency than was equivalent to 75 per cent of the member's quota. This meant in practice that even if all inconvertible currencies were to become immediately convertible, the only one acceptable to the Fund in repurchases, in addition to the U.S. dollars and US$15 million worth of Canadian dollars, would be $66 million worth of deutsche mark. This memorandum suggested that the practical solution to the difficulty of encouraging members to draw inconvertible currencies from the Fund was to induce a few members with large quotas to be ready to convert other members' holdings of their currencies into dollars to the extent that these other members needed to make repurchases from the Fund.

These three proposals were all before the Board when, on December 27, 1958, the Governments of the major European countries announced that they had taken steps to establish the nonresident convertibility of their currencies, as described below. As this in effect satisfied the requirement postulated in the Research Department's memorandum, it became unnecessary for the Board further to consider how to encourage drawings in inconvertible currencies, and the problem was not again discussed.

REPURCHASE OBLIGATIONS CLARIFIED

Apart from a number of voluntary repurchases and a number of requests to postpone repurchase commitments, none of which raised any fresh problems for the Board, there were two developments in connection with repurchases in 1957–59 which should be recorded. The first, a minor change in procedure, was brought about by a decision of the Board in November 1957 that repurchases of amounts under $500 would not be collected, but would be deferred until the next occasion on which a repurchase of more than $500 became due.[8]

The second development stemmed from a protest by Mr. Corominas-Segura (Argentina). He pointed out that Argentina had drawn $75 million from the Fund on April 16, 1957, but had incurred a repurchase obligation of $62 million at April 30, 1957, with the result that of the service charge of $375,000 which it had paid, $310,000 related to a sum to which it was theoretically entitled for 14 days only. (In fact, the repurchase obligation was not established until April 1958, and no repurchase was made by Argentina until 1960.) Mr. Corominas-Segura contended that it could not have been the intention of the Articles that such a charge should be made for so trifling a period. The repurchase obligation arose because the unused drawing was counted as part of Argentina's monetary reserves at April 30, 1957, and he believed that its inclusion was erroneous. He drew attention to what he considered to be analogous exceptions provided by Schedule B, viz.: the proceeds of loans borrowed but not used, and holdings set aside for a specific purpose but not yet disbursed, neither of which had to be counted as part of monetary reserves.

The matter came before the Board at the end of April 1958, when Mr. Corominas-Segura sought a postponement for the repurchase obligation which had been incurred. This was agreed to—Mr. de Largentaye (France) abstaining—and a fixed schedule of repurchases extending from April 1960 to April 1962 was substituted.

On the substance of Mr. Corominas-Segura's complaint, Mr. de Largentaye said that he thought the situation showed that the Board had been in error in deciding in effect, on January 22, 1947, that no attention should be paid in calculating repurchase obligations to changes in a member's monetary reserves that took place before it was eligible to use the Fund's resources.[9] Argentina's reserves had decreased sharply between April 1956 and January 1957, when, by paying its currency subscription, it became eligible to draw from the Fund. Mr. de Largentaye suggested that this decision should be changed, or alternatively that the Board should interpret "loans" in Schedule B as including drawings, especially drawings made under the Rooth Plan, which obligated members to complete repurchases within five years.

The Acting General Counsel advised the Board that the decision taken in January 1947 was based on the correct legal principle that the right to use the Fund's resources and the obligation to repurchase were related; the Board had accordingly decided that it would be unreasonable to base the possibility of

[8] E.B. Decision No. 705-(57/55), November 7, 1957; below, Vol. III, p. 245.

[9] E.B. Decision No. 124-2; see above, p. 188.

repurchase obligations on the state of affairs existing before a member was entitled to draw on the Fund.

Mr. Hockin (Canada) asked why a fixed schedule of repurchases was proposed as an alternative to the obligation which was being postponed. The Acting General Counsel replied that while the point had not been extensively discussed in the Board, there appeared to have grown up a tacit understanding that this procedure should be followed where the discharge of a repurchase obligation was postponed.

Subsequently the arguments put forward by Mr. Corominas-Segura and Mr. de Largentaye were answered in a memorandum by the staff, as follows.

(1) The principle underlying repurchase obligations was that the member should use its own reserves *pari passu* with drawings; if it did not do so, the repurchase obligation was intended to place it in the same position as if it had. Similarly, if the member enjoyed an increment in its monetary reserves while using the Fund's resources, the repurchase obligation ensured that it shared this increment with the Fund.

(2) Schedule B, paragraph 3, had been carefully drafted to include the exceptions mentioned by Mr. Corominas-Segura, but did not assimilate Fund transactions to loans. In fact, drawings on the Fund had none of the characteristic features of loans. Further, the drafters could not have intended to include among the exceptions in Schedule B any categories of transactions not there listed, since elsewhere they had used the phrase "without limitation" to indicate open-ended categories, and these words were not used in Schedule B.

(3) Mr. Corominas-Segura's proposal would not have obviated a repurchase obligation for Argentina as at April 30, 1957. The requirements laid down in Article V, Section 7 (*b*), were that a member should pay over in repurchase half of any increase during the fiscal year in the Fund's holdings of its currency, plus half of any increase, or minus half of any decrease, in the member's reserves of gold and convertible currencies. Argentina's reserves when it became eligible to use the Fund's resources had totaled $243 million, and at April 30, 1957, they had totaled $292 million. If the whole of the $75 million drawing had been deducted from the latter figure, Argentina's reserves would have shown a net decrease to April 30, 1957 of $26 million. But the Fund's holdings of Argentina's currency had increased by $75 million. Therefore Argentina would have incurred an obligation of $24.5 million ($37.5 million minus $13 million).

(4) Provided that a member did not delay so long in asking for a drawing to be transferred to it as to throw doubt on its having been "presently needed" when approved, a member might ask for a drawing to be effectuated when it was ready to use it. Argentina's remedy would have been to postpone accepting the drawing until it proposed to spend it.

CHARGES FOR DRAWINGS

The schedule of charges established in 1953 (see the right-hand side of Table 4) [10] was renewed for a year in December 1957, for three months in December 1958, and for a further month in March 1959. In April 1959 the Board undertook an extensive review of certain aspects of the schedule, based on a series of proposals by the staff, and Directors agreed that the general level of charges should remain at their existing point for the ensuing twelve months. Similar reviews in April 1960 and April 1961 led to similar decisions. The first of these reviews was, however, the occasion for considerable discussion of some details of the charges, including the amount of the charge to be levied after it had risen to the point at which the Fund and the member had to consult about ways of reducing the Fund's holdings of the member's currency, the extent to which drawing rights could be reconstituted by repurchases, the extent to which charges under a stand-by arrangement should be refunded against the service charge for drawings made under it, and the provision for the refund of charges if a stand-by arrangement was canceled.

Charge after consultation point

The staff drew attention to the fact that the charge payable by some members (rising as it did each half year and according to the proportion of the quota which the drawing represented) was approaching 4 per cent. Thereafter the charge would rise by ½ of 1 per cent each six months to 5 per cent. After 5 per cent had been charged for six months, and unless agreement was reached on ways to reduce the Fund's holdings of the member's currency, the Fund might charge what it would. The staff recommended that if agreement was reached between the Fund and the member, the rate to be charged should not exceed 4 per cent, being reduced to that amount if necessary.

This proposal led to an extended discussion in the Board. Mr. van Campenhout (Belgium) said that there was a real question whether the Fund had power to reduce charges below 5 per cent for individual members; he thought that it could only alter charges by way of general regulation. Mr. Southard (United States) said that the staff's proposal implied that 4 per cent would always be a fair level of charge; he would prefer that the Fund should retain discretion to charge up to 5 per cent even where agreement had been reached with the member. Mr. Guth (Germany), Mr. Jorge Hazera (Costa Rica), Alternate to Mr. Gómez, and Mr. Watanabe (Japan) also thought that the progression of charges should continue as provided in Article V, Section 8 (*d*), i.e., up to 5 per cent. On the other hand, Mr. Adarkar (India) and Mr. Jorge Marshall (Chile),

---

[10] Above, p. 372.

Alternate to Mr. Herrera, considered that 4 per cent was high enough for charges after agreement with the member had been reached.

In a memorandum distributed before the meeting, Mr. van Campenhout suggested that it was desirable to distinguish between agreements which would lead to the repurchase of the drawing within three to five years, and those which contemplated repurchase over a longer period. Mr. Hazera pointed out that drawings in the higher tranches would incur charges at the rate of 5 per cent per annum or more before the end of five years. He thought it wrong that a penalty rate of charge should be imposed on a member which succeeded in repurchasing a drawing within the period of three to five years set by the Board's decisions.

After considerable discussion, the Board rejected the staff's recommendation, and decided instead that the rate of charge should increase to 5 per cent in accordance with the scale. Thereafter, if the member agreed to repurchase within five years of the drawing, the rate of charge should remain at 5 per cent. If it agreed to repurchase within a longer period, the Fund might adopt higher maximum rates. If no agreement was reached with the member, the Fund might impose such charges as it deemed appropriate. Mr. de Largentaye (France) voted against this decision, on the ground that the Fund could not alter the rate of 5 per cent set in Article V, Section 8 (*d*), except in the event that no agreement could be reached with a member.

Revolving character of arrangements

Another issue raised by the staff concerned the provision by which a member repurchasing its currency while it had a stand-by arrangement in force was able to add the amount of the repurchase to whatever sum it had not drawn under the arrangement. The staff pointed out that this concession had been made in the stand-by arrangement with Belgium in June 1952. When the policy on stand-by arrangements had been revised late in 1953 much emphasis had been laid upon their possible use to facilitate the attainment of convertibility, and it was thought suitable that for such purposes the Fund should provide a revolving amount of assistance. However, it seemed likely that at that time Executive Directors were thinking only of the possibility that the ability to draw under a stand-by arrangement should be reconstituted by the repurchase of sums drawn under the arrangement itself. In practice, four members had been allowed to reconstitute their stand-by arrangements by making repurchases of drawings effectuated before their stand-by arrangements began. The staff proposed that in future a stand-by arrangement should normally be for a fixed amount, with exceptions for special cases. The exceptions could provide for reconstituting the arrangement either in respect of any repurchases, or in respect of repurchases of drawings under the arrangement. The staff pointed out that where repurchases were made under the provisions of Article V, Section 7, and

Schedule B, there was no link with any particular drawing, but suggested that this could be met by allotting such repurchases to the earliest drawing which the member had made. Any reconstituted drawing rights should, in the staff's view, attract a further charge of 1/4 of 1 per cent per annum for the remainder of the period of the stand-by arrangement.

Again the staff's proposals met with a mixed reception. The plan to impose a charge for a reconstituted drawing right was generally approved, but most of the Directors who spoke—Lord Cromer (United Kingdom), Mr. Guth, Mr. Marshall, Mr. Southard, and Mr. Watanabe—thought that it was desirable that drawing rights should continue to be reconstituted so far as they corresponded to repurchases of drawings made under the arrangement. This was both because of the inherent desirability of a revolving credit, and because in practice the Fund was likely usually to concede such reconstitution. They thought that the reconstitution of earlier drawings should normally not be conceded, but that this might be done in exceptional cases. Mr. de Largentaye, however, considered that the provision for the reconstitution of drawing rights had caused great difficulty, and he would have preferred that stand-by arrangements should always be made for a fixed amount. Mr. Asp (Finland) and Mr. Hockin (Canada) thought that a member should have the option of reconstituting drawing rights if it wished to do so.

In the event, the Directors' decision provided that drawing rights should be reconstituted to the extent of repurchases of drawings made under the stand-by arrangement, or at the same time as the stand-by arrangement was entered into, unless the member opted not to have them reconstituted in this way. Reconstitution of drawing rights in respect of the repurchase of earlier drawings was made possible in exceptional circumstances.[11] Mr. de Largentaye abstained.

Crediting of charges for stand-by arrangements

In 1953 the charge for a stand-by arrangement (1/4 of 1 per cent per annum) had been made payable in half-yearly installments in advance. It had been decided that if a drawing was made within the same or the following six months, the charge for the stand-by arrangement would be refunded up to the amount of the service charge (1/2 of 1 per cent) for the drawing. Thus, if a quarter or more of the amount available under the stand-by arrangement was drawn within six months of the date of the stand-by arrangement, the first half-year's installment of the stand-by charge could be recovered. Alternatively, if a half or more of the amount available under the stand-by arrangement was drawn between six and twelve months after the date of the arrangement, both installments of the stand-by charge would be refunded. But if the member drew all that it wished

[11] E.B. Decision No. 876-(59/15), April 27, 1959, par. II; below, Vol. III, p. 232.

to draw in the first six months after the date of the arrangement, the second half-year's stand-by charge could be recovered only if the member repurchased part of its drawing and drew again, thereby incurring a second service charge.

To deal with this, the staff recommended that the charge for the full period of a stand-by arrangement should be payable in advance. The staff also proposed a change of rule to cover the case of a member that (1) made a drawing under a stand-by arrangement, as a result of which it was credited with a proportionate part of the stand-by charge, (2) subsequently repurchased all or part of the drawing, and (3) wished to reconstitute a commensurate part of the drawing rights conferred by the stand-by arrangement. In such circumstances, the staff proposed that a further charge should be levied, proportioned to the remaining period of the stand-by arrangement.

When this proposal came before the Board, Directors generally agreed to it, but Mr. de Largentaye asked why the proposed amendment to the rule did not provide for a refund of the charge for a stand-by arrangement if, by repurchases or otherwise, the Fund's holdings of the member's currency were reduced below its quota, i.e., if the net amount that had been drawn did not exceed the "gold tranche." Directors agreed that this should also be done, and the rule was appropriately amended to cover both the staff's proposals and those of Mr. de Largentaye.[12]

Cancellation of stand-by arrangements

Finally, the staff pointed to a corollary of the decision just taken. The practice when a stand-by arrangement was canceled had been to refund a part of the charge proportionate to the unexpired period and to such part (if any) of the amount of the stand-by arrangement as had never been drawn. Thus, if a member drew the whole amount of a stand-by, then repurchased half of it, and then canceled the arrangement, it would not be entitled to any refund, because at one period nothing had been left of the drawing rights under the arrangement. This, the staff pointed out, would cease to be equitable once a charge was made for a reconstituted drawing right. It therefore proposed that in future the amount of the charge refunded should be proportionate to the unexpired period and to the part of the drawing rights under the arrangement (if any) which could still be drawn when the arrangement was canceled, and in respect of which the member had paid a charge. (This last clause was added to cover the case where the drawing rights under the stand-by arrangement fell within the gold tranche, since no charge was made for stand-by arrangements covering gold tranche transactions.) This recommendation was accepted by the Board.[13]

[12] *Ibid.*, pars. III. 1 and V.

[13] *Ibid.*, par. IV.

Repurchase of gold tranche drawings

Another question involving the rules on repurchases arose in December 1959, when Bolivia sought approval for a schedule which covered the repurchase of a drawing made in May 1953 and included the postponement for two years of repurchases of drawings made under a stand-by arrangement in December 1956 and January 1957. The staff recommended approval of the schedule, and suggested that Bolivia's proposal should be "deemed to be an agreement for the purposes of the second sentence of Rule I-4 (g). . . ." This meant that the rate of charge would not rise above 5 per cent per annum.

Mr. Toussaint (Belgium), however, pointed out that this sentence related only to agreements for repurchase within three to five years, whereas the schedule submitted by Bolivia provided for completing repurchase of the drawing made in May 1953 by July 1960, i.e., after seven years. He said that he understood that the staff was in effect arguing that because Bolivia's drawing in 1953 was within the gold tranche, and so did not incur any periodic charge, it could be ignored for the purpose of calculating the period within which repurchase was to be completed. He was unable to accept this view.

The representative of the Legal Department replied that the question whether an agreement with a member under Rule I-4 (g) had to relate to all of a member's drawings, or could relate to part only of them, had not been settled, and could perhaps remain open. The fact was that Bolivia had made a firm commitment to repurchase all its drawings and it seemed appropriate that the charge levied should not exceed 5 per cent. The Board agreed, but in order to meet Mr. Toussaint's point the decision taken was as follows:

> The Fund notes that commitments have been made by Bolivia for repurchase in respect of all its drawings on the Fund, and the rate of charges payable by Bolivia will not increase beyond 5 per cent per annum under Rule I-4 (g) . . . .

Since under present policies no drawing can remain outstanding for more than five years unless the member defaults, it has not subsequently been necessary to deal with the point which Mr. Toussaint raised.

General considerations

The discussion in the Board in April 1960 showed that Directors were still divided on the appropriateness of comparisons between charges and the rates of interest in financial markets. When the subject was resumed in April 1961 the Board had before it a staff memorandum covering three points:

(1) Market rates were undoubtedly substantially higher than the Fund's charges, and this would be true even if the charges were modified (as Mr. Southard had proposed in 1959) so as to average 3 per cent in the second year, instead of 2½ per cent. But the staff suggested that it was scarcely a time to make such

a change: the U.S. economy was slack, interest rates in Canada were falling, and several central banks in Europe had recently reduced their interest rates.

(2) When the charges were discussed in 1956, an Executive Director had questioned the rule by which, for the purpose of calculating charges, repurchases were deemed to be applied first to the most recent drawings, so that charges on earlier drawings continued to rise by 1/2 of 1 per cent each half year. In justification for this, the staff pointed out that it was consonant with the spirit of the Articles, and especially Article V, Section 4, that charges should be based on the period during which the member was continuously using the Fund's resources. Hence, LIFO (last in, first out) was appropriate to charges. It was true that, when deciding which drawing under a stand-by arrangement should be regarded as having been repaid by a given repurchase, it was appropriate to use FIFO (first in, first out), since otherwise the member would find itself obliged to repurchase all its drawings within three years from the date of the first drawing. But this did not invalidate the use of LIFO in connection with charges.

(3) Also in 1956 it had been suggested that when a new scale of charges was introduced it should be made applicable to holdings then in the possession of the Fund as a result of members' earlier drawings. The staff deprecated this, on the ground that it would constitute an *ex post facto* change, without prior notice being given of the possibility, in the terms on which the Fund's resources could be used. However, it would be appropriate to apply the new charges to drawings made after the date of their introduction, whether these drawings had been authorized earlier or not.

These proposals were generally approved, and after the Board had been reminded that a request for a reconsideration of the schedule of charges could be made at any time by any Executive Director, the Board agreed unanimously to continue the current schedule to April 30, 1962.

THE FUND IN THE BLACK: INVESTMENT PROGRAM

Investment continued

It will be recalled that as a result of a decision by the Board in January 1956 the Fund invested $200 million worth of gold in U.S. short-term securities, in order to produce an income toward defraying the accumulated operating deficit of the Fund, which at that time was some $14 million. The spate of transactions that began in October 1956 speedily transformed the financial situation. By April 30, 1957 the deficit had fallen to $6.29 million, and by August it became apparent that even this deficit would be eliminated by the time of the Annual Meeting. The opportunity was accordingly taken to charge the cost of the new building then in progress to income—instead of to a special account as had previously been done—with the result that the clearing off of the deficit was postponed until November. In the meantime the Managing Director appointed a staff working group to make recommendations on the future of the investment program.

This group suggested that it would be prudent to continue the investment in order to build up a Special Reserve against possible deficits in future years. No limit to the size of such a reserve need be set, but it should be segregated from any general reserve built up from an excess of ordinary income over expenditure, because it would not be a part of the Fund's net income that could be distributed by the Board of Governors under Article XII, Section 6. Subject to the concurrence of the United States, the group recommended that the program should continue unchanged.

The Executive Directors considered this report on November 27, 1957, and, except for Mr. de Largentaye (France), approved the continuation of the program.[14] Mr. de Largentaye recalled that he had opposed the original investment on the ground that the Fund had no power to make it; he felt that even if there were an implied power which would enable the Fund to invest its gold in order to eliminate a deficit (which he denied), it was not possible to infer the existence of such a power when the deficit no longer existed. Several Directors suggested that the program should be reviewed periodically by the Board, but they saw no difficulty in accepting the recommendation of the working group, and Mr. Southard (United States) said that his Government was prepared for the investment to continue. Accordingly it was decided to replace the words "reasonably related to the deficit of the Fund" in the decision of January 1956 by the phrase "reasonably related to the purpose of the investment," which was regarded as sufficiently elastic to cover any future contingency. The $200 million continued to be invested and reinvested and no change was made in the program until 1959, when it was expanded as shown below.

General Reserve

During the fiscal year 1957/58, the Fund's operational income totaled $20.3 million and income from its investments (excluding $2.83 million transferred to Special Reserve) was $3.33 million. Expenditure, including $5.62 million for the new building, totaled $11.34 million. After some minor adjustments there remained an excess of income over expenditure of $12.3 million, which extinguished the deficit of $6.3 million that had existed at the beginning of the fiscal year and left $6 million as a surplus.

The disposal of this surplus formed the subject of a submission by the staff to the Board on April 4, 1958, which was discussed on April 14. The Board decided as follows:

[14] E.B. Decision No. 708-(57/57), November 27, 1957; below, Vol. III, p. 276.

> On April 30, 1958 and at the end of each month thereafter until further action by the Executive Directors or the Board of Governors, the net income of the Fund shall be transferred provisionally to a General Reserve. At the next Annual Meeting it shall be recommended to the Board of Governors that it note with approval the establishment of the General Reserve and the allocation to such reserve of the net income for the fiscal year ended April 30, 1958.

The decision was not without its critics. Mr. Sol (El Salvador) reminded the Board that the Executive Directors had no legal power to transfer the Fund's net income to reserve, this being tantamount to a decision not to distribute the net income—a decision which was the prerogative of the Board of Governors. He felt that the point was an important one, especially for Executive Directors who represented several members, since they might be subject to criticism for an action possibly affecting members' basic rights. He thought that the most that the Executive Board could do would be to place net income to reserve on a provisional basis, and then refer the matter to the Board of Governors each year for a decision as to its disposal. Mr. de Largentaye supported Mr. Sol, with whose legal point he agreed.

On the other hand, Mr. Southard pointed out that it was a function of corporate boards and managements to make such recommendations as the decision proposed. Mr. Wilhelm Hanemann (Germany), Alternate to Mr. Emminger, agreed. Mr. Thorold (United Kingdom) also agreed, though he asked whether it was really necessary to make monthly transfers to reserve. To this, the representative of the Legal Department replied that to do so would simplify the Fund's accounts. It would also cover the situation which would arise if a member withdrew; such a member might claim a share in a surplus if there was one in the Fund's accounts, but there would be no surplus if net income had been transferred to reserve.

Mr. Southard and Mr. Sol suggested that the accounts should distinguish between annual transfers to reserve authorized by the Board of Governors and the monthly provisional transfers, and it was decided that this should be done.

At the Annual Meeting the Board of Governors approved the Board's action.

Investment increased

In June 1959 the Deputy General Counsel put forward a suggestion that the amount of the Fund's gold invested in U.S. Government securities should be increased from $200 million to $500 million, to give some relief to the United States in respect of the gold contribution ($343.75 million) which it would be making in connection with the increase in its quota. The Deputy General Counsel pointed out that recourse to Article VII, Section 2 (ii), which had twice been used to supplement the Fund's holdings of dollars, was now out of the question since the U.S. currency subscription would include over $1 billion as part of the increase in its quota. On the other hand, there would be no legal difficulties about an extension of the investment program for the purpose already approved, and this could be justified by the consideration that the increase in quotas was itself expected to reduce the Fund's income by some $10 million a year. (It increased quotas relative to drawings, and so shifted charges into lower brackets.) Such a decrease in income would reduce allocations to General Reserve, and a good case could be made for increasing the Special Reserve to offset this reduction.

Accordingly, a proposal was made to the Board on July 14, 1959 for an increase in the amount of gold invested from $200 million to $500 million. Citing the arguments put forward by the Deputy General Counsel, the staff also recalled that increases in the reserves of Western European countries and of Japan had led to repurchases totaling $510 million from July 1958 through June 1959, while drawings in the same period totaled only $156 million. This pointed to wide swings in Fund transactions, and consequently in its income, which would make it important to reinforce the Special Reserve so that the General Reserve (required to meet unforeseen contingencies, for which $100–200 million would not be in any way excessive) should not have to cover administrative deficits. On these grounds it would be prudent and conservative to increase the Special Reserve by $10–15 million a year, to reach, say, $100 million in six to nine years. The investment of $200 million was increasing the Special Reserve at a much smaller rate—by $4 million a year when interest on the amount invested was 2 per cent; by $6 million a year when it was 3 per cent. Moreover, the investment program was dependent upon the good will of the member in whose securities the investment was held; and it would be advisable to take advantage of that member's present willingness.

This willingness was no doubt a reflection of the substantial reduction in the U.S. gold stock that had been taking place. U.S. gold holdings declined by $2,294 million in 1958. In 1959 the reduction was still continuing, and indeed amounted to $1,041 million over the year. There can be no doubt that this was itself a factor conducing to favorable consideration of an increase in the Fund's investment.

A second recommendation put to the Board was that authority should be given to acquire securities of longer duration than three months, up to one year. The purpose of this recommendation was to increase the earning power of the investment, by enabling the Fund to take advantage of higher interest rates on longer-term securities.

When the staff's memorandum was discussed by the Board, on July 24, 1959, three aspects of the proposal came in for comment. Both the timing and the amount of the investment were questioned by Mr. Toussaint (Belgium) and Mr. Lieftinck (Netherlands). The latter doubted whether a boom was the right moment in which to add to an investment, and thought that a Special Reserve of $100–200 million was out of proportion to the Fund's expected administrative expenditure. On the other hand, Mr. Rasminsky (Canada) specifically supported a figure of $100–200 million, and Mr. B. E. Fleming (Australia), Alternate to Mr. Callaghan, thought that a period of rising prices was the best moment at which to consider accumulating a reserve against possible future deficits. The proposal to invest in longer-term securities was regarded with some doubt by Lord Cromer (United Kingdom) and Mr. Southard, who both thought that the amount so invested should represent only a moderate proportion of the total. With that proviso, however, the staff's plan was adopted by the Board, the only dissentient being Mr. André Feuché (France), Alternate to Mr. de Largentaye, who recalled Mr. de Largentaye's previous objection to the investment.[15]

After negotiations with the Federal Reserve Bank of New York to arrive at a convenient timing, the additional $300 million of gold was invested during the next three months, pursuant to a program designed to achieve a portfolio of approximately $200 million in three-month bills, $100 million in six-month bills, and $200 million in twelve-month bills. During the fiscal year ended April 30, 1960, the yield on the investment was $15.36 million.

EXTERNAL CONVERTIBILITY ACHIEVED

On December 27, 1958, the Executive Directors appointed or elected by ten European countries announced to the Board that their countries' currencies were being made externally convertible. These ten—Belgium, Denmark, France (which simultaneously agreed upon a new par value), Germany, Italy, Luxembourg, the Netherlands, Norway, Sweden, and the United Kingdom—were shortly afterward joined by Austria, Finland, Greece, Ireland, and Portugal. In addition, fifteen other member countries, most of which were associated in a monetary area with one or other of the European countries just mentioned, took steps to adjust their exchange control regulations to the new conditions. These were Australia, Burma, Ceylon, Ghana, India, Iraq, Jordan, Libya, Malaya, Morocco, New Zealand, Pakistan, the Sudan, Tunisia, and the Union of South Africa. Since none of the 30 countries mentioned was yet ready to accept the obligations of Article VIII, Sections 2, 3, and 4, their currencies remained unacceptable to the Fund in repurchases. However, the fact that nonresident holders of these currencies could obtain dollars or other convertible currencies for them meant that the major disadvantage of drawing such currencies from the Fund no longer existed. Two sequels to the announcement came before the Board during 1959.

[15] E.B. Decision No. 905-(59/32), July 24, 1959; below, Vol. III, p. 277.

Significance of external convertibility

At the first meeting of the Board in January 1959, Mr. Callaghan (Australia) proposed that Executive Directors should consider the implications for the Fund of the decision that had been taken in Europe. He suggested that it brought perceptibly nearer the time when important member countries would make their currencies convertible in the technical Fund sense, i.e., would move from Article XIV to Article VIII. The Board should accordingly turn its mind to consideration of the problems that it would face when deciding whether to approve the maintenance of restrictions by countries that had made this move.

Mr. Callaghan was disturbed that in discussing recent consultation reports the Board had failed to distinguish between exchange restrictions, which were its proper concern, and restrictions on imports. He did not wish at that juncture to discuss the limits of the Fund's responsibilities, but to point out that the blurring of these limits would make it difficult for a country that had accepted the obligations of Article VIII to foresee how the Fund would treat a request for the approval of restrictions.

Thanking Mr. Callaghan for his statement, the Managing Director said that the staff would study these problems. Mr. Jacobsson drew the attention of the Board to Article XII, Section 8, which empowered the Fund at any time to communicate its views informally to any member on any matter arising under the Articles of Agreement. As the same Article went on to refer to "monetary or economic conditions and developments which directly tend to produce a serious disequilibrium in the international balance of payments of members," it seemed clear that the Fund's powers of comment were wider than its strictly jurisdictional field. Thus the Fund could, if it wished, express views on such matters as a protective tariff, even though this fell within the sphere of the GATT.

Mr. Southard (United States) said that the view of the U.S. authorities had always been that the Fund had jurisdiction over restrictions maintained for balance of payments reasons, no matter what form these restrictions took. Moreover, he himself had always understood it to be the Fund's view that when a country could no longer claim balance of payments reasons for its restrictions, that country should be pressed to undertake the obligations of Article VIII. He recalled that in 1955 some Directors had taken the view that members should not be encouraged to move to Article VIII if thereafter the Fund would be asked to approve numerous restrictions.[16] However, the Board had reached no decision on the question whether it would prefer that member countries should not undertake the obligations of Article VIII unless they had virtually no restrictions.

[16] See above, p. 401.

A corollary of the foregoing discussion emerged in May during the review by the Board of a draft for the Exchange Restrictions Report. Mr. Southard proposed an amendment to the draft which contained the following sentences:

> With the coming of full nonresident convertibility, earnings in one currency can be freely converted into any other currency, including dollars. A logical consequence of the introduction of external convertibility is therefore to terminate the practice of discrimination.

While he believed that the Board was not yet able to reach agreement on an assertion that balance of payments reasons for discrimination no longer existed, he thought that the Executive Directors should discuss the matter in the near future, as it was clear that a decision would soon be necessary. Meanwhile, members should be urged to proceed as rapidly as possible toward the elimination of discrimination, including bilateralism.

Other Directors, while joining Mr. Southard in his general approach to the question of discrimination, did not find it possible to accept the second sentence quoted above, and this was accordingly deleted in the draft accepted for the Exchange Restrictions Report.

Discrimination

The Board's interest in the removal of discrimination was also recorded in the Annual Report for 1959,[17] and shortly before the Annual Meeting the staff produced an analysis of the extent to which member countries relied upon discrimination, including bilateral payments arrangements. This showed that about 20 of the "Article XIV" members had such arrangements and also discriminated against the dollar. About 20 others maintained such arrangements without otherwise discriminating against the dollar. A few countries discriminated against the dollar although they had no bilateral payments arrangements; some 15 neither had such arrangements nor discriminated. On the whole, the staff believed that bilateral relations were increasingly becoming matters of trade agreements rather than of payments agreements.

As to the future, the staff believed that most of the members that were still discriminating against the dollar could cease to do so in a reasonably short time without important repercussions on their balances of payments or reserves; with few exceptions, it appeared that these members could no longer justify discrimination on balance of payments grounds. As Mr. Jacobsson put it in his opening address to the Annual Meeting:

> In matters of international trade, the distinction between "hard" and "soft" currency countries has really become an anachronism. The traditional argument for continued discrimination has thus, by and large, been eliminated.[18]

---

[17] *Annual Report, 1959,* p. 30.

[18] *Summary Proceedings, 1959,* p. 15.

The staff's memorandum was considered by the Board on October 14, 1959, when Executive Directors had before them a draft decision prepared by Mr. Southard after discussion with a number of other Directors. This was generally supported by the Directors who spoke, though some—notably Mr. Asp (Finland), Mr. de Largentaye (France), and Mr. Saad (United Arab Republic, Egyptian Region)—felt that as regards bilateralism the Board should not go further than its decision of 1955. Mr. Watanabe (Japan) regretted that some members that had ended discrimination against dollar goods had maintained restrictions against imports from Japan. Mr. Fleming (Australia) called attention to the practical difficulty of ending discrimination; importers would be likely to build up stocks, creating a sudden drain on reserves. He also thought that the "dollar shortage" was so largely due to noneconomic disturbances that it might well recur; in his view the staff was too optimistic in this respect. Other Directors would have preferred a somewhat stronger decision, but after a further brief discussion a few days later the draft submitted was approved with the addition only of a preliminary sentence emphasizing that it dealt exclusively with discrimination for balance of payments reasons.[19]

As so approved, the decision recorded that the Fund considered there was no longer any balance of payments justification for discrimination by members whose current receipts were largely in externally convertible currencies. Members would be expected to proceed with all feasible speed to eliminate discrimination against member countries, including that arising from bilateralism. However, where a substantial part of current receipts was still subject to limitations on convertibility, particularly in payments relations with state-trading countries, the Fund was prepared to consider whether the balance of payments position would justify the maintenance of some degree of discrimination. But discrimination between countries having externally convertible currencies would not be acceptable.

Exchange dealings and margins

In his statement to the Board on December 27, 1958, dealing with the external convertibility of sterling, Mr. Thorold (United Kingdom) had stated that the British authorities would take steps to ensure that the sterling exchange rate remained between $2.82=£1 and $2.78=£1, i.e., within the limits set by the Articles of Agreement. However, this could mean that intra-European exchange rates derived from sterling might exceed these limits.

This contingency, among other consequences of the declaration of external convertibility for European currencies, was studied by the staff during the early part of 1959. In July the staff recommended that the Fund should declare that

[19] E.B. Decision No. 955-(59/45), October 23, 1959; below, Vol. III, p. 260.

it did not object to exchange rates within 2 per cent of par whenever such rates arose from the maintenance of margins of not more than 1 per cent for a convertible (including an externally convertible) currency.

When this was discussed at the Board, the General Counsel explained that, while exchange rates differing from par by as much as 2 per cent conflicted with the requirement of Article IV, Section 3, it was practicable for the Board to approve them as multiple currency practices. Further, the arrangements flowing from external convertibility were a contribution toward the objective expressed in Article IV, Section 4 (*a*), in which

> each member undertakes to collaborate with the Fund to promote exchange stability, to maintain orderly exchange arrangements with other members, and to avoid competitive exchange alterations.

The Board would therefore be thoroughly justified in declaring that the rates which could emerge would be consistent with the Articles of Agreement. This did not, he remarked, amount to amending Article IV, Section 3. On this understanding the staff's recommendation was accepted by the Board.[20]

BOARD-STAFF RELATIONS

The departure of Mr. Bernstein from the position of Director of Research, while it ended the connection with the Fund of one of the principal architects of its constitution, involved no considerable change in the relationship between the Board and the staff. Yet it may afford an occasion for a review of what that relationship had become—a review which will principally consist of weaving together threads which were spun in earlier pages of this Chronicle.

We may begin by recalling once again the contrasting affiliations of Board and staff as described at Savannah: Executive Directors responsible to the countries that had appointed or elected them; the Managing Director and the staff responsible to the Fund as a whole. This dichotomy had underlain the division of responsibility between the Managing Director and staff and the Executive Directors, which had been clarified in January 1948. The Board then broadly assumed the functions of formulating policies, taking decisions on major problems, and satisfying itself that its decisions were being carried out by the staff. It charged the Managing Director and staff with supplying to the Board analyses of the problems to be solved, with carrying out the Fund's policies, and with handling negotiations with members.

This does not, of course, imply that Board and staff kept one another at arm's length. On the contrary, the frequent contacts between individual members of the staff (especially, at first, Mr. Bernstein himself) and individual Executive

[20] E.B. Decision No. 904-(59/32), July 24, 1959; below, Vol. III, p. 226.

Directors were an important element in the nexus of relationships. On the one hand they enabled the staff to convey informally to the Board suggestions which might contribute to the improvement of Fund policy. On the other hand, they enabled the Board to gauge the quality of the staff and to develop that degree of confidence in it that was essential for a further devolution of responsibility. This tendency was strengthened by the appointment to the staff of several former Executive Directors and by the election to the Board of several ex-members of the staff.

By about 1951 a fresh element had been introduced by the Board's reliance on the staff to provide technical assistance and advice to member countries. The fact that this technical assistance had perforce to be given in the members' capitals, and without day-to-day recourse to the Board, meant that the staff had to make decisions as to the relative advisability of different courses, whether or not similar issues had been decided by the Executive Directors. It was not surprising that on occasion the judgment of the staff was questioned by individual Executive Directors, as for example when the staff advised Iran not to appreciate its currency further, or commended the introduction by Colombia of specific fiscal measures and a fluctuating exchange rate. Yet on the first of these occasions Mr. Southard (United States) had expressly reiterated his support for the independence of the staff, even while declaring that he could not agree that technical reports should be submitted by the Fund with which the Board disagreed.

Even so, the relation between the elements in the Fund remained inevitably a delicate one. It will be recalled that at the very end of his term as Managing Director, Mr. Rooth had emphasized this. He had in particular drawn attention to the tendency of Executive Directors to discuss the problems of their member countries with other Directors instead of with the management—a natural enough tendency, he might have added, since effective power lay with the Board rather than with the management, yet one contrary to the decision reached in 1948.

That in later years the influence of the staff tended to grow is undeniable. One reason was the large number of changes in the membership of the Board and the frequency with which these occurred. The increased size of the Board, which brought about some slowing down of its proceedings, was also a significant factor. On the other hand, the greater continuity of personnel among the staff, and its accumulated experience, strengthened its hand in tackling fresh issues. So, too, the international fame of Mr. Jacobsson, reflecting his personal prestige and supported by the large number of public speeches which he made during his years in the Fund, helped to bring the Managing Directorship more into the limelight. These speeches, and particularly the fact that they often commented on members' domestic policies, were in themselves a significant innovation.

But the principal reason for the strengthening of the staff's position was that it had opportunities for exercising initiative, and took them. Some of these emerged in Washington. For instance, the staff report on *International Reserves and Liquidity* was sent direct to members without being reviewed by the Board. On this occasion the reasons were partly pressure of time and partly a clash of views amongst Executive Directors, particularly on the question of gold, which might have made it impossible to present an agreed Board report. Subsequently, the reports which the staff rendered on the problems of quotas and charges went a long way toward presenting the Board with the complete analysis of these issues which was needed for their solution. A less important example was the attendance of the Deputy Managing Director and a member of the staff at the meeting of the World Bank Consortium on India—although this would have been unthinkable ten years earlier. But the major steps forward were two: the change of venue from Washington to members' capitals of staff inquiries in connection with consultations, and the increasing use made of the lapse of time procedure.

The former of these marked the end of the practice, adopted by some member countries, of nominating their Executive Directors to conduct the member's end of the discussions. It also led to the staff acquiring a much more intimate knowledge of the problems of each member country than was possible for any Executive Director except the one who had been appointed or elected by that country. It was a small step from this to the evolution by the staff, in discussions with members, of programs for the reform of their economies; and an even smaller step to the inclusion of conditions in stand-by arrangements which reflected these programs and the undertakings which members had given to observe them. Yet the result was that the Board came to be faced with draft stand-by arrangements and letters of intent that had been prepared by the staff in consultation only with the member country—or at most with the Executive Director immediately concerned—and which contained conditions drafted by the staff itself.

The progress of this revolution—for it was little less—did not pass without some protests from members of the Board. Mr. Callaghan (Australia) on more than one occasion suggested that the Board was treating consultations in too routine a fashion. He objected also, as did Mr. van Campenhout (Belgium), to the discussion in consultation reports of matters which he regarded as the prerogative of the GATT. Mr. Callaghan thought it "an unhappy development on several counts that it should be implied that the staff had corporate identity and corporate responsibility." [21] He also stressed that there was danger in the staff discussing a member's problems with individual officials, since that created

[21] Cf. the remarks of the Governor for Australia in 1951 (above, p. 270).

a risk of the Fund being placed in the position of associating with a particular pressure group or being used for political purposes.

But as time went on, and consultations multiplied, it became clear that their effectiveness depended upon thorough staff inquiries, and that these could only be assured in the member's own capital. Once there, the staff was of necessity treated as the representative of the Fund. Even though its recommendations were sometimes challenged by the Board, it yet remained the responsibility of the staff to communicate to the Board its appraisal of each member's attack on its problems, and to suggest the terms on which assistance should be given to members when needed. That these responsibilities were accepted will have become clear, for instance, from the descriptions in earlier chapters of the conclusions suggested for consultations and the special conditions devised by the staff to deal with individual members' difficulties. By a natural consequence, the Board came to rely upon the Managing Director for advice on prospective drawings—a development which went far to meet Mr. Rooth's complaint in 1956 that members tended to consult Executive Directors rather than the Managing Director before approaching the Board as a whole.

The extension of the lapse of time procedure was perhaps of secondary importance in relation to the development just described. Yet it led to many matters being handled by the staff, and approved by the Board without discussion, which in earlier years would have been placed on the agenda for debate. The procedure was, of course, a development of one first used to deal with the special problems of the Chinese exchange system and subsequently adopted to handle minor changes in multiple currency systems.

Over the years this procedure was more and more used. For instance, between the end of October 1958 and the end of September 1959 four requests were made by members for short extensions of stand-by arrangements in force, and three of these were approved without discussion in the Board. On eight occasions, modifications were made in ceilings prescribed in stand-by arrangements without any of them being debated. Similarly, of twelve requests made to the Board for approval of changes in members' exchange systems, ten were approved under the lapse of time procedure.

Too much must not be made of these developments. Obviously the Board remained ultimately responsible for the staff's work. Where Directors reached a decision on a particular issue, this decision guided the staff in all future circumstances where it was relevant. Obviously, also, there continued to be instances in which the Board introduced variations into draft stand-by arrangements, and even more frequently into the draft conclusions for consultations which the staff submitted. And yet when all this has been said, the relationship between the Managing Director and staff and the Executive Directors was to be very different in the days ahead from what it had been only a few years earlier.

CHAPTER

18

Convertibility and After (1959-61)

THE FORMAL ADOPTION by the major European countries of external convertibility for their currencies in December 1958 led on to their acceptance of the obligations of convertibility, in the Fund sense, in February 1961. Coincidentally there came about a marked increase in the influence which the Fund was able to exert, and in the degree to which its activities became central to the international monetary system. The present chapter, covering the two years from September 1959 to September 1961, will lay the foundation for the study of a more active period of the Fund's whole history than any hitherto recorded; that period will be described in Chapter 19.

MEMBERSHIP, BOARD, AND STAFF

Five new members joined the Fund during the two years now being reviewed, all of them in 1961. Portugal became a member on March 29, Nigeria on March 30, Laos on July 5, New Zealand on August 31, and Nepal on September 6. The number of members was thereby raised to 73. There was in prospect, moreover, a sharp further increase in membership: from Africa alone the applications of seven countries had been received by the end of August 1961 and inquiries were in hand from eleven others. It was clear that in the near future the size of the Fund would be greatly enlarged.

Annual Meetings

The Fifteenth Annual Meeting of the Board of Governors was held in Washington in September 1960, and the Sixteenth in Vienna in September 1961. The latter was the first occasion on which there was simultaneous interpretation of the addresses delivered during the Meetings; it provided for the rendering of the speeches in English, French, German, and Spanish. At all subsequent Meetings simultaneous interpretation in English, French, and Spanish has been furnished.

The speeches made both in Washington and in Vienna—perhaps especially in Vienna—were notable for the implicit acceptance by nearly all speakers of the role of the Fund as a key factor in the international monetary system, rather than as an isolated instrument with a specialized function of its own. The developments within the Fund that influenced this change of attitude are discussed below.

Executive Directors

There was an unusual number of changes among the Executive Directors in the two years. In November 1959 Mr. J. M. Garland (Australia), who had been Alternate to Messrs. McFarlane and Melville from March 1949 to March 1951, was elected to succeed Mr. Callaghan. In March 1960 Mr. Walter Müller (Chile) was elected in the place of Mr. Herrera, who had resigned on being elected President of the Inter-American Development Bank. In August 1960 Mr. Paranaguá (Brazil) died.

The Eighth Regular Election of Executive Directors was held on September 30, 1960. Mr. Thorhallur Ásgeirsson (Iceland) was then elected to succeed Mr. Asp, whose Alternate he had been for the two preceding years; Mr. Maurício Chagas Bicalho (Brazil) was elected to fill the place vacated by Mr. Paranaguá; Mr. Guillermo Walter Klein (Argentina) succeeded Mr. Müller; Mr. José Antonio Mayobre (Venezuela) succeeded Mr. Gómez; Mr. Sergio Siglienti (Italy) succeeded Mr. Gragnani; Mr. Soetikno Slamet (Indonesia) succeeded Soemarno; and Mr. Gengo Suzuki (Japan) succeeded Mr. Watanabe. Messrs. Garland, Lieftinck (Netherlands), Saad (United Arab Republic, Egyptian Region), and van Campenhout (Belgium) were re-elected.

The increases in quotas recorded in the last chapter resulted in China being replaced by Germany as one of the five members with the largest quotas. This meant that China's right to appoint an Executive Director passed to Germany, which appointed Mr. Guth (who had been elected in January 1959). Mr. Tann, who had been appointed by China in July 1950, was now elected by China. No country qualified under Article XII, Section 3 (*c*), to appoint a Director, and Mr. Rasminsky (Canada), who had been appointed by Canada in 1958 under the terms of this Section, was elected in 1960 by Canada and Ireland. There were no other changes in the groups electing Directors. However, in March 1961 Mr. Rasminsky undertook to look after Nigeria's interests in the Fund, and in September 1961 Mr. Garland similarly undertook to watch those of New Zealand.

In the first nine months of 1961 there were three changes among the appointed Directors: Mr. David B. Pitblado (United Kingdom) succeeded the Earl of Cromer from January 19; Mr. I. G. Patel (India), who had been Alternate to Mr. Adarkar since December 1958, was appointed to succeed him from June 22; and Mr. Jashwantrai J. Anjaria (India) was in turn appointed to succeed Mr. Patel from August 1. Mr. Patel then became Alternate to Mr. Anjaria.

Staff

The prospect that a number of newly independent African states would join the Fund prompted the Governor for Ghana, Mr. K. A. Gbedemah, to suggest at the Annual Meeting, 1960, that the time had come for the formation of an African Department.[1] In February 1961 Messrs. Saad and Slamet sent a memorandum to the Managing Director urging that effect should be given to this suggestion as soon as possible. Their memorandum added that it was essential that the new department should be headed by an African, and that the staff should be partly recruited from Africa in accordance with the arrangements in other departments.

Proposals along the foregoing lines were put to the Board by the Managing Director when presenting the budget for 1961/62, on April 10, 1961. The budget provided for an initial staff of 15 in the African Department. Mr. Jacobsson proposed that its sphere of activity should cover all African countries that should thereafter join the Fund, together with such of the existing members as preferred to be looked after by the new department instead of by those departments which had so far served them. It may be noted here that three countries which in 1961 were served by the European Department chose subsequently to be transferred to the African Department—Morocco in October 1963, Tunisia in November 1963, and Ghana in August 1964. South Africa, also looked after by the European Department, has preferred not to make a change, as have the four African countries served by the Middle Eastern Department, viz., Ethiopia, Libya, the Sudan, and the United Arab Republic.

Pending the appointment of an African, the new department was placed temporarily in the charge of Mr. Mládek. In August 1964 Mr. Hamzah Merghani (Sudan) was appointed Director.

Partly owing to the actual and prospective increase in membership, and partly because of the enhanced demands on the staff for consultations and for technical assistance, the number of Fund employees grew more in the fiscal year 1960/61 than in any previous year since 1948. On April 30, 1961 the staff numbered 474, of 52 nationalities; this compared with 451, from 51 countries, a year earlier.

---

[1] *Summary Proceedings, 1960,* p. 117.

The appointments of Mr. Jacobsson and Mr. Cochran, which were both due to expire in 1961, were extended until their seventieth birthdays, in February 1964 and July 1962, respectively. Later, Mr. Cochran's appointment was extended to October 31, 1962, to cover the 1962 Annual Meeting.

CONVERTIBILITY (ARTICLE VIII)

The previous chapter recorded the attainment in 1958–59 of external convertibility for 15 European currencies, and the introduction of corresponding arrangements in 15 other countries. It was noted that none of these 30 members had at that time accepted the obligations of Article VIII, Sections 2, 3, and 4, and none of their currencies was, therefore, convertible in the Fund sense. At the beginning of 1959 there were still only 10 countries that had taken the latter step—Canada, Cuba, the Dominican Republic, El Salvador, Guatemala, Haiti, Honduras, Mexico, Panama, and the United States. Nevertheless the Fund's Annual Report for 1959 spoke of the progress made by the 30 countries as promising further advances toward the ideal visualized by the Articles of Agreement.[2] This theme was taken up by a number of speakers at the Annual Meeting, 1959.

Article VIII and Article XIV

Even before the Annual Meeting, the staff had been already pressing on with an examination of the questions that would arise as members prepared to relinquish the privileges available to them under Article XIV and to accept instead the obligations of Article VIII, Sections 2, 3, and 4. It will be convenient at this point to summarize what those obligations are. Article VIII requires members not to impose restrictions on current payments (Section 2), to avoid discriminatory currency arrangements and multiple currency practices (Section 3), and to convert on request, under certain conditions, balances of their currencies held by other members into those members' currencies or into gold (Section 4). It will be remembered that this last-mentioned provision occasioned much concern to the United Kingdom at Bretton Woods, as a result of which it was there limited to the conversion of balances recently acquired as a result of current transactions, or of which the conversion was needed to make payments for current transactions. The requirement in Section 4 is also subject to five other limitations designed to ensure, for example, that conversion cannot be demanded for balances built up from transactions that were contrary to the exchange regulations of the member asked to make the conversion.

Staff studies of the implications of these obligations showed that some clarification was needed before the Board could decide whether, and if so how far, to

[2] *Annual Report, 1959*, p. 30.

press members to accept them. This clarification took the form of two memoranda, one from the Legal Department and one from the Exchange Restrictions Department, presented to the Board in November 1959 and February 1960, respectively. The former provided definitions of key terms in the two Articles—"maintenance," "adaptation," and "introduction" of restrictions (Article XIV, Section 2); the phrase "making of payments and transfers for current international transactions" (Article VIII, Section 2); and the "notification" which members had to give to the Fund under Article XIV, Section 3, when they were ready to accept the obligations of Article VIII. The department explained that it was not possible for the Board to terminate the transitional period; the most it could do would be to express the opinion that conditions were favorable for the withdrawal of restrictions on the ground that, in its opinion, postwar transitional conditions had disappeared.

Discussing the effect of Article VIII, Sections 2, 3, and 4, when members decided to accept them, the memorandum made four points: (1) Members must perform the obligations of all three Sections and must dispense with the practices listed in Sections 2 and 3 unless these were specifically approved by the Fund. (2) Once a member had accepted the obligations of Article VIII, it could not retract from them—once under Article VIII, always under Article VIII. (3) The currency of a member accepting Article VIII could be used at once by other members to make voluntary repurchases. (4) However, such a currency would not be included in calculations of the monetary reserves of other members until the Fund's financial year following that in which the acceptance of Article VIII took place, except that it would be included immediately in those calculations for the purpose of deciding under Article V, Section 8 (*f*), whether charges for the use of the Fund's resources might be paid in currency instead of in gold.

The memorandum by the Exchange Restrictions Department addressed itself to the policy questions whether it was desirable to encourage more members to accept the obligations of Article VIII, and how the Fund should treat restrictions applied by such members after they had moved from Article XIV to Article VIII.

On the first of these issues, the memorandum suggested as a precondition for the Fund's approval of a member's moving to Article VIII that the member should be able to convince the Fund that it would terminate within a reasonable period any restrictions on current transactions which it was maintaining. The memorandum pointed out that the use of restrictions was still widespread. There were, however, a limited number of member countries, mainly in Western Europe, with favorable balance of payments and reserve positions, which were making little use of exchange restrictions (confined mainly to quantitative restrictions maintained for other than balance of payments reasons, and bilateralism). There should be little difficulty for the Fund in approving the few minor restrictions which these countries would wish to retain, subject to agreement on a timetable for their removal.

The second major problem discussed in the Exchange Restrictions Department's memorandum involved the identification of restrictions. The most difficult technical problem was likely to be posed by quantitative restrictions on imports maintained by countries which automatically provided exchange for permitted imports. Certainly the Fund needed to know about such restrictions because it had to advise the GATT on them. However, about half the members of the Fund were not members of the GATT. The memorandum also pointed to the difficulty of distinguishing between controls on current transactions and controls on capital transactions, and to the problem of restrictions maintained by nonmetropolitan areas. The latter had not so far been investigated, although an inquiry into restrictions in the sterling area was in progress.

Thirdly, the memorandum recommended that the Board should determine in advance which restrictive practices would need approval under Article VIII, in order that when concurring in a member's decision to move to Article VIII the Fund would be able to specify which continuing restrictions it was approving. It would probably be unnecessary to include in such approvals any types of restriction which were in wide use but were unimportant in their effects. There might also be some restrictions over which the Fund's jurisdiction was uncertain and which, therefore, it might not wish expressly to approve.

The memorandum went on to express the hope that members that had accepted the obligations of Article VIII would thereafter seek alternative ways of correcting their balances of payments, rather than reintroduce restrictions. For such members the Fund would need to lay down stricter criteria to determine whether restrictions were permissible; this would raise in an acute form the problem, which had already given trouble, of the lack of time fully to examine members' proposals. Because of this problem it was suggested that approval given for restrictions should be for a limited time, say, a year. Eventually, the Fund's close contact with members should overcome these difficulties, and in this connection the memorandum proposed that the Fund should hold annual consultations with countries accepting Article VIII as it was doing with countries under Article XIV.

These two memoranda were considered by the Board at two meetings in March 1960. Most of the views expressed by the staff were supported by the Executive Directors. The greatest measure of dissent was expressed by Mr. de Largentaye (France), who challenged in particular the concept of countries continuing under Article XIV. He believed that the privileges provided by Article XIV were limited strictly to the postwar transitional period, which he thought could not be said still to exist. Moreover, he considered that the terminology of Article XIV was a source of great legal complications. In these views, however, Mr. de Largentaye appeared to be a minority of one, although Mr. Southard (United States) shared his discontent with the perpetuation of the transitional period.

Apart from Mr. de Largentaye's dissent, almost the only substantial differences of viewpont which emerged from the discussion related to the questions (*a*) whether it was necessary for a country accepting the obligations of Article VIII, Sections 2, 3, and 4, to have a par value—Lord Cromer (United Kingdom) and Mr. Guth (Germany) thought that it was, but Mr. Southard doubted this—and (*b*) whether consultations under Article VIII should result in conclusions. Mr. Guth and Mr. Southard thought that such consultations, if held, should not result in formal decisions or recommendations, but the idea that they would not yield the maximum benefit to members without such conclusions was expressed by Mr. Rasminsky (Canada) and Mr. Garland (Australia). At the end of the meetings, therefore, the Chairman proposed that the staff should draft a statement to be made along the lines of its memoranda and of the Board discussions. This would be brought to the Board for review in May.

For the next several weeks numerous attempts were made by the staff and by Executive Directors to formulate a decision on the transition from Article XIV to Article VIII which might express the views of the whole Board, and it was the seventh of these drafts which was brought before the Board on May 18. Four meetings were devoted to detailed consideration of the draft and to redrafting, and on June 1 the Board took its decision.[3]

After describing the improvement in balance of payments positions which had led to the achievement of external convertibility, the decision offered guidance to members that were considering accepting the obligations of Article VIII, Sections 2, 3, and 4. This was done in four paragraphs. The first paragraph described a "restriction on payments and transfers for current transactions" as one which "involves a direct governmental limitation on the availability or use of exchange as such." The second recommended that before a member gave notice that it was accepting the obligations of Article VIII it should eliminate, as far as possible, restrictions which would require the approval of the Fund, and should satisfy itself that it was not likely to need to use such measures in the foreseeable future. Warning was given that, before approving the restrictions for balance of payments reasons only, the Fund would require to be satisfied that the measures were necessary and that their use would be temporary. Measures requiring approval which were maintained or introduced for other than balance of payments reasons should be avoided to the greatest possible extent. Nothing was said about the need to have a par value. The third paragraph stressed that

[3] E.B. Decision No. 1034-(60/27), June 1, 1960; below, Vol. III, p. 260.

consultations under Article VIII were not mandatory, but indicated that there was "great merit in periodic discussions between the Fund and its members even though no questions arise involving action under Article VIII." This slight watering down of the proposal for annual consultations between the members and the Fund was introduced by the staff after discussions with Executive Directors who wished to emphasize that such consultations were voluntary.

The final paragraph referred to import restrictions for balance of payments reasons and urged members to continue to supply information about these to the Fund. Where members were also members of the GATT, this would enable the Fund to collaborate with the GATT in examining the members' positions.

Following the decision of the Board just cited, steps were immediately taken by the staff to elucidate with the European countries likely to move to Article VIII what restrictions they maintained that would need to be approved by the Board.

Article VIII achieved

The Annual Report for 1960 was in preparation when the Board took the decision described above. The Report reproduced the decision and commented that "The world is now closer to the attainment of a multilateral system of payments free from exchange restrictions than at any time since the beginning of World War II." [4] Reference to the subject was made by a number of speakers at the Annual Meeting, 1960—for example by Mr. Karl Blessing, Governor for Germany, who said, inter alia,

> We fully endorse the conclusions expressed in the Executive Board's decision. Some of us probably thought last year that we would attend this Annual Meeting already as new Article VIII members. Yet, as is true with other irreversible decisions, careful examination of all aspects of the intended step is certainly more important than a gain of a few months. Now, however, as the technical preparatory work has been completed with those countries which are likely to move first, the way is open for the acceptance of the formal obligations of Article VIII by these members in the next few months; and Germany is certainly prepared to take this step.[5]

Despite Germany's readiness, the wish of the main European countries to move in concert delayed the completion of the necessary formalities for another five months. However, when on February 6 and 8, 1961, Belgium, France, Germany, Ireland, Italy, Luxembourg, the Netherlands, Peru, Sweden, and the United Kingdom came to the Board to announce their acceptance of the obligations of Article VIII from February 15, a swift response was possible.

The decisions of the ten members were welcomed with few reservations. Mr. Suzuki (Japan) criticized the discrimination widely practiced against his

[4] *Annual Report, 1960*, pp. 29–31, 122.
[5] *Summary Proceedings, 1960*, pp. 64–65.

country, and he and some other Directors pointed out that some of the ten countries still had extremely complex trade regulations. Mr. Southard referred to the maintenance of exchange rates outside the permitted range of variation in Germany's free markets for security transactions. He shared the view expressed by the staff that these constituted a multiple currency practice over which the Fund had jurisdiction, but he did not press the point as he knew that some Executive Directors differed from the staff on the matter. (It will be remembered that this issue was left open when the Board decided, on July 25, 1956, that members were free to control capital movements.[6] It has not, in fact, ever been settled.) This said, the Board noted the intentions of the ten members to accept the obligations of Article VIII, Sections 2, 3, and 4, and approved the continuance of certain restrictions by Belgium, France, Luxembourg, and the Netherlands.

Six weeks later the number of countries moving to Article VIII was increased to 11, when Saudi Arabia also undertook the necessary obligations. This brought the number of members that had achieved convertibility in the Fund sense to 21. By the end of 1965 the number had grown to 27; Australia, Austria, Costa Rica, Jamaica, Japan, Kuwait, and Nicaragua had been added, but Cuba had dropped out, having left the Fund (as described in a later chapter). The list of "Article VIII" countries continues, of course, to grow as more members feel able to accept the responsibilities involved.

The first consultation with a member that had accepted the obligations of Article VIII was held in August 1961, with the United Kingdom. At the same time the Board discussed a British request for a drawing of $1,500 million, to which further reference is made later in this chapter. By the end of November 1962, consultations had been held with all 11 of the members whose currencies became convertible in 1961, except for Saudi Arabia, and in subsequent years they have been held with all other countries under Article VIII.

INTER-CENTRAL-BANK COOPERATION

During the two years with which we are now concerned, the Fund continued to be consulted about numerous changes in exchange systems. Initial par values were approved for Italy, Uruguay, and Greece. New monetary units were introduced in Chile, France, and the Union of South Africa. There were devaluations of the currencies in Iceland (twice), Korea (three times), China, Costa Rica, Ecuador, Turkey, and Venezuela. Minor changes were sanctioned in a number of other countries; extensive changes in the exchange system of Cuba, which the Board decided needed its approval as multiple currency practices, led to a protest by the member and proved to be the first step toward a severance of relations between Cuba and the Fund.

[6] See above, p. 404.

The most significant change in exchange rates during the two years, however, was an increase of some 5 per cent in the par value of the deutsche mark, proposed on Saturday, March 4, 1961 (i.e., three weeks after the deutsche mark became convertible). As there had been no previous change in the par value of the deutsche mark, the revaluation fell within the 10 per cent permitted by Article IV, Section 5 (*c*) (i), without the Fund's approval, and the Fund therefore merely noted Germany's decision. Immediately afterward, the Netherlands felt it necessary to make a nearly equal revaluation of the guilder because of the close relations between that currency and the deutsche mark. This necessitated the approval of the Fund, since the Netherlands had devalued the guilder by more than 10 per cent in 1949; approval was given on March 6.

The two revaluations, of the deutsche mark and the guilder, created speculative expectations that other similar changes would follow, as a result of which considerable pressure developed on sterling. The central bank governors of the European countries, meeting at the Bank for International Settlements on March 12, 1961, found it necessary to issue a statement denying that any more changes were contemplated. They added that the central banks were cooperating closely in the exchange markets. A further statement issued a week later explained that the central banks were acting with a view to discouraging speculation and minimizing the repercussions of "hot" money movements on countries' exchange reserve positions. Their cooperation was to take the form of holding each others' currencies to a greater extent than previously, instead of converting them immediately into gold or into dollars, and of short-term lending of needed currencies. The statement concluded:

> These procedures will be temporary, pending the evolution of more permanent techniques for dealing with the problems of international financial disequilibria, particularly short-term capital movements within the framework of, or through reform of, the International Monetary Fund.

From this so-called Basle Agreement much has stemmed, both as regards closer cooperation between central banks and as regards the supplementation of gold by alternative forms of international liquidity.

Assistance to the United Kingdom under the Agreement reached a peak of $900 million between March and July 1961. Most of this had been repaid by the end of September 1961, with the assistance of a drawing of $1,500 million from the Fund in August and September which is further discussed below.

Meanwhile, the United States, which took the lead in these inter-central bank arrangements, had entered into large forward sales of deutsche mark; by mid-June its commitments reached $340 million, but as the spot dollar rate gradually rose these commitments were reduced, and they had been extinguished by the end of 1961. In July 1961 the United States similarly undertook forward sales of Swiss francs to offset the effects of a flow of hot money into Switzerland, which was raising the reserves of the Swiss National Bank far above traditional levels. It also undertook operations in Italian lire and Netherlands guilders.

Beginning in February 1962 the Federal Reserve System entered into systematic "swap" arrangements with other central banks. By February 1964 these totaled $2.05 billion, viz.: $500 million with the Bank of England; $250 million each with the central banks of Canada, Germany, and Italy; $150 million each with the Bank of Japan, the Swiss National Bank, and the Bank for International Settlements; $100 million each with the Bank of France and the Netherlands Bank; and $50 million each with the central banks of Austria, Belgium, and Sweden. From March 1962 through August 1963 the total amount of drawings on these lines of credit by the Federal Reserve System and the other central banks was $978 million, and the total amount repaid was $876 million, generally within six months. It was the countries cited in this paragraph (except for Austria and Switzerland) that later formed the Group of Ten.

Cooperation between central banks in connection with the London gold market is described in the next section.

GOLD: MOVEMENTS AND PRICES

The price of gold

From the time when the London gold market was reopened, in March 1954, until the autumn of 1960, the price of gold in that market did not vary beyond the limits set by the Fund ($34.65–35.35 a fine ounce), and indeed for most of the time it fluctuated within the narrower margins of the U.S. Treasury's buying and selling prices for gold ($34.9125 and $35.0875, respectively). In October 1960, however, these limits were exceeded. On Monday, October 17, the price was $35.255 a fine ounce, which was approximately equivalent to the U.S. Treasury's selling price plus transatlantic shipping costs. Thereafter it rose sharply, and on Thursday, October 20, the price at the "fixing" was equivalent to $36.55 a fine ounce, while strong buying demand pushed the price for some sales up to $41 a fine ounce.

That afternoon the U.S. Secretary of the Treasury issued a statement as follows:

> The United States will continue its policy of buying gold from and selling gold to foreign governments, central banks and, under certain conditions, international institutions, for the settlement of international balances or for other legitimate monetary purposes at the established rate of $35 per fine troy ounce exclusive of handling charges. Treasury Secretary Anderson has stated many times in the past that it is our firm position to maintain the dollar at its existing gold parity.

Following this announcement the price of gold eased, but it was not until February 23, 1961, that it fell below the U.S. selling price. A contributing factor to the decline in February was a U.S. Executive Order dated January 14, 1961 prohibiting the purchase and holding of gold outside the United States by U.S. citizens and by corporations owned in the United States, and requiring U.S. residents to sell their existing holdings of gold, or of securities representing gold on deposit, by June 1, 1961. President Kennedy also declared firmly, in a Message to Congress on February 6, 1961, that the U.S. dollar would not be devalued.

Nevertheless, the demand for gold continued, and by the end of August 1961 had pushed the price up again to $35.20 a fine ounce. Until then the market had been supplied by the Bank of England, with the assistance of the U.S. monetary authorities. In October 1961 the latter proposed to the authorities in the United Kingdom and the European continent an informal arrangement to share the burden of intervention in the London market to keep price fluctuations within a reasonable range. This proposal was accepted, and the central banks of Belgium, France, Germany, Italy, the Netherlands, Switzerland, and the United Kingdom agreed, in case of need, to cooperate with the Federal Reserve Bank of New York in a sales consortium for the purpose of stabilizing the gold market. The "Gold Pool" thus constituted provided gold for the first time in November 1961. It remained in operation until March 1968, although France ceased to act in it in June 1967. The foregoing developments did not directly affect the Fund, although the philosophy behind the arrangements for the Gold Pool reflected the Fund's policy of international cooperation to prevent the appearance of a premium price for gold.

Fund investment

Meanwhile, however, the drain on the gold reserves of the United States continued. Net outward movements of gold from U.S. reserves during 1960 amounted to $1,669 million, of which some $550 million net was supplied to the United Kingdom. Just as in 1959, so in 1960 the decrease in the U.S. gold reserves was a factor predisposing the Board to consider favorably a proposal to increase the Fund's investment of gold in U.S. securities. Such a proposal, for an increase in the investment from $500 million to $800 million, was made by the staff on November 22, 1960.

Recommending this measure to the Board, the staff pointed out that the expected considerable growth in Fund membership was bound to bring about a sizable increase in costs. The Fund's operating income had declined over the three previous fiscal years and would drop very sharply indeed in 1960/61, while interest rates were appreciably lower than when the investment program was enlarged in the previous year; as a result, the rate of accumulation of reserves had slowed down. The staff urged that the Fund should have reserves of a size which the financial world would regard as appropriate, and that consequently there should be an acceleration in their growth, rather than a retardation. It therefore recommended the additional investment, in order that the resulting increase in the Special Reserve might give greater assurance that the General Reserve would be available, if necessary, for purposes other than meeting prospective deficits in the Fund's annual budget.

These arguments were supported in the Board by all the Directors who spoke, and the proposal was approved without dissent.[7] Mr. de Largentaye (France), who had opposed the investment of the original $200 million and the subsequent increase to $500 million, now said that on the legal basis of the Board's earlier interpretations, the French Government was prepared to agree.

A further release of gold by the Fund to members' reserves, in connection with a drawing by the United Kingdom in August 1961, is discussed in the next section.

USE OF THE FUND'S RESOURCES: PRECEDENTS SET

During the year from October 1959 to September 1960 comparatively little use was made of the Fund's resources, 13 members drawing a total of $247.25 million, while repurchases totaled $660.96 million. The following year, by contrast, was one of the most active that the Fund had known: 22 members drew a total of $2,503.68 million, and repurchases came to $596.32 million. In 1959–60 there was no drawing larger than $50 million, but in 1960–61 Australia drew $175 million, India $250 million, and the United Kingdom $1,500 million.

Stand-by arrangements followed a similar pattern. In 1959–60 there were 14 new or extended arrangements, for a total of $378.63 million; in 1960–61 there were 24 such arrangements, for a total of $1,459.88 million, including one for $500 million for the United Kingdom.

Some notes follow on drawings and stand-by arrangements that presented special features.

In February 1960 Iceland drew $2,812,500 (25 per cent of its quota) from the Fund, and was granted a stand-by arrangement for $5,625,000. Under this arrangement Iceland subsequently drew $4 million, including $800,000 in Danish kroner, the first time that this currency had been used in a Fund drawing.

In January 1961 Yugoslavia drew $45 million, of which it took $10 million in U.S. dollars and the remainder in five European currencies. This was the first

[7] E.B. Decision No. 1107-(60/50), November 30, 1960; below, Vol. III, p. 277.

occasion on which a drawing was so widely distributed between currencies, and anticipated the acceptance of the obligations of Article VIII by France, Germany, Italy, the Netherlands, and the United Kingdom in the following month. It also marked the first use of Italian lire in Fund drawings.

In February 1961 Chile drew $16 million in Argentine pesos and was granted a stand-by arrangement for $75 million. Thereby four precedents were established. The drawing was the first of a Latin American currency. It was also the first time that a member had drawn on the Fund for resources with which to terminate a bilateral agreement; the pesos drawn by Chile were used in partial settlement of the balance due to Argentina on a bilateral trade and payments agreement between the two countries, which had been wound up on January 31, 1961. Thirdly, the total made available to Chile in the drawing and stand-by arrangement, if fully utilized, would have raised the Fund's holdings of Chilean escudos to 189 per cent of Chile's quota; this was the first time that the Fund had accepted a commitment to increase its holdings beyond 175 per cent of a member's quota. Fourthly, the discussion of the stand-by arrangement led to the discontinuance, as described below, of the clause permitting the Fund to give notice to terminate drawing rights.

The acceptance of the obligations of Article VIII, Sections 2, 3, and 4, by the principal European countries in February 1961 made it possible for the Fund to receive their currencies in repurchases, provided that the Fund's holdings of these currencies did not exceed 75 per cent of the members' quotas. Use was first made of this facility by Burma, which in February 1961 repurchased the equivalent of $4 million of kyats with sterling.

In August 1961 Japanese yen were drawn for the first time as part of a drawing of $250 million in six currencies by India.

Also in August, in connection with the drawing of $1,500 million by the United Kingdom, use was made of Article VII, Section 2 (ii), which enables the Fund to replenish its holdings of currencies by requiring the issuing members to sell them to it for gold. This was the first occasion on which the Fund undertook such replenishment of several currencies simultaneously. Gold was used to purchase the nine currencies drawn by the United Kingdom to the extent of $500 million, being apportioned so as to provide one third of the amount drawn of each currency. One of the currencies so purchased was the Canadian dollar, for which no par value existed at the time. This necessitated amending the comprehensive decision on fluctuating currencies taken in 1954 so as to include, in the transactions there discussed, the sale of gold by the Fund under Article VII, Section 2.[8]

[8] E.B. Decision No. 1245-(61/45), August 4, 1961; below, Vol. III, p. 224.

CONDITIONS FOR STAND-BY ARRANGEMENTS AGAIN

THE "PRIOR NOTICE" CLAUSE

In connection with a stand-by arrangement for Paraguay, approved in August 1959, Mr. Saad (United Arab Republic, Egyptian Region) questioned the phrase "unless the Fund gives Paraguay prior notice to the contrary," which was included in the stand-by arrangement as a limitation on Paraguay's right to draw under the arrangement. On that occasion the Deputy General Counsel explained that because the ineligibility procedure in Article V, Section 5, was regarded as a severe sanction, two alternative provisions had been included in this and numerous other stand-by arrangements. One was a cross reference to an undertaking, usually given by the member in the letter of intent, that if it ceased to observe certain objective criteria it would not draw without consulting the Fund. The other was the clause permitting the Fund to give notice to terminate drawing rights, which might be done for reasons other than those which would bring into operation the undertakings in the letter of intent.

In February 1961 a reasoned study of the latter provision was presented to the Board by the Legal Department in response to questions by Mr. de Largentaye (France) in October 1960 and again in February 1961. The Legal Department recalled the provision which appeared in identical terms in paragraph 5 of the decision of October 1952 and paragraph 4 of that of December 1953 permitting the Fund to suspend a member's drawing rights after

> (b) a decision of the Executive Board to suspend transactions either generally (under Article XVI, Section 1 (*a*) (ii)) or in order to consider a proposal, made by an Executive Director or the Managing Director, formally to suppress or limit the eligibility of the member.

The memorandum referred also to the special provision for longer-term stand-by arrangements made in the decision of December 1953:

> With respect to stand-by arrangements for periods of more than six months, the Fund and the member might find it appropriate to reach understandings additional to those set forth in this decision.

Finally, it recalled the discussion which took place in connection with the stand-by arrangement with Peru in 1954. The staff pointed out that for members with fluctuating rates, uncertain economic conditions, or complex stabilization programs, the feeling persisted that protective clauses were needed to see that improper use was not made of the Fund's resources, and to give reasonable effect to the following clause in each stand-by arrangement:

> In consideration of the policies and intentions set forth in the annexed letter, the International Monetary Fund agrees to a stand-by arrangement for the support of those policies and intentions.

The outcome had been protective clauses of the two types mentioned by the Deputy General Counsel in August 1959. That now challenged—providing that the Fund might give prior notice to terminate drawing rights—had been included in some thirty stand-by arrangements before it was questioned in October 1960, and in one instance the Fund had given notice under it.

The legal basis for the clause might be found in one of three provisions, viz., (1) the reference in the decision of December 1953 to "additional understandings" for stand-by arrangements of more than six months; (2) the authority given to the Fund by Article V, Section 4, to impose "terms which safeguard its interests" (since almost all stand-by arrangements necessitated a waiver under that Section); and (3) paragraph 5 (b) of the 1952 decision (4 (b) of the 1953 decision), quoted above. Of these three, the Legal Department regarded the third as the most appropriate, especially as it was felt that relations between the Fund and its members had progressed to a point at which Article V, Section 5 (Ineligibility to use the Fund's resources), on which it was based, could be invoked without disturbing these relations. Since this Section read, in part, "Whenever the Fund is of the opinion that any member is using the resources of the Fund in a manner contrary to the purposes of the Fund," reliance on it meant that the member's eligibility could be withdrawn only if the member was actually using the Fund's resources. However, it seemed probable that if a member was not "using" the Fund's resources at all, any drawing which the member wished to make would fall wholly within the gold tranche, and so be permissible in any event under the Fund's policies for such drawings.

The conclusion at which the Legal Department arrived as a result of this argument was that the "prior notice" clause might be safely omitted from future stand-by arrangements, being replaced by a requirement that a member to whom notice had been given under clause (b) above should consult the Fund before making any further drawing. The memorandum concluded that this new requirement should be substituted for the "prior notice" clause in the 17 current stand-by arrangements which contained that clause, except in the one with Yugoslavia. In this, the Fund's right to give notice to the member suspending drawings was limited to certain objective developments in Yugoslavia's stabilization program. It was felt that to withdraw this clause and rely on more general suspensory powers might be regarded as a retroactive measure detrimental to Yugoslavia's interests.

The staff's proposals were approved by the Board on February 20, 1961, except that as drafted they covered that part of clause (b) which referred to a general decision to suspend transactions under Article XVI; it was agreed that there was no need to provide for special consultation before drawings were resumed if the decision to suspend them were a general one taken under the terms of Article XVI. Accordingly the decision was taken to withdraw the "prior notice" clause (except from the Yugoslav stand-by arrangement) as proposed by the staff, but in place of it to add to clause (b) the sentence:

> When notice of a decision of formal ineligibility or of a decision to consider a proposal is given pursuant to this paragraph, purchases under this stand-by arrangement will be resumed only after consultation has taken place between the Fund and the member and agreement has been reached on the terms for the resumption of such purchases.[9]

In consequence of the foregoing decision, the "prior notice" clause was not included in any subsequent stand-by arrangement. The next one approved, with Peru on February 27, 1961, contained only the usual undertaking, in the letter of intent, that Peru would consult the Fund before drawing further if it departed from its stabilization program in certain specific respects. This technique continued to be relied upon for stand-by arrangements with Latin American countries. It was not, however, appropriate where the letter of intent did not include quantified targets against which the achievement of the program could be measured. Such a situation arose shortly in connection with an arrangement for $100 million with Australia, approved on April 26, 1961. This was in addition to Australia's drawing of $175 million. The staff agreed with the Australian Government that the letter of intent should include a phrase as follows:

> Should any major shift in the direction or emphasis of policy become necessary during the currency of the stand-by arrangement the Australian Government would, at the request of the Managing Director, be ready to consult with the Fund and, if necessary, reach new understandings before any request for a further drawing is made.

Similar "major shift" clauses were included in the letters of intent annexed to stand-by arrangements approved for South Africa in July and for the United Kingdom in August, 1961.

Phasing

Another question about the terms of stand-by arrangements was raised by Mr. Jorge A. Montealegre (Nicaragua), Alternate to Mr. Mayobre, when a stand-by arrangement for $15 million with Guatemala was brought to the Board on August 11, 1961. This arrangement contained clauses providing (*a*) that not more than $5 million should be drawn within the first six months of the year for which the stand-by was granted, and (*b*) that not more than $10 million in all should be drawn (except to offset repurchases) without further consultation with the Fund and agreement on the terms on which the final $5 million would be made available. Mr. Montealegre took exception particularly to the second of these provisions. He felt that it detracted from the right to draw the $15 million of the stand-by arrangement and was in contradiction of the clause in the arrangement giving that right.

---

[9] E.B. Decision No. 1151-(61/6), February 20, 1961; below, Vol. III, p. 234.

The General Counsel said that the provisions had been included in a number of stand-by arrangements without being questioned by the Board. In the present instance the staff felt that if it became necessary for Guatemala to draw as much as $10 million under the arrangement, its stabilization program might not be working out as well as expected, so that a fresh look at the problem would be beneficial. Asked by Mr. Saad whether it was usual to include such a clause in all stand-by arrangements for sums equivalent to the quotas of the countries concerned, the General Counsel said that this was not so: the terms of stand-by arrangements were varied according to the conditions and problems of the members to which they were granted.

Several Executive Directors supported the staff, and while others were doubtful whether the clause was necessary in the circumstances, it was decided to let it stand. It may be added that when this type of clause was again questioned in 1964, in connection with a stand-by arrangement for the Dominican Republic, the Deputy General Counsel informed the Board that it had been used on a number of occasions but was regarded as somewhat exceptional; it was not standard practice.

INTERNATIONAL LIQUIDITY: THE PROBLEM EMERGES

It will be recalled that in the report *International Reserves and Liquidity*, written in 1958, the staff had argued that the more rapid growth of world trade than of world reserves made it doubtful whether the Fund's resources were sufficient to enable it to perform its duties under the Articles.[10] The attainment of external convertibility for the main European currencies at the end of 1958 added a new dimension to the problem by giving rise to massive short-term capital movements.

We have already noted two facets of the Fund's response to this situation. The first, a large increase in quotas, was recorded in the previous chapter; the second, the provision of access to its resources on an unprecedented scale, was described above. For the time being this was thought to be enough, especially as there were seen to be advantages in providing additional reserves on a conditional basis, as is done by the Fund, rather than unconditionally in the form of owned reserves. Nevertheless, international liquidity came to claim an increasing share of the Fund's attention. We may here trace this development through the Annual Reports and Annual Meetings of 1960 and 1961.

The Annual Report for 1960 took an optimistic view of the problem. While official reserves (apart from those of the U.S.S.R. and the countries associated

[10] See above, pp. 447–48.

with it) had fallen in 1959 by an estimated $700 million, this was offset on the one hand by an increase of about $1 billion in the gold holdings of the Fund, and on the other by a large increase in the foreign exchange holdings of commercial banks. As a whole, the Report observed, world liquidity actually improved. If account were taken of the increase in the Fund's holdings not only of gold but also of currencies suitable for international settlements, the growth in resources available through the Fund was several times that of the decrease in directly owned reserves.[11]

At the Annual Meeting, 1960, those Governors who referred to the matter expressed agreement with the Annual Report, and in his closing speech Mr. Jacobsson cited a consensus that there was "no lack of international liquidity." [12] This in fact remained the official view of the Fund for some time to come, but it was coupled both with an apprehension that the situation might not remain favorable and with an insistence on the important role to be played by the resources which the Fund controlled.

It was this last point which was mainly stressed in a brief reference to international liquidity in the Annual Report for 1961.[13] The volatility of the situation had been enhanced by the acceptance early in 1961 of the convertibility obligations of Article VIII by the major European countries. Favorable notice was taken of statements that had been made at about the same time by the Prime Minister of Australia, the British Chancellor of the Exchequer, and the President of the United States, all of whom called attention to their countries' drawing rights in the Fund as an integral part of their reserves. The Report pointed out that for all members of the Fund the aggregate of drawing rights was almost as large as the total foreign exchange components of their owned reserves.

Considerably more attention was paid to the problem during the Annual Meeting, 1961. Two or three Governors believed that, reinforced by the availability of the Fund's resources, international liquidity was adequate to meet the world's needs—one Governor (Mr. Holtrop, the Netherlands) even concluded that there had latterly been an oversupply of liquidity [14]—but the more general view was that care would be needed to ensure that no lack of reserves developed. In this connection Governors generally welcomed proposals made by the Managing Director for studying arrangements for the Fund to borrow needed currencies, and for reviewing the use of the Fund's resources to finance balance of payments deficits due to capital movements. These proposals form the main subject of Chapter 19.

---

[11] *Annual Report, 1960*, pp. 60, 64–65, 67.
[12] *Summary Proceedings, 1960*, p. 125.
[13] *Annual Report, 1961*, p. 114.
[14] *Summary Proceedings, 1961*, p. 113.

PART IV

Wider Horizons

CHAPTER

19

New Techniques, New Aims (1961-63)

AN INITIATIVE taken by the Managing Director in February 1961 led, during the ensuing two years, to three major advances in the Fund's techniques, facilitating the freer use of its resources. During the same period, the Fund took steps to offer larger drawings for the purpose of meeting fluctuations in the export earnings of the less developed countries. These decisions greatly strengthened the Fund's ability to deal effectively with current monetary problems. They enabled it increasingly to focus attention on the problem of international liquidity which, with its concomitant need for a reform of the international monetary system, became its major concern in subsequent years.

In this and the remaining chapters of this history, only brief references will be made to the continuing activity of the Fund in other directions. Nevertheless, the intricacy of the subjects that are here discussed is such that even a summary review of the years 1961–63 transcends reasonable limits for a single chapter. The present one will be concerned mainly with the three major advances in technique mentioned above. Other important aspects of the Fund's work in these two years will be considered in Chapter 20.

MEMBERSHIP AND BOARD

Membership

In October 1961 the Fund was notified that the union between the United Arab Republic and the Syrian Arab Republic had been terminated, and the Board decided that the two countries were separate members of the Fund.

During the two years October 1961 to September 1963 there was an unprecedented accession of members to the Fund, mainly because the ending of colonial rule in Africa created a large number of new nations, which all sought to join the Fund. The new members and the dates of their admission were as follows: Cyprus (December 1961), Liberia (March 1962), Senegal, Somalia, and Togo (August 1962), Kuwait, Sierra Leone, and Tanganyika (September 1962), Jamaica (February 1963), Ivory Coast (March 1963), Niger (April 1963), Upper Volta (May 1963), Cameroon, the Central African Republic, Chad, Congo (Brazzaville), and Dahomey (July 1963), Algeria, Burundi, Congo (Leopoldville, later Democratic Republic of Congo), Gabon, Guinea, the Malagasy Republic, Mali, Mauritania, Rwanda, Trinidad and Tobago, and Uganda (September 1963). These raised the total number of members from 73 to 102. Comments on the quotas allotted to certain of these countries will be found in Chapter 20.

Initial par values were agreed during the two years 1961–63 for Afghanistan, Cyprus, Jamaica, Kuwait, Liberia, Malaya, New Zealand, Nigeria, Portugal, and Somalia. The Board also agreed to the devaluation of the Israel pound from I£1.80=$1 to I£3.00=$1.

In January 1963 a change was made in the arrangements for the formal accession of members to the Fund. Previously this had taken place at the U.S. State Department, where the representatives of the new members had signed the Articles, of which the United States is the custodian, in the presence of photographers and with appropriate speeches. This procedure had been criticized by some new members as appearing to be an American, not a Fund, function. Accordingly the Secretary of the Fund, in conjunction with the Secretary of the World Bank, arranged that in future the representative of each new member would sign the Articles privately at the State Department and subsequently be escorted by the Secretaries to the Fund and Bank buildings, where the new member would be welcomed with appropriate ceremony.

Managing Director and Deputy Managing Director

Mr. Jacobsson died unexpectedly on May 5, 1963, while on a visit to London. An appreciation of his qualities appears at the end of this chapter. He was succeeded from September 5, 1963 by Mr. Pierre-Paul Schweitzer, who had been Deputy Governor of the Bank of France since 1960 and before that Director of the French Treasury. In 1947–48 he had been an Alternate Executive Director of the Fund.

On the expiration of Mr. Cochran's term of office as Deputy Managing Director, on October 31, 1962, he was succeeded by Mr. Southard, who since February 1949 had been the Executive Director of the Fund appointed by the United States. Prior to that appointment, Mr. Southard had held senior posts in the U.S. Treasury and Federal Reserve Board. Earlier, he had taught economics at the University of California and at Cornell University, where he became Chairman of the Department of Economics in 1946.

Pierre-Paul Schweitzer, Managing Director, 1963–

EXECUTIVE DIRECTORS

Mr. Wilhelm Hanemann (Germany) was appointed to succeed Mr. Guth from January 1, 1962. (Mr. Hanemann had been Alternate to Mr. Emminger and Mr. Guth from September 1956 to September 1959.) On May 16 Mr. Montealegre (Nicaragua) was elected to succeed Mr. Mayobre, whose Alternate he had been since April 1960. This election, necessitated by the appointment of Mr. Mayobre as an Under-Secretary of the United Nations, was unusual in that there were two candidates for the vacancy. Guatemala nominated and voted for Mr. Manuel Bendfeldt Jauregui, who had been its Alternate Governor of the Fund in 1954. Costa Rica, El Salvador, Mexico, Nicaragua, and Venezuela nominated Mr. Montealegre, and Costa Rica, Honduras, Mexico, and Nicaragua voted for him, giving him a majority of 3,174 votes to 400. Reporting Mr. Montealegre's election to the Board, the staff pointed out that he would be entitled to cast the votes of all the countries eligible to elect him, including those of Cuba, El Salvador, and Venezuela, which had not voted, and also those of Guatemala.

In June 1962 the Board set up a committee to establish the rules for the Ninth Regular Election of Executive Directors. This was to take place during the Annual Meeting, 1962, and the Directors elected would take office in November. In a report dated August 8, the committee recorded that since the previous increase in the membership of the Executive Board—to 18 in November 1958—eight countries with a total of 4,836 votes had joined the Fund, and many other applications were pending. It therefore recommended that the Governors should be invited to agree to the number of Directors being increased to 19 as soon as the votes of new members reached 8,000. So rapidly was membership increasing in the summer of 1962 that when, only five weeks later, the committee put forward a revised report, the number of new members that had joined since November 1958 had grown to 13, with total votes amounting to 7,135. In this second report the committee submitted a revised recommendation to the effect that a nineteenth Executive Director should be added to the Board within 90 days after the votes of members joining since 1958 reached 8,000, provided that at least 3,500 votes were available to be cast for the additional Executive Director. The proviso was prompted by the consideration that some members joining the Fund before September 1962 might vote for one of the 18 Executive Directors then being elected, as indeed six of them did (their votes totaled 4,112). The committee proposed that the Directors should be free to extend the period of 90 days to 120 days. By Resolution 17-5, the Governors approved the recommendation *in toto*.

The Ninth Regular Election, held on September 17, 1962, resulted in the re-election of Messrs. Bicalho (Brazil), Garland (Australia), Klein (Argentina), Lieftinck (Netherlands), Saad (United Arab Republic), Siglienti (Italy), Suzuki (Japan), Tann (China), and van Campenhout (Belgium). Mr. Práxedes Reina

Hermosillo (Mexico) was elected to succeed Mr. Montealegre, Mr. Arthur Fitzwalter Wynne Plumptre (Canada) to succeed Mr. Rasminsky, Mr. Karl Skjaeveland (Norway) to succeed Mr. Ásgeirsson, and Sumanang (Indonesia) to succeed Mr. Slamet. The new Executive Directors took office on November 1, and on the same date Mr. William B. Dale (United States) was appointed to succeed Mr. Southard.

The only changes in the groupings of countries for the purpose of electing Directors were additions caused by the accession of new members. New Zealand voted for Mr. Garland, Cyprus for Mr. Lieftinck, Kuwait for Mr. Saad, Portugal for Mr. Siglienti, Laos for Sumanang, and Nepal for Mr. Suzuki. Subsequently, Mr. Saad undertook to look after the interests in the Fund of Liberia and Somalia, neither of which voted in the election, and later also of Algeria. Mr. Plumptre agreed to look after those of Jamaica.

The requirements of the Governors' Resolution 17-5 were met on April 24, 1963, when Niger became a member of the Fund. (Niger's 325 votes brought the total of votes of members that had joined since the 1958 election to 8,310, of which 4,198 were eligible to be cast for the nineteenth Director.) However, it was clear that the countries eligible to elect the new Director would be primarily in Africa, and there were still 16 African countries whose applications for membership, while well advanced, had not become effective. It seemed undesirable to proceed with the election while this situation existed. If the election could be postponed until the next Annual Meeting, it was expected that all the applicants would by then have been able to fulfill the requirements for membership. The Board decided on May 29 to recommend to the Governors that the date should be postponed accordingly, and the Governors agreed. The Interim Election took place on October 3, 1963, Mr. Louis Kandé (Senegal) being elected by the votes of Burundi, Cameroon, the Central African Republic, Chad, Congo (Brazzaville), Congo (Leopoldville), Dahomey, Gabon, Guinea, Ivory Coast, Liberia, the Malagasy Republic, Mali, Mauritania, Niger, Nigeria, Rwanda, Senegal, Sierra Leone, Tanganyika, Togo, Trinidad and Tobago, Uganda, and Upper Volta.

On September 18, 1963, Sir Eric Roll, K.C.M.G., was appointed by the United Kingdom to succeed Mr. Pitblado.

ANNUAL MEETING ARRANGEMENTS

The 1962 Annual Meetings, in Washington, were attended by delegates from 81 member countries and observers from 17 other countries whose applications for membership were in process, as well as observers from 16 international organizations. Considerable congestion, both of the physical accommodation and of the timetable, resulted. Accordingly, the Annual Meetings Procedures Committees

> considered the difficulties of accommodating all activities of the Annual Meetings and directed the Secretaries of the Fund and Bank to review various aspects of the Annual Meetings and submit a report before the next Annual Meetings.[1]

The two Secretaries submitted reports, in identical terms, to the Boards of Directors of the Fund and the Bank on April 23, 1963. These reports recognized that, because the Meetings had become more crowded than formerly, there was less time available for private appointments, regional meetings, and informal exchanges of views—in short, for those discussions "in the corridors" which constituted a valuable aspect of the Meetings. They therefore suggested that the conduct of the Meetings should be eased by a number of changes in the organization of them, viz., (1) limiting the number of sessions devoted to the work of the Fund or the Bank separately, replacing them by joint sessions at which Governors would be invited to address their remarks to the work of both institutions; (2) restricting the formal sessions as far as possible to the mornings, leaving the afternoons free for other activities; (3) lengthening the duration of the Meetings (and scheduling sessions on Sundays), if necessary to achieve the foregoing; (4) encouraging Governors to extend their remarks in the record (as a preferred alternative to limiting the length of speeches).

The Secretaries also suggested that it might be well for speakers to address the meeting from a rostrum rather than from their seats in the body of the hall, thus avoiding the necessity for extensive amplification and public-address equipment. Finally, they called attention to the difficulty of arranging satisfactory social gatherings with so large a number of persons present, and suggested that there should be some curtailment of social activities.

The Board considered this report in May and approved most of the Secretaries' recommendations, taking exception, however, to the suggestions that sessions might be held on Sundays. Similar decisions were reached by the Board of the Bank. An amended report was accordingly submitted to the Governors.

The Executive Directors also agreed to a recommendation that before accepting an invitation from a member country to hold the Annual Meetings in its territory, the Fund should obtain satisfactory assurances that such facilities as the prompt provision of visas and the avoidance of undue customs delays would be accorded by the inviting government to all attending in an official capacity, together with their spouses. Such assurances having been received from the Japanese Government, the Board recommended to the Governors that the 1964 Annual Meetings should be held in Tokyo, and this was approved.

[1] *Summary Proceedings, 1962,* p. 217.

CANADIAN PAR VALUE RE-ESTABLISHED

A major event in the field of exchange rates during this period was the establishment of a new par value for the Canadian dollar in May 1962. Since 1950 the Canadian dollar had fluctuated, at first freely but since June 1961 under the influence of the operations of the Canadian Exchange Account, which had kept it within a range of 3–5 per cent discount on the U.S. dollar. During 1962, however, the rate had shown signs of weakening, and an expectation that it would depreciate had caused adverse speculative movements. As a result, reserves fell by over $400 million.

Describing this situation to the Board at an evening meeting on Wednesday, May 2, 1962, Mr. Rasminsky (Canada) said that the Canadian authorities had reached the conclusion that the time had come to re-establish a par value. The Government had considered proposing the existing rate of Can$1=US$0.95, but had decided that this would not eliminate uncertainty from the market; this rate might not carry conviction, since substantial reserve losses had been sustained at it. On the other hand, the Government believed that a rate of Can$1=US$0.90 would be lower than was needed for equilibrium, and therefore might not gain international acceptance; it had accordingly decided to propose a new par value of Can$1=US$0.925.

The Canadian proposal illustrated in a practical manner the problem for the Fund of handling the devaluation of a major currency. There had been extensive preliminary telephone conversations between Mr. Rasminsky and the Managing Director during the last week of April. But the relevant decision was not taken by the Canadian Minister of Finance until Tuesday, May 1, and although advance notice was given to the Managing Director late that afternoon by telephone, it was not until Mr. Rasminsky reached Washington at three o'clock on the afternoon of May 2, bringing with him the Order in Council that had been signed that morning, that sufficiently firm information was available to enable a notification of the proposal to be sent to Executive Directors. Thus, when they met at 6:00 P.M. that day to discuss the proposal, little time had been allowed them to consider the appropriateness of the new rate proposed. Some Directors felt that the request should be deferred until they had had an opportunity to consult their governments. Mr. Rasminsky, however, pointed out that where an active exchange market existed, as it did for the Canadian dollar, it was impossible to defer action once a decision to change the rate had been reached. While he regretted the short notice given to the Board, he suggested that in practice it was probably no less adequate than that allowed when, as sometimes happened, a proposal for a devaluation was put forward at a weekend.

The Managing Director reminded the Board that the Canadian Government had formally stated that the change was necessary to correct a fundamental disequilibrium, and that at a very early stage in the Fund's history it had been agreed

> that the extent of the change in par value, necessary to correct a fundamental disequilibrium, cannot be determined with precision and that in reaching a decision on a member's proposal to change its par value . . . the member should be given the benefit of any reasonable doubt.[2]

Executive Directors generally accepted the difficulties of the situation, and the Board approved the new par value proposed, adding a warm welcome for Canada's return to the par value system.

Unfortunately the new rate did not put an end to the losses of reserves. A cessation of investment from abroad had left the current account deficit uncovered, and a recurrence of speculation against the Canadian dollar in the early part of June led to the Government's taking emergency measures. One of these was an application to the Fund for a drawing of $300 million, which was brought to the Board on Sunday morning, June 24, 1962. Mr. Plumptre (Canada) explained that the Prime Minister would that afternoon be announcing fiscal measures designed to protect the balance of payments and to reduce to less than one half the budget deficit expected for the fiscal year. The Board agreed to the drawing, of which the amount was equivalent to that part of the Fund's holdings of Canadian dollars which was below 75 per cent of the Canadian quota (the "super gold tranche"), plus the gold tranche and the first credit tranche.

PREPARING FOR A CONVERTIBLE WORLD

On February 10, 1961 the Managing Director made an important statement to the Board on the subject of the future activities of the Fund. This statement immediately followed the announcement by ten member countries, including the major European ones, that they had accepted the obligations of Article VIII, Sections 2, 3, and 4. Mr. Jacobsson began by suggesting that the Fund should welcome the readiness of member countries (as recently voiced by Australia, the United Kingdom, and the United States) to regard access to the Fund's resources as a normal part of their reserves. He then remarked that the time had come when the Fund should not hesitate to allow members to make drawings that would raise the Fund's holdings of their currencies above 200 per cent of quota in appropriate circumstances. Finally, he indicated three fields in which progress was necessary if the Fund was to play a maximum part in international financial arrangements.

These three fields were the selection of currencies to be used in drawings and repurchases, the replenishment by borrowing of the Fund's resources of cur-

[2] E.B. Decision No. 278-3, March 1, 1948; see above, p. 203.

rencies needed for drawings, and the availability of drawings to assist members which had balance of payments difficulties owing to capital movements.

These ideas were discussed generally in informal sessions of the Board on February 24 and 27, 1961. Two months later, on the occasion of the Fund's annual report to ECOSOC, the Managing Director took the opportunity to expound them as forming the Fund's reactions to the needs of its members in "this new world of freer trade and convertible currencies." [3]

Beginning in May 1961 and continuing through July 1962, the Board considered the Managing Director's proposals at a series of meetings, in the course of which decisions were taken on each of the three subjects mentioned. These decisions were, however, reached in inverse order to that in which the topics had been introduced by the Managing Director, and it is in this inverse order that they will be discussed here. The major questions which each raised for the Fund can best be considered separately under each heading, but it must be remembered that the Board was at all times conscious of the mutual interaction of the three subjects, and that a strictly chronological study would deal sometimes with one and sometimes with another.

DRAWINGS FOR CAPITAL PURPOSES

Article VI, Section 1, of the Articles of Agreement reads as follows:

> *Use of the Fund's resources for capital transfers.*—(*a*) A member may not make net use of the Fund's resources to meet a large or sustained outflow of capital, and the Fund may request a member to exercise controls to prevent such use of the resources of the Fund. If, after receiving such a request, a member fails to exercise appropriate controls, the Fund may declare the member ineligible to use the resources of the Fund.
>
> (*b*) Nothing in this Section shall be deemed
>
> (i) to prevent the use of the resources of the Fund for capital transactions of reasonable amount required for the expansion of exports or in the ordinary course of trade, banking or other business, or
>
> (ii) to affect capital movements which are met out of a member's own resources of gold and foreign exchange, but members undertake that such capital movements will be in accordance with the purposes of the Fund.

In 1946, at the request of the United States, the Fund had interpreted the Articles, by Decision No. 71-2, as meaning that

> authority to use the resources of the Fund is limited to use in accordance with its purposes to give temporary assistance in financing balance of payments deficits on current account for monetary stabilization operations.[4]

[3] Per Jacobsson, *International Monetary Problems, 1957–1963* (Washington, 1964), p. 222.

[4] See above, p. 149.

Taken literally, this appeared to preclude the use of the Fund's resources by a member country whose balance of payments difficulties were due to a deficit on capital account. At Bretton Woods the general assumption was that capital movements would continue to be controlled. Since 1957, however, there had been a gradual movement toward freeing international capital movements from controls. Particularly within the six countries making up the European Economic Community, substantial progress had been made, by 1960, in permitting free movement of international capital. Although the official position within the OEEC was that capital movements were not necessarily in a desirable direction, so that the burden of proof in respect of their liberalization was on those who wished to liberalize, the advantages of freely moving international capital were becoming more widely recognized, and its movements less restricted. As a result, the danger of balance of payments difficulties arising from short-term capital movements of a speculative kind was again apparent. It was the possibility of permitting a member to draw on the Fund if it encountered difficulties of this nature that the Managing Director, in his statement on February 10, 1961, suggested should be examined.

In the initial informal sessions devoted to Mr. Jacobsson's statement, this proposal was in general favorably received. Mr. Rasminsky (Canada), recalling the Bretton Woods presumption mentioned above, said that he would like to see the Fund develop along lines that would allow short-term capital movements to take place without disturbing consequences, but he was doubtful whether that was legally possible. Should it be found necessary to amend Article VI, Section 1, to permit drawing on the Fund to offset short-term capital movements, he feared that this might encourage such movements to the point where it would also be necessary to widen beyond 1 per cent the margin on either side of par within which members were required, by Article IV, Section 3 (i), to maintain their exchange rates. Mr. de Largentaye (France) also believed that Article VI, as interpreted in 1946, precluded any use of the Fund's resources to assist members whose difficulties stemmed from capital movements. Mr. van Campenhout (Belgium), however, expressed doubts that the Bretton Woods formulation was intended categorically to debar drawings in such circumstances.

On May 24, 1961, the Legal Department sent to the Board the result of several months' study of the relevant provisions. It commented that the Governors did not discuss or pass upon the 1946 interpretation, which was made rather hurriedly in view of the imminence of the Annual Meeting; and that the decision had been taken on the basis of a staff memorandum, also prepared rather hurriedly, which further study had shown to be defective in a number of respects. It then pointed out (1) that the interpretation given at the request of the United States was incomplete because it ignored the provisions in Article VI, Section 1 (*b*) (i), permitting the use of the Fund's resources for certain capital transfers; (2) that Article V, Section 3 (*a*), did not specifically limit the use of the Fund's resources to the financing of current account deficits, but permitted them for making payments "which are consistent with the provisions of this Agreement"—i.e., inter alia, consistent with Article VI, Section 1, which barred only drawings to meet a "large or sustained outflow of capital"; and (3) that Article VIII, Section 4, which was not discussed in the 1946 memorandum, implied that it was permissible to use the Fund's resources for capital transfers.

In the light of this analysis, the staff concluded that the meaning of Article VI, Section 1, was that there were three purposes for which the Fund's resources might be used: (1) to meet current account deficits; (2) to meet deficits on capital account that were not large or sustained; (3) to meet deficits on account of the special types of capital transaction mentioned in Article VI, Section 1 (*b*) (i). The Legal Department therefore recommended that the interpretation of 1946 should be amended by adding to it the words "or to finance capital transfers in accordance with the provisions of the Articles, including Article VI."

A month later a companion paper was put to the Board by the Exchange Restrictions and Research Departments. This pointed out that to permit the use of the Fund's resources to meet deficits caused by international capital movements would assist members to avoid restrictions, which was desirable from the Fund's point of view. It proposed that requests for drawings necessitated by such movements should be dealt with in accordance with the general principles already established for evaluating requests to use the Fund's resources. For example, it should be ascertained whether the drawing would be likely to be repurchased within three to five years. Whether the originating outflow of capital was "large" should be judged in relation to the Fund's resources—possibly as augmented by borrowing. Members experiencing large or sustained outflows should use capital controls, consulting the Fund frequently, and the Fund should not seek to sway the member's decision by any application of its policy on the use of its resources.

Adverting to the inter-central-bank arrangements outlined in Chapter 18, the memorandum suggested that while these might suffice for a short period, Fund members might well need to draw on the Fund to repay their central bank creditors in order to convert such obligations from short term to medium term. In this way the Fund could aid the cooperation between monetary authorities that had been rendered necessary by the increased international mobility of capital.

These memoranda were considered by the Board at five meetings in June and July 1961. Mr. de Largentaye argued that the Fund had exhausted its interpretative powers by the 1946 decision, so that the only recourse was an amendment to the Articles as provided for by Article XVII; this involved a recommendation to the Governors, and would probably require member countries to pass supporting legislation. Mr. de Largentaye went on to contend that there were three conditions that had to be fulfilled before an interpretation could be reversed, and that none of these was present in the situation before the Board. One condition required that the 1946 interpretation contained an error in law, and such an error had been far from demonstrated; a second required that the desire to reverse the interpretation was not prompted by factors external to the interpretation itself, and the Managing Director's opening statement on February 10 showed that such factors were present; the third required that the effects of the interpretation had not been consolidated into a rule of which the benefit could be claimed by any member country, whereas the abstention by the Fund for fifteen years from permitting the use of its resources for capital transfers had reduced the claims made on the creditor countries.

Mr. de Largentaye's arguments were challenged by the General Counsel, Mr. Gold, who contended that, in fact, the three conditions postulated were all met. Since the interpretation, taken literally, ignored Article VI, Section 1, it constituted an error in law; a wish to correct this did not imply an external motive; and in practice the Fund had not denied the use of its resources to members suffering from an adverse balance of payments on capital account. On the contrary, the Fund had acted consistently with Article VI, Section 1.

This last point was supported by several Executive Directors, including Mr. Southard (United States), who referred especially to a drawing by Mexico in 1954.[5] He said that the U.S. authorities saw no need to alter the law to enable the Fund to conform to the provisions of the Articles.

The Board also discussed the nature of the corrective action to be taken. Although the General Counsel argued that Mr. de Largentaye was incorrect in his view that by its decision in 1946 the Fund had exhausted its powers of interpretation on this subject, the staff's suggestion of a "reinterpretation" created difficulties for some Directors. Mr. Saad (United Arab Republic) said that he agreed with Mr. de Largentaye that the Board's formal interpretation could not be changed except by appeal to the Governors. He himself, however, believed that this interpretation had been misunderstood. It could not go beyond the Articles which it interpreted; therefore it could not preclude the financing of capital transfers contemplated by Articles VI and VIII. Mr. Saad accordingly suggested that all that was needed was a clarification of the interpretation. This solution was accepted by the Board, and adopted in the following form:

> After full consideration of all relevant aspects concerning the use of the Fund's resources, the Executive Directors decide by way of clarification that Decision No. 71-2 does not preclude the use of the Fund's resources for capital transfers in accordance with the provisions of the Articles, including Article VI.[6]

[5] See above, p. 380.

[6] E.B. Decision No. 1238-(61/43), July 28, 1961; below, Vol. III, p. 245.

BORROWING BY THE FUND

Very soon after the general increase in quotas in 1959, the greater volatility of balances of payments created by the relaxation of controls on international transactions began to throw doubts on the adequacy of the Fund's holdings of usable currencies. In July 1960 the Director of Research, Mr. Polak, suggested to the Managing Director that

> the question of international liquidity will, inevitably, occupy the Fund for many years to come, albeit with varying degrees of intensity. In practice (excluding a revaluation of gold) this question now revolves around the method of operation and the resources of the Fund. It seems worthwhile, therefore, exploring any new techniques that might at some stage be helpful in this connection.

Mr. Polak then discussed the possibility of arranging for the Fund to accept deposits of gold from its members, these deposits being partly invested to earn interest enough to cover that paid by the Fund to the depositor. The remaining balances would be available to be sold for currencies if it became necessary to replenish the Fund's holdings of particular currencies.

Another suggestion considered at about the same time was to invite deposits of currencies. Although the General Counsel advised the Managing Director that the acceptance of such deposits would be legal provided that the currencies in question were genuinely needed for the Fund's operations, so that the deposits constituted borrowing by the Fund, the staff subsequently took the view that it would be more satisfactory to arrange something in the nature of a comprehensive stand-by borrowing arrangement, under Article VII, Section 2 (i). It was this that the Managing Director had in mind when making his statement in February 1961.

In preparation for the Board's discussion of the subject, the staff submitted on April 21, 1961 a detailed memorandum on the need for the Fund to borrow currencies, on the amount required, and on the conditions that would be applicable to such borrowing. After recalling the reasons given in the report entitled *Enlargement of Fund Resources Through Increases in Quotas* submitted by the Directors to the Governors in December 1958, the memorandum pointed out that, since then, the value of world trade had increased by 12 per cent, and convertibility had enhanced the mobility of funds. It was important that the Fund's resources should be adequate to check speculators. On the other hand, it was undesirable further to increase quotas because of the drain which this would cause on members' own reserves.

As to the amount of additional resources required, the memorandum reviewed possible demands from various groups of countries, bearing in mind that for some of the largest countries the loss of one tended to be the gain of another. The staff came to the conclusion that, in addition to its existing holdings, the

Fund might need some $2 billion in U.S. dollars and $3½–5 billion in currencies other than the U.S. dollar and sterling. The latter sum should be sought by way of credit arrangements with, say, Austria, Belgium, Canada, France, Germany, Italy, Japan, the Netherlands, and Sweden. Similar arrangements would be made with the United Kingdom and the United States for sterling and dollars, respectively, although the memorandum did not find it possible to estimate the extent of the need for sterling. The allocation of the total needed between the countries to be invited to participate would have to be negotiated. It would be inappropriate to relate the members' shares to their quotas, if only because part of the Fund's difficulties lay in the fact that quotas were not fully adjusted to the existing payments situation. One possibility would be to relate each country's contribution to its gross reserves less its quota in the Fund, although this would have the disadvantage of basing them on the relative position of the different countries at a single point of time. Alternatively, reference might be made to the potential surplus in each lender's international transactions. In any event, periodic renegotiation of the credit lines would be advisable.

On the conditions which might be relevant to such credit arrangements, the memorandum made the following points: (1) The Fund could not insist on a member lending to it, but if a member agreed to do so the Fund would be free to negotiate terms, which might, but presumably would not, be different for different members. It would be advisable for the arrangements to last for five years, to correspond to the period between general reviews of quotas. (2) When a prospective drawing made it necessary to utilize the credit arrangements, it would be best to borrow before entirely exhausting the Fund's holdings of any currency used, even though such borrowing would involve the payment of interest to the lender, whereas the use of the Fund's normal holdings would not do so. All the available currencies should be borrowed, not just one of them. (3) The sums borrowed should be repayable after five years, or earlier on the initiative either of the lender (on certain conditions) or of the Fund. (4) Claims on the Fund represented by loans under these arrangements should be transferable. (5) The Fund should guarantee the gold value of sums lent, just as the lenders guaranteed the gold value of the Fund's holdings of their currencies. (6) The rate of interest paid by the Fund should be less than that which the Fund received, on average, on drawings, i.e., less than 2 per cent. (7) The temporary increase in the Fund's holdings of a lender's currency which might occur before sums borrowed were used in drawings should not be allowed to affect adversely the lender's rights in the Fund.

These proposals were discussed by the Board at two meetings on May 10, 1961 and were generally approved, although Mr. de Largentaye (France) was not persuaded that the Fund required additional resources at that moment, and said that it was not possible to foresee what currencies would be needed if in the future the Fund's holdings proved inadequate. Mr. Lieftinck (Netherlands), who shared Mr. de Largentaye's doubts as to the need for borrowing, thought it would make a great deal of difference to the readiness of the Netherlands authorities to enter into a credit arrangement for five years or more, as the staff had suggested, if they could be assured that the Fund's existing holdings of guilders would first be drawn down to a large extent, and that they would always be consulted by the Fund before use was made of the additional credit sought. Mr. Rasminsky (Canada) was also unconvinced that additional resources were needed to deal with deficits on current account, but he believed that they would be required if the Fund had to cope with capital transfers as well. Mr. Guth (Germany) said that his country favored a collective borrowing arrangement in the form of a stand-by credit, provided that the availability of additional resources in this way did not cause the Fund to relax its standards for drawings.

Inquiries made in Europe during the summer showed that the point underlying Mr. Guth's proviso was troubling more than one of the EEC countries. They were particularly concerned at the recurrent weakness of the United Kingdom's position, and feared that if additional resources were made available to the Fund, drawings by the United Kingdom would be permitted on conditions less stringent than would be imposed, for example, if the United Kingdom sought to borrow from the European Fund. As a result, the staff reported, European countries were likely to stipulate that they should have control over the use made of any additional resources lent by them to the Fund.

In the Annual Report for 1961, a brief reference to a possible need, in certain contingencies, to reinforce the Fund's holdings of some currencies was followed by a statement that the Executive Board was considering the use of the Fund's borrowing powers, so as to prepare in good time for such contingencies as might arise.[7] In his statement presenting this Report to the Annual Meeting in September 1961, the Managing Director spoke at some length in support of the idea.[8]

Early in the Annual Meeting week Mr. C. Douglas Dillon, the Governor for the United States, convened a meeting of representatives of the main industrial powers to consider the Managing Director's proposals. This meeting disclosed wide agreement between the countries concerned on the conditions which they would regard as appropriate for a borrowing arrangement. As expressed by Mr. Dillon in his subsequent speech to the Governors, these were:

> First, the aggregate amount the participating countries should look forward to committing to the project should be large enough to add decisively to the Fund's capacity to play its essential role.
>
> Second, to be effective, the additional resources must be promptly available in case of need.

[7] *Annual Report, 1961*, p. 19.

[8] *Summary Proceedings, 1961*, pp. 27–29.

> Third, safeguards will be required to ensure that there will be effective consultation between the Fund and the lenders, and that the Fund will only actually borrow under the commitment arrangements after taking full account of the current reserve position of the lending country. In addition, each country which actually lends to the Fund should, in case the need develops, be able automatically to obtain repayment from the Fund.
>
> Fourth . . . there must be no weakening of the policies that have guided the Fund in the use of its resources; nor should the new arrangements change in any way the existing rights and duties of members of the Fund, both as drawers of currencies and as providers of currencies.[9]

The "safeguards" to which Mr. Dillon referred in his third point were spelled out more completely by other Governors. For example, Mr. Holtrop, Governor for the Netherlands, said that

> it would seem essential that the lending countries, when the Fund should make a call on them, shall have the opportunity, by a collective judgment, to confirm that also in their opinion the special emergency, for which the additional resources have been set aside, has indeed arisen.[10]

Mr. Wilfrid Baumgartner, Governor for France, went further.

> It seems to me necessary [he said] that . . . each country should remain judge of the advisability of the use of its own currency.[11]

In his concluding remarks, the Managing Director expressed satisfaction that the Governors had evinced a positive interest in having the Fund make suitable borrowing arrangements.[12] He went on to say that much work remained to be done in devising details of such arrangements. On his instructions, the staff immediately began work on a series of memoranda covering different aspects of the requirements for a borrowing arrangement, without at that stage attempting to draft a complete agreement.

Early in November Mr. Jacobsson had a discussion with Mr. Dillon, preparatory to visiting Paris to begin negotiations. Mr. Jacobsson said that the inter-central-bank credits had not, in his opinion, impressed the market, and that it would be necessary for the Fund to intervene. He wished to be assured that the United States would support proposals to provide the Fund with additional resources without impairing the Fund's authority. Mr. Dillon agreed that this should be the aim.

The position of the United States in the matter was, however, somewhat weakened by the fact that it expected to draw upon the Fund, and accordingly wished to see the Fund's resources increased; whereas the major European countries, and in particular France, were in a stronger bargaining position in that they

[9] *Summary Proceedings, 1961*, pp. 54–55.
[10] *Ibid.*, p. 117.
[11] *Ibid.*, p. 64.
[12] *Ibid.*, p. 158.

had no such expectation of calling on the Fund. When, therefore, as a result of discussions between U.S. and French officials, a draft of a comprehensive borrowing arrangement was prepared, its effect was stated to be

> the decision to lend special resources through the Fund to an applicant borrower and the determination of the financial circumstances warranting the transaction would be made by the Participating Countries.

On November 17, 1961 a meeting of seven European countries, the United States, and Canada was held in Paris to discuss this draft. Mr. Jacobsson and three members of the Fund staff were present and then saw the draft for the first time. At this meeting the philosophy behind the plan was explained by the chairman, Mr. Jean Sadrin (Alternate Governor of the Fund for France), as follows: The proposals put forward by the Fund were based on the idea that the Fund had insufficient resources to meet its commitments and should therefore borrow to supplement its resources. The proposals put forward in the draft under discussion were based on a system among the industrialized countries under which they would provide resources to assist one of their number, and in this way help all the countries of the world.

Two aspects of this plan were clearly inconsistent with the Articles of Agreement. In the first place, it would have substituted the judgment of a group of members for that of the Fund as a whole in a decision whether to permit the use of the Fund's resources. Secondly, it provided that the choice between meeting a drawing out of the Fund's own resources and meeting it by borrowing should be made by the member requesting the drawing. Accordingly, Mr. Jacobsson refused to accept the Franco-American draft and laid down three principles which would have to be observed in any draft that he was prepared to submit to the Fund Board:

(1) Any borrowing arrangement to which the Fund could agree must be fitted into the framework of the Fund according to the Articles.

(2) The authority of the Fund must not be impaired.

(3) The draft must provide for the decision whether to borrow to be made by the Fund, and the decision whether to lend to be made by the participating countries.

Mr. Jacobsson also insisted that an acceptable draft would have to be regarded as presenting ideas for further consideration rather than as a definitive document.

Subsequent drafts were prepared by the Fund staff along the lines of the memorandum submitted to the Board in April. These drafts were the subject of discussions between the Managing Director, assisted by staff members, and representatives of the nine countries (to which Japan was shortly added) at a series of meetings in Paris during December 1961. The fact that the negotiations were conducted in this way and not by the Board naturally caused difficulties.

Even though the Managing Director kept Directors informed about the progress of the discussions, and transmitted to them the successive drafts produced, the members of the Board appointed or elected by the ten countries represented in Paris (later known as the Group of Ten), and still more the remaining Directors, regarded the situation as unsatisfactory. The negotiations were not, however, prolonged. On December 18 the Managing Director was able to present a draft which he could recommend for the Board's acceptance. This comprised the agreement which became known as the General Arrangements to Borrow (GAB). It was supplemented by a letter addressed by Mr. Baumgartner (Minister of Finance, France) to the representatives of the other nine countries, detailing the procedure which would be followed if a request to borrow under the arrangements was made by the Fund.[13]

The commitments which the participants undertook were expressed in their own currencies. The amount of each commitment and its equivalent in millions of U.S. dollars at the then rate of exchange are shown in Table 6.

Table 6. GAB: Participants and Commitments

Participant	Units of Participant's Currency		Equivalent in Millions of U.S. Dollars
United States	US$	2,000,000,000	2,000
Deutsche Bundesbank	DM	4,000,000,000	1,000
United Kingdom	£	357,142,857	1,000
France	F	2,715,381,428	550
Italy	Lit	343,750,000,000	550
Japan	¥	90,000,000,000	250
Canada	Can$	208,938,000	200
Netherlands	f.	724,000,000	200
Belgium	BF	7,500,000,000	150
Sweden	SKr	517,320,000	100
		Total	6,000

Two formal changes were subsequently made in this schedule: when Canada agreed with the Fund on a new par value in May 1962 it increased its commitment so that the equivalent in U.S. dollars remained at $200 million; and the commitment of Sweden was subsequently transferred to the Sveriges Riksbank. Incidentally, the fact that Canada had no par value in December 1961 made it necessary to amend again the decision on fluctuating currencies taken in 1954 so as to cover borrowing and the repayment of sums borrowed.[14]

The principal provisions of the GAB, which reflect the studies which the staff from time to time presented to the Board, are as follows:

[13] For the text of the GAB and of Mr. Baumgartner's letter, see below, Vol. III, pp. 246–54.

[14] E.B. Decision No. 1283-(61/56), December 20, 1961; below, Vol. III, p. 224.

(*a*) Requests for drawings by participating countries, for which recourse to borrowing is necessary, are dealt with according to the Fund's established policies. Repayment has to be made to the Fund when the country's problem is solved, and in any event within three to five years.

(*b*) When the Fund receives repayment, it repays the countries from which it has borrowed; in any event it repays them not later than five years after a borrowing. Rights to repayment are backed by all the assets of the Fund.

(*c*) A country that has lent to the Fund can receive early repayment should it need and request this because its own payments position has deteriorated.

(*d*) Interest on sums borrowed by the Fund is based on a formula which has initially yielded a rate of 1½ per cent per annum; in addition, the Fund pays a charge of ½ of 1 per cent on each borrowing transaction.

(*e*) A preamble to the Arrangements stipulates that they are to be activated only "to forestall or cope with an impairment of the international monetary system" and paragraph 6 limits use of the Arrangements to drawings by a participant.

The procedure to be adopted to implement a borrowing under the arrangement is spelled out partly in the GAB and partly in the letter sent by Mr. Baumgartner to the other nine countries, to which the Fund was not a party. Briefly summarized, it is as follows:

By the GAB:

1. Before making a call on the participants, the Managing Director obtains their agreement and that of the Executive Board.

2. The amounts proposed to be lent are based on the present and prospective balances of payments and reserve positions of the participants.

By Mr. Baumgartner's letter:

3. A participant that proposes to seek a drawing from the Fund, or a refund of a loan made earlier to the Fund, if either may necessitate the Fund's borrowing, consults the Managing Director first and then the other participants.

4. When the Managing Director makes a call, the participants consult and inform him of the amounts of their currencies that they are prepared to lend, taking into account his proposals and their balance of payments positions. If unanimous agreement cannot be reached, a vote is taken by weighted voting. If this supports the Managing Director's proposal, an alternative selection of currencies, with a total of the same order of magnitude, is suggested.

When the draft of the GAB was discussed by the Board on December 18, 1961 there was general agreement that it represented a marked improvement on earlier drafts. Executive Directors appointed or elected by countries in the Group of Ten commended the plan as a big step forward. Mr. Pitblado (United Kingdom) remarked that while a casual reading of the GAB might suggest that the participants had acquired more rights, the fact was that they had acquired only more liabilities. Mr. Guth said that while he would have preferred that the right to use borrowed resources had not been limited to participants, he thought it probable that the Fund would always be able to provide for drawings by any other members from its own resources. Mr. Lieftinck described the plan as a compromise between the ideology of the Fund as a global monetary institution and a newer ideology which sought solutions by closer cooperation between the main industrial countries. Mr. Southard (United States) suggested that the consultations set out in Mr. Baumgartner's letter, on which some of the participants had insisted, did not differ greatly from the Fund's usual procedure before a large drawing.

The reception of the plan by Executive Directors appointed or elected by countries that were not participants was more guarded. Most expressed some disappointment and criticized the formation of what Mr. Garland (Australia) described as a "very exclusive club," which might have the result, as Mr. Anjaria (India) saw it, that the Board might find itself obliged to concur in decisions taken elsewhere. Mr. Bicalho (Brazil) said that it appeared to him that the proposed arrangement would result in the organization of a group of rich countries playing a large role within the Fund structure. He wondered why the Fund was concerned in the arrangements, since the participants were to decide how much to lend, and for what purpose. Mr. Slamet (Indonesia) thought that the original intention of formulating the borrowing arrangement as a Fund operation had not been achieved, and he regretted that in consequence several paragraphs of the draft were ambiguous. It would have been better, he said, to have faced up to the reality that the creditor countries were unwilling to delegate their powers to the Fund. However, Mr. Ásgeirsson (Iceland), Mr. Klein (Argentina), and Mr. Mansour (United Arab Republic), while finding the plan far from ideal, were prepared to welcome it as the best available.

At that meeting, and at a second meeting on December 20, a number of amendments to the draft were discussed, but as it was realized that to press these would necessarily delay the completion of the Arrangements, all were dropped, and the Board approved the plan. The formal decision was taken on January 5, 1962.[15] By October 24, 1962, enough of the participants had acceded to it to bring the GAB into operation. The last country to adhere was Canada, which notified the Fund of its agreement in January 1964.

Meanwhile, at the invitation of Mr. Dillon, Mr. Jacobsson had taken soundings in Switzerland to see whether the Swiss Confederation, which is not a member

[15] E.B. Decision No. 1289-(62/1), January 5, 1962; below, Vol. III, p. 246.

of the Fund, would cooperate in the GAB. The discussions resulted in a decision by Switzerland to provide support to countries drawing from the Fund at times when the Arrangements were activated, within a total equivalent to $200 million. To implement this plan, Switzerland undertook to enter into appropriate agreements with any of the participants if requested by them. It undertook also to lend Swiss francs directly to any participant with which it had an agreement, if asked to do so by the Managing Director when that participant was drawing on the Fund, provided that in Switzerland's view its own balance of payments permitted it to make the loan. Switzerland's undertaking was set out in an exchange of letters with the Managing Director, dated June 11, 1964.[16]

The first occasion on which the General Arrangements to Borrow were activated was in November 1964, to meet drawings by the United Kingdom under a stand-by arrangement for $1 billion approved in July 1964, as discussed in Chapter 21.

It may be mentioned at this point that shortly after this activation Mr. Lieftinck asked for an interpretation of paragraph 11 (f) of the GAB. Specifically, he inquired what was the legal character of a member's right to early repayment under that paragraph, which reads, in part, as follows:

> Before the [expiration of five years from a transfer under the GAB] a participant may give notice representing that there is a balance of payments need for repayment of part or all of the Fund's indebtedness and requesting such repayment. The Fund shall give the overwhelming benefit of any doubt to the participant's representation. Repayment shall be made after consultation with the participant in the currencies of other members that are convertible in fact, or made in gold, as determined by the Fund. If the Fund's holdings of currencies in which repayment should be made are not wholly adequate, individual participants shall be requested, and will be expected, to provide the necessary balance under their credit arrangements. If, notwithstanding the expectation that the participants will provide the necessary balance, they fail to do so, repayment shall be made to the extent necessary in the currency of the drawer for whose purchases the participant requesting repayment made transfers. . . .

In reply, the General Counsel said that, while there was nothing in the minutes of the Board to elucidate the paragraph, it was apparent that it gave the participant similar rights to those which governed drawings under the gold tranche; indeed, in some respects better rights—because the representation to be made was less specific and was not subject to challenge under the Articles; because while a member might be ineligible to draw, there was no provision for ineligibility under paragraph 11 (f); because no repurchase obligation attached to the use of paragraph 11 (f); and because no charges were payable. On the other hand it was true that while the Board had approved an expedited procedure for drawings

[16] E.B. Decision No. 1712-(64/29), June 8, 1964; below, Vol. III, p. 254.

in the gold tranche,[17] there was no corresponding procedure for quick repayments under the GAB, and if any such procedure were to be considered it would have to leave time for consultations on the medium for repayment and for an approach (if needed) to other participants.

SELECTION OF CURRENCIES

Before February 1961, when the currencies of the main European countries became convertible (in the Fund sense) by the acceptance by these countries of the obligations of Article VIII, Sections 2, 3, and 4, little use was made of any currency except the U.S. dollar in drawings on the Fund (Table 5).[18] Even when a wider selection of currencies became available, however, it did not follow that they would automatically be used in Fund drawings. Most member countries tended to keep their currency reserves in dollars, sterling, or French francs, and when faced with balance of payments difficulties considered that a drawing of one of these currencies would best suit their needs. Indeed, there was a question whether any other drawing would fit the requirement of the Articles.

The problem posed by these considerations, which threatened to immobilize a large part of the Fund's holdings of currencies other than the reserve currencies, had been the subject of study by the Fund staff from 1951 onward. A fresh look had been taken at the subject in 1959, in anticipation of convertibility. In November 1960 the Research Department prepared a draft memorandum which emphasized that members would be able, once convertibility had been achieved, to use a wide variety of currencies drawn from the Fund. It also discussed the influence of market exchange rates upon the currencies which members might choose to draw.

On March 22, 1961, a Legal Department memorandum was circulated to the Board. This considered the meaning of "needed" and "making in that currency payments" in Article V, Section 3 (*a*) (i), which reads:

> (*a*) A member shall be entitled to buy the currency of another member from the Fund in exchange for its own currency subject to the following conditions:
>
> (i) The member desiring to purchase the currency represents that it is presently needed for making in that currency payments which are consistent with the provisions of this Agreement. . . .

The memorandum recalled that at Bretton Woods the assumption was that international transactions would for some time continue to be conducted on a bilateral basis. The clause quoted was therefore drafted to ensure that a member drawing from the Fund would draw the currency needed to settle the particular bilateral deficit which it had incurred. It was feared that otherwise an undue

[17] See below, pp. 566–67.

[18] Above, p. 452.

burden would be placed upon the Fund's holdings of the one or two convertible currencies. Nevertheless, the delegates at Bretton Woods were well aware of the practice by which international balances were usually settled in one or other of the reserve currencies. The corollary that this would concentrate drawings from the Fund on the reserve currencies was squarely faced in a memorandum by the British delegation, which read in part:

> If Country A customarily carries on its international trade in terms of dollars, then a favorable balance of payments for Country A will be settled in dollars. The Fund should not be required to finance this favorable balance of payments with its resources of dollars. Instead, it should be possible for the Fund to use directly or indirectly its holdings of currency A to finance this favorable balance of payments with Country A.[19]

It was clear, therefore, that consideration had been given at Bretton Woods to the possibility that a country might draw from the Fund a currency that was not a reserve currency, convert this into its usual reserve currency, and use this to support its market. And, indeed, unless this was an acceptable procedure there would be no way in which a country whose currency was not a reserve currency could give credit through the Fund, no matter how large the surplus in its balance of payments. It must therefore be taken that the meaning of Article V, Section 3 (*a*) (i), was that a member might draw from the Fund any currency which it used, directly or indirectly, to support its exchange market. Alternatively, it could be allowed to achieve the same result by being given a waiver under Article V, Section 4, of the conditions of Article V, Section 3 (*a*) (i).

On the following day a parallel memorandum was presented by the Research Department. This, which was a development of the November 1960 draft mentioned above, reached the following conclusions:

(*a*) If the Fund was to act as an efficient source of additional liquidity, reserves should, through the Fund, flow from countries with strong balances of payments to countries with weak ones. Each member's position in the Fund (its quota less the Fund's holdings of its currency) should therefore move in parallel with the movements in its primary reserves, as that of the United States had done.

(*b*) The need for a specified currency was normal only when trade was conducted under bilateral agreements. To meet an over-all deficit in a world of convertible currencies and effective arbitrage, monetary authorities could support their currency with a wide variety of others.

(*c*) The currencies of countries accumulating reserves tended to be strong in exchange markets. If a drawing country was guided by exchange rates, therefore, it would tend to draw from the Fund the currencies of such countries. But this might be misleading. For example, the absolute level of the reserves of such a

[19] *Proceedings*, p. 462.

country might be low. Again, the official limits for intervention in exchange markets were wider in some countries than in others. Moreover, since all European countries based their currencies on the dollar, the price mechanism would never point to U.S. dollars so long as even one European country had a sufficiently large rate of reserve accumulation for its currency to be quoted at a premium over the dollar. Further, sterling area currencies reflected the position of the United Kingdom rather than that of any other sterling country. Finally, fluctuating currencies presented a problem.

The memorandum further commented that since the total of drawings would be fixed by the needs of members, what would have to be adjusted was the proportion between currencies used; this would require a composite judgment taking into account the circumstances of all the members concerned. As a first approximation, the memorandum suggested that the currencies to be selected for drawings should be those widely used and having a high degree of convertibility; that in deciding on them attention should be centered on the movements of each country's reserves over a recent period, together with the absolute adequacy of its reserves—the exchange rate of the currency, in relation to par, being also borne in mind. Rough and ready weights for distributing the total of drawings between the eligible currencies might be afforded by the size of the countries' total reserves (rather than that of their quotas).

The Legal and Research Departments' memoranda were discussed at meetings of the Board on April 26 and 27, 1961. Mr. de Largentaye (France) contended that the purpose of the Articles was clearly to provide for bilateral settlements, and that the currencies which members drew could therefore only be those of countries which had surpluses vis-à-vis the drawing members, unless—as Mr. van Campenhout (Belgium) also urged—use was made of the waiver provisions of Article V, Section 4. The other members of the Board, however, regarded the staff's proposals as constituting suitable guidelines for Fund action.

Review widened

When the discussion was resumed in April 1962 it was extended to cover also the selection of currencies to be used in repurchases. This was prompted by a revival by Mr. de Largentaye, in November 1961, of his contention that voluntary repurchases could be made only in gold, the occasion being a repurchase by the United Kingdom of £100 million with U.S. dollars in October. At that time the Managing Director had given Mr. de Largentaye a detailed legal justification for the acceptance of the repurchase in dollars, of which the crux was that the obligation of the United Kingdom to repurchase within three to five years was set by the Rooth Plan, but in setting it the Fund had not prescribed any particular media for the repurchase. The United Kingdom was therefore entitled to discharge its obligation in any media which were acceptable under the Articles. Since the member had not been required to repurchase its currency for gold, there was no obligation upon it to do so; Article V, Section 7 (*a*), which dealt with repurchases for gold, conferred a privilege, and not a duty.

A memorandum by the Research Department, which was before the Board when it resumed its discussion, described the procedure which had been adopted since early in 1961, by which countries seeking to draw had consulted the Managing Director before specifying the currencies which they wished to obtain, while the Managing Director had in turn discussed the proposed drawing with the Executive Directors appointed or elected by the countries whose currencies it was planned to use. Small drawings had normally been effected in one currency only (usually the member's reserve currency) and somewhat larger drawings in two or three currencies, the trade relations of the drawing country and other relevant factors being taken into account. For very large drawings (for example, that of the United Kingdom in August 1961) a wide range of currencies had been used. Broadly speaking, drawings had been directed toward the currencies of countries with strong balances of payments and reserves. In allocating drawings among such currencies, regard had been paid to the amount of each country's reserves, the magnitude of recent increases in its reserves and the likelihood of further increases in them in the near future, the size of its quota, and the extent to which net sales of its currency had been made in connection with earlier drawings.

As regards repurchases, the memorandum pointed out that it was only in February 1961 that a choice of currencies had become practicable. The first repurchase of any consequence after that date had been made by the United Kingdom in November 1961. This had included $85 million in deutsche mark, the position of which had previously weakened in the exchange markets, and $30 million in French francs. More recently, two large repurchases by the United Kingdom and Australia had together included seven different currencies.

The memorandum then went on to suggest a general policy for the use of currencies in drawings and repurchases. A reasonable and convenient starting point would be to prescribe that currencies for drawings should be selected in proportion to the reserves of the countries whose currencies were being used. Currencies for repurchases should be accepted proportionately to each member's position in the Fund, i.e., to the excess of its quota over the Fund's holdings of its currency. Such a rule would ensure that both drawings and repurchases were broadly distributed and also tend toward an equitable distribution over time, since it would make the ratios of members' positions in the Fund to their reserves converge. However, this could only provide an initial distribution of aggregate drawings and repurchases over a certain period. Normally the Fund would aim at encouraging repurchases in weak currencies.

The memorandum next discussed the problem of "conversion," by which was meant the right of Country A drawing currency B to obtain for it, from Country B, another currency which Country A needed for the purpose of settling its international accounts. The memorandum explained that although there had been some difficulties in this connection, drawing members' experience had usually been satisfactory. It suggested that countries whose currencies were to be drawn should inform the Managing Director of the method which they wished to employ to convert their currencies, at the request of a drawing country, into the latter's main reserve currency, at a rate approximating the prevailing market rate; and vice versa for currencies to be used in repurchases.

Finally, the memorandum discussed the "reversal" technique, which had been suggested by several Executive Directors as a solution to the problem of channeling drawings toward appropriate currencies. This technique consisted of allowing any member whose currency was being drawn, if it considered that this was being done to excess, to draw in its turn on the Fund so as to offset the use of its currency. Such arrangements, the memorandum commented, were of limited usefulness. If the second drawing was sought under Article VI, Section 2 (which made special provision for drawings by members whose currencies had been held by the Fund for at least six months in amounts less than 75 per cent of their quotas), the right could only be exercised to the extent that it raised the Fund's holdings of the drawing member's currency to 75 per cent of its quota, and did not lower the Fund's holdings of the currency desired to be drawn below 75 per cent of that member's quota. If, instead, the member which thought its currency was being drawn to excess sought to draw under Article V, Section 3, it would be necessary for it to represent that it had a present need for the currency which it sought to draw. In any event, the drawing would involve a service charge of ½ of 1 per cent. Altogether, the "reversal" technique must be considered too clumsy for normal use.

The staff's views were the subject of lengthy discussions in the Board on April 30 and May 7, 1962. Following these meetings, the staff prepared a draft decision along the lines of the policy proposed in its memorandum, and submitted this to the Board on July 13. Three meetings of the Board were devoted to consideration of drafting amendments, and on July 20, 1962, the Board reached its decision.[20] This was in form a description of the procedure which had previously been applied, but implicitly it approved for future guidance the principles that had been worked out.

In pursuance of this decision, a procedure has been evolved for the preparation of a quarterly budget of currencies to be used in purchases and in repurchases.[21]

[20] E.B. Decision No. 1371-(62/36), July 20, 1962; below, Vol. III, p. 235.

[21] Below, Vol. II, Chap. 19.

IN MEMORIAM, PER JACOBSSON

Mr. Jacobsson and the Fund

When Mr. Jacobsson died in May 1963, the then President of the United States, John F. Kennedy, said of him that "he combined with his incomparable professional talents a warmth and wit and depth of understanding that enabled him to give leadership to other men of goodwill in meeting the problems of our troubled times." This was a perceptive appreciation. Mr. Jacobsson was a big man, intellectually as well as physically, and his unique blend of experience, diplomacy, and good comradeship exactly fitted the needs of the Fund during the six and a half years that he was Managing Director.

An author of detective stories, a voracious reader who could quote appositely in several languages, a student of history who was constantly aware of the world-wide significance of financial activities, Mr. Jacobsson was an acute commentator on current affairs. During his tenure of office as Managing Director he made over a hundred speeches in public, and he rarely failed to stress the need for appropriate policies to combat inflation or to remove restrictions on the freedom of international transactions. His sense of the value of the past as a guide for the present was well expressed in a speech that he made three months before his death:

> . . . There is a great deal to be said for the notion that economics is a branch of history. . . . we have then to try to seek to distill out of our historical experiences what have been essential sequences of cause and effect to be used as guidance for the future.[22]

Mr. Jacobsson's connection with the Fund began at a moment when it was about to expand its activities to an unprecedented degree. Almost his first function as Managing Director was to announce the drawing and stand-by arrangement for the United Kingdom totaling $1.3 billion, although the negotiations for this had of course been well advanced before he arrived. Thereafter the Fund operated on a scale immensely greater than at any time during his predecessors' tenure of the chair. Further, the number of Fund members grew greatly, rising from 60 in September 1956 to 102 only a few months after his death.

Of course, this progress was not due solely to Mr. Jacobsson. By 1956 the Executive Board was functioning with a smoothness and a sense of purpose that had grown up under his predecessors, and its contribution to the subsequent success of the Fund was substantial and essential. So, too, the staff had developed both expertise and initiative, and the bold new forward steps which were

[22] *The Role of Money in a Dynamic Economy;* The Arthur K. Salomon Lecture, Graduate School of Business Administration, New York University, 1963, p. 3.

taken, such as those described in this chapter, were conceived by the Research and Legal Departments rather than by the Managing Director himself.

Yet with all this, Mr. Jacobsson's contribution was real and unique. He inspired all whom he met with his own vision and drive, and his personality helped greatly to weld the member countries, the Board, and the staff into a unity. Without this dynamism it is doubtful whether the Fund would have so quickly reached the point at which even the largest member countries came to treat its views with respect. The Fund which was entrusted in 1968 with the creation of Special Drawing Rights was a Fund which owed recognition of its strength very largely to Per Jacobsson.

As the Board of Governors put it in a memorial resolution:

> Under his leadership the Fund became better equipped than ever to realize the great ideals for which it was formed.[23]

The Per Jacobsson Foundation

The esteem in which Mr. Jacobsson was held prompted suggestions, put forward within a few months of his death, for a permanent memorial to him. These led to the incorporation on February 5, 1964 (which would have been Mr. Jacobsson's seventieth birthday) of The Per Jacobsson Foundation, to carry forward his contribution to international financial policies. The Foundation was sponsored by the Fund, the Bank for International Settlements, and a group of 45 former Finance Ministers, former Heads of central banks, and other friends of Mr. Jacobsson. Its President, who is also the Chairman of the Board of Directors, is Mr. W. Randolph Burgess, Chairman of the Atlantic Council and a former U.S. Ambassador to NATO and Under Secretary of the Treasury.

Contributions to the Foundation, totaling some $400,000, have provided an income with which it has been possible to arrange for, and to publish, annual lectures by eminent authorities on subjects in Mr. Jacobsson's fields of interest. The first such lectures were given in Basle in November 1964 on the general subject of "Economic Growth and Monetary Stability." In 1965 the lectures were given in Washington, the subject being "The Balance between Monetary Policy and other Instruments of Economic Policy in a Modern Society."

---

[23] Resolution 18-14, *Summary Proceedings, 1963,* p. 259.

CHAPTER

20

More New Techniques

(1961-63, concluded)

IN ADDITION to the three major advances described in the last chapter, the Fund in 1961–63 dealt with a number of questions concerning the use of its resources, and introduced new facilities for compensating fluctuations in export earnings, including selective increases in certain small quotas. As time went on, the Board became increasingly concerned with the problems of international liquidity. These aspects of its work are dealt with in the present chapter.

EXCHANGE TRANSACTIONS

During the year October 1961 to September 1962 drawings amounted to $614.8 million and repurchases to $1,729 million. The latter included repurchases totaling $1,282 million by the United Kingdom, which reduced the Fund's holdings of sterling to 75 per cent of the British quota. New or renewed stand-by arrangements amounted to $1,868.5 million. In the following twelve months transactions were comparatively small, drawings totaling $317.6 million and repurchases $346.2 million. New or renewed stand-by arrangements, however, were higher than in any previous October–September period, totaling $1,942.4 million. In both years the United Kingdom obtained a stand-by arrangement for $1 billion, and in the second year the United States was granted one for $500 million. The purpose of the latter is explained below.

DRAWINGS AGAINST GOLD COLLATERAL

In December 1958 the United Arab Republic (Egyptian Region) asked for a drawing of $4.3 million, and offered to provide an equal value in gold collateral as a guarantee that it would complete a repurchase within six months. The Board was advised by the staff that the offer could be accepted. It was true that

Article V, Section 4, which alone in the Articles discusses collateral, provides for the case where a waiver is required, whereas the proposed drawing by the Egyptian Region did not necessitate a waiver. However, the reference to collateral in Section 4 showed that its use would be consistent with the Articles, and power to accept it when offered could be found in Article IX, Section 2, which entitles the Fund to acquire and dispose of property. Moreover, the acceptance of the proffer of collateral could be justified because the maintenance of the revolving character of the Fund's resources was a fundamental principle of the Articles, and the purpose of the proposed pledge of gold was to promote this by ensuring repayment to the Fund within six months.

In view of the offer of collateral, the staff recommended that the proposed drawing should be treated as if it fell in the gold tranche, instead of (as it did) in the second credit tranche (125 to 150 per cent of quota). This recommendation conformed to the precedent set in 1952.[1] The Board accepted this reasoning and agreed to the drawing being made on the terms suggested. However, the request for it was subsequently withdrawn.

Three years later, the United Arab Republic again approached the Fund for a drawing for which it offered to deposit gold collateral. The first request was for a drawing of $22.4 million, which the Board discussed on January 5, 1962. The member offered to repay the drawing within a year, and meanwhile to make available to the Fund, in Cairo, gold of an equivalent value, as collateral security. The proposed drawing represented 25 per cent of the member's quota. The United Arab Republic had made a drawing of $10 million six months earlier, and in January 1962 the Fund's holdings of its currency amounted to 130 per cent of its quota. The breach of the 25 per cent per annum limitation imposed by Article V, Section 3 (*a*) (iii), necessitated a waiver; and as the drawing extended beyond the first credit tranche, the Fund would normally have required, as a condition for granting this waiver, that the United Arab Republic should put forward a "sound program aimed at establishing or maintaining the enduring stability of the member's currency at a realistic rate of exchange."[2] Putting the application to the Board, the Chairman regretted that such a program was not forthcoming, although the member country had expressed its willingness to receive a Fund mission, and one was being sent in mid-January. Nevertheless, an emergency situation existed in the United Arab Republic: the cotton crop had been extensively damaged by the cotton leaf worm, which had also reduced food crops, and a low flood by the Nile in the previous year had drastically reduced the supply of rice. Obviously the United Arab Republic urgently needed help, and if this was not forthcoming its stabilization problems would be even greater. He therefore recommended that the drawing should be approved.

---

[1] See above, p. 348.

[2] *Annual Report, 1959*, p. 22; see also above, p. 415.

Executive Directors expressed some hesitation because of the absence of a stabilization program, and some uneasiness about the acceptance of gold collateral as a substitute for such a program. Mr. Jacques Waïtzenegger (France), Alternate to Mr. de Largentaye, and Mr. van Campenhout (Belgium) abstained because they regarded the absence of a program as incompatible with the conditions that the Fund had laid down for a waiver in connection with a drawing reaching into the third credit tranche. Mr. Lieftinck (Netherlands) recalled that the approval of the drawing by the United Arab Republic in July 1961 had been based on an assurance that a stabilization program would be worked out with the staff. Mr. Southard (United States) was particularly concerned about the offer of gold collateral because the gold was not to be transferred to one of the Fund's normal gold depositories. Nevertheless, the majority of the Board agreed with the Chairman that the natural disasters which the United Arab Republic had encountered justified the drawing, and it was approved. At the same time the staff was requested to advise the Board on the conditions that should be attached to drawings when gold collateral was offered.

Two months later, on March 2, 1962, the United Arab Republic sought a second drawing, of $7.5 million, and again offered gold collateral. The purpose of this drawing was to offset a repurchase, amounting to $7.5 million, which had been made at the end of February in order to complete the winding up of drawings in 1956 and 1957. Mr. Raymond H. Bonham Carter (United Kingdom), Alternate to Mr. Pitblado, said that he could agree to the drawing only with reluctance because the offer of gold collateral did not justify the Fund's departing from its accepted policies for drawings in the higher credit tranches, because he was unsympathetic to the idea of drawing in order to finance a repurchase, and because what the Fund was actually doing was to agree to the postponement of a repurchase, which would have been acceptable had a stabilization program been adopted, but which could not be justified in the absence of such a program. He pointed out that Mr. Pitblado had agreed to the drawing in January on the understanding that a staff mission was about to visit the United Arab Republic to prepare a stabilization program; now, however, the Board was told that further visits would be needed before a program could be drawn up. He would therefore agree to the new drawing only on the understanding that the United Arab Republic was prepared to negotiate and agree on a real stabilization program. Other Directors also expressed concern, and Messrs. van Campenhout and Waïtzenegger said they would again abstain from the decision. Because of the reality and urgency of the United Arab Republic's problem, however, the Board as a whole approved the drawing.

Late in April 1962 the United Arab Republic made a third approach to the Fund, seeking a stand-by arrangement for $42.5 million. The letter of intent annexed to the draft stand-by arrangement intimated that the member was undertaking a comprehensive program to eliminate domestic inflation and to improve its balance of payments position. In the light of this, the Board agreed to the stand-by arrangement requested, which was subject to the condition that drawings should not exceed $20 million in the first three months, $30 million in the first six months, and $37.5 million in the first nine months. The United Arab Republic asked at the same time that it should be permitted to spread over three years the repurchase of the amounts drawn in January and March, instead of completing this within one year, as it had then undertaken to do; and that the gold which had been pledged as collateral for those two drawings should be released. The Board also agreed to these requests. Drawings were made under the stand-by arrangement to the full amount permitted.

The staff's examination of the problem of gold collateral drawings took a considerable time, and it was March 1963 before its recommendations were available to the Board. These were as follows: (1) The Fund had legal authority to accept gold collateral for a drawing. (2) Such collateral was no substitute for a satisfactory stabilization program. However, on rare occasions a drawing supported by such collateral might be justifiable, as for example if a member had an urgent need to use the Fund's resources, but had not yet adopted a program. In such, and perhaps in some similar, circumstances a gold collateral drawing for not more than six months would be appropriate if the member assured the Fund that it would persevere with preparing a program. If a member was able to establish a satisfactory program before the six months had expired, the gold collateral could be released. (3) The gold collateral should be equivalent to the full amount of the drawing, at $35 an ounce. (4) The gold collateral should be held outside the pledgor's territory, under earmark for the Fund, without notice being given to the depository that the gold was held under pledge. (5) The gold should be released *pro tanto* if the amount of the drawing outstanding was reduced. (6) If the drawing was not completely repurchased within thirty days after the expiration of the period for which it was granted, the remaining gold should become the property of the Fund. It could be sold to discharge the drawing. (7) All costs connected with the gold (moving, earmarking, etc.) should be borne by the pledgor. (8) The Fund's charges for drawings with gold collateral should be the same as for ordinary transactions. (9) The member should assure the Fund that the gold was free from, and would be kept free from, liens. Where the World Bank had an agreement with the member which included a prohibition on pledging its assets, there should be prior consultation between the Fund and the World Bank.

When these recommendations were considered by the Board in July, there was some disposition to question whether the charges for such drawings should not be less than for ordinary drawings, but the staff replied that these charges were believed to be less than would be imposed by other institutions making loans against a pledge of gold. On the understanding that the procedure would be adopted only in really exceptional circumstances, the staff's recommendations were accepted, and the Board also approved a draft letter which the staff had prepared for use when such a transaction was proposed.[3] However, during the remainder of the time covered by this volume no further drawing against gold collateral was sought.

CHARGES VARIED

The annual expiry of the schedule of Fund charges brought the problem of charges before the Board in April 1962 and April 1963. On both occasions the staff reported that during the previous twelve months there had been no widespread changes in rates of interest in short-term markets, and that there appeared to be no justification for any general change in the structure of charges. On both occasions the Board accepted this recommendation.

In April 1963, however, a minor change was made in the schedule. The staff pointed out that there was a considerable prospect that drawings would soon be made which would increase the Fund's holdings of a member's currency beyond 200 per cent of its quota (see below). The agreed schedule, however, made no provision for such drawings. The staff recommended that the charges applicable to drawings which increased the Fund's holdings to 175–200 per cent of the member's quota should in future be applied to drawings increasing these holdings to 200 per cent or more of quota. Drawings which fell within the 175–200 per cent tranche should attract the charges previously applied to the 150–175 per cent tranche. There were, in fact, only $20 million, drawn by two countries, which exceeded 175 per cent of quota, so that the reduction in charges occasioned by the latter proposal would be very small indeed. In any case, both the members concerned had applied for increases in their quotas which, if granted, would bring their drawings below 175 per cent of their quotas.

The staff drew attention to a second reason for not charging more on drawings which increased the Fund's holdings above 200 per cent of quota than had previously been charged for drawings reaching to 175–200 per cent of quota. The latter rate reached 4 per cent after two years, requiring members affected to consult the Fund at that time about ways of reducing the Fund's holdings of their currencies; to shorten this period would be unnecessary, and indeed undesirable. The Board agreed, and the changes proposed by the staff were adopted by 169,357 votes (i.e., unanimously).

Two other minor changes in connection with charges were introduced during the period with which we are now dealing. One was concerned with refunds

---

[3] E.B. Decision No. 1543-(63/39), July 1, 1963; below, Vol. III, p. 240.

of charges on stand-by arrangements. The other related to the charges to be imposed when no agreement could be reached with a member to repurchase a drawing within five years, or when such an agreement was made but not kept.

The former change was suggested by developments which had placed an unfruitful administrative burden upon both the Fund and members. It arose from the decision that charges on stand-by arrangements would be refunded if, after a charge for a stand-by arrangement had been paid, the Fund's holdings of the member's currency decreased in such a way that part of possible drawings under the arrangement lay within the gold tranche. An example may illustrate the procedure. If, at a time when the Fund held a member's currency to the equivalent of 95 per cent of quota, the member was given a stand-by arrangement for 25 per cent of quota, the charge which it would pay would relate to the 20 per cent by which, if the arrangement were fully drawn upon, the Fund's holdings would exceed 100 per cent of quota. No charge would be payable on the 5 per cent corresponding to the gold tranche. If now for any reason the Fund's holdings fell to 80 per cent of quota, a refund would become payable for the rest of the period covered by the stand-by arrangement, on the equivalent of 15 per cent of quota, since, if the arrangement were fully drawn upon, only 5 per cent would correspond to the credit tranche.

Such a refund was of course straightforward if the change in the Fund's holdings of the member's currency was a major one, as in the example just quoted. But there were many other reasons for changes in the Fund's holdings. For instance, a small administrative expenditure by the Fund in a member country—perhaps the purchase of a book—would reduce these holdings by a few dollars; and if the stand-by arrangement straddled the 100 per cent of quota, this would necessitate a refund of a few cents to the member country, a transaction uselessly burdensome both to it and to the Fund.

The staff therefore suggested that charges for stand-by arrangements negotiated in future should provide that changes in the Fund's No. 2 account (through which all administrative expenditures passed) should be ignored up to 1/100 of 1 per cent of quota. As regards existing stand-by arrangements, the staff proposed that refunds should be made once a quarter on the basis of changes in the Fund's holdings during the quarter, unless the Fund's holdings were so reduced that the stand-by arrangement came to fall wholly within the member's quota, in which event a refund would be made at once. These proposals were accepted.[4]

The other substantive decision on charges, dealing with those to be imposed in the event of the absence or nonperformance of an agreement to repurchase

[4] E.B. Decision No. 1345-(62/32), May 23, 1962; below, Vol. III, p. 233.

within five years, was designed to clear up a loose end that had been left when the matter was previously discussed. The staff pointed out that no decision had then been taken to vary the applicability of the normal scale in such instances, so that charges would automatically rise by 1/2 of 1 per cent each six months. This would presumably be satisfactory if no agreement to repurchase could be reached, although the Board might wish at some time to consider setting an upper limit to the rate. Nor would any difficulty arise if an agreement was reached, but not kept, at a time when the rate of charge had not yet reached 5 per cent; again the rate would rise automatically every six months. But suppose that at the moment when the member failed to keep such an agreement it had been paying 5 per cent for three months; should it continue to pay 5 per cent for six months thereafter, and subsequently be charged an additional 1/2 of 1 per cent each six months? The staff thought not; it suggested that after 5 per cent had been charged for a total of six months the rate should rise to 5 1/2 per cent. On the other hand, if the agreement was breached after the member had been paying 5 per cent for, say, nine months, the staff proposed that the rate should rise to 5 1/2 per cent from the date of default. In order to give effect to these proposals, the staff put forward suggested amendments to Rule I-4 (g).

The problem discussed in the staff's memorandum was not a merely theoretical one. As will be seen in the next chapter, Cuba had failed to repurchase a drawing of $25 million made in September 1958, although originally it had undertaken to repurchase this within six months.[5] In August 1962 the Cuban Government had written to the Fund asking permission to defer a first installment of the repurchase until March 1964. As this would have meant that the drawing remained outstanding for more than five years, the Managing Director had replied in November 1962 refusing the Government's request, and asking for repurchase to be completed not later than September 1963. No reply had been received to this letter. Meanwhile charges were rising, and would reach 5 1/2 per cent in March 1963.

When the staff's recommendation came before the Board in mid-February 1963, Mr. Saad (United Arab Republic) expressed concern that it made no provision for a maximum rate of charge. Mr. Saad himself thought that the Fund should be hesitant about charging more than 5 per cent; it should rely on ensuring the revolving nature of the Fund's resources more by cooperation between the Fund and its members than by charging higher rates. At the least he thought that provision should be made for the rate to be reviewed when it reached 6 per cent per annum. This view found general support in the Board, and the staff was asked to prepare a draft amendment to the Rule to give effect

[5] See below, pp. 548–49.

to it as well as to the staff's own recommendation. This was done, and after a minor clarification had been introduced the changed Rule was adopted by the Board.

REPURCHASES IN U.S. DOLLARS

The provisions of Article V, Section 7 (*c*) (iii), preclude repurchases with any currency if the effect would be to increase the Fund's holdings of that currency beyond 75 per cent of the relevant member's quota. In the Fund's early years, when most drawings were made in U.S. dollars and repurchases fell short of drawings, the Fund's holdings of U.S. dollars remained below 75 per cent of the U.S. quota—falling, indeed, as low as 28 per cent of that quota in 1957. But over several years down to 1962 repurchases in dollars largely exceeded purchases of dollars, with the result that by December of that year the Fund's holdings had risen to 74 per cent of the U.S. quota. Only another $33 million of repurchases in U.S. dollars could thereafter be accepted without increasing the Fund's holdings of dollars beyond 75 per cent.

This raised in an acute form the problem of ascertaining which of the repurchase obligations that would accrue at the end of the fiscal year (April 30, 1963) would be payable, and which would have to be abated. The relevant Rule, I-6, allowed member countries six months in which to compile and notify to the Fund their monetary reserves as at the end of the fiscal year. Until all these notifications had been received and processed by the Fund, the total repurchase obligations in dollars could not be known; meanwhile, therefore, it would be impossible to accept any repurchases in dollars. This meant that member countries wishing to repurchase in dollars, whether under Article V, Section 7 (*b*), or in fulfillment of obligations assumed in consideration of waivers having been granted, or voluntarily, would have to wait until the last quarter of 1963 before being able to do so.

Two measures were adopted to deal with this situation. The first was an alteration of the Rule governing the provision of monetary reserves data, insofar as it concerned members of whose currencies the Fund's holdings exceeded 75 per cent of the members' quotas. In future, such member countries were required to send to the Fund a provisional estimate of their monetary reserves as at April 30 each year, by the ensuing May 31; the Fund undertook to calculate from these each member's repurchase obligation and to notify the amount due by June 15; and repurchases would have to be effected within thirty days thereafter. If subsequently the original estimate was found to be inaccurate, adjustments would be made. This arrangement was adopted on May 3, 1963, being made subject to review at the end of 1964. It materially shortened the time of uncertainty during which no repurchases could be accepted. It did not, however, overcome the problem that only very limited repurchases in U.S. dollars could be accepted at all. Indeed, as the staff informed the Board on July 12, repurchase obligations accrued at April 30, 1963 would more than absorb the small margin of U.S. dollars that could still be accepted.

So long as repurchases were made in dollars, the Fund was in effect absorbing dollar holdings which reflected the adverse balance of payments of the United States. When dollars were no longer acceptable in repurchases, countries holding dollars and needing them to make repurchases could use them only to purchase, in the United States, either gold or currencies that the Fund could accept. Since the currencies would usually be those of European creditor countries, the result could be a similar drain on U.S. gold.

In this situation the United States came to the Fund for a stand-by arrangement for $500 million, offering to draw under this arrangement currencies acceptable to the Fund in repurchases, and to make them available at par to countries that held U.S. dollars and wished to fulfill repurchase obligations. The amount of the stand-by arrangement was calculated to cover all needs of this kind likely to arise within the next twelve months. The whole of the stand-by arrangement fell within the U.S. gold tranche, so that it was entitled to the "overwhelming benefit of any doubt" for its request, and the Board welcomed the arrangement proposed. The staff pointed out that as currencies drawn under the stand-by arrangement would normally be returned immediately to the Fund by the country making the repurchase, it was immaterial which currency the United States drew. In fact, during the twelve months of this first "technical" stand-by arrangement, the United States drew $129.75 million in deutsche mark, $114.75 million in French francs, and $5.5 million in Italian lire, a total of $250 million. As will be noted in the next chapter, the stand-by arrangement was renewed in July 1964. After it expired in July 1965 the United States continued to purchase currencies from the Fund, for the same purpose as well as for its own needs, but did not seek any further stand-by arrangement. It was felt that this had become unnecessary in view of the accelerated procedure for gold tranche drawings that the Board had meanwhile approved.

COMPENSATORY FINANCING OF EXPORT FLUCTUATIONS

While the Fund had always been prepared to accept shortfalls in the export receipts of countries producing primary products as part of the justification for drawings by such countries, it had no special arrangements for dealing with such shortfalls before 1963. The process of evolving such special arrangements brought into question the quotas allotted to primary producing countries, and standards for the revision of such quotas were extensively discussed. The following attempt to summarize a complicated story can do no more than sketch the highlights of a debate which lasted for nearly four years. Fuller details will be found in Volume II.

THE UN INQUIRIES

At the seventh session of the UN Commission on International Commodity Trade, in March 1959, the Commission "agreed to consider at its eighth session [in May 1960] international measures designed to compensate for fluctuations in foreign exchange receipts from the export of primary commodities." In this connection, the Commission recommended that "the International Monetary Fund be invited to inform the Commission about its policies and procedures as they bear on the subject under consideration."

In response to this invitation, the staff of the Fund drafted a report entitled "Fund Policies and Procedures in Relation to the Compensatory Financing of Commodity Fluctuations," which was submitted to the Commission as a staff report in April 1960.[6] The principal points made in the report were as follows:

Part I showed that fluctuations in export proceeds had been greater for primary producing countries than for industrial countries—perhaps 25–30 per cent greater in the period between the two World Wars, and as much as 45–55 per cent greater since World War II. Over the period 1900 to 1958 as a whole, the year-to-year variations in the export proceeds of primary producing countries were found to have been accounted for almost equally by variations in price and in volume; but variations in price appeared to be less important in the period since World War II than in the interwar period, mainly because of the diminished virulence of cyclical fluctuations in industrial countries. In the average primary producing country both instability in world demand and instability in domestic supply were important causes of variation in export proceeds.

Part II laid emphasis on the need to compensate for fluctuations in the balance of payments as a whole, on the need to keep such fluctuations reasonably short term, and on the need to adapt financial policies so as to keep imports in line with a medium-term trend in importing power. It was suggested that, in view of the problems involved, countries would find it difficult to do more, through compensatory financing, than alleviate the fluctuations in their importing power. Such financing should not be expected to eliminate fluctuations.

A description of the policies and practices of the Fund in connection with the use of its resources was followed by an explanation why it would be inappropriate for the Fund to pursue any sort of automatic financing, based perhaps on some mathematical formula, in connection with fluctuations in commodity exports. It was then argued that, since the financing of export shortfalls must be considered as part of over-all assistance rendered to member countries, it would

[6] Reproduced in *Staff Papers*, Vol. VIII (1960–61), pp. 1–76.

be undesirable to set up any special type of Fund financing distinct from its ordinary operations, either to compensate for commodity fluctuations or to finance buffer stocks.

A preamble concluded that

> members of the Fund that are taking appropriate steps to preserve internal financial stability and to maintain their balance of payments in equilibrium, taking good years with bad, and that are otherwise making satisfactory progress toward the fulfillment of the Fund's purposes can anticipate with confidence that financing will be available from the Fund which, in conjunction with a reasonable use of their own reserves, should be sufficient to enable them to overcome temporary payments difficulties arising from export fluctuations.[7]

At the eighth session of the Commission the Fund's report was in general well received, although a number of criticisms were expressed. It was suggested that the Fund's resources might not be adequate to cope with the needs of members suffering from shortfalls of export proceeds in a recession of the type experienced between the two World Wars. (As to this, the U.S. delegation expressed itself as confident that such a recession could be avoided in future.) Another suggestion was that the time limits placed on drawings from the Fund were too short; for example, a coffee producer would need more than three–five years to adjust his economy to adverse fluctuations in the coffee market. There was some feeling, also, that primary producing countries would be unwilling to add to their debt burden by borrowing from the Fund. Finally, the Fund's view that inflation was a main cause of trouble in primary producing countries was challenged by those who blamed instead the discriminatory trade policies of certain industrial countries, and by others who regarded anti-inflationary policies as injurious to development.

During the next two years a large number of proposals were put forward for dealing with the problem of export shortfalls.[8] Suggestions for increased assistance from the Fund were also being widely discussed in 1962. These included proposals that stand-by arrangements should be made available, without a waiver being needed, up to the point at which the Fund's holdings of the member's currency were equal to 200 per cent of its quota; and that the quasi-automatism applicable to drawings in the gold tranche should be extended to later tranches. As an alternative, it was suggested that an automatic right to compensation for export shortfalls should be granted either for the first credit tranche, or as an addition to drawing rights under the existing arrangements. Finally, the application by the Fund of qualitative criteria for drawings intended to compensate for export shortfalls was questioned; since shortfalls were

---

[7] *Ibid.*, p. 4.

[8] See Gertrud Lovasy, "Survey and Appraisal of Proposed Schemes of Compensatory Financing," *Staff Papers*, Vol. XII (1965), pp. 189–223, and below, Vol. II, Chap. 18.

objective phenomena, it was thought inappropriate that unsatisfactory financial policies should debar a country from receiving assistance.

THE FUND'S RESPONSE

Meanwhile the Fund staff had been examining exhaustively the problem of finding a formula which would measure the intensity of a shortfall in export receipts. In order to allow for a trend, the ideal, though unattainable, formula would have been one which gave equal weight to past and future years. Since data for future years would obviously not be forthcoming, the staff explored the effects of applying to past data various formulas based on current and recent years. Calculations from past experience showed that the best formula was one which compared export proceeds in the current year, x_t, with the sum of $0.25x_{t-2}$, $0.25x_{t-1}$, and $0.50x_t$. The staff also undertook an examination of 137 different schemes for compensating export shortfalls, varying among themselves in the weights given to the data for the current year and for two or three past years, in the proportion which each country's maximum permitted cumulative indebtedness under the scheme bore to the amount of its average exports over the three preceding years (20 per cent, one third, or no limit), and in the provisions governing the repayment of indebtedness under the scheme (six variants being considered).[9] Choice between these would depend upon the relative weight attached to such factors as the closeness with which the sums available to the country from exports plus compensatory financing approximated to the ideal, the smoothness over time of these available sums, and the maximum indebtedness that would be outstanding at any point of time.

At the beginning of November 1962, the staff submitted to the Board a draft report replying to an invitation, extended by the UN Commission to the Fund in May, to consider whether the Fund could play a larger part in providing compensatory financing, and if so in what way. This draft recalled the Fund's previous report and summarized the suggestions that had been made for it to play a larger part in compensatory financing. It then discussed whether the assistance given (*a*) should be made available automatically, and (*b*) should be related to the export shortfall alone or to the balance of payments as a whole. On the first point, the report concluded that the possibility that low export receipts in a given year might be due to a downward trend rather than to an abnormal shortfall indicated the need for the exercise of judgment rather than reliance on any formula. As regards the second point, the report suggested that it was essential to take into account the whole of the balance of payments, because the shortfall might well be due to the country's own inappropriate

[9] Both the papers described in this paragraph were reproduced in J. Marcus Fleming, Rudolf Rhomberg, and Lorette Boissonneault, "Export Norms and Their Role in Compensatory Financing," *Staff Papers*, Vol. X (1963), pp. 97–149.

policies, and because it was undesirable to disregard credit received from other sources.

This draft was considered by the Board at a series of informal sessions in November and December 1962. One of these was devoted wholly to the question of the adequacy of quotas, and this discussion is reported separately below. Apart from this, the informal sessions showed that the Board was ready to contemplate some extension of drawing rights beyond those normally made available. A new draft was accordingly put in hand, and was circulated in February 1963. This repeated much of the argument summarized above, and offered a series of conclusions. One was that the Fund was willing to give sympathetic consideration to requests for the adjustment of quotas, where needed to make them more adequate to deal with export fluctuations and other relevant criteria. A second conclusion embodied a description of the Fund's policies on the use of its resources, followed by the substantive concession which the Board had decided to offer, namely that a member might make a special drawing, normally not larger than 25 per cent of its quota, for the purpose of meeting shortfalls in export proceeds. Two provisos were attached, that these shortfalls were of a short-term character and largely attributable to circumstances beyond the control of the member, and that the member undertook to cooperate with the Fund in an effort to find, where required, appropriate solutions for its balance of payments difficulties. To permit the concession to operate, the Fund's holdings of the member's currency would if necessary be permitted to exceed the normal limit of 200 per cent of the member's quota. For the purpose of deciding whether a shortfall had occurred, the Fund, in conjunction with the member concerned, would make statistical estimates of the medium-term trend of the member's exports and combine these with qualitative information about its export prospects.

This draft was reviewed by the Board on February 27, 1963, and with very minor drafting changes was approved,[10] the report thus adopted being printed as *Compensatory Financing of Export Fluctuations: A Report by the International Monetary Fund.*[11]

The first request for a drawing under the new facility was made by Brazil in June 1963, the amount asked for being $60 million. (Brazil's quota was then $280 million.) Executive Directors examined with some care whether the proposed drawing fulfilled the conditions laid down in the foregoing report. There was general agreement with the staff view that the shortfall in Brazil's receipts was of a short-term character. Whether it was "largely attributable to circum-

---

[10] The conclusions were adopted as E.B. Decision No. 1477-(63/8), February 27, 1963; below, Vol. III, p. 238.

[11] Reproduced below, Vol. III, pp. 442–57.

stances beyond the control of the member" was a more difficult question, since it was apparent that Brazil's financial policies had had some effect on the level of exports. Nevertheless, Directors generally accepted that this condition also was fulfilled. On the third test, that Brazil had satisfied the Fund that it intended to cooperate to find solutions for its balance of payments difficulties, the Board believed that the evidence presented in the staff memorandum, combined with that in an initial statement made to the Board by Mr. Bicalho (Brazil), indicated that Brazil was in fact ready to cooperate with the Fund, in a serious and meaningful way, to try to meet its balance of payments problems. The drawing was accordingly approved.

In October 1963 the United Arab Republic sought and was granted a drawing of $16 million under the compensatory financing facility; this raised the Fund's holdings of Egyptian pounds to 215 per cent of the U.A.R. quota, the first time that the limit of 200 per cent had been breached. In June 1965 the Sudan drew $11.25 million (25 per cent of its quota). No further drawings under the facility were made during the period covered by this history. Commenting on this, the Fund's Annual Report for 1966 said:

> Downward fluctuations in the export receipts of the primary producing countries have been less numerous and milder than was expected at the time of the creation of the Compensatory Financing arrangements to be the normal pattern. It would, however, be imprudent to assume that this situation will hold for years to come.[12]

In fact, since the facility was enlarged and liberalized in September 1966,[13] extensive use has been made of it.

SOME QUOTAS REVIEWED

Requests for increases

It was an integral part of the Board's decision on compensatory financing that consideration would be given to requests for increases in quotas if members felt that their existing quotas were inadequate to enable them to deal with fluctuations in export proceeds, or in their balances of payments generally. The United Arab Republic had cited the variability of exports as a reason for requesting a larger quota as early as April 1962, when it asked for an increase from $90 million to $120 million. The Executive Directors recommended to the Governors that this increase should be granted, and the Governors concurred on June 22, 1962.

In July 1962 the Syrian Arab Republic requested an increase in quota from $15 million to $25 million, also on the grounds of instability of exports. When

[12] *Annual Report, 1966*, p. 8.

[13] See below, p. 612, and Vol. III, pp. 469–96.

this was discussed by the Board at the end of July, Mr. Southard (United States) said that many countries in the same quota range desired increases in their quotas, so that the increase sought by the Syrian Arab Republic raised very broad questions. In September a third application for an increase was received, El Salvador asking for its quota to be increased from $11.25 million to $15 million. When this was reviewed by the Board on October 3, Mr. Southard suggested that Executive Directors would find it difficult to give proper consideration to such requests unless criteria for guidance were first developed; he asked that the staff should prepare a study of the question. The Chairman then said that inquiries which he had made informally during the Annual Meeting suggested that increases in the quotas of small countries might be a useful way in which the Fund could assist these countries.

Staff studies

The study requested by Mr. Southard was distributed on November 8. It divided members into four groups, those having quotas of $30 million and under; those having quotas between $31 million and $60 million; the ten major industrial countries; and the remainder (excluding China). For each of these groups the aggregate of quotas was compared with three standards: the quotas as they would have been if the Bretton Woods formula had been applied to 1955–59 data; the countries' average exports for 1955–59; and the variation of exports from trend, 1950–61, calculated as was being done for purposes of the compensatory financing analysis. The first two of these comparisons showed that the quotas in the second group of countries—those between $31 million and $60 million—contrasted unfavorably with those in the other three groups, and especially with the fourth (miscellaneous) group. The third comparison was even more striking; both the under $30 million group and the $31–60 million group showed up very badly when set alongside the other two groups. The quotas of the ten industrial countries were shown to be equal to 2.92 times the variations in their exports, whereas those of the under $30 million group were only 1.39 times, and those in the $31–60 million group 1.32 times, their variations.

The staff's study was considered by the Board in an informal session on November 19. General agreement was reached that there was a case for selective increases in small quotas, but it became clear that Directors had no wish to adopt a formula to achieve such increases. Various suggestions for further studies by the staff were made, including one for a reworking of the Bretton Woods formula with some changes in its constituent elements.

Extensive calculations were accordingly undertaken, with the aid of a computer, to ascertain how changing some elements in the formula would affect individual quotas within a total of $19.1 billion (50 per cent of the total reached by applying the formula to 1957–61 data). The changes made were (*a*) reducing the relative weights applied to national income and reserves while retaining the structure of the Bretton Woods formula, and (*b*) eliminating from that formula the ratio between exports and national income while again reducing the weights applied to income and reserves. The purpose of the second procedure was to remove the anomaly produced by the inclusion in the formula of the ratio between exports and national income, viz., that when plotted with quotas measured vertically and national income measured horizontally, the quotas followed a U-shaped curve instead of one that rose from left to right. It was pointed out that the consequence of reducing the weights given to the national income and reserves in the formula was to increase the share of small countries in the total. The analysis suggested two lines of approach:

(1) The Bretton Woods formula should be reweighted to give less weight to national income (taken as a five-year average) and none to reserves. The weights applied to trade and to the variability of exports should be increased; the measure of the latter should be the standard deviation of exports from a five-year moving average.

(2) There would be some advantage in a formula with four additive components, viz., 0.45–0.50 per cent of national income, about 4 per cent each of imports and exports, and 100–130 per cent of the variability of exports.

The general conclusion of the earlier study was confirmed, the analysis showing that of the 33 countries with quotas under $30 million, 24 or 25 had quotas that were too small, as had all the 14 countries with quotas between $31 million and $60 million.

Informal calculations by the staff, not included in the paper, showed that if its suggestions were accepted, increases in quotas might amount to $475 million.

This paper was reviewed by the Board in May and June and was commended as an ingenious and helpful study. Executive Directors were agreed, however, that, as Mr. Plumptre (Canada) put it, "men were masters of formulae, not formulae of men"; the calculations put forward should be regarded as constituting a valuable point of reference in the consideration which would be given to quota increases when asked for by members, but not as explicit guidelines for decisions on such requests.

Gold subscription

Concomitantly with the foregoing discussions, the Board had been considering how to deal with a situation where a member desired an increase in quota and could justifiably be given one, but was unable to provide the necessary 25 per cent of the increase in gold. Proposals were put to the Board in April suggesting that a member in that position might be assisted in one of three ways: (1) By applying the second sentence of Article III, Section 4 (*a*), which reads:

> If . . . on the date when the member consents to an increase [in its quota], its monetary reserves are less than its new quota, the Fund may reduce the proportion of the increase to be paid in gold.

(2) By allowing the member to increase its quota by installments over, say, five years, paying in gold 25 per cent of each installment as it took effect. (3) By allowing the member to make a special drawing equivalent to the amount of gold to be provided. Recommending these courses, the staff pointed out that the first had not been applied in connection with the general increase in quotas in 1959 because at that time the Fund was engaged in a cooperative effort to provide larger resources against contingencies that might affect any member. This did not apply to increases granted in connection with compensatory financing arrangements. However, the Board preferred not to invoke Article III, Section 4 (*a*); it decided instead, on June 14, 1963, to offer the two other choices to any member which found difficulty in providing the gold needed for an increase in its quota, as had been done in connection with the general increase in quotas.[14]

Later requests

The first member to apply for an increase in quota under the compensatory financing decision was Honduras, which asked in July 1963 for an increase from $11.25 million to $15 million. Reporting this to the Board, the Acting Chairman said that he had explored with Directors the possibility of setting up a single committee to consider all such changes, instead of remitting each to a separate committee, as had been the custom. He had found, however, that Executive Directors appeared to prefer the existing system, so as to emphasize that any increases given were justified by the individual merits of each application.

The committees considering the requests from Honduras and El Salvador recommended to the Board on September 4 that these should be granted, and it was decided to submit these to the Governors. (The quota asked by El Salvador had meanwhile been revised to $20 million.) The committee that had been considering the request from the Syrian Arab Republic similarly reported favorably on September 20, and this also was recommended to the Governors. All three increases were approved.

Each of these countries paid 25 per cent of the increase in its quota in gold. In fact no country took advantage of the concessions offered by the Board until after the next general increase in quotas, recommended to the Governors in February 1965; this is discussed in Chapter 22.

---

[14] E.B. Decision No. 1529-(63/33), June 14, 1963; below, Vol. III, p. 222.

New members

Following the 50 per cent general increase in quotas in 1959, the normal minimum quota was $11.25 million. This represented the application of the 50 per cent increase to the figure of $7.5 million to which countries with quotas of $5 million or less had been allowed to increase their quotas by the Fund's decision in 1956. At the beginning of 1961 there were eight members with quotas of less than $11.25 million, but four of these increased their quotas to at least that figure during the year. The other four were Lebanon, which retained its original quota of $4.5 million until it was increased to $6.75 million in 1962; Libya and Jordan, which were increasing their quotas by installments but did not reach $11.25 million until September 1962 and July 1964, respectively; and Panama, which retained its original quota of $500,000 until it was increased to $11.25 million in 1965.

Figures like $11.25 million were, however, quite out of line with those which the Bretton Woods formula would have awarded to some of the newly emerging countries, especially the former dependent areas in Africa. For instance, an application of the formula to estimated data for Togo yielded a quota of approximately $1 million. For a number of the new members a lack of essential data, especially for national income, made it impossible to calculate a quota under the Bretton Woods formula at all. The expedient adopted, therefore, was to supply to the relevant membership committee of the Board a tabular comparison of the exports, imports, national income (where available), and estimated population for the new member and for a number of existing members with quotas ranging up to $11.25 million or $15 million. When the committee, on the basis of these comparisons, had decided on the approximate level of quota which would be appropriate, the representative of the member country was notified of this. Where the normal minimum of $11.25 million was clearly large in relation to the country's resources—remembering that normally 25 per cent of it would have to be paid in gold—the prospective member was advised that other small countries had found it useful to opt for a minimum quota of $7.5 million (as was done by Laos and Nepal in July and September 1961, respectively). Of the countries that joined the Fund during the two years now under review, nine accepted a quota of $7.5 million each—the Central African Republic, Chad, Congo (Brazzaville), Dahomey, Gabon, Mauritania, Niger, Senegal, and Upper Volta—and seven accepted $11.25 million each—Burundi, Cyprus, Liberia, Rwanda, Sierra Leone, Somalia, and Togo. The quotas of the rest were as follows: Algeria, $60 million; Kuwait, $50 million; Congo (Leopoldville), $45 million; Tanganyika and Uganda, $25 million each; Jamaica and Trinidad and Tobago, $20 million each; Cameroon, Guinea, Ivory Coast, and the Malagasy Republic, $15 million each; Mali, $13 million.

INTERNATIONAL LIQUIDITY: PRESSURE BEGINS

The year 1962 was a prosperous one for the world economy, while at the same time a further deficit in the U.S. balance of payments effected a substantial redistribution of gold reserves. International liquidity was also expanded by the measures of inter-central-bank cooperation described in Chapter 18. Meanwhile the Fund was actively engaged in removing obstacles to the more effective use of its resources. To its preoccupation with these domestic problems, and to the lack of strain experienced by a majority of the Fund's members, may be attributed the fact that in the Annual Report for 1962 international liquidity received only a short and noncommittal mention.[15]

Nevertheless, at the 1962 Annual Meeting the subject was featured by several speakers. A notable contribution was made by Mr. Reginald Maudling, the Governor for the United Kingdom, who put forward a proposal for a "mutual currency account." This would, in effect, have generalized, through the Fund, the arrangements for countries to hold one another's currencies in limited quantities which had been introduced on the initiative of the Federal Reserve System. Mr. Maudling described his plan in these terms:

> I have in mind an arrangement of a multilateral character under which countries could continue to acquire the currency of another country which was temporarily surplus in the markets and use it to establish claims on a mutual currency account which they could themselves use when their situations were reversed. Such claims on the account would attract the guarantee that attaches to holdings in the Fund.[16]

Very similar proposals were put forward by Mr. Xenophon Zolotas, the Governor for Greece.[17] In his closing remarks, however, the Managing Director, Mr. Jacobsson, was able to say that

> the consensus was, I think, that there is, at present, a sufficient degree of liquidity to finance expanding world trade, and many Governors emphasized the usefulness of the various steps already taken, whether through increased cooperation or otherwise, to strengthen the system.[18]

By the spring of 1963, the situation had changed considerably. Final figures for 1962 had shown that the aggregate of countries' official reserves (including their gold tranches in the Fund—see Chapter 21) had fallen, in contrast to increases averaging just over 3 per cent per annum in the previous three years. Meanwhile, world trade had risen by an average of 8 per cent per annum. It was clearly going to be necessary to discuss international liquidity fairly fully in the Annual Report for 1963, and the staff therefore included in the draft of the Report submitted to the Board in May a chapter entitled "International Reserves

[15] *Annual Report, 1962,* pp. 172–74.

[16] *Summary Proceedings, 1962,* pp. 67–68.

[17] *Ibid.,* pp. 111-12.

[18] *Ibid.,* p. 157.

and Liquidity." This chapter analyzed the constituents of official reserves as a prelude to a discussion of their adequacy, and put forward a guarded conclusion:

> On the assumption that liquidity of all kinds is freely used to deal with temporary swings in a country's balance of payments, available liquidity is large; but if a substantial proportion of it is, for one reason or another, considered to be available "for emergency use only," then the risk is correspondingly increased, not only of slowing down the world economy but also of being unable smoothly to deal with emergencies.[19]

In the light of this, the draft suggested that

> it may be more important, as well as more feasible, to concentrate attention on the use and, where necessary, the improvement or enlargement of existing arrangements than to seek supplementary or alternative arrangements among the industrial countries. In this connection, it should be evident that the Fund, in its further evolution, is capable of accommodating itself to the emerging needs for such enlarged facilities.

When this draft was discussed by the Board in June, two lines of thought emerged which had an important influence on the debate, not only in 1963 but in later years as well. One of these was a conviction that additions to conditional liquidity, such as those created by the Fund, were more to be desired than the expansion of unconditional liquidity. This view, which was held by several Executive Directors but was expressed most strongly by Mr. Lieftinck (Netherlands), stemmed from an apprehension that too great ease in the reserve situation would encourage inflationary policies. It will be recalled that a similar fear had motivated the European Executive Directors in connection with the General Arrangements to Borrow. It resulted in a strengthening of the reference to the Fund in the passage just quoted, which in the final version of the Report reads as follows:

> If improvement or enlargement of the credit facilities is needed, it may be more important and feasible to concentrate on the adaptation or enlargement of the existing multilateral arrangements through the Fund than to seek to establish supplementary or alternative arrangements outside. In this connection, it should be evident that the Fund, in its further evolution, would be capable of accommodating itself to the emerging needs for such enlarged facilities.[20]

The second line of thought related to the adequacy of such international liquidity as already existed. A majority of the Executive Directors believed that a more optimistic note was justified than had been struck by the staff in the conclusion quoted above. In the final version of the Report, therefore, the passage about "emergency use" is immediately followed by a statement that

---

[19] This was reproduced in the final version of the Report *(Annual Report, 1963)* on pp. 51–52.

[20] *Ibid.*, p. 51.

> if the problem of expansion of the world economy is approached as indicated here [i.e., through the Fund], lack of liquidity is unlikely, in the foreseeable future, to present a bar to the adoption of desirable policies.[21]

At the last meeting of the Executive Board before the 1963 Annual Meeting, Mr. Schweitzer—who had then been Managing Director for eighteen days—drew the attention of the Board to what he termed the "procedural aspects of the international liquidity problem." He said that the ten countries grouped in the General Arrangements to Borrow intended to discuss the matter during the Annual Meeting, and that he had been invited to attend some of these discussions. He thought that the efforts of any body or group of countries to consider these matters should be welcomed. Departing from precedent, he then read to the Board the last two paragraphs of the speech which he proposed to make at the Annual Meeting. These paragraphs described the expedients that had been adopted to supplement world reserves during the two preceding years, and expressed the view that the Fund would be found to be the instrument through which the bulk of any required expansion of international liquidity could most suitably be carried out. Mr. Schweitzer's belief was that

> the members of the Fund, taken as a whole, are not at present being prevented from adopting or carrying out desirable policies by any shortage of international liquidity. But it is wise and prudent [he said] to look into the future to consider what difficulties might arise and to devise ways of meeting them. This has been the habit of the Fund. . . . In the coming year the Fund will develop and intensify its studies regarding international liquidity. . . .

The speech concluded by inviting parallel inquiries by other bodies. Executive Directors welcomed the positive approach embodied in the Managing Director's remarks.

Mr. Schweitzer's speech, which was in form the presentation to the Governors of the 1963 Annual Report, was made on October 1.[22] On the following day a statement issued on behalf of the Group of Ten members of the Fund by Mr. Dillon, Governor for the United States, in his capacity as Secretary of the U.S. Treasury, noted that

> the present national reserves of member countries, supplemented as they are by the resources of the IMF, as well as by a network of bilateral facilities, seemed fully adequate in present circumstances to cope with possible threats to the stability of the international payments system.

The statement added, however, that it appeared to the Ministers and Governors of the Group of Ten

> to be useful to undertake a thorough examination of the outlook for the functioning of the international monetary system and of its probable future needs for liquidity,

---

[21] *Annual Report, 1963*, p. 52.

[22] *Summary Proceedings, 1963*, pp. 15–30. The passage quoted is on pp. 29–30.

and said that the Ministers and Governors

> have now instructed their Deputies to examine these questions, and to report to them on the progress of their studies and discussions over the course of the coming year.

In carrying out these studies, the Deputies were requested

> to maintain close working relations with the International Monetary Fund and with other international bodies concerned with monetary matters.[23]

It may be added that most of the 49 Governors who spoke at the Annual Meeting, whether or not they agreed that international liquidity was in need of reinforcement, welcomed the proposed inquiries by the Fund. Several Governors, and in particular Mr. Dillon and Mr. Maudling, referred to the problem created by the dependence of the international monetary system upon the deficits of the reserve currency countries for the provision of additional liquidity. Specific proposals for the reform of the system were made by Mr. Maudling, and also by Mr. Zolotas, who developed the idea that he had put forward a year earlier into a plan for members to deposit convertible currencies with the Fund in order to benefit from a gold guarantee on their currency reserves.[24]

Mr. Valéry Giscard d'Estaing, Governor of the World Bank for France, contended that the fundamental difficulties confronting the international monetary system were due not to any shortage of international liquidity but to three structural weaknesses in the system: the lack of corrective mechanisms; the lack of reciprocity in the holding of currencies between the reserve centers and other countries; and the uneven sharing of reserve risks between countries, depending upon the types of reserves that each held.[25] The more general view, however, was that expressed by Mr. Harold E. Holt, Governor for Australia, and others, who stressed the need to investigate international liquidity problems and for the Fund to take the decisions that might prove to be required.[26] Finally, Mr. T. E. Dönges, Governor for South Africa, called attention to the need to increase the share of gold in international liquidity, and for that purpose to raise its value in relation to currencies.[27]

Discussing the outcome of the Annual Meeting with the Executive Directors on October 16, 1963, the Chairman said that he visualized a very close working relationship between the Fund and the Group of Ten in the examination of international liquidity problems. There would be a full interchange of ideas; he himself would attend the Ministerial meetings of the Group of Ten, and the Fund would also be represented at the meetings of the Deputies. The staff would

---

[23] *Summary Proceedings, 1963,* pp. 285–86.
[24] *Ibid.,* pp. 44, 67, 69, 96–99.
[25] *Ibid.,* pp. 60–61.
[26] *Ibid.,* p. 71.
[27] *Ibid.,* p. 142.

be producing memoranda for the Board as their studies progressed, and copies of these would be available, through Executive Directors, to the Group of Ten. So the stage was set for the intensive examination of the problem of international liquidity which led, five years later, to the adoption by the Executive Board of the proposal for Special Drawing Rights. The progress made in 1964 and 1965 is reviewed in Chapter 22, and the outcome is summarized in Chapter 24.

STAFF ACTIVITIES

Technical cooperation

During the fiscal year 1961/62 visits were paid to 72 member countries by a total of 121 staff members, occupying in all 7,650 man-days. Many of these visits were concerned with annual consultations with the members, but there was also a continuing need to furnish technical assistance. For this purpose it was usually sufficient for the staff members concerned to be available to the member country for one or two weeks, but in an increasing number of instances prolonged stays became necessary. In the spring of 1963, for example, nine staff members were away on assignments lasting six months or more, and in four countries the Fund had been providing technical assistance by means of a resident staff member for consecutive periods of five to seven years.

Balance of payments studies

On April 13, 1962 the Board considered a memorandum presented by the staff which reviewed in detail the balance of payments situation of the United States, the United Kingdom, and Germany, and presented summary statistics for eleven other industrial countries. At the same time the staff submitted an analysis of the aggregate surpluses and deficits for all member countries, designed to bring out asymmetries in the concepts of these magnitudes.[28] Welcoming these analyses, the Board discussed four problems which they presented: the deficiencies in balance of payments statistics, the difficulty of presenting those available in appropriate categories, the limitations confronting attempts at a symmetrical presentation, and the problems involved in attempting to reconcile different presentations. Executive Directors suggested that it might be advisable to arrange a meeting of balance of payments experts from the major countries to discuss these problems and make recommendations which might be helpful both to the Fund and to national statisticians. Such a conference was accordingly convened in Washington on October 1, 1962, being attended by participants from Belgium, Canada, France, Germany, Italy, Japan, the Netherlands, Switzerland, the United

[28] Poul Høst-Madsen, "Asymmetries Between Balance of Payments Surpluses and Deficits," *Staff Papers*, Vol. IX (1962), pp. 182–201.

Kingdom, the United States, and the OECD. A report on the conference made later to the Board indicated that agreement was reached on the inadequacy of existing statistics, particularly of short-term capital and security transactions, and improvements in these statistics were discussed, although their practicability remained somewhat uncertain. The conference also reviewed balance of payments concepts, especially those of "balances," and prepared recommendations on some specific problems that had been presented to it by the Fund staff; these included errors and omissions and the calculation of seasonal adjustments as well as the problem of asymmetry in world aggregates. The conference recommended that similar discussions should be held at regular intervals.

Computers

Since 1959 the staff has made increasing use of computers for econometric calculations and for the tabulation of intricate data. Computer techniques were first applied on a major scale to the tabulation and analysis of monetary reserves in 1960; this program has since been repeated at annual intervals. Since 1962 the schedule of security holdings of the Investment Committee of the Staff Pension Plan has also been tabulated, four times a year, by computer. In addition, a number of major projects have been programmed for and carried out on computers. These include a world trade model.[29] Other uses have related to matters discussed in the present or preceding chapter, viz., the compensatory financing of export fluctuations, the calculation of quotas on the basis of hypothetical changes in the Bretton Woods formula, and the selection of currencies to be drawn or repurchased in connection with the use of the Fund's resources.

Computers have also been increasingly used in the preparation of the Fund's statistical compilations. The monthly *Direction of Trade*, published by the Fund in collaboration with the World Bank (which since 1964 has replaced the *Direction of International Trade*), has latterly been produced by a computer. The whole of the data presented in *International Financial Statistics* is now recorded in computer form.

---

[29] See Rudolf R. Rhomberg and Paola Fortucci, "Projection of U.S. Current Account Balance for 1964 from a World Trade Model," *Staff Papers*, Vol. XI (1964), pp. 414–33.

CHAPTER

21

New Problems, New Answers (1963-65)

"INTERNATIONAL LIQUIDITY is the business of the Fund." This claim, made by the Managing Director at the Annual Meetings in 1963 and 1965, sums up the principal preoccupation of the Executive Directors during the Fund's nineteenth and twentieth years, studied in this and the next chapter. Arising out of this study of liquidity were a second general increase in quotas, authorized by the Governors in 1965, and certain large drawings made during the two years. Meanwhile the other work of the Fund went on. Forty per cent or more of the Board's time was devoted to consultations, and substantial percentages to other regular duties, none of which are discussed here. There is room in these concluding pages only to describe some new features of the Fund's work and to outline the Board's activities in that minor fraction of its formal meetings which it was able to devote to the wider horizons that were opening before it.

The present chapter deals with some changes in the organization of the Fund and in its policies for the use of its resources, leaving the increase in quotas and the Fund's other activities in connection with international liquidity to be covered in Chapter 22.

CHANGES IN MEMBERSHIP

Three countries joined the Fund in 1963–65: Kenya in February 1964, Malawi in July 1965, and Zambia in September 1965. Malaya became Malaysia in September 1963 on its absorption of Singapore. The latter, however, subsequently left the Federation and applied for membership in the Fund, which it joined in August 1966. In April 1964 Zanzibar, whose application for membership was under consideration by the Fund at the time, joined with Tanganyika in the United Republic of Tanganyika and Zanzibar, which became Tanzania in

December 1964. Cuba withdrew from the Fund in April 1964 and Indonesia in August 1965; however, Indonesia rejoined in February 1967. At the end of 1965 the Fund had 103 members, with quotas totaling $19.4 billion.

Cuba leaves the Fund

The withdrawal of Cuba was the culmination of a long period of difficulty arising from Cuba's drawing of US$25 million from the Fund in September 1958. At the time, Cuba had undertaken to repurchase within six months. However, it repeatedly asked permission to defer repurchasing, and the Board agreed in March and April 1959, in March 1960, and in December 1961 to set new dates. During the three years 1959–61 the process of converting the island into a communist state disrupted both its internal organization and its relations with the Western world, resulting in a sharp deterioration of its economic position.

The agreement reached in December 1961 provided for Cuba to make three repurchases of $5 million each at half-yearly intervals beginning in September 1962, and to agree with the Fund before the latter date on arrangements for the repurchase of the final $10 million within the five-year period that ended in September 1963. However, in August 1962 Cuba wrote to the Fund asking for a further deferment, and undertook to make a first repurchase in March 1964. It drew attention to paragraph 2.d. of the Rooth Plan (Decision No. 102-(52/11) of February 13, 1952), which reads as follows:

> When unforeseen circumstances beyond the member's control would make unreasonable the application of the principles set forth . . . [that repurchases should be made within an outside range of three to five years], the Fund will consider extensions of time.

In a subsequent letter, Cuba supported this plea by pointing out that since December 1961, when it entered into its undertaking to repurchase, the United States had placed a total embargo on all interchanges of goods and services with Cuba, resulting in so marked a decline in Cuba's international assets as to prevent it from fulfilling its commitment. It hoped, however, that a prospective increase in 1963 in the output of its export products, especially sugar, together with a decline in its need for imports, would enable it to start repurchases in 1964.

In two letters replying to those from Cuba, the Managing Director stressed that five years was still regarded as the maximum period for repurchases. In his second letter, he pointed out that the paragraph on which Cuba relied could not be regarded as an effective part of the Fund's policy; only once in the whole period since February 1952 had the Fund agreed to prolong a repurchase period beyond five years, and even that was merely a technical extension, because the Fund was simultaneously granting a stand-by arrangement under which it would have been possible to "revolve" the postponed repurchase.[1] This letter was approved by the Board and sent on November 30, 1962. No reply was received.

In September 1963 the Managing Director sent a notification to Directors under Rule K-1, which requires him to "report to the Executive Board any case in which it appears to him that a member is not fulfilling its obligations under the Fund Agreement." He informed the Board that five years had elapsed since Cuba's drawing from the Fund, but no part of it had been repurchased, although all the charges due had been paid. Further, Cuba had supplied no monetary, banking, or balance of payments data, required under Article VIII, Section 5 (*a*), since July 1961, and no data on monetary reserves since the Fund's financial year 1959/60, despite the requirements of Rule I-6. Finally, Cuba had furnished no information about its exchange practices since June 1960, and did not appear to have removed the restrictions, imposed late in 1959, which it had been enjoined to discontinue. The Board agreed that the Managing Director should inquire into Cuba's intentions regarding these defaults, and he did so by letter on October 11, 1963. No reply was received to this letter, nor to a further one sent to Cuba on December 3, 1963.

The Managing Director therefore submitted to the Board, in January 1964, two memoranda dealing with the situation that had developed. One was concerned with the charges being paid by Cuba, which had increased to 6 per cent in September 1963 and, unless the Board decided otherwise, would rise to 6½ per cent in March 1964. Mr. Schweitzer suggested that no good purpose would be served by continuing to raise the rate, and recommended that it continue at 6 per cent. This was agreed by the Board.

The Managing Director's second memorandum recalled Cuba's persistent failure to fulfill its obligations, and recommended that the Board should consider taking action under Article XV, Section 2 (*a*), which would result in declaring Cuba to be ineligible to use the Fund's resources. Following the precedent set in connection with Czechoslovakia,[2] the procedure would be for the Board to take note of Cuba's failures and to set a future date to consider whether to declare it ineligible. The Board accepted the Managing Director's recommendation, and agreed that on April 15 it would consider whether to take action under Article XV, Section 2 (*a*). However, on April 2, 1964, Cuba announced that it had withdrawn from the Fund. The Government proposed to settle the sum due to the Fund by handing over title to its gold subscription ($12.5 million) and repaying the remainder in five annual installments of $2.5 million, with interest at 2 per cent per annum, beginning on July 1, 1964.

---

[1] The member whose repurchases were deferred was Bolivia (see above, p. 461), although no reference was then made to paragraph 2.d. of the Rooth Plan.

[2] See above, p. 361.

The Managing Director recommended that this proposal be accepted, even though 2 per cent was a low rate of interest, in order to secure a quick settlement. He pointed out that repurchase would be completed in 4¼ years from the date of Cuba's withdrawal, whereas, if Schedule D were applied, five years or more might be necessary. Further, the settlement with Czechoslovakia had provided for repayment over 6½ years, with interest at 2½ per cent subject to a reduction factor if repayment had been expedited; had Czechoslovakia repaid within 4¼ years, the effective rate of interest which it would have paid would have been about 2 per cent. The Board accepted this argument, and approved the settlement. Cuba completed payment under the settlement in January 1969.

EXECUTIVE DIRECTORS

In April 1964 the committee of the Board which had been set up to consider the rules for the Tenth Regular Election of Executive Directors recommended that the number of Directors should be increased at that election from nineteen to twenty. It pointed out that since 1958, when the number of Directors had been raised to eighteen, the membership of the Fund had grown by 34 countries, having a total of 16,064 votes. In 1962 the Governors had decided to expand the Board to nineteen Directors as soon as new members with a total of 8,000 votes had been admitted; thus, there was now a case for a further expansion to twenty Directors. The committee's recommendation was accepted by the Board and by the Governors.

There were two changes in the Board before the election was held. In April 1964 Mr. Ulrich Beelitz (Germany) was appointed to succeed Mr. Hanemann, and in June Mr. René Larre (France) succeeded Mr. de Largentaye. At the Tenth Regular Election, in September 1964, all except three of the Executive Directors were re-elected. The newcomers were Mr. Kurt Eklöf (Sweden) elected to succeed Mr. Skjaeveland, Mr. Luis Escobar (Chile) to succeed Mr. Klein, whose Alternate he had been since November 1963, and Mr. Alfonso Espinosa (Venezuela), who replaced Mr. Reina Hermosillo. The twentieth Executive Director, added to the Board at this election, was Mr. Semyano Kiingi (Uganda), who was elected by Burundi, Congo (Leopoldville), Guinea, Liberia, Mali, Nigeria, Sierra Leone, Tanganyika and Zanzibar, Trinidad and Tobago, and Uganda (all of which had previously voted for Mr. Kandé) together with the Sudan (which had previously voted for Mr. Saad) and Kenya, a new member. Mr. Kiingi had been Alternate to Mr. Kandé during the preceding year. Jamaica, another new member, voted for Mr. Plumptre, Somalia for Mr. Saad, and Algeria for Sumanang. Malaysia, which had previously voted for Sumanang, did not vote. The only other change in the groupings of members was the omission of Cuba from the countries voting for Mr. Espinosa.

In 1965 there were three further changes amongst the elected Directors: Mr. Espinosa resigned in February owing to ill health, and was succeeded by Mr. Enrique Tejera-Paris, also from Venezuela; Mr. Plumptre resigned in April, and was succeeded by Mr. S. J. Handfield-Jones (Canada), who had been his Alternate; and Sumanang resigned in June and was succeeded by Mr. Amon Nikoi (Ghana), who had likewise been his Alternate. In July Malaysia nominated Mr. Nikoi to look after its interests in the Fund, and in August Mr. Kiingi was similarly nominated by Malawi.

In January 1965 Sir Eric Roll resigned, and the United Kingdom appointed in his stead Mr. J. M. Stevens, who had been Director of the Fund's European Department in 1954–56.

THE CONGO

Technical assistance to the Congo (Leopoldville)—later known as the Democratic Republic of Congo—has been a major preoccupation of the Fund staff since June 1960, when representatives of the Fund were invited to Leopoldville to attend the Congo's independence ceremonies and to discuss possible membership of the Fund for the newly established country. One or more members of the staff were in Leopoldville almost every month for the ensuing two years and again during the winter of 1962–63. When, therefore, the United Nations, in May 1963, put forward a special UN program for technical assistance to the Congo, the staff was able to acquaint the Board fully with the difficulties in Leopoldville. To overcome these, the United Nations proposed to recruit and pay a number of high-level officials for key posts in the Congolese administration, and it invited the Fund to assist in these efforts. Specifically the Fund was asked to find and remunerate some twenty-five officials, of whom two would be placed in senior positions on the Monetary Council (which administered the country's foreign exchange resources), six in the Office of the Public Finance Controller, and twelve in the Bureau of Economic Coordination. The remuneration of these persons would amount to some $470,000 a year, and the Fund was asked to bear the foreign exchange element in this cost, which would be about $300,000 a year.

This request was considered by the Board on June 5, 1963. Its unusual nature raised doubts in the minds of some members of the Board. As Mr. Pitblado (United Kingdom), for example, observed, outside experts recruited by the Fund could not be expected to be familiar with the Fund's practices and principles, yet the Fund would be responsible for, and judged by, their activities. Moreover, if the Fund complied with the UN proposal it would be devoting significant amounts of its resources to general technical aid, for which other institutions rightly had the responsibility and received the resources provided by governments. He instanced the UN Special Fund and the expanded UN technical assistance program. He suggested that the Fund might make a special effort to second appropriately qualified members of its own staff for some directing positions for a limited period. Other Directors expressed similar disquiet, and the Board decided to leave the matter in abeyance pending further consideration.

In September 1963 the Congo (Leopoldville) became a member of the Fund, and forthwith approached the Fund for approval of an exchange reform. Recommending this to the Board, the staff again drew attention to the need to strengthen the new member's administrative structure. Recognizing the Board's difficulties, however, the staff now proposed that instead of participating in the UN technical assistance program, the Fund should undertake responsibility itself for the recruitment and remuneration of suitable persons, within the total of $300,000 a year previously mentioned. It recommended that experts for the positions which needed to be filled should be recruited gradually, as suitable persons became available, and that the Fund should assume no responsibility for their activities or advice.

This proposal was considered by the Board on November 8, and while Directors were still somewhat unhappy about the plan, the modifications introduced since June were regarded as making it acceptable, subject to the Managing Director reporting to the Board at intervals on its progress. It was approved accordingly.

FISCAL AND CENTRAL BANKING FUNCTIONS

The increased membership of the Fund brought with it many other requests for technical assistance, the more urgent in that many of the new members were not well equipped to deal with their difficult economic problems. As time went on, it became clear that a major need was for greater expertise in fiscal and central banking problems, and in the budget for the fiscal year 1963/64 provision was made for a modest start toward providing this. A Fiscal and Central Banking Group was created, initially in the Office of the Managing Director, and in the following year this was developed into a Fiscal Affairs Department and a Central Banking Service.

The Fiscal Affairs Department was staffed with experts available to visit member countries and advise on their problems. A panel of outside fiscal experts was established to carry out technical assistance assignments of long duration or a highly specialized nature. It was decided also that the staff of the department should participate in regular missions to member countries in selected cases. A program of applied research in fiscal problems, particularly those of the developing countries, was put in hand. The department was headed by Mr. Richard Goode, earlier a member of the Fund staff, who had since been working at the Brookings Institution. Under him it was divided into three divisions, dealing respectively with Budgets and Financial Control, Tax Administration, and Tax Policy.

The Central Banking Service, of which Mr. Mládek became Director, was organized as a liaison group whose function was to appraise requests for assistance in connection with central banking activities, and endeavor to arrange for an appropriate expert to be provided. For this purpose member countries were invited in August 1963 to make available suitable experts for temporary duty in central banks in less developed countries. It was decided that while the expert would be solely responsible to, and under the direction of, the requesting institution or government, the Fund would normally pay him salary and allowances and grant him benefits similar to those enjoyed by regular staff members. The Fund would also stand ready to pay the employer's contribution to his pension scheme. The requesting institution would normally be expected to pay the expert an allowance equal to the foreseen costs of subsistence, housing, medical care, and local transportation. Exceptionally, if the expert were filling a senior executive position (such as governor or general manager), the requesting institution or government would be expected to pay all or most of his salary.

By September 1965 a total of 21 requests had been met (including those from the Democratic Republic of Congo), and experts had been supplied to provide for central banks three governors, one president, four directors-general, two controllers, one general manager, one director of research, one consultant, three advisors, and five other experts. The periods of service given by the experts varied from a few weeks to two years.

In addition to the foregoing, assistance with central and other banking problems was rendered from time to time by the Fund's staff, chiefly by the Central Banking Service, in collaboration with members of the Legal Department. These advisory tasks have greatly increased since 1965.

Debt renegotiation

The Annual Reports for 1964 and 1965 contained passages dealing with debt renegotiation—the former briefly, the latter at some length.[3] It was pointed out that the Fund had never agreed to refinance debts directly, as that was an operation requiring longer-term financing than the Fund could provide. Nevertheless, there were a number of ways in which the Fund was able to assist a member country to negotiate a rearrangement of debt payments.

Where, as sometimes happens, the debt renegotiation was part of an over-all program of financial reform, the Fund might be able to permit a drawing to

[3] *Annual Report, 1964*, p. 19; *Annual Report, 1965*, pp. 23–30.

cover some other part of the program. If a stand-by arrangement was negotiated at the same time, the obligations assumed by the debtor might well include undertakings to limit the assumption of new short-term debt. While the Fund did not itself negotiate with creditors, it was able to support the debtor's case by providing an impartial assessment of the country's balance of payments prospects. It might also assist the debtor to formulate a revised schedule of debt service, for the purpose of its negotiations.[4] Fund staff members had attended a number of meetings between creditors and debtors, and on occasion it had been arranged that the Fund would obtain from a debtor, and transmit to the creditors, periodic reports on the progress of the debtor's efforts to limit new suppliers' credits.

IMF INSTITUTE

One consequence of the substantial growth in the membership of the Fund in 1961–63 was to increase sharply the need for training facilities in the Fund and, particularly, to emphasize the need for such facilities in French to enable citizens of the newly emerged French-speaking African countries to participate. A staff committee, set up in 1963 to survey the training program, recommended that this should be expanded so as to accommodate each year from 50 to 60 trainees in two regular English programs, from 30 to 40 in two regular French programs, and up to 15 special appointees for higher-level tuition. The committee considered that the importance of the program was such that it should be entrusted to a new department, for which it suggested the name Financial Institute or, for short, IMF Institute, by analogy with the World Bank's Economic Development Institute. The curriculum should include courses on the organization and operations of the Fund, and on the Fund's experience in the field of financial problems and policy; stress should be laid on the presentation of typical problems and the discussion of appropriate solutions by reference to the actual experience of the Fund. The object of the Institute should be to improve the capacities of public servants of high potential who were holding positions just below the policymaking level in member countries.

Proposals to implement these recommendations were put forward by the management during the discussions of the budget for 1964/65, and were generally welcomed by Executive Directors. The Institute was formally inaugurated at the beginning of the fiscal year. It was set up as a Fund department, of which Mr. F. A. G. Keesing became Director. The first two courses—high-level ones in French—were held from July 20 to August 28, and from October 26 to December 4, 1964. Its first regular English course began on March 15, 1965 and ran until the end of July. For this course, 69 candidates applied and 28 were

[4] For an example, see Moeen A. Qureshi, Yoshio Mizoe, and Francis d'A Collings, "The Liberian Economy," *Staff Papers*, Vol. XI (1964), at pp. 310–14.

invited, of whom 8 for various reasons could not come. The program for 1965–66, circulated to members in February 1965, listed five courses, two on balance of payments methodology (one in English and one in French), two on financial policy and analysis (one in English and one in French), and a special course, in English, for higher-level participants. Later a course in public finance was added.

PUBLICATIONS

It will be remembered that in 1948, in a review of the Fund's first two years, the Managing Director, Mr. Gutt, had suggested that a greater effort should have been made to publicize the Fund's work. The comparative lack of such effort at that time, and for some years to follow, may be attributed to three causes. One of them, the difficulty of explaining the technicalities of the Fund's operations, was mentioned by Mr. Gutt himself. A second seems to have been that the Board and staff were at first imbued with a belief that secrecy was an essential part of the Fund's duty toward its members. And a third undoubtedly was that for several years there was little to publicize; the Fund was functioning on a small scale, and had no such concrete results to show as facilitated the publicity given to the work of the World Bank.

As the years went on, however, Mr. Gutt's belief that too little had been done to explain the Fund's activities to the world at large was increasingly shared by members of the Board and by the staff. The feeling was intensified by a realization that misinterpretations widely diffused in the financial press reacted adversely on the Fund's effectiveness, especially as an advisory body. At the same time, the natural interest which the press and public took in an institution like the Fund, which had dealings with governments in difficulties, and which disposed of large sums of money, was thoroughly appreciated. Increasing efforts were therefore made to explain the Fund's operations and policies. This was done in speeches by the management, through Fund representation at meetings with other international organizations, and in briefings given to educational, business, banking, and labor groups, as well as to the press. But in its periodical publications, as distinct from these oral expositions, only the Annual Reports attempted to make the Fund's activities generally known; and it became evident that the usefulness of these Reports was limited by their small readership.

This is not to say that the Fund lacked a publications program. The information which it supplied in *International Financial Statistics, Direction of International Trade,* and the *Balance of Payments Yearbooks* provided essential statistics for the use of members. From 1950 onward the *Annual Report on Exchange Restrictions* offered increasingly complete surveys of the exchange systems and exchange controls of members and nonmembers. The *International Financial News Survey* made available extracts from the world press on matters of interest in the Fund's field, while *Staff Papers* offered a selection from the technical studies made by the Fund's own staff.

In and after 1961 these periodicals were supplemented by several new publications designed to meet the needs of members for information which the Fund was uniquely able to supply. One new departure was the publication of *Selected Decisions of the Executive Directors*, a collection of the major policy decisions taken by the Fund over the years. Another new step was to inaugurate a monograph series, of which the first was *Central Banking Legislation: A Collection of Central Bank, Monetary, and Banking Laws* (Volume I, 1961; Volume II, 1967), compiled by Mr. Hans Aufricht, a member of the Fund's legal staff; the second, *The Fund Agreement in the Courts* (1962), a reprint of a series of articles contributed to *Staff Papers* by Mr. Joseph Gold, the General Counsel of the Fund; and the third, *International Monetary Problems, 1957–1963* (1964), a selection of speeches made by Mr. Jacobsson during his tenure of office as Managing Director.

These publications were, however, exclusively in English, and even in the Fund's earliest days there were members to which material in that language was of limited value. Moreover, by a self-denying ordinance dating back to the original conceptions of the Fund's duties, none, except to a limited degree the last-mentioned, offered any explanation or discussion of the Fund's operating policies.

The access of new members in 1961–63, and especially the accretion of 18 African countries where French was the official language, stimulated a reconsideration of the Fund's policy in regard to publications. A first step was to append to each article in *Staff Papers*, beginning with the issue for March 1962, 300-word summaries in French and Spanish. With the same end in view, substantial extracts from the Annual Report for 1963 were published in French, and from the Annual Reports for 1964 and 1965 in French, Spanish, and German. More recently the whole of each Report has been published in the first two languages, and *International Financial Statistics* has been made available in a trilingual edition. Also, copies of the Fund's four subscription publications have been made available free of charge to university libraries in less developed countries, and at much reduced rates to other university libraries, faculty, and students.

It was realized, however, that the technical publications described above would not reach a wide audience, and that in order to make the Fund's work understood it would be necessary to break entirely fresh ground. As a result, it was decided, early in 1963, to produce a new quarterly journal, addressed to an interested but uninformed public, and to issue this free of charge in English, French, and Spanish. It was agreed that the task before this new journal was a delicate one; much of the Fund's work was, in detail, necessarily secret, and it would not be easy to explain its activities accurately and yet in language free from jargon. Nevertheless the need clearly existed and should be met.

A search for an editor for the new journal led to the engagement of an English writer, who was the author both of novels and of some studies in financial and business history, and early in 1964 preparations were begun for the issue of a trial number of *The Fund Review*. However, in March 1964 the President of the World Bank, hearing of the new venture, expressed a keen wish that the Bank should join with the Fund in it. This was welcomed by the Fund management for several reasons. One was that the participation of the Bank would enable the contents of the journal to be substantially diversified and therefore made more interesting. It would also show that the Fund was not blind to countries' needs for development, as was sometimes asserted. Finally, it seemed likely that the confusion in the public mind between the Bank and the Fund could be clarified if descriptions of the activities of the two institutions appeared side by side in the same journal. Publication plans were therefore overhauled, and a joint Fund and Bank editorial committee formed. The first public issue of *Finance and Development*, as the review was renamed, was made in June 1964, and it has since appeared quarterly in all three languages. Beginning in 1966 an annual number in Portuguese, containing a selection of articles translated from the monthly issues, has been published in Rio de Janeiro with the cooperation of the local Information Office of the United Nations.

One of the articles in the first number of *Finance and Development* was an "Introduction to the Fund," and this was later reproduced as a pamphlet, inaugurating a further publishing venture. In the pamphlet series which this began, the Fund has made available, free of charge, semitechnical descriptions of its role and activities, and also a number of legal studies bearing on its work. These pamphlets are also issued in English, French, and Spanish.[5]

Release of Fund documents

Two developments also connected with the provision of information by the Fund may here be mentioned. In March 1964 the Government of Trinidad and Tobago applied to the Fund for permission to circulate to members of the islands' Parliament copies of the report by the Fund staff on economic developments in Trinidad and Tobago, which the Government had found useful and informative. While it was not usual for reports made by Fund staff to be given such a wide distribution, the Board expressed no objection to this being done in the circumstances.

In August 1964 the Fund was asked to release to the UN Economic Commission for Africa copies of Part II of the consultation reports on African countries

[5] For a complete list of the Fund's publications, see below, Vol. III, pp. 545–49.

that were members of the Commission. Commending the request to the Board, the Managing Director mentioned that economic information about many of the newer African countries was difficult to obtain, and the data collected by the Fund would be most valuable to the Commission. He suggested at the same time that other UN regional economic commissions, and other international organizations, should also be allowed to have copies of Part II of relevant consultation reports if they asked for them.

The practice until then had been to release Part II of consultation reports only to the OECD and the GATT. Since the documents frequently included some confidential material, it was considered undesirable to make them generally available. Otherwise it might be difficult to ensure that the information supplied by members for inclusion in consultation reports was as full and frank as was necessary for the Fund's work. The Managing Director suggested, however, that this need not prevent the information being provided to appropriate organizations. Accordingly a procedure for the release of Part II was introduced which required the area department first to review the text to see whether any part of it should be deleted to preserve confidentiality, and then to check with the Executive Director elected or appointed by the country which was the subject of the report, and with any other Executive Directors whose constituents might in the department's view be affected, to decide how clearance for the release of the Part II was to be obtained.

TRANSLATION SERVICES

In 1963, as in the seventeen preceding years, translation of incoming documents into English from a dozen or so European languages for the information of Executive Directors and staff constituted the bulk of the translators' work at the Fund. Since 1961, however, an increasing volume of Fund documents has been translated into French and Spanish for the benefit of member countries. During the Annual Meeting in Tokyo in 1964 a number of the newly formed African countries presented to the management a memorandum urging, among other things, that French should be made an official language of the Fund. This memorandum emphasized a trend of which the management and staff had become especially conscious since the addition to the Fund's members of the 18 African countries in which French was the language mainly used. It was clearly no longer possible to maintain rigorously the principle, embodied in Rule C-13, that the language of Fund documents should ordinarily be English. Indeed, correspondence with these countries was already being conducted by the Fund in French. The decision to publish the Annual Reports, *Finance and Development*, and the pamphlet series in French and Spanish as well as in English was a natural outcome of this concern. In addition to this material, reports on consultations and stand-by arrangements with the French-speaking African countries, together with lectures for the IMF Institute, greatly increased the demand for translations.

As a result, it became necessary to strengthen the translation staff of the Fund. In March 1962 this consisted of 6 persons. By March 1965 the number had grown to 16, and yet, even so, a heavy backlog of work was developing. A further sharp increase in the size of the Language Services Division, which by then the Translation Section had become, was clearly necessary, and by the end of 1965 the division had grown to 27, the volume of French and Spanish translations having more than quadrupled since the end of 1963. The rapid growth of the division has continued.

In recent years, in addition to the publications already mentioned, the Articles of Agreement, the *Balance of Payments Manual*, Fund circulars, speeches by Fund officials, and papers on compensatory financing and other topics of current interest have been made available in French and Spanish. The Fund translators have collaborated with the World Bank translators to produce a trilingual glossary of special terminology, which is brought up to date periodically. The standardization of French and Spanish equivalents of the Fund's special terms is being gradually achieved, although certain phrases have presented great difficulties to the translators: "stand-by" is used in French and to some extent in Spanish; and "the overwhelming benefit of any doubt" cannot be exactly translated into the language of a country where the Roman law predominates.

NEW OFFICES

Office in Geneva

The United Nations Conference on Trade and Development (UNCTAD) was established as a permanent organ of the General Assembly of the United Nations on December 30, 1964. In 1965, after considerable debate, it was decided to establish the headquarters of the Secretariat of the Conference on a permanent basis at Geneva. It was apparent that the Fund as well as other international organizations would need to cooperate closely with the UNCTAD because of the purpose for which it was set up and the wide range of topics in the field of trade, aid, and development coming under discussion. A large number of meetings had been scheduled by the UNCTAD for the second half of 1965 and the first half of 1966. This meant that a Fund representative would need to be in Geneva almost full time. There were also other representational needs there in connection with the GATT, ECE, and ILO. The management accordingly recommended the establishment from October 1965 of a Fund office in Geneva with a Fund representative in charge. The Board agreed, and the office was set up with Mr. Edgar Jones, Deputy Director of the Exchange and Trade Relations

Department, as the Fund representative. By early in 1967 the effort to bring about closer coordination and collaboration between the Fund and UN economic organizations in Geneva through the setting up of an office there was regarded by the management as a successful experiment. In recognition of this the Board approved the establishment of the Office in Geneva on a permanent basis as from May 1, 1967 and appointed Mr. Edgar Jones as Director of the Office.

Headquarters building

The Fund's headquarters building, completed in 1958, had by 1961 been outgrown, and consideration was given to providing an addition. As the Fund's building abutted to the east on the World Bank building, to the north on H Street, and to the west on 19th Street, an extension to adjoin the existing building could be provided only on the south. Unfortunately the Fund was unable to purchase one of the existing properties on the site. It therefore enlisted, in August 1961, the assistance of the Secretary of State. With his cooperation an Act of Congress was secured in July 1962 empowering the U.S. Administrator of General Services to acquire the property by condemnation and to sell it to the Fund at the price paid.[6] In December 1962 the General Services Administration obtained an order for the possession of the property from the U.S. District Court for the District of Columbia. In the following month, however, the owners of the property claimed in the U.S. District Court that the Act of Congress was unconstitutional, in that the Federal Government's right of eminent domain could not be extended to the taking of property for use by international organizations. The U.S. District Court rejected this claim, and the owner appealed. In an order dated April 18, 1963, the Court of Appeals for the District of Columbia Circuit recognized the Fund's immunity and decided to hear arguments in June on the constitutional question.

Meanwhile the U.S. Government had obtained further appraisals of the property, and on the basis of these the Department of Justice undertook new negotiations with the owners, as a result of which agreement was reached on the withdrawal of their claim. Possession was obtained by the Fund at the end of 1963. In consequence it was possible, early in 1964, to let a contract for the new building, and this was occupied by the Fund by stages between November 1965 and May 1966. Further building operations by the World Bank have resulted in substantially the whole block between G Street and H Street, and between 18th Street and 19th Street, being occupied by one or other of the two institutions. The Fund has since been acquiring property on the west side of 19th Street, with a view to future expansion in that direction.

---

[6] Public Law 87-552: Joint Resolution authorizing the acquisition of certain property in the District of Columbia and its conveyance to the International Monetary Fund on a full reimbursement basis, for use in expansion of its headquarters, July 27, 1962 (76 Stat. 222).

Fund Offices, 19th Street, N.W., Washington, D.C. (1965)

USE OF THE FUND'S RESOURCES

Drawings on the Fund during the year from October 1963 to September 1964 amounted to $819.5 million, and repurchases to $404.9 million. In the following twelve months drawings totaled $3,506.2 million (including $2,400 million by the United Kingdom) and repurchases $401.0 million. During the last quarter of 1965 drawings were $104.7 million and repurchases $64.1 million. Some comments follow on a number of developments during the two years 1963–65, including the British transactions mentioned above.

The annual expiry of the decision fixing the charges to be made for the use of the Fund's resources led to reviews of these charges in April 1964 and April 1965. On both occasions the staff suggested that the time was not propitious to make any change in the schedule introduced in 1963, and on both occasions the Board agreed with that view. The discussion in April 1965 revealed again the underlying difference of view between those who wished the charges to be related to rates of interest in money markets and those who regarded these rates as irrelevant, but in the event the schedule was continued unchanged to April 30, 1966.

In January 1965 the Board reviewed the procedure inaugurated in May 1963 by which the provision of monetary reserves data to the Fund was expedited. It decided that this was operating satisfactorily, and confirmed it as a permanent arrangement, adding only a request that the notification by the member should be made "preferably by cable." [7]

DRAWINGS BY NEW MEMBERS

In January 1963 the Board had before it a proposal by Afghanistan to establish an initial par value for the afghani, and a request for a drawing of $5,625,000 (25 per cent of Afghanistan's quota). Paragraph 6 of the Membership Resolution admitting Afghanistan to the Fund provided for an interval of thirty days between the introduction of an initial par value and a first drawing from the Fund.[8] While approving both the initial par value and the drawing requested, Executive Directors questioned the need for this delay. The staff explained that the interval of thirty days had been prescribed in all Membership Resolutions since it was first introduced in that for Finland, approved by the Governors on September 17, 1947.

The reason for this time lag was that the Articles required that, in order to qualify to draw from the Fund, a member must have established a par value

[7] E.B. Decision No. 1813-(65/4), January 18, 1965; below, Vol. III, p. 245.

[8] Resolution 9-5, *Summary Proceedings, 1954*, pp. 107–109.

and completed its subscription (Article III, Section 3 (*a*), and Article XX, Section 4 (*c*)). The currency part of the subscription could not be calculated until the par value was known; hence a delay after the establishment of the par value had been thought desirable to enable the subscription to be calculated and paid. The Fund's initial relations with a new member also involved certain technical negotiations for which the thirty days' delay was intended to allow time. However, the staff recognized that in recent years all the issues for which the delay had been provided had tended to be settled before a member submitted its par value for approval; there was therefore no longer any need for a thirty-day interval. The staff accordingly suggested that in future Membership Resolutions, "thirty days" should be replaced by "one day," and that the Governors should be invited to amend retroactively in this way the Membership Resolutions of 26 existing members that had not yet established par values.

Recommending this course orally to the Board on March 8, the General Counsel said that the Articles envisaged that the right to draw from the Fund should be more or less concurrent with the establishment of a par value. Mr. Hanemann (Germany) was content with the change proposed by the staff, provided that a drawing was not permitted before the day after an initial par value had been not only agreed with the Fund, but actually put into operation. Mr. Toussaint (Belgium), however, inquired why a delay of even one day was necessary; why could not eligibility be concurrent with the establishment of a par value? The General Counsel agreed that there would be no difficulty in eliminating a delay altogether, and the Board so decided. The necessary Resolution to amend the 26 Membership Resolutions was put to the Governors and approved by them in April. To meet Mr. Hanemann's point the relevant paragraph in past and future Membership Resolutions was worded as follows:

> *Exchange Transactions with the Fund:* [Member] may not engage in exchange transactions with the Fund until both (*a*) the par value of its currency has been agreed . . . and put into operation and (*b*) its subscription has been paid in full.

The influx of new members in 1961–63, however, produced a situation in which a substantial proportion of the Fund membership had not agreed upon an initial par value and therefore could not draw upon the Fund at all. In January 1964 there were 28 members in this position, and the staff suggested to the Board that the ban on drawings by such members should be reconsidered.

The staff's memorandum recognized the danger of suggesting that the Fund's interest in par values was waning. It stressed, however, the anomalous effect of a rule which precluded drawing by a member with no par value but with a stable exchange rate, while permitting others to draw because they had par values, even though these par values were largely or even wholly ineffective as exchange rates. Recommending that members without par values should be permitted to draw on the Fund, the staff suggested that this might assist some members to establish par values that otherwise could not do so, and that in any case it would be better to allow such drawings than to encourage members to propose possibly untenable par values just in order to be able to use the Fund's resources.

Preliminary discussions of this recommendation with members of the Board showed that some were apprehensive about any weakening of the Fund's pressure for par values, and in April the staff put forward an amended recommendation. This suggested that Executive Directors should decide that the use of the Fund's resources, before an initial par value had been established, might on occasion serve the Fund's purposes, and that therefore:

(*a*) The Governors should be invited to amend past Membership Resolutions, where necessary, so as to give Executive Directors discretion to allow drawings before par values had been established.

(*b*) A similar clause should be inserted in future Membership Resolutions.

(*c*) In deciding whether to permit the use of the Fund's resources by members that had not yet established par values, Directors would encourage policies leading to the establishment of realistic exchange rates and the adoption at the earliest possible dates of effective par values. They would, however, give the overwhelming benefit of any doubt to requests for drawings in the gold tranche.

The Board considered this recommendation a few days later and approved it, the declaration of intention embodied in (*c*) satisfying those who had been perturbed at the thought that the principle of a fixed par value might be threatened by the Board's action.[9] In their turn, the Governors approved the changes in past Membership Resolutions, which took effect from June 1, 1964. The first transaction under the new provisions was a stand-by arrangement with Mali, for $9.9 million, approved by the Board on June 17, 1964. The whole sum was drawn, in three installments, raising the Fund's holdings of Mali's currency to 175 per cent of its quota.

GOLD TRANCHE DRAWINGS

During the formative stages of the Fund, its sponsors were urged to declare that a portion, at least, of members' subscriptions should be treated as part of their reserves. A provision to that effect was included in the final version of the proposal for a Stabilization Fund, but when the suggestion was repeated at Bretton Woods the U.S. delegate discouraged it on the ground that this was a matter for local legislation. In 1946, and again in 1947, the same point was put to the Board, but the Directors' decision on May 20, 1947 asserted the Fund's ownership of the gold subscribed by members and warned that members' accounts should be prepared "in such a way that misconceptions as to the owner-

[9] E.B. Decision No. 1687-(64/22), April 22, 1964; below, Vol. III, p. 243.

ship of the gold and currency subscribed to the Fund would be avoided." Consonantly with this, the Managing Director told Chile in September 1947 that there was no connection between a member's gold subscription and its first drawing.

The general increase in quotas recommended in 1958 brought about some reconsideration of these views, and the Directors' report to the Governors in December 1958 stressed that "the possibility of access to the Fund's resources serves in itself as a second line of reserves . . . ." [10]

In the Annual Report for 1961 the same thought was taken somewhat further. The Board remarked that

> when trends in world reserves are reviewed, countries' drawing rights in the International Monetary Fund, which are increasingly coming to be regarded as part of members' reserves, must also be considered. . . . it would seem reasonable for each country to regard the unused portion of its drawing rights as part of the foreign exchange resources which it may utilize. . . .[11]

Elsewhere in the Report, as in previous Reports, the Directors pointed out that "members are given the overwhelming benefit of the doubt in relation to requests for transactions within the 'gold tranche'," [12] the Fund's policy being in that respect more liberal than for transactions within the credit tranches. While thus differentiating between the gold tranche and other tranches as regards ease of access to the Fund's resources, the Directors did not, however, make any similar differentiation when evaluating this access as a contribution to reserves. That step was not taken until 1963, and may be said to have been a by-product of the Board's increasing preoccupation with the problems of international liquidity.

In the Annual Report for 1963, for the first time, the annual table of countries' monetary reserves was extended to include members' gold tranche positions.[13] Commenting on the table, the Directors remarked that

> the experience of member countries since [1952] has made it completely clear that these "gold tranche positions" are readily available to members whenever needed; and the clarification with respect to the use of the Fund's resources for capital transfers (decided in July 1961) removed any doubts that could have attached to the usability of these drawing rights within the limits of the Articles of Agreement. It therefore follows that members' reserves and their changes can usefully be measured as including gold tranche positions in the Fund.[14]

The point was not picked up by any Governor in the course of the 1963 Annual Meeting, but in December the staff drew the Board's attention to the

---

[10] *Enlargement of Fund Resources Through Increases in Quotas*; below, Vol. III, p. 426. See also above, p. 450.

[11] *Annual Report, 1961*, p. 114.

[12] *Ibid.*, pp. 16–17.

[13] *Annual Report, 1963*, p. 41; cf. *Annual Report, 1962*, p. 168.

[14] *Annual Report, 1963*, p. 40.

fact that there were still some limitations on members' access to their gold tranche positions, which might inhibit some members from treating them as part of their reserves. One factor was time: the procedure for handling requests for drawings occupied a week, including the preparation of a staff memorandum, its consideration by the Board, the dispatch of instructions to the Fund's depository to release the appropriate currency, and the actual transfer of the latter.

In January 1964 Mr. Saad (United Arab Republic) proposed that gold tranche drawings should be handled either automatically, under a general ruling from the Board, or on a lapse of time basis. He was supported by a number of other Directors, although Mr. Lieftinck (Netherlands) said that he had reservations about any procedure that would make a gold tranche drawing fully automatic. On that occasion the General Counsel pointed out that such an arrangement would conflict with the tradition that the Fund had the right to challenge any request to use its resources; the Board's decision on gold tranche drawings had established a strong *de facto* presumption that such drawings would not be challenged, but this was not the same thing as saying that *de jure* they were exempt from challenge.

Five months later the staff reverted to the subject. The discussions of international liquidity (reported in Chapter 22) had shown that there was a need to establish gold tranche positions as a part of monetary reserves. But they were not yet fully acceptable in this role, and the staff sought to overcome the remaining obstacles to their acceptance. One possibility considered was to try by semantic means to render them more suitable to be treated as reserves, but this was dismissed on the ground that it might unintentionally have the opposite effect to that desired. The only practicable alternative seemed to be to speed up drawings in the gold tranche to the point at which they could be regarded as available virtually on demand.

The staff proposed that when a request for such a drawing was received, it would be circulated to the Board, with the management's recommendation, on the day of receipt or on the following morning. Normally, no analytical memorandum would be distributed, though one might be circulated later if the drawing was one of sufficient interest. The Treasurer's Department would immediately inquire of the appropriate depositories whether they would be able to make the necessary transfers two business days later, on the understanding that instructions from the Fund would arrive on the day of transfer. Members of the Board would have until the close of the first business day after the receipt of the application to decide whether they wished the matter to come before the Board. If no one expressed such a wish, the instructions would be given to the depository on the following morning. This would represent a saving of three business days compared with the existing procedure. No difficulty need be expected as regards the selection of currencies to be drawn, since the great majority of members' drawings within the gold tranche did not exceed $25 million, and such drawings were usually executed in the currency in which the member held the bulk of its reserves. For larger drawings the Fund was usually aware of a member's intention to draw long enough in advance for arrangements to be made to select the currencies to be used.

This proposal was considered by the Board on August 3, 1964, and a decision taken which conformed to the staff's proposals.[15]

The United States considered whether to cancel the outstanding portion of the stand-by arrangement which had been approved a fortnight earlier, but decided not to do so. However, when this arrangement expired in July 1965 it was not renewed, and thereafter the United States made drawings in the gold tranche without a stand-by arrangement.

It should be added that the modification of procedure thus introduced did not satisfy all Fund members that it was proper to include in their reserves the equivalent of the gold tranche, or even the equivalent of the amount by which the Fund's holdings of their currencies fell short of 75 per cent of their quotas, sometimes known as the super gold tranche. It was perhaps the Belgian Government which was most concerned about the matter. Mr. van Campenhout (Belgium) had expressed his Government's views in the Board on several occasions, most recently when the draft of the Annual Report for 1964 was under consideration. They were reiterated at the Annual Meetings both in 1964 [16] and in 1965. On the latter occasion the Governor for Belgium, Mr. Hubert Ansiaux, said:

> The use of the gold tranche and even of the super gold tranche remains juridically and, therefore, potentially in fact, conditional. . . . It is, therefore, impossible for central banks to incorporate them in their reserves on the same footing as gold or convertible currencies.[17]

It was this defect that prompted the amendment of Article V, Section 3 (*a*) (iii), as part of the Reform of the Fund in 1968.

THE GAB ACTIVATED AND RENEWED

Activation of the GAB

In March 1964 the Director of Research, having reviewed the resources available to the Fund to meet drawings, gave it as his opinion that any substantial

[15] E.B. Decision No. 1745-(64/46), August 3, 1964; below, Vol. III, p. 243.

[16] *Summary Proceedings, 1964*, p. 77.

[17] *Summary Proceedings, 1965*, pp. 131–32.

drawing by a member of the Group of Ten would make it necessary to activate the General Arrangements to Borrow (GAB). In the event, this was first done in November 1964 on the occasion of a drawing by the United Kingdom, whose reserve position had deteriorated rapidly in the second half of the year.

In July 1963 the Board had sanctioned the third of a series of one-year stand-by arrangements for the United Kingdom, the amount covered being $1 billion. Before this was approved the question had been raised whether the GAB could be activated to meet drawings under a stand-by arrangement if the agreement of the participants to its possible activation had not been obtained before the stand-by arrangement went into effect. However, the General Counsel advised the Managing Director that paragraph 6 of the GAB left him free to seek to activate the GAB to meet drawings whether or not these were under a stand-by arrangement. This advice was mentioned by the Managing Director to the Ministers of the Group of Ten at a meeting on June 15, 1964, and although at a meeting of Working Party 3 of the OECD on July 16 the suggestion was made that the consent of the Group of Ten should be obtained before the stand-by arrangement was renewed, the point was not pressed. Executive Directors accepted the General Counsel's view when it was put to them by the Deputy Managing Director on July 24. The point was therefore not raised when the United Kingdom's request for a renewal of its stand-by arrangement came before the Board on July 27, 1964.

At that meeting the stand-by arrangement was duly renewed from August 8, but no drawing under it had been made up to the time when the Nineteenth Annual Meetings were held in Tokyo early in September. The Managing Director took an opportunity at a meeting of the Ministers and Governors of the Group of Ten, in Tokyo on September 7, to initiate an informal discussion of the possibility that the GAB might need to be activated. The matter was carried a stage further by the Director of the Research Department at a meeting of the Deputies of the Group of Ten on October 3, held primarily in connection with the discussions on international liquidity. On October 30, 1964 a formal proposal to activate the GAB in connection with any drawings that might be made by the United Kingdom was sent by the Managing Director to the participants. This was accepted at a meeting of the Group of Ten on November 7; confirmation from each participant reached the Fund during the following week. On November 16 the Managing Director put to the Board a proposal to provide for a possible drawing by the United Kingdom by a combination of three methods—using the Fund's existing resources, acquiring more of certain currencies by the sale of gold, and borrowing from the participants of the GAB. This proposal was approved by the Board on November 20.

Meanwhile speculative pressure on sterling was greatly intensifying, and although on Monday, November 23, the Bank of England raised the bank rate (normally changed only on Thursdays) from 5 per cent to 7 per cent, this did not check the drain on reserves. What appeared to be the imminent threat of a devaluation was averted only by the assembly, early in the morning of Wednesday, November 25, of an emergency package of credits totaling $3 billion put together under the leadership of the Federal Reserve Bank of New York. On November 24 the United Kingdom applied to the Fund to draw the whole $1 billion available under the stand-by arrangement, and on December 2 the appropriate sums were transferred to its account.

The currencies drawn were those of Austria, Belgium, Canada, France, Germany, Italy, Japan, the Netherlands, Spain, Sweden, and the United States.[18]

On November 30 the Fund was informed by the Swiss National Bank that an agreement had been signed between it and the Bank of England implementing the arrangements for the cooperation of Switzerland with the GAB. On December 1, accordingly, the Managing Director proposed to the National Bank that the Swiss Confederation should make available to the United Kingdom an amount in Swiss francs equivalent to $80 million, and this was done on December 3. The amount requested was based on a comparison of Switzerland's reserves with those of the members of the GAB.

The $3 billion of credits assembled by the Federal Reserve Bank of New York and made available to the United Kingdom were originally granted for three months only. However, in February 1965 the countries concerned agreed to extend the credits to the end of May. This suggested to the staff the likelihood that the United Kingdom would make a further drawing from the Fund in order to ensure the repayment of the credits used when they expired. The staff accordingly gave thought to a possible distribution of currencies to make up drawings of $1 billion or $1.5 billion.

On April 29 the United Kingdom, which by then had used up $1.1 billion of the $3 billion inter-central-bank credits, requested a drawing of $1.4 billion. On the same day the Managing Director had a further discussion with the Executive Directors from the countries that were members of the Group of Ten, and on April 30 he issued a formal proposal for the activation of the GAB.

The British request was circulated to the Board on May 3. By May 12 all the participants had agreed to the Managing Director's proposals, details of which are given in Volume II. The Board met on that day, and after a prolonged discussion of the situation of the United Kingdom, carried over into an afternoon meeting, it agreed to the drawing requested, to the proposed sales of gold, and to the activation of the GAB. Subsequently Switzerland agreed to make available $40 million worth of Swiss francs, under its parallel arrangements.

---

18 Details are given below, Vol. II, Chapter 19.

RENEWAL OF THE GAB

On April 28, 1965, the Chairman discussed with the Board the need to renew the General Arrangements to Borrow, which would expire on October 23, 1966 unless a decision to renew was taken by October 23, 1965. It seemed to him that the best course would be to propose a renewal unaltered, because while he could think of a number of desirable improvements in the terms of the Arrangements, it appeared unlikely that these would be acceptable to the participants. He mentioned two such improvements: the elimination of the requirement that the international monetary system should be in danger of impairment, and a simplification of the procedure for activating the Arrangements. While Messrs. Lieftinck (Netherlands) and Garland (Australia) supported the Chairman's suggestions for improvements, the Board agreed that the course which he proposed was best. The General Counsel explained that legally the participants had six months after the Fund had taken a decision to renew the GAB in which to decide whether to withdraw from it, and the Fund then had six months to consider what to do. In practice, however, it seemed more sensible to ascertain the participants' intentions before renewing the Arrangements.

Discussions within the Group of Ten during the summer showed that while all participants were willing to renew the GAB, there was a division of opinion as to whether the renewal should be for four years or for two. A compromise was arranged by which the participants agreed to a renewal for four years, subject to an effective review of the Arrangements within two years of the date of renewal and subject to the right of any participant to withdraw at any time during the three months ending October 24, 1968. Reporting this to the Board on October 15, 1965, the Chairman suggested that the Fund should agree to the proposed extension and review; as regards the right of participants to withdraw in 1968, while the participants themselves had agreed to this, the Fund had not been asked to do so, and there was no need to take a decision in advance. The Board concurred.

CONDITIONS FOR STAND-BY ARRANGEMENTS ONCE MORE

No major change was made between 1961 and 1965 in the conditions attached to stand-by arrangements. Before leaving the subject, however, we may bring together notes on a few arrangements authorized in that period which were of special interest.

In June 1962 India sought a stand-by arrangement for $100 million. At that time the Fund's holdings of rupees were equivalent to 131 per cent of India's quota ($600 million), and, if the stand-by arrangement had been fully drawn upon, the Fund's holdings would have risen to 148 per cent of quota. As Mr. de Largentaye (France) pointed out, however, the stabilization program embodied in the stand-by arrangement and letter of intent was less specific than was normally required for drawings in the second credit tranche. Only one quantitative limitation was included, viz., an undertaking that the fiscal deficit would not be allowed to grow any larger. Nevertheless, Mr. de Largentaye felt that the Fund's policy on the use of its resources should be more flexible when dealing with less developed countries; he was therefore prepared to approve the arrangement suggested. No other Executive Director commented on the point and the arrangement was duly approved.

Mr. de Largentaye's criticism was, however, revived by Mr. Waïtzenegger (France) and by Mr. Carlos Sansón (Nicaragua), Alternate to Mr. Reina Hermosillo, when India sought a similar stand-by arrangement a year later. On that occasion the Acting Chairman, Mr. Southard, said that consideration would be given to the question of quantitative limits in stand-by arrangements. Such limits have in consequence been included in subsequent arrangements for India.

In January 1963 a request for a stand-by arrangement for $40 million was made by Chile. The draft arrangement presented by the staff provided that drawings should be made at the rate of $2.5 million a month, cumulatively, with provision for an extra $10 million when import surcharges which had been recently imposed were removed. Mr. L. Denis Hudon (Canada), Alternate to Mr. Plumptre, questioned the desirability of this phasing, and the staff explained that unless the member's reserve needs showed a seasonal pattern, it was felt better to spread the availability of resources under the stand-by arrangement as evenly and over as long a period as possible.

In the same arrangement there were provisions dealing with advance import deposits (i.e., the proportions of the value of different types of imports that had to be deposited with the Chilean authorities before the imports were permitted) and with the compulsory deferment period for import payments (i.e., the obligatory delay between the date of the bill of lading and the date when foreign currency would be made available to pay for the goods). The stand-by arrangement provided that Chile should seek the approval of the Managing Director before making changes in the advance import deposits but should obtain the approval of the Fund before increasing the compulsory deferment period of 120 days. Mr. Lieftinck (Netherlands) asked why different authorizations were required for the two types of change. The staff explained that members sought whenever possible to be allowed to obtain the approval of the Managing Director, rather than of the Board, for changes in the stipulations set out in stand-by arrangements, since the former could be obtained more quickly. This tendency had to be resisted where it was not consistent with the requirements of the Fund Agreement. It was felt that a change in the deferment period for import payments fell clearly within the Fund's jurisdiction, and provision had accordingly been made for any change to be referred to the Board. Changes in the advance deposit requirements were, however, generally effected by administrative decisions, and it was felt unnecessary to refer such changes to the Board. Instead, the staff had adopted the expedient of stipulating only that the member should obtain the approval of the Managing Director for changes in advance deposit requirements, even though these contained elements of discrimination; in this, the staff had followed a precedent set in a stand-by arrangement with Ecuador in the preceding June. The staff's replies were accepted, and the stand-by arrangement was approved as put forward.

In 1964 the United Kingdom's requests for the considerable drawings described in a previous section were supported by letters of intent from the Chancellor of the Exchequer. These letters detailed the policies that the United Kingdom was pursuing, and would pursue, and undertook that if these policies did not succeed in their aims the Government would take such further action as might be necessary to ensure their success. In the first letter, which, as customary, formed part of the stand-by arrangement approved in August 1964, the Government's aim was described succinctly as "growth without inflation." In this letter the Chancellor stated that if any major shift in the direction or emphasis of British financial policy became necessary during the period covered by the arrangement, the Government would, at the request of the Managing Director, consult with the Fund and if necessary reach new understandings before any request for a drawing under the stand-by arrangement was made.

The second letter, provided in connection with the drawing of $1,400 million in May 1965, was more specific. The Government's aims were spelled out as achieving a strong balance of payments, sustaining expansion, avoiding inflation, and repaying debt, and the Chancellor undertook (*a*) to keep in close contact with the Fund in relation to the United Kingdom's balance of payments position and, if asked by the Managing Director, to discuss this position with the Fund; and (*b*) to notify the Fund if any shift in the direction or emphasis of financial policy became desirable at any time while the Fund's holdings of sterling exceeded 125 per cent of the British quota, and, at the request of the Managing Director, to consult the Fund about such shift in policy.

Relaxation of obligations

During the two years 1963–65 there was an increasing tendency for members which had undertaken obligations under stand-by arrangements to apply to the Fund for a relaxation of these obligations. Eighteen of the 37 members having stand-by arrangements in force during the period sought at one time or another to modify the terms of the letter of intent, or otherwise to adjust their undertakings to reflect a deterioration in their circumstances. Several of these members made applications more than once in the two years—Ecuador, the Philippines, and Turkey, for example, did so four times each. With few exceptions the changes were approved under the lapse of time procedure, without discussion in the Board.

Paralleling the adjustment of the conditions of stand-by arrangements, there was during 1963–65 an unusually large number of requests by members seeking to postpone repurchases due. Fifteen countries made a total of 27 applications to the Fund for permission to spread out repurchases over longer periods than had originally been agreed. While none of the new schedules provided for repurchases to be made over a longer period than five years from the date of the drawings, there were several instances where the repurchases and fresh drawings took place at roughly the same time. An examination of the extent to which members have by such means effectively made prolonged use of the Fund's resources will be found in Volume II.[19]

[19] Chapter 19.

CHAPTER

22

Unfinished Business

(1963-65, concluded)

UNTIL ABOUT 1963 the prospect of a deficiency in international liquidity was not considered a serious one by most countries. Thereafter, however, attitudes changed, and a possible need to supplement existing sources of international liquidity came increasingly to exercise the members of the Fund.

During 1963–65 the Board's deliberations on the subject had two main facets. One of these was concerned with the Fund's ability to meet the need for conditional liquidity; this resulted in a second general increase in quotas, which was in progress at the close of 1965. Concurrently the Board considered afresh the Fund's role in meeting the need for further unconditional liquidity; discussion of this was also in progress when the period covered by this volume came to an end. The present chapter deals successively with these two aspects of the problem of liquidity.

QUOTAS INCREASED AGAIN

During the latter part of 1963 and early in 1964 a number of members asked for increases in quotas. Some of these were requested under the terms of the compensatory financing decision; these are noted later in this section. Apart from these, Israel sought a special increase in quota from $25 million to $50 million, Italy one from $270 million to $500 million, Malaysia one from $37.5 million to $100 million, and Panama one from $500,000 to $11.25 million. These were all approved by the Board and authorized by the Governors.

Initiating a review

During 1964 the Board undertook a general review of quotas. While the fourth Quinquennial Review of Quotas was due in 1965, the immediate occasion for this general review was the study of the problem of international liquidity.

As part of this study, the staff prepared in March 1964 a survey which concluded that substantially larger quotas all round would be appropriate in 1964–65. The staff suggested that there should be a general increase of the order of 50 per cent, preceded by selective increases designed to reduce disparities in the quotas of different members.

The staff's memorandum was considered at an informal meeting of the Board in April, at which Directors expressed their personal views. With one exception, all who spoke favored an early increase in quotas, but they offered a wide diversity of comment on the details. Two Directors expressly approved both general and special increases, but two others voiced some doubts about the need for special increases, and two others again questioned the proposal that they should be granted before the general increase took effect. One Director proposed that increases should be spread over a period of years; two supported him, but a fourth disliked the idea. Two spoke about the subscriptions of gold which would have to be made when increases took effect; one of these stressed the importance of this gold to the Fund, and the other questioned whether the subscriptions of gold should not be waived altogether. While none of these proposals represented the considered opinions of the members that had appointed or elected the Directors concerned, they foreshadowed many of the controversial issues which arose as work on the matter proceeded.

At the end of the discussion the Chairman reminded the Board that while all aspects of international liquidity were interconnected, there could be no substitute for action by the Fund to increase quotas. This was an important area of responsibility for the Fund. He suggested that there were two reasons why selective increases were desirable: to correct anomalies in quotas, and to increase the supply of currencies potentially needed by the Fund—for example, those of some members of the Group of Ten. Concluding, the Chairman said that he thought it quite possible that at the forthcoming Annual Meeting in Tokyo the Governors might instruct the Board to put forward a proposal for increasing quotas. He recalled that in any event the fourth Quinquennial Review of Quotas would become due in the following year.

There was no further discussion of quotas in the Board until June 1964. Directors then had before them the draft of the Annual Report, including two chapters on international liquidity. In the second of these there was a passage arguing the case for an increase in Fund quotas. As eventually agreed by the Board, it referred to an increase in quotas as

> the normal way to make it possible to expand the operations of the Fund and to enable it to play a greater role in the provision of international liquidity of a more or less conditional kind.[1]

---

[1] *Annual Report, 1964*, p. 35.

The draft concluded that "the Fund should proceed to an early examination of quotas."

When this draft was about to be considered by the Board, a memorandum was distributed by five Executive Directors—Messrs. Beelitz (Germany), Larre (France), Lieftinck (Netherlands), Siglienti (Italy), and van Campenhout (Belgium)—which contended that it was premature to make any such recommendation. The five Directors urged that the Report should go no further in the direction of advocating an increase of liquidity than the Board had previously gone. Their intervention was not, however, accepted by the Board, and indeed, after extensive redrafting, the final text of the conclusion, replacing that quoted in the previous paragraph, was that "there is a case for an increase in Fund quotas."

From this premise the Report developed the argument that it would be advantageous for the Directors to consider quotas as promptly as possible after the Annual Meeting. For this, a number of reasons were given. The first consideration, the Report stated,

> is that in a world in which income and trade have expanded rapidly and are expected to continue to do so, the need for the type of liquidity provided by the Fund, like the need for international liquidity in general, may be expected to grow.

Other considerations included the desirability of providing conditional liquidity, of the type furnished by the Fund, rather than unconditional liquidity; the need to meet the strains created by short-term capital flows; and the need to enhance the liquidity of the Fund itself. Since a general expansion of quotas would not itself bring about a proportionate increase in drawings, it

> will increase the Fund's stock of gold and currencies relative to the calls that are likely to be made upon them and enhance confidence in the Fund's ability to meet all justifiable requests for drawings.

Gold and quota increases

The Report then went on to consider members' possible difficulties in finding the requisite 25 per cent of any increase in gold.[2] This was a problem which, it will be recalled, the Board had considered in 1958, on the occasion of the first general increase in quotas, and again in 1963 in connection with special increases under the compensatory financing decision. The relevant obligation stems from Article III, Section 4 (*a*), which reads as follows:

> Each member which consents to an increase in its quota shall, within thirty days after the date of its consent, pay to the Fund twenty-five percent of the increase in gold and the balance in its own currency. If, however, on the date when the member consents to an increase, its monetary reserves are less than its new quota, the Fund may reduce the proportion of the increase to be paid in gold.

[2] *Ibid.*, pp. 36–37.

Even before the review began this requirement had been discussed in the Board. It had been mentioned in a memorandum by the staff on "The Role of Gold in the Fund." When this memorandum was considered by the Board at informal meetings in January 1964, Mr. Saad (United Arab Republic) proposed that the terms of Article III, Section 4 (*a*), should be amended so as to permit the Directors at their discretion to accept convertible currencies instead of gold. If an amendment was not possible, or would prove a lengthy process, he suggested that the same result might be achieved by an interpretation by the Board. The General Counsel, however, pointed out that an interpretation in this sense would be difficult to justify, especially since the only decision of the Board that bore on the point required an obligation that had accrued in gold to be discharged in gold; this had been decided in relation to repurchases in 1951.[3] Messrs. Waïtzenegger (France) and van Campenhout took a similar line, remarking that while it might be possible to amend Article III, Section 4 (*a*), in that sense, this could not be done by interpretation. Most of the other Directors who spoke, however, indicated a willingness to consider means by which the requirement of a 25 per cent gold payment could be modified.

In the discussion of this subject in the Annual Report, two sources of difficulty were distinguished. Some countries, whose reserves of gold and convertible currencies were small, might consider that gold to the value of 25 per cent of the increases in their quotas was too much to relinquish from them. Others might have adequate reserves of convertible currencies, but would have to obtain gold for them from the reserve currency countries, which would impose a secondary drain upon the latter. The two types differed in their consequences: a country making a gold subscription to the Fund obtained, in exchange, an improvement in its Fund position, but this was not true of the conversion of reserve currencies into gold by the countries issuing these currencies; this "secondary" impact would involve an actual impairment of their reserves. The Report accordingly proposed that ways should be sought to mitigate the repercussions of gold payments not only (as in 1958) on the gold reserves of contributing members but also on those of the reserve centers that might be affected.

Following the completion of the Annual Report, the Managing Director placed before the Board a draft of a resolution which the Governors might be invited to pass, instructing the Executive Directors to "proceed to consider the question of adjusting the quotas of members of the Fund and submit an appropriate proposal to the Board of Governors." Inquiries made of individual Directors in advance of the meeting had shown that fairly strong, but diverse, views were held about the need to proceed quickly with the proposed review. The draft resolution was therefore offered in three versions, of which the first said nothing about timing,

[3] See above, p. 285.

the second instructed Executive Directors "promptly" to consider the question, and the third required them to submit their report "at an early date." The discussion at the Board showed that the third of these was an acceptable compromise, and it was accordingly adopted, the Chairman being requested to submit the resolution to the Governors "if in his judgment such action is warranted."

At the 1964 Annual Meetings the passage in the Report concerned with quotas received a great deal of attention. The reaction of Governors was almost unanimously favorable. Speaker after speaker commended the idea of an increase in quotas, and almost all who referred to the proposal to mitigate the impact of gold payments did so with approval.[4] The Ministers of the Group of Ten during their discussion of international liquidity had agreed that they would support a general increase of 25 per cent, and informal discussion among Governors showed that an increase of this size was most likely to be acceptable. During the Meetings the figure of 25 per cent was mentioned by five Governors. The first to speak of it, the Governor for the Netherlands, said that 25 per cent seemed "appropriate." There were, however, a few discordant notes. The Governors for Canada and the United Kingdom said that they would have preferred a larger figure, while on the other hand the Temporary Alternate Governor for Belgium and the Governor of the World Bank for France made it clear that 25 per cent was the maximum to which their countries could agree.[5]

Some differences of view were also expressed by Governors on the proposals to mitigate the impact of gold subscriptions. In this connection, the Governors for the United States and the United Kingdom naturally welcomed the proposals in the Report, and especially the references to the secondary impact on reserve centers. Many other Governors, particularly in less developed countries, also commended the proposals. But the Governors for Italy and France deprecated any mitigation of the primary impact on reserves, and the Governor for France disapproved of any easement even of the secondary impact on reserve centers.[6] While, therefore, the draft resolution, submitted by the Managing Director to the Governors in the course of the second session, on September 10, 1964, was carried *nem. con.*, the path before the Executive Directors, when they came to comply with the resolution, was clearly going to be a thorny one.

So indeed it proved. The Committee of the Whole which, in accordance with precedent, was set up to make the Quinquennial Review of Quotas, met eight times between November 1964 and February 1965 before it was able to agree upon a report to the Board, and it was not until February 24, 1965 that the Executive Directors were able to make their report to the Governors.

[4] See references listed in *Summary Proceedings, 1964*, p. 289.

[5] *Summary Proceedings, 1964*, pp. 69, 74, 165, 75, 208.

[6] *Ibid.*, pp. 45, 166, 106, 208.

Discussions begin

In preparation for the work of the committee the staff distributed two memoranda, both dealing with the question of mitigation. The first of these suggested seven ways of easing the strain on members' reserves, viz., (1) increasing quotas by installments, enabling members to spread their subscriptions over five years; (2) allowing members to make special drawings from the Fund to match gold subscriptions; (3) using the provisions of the second sentence of Article III, Section 4 (*a*), to reduce the amount of gold payable by members with low reserves; (4) amending Article III, Section 4 (*a*), so as to lessen the amount of gold payable by all members, regardless of the level of their monetary reserves; (5) replenishing the Fund's holdings of scarce currencies by purchasing them with gold, thus offsetting part or all of the gold subscriptions; (6) replacing gold subscriptions by gold certificates, analogous to the non-negotiable, non-interest-bearing notes which members use to make their currency subscriptions; (7) making general deposits of gold, similar to deposits made in a commercial banking account, as contrasted with the special deposits normally made by the Fund (which constituted the recipient, in effect, a bailee for the gold deposited).

Of these seven methods, the first two had been made available in connection with the general increase of quotas in 1959, and the fifth (replenishment) had been used on several occasions to reinforce the Fund's holdings of dollars and other needed currencies. The Board had, however, preferred not to make use of the second sentence of Article III, Section 4 (*a*). The substitution of gold certificates for gold had not previously been seriously considered. One reason was that it would involve an amendment of the Articles, since the first sentence of Article III, Section 4 (*a*), in conjunction with Article XIII, Section 2 (*b*)—requiring the Fund to hold assets other than currencies at certain depositories—made it necessary for the gold subscription to be paid in physical gold.

The final proposal, general deposits of gold—which was suggested only in connection with the secondary impact on reserve centers—was a new one. It was further developed in the staff's second memorandum, which explained that while the ownership of gold placed by the Fund on general deposits would pass to the depository, the Fund would remain able to require the gold to be restored on request. The Fund could continue to regard the gold as part of its gold holdings, for the purposes of Article XIII, Section 2 (*b*).

These proposals of the staff proved the nucleus around which the work of the Committee of the Whole centered. At its first meeting, on November 4, 1964, the problem which faced the reserve centers was squarely posed by Mr. Dale (United States), who said that in 1959 the secondary impact on U.S. gold reserves caused by converting dollars into gold to enable other members to pay their gold subscriptions was larger than the gold subscription of the

United States itself. This time, the United States wished to see measures introduced which would ensure that there should be neither an increase nor a decrease in the aggregate of monetary reserves, including in these both members' owned reserves and their positions in the Fund. Of the techniques suggested by the staff, Mr. Dale thought that the possible substitution of gold certificates for gold was attractive and deserved further study. He also found the idea of general deposits interesting and potentially helpful. None of the other proposals put forward, however, would meet the U.S. need. Mr. J. A. Kirbyshire (United Kingdom), Alternate to Sir Eric Roll, concurred in these views.

Among the other Executive Directors there was a disposition on the part of those representing less developed countries to advocate the use of the second sentence of Article III, Section 4 (*a*), or of special drawings, to mitigate the primary impact of gold subscriptions, coupled with general deposits to offset the secondary impact. Messrs. Larre, Beelitz, and Toussaint (Belgium), however, stressed the usefulness of gold to the Fund and argued that, ideally, 25 per cent of all increases in quotas should be paid in gold, although they were prepared to see some use made of installments or special drawings. All three expressed strong reservations about the proposed general deposits, and Mr. Larre suggested that the maximum drain on the United States (which might be a billion dollars) could be spread over several years, and in effect made good out of new production of gold.

The wishes of members as regards special increases were progressively made known to the staff by the Executive Directors concerned, and were tabulated in successive issues of a confidential draft table of increases, by means of which the Board was kept informed of developments. On these tabulations, in turn, were based estimates of the possible effect on gold subscriptions of recourse to the relief offered by the second sentence of Article III, Section 4 (*a*); one such estimate, at the end of November, found that the subscriptions waived for the one half of members who were eligible for relief under this sentence would amount to $721 million, including $258 million for the United States.

Opposing views

Most of this information was available to the Board when the Committee of the Whole met for a second time on November 23, 1964.

Opening the meeting, the Chairman suggested that the principal reliance for mitigating the primary effect should be placed on Article III, Section 4 (*a*). At a later stage the General Counsel explained that the use of this Section would enable the Fund to require that the payment of 25 per cent in gold should be completed within a stated period, and also to decide whether to insist on receiving gold or to be willing to accept convertible currencies instead. The

Chairman's proposal was supported by Directors representing some less developed countries, but was opposed by Mr. Lieftinck, who thought that reliance on Article III, Section 4 (*a*), would cause a "forest of difficulties," especially if it were applied selectively. Mr. Lieftinck urged that only the forms of mitigation approved in 1959 (installments and special drawings) should be considered.

The third meeting of the committee, on December 4, showed that an impasse had been reached. There was tacit agreement that the general increases in quotas should amount to 25 per cent and that there should be special increases for a limited number of countries, but there agreement ended. On the one side Mr. Kirbyshire believed that there was no need automatically to increase the Fund's gold stock, which was intended for use in emergencies only; he therefore advocated the application of Article III, Section 4 (*a*). In this he was supported by Mr. Anjaria (India), Mr. Kandé (Senegal), Mr. Saad, and Sumanang (Indonesia). But on the other side Mr. Beelitz said that the use of Article III, Section 4 (*a*), was opposed by his authorities as being discriminatory and a bad precedent. He recommended increasing quotas by installments—which he said did not constitute a hardship—or special drawings. Mr. Larre went even further; he saw no need to take any steps to mitigate the impact of gold payments. He pointed out that 25 per cent of an increase in quota represented only one sixteenth of the existing quota, and for many countries the gold subscription would replace gold in the member's own possession by a gold tranche position in the Fund. If mitigation was considered necessary he would agree to special drawings (but only in rare instances) or to increases by installments. He concurred with Mr. Beelitz in decrying the use of Article III, Section 4 (*a*).

In these circumstances the next meeting of the Committee of the Whole, which had been planned for the week before Christmas, was postponed to give time for negotiation, and the management and staff applied itself assiduously to the task of developing a compromise which would be acceptable to the committee. Such a compromise would clearly have to avoid recourse to Article III, Section 4 (*a*), but the less developed countries, which had expected that this provision would be used in their favor, would expect some compensation for being deprived of it. If, as seemed probable, the technique of special drawings was adopted instead, there might be pressure to relax the repurchase requirements for these drawings. This possibility was very disturbing to the staff, and it was felt essential to avoid any overt weakening of the three-to-five-year repurchase obligation which was established as Fund policy by the decision of February 1952 (the Rooth Plan). A difficulty here was that the 1952 decision itself, in paragraph 2.d., contemplated exceptions to this obligation, as had been pointed out by Cuba. However, in practice, paragraph 2.d. had become a dead letter, and the staff recalled that the Board had approved a communication from the Managing Director to Cuba refusing a plea based on it. Accordingly, the staff suggested that the best procedure was not to stipulate any specific period for repurchases of special drawings, but only to provide that repurchases would be made in accordance with the terms of the 1952 decision.

As regards those members that were objecting to the use of Article III, Section 4 (*a*), the hands of the staff were strengthened by the fact that the Ministers of the Group of Ten had accepted the need to mitigate the secondary impact on the reserve currencies. The staff therefore pressed the interested Executive Directors to accept a combination of measures to reduce this impact, including general deposits and some means of replenishment to offset the effect of special drawings. In order to make the use of general deposits more palatable, it was decided to suggest to the Committee of the Whole that the Fund should utilize these *pari passu* with its normal deposits of gold, as and when it had need to draw upon its gold holdings.

The committee resumes

By the middle of January 1965 the negotiations had shown that the Committee of the Whole might be able to agree on a report to the Governors which would include the compromise mitigation measures described above. The committee was accordingly convened on January 27, and the Chairman outlined to it the measures which the staff proposed. One known objection to the system of general deposits was removed by a statement by Mr. Dale, concurred in by Mr. Kirbyshire, that their respective authorities would invite the Fund to withdraw the general deposits if their balance of payments position improved sufficiently. This did not, however, satisfy Mr. Larre, who said that France was still dubious of the expedient of general deposits. He argued that the Chairman's proposals of such deposits plus a measure of replenishment would result in about one half of the gold due to the Fund, by reason of the increase in quotas, not being freely available to it. The Chairman, however, insisted that inquiries had shown that there was no other way of meeting the need to mitigate the secondary impact on the reserve centers, and Mr. Larre found no support in the Board.

The only other objection to the Chairman's statement came from Mr. Lieftinck. The Chairman had suggested that the mitigation measures might be applied to the general increase (25 per cent) in quotas, and also to that part of the special increases which was equivalent to 25 per cent of the members' existing quotas (i.e., to the equivalent of the general increase which the member would have received if it had not had a special increase). Mr. Lieftinck objected to any breach of the long-standing rule that 25 per cent of all special increases in quotas must be paid in gold.

Thereafter the staff prepared a draft report covering both the reasons for the increases and the amounts proposed. Two resolutions to be submitted to the

Governors were appended; a First Resolution providing for the 25 per cent general increase in quotas, and a Second Resolution embodying a list of sixteen special increases proposed. Merely to add 25 per cent to existing quotas would in many instances have produced new quotas extending to four places of decimals of a million. These would have greatly complicated subsequent calculations, and the staff therefore proposed to round the results to the next higher million dollars for all quotas up to $100 million, and to the next higher $5 million for larger quotas.

This draft was subjected to intensive examination by the committee at four more meetings. Requests for larger special increases for some members were pressed on the Board, but while sympathetically received were not accepted, mainly because Mr. van Campenhout, Mr. Walter O. Habermeier (Germany), Alternate to Mr. Beelitz, and Mr. Gérard M. Teyssier (France), Alternate to Mr. Larre, made it clear that their countries had accepted the increase in quotas on the understanding that the over-all effect would not greatly exceed an addition of 25 per cent to pre-existing quotas.

At a subsequent meeting, the method of presentation of the special increases was criticized by Mr. Beelitz and Mr. Larre, both of whom said that their countries would abstain from voting for the Second Resolution on this account; they believed that each special increase should have been considered separately in a committee, rather than that the Committee of the Whole should have been faced with a comprehensive list. Mr. Larre also objected to the method of rounding proposed by the staff, and suggested that quotas should be rounded to the next higher million dollars up to $500 million (instead of $100 million), being rounded to the next higher $5 million only above that figure. This was agreed.

It may here be noted that the special increases negotiated for members of the Group of Ten reflected a number of extraneous considerations. Substantial special increases were clearly appropriate for Canada, France, Germany, and Japan, but in all four instances there were restraining factors. France was unwilling to accept any special increase, which made it difficult for Germany, whose quota had previously been the same as that of France, to accept as large an increase as the data warranted. Appropriate increases for Canada and Japan would have given them quotas larger than that of India, which would have displaced India from its position as one of the members qualified to appoint an Executive Director. In the event, Germany accepted a new quota of $1,200 million while France, taking only the 25 per cent general increase, had a new quota of $985 million. Canada and Japan accepted new quotas of $740 million and $725 million, respectively, while India's increase (25 per cent only) brought it to $750 million.

THE GOVERNORS ACT

On February 24, 1965 the Committee of the Whole passed the draft report to the Board. There, Mr. Beelitz repeated his objections to the Second Resolution, and abstained from the vote on it. Mr. Teyssier said that while France agreed to the 25 per cent general increase and concurred in the measures to mitigate the primary impact of gold subscriptions, it had strong objections to general deposits and to the replenishment of currencies. He therefore voted against the First Resolution. He abstained from voting on the Second Resolution. There were no other dissentients, and the Board decided to approve the draft report and the First Resolution by 175,595 votes to 8,125, and the Second Resolution by 167,470 votes to nil. The report was then transmitted to the Governors, who were asked to vote separately on the two resolutions, and as regards the second to vote individually on each country's special increase.

The report and resolutions [7] were included in the Annual Report for 1965. Certain special features should be noted. (*a*) The quotas to which the general and special increases were to be applied were defined as "quotas as of February 26, 1965 or the maximum amount to which quotas could be increased under Resolutions adopted by or submitted to the Board of Governors before that date." (*b*) A member consenting to a special increase would be required to request an increase in its subscription to the capital of the World Bank equivalent to the special part of the increase in its quota (i.e., the excess of this increase over 25 per cent of its quota). (*c*) A member consenting to an increase under either Resolution might, if it wished, take this increase by installments over five years, or might request a special drawing not exceeding 25 per cent of the increase. (*d*) The Fund would suggest that certain of these special drawings, up to the equivalent of $150 million, should be made in currencies that the Fund would replenish by the sale of gold to the members concerned. (*e*) General deposits were limited to a maximum of $350 million, of which approximately $250 million would be deposited in the United States and approximately $100 million in the United Kingdom. These general deposits were subject to conditions which ensured that from the Fund's point of view they were demand deposits, and that the Fund would use "in appropriate proportions, earmarked gold and gold on general deposit in accordance with the good management of its assets." They were used for the first time in connection with a drawing by France in June 1968.

The provisions for implementing the increases in quotas were rather complicated. To give effect to the requirement of Article III, Section 2, that a four-fifths majority of the total voting power is necessary for any change in quotas, the report stipulated that the Resolutions would not become operative unless they were adopted by members representing 80 per cent of aggregate votes.

[7] Reproduced below, Vol. III, pp. 458–65.

This did not, however, mean that quotas would then be increased automatically. The Resolutions provided that this should not happen for any member until the latest of three events:

(i) The member had notified the Fund that it agreed to the increase;

(ii) The Fund determined that members having not less than two thirds of the total of quotas on February 26, 1965 had consented to the increases in their quotas; and

(iii) The member concerned had paid the full increase in its subscription.

It was also provided that notices under paragraph (i) should be received by the Fund by September 25, 1965, but that this date could be postponed by the Executive Directors.

The Resolutions were submitted to the Governors for a vote without meeting, and by April 1 had been approved by Governors exercising the necessary 80 per cent of votes. However, the acceptance of individual quotas, which in many countries required legislative action, was long drawn out, and it was not until February 17, 1966, that members holding the necessary two thirds of the total votes notified the Fund of their agreement. The effective date of the implementing decision of the Directors, declaring that the conditions laid down in the Resolutions had been fulfilled, was February 23, 1966. For those members that had already paid their additional subscriptions, February 23, 1966 was thus the date on which the increases in their quotas became effective; for the other members they became effective as subscriptions were paid.

China, Senegal, and Togo declined increases; Laos, having accepted an increase, subsequently preferred not to take it up, and the Governors rescinded the increase.

Special drawings under the mitigation plans were taken by 23 members for a total of $246 million, and the Fund replenished to a total of $148 million currencies bought by members for the purpose of obtaining gold with which to make subscriptions. Nineteen members opted to take the increases in quotas by installments. General deposits made by the Fund, as an offset to purchases of gold with reserve currencies by members not making drawings, amounted to $289.1 million, of which $244.7 million was deposited in the United States and the remainder in the United Kingdom.

The formal end of the fourth Quinquennial Review of Quotas was achieved in March 1966, when the Committee of the Whole recommended, and the Board agreed, that the Review had been completed.

Compensatory financing increases

The general and special increases in quotas approved by the Governors as above were stated to be without prejudice to members' rights to seek increases under the Fund's decision on the compensatory financing of export fluctuations. Such increases had been granted in 1964 to Ecuador, Costa Rica, the Dominican Republic, Ghana, Iraq, and the Sudan, and in February 1965 to Ceylon and Guatemala. Increases for Saudi Arabia, the Syrian Arab Republic, and Thailand were submitted to the Governors at the same time as the report on the general and special increases discussed above. All these members were therefore entitled to apply the 25 per cent general increase to a quota enlarged under the compensatory financing decision.

But applications for increases under this decision continued to be received, and it was necessary to decide how to relate these to the general increases recommended to the Governors. The first such application, received from Jordan on March 1, 1965, sought an increase from $11.25 million to $12.25 million, on the understanding that the latter sum would be increased by 25 per cent (and rounded to $16 million) if the general increase in quotas became effective. The request was referred to a committee of the Board, in accordance with the usual practice. By the time that the committee reported, it was known that the Governors had accepted the Directors' report recommending the general and special increases, but not whether or when these would become effective; the committee accordingly recommended an increase for Jordan in the terms in which this had been sought, and the Governors approved the increase in May. To achieve the necessary relationship with the Directors' report, it was decided to treat the application as if it had been received and submitted to the Governors before February 26, 1965. The same expedient was adopted for six other applications received during 1965, all of which were approved on similar terms: Iraq (a second increase), Jamaica, Liberia, Morocco, Nicaragua, and Tunisia.

INTERNATIONAL LIQUIDITY FURTHER CONSIDERED

When the Fund's twentieth year came to an end, in December 1965, the major item of unfinished business was the evolution of an acceptable plan to supplement international liquidity if and when existing sources of reserves proved insufficient to support the world economy. Little more than the groundwork for such a plan had indeed been laid, and a history that stops at December 31, 1965 cannot therefore attempt to discuss the full story that lies behind the Report of the Directors submitted to the Governors in April 1968.[8] A brief summary of this Report, and of the action that has flowed from it, is included in the Supplementary Chapter (Chapter 24), but for a full account of the unremitting

[8] See below, Vol. III, pp. 497–541.

struggle which led from the Fund's early exploratory studies to the achievement of the "New Facility Based on Special Drawing Rights" it will be necessary to wait until the next installment of the Fund's history is written.

Procedure

In an earlier chapter it was seen how, in September 1963, both the Fund and the Group of Ten were about to embark on studies of the problem of international liquidity. A first task of the Fund staff was to identify the areas of research in which work would be needed, and on October 31, 1963 the Managing Director sent to the Board a memorandum in which studies were proposed of four main subjects: the need for international liquidity; the supply and management of international liquidity; the liquidity of the Fund; and operational and policy issues arising in the Fund itself. The last-mentioned included reviews of the Fund's policy on the use of its resources, of the need for an increase in quotas, and of alternative methods of creating additional liquidity through the Fund. For the next two years much of the effort of the staff was devoted to examining these issues. For the Board, the review of the drafts of the Annual Reports in 1964 and 1965 formed the occasions for full-scale debates on the whole subject. Extensive contributions to the discussion were also made by the Governors at each of the Annual Meetings. The progress achieved in this way is summarized in Chapter 2 of the Annual Report for 1968.

The parallel inquiries by the Group of Ten, directed by the Ministers and Governors, were conducted mostly by their Deputies, who were furnished with copies of the Fund staff's studies as they became available. Meetings of the Ministers and Governors were attended by the Managing Director. The Deputies met informally during the winter of 1963–64 and thenceforward as representatives of their countries; senior members of the Fund staff took part in each meeting. In the summer of 1964 the Deputies set up a committee, under the chairmanship of Mr. Rinaldo Ossola, of Italy, to examine the various alternative proposals for the creation of additional liquidity which had been put forward. This committee, whose meetings were also attended by senior members of the Fund staff, reported on May 31, 1965.

On July 10, 1965 a new impetus was given to the debate by a proposal put forward by Mr. Henry H. Fowler, U.S. Secretary of the Treasury, in a speech to the Virginia State Bar Association. Mr. Fowler announced that the United States

> stands prepared to attend and participate in an international monetary conference that would consider what steps we might jointly take to secure substantial improvements in international monetary arrangements. . . .
>
> Our suggestion is that the work of preparation be undertaken by a Preparatory

> Committee which could be given its terms of reference at the time of the annual meeting of the International Monetary Fund this September.[9]

Following this initiative the Ministers and Governors, conferring at the Annual Meeting, 1965, instructed the Deputies to resume their discussions "on an intensified basis," and to "report to the Ministers in the spring of 1966 on the progress of their deliberations and the scope of agreement that they have found." [10]

The communiqué in which these instructions were given went on to say:

> 9. The Ministers and Governors recognize that, as soon as a basis for agreement on essential points has been reached, it will be necessary to proceed from this first phase to a broader consideration of the questions that affect the world economy as a whole. They have agreed that it would be very useful to seek ways by which the efforts of the Executive Board of the Fund and those of the Deputies of the Group of Ten can be directed toward a consensus as to desirable lines of action, and they have instructed their Deputies to work out during the coming year, in close consultation with the Managing Director of the Fund, procedures to achieve this aim, with a view to preparing for the final enactment of any new arrangements at an appropriate forum for international discussions.

As this statement recognized, the relationship of the Executive Board, on the one hand, to the Ministers and Governors and their Deputies, on the other, had become a difficult one. Those Executive Directors appointed or elected by members of the Group of Ten found themselves faced with the need to formulate in the Board policies that were being framed by their Ministers in meetings with the Managing Director, on the basis of discussions by other officials of their countries meeting with members of the Fund staff. The remaining Executive Directors were disturbed that negotiations on a matter of such general importance as international liquidity should be proceeding without any participation by the ninety-odd members of the Fund who were not in the Group of Ten. The situation resembled that which had arisen in connection with the negotiation of the General Arrangements to Borrow, but was regarded far more seriously by the excluded Directors, partly because it went on for many months instead of a few weeks, and partly because the subject matter was regarded as of wider-ranging importance than the GAB. The solution adopted, but not until 1966–67—after the end of the period with which this history deals—was to arrange for joint meetings of the Executive Directors and the Deputies.

Throughout the whole five years from 1963 until the emergence of the Executive Directors' Report on a "New Facility Based on Special Drawing Rights," differences of view persisted both within the Group of Ten and between the Group of Ten and the remaining members of the Fund. Nevertheless, a

---

[9] U.S. Treasury Department, Press Release, July 10, 1965.

[10] *Summary Proceedings, 1965*, pp. 280–81.

consensus gradually emerged. Its content, which it must be emphasized was not fully accepted until after the end of 1965, may be summarized as follows:

(*a*) That there was a contingent need for supplementary unconditional international liquidity, for which plans should be fully prepared in advance.

(*b*) That to provide the supplementary liquidity through the Fund was a more satisfactory method than to provide it through any of the alternative schemes that had been put forward.

(*c*) That the interests of the whole Fund membership, as prospective users of any supplementary liquidity that might be created, required that all members should participate on an equal basis in the distribution and in decision-making.

These three aspects of the problem, although not separated either chronologically or procedurally during the years 1963–65, can usefully be expounded seriatim, although it will be convenient to discuss (*b*) and (*c*) together.

NEED FOR INTERNATIONAL LIQUIDITY

The starting point of the discussions on this aspect was the Managing Director's distinction between the immediate sufficiency of liquidity and the possible long-term lack of it. This distinction, drawn in his speech at the Annual Meeting, 1963, was repeated at a meeting of the Board on January 10, 1964, at which he was reviewing the progress of the Fund's studies. It provoked two widely different reactions, typically expressed at the informal meetings of the Board on January 17 and 20, at which was discussed the staff's memorandum on "The Role of Gold in the Fund." The two viewpoints were indicated most clearly by Mr. Garland (Australia) and Mr. Klein (Argentina), who contended that a future shortage of liquidity was at least possible, and by Mr. Habermeier (Germany), who stressed that the urgent problem was a need not to reinforce liquidity, but to rectify the balance of payments deficit of the United States. From one point of view it was, indeed, this deficit which chiefly gave rise to apprehensions about a scarcity of liquidity. In the short run the deficit tended to reduce the acceptability of dollars as reserves, and in the long run the prospect of its elimination foreshadowed a drying up of the additions to reserves which U.S. dollars had provided annually since 1957.

The Annual Report for 1964 contained two chapters on international liquidity. Consideration of the drafts prepared by the staff precipitated a long-drawn-out debate in the Board on the whole question. As regards the aspect with which we are now dealing, the draft submitted to the Board described the general level of international liquidity as "broadly satisfactory," but added that this "does not mean that its distribution among countries or the supply of each type of liquidity is equally satisfactory."

Included in this draft was a recommendation for a review of quotas, based on the recognition that an increase in quotas was the normal way for the Fund to expand its contribution to international liquidity. The action taken on this recommendation was considered in the first section of this chapter.

On the general issue, the appraisal quoted above remained in the Report, and the Fund's views were summed up as follows:

> It must be assumed that payments deficits of the United States will not contribute to the formation of reserves in future on the same scale as in recent years. It therefore seems safe to forecast that in the future greater reliance than over the past decade will have to be placed on the provision of international liquidity, as needed, by other means. The Fund could make an essential contribution in this connection.[11]

At the 1964 Annual Meetings views similar to those of the five Executive Directors who had circulated a memorandum deprecating allusions to increases in liquidity were expressed by the Governors for the countries that had appointed or elected these Executive Directors. Mr. Blessing, Governor for Germany, and Mr. Emilio Colombo, Governor for Italy, urged the need to improve members' adjustment policies rather than to increase international liquidity. Mr. Giscard d'Estaing (Governor of the World Bank for France) and Mr. Cecil de Strycker (Temporary Alternate Governor for Belgium) stressed the risk of inflation. Mr. Holtrop (Governor for the Netherlands) and others welcomed the agreement of the countries of the Group of Ten on multilateral surveillance as a means of adapting credit facilities to the particular type of imbalance that might have to be financed.[12]

This last reference was to a recommendation of the Deputies presented to and adopted by the Ministers and Governors at their meeting on June 15–16, 1964. After speaking of the great gains to be drawn from such activities as the Fund's system of annual consultations, the Deputies recommended that

> these processes should be continued and intensified . . . in particular . . . the initiative already taken toward strengthening the multilateral character of the international monetary system should be further developed by bringing within the review and appraisal processes of multilateral surveillance the various elements in international liquidity—whether of a private or official character—available or created for the financing of surpluses and deficits.

The Deputies therefore proposed that all the countries in the Group of Ten should provide to the Bank for International Settlements statistical data bearing on the means utilized to finance surpluses or deficits in their external accounts;

---

11 *Annual Report, 1964,* p. 31.

12 *Summary Proceedings, 1964,* pp. 53, 108, 205, 76, 67–68.

and that these data, combined by the Bank for International Settlements, should be supplied confidentially to all participants and to Working Party 3 of the OECD.[13]

It may be added that multilateral surveillance, of which a good deal was heard during the Annual Meetings, was there defined by Mr. Reginald Maudling (Governor for the United Kingdom) as follows:

> This phrase was very carefully chosen because the possible alternative of "discipline" has a different significance in different languages. It is intended to represent a step forward along the road of increasing consultation and cooperation in monetary and economic affairs which we have been following ever since the end of the war. Our agreement does not give any member of the Group of Ten, or indeed the Group as such, a veto on the setting-up of new facilities within the Group or between members of it, or on the use of existing facilities. It does, however, recognize very clearly that agreements made between individual countries may well be of close interest to other members of the Group, and that the interest of these other members should be taken fully into account when new arrangements are made.[14]

Multilateral surveillance in this sense has, of course, been a feature of the work of the Fund from its outset.

The policy of the French Government, with its reliance on gold, was expounded more fully by Mr. Giscard d'Estaing in a speech in February 1965, and he remained opposed to any proposal even to contemplate a possible need to increase liquidity. However, the Managing Director, in a speech in Paris on June 2, 1965, drew attention to the danger that there might be a shortage of international liquidity when the United States and the United Kingdom rectified their balances of payments,[15] and it was this view, rather than that of France, which was reflected in the Annual Report for 1965. There the Fund's attitude to the problem was summed up as follows:

> . . . it is important that further progress be made toward an international consensus about the way in which the international monetary system should develop, including possible new techniques whereby the existing methods of reserve creation could be supplemented, if and when necessary, and to the extent required.[16]

At the 1965 Annual Meeting, Messrs. Blessing, Colombo, and Giscard d'Estaing repeated the warnings that they had given in 1964.[17] Mr. Colombo was particularly uncompromising. He said that, as his authorities saw it,

> the problem of strengthening the stability of the international monetary system really comes down to avoiding any decrease in unconditional liquidity. . . . In

[13] *Ministerial Statement of the Group of Ten and Annex Prepared by Deputies* (Paris, August 1964), Annex, pars. 36, 37.

[14] *Summary Proceedings, 1964*, pp. 166–67.

[15] Reproduced in *International Financial News Survey*, Vol. XVII (1965), pp. 209–16. Reference is to p. 214.

[16] *Annual Report, 1965*, p. 15.

[17] *Summary Proceedings, 1965*, pp. 117, 41–42, 124–26.

> other words, we believe that there is no case at present for any further increase in the volume of unconditional and conditional liquidity.

Mr. Holtrop, referring to a remark of Mr. Fowler's about the wisdom of repairing the roof while the sun shines, said:

> I found, in the light of Dutch experience of the past ten years, his simile all the more apt because in our country we are used to repairing roofs to protect our homes not against a shortage but against an overabundance of liquidity.[18]

However, the Ministers and Governors, in the communiqué in which they instructed the Deputies to resume their discussions "on an intensified basis," said that they had

> concluded that it is important to undertake, as soon as possible, contingency planning so as to ensure that the future reserve needs of the world are adequately met.[19]

And there, until the Deputies reported again in 1966, the question of the adequacy of liquidity remained.

A UNIVERSAL APPROACH OR A LIMITED GROUP

The question whether additional unconditional liquidity should be channeled through the Fund or should be provided by some other agency turned, in practice, on the parallel question whether the machinery provided should be a universal one or the prerogative of a limited group. It was decided on political, not on technical lines. It is therefore unnecessary to detail the technical issues which were so extensively discussed in 1964 and 1965. It will suffice to say that the ways in which the Fund could effectively meet the need for additional liquidity were set out in memoranda by the Fund staff in December 1963, December 1964, and February, March, May, and September 1965. They were explained further in the Annual Reports for 1964 and 1965, and in the speech of the Managing Director in June 1965 mentioned above.[20] The alternative plans that had been put forward outside the Fund—including those by Mr. Bernstein for a Composite Reserve Unit and others by Mr. Giscard d'Estaing and by Mr. Robert V. Roosa—were examined in memoranda by the staff in March 1964 and December 1965.

In the Annual Report for 1964 the case for a multilateral institutional approach was argued by way of contrast with the bilateral credit arrangements between central banks. Such arrangements, it was pointed out, are

> in practice open only to a relatively restricted group of countries. By contrast, multilateral institutions can extend the scope of their operations to a world-wide membership.

[18] *Ibid.*, p. 148.

[19] *Ibid.*, p. 280.

[20] *Annual Report, 1964*, pp. 34–39; *Annual Report, 1965*, p. 17; *IFNS*, cited above in note 15.

> The advantage of the multilateral institutional approach is still more marked with respect to ensuring that liquidity is made available to countries at appropriate times and on appropriate terms and conditions. . . .[21]

At the 1964 Annual Meetings the view that the Fund was the appropriate agency for administering international liquidity, because of its world-wide membership, was voiced by many Governors from less developed countries. For instance, the Chairman of the Annual Meetings, Mr. Francisco Aquino h., the Governor for El Salvador, remarked in his opening address that

> the problem of international liquidity is one which rightly concerns all members of the Fund. It is true, perhaps, that the efficiency of the international monetary system is largely dependent on the effective cooperation of a relatively small number of countries; but it serves the interests of all. . . .
>
> I should like, therefore, to urge that whatever action may be the outcome of the present deliberations in the Fund and elsewhere will be taken within a truly multilateral framework such as that provided by our meeting.[22]

Nevertheless, voices were heard against this view. Mr. Colombo suggested that the need for less developed countries to participate in the distribution of additional international liquidity should be satisfied by the increases in quotas which were being recommended.[23] Mr. Holtrop went further, saying:

> The creation of a new reserve asset is conceivable both within and outside the Fund. The Netherlands Government believes there are advantages in its introduction within a restricted group, albeit in close cooperation with the International Monetary Fund and with full recognition of the interests of the international community as a whole.[24]

By the time that the Annual Report for 1965 was being considered in the Fund, the issue, although still essentially political, had taken on economic overtones. Executive Directors representing some continental European members of the Group of Ten urged that increases in international liquidity should not be effected in such a way as to result in the transfer of real resources. Their wish was that such increases should be provided only to countries that, in general, would hold them as additions to their reserves; they therefore considered that the machinery evolved should exclude less developed countries from participating in any distribution of international liquidity. Somewhat naturally, Executive Directors representing the less developed countries were strongly opposed to this view. They suggested that the objective of increasing international liquidity, to ensure the smooth functioning of international trade, could best be achieved if the additional liquidity were moved into the hands of those who were prepared to spend it, rather than be confined to those who wished merely to hold it.

---

[21] *Annual Report, 1964*, p. 33.

[22] *Summary Proceedings, 1964*, pp. 10–11.

[23] *Ibid.*, p. 106.

[24] *Ibid.*, pp. 68–69.

At the 1965 Annual Meetings these views were strongly expressed by Governors from both groups of countries. Messrs. Blessing, Colombo, Giscard d'Estaing, and Holtrop all urged that the provision and distribution of any additional liquidity created should be confined to a limited group. As Mr. Blessing put it:

> . . . We should not create money artificially to assist the developing countries. What they need is not short-term money but long-term capital, and this can only come from savings and should not be created by the monetary machinery.[25]

Mr. Holtrop expounded the views of his Government as follows:

> In the first place, we agree with the conclusion of the Managing Director that the functioning of the international monetary system and the adequacy of the resources of international liquidity are matters of concern to all members. But we also agree with the statement of my distinguished fellow Governor for Italy that the responsibilities involved in the creation of new reserve assets should be borne mainly by those countries which are best able to shoulder the resulting burden.
>
> In the second place, the Netherlands Government strongly feels that the purpose of any new form of liquidity creation should not be to bring about a transfer of real resources to the countries that might, on the basis of some agreed formula, be the beneficiary of such creation, whether they are industrialized or developing nations. . . . We should . . . direct . . . the creation of the new reserve medium to the satisfaction of the desire for an increase of owned reserves. . . .[26]

The view of the less developed countries that they should be able to participate in the evolution of any plan for additional liquidity was perhaps expressed most clearly by Mr. Harold Holt, Governor for Australia, who said, in part:

> . . . It would not be acceptable to the great majority of members to have decisions on matters so vitally affecting every one of us determined in substance, if not also in form, by a small and strictly limited group. . . . I speak now as one of more than 90 countries who are not included in the membership of the Ten. I must say that it would be quite unacceptable to us to be confronted with a *fait accompli*, giving us no reasonable opportunities for expressing our views in a manner which permitted these views to make some impact.[27]

Mr. Holt also dealt, in similarly forthright fashion, with the proposal that any additional reserves created should be distributed only to a limited group of countries. Referring to the competing schemes mentioned above, he said:

> . . . A common feature of many of the proposals is that countries inside the Group could receive an immediate and direct increase in reserves. The benefit of this increased liquidity to countries outside the Group would be delayed and indirect. Some of those outside the Group are ready and able to assume the obligations involved. They would feel discriminated against if they were denied the oppor-

[25] *Summary Proceedings, 1965*, p. 117.
[26] *Ibid.*, pp. 148-49.
[27] *Ibid.*, p. 79.

> tunity to join in the arrangements made and share in the mutual extension of credits. Even where countries outside the Group were not in a position to accept the obligations involved in participation, they would wish to be assured that their legitimate interests were being taken into account. . . .
>
> I adopt, therefore, with warm approval the Managing Director's statement that "new facilities should be available to all countries which can meet reasonable and agreed tests." [28]

These views were repeated within the Board when, in November, it met for a preliminary discussion of the Fund's work in the following fiscal year. Mr. Beelitz (Germany) and Mr. Larre (France) voiced the views expressed by their countries' Ministers at the Annual Meetings, while Mr. Garland (Australia) took up the cudgels on behalf of the countries outside the Group of Ten.

Sentiment among the Deputies at that time remained strongly in favor of confining any new reserve creation to a small group, though not necessarily to the members of the Group of Ten. In December 1965 a discussion among the Deputies of the vexed question of decision-making centered on a proposed procedure which would have been similar to that for the activation of the GAB. Nevertheless, at this same December meeting a first concession was made to the view championed by the Australian representatives at the Annual Meetings and in the Board: the Deputies took into consideration a suggestion for a "parallel operation," to benefit countries outside the limited group.

Time was to show that this did not suffice to satisfy the "non-Ten," and that as a result of the negotiations between the Fund Directors and the Deputies which had been suggested in the communiqué of the Ministers and Governors of the Group of Ten in September 1965, the plan eventually adopted would embrace the whole of the Fund membership. The problem of decision-making was to be solved by providing that decisions should be taken by the members collectively, though the voting requirements would reserve for the Group of Ten—and indeed, within the Group, to the members of the EEC—a veto on the creation of additional liquidity. The details of these arrangements must, however, be left for some future historian to describe.

---

[28] *Ibid.*, pp. 80–82; cf. *ibid.*, p. 31.

CHAPTER

23

The Wood and the Trees

IN THE PRECEDING CHAPTERS we have been traversing a wood so full of undergrowth that the reader may not have been able to distinguish even the individual trees. It will perhaps be worthwhile, as we close, to look back very briefly at the path we have trodden since 1941, and to try to trace in the broadest outline the evolution of the Fund from the vision that inspired White and Keynes to the living organism of 1965. It will suffice to consider what has happened in five main areas: the size of the Fund, exchange rates, exchange restrictions, drawings, and administration.

SIZE OF THE FUND

The original plan for the Fund was more heavily influenced by the caution proper to the United States, whose resources would be chiefly in demand, than by the expansionist hopes of the United Kingdom and some other powers. It therefore took the form of a fixed subscription, rather than of an open-ended commitment to permit overdrafts, for which Keynes had hoped. And the total of quotas, $8.8 billion, while appreciably larger than the $5 billion originally mentioned by White, was only about one third the size of the resources which Keynes wished to make available.

Similarly, restraining influences have been brought to bear on the subsequent growth of the Fund. There have been only two general increases in quotas, although four quinquennial reviews have been made, as provided in the Articles. Further, while some disparities in quotas have been corrected by selective increases, the most important additions to the Fund's holdings of needed currencies have been provided in the qualified form of the General Arrangements to Borrow rather than in the unrestricted form of quota increases.

Use has been made of the powers given to replenish the Fund's holdings of needed currencies by the sale of gold and by drawing on the General Arrangements to Borrow. There has, however, been no recourse to the "scarce currency" clause. The way out of the danger of a scarcity of international liquidity has in fact been sought not through the provisions in the Articles drafted at Bretton Woods, but by the addition of new Articles since 1965.

EXCHANGE RATES

Both White and Keynes envisaged a postwar world in which each member country would have a par value for its currency. White was concerned to stress that these par values should remain as far as possible stable, and should be changed only with the consent of the world community. Keynes shared these views to a great extent, although he wished to retain some freedom for the individual country to change its rate if necessity arose. Both, therefore, expected that in the years to come the problem for the Fund would be to decide whether a member was justified in making a desired change in its par value. As it has turned out, formal devaluations have been fewer than anticipated, and the Fund has found its members reluctant to change their exchange rates even at times when such changes might be the best solution of their difficulties.

One reason for this difference between expectations and experience is, of course, that the par value system itself has been less universally adopted than had been planned. The system has been fully accepted, and indeed taken for granted, by all the major developed countries that are members of the Fund, so that the overwhelming bulk of world trade is conducted in currencies of fixed value. But among other Fund members the situation has been different. At the end of 1965 there were 23 member countries that had no par values, and 17 others whose par values were wholly or mainly ineffective. The attitude of the Fund toward par values for such members has been influenced by a realistic acceptance of the fact that a par value is of little usefulness if it is ineffective. It is symptomatic of this change of view that, whereas except for members that had been occupied by the enemy the Articles envisage a par value as a prerequisite to a drawing on the Fund, the Board in 1964 agreed that any member country might draw before it fixed a par value. One reason for this was that such a drawing might assist the country to achieve a par value; another, more significantly, that it would make it unnecessary for a member to declare a possibly ineffective par value merely in order to qualify to draw from the Fund.

A number of consequences have flowed from this greater flexibility in the exchange rate field. One was that in its early years the Fund was much involved with the problem of broken cross rates. Another, that the persistence of multiple currency practices has required the Fund to evolve sophisticated techniques for the evaluation of such practices. Thirdly, fluctuating exchange rates, although not contemplated by the Articles, have been found the best solution for certain difficult situations, and have been tolerated, and indeed encouraged, by the Fund where these situations existed.

Closely related to the problems of exchange rates has been the Fund's concern about the price of gold. Because par values are expressed in terms of gold, the Fund has been apprehensive that the establishment of premium prices in gold markets might undermine exchange parities, and during the first five years of its existence it sought actively to discourage such prices. In 1951 it became apparent that the Fund did not have the power to enforce a restriction of the price of gold in free markets to $35 an ounce, and its policy was changed to one of moral suasion. When in 1960 the price of gold again got out of control, its correction was left to the exertions of the Western European countries and the United States. The further change in policy in 1968 lies outside the scope of this history.

EXCHANGE RESTRICTIONS

The most significant variation between the plans of the founding fathers at Bretton Woods and the evolution of the postwar world has been the limited use made of Article VIII. At Bretton Woods the expectation was that all member countries would graduate to Article VIII after a comparatively short transitional period. The length of this period was nowhere specified, but the evidence suggests that Keynes was thinking of some five years, while White was expecting that soon after the end of hostilities members would begin to accept the obligations of convertibility. It was not, however, until 1961—more than sixteen years after Bretton Woods—that these obligations were accepted by the majority of the members whose currencies are important in international trade; and by the end of 1965, out of a total membership of 103, only 27 members had fully accepted the obligations of Article VIII, thereby making their currencies convertible in the Fund sense of the word.

As a consequence of the continued resort by members to Article XIV, the consultations with members which are prescribed under that Article have become one of the main activities of the Fund. And because the usefulness of such consultations rapidly became apparent, they were extended in 1961 to members that had accepted the obligations of Article VIII—although on a voluntary basis as regards members that have no restrictions requiring the Fund's approval. (Nothing was said about such consultations in the Bretton Woods Agreements.) As practiced today, the annual consultations deal not only with exchange restrictions but with all aspects of the member's economic life. They fulfill the function which White had envisaged as one of the most important for Executive Directors: to become closely acquainted with the circumstances of each member, so as to be able to make informed decisions on drawings or other requests which the member might put forward.

USE OF THE FUND'S RESOURCES

Of the several ambiguities in the Articles of Agreement—some intentional and some not—one stood out from the beginning as of prime importance. Some members understood that the Articles entitled each member to draw, without challenge from the Fund, up to 25 per cent of its quota each year. Others believed that the Fund had the right to require any member to justify any drawing. This issue—that of automatism versus conditionality in drawings—divided the Board for several years. For a time, small drawings—less than 5 per cent of a member's quota in any month—were effected automatically in accordance with the terms of Rule G-5. Very soon, however, the Board began as a matter of course to examine each request for a drawing. As its standards became better known, member countries tended to make informal inquiries before submitting a formal application; many tentative requests were not proceeded with as a result of discouragement received at that stage. In consequence, very few were actually refused, except that while the United States was priming the pump in Europe through Marshall Aid the Board declined to permit the European recipients of that aid to draw from the Fund.

The catalyst which ultimately precipitated agreement on a policy for the use of the Fund's resources was a realization that the repurchase provisions in the Articles of Agreement were ineffective to ensure that drawings would be repaid within a limited period. It followed that the temporariness of members' use of the Fund, which all agreed was intended at Bretton Woods, could be secured only if drawings were specifically limited in duration. This limitation, which was the essential part of the Rooth Plan for the use of the Fund's resources, requires that drawings shall be repaid within five years. In this aim the Rooth Plan has been largely successful—but not wholly so, because a few countries, by making repeated drawings, have been indebted to the Fund for substantially longer than five years at a time.

In one respect, however, the Fund's policy has been modified toward greater automaticity; there has been an increasing tendency for drawings within the gold tranche to be handled with a minimum of inquiry and a maximum of speed. The deliberate intention has been to encourage members to regard the right to draw in the gold tranche as a part of their exchange reserves. This culminated, after the period covered by this volume, in an explicit statement that drawings in the gold tranche would be granted automatically. Concurrently, the recourse to drawings by members has ceased to be regarded necessarily as a sign of weakness.

Drawing rights have also been extended by the provision of special assistance to compensate for fluctuations in export incomes, which (as devised in 1963 and 1966) has added 40 per cent to the range over which drawings by the members concerned can extend.

Of still greater importance to the Fund has been the evolution of stand-by arrangements. These were not specified in the Articles, but from small beginnings in 1952 they have grown to a major activity of the Fund. Only a few drawings today are not preceded by stand-by arrangements. And the Fund has found it possible, by stipulating conditions of increasing precision in such arrangements, to exert through them effective pressure on drawing members to follow appropriate policies.

It is right to add that, although the principle of automaticity has been conceded only for drawings in the gold tranche, the Board today would wish never to withhold approval of any drawing. At the most, Directors will make plain during the discussion of a request, for the future guidance of the staff, any features which they consider to be unsatisfactory. As a result, unwritten but clearly understood guidelines have been evolved, derived from the Board's consideration of past drawings. These enable the staff to recommend with confidence to members the steps which should be taken to ensure the acceptance of their requests, and permit of members putting forward requests with the assurance that they will be granted.

ADMINISTRATION

There is one more feature of the Fund's evolution which calls for comment: administration. It was never possible that, as Keynes had wished, the Fund should have been a purely technical institution, run by internationally minded experts; its functions have necessarily had political consequences of too far-reaching a kind. It has followed that the decisions of the Fund have perforce taken account of the national attitudes of the countries represented on the Board. It has followed, also, that the Board has remained the full-time supervisor of the Fund's work rather than the part-time court of appeal which Keynes had in mind.

Nevertheless, in at least three respects the work of the Board has been modified by experience. In the first place, formal voting, except on matters for which the Articles require such voting, has almost disappeared from the Board's practice. With it has gone some of the rigidity and formality of the Board's procedures—a development enhanced by the invention of different kinds of informal Board meetings for the preliminary exploration of sensitive subjects. In the second place, the extensive use of the lapse of time procedure has removed the need for debate in connection with a large proportion of the more routine decisions that the Board has to make. And in the third place, because the discussions preparatory to the annual consultations have been conducted by members of the Fund staff while visiting the countries concerned, the consultation procedure has necessarily enhanced the extent to which the permanent staff, rather than the Board (which has on the average turned over its membership about once every five years) has become the repository of detailed technical knowledge of members' economies and practices. As a result, the stand-by arrangements which are keyed to these practices have been devised by the Fund's technicians. Similarly, the selection of currencies to be used in purchases and repurchases has become the responsibility of the staff. Nevertheless, both these arrangements and the newer facilities which have been grafted on to the Articles—compensatory financing of export fluctuations, General Arrangements to Borrow, and most recently the Amendment of the Articles of Agreement—have been shaped by the staff under the guidance, and subject at all times to the decision, of the Board.

❖ ❖ ❖

It was made clear at the outset of this Chronicle that its objective is not to judge the success or failure of the Fund, but to recount its plans and its activities as they have unrolled from day to day. But the reader may well feel from the brief notes given in this chapter that if the Fund has succeeded, it is because of the flexibility which it has brought to its task. Without departing from the design of its founders the Fund has been able to add new dimensions to its scope. The new facilities that it has devised after the end of the period here covered represent only the latest in a series of developments which have led from the rigidity of a legal code to the flexibility of a living organism.

CHAPTER

24

Supplementary Chapter (1966-68)

THE PURPOSE OF THIS CHAPTER is to recount briefly the principal events in the work of the Fund since the end of 1965. No attempt will be made to explain the background of these events or to give the arguments adduced for and against the decisions taken. The intention is only to bring the reader up to date, in outline, about the Fund's progress since the end of the twenty years with which this history is mainly concerned.

MEMBERS, BOARD, AND STAFF

Eight countries joined the Fund during 1966–68: Singapore on August 3, 1966; Guyana on September 26, 1966; Indonesia (readmitted after withdrawing in 1965) on February 21, 1967; The Gambia on September 21, 1967; Botswana on July 24, 1968; Lesotho on July 25, 1968; Malta on September 11, 1968; and Mauritius on September 23, 1968. At the end of 1968, the Fund had 111 members and the total of quotas was $21,198,450,000. Applications for membership had been received from Cambodia, Southern Yemen, and Swaziland.

The Annual Meetings in 1966 and 1968 were held in Washington. In 1967 they were in Rio de Janeiro, Brazil. After consideration of invitations received from Denmark and Germany to hold the 1970 Annual Meetings in Copenhagen and Berlin respectively, the Executive Directors of the Fund and the Bank recommended to their respective Boards of Governors that the Meetings should be held in Copenhagen. The Governors of the two organizations so agreed.

In 1966 the Board met 90 times in formal sessions, once in Committee of the Whole on the Review of Quotas, and 21 times informally; in 1967 the corresponding figures were 112 formal and 30 informal sessions, and in 1968, 156 and four. In addition, in 1966 and 1967 there were 21 sessions at four joint meetings of the Executive Directors with the Deputies of the Group of Ten to discuss international liquidity and reserve creation.

At the request of some Executive Directors, the Board decided in August 1968 to provide facilities for simultaneous interpretation into English of major substantive statements made at Board meetings in French and Spanish.

There were biennial elections of Executive Directors in 1966 and 1968, and two individual elections in 1967, resulting in a large number of changes in the personnel of the Board. These, together with the changes in the appointed Directors, are shown in Appendix A.

The number of staff grew rapidly after 1965, and at the end of 1968 it had reached about 1,000, of whom about one half were in the professional grades. The broad geographical distribution of nationalities in the composition of the staff was maintained. Changes in the organization of the staff are shown in Appendix B. Some particulars of the Executive Directors and of the structure of the staff at the close of 1968 are given at the end of this chapter.

In order to provide recreational facilities for international personnel, especially those who had experienced difficulty in securing admission to privately owned facilities in the Washington area, the Fund in 1966 acquired some 280 acres of land in Maryland, about twenty miles from the Fund building. On this area there has been built the Bretton Woods Recreation Center, with a golf course, a swimming pool, tennis courts, picnic grounds, and other amenities. Membership is confined to the personnel of the Fund, the World Bank Group, and other international agencies. For Fund personnel the subscriptions vary with salaries, and the income from membership and other fees is intended to cover the running costs.

LIAISON WITH THE WORLD BANK

Agreement was reached with the World Bank early in 1966 on fresh arrangements for liaison between the two institutions, especially as regards missions to member countries. These provided for differing degrees of participation by a member of the staff of one institution in missions of the other, ranging from attending as observer or in a parallel mission to actual membership of the other institution's team.

An agreement was also worked out at about the same time to make clearer the spheres for which each institution has primary responsibility in dealings with member countries. While there had been few instances of divergent views being expressed, it was thought that such a clarification would assist, in particular, newly joined officers in both the Fund and the Bank. It was agreed that the Fund has primary responsibility for exchange rates and restrictive systems, for adjustment of temporary balance of payments disequilibria, and for evaluating and assisting members to work out stabilization programs as a sound basis for economic advance. On the matters thus identified, the staff of the Bank would inform themselves of the established views and position of the Fund and adopt these as a working basis for their own activities. On the other hand, the Bank was recognized as having primary responsibility for the composition and appropriateness of development programs and project evaluation, including development priorities. On these matters, the Fund staff would adopt the views of the Bank. In spheres which were not the primary responsibility of either institution, such as the structure and functioning of financial institutions, the staff of the Fund would acquaint itself, before visiting a member country, with the views of the Bank; and vice versa.

On the administrative side, arrangements were made in 1967 for a Joint Computer Center to be developed for both institutions. The Center is administered by the Bank, and the costs are shared equally between the Bank and the Fund. The Center's first computer went into operation late in 1968, and it is no longer necessary for the Fund to rent time on outside machines.

IMF INSTITUTE

The program of the IMF Institute for the fiscal year 1967/68 provided for five courses—three in Financial Analysis and Policy (one in English, one in French, and one in Spanish) and two in Balance of Payments Methodology (one in English and one in French). In 1968/69 and 1969/70 a course in Public Finance in English was added, but in 1968/69 the Balance of Payments course in French was not given. The courses given in Spanish, the first in that language, followed a successful experiment with a course in Balance of Payments Methodology given at San Salvador in 1966.

Until the early part of 1966, the participants attending courses at the IMF Institute were accommodated in an apartment house owned by the World Bank and adjoining its main building. This house was razed in 1966 in preparation for the building by the Bank of an extension to its premises. In its place the Fund arranged to rent, on behalf of both the Fund and the Bank, a newly built apartment house about half a mile from the Fund. The accommodation available is divided between the two institutions on a flexible basis so as to house participants in the IMF Institute and the Bank's Economic Development Institute and, if space is available, also newly joined staff members, temporary consultants, and others employed by either the Fund or the Bank who are in need of short-term accommodation.

Meanwhile the Fund was acquiring a site, immediately to the west of its present building, to accommodate the needs for expansion of both itself and the Bank. Negotiations to acquire some of the land were prolonged because the George Washington University owned several properties on it. However, after extended discussions and hearings before the zoning authorities, agreement was reached for the University to relinquish its plans for the site, and the Fund is to acquire practically all the square bounded by G Street, H Street, 19th Street, and 20th Street. The possibility is envisaged that the Fund may progressively complete a new building there and cede to the Bank the whole of its existing premises, in order to contribute to the Bank's expected needs for more space.

SPECIAL DRAWING RIGHTS

The major advance by the Fund during the three years 1966–68 resulted from the discussions of international liquidity reported in Chapters 20 and 22. After prolonged debate, the Executive Directors submitted to the Governors in September 1967 an "Outline of a Facility Based on Special Drawing Rights in the Fund." This was approved by the Governors at the Annual Meeting, 1967, by a resolution which requested the Directors to proceed with their work relating both to the establishment in the Fund of such a new facility, and to improvements in the existing rules and practices of the Fund.[1]

On April 17, 1968, detailed proposals for amending the Articles of Agreement, embodying both the special facility and modifications of the Fund's practices, were sent to the Governors. These were approved, by a vote without meeting, on May 31, 1968,[2] and entered into force on July 28, 1969, when they had been accepted by 69 members having 194,213 votes, thus fulfilling the requirement of acceptance by 60 per cent of the members having 80 per cent of the total voting power. A week later instruments of participation had been deposited by 50 members having 75 per cent of the total of quotas, and these 50 members became the first participants in the Special Drawing Account.

The following is a brief description of the new facility as given in the Annual Report for 1968.[3]

> Only members of the Fund can become participants in the facility. Allocations of special drawing rights will be made to individual participants in proportion to their quotas in the Fund. Decisions to allocate will normally be made for five-year periods ahead, with allocations being made at yearly intervals. A participant may, however, elect not to receive allocations made under a decision if it did not vote in favor of that decision.
>
> Countries will be able to use the special drawing rights unconditionally whenever they have a balance of payments or reserve need to do so. Correspondingly, participants will be obliged, whenever designated to do so, to accept special

[1] Resolution 22-8, *Summary Proceedings, 1967*, pp. 271–79.

[2] Resolution 23-5, *Summary Proceedings, 1968*, pp. 293–94. The proposals are reproduced below, Vol. III, pp. 497–541.

[3] A fuller description is given in Joseph Gold, *Special Drawing Rights*, IMF Pamphlet Series, No. 13 (Washington, 1969).

drawing rights and in exchange to provide currency convertible in fact, a term which is defined in the Proposed Amendment. A participant will normally be designated for this purpose only when its balance of payments and gross reserve position is sufficiently strong. The magnitude of the obligation to accept is determined by the total amount of special drawing rights allocated to the participant less any part thereof that has been canceled. This amount is termed the net cumulative allocation, and the participant's obligation to accept special drawing rights from other participants extends to the point where its holdings of special drawing rights equal the amount received as its net cumulative allocation, plus twice this amount. As a result of these provisions, participants will be able to use the new special drawing rights in much the same manner as they use their holdings of traditional reserves.

In the elaboration of the provisions for the facility, great care was taken that any decision to allocate special drawing rights should have broad support. Decisions on allocation can only be made on a proposal by the Managing Director of the Fund, concurred in by the Executive Directors, and approved by the Governors by an 85 per cent majority of the total voting power. The Proposed Amendment spells out the principles and considerations applying to any such proposal. The first decision to allocate special drawing rights will have to take into account a collective judgment that there is a global need to supplement reserves, and the attainment of a better balance of payments equilibrium, as well as the likelihood of a better working of the adjustment process in the future.

It has been provided that a participant's net use of its special drawing rights must be such that the average of its holdings of special drawing rights over a five-year period will not be less than 30 per cent of the average of its net cumulative allocations of special drawing rights over the same period. Participants that have, during some part of any five-year period, used more than 70 per cent of their average net cumulative allocation may, therefore, have to reconstitute their holdings in order to ensure that their average use does not exceed the specified proportion.

With the establishment of the new facility, the Fund will maintain and conduct its operations through two separate accounts. Operations and transactions involving special drawing rights will be conducted through the Special Drawing Account, and the present operations and transactions of the Fund will be conducted through the General Account. The Fund will meet the cost of conducting the business of the Special Drawing Account from the General Account, but these costs will be reimbursed to the General Account from time to time by assessments on participants to be paid in special drawing rights. Special drawing rights can also be acquired by the Fund in the General Account as a result of their use by members, in repurchases and in the payment of charges. The Fund will be able to use the special drawing rights which it holds in the General Account to replenish its holdings of currencies and to make special drawing rights available, against gold or convertible currencies, to participants that need to acquire them.

Each participant's holdings of special drawing rights are to be recorded in the Special Drawing Account. The account of each participant will be credited with the amount of special drawing rights allocated to it and debited in the event of a decision to cancel special drawing rights. The use by a participant of its special drawing rights will result in debits to its account and equivalent credits to the accounts of one or more other participants. It will be noted that the functioning of the special drawing rights facility, in contrast to the operations of the present Fund, will not be based on the Fund's holdings of gold and member currencies. Special drawing rights will thus derive their strength, not from a pool of assets held by the Fund, but from the acceptance obligations of participants to provide exchange from their own holdings to other participants entitled to use their special drawing rights.

The Special Drawing Account will also record the Fund's holdings of special drawing rights held in the General Account as well as those held by any other holder which the Fund may have prescribed.*

The value of special drawing rights is fixed in terms of gold. A participant will earn interest on its holdings of special drawing rights, and will pay a charge on the amount of its net cumulative allocation. The participant's position in the Special Drawing Account will determine whether, on balance, it will receive interest or pay charges. The rate of interest and the rate of charge will be the same; both will initially be 1½ per cent, with some room for later changes. Interest will be credited and charges debited to participants' accounts in special drawing rights.

REFORM OF THE FUND

The changes in the rules and practices of the Fund, approved concurrently with the new facility described above, have become known as "The reform of the Fund." The proposals were described in the Annual Report for 1968 as follows:[4]

> The changes in the rules and practices of the Fund proposed in the form of certain amendments to the existing 20 Articles of the Fund Agreement cover a number of provisions. First, there are changes in the majorities required for certain important Fund decisions. Changes in quotas, insofar as they are the result of a general review of quotas, will require a majority of 85 per cent of the total voting power, and the same majority will apply in respect of decisions on certain questions closely related to general quota increases, such as the question whether a member will be permitted to pay less than the standard 25 per cent of its additional subscription in gold.† An 85 per cent majority will also be required for decisions adopted by the Fund under the provisions in the Articles that relate to a uniform proportionate change in par values.
>
> Decisions requiring an 85 per cent majority under the Proposed Amendment, whether with respect to the General Account or the Special Drawing Account, are to be taken by the Board of Governors.

* These could include nonmember countries, members that are not participants, and institutions that perform one or more functions of a central bank for members.

[4] For a fuller description, see Joseph Gold, *The Reform of the Fund*, IMF Pamphlet Series, No. 12 (Washington, 1969).

† Changes in quotas other than those resulting from a general review of quotas will continue to require approval by the present majority of 80 per cent of the total voting power.

There are a number of proposed changes relating to the formal status of a member's entitlement to buy the currency of other members from the Fund. Gold tranche purchases, which are now practically automatic, will become legally automatic under the new provisions. At the same time, the Articles will be amended to make explicit what had been implicit before: that use of the Fund's resources must be temporary in character and that the Fund must adopt policies to this end. Under the new provisions, the Fund will no longer have the legal power to make the use of Fund resources outside of the gold tranche quasi-automatic and quasi-unconditional, in view of the availability of the new special drawing rights facility to take care of any need for additions to existing unconditional reserve assets. On the other hand, these proposed changes in the legal status of a member's entitlement to buy currency from the Fund in a transaction conducted through the General Account are not intended to make the rules with respect to use of the Fund's resources more restrictive than they are now.

The Proposed Amendment also provides for the payment of remuneration to members that hold what has become known as a super gold tranche position in the Fund.‡ The rate of remuneration will be 1½ per cent per annum, but the Executive Directors would be authorized to make changes in this rate.

In addition, the Articles as amended will permit the Fund to reduce or eliminate the service charge (presently at ½ per cent) on gold tranche purchases.

The Proposed Amendment calls for substantial changes in repurchases governed by Article V, Section 7. These changes involve, inter alia, the transition from a concept of monetary reserves net of currency liabilities to a gross concept. The changes can affect the amounts to be repurchased and also the media in which repurchases are to be made.

Finally, the Proposed Amendment envisages a change in the procedure to deal with questions of interpretation. Essentially, this change involves the creation of a Standing Committee on Interpretation of the Board of Governors, which will have to consider any question of interpretation referred to the Board of Governors at the request of a member. The decision of this Committee will be final unless the Board of Governors decides otherwise by an 85 per cent majority of the total voting power. Each member of the Committee on Interpretation will have one vote.

DISTRIBUTION OF NET INCOME

In 1968, for the first time, the Executive Directors recommended, and the Governors agreed, that part of the net income earned during the fiscal year should be distributed.[5] As provided in Article XII, Section 6, the distribution was made to members having super gold tranches. Of the total net income, amounting to $55,743,725 for the fiscal year ended April 30, 1968, the sum of $37,458,482 was distributed, in the members' own currencies, at the rate of

‡ The amount by which 75 per cent of a member's quota exceeds the Fund's holdings of its currency.

[5] *Annual Report, 1968,* p. 22; Resolution 23-12, *Summary Proceedings, 1968,* pp. 303–304.

1½ per cent on the average amount by which 75 per cent of the members' quotas exceeded the Fund's holdings of their currencies during the fiscal year. Provision for similar distributions in future years was made in the proposed revision of the Articles of Agreement by the addition of Section 9 to Article V. A consequential amendment of Article XII, Section 6, required such distributions to be taken into account when considering any general distribution of net income.

STABILIZING PRICES OF PRIMARY PRODUCTS

At the Annual Meeting, 1967, the Board of Governors was asked by the Governors of the Fund and the Bank for France and for thirteen African countries and the Malagasy Republic—all former French colonies—to arrange for a study to be made of the conditions in which the Fund, the World Bank, and the International Development Association could participate in the elaboration of mechanisms designed to stabilize the prices of primary products at remunerative levels. Recognizing the importance of the subject, the Board of Governors requested the staffs of the Fund and the Bank to prepare a study of the problem, its possible solutions, and their economic feasibility, which Executive Directors were asked to transmit to the Governors, with their comments, if possible by the time of the Annual Meeting, 1968.[6]

The study by the staffs of the Fund and the Bank fell into two parts, one discussing the nature of the problem and of possible solutions, and the other reviewing ways in which the two institutions could assist in stabilizing prices. The first part of this study was reviewed by the Directors early in September 1968, and was transmitted to the Governors. The second part of the study proposed that the Fund should assist its members in connection with the financing of international buffer stocks of primary products, by a facility somewhat similar to that for compensating export fluctuations. The Executive Directors decided, on June 25, 1969, that the Fund would be prepared to extend assistance in this way, within limits related to each member's quota.

EXCHANGE POLICIES

The principal events in 1966–68 in the field of exchange policies were the devaluations initiated by that of sterling on November 18, 1967. The amount by which sterling was devalued was 14.3 per cent. Devaluations to the same extent were approved for Ireland on November 18, for Guyana, Israel, and Spain on November 19, for Cyprus, Malawi, and The Gambia on November 20, for

[6] Resolution 22-9, *Summary Proceedings, 1967*, p. 280.

Jamaica on November 21, and for Trinidad and Tobago, Sierre Leone, and most British nonmetropolitan territories on November 22. Of these nonmetropolitan territories, Bahamas, Bahrain, Brunei, Rhodesia, and Tonga did not devalue, as their currencies were less closely linked with sterling than with other currencies that were not devalued, or with gold. Hong Kong and Fiji initially devalued by 14.3 per cent, but subsequently revalued, by 10 per cent and 6.2 per cent respectively, resulting in residual devaluations by 5.7 per cent in Hong Kong and 9.0 per cent in Fiji.

Other devaluations approved were for the currencies of New Zealand by 19.45 per cent and Denmark by 7.9 per cent on November 20, Ceylon by 20 per cent on November 21, and Iceland by 24.6 per cent on November 24. Somewhat later Nepal devalued by 24.75 per cent from December 11.

In October 1968 the United Kingdom informed the Fund that it had entered into arrangements designed to stabilize sterling balances. These arrangements included undertakings by overseas sterling area countries to hold specified proportions of their official exchange reserves in sterling, and a guarantee by the United Kingdom of the dollar value of all official sterling holdings by these countries in excess of 10 per cent of their reserves. Such features of these arrangements as required the United Kingdom to obtain the Fund's approval under Article VIII were approved by the Executive Board on November 8.

At the same time the "Basle Group" (Austria, Belgium, Canada, Denmark, Germany, Italy, Japan, the Netherlands, Norway, Sweden, Switzerland, the United States, and the Bank for International Settlements) undertook to provide foreign currencies, to be drawn by the United Kingdom from the Bank for International Settlements, to finance reductions in the sterling holdings of the overseas sterling area countries below certain levels. This undertaking applied both to official and to private sterling holdings. Sterling area countries were invited to deposit a proportion of their non-sterling reserves with the Bank for International Settlements, to be used in the first place to finance such reductions; but the "Basle Group" undertook to meet any ultimate drain for this purpose up to a total of $2 billion.

On December 4 the Board gave approval under Article VIII to France for restrictions on payments in connection with foreign travel, which were introduced as a temporary measure to guard against capital exports.

DRAWINGS AND REPURCHASES

The amounts drawn from the Fund during the three years were as follows: 1966, $1,448.2 million; 1967, $834.7 million; 1968, $3,552.4 million. The total for 1966 included $680 million for the United States, of which $250 million was drawn in Italian lire. As the Fund's holdings of lire were at that time only $74 million, the Fund borrowed $250 million worth of lire from Italy, by a special arrangement similar to, but outside of, the General Arrangements to Borrow. (The purpose of the U.S. drawing was to enable the United States to buy from Italy part of its substantial holdings of dollars.)

Also in 1966 the United Kingdom drew $122.5 million, Pakistan $9.5 million, and the United Arab Republic and Yugoslavia $7.5 million each, all in deutsche mark, in order to obtain from Germany gold with which to pay the gold subscriptions in connection with increases in their quotas. In pursuance of the special arrangements to meet the secondary impact of gold subscriptions, the Fund purchased equivalent amounts of deutsche mark from Germany, with gold, in connection with the drawings. A similar drawing of Belgian francs by Burundi was matched by the purchase of $937,500 worth of Belgian francs by the Fund with gold.

In 1967 the largest drawing was $166 million by Spain.

The total drawn in 1968 was almost 50 per cent larger than that in any previous calendar year. It included $1.4 billion for the United Kingdom and $745 million for France, both drawn in June 1968, for which purpose the Fund activated the General Arrangements to Borrow and borrowed a total of $741 million from Belgium, Germany, Italy, the Netherlands, and Sweden, bringing the total borrowed under the GAB to $1,571 million. The Fund also sold gold to thirteen countries for a total of $547 million of their currencies. Simultaneously France arranged, with the agreement of the Fund, to transfer its claim under the GAB, amounting to $140 million, to Belgium, Germany, Italy, and the Netherlands.

Canada was omitted from the participants called upon in June 1968 because in February 1968 it had drawn $391 million and had obtained a repayment from the Fund of its claim under the GAB, amounting to $35 million. The effect was to increase the Fund's holdings of Canadian dollars to 100 per cent of quota. The Fund, however, sold the equivalent of $121 million in Canadian dollars in the large June drawings, and additional sales of that currency were effected toward the end of the year.

In all, 21 currencies were used in the drawings during 1966–68, including for the first time Brazilian cruzeiros, Irish pounds, Malaysian dollars, Norwegian kroner, South African rand, and Venezuelan bolívares. All the other currencies that had previously been drawn were drawn again, except for Spanish pesetas.

Repurchases during the three years were as follows: 1966, $480.4 million; 1967, $920.4 million; 1968, $1,178.6 million. Of these totals, the United Kingdom repurchased $654.8 million in 1967 and $185 million in 1968, enabling the Fund to repay $590 million to the participants in the GAB. India repurchased $230 million during the three years and the United States, $185 million. Twelve currencies were used for the repurchases, including for the first time Australian dollars, Danish kroner, Mexican pesos, and Norwegian kroner.

By the end of 1968, the Fund's holdings of U.S. dollars had been reduced to 75 per cent of quota.

The mid-term review of the General Arrangements to Borrow was completed in October 1968. No participant proposed any change in the Arrangements, and the Board agreed that they should continue unchanged to October 1970. An exchange of letters with Switzerland extended the parallel arrangements with that country to the same date.

COMPENSATORY FINANCING OF EXPORT FLUCTUATIONS

By a decision of the Board in September 1966 the special drawings offered to compensate members for adverse fluctuations in export receipts were enlarged from a maximum of 25 per cent of quota to a maximum of 50 per cent of quota.[7] Except in the case of shortfalls resulting from disasters or major emergencies, not more than 25 per cent of quota may be drawn in any twelve months, and requests which would increase outstanding drawings under this facility beyond 25 per cent of the member's quota are met only if the Fund is satisfied that the member has been cooperating with the Fund in an effort to find, where required, appropriate solutions for its balance of payments difficulties.

Members making drawings under the terms of this decision are expected to undertake to repurchase within three to five years, in accordance with the decision of February 13, 1952; and the Fund recommends that, as soon as possible after the end of each of the first four years after a drawing, the member should repurchase its currency from the Fund to an extent approximately equal to one half of the amount by which its export receipts exceed the medium-term trend of its exports.

A member that makes an ordinary drawing—i.e., not under the special facility—may within six months reclassify the drawing as having been made under the facility, provided that the member's situation qualifies it for a drawing under the facility.

Special arrangements have been made to deal with the problem of "double compensation" which may arise when one or more ordinary drawings are made, or a stand-by arrangement is approved, after the beginning of the shortfall

[7] E.B. Decision No. 2192-(66/81). Reproduced in *Compensatory Financing of Export Fluctuations—Developments in the Fund's Facility: A Second Report by the International Monetary Fund;* below, Vol. III, pp. 469–96. The decision is on pp. 492–94.

period in respect of which a member may be entitled to a compensatory financing drawing and before such a drawing is requested.

Between the time when the facilities were enlarged, in September 1966, and the end of 1968, fourteen members drew a total of $290.5 million in order to meet difficulties caused by adverse fluctuations in export receipts. Four of these members made two drawings each.

CONDITIONS FOR USE OF THE FUND'S RESOURCES

In August and September 1968 the Board reviewed the practices of the Fund in relation to the use of its resources, and reached a comprehensive decision, of which the following is a summary. (*a*) Clauses requiring the member to remain in consultation with the Fund will be included in all stand-by arrangements. (*b*) Provision will be made for consultation with a member, from time to time, during the whole period in which the Fund's holdings of its currency exceed 125 per cent of its quota, whether or not a stand-by arrangement is in existence. (*c*) Clauses phasing the amounts that may be drawn, and requiring the achievement of certain performance criteria if drawings are to continue, will be omitted if the Fund's holdings, when augmented by the authorized drawings, would not exceed 125 per cent of the quota. (*d*) In all other stand-by arrangements phasing and performance clauses will normally be included, but will be applicable only to purchases which actually increase the Fund's holdings beyond 125 per cent of quota. (*e*) Exceptionally, phasing will not be stipulated in individual stand-by arrangements if it is essential that the full amount of the drawing should be available promptly. Where this is done, the performance clauses will require the member to consult the Fund about changes in the performance criteria even if there is nothing more to be drawn under the stand-by arrangement. (*f*) Performance clauses will be limited to stipulating criteria necessary to evaluate the implementation of the member's stabilization program, with a view to ensuring the achievement of its objectives.

In the course of the discussion leading to this decision, the General Counsel explained the nature of stand-by arrangements. He said that they were not international agreements, so that they did not require to be registered with the United Nations, nor were they subject to members' domestic laws dealing with such agreements. Neither was the member's letter of intent a contractual obligation; it was therefore not specifically approved by the Board. The stand-by arrangement itself, which the Board approved in detail, was a decision taken by the Fund under the legal authority of the Articles, establishing the circumstances under which the member could have the use of the Fund's resources without a further review of its requests, and the terms on which the member could draw from the Fund.

GOLD

On March 16 and 17, 1968, the Governors of the central banks of Belgium, Germany, Italy, the Netherlands, Switzerland, the United Kingdom, and the United States met in Washington. The Managing Director of the Fund and the General Manager of the Bank for International Settlements attended the meeting. The Governors agreed to discontinue the supply of gold from central banks to private gold markets. They also agreed that it was no longer necessary to buy gold from the market, and that they would not in future supply gold to monetary authorities to replace gold sold in private markets. These decisions were prompted by a sustained demand for gold which had kept its price through 1967 and the early part of 1968 near to $35.20 a fine ounce. They ended the arrangement known as the Gold Pool, established in 1961 to stabilize the supply of gold to the London gold market.

On June 17, 1968 South Africa sought to purchase from the Fund, for gold, $14.5 million in sterling. This was considered by the Board, and was also the subject of a conference of some Governors during the Annual Meeting. However, no agreement was reached, and at the end of 1968 the matter was still under study in the Fund and elsewhere.

THE FUND IN 1968

We may conclude this chapter with a brief survey of the structure of the Fund as it was at the end of 1968.

The Twenty-Third Annual Meeting of the Fund, held in Washington from September 30 to October 4, 1968, was attended by 234 Governors, Alternate Governors, and Temporary Alternate Governors, and by 486 Advisers. The Governors and Alternate Governors typically included the Minister of Finance or the Governor of the central bank, or both, of each member represented; the Advisers were usually senior officials of those Ministries or central banks. Most of the Executive Directors and Alternates were included in the delegations either as Temporary Alternate Governors or as Advisers. This yearly assemblage of so many persons responsible for the economic progress of their countries gives the Fund's Annual Meetings unique value and influence. Their impact on the work of the Fund during the remaining fifty-one weeks of each year is impossible to measure but is nonetheless highly significant.

In December 1968 the Managing Director and Chairman of the Executive Board, Mr. Schweitzer, had occupied that position for rather more than five years. (His appointment had been extended for a second five-year term from September 1, 1968.) Mr. Southard had been Deputy Managing Director for six years, after serving nearly fourteen years as the Executive Director appointed by the United States. Of the 20 Executive Directors, only Mr. Saad (United Arab Republic) had been a member of the original Board (see above, Chapter 7). Mr. Tann (China) had been an Executive Director for eighteen years, Mr. van Campenhout for fourteen, and Mr. Lieftinck for thirteen. No one else had had more than six years' service: one Executive Director joined the Board in 1962, three in 1966, five in 1967 (of whom one had previously been an Executive Director for two years), and seven in 1968 (of whom two had previously been Executive Directors for two years each). Six Executive Directors had had previous experience as Alternate Executive Directors, four had been members of the Fund staff, and one had attended a training course at the Fund.

The qualifications which Executive Directors brought to the Fund's work in 1968 were broadly similar to, though somewhat wider than, those of the twelve men who formed the original Board in 1946. Mr. Asp was Managing Director of the Finnish Export Guarantee Board and of Finnish Export Credit, Ltd.; Mr. Dale was Deputy Assistant Secretary for International Affairs in the U.S. Department of Commerce; Mr. Escobar was Minister of Economy, Development, and Reconstruction of Chile, and since his previous term as Executive Director of the Fund had been Executive Director of the World Bank; Mr. Johnstone was Deputy Chief of the Research Department of the Bank of Canada before joining the Fund staff in 1967; Mr. Kafka was Director of the Brazilian Institute of Economics and later Adviser to the Minister of Finance; Mr. Kharmawan was Chief Economic Adviser of the Central Bank of Indonesia, with the rank of Deputy Governor, and later an Executive Director of the Asian Development Bank; Mr. Lieftinck had been the Netherlands Minister of Finance from 1945 to 1952; Mr. Madan was Deputy Governor of the Reserve Bank of India and Vice-Chairman of the Industrial Development Bank of India; Mr. Maude was Deputy Secretary of the Department of Economic Affairs of the United Kingdom; Mr. Palamenghi-Crispi (Italy) was Managing Director and Deputy President of the Somali National Bank and a Director of the Bank of Italy; Mr. Phillips O. was sub-chief of the Department of Banks, Money, and Investment in the Mexican Ministry of Finance and Public Credit; Mr. Plescoff, Inspecteur des Finances, was Director of the French Caisse des Dépôts et Consignations; Mr. Saad had been Under-Secretary of Finance in Egypt and was later Governor of the National Bank of Egypt and President of its Board of Directors; Mr. Schleiminger was Deputy Head of the Department of International Affairs in the Deutsche Bundesbank; Mr. Stone was Assistant Secretary in the Australian Department of the Treasury; Mr. Suzuki was Special Adviser to the Japanese Minister of Finance and Special Assistant to the Minister of Foreign Affairs; Mr. Tann had been Vice-Minister of Finance in China and later Chairman of the Board of Directors of the Chinese Postal Remittance and Savings Bank; Mr. van Campenhout had been Head of the Belgian Economic Mission in London before joining the Fund staff as General Counsel in 1946; Mr. Williams was officer in charge of the Monetary Section of the Ministry of Finance of Trinidad and Tobago; and Mr. Yaméogo had been Director of the Treasury, Upper Volta, Commissioner for the Upper Volta Development Plan, and later Minister of National Economy in Upper Volta before joining the Fund staff early in 1963.

Under the Managing Director and the Deputy Managing Director, the staff included the Directors of the Legal Department and the Research Department, who were respectively designated the General Counsel and the Economic Counsellor. Eleven other Directors were in charge of five regional Departments (African, Asian, European, Middle Eastern, and Western Hemisphere), four functional Departments having relations with members (Administration, Central Banking Service, Exchange and Trade Relations, and Fiscal Affairs), and two other Departments (Secretary's and IMF Institute). The Treasurer's Department was without a head owing to the death of Mr. Altman in December 1968; the vacancy was filled in February 1969 by the appointment of Mr. Habermeier as Treasurer. Thereafter, six of the fourteen Heads of Departments were from the United States, two from the United Kingdom, two from the Netherlands, and one each from Chile, Germany, India, and Mauritania. The Bureau of Statistics and the two Offices in Europe completed the principal staff units.

Appendices

APPENDIX A

EXECUTIVE DIRECTORS AND ALTERNATES

Table A–1. Appointed Executive Directors and Their Alternates
Article XII, Section 3(*b*)(i)
1946–68

Countries Represented		Executive Director and Alternate[1]				
		Representation			Dates[2] of Service	
Name	Date[2] Became Member	Began	Ended	Name	Began	Ended
United States	12/27/45	1946		Harry D. White	5/6/46	6/1/47
				George F. Luthringer	*7/17/46*	
				Andrew N. Overby	7/1/47	2/8/49
				George F. Luthringer		*7/2/48*
				Henry J. Tasca	*10/21/48*	
				Frank A. Southard, Jr.	3/1/49	10/31/62
				Henry J. Tasca		*12/22/49*
				John S. Hooker	*1/3/50*	
				William B. Dale	11/1/62	
United Kingdom	12/27/45	1946		George L. F. Bolton	5/6/46	5/19/52
				A. P. Grafftey-Smith	*5/6/46*	*11/6/46*
				Maurice Henry Parsons	*11/7/46*	*11/17/47*
				Geoffrey Howson Tansley	*11/18/47*	*2/5/50*
				Leslie Frederick Crick	*2/6/50*	*3/15/51*
				Arthur Maxwell Stamp	*3/16/51*	
				Sir Edmund Hall-Patch	10/21/52	6/30/54
				Arthur Maxwell Stamp		*2/5/53*
				Leslie Frederick Crick	*2/6/53*	*12/30/53*
				F. J. Portsmore	*12/31/53*	
				Denis H. F. Rickett	7/1/54	9/30/54

				Viscount Harcourt	10/1/54	1/31/57
				F. J. Portsmore		*12/31/54*
				P. J. Keogh	*1/1/55*	*1/16/56*
				R. E. Heasman	*1/17/56*	
				Guy F. Thorold	2/1/57	1/31/59
				R. E. Heasman		*9/26/58*
				G. J. MacGillivray	*9/27/58*	
				The Earl of Cromer	2/2/59	1/18/61
				D. B. Pitblado	1/19/61	9/17/63
				G. J. MacGillivray		*2/26/61*
				Raymond H. Bonham Carter	*2/27/61*	*8/31/63*
				John A. Kirbyshire	*9/1/63*	
				Sir Eric Roll	9/18/63	1/14/65
				J. M. Stevens	1/15/65	8/8/67
				John A. Kirbyshire		*6/2/65*
				Douglas W. G. Wass	*6/3/65*	
				Evan W. Maude	8/9/67	
				Douglas W. G. Wass		*10/27/67*
				Guy Huntrods	*10/28/67*	
China [3]	12/27/45	1946	1960	Yee-Chun Koo	5/6/46	3/26/50
				Yueh-Lien Chang	*11/18/46*	*12/31/48*
				Tsoo Whe Chu	*2/3/49*	
				Beue Tann	7/11/50	10/31/60
				Tsoo Whe Chu		*1/2/51*
				Kuo-Hwa Yu	*1/3/51*	*5/31/55*
				Ching Yao Hsieh	*6/1/55*	*12/31/59*
				I-Shuan Sun	*1/1/60*	*10/31/60*

Table A–1 *(concluded)*. Appointed Executive Directors and Their Alternates
Article XII, Section 3(*b*)(i)
1946–68

Countries Represented				Executive Director and Alternate[1]		
		Representation			Dates[2] of Service	
Name	Date[2] Became Member	Began	Ended	Name	Began	Ended
France	12/27/45	1946		Pierre Mendès-France[4]	5/6/46	7/9/46
				Jean de Largentaye	*5/6/46*	*6/30/46*
				Jean de Largentaye	7/1/46	6/5/64
				T. de Clermont-Tonnerre	*9/17/46*	*3/22/47*
				Pierre-Paul Schweitzer	*10/23/47*	*7/15/48*
				Bernard de Margerie	*10/1/48*	*11/15/49*
				Guy de Lavergne	*11/16/49*	*11/18/50*
				François Bizard	*11/28/50*	*1/10/52*
				Albert Barraud	*1/11/52*	*2/5/53*
				Gabriel Ferras	*4/1/53*	*12/13/53*
				André de Lattre	*2/17/54*	*6/23/55*
				Daniel Dommel	*7/1/55*	*11/5/56*
				Jean-Maxime Lévêque	*11/6/56*	*3/15/58*
				Marcel Théron	*3/16/58*	*3/27/59*
				André Feuché	*4/15/59*	*3/31/60*
				Jacques Waïtzenegger	*4/14/60*	*5/24/64*
				René Larre	6/6/64	8/31/67
				Gérard M. Teyssier	*6/1/64*	*7/30/67*
				Paul Mentré	*7/31/67*	
				Georges Plescoff	9/1/67	
				Paul Mentré		*8/15/68*
				Bruno de Maulde	*8/16/68*	
India	12/27/45	1946		J. V. Joshi	5/6/46	10/31/48
				N. Sundaresan	*5/6/46*	*9/22/46*
				B. K. Madan	*9/22/46*	*10/31/48*
				B. K. Madan	11/1/48	1/10/50
				D. S. Savkar	*11/1/48*	
				J. V. Joshi	1/11/50	11/29/51
				D. S. Savkar		*10/31/51*
				W. R. Natu	*11/1/51*	*11/29/51*

			W. R. Natu	11/30/51	11/30/53
			B. R. Shenoy	*11/30/51*	*11/30/53*
			P. S. Narayan Prasad	12/1/53	6/10/57
			V. G. Pendharkar	*12/1/53*	*6/5/56*
			James Samuel Raj	*6/6/56*	*7/31/56*
			P. J. J. Pinto	*8/1/56*	
			B. N. Adarkar	6/11/57	6/21/61
			P. J. J. Pinto		*10/20/58*
			I. G. Patel	*12/8/58*	*6/22/61*
			I. G. Patel	6/22/61	7/31/61
			J. J. Anjaria	8/1/61	1/31/67
			I. G. Patel	*8/1/61*	*12/11/61*
			S. L. N. Simha	*12/12/61*	*6/30/64*
			Arun K. Ghosh	*7/1/64*	*6/30/66*
			Arun K. Banerji	*7/1/66*	
			B. K. Madan	2/1/67	
Germany [3]	8/14/52	1960	Wilfried Guth	11/1/60	12/31/61
			Helmut Koinzer	*11/1/60*	
			Wilhelm Hanemann	1/1/62	3/31/64
			Helmut Koinzer		*3/31/62*
			Walter O. Habermeier	*4/1/62*	
			Ulrich Beelitz	4/1/64	5/31/66
			Walter O. Habermeier		*10/31/65*
			Horst Ungerer	*11/1/65*	
			Ernst vom Hofe	6/1/66	4/30/68
			Guenther Schleiminger	5/1/68	
			Horst Ungerer		*8/25/68*
			Lore Fuenfgelt	*8/26/68*	

[1] Alternate Executive Directors (shown in italic type) are always appointed by the Executive Director.

[2] Dates are given in the following order: month/day/year.

[3] Executive Directors were appointed by China until 1960, when Germany replaced China as a member qualified to appoint an Executive Director.

[4] Did not come to Washington.

Table A–2. Elected Executive Directors and Their Alternates
Article XII, Section 3(*b*)(iii)
1946–68

Countries Represented		Executive Director and Alternate [1]				
		Representation			Dates [2] of Service	
Name	Date [2] Became Member	Began	Ended	Name	Began	Ended
China [3]	12/27/45	1960		Beue Tann (China)	11/1/60	
				I-Shuan Sun (China)	*11/1/60*	*10/4/65*
Korea	8/26/55	1966		*Chi-Ling Chow (China)*	*10/5/65*	*10/31/68*
Viet-Nam	9/21/56	1966		*Nguyen Huu Hanh (Viet-Nam)*	*11/1/68*	
Canada	12/27/45	1946		Louis Rasminsky (Canada) [4]	5/6/46	10/31/62
Norway	12/27/45	1946	1948	*Joseph F. Parkinson (Canada)*	*11/27/46*	*8/15/51*
				Harry L. Wolfson (Canada)	*8/30/51*	*3/31/52*
Iceland	12/27/45	1948	1952	*G. Neil Perry (Canada)*	*4/1/52*	*4/30/54*
				J. H. Warren (Canada)	*5/1/54*	*3/15/57*
Ireland [5]	8/8/57	1960		*Alan B. Hockin (Canada)*	*3/16/57*	*4/30/59*
				C. L. Read (Canada)	*5/1/59*	*6/30/61*
Jamaica	2/21/63	1964		*L. Denis Hudon (Canada)*	*7/1/61*	
				A. F. W. Plumptre (Canada)	11/1/62	4/13/65
Guyana	9/26/66	1966		*L. Denis Hudon (Canada)*		*7/31/64*
				S. J. Handfield-Jones (Canada)	*8/1/64*	*4/30/65*
				S. J. Handfield-Jones (Canada)	5/1/65	10/31/68
				Patrick M. Reid (Canada)	*7/1/65*	*10/31/68*
				Robert Johnstone (Canada)	11/1/68	
				Maurice Horgan (Ireland)	*11/1/68*	
Netherlands	12/27/45	1946		G. W. J. Bruins (Netherlands)	5/6/46	3/22/48
South Africa	12/27/45	1946	1948	*D. Crena de Iongh (Netherlands)*	*5/6/46*	*12/2/46*
				Willem Koster (Netherlands)	*1/9/47*	
Norway	12/27/45	1948	1952	Johan Willem Beyen (Netherlands)	4/16/48	9/30/52
				Willem Koster (Netherlands)		*4/30/49*
Israel	7/12/54	1954		*H. M. H. A. van der Valk (Netherlands)*	*5/23/49*	
Yugoslavia	12/27/45	1954		A. M. de Jong (Netherlands) [6]	11/1/52	1/1/53
				D. Crena de Iongh (Netherlands)	1/1/53	9/30/55
Cyprus	12/21/61	1962		Pieter Lieftinck (Netherlands)	10/1/55	
				H. M. H. A. van der Valk (Netherlands)		*11/30/68*
				Pieter C. Timmerman (Netherlands)	*12/1/68*	

Czechoslovakia [7]	12/27/45	1946	1950	J. V. Mládek (Czechoslovakia)	5/6/46	10/17/48
Poland [8]	1/10/46	1946	1950	*Zygmunt Karpinski (Poland)*	*5/29/46*	*7/24/46*
Yugoslavia	12/27/45	1946	1952	*Mihailo Kolovic (Yugoslavia)*	*9/5/46*	
				Bohumil Sucharda (Czechoslovakia)	11/1/48	10/31/50
Finland	1/14/48	1948	1950	*Mihailo Kolovic (Yugoslavia)*		*10/31/50*
				Nenad Popovic (Yugoslavia)	11/1/50	10/31/52
Ceylon	8/29/50	1950		*W. D. Gunaratna (Ceylon)*	*11/10/50*	*4/6/51*
Thailand	5/3/49	1950		*D. W. Rajapatirana (Ceylon)*	*4/9/51*	
Turkey	3/11/47	1950	1952	Takeo Yumoto (Japan)	11/1/52	10/31/56
				D. W. Rajapatirana (Ceylon)		*8/14/53*
Burma	1/3/52	1952		*William Tennekoon (Ceylon)*	*8/15/53*	*10/31/54*
Japan	8/13/52	1952		*Boonma Wongswan (Thailand)*	*11/1/54*	*10/31/55*
				U San Lin (Burma)	*11/1/55*	*10/31/56*
Nepal	9/6/61	1962		Takeshi Watanabe (Japan)	11/1/56	10/31/60
				Prayad Buranasiri (Thailand)	*11/1/56*	*10/31/57*
				Tun Thin (Burma)	*11/1/57*	*9/25/59*
				Prayad Buranasiri (Thailand)	*10/1/59*	*10/31/59*
				P. M. Jayarajan (Ceylon)	*11/1/59*	*10/31/60*
				Gengo Suzuki (Japan)	11/1/60	10/31/66
				M. Kumashiro (Japan)	*11/1/60*	*10/31/62*
				William Tennekoon (Ceylon)	*11/1/62*	*10/31/64*
				Chalong Pungtrakul (Thailand)	*11/1/64*	*6/30/65*
				Eiji Ozaki (Japan)	*7/1/65*	
				Hideo Suzuki (Japan)	11/1/66	
				Eiji Ozaki (Japan)		*4/26/68*
				Seitaro Hattori (Japan)	*4/27/68*	

Table A–2 *(continued)*. Elected Executive Directors and Their Alternates
Article XII, Section 3(*b*)(iii)
1946–68

Countries Represented		Executive Director and Alternate[1]				
		Representation			Dates[2] of Service	
Name	Date[2] Became Member	Began	Ended	Name	Began	Ended
Egypt—see also 1958 and 1962	12/27/45	1946	1958	Ahmed Zaki Saad (United Arab Republic)	5/6/46	
				Mahmoud Saleh El Falaki (U.A.R.)	*9/6/46*	*11/15/51*
Ethiopia	12/27/45	1946		*Albert Mansour (U.A.R.)*	*11/16/51*	*7/31/68*
Greece	12/27/45	1946	1948	*Albert Mansour (U.A.R.)*	*12/26/68*	
Iran	12/29/45	1946				
Iraq	12/27/45	1946				
Philippines	12/27/45	1946				
Lebanon	4/14/47	1948				
Syria—see also 1958 and 1962	4/10/47	1948	1958			
Turkey	3/11/47	1948	1950			
Pakistan	7/11/50	1950				
Jordan	8/29/52	1952				
Afghanistan	7/14/55	1956				
Saudi Arabia	8/26/57	1958				
Sudan	9/5/57	1958	1964			
United Arab Rep. (formerly Egypt and Syria)—see also 1962		1958	1962			
Kuwait	9/13/62	1962				
Syrian Arab Rep. (formerly in U.A.R.)		1962				
United Arab Rep. (now Egypt only)		1962				
Somalia	8/31/62	1964				

Belgium	12/27/45	1946		Camille Gutt (Belgium) [9]	5/6/46	5/6/46
Iceland	12/27/45	1946	1948	*Louis Gaffin (Belgium)*	*5/6/46*	*6/15/46*
Luxembourg	12/27/45	1946		Hubert Ansiaux (Belgium)	6/19/46	10/31/48
				Ernest de Selliers (Belgium)	*6/18/46*	*10/31/48*
Denmark	3/30/46	1948	1952	Ernest de Selliers (Belgium)	11/1/48	3/22/54
				Jean C. Godeaux (Belgium)	*5/1/50*	
Finland	1/14/48	1950	1952	Hubert Ansiaux (Belgium)	4/2/54	10/31/54
				Jean C. Godeaux (Belgium)		*10/31/54*
Austria	8/27/48	1954		Jean C. Godeaux (Belgium)	11/1/54	11/30/54
Turkey	3/11/47	1954		*Maurice Toussaint (Belgium)*	*11/1/54*	
				André van Campenhout (Belgium)	12/1/54	
Korea	8/26/55	1956	1966	*Maurice Toussaint (Belgium)*		*11/23/65*
				Herman Biron (Belgium)	*11/24/65*	*11/15/68*
				Jacques Roelandts (Belgium)	*11/16/68*	
Denmark	3/30/46	[1947] [10]	1948	Guido Carli (Italy)	6/24/47	10/31/52
Italy	3/27/47	[1947] [10]		*Giorgio Cigliana-Piazza (Italy)*	*6/3/47*	*10/31/52*
Turkey	3/11/47	[1947] [10]	1948	Carlo Gragnani (Italy)	11/1/52	10/31/60
Venezuela	12/30/46	[1947] [10]	1948	*Costa P. Caranicas (Greece)*	*11/1/52*	
				Sergio Siglienti (Italy)	11/1/60	11/30/67
Austria	8/27/48	1948	1954	Francesco Palamenghi-Crispi (Italy) [11]	12/1/67	
Greece	12/27/45	1948 [12]		*Costa P. Caranicas (Greece)*		*10/31/68*
				Carlos Bustelo (Spain)	*11/1/68*	
Turkey	3/11/47	1952	1954			
Indonesia	4/15/54	1954	1958			
Spain	9/15/58	1958 [12]				
Portugal	3/29/61	1962 [12]				
Malta	9/11/68	— [12]				

Table A–2 *(continued)*. Elected Executive Directors and Their Alternates
Article XII, Section 3(*b*)(iii)
1946–68

Countries Represented		Executive Director and Alternate [1]				
		Representation			Dates [2] of Service	
Name	Date [2] Became Member	Began	Ended	Name	Began	Ended
Australia	8/5/47	[1948] [10]		Stuart G. McFarlane (Australia)	3/4/48	10/31/50
Lebanon	4/14/47	[1948] [10]	1948	*Roland Wilson (Australia)*	*3/5/48*	*2/28/49*
Syria	4/10/47	[1948] [10]	1948	*J. M. Garland (Australia)*	*3/1/49*	
				Leslie Galfreid Melville (Australia)	11/1/50	10/31/53
South Africa	12/27/45	1948		*J. M. Garland (Australia)*		*3/11/51*
				Leslie Harry Ernest Bury (Australia)	*3/12/51*	*10/31/53*
Viet-Nam	9/21/56	1956	1966	Leslie Harry Ernest Bury (Australia)	11/1/53	2/19/57
				Horace A. Fuller (Australia)	*11/16/53*	*2/10/54*
New Zealand	8/31/61	1962		*B. B. Callaghan (Australia)*	*2/11/54*	*3/8/57*
				B. B. Callaghan (Australia)	3/9/57	11/10/59
Lesotho	7/25/68	1968		*B. E. Fleming (Australia)*	*6/27/57*	
				J. M. Garland (Australia)	11/11/59	1/17/66
				B. E. Fleming (Australia)		*6/10/60*
				A. W. McCasker (Australia)	*6/11/60*	*9/19/60*
				F. C. Pryor (Australia)	*9/20/60*	*1/9/64*
				Roy Daniel (Australia)	*1/10/64*	
				M. W. O'Donnell (Australia)	1/18/66	2/1/67
				Roy Daniel (Australia)		*2/1/66*
				A. M. de Villiers (South Africa)	*2/2/66*	
				J. O. Stone (Australia)	2/2/67	
				A. M. de Villiers (South Africa)		*8/31/68*
				G. P. C. de Kock (South Africa)	*9/1/68*	
Germany [13]	8/14/52	1952	1960	Otto Pfleiderer (Germany) [6]	11/1/52	8/1/53
Yugoslavia	12/27/45	1952	1954	*Otto Donner (Germany)*	*11/1/52*	
				Otmar Emminger (Germany)	8/27/53	1/15/59
				Otto Donner (Germany)		*9/14/56*
				Wilhelm Hanemann (Germany)	*9/15/56*	
				Wilfried Guth (Germany)	1/16/59	10/31/60
				Wilhelm Hanemann (Germany)		*9/13/59*
				Helmut Koinzer (Germany)	*9/14/59*	*10/31/60*

Denmark	3/30/46	1952		Alf Kristian Eriksen (Norway)	11/1/52	10/31/54
Finland	1/14/48	1952		*S. T. Gunnar Åkermalm (Sweden)*	*11/1/52*	*10/31/54*
Iceland	12/27/45	1952		S. T. Gunnar Åkermalm (Sweden)	11/1/54	10/31/56
Norway	12/27/45	1952		*Torben Friis (Denmark)*	*11/10/54*	*10/31/56*
Sweden	8/31/51	1952		Torben Friis (Denmark)	11/1/56	10/31/58
				Jouko J. Voutilainen (Finland)	*11/1/56*	*10/31/58*
				Eero Asp (Finland)	11/1/58	10/31/60
				Thorhallur Ásgeirsson (Iceland)	*11/1/58*	*10/31/60*
				Thorhallur Ásgeirsson (Iceland)	11/1/60	10/31/62
				Gabriel Kielland (Norway)	*11/1/60*	*10/31/62*
				Karl Skjaeveland (Norway)	11/1/62	10/31/64
				Lennart Olofsson (Sweden)	*11/1/62*	*10/31/64*
				Kurt Eklöf (Sweden)	11/1/64	10/31/66
				Otto Schelin (Denmark)	*11/2/64*	*10/31/66*
				Torben Friis (Denmark)	11/1/66	10/31/68
				Jorma Aranko (Finland)	*11/1/66*	
				Eero Asp (Finland)	11/1/68	
				Jorma Aranko (Finland)		*12/12/68*
				Sigurgeir Jónsson (Iceland)	*12/13/68*	
Ghana	9/20/57	1958		Soemarno (Indonesia)	11/1/58	10/31/60
Indonesia [14]	4/15/54	1958	1965	*Aly Jumaa Mouzughi (Libya)*	*10/1/59*	*10/31/60*
Libya	9/17/58	1958		Soetikno Slamet (Indonesia)	11/1/60	10/31/62
Malaysia [15]	3/7/58	1958		*Amon Nikoi (Ghana)*	*12/30/60*	
Morocco	4/25/58	1958		Sumanang (Indonesia)	11/1/62	5/31/65
Tunisia	4/14/58	1958		*Amon Nikoi (Ghana)*		*6/14/65*
				Amon Nikoi (Ghana)	6/15/65	10/31/68
Laos	7/5/61	1962		*Muhamed Barmawie Alwie (Indonesia)*	*1/16/67*	*2/16/68*
				Byanti Kharmawan (Indonesia)	11/1/68	
Algeria	9/26/63	1964		*Abdoel Hamid (Indonesia)*	*11/1/68*	*12/4/68*
				Malek Ali Merican (Malaysia)	*12/5/68*	
Singapore	8/3/66	1966				
Indonesia [14]	2/21/67	1968				

Table A–2 *(concluded)*. Elected Executive Directors and Their Alternates
Article XII, Section 3(*b*)(iii)
1946–68

Countries Represented		Executive Director and Alternate[1]				
		Representation			Dates[2] of Service	
Name	Date[2] Became Member	Began	Ended	Name	Began	Ended
Burundi	9/28/63	[1963] [10]	1964	Louis Kandé (Senegal)	10/3/63	10/31/66
Cameroon	7/10/63	[1963] [10]		*Semyano Kiingi (Uganda)*	*11/1/63*	*10/31/64*
Central African Rep.	7/10/63	[1963] [10]		*Antoine W. Yaméogo (Upper Volta)*	*11/1/64*	*10/31/66*
Chad	7/10/63	[1963] [10]		Antoine W. Yaméogo (Upper Volta)	11/1/66	
Congo (Brazzaville)	7/10/63	[1963] [10]		*Léon M. Rajaobelina (Malagasy Rep.)*	*11/1/66*	
Congo, Dem. Rep. of	9/28/63	[1963] [10]	1964			
Dahomey	7/10/63	[1963] [10]				
Gabon	9/10/63	[1963] [10]				
Guinea	9/28/63	[1963] [10]	1964			
Ivory Coast	3/11/63	[1963] [10]				
Liberia	3/28/62	[1963] [10]	1964			
Malagasy Rep.	9/25/63	[1963] [10]				
Mali	9/27/63	[1963] [10]	1964			
Mauritania	9/10/63	[1963] [10]				
Niger	4/24/63	[1963] [10]				
Nigeria	3/30/61	[1963] [10]	1964			
Rwanda	9/30/63	[1963] [10]				
Senegal	8/31/62	[1963] [10]				
Sierra Leone	9/10/62	[1963] [10]	1964			
Tanzania (formerly Tanganyika)	9/10/62	[1963] [10]	1964			
Togo	8/1/62	[1963] [10]				
Trinidad and Tobago	9/16/63	[1963] [10]	1964			
Uganda	9/27/63	[1963] [10]	1964			
Upper Volta	5/2/63	[1963] [10]				
Congo, Dem. Rep. of	9/28/63	1966				
Mauritius	9/23/68	1968				

Burundi	9/28/63	1964		Semyano Kiingi (Uganda)	11/1/64	10/31/66
Congo, Dem. Rep. of	9/28/63	1964	1966	*Paul L. Faber (Guinea)*	*11/1/64*	*10/31/66*
Guinea	9/28/63	1964		Paul L. Faber (Guinea)	11/1/66	10/31/68
Kenya	2/3/64	1964		*Leonard A. Williams (Trinidad & Tobago)*	*11/1/66*	*10/31/68*
Liberia	3/28/62	1964		Leonard A. Williams (Trinidad & Tobago)	11/1/68	
Mali	9/27/63	1964		*Maurice Peter Omwony (Kenya)*	*11/1/68*	
Nigeria	3/30/61	1964				
Sierra Leone	9/10/62	1964				
Sudan	9/5/57	1964				
Tanzania	9/10/62	1964				
Trinidad and Tobago	9/16/63	1964				
Uganda	9/27/63	1964				
Malawi	7/19/65	1966				
Zambia	9/23/65	1966				
Botswana	7/24/68	1968				
The Gambia	9/21/67	1968				

[1] Alternate Executive Directors (shown in italic type) are always appointed by the Executive Director.

[2] Dates are given in the following order: month/day/year.

[3] Executive Directors were appointed by China until 1960, when Germany replaced China as a member qualified to appoint an Executive Director.

[4] In 1958 Mr. Rasminsky was appointed by Canada under the terms of Article XII, Section 3(*b*)(ii).

[5] Ireland, which was eligible to vote in the 1958 Regular Election of Executive Directors, abstained, but its interests were represented during that term by the Executive Director appointed by Canada.

[6] Did not come to Washington.

[7] Czechoslovakia did not participate in the 1950 Regular Election of Executive Directors, was declared ineligible to use the Fund's resources on November 4, 1953, and ceased to be a member of the Fund on December 31, 1954.

[8] Poland withdrew from the Fund, effective March 14, 1950.

[9] Mr. Gutt was elected Managing Director at the first Executive Board meeting, on May 6, 1946.

[10] Interim election.

[11] In 1968 Mr. Palamenghi-Crispi was appointed by Italy under the terms of Article XII, Section 3(*b*)(ii).

[12] Greece, Malta, Portugal, and Spain, which were eligible to vote in the 1968 Regular Election of Executive Directors, abstained, but asked that their interests be represented by the Executive Director appointed by Italy.

[13] In 1960 Germany replaced China as a member qualified to appoint an Executive Director.

[14] Indonesia withdrew from the Fund, effective August 17, 1965, and rejoined on February 21, 1967.

[15] The Fund was notified in September 1963 of the change of name from Malaya to Malaysia. Malaysia, though eligible to participate in the 1964 Regular Election of Executive Directors, abstained from voting in that election and was looked after specifically by Mr. Nikoi, then the Alternate Executive Director from Ghana and later to be elected to take the seat vacated by the Executive Director from Indonesia.

Table A–3. Elected Executive Directors and Their Alternates
Article XII, Section 3(*b*)(iv)
1946–68

Countries Represented		Executive Director and Alternate[1]				
		Representation			Dates[2] of Service	
Name	Date[2] Became Member	Began	Ended	Name	Began	Ended
Bolivia	12/27/45	1946	1956	Francisco A. dos Santos-Filho (Brazil)	5/6/46	10/31/48
Brazil	1/14/46	1946		*Octávio Bulhões (Brazil)*	*5/29/46*	*1/1/47*
Chile	12/31/45	1946	1956	*Octávio Paranaguá (Brazil)*	*1/1/47*	*10/31/48*
Ecuador	12/28/45	1946	1948	Octávio Paranaguá (Brazil)	11/1/48	8/21/60
Panama	3/14/46	1946	1948	*Walter Blomeyer (Brazil)*	*4/1/49*	*4/30/51*
Paraguay	12/28/45	1946	1956	*Herculano Borges da Fonseca (Brazil)*	*5/1/51*	*11/16/51*
Peru	12/31/45	1946		*Charles P. Hargreaves (Brazil)*	*11/20/51*	*1/24/53*
Uruguay	3/11/46	1946	1956	*J. C. Gouvêa Filho (Brazil)*	*1/25/53*	*10/14/56*
				Helvécio Xavier Lopes (Brazil)	*10/15/56*	*4/10/59*
Dominican Rep.	12/28/45	1948		*Gabriel Costa Carvalho (Brazil)*	*5/15/59*	
Honduras	12/27/45	1948	1952	Maurício Chagas Bicalho (Brazil)	11/1/60	10/31/66
Nicaragua	3/14/46	1948	1952	*Gabriel Costa Carvalho (Brazil)*		*11/20/61*
				Gabriel Costa Carvalho (Brazil)	*6/20/62*	*10/31/62*
Ecuador	12/28/45	1952	1956	*Antonio de Abreu Coutinho (Brazil)*	*11/1/62*	*4/18/66*
Panama	3/14/46	1952		*Alexandre Kafka (Brazil)*	*6/5/66*	*10/31/66*
				Alexandre Kafka (Brazil)	11/1/66	
Haiti	9/8/53	1954		*Paulo H. Pereira Lira (Brazil)*	*11/13/66*	*3/4/68*
				Eduardo da S. Gomes, Jr. (Brazil)	*3/29/68*	
Colombia	12/27/45	1956				

Colombia	12/27/45	1946	1956	Rodrigo Gómez (Mexico)	5/6/46	10/31/48
Costa Rica	1/8/46	1946		*Raul Martinez-Ostos (Mexico)*	*5/6/46*	*10/31/48*
Cuba [3]	3/14/46	1946	1964	Carlos A. D'Ascoli (Venezuela)	1/28/49	10/31/50
Dominican Rep.	12/28/45	1946	1948	*Eduardo Montealegre (Guatemala)*	*11/1/48*	*1/31/49*
El Salvador	3/14/46	1946		*Hector Santaella (Venezuela)*	*2/7/49*	*10/31/50*
Guatemala	12/28/45	1946		Raul Martínez-Ostos (Mexico)	11/1/50	10/31/52
Honduras	12/27/45	1946	1948	*Rodrigo Facio (Costa Rica)*	*11/1/50*	*2/9/51*
Mexico	12/31/45	1946		*Javier Márquez (Mexico)*	*4/12/51*	*10/31/52*
Nicaragua	3/14/46	1946	1948	Enrique Delgado (Nicaragua)	11/1/52	10/31/54
				Manuel F. Chavarría (El Salvador)	*11/1/52*	*10/31/53*
Ecuador	12/28/45	1948	1952	*Alejandro Baca-Muñoz (Nicaragua)*	*11/1/53*	*5/28/54*
Panama	3/14/46	1948	1952	*José Luna-Guerra (Mexico)*	*10/15/54*	*10/31/54*
Venezuela	12/30/46	1948		José Luna-Guerra (Mexico)	11/1/54	10/31/56
				Jorge Sol (El Salvador)	*11/1/54*	*10/31/56*
Honduras	12/27/45	1952		Jorge Sol (El Salvador)	11/1/56	10/31/58
Nicaragua	3/14/46	1952		*Jorge Hazera (Costa Rica)*	*2/12/57*	
				Rodrigo Gómez (Mexico)	11/1/58	10/31/60
				Jorge Hazera (Costa Rica)		*3/31/60*
				Jorge A. Montealegre (Nicaragua)	*4/1/60*	
				José Antonio Mayobre (Venezuela)	11/1/60	5/15/62
				Jorge A. Montealegre (Nicaragua)		*5/15/62*
				Jorge A. Montealegre (Nicaragua)	5/16/62	10/31/62
				Lempira E. Bonilla (Honduras)	*5/16/62*	*10/31/62*
				Práxedes Reina Hermosillo (Mexico)	11/1/62	10/31/64
				Carlos Sansón (Nicaragua)	*11/1/62*	*10/31/64*
				Alfonso Espinosa (Venezuela)	11/1/64	2/11/65
				Jorge González del Valle (Guatemala)	*11/1/64*	
				Enrique Tejera-París (Venezuela)	3/2/65	10/31/66
				Jorge González del Valle (Guatemala)		*10/31/66*
				Jorge González del Valle (Guatemala)	11/1/66	10/31/68
				Alfredo Phillips O. (Mexico)	*11/1/66*	*10/31/68*
				Alfredo Phillips O. (Mexico)	11/1/68	
				Marcos A. Sandoval (Venezuela)	*11/1/68*	

Table A–3 *(concluded)*. Elected Executive Directors and Their Alternates
Article XII, Section 3(*b*)(iv)
1946–68

Countries Represented				Executive Director and Alternate[1]		
		Representation			Dates[2] of Service	
Name	Date[2] Became Member	Began	Ended	Name	Began	Ended
Argentina	9/20/56	1956		Rodolfo Corominas-Segura (Argentina)	11/1/56	10/31/58
Bolivia	12/27/45	1956		*Julio González del Solar (Guatemala)*	*11/1/56*	*9/30/57*
Chile	12/31/45	1956		*Carlos Luzzetti (Argentina)*	*10/1/57*	*10/31/58*
Ecuador	12/28/45	1956		Felipe Herrera (Chile)	11/1/58	2/23/60
Paraguay	12/28/45	1956		*Jorge Marshall (Chile)*	*11/1/58*	*10/15/59*
Uruguay	3/11/46	1956		*Javier Urrutia (Chile)*	*10/16/59*	
				Walter Müller (Chile)	3/31/60	10/31/60
				Guillermo Walter Klein (Argentina)	11/1/60	10/31/64
				Javier Urrutia (Chile)		*11/15/63*
				Luis Escobar (Chile)	*11/16/63*	*10/31/64*
				Luis Escobar (Chile)	11/1/64	10/31/66
				Enrique Domenech (Argentina)	*11/1/64*	*10/31/66*
				Adolfo C. Diz (Argentina)	11/1/66	10/31/68
				Yamandú S. Patrón (Uruguay)	*11/1/66*	*10/31/68*
				Luis Escobar (Chile)	11/1/68	
				Ricardo H. Arriazu (Argentina)	*11/1/68*	

[1] Alternate Executive Directors (shown in italic type) are always appointed by the Executive Director.
[2] All dates are given in the following order: month/day/year.
[3] Cuba withdrew from the Fund, effective April 2, 1964.

APPENDIX B

STAFF AND OFFICES

Headquarters Organization
1946–1968

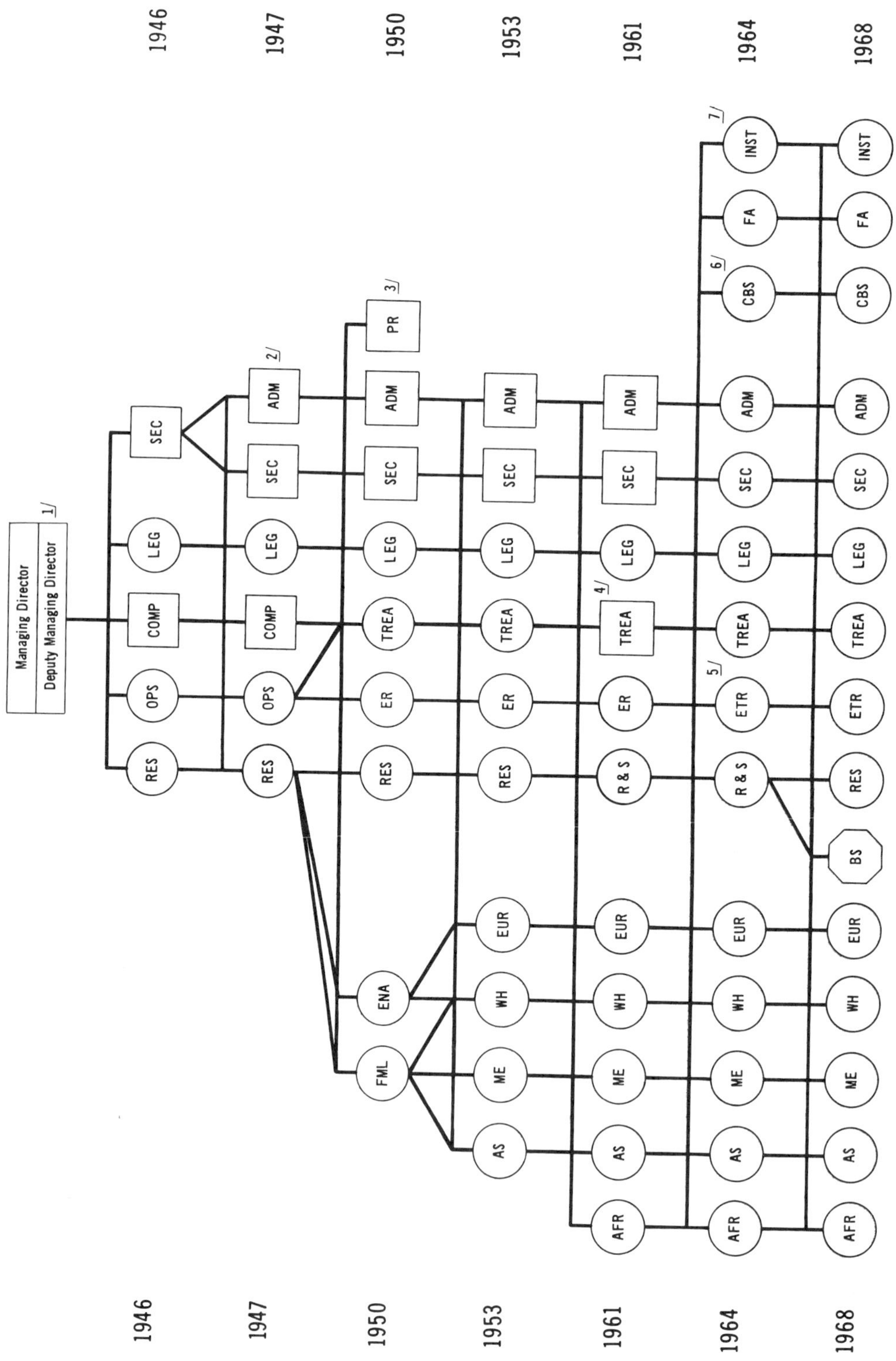

○ Department ☐ Office ⬡ Bureau

ADM	Administration
AFR	African
AS	Asian
BS	Bureau of Statistics
CBS	Central Banking Service
COMP	Comptroller
ENA	European and North American
ER	Exchange Restrictions
ETR	Exchange and Trade Relations
EUR	European
FA	Fiscal Affairs
FML	Far Eastern, Middle Eastern, and Latin American
INST	IMF Institute
LEG	Legal
ME	Middle Eastern
OPS	Operations
PR	Public Relations
R&S	Research and Statistics
RES	Research
SEC	Secretary's
TREA	Treasurer's
WH	Western Hemisphere

1 The position of Deputy Managing Director was established in February 1949.

2 From 1947 to 1950 the Director of this Office was entitled Administrative Assistant to the Managing Director.

3 Function retained after 1952 as part of the Office of the Managing Director.

4 Treasurer's was a Department until May 1956, and an Office until 1964.

5 In May 1965 Exchange Restrictions became Exchange and Trade Relations. The work of ER in the area of exchange restrictions had diminished; however, new responsibilities appropriately centered in the Department had developed.

6 Originally established as part of the Office of the Managing Director.

7 The Training Program originated in 1950 as part of the Office of Administration, and subsequently came under the Office of the Managing Director.

Departments and Offices
1946–December 31, 1968

	Name	Term of Service (month/year)
The Managing Director	Camille Gutt	5/46–5/51
	Ivar Rooth	8/51–10/56
	Per Jacobsson	11/56–5/63
	Pierre-Paul Schweitzer	9/63—
The Deputy Managing Director	Andrew N. Overby	2/49–1/52
	H. Merle Cochran	3/53–10/62
	Frank A. Southard, Jr.	11/62—

Department or Office		Head of Department or Office	
Name	Period	Name	Term of Service (month/year)
Administration (formed out of Secretary's Office as an Office; became Department in 1964)	1947—	Oscar L. Altman	3/50–4/54
		Phillip Thorson	5/54—
African	1961—	Jan V. Mládek (acting)	5/61–4/64
		Hamzah Merghani	8/64–8/66
		Mamoudou Touré	4/67—
Asian (formed out of Far Eastern, Middle Eastern, and Latin American Department)	1953—	Hirendra Lal Dey	5/53–7/56
		James Samuel Raj	8/56–5/59
		D. S. Savkar	6/59—
Bureau of Statistics (formed out of Research and Statistics Department)	1968—	Earl Hicks	5/68—
Central Banking Service	1964—	Jan V. Mládek	5/64—
Comptroller's (became Treasurer's Office in 1950; see Treasurer's)	1946–1950	Charles M. Powell	11/46–4/50
European (formed out of European and North American Department)	1953—	A. M. Stamp	3/53–2/54
		John M. Stevens	3/54–6/56
		Gabriel Ferras	7/56–1/63
		L. A. Whittome	8/64—
European and North American (formed out of Research Department; split in 1953, forming European and Western Hemisphere Departments)	1950–1953	G. A. Ph. Weyer	12/50–8/52

Department or Office Name	Period	Head of Department or Office Name	Term of Service (month/year)
Exchange and Trade Relations (name changed from Exchange Restrictions Department in 1965)	1965—	Ernest Sturc	1/65—
Exchange Restrictions (formed out of Operations Department; became Exchange and Trade Relations Department in 1965)	1950–1964	Irving S. Friedman	3/50–10/64
Far Eastern, Middle Eastern, and Latin American (formed out of Research Department; split in 1953, forming Asian, Middle Eastern, and Western Hemisphere Departments)	1950–1953	George F. Luthringer	3/50–4/53
Fiscal Affairs	1964—	Richard Goode	3/65—
IMF Institute (prior to 1964, responsibility for training was in Office of Administration and, later, in Office of the Managing Director)	1964—	F. A. G. Keesing	5/64—
Legal (General Counsel)	1946—	André van Campenhout J. E. S. Fawcett Joseph Gold	7/46–11/54 9/55–3/60 3/60—
Middle Eastern (formed out of Far Eastern, Middle Eastern, and Latin American Department)	1953—	Abol Hassan Ebtehaj Anwar Ali (on leave of absence since 1965) John Gunter (acting)	5/53–7/54 10/54— 5/66—
Operations (see Treasurer's and Exchange Restrictions)	1946–1950	John L. Fisher Maurice L. Parsons	8/46–10/47 11/47–1/50
Public Relations (function retained after 1952 as part of Office of the Managing Director)	1950–1952	David H. Wills	3/50–1/52
Research (named Research and Statistics, 1956–68)	1946–1956 1968—	Edward M. Bernstein J. J. Polak	6/46–4/56 5/68—
Research and Statistics (renamed Research in 1968)	1956–1968	Edward M. Bernstein J. J. Polak	5/56–1/58 6/58–4/68

Department or Office		Head of Department or Office	
Name	Period	Name	Term of Service (month/year)
Secretary's (Office became Department in 1964)	1946—	V. Frank Coe Roman L. Horne W. L. Hebbard	6/46–12/52 1/53–12/66 1/67—
Treasurer's (formed out of Comptroller's Office and Operations Department; a Department until 4/56 and from 5/64)	1950—	Frederick W. Gray Y. C. Koo Oscar L. Altman	4/50–4/53 5/53–2/66 5/66–12/68
Western Hemisphere (formed out of Far Eastern, Middle Eastern, and Latin American Department and European and North American Department)	1953—	George F. Luthringer Jorge Del Canto	5/53–3/55 5/57—

Overseas Offices

Location	Period (month/year)	Head	Term of Service (month/year)
Bombay [1]	12/48–6/50	B. R. Shenoy	7/49–6/50
Cairo	10/48–5/50	A. M. El Kaissouni	10/48–5/50
Geneva [2]	5/67—	Edgar Jones	5/67—
Paris [3]	7/48—	Robert Triffin Albin Pfeifer Jan V. Mládek Jean-Paul Sallé	7/48–1/51 1/51–6/52 1/53–5/61 5/61—

[1] Authorized 12/48 but not opened until 7/49.
[2] Established on a provisional basis in 10/65 with Mr. Jones in charge.
[3] Temporarily at Brussels 5/48 to 7/48 with Mr. Triffin in charge.

Office Buildings, Washington

The buildings occupied in whole or in part by the Executive Directors and staff in Washington have been as follows:

1946 [1]	Washington Hotel, Pennsylvania Avenue
1946–1958	1818 H Street (shared with World Bank)
1948–1958	Premier Building, 18th Street
1955–1958	Hurley Wright Building (rented offices)
1958—	19th and H Streets
1961–1966	1901 Pennsylvania Avenue (rented offices)
1963–1965	801 19th Street (rented offices)
1963–1965	Hurley Wright Building (shared with World Bank)
1964–1966	Equitable Building, 1809 G Street (rented offices)
1965–1966	Northwestern Building, 1800 G Street (rented offices)
1965 [2]—	Annex,19th Street between G and H Streets

[1] April to June.
[2] October.

Indexes

INDEX A. SUBJECTS

References in this index are in general arranged in alphabetical order of subject within each main heading. There are three exceptions to this: (1) References to the subjects in the first five chapters (through Bretton Woods) are frequently grouped together as "prehistory" at the beginning of each entry. (2) In certain main headings where chronological order is of importance, the subjects within that heading are listed in the order in which they first appear in this volume; these headings are marked with a dagger (†). (3) Where a number of countries appear among the subjects, they are listed first.

References are to pages; page numbers marked with an asterisk (*) are references to tables, and references including the letter n *are to footnotes.*

A

B

C

M

N

O

P

Q

Index B. Persons

The following abbreviations are used in this index: AED = Alternate Executive Director of the Fund; AGF = Alternate Governor of the Fund; ED = Executive Director of the Fund; GF = Governor of the Fund. Governors and Alternate Governors are those who held these positions at the time of the Inaugural Meeting or the Annual Meeting in the year or years shown. Dates are given through 1968 only. Where those named were members of the Fund Boards, no other positions that they may have held outside the Fund are shown. Numbers refer to pages. Persons listed in Appendix A or Appendix B, but not named in the text, are not indexed.

A

B

C

I

J

K

L

M

N

O

P

Q

R

S

T

V

W

GOVERNORS

Governors and/or Alternate Governors for the following countries are mentioned, but not necessarily named, on the pages shown.

Index C. Countries

The entries for each country are arranged in the order in which the subject first appears in the volume. Entries for the first five chapters (through Bretton Woods) which are not significant for later periods are grouped as "prehistory." References are to pages; page numbers marked with an asterisk (*) refer to tables.

A

B

C

K

L

M

N

P

R

S

Index D. Articles of Agreement

The page numbers given for an Article may also refer to individual Sections of that Article. References given for Sections of an Article are not necessarily repeated against the Article itself.

The text of the Articles will be found in Volume III of this history. Those adopted at Bretton Woods are on pages 185-214 of Volume III; those embodied in the Amendment that came into force in July 1969 are on pages 521-38 of that volume.

INDEX E. EXECUTIVE BOARD DECISIONS

Decisions Cited by Number

The citation is usually in a footnote. The text of these decisions is given in full in Volume III of this history, pp. 219-77, 492-94.

Other Major Decisions

Index F. Publications Cited

Numbers refer to pages. The publication is usually cited in a footnote.

J

K

L

M

N

O

P

Q

THE INTERNATIONAL MONETARY FUND

1945-1965

Volume II: Analysis

THE INTERNATIONAL MONETARY FUND 1945-1965

Twenty Years of International Monetary Cooperation

VOLUME II: ANALYSIS

By
Margaret G. de Vries *and* J. Keith Horsefield
with the collaboration of
Joseph Gold, Mary H. Gumbart, Gertrud Lovasy,
and Emil G. Spitzer

Edited by
J. Keith Horsefield

INTERNATIONAL MONETARY FUND
WASHINGTON, D. C.
1969

ISBN 0-939934-06-x (v.II)
ISBN 0-939934-08-6 (set)

Second printing, February 1972
Third printing, May 1981
Fourth printing, March 1986

CONTENTS

PART III: EXCHANGE RESTRICTIONS

PART V: CONSTITUTIONAL DEVELOPMENT AND CHANGE

INDEXES

TABLES

PREFACE TO VOLUME II

The first four parts of this volume deal successively with the process of policy formation and the objectives of the Fund, and with its policies in three main aspects of its work. These chapters are concerned wholly with the period covered by this history, viz., the twenty years 1945–65. Part V differs from the rest of the volume in two respects: in this, the General Counsel of the Fund deals with the constitutional development of the Fund rather than with its economic activities; and he includes a brief description of the amendments to the Articles which entered into force in July 1969, in order to relate past constitutional developments to special drawing rights and the reform of certain features of the Fund.

As indicated in the title, *Analysis*, given to this volume, the intention is to examine here, more intensively than was possible in Volume I, the Fund's activities in the various fields chosen for study. The additional dimension here provided has several facets. By bringing together the Fund's decisions on a given subject, instead of discussing them seriatim as they were taken, it has been possible to bring into sharper focus the reasoning which led to the Fund's actions. Similarly, where its decisions have been diffused among discussions with a number of different countries, the underlying policy has here been brought out. Further, an attempt has been made to take into account the economic background against which the Fund's decisions were taken. Finally, some reference has been made to comments on and criticisms of the Fund's actions by officials and economists not connected with it.

The foundation for this volume was laid by the late Oscar L. Altman, then Historian of the Fund, with the assistance of Mrs. Margaret G. de Vries, Mr. Allan G. B. Fisher, and Miss Mary H. Gumbart. Half of the final text has been written by Mrs. de Vries. Other contributors are Mr. Joseph Gold, the General Counsel of the Fund, who wrote Chapters 22 through 27; Miss Gumbart, who wrote Chapter 8 and contributed preparatory work for parts of Chapters 11, 15, and 17; Mr. Emil G. Spitzer, who wrote Chapters 20 and 21 and prepared early drafts of parts of Chapters 18 and 19; and Mr. J. Keith Horsefield, Mr. Altman's successor as Historian of the Fund, who wrote Chapters 9, 17, 18, and 19 and has also edited the volume. A part of Chapter 18 was written by Miss Gertrud Lovasy, and Mr. Evan B. Hannay prepared early drafts for some other sections. All those mentioned are or have been members of the staff of the Fund.

At all stages the authors have been greatly assisted by advice and comments from present and former members of the Executive Board and of the staff of the Fund. In particular, Mr. Fisher has made most helpful comments on the draft of each chapter in Parts II, III, and IV. Mrs. de Vries expresses appreciation to Professor Gerard Curzon, of the Graduate Institute of International Studies, University of Geneva, and to Professor Gardner Patterson, of Princeton University, for sharing with her some of their experiences as authors of volumes in related fields and for making suggestions for the contents of this volume. She is grateful also to Professor Robert A. Mundell, of the University of Chicago, for his encouraging interest in the project.

The staffs of the Archivist of the Fund and of the Joint Bank-Fund Library have much facilitated the task of identifying and consulting the relevant documents and volumes.

Mrs. Jane B. Evensen, Assistant Editor of the Fund, has greatly assisted in clarifying the final text.

Mrs. Margaret P. Estes has helped with some of the statistical material and has patiently typed several versions of the manuscript.

Responsibility for the contents of this volume is, however, that of the authors and editor alone.

M. G. de V.
J. G.
M. H. G.
J. K. H.
G. L.
E. G. S.

ABBREVIATIONS AND DEFINITIONS

Annual Meetings, 19—	Annual Meetings of the Boards of Governors of the Fund and the Bank, in the year specified. The Meetings of the two institutions are held at the same time and in the same place, and some of the sessions are held jointly. Other sessions, however, are held separately by the Fund and the Bank. When the term Annual Meeting (in the singular) is used, the reference is to a Meeting of the Fund Governors.
Annual Report, 19—	*Annual Report of the Executive Directors for the Fiscal Year Ended April 30, 19—*
Articles of Agreement; Articles; Fund Agreement	*Articles of Agreement of the International Monetary Fund*
Bank; World Bank	International Bank for Reconstruction and Development
BIS	Bank for International Settlements
Bretton Woods	[Site of] United Nations Monetary and Financial Conference, July 1944
Consultations	Annual consultations with members by the Executive Board under Article XIV, and parallel consultations with members that have accepted the obligations of Article VIII
Drawing	Purchase from the Fund by a member of another member's currency (or other members' currencies). Amounts are always expressed in U.S. dollars.
E.B. Decision	Decision of the Executive Board. Until Meeting 630 (at the beginning of 1951), the formal decisions and policy actions of the Executive Board were numbered *x-y*, where *x* was the number of the meeting and *y* that of the decision taken at that meeting (e.g., 2-1 was the first decision taken at Executive Board Meeting 2). Beginning with Meeting 630, the decisions were numbered consecutively; thereafter

	the number was *z*-(*x*), where *z* was the consecutive number of the decision and *x* that of the meeting (e.g., 7-(648) was the seventh policy decision taken since Meeting 630, and was taken at Meeting 648). From January 1, 1952, the number of the decision has been followed by the last two figures of the year and the number of the meeting in that year in parentheses (e.g., Decision No. 102-(52/11) was the 102nd decision since Meeting 630, and was taken at the eleventh meeting in 1952).
ECA	Economic Cooperation Administration (U.S.)
ECOSOC	Economic and Social Council (UN)
EEC	European Economic Community
EMA	European Monetary Agreement
EPU	European Payments Union
ERP	European Recovery Program (U.S.)
FAO	Food and Agriculture Organization (UN)
FIFO	First in, first out (pertaining to Fund transactions)
GAB	General Arrangements to Borrow
GATT	General Agreement on Tariffs and Trade. The term CONTRACTING PARTIES in capital letters denotes the adherents to the General Agreement acting in concert. The terms contracting parties and contracting party in lower case letters refer to the individual adherents to the General Agreement.
Group of Ten	The countries associated in the General Arrangements to Borrow, viz., Belgium, Canada, France, Germany, Italy, Japan, the Netherlands, Sweden, the United Kingdom, the United States
IDB	Inter-American Development Bank
IFNS	*International Financial News Survey*
IFS	*International Financial Statistics*
ITO	International Trade Organization

Joint Statement	*Joint Statement by Experts on the Establishment of an International Monetary Fund*
Keynes Plan	Proposals for an International Clearing Union
LIFO	Last in, first out (pertaining to Fund transactions)
OAS	Organization of American States
OECD	Organization for Economic Cooperation and Development
OEEC	Organization for European Economic Cooperation
Proceedings	*Proceedings and Documents of the United Nations Monetary and Financial Conference, Bretton Woods, New Hampshire, July 1–22, 1944*, 2 vols. (Washington, 1948)
Repurchase	Purchase of its own currency from the Fund by a member country, in reduction of the Fund's holdings of that currency. Amounts are always expressed in U.S. dollars.
Resolution	Resolution of the Board of Governors of the Fund. Resolutions at the Annual Meetings of Governors are referred to by the number of the Annual Meeting followed by a dash and the number of the resolution. Resolutions passed at the Inaugural Meeting (Savannah, March 1946) are listed as IM-1, etc., those at the First Annual Meeting (Washington, September 1946) as 1-1, and so on. Resolutions passed by Governors between Annual Meetings are given the number of the next succeeding Annual Meeting.
Selected Decisions	*Selected Decisions of the Executive Directors and Selected Documents*, 3rd issue, January 1965
Selected Documents	*Selected Documents, Board of Governors Inaugural Meeting, Savannah, Ga., March 8 to 18, 1946* (compare *Summary Proceedings* below)
Summary Proceedings, 19—	*Summary Proceedings of the . . . Annual Meeting of the Board of Governors* (issued after each Annual Meeting). In early years *Summary Proceedings* were really summaries, but latterly most speeches made at the Annual Meetings have been printed in full. In these printed

	reports Governors are named, but in the records maintained in the Fund's files they are not, being referred to as "Governor" whether they were in fact Governors, Alternate Governors, or Temporary Alternate Governors. Unless, therefore, the speaker can be identified in other ways, it has been necessary, in those parts of this volume that are drawn from unpublished reports, to cite only "Governor for . . . ".
UN	United Nations
UNCTAD	United Nations Conference on Trade and Development
White Plan	Proposals for an International Stabilization Fund
World Bank; Bank	International Bank for Reconstruction and Development

PART I

The Formation and Objectives of Fund Policy

CHAPTER

1

The Process of Policymaking

Margaret G. de Vries

ONE OF THE DISTINGUISHING CHARACTERISTICS of the international economic scene since World War II is the existence of multi-member economic institutions, such as the International Monetary Fund. The Fund was established to substitute cooperation and consultation in monetary and financial affairs for the unilateral and independent decision-making concerning these matters in which countries had previously engaged. Subsequently, in accordance with its Articles of Agreement, the Fund has been evolving policies in the fields for which it has responsibility that are of considerable significance to its members.

IMPORTANCE OF THE FUND'S POLICIES

The Fund's attitudes and policies are an important factor circumscribing the monetary and financial policies of each member country. For several of its policies, a member is accountable to the Fund. Regular consultations between the Fund and the member provide the Fund with an opportunity to review and to criticize the monetary and financial policies being pursued by the member. Some actions contemplated by the monetary authorities of a member—such as a change in the exchange rate or the imposition of exchange restrictions—must receive the concurrence of the Fund even before these steps can be taken.

A member has a vested interest in securing the Fund's approval: not only may the member then be regarded as one in good standing in the international economic community, but it is enabled should the need arise to draw upon the pool of resources which the Fund has at its disposal. Through the medium of the Fund, a member has opportunities to comment upon the policies of other members and, should it feel that its interests are adversely affected by the policies of another, it has the right to object.

Just as the Fund's policies are of concern to a member individually, so are they important to its members collectively. These policies aim at making harmonious the conduct of trade and payments among all members. And, through the Fund, members as a group have worked out additional forms and techniques of international monetary cooperation as new problems in international trade and payments have arisen.

The upcoming chapters in this volume are devoted to explaining many of the specific policies of the Fund. This chapter provides background by describing the process by which these policies are formed. As an example of the machinery of international organizations, the process of policymaking in the Fund is, in fact, a subject of interest in itself. Because this process has changed significantly over the years, note is also taken of some of the important ways in which the process differs from that in the early years.

INSTRUMENTS OF POLICYMAKING

The process of policymaking in the Fund consists of a complex of relations between member governments, the Board of Governors, the Board of Executive Directors, the Managing Director, and the international staff, and the line of formal authority moreover proceeds in that order.

Members

The Fund is, of course, an entity composed of its members. It is the members who determine the Fund's policies. Thus the Fund can go only as far in fulfilling its objectives and deciding what policies will be pursued as its members will allow.

At the end of 1965 there were 103 members, compared with 40 at the end of 1946. Until 1960 the growth of membership was relatively slow; on average, there were about two new members each year. Thereafter membership increased sharply, as former colonial territories which had achieved their independence joined. These countries were especially eager to be admitted to the Fund, not only because of the benefits of such membership itself, but also because Fund membership is a condition for membership in the International Bank for Reconstruction and Development (the World Bank). Of the Fund's 103 members at the end of 1965, 48 had not existed as sovereign states when the Fund was formed. Apart from the U.S.S.R., mainland China, and some countries closely associated with one or the other of these, the only considerable countries that were independent at the end of 1965 and had not joined the Fund were Cambodia, Switzerland, and Yemen.[1]

The composition of the Fund's membership at the end of 1965, although roughly the same as that of the United Nations, differed in some important

[1] Switzerland does, however, have an agreement with the Fund parallel to the Fund's General Arrangements to Borrow.

respects. Among the member countries of the Fund were some, such as Germany, Korea, and Viet-Nam, that were not members of the United Nations. On the other hand, the U.S.S.R. and states associated with it that were members of the United Nations were not members of the Fund. The U.S.S.R. sent a delegation to the Bretton Woods Conference and took an active part in the deliberations there; indeed, some of the Articles of Agreement were reworded in an effort to meet the points of view of the U.S.S.R. A member of the staff of the U.S.S.R. Purchasing Commission in Washington also attended as an observer the Inaugural Meetings of the Boards of Governors of the Fund and the Bank in March 1946. By that time, however, relations between the Soviet bloc and its wartime allies had sharply deteriorated, and the U.S.S.R. never joined the Fund. Poland, Cuba, and Czechoslovakia were original members, but the first two withdrew in 1950 and 1964, respectively, and Czechoslovakia's membership terminated at the end of 1954.[2]

This composition of membership meant, inter alia, that the tensions of the cold war did not cause the same conflict among the Fund's members as had occurred in the United Nations. On the contrary, rather quickly after the Fund's establishment, members developed harmonious working relationships and a sharing of confidences concerning their economic situations and policies that, in all probability, would not have been possible if there had been acute political differences among the membership.

At the time that it joins the Fund, each member country agrees to a *quota.* These quotas play a unique role in the organization and operation of the Fund: they determine the contribution that a member makes to the Fund (and hence the size and composition of the Fund's resources), the drawings permitted to members and the charges and repayments on these drawings, and members' voting power.

No formal principles have been laid down for the determination of quotas. The quotas agreed at Bretton Woods for the original members were based on a complicated formula which employed various percentages of the member's national income, its holdings of gold and U.S. dollars, and its average annual exports and imports. The idea was that quotas would be in accordance with the relative economic circumstances of members.

Although quotas of subsequent members have continued to be based primarily on their economic circumstances, a good deal of consideration is also given to fitting the quota into the existing structure of quotas. In accordance with its Articles, the Fund conducts a comprehensive review of quotas every five years. In 1958–59 and 1965–66, general increases for all members were proposed and

[2] The membership at the end of 1965 and the date that each member joined are listed in Table 2 of Chapter 4 (below, pp. 87–89).

accepted. There have also been many special increases in the quotas of individual countries. By early in 1966, the total of the Fund's quotas had reached nearly $21 billion.

Unlike the United Nations and some other international organizations, members do not have to make periodic contributions for the administrative expenses of the Fund: these are met from the charges the Fund receives from its members for drawings from its resources. Although in its first ten years the Fund ran an annual deficit, subsequently there was a sharp rise in transactions, which increased the Fund's income.

Board of Governors

As its highest-ranking representatives in the Fund, every member appoints a Governor (usually the Minister of Finance or the Governor of the central bank) and an Alternate Governor. In late September or early October of each year there is a meeting attended by all the Governors and Alternate Governors, held jointly with that of the World Bank. Because of the high-level representation of member countries at the Joint Bank-Fund Meetings, these meetings have become the occasion not only for conducting the immediate business of the Fund but also for holding informal discussions among members on a variety of financial matters of mutual concern. Such informal discussions have become part of the process by which international monetary cooperation has gradually been extended.

Although the Articles of the Fund provide also for special meetings of the Board of Governors, such meetings have never been called. Convening Governors—and by 1965 there were more than one hundred—from all over the world would be a cumbersome way to make decisions. When a vote of the Governors is needed, they are polled by mail or cable.

Executive Directors

The Articles also provide for Executive Directors who are to exercise whatever powers are delegated to them by the Board of Governors. At its Inaugural Meeting in 1946, the Board of Governors delegated to the Executive Directors all its powers except for a few reserved subjects, notably the admission of members and changes in quotas. The Board of Governors, however, retains authority to issue policy decisions for the guidance of the Executive Directors, and all decisions and actions of the Executive Directors may, upon the proposal of any member, be reviewed by the Board of Governors.

On December 31, 1965, the Executive Board consisted of twenty Executive Directors.[3] The five members with the largest quotas—the United States, the

[3] For a list of the Executive Directors and their Alternates from the Fund's inception to the end of 1968, see above, Vol. I, Appendix A.

United Kingdom, France, Germany, and India—are each entitled to appoint one Director. The two countries whose currencies are drawn on the most in the preceding two years are also entitled to appoint a Director each, on the occasion of the biennial elections of Executive Directors. Usually these countries are among the five with the largest quotas, but Canada appointed a Director under this provision for the two years beginning November 1958.

The remaining Directors are elected for two-year terms by the other members. Three seats are specifically reserved for the Latin American Republics. The other members arrange themselves informally into groups. For example, the five Nordic countries customarily form a single group. Some members are, however, represented by an Executive Director from a country which is not geographically close. For example, at the end of 1965 eight Middle Eastern countries were represented by Mr. Saad (from the United Arab Republic), but Mr. Saad also represented Afghanistan, Ethiopia, Pakistan, Somalia, and the Philippines; Mr. Lieftinck (a Dutch national) cast the votes of Cyprus, Israel, the Netherlands, and Yugoslavia; and Mr. van Campenhout (from Belgium) those of Austria, Belgium, Korea, Luxembourg, and Turkey. The groupings of countries that combine to elect Directors have changed little since 1954.

Voting in the Fund is not conducted, as in most other international organizations, on the basis of one country, one vote. The system in the Fund is one of weighted voting, that is, the voting strength wielded by each member's representative is based on the quotas of the members (or quota of the member) which he represents. The intent is to give the greatest "say" to those countries which have contributed the most to the Fund's assets.

On April 30, 1966, the U.S. Director had 23.82 per cent of the total voting power in the Fund, the British Director 11.33 per cent, the Directors from France and Germany 3.73 per cent each, and the Indian Director 3.56 per cent. With the steady increase in the number of members and the disproportionate increases in many quotas in 1959–60, these percentages were somewhat smaller than when the Fund was first established. The voting power of the elected Directors in April 1966 ranged from 5.53 per cent of the total (Mr. Saad) to 1.89 per cent.

Some of the Directors have served for long periods of time. Among appointed Directors, for example, Mr. de Largentaye was the French Director from June 1946 until June 1964 and Mr. Southard represented the United States from March 1949 to October 1962 (the United States has had only four Directors since 1946). Among elected Directors, Mr. Saad has been a Director since the establishment of the Fund; Mr. Rasminsky (Canada) served from 1946 to 1962; Mr. Lieftinck has been on the Board since 1955, Mr. Tann (China) since 1950, and Mr. van Campenhout since 1954. Other groups, for example, the Nordic countries and sometimes the countries of Central America, vary the countries from which their Directors are elected.

Usually the Directors are experts in international monetary affairs. Most of them have been officials of treasuries, ministries of economics, or central banks; a number have been former Ministers of Finance or Governors of central banks. Many are highly qualified economists; some have already been on the senior staff of the Fund and some have been appointed later to senior staff posts.

The Executive Board functions in continuous session, meeting as often as Fund business requires. Through the Executive Directors, members exercise a closer control over the day-to-day activities of the Fund than is generally the case with international organizations, with one or two exceptions such as the Organization for Economic Cooperation and Development (OECD).

A few countries formerly made it a practice to appoint as Executive Director a high official whose main work was at home, and who visited Washington on Fund business only at irregular intervals. But nowadays the Directors usually devote full time to their Fund duties. Some also represent their countries on the Executive Board of the World Bank, or combine with their work as a Director of the Fund other duties in Washington on behalf of their governments. Mondays, Wednesdays, and Fridays are reserved for meetings of the Fund Board; this permits Executive Directors who also serve on the Board of the Bank to attend its meetings on Tuesdays and Thursdays. When business demands it, meetings are also held on holidays and on week-ends.

Each Executive Director appoints an Alternate from the country or countries which appointed or elected him. Some of the elected Directors appoint Alternates from member states other than those from which they themselves come. The presence of Alternates in Washington makes it possible to maintain the principle of continuous session for the Board, even though some Executive Directors may not themselves be continuously available. A member not entitled to appoint an Executive Director may send a special representative to an Executive Board meeting when a matter particularly affecting the member is under consideration. The representative may speak at meetings but may not vote.

With a few exceptions, such as a change in quota, a simple majority of votes cast is all that is necessary to carry a decision. But some actions—for instance, changes in quotas or in par values—must have the concurrence of the member concerned as well.

In practice, nearly all decisions of the Executive Board are taken without a vote. Down to the end of 1965, only 45 recorded votes were taken; of these, many were purely a matter of form, relating to changes in the Fund's schedule of charges, for which a three-fourths majority of the Directors is required by the Articles. Several more of the 45 recorded votes dealt with administrative and personnel matters. Since 1953 votes on substantive issues have occurred only infrequently. Apart from the approval of changes in the schedule of Fund charges, there was, between 1953 and the end of 1965, only one issue on which a vote was taken. Instead, the Chairman of the Board customarily obtains what is agreed to be *the sense of the meeting.* These words were explicitly defined by the Directors in 1947 to be a position supported by those Directors having sufficient votes to carry the question if a vote were to be taken.

One other special attribute of the Executive Board should be noted—the responsibility for interpreting the Articles of Agreement. Indeed, the Articles give the Executive Directors the power to interpret questions relating to the range and limits of their own authority.[4]

Managing Director

The Managing Director is Chairman of the Executive Board as well as chief of the international staff. He is appointed by the Board for a five-year term. He presides over meetings of the Board but has no vote. He is also in charge of the organization, appointment, and dismissal of the staff, and is responsible for the work of the staff and for the formulation of staff positions on policy matters.

The Managing Director is the principal representative of the Fund; for example, he addresses the Board of Governors at Annual Meetings, and gives formal statements on behalf of the Fund to other high-level international gatherings. When the Fund is invited to meetings at the ministerial level, it is the Managing Director who attends.

The Fund has been under the leadership of four Managing Directors: Camille Gutt, from Belgium (May 1946–May 1951); Ivar Rooth, from Sweden (August 1951–October 1956); Per Jacobsson, also from Sweden (November 1956–May 1963); and Pierre-Paul Schweitzer, from France (September 1963 to the present). Each has been well known in the fields of money, banking, and finance. Mr. Gutt had been Minister of Finance in Belgium; Mr. Rooth, Governor of the Sveriges Riksbank; Mr. Jacobsson, Economic Adviser and Head of the Monetary and Economic Department of the Bank for International Settlements; and Mr. Schweitzer, Deputy Governor of the Bank of France.

Since 1949 there has also been a Deputy Managing Director. So far three persons, all from the United States, have served in this capacity: Andrew N. Overby (February 1949–January 1952); H. Merle Cochran (March 1953–October 1962); and Frank A. Southard, Jr. (November 1962 to the present). The Deputy Managing Director assists the Managing Director and, in his absence, chairs the meetings of the Executive Board and directs the staff.

[4] On the significance of this feature, see Chapter 25 below and Joseph Gold, *Interpretation by the Fund*, IMF Pamphlet Series, No. 11. For an earlier study, see Ervin P. Hexner, "Interpretation by Public International Organizations of their Basic Instruments," *American Journal of International Law*, Vol. 53 (1959), pp. 341–70.

Staff

The Fund is relatively small as organizations go these days: on April 30, 1966, the staff consisted of 750 persons in total. About half were professional staff—economists, lawyers, statisticians, and fiscal experts—drawn from 69 member countries. The staff is selected with a view to securing the highest standards of efficiency and technical competence, with due regard to the importance of having as wide a geographical basis as possible. Because it has often been difficult to recruit from the less developed countries staff members who have the necessary qualifications and who can be spared from duties in their home countries for several years, a high proportion of the staff—especially of the senior staff—has come from the United States, the United Kingdom, other European countries, Canada, and Australia. However, many of the less developed countries have also been represented on the senior staff; in 1965, for example, senior staff officers included persons from Burma, Chile, Ghana, India, Pakistan, and Paraguay. Senior staff appointments are subject to the approval of the Executive Directors, who also pass on the annual administrative budget.

Members of the staff owe their duty entirely to the Fund; each staff member is, on appointment, required to sign a statement that he will accept no instruction from any country. The majority of staff members stay with the Fund for long periods; most of the senior staff, in April 1966, had been with the Fund for close to fifteen years, and many for twenty years. Hence, over time, the Fund's staff has become part of an international civil servant group, similar to staff serving in other international organizations, such as the United Nations, the World Bank, the GATT, and the FAO.

The staff at the end of 1965 was organized into fourteen departments–five functional departments (Exchange and Trade Relations, Fiscal Affairs, Legal, Research and Statistics, and Treasurer's) and five area departments (African, Asian, European, Middle Eastern, and Western Hemisphere). Two departments (the Central Banking Service and the IMF Institute) were devoted to technical assistance and training, and in addition there was an Administration Department, for internal administration, and a Secretary's Department, to provide services to the Executive Directors and to Governors. In addition to the headquarters in Washington, there were small offices in Paris and Geneva.

EVOLUTION OF THE PROCESS OF POLICYMAKING

As early as the Inaugural Meeting in Savannah in 1946, a distinction was made between the roles of the Executive Directors on the one hand and of the Managing Director and the staff on the other: the Executive Directors are responsible to the countries that appointed or elected them; the Managing

Director and the staff to the Fund as a whole. This division of responsibility has persisted, although, over time, the implementation has changed substantially.

In the Fund's first two years, Executive Directors headed field missions to member countries, frequently accompanied by senior staff. In 1948, after the Board took a decision clarifying the division of responsibility, Directors ceased as a rule to head such missions, and these were now headed by members of the staff. Mr. Saad (Egypt) continued until 1955 to act as head of the Fund's missions to the meetings of the GATT, but since then the Fund has been represented at international meetings by members of the staff, or, on occasion, by the Managing Director or Deputy Managing Director.

From 1948 until well into the 1950's, the composition of each staff mission was subject to Board approval, and the Board outlined detailed instructions for them. Sometimes the Board would pass a general decision outlining the Fund's official position; at other times Board meetings were held so that, prior to the staff's departure, Directors could indicate their points of view on a particular topic. Several instances of this process can be noted in the forthcoming chapters.

There was also a tendency for member governments, before submitting a formal proposal or request to the Fund, to ask their Executive Directors to discuss it with other Directors first. Quite frequently the Executive Director for the member concerned went to the Director of the United States—the country with the largest quota. If the U.S. Director concurred with the proposal or request, the member would then continue with the formal procedures of the Fund. It was in this sense that some observers commented that the United States "dominated" the Fund. By 1952 this practice had begun to wane and by 1956 it had virtually ended.

What emerged by the late 1950's and early 1960's, and has continued, is a process in which the five instruments of policymaking are closely interwoven, but in which the management and the staff have a large measure of responsibility. There were several reasons for the change. Increasing contacts between individual members of the staff and individual Directors, frequently on a first-name basis, both enabled the staff to convey informally to the Directors suggestions for the improved operation of the Fund and gave Directors greater confidence in the staff. As the staff conducted missions and technical assistance to member countries, it had to make on-the-spot decisions, subject only later to Board review and confirmation. As missions became more frequent, and a regular part of the Fund's procedures, members themselves were inclined to place more confidence in the staff. In addition, members became less concerned that the presence of a staff mission would be interpreted by the press or outsiders as a sign of pending exchange devaluation: the extreme secrecy which had attended missions could be dispensed with. Henceforth, representatives of member governments and the Fund staff could have more open contacts and exploratory discussions that did not commit the Board.

The public speeches commenting on countries' domestic policies made by Mr. Jacobsson during his tenure gave separate and important identity to the Managing Director. Furthermore, as the membership grew, the Board grew, and the new Directors did not have the accumulated experience of their predecessors. Meanwhile, the staff was gaining experience, especially as senior staff stayed on in the service of the Fund. As the same staff representatives returned time and again to member countries, the staff developed insight into the problems of members and an intimate acquaintance with their officials; indeed, several members of the staff, in the course of providing technical assistance to the member, have resided for long periods in a country.

Now as the Fund's policies are gradually worked out, an almost continuous interchange of ideas, both formally and informally, takes place between the members, the Governors, the Executive Directors, the Managing Director, and the staff. The nature of this interchange is somewhat different for policies pertaining to individual member countries and for general policies.

POLICIES FOR INDIVIDUAL MEMBERS

Day-to-day work

In the day-to-day operations of the Fund, the procedure is almost the inverse of the formal line of authority described above. Preparatory work is done by the staff, whose appraisal and recommendations are approved by the Managing Director; and the agreed staff position is then reviewed and decided upon by the Executive Directors. Only after decision by the Board do proposals become official Fund policy. Later action is taken by the Governors, if required, and then, if need be, by the members. As noted above, the Governors must approve quota changes and applications for membership. They have also passed several resolutions requesting the staff and the Executive Board to look into broad general policy questions facing the Fund. Action at the member level is also necessary for certain procedural changes, as, for example, the ratification of amendments to the Articles by the legislatures of member governments.

The primary responsibilities of the staff are to keep abreast of developments in member countries, especially of those financial and monetary developments directly pertinent to the Fund's interests; to carry out the Fund's policies vis-à-vis members; and to handle negotiations with members. The staff examines a regular inflow of documentary and statistical material from member countries. But in addition, both junior and senior staff make frequent visits to the member countries to gather data, to confer with technicians, to evaluate economic trends, and to conduct discussions with the authorities concerning the member's monetary and financial policies, as part of the policy of annual consultation with members. (The evolution of these consultations and the way in which they are conducted forms the subject of Chapter 11.)

As a result, the staff is often engaged not only in becoming familiar with members' economies, but in assisting them to work out monetary and financial policies. For example, if a member is trying to stabilize its economy, the staff may help the government team to formulate monetary and credit measures, or budget and tax policies, or both. If the country wishes to relax restrictions on international payments or to move to an alternative exchange rate, the staff may help to analyze the impact of these actions and to judge the need and nature of supporting measures. Not infrequently, high-ranking officials of member countries, at an early stage in their deliberations on new monetary and financial policies, explore informally the likely reactions of the Fund management and staff.

Most of the work with the countries is carried on by the area departments. But functional departments also perform specialized day-to-day work that helps to shape the Fund's policies vis-à-vis individual countries. The Exchange and Trade Relations Department, for example, analyzes developments in members' restrictive systems. The Fiscal Affairs Department concerns itself with tax and budgetary problems. The Research and Statistics Department has, among its other duties, the making of calculations and projections for the operation of the compensatory financing facility, and the important job of collecting from members the basic financial, monetary, and balance of payments statistics essential for assessing the nature and magnitude of a member's problems. The Treasurer's Department undertakes the Fund's financial operations, including drawings, repurchases, and charges, and is responsible also for quotas and calculations of monetary reserves. The Legal Department ensures that the Fund and its members are fulfilling their obligations under the Articles of Agreement. The Central Banking Service provides advice and technical assistance on the setting up and operating of central banks, especially in less developed countries. The Joint Library, to provide the basic source materials needed by both the Fund and the Bank, is continuously adding to its collection of documents, reports, books, and periodicals in more than thirty languages. Indeed, there is virtually no staff member whose work is not in some way or another pertinent to the Fund's dealings with its member countries.

Generally, an attempt is made to avoid having a staff member negotiate with his own country. The availability of staff from the functional departments makes this task easier, while at the same time giving the member countries the benefit of the specialized experience of the staff of functional departments and keeping this staff informed on the current problems of members.

In carrying on these functions, the staff has close discussions, which take place before field missions as well as immediately thereafter, with the Managing Director and his Deputy. Senior staff officials from various departments are also frequently involved in these discussions, as part of many informal interdepartmental meetings between staff and management.

Staff recommendations

Upon return from a mission, the staff team reports directly, within forty-eight hours, to the Managing Director and the Deputy Managing Director. Should any issues need to be resolved, meetings of the staff team and senior staff officers are called by the Managing Director. The staff team then prepares a detailed report of its activities and discussions with the member, and drafts recommendations for action by the Fund. This report is considered by an informal interdepartmental committee, which includes at least some of the members of the mission. In any case, the reviewing committee includes members of the relevant area department, the Exchange and Trade Relations Department, and the Legal Department.

In formulating an agreed position, the staff is guided by previous decisions taken by the Executive Directors. As time has gone on, and general guidelines have emerged delimiting what the Board will or will not approve, the staff has been able to work informally with member countries in drafting programs and requests that are likely to be acceptable to the Board. As a result, for example, no request for a drawing which reached the Board for several years before 1965 was rejected, although a considerable number of requests which members would have liked to make were not made because the staff advised them that the attendant circumstances were not in line with the Fund's policy.

The Managing Director, in his continuous contacts with the Executive Directors, may well have explored informally with the Director of the country concerned his reactions to the staff's appraisal and recommendations. In some instances, the Executive Director may even have attended, as an observer, the discussions in the member country between the staff and the member's representatives.

Board decisions

Once a staff report has been written and approved and an agreed staff and management position has been formulated, the subject is ready for the agenda of the Board of Executive Directors. Although any Director may propose items for the agenda, usually it is determined by the Managing Director after informal consultation with individual Directors.

The meetings on the topics on the agenda are formal ones, of which detailed minutes are kept. In discussions concerning a particular country, the Director appointed or elected by that country customarily speaks first, presenting his (or the government's) views of the staff's evaluation and recommendations and any additional explanations and comments he wishes. Comments by virtually all of the Directors on most topics are common. The positions taken by an appointed Director naturally reflect closely those of his government. He keeps his government more or less continuously informed about the Fund's deliberations and receives appropriate instructions, although he may also have participated within his government in the formulation of those instructions. An elected Director, too, does his best to accommodate the views and suggestions of all his constituents, including the one which nominated him. In fact, placing an important item on the agenda may be delayed for a while if a Director does not receive instructions from his home country. Usually, too, the Managing Director attempts to iron out important controversies between Directors prior to placing an item on the agenda.[5]

Although in the first few years of the Board's deliberations, many Directors were concerned primarily with safeguarding the legal rights of their members against the Fund's overstepping its bounds, or with preventing the Fund from jeopardizing the vested financial interests of members, an international viewpoint quite rapidly evolved. Directors soon began to express points of view that took into account the interests of all members or of the Fund as a whole. The changes in the process of policymaking just described were also part of the process by which the Fund became more truly international, with members gradually submerging many of their conflicting national interests.[6] Frequently Directors speak as technical experts on a particular problem on which they have expertise.

Staff members concerned with a particular country or a general topic are present at Board meetings. Senior staff members explain and defend the staff position, and answer specific questions raised by the Directors. Even if a Director disagrees with a staff appraisal or recommendation, he usually values an independent staff position. Directors often make minor changes in the wording of draft stand-by arrangements or draft conclusions to consultations. Discussion of items in which there is little interest or controversy may last for only a few minutes; discussions of other items may go on for two or three hours—the usual length of a meeting—or even be extended to two or three sessions.

---

[5] Further details on the functioning of the Executive Board can be found in articles by two former members of the Fund staff: Allan G. B. Fisher, "The Political Framework of an International Institution," *The Manchester School*, Vol. XXX (May 1962), pp. 121–51; and Ervin P. Hexner, "The Executive Board of the International Monetary Fund: A Decision-Making Instrument," *International Organization*, Vol. XVIII (1964), pp. 74–96.

[6] See below, pp. 31–33.

Final decisions of the Board are drafted with great care. Terms which might adversely affect the prestige or domestic affairs of a member are avoided. Recommendations for action are couched in phrases which carefully reflect the limits of the Fund's authority. Efforts are made to incorporate the points of view of as many Directors as possible, consistent with a meaningful decision. Once a decision is taken by the Board, it becomes the decision of the Board as a whole. No publicity is given to the dissenting view of individual Directors.

Decisions on individual countries are communicated to the members by the Managing Director. Some, such as recommendations concerning changes in quotas or membership resolutions, require action by the Board of Governors. The precise language submitted to the Governors for consideration is drafted by the staff and approved by the Board of Executive Directors before being taken to the Governors. The relations between the Governors and Executive Directors make it unlikely that the Governors will vote differently from the Directors; only rarely, and not since 1951, have Governors even made statements critical of Directors.

To complete the policymaking circle, after decisions have been taken by the Executive Board or resolutions have been adopted by the Board of Governors, the staff has the responsibility for carrying out these instructions in its day-to-day work with the member countries.

There are several advantages to these procedures. First, efficient use is made of the staff. A field mission is competent to deal with a wide range of topics and is treated by the member country as a negotiating team. Also, a minimum amount of time is involved in eliciting and reconciling the views of the staff, so that an agreed staff position can be formulated. Thus, the Fund's operations with over a hundred member countries have been handled by a relatively small staff. Second, Fund actions, such as drawings or exchange rate changes, can be taken quickly. Close acquaintance with the problems of members means that staff position papers can be prepared at short notice. The fact that the Executive Board is in continuous session, meeting as the occasion requires; the periodic review by the Board of member countries' economic situations; and the rapid preparation by the staff of papers to be considered, together make possible the taking of decisions by the Fund very promptly.

GENERAL POLICIES

In the formation of the general policies of the Fund on such subjects as restrictions, exchange rates, changes in quotas, and use of resources, the procedures differ somewhat from those followed in respect of individual countries. An issue may arise in the course of Executive Board discussions, which is then pursued by an ad hoc committee of officials from the departments immediately concerned. Or an issue may arise during the course of a discussion by senior staff of some other problem. The small group of senior officials which first explores a general problem usually consists of the Managing Director, the Deputy Managing Director, the General Counsel (the head of the Legal Department), the Economic Counsellor (the head of the Research Department), and, depending on the issue at hand, possibly the Directors of the Exchange and Trade Relations Department, the Fiscal Affairs Department, the Treasurer's Department, and some of the area departments. Then if, after discussion, the group decides that further study is desirable, the topic is assigned to one of the departments, usually a functional department, or an interdepartmental working group. There is then intensive study by the staff, and general analytical papers are circulated to the Board, for information only. The possibilities of compensatory financing through the Fund were, for example, exhaustively investigated by the staff for two years prior to the Board's decision.

The Executive Directors frequently hold preliminary meetings to explore a general issue and possible alternative policies. The technique of informal sessions of the Board was introduced in January 1950, when the Board adopted a proposal by Mr. Southard (United States) that it meet from time to time to discuss multiple currency policy. The purpose of informal sessions is to allow Directors to express their views without necessarily committing the countries which they represent. Minutes are not circulated, though an unofficial record is kept in the Secretary's Office for reference. The discussions are purely between the management, the Directors, and the senior staff. The Managing Director, meanwhile, may be exploring with various Governors their reactions and views, including discussions in meetings of the Group of Ten (see below). Only after a considerable sorting out of ideas and views has taken place, and virtual agreement by the Governors has been assured, are proposals considered formally by the Board of Executive Directors.

Here, again, the process of formulating general policy differs significantly from the process in the Fund's early days. In 1947, for example, examination of the major policy problem facing the Fund—what action to take concerning multiple exchange rates—had been undertaken by an Ad Hoc Committee of Executive Directors, and it had been that committee which made policy proposals to the Board.

THE GROUP OF TEN

What has come to be known as the Group of Ten is not part of the structure of the Fund; however, because of the close relations involved, a few words about the nature of this group are appropriate. In October 1962 the General Arrangements to Borrow came into effect. Under these Arrangements, ten major industrial countries—Belgium, Canada, France, Germany, Italy, Japan, the Netherlands, Sweden, the United Kingdom, and the United States—agreed to stand ready to lend their currencies to the Fund up to specified amounts when the Fund and these countries considered that supplementary resources were needed by the Fund to forestall or cope with an impairment of the international monetary system. The total of the supplementary resources made available was equivalent to $6 billion. On October 15, 1965, the Executive Directors approved a four-year renewal of these Arrangements for the period October 1966–October 1970.

The Ministers of Finance and Governors of central banks of the ten countries concerned have met on several occasions to discuss major international monetary and financial problems of mutual interest. The Managing Director has been invited to attend these meetings. Deputies of the Group of Ten meet at the official level; senior staff members of the Fund participate in these meetings. In addition, shortly after the end of the period covered by this volume, in 1966–67, four joint meetings were held between the Executive Directors and the Deputies of the Group of Ten.

CHAPTER

2

Objectives

Margaret G. de Vries

WHEN THE FUND was established, the founders had six purposes in mind. These were, as stated in Article I of the Fund Agreement:

(i) To promote international monetary cooperation through a permanent institution which provides the machinery for consultation and collaboration on international monetary problems.

(ii) To facilitate the expansion and balanced growth of international trade, and to contribute thereby to the promotion and maintenance of high levels of employment and real income and to the development of the productive resources of all members as primary objectives of economic policy.

(iii) To promote exchange stability, to maintain orderly exchange arrangements among members, and to avoid competitive exchange depreciation.

(iv) To assist in the establishment of a multilateral system of payments in respect of current transactions between members and in the elimination of foreign exchange restrictions which hamper the growth of world trade.

(v) To give confidence to members by making the Fund's resources available to them under adequate safeguards, thus providing them with the opportunity to correct maladjustments in their balance of payments without resorting to measures destructive of national or international prosperity.

(vi) In accordance with the above, to shorten the duration and lessen the degree of disequilibrium in the international balances of payments of members.

INTERDEPENDENT OBJECTIVES

The intention was that countries which joined the Fund would conform to certain standards of behavior in international financial matters. An elaborate and detailed code of what was considered good conduct was drawn up; it called for exchange stability, orderly exchange arrangements, the avoidance of competitive exchange depreciation, and a liberal regime of international payments—that is, convertibility of currencies and freedom from exchange restrictions.

Adherence to this code of conduct was not an end in itself. The specific goals of exchange rate stability, freedom from exchange restrictions, and convertibility of currencies were rather viewed as essential for the achievement of full employment and the maximum development of productive resources—objectives which were regarded by practically all countries at the close of World War II as primary.

The logic was that good conduct in international financial relations would foster a high level of international trade and investment. More specifically, the Fund's purposes implied that fixed exchange rates, freedom from exchange restrictions, and multilateral trade and payments were the best basis for international financial cooperation and for promoting world trade and investment. Expanding world trade and investment were, in turn, regarded as essential for the attainment of the even broader objectives of full employment and economic development in all member countries.

In the past, national economic policies had frequently led to restrictive measures in the international field, and thereupon to international economic conflict. The purpose of the new cooperation to be achieved through the Fund was to reconcile domestic and international objectives.

It was recognized that such reconciliation could not be assumed. In the forefront of economists' attention at the time were the questions whether full employment and balance of payments equilibrium could be attained simultaneously and, if so, what policies in the international field were compatible with the maintenance of full employment at home.[1] There were those who argued that, under certain assumptions, multilateral trade and payments might not maximize world trade.[2] The issue of the consistency of economic development—especially in what were only later to be called "the less developed countries"—with the international objectives of exchange stability and free trade and payments was still in the wings, rather than on stage, in economists' thinking.[3] While these questions were being debated, those who were proceeding with setting up and operating the International Monetary Fund took the view that these goals were not only compatible but even mutually reinforcing.

However, the architects of the Fund were fully aware that a permanent institution would be needed if the specified aims were to be accomplished. International

---

[1] These questions were discussed, for example, at the 59th annual meeting of the American Economic Association in January 1947; see "Papers and Proceedings," *American Economic Review*, Vol. XXXVII, No. 2 (May 1947), pp. 560–94. And they formed the subject of James Meade's *The Theory of International Economic Policy*; Vol. I, *The Balance of Payments*.

[2] Ragnar Frisch, "On the Need for Forecasting a Multilateral Balance of Payments," *American Economic Review*, Vol. XXXVII, No. 4 (September 1947), pp. 535–51.

[3] The second volume of James Meade's *The Theory of International Economic Policy*, entitled *Trade and Welfare*, was, however, devoted to the related question of how direct trade and payments controls can increase welfare.

cooperation was now to replace the exclusive authority of governments in fields in which decisions had previously been taken solely in the national interest. Resolving the conflicts that would arise and making the necessary day-to-day decisions would inevitably require continuous consultation and collaboration among the member countries. The Fund was thus intended as part of the permanent machinery of international monetary cooperation to be set up after World War II, rather than as an emergency agency to meet the temporary needs associated with the aftermath of war.

But it was also realized that the Fund would need to do more than enforce a code of conduct. The harmful financial practices which had characterized international relations prior to the Fund's establishment had been adopted because countries were short of foreign exchange. The Fund was, therefore, provided with large resources which it could make available to its members. Consequently, while countries joining the Fund agree to strict rules for the conduct of their international financial relations, they become members of an institution that possesses a large reserve of gold and foreign currencies with which it can assist any member that gets into payments difficulties.

The Fund can thus be thought of as having two types of function. What are sometimes called its regulatory functions consist of determining and enforcing the code of behavior in international financial and monetary matters. Its financial functions consist of making available to its members the resources to which it has access.

Other agencies of international cooperation were to supplement the Fund's functions. The International Bank for Reconstruction and Development was established to assist countries in obtaining funds for long-term investment. The International Trade Organization was planned—but never came into being—to reduce barriers to international trade, such as tariffs and trade quotas, and to set standards of behavior in the international trade field analogous to those established by the Fund in international financial matters.

We now turn to a brief description of the code of conduct administered by the Fund and of its financial assistance, as envisaged in the Articles.

Exchange rate stability

The first part of the code of conduct consists of rules about exchange rates. Article IV provides for fixed exchange rates. Members agree to decide through the Fund on a system of exchange rates—that is, par values—for their currencies, and not to change these rates without consulting the Fund. Related obligations concern the price of gold.

Exchange rate stability is not, however, tantamount to rigidity. On the contrary, the exchange rate is to be adjusted when necessary to correct a fundamental disequilibrium in the member's balance of payments. But it is implicit in the Articles that exchange rates should be adjusted at only infrequent intervals: fundamental disequilibrium (although it has never been formally defined) is distinguished from merely ephemeral balance of payments disequilibria, such as those associated with seasonal, speculative, or possibly even short cyclical, disturbances.

The initiative for changing an exchange rate is reserved to the member concerned: the Fund cannot propose it. With minor exceptions, however, the member must seek the Fund's approval for the proposed change, and the Fund concurs if it is satisfied that the change is necessary and sufficient to correct a fundamental disequilibrium. If a member changes the par value of its currency despite the Fund's objection, the Fund may declare the member ineligible to use its resources and, subsequently, may even require the member to withdraw from membership.

The principal intention is to empower the Fund to prevent undue fluctuation or undue depreciation of exchange rates, or both. It is one of the explicit purposes of the Fund to outlaw competitive exchange depreciation—that is, depreciation in excess of that required to remove a fundamental disequilibrium.

Currency convertibility and freedom from exchange restrictions

The second part of the code of conduct consists of rules about exchange restrictions and similar practices, and requires members to establish and maintain a multilateral system of payments. It is envisaged that each member, after a transitional period of varying duration, will accept certain obligations set out in Article VIII. This Article provides that no member may, without the approval of the Fund, impose restrictions on the making of payments or transfers for current international transactions, or engage in discriminatory currency arrangements or multiple currency practices. Article VIII further provides for the convertibility of currencies—namely, for arrangements by which any trader exporting from one member country to another can secure effective payment in his own currency, and by which a member is free to use a payments surplus with any other member to pay for its deficit with a third country.

The aim of the Articles is that exchange restrictions shall be minimized—indeed eliminated—in the conviction that they are harmful to the growth of world trade and result in distortions in the domestic economies of members which discourage maximum economic growth and rising standards of living.

However, it was recognized at Bretton Woods that conditions after World War II would probably be such as to make it impossible, for some time to come, for many countries to accept in full the obligations pertaining to abolition of restrictions and establishment of convertibility. A transitional period, during which members might maintain and adapt their exchange restrictions, was therefore provided by Article XIV. But even members taking advantage of this

Article were to do their best to remove restrictions as soon as possible. After five years they were to consult with the Fund annually regarding any remaining restrictions, and the Fund was given authority to apply pressure on them to withdraw such restrictions.

Financial assistance

The Fund's financial assistance to a member takes the form of an exchange of currencies. When a member wishes to draw on the Fund's resources, it purchases from the Fund some foreign currency that it can use and pays in a corresponding amount of its own currency, which the Fund then holds. Conversely, when a member pays back the drawing, it repurchases its own currency from the Fund with gold or some currency acceptable to the Fund. Such transactions are analogous to borrowing and repaying.

These transactions affect the Fund's holdings not only of the currency of the drawing or repurchasing member, but of the currencies of other members as well. While a drawing, for instance, increases the Fund's holdings of the currency of the member making the drawing, it reduces the holdings of the currency drawn. The Articles provide that the Fund shall be a revolving fund; that is, whatever the Fund pays out to its member countries is sooner or later to be returned to it. The drafters at Bretton Woods planned that in ideal conditions the Fund would hold 75 per cent of each member's quota in that member's currency.

The purpose for which the Fund's resources are to be made available is stated in Article I (v) to be that of providing members "with the opportunity to correct maladjustments in their balance of payments without resorting to measures destructive of national or international prosperity." This purpose implies *temporary* use of the Fund's resources.

The provisions for repurchase and for charges on drawings also indicate the temporary nature of the Fund's assistance. The idea on which the repurchase provisions in the Agreement are based is that an increase in a member's monetary reserves indicates an improvement in its balance of payments position. Any member that has drawn from the Fund an amount equal to more than half of its balance of payments deficit in any one year has to pay back the excess; thereafter, half of any payments surplus, or rise in reserves, has to be paid to the Fund in the form of a repurchase of the member's currency, although such repurchases are not required of a member whose reserves have fallen sharply or are less than its quota. Charges on drawings increase not only with the amount of the drawing outstanding relative to quota, but also with the time for which the drawing has been outstanding.

The concept of the Fund's assistance is that the Fund's resources form a secondary source of reserves for a member with a temporary balance of payments deficit; the member's own reserves constitute its first line of defense. Use of the Fund's resources makes it unnecessary for a member, in the absence of adequate reserves of its own, to resort to other means for coping with a temporary payments deficit. The solutions especially to be avoided for short-term deficits are exchange rate devaluation—reserved by the Fund's Articles for balance of payments deficits of a *fundamental* character—and exchange restrictions which curb the flow of trade and payments.

WORKING TOWARD THE OBJECTIVES

So much for the Fund's objectives as intended by its Articles. In working toward these goals the Fund has encountered many problems and a series of ever-changing circumstances in the world economy. Questions have continually arisen as to how the Fund should go about implementing its code of conduct. Examples during the years 1945 to 1965 were: What should the Fund do about members that did not believe that they could establish par values? What initiative could, and should, the Fund take if members did not of their own accord adjust their par values? What attitude should the Fund take toward countries that maintained multiple exchange rates rather than a single one? Since the convertibility of European currencies did not appear feasible for many years, what other exchange restrictions could be removed? The Fund also had to decide whether to permit the use of its resources in the absence of ready compliance with its code of conduct. Should drawings from the Fund, for example, be automatic, on the strength of a member's representation that the currency was needed for payments consistent with the Fund's Articles? Or could the Fund reject a request or impose conditions on drawings? If so, what should the conditions be?

The policies formulated to answer the foregoing and many similar questions form the subjects of the subsequent chapters of this volume. The evolution from 1945 to 1965 of the Fund's policies on exchange rates is traced in Chapters 3–7; Chapters 8 and 9 describe the related policies for transactions in gold. The policies adopted as regards exchange restrictions are surveyed in Chapters 10–14. Separate accounts of the Fund's relations with the European Payments Union (EPU) and with the CONTRACTING PARTIES to the General Agreement on Tariffs and Trade (GATT) are given in Chapters 15 and 16 respectively. Chapters 17–19 explain how the size and composition of the Fund's resources have changed over the years, and how access to the Fund's resources has gradually been implemented by the enunciation of various drawing policies and by the introduction of stand-by arrangements. Chapters 20 and 21 discuss the relation between stand-by arrangements and stabilization programs; these programs emerged as part of the Fund's objective of internal financial stability for its member countries, immediately discussed below. Finally, Chapters 22–27 study the constitutional development of the Fund from 1945 to 1968.

THE OBJECTIVE OF INTERNAL FINANCIAL STABILITY

As the Fund began to evolve precise principles and detailed procedures, it soon became apparent that one facet of economic policy which had not been an explicit feature of the Articles was a prerequisite for the implementation of the Fund's objectives, namely, the maintenance of internal financial stability. Domestic financial policy had not been made a matter of international obligation. On the contrary, care had been taken to ensure that the obligations laid upon countries with respect to international transactions should not impede the use of internal monetary and financial policies to achieve national goals.

Shortly after the Fund commenced operations, it was evident that the problem of inflation was creating serious economic difficulties. Though the fundamental forces of inflation had had their origins in World War II, their effects became more apparent after the war. The public, long deprived of the goods to which it had been accustomed, had expectations far beyond the capacity of the war-depleted economies; and large-scale investments to restore and increase productive capacity further limited the supply of consumer goods. Government expenditure was expanded on an unprecedented scale, and in many countries the extension of credit to finance investment was excessive.

It soon became clear, and the Fund began to emphasize, that achievement of the international goals of free exchange and exchange stability would be frustrated unless government and monetary authorities took appropriate measures to prevent inflation.[4] The next step was that the Fund, while recognizing that there was no single program of fiscal, credit, and monetary measures which could be applied to every country, began to enunciate general principles for the attainment of internal monetary stability.[5] These principles related to a wide range of fiscal and financial policies, involving inter alia the level of government expenditure, the rate of domestic taxation, the measures to promote domestic savings, and the rate and nature of bank credit expansion.

Because the Fund had no authority or jurisdiction over these matters, it had to proceed with caution. The Fund cannot impose any particular domestic policies upon its members. It can, of course, refuse to provide financial assistance to a member whose policies are conducive to acute and persistent balance of payments difficulties. But the Fund has preferred a more positive role.

In the circumstances, much of the work of the Fund in its formative years consisted of securing a wider recognition of the close relationship between the domestic financial policies of a member and that member's balance of payments. In later years, as inflation continued to prevail in many countries, the Fund devoted a great deal of attention to studying the internal financial problems of

[4] *Annual Report, 1948*, pp. 19–20.

[5] *Ibid.*, p. 20.

its members, to advocating particular policies to cope with these problems, and to providing technical assistance in the application of such policies.

From time to time fears have been expressed that the Fund was overstepping its jurisdictional bounds. These fears have lessened in recent years, however, and attacks have more frequently been made on the Fund's emphasis on sound monetary management, the term often used for anti-inflationary measures, sometimes derogatorily. Indeed, not a few economists and government officials have continued to contend that moderate amounts of inflation are necessary to achieve full employment or rapid economic development, although this is a view which the Fund's experience makes it difficult to support.

Despite periodic debates among economists, both within and outside the Fund, about the degree of inflation that is compatible with broader economic objectives, and even about the nature and causes of inflation,[6] the working out with members of programs of internal financial stabilization has gradually become one of the main activities of the Fund. These stabilization programs go fairly deeply into internal policies; they include, for example, rather precise undertakings by members with respect to public finance, quantitative limitations on expansion of central bank credit, and minimum reserve requirements for commercial banks.

Linking activities to objectives

Another theme which has emerged as the Fund has developed its policies is that all of the Fund's activities should be aimed toward a common set of objectives. In other words, the Fund's regulatory functions should be unified, and the operation of its financial functions—that is, the use of its resources—should be made conditional on a member's progress toward the Fund's objectives or toward compliance with the Fund's code of conduct.

Article I provides that the resources of the Fund be made available to members "under adequate safeguards." In effect, Fund assistance is to be made available to countries that make efforts to eliminate those aspects of their exchange and monetary policies that are detrimental to their own interests or those of other members. The degree and nature of the conditions that could and should be attached to drawings must, however, be determined. And much of the Fund's history pertaining to its resources is concerned with the determination of the type and degree of conditionality that should govern access to its resources.

The formal linking of the use of its resources with practical programs of action was an important step in the Fund's policy, taken in 1951. But the search for a means of reducing the uncertainty about the conditions of access to its resources continued. Eventually, conditions for some drawings were to become

[6] See, for example, Martin Bronfenbrenner and Franklin D. Holzman, "A Survey of Inflation Theory," in *Surveys of Economic Theory; Vol. I, Money, Interest, and Welfare*, pp. 46–107.

very specific indeed. They have included, for example, reduction or removal of exchange restrictions, simplification of a multiple rate system, and adoption of a detailed program of internal financial stabilization.

By the mid-1960's, support of stabilization programs designed to eliminate inflation and reduce reliance on restrictions had become the most common purpose of Fund assistance. Members using the Fund's resources were thus encouraged to adopt measures consistent with the Fund's basic objectives.

Developing the necessary procedures

As the Fund worked toward its objectives, various procedures which had not been envisaged in the Articles also had to be developed. One procedure that has evolved over the years has been the annual consultations with all members, including those with no exchange restrictions requiring the Fund's approval. Another is the stand-by arrangement.

The Articles provide for annual consultations, after the Fund has been in operation for five years, covering exchange restrictions still maintained by members under Article XIV. Accordingly, consultations under Article XIV commenced with most member countries in 1952. Intense debates took place at that time about the conduct of these consultations and the subjects to which the discussions should be confined. Within a few years, however, these consultations had become the principal vehicle by which the Fund and its members explored a whole range of topics of mutual interest, including exchange rates and par values, multiple currency practices, exchange restrictions, internal financial policies, use of the Fund's resources, and quotas. In 1961 it was agreed that annual consultations would take place with members that had discarded the transitional regime of Article XIV as well as with those which still availed themselves of that regime.

These periodic exchanges of views have become of key importance to the Fund and its members and have proved to be a valuable instrument of international monetary cooperation. Indeed, they have become essential instruments for promoting the purposes of the Fund, paving the way to the use of its resources where appropriate and facilitating adjustments in payments imbalances where these have existed. The consultations have made members' policies more responsive to the aims of the international community, and have equipped the Fund to be more fully appreciative of the problems of its individual members.

The other innovation is the stand-by arrangement. These arrangements are not expressly provided for in the Fund's Articles. They were introduced because of the need for some procedure by which members could be sure of being able to purchase exchange during an agreed period, if they needed to do so. Under a stand-by arrangement a country is assured that, following a review of its policies and position, and subject to such conditions as are included in the arrangement, it can, without further consideration of its position by the Fund, purchase from the Fund the currencies of other members up to an agreed amount during a stated period. Such an arrangement is usually granted for twelve months (or six months if the member's request is purely seasonal), but is renewable. In considering a request for a stand-by arrangement, the Fund applies the same policies as it applies to requests for immediate drawings. The arrangement is usually accompanied by a precise agreement between the Fund and the member specifying the policies the member will pursue and how the drawings conferred by the stand-by arrangement are to be phased over time.

ATTAINMENTS BY 1965

Although at the end of 1965 important problems persisted in the international monetary system, and others were already on the horizon, it was nonetheless evident that considerable progress toward the Fund's initial objectives had been made since 1945. Exchange rates, exchange arrangements, exchange restrictions, and currency convertibility, all afforded many favorable contrasts with those prevailing at the end of World War II.

The starting point

When the Fund opened its doors in May 1946, international economic relations were very much restricted. One of the legacies of World War II had been the imposition of additional problems on the already burdened flow of international commerce. For countries in Europe and for Japan, the war had left difficulties arising from destruction and disruption, the loss of overseas resources, and the rupture of long-established trade connections. Not only did most of these countries have sizable trade and payments deficits, but the whole pattern of world trade was seriously unbalanced. This imbalance reflected the sharp contrast between the capacity of the Western Hemisphere to produce for export and that of other areas, where postwar productive facilities were inadequate to meet the greatly increased demands of their populations for goods and services.

In these circumstances, many countries in Europe, the Middle East, and Asia were compelled to ration available supplies of domestically produced goods and to continue and even to extend their stringent wartime restrictions on imports. Only a handful of members—all in the Western Hemisphere—assumed the obligations of Article VIII of the Fund Agreement.

Moreover, by 1947 the payments problem, which was shortly to become generally known as the "chronic world dollar shortage," had forced many countries to change the character of their restrictions. Where before restrictions had been placed on imports of certain goods, such as nonessential and luxury items, rather than on imports from specific currency areas, during 1947 the restrictions of most countries were altered so as to reduce their deficits in U.S. dollars and save their gold and dollar reserves. In short, restrictions commonly became discriminatory against the dollar area—that is, against imports from the United States, Canada, and parts of Latin America. In addition, the attempt to render convertible all sterling accruing from current transactions, under the terms of the Anglo-American Financial Agreement of 1945, had failed by the summer of 1947. All European currencies were still inconvertible.

Restrictions also prevailed elsewhere. In many Latin American countries the demand for imports—swollen partly because of deferred demand and partly because of postwar inflation—had made necessary an intensification of restrictions, even though foreign exchange receipts were large. In several Eastern European countries exchange restrictions, although severe, were themselves subordinated to even more direct and comprehensive state intervention through state trading and barter arrangements.

As regards exchange rates, although most original members agreed par values with the Fund at the end of 1946, some did not, and others had multiple exchange rate systems which made their par values more or less nominal. Of the 40 countries that were Fund members at the end of 1946, some 13 were using multiple rates. And within a few years several members gave up conducting transactions at exchange rates based on their par values and adopted fluctuating rates of exchange.

Progress by 1965

By the end of 1965, the great majority of the Fund's 103 members were adhering to a regime of parity exchange rates: if they did not have institutionally agreed par values, they at least maintained exchange rates which were fixed or had been stable for several years. The extent and complexity of multiple exchange rate systems had also vastly diminished, and restrictions on current payments in the world as a whole were far fewer in the early 1960's than they had been for some decades.

Convertibility of the currencies of the European countries had been fully maintained since 1961, when 10 European members had given up the transitional arrangements of Article XIV. By the end of 1965, 27 of the Fund's members, from all geographic regions, had assumed the obligations of Article VIII. The introduction and successful maintenance of widespread currency convertibility had also brought about a virtual end to discriminatory exchange restrictions.

Many countries had gone even farther in reducing restrictions on payments than they were obliged to do; although the Articles permitted controls on capital movements, liberalization of restrictions was gradually extended even to these. Moreover, the industrial countries had begun to concentrate on the liberalization of trade as well as of payments. In particular, in 1962–63 efforts were initiated to reduce tariffs which eventually culminated in the "Kennedy Round" of tariff cuts effected through the GATT in 1967.

At the same time as countries had progressed toward following the Fund's code of conduct, there had been a signal expansion of the world economy and of international trade, and although only modest progress had been made in raising the incomes of the developing countries, relatively high levels of employment had been maintained in most countries.

Since the intra-European trade liberalization program of the OEEC and several consultations of the GATT were going forward simultaneously with the activities of the Fund in the field of restrictions, it is difficult, if not impossible, to disentangle the precise role of the Fund in the substantial liberalization of restrictions that occurred. Three contributions of the Fund may, nonetheless, be noted: it repeatedly stressed the dangers of permanent regional blocs; it emphasized the need for freeing trade and payments on a world-wide nondiscriminatory basis; and, by highlighting the importance of countries' domestic financial policies and by making its resources available, it helped to create the conditions essential for the restoration of currency convertibility and the relaxation of restrictions.

The other side of the picture

Admittedly the picture was not entirely unmixed, and the Fund was not without its problems or its critics. Not all countries had been able to abolish their exchange restrictions. By and large the less developed countries, hampered by structural problems, notably the unsatisfactory expansion of their export earnings, had found it difficult to achieve simultaneously the goals of rapid economic growth and internal and external stability. Hence, although by the 1960's the industrial countries were generally able to maintain their external economic relations with few limitations on the acquisition or use of foreign exchange, many less developed countries continued to rely on exchange restrictions, and some still had multiple or fluctuating exchange rates. Many that had reduced their exchange restrictions had turned to other devices, frequently in the trade field, to stem imports, and had introduced export bonuses and subsidies to encourage exports. Possibly worst of all, in some less developed countries restrictions seemed to have lost their temporary character.

The mid-1960's also saw the reintroduction of exchange controls on capital movements by some of the leading industrial countries. After restrictions on capital movements had been lifted in the early years of the decade, transfers of short-term capital had become sizable and frequent. Because such capital movements were often speculative and disequilibrating rather than equilibrating, they presented the financial authorities, especially in industrial countries, with new problems. Sterling, for example, was subjected from time to time to severe strains in the world's exchange markets, at least partly because of rather sharp movements of short-term capital. The unexpected magnitudes of capital flows from the United States were also responsible in part for the emergence and persistence of a sizable deficit in the balance of payments of that country.

These disturbances often necessitated official intervention—sometimes on a large scale—to enable countries to maintain their exchange rates within the margins specified by the Fund. In order to avoid impairing the freedom already allowed to foreign payments, large amounts of reserves were utilized, and there was heavy resort to the Fund.

Devaluations and rumors of devaluation of important European currencies were recurrent. Consequently, the principal industrial countries took special measures to curb capital flows. In 1964, the United States imposed a tax on purchases of foreign stocks and bonds. This tax was extended in February 1965, at which time the United States also introduced a voluntary program to discourage capital exports by banks and other financial institutions. As one of several steps to correct its balance of payments in 1964–65, the United Kingdom made changes in its exchange control regulations affecting capital movements.

As one international monetary crisis after another occurred, and were solved by ad hoc decisions, the Fund's mechanisms began to be criticized as unequipped to deal with the problems at hand. Major reforms, especially in the field of exchange rates, were suggested. Some critics were disappointed that the Fund had not itself come forward with proposals for exchange reform. Others cited as evidence of the deficiencies of the Fund the fact that since 1962 the Ministers of the Group of Ten had considered several key questions of international finance prior to their discussion by the Executive Board of the Fund.[7]

THE GROWTH OF INTERNATIONALISM

Over a considerable part of its field, therefore, the Fund's achievements by 1965 were partial rather than complete. But in one important direction the aim of its founders, as expressed in Article I, had been fulfilled with conspicuous success. By the mid-1960's the Fund had developed a system of international cooperation and consultation in the monetary and financial field which was in sharp contrast to the situation of the interwar period, particularly the 1930's, when countries had pursued their financial policies with little regard for, and little understanding of, the effects of these policies on other countries. Indeed, the way in which countries were working together in the Fund by 1965 was in sharp contrast to that prevailing during the Fund's first decade.

[7] See, for example, Fritz Machlup, *Plans for Reform of the International Monetary System*; Fritz Machlup and Burton G. Malkiel, eds., *International Monetary Arrangements: The Problem of Choice*; and Harry G. Johnson, *The World Economy at the Crossroads*, Chap. 3.

At the outset of the discussions on the organization of the Fund, it was evident that countries had profoundly conflicting views as to how vital and effective a force in international monetary affairs the Fund should be. Sharply conflicting views surfaced as early as the Inaugural Meeting of the Board of Governors at Savannah in March 1946: White argued for a strong, currently informed Board of Executive Directors, which would take the initiative and make decisions, while Keynes envisaged the Board more as an arbiter of disputes, meeting as the occasion required.[8] Conflicts of national interests were, in the next several years, to occasion many debates among Directors. Especially contended were questions about the Fund's jurisdiction and how it should be implemented. The United States, eager to restore normal international relations as quickly as possible, sought to enhance the authority and activities of the Fund, while European countries, faced with reconstruction and major readjustments of their economies and of their trading relations, had much narrower ideas as to what the Fund should or could do.

There was also a sharp division in the Board between those who believed that members had automatic rights to draw on the Fund's resources and others, notably the U.S. Directors. The European countries, with urgent needs for U.S. dollars, clung strongly to conceptions of "automaticity" about the Fund's resources, while the United States, deluged with requests for aid, and with a Congress anxious to keep close watch over disbursements, took the line that access to the Fund's holdings of dollars should be made subject to fairly strict conditions.

This atmosphere resulted in many decisions by the Board which in effect tied the Fund's hands in its initial years: there were to be few transactions, no participation in European payments arrangements, and little action against restrictions. The Fund's attention was given mainly to broken cross rates and multiple currency practices. Moreover, as effective power lay with the Board, there was little that management and staff could do to alter the situation. The morale of the staff, already low, was further depressed by curbs on administrative expenditures necessitated by the Fund's persistent budgetary deficits. Following the suggestion of the Governor for the United Kingdom in 1951 that ways be found for cooperation with the World Bank so as to reduce the Fund's expenditures, there were even fears that some of the Fund's functions might be eliminated or absorbed by the World Bank, which was operating very profitably.

This story, in detail, is clearly traceable in the chronicle related in Volume I, as is the subsequent turnaround after 1952–53 and the growth of the Fund into an effective organization. By the 1960's the Fund was operating with relatively little controversy in all its fields of responsibility: practically all members, including the largest ones, the United States and the United Kingdom, had concluded

---

[8] See above, Vol. I, pp. 130–34.

stand-by arrangements or had made drawings; the Fund's resources had been enlarged; all the major European countries had undertaken the obligations of Article VIII; and all members, including those under Article VIII, were regularly consulting with the Fund concerning a wide range of economic policies. A by-product of the extensive use of the Fund's resources has been that, despite a severalfold increase in the size of the staff, there have been budgetary surpluses in each year since 1955–56.

A number of factors, political as well as economic, contributed to the dramatic change. Many of these are described in Volume I, some of them have been mentioned in the previous chapter, and still more are considered in Part V of this volume. But two elements making for improved relations between the Fund and its members may here be mentioned; they are (1) the development from 1952 onward of policies opening up use of the Fund's resources, and (2) the successful conduct of the annual consultations which commenced in March 1952. Both of these factors gave new and meaningful form and substance to collaboration among members, Executive Directors, the management, and the staff.

PROGRESS AND CHANGE

In the last resort, any attempt to assess the over-all achievements of the Fund necessitates the weighing of intangibles. One would need to discover what the postwar world would have been like without the Fund, or with a Fund that had acted in a different way. Moreover, one must keep in mind that the complex of political considerations that determine relations between governments inevitably affects the operations and policies of specialized international agencies. In addition, there is a reverse flow of effects from international agencies to governments. Finally, the operations and policies of the international agencies are themselves influenced by contacts and discussions between these agencies and between their staffs.

In attempting to strike a balance it is also necessary to take into account that the Fund has shown a capacity to adapt to new situations which may not have been anticipated by its founding fathers. For example, in the 1960's new and wider solutions were being sought for the trade and payments problems of the less developed countries. In 1963 a decision on compensatory financing introduced a new drawing policy, chiefly for the benefit of these countries. Under this decision, members can draw on the Fund's resources to meet payments difficulties arising out of temporary export shortfalls, provided that the shortfall is largely attributable to circumstances beyond the control of the member, and provided that the member is willing to cooperate with the Fund in seeking appropriate solutions for its balance of payments difficulties where such solutions are called for. This second provision is much less strict than the conditions generally stipulated for drawings of a substantial amount—that is, in the technical terminology of the Fund, for drawings beyond the first credit tranche (see Chapter 18). In other words, there was recognition that even countries which had difficulty in meeting the Fund's standards should be able to obtain assistance to meet difficulties arising out of genuinely short-term export fluctuations.

Technical assistance to the less developed countries has also been expanded in many areas within the Fund's competence—the improvement of statistics, taxation, budgeting, central banking operations, banking legislation, exchange reforms, and programs of monetary stabilization—and the Fund has established a special institute for the training of technicians from the less developed countries.

Even more significantly, the Fund has increasingly recognized that, while monetary stability is a prerequisite for sustained economic development, resolute efforts by developing countries to increase productivity and capital formation, and to reallocate productive resources, are equally essential. Moreover, the Fund has taken an active interest in such matters as the level of external indebtedness of primary producing countries and the impact on them of the hard-core trade barriers of the industrial countries, especially on imports of agricultural commodities from the less developed countries. These activities have expanded further since 1965. To help to alleviate the continuing difficulties of the less developed countries, the compensatory financing scheme has been expanded and the Fund has put forward proposals to deal with the instability of prices of primary commodities in world markets.

In the same vein, when, after convertibility had become widespread, it became obvious that capital transfers would be an important feature of the payments scene, the Fund took steps to deal with the problems then presented. First, in 1962 it augmented its resources through the General Arrangements to Borrow (GAB), under which ten main industrial countries agreed to stand ready to lend their currencies to the Fund up to specified amounts when the Fund and the countries considered that supplementary resources were needed to forestall or cope with an impairment of the international monetary system, especially because of sizable short-term capital movements.

Second, during the early 1960's the Fund re-examined the legal and policy aspects of the provisions of its Articles respecting the use of its resources to finance capital movements.[9] The Articles preclude use of the Fund's resources "to meet a large or sustained outflow of capital" (Article VI, Section 1 (*a*)). Immediately after World War II, there had been great apprehension lest the

[9] E.B. Decision No. 1238-(61/43), July 28, 1961; below, Vol. III, p. 245.

resources of the Fund be wasted in financing capital flight from countries whose currencies were overvalued. But as the years passed and circumstances changed, it came to be appreciated that disturbances to the normal flow of capital, provided they are temporary, are eminently suitable for Fund financing. Hence, in 1962 the Fund announced that it should not, on account of its Articles, be precluded from assisting a member because the latter's difficulties are caused or accentuated by an outflow of short-term capital that could not be deemed large or sustained. The Fund let it be known that, if a country facing an outflow of capital turned to the Fund for assistance, the test to be applied by the Fund would be in accordance with its accepted principles, i.e., that appropriate measures were being taken to restore equilibrium in the balance of payments, and that assistance provided by the Fund would be repaid within a maximum period of three to five years.[10]

The possible need for greater Fund resources which evoked the GAB stemmed from a more general concern for international liquidity—that is, the stock of the world's gold and foreign exchange reserves and other assets with which countries can finance payments deficits, such as facilities to draw on the Fund or to borrow from other international institutions, or various arrangements to borrow from foreign central banks or governments. For several years the Fund debated whether these resources were adequate. Searching questions were raised, e.g.: Was international liquidity increasing fast enough to keep pace with the rising levels of world trade, investment, and capital movements? How great was the danger that additional liquidity in the international monetary system would cause countries to pursue excessively inflationary policies? Was the stock of international liquidity so low that countries encountering payments deficits would again have to resort to exchange restrictions?

The gradual recognition of a possible inadequacy of reserves had led to a long process of international discussion and negotiation, both in the Fund and among the ten countries that had signed the GAB. In 1964–65 there had been a wide-ranging exploration of a variety of possible techniques of reserve creation, and, as 1965 came to a close, discussions were proceeding which aimed at finding a basis for agreement among governments on contingency plans for deliberate reserve creation.

The outcome of these discussions was to produce perhaps the greatest evidence that the Fund contained capacity for growth and change—that is, agreement among its members at the Annual Meeting in 1967 on an Outline of a Facility Based on Special Drawing Rights. This system of special drawing rights—which was agreed to by the Board of Governors shortly after the close of the period here reviewed—was sufficiently new and different as to require significant modifications in the Articles of Agreement of the Fund.

---

[10] *Annual Report, 1962*, p. 33.

PART II

Exchange Rates and Gold Markets

CHAPTER

3

The Par Value System: An Overview

Margaret G. de Vries

SINCE THE PAR VALUE SYSTEM was initiated in 1945, there have been several ups and downs—or, more literally, downs and ups—in the extent to which it has been adhered to. In the first decade of the Fund's life—that is until about 1955—several countries found it necessary to deviate from parity exchange rates. Some suspended their parities; others resorted to one or more of the myriad types of multiple exchange rate systems which made meaningless the par values to which they had originally agreed.

In the second decade of the Fund's operations, however, a pronounced trend toward adherence to agreed par values appeared. Par values were agreed by most countries which had not previously had them; fluctuating exchange rates were abolished in favor of agreed parities; and many multiple rates were eliminated. In many countries where par values had not been established, exchange rates of a fixed nature were introduced.

This trend toward par values, or at least toward fixed exchange rates, became especially marked after 1960. By the end of 1965, some 57 of the Fund's 103 members were using their par values for all transactions; another 4 had only minor deviations from the par value system; and 28, although without par values, were using fixed or stable single rates of exchange. In this sense, by the mid-1960's the par value system was for the first time operating in the great majority of countries.

These broad trends are traced in this chapter, following a brief description of the genesis of the par value system and how it was meant to work. Focus on these general trends, however, is merely introductory to the main story of exchange rates in the twenty years reviewed here. Much occurred quietly and behind the scenes, as it were. As the Fund administered the par value system, a variety of policies on different aspects of exchange rates had to be formulated and implemented. Answers had to be provided, for example, to such questions as the circumstances in which par values should be instituted or when they might be delayed; and policies had to be worked out governing the adjustment of par values in instances of fundamental disequilibrium. In the same way, it was essential that policies on multiple rates and on fluctuating rates be developed.

These matters are covered in detail in the next four chapters. Chapter 4 elaborates the policies that the Fund evolved from 1945 to 1965 on the establishment and maintenance of the par value system. Chapter 5 is concerned with policies on exchange rate adjustment—that is, with the alteration of par values or, where no par values exist, with the changing of existing exchange rates—and also contains a statistical picture of the extent to which exchange rates were actually altered between the time the Fund was established and the end of 1965. Chapter 6 traces the policies of the Fund as regards multiple rates, and Chapter 7 as regards fluctuating rates.

GENESIS OF THE PAR VALUE SYSTEM

From very early in World War II, there had been extensive discussion about the nature of the exchange rate system which would be appropriate after the war. What was believed to be needed was some sort of international mechanism by which an individual country's exchange rate could be set and altered under mutually agreed conditions. The interwar years seemed to have demonstrated two primary needs as regards exchange rates. First, exchange rates should be established and changed in the context of an international review, rather than by countries acting alone. Since countries had a vital interest in each other's exchange rates, international cooperation was essential. It was unilateral action that had led to the economic chaos of the 1930's. Second, stable exchange rates were regarded as more likely than fluctuating or frequently changing rates to produce good financial relations between countries and an orderly working of the international monetary system. Following the "beggar-my-neighbor" experiences of the 1930's, exchange rates that were frequently changed were thought to run the risk of creating opportunities for competitive exchange depreciation and of exporting unemployment.

Some influential economists, then as now, believed in the merits of fluctuating exchange rates, at least in certain circumstances. In the forthcoming years much ingenuity was to be devoted to producing schemes for almost automatic fluctuations in exchange rates which, it was hoped, would not involve competitive exchange depreciation. Nonetheless, the par value system was generally accepted as a central core of the new international cooperation.

Procedures are set out in the Articles, first for establishing and then for maintaining an international par value system. The principal Article in this regard is Article IV, of which the contents, partly quoted and partly summarized (in brackets) follow:

SECTION 1. *Expression of par values.*—(*a*) The par value of the currency of each member shall be expressed in terms of gold as a common denominator or in terms of the United States dollar of the weight and fineness in effect on July 1, 1944.

(*b*) [All computations relating to members' currencies necessary for carrying on Fund activities are to be based on par values.]

SEC. 2. [Gold purchases and sales are to be based on par values.]

SEC. 3. *Foreign exchange dealings based on parity.*—The maximum and the minimum rates for exchange transactions between the currencies of members taking place within their territories shall not differ from parity

(i) in the case of spot exchange transactions, by more than one percent; and

(ii) in the case of other exchange transactions, by a margin which exceeds the margin for spot exchange transactions by more than the Fund considers reasonable.

SEC. 4. *Obligations regarding exchange stability.*—(*a*) Each member undertakes to collaborate with the Fund to promote exchange stability, to maintain orderly exchange arrangements with other members, and to avoid competitive exchange alterations.

(*b*) [Provisions for exchange of currencies based on par values.]

SEC. 5. *Changes in par values.*—(*a*) A member shall not propose a change in the par value of its currency except to correct a fundamental disequilibrium.

(*b*) A change in the par value of a member's currency may be made only on the proposal of the member and only after consultation with the Fund.

(*c*) When a change is proposed, the Fund shall first take into account the changes, if any, which have already taken place in the initial par value of the member's currency as determined under Article XX, Section 4. If the proposed change, together with all previous changes, whether increases or decreases,

(i) does not exceed ten percent of the initial par value, the Fund shall raise no objection;

(ii) does not exceed a further ten percent of the initial par value, the Fund may either concur or object, but shall declare its attitude within seventy-two hours if the member so requests;

(iii) is not within (i) or (ii) above, the Fund may either concur or object, but shall be entitled to a longer period in which to declare its attitude.

(*d*) . . .

(*e*) A member may change the par value of its currency without the concurrence of the Fund if the change does not affect the international transactions of members of the Fund.

(*f*) The Fund shall concur in a proposed change which is within the terms of (*c*) (ii) or (*c*) (iii) above if it is satisfied that the change is necessary to correct a fundamental disequilibrium. In particular, provided it is so satisfied, it shall not object to a proposed change because of the domestic social or political policies of the member proposing the change.

> SEC. 6. *Effect of unauthorized changes.*—If a member changes the par value of its currency despite the objection of the Fund, in cases where the Fund is entitled to object, the member shall be ineligible to use the resources of the Fund unless the Fund otherwise determines; and if, after the expiration of a reasonable period, the difference between the member and the Fund continues, the matter shall be subject to the provisions of Article XV, Section 2 (*b*) [that is, the member may be expelled from Fund membership].

In addition, Article XX, Section 4, specifies the procedures for the determination of initial par values. This Article states in part (summarized portions in brackets):

> SEC. 4. *Initial determination of par values.*—(*a*) When the Fund is of the opinion that it will shortly be in a position to begin exchange transactions, it shall so notify the members and shall request each member to communicate within thirty days the par value of its currency based on the rates of exchange prevailing on the sixtieth day before the entry into force of this Agreement. [Enemy-occupied members still in the midst of hostilities were to be given extra time.]
>
> (*b*) [The par value so communicated, except for enemy-occupied countries, is to become the par value unless, within ninety days after the Fund's request for communication of a par value, the member notifies the Fund that it regards that par value as unsatisfactory or the Fund notifies the member that the par value is likely to cause undue use of the Fund's resources. If such notification is given either way, the Fund and the member are to agree on a par value within a period determined by the Fund.]
>
> (*c*) When the par value of a member's currency has been established under (*b*) above, either by the expiration of ninety days without notification, or by agreement after notification, the member shall be eligible to buy from the Fund the currencies of other members to the full extent permitted in this Agreement, provided that the Fund has begun exchange transactions.
>
> (*d*) In the case of a member whose metropolitan territory has been occupied by the enemy, the provisions of (*b*) above shall apply [but, (i) the period of ninety days shall be extended to a date fixed by agreement between the Fund and the member; meanwhile, (ii) the member may have recourse to Fund resources, under conditions and in amounts prescribed by the Fund and, (iii) may, by agreement with the Fund, change its par value].
>
> (*e*) [Provision for an enemy-occupied country to adopt a new monetary unit.]
>
> (*f*) Changes in par values agreed with the Fund under this Section shall not be taken into account in determining whether a proposed change falls within (i), (ii), or (iii) of Article IV, Section 5 (*c*).
>
> (*g*) [Provision for par values for separate currencies of nonmetropolitan territories.]
>
> (*h*) The Fund shall begin exchange transactions at such date as it may determine after members having sixty-five percent of the total of the quotas set forth in Schedule A have become eligible . . . to purchase the currencies of other members [that is, after they have agreed initial par values with the Fund]. . . .

The par value technique can be characterized as one of managed flexibility of exchange rates; it stands between permanently fixed exchange rates, such as would exist under the gold standard, and freely fluctuating rates. In recent years, economists have come to refer to it as the "adjustable peg" system, par values being thought of as pegs that can be changed under specified conditions.

Late in 1946, for reasons made clear in the next chapter, the Fund decided to go ahead with the establishment of initial par values for its 39 members. All but seven of these members set such par values in December 1946. However, several problems already existed in connection with the system established. Most of the exchange rates prevailing were those that had been operative during World War II; some had been in use even earlier. It was, of course, known—and the Fund's studies of individual countries at the time also revealed—that on the basis of price, wage, and cost of living comparisons, the rates for many currencies were out of line with the U.S. dollar and a few other currencies. In addition, it was explicitly recognized that the initial par values for some countries might later be found to be incompatible with the maintenance of full employment in those countries. The possibility was also envisaged that the initial par values agreed might have an unduly contractionist effect, reducing the exports of several countries and adversely affecting the flow of world trade. In this regard the Fund noted that the continuation of price inflation in a number of countries threatened to impair their ability to compete in world trade. Inflationary fiscal and credit policies, warned the Fund, would undermine the parities just established.[1]

Nevertheless, the Fund believed it preferable to make a start with these exchange rates rather than to wait until a better set of initial par values could be agreed. Many parities were thus accepted which the Fund was fully cognizant could not long be held. Some of them were already used in conjunction with other effective rates. For example, among the countries for which par values were accepted, eleven had various forms of multiple exchange rate systems. Ten of these—Bolivia, Chile, Colombia, Costa Rica, Cuba, Ecuador, Honduras, Nicaragua, Paraguay, and Peru—were in Latin America; the eleventh was Iran. Venezuela joined the Fund in December 1946 but did not establish a par value until 1947; it too had multiple rates.

EARLY BREAKS WITH THE SYSTEM

Establishing and maintaining the par value regime just after World War II was not an easy task. The Fund was immediately confronted with three kinds of deviations from the system of agreed par values. First, because of concern with the uncertainties in their economies, a few countries delayed setting initial par values at all. This postponement involved large countries, such as Italy, as well as small ones. Second, because of the inconvertibility of European currencies, broken cross rates—an exchange rate between two currencies in a third

[1] *Annual Report, 1947*, p. 27.

market which differs from that derived from their par values—were to emerge in several markets throughout the world. The third deviation from the par value system occurred almost at once. France, Mexico, Peru, and Canada took measures between 1948 and 1950 which suspended all transactions at their par values. The last three introduced fluctuating rates; France set up a limited free market.

The French proposal, in January 1948, to change its par value was a significant one: France was the first nation under the new international regime to propose a change in its exchange rate. Instead of making the change unilaterally, as it would have done before the days of the Fund, it came to an international organization to ask its opinion and concurrence. Subsequent developments, however, led to disagreement between France and the Fund. In addition to the change in the par value, France proposed a concurrent free market. In the free market were to be sold half the export proceeds and all receipts from investments in U.S. dollars and Portuguese escudos, and these currencies were to be bought in this free market for certain transactions. While the Executive Directors were prepared to concur in a devaluation of the franc to a realistic rate which would be applicable to transactions in all currencies, they objected to the proposed free market for a few currencies.

In July 1948 the Mexican Government informed the Fund that, unless Mexico could obtain substantial financial support, its par value could not be held. When this assistance was not forthcoming, Mexico suspended its par value in favor of a fluctuating rate; this rate lasted until June 1949, when a new par value was established. In November 1949 Peru proposed to abandon its official parity for the sol and to permit the exchange rate to fluctuate freely until it found its natural and stable level. In September 1950 Canada introduced a fluctuating rate.

ATTITUDES TOWARD DEVALUATION IN THE LATE 1940's

Another stumbling block for the Fund and the par value system in these early years was the discovery, shortly after the Fund commenced operations, that members were reluctant to devalue their currencies. At the time of Bretton Woods it had been the fear in some circles that countries would resort to frequent exchange rate changes in the postwar period. Indeed, one of the objectives of the Fund was to be the curbing of excessive devaluation. By 1948, however, it had become apparent that these fears were misplaced. Countries had in fact tended to lean in the opposite direction, maintaining exchange rates which should have been changed. Apart from a devaluation by Italy in 1947, and the devaluations of France, Mexico, and Peru just noted, only Colombia and French Somaliland had altered their par values by mid-1949.[2]

[2] For statements on the devaluations of Italy, Colombia, and French Somaliland, see *Annual Report, 1948*, pp. 63–64, and *1949*, pp. 57, 58.

Many reasons explain the lack of shifts in exchange rates in these initial years. Prior to 1949 there was still considerable concern that supply and production facilities had not yet been sufficiently restored in Western Europe to make relative prices a key factor in world trade. Inability to produce enough exportable goods remained the principal limitation on exports, and devaluation would not reduce imports, which were already held in check by restrictions. Moreover, inflation in European countries, as well as in much of the rest of the world, had not yet been brought under control. Until these countries achieved a reasonable amount of internal stability, any improvement in their balances of payments brought about by devaluation would be quickly dissipated by price rises.

By the latter part of 1948 and early in 1949, production in Western Europe had recovered and a reasonable degree of internal financial stability had been attained. Debate among economists then arose as to the need for an adjustment of European currencies. In a world which seemed to be increasingly characterized by controlled economies and imperfect markets, some economists questioned the relevance of the price mechanism for restoring balance of payments equilibrium. Others believed that the world dollar shortage was due to deep-seated differences in productivity between the United States and Western Europe. These economists argued that, until these differences in productivity were reduced, the devaluation required to achieve equilibrium would cut real incomes and consumption to intolerable levels. There was also a widely held belief that the U.S. demand for imports was inelastic with respect to relative price changes for imports and domestic commodities. Hence it was argued that devaluation by European countries would not increase their dollar earnings sufficiently to make the devaluation successful.[3] Many economists, including some on the Fund staff, focused attention on and debated all these arguments.

Eventually the pound sterling was devalued, on September 17, 1949, from £1 = $4.03 to £1 = $2.80, or by 30.5 per cent, and this set off a series of devaluations literally around the world. Some countries had been waiting for sterling devaluation in order to adjust their own exchange rates. Others recognized that they had no alternative but to follow sterling.

INSTITUTION OF PROCEDURES

One of the consequences of the week of devaluations in September 1949 was an important institutional one for the Fund, for it brought to light the need for quick-acting procedures for handling changes in par values. Many such changes would have to be effected over week-ends, while exchange markets were closed.

---

[3] The various economic and political arguments against devaluation at this time can be found in Raymond F. Mikesell, *Foreign Exchange in the Postwar World*, pp. 136–44.

Speedy consideration and decision by the Fund was crucial. The Fund therefore instituted rush procedures for dealing with cables coming in late on Friday afternoons, for the preparation on Friday night and Saturday morning of reports by the staff, and for their immediate distribution to the Executive Directors. It was established that the Board would meet to consider the request on Sunday or at the latest Monday morning, depending on the circumstances.

The effects of the 1949 exchange devaluations on trade, payments, and prices became the object of special study by the Fund staff.[4] The data were intensively examined as well for the lessons that might be learned for economic analysis,[5] and for the estimation of trade elasticities.[6] Appraisal of the immediate impact of the devaluations on international trade and the world dollar shortage was, however, made difficult by the host of other factors which came into play in 1950. These included recovery of the U.S. economy, a rapid acceleration of imports by the United States, and large increases in world demand and prices for raw materials after the middle of 1950, in connection with the outbreak of hostilities in Korea.

By the mid-1950's many of the debates among economists and government officials concerning the benefits of the 1949 exchange rate devaluations had subsided. It was generally agreed that these devaluations and the subsequent expansion in dollar earnings by the countries of Western Europe had helped to lay the basis for the restoration of convertibility of European currencies which was achieved in 1958. Indeed, the expansion of European exports was so successful that by the mid-1960's the view had emerged in some circles that the 1949 devaluations had been too great.

FURTHER FRACTURES IN THE PAR VALUE REGIME

During the early 1950's more departures from the par value system took place. True enough, the Fund had gained several new members, most of which agreed initial par values: Burma, Ceylon, Germany, Haiti, Japan, Jordan, Pakistan, and Sweden. However, by this time there were several countries—

[4] See, for example, J. J. Polak, "Contribution of the September 1949 Devaluations to the Solution of Europe's Dollar Problem," *Staff Papers*, Vol. II (1951–52), pp. 1–32; and Barend A. de Vries, "Immediate Effects of Devaluation on Prices of Raw Materials," *ibid.*, Vol. I (1950–51), pp. 238–53.

[5] See Sidney S. Alexander, "Devaluation versus Import Restriction as an Instrument for Improving Foreign Trade Balance," *Staff Papers*, Vol. I (1950–51), pp. 379–96.

[6] Barend A. de Vries, "Price Elasticities of Demand for Individual Commodities Imported into the United States," *Staff Papers*, Vol. I (1950–51), pp. 397–419; Sidney S. Alexander, "Effects of Devaluation on a Trade Balance," *ibid.*, Vol. II (1951–52), pp. 263–78; and Ta-Chung Liu, "The Elasticity of U.S. Import Demand," *ibid.*, Vol. III (1953–54), pp. 416–41. For a listing of other statistical studies dealing with trade elasticities, see Hang Sheng Cheng, "Statistical Estimates of Elasticities and Propensities in International Trade," *ibid.*, Vol. VII (1959–60), pp. 107–58.

Canada, Lebanon, Peru, Syria, and Thailand—which, instead of adhering to par values or even to fixed exchange rates, had turned to fluctuating rates. Moreover, there was considerable speculation that other countries—including the United Kingdom—were seriously contemplating the use of fluctuating rates. The advantages and disadvantages of fixed versus fluctuating exchange rates were intensively discussed, not only in academic circles but by highly placed government officials. In part because a few countries already had fluctuating rates, and in part because from time to time there emerged exchange difficulties with other currencies, there was some advocacy not only of fluctuating exchange rates for a particular country, but even of a large number of fluctuating rates.[7]

The Fund continued to defend the par value system, and contended that in the circumstances of the early 1950's it was essential that the cooperative endeavor represented by the Fund be extended and improved, rather than undermined; but it was evident that a universal system of fixed par values was far from being achieved. Problems arising from the world dollar shortage—bilateralism and currency inconvertibility—had led to the temporary use of a variety of practices in Western Europe which deviated from the concept that all transactions should take place at rates based on par values. These practices included separate free markets for tourist receipts or other invisibles or capital transactions, and arrangements to increase dollar export earnings, such as retention quotas, import entitlement schemes, or "transit dollar" arrangements. In addition, multiple exchange rates, which had been introduced in the 1930's in a few Latin American countries to cope with depression-oriented situations, were increasingly being used to cope with the postwar problems of currency inconvertibility, severe inflation, and economic development. As a result, there had been a continued spread of multiple rates.

By the end of 1956—a decade after the initial par values had been established in 1946—the Fund had 60 members. Eleven of these (Afghanistan, Argentina, China, Greece, Indonesia, Israel, Italy, Korea, Thailand, Uruguay, and Viet-Nam) had not yet established initial par values. France, having given up its initial par value in January 1948, had not yet set a new one. Canada continued to rely on a fluctuating rate. Twelve countries (Brazil, Colombia, Costa Rica, Ecuador, Finland, Iceland, Iran, Jordan, Nicaragua, Syria, Venezuela, and Yugoslavia) had multiple rate systems of some significance. Five (Bolivia, Chile, Lebanon, Paraguay, and Peru) that had abolished their multiple rates did so in favor of fluctuating rather than fixed rates. Six others (Cuba, Denmark, Egypt, the Netherlands, Sweden, and Turkey) had various minor multiple currency practices for some current transactions (many more had such practices for capital transactions). This left only 24 members out of 60 conducting all their

[7] A summary of the arguments for and against fluctuating exchange rates, as presented at that time, can be found in Bank for International Settlements, *Twenty-Second Annual Report* (Basle, 1952), pp. 142–49.

current transactions at exchange rates within 1 per cent of their par values. In other words, only these had what can be defined as "fully effective par values," that is, par values agreed with the Fund and all transactions (except certain minor practices affecting only capital transactions) conducted at parity rates.[8] The first decade of the Fund's existence had proved to be a most difficult environment for the attainment of its exchange rate objectives.

ACCELERATED TRENDS TOWARD PAR VALUES, 1957–65

In the next decade the setback to the par value system was to be overcome. In the second half of the 1950's countries began to return to fixed exchange rates and to agree with the Fund on par values for their currencies. Once par values were set, they were effectively maintained for long periods of time. These trends, apparent by 1960, became even stronger thereafter.

A series of events brought about the gradual re-establishment of effective parity exchange rates. First was a progressive elimination of the minor multiple currency practices and retention quotas that had been maintained earlier by Western European countries. By 1958 the Fund was able to report that, for the most part, Western European currencies were traded in official exchange markets at rates fluctuating within official limits, and that in view of the closeness of the free market rates to the official market quotations, the problem of broken cross rates in these currencies was no longer important. Thus the Annual Report for 1958 was able to state that

> most Fund members maintain exchange systems in which for the most part transactions take place within the prescribed margins of their respective par values agreed with the Fund. The currencies of these members include all that are most used as means of payment in international trading and financial transactions.[9]

Second, the major countries which had not previously established par values did so. On March 31, 1960, Italy agreed a par value of 625 lire = $1. In March 1961 Greece declared a par value (30 drachmas = $1). In May 1962 Canada, after nearly twelve years with a fluctuating rate, established a new par value of 1 Canadian dollar = 92.5 U.S. cents.

Third, beginning in 1955–56 a series of exchange reforms led to the elimination of many multiple rate systems in the less developed countries. For some of these countries the setting of new par values took place immediately. For others, experimentation with different rates of exchange was to occur before a new parity was finally selected and established.

Fourth, during 1958–65 initial par values were set for many of the countries then joining the Fund—twenty in all.

---

[8] This definition is used here for statistical purposes only; it does not represent the official definition of the Fund.

[9] *Annual Report, 1958,* p. 20.

By 1965 there had been attained a regime in which the majority of Fund members had par values. By December 31 of that year, 57 of the Fund's 103 members (55 per cent) were carrying out all their transactions at "fully effective par values," [10] viz., the United States and Canada; all 19 European members; Australia, New Zealand, Jamaica, and Trinidad and Tobago; 6 out of 12 members in the Far East; 12 out of 34 in Africa; 6 out of 13 in the Middle East; and 8 out of 19 in Latin America.[11] Nine years earlier, as previously noted, only 24 members out of 60 (40 per cent) had been in such a position, and the proportion had been even lower (36 and 38 per cent) in 1954 and 1955.

Because of the addition over time of many new members, the trend from 1954 to 1965 toward par values may be more clearly seen by use of a constant sample. At the end of 1954, out of a total of 56 member countries, 36 were without "fully effective par values," although 10 of these had only minor deviations from the Fund's standard. Among these 36 members, 21 had, by December 31, 1965, attained "fully effective par values." This included many countries which had previously had systems of multiple rates, fluctuating rates, or long-standing absence of par values: Canada, Costa Rica, Finland, Greece, Iceland, Iran, Israel, Italy, Jordan, Nicaragua, the Philippines, and Yugoslavia.

The trend toward adherence to fixed exchange rates was even more marked than that toward legally instituted par values. By December 1965, more than 86 per cent of Fund members (89 out of 103) had fixed exchange rates or rates which, while nominally fluctuating, had been stable for several years; the comparable figure for the end of 1954 was 59 per cent (33 out of 56 members).

Furthermore, members with "fully effective par values" accounted for by far the bulk of world exports. Even in 1954, the approximately one third of Fund members that continued to adhere fully and formally to the par value regime had accounted for 76 per cent of world (noncommunist) exports; by 1965, the share in world exports of countries with par values had risen to 91 per cent.

CRITICISM AND DEFENSE OF THE SYSTEM IN THE 1960's

By one of the ironies of international economic life, the effective attainment of a par value system and of stable unitary exchange rates coincided with renewed attacks by several economists on the par value regime. Their complaint was that par values were too infrequently altered; "adjustable pegs" were rarely adjusted. As a result, exchange rate changes were no longer an important instrument of balance of payments policy.

---

[10] As defined above, p. 48.

[11] Details concerning the gradual attainment of the par value system can be found in Margaret G. de Vries, "Fund Members' Adherence to the Par Value Regime," *Staff Papers*, Vol. XIII (1966), pp. 504–32.

In the mid-1960's, a number of economists, especially in academic circles but also in some official and semiofficial groups, were once again recommending fluctuating exchange rates for the major currencies of the world. But other specific suggestions for enhancing the flexibility of exchange rates were also forthcoming. A proposal was advanced for widening the range of fluctuations permitted under the par value regime to something like 5–7 per cent either side of the par value rather than the 1 per cent required by the Fund's Articles. The necessary width of the band under this "band proposal" was said to depend on whether the effects of exchange rate changes on trade or capital were stressed; doubling the range of fluctuation from the present 2 per cent to 4 per cent was thought to be possibly sufficient for capital. Several economists favored a "shiftable-parity" or "crawling peg" arrangement: automatic adjustments in par values could be made at intervals which might be annual or, conceivably, even quarterly.[12]

The system of par values was, of course, not without academic defenders. In addition, the official views of the Fund and also of practically all central banks continued to favor—strongly—fixed exchange rates. Accordingly, when the Group of Ten agreed in August 1964 to study proposals for the reform of the international monetary system, changes in the exchange rate system were explicitly ruled out.[13]

Reluctance to tamper with the par value system reflected at least in part the experience of the Fund and its members during the previous twenty years. The greater use by Fund members of fully effective par values, described in this chapter, could be attributed to a variety of factors. Decisive among these, as is made clear in the next chapters, were the unsatisfactory results encountered with alternative exchange rate systems.

But there were other arguments in favor of fixed exchange rates—that they put national monetary authorities under pressure to integrate their policies; that they have to be defended by anti-inflationary measures; that they eliminate the danger of competitive depreciation. In addition to these arguments in favor of fixed exchange rates, the Fund had yet another reason for preferring the par value system: in the Fund's view an alternative exchange rate system would make the process of international collaboration far more difficult.

As the year 1965 drew to a close, the debates over exchange rates were continuing and becoming even more heated.

---

[12] The literature on these proposals is extensive. Summaries of the arguments of academic economists may be found in *International Monetary Arrangements: The Problem of Choice*, Fritz Machlup and Burton G. Malkiel, eds., pp. 94–100; and in William Fellner, "On Limited Exchange-rate Flexibility," in Fellner, Machlup, Triffin, and others, *Maintaining and Restoring Balance in International Payments*, pp. 111-22. An illustration of official argumentation may be found in Federal Republic of Germany, Sachverständigenrat zur Begutachtung der gesamtwirtschaftlichen Entwinklung, *Jahresgutachten*, 1964, par. 240.

[13] *Ministerial Statement of the Group of Ten and Annex Prepared by the Deputies* (Paris, August 1964), Ministerial Statement, par. 2.

CHAPTER

4

Setting Par Values

Margaret G. de Vries

AS THE PAR VALUE SYSTEM has evolved, many questions have confronted the Fund. Since par values are central to the Fund Agreement, one set of questions has concerned their establishment. How quickly should initial par values be agreed? What should be the attitude of the Fund toward delays by members in proposing parities? How much pressure should the Fund put on countries to set parities? What exceptions might be made to the requirement of the Articles that an initial par value must be set before a country may draw on the Fund's resources? What considerations ought to govern appraisal of a proposed parity? Once initial par values are no longer used for any transactions, when should a new effective par value be instituted? Can a country be regarded as having a fully convertible currency—that is, subject to the requirements of Article VIII—if it does not have a par value?

Still other questions have arisen in connection with the adjustment of par values and exchange rates. By what criteria should the need for a change in an exchange rate be determined? Inasmuch as the Articles provide that devaluations shall be proposed only by members, what informal role might the Fund play in suggesting to members the advisability of changes in exchange rates? What constitutes *fundamental disequilibrium* and what *competitive exchange depreciation,* the two concepts of the Articles relating to changes in exchange rates?

The ways in which the Fund has attempted to find answers to these questions make up, in part, the policy of the Fund on exchange rates. A few of the issues involved have been covered by decisions of general applicability taken by the Executive Board. But for most of these issues, no broadly stated policy lines have been formulated. Rather, as is customary in most fields, policy is mainly an accretion of the attitudes and actions taken in particular situations over the years.

This chapter and the next three provide some generalizations of the Fund's policies on par values and exchange rates. These generalizations are based on an examination of the decisions taken by the Board and the views expressed by several Directors in a variety of individual country situations; in a number of instances the reasoning of the staff, reflected in the papers prepared for the discussions in the Board, has also been included. The present chapter covers those policies which have applied to the setting of par values. It describes considerations which have guided the Fund in timing the introduction of par values, the criteria used for approving the parities proposed, and the views of the Fund as to whether a par value must first be agreed if a member is to draw on the Fund's resources.

Several countries, after they had established initial par values, took measures which meant that these par values were no longer applied to any transactions. The Fund, therefore, has also had to consider the extent to which it should urge countries to institute effective par values, and whether countries without effective par values may assume the convertibility status of Article VIII. Moreover, once par values have been established, certain requirements follow for cross rates with third currencies, for the margins within which exchange rates may move around parities, and for rates in forward exchange markets. These matters are also discussed in this chapter. Policies relating to the adjustment of par values and of exchange rates are deferred until Chapter 5.

Tracing the growth of the Fund's exchange rate policies over the years reveals the flexibility and adaptability with which the Fund has administered the par value system. Yet adaptability and flexibility have not meant the absence of basic policies. Some general guidelines can be discerned, demonstrating that the policies have not been merely a series of ad hoc reactions to particular situations. Nonetheless, since generally formulated policies cannot always be applied to the particulars of individual situations, some anomalies and inconsistencies in the application of policy have inevitably occurred.

ESTABLISHING INITIAL PAR VALUES

Immediate parities in early years

In the first years the Board was anxious that members should establish par values as soon as possible. This was manifested when the initial par values for original members were agreed at the end of 1946. Although both the Board and member countries recognized the many uncertainties then attending exchange rate determination, initial par values were quickly set for most original members.

Weighty arguments could have been marshaled against setting initial par values in 1946. Many members had been devastated by the war and had to undergo extensive reconstruction. These countries, and others, were in the grip of serious inflation. Shortages of goods and services were widespread and international trade was badly distorted.

However, the Board wished to go ahead. In the first place, Article XX, Section 4, provided that initial par values for members having at least 65 per cent of the total of quotas must be established before exchange transactions could begin, and that (except for countries that had been occupied by the enemy) a par value must be agreed with the Fund before a member could use the Fund's resources. Moreover, the Board recognized the desire of the drafters of the Articles to put the par value regime into operation at an early stage. It had been foreseen at Bretton Woods that the Fund would have to begin in a period of disorder, but the conferees were convinced that a start toward an improved world exchange rate structure could be made.

On September 12, 1946, therefore, the Fund called upon its 39 members to communicate par values, and on December 18, 1946 the initial par values of 32 countries were announced, viz., Belgium, Bolivia, Canada, Chile, Colombia, Costa Rica, Cuba, Czechoslovakia, Denmark, Ecuador, Egypt, El Salvador, Ethiopia, France, Guatemala, Honduras, Iceland, India, Iran, Iraq, Luxembourg, Mexico, the Netherlands, Nicaragua, Norway, Panama, Paraguay, Peru, the Philippines, the Union of South Africa, the United Kingdom, and the United States.

Initial par values were also agreed with Belgium for the Belgian Congo; with France for Algeria, Cameroun, French Antilles, French Equatorial Africa, French Guiana, French possessions in India, French possessions in Oceania, French Somaliland, French West Africa, Madagascar and dependencies, Morocco, New Caledonia, New Hebrides, Réunion, St. Pierre and Miquelon, Togoland, and Tunisia; with the Netherlands for Curaçao and Surinam; and with the United Kingdom for Bahamas, Barbados, Bermuda, British Guiana, British Honduras, Burma, Ceylon, Cyprus, Falkland Islands, Fiji, Gambia, Gibraltar, Gold Coast, Hong Kong, Jamaica, Kenya, Malaya (Singapore and Malayan Union), Malta, Mauritius, Nigeria, Northern Rhodesia, Nyasaland, Palestine, Sarawak (British North Borneo), Seychelles, Sierra Leone, Southern Rhodesia, Tanganyika, Tonga, Trinidad, Uganda, and Zanzibar.

The determination of par values for six members (Brazil, China, the Dominican Republic, Greece, Poland, and Yugoslavia) was deferred at their request because their domestic monetary situation was not sufficiently stable to warrant the adoption of par values. The Uruguayan submission of a par value was not definite enough to permit its formal acceptance. The determination of initial par values for the French dependent territories in Indo-China and for the Netherlands Indies was also deferred.

Since imports were subject to controls by nearly all countries, the main criterion for judging the rates proposed was their effect on exports. So long as exports continued to flow, it could fairly be assumed that the prevailing exchange rate would help to attain by the end of the transitional period a "tolerable balance of payments."[1] Existing exchange rates did not seem to be impairing the ability of any country to export. Supply shortages were so acute that, despite the current exchange rates and despite the import controls, there was no difficulty in disposing of any exports that a country was in a position to offer. Difficulties of production and transport and other prevalent obstacles to a smooth supply of goods were by far the most serious impediments to an expansion of exports. The Executive Directors were also aware that to encourage a general revision of exchange rates would have been quite unacceptable to member countries. Such a revision "would have gravely dislocated exchange relationships which were already working in practice and enabling trade to be carried on."[2]

For members subsequently joining the Fund, a procedure for the establishment of an initial par value is prescribed which gives the Fund the right to initiate the process. The standard membership resolution provides (paragraph 5) that the Fund is to request the member to communicate, within thirty days of receipt of the Fund's request, a proposed par value for its currency. Within sixty days of receipt of the proposed par value by the Fund, the Fund and the member must agree on an initial par value. In practice, the period of thirty days is not introduced until the member is known to be ready to establish a par value, and the sixty-day period is extended if this is found to be necessary. Should no agreement be reached at the end of the extended period, the member will be deemed to have withdrawn from the Fund.

In the late 1940's and early 1950's, the Fund made persistent efforts to get original members to agree initial par values if they had not already done so. Brazil and the Dominican Republic, having postponed theirs in 1946, set them in 1948; Yugoslavia's par value was agreed in May 1949. Most countries that joined the Fund in these years very quickly agreed initial par values. These included Australia, Lebanon, Syria, Turkey, and Venezuela in 1947, Sweden and Pakistan in 1951, Ceylon in 1952, Burma, Germany, Japan, and Jordan in 1953, and Haiti in 1954. Table 1 at the end of this chapter lists the initial par values agreed with the Fund for each year from 1946 through 1965.

Delayed parities

There were, of course, some instances of initial parities being delayed. Two illustrations of relatively short delays are provided by Finland and Austria. Both joined the Fund in 1948 but Finland did not set its first parity until 1951 and Austria not until 1953. Finland agreed as an initial par value the exchange rate which had been in effect since the devaluations of September 1949. The establishment of Austria's parity, however, was dependent on further drastic devaluation. The rate adopted for the schilling after the war was S 10 = $1. In Novem-

[1] Camille Gutt, *The Practical Problem of Exchange Rates*, p. 4.

[2] *Annual Report, 1947*, p. 27.

ber 1949 Austria introduced multiple rates; these were replaced by a single rate in May 1953, at which time an initial par value of S 26 = $1 was established.

As to long delays in establishing initial parities, Italy is a case in point, and also serves to illustrate the caution exercised both by members in communicating par values and by the Fund in not applying strong pressure to do so. Italy joined the Fund in March 1947. The Membership Resolution, drafted soon after the Fund came into being, contained terms similar to those in the Articles of Agreement. In effect, Italy was declared a country whose metropolitan territory had been occupied by the enemy.[3] It was specifically granted the privileges of Article XX, Section 4 (*d*) (ii), which provided that an enemy-occupied country could, with the permission of the Executive Board, draw on the Fund's resources prior to establishing an initial par value.

On April 24, 1947, in accordance with its usual procedure, the Board requested the Government of Italy to communicate within thirty days a par value for the lira based on the exchange rate prevailing on March 27, 1947, the date on which Italy joined the Fund. The Italian economy was then encountering several difficulties. Prices were rising rapidly, owing to inflation, and the balance of payments was in marked disequilibrium. Production was stagnating and the rate of unemployment was high. Multiple currency practices existed: there was an official rate of Lit 225 = $1 and a free rate of Lit 585–600 = $1. A rate of Lit 410 = $1 seemed to the Italian Government at the time as the only rate which could reasonably be proposed as a par value. But this rate could not be considered definitive. Moreover, the Fund's request was for a rate based on the rate on March 27, 1947, which was presumably already outdated.

Therefore, on May 23, 1947 the Government requested an extension of the usual period of ninety days for agreeing on a par value with the Fund, and on May 28 the Board informed the Government that it had extended the period indefinitely and was prepared to discuss with a representative of the Government a new date for communication of a par value.

During the following three years Italy made great progress in the achievement of economic stability, as a result of the adoption in November 1947 of a comprehensive anti-inflationary program and of financial assistance from the United States. By mid-1950 a reasonable degree of monetary stability had been attained, production had expanded beyond the prewar peak, and the increase in exports had helped to reduce substantially the balance of payments deficit. In 1949 the exchange rate for the lira, only theoretically a fluctuating rate, had been devalued from Lit 575 = $1 to about Lit 625 = $1. This rate applied to all transactions in the official market, there was no currency discrimination, and the rates of various other currencies were pegged to the lira-dollar rate.

[3] Resolution No. 1-6; *Summary Proceedings, 1946*, pp. 49–50.

During the 1950's, consequently, there were frequent contacts between the Italian Government and the Fund to explore the possibility of agreement on a par value. The Board's belief was that the setting, and defense, of a par value would help to consolidate the strength of the lira both internally and externally. On all these occasions the Government showed extreme caution and suggested that continuing uncertainties, such as the process of trade liberalization under the OEEC and the establishment of a new tariff system, counseled delay. Between September 1949 and the establishment of external convertibility for the lira on December 29, 1958, Italy maintained a unitary exchange rate of between Lit 624.60 and Lit 625.10 = $1. The Italian authorities, nonetheless, argued for the need to maintain a rate for the lira which was, at least potentially, a fluctuating one.

In September 1959 the Government asked the Fund to agree to a rate of Lit 625 = $1 for determination of the amount of Italy's currency subscription in connection with the increase in its quota. The Board took the occasion to suggest again that a par value be instituted. A few months later, on March 15, 1960, Italy proposed an initial par value of Lit 625 = $1. Foreign trade had been liberalized. Reserves had increased fivefold since 1950. The national product was growing at an average annual rate of more than 5 per cent. It was difficult, if not impossible, to justify any further delay in setting a par value. The Board agreed with the communicated par value, expressing satisfaction that the rate prevailing for many years had at last become the par value.

The instance of Italy is by no means unique. Greece, Thailand, and Uruguay, among others, joined the Fund early on but set their par values only many years thereafter. Table 2 at the end of this chapter gives the date of membership and the date that the initial par value became effective for all countries that were Fund members in the years 1945–65.

A variety of circumstances help to explain delays in establishing par values: chronic inflation, a multiplicity of rates, the need to experiment with devaluation. The continuous ebb and flow of opinion about fluctuating rates no doubt also contributed, at least in part. Countries that already had fluctuating rates, albeit nominally, were reluctant to give them up. Their hesitation did not stem from the fact that they gained any advantages from their fluctuating rates; in most instances rate fluctuations were smoothed out by official intervention in the exchange market. Rather, the authorities concerned believed that it would be easier to change a rate if it had not been instituted as a par value. This consideration became less important as the Fund established its authority over changes in all exchange rates.

What motivated Fund concurrence in these delays was not any weakened faith in the system of par values. In part the Board concurred because of the realization as time went on that it was preferable to have parities set at realistic and maintainable levels rather than to have them established prematurely. By the late 1940's it had become apparent that par values would not be adjusted frequently; the appropriateness, therefore, of a particular parity was of greater significance than its timing. In part, too, the Fund did not wish to jeopardize the improving Fund-member relations in the exchange rate field. As Chapter 5 indicates, the Fund had managed to bring under its jurisdiction virtually all changes in exchange rates, whether par values or not, and the Fund's views were frequently being sought. In this environment, to attach excessive significance to the formal status of a par value at the expense of workable, even affable, member relations might be foolhardy.

Short-lived parities

Despite the pragmatism of the Fund's policy on the establishment of initial parities, a few par values were set which quickly proved untenable. Because countries changed the multiple rates that coexisted with their par values, their par values were within a short time not meaningful. The examples of Argentina and Uruguay best illustrate this phenomenon.

The Fund agreed in January 1957 to an initial par value for Argentina. An exchange rate of M$N 18 = US$1 had been introduced in October 1955 in connection with a devaluation and as part of a major effort to liberalize and stabilize the economy. The Argentine authorities now proposed this rate as a par value. At the time, this exchange rate applied to the bulk of exports and imports (approximately 85 to 90 per cent of total trade transactions), although retention taxes applied to most exports and a free market also existed.

The staff found it difficult to make any analysis of the appropriateness of the proposed par value based on a comparison of prices, and believed that the rate of M$N 18 = US$1 had not been in effect long enough to judge whether it was an equilibrium rate. Nonetheless, the staff recommended to the Board that it should agree to the proposed par value. This recommendation was based on the expectation of the Argentine authorities that the rate would prove to be appropriate in the light of their domestic financial policies and the anticipated improvement of exports. Relying on this expectation, the Board accepted the rate, but with some misgivings.

It soon became doubtful whether the par value could be maintained. Already by May 1957, changes in the effective exchange rates for imports were being made by transfers of certain commodities to the free market, and throughout 1958 the exchange rates for exports were frequently adjusted. On January 12, 1959, the Argentine authorities introduced a single, free, exchange market for all transactions; at the outset the rate in this free market was M$N 66.60 = US$1. The par value of M$N 18 = US$1 thereafter applied only to the proceeds of exports effected before December 30, 1958, and to payments for imports contracted for before that date.[4] No new par value had been suggested by Argentina down to the end of 1965, and no transactions were then taking place at the par value agreed in 1957.

The Uruguayan par value agreed in 1960 provides another example of a short-lived initial parity. In connection with a stabilization plan supported by a stand-by arrangement, the Fund in October 1960 agreed to an initial par value for the peso of Ur$7.40 = US$1. This rate was the effective one for exports of greasy wool; it resulted from the application of a retention tax of approximately 25 per cent to the sale of exchange receipts for this product at the free market rate (at that time approximately Ur$11.42 = US$1). The Uruguayan authorities believed that this rate was adequate and viable for the wool exports to which it was applicable (wool accounted for somewhat more than half of the country's total exports). Hence, although the staff had been pressing for the adoption of the free market rate as the basis for an initial par value, it recommended that the Fund should concur in the rate proposed by Uruguay. The Board agreed. However, by January 1, 1961—only a few months later—all exchange transactions were moved to a free market with a fluctuating rate, where the prevailing rate was about Ur$11.00 = US$1.[5]

Criteria for accepting proposed par values

According to the Articles of Agreement (Article XX, Section 4 (*b*)), the criterion for Fund concurrence in a proposal for an initial parity is a negative one: the par value must not in the Fund's opinion cause "recourse to the Fund on the part of that member or others on a scale prejudicial to the Fund and to members." In practice, the prospects for a country's exports have been a crucial factor in the consideration of a proposed parity. As noted above, in the selection of initial parities for original members in 1946, considerable emphasis was given to the effect on exports; [6] and for the next several years this consideration continued to be given the most weight. "So long as an exchange rate does not hamper a country's exports, there is little to be said in present world conditions for altering it." [7] The Fund has continued to rely heavily on the effect-on-exports test. However, once world markets again became competitive, in the 1950's, the Fund was more inclined to accept a par value that differed from the existing exchange rate.

Since the middle of the 1950's, members have generally not proposed par values unless they were fairly certain that the rate suggested would be

[4] *Ninth Annual Report on Exchange Restrictions* (1958), pp. 23–31; *Tenth Annual Report on Exchange Restrictions* (1959), pp. 29–33.

[5] *Twelfth Annual Report on Exchange Restrictions* (1961), pp. 360–63.

[6] "Statement Concerning Initial Par Values," December 18, 1946, *Annual Report, 1947*, pp. 70–71.

[7] *Annual Report, 1948*, p. 23.

acceptable to the Fund and that they could maintain that rate. The nature of the circumstances prevailing when countries have proposed parities suggests some of the criteria the Fund has developed for accepting them. One such circumstance is that exchange rates proposed as par values have commonly been in effect for a number of years. From 1957 to the end of 1965, twenty-seven countries proposed initial par values shortly after they accepted membership. Most of these countries, especially those in the sterling area, selected as initial parities the exchange rates that had been in effect since the devaluations of September 1949. Both more and less developed countries were among those that proposed as par values exchange rates that had already been in effect for some eight to fifteen years: Cyprus, Ghana, Ireland, Jamaica, Kuwait, Liberia, Libya, New Zealand, Nigeria, Portugal, Sierra Leone, Somalia, and the Sudan.

Because it was known that the Fund wished to approve as par values only exchange rates which were clearly stable, only countries which had such rates offered them as par values. Indeed, assuming that the rate proposed is appropriate for a member's exports, stability has often been the principal factor noted in the Board's discussions of proposed par values. This is, of course, in accordance with the Fund's emphasis on the achievement of general economic stability. In addition, a stable exchange rate usually has had a close link with other currencies. Thus, for example, when the Fund considered an initial par value for New Zealand, the long-standing relation of the New Zealand pound to the pound sterling was recognized. Another reason why the Fund has used the test of stability for judging a proposed par value is that a stable rate provides good evidence that the authorities can maintain the par value proposed. Still a further reason for adopting the criterion of stability has been that where an exchange rate has not been stable, the correct level for a par value has been extremely hard to gauge. The difficulties of finding an appropriate rate, in the absence of an already stable rate, was evident, for example, in the Canadian experience of the early 1960's. After the authorities had decided to give up the fluctuating rate they still delayed the institution of an effective par value, partly because of the difficulty of choosing an exchange rate satisfactory for both current and capital account. (The details of Canada's fluctuating rate are discussed in Chapter 7.)

In addition to stability, the Fund has, since the mid-1950's, considered the uniformity and general applicability of the exchange rate suggested as a par value. When a member proposes a parity, exchange reform has usually already been completed. Few, if any, transactions continue to be carried out at exchange rates other than the proposed one. In this sense the par value must be an effective one. Austria, Saudi Arabia, and Spain, for example, all introduced par values only after exchange reform had been made fully effective. This policy, emerging after 1955, was in contrast to that followed earlier when the Board had been eager that members should establish par values even if multiple rates coexisted with these par values.

A final criterion of the suitability of a proposed par value is that the country concerned should have a strong balance of payments and reserve position, and few restrictions. Malaysia and Nigeria, for example, had few restrictions and the former had been contemplating coming under Article VIII. Preferably, the country should be able to relax any prevailing restrictions. Thus, simultaneously with their new parities, Jamaica and Kuwait accepted the obligations of Article VIII.

SOME TROUBLESOME EPISODES

Although generally the initial par values of member countries have been agreed with little controversy, some problems have attended the establishment of a few initial parities. One such instance involved a dispute in which one country believed itself to be adversely affected not by the devaluation of another country's currency but by that other country's abstaining from devaluation. Such a situation is, in effect, the opposite of competitive devaluation. Difficulties have also arisen in connection with the establishment of, or alteration of, par values for totally planned economies. One such instance was the establishment of a par value by Yugoslavia in 1949; another involved a change in par value by Czechoslovakia in 1953.

A CONTROVERSIAL PARITY—PAKISTAN

A dispute about an exchange rate arose when the Fund deliberated on an initial par value for the Pakistan rupee, after Pakistan had become a member early in 1950. In September 1949 Pakistan had elected not to follow the United Kingdom and the rest of the sterling area in devaluation, and maintained the rate for the Pakistan rupee at PRs 1 = $0.30225. This was the same as the rate for the Indian rupee before the 1949 devaluation, and Pakistan proposed this rate to the Fund in 1950 as an initial par value. India's new rate was Rs 1 = $0.21.

India refused to trade with Pakistan at its current rate of exchange and Pakistan was adamant that it would not devalue. Consequently, trade between the two countries—which had previously been extensive and essential to both—had come to a virtual halt. The balance of payments of both countries was being seriously harmed. Pakistan's exports at the time consisted almost entirely of raw jute, most of which went to India for the manufacture of burlap. Inasmuch as India produced most of the world's burlap, Pakistan had no other outlet for its jute. And India had no other source of supply.

Pakistan's position was that, on the basis of price comparisons, exchange devaluation would not help to expand raw material exports; nor would it aid in diversifying exports, whether in composition or trading pattern, as industrialization progressed. Devaluation would also turn the terms of trade against imports—which were mainly consumer goods—and especially textiles from India. India's position was that Pakistan's exchange rate made it impossible for India's burlap producers to operate profitably.

A special staff working party was set up in the Fund to examine the economic merits of Pakistan's proposed par value. In September 1950 the Executive Board, at a special meeting in Paris during the Fifth Annual Meeting, discussed the problem. Not wishing to add to the contention between the two members, the Board agreed to postpone indefinitely the establishment of a par value for Pakistan, and reserved the right to fix the date when the matter would be further considered.

The issue was settled in March 1951, when the Board agreed with Pakistan on an initial par value of PRs 1 = $0.30225. The upward movement of world prices following the outbreak of hostilities in Korea, together with an increasing demand for Pakistan's exports, had strengthened the case for maintaining the original exchange rate of the rupee. But intrinsic to the Fund's action was that in February 1951 the Governments of India and Pakistan had concluded a new trade and payments agreement, providing for the purchase and sale of each other's currencies and for conversion of balances at the par value of the Pakistan rupee as declared to the Fund. Therefore, the Indian Government no longer pressed its objection to acceptance by the Fund of the par value proposed by Pakistan.

This rate for the Pakistan rupee was maintained until July 1955, when the Board concurred in a devaluation of 30.5 per cent, bringing the Pakistani rate into line with other sterling area currencies. This move followed a period in which the prices of Pakistan's exports had been declining under the impact of increased competition in agricultural markets, while at the same time the prices of home-consumed goods had risen because of the monetary expansion induced by the financing of large capital expenditures.

An exchange rate for a planned economy—Yugoslavia

One of the questions about exchange rates which was receiving heightened attention toward the end of 1965, especially in discussions about Eastern European economies, was one with which the Fund had grappled in its early days: what is the role of the exchange rate in a centrally planned economy? This question had arisen at Bretton Woods. The delegation of the U.S.S.R. had proposed the provision which became Article IV, Section 5 (*e*), that a member may change the par value of its currency without the concurrence of the Fund *if the change does not affect the international transactions of members of the Fund.* The question of the significance of the exchange rate in a socialist economy became a practical one for the Fund in August 1947 when Yugoslavia, an original member, requested the Fund to consider a par value for the dinar. The establishment of a par value had been postponed in December 1946 because Yugoslavia had found it difficult to supply adequate basic data to the staff.

The Yugoslav authorities communicated a rate of Din 50 = $1. A report by the staff on the Yugoslav proposal commented that comparisons with the cost of living in other countries and with wholesale prices in the United States showed the dinar only slightly overvalued at this rate, but pointed out that these comparisons were of doubtful validity since supply, demand, prices, and wages in Yugoslavia were all governmentally controlled. But the staff also noted that devaluation of the dinar would not help to increase that country's exports in the short run. The Executive Board considered the staff's findings, but believed that more information was required before a par value could be agreed.

It was not until May 1949 that the Board again considered this matter. Meanwhile, in the course of 1948 the staff examined the significance for the Fund of an exchange rate in a state-controlled economy. Two main conclusions were reached. One was that a state-controlled economy could have a fundamental disequilibrium in the Fund sense of that term. The second was that a member could alter its par value in order to correct a fundamental disequilibrium only after consultation with the Fund; this obligation applied to all members.

When the par value for the dinar was discussed by the Board in May 1949, the Fund agreed to the communicated rate of Din 50 = $1. Mr. Kolovic (Yugoslavia), Alternate to Mr. Sucharda, argued that, although the function of the par value in a planned economy was somewhat different from its function in a free economy, it was of equal importance for either type of economy. He contended that, although in Yugoslavia imports were limited by an economic plan, in drawing up that plan the calculations of trade items were based on the purchase prices of these items expressed in terms of foreign currencies at existing parities plus distribution costs. Hence, the exchange rate played the same role for trade items in a planned economy as in a free one.

Mr. Southard (United States) questioned this line of reasoning. In his view, the real function of a par value in a centrally controlled economy was difficult to understand. The exchange rate was probably a subordinate policy instrument, the main adjustments being made through internal controls. Because of the unusual nature of the economy and the absence of the usual criteria, Mr. Southard could not regard the acceptance by the Board of the Yugoslav par value as implying that the economy was in complete equilibrium.

Mr. Sucharda (Czechoslovakia) insisted that any reservations about the par value for Yugoslavia were unnecessary. He asked that the staff make comprehensive studies so as to dispel any doubts about the Yugoslav parity.

These antipodal views were in practice fused on January 1, 1952, when the par value for the dinar was altered from Din 50 = $1 to Din 300 = $1. This change in the exchange rate not only represented a drastic devaluation but also signified a far-reaching reform of the Yugoslav economic system, a reform which gave a much greater role to the exchange rate. It had been the Fund's view that, under the previous system, the exchange rate had not been one of the determinants of foreign trade transactions.[8] Such transactions were carried out by the state foreign trade monopoly according to a plan, without much regard to the relations between prices in Yugoslavia and abroad. Now, as a result of a process of reorganizing and liberalizing the Yugoslav economic system and equilibrating Yugoslav prices, begun in 1950, a new rate came into being.

The Fund concurred in the devaluation. Explaining its action, the Board stated that the new exchange rate would help to forge a link between domestic and foreign prices, and put the exchange rate in line with the intended level at which prices were to be unified and stabilized.[9]

Later on, Yugoslavia was to encounter serious difficulties in synchronizing domestic and foreign prices while at the same time attempting to use relative domestic prices both as incentives to producers and as taxation of consumers. This use of the price system was made inordinately difficult because of the absence of customs tariffs in Yugoslavia. Utilization of the exchange system for too many objectives led to the emergence of a complex maze of multiple rates: by 1955 the Yugoslav exchange rate system had become one of the most complicated of any maintained by a Fund member. By 1961, however, following a series of steps closely worked out between Yugoslavia and the Fund, this rate system had gradually been unified.

A DISPUTE WITH CZECHOSLOVAKIA

The issue of the role of the exchange rate in a totally controlled economy came up again in 1953. But this time the circumstances were entirely different. On a minor level, the Czechoslovak proposal in 1953 was not for the establishment of an initial par value but for a change in its par value. On a major level, the Fund's relations with the member were in great contrast. Whereas cordial and friendly relations between Yugoslavia and the Fund had developed very early, the Fund's relations with Czechoslovakia had by 1953 become extremely stiff.

On June 2, 1953, the State Bank of Czechoslovakia sent a cable informing the Fund of a change in the par value of the koruna that had become effective the day before. On July 1, the Managing Director, Mr. Rooth, notified the member that since it had not consulted the Fund on this matter, the item would be placed on the agenda of the Board for July 20, 1953, that the member

[8] *Annual Report, 1952*, pp. 64–65.

[9] *Ibid.*

was entitled to send a representative, and that the Fund would wish information on the reasons for the lack of consultation. Czechoslovakia replied that it would be represented by its Ambassador in Washington.

At the meeting on July 20, the representative of Czechoslovakia took the position that his Government's action was covered by Article IV, Section 5 (*e*), of the Fund Agreement. Since Czechoslovakia conducted the overwhelming majority of its international transactions in foreign currencies, the change in the par value of the koruna did not and could not in any way affect international transactions.

Mr. Southard emphasized that consultation with the Fund was to take place *before* changes in the par values were made, and that such consultation was more than a matter of form. In his view, there was no basis for arguing that changes in par values which members claimed did not affect international transactions were not subject to the obligation of advance consultation. No such exception was stated in the Fund Agreement; on the contrary, advance consultation was required even where the Fund had no right to object (Article IV, Section 5 (*c*) (i)).

A salient question was whether the change in the exchange rate did in actuality affect international transactions. Unless the rate had some international effect, why was it being changed? The Executive Directors took the view that, before the Fund could judge the impact of the alteration in the par value on international transactions, it would have to have information on how the country's foreign trading system operated. Were any of the outstanding debts which were altered by the monetary reform owed to foreign countries or their residents? At what exchange rates were the koruna clearing balances of foreign countries converted from old to new korunas? At what rates were other koruna debts to foreign countries converted? What were the total balances, both in korunas and in foreign currencies, between Czechoslovakia and other countries before the exchange rate was changed, how were they distributed between countries, and how were they affected by the revaluation of the rate?

The representative of Czechoslovakia forwarded these questions to his Government. Temporary postponements of the date set for further consideration by the Board were granted, and it was the middle of September 1953 before Czechoslovakia was ready to reply. The representative of Czechoslovakia then read a prepared statement in which he argued that the economy of his country was very different from that of other Fund members and that the change in par value did not affect international transactions. The gist of his contention was that the Czechoslovak balance of payments was the result of a national economic plan. The balance of payments expressed the country's foreign trade plan; equilibrium in the balance of payments was always maintained. The principal motives for the change in par value were internal. The change in no way affected either the current or the capital transactions of other members of the Fund. The Czechoslovak representative thought it was significant that some Fund members—in their payments agreements with Czechoslovakia—had already recognized the new par value. He further supplied brief information on the questions asked by the Fund but did not provide basic background material.

Meanwhile Mr. Southard had suggested that action be taken under Article XV, Section 2 (*a*), to make Czechoslovakia ineligible to use the Fund's resources. He noted the several occasions on which the member had failed to supply adequate information to the Fund, and pointed out that in its financial relations with the Fund Czechoslovakia was using an unauthorized exchange rate which reduced the number of korunas due to the Fund. However, by October 1953 the issue of the par value was just one of several controversies between Czechoslovakia and the Fund. From September until mid-December 1953, the Directors repeatedly deliberated the par value issue per se. Representatives of Czechoslovakia were present at a series of meetings. Their contention continued to be that, as the change in the par value was not intended to correct a fundamental disequilibrium, and did not affect international transactions, it had not been necessary for Czechoslovakia to consult the Fund. The representatives discussed detailed items of the balance of payments accounts in an effort to prove that the change in parity had not affected these accounts. They explained how foreign trade was conducted in Czechoslovakia. However, such important information as data on the levels and composition of exports and imports, or quantitative estimates for the balance of payments and for national income, could not, they insisted, be revealed for security reasons.

The Executive Directors were unable to accept the arguments put forward by Czechoslovakia. The staff had shown that diplomats and tourists were affected by the new rate. That being the case, Czechoslovakia was not justified in claiming the right to alter its exchange rate without Fund approval. The contrast with the position taken by Yugoslavia, also a socialist economy, on the relevance of its exchange rate was especially noted.

On December 16, 1953, the Board took the following decision:

> The Government of Czechoslovakia on June 1, 1953, changed the par value of its currency, the koruna, and subsequently informed the Fund that concurrence of the Fund with this change was not required because Czechoslovakia had taken the action in accordance with the provisions of Article IV, Section 5 (*e*). Having considered the arguments offered by Czechoslovakia, and such information as was made available, the Fund concludes that the change of par value by Czechoslovakia does not come under Article IV, Section 5 (*e*).

PAR VALUES AND FUND RESOURCES

The establishment of an initial par value is, by Article XX, Section 4 (*c*), a prerequisite to the use of the Fund's resources. Hence, countries without initial par values are, in the absence of any further Fund decision or action, ineligible to draw upon the Fund. Prima facie, this deprives members of financial support from the Fund even when they are, for example, contemplating extensive exchange reforms or coping with a temporary balance of payments problem.

Thailand queries its position

Exceptions to the above provisions were possible to members whose metropolitan territory had been occupied by the enemy. Such a member was granted certain privileges under Article XX, Section 4 (*d*). According to subsection (i) of this Section, the ninety-day period prescribed by Article XX, Section 4 (*b*), could be extended. Subsection (ii) further provided that:

> Within the extended period the member may, if the Fund has begun exchange transactions, buy from the Fund with its currency the currencies of other members, but only under such conditions and in such amounts as may be prescribed by the Fund.

The privileges of Article XX, Section 4 (*d*), had been automatically accorded to original members whose metropolitan territories had been occupied by the enemy. When Italy became a member in 1947, the Membership Resolution incorporated references to Article XX, Section 4 (*d*), thus making explicit the possibility that Italy could draw on the Fund prior to agreeing a par value. The question of drawings for countries without parities was queried rather forcefully at the Annual Meeting, 1952, by the Governor for Thailand, Prince Viwat. The Membership Resolution for Thailand, which became a member in 1949, had contained no provision to the effect that the privileges of Article XX, Section 4 (*d*) (ii), be accorded to that country. Therefore, the Executive Directors were not authorized to permit exchange transactions with Thailand under that provision. Furthermore, paragraph 5 of the Resolution stated categorically that the member "may not engage in exchange transactions with the Fund before the thirtieth day after the par value of its currency has been agreed."

This particular clause relating to exchange transactions with the Fund had appeared for the first time in 1948 in the Membership Resolution for Finland and had subsequently been repeated for Austria and Burma, as well as for Thailand; the same paragraph also occurred in the Membership Resolution for Indonesia, which was, in 1952, in the process of joining the Fund. The staff explained to the Board that the wording for those countries joining the Fund after Italy had been changed because it had been cumbersome to draft membership resolutions in such detail as that for Italy. Now, in 1952, Thailand was asking whether there were any circumstances which would prevent Thailand from enjoying the privileges of Article XX, Section 4 (*d*) (ii), and, if so, whether these obstacles could be removed by any action of the Fund.

Prince Viwat, in September 1952, pointed to the nature of the balance of payments difficulties of Thailand. His country's deficits, when they occurred, seemed to exemplify the classic textbook case for use of the Fund's resources. Thailand was a large exporter of rice and normally had little balance of payments problem. But since the successful production of rice depended upon the quantity of rainfall, he expressed Thailand's potential predicament in 1952 in four words—"no rain, no rice." [10] Any balance of payments difficulty would be temporary and likely to be self-correcting, since a two-year failure of the monsoon was a rarity. Therefore, he asked, should a country which is creditworthy and has a good record as a debtor, if faced with a temporary and self-correcting balance of payments difficulty, be barred from using the Fund's resources simply because it has not been able to declare a par value? The Managing Director replied that he hoped that countries in positions similar to that of Thailand would soon be able to agree with the Fund on par values for their currencies. Should an emergency develop, however, the Fund and the member would endeavor to find a practical solution for the problem.[11]

The question of the need for par values prior to Fund drawings was carefully considered by the Board beginning in mid-1953. Mr. Rajapatirana (Ceylon), Alternate to Mr. Yumoto (who had been elected by Thailand) called attention to Prince Viwat's statement of several months before and urged the Directors to reconsider whether the relevant paragraph of the Membership Resolution for Thailand was the correct condition to be imposed. In his opinion, an injustice had been done to Thailand and should not be perpetuated because that country, owing to circumstances beyond its control, could not comply with the technicality of declaring a par value. (These circumstances concerned cross rates, which are discussed later in this chapter.)

Action considered for a few countries

The staff's first recommendations on this subject were considered by the Board in June 1953. The conclusion of the staff was that, under the Articles of Agreement and paragraph 5 of the Membership Resolution for Thailand, the Executive Directors could not permit Thailand to buy exchange from the Fund before a par value for its currency was agreed. However, the Board of Governors could authorize the Executive Directors to permit exchange transactions with Thailand, or any other member in similar circumstances, on terms substantially similar to those prescribed in Article XX, Section 4 (*d*) (ii), notwithstanding any provision of the original membership resolutions for such countries.

A draft text of a resolution for adoption by the Governors was therefore submitted by the staff to the Executive Board for consideration. This draft resolution covered Thailand and Burma, and would cover Indonesia if it accepted membership under the terms of its Membership Resolution. For addi-

[10] *Summary Proceedings, 1952,* p. 65.

[11] *Ibid.,* p. 124.

tional new members the staff proposed that the problem be handled in the drafting of the membership resolutions.

When this draft resolution came before the Board, a few Directors insisted that the communication of a par value should be retained as a requirement for drawings. But several Directors believed that new members without par values should have at least the same privileges for drawings as those members which, while having agreed par values with the Fund, were not necessarily maintaining them.

Mr. Southard went further and wondered whether the staff suggestions were too limited. He questioned the wisdom of the distinction, implicit in the staff approach, between enemy-occupied countries and those not so occupied; the draft resolution would, moreover, provide a solution only for Thailand, Burma, and possibly Indonesia. There still remained the problem of Uruguay, an original Fund member without an initial par value, which could not be accorded the privileges of Article XX, Section 4 (*d*) (ii), since its territory had not been occupied by the enemy in World War II. The Board thereupon agreed to postpone discussion of the draft resolution pending a further review by the staff.

General action considered

The next discussions by the Executive Board weighed the pros and cons of action on this issue for a great number of countries. Directors recognized that the Board of Governors had the legal authority to provide in a membership resolution for exchange transactions between the Fund and a new member prior to agreement on a par value, even in those instances where the member had not been occupied by the enemy within the meaning of the Articles. But several Directors were concerned that any general action might grant new members which had not been occupied by the enemy a privilege which some original members did not have. Several Directors recognized that with the passing of time there was a diminution of the original significance of occupation by the enemy. However, they doubted the wisdom of proposing at this time any action by the Governors which would be generally applied to all new members; such action would amount to discrimination against original members that had not yet set par values.

On the other hand, some Directors noted that there was only one original member, namely Uruguay, that did not have the right to purchase exchange from the Fund because it had not agreed a par value with the Fund.[12] Perhaps some solution might be found for that case. These Directors stressed that the Fund already seemed to have a new category of members not mentioned in the Articles, namely those which did not make their par values effective. They

[12] China was also an original member without a par value, but had not paid its subscription (also a prerequisite to the use of the Fund's resources).

suggested that there seemed to be no point in requiring new members to declare a par value as a prerequisite to using the Fund's resources if original members did not live up to their obligations under Article IV, Section 3, and yet remained eligible to engage in transactions with the Fund.

In line with this reasoning, the staff then proposed a broad approach, viz., that the Board of Governors should be asked to give the Executive Directors discretion to engage in transactions on an ad hoc basis before a par value was agreed, when the circumstances of a particular country justified assistance from the Fund. If this approach was too comprehensive, the staff recommended as a minimum that a proposal be made to the Board of Governors covering new members whose territories had been occupied by the enemy.

Although two Directors favored the general approach suggested by the staff, most had difficulties with any broadly applying resolution. Universal action would grant the privileges of Article XX, Section 4 (*d*) (ii), to countries never occupied by the enemy, thereby granting greater privileges to some new members than were given to original members. A clear-cut distinction between old and new members raised many delicate points which would provoke lengthy debate in the Governors' Meeting.

Agreement for Thailand and Indonesia

Accordingly, the Board went back to considering a limited action which would apply only to Thailand and Indonesia. (Burma, in the meantime, had agreed an initial par value.) No new category of members would thus be set up. The Board, aware of the economic situations in Thailand and Indonesia, acknowledged that the establishment of par values might not be possible for some time. It was clear that special action for Thailand and Indonesia could not be regarded as discriminatory against Uruguay, and that such special action for two countries would not set a precedent.

In August 1953, the Executive Directors approved a report to the Board of Governors and two draft resolutions amending the Membership Resolutions for Thailand and Indonesia.[13] The draft resolution for Thailand read as follows (that for Indonesia was similar):

> Resolved:
>
> That paragraph (5) of Resolution No. 3-4 of the Board of Governors on Membership for Siam [Thailand] be amended to read as follows:
>
> (5) That Siam may not engage in exchange transactions with the Fund before the thirtieth day after the par value of its currency has been agreed in accordance with (4) above and its subscription shall be paid in full before such thirtieth day; provided, however, that at any time before such thirtieth day the Executive Directors are authorized to permit exchange transactions with Siam on the same terms

[13] *Summary Proceedings, 1953,* Appendix VI, Annex A, pp. 120–22.

and conditions as those prescribed by Article XX, Section 4 (*d*) (ii), of the Articles of Agreement.

These two resolutions were passed by the Board of Governors in September 1953.[14] The amended paragraph 5 has served as an archetype for later membership resolutions.

Agreement for all new members

The Governors' resolutions on Thailand and Indonesia were precursors to much broader action ten years later. The question of the need for initial par values prior to drawings again came up in 1962–63 following the admission to Fund membership of 24 new African countries. The circumstances of these countries suggested that many of them might not be able to establish initial par values for some years. Would they, on that account, not be eligible to draw on the Fund? When, in 1964, the Executive Directors considered this question for a second time, they were no longer disturbed at the idea that countries might use the Fund's resources prior to the establishment of par values, and thus were able to accept a general change in the Fund's policy that they had rejected eleven years earlier.

The first step taken to make new members eligible to use the Fund's resources without waiting for the establishment of initial par values was to reduce the waiting period between the time when a member country had agreed to a par value with the Fund and had paid its subscription and the time when it was eligible to use the Fund's resources. The standard provision in membership resolutions had been a waiting period of at least thirty days.

Mr. Saad (United Arab Republic), who had been elected by Afghanistan, in a discussion of a proposed par value for Afghanistan in January 1963, made the suggestion that there be an "acceleration of eligibility" by reducing this period to one day. In March 1963 the Board agreed to eliminate the delay altogether and recommended to the Board of Governors that the change should apply both to future membership resolutions and to all past ones. This was agreed by the Governors in April 1963.[15] The countries for whom membership resolutions were retroactively amended in this way were Cameroon, Central African Republic, Chad, Congo (Brazzaville), Dahomey, Gabon, Guinea, Ivory Coast, Jamaica, Korea, Kuwait, Laos, Liberia, Nepal, Niger, Nigeria, Sierra Leone, Somalia, Tanganyika, Togo, Tunisia, Upper Volta, and Viet-Nam.

On April 22, 1964, in a series of three decisions, a much more sweeping policy was formulated. First, the Executive Directors recommended to the Board of Governors an amendment of the membership resolutions for all those members

---

[14] Resolutions 8-4 and 8-5, *Summary Proceedings, 1953*, pp. 96–97.

[15] Resolution No. 18-2, *Summary Proceedings, 1963*, p. 227.

that had paid their subscriptions but had not yet agreed initial par values with the Fund, viz., Algeria, Burundi, Cameroon, Central African Republic, Chad, Congo (Brazzaville), Congo (Leopoldville), Dahomey, Gabon, Guinea, Ivory Coast, Kenya, Korea, Laos, Malagasy Republic, Mali, Mauritania, Nepal, Niger, Rwanda, Senegal, Sierra Leone, Tanganyika, Togo, Trinidad and Tobago, Tunisia, Uganda, Upper Volta, and Viet-Nam. This amendment authorized the Executive Directors to permit exchange transactions with any of these members prior to establishment of an initial par value, under such conditions and in such amounts as might be prescribed by the Executive Directors. The Board of Governors approved the amendment on June 1, 1964.[16]

The second decision was to the effect that the provision permitting transactions with new members prior to the setting of par values should be incorporated in all future membership resolutions, and the Directors agreed on guidelines for implementing this provision.

In the third decision, the Board emphasized that the two foregoing decisions should not be interpreted as a sign of weakened emphasis on the par value system. It was agreed that, when considering requests to draw by members that had not established par values, the Fund would be guided by the purposes of the Articles. Moreover, the Fund would encourage members to follow policies leading to the establishment of realistic exchange rates and to the adoption at the earliest feasible date of effective par values, and would take into account the efforts being made to achieve these objectives.

However, the Fund would give the overwhelming benefit of the doubt to requests for exchange transactions within the gold tranche. Further, members might expect that requests for drawings would be met where they were made in accordance with the decision on compensatory financing of shortfalls in export receipts.[17] A further condition for transactions with a member without an initial par value was that the member should complete the payment of its subscription on the basis of a provisional rate of exchange agreed with the Fund.[18]

Why had such comprehensive action finally been taken? First, the terms on which Fund resources would be made available were becoming more liberal. At about this time the Fund was increasing the availability of the gold tranche to members in general. Also, in 1963 the Fund had introduced facilities for compensatory financing of export fluctuations and wished to permit the use of these facilities by members who, although otherwise eligible, had not declared par values.

Second, the staff presented several arguments in favor of permitting exchange transactions before par values were agreed. The use of the Fund's resources by

[16] Resolution No. 19-8, *Summary Proceedings, 1964*, p. 260.
[17] See below, pp. 403, 421.
[18] E.B. Decision No. 1687-(64/22), April 22, 1964; below, Vol. III, p. 243.

members suffering temporary payments difficulties could encourage them to follow policies leading to the establishment of adequate exchange rates and, ultimately, to realistic par values. Moreover, allowing members to draw on the Fund before they had established par values would make it unnecessary for them to propose possibly unrealistic par values in order to become eligible to draw. The staff argued that unrealistic par values should be avoided because, once set, they were often adjusted only after severe damage had been done to the economy of the country concerned. Also, the acceptance by the Fund of unrealistic par values for some members might discourage other members from adopting appropriate ones, or make it difficult for them to do so.

Third, to preclude transactions with new members which had not established initial par values, while permitting transactions with other members which did not use their par values or whose par values were not realistic, might also be regarded as unfair.

Finally, the staff found little logic in the practice of withholding the right to use the Fund's resources from countries that had joined the Fund after Indonesia and Thailand and which had also been occupied by the enemy, for example, Korea and Viet-Nam.

On the other side of the argument, the staff recognized the need to bear in mind the risk of weakening the authority of the Fund in the field of par values. Any concession might be interpreted as a departure from the Fund's general policy of encouraging members to establish realistic and effective par values. It might also lead to the relaxation by some members of their efforts to establish such par values at an early date.

At the Board meeting at which these staff recommendations were discussed, the Directors focused on the question: If general action was taken permitting drawings by countries without parities, would the principle of fixed par values, so important to the Fund, be threatened? The Directors indicated a strong awareness of the likelihood that the establishment of par values in many developing countries might take a long time. They agreed that where a developing country could establish an initial par value at an early stage in its membership, it should do so, their reasoning being that where countries had reached an appropriate stage of development par values were desirable. At the same time, some Directors voiced the thought that the establishment of a par value could not be regarded as a precondition of economic progress, and in certain circumstances might even be detrimental.

Both the Managing Director and Mr. Saad reminded the Board that the proposed third decision was really a reaffirmation of the Articles. Stress was placed on the statement in the draft that the Fund would "encourage members to follow policies leading to the establishment of realistic exchange rates." The purpose of the decision would be to avoid any impression that the Fund was no longer giving the same pre-eminence as in the past to the par value principle.

Directors also agreed that the impact of the proposed decisions was that exchange transactions should not *generally* be permitted prior to the establishment of an initial par value, but only in appropriate cases. The Board recorded its obligation to make a careful and individual approach to requests for drawings, considering the particular aspects of each application and not losing sight of the purposes of the Articles of Agreement, in which the establishment of an initial par value was a basic principle.

Mr. Kiingi (Uganda), Alternate to Mr. Kandé, emphasized that while the adoption of these decisions would make it possible for the 29 member countries which had not yet established par values, and any countries which later joined the Fund, to participate fully in the major benefits to be derived from Fund membership, this possibility did not mean that the African countries would not try to establish realistic par values whenever possible.

Another problem which concerned the Directors as they reached the decisions mentioned was that the Board might be more lax in granting requests to use the Fund's resources from the new members affected by the decisions than requests from old members, some of which also did not have par values, or did not have effective par values. For these reasons, some Directors suggested that it might be desirable later to review this departure from past Fund policy. The Managing Director emphasized that no discrimination between old and new members was intended.

Par values and stand-by arrangements

The Directors have agreed to stand-by arrangements with several member countries which had not established par values or did not have effective par values. The first such member was Peru, in February 1954.[19] This arrangement was approved by the Directors even though, in the view of the staff, Peru's economic circumstances seemed favorable for setting a par value and its current exchange rate appeared stable.

REINSTITUTING PARITIES

The Fund's policies toward the setting of new par values by members that had suspended parities agreed earlier, or had made them nominal by subsequent changes in their exchange systems, have been as pragmatic as its policies toward initial par values.

---

[19] See below, p. 471.

Par values and multiple rates

In the Fund's early years, it was not prepared to see initial par values remain unaltered while members made changes in their *de facto* exchange rates. Consequently, many countries with multiple rates not only established initial par values despite the multiplicity of their exchange rates; they also altered those par values when they changed their exchange systems. In effect, countries made an effort to keep their par values in line with their current exchange rate structures. For example, until 1956 Bolivia from time to time introduced new parities as it made alterations in its multiple rate system. Similarly, Ecuador adjusted its par value in 1950 when making changes in the rate structure. An extreme example is offered by Paraguay, which changed its par value once in 1951, twice within eight months in 1953–54, and again early in 1956—all of these par values being accompanied by a continued multiplicity of exchange rates. The logic of changing par values in these instances was that changes in the exchange system represented genuine steps toward more realistic rate patterns; hence par values should be moved in line with the improved exchange rate structures.

After the mid-1950's, however, as the difficulties of final elimination of multiple exchange rates became more apparent, there was less resetting of par values in line with frequent adaptations of multiple rates. Most changes in multiple exchange rate systems, and even unifications of multiple rates, took place without the establishment of new par values, either immediately or even for some years thereafter. Only after the new system had proved itself to be enduring did new par values tend to be proposed.

Paraguay again provides an interesting example. In 1957, it replaced its multiple rate system with a fluctuating rate of exchange. Subsequently, although the guaraní has depreciated by some 50 per cent, Paraguay has not declared a new par value. Similarly, several other countries which had eliminated their multiple rate systems and had had stable, unitary rates for many years, still had not instituted new par values by the end of 1965. These included Bolivia, Lebanon, and Peru. Still others—for example, Venezuela—had considerably simplified their exchange systems but had not yet set a new parity.

Urging par values

Where conditions have been considered eventually to have become appropriate, the Fund has urged countries to set par values—either initial parities or realigned parities in accordance with their *de facto* exchange rates. Thailand provides an example of such action by the Fund. After Thailand had eliminated multiple rates in favor of a fluctuating rate, and after the fluctuating rate had been stabilized, the Fund urged the Thai authorities to set a par value: from early in 1960 until late in 1963, when a par value was agreed, several statements were made in Board decisions on Article XIV consultations to the effect that the Fund would welcome the establishment of a par value.

Par values and convertibility status

The facts that some countries did not establish an initial par value, and that others did not establish a new parity after their earlier ones had become outdated, raised a further question: Should such countries be permitted to undertake the obligations of Article VIII? Canada, which had suspended transactions at its par value in 1950, had come under Article VIII in 1952. At that time, however, the question of the need for a member to have an effective par value prior to assuming Article VIII status had not been pointedly discussed. In 1960 this question was one of several considered by the Board at length.

The preparatory paper by the staff had suggested that countries assuming Article VIII status should conduct their international transactions through a uniform rate system based on a par value agreed with the Fund. This paper outlined various categories of countries which should probably not assume Article VIII status. One such category was of countries which had few or virtually no restrictions but where considerable uncertainty prevailed concerning balance of payments prospects. Doubt was cast on the ability of such countries to cope with a deterioration of the balance of payments without resort to restrictions. Countries which had been unable to establish effective par values were included in this category, on the ground that avoiding restrictions was not a sufficient test of the strength of a country's external position; what was needed as well was a demonstration that the country's exchange rate could remain stable.

As the Board considered the possible requirements of Article VIII status, some European Directors expressed the conviction that the establishment of an effective par value was an essential qualification for a country moving to Article VIII. Mr. Southard, however, although wholeheartedly supporting the par value system, argued that the Fund should not put undue emphasis on this point. He agreed that where a country seemed to have no justifiable reason for not having a par value, the Fund should try to convince the member that it should establish one. But he also believed that the Board should recognize that there were instances where it was to a member's advantage to have a fluctuating rate.

Other Directors also believed that it was desirable for the Fund to keep open the possibility that a country could come under Article VIII even if that country had no par value. They recognized that many countries which did not have par values were, nonetheless, relatively free of restrictions. These countries maintained dual exchange rates on the premise that they could keep capital movements unrestricted provided that a free exchange rate was applied to those transactions. Although in the 1950's many countries that had dual exchange rates also had par values, countries that established par values in the 1960's usually had first unified their exchange systems.

The question of whether a country coming under Article VIII should have a par value came to the fore in a specific instance in February 1961. Ten European countries and Peru had indicated to the Fund that they intended to accept the obligations of Article VIII; but Peru's situation was somewhat different from that of the others in that it did not have a par value and, in fact, had a fluctuating rate. Some Directors believed that the significance of Peru's move to Article VIII was reduced by the fact that its exchange rate situation was irregular. They stressed that fulfillment of the Fund's purposes required the removal of two obstacles, variations in exchange rates and restrictions on current transfers. The attainment of Article VIII status, in their view, should be indicative of economic stability, which should be reflected in a fixed rate of exchange. Several Directors, however, were especially gratified that Peru could join the list of Article VIII countries together with the European countries. Mr. Klein (Argentina), who had been elected by Peru, argued that a country could not always fix a parity without at the same time adopting a number of restrictive regulations. Some of the other countries then moving to Article VIII had at least some restrictions, while Peru did not.

The Board decided to note Peru's intention of accepting the obligations of Article VIII from February 15, 1961, the same action as was taken for the other ten countries then assuming Article VIII status.

CROSS RATES

Once an economic issue has been closed, the passions that it once engendered are difficult to recapture or even to imagine. Such is the situation with regard to the Fund's actions in connection with cross rates. The existence of "broken" or "disorderly" cross rates was the source of repeated discussions between the Fund and its members and among Board members from 1946 until about 1952–53, after which the prevalence of broken cross rates diminished. By 1958, most of such problems had disappeared, largely because the general economic environment which had occasioned them had changed.

Causes and the Fund's early position

Broken cross rates are rates of exchange between two currencies which differ from the parity relationships between these currencies. If, for example, in 1948 in a free market in a third country, the U.S. dollar sold for 10 pesos and the pound sterling for 35 pesos, the cross rate between dollars and sterling would have been $3.50 rather than the official $4.03. In the late 1940's and in the early 1950's, even after the devaluation of sterling, broken cross rates occurred almost everywhere that limited free market rates or fluctuating rates prevailed.

These broken cross rates resulted from the inconvertibility of currencies. In normal circumstances, where currencies are freely interchangeable, their values in terms of each other are as a rule the same in exchange markets throughout the world. Any temporary divergence which may appear is quickly eliminated by arbitrage operations. However, when currencies are inconvertible, exchange dealers are prevented from carrying out the necessary arbitrage transactions. If the exchange control authorities do not cooperate to maintain agreed exchange rates, the rate for each currency is affected by the special circumstances of local supply and demand or by unilateral controls, and the resulting cross rates may have little relation to the parities agreed with the Fund.

Deviations from an orderly pattern of cross rates in the late 1940's and early 1950's were part of the abnormal circumstances of the times. Not only were currencies inconvertible, but transactions in exchange markets were very limited. Most central banks fixed exchange rates unilaterally and based their official quotations on parities, maintaining a small and usually uniform spread between their buying and selling prices for each currency. There was little scope for even minor movements of exchange rates. Exchange markets for transactions in the same currency in different countries were not interrelated.

Countries that had free markets in which broken cross rates existed usually had an excess supply of inconvertible currencies—some of which had accumulated during the war years—and a shortage of convertible currencies (mainly U.S. dollars). Broken cross rates helped these countries to encourage imports requiring inconvertible currencies and to make it more profitable to export to the dollar area than to countries with inconvertible currencies.

On the other hand, given the world shortages of goods and the buyers' markets then prevailing, the trade effects produced by broken cross rates were adverse for the countries whose currencies were sold at implicit discounts. The discounted rate, while making it easier for the country with an inconvertible currency to sell goods to countries in which cross rates were broken, made it more expensive to buy from them. In the circumstances of the late 1940's, the latter consideration was the more important one: shortages of supplies so limited exports that an exchange rate inducement was considered of no value. Instead, countries were eager to obtain an abundant flow of imports as cheaply as possible.

The United Kingdom was particularly concerned about broken cross rates for sterling. When, for example, the Italian authorities indicated to the Fund in 1947 that Italy would have a broken cross rate between sterling and the U.S. dollar because of its fluctuating rate, the British Government made a formal protest to Italy.

Partly, the United Kingdom was troubled by the adverse effects of broken cross rates, wherever they existed, on confidence in the sterling rate. But the unfavorable implications for British imports were also of consequence. In addition, broken cross rates induced traders to buy British goods for resale in the United States and thus diverted part of the dollar receipts which would otherwise have accrued to the United Kingdom and other countries in the sterling area. And broken cross rates diminished the incentive of countries in whose markets broken cross rates prevailed to seek to earn dollars directly.

The Fund Agreement contains no express provisions regarding cross rates. But as a matter of interpretation and policy, the Fund's approaches at the outset were based on an insistence on orderly cross rates. The Fund recognized the adverse consequences for some members of broken cross rates, and also had various legal arguments against these rates. The General Counsel's view was that to comply with the Fund Agreement a country with a single rate should not have cross rates differing from parity. Where such cross rates resulted from multiple rates, they were discriminatory. And, clearly, the general philosophy of the Fund Agreement made discriminatory practices undesirable.

In addition, in formulating policy on cross rates, the Fund used a broader test: What would be the implications of broken cross rates for the quick restoration of the convertibility of currencies? It was the Fund's view at the time that disorderly cross rates distorted trade relations and made future convertibility even more difficult to attain. Changes in the direction of trade in response to the movements of disorderly cross rates were likely to be determined by short-run considerations and local peculiarities which had little to do with the fundamental influences by which a new pattern of world trade should be determined. Hence, the Fund attached great importance to the maintenance of orderly cross rates based on parities (1) because of its Articles, (2) as a means of protecting its members, and (3) as a way to encourage the appropriate reorientation of trade on a multilateral basis.[20]

Debates over policy

By March 1949 a few Directors, while recognizing the importance in the long run of orderly cross rates, had begun to question the extent to which the Fund should continue to insist on orderly cross rates in the circumstances then prevailing. Mr. Tasca (United States), Alternate to Mr. Southard, pointed out that in many cases the only alternative to breaking the cross rates was overt discrimination through quantitative restrictions against imports from the United States. In his view, therefore, the Fund could press for parity cross rates only as part of a larger program looking toward the elimination of all currency discrimination and inconvertibility. When after the devaluations of September 1949 a few countries continued to have problems in maintaining orderly cross rates, some Directors again queried whether the Fund should press the matter.

[20] See, e.g., *Annual Report, 1948*, pp. 26–27.

These Directors were beginning to believe that some revision of Fund policy might be desirable. The issues raised are exemplified by the cross-rate problem of Thailand.

In March 1950 Thailand, which had a multiple exchange rate system, proposed a new exchange market in which broken cross rates would prevail. The argument was that broken cross rates in markets in other Far Eastern countries made it impossible for Thailand to maintain parity cross rates. The cross rates in these other markets fluctuated a great deal; however, by buying and selling dollars in the free market, the Thai authorities could compensate for these fluctuations, hold the free market rate stable, avoid large changes in the cost of living, and maintain a fairly satisfactory payments position. The staff thought that within eighteen months, or earlier if the sterling-dollar cross rate improved, Thailand might establish a par value.

The majority of Directors acknowledged that any attempt by Thailand to maintain orderly cross rates would result in Thailand's reserves ending up in Hong Kong or other Far Eastern free markets. Certainly the system proposed would put little pressure on sterling. In the future, should the position of sterling in the Far East improve sufficiently, Thailand would, after unification of its rates, be in a good position to establish a par value and maintain regular cross rates. If, on the other hand, the sterling cross-rate problem was not solved for a considerable time, the arrangement proposed should still make it possible for Thailand to look forward to establishing a par value, even though a disparate cross rate would remain. These Directors reasoned that no member should be expected to undertake a stabilization of cross rates which was beyond its ability to achieve, nor should the objective of orderly cross rates be allowed to prejudice a member's efforts to achieve and maintain an appropriate parity.

On the opposite side were Directors who had grave misgivings about any change in the Fund's policy on cross rates. They contended, for example, that a broken cross rate in Thailand might afford the country an unfair competitive advantage over other areas, such as Latin America, exporting similar products. Mr. Crick (United Kingdom), Alternate to Sir George Bolton, was especially concerned about the prospect that the volume of transactions taking place at broken cross rates would increase considerably. To support his concern, Mr. Crick cited the major discounts for sterling which continued to prevail in markets other than the one in Thailand—those in Peru, Lebanon, and Hong Kong.

Because of these conflicting views, the Board, in 1950, 1951, and 1952, undertook a general reassessment of the Fund's cross-rate policy. The staff paper prepared for these discussions suggested that the Fund should not sanction any exceptions to the obligations of orderly cross rates except in situations where it was clearly evident that a particular problem faced by members had no acceptable solution other than a break in cross rates. In general, Fund policy would continue to be not to approve of broken cross rates, but for the first time the Fund would recognize some exceptional cases.

After consideration, the Board concluded that a general decision on cross rates would not be desirable; rather, each case should be determined on its merits. The Board's public statement ran as follows:

> The area within which broken cross rates threaten to distort the normal flow of trade is now much narrower than it was two or three years ago. The cross rates of greatest significance are the sterling-dollar rates, and the increased relative strength of sterling has been the basic reason for the improvement. There are, however, still a number of countries, including Hong Kong, Peru, Syria, Lebanon, and Thailand, where cross rates have not been brought under control, and countries confronted with special exchange problems are still sometimes disposed to look for an easy solution to practices that involve broken cross rates.[21]

Thereafter it was increasingly recognized, by both the Board and the staff, that broken cross rates for inconvertible currencies could not be avoided in free exchange markets. The only way to eliminate them was to abolish the free markets; yet most free markets were regarded as desirable both by the country concerned and by the Fund.

The extent of broken cross rates subsequently decreased further. In 1953, under the EPU agreement, eight European countries—Belgium, Denmark, France, Germany, the Netherlands, Sweden, Switzerland, and the United Kingdom—set up a multilateral arbitrage system. These countries allowed their banks (when authorized) to buy from and sell to authorized banks in the other cooperating countries any of their currencies in exchange for the currency of any of the other cooperating countries. The central banks concerned undertook to intervene at stated margins, usually ¾ of 1 per cent either side of parity. Cross rates between the eight currencies involved henceforth became approximately the same in all eight markets. After the establishment of external convertibility for sterling and other major European currencies in 1958, the U.S. dollar also came into the circuit of multilateral arbitrage facilities. Hence, there were no longer any broken cross rates involving European currencies and the U.S. dollar. Earlier that year the Fund had specifically noted the marked decline in broken cross rates for sterling and other key currencies.[22] Thus, although some broken cross rates have continued to prevail in free markets, they no longer constitute a serious issue for the Fund.

MARGINS AROUND PARITY

Once countries have set par values, they are obliged under the Articles to keep their spot exchange rates within a margin of 1 per cent on either side of

21 *Annual Report, 1951,* p. 48.
22 *Annual Report, 1958,* p. 127.

parity. If two countries fix margins for their currencies in terms of the U.S. dollar, the cross rate between their two currencies can, under the Articles, vary up to 2 per cent from that calculated on the basis of their parities. After European countries introduced external convertibility (in 1958), although they did not in fact allow their currencies to move all the way to the 1 per cent margin—stopping at ¾ per cent—the possibility of an illegal cross rate still arose. This was because the margins from par for the exchange rates between EPU currencies in the market were the sum of the margins prevailing for each currency against the U.S. dollar. In the extreme case, if one currency moved to the maximum permitted premium against the U.S. dollar while another currency moved to the maximum discount, the rate of exchange between the two currencies would move to a point approximately 1.5 per cent from parity. Because of this potential margin of 1.5 per cent, the central bank whose currency was involved in the differential would find it useful to buy and sell interchangeable currencies at exchange rates related to their quotations in foreign exchange markets. Central banks would thereby be engaging in transactions at exchange rates of more than 1 per cent from parity.

In recognition of such situations, and to avoid the possibility of excessive rate movements, the staff recommended to the Board that countries should fix the margin vis-à-vis the currency which they selected within 1 per cent and then ensure that the cumulative margins on either side of parity in relation to other convertible currencies would not exceed 2 per cent. This approach, the staff believed, would in general meet member countries' needs; any exceptional problems could be dealt with by the Fund on an individual basis.

When the Executive Board considered this recommendation, most Directors agreed with the staff's analysis. The question arose, however, as to the legal basis for the Fund to allow larger margins than those prescribed by Article IV, Section 3 (*a*). Was the Fund departing from its Articles either by amendment or by interpretation? The view of the General Counsel was that the proposed margins were technically multiple currency practices and could be approved by the Board under Article VIII, Section 3, which states that "no member shall engage in . . . any discriminatory currency arrangements or multiple currency practices except as authorized under this Agreement or approved by the Fund." Moreover, and even more important, the exchange systems in which these rates might develop already met or went far to meet the standards laid down in Article IV, Section 4 (*a*). Therefore, the General Counsel contended that the Fund could declare rates within a 2 per cent margin to be consistent with the Fund Agreement.

A few Directors noted that if rates outside the 1 per cent margin were legally approved under the authority of the Fund to deal with multiple currency practices, there might be some question that, like multiple currency practices, these rates were approved "on a temporary basis." But the decisive element, in the Board's view, was that the decision on margins about to be taken could not be interpreted as a violation of Article IV, Section 3. In any event, this decision could always be reversed later.

With these considerations in mind, the Board took the following decision on July 24, 1959:

> The Fund does not object to exchange rates which are within 2 per cent of parity for spot exchange transactions between a member's currency and the currencies of other members taking place within the member's territories, whenever such rates result from the maintenance of margins of no more than 1 per cent from parity for a convertible, including externally convertible, currency.[23]

FORWARD EXCHANGE RATES

Quite early in the Fund's existence, the question of the relation of forward to spot exchange rates arose. That the Fund was obliged to see that forward exchange rates bore a proper relation to spot rates was immediately recognized by both the staff and the Board. Provision had been made in Article IV, Section 3 (ii), for the Fund to determine what constituted a "reasonable" spread between spot and forward rates.

In 1946 the Board discussed a proposed section for the Rules and Regulations to the effect that agreed parities should not be circumvented by rates for forward exchange transactions. However, it was decided that it was not necessary for the Board to adopt a special regulation concerning forward transactions.

During the early 1950's concern about the relation of forward to spot rates was somewhat intensified. Spreads in forward rates from spot rates began to emerge after free markets in forward exchange had been re-established in a number of countries. When the Exchange Restrictions Report was discussed in the Board in 1953, attention focused on exchange arrangements which had recently gone into effect in some countries. These arrangements limited the purchase and sale of certain currencies at spot rates. As a result, transactions in forward markets had increased at the same time that there was little, if any, official intervention to support forward exchange rates.

While the Directors agreed that the Fund should not at the time attempt to take a position with respect to forward exchange arrangements, they recognized that an increase in forward transactions might constitute a rather significant development. Traders would naturally deal in the forward market if they could obtain more favorable exchange rates for certain currencies than the rate within 1 per cent of parity available in the spot market. Possibly forward market arrangements could even put in jeopardy the principle of orderly cross rates.

[23] E.B. Decision No. 904-(59/32), July 24, 1959; below, Vol. III, p. 226.

It was noted that discounts for certain currencies already existed in the forward exchange markets of some countries.

This problem was examined further during the course of 1953. The specific question of how the Fund was to determine a "reasonable" spread between a forward and a spot rate had arisen during the 1953 consultations under Article XIV with Belgium, in connection with the forward rate for Egyptian pounds. In first analyzing the factors responsible for a spread between spot and forward rates, the staff related premiums (or discounts) of forward rates over spot rates to interest rates. According to this analysis, at any given time the forward rate of exchange between two currencies is determined by the conditions of supply and demand in the forward market. But if, for example, the premium of the forward rate over the spot rate exceeds a certain margin, it becomes profitable for a bank to undertake interest arbitrage—that is, to sell the foreign currency forward and cover the exchange risk by buying the currency involved at the spot rate and investing that currency abroad. Therefore, under conditions of free competition, interest arbitrage will narrow down the forward premium (or discount) until it equals the difference in short-term (open market) interest rates in different countries.[24]

Wider spreads between forward and spot exchange rates resulted from limitations on access to spot markets, expectation of devaluation, or intervention in the forward market by monetary authorities. The Fund would, so the staff thought, have to judge instances of wider spreads in relation to the particular factor responsible for such a spread. For example, if an excessive spread between a forward rate and a spot rate resulted from controls on spot transactions, the Fund might treat the forward rate as a multiple currency practice.

The problem of spreads between forward and spot exchange rates diminished in the late 1950's as external convertibility was established. Subsequently, the staff undertook studies of the implications of government intervention in forward markets.[25] Later, as the world became more concerned about the role of interest rates in stimulating short-term capital movements and hence in facilitating balance of payments adjustment, the staff also examined the scope for movements of short-term funds in response to changes in forward rates.[26] But in the absence of the need for policy decisions, these analyses, while of interest to the Board, were not generally discussed.

---

[24] For a detailed exposition of forward exchange theory, see Paul Einzig, *A Dynamic Theory of Forward Exchange.*

[25] S.C. Tsiang, "The Theory of Forward Exchange and Effects of Government Intervention on the Forward Exchange Market," *Staff Papers,* Vol. VII (1959–60), pp. 75–106; J. Marcus Fleming and Robert A. Mundell, "Official Intervention on the Forward Exchange Market," *ibid.,* Vol. XI (1964), pp. 1–19.

[26] William H. White, "Interest Rate Differences, Forward Exchange Mechanism, and Scope for Short-Term Capital Movements," *Staff Papers,* Vol. X (1963), pp. 485–503.

Table 1. Initial Par Values Established, 1946–65

Date [1]	Member [2] and Rate
1946	
Dec. 18	Belgium — 2.28167 U.S. cents per franc
Dec. 18	Bolivia — 2.38095 U.S. cents per boliviano
Dec. 18	Canada — 100.000 U.S. cents per dollar
Dec. 18	Chile — 3.22581 U.S. cents per peso
Dec. 18	Colombia — 57.1433 U.S. cents per peso
Dec. 18	Costa Rica — 17.8094 U.S. cents per colón
Dec. 18	Cuba — 100.000 U.S. cents per peso
Dec. 18	Czechoslovakia — 2.00000 U.S. cents per koruna
Dec. 18	Denmark — 20.8376 U.S. cents per krone
Dec. 18	Ecuador — 7.40741 U.S. cents per sucre
Dec. 18	Egypt — 413.300 U.S. cents per pound
Dec. 18	El Salvador — 40.0000 U.S. cents per colón
Dec. 18	Ethiopia — 40.2500 U.S. cents per dollar
Dec. 18	France — 0.839583 U.S. cent per franc
Dec. 18	Guatemala — 100.000 U.S. cents per quetzal
Dec. 18	Honduras — 50.0000 U.S. cents per lempira
Dec. 18	Iceland — 15.4111 U.S. cents per króna
Dec. 18	India — 30.2250 U.S. cents per rupee
Dec. 18	Iran — 3.10078 U.S. cents per rial
Dec. 18	Iraq — 403.000 U.S. cents per dinar
Dec. 18	Luxembourg — 2.28167 U.S. cents per franc
Dec. 18	Mexico — 20.5973 U.S. cents per peso
Dec. 18	Netherlands — 37.6953 U.S. cents per guilder
Dec. 18	Nicaragua — 20.0000 U.S. cents per córdoba
Dec. 18	Norway — 20.1500 U.S. cents per krone
Dec. 18	Panama — 100.000 U.S. cents per balboa
Dec. 18	Paraguay — 32.3625 U.S. cents per guaraní
Dec. 18	Peru — 15.3846 U.S. cents per sol
Dec. 18	Philippines — 50.0000 U.S. cents per peso
Dec. 18	South Africa — 403.000 U.S. cents per pound
Dec. 18	United Kingdom — 403.000 U.S. cents per pound
Dec. 18	United States — 100.000 U.S. cents per dollar
1947	
Apr. 18	Venezuela — 29.8507 U.S. cents per bolívar
June 19	Turkey — 35.7143 U.S. cents per lira
July 29	Lebanon — 45.6313 U.S. cents per pound
July 29	Syrian Arab Republic — 45.6313 U.S. cents per pound
Nov. 17	Australia — 322.400 U.S. cents per pound
1948	
Apr. 23	Dominican Republic — 100.000 U.S. cents per peso
July 14	Brazil — 5.40541 U.S. cents per cruzeiro

Footnotes on page 86.

Table 1 *(continued).* Initial Par Values Established, 1946–65

Date [1]	Member [2] and Rate
1949	
May 24	Yugoslavia — 2.00000 U.S. cents per dinar
1951	
Mar. 19	Pakistan — 30.2250 U.S. cents per rupee
July 1	Finland — 0.434783 U.S. cent per markka
Nov. 5	Sweden — 19.3304 U.S. cents per krona
1952	
Jan. 16	Ceylon — 21.0000 U.S. cents per rupee
1953	
Jan. 30	Germany — 23.8095 U.S. cents per deutsche mark
May 4	Austria — 3.84615 U.S. cents per schilling
May 11	Japan — 0.277778 U.S. cent per yen
Aug. 7	Burma — 21.0000 U.S. cents per kyat
Oct. 2	Jordan — 280.000 U.S. cents per dinar
1954	
Apr. 9	Haiti — 20.0000 U.S. cents per gourde
1957	
Jan. 9	Argentina — 5.55556 U.S. cents per peso
Mar. 13	Israel — 55.5556 U.S. cents per pound
1958	
May 14	Ireland — 280.000 U.S. cents per pound
July 23	Sudan — 287.156 U.S. cents per pound
Nov. 5	Ghana — 280.000 U.S. cents per pound
1959	
July 17	Spain — 1.66667 U.S. cents per peseta
Aug. 12	Libya — 280.000 U.S. cents per pound
Oct. 16	Morocco — 19.7609 U.S. cents per dirham
1960	
Jan. 8	Saudi Arabia — 22.2222 U.S. cents per riyal
Mar. 30	Italy — 0.160000 U.S. cent per lira
Oct. 7	Uruguay — 13.5135 U.S. cents per peso
1961	
Mar. 29	Greece — 3.33333 U.S. cents per drachma
Oct. 27	New Zealand — 278.090 U.S. cents per pound
1962	
June 1	Portugal — 3.47826 U.S. cents per escudo
July 20	Malaya — 32.6667 U.S. cents per dollar
July 25	Cyprus — 280.000 U.S. cents per pound

Table 1 *(concluded)*. Initial Par Values Established, 1946–65

Date [1]	Member [2] and Rate
1963	
Mar. 8	Jamaica — 280.000 U.S. cents per pound
Mar. 13	Liberia — 100.000 U.S. cents per dollar
Mar. 22	Afghanistan — 2.22222 U.S. cents per afghani
Apr. 17	Nigeria — 280.000 U.S. cents per pound
Apr. 26	Kuwait — 280.000 U.S. cents per dinar
June 14	Somalia — 14.0000 U.S. cents per shilling
Oct. 20	Thailand — 4.80769 U.S. cents per baht
1964	
Sept. 28	Tunisia — 190.476 U.S. cents per dinar
1965	
Jan. 26	Burundi — 1.14286 U.S. cents per franc
Feb. 10	Trinidad and Tobago — 58.3333 U.S. cents per dollar
Aug. 6	Sierra Leone — 140.000 U.S. cents per leone

[1] The date given is that on which the initial par value became effective, usually a few days later than that on which the par value was agreed with the Fund.

[2] Excludes nonmetropolitan territories.

Table 2. Dates of Membership and of Initial Par Values, December 27, 1945–December 31, 1965 [1]

Member [2]	Date of Membership	Effective Date of Initial Par Value [3]
1. Afghanistan	July 14, 1955	Mar. 22, 1963
2. Algeria	Sept. 26, 1963	Not established
3. Argentina	Sept 20, 1956	Jan. 9, 1957
4. Australia	Aug. 5, 1947	Nov. 17, 1947
5. Austria	Aug. 27, 1948	May 4, 1953
6. Belgium	Dec. 27, 1945	Dec. 18, 1946
7. Bolivia	Dec. 27, 1945	Dec. 18, 1946
8. Brazil	Jan. 14, 1946	July 14, 1948
9. Burma	Jan. 3, 1952	Aug. 7, 1953
10. Burundi	Sept. 28, 1963	Jan. 26, 1965
11. Cameroon	July 10, 1963	Not established
12. Canada	Dec. 27, 1945	Dec. 18, 1946
13. Central African Republic	July 10, 1963	Not established
14. Ceylon	Aug. 29, 1950	Jan. 16, 1952
15. Chad	July 10, 1963	Not established
16. Chile	Dec. 31, 1945	Dec. 18, 1946
17. China	Dec. 27, 1945	Not established
18. Colombia	Dec. 27, 1945	Dec. 18, 1946
19. Congo (Brazzaville)	July 10, 1963	Not established
20. Congo, Democratic Republic	Sept. 28, 1963	Not established
21. Costa Rica	Jan. 8, 1946	Dec. 18, 1946
22. Cuba	Mar. 14, 1946	Dec. 18, 1946
23. Cyprus	Dec. 21, 1961	July 25, 1962
24. Czechoslovakia	Dec. 27, 1945	Dec. 18, 1946
25. Dahomey	July 10, 1963	Not established
26. Denmark	Mar. 30, 1946	Dec. 18, 1946
27. Dominican Republic	Dec. 28, 1945	Apr. 23, 1948
28. Ecuador	Dec. 27, 1945	Dec. 18, 1946
29. El Salvador	Mar. 14, 1946	Dec. 18, 1946
30. Ethiopia	Dec. 27, 1945	Dec. 18, 1946
31. Finland	Jan. 14, 1948	July 1, 1951
32. France	Dec. 27, 1945	Dec. 18, 1946
33. Gabon	Sept. 10, 1963	Not established
34. Germany	Aug. 14, 1952	Jan. 30, 1953
35. Ghana	Sept. 20, 1957	Nov. 5, 1958
36. Greece	Dec. 27, 1945	Mar. 29, 1961
37. Guatemala	Dec. 27, 1945	Dec. 18, 1946
38. Guinea	Sept. 28, 1963	Not established
39. Haiti	Sept. 8, 1953	Apr. 9, 1954
40. Honduras	Dec. 27, 1945	Dec. 18, 1946
41. Iceland	Dec. 27, 1945	Dec. 18, 1946
42. India	Dec. 27, 1945	Dec. 18, 1946
43. Indonesia	Apr. 15, 1954	Not established
44. Iran	Dec. 29, 1945	Dec. 18, 1946
45. Iraq	Dec. 27, 1945	Dec. 18, 1946

Footnotes on page 89.

Table 2 *(continued)*. Dates of Membership and of Initial Par Values, December 27, 1945–December 31, 1965 [1]

Member [2]	Date of Membership	Effective Date of Initial Par Value [3]
46. Ireland	Aug. 8, 1957	May 14, 1958
47. Israel	July 12, 1954	Mar. 13, 1957
48. Italy	Mar. 27, 1947	Mar. 30, 1960
49. Ivory Coast	Mar. 11, 1963	Not established
50. Jamaica	Feb. 21, 1963	Mar. 8, 1963
51. Japan	Aug. 13, 1952	May 11, 1953
52. Jordan	Aug. 29, 1952	Oct. 2, 1953
53. Kenya	Feb. 3, 1964	Not established
54. Korea	Aug. 26, 1955	Not established
55. Kuwait	Sept. 13, 1962	Apr. 26, 1963
56. Laos	July 5, 1961	Not established
57. Lebanon	Apr. 14, 1947	July 29, 1947
58. Liberia	Mar. 28, 1962	Mar. 13, 1963
59. Libya	Sept. 17, 1958	Aug. 12, 1959
60. Luxembourg	Dec. 27, 1945	Dec. 18, 1946
61. Malagasy Republic	Sept. 25, 1963	Not established
62. Malawi	July 19, 1965	Not established
63. Malaysia	Mar. 7, 1958	July 20, 1962
64. Mali	Sept. 27, 1963	Not established
65. Mauritania	Sept. 10, 1963	Not established
66. Mexico	Dec. 31, 1945	Dec. 18, 1946
67. Morocco	Apr. 25, 1958	Oct. 16, 1959
68. Nepal	Sept. 6, 1961	Not established
69. Netherlands	Dec. 27, 1945	Dec. 18, 1946
70. New Zealand	Aug. 31, 1961	Oct. 27, 1961
71. Nicaragua	Mar. 14, 1946	Dec. 18, 1946
72. Niger	Apr. 24, 1963	Not established
73. Nigeria	Mar. 30, 1961	Apr. 17, 1963
74. Norway	Dec. 27, 1945	Dec. 18, 1946
75. Pakistan	July 11, 1950	Mar. 19, 1951
76. Panama	Mar. 14, 1946	Dec. 18, 1946
77. Paraguay	Dec. 27, 1945	Dec. 18, 1946
78. Peru	Dec. 31, 1945	Dec. 18, 1946
79. Philippines	Dec. 27, 1945	Dec. 18, 1946
80. Poland	Dec. 27, 1945	Not established
81. Portugal	Mar. 29, 1961	June 1, 1962
82. Rwanda	Sept. 30, 1963	Not established
83. Saudi Arabia	Aug. 26, 1957	Jan. 8, 1960
84. Senegal	Aug. 31, 1962	Not established
85. Sierra Leone	Sept. 10, 1962	Aug. 6, 1965
86. Somalia	Aug. 31, 1962	June 14, 1963
87. South Africa	Dec. 27, 1945	Dec. 18, 1946
88. Spain	Sept. 15, 1958	July 17, 1959
89. Sudan	Sept. 5, 1957	July 23, 1958
90. Sweden	Aug. 31, 1951	Nov. 5, 1951

Table 2 *(concluded).* Dates of Membership and of Initial Par Values, December 27, 1945–December 31, 1965 [1]

Member [2]	Date of Membership	Effective Date of Initial Par Value [3]
91. Syrian Arab Republic	Apr. 10, 1947	July 29, 1947
92. Tanzania	Sept. 10, 1962	Not established
93. Thailand	May 3, 1949	Oct. 20, 1963
94. Togo	Aug. 1, 1962	Not established
95. Trinidad and Tobago	Sept. 16, 1963	Feb. 10, 1965
96. Tunisia	Apr. 14, 1958	Sept. 28, 1964
97. Turkey	Mar. 11, 1947	June 19, 1947
98. Uganda	Sept. 27, 1963	Not established
99. United Arab Republic	Dec. 27, 1945	Dec. 18, 1946
100. United Kingdom	Dec. 27, 1945	Dec. 18, 1946
101. United States	Dec. 27, 1945	Dec. 18, 1946
102. Upper Volta	May 2, 1963	Not established
103. Uruguay	Dec. 27, 1945	Oct. 7, 1960
104. Venezuela	Dec. 30, 1946	Apr. 18, 1947
105. Viet-Nam	Sept. 21, 1956	Not established
106. Yugoslavia	Dec. 27, 1945	May 24, 1949
107. Zambia	Sept. 23, 1965	Not established

[1] As 4 of the 107 countries listed in this table withdrew from membership (Cuba, Czechoslovakia, Indonesia, and Poland), the actual membership on December 31, 1965 was 103.

[2] Excludes nonmetropolitan territories.

[3] The date given is that on which the par value became effective, usually a few days later than that on which the par value was agreed with the Fund.

CHAPTER

5

Exchange Rate Adjustment

Margaret G. de Vries

JUST AS THE FUND has had to develop policies pertaining to the establishment and maintenance of par values, so it has had to evolve policies relating to changes in those par values and in other exchange rates. The issues which have come to the fore include the reasons for devaluation, the magnitudes of the changes, and the possibility of adverse consequences for other members. The role of the Fund in a matter explicitly stated by the Articles to be reserved to the initiative of members has also had to be clarified. Furthermore, the Fund has had to decide what to do when members change exchange rates that have not been agreed as par values: adjustment of exchange rates is not always effected by the simple mechanism set up in the Articles—that is, from one unitary par value to another.

The major examples of rate adjustment between 1946 and 1965 through what, in the parlance of economists, is called "altering the pegs" were the devaluations of the major currencies in September 1949, devaluations by Mexico (1954) and Pakistan (1955), and the German and Dutch revaluations of 1961. These rate adjustments form the subject of this chapter. Exchange rates have also been altered in three other ways. The first comprises partial and selective devaluations through the alteration of multiple rates; these were very frequent until the late 1950's. The reasons for devaluation in this manner, and the Fund's views, are discussed in Chapter 6. Second, in a few countries devaluation has been effected by the temporary institution of a fluctuating exchange rate; only later was a new par value established. Canada, the Philippines, and Thailand afford noteworthy examples of this type of devaluation. Third, devaluation has occurred through the use of steadily depreciating fluctuating rates. Some countries which had introduced fluctuating rates subsequently undertook to support these rates. Later, they were obliged to devalue again. These last two types of devaluation are discussed in Chapter 7.

TWO BASIC CONCEPTS

The Fund's Articles contain two basic concepts applicable to changes in par values. The first provides a criterion by which to judge the *need* for a change in par value: par values are to be altered only to correct a fundamental disequilibrium. The second relates not only to the need for devaluation but also to its *size:* competitive depreciation is to be avoided.

In the twenty-odd years since these concepts were formulated, the Fund has never attempted to define precisely either "fundamental disequilibrium" or "competitive depreciation." In its first years, in response to members' requests, the Fund did make two interpretations of its Articles involving the first term. And in the early 1950's some sizable devaluations excited in at least one Executive Director the fear of excessive, if not competitive, depreciation.

Subsequently, the need for exact definitions of these terms has not been a pressing one; therefore such definitions, which could limit the leverage of future Fund actions, have been avoided. In fact, even when the Fund has taken decisions denoting its concurrence with the proposed rate changes of individual countries, it has rarely used these terms. But the absence of definitions has not meant that the conditions described could not be recognized when they were thought to occur. Over the years member countries have proposed a number of changes in par values and, where par values did not exist, in their prevailing exchange rates, and the Fund has generally concurred. In these instances, several different reasons for devaluation can be discerned, all tending to suggest the nature of fundamental disequilibrium.

In a postwar world in which economic conditions have been in direct contrast to those of the interwar period, there has been little temptation to indulge in competitive depreciation of exchange rates. Whereas unemployment had been widespread in the 1930's, high levels of employment have prevailed in most countries since the end of World War II. The economic dangers have stemmed from inflation rather than from deflation. Consequently, countries have been less, rather than more, inclined since the war than in the interwar period to use devaluation as an instrument of balance of payments policy. In this environment it is understandable that the Fund has not found it necessary to disapprove, certainly not formally, any proposed change in exchange rates as constituting competitive depreciation.

EARLY INTERPRETATION OF FUNDAMENTAL DISEQUILIBRIUM

While the plans for a postwar international monetary organization were being drawn up, considerable interest centered on how to limit the frequency of exchange rate adjustments. To this end many economists distinguished fundamental disequilibrium—for which rate adjustments were appropriate—from cyclical or seasonal disequilibrium—for which rate adjustments were not suitable. Furthermore, a prime concern, both for Fund member countries and for economists, was how to reconcile domestic objectives, especially the attainment of full employment, with the requirements of external balance. Therefore, the question raised by the United Kingdom at the outset of the Fund's activity in 1946 could be expected. The British Government stated its intention to maintain full employment and asked whether steps necessary to protect a member from unemployment of a chronic or persistent character, arising from pressures on its balance of payments, would be considered measures necessary to correct a fundamental disequilibrium.[1] In other words, would countries threatened by unemployment due to loss of exports, now (with the advent of the Fund) have the option of devaluing their currency with the approval of an international body? Their choice had previously been restricted to deflation, as required by the gold standard, or to devaluation in circumstances likely to induce retaliatory depreciation, as during the 1930's.

In answer to the British request for an interpretation of fundamental disequilibrium, the Executive Directors took what proved to be one of two unique decisions pertaining to that expression—that steps necessary to protect a member from unemployment of a chronic or persistent character, arising from pressure on its balance of payments, were indeed among the measures necessary to correct a fundamental disequilibrium. The Board further decided that, in each instance in which a member proposed a change in the par value of its currency to correct a fundamental disequilibrium, the Fund would be required to determine, in the light of all relevant circumstances, whether in its opinion the proposed change was necessary to correct the fundamental disequilibrium.[2]

THE FUND'S AUTHORITY

Another early issue in connection with the interpretation of fundamental disequilibrium focused on the question of the exact powers of the Fund. Although the Fund Agreement specified that exchange rate changes could be proposed only by members—not by the Fund—and only where there was fundamental disequilibrium, this still left scope for wide differences in view as to how much of a role the Fund might play, and in what way. How much informal initiative could the Fund take in suggesting exchange rate changes? Who in the Fund—the Executive Board, the Managing Director, or, informally, the staff—might take such initiative, and in what ways and to what degree?

[1] Resolution IM-5, *Selected Documents*, p. 19.

[2] E.B. Decision No. 71-2, September 26, 1946; below, Vol. III, p. 227.

In fact, as the Fund and its members learned to work closely together, a *modus operandi* was evolved without any formalized arrangements having been agreed. However, at the outset of the Fund's deliberations in the late 1940's, countries were understandably jealous of their sovereignty in this important field. This was the first time that such a previously unilateral matter had been turned over to an international body. Moreover, there was much mistrust of the Fund, especially among Western European countries. They feared especially that changes in exchange rates or relaxation of restrictions might be forced upon them. They doubted that the Fund was adequately aware of the difficulties of postwar reconstruction. And in their fears and concerns they were mindful of the strong voting position in the Fund of the United States and of the eagerness of the U.S. authorities to have international trade and payments relations restored to normal. In these circumstances the power of the Fund even to object to a proposed par value had to be agreed upon explicitly by the Board.

An insufficient devaluation

In the course of the Executive Board's discussion concerning the first devaluation referred to the Fund—that of the French franc early in 1948 [3]—Mr. de Largentaye (France) brought up an ancillary, but crucial, question. Although under its Articles the Fund could object to a change in par value if no fundamental disequilibrium existed, could the Fund also object if it considered the proposed degree of change in par value not sufficient to correct that disequilibrium? Did the Fund not have to concur in a proposed change of parity if (*a*) there was a fundamental disequilibrium, and (*b*) a change in the par value was necessary to correct the fundamental disequilibrium?

Mr. de Largentaye believed that the Fund had no power to object to an insufficient change in parity. His reasoning was that if the Fund had the right to object to a proposed change in a par value because it found the change insufficient, the Fund would, in the long run, force the member to accept an additional depreciation of its currency. The Fund, rather than the member, thereby would initiate a change in the par value. The purpose of the Fund was to oppose competitive alterations of par values. In order to prevent competitive depreciation, it was not necessary for the Fund to be able to object to an insufficient alteration; it was enough to empower it to object to an excessive alteration.

The question at stake was vital. The Board, in addition to discussing France's devaluation, held extra sessions to consider this matter of the Fund's authority. In the preparatory staff paper for these discussions, the General Counsel expressed the opinion that the Fund could object if the degree of proposed devaluation was insufficient. In effect, the Fund must be satisfied that not just two but three conditions existed before it was required to concur in a change in

[3] See below, pp. 129–30.

par value: first, a fundamental disequilibrium must exist; second, the fundamental disequilibrium could not be corrected without a change in par value; and third, *the change would, in fact, correct the disequilibrium.*

The Directors, however, did not consider the question resolved so simply. Mr. de Selliers (Belgium) concurred with Mr. de Largentaye in his belief that the Fund had no power to object to an insufficient devaluation. Article IV, he contended, was intended to avoid competitive devaluations. Its whole emphasis was on keeping changes in par values as small as possible. There was no indication that members could be made to devalue further than they wished because the Fund thought that only a greater change would correct a fundamental disequilibrium.

Mr. Martínez-Ostos (Mexico), Alternate to Mr. Gómez, agreed with Mr. de Largentaye and Mr. de Selliers on purely legal grounds. He recalled that the Fund was debarred from objecting to a change in par value amounting to less than 10 per cent of the original parity. If a member could make a change of up to 10 per cent with freedom, he doubted that the Fund could object to an even greater change on the ground that it was insufficient.

Other Directors had a broader view of the Fund's powers. Mr. Overby (United States) thought that the Fund would be in a ridiculous position if it was forced to concur in a change in par value which it was convinced was not adequate. The acceptance of an inadequate change would jeopardize exchange stability for the member and endanger orderly exchange arrangements for all members. He emphasized that, with the establishment of the Fund, a new regime had come into being. Par values were no longer matters of unilateral decision. They were now subject to agreement with the Fund. And the term *agreement* necessarily meant that the parties must have the power to concur or reject. Consultation and collaboration in the true sense involved more than mere form.

Although he did not ordinarily intervene in discussions such as this, the Chairman, Mr. Gutt, believed the issue to be so significant that he wished to express his opinion. From the practical point of view, he believed that the Fund would be placed in an absurd position before the public if it was forced by interpretation to concur in inadequate changes. To protect its integrity, the Fund would have to declare that the concurrence was purely formal, and that it really opposed the new par value; such a declaration would be confusing to the public and would bring discredit on the Fund.

The concept of "reasonable doubt"

Mr. Saad (Egypt), who was away from headquarters at the time, cabled a statement of his position and successfully resolved the debate with a concept of "reasonable doubt." He believed that the Fund, which could not legally require a member to change its par value in order to correct a fundamental disequilibrium, could not justifiably express disagreement with a proposed depreciation merely because it questioned whether the depreciation was sufficient to correct the fundamental disequilibrium. However, he thought that a different situation prevailed if it was *proved beyond doubt* that the proposed depreciation would not correct even partially the fundamental disequilibrium, or that the damage done to a member's interest by such a depreciation would absorb any possible advantage that the depreciation would give to the member. In such circumstances, the Fund could rightly consider that a proposed depreciation could not be justified as correcting a fundamental disequilibrium.

In effect, Mr. Saad's concept acknowledged the Fund's power to object to a proposed devaluation if the inadequacy of that devaluation could be proved beyond doubt; if it could not, the Fund could not object. Moreover, in its deliberations, the Fund must give the member the benefit of any reasonable doubt.

On this basis the Board was able to take the second of two decisions on fundamental disequilibrium. On March 1, 1948, it decided that the Fund had authority under Article IV, Section 5, to object to a change in par value proposed by a member when the extent of the proposed change, in the judgment of the Fund, was insufficient to correct a fundamental disequilibrium. The Fund recognized, however, that the extent of the necessary change could not be determined with precision, and that, in reaching a decision on a member's proposal to change its par value, whether during the transitional period or thereafter, the member should be given the benefit of any reasonable doubt. In addition, due consideration should be given to the views of the member regarding the political and social consequences of a change in par value greater than the one proposed.[4]

Changes in rates other than par values

Since members did not always devalue their currencies by altering an agreed par value, the Fund found it necessary to establish its authority to agree to other kinds of exchange rate changes. From 1947 to 1951, the Executive Board took a series of decisions to the effect that all alterations of exchange rates, regardless of whether par values were involved or not, were subject to review by the Fund. In December 1947 procedures and policies were outlined for reviewing changes in multiple rates, to apply to all members including those for whose currencies par values had not been established.[5] In April 1951, the Board took a further decision requiring new members that had not yet agreed initial par values to consult with the Fund and obtain its agreement before changing the exchange rates which had prevailed when they accepted membership. Thus, as countries

---

[4] E.B. Decision No. 278-3, March 1, 1948; below, Vol. III, p. 227.

[5] Footnote to E.B. Decision No. 237-2, December 18, 1947; below, Vol. III, p. 264.

joined the Fund, they were required to consult with the Fund before changing their exchange rates, even though they might not yet have set par values.

THE DEVALUATIONS OF 1949

A TEST FOR THE FUND

Both the staff and the Executive Directors were well aware of the arguments against devaluation being advanced by many economists in the late 1940's. Differences of opinion as regards the need for exchange rate adjustment in Western Europe also occurred among the staff, who had been studying the need for devaluation, and among the Directors. Nevertheless, in their Annual Report for 1948 the Executive Directors distinguished between exchange stability and exchange rigidity:

> The Fund Agreement makes it clear that the provisions for the regulation of exchange rates are not intended to impose upon the Fund the duty of perpetuating in the name of stability exchange rates which have lost touch with economic realities.[6]

By that time there were indications that in some countries the exchange rate was restraining exports and adding to the difficulty of earning convertible currencies. The Fund stressed that in the timing of an exchange rate adjustment, the function of the rate in promoting exports, which had been a major element in the determination of the initial par values, was still of great importance.[7]

Significantly, the Directors also said that

> although the Fund is not entitled to propose a change in the par value of a currency it has an obligation to keep the exchange rate situation constantly under review, and its views may properly find expression in its informal consultations with members. When an exchange rate is no longer appropriate the Fund will, of course, give prompt and realistic consideration to a member's request for adjustment in the par value of its currency.[8]

But this statement was as far as the Directors, as a whole, were prepared to go. The European Directors especially were unready, even by mid-1949, for any decision by the Fund to review countries' exchange rates. Some did not want the Board even to discuss the problem. Jealous of members' sovereignty in this field, they believed that a decision by the Board to study exchange rates was unnecessary and likely to be detrimental to the interests of both the Fund and members. They were especially fearful that the Fund might *propose* a devaluation and thereby usurp a prerogative of members.

---

[6] *Annual Report, 1948,* p. 21.

[7] *Ibid.,* p. 23.

[8] *Ibid.,* p. 24.

The position of the U.S. Executive Director was exactly the opposite. In the U.S. Government the conviction had gradually grown that the establishment of a stronger economic structure in Europe required a substantial depreciation of sterling and other Western European currencies. Early in 1949 this attitude found public expression. The U.S. National Advisory Council proposed that "the exchange rate question should be reviewed with a number of European countries in the course of the next year." [9] In discussions in the Executive Board of the position of individual members during the first eight months of 1949, Mr. Overby and Mr. Southard (who succeeded him in March 1949) found frequent opportunities to raise the question of exchange rate adjustment.

At the suggestion of Mr. Southard, an Ad Hoc Committee of the Board was established in August 1949 to consider the problems arising out of the international payments situation and the relation of exchange rates to these problems. Some Directors objected to the establishment of such a committee and took a very unfavorable view of its discussions. The last meeting of this committee was held on September 8, about a week before the devaluation of sterling. The committee's report advocated that member countries in Western Europe review their rate structures and determine, in consultation with the Fund, to what extent adjustment should be made in each individual case where it was appropriate. Several Directors, among them Mr. Beyen (Netherlands), Mr. Bolton (United Kingdom), Mr. de Largentaye, Mr. Madan (India), Alternate to Mr. Joshi, Mr. McFarlane (Australia), and Mr. Rasminsky (Canada), opposed adoption of any formal report in which members were "invited" to change their exchange rates. Their opposition continued even after the devaluations of September. In their view the Fund should refrain from coming to formal decisions in advance on the exchange rates of its members. Eventually, the committee's report was adopted by formal vote of the Directors.

The devaluation of sterling

What finally precipitated the devaluation of sterling was a large outflow of sterling reserves during the summer of 1949, such as had occurred in the attempt at convertibility in 1947. In the three months April–June 1949, gold and dollar reserves of the sterling area fell by 14 per cent, to $1,650 million. This level of reserves was less than half the amount of gold alone held at the beginning of 1938, and less than a quarter of that amount in terms of purchasing power, after making allowance for the increase in U.S. prices in the intervening decade. As anticipations of devaluation grew, speculative action increased. In the eleven weeks from June 30 to September 18 reserves declined by nearly 20 per cent, to $1,340 million, and the British authorities came to look

[9] U.S. Congress, Senate, Committee on Foreign Relations, *Extension of European Recovery*, Hearings . . . on S. 833, a Bill to Amend the Economic Cooperation Act of 1948, 81st Cong., 1st sess., 1949, p. 388.

upon devaluation as an unavoidable step in order to end a situation which was being made more difficult by the expectation of devaluation.

The choice of an appropriate new rate presented a most difficult problem. Obviously, the lower the new rate, the more expensive in sterling terms American imports would be, and the greater, therefore, the difficulty of controlling increases in manufacturing and living costs; in addition, the lower the rate, the greater the difficulty of servicing the dollar debts of the United Kingdom. On the other hand, the disparity in export price levels was such as to call for a drastic change. Perhaps even more important was the need to establish a rate low enough to create expectations that the British Government would be able to maintain it.

The Managing Director of the Fund was informed by the Chancellor of the Exchequer on September 15, 1949, the penultimate day of the Fund's Fourth Annual Meeting, that the U.K. Government intended to devalue sterling by approximately 30.5 per cent. The exchange rate of £1 = $4.03 which had been accepted by the Fund as the initial par value for sterling would be replaced by a new rate of £1 = $2.80. Formal notification of the proposal to establish a new par value was submitted to the Fund on Saturday, September 17, and on the afternoon of that day the Executive Board concurred in the proposal.

The Directors considered that the causes of the devaluation of sterling were to be found both in the United Kingdom itself and in other countries of the sterling area. Among the long-term factors that had shaped the problem of the United Kingdom in 1949, the most important were the severe deterioration of its external position on capital account compared with ten years earlier, the deterioration in its terms of trade, the difficulties it had experienced in recapturing an adequate share of the dollar markets, its abnormal dependence on dollar imports, the persistence of inflationary pressures in its economy, and the existence of large sterling balances.

Subsequently the role of the Fund in the devaluation of sterling was, variously, questioned, criticized, and defended. Had not the Fund been merely a "rubber stamp"? Had not the Fund been too passive—some said "by-passed"—in this devaluation?

Clearly the magnitude of the devaluation as well as the timing had been determined by the British authorities before the Fund was notified. However, the test had been met that plans to change the rate were presented to an international body prior to action. The Fund, recognizing the need for devaluation, and that the extent ought to be large, agreed to the proposed change. The Fund could therefore be regarded as putting into operation the guidelines of the general decision taken a year and a half earlier. At that time, as noted above, it had stated that the extent of a necessary change in par value could not be determined with precision and that, as the Fund reached a decision on a member's proposal to change its par value, the member should be given the benefit of any reasonable doubt. Also the Fund might, and did, stress the need for monetary and fiscal policies to back up the new exchange rate.

Devaluations of other currencies

The devaluation of sterling was immediately followed by devaluations of several other currencies—those of the sterling area and of all the Western European countries. This was indeed a week in which the Fund's machinery—Board and staff—went into operation. A detailed staff study evaluating the new exchange rate was prepared for each of the several countries and was discussed by the Executive Board. Much relevant preparatory work had laid the basis for expediting the staff's papers and the Board's consideration of them. Nonetheless, much preparation and discussion still had to be done quickly—within the course of four days and mostly over a week-end. Furthermore, complete secrecy was mandatory. Those who were closely involved at the time recall several measures to maintain secrecy and to keep up the pace of staff preparation and Board consideration of the exchange rate changes being proposed. The staff, for example, was not permitted to leave the building for any purpose on Saturday, September 17, meals being brought in. And senior officials did not go home for three days, sleeping at a nearby hotel.

Most of the currencies involved, including not only those of other countries in the sterling area (Australia, Iceland, India, Iraq, and the Union of South Africa), but those of Egypt, Denmark, and Norway, were also devalued by 30.5 per cent. The Netherlands guilder was devalued from f. 2.65285 to f. 3.80 = $1, i.e., by 30.2 per cent.

The devaluation of the currencies of Belgium and Luxembourg from 43.8275 francs to 50.000 francs = $1 involved a depreciation of only 12.3 per cent. For a few days the Belgian Government had considered the possibility of introducing a fluctuating rate. After discussion with the Fund, however, the Government concluded that the disadvantages of a floating rate were too grave to be worthwhile, and proposed a new par value. The rate chosen was designed to adjust the export and import prices of the Belgian-Luxembourg Economic Union (BLEU) to the trend of world prices which was expected to follow the devaluations, and to improve the payments position of the BLEU vis-à-vis the dollar area. Since the end of World War II the international financial position of the BLEU had been strong; its current account deficit with the dollar area had been declining and its surplus with other countries had increased. The position of the Belgian steel industry was also relatively strong. However, the Belgian authorities believed it necessary to adjust the parity of the Belgian franc somewhat in the face of the general devaluation. These considerations led the Belgian Government to adopt a middle course between maintenance of the former parity and devaluation to the same extent as sterling.

The problem of the appropriate rate for Canada was dominated by two considerations. Had the rate been left unchanged, Canada would have been subjected to the strains arising from the improved competitive position of the devaluing countries, although still needing to alleviate the imbalance in its trade with the United States. On the other hand, a devaluation equal to that of sterling would not have helped to expand imports from the devaluing countries, which was required if such countries were to correct the serious disequilibrium in their payments position vis-à-vis Canada. In light of these considerations, the Canadian dollar was devalued by 9.1 per cent.

The Fund also agreed to changes in the exchange rates of Finland and Greece, for which no par values had been agreed, and to a change in the exchange rate for France, for which the agreed par value had been suspended. In July 1949, Finland had devalued the markka by 15 per cent, from Fmk 135 = $1 to Fmk 160 = $1. The devaluation in September 1949 was to Fmk 230 = $1. The Government of Greece, on September 22, changed the effective exchange rate for the drachma to Dr 15,000 = $1 and Dr 42,000 = £1, a depreciation of 33.3 per cent in respect of the dollar.

The French Government proposed to unify its system as well as adjust the exchange rate. Since October 1948 the free rate for the franc had applied only to nontrade transactions in certain currencies. For commercial transactions the daily average of the free rate and the previous fixed official rate of 214.392 francs per U.S. dollar had been used. Financial as well as commercial transactions in all other currencies except the Italian lira were conducted at exchange rates based on this average dollar rate. The rates for financial transactions were approximately 20 per cent more depreciated than the rates for commercial transactions. After unification in September 1949, the exchange rate applicable to transactions in U.S. dollars was allowed to rise from F 330.80 to F 350.00 = $1. This represented a depreciation vis-à-vis the dollar of 5.7 per cent for financial transactions and 21.8 per cent for commercial transactions, but it represented an appreciation vis-à-vis sterling of about 12.5 per cent.

COMPETITIVE DEPRECIATION

THE ISSUE ARISES

The onset of the first devaluations—those of September 1949—demonstrated that differences in points of view about the need for and magnitudes of devaluation were inevitable. The Latin American Directors, exercised lest the devaluations of the outer sterling area in line with that of the pound sterling should harm the export prospects of their countries, thought that there was a need for a "definitional examination" of competitive depreciation. Both Mr. Paranaguá (Brazil) and Mr. D'Ascoli (Venezuela) doubted whether a clear case of fundamental disequilibrium could be made in support of the devaluations of the dependent territories, and felt certain that no such case could be made for a devaluation by 30 per cent.

This objection raised a related legal question. When a member proposed to the Fund a change in the par value of its metropolitan currency and corresponding changes in the par values of the separate currencies of its nonmetropolitan areas, could the Fund consider the various pieces of the proposal separately or did the Fund have to deal with the proposal as a whole? The Legal Department's opinion in the preparatory staff paper was that the Fund was required to consider and decide on such proposals as a unit. It could object to the entire proposal if it was not satisfied that the changes proposed in the par value of the metropolitan currency or in the par value of one or more of the separate currencies were necessary to correct a fundamental disequilibrium. But it was not required to decide on the proposal as a unit if the intended changes in the par values of the separate currencies did not correspond to that in the metropolitan currency.

Several Directors did not concur. Mr. D'Ascoli thought that the conclusion that the Fund had to accept or reject the entire proposal of a country was wholly impractical. It put the Board in the situation of either (*a*) accepting an unjustified change in the par value of a separate currency (i.e., a colonial currency) purely for the sake of not having to reject at the same time a justified and even very necessary change in the par value of a metropolitan currency, or (*b*) rejecting both proposals, even if the member making the proposal was taking the very action that the Board thought it should have taken long before with respect to the metropolitan currency.

There seemed, Mr. D'Ascoli stated, to be an assumption that colonial empires possessed economic uniformity. In actuality, the differences between metropolitan and dependent territories were so great that separate currencies had been created for many dependent territories. The Fund should be entitled to decide upon the changes in those separate currencies without being influenced by considerations independent of the payments position of the territory concerned. Mr. Hooker (United States), Alternate to Mr. Southard, supported Mr. D'Ascoli's position. But he commented that, as a practical matter, if the Fund had any doubts on a joint proposal, these doubts could be expressed to the member during the course of the Fund's preliminary discussions with that member.

Most of the European Directors, on the other hand, agreed with the interpretation put forward by the staff. Mr. Tansley (United Kingdom) and Mr. McFarlane (Australia) argued that a member which proposed a change in the par values of its metropolitan currency and its separate currencies made a single proposal which the Fund had to accept or reject as a whole, although the

Fund had the right to look at each separate currency. Mr. de Largentaye's opinion was that the drafters of the Articles of Agreement could not have intended to give the Fund the right to object or concur in only part of a proposal. The Fund's rejection of a part of the proposal would amount to a change in the par value of the separate currency in terms of the metropolitan currency which the member had not proposed.

Mr. Southard's reasoning was that on economic grounds there was no necessity for a separate currency to follow the metropolitan currency. The Fund should consider each currency independently after economic analysis of each proposal. He did not believe that the Articles of Agreement denied the Fund the right to concur in part of a proposal if it had arrived at the conclusion that only a portion of a proposal was justified and other portions were not. Mr. Southard's argument was also that the Fund was not necessarily serving the best interests of members that administered dependent territories by treating a joint proposal as a unit. It was of more help to the metropolitan members for the Fund to examine carefully the exchange rates of dependent territories. Accordingly, Mr. Southard suggested and the Board agreed that further discussion should be postponed until the Directors for these members had had an opportunity to consider the problem further.

There has not, however, been any further discussion in the Board of the question whether devaluation of nonmetropolitan currencies should be considered separately from that of the member. Another instance of devaluation of nonmetropolitan currencies occurred in December 1958. After France had devalued and proposed a new par value for the franc, it also proposed parities for the separate currencies of its nonmetropolitan territories, but the rates proposed were not uniform. The new par value established for the franc for Algeria, the French Antilles, and French Guiana was the same as that for the French franc, 0.202550 U.S. cents per franc. The par value of the CFA franc, for Cameroun, French Equatorial Africa, French West Africa, Madagascar and dependencies, Réunion, St. Pierre and Miquelon, and Togoland, was 0.405099 U.S. cent per CFA franc; the CFA franc was thus equal to 2.00 French francs. The par value agreed for the CFP franc, applying to the French possessions of Oceania, New Caledonia, and New Hebrides, was 1.11402 U.S. cents per CFP franc, equal to 5.50 French francs. But, in any event, no question was raised in the Board about these devaluations, and the decision was taken without discussion.

What is competitive depreciation?

The possibility that competitive depreciation might be involved in a member's proposal to devalue has come up on only a few occasions. One such occasion was when Iceland, which had already devalued by 30.5 per cent in September

1949, proposed to devalue by another 42.5 per cent in February 1950. The problem posed for the Fund was made the more difficult by the fact that the second devaluation, according to the member, was not needed to sustain exports; in fact, in order to prevent excessive export price cutting, sizable export taxes were being introduced. The extra depreciation was necessary rather to curb imports: import demand was swollen and the country could not introduce import duties. Inasmuch as European markets for fish, the chief Icelandic export, had become much more competitive, concern by several European Directors over this devaluation was more pronounced than it might otherwise have been.

Several questions confronted the Fund: Should a country be permitted, because of import considerations, to cut its par value below a point adequate to move exports? Could devaluing a currency so as to balance imports with exports be regarded as competitive depreciation? If export taxes were to be applied after devaluation because otherwise the profits to exporters would be too great, could such a devaluation be considered necessary to correct a fundamental disequilibrium?

In effect, the Icelandic devaluation had raised the question of the nature of competitive depreciation. How could it be defined or identified? The staff undertook a careful examination of the subject.

Meanwhile, a decision on Iceland's exchange rate could not wait. When the Board considered the proposal, several Directors agreed that a devaluation was necessary and saw no reason to object to the degree proposed. In their view, because of its payments deficits, Iceland needed some protection for its exports. And they were pleased at the well thought out program of fiscal measures that would accompany devaluation. However, Mr. de Largentaye believed that the devaluation should be held to the lowest possible level so as to keep down the inflationary and other undesirable effects that would follow. He also questioned whether the country was taking all possible steps to deflate the economy, which, in his view, was a better alternative than devaluation where it was possible.

Mr. van der Valk (Netherlands), Alternate to Mr. Beyen, and Mr. Santaella (Venezuela), Alternate to Mr. D'Ascoli, had similar doubts about the degree of devaluation proposed. So large a devaluation as was proposed might mean that other countries would be subjected to unjustified competition from Icelandic exports only because of Iceland's need to curb imports.

After an assurance by Iceland that it was not intending to engage in competitive depreciation, the Fund concurred in the proposed change in the par value, noting with approval the intention to impose export taxes which would help to prevent undue pressure on highly competitive markets for particular exports. A year later, to cope with a similar set of circumstances, Iceland introduced a multiple rate system which lasted for several years.

Search for a definition

After studying the question of a definition of competitive depreciation, the consensus of the staff was that a devaluation which merely corrected the payments position of a country could not be considered competitive, even if that devaluation had adverse effects on other countries. Admittedly, devaluation might be disturbing to other countries exporting the same goods, and even to countries importing such goods if they competed with home output, but this did not make the devaluation competitive. Only an excessive devaluation—that is, one that overcorrected for a fundamental disequilibrium—could be regarded as competitive depreciation in the sense of the Fund Agreement. The question was how to determine an excessive devaluation.

The staff approach to this question was to measure an excessive devaluation in terms of its departure from a "correct" exchange rate. The "correct" level of an exchange rate was defined to be one that over a period of years tended to restore external balance *and* to yield a moderate increase in reserves if these were previously deficient. In this light, devaluation was competitive only when it resulted in so marked a surplus in the devaluing country that reserves grew at an excessive rate.[10] This definition was, of course, influenced heavily by the circumstances of the time, when all countries except the United States were suffering from low foreign exchange reserves. But this definition also made clear that, in order to judge whether a proposed exchange adjustment is correct, the Fund must have a broad concept of (1) the appropriate distribution of reserves in the world, (2) the effects on the world pattern of exchange rates and the need for continuing direct controls that the proposed adjustment would involve, and (3) the extent to which the new exchange rate would enable the devaluing country, over a period of years, to acquire reserves.

From time to time other devaluations aroused some concern, at least for one or two Directors; these are discussed immediately below. On these occasions, although some members of the staff suggested a general discussion by the Board of competitive depreciation, one was never held. The need for a definition of competitive depreciation had waned.

OTHER DEVALUATIONS OF CONCERN

In the next few years the magnitudes of some other proposed devaluations, although acceptable to nearly all the Executive Directors and defensible as far as staff analysis was concerned, were to elicit expressions of disapproval from at least one Director when the proposals were discussed by the Board.

---

[10] See Walter R. Gardner and S.C. Tsiang, "Competitive Depreciation," *Staff Papers*, Vol. II (1951–52), pp. 399–406.

Greece and Austria

In 1953 two countries—Greece and Austria—both of which had devalued in late 1949, again proposed sizable devaluations in moves to unify their multiple rates. When Greece proposed to unify its exchange structure at a new rate of Dr 30,000 = $1, Mr. de Largentaye (France) queried the rate. The free rate in New York was only 16,000 to 17,000 drachmas per U.S. dollar. According to staff calculations, the average effective rate for all exports under the multiple rate system was approximately 20,000 drachmas per U.S. dollar. The average effective rate for imports subject to tax was also estimated at about 20,000 drachmas per U.S. dollar. Mr. de Largentaye was of the opinion, therefore, that a devaluation to Dr 30,000 = $1 was extreme, especially for a country which was in near equilibrium. Such a sizable devaluation would, he believed, be apt to bring a considerable reflux of capital, which might well destroy the newly won internal economic stability and might ruin the deflationary efforts of the Government.

The consensus of the Board did not coincide with this view. As had the staff, the Directors reasoned that the inflation which continued in Greece after the devaluation of September 1949 had made the drachma by 1953 again considerably overvalued. Moreover, Greece had had great difficulty in moving its principal exports, even at exchange rates of 20,000 drachmas per U.S. dollar and more. Additionally, Greece was proposing to remove virtually all quantitative restrictions on imports, except for those on some luxury goods. Therefore, the new rate had to be high enough to keep in check the hitherto suppressed import demand which might otherwise emerge. But because of the point made by Mr. de Largentaye, the Board, in its decision, impressed upon the Greek authorities the importance of firm anti-inflationary measures.

In May 1953 Austria similarly proposed a unification of its multiple rates and a devaluation to S 26 = $1. Austria also proposed this rate as an initial par value. Once again Mr. de Largentaye commented that the proposed devaluation was rather severe. He was not convinced that a smaller devaluation would not have been possible: Austria's reserves had doubled in one year, its credit in the EPU had increased, and its exports had been expanding.

The majority of Directors, however, were in favor of sizable devaluation. A new price-wage spiral which had developed after the outbreak of the Korean War had weakened the competitive position of Austria's exports, and the country was liberalizing restrictions.[11]

Bolivia and Mexico

About the same time Bolivia also proposed a large devaluation of its currency. This was the second change in its par value in three years. Mr. de Largentaye

[11] *Annual Report, 1953,* pp. 63–64.

again questioned the size of the devaluation. In his view, the fundamental disequilibrium involved could be corrected by a much smaller devaluation, provided wages and salaries were held at their then-current levels rather than being permitted to rise. However, the Board concurred in the Bolivian proposal on several grounds. The country's exchange earnings had declined, both because of a drop in the price of its main export (tin) from the level reached during the Korean War, and from adjustments in connection with the nationalization of various industries. Meanwhile, import demand had remained high. Bolivia's system of multiple rates had become most complex, and the new devaluation would enable a simplification of the exchange rate structure.

In answer to Mr. de Largentaye, some Directors commented that the devaluation could scarcely be considered excessive when quantitative restrictions were still required. Interestingly enough, at this time some Directors thought that the Fund was not required to pass judgment on the entire stabilization program, but only on the devaluation; it was later that the Fund adopted the policy of assessing the over-all stabilization programs of its members.

Another example of a unitary rate change which seemed to some Directors to be possibly unnecessary or excessive was that of Mexico in 1954. That country proposed a devaluation of 30.8 per cent from its par value, although it had devalued substantially just five years earlier. As in the Icelandic case in 1950, the evidence of a fundamental disequilibrium was not to be found in a falling off of exports. Although the demand for the country's exports had slackened, this was attributable to a decline in world demand and prices.

As the staff pointed out, the more difficult part of Mexico's problem was twofold. First, because of the decline in exports, business conditions had become depressed. The Government wished to neutralize the export decline through compensatory fiscal policies, but without a devaluation such fiscal policies would have tended to place additional pressure on the monetary system and the balance of payments. Second, there had been massive speculative capital outflows—the largest in Mexico's history. The gradual reduction over three years of the country's reserves had impaired Mexico's ability to cope with balance of payments deficits or with recurrent sizable outflows of capital. A foreign exchange crisis had in fact emerged.

To cope with these developments, the country was proposing a devaluation which it expected would restrain imports, give a stimulus to foreign tourist receipts, and encourage an inflow of private investment. Simultaneously, the Government planned to impose a special 25 per cent ad valorem tax on all exports to absorb the windfall profits on exports and to increase government revenues.

Mr. Martínez-Ostos, a former Executive Director, attended the Board meeting as the representative of Mexico. He stressed that his Government was not resorting to this exchange rate depreciation as a competitive device to increase Mexican exports at the expense of other countries. Not only had Mexico always deprecated such practices as unfair, but it considered that competitive depreciation would be self-defeating: competitive depreciation would impair the country's terms of trade without bringing any significant gains in the volume of exports.

The Directors reviewed the reasons why devaluation seemed the only alternative. Since Mexico had relatively small reserves, the peso was susceptible to speculative pressures. Again the point was made that the Mexican authorities wished to avoid exchange controls; they were not certain that such controls could be enforced. These characteristics of Mexico's situation had been impressed upon the Directors in 1948–49, when Mexico had previously devalued the peso. Thus what Mr. Southard referred to as a "premature devaluation" seemed the only solution.

Mr. Southard also commented that he was prepared to accept the judgment of the Mexican authorities about the degree of devaluation required. It had to be large enough to provoke a backflow of capital and to meet the country's needs for some years hence. However, the danger of competitive depreciation in the years ahead was increased, and he reserved the right of the United States to take appropriate action if unfair competition resulted from Mexico's action. After expressing similar concerns, but with a recognition that no alternative was open to Mexico, the Directors took a decision noting the Fund's concurrence with the devaluation.

FEARS OF COMPETITIVE DEPRECIATION THROUGH MULTIPLE RATES

Multiple rates have also given rise to fears of competitive depreciation, especially insofar as they have suggested that certain exports were being subsidized. There was grave concern about this prospect in the middle 1950's, when several countries intensified their use of multiple rates for exports. The intention of these countries was to promote exports at a time when their particular products were encountering stiffer competition in world markets. Early in 1955, Brazil introduced a series of export bonuses and gradually added to the number of its effective exchange rates, eventually ending up with a complex system. Indonesia considerably revised its exchange system in order to assist its exports. Uruguay announced a special premium for exports of wool, including wool tops. Israel devised a system in which export premiums were applied to various commodities on the basis of net domestic value added.

THE STORMS OF THE 1950'S

As world export markets in the mid-1950's were becoming increasingly competitive for all countries, the alarm of the Executive Directors from nearly all the major countries at any exchange rates which favored exports became more vocal. Were multiple rates subsidizing the exports of certain countries? How could a subsidy within a multiple rate system, which also included penalty rates, be identified? At one time Mr. Southard, for example, announced that he reserved the right of his Government to impose countervailing duties if export subsidies were found to be involved in new export rates introduced in Brazil. Mr. Warren (Canada), Alternate to Mr. Rasminsky, drew attention to the interest of the GATT, as well as of the Fund, in export measures, because of their commercial aspects.

Requests for the Fund's approval to shift individual commodities from one exchange rate category to another within a complex rate structure were regarded by both the Board and the staff as especially difficult to appraise. The mere fact that the rate for a given export was being devalued did not suggest competitive depreciation. Indeed the Fund, in its informal contacts with members, had been encouraging—or at least not discouraging—countries to alter their exchange rates toward more depreciated rates where exports were not moving satisfactorily and where it appeared likely that a unification of multiple rates would involve further depreciation.

The criterion by which the staff judged a change in an export rate was whether the change was in the direction of an exchange rate at which future unification might take place. If so, no subsidy was considered to be involved; shifting an export to such a rate was really equivalent to reducing an export duty. If, however, a subsidy was involved, the staff was guided by the Board's view that the exchange system was not an appropriate instrument for providing subsidies. Straight budgetary subsidies were usually preferable, as they made clear the costs of the subsidy and avoided misuse of the exchange system.

This anxiety over multiple export rates brought about renewed attempts by the Fund to assist countries to eliminate multiple rates more quickly, and by the late 1950's the number of multiple rates was greatly reduced and the problem of export subsidies—and of possible competitive depreciation via multiple rates—much diminished.[12]

New views in the 1960's

A changed climate had emerged by the 1960's. The gravity of the problem faced by the less developed countries in exporting primary products had become more apparent. Empirical evidence had revealed that the exports of the less developed countries had been expanding much less rapidly than those of the industrial countries. During the 1950's, the former had increased at an annual rate of 3.6 per cent; this was only about one-half the rate at which the exports of the industrial countries had advanced. Moreover, since there had been a

[12] See Chapter 6 above, especially pp. 143–44.

deterioration in the terms of trade of the less developed countries, the purchasing power of their exports had risen at an annual rate only slightly above 2 per cent.[13] Trade in primary products had fallen even farther behind that of manufactured goods. In the three decades between 1928 and 1955–57, the increase in total world trade of primary commodities had been less than one-third that in manufactured goods; excluding petroleum, a special case since it is exported by only a few countries, the growth of world trade in primary products had amounted to only about one-seventh that in manufactures.[14]

But another factor contributed even more to a new attitude toward the exports of the less developed countries. This was the growing realization that exports were the key to successful economic development. Several studies by the United Nations, the Economic Commission for Latin America, the Economic Commission for Asia and the Far East, and the World Bank, as well as various private studies, pointed up a striking correlation between the expansion of exports of developing countries and the rates of growth of their economies. The trade and exchange policies of the less developed countries shifted markedly away from policies which emphasized restriction of imports to those which stressed stimulation of exports.[15]

There was a parallel change in emphasis away from the policies of individual countries to the policies of international bodies or of groups of countries acting in unison. A new general awareness emerged that, except for possible temporary and unusual circumstances, the problems of expanding the exports of the less developed countries could be tackled only as a cooperative venture. Various new exceptions to its rules for the less developed countries were worked out by the GATT. A United Nations Conference on Trade and Development (UNCTAD) was held in March 1964 to consider proposals for dealing with their special trade problems. Shortly thereafter, UNCTAD was set up on a permanent basis to give continuing attention to the trade problems of these countries. The Fund itself, in 1963, introduced a new facility known as "compensatory financing," to provide short-term financial assistance to countries suffering from fluctuations in exchange receipts from exports of primary products (see Chapter 18).

The widespread search for new ways to promote the exports of the less developed countries caused some changes in the Fund's policies on exchange rates, stress being placed on the close relation between realistic rates of exchange and exports. Where exchange rate flexibility was thought useful and feasible, countries were encouraged to adjust their exchange rates periodically, or even, temporarily, to institute fluctuating exchange rates. The widespread prevalence of inflation had caused Executive Directors to fear that, in the

[13] United Nations, *World Economic Survey, 1961*, p. 7, and *1962*, p. 1.

[14] United Nations, *World Economic Survey, 1958*, pp. 17–18.

[15] For details on these trends see Margaret G. de Vries, "Trade and Exchange Policy and Economic Development," *Oxford Economic Papers*, Vol. 18 (1966), pp. 19–44.

absence of exchange rate adjustments, domestic price increases would affect exports adversely and shift demand to imports. Increasingly, the Fund placed emphasis on the benefits to exports likely to accrue from exchange depreciation, and by 1965 had come to the view that possibly the most important gain from devaluation was the effect on exports of the realignment of external prices with domestic prices.[16]

Export promotion programs were introduced by a number of countries. In part because of the general world emphasis on the need for developing countries to increase their exports, but probably even more because many developing countries were eliminating multiple rates and devaluing to unitary rates, these export promotional devices no longer occasioned the adverse reactions among Executive Directors that similar schemes in the 1950's had done. And some Directors recognized the usefulness of many of these arrangements: they frequently did give a pronounced fillip to exports.

Nonetheless, the Board continued to be very cognizant of the undesirable consequences of promoting exports through special export schemes or multiple currency practices favoring exports. Indeed, when such arrangements became complex and yielded exchange rates widely different from the par value, the Board urged their elimination. Moreover, export promotion schemes were still regarded as temporary palliatives. The Fund called the attention of its developing members specifically to two more enduring solutions: improving the supply and the quality of their exports by altering resource allocation patterns, and maintaining the competitiveness of their exports.[17] But by the mid-1960's all methods of enlarging the export earnings of the less developed countries were certain to receive serious discussion and consideration by both the Fund staff and the Board.

REVALUATION BY GERMANY AND THE NETHERLANDS

In the early 1960's the exchange rates of two of the major currencies that had been devalued in 1949 were adjusted upward—that is, they were appreciated. On March 4, 1961, Germany proposed to the Board a change in the par value of the deutsche mark from DM 4.20 to DM 4.00 = \$1, effective on March 6. Germany argued that it wished to make a useful contribution to the common task of reaching a better equilibrium in international payments. Some steps had already been taken in the monetary field. Moreover, considerable speculative capital had come to Germany. The appreciation of the deutsche mark by 5 per cent—chosen to allow some leeway for internal adjustment—was

---

[16] *Annual Report, 1966,* p. 25.

[17] *Annual Report, 1963,* pp. 71–72.

believed to be sufficient to bring down the current balance of payments surplus, and to cheapen imports so as to offset excessive inflationary tendencies.

Because the change in the value of the currency was less than 10 per cent of the initial par value, and because no previous change had been made in the initial par value, the proposal did not require a decision by the Fund. The Board, however, recorded its view that the move was a useful one because it reflected the improvement in Germany's competitive position.

On March 6, 1961—two days later—the Netherlands Government took a similar decision, to be effective on March 7. As the guilder had already been devalued in 1949 by more than 10 per cent of its initial par value, this change required the approval of the Fund. Mr. Lieftinck (Netherlands) laid stress on the surplus in the Dutch balance of payments on current account and the increased liquidity in the domestic economy. He contended, moreover, that the labor market in particular had become excessively strained by the continuing boom. Before the revaluation of the deutsche mark there had already existed a large and growing discrepancy between the wage levels in the Netherlands and in Germany, resulting in a significant outflow of Dutch workers across the eastern frontier. The Fund accepted the Netherlands' proposal and a new par value of f. 3.62 = $1 was set.

Table 4, at the end of this chapter, presents a chronological list of all changes in par values from 1948 through 1965.

MAGNITUDES OF DEPRECIATION

As shown in the foregoing sections, the years 1948 through 1965 witnessed a number of changes in par values. Briefly, the industrial countries undertook relatively little devaluation of their exchange rates. Of the fourteen members of the Fund classed as industrial countries in 1965, only five altered their exchange rates between September 1949 and the end of 1965.[18] The adjustments of two of these countries—Germany and the Netherlands in March 1961—were appreciations. Austria devalued by stages until 1953. France devalued twice. Canada devalued once, by a small amount, in the course of its return to parity from a fluctuating rate in 1962. (The Canadian dollar had appreciated by some 5 per cent while it was fluctuating.)

However, many less developed countries experienced a greater frequency and degree of exchange depreciation than often is realized. Countries in Africa, Asia, Latin America, and the Middle East undertook several exchange rate adjustments. Among a third group of countries, classed as primary producing but

[18] The member countries specified here as industrial are those listed in the *Annual Report, 1967*, p. 55: Austria, Belgium, Canada, Denmark, France, Germany, Italy, Japan, Luxembourg, the Netherlands, Norway, Sweden, the United Kingdom, and the United States.

more developed,[19] exchange devaluation was not uncommon. Finland and Iceland each devalued twice again between 1949 and 1965, and Turkey and Yugoslavia once.

This section presents some measurements of the extent of these devaluations. The focus is on the accumulated magnitudes over a long period of years.

Measuring the magnitudes

Percentage changes in the exchange rates for 105 countries for the seventeen years from the end of 1948 to the end of December 1965 are summarized in Table 3. The 105 countries comprise the membership of the Fund at the end

Table 3. Magnitudes of Exchange Depreciation, End 1948 to End 1965: Distribution of 105 Countries by Degree of Depreciation

(Magnitudes in per cent)

Category [1]	Magnitude of Depreciation	Number of Countries
A	Appreciation	1
B	Zero	10
C	Less than 30.5	14
D	30.5	29
E	31–65	13
F	66–90	28
G	More than 90	10
Total		105

[1] The countries are distributed among the categories as follows (for each category they are listed in order of increasing depreciation, or in alphabetical order where the depreciation was the same for all countries in the group):

A. Lebanon

B. Cuba, Dominican Republic, El Salvador, Guatemala, Haiti, Honduras, Japan, Liberia, Panama, United States

C. Ethiopia, Canada, Italy, Belgium, Luxembourg, Ecuador, Costa Rica, Germany, Syrian Arab Republic, Saudi Arabia, Portugal, Venezuela, Netherlands, Nicaragua

D. Australia, Burma, Ceylon, Cyprus, Denmark, Ghana, Iraq, Ireland, Jamaica, Jordan, Kenya, Kuwait, Libya, Malawi, Malaysia, New Zealand, Nigeria, Norway, Pakistan, Sierra Leone, Somalia, South Africa, Sudan, Sweden, Tanzania, Trinidad and Tobago, Uganda, United Kingdom, Zambia

E. Burundi, United Arab Republic, Nepal, Afghanistan, Philippines, Rwanda, Thailand, India, Iran, France, Austria, Finland, Mexico

F. Turkey, China, Cameroon, Central African Republic, Chad, Dahomey, Gabon, Guinea, Ivory Coast, Malagasy Republic, Mali, Mauritania, Niger, Senegal, Togo, Upper Volta, Viet-Nam, Peru, Algeria, Tunisia, Democratic Republic of Congo, Morocco, Spain, Congo (Brazzaville), Colombia, Greece, Iceland, Laos

G. Israel, Yugoslavia, Uruguay, Paraguay, Argentina, Chile, Brazil, Bolivia, Indonesia, Korea

[19] Australia, Finland, Greece, Iceland, Ireland, New Zealand, Portugal, South Africa, Spain, Turkey, and Yugoslavia.

of 1965 plus Cuba and Indonesia, which were Fund members during part of the period. As a starting date, the end of 1948 has been preferred to an earlier postwar date (that is, the end of 1945, or of 1946, when the Fund set initial parities for its original members) because the exchange rates of several countries were more settled by that year (or by early in 1949) than they were immediately after World War II. Moreover, data for 1948 are readily available.[20]

Because the results depend on the particular exchange rate used, and because in some instances (e.g., for countries with multiple exchange rates) there was a choice of rates, an endeavor has been made to select exchange rates that were currently used for most transactions. For most countries par values, or at least fixed official rates, could be used for both initial and end years. For other countries, a free market rate or one of the multiple rates was used for either the initial or end year, and in some instances midpoints among multiple rates were used. Table 5, at the end of this chapter, specifies which rates were used for each country.

Exchange rate changes were measured relative to gold; that is, with the initial period as the base, the percentage was calculated of the change in the exchange rate expressed in terms of grams of fine gold per local currency unit. This is the customary Fund way of measuring exchange rate changes: it produces, for example, the familiar 30.5 per cent devaluation of the pound sterling in September 1949. Measured in this way, 100 per cent is the maximum that a currency can depreciate. Inasmuch as the gold content of the U.S. dollar has remained unchanged, measurements relative to gold are, of course, identical with measurements relative to the U.S. dollar.

How much depreciation?

In Table 3 the countries covered are distributed over seven categories according to the degree of their exchange depreciation from the end of 1948 to the end of 1965. In Lebanon a slight appreciation occurred. Group B comprises 10 countries which did not devalue at all: the United States, 7 Central American countries, Liberia, and Japan.[21] Group C comprises 14 countries that devalued less than 30.5 per cent—that is, less than the amount by which sterling was devalued in September 1949; in this group are several industrial nations (Belgium, Canada, Germany, Italy, Luxembourg, and the Netherlands), 4 Latin American countries (Costa Rica, Ecuador, Nicaragua, and Venezuela), and Ethiopia, Portugal, Saudi Arabia, and the Syrian Arab Republic. Germany and the Netherlands, after depreciating by approximately 30 per cent in September 1949, both appreciated their currencies by 5 per cent in 1961.

[20] The annual supplement to *International Financial Statistics* regularly presents series beginning with 1948.

[21] Japan's official rate was set in April 1949, and has since remained unaltered.

Group D comprises 29 countries which devalued by 30.5 per cent in September 1949, or (Pakistan) some years later. These countries are mainly those of the sterling area, plus Denmark, Norway, and Sweden.

What is often not fully realized is that for 50 countries (groups E, F, and G), the magnitude of exchange depreciation in these years exceeded 30 per cent. Thirteen countries devalued by between 31 and 65 per cent; these included Austria, Finland, France, India, Mexico, and the Philippines. For another 28 countries devaluation ranged from 66 to 90 per cent. Among European countries in this group were Greece, Iceland, Spain, and Turkey. Other countries devaluing by these large amounts were two Latin American countries (Colombia and Peru), much of the French franc area of Africa, and Viet-Nam. Finally, there were 10 countries—6 Latin American countries plus Indonesia, Israel, Korea, and Yugoslavia—for which depreciation exceeded 90 per cent.

Developed countries, even in Europe, are distributed among all the five groups C through G. Among less developed countries two patterns of depreciation are apparent. One follows that of the major currencies. Countries in Central America conformed generally to the U.S. dollar and devalued either not at all or very little. Many others in Asia and Africa followed the lead of either sterling or the French franc. The second pattern was related to the price and balance of payments experiences of the individual country. Quite a number of countries, in all geographic regions, devalued independently of the major currencies, by from 40 to nearly 100 per cent.[22]

THE FUND AS A PARTICIPATOR

The role of the Fund in exchange rate adjustments has grown appreciably over the years. By 1965 the Board could, as it discussed a member's economic situation, consider the exchange rate without setting off the same touchy debates among Directors about the Fund's jurisdiction as had characterized 1948 and 1949. Individual Directors had become less desirous of defining the precise limits of the Fund's authority in this field.

This change in attitude had come about mainly because Fund-member relations in general had grown easier. One of the primary benefits of the annual consultations, begun in 1952, was that the Fund and its members learned how to talk to each other informally and quietly about a range of topics of mutual concern (see Chapter 11). In addition, precedents had gradually been set for the inclusion in Board decisions of sentences relating to exchange rates. When the atmosphere first tended to become more relaxed—about the mid-1950's—decisions merely reminded countries to keep their exchange policies under

[22] Further details can be found in Margaret G. de Vries, "Exchange Depreciation in Developing Countries," *Staff Papers*, Vol. XV (1968), pp. 560–78.

review. But individual Directors went so far as to note freely at Board meetings that they considered certain currencies overvalued, or at least questionable. Later, increasingly stronger sentences were incorporated into decisions. It became commonplace for decisions to contain phrases urging countries to adopt more realistic exchange rates or policies which would permit unification of multiple rates at realistic levels. In one instance in 1964 the Board went so far as to comment explicitly, in its decision, on the overvaluation of the currency of a member and its unrealistic exchange rate.

Some Directors have continued to be fearful that the Fund might overstep its bounds. A few, for instance, have questioned the propriety of inserting in a decision any exhortations to a country to correct a growing disparity between external and internal prices, or have wanted to know precisely the precedents for inclusion of the term overvaluation in decisions. As time has gone on, however, anxieties over the Fund's jurisdiction in exchange rate matters have tended to diminish. This lessening of the sensitivities of the Executive Directors, and in effect of the members they represented, concerning the Fund's role in deliberations of exchange rate policy, also had implications for the work of the staff. Staff discussions with authorities in member countries could increasingly include consideration of exchange rate policies. Over time the staff has undertaken informally to explore with members the need for exchange rate adjustment or the likely consequences of devaluation, and, at times, even to suggest specific exchange reforms. Nonetheless, both the staff and the Board have proceeded cautiously in these matters, mindful both of the paramount need for secrecy concerning possible exchange rate changes and of members' prerogatives in this field.

By the 1960's, a more serious problem for the Fund than that of immediate jurisdiction was the onset of new debates about exchange rates in general. To many economists, countries seemed to be eschewing devaluation. The experience of the Fund had revealed a variety of reasons why, since World War II, countries often avoided or at least postponed devaluation. Domestic political resistance to reductions in the external values of currencies, especially if elections were to be held in the near future, was a factor. In a world of general inflation, the danger of further price advances following devaluation was another. Authorities were often preoccupied with the effects of devaluation on the prices of imported goods, and hence on the cost of living. There was also a strong apprehension that, where the country was an important supplier to world markets, and where the demand for its exports was inelastic, devaluation would lower world market prices and yet not enhance the country's export earnings.

The environment in which the Fund operated in the 1960's was made even more complex by the re-examination of questions central to the operation of the international monetary system. What was the mechanism by which balance of payments adjustment took place? Could fundamental disequilibrium be corrected by a change in the exchange rate? Had it not been demonstrated that policies of several kinds—exchange rate, monetary, fiscal, and, more recently, incomes policies—worked together to alter a given balance of payments situation? What was the appropriate "policy mix" for attaining external equilibrium? What was the function of international capital flows in balance of payments adjustment? Were capital movements equilibrating, as had once been thought, or disequilibrating? Finally, new proposals were being advanced for enhancing the liquidity of the international monetary system.

In this climate, steering between the Scylla of taking upon itself the initiative that rightfully belongs to its members, and the Charybdis of ignoring exchange rate adjustment as a vital policy tool, was not easy for the Fund. Indeed, the passive role in exchange rate changes assigned to the Fund, and the continued sensitivities of several members, had the result that, in the midst of the crucial concerns of the middle 1960's—the balance of payments deficits of major nations and the problem of international liquidity—the Board had not, by the end of 1965, discussed the general role of exchange rates in balance of payments adjustment.

Table 4. Changes in Par Values, 1948–65 [1]

Date [2]	Country	Change in Par Value
1948		
Jan. 26	France	Initial par value suspended
July 22	Mexico	Initial par value suspended
Dec. 17	Colombia	Par value changed to 51.2825 U.S. cents per peso
1949		
June 17	Mexico	New par value set at 11.5607 U.S. cents per peso
Sept. 18	Australia	Par value changed to 224.000 U.S. cents per pound
Sept. 18	Denmark	Par value changed to 14.4778 U.S. cents per krone
Sept. 18	Norway	Par value changed to 14.0000 U.S. cents per krone
Sept. 18	South Africa	Par value changed to 280.000 U.S. cents per pound
Sept. 18	Egypt	Par value changed to 287.156 U.S. cents per pound
Sept. 18	United Kingdom	Par value changed to 280.000 U.S. cents per pound
Sept. 19	Canada	Par value changed to 90.9091 U.S. cents per dollar
Sept. 20	Iraq	Par value changed to 280.000 U.S. cents per dinar

Footnotes on page 118.

Table 4 *(continued)*. Changes in Par Values, 1948–65 [1]

Date [2]	Country	Change in Par Value
Sept. 21	Iceland	Par value changed to 10.7054 U.S. cents per króna
Sept. 21	Netherlands	Par value changed to 26.3158 U.S. cents per guilder
Sept. 22	Belgium	Par value changed to 2.00000 U.S. cents per franc
Sept. 22	Luxembourg	Par value changed to 2.00000 U.S. cents per franc
Sept. 22	India	Par value changed to 21.0000 U.S. cents per rupee
Nov. 15	Peru	Par value suspended
1950		
Mar. 20	Iceland	Par value changed to 6.14036 U.S. cents per króna
Apr. 8	Bolivia	Par value changed to 1.66667 U.S. cents per boliviano
Sept. 30	Canada	Par value suspended
Dec. 1	Ecuador	Par value changed to 6.66667 U.S. cents per sucre
1951		
Mar. 5	Paraguay	Par value changed to 16.6667 U.S. cents per guaraní
1952		
Jan. 1	Yugoslavia	Par value changed to 0.33333 U.S. cent per dinar
1953		
May 14	Bolivia	Par value changed to 0.52632 U.S. cent per boliviano
Oct. 5	Chile	Par value changed to 0.90909 U.S. cent per peso
1954		
Jan. 1	Paraguay	Par value changed to 6.66667 U.S. cents per guaraní
Apr. 19	Mexico	Par value changed to 8.00000 U.S. cents per peso
Aug. 18	Paraguay	Par value changed to 4.76190 U.S. cents per guaraní
1955		
July 1	Nicaragua	Par value changed to 14.2857 U.S. cents per córdoba
July 30	Pakistan	Par value changed to 21.0000 U.S. cents per rupee
1956		
Mar. 1	Paraguay	Par value changed to 1.66667 U.S. cents per guaraní

Table 4 *(concluded)*. Changes in Par Values, 1948–65 [1]

Date [2]	Country	Change in Par Value
1957		
May 22	Iran	Par value changed to 1.32013 U.S. cents per rial
Sept. 15	Finland	Par value changed to 0.31250 U.S. cent per markka
1958		
Dec. 29	France	New par value set at 0.20255 U.S. cent per franc
1960		
Jan. 1	France	Par value changed to 20.2550 U.S. cents per (new) franc
Feb. 22	Iceland	Par value changed to 2.63158 U.S. cents per króna
Aug. 20	Turkey	Par value changed to 11.1111 U.S. cents per lira
1961		
Feb. 14	South Africa	Par value changed to 140.000 U.S. cents per rand
Mar. 6	Germany	Par value changed to 25.0000 U.S. cents per deutsche mark
Mar. 7	Netherlands	Par value changed to 27.6243 U.S. cents per guilder
July 14	Ecuador	Par value changed to 5.55556 U.S. cents per sucre
Aug. 4	Iceland	Par value changed to 2.32558 U.S. cents per króna
Sept. 3	Costa Rica	Par value changed to 15.0943 U.S. cents per colón
1962		
Feb. 9	Israel	Par value changed to 33.3333 U.S. cents per pound
May 2	Canada	New par value set at 92.5000 U.S. cents per dollar
1963		
Jan. 1	Finland	Par value changed to 31.2500 U.S. cents per (new) markka
Dec. 31	Ethiopia	Par value changed to 40.0000 U.S. cents per dollar
1965		
July 26	Yugoslavia	Par value changed to 0.080000 U.S. cent per dinar
Nov. 8	Philippines	Par value changed to 25.6410 U.S. cents per peso

[1] Excludes nonmetropolitan territories.

[2] Dates specified are those on which the change took effect, which is not necessarily the same date on which the change was agreed with the Fund.

Table 5. Exchange Rates Used in Table 3

Country	1948 [1]	1965
1. Afghanistan	Free	Free
2. Algeria	Official	Official
3. Argentina	Free	Free
4. Australia	Par value	Par value
5. Austria	Official	Par value
6. Belgium	Par value	Par value
7. Bolivia	Par value	Free
8. Brazil	Free	Free
9. Burma	Par value	Par value
10. Burundi	Official	Par value
11. Cameroon	Official	Official
12. Canada	Par value	Par value
13. Central African Republic	Official	Official
14. Ceylon	Official	Par value
15. Chad	Official	Official
16. Chile	Free	Free
17. China	Official	Official
18. Colombia	Free	Free
19. Congo (Brazzaville)	Official	Official
20. Congo, Democratic Republic	Par value	Official
21. Costa Rica	Par value	Par value
22. Cuba	Par value	Official
23. Cyprus	Par value	Par value
24. Dahomey	Official	Official
25. Denmark	Par value	Par value
26. Dominican Republic	Par value	Par value
27. Ecuador	Official [2]	Official [2]
28. El Salvador	Par value	Par value
29. Ethiopia	Par value	Par value
30. Finland	Official	Par value
31. France	Official	Par value
32. Gabon	Official	Official
33. Germany	Official	Par value
34. Ghana	Par value	Par value
35. Greece	Official	Par value
36. Guatemala	Par value	Par value
37. Guinea	Official	Official
38. Haiti	Official	Par value
39. Honduras	Par value	Par value
40. Iceland	Par value	Par value
41. India	Par value	Par value
42. Indonesia	Free	Free
43. Iran	Par value	Par value
44. Iraq	Par value	Par value
45. Ireland	Official	Par value

Footnotes on page 121.

Table 5 *(continued)*. Exchange Rates Used in Table 3

Country	1948 [1]	1965
46. Israel	Official	Par value
47. Italy	Official	Par value
48. Ivory Coast	Official	Official
49. Jamaica	Par value	Par value
50. Japan	Official [3]	Par value
51. Jordan	Official	Par value
52. Kenya	Par value	Par value
53. Korea	Official	Official
54. Kuwait	Official	Par value
55. Laos	Official	Free
56. Lebanon	Free	Free
57. Liberia	Official	Par value
58. Libya	Official	Par value
59. Luxembourg	Par value	Par value
60. Malagasy Republic	Official	Official
61. Malawi	Par value	Par value
62. Malaysia	Par value	Par value
63. Mali	Official	Official
64. Mauritania	Official	Official
65. Mexico	Par value	Par value
66. Morocco	Official	Par value
67. Nepal	Official	Par value
68. Netherlands	Par value	Par value
69. New Zealand	Official	Par value
70. Nicaragua	Par value	Par value
71. Niger	Official	Official
72. Nigeria	Par value	Par value
73. Norway	Par value	Par value
74. Pakistan	Official	Par value
75. Panama	Par value	Par value
76. Paraguay	Free	Free
77. Peru	Principal	Free
78. Philippines	Par value	Par value
79. Portugal	Official	Par value
80. Rwanda	Official	Par value
81. Saudi Arabia	Official	Par value
82. Senegal	Official	Official
83. Sierra Leone	Par value	Par value
84. Somalia	Official	Par value
85. South Africa	Par value	Par value
86. Spain	Official	Par value
87. Sudan	Official	Par value
88. Sweden	Official	Par value
89. Syrian Arab Republic	Free	Free
90. Tanzania	Par value	Par value

Table 5 *(concluded).* Exchange Rates Used in Table 3

Country	1948 [1]	1965
91. Thailand	Official	Par value
92. Togo	Official	Official
93. Trinidad and Tobago	Par value	Par value
94. Tunisia	Official	Par value
95. Turkey	Par value	Par value
96. Uganda	Par value	Par value
97. United Arab Republic	Par value	Official
98. United Kingdom	Par value	Par value
99. United States	Par value	Par value
100. Upper Volta	Official	Official
101. Uruguay	Free	Free
102. Venezuela	Non-oil exports	Non-oil exports
103. Viet-Nam	Principal	Free
104. Yugoslavia	Official	Par value
105. Zambia	Par value	Par value

Sources: *International Financial Statistics,* monthly issues and Supplement to 1966–67 issues; and *Annual Report on Exchange Restrictions,* various years.

[1] For some members the par values used here were those that had been established for them while they were nonmetropolitan areas.

[2] Selling rate.

[3] 1949.

CHAPTER

6

Multiple Exchange Rates

Margaret G. de Vries

MULTIPLE EXCHANGE RATES were one of the first problems that faced the Fund in 1946, and have probably been its most common problem in the field of exchange rates. An impressive number and diversity of countries in the last twenty years have experimented with one form or another of what the Fund has called *multiple currency practices,* at least for a few, if not for most, of their transactions.[1] And, although the use of such practices has been much reduced in recent years, a succession of countries that had not previously tried multiple rates has been experimenting with them. In the mid-1960's, some new suggestions for multiple exchange rates were put forward. Economists, especially those outside official circles, have continued to propose exchange rate schemes as a means of assisting primary producing countries. Moreover, a few have suggested that subsidies-cum-tariffs—in a sense a form of multiple rates—or two exchange rates, one a floating rate for capital, might be possible compromises between fixed and fluctuating rates for the industrialized nations. The problem of multiple rates, then, never seems entirely at an end.

THE BACKGROUND

The interwar period

Multiple rates originated in the exchange control mechanisms of the 1930's. First used by Germany in 1934 in dealings with its bilateral agreement partners, multiple rates allowed considerably more exchange rate manipulation than did

[1] The established technical term of the Fund for any multiple rate is *multiple currency practice.* In what follows, the terms *multiple exchange rate* and *multiple currency practice* are used interchangeably.

ordinary clearing agreements with a fixed exchange rate.[2] German exports to a particular country could enjoy the benefits of sudden exchange depreciation. Through such devices, Germany succeeded in expanding its trade with certain countries in southeastern Europe and with a number of Latin American countries, especially those which had their own exchange controls, for example, Brazil, Chile, and Peru. Brazil's imports from Germany rose from 13 per cent of its total imports in 1929 to 25 per cent in 1938, and its exports to Germany rose from 9 per cent to 19 per cent. In the same period, Peru's imports from Germany rose from 10 per cent to 20 per cent of the total.[3] Although Germany's methods met with increasing resistance, Latin American countries tended to encourage bilateral transactions with Germany, even at unfavorable exchange rates, when raw material prices were low and exports to free exchange countries were depressed.

Multiple rates also began to be employed by other countries during the Great Depression. After 1932, the majority of European countries with exchange controls resorted eventually to some form of currency devaluation. Although some countries, like Czechoslovakia and Italy, devalued in one step, other countries passed through a period of gradual depreciation, usually through the use of multiple rates. Black markets developed, and later became legal free markets: Austria, Hungary, Yugoslavia, and Rumania were among the countries in Europe which, after a time, gave official recognition to black markets and thus to the multiple exchange rates prevailing in them.

Several Latin American countries similarly embarked on programs of multiple rates, essentially as exchange control devices. The purposes in Latin America, however, differed from those in Europe in two respects. Although the initial purpose of exchange controls in Europe was to control capital movements, this was taken less seriously in Latin America: several countries there permitted capital transactions through free markets. Secondly, in Latin America one of the main objectives of differentiated rates of exchange was to secure, at preferential rates, foreign exchange to service the government debt. Exchange depreciation had increased the cost of this service in terms of domestic currency, and the compulsory surrender of part of export proceeds at official rates operated in effect as a special tax to meet that cost. The obligation of exporters to surrender exchange receipts was sometimes confined to one or a few of the chief export products, to make it easier to enforce. In European countries, on the other

[2] Further details of the interwar experiences with multiple rates can be found in Margaret S. Gordon, *Barriers to World Trade*, Chapters V and VII; and in League of Nations, *International Currency Experience*. A detailed description of European exchange controls in the interwar period is in Howard S. Ellis, *Exchange Control in Central Europe*. League of Nations, *Report on Exchange Control*, briefly examines the economic effects of exchange controls, especially on the domestic economies of the countries concerned.

[3] League of Nations, *World Economic Survey, 1938/39*, p. 202.

hand, generally because of their creditor status, debt service was not an important stimulus to exchange control.

What precipitated international concern about these practices was that the trend in most countries with multiple rates was toward discrimination. The discrimination was seldom explicit. More often the allocation of foreign exchange among different countries became subject to administrative discretion, and in these circumstances some form of discrimination, or "preferential allotment," became virtually inevitable. The objective of discrimination was usually to evade the most-favored-nation clause of trade agreements and to force trade into bilateral channels.

Free exchange countries, therefore, when concluding trade agreements with exchange control countries, frequently insisted on the insertion of various formulas to ensure a "fair and equitable share" in any allotment of foreign exchange. However, because such formulas were difficult to prescribe in such a way as to give real equality of treatment, most of them had in practice little real meaning.

Multiple rates at Bretton Woods

Against this background the delegations at Bretton Woods treated multiple currency practices in the same way as they treated quantitative exchange restrictions. In the Keynes Plan no specific mention had been made of multiple currency practices. But in the White Plan, one of the stated purposes of the Fund was

> 5. To reduce the use of such foreign exchange restrictions, bilateral clearing arrangements, multiple currency devices, and discriminatory foreign exchange practices as hamper world trade and the international flow of productive capital.[4]

Clause IX of the *Joint Statement by Experts on the Establishment of an International Monetary Fund*, paragraphs 2 and 3, under the heading The Obligations of Member Countries, contained statements to the effect that each member country is

> 2. Not to allow exchange transactions in its market in currencies of other members at rates outside a prescribed range based on the agreed parities.
>
> 3. Not to impose restrictions on payments for current international transactions with other member countries (other than those involving capital transfers or in accordance with VI, above) or to engage in any discriminatory currency arrangements or multiple currency practices without the approval of the Fund.[5]

"VI, above" referred to the provisions for allocating a scarce currency.

In June 1944, the scope of these provisions was interpreted by the U.S. Treasury in *Questions and Answers on the International Monetary Fund*. Ques-

[4] Vol. III below, p. 86.
[5] Vol. III below, p. 135.

tion 20 was: Would differential rates of exchange for different classes of imports and exports (visible and invisible) be permitted by the Fund? The answer suggested that what was considered most objectionable in multiple currency practices was the uses to which such devices might be put, rather than the multiplicity of rates itself. Multiple rates should be avoided because they might so easily become the means for discrimination in trade relationships, and because they usually involved control of the exchanges so complete as to offer a strong temptation to restrict transactions on current account. Nonetheless, it was made clear that, conceivably, the Fund might decide that a member's multiple currency practices did not conflict with the principles of the Fund. Moreover, where conflict did occur, the Fund would allow adequate time for the abolition of multiple currency practices.[6]

As finally drafted, Article VIII of the Articles of Agreement obliges members (Section 2 (*a*)) not to "impose restrictions on the making of payments and transfers for current international transactions," nor (Section 3) to

> engage in, or permit any of its fiscal agencies . . . to engage in, any discriminatory currency arrangements or multiple currency practices except as authorized under this Agreement or approved by the Fund. If such arrangements and practices are engaged in at the date when this Agreement enters into force the member concerned shall consult with the Fund as to their progressive removal unless they are maintained or imposed under Article XIV, Section 2, in which case the provisions of Section 4 of that Article shall apply.

Article XIV makes no explicit reference to multiple currency practices.

Prevalence of multiple rates in 1946

By the time the Fund was organized, multiple rates were in use not only in the six countries of Latin America that had used them during the 1930's (Argentina, Brazil, Chile, Ecuador, Peru, and Venezuela), but also in Bolivia, Colombia, Costa Rica, Nicaragua, and Uruguay; and Cuba and Honduras had introduced small exchange taxes that had somewhat the same effect as multiple rates.[7] The use of multiple rates in Iran suggested that the problem might not remain confined to Latin America.

The countries adopting multiple currency practices had problems which did not seem to be solvable in any other way. Mr. (now Professor) Robert Triffin, then with the Board of Governors of the Federal Reserve System, had in fact, when helping a number of Latin American countries to overhaul their monetary, exchange control, and banking systems, suggested policies which, in his own

[6] Vol. III below, pp. 160–61.

[7] Argentina was not an original Fund member; the other Latin American countries mentioned were.

words, were "highly unorthodox . . . for the newly born International Monetary Fund." [8]

The problem to which Mr. Triffin was seeking a solution was that of a primary producing country facing balance of payments disequilibrium due to a cyclically depressed world market for raw materials or for its own particular exports. This situation, in which over-all exchange depreciation was regarded as ineffective, was distinguished from that of fundamental disequilibrium, where an over-all exchange rate adjustment was required. For the cyclical problem, Mr. Triffin advocated two markets—a normal market and an "auction" market. Exchange proceeds from exports or other easily controllable sources would be channeled into the normal market, and be available for essential imports and current invisibles. Exchange proceeds from less controllable transactions, such as capital movements, would be sold in a free or "auction" market; purchasers could use these proceeds to make payments for nonessential imports or for outgoing capital. Such a dual exchange system would, Mr. Triffin argued, prevent the emergence of a black market and the need for administrative allocations, and would provide an escape valve: capital movements could take place without upsetting the markets or rates for normal transactions.[9]

These arguments were not merely theoretical; they expressed the objectives of countries' actual policies. They explained, for example, the initial establishment of multiple rates in Argentina and of dual markets in several other countries, e.g., Chile, Costa Rica, Ecuador, and Paraguay.

THE FUND'S POLICIES INAUGURATED (1946–51)

Initial questions for the Fund

When the Fund opened its doors, 13 of its 39 members were using multiple exchange rates. Specific questions began to arise almost immediately. Even before concluding membership formalities, Venezuela (in September 1946) asked for assurance from the Fund that adherence to the Articles would not prevent it from taking a suitable period to eliminate its multiple currency practices. When the establishment of initial par values was considered at the end of 1946, the question arose as to what rates could be used as par values where multiple rates existed. When, in the early months of 1947, the Fund asked countries to state whether or not they were going to take advantage of the transitional arrangements, the significance of multiple rates again came to the fore. Cuba indicated that it would avail itself of the transitional arrangements primarily because of its small exchange tax.

[8] Robert Triffin, *The World Money Maze*, p. 141.

[9] *Ibid.*, pp. 142–77.

Questions of definition hampered consideration of these practices. What precisely constituted a multiple currency practice under the Fund Agreement? Could the small exchange taxes of Cuba and Honduras be so defined? Did an unusually large difference between the effective buying and selling rates for a currency constitute a multiple currency practice? Were multiple currency practices to be regarded as a restriction and therefore subject to the Fund's transitional arrangements, or were these practices to be considered solely as exchange rates?

More basic were questions pertaining to the Fund's authority in this field. Could a member maintaining a multiple currency practice under the transitional arrangements introduce a new multiple rate without Fund approval? Could a member with a multiple currency practice change the classifications of commodities subject to different multiple rates without prior consultation with the Fund? Could a member which did not have any multiple currency practices, but which took advantage of the transitional arrangements, introduce a multiple currency practice without the Fund's approval?

Important questions of policy also had to be answered: What was the economic significance of these practices? What should be the Fund's attitude toward the multiple rates already in existence? Under what conditions might these rates be temporarily retained? What should be the view of the Fund toward new practices?

The December 1947 letter

During its first year, the Fund studied these questions at great length. Moreover, a review of individual country situations in 1947 made it clear that the extent of multiple currency practices warranted early discussion between members and the Fund; the Board agreed that most of these discussions should be held in the territory of the members concerned.

In order that a detailed examination could be made of the economic, legal, and procedural issues raised by all the questions on multiple rates, the Board set up an Ad Hoc Committee on Spreads and Multiple Currency Practices in the middle of 1947. The members of the committee were Mr. Mládek (Czechoslovakia), Chairman; Mr. Bruins (Netherlands); Mr. Joshi (India); Mr. Luthringer (United States), Alternate to Mr. Overby; and Mr. Martínez-Ostos (Mexico), Alternate to Mr. Gómez. This committee held many meetings and undertook a careful assessment of the extent of the multiple rate problem, of the Fund's powers in this field, and of possible policies. In its report to the Board the committee urged moderation in the Fund's approach to multiple rates. It emphasized that the Fund was especially interested in multiple rates because they were not simply restrictive practices but rates of exchange as well, and hence could be a primary source of exchange instability. Exchange rate stability, the report stressed, was one of the Fund's main objectives. In order to make a start toward this objective the Fund had already, late in 1946, decided to set initial par values. While the mere existence of multiple exchange rates might not endanger exchange stability, frequent changes and extensions of such rates could well undermine the whole par value system. Moreover, multiple rates might also endanger the Fund's objective of the avoidance of competitive depreciation.

A multiple currency practice was defined as any practice which, as a result of official action, gives rise to an effective buying or selling rate differing from the par value by more than 1 per cent. Such a practice was explicitly recognized to include any of a series of fixed exchange rates, exchange taxes, exchange surcharges, free markets, and auction systems. Although on several future occasions debates were to occur between a member and the Fund, and even within the Fund, as to whether particular exchange systems did in fact constitute multiple currency practices, this definition proved to be sufficiently comprehensive to cover the vast majority of cases for the next twenty years.

After deliberation, the Board adopted the committee's recommendations unanimously. It agreed with the committee that the Fund had broad powers over the introduction of new practices and the adaptation of old ones, even during the transitional period; and decided that member countries should, as a minimum, consult the Fund before introducing a multiple currency practice, before making any change in a multiple exchange rate, before reclassifying transactions subject to different rates, and before making any other significant change in their exchange systems.

The Board also spelled out the policies to be followed. It recommended that early steps should be taken toward the removal of multiple currency practices that were not necessary for balance of payments reasons, although ample time should be provided for members to take these steps and to install appropriate substitutes where necessary. The Fund would encourage members engaging in multiple currency practices for balance of payments reasons to establish, as soon as possible, conditions which would permit the removal of these practices, with the general objective of seeking this removal not later than the end of the transitional period. Where complete removal by the end of the transitional period proved impossible, the Fund would assist the members concerned to eliminate the most dangerous aspects of their multiple currency practices and to exercise reasonable control over those retained.

As a consequence, there was circulated to the members in December 1947 a letter and memorandum outlining the Fund's powers and policies in the matter of multiple rates. This letter and memorandum, which together came to be known as "the December 1947 letter on multiple currency practices,"[10] laid

[10] Reproduced below, Vol. III, pp. 262–65.

the basis for relations with members in this field, although there have subsequently been modifications in the policies and procedures which it set forth.

A few Directors had had some difficulty with the terms of the letter. Mr. de Largentaye (France), among other points of disagreement, was of the opinion that members which had been occupied by the enemy and which were availing themselves of Article XIV could independently (i.e., without authorization from the Fund) introduce and modify multiple currency practices. In his view, such a member's only obligation was to consult the Fund. And this obligation did not mean that the Fund could object. Some weeks later (in January 1948) this difference of opinion led to the vexing difficulties between France and the Fund described below.

Mr. Martínez-Ostos, while not disagreeing with the committee's conclusions, pointed out two factors not mentioned in its analysis which he thought would have to be taken into consideration when specific courses of action were considered: the importance of the monetary management (nontrade) functions of multiple rates, and the negligible amount of world trade conducted by a few Latin American countries which maintained multiple rates.

It is noteworthy, in retrospect, that despite the importance that other Executive Directors attached to exchange rate stability *during* as well as *after* the transitional period, Mr. Martínez-Ostos stressed at this time that fixed multiple rates were not to be preferred over multiple rate systems with a floating rate (that is, a fluctuating or free market rate). He believed the opposite: since floating rates did not freeze particular rates into the economy, members would have less difficulty in moving to a single rate later on. Thus, floating rate mechanisms tended to be self-liquidating. This point is the more memorable because some ten years later, as noted below, this was to be the road by which many members were to move to unitary rates and a gradual change in Fund policy became necessary.

Disagreement with France

Immediately after the December 1947 letter—that is, in January 1948—the first example of a multiple currency practice was brought to the Board and led to disagreement with a major member. France proposed a devaluation of the franc from 119.107 francs to 214.392 francs per U.S. dollar. In addition, France proposed a free market for certain convertible currencies—namely, U.S. dollars and Portuguese escudos; Swiss francs were added subsequently.

The French authorities were willing to maintain orderly cross rates between all inconvertible currencies and between all convertible currencies. Thus, there would be only one case of disorderly cross rates—between the official rates of all currencies and the free rates of the convertible currencies. Mr. de Largentaye adduced two arguments in support of the French proposal. Legally, Article XIV,

Section 2, permitted France, as an enemy-occupied country, to introduce a multiple currency practice. Economically, the free market in certain currencies would help to meet the deficit in the French balance of payments. A premium on exports to the dollar area would encourage such exports, while the penalty on dollar imports would encourage the substitution of European imports for dollar imports. In addition, the repatriation of French assets held abroad would be encouraged, and tourist receipts and other invisibles would be diverted from black markets into a legal free market.

The Executive Directors objected to the free market. In the first place, they thought that it was an introduction of a multiple currency practice which was not necessary to achieve the trade objectives sought by France. In the second place, many Directors thought that the free market would be liable to have adverse effects on other members. There would be scope for competitive depreciation. Trade could be distorted by French traders purchasing goods in soft currency areas and selling them for hard currencies. France would be able to buy raw materials for soft currencies and sell finished goods for dollars, thereby giving French manufactures a substantial price advantage. This would hamper the eventual achievement of multilateral trade.

As an alternative to its proposal, France was prepared to institute a free market for all currencies, but this was also objected to by the Fund, as in effect destroying the whole system of fixed and stable par values. The Directors proposed that the free market should be limited to nontrade transactions, but this was not acceptable to the French authorities. A considerable effort was made by the Executive Directors to work out some alternative acceptable to all countries, but without success. France proceeded with its measures, and the Fund declared France ineligible to use its resources.

These difficulties between the Fund and France were, however, short-lived. In October 1948 France made changes in its exchange system which restored orderly cross rates for trade transactions. In September 1949, following the devaluation of sterling, the French Government consulted the Fund on a proposal to unify its exchange system at the exchange rate for the U.S. dollar prevailing in the free market—350 francs per U.S. dollar—which involved a further depreciation of the franc against the dollar. The Fund welcomed the modifications proposed by the French Government. Between September 20, 1949 and May 1950, the range of fluctuation in the franc-dollar rate was less than 0.3 per cent. Thus France had introduced a stable unitary exchange rate, although not a new par value.

Implementing the December 1947 letter

In the next few years, a flood of multiple exchange rates was proposed for consideration and action by the Executive Board. There were, for example, some twenty occasions in 1948 and some twenty-five in 1949 on which broad changes in their exchange systems were proposed by members, and several smaller changes of rates or shifts of commodities from one rate to another.

Ways of implementing the general policies laid down in the December 1947 letter had to be worked out to deal with individual cases. Formulas had to be found for approving or disapproving specific practices. In addition, some procedure had to be developed for dealing with countries—although these were a minority—which did not consult the Fund at all.

The member's action in one or two instances seemed almost like deliberate flouting of the Fund. But in most cases the lack of consultation was due to misunderstanding. Changes were sometimes made after informal discussion with the staff, or after a visit to the member country of a staff mission, which the member had regarded as "consulting" the Fund. Other changes represented progress toward a unitary rate structure, and some members believed that steps of this sort should not be subject to prior consultation and approval. In instances of nonconsultation, the Directors either communicated with the member in an informal way, calling the member's attention to its obligations and requesting an explanation, or took a decision drawing the member's attention to the need for prior consultation.

A question related to nonconsultation arose where the member did not allow adequate time for the Fund to consider a measure before it went into effect: What constitutes effective consultation? In December 1949, the Board sent a letter to all members carefully explaining the need for time for the staff to prepare economic and legal analyses, as well as time for consideration by the Executive Directors, and specifically requesting members to notify the Fund at least seven days before multiple rate changes were to go into effect.

From time to time the details of a particular practice had to be examined by both the economic and the legal staff in order to determine whether or not a multiple currency practice as defined by the Fund existed. Many different practices, in addition to straightforward fixed or free market rates, were soon uncovered, some of which gave rise not to explicit but to implicit rates. Among these practices were "mixing" rates, import surcharges, compensation arrangements, *aforo* techniques, negotiable and nonnegotiable exchange certificates, a variety of export bonus and import entitlement schemes, and "cheap currency" schemes. Of these, "mixing" rates were by far the most common. A "mixing" rate occurs when a specified proportion of exchange proceeds is sold at the official rate and the remainder is sold in a free market, resulting in an effective rate of exchange which is a weighted average of the two rates at which the exchange has been sold.[11]

[11] Detailed descriptions of all these various arrangements can be found in the individual country surveys of the *Annual Report on Exchange Restrictions*, especially for the years 1950–55, and in the monthly issues of *International Financial Statistics*.

Because of the number of multiple exchange rate changes it had to consider, the Executive Board, early in 1949, requested the staff to study and recommend a procedure by which at least some changes in multiple currency practices—for example, "minor" ones—might be acted upon simply. Several Directors, however, were uneasy lest a procedure might be adopted which would result in changes in multiple rates being made without Directors having adequate time to consult their governments, or without their even being informed of the changes. How, they asked, would it be decided what was a "minor" change? What appeared to be a minor change on the surface might be of material significance to a particular country exporting a given commodity. And certainly it must not appear to members that the Board was relinquishing any authority in this field.

Nevertheless, a procedure for dealing with minor changes in multiple rates had finally been worked out by May 1951. When a member country proposed to the Fund a change in its multiple currency practices which the Managing Director (with the assistance of the staff) regarded as minor, the Managing Director was to inform the Executive Directors, stating that he did not intend to place the matter on the agenda unless a Director so requested by a specified date. In the absence of any such request, the minutes of the next Board meeting would record the proposal as being approved. This gradually became known internally in the Fund as the "minor change procedure" or the "lapse of time procedure."

This procedure was similar to one that had been worked out earlier for China's multiple rates. While still on the mainland, the Chinese authorities began to maintain a series of multiple exchange rates which were, in the midst of civil war and severe inflation, almost continuously being altered. In view of the unusual difficulties that confronted the exchange authorities in China, a special procedure for dealing with them was evolved in 1948 by which China would inform the Fund of changes in advance where possible, or in any case at the earliest possible time, and the Managing Director would reply to China promptly on behalf of the Fund, without a Board meeting, unless the Managing Director preferred to raise the matter with the Board.

In addition to problems of procedure, issues of substance, even more intractable, concerned the Board. Member countries, and also economists who were closely concerned with the subject, came to realize that cogent arguments might be advanced for multiple rates. Some of these were economic, others administrative. It was contended, for example, that multiple currency practices represented an attempt to use the exchange rate mechanism to adjust the balance of payments when it was not politically possible to change the par value.

There were even times when selective exchange rate devaluation was preferable to general devaluation—when general devaluation would be inflationary, or would raise the cost of living of essential items, or would bring excessive windfall profits to exporters but would not help significantly to solve the balance of payments deficit. In regard to the last mentioned, much was made of the price inelasticity of both the demand for and the supply of primary products. It was argued that these inelasticities made multiple rates necessary so that import demand might be restrained without the export rate being depreciated. In these circumstances, use of an exchange spread—that is, maintenance of the exchange rate for exports but depreciation of the effective rate for imports—might be preferred to the depreciation of a single rate.[12]

Multiple rates were also defended as merely another form of exchange control, like quantitative restrictions. Here it was important that they were easier to administer than quantitative controls. A multiple rate system could be handled by a small group of trained bankers who bought and sold foreign exchange, whereas quantitative controls required a comprehensive system of licensing, exchange budgeting, and exchange allocation. It was argued, in addition, that if a choice had to be made, multiple rates were preferable to quantitative restrictions because they distributed foreign exchange on a basis of price rather than of ability to obtain a license. They constituted a mechanism by which the arbitrary decisions of exchange control authorities, inherent in quantitative restrictions, were thought to be avoided. They imposed less interference on consumer choice

Another rationale of multiple rates was that they might have monetary effects which would alleviate inflation. Multiple rate systems usually yield profits in local currency to the exchange authorities: exchange is sold to importers at higher rates (that is, more units of local currency per unit of foreign exchange) than the authorities pay out to the exporters surrendering foreign exchange. If these profits are spent by the authorities, no money is withdrawn from circulation. But to the extent that the authorities refrain from spending these profits—that is, if they freeze them—a decline in money occurs. This anti-inflationary effect of a multiple rate system has repercussions on the balance of payments of the country concerned additional to the effects of devaluation. Both help to restrain import demand.

In these early years the objections of the Fund to multiple rates were of several types. Most frequent were the fear of harmful effects on other countries, especially through broken cross rates, and, although to a lesser extent, the fear of competitive depreciation. Another was that multiple exchange rates tended to perpetuate themselves, as vested interests in their continuation developed: complicated exchange systems had not, in practice, led eventually to a unitary rate; multiple rates had, in fact, proliferated.

12 These economic objectives of multiple exchange rates are explained by E. M. Bernstein in "Some Economic Aspects of Multiple Exchange Rates," *Staff Papers*, Vol. I (1950–51), pp. 224–37.

Another objection to multiple currency practices was that, by making official rates nominal, multiple rates tended to undermine par values. Because most of the countries using multiple rates were subject to strong inflationary pressures, their exchange rates had to be adjusted frequently. Experience had demonstrated that, shortly after a country instituted multiple rates, its official exchange rates or its agreed par value no longer applied to many transactions.

Many Directors objected to multiple currency practices on yet another ground: they did not help to overcome the underlying economic problems of the countries employing them. Devaluation via multiple rates was usually inadequate and partial. Resort to multiple rates in many instances had not avoided the need for quantitative controls to curb import demand. When used for their anti-inflationary effects, multiple rates were insufficient to restrain inflationary pressures; primary reliance still had to be placed on the usual monetary and fiscal policies.

The Fund was, in the next few years, to learn even more about the adverse consequences of multiple rates, as well as the circumstances in which they might be useful; these are discussed below.

Adaptation of policies

As the arguments about the relative merits of multiple rates continued, it became evident that multiple rates usually resulted from balance of payments deficits, which in turn were most often caused by inflation. Until inflation was brought under control, the removal of multiple rates would necessitate, in their place, the introduction or tightening of quantitative restrictions on imports and payments. Since quantitative restrictions were themselves a form of control, and gave rise to many difficulties, the replacement of multiple rates by such restrictions would achieve little. (The Fund's first Exchange Restrictions Report, dated March 1, 1950, used the term *cost restrictions* for multiple currency practices and referred to quantitative restrictions as *supply-type* restrictions. These expressions did not subsequently become common Fund usage, although they occur in unofficial discussions of multiple rates.)

There was also increasing evidence of the widespread use of multiple rates for purposes not concerned with the balance of payments, such as taxation and protection. Therefore, the Fund realized that insistence on the immediate discontinuation of multiple rates might compel members to put into effect hastily devised tax substitutes, different in form but no better in practice than the existing systems of multiple rates. Preferable substitutes would require comprehensive reforms of fiscal systems and customs tariff schedules, and these had first to be carefully designed and then had to go through prolonged legislative procedures.

In these circumstances the general principles outlined in the 1947 letter had to be adapted to deal with specific problems. This adaptation took several forms.

One, rather than insisting on the immediate elimination of multiple rates, the Fund came to put stress on the achievement of general economic conditions which would facilitate this elimination as soon as practicable. Most important among these conditions was domestic financial stability. Thus, as part of its early consideration of multiple currency practices, the Fund came to concentrate heavily on the domestic inflation of its members.[13]

Two, there was gradually evolved what was in effect a case-by-case approach: each member's request for approval of multiple rates was decided on its own merits. In certain inflationary conditions, for example, members' exchange difficulties were considered to be related to the inadequacy of their import rates for restraining excessive import demand. Among the recommendations which the Fund made to members, along with anti-inflationary measures, were higher penalty selling rates for nonessential imports. At times the further restriction of import demand—including, occasionally, tightened quantitative restrictions—was advised.

Members were also encouraged to avoid the use of many particular practices—such as auction systems, compensation arrangements, and "mixing" rates, especially for exports—which might unduly complicate their exchange rates or harm other countries. "Mixing" systems were considered to be unduly susceptible to pressure from exporters for further rate multiplicity, as well as to administrative juggling. Compensation arrangements also gave rise to extensive multiplication of rates. In order to keep exchange rates as stable as possible, the Fund urged that free market rates be limited to balance of payments items other than trade, such as capital or invisibles. This sort of "code of fair practices," it was thought, would keep continuing systems within tolerable limits.

Despite these difficulties, the Fund still hoped for progress in the elimination of multiple rates. Not wishing to disapprove multiple rates or to approve them outright, the Board gave approval to those proposed by individual countries as "temporary measures," and remained in consultation with the members concerned.

During these early years, the Fund worked intensely with its members on multiple rate problems. Innumerable informal contacts were made, many staff missions were sent out, sundry reports were written, and frequent discussions took place in the Board. All this activity was almost entirely concerned with the Fund's Latin American members, especially Chile, Colombia, Costa Rica, Ecuador, Honduras, Nicaragua, and Paraguay.

In many respects, these years were frustrating ones. The Fund was criticized at times for too much and at times for too little attention to multiple rates.

[13] *Annual Report, 1948*, p. 28.

Some of the Latin American countries began to ask whether the Fund, in a world of extensive exchange controls and the continued inconvertibility of key currencies, was not devoting excessive attention to the multiple rates of a few countries that contributed little to total world trade. On the other hand, some economists, both in academic and in some official circles, anxious for evidences of successful international monetary cooperation within the new organization, frequently lamented the lack of progress, even in the field of multiple rates, which was thought to be easier than that of other controls.

Reassessment of policies

In January–February 1950 these problems were brought to a head in the Executive Board, which undertook a series of informal sessions on multiple currency practices. In these sessions it was stressed that the Fund had been willing to approve multiple rates *only* for balance of payments reasons. Much discussion centered, therefore, on the other reasons for multiple rates, including the use of such rates for taxation and subsidization and for protection.

To assist in formulating a new policy, Directors considered a model system of multiple rates. This model was designed to take account of balance of payments deficits without making concessions to the other purposes of multiple rates. The model had one import and one export rate with a fixed spread in excess of 1 per cent, and a free market as a safety valve for excessive import demand. The various advantages and disadvantages of the model were debated. But the basic question remained, and was left unanswered: Would such a model imply the *permanent* use of multiple rates? No firm consolidation of views among Directors took place even after these informal sessions.

THE MIDDLE YEARS (1952–55)

Second phase in the Fund's approach

The beginning of consultations under Article XIV in 1952 led to what may be seen as a second phase in the Fund's policies on multiple exchange rates. This phase continued until about the end of 1955. Although the legal obligation of members to consult the Fund in advance of multiple rate changes, set forth in the December 1947 letter, continued to apply, the Board's operating procedures were altered in important respects. The Directors no longer reviewed changes in multiple exchange rates when such changes were made. Instead, they gave temporary approval to a proposed change in a multiple rate system without immediate review of a particular practice, pending the forthcoming annual Article XIV consultation. In the course of that consultation a review of the total exchange rate system was undertaken and a final decision reached on the particular rate changes made.

This change in procedure had two important advantages. First, it enabled the Fund and the member country to consider the reasons for, and possible alternatives to, multiple rates in a broad, regular (annual) context, and eventually to work together toward the elimination of multiple rates. Second, as such consultations came to be held with practically all members, including the major European ones, the dualism in the Fund's policy between multiple exchange rates and other types of exchange restrictions seemed more or less at an end. After 1952, the consultations became the main activity of the Fund, in contrast to the previous situation, when multiple currency practices had been the great generator of the work of the Fund.

This switch in procedure—from considering multiple currency practices as they were introduced to considering them more fully in the course of the Article XIV consultations—culminated in a decision of the Executive Board, taken in February 1956, to use much more extensively the so-called lapse of time procedure for changes in multiple rates. The changes approved by the Managing Director under this procedure were, of course, more fully examined at the time of the Article XIV consultations. However, it was understood that this procedure would not be used for multiple rate changes involving shifts of payments from an official market to a new or narrow free market or to a free market in which the prevailing exchange rates were far out of line with the official rate at which most exports were handled. The Directors were particularly sensitive to multiple rate changes that jeopardized fixed exchange rates or that might in effect subsidize exports.

During this second phase, it was still evident that multiple currency practices could not be eradicated easily or quickly, and that the case-by-case approach would have to be continued for some time. A search was therefore begun for some new policy that could be implemented on a case-by-case basis.

Spread of multiple rates

The question of what policy to apply had been made even more difficult by an increasing divergence in practice between the Fund's ultimate goal of unification of exchange systems and the existing situation. Despite the Fund's efforts, multiple currency practices continued to spread.[14] Several countries that were already employing multiple exchange rates joined the Fund: Afghanistan, Indonesia, Israel, and Korea. Many countries that were already members introduced multiple currency practices: China, Egypt, Finland, Greece, Iceland, the Philippines, Turkey, and Yugoslavia. Even a number of Western European countries, although retaining unitary fixed rates for the bulk of their transactions, felt compelled to open free markets for the sale of certain bilateral or EPU currencies, or for certain capital flows. Belgium, for example, established a free

[14] *Fourth Annual Report on Exchange Restrictions* (1953), pp. 40–50.

market for EPU currencies; Germany introduced a free market for "Brazilian accounting dollars." Multiple rates were thus no longer confined to Latin America; they had spread to Asia, the Middle East, and Western Europe. Table 6 at the end of this chapter, which provides a detailed chronological summary of the principal developments in multiple rates, shows this extension.

Reasons for extension of multiple rates

The increased use of multiple currency practices during these years reflected two distinct kinds of problem, each of which gave rise to different practices. One problem was what was commonly known at the time as the world dollar shortage. The currencies of the world had become divided into "hard" currencies, mainly the U.S. and Canadian dollars, which were convertible, and "soft" currencies, including the pound sterling, the French and Belgian francs, the deutsche mark, and the guilder, which were inconvertible. Although a country might have achieved equilibrium in its aggregate balance of payments, a surplus in an inconvertible currency could not be used to settle deficits where convertible currencies were needed.

This situation had led, in Western Europe as elsewhere, to some multiple currency practices—such as limited free markets and broken cross rates in broader free markets—and to retention quotas, which aimed at increasing a country's supply of "hard" currencies and decreasing its holdings of "soft" ones.

The trend to such practices began to be reversed in 1954–55 as a result of the marked general improvement in the international payments situation which had started to take place. On January 23, 1954, the Report of the Randall Commission of the U.S. Government noted, for example, that the conditions prerequisite to currency convertibility were more nearly in prospect at that time than at any previous time since the war.[15]

By the spring of 1954 the Fund was able to discern a general tendency toward the removal of barriers to trade and payments; restrictive practices had been considerably reduced or modified.[16] The Exchange Restrictions Report for 1955 called attention to continued—although more gradual—progress in relaxing restrictions and, in particular, to increased facilities for nonresidents to convert inconvertible currencies into dollars.[17]

The second reason for the spread of multiple rates, applying to the less developed countries, was a more difficult one to counter. Multiple exchange rates, originally introduced to alleviate the depression-based payments problems of the 1930's, now seemed useful instruments to support economic development

---

[15] U.S. Commission on Foreign Economic Policy, *Report to the President and the Congress*, p. 470.

[16] *Annual Report, 1954*, p. 74.

[17] *Sixth Annual Report on Exchange Restrictions* (1955), pp. 2–6.

efforts, particularly in the economic and institutional environment of developing countries.

The problems of establishing or maintaining internal monetary stability were often intensified by the pressing claims of development programs. Multiple rates could, as described above, have an anti-inflationary effect if exchange profits were frozen. Dual exchange markets could isolate speculative capital from trade transactions. Alternatively, dual markets could separate exports of primary products, which might not benefit from devaluation, from exports of manufactured goods, where an exchange rate incentive might induce new export industries, so essential to development. On the import side, multiple rates might offer protection to some domestic industries; or they might provide subsidies to essential consumer goods, thereby keeping down the cost of living. Additional arguments for multiple rates as an aid to development were also advanced by member countries.

Multiple rates thus persisted in developing countries. Several countries, dissatisfied with the results of quantitative controls, switched to multiple rates. The Annual Report of the Executive Directors for 1955, after noting that world trade and payments were less subject to restriction than they had been a year earlier, commented that much less progress had been made in the elimination of multiple currency practices.[18]

At the same time, the problem of multiple export rates had become of added concern to countries not employing them. The less developed countries had begun to increase their use of multiple rates for exports, and keener competition in international markets made countries with unitary rates increasingly fearful that competitors using multiple rates might derive unfair advantages in export markets. It seemed certain that tension between the Fund's members concerning multiple rates might again increase, as it had in the Fund's first days.

In these circumstances both the staff and the Board began to consider even more intensively the economic functions and effects of multiple rates, especially the relation between multiple rates and economic development. The conclusion was that the use of exchange restrictions and multiple rates to foster economic development would be unnecessary if substitute measures were introduced. Since multiple rates were, for example, often used in place of customs duties or taxes, they could be eliminated if equivalent revenue was raised in another way. Similarly, multiple rates that provided protection to domestic producers could be abolished if protective tariffs were appropriately raised. Increasingly the devising of acceptable alternative measures for multiple rates became a main problem for the Fund. Meanwhile, the questions facing the Fund were these: Should it condone, or at least not object to, these uses of multiple

[18] *Annual Report, 1955*, p. 76.

rates for reasons other than the balance of payments? Should it recommend specific alternatives?

As background for the Board's consideration of these problems, the staff also prepared studies of the revenue-raising functions of multiple currency practices [19] and of the desirability of substituting increases in tariffs for exchange surcharges. In the latter study, a series of propositions was advanced as to the economic circumstances for which tariffs and surcharges, respectively, were most appropriate. Essentially, surcharges were considered best suited to meet temporary balance of payments deficits. Consequently, when surcharges were used to help cope with temporary payments deficits, they should not be incorporated in the customs tariff schedule. When, however, surcharges were serving a longer-run balance of payments purpose, the study deemed it advisable for the country concerned to introduce anti-inflationary measures or to adjust its exchange rate rather than to revise its customs tariff rates. On the other hand, the study concluded that tariffs were preferable to surcharges as a long-run source of revenue and for protection.

Consideration of these staff suggestions showed that Directors held widely differing views. After much discussion the Board came to the conclusion that generalizations on alternative measures for multiple rates were difficult and dangerous, and that it was preferable to consider the individual circumstances of each country.

By the end of 1955, membership of the Fund had grown to 58. But, despite some lessening of multiple rates, there were still 36 members that had some kind of practice which the Fund considered a multiple currency practice. Many of these practices, especially in Europe, were minor, and most transactions were still conducted at exchange rates based on par values. But there remained very complex systems with many different rates in many countries throughout the world.

EVENTUAL BREAKTHROUGH (1956–62)

Toward the end of 1955, a third phase in the history of the Fund's dealings with multiple rates began. In the Exchange Restrictions Report for 1956, the Fund was able to report considerable progress toward the lessened use of multiple rates:

> In the past year, many countries maintaining multiple exchange rates and similar practices made some changes in these practices, which varied considerably in character and significance. The countries that did not change their multiple currency practices are, for the most part, those in which the practice is only a

[19] W. John R. Woodley, "The Use of Special Exchange Rates for Transactions with Foreign Companies," *Staff Papers*, Vol. III (1953–54), pp. 254–69; Joyce Sherwood, "Revenue Features of Multiple Exchange Rate Systems," *ibid.*, Vol. V (1956–57), pp. 74–107.

minor element in the exchange rate structure. The number of countries in which multiple currency practices were simplified appreciably exceeded those in which there was an increase in multiple rates.[20]

The intensive postwar investment programs, especially in Western Europe, had borne fruit, and production was rising rapidly. Increased supplies of goods, together with the improved domestic financial and monetary positions of Western European countries following the realignment of exchange rates in 1949, brought the world dollar shortage to an end. Hence, from 1956 onward, the main industrial countries relaxed many of the barriers to trade and payments and made their currencies convertible. Multiple currency practices, as well as discriminatory quantitative restrictions, which distinguished between "hard" and "soft" currencies could be, and were, quickly removed. By 1958 the free markets in which some but not all transactions took place, broken cross rates, retention quotas, and other special devices of a number of Western European countries had all been discontinued.

Toward the end of 1955 and in 1956 events occurred which were, in some ways, even more unexpected. Three less developed countries—Bolivia, Chile, and Paraguay—which had maintained multiple rates since the 1930's and had believed them imperative for primary producing economies, undertook comprehensive exchange reforms, eliminating multiple rates at a single stroke and introducing unitary fluctuating rates. Thailand also achieved a unitary fluctuating rate, but gradually. In addition, several other multiple rates, such as an exchange tax in the Philippines and the application of an official rate to oil company transactions in Syria, were eliminated.

New Fund approaches

The time was ripe for an intensification of the Fund's efforts to eliminate multiple rates. The countries employing them now were less convinced of their usefulness than they had been several years before. Greater emphasis was being placed on the practical difficulties of eliminating multiple rates than on a preference for them over unitary rates.

The experiences of the Fund in the previous ten years had demonstrated that, for most countries with complex systems, unification of the exchange system required the mapping out of a special course of action. The elimination of multiple rates could not be expected to come about automatically as internal monetary conditions were brought satisfactorily under control, or even as balance of payments positions were strengthened. Moreover, in many countries, unification at a realistic par value was not likely to be attained in one step: what was required was either a process of simplification to a few fixed rates or to one fixed and one free rate, or, alternatively, unification at a fluctuating rate.

[20] *Seventh Annual Report on Exchange Restrictions* (1956), p. 5.

The Fund had also learned that it was much easier for a country to simplify its exchange rate structure than to unify it. The necessary degree of stringency in internal monetary policies was significantly smaller for simplification than for unification, and fewer reserves were required if a simplified system included a fluctuating rate. Over the years it had become evident that floating rate mechanisms were often more self-liquidating than a group of fixed rates. Another advantage of simplification as against unification was that an exchange spread, such as often characterized simple multiple rate systems, might absorb part of any internal monetary expansion; such absorption was not possible with a unitary rate.

Moreover, it had been learned that it was the *complexity* of multiple rates that was especially at fault. Complex exchange systems brought into economic decisions many more elements of arbitrariness and uncertainty. Extensive differentiation of rates among export and import commodities was particularly likely to distort domestic prices and output and made it more difficult for the authorities to resist pressures for special treatment of a given commodity. Further, an excessive number of rates increased the possibilities of hidden subsidization and encouraged the continuation of overvalued rates. But perhaps the most important condemnation of complex rate systems was that they tended to perpetuate themselves until the countries using them experienced crises which might well have been avoided.

For several months in 1957 the Board carefully considered the possibility of making new and intensified efforts to reduce multiple rates. All the Directors were anxious to reach a decision that would be widely supported, especially by the developing countries that maintained multiple rates. In June 1957 this consensus was reached, and the Board decided to send to the members a new communication on multiple currency practices.[21] This memorandum urged countries using such techniques to simplify considerably their existing rate structures. Such a simplification meant more than a mere reduction in the number of existing rates: emphasis was placed on limiting the system to two or three rates which would be sufficiently realistic to maintain a satisfactory balance of payments with a minimum of restrictions. A simpler system could include, where necessary, the temporary use of a widened free market or of a fluctuating rate as a step toward a stable unitary rate.

The Fund undertook to help countries to plan specific exchange systems. Technical assistance could also be made available to cover the formulation, where appropriate, of substitute fiscal arrangements. Most important of all, where the exchange reform was sufficiently broad and was accompanied by a domestic stabilization program, the Fund was willing to consider permitting

[21] Reproduced below, Vol. III, pp. 265–66.

members to use its resources in support of exchange reforms. Meanwhile, the Board would be reluctant to approve changes in multiple rate systems which would make them more complex.

While not insisting on the immediate unification of exchange rates, this communication sounded a warning that the Board would no longer approve complex systems except in certain circumstances.

Accelerated elimination of multiple rates

For several years after the issue of the June 1957 memorandum, there was a strong trend toward elimination of multiple exchange rates by the developing countries. Significantly, the countries abandoning multiple rates included Argentina (1958), which in the 1930's had been one of the first Latin American countries to use them, and Yugoslavia (1961), which had had in the mid-1950's an exchange system often regarded as the most complex of all. Table 6 at the end of this chapter gives additional details of the decline in the use of multiple rates.

Some countries devalued, eliminated multiple rates, and set a new fixed rate, all at the same time. Generally these were the European countries, but they included Israel. This was the pattern in Finland, Spain, and Turkey. Many of these countries also set new par values. Others—especially the less developed countries—reached a par value by stages, first eliminating multiple rates and introducing a unitary fluctuating rate, then gradually stabilizing the fluctuating rate, and eventually converting it into a par value. Costa Rica, Iran, Jordan, Korea, Nicaragua, the Philippines, Saudi Arabia, and Thailand attained fixed rates (or even par values) via fluctuating rates, at least for some transactions.[22]

A few countries eliminated multiple rates when they were enjoying a favorable balance of payments; usually the strong payments situation was the result of peak production or high world prices for exports, or both. More frequently, however, countries reshaped their exchange rate structures as part of a broad program to meet balance of payments crises. These general reforms of the exchange system were usually accompanied by exchange devaluation and by internal policies designed to remove price distortions and to restrain inflation.

Frequently also tariff adjustments, usually upward, were undertaken simultaneously with exchange reform. In some countries, comprehensive fiscal reforms were carried out. Other countries, introducing a single fluctuating rate, temporarily applied taxes or surcharges to some imports. Apart from whether or not these taxes and surcharges were different from multiple rates insofar as the Fund's Articles were concerned, their economic function was different. Because

[22] These alternative approaches have been described in Margaret G. de Vries, "Fund Members' Adherence to the Par Value Regime," *Staff Papers*, Vol. XIII (1966), at pp. 516–20.

they were now superimposed on unitary exchange rates that were unrestricted and hence presumably realistic, these taxes and surcharges were regarded purely as fiscal devices; previously, because they comprised part of the exchange system, they had been considered at least in part as balance of payments measures. The main reason why countries used taxes and surcharges, after exchange reform, was that alternative revenue sources could not be quickly developed. Some countries proposed explicitly to undertake tariff revision at a later date, at which time these taxes and surcharges were to be incorporated into the tariff structure.[23]

In sum, between 1955 and 1962, not only did several Western European countries eliminate their minor exchange practices, but major systems of multiple rates were unified in many other countries as well, in every geographic region. By the end of 1962, only 15 Fund members out of a total of 82 had multiple rates of any type, in contrast to 36 out of 58 members seven years earlier.

Explanations of decline in multiple rates

One of the principal reasons for the decline in multiple rates was the adverse experiences with these practices that many countries had had. Although some countries had been able to use them to advantage, the experiences of most had been disappointing and frustrating. In order to achieve any of the professed purposes of multiple exchange rates—that is, to tax a major export, to restrain imports of luxury commodities, to raise revenue, to alleviate inflation, to stimulate minor exports, or to isolate capital movements from trade transactions—countries had found that certain conditions had to prevail.

First, it was essential that the exchange system be simple; that is, there should be only a few exchange rates rather than many. Complex systems worked out much less well; they rarely achieved several objectives concurrently. Finding a rate structure suitable for such diverse purposes as holding down external deficits, redistributing internal income, and checking inflation seemed to be virtually impossible, even where several rates existed. Seeking to make multiple rates perform both balance of payments and taxation functions, especially under conditions of chronic inflation, led to complex systems and the dissipation of the initial objectives.

Second, periodic adjustments had to be made in the exchange system or else fluctuating rates had to be used in order to keep at realistic levels the exchange rates applicable to most exports and imports; otherwise, there was a danger that the exchange rates prevailing would become overvalued.

---

[23] A discussion of the techniques of unification of multiple rates is to be found in F. d'A. Collings, "Recent Progress in Latin America Toward Eliminating Exchange Restrictions," *Staff Papers*, Vol. VIII (1960–61), pp. 274–86.

Third, a reasonable amount of domestic monetary stability had to be maintained.[24] Under conditions of inflation, traditional export industries were harmed by being subjected to penalty rates of exchange at overvalued levels. New and potential export industries were neglected, even where special exchange rates for so-called minor exports existed. Multiple import rates had adverse effects on the structure of domestic production and investment.

These conditions for successful use of multiple rates had not always, or even frequently, been fulfilled in the countries that had employed multiple rates, and multiple rates had then proved worse than practicable alternatives.

Following the memorandum of June 1957, the Fund vigorously encouraged countries to eliminate multiple rates. On many occasions the Fund urged countries not to be unduly cautious in moving toward simplified exchange systems. It drew attention to specific circumstances where, in the Fund's view, greater simplification was feasible and even essential. Frequently it singled out for comment to a member exchange rates that were considered especially troublesome. The Fund provided technical assistance to work out specific exchange reforms and internal stabilization programs. Finally, there were stand-by arrangements to bolster countries' reserves.

Once some countries had eliminated complex systems of multiple rates, the Fund could point to the favorable aftermath. In their Annual Report for 1961 the Directors had this to say:

> In arguing the advantages of [the removal of multiple rates], the Fund has been able to point to the generally favorable experience of several members that have eliminated complex multiple exchange rate systems in the recent past. In general, these countries have found that their economies are better able than previously to deal with both domestic and balance of payments problems. In some countries, this improvement occurred despite lower prices for major export products upon which they largely depend for foreign exchange. In several of the countries which adopted freely fluctuating exchange rates when they abolished their multiple exchange [rate] systems, these rates remained virtually unchanged for long periods. For some, moreover, the initial, sometimes difficult, period of adjustment to the new conditions that inevitably follows a major economic reform has been succeeded by a period of renewed progress, accompanied at the same time by monetary and exchange rate stability and an increasingly satisfactory reserve position.[25]

SOME CONTINUING PROBLEMS (1963–65)

Developments in multiple exchange rates in the eighteenth to twentieth years of the Fund's history were of three types.

---

[24] A fuller account of the economic experiences of countries with multiple rates can be found in Margaret G. de Vries, "Multiple Exchange Rates," *Staff Papers*, Vol. XII (1965), pp. 282–313.

[25] *Annual Report, 1961*, p. 117.

(1) Countries which had long made use of multiple rates continued to join others which had considerably simplified or unified their exchange rates. In 1964–65 Venezuela and Brazil simplified their exchange systems in a series of steps. The Philippines, which had introduced multiple rates with a fluctuating rate in 1962, eliminated them and set a new par value in November 1965. Also in 1965, Korea replaced its multiple rates with a unitary fluctuating rate.

(2) A few countries, including Afghanistan, Colombia, Indonesia, and Viet-Nam, continued to maintain significant multiple rate systems, although some of these became somewhat less complex.

(3) On the other hand, certain countries where multiple rates had been eliminated or very much simplified reintroduced them or reverted to complex systems. And in some countries which previously did not have them, multiple rates appeared. Chile, for example, following a virtual unification of its exchange rate in 1956, introduced in 1962 a dual market system which still continued at the end of 1965. Multiple rates were adopted in several countries where they had not been used previously. Pakistan, to assist exports of all except its major primary products, had in 1959 introduced an export bonus scheme patterned along the lines of the retention quota employed by Germany in the mid-1950's. This system was still in use at the end of 1965, and its scope and complexity had been increased. A few new African countries had begun to use devices reminiscent of those used in Latin America in the 1940's.

Some other devices, such as import surcharges and advance deposit requirements, which are in many respects similar to multiple currency practices, were instituted by several countries to deal with recurrent payments or fiscal deficits. Among these countries were Argentina, Brazil, Ceylon, Colombia, Ecuador, India, Iran, Ireland, Japan, Pakistan, and Uruguay. Moreover, among the measures introduced by a number of industrial countries to reduce the outflow of capital were special taxes or markets with premiums for investment currencies, as in the United Kingdom.[26]

The problem of multiple exchange rates may never be entirely solved. The nature of and reasons for the practices used differ, their locale shifts, and there is a constant need for vigilance by the Fund. Despite some continued and some newly emerging problems, however, the extent and complexity of multiple rates were clearly less at the end of 1965 than they had been twenty years earlier.

[26] See *Seventeenth Annual Report on Exchange Restrictions* (1966), p. 6.

Table 6. Principal Developments in Multiple Exchange Rates, 1946–65

1946

Sept. *Venezuela* asked Fund assurance that membership would not prevent it from taking suitable time to eliminate multiple currency practices.

Nov. The question arose whether an initial par value could be agreed if multiple rates prevailed.

1947

Jan.–Feb. The Board discussed several matters pertaining to multiple rates. Do differences exceeding 2 per cent between buying and selling rates constitute a multiple currency practice? Are multiple rates subject to Article XIV? How prevalent are they?

May The Board set up an Ad Hoc Committee on Spreads and Multiple Currency Practices to study the application of the Articles to multiple rates.

June–Aug. The Board considered the recommendations of the Ad Hoc Committee.

Dec. A letter setting forth the decisions on policy and procedures for multiple currency practices was sent to all members.

1948

Jan. *France* devalued the franc and instituted a multiple currency practice, to which the Fund objected.

June The Fund agreed to a special simple procedure for changes in *China's* exchange system because of special problems in the case: the Managing Director approved in writing changes proposed by the Chinese authorities, and circulated the correspondence to the Board for information, Board consideration of the change not being first required.

Oct.–Nov. The Fund reviewed Latin American exchange problems and policies. No Board decision was taken but it was stressed that continuing inflation had been found to be a major cause of exchange difficulties and that, in view of the diversity of conditions in Latin America, proposals by each country would have to be considered separately.

1949

Feb. During a review of the exchange position of one country, the question first arose whether a member could properly maintain multiple rates if they were not necessary for balance of payments reasons.

Apr. Instructions given to a Fund mission to one country required it to investigate the possibility of substituting nonexchange measures for the existing exchange surcharges in order to restrain imports.

1950

Jan.–Feb. The Board held a series of informal sessions on multiple currency practices.

Mar. A separate Multiple Currency Practices Division was created in a staff reorganization.

Table 6 *(continued).* Principal Developments in Multiple Exchange Rates, 1946–65

1951	
Mar.	*The Philippines* imposed a 17 per cent tax on sales of foreign exchange.
Mar.–Apr.	*Paraguay* devalued the guaraní, removed taxes on sales of exchange, and transferred various transactions to the free market in an attempt to meet objections of the Fund to its exchange system.
May	An internal Fund procedure for minor changes in multiple rates was established to lessen the need for consideration by the Board of all changes in multiple rate systems.
Sept.	*Costa Rica* abolished surcharges, reducing the complexity of its multiple rate structure; the abolition was facilitated by upward revisions in its tariffs. It was agreed by the Board that the staff should look into the general problem of surcharges versus tariffs.
1952	
Jan.	After consideration of a staff paper on tariffs versus surcharges, the Board decided that no general line either favoring or disapproving elimination of multiple rates through upward tariff revisions could be taken and that each case must be considered on its merits.
Jan.–June	*Yugoslavia,* in a series of steps, introduced a complex system of multiple rates.
Feb.	*Ecuador* simplified its exchange system by abolishing its compensation system.
Sept.	*Germany* introduced a free market for "Brazilian accounting dollars" (used in payments transactions under the payments agreements between Germany and Brazil).
1953	
Feb.	*Brazil* inaugurated a free market for invisibles and most capital transactions and for certain trade items.
Apr.	*Greece* unified its exchange structure and devalued the drachma.
May	*Austria* unified its exchange structure and set an initial par value.
Aug.	*Brazil* reduced the list of export products subject to a "mixing" arrangement, but a complex system remained.
1954	
Jan.	*Israel* (not yet a member) substituted a single official rate for three fixed official rates, but for certain transactions either one of two premiums or a surcharge applied.
July	*The Netherlands, Belgium,* and *Luxembourg,* in connection with arrangements to facilitate capital movements between them and other EPU countries, extended the free market for capital to residents of other EPU countries; previously the free market had been confined to transactions between their own residents.
Aug.	*Paraguay* depreciated to a new par value and made other substantial alterations in its exchange system, but a complex system remained.
	Israel (now a Fund member) extended its surcharge to all imports.

Table 6 *(continued).* Principal Developments in Multiple Exchange Rates, 1946–65

1955

Jan.–Feb.	*Brazil* established export bonuses.
Feb.–May	*Colombia* abolished a differential rate for coffee exports and introduced a broad free market; imports were made subject to stamp taxes.
Mar.	*China* introduced a system of negotiable exchange certificates.
May	*Chile* eliminated the special exchange rate for copper companies.
July	*Nicaragua* removed surcharges and depreciated its par value but retained an exchange spread.
	Belgium's free market was opened to capital transfers to all destinations.
July–Oct.	*Indonesia* considerably revised its system in an attempt at simplification, but a wide range of rates, especially on imports, continued.
Sept.–Dec.	*Uruguay* announced a special premium for exports of wool, including wool tops.

1956

Jan.	*Thailand* completed unification of its exchange system; all transactions were to be effected at a fluctuating free market rate.
Mar.	*Paraguay* depreciated its par value and greatly simplified its complex multiple rate system. A broad internal monetary stabilization program was introduced.
	The Board agreed to more extensive use of the lapse of time procedure for multiple rates: it could now be used for all changes that did not, in the opinion of the Managing Director, seem to require immediate discussion by the Board.
Apr.	*Chile* considerably simplified its multiple rate system, abolished the import licensing system, and instituted a fluctuating free market for all commodity transactions.
Dec.	*Bolivia* undertook an exchange reform and comprehensive economic stabilization measures, replacing the complex multiple rate system with a single fluctuating rate.

1957

Mar.	The Board began consideration of a staff paper on a change in policies for multiple currency practices which would put an end to Fund approval of complex systems and would encourage genuine and substantial simplification.
May	*Iran,* as a final step in unifying its multiple rates, changed its par value to what was the *de facto* unitary exchange rate.
June	The Board reached a second general decision on multiple currency practices. The Fund notified countries that it would no longer approve complex systems unless the countries maintaining them were making reasonable progress toward simplification.
Aug.	*Paraguay* gave up all transactions at the par value, eliminated all multiple rates and quantitative restrictions, and adopted a freely fluctuating rate.
	France introduced a 20 per cent surcharge and premium on most transactions, which was extended to all transactions shortly thereafter.
Sept.	*Finland* depreciated its par value and abolished its multiple currency practices.
Nov.	*Nicaragua* applied the official rate to exports of cotton and minor exports, thus moving toward unification.

Table 6 *(continued).* Principal Developments in Multiple Exchange Rates, 1946–65

1958

Jan.–Dec.	*Uruguay* made various changes in its rate structure, making it more complex.
Apr.	*China* simplified its exchange system, abolishing its 20 per cent defense tax and other rates. There were now two effective rates.
May	*Iceland* introduced three exchange premiums on export proceeds, replacing the assistance previously granted to exports through different forms of subsidization. Discrimination as to country destination was terminated.
July	*Yugoslavia* continued to simplify its complex rate structure by reducing the number of export and import coefficients.
Aug.	*Turkey* replaced its complex system with a simpler one.
Oct.	*Nicaragua* extended the par value rate to coffee exports; thus by the end of the crop year all trade transactions were unified at a rate based on the par value.
Dec.	*Argentina,* as part of an economic stabilization program, abolished multiple rates and introduced a single fluctuating rate.

1959

Jan.	*Chile* combined its two fluctuating exchange markets.
	Pakistan introduced an export bonus scheme.
July	*Spain* set a par value and abolished all multiple rates.
Aug.	*China* established a single fluctuating rate for all transactions except government payments.
	Indonesia abolished its exchange certificate system and introduced other multiple rates.
	Turkey modified its export premiums so that a single rate applied to all transactions except exports of two commodities.

1960

Feb.	*Iceland* eliminated its multiple rate system, and depreciated its par value.
Apr.	*The Philippines* introduced a fluctuating free market for most transactions, with a "mixing" rate for exports.
May	*Peru* unified its two exchange markets.
Dec.	The special procedure for changes in *China's* exchange system arranged in June 1948 was discontinued.

1961

Jan.	*Yugoslavia* abolished its multiple rate system and introduced a unified fixed rate for all transactions except receipts from tourism.
May–July	*Brazil* introduced new exchange arrangements for coffee export proceeds and transferred to the free market all imports previously at preferential rates.
June	*China* introduced a fixed rate for all transactions.
July	*Ecuador* replaced a complex multiple rate system with a new par value applying to most transactions; only a minor free market with a fluctuating rate was retained for some transactions in invisibles and unregistered capital.
Sept.	*Costa Rica* set a new par value and except for temporary arrangements abolished all multiple rates.

Table 6 *(concluded).* Principal Developments in Multiple Exchange Rates, 1946–65

1962

Jan.	*Chile* again instituted two exchange markets.
	The Philippines introduced a fluctuating rate for all transactions except merchandise exports, to which a "mixing" rate would apply.
Feb.	*Israel* set a new par value and eliminated multiple rates.
May	*The United Arab Republic* replaced its multiple rates with a single rate.
Aug.	*Costa Rica* removed its last multiple rate.
Oct.	*Indonesia* reclassified imports in its complex rate structure.

1963

Mar.	*Nicaragua* transferred the remaining items from the free to the official market, so that a single rate of exchange applied to all transactions.
	Afghanistan devalued its official rate, set an initial par value, and greatly simplified its complex rate structure.

1964

Jan.	*Laos* devalued its official rate and established a legal free market for imports other than aid goods, and for tourism, capital transfers, and other payments.
	Venezuela considerably simplified its exchange system through a series of steps worked out with the Fund.
Mar.–July	*Brazil* undertook several simplifications of its exchange system.
May	*Korea* established a unitary rate which was only nominally fluctuating, and abolished multiple rates.

1965

Jan.–Dec.	*Brazil* changed the effective rates applicable to coffee exports on several occasions throughout the year.
Mar.	*Korea* established an exchange market in which the rate was allowed to fluctuate, and substantially liberalized its restrictive system.
Nov.	*The Philippines* unified its exchange system, and set a new par value of ₱ 3.90 = US$1.
Dec.	*Somalia* introduced a temporary 3 per cent exchange tax for revenue purposes.

CHAPTER

7

Fluctuating Exchange Rates

Margaret G. de Vries

IN NO FIELD of the Fund's endeavor have principle and expediency been more thoroughly interwoven than in that of fluctuating rates. Fixed exchange rates have remained the Fund's main principle; but temporarily, and in certain circumstances, fluctuating rates have been recognized as useful expedients.

Reconciliation between the aim of exchange rate stability and awareness of the need for flexibility of exchange rates has come by degrees: over the years it is possible to discern almost step-by-step movements in the Fund's policy in this regard. In its very early days the Fund put primary stress on the fact that fluctuating rates were inconsistent with the Articles. Quite soon, however, pragmatic considerations began to overshadow the more technical ones, and a less rigid approach was adopted. Hoping that a few exceptions would not cause a general return to the unstable rates of the pre-Fund era, the staff and the Board recognized the possibility that unusual circumstances might justify temporary departures from the standard prescribed by the Articles.

This toleration was not entirely a mere giving in to circumstances. Already the useful possibilities of less exacting policies toward exchange rates could be envisaged. Consequently, as successful experiences mounted, the Fund's policy gradually extended to outright advocacy of fluctuating rates for those situations where they seemed especially fitting.

Nevertheless, these shifts in the Fund's attitude toward flexible rates from 1948 to 1965 were not at the expense of the Fund's belief in exchange rate stability. There were two reasons why the Board could accept fluctuating rates on a number of occasions without surrendering the prime objective of rate stability. First, fluctuating rates have, for several countries, turned out to be part of the journey to a fixed exchange rate. Second, the circumstances in which fluctuating rates could meet with Fund approval have been carefully delineated. Although liberalizing its policies on flexible rates, the Fund opposed all suggestions that a general scheme of fluctuating rates be instituted.

CONCERN WITH THE ARTICLES

Mexico in 1948

That members of the staff and nearly all the Directors were anxious about the status under the Articles of a country that had suspended its par value, is clear from the action taken when the first such example came up for the Fund's consideration. In July 1948 Mexico suspended all transactions at the par value, and proposed to allow exchange transactions to take place at whatever exchange rates the market set. Although imports were to some extent excessive, the country's payments difficulty was due not so much to the balance of trade as to capital flight.

When the Mexican proposal was considered, the legal staff made much of the point that the Fund had no authority, under the terms of the Agreement, to *approve* a fluctuating rate. Not wishing to disapprove the Mexican action, the Board therefore did not take any decision, on the understanding that Mexico would establish a new parity "within three weeks." It soon became evident that a new parity would not be so quickly set, and the situation then posed for the Fund, as a new international agency, was a most difficult one. The two questions regarded as basic were: Could the Fund *agree* to a continued violation of the Articles? Could access to the Fund's resources be permitted during the period in which the par value was ineffective?

Mr. Gómez (Mexico), when explaining to the Board Mexico's request for an extension of time, argued the necessity for Mexico to ascertain the level at which a new rate could be maintained before agreeing a new parity. The Mexican Government had adopted all the strict internal stabilization measures the Fund had recommended, but more time was still required. Although it was possible that a stable exchange rate might be maintained if exchange controls were introduced, Mr. Gómez made it clear that the Mexican authorities were especially reluctant to resort to exchange controls. It was not even certain that the authorities could enforce exchange controls.

Nonetheless, Mexico did not wish to place itself in the position of violating the Articles of Agreement. Mr. Gómez suggested, therefore, that Mexico's situation might be considered as falling within the provisions of Article IV, Section 5 (*c*) (iii), which entitles the Fund to "a longer period in which to declare its attitude" concerning a proposed change in par value. Recognizing that this Section might not have been intended to cover the exact circumstances of the Mexican case, he urged that the Fund and Mexico should be guided by the principles rather than by the strict letter of the Articles.

Most Executive Directors feared dangerous implications in an interpretation of the Fund's Agreement which would permit a member to change its par value by introducing a free rate. Although the staff and the Directors considered at some length the economic feasibility of fixing a new parity, they were even more concerned about Mexico's formal status under the Articles. Mexico was not meeting the basic obligations of Article IV, Section 3, which required members to maintain exchange transactions within 1 per cent of parity. The request for an extension of time under Article IV, Section 5 (*c*) (iii), amounted to a request that the Fund condone a technical violation of its Agreement during the extended period of time.

Arguments for a new parity for Mexico

In the next several months a number of staff missions went to Mexico and the situation was discussed by the Board several times. The reasons why Mexico hesitated to set a new par value were considered, and each time the Fund stressed the economic advantages to Mexico of quickly doing so—the promotion of exports, the encouragement of foreign capital inflow, the return of domestic funds held abroad, and support for the determination of the Government to take the strong fiscal and credit measures necessary to redress Mexico's economic difficulties.

In the early part of 1949 the United States was in the midst of a recession. Hence, one issue to which special attention was given was whether a country closely affected by business conditions in the United States could determine a new par value so long as the recession there continued. Following the experiences of the 1930's, the fear continued to prevail in the late 1940's that fluctuations in U.S. business conditions would seriously harm the United States' trading partners.

The Fund took the view that the fixed rate system of its Agreement had already taken into account the possibility of changing business conditions in its largest member countries. Swings in business conditions should, therefore, not be the occasion for members to break away from the par value regime. Depressions and recessions were, instead, to be relieved by use of the Fund's resources.

What disturbed the legal staff and several Directors most was the continuation of Mexico's anomalous formal position in the Fund. Mexico's exchange system remained unapproved by the Fund. Accordingly, in January 1949 a proposal was made in the Board, which received general support, to write to Mexico urging the establishment of a new par value by the end of March.

Another staff mission to Mexico followed the dispatch of this communication and intensive consideration by the Board was renewed. In July 1949—one year after suspension of the initial par value—a new par value was agreed and Mexico was declared again eligible to use the Fund's resources.

EROSION OF FORMAL APPROACHES

THE BELGIAN PROPOSAL

Preoccupation with the formal status under the Articles of members with fluctuating rates was short-lived. In September 1949, at the time of the general European devaluations, the Belgian Government requested the Fund to agree to its abandoning its existing par value and delaying establishment of a new one until an appropriate rate could be determined. The Executive Directors raised no objection to the plan, there being a general feeling that the Fund had to recognize the difficulties facing Belgium. Nonetheless, deliberation took place over the precise wording of a decision. The Fund could not *agree* to the Belgian proposal because it had no authority to *approve* the adoption of fluctuating rates. There was the further question as to how far the Fund should go in condoning Belgium's action. The problem seemed simple: if Belgium found that circumstances made a fluctuating exchange rate imperative, the Fund should not try to prevent the introduction of that rate. However, it was quite another matter for the Fund to lend moral support to a fluctuating rate by formally expressing "approval" or "no objection." Mr. Rasminsky (Canada), for example, was disturbed at the change in the attitude of the Directors toward fluctuating exchange rates. Previously, the Fund had held strictly that fluctuating rates were illegal under the Articles; now the Board was considering a decision in which the Fund would agree to the need for a fluctuating rate, or at least would not object. In his view, the Fund should only note the Belgian proposal, treat it as a situation of *force majeure*, and refrain from imposing any sanctions against the member.

Mr. Tansley (United Kingdom) agreed with Mr. Rasminsky. He was especially uneasy lest the decision be taken as an invitation to other members to have recourse to fluctuating rates for indefinite periods. Moreover, he thought that any intimation of approval would be unfair to those members who had taken the risks of deciding on a new par value.

Because of these considerations, the Board discussed imposing a one-month time limit, but decided that such a limit would be unwise. A draft decision in which the Fund agreed to Belgium's plan was withdrawn. Two other alternatives—one in which the Fund *raised no objection* to Belgium's proposal, and a second in which the Fund merely *noted the Belgian measures*—were formally voted upon. The first of these two won, by a vote of 53,600 to 38,490. The final decision was, therefore:

> 1. Belgium has informed the Fund that it proposes to abandon the existing par value of the Belgian franc, beginning September 20, 1949, and, until the situation in the monetary field can be properly assessed so as to make possible a decision on the appropriate level for a new par value, no new fixed par value would be estab-

> lished; instead a free market for the U.S. dollar would be established in Brussels for the time being. Cross rates between the dollar and other currencies would be maintained and the normal operation of payments agreements would not be affected. The firm resolve of the Belgian Government would be to propose a new fixed par value for the Belgian franc as soon as circumstances warrant it. In the meantime the member would keep in close contact with the Fund concerning developments in the free market. The Fund has been requested to concur in the plan as an appropriate step in the light of existing circumstances. . . .
>
> 2. The Fund recognizes that the plan proposed by the Government of Belgium is an appropriate step in view of the exigencies of the situation. The Fund therefore raises no objection to the plan and takes note of the intention expressed by the Belgian Government to consult with the Fund and to propose a new parity as soon as circumstances warrant.

Two days later, on September 21, 1949, Belgium, fearful of the dangers of a fluctuating rate, proposed a new par value and the Fund agreed. The decision quoted above was revoked.

Peru turns to fluctuating rates

That the Fund's views on fluctuating rates had been considerably modified was further evidenced in November 1949, when Peru suspended all transactions at the par value. The country had had an exchange system consisting of three separate markets, the rates in one of which were fixed on the basis of the par value. It now proposed that the market with fixed rates should be abolished and all transactions should be conducted in two markets, one for trade and the other for nontrade transactions. Although the rates in both markets would fluctuate, they were expected to remain close to each other.

The Peruvian authorities explained that the weakening of demand abroad had created problems for Peru's metal exports. In addition, the accumulation of more sterling than could be used under Peru's import restrictions had caused difficulties for exports to the sterling area. The authorities contended that the parity rate had thus become unrealistic but that it was impossible for the time being to determine the level at which a new rate should be fixed. A prestabilization period was needed.

In a preparatory paper, the staff, guided by the less rigid view toward fluctuating rates that the Board had taken in the Belgian instance, suggested that the Fund should merely note the Peruvian proposal and take no further action. The staff reasoned that, since a system of unitary, fixed rates was fundamental to the Fund Agreement, the Fund should do no more than recognize the circumstances in which a fluctuating rate was introduced and refrain from applying sanctions. It was to be understood that Peru could not use the Fund's resources. The staff suggested that a time limit should be set within which a new par value should be proposed; otherwise, the Peruvian authorities might not have sufficient incentive to take the difficult steps necessary to stabilize the internal economy.

Several Directors, including Mr. Southard (United States), wished to go further in support of Peru's action, and suggested that the Board should commend Peru's new rate system as an effective step toward realizing the Fund's objectives. Observing that the exchange system was essentially unified and that the new rates seemed realistic, they viewed Peru's action as a substantial improvement on the complex multiple rate systems of many other countries.

As described in the preceding chapter, the Fund was becoming increasingly aware at this time that multiple rates would be difficult to abolish. Many countries had complex exchange systems based on par values which were clearly overvalued. By contrast, Peru's simple dual market system with two fluctuating rates seemed much closer to a unitary, realistic exchange rate.

Emergence of a case-by-case approach

Not all Executive Directors shared this favorable view of Peru's fluctuating rates. Recalling that a fluctuating rate had been under discussion only two months earlier when proposed by Belgium, some Directors insisted that the Fund's action on Peru should not be taken as introducing a new general policy on fluctuating rates; as in the field of multiple rates, so with fluctuating rates, a preferable solution lay in a policy which considered each country's situation on its merits.

The Board accepted this view and, on the understanding that the purpose of Peru's fluctuating rates was the establishment of a unitary exchange system on a more appropriate level, decided not to object to the use of fluctuating rates as a temporary measure. It asked the Peruvian Government to remain in close consultation with the Fund in order to fix a new par value when circumstances permitted. Meanwhile, the Board considered it urgent that Peru should adopt appropriate fiscal and credit policies in order to restrain inflationary forces and assure internal financial stability, and instructed the staff to submit a complete review of Peru's problems within six months.

The requirements of the Articles once again

During the foregoing discussion of the Peruvian proposal, the status under the Articles of a country with a fluctuating rate was again reviewed. This time some Directors considered it possible for the Fund to *approve* a fluctuating rate. They argued that Sections 6 and 8 of Article IV envisaged the eventuality that some members would have to abandon existing par values without immediately fixing new ones. Section 6 provided for sanctions against members who fixed par values over the Fund's objection, but not against members who abandoned par values without moving to new ones. Section 8 provided for interim payments to maintain the value of the Fund's assets by countries without par values.

The General Counsel did not agree. His view was that, although Article IV, Section 6, did give evidence that the Fund Agreement envisaged situations in which a member might operate temporarily without a par value, these situations would remain unauthorized and thus inconsistent with the Agreement. The member would be required to agree with the Fund on a par value within a reasonable period or the sanctions provided in Article XV, Section 2, might have to be invoked.

Also in November 1949, the Board considered the procedure for dealing with the exchange system of Thailand, which had a fluctuating rate as part of a multiple rate system. A staff mission was then in Thailand; and the Thai authorities, presumably prompted by its presence, had cabled the Fund requesting authorization for its then prevailing policies, and for a change in one of its rates. Mr. de Largentaye (France) questioned whether a member that had no par value but had a fluctuating rate needed to secure the Fund's approval for changes in that rate. He did not accept that the Fund was to be the judge of whether circumstances required a change in the fluctuating rate. If it had been intended by the drafters of the Articles that the Fund's approval was required, Article XIV would have so specified. Accordingly, he abstained from any decision on the change in the Thai rate. The decision taken was in fact quite limited. In view of the lack of information at the time on Thailand's exchange system, the Fund did not object to the continuance of Thailand's existing policies, pending the return of the staff mission and consideration of its report.

Continued deferment of a par value for Peru

At the end of 1950, the Board took up a first request from Peru to defer establishing a new par value. The country's two fluctuating rates had been close together and had remained stable, but in the Government's view a new parity could not yet be fixed. The Board discussed setting a time limit within which Peru must take action on a par value. Mr. Southard questioned the desirability of this. He thought that the Fund should not take an inflexible attitude toward such cases, particularly since most members seemed convinced of the advantages of stable exchange rates and the use of fluctuating rates did not seem especially contagious. The most important consideration was to find amicable ways of genuine consultation with members having such arrangements, so that the Fund could periodically review with them the feasibility of establishing a formal parity. Mr. Crick (United Kingdom) similarly questioned a proposed six-month deadline. Hence, the decision was merely to the effect that the Fund would from time to time review with Peru its exchange situation, with a view to determining whether action respecting a new parity would be feasible.

In 1960, by combining its two markets, Peru introduced a unitary fluctuating rate. This rate was still in existence on December 31, 1965, having remained, or been held, stable at 26.8 soles per U.S. dollar. In the intervening years, the Fund had permitted Peru to draw on the Fund's resources and to assume the obligations of Article VIII—that is, to be regarded as a country which has a convertible currency.[1]

FLUCTUATION OF A MAJOR CURRENCY

Why Canada turned to a fluctuating rate

A further example of the Fund's acceptance or toleration of a fluctuating rate in exceptional circumstances is afforded by Canada. At the end of September 1950, Mr. Rasminsky informed the Fund that Canada had decided for the time being to suspend the par value of the Canadian dollar and to allow its foreign exchange value to fluctuate in response to market forces. The main purpose was to restrain a heavy inflow of capital, especially of speculative capital and mainly from the United States. This inflow, which had become especially great in 1950, was adding to the money supply and tending to depress interest rates, thus augmenting inflation. The object of the Canadian proposal was thus in contrast to most other exchange rate adjustments, which are intended to rectify an unfavorable balance of trade and to check an outflow of capital. In the view of the Canadian Government, it was impossible to determine in advance with any reasonable assurance what new rate level would be appropriate.

When the Canadian proposal was received, the staff recommended that one or both of two alternatives to the contemplated fluctuating rate should be considered: (1) the absorption of additional reserves by open market operations; (2) the introduction of additional controls to restrain the inflow of capital. In the staff view, a basic principle of the Fund was that exchange rates should not be used as an instrument of domestic monetary policy. The rationale of the Canadian proposal was the hope that a small appreciation of the exchange rate would have a minor effect on the current payments position but would have an important restraining effect on the capital inflow; the absorption of the residual dollar inflow could be handled by open market operations.

The staff, however, believed that it was unlikely that small changes in the exchange rate would have important effects on capital flows. Continued fluctuation of the rate would encourage and even justify the expectations of speculators. The Canadian problem was a fundamental one: capital movements had recurrently led to pressures on the exchange rate. The Canadians should act on the

[1] See p. 76 above.

assumption that the world-wide instability leading to pressures on its exchange rate would continue and might even grow worse.

Mr. Rasminsky explained to the Directors that the suggestions made by the staff had already been submitted to the Finance Minister for consideration and had been referred to the Canadian Cabinet. The Canadian authorities, however, had rejected these alternatives as inadequate. As for open market operations, the Government could not take on additional debt of an unpredictable amount. And there were technical and political difficulties in controlling capital movements: direct controls would impose a tremendous, if not impossible, administrative burden; they might create hostility toward American capital; and, in addition, the Canadian Government was opposed to exchange controls of any kind.

The Fund's immediate response

The decision which the Executive Directors took at the time was that the Fund, unable under its Articles of Agreement to approve a fluctuating rate, recognized the exigencies of the situation and took note of the intention of the Canadian Government to remain in consultation with the Fund and to re-establish an effective par value as soon as circumstances warranted. This decision reflected the position of the majority of Directors that Canada should, in the light of its special circumstances, be permitted to try a fluctuating exchange rate for a short period. If, at the end of that period, the Canadian Government had to conclude that the alternatives were either to declare a new par value at parity with the U.S. dollar or to restore the old par value and impose effective capital controls, at least there was a better prospect of reaching general agreement that no other alternatives existed. At the same time, the language of the decision was not as forthright as in the Belgian case in 1949; it made no reference to "an appropriate step."

A few Directors again commented that possibly the Articles had been somewhat deficient: they made no provision for the case of a country which could not immediately propose a new par value. It was the view of Mr. Beyen (Netherlands), for example, that where a country could not propose a new parity, the Board could not ask the government to take the responsibility of doing so; the Fund had to give the member the benefit of the doubt in instances of this kind, since the responsibility for the action was the government's.

The Chairman, however, stressed that the position taken by Mr. Beyen called for very definite qualification because, if too widely interpreted, it might amount to a negation of one of the main principles of the Fund. He could not agree that the Fund was obliged to accept any proposal submitted by a member, on the theory that the responsibility for the proposed action and its effect were the government's alone. The Fund also had a responsibility to all its members, and each member in turn had a responsibility to other members.

Debates over the Canadian rate

For the next decade, until Canada returned to the par value system, there were intensive discussions among the staff and in the Board about the Canadian rate. The discussions in the Board began only a few months after the introduction of the fluctuating rate. In April 1951, in the course of a review by the Board of the Canadian economy, Mr. Rasminsky defended the fluctuating rate. He stressed that the excessive capital inflow had been reduced and import and exchange restrictions had been liberalized. Mr. de Largentaye insisted, however, that the Canadian Government could have used alternative arrangements to deal with the capital inflow. Mr. Melville (Australia) believed that the Canadian example, and the fact that the Fund had not objected, had made it difficult for the Fund to refuse other requests for fluctuating rates.

In another review in February 1952, several Directors inquired what economic factors, if any, prevented Canada from establishing a par value and whether the fluctuating rate had not had greater disadvantages than a fixed rate even for a member in Canada's circumstances. Mr. Rasminsky replied that the Canadian experience had been that a fixed rate of exchange produced wide swings in capital movements: foreign capital came in when the fixed rate looked too low and tended to leave when the rate looked high. The Canadian Government believed that, where foreign capital movements were large, a fluctuating rate controlled them better than a fixed rate. A fluctuating rate discouraged oscillations in capital flows because of its own fluctuations. Moreover, the size of the capital flows was not enhanced by further speculative capital movements in anticipation of a change in a pegged exchange rate.

Several Directors were concerned that the Canadian problem was not a temporary one, and that the fluctuating rate, also, was not temporary. Therefore, Mr. Stamp (United Kingdom) argued that the Fund should review the general policy at issue, with emphasis on the possible result if the practice of exchange rate fluctuation spread more widely.

Mr. Rasminsky argued, in rebuttal, that Canada's current circumstances were abnormal. Moreover, Canada's adaptation to these circumstances had contributed to its attainment of two of the three main Fund objectives—the elimination of exchange restrictions and the establishment of a convertible currency with no discrimination. Some Directors supported his position. They believed that the world's exchange situation had been abnormal for some time and in such circumstances fluctuating exchange rates were of great help to countries, particularly in permitting the removal of restrictions.

By 1956 the Fund had come to regard Canada's relative success with a fluctuating rate as reflecting the uniqueness of that country's circumstances. Canada had a trade deficit with a large capital inflow. There was confidence in the Canadian dollar because of the fiscal and credit policies being followed; Canada was relatively free of restrictions and had a convertible currency. Moreover, the institutional background led many to regard as natural a parity for the Canadian dollar somewhere near that of the U.S. dollar. Close interdependence between short-term capital movements and movements of the exchange rate had caused capital flows on the whole to be equilibrating rather than disturbing. Finally, the exchange rate fluctuated by only about 3–5 per cent, despite the absence of intervention by the authorities except to maintain an orderly exchange market.

For all these reasons, Canadian trade and normal capital transactions had not lost the important benefits commonly associated with exchange rate stability. The Canadian example was not a precedent, for the circumstances of other countries were quite different.

At the crossroads

Thus, from 1950 until about 1956, Canada's fluctuating rate had achieved the primary objectives for which it had been established. Massive inflows of long-term capital had continued and had provided net additional savings with which Canada had been able to finance a high rate of investment and growth. Yet the potentially disequilibrating effects of these long-term capital inflows on the balance of payments had been sufficiently offset by current account balances and compensating short-term capital movements. Exchange stability had been preserved. Short-term capital movements appeared to have responded much more to changes in the exchange rate than to relative interest rates in Canada and the United States.

After 1957, however, Canada began to encounter several difficulties. A very large current account deficit emerged and persisted; at 3–4 per cent of the gross national product, it was among the largest in the world. The rate of growth of the economy had slowed down measurably, and unemployment was high—7½ per cent by mid-1961. By then disenchantment with the way the Canadian rate had been operating since the late 1950's was discernible both among Canadian authorities and in the Fund.

The Canadian authorities attributed the country's economic reverses in large part to the now unduly appreciated level of the exchange rate; the inflow of capital had caused the rate to reach a point at which it acted as a stimulus to imports and as some deterrent to exports. In presenting his budget to Parliament on June 20, 1961, the Minister of Finance announced several new policies, including a switch in exchange rate policy. Whereas the Government previously had had a neutral attitude toward the level of the exchange rate, there was now to be some direct official intervention in the exchange market. Canada was thus to have a *managed* flexible rate.

Describing the Canadian policy to the Board in the middle of 1961, Mr. Rasminsky recognized that the shift in the exchange rate policy of the Canadian

Government might create some special problems for the Fund. Other Fund members might well have anxiety about the degree to which the Canadian Government would devalue the Canadian dollar, but would not have an opportunity to sanction, or object to, the rate that emerged. Mr. Rasminsky sought to reassure the other Fund members by stating that Canada did not intend to operate its rate policies so as to cause competitive depreciation. The intention of the Canadian Government was not to determine the level of the exchange rate in the market but rather to reduce the inflow of capital and the size of the current account deficit.

The assessment of the Canadian exchange rate situation which the Fund staff made differed from that of the Canadian authorities. The staff agreed with the authorities that the period prior to 1956–57 had shown the usefulness of the fluctuating rate, and that the post-1956 experiences had been more disturbing than equilibrating. But the explanation offered by the staff for what had gone wrong since 1956–57 differed from that of the authorities.

In the staff view, the primary cause of the unsatisfactory results of the fluctuating exchange rate after the first few years was not any change in the mechanism of the Canadian balance of payments, but the effect of governmental policy on that mechanism. Governmental policy had resulted in the emergence of a wide differential between Canadian interest rates and those of the United States. A spread in which interest rates in Canada were higher than those in the United States had attracted liquid funds into Canada. The inflow of these funds kept the exchange rate appreciated during a period when basic trade and long-term capital flows that were normally motivated would have tended to push it downward.

The staff pointed out that after 1956–57 the size and composition of the long-term capital inflow into Canada had changed markedly. While direct investment inflows had continued on a more or less steady and generally upward course, they had been supplemented by huge and erratic movements of portfolio capital. Various types of capital flowed in unevenly at different times. Many of these flows seemed to have been highly sensitive to divergences between monetary and credit conditions in Canada and the United States. By the late 1950's capital movements which were induced primarily, or solely, by interest differentials were much larger than they had been in the early 1950's. Another factor which had made the fluctuating rate increasingly difficult to handle by 1960 had been the mounting uncertainties as to the prospects for the Canadian economy and as to the Government's economic policies. The staff concluded, therefore, that "Canada should re-establish an effective par value as soon as circumstances permit."

The foregoing report by the staff was before the Board when, in February 1962, it undertook the first consultation with Canada under Article VIII. At this consultation, the uneasiness of most of the Executive Directors concerning the continuance of the fluctuating rate was readily manifest. The Board did not press for an immediate re-establishment of a par value. But many Directors questioned whether Canada still had a plausible case for continued noncompliance with the Fund Agreement. What economic situation would enable a par value to be restored? Were not Canada's special circumstances, in effect, permanent? Did not Canada's large reserves seem sufficiently ample to enable the authorities to defend a fixed rate? How should the Fund assess the declared intention of the Canadian authorities to bring the rate down to a lower level? How far would the rate actually be depreciated? How could depreciation be achieved without endangering exchange rate stability, if large fiscal deficits and low interest rates were permitted?

The Directors observed that Canada presented a rare example of an exchange depreciation being undertaken largely to stimulate the growth of national income rather than to influence the current balance of payments. They also expressed considerable concern over the possibility that Canada's internal policies were too expansionary.

From Canada's experiences the Directors drew conclusions regarding fluctuating rates in general. Had not Canada's experience demonstrated that it was difficult and potentially harmful for a country to conduct a monetary policy isolated from that of other countries? Even a flexible exchange rate had not given Canada freedom in its internal monetary policy. Had not another danger of flexible rates also been revealed—that feeling safe under the shelter of a flexible rate and deprived of the symptoms of movements in reserves, the authorities tended to disregard the external repercussions of their domestic policies? It was significantly noted that Mexico, like Canada a neighbor of the United States and a recipient of heavy inflows of U.S. capital, had also found a fluctuating rate unworkable.

Several Directors, therefore, supported the conclusions of the staff that Canada should re-establish an effective par value as soon as circumstances permitted. Some of the Directors were fairly specific that the new par value should be introduced as soon as the Canadian Government's policies were clearly established and the authorities had reached a conclusion as to the appropriate level for the new parity.

On May 2, 1962, in the midst of exchange difficulties, Canada gave up its fluctuating rate and proposed a new par value to the Fund. The authorities stated that the new par value was necessary to correct a fundamental disequilibrium. Moreover, they expressed their awareness, deriving from the discussions at the meetings of the Board in July 1961 and February 1962, of the widespread international concern at Canada's deviation from the established exchange system.

Having decided to re-establish a par value, the Canadian authorities faced the question of selecting a rate. Mr. Rasminsky explained that a par value at the current rate of 95 U.S. cents per Canadian dollar was thought to be too high to eliminate uncertainty in the market; the Government had already lost substantial reserves in defending that rate. Alternatively, a rate of 90 U.S. cents per Canadian dollar was rejected as being lower than the Canadian economy required. Furthermore, Canada could not count on international acceptance of such a depreciated rate. Consequently, the authorities proposed a new rate of 92.5 U.S. cents per Canadian dollar.

The Directors, agreeing with the new par value, welcomed the return of Canada to the par value system.

A REMAINING HURDLE

With the acceptance by the Board during the 1950's of Canada's fluctuating rate, the formal objections of the Fund to fluctuating rates had quietly come to an end. But yet another hurdle had had, in the meantime, to be surmounted. This concerned the valuation of the Fund's holdings of currencies of countries where fluctuating rates prevailed. Article IV, Section 8, of the Agreement requires countries to maintain the gold value of the Fund's assets. Hence, in the event of a depreciation in its par value, a member has to pay additional local currency to the Fund. Was there not a need for such payments to be made by countries without par values and with fluctuating rates? If payments were required, what rate of exchange should be applied? The staff pointed out that a similar difficulty covering the exchange rate to use for computations would arise if another member wished to draw from the Fund the currency of the country with the fluctuating rate.

These questions became a matter for consideration and decision by the Board in 1954. At that time members with fluctuating rates included not only Canada but also Lebanon, Peru, Syria, and Thailand. Even if only for the purposes of the auditors, some rules were essential. In addition, it was imperative to preserve the gold value of the Fund's assets. And it was desirable to ensure that the Fund was not used in lieu of the outside market for short-term arbitrage gains.

With little debate the Board decided that for currencies with a single fluctuating rate, computations were to be based on the mid-point between the highest and lowest exchange rates for the U.S. dollar for cable transfers for spot delivery in the main financial center of the country of the fluctuating currency on specified days. If a mid-point could not be determined in the main financial center of the country of the fluctuating currency, rates quoted in New York could be substituted.[2]

[2] E.B. Decision No. 321-(54/32), June 15, 1954; below, Vol. III, p. 222.

The Directors had, however, some difficulty in deciding upon the scope of application of these rules. How should they be applied to currencies with multiple exchange rates, some of which might fluctuate? The Directors from Latin America stressed that it was vital that the Fund should not embarrass a country which was struggling to maintain a par value. Such embarrassment might result from the Fund's computing an effective rate other than the par value for use in Fund transactions in the currency of that country. Hence, a preamble to the decision on computed exchange rates explicitly specified that multiple rate systems were not to be covered by these special rules, and that the Fund would not determine computed rates except where there was a practical interest for the Fund or its members to do so.

These rules have the practical purpose of facilitating the operations of the Fund. They make it possible for the Fund to engage in transactions in the currencies of members with fluctuating exchange rates on an equitable basis and to make the computations required by the Fund Agreement—that is, to facilitate the periodic revaluations of the Fund's holdings of fluctuating currencies, as well as their valuation for the purpose of actual transactions. Other members of the Fund are thus not precluded by the fluctuations in the rate for a member's currency from purchasing it from the Fund, nor is a member whose currency fluctuates necessarily deprived of its right to purchase the currencies of other members. These rules become operative in any given case only after the Fund has decided to apply Article IV, Section 8, to its holdings of a fluctuating currency.

In July 1954, this general decision on computed rates for fluctuating currencies was made applicable to Canada and Peru. Canada, of course, had had a single fluctuating rate since September 20, 1950, and this rate was used as the basis for the rate computed for Fund transactions.

Peru had had two exchange markets since November 1949; the par value of 6.50 soles per U.S. dollar no longer applied to any transactions. The exchange rates in the two markets fluctuated freely and there was only a small spread between the rates. The Fund's holdings of Peruvian soles had been adjusted under Article IV, Section 8 (*b*) (ii), in April 1951. This adjustment had been made on the basis of a rate of 15 soles per U.S. dollar, a rate which had been proposed by Peru and accepted by the Board "subject to further adjustment in the event of a significant change in the foreign exchange value of the currency or when a new par value for the sol is established in agreement with the Fund." The rate in the certificate market—more important than the free market as measured by the volume of transactions—had been adopted as the rate for purposes of a stand-by arrangement with the Fund approved in February 1954. Paragraph 2 of the stand-by arrangement had specified that "currencies drawn from the Fund shall be used only for the support of the certificate market rate."

Paragraph 19 of the arrangement had specified that the rate of exchange to be used for drawings and repurchases would be the rate determined from time to time under Article IV, Section 8. In computing this rate for the currency of Peru, the mid-point stated in the general rules was to be that of the rate in the certificate market.

Computations under the general decision have been made only for countries where no transactions any longer take place at the par values. At the end of 1965, for example, computed effective rates applied only to Argentina, Bolivia, Brazil, Chile, Colombia, Paraguay, and Peru.[3]

The question of a country's formal status in the Fund if it had no par value, while quiescent, was not entirely dead in 1954. Discussing the application to Canada of the decision on computed rates, Mr. Saad (Egypt) said that he had serious difficulty with the Fund's adopting rules which in a sense helped to perpetuate a member's technical violation of the Articles. However, the decision passed without objection by other Directors.

Subsequently, two technical amendments were made to the decision on the determination of rates for transactions in currencies of countries with fluctuating rates.[4] The first was introduced in August 1961 when the Fund decided that it should sell gold to replenish its holdings of certain currencies. Because the currencies of some countries with fluctuating rates were involved—for example, the Canadian dollar—the earlier decision on transactions and computations involving fluctuating currencies was amended to cover such sales of gold by the Fund. The second amendment was made in December 1961 when the Board took a decision on the General Arrangements to Borrow. At that time, the decision on computed rates for fluctuating currencies was amended to cover such borrowing and the repayment of borrowing in fluctuating currencies.

FLUCTUATING RATES AND EXCHANGE REFORM

The gradually evolving policies in connection with the fluctuating rates of Mexico, Peru, and Canada illustrate one major direction in which the Fund's attitude toward fixed rates was not immutable. In these instances, the Fund, in effect, tolerated fluctuating rates; later, it went somewhat further.

Beginning in 1956, the Fund has supported programs which, in conjunction with exchange reforms and stabilization plans, have included a fluctuating rate. To some extent Peru's fluctuating rate, described above, had been introduced as part of an exchange reform. But even before reform, Peru's exchange system had been fairly simple, inflation had not been massive, and the devaluation involved was modest. In the late 1950's, however, the technique of using a

[3] *Schedule of Par Values*, February 15, 1966.

[4] E.B. Decision No. 1245-(61/45), August 4, 1961, and E.B. Decision No. 1283-(61/56), December 20, 1961; below, Vol. III, p. 224.

fluctuating exchange rate to effect reform of a complex exchange system became widely used.

The circumstances

Many of the less developed countries in which there has been prolonged inflation have found it necessary to change their exchange rates frequently. Several of these countries, for various reasons, have instituted fluctuating rates. Countries undertaking stabilization of their economies are frequently uncertain about the effects of the internal measures being adopted. Future movements in prices and wages have been difficult to estimate. In these circumstances, countries have been unable to determine in advance an appropriate level for the exchange rate. Where a combination of restrictions and multiple rates exist, it is difficult to ascertain even the average effective exchange rate being applied. Determination of an equilibrium rate is virtually impossible. In still other instances, a new par value cannot be determined until after a new tariff system has been established. For these reasons, as exchange reforms have been undertaken, several countries have instituted single fluctuating rates.

The changing Fund policy

Bolivia was among the first, in 1956, to effect exchange reform via a fluctuating rate. Its example was soon followed by Chile, Paraguay, and Argentina. At first, the Fund merely agreed to these fluctuating rates. But as more instances occurred, it was clear that the Fund had, in effect, adopted a general policy of permitting fluctuating exchange rates as a temporary instrument of exchange depreciation and liberalization of restrictions.

This policy was made manifest in the Board's reaction to a proposal put forward by the Philippines in 1962. At this time the Philippines, which had had a fixed exchange rate, introduced a fluctuating one. When presenting to the Board the Philippine proposal for exchange reform and request for a drawing from the Fund, Mr. Saad (who had been elected by the Philippines) emphasized that the proposed fluctuating rate was clearly in line with the Fund's policy. The Government of the Philippines was resorting to a fluctuating rate just as had other countries as a means of eliminating restrictions on payments and of finding a realistic level for the exchange rate. The proposed change in the exchange rate represented the culmination of a program, which the Philippines had been following for the previous two years, of steadily simplifying its exchange system and of reducing reliance on quantitative restrictions. The Philippine authorities regarded the fluctuating rate as temporary and looked forward to the establishment of an appropriate new par value.

The Directors agreed that the proposed exchange reform, except for a few transitional features, followed a plan with which they were already familiar.

They would have preferred that the Philippine authorities move to a single fixed rate system, but they recognized the circumstances which necessitated delay in introducing a new par value. These circumstances included the persistence of a great deal of inflationary pressure, a change in government administration, and a need to revise the tariff. The Managing Director, Mr. Jacobsson, while reasserting that a floating rate was not, in general, desirable, emphasized the difficulty which a country with slender reserves experienced in adopting a fixed rate without imposing exchange restrictions. Were restrictions to be instituted, a black market would inevitably emerge.

Some Directors questioned how capital movements, both in and out of the Philippines, would react to a fluctuating exchange rate. The effect of the new rate on capital was important, especially because capital outflows had been partly responsible for the deterioration in the balance of payments. These Directors hoped that the proposed exchange reform would help to curb capital flight and even to stimulate capital repatriation. They favored a fixed rate, which in their view was more likely to make capital movements normal. Therefore, they placed a great deal of emphasis on the intention of the Philippine authorities to use the fluctuating rate only temporarily.

Experiences with temporary fluctuating rates have, in general, proved quite successful. Several such rates were eventually stabilized and furnished the basis for new par values. Indeed, by 1962–63 the Fund had even begun to initiate suggestions for fluctuating rates as temporary ways of altering exchange rates and of achieving exchange reforms. Several countries were advised—even urged—to take this road to depreciation and exchange reform. Where countries introduced greater rate flexibility, the Fund welcomed the action.

Appropriate conditions for a fluctuating rate

The questions that have come up as the Fund has considered individual fluctuating rates reveal the difficulties of deciding the circumstances in which fluctuating rates are appropriate. Many of these questions have concerned reserves and reserve policy. What is the level of reserves required before an exchange rate can be maintained? When should the central bank enter the market in order to accumulate reserves? Do not central bank purchases in the market to repay short-term liabilities differ from purchases for reserves? (The former may be treated as a genuine market force, while the demand for foreign exchange for reserve accumulation represents a policy decision of the authorities rather than a market force.) May it not be best to accumulate reserves by taking advantage of special occurrences in the exchange market rather than by exerting a continuous downward pressure on the rate?

Another group of questions has concerned the reactions of capital movements to a fluctuating exchange rate. For example, is a fluctuating rate appropriate where underinvoicing and smuggling as well as an excessive outflow of capital have been a problem? The use of fluctuating rates in circumstances of continuous inflation has given rise to still other questions. For, if internal prices are not stabilized, flexible rates are necessary to prevent overvaluation. Yet under conditions of unstable internal prices, the rate depreciates regularly; this depreciation in turn contributes to continued instability of internal prices, and also possibly induces speculative capital movements.

One situation in which a unitary fluctuating exchange rate has been found unworkable is that in which a particular exchange rate is required for a given commodity. When Colombia, for example, attempted to introduce a fluctuating rate in 1957–58, it was found to be inappropriate because of the need for a special exchange rate for coffee exports.

Pegging of fluctuating rates

The Fund's view has been that, once a fluctuating rate is introduced, the authorities should let the rate change freely in response to market forces, intervening only to maintain orderly market conditions. The Board has, therefore, often warned against pegging of fluctuating rates. Similarly, the Board has suggested that, where two markets exist, sales of exchange by the central bank in the free market should not result in a spread of fixed size between the official rate of exchange and that in the free market. The fear of the Board has been that intervention by the central bank could lead to an undue loss of foreign exchange reserves as well as establish an inappropriate exchange rate. Where the member has drawn on the Fund, the Board has been concerned lest the Fund's resources be used to peg a potentially unrealistic exchange rate.

In some countries where a flexible exchange rate policy is considered essential, certain "balance of payments tests" have been developed and have become part of stabilization programs.[5] The object of these tests is to ensure that an exchange rate will be maintained which conforms to the basic trends in the economy. A level at which the country's foreign exchange reserves are to be maintained during a stated period is prescribed. The country undertakes that if there is a danger that reserves will fall below this level, it will take appropriate action, for example, by allowing the exchange rate to fall. Even so, since most countries have been reluctant to see their exchange rates depreciate excessively, the Fund has frequently had to call upon countries with flexible rates not to stabilize prematurely.

FIXED RATES AS AN OBJECTIVE

Nonetheless, the Fund's ultimate objective in cases of exchange reform has been to create the conditions for the restoration of a stable and unified exchange

[5] See below, pp. 506–10.

rate. The fluctuating rate has been regarded as a temporary means to an end. The Fund has also continued to regard a general system of fixed rates and institutionally agreed par values as decidedly superior to a system of fluctuating rates.

As early as 1951 the Fund gave several reasons for its belief that a system of fluctuating rates would not be a satisfactory alternative to the par value system. To those who advocated allowing rates to find their "natural" level it replied that there was no such thing as a natural level for the rate of exchange of a currency. The "natural" rate differed in each case, as it was dependent upon the economic, financial, and monetary policies followed by the country concerned, and by other countries with whom it had important economic relationships. In addition, whether a given exchange rate was at the correct level could be determined only after there had been time to observe the course of the balance of payments in response to that rate.

Furthermore, implicit in the arguments for fluctuating rates was the assumption that some major currency would remain stable as a point of reference. The limited number of countries that had used flexible rates had done so within the framework of fixed parities for the currencies of well-nigh all the industrial countries. Chaos would result if a substantial number of rates were allowed to fluctuate.[6]

By 1958 the Fund's views were based on its widening experiences. As in the 1930's, so in the 1950's, fluctuating rates had been found to be inappropriate where outflows of capital were excessive or underinvoicing and smuggling were troublesome. Fluctuating rates often induced additional capital inflows which were prompted by speculation on exchange rate movements. It had also become clear that countries preferred to make adjustments in their exchange rates in some manner other than through fluctuating rates, so as to minimize speculation. Most countries seemed to recognize, in practice, the importance of orderly exchange arrangements and exchange stability. Even in countries where the authorities were not prepared formally to stabilize the exchange rate on the basis of a realistic parity, *de facto* stable rates, the Board observed, were often maintained for long periods of time.[7]

In its Annual Report for 1962 further examples were cited of the Fund's postwar experience with fluctuating exchange rates.[8] The conclusion was that a short period of fluctuation might be a means of reaching a rate which could subsequently be maintained. But in other circumstances fluctuating rates gave rise to difficulties. In exceptional circumstances, such as the large capital inflows into Canada in the early 1950's and into Peru for brief periods, a fluctuating rate might have an upward tendency. The more general experience, however, was

[6] *Annual Report, 1951*, pp. 36–41.

[7] *Annual Report, 1958*, p. 20.

[8] *Annual Report, 1962*, pp. 62–67.

that if a country did not clearly and quickly adopt a monetary policy aimed at stability, the movements of its fluctuating rate were likely to be oscillations not around a stable value but around a declining trend.

If an exchange rate fluctuated widely, it might be expected to depreciate over time. Any circumstance leading to a temporary depreciation of the rate raised the domestic currency cost of imports and directly and indirectly led to price increases. These increases encouraged demands for higher money wages, at least some of which were met. Hence, depreciations were likely to induce increases in domestic costs. On the other hand, institutional rigidities limited reductions in money wages, so that exchange appreciations were unlikely to lead to any significant lowering of domestic costs. Therefore, a fluctuating rate might be expected to encourage a rising trend in domestic costs, which in turn put downward pressure on the rate.

Pegging of a fluctuating rate had still other disadvantages. A fixed rate subject to frequent changes, or a temporarily pegged fluctuating rate, was likely to encourage destabilizing speculation which would create even more serious problems than those which arose under a system of freely fluctuating rates.

It was concluded therefore that it was an illusion to expect a fluctuating rate to ease the problems facing monetary authorities. On the contrary, by eliminating the rallying point of the defense of a fixed par value, a fluctuating rate made it necessary for the authorities to exercise greater caution in determining monetary policy.

In 1964 the Deputy Managing Director summarized the Fund's position as follows:

> Some economists argue the case for freely fluctuating rates of exchange as an instrument for balance of payments adjustment. But financial officials in most countries today—even in those developing countries which temporarily have fluctuating rates—have been convinced by experience that greater flexibility than that sanctioned by the Fund's Articles of Agreement would be undesirable and impractical. Fluctuating rates create great uncertainty for traders and investors and set up stresses in the financial and economic relationships within a country and in its international position. Moreover, far from being simple, the problems of managing a flexible rate are no less complex than those which arise in maintaining an effective par value, and in addition present their own mixture of financial, economic, and political difficulties. Indeed, countries which have endeavored to conduct their affairs on the basis of a fluctuating rate have found it extremely hard to let the exchange rate perform its intended functions. It also is generally true that exchange rate policy under a system of flexible rates tends to become much more a matter of unilateral action, which would make the whole process of international collaboration in financial matters far more difficult.[9]

[9] Speech by Frank A. Southard, Jr., Dallas, Texas, March 27, 1964, in *International Financial News Survey*, April 3, 1964, pp. 115–16.

Thus, while the Fund's policy as regards fluctuating rates became more flexible, the Fund continued, strongly, to favor a system of fixed exchange rates. Nonetheless, events on the horizon forewarned that the debates concerning the merits of fluctuating rates would, shortly, be intensified. Among the suggestions being made in the mid-1960's for ways to improve the system of par values was that fluctuating rates, at least for major currencies, should be substituted for par values. When, in 1964 and 1965, one large industrial country after another began to be plagued by balance of payments stresses for which there seemed no adequate solutions, the advocates of fluctuating rates were able to muster additional adherents.

Changes in fixed rates seemed ruled out because the authorities of the major countries concerned found it difficult politically to alter the exchange values of their currencies. Further, in the absence of adequate world gold stocks, most countries had come to hold sizable amounts of the currencies of the major countries as foreign exchange reserves. Therefore, among other effects of exchange rate alteration, the authorities in charge of the currencies used as reserves were concerned with the implications of changes in exchange rates for the reserve holdings of all trading nations. Tighter monetary and fiscal policies had already been introduced in most of the large industrial nations; the imposition of still more stringent internal measures to alleviate or reverse external deficits was considered contrary to the domestic objectives to which these countries were committed. Stricter credit or tax measures might jeopardize employment; reduced public expenditure might mean that urgent domestic programs would have to be postponed or foregone. Some countries had reintroduced, or enacted for the first time, controls on capital movements, but they shunned controls on current transactions.

All these difficulties with alternative solutions strengthened the arguments for enhanced flexibility of exchange rates. Nevertheless, the monetary authorities of all the large industrial nations, and especially the central bankers, as well as the officials of the Fund, continued to view as untenable any general system of fluctuating rates.

CHAPTER

8

Gold Transactions at Premium Prices

Mary H. Gumbart

THE OBLIGATIONS OF FUND MEMBERS in connection with the price of gold are set out in Article IV, Section 2, of the Fund Agreement, which reads as follows:

> *Gold purchases based on par values.*—The Fund shall prescribe a margin above and below par value for transactions in gold by members, and no member shall buy gold at a price above par value plus the prescribed margin, or sell gold at a price below par value minus the prescribed margin.

Because of this link between par values and the price of gold, the Fund's policy on gold transactions at premium prices has sought to prevent international transactions in gold being effected at prices substantially above par values. (Transactions below par values have never been at issue.) The purposes of the policy were twofold: first to prevent such sales from undermining the stability of members' exchange rates, and second to minimize the loss to monetary reserves resulting from private hoarding, which was the main source of demand in the premium market. The achievement of both aims required the prevention of premium gold sales.

The dilemma facing the Fund was as follows: If the premium market was kept supplied in order to lower or eliminate the premium, this would result in a larger portion of newly mined gold going into private hoards and, possibly, in the diversion of official gold holdings to hoards. As long as newly mined gold was sold at a premium above the margin set by the Fund, the monetary authorities of Fund members would be precluded, under Article IV, Section 2, from purchasing the new gold. This would reduce the amount of international liquidity (i.e., gold) available to monetary authorities. If, on the other hand, the supply to the premium gold market was not maintained, the premium would continue and might increase, thus possibly leading to instability of exchange rates. The reason that exchange rates might be undermined was that they are denominated in terms of gold, so that international transactions in gold at other than official rates must affect the established rates; premium transactions at least establish another rate for the currency in which the transactions take place.

FIRST STATEMENT ON GOLD TRANSACTIONS AT PREMIUM PRICES

History of first statement

The first time that the issue of premium gold sales was raised in the Board was in August 1946, when Peru inquired whether its Central Reserve Bank might, after the par value for the sol had been fixed, sell gold coins at a premium price in any market for the account of private concerns. The divergences of opinion on the economic, legal, and political aspects of the problem that characterized all considerations of it by Executive Directors emerged during a discussion of a draft reply to Peru. The minutes of the Board meeting include the following:

> It was generally agreed that [Peru's] project . . . was not specifically prohibited by any provision of the Fund Agreement. One view was that the Fund's reply should not appear to condone the practices, which resulted in smuggling of gold against the laws of various governments. . . . such a position would give the impression that the Fund approved dual prices for gold, whereas such dual prices were harmful to exchange stability.
>
> The other view was that in its infancy, the Fund should avoid any impression of rendering opinions on matters beyond its actual authority, and for the sake of its relations with members should not attempt to enforce a broad interpretation, where such might properly be disputed.
>
> It was agreed that the Ad Hoc Drafting Committee should prepare a final draft letter indicating that while the proposed project could not be said to contravene the Fund Agreement, the Fund did not wish this opinion to be construed as encouragement of the proposed action.

Such a letter was produced and sent to Peru on September 11, 1946.

Six months later Colombia asked (*a*) whether the Fund Agreement would permit mine owners to sell their output at a premium price (i) on the free international market, or (ii) on the local market for industrial purposes, and (*b*) in either event, whether the Colombian central bank could intervene in the prospective markets for purposes of control and management.

At the first discussion of this request, Mr. Gómez (Mexico), who had been elected by Colombia, urged that the Fund should reply to Colombia, as it had to Peru, that, with appropriate qualifications, the proposed actions would not in themselves "be inconsistent with any particular provision of the Fund Agreement." There was considerable opposition to Mr. Gómez' proposal, mainly on the ground that the Fund Agreement enabled the Fund to intervene against a member's permitting external gold sales at premium prices, if official rates of exchange were likely to be undermined. Any action that siphoned newly mined gold into private hoards and away from monetary systems where it could support exchange rates and finance world trade should be opposed. On the other hand, it was argued that the effects of premium gold sales might not, in fact, be as bad as assumed.

The discussion also touched on the problem of nonmember countries, which the Fund could not control, and on the question whether responsibility for stopping the trade should not rest with the buying nations rather than the selling. The discussion ended when, at the Managing Director's suggestion, the Directors agreed to set up a Committee on External Sales of Gold to study the question. The committee members were Messrs. Luthringer (United States), Chairman, Bolton (United Kingdom), Bruins (Netherlands), de Selliers (Belgium), Gómez, and Rasminsky (Canada).

The committee's first report to the Board, on May 19, 1947, was agreed by all members of the committee except Mr. Gómez, whose views were presented to the Board in writing by his Alternate, Mr. Martínez-Ostos (Mexico). The report made the following main points:

1. *General policy.* In the interest of world monetary stabilization and in view of the purposes of the Fund, the Fund should take a strong position deprecating external sales of gold at premium prices. It was recognized, as pointed out by Mr. Gómez, that the immediate value of the Fund's taking such a position might be limited owing to the action of nonmember countries. But the moral and psychological effect of the Fund's action would be internationally favorable. The committee felt that exchange stability would be undermined by continued external sales of gold at premium prices and there would be increased pressure by producers on governments of large gold producing countries to permit their production to be sold at premium prices.

2. *Authority of the Fund.* The Fund has authority under Article I and Article IV, Sections 2 and 4 (*a*), of the Fund Agreement to take action to prevent members from engaging in gold sale practices which would undermine exchange stability.

3. *Recommended action.* The committee was of the opinion that a general statement of policy should be prepared and circulated to the members recommending the adoption of effective measures by member countries to prevent exports and imports of gold at premium prices. It was felt that a legalistic statement of interpretation of the Articles of Agreement would not be desirable.

On the questions raised by Colombia, the report suggested that no reply should be sent until the general policy had been settled, and that Colombia should then be told that further consideration would be given to the question of intervention by the central bank if Colombian producers were allowed to sell their gold at a premium in the domestic market.

The committee's report was twice discussed in the Board. At the first of these meetings, some Directors urged that the question of whether the Fund had the legal authority to prevent members and/or their nationals from engaging in external gold transactions at premium prices be referred to the Committee on Interpretation, and the discussion was confined to questions of substance. These questions included the following: whether continued sales of gold at premium prices would in fact undermine exchange rate stability; the status under the Fund Agreement, and the effects of, official versus private transactions in gold; the volume and character of the premium gold trade; and whether continued premium gold sales by some members would lead to irresistible pressures on other members to permit such sales.

The only two points on which Directors were generally agreed were, first, that official agencies of members would not be permitted, under the Fund Agreement, to engage in international gold transactions outside official rates; and, second, that (as the committee proposed) the Fund should not object to internal sales of gold above parity, provided that such sales did not in effect establish new rates of exchange or undermine existing rates of other members. Opposing views were expressed in the Board on the question whether members' obligations under the Fund Agreement extended to private transactions in gold, as well as on the other points discussed.

However, at the next meeting of the Board it was decided to waive the problem of a formal interpretation of the Articles and instead to approve point 2 (Authority of the Fund) in the committee's report.

Mr. Martínez-Ostos opposed the committee's recommendations. He said that while he did not deny the obligation of members regarding exchange stability, this obligation rested on buyers of gold as much as on sellers, and premium sales were permitted under Article IV, Section 2. Perhaps as a result of these representations, the decision of the Board departed from the committee's proposals by making no reference to Article IV, Section 2, and by altering the phrase "gold sale practices" to "gold transactions."

The Board also approved points 1 and 3 of the committee's report, and agreed that a statement expressing the policy of the Fund and recommending action to members should be prepared by the staff and transmitted to members after approval by the Board. It was also decided that, before the statement was transmitted, the Board should prescribe the margins for members' gold transactions as required in Article IV, Section 2.

The decision setting the margin for members' gold transactions at ¼ of 1 per cent, plus certain handling charges, was adopted on June 10, 1947. Colombia then requested that its inquiry be withdrawn, and the letter in which the inquiry had been made be returned. The Board noted the request for withdrawal, agreed to return the original letter to Colombia, and decided that the other records of the Fund on the matter would not be altered.

The Board then approved the drafts of the proposed general statement on premium gold transactions and the letter of transmittal to members. The discussion of the latter document was chiefly concerned with the question whether the Fund itself would make the statement public. The committee had previously suggested that the Fund should not do so, although the letter of transmittal would make it clear that members could make such use of the statement as they considered desirable. This position was the one finally adopted, being apparently influenced by Mr. Martínez-Ostos' statement that Colombia's withdrawal of its inquiry might have depended to a certain degree on his personal assurance that no public statement would be made by the Fund, and that if a Fund statement were to be made, he would want to make a general reservation on the whole problem.

Text of first statement

The text of the statement, which was communicated by the Fund to all members in a letter of June 18, 1947 from the Managing Director, is set out in Volume III of this history.[1] The operative paragraphs were the following:

> A primary purpose of the Fund is world exchange stability and it is the considered opinion of the Fund that exchange stability may be undermined by continued and increasing external purchases and sales of gold at prices which directly or indirectly produce exchange transactions at depreciated rates. From information at its disposal, the Fund believes that unless discouraged this practice is likely to become extensive, which would fundamentally disturb the exchange relationships among the members of the Fund. Moreover, these transactions involve a loss to monetary reserves, since much of the gold goes into private hoards rather than into central holdings. For these reasons, the Fund strongly deprecates international transactions in gold at premium prices and recommends that all of its members take effective action to prevent such transactions in gold with other countries or with the nationals of other countries. . . .
>
> The Fund has not overlooked the problems arising in connection with domestic transactions in gold at prices above parity. The conclusion was reached that the Fund would not object at this time to such transactions unless they have the effect of establishing new rates of exchange or undermining existing rates of other members, or unless they result in a significant weakening of the international financial position of a member which might affect its utilization of the Fund's resources.
>
> The Fund has requested its members to take action as promptly as possible to put into effect the recommendations contained in this statement.

That the statement is in the form of an expression of the Fund's views and recommendations rather than a formal interpretation of the Articles of Agreement, reflects the fact that there were conflicting points of view among Directors as to the legal basis for the Fund's authority. It should be noted also that, while

[1] Below, Vol. III, p. 310.

external and internal transactions are distinguished, the statement makes no distinction between monetary gold and nonmonetary (processed) gold. This point was to be of importance later in connection with South Africa's proposals for sales of semiprocessed gold at premium prices. However, Mr. Martínez-Ostos later commented that although he and Mr. Gómez had pointed out the problems that would arise from the exclusion of processed gold from the Fund's statement of June 1947, the Fund had exempted such transactions in August of the same year. Other Executive Directors then recalled that processed gold had been excluded from the Fund's statement because the Fund did not wish to curtail normal commercial enterprises. However, where it appeared that an increase in commercial activity was in reality a negation of the Fund's policy statement, the Fund would have to be concerned.

The Mexican inquiry

Shortly after the statement was issued, Mexico asked (*a*) for the legal grounds of the Fund's statement, and (*b*) whether members were required to suspend gold sales to nonmember countries.

When this inquiry was considered on July 28, 1947, the Executive Board approved a reply to (*a*) in the following terms:

> The legal basis of the statement in connection with Transactions in Gold at Premium Prices is to be found in Article I (iii), and Article IV, Section 4 (*a*). Article I makes it the duty of the Fund to promote exchange stability, maintain orderly exchange arrangements, and avoid competitive exchange depreciation. Where the Fund finds a threat to exchange stability or orderly exchange arrangements, Article IV, Section 4 (*a*), gives the Fund the right to call for collaboration by members to eliminate the threat.

As regards (*b*), the Legal Department suggested that the reply might explain that "the reference to 'other countries' in [the Fund's statement of June 18, 1947] was intended and should be interpreted to embrace both members and nonmembers."

However, on this second issue the Board disagreed. In the discussion, Executive Directors raised two further problems. The first was whether the Fund's statement covered transactions with nonmembers clearly and satisfactorily: nonmembers necessarily had no par value, which created a possible ambiguity as to the meaning of premium prices. The special case of a nonmember with multiple rates of exchange was also considered. The second problem was whether the June 18 statement applied or should apply to sales of gold for manufacture into jewelry, or sales of gold in the form of jewelry. It was agreed to defer an answer to Mexico until these matters had been further studied.

At a further Board meeting on August 26, Mr. Gómez observed that there was no indication that the gold which Mexico sold returned to international channels where it might affect par values. For that reason he could not support the proposed draft reply on this point.

Other Directors, however, pointed out that stable exchange rates could be weakened by premium sales even if the gold did not move out of the buying country. If Mexico sold gold at a premium for a particular currency, it would be getting that currency at a more favorable rate than other Fund members. Cross rates for member currencies might result which would be significantly different from the pattern of rates established by the Fund. Thus there might be a tendency to undermine the stability of members' currencies. The Fund's concern would certainly extend to such cases. Mr. Gómez accepted that the argument about disorderly cross rates was valid; it was therefore embodied in a reply sent to Mexico covering both points in the member's letter.

Results of first statement

Parallel with the consideration of the letter from Mexico just discussed, the Board had under consideration a further inquiry from Peru. This described the adverse effect that the Fund's statement would have on the prospects of gold mines in Peru, and asked advice on ways of protecting the industry. The Board decided to request the Committee on External Sales of Gold to study the question of what measures, acceptable to the Fund, could be taken to encourage domestic gold production. In preparation for the work of the committee, the staff was asked for "studies of the developments and results which had occurred since the Fund's policy on premium transactions had been announced, the movements of gold in recent years, and the nature of the 'underground' gold traffic." A further general statement about the price of gold which emerged from the committee's work dealt primarily with subsidies to gold producers, and is therefore reported in the next chapter. However, it is appropriate here to set out the result of the staff's studies, as summarized in a memorandum circulated in January 1948.

The staff found that the Fund's requests had been anticipated in India, China, and Hong Kong, and had been followed by immediate action in Mexico and the Philippines toward ending gold exports at a premium. In the United Kingdom, the United States, and Canada, supplementary measures had been taken to tighten controls having the same purpose. Following these measures there had in general been an upward movement in the price of gold in Eastern free markets, and there might also have been a shrinkage in the volume of transactions in those markets.

During the discussion of this memorandum, Mr. Overby (United States) told the Board that U.S. mining and smelting interests had complained that they were at a disadvantage because the Fund's policy was enforced in the United States, whereas it did not seem to be in certain other countries. Another Director pointed out that cooperation by the large producing countries was essential to any reduction of premium transactions in gold, as the number of receiving countries and their tendency toward lax administration made effective control unlikely at the receiving end.

Mr. Martínez-Ostos doubted that the Fund's policy was having any beneficial effect. He believed that unless there was a noticeable drop in the volume of premium transactions, the Fund's policy could be regarded as having increased the premiums and hence the incentives for trade in the black markets. The premiums had in fact continued to rise since the date of the Fund's statement, and apparently the amounts involved in the transactions were not less than when the Fund made the statement.

The Director of Research replied that the volume of transactions had probably decreased somewhat. Measurement of the drop was difficult. However, the very fact that the prices for gold were going up in black markets was evidence that the Fund's policy and members' actions were having a noticeable effect.

Mr. de Largentaye (France) believed that the Fund would have done better to urge that gold be made available in plentiful supply at the official price. He felt that this would soon have eliminated the premium in terms of dollars on the free markets. The Director of Research said that sales above $35 an ounce probably could be eliminated in this way without excessive offerings. However, he doubted that the same would be true of the premium prices in inconvertible currencies.

At the conclusion of the meeting, the Board decided that the Fund should ask its members, through a letter from the Managing Director, for information on their laws, decrees, administrative practices, etc., concerning monetary, processed, and nonprocessed gold; those measures that were taken subsequent to the Fund's first statement; recent data on trade in such gold; and other pertinent details relating to the implementation of the first statement. The letter together with a questionnaire was sent out on April 6, 1948.

SUBSEQUENT DEVELOPMENTS—BELGIUM AND CHILE

The evolution of the Board's policy on gold during the years 1948–51 was closely connected with developments in South Africa. In order not to interrupt the discussion of these developments, we may here mention briefly the Board's attention to practices bearing on the price of gold introduced in Belgium and Chile during 1948 and 1949.

The Belgian Government informed the Fund in October 1948 that it was considering an arrangement for an internal free gold market. It gave two reasons: (1) it believed that the black market in gold which already existed and was tolerated should be legalized, and (2) certain gold producers in the Belgian Congo needed relief because of increased costs of production. After some discussion, the Board decided on a reply to Belgium which stated that sales in a member's metropolitan territory of gold produced in a nonmetropolitan territory in respect of which the member had accepted the Fund Agreement were not international transactions, and that the proposed arrangement would not be in conflict with the Fund's first statement on premium gold transactions because the Belgian Government intended to prevent international transactions. However, the reply also drew attention to a number of unfavorable comments by Executive Directors. Some doubted that international transactions could be entirely prevented. Furthermore, the establishment of a free market would divert gold from central reserves and put pressure on other countries to take the same step. The reply concluded by asking Belgium to consider these unfavorable views carefully before coming to a decision on the proposal.

As a result of this reply, the Belgian Government revised its proposal so as to limit sellers in the free market to Belgian Congo gold producers, and buyers to bona fide dentists, industrialists, and goldsmiths residing in Belgium or the Congo; the price in Belgian francs was to be fixed by the seller. Buyers would not be allowed to resell the gold except in processed form. No imports of semi-processed or fabricated gold would be allowed. When the Board discussed the revised proposal, Mr. Southard (United States) said that he believed the proposal represented an effort to bring a gold subsidy arrangement within a range to which the Fund would not object, and he appreciated the effort made to eliminate the monetary implications. His Government, however, believed that all premium sales arrangements would necessarily have monetary aspects, and it continued to oppose them. It was also concerned at the apparent intention to increase Congolese gold production by this means. Mr. de Selliers defended the plan, saying that it was not intended to expand output but to protect a major Congolese industry. The Board's decision on the matter did not specifically approve the plan; after describing the revised arrangements it stated as follows:

> 2. Considering its previous decision . . . the Fund notes the proposal and the revisions from the previous plan. It will expect to review developments under the arrangement from time to time and to receive current statistics on the operation of the market.

In November 1949 access to the market was extended to buyers of the specified occupations who were resident in the Belgian Trust Territory of Ruanda Urundi.

Another relevant decision taken at this time arose from a consideration of the multiple currency system of Chile, which included an import rate fluctuating around 125 pesos = \$1 (compared with a par value of 31 pesos = \$1) resulting from the method of marketing newly mined gold; this applied to authorized nonessential imports. The Board's decision included the following:

5. While it regrets that the gold practice authorized by the Chilean law of December 2, 1948, results in creation of a new effective rate of exchange for nonessential imports, the Fund approves this aspect of the gold practice. However, because of the inconsistency with the Fund's established policy on external transactions in gold at premium prices, the Fund disapproves the practice of permitting exportation of gold from Chile at premium prices.

SOUTH AFRICAN SALES

During 1948 and 1949 the Fund had a prolonged discussion with South Africa on a proposal to sell semiprocessed gold at premium prices. South Africa was in balance of payments difficulties at the time because of excessive import demand, and in fact drew on the Fund's resources.

September-October 1948

In September 1948, South Africa requested an opportunity for Mr. M. H. de Kock, the Alternate Governor for South Africa, to discuss, at the time of the forthcoming Annual Meeting, a proposal made to the South African Mint that it sell for export, at a premium price, a considerable quantity of semiprocessed gold. The gold would be in the shape and form normally used by manufacturing goldsmiths and jewelers and would be alloyed to required standards and hall-marked to show the actual fineness. All the gold would be exported, and all payments would be made in dollars. The proposal had been made to the South African Mint by a London firm. It was the intention of the Government to share any financial benefit from the transaction with the producers of gold.

The Legal Department advised the Board as follows:

(i) External transactions in semiprocessed gold at premium prices are within the scope of the Fund's Statement on Transactions in Gold at Premium Prices if such gold will be held, used, or disposed of for monetary purposes and not for industrial, professional or artistic purposes.

(ii) The contemplated profit-sharing with producers might involve a price paid for gold by the Government in violation of Article IV, Section 2, or, depending on the form of profit-sharing arrangements, constitute a subsidy which, under the Fund's Statement on Gold Subsidies [see p. 205 below], would be regarded as an increase in the purchase price beyond that permitted by Article IV, Section 2. Even though the additional payments might not have these effects, they might be subsidies which, as pointed out in the Statement on Gold Subsidies, would, directly or indirectly, undermine or threaten to undermine exchange or monetary stability and thus be of concern to the Fund.

These two conclusions were incorporated in a letter that the Managing Director sent to the South African Government on October 5, 1948 following the Board's discussion of the proposal with Mr. de Kock. In addition, the letter made further points that indicated, but did not state explicitly, the Fund's general disapproval of the proposal. First, the letter stated that members of the Executive Board were "disturbed by the fear that the proposed transactions would involve considerable sales of gold for purposes other than legitimate industrial, professional, or artistic uses," a consequence that would almost certainly occur if the scale of the proposed transactions was large enough to ensure an appreciable profit to South African gold producers. Accordingly, the letter went on to say that

> in these circumstances, the Fund believes that South Africa should not engage in the proposed plan unless it is satisfied that it can take effective measures to ensure that gold sold under the plan will in fact be used for bona fide and customary industrial, professional or artistic purposes

Second, the letter noted the Fund's pleasure at Mr. de Kock's statement that South Africa had no specific plan in mind for sharing any profit with producers and would consult with the Fund before putting any plan into effect.

During the discussions that preceded the dispatch of this letter, the principal opposition to the South African proposal came from Mr. Overby and Mr. Tansley (United Kingdom). Mr. Overby believed that any substantial sales of semiprocessed gold by South Africa would be destined for private hoards, because the United States and the United Kingdom were prepared to supply, at prices based on $35 an ounce, all the gold needed for legitimate industrial, professional, and artistic purposes. In reply Mr. de Kock said that his Government had been told that the sales by the United States and the United Kingdom were so restricted that the real demand for processed and semiprocessed gold was by no means met. He believed that "legitimate" demands were hard if not impossible to define. However, Mr. de Kock added that "the demand for gold in artistic forms had always included a large element of desire for gold as a store of value."

Mr. Martínez-Ostos again stated his belief that the Fund had never given adequate consideration to the theoretical and factual background of its whole policy on premium gold transactions, and that a full study was necessary before action could be taken in the South African case. Some other Directors supported Mr. Martínez-Ostos by urging that a full review of the Fund's gold policies be undertaken, and Mr. Martínez-Ostos said he would abstain from taking a position on South Africa's question until such a general discussion could be held.

February-March 1949

On Saturday, February 5, 1949, the South African Legation in Washington handed to the Managing Director a cable from its Government in which the Fund was informed of the outline of a plan to sell for dollars 100,000 ounces of semiprocessed gold at a price of $38.20 an ounce, over a period of eight weeks beginning on that day. The cable indicated that the gold would be sold to a firm of London bullion brokers, on the understanding that the gold would be used for specific and customary industrial, professional, and artistic purposes. The method of transferring the premium benefit to the gold producers would be settled later in a way that would not conflict with the Fund's purposes. The arrangement was regarded as an experiment, and any subsequent sales would be subject to new negotiation.

The staff advised the Board that as South Africa appeared to be already fully committed to the initial transaction, no useful purpose would be served by asking the Government to consult further with the Fund before entering into the contract. Instead, South Africa might be requested to enter into discussions with the Fund before further negotiations for the sale of semiprocessed gold were undertaken. However, on February 9 the Managing Director circulated to the Board a memorandum that he had received from Mr. Tansley. This stated that the South African gold was to be sold for delivery in Switzerland (the London brokers acting as agents for a Swiss-French syndicate) and that such a transaction could not be carried out in the United Kingdom. Mr. Tansley added that unless the Fund took a strong position regarding premium sales, his Government would be compelled to open the London bullion market to unlimited transactions in industrial gold. He said that the British Government asked to be informed by the evening of the next day, i.e., Thursday, February 10, of the action the Fund proposed to take.

Accordingly, a Board meeting was held on Thursday morning. It revealed that the South African proposal aroused strong feelings, both pro and con. Two questions were raised: first, whether South Africa should have consulted the Fund before entering into the contract, and second, whether there was adequate assurance that the gold would in fact be used only for legitimate industrial purposes.

On the first question, Mr. McFarlane (Australia), who had been elected by South Africa, pointed out that the Fund had not asked the member to consult again before engaging in any premium gold sales, but had only asked that it satisfy itself on the proposed uses of the gold. Mr. Tasca (United States), on the other hand, thought that the spirit if not the letter of the Fund's recommendation had been violated. He repeated Mr. Overby's doubts that any gold sold would be used for legitimate industrial purposes, as the buyers would be paying a premium price whereas the United States and the United Kingdom would meet any such legitimate demand at a price of $35 an ounce. Mr. Parkinson (Canada) supported the U.S. view, but Mr. de Largentaye dissented, saying he was not satisfied that all bona fide demands were being met by the United States and the United Kingdom, especially as part of the demand for industrial gold had been supplied through the free market.

At the end of the meeting, the Board took a decision which expressed doubts similar to those which had been brought forward during the meeting, and asked

South Africa to take all practicable steps to ensure that the gold sold was in fact used for bona fide industrial, professional, or artistic purposes.

At a further meeting that afternoon the Board approved a reply to South Africa and a press release. The reply, sent on the same day, incorporated the substance of the Board's decision and also requested South Africa to provide the Fund with a copy of the contract or the text of the relevant terms. The press release referred to news reports about a gold sale at premium prices made by South Africa, and emphasized that the Fund had never approved any specific gold sale at a premium price. It then recited the Fund's view of the undesirability of such sales as those which South Africa was making, and explained that the Government was being asked for further information to enable the Fund to judge whether the safeguards in the contract were adequate.

An answer from South Africa to the Fund's inquiries, dispatched by airmail on February 16, failed to arrive. Meanwhile the South African Legation stated that Mr. Havenga would make a public statement on the premium gold sale in the South African Parliament before it recessed in the following week. On February 22 a copy of the letter of February 16 was received by cable and at the same time Mr. Havenga undertook to postpone his speech until February 24, the last day before the recess. On February 23 the Board met to consider a draft reply to South Africa. The Managing Director commented that consideration of the matter was urgent, since receipt of the member's explanation had been delayed, and since the Fund had been informed that South Africa's Finance Minister would make a statement in Parliament on the matter in less than twenty-four hours.

South Africa's reply was summarized by Mr. McFarlane as follows:

(1) The text of the agreement South Africa had made with the London brokers was being sent to the Fund as requested.

(2) This agreement put into effect safeguards which were considered as meeting the requirements of the Fund's letter of October 5, 1948. If any breach of the undertakings came to the member's attention, the defaulting house would be debarred from further participation.

(3) In fact the legitimate and bona fide market for semiprocessed gold had expanded very considerably in recent years, so that an increased supply was appropriate.

(4) The contract could not be broken or postponed without exposing South Africa to action for breach of contract.

(5) South Africa would give serious consideration to any further practicable precautions that the Fund might suggest during the period of the present contract.

(6) The South African authorities would consult with the Fund regarding the plan for distributing the premium among gold producers.

The discussion that followed was concerned principally with the point that South Africa's safeguards relied mainly on the argument that the use of the gold would be controlled until it was fabricated. Directors felt that effective safeguards against hoarding would control the volume of sales, not the form of the gold. Accordingly, the reply to South Africa approved by the Board stated that the Fund was still not satisfied with South Africa's safeguards and recommended more effective procedures, citing regulations enforced by the United States.

Two days later, the Board met twice to consider a draft press release explaining the Fund's position in reply to the Finance Minister's statement to Parliament. The speech had included criticism of the Fund's gold policies and the maintenance of the dollar price of gold, and stigmatized as a "fiction" that gold was worth only $35 an ounce. The press release, a long one, added further details to what had been said in the previous release, and defended the Fund's position on premium sales and on the price of gold. Several Directors questioned the wisdom of the Fund's issuing a press release, and Messrs. McFarlane, de Largentaye, and D'Ascoli (Venezuela) recorded their objections to its terms.

The Managing Director had become increasingly unhappy about the situation and accordingly, with Board approval, sent personal and private letters on March 9 to Mr. Havenga and Mr. Holloway (Secretary for Finance in the South African Treasury), proposing direct, face-to-face talks either in South Africa or in Washington. Mr. Havenga accepted the proposal and expressed his preference for a meeting in South Africa and his hope that the Managing Director himself would come.

April-May 1949

Before the Managing Director went to South Africa, the Board in April 1949 had two discussions on the $35 an ounce price of gold, on premium transactions in gold, and on the Fund's gold policy, based on a number of staff memoranda. At the first discussion Mr. de Largentaye made a long statement in favor of increasing the price of gold, a proposal with which Mr. Southard disagreed, saying that his Government opposed a change in the price of gold. At the end of the second discussion the Managing Director summed up the views expressed, particularly as they bore on his coming talks with the South African authorities. He discerned no desire to stiffen the Fund's policy on international gold transactions at premium prices. At the same time only one Executive Director had proposed a reversal of that policy. Thus the matter appeared to come down to presenting the Fund's view that it was in the interest of all members, including South Africa, to carry out the spirit and purpose of the policy which had been established; also that there should be discussion on the arrangements that should govern any sales of semiprocessed and fabricated gold. Mr. Gutt believed that the aim of the talks should be to arrive at a full understanding on principles, so that both the Fund and the member could be assured of each other's continuing cooperation.

During his ensuing visit to South Africa in May the Managing Director cabled to the Fund the terms of some further proposals for the sales of semiprocessed gold which had been communicated to him by the Government. These included additional precautions to ensure that the gold was confined to legitimate industrial uses. When the Managing Director's cable was discussed at the Board, however, some Directors still had misgivings about the adequacy of these precautions, and the Board asked the Managing Director to convey these misgivings to the Government.

Mr. Gutt issued a public statement during his stay in South Africa, and Mr. Havenga made a statement in Parliament on their discussions. Mr. Gutt stressed the cordial atmosphere and desire of South Africa to reach agreement with the Fund, the safeguards that had been adopted, the undertaking of South Africa to keep a watch on developments, and the intention of the Fund to keep premium gold sales under review with all its members. Mr. Havenga referred not only to the discussions on premium gold sales (and subsidies), but also to the discussions held at the same time on South Africa's economic and foreign exchange position, both of which he noted had been cordial. However, he also implied that the question of the price of gold would have to be taken up again in view of the world exchange position. These statements ended the matter until the Annual Meeting in September 1949, except for a short factual report made to the Board, in the absence of the Managing Director, by the Director of Operations, who had also been in South Africa.

SOUTH AFRICAN RESOLUTION

At the Fourth Annual Meeting, in September 1949, Mr. Havenga, Governor for South Africa, introduced a resolution [2] that mentioned a number of factors, among them the long period during which the price of gold had remained fixed while prices of other commodities had risen, and proposed that the Governors resolve

> that nothing in the Articles of Agreement of the Fund shall be interpreted to prevent the sale, by the Government of any member, of newly-mined gold in any market at such premium prices as may be ruling in that market *provided* the said member sells to the Fund or to one or more members of the Fund, or transfers to its own monetary reserves at least fifty percent of its newly-mined gold at the price from time to time current in terms of the Articles of Agreement of the Fund.

[2] *Summary Proceedings, 1949,* p. 34.

The Board of Governors referred this proposal to a Committee on Gold, which reported back to the Governors a resolution, which was adopted, that the

> resolution of the Governor for the Union of South Africa be referred to the Executive Directors of the Fund for study of all relevant considerations and report to the Board of Governors.[3]

It will, of course, be realized that the devaluations which immediately followed the Annual Meeting, 1949, and included that of the South African pound, materially improved the position of the gold producers.

The Executive Board took up the Governors' resolution at two meetings in October 1949, and at the second meeting directed the staff to prepare a study for Executive Directors' consideration. The decision provided that a determination as to the scope of the phrase "all relevant considerations" should be reserved until the staff study was considered by the Board.

First staff report

A lengthy report by the staff and a draft of a public statement on the report's recommendations were circulated to the Board on February 2, 1950. The report was in two parts: the first, an examination of the Fund's policy on external transactions in gold at premium prices and related matters, and the second, a country-by-country analysis of premium gold markets and regulations on gold transactions. In a brief consideration of the appropriateness of the $35 price of gold, the report touched on the extent to which the purchasing power of gold and the profitability of gold mining had fallen out of line with that of other industries and other commodities, and reviewed the extent to which these were suitable criteria for determining the price of gold.

While in form the report was one by the staff to the Executive Board, it had been so written that it could be converted into a report from the Executive Board to the Governors. The principal alternatives confronting the Fund at the time were stated to be (1) continue the present policy; (2) strengthen the policy by calling on members to tighten their regulations covering international gold trade in a number of fields (i.e., exports of processed gold, gold transit trade and agency deals, re-exports of gold imported for refining, and gold imports); (3) adopt the South African proposal; (4) permit all newly mined gold to be sold in premium markets but continue the policy with respect to all other gold; and (5) modify the present policy.

The report concluded that the preferable alternative was to modify the present policy. The following summary of the principal arguments for this course is taken from a paper prepared by the staff working party at a later stage in the discussions:

[3] See *ibid.*, pp. 34–36, for the text of the committee's report.

(1) While the Fund's policy helped to limit the flow of gold into hoards, it was not the only or the most important limitation, other limitations being the import restrictions and the exchange control machinery of importing countries, the demand in the gold markets in these countries, and the national policies of exporting countries to the extent that these would be maintained independently of the Fund's premium gold policy.

(2) A relaxation of the Fund's policy might be expected to lower the dollar price of gold in premium markets and thus to strengthen confidence in the basic parity between the dollar and gold.

(3) The limited extent to which the policy was implemented (or such degree of implementation as might reasonably be hoped to be achieved on the most optimistic assumption) left serious inequities, and the persistence of such inequities would be a source of international irritation and would be likely to set up increasing pressures within countries that might lead to the ultimate collapse of the policy.

The staff report proposed that the Fund's policy should be modified so as to leave the countries exporting gold substantial freedom of action, subject to the provisions of Article IV, Section 2, of the Fund Agreement, and subject (1) to the undertaking of members to cooperate with the Fund to maintain orderly exchange arrangements with other members; (2) to the unenforceability in members' courts, pursuant to Article VIII, Section 2 (*b*), of contracts involving the currency of any member which are contrary to the exchange control regulations of that member maintained or imposed consistently with the Articles of Agreement; and (3) to any accord between members under Article VIII, Section 2 (*b*), to cooperate in any further measures for the purpose of making each other's exchange control regulations more effective.

Consideration of staff report

The Board first discussed the staff report, shortly after it was issued, at two informal sessions. The recommendations were given a generally cool reception, suggesting that Directors representing a majority would oppose changing the Fund's policy.

The Board's first formal session on the staff's report was held on April 11, 1950, when the only speaker was Mr. Holloway, who made a statement as the representative of South Africa. Describing and defending South Africa's position, Mr. Holloway made, inter alia, the following points: South Africa had understood at Bretton Woods that Article IV, Section 2, of the Fund Agreement gave members a legal right to sell gold at premium prices and had accepted this Article with that understanding. However, while South Africa still took the position that members had this legal right, it was prepared to reserve the legal question for the purposes of the discussion and deal instead with the policy. On this he stated that South Africa challenged not only the Fund's policy on premium gold sales but also the official price of gold. The Fund had evaded this latter challenge, and if it could not prove that the present official price for gold was the right one, it would have failed to meet the challenge.

At the next discussion of the staff report, a number of Directors supported the continuation, or even the strengthening, of the Fund's policy rather than its modification. Mr. Southard said that while there were admissible arguments for modifying the policy, the U.S. Government had decided that on balance there was no conclusive reason for changing the policy as it now stood. As to South Africa's proposal for a uniform change in par values, he said that he believed that discussion by the Executive Directors was appropriate, but he made it clear that the policy of the U.S. Government was still the same as it had been a year earlier. Although the United States was mindful of the gains that a uniform change in par values would bring to gold producers and gold holding countries, it had decided against a change in the present period of struggle against disequilibrium and inflation. He added that the U.S. Government was aware of the imperfect enforcement of the policy and the loopholes in its own and other members' regulations, which were the main reason for the recommendation of the staff report, but it believed that the present policy was still serviceable.

Mr. Crick (United Kingdom) indicated that his Government could not contemplate an abandonment of the Fund's policy; he supported maintaining and, if possible, strengthening it. Messrs. Falaki (Egypt), Joshi (India), and Rasminsky also supported the policy.

On the other hand, Mr. de Largentaye favored modification of the policy because he thought it was legally untenable, and because he did not agree that premium gold transactions undermined exchange stability and tended to reduce official reserves. Mr. de Selliers supported Mr. de Largentaye's position.

The Board's decision

At a further meeting, on April 13, 1950, the Board decided to recommend to the Governors that they should *not* adopt the South African resolution. The votes were 51,740 for so recommending, and 7,280 against, seven Directors abstaining. Mr. de Largentaye was the only one to state his reason for abstaining, which was that he could not see any legal basis on which different rules could be applied to various parts of gold production.

Following the vote, Mr. Holloway made a number of criticisms of the Fund's treatment of South Africa, and stated that he assumed that the Executive Board, in view of the trend of previous discussions, would reaffirm the 1947 policy. This, he said, would pose a question of high policy for his Government. The Government would have to decide whether, in the spirit of altruistic, international cooperation, it would still adhere to the Fund's policy and its agreement of 1949, or whether it would act solely on the basis of self-interest. His Government had instructed him to inform the Executive Board that this question would be decided only after his report had been submitted; meanwhile South Africa reserved all its rights under Article IV, Section 2, of the Articles of Agreement.

At its next meeting, on April 14, the Executive Board, without further discussion of the staff report, voted against the recommendations in that report and decided by 55,290 votes to 16,530 that the policy expressed in the first statement (June 1947) should be continued. While no Director changed his position from the preceding vote, three who had previously abstained voted this time, one to continue the policy and two against the decision.

Discussion of uniform change in par values

Following the vote, the Board took up the question of a uniform change in par values. Mr. Holloway stated that discussion of this matter was called for if the Executive Directors were to meet the requirements of the Governors' resolution. While South Africa accepted the provisions of Article IV, Section 7, which gave any member having 10 per cent or more of the total of the quotas the power to veto a uniform change in par values, it thought that the exercise of the power in the face of an approval of such a change by a majority of the Board of Governors would be undemocratic. Mr. Southard took exception to the word "undemocratic," and said that the question could not be considered a substantive one in the light of the U.S. Government's position.

In reply to a question, the staff representative said that Article IV, Section 7, had not been intended to grant undemocratic veto powers to any members but had merely recognized that exchange rates would move with those of the countries having the largest quotas, not because of votes but because of economics.

The staff then commented on the principal economic arguments used by the proponents of a uniform change in par values, as follows:

A premium price in gold markets did not prove that gold was worth more than $35 an ounce. The recent sharp fall in the dollar premium price of gold reflected much more the better pattern of exchange rates after devaluation. If the dollar premium price of gold should rise again, the fundamental reason for it would be further inflation in gold hoarding countries and a worsening of the balance of payments situation.

The argument that a change in the price of gold was needed to give the world more liquidity was generally advanced because the public ordinarily thought of liquidity in terms of gold. But national liquidity in terms of gold had not been a factor in any major country. As for other countries, the ratio of money supply and national income to gold would be inconsequential even if gold stocks were doubled.

International liquidity, however, was a more important element. With a uniform change in par values, the ratio of gold to total world liquidity would increase somewhat, but the countries with the greatest shortage of reserves would benefit least. In fact, it would be quite impossible to increase international liquidity substantially unless the balance of payments of countries outside the United States were improved simultaneously.

Those favoring a uniform change in par values argued that an increase in the price of gold would correct the present balance of payments disequilibrium of the world. However, the payments difficulties of the world did not arise from the $35 price of gold and a change in the price would merely postpone solution of the real problem, which could be satisfactorily met only by an increase in production for export at competitive prices.

Moreover, a change in the price of gold was not needed to do justice to the gold producers of the world. Profitability for gold producers, while lower than in 1934, was considerably higher than in the years prior to 1934. There was no special obligation to keep the return to gold producers constant.

Mr. de Largentaye, and Messrs. Holloway and Busschau, who represented South Africa, indicated at the next meeting that they did not accept the staff's arguments. The Managing Director asked the Directors whether they wished to report to the Governors on the question of a uniform change in par values, and it was agreed that the Board would decide later the nature of its report to the Governors and what, if anything, should be included on the par value question.

The Board's report

The Research Department then produced for the Board a revised draft of a report to the Governors. The Board's discussions of this draft, from April 21 to 25, 1950, revolved principally around two questions: the extent to which dissenting or minority views should be given, and whether a reference to uniform changes in par values should be included. On the former point the Board decided that its report would contain the decisions on the South African resolution and on the continuance of the policy on premium gold transactions taken on April 13 and 14. It would also set out the various considerations which led to those decisions, but would not give a minority view or indicate that the decisions were not unanimous.

On the question of a reference to the Board's consideration of a uniform change in par values, Mr. Parkinson proposed the omission of this paragraph in the report. When it was agreed to include the paragraph, in view of South Africa's desire to have it and the fact that the South African resolution contained a reference to it, he expressed formal dissent. Further difficulties arose over the inclusion of the word *present* in the draft sentence giving the Executive Directors' view of the par value question: "In their view there is no present economic justification for recommending such a change to the Board of Governors." The word was deleted from the report as approved by the Executive Directors, but Mr. McFarlane asked at the following meeting that it be reinstated, saying that the deletion made the sentence unsatisfactory to the South African representative, who had not been in attendance when the report was adopted. However, the sense of the meeting opposed changing the previous decision.

The Executive Board's report, as approved, quoted part of the Fund's first statement on premium gold transactions, the resolution of the Board of Governors, and the resolution proposed by the South African Governor, recorded that after full consideration the Directors were not in favor of changing the policy, and then developed in full the arguments for that policy which have been indicated above.

The Executive Board decided that its report should be sent to the Governors without delay and released to the public on May 3, 1950. The report was reproduced as an Appendix to the Annual Report of the Executive Directors for 1950, and was discussed in a chapter on Gold Policy in that Report.[4] At the ensuing Annual Meeting, in September 1950, Mr. Havenga, as Governor for South Africa, criticized the Executive Directors' treatment of the matter in a speech on September 7.[5] Four days later the Governors' Committee on Gold discussed the report and the related chapter in the Annual Report. Some Governors agreed with the Executive Board and others did not.[6] This divergence of views was reported by the committee to the Governors, who accepted the committee's report without comment. The South African resolution, as such, was not formally considered by the Governors.

TWO MINOR ISSUES

During 1949 and 1950 two minor questions concerning South Africa's gold sales were dealt with by the Executive Board. Both involved, in somewhat different ways, problems created by the Fund's policy.

---

[4] *Annual Report, 1950,* Appendix II, pp. 90–95, and Chap. IV, pp. 70–74.

[5] *Summary Proceedings, 1950,* pp. 93–98.

[6] *Ibid.,* pp. 42–43.

Among the measures of control adopted by the United States, and recommended to South Africa, was a rule that not more than 80 per cent of the value of fabricated gold sold abroad might represent the value of the gold itself. Adapting this rule to local conditions, the South African Government prescribed that the elements of the cost of any fabricated gold article which represented labor and overhead must represent at least 25 per cent of the value of the gold (at $35 an ounce) included in it. This meant a minimum of £2 3s. 1½d. for labor and overhead added for each ounce of gold used. Announcing this to the Fund in August 1949, however, the South African authorities said that they regarded it as an unsatisfactory requirement because it put a premium on inefficient manufacturing processes, and because mark-ups arising from intercompany sales afforded an easy way of escaping it. They preferred to rely upon inspection of all consignments of gold articles by the police. Three months later, Mr. Holloway wrote to the Fund to say that the revision of the price of gold due to the devaluation of the South African pound had raised the value of 25 per cent of an ounce of gold to £3 2s. 0d. To require manufacturers to incur minimum costs of this order would, however, run counter to South Africa's anti-inflationary policy. The Government had accordingly decided to change the requirement to a minimum of £1 10s. 0d. for labor and overhead per ounce of gold.

In May 1950, however, Mr. Holloway sent a further letter, announcing that his Government had decided to abandon the imposition of a minimum mark-up for labor and overhead, partly because it was so easily evaded and partly because of the inducement to inefficiency. South Africa intended for the future to rely solely upon police inspection. This letter was considered by the Board in July, and a reply was sent explaining that the purpose of the "80 per cent test" applied in the United States was to distinguish between fabricated gold and semi-processed gold, which was subject to export licensing. The reply expressed the hope that, in the absence of a similar test, South Africa would take special precautions to avoid semiprocessed gold being exported as fabricated gold.

The second question raised by South Africa's gold transactions concerned a proposed sale of gold sovereigns equivalent to 1,800,000 ounces of gold to the Arabian American Oil Company for use in payment of oil royalties to the King of Saudi Arabia. Mr. Holloway consulted the Fund in December 1949 about the transaction, which involved payment by the company of handling, conversion, transport, and minting charges equivalent to $1.3175 per fine ounce. Following discussion of the matter in the Board, Mr. Overby (Acting Chairman) replied, drawing attention to Rule F-4 of the Fund's Rules and Regulations. Inquiries made by the staff had shown that normal charges for the operations proposed by South Africa would be approximately $0.90 an ounce less than the figure quoted by Mr. Holloway. The Fund would therefore have to regard the proposed sale of sovereigns as a premium transaction.

SECOND FUND STATEMENT

Establishment of staff Working Party

The flow of gold to private hoards, after declining in 1949 and the first half of 1950, increased sharply in the second half of 1950, following the outbreak of the Korean War, to an annual rate of 60 per cent of world gold production. The staff became concerned about the possibility that gold from official reserves was reaching private hoards through the premium markets. The Managing Director therefore wrote to all members on February 9, 1951, requesting information on any sales made recently from their reserves to nonmonetary authorities.

Shortly after the inquiry had been sent, the staff circulated to the Board two memoranda on gold transactions. The first, dated February 14, 1951, drew the Board's attention to the large increase in the volume of gold exports at premium prices authorized by South Africa since the outbreak of the Korean War. The second, dated February 26, described the large increase in hoarding, expressed the fear that continued hoarding on such a scale would in time lead to a complete breakdown of attempts to conserve gold for central reserves, and gave as the staff's judgment that the amount of gold exported by South Africa at a premium far exceeded what was required for arts and industries. It therefore recommended that the Board should review the arrangement with South Africa reached in May 1949, and also that the Managing Director should be authorized to consult appropriate gold producing and gold importing countries to ascertain whether further steps could be taken to make the Fund's policy more effective.

The staff memoranda and recommendations were discussed at a number of Board meetings in February and early in March 1951, at which the main points at issue were (1) the legal authority for the Fund's gold policy, (2) whether there was, in fact, any agreed arrangement between the Fund and South Africa, and (3) whether any Board decision on the staff's recommendations should single out South Africa.

The legal question was raised again by Mr. Martínez-Ostos, but he agreed to defer it for the time being to enable the Board to consider questions of substance. Mr. Melville (Australia), who had been elected by South Africa, on the other hand, asked that the legal authority should be clearly established, e.g., by Board interpretation, before any decision was taken that involved a question of a member's compliance with the Fund Agreement. Mr. Melville sharply attacked not only the Fund staff for concentrating on South Africa in its memorandum of February 14, but also the Fund's premium gold policy, stating that it was impracticable. He advocated flooding the premium markets to destroy them as the only possible policy, if the price of gold was not to be increased. Referring to the two countries that had elected him, he said, "As a South African I am, of course, in favour of premium sales of gold. As an Australian I must add that my instructions are to oppose them."

After some discussion, in which differences of opinion were expressed as to the terms in which the decision should refer to South Africa, the Board decided on March 7, 1951 as follows, agreeing at the same time that the text should be made public:

> Since the amount of sales and purchases in the world markets of gold for jewelry, artistic and industrial purposes has recently been increasing at a rate indicating that at least a part of it finds its way to private hoards, contrary to the gold policy of the Fund established in June 1947, the Executive Board considers the existing arrangements and practices of several countries, including South Africa, are no longer a satisfactory basis to implement the Fund's gold policy and directs the staff of the Fund urgently to elaborate, after consultation with the countries concerned, more effective methods than the existing ones.

The Managing Director appointed a committee of four staff members to plan action to carry out the Board's decision. However, the committee was unable to agree on a report, one plan being advocated by the Treasurer and a member of his Department, and another by the other two members of the committee, who were drawn from the Legal and Research Departments. The Acting Chairman (Mr. Overby) then appointed a staff Working Party on Gold with terms of reference which included the stipulation that the Fund's gold policy was to be taken for granted. The Working Party was to have unlimited scope to investigate what measures might be taken to make the policy more effective. To this end, major gold producers and importers were to be consulted on existing practices and arrangements. Following such consultation, the Working Party might make recommendations to the Executive Board in accordance with its decision of March 7. The Working Party was also to consider the question of sales of gold from monetary reserves and, in this connection, was to study the replies received from members to the general letter of February 9.

Report of staff Working Party

The Working Party held discussions in Washington during April and May 1951 with technical representatives from Canada, France, Mexico, the Netherlands, South Africa, the United Kingdom, and the United States.[7] The discussions, which included both separate conversations with the representatives from each member and joint meetings, were concerned with the members' regulations and practices for dealing with gold transactions, and their experience in carrying

[7] Italy and Egypt had also been invited to send representatives. However, Italy did not nominate a representative until after the discussions had been held, and the information supplied by him was received too late to be included in the Working Party's report. Although Egypt stated that it would supply written information, this had not been received by the time the report was issued.

them out. In addition to the discussions, the Working Party obtained statistical and other information from the representatives and supplemented its discussions with further studies and inquiries on the subject.

The Working Party's report, which was prepared on the basis of all the information received, was issued on July 18, 1951. The report was circulated to the Board with a covering note by the Acting Managing Director, which emphasized that the Board's decision required that the Fund's gold policy as it stood should be the basis of the report and that the report therefore dealt with more effective measures for implementing the existing policy, which deprecated external premium gold sales. Accordingly, the main recommendations of the report were as follows:

> Countries should permit exports and imports of gold only in accordance with the following principles:
>
> (1) Except for movements of gold between monetary authorities, gold in whatever form, such as gold-bearing materials, raw gold, semiprocessed gold, bullion, coin, fully fabricated gold, or scrap gold, should not be imported into any country from any source except
>
> (*a*) for the purpose of satisfying the demand for gold required for local industrial, professional, or artistic consumption, and not for re-export; or
>
> (*b*) for the purpose of refining, processing, or fabrication of the gold for export in accordance with paragraph 2 below:
>
> (2) Except for movements of gold between monetary authorities, no gold in whatever form should be exported from a country to any other country, whether a member or nonmember of the Fund, unless the importing country has agreed to subscribe to the principles outlined in paragraph 1 above.

The Board considered the Working Party's recommendations on September 18, 1951. During the course of the discussions, it became clear that for a variety of reasons the Board was unwilling to recommend the adoption of the much more stringent measures that the Working Party's report had shown would be necessary, if the Fund's existing gold policy was to be better implemented. Among the reasons were that enforcement of the policy required the cooperation of all members and a general will to support the policy, whereas certain members were opposed to the policy and to the imposition of further controls. Also, more stringent measures would probably fail, especially in times of uncertainty; gold premiums were only a symptom of financial ills, and the Fund would do better to attack the disease rather than trying to control the symptoms.

Other Directors argued that the Fund's policy was mistaken because a curtailment of premium markets raised the premium in them, and this reduced public confidence in currencies. Another view expressed again was that the proper course was for importing countries to stiffen their controls against gold imports, and not for exporting countries to be required to limit their exports. Finally, Mr. Melville made it clear that South Africa was still wholly opposed to the Fund's policy, and was in any event unwilling to go beyond the arrangement reached in May 1949. However, Mr. Southard said that he did not believe that the Fund could solve the problem by throwing the gold policy overboard on the ground that it was unenforceable.

Accordingly, the Board decided that "the recommendations [of the Working Party report] are not adopted and the staff is asked to prepare further recommendations."

Staff recommendation

In accordance with this decision, the Working Party prepared another memorandum which included a brief review of the premium gold policy and a new recommendation. The staff had considered whether it should explore alternative techniques of enforcing the policy that would be more acceptable to members, but had concluded that this would not be fruitful in the present circumstances. The fact was that the Fund's policy was bound to be ineffective so long as there remained a strong demand for gold at prices above parity, with payment to be made in dollars. Accordingly, the staff's new recommendation was that "the Fund, while reaffirming its belief in the economic principles underlying its premium gold statement, should withdraw its request to members to prevent external transactions in gold at premium prices" because it had become clear that the flow of gold into hoards could not effectively be checked except by much more extensive and hence much more onerous controls, which members did not feel able to accept. The memorandum also discussed briefly the likely consequences of the proposed change in policy, finding them not wholly adverse to the Fund's objectives.

Second Board statement

The staff also prepared a draft statement incorporating its new recommendation. This proposal was not acceptable to Mr. Southard and was considered too drastic by other Directors. Mr. Joshi stated that his Government was completely opposed to scuttling the Fund gold policy. Accordingly, the Board's discussions were mainly based on alternative drafts put forward by Mr. Southard and Mr. Saad (Egypt).

Mr. Southard's draft was specific about the controls members should maintain to distinguish between transactions in monetary and nonmonetary gold, whereas Mr. Saad's did not mention any, nor did the final statement. Both drafts contained the essential paragraph of the statement finally adopted on September 28, 1951, which read as follows:

> . . . the Fund's continuous study of the situation in gold-producing and -consuming countries shows that their positions vary so widely as to make it impracticable to expect all members to take uniform measures in order to achieve the objectives of the premium gold statement. Accordingly, while the Fund reaffirms its belief in the economic principles involved and urges the members to support them, the Fund leaves to its members the practical operating decisions involved in their implementation, subject to the provisions of Article IV, Section 2 and other relevant Articles of the Articles of Agreement of the International Monetary Fund.[8]

Mr. de Largentaye said he would have to object to the proposed statement and could take no responsibility for it, having never agreed with the Fund's gold policy. He offered a different statement that he thought would be a better way out of the difficulty; this put the primary burden for preventing premium transactions in gold on importing countries and also stressed the need for tight monetary policies.

Mr. Rasminsky, in a statement highly critical of the proposed decision, said that it was misleading to suggest that members had obligations other than those imposed by Article IV, Section 2. The Canadian Government would not feel obliged to pretend otherwise, and would take the decision to mean that it would cover such actions as the Government thought necessary to pursue.

Mr. de Selliers disliked the fact that the paragraph did not clearly indicate what the Fund expected of its members, and said that he would have to reserve the position of Belgium because of the vague wording.

In reply to Sir George Bolton (United Kingdom), Mr. Southard said that he believed the intent of the new statement to be that members would make effective as far as possible an operating distinction between hoarding and nonhoarding sales. Other Directors indicated their views that the new statement meant that the judgment as to whether it was desirable to sell gold bars and coins was left to the discretion of each member.

The Managing Director stated his understanding of what the new statement involved so that those who would be working with it would know exactly what its implications were. His statement, on which no Director commented, read in part as follows:

> I take it that we are not withdrawing the Fund's gold statement of June 1947. What we are doing instead is to modify that statement in certain important respects. For example, where the original statement requested members to take effective measures to prevent external transactions in gold at premium prices, the new statement will urge members to support the basic principles underlying the policy under which, to the maximum extent practicable, gold should be held in

[8] For the full text of the statement, see E.B. Decision No. 75-(705), September 28, 1951; below, Vol. III, p. 225.

official reserves rather than go into private hoards, so that it should contribute to monetary and exchange stability.

I understand that it is left to members to decide what measures they consider practicable. Some members may take strong measures, others weaker measures, and yet others, perhaps, no measures at all. Each member will be the judge of just how and to what extent it will implement this statement. So far as premium sales are concerned they do not come within the purview of the statement as long as they are not designed to direct gold into private hoards.

Finally, it should be clear that although the Fund will continue to study all aspects of gold transactions, and will remain the instrument of collaboration available at all times to its members to discuss any question relating, for instance, to gold, the Fund will not be expected to represent to any member which sells significant amounts of gold for any nonmonetary purpose that for this reason it is failing to support the statement. Of course, if at any time the failure of gold to enter or remain in official reserves threatens to become dangerous to its members or to some of them, the Fund will review the whole situation, and this statement will not prevent it from performing this normal function or from taking the initiative in consulting with members on any problems which may arise.

This was the last occasion during the period covered by this history on which the Board discussed the problem of the sale of gold at premium prices.

REVIEW OF POLICY

During the years 1947–51, the Fund was faced with the alternatives of attempting to maximize the accretion of gold to reserves, or attempting to drive down the price of gold in premium markets. Had the latter course been followed, it seems likely that most of the flow of newly mined gold ($800 million a year), apart from that needed for legitimate industrial or artistic demands, would have been absorbed by hoarders. In the event, the Board decided to disregard the possibility of reducing the premium, and concentrate on securing as much gold as possible for reserves. There is little doubt that this was the right choice. At least, some $1.5 billion of gold was added to world reserves in the four years 1948 through 1951, whereas if the Fund had been inactive it seems likely that little of this would have been secured.

It is arguable, also, that the contribution made by this increase in reserves to the stability of exchange rates itself helped, in the longer run, to lessen the premium in gold markets. Nor did this influence cease with the Board's decision to leave the implementation of its policy to individual member countries. Its known views assisted members to continue to encourage the accretion of gold to reserves, and to discourage premium markets, so that as the demand for gold for hoarding diminished, reserves were able to benefit increasingly from the steadily growing output from the mines.

SUBSEQUENT ACTION

In their Annual Reports since 1951 the Executive Directors have continued to pay attention to the price of gold. The Reports for 1953 and 1954 recorded the gradual removal of restrictions on the sale and movement of gold, and a fall in the premium.[9] The reasons for this fall were given in the 1953 Report as being the relaxation of controls and the creation of new marketing facilities; the continuance of the legal restrictions imposed in certain countries on the purchase and holding of gold; and the general tightening of monetary policy and the decline of inflationary pressures.[10] The Report for 1954 recorded the reopening of the London gold market on March 22, 1954.[11]

In September 1954, at the instance of Lord Harcourt (United Kingdom), the Board agreed to amend Rule F-4, which set the margins above and below $35 an ounce outside which members may not buy and sell gold, because the existing margins made it impossible for the Bank of England to intervene to regulate the London market when the price moved outside $35 plus/minus ¼ per cent.[12] The new rule, which was established for a month on a temporary basis and then made permanent, sets an alternative margin of 1 per cent including all charges.

The Annual Report for 1956 stated that there had been virtually no premium obtainable by several members that had previously obtained relief for their mining industries by selling part of their output at a premium, and the 1957 Report recorded that there had actually been some dishoarding during the year.[13]

After 1954 the price of gold on the London market remained within limits close to the gold points based on the buying and selling prices of the U.S. Treasury ($35.0875 and $34.9125) until the winter of 1960–61, when the price rose briefly to a maximum of $40. Recording this in its Annual Report for 1961, the Board also referred to the measures taken in several countries to reduce the abnormal demand for gold that had caused the increase.[14] No other major disturbance occurred during the period covered by this chapter.

Prices in other markets, which continued to show substantial premiums above $35 an ounce, were recorded annually with some indication of the probable cause of fluctuations, but with no general comment.[15]

---

[9] *Annual Report, 1953,* pp. 58–60, and *1954,* pp. 114–19.

[10] *Annual Report, 1953,* p. 60.

[11] *Annual Report, 1954,* p. 116.

[12] *Annual Report, 1955,* pp. 97–98.

[13] *Annual Report, 1956,* p. 112, and *1957,* p. 109.

[14] *Annual Report, 1961,* pp. 128–29.

[15] See, e.g., *Annual Report, 1966,* p. 118.

CHAPTER

9

Subsidies to Gold Producers

J. Keith Horsefield

THE FUND'S POLICY of discouraging sales of gold at premium prices, described in the last chapter, has had a parallel in connection with the payment of subsidies to gold producers. This practice too has been held by the Board to run the risk of infringing Article IV, Section 2, which reads as follows:

> *Gold purchases based on par values.*—The Fund shall prescribe a margin above and below par value for transactions in gold by members, and no member shall buy gold at a price above par value plus the prescribed margin, or sell gold at a price below par value minus the prescribed margin.

The margin referred to was fixed by the Board in June 1947 at ¼ of 1 per cent plus certain handling and transportation charges. In October 1954 this was altered to either ¼ of 1 per cent plus handling and transportation charges, or 1 per cent, at the option of the member.

FORMULATION OF POLICY

The problem of subsidies to gold producers first came to the notice of the Board in August 1947, when Peru, having been discouraged from assisting its gold miners to profit from the premium on gold available in free markets, asked the Fund to suggest what alternative methods of aiding its producers were open to it. This problem was remitted to the Committee on External Sales of Gold, which had been set up in May 1947 to consider a request from Colombia for the Board's views on a plan similar to that originally proposed by Peru.[1] (It may be noted that at Bretton Woods Colombia had offered an amendment—which was not accepted—authorizing member countries to pay bonuses in order to promote gold production within their territories.)[2]

[1] See above, p. 175.

[2] Alternative C, *Proceedings*, p. 432.

Before the committee was able to consider the matter, the need for a decision was precipitated by an announcement by the Canadian Minister of Finance that his Government proposed to offer to each Canadian gold mine a subsidy of Can$7 for each ounce of gold produced in excess of the output for the year ended June 30, 1947. When communicating this to the Board in November 1947, Mr. Rasminsky (Canada) explained that he was in effect informing the Fund what his Government intended to do, leaving it up to the Fund to take what action it thought necessary.

Meanwhile the committee, having made a preliminary examination of the question posed by Peru, had some doubts whether it was competent to give an answer; the view was expressed that it could not give useful advice to members without having consulted, for example, gold mining experts. It therefore came back to the Board and asked for clarification of its terms of reference. This was given in the form of an instruction to examine whether the Canadian scheme or a variant of it was consonant with the provisions of the Fund Agreement, and what general methods of encouraging gold production in Peru would meet the same test. In its considerations, the committee was enjoined to pay due attention to the implications of these questions for general monetary policy, and to their effect upon the policies and actions of other members.

The discussion of the Canadian plan in the committee showed that there was a difference of opinion between Mr. Overby (United States) and Mr. Martínez-Ostos (Mexico) on the one hand, and Mr. Bolton (United Kingdom) and Mr. Bruins (Netherlands) on the other. Messrs. Overby and Martínez-Ostos believed that the proposed subsidy amounted to an increase in the price of gold, and therefore contravened Article IV, Section 2. Mr. Overby also contended that the economic effects could be serious, and in particular that the subsidy would cause irresistible pressure on the governments of other gold producing countries to assist their gold miners in similar ways. Mr. Bolton and Mr. Bruins, on the other hand, regarded the Canadian proposal as a domestic matter, and not tantamount to an increase in the official price of gold. Mr. Bruins, however, deplored the probable effect, mentioned by Mr. Overby, on other gold producing countries.

Shortly afterwards the Canadian Government, responding to the criticisms in the committee, put forward a new proposal. This provided for a subsidy comprising some percentage (e.g., 30 per cent, 40 per cent, 50 per cent) of the amount by which a mine's actual production costs per fine ounce of gold exceeded a stated basic cost (e.g., $18, $20, $25) per fine ounce. This would be paid on the amount by which the production in any year exceeded a certain percentage (e.g., 66⅔ per cent, 75 per cent) of gold production in the base year. For new mines the subsidy would be paid on the entire production for the first year, and on the amount by which output exceeded a certain percentage (e.g., 66⅔ per cent, 75 per cent) of the first year's production in subsequent years.

The staff advised the committee that this revised plan need not be objected to, particularly in the light of the comment by the reporting delegate of Committee 1 of Commission I at Bretton Woods, to the effect that members were free to encourage their local gold mining industries by means other than paying a higher price for gold.[3] At the instance of Mr. Overby, however, the committee decided that it would be preferable first to draft a general statement on the Fund's attitude toward subsidies, and after three meetings of the committee and three of the Board, at which drafts were discussed, a detailed statement was adopted on December 11, 1947.[4] The following are the operative paragraphs:

> The International Monetary Fund has a responsibility to see that the gold policies of its members do not undermine or threaten to undermine exchange stability. Consequently every member which proposes to introduce new measures to subsidize the production of gold is under obligation to consult with the Fund on the specific measures to be introduced.
>
> Under Article IV, Section 2, of the Articles of Agreement of the Fund members are prohibited from buying gold at a price above parity plus the prescribed margin. In the view of the Fund, a subsidy in the form of a uniform payment per ounce for all or part of the gold produced would constitute an increase in price which would not be permissible if the total price paid by the member for gold were thereby to become in excess of parity plus the prescribed margin. Subsidies involving payments in another form may also, depending upon their nature, constitute an increase in price.

Some reservations to this statement were expressed by Executive Directors. Mr. Tansley (United Kingdom), who had objected to a provision in an earlier draft requiring members to consult the Fund about proposed changes in regulations and practices relating to external transactions in gold, expressed similar concern at the terms of the statement as issued, because there was in it no definition of subsidies. Mr. de Largentaye (France) would have preferred the Board to state that the Fund disapproved of subsidies on gold production, but contended that the Fund Agreement did not empower it to object, since Article IV, Section 2, referred only to price. Mr. Martínez-Ostos sought, and obtained, an assurance that the issuance of the statement would not prevent members from asking the Fund to reconsider any of the related questions involved, or from requesting a formal interpretation by the Executive Directors.

In the light of the general policy just expressed, the Board considered the Canadian plan as acceptable, and took the following decision:

> The Canadian Government has consulted with the Fund regarding its proposed gold production subsidy and has today made an announcement on this subject. The Fund has examined the present Canadian proposal in the light of its own

[3] *Proceedings*, p. 575.

[4] E.B. Decision No. 233-2, December 11, 1947; below, Vol. III, p. 225.

general statement of policy published today. The Fund has determined that in the present circumstances the proposed Canadian action is not inconsistent with the policy stated by the Fund.

The crucial element in the policy formulated in the statement quoted above was that it brought within the prohibition in Article IV, Section 2, all subsidy schemes providing for uniform payments per ounce. It is arguable that the consequential recourse by gold producing countries to subsidies adapted to the circumstances of individual producing units stimulated gold production more than uniform subsidies would have done.

APPLICATION OF POLICY

The next opportunity to apply the newly framed policy came in March 1948, when Mr. McFarlane (Australia) sought the approval of the Board for a plan prepared by the Australian Government. This was designed to enable certain marginal gold mines in Western Australia to remain in production despite rising costs—a socially necessary measure since the local population was economically dependent on their continuance. The Government proposed to determine the amount of assistance to be given to each mine individually, on the basis of its costs, ore reserves, value, and dependent population. Mr. McFarlane said that the measures would not affect the price of gold, nor increase output; the Government was opposed to any subsidies for the latter purpose.

Mr. Overby called attention to a statement issued by the U.S. National Advisory Council on the day after the enunciation of the Board's general policy. This expressed the view, inter alia, that there were no grounds which would justify instituting a subsidy to encourage the production of gold in the United States. Mr. Overby said that, in the light of this, he would have to object to any proposal by another member country to subsidize gold production in order to increase it. However, as this feature was absent from the Australian proposal, he would not oppose its approval. The Board then decided that the plan as put forward was consistent with the principles enunciated in its statement of December 11, 1947; therefore the Fund would not object to it.

Six months later the Board considered a staff report on subsidy arrangements in Southern Rhodesia. These had come to light as a result of an article in the London *Economist* in May 1948.[5] Mr. Tansley, having made inquiries, explained to the Board in June that the Government of Southern Rhodesia, which was a self-governing territory, had included the proposal in good faith in its budget for the year. The plan provided for a minimum payment of £1 7s. 6d. an ounce for all gold produced, with additional benefits up to £1 0s. 0d. an ounce for mines of economic benefit to Southern Rhodesia which otherwise would have to close.

[5] "Rhodesia's Gold Subsidy," *The Economist*, Vol. CLIV (January-June 1948), p. 855.

It was regarded as a cost of living payment to the industry to compensate for sharply increased costs. The Government had considered that a system of subsidies to individual mines, such as the Canadian Government had instituted, would be impracticable because of the large number of small mines whose costs would be difficult to determine. Mr. Tansley concluded by saying that the British Government felt that it had gone as far as it could in drawing the attention of Southern Rhodesia to the difficulties inherent in the proposal.

Mr. Overby suggested that Mr. Tansley's last statement raised serious questions about responsibilities to the Fund, since the United Kingdom had included Southern Rhodesia in the nonmetropolitan territories for which it had accepted the Articles of Agreement. He asked that the question should be further studied, and discussions between the staff, the U.K. delegation, and representatives of Southern Rhodesia were held during the Annual Meeting in Washington. As a result, Mr. Tansley reported to the Board on October 5 that the British Government accepted responsibility vis-à-vis the Fund.

Mr. Tansley went on to say that the British Government realized that Southern Rhodesia had unwittingly adopted measures which were not consistent with Article IV, Section 2, and with the Fund's statement of December 11, 1947. Southern Rhodesia was unable to modify the arrangements during the current budget year, but had undertaken to introduce legislation to remove the inconsistency at the next session of the Southern Rhodesian Parliament. Mr. Overby pointed out that the measures criticized had been introduced in Southern Rhodesia without consultation with the Fund, and suggested that the Fund's disapproval be made clear. This was done in the ensuing Annual Report.[6]

In April 1949 the promised legislation was introduced. It replaced the flat rate subsidy by assistance on a graduated scale related to the gold content of the ore processed. The new scale rose from 1s. 0d. a ton for ore yielding 0.75 dwt. per ton to 5s. 0d. a ton for ore yielding 4.0 dwts., and then fell off to zero for ore yielding 10 dwts. This was considered by the Board on May 4. The discussion raised for the first time the significance of the phrase in the statement of December 11, 1947, "a uniform payment per ounce for . . . part of the gold produced. . . ." The Legal Department advised the Board that the broad intention of the statement had been to prohibit a flat rate subsidy for all gold produced or for such a substantial part of it as to violate the spirit. The Southern Rhodesian plan could not, the Department thought, be said to set up a uniform payment for all or for a substantial part of the gold produced.

Mr. Southard (United States) again referred to the U.S. Government's disapproval of gold subsidies instituted for the purpose of expanding gold production to enhance a country's balance of payments position. Commenting on this, Mr. Parkinson (Canada) said that Canada's subsidy continued to be for the

---

[6] *Annual Report, 1949*, p. 36.

purpose of maintaining production in an industry whose output was substantially below normal. In 1948 the value of gold produced was some $10–15 million higher than in 1947, but this was only a negligible part of the improvement in the Canadian balance of payments during the year. Mr. McFarlane said that the purpose of the Australian subsidy plan was similar, and that output in 1948 had not increased at all. Mr. Tansley said that in Southern Rhodesia the previous subsidy scheme, which the Fund did not approve, had done no more than slow down the rate of decline of gold production, and as the new system would cost little, if anything, more than the previous one, it was clear that the Government's objective remained a modest one. The Board then decided that the proposed subsidy did not contravene the requirements of Article IV, Sections 2 and 4, or of the Board's statement of December 11, 1947.

Following the devaluations in September 1949, Australia and Southern Rhodesia canceled their subsidies and Canada reduced the amount of its subsidy, while still avoiding payment of a uniform amount per ounce.[7] When in September 1950 Canada adopted a fluctuating exchange rate, its subsidy was increased by 10 per cent, but in the rush of events the Government overlooked obtaining the Fund's consent, for which Mr. Parkinson subsequently expressed the Government's regret.

Shortly thereafter Canada sought the Fund's approval for a change in the cost limits used for the calculation of the subsidy for individual mines, raising the minimum limit and lowering the maximum one. It also proposed to change the base year to 1949. The cost to the Government was expected to fall from $9.4 million in 1950 to $7 million in 1951. Asked under what conditions Canada could visualize that the subsidy could be eliminated, Mr. Parkinson said that this would probably have to depend primarily upon increased efficiency and declining costs in the industry. He agreed that the latter development did not seem likely, at least for some time to come. The Board accepted the proposed change in the subsidy arrangements as being within the terms of its statement of December 11, 1947. A minor change in the plan, introduced early in 1951, was similarly accepted, the Board referring in its decision to the continuing rise in operating costs. A further minor change was approved in June 1951.

Up to this time the Canadian subsidy had been renewed from year to year; but in December 1951 the Government sought the Board's concurrence in its extension for two years. Mr. Wolfson (Canada) explained that Canadian producers had been given the option of continuing to receive the subsidy or of selling their output in the free market; this had followed from the Board's statement of September 28, 1951.[8] (When that statement was prepared, Mr. Rasminsky had said that his Government would not "feel obligated . . . to resort

[7] *Annual Report, 1950*, p. 74.

[8] See above, p. 200.

to any form of pretence with regard to gold transactions at premium prices.") Some Executive Directors questioned whether, in view of the option available to gold producers, there was any justification in continuing the subsidy; insofar as this kept gold off the free market, it would lessen the desirable tendency for the free market price to fall. Pressing this argument, Mr. Martínez-Ostos said that he still believed that any subsidy contravened the requirements of Article IV, Section 2. However, as the Board had so frequently approved the Canadian plan, he would not vote against it.

Mr. Southard denied that the intention of the Board's statement of September 1951 was to channel more gold into free markets; on the contrary, it was the Fund's wish that as much as possible should find its way into monetary reserves. He therefore saw no contradiction between that statement and the Canadian subsidy. While he himself thought that subsidies for gold production were unwise, the Canadian plan had previously been approved, and the Board's decision of September 28 made no difference. He therefore supported the Canadian request. The Board then agreed to it.

In November 1952 the Canadian Government decided that it would be necessary to increase the scale of its subsidy. Rising costs and declining yields had led to the closing of ten mines during the previous eighteen months, and more were threatened with closure. Executive Directors commented in terms similar to those used on previous occasions, but the Board decided again that the plan was compatible with the Fund's policy.

Later developments in connection with the Canadian subsidy may be briefly noted. It was prolonged without alteration in December 1953, the Government at that time still regarding it as a temporary measure. In January 1955 the rate of subsidy was reduced to two thirds of the excess of costs of production over Can$26.50 an ounce, up to a maximum of Can$12.33 an ounce.[9] It was payable on two thirds of the amount produced. This new plan was initially to be limited to two years, but in 1956 it was extended for a further two years.[10] In 1958 the rate of subsidy was increased by 25 per cent (to offset the decline in the gold price corresponding to the appreciation of the Canadian dollar), and the arrangement was extended for a further two years.[11] In June 1960 it was further extended through 1963.[12] Finally, in April 1964 it was extended to the end of 1967, with a modification excluding new lode mines commencing production after June 1965 unless they provided direct support to an existing gold mining community.[13] These successive adjustments were all considered by the Board, and the schemes as revised were deemed consistent with Fund policy.

---

[9] *Annual Report, 1955*, p. 95.

[10] *Annual Report, 1957*, p. 105.

[11] *Annual Report, 1959*, pp. 149–50.

[12] *Annual Report, 1961*, p. 125.

[13] *Annual Report, 1964*, p. 109.

MODIFICATION OF POLICY

In 1954 three other countries joined Canada in offering subsidies for gold production—Australia, Colombia, and the Philippines. The first of these to submit a proposal was the Philippines, which consulted the Fund in June 1954 about a proposal to provide subsidies at three levels, to corresponding categories of mines, classified on the basis of profits and production costs.

Commenting on this proposal, the staff suggested that it was scarcely consistent with the policy enunciated on December 11, 1947, since uniform payments per ounce would be made to the mines in each group. Nevertheless the staff recommended that the proposal should be approved, being influenced by the belief that in the past the application of the 1947 policy had led to the drawing of fine distinctions which were difficult to defend. Since the number of mines in the Philippines to be assisted was in any case quite small, there would be no large groups receiving identical assistance. While it could not be denied that the contemplated subsidy would amount to "a uniform payment per ounce for . . . part of the gold produced," the structure of the subsidy was so similar to others which had been approved that the staff believed the Board could consent.

Discussing the proposal, Executive Directors recognized that gold mines in the Philippines were gravely disadvantaged by high production costs. Mr. Saad (Egypt), who had been elected by the Philippines, supported the recommendation of the staff, while recognizing that the phrase quoted from the 1947 decision created a problem. He agreed with a suggestion by the staff that the policy should be re-examined. Mr. Eriksen (Norway) agreed with the proposal but suggested that meanwhile the Philippine plan should be approved for one year only. Other Directors, however, observed that the Philippines had proposed to apply the subsidy for two years, and it seemed inappropriate to refuse this request merely in order that the policy might be re-examined. One Director indeed suggested that experience with the Canadian subsidy suggested that there was no good purpose to be served by approving such a plan for a fixed term; he thought it would be better to approve the Philippine proposal without a time limit, on the understanding that any changes would be brought before the Board.

Mr. Southard believed that the plan met the test of a subsidy and not an increase in the monetary price of gold. Mr. de Lattre (France) recalled that Mr. de Largentaye had frequently indicated his dislike of subsidies, but considering the small number of mines involved in the Philippines he would not object to the proposal. Mr. Bury (Australia) saw no advantage in re-examining the Fund's policy; he thought it was clear that it would be unreasonable to deny the Philippine request to meet their serious problems. He and Mr. Warren

(Canada) both welcomed the implicit change in the application of the Fund's policy. On this footing the Board decided that the Philippine proposal was deemed to be consistent with the objectives of the Fund's statement of December 11, 1947. The plan was subsequently modified on two occasions and approved by the Board for continuance until July 1957, when it was allowed to expire.[14] For some years thereafter producers were assisted through the Philippines' exchange system. The resulting multiple currency practice was considered by the Board in January 1958 and not objected to.

In June 1961, however, the Philippines reintroduced subsidies. This time, producers were divided into two categories only—marginal and over-marginal—depending on whether or not their profits fell short of "base profits" calculated separately for each mine.[15] The Board agreed that these arrangements were consistent with the Fund's policy. This plan was modified in the following year as a result of the inauguration of a floating exchange rate on January 22, 1962. While the rates of subsidy remained unchanged, it was proposed that the total of the official price plus the subsidy should not exceed ₱ 200 an ounce nor fall below ₱ 160 an ounce for both classes of producers. (At the free rate, these figures were approximately equivalent to $55 and $44.) As there appeared to be a danger that these arrangements might lead to the payment of a uniform premium price for gold should the exchange rate appreciate or depreciate sufficiently far, the Board asked for assurances that, if this seemed likely to happen, corrective measures would be taken in consultation with the Fund. These assurances were forthcoming, and the Board then accepted the plan, which has since been maintained in operation.[16] A new par value for the Philippine peso was agreed with the Fund on November 8, 1965.

In June 1954 Colombia also introduced a subsidy for gold producers. The Government then set aside the sum of Col$80,000 a month to assist certain small mines and gold-pan miners whose production had not exceeded 180 ounces of gold during the first six months of 1953.[17] Provided that these mines and miners agreed to sell their gold to the central bank, they would be eligible to receive not more than Col$20 per fine ounce (equivalent at the official rate to US$8) on not more than 30 ounces a month. This plan was brought to the notice of the Board in January 1955, during the 1954 consultation with Colombia, and was deemed to be consistent with Fund policy. The subsidy was discontinued in 1962, but since then Colombian gold producers have been assisted through the exchange market and fiscal incentives.

Australia reintroduced subsidy arrangements in October 1954.[18] Its gold

[14] *Annual Report, 1958*, p. 144.

[15] *Annual Report, 1962*, p. 164.

[16] *Annual Report, 1963*, p. 181, *1964*, p. 109, *1965*, pp. 102–103, and *1966*, p. 119.

[17] *Annual Report, 1955*, pp. 94–95.

[18] *Ibid.*, p. 94.

producers were divided into two groups. Those with an output exceeding 500 ounces a year and satisfying certain conditions were to be eligible during the two financial years 1954/55 and 1955/56 for a subsidy equal to three fourths of the excess cost of production over £A 13 10s. 0d. (US$30) an ounce, subject to a maximum subsidy of £A 2 0s. 0d. an ounce. Producers whose output was less than 500 ounces a year were to be eligible for a flat rate subsidy of £A 1 10s. 0d. an ounce. This flat rate was adopted for administrative convenience because of the great number of small mines affected and the possible imperfection of their records. The output of the small mines represented only 4 per cent of Australia's total production. Mr. Southard commented that a good case had been made out for the flat rate subsidy to small producers, and he believed that it would not result in any measurable breaking down of the Fund's policy; he therefore supported the Australian request for approval of the plan. The Board accepted it as being consistent with the objectives of Fund policy.

In September 1957 and May 1959 the rates of subsidy paid to both classes of producer were increased.[19] With these alterations the scheme remained in operation until October 1961, when it was modified to remove the sharp distinction between large and small producers. Under the revised plan producers with an annual output of between 500 and 1,075 ounces could opt to be paid a flat rate subsidy at a rate diminishing from £A 2 8s. 0d. an ounce at 500 ounces to zero at 1,076 ounces a year.[20]

In August 1962 Australia granted a subsidy for developmental purposes to mines not previously eligible; the allowance was not to exceed the amount by which their expenditure on development in any year exceeded their annual rate of expenditure on development in a selected base period.[21] The latter provision was removed in 1965, when the rates of subsidy were again increased.[22] All these changes were submitted to the Board and were accepted as consistent with the Fund's policy.

It may be added that the possibility of revising the statement of policy enunciated in December 1947, suggested during the discussion of the original Philippine proposal mentioned above, was reviewed by the staff in December 1954 and January 1955. In view of the legislative history of Article IV, Section 2, however, the Legal Department formed the view that any payments made in addition to the official price of gold must be construed as additions to its price. No reformulation of the 1947 decision which would be consistent with the Articles could therefore be found, and the matter was not again submitted to the Executive Board.

---

[19] *Annual Report, 1958,* p. 145, and *1960,* p. 144.

[20] *Annual Report, 1962,* pp. 163–64.

[21] *Annual Report, 1963,* p. 181.

[22] *Annual Report, 1965,* p. 103.

LATER DEVELOPMENTS

For nearly ten years after 1954 the only new plan to subsidize gold production brought to the notice of the Board was one introduced by Fiji for the three fiscal years 1958/59, 1959/60, and 1960/61. In these years the Fiji Government undertook to pay an annual subsidy not exceeding £150,000 a year to the one mining company in the colony, on condition that the company would expend an equal or greater amount on development. The maximum subsidy was to be reduced by £2 for each ounce that output fell below 75,000 ounces in any one of the three years. This plan was accepted by the Board at the instance of the United Kingdom, of which Fiji was a nonmetropolitan territory, in February 1959.[23]

In August 1963 South Africa obtained the Board's approval for a plan to assist twelve marginal gold mines to meet the cost of pumping out underground water in order that they might remain in production. The total cost for the year 1963–64 was not to exceed R 1 million. In April 1964 this assistance to the marginal mines was supplemented by the grant of unsecured loans by the state to cover working losses up to 10 per cent of revenue, plus certain capital expenditures approved by the Government Mining Engineer.[24] These arrangements have since been continued from year to year.[25]

The only other subsidy plan introduced during the period covered by this history was a new arrangement by Southern Rhodesia in December 1963. This was designed to subsidize potentially economic mines that otherwise would for the time being operate at a loss and possibly have to close down. The amount of assistance to be given was left to the discretion of the Minister of the Treasury.[26] The plan was accepted by the Fund as being consistent with its objectives, and has since remained in force.[27]

RESULTS OF SUBSIDIES

The size of the output of gold is determined by a number of factors, including the availability and yield of ores, the ability of the mines to compete for necessary resources of labor and capital, and the attractiveness of the price of gold in relation to its cost of production. Compared with these three factors, the effects of a subsidy can only be marginal, so that one can hardly expect to detect it from the figures of output.

[23] *Annual Report, 1959*, pp. 150–51.

[24] *Annual Report, 1964*, p. 109.

[25] *Annual Report, 1965*, pp. 102–103, and *1966*, p. 119.

[26] *Annual Report, 1964*, p. 109.

[27] *Annual Report, 1965*, p. 103, and *1966*, p. 119.

In general, however, it appears that subsidy arrangements have at best succeeded in maintaining output at the level at which it stood when they were introduced. The exceptions have been Canada, from 1948 to about 1955, and South Africa. Canadian output rose from $124 million in 1948 to $159 million in 1955, fluctuated around the latter figure until 1961, but then fell off, to $126 million in 1965. South Africa's production rose from 58 per cent of world output (excluding communist countries) in 1945 to 75 per cent in 1965, but its subsidies affected only about 4 per cent of its output. Colombia's output was a little larger than usual in 1956 and 1960, but if the former year is averaged with 1957 the improvement disappears, and the higher figure achieved in 1960 has not been repeated. Figures for the most recent years show a decline also in Australia, despite the continuance of the subsidy. It seems clear, therefore, that subsidies have not led to any material increase in the output of gold.

On the other hand, the spread of subsidy payments has certainly slowed the pace of mine closures and thereby averted a significant fall in output from a growing number of marginal and submarginal mines. The proportion of gold produced from mines with reported production costs above the equivalent of $35 an ounce was perhaps 30 per cent in Canada in 1965 and some 45 per cent in Australia in the year ended June 30, 1966. On less complete information it may be inferred that the proportion of gold produced from such mines in Ghana was about one fourth, in the Philippines a large proportion, and in Rhodesia a substantial part. In all, among gold producers other than South Africa, somewhere between 22 per cent and 27 per cent of output may have been made economic by subsidy payments. This would represent between 5½ and 7 per cent of world production outside the communist countries; without subsidy payments, most if not all of this output might have been expected to cease.

PART III

Exchange Restrictions

CHAPTER

10

Exchange Restrictions: The Setting

Margaret G. de Vries

THE SECOND PART of the code of conduct implicit in the Articles of Agreement (as described in Chapter 2) concerns exchange restrictions and convertibility of currencies. When the Articles were signed at the end of 1945, the flow of international commerce and payments was very much restricted. The preceding fifteen years had seen the introduction and extension of fairly rigid controls over international trade and payments by all except a few countries, mainly in the Western Hemisphere. The depression of the 1930's had forced most countries to abandon the gold standard. Faced with drastically reduced supplies of foreign exchange, countries had had to take measures to curb the demand for exchange. Many adopted exchange controls.[1]

THE BREADTH AND DEPTH OF RESTRICTIONS IN 1945

By 1945, European countries could be classified in three groups. (1) A first group of countries had formed a "sterling bloc." In September 1931 Denmark, Finland, Norway, Portugal, and Sweden devalued along with the United Kingdom, and thereafter their currencies were pegged to the pound sterling, the rate for which fluctuated. They retained their free markets and, with minor exceptions, did not impose exchange controls. (2) Another group of countries—Belgium, France, the Netherlands, and Switzerland—had constituted a "gold bloc."[2] These countries in general maintained both the pre-1931 parities for their exchange rates and the convertibility of their currencies into gold until 1936, after which they departed from the gold standard but avoided introducing

[1] The term *exchange controls* in this volume is used to designate a broad course of action and an entire apparatus of control, which usually includes *exchange restrictions*.

[2] Italy was part of the gold bloc until 1934, and Poland until 1936.

exchange controls.[3] (3) A third group of countries in Central and Eastern Europe had taken the exchange control route. Germany adopted controls in August 1931, and shortly thereafter Austria, Bulgaria, Czechoslovakia, Greece, Hungary, Rumania, and Yugoslavia did likewise. Italy held out until 1934, and Poland until 1936, when exchange controls were adopted by those two countries also.[4]

Exchange controls had also been adopted by countries outside Europe. Japan resorted to controls in July 1932; and in 1931–32 several Latin American countries, notably Argentina, Bolivia, Brazil, Chile, Colombia, Paraguay, and Uruguay, found it necessary to restrict transactions in foreign exchange. The exchange depreciation already undertaken by most of these Latin American countries had failed to alleviate sufficiently the acute shortages of foreign exchange brought about after 1929 by severe declines in the demand for their exports and a marked deterioration in their terms of trade.

With the outbreak of World War II, practically all countries had been compelled to bring their international payments and reserves under strict regulation. In September 1939 the United Kingdom had set up a comprehensive system of controls over foreign exchange transactions. Moreover, what had been the informal and voluntary arrangements of the "sterling bloc" had become the formal and legal arrangements of the "sterling area." Regulations similar to those of the United Kingdom had been put into effect in the British Dominions (except for Canada and Newfoundland) and throughout the British colonies, protectorates, and mandated territories. Thus exchange controls had been put in force in what were then—or were to become after the war—Australia, Burma, Ceylon, Egypt, India, Iraq, Ireland, Israel, Jamaica, Jordan, Kenya, Kuwait, Malaysia, New Zealand, Nigeria, Pakistan, Sierra Leone, South Africa, the Sudan, and Uganda. Furthermore, as Germany had occupied the continent of Europe, the system of German controls and clearing arrangements had been extended. By early 1942, some seventeen countries, including Belgium, Denmark, France, the Netherlands, and Norway, had been linked to the German arrangements.[5]

Exchange controls and quantitative restrictions on trade had become major instruments of national policy, and their manipulation had become a plausible new alternative to exchange rate adjustment when a country's balance of payments fell into disorder. Moreover, exchange controls had become not only a method of adjusting the external financial position of a country, but also a way

---

[3] Belgium introduced controls in March 1935 but rescinded them soon afterward.

[4] Details of the introduction, extent, and nature of controls in Europe during the 1930's can be found in League of Nations, *Report on Exchange Control.*

[5] Details of the extension of exchange controls as a result of World War II can be found in Raymond F. Mikesell, *Foreign Exchange in the Postwar World,* pp. 3–21.

in which countries could pursue internal monetary policies in their own interests independent of external considerations. Behind a protective wall of controls, countries could, for example, employ expansionary monetary policies aimed at stimulating full employment.[6]

It was hoped by many economists and government officials that, once the war was over, most of these controls would be removed. They favored a return to some mechanism which would again permit freedom of international transactions on a multilateral rather than a bilateral basis. To this end, the convertibility of sterling was looked upon as a key element. The Anglo-American Financial Agreement of 1945 had, therefore, envisaged an early restoration of sterling convertibility: under the terms of this Agreement, sterling was to be made convertible by July 16, 1947.

The problem of eliminating exchange restrictions—and of subsequently maintaining freedom of international payments—was, however, inextricably bound up with the question of how reconcilable was the pursuit of domestic full employment with the maintenance of free and multilateral international trade and payments—a question discussed in Chapter 2. Countries agreed to the code of conduct of the Fund in the realization that much harm had been wrought both to the system of international payments and to their own domestic economies by the wide use of exchange controls. But they were by no means confident that they could live without such controls. It was evident that the Fund's task in this field would not be an easy one. Controls would not wither away merely because World War II had come to an end, or because the Fund's Articles had come into effect.

THE FUND'S ASSIGNMENT

This was the environment in which the Fund came into being. One of its major purposes, as noted in Chapter 2, is "to assist in the establishment of a multilateral system of payments in respect of current transactions between members and in the elimination of foreign exchange restrictions which hamper the growth of world trade" (Article I (iv)). Beyond that, its Articles spell out several obligations that members must assume. Article VIII defines the general obligations of members; Sections 2, 3, and 4 specify those regarding exchange restrictions and convertibility of currencies. These are, in part:

> SEC. 2. *Avoidance of restrictions on current payments.*—(*a*) Subject to the provisions of Article VII, Section 3 (*b*), and Article XIV, Section 2, no member

[6] The details of how countries had learned to use controls and of their harmful consequences are given in League of Nations, *International Currency Experience;* in Margaret S. Gordon, *Barriers to World Trade;* and in Howard S. Ellis, *Exchange Control in Central Europe.*

shall, without the approval of the Fund, impose restrictions on the making of payments and transfers for current international transactions.[7]

(*b*) Exchange contracts which involve the currency of any member and which are contrary to the exchange control regulations of that member maintained or imposed consistently with this Agreement shall be unenforceable in the territories of any member. . . .[8]

SEC. 3. *Avoidance of discriminatory currency practices.*—No member shall engage in, or permit any of its fiscal agencies . . . to engage in, any discriminatory currency arrangements or multiple currency practices except as authorized under this Agreement or approved by the Fund. . . .

SEC. 4. *Convertibility of foreign held balances.*—(*a*) Each member shall buy balances of its currency held by another member if the latter, in requesting the purchase, represents

(i) that the balances to be bought have been recently acquired as a result of current transactions; or

(ii) that their conversion is needed for making payments for current transactions.

However, these obligations did not have to be fulfilled immediately. Article XIV, Sections 2, 3, 4, and 5, provided for a transitional period:

SEC. 2. *Exchange restrictions.*—In the post-war transitional period members may, notwithstanding the provisions of any other articles of this Agreement, maintain and adapt to changing circumstances (and, in the case of members whose territories have been occupied by the enemy, introduce where necessary) restrictions on payments and transfers for current international transactions. . . . members shall withdraw restrictions maintained or imposed under this Section as soon as they are satisfied that they will be able, in the absence of such restrictions, to settle their balance of payments in a manner which will not unduly encumber their access to the resources of the Fund.

SEC. 3. *Notification to the Fund.*—Each member shall notify the Fund before it becomes eligible under Article XX, Section 4 (*c*) or (*d*), to buy currency from the Fund, whether it intends to avail itself of the transitional arrangements in Section 2 of this Article, or whether it is prepared to accept the obligations of Article VIII, Sections 2, 3, and 4. . . .

SEC. 4. *Action of the Fund relating to restrictions.*—Not later than three years after the date on which the Fund begins operations and in each year thereafter, the Fund shall report on the restrictions still in force under Section 2 of this Article. Five years after the date on which the Fund begins operations, and in each year thereafter, any member still retaining any restrictions inconsistent with Article VIII, Sections 2, 3, or 4, shall consult the Fund as to their further retention.

---

[7] Article VII, Section 3 (*b*), refers to the special situation when the Fund has formally declared its holdings of a given currency to be scarce; see Vol. I, p. 193. Article XIV, Section 2, provides for a postwar transitional period. For the full text of the Articles, see below, Vol. III, pp. 185–214.

[8] For a discussion of the interpretation of this provision and of the legal proceedings involved in the courts of member countries in enforcing this provision, see Joseph Gold, *The Fund Agreement in the Courts.*

> The Fund may, if it deems such action necessary in exceptional circumstances, make representations to any member that conditions are favorable for the withdrawal of any particular restriction, or for the general abandonment of restrictions, inconsistent with the provisions of any other article of this Agreement. The member shall be given a suitable time to reply to such representations. If the Fund finds that the member persists in maintaining restrictions which are inconsistent with the purposes of the Fund, the member shall be subject to Article XV, Section 2 (*a*).
>
> Sec. 5. *Nature of transitional period.*—In its relations with members, the Fund shall recognize that the post-war transitional period will be one of change and adjustment and in making decisions on requests occasioned thereby which are presented by any member it shall give the member the benefit of any reasonable doubt.

Not only did these Articles specify the obligations of members, but they made clear that despite the considerable powers of the Fund, there were certain limitations on its objectives and on its jurisdiction in the field of exchange restrictions.

LIMITATIONS ON THE FUND

Restrictions on payments

The first point to be noted about the obligations of Article VIII is the phrase in Section 2 (*a*), *restrictions on the making of payments and transfers* (referred to in this volume as exchange restrictions). This phrase has the effect of demarcating the Fund's authority.

At the time of the Bretton Woods Conference in 1944, it was expected that two agencies would be established in the international economic field: one, a trade organization, to deal inter alia with restraints on international *trade,* such as tariffs, quotas, import controls, and the like; the other, the International Monetary Fund, to deal with restrictions on international *payments and transfers.* Later, in its first Annual Report, the Fund stressed that it "was conceived as one element in a many-sided approach to the task of re-establishing a functioning world economic system," and pointed reference was made to the plans for a parallel International Trade Organization.[9]

For a variety of reasons, the trade organization was not in fact ever set up. But most of the matters that were to have been under its jurisdiction eventually came to be handled through the Contracting Parties to the General Agreement on Tariffs and Trade (GATT). The GATT, accordingly, has jurisdiction over *trade* and *import* restrictions. Many economists have argued that distinctions between the various types of obstacles to international transactions—and in particular between restraints labeled "import restrictions" and others called "exchange

[9] *Annual Report, 1946,* p. 15.

restrictions"—have little economic significance. Nonetheless, the Fund's competence was delimited by the specific words of Article VIII, Section 2 (*a*).

In the Fund's early years there were repeated discussions among both the staff and the Executive Directors as to the extent of the Fund's jurisdiction. Frequently, such internal discussions focused on the questions of just how an *exchange* restriction should be defined and how it should be differentiated from a *trade* restriction. Clearly, something called restrictions on trade—including import licensing—were to be the concern of the GATT, while restrictions on payments —including payments for imports through an exchange licensing procedure— were the proper province of the Fund. It was to prove difficult in practice, however, to distinguish trade restrictions from payments restrictions. Differences between the exchange control systems of one country and another often seemed to result more from variations among countries' legal requirements and administrative procedures than from the economic intent of the controls. In some countries—including those of the sterling area—goods could not be imported without import licenses; and such licenses were not freely issued. However, once an import license had been obtained, foreign exchange could be automatically obtained for the permitted import. On the surface of things, this type of regulation seemed to constitute a restriction on trade but not a restriction on foreign exchange payments. The converse, a restriction on foreign exchange payments but not on trade, seemed to exist in other countries, where it was the foreign exchange which was subject to license and where such exchange licenses were limited in issue but, once obtained, conferred an automatic right to import or to obtain an import license.

Hence, important questions had to be answered: Was there an essential difference between a situation where an importer was unable to import a commodity because he could not obtain an import license, and one where he was denied the foreign exchange with which to purchase it? Was the point at which a restriction was applied—i.e., on imports or on exchange—an adequate basis for deciding which countries would have to consult the Fund or obtain the Fund's approval for their restrictions? If so, were many of the Fund's principal members that applied controls to imports, such as those in the sterling area, to be left free of the Fund's code of conduct as regards restrictions?

If the *form* alone of a restriction did not constitute a sufficient basis for differentiating an exchange restriction from a trade restriction, it quickly became evident that neither did the *purpose* for which a given restriction might be applied. Licensing of imports could easily be used as a means of restricting payments in foreign exchange—that is, import restrictions could be introduced to restrain deficits in the balance of payments. In fact, the GATT charter explicitly recognized the possibility of "quantitative restrictions for balance of payments purposes." Similarly, restrictions on payments originally applied in order to conserve foreign exchange could be retained, after the need to conserve foreign exchange no longer existed, for the benefit of domestic industry that had grown up under its protection. Thus, a division of the jurisdiction between the Fund and the GATT using the purpose of the restrictions as a guide was not feasible.

Debates within the Fund over how to define and characterize an exchange restriction became especially intense early in 1952, just before the first consultations under Article XIV were to take place. For it was then that it had to be decided what types of restrictive and other policies of members would be made subject to consultation. Although an explicit definition of an exchange restriction was not agreed until 1960,[10] the Directors, the member countries, and the staff worked out arrangements by which, in the meantime, the Fund could discuss, even if it did not comment formally on, a wide range of members' restrictions.

Although on other occasions the problem of a clear differentiation between the jurisdiction of the Fund and of the GATT has been a subject of discussion by the Executive Directors, the Fund and the GATT have not had any actual disputes over jurisdiction; on the contrary, cooperation has been close and substantive.

The European Payments Union

Shortly after its establishment, the Fund found itself operating in a world that contained not only the GATT but also various regional groupings which, like the Fund, concerned themselves with payments arrangements across national boundaries. The most important of these was the European Payments Union (EPU), which was founded in Paris in September 1950 under the auspices of the Organization for European Economic Cooperation (OEEC), also relatively new. The EPU led to the creation of a new monetary area known as the "EPU monetary area," the main features of which were that currencies of EPU members (as well as currencies of the countries in the members' own monetary areas) held by residents of other EPU members became, in practice, transferable, i.e., convertible within the EPU area. Intra-EPU payments hence became "multilateralized." Furthermore, members of the EPU were committed to liberalize their restrictions on intra-European trade and payments. Trade liberalization ratios were established which applied to each member's total trade with the whole area rather than to trade with each member separately.

The Fund's task of achieving liberalization of exchange restrictions and convertibility of currencies was thus made both more complex and easier. It was more complex because there was now another formal organization in the same field, and the loyalties of countries that were members of both organizations

---

[10] E.B. Decision No. 1034-(60/27), June 1, 1960; below, Vol. III, pp. 260–61.

might be divided. Initially, the establishment of the EPU monetary area gave rise to anxiety among the staff, the management, and some of the Executive Directors, who feared that the EPU might become a permanent monetary area and that discrimination against outside countries, especially those in the dollar area, might be prolonged. At the same time, however, the achievement of the Fund's objectives was facilitated by the corresponding efforts of the OEEC in liberalizing the restrictions of the members of the EPU and in restoring the convertibility of their currencies.

Current transactions

In addition to the limitations described above, the Fund's regulatory functions apply only to certain kinds of international transactions, some kinds being deliberately left out. The Articles recognize that members might find it necessary to control capital movements. The obligation of members under Article VIII, Section 2, with respect to freedom of exchange transactions is explicitly limited to the avoidance of restrictions on payments and transfers on *current* international transactions. To underscore the point, Article VI, Section 3, explicitly provides that "members may exercise such controls as are necessary to regulate international capital movements," although it goes on to provide that, with certain exceptions, "no member may exercise these controls in a manner which will restrict payments for current transactions or which will unduly delay transfers of funds in settlement of commitments. . . ."

As the Fund's Articles were drafted against the background of the disturbing capital movements that had taken place during the 1930's, there was an understandable desire to prevent movements of "hot" money and to minimize the risk that inadequate foreign exchange reserves would be depleted by more or less panic-inspired capital transfers. Hence, it was thought that controls over capital movements might be necessary and beneficial.

The freedom of the members of the Fund to exercise such controls as are necessary to regulate capital movements for any reason, without prior Fund approval, was restated in a decision by the Executive Board interpreting Article VI, Section 3.[11]

Transitional arrangements

Finally, the Articles provided that the Fund was not to pursue to the full its objectives in the field of restrictions during a "transitional period." This limitation affected the Fund's activities in a very important way in the early years, and has continued to be relevant until the present time for the majority of the Fund's members. As quoted above, Article XIV provides for the retention

[11] E.B. Decision No. 541-(56/39), July 25, 1956; below, Vol. III, p. 246.

of restrictions during this transitional period. After World War II, when supplies of foreign exchange nearly everywhere were running far short of probable demands for imports, it was obviously impossible to expect any country to abandon at once the elaborate control machinery which had been built up; and it was certain that, at least during an interim period whose length no one could predict, countries where the whole economic structure had to be painfully reconstructed after enemy occupation would feel obliged to impose strict controls upon their international trade and payments.

No period of time was set by the Articles for this transitional period. No definitional criteria of any kind were given. The Fund was merely admonished to recognize that the "post-war transitional period" would be a period "of change and adjustment" and in making any decisions to "give the member the benefit of any reasonable doubt." Two periods were mentioned in Article XIV—three years between the time the Fund started operations (i.e., March 1947) and the time when it was required to make a report to its members on any exchange restrictions still in force, and five years between the time the Fund began operations and the start of consultations on restrictions maintained under Article XIV. But neither of these periods was intended to define the transitional period.

The provision for a transitional period has had several implications for the formation of the Fund's policies on restrictions. First, for several years, the Fund hesitated to take much, if any, action concerning the exchange restrictions maintained by its members. Indeed, prior to the publication of the first Exchange Restrictions Report, in 1950, the only time that the Executive Directors undertook to make any general pronouncements on exchange restrictions was in the course of agreeing on their Annual Reports to the Board of Governors. Second, inasmuch as the Fund had already subjected multiple currency practices to its review (as early as 1947), it seemed to many members, especially those in Latin America, that there was an unfair dichotomy in the Fund's policies. With other forms of control so prevalent and the Fund doing little about them, harping on the elimination of multiple rates which seemed to many relatively minor was a source of irritation to a lot of members. Third, most members were to continue to take advantage of the transitional arrangements for a number of years. Before 1961, only Canada, Cuba, the Dominican Republic, El Salvador, Guatemala, Haiti, Honduras, Mexico, Panama, and the United States had accepted the obligations of Article VIII.

Therefore, from time to time the question arose whether the Fund should not declare the transitional period ended. The Legal Department, in 1959, advised that the Board had no power to terminate the transitional period. By 1965 the issue was no longer much debated, although all but 27 of the Fund's members still took advantage of these arrangements.

THE GENERAL VERSUS THE PARTICULAR

In addition to the limitations imposed by the Articles, Article VIII defines a general and ultimate objective. It does not catalog the particular types of restrictions that usually make up an exchange control system. No differentiation is made, for example, between *payments made* by a member's residents, and *payments received* by residents, e.g., payments made by nonresidents.

Of course, when the Fund began to take action concerning restrictions on payments and transfers, it had to seek to apply these general principles to individual restrictions. Moreover, it became necessary to formulate separate lines of action in respect of certain *particular* forms of restrictions or payments arrangements. Additionally, as the Fund specified its goals from time to time, it had to formulate a lesser objective than the total elimination of restrictions. Only gradually could its ultimate objectives be attained.

Three particular aspects of exchange restrictions were to become the focus of the Fund's attention during the years 1945 to 1965: partial (or external) convertibility, discrimination, and bilateralism.

Partial convertibility

In the exchange control regulations with which the Fund was faced when it undertook consultations on restrictions in 1952, various monetary or currency areas were usually differentiated. Payments by residents of one monetary area to those of another were subject to restrictions of varying degrees. For instance, countries in the sterling area applied much stricter rules to payments to countries in the dollar area than to payments to other sterling area countries.

After the Fund had been in operation for some eight or nine years, the concepts of *external* and *internal* convertibility became regularly used to distinguish different degrees of convertibility. Such concepts had not been part of the Articles. When convertibility of sterling was attempted in 1947, total convertibility, not partial, was the aim. Yet as time went on, it became evident that currencies would be made convertible by degrees, and not all at once. Hence the distinction between external and internal convertibility became a useful one.

The payments system of a country whose currency is *externally* convertible has two important characteristics. First, all holdings of that currency by nonresidents are freely exchangeable into any foreign (nonresident) currency at exchange rates within the official margins. Second, all payments that residents of the country are authorized to make to nonresidents may be made in any externally convertible currency that residents can buy in foreign exchange markets. On the other hand, if there are no restrictions on the ability of a country's residents to use their holdings of domestic currency to acquire any foreign currency and hold it, or transfer it to any nonresident for any purpose, the country's currency is said to be *internally* convertible. Thus *external* convertibility alone is tantamount to *partial* convertibility whereas *total* convertibility involves both *external* and *internal* convertibility.

The Fund members that initially opted for Article XIV and that subsequently moved to Article VIII (mainly countries in Western Europe), in general established external convertibility first and internal convertibility later. Only a few countries—Germany, for example—established the two simultaneously. Both types of convertibility were achieved gradually by most of the European countries, and not without setbacks. Formal recognition was usually eventually given to the *de facto* convertibility established by a series of administrative acts which had in successive stages liberalized the country's system of restrictions. In this process, a number of stages of less than total convertibility were reached.

Discrimination

The second distinction of which the Fund has had to take account is that between *discriminatory* and *nondiscriminatory* restrictions. Prior to the establishment of external convertibility, there was considerable discrimination in the restrictions applied to different monetary or currency areas. Again, as an illustration, the tighter restrictions imposed on transactions in dollars than on transactions in sterling constituted discrimination against the dollar area. In general, discrimination refers to a situation where a country treats its international transactions differently depending on which foreign countries, or which currencies, or both, are involved.

The issue of discrimination in international trade and finance has been a long-standing one, extending far beyond the payments restrictions falling under the jurisdiction of the Fund. Discrimination may be involved, for example, in trade restrictions, in regional arrangements, in customs unions, and in customs tariffs.[12] Discrimination in payments was for many of the years reviewed here especially pronounced and prolonged against countries in the dollar area; transactions with the dollar area were, as a rule, the last to be freed from restrictions.

Thus, the field of discrimination was a *particular* aspect of exchange controls that the Fund also had to tackle. Indeed, discrimination was one of the first problems pertaining to exchange restrictions considered by the Fund; the question of discrimination arose as early as 1949 in connection with South Africa's restrictions. The problem of discrimination against the dollar area persisted to some extent even after the establishment of the external convertibility of European currencies at the end of 1958. Hence, in 1959 the Executive Board took a special decision pertaining to discrimination in exchange restrictions.

[12] For a study of discrimination in these broader aspects covering the same years as this volume, see Gardner Patterson, *Discrimination in International Trade.*

BILATERALISM

Another feature of restrictive systems consists of bilateral payments agreements, i.e., agreements between two countries on how payments between them will be settled. Under a typical bilateral agreement, payments between the partner countries have to be made through the bilateral accounts held by the countries' central banks with each other. The outstanding balances on these accounts are generally subject to limits which represent the amount of credit each country is willing to extend to the other; when one of the limits is reached, further amounts accruing to the creditor are to be settled in gold or convertible currencies. The Fund has often used the term *bilateralism* to mean the use of such agreements.

Although the Articles of Agreement do not refer specifically to bilateral payments agreements, they do specify as one of the aims of the Fund the attainment of a multilateral system of payments. Consequently, the Executive Directors have had no difficulty in accepting the view that bilateral payments agreements fall within the Fund's jurisdiction. In 1955 the Board took a special decision stating the Fund's policy on bilateralism.

OUTLINE OF THE DETAILED CHAPTERS

Against this background, the next several chapters have been organized. Chapter 11 explains in detail how the Fund carries on its consultations with individual members. In addition, there are described the reasons why the present procedures were agreed, and the way in which the Fund resolved the question of which restrictions should be the subject of consultation. The chapter also explains how the consultations, which started as consultations on exchange restrictions under Article XIV, evolved into full-blown discussions on many other topics, even with countries not under Article XIV.

Chapter 12 traces developments in the Fund's policies on restrictions from 1945 to the end of 1958 when European countries established external convertibility for their currencies. This chapter interweaves the related developments in world economic conditions during these years and the process by which restrictions were gradually liberalized. Chapter 13 explains these same developments from 1959 to 1965, as well as some special problems of the 1960's, such as those of the less developed countries and some newly emerging difficulties with regard to capital movements among industrial nations. Chapter 14 relates the separate story of bilateral payments agreements. The Fund's relations with the EPU are briefly described in Chapter 15. The discussion of exchange restrictions is then concluded with a résumé of the Fund's relations with the GATT in Chapter 16.

CHAPTER

11

The Consultations Process

Margaret G. de Vries

THE FIVE YEARS specified by Article XIV as the period after which the Fund was to consult annually with members on exchange restrictions came to an end on March 1, 1952. The staff and the Executive Board spent some months prior to that date working out how to conduct the consultations. At that time, the climate for the initiation and acceptance of effective consultations was anything but propitious. Hence, although consultations commenced on schedule, many issues concerning their pattern and content remained to be resolved, and the initial procedures were viewed as experimental. In the course of the next few years discussions in the Board, especially during the annual reviews of the procedures for the consultations, focused on these issues. The basic procedures were, with some adaptations, retained. By 1955 the process was working smoothly.

In subsequent years few changes have been made in the procedures, but over time the scope of the consultations has been very much broadened and they have come to serve a growing number of purposes and to involve the effective international scrutiny of members' policies. Significantly, both the Fund and its members decided in 1960 to institute similar annual consultations for members accepting the obligations of Article VIII, although such consultations are not required by the Articles.

Toward the end of 1965 the Fund re-examined its consultations procedures. A few minor alterations were made, but essentially the process was retained unchanged.

A CAUTIOUS BEGINNING

AN UNEASY ENVIRONMENT

In 1952 the Fund's reputation and its relations with many of its members were at a low ebb. The Fund had not yet developed close and frequent contacts with the senior officials of the member governments. While some contacts had been made with the less developed countries, these were not on a regular basis, and some of them had been characterized by friction. In particular, a few less developed countries resented the greater attention being paid to their restrictions than to those of the major powers. Furthermore, the use of the Fund's resources had been minimized by, among other things, the decision of the Fund in April 1948 to limit the use of its resources by European recipients of Marshall Plan Aid (see Chapter 18).

Other elements contributing to disquietude among Fund members with the onset of consultations were uncertainty about the policies on restrictions that the Fund might evolve, and disagreement over the Fund's authority in this field. Little if any progress had been made since 1945 toward the achievement of the objectives of currency convertibility and the elimination of exchange restrictions, and a number of members feared a push by the Fund for a more rapid relaxation of restrictions.

Disagreements in the Board in 1950 on the occasion of the Fund's participation in the Torquay Session of the GATT had already foreshadowed the kind of struggle that could arise. Anticipating that the Fund's own consultations were to commence in 1952 and were likely to take place with practically all of the Fund's members, several Executive Directors sought to create precedents that would circumscribe the Fund's activities vis-à-vis restrictions. It was argued that the Fund's advice to the GATT could not be based on current economic conditions; rather, it should be limited to an appraisal of the circumstances at the time that the member imposed the restrictions. In other words, the Fund was merely to determine whether the initial restrictions had been justified and not to appraise whether such restrictions were currently necessary. Some Directors also contended that the Fund's reports to the GATT should be limited to the facts of the situation, and that the Fund should not draw from these facts any conclusions about the need for restrictions. The very participation of the Fund in these GATT consultations was challenged by Australia, which went so far as to refuse to allow the GATT secretariat to send to the Fund certain documents necessary to the Fund's preparations for the consultations.

The reports that the staff had prepared added to the difficulties among the Executive Directors. The staff had found that while further relaxation of dollar imports by Chile, India, and Pakistan did not then seem practicable, it would be feasible for Australia, Ceylon, New Zealand, Southern Rhodesia, and the United Kingdom to begin a progressive relaxation of their restrictions on imports from "hard" currency areas, although it was recommended that this should be undertaken with due caution.[1] It became necessary to vote formally on the decisions

[1] Fund Press Release of December 13, 1950, reprinted in the *Second Annual Report on Exchange Restrictions* (1951), p. 159.

before the Board, and in two series of votes the Directors decided that the Fund should both analyze current conditions and put forward conclusions.

Instituting procedures

Against this background, the Fund's consultations were started in an experimental way. Certain procedures were proposed by the staff and accepted by the Board in January 1952 as a way to get going. Later these same procedures continued to be the crux of the Fund's consultations process, but only after several troublesome issues had been ironed out. The decisions taken in January 1952 were as follows:

First, the consultations should begin on time, that is, on March 1, 1952, and not, for any reason, be delayed.

Second, the staff should hold discussions with representatives of the members concerned and then prepare recommendations for consideration by the Board.

Third, consultations should be far-reaching. They should cover not only the detailed characteristics of the restrictive system, but the factors necessitating the retention of restrictions as well. And "for appropriate situations" the consultations were to go further. They could include consideration of the ways and means of eliminating or adapting restrictions, the feasibility of substituting alternative measures, and possible technical and financial assistance from the Fund.

That these proposals, with their broad terms of reference, were accepted by the Board was most auspicious for the future development of consultations. But agreement was not reached without anxieties being expressed.

One Executive Director suggested postponing the consultations altogether, on the ground that the requirement for consultations might have been the result of a miscalculation at Bretton Woods of the postwar conditions of the world, which were far different from what had been envisaged at that time. This point was not, however, seriously debated, as the Board as a whole agreed that the consultations were clearly required under Article XIV. Another suggestion was that the procedure should explicitly recognize that the initiative for a consultation had to come from the member rather than from the Fund: some Directors were eager that the Fund should not give the impression that it was exercising the initiative. Had this approach been accepted, members might have avoided consulting the Fund. However, as discussed below, the question of initiative was among those resolved most readily.

Several Directors also expressed a caveat about the Fund's power to communicate its views after a consultation had taken place. They pointed to the terms of Article XIV, Section 4: before the Fund could make formal "representations" to a member about removing restrictions, there would have to be a finding by the Board that "exceptional circumstances" existed. These remarks on "representations" disclosed the fears of a number of countries that the Fund might make representations to many members, in order to end the transitional period. Without coming to any agreement as to their form or content, the Executive Directors tentatively agreed that some conclusions could probably be reached that would be "appropriately notified to the members."

RESOLVING THE ISSUES

Desirous as some Directors had been that vexing issues should be settled in advance, this did not prove possible. Various troublesome questions kept coming up during the next three to four years as the Fund consulted with individual countries, and to a greater extent as annual reviews of consultation procedures took place in the Board. How and by whom—the member or the Fund—should the consultation be initiated? Are annual consultations necessary and worthwhile, or should they be held less frequently? What should be the form and content of the Fund's conclusions for each country's consultation? If the Fund does not make representations, is the Fund in effect giving "approval" to the retention of restrictions? What particular restrictions can the Fund ask members to consult about? Precisely which restrictions does the Fund have authority to "approve"? To what extent can the Fund, in the process of consulting about exchange restrictions, probe into—and comment on—the domestic policies of its members?

Recurrent discussion, widening experience, and improving Fund-member relations were gradually to settle these questions, or at least to make them quiescent.

Who should initiate the consultation?

A formula was quickly found to answer the question whether the Fund or the member should take the initiative in setting up the consultation each year. It was readily recognized that consultations had to be a two-way action, involving cooperation between the Fund and the member, and that practical procedures were of greater importance than the formal rights of initiative.

Nowadays the Fund starts the process by sending letters each year to members announcing the beginning of another round of consultations. But in these letters the Fund recognizes the members' right to initiate them. Simultaneously, the Fund proposes to individual members through their Executive Directors, or after conferring with them, a specific date for the consultations. Over the years, a convenient time of the year has come to be settled upon for most members, governed by such considerations as when the budget is prepared, when legislative sessions are held, and the season of the year. But the date has often been put forward or postponed because of special factors, such as changes in members' governments (due, e.g., to elections), variations in members' attitudes toward the Fund and its usefulness, and sudden crises in a member's balance of payments situation giving rise to a need for the member to use the Fund's resources. Proposals for an alteration in the consultation date have usually been made by the member. Sometimes changes in a member's situation have prevented a consultation being held at all for that year.

How frequently should consultations be held?

Closely related to the foregoing was the question of how frequently consultations should be held. Were annual consultations useful? In the early years, some Executive Directors expressed the view that the consultations could not be expected to achieve any results until there was a change in basic economic conditions, that is, until the problems created by World War II had been overcome. They reiterated that so long as key currencies, especially sterling, remained inconvertible, there was little hope for the elimination of restrictions. Why then was it necessary to have elaborate machinery for annual consultations with the Fund, especially if no changes had taken place in a member's restrictive system since the previous year's consultation? Had not experience shown that the Fund could hardly expect to have a profound consultation with every member more than once every two years? Implicit in these queries was the assumption that the Fund could not help to overcome the fundamental difficulties restricting international commerce.

On the other hand, even in those early years, some Executive Directors—especially the U.S. Director—took exception to the idea that annual consultations were not profitable. These Directors did not wish to limit the frequency of consultations. In their view, if the Fund did not take a rather intensive look at the situation in each member country about once a year through the consultations, some other way would have to be devised to keep up with the developments in each country.

Because of the expressed skepticism about the usefulness of the consultations, and even more because of the considerable work and expense involved for both Fund and members, the staff and management made several suggestions in 1953 and 1954 for simplifying the procedures. Consultations would be advanced, wherever possible, by a preliminary exchange of correspondence—or, in some instances, conducted entirely by correspondence—and the number of formal discussions would be reduced. However, 1954 was also the year when several Directors, during consideration of the Fund's annual budget, suggested that, while expenditures should be limited, more travel by senior staff to member countries should be allowed for. These conflicting views could not easily be reconciled.

Shortly thereafter, however, annual consultations began to be more generally accepted, with due regard to timing problems. It was evident that the regularity of the consultations was not only helping to keep the Board informed of developments, but was also enabling the Fund to avoid any air of crisis in arranging staff contacts with the authorities of its members. The Fund had become much more able than before to act quickly on exchange reforms, drawings, and stand-by arrangements; the consultations had, in fact, frequently led directly to action by the Fund on these matters.

Should the Fund "approve" restrictions?

Despite the initial concern of some members that the Board might make formal representations under Article XIV, Section 4, the Directors did not in fact do so. The closest they came to making representations was in the decision taken on the first consultation, with Belgium-Luxembourg in August 1952. In this decision, the Board expressed the opinion that the strong balance of payments and reserve position of Belgium-Luxembourg made relaxation of restrictions feasible. Accordingly, it requested Belgium-Luxembourg to reconsider the necessity for the level of restrictions maintained on dollar imports.

This decision had been reached by vote after extensive discussion, during which some Directors urged that the decision was tantamount to a representation and, more important, a dangerous precedent. This was the only time in the period covered by this history that a formal vote was taken on a decision after a consultation, although there have been a number of abstentions from decisions. After 1952 the question of making representations did not come up again.

Nonetheless, once it was clear that no representations were to be made, the related questions emerged: Would the Fund then "approve" a member's restrictions, in whole or in part? If so, what language should be used? This problem of approval first came up during the Board's discussion of the draft decision on the first consultation with Denmark, the seventh to be considered by the Board in 1952. The staff had recommended that the Fund "agree" to the temporary retention of Denmark's transitional arrangements and that, if Denmark introduced new restrictions on payments or substantially adapted existing ones, the changes should be made in consultation with the Fund. A number of Directors, especially the Europeans, had difficulties over the implication of this recommendation. Did "agree" mean that the Board was authorizing the continuance of restrictions? Had the Fund any such authority? The Director appointed by the United States had difficulties of an opposite nature with the staff recommendation: How could the Fund question certain restrictions and yet "agree" to their retention?

The issue that had to be resolved can be simply stated: Should the conclusions following a consultation make explicit that the Fund had, in essence, decided *not* to make representations? If there were to be no representations, should the words "agree to" be used, with their implications of Fund approbation of continuing restrictions? The first question—that of representation—was laid to rest by a decision on August 15, 1952, on the basis of a proposal by Mr. Southard (United States). It was agreed that, except under special circumstances, two sentences would be used to open and close, respectively, all decisions taken in the 1952 Article XIV consultations:

> 1. The Government of [*name of country*] has consulted the Fund under Article XIV, Section 4, of the Fund Agreement concerning the further retention of its transitional arrangements.
>
> 2. In concluding the 1952 consultations, the Fund has no further comments to make on the transitional arrangements maintained by [*name of country*].

These innocuous sentences were a way of saying that, after considering the country's restrictions, the Fund did not wish to make any representation.

The second question—of "agreeing" to a country's restrictions—was not dealt with but was left in abeyance. Any conclusions embodied in an Article XIV decision had the status of advice and recommendation rather than of approval by the Fund. Thus, the question of whether the Fund was legally approving a country's restrictions had been skirted. The decisions on Article XIV consultations for several countries taken before August 15, 1952 were correspondingly revised. And the two sentences continued to be used for all Article XIV consultation decisions until early in 1966.

WHAT RESTRICTIONS SHOULD BE REVIEWED

It had been generally understood—by the staff, the management, and the Executive Directors—that the "approval" jurisdiction of the Fund did not go beyond restrictions on current payments and transfers, multiple currency practices, and discriminatory currency arrangements. Nevertheless, difficult definitional and jurisdictional questions still remained. When the consultations began in 1952, a *restriction on payments* (i.e., an exchange restriction) had not yet been defined. Just what restrictions the Fund could discuss with its members remained uncertain. Similarly, whether the Board could comment to its members on what were mutually regarded as trade policies and practices, as distinct from exchange policies and practices, was undetermined.

DEBATES AND DEFINITIONS

Not only did various Directors hold opposing views on these questions, but so did members of the staff. For this reason, and because of the GATT's jurisdiction over trade restrictions, it was only to be expected that the question of what types of restrictions should be covered by the consultations, and by the Executive Board's decisions on them, would frequently plague the Board in the early years of consultations. Even before the Article XIV consultations had begun, such debates had occurred. The Australian Director had held the extreme view that since the Fund had no jurisdiction over quantitative restrictions on imports, a case could be made for limiting consultations to restrictions on current payments for transactions in invisibles only. On the occasion of considering one of the early Exchange Restrictions Reports, Mr. Melville (Australia) had objected to the proposed description of Australia's restrictive system. Distinguishing between import licenses and exchange licenses, he wished the description to make it abundantly clear that Australia's restrictions on imports were exercised only through import licenses and not through exchange licenses. Mr. Saad (Egypt), who had represented the Fund at the General Sessions of the GATT, argued in rebuttal that import licenses in the Australian system implemented *both* trade and exchange restrictions. He pointed out that many countries had mixed systems of trade and exchange restrictions, and any form of licensing technique might be used to enforce the two kinds of restrictions simultaneously.

With the support of Mr. Stamp (United Kingdom) and Mr. Savkar (India), whose countries had similar control systems, Mr. Melville requested an opinion from the General Counsel on what constitutes an exchange restriction. Mr. Saad, in his capacity as Governor of the Fund for Egypt, then requested a decision by the Executive Board giving a formal interpretation of the meaning in Article VIII, Section 2, of the phrase *restrictions on the making of payments and transfers for current international transactions.* The Board, in a sense-of-the-meeting decision, approved for inclusion in the Exchange Restrictions Report the staff's description of Australia's restrictive system, and referred Mr. Saad's request to the Committee on Interpretation. However, neither the committee nor the Board was able to reach agreement on the question, and after the Board had discussed the question in executive session, general consideration of the matter was, at least temporarily, dropped.

The issue of jurisdiction, therefore, had not really been decided. And it recurred persistently in the Board's consultations during the next several years. On various occasions the Directors for Australia and the United Kingdom pointed out that Fund decisions must be limited to restrictions on payments. Or that while the Fund, as a party to a GATT consultation, could *comment* on any restrictive measures affecting a country's balance of payments, any *recommendations* in Article XIV consultations should be confined to restrictions on current payments and transfers. Mr. Bury (Australia) opposed "any attempt to bring trade matters into a Fund decision," because it would "raise the fears of certain governments that the Fund was going beyond its proper sphere." In the view of Sir Edmund Hall-Patch (United Kingdom), for the Fund to give advice in areas where its jurisdiction was not clear would tend to weaken its influence in areas where it was intended to have authority. The sensitivity of these Directors on such points was evidenced, for example, when Mr. Southard proposed, for the conclusions to the first consultation with Colombia, a reference to the adjustment of import prohibitions. And it was apparent again in 1954 and 1955, when during the first two consultations with Germany comments were made on import restrictions to protect agriculture. Subsequently, the issue has recurred from time to time but has not been so intensely debated as in those early years.

A closely related question was how far the Fund could go in suggesting specific ways of reducing restrictions. This problem had arisen during the first consultation with Burma. The staff's draft decision contained the suggestion that "wherever possible, Burma should increase the proportion of imports under open general license." Mr. Crick (United Kingdom) and Mr. Melville argued for the deletion of this reference, on the ground that the Fund should not comment on one particular type of licensing technique. In contrast, Mr. Southard and Mr. Perry (Canada) urged that on grounds of principle the Fund had not only the right but the duty to transmit technical advice, especially in the area of exchange controls.

Emergence of broad discussions

In the course of time jurisdictional disputes and fears of the Fund's overstepping the mark subsided, allowing the economic realities to guide the Fund's activities. These realities were that various forms of restrictions were interrelated both in their operation and in their effects on the domestic situation and on other Fund members, and that it was impossible to make sensible judgments regarding a particular restriction on payments without taking account of the totality of restrictive practices of a member. Practice began to demonstrate that jurisdiction was not being usurped. Without further debate, the staff's discussions with members came gradually to cover all quantitative and other trade restrictions operated for the purpose of restricting exchange payments. Eventually, restrictions maintained for protective as well as for balance of payments reasons were also included in these discussions.

At the same time, however, the decisions on restrictions taken by the Board at the end of each consultation were made more precise. For a time, the working principle used for Board decisions was that only restrictions for balance of payments purposes could be maintained under Article XIV, whereas restrictions for other reasons would have to be approved under Article VIII. This principle had been enunciated as an ad hoc guide during the first consultation with Italy. It was made explicit in the decision on the 1952 consultation with Cuba: Cuba's 2 per cent exchange tax on remittances abroad was not maintained for balance of payments purposes and consequently was maintained in accordance with the provisions of Article VIII.

Later, for the same reasons that staff discussions with the member encompassed the broad range of restrictions, Executive Board decisions also came to include statements of views regarding the general level of restrictions and the possibility of removing them, but did not "approve" or "disapprove" them. The language used over the years ranged from urging action to suggesting re-examination of the practices, depending upon the severity of the restrictions and their harmfulness to the international community.

COMMENTING ON TRADE POLICY

The authority of the Fund

The legal authority of the Fund to consider and comment on trade policies and practices—as distinct from the jurisdictional character of its authority with respect to exchange practices—was finally formulated in 1960. At that time the Legal Department, distinguishing between the Fund's official authority to consider and comment on the trade policies and practices of its members and its power to approve exchange practices, worked out a legal position which met with little opposition. While members are not required to submit their trade policies and practices as such to the Fund for its approval, and the Fund cannot disapprove these policies and practices in the sense that if members persist in them they can be regarded as violating international obligations under the Fund's Articles, these trade policies and practices can be evaluated in the light of the Fund's purposes.

In defense of its reasoning, the legal staff cited various provisions of the Articles. Since Article I (ii) specified as a purpose of the Fund "to facilitate the expansion and balanced growth of international trade," the Fund can consider and comment on the extent to which the policies and practices of its members conduce toward the realization of this purpose. Moreover, Article XII, Section 7 (*b*), provides that "the Fund may publish such . . . reports as it deems desirable for carrying out its purposes," and the first sentence of Article XII, Section 8, declares that "the Fund shall at all times have the right to communicate its views informally to any member on any matter arising under this Agreement." The broad scope of the Fund's authority under these provisions, said the Legal Department, is established by the words "purposes" in Section 7 (*b*) and "any matter arising under this Agreement" in Section 8. All that needed to be added—and this was then made explicit—was that the authority to publish reports and communicate views embraces authority to consider the policies and positions of members in order to decide whether to publish reports or communicate views.

Finally, Article XIV, Section 2, expected members "to develop such commercial and financial arrangements with other members as will facilitate international payments and the maintenance of exchange stability." Hence, the Fund could consider and comment on commercial and financial measures. Significantly, it was also the legal view that although this objective appeared in Article XIV, it was not confined to the period of transitional arrangements, but connoted a permanent objective.

Need for clarification

The reason why the Fund's legal position as regards trade restrictions could be established in 1960 was in part that a greater area of common ground existed between members then than in the early 1950's. But more compelling was the need, as members ceased to avail themselves of the transitional arrangements of Article XIV, to elucidate the Fund's authority under Article VIII. Not only was there the question whether the Fund should hold regular consultations with members once they had assumed the obligations of Article VIII, but also the question whether the Fund could, once a member was under Article VIII, consider and comment on its policies other than its exchange policies. Specific answers to these questions had been postponed while consultations were being conducted under Article XIV. It became especially necessary to settle the long-standing question about trade restrictions when consultations with the GATT showed that it was possible for the Fund effectively to comment on the trade restrictions of GATT members. The difficulty was that half of the Fund's members were not GATT members.

The immediate problem at hand was to work out a procedure for discussing with members under Article VIII their *import restrictions for balance of payments reasons.* The staff proposed a duality of treatment between the Fund's members which were also GATT members and those which were not. GATT members would be asked merely to send information concerning their restrictions directly to the Fund as well as to the GATT; since such information was already being sent to the Fund by most GATT members, this provision merely ensured that other members of the Fund which were also GATT members would do likewise. As regards non-GATT members, the staff proposed that the Fund should seek to "reach agreement" with those members which imposed import restrictions for balance of payments reasons, "to obtain information on these restrictions, thus facilitating the preparation of studies designed to assist members in developing principles which further the purposes of the Fund."

Agreement by the Board

In 1960, the Executive Directors reached, with relative ease, a working agreement on the very question—that is, the Fund's authority on trade matters—

which had, in years gone by, provoked almost open discord. But, although a *modus operandi* could now be articulated in written agreement, some of the old concerns, long dormant, were again expressed.

Once again the Australian Director—now Mr. Garland—referred briefly to his country's well-known views about the Fund's jurisdiction over import restrictions, discriminatory or nondiscriminatory, and whether for balance of payments reasons or not. But this time he conceded that import restrictions and trade discrimination fall within the Fund's sphere of general interest and properly form the subject of general comment by the Fund. However, he was troubled about "reaching agreement" with non-GATT members; if such agreements were to vary, an unwanted differentiation between Fund members would occur.

In addition, a definition of an exchange restriction—which had been incorporated as a guiding principle in the proposed decision—caused much uneasiness among authorities of the United States. This guiding principle was that a restriction on payments and transfers for current transactions under Article VIII, Section 2, was one which involved a direct governmental limitation on the availability or use of exchange as such. It appeared to the U.S. authorities that by this definition the Fund's role in the broad field of balance of payments restrictions was reduced. Concern about explicit limitations on the Fund's "approval" jurisdiction had been abated by realization that the Fund, through its role with the GATT, could be effective in this field. However, would not non-GATT members escape a similar determination for their import restrictions? The United States, therefore, was hopeful that they would not really mind acquiescing in a Fund examination; such examination would not be for the purpose of a determination by the Fund but merely to collect and provide useful information, especially for the benefit of other Fund members which might be injured by such restrictions.

It was finally agreed that Fund members which are contracting parties to the GATT and which impose import restrictions for balance of payments reasons would continue to send information concerning such restrictions to the Fund. Such information would enable the Fund and the member to join in an examination of the balance of payments situation in order to assist the Fund in its collaboration with the GATT. It was also agreed that the Fund, by consent of its members which are not contracting parties to the GATT and which impose import restrictions for balance of payments reasons, would seek to obtain information relating to such restrictions.

BROADENING THE SCOPE OF CONSULTATIONS

The Fund's consultations on restrictions under Article XIV became, relatively quickly, a vehicle for purposes additional to an examination of restrictions.

A technique and language were soon developed for giving advice to members that was acceptable, or even desired, by them on policies that might not be strictly within the Fund's jurisdiction. The Executive Board minutes or the staff report came to be used to record comments on policies not considered appropriate to Board decisions. Some topics that were at first considered taboo or suspect by some Directors even came, within a few years, to be stressed.

As an illustration, one of the most persistent and pervasive themes to emerge almost as soon as consultations began was the need for the Fund's members to pursue what are called "sound" fiscal and monetary policies in order to overcome or to avoid inflation. In the early years the extent to which the Fund could appropriately comment and give advice on a member's domestic policies had been seriously questioned by many Directors. In the years 1952–55, for example, several Directors queried the propriety of the Fund's calling attention to the importance of fiscal and monetary policies that would maintain stability, although from the outset some other Directors had believed that the Fund might comment on purely domestic matters. Agreement was eased by the understanding that no general precedents were being set. Moreover, it was recognized that comments from the Fund might be helpful to the authorities of some countries in putting through politically unpopular policies.

Almost immediately the occasion of the consultations was used as an opportunity for the Fund and its members to work out exchange reforms. An early example of this is the agreement reached on a new exchange rate for Paraguay during the 1952 consultation with that member. Paraguay proposed a rate which corresponded quite closely to recommendations made by the Fund's staff during the discussion preceding the consultation, and the Executive Directors agreed to the proposal.

THE PROCESS ESTABLISHED

By 1955 the pattern of consultations had become firmly established. Three distinct stages had evolved: (1) preliminary work by the staff, (2) discussions between representatives of the staff and of the member country, and (3) the consultation proper, i.e., the consideration by the Executive Board of the staff report on the discussions and the taking of a Board decision on the consultation if with an Article XIV member or with an Article VIII member that maintains exchange measures requiring the Fund's approval. No decision is taken on consultations with other Article VIII members (see below).

Preliminary work by the staff

The work of the staff proceeds according to a tentative schedule based on past experience with the particular country. The team selected generally consists of three or four professionals and a secretary. The professionals include staff members from the Area Department handling the country concerned, and from the Exchange and Trade Relations Department, although the latter is not usually involved in an Article VIII consultation. Staff members from the Fiscal Affairs Department and the Research Department may be on the team if matters relevant to these departments are to be taken up, and from the Legal Department if complex legal issues are at stake.

As a first step, the staff writes a background study of the member's economic situation and of its restrictive system. These background papers have become widely known as Part II of the Fund's consultation reports. For a few members much of the material included is available in published form. For most, however, technical discussions and policy reviews between the members and the staff result in reports and surveys with a considerable amount of information not found elsewhere. These reports contain a detailed description and analysis of internal and external economic developments and of the restrictions still in force. Systematic reviews of trends in production, of wage and price developments, of credit and monetary flows, and of the budget and fiscal situation are nearly always included. The main focus on the external side is usually the current balance of payments position and the short-run outlook for the balance of payments; but details of the magnitude and composition of exports and imports, of capital movements, of foreign indebtedness, and of foreign aid, are often included.

Differences in the situations of countries lead to variations in treatment. For example, when an exchange reform has taken place or is in process, the exchange system both before and after reform is usually described fully. Similarly, the issuance of a new long-term development plan has frequently been the occasion for a more thorough description of the country's development policies and their relation to its policies in the monetary, fiscal, and exchange fields.

As regards restrictions, the complete system—that is, all forms of restrictions, including those both within and outside the "approval" jurisdiction of the Fund—is described. Such broad coverage has been found necessary in order to relate the general level of restrictions to the balance of payments position of the country, and to the policies being used to equilibrate the balance of payments. Although the first consultations in 1952 required the use of general questionnaires to members in order to ascertain the complete nature of the restrictions actually being applied, these are no longer needed.

A preliminary version of the background paper is customarily sent to the member before discussions take place. Because of its comprehensiveness, Part II of the consultation report has proved a valuable source of information to all member governments interested in the member being consulted. At first, even Part II of a consultation report was only for the internal use of the Fund; now, however, these reports are supplied to the GATT and from time to time to some other international agencies, with the consent of the member country.

For some countries, where data have been scarce and available statistical series have not proved to be reliable indicators of significant economic trends, draft Part II reports have not been prepared in advance; sending questionnaires ahead of a staff mission has also not been found useful. In such instances the preparation of useful statistical tables has become a major concern of the mission, and has often necessitated extending the discussions or sending some staff members in advance of the policy discussions. Technical advice has also been given in the process of preparing such tables; such advice has sometimes resulted in the initiation of new statistical series or in arrangements for the Fund to give technical assistance to the member in the compilation of its statistics.

Preparations for discussions with the member include a draft agenda and a briefing paper. The latter, which is seen only by the staff concerned and the management, reviews the last consultation decision and any developments in the Fund's policy which may be of particular concern for the country being consulted, and suggests the main lines of inquiry for the forthcoming discussions, the emphasis to be placed on various subjects, and the attitudes that the staff proposes to adopt on the principal policy questions. The proposed agenda for the meetings and the briefing paper are approved by the Director of the Area Department concerned; by the Director of the Exchange and Trade Relations Department; by the Managing Director or his Deputy; and, where issues of concern to them are involved, by the Fiscal, Legal, Research, and Treasurer's Departments. The agenda is then forwarded to the member concerned.

Discussions with the member

The most important change in the consultation procedure since consultations were initiated in 1952 has been the shift in locale. Whereas in the beginning it was specified that as far as possible staff discussions with member governments should be held in Washington, such discussions today nearly always take place in the member country. The ostensible reasons for holding the discussions in Washington were the limited number of staff members available and, to some extent, the belief that the Fund should restrict expenditures in view of its low income and the budget deficits that prevailed during the early 1950's. One consequence of meetings being held in Washington was that the members tended to designate their Executive Directors or staff from their embassies in Washington to represent them, or to request that the discussions be held at the time of the Annual Meetings so that the Governors themselves or their technical advisors could attend.

The greatest disadvantage of conducting the discussions in Washington was the limited number of members' representatives who could be interviewed.

Moreover, where the representatives were Executive Directors or embassy staff, they had frequently not been in very close or recent contact with the policy-making authorities of their governments, and it was rarely possible for the Washington people to be supported by technicians from their home countries.

Furthermore, although a larger number of the Fund's staff members could attend discussions held in Washington, this advantage of acquainting more staff members with countries' problems was offset by the lack of opportunity to become well acquainted with the country itself and with a number of its officials. Also, the concentration of discussions about the time of the Annual Meetings could not help but adversely affect the efficiency of the staff; 11 of the 22 discussions held in Washington in 1953 and 10 of the 14 in 1954 took place near the time of the Annual Meeting. Subsequent experience confirmed that holding the discussions abroad reduced the burden on the senior officials of the country as well. And it permitted the Fund's staff to work closely with the country so as to produce a more authoritative report.

Consequently, although the practice of holding the staff discussions in Washington was at first closely followed, it died under the weight of its disadvantages and of a growing awareness of the usefulness of visits by Fund staff missions to member countries. While two thirds of the staff discussions with members in 1952 and 1953 were held in Washington, the proportion dropped sharply over the next three years, amounting to about one fourth in 1956. In all succeeding years, no more than two a year have been held in Washington and then, as a rule, because of unusual circumstances.

Thus, one of the features of the Fund's consultations which has come to differentiate them from the annual review techniques of a number of other international organizations is that they rely more heavily on regular staff visits to the countries concerned, and on intensive discussions in the field with officials of the member countries.

Staff teams usually stay in the country for about two weeks, but there is a wide range, from as little as four or five working days to as much as five weeks.

The member's team for the discussions includes representatives of the financial agencies of the government, e.g., the treasury, the central bank, and economic ministries; the Executive Director elected or appointed by the member often attends as an observer. These discussions have taken many forms, depending upon the problems facing the government, the working practices of the officials, the availability of statistical and other information, and the staff's familiarity with the situation. Discussions in some countries are more formal than in others. Sometimes the Minister of Finance or the Governor of the central bank attends; but in any event, the staff usually interviews these persons and often has informal discussions with them on matters outside the consultation proper. Sometimes the staff is received by the Prime Minister or the Head of State.

The staff team may also, with the knowledge and consent of the government, meet members of the parliamentary opposition, the press, the business community, and labor representatives, although this varies with the circumstances and traditions of the country.

Usually the discussions begin with a systematic review of the country's economic situation. Then the discussions center on major policies—that is, policies to promote internal financial stability and equilibrium in the balance of payments and to facilitate economic growth. With regard to the restrictive system, the staff has usually sought to understand how the restrictions operate and their principal effects, and has given special emphasis to alternative measures for correcting balance of payments difficulties.

Generally, the staff prepares detailed minutes of the discussions which, after agreement with the government concerned, are used to prepare the report to the Executive Directors. This report, which includes an appraisal of the situation in the member country, has come to be known as Part I of the consultation report. Before being circulated to the Executive Directors, this report is reviewed by a committee of representatives from several departments in the Fund and is approved by the management. During the first few years of consultations, this committee discussed and approved both the preliminary papers and the final reports, but later the practice was developed of circulating to the committee for comment only the drafts of final reports. Although the opinions expressed by the staff in the reports are attributed to the staff team, the management and staff collectively are responsible for the appraisal and the recommended draft decision.

The length of the report varies considerably, depending upon the information available and the analytic techniques that can be used effectively; in general, the more sophisticated the arsenal of economic measures available to the authorities, the longer is the description of the actual policy measures selected by the authorities, and the reasons for such choice. Part I is usually much shorter than Part II. The report is normally completed within a few weeks after the return of the mission to Washington.

Consultation in the Board

After the report has been approved, it is circulated to the Board and scheduled for consideration after a period—usually about four weeks—which permits Executive Directors to be in contact with their governments. Most consultations take only one meeting, although some have required two or more.

The decision taken by the Board represents the official views of the Fund. The Board may confirm or disagree with the views of the staff, which may have been informally communicated earlier to the country's representatives. This procedure has allowed the staff freedom while in the field to appraise or comment informally and unofficially on a country's policies or economic situation, without the need to obtain prior approval by the Board for the views expressed.

The Board's decisions have varied from country to country and from time to time. Most decisions give a capsule description of the economic situation and the current policies of the member; they sometimes indicate that excellent progress has been made, and at other times recommend that policies be changed. There is also usually a statement of the Fund's views regarding the member's monetary and fiscal policies as they relate to the country's internal financial stability and to balance of payments position. Finally, the decisions regularly comment on the country's exchange system, exchange restrictions, discrimination, and use of bilateral payments agreements. Changes in exchange systems and recent relaxations or eliminations of restrictions have often been welcomed; frequently further action has been suggested. The Fund's views on the general level of and the possibility of removing quantitative restrictions and other devices which impede the free flow of trade and payments are also included.

The decision is transmitted to the member. There is no formal follow-up. But when the country subsequently encounters serious payments problems, or requests the use of the Fund's resources, or undertakes exchange reform, further contacts take place. And in the next consultation, a review is undertaken of the progress made toward implementing the decision adopted in the previous one.

The length of time involved in the consultation process is one of the reasons, if not the principal one, why the number of consultations completed every year has been less than the number of Article XIV members, and also less than the number of Article VIII members (after they began to consult in April 1961). If a consultation has not been held with a member in the course of a given consultation year, a special effort is usually made to consult early in the following year. Details of the number of consultations held in relation to the number of members, from April 1, 1952 to March 31, 1966, are given in Table 7 at the end of this chapter.

CONSULTATIONS UNDER ARTICLE VIII

The success of consultations under Article XIV was clearly reflected in the institution in 1960 of similar consultations under Article VIII, although these are not required by the Articles. The staff suggested that such consultations should be held because they provided a method whereby the Fund could maintain contact with the officials of the countries concerned and provided also the machinery for collaboration on international monetary problems. Thoroughgoing annual reviews of economic policies were useful both to members and to the Fund. The Directors agreed on the usefulness of consultations. Some even went so far as to state that the removal of restrictions on payments created a new degree of interdependence among members and that consultations with the Fund were therefore just as important as when restrictions had been widespread. Mr. Southard stated that the U.S. Government, which had never been under Article XIV and hence not previously required to consult the Fund, was willing to consult annually with the Fund under Article VIII.

After some discussion, however, it was agreed that consultations under Article VIII would not end in formal decisions by the Board. That the Fund should not come to some conclusion about the affairs of the member concerned was in line with the philosophy that consultations under Article VIII were voluntary on the part of the member.

The Board thereupon took the following decision implementing consultations under Article VIII:

> If members at any time maintain measures which are subject to Sections 2 and 3 of Article VIII, they shall consult with the Fund with respect to the further maintenance of such measures. Consultations with the Fund under Article VIII are not otherwise required or mandatory. However, the Fund is able to provide technical facilities and advice, and to this end, or as a means of exchanging views on monetary and financial developments, there is great merit in periodic discussions between the Fund and its members even though no questions arise involving action under Article VIII. Such discussions would be planned between the Fund and the member, including agreement on place and timing, and would ordinarily take place at intervals of about one year.[2]

Consultations under Article VIII represented a new procedure that had not been contemplated at Bretton Woods. Agreement to such consultations reflected the widely held belief that the Fund's Article XIV consultations had been most helpful to members and that similar discussions with countries under Article VIII would be useful both to the Fund and to the members concerned.

In 1961–62—the first year of the new Article VIII regime—consultations under that Article were held with eleven members; these included the first consultations held with Canada, the United States, and El Salvador. The staff discussions, as in the case of Article XIV consultations, involved visits by staff missions to the capitals of the countries concerned.

In the next few years, the Article VIII consultations were found to be increasingly useful as, together with those under Article XIV, they enabled the Fund to inform itself of policy problems and attitudes throughout the world, to appreciate more fully the peculiar circumstances and needs of individual countries, and to anticipate their payments problems. It is the belief of the Fund also that these consultations serve to make members' policies more responsive to the aims of the international community.

---

[2] E.B. Decision No. 1034-(60/27), June 1, 1960; below, Vol. III, p. 261.

THE PROCESS REAFFIRMED

Between the time when the consultations started in 1952 and the end of 1965, the membership of the Fund rose from 51 to 103, and the burden of work on the staff and on the Executive Directors increased proportionately. Therefore, when the Fund reviewed its procedures late in 1965 and early in 1966, it sought ways of reducing this burden. The staff put forward proposals for abbreviating Part I of the reports, and the Board made some suggestions for shortening its consideration of the reports. It was decided that Part I of the reports should be shortened; but the basic structure of the procedures was kept intact. The opening and closing sentences of Article XIV consultations, as agreed in 1952, were dropped; instead, a simple factual statement was to be made:

> This decision is taken by the Executive Directors in concluding the [*year*] consultations with [*member*], pursuant to Article XIV, Section 4, of the Articles of Agreement.

The staff now proposed that Article VIII consultations should put forward conclusions, but the Board decided against this.

Table 7. Fund Members by Article VIII or Article XIV Status, and Completed Consultations, April 1, 1952–March 31, 1966

Consultations Year (beginning April 1)	Number of Members at Beginning of Consultations Year: Total	Status Not Yet Notified	Article VIII Members	Article XIV Members [2]	Number of Completed Consultations [1]: During Year: Article XIV	During Year: Article VIII	During Year: Total	Cumulative Total
1952	51	—	7	44	35 [3]	—	35	35
1953	54	—	7	47	35	—	35	70
1954	55	—	9	46	34 [4]	—	34	104
1955	56	—	10	46	37	—	37	141
1956	58	—	10	48	36 [4]	—	36	177
1957	60	—	10	50	37 [5]	—	37	214
1958	65	—	10	55	38 [4]	—	38	252
1959	68	—	10	58	42 [4]	—	42	294
1960	68	—	10	58	44 [6]	—	44	338
1961	70	1	21	48	36 [4]	11	47	385
1962	76	3	21	52	38 [5]	14	52	437
1963	84	4	23	57	49 [5]	12	61	498
1964	102	12	25	65	40	22	62	560
1965	102	1	26	75	36	19	55	615

[1] A consultation is completed when the Board has discussed the staff report.

[2] Includes Venezuela for all years, although it did not have Article XIV restrictions and did not consult with the Fund during the years 1953–62.

[3] Includes a consultation with Germany, which did not become a member until August 1952, but excludes one with Southern Rhodesia in 1952, the only occasion on which the Board had a separate consultation with a nonmetropolitan territory.

[4] Includes two consultations with one member.

[5] Includes two consultations each with two members.

[6] Includes two consultations each with four members.

CHAPTER

12

Progress Toward Liberalization

Margaret G. de Vries

THE CONSULTATIONS PROCESS just described has become the principal instrument through which the Fund's policies on exchange restrictions have been implemented. These policies have varied a great deal—as have the Fund's policies in other fields—reflecting the ever-changing panorama of international economic and monetary conditions.

From 1946 to 1958, when external convertibility of European currencies was finally attained, the Fund's policies on restrictions were directed mainly toward the liberalization of the severe restrictions which were in force when the Fund was established. This chapter recounts the developments in those policies, and depicts also the international economic situation prevailing at the time they were formulated and which therefore influenced them. Three periods, of four to five years each, may be distinguished.

TIME PATH OF POLICY DEVELOPMENTS

The first period began in 1946, with the inception of the Fund, and lasted roughly through September 1949, when the realignment of currencies necessary to the lessening of the strict controls over international payments which prevailed after World War II took place. Apart from the working out of procedures and policies for handling multiple exchange rates, the Fund did relatively little during this period to reduce restrictions, its philosophy being that it was premature to press for any reduction.[1] Instead, it stressed to its members the importance of measures—such as exchange depreciation and domestic monetary policies—that would be likely to improve their payments positions over the longer run and would lay the basis for an *eventual* reduction of restrictions.

[1] *Annual Report, 1947*, pp. 2, 35, and *1948*, p. 30.

In the second period, 1950 to 1954, the international economic climate became propitious for some reduction of restrictions, and there was a tremendous upsurge in the Fund's activities. In March 1950 the *First Annual Report on Exchange Restrictions* appeared. Later in that year, in Torquay, England, the Fund participated in the consultations with several of the contracting parties to the GATT. The Fund's own consultations under Article XIV were begun in 1952, and within a few years were being hailed as successful points of contact between the Fund and its members. Nevertheless, the Fund continued to postulate its policies as regards restrictions on the premise that it was preferable not to push its members too hard. Recognizing that relaxation of restrictions and establishment of convertibility could be brought about only gradually, its principal aims during this period were to ensure the maintenance of the then-current momentum in the relaxation of restrictions and to prevent their reintensification.[2]

By 1955 it was evident that the abnormal postwar economic difficulties of European countries had come to an end. Large gains had been made both in productivity and in the attainment of internal financial stability. Still a third phase of the Fund's policy as regards restrictions began. Although many countries relaxed restrictions, the Fund, aware of their cautious attitudes, urged them to go further, and especially to reduce discriminatory restrictions. Western European countries undertook, under the aegis of the OEEC liberalization program, to free from restrictions most of the trade and payments which they conducted among themselves. But the Fund, anxious to hasten the convertibility of European currencies into gold and U.S. dollars, repeatedly stressed the need for an equal lessening of restrictions against imports from the dollar area. In 1955, as European countries began to take steps to widen further the transferability of their currencies, the Fund, eager to obtain greater multilateralization of world payments, also took a decision calling upon its members to reduce their use of bilateral payments agreements. By the end of 1958, external convertibility of the major European currencies had been attained.

AN INCUBATING PERIOD, 1946–49

In 1946 all the Fund's members except El Salvador, Guatemala, Mexico, Panama, and the United States had opted for the transitional arrangements of Article XIV. Although there were wide differences in the nature and severity of the restrictions maintained, most countries applied an impressive array of restrictions to virtually all foreign exchange transactions. The underlying assumption of their exchange controls was that all payments were prohibited unless specifically authorized.

[2] *Annual Report, 1955*, p. 77.

Troubled economies

These restrictions mirrored the troubled economic conditions of many countries after World War II. Supply fell very much short of demand. In the countries whose economic position had been seriously impaired by the war, the amounts of goods needed for reconstruction and to meet minimum consumption requirements were in excess of their limited productive capacity. Much of the current output was being used to repair the damage and deficiencies caused by the war. Demand, however, was high as incomes were inflated by intense economic activity, including reconstruction, which did not result immediately in a flow of consumer goods. There was also a latent inflationary pressure in most countries as a result of wartime finance, the resultant build-up of liquid funds in the hands of consumers, and the sizable pent-up demand.

In these circumstances, the countries concerned, especially in Europe but also in parts of Asia and the Middle East, felt compelled to ration available supplies of domestically produced goods. The urgency of conserving foreign exchange for the most essential imports necessitated the continuation and even the extension of heavy wartime exchange restrictions. Of the alternative methods available for limiting the demand for imports, quantitative import controls and exchange restrictions appeared to most of these countries to be preferable to exchange depreciation. The disequilibrium in their balance of payments, while large, was considered to be due more to special factors connected with the war, which would in time be overcome, than to fundamental disparities in costs and prices.

Another reason for restrictions was that the pattern of world trade that emerged was seriously unbalanced. In 1947 this imbalance, which was soon to be generally referred to as the world dollar shortage, had forced many countries to change the character of their restrictions. Whereas restrictions had in general been placed on imports of certain goods—e.g., nonessential and luxury items—rather than on imports from specific currency areas, restrictions during 1947 were in most instances imposed with the intentions of reducing an existing or prospective deficit in U.S. dollars and of safeguarding gold and dollar reserves.

In many Latin American countries the huge demand for imports also necessitated the intensification of exchange restrictions after World War II, even though foreign exchange receipts were high. Their large demand for imports was a result partly of deferred wartime demand and partly of postwar inflation. In several Eastern European countries exchange restrictions, although severe, were themselves subordinated to even more direct and comprehensive state intervention through state-trading and barter arrangements.

Deciding on an approach

In these early years, the Fund recognized that it was not possible to effect any considerable relaxation of restrictions. The Executive Board, in fact, discussed the general problem of reducing exchange restrictions chiefly in the course of agreeing on its Annual Reports; hence, these Reports provide an indication of the Fund's attitudes during these years.

The Reports for 1946–49 were not on the whole optimistic about the possibilities for the early elimination, or even the reduction, of exchange restrictions. The severe shortages of goods of all kinds in most countries were believed to make exchange restrictions on current transactions unavoidable for some time, in order to ensure that limited foreign exchange reserves could finance imports to meet the most essential requirements for consumption and reconstruction. The first Report did, however, strike a note of optimism over the prospects of an early restoration of sterling convertibility for current transactions under the terms of the Anglo-American Financial Agreement of 1945, and the United Kingdom's intention to make agreements for early settlement of accumulated sterling balances. The Report noted that these developments would help in restoring the convertibility of currencies and freedom in current transactions in accordance with the provisions of the Fund's Agreement.[3]

By the terms of the Anglo-American Financial Agreement, the Government of the United Kingdom had undertaken that after July 15, 1947, unless an extension were agreed with the Government of the United States, it would impose no restrictions upon payments and transfers for current transactions and would permit the current sterling receipts of sterling area countries to be used in any currency area without discrimination.

During the months preceding that date the United Kingdom took a series of steps to extend the degree of transferability of sterling already existing and to fulfill its convertibility commitments; it announced from time to time the relaxation of certain wartime restrictions on the transferability of sterling. By July 1947 these arrangements covered the greater part of the trading world, negotiations being unfinished with only a few countries. Convertibility for current sterling did not, of course, obligate the United Kingdom to remove all trade and exchange controls. Exports and imports were still subject to license, and controls were retained on capital movements and on the large sterling balances which had accumulated during and immediately after the war.

Nonetheless, the deficit with the dollar area both of the United Kingdom and of the rest of the sterling area was growing as a result of the large rate of dollar expenditure by the sterling area as a whole. This deficit, the greater part being attributable to the deficit of the United Kingdom itself, was occasioning large use of reserves and dollar credits.[4]

So great was the drain on its exchange resources that on August 21, 1947 the United Kingdom, by agreement with the United States, withdrew the facility of

[3] *Annual Report, 1946,* p. 12.
[4] *Annual Report, 1948,* p. 31.

freely transferring sterling from Transferable Accounts to American or Canadian Accounts, and at the same time eliminated Canadian Transferable Accounts. In effect, although sterling remained transferable over a wide area, the convertibility of sterling into dollars was suspended.

ESTABLISHING THE PRECONDITIONS

The Fund's attitude toward the difficulties encountered by its members in relaxing restrictions and establishing convertibility was mixed. On the one hand, the Fund was aware that the balance of payments problems of its members were not easy of solution. But on the other, the Fund did not wish its members to abandon the objective of eventually freeing their international transactions from restrictions. It was unrealistic for the Fund to call for the abandonment of restrictions; but it was capitulation for the Fund to succumb entirely to adverse economic conditions. In these circumstances the Fund began to work out policies which stressed the need for members to lay the proper foundation for a future relaxation of restrictions. This philosophy of *establishing the preconditions* for relaxation of restrictions was exemplified by the remarks of the Managing Director, Mr. Gutt, to the Governors as he presented to them the Annual Report for 1947. The Report had been approved by the Executive Directors before failure of the attempt to restore convertibility of sterling; although the Directors considered modifying the Report to take account of this development, they decided that, instead of doing so, the Managing Director should make reference to it in his presentation of the Report to the Governors. In so doing, he commented on the difficult postwar economic and political problems, the Marshall Plan proposals of the U.S. Government, and the failure of sterling convertibility. His attitude toward restrictions was as follows:

> I have indicated . . . how much, in the monetary field as in others, the disruption of the war still makes itself felt. But that is no reason for abandoning or modifying the objectives of the Fund. Rather, concerted effort must be made to establish the conditions under which these objectives can be attained. A premature attempt to force the acceptance of exchange and trade practices suited for a balanced world economy can do much harm and even endanger the attainment of these objectives.[5]

The Annual Report for 1947 had begun to foreshadow in greater detail the main features of what would become the Fund's approaches to exchange restrictions for the next several years. First, the Fund's attitude toward restrictions would not be doctrinaire; in particular, account would be taken of the differing circumstances of member countries. Second, the criteria for judging the need for restrictions were to be whether these were warranted by balance

[5] *Summary Proceedings, 1947*, p. 10.

of payments considerations and whether they had harmful effects on the balances of payments of other countries. Finally, for the foreseeable future, emphasis was to be placed on the necessity of establishing the preconditions for a return to convertibility and the elimination of restrictions.[6] In the 1948 Annual Report the Executive Directors reiterated that the British experience in failing to restore convertibility showed that convertibility could succeed only when the underlying conditions were favorable to a system of multilateral trade and payments.[7]

Characteristics of the preconditions

The preconditions on which the Fund placed emphasis were the restoration of productive capacity, the establishment of a better pattern of international payments, and elimination of inflation through proper credit and fiscal policies. What was especially required was an expansion of exports in general and in particular an enhanced flow of exports in the directions most likely to diminish dollar deficits. Preference should be given to investment which would have relatively prompt effects upon the balance of payments. An improvement in the capital accounts of many countries, while not a prerequisite for the removal of restrictions from current transactions, was also considered important for strengthening their balance of payments. Changes in international indebtedness had aggravated the payments problems of several trading countries, especially those in Western Europe. In less than forty years, the United Kingdom, for example, had passed from the position of leading international creditor to that of the largest international debtor.

It also became apparent that another essential condition for the relaxation of restrictions and the restoration of currency convertibility was some building up of the non-dollar world's monetary reserves. Most of the members of the Fund that had taken advantage of the transitional arrangements did not, in 1947–48, have reserves adequate to enable them to meet large current deficits for even a short period, or to meet persistent deficits, even of a moderate size, for an extended period. By 1948, in their Annual Report, the Directors were also suggesting that some adjustments of exchange rates might sooner or later be necessary before adequate progress could be made.[8]

The Fund was also mindful that the elimination of exchange restrictions would be illusory if direct trade controls were to take their place. The mere substitution for exchange restrictions of other measures, such as direct quantitative restrictions or excessive tariffs, would not reduce the magnitude of existing restraints on international trade. Moreover, the Fund recognized that while international organizations could make an important contribution in helping to achieve these

[6] *Annual Report, 1947*, p. 35.

[7] *Annual Report, 1948*, p. 32.

[8] *Ibid.*, p. 23.

preconditions, basically it was national policies that would determine the kind of world economy which would ultimately emerge.

Dangers of prolonged restrictions

Despite the continuing consensus that early relaxation of exchange restrictions could not be expected, there was, by 1949, some change of tone in the Fund's pronouncements on restrictions. The dangers of a prolonged period of severe restrictions and inconvertible currencies began to be perceived. In discussing the transitional period, the Annual Report for 1949, for example, drew attention to the Board's view that if the earliest reasonable opportunity was not seized to modify restrictive policies, the difficulty of resuming trade under more normal conditions would be greatly aggravated and world trade would tend more and more to be conducted with inconvertible currencies on the basis of bilateral bargains.[9]

At the Annual Meeting, 1949, the Board of Governors adopted a procedure for considering selected topics, on the basis of chapters in the Annual Reports, in separate discussion groups or committees. The discussion groups at the 1949 Meeting covered two topics: (1) exchange and monetary policy, and (2) exchange restrictions and monetary reserves. The Managing Director, who chaired both discussions, noted in his report on the second discussion that the Governors generally subscribed, but with differing emphasis, to the ideas expressed by the Executive Directors in the Annual Report, that early removal of restrictions could not be expected because of difficult payments problems and low reserves, but that the improvement in the underlying economic situation over the last few years, though inadequate, provided an environment for progress toward convertibility.[10]

PROGRESS FORESEEN, 1950–54

The first signs of improving world economic conditions had appeared by 1950. The financial aid provided to European countries by the United States through the Marshall Plan had immensely facilitated the reconstruction of the economies of these countries. Production throughout Western Europe had greatly increased, exportable goods from the deficit countries had become more plentiful, and the abnormal need for imports for reconstruction had become much smaller. Inflationary pressures had, in most countries, also become more moderate. Lastly, the devaluations of September 1949 had corrected many distortions in international prices. These improvements had made it possible for some countries to achieve equilibrium in their over-all balances of payments, although not in their dollar accounts. This equilibrium was, however, maintained only with the

[9] *Annual Report, 1949*, p. 30.
[10] *Summary Proceedings, 1949*, pp. 37–39.

support of import and exchange restrictions and, in several countries, of extraordinary external financial aid.

Some countries made a start toward freeing their trade and payments from restrictions, but in general, even after the devaluations of 1949, countries moved slowly in removing restrictions. Economists debated whether, in view of the "chronic dollar shortage," substantial liberalization of restrictions would ever be feasible. Some argued that the difference in productivity between European countries and the United States was deep-seated; structural changes, including modernization of industrial techniques, were required in the economies of European countries if they were to overcome their persistent dollar deficits. Others argued that European countries needed mainly to pursue orthodox monetary policies; they contended that, with the restoration—indeed the expansion—of European productive capacity, these countries need only attain internal financial stability to be able to earn sufficient dollars to cover their outgo in dollars.

First Exchange Restrictions Report

This was the situation when the Fund, in accordance with Article XIV, Section 4, issued the first of its Annual Reports on Exchange Restrictions. That Article states in part that "not later than three years after the date on which the Fund begins operations and in each year thereafter, the Fund shall report on the restrictions still in force under Section 2 of this Article," i.e., restrictions maintained under transitional arrangements. The three-year period ended on March 1, 1950.

The first Report was drafted by the Operations Department; the Exchange Restrictions Department, which was responsible for drafting subsequent reports, was not set up until March 1950. The Report was presented in two parts. The first consisted of a general account of the forms of exchange restrictions, some historical background, and the current situation and problems; the second part was a country-by-country description of the exchange restrictions maintained by Fund members under Article XIV. The same basic structure has been followed in all subsequent reports, although in later reports the first part omitted the description of forms of exchange restrictions and historical background, and was addressed more to changes during the past year and to the current situation. The second part has also changed over the years, both in form and in countries covered, a number of nonmember countries being included in the Reports after 1951 and all Article VIII members in Reports after 1955.

The first Exchange Restrictions Report reflected the Fund's awareness of the several factors which had, since World War II, necessitated the maintenance of restrictions, and the Fund's realization that, though some of the postwar economic disturbances had been brought under control, others were still in evidence.

By 1950, the factor with which the Fund had become most concerned was continued inflation. It was apparent that increased supplies for export would shortly be forthcoming as reconstruction was completed and productive facilities were restored. However, inflation could undermine those exports: it raised internal costs and caused products to be shifted from export markets to domestic consumption.

The Fund's policy, as exemplified by this Report, was postulated on two general considerations. One, relaxation of restrictions and the establishment of convertibility should be a *progressive* action over time. Member countries could undertake gradual programs of decontrol without incurring unnecessary risks. Three ways in which restrictions could be relaxed on a step-by-step basis were specified: by categories of international transactions, by particular foreign currencies, and by types of international payments.[11] Members proceeding along these lines could test their balance of payments positions by degrees and could appropriately time the next stage of their program to remove restrictions.

Two, actions of members were interdependent: the ability of one member to eliminate restrictions was often a function of the policies and actions of other members. In many instances, members had joint responsibilities if exchange restrictions were to be effectively reduced. For example, some countries could remove their restrictions only when the main currencies which they earned had become convertible. Hence there was a need for a coordinated program so that the policies and practices of every country would, to the maximum extent, assist rather than frustrate the efforts of others.[12]

The Executive Directors had indeed agreed, when they considered the draft of this Report, that a proper and useful role for the Fund was to assist its members *to work together* in eliminating restrictions: the Fund could contribute to the progress toward relaxation of restrictions by initiating, encouraging, and coordinating appropriate concerted action among its members. Some Directors had been specific: in their view, the Fund should, as necessary, consult member countries individually as to the measures which those maintaining restrictions might take, consider with creditor countries what they might do to assist the payments position of the debtors, help to work out the proper timing of actions, and examine the possibility of making Fund resources available to cushion the shocks for countries moving toward convertibility.

Intensified Fund efforts

A few months later, when the Annual Report for 1950 appeared, the Board further clarified its specific concerns. Although the improvement in the world economic situation had been substantial, many difficulties had still to be over-

[11] *First Annual Report on Exchange Restrictions* (1950), p. 35.
[12] *Ibid.*, pp. 36–37.

come before countries could, without facing serious risks, remove restrictions and assume the obligations of convertibility. Inflationary pressures had been brought under more effective control by many countries, but it remained to be seen whether the stability achieved could be maintained. The correction of international price distortions was far from complete. While the strengthening of reserves was progressing, it was too early to judge whether the increase in reserves was due to permanent factors or was just a temporary aftermath of the devaluations of 1949.

Along with its concern about inflation, the Fund was anxious that countries should improve their ability to compete in the U.S. market and expand their exports to the dollar area. The reasoning underlying this position was as follows: Both the staff and the Directors recognized that the dollar reserves of most Fund members were low. But they believed that, even more than reserves, members needed to improve their *current* dollar payments position. Mindful of the large loss of reserves suffered by the United Kingdom in mid-1947 when it had attempted to make sterling convertible, both staff and Directors were cognizant of the fact that even sizable reserves might be quickly dissipated if countries relaxed restrictions before they had obtained satisfactory balance in their *current* dollar accounts. Indeed, concern with the need for countries to strengthen their current dollar earnings led several members of the staff and some of the Directors to fear that the maintenance of protected markets at home and abroad, such as was possible through the intra-European payments arrangements then being organized, would provide outlets in Europe for relatively high-cost output. The dollar positions of European countries would, in that event, remain relatively weak.

In addition, in the Annual Report for 1950, the Board was somewhat more definite on the possibilities of removing restrictions. While recognizing that it could not press members too hard, it argued that greater progress in decontrol was feasible and should be made.[13] Regretting that the 1949 devaluations had not been followed by more freeing of trade and payments, the Board warned that waiting for convertibility until all obstacles in the path had been removed might become the most effective means of ensuring that the path would always remain blocked. The danger had to be recognized that the continuation of restrictions might create a situation in which some condition for convertibility would always be absent; thereby any effective move toward the relaxation of restrictions could always be prevented.

Pointing to the further disadvantages of continuing restrictions, the Board called attention to the way in which they supported high costs and prices in the countries using them, distorted the allocation of resources, reduced competitive ability, and discouraged private capital. Accordingly, the Fund intended to press

[13] *Annual Report, 1950*, pp. 55–69.

forward with a continuing examination of the need for, and the effects of, existing exchange restrictions in order to make sure that no reasonable opportunity for their removal was lost.

Restrictions on security grounds

Meanwhile, the Korean conflict, which broke out in June 1950, complicated the picture by introducing strategic and military considerations into the field of restrictions. In December 1950 the United States, for reasons of national security and international emergency, placed a virtual embargo on exports to certain Far Eastern destinations and froze assets and restricted payments in the United States of residents of the Chinese mainland and North Korea. In July 1951 Cuba introduced controls similar to those of the United States. As a way of rationing scarce supplies, many other countries introduced export controls, and these became increasingly important determinants of the composition, volume, and direction of international trade.

The imposition of these restrictions raised the issue of the Fund's authority over restrictions imposed not for economic or financial reasons but on security grounds. The view of the U.S. Executive Director was that the Articles of Agreement were not explicit, and that probably the Fund would not have to act; nonetheless, the United States had informed the Fund of its measures. The Board formally noted the actions of the United States and Cuba, and deferred judgment on the questions of the Fund's authority and of how it should be exercised.

In August 1952, after extensive consideration by the staff and by the Board, the Board took a decision to the effect that Article VIII, Section 2 (*a*), applies to *all* restrictions on current payments and transfers, irrespective of their motivation and the circumstances in which they are imposed. However, recognizing that the Fund does not provide a suitable forum for discussion of restrictions imposed solely for the preservation of national or international security, certain policy guidelines were formulated for such situations. First, when a member proposed to impose restrictions on security grounds, it was to notify the Managing Director, preferably in advance but ordinarily not later than thirty days afterward; such notification was to be circulated to the Executive Directors. The member could assume that the Fund had no objection to the imposition of the restrictions, unless the Fund informed the member otherwise within thirty days. Second, the Fund would thereafter review the restrictions periodically and reserve the right to modify or revoke, at any time, its approval or the effect of this approval on any restrictions that might have been imposed under it.[14] The Board applied this decision retroactively to the measures taken earlier by the United States and Cuba.

[14] E.B. Decision No. 144-(52/51), August 14, 1952; below, Vol. III, p. 257.

This procedure was to be followed again late in 1965 when the United Kingdom, by a series of steps, subjected to exchange control all transactions with Rhodesia. Beginning on November 11, 1965, following its unilateral declaration of independence, Rhodesia was excluded from the sterling area, all transfers of capital from the United Kingdom to Rhodesia were prohibited, a stop was placed on practically all current payments from the United Kingdom to Rhodesia, imports into the United Kingdom from Rhodesia were subjected to license and virtually prohibited, and no credit was to be allowed for U.K. exports to Rhodesia.[15] In accordance with the Board's decision in 1952, the United Kingdom informed the Fund of these measures as measures solely related to the preservation of national security.

TIME TO LESSEN RESTRICTIONS

By the end of 1950, the Fund recognized that some of the essential characteristics of the problem of exchange restrictions were being altered as the largest trading countries diverted an increased proportion of their productive efforts to rearmament. For many countries, the problem had become more one of shortage of supplies and less one of inability to finance foreign expenditures. Export controls were becoming increasingly important in determining the pattern of world trade and payments. Greater attention was being given to the obtaining of strategic commodities and raw materials. Some international agreements were being worked out to ration these commodities.

At the same time the Fund continued to press for a reduction of restrictions. It was noted that during the year 1950, before the Korean hostilities, there had been a remarkable improvement in the world payments situation, especially vis-à-vis the United States, and an accelerated increase in the gold and dollar exchange reserves of countries other than the United States. The new security considerations were regarded as essentially independent of balance of payments requirements. The Fund continued to believe that the general improvement in the balance of payments positions and prospects of most of its members, stemming at least partly from the Korean crisis, justified a relaxation of restrictions, especially of discriminatory ones. Therefore, countries limiting imports of available goods for financial or protectionist reasons might well be able to relax or remove restrictions on imports despite the need for emergency measures on exports.

Not only was it feasible for countries with improved balance of payments conditions to relax restrictions, but it was in their interest as well. Relaxation of restrictions would increase the quantity of goods available for domestic consumption, and hence restrain inflation, and would permit a more economic use of resources.

---

[15] *Seventeenth Annual Report on Exchange Restrictions* (1966), pp. 588–91.

These arguments, as expressed in the Fund's public statements, reflected the concern of the Managing Director and the Governors during the Fifth Annual Meeting, held in Paris in September 1950, just three months after the outbreak of the Korean conflict. A committee of Governors was again set up to consider the Directors' views on exchange restrictions as expressed in the Annual Report and also in the first Exchange Restrictions Report. The Governor for the United States, Mr. Snyder, stressed the dangers of maintaining exchange restrictions indefinitely, their tendency to perpetuate themselves, and the desirability of the Fund's persisting in its efforts to promote relaxation of restrictions or at least to prevent unnecessary tightening, even though new difficulties would arise out of rearmament. The Governor for the United Kingdom, Mr. Gaitskell, again indicated that there was little chance of the United Kingdom's removing restrictions or dropping exchange control as a whole, but stated that the United Kingdom would remove all unnecessary restrictions. The Governor for Belgium, Mr. Frère, pointed out that the necessity for restrictions was a consequence of inadequate monetary and credit policies, and that it was idle to talk about removing restrictions if inflation was not dealt with first. The Managing Director, noting that the first Exchange Restrictions Report had been drafted before the Korean crisis, repeated in presenting the Annual Report his alarm concerning the dangers of inflation. He also expressed worry about increased restrictions as a result of the Korean hostilities. These views, except for those of the Governor for the United Kingdom, were reflected in the Report of the committee.[16]

Following its Fifth Annual Meeting, the Fund participated in the consultations held in connection with the Fifth (Torquay) Session of the CONTRACTING PARTIES to the GATT on recent changes in the import policies of Australia, Ceylon, Chile, India, New Zealand, Pakistan, Southern Rhodesia, and the United Kingdom.[17] The Fund's reports for these consultations similarly reflected a hardening of its attitude toward prolonged restrictions. These reports had concluded that it would be feasible for several countries in the sterling area to relax their restrictions, a recommendation resisted by those countries.

A START TOWARD RELAXATION

For the first time there was progress toward lessened restrictions. In Europe, after the European Payments Union (EPU) had been established, liberalization of both intra-European trade and transactions in invisibles started to move forward.[18] For example, in regard to the liberalization of intra-European visible

[16] *Summary Proceedings, 1950*, pp. 44–45.

[17] The first such consultation in which the Fund participated was on South Africa's import policy at the Fourth (Geneva) Session in the spring of 1950.

[18] Details are given in Frederic Boyer and J. P. Sallé, "The Liberalization of Intra-European Trade in the Framework of OEEC," *Staff Papers*, Vol. IV (1954–55), pp. 179–216.

trade, OEEC members agreed in 1950 to take measures for the progressive elimination of restrictions on nongovernmental imports from other members and to provide for the automatic allocation of foreign exchange to pay for such imports. This relaxation was originally (from December 15, 1949) applied to 50 per cent of imports on private account from other OEEC countries, using the year 1948 as a base. From October 4, 1950, the percentage was raised to 60 (with exceptions for certain countries); these percentages were calculated separately for each of three categories—food and feeding stuffs, raw materials, and manufactured goods. It was proposed that the 60 per cent liberalization requirement be raised, by February 1, 1951, to 75 per cent of all nongovernmental imports from participants regardless of category.

The OEEC countries varied in their ability to achieve these goals. Italy and Belgium, which had become creditors to the EPU, had, by the end of 1951, freed from restrictions commodities which in 1948 had formed over 90 per cent of their total imports on private account from other OEEC countries. But France and the United Kingdom, which had accumulated considerable deficits with the EPU, were forced during 1951–52 to reintroduce many of their import restrictions: by measures taken at the end of 1951, the United Kingdom reduced its percentage of liberalized imports to 44, and France in early 1952 again subjected all OEEC imports to quantitative restrictions.

Despite this setback, some European countries began to increase the amount of their imports not only from each other but from the dollar area as well. Some countries in the sterling area also expanded their imports, including imports from the dollar area. India, in March 1951, doubled the value of import licenses issued for the first half of 1951 and extended the validity of licenses to the end of the year. Both India and the United Kingdom placed additional raw materials under "world open general license," allowing their unrestricted import from any country. The same trend toward attempting to increase imports and relax restrictions also occurred in the Western Hemisphere and in some countries in the Middle and Far East.[19] Canada abolished its exchange control system on December 14, 1951. Some of the easing of restrictions in 1950 and 1951 took the form of formal removal or relaxation of restrictions. Much, however, was done by administrative action within existing control mechanisms: more licenses for imports were granted, for example, and some goods were freed from licensing requirements.

The Fund saw these developments as indications that the acceptance of restrictions as more or less unavoidable and well-nigh permanent features of the international economic scene was at least being challenged. Anticipating important further developments, the Fund noted that the distinction between "hard"

[19] *Second Annual Report on Exchange Restrictions* (1951), pp. 31–32.

and "soft" currencies had been greatly narrowed and suggested that this should lay the basis for a reduction of restrictions, and especially of discrimination. The Fund stressed an international approach to the relaxation of restrictions, as against uncoordinated and self-defeating national action.[20]

It was nonetheless apparent from the first round of the Fund's consultations under Article XIV, beginning in March 1952, that dependence on restrictions was still widespread. Most members contended that they continued to need restrictions in order to restrain aggregate import demand. The inconvertibility of many currencies, the inadequacy of reserves, the fear of capital flight, and the persistence of dollar deficits in balances of payments were repeatedly mentioned as reasons. Moreover, many members had come to regard the diminution of inflationary pressures as a very important condition for the removal of restrictions. They recognized that external balance, and particularly balance with the dollar area, could not be achieved unless the prices for their exports were competitive and unless their domestic industries could compete with imported commodities.

Thus the Fund, while recognizing the existence of other factors which still necessitated restrictions, retained its previously expressed conviction that further action in the monetary and fiscal fields was especially important if restrictions were to be reduced. Specific reference was made to monetary and fiscal policies in about two thirds of the decisions of the Executive Board in the 1952 consultations.[21]

RETENTION QUOTAS

The nature of the problem

As supplies of goods increased, export markets gradually became more competitive. Countries were especially anxious to penetrate the heretofore difficult dollar market, especially in the United States. Hence, in the early 1950's another problem suddenly emerged, which was just as suddenly to disappear by 1954–55. This was the problem of "retention quotas." Exporters in many Western European countries were allowed to retain specified proportions of their earnings of convertible currencies, and sell them or use them to import from the dollar area commodities that could be sold profitably (usually at premium prices) in the exporter's country, where their supply was limited by discriminatory import restrictions.

There were two kinds of retention quotas, according to purpose: to foster direct exports or to promote indirect trade. The first was relatively simple in concept and operation. An exporter was induced to sell goods to the dollar area

[20] *Ibid.*, pp. 19–21.

[21] *Fourth Annual Report on Exchange Restrictions* (1953), p. 12.

in return for special privileges: either he could retain some of the exchange earned and sell it in a premium market or he could use such exchange to purchase imported goods which he could sell at a substantial profit. The second kind of retention quota, to boost indirect trade, had been devised to keep transit trade going in the presence of adverse conditions. Transit trade, by which traders in one country sell goods originating in another country to a third country, had tended to come to an end because of the absence of convertibility. Traders could not buy goods in a hard currency country for resale (presumably at a profit) in a soft currency country; the exchange control authorities in the trader's country would not make hard currency available for such purchases. The opposite type of transit trade transaction (buying in a soft currency country and selling in a hard currency country) would have been attractive to the exchange control authorities, but there was no profit in it for the trader at the official exchange rate.

Retention quotas made transit trade possible in these circumstances. A trader could get a license to use hard currency for the purchase of goods to be sold in a soft currency country provided that the hard currency required had been obtained as the result of a previous transit transaction effected in the opposite direction. The earlier one (sometimes called the "first leg of a switch transaction") might entail a loss; but the latter transaction (sometimes called the "second leg") yielded a profit. As the combination was attractive only if the profit on the second leg more than offset any loss on the first, the dealer who completed the unprofitable first leg of the transaction was given the right to retain part of the hard currency obtained in order to use it for the second leg. This right might or might not be negotiable. The reason why the authorities of the transit trader's country were interested in this kind of deal was that the part of the hard currency proceeds of which they demanded surrender helped to increase their hard currency holdings.

Although the Fund's staff had been concerned about retention quotas as early as 1947, it was only later, when the practice began to spread, that they became troublesome. A survey by the staff in 1952 had indicated that retention quotas were in use at least in Austria, Denmark, Finland, France, Germany, Greece, Iceland, Indonesia, Italy, Japan, the Netherlands, Norway, Sweden, Turkey, and Yugoslavia. As the Executive Board began consultations with individual countries, early in 1952, it became apparent that retention quotas were symptoms of a wider problem and that it would be desirable for the Fund to formulate a general approach to their removal. However, some countries had already indicated to the Fund that they could not see their way clear to removing such practices unless such removal was part of a general action by several countries; the Board therefore deferred any decision regarding these practices pending an over-all study.

The analysis by the staff revealed several dangers in the use of retention quotas and similar arrangements. A retention quota for the purpose of expanding direct exports was a partial *de facto* devaluation, as it made possible a cut in the price of the export product. Such devaluation might set off a chain of competitive actions. Retention quotas for transit trade were even more worrisome. Hard currency earnings were channeled from the soft currency country in which the goods originated to the country whose trader effected the final sale. The commodities marketed competed advantageously in the hard currency market with the same goods sold in that market by the original producer, since the transit trader could afford to accept a loss which the direct exporter could not. Trade was diverted, by an intermediary, from its normal channel direct from the country of production to the country of consumption; and the intermediary, not the country of production, received the precious dollar earnings.

Taking action

The importance of the retention quota problem at the time prompted the Board of Governors, at its Seventh Annual Meeting in September 1952 in Mexico City, to adopt a resolution to the effect that the Fund should make a special study of dollar retention quotas and similar practices in member countries, and make recommendations. This study was to take into account the situations which give rise to these practices, their magnitude in each country, the methods used for their application, their impact on other members of the Fund, and possible alternative measures.[22]

In judging these practices, the staff, while taking into account the point of view of the individual countries using them, employed primarily international criteria: Did they cause undue harm to the economic interests of other members? What implications did they have for international monetary cooperation? What were the consequences of these devices for existing exchange rates? Were they likely to shorten the period of inconvertibility? Essentially the staff's findings were that retention quotas constituted a break with the principle of unitary rates, that they did not add significant flexibility to the exchange rate system of the countries concerned, and that they did not help to achieve convertibility or a substantial relaxation of restrictions. Accordingly, it was suggested that the Fund should seek the simultaneous removal of these practices by all countries.

The Executive Board had considerable difficulty in agreeing on a course of action. The Directors from those countries that were condemning retention quotas and similar practices argued that such practices involved competitive exchange depreciation, undermined otherwise appropriate exchange rates, encouraged unfair commercial practices, and resulted in diverting dollar earnings from already dollar-scarce countries. On the other hand, the Directors from those countries that were using the practices argued that the real problem was the

[22] *Summary Proceedings, 1952,* pp. 169–70.

general dollar shortage and the fact that some countries had over-all balance of payments equilibrium while others did not. Because of the inconvertibility of currencies, the former could not use their surpluses in one currency to settle deficits in another. Meanwhile, retention quotas were useful parts of dollar export promotion programs which helped to expand dollar earnings and made the export business competitive.

This difference of view made it necessary for the Board to give intensive consideration to numerous drafts of a decision. On May 4, 1953, the following decision was taken, without dissent but with one abstention:

> In concluding consultations on restrictions on current payments and transfers as required under Article XIV of the Fund Agreement, the Fund postponed consideration of retention quotas and similar practices through which some members have sought to improve their earnings of specific currencies. The Fund has now examined these practices more fully than was possible at the consultations referred to above. The Fund has extended this examination to cover the terms of reference of the resolution adopted on September 9, 1952, by the Board of Governors, and has come to the following conclusions:
>
> 1. Members should work toward and achieve as soon as feasible the removal of these retention quotas and similar practices, particularly where they lead to abnormal shifts in trade which cause unnecessary damage to other countries. Members should endeavor to replace these practices by more appropriate measures leading to currency convertibility.
>
> 2. The Fund will enter into consultation with each of the members concerned with a view to agreeing on a program for the implementation of 1 above, including appropriate attention to timing of any action which may be decided upon.
>
> 3. The Fund does not object to those practices which, by their nature, can be regarded as devices designed solely to simplify the administration of official exchange allocations.[23]

Subsequently the Executive Board considered the retention quotas of several European countries, making suggestions where they might be reduced. During later 1953 and early 1954 the use of retention quotas declined substantially and no longer presented such an acute problem as they had a year or two earlier. They were abolished in France, Germany, the Netherlands, Sweden, and Turkey. In March 1955 Japan reduced its use of the practice.

CONVERTIBILITY OF EUROPEAN CURRENCIES CONSIDERED

Prospects for sterling convertibility

By the early 1950's the establishment by the United Kingdom of convertibility for sterling had come to be regarded by many as a necessary condition for the

[23] E.B. Decision No. 201-(53/29), May 4, 1953; below, Vol. III, p. 258.

introduction of convertibility by other countries where economic conditions were already favorable. Much attention, therefore, centered on the prospects for making the pound sterling convertible.

After the abortive attempt in 1947, no consideration was given to the problem of restoring sterling convertibility until the autumn of 1951, when the Conservative Party returned to power in the United Kingdom. A statement issued in London in January 1952 by the Conference of Commonwealth Finance Ministers following their discussions on the problems confronting the sterling area stated that "it is our definite objective to make sterling convertible and to keep it so." But convertibility was not imminent—rather a goal to be achieved gradually. "We intend to work towards that goal by progressive steps aimed at creating the conditions under which convertibility can be reached, and maintained." The statement noted that while the sterling area countries had the primary responsibility for creating the conditions required to reach this objective, the cooperation of other countries, especially countries in surplus, was imperative. No mention was made of the Fund or of any other international financial organization, such as the EPU.[24]

Discussions by the British Government and the Governments of the other Commonwealth countries about the prospects for convertibility were accelerated in 1952 and 1953. These discussions were more practical and pointed than those of the past: they were less in terms of whether convertibility ought to be established and more in terms of how and when the specific necessary conditions could be established and the forms which convertibility might take. Keen interest in the prospects for sterling convertibility was also expressed in meetings of the EPU and the OEEC.

In a communiqué issued at the end of the Commonwealth Economic Conference (attended by Prime Ministers) in December 1952, it was stated that the conference had agreed that it was important not only for the United Kingdom and the rest of the sterling area but also for the world that sterling should resume its full role as a medium of world trade and exchange. The communiqué reiterated that, while an integral part of any effective multilateral system was the restoration of the convertibility of sterling, this could only be achieved in progressive stages.

The stages were now made more explicit. Three conditions were outlined for the achievement of convertibility: (1) the continuing success of actions by the sterling Commonwealth countries themselves, (2) the adoption by trading nations of trade policies conducive to the expansion of world trade, and (3) the availability of adequate financial support through the Fund or otherwise.[25] Subsequent talks were held between the British Government and the new U.S. Administration

[24] *Third Annual Report on Exchange Restrictions* (1952), pp. 188–91.

[25] *Department of State Bulletin*, March 16, 1953, p. 399.

early in March 1953. It was agreed that while full multilateral trade and general convertibility of currencies were ultimate objectives, firm commitments on either side were then impossible.

Position of other European currencies

Meanwhile, the continental members of the OEEC had become somewhat disturbed at the prospect of sterling convertibility. They feared both that it might be established at the expense of the trade liberalization program of the OEEC and that it would mean the end of the EPU. Conceivably, a degree of convertibility might be established accompanied by the tightening of other restrictions. At the OEEC Ministerial Council Meeting held in Paris on March 23 and 24, 1953, the United Kingdom allayed these fears by supporting the consensus of the continental members that progress toward trade liberalization should proceed *pari passu* with progress toward convertibility.

During the first half of 1954, a number of official reports and statements discussed the need for, and possibilities of, establishing convertibility for several European currencies. In January the report of the U.S. Commission on Foreign Economic Policy (the Randall Commission) had stated that the general economic conditions prerequisite to currency convertibility were more nearly in prospect at that time than at any previous time since the war. The decision, the methods, the timetable, and the responsibility for introducing currency convertibility should rest with the countries concerned; the commission believed, however, that its recommendations on commercial policy and for strengthening the gold and dollar reserves of European countries, as their currencies became convertible, would assist these countries in removing restrictions.[26] These recommendations were subsequently approved by the President in his Message to the Congress on foreign economic policy on March 30. Also in March 1954 the U.S. and Canadian Ministers who had been members of the Joint United States-Canadian Committee on Trade and Economic Affairs welcomed the evidence of a desire in many countries to take decisive steps toward convertibility.[27]

Several European central banks, in the early months of 1954, pointed to the steps being taken toward convertibility.[28] On February 22, 1954, the Governor of the National Bank of Belgium, after emphasizing that convertibility required strict financial discipline, stated that the National Bank believed that Belgium had attained the necessary conditions for introducing convertibility of the Belgian franc. The Board of Governors of the Bank deutscher Länder stated that convertibility of the deutsche mark had already in large measure been established,

---

[26] U.S. Commission on Foreign Economic Policy, *Report to the President and the Congress* (January 1954), pp. 72–73.

[27] U.S. Department of State, Press Release No. 143, March 17, 1954.

[28] *Annual Report, 1954*, pp. 8–10.

expressed the opinion that the conditions for instituting a fully convertible system of payments in Europe had been better in 1953 than at any other time since the end of World War II, and urged that any monetary decisions being taken should aim at convertibility. The President of the Netherlands Bank said that the Netherlands was standing on the threshold of convertibility. The approach to convertibility had therefore been broadened to include not only sterling but the French franc, the deutsche mark, the Dutch guilder, the Belgian franc, the Italian lira, and possibly other currencies as well.

A Ministerial Examination Group on Convertibility was established at an OEEC Council Meeting in May 1954 to consider the problems that might arise for intra-European trade and payments if and when convertibility was introduced for one or more European currencies. At a meeting of this group in London in July 1954, the United Kingdom suggested the establishment of a European Fund, and this suggestion led in time to the European Monetary Agreement.

Deliberations in the Fund

As they began to consider the prospects for convertibility, both the United Kingdom and the OEEC Group on Convertibility made informal inquiries seeking the Fund's views; moreover, in their Annual Report for 1954, the Executive Directors took note of the discussions going on in Europe concerning convertibility: "Formal statements made by several Fund members in recent months have indicated a widespread interest in the possibility of more rapid movement in the direction of currency convertibility and the further removal of restrictions." [29]

While the Board welcomed both the general trend of opinion and the policy decisions made by individual countries and by groups of countries as regards convertibility, it was aware of the problems posed by the fact that not all European currencies were equally strong. Countries returning to convertibility might impose or intensify restrictions on imports from countries with weaker currencies that remained inconvertible for the time being; countries whose currencies remained inconvertible might intensify restrictions on imports from countries with newly convertible currencies in order to increase or create balances available for conversion into dollars. It was essential, therefore, that relaxation of restrictions and restoration of convertibility should go hand in hand, and that most if not all European countries should undertake convertibility simultaneously; on the other hand, the countries which had already attained strong payments positions could not wait indefinitely.

At the Ninth Annual Meeting, in September 1954, some of the Governors expressed the belief that conditions necessitating the postwar transitional

[29] *Ibid.*, p. 8.

arrangements of the Articles of Agreement were drawing to an end. The Governor for the United Kingdom warned that "there may well be danger in continuing for too long a transitional provision," and he asked the Fund to study the question of the best means of shifting from the transitional arrangements under Article XIV to Article VIII. The Governor for the United States supported this request.[30]

Meanwhile, the staff had been considering how the Fund might assist in a move to convertibility, both by giving financial assistance and by formulating relevant policies and procedures. Among the questions being considered was whether the Fund should announce the end of the transitional period. Did the Fund, in fact, have the power to do so? On whose initiative—the Fund's or the country's—should the decision be taken to give up Article XIV and take up the obligations of Article VIII? What restrictions, if any, might the Fund approve under Article VIII? How was Article VIII stricter than Article XIV?

From the Fund's inception, it had generally been assumed that Article XIV was somehow more permissive than Article VIII—that is, countries could presumably maintain a greater degree of restriction under Article XIV than would be permitted under Article VIII. But the precise extent to which Article VIII was stricter, and the exact nature of the restrictions that might be approved under that Article, remained uncertain. Accordingly, the policies and procedures of the Fund in these matters began to be explored.

In informal session in November 1954 the Executive Directors considered a possible shift of several member countries to Article VIII. This preliminary discussion did more to point up problems and differences among members than to resolve them. Attention tended to concentrate on two important legal issues. First, was formal notification to the Fund of acceptance of Article VIII by a member required before Article VIII could become binding on a member? Inversely expressed, could the Fund find that a member was under Article VIII by virtue of that member's having no restrictions that were maintained for balance of payments reasons? Second, did the Fund have the legal power to end the transitional period, either for all members or with exceptions for some members still in need of transitional arrangements?

Consideration of the stage at which members would come under Article VIII was also an important part of the 1954 discussions. As the staff saw it, even with the restoration of convertibility some restrictions—possibly a great many—would remain. While countries might establish "external" convertibility, it might be only at some later time that "internal" convertibility could be undertaken as well. Until then, while nonresidents could convert their earnings of a given currency, restrictions on residents would continue. The establishment of convertibility was, therefore, envisaged as occurring in two stages.

---

30 *Summary Proceedings, 1954,* p. 44.

PROGRESS ACHIEVED, 1955–58

Improved world payments situation

The sudden and extensive decline in the use of retention quotas may, in part, have been occasioned by the adverse reactions of the Fund and of several of its largest members; but the virtual abolition of these practices, and the talk about prospects for convertibility, were due even more to the vast improvement in the world payments situation that had become apparent by the mid-1950's.

World industrial production was expanding rapidly and world trade even more quickly. As increased production of both agricultural and industrial commodities had made many countries less dependent on dollar imports, the volume of these imports had tended to fall despite a considerable decline in the degree of discrimination applied against imports requiring payment in dollars. The sterling area had achieved an aggregate surplus as well as a surplus with the dollar area; and several countries in Western Europe had attained, or had continued in, total balance of payments surplus. The previously difficult U.S. market had been penetrated by the exports of other industrial countries; and exporters from Western Europe and Japan were competing successfully in third markets with exports from the United States. The shares in world exports of manufactured goods of Japan, Germany, Italy, Belgium, and Sweden had sharply increased, and smaller rises had been experienced by the Netherlands, Switzerland, and France; the shares of the United States, and also of the United Kingdom, had diminished.[31]

The improvement in the international payments situation was signalized by an expansion of gold and dollar reserves outside the United States. These reserves had been rising steadily and by the end of 1954 totaled $25 billion, as against $15 billion held at the end of 1948.[32] Further testimony to the strength of the balance of payments of the non-dollar world was that the recession in the United States in 1953–54, unlike those of 1945–46 and 1948–49, did not lead to a recrudescence of payments difficulties elsewhere. In fact, the reserves of non-dollar countries in 1953 and 1954 had risen by approximately $4.8 billion.[33] In contrast, the recession of 1948–49, of about the same magnitude, had helped to precipitate the currency devaluations of September 1949.

Thus, by 1955 most of the *abnormal* postwar difficulties had faded into the past and with them had gone the acute payments problems that had given rise to severe restrictions. In addition, the improvement in the world payments situation between 1951–52 and 1954–55—in contrast to the period after the

[31] *Annual Report, 1957*, pp. 20–21.

[32] *Annual Report, 1955*, p. 33.

[33] *Ibid.*, p. 13.

outbreak of hostilities in Korea, when there had also been a rapid rise in the non-dollar world's reserves—was associated with stable prices and a greater freedom from inflationary pressures than in earlier years. It had been possible for countries to pursue credit policies which were more cautious than those previously employed without unduly hampering the expansion of production or creating any serious problems of unemployment.

Debates by members of the staff and by the Executive Board with representatives of member governments on the need for, and effectiveness of, anti-inflationary policies in improving balances of payments lessened in intensity and in frequency. In its 1955 consultations, for example, the Fund found in its members a much greater readiness to take measures for the correction and prevention of monetary instability. Although the authorities of practically all members made it clear that they regarded the maintenance of satisfactory levels of productive employment as a major objective of their economic policies, there was increasing recognition of the value of flexible monetary and fiscal policies as a major means of achieving stability. Differences of opinion now centered on such questions as at what point current changes in economic activity required the institution of tighter monetary, credit, and fiscal policies, the extent to which fiscal measures should be combined with monetary measures, and to which sectors of the economy stricter monetary policies should be applied.

In order to facilitate the attempts by central banks to prevent or at least counteract any inflationary or deflationary developments of sufficient magnitude to create a threat to the long-run stability of the internal and external purchasing power of their currencies, special attention was given to the problem of how to detect inflationary or deflationary developments. As part of the proceedings of the Eleventh Annual Meeting of the Board of Governors, an Informal Session on Recent Developments in Monetary Analysis was held on September 25, 1956.[34] Three papers were presented, by Dr. M. W. Holtrop, President of the Netherlands Bank, Dr. Paolo Baffi, Economic Adviser to the Bank of Italy, and Dr. Ralph A. Young, Director of the Division of Research and Statistics, Board of Governors of the Federal Reserve System of the United States.[35]

The easing of restrictions

In response to the more satisfactory balance of payments positions of many countries, notable steps were taken, particularly in Western Europe and the sterling area but also elsewhere, to accelerate the reduction of restrictions. Although the elimination of controls was sometimes delayed because authorities

---

34 *Summary Proceedings, 1956,* p. 125.

35 The papers presented by the principal speakers and the background paper on Monetary Analysis prepared by the Fund's staff are to be found in *Staff Papers,* Vol. V (1956–57), pp. 303–433.

hesitated to dismantle a control apparatus which they feared they might have to re-establish in the event of a deterioration of the payments situation, controls were applied less rigorously or regulations were made less rigid and formalistic. The result was a considerable relaxing of restrictions. The trade liberalization policy of the OEEC had become a driving force in the freeing of trade between Western European countries. These countries had, by January 1954, freed from quantitative restrictions three fourths of the trade conducted with each other and in 1955 they began to relax restrictions on the granting of exchange for transactions in invisibles within the OEEC. Liberalization of trade restrictions was also frequently extended to imports from other non-dollar sources. Outside Europe, where countries' policies on restrictions were not in general subject to joint agreement, there was also extensive relaxation of restrictions.

There was a tendency, as well, to give more equal treatment to imports from different countries or paid for in different currencies, i.e., to reduce the degree of discrimination. By 1955, ten members outside the dollar area (Belgium, Ethiopia, Greece, Indonesia, Luxembourg, the Netherlands, Pakistan, Peru, Thailand, and the Union of South Africa) made little significant distinction between their treatment of the dollar area and of other countries; and during the next year, dollar import lists were further enlarged by many countries, and the OEEC countries continued their efforts to extend dollar liberalization.

Moreover, in the summer of 1955 Western European countries began to terminate some of their bilateral payments arrangements with countries outside Europe and to broaden their payments arrangements with non-European countries. Under arrangements known as the "Hague Club," Belgium, Germany, Luxembourg, the Netherlands, and the United Kingdom terminated their bilateral agreements with Brazil and the degree of multilateralization of trade and payments between Brazil and their monetary areas was widened. Brazil undertook to apply to exports to the monetary areas of the participants the same exchange rate treatment as exports paid for in convertible currencies; to accept payment in any of the participants' currencies without regard to the country of destination; not to discriminate between the European currencies in respect of payments for imports; and to maintain orderly cross rates among these currencies. In addition, Brazil was permitted to transfer its earnings of these currencies to other non-dollar countries. In 1956, the arrangement was extended to include Austria, France, and Italy.

In July 1956 similar arrangements, called the "Paris Club," were established between Argentina and a number of European countries which by 1957 had increased to eleven—Austria, Belgium, Denmark, France, Italy, Luxembourg, the Netherlands, Norway, Sweden, Switzerland, and the United Kingdom. Under this regime, Argentina could freely transfer the currencies of the European participants from one participant to another.

Meanwhile, from 1955 to 1957, the areas of transferability were increasingly being extended for the pound sterling, the deutsche mark, the Belgian franc, the Italian lira, the Netherlands guilder, and the Swedish krona. There was thus a continued movement to ease the requirements of bilateral arrangements. There were new arrangements by which one partner country made its currency transferable, and arrangements in which the two partners agreed to conduct transactions in the transferable currency of a third country.

Many of these measures, considered in isolation, were of no great significance; but their result in the aggregate was an impressive relaxation of restrictions. By early in 1956, the Fund was able to report that "foreign exchange restrictions impose a less serious obstacle to international commerce today than at any time since the outbreak of World War II." [36]

Continued inconvertibility

On the other hand, relations between European currencies and fully convertible currencies, especially the U.S. and Canadian dollars, remained unchanged. It had become fairly well established that no general move to convertibility by European countries or to the Fund's Article VIII could be made before sterling became convertible. The need for countries to move together to the Fund's Article VIII had been reiterated by the Governor of the Fund for Belgium, Mr. Frère, at Mr. Rooth's luncheon for Governors at the Tenth Annual Meeting in Istanbul in September 1955, but hopes for establishment of sterling convertibility were dimming. At the Annual Meeting in Istanbul, the Governor for the United Kingdom, Mr. Butler, noted that "in the United Kingdom a too buoyant economy has called for measures to control the surge of expansion" and that "my Government has taken no decision on the timing of the convertibility of sterling." Referring to his remarks at the previous Meeting, the Governor for the United Kingdom went on to say that the Executive Directors had found that the difficulties of a move to Article VIII were considerable and that it would be a mistake "to reach a rushed decision." [37] When sterling area reserves declined in the second half of 1955, it became clear that there would be no early action by the U.K. authorities to extend general authorization to all nonresidents to convert their current sterling earnings into convertible currencies at the official rate of exchange. Thus were ended, for the time being, any expectations of an early move to convertibility for European currencies or of members shifting to Article VIII. It is noteworthy that a few months earlier, in July 1955, the Managing Director, Mr. Rooth, had recorded in his own notations his personal view that no decision should be taken at that time to end the transitional period.

[36] *Annual Report, 1956*, p. 89.

[37] *Summary Proceedings, 1955*, pp. 37, 39, 41.

SHAPING THE FUND'S POLICY

These were not easy years for the Fund. First, the great majority of members continued to apply restrictions under Article XIV. Second, most countries still retained some discrimination against the dollar area. Third, almost two thirds of the Fund's members had bilateral payments arrangements of some kind, though some were of little more than marginal significance. Finally, administrative machinery for applying restrictions was maintained by four fifths of the Fund's members, even though the improvements in their economic situations suggested that many could dismantle their exchange controls.

Increasing concern about discrimination

The fact that most members, including those in Europe, still applied restrictions that discriminated against imports from the dollar area had, by the mid-1950's become of increasing concern, especially to the Directors for the United States and Canada. Part of the problem was that the way in which EPU settlements were arranged tended to encourage tighter restrictions against the dollar area. The participating countries extended credits to each other for part of the net payments due to them; consequently, they did not receive in gold or convertible currencies the full value of whatever balance of payments surplus they acquired inside the Union. They were, therefore, not able to apply the full value of surpluses within the Union to meet deficits with other areas. This settlement arrangement was of particular importance in relation to the dollar area, and, indeed, was one of the reasons given to the Fund for the retention of restrictions which discriminated against imports of dollar goods.

The U.S. and Canadian Directors were especially disturbed by discrimination against dollar imports when the country under discussion had already attained equilibrium in its aggregate balance of payments, or had achieved a surplus in its accounts with the dollar area whether or not it had reached total equilibrium. At least two of the OEEC countries which in the mid-1950's had deficits in their accounts with EPU countries were in surplus with the dollar area, and were using the resulting dollar proceeds to finance their EPU deficits. Yet these countries maintained restrictions which were more severe against imports from the dollar area than against imports from other EPU participants. Noting that other OEEC countries had liberalized to a considerable extent without discriminating between EPU liberalization and dollar liberalization, the U.S. and Canadian Directors questioned the reasons for the discriminatory restrictions given by some of the individual members of the OEEC. They disagreed, for example, with the argument presented by the representatives of one of the OEEC countries that a certain amount of discrimination against dollar imports was required if European integration was to be achieved. They doubted that the Fund could tolerate indefinitely the policy followed by EPU countries of earmarking dollar earnings for settlement of their deficits within the EPU.

In the hope and expectation that a push by the Fund against bilateral payments agreements might help to end the discrimination resulting from those agreements, and might also hasten convertibility and thus put an end to currency discrimination, the Board, in June 1955, took a decision urging members to re-examine the need for their bilateral agreements and calling upon them to reduce their use of these agreements.[38]

In addition, in September 1955, preparatory to a Board discussion of the general problem of discriminatory restrictions, the staff undertook a survey of the extent of discrimination still being applied by members. The staff study concluded that the degree of discrimination against dollar imports had diminished and was continuing to diminish, and that this was in line with the improved balance of payments and reserve positions of most members. Late in 1955 and early in 1956 the Directors held an intensive series of meetings on the topic of discriminatory restrictions. But it was evident that there remained considerable differences of opinion among them concerning whether greater progress toward reducing discrimination could be made by the majority of the Fund's members.

During the Board's discussion, Mr. Rasminsky (Canada) took strong issue with the position of the staff that some Western European countries felt obliged to maintain a significant degree of restriction because of a sense of European solidarity, or to discriminate against dollar imports in view of the nature of the EPU settlement arrangements. He believed it was becoming increasingly clear that the basic reasons for continued discrimination were commercial policy considerations, including special export advantages gained by European countries through their regional or bilateral arrangements.

Drawings to avoid intensifying restrictions

Meanwhile, the Fund's immediate aim was to ensure that relaxation of restrictions continued or, at a minimum, that countries avoided tightening their restrictions. The Fund was especially concerned that any retrogression would be likely to delay movements toward convertibility. To this end, it began to apply the policies regarding the use of its resources which it had been developing since 1952. These new policies, involving gold tranche drawings, stand-by arrangements, and the application of the waiver provisions of the Articles of Agreement, had been worked out so as to provide additional exchange resources to members that undertook to make their currencies convertible. The policies were also intended to assist members through renewed balance of payments crises without their having to tighten restrictions which they had previously relaxed.[39]

---

[38] See below, p. 304.

[39] *Annual Report, 1955*, pp. 77–78.

These policies of the Fund relating use of the Fund's resources to relaxation of restrictions and steps to convertibility proved useful in the latter part of 1956 and in 1957, when both industrial and primary producing countries experienced a new round of financial difficulties. Boom conditions and overspending, aggravated by the Suez Canal crisis, led to various strains and stresses. The Fund, in two exceptional years ending April 30, 1958, lent resources totaling $1,780 million, including substantial sums to the United Kingdom, France, India, Japan, the Netherlands, and Argentina. In general an intensification of restrictions was avoided. Countries were enabled to gain the time required for putting into effect the measures contemplated or already initiated to check deteriorations in their payments positions.

But the Fund also considered these crises as temporary and hoped to encourage greater movement toward the further relaxation of restrictions and the establishment of convertibility. It recognized that governments, anxious to avoid being compelled by unfavorable developments to reverse decisions already made, must proceed cautiously in relaxing restrictions. But at the same time, the Fund did not wish to see progress delayed unduly. Hence, in its decisions on consultations, especially in the years 1957–58, the Board pressed for more rapid progress by members in eliminating their restrictions, and especially in reducing discrimination and bilateralism.

EXTERNAL CONVERTIBILITY ATTAINED

The year 1958 witnessed the most signal achievement of the postwar period in the field of exchange restrictions. On December 29, 1958, fourteen Western European countries—Austria, Belgium, Denmark, Finland, France, Germany, Ireland, Italy, Luxembourg, the Netherlands, Norway, Portugal, Sweden, and the United Kingdom—made their currencies externally convertible for current transactions; that is, nonresidents would now be freely permitted to exchange their earnings of these currencies from current transactions into any other currency at rates within the official margins. Greece took the same step on May 25, 1959. Fifteen other countries, most of which were associated in a monetary area with one or another of these Western European countries, adjusted their exchange control regulations to the new conditions; these were Australia, Burma, Ceylon, Ghana, India, Iraq, Jordan, Libya, Malaya, Morocco, New Zealand, Pakistan, the Sudan, Tunisia, and the Union of South Africa. It thus became a matter of indifference to the exchange control authorities in what currency or to what account authorized payments to nonresidents were made by the residents of their country.

Except for Germany, however, none of the other countries with newly restored external convertibility granted nonresident convertibility, at rates within the official margins, for all payments of a capital nature. In some of the countries, a free exchange market existed in which capital transactions were unrestricted. Germany also took the opportunity provided by the moves toward nonresident convertibility—and the very strong gold and foreign exchange reserve position of Germany justified this—to announce convertibility of the deutsche mark for residents. By a series of general licenses, the German public was given complete freedom in foreign exchange transactions. The connection between licensing of imports (and of service transactions) and foreign exchange transactions was eliminated.

Before 1958 only ten member countries had been maintaining fully convertible currencies. But a number of other members had, for varying lengths of time, maintained free exchange markets in which their currencies could be converted at will into the major trading currencies. The decision taken in December 1958 was, therefore, very significant; it meant that a majority of the Fund's members now permitted nonresidents to transfer current earnings of their currencies to any other country. A system had been formally established in which the currencies used for the great bulk of international payments were convertible into other currencies or into gold. By and large, this was true whether the payments were received from residents of countries whose currencies were externally convertible or from residents of other countries, since the foreign trade of the latter was, to a very great extent, financed in currencies which were now convertible.

Significance for the Fund

Since none of the 30 countries that had made their currencies externally convertible was yet ready to accept the obligations of Article VIII, Sections 2, 3, and 4, of the Fund Agreement, their currencies were still inconvertible in the technical meaning of the Fund's Articles; that is, their currencies remained unacceptable to the Fund in repurchases. Nonetheless, the currency moves in Europe at the end of 1958 had immediate and long-run significance for the Fund. The introduction of external convertibility followed the substantial strengthening, during the past few years, of the reserve and balance of payments positions of the Western European countries taken as a group, and the considerable improvement in the position of sterling during 1958. External convertibility, plus the subsequent favorable developments in early 1959 in the external financial situations of the European countries concerned, reflected the fact that these countries had, on the whole, attained a balanced position internally and increased strength in relation to other countries. And it was expected that, should that improvement continue, one country after another would be able to eliminate restrictions still further.

Indeed, the Managing Director, Mr. Jacobsson, in addressing the Governors at the Fourteenth Annual Meeting in Washington on September 28, 1959, spoke of the introduction of external convertibility as "the consummation of the first stage of a process extending over many years for strengthening the economic and financial position of countries all over the world." Long an advocate of the importance of monetary and credit policies for overcoming the balance of payments deficits of European countries, Mr. Jacobsson also saw in these developments some vindication of his beliefs:

> The monetary disturbances which were brought about by the Second World War could not be easily overcome; but through increases in national income and the more effective application of flexible fiscal and credit policies, the excessive liquidity which weighed on many economies in the postwar years has gradually been worked off, so that by now the authorities in many countries have got a firm grip on the monetary position.[40]

While nonresident convertibility by itself did not necessarily produce a reduction of trade restrictions, it had important repercussions upon trade relations, and countries were thereby brought closer to the time when the Fund's objective of avoiding restrictions on current payments would be fully achieved.

All in all, the Fund warmly welcomed the establishment of nonresident convertibility, especially the remarkable cooperative effort of European countries in making a concerted move.[41]

---

40 *Summary Proceedings, 1959*, p. 13.

41 *Annual Report, 1959*, pp. 3–4.

CHAPTER

13

A Convertible Currency World

Margaret G. de Vries

AFTER EXTERNAL CONVERTIBILITY was established by the European countries at the end of 1958, another period of the Fund's policy as regards exchange restrictions began. It was the opinion of many of the Directors and staff that the time was ripe to push for the elimination of discriminatory restrictions, at least by the European members, and for the assumption of the obligations of Article VIII. To this end, two decisions were taken by the Executive Board, late in 1959 and in mid-1960. These decisions were followed by the acceptance of the obligations of Article VIII early in 1961 by 11 members. Since 10 others, all in the Western Hemisphere, had previously done so, 21 now had currencies that were fully convertible in the Fund sense of the word.

DECISION ON DISCRIMINATION

Pressure for action

One of the cardinal principles on which both the Fund and the GATT had been founded was that trade and exchange restrictions, as well as any other trade barriers, should be applied in a nondiscriminatory manner.[1] However, it was generally conceded that so long as a chronic dollar shortage prevailed—that is, while many countries had serious payments deficits with the dollar area—and so long as European currencies remained inconvertible, discriminatory restrictions might have to be employed.

But while recognizing the inevitability of discrimination in the application of restrictions so long as inconvertibility prevailed, many economists feared that protected markets might thereby be developed in countries that continued, for many years, to discriminate. The industries growing up in these sheltered

[1] For a brief description of the origins of the principle of nondiscrimination, see Gardner Patterson, *Discrimination in International Trade*, Chap. 1. For some criticisms of this principle, see Harry G. Johnson, *The World Economy at the Crossroads*, Chap. 4.

markets would be unable to compete with the industries of countries, such as the United States, that were highly competitive. Discrimination might therefore be long lasting. In addition, producers in countries such as the United States and Canada, whose products were being discriminated against in foreign markets, were complaining about their unequal export opportunities. This concern had already found expression in statements to the Board by the Executive Directors for the United States and Canada.

Among the countries continuing to maintain discriminatory restrictions, there had been increasing recognition of the costs to their economies of such discrimination. But there were a great many anxieties about eliminating practices that had been in effect for several years. In particular, these countries were uncertain whether their industries could compete in a world without discriminatory restrictions; and, if their industries were not competitive, what would be the effects on domestic employment and on their balance of payments positions?

Once the dollar shortage was over, therefore, and after external convertibility of European currencies was established, the Fund began to examine the questions raised by the remaining discriminatory restrictions. In mid-1959, however, the Executive Directors still could not agree on just what steps against discriminatory restrictions the Fund might take. They disagreed, indeed, on whether the establishment of external convertibility meant that discriminatory restrictions for balance of payments reasons had now become unnecessary. Even if the currency inconvertibility argument for discriminatory restrictions had been destroyed, commercial reasons remained. It was also evident that, where discriminatory restrictions had been maintained for a long time, a reasonable period would have to be allowed before countries could eliminate them completely.

Hence, it was not until late in 1959 that agreement among the Directors on a general decision on discrimination could be reached. A study by the staff concentrated on two types of discrimination—that against transactions with the dollar area and that arising out of bilateral arrangements. A survey of the extent of discrimination revealed that late in 1959 about twenty of the members that were taking advantage of the transitional arrangements of Article XIV discriminated against dollar imports and also had bilateral agreements, and about twenty other members discriminated against the dollar but had no bilateral arrangements. Only about fifteen members that were still under Article XIV had neither discrimination against dollar imports nor bilateral payments agreements.

The staff study also concluded that most of the members that still maintained discriminatory restrictions could eliminate them without important repercussions on their balance of payments or reserve positions. Either the remaining discrimination was slight, or their balance of payments and reserve positions were satisfactory, or, perhaps most important of all, the existing degree of liberalization vis-à-vis other countries was so great that the impact of the removal of discrimination could not really be expected to be onerous in its effects on the balance of payments. Therefore the staff believed that these members no longer had a balance of payments reason for discrimination.

The staff, nonetheless, recognized the existence of other considerations which might cause difficulties for members in withdrawing discriminatory restrictions, particularly if those restrictions had been in force for some decades. There might be practical problems, such as the need to formulate new regulations or to dismantle administrative machinery. International commitments might have been made to import specific goods from some other country or group of countries. Alternative ways had to be found to liquidate credits built up under bilateral arrangements. Most difficult of all was likely to be the impact of the removal of discriminatory restrictions on industries that had been operating under a mantle of protection.

Consideration by the Executive Board of the problem of discrimination, and the related staff study, followed by a few weeks the Annual Meeting, 1959. At that Meeting, Mr. Jacobsson said that the essence of the problem of the remaining discriminatory restrictions was that they were now seen to be "protectionist devices." They had thus become a problem of commercial policy and were no longer to be considered a balance of payments problem. He expressed concern for future trade relations should such discrimination remain:

> The maintenance of discrimination, moreover, undoubtedly acts as a strong irritant, liable to bedevil commercial relations; it may provoke a resurgence of protectionist sentiment, especially when the business trend turns downward; and if such possibilities are not guarded against, the result might well be a dangerous disruption of trade relations in general.[2]

It was his personal conviction that for the vast majority of countries there were no longer any balance of payments reasons for the maintenance of discrimination, and he thought that the time had come when, for many reasons, the practice of discrimination should be abandoned with the least possible delay.

The Governors for Canada (Mr. Fleming) and the United States (Mr. Anderson) endorsed these views of the Managing Director.[3] They believed very strongly that the Fund should take early action to declare a position to the effect that there was no longer any balance of payments justification for discrimination.

Other Governors—for example those for Australia and the United Kingdom—while agreeing that the stage had been set for "the progressive removal of discrimination, including that arising from bilateralism," called attention to

[2] *Summary Proceedings, 1959*, p. 16.

[3] *Ibid.*, pp. 42, 52.

various complications. The Governor for the United Kingdom (Sir Roger Makins) stressed that discriminatory restrictions had long been maintained and that many member countries would require a reasonable time to deal with the political, social, and economic problems associated with their removal.[4] The Governor for Australia (Mr. Holt) expressed concern about the dangers of agricultural protectionism.[5]

A DECISION TAKEN

After a relatively short discussion, the Executive Board took this decision in October 1959:

> The following decision deals exclusively with discriminatory restrictions imposed for balance of payments reasons.
>
> In some countries, considerable progress has already been made towards the elimination of discriminatory restrictions; in others, much remains to be done. Recent international financial developments have established an environment favorable to the elimination of discrimination for balance of payments reasons. There has been a substantial improvement in the reserve positions of the industrial countries in particular and widespread moves to external convertibility have taken place.
>
> Under these circumstances, the Fund considers that there is no longer any balance of payments justification for discrimination by members whose current receipts are largely in externally convertible currencies. However, the Fund recognizes that where such discriminatory restrictions have been long maintained, a reasonable amount of time may be needed fully to eliminate them. But this time should be short and members will be expected to proceed with all feasible speed in eliminating discrimination against member countries, including that arising from bilateralism.
>
> Notwithstanding the extensive moves toward convertibility, a substantial portion of the current receipts of some countries is still subject to limitations on convertibility, particularly in payments relations with state-trading countries. In the case of these countries the Fund will be prepared to consider whether balance of payments considerations would justify the maintenance of some degree of discrimination, although not as between countries having externally convertible currencies. In this connection the Fund wishes to reaffirm its basic policy on bilateralism as stated in its decision of June 22, 1955.[6]

POLICY AND PROCEDURAL ASPECTS OF ARTICLE VIII STATUS

During 1959 and the early part of 1960, further substantial progress was made by many countries in reducing or eliminating their exchange restrictions. The

---

[4] *Ibid.*, p. 79.

[5] *Ibid.*, pp. 68–69.

[6] E.B. Decision No. 955-(59/45), October 23, 1959; below, Vol. III, p. 260. On the decision of June 1955, see Chapter 14 of this volume, pp. 304–305.

beneficial effects of the widening scope of external currency convertibility were felt in many areas, and there was an evolution toward freer, more orderly, and less discriminatory trade and payments. By early in 1960 the currencies of about half of the Fund's members were convertible for virtually all nonresidents. In a number of countries, the remaining restrictions on current payments had dwindled to the point of insignificance.

Under these conditions, it was becoming increasingly possible to visualize for many of the Fund's members the establishment of the multilateral system of current payments, without foreign exchange restrictions, that was foreseen in Article I of the Fund Agreement. It appeared that a number of members which had been availing themselves of Article XIV would soon be able to implement in full the obligations of Article VIII. Accordingly, the Fund began again to examine the legal, policy, and procedural aspects connected with a member's formal acceptance of the obligations of Article VIII.

Some suggested definitions

Answers to the questions concerning the assumption of Article VIII status which had proved controversial or difficult in the past could no longer be postponed. Accordingly, the staff prepared some suggested solutions and presented these to the Board. First came the question of whether the Fund should—or even could—announce the end of the transitional period generally. The legal staff reached the conclusion that the Fund had no such legal authority. This meant that some countries could, if they so wished, continue under Article XIV more or less indefinitely. Second, the legal staff advised the Board that the initiative to give up Article XIV and to assume the obligations of Article VIII rested solely with the member, not with the Fund. Any restrictions that the member might have would of course have to be approved under Article VIII if the member accepted the obligations of that Article. Third, a decision by a member to take up Article VIII status was irreversible: if a country moved to Article VIII, it could not revert to Article XIV should the Fund disapprove of its remaining restrictions, or should it later wish to reintroduce restrictions.

Next came the matter of the long-debated definition of a "restriction on payments" that the Fund was called upon to approve under Article VIII. The controversy was not yet dead. In January 1959—immediately after the main European currencies had become externally convertible—Mr. Callaghan (Australia) had raised the jurisdictional question once more. In calling to the attention of the Directors the need to turn their minds again toward the transition from Article XIV to Article VIII, he was interested especially in seeking to get the Fund to clarify its "approval" authority.

The staff pointed out that the language of the relevant Articles was broad and comprehensive, not narrow and restrictive. Therefore, a good case had to be made before anything that appeared to be a qualification of this general language could be accepted as having been within the intention of the drafters of the Agreement. Secondly, any doubt about the Fund's jurisdiction had to be resolved in the light of the wide purposes of Article I. Thirdly, no formula would provide automatic answers for all cases in which jurisdictional issues arise. Given these qualifications, the staff suggested that the guiding principle for determining whether a given measure was a restriction on current payments should be simply whether it "involves a direct governmental limitation on the availability or use of exchange as such." Even so, members would often need to consult the Fund, not only where it was obvious that a measure was covered by the definition, but also where this was not clear until there had been adequate study of the underlying facts.

Proposed standards

Next came the question of the standards which the Fund should use for approving restrictions under Article VIII: how many and which restrictions would countries be permitted to retain when they gave up Article XIV and came under Article VIII? First, noting that the use of restrictions was still widespread, the staff commented that any general move to Article VIII would create the serious dilemma discussed by the Board in the past. On the one hand, there would be pressure on the Fund to give approval to many existing restrictions. This would tend to make approval of restrictions under Article VIII a mere formality. From a practical point of view, there would also be great difficulties in the Fund's administering an "approval" jurisdiction in such conditions. Frequent changes in restrictive systems would require Board approval on the merits of particular restrictive practices, with all the difficulties of deciding in haste because of the emergency conditions in which restrictions are usually introduced. Alternatively, if strict standards were applied under Article VIII, many member countries would find themselves with restrictive practices not approved by the Fund.

The staff further noted that, in practice, the Fund had been attempting to develop the concept of Article VIII as a substantive goal—a goal which involved the *elimination* of restrictions on current payments, of multiple exchange rates, and of other practices. The Fund had been greatly facilitated in this endeavor by the fact that the ten member countries which had assumed Article VIII status prior to 1960—Canada, Cuba, the Dominican Republic, El Salvador, Guatemala, Haiti, Honduras, Mexico, Panama, and the United States—had very few or no exchange restrictions. Indeed the existing Article VIII countries had, in general, gone beyond the formal requirements of the Fund Agreement in that they had avoided capital controls as well as restrictions on current payments. Of even greater significance, Article VIII status had come to signify over the years either that a country had a sound international balance of payments position or that, if its payments position was threatened, it would avoid the use of exchange restrictions and take other corrective measures including, where appropriate, the use of the Fund's resources. The record of Article VIII countries in this respect had been remarkably good.

The Article VIII countries, with one small exception, had not introduced restrictions. The exception had been Cuba, which had introduced a new multiple rate arrangement in September 1959. Because the multiple rate measures were one of a series of tax measures adopted by the Cuban authorities to deal with their balance of payments difficulties, and because the measure was intended to be provisional, the Fund did not object; but approval was specified for a limited time (until June 30, 1960) and meanwhile the Fund was to have further discussions with Cuba.

The staff further reasoned that the achievement of Article VIII status had come to be the objective of the consultations under Article XIV. To this end, there had developed an attitude that the Fund's approval of restrictions must be based on a close scrutiny of the country's over-all economic position—domestic as well as external—and of the possibility of alternative corrective measures, particularly in the monetary and fiscal fields.

Recommended strategies

On the basis of this analysis, the staff recommended to the Executive Directors that a selective course of action be adopted for the assumption of Article VIII status. Those countries which made little use of restrictions and whose balance of payments and reserve positions and prospects were good might advantageously move to Article VIII. There were a limited number of such countries, mainly in Europe. For these countries, approval by the Fund of any existing exchange restrictions would require relatively few difficult policy decisions. Since the prospects for the removal of any remaining restrictions for balance of payments purposes would, by definition, be good, the member could commit itself to some program or time schedule for their elimination. In this way there would be a period of grace under Article VIII during which some further few restrictions might be eliminated, but that period would be short and definite. Were such countries to assume formal Article VIII status, the paradox would be ended that their currencies were treated by the Fund, for various purposes and in the technical sense of the Articles, as inconvertible, although these currencies were fully, or largely, convertible in actual foreign transactions.

This procedure would also make it clear, the staff argued, that countries having multiple exchange rates, bilateral payments arrangements, or discriminatory restrictions should not aspire to Article VIII status unless they were able to eliminate these practices promptly. Perhaps some exceptions might be made for bilateral arrangements that were maintained for other than balance of payments reasons or that discriminated solely against countries that were not members of the Fund. Furthermore, countries which had few or virtually no restrictions, but which experienced considerable uncertainty about their balance of payments outlook and reserve positions, should also refrain from undertaking Article VIII status; in their situations there would be concern about their inability to cope with deterioration in their payments positions without recourse to restrictions.

The staff further suggested that countries giving up Article XIV and coming under Article VIII should agree to periodic reviews under Article VIII similar to the consultations they had been having under Article XIV. In consultations under Article VIII there would be relatively little concern with restrictions; but, even more than in the past, attention would be devoted to the general economic and financial situation of the country. Holding consultations with countries shifting from Article XIV to Article VIII would also raise the question of holding consultations with countries already under Article VIII, such as the United States; consultations had not heretofore been conducted with countries that had never been under Article XIV.

Board concurrence and decision

The Executive Board considered these staff suggestions at two meetings in March 1960. Most of the definitions and strategies presented by the staff were supported by the Directors. Mr. Southard (United States), Lord Cromer (United Kingdom), and Mr. Guth (Germany) were especially in agreement with the line of action proposed. Mr. de Largentaye (France) did not, however, assent to the idea that some countries, maybe even many, would continue to remain under Article XIV. In his view, Article XIV applied strictly to a postwar transitional period which, he thought, no longer existed.

With respect to the Fund's jurisdiction, Mr. Southard accepted the opinion of the legal staff that the Fund does not have "approval" jurisdiction for nondiscriminatory import restrictions imposed for balance of payments reasons. He concurred with the legal staff that where a country imposes discriminatory import restrictions for balance of payments reasons, the currency considerations are so clear that the restrictions partake of exchange as well as trade, and fall under the parallel jurisdiction of the Fund and the GATT.

Two related questions concerning the requirements which the Fund would impose for the assumption of Article VIII status were discussed in the Executive Board at this time: (1) whether a country needed to have an effective par value before assuming Article VIII status, and (2) whether consultations under Article VIII should result in conclusions. The issues involved, and the Board's decisions on both these questions in the negative, have been considered, respectively, in Chapters 4 and 11.[7]

For the next two to three months, efforts were made to draft a decision which would outline in some detail the Fund's policies and procedures on the move from Article XIV to Article VIII. On June 1, 1960 such a detailed decision was finally taken.[8]

The decision contained four basic points. The first stated that the guiding principle to determine a "restriction on payments and transfers for current transactions" under Article VIII would be that the measure "involved a direct governmental limitation on the availability or use of exchange as such." Members in doubt as to whether any of their measures did or did not fall under Article VIII were urged to consult the Fund.

The second point of the decision was that before members gave notice to the Fund that they were accepting the obligations of Article VIII, they should eliminate measures which would require the approval of the Fund and satisfy themselves that they were not likely to need to have recourse to such measures in the foreseeable future. The Fund would grant approval under Article VIII to measures for balance of payments reasons only where it was satisfied that the measures were necessary and temporary; exchange measures for other than balance of payments reasons should be avoided.

The second paragraph of the decision also stated that "members may at any time notify the Fund that they accept the obligations of Article VIII, Sections 2, 3, and 4, and no longer avail themselves of the transitional provisions of Article XIV." No mention was made of the Fund's ending the transitional period, nor was there any hint that members should be in a hurry to accept Article VIII. That countries should be cautious about undertaking the obligations of Article VIII reflected the strict standards adopted. But it also reflected the general recognition among the Directors of a difference between the industrial countries and the less developed countries—a difference in their attitudes toward policies as well as in their economic positions. Countries that found it difficult to discard restrictions would wish to remain under Article XIV. The consensus of the Board was that the wisest course would be to treat the continuation of the postwar transitional period as a sleeping dog, letting it continue without taking any action on it.

The third topic of the Article VIII-Article XIV decision concerned the matter of consultations; this is discussed in Chapter 11.[9] The fourth paragraph concerned methods of dealing with import restrictions for all members, whether or not they are also members of the GATT; this is also discussed in Chapter 11.[10]

---

[7] Above, pp. 75–76, 247.

[8] E.B. Decision No. 1034-(60/27), June 1, 1960; below, Vol. III, p. 260.

[9] Above, pp. 246–48.

[10] Above, p. 240.

IMPLEMENTATION OF DECISION ON ARTICLES VIII AND XIV

Actions of 1961

The Fund's decision on Article VIII status was followed by the acceptance of the obligations of Article VIII by nine European countries and Peru, effective February 15, 1961, and by Saudi Arabia, effective March 22, 1961. The European countries were Belgium, France, Germany, Ireland, Italy, Luxembourg, the Netherlands, Sweden, and the United Kingdom. This move resulted in all the major currencies which had been considered inconvertible in the sense of the Fund Agreement becoming convertible in the meaning of that term.

The undertaking of the obligations of Article VIII by these countries was preceded by intensive consultations and discussions, both formal and informal, between the members and the Fund. These were necessary to decide whether the arrangements for external convertibility that had been established by European countries could be maintained during the foreseeable future, and what the country's remaining restrictions were that would require, and could probably obtain, Fund approval under Article VIII. Since a notice that a member accepts the obligations of Article VIII is irrevocable, an awkward situation would have arisen if a member had given notice and then found that the Fund withheld approval of a practice that the member wished to keep. In fact, because of these consultations and discussions, and the delay in the move to come under Article VIII, by the time the move took place only four of the European countries—Belgium, France, Luxembourg, and the Netherlands—had any measures requiring Fund approval under Article VIII, and these measures were not extensive.

The precise *timing* of the move by these countries to Article VIII had also been a question of considerable importance. The staff had argued that Fund action on any measures requiring approval should be taken *before* the effective date of Article VIII status. A certain amount of time had to be allowed, therefore, for preparation of staff papers on each country's remaining exchange restrictions, if any, including the staff's recommendations to the Executive Board. These papers were also agreed by the staff with the country concerned before submission to the Board.

However, the time needed for this preparation was not the only reason for the delay of several months between the Board's general decision of June 1960 and the assumption of the obligations of Article VIII by the European countries. The staff's reports were actually agreed by the end of October 1960; the subsequent delay was due to political difficulties. First, there was the question of whether or not the undertaking of Article VIII status would be a concerted one, carried out by several European members. So far it had appeared that European countries were hesitant to be first and alone, because of the strains such a position might place on their currencies; yet none of them wished to be a laggard, for reasons of prestige and also because of intra-European ties.

By early in September 1960, before the Fund's Annual Meeting (September 26–30), the six countries of the European Economic Community (EEC) had apparently agreed to move simultaneously but had not yet agreed on the exact date. The United Kingdom, together with Ireland and Sweden, evidently intended to move when the EEC countries did. As Germany no longer had any exchange restrictions and was, it seems, the most eager of the six to come under Article VIII, the initiative for pressing for it lay with that country.[11] However, although there are indications that Germany hoped to get agreement with other countries on the exact timing of such a step at an October meeting of the EEC, no decision was reached. Other countries were not yet ready to go ahead. A press report, for example, indicated that the French Government had postponed taking the Article VIII step until after the presidential elections in the United States in November 1960.[12] By that time, the delay in making the move was causing increasing concern in the Fund, both to the staff and to certain Executive Directors, especially Mr. Southard. The fear was that the impetus toward a general shift to Article VIII status for European countries given by the Board decision of June 1960 might be lost and the decision itself might become inoperative.

However, shortly after the end of the year the difficulties that had inhibited concerted action were overcome. The Managing Director was informed between January 27 and February 2 by the Executive Directors of the countries concerned of these countries' intentions to assume the obligations of Article VIII on February 15, 1961. The Board's discussions of the countries' intentions and remaining restrictions, if any, took place on February 6 and 8. As had been expected, Peru joined the nine European members. A few weeks later, in March 1961, Saudi Arabia also assumed the obligations of Article VIII. This brought the number of members that had achieved formal convertibility under the Fund Agreement to 21.

This widening of the area of formal convertibility had implications of consequence for the Fund's general activities. Although drawings from the Fund had, from 1959 to 1961, included the use of the currencies of some of the countries which, in 1961, assumed the obligations of Article VIII, it had not been permissible under the Fund Agreement to use such currencies to make repayments to the Fund. The removal of this limitation proved an added encouragement to the use of a larger number of currencies in Fund transactions. Indeed, the

[11] See, for example, the statement by Mr. Blessing, Governor for Germany, in *Summary Proceedings, 1960*, p. 65.

[12] *Agence Economique et Financière* (Paris), October 28, 1960.

question of which particular currencies should be drawn from the Fund was to become a vital one in the next few years.[13]

As stated above, the member countries that assumed Article VIII status early in 1961 had by that time eliminated all, or nearly all, restrictions on current payments and transfers. However, these countries in most cases restricted the making of some capital payments at official rates of exchange. Only Germany and Saudi Arabia permitted all current and capital payments to be made at market rates of exchange maintained within the limits permitted by the Fund Agreement. Peru had similar arrangements except that the exchange rate was a unitary fluctuating one.

By 1961 the European countries that had established external convertibility—and defended it against something of a crisis in 1960–61—had been joined by others. The Exchange Restrictions Report for 1961 recorded that two thirds of the Fund's members permitted nonresidents to transfer freely to other nonresidents the local currency they acquired from current transactions.[14] Most of these countries believed that their balance of payments prospects or remaining restrictions, or both, made it advisable for them to await further developments before assuming formal Article VIII status. Nevertheless, virtually every currency used in financing international trade was now convertible in terms of the Fund Agreement, and virtually all of the trade of the other Fund members was conducted in these convertible currencies. Thus, while important obstacles to international trade persisted, relatively few impediments remained to conducting that trade on the basis of a multilateral payments system.

CONTINUED RELAXATION OF RESTRICTIONS

The successful maintenance of widespread convertibility provided, in the next few years, the basis and incentive for further reductions in restrictions. Import restrictions were reduced or simplified in many countries in addition to those that had moved to Article VIII in 1961. Countries relaxing their import restrictions included Austria, Burma, Finland, Pakistan, Portugal, Spain, Turkey, and Yugoslavia. Discrimination against imports from Canada and the United States was eliminated, or virtually eliminated, by Australia, Austria, Finland, France, Greece, Italy, Japan, Malaysia, Norway, and Sweden. Several countries—France, Iceland, Italy, Japan, the Netherlands, Pakistan, Spain, Sweden, and the United Kingdom—were able to liberalize further the granting of exchange for payments for invisibles. By 1962, restrictions on trade and payments for the world as a whole were less than they had been for some decades.

---

[13] See below, Chapter 19, p. 451.

[14] *Twelfth Annual Report on Exchange Restrictions* (1961), pp. 4–5.

Other members also accepted Article VIII status. In 1962–63 Austria, Jamaica, and Kuwait came under Article VIII. Japan and Nicaragua joined the list in 1964 and Australia and Costa Rica during 1965. Meanwhile, Cuba—an Article VIII member—had withdrawn from Fund membership. Thus, 27 countries had made their currencies convertible under the Articles of Agreement by the end of 1965; these are listed in Table 8.

As the decade of the 1960's got under way, many countries went even further in reducing their restrictions on payments than they were obliged to do under the Articles: although the Articles permitted controls on capital movements,

Table 8. Countries with Article VIII Status, as at December 31, 1965

Member	Date [1]	Member	Date [1]
Australia	July 1, 1965	Jamaica	Feb. 22, 1963
Austria	Aug. 1, 1962	Japan	Apr. 1, 1964
Belgium	Feb. 15, 1961	Kuwait	Apr. 5, 1963
Canada	Mar. 25, 1952	Luxembourg	Feb. 15, 1961
Costa Rica	Feb. 1, 1965	Mexico	Nov. 12, 1946
Dominican Republic	Aug. 1, 1953	Netherlands	Feb. 15, 1961
El Salvador	Nov. 6, 1946	Nicaragua	July 20, 1964
France	Feb. 15, 1961	Panama	Nov. 26, 1946
Germany	Feb. 15, 1961	Peru	Feb. 15, 1961
Guatemala	Jan. 27, 1947	Saudi Arabia	Mar. 22, 1961
Haiti	Dec. 22, 1953	Sweden	Feb. 15, 1961
Honduras	July 1, 1950	United Kingdom	Feb. 15, 1961
Ireland	Feb. 15, 1961	United States	Dec. 10, 1946
Italy	Feb. 15, 1961		

[1] I.e., the date on which the country's acceptance of the obligations of Article VIII became effective.

liberalization was gradually extended even to these. A view that had been dominant before 1930 began to gain ground, namely, that freedom of capital movements was highly desirable in itself: the movement of short-term funds might be regarded as an equilibrating factor in international payments, diminishing the need for reserves.

Liberalization of capital movements, both for direct investment and for portfolio investment, was therefore undertaken in the countries of Western Europe and certain others, including Japan, New Zealand, and South Africa. Complete freedom to transfer capital among the member countries of the EEC, for example, was achieved in 1963 for direct investments, personal transfers, short- and medium-term commercial loans, and operations in marketable securities. Also, the United Kingdom permitted transactions in foreign securities, and in domestic securities by nonresidents, to be carried out in exchange markets separate from the market for current transactions. In 1964 restrictions on outward capital transfers were further relaxed by European countries. In most

OECD countries, direct investment (both incoming and outgoing) was completely, or almost completely, liberalized or was treated liberally in practice; much the same was true of portfolio investment, other than new issues of securities.

The reductions in restrictions that had taken place were mirrored even in changes in the internal organization of the Fund's staff. In 1965, the Exchange Restrictions Department, which had been set up in 1950 especially so that the Fund might center its attention on the problems of restrictions, became the Exchange and Trade Relations Department. Its functions were now broadened to include assessments of the aggregate international trade and payments situation and of programs for stabilizing the economies of Fund members.

RESTRICTIONS OF LESS DEVELOPED COUNTRIES

Nonetheless, problems of restrictions were not entirely ended. In fact, the elimination of restrictions and even the dismantling of controls that occurred laid bare one problem and created another. The problem that remained concerned the general persistence of restrictions among the less developed countries, which were now generally called developing countries. Several of these countries shared in the progress made between 1955 and 1965 toward the establishment and maintenance of a relatively free international payments system. Of the 27 members that had by 1965 accepted the obligations of Article VIII, about one half were among the developing countries.

Most developing countries, however, still had serious balance of payments problems, and continued to apply an extensive array of restrictions. In addition, from 1960 to 1965, 35 new members, practically all of which were newly independent states and in the early stages of economic development, joined the Fund; all but one chose to avail themselves of the provisions of Article XIV (the transitional arrangements).

The developing countries also began to use a greater range of practices. The use of advance import deposit requirements spread, and more countries applied surcharges to imports. A wide variety of arrangements began to be used to encourage exports—the granting of export credits on concessionary terms, refunds of import duties paid on materials imported for use in the production of exports, certain fiscal measures (including tax refunds and rebates), and export subsidies. A number of countries supported exports through export bonus schemes, whereby exports were granted import entitlements; these arrangements were, in many respects, similar to the retention quotas employed earlier by some of the industrial countries, discussed in the preceding chapter. While in some countries these techniques for exports were introduced as an alternative to other practices, in many countries they supplemented restrictions already in force.

Although many of the developing countries requested and received assistance from the Fund in order to avoid intensification of exchange restrictions, some, in an attempt to avoid undue pressure on their exchange rates and drains on their reserves, did intensify restrictions. In sum, while the industrial countries were able to maintain their external economic relations with few limitations on the acquisition or use of foreign exchange, many of the developing countries continued to rely on restrictions, sometimes in combination with multiple exchange rates. Possibly worst of all, in some of the developing countries restrictions seemed so entrenched as to offer little prospect of rapid removal.

As the Fund explored the trade and payments problems of the developing countries in greater depth, it increasingly recognized that there was no simple solution for the continuing restrictions of these countries. Their situations were very diverse. Many were primarily dependent on the export of a few commodities to provide the imports which accounted for a large part of their consumption and investment, but others had already achieved a high degree of self-sufficiency. Some were faced with serious population pressures, whereas others were able to absorb a fairly large number of immigrants. In many, export products were subject to wide price fluctuations, which made the determination of the prospective profitability of investment uncertain and the maintenance of balance of payments equilibrium difficult. Many had attained internal financial stability, but for a few inflation was almost endemic. By 1964, moreover, increasing international indebtedness and difficulties in servicing existing debt had added to the payments burdens of these countries.

The Fund's policies toward restrictions reflected its awareness of the complexity of the problems of developing countries. Some years earlier (in 1955) the Executive Directors, in considering the impact that the restoration of the convertibility of European currencies would have on the developing countries, had been mindful that these countries might continue to apply restrictions for a long time despite the convertibility of European currencies. Although the revision of the GATT then being discussed contemplated more lenient treatment of restrictions imposed for purposes of speeding up economic development by "countries which can only support low standards of living and are in the early stages of development," the Executive Directors of the Fund had attached significance to the fact that no such distinction had been made in the Fund's Articles, which contemplated the use of generally applicable criteria. Nonetheless, in implementing its policies, the Fund was careful to take into consideration the particular problems of individual countries; these included problems related to economic development.

The staff and the Directors, therefore, stressed alternative measures to restrictions and put considerable effort into working out specific alternatives. In brief, in its consultations with individual members and in its technical assistance, the

Fund argued against temporary expedients—such as price controls, import restrictions, currency overvaluation, multiple rates, and protectionist devices—and in favor of exchange rate adjustment, internal stabilization programs, freer trade and payments, and export promotion and diversification.

There was also, by the 1960's, an enhanced appreciation by the Fund that financial problems—in which the Fund is necessarily most directly interested—account for only part of the difficulties of the developing countries. The Fund recognized, for example, that the search for broader solutions to their trade and payments problems had to include action by the industrial countries: industrial nations had to maintain a high level of economic activity and to reduce their own trade barriers, both tariff and nontariff restraints, against imports from developing countries, as well as export capital to the developing nations.[15]

NEED TO RESTRAIN CAPITAL MOVEMENTS

The second problem of the mid-1960's concerned the massive revival of capital movements among the industrial countries which took place once European currencies had become convertible and restrictions on these movements had been eased. Prior to the late 1950's any capital movements that might have been induced by international monetary developments, such as the emergence of differences in interest rates between countries, had been restrained by restrictions or by special exchange rates applied to capital transfers. But by the early 1960's, either differential interest rates or the prospect of a change in the foreign exchange value of any leading currency—or even political changes—tended to cause large movements of capital. Transfers of short-term capital, in particular, became large and frequent. As these short-term capital movements were often speculative and disequilibrating, they presented the financial authorities, especially in industrial countries, with new problems. Sterling, for example, from time to time in the 1960's was subjected to severe strains in the world's exchange markets, at least partly because of rather sharp movements of short-term capital. For a while in 1962, severe pressures on Canada's balance of payments could be traced mainly to capital flows. The unexpected magnitudes of capital flows from the United States were also responsible in part for the emergence and persistence of a sizable deficit in the balance of payments of that country.

These disturbing occurrences often necessitated official intervention—sometimes on a large scale—to enable countries to maintain their exchange rates within the margins specified in the Articles of Agreement. In order to avoid impairing the freedom already allowed to foreign payments, large amounts of reserves were utilized. There was heavy resort to the Fund. New forms of cooperation arose among the monetary authorities of the industrial countries,

[15] *Annual Report, 1963*, p. 71, and *1964*, pp. 68–69.

including mutual assistance to support each other's currencies and the setting up in the Fund of the General Arrangements to Borrow (GAB).[16]

Despite these arrangements, the principal industrial countries had, by 1964, to take special measures to curb capital flows. On September 2 of that year, the United States enacted a tax to be applied to purchases by U.S. residents of foreign stocks and bonds. Only a relatively few transactions—such as direct investments, investments in less developed countries, purchases of stocks and bonds from other U.S. holders, and purchases of Canadian stocks and bonds—were exempted. In February 1965, this tax was extended to bank loans with a maturity of one year or more made to residents of countries other than the developing countries; and still later, the tax was further extended to nonbank lending of one to three years' maturity. The United States also introduced a voluntary program to discourage capital exports by banks and other financial institutions.

As part of a series of steps to correct its balance of payments in 1964–65, the United Kingdom made changes in its exchange control regulations affecting capital movements. These included making slightly more stringent the criteria for the use of official exchange for direct investment outside the sterling area, and a strengthening of controls on travel expenditure so as to prevent evasion of the controls on capital movements.

True, the major industrial countries, while resorting to controls on capital movements, had avoided recourse to restrictions on current payments and transfers. Nonetheless, as 1965 came to a close there were evidences of continuing difficulties in the international monetary system. Some searching questions were being asked. Was there a risk that the large trading nations would go their own separate ways, introducing controls as needed? Might not the international monetary system thus even "collapse"? How could the functioning of the international monetary system best be improved? Would the introduction into the system of new liquidity solve the problems arising from capital movements? Should some procedure be arranged for enhancing the flexibility of exchange rates?

Debates on these, and similar questions, become more intensive after 1965, when the United Kingdom and the United States further tightened controls on capital movements and when other industrial countries—for example, France—began to reinstitute controls on capital movements.

---

[16] See below, pp. 375–76.

CHAPTER

14

The Retreat of Bilateralism

Margaret G. de Vries

WHEN THE MACHINERY for international monetary cooperation was being set up in 1943 and 1944, bilateral trade and payments agreements were not as extensively used as they were later to be. During the interwar period, these kinds of agreement had been employed mainly by Germany and by countries in Central and Eastern Europe.[1] However, because bilateral agreements had been manipulated so as to promote exports, and hence domestic employment, and to protect agriculture and manufacturing industries against imports that threatened to increase domestic unemployment, bilateral agreements had come to be regarded as synonymous with aggressive commercial policies. Another difficulty with bilateral agreements, as revealed by earlier international experiences, was that imports might be curtailed in order to force the partner to repay past debts.[2] A few economists, anticipating in the postwar period the widespread unemployment that had prevailed before the war, were fearful that bilateralism might become more prevalent.[3] Consequently, one of the major purposes of the Fund, as noted in Chapter 2, is to assist in the establishment of a multilateral system of payments in respect of current transactions between members.

THE EXTENSION OF BILATERALISM

Rapid spread after World War II

Because virtually all non-dollar countries had balance of payments difficulties in the late 1940's and early 1950's, bilateral payments arrangements spread more rapidly and became much more widespread than in the 1930's. Such arrangements provided a mechanism by which the partner countries could effect their

[1] The bilateral arrangements of the interwar period are described in Margaret S. Gordon, *Barriers to World Trade*, and Howard S. Ellis, *Exchange Control in Central Europe.*

[2] See, for example, Henry J. Tasca, *World Trading Systems*, Chaps. IX and X.

[3] See, for example, Howard S. Ellis, *Bilateralism and the Future of International Trade.*

reciprocal current settlements with a minimum use of convertible exchange and gold. In a typical case, the two central banks opened accounts in their respective currencies in each other's name, and all permitted payments were channeled through these agreement accounts; settlements in convertible currencies or gold had to be made only for balances within limits agreed in advance, that is, for amounts specified in what were called the "swing." [4]

The models for postwar payments agreements were the Belgo-Dutch (1943) and the Anglo-Belgian (1944) agreements.[5] Toward the end of 1944, the United Kingdom started negotiations with a number of continental countries with a view to the signing of payments agreements. Several of these were concluded between October 1944 and May 1946, with—in chronological order—Belgium, Sweden, France, Denmark, the Netherlands, Czechoslovakia, Norway, Switzerland, and Portugal.

What happened to the number of agreements into which Switzerland entered serves as an illustration. At no time before World War II did Switzerland have more than 14 clearing systems in force; but in 1945 and 1946 alone Switzerland signed 12 new payments agreements, and by the end of May 1947 it had 19 such agreements. Other countries had similar experiences. By the end of 1946 France was already a partner to 20 payments agreements, Belgium to 17, and the Netherlands to 14. By June 1947, the number of bilateral payments agreements in effect was estimated at 200.[6]

Shortly thereafter came a further series of agreements by the United Kingdom. While using bilateral payments agreements after the war, the United Kingdom had at first made little use of bilateral trade agreements. However, following the failure to establish sterling convertibility in mid-1947, it concluded bilateral trade agreements with countries with which it already had payments agreements. In 1948, Germany started to enter into trade and payments agreements with Latin American countries. Also in 1948, the Supreme Commander for Allied Powers in Japan embarked on a policy of bilateralism. A number of agreements were concluded between Japan and European countries, followed in 1949 by the first series of trade and payments agreements between Japan and Latin American countries.

In addition, in the late 1940's European countries rounded out their systems of agreements by concluding agreements with their smaller European trading

---

[4] The main features of postwar bilateral payments agreements, their purposes, and how they operated, are described in considerable detail by Johan H. C. de Looper in "Current Usage of Payments Agreements and Trade Agreements," *Staff Papers*, Vol. IV (1954–55), at pp. 339–50.

[5] The contrast between the type of bilateral agreements used after World War II and those used earlier is described by J. W. Beyen in *Money in a Maelstrom*. The genesis and spread of postwar agreements is recounted by Judd Polk and Gardner Patterson in "The Emerging Pattern of Bilateralism," *Quarterly Journal of Economics*, Vol. 62 (1947–48), pp. 118–42.

[6] Bank for International Settlements, *Seventeenth Annual Report* (Basle, 1947), p. 75.

partners. The establishment of the sovereign states of Israel in 1948 and Indonesia in 1949 also led to a series of bilateral payments agreements.

Similarly, the number of payments agreements of the Latin American countries gradually became larger than the number of agreements which they had had before World War II. European countries arranged a number of payments agreements with those Latin American countries that were *not* in the dollar area—that is, with Argentina, Brazil, Paraguay, and Uruguay. (The dollar area included the Republics of Central America and the Caribbean, and Bolivia, Chile, Colombia, Ecuador, Mexico, Peru, and Venezuela.) European countries were also anxious to enter into payments agreements with Latin American countries that *were* in the dollar area, as these enabled European countries to purchase, for inconvertible currencies, commodities for which they previously had been paying dollars, and facilitated their exports to these countries. The Latin American countries in the dollar area, in turn, were induced to enter into agreements with European countries in order to overcome the effects of discriminatory import licensing in countries with inconvertible currencies, and thus to recapture or to expand markets in Europe. European countries tended to discriminate against any Latin American country that did not enter into a payments agreement, particularly with regard to commodities which the former were able to obtain without financial problems from their dependent or associated territories. There were relatively few intra-Latin American bilateral trade and payments agreements.[7]

Not only did inconvertibility and the virtually universal existence of balance of payments deficits induce the onset of so many bilateral agreements, but bilateralism, once started, tended to generate more bilateralism. Once a number of important payments agreements had been signed, countries had an incentive to conclude additional agreements. First, because of the "swing" arrangements, bilateral agreements offered a means of obtaining or giving a tied credit. Second, countries that already had payments agreements adopted import licensing techniques and policies discriminating against the dollar area and favoring their bilateral payments and trade agreement partners; hence rather than be discriminated against, even some countries in the dollar area became partners to new agreements.

Dimension of the problem by 1954

At the end of 1954, the Fund began to take measures to reduce the use of bilateral agreements by its members. At the time, over 400 bilateral payments and similar arrangements were believed to be in force. Of these, approximately

[7] Latin America's bilateral arrangements after World War II are described by Johan H. C. de Looper in "Recent Latin American Experience with Bilateral Trade and Payments Agreements," *Staff Papers*, Vol. IV (1954–55), pp. 85–112.

235 were between pairs of European countries. Next in numerical importance was the network of approximately 100 agreements between European and Latin American countries. European countries also had about 60 agreements with countries in the Middle East and the Far East. Finally, a much smaller number of intraregional agreements existed within Latin America and among the Middle Eastern and Far Eastern countries. At least 18 countries were maintaining 15 or more bilateral payments agreements each: Argentina, Belgium-Luxembourg, Brazil, Denmark, Egypt, Finland, France, Germany, Greece, Israel, Italy, Japan, the Netherlands, Spain, Turkey, Uruguay, and Yugoslavia.

The number of agreements alone is not, however, a sufficient measure of their importance. The estimated amount of trade affected is perhaps even more indicative. The total value of exports in 1954 by members of the Fund with countries with which they had bilateral agreements reached $6.4 billion, which was about 8.5 per cent of aggregate world exports. For some individual countries, the significance of bilateralism for their exports was much higher. Over half of the exports of Argentina, Brazil, China, Egypt, Finland, Uruguay, and Yugoslavia were conducted with countries with which they had bilateral agreements. From one quarter to one half of the exports of Chile, Iceland, Indonesia, Iran, Israel, Japan, Korea, Spain, and Turkey, and from 10 to 25 per cent of the exports of another 15 countries—including several large ones in Western Europe (Austria, Denmark, France, Germany, Italy, the Netherlands, and Norway)—were with bilateral partners.

At the end of 1954, 41 out of the 56 members of the Fund conducted at least 10 per cent of their exports under bilateral arrangements. Much of the trade between Western European countries and the Soviet bloc in Eastern Europe was still conducted bilaterally, as well as a large part of the trade between Western Europe and Latin America and a substantial part of the trade between Latin America and Asia.

On the other hand, there was evidence that some bilateral arrangements tended to be construed less strictly. European countries had developed techniques to widen the scope of their payments arrangements. Although the United Kingdom had been a partner to many bilateral agreements, these usually gave the partner access to the whole sterling area. The existence of the sizable sterling area, the wide international use of sterling, although inconvertible, for financing trade and payments between countries unwilling or unable to finance their trade or payments in dollars, and the widening transferability of sterling, accordingly made the payments agreements of the United Kingdom much more plurilateral than bilateral.

In addition, with the establishment in 1950 of the European Payments Union (EPU),[8] the payments agreements between pairs of participating European coun-

[8] See Chapter 15 below.

tries were left with nothing but a technical function.[9] Since all member currencies had become transferable among EPU members, they were all equally "hard" (or "soft") to any one of them. In these circumstances, while some European countries were concluding new bilateral payments agreements, the general tendency after 1953 was for the important trading countries to place a decreasing reliance upon bilateralism.

Propitious circumstances for Fund action

Not only had European countries, by 1954, decreased their reliance on bilateral agreements, but other circumstances were also propitious for the Fund to take action against bilateralism. By 1953–54, the balance of payments positions of the European countries vis-à-vis their bilateral partners outside Europe, including Latin America, the Middle East, and the Far East, had become very different from that immediately after the war. Whereas earlier the Latin American and other countries had acquired substantial balances of European currencies, especially sterling, and their inability to convert these currencies had given them a strong incentive to form bilateral arrangements with Europe, by 1953–54 accumulated balances had been used up.

Additionally, there were limits to the amount of bilateral credits that European countries were willing to grant to countries outside Europe. When these limits were reached, their bilateral partners had either to restrict imports under their agreements or to pay acceptable currencies, such as U.S. dollars. When bilateral credit margins were exhausted and settlements with the bilateral partner had to be made in dollars, the inducement on the part of countries outside Europe to discriminate against dollar imports through bilateral agreements with European countries was greatly reduced.

At the same time, the more liberal trade policies emerging in Western Europe, as described in Chapter 12, made less acceptable the artificial and noncompetitive prices which frequently had to be paid for the commodities which the European countries imported under bilateral agreements. Many creditor countries started to restrict their exports, and sometimes refused to convert export proceeds into local currency. Furthermore, the reduced scope of government purchasing and the relaxation of restrictions on imports into certain countries increased the difficulties of operating some payments agreements.[10] Bilateral agreement currencies were being sold at discounts in an effort to evade the strict bilateral balancing of accounts.[11]

[9] European experience with trade and payments agreements prior to the EPU is described in William Diebold, *Trade and Payments in Western Europe*.

[10] The ways in which it gradually become more difficult for countries to operate bilateral agreements are spelled out in *Fifth Annual Report on Exchange Restrictions* (1954), pp. 17–18.

[11] See Barend A. de Vries and F. A. G. Keesing, "The Use of Bilateral Agreement Currencies for Trade with Third Countries," *Staff Papers*, Vol. V (1956–57), pp. 170–99.

All these developments had begun to reduce the flow of trade taking place under bilateral arrangements.

At the same time, it could not be assumed that bilateralism would come to an end easily, even though convertibility might be imminent. The Japanese authorities had, for example, already suggested to the staff of the Fund that a return to convertibility might decrease rather than increase the volume of world trade; therefore, bilateral agreements would be necessary to prevent increased unemployment. The subsequent discussion in the Executive Board on the occasion of the annual consultation with Japan had revealed that Japan was not alone in such fears. In several countries bilateral agreements had become motivated more by the desire to safeguard export industries than by balance of payments considerations.

FORMULATION OF THE FUND'S POLICY

Staff initiative

In these circumstances the staff of the Fund, toward the end of 1954, decided that it was time to bring to the Executive Board the general issue of bilateral payments agreements. This staff action may have been prompted in part by the facts that the United Kingdom had, in June 1954, suggested to the OEEC Ministerial Group on Convertibility a concerted move by OEEC countries to abolish bilateral agreements and that the United Kingdom's paper had been accepted by the Group in September 1954 as a basis for study. But a stronger reason for the decision of the Fund staff to suggest that the Fund take action against bilateralism was that, in the improving world payments situation, bilateralism seemed to be much less warranted than it had been earlier. Even more compelling was the belief, held by some members of the staff and by some Executive Directors, that a stronger line by the Fund against bilateralism might hasten the establishment of convertibility of European currencies.

The staff first suggested a three-phase policy, the timing of which would depend on the progress made by the major countries toward the convertibility of their currencies. The first phase was to extend from 1954 until the several countries then approaching convertibility had actually taken this decisive step. In this phase, the Fund would use its annual consultations to explore in greater detail than hitherto the scope and content of bilateral agreements and the reasons for their retention. Such action, it was argued, not only might help to shorten the life of some agreements, but also would build up an important body of experience, and enable the Fund to move effectively in the following phases.

The second phase would arise if not all the main currencies became convertible. In these circumstances some of the countries whose currencies were newly convertible might be faced with new restrictions by other industrial countries, with currencies still inconvertible, which continued to practice discrimination. The former might then feel the need to enter into some bilateral agreements. The Fund would have to pay careful attention to any restrictions which it was asked to approve under Article VIII by countries opting to accept the obligations of this Article. The reasons given by countries for not making their currencies convertible would also have to be carefully scrutinized. But it was recognized that this second phase might never occur.

The third phase would be reached when the largest members of the Fund—and particularly all the industrial countries—had convertible currencies. The countries whose currencies remained inconvertible might still find it useful in certain instances to conclude bilateral agreements among themselves, but these were expected to be of minor importance in world trade. During this third phase the Fund would have to ensure that, except for such minor exceptions, bilateralism would be abandoned by all countries; its jurisdiction under Article VIII would provide it with the necessary means.

The Board had no difficulty in accepting that bilateral payments agreements, having a restrictive character and an inherent bias toward discrimination, clearly fell within the Fund's jurisdiction. However, the emphasis to be given to bilateralism was subject to considerable debate. A few Directors believed that the staff's approach, which based the need for bilateralism on the absence of convertibility and which would intensify the Fund's action against bilateralism as steps were taken toward convertibility, was too narrow. These Directors pointed to additional reasons why countries resorted to bilateralism. Primary producing countries used bilateral agreements because they had special problems in sustaining their basic exports or stabilizing their export earnings, or both. Other agreements were used to avoid or to repay commercial debts. Bilateral agreements also had a function for trade with countries which were not members of the Fund, such as state-trading countries.

The majority of Directors—including those from the United States, Canada, the United Kingdom, and Germany—believed, nonetheless, that the only practical course for the Fund was the pursuit of the aims of the Articles, including that of multilateralism. They advocated an even stronger line against bilateralism than that proposed by the staff. The Directors therefore agreed that the staff should ascertain the nature and extent of the bilateral arrangements then prevailing and draft a decision for the consideration of the Board.

Decision of 1955

The staff reported back to the Directors in May 1955. The Western European countries had been found to be in the process of multilateralizing their bilateral payments relationships by resort to transit trade, by acceptance of third currencies such as transferable sterling and transferable deutsche mark, and by granting permission to effect transfers to and from certain payments agreement partners through the accounts established under payments agreements with other countries. However, a significant measure of bilateralism remained in the Eastern European countries, the Latin American non-dollar countries, and the Far Eastern and Middle Eastern countries. The staff still related the proposed policy of the Fund to convertibility. With the attainment of convertibility of the major European currencies, the balance of payments justification for bilateralism would diminish, if not disappear. Another reason why the staff tied the proposed policy against bilateralism to the prospects for convertibility was its belief that countries with newly convertible currencies would require safeguards against the use of bilateral arrangements by other countries.

The ensuing discussion in the Executive Board revealed that many Directors did not accept the staff's view that convertibility would result in the abolition of bilateral agreements by members. These Directors feared that members would still retain bilateral agreements for commercial reasons. Since members would always defend bilateralism on balance of payments grounds, would not an emphasis by the Fund on the balance of payments justification for bilateralism in effect make all bilateralism defensible? What criteria could be used to determine a "balance of payments need"? What would be accomplished if the Fund's efforts to wipe out bilateral *payments* agreements were accompanied by an intensification of bilateral *trade* agreements? Was it not necessary for the Fund and the GATT to work together? Could not the Fund do more than merely explore with members their need to continue bilateral arrangements and the possibilities of removing these arrangements? Should not countries in surplus as well as those in deficit review their policies so as to improve the system of multilateral payments?

On the other hand, a number of Directors were concerned about too strong a push against bilateralism. They reiterated their view that the composition of the exports of a number of the less developed countries made them particularly dependent on bilateralism, and that trade with state-trading countries posed some special problems. These concerns led to the inclusion in the decision finally taken of a statement that

> in its examination of the justification for reliance on such bilateral arrangements the Fund will, without excluding other considerations, have particular regard to the payments position and prospects of the members concerned.

The decision against bilateralism was adopted in June 1955.[12] The Board strengthened the text suggested by the staff. Where, for example, the draft had called on members "eventually" to eliminate bilateral arrangements, the Board substituted "as rapidly as practicable."

[12] E.B. Decision No. 433-(55/42), June 22, 1955; below, Vol. III, p. 258.

The essential elements of the decision were that the Fund's policy on bilateralism was an integral part of its policy on restrictions, that the Fund urged the full collaboration of all its members to reduce, and to eliminate as rapidly as practicable, reliance on bilateralism, and that the Fund would explore with all countries which were parties to bilateral arrangements which involved the use of exchange restrictions the need for continuation of these arrangements, the possibilities of their early removal, and ways and means, including the use of the Fund's resources, by which the Fund could assist in this process. A letter from the Managing Director transmitting the decision to members indicated that bilateral payments agreements would receive special attention in the forthcoming round of Article XIV consultations; as a preparation, members were requested to review their bilateral agreements.[13]

REAFFIRMATION OF POLICY

On three subsequent occasions the Fund reaffirmed that it would persist in its efforts to secure the speedy elimination of bilateral arrangements. Further ways in which this elimination might be accomplished were made explicit.

Specification of immediate goals

The first reaffirmation of the Fund's general policy against bilateralism came in mid-1956, when the Directors reviewed the progress that had been made since the general decision of the year before. The staff was able to report that there had been considerable progress in widening the payments arrangements under existing bilateral agreements in the intervening year. The United Kingdom and Germany had, for example, facilitated the use, under their bilateral payments agreements, of certain inconvertible currencies of third (nonpartner) countries. The "Hague Club" had been formed to multilateralize the payments relations of most Western European countries with Brazil. The "Paris Club," just being instituted, would effect virtually the same multilateralization of payments between Europe and Argentina (Chapter 12).

Nonetheless, in their consultations with the Fund several member countries were advancing a number of reasons why they had to go slowly in abolishing their bilateral arrangements. Some argued that they needed special arrangements vis-à-vis the state-trading countries of Eastern Europe. Even more common was the contention that bilateral arrangements were necessary to protect or promote exports. Some countries feared that the elimination of a bilateral agreement with a specific partner would put them at a disadvantage compared with other suppliers which still maintained preferential access to the markets of

[13] The letter was published in *Annual Report, 1955*, Appendix I, p. 123.

that partner. For a few countries, the inadequacy or unsatisfactory composition of foreign exchange reserves made bilateral swing credits still of some importance. For one or two others, bilateral agreements were the means for the gradual unfreezing of capital claims.

In these circumstances the staff proposed, and the Board agreed, that during the 1956 round of consultations the Fund should continue to press the issue of bilateralism. Specific goals were to be the termination of those bilateral arrangements which no longer seemed essential; the renegotiation of unnecessarily restrictive or discriminatory agreements; the replacement of bilateral swing credits by other forms of credit, including the Fund's resources; and the abandonment of bilateralism as the use of transferable currencies became possible. It was also agreed that, where the situations so merited, the Fund would make a simultaneous approach to two or more member countries, perhaps through their Executive Directors, to end a particular agreement.

THE POLICY FURTHER ELABORATED

Some three and a half years later, in October 1959, the Fund's policy on bilateralism was again restated. The occasion was the decision on discrimination for balance of payments reasons (Chapter 13). By then bilateral payments agreements had been considerably reduced, and in the Western European countries virtually eliminated except for those with state-trading nations. It had become the Fund's view that there was no longer any justification for bilateral agreements between countries having externally convertible currencies. However, several countries—although by no means all—were still using bilateral payments agreements for trade with Soviet bloc countries, and with other state-trading countries, most of which were not members of the Fund.

This situation called for a new elaboration of the Fund's policy. The original decision in 1955 had not differentiated those bilateral payments agreements arranged between two members of the Fund from those agreements arranged by a Fund member with a nonmember. This distinction had now become important. The Board decision on discrimination of October 1959, therefore, clarified the Fund's position on bilateral payments agreements between members and nonmembers. Member countries were expected to proceed with all feasible speed to eliminate discrimination against other members, including discrimination arising from bilateralism. However, some concession was thought necessary regarding the bilateral arrangements of members of the Fund with nonmembers. For such arrangements the Fund stated that it would be "prepared to consider whether balance of payments considerations would justify the maintenance of some degree of discrimination, although not as between countries having externally convertible currencies." [14]

[14] E.B. Decision No. 955-(59/45), October 23, 1959; below, Vol. III, p. 260.

This specification represented an elaboration—not a change—in the Fund's attitude toward bilateral payments arrangements. As expressed by the Chairman of the Executive Board at the time, the statement being made by the Fund in 1959 was that those members still engaging in bilateralism should be mindful of the fact that many other members had been able to eliminate reliance on bilateralism, and aware also of their obligation not to harm the interests of other members of the Fund by their bilateral arrangements, including those with nonmembers.

At the same time the Fund would not concern itself directly with bilateral payments agreements with nonmembers; the 1959 decision did not condemn such agreements. Rather, stress was laid on the *discrimination against other members of the Fund* that might be involved in any bilateral arrangements with nonmembers. The question whether bilateral agreements with state-trading countries did or did not actually involve discrimination against members remained open and, as discussed below, was to come up on various occasions in the next few years.

The third occasion on which the general problem of bilateralism was reviewed by the Executive Board was in June 1960, when the Board determined the conditions necessary for a country to accept the obligations of Article VIII (Chapter 13). Bilateralism was specifically covered by the preamble to the decision on Articles VIII and XIV, which states that

> previous decisions taken by the Fund, such as those on multiple currency practices, bilateral arrangements, discriminatory restrictions maintained for balance of payments purposes, and payments restrictions for security reasons, indicate the Fund's attitude on these matters.[15]

It was further agreed that bilateral payments agreements were included as "measures" in the statement in paragraph 2 of that decision:

> As regards measures requiring approval under Article VIII and maintained or introduced for nonbalance of payments reasons, the Fund believes that the use of exchange systems for nonbalance of payments reasons should be avoided to the greatest possible extent, and is prepared to consider with members the ways and means of achieving the elimination of such measures as soon as possible.[16]

Even more significant was the consensus of the Directors that, because bilateral payments agreements involved both restrictions and discrimination, members should have eliminated *all* such arrangements before moving to Article VIII status, or should be prepared to get rid of them within a stated time, e.g., at the expiry of the current agreement.

---

[15] E.B. Decision No. 1034-(60/27), June 1, 1960; below, Vol. III, p. 260.

[16] *Ibid.*

IMPLEMENTATION OF POLICY

The general policy of the Fund against bilateral payments agreements, like other policies of the Fund, has been implemented on a case-by-case basis. In particular, as countries consulted the Fund under Article XIV, the Fund has been able to apply the above pronouncements to specific country situations. Since 1955 the reports on the staff's discussions with member countries have regularly contained descriptions of bilateral payments agreements, the results of the discussions pertaining to bilateralism between the representatives of the member government and the staff, and a staff appraisal of the possibilities of ending any bilateralism still remaining.

The Executive Board decisions in Article XIV consultations have also usually included recommendations as regards the member's bilateral payments agreements. During 1964 and 1965, for example, out of 62 countries for which Article XIV consultations were concluded, 42 had some bilateral agreements; of these the Fund made recommendations on bilateralism to 27. The countries for which no recommendations were made were mainly those with only one or two agreements, sometimes involving an element of doubt about whether the arrangements could be considered as bilateral payments agreements, and sometimes covering a negligible volume of transactions. There were also a few countries which had agreements only with nonmembers and these were not important in terms of the total amount of trade.

The recommendations made to members have varied, depending on the number of agreements, the proportion of trade financed under them, the possibility of alternative outlets for exports, the degree of discrimination practiced on the import side, and the size of the accumulation of inconvertible balances. Consideration has also been given to the measures which the government was taking to deal with the problems which gave rise to the reliance on bilateralism. When there were objectionable features in the exchange systems—for example, an unrealistic exchange rate supported by heavy dependence on restrictions—the recommendations have frequently put major emphasis on these factors, and the removal of bilateralism has been linked to the need for more fundamental reform. Where progress has already been made in removing bilateral agreements, the recommendation for further action has been less forceful.

A second way in which the Fund's general policy on bilateralism has been implemented is through the exercise of the Fund's powers of approval under Article VIII. As countries have assumed the obligations of Article VIII, additional pressure has been applied. When the European countries began to undertake the obligations of Article VIII in the early 1960's, the number of bilateral payments agreements which they still retained were few, and these agreements no longer reflected inconvertibility or balance of payments problems. The arrangements being maintained between Belgium-Luxembourg and the Congo, Rwanda, and Burundi, and those between the Netherlands and Indonesia, for example, were outgrowths of past relations with former overseas territories. When Belgium and the Netherlands accepted Article VIII obligations, the Fund approved these agreements.

When discussing members' plans to move to Article VIII, the Fund also reviewed the bilateral payments arrangements maintained by some of these countries with nonmembers. Austria, Belgium-Luxembourg, France, Italy, the Netherlands, and Sweden all argued that their bilateral arrangements with nonmembers did not result in restrictions or discrimination against any member of the Fund. Sweden argued that its payments arrangements were, in fact, supplementary to parallel bilateral trade agreements, and that most imports from nonmembers were subject to licensing requirements while most imports of similar goods from other countries were free from such requirements. As a consequence, there was no mechanism by which the authorities could favor imports from bilateral countries to the detriment of imports from Fund members.

Still a third way in which the Fund has implemented its policy on bilateralism has been through stand-by arrangements. These arrangements have involved commitments to carry out the Fund's policy regarding the use of bilateral agreements; however, in all but those exceptional cases where bilateral payments agreements have dominated the restrictive system, commitments concerning bilateralism have been of the second order of priority and not central elements in the program for which the stand-by arrangement was granted.[17] Frequently the Fund has expected that general programs for achieving internal and external equilibrium would ensure a substantial improvement in the balance of payments and would, in due course, permit elimination of undesirable restrictive practices, including bilateral agreements.

By the end of 1965, the Executive Board had approved 167 stand-by arrangements with 50 governments; 104 of these had been concluded with 37 member countries maintaining bilateral payments agreements, some of which still had several agreements. There had also been 31 letters of intent from 17 countries, submitted in support of requests for stand-by arrangements, which contained specific policy statements regarding bilateral payments agreements. Some of these stated the government's intent to eliminate bilateral agreements "shortly" or within a specified time period; more stated "as soon as possible," or words to that effect. In 1965 two stand-by arrangements had "binding commitments" on bilateralism; many have included binding commitments with respect to the introduction of exchange restrictions, which have thus inhibited the introduction of bilateral agreements.

[17] The provisions of stand-by arrangements are described below in Chapter 20.

BILATERALISM DUE TO INCONVERTIBILITY DIMINISHED

Well before the end of 1965 the use of those bilateral payments agreements which stemmed from the inconvertibility of major currencies had all but disappeared. This elimination of bilateralism had come in surges. By the mid-1950's, European bilateralism was on the wane. The establishment of the "Hague Club" and the "Paris Club" in 1955 and 1956 led soon after to the elimination of a group of bilateral agreements between Brazil and Argentina, on the one side, and European countries on the other. By the late 1950's other Latin American countries had also reduced their agreements. The remaining European bilateralism had greatly diminished as the countries moved to Article VIII status in 1960 and 1961.

Statistically, by the end of 1964 more than 80 per cent of the total number of bilateral payments agreements that had been in effect in 1955 when the Fund's decision was taken had been abolished. The number of agreements abandoned by individual countries was impressively large. From 1955 to 1964 Argentina, Belgium-Luxembourg, Finland, Germany, Italy, Japan, the Netherlands, and Uruguay eliminated 15 or more agreements each; and at least 6 agreements each were given up by a number of other countries, including Brazil, Chile, Denmark, Norway, Paraguay, Spain, Sweden, and Turkey.

Looked at more generally, rather than in terms of the number of agreements that individual countries had given up, in 1955 some 165 bilateral payments agreements were maintained by those 26 countries that had, by the end of 1964, accepted the obligations of the Fund's Article VIII; but by the end of 1964 these countries had only 16 such agreements. In other words, they had eliminated over 90 per cent of their agreements. The agreements still remaining were maintained by only 7 of the 26 countries concerned, 4 of which had agreements exclusively with state-trading countries. Taking the whole of the Fund's membership into account, by the end of 1964 more than one third had no bilateral payments agreements at all and nearly one half had no agreements with other members of the Fund.

The value of exports being conducted under bilateral payments agreements had, of course, also fallen—by about one half between 1954 and 1964—so that only 2 per cent of world exports, instead of 8.5 per cent, was involved.

Usually a country gave up its bilateral payments agreements prior to assuming Article VIII status. But in a few instances agreements were maintained which were eliminated later. For example, in 1964 France and Japan gave up the last of their agreements and Sweden ended two of its remaining agreements.

The elimination in 1965 of an agreement between Argentina and Uruguay left only two intra-Latin American agreements. One of these, between Bolivia and Brazil, was little used in practice; however, a new one between Mexico and Argentina had come into effect.

CONTINUED RELIANCE ON BILATERALISM BY LESS DEVELOPED COUNTRIES

Despite the sharp drop in the use of bilateral payments agreements, especially by Western European countries, Japan, and Latin American countries, some other less developed countries have continued to arrange bilateral payments agreements, especially among themselves. A tendency to conclude bilateral payments agreements, even though little trade was covered, has been particularly prevalent among the newly independent countries in Africa. In addition, many less developed countries still conduct much of their trade with state-trading countries under bilateral arrangements.

As a result, the total *number* of bilateral payments agreements in the world declined little from 1954 to 1964. While four fifths of the agreements that had been in effect in 1954 had disappeared by 1964, many new agreements had come into being, and in December 1964 there were still 322 agreements in force. The number of bilateral payments agreements within Africa (including those of the United Arab Republic) had risen from nil to 20; and the number of agreements between African countries and state-trading countries had increased from 7 to 81. No agreements had been signed between African countries and Latin American countries or the European countries that had moved to Article VIII.

As did the African countries, so less developed countries in other regions entered into new bilateral agreements. A number of such countries (for example, Ceylon, India, Portugal, Spain, and the Syrian Arab Republic) which had had no agreements with state-trading countries in 1954, subsequently concluded several. At the end of 1964, seven Fund members—Brazil, Ghana, Guinea, Mali, Spain, the United Arab Republic, and Yugoslavia—still had 15 or more bilateral payments agreements each.

The implications of these agreements for the volume of trade conducted under bilateral arrangements were not uniform among the countries concerned. Many of the countries that had joined the Fund after 1954 and that had entered into new bilateral payments agreements had previously used the payments arrangements provided by their metropolitan centers in Europe, which, except for the United Kingdom, had been using some bilateral agreements in 1954. Hence, many of the new agreements of the African countries—e.g., those of Algeria, Burundi, Cameroon, the Central African Republic, Congo (Brazzaville), Dahomey, Laos, Mauritania, Niger, Senegal, Somalia, and Tunisia—did not necessarily involve an expansion of bilaterally conducted trade.

For other countries, however, including Afghanistan, Ceylon, Ghana, Guinea, India, Jordan, Mali, Morocco, the Syrian Arab Republic, and Upper Volta, trade under bilateralism had risen sharply. Most important of all, in 1964 more than

25 per cent of the total exports of some nine countries—Afghanistan, Greece, Guinea, Korea, Mali, the Syrian Arab Republic, the United Arab Republic, Upper Volta, and Yugoslavia—were still being sold to bilateral partners.

Changed character of bilateralism

This marked change in the *distribution* of bilateral agreements from early 1955 to late 1964—which was to have implications for the Fund's policies—is shown in Table 9. While there was a reduction of one half in the arrangements between Fund members, bilateral payments agreements between members of the Fund and nonmembers (primarily state-trading countries) rose by more than 50 per cent. Agreements with nonmembers, which had constituted 44 per cent of the total number of agreements in April 1955, had become 70 per cent of the total remaining agreements in December 1964.

Table 9. Bilateral Payments Agreements Maintained by Fund Members in 1955 and 1964

	Number of Agreements	
	April 1955	December 1964
Agreements with other members	189	95
Agreements with nonmembers	146	227
Total	335	322

The important increase in bilateral payments agreements between members of the Fund and state-trading countries had to some extent been the result of new agreements with state-trading countries by Western European countries. But to a much larger extent it had been the less developed members in Africa, Asia, and the Middle East that had been partners to the new agreements. A few statistics suggest the magnitudes involved. At the end of 1964, bilateral payments agreements between European members of the Fund—which here include Cyprus—and state-trading countries totaled 74; eight European members—Austria, Cyprus, Finland, Greece, Iceland, Spain, Turkey, and Yugoslavia—each maintained more than 5 agreements apiece. Less developed countries elsewhere had some 140 agreements with state-trading countries. Several of these countries—Algeria, Brazil, Ceylon, Colombia, Ghana, Guinea, India, Morocco, Tunisia, and the United Arab Republic—still maintained a number of agreements.

Reasons for persistence of bilateralism

The Fund's consultations with members have revealed three main reasons why the less developed countries have continued, in the 1960's, to arrange bilateral agreements despite the absence of a currency convertibility problem such as had prevailed in the 1950's.

First, one of the principal motivations impelling the less developed countries to enter into bilateral payments agreements has been their need to promote additional exports of primary products. Brazil, Ceylon, Colombia, Ghana, India, and the United Arab Republic, for example, have maintained agreements to boost sales of coffee, cocoa, tea, or cotton. Certain countries—for instance, Denmark, Finland, Spain, Yugoslavia, and most state-trading countries—purchased coffee under bilateral arrangements as late as 1964–65. Since many of the producing countries have exportable supplies in excess of their quotas under the International Coffee Agreement, since attempts to reach an international commodity agreement for cocoa have been unsuccessful, and since storage is costly and has inflationary implications, the pressure on exporters of primary products, such as coffee and cocoa, to enter into bilateral arrangements has been strong.

The main argument of Fund members which have been relying on bilateral arrangements with state-trading countries has been that sales to these countries must be made bilaterally because commodities such as coffee and cocoa are given low priority in the plans of state-trading nations. But the member governments concerned have also argued that to open up important new markets by fostering changes in consumption patterns in these countries will make easier of solution the structural problem of excess supplies of primary products in world markets. Moreover, imports from bilateral partners, even if obtained on unfavorable terms, are considered a net gain to the economies of the less developed countries so long as these countries are themselves unable to produce the kind of products imported. In other words, as long as the factors of production are fairly immobile, and in particular cannot be moved out of the major export industries, less developed countries have considered bilaterally conducted trade as useful for disposing of surplus exports in return for needed imports.

The magnitudes involved in such bilateral trade, although marginal, have not been unimportant. In 1964, for example, Brazil and Colombia, which together accounted for about 60 per cent of world exports of coffee, sold 9 per cent and 7 per cent, respectively, of their total exports to countries with which they had bilateral agreements; and Brazil and Ghana, which accounted for almost half of the world's cocoa exports, sold about 20 per cent of their cocoa exports under such agreements. Exports of tea by Ceylon and India under bilateral agreements, however, involved less than 3 per cent of India's exports of tea in 1964 and less than 2 per cent of Ceylon's.

A second reason for prolonged bilateralism, according to the authorities of a number of Fund members, is to assist the minor exports of the less developed countries. Some less developed countries have argued that they need the special export arrangements provided by bilateralism because of the trade barriers against their products, especially nontariff restrictions, prevailing in several industrial nations of the West. The Tunisian and Jordanian authorities have, for example, used bilateral agreements for exports of phosphates. Chilean nitrates have also been exported bilaterally, as have fruits, nuts, and tobacco by a number of Mediterranean countries. A few of the less developed countries which have traditionally sold manufactured goods to markets in state-trading countries have financed that trade through bilateral agreements in an effort to avoid the difficult processes of finding alternative markets or of shifting productive factors.

Finally, the increased use of bilateral arrangements to finance mutual trade among the less developed countries has reflected the desire, partly for political reasons, for some type of regional cooperation. Not only have agreements been fostered by the central banks concerned with international payments, and by the trade ministries interested in promoting exports, but the ministries of foreign affairs of the countries concerned have often also urged bilateral agreements in order to foster political or diplomatic ties between countries. Thus, for several of the less developed countries bilateral payments agreements have been only one part of a complex of arrangements.

FUND'S REACTION TO CONTINUED BILATERALISM

The Fund's general policy decisions of 1955–60 foreshadowed the changing character of bilateralism, and hence have continued to be relevant to the altered circumstances. Thus the Fund has continued to try to reduce the use of bilateral agreements by individual members when annual consultations have been undertaken and when stand-by arrangements have been agreed.

Stressing discrimination against members

Immediately after the Board's decision on discrimination in October 1959, the Fund's primary concern as regards the bilateral agreements of some of its members with state-trading countries centered on the possible harm to other members. The Directors, however, had differing opinions about whether the agreements of Fund members with state-trading countries really did discriminate against other members of the Fund.

The Board's concern with such agreements may be illustrated by its discussion in 1960 of the agreements maintained by Ceylon. These were all with nonmembers and affected mainly food items imported by the Government. The most important agreement was with mainland China; under this agreement, the two countries had undertaken to import certain items up to specified quotas and to endeavor to keep the balance of trade and payments between them as nearly equated as possible. Mr. Jayarajan (Ceylon), Alternate to Mr. Watanabe, stated that his Government believed that the bilateral agreements of Ceylon with state-trading countries did not conflict with the Fund's objectives; in particular, these agreements did not contain any discriminatory features. Ceylon's view was that bilateral trade agreements continued to be the only way in which Ceylon could maintain and foster trade with state-trading countries until these countries were willing to pay for their imports in convertible currencies.

Both Lord Cromer (United Kingdom) and Mr. Southard (United States), nonetheless, had reservations about the inoffensiveness of these agreements. In their view, some kind of *de facto* discrimination against private traders might well arise from these arrangements. Bilateral agreements of this type, they thought, gave rise to discrimination against other members of the Fund by requiring Ceylon to import from partner countries certain quantities of goods which could not therefore be imported from other countries. Mr. Southard wished to retain in the Board's decision on the consultation with Ceylon a sentence urging Ceylon to re-examine the need for its bilateral agreements. Mr. Jayarajan argued against the inclusion of this sentence on the grounds that, as there had been no increase in the scope of bilateralism since the previous year's consultation, and as no mention of Ceylon's bilateralism had then been made, it was unnecessary for the Fund to say anything now. After considerable discussion, in which it was noted that Ceylon had declared its willingness to re-examine its agreements, the Directors agreed on a sentence for the decision as follows: "The Fund notes the intention of Ceylon to keep under review its bilateral trade and payments arrangements, especially as to their possible discriminatory aspects."

Emphasizing the costs of bilateralism

In more recent years the Fund has taken special pains to point out to the individual countries concerned the economic disadvantages likely to flow from bilateral agreements. In general the Fund has conceded that, in the short run, such agreements often seem to achieve the objectives sought, which may include economizing convertible exchange, seeking more outlets for traditional exports or opening up markets for new ones (e.g., manufactures produced by emerging industries), or merely postponing settlements in convertible currencies until swing credits are overdrawn. The Fund has stressed, however, that in the longer run serious drawbacks become apparent where an attempt is made to divert trade into new channels. The most common and most obvious one is that it is difficult to find in the partner country a sufficient variety of goods of the right qualities, at attractive prices, and on acceptable delivery terms, to avoid a one-way development of the clearing account to the point where an excessive bilateral claim arises. Thus, less developed countries may find themselves granting credits which they cannot afford, rather than receiving them; alternatively, trade under the agreement may stagnate.

A less apparent drawback that the Fund has pointed out is that, in the longer run, bilateralism actually tends to harm the exports of a less developed country. Exports effected bilaterally may cause upward pressures on prices, wages, and costs; or may distort the structure of domestic production. What is more, the Fund has argued, the other party to the bilateral agreement may well experience similarly adverse economic effects, and is likely to feel obliged to maintain more discriminatory trade and exchange policies than would be required in the absence of the agreement.[18]

The Fund has often pointed out to members that it is doubtful that imports by other Fund members of products such as cocoa and coffee are determined by the availability of bilateral financial arrangements or by preferential access to the import markets of the producing countries. Such small amounts of trade are involved, so the Fund's argument has run, that they could readily be handled on a convertible basis. As regards sales to state-trading countries, the Fund has also noted that the actual increase in exports by primary producers may be exaggerated; time and again evidence has been found of substantial re-exports of these commodities by state-trading countries to established markets, often with unfavorable effect on the prices of the commodities. As regards the problem of bilaterally conducted sales by member countries of minor exports, the staff of the Fund has used mainly the approach of suggesting to members alternative ways to promote minor exports.

Thus the Fund's efforts to diminish the use of bilateral agreements, even those of members of the Fund with state-trading countries, have continued. Members have been encouraged to implement the Fund's general policy whenever the opportunity to dispense with bilateral agreements arises.

---

[18] See, for example, *Annual Report, 1963*, pp. 69–70.

CHAPTER

15

The Fund and the EPU

Margaret G. de Vries

THE STORY OF THE FUND'S REACTIONS to plans in the late 1940's for European payments arrangements, and of its relations with the European Payments Union (EPU) which was formed in 1950, belongs to an era of the Fund's history which has little relevance to the present. The EPU was terminated in 1958, and long before that—in fact after 1952—relations had distinctly improved.

However, this period of the Fund's history has, time and again, been the subject of possibly the severest attacks that the Fund has experienced. It has been contended, for example, that as the EPU became the main instrument by which the trade and exchange restrictions of European countries were reduced, the Fund, by failing to organize under its own aegis a multilateral system of European settlements, "missed the bus." [1] And the Fund has been characterized as having been thenceforth outside the principal stream of important international economic events.[2]

The critics stress that, once European countries had developed the habit of intraregional cooperation on economic questions, they continued to make their most crucial financial and monetary decisions in small meetings among themselves rather than through the wider framework of the Fund. In some respects, the EPU thus formed the nucleus of the Group of Ten.

Whether or not these criticisms are wholly valid, it did appear to many observers that for some years following the establishment of the EPU the focal point of important monetary decisions was that organization rather than the Fund. Only after the Fund commenced to have large-scale financial operations with European countries in 1956 did this impression begin to change.

---

[1] See, for example, Robert Triffin, *The World Money Maze*, p. 406.

[2] Harry G. Johnson, *The World Economy at the Crossroads*, Chap. 3.

Accordingly, it is worthwhile to take a brief look at what the Fund's records show about its reactions to proposals for intra-European payments arrangements, including the EPU itself. A reading of these records suggests that the story was neither so simple nor so one-sided as the one heretofore publicly revealed.

THE NEED FOR INTRA-EUROPEAN CLEARING[3]

The EPU, established in September 1950, was the outgrowth of discussion and experimentation from 1947 to 1950 among European countries, looking to some sort of clearing union to facilitate trade and payments between them. Meetings to explore European payments arrangements were held as early as August 1947, shortly after General George C. Marshall (in June 1947) proposed that the U.S. Government should undertake a special program to help in reconstructing the economies of Europe. Although intra-European trade had made a remarkable recovery after World War II, that trade had expanded much less rapidly than either the industrial or the agricultural output of most European countries; and a much greater expansion of trade was considered necessary for the general economic recovery of Europe.

A number of officials, both in the U.S. Government and in several of the governments in Europe, had come to the conclusion that, although the bilateral payments agreements established among European countries immediately after the war had facilitated the restoration of intra-European trade, these payments arrangements were preventing further increases in that trade. Trade deficits in excess of the credit limits specified in bilateral payments agreements had to be financed with gold or convertible currencies. European countries with such deficits tended to restrict imports from other European countries in order to conserve their scarce supplies of gold and convertible foreign exchange for payments to the dollar area.

These misgivings about the existing payments arrangements were reinforced by developments in the fall of 1947. By that time, the effective credit or debit balances under existing payments agreements were tending more and more to exceed the bilateral ceilings, and had forced a resumption of gold settlements. Simultaneously, there had been an actual decline in the volume of intra-European trade. Illustrative of the thinking which related these two events was that of Mr. Robert Triffin, a staff member, who in July 1948 was to take charge of the Fund's Paris Office; Mr. Triffin regarded the decline in European trade as

---

[3] A comprehensive description of the development of the EPU can be found in William Diebold, *Trade and Payments in Western Europe*, and in Raymond F. Mikesell, *Foreign Exchange in the Postwar World*. The first three sections of this chapter are based largely on Mikesell's volume, Chap. 6, pp. 100–102, 108–23.

probably due in part to the progressive paralysis of the payments agreements mechanism.[4]

A number of officials believed that intra-European trade could be expanded by the institution of some system of multilateral compensation and a multilateralization of credits among European countries. What was required was a mechanism by which European countries having bilateral surpluses with other European countries could use these surpluses to finance (or to offset) their deficits with third countries in Europe. Payments in gold and convertible currencies between European countries could thereby be held to a minimum.

In addition, some way was needed to finance any over-all deficit a European country might have with its European trading partners as a group. The fact that some European countries, such as France and the Netherlands, had tended to have deficits with nearly all their European trading partners, while other countries, such as Belgium, tended to have surpluses, made it extremely difficult to establish a payments system through which even the bilateral positions that in theory could be offset against one another could, in practice, be cleared. Since all European countries had deficits with the dollar area, there were no dollar surpluses with which a European country could finance its deficit on intra-European account. By the same token, creditor countries, such as Belgium, that tended to have persistent surpluses with their European partners were anxious to receive convertible exchange with which to cover deficits with the Western Hemisphere.

FORERUNNERS OF THE EPU

Following meetings in London and Paris in the late summer and early fall of 1947, Belgium, France, Italy, Luxembourg, and the Netherlands signed a five-nation agreement on multilateral compensations in November 1947. The successful operation of compensation machinery of this kind was dependent, however, upon the balance of creditor-debtor relations between the participants in the system. The predominant creditor position of Belgium among European countries at the time, and the few participants in the scheme, narrowly limited the scope for compensation. It became apparent before long that, if any clearing system was to succeed, all the sixteen countries that had by then formally come together in the Organization for European Economic Cooperation (OEEC) would have to be brought into the system. Further, some way would have to be found to deal with those countries that were predominantly creditors or debtors of most of the other European countries.

There was considerable divergence of opinion among European countries as to what arrangements for multilateral clearing were preferable. Differences of

[4] Triffin, *World Money Maze*, p. 408.

view prevailed as well between European countries and officials of the Economic Cooperation Administration (ECA), an arm of the U.S. Government that had been set up in April 1948 to administer the European Recovery Program (ERP) on the U.S. side. Much debate concerned, for example, the arrangements to be made for the settlement of payments between debtors and creditors that were in excess of agreed limits. Especially basic was the question of how liberal should be the terms under which credits to debtors would be extended. If credit terms were too liberal, the pressure on debtor countries to correct the causes of their balance of payments deficits might not be sufficient.

In addition, creditor countries did not like the prospect of extending further substantial credits to their European neighbors; such credit extension not only entailed the loss of current receipts of convertible exchange, but also had an inflationary impact on the economies of the creditors. Belgium, therefore, as well as some other countries—including France, Italy, Luxembourg, and the Netherlands—favored a completely multilateral payments system, with excess credit positions being covered by an arrangement for U.S. aid. Belgium in fact did not like any arrangement which did not provide for the conversion of credit positions into gold or dollars. The United Kingdom and the other OEEC countries, however, hesitated to adopt such a scheme, on the ground that it would introduce too much dollar competition into intra-European trade.

The United States, for its part, was unwilling in the initial stages of the ERP to allocate aid to a special clearing fund from which it would be used automatically. The intent of the U.S. Congress in passing the Economic Cooperation Act in April 1948 had been that ECA aid should cover specific dollar deficits of European countries for programs to achieve particular recovery goals. Moreover, the ECA wished to stimulate competition in intra-European trade, so that European industries would be induced to improve their productivity vis-à-vis both the industries of other European countries and the industries of the Western Hemisphere.

On October 14, 1948, the sixteen OEEC countries signed an Agreement on Intra-European Payments and Compensations, covering the year July 1948 to June 1949. This agreement had been made possible by the adoption by the ECA of a new arrangement for the settlement of intra-European deficits. Under a system of "conditional aid," part of the ECA's assistance to European countries was based upon the amount of each country's planned bilateral surplus with each of the other members. Recipients of conditional aid were, in turn, required to provide drawing rights to each bilateral partner with whom they expected to have a surplus during a specified period. Thus each ERP country would receive drawing rights on the member countries with which they were expected to have bilateral deficits, entitling them to incur a given amount of deficit without being required to pay gold or to accumulate an indebtedness. By this device, nearly every country entitled to ECA aid both extended drawing rights to other members (equal to the amount of conditional aid received) and received drawing rights from others.

With some relatively minor changes, a second such agreement was adopted in September 1949, for the year ending June 30, 1950. But, because these agreements did not permit the full offsetting of deficits against surpluses among participating countries, and because their operation required estimating the anticipated bilateral surpluses and deficits, they, like the earlier five-nation clearing scheme of 1947–48, were not wholly satisfactory. The system remained basically bilateral.

ESTABLISHMENT OF THE EPU

Late in 1949, at the suggestion of the ECA, the countries in the OEEC began to discuss again ideas for a payments arrangement for Western European and related currencies that would provide a better solution to intra-European trade and payments problems. In December 1949, the ECA and a number of European countries submitted to the OEEC proposals for a European clearing union.

There were long negotiations over numerous difficult problems. One problem, for example, concerned the treatment of the pound sterling. Should sterling be treated differently from other European currencies because of its international character—that is, because sterling was widely used in third country settlements and as a form in which monetary reserves were held? Additional complications arose from the fact that the sterling area encompassed a large number of independent monetary authorities, whereas each of the continental European currencies was controlled by a single monetary authority. What, for example, would be the relations between an independent country like Australia and the European members of the EPU? Accounts within the sterling area were already settled between the member countries; if the sterling area settled its accounts with the EPU on an aggregated net basis, the United Kingdom would have to cover with gold and dollar payments the EPU deficits of the rest of the sterling area as well as those of Britain alone.

There was also the problem that some OEEC members held sizable accumulated sterling balances. If these countries were permitted to use such balances to settle EPU deficits, Britain might be required to pay gold to the EPU on account of large transfers of sterling to the EPU by these OEEC members. To settle these difficulties, the ECA agreed to reimburse the United Kingdom for any net payment of dollars to the EPU which might result from the use of accumulated sterling holdings by participating EPU countries to cover their deficits with the Union.

The agreement setting up the EPU was finally signed on September 19, 1950, to be effective for a period of two years from July 1, 1950 to June 30, 1952. The new Union was designed to facilitate liberalization of intra-European trade on a nondiscriminatory basis; to assist its members in their progress toward viable economies, especially by supplying credit and providing incentives; and to encourage them to achieve or maintain high and stable levels of trade and employment. Like the Fund, the EPU also stood for the maintenance of internal and external financial equilibrium and the need for European countries to return to full multilateral trade and to currency convertibility.

There were two important features of the arrangements: the full multilateralization of payments among members of the OEEC and their associated monetary areas through a compensation mechanism, and a means of facilitating the net payments due from debtors after the compensations were effected. The first feature came from provision for a complete netting of all bilateral payments positions at the end of each accounting period. Each member country was to report its position with every other member to the Bank for International Settlements (BIS) at the end of each month. The BIS was then to determine for each country its "accounting surplus or deficit" for that month. The bilateral positions with other members were thus eliminated in exchange for a position with the EPU.

The complicated nature of the EPU derived from the method of net settlement—not from the clearing operation. Within certain limits, the settlement of accounting surpluses and deficits was to consist merely of the crediting or debiting of each member's account. EPU credits were to be available for use in covering a deficit with other EPU members, since each member agreed to accept EPU credits in settlement of a credit against any other member. When a member's accounting credit or debit reached a certain level, additional amounts had to be settled partly in gold. Schedules fixing the proportions of the monthly settlements to be made in gold by debtors and to be received in gold by creditors provided for the payment of an increasing proportion by debtors as their cumulative deficits rose and the receipt of a decreasing proportion by creditors as their cumulative surpluses, for which a quota was set, rose.

While most of the liquidity of the payments system was provided by the members themselves through the extension of credits, some working capital was provided by the ECA. At the beginning of the EPU's operations in the middle of 1950, the ECA made available to the EPU $350 million to be used in the event that gold payments to creditor countries exceeded gold receipts from debtors.

The EPU was to be administered by a Managing Board, whose policymaking power was, however, limited to making proposals to the OEEC Council, by which it was appointed. The EPU remained in existence until December 1958, when it was terminated following the establishment of external convertibility for the major European currencies. In accordance with an agreement reached by the OEEC in July 1955, the European Monetary Agreement (EMA) then came into force.

THE FUND'S INITIAL REACTIONS [5]

In view of the similarity of the objectives of the European payments arrangements, and those of the EPU as established, with those of the Fund, it might have been expected that the Fund's reactions to these arrangements would have been at least favorable, if not enthusiastic. Indeed, in the early stages, the Board agreed to send observers to the meetings of the Financial Committee of the Committee on Cooperation of European Countries, held in London in the fall of 1947. However, several Directors were anxious that the Fund should not become committed to any particular clearing scheme, especially as a number of proposals were just beginning to be discussed among the European countries.

Fund observers did attend meetings in London. However, although the report of the participants in the London meetings had indicated that the Fund was invited to send an observer to the next series of meetings in Paris in October 1947, the Fund was not in fact represented. The absence of a Fund observer at these meetings was to have lasting consequence. For it was then and there that Belgium, France, Italy, Luxembourg, and the Netherlands signed the first European payments agreement. While the Fund was not represented, the BIS was. The first draft of the payments agreement signed by these five nations had provided for the Fund to act as a clearing agent, but, in the absence of a representative from the Fund, the BIS's offer of its services as a clearing agent was accepted. The BIS remained the agent for all later intra-European payments organizations, including the EPU and the subsequent EMA.

The Fund has at times been criticized for failing to become at least the clearing agent for the EPU. However, as far as the Fund's records show, its absence from the Paris meeting in October 1947 was accidental, although how the accident happened is not clear. In a statement to the Board on November 12, 1948, the Managing Director stated that it had been due to a "genuine misunderstanding." Actually, the Managing Director, some Executive Directors, and most staff members were inclined to advocate a stronger role for the Fund than that of clearing agent. As early as December 1947 the staff suggested to the Executive Board that additional credits were essential to enable a European clearing mechanism to work and that the Fund could and should provide them. In May 1948, the Board discussed a specific staff plan for the Fund's participation in European multilateral clearing arrangements; this plan would have had the

[5] Details of the Executive Directors' discussions of the various plans for European payments arrangements may be found in Vol. I above, pp. 212–23, 288–90.

Fund make available resources of $338 million, in the form of drawings of Belgian francs or other European currencies.

But, although some Directors believed that the aims of multilateral clearing in Europe were in accord with the Fund's objectives, other Directors had misgivings. Would European payments schemes, in fact, help to lay the basis for eventual convertibility of European currencies? Would a clearing arrangement not tend to postpone the solution of Europe's problems rather than help to solve them? Was there not a danger that increasing the means of payment in Europe would encourage nonessential and luxury imports more than essential trade? In addition, since the Fund had in the previous month taken a decision (the "ERP Decision" of April 1948) limiting European members' access to the Fund's dollar resources during the life of the ERP, several Directors inquired specifically about those portions of any plan which called for use of the Fund's dollar resources.[6] Would not a contribution from the Fund to clearing arrangements be counter to the Fund's "ERP Decision"? What guarantee could there be that the Fund's commitments under the clearing arrangements proposed would not be excessive, using up in a few months resources which should be made available over several years?

Concern of the kind indicated by these questions led the Directors to take, on June 4, 1948, a decision which limited the Fund's involvement in European payments arrangements.[7] The decision stated that the Fund hoped that an arrangement could be made for multilateralizing European payments. The Fund also hoped that a revision of and a moderate rise in credits could be agreed for use in multilateral payments and, reiterating the Fund's "ERP Decision" on the use of its own resources, hoped that any increase in credits could be financed by the creditor countries. The Fund was also willing to place its advice and technical facilities at the disposal of its members in connection with the formulation and administration of any multilateral payments arrangements and for other purposes related to their payments problems.

Mr. Triffin, as head of the Fund's Paris Office, strongly advocated participation by the Fund in European multilateral clearing arrangements. Early in 1949 he submitted to the Executive Board a second specific proposal for a modification of the European payments arrangements then being discussed; this proposal again envisaged the possible use of the Fund's resources as an aid to multilateralizing payments in 1949–50. However, the proposal was not accepted by the Board.

The Managing Director of the Fund, Mr. Gutt, was also very much in favor of the Fund's cooperating actively with the plans for multilateral clearing which

[6] The "ERP Decision" is reproduced in Chapter 18 below (pp. 395–96). Other implications of the decision are discussed later in this chapter (p. 328).

[7] See above, Vol. I, p. 221.

were continuing to go forward in Europe. On one occasion, in November 1948, he made a powerful plea to the Executive Board for the Fund to take an active share in these plans. He was concerned, inter alia, that if the sixteen nations assembled together in Europe did not have enough contact with the rest of the world, they might tend to build up a so-called European monetary policy, which might be different from, or opposed to, an international monetary policy. Again in January 1950 he recommended to the Board that the Fund participate in the discussions for the setting up of the EPU.

Anticipating that the Managing Director's appeal might bring favorable response from the Board, the staff came up with new suggestions as to how European clearing could be conducted through the Fund. While recognizing that the Fund had been used very little for the purchase of European currencies, the staff believed that the Fund constituted suitable machinery to facilitate payments within Europe if a large group of European countries decided jointly to use the Fund for this purpose. However, for reasons discussed in the next section the Board was unwilling to proceed along these lines.

SOME DIFFERING OPINIONS

Throughout these years, the Board was kept informed by the Paris Office of the various proposals for clearing arrangements which were put forward in Europe. After studying these, however, tne staff formed the view that the clearing mechanisms being considered would be more likely, at least in the short run, to impede than to advance convertibility and a solution of the dollar problem. The argument was that, while the progressive removal of trade and payments restrictions within Europe as called for by the planned arrangements was an objective of great importance, it could not be regarded as transcending the basic need that must dominate European policy: a tenable *dollar* payments position.

It was pointed out that even for the countries participating in the OEEC, intra-European trade as measured by imports was only 46 per cent of their total trade; and that the magnitudes of the payments deficits within Europe were quite small compared to the dollar deficits. The staff stressed that the restrictions from which European countries suffered most were not those against one another, but those which they had to impose on their dollar imports because of their own inadequate dollar earnings, and concluded that it was in the interest of European countries to reduce restrictions on trade and payments between them to that minimum *which was consistent with positive progress in the solution of the dollar problem.*

Elaborating this argument, the staff reasoned that before September 1949 Fund members had tended to concentrate on exporting to the high-priced markets of Europe. This was because inflated demand within Europe had made these markets, despite restrictions, more attractive than dollar markets. Under such conditions, the general removal of trade and payments restrictions within Europe could only have added to the difficulties that European countries already faced in instituting positive measures to meet their dollar problems. Since the devaluations of September 1949, there had been a great change in the relative attractiveness to exporters of dollar markets and of markets in Europe and associated currency areas. If the active and latent inflation within Europe and in the associated currency areas could be eliminated, the case would be exceptionally strong for the removal of nearly all trade and payments restrictions in the countries participating in any intra-European payments scheme. But until inflation had been at least sharply reduced, liberalization of European trade would not be likely to solve the dollar problem.

Recognizing that their conclusions were contrary to the usual opinions about European clearing arrangements and the liberalization of intra-European trade, staff members added some qualifications to their analysis. Their conclusions would be affected if the tendency that had been occurring among European countries for exports to the dollar area to be reduced were to be reversed after a new payments scheme had gone into effect. Furthermore, their conclusions could be altered depending on what happened to the productivity of European industries as trade barriers were relaxed and greater competition among European countries was induced. In the longer run, greater productivity might result in lower costs and prices which, in turn, would help to solve Europe's dollar problem.

Thus there were genuine differences of opinion, both in the staff and in the Executive Board, from the views being expressed in Europe concerning the advantages and disadvantages of the various proposed mechanisms.

The official policy of the Fund early in 1950 was exemplified by the Board's instructions to a staff mission which was to participate in discussions in Europe on the proposals for an EPU. The position of the Fund was that European countries needed primarily to overcome their inflationary difficulties and that, while inflation remained a threat, the role of credit, particularly of long- and medium-term credit, in the settlement of intra-European current balances should be restrained. Settlement in gold or dollars should be relatively large and should become the rule whenever possible.

The Fund considered that, in any European payments arrangement, credit had two functions as regards debtors and one as regards creditors. As regards debtors, credits were a substitute for grants insofar as they tended to undo the deterrent effect of any payments scheme on a debtor's building up of deficits. On the other hand, if credits were a substitute for required gold payments, they acted as a safety valve to prevent a scheme from acting too rigorously and perhaps from breaking down. As regards creditors, the function of credit was to make earnings inside Europe less attractive than gold, in order to discourage undue attempts by creditors to earn dollars by trading with European countries rather than by exporting to the dollar area. Moderate amounts of credit, with large amounts of settlements required in gold or dollars, would best reconcile these conflicting functions of credit.

THE QUESTION OF LIAISON

Apart from the merits of European clearing arrangements, the question of liaison with any European organization that might be established was also carefully weighed in the Fund. Once it had become evident that the EPU was to come into being, the question of liaison became, for the Fund, a more pertinent issue than the nature of the particular clearing mechanism to be set up.

Need for collaboration

Many, both among the Fund staff and on the Board, believed that the closest possible relationship should be established between the Fund and the EPU. The fact that the EPU involved a number of the Fund's members was itself sufficient, several thought, to argue for close collaboration. The provisions agreed upon by the OEEC Council could lead to actions by European members of the Fund which would be inconsistent with their obligations under the Fund Agreement. To avoid such situations, and to protect other members of the Fund from the consequences thereof, the Fund should be in close touch with the EPU and make its views known to its European members. Moreover, the shape which the EPU had taken might be changed from time to time, and the Fund had a duty to all of its members, including those in Europe, to do its best to assist in improving the system and in bringing about as rapidly as possible conditions under which the purposes of the Fund Agreement could be achieved.

The Fund also believed that it had a vital stake in any decisions taken by the EPU Managing Board. The Fund's attitude, prior to the establishment of the EPU, had been that the degree of its interest in the management of any European clearing arrangement depended greatly on the purposes of that management. If such management was to deal only with the financial terms on which credits were extended, such as the conditions for repayment and the rate of interest, the Fund had no concern with it. The Fund would have some concern if an EPU management was to deal with the amounts of credit granted; and if that management was to prescribe the policy conditions on which credits were granted, the Fund believed it was vitally concerned.

Once it was evident that the Managing Board of the EPU would have broad powers and would be discussing the policies of the OEEC members, the Fund believed its interests were definitely involved and that collaboration was important. The Board decided that, although the Fund's representatives should not seek to secure any special arrangements with the EPU, these representatives might ask to attend meetings of the EPU Managing Board. The Managing Director, Mr. Gutt, and the Deputy Managing Director, Mr. Overby, visited Paris several times in the last planning stages of the EPU in April, May, and June, 1950. The Managing Director went to Europe again prior to the Annual Meeting in Paris in September 1950, and simultaneous and subsequent visits to European countries were also made by the staff. The suggestions made by these Fund representatives were that the Fund might have a permanent observer on the EPU Board; then, after experience in Fund-EPU cooperation had been gained, a more formal relationship between the two organizations might be established.

Opposition to the Fund's participation

Several circumstances, however, operated against the possibilities of close cooperation, at least in the early years, between the Fund and the EPU. European countries were not necessarily eager for the Fund to have much, if any, participation in their arrangements. European countries had, to some extent, been disturbed by the Fund's "ERP Decision" on the use of its resources. They apparently did not take seriously the possibility, which was mentioned during the Board's discussions, that the amount of ERP aid might be reduced to the extent that Europe received dollar resources from the Fund. They therefore viewed the Fund's decision as a curtailment of the amount of dollar resources that might have been available to Europe. The Fund's non-dollar resources were of less interest to them, because these currencies were inconvertible at that time and repurchases would have to be made in gold or dollars. There was also some feeling in Europe that the Fund was dominated by the U.S. Government, with which the Europeans already had to deal through the ECA.

That the European countries hesitated to have close participation by the Fund in their arrangements was manifested as early as the summer of 1948, when the Fund's representative in Paris was endeavoring to obtain representation for the Fund in the OEEC and a role in the proposed first Intra-European Payments Agreement. He was then told by Mr. Hubert Ansiaux, Chairman of the Financial Committee of the OEEC as well as an Executive Director of the Fund, that there was a great deal of resistance in the OEEC toward inviting international organizations to be represented officially at its regular meetings, as the OEEC considered itself primarily a European organization. Again, at the end of January 1950, Mr. Ansiaux wrote to the Managing Director about the EPU proposals and, especially, about European attitudes toward the Fund's participation in such a Union and in the OEEC. He indicated that while it would be possible for the Fund to have an observer to follow the discussions in the OEEC on the EPU proposals, it appeared impossible, for both political and practical reasons, that the Fund should participate either in the discussions of the plans or in their implementation.

Later in 1950, discussions with the continental European countries showed that they were willing to have an observer from the Fund on the EPU Board. However, discussions with the British representative in the OEEC and the EPU showed that the United Kingdom opposed the idea of any Fund observer. The reasons given were as follows: First, the United Kingdom wanted to keep the number of people around the table very small. Second, the discussions of the EPU Board were confidential even vis-à-vis members of the EPU not represented on the EPU Board. Third, some countries in the EPU were not members of the Fund. Finally, the British representative argued that the Fund was unable to maintain the necessary confidentiality in view of the insistence of its Board on receiving all information given to the staff and of the right of the Executive Directors to report to their governments.

Still another political consideration militated against the Fund, with its world-wide membership, taking much of a role in European arrangements. The U.S. Government, in particular the ECA and the State Department, had become committed to an independent EPU as an essential means of promoting European political integration. Integration was expected to be furthered principally by getting the European countries to coordinate their monetary policies toward the common end of balance of payments equilibrium.

In addition to the political considerations that made it difficult for the Fund to participate effectively either in the discussions for European clearing or in their implementation, there were two practical difficulties which precluded any effective role for the Fund. One was that it appeared inconceivable that decisions taken at a ministerial level in the OEEC should be subject to review by the ministers' own representatives on the Fund's Board. The other was that EPU operations had to be directed from Paris, not from Washington, and if decisions made in Paris had to be approved by the Fund's Board, there would inevitably be delays.

All these circumstances, taken together, had the result that a representative from the Fund was not invited to attend meetings of the EPU Managing Board until 1952.

IMPROVEMENT IN RELATIONS

Improvement in Fund-EPU relations, when it came, resulted not from any formal decisions but rather from the more favorable attitudes in Europe toward cooperation with the Fund which followed the Fund's agreement in June 1952 to a request from Belgium for a stand-by arrangement.

In June 1952, the OEEC Council agreed to extend the EPU for another year, until June 30, 1953. But among the problems that had to be solved was the emergence of Belgium as a large creditor. It was necessary for the EPU to reach agreement concerning payment to Belgium for its past surplus and to arrange for new credits for the coming year. Part of the settlement worked out between the EPU and Belgium was that $50 million would be paid to Belgium in five annual installments. But Belgium was reluctant to agree to this arrangement unless it was, meanwhile, safeguarded against a possible dollar drain, and the U.S. Government had decided not to commit any more funds to the EPU. A way was found around this impasse when the Fund agreed to a stand-by arrangement with Belgium for $50 million which was automatically renewable for five years unless canceled by either party. The commitment from the Fund gave the National Bank of Belgium assurance that, if necessary, it could mobilize in advance the dollar debt owed to Belgium by the EPU.

The OEEC Council, in its meeting of July 11, 1952, formally expressed its appreciation of the prompt and favorable response of the Fund to the Belgian request, and declared its hope that "it may also be possible to have fruitful collaboration in the future between the Fund and the Organization in connection with problems of mutual concern." As a result, members of the Fund's Office in Paris were invited with increasing frequency to meetings of the EPU Managing Board.

In the spring of 1953, the EPU Managing Board's recommendations for the extension of the Union contained three paragraphs on relations with the Fund. It was stated that close cooperation with the Fund was increasingly necessary and practical, especially as European countries needed more reserves to continue their progress toward derestriction. Examples were listed of circumstances in which EPU members could usefully draw on the Fund, which seemed to raise no problems except for one which suggested the possibility that the Fund and the EPU open joint credits for European countries so as to stabilize their currencies. Also suggested were a joint examination of problem countries and coordinated decisions on the measures to be taken. These suggestions were discussed by the two staffs, but no formal proposals were made to the Fund.

In the summer of 1953, the Fund staff suggested, and the Executive Board approved, the formal transmittal of certain Fund documents, including Part II of the Fund's consultation reports, for the use of the OEEC, subject to approval in each case by the Executive Director concerned. In April 1956, the Board also agreed to transmit to the OEEC Part I of the Fund's consultation reports, again subject to the right of any Executive Director to object to the transmission of any report in which he was interested.

Closer liaison between the Fund and the OEEC also developed as the latter assumed responsibilities for supervising the progress of its members toward liberalization of trade. As the trade of OEEC countries began to be freed from restrictions, the objectives of the OEEC and of the EPU came closer to those of the Fund than had been thought likely when the EPU was set up. The result was that Fund-EPU relations steadily improved.

Some doubts remained as to whether the EPU made restrictions against dollar area imports more discriminatory than they would otherwise have been. A few Directors argued that the EPU actually contributed to reduce such discrimination, but others continued to have misgivings. After the EPU had come to an end, the Managing Director of the Fund, Mr. Jacobsson, stated that "the European Payments Union, for eight and a half years up to the end of 1958, made a most useful contribution to progress in Europe by assuring prompt payments and by giving an impetus to the relaxation of trade restrictions." [8]

One final word may be added about the Fund's reactions in 1947–50 to European payments arrangements. The Fund itself was a young institution. It was just beginning to formulate general policies to guide it in its relations with members. Moreover, it was having difficulty in establishing its own authority, especially in the field of exchange rates. In these circumstances, it is understandable that the prospect of a European financial organization dealing with many of the subjects in the Fund's field, and including many of the Fund's important members, was viewed with some anxiety.

During the next several years the Fund was able to work out the policies it would pursue—toward exchange rates, the use of its resources, the transitional period, restrictions, and the restoration of convertibility. By 1952 its own consultation program with its members had also commenced. Hence it is not unlikely that, had the whole matter of European payments arrangements come up five years later than it did, the outcome might have been quite different from what it was.

[8] *Summary Proceedings, 1959*, p. 15.

CHAPTER

16

Collaborating with the GATT

Margaret G. de Vries

WHEN THE FUND WAS PLANNED it was expected that there would be some international body responsible for trade relations. Resolution VII passed at Bretton Woods recommended to the governments participating in the Conference that they seek to reach agreement as soon as possible on ways and means to reduce obstacles to international trade and in other ways to promote mutually advantageous international commercial relations.[1] Originally it had been thought that the Fund and the proposed International Trade Organization (ITO) would have a common membership.

Thereafter—in the planning for an ITO, in the provisions of the General Agreement on Tariffs and Trade (GATT), and in the GATT's subsequent activities—the Fund has continuously and overtly recognized that it has a vital stake in the regulation of barriers to world trade in any form. The attainment of the Fund's own objectives has been regarded as intertwined with the successful operation of some international mechanism for achieving the same freedom from restrictions in relation to international trade as the Fund seeks to achieve with respect to international payments. In its relations with the GATT, therefore, the Fund has been guided by a conviction that the freeing of trade and the freeing of exchange are complementary, if not interdependent, objectives.

The GATT provides that any contracting party to it that is not a member of the Fund must enter into a Special Exchange Agreement with the Fund so that the Fund can, for those countries, fulfill its responsibilities to the GATT. Such Special Exchange Agreements were used for a time for one or two countries, notably for New Zealand until that country joined the Fund in 1961. More recently, contracting parties to the GATT that are not Fund members have been given waivers of the applicability of the relevant provisions of the GATT, and have agreed to provide the Fund with the information and documentation

[1] *Proceedings*, p. 941.

necessary for the Fund to make its presentation to the GATT, should such presentation be required.

FUND PARTICIPATION IN SETTING UP THE GATT

Meetings for the proposed ITO

Shortly after its establishment, the Fund participated in the meetings which were called by the United Nations in 1946 to plan for the ITO. The Preparatory Committee for an International Conference on Trade and Employment had two meetings, one in London from October 15, 1946 to November 20, 1946, and a second in Geneva from April 10, 1947 to August 25, 1947. Between these periods a drafting committee met in Washington from January 20 to February 25, 1947. In the following winter a third session of the Preparatory Committee was held in Havana.

The Fund's acute interest in whatever plans were drawn up was immediately made clear by the Executive Directors. The field of activity of the proposed ITO would, at the least, run parallel to that of the Fund. It might even be so formulated as to encroach upon the Fund's responsibilities; indeed, the rules of the ITO might provide for its members a means of escape from the jurisdiction of the Fund. In either case, the Fund's influence would be impaired. How to prevent this formed a major preoccupation of the Executive Directors as they considered the Fund's participation in the Preparatory Committee's sessions. The Directors were especially mindful of the wide differences in attitude among the major countries planning the trade organization. While the United States sought, for example, the outright prohibition of trade restrictions, especially discriminatory ones, except when members had large or prolonged balance of payments deficits, the United Kingdom and Australia were less desirous of erecting a strong trade organization. At the same time, the Executive Board wished to assert the Fund's right under its Articles to supervise any issues pertaining to exchange rates, multiple rates, exchange restrictions, or exchange controls, regardless of the purpose for which they were used.

At the first session of the Preparatory Committee in London, the Fund's representative, Mr. Luthringer (United States), Alternate to Mr. White, made several suggestions: that in the charter being drafted the use of quantitative restrictions under the ITO should be subject to provisions similar to those of Article XIV of the Fund Agreement; that the charter should seek, once the transitional period had been passed, to limit the use of quantitative restrictions to circumstances in which other techniques had been exhausted; and that, in these conditions, the ITO should request the Fund to make a finding as to whether the member's foreign exchange reserves warranted the imposition of the proposed restrictions, and should subsequently consult the Fund on the possibilities for the progressive removal of restrictions that had been authorized.

At the session in Geneva, the Fund's representative, Mr. Saad (Egypt), saw to it that the provisions concerning multiple exchange rates and control of capital movements which were in the draft ITO charter were in accord with the Fund Agreement, and that the draft charter for the ITO provided for close coordination of policy between the two organizations, both on exchange questions and on quantitative restrictions. The activities of the Fund's representatives at these preparatory sessions helped to ensure that the charter of the ITO would be compatible with the Fund's interests.

Following the Havana Conference of 1947–48, Mr. Saad emphasized to the Fund's Board that the interdependence of the roles of the Fund and the ITO made it imperative that there should be full cooperation between the two bodies. He suggested that the Fund's Board should immediately consider the terms of a possible agreement for cooperation with the ITO. Hence, in July 1948 a Committee of Directors on Liaison with the ITO, with Mr. Saad as its first chairman, was formed. When the ITO failed to materialize, this committee was reconstituted as the Committee on Liaison with the CONTRACTING PARTIES to the GATT, and in that form has continued to be one of very few standing committees of the Executive Board.

THE GATT EMERGES

Pending action by the prospective members of the ITO, a multilateral trade agreement, called the General Agreement on Tariffs and Trade, which had been agreed at the second session in Geneva, was put into provisional application during the summer of 1948. Fortunately for the Fund, many of the relationships with the Fund that had been so carefully defined for the proposed ITO were contained in the GATT.

The GATT consists of tariff provisions and of regulations concerning general commercial policy. A multilateral trade agreement of such comprehensive scope, covering not only tariffs but also the general principles of commercial policies, is without precedent. The participating governments deliberately avoided the traditional pattern of an international organization; they merely established contractual relations among themselves. The participants in the GATT attempt to achieve their purpose of reducing excessive trade barriers through a number of consultative arrangements.[2] In September 1948, the Board of the Fund approved proposals by the Chairman of the CONTRACTING PARTIES for informal cooperation between the GATT and the Fund. Between 1948 and

[2] For a detailed explanation of how the GATT is organized and how it works, see Gerard Curzon, *Multilateral Commercial Diplomacy*, Chap. II, p. 53.

1950 thirty-one countries, most of which were members of the Fund, became contracting parties to the GATT.

PROVISIONS OF THE GATT RELATING TO THE FUND

The Fund's close ties with the GATT are made explicit by three basic provisions contained in Article XV of the GATT. Paragraph 1 provides:

> The CONTRACTING PARTIES shall seek co-operation with the International Monetary Fund to the end that the CONTRACTING PARTIES and the Fund may pursue a co-ordinated policy with regard to exchange questions within the jurisdiction of the Fund and questions of quantitative restrictions and other trade measures within the jurisdiction of the CONTRACTING PARTIES.

The first sentence of paragraph 2 states:

> In all cases in which the CONTRACTING PARTIES are called upon to consider or deal with problems concerning monetary reserves, balances of payments or foreign exchange arrangements, they shall consult fully with the International Monetary Fund.

Later in the same paragraph the CONTRACTING PARTIES are required

> in cases involving the criteria set forth in paragraph 2 (*a*) of Article XII or in paragraph 9 of Article XVIII [to] accept the determination of the Fund as to what constitutes a serious decline in the contracting party's monetary reserves, a very low level of its monetary reserves or a reasonable rate of increase in its monetary reserves, and as to the financial aspects of other matters covered in consultation in such cases.

In sum, the general effect of the GATT is that countries are to coordinate their exchange policies (under the jurisdiction of the Fund) and their trade policies (under the jurisdiction of the GATT). The CONTRACTING PARTIES must consult the Fund on all matters dealing with reserves and balances of payments and must accept the Fund's findings. The CONTRACTING PARTIES themselves, of course, determine whether or not the subject with which they are dealing involves monetary problems, and consequently whether consultations with the Fund are required. Legal opinion is that, in the final analysis, the GATT is sovereign in these matters. Moreover, the Fund's findings are only part of the material on which the GATT's decisions are taken.[3]

The provisions of the GATT relating to the Fund are the more significant because the GATT bases any permission given to a contracting party to institute or maintain import restrictions on the state of that country's reserve and balance of payments positions. The specific provisions of the GATT governing the use of import restrictions were revised in 1954–55 during a

---

[3] Ervin Hexner, "The General Agreement on Tariffs and Trade and the Monetary Fund," *Staff Papers*, Vol. I (1950–51), pp. 448–52.

Review Session of the CONTRACTING PARTIES; the improvement in the balances of payments of most countries by the mid-1950's had produced a desire to put an end to the provisional character of the GATT and to transform it into a permanent international organization.[4] It is the revised rules, operative since October 1957, to which we refer in this chapter.[5]

All restrictions are subject to a system of periodic consultations, based on a detailed examination by the CONTRACTING PARTIES of the level, methods, and effects on trade of the restrictions in use by the various countries. The General Agreement also makes the purpose of these consultations fairly explicit. The CONTRACTING PARTIES, finding that a country's restrictions are inconsistent with the provisions of the GATT, can advise that the restrictions be suitably modified. They can even make appropriate recommendations for securing conformity with GATT provisions within a specified period, and sanctions against noncompliance with such recommendations are provided for in the form of a suspension of obligations by any adversely affected contracting party.

More specifically, provision is made for the introduction or maintenance of restrictions to safeguard a contracting party's balance of payments at two points—in Article XII, and in Section B of Article XVIII, the latter applying to less developed countries. By paragraph 2 (*a*) of Article XII, import restrictions imposed by a contracting party under that Article may not exceed those necessary

> (i) to forestall the imminent threat of, or to stop, a serious decline in its monetary reserves, or
>
> (ii) in the case of a contracting party with very low monetary reserves, to achieve a reasonable rate of increase in its reserves.

Paragraphs 9 and 11 of Article XVIII:B provide broadly the same facilities, but with some changes in phraseology, such as the elimination of the word "imminent" from clause (i), and the replacement of "very low" in clause (ii) by the word "inadequate."

The two Articles go on to provide for consultations on restrictions imposed or maintained. The text in Article XII is:

> 4. (*a*) Any contracting party applying new restrictions or raising the general level of its existing restrictions by a substantial intensification of the measures applied under this Article shall immediately after instituting or intensifying such restrictions (or, in circumstances in which prior consultation is practicable, before doing so) consult with the CONTRACTING PARTIES as to the nature of its balance of payments difficulties, alternative corrective measures which may be available, and the possible effect of the restriction on the economies of other contracting parties.
>
> (*b*) On a date to be determined by them, the CONTRACTING PARTIES shall review all restrictions still applied under this Article on that date. Beginning one year

[4] Curzon, *Multilateral Commercial Diplomacy*, p. 136.

[5] The provisions of the earlier rules can be found in Hexner, "General Agreement on Tariffs and Trade and the Monetary Fund," pp. 436–43, 445–48.

> after that date, contracting parties applying import restrictions under this Article shall enter into consultations of the type provided for in sub-paragraph (*a*) of this paragraph with the CONTRACTING PARTIES annually.

Similar provisions are included in Article XVIII: 12 (relevant to less developed countries), except that the consultations provided for in subparagraph (*b*) are to take place at intervals of two years instead of annually.

QUESTIONS CONCERNING THE FUND'S ROLE

At first the Executive Directors had doubts about the precise way in which the Fund should implement the provisions called for by the GATT. In May 1949 South Africa sought approval under the GATT for some new import restrictions, and the CONTRACTING PARTIES consulted the Fund on the question whether these restrictions were justified by South Africa's balance of payments. The request for the Fund's advice led some Executive Directors to inquire into the extent of the Fund's responsibility. Specifically, the question was raised whether the Fund should merely report facts to the GATT, or whether the Fund should also provide an evaluation of the facts. Mr. Southard (United States) thought that full consultation, such as the agreement with the GATT visualized, necessarily implied an evaluation. On the other hand, Mr. McFarlane (Australia), who had been elected by South Africa, suggested that only the GATT could decide on the implications of import restrictions for its other members; the Fund should not risk an independent opinion which might clash with that of the GATT.

Since the exact nature of the South African proposals was not made clear at first, and since the issue of discriminatory restrictions was involved and several Directors doubted whether enough data was available to conclude that discrimination was justified, the issue was not really resolved. Rather, it was decided to transmit to the GATT a staff study of the balance of payments of South Africa, which justified import restrictions, but to omit the last paragraph of the study, which would have advised the GATT that some discrimination was not unreasonable.

Something of a major conflict on these issues was still to come. Mr. McFarlane continued to urge that the Board should be very cautious in such matters. As the representative of Australia, he stated that his Government had understood when joining the Fund that the Fund would not intervene in matters of import restrictions. But Mr. Saad, who had been representing the Fund at the consultations with the GATT, pointed out that, where import restrictions were imposed for balance of payments reasons, the responsibilities of the Fund and the GATT were necessarily interlocked. No final decision on this issue was reached during the year, and the discussion was resumed in 1950, when further restrictions were submitted by South Africa for approval under the GATT and a fresh consultation took place.

There were various reasons why countries, such as Australia, that were apprehensive about subjecting their import restrictions to international review tended to fear the Fund's scrutiny more than they did that of the CONTRACTING PARTIES to the GATT. For one thing, the Fund had a large professional staff to prepare for consultations whereas the GATT did not. For another, since the Board of the Fund was in continuous session, while the CONTRACTING PARTIES met only periodically in General Session, the Fund's Directors had frequent opportunity to review and comment on the restrictions of its members. More importantly, the Fund's system of weighted voting gave such countries less of a vote in the decision-making process than did the GATT's one country, one vote system. Finally, until the GATT was revised in the middle 1950's, its powers were clearly less than those of the Fund: no provision was made in the GATT for the organization to make representations to its members and it had no financial resources of which to dispose. After all, the GATT had come into being because countries had not been able to agree on an international trade organization. For all these reasons, the GATT was less able than the Fund to take action against the restrictions of its members. There were some observers who went even further, believing that the role of the Fund as a fact-finding agency for the GATT would have little influence on the attitudes of the CONTRACTING PARTIES.[6]

CONTROVERSY AT TORQUAY

The controversies concerning the Fund's role in the consultations under the GATT came to a head in 1950, when several countries in the sterling area undertook such consultations. In July 1949 the Commonwealth Finance Ministers had agreed that, because of a continuing and growing drain on the dollar reserves of the sterling area,[7] each member of the sterling area would reduce its dollar expenditures by 25 per cent of their total in calendar 1948. The GATT permitted contracting parties temporarily to *intensify* restrictions—including making their restrictions more discriminatory—in order to forestall or stop a serious decline in monetary reserves or to permit a reasonable rate of increase in reserves; consultations were, however, required. The CONTRACTING PARTIES, therefore, in accordance with Article XV of the GATT, invited Australia,

[6] Michael A. Heilperin, *Answer to the State Department's Comments on the Document, Basic Criticisms of the Havana Charter* (October 1948), as cited in Curzon, *Multilateral Commercial Diplomacy*, pp. 134–35.

[7] See Chapter 4 above, pp. 97–98.

Ceylon, India, New Zealand, Pakistan, South Africa, Southern Rhodesia, and the United Kingdom (as well as Chile, which had also intensified its restrictions) to consult. The Fund was invited by the GATT to take part in these consultations, which took place at the Fifth Session held at Torquay, England, in the autumn of 1950.

Debates within the Fund

As the Fund's staff began to prepare the documentation for these consultations, the deep differences of opinion among the Executive Directors on just what the Fund should submit to the GATT came to the surface. Should the Fund's documentation focus only on the justification for the restrictions when they were initially imposed—that is in July 1949—or should emphasis be placed on the need for the restrictions at the time of the consultations, that is, late in 1950? (Since the devaluations of September 1949 had occurred in the meantime, and presumably alleviated the need for some of the restrictions, the difference in the date to be used was significant.) Should the Fund supply to the GATT only facts, especially statistical material, or should an evaluation and conclusions, particularly conclusions passed by the Fund's Board, be transmitted as well?

Eventually these questions had to be answered by vote.[8] The Board decided that the Fund was to supply to the GATT not only relevant statistical data but also conclusions as to the current need for restrictions. The information supplied to the GATT on behalf of the Fund thus covered the restrictive systems and the balance of payments and presented analyses of the causes and effects of the import restrictions in the light of the existing situation. Separate reports to the GATT contained the Fund's conclusions with respect to the import restrictions of each country. The results of the Fund's analyses varied from case to case. For some countries, balance of payments conditions did not seem to warrant further relaxation of import restrictions. For others, the conclusion was that circumstances were such that a progressive relaxation of discriminatory import restrictions could begin, having due regard to the uncertainties of the situation.

That separate reports and conclusions were prepared for each country was significant in itself. By judging the need for restrictions of each sterling area country in the light of its own balance of payments situation, the Fund was in effect challenging the principles by which the sterling area hung together. The two basic tenets of the sterling area were the institution of common policies by all its members and the combining of dollar reserves in a central pool, regardless of the balance of payments position of the individual sterling area member. Sterling area members, especially the United Kingdom, were anxious to preserve the sterling area for both economic and political reasons. For all members it

[8] See Chapter 11 above, pp. 230–31.

provided a sheltered export market; for the United Kingdom it helped to provide non-sterling earnings, and for the "outer sterling area," easy access to the London capital market. In addition, the sterling area preserved political ties within the British Commonwealth. The Fund's position was the same as it was later to take in its own consultations, as regards members both of the sterling area and of the EPU—namely, that groupings of these types were not members of the Fund or of the GATT, and that each member of these groupings as a member of the Fund (or a contracting party to the GATT) was individually responsible for its international commitments.

Deliberations at Torquay

Mr. Saad led the Fund's delegation to Torquay. The actual consultations with the GATT were protracted and at times acrimonious. The method, the findings, and the recommendations of the Fund were supported in the GATT by the delegates of Belgium, Cuba, Canada, and the United States—mainly nations whose exports were the subject of discrimination. But the Fund's findings were bitterly contested by representatives of the United Kingdom, Australia, and New Zealand. They argued that the Fund had to recognize the existence of the sterling area and that it was unrealistic and unhelpful to look at individual nations apart from their membership in the regional system. Beyond this, they asserted that the discrimination resulting from the dollar pool was defensible because such discrimination enhanced the hard currency reserves of the sterling area and thereby helped to create conditions under which sterling could be made convertible and discrimination eventually eliminated. Australia also continued to argue, with considerable acerbity, that the Fund's concern was exclusively with exchange and other financial matters, and not at all with import restrictions or trade controls; that the Fund's advice should have been directed only to the need for intensifying restrictions at the time that the step was taken and not with the current position; and that the Fund's contribution to GATT consultations should be limited to detailed factual information.

Gradually, debates over these issues tended to subside, especially after the Fund began its own annual consultations program in March 1952. The Fund continued to be concerned that temporary regional arrangements, such as the sterling area and the EPU, might not be the road to convertibility and might become permanent economic blocs, but it confined itself to pointing out the dangers, such as prolonged inconvertibility, that could result from regional arrangements and to urging countries individually to reduce their restrictions. The Australian representatives did not push their position as strongly as before. A working party set up in Geneva in October 1951, under Australian chairmanship, to draft a procedure for consultations in and after March 1952 recommended only that a consultation under the GATT should not take place until the Fund had completed its consultation under Article XIV with the same country, and that the Fund should make available to the CONTRACTING PARTIES the results of its consultation with that member. In later years, in recognition of Australia's interest in GATT matters, the Australian Executive Director was appointed chairman of the Fund's Board Committee on Liaison with the CONTRACTING PARTIES to the GATT.

THE PROCEDURES REGULARIZED

Over time a regular procedure emerged for the Fund's participation in the GATT's consultations. Significantly, one of the reasons why the Fund wished to retain annual consultations with its members even after they had given up Article XIV of the Fund Agreement was that the Fund could implement its responsibilities to the CONTRACTING PARTIES to the GATT. Moreover, the Fund's decision of 1960 on the transition from Article XIV to Article VIII had a fourth paragraph concerning the Fund's coordination with the GATT.[9] In the interest of Fund-GATT collaboration, those Fund members which were also contracting parties to the GATT were requested to continue to send to the Fund information about their import restrictions maintained for balance of payments reasons. For countries which were not parties to the GATT, the Fund would seek to obtain information about such restrictions.

Certain changes in the GATT rules concerning discriminatory restrictions also came into effect as countries which were members of the Fund assumed the obligations of Article VIII. In general, the rules under which a contracting party could continue to have discriminatory restrictions were greatly simplified. A contracting party was now allowed to have discrimination in the application of its balance of payments restrictions only in a manner having equivalent effect to its restrictions maintained under the Fund Agreement, either Article XIV or Article VIII. These changes in the GATT rules took effect in February 1961. However, the practical significance of these changes in GATT rules was limited, since no contracting party had had discriminatory restrictions since October 1960.

GATT PROCEDURE

The actual process by which the CONTRACTING PARTIES conduct their consultations is different from that of the Fund.[10] Under the GATT, consultations are typically conducted by a working party or committee consisting of representa-

[9] E.B. Decision No. 1034-(60/27), June 1, 1960; below, Vol. III, p. 261.

[10] The process of Fund consultations is described in detail in Chapter 11 above. A brief statement contrasting Fund and GATT consultations procedures can also be found in Gardner Patterson, *Discrimination in International Trade*, footnotes 77 and 78 on pp. 62–63.

tives of individual contracting parties. Recently, this has been the Committee on Balance of Payments Restrictions.

To facilitate the conduct of the consultations provided for in the GATT, the CONTRACTING PARTIES agree from time to time on certain plans, on the basis of which the consultations are conducted. Generally the plan for consultations under Articles XII:4 (*b*) and XVIII:12 (*b*) contains the following major headings:

I. Balance of payments position and prospects
II. Alternative measures to restore equilibrium
III. System and methods of restrictions
IV. Effects of the restrictions

Also considered under the heading "Balance of payments positions and prospects" are the level of and expected movements in monetary reserves, and any special factors affecting the availability of or the need for reserves. Under the topic "Alternative measures to restore equilibrium" are examined the internal monetary and fiscal situation and other relevant matters which may affect the balance of payments, and any internal action necessary to preserve or restore equilibrium. Such action may include long-term measures designed to raise productivity and expand capacity or to reduce structural rigidities. In discussing the "System and methods of restrictions" the legal and administrative bases for the restrictions are examined, as well as the particular categories of goods and the proportion of imports restricted. Variations in the treatment given to imports from different countries or currency areas are given special attention. Finally, under the last heading, the protective effects of restrictions on domestic production are closely considered, as well as the difficulties that may be expected upon relaxation or elimination of the restrictions.

Written material on these topics, or on other topics considered relevant, is examined by the Committee on Balance of Payments Restrictions; high-level technicians from the contracting party having the consultation are then expected to explain at some length to the committee their country's position. Finally, the GATT secretariat prepares a draft report on the committee's discussion with respect to each consultation; after agreement by the committee on a final version, the report is submitted to the CONTRACTING PARTIES for adoption.

FUND PROCEDURE

Under the procedure which has been evolved in the Fund, and by agreement with the GATT, the Fund provides for each GATT consultation, when notified of it, background material (such as Part II of a Fund paper prepared for a recent consultation under Article XIV or Article VIII with the country concerned, if this is available) together with the recent Article XIV consultation decision, if there is one. The right of any Executive Director concerned to object to the transmission of any of these documents is reserved. Supplementary or special background papers are transmitted only with the agreement of the Executive Board.

In addition to the provision of this background material, the Fund representative at a GATT consultation (nowadays always a member of the staff) is customarily invited by the chairman of the GATT Committee on Balance of Payments Restrictions to make a statement supplementing the documentation with respect to the position of the consulting country. This statement, which is approved by the Board in advance, is in two parts. The first relates to the balance of payments need for, and to the form of, the restrictions, i.e., to items I and III of the plan for the GATT consultations. The second part of the statement relates to "Alternative measures to restore equilibrium," in the language of item II of the plan, or to "alternative corrective measures which may be available" in the language of Article XII:4 (*a*) or Article XVIII:12 (*a*).

Somewhat different statements are made on behalf of the Fund at GATT consultations under Articles XII:4 (*a*) and XVIII:12 (*a*)—"intensification" consultations—on the one hand, and at annual or biennial consultations under Articles XII:4 (*b*) and XVIII:12 (*b*), on the other. For the former, the formula which has been evolved to present the Fund's views, if it is of the opinion that the level of restrictions is not excessive in relation to the balance of payments and reserve developments (the normal case), is:

> The general level of restrictions of [*country*] which are under reference does not go beyond the extent necessary at the present time to stop a serious decline in its monetary reserves.

When an earlier version of this statement was being worked out in 1952, the staff and the Board of the Fund believed that a determination in terms only of the last sentence of Article XV:2 (i.e., "as to what constitutes a serious decline in the contracting party's monetary reserves, a very low level of its monetary reserves or a reasonable rate of increase in its monetary reserves") would be difficult to formulate and probably not very helpful if it were presented in a flat, absolute form without a reference to the impact of the restrictions under consideration. Thus an attempt was made to relate the level of restrictions to the balance of payments or reserve problem, but still to keep as close as possible to the GATT criteria.

At the regular annual or biennial consultations, the statements made have varied according to circumstances. Some have been in terms similar to the one quoted above, while some have drawn attention to recent decisions taken in connection with Fund consultations under Article XIV and quoted passages from these decisions. These passages range from expressing the Fund's hope that progress in reducing discrimination and bilateralism will continue and that progress in reducing restrictions will be resumed as soon as practicable, to stating that the Fund considers that restrictions on a country's imports are no longer necessary to safeguard a country's monetary reserves and balance of payments.

The quotation of passages from Article XIV consultation decisions is particularly appropriate if the Fund wishes neither to suggest that the country has no balance of payments need for restrictions nor that its situation is such as to warrant the retention of restrictions. In such circumstances the standard form quoted above ("The general level . . . does not go beyond the extent necessary . . .") is clearly inappropriate, and the exact nuance of the Fund's views can best be conveyed by using the words of the Article XIV decision.

A third type of statement has been necessary where the Fund is not in a position to offer firm advice, either because the current year's consultation with the country under Article XIV has not been completed, or because the situation in the country has recently changed so substantially that a judgment on it is not yet possible.

As regards alternative measures (item II of the plan of the GATT consultations), the practice has been to notify the GATT that the Fund has no alternative measures to suggest. This wording has been taken to mean "no measures additional to the whole complex of measures discussed in the documentation" and not just the restrictions maintained by the country.

The provision of advice to the GATT is thus greatly dependent upon the smooth progress of the Fund's own program of consultations under Article XIV or Article VIII. The GATT secretariat seeks, after informal contact with the Fund staff, to arrange the CONTRACTING PARTIES' consultation schedules so that GATT consultations follow with a minimum of delay those which the Fund conducts with the same countries. Despite these efforts, however, GATT consultations sometimes take place without a recent Fund consultation decision and related background material being available. There are two main reasons why the Fund may not have completed a consultation with the country in question in the year since the preceding GATT consultation: (1) GATT consultations normally take place in brief semiannual meetings of the Committee on Balance of Payments Restrictions; (2) the contracting party may wish to have its GATT consultation scheduled at a particular time which does not fit the Fund's schedule. For these reasons, the Fund has devised a variety of "holding" or "delaying" statements.

The preparation of advice to be given to the GATT can therefore not be a routine matter. It is handled at Executive Director level by the Committee on Liaison with the CONTRACTING PARTIES to the GATT. As meetings of this committee are in practice attended by all Executive Directors with an interest in the matters on its agenda, it is usually possible to dispose of the committee's reports, when they reach the Board, under the lapse of time procedure.

CONSULTATIONS HELD AND THEIR SIGNIFICANCE

By the process described above, the CONTRACTING PARTIES undertook well over a hundred consultations from 1949 to 1965. After those in Torquay in November 1950, the next were held in Geneva in October-November 1952. These included consultations with Italy and the Netherlands on the continuance of discrimination, with France and Pakistan on the intensification of restrictions, and with Australia, Ceylon, and the United Kingdom on both discrimination and intensification. The revision in 1954–55 of the provisions of the GATT governing the use of import restrictions was undertaken principally to meet the emerging situation in which most countries no longer had balance of payments deficits of any consequence. But these provisions did not come into force until late in 1957 because the necessary number of acceptances had not been received earlier. Since several countries still maintained various import restrictions despite their strong balance of payments positions, the CONTRACTING PARTIES made use of a clause in the old provisions, and in 1956 invited twenty-one countries to consult: Australia, Austria, Brazil, Ceylon, Denmark, Finland, France, Germany, Greece, India, Italy, Japan, the Netherlands, New Zealand, Norway, Pakistan, the Federation of Rhodesia and Nyasaland, Sweden, Turkey, the Union of South Africa, and the United Kingdom. These consultations took place in the second half of 1957.

After the revised rules had come into effect, a broad general review of outstanding quantitative restrictions was initiated in 1958, and the first annual consultations under the new rules took place with thirteen countries in 1959. Biennial consultations were begun in 1960 with several less developed countries that maintained import restrictions for balance of payments reasons under Article XVIII of the GATT.[11]

Inasmuch as the Fund has assisted the GATT in all these consultations, Fund collaboration with the GATT has become a significant part of the Fund's work on restrictions. Cooperation between the two organizations has been close from the beginning, and the Fund's findings have always been accepted. Staff of the Fund have not only participated in the General Sessions but also have frequently attended meetings of the Committee on Balance of Payments Restrictions and of various working parties. To facilitate the Fund's participation in these various GATT activities, as well as to establish close contact with the UNCTAD, the Fund in 1965 set up its own office in Geneva.

This is not the place to consider just how effective the consultations held under the GATT have been in eliminating restrictions; but in view of the Fund's interest, a few observations may be made. An independent appraisal of the

[11] A list of the countries involved in GATT consultations from 1949 to 1963 is to be found in Curzon, *Multilateral Commercial Diplomacy*, Table 10, pp. 141–43.

GATT consultations held up to 1963 has come to the conclusion that they were blunt and hard-hitting, that they made European countries accountable for significant restrictions left untouched by the OEEC code of liberalization, and that they served to bring pressure on some European countries to remove import restrictions no longer needed in view of their balance of payments positions.[12] From the Fund's point of view, the last conclusion is the most important one: it seems safe to infer that, for the most part, countries which had relaxed restrictions covered by the Fund's Articles did not substitute restrictions falling under the jurisdiction of the GATT.

---

12 Curzon, *Multilateral Commercial Diplomacy*, pp. 145–65.

PART IV

The Fund's Resources and Their Use

CHAPTER

17

Derivation and Significance of the Fund's Resources

J. Keith Horsefield

THE FINANCIAL RESOURCES which the Fund can make available to its members originate in three ways. The first and largest source is the subscriptions paid by members when they join the Fund; the second is the excess of the Fund's income—mainly consisting of charges levied by the Fund for the use of its resources plus its income from investments—over its expenditures; the third is borrowing from members. For the purposes of the present chapter it is the total rather than the constitution of the Fund's holdings of members' currencies that is relevant. The replenishment of the Fund's holdings of individual currencies by the sale of gold is reviewed in Chapter 19.

QUOTAS AND SUBSCRIPTIONS

Provisions of the Articles

The principal Article in connection with quotas and subscriptions is Article III, of which the contents, partly summarized (in brackets), follow:

> Section 1. *Quotas.*—Each member shall be assigned a quota. [Members represented at Bretton Woods have quotas set out in Schedule A to the Articles.] The quotas of other members shall be determined by the Fund.
>
> Sec. 2. *Adjustment of quotas.*—The Fund shall at intervals of five years review, and if it deems it appropriate propose an adjustment of, the quotas of the members. It may also, if it thinks fit, consider at any other time the adjustment of any particular quota at the request of the member concerned. A four-fifths majority of the total voting power shall be required for any change in quotas and no quota shall be changed without the consent of the member concerned.
>
> Sec. 3. *Subscriptions: time, place, and form of payment.*—(*a*) The subscription of each member shall be equal to its quota and shall be paid in full to the Fund

at the appropriate depository on or before the date when the member becomes eligible under Article XX, Section 4 *(c)* or *(d)*, to buy currencies from the Fund.

(b) Each member shall pay in gold, as a minimum, the smaller of

(i) twenty-five percent of its quota; or

(ii) ten percent of its net official holdings of gold and United States dollars as at the date when the Fund notifies members under Article XX, Section 4 *(a)* that it will shortly be in a position to begin exchange transactions.

Each member shall furnish to the Fund the data necessary to determine its net official holdings of gold and United States dollars.

(c) Each member shall pay the balance of its quota in its own currency.

(d) [Provision for countries occupied by the enemy]

SEC. 4. *Payments when quotas are changed.—(a)* Each member which consents to an increase in its quota shall, within thirty days after the date of its consent, pay to the Fund twenty-five percent of the increase in gold and the balance in its own currency. If, however, on the date when the member consents to an increase, its monetary reserves are less than its new quota, the Fund may reduce the proportion of the increase to be paid in gold.

(b) [Provision for reduction in quota]

SEC. 5. *Substitution of securities for currency.*—[The Fund must accept non-negotiable noninterest-bearing securities in place of currency to the extent that it deems the currency not to be needed for its purposes.]

Two provisions elsewhere in the Articles safeguard members' rights in relation to quotas. By Article XII, Section 2 *(b)* (ii), only the Governors (not the Executive Directors) can approve a revision of quotas. By Article XVII *(b)* (ii), the provision in Article III, Section 2, that no change in a quota shall be made without the consent of the member concerned, can be revoked only with the consent of every member.

The only interpretation that the Board has found it necessary to give in connection with the foregoing provisions was the following, decided on July 20, 1950:

> It is determined as a matter of interpretation that Article III, Section 4, and not Article III, Section 3, applies to all changes in quotas.[1]

The occasion for this interpretation arose when France received an increase in its quota before it had paid its subscription. Because of the low level of its reserves, its gold subscription was to be 10 per cent of its net official holdings of gold and dollars instead of 25 per cent of its quota. The question was whether this subscription would suffice for the enlarged quota, or whether 25 per cent of the increase would have to be paid in gold. The Board decided, in principle, that the latter was right; but as France had been given to understand the contrary, it accepted 10 per cent of France's net official holdings of gold and

[1] E.B. Decision No. 595-3, July 20, 1950; below, Vol. III, p. 222.

dollars as sufficing for the whole gold subscription. (Subsequently France reduced the Fund's holdings of its currency to 75 per cent of its quota, as has been done by most members that originally subscribed less than 25 per cent of their quotas in gold.)

Basis of quotas

The quotas negotiated at Bretton Woods and listed in Schedule A to the Articles of Agreement bore some relation to a formula devised by the U.S. Treasury, as follows:

> 90 per cent of
> 2 per cent of national income, 1940,
> *plus* 5 per cent of gold and dollar balances on July 1, 1943,
> *plus* 10 per cent of maximum variation of exports, 1934–38,
> *plus* 10 per cent of average imports, 1934–38,
>
> increased for each country in the same ratio as average exports, 1934–38, bore to national income.

The extent to which the quotas negotiated actually conformed to this formula has been discussed in Volume I.[2] It is sufficient here to note that when considering quotas for new members in the early years of the Fund, the data yielded by this formula were used as a starting point for the discussion. Some anomalies produced by the formula were reviewed in 1962, and are considered below.

In accordance with Article III, Section 2, a general review of quotas took place in 1950, 1955, 1960, and 1965. Although there have been only two general revisions of quotas during the twenty years covered by this volume, and one of these did not coincide with the date for a general review, it will be convenient to divide our study of quotas into four parts corresponding to the periods between the general review dates.

Table 14 at the end of this chapter lists the quotas for all member countries as shown in Schedule A to the Articles of Agreement and as they stood at the end of 1950, 1955, 1960, and 1965.

Significance of quotas[3]

For the Fund as a whole, the size of quotas determines the volume of currencies and of gold which is available to it. Quotas have two other functions, both applying to individual members: they determine the member's basic voting rights and they influence the amount that it can draw from the Fund.

---

[2] See above, Vol. I, pp. 97–98.

[3] See also Oscar L. Altman, "Quotas in the International Monetary Fund," *Staff Papers*, Vol. V (1956–57), pp. 129–50.

A member's basic votes comprise 250 votes plus one additional vote for each part of its quota equivalent to $100,000 (Article XII, Section 5 (*a*)). For the purpose of voting under Article V, Sections 4 and 5, relating to the use of the Fund's resources (waiver of conditions and declaration of ineligibility), these votes are increased by one for each $400,000 of net sales by the Fund of the member's currency, or decreased by one for each $400,000 of its net purchases from the Fund, as the case may be (Article XII, Section 5 (*b*)).[4] Executive Directors cast the votes of the members that have appointed or elected them. They must cast these votes as a unit (Article XII, Section 3 (*i*)). On most matters, a majority of votes is sufficient to carry a Board decision. In recent years votes have seldom been formally counted, except where required by the Articles in connection with changes in the scale of charges. Nevertheless, the voting power of Executive Directors still operates as the means by which a consensus is arrived at.

Table 10 shows the proportion of the total votes that could be cast, at five selected dates, by each Executive Director. The changes between the columns reflect principally the effects of (*a*) the quotas of countries joining the Fund, and (*b*) disproportionate changes in members' quotas, particularly the special increases approved by the Governors in 1959 and the increases granted under the decision on the compensatory financing of export fluctuations.[5] As new countries have joined the Fund the number of Executive Directors has increased, although not in proportion to the growth in total membership or total quotas. As a result of all the foregoing, the proportion of total votes which can be cast by the five appointed Executive Directors declined from 67.33 per cent in 1946 to 45.67 per cent in 1964.

The stability of the Executive Board in terms of the nationality of the Directors is indicated in Table 10 and shown in more detail in Appendix A to Volume I. The latter also shows the stability of the groupings of countries electing Directors, which has been almost complete since 1954. The lack of change in these respects reflects the interweaving of four factors: (1) the relative sizes of members' quotas; (2) the rules of election laid down in the Articles of Agreement (Schedule C), as modified from time to time by the Board of Governors; (3) economic, political, social, and cultural affinities; and (4) pre-election negotiation among members and Executive Directors, influenced by the relative voting powers of the members.

Two limits are imposed by Article V, Section 3 (*a*) (iii), on the amounts that a member may draw from the Fund. Unless the Fund agrees to waive these limits, the member may not draw in any twelve months more than 25 per cent of its quota plus any amount needed to increase the Fund's holdings of its

---

[4] For a discussion of the interpretation of this provision, see above, Vol. I, pp. 367–68.

[5] See Chapter 18 below, pp. 421–22.

Table 10. Voting Power of Executive Directors as Percentage of Total Votes, at Selected Election Dates

	Years in Which Elections Held				
	1946	1950	1956	1960	1964
	Number of Executive Directors				
Executive Directors	12	14	16	18	20
Appointed by:					
United States	33.52	30.46	26.62	25.63	22.63
United Kingdom	16.00	14.54	12.71	12.18	10.77
China	6.95	6.31	5.52	—	—
France	5.73	6.04	5.28	5.02	4.43
India	5.13	4.66	4.08	3.86	3.41
Germany	—	—	—	5.02	4.43
Elected from: (Article XII, Section 3 *(b)* (iii))					
Belgium	3.75	4.84	4.46	4.03	3.58
Canada	4.83	3.85	3.12	3.98	3.76
Czechoslovakia/Yugoslavia/Germany	4.65	2.53	3.41	—	—
Netherlands	5.13	4.12	3.98	3.57	3.78
United Arab Republic	3.48	4.77	4.78	4.86	5.20
Australia	—	3.84	3.72	3.95	4.35
Italy	—	3.79	3.88	3.43	4.74
Denmark/Iceland/Sweden	—	—	3.66	3.54	3.13
Japan	—	—	3.77	4.36	4.10
China	—	—	--	3.55	3.14
Indonesia	—	—	—	2.81	2.90
Senegal	—	—	—	—	2.74
Uganda	—	—	—	—	3.09
Elected from: (Article XII, Section 3 *(b)* (iv))					
Brazil	5.53	5.33	3.72	3.61	3.30
Mexico/El Salvador/Venezuela	5.28	4.92	3.57	3.08	3.17
Argentina/Chile	—	—	3.73	3.50	3.35
Total [1]	100.00	100.00	100.00	100.00	100.00
Number of members	38	49	60	68	101
Total quotas *($ million)*	7,329.5	8,036.5	8,750.5	14,740.7	15,849.5

[1] The sums of the items may not equal the totals because of rounding.

currency to 75 per cent of its quota; and the Fund's holdings may not exceed 200 per cent of the quota.

Quotas, 1946–50

Among the earliest tasks undertaken by the Executive Board when it began work in 1946 was to review the quotas of certain members that had protested at Bretton Woods that the amounts allotted to them were too small. One of these members was Paraguay, which had been allotted $2 million at Bretton Woods but sought a quota of $5 million. Its representative argued that the formula showed that $5 million would have been the correct figure, but the Board, viewing the formula as having no official standing, decided to increase Paraguay's quota to $3.5 million only.

A request by France for an increase from $450 million to $675 million was also supported by a reference to the formula. This request, however, would have raised the French quota above that of China, whereas it had been understood between the U.S. and Chinese delegations at Bretton Woods that China should have the fourth largest quota (after the United States, the United Kingdom, and the U.S.S.R.). China therefore made a counter-request for an increase in quota from $550 million to $715 million. The Governors decided to increase the French quota only to $525 million,[6] and China then withdrew its request.

Australia, which had been allotted a quota of $200 million at Bretton Woods, delayed its application for membership until 1947. When this came before the Board, Mr. Saad (Egypt) pointed out that the formula would have yielded a quota for Australia of $134 million only. He was reminded that the formula had no binding force, and that Australia's quota had been settled at the same time as those of the other original members. He suggested, however, that if Australia was to receive a quota so appreciably larger than that yielded by the formula, Egypt and Iran, which had protested at Bretton Woods against the amounts allotted to them, should also be given larger quotas. The Executive Directors therefore considered the cases of these two members, and recommended to the Governors that their quotas should be revised. The Governors agreed, and accordingly the quota for Egypt was increased from $45 million to $60 million and that of Iran from $25 million to $35 million.[7]

There were no further increases in quotas during the years 1946 through 1950. However, on the partition of India in 1947 the quota for India was maintained unaltered, thus affording the member, in effect, an increase in quota per capita;[8] India had protested at Bretton Woods that its quota was too small. Honduras, because of a difficulty in providing its gold subscription, asked that

---

[6] Resolution 1-13, *Summary Proceedings, 1946,* p. 56.

[7] Resolutions 2-3 and 2-4, *Summary Proceedings, 1947,* pp. 35–36.

[8] *Summary Proceedings, 1947,* p. 20.

its quota should be reduced from $2.5 million to $0.5 million. The Governors agreed.[9]

Rule D-3 requires the Board, at least one year before the time when a quinquennial review of quotas is due, to appoint a committee to study what should be done and prepare a written report. Accordingly, in December 1949 the Board agreed, on the proposal of the Managing Director, to set up a Committee of the Whole on Review of Quotas. A staff committee, appointed to advise the Committee of the Whole, recommended that quotas should be doubled to correspond to the general economic growth since the dates on which the formula was based. However, the Managing Director suggested to the Board that, in view of the uncertain conditions prevailing in the world late in 1950, the time was inopportune to make any change. The Committee of the Whole agreed with the Managing Director, and the Board formally closed the general review in March 1951 with a decision that no increase should be proposed at that time.

The total of quotas, which in Schedule A was $7,600 million (excluding the U.S.S.R.), had risen by the end of 1950 to $8,036.5 million, principally because of the addition of nine new members, offset by one (Poland) that left the Fund.

Proposals to entrust the Fund with additional resources were made by a group of experts appointed by the United Nations in 1949 to recommend national and international measures to achieve full employment. The inflationary dangers inherent in their proposals, however, caused these to be disregarded.

Quotas, 1951–55

A second group of experts, asked by the United Nations to propose measures to achieve international economic stability, including the reduction of fluctuations in primary product markets, reported late in 1951.[10] The report included a number of proposals affecting the Fund, including a recommendation that its resources should be increased to the point at which it could meet its share of a decline in the supply of dollars which might amount to $10 billion over two years. The Board considered this report in April 1952, and decided that the Fund's representatives to the meeting of ECOSOC at which the report was to be presented should make two points that concern the subject of this chapter. One was that the Fund regarded it as its function to make its resources available, to make known that they were available, and to provide a forum for the discussion of economic problems. A second point was that the Fund's resources were limited, and although there had for some time been discussions of the possibility of increases in quotas, these seemed likely to be frustrated by members' inability to find the necessary 25 per cent of any increase in gold.

[9] Resolution 3-5, *Summary Proceedings, 1948,* p. 48.

[10] *Measures for International Economic Stability.*

Toward the end of 1952 the Board discussed a request from Ethiopia for an increase in its quota (which was not, however, proceeded with). At the request of Directors, the staff then prepared a general study of the adequacy of quotas. Because it was less than two years since the Board had decided that no general increase was needed, the staff concentrated on a possible need for relative increases. In a report to the Board in January 1953 the staff pointed out that, while the value of world trade in general had increased by approximately three times since 1937–38, there were eleven members whose trade had increased by more than four times in the interval. The staff also pointed to three members whose quotas as fixed at Bretton Woods appeared to be badly out of line with the formula. To amend these discrepancies an increase in aggregate quotas of some $250 million would be needed. The Managing Director commented, however, that it appeared from the staff's inquiries that the quota structure as a whole was not badly distorted, and for this reason, and because quotas could not be fixed on statistical grounds alone, he proposed that no action should be taken. The Board tacitly agreed.

The Fund's views were noted at the meeting of ECOSOC at which the report on measures for international economic stability was considered, and the Fund was invited to keep under review the adequacy of monetary reserves and to furnish a report on the subject for the meeting of ECOSOC in 1953.[11] In response to this invitation the staff prepared in April 1953 a draft study which, after discussion in the Board and some consequential revision, was forwarded to ECOSOC in June 1953.[12] Its conclusions were presented in the form of four alternative definitions of "adequacy," coupled with the statement that while many countries would have adequate reserves on the least exacting definition, only a few would do so if reserves were to be expected to maintain currency stability without restrictions even in a severe depression—falling short, however, of the severity of the 1930's.

Thereafter the staff continued to study the subject, with particular reference to a possible need to expand the Fund's resources in order to enable it adequately to supplement members' owned reserves.

In December 1954 the Board set up a Committee of the Whole to undertake the Second Quinquennial Review of quotas, due in 1955. It became clear at an early meeting of the committee that some of the primary producing countries, especially in Latin America, were seeking increases in their quotas. Mr. Southard (United States), however, suggested that no over-all increase in quotas was justified because the Fund's resources were already large and had remained relatively unused. He and Lord Harcourt (United Kingdom) announced that their

---

[11] Resolution 427(XIV), July 8, 1952.

[12] An updated version was printed in *Staff Papers*, Vol. III (1953–54), pp. 181–227, and is reproduced below, Vol. III, pp. 311–48.

Governments were unwilling to increase their quotas. As this meant that the necessary 80 per cent majority for an increase in quotas would not be forthcoming, the Board decided instead to invite individual member countries to approach it if they wished their quotas increased.

Meanwhile several attempts were made to evolve a formula which would permit members with the smallest quotas to increase them, although any such formula was opposed by some Directors as tending to impair the liquidity of the Fund by increasing only its supply of currencies not likely to be needed for drawings. The Committee of the Whole was reluctant, in any case, to suggest an increase in any quota that already exceeded $20 million, and as it turned out a number of Latin American countries seeking increases had quotas in that category. Taking everything into account, the committee recommended in January 1956 that there should be no general increase in quotas, but that the Board should look with favor upon requests by members with small quotas to increase them. The Board accepted this recommendation, thereby ending the Second Quinquennial Review. Within the five years 1951–55 only one increase in quota was granted, Honduras being permitted to restore its quota from an initial figure of $0.5 million to the $2.5 million agreed at Bretton Woods.

During the five years 1951–55 the aggregate of quotas increased by $714 million as the result of the addition of ten new members, offset by the departure of Czechoslovakia.

Quotas, 1956–60

In contrast to the preceding five years, the quinquennium 1956–60 saw major changes in quotas. During 1956 and 1957 a number of increases were granted, following the recommendation of the Committee of the Whole in January 1956. These were based on a scale which was worked out in the course of informal discussions among Executive Directors and was officially known as the "Small Quotas Policy." It provided that quotas below $5 million could be increased, on request, to $7.5 million, those of $5–8 million to $10 million, those of $10 million to $15 million, and those of $15 million to $20 million.

First signs of pressure on the Fund's resources also developed in 1957. The Managing Director and some Governors at the Annual Meeting, 1957, pointed out that almost all drawings during the year had necessitated waivers of the quantitative limits set by Article V, Section 3 (*a*) (iii), and suggested that this implied that quotas were too small.[13] Pursuing this point, the staff provided the management in April 1958 with an interim report on a possible need to increase quotas. This argued that the recession in the United States, and the related decline in raw material prices, were likely to induce primary producing

[13] *Summary Proceedings, 1957*, pp. 22, 42, 62, 86, 139.

countries to seek drawings from the Fund on a scale which it might be difficult for the Fund to meet. After further review, the staff produced in August 1958 a report entitled *International Reserves and Liquidity*, which concluded that it was doubtful whether the Fund's resources were adequate fully to perform its duties under the Articles in the conditions likely to be met in coming months.[14]

Meanwhile a decision was reached in the U.S. Government on the basis of which the President instructed the U.S. Governor to propose, at the forthcoming Annual Meeting in New Delhi, that prompt consideration should be given to a general increase in quotas. A resolution to that effect was adopted on October 7,[15] and on the Board's return to Washington from New Delhi consideration was given to it.

The outcome of the Board's deliberations was a report to the Governors entitled *Enlargement of Fund Resources Through Increases in Quotas*, which was printed and distributed at the end of December 1958. In this, the Directors announced their conclusion that an increase in quotas was highly desirable, and suggested that an increase by 50 per cent was a reasonable basis for a general increase.[16] At the same time, the Board proposed that special increases should be given to Canada, Germany, and Japan, and to members with particularly small quotas. The report concluded with three draft resolutions, the first providing for a general increase of 50 per cent in quotas, the second for increasing the quotas of twenty-four members to which the Small Quotas Policy applied to levels 50 per cent above those provided by that formula, and the third for special increases for Canada, Germany, and Japan. At the time that this report was completed the Board had not finished reviewing the requests for special increases submitted by some other members, and in February 1959 the Governors were invited to consider a fourth resolution providing for such increases for fourteen members other than those covered by the second and third resolutions.

The justification for these special increases rested on two alternative arguments. Some members sought such increases because at Bretton Woods they had been offered smaller quotas than they wished for, or quotas not in line with the formula, or quotas based on incomplete or inaccurate data. Other members requested increases because their economies had grown appreciably faster than the general run in the postwar period.

The difficulty expected to be experienced by some members in finding gold to pay for 25 per cent of the increase in their quotas, mentioned to ECOSOC in 1952, was met by the offer of two concessions. Members in that position were

---

[14] The report was published on September 16; see below, Vol. III, pp. 349–420.

[15] Resolution 13-10, *Summary Proceedings, 1958*, p. 178.

[16] *Enlargement of Fund Resources Through Increases in Quotas*, pp. 11, 12; below, Vol. III, p. 427.

to be allowed to increase their quotas by installments over five years, paying in gold 25 per cent of each installment annually; or, if they preferred, they might provide the gold subscription by making a special drawing, which would have to be repurchased in three annual installments. These arrangements applied only to the general increase in quotas; members having special increases were expected to pay 25 per cent of their increases in gold.

All four resolutions were adopted by the Governors, the first three on February 2, 1959 and the fourth on April 6.[17] The new quotas became operative on September 9, when members aggregating more than 75 per cent of total quotas had accepted their increases.

During 1960 special increases were approved for four other countries, Australia, Chile, Colombia, and Yugoslavia.[18]

A Committee of the Whole appointed by the Board in December 1959, in preparation for the quinquennial review of quotas due in 1960, recommended that no further increases were necessary. The Board agreed on December 16, 1960.

As a result of the foregoing changes, and of the addition of eleven new members, the total of quotas at the end of 1960 was $14,740.7 million, an increase of almost $6 billion compared with five years earlier.

Quotas, 1961–65

During the Fund's fourth quinquennium, as during the preceding one, much attention was focused on small quotas. The period ended with a recommendation for a second general increase in quotas, together with a further group of special increases, all of which took effect after 1965.

Apart from one or two belated increases stemming from the general review described in the previous section, the first occasion when the Board's attention was directed to quotas during the period 1961–65 was in April 1962, when the United Arab Republic sought an increase from $90 million to $120 million. Among the reasons which the member cited for the increase was the instability of its export receipts, and the same reason was given three months later when the Syrian Arab Republic asked for an increase from $15 million to $25 million. The United Arab Republic's request was approved by the Board and in due course by the Governors.[19] When that of the Syrian Arab Republic was discussed by the Board, Mr. Southard said that he understood that many countries in the same quota range desired increases in their quotas, and the increase sought therefore raised very broad questions. Shortly afterward, El Salvador asked for its quota to be increased from $11.25 million to $15 million.

[17] Resolutions 14-1, 14-2, 14-3, 14-4, *Summary Proceedings, 1959,* pp. 158–62.

[18] Resolutions 15-2, 15-3, 15-4, 15-11, *Summary Proceedings, 1960,* pp. 158–60, 169.

[19] Resolution 17-2, *Summary Proceedings, 1962,* p. 221.

During the Annual Meeting, 1962, the Managing Director discussed the problem of small quotas with a number of Governors, and subsequently reported to the Board that he believed that increases in such quotas might be a useful way in which the Fund could assist the members concerned. The staff was asked to prepare a study suggesting the lines along which the Board might proceed.

In the meantime the Board had before it an invitation from the UN Commission on International Commodity Trade to consider whether the Fund could play a larger part in providing compensatory financing for export fluctuations, and if so in what way. By the time that the staff study just mentioned was ready, the Board was engaged in considering its reply to the UN Commission, and the two subjects thereafter were dealt with together.

The staff analysis divided members into four groups, (1) those having quotas of $30 million and under, (2) those having quotas between $31 million and $60 million, (3) the ten industrial countries, and (4) the remainder (excluding China). Comparisons of existing quotas with the Bretton Woods formula applied to 1955–59 data, with average exports for 1955–59, and with the variation of exports from trend in 1950–61, showed that the quotas of the second group of countries compared unfavorably with those of the countries in the other three groups. Using the comparison with variation of exports from trend, the under $30 million group also appeared to have quotas that were too small in relation to the ten industrial countries and the remainder. Fresh calculations, made a little later with more up-to-date data, confirmed these results.

The staff then undertook extensive research into possible variations in the formula underlying quotas, in the hope of discovering a version of it which would avoid certain unsatisfactory features. A first report pointed out that the inclusion of the ratio between exports and national income in the formula had the effect, if quotas were plotted on a graph measuring quotas vertically and national income horizontally, of producing a U-shaped curve instead of one that rose consistently from left to right. The staff also commented that if the weights allotted to national income and to reserves in the formula were lessened, the quotas for small countries would be increased relative to those of large countries. The Board considered with interest these results of the staff's work, but was unwilling to accept any alternative formula, preferring to continue to regard the original one as a point of reference when the calculation of quotas was being undertaken.

It may be noted here that a substantial departure from the formula as applied to small countries followed from the resolutions taken in 1959 and reported above. The combined effect of the Small Quotas Policy and the 50 per cent general increase in quotas in 1959 was to raise the minimum quota to $11.25 million. This, however, was greatly in excess of the figure reached by applying the Bretton Woods formula to data for a large number of the newly established

African countries which joined the Fund in 1963. It was accordingly suggested to some of these countries that they might prefer to accept a quota of $7.5 million, and nine of them did so, as Laos and Nepal had done in 1961.

Meanwhile the Fund's reply in February 1963 to the inquiry from the UN Commission included a statement that consideration would be given to increases in quotas if members felt that their existing quotas were inadequate to enable them to deal with fluctuations in export proceeds, or in their balances of payments generally.[20]

Any increases in quotas, and particularly those of small countries, were likely to raise again the question whether the members concerned were able to contribute 25 per cent of the increases in gold. The Board accordingly offered again the options of increasing the quotas by installments over five years or of taking special drawings from which to provide the needed gold.[21] It considered, but rejected, a suggestion by the staff that the Fund might also be prepared to reduce the proportion of increases required to be provided in gold, as contemplated by Article III, Section 4 (*a*).

The increase requested by the Syrian Arab Republic, that by El Salvador (which had since been revised upward to $20 million), and one asked for by Honduras (from $11.25 million to $15 million) were recommended to the Governors under the terms of the compensatory financing facility, and were approved.[22] Six similar increases were approved in 1964, and a further five in the first two months of 1965.[23]

Apart from these increases under the compensatory financing facility, the quotas of four countries were enlarged in the latter part of 1963 and the early part of 1964—those of Israel ($25 million to $50 million), Italy ($270 million to $500 million), Malaysia ($37.5 million to $100 million), and Panama ($0.5 million to $11.25 million).[24]

In March 1964, as part of its study of the problems of international liquidity, the staff prepared a study of quotas which suggested that substantially larger ones would be appropriate in 1964–65. An increase of the general order of 50 per cent was suggested, together with special increases larger than this for certain members in order to reduce disparities between the existing quotas. This recommendation was discussed by the Board in April, and again in connection with the drafting of the Annual Report in June. In the Annual Report the

[20] *Compensatory Financing of Export Fluctuations: A Report by the International Monetary Fund;* below, Vol. III, pp. 442-57.

[21] E.B. Decision No. 1529-(63/33), June 14, 1963; below, Vol. III, p. 222.

[22] Resolutions 18-19, 18-20, 18-21, *Summary Proceedings, 1963*, pp. 264–65.

[23] Resolutions 19-1, 19-4, 19-5, 19-16, 19-17, 19-19, *Summary Proceedings, 1964*, pp. 254, 256–58, 266–67, 268; Resolutions 20-1 through 20-5, *Summary Proceedings, 1965*, pp. 241–45.

[24] Resolutions 19-2, 19-3, 19-7, 19-18, *Summary Proceedings, 1964*, pp. 255–56, 259, 267–68.

Directors commented that increases in quotas were the normal way to expand the operations of the Fund, and suggested that it would be advantageous to consider quotas as promptly as possible after the Annual Meeting.[25]

Once more the problem of the payment in gold for 25 per cent of any increase came to the fore. On this occasion the Annual Report distinguished two types of difficulty.[26] One, which had previously been provided for, was that some members' reserves of gold and foreign exchange were too low for them to be able to afford the gold payment. The other, which was considered for the first time, was that other members having reserves of convertible currencies but not gold would be apt to request the issuers of these currencies (mainly the United States and the United Kingdom) to convert appropriate amounts into gold for use in providing the necessary 25 per cent of quota increases. While gold found from a member's own reserves entailed only an exchange of one type of reserve for another (an improved position in the Fund), gold provided by the issuers of reserve currencies in exchange for their currencies would adversely affect their reserve positions.

On the invitation of the Executive Board, the Governors passed a resolution instructing the Executive Directors to consider adjusting members' quotas and to submit an appropriate proposal to the Board of Governors at an early date.[27] Pursuant to this resolution there was prolonged consideration in the Executive Board [28] which culminated in a recommendation for a general increase of 25 per cent all round, together with special increases for sixteen countries whose quotas were disproportionately small.[29] Provision was made for the increases in quotas to be taken in installments, and for special drawings, as on previous occasions. In addition the Board, after much debate, proposed two procedures to mitigate the drain on those members whose currencies were converted to provide gold. One was that certain of the special drawings, up to the equivalent of $150 million, would be directed by the Fund to specific members' currencies; the Fund would then replenish its holdings of these currencies by the sale of gold to the members concerned. The second was that the Fund would make general deposits of gold with the United States (maximum $250 million) and the United Kingdom (maximum $100 million) in respect of gold sold by those countries. The deposits would be demand deposits, and the Fund would propose to draw on them and on earmarked gold, in appropriate proportions, when it had need of gold.

Resolutions embodying the Directors' proposals were submitted to the Governors for a vote without meeting and by April 1, 1965 had been approved by

[25] *Annual Report, 1964*, pp. 35–36.
[26] *Ibid.*, pp. 36–37.
[27] Resolution 19-20, *Summary Proceedings, 1964*, p. 269.
[28] See Vol. I above, pp. 579–83.
[29] *Annual Report, 1965*, pp. 124–32. See also below, Vol. III, pp. 458–65.

the necessary 80 per cent of votes.[30] However, the acceptance of individual increases, which in many countries required legislative action, was protracted, and it was not until February 23, 1966 that the Directors were able to decide that members holding two thirds of the total votes had notified their acceptance, this being the minimum stipulated in the resolutions to bring the increases into effect. Shortly afterwards the Fourth Quinquennial Review was formally terminated.

The concessions offered in connection with the 25 per cent gold subscription were utilized by forty-two members; of these, twenty-three took special drawings totaling $246 million and nineteen opted for increases by installments. Gold deposits of $289.1 million were made, of which $244.7 million were in the United States and the remainder in the United Kingdom. Gold to the value of $148 million was used to replenish currencies. Four members declined the offered increases, and three others had not decided whether to accept at the expiration of the period allowed for the purpose.

Seven members that applied for increases under the compensatory financing facility after the Directors' recommendations had been submitted to the Governors were permitted to superimpose the general increase upon the special increases which they sought.[31]

As a result of the influx of new members and of the various special increases (including compensatory financing increases) mentioned above, the aggregate of quotas rose between 1961 and the end of 1965 to $15,976.6 million, an increase of $1,236 million. But the effect of the general increase was felt progressively after 1965. By the end of 1968 the total had risen to $21,198.4 million; and it continues to rise as the quotas being increased by installments progressively attain higher levels.

INCOME AND EXPENDITURE

The Fund's income is mostly derived from charges, and is therefore closely related to the volume of transactions. It will be convenient to summarize the figures (set out in Table 11) by the same five-year periods as were used in the previous section.

During the first five years of the Fund's life drawings were small, except in 1947. Correspondingly, the addition to its resources arising from charges was also small. For the five financial years 1946/47 through 1950/51 the Fund's income totaled $11.4 million, of which $9.3 million was paid in gold and the

[30] Resolutions 20-6 and 20-7, *Summary Proceedings, 1965*, pp. 245–49.

[31] Resolutions 20-9 through 20-13, *Summary Proceedings, 1965*, pp. 252–57; Resolutions 21-1 and 21-2, *Summary Proceedings, 1966*, pp. 236–38.

Table 11. International Monetary Fund: Income, Expenditure, and Reserves, Fiscal Years 1947–66

(In millions of U.S. dollars)

Fiscal Year[1]	Income Excluding Investments: Charges on Drawings: Paid in gold	Income Excluding Investments: Charges on Drawings: Paid in currencies	Income Excluding Investments: Other[2]	Income Excluding Investments: Total	Expenditure	Investment Income: Applied to Deficit	Investment Income: To Special Reserve	Accumulated Deficit (−) or General Reserve	Accumulated Total of Special Reserve
1946/47	0.47	—	—	0.47	2.17[3]	—	—	−1.70	—
1947/48	4.16	0.03	—	4.19	2.63	—	—	−0.15	—
1948/49	1.38	0.41	0.01	1.80	3.81	—	—	−2.16	—
1949/50	1.59	0.72	0.01	2.32	3.97	—	—	−3.81	—
1950/51	1.76	0.90	0.01	2.68	4.60	—	—	−5.72	—
1951/52	2.52	0.71	0.02	3.25	4.77	—	—	−7.24	—
1952/53	2.96	0.92	0.28	4.16	4.89	—	—	−7.96	—
1953/54	4.41	0.51	0.07	4.99	5.01	—	—	−7.99	—
1954/55	2.16	0.13	0.06	2.47	4.99	—	—	−10.51	—
1955/56	1.30	0.02	0.23	1.53	5.35	0.12	—	−14.21	—
1956/57	4.63	3.57	0.19	8.40	5.38	4.90	—	−6.30	—
1957/58	13.47	5.50	1.29	20.30	11.34[4]	3.33	2.83	5.99	2.83
1958/59	20.57	4.55	2.05	27.17	6.68	—	4.11	25.58	6.94
1959/60	12.57	5.16	3.27	21.00	6.88	—	15.36	39.76	22.30
1960/61	10.72	3.18	0.65	14.55	7.36	—	19.87	46.99	42.16
1961/62	20.59	11.98	0.54	33.11	8.16	—	22.78	71.81	64.94
1962/63	22.72	4.66	3.66	31.04	9.57	—	25.09	93.29	90.04
1963/64	27.95	6.68	1.72	36.35	13.12[5]	—	27.49	116.52	117.52
1964/65	27.36	18.03	2.36	47.75	22.20[6]	—	30.75	141.81	148.27
1965/66	27.65	52.18	1.49	81.32	36.77[7]	—	33.91	186.36	182.18
Totals[8]	210.94	119.84	17.91	348.85	169.65	8.35	182.19		

[1] Ending June 30 for 1946/47 and April 30 for 1947/48–1965/66.
[2] Mainly charges on stand-by arrangements, and mainly paid in currencies.
[3] Includes excess of expenditure over income from inception to June 30, 1946, amounting to $0.10 million.
[4] Includes building costs to end of fiscal year 1957/58 ($5.62 million).
[5] Includes building costs, $2.18 million.
[6] Includes building costs, $4.64 million, and payments under the GAB, $4.56 million.
[7] Includes building costs, $5.66 million, and payments under the GAB, $16.07 million.
[8] Totals do not exactly agree because of rounding and of certain administrative adjustments.

remainder in drawing members' currencies. As total expenditure in the five years was over $17 million, the Fund's resources were reduced, on income and expenditure account, by some $5.7 million.

During the five financial years 1951/52 through 1955/56, income totaled $16.4 million and expenditure amounted to $25 million. By the end of the Fund's first ten years, therefore, there had been a net loss of resources on income and expenditure account of $14.2 million.

The year 1956 was, however, the turning point. Since then much greater drawings have produced a large increase in the Fund's income. During the five financial years 1956/57 through 1960/61 charges totaled almost $84 million, of which three fourths was paid in gold. Total income apart from that derived from investments was over $91 million, and as expenditure was only $37.3 million a substantial increment to the Fund's resources resulted. During the same period the income from the Fund's investments (see the immediately following section) totaled $50.5 million.

During the five financial years 1961/62 through 1965/66, the Fund's income rose steeply to a total of $229.6 million, exclusive of $140 million from investments. Charges totaled $220 million, of which $126 million was paid in gold. Expenditure was $88 million. At the end of the five years the General Reserve amounted to $186.4 million and the Special Reserve (resulting from investment income) to $182.2 million.

INVESTMENT OF THE FUND'S ASSETS

Provisions of the Articles

Article XII, Section 2 (*g*), provides that

> The Board of Governors, and the Executive Directors to the extent authorized, may adopt such rules and regulations as may be necessary or appropriate to conduct the business of the Fund.

This has been held to recognize the principle of implied powers, by virtue of which the Executive Board may perform any act that it judges to be necessary or appropriate to the proper administration of the Fund's assets, unless a specific provision of the Articles prohibits it.

Article IX, Section 2, states in part that "the Fund shall possess . . . the capacity . . . to acquire and dispose of immovable and movable property," and Article IV, Section 8 (*a*), provides that "the gold value of the Fund's assets shall be maintained notwithstanding changes in the par or foreign exchange value of the currency of any member." It should be noted that the latter provision covers not only the Fund's holdings of currencies but all its assets.

A limit to the Fund's operations is set by Article V, Section 2, which reads:

> Except as otherwise provided in this Agreement, operations on the account of the Fund shall be limited to transactions for the purpose of supplying a member, on the initiative of such member, with the currency of another member in exchange for gold or for the currency of the member desiring to make the purchase.

This has been held to limit operations to those specifically provided for in the Articles, but not to prohibit transactions of an administrative character.

Early proposals

In October 1946 Mr. White (United States) sent to the Board a memorandum stating that he had asked the Legal Department to investigate whether the Articles would prohibit investment by the Fund in U.S. Government securities. The Legal Department's reply to this inquiry contained the explanation of Article XII, Section 2 (*g*), and of Article V, Section 2, and drew attention to the significance of Article IX, Section 2, and Article IV, Section 8 (*a*). It suggested that in the light of these provisions the Executive Directors were entitled to invest the Fund's assets and to use the income from the investment for administrative purposes. However, a prior understanding with the United States concerning the application of Article IV, Section 8 (*a*), would be advisable. If possible, any arrangements for an investment should include a guarantee of conversion into gold at the price received by the Fund for its gold.

Mr. White's proposal, and the Legal Department's comments, were considered by the Board in November 1946. Directors accepted the legal arguments that an investment in short-term U.S. Government securities, such as Mr. White proposed, could be made by the Fund, and agreed that it could be so arranged as to be practically riskless. Some Directors, however, deprecated an investment on the grounds that it might be misunderstood and even impair confidence in the Fund. The Board accordingly decided not to take any decision at that time.

During the discussion the Research Department was asked to review the possible effects on the U.S. money market of the suggested investment. In a memorandum distributed shortly afterward, the Department replied that an investment of a substantial size, and its subsequent liquidation, would have important effects on money and credit in the United States—which effects could, however, be offset by the Federal Reserve System.

Four years later Mr. Overby, Deputy Managing Director, asked the Legal Department for an opinion on the legality of investing in U.S. Government securities (*a*) part of the Fund's gold holdings and (*b*) part of the dollar subscription of the United States. The Legal Department's reply was confined to the question of investing gold. After confirming the opinion that it had expressed in reply to Mr. White, the Legal Department proposed three safeguards to which any investment should conform:

(i) The amount of the investment should be reasonably proportioned to the expenditures for which income was intended to be produced;

(ii) the amount and duration of the investment should be such as not to hamper sales of currencies by the Fund to its members; and

(iii) risks of loss should be avoided by a U.S. guarantee that the Fund could reacquire at any time the same amount of gold, and by an interpretation of the Articles that would establish the responsibility of the United States to maintain the gold value of the investment should the par value of the dollar be changed.

In April 1951 the Board again considered the question of investment, and this time appointed an Ad Hoc Committee consisting of Mr. Martínez-Ostos (Mexico), chairman, Mr. Beyen (Netherlands), Sir George Bolton (United Kingdom), Mr. Melville (Australia), and Mr. Southard to investigate the possibilities of investing some of the Fund's assets in order to yield an income to offset the operating deficit. This committee met for the first time in May 1951. Mr. Southard then said that he could not state the U.S. Government's position on either the legal or the policy issues involved, since the U.S. legal advisors were still reviewing the matter. For himself, while he agreed with the staff that legally the Fund could make such an investment, he had doubts about the wisdom of doing so. He also doubted whether the U.S. Government would be willing to give a repurchase guarantee, or would accept that it was obliged to maintain the gold value of the investment. Other members of the committee also expressed doubts on both the legal and the policy issues.

The committee did not meet again until July 1952. The chairman then reported that the U.S. Government had still not reached any definite decisions. He had examined the possibility that the Fund might purchase government bonds from some members' central banks, with a guarantee of the convertibility of the earnings, but the interest shown earlier by some Latin American banks in such a proposal had waned. He had also looked into a suggestion that the Fund might acquire World Bank bonds, but discussions with the World Bank had shown that this would not be feasible. In view of these negative results, and of the continuing differences of view among Directors, the committee recommended to the Board that no action be taken and that it be discharged; this was done in August 1952.

First investment

In April 1955 Mr. Southard suggested that, in view of the Fund's growing deficit, further consideration should be given to investing part of its gold. When this was discussed at three meetings in May, the legality of an investment was debated but no decision was reached. Mr. Southard indicated that the U.S. Government was willing to accept $200 million of the Fund's gold for investment in U.S. securities, but while Lord Harcourt expressed appreciation of this offer and said that in the British view the Fund could legally make such an investment, he reported that the British Government doubted the wisdom of making one: the Fund's prestige might be damaged, and its influence impaired, if the impression was given that it was not functioning as had been intended. Other Directors, including Mr. Crena de Iongh (Netherlands), Mr. van Campenhout (Belgium), and Mr. de Largentaye (France), also opposed an investment, citing both legal and policy objections. However, at a fourth meeting, in July, some change of view appeared. Mr. Southard and Mr. Rasminsky (Canada) urged that a favorable decision should be taken because it was vital that the Fund should not continue to run a deficit. Lord Harcourt agreed to take the matter up again with his authorities.

One of the reasons urged at these meetings against making an investment was that there was a possibility that in the near future convertibility of some of the major non-dollar currencies would be restored, which might alter the Fund's situation in an unforeseeable way. This reason was undermined at the Annual Meeting, 1955, when the Governor for the United Kingdom announced that for the time being sterling would not be made convertible. After the Meeting, Lord Harcourt informed the Managing Director that the United Kingdom was now willing to agree to the Fund's investing part of its gold on the conditions that (1) the amount and terms of the investment must be such as not significantly to impair the Fund's liquidity; (2) the U.S. Treasury must recognize the Fund's right to repurchase the gold; (3) the Fund must not bear an exchange risk on the dollars that it acquired; and (4) the amount to be invested should be subject to review by the Board from time to time. Some two months later, in December 1955, Mr. Southard notified the Board that he was now in a position to return to the question of investment, and Lord Harcourt then repeated these conditions to the Board.

Three further meetings were needed before Executive Directors were satisfied that the proposal should be implemented. Mr. de Largentaye still contended that the investment was *ultra vires* because of Article V, Section 2, but he was alone in dissenting from the eventual decision, which set out the purposes and the rationale of the investment in the following terms:

> The Executive Board, observing that the Fund has had and may continue to have an excess of expenditure over income and that the greater part of the Fund's administrative expenditures has been and will continue to be in United States dollars, considers that in the interest of good administration and conservation of the Fund's resources it would be appropriate to raise income towards meeting the deficit by the investment of a portion of the Fund's gold. . . .[32]

The decision also noted the willingness of the United States to consent to the investment, and embodied two interpretations under Article XVIII (*a*) of the

[32] E.B. Decision No. 488-(56/5), January 25, 1956; below, Vol. III, p. 275.

Articles of Agreement. The first of these specified the conditions under which the sale of gold for investment would be legal:

(1) The amount of gold to be sold for investment:

(a) will not be such as to limit the ability of the Fund to make its resources available to members in accordance with the Articles of Agreement; and

(b) will be such as to produce an amount of income reasonably related to the deficit of the Fund;

(2) Whenever the Fund decides to reacquire gold after the sale or maturity of any United States Treasury bills invested in, it will be able to reacquire the same amount of gold as was sold for investment in such bills; and the United States, at the request of the Fund, will sell the said amount of gold to the Fund for U.S. dollars at the United States selling price at the time of the sale to the Fund;

(3) In any computations for the purpose of applying the provisions of the Articles of Agreement the Fund will treat the following assets as representing gold and not as holdings of United States currency;

(a) the dollar proceeds of the sale of gold before investment in the United States Treasury bills; and

(b) the United States Treasury bills invested in; and

(c) the dollar proceeds resulting from the sale or maturity of any such bills before the purchase of gold therewith.[33]

The second interpretation was to the effect that Article IV, Section 8 (*a*), required the United States to maintain the gold value of the assets mentioned in paragraph (3) above, notwithstanding changes in the par or foreign exchange value of the U.S. dollar. It continued:

> This obligation of the United States shall be fully discharged by its maintaining the gold value of the dollar proceeds resulting from the sale of the gold or from the sale or maturity of the U.S. Treasury bills purchased therewith.

Mr. Southard had indicated earlier that the U.S. Secretary of the Treasury was prepared to give the assurances required by this interpretation, and also to recommend to the President a waiver of the customary ¼ of 1 per cent handling charge on the sale and ultimate repurchase of gold. Both of these arrangements were carried through.

When it became evident in December 1955 that the Board would probably approve the investment, the staff began to make arrangements for the gold to be sold and the resulting investment to be made through the Federal Reserve Bank of New York. The latter approached the transaction with some reluctance. Its President, Mr. Allan Sproul, looked on it unfavorably, believing that the investment would be more severely criticized in Congress than the Fund's deficit had been. The Federal Reserve Bank's advisors were also apprehensive that the

[33] *Ibid.*, pp. 275–76.

Bank might be subjected to lawsuits on the ground that the investment was illegal. Although the advisors of the Fund and of the U.S. Treasury held that the legality of the transaction was fully established, the Fund's letter to the Federal Reserve Bank of New York instructing it to carry out the operation—the terms of which were agreed with the Bank—stated that the Fund would indemnify the Bank for any claims, losses, damages, or charges that it might incur or for which it might become liable in connection with the operation.

The Federal Reserve Bank's letter to the Fund included the following paragraph, accepted by the Fund in recognition of the Federal Reserve System's responsibilities in the monetary field:

> We hold to the principle that in this market operations of foreign central banks and international organizations should conform in a general way to the monetary and credit policy of the Federal Reserve System, as otherwise it might be necessary for us at times to magnify our own operations in order to offset those here of such banks and organizations. Accordingly, we are sure that you will understand that, if at any time in the future the investment of your dollar balances should run counter to the Federal Reserve System policy, we would wish to feel free to advise you to that effect and, if we deem it necessary, to request that you allow your investments to run off at maturity.

To comply with the Federal Reserve Bank's wishes, the investment of the Fund's gold was made gradually, being completed in October 1956.

Change of purpose

A sharp increase in drawings during the winter of 1956–57 produced a steep rise in the Fund's income, and by the middle of August 1957 it became clear to the staff that the Fund's accumulated deficit was likely to be eliminated by the time of the Annual Meeting. As the decision taken in 1956 restricted the investment to the purpose of dealing with the accumulated and current deficit, the Acting Managing Director, Mr. Cochran, decided that the cost of the new Fund building, then under construction, should be charged to income instead of to a special account as had been done previously. This delayed the elimination of the deficit on income account until November 1957.

After the Annual Meeting, 1957, the Managing Director submitted to the Board a proposal that the investment should be continued to provide a reserve against possible future deficits. He pointed out that there could be no guarantee that drawings would continue at the level they had reached, so that the Fund's future income could not be relied upon to cover expenditure. He recommended that the purpose of the investment be altered from "to raise income towards meeting the deficit" to "to raise income and provide a reserve towards meeting possible future deficits." The income from the investment should be placed in a special reserve. It was unnecessary to set a limit to the size of the reserve.

This proposal was discussed by the Board at the end of November 1957 and approved, Mr. de Largentaye being the only dissentient. Mr. Southard expressed the view that a reserve of at least $100 million would be sensible, and that the program should be reviewed annually. Following this decision, the Special Reserve was set up (see Table 11).

Other possible purposes for an investment were discussed in a memorandum prepared by the Director of Research and the Deputy General Counsel in February 1959 which suggested that the Fund should embark upon a long-term policy of investing a substantial amount of the Fund's gold, not limited to U.S. securities. The memorandum pointed out that the Fund's gold holdings would increase substantially as a result of the general quota increase just then approved by the Governors, and suggested that the disadvantages of the resulting decrease in members' owned reserves could be counteracted if the Fund were able to channel back some of the gold to them by means of an investment. However, the memorandum recognized that an investment for this purpose would be *ultra vires*, because of the prohibition in Article V, Section 2.

One particular aspect of members' loss of gold was the subject of a further memorandum in June 1959. In this, the Deputy General Counsel pointed out that the gold holdings of the United States had been declining sharply, and he observed that if the Fund were to make a further investment of gold in U.S. securities—perhaps increasing the existing $200 million to $500 million—this would ease for the United States the payment of $343.75 million in gold due in connection with the increase in the U.S. quota.

Increase in amount and maturity

In July 1959 the Managing Director proposed to the Board that the amount of gold invested should be increased from $200 million to $500 million, and that part of the larger sum should be invested in securities having a term to maturity of more than three months but not more than twelve months. He pointed out that the effect of the increases in quotas then being implemented would be to reduce the Fund's income (1) by relating existing drawings to lower tranches of the quotas and (2) in particular, by shifting some drawings into the gold tranche, thereby ending charges on that drawing. Such changes were expected to lower income by $10 million a year. Income might also be expected to decline as the large drawings then outstanding were repurchased. The result would be a decline in the rate of growth of the General Reserve, to which the operating surplus was carried. This Reserve totaled about $26 million at that time. In relation to the Fund's capital, increased by the changes in quotas to about $15 billion, total reserves (General and Special together) of $100–200 million would not be excessive. In these circumstances an increase in the rate of growth of the Special Reserve was desirable. At that time the Special Reserve totaled about

$8 million and was increasing at a rate of $4–6 million a year, depending on the rate of interest earned. Under the new proposal it would increase by $10–15 million a year. This figure resulted partly from the larger amount of the investment and partly from the higher rate of interest which would be obtainable on securities with a longer term than three months; recourse to the latter would require an amendment to the interpretation of the Articles set out in the first decision on investment, and a draft decision provided to the Board embodied this.

When this proposal came before the Board, Mr. Southard said that the U.S. Government was willing to extend its guarantee of the gold value of the investment to cover the enlarged sum. Mr. Rasminsky stressed the desirability of cooperation with the U.S. monetary authorities, and commented that since the investment was useful to the Fund, advantage should be taken of the authorities' willingness so long as this continued. Mr. Feuché (France) again stated the French objections, explained on previous occasions by Mr. de Largentaye. Messrs. Lieftinck (Netherlands) and Toussaint (Belgium), while not objecting to the proposal, expressed concern at the proposed size of the reserves in relation to the Fund's prospective expenditure, and also questioned the wisdom of increasing the investment in a period of boom. The investment was, however, approved.

Second increase in amount

In November 1960 the Managing Director proposed to the Board that the amount invested should be further increased, from $500 million to $800 million. His reasons were that the continuous growth in the number of Fund members was necessarily expanding the Fund's expenditure, while its operating income had been declining. Further, the rate of interest earned on the investment was appreciably less than it had been at the time of the increase from $200 million to $500 million. The increase in the Special Reserve (then about $32 million) which would result from a larger investment would give greater assurance that the whole of the General Reserve (then about $43 million) would be available for purposes other than financing administrative deficits.

Mr. Southard told the Board that the U.S. authorities would agree to the proposed increase in the investment, and would give the necessary guarantee. While the continued decline in the U.S. gold reserves (from $20.58 billion at the end of 1958 to $18.44 billion in October 1960) was not mentioned in the discussion, it may be assumed that this played a part in influencing the U.S. Government's decision.

The Board accepted the Managing Director's proposal. On this occasion Mr. de Largentaye agreed with the decision, on the footing that the Board's interpretations had made the investment legal. Mr. Reid (Canada) suggested that it might be desirable to give some consideration in the future to permitting investment in longer-term (say 3-year) securities. The Managing Director undertook that the suggestion would be borne in mind, and that if such an investment seemed desirable a recommendation would be made to the Board. However, no general recommendation has been made, and the only securities for longer than 12 months that have been held by the Fund have been U.S. Treasury notes in which investments of about $62 million were twice authorized, in July and November 1961. Both investments were suggested by the U.S. authorities, the first in 15½-month notes to facilitate a Treasury refinancing operation, and the second in 15-month notes because no 12-month securities were being issued at a time when the Fund had $62 million of 12-month securities coming to maturity.

BORROWING BY THE FUND

The powers of the Fund to borrow currencies that it needs for its operations are contained in Article VII, Section 2—which forms part of the Article making provision for action by the Fund should a currency become scarce, and is the only part of that Article of which the Fund has so far made use. Section 2 reads as follows:

> The Fund may, if it deems such action appropriate to replenish its holdings of any member's currency, take either or both of the following steps:
>
> (i) Propose to the member that, on terms and conditions agreed between the Fund and the member, the latter lend its currency to the Fund or that, with the approval of the member, the Fund borrow such currency from some other source either within or outside the territories of the member, but no member shall be under any obligation to make such loans to the Fund or to approve the borrowing of its currency by the Fund from any other source.
>
> (ii) Require the member to sell its currency to the Fund for gold.

The provisions of Section 2 (ii) involve, of course, the exchange by the Fund of one type of asset for another. They are accordingly dealt with in Chapter 19 below. In the present chapter we shall be concerned only with Section 2 (i).

Very soon after the first general increase in quotas had taken effect in 1959, the increasing volatility of balances of payments resulting from the restoration of external convertibility by European countries began to make the staff question whether the Fund's resources would be adequate for the greater demands likely to be made upon them. Outside the Fund also, questions of the same sort were being raised. In testimony before the U.S. Congress in January 1960 Mr. Bernstein (former Director of the Fund's Research Department) suggested that the Fund should take steps to issue debentures for, say, $6 billion to add to the resources available to it in case of emergency.

In February 1961 the Managing Director presented to the Board three proposals for enhancing the Fund's ability to serve the purposes of the Articles; one of these was a suggestion that use might be made of Article VII, Section 2 (i), to borrow currencies likely to be needed in the event of large drawings. Following up this proposal, the staff submitted to the Board in April a detailed memorandum on the need to borrow currencies, on the amounts likely to be required, and on the conditions under which such borrowings might be made.

Two meetings in May 1961 were devoted to a discussion of these proposals, and showed that the Board was in general favorably disposed toward them but that some Directors felt that it would be important to stress that drawings involving the use of borrowed currencies should be made on terms no less strict than those applied to drawings on the Fund's own resources. Inquiries made by the staff in continental European countries during the summer showed that there was considerable anxiety on this point, and that the members concerned feared that if their currencies were lent to the Fund, and by the Fund lent, for example, to the United Kingdom, the latter might obtain them on less stringent terms than if it had had recourse to the European Fund controlled by its partners in the OEEC.

The Annual Report for 1961 referred to the possible need for the Fund to utilize Article VII, Section 2 (i); [34] and in his speech at the Annual Meeting the Managing Director expanded at some length on the possibility.[35] At the same Meeting, however, a discussion among representatives of the main industrial powers, convened by the Secretary of the U.S. Treasury, Mr. Dillon, showed that the apprehensions detected by the staff in Europe were likely to influence the terms on which the members whose currencies would be most needed would be willing to make them available to the Fund. These terms were likely to include a measure of control over the use to which the borrowed funds were put.[36]

During the last quarter of the calendar year 1961, negotiations for a borrowing arrangement—involving Belgium, Canada, France, Germany, Italy, Japan, the Netherlands, Sweden, the United Kingdom, and the United States—were undertaken by the Managing Director and members of the staff at a series of meetings with representatives of these countries in Paris. Some difficulty was found in reconciling the philosophy behind the plan, as originally conceived and expressed in a Franco-American draft handed to the Managing Director on November 17, with the provisions of the Fund Agreement. The Franco-American draft would have transferred from the Fund to the member providing borrowed funds the responsibility for deciding whether to permit the use of the Fund's resources, if borrowed funds were involved. It would also have permitted the

---

[34] *Annual Report, 1961*, p. 19.

[35] *Summary Proceedings, 1961*, pp. 27–29.

[36] *Ibid.*, pp. 54–55, 64, 117.

member requesting the drawing, and not the Fund, to decide whether the member's needs should be met from borrowed funds or from the Fund's own resources. Both these provisions were inconsistent with the principles of the Fund, and were rejected by the Managing Director.

Subsequent drafts of a borrowing arrangement were prepared by the Fund staff. They were communicated to the Executive Directors, but the exclusion of the latter from the actual negotiations was regarded as unfortunate, and the eventual text, although accepted as containing probably the best conditions that could be arranged, still seemed to some Directors to fall short of what was desirable. The General Arrangements to Borrow (GAB), as they were termed, are set out in full in Volume III.[37] Here it will suffice to note the main features.

(1) The Arrangements were to be implemented only "to forestall and cope with an impairment of the international monetary system" and only for the purpose of meeting a request to draw on the Fund by one of the participants in the Arrangements.

(2) A participant that proposed to make a drawing, or to seek the repayment of a loan made previously under the Arrangements, if either might necessitate activating the Arrangements, would consult the Managing Director first and then the other participants.

(3) Before making a call on the other participants, the Managing Director would consult the Executive Directors and the participants.

(4) The amount that each participant would lend on a given occasion would be based on its (or its country's) existing and prospective balance of payments and reserve position.

(5) When the Managing Director made a call on the participants, they would consult and inform him of the amounts of their currencies that they were prepared to lend. If they could not agree on the distribution proposed by the Managing Director, they would propose an alternative one of the same order of magnitude as his call.

(6) Each request for a drawing which would require the activation of the Arrangements would be dealt with in accordance with the Fund's established policies.

(7) When such a drawing was repurchased, the Fund would repay the countries from which it had borrowed; in any event it would repay them within five years of the transfer of funds by them for that drawing.

(8) A participant that had lent to the Fund could receive early repayment should it need and request this because its own payments position had deteriorated.

[37] E.B. Decision No. 1289-(62/1), January 5, 1962; below, Vol. III, pp. 246–52.

(9) Interest would be payable on sums borrowed, in accordance with a formula which initially yielded a rate of 1½ per cent per annum. The Fund would also pay a charge of ½ of 1 per cent on each borrowing transaction.

Not all these provisions were spelled out in the Arrangements themselves; those summarized in paragraphs (2) and (5) above were contained in a letter sent to the other participants by Mr. Baumgartner, the French Minister of Finance.

The commitments which the participants undertook, adjusted to allow for two minor changes effected in 1962, are set out in Table 12.

The plan was formally adopted by the Board on January 5, 1962. By October 24, 1962, enough of the participants had acceded to it to bring the Arrangements into operation. The last country to adhere was Canada, which notified the Fund of its agreement in January 1964. The Managing Director subsequently negotiated an arrangement with Switzerland, which is not a member of the Fund, by which Switzerland undertook to lend to a country

Table 12. General Arrangements to Borrow: Participants and Commitments as at December 31, 1965

Participant	Units of Participant's Currency		Equivalents in Millions of U.S. Dollars at 1962 Rates
United States	US$	2,000,000,000	2,000
Deutsche Bundesbank	DM	4,000,000,000	1,000
United Kingdom	£	357,142,857	1,000
France	F	2,715,381,428	550
Italy	Lit	343,750,000,000	550
Japan	¥	90,000,000,000	250
Canada	Can$	216,216,216	200
Netherlands	f.	724,000,000	200
Belgium	BF	7,500,000,000	150
Sveriges Riksbank	SKr	517,320,000	100
Total			6,000

drawing on the Fund on occasions when the General Arrangements were activated, subject to the completion of an agreement with that participant.[38]

The first occasion on which the General Arrangements were activated was in December 1964, when the United Kingdom drew under its stand-by arrangement for $1 billion. The amounts borrowed then and for another drawing by the United Kingdom in May 1965 are summarized in Table 13.

The Arrangements were originally introduced for four years, with the proviso that they could be renewed if the decision to this effect was taken by October 23, 1965. The question of renewal was discussed in the Board on April 28, 1965. A number of changes were then mentioned as desirable, including the elimination

[38] E.B. Decision No. 1712-(64/29), June 8, 1964; below, Vol. III, p. 254.

of the requirement that the international monetary system should be in danger of impairment and of the limitation of borrowings to drawings by participants. Some simplification of the method of activating the Arrangements was also suggested. As, however, it seemed likely that such changes would not be approved by the participants, the Chairman proposed, and the Board approved,

Table 13. General Arrangements to Borrow: Borrowings by the Fund, 1964–65
(In millions of U.S. dollars)

Participant	Amounts Borrowed		Amount Still Available
	Dec. 1964	May 1965	Dec. 1965
Belgium	30.0	37.5	82.5
Canada	15.0	35.0	150.0
France	100.0	140.0	310.0
Deutsche Bundesbank	180.0	167.5	652.5
Italy	5.0	65.0	480.0
Japan	20.0	25.0	205.0
Netherlands	40.0	37.5	122.5
Sveriges Riksbank	15.0	17.5	67.5
United Kingdom	—	—	1,000.0
United States	—	—	2,000.0
Totals	405.0	525.0	5,070.0

that the Fund should seek a continuation of the Arrangements without amendment.

After consultation with the participants, it was agreed that the Arrangements should continue until October 23, 1970, subject to a review within two years from the expiry of the original four years (October 23, 1966), and subject to the right of any participant to withdraw at any time during the three months ending October 23, 1968.

Table 14. Quotas of Members at Selected Dates [1]

(In millions of U.S. dollars)

Member Country	Dec. 31 1945	Dec. 31 1950	Dec. 31 1955	Dec. 31 1960	Dec. 31 1965
Afghanistan	•	•	10.0	22.5	22.5
Algeria	•	•	•	•	60.0
Argentina	•	•	150.0[2]	280.0	280.0
Australia	200.0	200.0	200.0	400.0	400.0
Austria	•	50.0	50.0	75.0	75.0
Belgium	225.0	225.0	225.0	337.5	337.5
Bolivia	10.0	10.0	10.0	22.5	22.5
Brazil	150.0	150.0	150.0	280.0	280.0
Burma	•	•	15.0	30.0	30.0
Burundi	•	•	•	•	11.25
Cameroon	•	•	•	•	15.0
Canada	300.0	300.0	300.0	550.0	550.0
Central African Rep.	•	•	•	•	7.5
Ceylon	•	15.0	15.0	45.0	62.0
Chad	•	•	•	•	7.5
Chile	50.0	50.0	50.0	100.0	100.0
China	550.0	550.0	550.0	550.0	550.0
Colombia	50.0	50.0	50.0	100.0	100.0
Congo (Brazzaville)	•	•	•	•	7.5
Congo, Dem. Rep.	•	•	•	•	45.0
Costa Rica	5.0	5.0	5.0	5.5	20.0
Cuba	50.0	50.0	50.0	50.0	•
Cyprus	•	•	•	•	11.25
Czechoslovakia	125.0	125.0	•	•	•
Dahomey	•	•	•	•	7.5
Denmark	•	68.0	68.0	130.0	130.0
Dominican Rep.	5.0	5.0	5.0	15.0	25.0
Ecuador	5.0	5.0	5.0	15.0	20.0
El Salvador	2.5	2.5	2.5	11.25	20.0
Ethiopia	6.0	6.0	6.0	9.6[3]	15.0
Finland	•	38.0	38.0	57.0	57.0
France	450.0	525.0	525.0	787.5	787.5
Gabon	•	•	•	•	7.5
Germany	•	•	330.0	787.5	787.5
Ghana	•	•	15.0[4]	35.0	55.0
Greece	40.0	40.0	40.0	60.0	60.0
Guatemala	5.0	5.0	5.0	15.0	20.0
Guinea	•	•	•	•	15.0
Haiti	5.0	•	2.0	11.25	11.25
Honduras	2.5	0.5	2.5	11.25	15.0
Iceland	1.0	1.0	1.0	11.25	11.25
India	400.0	400.0	400.0	600.0	600.0
Indonesia	•	•	110.0	165.0	•
Iran	25.0	35.0	35.0	70.0	70.0
Iraq	8.0	8.0	8.0	15.0	64.0

Footnotes on page 380.

Table 14 *(continued)*. Quotas of Members at Selected Dates [1]
(In millions of U.S. dollars)

Member Country	Dec. 31 1945	Dec. 31 1950	Dec. 31 1955	Dec. 31 1960	Dec. 31 1965
Ireland	•	•	30.0[5]	45.0	45.0
Israel	•	•	4.5	25.0	50.0
Italy	•	180.0	180.0	270.0	500.0
Ivory Coast	•	•	•	•	15.0
Jamaica	•	•	•	•	20.0
Japan	•	•	250.0	500.0	500.0
Jordan	•	•	3.0	4.5[3]	12.25[3]
Kenya	•	•	•	•	25.0
Korea	•	•	12.5	18.75	18.75
Kuwait	•	•	•	•	50.0
Laos	•	•	•	•	7.5
Lebanon	•	4.5	4.5	4.5	6.75
Liberia	0.5	•	•	11.25[6]	16.0
Libya	•	•	5.0[7]	9.0	15.0
Luxembourg	10.0	10.0	10.0	11.0[3]	15.0
Malagasy Rep.	•	•	•	•	15.0
Malawi	•	•	•	•	11.25
Malaysia	•	•	25.0[8]	30.0[3]	58.33[3]
Mali	•	•	•	•	13.0
Mauritania	•	•	•	•	7.5
Mexico	90.0	90.0	90.0	180.0	180.0
Morocco	•	•	35.0[9]	52.5	72.0
Nepal	•	•	•	•	7.5
Netherlands	275.0	275.0	275.0	412.5	412.5
New Zealand	50.0	•	•	•	125.0
Nicaragua	2.0	2.0	2.0	11.25	11.25
Niger	•	•	•	•	7.5
Nigeria	•	•	•	•	50.0
Norway	50.0	50.0	50.0	100.0	100.0
Pakistan	•	100.0	100.0	150.0	150.0
Panama	0.5	0.5	0.5	0.5	11.25
Paraguay	2.0	3.5	3.5	10.0[3]	11.25
Peru	25.0	25.0	25.0	30.0[3]	37.5
Philippines	15.0	15.0	15.0	75.0	75.0
Poland	125.0	•	•	•	•
Portugal	•	•	•	•	60.0
Rwanda	•	•	•	•	11.25
Saudi Arabia	•	•	10.0[5]	55.0	72.0
Senegal	•	•	•	7.5[10]	25.0
Sierra Leone	•	•	•	•	11.25
Somalia	•	•	•	•	11.25
South Africa	100.0	100.0	100.0	150.0	150.0
Spain	•	•	100.0[7]	150.0	150.0
Sudan	•	•	10.0[4]	15.0	45.0
Sweden	•	•	100.0	150.0	150.0

Table 14 *(concluded)*. Quotas of Members at Selected Dates [1]

(In millions of U.S. dollars)

Member Country	Dec. 31 1945	Dec. 31 1950	Dec. 31 1955	Dec. 31 1960	Dec. 31 1965
Syrian Arab Rep.	•	6.5	6.5	[11]	25.0
Tanzania	•	•	•	•	25.0
Thailand	•	12.5	12.5	45.0	76.0
Togo	•	•	•	•	11.25
Trinidad & Tobago	•	•	•	•	20.0
Tunisia	•	•	12.0[9]	14.1[3]	22.5
Turkey	•	43.0	43.0	86.0	86.0
Uganda	•	•	•	•	25.0
United Arab Rep.	45.0	60.0	60.0	105.0[12]	120.0
United Kingdom	1,300.0	1,300.0	1,300.0	1,950.0	1,950.0
United States	2,750.0	2,750.0	2,750.0	4,125.0	4,125.0
Upper Volta	•	•	•	•	7.5
Uruguay	15.0	15.0	15.0	15.0	30.0
Venezuela	15.0	15.0	15.0	150.0	150.0
Viet-Nam	•	•	12.5[2]	16.5[3]	22.5
Yugoslavia	60.0	60.0	60.0	120.0	120.0
Zambia	•	•	•	•	50.0
Totals	7,600.0[13]	8,036.5	8,750.5[14]	14,740.7[15]	15,976.6[16]

[1] The column headed Dec. 31, 1945 lists the quotas decided on at Bretton Woods and listed in Schedule A to the Articles of Agreement. The other columns show the quotas at the end of each year in which there was a quinquennial review of quotas. A dot (•) indicates that the country was not a member at the time.

[2] Initial quota (September 1956).

[3] Increasing quota by installments; not yet completed.

[4] Initial quota (September 1957).

[5] Initial quota (August 1957).

[6] Initial quota (March 1962).

[7] Initial quota (September 1958).

[8] Initial quota (March 1958).

[9] Initial quota (April 1958).

[10] Initial quota (August 1962).

[11] At this date Syria was part of United Arab Republic.

[12] Including Syria.

[13] Excluding U.S.S.R.

[14] Excluding the eleven countries designated by footnotes 2, 4, 5, 7, 8, and 9.

[15] Excluding Liberia and Senegal.

[16] The Fourth Quinquennial Review was not formally terminated until early in 1966 (see p. 363 above), so that the resulting increase in quotas is not reflected in the December 31, 1965 total. On December 31, 1968 the total of quotas was $21,198.4 million.

CHAPTER

18

Evolution of the Fund's Policy on Drawings

J. Keith Horsefield and Gertrud Lovasy *

THE ORIGIN AND MAGNITUDE of the Fund's resources (which are so far derived mainly from subscriptions) were described in Chapter 17. For the purpose of the following discussion it should be kept in mind that each member has a quota in the Fund; that its subscription, which is paid partly in gold and partly in the member's own currency, is equal to its quota; and that the normal quantitative limitations on the use of the Fund's resources by each member are determined by its quota.

The basic mechanism of a drawing from the Fund consists of an exchange of the drawing member's currency for an equivalent amount of other currencies. The effect is therefore to increase the Fund's holdings of the drawing member's currency and to decrease its holdings of the currencies that are drawn. The Articles contain provisions the effect of which is to tend to restore the Fund's holdings of each member's currency to a level equal to 75 per cent of that member's quota—i.e., to the level at which the Fund's holdings would stand if the member had paid the required 25 per cent of its subscription in gold, and the Fund had effected no transactions in that currency (or any transactions effected had canceled one another out).

Annual figures for drawings are given in Table 22 at the end of Chapter 19.

LEGAL PROVISIONS

The provisions in the Articles of Agreement governing the use of the Fund's resources are extensive and complicated. Since much of the evolution of the

* The first three sections of this chapter were written by Mr. Horsefield; the last section, on the Compensatory Financing of Export Fluctuations, by Miss Lovasy. In the earlier parts of the chapter, use has been made of an article by Mr. Subimal Mookerjee entitled "Policies on the Use of Fund Resources," *Staff Papers*, Vol. XIII (1966), pp. 421–42.

relevant policies hinged on the text of these Articles, it is necessary to start by setting them out in some detail. The reader will need to refer back to the following extracts as the argument proceeds.[1]

Articles of Agreement

The Fund's resources are to be used in accordance with the purposes of the Fund, which are set out in Article I of the Fund Agreement. Among these purposes are:

(v) To give confidence to members by making the Fund's resources available to them under adequate safeguards, thus providing them with opportunity to correct maladjustments in their balance of payments without resorting to measures destructive of national or international prosperity.

(vi) In accordance with the above, to shorten the duration and lessen the degree of disequilibrium in the international balances of payments of members.

The conditions governing the use of the Fund's resources are set out more precisely in Article V, Section 3, which reads as follows:

(a) A member shall be entitled to buy the currency of another member from the Fund in exchange for its own currency subject to the following conditions:

(i) The member desiring to purchase the currency represents that it is presently needed for making in that currency payments which are consistent with the provisions of this Agreement;

(ii) The Fund has not given notice under Article VII, Section 3, that its holdings of the currency desired have become scarce;

(iii) The proposed purchase would not cause the Fund's holdings of the purchasing member's currency to increase by more than twenty-five percent of its quota during the period of twelve months ending on the date of the purchase nor to exceed two hundred percent of its quota, but the twenty-five percent limitation shall apply only to the extent that the Fund's holdings of the member's currency have been brought above seventy-five percent of its quota if they had been below that amount;

(iv) The Fund has not previously declared under Section 5 of this Article, Article IV, Section 6, Article VI, Section 1, or Article XV, Section 2 *(a)*, that the member desiring to purchase is ineligible to use the resources of the Fund.

(b) A member shall not be entitled without the permission of the Fund to use the Fund's resources to acquire currency to hold against forward exchange transactions.

Other relevant provisions of the same Article are as follows:

Sec. 4. *Waiver of conditions.*—The Fund may in its discretion, and on terms which safeguard its interests, waive any of the conditions prescribed in Sec-

[1] In what follows no account is taken of the amendments to the Articles effected in 1969, of which a summary appears in Part V of this volume. The full text of the Articles of Agreement as approved at Bretton Woods is reproduced below, Vol. III, pp. 185–214. The amendments to the Articles are reproduced in Vol. III, pp. 521–41.

tion 3 *(a)* of this Article, especially in the case of members with a record of avoiding large or continuous use of the Fund's resources. In making a waiver it shall take into consideration periodic or exceptional requirements of the member requesting the waiver. The Fund shall also take into consideration a member's willingness to pledge as collateral security gold, silver, securities, or other acceptable assets having a value sufficient in the opinion of the Fund to protect its interests and may require as a condition of waiver the pledge of such collateral security.

SEC. 5. *Ineligibility to use the Fund's resources.*—Whenever the Fund is of the opinion that any member is using the resources of the Fund in a manner contrary to the purposes of the Fund, it shall present to the member a report setting forth the views of the Fund and prescribing a suitable time for reply. After presenting such a report to a member, the Fund may limit the use of its resources by the member. If no reply to the report is received from the member within the prescribed time, or if the reply received is unsatisfactory, the Fund may continue to limit the member's use of the Fund's resources or may, after giving reasonable notice to the member, declare it ineligible to use the resources of the Fund.

Article V, Section 7, contains provisions designed to restore a member's position in the Fund after it has made use of the Fund's resources. These are set out in full in Chapter 19. They may be summarized as follows:

(1) At the end of each of the Fund's financial years each member must use in repurchase of its own currency from the Fund an amount of its monetary reserves equal in value to one half of any increase that has occurred during the year in the Fund's holdings of its currency plus one half of any increase, or minus one half of any decrease, that has occurred during the year in the member's monetary reserves (Section 7 *(b)* (i)).

(2) But repurchases are *not* to be made at all if the member's monetary reserves have decreased more than the Fund's holdings have increased during the year (Section 7 *(b)* (i)); or to an extent that would *(a)* reduce the member's monetary reserves below its quota (Section 7 *(c)* (i)), *(b)* reduce the Fund's holdings of the member's currency below 75 per cent of its quota (Section 7 *(c)* (ii)); *(c)* increase the Fund's holdings of any other member's currency above 75 per cent of that member's quota (Section 7 *(c)* (iii)).

The make-up of repurchase requirements, in terms of gold and particular currencies, is stipulated in detail in Schedule B.

Article V, Section 8, details the charges which the Fund makes for the use of its resources. These are discussed in Chapter 19, but mention must be made here of Section 8 *(d)*, which reads in part:

> Whenever the Fund's holdings of a member's currency are such that the charge applicable to any bracket for any period has reached the rate of four percent per annum, the Fund and the member shall consider means by which the Fund's holdings of the currency can be reduced.

Elsewhere in the Articles there are a number of other provisions relevant to the use of the Fund's resources, as follows:

(a) Drawings to finance capital transfers are subject to limitations (Article VI). This is the subject of a later section in this chapter.[2]

(b) The Fund was not intended to provide facilities for relief or reconstruction or to deal with the international indebtedness arising out of World War II. (Article XIV, Section 1).

(c) The Fund may postpone exchange transactions with any member if its circumstances are such that, in the opinion of the Fund, they would lead to use of the resources of the Fund in a manner contrary to the purposes of the Fund Agreement or prejudicial to the Fund or its members (Article XX, Section 4 *(i)*).

(d) If a member changes the par value of its currency despite the objection of the Fund, in cases where the Fund is entitled to object, the member shall be ineligible to use the resources of the Fund unless the Fund otherwise determines (Article IV, Section 6).

(e) If a member fails to fulfill any of its obligations under the Articles of Agreement, the Fund may declare the member ineligible to use the resources of the Fund (Article XV, Section 2 *(a)*).

(f) In its relations with members, the Fund was enjoined to recognize that the postwar transitional period would be one of change and adjustment, and in making decisions on requests occasioned thereby which were presented by any member it must give the member the benefit of any reasonable doubt (Article XIV, Section 5).

(g) In the event of an emergency or the development of unforeseen circumstances threatening the operations of the Fund, the Executive Directors by unanimous vote may suspend for a period of not more than one hundred and twenty days the operation of certain provisions, including those in Article V, Sections 3 and 7. Such suspension may be extended by not more than two hundred and forty days by the Board of Governors, by a vote of four fifths of the total voting power (Article XVI, Section 1 *(a)* and *(c)*).

Interpretations

Over the years, these provisions of the Articles of Agreement have been the subject of much discussion in the Executive Board, and many of the relevant phrases have had to be interpreted by decisions of the Executive Directors. Some, but not all, of these were formal interpretations under Article XVIII.[3] The most important of these decisions may be summarized as follows:

---

[2] Below, pp. 410–16.

[3] For an explanation of the Fund's powers of interpretation, see below, pp. 567–73.

General purposes of provisions

The U.S. Bretton Woods Agreements Act required the Governor of the Fund for the United States

> to obtain promptly an official interpretation by the Fund as to whether its authority to use its resources extends beyond current monetary stabilization operations to afford temporary assistance to members in connection with seasonal, cyclical, and emergency fluctuations in the balance of payments of any member for current transactions, and whether it has authority to use its resources to provide facilities for relief, reconstruction, or armaments, or to meet a large or sustained outflow of capital on the part of any member.[4]

This question was put by the Governor for the United States to the Governors at the Inaugural Meeting at Savannah, and was by them referred to the Executive Directors.[5] The Directors discussed it in September 1946. The answer was complicated by the consideration that the Articles of Agreement provided for the Fund to finance balance of payments deficits as a whole, and not particular types of imports. However, the Directors agreed to report to the Governors at the First Annual Meeting that

> authority to use the resources of the Fund is limited to use in accordance with its purposes to give temporary assistance in financing balance of payments deficits on current account for monetary stabilization operations.[6]

The key words in this interpretation were "temporary" and "current account." The significance of the former will become apparent in the next section of this chapter; the latter assumed importance, after some years, in connection with the possible use of the Fund's resources to cope with deficits due to capital transactions, and is discussed in that connection in the next section but one.

Meaning of "the member . . . represents" (Article V, Section 3 (a) (i))

That the Fund was not obliged to accept the representation of a member had been the view of the U.S. delegation at Bretton Woods.[7] The point was discussed in the Board on May 6, 1947, and the conclusion reached (after a slight change of wording on May 29) was as follows: [8]

> The word "represents" in Article V, Section 3 *(a)* (i), means "declares." The member is presumed to have fulfilled the condition mentioned in Article V, Section 3 *(a)* (i), if it declares that the currency is presently needed for making payments in that currency which are consistent with the provisions of the Agreement. But the Fund may, for good reasons, challenge the correctness of this declaration, on the grounds that the currency is not "presently needed" or because

[4] Public Law 171, 79th Cong., 1st sess., Sec. 13.(a); *Selected Decisions*, p. 155.

[5] Resolution IM-6, *Selected Documents*, p. 19.

[6] E.B. Decision No. 71-2, September 26, 1946; below, Vol. III, p. 245.

[7] See above, Vol. I, p. 72.

[8] E.B. Decision No. 284-4, May 29, 1947, reaffirmed March 10, 1948; below, Vol. III, p. 227.

> the currency is not needed for payment "in that currency," or because the payments will not be "consistent with the provisions of this Agreement." If the Fund concludes that a particular declaration is not correct, the Fund may postpone or reject the request, or accept it subject to conditions. . . .

Meaning of "presently needed" (Article V, Section 3 (a) (i))

The decision just quoted concludes with the following sentence:

> The phrase "presently needed" cannot be defined in terms of a formula uniformly applicable to all cases, but where there is good reason to doubt that the currency is "presently needed," the Fund will have to apply the phrase in each case in the light of all the circumstances.

This pronouncement followed a short discussion of the meaning of the phrase, during which it was stated that it implied an intent by the drafters of the Articles of Agreement that members should draw in limited amounts as necessary for immediate payments. When, on April 23, 1947, the first member to apply for a drawing, Ethiopia, sought to obtain $900,000, some Directors thought that since this amount was 15 per cent of the member's quota, it was more than could be "presently needed," and Ethiopia was asked to justify the request. As, instead, the request was withdrawn, the point was never cleared up. However, since then the Board's views on what can be "presently needed" have undergone much change, so that, when in February 1956 Burma asked to draw $15 million (100 per cent of its quota), this was allowed, the question whether the amount was "presently needed" not being raised.

Meaning of "making in that currency" (Article V, Section 3 (a) (i))

The question raised by this phrase was whether a member that conducted its international transactions wholly in terms of a reserve currency could be allowed to draw some other currency from the Fund, in order to convert this other currency into the reserve currency which it needed to settle its international accounts. This question was considered by the Board in April 1961, and although the point was not formally decided, the practice of the Fund has since conformed to the view of the Legal Department that the meaning of Article V, Section 3 (*a*) (i), is that a member may draw from the Fund any currency which it uses, directly or indirectly, to support its exchange market.

Meaning of "consistent with the provisions of this Agreement" (Article V, Section 3 (a) (i))

The Board decided in March 1948 that the phrase meant

> consistent both with the provisions of the Fund Agreement other than Article I and with the purposes of the Fund contained in Article I.[9]

---

[9] E.B. Decision No. 287-3, March 17, 1948; below, Vol. III, p. 228.

The significance of this decision, as is explained below, was that it required that a member seeking to draw from the Fund should not only fulfill the specific stipulations of Article V, Section 3, but also be conforming to the general purposes of the Fund, as set out in Article I.

Meaning of "twenty-five percent" (Article V, Section 3 (a) (iii))

In 1955 the Board interpreted the quantitative limit of 25 per cent of quota in relation to drawing rights under Article V, Section 3 (*a*) (iii), as follows:

> Where the Fund's holdings of a member's currency are not less than seventy-five per cent of its quota, and to the extent that such holdings would not be increased above two hundred per cent of its quota, the purchases which the member may make during a period of twelve months ending on the date of a proposed purchase shall be determined as follows:
>
> (a) The total purchases shall not exceed twenty-five per cent of its quota;
>
> (b) Provided that, if the member has made purchases during the period, it may then purchase an amount equal to the difference between twenty-five per cent of its quota and the total of such purchases adjusted on the basis that a repurchase by the member or sale of its currency during the period is deducted from a previous, but not subsequent, purchase or purchases during the period.[10]

Meaning of "is using" (Article V, Section 5)

In March 1948 the Board decided that

> a member "is using" the resources of the Fund within the meaning of Article V, Section 5, where it is either actually disposing of the exchange purchased from the Fund, or, having purchased exchange from the Fund, the Fund's holdings of its currency are in excess of 75 per cent of its quota.[11]

There have been two decisions explaining the Fund's right to use the powers provided by Article V, Section 5. Three weeks before the decision just quoted, the Board affirmed that

> The Fund has, in the case of a member which has had a previous exchange transaction with the Fund, power to declare the member ineligible or limit its use of the resources of the Fund if the member is, in the opinion of the Fund, using the resources of the Fund in a manner contrary to the purposes of the Fund.[12]

Two meetings later, the Board decided that

> if the Fund receives a request from a member to purchase exchange and either, (1) the Fund is considering sending the member a report pursuant to Article V, Section 5, or (2) the Fund finds when the request is before it that action pursuant to that Section should be considered; then the Fund has the authority, pursuant

[10] E.B. Decision No. 451-(55/52), August 24, 1955; below, Vol. III, p. 228.

[11] E.B. Decision No. 292-3, March 30, 1948; below, Vol. III, p. 235.

[12] E.B. Decision No. 284-3, March 10, 1948; below, Vol. III, p. 234.

> to Article V, Section 5, of the Fund Agreement, to postpone the transfer as permitted under the provisions of Rules and Regulations G-3 for such time as may reasonably be necessary to decide the question of applying Article V, Section 5, and, if it decides to apply it, to prepare and send to the member a report and subject its use of the Fund's resources to limitations. Under such circumstances the limitations imposed will apply to the pending request for the purchase of exchange as well as to future requests.[13]

Nevertheless, the Board was reluctant to apply Article V, Section 5, considering this rather a drastic sanction. It had in any case provided, by Rule K-2, that whenever the Board would be authorized to declare a member ineligible to use the Fund's resources, it could exercise less extreme powers—i.e., it could "indicate the circumstances under which, and/or the extent to which" drawings would be permitted.

Use for "reconstruction" (Article XIV, Section 1)

In July 1947 the Board agreed that

> the prohibition in the Fund Agreement, Article XIV, Section 1, was not meant to prevent countries which were undergoing reconstruction from using the Fund's resources.[14]

It should be noted that the prohibitions in Article XIV, Section 1, were based on two considerations discussed at Bretton Woods. The first was that long-term tasks of reconstruction were to be undertaken by another agency than the Fund, viz., the World Bank. The second was that the United Kingdom had asked that the possibility of using the Fund's resources to repay blocked sterling balances should be omitted from the Fund Agreement.[15]

Postponement under Article XX, Section 4 (i)

The Board has interpreted its powers under Article XX, Section 4 (*i*), as follows:

> The Fund has, in the case of a member which has had no previous exchange transaction with the Fund, the power to postpone exchange transactions with it if its circumstances are such that, in the opinion of the Fund, they would lead to the use of the resources of the Fund in a manner contrary to the purposes of the Agreement or prejudicial to the Fund or its members. This power did not lapse as of the date the Fund began exchange transactions.[16]

This conclusion was reached in two stages. In February 1947 the Board agreed, in effect, on the decision embodied in the last sentence quoted above;

---

[13] E.B. Decision No. 286-1, March 15, 1948; below, Vol. III, p. 234. For Rule G-3 see below, Vol. III, p. 292.

[14] E.B. Decision No. 196-2, July 31, 1947; below, Vol. III, p. 268.

[15] See discussion in Vol. I above, p. 52.

[16] E.B. Decision No. 284-2, March 10, 1948; below, Vol. III, p. 272.

a year later the Directors considered the related problem whether the Fund's powers lapsed once a member had drawn on the Fund, and decided by a majority that they did.

Use of ineligibility provisions

It will be convenient to note here the few occasions on which members have become ineligible to use the Fund's resources, or the Board has considered using the provisions of the Articles to render them ineligible.

Before beginning transactions, the Board considered whether to invoke its powers under Article XX, Section 4 (*i*), to restrain members from drawing if their circumstances were such as to make the short-term use of the Fund's resources by them unlikely. The Board decided not to invoke its formal powers, but to notify the affected members informally. Ten members were so notified in the winter of 1946–47, although the ban was removed from three of them after a short time.

The first occasion on which a member became ineligible to use the Fund's resources was in January 1948, when the French Government devalued the franc and introduced measures which created multiple currency practices. The Board was unable to approve these measures and accordingly, under the terms of Article IV, Section 6, France became ineligible to draw upon the Fund. Eligibility was restored by a decision of the Board in October 1954.[17]

The next occasion was in October 1953, when Czechoslovakia's unauthorized change in the value of the koruna, and its failure to cooperate with the Fund in other ways, led the Board to invoke Article XV, Section 2 (*a*), and declare Czechoslovakia ineligible to use the Fund's resources.[18] The ban had not been removed when Czechoslovakia left the Fund early in 1955.

The use of Article XV, Section 2 (*a*), was again considered by the Board in January 1964, in connection with Cuba's failure to repurchase a drawing within five years, its failure to supply essential data, and its continuance of exchange restrictions which the Fund had disapproved. However, the provisions of the Article were not, in fact, applied, because Cuba resigned from the Fund before the date set for a meeting at which it was to be given the opportunity to answer the Fund's complaints.[19]

In September 1958 Bolivia found itself unable to carry out the conditions under which it had been granted a stand-by arrangement. By that time $2 million out of a total of $3.5 million authorized by the stand-by arrangement had been drawn. The staff recommended to the Board, which agreed, that in the

---

[17] See above, Vol. I, pp. 202, 412.

[18] See above, Vol. I, p. 361.

[19] See above, Vol. I, p. 549.

circumstances Bolivia should not be allowed to draw further until it had agreed with the Fund on revised conditions for the stand-by arrangement. Satisfactory new undertakings were given by the member in November, and it was authorized to resume drawing.

The Fund's powers under Article V, Section 5, and Article XX, Section 4 (*i*), have never been used expressly, although, as noted above, they have been regarded as authorizing the Fund to impose less drastic conditions than the exclusion of a member from the use of its resources.

FORMATION OF POLICY

Background

The difference of view between Keynes and White on the attitude of the Fund toward applications to draw has been examined in detail in Volume I, and need not be recapitulated here.[20] It will suffice to say that White was convinced that the Fund must have the power to question any request to draw on its resources, in order to prevent unjustified drawings which, in the circumstances of 1945, would necessarily have been drawings of U.S. dollars. Keynes, on the other hand, sought to ensure that members would have the right (at least, once convertibility had been achieved) to draw from the Fund, without question, the equivalent of 25 per cent of their quotas annually, up to the point at which the Fund's holdings of their currencies were equal to 200 per cent of their quotas.

This difference of view found expression in the Articles of Agreement in juxtaposition of Article V, Section 3 (*a*) (i) and (iii), which are permissive, and Article V, Section 3 (*a*) (iv), which gives the Fund power to declare a member ineligible to use its resources. The latter subsection was reinforced, among other provisions, by Article XX, Section 4 (*i*), which empowers the Fund to postpone transactions before a member has drawn, and by Article V, Section 5, which elaborates the powers in Article V, Section 3 (*a*) (iv), for application once a member has used the Fund's resources.

After the Board had begun work, the significance of the Sections just quoted led to extensive discussions, in the course of which the issue came to be seen as one between automatic rights to draw on the one hand and conditional rights on the other. Those Directors who took the point of view of Keynes protested that members should be able to draw without question the annual 25 per cent of quota provided by Article V, Section 3 (*a*) (iii); those who were of White's opinion claimed that no member should be able to draw from the Fund without the Fund's explicit consent.

---

[20] See above, Vol. I, pp. 67–77.

For a short time in 1947 it became the practice for a member to be allowed to draw without the Board's specific approval sums not exceeding 5 per cent of its quota in any thirty days.[21] However, for reasons discussed below, this practice did not last.

The stumbling block which eventually frustrated the application of the principle of automaticity to drawings was the ineffectiveness of repurchase obligations.[22] It was generally agreed by Executive Directors that the Fund's resources were to be used for short-term advances, unlike those of the World Bank. But the provisions of Article V, Section 7, and Schedule B proved inadequate to ensure the brevity of use which was desired.[23] The main cause of this was the limitations set out in Article V, Section 7 (*c*), and especially, at first, the elimination of any repurchase obligation which would bring the member's monetary reserves below its quota. In the early postwar period many members' reserves were already below their quotas. This was particularly true of the United Kingdom, whose reserves were offset by such large liabilities that the net amount was below its quota. It was also true of the other countries in the sterling area, because most of their monetary reserves were held in sterling, which was not (until 1961) convertible and so was not included in reserves calculated for the purposes of the Fund.

The Board also realized that the size of a member's monetary reserves was to a considerable extent within its own power to determine, and accordingly, if a member wished to avoid a repurchase obligation, it had a fairly ready method of doing so.

It was true that the Articles of Agreement provided, in Article V, Section 8 (*d*), for consultation between the Fund and the member as to means of reducing the Fund's holdings of the member's currency after charges had reached 4 per cent. Quite apart from uncertainty as to the outcome of such consultations, however, 4 per cent would not be payable for drawings in the lower credit tranches until they had been outstanding for 6–7 years, and the provision cited would not apply at all to drawings in the gold tranche. The Section was therefore not regarded as adequately ensuring that the Fund's resources would be revolving.

THE FIRST YEAR

Before the Fund could begin transactions, a number of preliminary procedures had to be gone through. Among these was the determination of par values for countries having at least 65 per cent of the total of quotas. For this and other

---

[21] See above, Vol. I, pp. 190–92.

[22] See above, Vol. I, pp. 276–77.

[23] See below, pp. 441–43.

reasons,[24] it was not until March 1, 1947 that the Fund was ready to begin to permit the use of its resources. During the previous ten months, two points calling for comment arose in connection with the formation of policy.

In the Annual Report for 1946 (the Board's first report, which was written in September 1946) emphasis was laid on the temporary nature of the assistance which the Fund could give:

> The essential test of the propriety of use of the Fund's resources is . . . whether the prospective balance of payments position of the country concerned (including long-term capital movements) will be such that its use of the Fund's resources will be of relatively short duration.[25]

At the same time, the Fund would run the risk that some of its resources would be used for other than temporary assistance, and the Directors considered it their duty to bring this risk to the notice of the Board of Governors. This did not, however, mean that the Fund would be undiscriminating. On the contrary, the Directors remarked that "there are certain to be disappointments because of the restraints placed on use of the Fund's resources by some members." [26] (The ambiguity of this sentence was resolved by the context, which referred to restraints placed by the Fund, not by members.) Mention of these "restraints" was made earlier in this chapter.

References to the Fund's policy on the use of its resources in the Annual Report for 1947 were confined to two points. One was an exposition of the decision about the meaning of "the member . . . represents," which stated that the Board would implement its responsibility for adjudicating on the correctness of representations by keeping itself closely informed at all times of developments in each member country.[27] The other pointed out that the Fund was not intended to give assistance for reconstruction, and that, while it could and would provide temporary assistance to members even during the transitional period, in order to attain the objectives of the Fund it must be in a position to provide financial assistance after the transitional period.[28] The implicit suggestion that the Fund should meanwhile conserve its resources assumed greater importance six months later.[29]

Early disagreements

The interpretation by the Board of a number of phrases in Articles V and XX, summarized in an earlier section of this chapter, was not achieved without

---

[24] See details in Vol. I, pp. 157–60.

[25] *Annual Report, 1946,* p. 13.

[26] *Ibid.*

[27] *Annual Report, 1947,* p. 31.

[28] *Ibid.,* p. 18.

[29] See below, pp. 394–96.

dissent being expressed. Mr. de Largentaye (France) challenged the advice given by the staff to the Board on the subject of the meaning of "consistent with the provisions of this Agreement" (Article V, Section 3 (*a*) (i)); he and Mr. de Selliers (Belgium) did not see how a member could be required to make a representation that a drawing was for the purpose of making payments which would be consistent with the purposes of the Fund when it did not know how the Fund would interpret Article I. Mr. de Largentaye also believed that Article V, Section 5, could not be used to postpone a drawing once the member had made application for one. Mr. Overby (United States), on the other hand, could not accept that the Fund's powers were so limited. The view which the Board adopted of Article XX, Section 4 (*i*)—that its powers under this Section lapsed when a member drew—was also disputed; Messrs. Overby and Saad (Egypt) argued that the Section remained in force, and was a more suitable sanction for the Board to use than Article V, Section 5.

It was problems like these which the Managing Director had in mind when in January 1948 he sent to the Board a memorandum on the interpretation of the Articles of Agreement. He referred to the ambiguities and inconsistencies that could be found in them, and urged the Board to resolve such questions (where appropriate) by interpretations. His view, as he explained it to the Board, was that where the wording of the Agreement was clear it had to be applied or else a constitutional change had to be sought. However, where the text was ambiguous or even inconsistent, the interpretation should be guided by common sense and the broad principles and purposes of the Fund such as were expressed in Article I.

A similar view was expressed by Mr. Rasminsky (Canada). The minutes of the meeting report him to have said that

> he had been Chairman of the Drafting Committee at Bretton Woods. Because of the shortage of time and the conditions of work at the Conference, the result had not always been the optimum. He would be the first to admit that there were ambiguities in the text, some intended and others not. There also were inconsistencies. Hence, he thought, to a greater degree than usual the meaning had to be interpreted in terms of the general principles underlying the Fund. He pointed out the undesirability of reliance on shaky legal interpretations to secure action by members. In such cases, he thought, general statements of the Fund's policy on nonlegal bases would be preferable as means of securing member support.

These ideas were not, however, shared by all Executive Directors. One view was that

> in some cases of interpretation by the Executive Board there had been a tendency to overrule the evident meaning of precise provisions in favor of some general provision in Article I. This was not proper, especially since there might even be conflicts between certain of the enumerated purposes in Article I, such as high levels of employment and expanded international trade.

It was also pointed out that

> some members had thought their particular needs had been safeguarded by one specific provision or another in the Agreement. They would be alarmed if they found these particular provisions being overturned by some general phrasing.

Mr. Gutt's memorandum had stressed the significance of inflation as evidence of a member's likely inability to qualify for a drawing from the Fund. This point was also made by Mr. Overby in a contemporary memorandum, in which he proposed that four specific questions should be asked when a member sought to draw from the Fund: (*a*) Is its exchange rate increasing its balance of payments difficulties, and would an adjustment of the rate reduce them? (*b*) What are the prospects of the member's repurchasing? (*c*) Will the drawing be used for relief, reconstruction, or development? (*d*) Are the member's monetary or fiscal policies leading to fundamental disequilibrium? This attempt to categorize the conditions under which a member might have access to the Fund's resources led to a debate on whether the Board should attempt to establish general policies to follow when considering members' requests to use the Fund's resources, or should base its determination on the particular circumstances of the member concerned. The decision reached was that certain broad considerations—such as the existence of inflation and the current general disequilibrium—would in all probability influence the Executive Board's opinion as to the use of the Fund's resources by particular members. However, in any case, the particular position of the member would have to be examined. It was probable, the Board concluded, that policies on general aspects would tend to develop as the individual reviews proceeded.

The foregoing discussions, which took place early in 1948, led to a number of interpretations set out at the beginning of this chapter. In reaching these decisions, the Board as a whole moved further away from the concept of an automatic right to the use of the Fund's resources—a movement that had been started by the interpretation of the phrase "the member . . . represents" in May 1947.

ERP Decision

The elucidation of general principles was, however, interrupted shortly afterward by the intervention of U.S. aid to Europe through the European Recovery Program (ERP). Expounding the Program to the Board, the U.S. Executive Director and his Alternate explained that the data upon which the U.S. proposals for the ERP had been predicated did not assume any assistance from the Fund to European participants during the four-year period which it covered, chiefly because the data were concerned with the needs of Europe for relief and reconstruction, for neither of which the Fund was intended. They cited several reasons why, in their view, the Fund's resources should not be used, during the course of the Program, by the countries assisted:

(*a*) By making dollars available, the ERP would substantially reduce the pressure for dollar currencies to balance the international payments of the receiving countries.

(*b*) The determination by Congress of the dollar limits of ERP aid implicitly indicated the amount of U.S. production which should be shipped to Europe during the program. Any substantial provision of dollars through the Fund might result in a reconsideration of the amount of ERP aid.

(*c*) The balance of payments estimates for Europe showed a dollar disequilibrium of $3.5 billion still to be expected in 1952, so that the prospects for repurchase within five years were not bright. (This seems to have been the first occasion on which repurchase within five years was assumed to be normal.)

These arguments were countered by other Directors, who appealed to general principles. Even if the ERP would tend to reduce the need for members to call on the Fund for dollars, these Directors doubted whether this justified a policy limiting the members' access to the Fund. They believed that under the Articles of Agreement members had certain rights to purchase exchange, and the existence of programs such as the ERP could not diminish members' legal rights to use the Fund's resources. Moreover, because the ERP was assisting all European countries, it did not follow that each of them would be in deficit in 1952.

Nevertheless, Mr. Overby pressed the point that the Board's decision on any request to draw must take into account all the circumstances, and the existence of the ERP was a factor which could not be ignored. While there might be individual circumstances in which a drawing could be justified, he felt that the general effect of the new situation in Europe must be to tighten the Fund's evaluation of "reasonable doubt."

The formal decision of the Board was deferred until the ERP was actually in operation, and was then taken in the following terms, Mr. Tansley (United Kingdom) alone dissenting:

> Although the Fund recognizes that a general rule is not sufficient basis for all cases, the Fund must, in examining requests for the use of its resources, take into account the European Recovery Program. . . . Since the ERP is to be handled year by year, related policies on use of the Fund's resources should be developed at similar intervals. For the first year the attitude of the Fund and ERP members should be that such members should request the purchase of United States dollars from the Fund only in exceptional or unforeseen cases. The Fund and members participating in ERP should have as their objective to maintain the resources of the Fund at a safe and reasonable level during the ERP period in order that at the end of the period such members will have unencumbered access to the resources of the

> Fund. This objective conforms with the intention of Article XIV, Section 1, that during the transitional period members should not impair the capacity of the Fund to serve its members or impair their ability to secure help from the Fund after the transitional period.[30]

At the same meeting as that at which the foregoing decision (generally known as the "ERP Decision") was adopted, Mr. de Selliers asked what would be the Fund's view of drawings of currencies other than the U.S. dollar. Mr. de Selliers was concerned about this because Belgium was the principal European creditor. The Belgian franc was therefore most likely to be in demand, but extensive drawings of that currency might place a severe strain on Belgium's balance of payments. Taking this into account, the Board decided as follows:

> During the European Recovery Program members of the Fund may wish to use the Fund's holdings of the currency of a country participating in ERP. No member has the right to veto or limit the Fund's sales of its currency to other members for use in accordance with the Fund Agreement. The Fund recognizes, however, that such sales should not have the effect of compelling a country to finance a large bilateral surplus with some countries, while it has to make net drawings on its gold and convertible currency reserves for current payments. Such circumstances would fall within the meaning of the "exceptional or unforeseen cases" mentioned in the policy decision of April 5, 1948, made by the Fund concerning the use of the Fund's resources by ERP countries and would justify requests by a country to purchase foreign exchange from the Fund to make to other members current payments or payments authorized by Article VI, Section 2, but not to build up its monetary reserves. This is in fact the manner in which the Fund is intended to facilitate a system of multilateral payments.[31]

The foregoing decisions were reproduced in full in the Annual Report for 1948, and the Board took the opportunity to make some general statements bearing on its attitude toward requests to use the Fund's resources. Having explained that certain members had been asked to refrain from seeking to draw because their situation was "not conducive to the proper use of the Fund's resources," and that judgment was necessary to determine whether a particular drawing was likely to be outstanding for a relatively short or a relatively long period, Directors went on:

> The Board has had, moreover, within the limits of the Fund Agreement, to weigh the advantages from both its own point of view and the point of view of its members of conserving the resources of the Fund for use in the post-transitional period against the advantages which members could derive from some immediate use of the Fund's resources. In the grave and unsettled conditions which prevailed, the Fund reached the conclusion that in some doubtful cases there were in general more disadvantages involved in denying members access to its resources than in allowing them such access.[32]

---

30 *Annual Report, 1948,* p. 74.

31 *Ibid.,* p. 75.

32 *Ibid.,* p. 47.

The last sentence of this quotation was addressed to the point that the Fund was prepared to take risks—a point which, it will be recalled, was made in its first Annual Report. It did not imply that the Board's attitude to drawings by members in receipt of ERP aid would similarly give them the benefit of the doubt, for immediately after this statement the Board explained its attitude to such drawings along the lines of the U.S. arguments mentioned above, and of the terms of the ERP Decision.[33]

Formulating criteria

As a result of the ERP Decision, the volume of Fund transactions, which had totaled $606.0 million in the financial year 1947/48, fell in the three ensuing years to $119.4 million, $51.8 million, and $28.0 million, respectively. Such requests as were made by European countries to draw on the Fund while the ERP was in force gave rise to sharp differences of opinion in the Board. The first occasion for such a discussion was a preliminary inquiry from the Netherlands, in October 1948, as to the possibility of drawing Belgian francs. Mr. Beyen (Netherlands) explained that if the Fund's resources were used in this way it would be to tide his country over temporarily in anticipation of U.S. aid.

Mr. Overby then raised two questions: (1) whether the Fund could properly provide "temporary" financing to a country whose payments deficit arose essentially from a large reconstruction program and other nontemporary needs, and (2) whether a drawing could be considered as being for a relatively short term when all the indications were that the Netherlands' balance of payments deficit, particularly in convertible currencies, would continue long after 1952. Mr. Beyen's response was that if the Netherlands did apply to the Fund for a drawing it would be for purposes in accordance with the Articles of Agreement; should the Netherlands wish to finance reconstruction, it would seek assistance elsewhere.

The Director of Research, intervening, drew attention to the fact that the Fund's decision on dollar drawings by ERP countries indicated that the proper test would be quantitative. So far the drawings by the Netherlands had been very limited, and any need for Belgian francs should be small—probably not over 6 per cent of quota. As for repayment, he believed that the Netherlands' international accounts would be in balance long before 1955; while they would probably still be short of dollars, they would be long of other currencies which would be convertible for the Fund's purposes. Some Executive Directors pointed out that in the past the Fund had never required a precise demonstration of the arrangements for repayment; they felt that the burden of proof concerning the prospects of repurchase would be on the Fund. Mr. Ansiaux (Belgium)

[33] *Ibid.*, pp. 48–50.

said that he agreed with that view and noted that Belgium would not object to drawings of its currency from the Fund for the purpose indicated. Mr. Bolton (United Kingdom), expressing his views on the Fund's policy in more general terms, opposed the increasing number of interpretations reading into the Fund Agreement limitations which were not in the text. Because of such limitations, he said, the Fund was now of no use to its European members; it carried obligations but no benefits.

The occasion for the Netherlands' request was that it had given an informal undertaking not to draw on the Fund, which it now wished to withdraw. At the conclusion of the discussion Mr. Overby agreed to this course, on the understanding that if a request for a drawing from the Netherlands reached the Board, Executive Directors would be free to challenge it in accordance with Article V, Sections 3 and 5. However, he intervened also when some subsequent requests for drawings, not connected with the ERP, were made (e.g., by Nicaragua and South Africa), questioning either the temporary character of these drawings or the prospects for repurchase.

The differences of opinion which had emerged in the discussions of these transactions contributed to a growing feeling in the Executive Board that a further clarification of the Fund's policy on the use of its resources was urgently needed. It was obviously desirable that members should know how they stood with the Fund. It was also clear that the confidence which the Fund intended to give to its members would not be assured if the fate of a request for use of its resources were left uncertain while the Fund engaged in a lengthy review of the member's position.

For the moment, however, the clarification took the form of a restatement of the U.S. position. In a memorandum circulated to the Executive Directors on May 20, 1949, Mr. Southard, who had succeeded Mr. Overby as Executive Director for the United States, reported on the outcome of a review within the U.S. Government of the Fund's policy and practices on the use of its resources. The position of the United States was that

> the use of the resources of the Fund by any member should be subject to close scrutiny to assure that any purchases conform strictly to the general principles and purposes of the Fund, as well as to the specific provisions of the Articles of Agreement. Any doubt should be resolved in favor of the Fund rather than in favor of the member.

The practical principles and criteria which the U.S. authorities had evolved from this position were that drawings by a member which applied exchange restrictions on current transactions or quantitative import controls should not be permitted without four specific determinations by the Fund: (*a*) that the par value of the member was appropriate; (*b*) that the circumstances which gave rise to the proposed drawing were due to a temporary rather than to a fundamental disequilibrium; (*c*) that the proposed drawing could not primarily be attributed, directly or indirectly, to requirements engendered by programs of rehabilitation or development; and (*d*) that the member was taking all the steps essential to assume, as soon as possible, its full obligations under the Articles of Agreement.

The first occasion on which these tests were applied to a prospective drawing occurred on May 31, 1949, when Brazil sought to draw $15 million. Mr. Southard then accepted that the first of his criteria was satisfied, but said that he wished to be assured that Brazil's request was prompted neither by a fundamental disequilibrium nor by the requirements of development. Other Executive Directors deprecated this approach, believing that Brazil was entitled to the benefit of "any reasonable doubt" during the transitional period, and questioning whether Mr. Southard's tests were justified in terms of the Articles of Agreement. At the end of the discussion, Mr. Paranaguá (Brazil) said that Brazil would defer its request.

In the middle of July an application by the Netherlands to purchase Belgian francs was deferred after Mr. Southard said that he doubted whether the circumstances satisfied the criteria which he had laid down. By then the probability that European currencies would have shortly to be devalued was becoming increasingly recognized, and this underlay the Board's attitude not only to the Netherlands' request but to drawings in general.

In these conditions the Directors did not attempt any fresh description of the Fund's policies on the use of its resources when they came to write the Annual Report for 1949; they contented themselves with referring to the passage in the Annual Report for 1948 cited above.[34]

COUNTERPROPOSALS, 1949–51

After the Annual Meeting and the group of major devaluations which immediately followed, Mr. Southard again took the initiative. In a memorandum to the Managing Director dated October 17, 1949, he requested that the following proposal should be placed on the Board's agenda:

> . . . in the future dollar drawings should be objected to unless the member proposing to draw on the resources of the Fund is willing to make an agreement, or to give a firm commitment, to repurchase its currency from the Fund within a maximum period of five years, preferably according to a definite schedule of repayment.

Underlying this proposal was the realization, explained earlier, that the repurchase provisions in the Articles of Agreement were inadequate to ensure the prompt repayment of sums drawn from the Fund. Mr. Southard called attention in particular to the position in the sterling area and in member countries with

[34] *Annual Report, 1949*, p. 43.

centrally planned balances of payments. He agreed that his proposal would apply logically to drawings in all currencies, and not only in dollars, and suggested that it should be considered in those terms.

A counter memorandum by Mr. Beyen pointed out that while the Articles of Agreement defined, although negatively, the purposes for which drawings might be made, they said nothing about the period for which they might be held by the member. Mr. Southard's proposal therefore, in Mr. Beyen's view, cut right across the provisions of the Agreement. Mr. Beyen also argued that the repurchase provisions of Article V, Section 7, and Schedule B were not meant to be the normal mechanism for securing repurchases, but rather to become operative if members failed to repurchase spontaneously.

A discussion of Mr. Southard's and Mr. Beyen's memoranda on December 19, 1949 showed that most Executive Directors shared Mr. Beyen's point of view. Several questioned the legality and propriety of the Fund's imposing requirements as to the time of repurchase. Some went further, and believed that most members would be much concerned at a proposal like Mr. Southard's. Before accepting the Articles of Agreement, members had carefully weighed the benefits and obligations which were entailed, and many, at least, had never believed that the Articles involved such a severe limitation of drawing rights as was suggested. While agreeing that the use of the Fund's resources should be temporary, Directors thought that the proper course was for the Fund to work out ways to ensure this without imposing conditions which might force members, in order to repurchase drawings, to introduce measures which would be inimical to the Fund's basic aims. The debate was continued at two further meetings in January 1950.

Early in December the staff had put before the Board a recommendation that a circular letter should be sent to all members pointing out that proper use of the Fund's resources required that members should adopt corrective measures to ensure repayment. The staff suggested that as a general rule members should consult the Fund before drawing; however, the Board should as soon as possible review each member's prospects, and if these were satisfactory the request to consult before drawing could be canceled. This proposal was refined and elaborated by a staff Working Party which reported in May 1950. The Working Party emphasized the need for member countries to know in advance whether they could draw on the Fund. To enable the Board to inform them on this point, the Working Party proposed a system of prior review and assessment of the eligibility of each member, coupled with criteria on the basis of which it could be determined whether the member was following appropriate policies with regard to its exchange rate, etc.

The Board discussed this report at several informal sessions, but it was not favorably received. Objections were raised on various grounds. It was argued, in particular, that the procedure might lead to a kind of blacklisting of members, and that unless the reviews were frequently repeated they would be ineffective. In July the Board agreed to resume discussion of the problem after the Annual Meeting. No reference to the controversy was made in the Annual Report for 1950. A further informal session held in October showed that the Directors' views were unchanged.

In an attempt to break the deadlock, the Managing Director proposed early in November a procedure which would tie drawings to programs of action by the drawing members. He suggested that where a member was in difficulties the staff might assist it to work out a suitable policy for the recovery of equilibrium, and that this policy might then be supported by a drawing. This was discussed at several meetings during the ensuing six months and eventually accepted by the Board for use "in addition to and without prejudice to existing procedures, or policies." Objections to it were, however, maintained by Mr. de Largentaye and by Mr. Stamp (United Kingdom), the former on both legal and practical grounds, and the latter because the British Government objected to "any suggestion that the right of members to come to the Fund would in any way depend upon their carrying out policies with which they did not agree." As it turned out, the new procedure had little practical result, partly because discussions aimed at designing a program of action for a member in difficulties were bound to be lengthy.

The change of attitude toward drawing rights which was implicit in the Managing Director's proposal was brought into the open by Mr. Beyen. In the discussion in the Board in November 1950, and again in a memorandum three months later, he pointed out that the plan to tie drawings to programs of action involved changing the concept of eligibility from automaticity to conditionality. It was on this note that Mr. Gutt's tenure of the Managing Directorship ended.

The Rooth Plan

After the arrival of Mr. Rooth as Managing Director, the search for an effective policy for the use of the Fund's resources was actively resumed. On October 19, 1951, Mr. Rooth proposed to the Board a revision of the scale of charges for drawings. These changes, and the resulting new scale, are discussed in Chapter 19; here it will suffice to say that the general effect of the changes proposed was to emphasize the short-term character of drawings by reducing the cost of using the Fund's resources for a very short period, and increasing the cost for longer periods. It was even more important that the changes also reduced the length of time for which a drawing could remain outstanding before the member was required to consult the Fund about ways of reducing the Fund's holdings of its currency.

Three weeks later Mr. Rooth outlined to the Board some principles which in his view would enable the Fund to make its resources more readily available. He suggested that, in order to preserve the revolving character of the Fund, the time limit for repurchases should normally be three years, with an outside limit of five years. He proposed also that there should be special terms for drawings within the gold tranche (i.e., drawings which increased the Fund's holdings of the member's currency to not more than 100 per cent of its quota), and for very short-term drawings (i.e., drawings for not more than eighteen months).

In the discussion that followed, most Executive Directors commented favorably on Mr. Rooth's proposals. The only strong objection came from Mr. de Largentaye, who argued that the Articles of Agreement permitted the imposition of special conditions as to repurchases in accordance with Article V, Section 4, only for drawings above the limits of 25 per cent of quota a year and 200 per cent of quota in all. Where such special circumstances did not exist, members would find it very difficult to give up their rights under Article V, Section 3. Mr. de Largentaye also made a comment on the Managing Director's proposal for special terms for drawings in the gold tranche; while he regarded these as commendable, his own view was that such drawings were a matter of right, and not one of special privilege.

Encouraged by the general support of the Board, the Managing Director appointed a new staff Working Party to make definite recommendations. This Working Party's report was circulated on January 19 and was debated at two informal and two formal sessions of the Board, resulting on February 13, 1952 in a decision approved by all the Directors present except Mr. de Largentaye, who abstained on legal grounds. This decision became known as the Rooth Plan, and with only minor changes it has governed the use of the Fund's resources ever since. The text will be found in Volume III.[35] The following features of the decision should, however, be specially noted:

(1) An introductory statement by the Managing Director suggested that sometimes "discussions between the member and the Fund may cover its general position, not with a view to any immediate drawing, but in order to ensure that it would be able to draw if, within a period of say 6 or 12 months, the need presented itself." This proposal contained the germ of the stand-by arrangements which have since become one of the most important features of the Fund's work; these arrangements are discussed in detail in Chapters 20 and 21.

(2) By paragraph 2.a., "exchange purchased from the Fund should not remain outstanding beyond the period reasonably related to the payments problem for which it was purchased from the Fund. The period should fall within an outside range of three to five years."

---

[35] E.B. Decision No. 102-(52/11), February 13, 1952; below, Vol. III, p. 228.

(3) By paragraph 3, a "member can count on receiving the overwhelming benefit of any doubt respecting drawings which would raise the Fund's holdings of its currency to not more than its quota"—i.e., for drawings in the gold tranche.

(4) By paragraph 2.e., a member seeking to draw from the Fund "will be expected to include in its authenticated request a statement that it will comply" with the principles of the decision.

Waivers

Six months later, on October 1, 1952, the Board adopted a decision which made detailed provision for stand-by arrangements.[36] The details of this decision are discussed in Chapter 20. Here it need only be noted that while such arrangements were expected to be, in general, for not more than a quarter of the member's quota—the limit mentioned in Article V, Section 3 (*a*) (iii)—the decision provided that the Fund would not regard itself as precluded from granting stand-by arrangements for a larger proportion of the quota. This would be done, of course, by invoking the provisions in Article V, Section 4, for a waiver.

The first waiver granted was to Turkey in August 1953, in connection with a drawing equivalent to 47 per cent of its quota. At first, recourse to a waiver was regarded as exceptional, and indeed as late as December 1954 the granting of a waiver was described as "unusual in itself." But in 1956 waivers were granted for all the 8 stand-by arrangements approved, and for all the 8 drawings not made under stand-by arrangements, and during the ten years 1956 through 1965 only 11 out of 157 stand-by arrangements and 32 out of 76 direct drawings did not involve a waiver.

The first drawing equivalent to 100 per cent of quota was made, as already mentioned, by Burma in 1956.[37] In 1961 Chile was given a drawing and stand-by arrangement which together committed the Fund, for the first time, to increase its holdings of a member's currency beyond 175 per cent of the member's quota. In October 1963 the United Arab Republic, by drawing $16 million, increased the Fund's holdings of its currency to 215 per cent of quota. This was the first time that the limit of 200 per cent had been exceeded, and resulted from the Fund's new policy for the compensation of export fluctuations, described in the final section of this chapter. The largest drawing by any member down to the end of 1965 was one of $1,400 million (72 per cent of quota) by the United Kingdom in May of that year.

Credit tranche policy

The decision of February 13, 1952 differentiated only between drawings in the gold tranche and all other drawings. During the next three years the Board

---

36 E.B. Decision No. 155-(52/57), October 1, 1952; below, Vol. III, p. 230.

37 See above, p. 386.

was cautiously exploring the possibilities opened up by the decision, and especially by the introduction of stand-by arrangements. By 1955, sufficient experience had been gained to enable the Board to begin to refine upon its policies in respect of drawings beyond the gold tranche. In its Annual Report for 1955 the Board first stated that "unless there are overwhelmingly strong reasons for not doing so, the Fund will invariably grant members' requests for gold tranche drawings,"[38] and then went on to distinguish among larger drawings, as follows:

> . . . The larger the drawing in relation to a member's quota the stronger is the justification required of the member.
>
> In practice, the Fund's attitude toward applications for drawings within the first credit tranche (i.e., drawings that raise the Fund's holdings of a member's currency above 100 per cent but not over 125 per cent of its quota) is a liberal one. Members are aware that, if they face balance of payments problems of a temporary nature, they may confidently expect a favorable response from the Fund to a request for a drawing within the first credit tranche, provided they are themselves making reasonable efforts to solve their problems.[39]

For drawings beyond the first credit tranche, the Report explained, there was not as yet the same body of precedent, but "should the need arise, and should the justification be substantial, members need not doubt that drawings on subsequent tranches will be permitted."[40]

By 1958 the necessary experience had been gained, and in the Annual Report for that year the Board set out its policy toward drawings beyond the first credit tranche. This was repeated in the following year in a recapitulation which has since served as the classic statement of policy on the use of the Fund's resources:

> Members are given the overwhelming benefit of the doubt in relation to requests for transactions within the "gold tranche". . . . The Fund's attitude to requests for transactions within the first credit tranche . . . is a liberal one, provided that the member itself is also making reasonable efforts to solve its problems. Requests for transactions beyond these limits require substantial justification. They are likely to be favorably received when the drawings or stand-bys are intended to support a sound program aimed at establishing or maintaining the enduring stability of the member's currency at a realistic rate of exchange.[41]

The undertaking to give gold tranche drawings "the overwhelming benefit of any doubt" was intended to encourage members to regard the right to draw in the gold tranche as part of their reserves. In the Annual Report for 1963, in a table showing monetary reserves, the Board included for the first time members' gold tranche drawing rights as part of these reserves.[42] Some mem-

---

[38] *Annual Report, 1955*, p. 84.

[39] *Ibid.*, pp. 84–85.

[40] *Ibid.*, p. 85.

[41] *Annual Report, 1959*, p. 22.

[42] *Annual Report, 1963*, pp. 40–41.

bers were, however, unable to accept this concept; opposition to it was expressed on several occasions, notably by Mr. van Campenhout (Belgium)—chiefly on the ground that requests to draw in the gold tranche were not legally immune from challenge.

Considering what could be done to strengthen the claim of gold tranche drawing rights to be regarded as reserves, the staff suggested in December 1963 that steps should be taken to streamline the procedure for such drawings. Up to that time they had been handled by the normal drawing procedure, which involved the preparation of a staff recommendation to the Board, its consideration at a Board meeting, and the subsequent giving of instructions to the relevant depositories to transfer the required currencies to the drawing member. The whole procedure took about a week.

As the General Counsel pointed out at an informal session in January 1964, to go further and make such drawings wholly automatic (as was suggested by Mr. Saad) would conflict with the tradition, founded on the interpretation of "the member . . . represents," that the Fund had the right to challenge any request for a drawing. However, the opportunity for a challenge could be given by a brief notification by the Managing Director to Executive Directors that a request for a gold tranche drawing had been received, on the understanding that if no objection was raised within, say, twenty-four hours, the drawing would proceed. This proposal was further considered by the Board in August 1964 and was approved. The decision was:

> When a duly authenticated request to draw in the gold tranche is received from a member, the request shall be notified to the Executive Board on the day it is received, whenever possible, or on the next business day, and unless, by the close of that business day, the Managing Director decides or an Executive Director requests that the matter be placed on the Board's agenda for discussion, the Fund shall, at the close of the first business day following the date of the receipt of the request, instruct the appropriate depository to make the transfer on the next business day after the instruction or as soon as possible thereafter.[43]

It should be added that while this change in procedure shortened the time needed to effect a gold tranche drawing to about three days, it did not satisfy those members that had hesitated to regard the rights to such drawings as reserves. Their doubts were expressed, for example, by Mr. Ansiaux, Governor for Belgium, at the Annual Meeting in 1965. As will be seen, these doubts expressly included drawings that raised the Fund's holdings of the member's currency from below 75 per cent to 75 per cent of quota (sometimes known as the "super gold tranche"). Mr. Ansiaux said:

> . . . The use of the gold tranche and even of the super gold tranche remains juridically and, therefore, potentially in fact, conditional. . . . It is, therefore,

[43] E.B. Decision No. 1745-(64/46), August 3, 1964; below, Vol. III, p. 243.

impossible for central banks to incorporate them in their reserves on the same footing as gold or convertible currencies.[44]

It was a recognition of this difficulty that prompted the change in the Articles of Agreement, effected in 1969, which made gold tranche drawings legally immune from challenge.[45]

There was, as time went on, a natural tendency for drawings to reach higher tranches in members' quotas—i.e., for the Fund's holdings of the members' currencies to increase relative to quotas. On the other hand, in 1961, 1962, and 1964, there were drawings in the "super gold tranche." These tendencies are summarized in Table 15.

Table 15. Fund Transactions by Tranches, 1947–65
(In per cent)

Calendar Years	Annual Average of Amounts Drawn (*$ million*)	Percentage of Amounts Drawn That Increased the Fund's Holdings to the Following Percentages of Quotas				
		0–100	101–125	126–150	151–175	Over 175
1947–51	162	68	32	—	—	—
1952–56	219	48	45	6	1	—
1957–61	851	31[1]	36	30	2	—
1962–65	1,325	38[2]	16	20	14	12[3]

Source: Mookerjee, *op. cit.*, p. 430, supplemented by *IFS*, December 1965–February 1966.
[1] Includes 1 per cent in the member's "super gold tranche."
[2] Includes 3 per cent in the member's "super gold tranche."
[3] Includes 0.3 per cent, raising the Fund's holdings above 200 per cent of quota.

Drawings against gold collateral

It will be remembered that Article V, Section 4, requires that the Fund, when deciding whether to waive any of the requirements for a drawing set out in Section 3 (*a*), shall take into consideration "a member's willingness to pledge as collateral security gold, silver, securities, or other acceptable assets having a value sufficient in the opinion of the Fund to protect its interests," and empowers the Fund to require such collateral security if it so wishes. The power to require collateral security has never been exercised. When the request by Burma to draw the equivalent of 100 per cent of its quota was being considered, Mr. Lieftinck (Netherlands) suggested that the Fund should call for collateral security to cover one third of the sum, but this was not adopted by the Board.[46] This appears to have been the only time that an Executive Director has suggested that the Board should require the deposit of collateral security. However, a deposit of gold as security has on four occasions been offered by members wishing to draw from the Fund, and such a deposit has three times been accepted.

[44] *Summary Proceedings, 1965*, pp. 131–32.
[45] See below, p. 601.
[46] See above, p. 386.

On the first occasion when an offer was made, by Iran in February 1953, it was withdrawn before a decision had been reached in the Board. In the three other instances, the proposal was made by the United Arab Republic. The first time was in December 1958, but the member then decided, after its offer had been accepted by the Board, to withdraw its request for a drawing. The other two offers were made in 1962, and both were carried through. The relevant drawings increased the Fund's holdings of Egyptian pounds to 155 per cent of the member's quota.

It was, however, not without some hesitation that the Board approved the United Arab Republic's proposals. In the first place, Directors considered that gold collateral was not an adequate substitute for a stabilization program, such as would normally have been required as a condition for permitting a drawing reaching into the third credit tranche. Secondly, the offer made by the member was to earmark gold in Cairo, whereas the Board felt that gold accepted as collateral should be deposited in one of the Fund's own gold depositories (which did not include Cairo). The Board therefore readily agreed to the release of the gold when in April 1962 the United Arab Republic sought a stand-by arrangement in connection with which it undertook to implement a stabilization program.

As a result of the foregoing experience, the staff was asked to draft standard terms for drawings against gold collateral. Proposing these to the Board in March 1963, the staff suggested that such drawings should be regarded as exceptional, but that they might have a value in special circumstances, as for example if the member was planning a stabilization program but had not yet been able to bring it into effect and needed assistance meanwhile. The terms for a drawing against gold collateral should be the same as for an ordinary drawing, except that the drawing would normally be expected to be repurchased within six months. The member should pay any incidental charges in connection with the transfer of the gold to a depository named by the Fund, where it should be retained until the drawing was repurchased. If the repurchase was not completed in the agreed time, the gold would be used by the Fund to repurchase the drawing. These proposals were accepted by the Board and embodied in a decision taken on July 1, 1963.[47] There was, however, no other drawing against gold collateral during the period covered by this volume.

Drawings by new members

On three occasions during the twenty years 1945–65 the Board reviewed the link between the establishment of a par value and the right to use the Fund's resources. This link, and in particular the problems of new members in this respect, have been discussed in detail in Chapter 4 of this volume (pages 65–73).

[47] E.B. Decision No. 1543-(63/39), July 1, 1963; below, Vol. III, p. 240.

A brief recapitulation here will be sufficient to round out the discussion of the Fund's policy on the use of its resources. It will be remembered that the link in question was created by Article XX, Section 4 (*c*), which reads, in part:

> When the par value of a member's currency has been established . . . the member shall be eligible to buy from the Fund the currencies of other members to the full extent permitted in this Agreement. . . .

This is modified by Article XX, Section 4 (*d*) (ii), to permit members that had been occupied by the enemy to use the Fund's resources after they had proposed a par value, even though this had not been accepted by the Fund. Original members—that is, countries that had signed the Articles of Agreement by December 31, 1946—could utilize Article XX, Section 4 (*d*) (ii), automatically, but new members could do so only if an appropriate reference was made, in the Membership Resolution admitting them to the Fund, to the privileges accorded by that Section. Such a reference was made in the Membership Resolution for Italy, but it was thought cumbersome to repeat it for members joining later, and this was not done. This omission gave rise to the first review by the Board of the conditions under which new members might draw on the Fund.

The occasion for this review arose in 1952, when at the Annual Meeting the Governor for Thailand asked that consideration should be given to permitting his country—which was not an original member—to draw on the Fund even though it did not have, and was not able to propose, a par value.[48] When the Board looked into the matter, it appeared that Thailand and Indonesia were unique in that their Membership Resolutions made no provision for utilizing Article XX, Section 4 (*d*) (ii). (Burma would have been in a similar position except that it was on the point of agreeing with the Fund a par value for the kyat.) The Board accordingly decided to invite the Governors to amend the Membership Resolutions for Thailand and Indonesia so as to include a reference to Article XX, Section 4 (*d*) (ii), and this was done.[49]

Ten years later a new point arose. The Membership Resolutions for all members from 1947 onward had provided that the member should not draw until thirty days after a par value for its currency had been agreed. The original purpose of this provision had been to allow time for the completion of formalities, such as the calculation of the member's net official holdings and of its gold and currency subscriptions, the last of which could not be determined until the par value was known. When, however, Afghanistan sought the Fund's agreement to a par value at the beginning of 1963, and wished also to draw from the Fund, Executive Directors questioned whether the interval of thirty days was necessary. The staff then agreed that since 1947 it had become the custom to

---

[48] *Summary Proceedings, 1952*, p. 65.

[49] Resolutions 8-4 and 8-5, *Summary Proceedings, 1953*, pp. 96–97.

settle all technical points before a par value was actually agreed, so that the need for the interval no longer existed. The Board accordingly recommended to the Governors that the Membership Resolutions should be amended so as to permit members to draw as soon as a par value had been agreed and put into operation. The Governors agreed.[50]

So far, it will be observed, eligibility to draw on the Fund remained linked to at least the proposal of a par value; members that had not been occupied by the enemy had to have a par value established before a drawing could be permitted. The third review by the Board of this subject was concerned with the necessity for retaining this link at all.

The proposal that it should be discarded was made by the staff early in 1964. There were then 28 members, including most of the newly joined African members, that had not established a par value, and the staff suggested that it was anomalous that such members might not draw from the Fund, even if they had a stable exchange rate, while other countries, having par values, were permitted to do so, even though their effective exchange rates departed widely from their par values. The staff also believed that there would be positive advantages in severing the link between par values and eligibility to draw on the Fund. For one thing, it would discourage members from proposing possibly unrealistic exchange rates as par values in order to qualify for a drawing; for another, a drawing might in some instances assist a member to achieve a stable exchange rate, and a viable par value, which might otherwise be beyond its power to attain.

Preliminary discussions of the matter with Executive Directors showed that the Board was sensitive to the need to avoid diminishing the importance which the Fund attached to the establishment and maintenance of par values. The staff therefore amended its proposal by adding to the proposed decision a declaration safeguarding this point. In this amended form the Board accepted the staff's recommendation, and decided as follows:

> *(a)* Where the Fund prescribes the conditions and amount of an exchange transaction by a member before the establishment of an initial par value, the member will be required to complete the payment of its subscription on the basis of a provisional rate of exchange for its currency proposed by the member and agreed by the Fund.
>
> *(b)* In deciding whether to permit exchange transactions before the establishment of an initial par value, the Fund, in accordance with the last sentence of Article I, will be guided by the purposes of the Articles; the Fund will encourage members to follow policies leading to the establishment of realistic exchange rates and to the adoption at the earliest feasible date of effective par values, and will take into account the efforts that are being made to achieve this objective. . . .[51]

---

[50] Resolution 18-2, *Summary Proceedings, 1963*, pp. 227–29.

[51] E.B. Decision No. 1687-(64/22), April 22, 1964; below, Vol. III, p. 243.

The decision concluded with an assurance that the Fund would give the overwhelming benefit of any doubt to a request for a gold tranche drawing, and would implement drawings under the compensatory financing decision (see the final section of this chapter). Appropriate amendments to the Membership Resolutions of members without par values were proposed to the Governors and accepted on June 1, 1964.[52]

The Fund's attitude today

It is right to conclude this description of the evolution of the Fund's policy on drawings by saying that in recent years the legal limitations on members' rights to draw have ceased to preoccupy the Board. This development has been made possible by three things: the decision of February 13, 1952, with its specific provisions for repurchases within three to five years; the increasingly detailed knowledge of members' situations which has been built up over the years; and the emergence of unwritten but clearly understood guidelines as a result of the Board's consideration of the several hundred drawings already made. The existence of these guidelines has enabled the staff to advise member countries, when they wish to draw, what steps they should take in order to ensure favorable consideration for their requests. This in turn enables members to make formal requests for drawings with confidence that they will not be rejected. It can be fairly said that in present circumstances the Board would wish never to withhold approval of a drawing; at the most, Directors would criticize during the discussion any features which they considered to be unsatisfactory, in order to guide the staff in its future advice to members.

DRAWINGS FOR CAPITAL TRANSFERS

The terms of the Articles

The principal provisions of the Articles of Agreement on the subject of capital transfers are as follows:

> *Article VI. Capital Transfers*
>
> Section 1. *Use of the Fund's resources for capital transfers.—(a)* A member may not make net use of the Fund's resources to meet a large or sustained outflow of capital, and the Fund may request a member to exercise controls to prevent such use of the resources of the Fund. If, after receiving such a request, a member fails to exercise appropriate controls, the Fund may declare the member ineligible to use the resources of the Fund.
>
> *(b)* Nothing in this Section shall be deemed
>
> (i) to prevent the use of the resources of the Fund for capital transactions of reasonable amount required for the expansion of exports or in the ordinary course of trade, banking or other business, or

[52] Resolution 19-8, *Summary Proceedings, 1964*, pp. 260–61.

(ii) to affect capital movements which are met out of a member's own resources of gold and foreign exchange, but members undertake that such capital movements will be in accordance with the purposes of the Fund.

SEC. 2. *Special provisions for capital transfers.*—If the Fund's holdings of the currency of a member have remained below seventy-five percent of its quota for an immediately preceding period of not less than six months, such member, if it has not been declared ineligible to use the resources of the Fund under Section 1 of this Article, Article IV, Section 6, Article V, Section 5, or Article XV, Section 2 *(a)*, shall be entitled, notwithstanding the provisions of Section 1 *(a)* of this Article, to buy the currency of another member from the Fund with its own currency for any purpose, including capital transfers. Purchases for capital transfers under this Section shall not, however, be permitted if they have the effect of raising the Fund's holdings of the currency of the member desiring to purchase above seventy-five percent of its quota, or of reducing the Fund's holdings of the currency desired below seventy-five percent of the quota of the member whose currency is desired.

SEC. 3. *Controls of capital transfers.*—Members may exercise such controls as are necessary to regulate international capital movements, but no member may exercise these controls in a manner which will restrict payments for current transactions or which will unduly delay transfers of funds in settlement of commitments, except as provided in Article VII, Section 3 *(b)*, and in Article XIV, Section 2.

Article XIX *(i)* defines, though not exhaustively, payments for current transactions as "payments which are not for the purpose of transferring capital," and includes certain items which in ordinary parlance would be regarded as capital transactions, viz., "payments of moderate amount for amortization of loans or for depreciation of direct investments." The paragraph also empowers the Fund to determine, after consultation with the members concerned, whether certain specific transactions are to be considered current transactions or capital transactions.

We are not here concerned with the main purpose of this definition, which was to clarify the obligations of members, set out in Articles VIII and XIV, in connection with exchange restrictions. It is sufficient to note that the special definition of current transactions given in Article XIX *(i)* does not invalidate the prohibition, in Article VI, Section 1, on the use of the Fund's resources to meet large or sustained outflows of capital.

APPLICATION OF THE ARTICLES

The Board has not formally adopted any rules or guiding principles to help it to apply the prohibition in Article VI, Section 1, or the interpretation given, in response to the United States in 1946 (quoted above), to requests to use the Fund's resources. In practice emphasis has been laid, in discussing requests for drawings, upon the existence of a current account deficit, whether or not a capital account deficit also existed. In 1961 the position was transformed, as described below, by the clarification of the interpretation given in 1946. Before then there had been a number of transactions where the presence of a capital account deficit was taken into consideration in reaching the Board's decision.

The first example of such a transaction was one with Mexico in connection with the devaluation of the peso in 1954. Mexico had never employed exchange controls, and its representatives had several times informed the Board that it would be impracticable to do so. As a result, when a strong speculative outflow of capital funds was added in 1954 to the current account deficit which had persisted since 1951, an exchange crisis developed. It was at this point that Mexico approached the Fund with a proposal to devalue the peso by 30 per cent in order to correct a fundamental disequilibrium, and asked at the same time for a stand-by arrangement for $50 million (about 55 per cent of Mexico's quota at that time).

During the discussion of this request, Mr. Southard observed that the degree of devaluation had to be large enough to provoke a backflow of capital (thus implying that the Fund's resources would not be used to finance a further capital outflow), and supported the stand-by request in view of the assurances given by Mexico with regard to the financial policies it would pursue. When some other Directors questioned the need for a stand-by arrangement as well as the devaluation, the representative of Mexico explained that the authorities believed that a second line of reserves was needed to strengthen the exchange position. Mr. Saad supported the request for a stand-by arrangement because, as he said, he had always understood that one of the purposes to be served by such an arrangement was to provide psychological assistance to a member in circumstances such as those of Mexico. The approval of the stand-by arrangement thus appeared to establish the principle that such arrangements could assist a member in dealing with the problems of capital outflow by helping to restore and maintain confidence in its currency.

Somewhat similar considerations arose when Cuba came to the Fund for a gold tranche drawing and a stand-by arrangement in December 1956. Cuba, which was also without exchange controls at that time, feared that too large a decrease in reserves, which might result from the imminent settlement of some short-term and medium-term debts incurred to meet past deficits on current account, would lead to capital flight. Some doubts were expressed by members of the Board as to the need for the stand-by arrangement, but it was in fact approved.

Four days later the United Kingdom came to the Fund for a drawing of $561.47 million and a stand-by arrangement for $738.53 million, amounting together to 100 per cent of the British quota. The request was prompted by the crisis of confidence in sterling which resulted from the Suez Canal conflict.

While the British authorities believed that measures already taken should ensure a satisfactory current account balance for 1956–57, they were afraid that this result would be endangered if the loss of confidence in sterling were not overcome. Both in the staff's memorandum to the Board and in the discussion of it by Executive Directors, the need to restore confidence in sterling was cited as the most cogent justification for the drawing and the stand-by arrangement, which were approved.

In March 1958 the Union of South Africa approached the Fund for a gold tranche drawing and a stand-by arrangement covering the first credit tranche. At that time, South Africa's reserves had been drawn down because of balance of payments deficits on both current and capital account, that on capital account being the more important. The current account deficit resulted mainly from a sharp expansion of imports, which had reached a high stage of liberalization following relaxation of import restrictions in 1957. The capital outflow was primarily connected with a reduction in the intake of foreign investments and the sharp increase in interest rates abroad, particularly in the United Kingdom. Mr. Fleming (Australia), Alternate to Mr. Callaghan, who had been elected by South Africa, explained that the drawing and stand-by arrangement were needed to enable the South African Government to avoid reimposing import restrictions. The request was approved on these grounds.

In March 1960 the Fund agreed to a one-year stand-by arrangement for Venezuela which would, if fully utilized, raise the Fund's holding of bolívares to 142 per cent of Venezuela's quota, as this would be when the first general increase in quotas took effect.[53] Venezuela's international reserves had been drawn down by substantial amounts in 1958 and 1959, in contrast to large gains in 1956 and 1957. However, the deficits on current account in its balance of payments were not large, the principal cause of the decline in reserves being a substantial outflow of capital. This was due in part to repayment of foreign-held floating debt created by the preceding Government.

On this occasion the prohibition in the Articles against financing "large or sustained" outflows of capital was expressly introduced into the discussion in the Board. Mr. Toussaint (Belgium) pointed out that if a continuation of such substantial capital exports as had been observed recently was to be expected in the coming months, it would not be appropriate, in view of the language of Article VI, Section 1 (*a*), that the Fund's resources should be used to cover the deficit. However, he took note of the special and nonrecurrent character of a large part of the capital outflow over the previous two years, and of the staff's judgment that the effect of the stabilization measures then being taken by the Venezuelan authorities would be to reduce the net sales of exchange by the

[53] On the first general increase in quotas, see above, pp. 358–59.

Central Bank in the coming months to an amount which could be financed from foreign bank credits then under negotiation.

It will be observed that Mr. Toussaint's intervention was based on Article VI, Section 1 (*a*), and not on the interpretation given in response to the request from the U.S. Government in 1946. The General Counsel commented on this in a memorandum to the Managing Director later in 1960. Surveying the Board's practice in connection with drawings which involved consideration of capital transfers, he said:

> It has been the growing tendency of the Fund not to examine closely whether there exists a current account deficit in the case of drawings within the gold tranche or, to some extent, in the first credit tranche. However, the Board has never said that the [1946] interpretation does not apply to such drawings. In the case of Venezuela, on the other hand, where drawing rights in upper tranches were involved, the question of capital outflow was raised.

By the time that this memorandum was written, international short-term capital movements were again threatening to cause serious dislocation on the international monetary scene. The restoration of external convertibility for European currencies at the end of 1958 had partially opened the way for such movements, and it was apparent that when the major countries which were relying on Article XIV came to accept the obligations of Article VIII, Sections 2, 3, and 4 (as they were shortly expected to do), the risk of such movements would be enhanced. It was, indeed, very shortly after ten countries had accepted these obligations, in February 1961, that the problem created by the 1946 interpretation was raised in the Board.

Before then there was one more transaction which involved a deficit on capital account. Late in December 1960 South Africa, which had repaid its earlier drawing from the Fund, sought to draw $18.75 million, which would raise the Fund's holdings of its currency from 75 per cent to 87.5 per cent of its quota. On this occasion, South Africa's balance of payments on current account was in surplus, and the large decline in reserves which prompted the member's request was caused by a substantial outflow of capital. A large part of the outflow consisted of the withdrawal of foreign capital invested in South Africa, both portfolio and direct investment, and of contractual repayments on loans. It appeared doubtful whether the capital outflow would end during the ensuing year, especially in view of further contractual repayments falling due. As the Managing Director pointed out to the Board, such repayments would count as current transactions under the definition in Article XIX (*i*).

Commenting on the request, Mr. Lieftinck said that everyone would agree that the case would have been stronger if the strain on the balance of payments had been concentrated on the current account instead of the capital account. However, the drawing would be within the gold tranche, which the Fund had agreed belonged to the free reserves of the member countries. For that reason he supported the drawing, which was approved. It would appear that the consideration which Mr. Lieftinck advanced was regarded as decisive.

Clarification of 1946 decision

On February 10, 1961, the Managing Director proposed to the Board for consideration five issues concerned with the future activities of the Fund. The fifth of these was set out by Mr. Jacobsson as follows:

> In recent years there have been a number of movements of international reserves between monetary centers, for which capital as well as current transactions have been responsible. Some of these movements are a normal feature of international business under conditions of widespread convertibility and freedom of transfers, which are most certainly welcomed by the Fund. The manner in which the Fund's resources can be made available to countries whose reserves are temporarily reduced by certain of these movements involves a number of questions. Some of these questions have arisen from time to time during discussions in the Board and it has been pointed out that the concept of "current" transactions under the Articles is a good deal wider than it is in common statistical usage. These questions merit examination in the light of the needs of the member countries under present-day circumstances.

In two informal sessions, on February 24 and 27, the Board discussed the Managing Director's statement. It was generally agreed that the Fund should consider the problem of capital transfers, and several Directors expressed the view that the use of the Fund's resources in the conditions described by the Managing Director would be proper and useful. However, the three Executive Directors who had been on the Board when the 1946 interpretation was given—Messrs. de Largentaye, Rasminsky, and Saad—drew attention to the legal difficulties which would arise if it was proposed to change that interpretation. The Legal Department was therefore asked to prepare a memorandum on the subject.

The results of the Legal Department's researches were distributed to the Board on May 24, 1961. The Department's memorandum threw doubt on the adequacy of the 1946 interpretation, since this ignored the provisions in Article VI, Section 1 (*b*) (i), permitting the use of the Fund's resources for certain capital transfers. The interpretation also failed to allow for the fact that Article V, Section 3 (*a*), did not specifically limit the use of the Fund's resources to the financing of current account deficits, but permitted them for payments "which are consistent with the provisions of this Agreement." These provisions included Article VI, Section 1, which barred only drawings to meet a "large or sustained outflow of capital." Thirdly, the interpretation overlooked that Article VIII, Section 4, implied that it was permissible to use the Fund's resources for capital transfers, since it provided that a member might be required to convert foreign-held balances of its currency subject to certain conditions, one of which was that the holder of the balances was entitled to use the Fund's resources (and therefore presumptively to draw from the Fund to finance the conversion of its balances).

Taking into account all the provisions in the Articles, the staff concluded that there were three purposes for which the Fund's resources might be used: (1) to meet current account deficits; (2) to meet deficits on capital account that were neither large nor sustained; and (3) to meet deficits stemming from the special types of capital transaction mentioned in Article VI, Section 1 (*b*) (i).

A second memorandum, submitted to the Board by the Exchange Restrictions Department and the Research Department, pointed out the desirability, from the Fund's point of view, of its resources being available to meet deficits caused by international capital movements. The two Departments proposed that such drawings should be approved on the same terms as had been established for other drawings; and that whether the capital outflow was "large" should be judged in relation to the Fund's resources, possibly augmented by borrowing, rather than in relation to the member's balance of payments.

The Board devoted five meetings to a consideration of these memoranda. Four different solutions to the problem created by the 1946 interpretation were suggested: (1) widening the definition of current transactions; (2) amending the Articles of Agreement; (3) revising or repealing the interpretation by a new decision; and (4) adding a sentence to the interpretation to clarify the Board's understanding of what it meant. The first three of these were rejected. Little reference was made to the first possibility, but the Board appears to have felt that any distinction between current and capital transactions would be difficult to apply. The second was discarded because, in the words of Mr. Pitblado (United Kingdom), "there appeared to be no desire on the part of anyone to change the Articles of Agreement." The third possibility—revising or repealing the earlier interpretation—was regarded as impracticable, if only because there was no agreement whether the powers of the Board would permit it to amend an interpretation. This left the solution that was ultimately adopted—the clarification of the interpretation.

A proposal to this effect was tabled by Mr. Saad at the first of the five meetings, and a streamlined version of it was eventually accepted. The Board's decision was:

> After full consideration of all relevant aspects concerning the use of the Fund's resources, the Executive Directors decide by way of clarification that Decision No. 71-2 [the 1946 interpretation] does not preclude the use of the Fund's resources for capital transfers in accordance with the provisions of the Articles, including Article VI.[54]

[54] E.B. Decision No. 1238-(61/43), July 28, 1961; below, Vol. III, p. 245.

COMPENSATORY FINANCING OF EXPORT FLUCTUATIONS

The term "compensatory official financing" was originally used by the Fund to mean transactions undertaken by monetary authorities for the purpose of meeting temporary balance of payments disequilibria regardless of their origin.[55] In this sense it covers, for example, reserve movements, drawings from the Fund, and official borrowing from official or private sources. Compensatory financing of this kind has been the domain of the Fund since its inception. The present section, however, refers to the narrower concept of compensatory financing provided by the Fund and intended specifically to offset the effects of fluctuations in export earnings of primary producing countries.

Early plans

Efforts to deal with instability of exports of primary products have a long history; the traditional means to cope with the problem have been commodity agreements designed to maintain prices and/or export receipts within agreed ranges. The fact that such agreements could be applied to a limited number of commodities only, that negotiations have generally proved difficult and often abortive, and that even where established such agreements have not always been successful, has prompted the search for a different approach. Reducing the effects of export fluctuations by compensatory financing could take the place of, or could supplement, commodity agreements. Discussions along these lines have been held, and various proposals have been made, within the framework of the United Nations and that of the Organization of American States, in both instances with the active participation of the Fund itself. What emerged in the end was what has become known as "the special compensatory facility" established in 1963 by the Fund—less ambitious than some of the schemes proposed, but readily available to member countries experiencing export shortfalls which endanger their balance of payments.

Establishment of the "facility" came just one decade after the first suggestion for compensatory financing had been made by a group of experts convened by the United Nations in 1953. This group, in its report,[56] proposed compensatory financing in the form of countercyclical lending, intended to avoid disturbances arising from fluctuations in industrial countries' import demand. The authors suggested that such lending might be channeled through the Fund; though conceptually not distinct from current operations by the Fund, it "would involve

[55] For a discussion of this concept, see above, Vol. I, pp. 345–47.

[56] *Commodity Trade and Economic Development;* Submitted by a Committee appointed by the Secretary General, United Nations, Department of Economic Affairs (New York, 1953), pp. 67 ff.

a radical change in scale of action" and would necessitate extension of the Fund's resources.

The Board of the Fund responded to this suggestion by confirming that it was one of the Fund's "important functions to make available to its members temporary assistance in meeting a decline in their international receipts arising out of a fall in the value of their exports in time of depression." [57] This was consistent with the Articles of Agreement; rules and procedures governing transactions were intended to allow countercyclical lending. While there were various other important uses for the Fund's resources, these resources could be a significant factor in connection with a (world) depression; moreover, it might be expected that in the case of a severe depression the Fund would consult with its members on the desirability of additions to its resources.

THE FUND'S FIRST REPORT

Postwar recessions have so far been mild, and the need for countercyclical lending on a wide scale has not arisen. But fluctuations in export proceeds resulting from various other causes have continued to plague primary producing countries. The general decline in the prices of primary products, which started in the second half of the 1950's, aggravated their problems. The question of providing compensatory financing in order to alleviate the effects of export shortfalls was taken up again, in March 1959, by the UN Commission on International Commodity Trade (CICT). It was decided, as a first step, to explore the role of the Fund in this connection, and the Fund was invited to inform the Commission about its policies and procedures as they bore on the subject.[58] In response to this request the staff prepared a report, "Fund Policies and Procedures in Relation to Compensatory Financing of Commodity Fluctuations." [59] Though this report has been superseded by later documents announcing the Fund's decision to establish a special compensatory facility, it contributed much by way of clarifying issues and explaining the Fund's attitude; it also laid the foundation for methods of measuring export shortfalls. It is, therefore, worthwhile to recall here some of its findings and conclusions.

In the first part of the report attempts were made to determine the magnitude of fluctuations in export receipts of primary producing countries in the interwar and postwar (1948–58) period; for that purpose deviations were measured relative to a five-year moving average centered on the current year. However, the report recognized that for practical purposes of compensatory financing this norm cannot be derived from export data known at the time action has to be taken. In consequence, subsequent studies have attempted to develop statistical approaches for estimating the norm on the basis of exports in past years.

---

[57] ECOSOC: Official Records, 17th Session, 765th meeting, April 7, 1954, p. 55.

[58] ECOSOC: Official Records, 28th Session, Supplement No. 6 (E/3225), p. 15.

[59] Reproduced in *Staff Papers*, Vol. VIII (1960–61), pp. 1–76.

Part II of the report discussed the concept of compensatory financing in the broad sense, as understood by the Fund, and its implications for the policies of countries making use of it; the principles guiding the use of the Fund's resources; and the attitude of the Fund to automatic access to these resources in the event of export shortfalls. The report explained that compensatory financing, as understood by the Fund, was not confined to international transfers in the form of loans or grants, but encompassed, in addition, the use of a country's own reserves. The need for compensatory financing did not stop at export shortfalls; it applied to the balance of payments as a whole. If countries wished to mitigate the effect of short-term fluctuations in their exports, they could do so by drawing on their reserves, supplemented by short-term borrowing; the Fund was among the principal sources for such temporary assistance. But reserves have to be replenished and loans have to be repaid. Hence countries needed to aim at maintaining approximate equilibrium in their international accounts over a reasonable period of time. The report then described the criteria for the use of the Fund's resources which had been developed in the course of the years: the larger the drawing in relation to the member's quota, the higher the degree of justification for it that was expected. This policy constituted one reason for rejecting automatic access to the Fund's resources in the event of export shortfalls: the causes of such a shortfall, as well as the country's balance of payments situation as a whole, had to be taken into account.

However, in its concluding remarks the report stressed that member countries that were taking appropriate steps to preserve internal financial stability and to maintain their balance of payments in equilibrium, taking good years with bad, and that were otherwise making satisfactory progress toward the fulfillment of the Fund's purposes, could anticipate with confidence that financing would be available from the Fund which, in conjunction with a reasonable use of their own reserves, should be sufficient to enable them to overcome temporary payments difficulties arising from export fluctuations.

The report was presented to the May 1960 session of CICT. Discussions at this session centered around the question whether assistance by the Fund could adequately solve the problem arising from export fluctuations. Doubts were expressed in various respects: the Fund was limited to short-term operations; a country might be ineligible on account of earlier drawings or because it was not fulfilling Fund requirements concerning internal stability; the resources the Fund could devote to compensation of export fluctuations might not be adequate.

UN AND OAS PROPOSALS

A group of experts appointed for the purpose of "assisting CICT in its consideration of commodity problems . . . with special reference to compensatory financing"[60] suggested that enhancement of the compensatory role of the Fund was desirable; member countries had not fully tested the Fund's willingness to provide resources in order to meet difficulties arising from commodity fluctuations and should be encouraged to do so. But, unless the basic structure of the Fund was altered, a large increase in automatic drawing rights was not practicable. One of the experts added a note which suggested that primary producing countries should be entitled to look to the Fund for automatic compensation of export shortfalls, determined by a formula estimating the trend on the basis of a moving average of the preceding three years. In that event the Fund should make available resources up to "say, an amount which causes the Fund's holdings of the country's currency to equal 125 per cent of its quota."[61] When, subsequently, export proceeds were above trend, the excess earnings should be used automatically to repay the drawings. Nevertheless, the group as a whole shared the doubts expressed by CICT members and proposed the setting up of a special scheme called a Development Insurance Fund (DIF) which would provide automatic compensation to countries experiencing export shortfalls. Compensation would take the form of loans, repayable if (and within the limits to which) exports within the next three years exceeded the trend; any balance outstanding after three years would be written off. An alternative variant of the scheme would give compensation in the form of outright grants.[62]

The Conference of the Organization of American States (OAS), held in Punta del Este in August 1961, also concerned itself with compensatory financing and the Fund's possible contribution to the problem. In pursuance of a resolution taken by this Conference, an expert group developed yet another scheme for automatic compensation of export shortfalls, in the form of loans to be repaid not later than five years from the date of extension.

Both the DIF and the OAS schemes were discussed by CICT[63] and were referred for further study to a technical working group with which the Fund would be closely associated. At the same time, the Fund was requested to prepare a report on any possible expansion of its own role with respect to compensatory financing. Hope was expressed that the Fund might be persuaded to play a more active part in the compensation of export shortfalls.

The Board had closely followed the emergence of the schemes developed and the staff undertook extensive studies on their technical aspects.[64] Statistical

---

[60] General Assembly Resolution 1423 (December 1959).

[61] *International Compensation for Fluctuations in Commodity Trade*, United Nations (New York, 1961), p. 81.

[62] *Ibid.*, pp. 39 ff.

[63] Tenth Session of CICT, held in Rome in May 1962.

[64] The main results of these studies have been reported in Marcus Fleming, Rudolf Rhomberg, and Lorette Boissonneault, "Export Norms and Their Role in Compensatory Financing," *Staff Papers*, Vol. X (1963), pp. 97–149.

methods of estimating the medium-term trend value of exports in any given year, with a view to measuring shortfalls from this trend, were explored in great detail and a number of variants of repayment conditions were analyzed, with regard to their bearing on both benefits derived and cost involved. Experience gained in the course of these studies proved valuable not only for appraising the proposed schemes but also for revising the Fund's own policy.

Establishment of Fund facility

While the Fund staff was actively participating in the work of the technical working group, the Board proceeded to consider ways in which it could extend special assistance to members experiencing balance of payments difficulties arising from temporary export shortfalls. The result was the development of what has become known as the Fund's "compensatory financing facility." The Fund report announcing its establishment, with immediate effect, was issued late in February 1963 and presented to CICT at its meeting in May 1963.[65]

In essence the new facility, set out in Part V of the report, provided that a compensatory drawing would be made available where (*a*) a shortfall in export receipts was of short-term character and largely caused by circumstances beyond the member's control, and (*b*) the member was willing to cooperate with the Fund in an effort to find appropriate solutions for its balance of payments difficulties, where such solutions were needed.

In order to identify shortfalls of a short-term character, the Fund, in conjunction with the member concerned, would seek to establish reasonable estimates of the medium-term trend of the country's exports; such estimates would be based partly on statistical data and partly on qualitative information regarding export prospects.

Provided conditions (*a*) and (*b*) above were satisfied, a country was assured that its request for a compensatory drawing would be met in amounts not normally exceeding 25 per cent of its quota. Such drawings would be subject to the Fund's established policies and practices on repurchase, i.e., exchange purchased from the Fund should not remain outstanding beyond a period reasonably related to the payments problem for which it was purchased, which period should normally fall within an outside range of three to five years.

In order to enable members to have the full benefit of the facility, the Board declared its willingness to waive the provision in the Articles limiting the Fund's holdings of a member's currency to 200 per cent of quota.

The report also announced that in those instances where adjustments of quotas would be appropriate to make them more adequate in the light of fluctua-

---

[65] *Compensatory Financing of Export Fluctuations*, February 1963 (E.B. Decision No. 1477-(63/8)); below, Vol. III, pp. 238, 442–57.

tions in members' export proceeds, the Fund would be willing to give sympathetic consideration to requests for such adjustments.

Reflections on the decision

Over the previous decade the Fund had been dealing increasingly with the specific problems of primary producing countries. The establishment of the compensatory facility marked a further step in that direction. It has been said that the Fund's decision represented a development in thought but not a departure from its major principles.[66] The report repeated the Fund's rejection of automatic recourse to its resources. It explained that the exercise of judgment based on an analysis of causal factors was required when appraising the nature of a shortfall and deciding whether it was temporary. Moreover, the country's balance of payments position as a whole had to be examined. Automatic access to the Fund's resources in case of an export shortfall would ignore such requirements. Hence the indication of an export shortfall by a mathematical formula could not, per se, entitle a member to make a drawing.

The report also reiterated that the Fund's resources should supplement the use of domestic reserves and should not be regarded as the sole source of finance to meet short-term needs. However, the Board recognized that declining trends in the prices of primary products over a number of years had adversely affected the export earnings of many of the Fund's members and thus increased the strain on their reserves. The special facility was designed to assure effective support to members faced with fluctuations in exports.

The main respects in which the new facility involved a change in established procedures were the following: (1) A member with an export shortfall due mainly to factors beyond its control might draw on the Fund, if it was willing to cooperate with the Fund in an effort to find solutions, where required, to its balance of payments difficulties. It would not be necessary for such a country, even if it had already drawn the equivalent of a substantial part of its quota, to have an approved program worked out and agreed with the Fund before the drawing took place, as would be required under the Fund's normal policies for drawings in higher tranches. (2) The Board's willingness to waive the 200 per cent limit on drawings would permit a member to obtain compensatory financing of an export shortfall even if the Fund's holdings of its currency had already reached that limit.

Experience with the facility

Up to the end of 1965 experience with the new facility was limited. Export developments for primary producers were favorable. Prices rose through 1963

[66] Statement of the Fund observer in presenting the report to CICT.

and well into 1964; in spite of a subsequent downturn, part of the previous gain was still maintained in 1965. As a result, only three countries—Brazil, the United Arab Republic, and the Sudan—applied for and made compensatory drawings. Export shortfalls were calculated *ex post* for the latest twelve-month period for which, at the time of the request, relevant data were available. The trend value against which shortfalls were measured has been defined as the five-year moving average of exports, centered on the shortfall year. This trend value was estimated, in part, by forecasting exports in the two years following the shortfall year and, in part, on the basis of a formula developed by the Fund, using a weighted average of exports in the shortfall year (with a weight of 50 per cent) and in the preceding two years (each with a weight of 25 per cent). For two of the three members the shortfall so derived was less than 25 per cent of the country's quota and was met in full; for the third, where the shortfall exceeded the limit, compensation was confined to 25 per cent of the country's quota.

Sixteen countries applied for quota increases so as to make their quotas more adequate, as suggested in the Fund's report. In all cases the increase was granted.

Reactions to the facility

The new facility attracted many comments and some suggestions. It was hailed by CICT as a significant contribution toward the problems arising for primary producing countries through short-term fluctuations in their export proceeds. Similarly the OAS Committee on Basic Products welcomed the facility, although it suggested that it should be widened and further liberalized. The facility was again discussed in the wider framework of compensatory financing at the UN Conference on Trade and Development (UNCTAD) in 1964; earlier proposals were reiterated and a resolution was passed suggesting to member governments of the Fund that consideration should be given to revising the decision along the following lines: (1) increasing the amount allocated to compensatory financing from 25 per cent to at least 50 per cent of quota; (2) placing compensatory credits entirely outside the structure of the gold and credit tranches, ensuring that such credit would in no way prejudice a member's ability to make an ordinary drawing; (3) exploring ways of possible refinancing of drawings in the event of a persistent export shortfall beyond the control of the country affected; (4) giving greater weight to the country's actual experience in the preceding three years when determining the export shortfall.

Suggestions along similar lines, particularly with respect to raising the amount allocated for compensatory financing and to placing drawings under that title entirely outside the tranche structure, were put forward at the Annual Meeting in 1965. It also was suggested, in the course of this Meeting, that compensatory assistance should be tied to a deterioration in the terms of trade rather than to an export shortfall.

Review and suggestions by the staff

In the course of 1965 the staff reviewed the experience gained so far, as well as problems deemed likely to arise in the future. Policies and procedures embodied in the decision of 1963 were re-examined and various possible alterations were considered, taking into account the suggestions made at the Annual Meeting and at the UNCTAD Conference. As a result, a memorandum entitled "The Fund's Compensatory Financing Facility Reconsidered" was prepared and sent to the Board on December 10, 1965. The main changes suggested concerned (1) the relationship of compensatory to other drawings and (2) the limit of compensation in relation to quota.

(1) The separation of compensatory from other drawings, in a quantitative sense, had already been provided for under the decision; as pointed out earlier, the Fund had declared its willingness to waive the 200 per cent limit on holdings of a member's quota in order to accommodate compensatory drawings above that limit. However, such drawings, which were likely to be made after a country had used its gold tranche, and probably its first credit tranche, would be taken into account when subsequent requests for drawings were received. Accordingly, these further requests would be subject to the increasingly stringent criteria applicable to drawings in the higher tranches. To follow the suggestion made by UNCTAD, and again at the Annual Meeting, that compensatory drawings should be treated as entirely outside the tranche structure, would eliminate this effect, so that compensatory drawings would become additional in both a quantitative and a qualitative sense. Even though such a concession would obviously weaken somewhat the Fund's ability to secure satisfactory corrective programs in connection with ordinary drawings, the staff expressed itself in favor of accepting this proposal.

(2) The second suggestion made by UNCTAD and at the Annual Meeting was to extend the limit on compensatory drawings from (normally) 25 per cent of a member's quota to a straight 50 per cent of the quota. Commenting on this proposal, the staff pointed to the qualifying word "normally" in the decision, which would permit the Board at its discretion to exceed the limit of 25 per cent of quota. This was not, however, sufficient to assure a country that it could depend on compensatory drawings beyond that limit. That a larger drawing might sometimes be desirable was shown by the experience of the three drawings made before the end of 1965. In connection with one of these, as mentioned above, the shortfall as determined by the Fund actually exceeded the limit of 25 per cent of the member's quota; in one of the other two 86 per cent of that limit was absorbed, and in the other 71 per cent.

Moreover, larger drawings might bring "export availabilities," defined as export proceeds plus compensatory drawings or minus repurchases, closer to the desired goal, the true trend value; statistical tests covering 48 countries and 15 years (1951–64) showed that schemes allowing drawings up to 50 per cent of quota would be superior in this respect. On the other hand, to extend the maximum from 25 per cent of quota to 50 per cent would further weaken the "conditionality" of drawings, which would already be somewhat reduced by placing compensatory drawings outside the ordinary tranche structure.

The staff nevertheless suggested that the limit should be extended to 50 per cent of quota, subject to the following two qualifications: (*a*) the net expansion of compensatory drawings outstanding should not, in any twelve-month period, exceed 25 per cent of quota, and (*b*) a compensatory drawing which would raise the increase in the Fund's holdings of a member's currency, caused by compensatory drawings, beyond 25 per cent of quota, would be granted only if the member had been following policies "reasonably conducive to the development of its exports."

The foregoing recommendations by the staff were both adopted, and were incorporated, with some minor modifications in wording, in *Compensatory Financing of Export Fluctuations: A Second Report by the International Monetary Fund*, published in September 1966.[67]

A third suggestion put forward by UNCTAD was that the Fund should give consideration to ways of refinancing members' obligations in the event of a persistent shortfall in export receipts beyond the country's control. In this connection the staff pointed out that refinancing was entirely possible under existing procedures: repurchase at any time would restore the compensatory facility, and if an export shortfall of the type mentioned persisted, the member would be able to apply immediately for a new drawing.

In the broader context of repayments provisions, the staff raised the more fundamental issue whether repayment should be requested in any year in which exports exceeded the estimated trend value. Under such a system repurchases might be made exclusively in years (and to the extent) of such excesses; alternatively, under a "mixed" system any outstanding balance would have to be repaid before the end of the fifth year. In testing these two variants—a fully and a partially "compensatory" repayment system—it was assumed that for the purpose of repurchases the trend value would be determined by the mathematical formula only; that the full amount of an excess (unless it exceeded the outstanding drawing) would be used for repurchase and, in the second variant, that amounts outstanding after three years (if any) would be repaid in the fourth and/or fifth year. The statistical tests indicated that the results of either variant would be superior to those under existing repurchase provisions—superiority

[67] Reproduced below, Vol. III, pp. 469–96.

being again measured by success in bringing export availabilities closer to the trend value.

This concept of "compensatory" repurchases, and the statistical evidence in its favor, were brought to the attention of the Board, but no specific recommendation was made by the staff. The Board decided not to include any mandatory provision along these lines, but to suggest that exports in excess of the trend value should in fact be used for the repurchase of compensatory drawings. A recommendation to that effect was included in the second report.

A fourth recommendation made by UNCTAD, that in the formula for calculating the trend greater weight should be given to the three years preceding the shortfall, was also examined by the staff. Statistical tests, however, indicated that the formula devised by the staff was superior, and no change was suggested.

The related issue, of substituting fully automatic determination of the trend value for a combination of statistical and qualitative estimation, was not re-examined. However, the staff gave some thought to the problem of the relative weight to be given to the statistical evidence and to the element of judgment when determining the trend. It was found by experience that short-term forecasts by the Fund and by other expert bodies had yielded results that were closer to the truth than even the best statistical formula. On the other hand, statistical calculations, if taken by themselves, would enable member countries to foresee more accurately what compensatory financing they would be able to rely upon. Thus the weight to be given to the automatic element would itself be a matter of judgment, and might well differ in individual cases.

Commenting on the suggestion that compensation should be provided for a deterioration in the terms of trade rather than in export proceeds, the staff pointed out that such compensation would not cover changes in the volume of exports, such as those arising, not infrequently, from crop failures. Such a change might, therefore, do more harm than good. It was true that there was much to be said for taking account of variations in import prices in the determination of export shortfalls, thus aiming at compensating for a decline not in their money value but in their real value. This was not, however, practicable; for a number of countries import price indices are lacking, for others they are not reliable, and for yet others they become available only after great delay.

For the reasons given in the preceding paragraphs the staff suggested no changes in the procedure for determining the magnitude of shortfalls, or in the nature of the shortfalls to be compensated.

One further point taken up by the staff concerned the problem of double compensation for shortfalls. This might arise in the event of a country making two consecutive compensatory drawings or, more probably, making an ordinary drawing, perhaps under a stand-by arrangement, followed within less than twelve months by a drawing under the compensatory financing decision. It was conceivable, under these conditions, that the payments situation leading to the first drawing was caused, in part, by a shortfall in exports for which a compensatory drawing was subsequently claimed. The staff pointed out that there was no way of determining to what extent such a shortfall had been responsible for the payments difficulties experienced; or, consequently, what proportion of the shortfall should be regarded as met by the original drawing. For practical purposes, however, standard procedures have been laid down which provide guidelines for determining what part of such a shortfall should be deemed to have been covered by the original drawing, and not eligible for additional compensation.

It may be added, in conclusion, that the years 1963 to 1965 were the formative years of the compensatory financing facility. It was not until after the end of 1965 that this type of financial assistance from the Fund became a routine source of drawings, widely used by member countries.

CHAPTER

19

Charges, Repurchases, Selection of Currencies

J. Keith Horsefield

THE MAIN LINES OF THE FUND'S POLICIES on the use of its resources were discussed in Chapter 18; those for stand-by arrangements are dealt with in Chapters 20 and 21. Incidental references have necessarily been made already to charges on drawings and to the repurchase obligations. These subjects are more fully discussed in the present chapter, which also describes the Fund's policy for the selection of currencies to be used in purchases and repurchases. A statistical section is appended.

CHARGES

When a member uses the resources of the Fund, it becomes subject to certain charges which are uniform for all members. These charges provide the Fund with an income. At the same time, they are designed to act as a deterrent against excessive or prolonged use of the Fund's resources.

Nature of charges

Article V, Section 8, the relevant provisions of which are reproduced below, provides for two kinds of charges on drawings, viz.: (1) A service charge which is levied on the amount drawn without reference to the time that a drawing remains outstanding; this may be varied within narrow limits and was in fact reduced from 3/4 of 1 per cent to 1/2 of 1 per cent in 1951. (2) Periodic charges on the Fund's holdings of a member's currency in excess of the member's quota, varying with the relation of the holdings to quota and with the length of time that the drawings have been outstanding; these may also be varied, and were in fact altered in 1951, 1953, and 1963. There are supplementary provisions for the calculation of charges in Rules and Regulations I-4 and I-5.

The pertinent provisions of Article V, Section 8, are as follows:

(*a*) Any member buying the currency of another member from the Fund in exchange for its own currency shall pay a service charge uniform for all members of three-fourths percent in addition to the parity price. The Fund in its discretion may increase this service charge to not more than one percent or reduce it to not less than one-half percent.

(*c*) The Fund shall levy charges uniform for all members which shall be payable by any member on the average daily balances of its currency held by the Fund in excess of its quota. These charges shall be at the following rates:

(i) *On amounts not more than twenty-five percent in excess of the quota:* no charge for the first three months; one-half percent per annum for the next nine months; and thereafter an increase in the charge of one-half percent for each subsequent year.

(ii) *On amounts more than twenty-five percent and not more than fifty percent in excess of the quota:* an additional one-half percent for the first year; and an additional one-half percent for each subsequent year.

(iii) *On each additional bracket of twenty-five percent in excess of the quota:* an additional one-half percent for the first year; and an additional one-half percent for each subsequent year.

(*d*) Whenever the Fund's holdings of a member's currency are such that the charge applicable to any bracket for any period has reached the rate of four percent per annum, the Fund and the member shall consider means by which the Fund's holdings of the currency can be reduced. Thereafter, the charges shall rise in accordance with the provisions of (*c*) above until they reach five percent and failing agreement, the Fund may then impose such charges as it deems appropriate.

(*e*) The rates referred to in (*c*) and (*d*) above may be changed by a three-fourths majority of the total voting power.

(*f*) All charges shall be paid in gold. If, however, the member's monetary reserves are less than one-half of its quota, it shall pay in gold only that proportion of the charges due which such reserves bear to one-half of its quota, and shall pay the balance in its own currency.

In computing charges on drawings, the Fund treats reductions in its holdings of a member's currency as canceling the portions of these holdings that have most recently accrued—i.e., those resulting from the member's most recent drawing. The Fund thus applies the LIFO (last in, first out) principle to the calculation of charges. If it did not do this, a member that obtained a succession of drawings from the Fund could in effect acquire very cheaply a continuously revolving sum. The effect of this procedure is that charges on the portions of a member's currency that the Fund has held longest continue to rise in accordance with the scale of charges, even though for the purpose of allocating reductions in the Fund's holdings (to which, as mentioned in the next section of this chapter, the FIFO principle applies) those holdings are considered to have been repurchased. Not until the Fund's holdings of a currency have been reduced to the level of the member's quota for at least one calendar month is the progression of charges broken. Once that has been done, any subsequent drawing attracts charges at the lowest end of the scale once more.

Stand-by arrangements are not expressly provided for in the Articles, but when these are approved the Fund makes a commitment charge similar to a service charge, acting under its general powers (Article XII, Section 2 (*g*)). This charge (¼ per cent per annum) has to be paid in gold or U.S. dollars, except that where Article V, Section 8 (*f*), would permit a member to pay in its own currency part of the charges for a drawing, the commitment charge may similarly be paid partly in a member's own currency. No commitment charge is made for such part of a stand-by arrangement as would permit the member to make drawings within the gold tranche.

Changes in charges

The charges originally imposed by the Fund were those laid down in Article V, Section 8, but on three occasions the Board has exercised its powers to alter the rates contained in this schedule. Table 16 summarizes the changes made. As a consequence of the system of progressively rising charges, there is a spread between the rate currently being paid on the Fund's holdings resulting from any drawing and the average rate which has been paid on those holdings during the time that they have been outstanding. The lower half of the table shows the latter average (which includes the service charge) corresponding to each rate in the upper half. For example, if since May 1, 1963 the Fund's holdings of a member's currency have for three years been between 100 per cent and 150 per cent of the member's quota, the charge payable will have risen to 3.5 per cent per annum on the amount drawn. The table shows that the average rate which the member will have paid during the three years was 2.5 per cent. On any part of the Fund's holdings of the member's currency which exceeds 150 per cent but is not over 200 per cent of the member's quota, the corresponding figures will be 4.0 per cent and 2.83 per cent.

The first occasion on which a change was introduced in the schedule of charges was in November 1951, as the first step toward a policy of encouraging the short-term use of the Fund's resources. The changes made were as follows: (*a*) The service charge was reduced from ¾ per cent to ½ per cent. (*b*) The charge on the Fund's holdings of a member's currency lying between 100 per cent and 125 per cent of quota and maintained for between three and six months was deleted. (*c*) The intervals at which the charges rose by ½ of 1 per cent per annum were reduced from a year to six months, so that the charges on all other holdings maintained for periods longer than six months were increased by progressively larger amounts. (*d*) The point at which it becomes obligatory for the Fund and the member to discuss means of reducing the member's outstanding drawings was lowered from that at which the charge reached 4 per cent to that at which it reached 3½ per cent. (*e*) The point at which charges ceased to be expressly prescribed and were left to the discretion of the Fund was put at 4 per cent, not 5 per cent. There was, however, a limit of 4½ per cent to the rate which might be charged during the ensuing six months, and a limit of 5 per cent to the rate for the six months after that.

As will be seen from the lower half of Table 16, the effect of these changes was as follows: For a drawing which increased the Fund's holdings of the member's currency to not more than 125 per cent of quota, the average rate of charge was reduced if these holdings were maintained for not more than a year. For drawings in higher tranches, the average rate of charge was reduced if the Fund's holdings were maintained for not more than six months. If the Fund's holdings of the member's currency remained above the member's quota for eighteen months or longer, the average rate of charge was increased. This effect was designed: it was related to the Managing Director's wish to encourage small and ultra short-term drawings, and to discourage long-term drawings. Moreover, the shortening of the period before the member was required to consult the Fund about ways of reducing the Fund's holdings of its currency was deliberately intended to ensure that repurchases were made sooner than was implicit in the schedule adopted at Bretton Woods.

In accordance with the requirements of Article V, Section 8 (*e*), the minute recording the foregoing decision noted that a vote was taken. The decision was supported unanimously by the Directors present at the meeting, who cast 78,455 votes out of a possible maximum for the whole Board of 91,115 votes. Similar votes were taken on the occasion of all the later changes noted below.

The decision taken in November 1951 determined the new schedule only for the period ending December 31, 1952. In November 1952 its currency was extended to June 30, 1953; in June 1953 it was further extended to the end of October 1953; and in October it was again extended to December 31, 1953.

The reason for these piecemeal prolongations was that some Executive Directors, and notably Mr. Southard (United States), were dissatisfied with the schedule but were unable to reach agreement with their colleagues on a new set of charges. Some Directors believed that the charges were too high. The U.S. view was that the rate of charge arranged in 1951 on drawings which raised the Fund's holdings of the member's currency to 125 per cent of quota was too low, but that some reduction would be practicable in charges on drawings in higher tranches. Eventually, after negotiations lasting several months, Mr. Southard proposed to the Board a new scale which represented a compromise between the views of his Government and those of other members. The principal feature of his proposal was the abandonment of a separate rate of charge for holdings in the 100–125 per cent bracket, and the application to such holdings of the charge

Table 16. Charges on the Fund's Holdings of a Member's Currency in Excess of the Member's Quota Resulting from Transactions Effected

	Prior to December 1, 1951				From December 1, 1951 through December 31, 1953				From January 1, 1954 to April 30, 1963			From May 1, 1963 to December 31, 1965		
	Holdings Equivalent to the Following Percentages of Quota													
More than	100	125	150	175	100	125	150	175	100	150	175	100	150	200
But not more than	125	150	175	200	125	150	175	200	150	175	200	150	200	
	Charges in Per Cent Per Annum [1]													
Service charge	0.75	0.75	0.75	0.75	0.5	0.5	0.5	0.5	0.5	0.5	0.5	0.5	0.5	0.5
Duration:														
0–3 months	0.0	1.0	1.5	2.0	0.0	1.0	1.5	2.0	0.0	0.0	0.0	0.0	0.0	0.0
3–6 "	0.5	1.0	1.5	2.0	0.0	1.0	1.5	2.0	2.0	2.0	2.0	2.0	2.0	2.0
6–12 "	0.5	1.0	1.5	2.0	1.0	1.5	2.0	2.5	2.0	2.0	2.5	2.0	2.0	2.5
1–1½ years	1.0	1.5	2.0	2.5	1.5	2.0	2.5	3.0	2.0	2.5	3.0	2.0	2.5	3.0
1½–2 "	1.0	1.5	2.0	2.5	2.0	2.5	3.0	3.5[2]	2.5	3.0	3.5	2.5	3.0	3.5
2–2½ "	1.5	2.0	2.5	3.0	2.5	3.0	3.5[2]	4.0	3.0	3.5	4.0[2]	3.0	3.5	4.0[2]
2½–3 "	1.5	2.0	2.5	3.0	3.0	3.5[2]	4.0	4.5[3]	3.5	4.0[2]	4.5	3.5	4.0[2]	4.5
3–3½ "	2.0	2.5	3.0	3.5	3.5[2]	4.0	4.5[3]	5.0[3]	4.0[2]	4.5	5.0[3]	4.0[2]	4.5	5.0
3½–4 "	2.0	2.5	3.0	3.5	4.0	4.5[3]	5.0[3]		4.5[3]	5.0[3]		4.5	5.0	
4–4½ "	2.5	3.0	3.5	4.0[2]	4.5[3]	5.0[3]			5.0[3]			5.0		
4½–5 "	2.5	3.0	3.5	4.0	5.0[3]									
5–6 "	3.0	3.5	4.0[2]	4.5										
6–7 "	3.5	4.0[2]	4.5	5.0										
7–8 "	4.0[2]	4.5	5.0											
8–9 "	4.5	5.0												
9–10 "	5.0													

Average Effective Rates in Per Cent Per Annum [4]

Duration:															
3 months	3.00	4.00	4.50	5.00	2.00	3.00	3.50	4.00	2.00	2.00	2.00	2.00	2.00	2.00
6 "	1.75	2.50	3.00	3.50	1.00	2.00	2.50	3.00	2.00	2.00	2.00	2.00	2.00	2.00
1 year	1.12	1.75	2.25	2.75	1.00	1.75	2.25	2.75	2.00	2.00	2.25	2.00	2.00	2.25
1½ years	1.08	1.67	2.17	2.67	1.17	1.83	2.33	2.83	2.00	2.17	2.50	2.00	2.17	2.50
2 "	1.06	1.62	2.12	2.62	1.38	2.00	2.50	3.00	2.12	2.38	2.75	2.12	2.38	2.75
2½ "	1.15	1.70	2.20	2.70	1.60	2.20	2.70	3.20	2.30	2.60	3.00	2.30	2.60	3.00
3 "	1.21	1.75	2.25	2.75	1.83	2.42	2.92	3.42	2.50	2.83	3.25	2.50	2.83	3.25
3½ "	1.32	1.86	2.36	2.86	2.07	2.64	3.14	3.64	2.71	3.07	3.50	2.71	3.07	3.50
4 "	1.41	1.94	2.44	2.94	2.31	2.88	3.38		2.94	3.31		2.94	3.31	
4½ "	1.53	2.06	2.56	3.06	2.56	3.11			3.17			3.17		
5 "	1.62	2.15	2.65	3.15	2.80									
6 "	1.85	2.38	2.87	3.38										
7 "	2.09	2.61	3.11	3.61										
8 "	2.33	2.84	3.34											
9 "	2.57	3.08												
10 "	2.81													

[1] Except for the service charge, which is payable once per transaction and is expressed as a percentage of the amount of the transaction.

[2] Point at which consultation between the Fund and the member becomes obligatory.

[3] Maximum charges.

[4] Total charges payable by the member cver the stated period, expressed as a percentage and divided by the number of years of the period. Includes service charge.

on holdings in the 125–150 per cent bracket. Another change was the abandonment of any charge except the service charge on holdings maintained for not more than three months; this overcame the difficulty that under the earlier scales the annual rate of charge (including the service charge) was greater on holdings maintained for not more than three months than on holdings maintained for substantially longer periods. At the same time, the point of time at which a member was required to consult the Fund about ways to reduce the Fund's holdings of its currency was left unaltered. Because charges had risen, this point again became that at which the rate of charge reached 4 per cent. The new scale was approved on December 23, 1953, to be applied to drawings on or after January 1, 1954.

The discussion of Mr. Southard's proposal raised a question which was subsequently to feature in most discussions of charges: Should the rates take account of the rates of interest ruling in the world's principal money markets? Executive Directors' views on the point have continued to differ, and the lack of unanimity has contributed to the subsequent stability of charges. While the schedule of rates has been reviewed annually since 1954, the only change introduced has been necessitated by the emergence of a new factor. This was the decision that a drawing under the compensatory financing plan might be permitted to increase the Fund's holdings of a member's currency beyond 200 per cent of quota,[1] whereas the scale previously in force made no provision for such drawings.

The staff recommended in April 1963 that for the future the charges applicable to holdings in the 175–200 per cent bracket should be applied to drawings which raised the Fund's holdings above 200 per cent of quota. Drawings which raised the Fund's holdings to between 175 per cent and 200 per cent of quota should in future attract the rate charged in the next lower bracket (150–175 per cent of quota). One argument for the proposal not to charge more on holdings above 200 per cent of quota than had previously been charged on holdings in the 175–200 per cent bracket was that under the previous scale the point at which the Fund and the member had to discuss ways to reduce the Fund's holdings of the member's currency was reached after only two years; there seemed to be no point in setting rates of charge which would shorten even more the time before such discussions became obligatory. The Board approved the proposal, with effect from May 1, 1963.

It will be observed that the maximum rate of charge shown in Table 16 is 5 per cent per annum. This would be reached, for drawings effected after January 1, 1954, one year after the point at which the Fund and the member were required to enter into discussions. Neither Article V, Section 8, nor the relevant Rule prescribed what rate of charge was to be levied on drawings held still longer. This deficiency was remedied in two stages.

---

[1] See above, pp. 421–22.

In April 1959 the Board decided that if the member agreed with the Fund on a schedule which would complete repurchases within five years of the date of a drawing, the maximum rate of charge should be 5 per cent. If agreement on a schedule was reached, but repurchases under this schedule would not extinguish the drawing within the five years, the Fund might adopt higher maximum rates. If no agreement was reached with the member at all, the Fund might impose such charges as it deemed appropriate, after the 5 per cent rate had been reached.

Four years later the question of such charges became an imminent one, as Cuba had failed to agree on a schedule of repurchases which would extinguish a drawing which it had had five years earlier. The staff then proposed that so long as a member in Cuba's position failed to reach an agreement, the charge should continue to rise by ½ of 1 per cent each six months; but it also suggested that the Board might wish to consider imposing a maximum rate of charge. The staff also proposed a procedure to deal with the case, hitherto unprovided for, of a member that agreed to a schedule which would complete repurchase within five years, but failed to keep the agreement. The staff suggested that for such a member the rate of charge should rise to 5½ per cent six months after it had reached 5 per cent, and thereafter increase by ½ of 1 per cent each six months; except that if the member broke the agreement at a time when it had already been paying 5 per cent for more than six months, the rate should rise to 5½ per cent immediately. These recommendations were approved when they came before the Board, and at the instance of Mr. Saad (United Arab Republic) provision was made for reviewing the rate of charge when this had reached 6 per cent.

Also in 1959 a change was made in the rules governing the commitment charge on stand-by arrangements, as a result of which it was made payable in advance but became available to be offset against the service charge on any drawing made while the stand-by arrangement was in force.[2] (Previously the commitment charge had been payable in half-yearly installments, and that for the second half of a year had not been available to be offset against a drawing in the first half of the year.) At the same time, appropriate arrangements were made to cover such complications as arose if a member (*a*) made a drawing under a stand-by arrangement, as a result of which it was credited with a proportionate part of the commitment charge, (*b*) subsequently repurchased all or part of the drawing, and (*c*) wished to reconstitute a commensurate part of the drawing rights conferred by the stand-by arrangement. It was also decided that when a member canceled a stand-by arrangement it should be entitled to a refund of the commitment charge proportionate to the unexpired period of the arrangement in respect of the part of the drawing rights under the arrangement (if any) which could still be drawn when the arrangement was canceled, and in respect of which the member had paid a charge.

[2] E.B. Decision No. 876-(59/15), April 27, 1959; below, Vol. III, p. 232.

The reason for the final clause of the last-mentioned decision was that commitment charges are not levied in respect of such part of a stand-by arrangement as covers the member's gold tranche. In the same decision, the Board agreed that where the Fund's holdings of the currency of a member that had a stand-by arrangement were reduced, so that the excess of these holdings over the member's quota was less than the undrawn amount of the stand-by arrangement, the commitment fee would be pro rata refunded. Three years later, this was modified to exclude changes in the Fund's holdings of a member's currency in a special account for administrative expenditures, provided that these did not exceed 1/100 of 1 per cent of the member's quota.[3] This avoided trifling refunds which became due if the Fund or a member made a small payment (e.g., for a book) at a time when the member had a stand-by arrangement straddling its quota.

REPURCHASES [4]

Provisions in Articles of Agreement

The provisions in the Articles of Agreement that relate to repurchases may be divided into six categories, as follows:

(1) Provision for the automatic repurchase of the Fund's holdings of the member's currency in excess of 75 per cent of its quota (Article V, Section 7 (*b*) (i)).

(2) Provision for the automatic repurchase of additional segments of the Fund's holdings in excess of 75 per cent of the member's quota, in particular circumstances (Article V, Section 7 (*b*) (ii)).

(3) Limitations on the foregoing (Article V, Section 7 (*c*)).

(4) Detailed provisions for identifying the particular currencies, or gold, to be used for obligatory repurchases (Schedule B).

(5) Provisions for voluntary repurchases of the Fund's holdings in excess of the member's quota (Article V, Section 7 (*a*)).

(6) Provision for the emergency suspension of all the foregoing (Article XVI, Section 1).

The full text of Article V, Section 7, is as follows:

> *Repurchase by a member of its currency held by the Fund.*—(*a*) A member may repurchase from the Fund and the Fund shall sell for gold any part of the Fund's holdings of its currency in excess of its quota.
>
> (*b*) At the end of each financial year of the Fund, a member shall repurchase from the Fund with gold or convertible currencies, as determined in accordance

[3] E.B. Decision No. 1345-(62/32), May 23, 1962; below, Vol. III, p. 233.

[4] Only the highlights of the Fund's policy on repurchases are described in this section. For a full description of the relevant technicalities the reader is referred to Fund Circular No. 9.

with Schedule B, part of the Fund's holdings of its currency under the following conditions:

(i) Each member shall use in repurchases of its own currency from the Fund an amount of its monetary reserves equal in value to one-half of any increase that has occurred during the year in the Fund's holdings of its currency plus one-half of any increase, or minus one-half of any decrease, that has occurred during the year in the member's monetary reserves. This rule shall not apply when a member's monetary reserves have decreased during the year by more than the Fund's holdings of its currency have increased.

(ii) If after the repurchase described in (i) above (if required) has been made, a member's holdings of another member's currency (or of gold acquired from that member) are found to have increased by reason of transactions in terms of that currency with other members or persons in their territories, the member whose holdings of such currency (or gold) have thus increased shall use the increase to repurchase its own currency from the Fund.

(*c*) None of the adjustments described in (*b*) above shall be carried to a point at which

(i) the member's monetary reserves are below its quota, or

(ii) the Fund's holdings of its currency are below seventy-five percent of its quota, or

(iii) the Fund's holdings of any currency required to be used are above seventy-five percent of the quota of the member concerned.

The provisions of Article V, Section 7 (*b*) (ii), which were intended to deal with the case of a member building up reserves in a reserve currency by operations in that currency in a third country, have proved impracticable and have never been applied by the Fund.

The principal provisions of Schedule B are as follows:

1 (*a*). If the member's monetary reserves have not increased during the year, the amount payable to the Fund shall be distributed among all types of reserves in proportion to the member's holdings thereof at the end of the year.

1 (*b*). If the member's monetary reserves have increased during the year, a part of the amount payable to the Fund equal to one-half of the increase shall be distributed among those types of reserves which have increased in proportion to the amount by which each of them has increased. The remainder of the sum payable to the Fund shall be distributed among all types of reserves in proportion to the member's remaining holdings thereof.

1 (*c*). If after all the repurchases required under Article V, Section 7 (*b*), had been made, the result would exceed any of the limits specified in Article V, Section 7 (*c*), the Fund shall require such repurchases to be made by the members proportionately in such manner that the limits will not be exceeded.

3. . . . No account shall be taken . . . of any increase in [a member's] monetary reserves which is due to currency previously inconvertible having become convertible during the year; or to holdings which are the proceeds of a long-term or medium-term loan contracted during the year; or to holdings which have been transferred or set aside for repayment of a loan during the subsequent year.

The principal elements in the definition of monetary reserves, which is of course basic to the calculations needed to assess repurchase obligations, are as follows:

> A member's monetary reserves means its net official holdings of gold, of convertible currencies of other members, and of the currencies of such non-members as the Fund may specify. (Article XIX (*a*)) [*Note:* The Fund has never "specified" any non-member currency.]
>
> A member's monetary reserves shall be calculated by deducting from its central holdings the currency liabilities to the Treasuries, central banks, stabilization funds, or similar fiscal agencies of other members . . . together with similar liabilities to other official institutions and other banks in the territories of members. . . . (Article XIX (*e*))

INTERPRETATIVE DECISIONS

In the early days of the Fund's work the calculation of members' monetary reserves gave rise to a large number of problems, and various decisions were taken which generalized the answers given.[5] For our purposes the following are the most important of these decisions.[6]

Timing of repurchase obligations

Three questions concerning the application of time limits to the calculation of monetary reserves, and hence of repurchase obligations, have been decided by the Board. The first one dealt with the question when the initial calculation of monetary reserves was to be made. The Board decided that

> for the purpose of the repurchase obligations prescribed by Article V, Section 7, increases and decreases in the monetary reserves of a member shall not be considered if they occur on or before the latest date on which the member's subscription must be paid . . . ; and the payment of subscriptions, whether actually made before or after such latest date for payment, shall not be regarded as resulting in a decrease in monetary reserves.[7]

The second decision settled at what point of time the decrease in monetary reserves resulting from a repurchase would be deemed to take effect for the purpose of the next calculation under this provision:

> Whenever a member uses its monetary reserves to repurchase its currency from the Fund in accordance with the provisions of Article V, Section 7 (*b*) (i) or (ii), the resulting reduction in its monetary reserves and in the Fund's holdings of its currency must be regarded as having occurred, for the purpose of calculating subsequent repurchase obligations under the same provisions of the Fund Agreement, at the end of the financial year of the Fund in respect of which the obligation to make the repurchase arose.[8]

[5] See, e.g., in Vol. III below, pp. 220, 243–44, 269–73.

[6] See also E.B. Decision No. 493-3, November 4, 1949; below, Vol. III, p. 272.

[7] E.B. Decision No. 124-2, January 22, 1947; below, Vol. III, p. 244.

[8] E.B. Decision No. 447-5, June 17, 1949; below, Vol. III, p. 244.

The third decision determined the point of time at which the limits set out in Article V, Section 7 (*c*), were to be regarded as applying:

> In the application of the repurchase obligations of the Fund Agreement the limits specified in Article V, Section 7 (*c*), apply solely as of the end of the financial year for which the repurchase obligations are calculated.[9]

Abatement of repurchase obligations

The Board considered in 1950 what should be done when a repurchase obligation calculated in accordance with Article V, Section 7, and Schedule B included an amount of a currency which the Fund could not accept because of the terms of Article V, Section 7 (*c*) (iii), and decided as follows:

> If part of a member's gross repurchase obligation for any financial year is allocated to a currency which the Fund cannot accept because of Article V, Section 7 (*c*) (iii), that part of the gross obligation is abated for that year under Schedule B, Paragraph 1 (*c*), and is not required to be discharged in gold or some other currency.[10]

Voluntary repurchases

On several occasions the question has arisen whether the Fund might accept a voluntary repurchase. Provision was made in Article V, Section 7 (*a*), for a member wishing to repurchase from the Fund the Fund's holdings of its currency in excess of its quota. However, a difficulty arose (as explained below) in connection with other repurchases that were neither (1) required by Article V, Section 7 (*b*), nor (2) arranged following consultations prescribed by Article V, Section 8 (*d*), nor (3) made in pursuance of an undertaking given at the time of a drawing (e.g., under a stand-by arrangement or in consideration of the Board's waiving the limits set out in Article V, Section 3 (*a*)).

The decision eventually reached was as follows:

> (1) Subject to paragraph 3 below, a member may offer in voluntary repurchase, and the Fund has the power to accept, if it so decides, gold or convertible currencies to the extent that (a) the Fund's holdings of the convertible currency of a member which is offered would not be increased above 75% of the quota of that member, and (b) the Fund's holdings of the repurchasing member's currency would not be decreased below 75% of its quota.
>
> (2) As a matter of legal interpretation it is determined that the consent of the member whose currency is offered in voluntary repurchase is not necessary as a condition precedent to the acceptance by the Fund of such currency.
>
> (3) Where a member has an accrued and undischarged repurchase obligation under Art. V, Sec. 7 (*b*), and Schedule B in respect of any financial year of the

[9] E.B. Decision No. 419-1, April 11, 1949; below, Vol. III, p. 244.

[10] E.B. Decision No. 521-3, January 16, 1950; below, Vol. III, p. 273.

Fund, the member must discharge the obligation in accordance with those provisions; provided, however, that the payment of currency under those provisions may be combined with the sale of gold to the Fund for the currency under Art. V, Sec. 6 (*a*).[11]

COLLECTION OF MONETARY RESERVES DATA

The information needed to calculate repurchase obligations under Article V, Section 7, consists of figures for the member's monetary reserves, as defined in the Articles and in the Board's decisions, together with the Fund's holdings of the members' currencies. The latter data are, of course, in the Fund's possession, but for the former it is dependent upon reports from the members. The original Rules and Regulations provided (Rule I-6) that each member should furnish to the Fund the necessary data about its monetary reserves "at the end of each financial year." At first, however, it proved difficult to secure the data, and in July 1950 the Board altered the Rule to require the provision of the information within six months of the end of each financial year. Despite this, the staff had to report in November 1950 that, out of the 49 members of the Fund at that time, 20 had failed to provide information about their monetary reserves as at April 30, 1950, and 14 of these had also failed to provide figures for earlier years.

Thereafter matters improved, and as time went on the staff was able to make the necessary calculations with reasonable promptitude. The provisions of Article V, Section 7 (*b*) (i), Section 7 (*c*) (i), and Section 7 (*c*) (ii), affect only the monetary reserves of the member concerned. As soon, therefore, as data of these reserves is available, the member's repurchase obligation, so far as it is affected by these provisions, can be calculated. Article V, Section 7 (*c*) (iii), introduces into the calculation a limit related to the Fund's holdings of another member's currency. If there is any doubt whether repurchase obligations in the aggregate exceed the amount of that currency which can be accepted within the limit, none of the calculations can be finalized until this point has been cleared up. Before 1961 this did not much matter, as only a few countries had accepted the obligations of Article VIII, Sections 2, 3, and 4 (thereby making their currencies acceptable in repurchases). Of these few, the only one in whose currency substantial repurchases became due was the United States, and the Fund's holdings of U.S. dollars were well below 75 per cent of the U.S. quota.

In 1961 the calculations became complicated by the acceptability of a number of other currencies, but there was little doubt that the relatively small repurchase obligations accruing in them could be accepted by the Fund. By the end of 1962, however, the position had radically changed. The Fund's holdings of U.S. dollars had risen to 74 per cent of the U.S. quota, and it would not be possible, under the limitation imposed by Article V, Section 7 (*c*) (iii), to accept

[11] E.B. Decision No. 7-(648), March 8, 1951; below, Vol. III, p. 244.

more than US$34 million in repurchases thereafter. As repurchase obligations arising at April 30, 1963 were bound to include much more than this sum, there would have to be a scaling down of the obligations of all members who were due to repurchase their currencies with U.S. dollars. By how much each obligation would have to be scaled down, however, could not be known until all obligations had been calculated. If the Fund was to wait for six months for members to supply monetary reserves data, then make the requisite calculations, and only then notify all repurchasing members how much they were due to pay, no member would be able to make any repurchase, in respect of the year ended April 30, 1963, until late in that year. This could well have been awkward, as by that time a member's monetary reserves might (as experience in the past had shown) have been depleted to a point at which a repurchase would be embarrassing.

The Board accordingly decided to require members to expedite the provision of monetary reserves data, taking for that purpose the following decision:

> 1. Where on any April 30 the Fund holds a member's currency in an amount exceeding 75 per cent of the member's quota, the member shall make a provisional monetary reserves report to the Fund not later than May 31, preferably by cable.
>
> 2. The Fund will make a provisional calculation of the amount and distribution of the repurchase obligations of such members and will inform them of the results of the calculation not later than June 15. Members shall discharge within thirty days any repurchase obligations as thus provisionally calculated and agreed with the member.
>
> 3. All provisional repurchases shall be subject to adjustment by members and the Fund in accordance with Rule I-6 of the Fund's Rules and Regulations.[12]

While each member of whose currency the Fund holds more than 75 per cent of its quota is thus required to supply information annually about its monetary reserves, the Board decided in 1957 that it was not necessary actually to collect repurchases if the amount involved was small. It accordingly decided:

> In cases where a repurchase obligation of less than the equivalent of $500 is calculated the member will be notified, and the obligation collected, on the next occasion thereafter that a repurchase obligation accrues which, together with the first one, will total the equivalent of $500 or more.[13]

Limitation of repurchase obligations

Throughout the Fund's life, repurchase obligations under Article V, Section 7, have been prevented from arising because of Section 7 (*c*) (ii) and have been substantially reduced by Section 7 (*c*) (i) and (iii). The effects of these limitations are described in the immediately following paragraphs.

---

[12] E.B. Decision No. 1813-(65/4), January 18, 1965; below, Vol. III, p. 245.

[13] E.B. Decision No. 705-(57/55), November 7, 1957; below, Vol. III, p. 245.

The member most affected by Article V, Section 7 (*c*) (i), has been the United Kingdom. For instance, between April 1961 and May 1965 the United Kingdom drew over $4 billion from the Fund and repurchased $1.28 billion, but it incurred no repurchase obligation under Article V, Section 7 (*b*), because of the operation of Article V, Section 7 (*c*) (i): its monetary reserves were at all times less than its quota. In addition, the limitations contained in the last sentence of Article V, Section 7 (*b*) (i), and in Article V, Section 7 (*c*) (ii), applied at April 30, 1963 and April 30, 1964.

As regards Article V, Section 7 (*c*), it is convenient to consider two periods, the first comprising the twelve financial years 1948/49 through 1959/60, and the second, the six financial years 1960/61 through 1965/66. For the first twelve years it is sufficient to say that actual repurchases, which began in 1949/50, totaled $2,179 million,[14] while repurchase obligations arising at April 30 in each year from 1948 to 1959 (which will normally have become payable in the ensuing fiscal year) totaled less than 60 per cent of this figure, viz., $1,235 million.[15]

For the six years 1960/61 through 1965/66, during which the Fund's operations were on a much larger scale, actual repurchases totaled $4,029 million.[16] But repurchase obligations accruing under Article V, Section 7 (*b*), totaled only 12 per cent of this sum, viz., $491 million. A total of $1,621 million did not emerge as an obligation or was abated as a result of the impact of Article V, Section 7 (*c*). This total was made up as follows:

Under Section 7 (*c*) (i)	$198 million, affecting 11 countries
Under Section 7 (*c*) (ii)	$1,106 million, affecting 20 countries
Under Section 7 (*c*) (iii)	$317 million, affecting 26 countries

Of the 67 repurchase obligations, amounting to $2,112 million, which arose during the six years, 16 were affected by Section 7 (*c*) (i), 35 by Section 7 (*c*) (ii), and 55 by Section 7 (*c*) (iii).

The abatements under Section 7 (*c*) (i), representing the elimination of repurchases which otherwise would have reduced the member's monetary reserves below its quota, largely affected Argentina, Chile, and Spain ($76 million).

Section 7 (*c*) (ii), which precludes repurchases which would reduce the Fund's holdings of the repurchasing member's currency below 75 per cent of its quota, affected principally France ($253 million). But quite substantial sums were also involved for a number of the other 19 countries concerned. The chief reason was that the members' reserves increased so much that 50 per cent of the increase was greatly in excess of the amount needed to reduce the Fund's holdings of their currencies to 75 per cent of their quotas.

[14] *Annual Report, 1966*, Table 55, p. 131.
[15] *Annual Report, 1965*, Table 55, p. 114.
[16] *Annual Report, 1966*, Table 55, p. 131.

Section 7 (*c*) (iii) precludes the acceptance by the Fund in repurchases of any currency of which its holdings had reached 75 per cent of the issuing member's quota. The effect of this provision was greatly increased during the six years 1960/61 to 1965/66 by two circumstances. The first was the acceptance of the obligations of Article VIII, Sections 2, 3, and 4, by the United Kingdom and 17 other countries. The effect of this was to make their currencies available, in principle, for repurchases. However, as the Fund's holdings were at 75 per cent or more of the British quota except between February and August 1961 and between August 1962 and April 1963, there was little scope for using sterling in repurchases, and most of the other countries' obligations in that currency were abated, to a total equivalent to $45 million. The other factor was that the Fund's holdings of U.S. dollars reached 75 per cent of the U.S. quota during 1963 and subsequently remained above that figure, so that the other countries' obligations in U.S. dollars were also abated, to a total of $268 million.

Alternative repurchase procedures

In addition to the obligatory repurchases called for by Article V, Section 7 (*b*), and to the voluntary repurchases permitted by Article V, Section 7 (*a*), four other methods of repurchase have evolved: (1) repurchases called for by the Board's decision of February 1952 (the Rooth Plan), which limits the retention of drawings to "the period reasonably related to the payments problem for which [the currency] was purchased from the Fund" and requires this period to "fall within an outside range of three to five years"; (2) repurchases of drawings under stand-by arrangements, for which the time limit is three years; (3) repurchases in accordance with a schedule agreed with the member, usually after it has been unable to repurchase within three years; and (4) voluntary repurchases.

The effect of repurchases is, of course, also achieved if other members draw from the Fund the currency of a member that has a repurchase obligation. This process has gained in importance in recent years as a result of the widening of the range of currencies drawn from the Fund—see the next section of this chapter.

Repurchases in fluctuating currencies

In September 1950 Canada abandoned the par value of the Canadian dollar, which thereafter was allowed to fluctuate. The Articles of Agreement make no provision for a fluctuating currency, so that when in 1952 Canada accepted the obligations of Article VIII, Sections 2, 3, and 4, thereby making its currency eligible for use in repurchases, it became necessary to stipulate at what exchange rate the Canadian dollar should be accepted in repurchases.

This was settled by the Board in the course of a comprehensive decision on "Transactions and Computations Involving Fluctuating Currencies" taken on June 15, 1954. The decision provided for the exchange rate for fluctuating currencies offered in repurchases to be the midpoint between the highest rate and the lowest rate for the U.S. dollar quoted, for cable transfers for spot delivery, in the main financial center of the country of the fluctuating currency, on the last business day before the Fund instructed its depository to receive the fluctuating currency.[17]

Voluntary repurchases

It will be recalled that the provision in the Articles of Agreement for voluntary repurchases (Article V, Section 7 (*a*)) relates only to repurchases of the Fund's holdings in excess of quota, and provides for such repurchases in gold. It was for long disputed whether the Fund was entitled to accept voluntary repurchases in other circumstances. Mr. de Largentaye (France), who was the principal opponent of such voluntary repurchases, based his argument on Article V, Section 2, which reads:

> *Limitation on the Fund's operations.*—Except as otherwise provided in this Agreement, operations on the account of the Fund shall be limited to transactions for the purpose of supplying a member, on the initiative of such member, with the currency of another member in exchange for gold or for the currency of the member desiring to make the purchase.

He also objected that voluntary repurchases other than in gold, such as were in the main offered, might deprive the Fund of gold which otherwise would have had to be provided by the member in making repurchases under the terms of Article V, Section 7 (*b*), and Schedule B.

The Board, however, believed that it was in principle desirable to encourage voluntary repurchases, and that the correct view of the limitations set out in Article V, Section 2, did not debar such repurchases. This view, as expounded by the General Counsel in February 1950, was that the "operations" referred to in Section 2 could be simple or complex. They could, for instance, consist of a combination of a purchase of dollars from the Fund and a repurchase of the member's currency with dollars. For if "operations" did not mean this, the Fund would be precluded from accepting any repurchase (other than under the provisions of Article V, Section 7 (*b*)) which would reduce the Fund's holdings of the member's currency below 100 per cent of quota; and this was clearly inconsistent with the emphasis in the Articles of Agreement on the desirability of the Fund's holdings of members' currencies being equal to 75 per cent of their quotas.

There remained the possibility that a member having an accrued obligation under Article V, Section 7 (*b*), might forestall the payment to the Fund of gold due under that obligation, by making a voluntary repurchase in some currency which might be of less use to the Fund. To prevent this, the Board decided—as set out in full earlier in this section—that any accrued and undischarged obliga-

[17] E.B. Decision No. 321-(54/32), June 15, 1954; below, Vol. III, p. 222.

tion under Article V, Section 7 (*b*), must be fulfilled in accordance with the stipulations of Schedule B, except that it could be paid in gold.

Ten years later the subject recurred. In November 1961 the United Kingdom made a voluntary repurchase of £100 million sterling with U.S. dollars. Mr. de Largentaye argued that the repurchase, being a voluntary one, should have been made in gold. He was answered in a memorandum from the Managing Director which pointed out that the Rooth Plan had imposed on the United Kingdom an obligation to repurchase its drawing within three to five years; that the Fund had made no stipulation at any time as to the medium in which it should be repurchased; and that therefore the United Kingdom was entitled to repurchase with any convertible currency. Article V, Section 7 (*a*), to which Mr. de Largentaye had referred, offered a privilege, and did not constitute a duty. When the matter came before the Board, Mr. de Largentaye's view was not shared by other Directors, and the Managing Director's answer was approved.

Of the total sum repurchased down to the end of 1965 (including transactions for the purpose of reducing initial currency subscriptions to 75 per cent of quota), about one eighth was voluntarily repurchased as described on page 439. A further 3½ per cent of the total sum was originally repurchased voluntarily, but was subsequently applied to extinguish liabilities arising under Article V, Section 7 (*b*).

Allocation of repurchases

The fact that, as mentioned above, the reductions in the Fund's holdings of a member's currency can be effected in a number of different ways, not all of which are related to specific drawings, makes it necessary to allocate such reductions according to fixed principles. (The need for such principles was crystallized by the obligations assumed by the Fund, under the General Arrangements to Borrow (GAB), to repay participants as members repurchased drawings for which the GAB had been activated.) The following are the principles which the Fund has adopted:

Repurchases not accruing under Article V, Section 7 (b). When such a repurchase is made, the member may specify which drawing is being repurchased; if so, its decision is accepted. If it does not specify which drawing is being repurchased, it is invited to do so. If it does not do so, the repurchase is regarded as extinguishing in whole or in part the commitment which matures first.

Repurchases accruing under Article V, Section 7 (b). Where it is practicable to identify which drawing is being repurchased, this is done (e.g., where only one drawing is outstanding in that financial year, or where several drawings are outstanding, but only one was made in the year, and the repurchase obligation arises solely because of the increase in the Fund's holdings of the member's currency). Where it is not possible to identify the drawing, the repurchase is regarded as relating to the drawing which matures first.

Sale by Fund of member's currency. This is regarded as extinguishing, in whole or in part, the drawing by the member concerned that has the earliest maturity.

In effect, the arrangements ensure that the earliest drawings are normally repurchased first, in accordance with the FIFO (first in, first out) principle, in contrast to the LIFO (last in, first out) principle applied to the determination of charges. If the FIFO principle were not used in allocating reductions in holdings, a member making a series of drawings might find itself due to repurchase some of the earliest amounts all at once in order to ensure that none of them remained outstanding for longer than five years.

A related issue was discussed by the Board in 1959, when the staff brought to its notice the question of the extent to which a member could reconstitute a stand-by arrangement by repurchasing a drawing while the arrangement was in force. This feature had been introduced in the stand-by arrangement with Belgium in 1952 [18] and implicitly approved when the Board revised the conditions for stand-by arrangements in 1953.[19] Since then, members had been allowed to reconstitute stand-by arrangements that had been wholly or partially exhausted, by repurchasing not only drawings made under the stand-by arrangement but also drawings made before the arrangement began. The staff suggested that this was probably not the Board's intention, and proposed that in the revision of conditions then in preparation this should be made clear. The Board agreed, and its decision accordingly included the following passage:

> A stand-by arrangement shall provide for a fixed amount that can be purchased under it augmented by amounts equivalent to repurchases in respect of drawings made under the stand-by arrangement or made at the time when the stand-by arrangement is entered into, unless when any such repurchase is made the member informs the Fund that it does not wish the stand-by arrangement to be augmented by the amount of that repurchase.[20]

Effectiveness of repurchase arrangements

Since 1952 it has been the declared policy of the Fund that drawings shall be repurchased within three to five years. As with any other drawing, a member wishing to draw further before it has completed the repurchase of an existing drawing is required to justify the further drawing in accordance with the terms of the Board's decision of February 1952. It is not surprising that there has been some increase in the total of drawings outstanding during the later years of the

---

[18] See below, p. 469.

[19] E.B. Decision No. 270-(53/95), December 23, 1953; below, Vol. III, pp. 231–32.

[20] E.B. Decision No. 876-(59/15), April 27, 1959; below, Vol. III, pp. 232–33.

period covered by this volume, but it is of interest to inquire how far the repurchase requirements have succeeded in limiting the period for which members have had continuous use of the Fund's resources. The following analysis results from such an inquiry.

During the twenty years 1946–65 there were twenty-seven members of whose currencies the Fund held more than the equivalent of 75 per cent of their quotas for more than five consecutive years. Fourteen of these, however, were members whose original gold subscriptions were less than 25 per cent of their quotas, and who took more than five years to reduce the Fund's holdings of their currencies to 75 per cent of quota. These members, because of the relative smallness of their monetary reserves, did not incur repurchase obligations for at least a part of the time. For four other members the Fund's holdings, while in excess of 75 per cent of quota for more than five years, did not exceed 100 per cent of quota for that length of time. Since access to drawings in the gold tranche is quasi-automatic, the position of these members scarcely gives cause for concern.

There remain nine members of whose currencies the Fund had held, during the twenty years down to December 31, 1965, more than the equivalent of 100 per cent of their quotas for more than sixty consecutive months. These members are shown in Table 17. For seven of the nine members listed, the Fund's holdings were still in excess of 100 per cent of the member's quota at the end of the period, indicating that, as might have been expected, the members'

Table 17. Continuous Use of the Fund's Resources, 1946–65

Member	Number of Months During Which the Fund's Holdings of the Member's Currency Continuously Exceeded: 75 per cent of quota	100 per cent of quota
United Arab Republic [1]	111	106
Argentina	104	104
Turkey	161	101
Brazil [1]	200	98
Yugoslavia	195	95
Bolivia	151	93
Paraguay	160	69
Syrian Arab Republic	67	67
Honduras	68	64

[1] To disregard the special drawings under the arrangements for the compensatory financing of export fluctuations, granted to the United Arab Republic and Brazil, would make no difference to the table.

difficulties were cumulative. The total amount drawn by these seven members in excess of 100 per cent of their quotas was, at December 31, 1965, $388.1 million (equal to 1.9 per cent of the aggregate of Fund quotas).

SELECTION OF CURRENCIES

Drawings in inconvertible currencies

Before 1952 the only currencies that were convertible in the Fund sense, and therefore acceptable by the Fund in repurchases, were the Cuban peso, Guatemalan quetzal, Honduran lempira, Mexican peso, Panamanian balboa, Salvadoran colón, and U.S. dollar. In 1952 the Canadian dollar was added to the list, and in 1953 the Dominican peso and the Haitian gourde. No further currencies became convertible until 1961. Of those listed, only the U.S. dollar, and to a much more limited extent the Canadian dollar, are used in international trade. In consequence, drawings down to the end of 1960 were concentrated largely on the U.S. dollar, since members did not wish to obtain a currency that was inconvertible, especially since it could not be used in repurchases. Indeed, of the currencies mentioned above, the only ones drawn at all were Canadian and U.S. dollars. This meant that the Fund's holdings of all the other convertible currencies were consistently at or above 75 per cent of their quotas. No repurchases could therefore be made in any currencies except the two dollar currencies.

Of total drawings down to December 31, 1960 amounting to $3,683 million, 87 per cent were drawn in U.S. dollars, 8 per cent in sterling, and 3 per cent in deutsche mark; the remaining 2 per cent were divided between Belgian francs, Canadian dollars, Danish kroner, French francs, and Netherlands guilders (Table 18). Total repurchases amounted to $2,748 million, of which $628 million was repurchased with gold, $2,120 million with U.S. dollars, and $0.1 million with Canadian dollars.

This heavy concentration of drawings and repurchases on one currency had not been intended by the drafters of the Articles of Agreement, who had expected that the majority of countries would accept the obligations of Article VIII, Sections 2, 3, and 4, at a fairly early stage in the Fund's life, thereby making their currencies acceptable in repurchases once they had been drawn. On two occasions before 1961, accordingly, attempts were made to devise means by which members could be encouraged to draw inconvertible currencies.

This subject was among those remitted to the staff Working Party which was set up in November 1951 to draft the proposals for the use of the Fund's resources which were adopted in February 1952.[21] A suggestion was made to the Working Party by Sir George Bolton (United Kingdom) that the disadvantages of drawing an inconvertible currency might be overcome if two members, A and B, mutually agreed that if A drew B's currency, B would (after a specified lapse of time) draw a corresponding amount of A's currency, which it would sell to A for its own (B's) currency. These arrangements would, of course, restore the Fund's

[21] See above, p. 402.

holdings of both A's and B's currencies to what they had been before the drawing took place; and provided that the Fund's holdings of neither currency was, at the end of the double transaction, above 75 per cent of quota, neither would finish with a repurchase obligation (although A might have incurred one when it originally drew). Sir George's proposal was commended to the Board by the staff, who added that it would be still more attractive to members if the arrangements, instead of being bilateral, were multilateral—though this would, of course, be much more difficult to arrange.

The staff's recommendation was discussed in the Board on two occasions in 1952, but was not in general favorably received. Some Executive Directors suggested that drawings in inconvertible currencies were to be deprecated

Table 18. Drawings and Repurchases by Currency, 1946–65
(In millions of U.S. dollars or equivalents)

Currency	Drawn 1946–60	Drawn 1961–65	Total Drawn 1946–65	Repurchased 1946–65
Argentine pesos	—	16.0	16.0	—
Australian pounds	—	35.0	35.0	—
Austrian schillings	—	73.0	73.0	11.6
Belgian francs	11.4	360.5	371.9	61.8
Canadian dollars	15.0	474.5	489.5	157.8
Danish kroner	0.8	30.0	30.8	—
Deutsche mark	116.2	1,792.8	1,909.0	709.8
French francs	17.5	1,195.0	1,212.5	267.4
Italian lire	—	753.4	753.4	94.1
Japanese yen	—	241.5	241.5	49.9
Mexican pesos	—	9.5	9.5	—
Netherlands guilders	22.5	469.0	491.5	133.0
Spanish pesetas	—	128.5	128.5	—
Swedish kronor	—	157.0	157.0	22.5
Pounds sterling	297.4	353.6	651.0	96.3
U.S. dollars	3,202.8	1,689.3	4,892.1	3,572.0
Totals in currencies	3,683.5	7,778.9	11,462.4	5,176.0
Repurchases in gold				858.1
Total repurchases				6,034.1

because a country whose currency was inconvertible was *ipso facto* not in a position to extend credit to others. These Directors also thought it unlikely that bilateral balances could be reversed as quickly as would be necessary to enable the drawing to be extinguished within three to five years. Some other Directors, however, welcomed the proposal, believing that some countries with inconvertible currencies could, in fact, afford to assist other members. This point was taken up especially by Mr. de Selliers (Belgium), whose country was then extending credit through the EPU to much of Europe. However, when Mr. de Selliers commended the plan from the point of view of the country with the inconvertible currency, remarking that the drawing of its currency would enable that country to come to the Fund to draw dollars, Mr. Southard objected. He said that a member acquired the right to draw a convertible currency from the Fund by virtue of having contributed gold or convertible assets to its holdings. He also argued that it was implicit in the concept of gold tranche drawings [22] that they should be reversed by repurchases with convertible currencies.

The next occasion for a discussion of the possibility of making more use of inconvertible currencies in drawings arose in 1958. At the Annual Meeting in New Delhi that year the Governors had passed a resolution requesting the Executive Directors to examine the question of enlarging the resources of the Fund.[23] A related issue, which the Board also examined, was whether fuller use could not be made of the resources which the Fund already possessed. To assist in the examination of this question, the staff made two suggestions. One was that the Fund should apply Article XIX (*g*), which reads as follows:

> The Fund, after consultation with a member which is availing itself of the transitional arrangements under Article XIV, Section 2, may deem holdings of the currency of that member which carry specified rights of conversion into another currency or into gold to be holdings of convertible currency for the purpose of the calculation of monetary reserves.

If the Fund, using this provision, "deemed" members' holdings of specific currencies to be convertible, these holdings could be accepted in repurchases (subject to the limits set out in Article V, Section 7 (*c*)).

The other suggestion by the staff was an elaboration of that made in 1952 by Sir George Bolton; it set out a series of steps by which the Fund's holdings could be restored, after a drawing and repurchase in inconvertible currency, to exactly the same position as before the drawing.

Simultaneously, however, a further staff memorandum pointed out that in practice the use which could be made of inconvertible currencies in repurchases, even if the legal difficulties could be overcome in this way, was effectually limited by the provisions of Article V, Section 7 (*c*) (iii). The only inconvertible currency which could be accepted by the Fund without infringing the limits in that Section was the deutsche mark (to the extent of $66 million). The Research Department, which had written this last memorandum, suggested that the practical solution was to encourage a few members with large quotas to be ready to convert other members' holdings of their currencies into dollars to the extent that these other members needed to make repurchases from the Fund.

While the foregoing proposals were before the Board, the major European countries announced, on December 27, 1958, that they had taken steps to

[22] See above, pp. 402–406.

[23] Resolution 13-10, *Summary Proceedings, 1958*, p. 178. See above, p. 358.

establish the nonresident convertibility of their currencies. This in effect achieved what the Research Department had in mind, and it became unnecessary for the Board to consider further how to encourage the use of inconvertible currencies. The problem thus minimized vanished altogether when in February 1961 the main European countries accepted the obligations of Article VIII, Sections 2, 3, and 4.

Effects of convertibility

An analysis of drawings from the Fund during the calendar years 1961 through 1965 shows an entirely different picture from that prevailing in the years 1946–60, as described above. During the years 1961–65 only 22 per cent of drawings were taken in U.S. dollars. As will be seen from Table 18, the currency most used was the deutsche mark (23 per cent of all drawings), and there were also extensive drawings in French francs (15 per cent) and Italian lire (10 per cent). Repurchases were also widely spread.

Principles of selection

The distribution of drawings shown in Table 18 did not come about spontaneously. Because a large proportion of international trade is carried on in the reserve currencies, the currency which a member would normally need in the terms of Article V, Section 3 (*a*) (i), is likely to be either U.S. dollars or sterling. As soon, therefore, as the assumption of convertibility by the major European countries opened up the possibility of using other currencies for repurchases, the Managing Director represented to the Board the need to guide drawings and repurchases toward a range of currencies.

The first step was for the Legal Department to remove any doubts about the meaning of "needed for making in that currency" in Article V, Section 3 (*a*) (i). Its advice was that the phrase, interpreted against the background of Bretton Woods, must be taken to mean that a member was entitled to draw any currency which it could use, directly or indirectly, to support its exchange market. It could therefore draw a currency which was not a reserve currency in order to obtain for it, from the country issuing it, a reserve currency with which to settle its international accounts. This view was tacitly accepted by the Board.

A parallel memorandum prepared by the Research Department proposed a series of principles which should govern the Fund's use of the currencies at its disposal. This concluded that the overriding concept should be that reserves should, through the Fund, flow from countries with strong balances of payments to countries with weak ones. Ideally, therefore, each member's reserve position in the Fund (its quota less the Fund's holdings of its currency) should move in parallel with the movements in its primary reserves. In order to influence the constitution of drawings and repurchases in this direction, the Fund should

(1) ensure that future drawings were preceded by consultation as to the currencies to be drawn; (2) arrange for facilities to be available to convert currencies that were drawn into the currency directly needed by the drawing country; (3) apply the policy not necessarily to individual drawings, but in such a way as to secure the desired result from drawings in general; (4) include more currencies, rather than fewer, in any arrangements set up. At this stage the emphasis was primarily on policy with respect to drawings, and during the ensuing twelve months the members that drew from the Fund were asked to draw individual currencies in such a way as to move toward the goal outlined by the staff.

The Board returned to the subject in April 1962, and attention was then focused also on repurchases, partly as a result of Mr. de Largentaye's protest against a voluntary repurchase by the United Kingdom in U.S. dollars.[24] The staff then suggested that a reasonable starting point for future policy would be to prescribe that currencies to be used in drawings should be selected in proportion to the primary reserves of the countries whose currencies were being used, and that currencies for repurchases should be accepted proportionately to each member's position in the Fund.

Some attention was devoted in the discussion of these proposals to the "reversal" technique, which had been suggested as a solution to the problem of directing drawings toward appropriate currencies. This technique consisted in allowing a member whose currency was drawn, if it considered that this had been done to excess, to draw in turn on the Fund, so as to offset the use of its currency. The staff deprecated this plan because of its limited usefulness. For one thing, the member that sought to draw in order to offset a drawing would itself have to make representations to the Fund within the terms of Article V, Section 3 (*a*), except to the limited extent that it might be able to have recourse to Article VI, Section 2.[25] Also, any drawing would involve the member concerned in paying a service charge.

In the event, the Board agreed in July 1962 on a lengthy statement which included an explanation of the technique that had been adopted and an elaboration of the criteria used in the selection of currencies.[26] The technique of selection, as it has since been used, may be summarized as follows:

(1) A quarterly budget of currencies to be used in purchases and to be received in repurchases is formulated as described in (5) to (10) below. The basis for this budget is a rough estimate of the requests for drawings that might be made in the coming quarter, and a forecast of the repurchase obligations which are due to be fulfilled during the quarter.

(2) The budget thus evolved is discussed by the Managing Director with the Executive Directors appointed or elected by the countries whose currencies are

[24] See above, p. 445.
[25] See above, p. 411.
[26] E.B. Decision No. 1371-(62/36), July 20, 1962; below, Vol. III, p. 235.

included in it. Subject to any modifications made as a result of these discussions, the figures are used to guide members, when drawing or repurchasing, toward the use of the listed currencies in such a manner as to approach the budget targets, taking the transactions for the period as a whole.

(3) Any drawings or repurchases that are too large to be accommodated in the budget are the subject of separate consultations with respect to the currencies to be used. For very large drawings other considerations arise—for example, it may be decided to replenish the Fund's holdings of certain currencies by the sale of gold,[27] or to activate the General Arrangements to Borrow.[28] Even for these transactions, however, the principles in (5) to (10) below guide the decisions taken.

(4) For drawings that are large, but not too large to be met within the budget, a distribution of currencies is worked out individually along the same lines. Very small drawings are arranged in the reserve currency of the member drawing; this is not only operationally convenient, but makes it unnecessary for a small country to handle an unfamiliar currency. For intermediate drawings the procedure is regarded as applying to the transactions of the quarter as a whole rather than to any individual drawing; the currencies used in any one such drawing, therefore, have no great significance.

The principles which guide the selection of currencies, and the decision as to the amounts of each to be used, are as follows:

(5) A relatively short, but growing, list is maintained of countries whose balances of payments and reserves would normally permit them to see a gradual increase in their reserve positions in the Fund, and with which suitable arrangements have been worked out for conversion of amounts of their currencies when drawn. For the most part, these countries have accepted Article VIII and have reserves which exceed $500 million and (except for those of the United Kingdom) are large in relation to their quotas.

(6) On the occasion of any particular budget or large drawing, a few countries may be eliminated from this list on short-term balance of payments grounds, as indicated by the exchange rates and by changes in their reserves. Current and long-term capital accounts are watched as a check. Such countries are eliminated, however, only if they appear likely to have to draw on the Fund.

(7) As between the different currencies thus available, drawings are allocated in proportion to the size of the members' reserves (excluding their reserve positions in the Fund).

(8) Some restraint may be imposed should the Fund's holdings of a particular currency fall very low, but this is disregarded if it is possible to borrow that currency under the GAB.

---

27 See below, p. 455.

28 See above, p. 376.

(9) The currencies thus selected will also be available for use in repurchases, if and when the Fund's holdings of them fall below 75 per cent of the quotas of the members issuing them, provided that these members have accepted Article VIII. The budget for repurchases allocates the aggregate commitments expected to arise during the quarter among the acceptable currencies in proportion to each member's reserve position in the Fund.

(10) The long-term aim is to equalize the ratios between each member's reserve position in the Fund on the one hand and its official gold and foreign exchange holdings on the other. The former quantity is defined as the gold tranche drawings which the member could make plus the amount of any indebtedness of the Fund which is readily repayable to the member under a loan agreement (including the GAB and any similar arrangement with one or more members).

U.S. technical drawings

At an early stage, the application of the foregoing procedure to repurchases came up against the difficulty that the Fund's holdings of U.S. dollars had reached 75 per cent of the U.S. quota. When dollars thus became no longer acceptable in repurchases, countries holding dollars and needing to make repurchases could do so only by exchanging them for gold in the United States, or by purchasing with them currencies which the Fund could accept. Since these purchases would usually be those of European creditor countries, the result could be a similar drain on U.S. gold.

In these circumstances the United States offered to draw on the Fund, not for its own needs but in order to obtain a supply of currencies which the Fund could accept; these it would exchange for dollars at the request of members that had repurchases to make and wished to do so. Since currencies thus drawn by the United States would be promptly repaid to the Fund by the member making the repurchases, it was immaterial which currencies were drawn, provided that the Fund's holdings of them were not in excess of 75 per cent of the issuing members' quotas. The United States first drew from the Fund early in 1964, and from then until the end of 1965 it drew and made available for conversion a total equivalent to $660 million in eight different currencies. The arrangement was terminated at the end of 1966.

Replenishment

Passing reference was made above to the possibility that the Fund might acquire additional supplies of currencies needed to meet requests for drawings by replenishing its holdings of these currencies and by activating the GAB. The Fund's powers for these purposes have been discussed in Chapter 17. Here we shall be concerned with the principles by which the Fund has selected the amounts of currencies to be acquired.

Until 1961 the only currency of which any substantial use was made was, as has been shown, the U.S. dollar. As a result of heavy drawings in 1956, the Fund's holdings of U.S. dollars fell to $1,142 million at the end of that year, while at the same date commitments under stand-by arrangements totaled $1,117 million. The Board decided that it was desirable to replenish the holdings of dollars, and sold $300 million of gold to the United States for this purpose in January 1957. Four months later, when the Fund's holdings of U.S. dollars had been further reduced to $977 million, and commitments under stand-by arrangements totaled $969 million, a second sale of $300 million of gold was authorized. Those were the only occasions on which the Fund has replenished its holdings of a single currency, until it borrowed Italian lire in 1966.

In August 1961 the United Kingdom came to the Fund for a drawing of $1,500 million. The Board then decided that it would replenish the Fund's resources of each of the nine currencies being used to meet the drawing (Belgian francs, Canadian dollars, French francs, deutsche mark, Italian lire, Japanese yen, Netherlands guilders, Swedish kronor, and U.S. dollars) to the extent of one third of the use made of each. This was done by purchasing these currencies for gold.

In July 1964 the United Kingdom renewed a stand-by arrangement for $1 billion from the Fund, and within a few weeks it became apparent to the staff that a substantial drawing under that arrangement was to be expected. The Fund's holdings of the principal continental European currencies were at a low ebb, and there would clearly have to be some reinforcement of them if the drawing was to be met without reducing the holdings to injudiciously low levels. In contrast to the situation in 1961, the GAB had become available in 1963, and during the Annual Meeting, 1964, the Managing Director discussed with the participants in the GAB the possibility of activating these Arrangements when the British request for a drawing should eventuate.

When, therefore, the United Kingdom presented its request to draw the whole amount under the stand-by arrangement late in November, a comprehensive plan was worked out, as shown in Table 19. The principal points to be noted in the table concern the proportions between the constituent columns and the totals.

(*a*) The proportion of the total obtained from sales of gold was one fourth. At the meeting of the Board on November 20, Mr. Garland (Australia) and Mr. Anjaria (India) questioned whether it was necessary to sell as much as $250 million of gold since, in contrast to 1961, currencies could be obtained by drawing on the GAB. The Managing Director, in reply, said that the proportion obtained by the sale of gold was a matter of judgment; he and the staff believed that one fourth was appropriate. No other Director raised the point. As between the different currencies, the amounts obtained by the sale of gold were related not to the amounts drawn on this occasion but to the cumulative total of net drawings outstanding, including those to be provided for the United Kingdom.

(*b*) The $750 million needed in addition to the currencies obtained by the sale of gold was apportioned among the countries whose currencies were to be drawn in a rough ratio to their holdings of gold and foreign exchange. As

Table 19. Constitution of Drawing by United Kingdom, December 1964
(In millions of U.S. dollars or equivalents)

Currencies	From Fund Holdings	From GAB	From Sales of Gold	Total
Austrian schillings	20	—	8	28
Belgian francs	10	30	17	57
Canadian dollars	45	15	9	69
Deutsche mark	—	180	93	273
French francs	—	100	63	163
Italian lire	15	5	3	23
Japanese yen	20	20	14	54
Netherlands guilders	—	40	26	66
Spanish pesetas	30	—	10	40
Swedish kronor	5	15	7	27
U.S. dollars	200	—	—	200
Total	345	405	250	1,000

between the Fund's holdings and borrowings under the GAB, the original intention had been to borrow the full amount of the five currencies of which the Fund's holdings were lowest (Belgian francs, deutsche mark, French francs, Netherlands guilders, and Swedish kronor), and to obtain what was required of the other currencies wholly from the Fund's holdings. The signatories of the GAB, however, preferred that the Fund should borrow from each participant except the United Kingdom itself, even if only a token sum were borrowed. The reason for this was partly a wish for solidarity among the participants, and partly a doubt whether the terms of the agreement between the participants which was embodied in Mr. Baumgartner's letters [29] would permit a member of the Group of Ten to vote on the proposal to activate the GAB if its currency was not borrowed.

The Managing Director was prepared to agree to the proposal that the currency of each participant should be borrowed to a greater or lesser degree, except that he demurred at the Fund's borrowing any currency of which its holdings would exceed 75 per cent of the member's quota after the drawing. Until October this would have excluded any borrowing of Canadian dollars, as well as of U.S. dollars, but at the end of that month, prompted by a large increase in its reserves, Canada repurchased its currency from the Fund to an extent that reduced the Fund's holdings to 75 per cent of quota. The final

[29] See above, Vol. I, p. 512; below, pp. 520–21 of this volume; and below, Vol. III, p. 252.

allocation of currencies between the Fund's holdings and borrowings under the GAB was made on a sliding scale. For the three currencies of which the Fund's holdings were smallest in relation to quota (ranging from 20 per cent to 42 per cent), the whole sum needed was borrowed; for two currencies, of which the Fund's holdings were 52–55 per cent of quota, the percentage borrowed was 75; for one, of which the Fund's holdings were at 64 per cent of quota, the percentage borrowed was 50; and for the other two, of which the Fund's holdings were at 75 per cent, the percentage borrowed was 25. The appropriate sums were transferred to the United Kingdom's account on December 2.

In February 1965 it became known to the Fund staff that some $3 billion of credits to the United Kingdom, which had been arranged in the previous November concurrently with the drawing, would expire in May. This made it likely that the British authorities would then seek a further drawing to enable them to repay such of the credits as had been used. The staff accordingly gave thought to a possible distribution of currencies to make up a drawing of $1 billion or $1.5 billion.

On April 21 the Managing Director handed to the Executive Directors appointed or elected by the ten countries in the GAB a possible schedule of currencies to be drawn from the Fund's holdings, to be borrowed, and to be obtained from the sale of gold. As it appeared probable that the United Kingdom would wish to draw as much as it could without increasing the Fund's holdings of sterling beyond 200 per cent of the British quota, the draft schedule assumed a drawing of $1,400 million. The main proposal was that the amount of gold sold should be one fourth of the total, as in 1964. This would yield $350 million. It was planned to use $200 million from the Fund's holdings of U.S. dollars, and $25 million each from its holdings of Danish kroner and Spanish pesetas—the substitution of the kroner for Austrian schillings being due to the improvement in the Danish balance of payments, and the deterioration of that of Austria, since the 1964 drawing. The remainder ($800 million) of the drawing would be found in the currencies of the members of the GAB other than the United States and the United Kingdom. The division between drawings on the Fund's holdings and drawings on borrowed funds would depend (as in 1964) on the proportion of the Fund's holdings of each currency to that country's quota.

On April 29 the United Kingdom, which had by then used up $1.1 billion of the $3 billion of inter-central-bank credits, requested a drawing of $1.4 billion. On the same day the Managing Director had a further discussion with the Executive Directors from the countries that were signatories of the GAB, preparatory to issuing a formal proposal for its activation. At this meeting some criticism developed of the plans put forward on April 21. Specifically, it was urged that a larger proportion of the total should be found by the sale of gold, preferably one third, as had been done for the British drawing in August 1961. Directors also wished more use to be made of the Fund's holdings and less of currencies borrowed through the GAB. In consequence, a revised plan was immediately prepared and cleared with the Executive Directors concerned. This provided for a sale of gold amounting to $400 million and for an increase from $187 million (out of $800 million) to $225 million (out of $750 million) in the amount to be taken from the Fund's holdings of the currencies of the GAB countries other than the United States. The proportion of the total needed of each currency that was borrowed under the GAB was again related inversely to the proportion of the Fund's holdings of that currency to the country's quota; it varied from 93 per cent for France and Germany down to 44–45 per cent for Canada, Italy, and Japan. The drawing was approved on May 12; its constitution is shown in Table 20.

Table 20. Constitution of Drawing by United Kingdom, May 1965
(In millions of U.S. dollars or equivalents)

Currencies	From Fund Holdings	From GAB	From Sales of Gold	Total
Belgian francs	17.5	37.5	27.5	82.5
Canadian dollars	45.0	35.0	27.5	107.5
Danish kroner	25.0	—	5.0	30.0
Deutsche mark	12.5	167.5	132.5	312.5
French francs	10.0	140.0	92.5	242.5
Italian lire	85.0	65.0	32.5	182.5
Japanese yen	30.0	25.0	22.5	77.5
Netherlands guilders	17.5	37.5	32.5	87.5
Spanish pesetas	25.0	—	15.0	40.0
Swedish kronor	7.5	17.5	12.5	37.5
U.S. dollars	200.0	—	—	200.0
Total	475.0	525.0	400.00	1,400.0

Results of policy

Despite the difficulty created by the unavailability of U.S. dollars, the policy worked out in 1961 has been successful in reducing the disparities which previously existed between the ratios of the reserve positions in the Fund to official gold and foreign exchange reserves for those members whose currencies have been used for repurchases. Table 21 shows these ratios as they were shortly before the Managing Director made his statement and as they were at the end of the period covered by this volume. It will be seen that, before the policy for the selection of currencies was introduced, the ratios between the members' positions in the Fund and their gold and foreign exchange reserves varied from 2 to 10 per cent. By 1965 the range of ratios had been narrowed, for most of the countries concerned, to 13–17 per cent. The low ratios for the other two countries, Austria and Spain, were due to the imminent exhaustion of the Fund's holdings of their currencies.

Table 21. Ratio of Reserve Position in the Fund to Official Gold and Foreign Exchange Holdings: Selected Countries, as at December 31, 1960 and 1965 [1]

(In per cent)

Country	Ratio, 1960	Ratio, 1965
Austria	3	6
Belgium	6	15
Canada	8	13
France	10	16
Germany	5	17
Italy	2	13
Japan	7	13
Netherlands	7	17
Spain	—	11
Sweden	8	17

[1] The countries selected are those whose currencies have been used regularly, during most of the period, for drawings in accordance with the criteria for the selection of currencies. The United Kingdom and the United States are excluded because of balance of payments weakness. Australia, Denmark, and Mexico are omitted because their currencies were not considered for use until 1965.

STATISTICAL APPENDIX

Table 22 details the amounts drawn by each member of the Fund in each calendar year from 1947 through 1965.

Table 23 shows the amounts of the drawings listed in Table 22 that were repurchased by each member in each year. The final column shows the amount (if any) of the drawings which was still outstanding on December 31, 1965. The following points should be noted:

(*a*) The figure in the last column does not necessarily represent the difference between the amounts drawn and the amounts repurchased by the member. The reason is that if any member A's currency is drawn by another member, the Fund's holdings of A's currency are reduced; if A has itself drawn, the amount that it has to repurchase is correspondingly reduced. (This has affected especially the United States.)

(*b*) The absence of a figure in the last column means only that any drawings have been wholly repurchased. The Fund's holdings of the member's currency may be below, at, or above 75 per cent of the member's quota. They may be below 75 per cent if other members have drawn that currency, or above 75 per cent if the member concerned has not yet paid 25 per cent of its subscription in gold.

Details of stand-by arrangements are appended to Chapter 20.

Table 22. Drawings from the Fund, Calendar Years 1947–65 [1]
(In millions of U.S. dollars)

Member	1947	1948	1949	1950	1951	1952	1953	1954	1955	1956
Afghanistan	•	•	•	•	•	•	•	•	—	—
Algeria	•	•	•	•	•	•	•	•	•	•
Argentina	•	•	•	•	•	•	•	•	•	—
Australia	—	—	20.0	—	—	30.0	—	—	—	—
Austria	•	—	—	—	—	—	—	—	—	—
Belgium	11.0	22.0	—	—	—	—	—	—	—	—
Bolivia	—	—	—	—	—	—	2.5	—	—	3.0*
Brazil	—	—	37.5	—	28.0	37.5	65.5	—	—	—
Burma	•	•	•	•	•	—	—	—	—	15.0
Burundi	•	•	•	•	•	•	•	•	•	•
Cameroon	•	•	•	•	•	•	•	•	•	•
Canada	—	—	—	—	—	—	—	—	—	—
Central African Rep.	•	•	•	•	•	•	•	•	•	•
Ceylon	•	•	•	—	—	—	—	—	—	—
Chad	•	•	•	•	•	•	•	•	•	•
Chile	8.8	—	—	—	—	—	12.5	—	—	—
China	—	—	—	—	—	—	—	—	—	—
Colombia	—	—	—	—	—	—	—	25.0	—	—
Congo (Brazzaville)	•	•	•	•	•	•	•	•	•	•
Congo, Dem. Rep.	•	•	•	•	•	•	•	•	•	•
Costa Rica	—	1.2	—	—	—	—	—	—	—	—
Cuba	—	—	—	—	—	—	—	—	—	12.5
Cyprus	•	•	•	•	•	•	•	•	•	•
Czechoslovakia	—	6.0	—	—	—	—	—	—	—	•
Dahomey	•	•	•	•	•	•	•	•	•	•
Denmark	3.4	6.8	—	—	—	—	—	—	—	—
Dominican Rep.	—	—	—	—	—	—	—	—	—	—
Ecuador	—	—	—	—	—	—	—	—	—	—
El Salvador	—	—	—	—	—	—	—	—	—	2.5
Ethiopia	—	0.3	0.3	—	—	—	—	—	—	—
Finland	•	—	—	—	—	4.5	5.0*	—	—	—
France	125.0	—	—	—	—	—	—	—	—	—
Gabon	•	•	•	•	•	•	•	•	•	•
Germany	•	•	•	•	•	—	—	—	—	—
Ghana	•	•	•	•	•	•	•	•	•	•
Greece	—	—	—	—	—	—	—	—	—	—
Guatemala	—	—	—	—	—	—	—	—	—	—
Guinea	•	•	•	•	•	•	•	•	•	•
Haiti	•	•	•	•	•	•	—	—	—	—
Honduras	—	—	—	—	—	—	—	—	—	—
Iceland	—	—	—	—	—	—	—	—	—	—
India	—	68.3	31.7	—	—	—	—	—	—	—
Indonesia	•	•	•	•	•	•	•	15.0	—	55.0
Iran	—	—	—	—	6.6	2.2	—	—	17.5	19.7*
Iraq	—	—	—	—	—	—	—	—	—	—
Ireland	•	•	•	•	•	•	•	•	•	•
Israel	•	•	•	•	•	•	•	—	—	—
Italy	—	—	—	—	—	—	—	—	—	—
Ivory Coast	•	•	•	•	•	•	•	•	•	•
Jamaica	•	•	•	•	•	•	•	•	•	•
Japan	•	•	•	•	•	—	124.0	—	—	—
Jordan	•	•	•	•	•	—	—	—	—	—
Kenya	•	•	•	•	•	•	•	•	•	•
Korea	•	•	•	•	•	•	•	•	—	—
Kuwait	•	•	•	•	•	•	•	•	•	•

Footnote on page 462.

Table 22. Drawings from the Fund, Calendar Years 1947–65 [1]

(In millions of U.S. dollars)

1957	1958	1959	1960	1961	1962	1963	1964	1965	Total	Member
—	—	—	—	—	—	5.6	5.6	1.7*	12.9	Afghanistan
—	—	—	—	—	—	—	—	—	—	Algeria
75.0	—	72.5*	70.0*	60.0*	50.0*	50.0*	—	—	377.5	Argentina
—	—	—	—	175.0	—	—	—	—	225.0	Australia
—	—	—	—	—	—	—	—	—	—	Austria
50.0	—	—	—	—	—	—	—	—	83.0	Belgium
1.0*	2.0*	3.4*	1.0*	2.0*	3.5*	4.0*	—	—	22.4	Bolivia
37.5	54.8*	—	47.7	60.0*	—	60.0	—	75.0*	503.4	Brazil
—	—	—	—	—	—	—	—	—	15.0	Burma
•	•	•	•	•	•	—	—	2.0*	2.0	Burundi
•	•	•	•	•	•	—	—	—	—	Cameroon
—	—	—	—	—	300.0	—	—	—	300.0	Canada
•	•	•	•	•	•	—	—	—	—	Central African Rep.
—	—	—	—	11.2	11.2	—	—	23.0*	45.5	Ceylon
•	•	•	•	•	•	—	—	—	—	Chad
31.1*	10.6*	0.7*	—	76.0*	—	40.0*	20.0*	36.0*	235.7	Chile
—	—	—	—	—	—	—	—	—	—	China
5.0*	10.0*	—	—	65.0*	7.5*	48.5*	7.5*	—	168.5	Colombia
•	•	•	•	•	•	—	—	—	—	Congo (Brazzaville)
•	•	•	•	•	•	—	—	—	—	Congo, Dem. Rep.
—	—	—	—	7.5*	2.5*	10.0*	—	10.0*	31.2	Costa Rica
35.0*	25.0	—	—	—	—	—	—	•	72.5	Cuba
•	•	•	•	—	—	—	2.0	—	2.0	Cyprus
•	•	•	•	•	•	•	•	•	6.0	Czechoslovakia
•	•	•	•	•	•	—	—	—	—	Dahomey
34.0	—	—	—	—	—	—	—	—	44.2	Denmark
—	—	—	9.0*	—	—	—	15.0*	5.0*	29.0	Dominican Rep.
5.0	—	—	—	14.0*	4.0*	—	—	11.0*	34.0	Ecuador
—	—	5.5*	13.2*	8.0*	—	—	—	—	29.2	El Salvador
—	—	—	—	—	—	—	—	—	0.6	Ethiopia
—	—	—	—	—	—	—	—	—	9.5	Finland
262.5*	131.2*	—	—	—	—	—	—	—	518.8	France
•	•	•	•	•	•	—	—	—	—	Gabon
—	—		—	—	—	—	—	—	—	Germany
—	—	—	—	—	14.2	—	—	—	14.2	Ghana
—	—	—	—	—	—	—	—	—	—	Greece
—	—	—	—	—	5.0*	—	—	5.0	10.0	Guatemala
•	•	•	•	•	•	—	—	—	—	Guinea
1.0	2.5*	1.9*	—	1.5*	3.2*	5.0*	3.0*	2.5*	20.7	Haiti
6.2*	—	3.8*	5.0*	2.4*	5.0*	2.5*	5.0*	—	30.0	Honduras
—	—	—	6.8*	—	—	—	—	—	6.8	Iceland
200.0*	—	—	—	250.0	25.0*	—	—	200.0*	775.0	India
—	—	—	—	61.2*	21.2*	20.0*	—	—	172.5	Indonesia
—	—	5.0	45.0*	7.5*	—	—	17.5	—	121.0	Iran
—	—	—	—	—	—	—	—	—	—	Iraq
—	—	—	—	—	—	—	—	—	—	Ireland
3.8	—	—	—	—	—	—	12.5	—	16.2	Israel
—	—	—	—	—	—	—	225.0	—	225.0	Italy
•	•	•	•	•	•	—	—	—	—	Ivory Coast
•	•	•	•	•	•	—	—	—	—	Jamaica
125.0	—	—	—	—	—	—	—	—	249.0	Japan
—	—	—	—	—	—	—	—	—	—	Jordan
•	•	•	•	•	•	•	—	—	—	Kenya
—	—	—	—	—	—	—	—	—	—	Korea
•	•	•	•	•	—	—	—	—	—	Kuwait

Table 22 *(concluded)*. Drawings from the Fund, Calendar Years 1947–65 [1]
(In millions of U.S. dollars)

Member	1947	1948	1949	1950	1951	1952	1953	1954	1955	1956
Laos	•	•	•	•	•	•	•	•	•	•
Lebanon	—	—	—	—	—	—	—	—	—	—
Liberia	•	•	•	•	•	•	•	•	•	•
Libya	•	•	•	•	•	•	•	•	•	•
Luxembourg	—	—	—	—	—	—	—	—	—	—
Malagasy Rep.	•	•	•	•	•	•	•	•	•	•
Malawi	•	•	•	•	•	•	•	•	•	•
Malaysia	•	•	•	•	•	•	•	•	•	•
Mali	•	•	•	•	•	•	•	•	•	•
Mauritania	•	•	•	•	•	•	•	•	•	•
Mexico	22.5	—	—	—	—	—	—	22.5*	—	—
Morocco	•	•	•	•	•	•	•	•	•	•
Nepal	•	•	•	•	•	•	•	•	•	•
Netherlands	52.0	23.3	—	—	—	—	—	—	—	—
New Zealand	•	•	•	•	•	•	•	•	•	•
Nicaragua	—	0.5	—	—	—	—	—	—	—	1.9*
Niger	•	•	•	•	•	•	•	•	•	•
Nigeria	•	•	•	•	•	•	•	•	•	•
Norway	—	9.6	—	—	—	—	—	—	—	—
Pakistan	•	•	•	—	—	—	—	—	—	—
Panama	—	—	—	—	—	—	—	—	—	—
Paraguay	—	—	—	—	—	0.9	—	—	—	1.5
Peru	—	—	—	—	—	—	—	—	—	—
Philippines	—	—	—	—	—	—	—	—	10.0	5.0
Poland	—	—	—	—	•	•	•	•	•	•
Portugal	•	•	•	•	•	•	•	•	•	•
Rwanda	•	•	•	•	•	•	•	•	•	•
Saudi Arabia	•	•	•	•	•	•	•	•	•	•
Senegal	•	•	•	•	•	•	•	•	•	•
Sierra Leone	•	•	•	•	•	•	•	•	•	•
Somalia	•	•	•	•	•	•	•	•	•	•
South Africa	—	10.0	—	—	—	—	—	—	—	—
Spain	•	•	•	•	•	•	•	•	•	•
Sudan	•	•	•	•	•	•	•	•	•	•
Sweden	•	•	•	•	—	—	—	—	—	—
Syrian Arab Rep.	—	—	—	—	—	—	—	—	—	—
Tanzania	•	•	•	•	•	•	•	•	•	•
Thailand	•	•	—	—	—	—	—	—	—	—
Togo	•	•	•	•	•	•	•	•	•	•
Trinidad & Tobago	•	•	•	•	•	•	•	•	•	•
Tunisia	•	•	•	•	•	•	•	•	•	•
Turkey	5.0	—	—	—	—	10.0	20.0	—	—	—
Uganda	•	•	•	•	•	•	•	•	•	•
United Arab Rep.	—	—	3.0	—	—	—	—	—	—	15.0
United Kingdom	240.0	60.0	—	—	—	—	—	—	—	561.5
United States	—	—	—	—	—	—	—	—	—	—
Upper Volta	•	•	•	•	•	•	•	•	•	•
Uruguay	—	—	—	—	—	—	—	—	—	—
Venezuela	—	—	—	—	—	—	—	—	—	—
Viet-Nam	•	•	•	•	•	•	•	•	•	—
Yugoslavia	—	—	9.0	—	—	—	—	—	—	—
Zambia	•	•	•	•	•	•	•	•	•	•
Totals	467.7	208.0	101.5	—	34.6	85.1	229.5	62.5	27.5	692.6

[1] A dot (•) indicates that the country was not a member at the time; a dash (—) indicates that no drawing was made; an asterisk (*) designates drawings made wholly or partly under stand-by arrangements.

Table 22 *(concluded)*. Drawings from the Fund, Calendar Years 1947–65 [1]

(In millions of U.S. dollars)

1957	1958	1959	1960	1961	1962	1963	1964	1965	Total	Member
•	•	•	•	—	—	—	—	—	—	Laos
—	—	—	—	—	—	—	—	—	—	Lebanon
•	•	•	•	•	—	3.6*	3.8*	3.0*	10.4	Liberia
•	—	—	—	—	—	—	—	—	—	Libya
—	—	—	—	—	—	—	—	—	—	Luxembourg
•	•	•	•	•	•	—	—	—	—	Malagasy Rep.
•	•	•	•	•	•	•	•	—	—	Malawi
•	—	—	—	—	—	—	—	—	—	Malaysia
•	•	•	•	•	•	—	5.0*	5.0*	9.9	Mali
•	•	•	•	•	•	—	—	—	—	Mauritania
—	—	22.5*	—	45.0*	—	—	—	—	112.5	Mexico
•	—	—	—	—	—	—	13.1	—	13.1	Morocco
•	•	•	•	—	—	—	—	—	—	Nepal
68.8	—	—	—	—	—	—	—	—	144.1	Netherlands
•	•	•	•	—	—	—	—	62.0	62.0	New Zealand
3.8*	1.9*	—	—	6.0*	—	11.5*	12.0*	—	37.5	Nicaragua
•	•	•	•	•	•	—	—	—	—	Niger
•	•	•	•	—	—	—	—	—	—	Nigeria
—	—	—	—	—	—	—	—	—	9.6	Norway
—	—	—	12.5	—	—	—	—	53.5*	66.0	Pakistan
—	—	—	—	—	—	—	—	2.7	2.7	Panama
4.0*	0.8*	—	1.0*	—	—	—	—	—	8.1	Paraguay
—	10.0*	4.5*	—	—	—	—	—	—	14.5	Peru
—	—	8.8	6.2	—	28.3	—	—	—	58.3	Philippines
•	•	•	•	•	•	•	•	•	—	Poland
•	•	•	•	—	—	—	—	—	—	Portugal
•	•	•	•	•	•	—	—	—	—	Rwanda
—	—	—	—	—	—	—	—	—	—	Saudi Arabia
•	•	•	•	•	—	—	—	—	—	Senegal
•	•	•	•	•	—	—	—	—	—	Sierra Leone
•	•	•	•	•	—	—	4.7*	5.6*	10.3	Somalia
—	36.2*	—	12.5	25.0	—	—	—	—	83.7	South Africa
•	—	50.0	—	—	—	—	—	—	50.0	Spain
—	5.0	1.2	—	—	—	—	5.4	18.8	30.4	Sudan
—	—	—	—	—	—	—	—	—	—	Sweden
—	—	—	15.0*	—	5.6*	—	18.5*	—	39.1	Syrian Arab Rep.
•	•	•	•	•	—	—	—	—	—	Tanzania
—	—	—	—	—	—	—	—	—	—	Thailand
•	•	•	•	•	—	—	—	—	—	Togo
•	•	•	•	•	•	—	—	—	—	Trinidad & Tobago
•	—	—	—	—	—	—	5.2*	11.8*	17.0	Tunisia
13.5	25.0	—	—	16.0*	15.0*	21.5*	19.0*	—	145.0	Turkey
•	•	•	•	•	•	—	—	—	—	Uganda
15.0	—	—	34.8	10.0	67.4*	21.0	25.0*	15.0*	206.2	United Arab Rep.
—	—	—	—	1,500.0	—	—	1,000.0*	1,400.0*	4,761.5	United Kingdom
—	—	—	—	—	—	—	525.0*	435.0*	960.0	United States
•	•	•	•	•	•	—	—	—	—	Upper Volta
—	—	—	—	—	15.0*	—	—	—	15.0	Uruguay
—	—	—	—	—	—	—	—	—	—	Venezuela
—	—	—	—	—	—	—	—	—	—	Viet-Nam
—	22.9	—	—	75.0*	—	30.0	—	50.0*	186.9	Yugoslavia
•	•	•	•	•	•	•	•	—	—	Zambia
977.1	337.9	179.8	279.8	2,478.5	583.8	333.2	1,949.8	2,433.5	11,462.4	Totals

Table 23. Repurchases of Drawings, Calendar Years 1947–65 [1]

(In millions of U.S. dollars)

Member	1947	1948	1949	1950	1951	1952	1953	1954	1955	1956
Afghanistan	•	•	•	•	•	•	•	•	—	—
Algeria	•	•	•	•	•	•	•	•	•	•
Argentina	•	•	•	•	•	•	•	•	•	—
Australia	—	—	—	—	—	—	12.0	24.0	14.0	—
Austria	•	—	—	—	—	—	—	—	—	—
Belgium	—	—	0.9	20.7	—	—	—	—	—	—
Bolivia	—	—	—	—	—	—	—	—	—	—
Brazil	—	—	—	—	—	65.5	37.5	—	—	28.0
Burma	•	•	•	•	•	—	—	—	—	—
Burundi	•	•	•	•	•	•	•	•	•	•
Cameroon	•	•	•	•	•	•	•	•	•	•
Canada	—	—	—	—	—	—	—	—	—	—
Central African Rep.	•	•	•	•	•	•	•	•	•	•
Ceylon	•	•	•	—	—	—	—	—	—	—
Chad	•	•	•	•	•	•	•	•	•	•
Chile	—	—	—	—	3.4	3.7	1.7	—	—	0.2
China	—	—	—	—	—	—	—	—	—	—
Colombia	—	—	—	—	—	—	—	—	—	—
Congo (Brazzaville)	•	•	•	•	•	•	•	•	•	•
Congo, Dem. Rep.	•	•	•	•	•	•	•	•	•	•
Costa Rica	—	—	0.9	0.3	—	—	—	—	—	—
Cuba	—	—	—	—	—	—	—	—	—	—
Cyprus	•	•	•	•	•	•	•	•	•	•
Czechoslovakia	—	—	—	—	—	—	—	—	2.0	0.7
Dahomey	•	•	•	•	•	•	•	•	•	•
Denmark	—	—	—	—	—	—	—	—	10.2	—
Dominican Rep.	—	—	—	—	—	—	—	—	—	—
Ecuador	—	—	—	—	—	—	—	—	—	—
El Salvador	—	—	—	—	—	—	—	—	—	—
Ethiopia	—	—	—	0.3	0.3	—	—	—	—	—
Finland	•	—	—	—	—	—	2.0	4.5	3.0	—
France	—	—	—	—	—	—	—	20.0	60.0	45.0
Gabon	•	•	•	•	•	•	•	•	•	•
Germany	•	•	•	•	•	—	—	—	—	—
Ghana	•	•	•	•	•	•	•	•	•	•
Greece	—	—	—	—	—	—	—	—	—	—
Guatemala	—	—	—	—	—	—	—	—	—	—
Guinea	•	•	•	•	•	•	•	•	•	•
Haiti	•	•	•	•	•	•	—	—	—	—
Honduras	—	—	—	—	—	—	—	—	—	—
Iceland	—	—	—	—	—	—	—	—	—	—
India	—	—	—	—	—	—	—	46.7	40.7	12.5
Indonesia	•	•	•	•	•	•	•	—	—	15.0
Iran	—	—	—	—	—	—	—	—	8.7	11.9
Iraq	—	—	—	—	—	—	—	—	—	—
Ireland	•	•	•	•	•	•	•	•	•	•
Israel	•	•	•	•	•	•	•	—	—	—
Italy	—	—	—	—	—	—	—	—	—	—
Ivory Coast	•	•	•	•	•	•	•	•	•	•
Jamaica	•	•	•	•	•	•	•	•	•	•
Japan	•	•	•	•	•	—	61.6	—	62.4	—
Jordan	•	•	•	•	•	—	—	—	—	—
Kenya	•	•	•	•	•	•	•	•	•	•
Korea	•	•	•	•	•	•	•	•	—	—
Kuwait	•	•	•	•	•	•	•	•	•	•

Footnotes on page 466.

Table 23. Repurchases of Drawings, Calendar Years 1947–65 [1]

(In millions of U.S. dollars)

1957	1958	1959	1960	1961	1962	1963	1964	1965	Total	Member	Outstanding [2]
—	—	—	—	—	—	—	—	—	—	Afghanistan	12.9
—	—	—	—	—	—	—	—	—	—	Algeria	
—	—	—	21.5	13.0	59.0	36.0	42.0	44.0	215.5	Argentina	146.0
—	—	—	—	—	175.0	—	—	—	225.0	Australia	
—	—	—	—	—	—	—	—	—	—	Austria	
—	50.0	—	—	—	—	—	—	—	71.6	Belgium	
—	—	1.0	2.5	4.0	2.3	2.9	4.8	1.0	18.4	Bolivia	4.0
—	17.2	20.2	—	20.0	17.5	55.5	28.0	55.0	344.5	Brazil	159.0
—	3.0	4.0	4.0	4.0	—	—	—	—	15.0	Burma	
•	•	•	•	•	•	—	—	2.0	2.0	Burundi	
•	•	•	•	•	•	—	—	—	—	Cameroon	
—	—	—	—	—	—	79.7	166.0	—	245.7	Canada	
•	•	•	•	•	•	—	—	—	—	Central African Rep.	
—	—	—	—	—	—	—	—	7.5	7.5	Ceylon	38.0
•	•	•	•	•	•	—	—	—	—	Chad	
12.3	—	0.7	12.4	16.7	12.7	—	10.0	37.0	110.7	Chile	125.0
—	—	—	—	—	—	—	—	—	—	China	
5.0	5.0	15.0	15.0	—	—	—	20.0	24.0	84.0	Colombia	84.5
•	•	•	•	•	•	—	—	—	—	Congo (Brazzaville)	
•	•	•	•	•	•	—	—	—	—	Congo, Dem. Rep.	
—	—	—	—	—	6.6	0.4	1.3	1.7	11.3	Costa Rica	20.0
22.5	25.0	—	—	—	—	—	15.0	2.5	65.0	Cuba	7.5
•	•	•	•	—	—	—	—	—	—	Cyprus	2.0
0.7	0.7	0.7	0.7	0.7	•	•	•	•	6.0	Czechoslovakia	
•	•	•	•	•	•	—	—	—	—	Dahomey	
—	25.5	8.5	—	—	—	—	—	—	44.2	Denmark	
—	—	—	—	—	—	9.0	—	—	9.0	Dominican Rep.	20.0
—	5.0	—	—	—	6.2	3.3	6.6	2.0	23.0	Ecuador	11.0
2.5	—	—	7.5	11.2	8.0	—	—	—	29.2	El Salvador	
—	—	—	—	—	—	—	—	—	0.6	Ethiopia	
—	—	—	—	—	—	—	—	—	9.5	Finland	
—	—	200.0	181.1	—	—	—	—	—	506.1	France	
•	•	•	•	•	•	—	—	—	—	Gabon	
—	—	—	—	—	—	—	—	—	—	Germany	
—	—	—	—	—	—	—	—	5.6	5.6	Ghana	8.6
—	—	—	—	—	—	—	—	—	—	Greece	
—	—	—	—	—	—	1.1	3.9	—	5.0	Guatemala	5.0
•	•	•	•	•	•	—	—	—	—	Guinea	
—	—	—	1.3	2.8	1.3	1.5	2.5	2.3	11.7	Haiti	9.0
2.5	3.8	—	3.7	1.2	3.8	2.5	2.5	2.5	22.5	Honduras	7.5
—	—	—	—	—	4.0	2.8	—	—	6.8	Iceland	
—	—	—	72.5	127.5	—	25.0	50.0	75.0	449.9	India	325.1
—	—	9.0	18.5	27.5	—	—	—	39.1	109.0	Indonesia	63.5
—	8.4	16.9	—	19.5	37.9	—	—	3.5	106.9	Iran	14.0
—	—	—	—	—	—	—	—	—	—	Iraq	
—	—	—	—	—	—	—	—	—	—	Ireland	
—	3.8	—	—	—	—	—	12.5	—	16.2	Israel	
—	—	—	—	—	—	—	65.3	—	65.3	Italy	
•	•	•	•	•	•	—	—	—	—	Ivory Coast	
•	•	•	•	•	•	—	—	—	—	Jamaica	
—	125.0	—	—	—	—	—	—	—	249.0	Japan	
—	—	—	—	—	—	—	—	—	—	Jordan	
•	•	•	•	•	•	•	—	—	—	Kenya	
—	—	—	—	—	—	—	—	—	—	Korea	
•	•	•	•	•	—	—	—	—	—	Kuwait	

Table 23 *(concluded).* Repurchases of Drawings, Calendar Years 1947–65 [1]

(In millions of U.S. dollars)

Member	1947	1948	1949	1950	1951	1952	1953	1954	1955	1956
Laos	•	•	•	•	•	•	•	•	•	•
Lebanon	—	—	—	—	—	—	—	—	—	—
Liberia	•	•	•	•	•	•	•	•	•	•
Libya	•	•	•	•	•	•	•	•	•	•
Luxembourg	—	—	—	—	—	—	—	—	—	—
Malagasy Rep.	•	•	•	•	•	•	•	•	•	•
Malawi	•	•	•	•	•	•	•	•	•	•
Malaysia	•	•	•	•	•	•	•	•	•	•
Mali	•	•	•	•	•	•	•	•	•	•
Mauritania	•	•	•	•	•	•	•	•	•	•
Mexico	—	—	—	—	22.5	—	—	—	22.4	—
Morocco	•	•	•	•	•	•	•	•	•	•
Nepal	•	•	•	•	•	•	•	•	•	•
Netherlands	—	—	—	—	—	27.3	48.0	—	—	—
New Zealand	•	•	•	•	•	•	•	•	•	•
Nicaragua	—	—	0.5	—	—	—	—	—	—	—
Niger	•	•	•	•	•	•	•	•	•	•
Nigeria	•	•	•	•	•	•	•	•	•	•
Norway	—	—	—	—	9.6	—	—	—	—	—
Pakistan	•	•	•	—	—	—	—	—	—	—
Panama	—	—	—	—	—	—	—	—	—	—
Paraguay	—	—	—	—	—	—	—	0.4	—	—
Peru	—	—	—	—	—	—	—	—	—	—
Philippines	—	—	—	—	—	—	—	—	—	—
Poland	—	—	—	—	•	•	•	•	•	•
Portugal	•	•	•	•	•	•	•	•	•	•
Rwanda	•	•	•	•	•	•	•	•	•	•
Saudi Arabia	•	•	•	•	•	•	•	•	•	•
Senegal	•	•	•	•	•	•	•	•	•	•
Sierra Leone	•	•	•	•	•	•	•	•	•	•
Somalia	•	•	•	•	•	•	•	•	•	•
South Africa	—	—	—	—	10.0	—	—	—	—	—
Spain	•	•	•	•	•	•	•	•	•	•
Sudan	•	•	•	•	•	•	•	•	•	•
Sweden	•	•	•	•	—	—	—	—	—	—
Syrian Arab Rep.	—	—	—	—	—	—	—	—	—	—
Tanzania	•	•	•	•	•	•	•	•	•	•
Thailand	•	•	—	—	—	—	—	—	—	—
Togo	•	•	•	•	•	•	•	•	•	•
Trinidad & Tobago	•	•	•	•	•	•	•	•	•	•
Tunisia	•	•	•	•	•	•	•	•	•	•
Turkey	—	—	—	—	—	5.0	—	6.0	9.0	—
Uganda	•	•	•	•	•	•	•	•	•	•
United Arab Rep.	—	—	—	3.0	—	—	—	—	—	—
United Kingdom	—	—	—	—	—	—	—	108.3	—	—
United States	—	—	—	—	—	—	—	—	—	—
Upper Volta	•	•	•	•	•	•	•	•	•	•
Uruguay	—	—	—	—	—	—	—	—	—	—
Venezuela	—	—	—	—	—	—	—	—	—	—
Viet-Nam	•	•	•	•	•	•	•	•	•	—
Yugoslavia	—	—	—	—	—	—	—	—	—	—
Zambia	•	•	•	•	•	•	•	•	•	•
Totals	—	—	2.3	24.3	45.8	101.5	162.8	210.0	232.4	113.3

[1] A dot (•) indicates that the country was not a member at the time; a dash (—) indicates no repurchase; a blank in the last column means that any drawings made have been wholly repurchased.

[2] At December 31, 1965.

Table 23 *(concluded)*. Repurchases of Drawings, Calendar Years 1947–65 [1]
(In millions of U.S. dollars)

1957	1958	1959	1960	1961	1962	1963	1964	1965	Total	Member	Outstanding [2]
•	•	•	•	—	—	—	—	—	—	Laos	
—	—	—	—	—	—	—	—	—	—	Lebanon	
•	•	•	•	•	—	—	—	—	—	Liberia	10.4
•	—	—	—	—	—	—	—	—	—	Libya	
—	—	—	—	—	—	—	—	—	—	Luxembourg	
•	•	•	•	•	•	—	—	—	—	Malagasy Rep.	
•	•	•	•	•	•	•	•	—	—	Malawi	
•	—	—	—	—	—	—	—	—	—	Malaysia	
•	•	•	•	•	•	—	—	—	—	Mali	9.9
•	•	•	•	•	•	—	—	—	—	Mauritania	
—	—	22.5	—	—	45.0	—	—	—	112.5	Mexico	
•	—	—	—	—	—	—	—	5.9	5.9	Morocco	7.2
•	•	•	•	—	—	—	—	—	—	Nepal	
—	63.7	—	—	—	—	—	—	—	139.1	Netherlands	
•	•	•	•	—	—	—	—	—	—	New Zealand	62.0
1.9	3.8	1.9	—	1.5	—	5.5	11.2	—	26.3	Nicaragua	11.2
•	•	•	•	•	•	—	—	—	—	Niger	
•	•	•	•	—	—	—	—	—	—	Nigeria	
—	—	—	—	—	—	—	—	—	9.6	Norway	
—	—	—	—	—	—	12.5	—	—	12.5	Pakistan	53.5
—	—	—	—	—	—	—	—	—	—	Panama	2.7
0.5	—	1.5	0.9	1.6	1.8	0.5	0.5	0.5	8.1	Paraguay	
—	—	14.5	—	—	—	—	—	—	14.5	Peru	
—	—	15.0	2.9	2.9	2.9	—	6.2	14.0	44.0	Philippines	14.3
•	•	•	•	•	•	•	•	•	—	Poland	
•	•	•	•	—	—	—	—	—	—	Portugal	
•	•	•	•	•	•	—	—	—	—	Rwanda	
—	—	—	—	—	—	—	—	—	—	Saudi Arabia	
•	•	•	•	•	—	—	—	—	—	Senegal	
•	•	•	•	•	—	—	—	—	—	Sierra Leone	
•	•	•	•	•	—	—	—	—	—	Somalia	10.3
—	—	36.2	—	—	37.5	—	—	—	83.7	South Africa	
•	—	—	—	50.0	—	—	—	—	50.0	Spain	
—	—	—	0.4	2.9	2.9	—	—	—	6.2	Sudan	24.2
—	—	—	—	—	—	—	—	—	—	Sweden	
—	—	—	—	0.7	2.2	1.2	3.9	7.0	15.0	Syrian Arab Rep.	24.1
•	•	•	•	•	—	—	—	—	—	Tanzania	
—	—	—	—	—	—	—	—	—	—	Thailand	
•	•	•	•	•	—	—	—	—	—	Togo	
•	•	•	•	•	•	—	—	—	—	Trinidad & Tobago	
•	—	—	—	—	—	—	—	—	—	Tunisia	17.1
7.0	8.0	3.0	3.0	5.5	9.5	17.5	16.0	15.0	104.5	Turkey	40.5
•	•	•	•	•	•	—	—	—	—	Uganda	
—	—	2.7	9.6	12.7	10.0	2.5	12.0	28.5	81.0	United Arab Rep.	125.2
—	—	200.0	296.8	420.0	852.2	—	—	—	1,877.4	United Kingdom	2,370.4
—	—	—	—	—	—	—	—	—	—	United States	383.5
•	•	•	•	•	•	—	—	—	—	Upper Volta	
—	—	—	—	—	—	—	—	—	—	Uruguay	15.0
—	—	—	—	—	—	—	—	—	—	Venezuela	
—	—	—	—	—	—	—	—	—	—	Viet-Nam	
9.0	—	—	—	7.5	7.5	7.9	30.0	15.0	76.9	Yugoslavia	110.0
•	•	•	•	•	•	•	•	—	—	Zambia	
63.8	347.7	573.3	654.3	753.6	1,305.8	267.1	510.2	390.5	5,758.6	Totals	4,354.1

CHAPTER

20

Stand-By Arrangements: Purposes and Form

Emil G. Spitzer

COMBATING INFLATION by monetary and fiscal policies has been a recognized task of governments, especially since World War I, even though for much of the interwar period the major economic problems which countries had to face derived from the deflationary consequences of the Great Depression rather than from inflationary pressures. The generally expansionary environment which has prevailed in most parts of the world since World War II has intensified the need for anti-inflationary policies, and has encouraged their embodiment in comprehensive stabilization programs. In its work with its members the Fund has devoted much time and thought to fostering such programs.

The link between stabilization programs and the support of them by the Fund has been provided by the Fund's policies on the use of its resources (described in previous chapters), and especially by those governing stand-by arrangements. The importance of these arrangements has grown with time. Nowadays a high proportion of all drawings is made under stand-by arrangements. Table 24 at the end of this chapter lists the arrangements inaugurated or renewed down to the end of 1965.

ORIGINS OF STAND-BY ARRANGEMENTS

The Board's decision of February 13, 1952 establishing the policy for the use of the Fund's resources contained a reference to arrangements by which a member might "ensure that it would be able to draw if, within a period of say 6 or 12 months, the need presented itself." [1] Such an arrangement had, excep-

[1] E.B. Decision No. 102-(52/11), February 13, 1952, par. 1; below, Vol. III, p. 228. For the background of this decision see above, p. 402.

tionally, been made with Mexico in May 1949, when the Board decided to inform the member that the Fund would not object to its drawing $22.5 million within the ensuing twelve months. The passage quoted above was also in the Board's mind in April 1952 when Australia came to the Fund for a drawing of $30 million and it was decided to permit this to be made at any time before September 30, 1952. However, in neither of these instances was it thought that the right to draw might be, in itself, sufficient to satisfy the member's requirements without a drawing actually being made. This feature has since been characteristic of stand-by arrangements, even though in many—indeed in most—instances the member has in fact drawn under the arrangement. It was first introduced when Belgium sought the Fund's assistance in June 1952. As explained to the Board by Mr. de Selliers (Belgium), his country

> wished to be able to consider the Fund's resources as a second line of reserves to help meet any sizable dollar deficit without having to resort to measures that would move away from convertibility. . . . The request for the stand-by credit . . . should help give the authorities the confidence they needed to help maintain a liberal economic policy.

The immediate occasion for Belgium's request was that negotiations in Paris to continue the European Payments Union and to settle the Belgian surplus in the Union had included the consolidation of a $50 million debt to be repaid to Belgium at the rate of $10 million a year starting on June 30, 1953. It was this $50 million for which a stand-by arrangement was asked. The Board's decision was:

> 1. The Fund assures Belgium the right for an initial period of six months to purchase the currencies of other members from the Fund in exchange for its own currency so long as such purchases do not bring the Fund's holdings of Belgian francs above their present level increased by the equivalent in Belgian francs of 50 million United States dollars; provided, however, that the amounts Belgium may purchase under this arrangement shall not be increased by reason of any purchases of Belgian francs by other members.
>
> 2. Belgium will pay a charge of one-quarter of one per cent fifteen days after this arrangement is concluded. This charge will be in addition to any charge that may become due under Article V, Section 8 (*a*).[2]
>
> 3. Belgium's right to purchase under this arrangement shall be subject only to the eligibility provisions of the Articles of Agreement.
>
> 4. Belgium will remain in consultation with the Fund from time to time on its payments situation and its general policies. The arrangement will be renewed for subsequent periods of six months each, unless either Belgium or the Fund determines that conditions have been basically altered so that the arrangement should be terminated. The arrangement will, in any case, be terminated when it has been in effect for five years.

[2] See above, p. 429.

In the event, Belgium drew nothing under the stand-by arrangement until almost the end of the five-year period, when it drew the whole $50 million.

At the conclusion of the meeting which approved the Belgian request, the Managing Director undertook that the staff would submit proposals for standard conditions for stand-by arrangements. These were presented in August 1952, and after considerable debate resulted in the Board's first general decision on such arrangements, taken on October 1, 1952.[3] This dealt only with stand-by arrangements for six months, as some Executive Directors had expressed the view that it would not be possible to foresee conditions in a member country for more than six months, and it was therefore inadvisable for the Fund to commit itself for a longer period. The preamble to the decision contained the following general statement concerning drawing rights:

> The Fund is prepared to consider requests by members for stand-by arrangements designed to give assurance that, during a fixed period of time, transactions up to a specified amount will be made whenever a member requests and without further consideration of its position, unless the ineligibility provisions of the Fund Agreement have been invoked.

Other clauses in the decision introduced conditions similar to those in the stand-by arrangement with Belgium, covering charges and the possibility of renewing the arrangement after six months. It was also provided that a stand-by arrangement would be for a sum not larger than the member could draw under the terms of Article V, Section 3, subject to the Fund's powers to waive these limits by the exercise of Article V, Section 4.

In paragraph 5 of the decision the conditions for drawings and for the suspension of drawing rights were elaborated as follows:

> A member having a stand-by arrangement would have the right to engage in the transactions covered by the stand-by arrangement without further review by the Fund. This right of the member could be suspended only with respect to requests received by the Fund after: (a) a formal ineligibility, or (b) a decision of the Executive Board to suspend transactions either generally (under Article XVI, Section 1 (*a*) (ii)) or in order to consider a proposal, made by an Executive Director or the Managing Director, formally to suppress or to limit the eligibility of the member.

A clause embodying this paragraph has been included in all stand-by arrangements.

In December 1952 the terms of the decision were made applicable for the first time. Finland requested a stand-by arrangement for six months permitting drawings up to $5 million, and undertook to abide by the terms of the decision. It also undertook to repurchase any drawings under the arrangement within three years of the date of drawing.

---

[3] E.B. Decision No. 155-(52/57), October 1, 1952; below, Vol. III, p. 230.

A second policy decision on stand-by arrangements, taken on December 23, 1953,[4] recognized that arrangements might be for periods of more than six months. Although the preamble and paragraph 5 of the first decision (which became paragraph 4 in the second decision) remained unchanged, the following sentence was added to paragraph 1 of the second decision:

> With respect to stand-by arrangements for periods of more than six months, the Fund and the member might find it appropriate to reach understandings additional to those set forth in this decision.

In the course of the discussion in the Board, the need for this sentence was explained by the staff as follows:

> Because of the difficulty of foreseeing a member's situation for a long time in advance, a stand-by beyond 6 months might have to be based on the expectation that the member would maintain certain policies. If the member changed those policies so as to impair the character of the understanding with the Fund, the Fund should have the possibility of cancelling its guarantee. For example, if a stand-by was arranged for the purpose of supporting an attempt at convertibility and the country later called off the attempt, the basis for continuing the stand-by would be gone. Such a situation might be handled by formal ineligibility proceedings as provided in paragraph 5 of the decision, but in most cases such an extreme action would probably not be desirable. Moreover, there might be cases where there would be no basis for a declaration of ineligibility, but nevertheless the stand-by should be terminated.

The provision for stand-by arrangements for more than six months was first utilized in February 1954, when an arrangement for one year was agreed with Peru. The special conditions incorporated in this arrangement are discussed later in this chapter.[5] Here we should note that the arrangement with Peru set a precedent by including as a requirement the offer made by Finland, viz., that drawings under it should be repurchased within three years instead of "within an outside range of three to five years" as prescribed in the decision of February 13, 1952.

It has not been possible to trace a connection between the undertaking offered by Finland and that required of Peru. On the contrary, the immediate reason for stipulating that Peru should complete repurchase within three years appears to have been that Peru had negotiated an arrangement with the U.S. Government parallel to the stand-by arrangement with the Fund, and the U.S. authorities required drawings under that arrangement to be repaid within three years. Mr. de Largentaye (France) suggested, when the Board discussed Peru's request, that it should be possible for Peru to repurchase more quickly than in three years, since it had a fluctuating exchange rate, which should enable it to rectify its balance of payments more quickly. But Mr. Southard (United States) urged

[4] E.B. Decision No. 270-(53/95), December 23, 1953; below, Vol. III, p. 231.

[5] Below, p. 478.

that it would be better for the obligations to the Fund and to the United States to be similar, and the Board agreed.

There has been no formal decision by the Board stipulating that repurchases of drawings under stand-by arrangements should be completed within three years, but this has, in fact, been the practice in all subsequent arrangements. It has been rationalized as follows. Drawings under a stand-by arrangement may take place at any time up to a year from the date when the arrangement is agreed, while the Fund's commitment begins as soon as the arrangement comes into force. It is therefore desirable that repurchases should be completed within a shorter time than five years, so that the total time that elapses between the date of the Fund's commitment and the date when repurchase is completed shall not exceed five years. To require drawings to be repurchased within three years ensures, in the circumstances envisaged, that the Fund's position will be fully restored within four years—i.e., by the mid-point of the period of three to five years applicable to drawings not made under a stand-by arrangement.

STABILIZATION PROGRAMS

Before detailing the process by which stand-by arrangements have been adapted to the varying circumstances of members, and especially to the support of stabilization programs, we should consider briefly the value of stabilization programs in encouraging progress toward the Fund's objectives.

It has been the experience of the Fund that in most of its member countries the need for a stable financial base is recognized, and that repeated efforts are made to bring about and maintain this stability. The generic term *stabilization program* is used for such efforts when concerted with the Fund, although this is, in fact, a partial misnomer: the aim both of the country and of the Fund is steady development, not stabilization of the current situation.

Purposes

Stabilization programs supported by the Fund have been designed to cope with a great variety of balance of payments difficulties and internal financial problems. The policies incorporated in such programs have naturally differed according to the source and duration of these difficulties and the magnitude of the problems involved. Frequently the foreign exchange reserves held by member countries have been too low to absorb pressures on their payments position arising from temporary or seasonal variations in export earnings. Such variations may follow, for example, a decline in export prices, or a decline in domestic production for export resulting from a drought or some other factors beyond the control of the authorities. In such instances, the stabilization programs adopted have been able to be limited to short-term correctives.

In many countries, however, the problems have been more serious and more complex, especially where the balance of payments difficulties have resulted from persistent inflation. Excessive credit expansion to finance private investment or consumption has sometimes been an important factor in generating inflation; but large fiscal deficits financed by bank credit have been by far the most common cause of inflationary pressure. These deficits have arisen for a variety of reasons. Some have been caused by financing subsidies to producers or consumers through the budget. Others have arisen from increases in the operating losses of public enterprises or from increases in public investment expenditures at a time when consumption expenditures were rising. Frequently the situation has been aggravated by serious deficiencies in the tax structure and the tax collection mechanism. Sometimes, the simultaneous occurrence of droughts or other natural calamities, political disturbances, or adverse movements in the terms of trade have further weakened the fiscal position by reducing revenues and increasing expenditures.

In some countries the process of economic development itself has generated serious pressures on the balance of payments. There has been a tendency for domestic expenditures to outstrip available resources, as countries have attempted to provide desirable public services to their growing populations and to accelerate economic growth. Development plans have frequently called for a considerable increase in public investment expenditures, but the mobilization of additional resources through taxation or other noninflationary means, to finance the rising levels of both current and investment expenditures, has proved difficult. The absence of appropriate institutions for mobilizing private savings has also been a constraining factor. In these circumstances, recourse to inflationary financing has been substantial.

Elsewhere the balance of payments difficulties have been caused by a concentration on investment in industries with a high import content but with little export potential in the near future, while agriculture and the traditional export sectors have received inadequate attention.

The objective of stabilization programs in inflationary situations has been not only to control inflation, to arrest the decline in foreign exchange reserves, and to prevent an increase in debt service, but also to sustain an improvement in the payments position and lay the foundation for sustained economic growth.

The programs have not necessarily aimed at an unchanged price level or the establishment of a balance of payments equilibrium during the period of the program. Some programs have involved a general upward adjustment of prices, resulting from exchange rate depreciation, and other measures aimed at correcting price distortions. Because most domestic prices tend to be inflexible downward, relative price adjustments have usually entailed a general rise in prices. In circumstances of severe and protracted inflation the programs have not attempted to arrest the rise in prices within one year, but to taper it off over several years.

As to the balance of payments, an essential step in formulating a program has been to examine to what extent the exchange rate needs to be adjusted to correct disparities between domestic and foreign prices. Sometimes, if the necessary financing is available, a large increase in imports is planned, in order to reduce inflationary pressures. Much more commonly, however, it has been reasonable to assume that there would be an immediate lessening of pressures on imports and other payments as aggregate demand was controlled, and as inventories built up during the inflationary period were dishoarded. Another general expectation has been that there would be a return of domestic capital that had sought refuge abroad and an increased inflow of public and private foreign capital.

Problems

A prolonged inflation derives, to a large extent, from a failure to resolve by other means the conflicting claims of different social groups, each aiming at a larger share of the national income. The retrenchment of consumption often proves to be difficult, particularly in developing countries, where public expenditures, for example on welfare, tend to increase with the growth of population and urbanization. In such a situation, not only do the distortions of the price-cost structure deepen with the passage of time, but also the antagonisms become more intransigent, magnifying the difficulty of implementing a stabilization program. The success of a stabilization program in this situation depends largely on the broad acceptance of its objectives (including an appropriate policy for incomes) by the main social, political, and economic forces in the country.

Equally important, in very difficult situations, is the continuity of action over a period of years. A program may be carried through for a year or so, but evolving political and social pressures or unexpected economic difficulties may lead to an eventual slackening of the efforts or even to a reversal of policies. These considerations underscore the obstacles which the authorities face when they feel forced to adopt a gradual attack on inflation—i.e., one which is planned to extend over several years.

The implementation of major policy changes also calls for efficient and stable administrative machinery. The most complex administrative problems have arisen in the fiscal field and have frequently prevented countries from attaining their revenue goals and controlling expenditures. Difficulties have also been experienced in collecting the government's share in the profits of public enterprises or in obtaining repayment of budgetary loans. Furthermore, when budget receipts have not materialized as planned, many governments have not been able to bring about a corresponding reduction in expenditures.

One major problem, with which the Fund is particularly concerned, is the adjustment of the exchange rate. In an acute inflationary situation it is difficult to determine the extent of the necessary change. For one thing, the increase in prices and costs resulting from a devaluation and other measures must be allowed for in determining the extent of the devaluation itself. Some countries do not realize how large an adjustment may for this reason be needed, with the result that the benefits of devaluation are largely offset by consequential price increases. Unless exports receive the stimulus needed to sustain an adequate level of activity, restrictions on imports may have to remain severe, thus perpetuating structural or price distortions. Moreover, expectations about a further change in the rate may adversely affect the movement of capital. Control over suppliers' and other short-term and medium-term foreign credits often proves extremely difficult, in both debtor and creditor countries.

STAND-BY ARRANGEMENTS: GENERAL PRINCIPLES

When introducing or pursuing a stabilization program a country often feels the need to reinforce its reserves, not necessarily for immediate disbursement but as a precaution against pressure on the balance of payments. It was to meet such needs that the Fund's stand-by arrangements were devised. Since the introduction of the technique in 1952, there have been some two hundred stand-by arrangements, most of which have been associated with stabilization programs.

In negotiating a stand-by arrangement, the Fund determines the appropriate degree of conditionality to be applied to drawings under the arrangement in accordance with the particular circumstances, and within the framework of the Fund's tranche policy. This policy, which relates to stand-by arrangements as well as to outright drawings, was described in Chapter 18.[6] In the context of the present discussion it is sufficient to refer to the basic principle of that policy, viz., that "the larger the drawing in relation to a member's quota the stronger is the justification required of the member";[7] and, further, that "requests for such drawings or stand-by arrangements [in the higher credit tranches] are likely to be favorably received where they are intended to support well-balanced and adequate programs. . . ."[8]

The choice of policy instruments for the implementation of these programs has depended not only on the problems facing the country, but also on the stage of its development and the institutional features of its economy. In order for

---

[6] See above, p. 404.

[7] *Annual Report, 1955*, pp. 84–85.

[8] *Annual Report, 1957*, p. 120.

the Fund to be assured of the effective implementation of a program, it has been necessary to formulate the appropriate policies, as far as possible, in quantitative terms. Thus the practice has developed of placing quantitative limits on the expansion of domestic credit by the central bank or the banking system or on the growth of certain types of foreign debt; or of establishing specific goals for the budgetary or balance of payments position or for the level of foreign exchange reserves during the period of the program. These quantitative limits and specific goals have at the same time provided the authorities of the country concerned with a basis for appraisal of monetary, fiscal, and balance of payments developments, which has enabled them, if necessary, to make adjustments in their policies to conform to the objectives. In such arrangements certain protective clauses (detailed below) are used; these clauses call for consultation with the Fund and frequently also for agreement on new terms in the event that the commitments expressed in quantitative terms or the other specific policy intentions of the member are not observed, or that the policies pursued do not appear to be adequate to achieve the objectives of the program. (The problems experienced in defining the factors to be quantitatively expressed are considered in Chapter 21.)

Where there is strong evidence that the problems have arisen from serious weaknesses in policy and that the member has not made reasonable efforts to cope with them, the Fund applies a high degree of conditionality. This is of particular importance if the member chooses a gradual approach to stability and if the expected price and cost increases during the period of the stand-by arrangement are likely to be incompatible with the maintenance of the existing exchange rate. In such instances, drawing rights are generally made contingent upon the observance of binding conditions expressed in quantitative terms, which may call for a flexible exchange rate policy, i.e., periodic exchange rate adjustments when certain balance of payments goals are not reached.

If the member has not yet established a par value, particular attention is given to the efforts that it is making toward the establishment of a realistic exchange rate and the early adoption of an effective par value.[9] In such a situation, it is normally required that the granting of financial assistance be preceded by a reasonably adequate exchange rate adjustment that will enable the country to make progress toward the establishment of an effective par value. In some instances, however, immediate action in the exchange field may not be feasible and a better course of action may be to make the change over time. In either event, if the balance of payments problem of the member indicates a need for continuing policy adjustments, the member has to present a detailed quantitative program and the stand-by arrangement contains an appropriate clause requiring consultation between the Fund and the member.

[9] E.B. Decision No. 1687-(64/22), April 22, 1964; below, Vol. III, p. 243.

FORM OF STAND-BY ARRANGEMENTS

From the legal point of view a stand-by arrangement embraces two documents: (1) The stand-by arrangement proper, containing certain legal clauses, is designed to fit the operation into the framework of the Articles of Agreement and the Fund's mechanism of financing. (2) The letter of intent, usually signed by the Minister of Finance and the Governor of the central bank, describes in precise terms the policies and measures comprising the stabilization program, especially in the credit, fiscal, balance of payments, and exchange fields. The letter of intent is annexed to the stand-by arrangement proper, and is referred to in the first paragraph of the latter as a "consideration." It frequently contains specific commitments on various aspects of these policies, and whenever these commitments involve legally binding undertakings which are not fulfilled, the member is not entitled to make further drawings under the stand-by arrangement until it consults with the Fund and, where necessary, agrees on new terms. During the period of the stand-by arrangement the Fund maintains close and continuing contact with the country through frequent visits by the staff. Sometimes, at the request of the member, the Fund may station one of its officials in the country as a representative accredited to the central bank or the government, or both.

PROTECTIVE CLAUSES

One of the recurrent problems in the development of the Fund's policy on stand-by arrangements has been to know how to reconcile the assurance to members of their right to draw on the Fund with the duty of the Fund to ensure that proper use will be made of its resources. The general conditions governing all stand-by arrangements, as decided in October 1952 and December 1953, left this matter open; but it will be recalled that the Board's hesitation about entering into arrangements for longer than six months stemmed from a doubt whether a member's economic situation could be foreseen for a longer period. Viewed in historical perspective it was this doubt, and the consequential provision in the December 1953 decision that for stand-by arrangements lasting longer than six months "the Fund and the member might find it appropriate to reach understandings additional to those set forth in this decision," which initiated the Fund's current policies and practices in connection with stand-by arrangements associated with stabilization programs. Such arrangements are usually concluded for periods of one year. But in the first one-year arrangement—with Peru, in 1954—a provision was included permitting the Fund to give notice of the interruption of drawing rights, although certain reservations were expressed about this provision by some Executive Directors. In the course of time, as stand-by arrangements were adopted increasingly for a period of one year and for members with fluctuating rates, uncertain economic conditions, or complex stabilization programs, the feeling persisted that protective clauses were needed to prevent improper use of the Fund's resources and to give reasonable effect to the following standard clause, which appears in all stand-by arrangements:

> In consideration of the policies and intentions set forth in the annexed letter, the International Monetary Fund agrees to this stand-by arrangement to support these policies and intentions.

The need for effective protective clauses was felt all the more strongly because the Executive Board did not wish to resort to procedures associated with ineligibility under paragraph 5 of the first and paragraph 4 of the second policy decisions on stand-by arrangements.

The "prior notice" clause

As a result of these considerations various types of clauses for stand-by arrangements have been developed. One is the "prior notice" clause, which was first used in paragraph 7 of the 1954 stand-by arrangement with Peru and was then worded as follows:

> If the Fund should indicate that developments had occurred that would no longer justify the belief that the Exchange Stabilization Program could be made effective, Peru would not draw further amounts under the stand-by arrangement before consulting the Fund and securing its consent. Under such circumstances Peru would, of course, be free to approach the Fund for financial assistance, but without relying upon the stand-by arrangement.

In presenting the proposed arrangement with Peru to the Executive Board, the management emphasized that "the proposed text of the agreement including paragraph 7 had been adapted to the particular needs of Peru" and that the management "did not want to feel that any fixed pattern had been developed for all countries as a result of the negotiations with Peru. It would not want to regard the Peruvian arrangement as constituting a standard to be followed in other cases." In the ensuing discussions most Executive Directors stressed the point that the arrangement with Peru did not establish a precedent. Mr. Southard, who strongly supported the arrangement, agreed that it would "still be understood that Fund stand-by arrangements generally should involve irrevocable lines of credit as indicated in the December 1953 decision." Nevertheless, several Executive Directors remained unconvinced that the arrangement with Peru could properly be called a stand-by arrangement; they felt that the conditions contained in paragraph 7 of the arrangement could be justified in this particular instance only because the arrangement involved a waiver of the quantitative limits on drawings set out in Article V, Section 4, of the Fund Agreement. (This refers to the provision that the Fund may grant a waiver "on terms which safeguard its interests.")

Under the "prior notice" clause, further drawing rights could be interrupted if, pursuant to a decision of the Board, the Fund gave the member notice to that effect. In most cases, the criteria for giving notice were not made explicit, but were tacitly assumed to be the observance of the policies and intentions in consideration of which the stand-by arrangement was entered into, and the observance of which would ensure that a proper use was made of the Fund's resources. The clause was included in more than thirty arrangements before the end of 1960; and in one instance, that of Bolivia, the Board decided to give notice.[10]

There have been variations in the wording of the "prior notice" clause, as the following examples indicate. A typical formulation (more general than that shown above) has been as follows:

> [The member] will have the right, unless the Fund gives [the member] prior notice to the contrary, to purchase the currencies of other members.

Or, if the clause was to become operative only after the Fund's holdings of the member's currency had reached a certain level:

> If the Fund's holdings of [the member's] currency are increased to the level described in paragraph —, [the member] will have the right, after 30 days from the date when this level is reached, to make further purchases under this arrangement unless the Fund notifies [the member] to the contrary within the period of 30 days. . . .

The details of the decision of September 17, 1958 to give notice to Bolivia under the "prior notice" clause are of some interest as showing the kind of criticism to which it was subjected. The decision was:

> 1. In December 1957 the Fund agreed to a stand-by arrangement with Bolivia to support the stabilization program of the Government of Bolivia as described in the Annex to the stand-by arrangement. During the course of 1958 there were substantial deviations from this program which have created conditions under which it is no longer possible for the Government of Bolivia to use the Fund's resources under the stand-by arrangement for the stabilization purposes indicated in the stand-by.
>
> 2. In these circumstances and in order to establish conditions under which further drawings under the stand-by arrangement will be for the purposes set forth in it, the Fund shall notify Bolivia, pursuant to paragraph 6 of the stand-by arrangement, that no further drawings may be made until the Bolivian Government and the Fund agree on terms for such further drawings.

In the course of the discussion in the Board, Mr. Luzzetti (Argentina), Alternate to Mr. Corominas-Segura, called attention to the fact that when the extension of the stand-by arrangement with Bolivia was discussed by the Board, Mr. Corominas-Segura, as Executive Director of the Fund elected by Bolivia, had objected to the text of the proposed agreement and had pointed out the

[10] See above, pp. 389–90.

danger of including, as part of the arrangement with the Fund, government measures which unforeseen circumstances might cause to be modified at any moment. Mr. Luzzetti wished to reiterate Mr. Corominas-Segura's position and express his concern about the way the Fund was handling the Bolivian case. He saw no reason for taking the drastic measure the staff had proposed.

The Deputy Managing Director (Mr. Cochran) commented that

> paragraph 6 of the stand-by arrangement with Bolivia provided that notice for a suspension of further drawings shall be given within 30 days of the date on which Bolivia's drawings under the stand-by reach a level of 140 per cent of quota, increased by the equivalent in Bolivian currency of US$2 million. This level was reached on September 4.

The "prior notice" clause came in for criticism also on various other occasions on the ground that it had not been incorporated in all stand-by arrangements and that when it had been adopted it had not indicated with sufficient clarity the circumstances in which it could be applied. Moreover, the "prior notice" clause gave the Fund the right to stop drawings that had not yet been requested, apparently for any reason that the Fund thought proper. When these controversial features were discussed in 1961, the Executive Board felt that this formulation did not give members an adequate assurance of their ability to draw. The staff accordingly proposed the elimination of the "prior notice" clause and the addition of the following sentence to the provision in the stand-by arrangement dealing with ineligibility (paragraph 5 of the decision of October 1, 1953 and paragraph 4 of that of December 23, 1953):

> When notice of a decision [on ineligibility] is given pursuant to clause (b) of this paragraph, the member will consult the Fund and prior to any further drawings will agree with it the terms on which such further drawings may be made.

This text was not accepted by the Board because some Executive Directors felt that there was no good reason for requiring a member to consult when it had no intention of making further drawings under the stand-by arrangement.

Discussions in the Executive Board led to the conclusion that thenceforth references to the "prior notice" clause in stand-by arrangements should be eliminated in favor of a new official formulation of Fund policy by amendment of the ineligibility provisions; but in formulating the amendment, the Board took into account the objections to the staff proposal mentioned above. The decision agreed on February 20, 1961 included the following:

> 1. There shall be added to the end of paragraph II.4 of Executive Board Decision No. 270-(53/95) the following sentence for use in all future stand-by arrangements:
>
> > When notice of a decision of formal ineligibility or of a decision to consider a proposal is given pursuant to this paragraph, purchases under this stand-by arrangement will be resumed only after consultation has taken place between

> the Fund and the member and agreement has been reached on the terms for the resumption of such purchases.
>
> 2. "Prior notice" provisions appearing in existing stand-by arrangements, except for the one approved [for Yugoslavia] shall be understood as if the sentence set forth in paragraph 1 above were substituted for such provisions.[11]

By this decision, the "prior notice" clause was replaced by a clause which called for "consultation and agreement" on new terms when a member had become unable to draw, either because it had become ineligible or because the Board had decided to consider a proposal that the member be declared ineligible. At the time when the decision was taken there were seventeen stand-by arrangements in effect which contained "prior notice" clauses in the old form. In all instances but one the new decision involved no disadvantage to the members. An exception had, however, to be made for the stand-by arrangement with Yugoslavia, because in agreement with Yugoslavia the standards for the application of the "prior notice" clause in that arrangement had been spelled out in detail, and an amendment of these precise provisions might have been regarded as an action detrimental to Yugoslavia's interests.

Phasing of drawing rights

Very soon after one-year stand-by arrangements began to be approved, the practice was developed of relating drawings under the arrangements not only to the implementation of certain policies, but also to the period of time during which the need for using the Fund's resources might be experienced.

This new technique was used for the first time in a stand-by arrangement with Chile, approved by the Executive Board in March 1956, which was the first arrangement granted in support of a comprehensive stabilization program. At that time the Chilean exchange system was being modified to include two free markets with fluctuating rates, viz., (1) a banking free market for permitted imports and exports and associated invisibles and government transactions, and (2) a brokers' free market for transactions not permitted in the banking free market. Paragraph 1 of the stand-by arrangement, containing a general outline of the stabilization program, stated inter alia:

> Chile is undertaking a comprehensive economic stabilization program which includes certain fundamental changes in its exchange system approved by the Fund March 2, 1956. Steps have already been taken toward breaking the wage-price spiral by enactment of legislation providing for the eventual discontinuation of the automatic wage and salary adjustments in relation to changes in the cost of living. Quantitative ceilings have been established on the permissible expansion in bank credit and steps have been taken to limit the use of Central Bank rediscount facilities. The Government of Chile intends to maintain firmly this new restrictive credit policy. As an essential part of the over-all stabilization effort,

[11] E.B. Decision No. 1151-(61/6), February 20, 1961; below, Vol. III, p. 234.

> the Government intends to take measures to increase revenue and reduce public expenditures. . . . The Government of Chile realizes that the success of the stabilization program requires continued efforts to reduce further the budgetary deficit.

The Fund agreed "in consideration of the stabilization policies and intentions of the Government of Chile" to a stand-by arrangement whereby up to $35 million could be drawn during the period of a year beginning April 1, 1956. Chile's quota in the Fund at that time was $50 million. The right to draw under the stand-by arrangement was, however, subject to certain conditions which were contained in paragraphs 5 and 6 of the arrangement. In essence, these conditions were that after drawings under the stand-by arrangement had reached an amount of $12.5 million further drawings could not exceed, without the consent of the Fund, an amount of $6.25 million within any thirty-day period.

Parallel arrangements made by the U.S. Treasury and various commercial banks provided supplementary credits of $75 million in support of Chile's stabilization program.

In the Board discussion several Executive Directors stressed the point that the arrangement should not be regarded as a precedent. As Mr. Luna-Guerra (Mexico) put it, there was no doubt, to his way of thinking, that the conditions attached to the stand-by arrangement modified the generic and essential features of an irrevocable line of credit intended in the original decision, to convert it into a *sui generis* contract suitable to the specific circumstances in the Chilean case.

Although it cannot be said that the arrangement with Chile was intended to set a pattern for future stand-by arrangements associated with stabilization programs, it did, in fact, initiate the process of adapting the stand-by techniques to the implementation of such programs and of developing the policy instruments used in the supervision of such programs by the Fund.

In the following two years phasing was used infrequently, but since the middle of 1958 phasing clauses have been included in the majority of stand-by arrangements, especially those with Latin American countries: of 141 stand-by arrangements approved between the end of 1957 and the end of 1965, 117 included phasing clauses. In the latter part of this period the use of phasing was even more common: of 101 stand-by arrangements approved between the end of 1960 and the end of 1965, 89 included phasing clauses. The 12 stand-by agreements without phasing which were approved during that period involved only six countries (Iceland, Japan, Pakistan, the Philippines, the United Kingdom, and the United States). In these arrangements the circumstances were such that either the whole amount of the stand-by credit should be available to the members at any time during the period of the arrangement, if needed, or the amount of the drawing was very small or fell within the first credit tranche.

The amounts available for drawings under each phase of a stand-by arrangement have been determined in accordance with the needs of each particular program. In many instances a large proportion of the total amount of the stand-by arrangement has been made available for drawing within a relatively short period. Some typical examples of phasing clauses are shown below to illustrate this point:

(A) Clause limiting amounts of purchases in any thirty-day period (without cumulation):

> For a period of one year from _____ [the member] will have the right . . . to purchase from the Fund the currencies of other members in exchange for its own currency in an amount equivalent to US$___ provided that purchases under the stand-by arrangement shall not, without the consent of the Fund, exceed the equivalent of US$___ within any thirty days.

(B) Clause limiting amounts of purchases in any ninety-day period (without cumulation):

> For a period of one year from _______ [the member] will have the right . . . to purchase the currencies of other members from the Fund in exchange for its own currency in an amount equivalent to US$___ provided that purchases under this stand-by arrangement shall not, without the consent of the Fund, exceed the equivalent of US$___ in any ninety-day period.

(C) Clause limiting amounts of purchases in any three months and permitting cumulation:

> For a period of one year from _______ [the member] will have the right . . . to purchase the currencies of other members from the Fund in exchange for its own currency in an amount of US$___; provided that purchases under this stand-by arrangement shall not, without the consent of the Fund, exceed the equivalent of US$___ in the first three months of the stand-by arrangement and a cumulative total equivalent to US$___ for each subsequent ninety-day period.

(D) Clause limiting amounts of purchases per month and permitting cumulation:

> For a period of one year from _______ [the member] will have the right . . . to purchase the currencies of other members from the Fund in exchange for its own currency in an amount of US$___; provided that purchases under this stand-by arrangement shall not, without the consent of the Fund, exceed at any time a cumulative total equivalent to US$___ plus US$___ per month. . . .

(E) Clause limiting amount of purchases by specified time periods:

> For a period of one year from _______ [the member] will have the right . . . to purchase the currencies of other members from the Fund in exchange for its own currency in an amount equivalent to US$___; provided that purchases under this stand-by arrangement shall not, without the consent of the Fund, exceed the equivalent of US$___ in the first three months, US$___ in the first six months, and US$___ in the first nine months.

An analysis of stand-by arrangements approved between the end of 1960 and the end of 1965 that included phasing shows that in 40 per cent of these arrangements, 50 per cent or more of the amount could be drawn immediately; in 82 per cent of them, 50 per cent or more of the amount could be drawn within three months; and in 83 per cent of them, 75 per cent or more of the amount could be drawn within six months. Moreover, it should be noted that all stand-by arrangements permit acceleration of the use of resources if the member requests it and the Fund agrees.

"Binding" performance conditions

By the time the "prior notice" clause was abandoned, another type of technique had come into use which made drawings under stand-by arrangements dependent on the observance of certain specified policies, frequently expressed in quantitative terms. This technique (which is usually combined with the phasing of drawing rights) involves an undertaking by members committed to such "objective" policies as limiting credit to a fixed amount or maintaining specified reserve requirements, that if they should deviate from those policies they would not request drawings under the stand-by arrangement without first consulting the Fund and agreeing on new terms for further drawings. This type of clause, based on the "additional understandings" provision in the second policy decision on stand-by arrangements quoted above, has appeared, according to the member's preference, either in the text of the stand-by arrangement or in the annexed letter of intent. Whichever alternative was adopted, appropriate cross references have been made in the relevant provisions of the arrangement.

The practice of making some of the policy intentions legally binding originated in stand-by arrangements with Latin American countries, and has evolved gradually. The first stand-by arrangement in which binding policy commitments in the credit and fiscal fields (expressed in quantitative terms) were included was that with Paraguay, approved by the Executive Board on July 29, 1957. This arrangement included the following two clauses:

> If, at any time before January 1, 1958, the credit ceiling as described in _____ is exceeded, Paraguay will not draw further amounts under this stand-by arrangement before consulting the Fund and obtaining its consent.

and

> If, at any time before January 1, 1958, the Government of Paraguay exceeds the maximum commitment level for ordinary budget expenditures or the maximum level for the implementation of the four-year public works program as described in the annexed Report, Paraguay will not draw further amounts under this stand-by arrangement before consulting the Fund and obtaining its consent.

A number of Executive Directors expressed misgivings about the inclusion of such specific performance conditions in the proposed arrangement. Mr. Thorold

(United Kingdom) stated that he "would wish the record to show that the decision taken was on the merits of the particular case and was not to be regarded as a precedent for general application," but did not press for the deletion of these provisions. Several other Directors expressed similar views. Mr. Southard, who favored the inclusion of these specific conditions, stated that in the light of its experience the Fund had learned the advisability of adjusting the terms of its stand-by arrangements to the situation of each country and to the circumstances in which the situation had developed. He emphasized the point that the Paraguayan authorities and the Fund had examined the practical situation and concluded that these provisions were essential and that if the authorities were unable to meet them they would consult with the Fund. Following the discussion, the arrangement with Paraguay (which required a waiver under Article V, Section 4, of the Fund Agreement) was approved by the Board.

A subsequent stand-by arrangement with Haiti, approved by the Executive Board about a year later, contained a wider range of specific policy commitments, including the following clause:

> If Haiti, without consultation and agreement with the Fund, departs from the budgetary or credit or other policies and intentions set forth in the annexed letter, Haiti will not draw further amounts under this stand-by arrangement before consulting the Fund and agreeing with it the terms on which further drawings may be made.

Several Executive Directors again expressed misgivings about the conditions attached to the arrangement. Mr. Luzzetti stated that Mr. Corominas-Segura, for whom he spoke, wished to reserve his position with respect to the specific conditions recommended by the staff. Mr. Hockin (Canada) objected to the particularly detailed nature of the specific conditions in the monetary and fiscal fields which, he felt, "went too far, involving as it did judgments of specific detail which the Board had not discussed." After further debate, in which Mr. Southard supported the arrangement, the Chairman (Mr. Jacobsson) expressed his feeling that there was a definite advantage in having the members submit a detailed program. He added that if the member felt that it would not be able to meet a particular commitment, the staff would submit its recommendations to the management, which in turn would bring any proposal for a major change to the Board for its consideration.

The Board discussions mentioned above illustrate the point that binding specific performance conditions for drawings under stand-by arrangements in their early days had to be defended against the charge that they were not in accordance with the concept of an assured line of credit. It was, therefore, considered advisable to make it clear that if there was a deviation from a condition, this did not necessarily mean that there was no possibility of making further drawings during the remaining period of the stand-by arrangement. For this reason, it was made explicit that the member could resume drawings if it consulted and agreed on new terms. The "consult and agree" clause itself did not interrupt drawings because the interruption of drawing rights had already occurred as a result of the deviation from a condition. The main purpose of the clause was, therefore, at that time to draw attention to the possibility of restoring drawing rights.

The use of legally binding specific performance conditions in stand-by arrangements spread quickly. Since 1959 most stand-by arrangements in the higher credit tranches (and even some arrangements confined to the first credit tranche) have included specific policy commitments and an appropriate protective clause which refers to these commitments. This clause, as included in letters of intent, has been most frequently worded as follows:

> During any period in which [the specified limits are exceeded, etc.] [the member] will not request any further drawing under the stand-by arrangement, except after consulting with the Fund and agreeing with it on the terms on which further drawings may be made.

Sometimes, in addition to the above clause, which is designed to interrupt drawings when specific commitments are not observed, another clause is included, in the stand-by arrangement itself, which calls for "consultation and agreement" with the Fund on terms for further drawings when the total drawn reaches a specified amount or increases the Fund's holdings of the member's currency to a certain level, as shown in the following examples:

> . . . when purchases under this stand-by arrangement reach a total equivalent to US$__ million [the member] will consult the Fund and agree with it on the terms for further purchases under this arrangement.

or

> If . . . the Fund's holdings of [the member's currency] are increased to ______ per cent of the present quota, [the member] will consult with the Fund before requesting any further purchases under this arrangement and will agree with it on the terms on which such further purchases may be made.

The specific policies referred to in stand-by arrangements have varied widely in numbers and range of coverage. In addition to a ceiling (or a number of ceilings) on the domestic assets of the central bank, they have frequently included fiscal, exchange rate, and balance of payments policies. There has been a tendency toward the proliferation of specific limitations and targets, especially in stand-by arrangements with certain Latin American countries which have adopted a gradual approach toward stabilization. When a stabilization program is aimed only at a deceleration of the inflationary process, it has been necessary to maintain a flexible exchange rate policy based on certain balance of payments tests and the achievement of certain net foreign exchange reserve targets. In such arrangements, failure to observe the net foreign exchange reserve target generally carries only the standard obligation "not to request any further drawing under the stand-by arrangement, except after consulting with the Fund and agreeing with it on the terms on which further drawings may be made." The link of the balance of payments performance test with exchange rate flexibility is provided by the declared intention of the authorities concerning their exchange rate policy. For example, in a stand-by arrangement with Brazil, approved by the Board on February 2, 1966, the letter of intent included the following statement:

> The Brazilian Government intends to maintain the unification of the exchange rate structure achieved in 1965 and it intends to continue to place major reliance on the exchange rate to achieve a sound improvement in its balance of payments and foreign exchange reserve position. Accordingly the exchange rates quoted by the Central Bank and the Bank of Brazil will follow the fundamental market trends. . . . (*b*) In carrying out its policy with regard to foreign exchange commitments, the authorities will ensure that their net foreign exchange assets at the end of each month in 1966 will be, in U.S. dollar terms, equal to, or higher than, those existing at the end of October 1965. . . .

In some arrangements, however, an explicit link between the balance of payments performance and the exchange rate policy has not been established. For instance, in the letter of intent provided by Paraguay in connection with a stand-by arrangement approved by the Board on November 20, 1964, it was stated that

> the Paraguayan authorities believe that the policies described in this letter will be sufficient to avoid an over-all balance of payments deficit during the forthcoming year, although seasonal fluctuations are expected in the level of the international reserves. Accordingly, during the period of the requested stand-by arrangement it will be their policy to avoid a reduction of more than $3.5 million in the net international reserves of the Central Bank below the level of October 23, 1964. . . .

The letter of intent attached to a stand-by arrangement with Colombia, approved by the Board on December 15, 1965, unlike others before, included a specific reference to what could appropriately be done after failure of a quarterly balance of payments test:

> Any shortfalls from the balance of payments targets for 1966 described in paragraph 6 above will be corrected as quickly as possible by (i) appropriate adjustments of the exchange rate in the intermediate official market; (ii) shifts of payments from the preferential to the intermediate official selling rate; (iii) increases in tariff duties; or (iv) any combination of these measures. Also, monetary policies could be tightened more than is contemplated in paragraph 9 below.

Circumstances in Colombia and Paraguay, however, were somewhat different from those considered above, in that inflation was less acute and the stabilization program could conceivably be implemented without exchange rate adjustment.

(There was disagreement on this point between the staff and the authorities of the countries concerned.)

THE "MAJOR SHIFT" CLAUSE

Following the rejection of the "prior notice" clause by the Board, another technique was developed to fill the gap resulting from the fact that not all policies can be made the subject of specific "objective" conditions. In contrast to the discarded "prior notice" clause, the "major shift" clause which was then introduced has not been given legal force.

In the letter of intent provided in connection with a stand-by arrangement approved by the Board on April 26, 1961, Australia stated:

> Should any major shift in the direction or emphasis of policy become necessary during the currency of the stand-by arrangement the Australian Government would, at the request of the Managing Director, be ready to consult with the Fund and, if necessary, reach new understandings before any request for a further drawing under the stand-by arrangement is made.

The arrangement with Australia and certain other arrangements in which the "major shift" clause has been used did not contain any "objective" conditions, and originally the clause was undoubtedly intended to be a moral equivalent for those conditions. However, sometimes the clause has been used also in stand-by arrangements which contained numerous "objective" performance conditions. There has even been a tendency to stiffen the clause in some cases. For example, in the letter of intent annexed to the stand-by arrangement with Chile, approved by the Board on February 14, 1964, the clause was worded as follows:

> Should any major shift in the direction or emphasis of any of the policies outlined in this letter become necessary during the period of the requested stand-by arrangement, the Government of Chile will consult with the International Monetary Fund and, if necessary, reach new understandings before any request for a drawing under the stand-by arrangement is made.

In the stand-by arrangement with the United Kingdom approved by the Board on July 27, 1964, the formulation was substantially the one quoted above for Australia. The staff memorandum contained the following explanation:

> The staff's understanding of this formulation is that the member will inform the Fund of any major shift, whatever may be the reason for it. In addition, the staff understands that the member would give the Managing Director such information in sufficient time to enable him to decide whether to request consultation in accordance with the paragraph.

This type of clause calls for consultation if there is a "major shift" of policy, whether or not the member intends to draw again. This is a reasonable requirement in view of the serious implications of a major shift of policy, particularly if there are no "objective" performance conditions that bring about an automatic interruption of drawings. More recently, however, the "major shift" clause has been subject to criticism because of the difficulty of deciding what constitutes a major shift in policy. Although in 1965 the clause was still being used, it was tending to give way to another type of clause which called for consultation when the objectives of the program were not achieved rather than when a shift in policies occurred.

If the amount made available under the stand-by arrangement did not exceed the amount of the first credit tranche, it became the practice to include two clauses, as follows:

(A) If at any time during the period of the stand-by arrangement (*a*) the limits specified in paragraphs ________ of this letter are exceeded, or (*b*) the intentions set forth in paragraphs ________ of this letter are not carried out, the Government of [the member] will consult with the International Monetary Fund regarding measures to be adopted in order to achieve the objectives of the program described above.

(B) If in the opinion of [the member] Government or the Managing Director the policies outlined in this letter turn out to be inadequate to achieve the objectives of the program described above, the Government of [the member] will consult with the International Monetary Fund regarding additional measures to be adopted in order to achieve the objectives of the program of [the member] described above.

Thus, if the amount available under a stand-by arrangement would not raise the Fund's holdings of the member's currency above the first credit tranche, the member's obligation, should the specified limits be exceeded, was to consult the Fund on ways in which to improve its program. In stand-by arrangements above the first credit tranche, on the other hand, the observance of specific policy commitments was normally made binding: if the member deviated from the quantitative limits or targets or other policies specified, it had to consult with the Fund prior to any further drawings and agree with it on the terms on which such further drawings might be made. In addition, the clause shown above in paragraph (B) was used in such arrangements.

Table 24. Stand-By Arrangements Inaugurated or Renewed, Calendar Years 1952–65 [1]
(In millions of U.S. dollars)

Member	1952	1953	1954	1955	1956	1957	1958	1959	1960	1961	1962	1963	1964	1965
Afghanistan	•	•	•	—	—	—	—	—	—	—	—	—	—	6.7
Argentina	•	•	•	•	—	—	75.0	100.0	100.0	100.0	100.0	100.0	—	—
Australia	—	—	—	—	—	—	—	—	—	100.0	—	—	—	—
Belgium	50.0*	50.0*	50.0*	50.0	50.0	—	—	—	—	—	—	—	—	—
Bolivia	—	—	—	—	7.5	3.5	3.5*	1.5	1.5*	7.5	10.0	10.0	12.0	14.0
Brazil	—	—	—	—	—	—	37.5	—	—	160.0	—	—	—	125.0
Burundi	•	•	•	•	•	•	•	•	•	•	•	—	—	4.0
Ceylon	—	—	—	—	—	—	—	—	—	—	—	—	—	30.0
Chile	—	—	—	—	35.0	35.0	10.0	8.1*	—	75.0	—	40.0	25.0	36.0
Colombia	—	—	—	—	—	25.0	15.0	41.2	75.0	—	10.0	52.5	10.0	—
Costa Rica	—	—	—	—	—	—	—	—	—	15.0	11.6	—	—	10.0
Cuba	—	—	—	—	12.5*	—	—	—	—	—	—	—	—	•
Dominican Rep.	—	—	—	—	—	—	—	11.2	—	—	—	—	25.0	—
Ecuador	—	—	—	—	—	—	—	—	—	10.0	5.0	6.0	13.0	12.0
El Salvador	—	—	—	—	—	—	7.5*	7.5*	11.2*	11.2	11.2	5.0	—	20.0
Finland	5.0*	—	—	—	—	—	—	—	—	—	—	—	—	—
France	—	—	—	—	262.5	—	131.2	—	—	—	—	—	—	—
Guatemala	—	—	—	—	—	—	—	—	15.0	15.0	—	—	—	—
Haiti	•	—	—	—	—	—	5.0	4.0	6.0	6.0	6.0	4.0	4.0	4.0
Honduras	—	—	—	—	—	3.7*	—	4.5	7.5	7.5	7.5	7.5	7.5	—
Iceland	—	—	—	—	—	—	—	—	5.6	1.6*	1.6	—	—	—
India	—	—	—	—	—	72.5	—	—	—	—	100.0	100.0	—	200.0
Indonesia	•	•	—	—	—	—	—	—	—	41.2	—	50.0	—	—
Iran	—	—	—	—	17.5*	—	—	—	35.0	35.0	—	—	—	—
Jamaica	•	•	•	•	•	•	•	•	•	•	•	10.0	—	—

Japan	—	—	—	—	—	—	—	—	—	—	305.0	—	305.0	—
Korea	•	•	•	—	—	—	—	—	—	—	—	—	—	9.3
Liberia	•	•	•	•	•	•	•	•	•	•	—	5.7	4.4	4.0
Mali	•	•	•	•	•	•	•	•	•	•	•	—	9.9	—
Mexico	—	—	50.0*	50.0	—	—	—	90.0*	—	90.0	—	—	—	—
Morocco	•	•	•	•	•	•	—	25.0	—	—	—	—	—	45.0
Netherlands	—	—	—	—	—	68.7	—	—	—	—	—	—	—	—
Nicaragua	—	—	—	—	3.7*	7.5*	7.5*	—	7.5	—	—	11.2	11.2	—
Pakistan	—	—	—	—	—	—	25.0	—	—	—	—	—	—	37.5
Panama	—	—	—	—	—	—	—	—	—	—	—	—	—	7.0
Paraguay	—	—	—	—	—	5.5	1.5	2.7	3.5	5.0	5.0*	—	5.0	—
Peru	—	—	12.5	12.5	12.5	12.5	25.0	13.0	27.5	30.0	30.0	30.0	30.0	30.0
Philippines	—	—	—	—	—	—	—	—	—	—	40.4	40.4	40.4	40.4
Somalia	•	•	•	•	•	•	•	•	•	•	—	—	4.7	5.6
South Africa	—	—	—	—	—	—	25.0	—	—	75.0	—	—	—	—
Spain	•	•	•	•	•	•	—	25.0	25.0	—	—	—	—	—
Syrian Arab Rep.	—	—	—	—	—	—	—	—	7.5*	—	6.6*	—	18.5*	—
Tunisia	•	•	•	•	•	•	—	—	—	—	—	—	14.2	5.6
Turkey	—	—	—	—	—	—	—	—	—	37.5	31.0*	21.5*	21.5*	21.5*
United Arab Rep.	—	—	—	—	—	—	—	—	—	—	42.5	—	40.0	—
United Kingdom	—	—	—	—	738.5	738.5	738.5	—	—	500.0	1,000.0	1,000.0	1,000.0	—
United States	—	—	—	—	—	—	—	—	—	—	—	500.0	500.0	—
Uruguay	—	—	—	—	—	—	—	—	—	30.0	30.0	—	—	—
Venezuela	—	—	—	—	—	—	—	—	100.0	—	—	—	—	—
Yugoslavia	—	—	—	—	—	—	—	—	—	30.0	—	—	—	80.0

[1] A dot (•) indicates that the country was not a member at the time; a dash (—) indicates that no stand-by arrangement was in effect; an asterisk (*) indicates that the stand-by arrangement was for less than one year (usually for six months).

CHAPTER

21

Factors in Stabilization Programs

Emil G. Spitzer

THE PURPOSES OF STABILIZATION PROGRAMS and the evolution of stand-by arrangements as a means by which the Fund is able to assist members undertaking such programs have been described in Chapter 20. It has been shown that in considering members' proposals, the Fund focuses attention on certain critical factors by which the success of a program can be tested.

The main considerations in the selection of the criteria of performance have been (1) that they are capable of being expressed in quantitative or objective terms, (2) that actual performance can be compared with the criteria without delay due to time lags, and (3) that the criteria are significant enough to serve as a basis for an appraisal of the economy as a whole. The present chapter examines typical policy objectives in detail and describes the difficulties experienced in defining them.

CREDIT CONTROLS

Domestic credit ceilings

In the majority of financial programs the control of domestic bank credit has been of particular importance. The major instrument used for this purpose is a ceiling on the expansion of the domestic assets of the central bank during the period of the stand-by arrangement. An over-all ceiling is capable of being defined and administered easily; it also has the advantage of providing operational flexibility to the central bank. Frequently, however, separate ceilings have been applied to different categories of central bank credit. For example, in some programs there has been one ceiling on credit to the government and another on credit to the private sector; when budget deficits have been the primary cause of financial instability, this has been useful in indicating the magnitude of the government's share in the total credit expansion. Sometimes there are separate ceilings for central bank credit to the government, to various official agencies or state-owned enterprises, and to the banking system; the use of this technique has been based on the view that separate ceilings on each major category of central bank credit would facilitate the control of over-all credit expansion. Sometimes ceilings on credit to particular official agencies have been not so much an element in the over-all program of credit control as a means of encouraging changes in the financial operations and pricing policies of the agencies concerned or of ensuring that compliance with the over-all ceiling does not involve undue restraint on credit to the private sector.

Credit ceilings have frequently been phased in order to take account of seasonal changes in the demand for bank credit; it has also been necessary to provide some accommodation for the government where revenues or expenditures are subject to significant seasonal variation.

A ceiling on the domestic assets of the central bank has usually been supplemented by provisions regarding the policy to be followed in respect of changes in the legal requirements governing the minimum reserves of the commercial banks. Where, at the beginning of a program, the commercial banks were in a highly liquid position, programs have provided for an increase in reserve requirements in order to reduce excess liquidity and keep the expansion of credit within the desired limit. In some other programs, marginal reserve requirements (i.e., requirements applying only to an expansion of bank deposits after a certain date) have been introduced to increase the control over monetary expansion. On some occasions the amount of rediscounts to the commercial banks has been limited, in order to achieve the desired effect on commercial bank credit. Some programs, however, have aimed at a more comprehensive control of credit by establishing additional ceilings on commercial bank credit to the government or even broader limits on government indebtedness to commercial banks and to the private sector.

Provisions of a more selective nature, regulating the flow of credit to particular purposes or industries, have been part of a number of programs but only rarely have they been quantified. The central bank has exercised such selective controls either by establishing quantitative limits on the amount of the various types of bills which are eligible for rediscounting or by changing the eligibility requirements, or by fixing subceilings for credits to particular industries or purposes under the broader ceiling on credit to the private sector.

In some situations an increase in the central bank's rediscount rate has been used as a supplement to quantitative limits on the supply of credit. However, where the rate of inflation is rapid, it is difficult to use interest rate policy as a credit control device; in such conditions, an adequate interest rate in real terms would necessitate a very considerable increase in the nominal interest rate.

The policy instruments mentioned above are aimed at controlling the total expansion of bank credit indirectly by reducing the liquidity of the commercial banks. Because of particular institutional arrangements, some countries have preferred to regulate the amount of credit extended by the banking system as a whole. This regulation has taken different forms, depending largely upon the degree of flexibility desired by the monetary authorities and the legal powers they possess for controlling commercial bank operations. For example, in some programs a ceiling has been placed on total credit extended by the banking system. In others, a ceiling has been placed on credit extended by the commercial banks, either with or without a ceiling on credit by the central bank. In some circumstances a ceiling has been established for each bank, allowing it to expand its lending by a specified percentage over the level existing as of a base date.

The choice between a ceiling on credit of the banking system as a whole and a ceiling on central bank credit only is influenced largely by institutional factors. Use of the former has usually been confined to countries where commercial banks are relatively few in number and are subject to strong central bank control. Another important consideration in deciding whether a ceiling should cover commercial bank assets has been the promptness with which the relevant data become available. Credit ceilings covering commercial bank credit may prove ineffective as a guide to policy if there are substantial lags in reporting data.

In the formulation of credit ceilings, various problems have arisen with regard to the inclusion or exclusion of certain central bank assets. The practice of covering credit to the central government, to state and local governments where applicable, and to other official entities has been fairly uniform. Further, the inclusion in credit ceilings of loans or discounts to commercial banks and other banking institutions, such as development banks and agricultural banks, has posed no particular problem. In many countries central banks do not lend directly to the private sector, but where they do (i.e., where they engage in commercial banking activities) the ceilings have covered such credit.

In several instances credit for the marketing of major agricultural crops has had to be excluded from domestic credit ceilings because the financial requirements depended on the size of the crops and therefore could not be predicted. For example, in a program for Ceylon the ceiling excluded finance for rice marketing, and in a program for Ghana it excluded financing of cocoa purchases by the Cocoa Marketing Board. In several other programs (e.g., those for the Sudan and the United Arab Republic), such problems have led to the establishment of separate ceilings on the financing of agricultural crops. The advantage of this technique is that it prevents the use of such credit for other purposes. Sometimes the letter of intent has specified the estimated size of the agricultural crop on which the ceiling on marketing finance is based and has provided for an adjustment in the ceiling, if necessary, after consultation and agreement with the Fund.

In the majority of programs, domestic credit ceilings have not covered items which in the balance sheets of the central bank are included in "other assets" (fixed assets, etc.). The smallness of such "other assets" has been sufficient reason for their exclusion. In addition, delays in the availability of data covering "other assets" and their tendency to exhibit random short-term fluctuations would have complicated the task of setting ceilings.

With regard to the coverage of central bank assets, it should be noted that two different approaches have been adopted in defining the assets subject to domestic credit ceilings. The more common method, called the "selected assets" approach, has been to specify for inclusion certain balance sheet items which cover the main domestic assets of the central bank. The alternative method, the "residual" approach, has been to define domestic assets as the difference between the total assets of the central bank and specified assets, primarily foreign assets, which have been excluded from the ceiling. The "residual" approach has been used mainly in programs for countries in the Western Hemisphere. Both the "selected" and the "residual" approach have also been applied to the liability side of the balance sheet. Where the "residual" approach has been adopted on both sides of the balance sheet, the ceiling has sometimes been defined as the difference between the currency issue and the net foreign assets of the central bank.

"Residual" ceilings have tended to be more comprehensive, covering in most cases "other assets" as well as the main credit operations of the central bank. The main argument for adopting the "residual" approach has been that it is likely to reduce the chances of credit being extended outside the coverage of the ceiling; any new type of domestic operation of the central bank, unforeseen at the time of the establishment of the ceiling, is automatically covered. On the other hand, ceilings on "selected assets" have usually been more meaningful to the authorities of the country concerned; when the ceilings are applied to such specific central bank assets as credit to the government and credit to the commercial banks, which are subject to the direct control of the authorities, there is a greater chance of compliance. The "residual" approach, however, does not necessarily preclude the use of additional ceilings on specific components of domestic credit. In some programs, for example, a global ceiling arrived at on a "residual" basis has been supplemented by a ceiling on credit to the government sector, or by a number of separate ceilings each covering an important component of central bank credit.

Some problems in the formulation of credit ceilings have been related to the fact that monetary expansion or contraction may result not only from movements in the domestic assets of the central bank, but also from movements in its domestic liabilities. For instance, the monetary consequences of a reduction in the government's deposits with the central bank are the same as those of an increase in the central bank's advances to the government. Netting of assets and liabilities has therefore been an important aspect of the formulation of credit ceilings.

In establishing most domestic credit ceilings, the government's deposits are netted against its liabilities to the central bank. This is not done, however, when government deposits are low, with little scope for further reduction, or when the government has given other undertakings directly related to its revenue and expenditure.

In the majority of instances, deposits of the commercial banks with the central bank have not been netted, particularly in those programs in which the ceilings have been related to over-all credit operations of the banking system, interbank claims being excluded. However, the freedom of the commercial banks to reduce their deposits with the central bank has been limited by undertakings to maintain specified reserve ratios. This has also been the practice in programs where the ceilings have been applied only to the central bank. Sometimes, commercial banks' deposits with the central bank have been excluded from the ceiling even without a commitment on reserve requirements, either because these deposits were relatively small or because an excessive expansion of commercial bank credit was considered unlikely. In some instances, these deposits have been netted because of the unsatisfactory record of the commercial banks in complying with reserve requirements. In other instances, the authorities of the country concerned have preferred this arrangement because of its greater operational flexibility compared with a commitment to maintain specified reserve requirement ratios.

Other arrangements involve the compulsory holding of deposits with the central bank. The most common practice requires the commercial banks to make advance deposits for imports. Although these deposits are maintained primarily for balance of payments reasons, they also have some monetary effects: an increase in them represents a contractionary factor while a decrease is a source of monetary expansion.

In most programs for countries with compulsory deposit arrangements such deposits have not been netted against liabilities, mainly because the amounts involved were small or were not likely to change substantially. In several programs, however, where compulsory deposits have not been so netted, they have, nevertheless, been taken into account: for example, some items, such as losses on official foreign exchange transactions, have been excluded from the ceilings in the expectation that they would be a source of monetary expansion offsetting the contractionary effects of expected increases in advance deposits for imports.

Foreign transactions

The majority of countries that have stand-by arrangements associated with stabilization programs are recipients of foreign aid as well. As the commodities imported under the various aid arrangements are sold, they generate counterpart funds which in some countries have a significant effect on the monetary situation. While counterpart funds are being accumulated the effect is contractionary, but when the funds are spent they represent a source of monetary expansion. The monetary effects of significant movements in counterpart funds are usually taken into account in the formulation of credit ceilings by netting the counterpart fund accounts. In a few countries where counterpart funds are not deposited with the central bank but with commercial banks, they have not been covered by a ceiling because the amounts involved have not been significant.

In some countries characterized by exchange rate instability, foreign exchange operations have been the source of substantial central bank profits or losses. These may be divided into two groups, those arising from the revaluation of foreign assets and foreign liabilities in connection with exchange rate adjustments, and those arising from a variety of other foreign exchange operations.

As a result of devaluing the exchange rate, the domestic currency value of the central bank's foreign assets and liabilities is increased. If the assets exceed the liabilities, a profit is earned, and if the liabilities are greater, there is a loss; but as revaluation of the assets and liabilities involves only book entries, the profits and losses arising during the period of the stand-by arrangement are not included in credit ceilings. Profits arising from revaluations may, however, pose a problem if they are transferred to the government; in the absence of provisions to the contrary, this increases the margin available for credit expansion under the ceiling. In such cases the stand-by arrangement may specify that the ceiling will be reduced by the amount of any transfer of profits from the exchange revaluation account to the government.

The other category of profits and losses arises from a variety of foreign exchange operations other than revaluations of foreign assets and liabilities. Sometimes, there have been substantial losses on swap arrangements entered into at contractual exchange rates below those prevailing at the time of repayment of the swap. Losses on liquidation of forward exchange contracts have also occurred. In a number of countries, profits or losses (generally the former), have resulted from the existence of multiple currency practices. In some countries, for instance, such practices have yielded substantial profits owing to the application of penalty exchange rates to major export items.

An important characteristic of these profits and losses is that they involve real monetary effects; they have, therefore, usually been covered by the ceiling. In some instances, while the exchange profit accounts as such have not been included, profits yielded by the exchange system have been credited directly to the government's accounts with the central bank and in this way have been covered by the ceiling. In a few instances, where exchange operations have been a source of loss, the accounting system has not permitted an accurate identification of the items involved, but it has been possible to take account of their estimated expansionary effects in constructing the ceiling.

There have usually been excluded from the ceiling domestic loans by a central bank which represent the counterpart of certain foreign loans, such as development loans from the World Bank and the Inter-American Development Bank. In these instances the central bank becomes involved in a credit operation only as an intermediary. Accordingly, the exclusion of such credit from the ceiling has the same result as if the foreign credit had been extended directly to the government or the private sector. However, for the counterpart of the loan to qualify for exclusion from the ceiling, the foreign credit must exceed a specified maturity, generally five years. This minimum maturity limit serves to ensure that exclusion from the ceiling does not extend to the lending of the counterpart of short-term foreign borrowings undertaken by the central bank for balance of payments reasons. The absence of provisions regarding the treatment of loans representing the counterpart of foreign credits channeled through the central bank has generally reflected a judgment that no such credits were likely during the period of the stand-by arrangement, rather than a different view on how they should be treated. However, if the amount of foreign credits to be channeled through the central bank is known when a financial program is drawn up, the ceiling can be set correspondingly higher and the need to provide for the exclusion of counterpart loans will not arise.

Where the government or the private sector has been engaged directly in short-term borrowing abroad, the level of the ceiling has sometimes varied inversely with the amount of foreign borrowing. Thus, the letter of intent has, for example, provided that the ceiling on credit operations of the central bank is to be reduced by the amount of any Treasury bills placed abroad. Some programs have contained provisions setting ceilings on specified forms of short-term and medium-term foreign indebtedness.

The Fund has applied such limitations where a rapid accumulation of foreign debt has threatened to disrupt financial stability and the burden of servicing has become critical, and in the context of multilateral debt renegotiations. In other instances such limitations have been applied in order to reinforce the effectiveness of domestic credit and fiscal policies. The insertion of such provisions has, however, more often been motivated by the desire to avoid external debt problems than by the need to limit domestic credit expansion.

Provisions concerning foreign debt obligations were first included in stand-by arrangements in 1958, when Argentina and Chile decided to curtail authorizations of government imports under deferred payments arrangements. While in early stand-by arrangements no quantitative commitments were undertaken, in later arrangements specific commitments were made with regard to the amount of certain categories of foreign credits that could be contracted, or for which official guarantees could be given during the period of the stand-by arrangement. Access to the Fund's resources was made contingent on the fulfillment of these commitments.

The degree of restrictiveness applied to borrowing abroad has varied considerably. The most restrictive debt limitation used in stabilization programs has been the prohibition of certain categories of foreign credits for a given period. Its effect has been to reduce the level of such foreign indebtedness by the amount of repayments falling due during the period of the stand-by arrangement. Less restrictive have been ceilings permitting new credits, but limiting them to less than net repayments (i.e., repayments less refinancing). In some other programs, ceilings on new credits equal to repayments have been used to ensure that the outstanding level of indebtedness would not increase. In some instances when this method has been used, however, the level of indebtedness has still tended to decline because disbursements have lagged behind the authorization of new credits. The least restrictive limitation on foreign credits has been one which has permitted the total outstanding debt subject to control to increase by a specified amount during the period of the program.

The prohibition of certain types of credit has been used in two situations. First, where an excessive debt servicing burden has emerged, or has threatened to emerge, as a result of a rapid accumulation of debts, a prohibition has been applied to provide a breathing spell in which the magnitude of the debt problem could be assessed and guidelines for the contracting of new debts as well as procedures for the orderly repayment of past debt obligations could be established. The second kind of prohibition has been related to the enforcement of domestic credit ceilings or the strengthening of fiscal measures. This has been necessary when the public or private sector, by borrowing abroad, has tended to circumvent a ceiling imposed on domestic credit expansion.

Sight drafts and letters of credit at the lower end of the time spectrum, and long-term credits at the upper end, have generally been excluded from limitations. The credits most frequently subjected to limitations have been short-term and medium-term suppliers' credits and, to a lesser extent, short-term bank credits not related to commercial transactions. Experience has shown that because of the relatively easier circumstances under which suppliers' credits can be obtained, fairly substantial indebtedness can be incurred in a short time. Moreover, the fact that such credits are frequently handled through private channels on both sides often conceals their magnitude from the authorities unless contingent government liabilities are involved.

Stabilization programs supported by stand-by arrangements have sometimes contained limitations on certain new foreign credits contracted by both the public and private sectors, but in most instances the limitations have been applied only to credits contracted by the government and its agencies. Credits contracted by the private sector have usually been controlled by denying them the benefit of official guarantees. For example, in Chile's 1959 stabilization program the contracting of new suppliers' credits by the public sector was prohibited, while the contracting of such credits by the private sector without official guarantee was permitted. However, in connection with Chile's 1965 multilateral debt rearrangement, the contracting of new suppliers' credits by both sectors was made subject to limitations. The 1965 and 1966 Brazilian stabilization programs prohibited the Bank of Brazil and the commercial banks from guaranteeing short-term and medium-term foreign loans unless these were used to finance foreign trade.

Unguaranteed private sector credits have been subject to reporting in some programs; this has helped the authorities to secure better information on the foreign debt situation of the private sector.

The types of suppliers' credits to be controlled have usually been identified in terms of the number of years to final maturity. The maturity limit has often been placed at eight years on the ground that this period is long enough to account for the bulk of credit transactions which are to be brought under control. The fixing of a maturity limit has, however, created some problems.

The terms traditionally applied to exports of light capital goods and durable consumer goods tend to be of shorter duration than those relating to heavy capital goods. There has been some concern that the exclusion from ceilings of long maturities geared to imports of heavy capital goods may exert pressure on suppliers to extend the terms for other types of goods beyond their typical shorter maturities. It has also been felt that limitations applied to suppliers' credits of less than a certain number of years may discriminate against suppliers who are not able to offer longer terms. The risk of curtailing competition or discriminating against certain suppliers exists in any arrangement prescribing upper time limits on credit.

Limitations on foreign credits applied for the purpose of making domestic credit controls more effective have been placed only on short-term borrowing abroad, defined as credits with maturities up to five years. Longer-term credits not subject to limitations are often extended by foreign governments or government agencies, or by international institutions after scrutiny and evaluation whereby the chances of an unduly large accumulation of such long-term debts are reduced.

Moreover, an important objective of stabilization programs is to create conditions conducive to an orderly growth of the economy, which requires the inflow of long-term capital. Consequently, far from placing limitations on the inflow of long-term capital, stabilization programs are designed to encourage the financing of development by long-term loans. Development loans usually involve relatively small debt servicing obligations in the early years because the terms of such loans usually include grace periods. Hence, there is less immediate danger of a sharp rise in debt servicing obligations resulting from long-term development loans than from short-term and medium-term suppliers' credits.

The complete prohibition of new foreign indebtedness has been regarded as an exceptional debt control procedure to be reserved for extreme situations. Even though short-term commercial credits from abroad (up to one year) are usually exempted, such prohibitions impede the financing of the movements of goods by longer-term credits. Also, domestic enterprises often depend on foreign credits for supplementing their working capital. Some degree of flexibility has been provided in some arrangements by permitting exceptions from the prohibitions through consultation with the Managing Director of the Fund. However, in dealing with such requests, difficult problems are likely to arise. For example, it may be necessary to determine whether the project to be financed will make a direct contribution to the balance of payments and whether the amortization schedule proposed is consistent with the project's earning capacity. It may also be necessary to determine whether financing at lower cost could be obtained from other sources.

Limitations aimed only at some debt reduction are less onerous. Limitations which permit the contracting of new credits up to the amount of repayments during the period of the stand-by arrangement are no more than a standstill device, designed to prevent the level of indebtedness in the restricted category from rising. For administrative and planning purposes, a limitation permitting a specified amount of new credits may be preferable to one which links the contracting of new credits to the irregular flow of repayments. Limitations permitting a certain amount of new credits to be contracted as old credits are repaid have the advantage that they enable the authorities to keep the debt situation under control without disrupting the country's established commercial relations with its creditors.

Some member countries have undertaken, with the support of the Fund, to implement a stabilization program designed to eliminate inflationary conditions at a time when their external debt was large but on the whole sustainable. Limitations on foreign credits have then been applied to strengthen confidence in the creditworthiness of the country by keeping foreign borrowing under careful control. Such limitations have not aimed at reducing foreign indebtedness but rather at restraining its rate of growth, while the main stabilization effort has been directed toward restoring domestic financial stability.

In most stabilization programs containing limitations on foreign credits these limitations have been applied to the public sector as a whole, including public enterprises. As their borrowing capacity is enhanced by the implicit or explicit guarantee of the government, public enterprises have tended to shift to foreign borrowing in order to escape the pressures exerted by domestic financial restraints. A limitation on foreign borrowing by public enterprises is therefore necessary in most instances.

Sometimes domestic credit ceilings have been adjusted for subscriptions to international organizations. This problem has arisen mostly in connection with a prospective increase in a country's quota in the Fund. If the government makes the subscription, the ceiling excludes credit to the government to finance it. If the central bank makes the subscription, there is no need for an adjustment in the ceiling as the subscription to the Fund affects only the foreign assets and liabilities of the central bank and has no effect on the ceiling on domestic assets.

In programs for some Central and South American countries, it has also been necessary to take into account in constructing the ceilings subscriptions to such international organizations as the Central American Bank for Economic Integration (CABEI) and the Inter-American Development Bank (IDB). As far as the gold or foreign exchange component of any subscription has been concerned, the view has been taken that the making of such a subscription should lessen the permissible domestic credit expansion. Accordingly, the usual practice has been to include in the ceiling the credit to the government to finance the subscription where the government rather than the central bank subscribes.

On occasions, the net position on local currency subscriptions to international organizations has been of some importance. The making of a subscription in local currency by the central bank raises both its assets and its liabilities without affecting its net position. However, the net position is affected where the international organization subsequently uses the local currency subscription to finance projects or to lend to other borrowers in the subscribing country. The use by CABEI of the local currency component of subscriptions has been an important source of monetary expansion. Accordingly, in some arrangements with members of that institution (e.g., Costa Rica, Guatemala, and Honduras) the net position on local currency subscriptions has been included in the ceiling. Sometimes the net position on local currency subscriptions to the IDB has also been included in the ceiling, but only when domestic financing from this source has been significant.

Drawings on the Fund or repurchases may have to be taken into account in the formulation of credit ceilings. In the majority of countries, such transactions are carried out by the central bank. Their effect is simply to raise the foreign assets and liabilities of the central bank, and they have no implications for credit ceilings covering domestic assets of the central bank. It makes also no difference whether the central bank records its liability to the Fund in its balance sheet as a noninterest-bearing note or as a deposit. Neither does the meeting of repurchase obligations have any implications for the credit ceiling when effected by the central bank.

In some countries, however, it is the government rather than the central bank which draws on the Fund, and the foreign exchange drawn is usually sold to the central bank for national currency. Some governments leave the proceeds on deposit with the central bank. This may reflect either a voluntary decision on the part of the authorities concerned or the requirements of the national legislation governing transactions with the Fund. In order to cover this aspect, a provision may be included in the letter of intent that the counterpart of Fund drawings will be sterilized. The alternative to leaving the currency on deposit with the central bank is for the government to substitute noninterest-bearing notes, thereby making the national currency counterpart available to the government. Where this has been the practice, one of two measures has been adopted in the relevant programs to take account of this additional source of funds to the government. In some programs where it was considered likely that the amount of drawings available under the stand-by arrangements would be fully utilized, the ceilings have been set at levels lower by this amount than they would have been if the counterpart funds had not been available to the government. Another approach has been to permit the local currency counterpart to be used to meet the needs of the government but to word the letter of intent so that, in effect, the limit on other forms of credit expansion is reduced by the amount of any use of counterpart funds. This has served to ensure that drawings on the Fund do not affect the margin for credit expansion under the ceiling but at the same time has left the government free to use the counterpart funds rather than borrow from the central bank to meet its financial needs. The need to maintain this freedom of choice may exist, for example, because of a statutory limitation on government borrowing from the central bank.

FISCAL CONTROLS

As mentioned before, major inflationary pressures frequently originate in public sector deficits. In such situations it has not been sufficient to place global ceilings on the expansion of bank credit, or separate ceilings on central bank credit to the government or the public sector as a whole. These indirect methods of controlling public finances do not go to the root of the problem; moreover, being subject to strong pressure from the government, the central bank authorities cannot always enforce these credit ceilings. Therefore, more direct fiscal measures have been stipulated in many programs (in addition to limiting access to bank credit).

In order to keep the deficit of the public sector within limits compatible with the monetary objectives, these fiscal measures have been designed to increase budgetary receipts, to reduce the growth of current or capital expenditures, and to strengthen the financial position of public enterprises.

For the most part, measures designed to increase revenue have involved additional taxation, mainly in areas where taxes can be introduced quickly and where they can be easily collected. The most common measure has been the imposition of taxes on foreign trade transactions, especially in connection with exchange rate adjustments. In situations of prolonged inflation, devaluation of the currency (or, where a multiple exchange rate system had existed, unification of the rates at a realistic level) has been a major policy instrument, frequently leading to the removal or the liberalization of restrictions on trade and payments.

Such exchange rate adjustments have often been accompanied by the introduction of new, or the increase of existing, export taxes or import subsidies. For certain primary export commodities the supply is inelastic in the short run, and devaluation may therefore generate excessive profits. An export tax designed to absorb part of these profits has frequently been imposed as a temporary measure. In some instances, the liberalization of quantitative restrictions following the unification of multiple rates has been facilitated by an increase in import duties or, pending an adjustment in the tariff structure, by the imposition of import surcharges. On the other hand, import subsidies for certain items of general consumption have sometimes been granted for a transitional period to minimize the impact of the devaluation on the cost of living; but in view of the distorting effects of import subsidies on the production and consumption of the commodities concerned, and of the burden on the budget, the use of such subsidies has been far less common.

Another frequently used tax measure has been the imposition of indirect taxes on nonessential commodities. Action in the field of direct taxation has been less frequent because it has been difficult to obtain quick and effective results. However, various programs have aimed at improvements in the income tax structure or stricter enforcement of existing income taxes, and the collection of tax arrears.

Measures to restrain the growth of government expenditures have been an important feature of many stabilization programs. For example, limits have been placed on government expenditures by establishing a ceiling on the fiscal deficit, or on current or total government spending. Sometimes also a certain revenue target has been stipulated. These measures have aimed not only at improving the current budgetary situation but also at providing additional resources for the financing of public investment expenditures. This has been done in some programs by establishing minimum targets for the achievement of savings in the public sector, i.e., minimum targets for surpluses of current revenues over current expenditures. In some instances, the program has provided that, in order to comply with the over-all credit policy, the government would refrain from initiating new investment projects unless foreign aid was actually forthcoming, or some other form of noninflationary financing was available. Sometimes new taxes have been imposed to provide the financial resources required to cover the domestic costs of investment projects without undue resort to bank financing.

In several instances an improvement in the over-all budgetary situation has been achieved by bettering the financial position of public enterprises. Some programs, for example, have introduced substantial upward adjustments in the charges for the services of various public utilities, such as electricity, gas, and water, state-owned railroads, or urban transportation, thereby reducing their dependence on budgetary support. Again, some programs have specified measures directed toward raising the efficiency of these enterprises through better management control, more efficient work rules, or the discontinuation of certain uneconomic operations.

EXCHANGE RATE ADJUSTMENT

Sometimes, where a substantial adjustment in the exchange system has been necessary, a gradual approach has been adopted to ease the problems of transition. For example, the devaluation of exchange rates to realistic levels has been carried out in more than one step; in the intervening period subsidies have been given to provide added incentives to some exports, and the demand for imports has been limited by maintaining quantitative restrictions, which have on occasion been reinforced by import surcharges. Similarly, some multiple rate systems have been gradually unified through a succession of simplifying measures.

In a number of instances, the political and administrative difficulties encountered in adjusting a highly complex exchange system have been so great that only a partial or selective adjustment could be made at the initial stage, although the ultimate objective has always been the achievement of a single realistic exchange rate. In these circumstances, the existing rate of exchange has been maintained for certain transactions such as traditional exports, essential imports, and some invisibles, while the rate for other transactions has been devalued either directly or indirectly through exchange taxes and subsidies. Alternatively, a complex multiple rate system has been simplified so as to consist of only a few rates; this has usually involved a devaluation on both the buying and selling sides through the elimination of the more appreciated rates. In general, the provision of a subsidy through the exchange system, i.e., through the maintenance of a more depreciated rate for exports than for imports, has been avoided.

Adjustment of the exchange system to a realistic single rate has not always involved the immediate establishment of a fixed rate. Many programs have provided for a fluctuating exchange rate as a temporary device, because of the difficulty of determining in advance the rate that would be appropriate after the stabilization measures have taken effect. When a combination of restrictions and multiple rates has existed, the effectiveness of the immediate measures to bring inflation under control has frequently been in doubt. A fluctuating rate used in these situations has carried with it a commitment that the rate would be allowed to move in accordance with the market forces, and that the authorities would intervene in the exchange market only to maintain orderly market conditions.

In some programs, the purpose of such a commitment was to ensure that gross foreign exchange reserves would not fall below the level maintained at the beginning of the program. The assumption was that observance of a minimum level for gross reserves would cause the exchange rate to be determined in the market, free from government intervention. This commitment was, however, not sufficiently precise and sometimes proved to be ineffective, because the gross reserve position could be improved by external borrowing. It was also very difficult to distinguish between temporary fluctuations and a long-term trend, especially in countries where export earnings are subject to wide fluctuations.

In recent years, as an alternative to fluctuating rates, exchange rate flexibility through periodic rate adjustment has been introduced in some programs which could not aim at an early restoration of stability. In several countries, inflation has been so acute and prolonged that it has not been feasible to restore financial stability in the immediate future. In such circumstances, the stabilization programs have been aimed at the gradual deceleration of inflation. Continuing domestic inflation, however, is likely to wipe out rapidly the beneficial effects of an exchange rate adjustment, and the exchange rate must therefore be adjusted periodically in order to counteract the adverse effects of domestic price increases on the balance of payments.

Experience has shown that some mutually agreed objective criteria are required to judge the compliance with the commitment on the flexibility of the exchange rate during the period of the stabilization program. Such programs have, in most instances, included certain "balance of payments tests" to ensure that official support does not cause the exchange rate to diverge significantly from the basic market trend. By these tests the minimum level at which the net foreign exchange reserves of the central bank or the banking system are to be maintained during the period of the program has been specified, thus setting limits within which the authorities would intervene in the market to smooth out fluctuations. The minimum limits to the net foreign exchange position of the monetary authorities, as defined in the arrangement, have usually been phased over the period covered by the program. The commitment not to let the net foreign exchange reserves fall below the agreed level (or levels) during the period of the program is binding, and compliance with this commitment is checked periodically.

In some programs the periodic exchange rate adjustments have been linked to movements in the domestic price index rather than to balance of payments performance, i.e., the programs have provided that a specified increase in the price index would be followed by an appropriate adjustment in the exchange rate.

The commitment to follow a flexible exchange rate policy has the advantage of being applicable to countries maintaining a fixed exchange rate. The setting of a minimum level for net reserves aims at preventing the authorities from maintaining an exchange rate which does not yield, in the context of the stabilization program, the desired balance of payments performance. The balance of payments adjustment through exchange rate action becomes necessary when other means of adjustment are judged to be insufficient. Thus, the level of net foreign exchange reserves is used both as a guide for the determination of the exchange rate adjustment and as a test of the effectiveness of this action.

The inclusion of a balance of payments performance test as an additional binding commitment in a stand-by arrangement increases the stringency of the conditions applied to the use of the Fund's resources, and has important policy implications. The main problems involved in the formulation of the test are the definition of net foreign exchange reserves, the choice of the minimum level for reserves, and the linking of the test to the required exchange rate adjustment.

The definition of net foreign exchange reserves has to draw a line between those operations which do not influence the performance under the test, and those which should yield the desired performance. If a foreign credit facility is included in the definition of net reserves as a liability of the monetary authorities, the performance under the test is not affected by the receipts from this source, as the minimum reserves level covers both assets and liabilities of the monetary authorities. If the proceeds from such a foreign loan are redisbursed to meet current obligations, there is a net loss in the reserves as defined. If the proceeds are redisbursed in order to repay an obligation listed as a liability of the monetary authorities, there is no change in the net reserve position. Similarly, any movement in gross reserves may or may not affect the performance under the test depending on whether there is a simultaneous change in the liabilities of the monetary authorities. This does not mean, however, that foreign assistance cannot be used without impairing the results of the test, except to repay a liability of the monetary authorities. To the extent that the amount of foreign assistance was known in advance, it may have been taken into account by lowering the performance target by an equivalent amount when it was fixed. For example, if a balance of payments surplus would have been required in order to meet short-term obligations coming due, a foreign credit (or a drawing on the Fund) may allow the authorities to aim at equilibrium rather than a surplus in the balance of payments. However, once a performance target has been chosen, and unless this target is a deficit, resources from foreign borrowing can be used only to be added to gross reserves or to consolidate the debt of the monetary authorities.

Generally, the performance target has covered the amount of foreign assets and short-term liabilities of the central bank. In one arrangement the liabilities of the central bank were defined as "its liabilities to nonresident banks and other financial institutions, excluding loans with a maturity of over five years granted for development purposes." Sometimes, however, the over-all amount of foreign assets and liabilities of the Treasury and other official agencies has been included when they have formed an important part of foreign indebtedness. In one instance, the performance target covered the net position of the whole banking system, including the commercial banks, because the commercial banks had tended to borrow heavily abroad in order to ease the tightness of domestic credit restrictions. Suppliers' credits have on occasion been taken into account, either by a separate commitment to limit the amount of such credits, or by a clause providing for a reduction or increase in the target in accordance with any decrease or increase in suppliers' credits.

The choice of a level for net reserves involves a projection of the payments and receipts of the monetary authorities as defined; the receipts are estimated as accurately as possible and a certain amount is allowed for payments in order to yield a performance considered as desirable and feasible. If heavy short-term obligations fall due during the program period, the level of gross reserves and of foreign assistance available may indicate that a certain minimum surplus will be necessary in order to meet the payments coming due. Some basic elements in the balance of payments projection, such as the prospective foreign exchange receipts and payments of the government, may be known with some degree of certainty, while some other elements, such as exports, imports, and private capital movements, are difficult to estimate. It is on these elements that certain assumptions have to be made and targets have to be established through negotiation and agreement with the authorities. In general the stabilization program aims at achieving a balance of payments surplus or at least an equilibrium over the whole period, and the rest of the financial program has to be consistent with that target.

After an over-all net reserves target has been chosen, it may be necessary to phase it according to the seasonal pattern of receipts and payments, taking into account any predictable elements that may temporarily affect the level of reserves. The establishment of phased net reserves targets, usually on a quarterly basis, is a difficult task, as foreign exchange reserves may be subject to wide short-term fluctuations, especially in countries where receipts from exports are largely dependent on agricultural crops. The seasonality of such receipts may not be clearly apparent or there may be some leads or lags from one year to the other. In some instances, a fixed margin of deviation from the target for seasonal or accidental factors has been allowed or a more elaborate phasing has been used.

Unexpected circumstances such as strikes, droughts, or fluctuations in world market prices for major export commodities may also temporarily affect the level of receipts. Consequently, some arrangements have included a safeguarding clause for situations where receipts from exports rose above or fell below the estimated level as a result of a change in the export volume or in export prices. The target could then be adjusted downward by the amount of the shortfall, or adjusted upward by an amount equivalent to the excess of receipts over the projected level. These safeguarding clauses, however, change the nature of the test by eliminating certain types of transactions from the balance of payments performance which is tested. If, for instance, compensation is given for some major receipts, the test primarily affects payments, and failure to pass the test may occur only if actual payments differ significantly from estimated payments irrespective of the level of receipts. Therefore, such safeguarding clauses, like the definition of foreign exchange reserves, are closely related to the problem of deciding for which type of transaction a certain performance is desired.

Agreement to submit to a balance of payments performance test implies that appropriate corrective action has to be taken before rather than after the points in time when the performance is checked, since failure to pass the test makes the country ineligible for drawings under the stand-by arrangement. Although the type of appropriate action is not always specified, it is generally understood that the achievement of the target should essentially result from an exchange rate adjustment. Thus, the staff report concerning the stand-by arrangement with Uruguay, of May 25, 1966, contained the following statement:

> Attainment of the balance of payments performance targets will clearly depend on the implementation of the other policies embodied in the program. . . . Any necessary corrections will have to come through movements of the exchange rate, a tightening of monetary policies, or a combination of the two.

Other types of action, such as an increase in quantitative import restrictions or in exchange restrictions, may be specifically barred, but a tightening of monetary policy or of fiscal policy is never specifically ruled out. The timing and magnitude of the corrective action are left to the authorities to the extent that their action is successful in keeping the net foreign exchange reserves above the stipulated minimum limit. In the case of failure to pass the test, their decisions become a subject of the consultations with the Fund in order to agree on "the terms on which further drawings may be made."

If the balance of payments performed better than the net foreign exchange reserve target required, the authorities could, in theory, either accumulate additional reserves or let the exchange rate appreciate. However, sometimes other conditions in the stand-by arrangement prevent any appreciation of the exchange rate, or the further improvement in the net reserves position may be considered preferable in view of the general indebtedness of the country. Thus the flexible exchange rate policies involving a balance of payments performance test have, in practice, resulted in the periodic devaluation of fixed exchange rates.

PRICE AND WAGE CONTROLS

In most programs appropriate monetary and fiscal measures have been sufficient to restore internal financial stability. In some instances, however, direct action in the field of prices and wages has been considered necessary. Thus, some programs have provided for the immediate or gradual removal of price controls where these were hampering production and distorting the allocation of resources. Some other programs have included specific price adjustments, such as the increases in public utility rates mentioned above, within the context of commitments made in the fiscal field.

Wage policies have frequently been of particular concern because the effectiveness of monetary and fiscal measures designed to combat inflation is greatly affected by wage movements. However, the ability of the authorities to influence wage movements differs widely, depending on the institutional framework within which labor unions operate. Consequently, stand-by arrangements have frequently contained general declarations of wage policies, but rarely are these policies made binding commitments. Where the stabilization measures have resulted in a significant upward adjustment of prices, the programs have sometimes provided for an initial increase in wages in the public sector to be followed by a period without change. In the 1959 stand-by arrangement with Bolivia, the adjustment of prices of commissary goods to market levels and certain specific wage increases for workers employed by the Mining Corporation were made binding commitments (and subsequently modified). In the 1965 Brazilian arrangement, the fiscal program included an undertaking not to increase wages and salaries of government employees beyond the budgeted amount, unless further financial resources should be made available through additional taxation. With regard to the private sector, in countries where the government exercises control over wage policy through its role as arbitrator in wage negotiations, some undertakings on wage policy have been included. Where the government has little direct role in connection with wages, some programs have attempted to implement wage policy by moral suasion.

PART V

Constitutional Development and Change

CHAPTER

22

The Institution

Joseph Gold

THE ARTICLES OF THE FUND are one of the great law-making charters of the postwar world. "Something very important happened at Bretton Woods in 1944, and that was that the world consciously took control of the international monetary system." [1] The Articles drafted at Bretton Woods have had the strength and suppleness to permit the institution, by interpretation, rule-making, policy, and practice, to adapt to a world of change.[2] This part of this volume will deal with the Articles as a dynamic instrument of international law. It begins with an account of the career of certain provisions, in the course of which there will be some attempt to compare experience with expectation. The survey must be selective in the choice of both provisions and the episodes in which they have been involved. As is common in the literature on the Fund, the subject is divided into topics dealing with the institution, the resources (Chapter 23), and the code of conduct (Chapter 24). Chapter 25 deals with the techniques that have been employed by the Fund for flexible response to new needs, and Chapter 26 examines some characteristics of the Fund in action. Finally, there is a chapter on the amendments that entered into effect in July 1969. This stresses the uses of the past not only in the transformation of some of the original provisions but also in the fashioning of many of the new provisions.

Two preliminary remarks by way of apologia are in order. In the course of these chapters it is sometimes said that certain influences were responsible for certain developments, but, in the words of Francis Bacon, the causes of causes are infinite and their impulsion one of another. Again, there may be an undue emphasis on the difficulties that have arisen in the application of certain provisions, but no disparagement is intended. If we can see further than the drafters of the original Articles, it is because we are standing on their shoulders.

---

[1] Louis Rasminsky, speech at Guildhall, London, February 3, 1969.

[2] For the text of the Articles, see below, Vol. III, pp. 185–214 and 521–38.

THE ORGANIZATION

The great growth in the membership of the Fund has caused no grave constitutional problems. Membership is not available to countries as of right, but the criteria that the Fund has applied in permitting membership are few. The Fund satisfies itself that an applicant is in full charge of its external affairs and that all of the obligations of the Articles can be observed. The U.S.S.R. participated in the Bretton Woods Conference and influenced the drafting of certain provisions [3] but has not joined the institution. Poland and Cuba have been members but withdrew. Indonesia withdrew and was readmitted. Czechoslovakia withdrew after a decision of the Fund requiring it to withdraw.

The admission of small states has not given rise to the concern that has been felt in some other international organizations. This is largely the result of the system of weighted voting which exists in the Fund.[4] There have been consequences, however, of the membership of small states. One of them has been the necessity to modify the Fund's policies on minimum quotas. Another has been the need to solve legal problems and make special arrangements because of some unusual circumstance in the country's situation, such as its use of the currency of another member as its own legal tender.

The senior organ of the Fund, the Board of Governors, has held only annual sessions. Its meetings have given governors the opportunity to express opinions on the conduct of the Fund and the policies that should guide it, but the actions of the Board are taken normally on the basis of preparatory work or recommendations by the Executive Directors. One consequence of the great increase in the size of the Board of Governors has been a tendency towards the expression of regional views in meetings of the Board.

The powers of the Fund are vested in the Board of Governors, but the Board can delegate all but a small number of reserved powers to the Executive Directors. All the powers that are not reserved were delegated to the Executive Directors by the Board of Governors when it adopted Section 15 of the By-Laws on March 16, 1946. Under the Articles of Agreement as amended, the Board of Governors will have additional reserved powers, some of which are connected with the original powers of the Fund and others with special drawing rights.

The Executive Directors have grown in number from the original twelve to the present twenty. They meet frequently and still retain the camaraderie of an executive committee, although as the number grew with the increase in the membership of the Fund fears were expressed that this spirit might be jeopardized. Under the Articles, five executive directors [5] were appointed by

[3] E.g., Article IV, Section 5 (*e*); Article XIX (*c*).

[4] Article XII, Section 5.

[5] In this and the following chapters the distinction drawn in the Articles between individual executive directors and the Executive Directors as an organ of the Fund is followed by reserving the use of capital letters for the latter.

the five members with the largest quotas, two were elected by the American Republics not entitled to appoint directors, and five were elected by the rest of the members. The Board of Governors may decide by a four-fifths majority of the total voting power to increase the number of executive directors when new members join the Fund,[6] and the Board has exercised this power in accordance with a policy based on the voting power of new members. By the time of the 1966 election, the number of executive directors elected by the American Republics had been increased to three and the other elected executive directors had been increased from five to twelve. The biennial election of executive directors by members not entitled to appoint executive directors is settled by negotiations among members in which the Managing Director and staff take no part.

The Articles provide for an increase, in certain circumstances, in the number of appointed executive directors.[7] The drafters wanted to be certain that the members which were providing assistance through the Fund because of the net sales of their currencies by the Fund would be able to express their views directly in the Executive Directors and, as a minimum, balance the views of the members making a net use of the Fund's resources. It was provided, therefore, that if the two currencies that had been used in the largest absolute amounts during the two years preceding a biennial election were the currencies of members that were not among those already entitled to appoint executive directors, these two members also were to be entitled to make appointments. Canada was entitled to exercise this right in 1958 and Italy in 1968. In 1950, the question arose whether a member entitled to appoint an additional executive director was bound to exercise the right. The reluctance to exercise it resulted from the fact that the executive director appointed by a member in this position would speak no longer for the other members that had voted for him in earlier elections, and the number of votes that he could cast would be reduced correspondingly. It was concluded that the right was also a duty, and on both occasions the other members, in order to maintain the earlier associations, refrained from participating in the election of executive directors, with the result that no executive director could cast votes corresponding to the votes allotted to these members. Instead, an informal procedure was followed by which these other members have requested the Canadian and Italian executive directors to take care of their interests in the Executive Directors.

The Articles do not define the status of executive directors, but in some ways the silence of the Articles is the most interesting contribution to the definition of their position. For example, the word "representative" is not used in the Articles although it appeared in some earlier drafts. It is not said, as it is in the

[6] Article XII, Section 3 (*b*).

[7] Article XII, Section 3 (*c*).

case of the Managing Director and the staff, that they owe their duty entirely to the Fund and to no other authority, but they are officials of the institution and are paid by it. The absence of definition has enabled executive directors to work out their own relations with the members that appointed or elected them, and there is much variety in those relations. Only the United States [8] and a few other members [9] have provided by law for the way in which an executive director shall receive instructions on the positions he is to take on issues arising in the Fund.

It is impossible to understand the Fund without some discussion of voting. All members have an equal number of basic votes in deference to the classical principle of the equality of sovereign states, and further votes weighted according to quota in recognition of the fact that they belong to a financial institution and have made varying contributions to its resources. For two kinds of financial decisions, weighted voting power is adjusted on the basis of a member's net purchases from the Fund or the net sales of a member's currency to other members. In the drafting of the Articles and in legislative discussions of their acceptability, relative voting strength, possible blocs, and possible alignments on particular issues were a major preoccupation. This concern is apparent in the provisions of the Articles on voting and decisions. Although the basic rule is that decisions are taken by a majority of votes cast, there is an elaborate network of special majorities and safeguards.

In the Board of Governors voting is unavoidable because most issues are put to the Board by correspondence. It is remarkable, however, that voting by the Executive Directors, who are in continuous session, has been almost nonexistent. This has been the result of deliberate policy. As early as September 25, 1946, a rule was adopted declaring that "the Chairman will ordinarily ascertain the sense of the meeting in lieu of a formal vote," although any director is entitled to call for a vote.[10] It did not follow that voting strength became irrelevant, and it was decided on May 28, 1947 that in ascertaining the sense of the meeting the Chairman must take account of voting power, but the avoidance of formal voting has tended to moderate the effect of discrepancies in voting strength.

Most of the votes that have occurred took place in the early years of the Fund before satisfactory procedures were developed by which individual executive directors could record their views. If an executive director was not able to concur in a decision without qualification, almost the only way in which he could record his reservations was by voting against the decision. Many of the early votes

---

[8] Bretton Woods Agreements Act, P.L. 171, 79th Congress, 1st Session (59 Stat. 512 (1945)), Sec. 4 (*Selected Decisions*, pp. 147–50).

[9] For example, Germany, *Bundesgesetzblatt*, Part II, No. 21, July 13, 1956, page 747, Article 5.

[10] Rules and Regulations, Rule C-10; below, Vol. III, p. 290.

were on successive motions on the same issue, so that the number of occasions on which there has been resort to voting has been much smaller than the number of votes. There has been no pattern in these votes, and certainly they have not all been on major issues.

For some years the threat of a vote has been regarded as regrettable. The effect of this distaste for voting on the operation of the institution has been profound. It has helped to avoid blocs or at least not to intensify any drive towards routine coalition. On any important question, the Managing Director and executive directors try to reach a decision which all can accept or at least not oppose, and they persist in this effort while there is still reasonable hope that it will succeed. Naturally, there are abstentions or dissents on occasion, but in an atmosphere in which normally more attention is given to the weight of argument than to the weight of voting power the minority does not feel that it has been overborne by force. It would be disingenuous to pretend that the influence of all members is the same, but a policy of not voting has given even members with small voting strength a sense of participation in the process of reaching decisions. In addition, the policy has induced members with great voting power to be restrained in working towards a decision. An incident which involved one of the few votes is revealing. A decision was taken on the morning of March 2, 1951 by 44,510 to 33,155 votes, but the majority consisted only of the U.S., British, and Canadian executive directors, whereas eight executive directors voted against the decision and three abstained. In the afternoon session one of the three executive directors asked that the discussion of the subject be resumed at a later date, and on March 7 there was general agreement on the minority position. The significance of any one incident must not be exaggerated, but it is a defensible proposition that the larger voting power of some members gives them an assurance that enables them to act with moderation. It is the desire for this assurance that has made relative voting power a continuing concern of members, particularly in the negotiation of the amendments to the Articles, even if voting power is exercised only on rare occasions.

One reason why voting has been avoided as a deliberate policy is that, in some of its functions, the Fund, in the international field, closely resembles the regulatory or administrative agency of national law.[11] The exercise of the Fund's functions as an international regulatory agency has an impact on the rights and

[11] "Present-day administrative agencies are vested with authority to prescribe generally what shall or shall not be done in a given situation (just as legislatures do); to determine whether the law has been violated in particular cases and to proceed against the violators (just as courts do); to admit people to privileges not otherwise open to members of the public (as the Crown once could do); and even to render what amount to money judgments. Agencies vested with such powers are usually called 'regulatory agencies' in the United States, because their activities impinge upon the personal or property rights of private individuals and regulate the manner in which such rights may be exercised." Bernard Schwartz, *An Introduction to American Administrative Law*, p. 8.

duties of its members. It must have been clear at an early date that members would be more likely to accept the decisions and rules of the Fund if the Fund strove for consensus, at least on important issues. It must have been clear also that the objective of consensus would tend to deter the formation of permanent combinations among members and encourage a more fluid procedure for reaching decisions. The policy of seeking consensus does much to explain the authority of the Executive Directors, because it is largely through them that consensus, or at least widespread agreement, is reached.

THE ORGANIZATION IN THE WORLD

The place of the Fund in international organization at large has helped to shape its role. Two aspects of international organization have had unusual importance. One of them has been the intention to establish an international trade organization, and the other has been the advent of additional institutions or groups with international monetary functions.

At the Bretton Woods Conference it was contemplated that the Fund and the International Bank for Reconstruction and Development (the World Bank) would be joined by a trade organization, and it was resolved that participating governments should reach agreement as soon as possible on the ways in which obstacles to international trade could be reduced, the orderly marketing of staple commodities at fair prices could be ensured, and other related objectives attained. The intention to create an international trade organization and the subsequent history of efforts to carry out this intention affected the Fund in various ways. The effects on the definition of "restrictions on payments and transfers for current international transactions," on which much of the Fund's jurisdiction in bringing about a multilateral system of payments and transfers depends, and on the scope of the Fund's consultations with members, are discussed elsewhere in these chapters.

In the scales of history the emergence of other international entities with authority in monetary matters will probably have greater weight. There is no evidence that at the time of Bretton Woods the world contemplated more than one international monetary entity. A generation later, the Fund is the central but not the sole monetary institution. The Bank for International Settlements is not a newcomer, but its activities are broader now than in the past. Certain committees of the Organization for Economic Cooperation and Development and of the European Economic Community, the Group of Ten, and the members of the Gold Pool are among the entities that have taken an active part or exercised authority in international monetary matters. The Fund is the central institution in the sense that its resources are the most considerable, but, more to the present point, its formal authority is the broadest and its membership the largest of all of the monetary entities. As a result, as was seen in the liquidity debate which led finally to the amendments of the Articles, smaller combinations of members sometimes seem to be exclusionary and for this reason provoke political reactions.

The obligations involved in participation in other organizations or less formal bodies cannot derogate in law from the obligations of membership in the Fund. Inevitably, however, decisions have been taken in other entities that have had major importance for the Fund. The provisions of the Articles are extensive enough to have permitted the adoption of at least some of these decisions within the Fund even if there was no legal necessity that the decisions be taken there. Examples of decisions affecting the international monetary system taken outside the Fund are the establishment of the Gold Pool, the introduction of the two-tier gold system, the Basle Agreements relating to sterling, and the increases in swap arrangements. In some but not in all of the other entities the Managing Director or his representative has participated in the deliberations leading to decisions.

Observers may disagree on the reasons for the proliferation of other entities in international monetary matters. Some of the reasons that may be suggested are related more or less closely to the Fund itself. One of them may be the great growth in the membership of the Fund and the belief that other entities are needed that are based on more homogeneous interests or simply on geography. The original reaction in the Fund that the European Payments Union was an unwelcome discriminatory currency arrangement may have left a residual feeling that the reconciliation between particular interests and universal objectives is not always easy. Inequality of voting power in the Fund, even though voting power is not brandished, may have spurred some members to find an environment in which this disparity would be absent or less marked. The continued deficit in the balance of payments of the United States and its need to find acceptable forms of financing have made it easier to suggest that some other environment would be more convenient. The tranche policies of the Fund may have led the United States to conclude that the Fund was *forum non conveniens*. From time to time, the theory of the special responsibility of certain members for the monetary system has been heard. This is probably not an autonomous influence, but then most of the other reasons that have been suggested are related to each other in one way or another.

In the history of the effect on the Fund of other entities the greatest interest attaches to the Group of Ten. It came into being as part of the search by the United States for financing for its balance of payments deficit and as a result of the fear that the resources of the Fund would be inadequate to enable the United States to make a substantial use of them. As the result of complex negotiations, the Fund adopted the decision which is called the General Arrangements to Borrow.[12] Under it, eight members and the central banks of two other members were invited, and by adherence to the decision have agreed, to lend the currencies

[12] E.B. Decision No. 1289-(62/1), January 5, 1962; below, Vol. III, pp. 246–52.

of these members to the Fund to supplement the resources of the Fund for the financing of exchange transactions by any of the ten members with the Fund. The decision, which is also an agreement between the Fund and the participants, became effective on October 24, 1962 for a period of four years, and has been renewed for a further period of four years. The intention of the Fund was to establish a ring of lenders to the Fund and the decision retains evidences of a bilateral nexus between the Fund and individual participants.[13] It became apparent early in the negotiations, however, that a more corporate spirit was intended and that a certain amount of authority would be exercised elsewhere by the incipient collectivity.

The substructure of the Group of Ten consists of the General Arrangements to Borrow and identical letters addressed on December 15, 1961, by Mr. Baumgartner, the then Minister of Finance of France, to the other nine participants.[14] These letters, to which the Fund was not a party, established the procedures for consultation and decision among the Ten. It must be understood that under the General Arrangements participants are not obligated to lend to the Fund but only to consider whether they will accept calls on them by the Fund to lend. The letters establish the procedures by which the participants will reach their conclusions collectively, although each participant responds individually to the call on it made by the Fund. The desideratum stated in the letters is unanimity, but if that is not attainable, decisions are taken by a system of weighted voting that is unrelated to voting power in the Fund. Voting power according to the letters is weighted in relation to the total amount that each participant may be called on to lend under the General Arrangements. Two majorities are needed for a decision: two thirds of the participants voting and three fifths of the weighted votes. The participant requesting a transaction with the Fund, for the purpose of which the Fund seeks to borrow, is not entitled to vote on the question whether the participants asked to lend will agree to lend.

The Baumgartner letters state the understanding that a consultative meeting will be held if proposals for calls are made "or if other matters should arise under the Fund decision requiring consultations among the participants." They also state that to further these consultations participants, to the fullest extent practicable, should use the facilities of the international organizations—the plural is used—to which they belong to keep each other informed of developments in their balances of payments that could give rise to a need to lend under the General Arrangements. The Ministers of Finance and Central Bank Governors of the Group of Ten, however, have given mandates to their deputies to perform other tasks. The work by the Group of Ten in connection with international liquidity is the leading example of an activity that goes beyond the General

[13] Paragraph 7 (a); *ibid.*, p. 248.

[14] Below, Vol. III, pp. 252–54.

Arrangements and the Baumgartner letters. The United States has not attempted so far to make a use of the Fund's resources beyond the gold tranche, and the Fund has not found it necessary to invoke the General Arrangements for the purpose of a transaction with the United States, although it has borrowed under them for transactions with the United Kingdom and France.

The General Arrangements caused uneasiness among some members of the Fund. The agreement establishing the General Arrangements seemed to them to be a preferential facility because it was not for the benefit of transactions with the Fund by nonparticipants. One reason why they could not welcome the agreement was that they could discern no convincing principle by which to explain the selection of the Ten as a distinctive group. The reaction of members outside the Ten may have contributed something to the willingness of the Fund community to establish the compensatory financing facility which on its face is available to all members but in practice is likely to be used only by the exporters of primary products.

In time, the disquiet of some members outside the Ten took another form because of the movement towards the deliberate control of more elements in the international monetary system. These members felt that decisions were being reached on problems affecting the international monetary system as a whole by a process in which the rest of the members of the Fund had no direct voice although their views could be communicated to the Ten by the Managing Director or his representative. Even if decisions had to be taken in the Fund on these matters, the outcome might be predetermined by the Ten because of their dominating voting power in the Fund. In the liquidity debate a solution was sought by holding four joint meetings of executive directors and the deputies of the Group of Ten. The problem of a *modus vivendi* remains.

CHAPTER

23

Use of the Fund's Resources

Joseph Gold

THE POWER TO CHALLENGE

It is in connection with its financial operations and transactions that the Fund has shown the greatest virtuosity and imagination even though the overture began with discord. "For legal purposes it is normally necessary to try to get rid of ambiguities. . . . In poetry the ambiguities can happily remain." [1] The negotiators of treaties are sometimes more like poets than lawyers in their drafting. It is possible that the dissonant effect of declaring in Article V, Section 3 (*a*) that a member is "entitled" to make purchases from the Fund subject to certain conditions, but that one of the conditions is that the member "represents" that the currency is needed and so on, is not fortuitous. The words permitted two understandings of the right to make purchases from the Fund and each had vigorous supporters. One version, based on the word "entitled," was that, if a member was eligible to use the Fund's resources, it had the right to make purchases without hindrance if they did not require a waiver under Article V, Section 4. "Drawing rights" were often said to be "automatic" according to this view. The other version, based on the word "represents," was that the representation that the currency requested "is presently needed for making in that currency payments which are consistent with the provisions of this Agreement" could be challenged by the Fund if it thought the representation to be incorrect in some respect. The acceptance of this second understanding would reduce the need for the Fund to employ the procedures of ineligibility in order to defend the Fund's resources against an improper use of them. The Fund would be able to challenge the representation made when a member requested a purchase without taking the more disagreeable action of imposing a status on the member which made it ineligible to use the Fund's resources in general or beyond a limited amount prescribed by the Fund.

---

[1] Roy Fuller, "The Lawyer as Poet," *The New Law Journal*, December 19, 1968, p. 1205.

A decision in favor of the second understanding of Article V, Section 3 (*a*) was adopted in May 1947, and, after further examination, this conclusion was confirmed by a decision of March 10, 1948.[2] The later decision states that there is a presumption in favor of the correctness of a representation, but that the Fund may challenge any element in it if the Fund has good reasons to doubt its correctness. If the Fund concludes that a representation is not correct, the Fund may postpone or reject the request or accept it subject to conditions. This decision is one of the major influences in the development of the Fund's law and practice on the use of its resources because in rejecting the theory of "automaticity" the decision opened the way to the tranche policies and "conditionality."

The power to challenge representations was not a substitute for ineligibility if there were grounds for ineligibility, but no member has ever submitted repeated requests that forced the Fund to declare the member ineligible in order to avoid repeated challenges. In fact, there has never been a decision by the Executive Directors to challenge a representation on the occasion of a request. Members seem to feel that even a challenge would convey stigma, and, therefore, once it became clear that the Fund had the power to challenge representations, there developed the tacit understanding that it was wise for a member to consult the Managing Director before it submitted a request to the Fund. Even Rule G-5 of the Rules and Regulations has become a dead letter insofar as it was intended to facilitate small purchases. One purpose of this rule, which was adopted on February 7, 1947, was to allow members an automatic right to make a limited use of the Fund's resources by permitting a member to make a purchase without the need for consideration by the Executive Directors if the purchase would increase the Fund's holdings of the member's currency by no more than 5 per cent of quota during the thirty days ending with the purchase.

The decision establishing the Fund's power to challenge a representation when an eligible member requests an exchange transaction was one of a number taken during March 1948 in order to clarify the Fund's powers to prevent an improper use of its resources,[3] but it is not necessary to say more about the other decisions. The central decision was the one affirming the power to challenge, and the uncertainty which it produced about the circumstances in which the power might be exercised, apart from the notice given in the decisions of April 5 and June 4, 1948 on the use of the Fund's resources by members benefiting under the European Recovery Program, led to an almost complete paralysis in the financial operations of the Fund.

If the decision of March 10, 1948 on the power to challenge representations is a landmark, the decision of February 13, 1952 is the Mount Everest that towers

---

[2] E.B. Decision No. 284-4; below, Vol. III, p. 227.

[3] E.B. Decisions Nos. 287-3, 284-3, 286-1, 292-3; below, Vol. III, pp. 228, 234–35.

over all other decisions on the use of the Fund's resources.[4] The decision of February 13, 1952 was intended to reinvigorate the Fund by encouraging members to believe that they would be able to use its resources. The decision clarified what the Fund regarded as an appropriately temporary use of its resources; initiated the policy of representations of intention as to repurchase; foreshadowed the stand-by arrangement; and invented the concept of the gold tranche. The discussion will deal with these elements in the decision and then other developments in the Fund's law and practice on the use of its resources.

TEMPORARY USE AND REPURCHASE

The topics of temporary use and repurchase are related and can be considered together. The word "temporary" in connection with the use of the Fund's resources does not appear in the original Articles, although there were clear indications that only temporary use was proper. This was inherent, of course, in the idea that the Fund provided an addition to a member's monetary reserves during periods of balance of payments difficulty. In order to pacify those critics in the United States who feared that the Fund might engage in long-term financing and undermine the lending practices of the World Bank, the United States provided in its Bretton Woods legislation that it would seek an interpretation from the Fund on the proper use of the Fund's resources, and that it would propose an amendment of the Articles if the interpretation was unsatisfactory.[5] This led to the interpretation of September 26, 1946 on the use of the Fund's resources, on which more will be said later in this chapter, but which, it is sufficient to note here, emphasized that the Fund gave no more than "temporary assistance" in making its resources available.[6]

There could be no quarrel with that conclusion but it was not specific. What was meant by "temporary"? The Articles did not declare that use must be temporary and, therefore, they did not define what period could be regarded as temporary, but nevertheless there was some evidence of the attitude of the drafters. Article V, Section 8 sets forth a system of charges on the Fund's holdings of a currency in excess of quota, which increased in relation to both time and amount, and provided that when the rate of charge on any part of those holdings reached 4 per cent per annum the Fund and the member must consider means by which the Fund's holdings could be reduced. The stage of compulsory consultation might not be reached until seven years had passed after a purchase on which periodic charges were payable, and therefore it was argued

[4] E.B. Decision No. 102-(52/11); below, Vol. III, p. 228.

[5] Sec. 13 (see above, Chapter 22, footnote 8).

[6] E.B. Decision No. 71-2; below, Vol. III, p. 245.

by some that the maximum period of temporary use could not be less than seven years. Their view of the Articles was that the repurchase provisions of Article V, Section 7 (*b*) were a mechanism under which repurchase obligations were to accrue, and if they did not accrue there would then be consultation on the means to reduce the Fund's holdings under Article V, Section 8 (*d*), and finally ineligibility could be declared under Article V, Section 5 if a member's use of the Fund's resources was so protracted as to be adjudged "contrary to the purposes of the Fund."

The opponents of this view considered seven years, followed by whatever period was agreed in the consultation for the reduction of the Fund's holdings, to be too lengthy. Moreover, they were troubled by the fact that the provisions of Article V, Section 7 (*b*) would not produce repurchase obligations for some members. Obligations under that provision depended on monetary reserves and increases in them. A member's monetary reserves were defined substantially as the holdings of gold and convertible currencies of its central institutions minus currency liabilities, i.e., the holdings of the member's currency by the central institutions and other official institutions of other members and by other banks within their territories. A member like the United Kingdom tended to have negative monetary reserves under this formula because its central holdings were less than its currency liabilities. For certain other members, repurchase obligations would not accrue because a large part of their reserves was held in the form of inconvertible currencies which were not included in the calculation of monetary reserves.

Discouraged by the probable ineffectiveness of the repurchase provisions, the U.S. executive director proposed in October 1949 that whenever a member sought to use the Fund's resources it should undertake to make a repurchase equivalent to its purchase not later than five years after the event. The dissenters argued, correctly, that the "conditions" on which a member could make purchases were set forth in Article V, Section 3 (*a*) and they could not be added to by fiat. The Articles did not establish a fixed term for use of the Fund's resources, and this was one of the ways in which the use of the Fund's resources differed from a loan. The attempt to impose repurchase conditions failed.

A related development was in process at this time. The Fund could not impose repurchase conditions, but could it accept a repurchase that was voluntary because the member was not obligated to make it and the Fund was not obligated to receive it? The question in other words was whether a repurchase could be made by agreement between the Fund and a member. Probably there would have been no dispute about the validity of "voluntary" repurchases in gold, but for a time there was stiff resistance by some to the acceptability of currencies. It was understood that voluntary repurchases would have to be compatible with the concept of repurchase as elaborated in the Articles, and that they could be made, therefore, only in convertible currencies and only to the extent that they did not increase the Fund's holdings of any member's currency above 75 per cent of that member's quota or reduce the Fund's holdings of the repurchasing member's currency below 75 per cent of its quota. Nevertheless, it was argued by a minority that voluntary repurchases in this form were unacceptable. In part, the objection was based on a suspicion of the doctrine of implied powers, on which part of the argument for voluntary repurchases rested. This was not the only occasion on which implied powers have been resisted, but this resistance has not prevented them from making their due contribution to the growth of Fund law. However, the objection to voluntary repurchases in currency was based on more than textual or doctrinal considerations. For example, according to one view, it would be advantageous for the Fund to obtain as much gold as possible, and therefore voluntary repurchases in gold should be encouraged by refusing to recognize that they could be made in currency. Another reason for opposition was that the amount of currency that a member would be able to purchase from the Fund would be reduced by voluntary repurchases made with its currency. This consideration was related more to the future operation of the Fund because when the validity of voluntary repurchases in currency was discussed few currencies were convertible and therefore acceptable in repurchase. It was not then as clear as it became in later years that if the Fund receives a member's currency in repurchase this can be as helpful to the member as an equivalent purchase by it, because it eliminates a claim against the member's resources. Indeed, the repurchase is a less expensive form of assistance because a repurchase, unlike a purchase, involves no service charge. The lengthy debate terminated with a decision of March 8, 1951 which recognized the validity of voluntary repurchases on the ground that, like repurchase obligations, they promoted the revolving character of the Fund's resources, and they were not prohibited by any provision of the Articles.[7] Again, as in the case of repurchase obligations, a voluntary repurchase could be made in a member's currency without the necessity for getting the consent of that member.

When the time arrived for ending the Fund's financial inactivity, it was possible to build on the basis of the decision on voluntary repurchases. The decision of February 13, 1952 relied upon the classic theory of the purpose of the use of the Fund's resources. It is to give a member the time in which to pursue the policies that will correct its balance of payments problem and thereby enable the member to accumulate resources with which to repurchase. Therefore, the appropriate period of use is one that is reasonably related to the problem for which the member makes its purchase. Some term had to be placed on the period of use, and as there were different views on what it should be, the limping phrase of "an outside range of three to five years" was adopted as a compromise

[7] E.B. Decision No. 7-(648); below, Vol. III, p. 244.

in the drafting of the decision. Lack of style has not impaired its career. It has become firm practice that if the Fund's holdings of the currency of a purchasing member have not been reduced within three years after a purchase, there must be an understanding under which repurchase will be completed not later than five years after the purchase. Even the paragraph in the decision which was introduced because the new policy was an experiment and which said that the Fund would "consider" some extension beyond five years if "unforeseen circumstances beyond the member's control" made it "unreasonable" to insist that the member repurchase in accordance with the decision [8] has never been applied, although there have been a few attempts to obtain a longer period. There is a strong feeling that there should be no extensions of the period of use beyond five years, either in particular cases or under general policies, even though from time to time those who would like a longer period recall that the determination of what is temporary is a policy decision. Notwithstanding its strict adherence to the limit of five years, the Fund has permitted a small percentage of members to make an effectively longer use of the Fund's resources by allowing these members to make new purchases after they have repurchased. Each stand-by arrangement or purchase in the series has required consultation with the Fund on a new program, and in this way the Fund has been able to stay in close contact with members that have had persistent balance of payments difficulties notwithstanding their efforts to solve their problems.

The technique for putting the understanding on temporary use to work, without stumbling over the objection that the "conditions" in Article V, Section 3 (*a*) are exhaustive, was as follows. The rates of charge on the Fund's holdings of a member's currency in excess of quota were altered so that the date for consultation under Article V, Section 8 (*d*) on means to reduce the Fund's holdings of a member's currency would arrive not later than three years after the member's purchase. When making a request for a purchase, a member would be expected, although not required, to declare that in the consultation the member would agree with the Fund on appropriate arrangements to ensure that the Fund's holdings would be reduced by the amount of the purchase as soon as possible and not later than five years after the purchase. The "conditions" of Article V, Section 3 (*a*) did not preclude a representation of intention as to repurchase, and nothing else in the Articles prevented a member from declaring that it intended to make a voluntary repurchase not later than a date that met the test of temporary use. It was never made clear what would happen if a member refused to make the representation of intention as to repurchase. In practice, this representation has been made in connection with all purchases, and, on the rare occasions when it was omitted as part of the request, this was an oversight that was remedied immediately when it was drawn to the member's attention.

[8] E.B. Decision No. 102-(52/11), February 13, 1952, paragraph 2.d; below, Vol. III, p. 229.

A representation as to repurchase became standard practice very quickly, but the original conception of it has been transformed to a very great extent. It has been seen that a representation of intention as to repurchase is not a "condition" of a purchase, and it does not create an obligation of repurchase in any other way. It is a representation of the member's intention to make a repurchase in due time. Members began to make these representations at a time when modest uses of the Fund's resources were foreseen after a period of virtually no use. As the volume of transactions grew under the influence of decisions that gave increasing precision to the Fund's policies on the use of its resources, it became possible for the Fund to employ certain powers which enabled it to insist on binding commitments with respect to repurchase instead of being content with representations of intention. For example, the Fund can grant a waiver under Article V, Section 4 of the conditions in Article V, Section 3 (*a*) under which members may make purchases, including the condition of use not in excess of 25 per cent of quota during any period of twelve months.[9] It will be seen later that the grant of a waiver permitting use in any period of twelve months beyond this "normal" amount has become common practice. When the Fund grants a waiver, it can impose terms that safeguard its interests, and it invariably makes the repurchase provisions of the decision of February 13, 1952 a term safeguarding its interests. This is not the only way in which repurchase commitments, which differ from representations because they are legally binding, are entered into. For example, when the Fund approves a stand-by arrangement, a term is always included which obligates the member to make a repurchase corresponding to each purchase under the stand-by arrangement, unless the Fund's holdings resulting from the purchase are reduced in some other way, not later than three years after the purchase. The result, therefore, is that in every case in which a purchase is requested the member makes a representation as to repurchase or assumes a commitment to repurchase if there is a legal basis for an obligation. In view of the frequency with which the Fund now grants waivers or approves stand-by arrangements, commitments are far more common than representations.

These developments in Fund practice represent a transformation of certain features of the original theory of the Fund. For example, the practice on repurchase makes the doctrine that the Fund's operations are not for a fixed term somewhat unreal. Repurchase representations and commitments do not replace the provisions of Article V, Section 7 (*b*), to which they can be regarded as ancillary, but there is now a precise final date for repurchase, which may not be obligatory but usually is. Although this practice was first introduced as a result of the initiative of the United States, it has had widespread support for some years, and not merely from the expanding group of members whose currencies are used in the Fund's operations.

---

[9] For the meaning of 25 per cent of quota in Article V, Section 3 (*a*) (iii), see E.B. Decision No. 451-(55/52), August 24, 1955; below, Vol. III, p. 228.

The slogan that the Fund's resources should be a "second line of reserves" is another example of the divergence between theory and practice.[10] It was intended that if a member wishes to use the Fund's resources in order to meet a balance of payments problem, it should use its own reserves and the Fund's resources in equal proportions and should not throw the whole burden on the Fund. There is no obligation to make an equal current use, but the object of the repurchase provisions is to bring this about if the member has made a disproportionate use of the Fund's resources. Subject to certain refinements which need not be recalled here, the repurchase provisions are constructed on the principle that if in any year in which a member, in order to meet a deficit, makes a purchase from the Fund in a greater amount than it uses its own reserves, the member will have a repurchase obligation at the end of that year that will put it in the same position as if it had made that equal use. Moreover, if in any year in which a member is making use of the Fund's resources it enjoys an increase in its monetary reserves, it will have to share that increase with the Fund, so as to reduce or eliminate its outstanding use of the Fund's resources. In recent years, for a number of reasons, including the unacceptability in repurchase of both U.S. dollars and sterling because the Fund's holdings of those currencies were at or above the level of 75 per cent of quota, no more than about one fourth by value of repurchases have been the result of obligations that accrued under Article V, Section 7 (*b*). All other repurchases have been made in accordance with representations or commitments. This phenomenon, coupled with widespread waivers, means that the concept of the second line of reserves as an equal use of a member's own reserves and the Fund's resources has not operated as it would have if the repurchase provisions had been effective on a broad scale. The Fund's resources have been a second line of reserves in a less precise sense because of the condition that a member must "need" the currency that it purchases, which implies in many cases some reduction in its reserves in the recent past, the present, or the immediate future.

Equally little significance remains in the distribution theory of repurchase obligations as written into the Articles. Article V, Section 7 (*b*), and Schedule B were drafted on the principle that repurchase obligations should be discharged in the types of reserve assets that constitute monetary reserves in proportion to a member's holdings, or increases in its holdings, of each type of reserve asset. The rationale of the distribution rules was that reserve assets might not be of equal quality. For example, a currency would still be "convertible" under the Articles even though the Fund approved many restrictions on its use. This consideration led to the interpretative decision under which if part of an obliga-

[10] See, e.g., *Hearings Before the Committee on Banking and Currency of the U.S. Senate on H.R. 3314* (79th Cong., 1st sess.) (Bretton Woods Agreements Act), p. 575. *Hearings Before the Committee on Banking and Currency, U.S. House of Representatives, on H.R. 2211* (79th Cong., 1st sess.), p. 88.

tion had to be discharged under the distribution rules in a member's currency that could not be accepted by the Fund because its holdings of the currency were already at 75 per cent of quota, that part of the obligation was abated and there was no obligation to discharge it in gold or some other currency that the Fund could accept.[11] The drafters thought that if an obligation allocated to a currency which the Fund could not accept had to be discharged by the automatic reallocation of the obligation to another and more usable currency, the distribution formulas would work too inflexibly and perhaps inequitably. Repurchases under representations and commitments are not based on any formulas for distribution among types of reserve assets, and repurchases of this kind may have to be made on occasion because abatement has operated under the fixed formulas of the Articles. The Fund has developed policies, which are discussed a little later, on the currencies in which repurchases should be made under representations or commitments. It will also be seen in Chapter 27 that the principle of abatement has been abrogated under the amendments, but there will be no automatic redistribution of any repurchase obligation that is distributed to an unacceptable currency. The greater flexibility that developed in practice has been preferred, and the new rule is that the Fund will determine the convertible currencies in which the obligation is to be discharged.[12]

WAIVERS

In the discussion of repurchase there was a reference to the Fund's practice on waivers under Article V, Section 4, and an excursus on that subject will be useful before stand-by arrangements are considered. Under Article V, Section 4, the Fund has the discretion to waive any of the conditions governing use of the Fund's resources, and it may grant a waiver on terms which safeguard the Fund's interests. The provision declares that the Fund may grant a waiver especially in the case of members with a record of avoiding large or continuous use of the Fund's resources. In making a waiver, the Fund is to take into consideration "periodic or exceptional requirements" of the member requesting the waiver. Although the Fund is not required by the provision to confine waivers to members that avoid a large or continuous use of the Fund's resources or to members that have periodic or exceptional requirements, the drafters undoubtedly thought that waivers would be unusual. In particular, they regarded the condition limiting use of the Fund's resources in any period of twelve months to 25 per cent of quota as an indication of the "normal" rate of use of the Fund's resources. The Fund has not developed in accordance with these expectations. The first waiver of the 25 per cent limit was not granted until August 1953, but

[11] E.B. Decision No. 521-3, January 16, 1950; below, Vol. III, p. 273.

[12] Schedule B, paragraph 1 (*d*); below, Vol. III, p. 534. Cf. E.B. Decision No. 1371-(62/36), July 20, 1962; below, Vol. III, pp. 235–36.

it is now granted with great frequency. It is still uncommon for the Fund to waive the limit of 200 per cent on its total holdings of a member's currency, but there is evidence of an attitude towards the waiver of that limit also which is different from that of the drafters. For example, in the decision on the compensatory financing of export fluctuations, the Fund has announced in advance its willingness to waive the latter limit in order to make the decision workable.[13]

The almost routine grant of waivers suggests that it would be possible to realize the expectations of the drafters in connection with waivers only if all quotas were considerably larger. A general increase in quotas of 50 per cent was approved in February 1959 and a further increase of 25 per cent in March 1965. These general increases, together with numerous increases in individual quotas throughout the life of the Fund, have expanded total quotas from under $8 billion to the equivalent of approximately $21 billion, but this has not led to a diminished grant of waivers.[14] The effect of the size of quotas and resources on the development of the Fund is not confined to waivers. The General Arrangements to Borrow and all that has followed on that decision are other consequences. This may be true also, at least to some extent, of other forms of financing balance of payments difficulties that have been negotiated outside the framework of the Fund. Some of these are now recognized by the amendments to the Articles.[15]

The Fund has been modest in its recourse to terms safeguarding its interests when granting waivers. The only terms that it has imposed, apart from the rare exceptions mentioned in the next paragraph, have dealt with repurchase. Whenever a member receives the benefit of a waiver, it is required to undertake a commitment to repurchase either as a term under the waiver provision or as a term in a stand-by arrangement.

Under Article V, Section 4 a further consideration that the Fund is to take into account when deciding whether to grant a waiver is "a member's willingness to pledge as collateral security gold, silver, securities, or other acceptable assets having a value sufficient in the opinion of the Fund to protect its interests" and the Fund may require "the pledge of such collateral security." There has always been resistance to the idea that the Fund should relax the standards of its tranche policies merely because of a member's willingness to give security. In addition, the Fund has drawn back from the prospect that, if a pledgor could not repurchase because of continuing difficulties, the Fund would have to decide either to pursue its remedy against the pledged property or, by foregoing its remedy, admit that the pledge was an illusory security. For these and other reasons, the Fund has shown no more than a glimmer of willingness to accept collateral.

[13] E.B. Decision No. 1477-(63/8), February 27, 1963; below, Vol. III, p. 239.

[14] The amendment by which 150 per cent of quota is substituted for quota in Article V, Section 7 (c) should be noted; see below, Vol. III, p. 523.

[15] Schedule B, paragraph 5, below, Vol. III, p. 535

There have been only three decisions by the Fund to accept gold collateral, and one of them was abortive. It is interesting, however, that one of the cases did not involve a waiver but rested on the proposition that the Fund and a member could agree on the pledge of collateral in any circumstances. As a result of the reaction to some of the features of these three cases, the Fund adopted a general decision on July 1, 1963 which declared that it would be willing to enter into a gold collateral transaction in exceptional circumstances if this would promote the purposes of the Fund and give the member time to work out a program in consultation with the Fund. Certain restrictive conditions were established in order to enforce this objective, including the condition that normally the transaction would not be outstanding for more than six months.[16] There has been no transaction in which this decision has been tested.

The Fund itself, however, has given a negative pledge. When the General Arrangements to Borrow were being negotiated the participants feared that the Fund's liquidity would be enhanced unduly by its receipt of the currency of the participant in an exchange transaction made possible by a loan to the Fund. The Fund might then use that currency in transactions with other members, including nonparticipants. The Fund could not agree that some of its holdings could not be used in its operations, but it was a legitimate use to retain adequate satisfactory resources with which to repay its creditors. It is, therefore, a term of the General Arrangements to Borrow that the Fund shall not reduce its holdings of the currency of a participant below the amount that the Fund has borrowed under the General Arrangements to Borrow in order to finance a transaction with the participant.[17]

STAND-BY ARRANGEMENTS

The stand-by arrangement is the most original instrument of financial policy that the Fund has created. It is wholly an invention because no suggestion of it can be found in the Articles. Among the forces that produced it, as well as the tranche policies, were the affirmation of the Fund's power to challenge representations when members request the use of the Fund's resources, the absence of any clear definition of the circumstances in which there might be a challenge, and the Fund's determination early in 1952 to end its financial inactivity. The possibility of the stand-by arrangement was suggested, therefore, as a technique by which a member could be given an assurance that it would be able to make purchases not going beyond a prescribed limit during a defined period. The essential characteristic of a stand-by arrangement is that a member is given the assurance that it will be able to use the Fund's resources without any further

[16] E.B. Decision No. 1543-(63/39); below, Vol. III, pp. 240–42.

[17] E.B. Decision No. 1289-(62/1); below, Vol. III, p. 250.

review of its position and policies. This assurance means that there will be no challenge of a representation when there is a request to make a purchase under a stand-by arrangement, because it is a review which shows whether there is the basis for a challenge.

The idea imbedded in the decision of February 13, 1952 germinated in the first general decision on stand-by arrangements of October 1, 1952, and it has flourished with ever increasing vigor under the four major decisions of December 23, 1953, April 27, 1959, February 20, 1961,[18] and September 20, 1968. Each decision has been taken after a period in which it had become apparent as the result of experience that the stand-by arrangement could be made to serve the interests of members and the Fund even more effectively than it already had. There has been and continues to be great scope for the adaptation of policy on stand-by arrangements without running athwart the Articles.

There is no need to resume the stages by which the stand-by arrangement has been improved to the point of its present flexibility and variety. A few general reflections on its intricate history are appropriate, however, in a survey of development and change. The first comment must be that the concept of the stand-by arrangement has undergone a complete metamorphosis. Originally, it was considered as something in the nature of a confirmed line of credit that gave a member an absolute right to make purchases subject only to those provisions of the Articles on ineligibility and the general suspension of operations that were *lex cogens* and therefore necessarily applicable. At the present date it has become the main instrument for conditionality, and, in particular, for making the Fund's resources available beyond the first credit tranche only if the member observes certain policies. Annexed to each stand-by arrangement is a letter of intent from the member's authorities in which they set forth the program they will pursue. The stand-by arrangements that permit purchases beyond the first credit tranche include performance clauses establishing criteria on the nonobservance of which the member's right to make purchases under the stand-by arrangement will be interrupted without the need for a decision by, or even notice to, the Executive Directors. Performance criteria are invariably objective in character, in the sense that a subjective judgment is not necessary in order to ascertain whether they are being observed, with the result that a member will know at all times whether it is able to make purchases. The movement, therefore, has been from the assurance of use without the review of requests to the definition of the circumstances in which there is assured use without review. It is still proper to speak of assured use because no evaluation is necessary in order to determine whether performance criteria are being observed. No subjective judgment is necessary to determine whether, for example, a limit on

[18] E.B. Decisions Nos. 155-(52/57), 270-(53/95), 876-(59/15), 1151-(61/6); below, Vol. III, pp. 230–33, 234.

credit has been transcended or a restriction on payments and transfers for current international transactions has been introduced. Therefore, if a member is unable to make purchases under its stand-by arrangement, it will not be able to complain that its legitimate expectations have been frustrated by a surprise decision of the Fund.

There are a number of reasons why the stand-by arrangement has been transformed into an instrument of conditionality. One reason has been the willingness of the Fund to take into account the fact that quotas are less than they might be and therefore to allow members to make a large outstanding use of the Fund's resources in terms of quota, provided, however, that there are adequate safeguards that the use will be proper. The continuous refinement of protective clauses in stand-by arrangements providing for consultation, review, and performance has made it possible to protect the Fund's resources against improper use. This should not be understood to mean that the provisions of stand-by arrangements have become progressively stricter for members with each development in the Fund's policies on stand-by arrangements. On the contrary, a dominant theme in the history of these arrangements has been an equitable reconciliation of the assurance to members that they will be able to use the Fund's resources with the assurance to the Fund that use by members will be consistent with the Articles and the policies of the Fund. Great care has been taken to ensure that the balance between the two assurances is not disturbed by being tilted unfairly in either direction, with the result that there have been changes in policy that were designed to reduce the severity of certain protective clauses. For example, the Fund does not insist on performance criteria for purchases in the gold tranche or the first credit tranche, and the "prior notice" clause, which was in common use at one time and which enabled the Fund to interrupt the right to make purchases under a stand-by arrangement on the basis of its subjective judgment of performance, has been banished since February 1961. More recently, in September 1968, the Fund has decided that the number of performance criteria affecting purchases beyond the first credit tranche should be confined to those that are truly necessary for determining whether the objectives of the member's program are being achieved.

It must not be assumed that the stand-by arrangement could have become an effective instrument of conditionality without the support of members. It is true that from time to time there have been debates leading to a revision of policy in order to strike a more acceptable balance between the two basic assurances and between the desiderata of flexibility in dealing with the idiosyncrasies of particular cases and the uniform treatment of all members. The stand-by arrangement has had the endorsement of members since its conception, and the Fund's efforts to improve the efficacy of the instrument have had the same response. The Fund's approval of a stand-by arrangement is commonly regarded by other sources of finance as a seal of approval on the member's program as set forth in its letter of intent, although it should be understood that the standards for this judgment depend upon the amount in terms of tranches that is made available by the stand-by arrangement. Other lenders, international, governmental, or private, often await the Fund's decision to approve a stand-by arrangement before entering into their own financial arrangements with the member, sometimes in a total amount exceeding the amount that the member can purchase under the stand-by arrangement. This is one of the reasons why most of the exchange transactions of the Fund now take place under stand-by arrangements and they account for the larger proportion by value as well. Moreover, there are cases in which stand-by arrangements are approved although there is no great likelihood that any purchases will be made under them. Sometimes a member fears that it is not the presence of a stand-by arrangement but its absence that may be interpreted as a criticism of the member's program. This is an unexpected form of testimony by some members to the success of the Fund's erstwhile campaign to encourage a more routine use of the Fund's resources in order to dispel the impression that members resort to the Fund only in a crisis. Now, if one or another member is reluctant to use the Fund's resources the reason is less likely to be the fear that the public will be alarmed than the reluctance of the member to measure its program against the Fund's tranche policies.

The stand-by arrangement has become the main instrument by which the Fund makes a practical contribution to the adjustment process because all stand-by arrangements are approved on the basis of a letter of intent in which the member sets forth its policies after they have been discussed with the representatives of the Fund. The legal character of the stand-by arrangement and letter of intent as clarified by the Fund is itself evidence of the responsiveness of the Fund. In its letter of intent a member states the program that it will pursue during the period of the stand-by arrangement. The stand-by arrangement is the Fund's decision which prescribes the terms on which the member may make purchases consistently with the Articles, including those specific or quantified policies, targets, or ceilings that are to be performance criteria, i.e., the criteria that the member must observe in order that there will be no interruption of its right to make purchases. There are many reasons why a member may not be able to observe a performance criterion, and sometimes the circumstances responsible for non-observance may be beyond the member's control. The Fund has made it clear that a letter of intent does not have contractual effect, and the non-observance of a performance criterion is not the violation of an international agreement. If a member fails to observe a performance criterion, its access to the Fund's resources under a stand-by arrangement will be interrupted not because it is breaking a contractual commitment but because the Fund has decided in the stand-by arrangement that the non-observance may result in an improper use of the Fund's resources and therefore that there should be consultation with the

Fund to determine the circumstances in which further purchases may be made. This analysis is consistent with the disposition of the Fund to avoid actions that may harm the reputation of members. The analysis has made it easier for members to formulate effective programs and accept performance clauses as a basis for access to the Fund's resources. The stand-by arrangement is a wholly original contribution to international finance and international monetary law.

THE GOLD TRANCHE

One of the main purposes of the decision of February 13, 1952 was to give members the maximum assurance that was possible under the Articles that they would be able to make certain purchases without challenge. The purchases for which there was the strongest case were those that would not raise the Fund's holdings of a member's currency above its quota. These purchases would not exceed the net contribution in economic terms that the member had made to the Fund because they would be no more than the member's gold subscription and the net use of the member's currency by the Fund in its operations and transactions. In the first instance, the amount of this contribution was equal to the member's gold subscription, and for this reason it was called the gold tranche. The Fund could not bind itself validly to surrender the right to challenge the representation of a member requesting a transaction, but in order to convey the idea that a challenge was highly unlikely in practice, even though it remained possible in law, the decision informed members that they could count on "receiving the overwhelming benefit of any doubt" if they requested gold tranche purchases. The concept of "adequate safeguards" in Article I (v), under which the Fund makes its resources available, enables it to graduate safeguards according to financial risk. For gold tranche purchases, the Fund could adopt minimum safeguards because its risk would not exceed the member's own net economic contribution to the Fund.

The gold tranche policy thus began as an attempt to encourage a limited use of the Fund's resources, but from this modest origin it has developed into yet another original contribution to international monetary law and financial arrangements. Once the Fund had formulated its full tranche policies and had become an active financial institution, the gold tranche policy ceased to be an experimental first step in the use of the Fund's resources. The Fund and many of its members began to see in the gold tranche a facility that could be treated as a reserve asset under central bank statutes or at least in the public presentation of a member's reserves. One advantage of this treatment of the gold tranche was that it would counteract the decline in reserves that would follow from the payment of a gold subscription to the Fund or from the Fund's sale of a member's currency and the member's conversion of it into a reserve currency. The latter effect would have special importance in connection with the Fund's efforts to bring about the use of a broader range of currencies in its transactions.

The Fund urged its members to regard the gold tranche as an asset, notwithstanding an occasional resistance provoked by the novelty of the idea, and did what it could to emphasize the asset-like character of the gold tranche. In order to facilitate gold tranche purchases, the Fund refrained from making an examination of the member's policies as it did in the case of purchases beyond the gold tranche, and on August 3, 1964 the Fund adopted a further simplification of procedure for dealing with requests for gold tranche purchases. They were not placed on the agenda of the Executive Directors, unless there was a prompt call for discussion, and arrangements were made for an accelerated transfer of currency.[19] There remained, however, certain shortcomings of the gold tranche in the view of some members. Although in practice it had the quality of ready availability, often described as "*de facto* automaticity" or "virtual automaticity," it could not be given this quality *de jure*. It had to remain subject in principle to the possibility of challenge, although it was never necessary for the Fund to clarify in what circumstances it would feel constrained to challenge a representation because even the overwhelming benefit of any doubt would not be an adequate presumption of propriety. The legal possibility of challenge was not the only shortcoming. It was pointed out that, in addition, the gold tranche policy could be abrogated because it was no more than a policy, and again it was not a formal rebuttal of the objection to aver that this was unlikely to occur. These criticisms of the gold tranche became more troublesome as the Fund sought to promote a policy on the use of an increasing number of currencies in its transactions, one result of which would be to produce gold tranches for more members. There was some sympathy for a more solid legal foundation for the gold tranche even before the principle of amendment was accepted at Rio de Janeiro, and it is not surprising, therefore, that a number of the amendments concentrate on the legal status of the gold tranche and its characteristics. Under the amendments, representations by a member when requesting gold tranche purchases will be immune from challenge by legal prescription, and the gold tranche will enter yet another stage in its evolution.

The Fund's success in achieving widespread recognition of the gold tranche as a reserve asset even before the proposals to amend the Articles led it to make a similar effort in connection with the claims of its creditors to repayment under loan agreements negotiated by the Fund in order to replenish its holdings of currencies. The terms of the General Arrangements to Borrow [20] and the bilateral loan agreement with Italy [21] provide that if before the due date for repayment a lender gives notice to the Fund representing that it has a balance of payments

[19] E.B. Decision No. 1745-(64/46); below, Vol. III, p. 243.

[20] E.B. Decision No. 1289-(62/1), January 5, 1962, paragraph 11 (f); below, Vol. III, p. 250.

[21] See below, p. 544.

need for repayment, the Fund will give "the overwhelming benefit of any doubt" to the representation and will make prompt repayment. Members lending to the Fund under these agreements have concluded that the characteristics of their claims to repayment warranted recognition of them as reserve assets. It will be seen later that once again the reserve character of these claims will have legal endorsement under the amendments to the Articles.

CREDIT TRANCHE POLICY AND COMPENSATORY FINANCING

The Fund's policies for the use of the "credit" tranches, i.e., for members' purchases beyond the gold tranche, developed after 1952 on the legal basis of the Fund's power to challenge representations and the concept of adequate safeguards. By 1955 the Annual Report could state the policy for the first credit tranche and by 1957 the Annual Report could formulate the policy for the higher tranches.[22] These declarations are the framework within which the Fund supports the policies of members by making its resources available as conditional liquidity. Members have come to recognize the credit tranche policies as applied to both purchases and stand-by arrangements as more than the safeguards by which the Fund attempts to protect its resources against improper use. In a world in which the adjustment process is still largely unregulated by international agreement, the credit tranche policies perform part of the task, although only for members in balance of payments deficit.

The greater part of the financial activity of the Fund is now conducted under its credit tranche policies, but the Fund has been prolific in establishing more specialized operations. Although the Fund still subscribes to the doctrine that its financial operations are entered into for the purpose of assisting members to overcome difficulties in the balance of payments taken as a whole, the Fund has felt that this did not prevent it from identifying the specific character of the difficulty and providing assistance more closely related to the difficulty.

The compensatory financing facility is one of the results of this approach that deserves special notice not only because of the intrinsic interest of the facility but also because it has had an effect on the amendments to the Articles. On February 27, 1963 the Fund adopted a decision under which it declared its willingness to assist all members, but particularly primary producers, by compensating them for temporary shortfalls in their export receipts that were largely attributable to circumstances beyond their control. The Fund had been making its resources available to members suffering from these difficulties under its tranche policies but now it was prepared to give special assistance. Compensation was to be limited normally to 25 per cent of quota and was to be additional to

[22] *Annual Report, 1955*, p. 85; *Annual Report, 1957*, p. 119.

the amounts that a member could purchase under the tranche policies. For purchases under the new facility special criteria were prescribed that were less severe than those that applied to the credit tranches or at least the higher credit tranches.[23] On September 20, 1966 the facility was liberalized in amount and in other ways,[24] one of which was the introduction of the "floating" feature. Under the earlier policy, the compensatory financing facility was not separated from the ordinary tranches, with the result that a purchase under the facility might exhaust the gold tranche or the first credit tranche as well and thus deprive the member of the opportunity to make other purchases under the relaxed criteria that apply to those tranches. The revised policy introduced an original development in Fund practice by providing that the facility was to exist alongside the ordinary tranches without overlapping them, so that purchases under the facility would not affect the tranches. The facility has been given statutory recognition in a form that will be mentioned later.

USE OF RESOURCES FOR CAPITAL TRANSFERS

On September 26, 1946 the Executive Directors adopted an interpretation in response to a request made by the Governor for the United States in accordance with the U.S. Bretton Woods Agreements Act.[25] The question was drafted somewhat infelicitously and seemed to ask whether the Fund's authority went beyond the financing of deficits on current account to the length of meeting a large or sustained outflow of capital. The reply to the question was that "authority to use the resources of the Fund is limited to use in accordance with its purposes to give temporary assistance in financing balance of payments deficits on current account for monetary stabilization operations."[26] This appeared to exclude all possibilities for the use of the Fund's resources in respect of an outflow of capital under Article VI ("Capital Transfers"). Section 1 (*a*) of that Article declares that a member may not make net use of the Fund's resources to meet a large or sustained outflow of capital, and Section 1 (*b*) provides that this rule does not prevent the use of the Fund's resources for certain capital transactions of reasonable amount. According to these provisions, therefore, it would seem that the Fund's resources could be used to deal with difficulties created by a capital outflow that was not large or sustained or by certain specified capital transactions of reasonable amount.

There was no doubt that the drafters had placed primary emphasis on the financing of deficits on current account but they had left room in Article VI

[23] E.B. Decision No. 1477-(63/8); below, Vol. III, p. 238.

[24] *Compensatory Financing of Export Fluctuations: A Second Report by the International Monetary Fund*; below, Vol. III, pp. 469–96.

[25] Sec. 13; see above, Chapter 22, footnote 8.

[26] E.B. Decision No. 71-2; below, Vol. III, p. 245.

for the financing of difficulties caused by capital transactions in certain circumstances. The interpretation of September 26, 1946 had not been applied so as to preclude this form of financing, and indeed it gave so little difficulty that virtually no reference was made to it in the Fund's conduct of its operations. By 1961 widespread convertibility had been restored for the currencies of members that had major roles in world trade and payments and this movement had been accompanied by a freedom for exchange markets that permitted great mobility for capital movements. This probably involved a greater freedom for capital movements than the drafters had expected. They had assumed that capital transfers would be suppressed by controls if they became troublesome, and this assumption was carried to the point of empowering the Fund to call for capital controls in certain circumstances. The view which developed, however, was that greater freedom was beneficial and would bring about a greater integration among markets, even though there were dangers of disequilibrating movements. As a result, the Fund has never exercised its power to call for capital controls.

Greater permissiveness for capital movements made it more difficult to decide contemporaneously to what extent payments problems were in the current or in the capital account. In these circumstances, it became advisable to ascertain the exact effect of the 1946 interpretation. Studies of the legislative history of the Articles confirmed what seemed apparent from the text of Article VI: use of the Fund's resources for capital outflows was not proscribed if the outflows were not "large or sustained." These terms were not self-executing, and in the application of them the Fund could take a number of factors into account, including the resources, whether subscribed or borrowed, available for its transactions and its continued capacity to help members deal with deficits on current account. Certain special difficulties might have arisen if it had been necessary to rescind or amend the interpretation, but it was decided ultimately that a clarification would suffice because it could not have been intended that the interpretation should reject what seemed so clear on a reading of Article VI. On July 28, 1961 the Executive Directors decided "by way of clarification" that the interpretation of September 26, 1946 "does not preclude the use of the Fund's resources for capital transfers in accordance with the provisions of the Articles, including Article VI." [27]

The clarification did not initiate use of the Fund's resources to meet difficulties occasioned by capital transfers. That kind of use had already occurred. It is probable, however, that it has led to a greater volume of use for this purpose than would have occurred without provoking the anxiety that this could not be defended under Fund law. The reason for this in large part is that the General Arrangements to Borrow became effective on October 24, 1962 "in order to

[27] E.B. Decision No. 1238-(61/43); below, Vol. III, p. 245.

enable the . . . Fund to fulfill more effectively its role in the international monetary system in the new conditions of widespread convertibility, including greater freedom for short-term capital movements." [28] The participants in the General Arrangements to Borrow stand ready, in accordance with the terms of the General Arrangements, to make their currencies available to the Fund to supplement its resources for financing the exchange transactions of these members in order to deal with their balance of payments difficulties, including, but not limited to, those produced by short-term capital movements.

THE WIDER USE OF CURRENCIES

The last of the leading decisions on the use of the Fund's resources to be considered here is the decision of July 20, 1962 entitled "Currencies to be drawn and to be used in repurchases." [29] It is a decision approving a statement that sets out "what may be regarded as appropriate practices to be followed for the time being." The tentative note in this language reflects the novelty of the synthesis that was being attempted. Nevertheless, the statement has not been amended since it was adopted, although, as in the case of most important declarations of policy, it has become the nucleus around which conventions and procedures are constantly forming.

For ten years or more, almost all purchases from the Fund were of U.S. dollars, but in 1958 the Fund began to suggest that other currencies might enter into its transactions. As the deficit in the balance of payments of the United States continued, it became less justifiable to concentrate on the dollar in the Fund's exchange transactions with other members while the United States itself was reluctant to use the Fund's resources. If the United States had been more willing to purchase the currencies of other members, it would have been possible to continue to sell substantial amounts of dollars to other members. This procedure would have produced fewer problems in applying the provisions of the Articles. With the reluctance of the United States to resort to the Fund, it became necessary to sell non-reserve currencies to other members. This process was encouraged by the *de facto* convertibility of many European currencies and the protracted payments difficulties of both of the main reserve currency countries. The practices that grew up in the period after 1958 were the main content of the decision of July 20, 1962.

A policy of a wider use of currencies in Fund transactions had to be considered in relation to Article V, Section 3 (*a*) (i), which speaks of the sale of a currency that is needed by the purchasing member for making payments "in that currency." The language could be read to mean that a member is entitled to

---

[28] E.B. Decision No. 1289-(62/1), January 5, 1962; below, Vol. III, p. 246.
[29] E.B. Decision No. 1371-(62/36); below, Vol. III, pp. 235–38.

purchase the currency that the member needs to support its exchange market or that its residents need in order to make international payments. On this view, the member would be able to purchase its intervention currency or the currency demanded by payees, which might be the intervention currency in its role of transactions or "vehicle" currency. This version would preclude the sale by the Fund of currencies that would have to be converted by the currency issuer for the benefit of the purchasing member. In reply to this view, it was argued that in a regime of widespread convertibility a member could be said to need any currency that would be converted in order that the proceeds could be put into the market. There was, however, a different approach to the provision which did not require the elucidation of its language. Whatever the words "for making in that currency payments" meant, the Fund could waive them as one of the conditions that were subject to waiver under Article V, Section 4, and in this way the Fund could eliminate any restrictive effect of the words on the sale of currencies. The choice between these theories was never formally settled. It was sufficient that the sale of currencies that would be converted by the currency issuers into a reserve currency for the benefit of purchasing members could be defended under the Articles. Moreover, the question whether there is an obligation on a member to convert its currency for the benefit of a purchasing member also has been left unresolved. Members have been willing to convert their currencies in the conviction that a policy of collaboration of this kind benefited the whole membership of the Fund. The evolution of procedures satisfactory to members for consulting them on the use of their currencies has encouraged the collaboration on which the wider use of currencies depends.

The decision of July 20, 1962 rests on the principle that the selection of currencies for use in the Fund's transactions should be based on the balance of payments and reserve positions of members as well as on the level of the Fund's holdings of their currencies. The Fund seeks to maintain an equitable proportion among members in the sale of their currencies, but the motive for this now is not so much equality of sacrifice as the fair distribution of a reserve asset resulting from Fund transactions, the gold tranche. It is a desirable asset because it is guaranteed as to gold value and to some extent carries remuneration.

It is now standard practice for a member contemplating a purchase to consult the Fund on the currency or currencies it should select. A similar practice has become established in connection with the choice of currencies to be used in repurchases that do not accrue under Article V, Section 7 (*b*), and the decision of July 20, 1962 includes criteria for this purpose also. The impact of the decision has extended even beyond the wider use of currencies in purchases and repurchases because the criteria which it established have affected the drafting of the provisions of the General Arrangements to Borrow on the selection of the currencies that should be lent to the Fund to supplement its resources and, more recently, the drafting of the amendments on special drawing rights.

The practices that are described in the decision of July 20, 1962 and that have grown up under it have had a fundamental effect on the operation of the Fund. These practices have made it possible for members to give assistance through the Fund whenever their position warrants this, and to give assistance on a multilateral basis that eliminates any need to link deficits and surpluses bilaterally. Another result is that to a large extent the subscription paid by a member in its currency has become a token of the reserve currency, or even gold, into which the member will convert its currency for use by purchasing members.

The policy has had another interesting effect. The drafters of the Articles were worried that the traditional practice by which trade and payments are conducted largely in a few transactions currencies might lead to the immobilization of the Fund's holdings of many or even most currencies.[30] For example, a member might require that payments to it or to its residents be made in dollars, with the result that the Fund's holdings of the member's currency would not be in demand from the Fund for making payments to it. At the same time, there might be additional pressure on the Fund's holdings of U.S. dollars because other members might have to purchase dollars for making payments to the member or its residents. A member is free to prescribe the currency in which payments must be made to the member or its residents. This is not a restriction on the *making* of payments and transfers. The drafters did not want to interpose any impediment to the traditional use of transactions currencies, and so they adopted a special, although partial, solution for the effect that this practice might have on the Fund's currency holdings. They imposed an additional repurchase obligation on a member that required payments to be made in a "third" currency if it was itself using the Fund's resources. A formula was adopted under which the proceeds of transactions which a member had received in a third currency had to be used for the repurchase of that member's currency from the Fund even beyond the standard repurchase obligation if that obligation did not reduce the Fund's holdings to 75 per cent of the member's quota.[31] But this was a case in which the drafters' reach exceeded the administrators' grasp, because no way was found by which the provision could be made to work. The Fund's policy on the wider use of currencies in its transactions provides a more satisfactory solution. If a member is in an economic position that justifies the use of its currency under the decision, other members can purchase the currency for conversion by the member into its reserve currency and they can use that currency for making international payments. Moreover, these sales by the Fund of the member's currency can be more extensive than the member's repurchases. A member cannot reduce the Fund's holdings of its currency below 75 per cent

[30] *Proceedings*, pp. 461–63.

[31] Article V, Section 7 (*b*) (ii); below, Vol. III, pp. 192–93.

of quota by repurchase, but the Fund can sell any of the member's currency which it holds without observing that or any other limit.

It is convenient to refer here to another financial provision that has been dormant most of the time, although it has not become a dead letter. This is Article VIII, Section 4, which created a new form of convertibility. If a member undertakes the obligations of convertibility under the Articles it must convert balances of its currency that are presented to it by the monetary authorities of another member if the balances were recently acquired as the result of current transactions or their conversion is needed for making payments for current transactions. The currency issuer may choose to make the conversion with either gold or the currency of the other member, but the currency issuer will not be obligated to make a conversion unless it is entitled to purchase the currency of the other member from the Fund. This was a new form of convertibility because it is convertibility through the Fund on the theory that if the currency issuer purchases from the Fund the currency of the holder of the balances, the extent to which the latter will be able to make purchases of currencies from the Fund will be increased correspondingly. The provision is based on the assumption of a bilateral balancing of payments that has not occurred among members having convertible currencies.[32] With the restoration of free exchange markets, most conversions take place in the market on an even broader scale than is required by Article VIII, Section 2 (*a*), under which members must refrain from restricting payments and transfers for current international transactions. In the result, there has been only one occasion on which there was an overt reference to Article VIII, Section 4 as the basis of a transaction. This was a sale by the Fund in August 1966 of lire to the United States in an amount equivalent to one quarter of a billion dollars in order to enable it to convert dollars held by Italy. The sale was contemporaneous with an equivalent loan of lire by Italy to the Fund.

The Fund's policy on the selection of the appropriate currencies for its exchange transactions has not departed from the drafters' theory of a "passive" Fund. The main expression of that theory is Article V, Section 2, which places a "limitation on the Fund's operations" by declaring that, except as otherwise provided in the Articles, the Fund's operations are to be confined to transactions for the purpose of supplying a member, "on the initiative of such member," with the currency of another member in return for gold or for the purchasing member's currency. Under this provision, the Fund cannot initiate an exchange transaction, either with a member or in the market. Under the policy on the selection of currencies, the Fund does not initiate exchange transactions, but it is the active party in indicating the currencies that are to be purchased in transactions initiated by members.

[32] See *Questions and Answers on the International Monetary Fund*, Question 24; below, Vol. III, pp. 164–65.

Another effect of Article V, Section 2 is that the Fund cannot sell currency A to member A in return for currency B, except under the repurchase provisions, if, for example, the Fund wishes to acquire currency B because member C wishes to purchase it from the Fund. Under the Fund's policy on the selection of currencies, however, the Fund has been able to sell currency A to member C and member A has converted currency A into currency B for the benefit of member C. In this example, it is assumed, of course, that currency B is a reserve currency of A and needed by C. Because the conversion is not carried out in a direct operation with the Fund it need not be made at the par values.[33] Once there is a departure from par values, however, the question of the ultimate value received by the purchasing member C arises, and this consideration has not been absent in the selection of currencies under the policy. The experience with exchange rates in conversions under the policy has been taken into account in the drafting of the provisions dealing with special drawing rights. In transactions between participants in the special drawing rights facility, currency is not provided at the par value, and the exchange rates that are used must be such that the transferor of special drawing rights receives the same value whatever the currencies that are provided.[34]

A BACKWARD GLANCE

In retrospect, there seem to have been two major and related themes in the evolution of the Fund's practice on the use of its resources. The first has been the development of the two forms of liquidity, conditional and unconditional, that the Fund makes available to its members. Once it was accepted that the Articles give the Fund a power to challenge the representation made by a member when requesting the use of the Fund's resources, it became desirable to encourage members to use the Fund's resources by creating the concept of a gold tranche that was to be available as nearly automatically as possible. Because of this and other attributes, the gold tranche became recognized eventually as a new reserve asset. Meanwhile, the tranche policies based on an ascending scale of conditionality were being elaborated, while constant experiment was being devoted to the stand-by arrangement in order to improve it as the main instrument for putting this conditionality to work. A prerequisite of development in this part of the Fund's constitutional history was the solution of the problems of temporary use and repurchase. Both the tranche policies and stand-by arrangements have entered on the scene and played their leading parts without the benefit of express mention in the Articles.

[33] Article IV, Section 1 (*b*). E.B. Decision No. 1371-(62/36), July 20, 1962; below, Vol. III, pp. 237–38.

[34] Article XXV, Section 8; below, Vol. III, p. 530.

The second main theme has been the extension of the Fund's financial operations in both volume and character. The "adequate safeguards" of tranche policies and stand-by arrangements and the liberal approach to waivers have made it possible to permit large individual transactions and large outstanding use of the Fund's resources in terms of quota. Borrowing by the Fund and the employment of a wider range of currencies in its transactions are other techniques that have made this greater use possible. Clarification of the Fund's authority to permit the use of its resources to meet difficulties caused by capital outflows in certain circumstances and the creation of the compensatory financing facility are leading examples of the adaptability of the Fund in helping members to deal with pressing new problems.

The position of the United States in the world and in the Fund has dominated much of the history of this part of the Fund's affairs. For many years it was the member which provided virtually the only currency purchased from the Fund, and it used its influence to insist on adequate safeguards. In a later stage, the United States was in a persistent and troubling deficit in its balance of payments, and the Fund then sought to adjust itself to a situation in which the United States would need to receive assistance in financing its deficit, in greater or less degree through the Fund according to the willingness of the United States itself. It is not surprising that in this stage the members that did not readily accept the caution of the United States in the earlier period are now the most determined advocates of it. This change of opinion has had a decisive effect on the amendments of the Articles that deal with the use of the Fund's resources.

CHAPTER

24

The Code of Conduct

Joseph Gold

PAR VALUES AND EXCHANGE RATES

The basic premise of the provisions dealing with par values and rates of exchange, sometimes referred to as the par value system, was the novel idea that rates of exchange are matters of international concern and therefore should be the subject of international scrutiny and endorsement. It was provided that each member should agree on a par value for its currency with the Fund.[1] Exchange rates should be fixed, and therefore should not fluctuate beyond narrow margins around the par value,[2] and multiple currency practices should be avoided.[3] To ensure stability without rigidity, it was agreed that a par value should be subject to change but only to correct a fundamental disequilibrium. Each member was to have the exclusive privilege of proposing a change in the par value of its currency, but it was required to consult the Fund and in most cases obtain its concurrence before making a change. In deciding whether to concur in or object to a change, the Fund would seek to deter a member from making a change that would be competitive.[4]

The Fund has had to deal with a world for which this model was not completely appropriate, with the result that the model has been adapted in some respects, although without any compromise of the principle that rates of exchange are matters of international concern. The most crucial issue of interpretation in which this principle was involved in the early years of the Fund was the question whether a member could adapt multiple currency practices, or in the case of some members introduce them, without the approval of the Fund because the member was availing itself of the transitional arrangements of Article XIV. Section 2 of that Article enables a member availing itself of the

[1] Article XX, Section 4; below, Vol. III, p. 208.

[2] Article IV, Sections 3 and 4 (*b*).

[3] Article VIII, Section 3.

[4] Article IV, Section 5.

transitional arrangements to adapt restrictions on payments and transfers for current international transactions to changing circumstances, and introduce them where necessary if the member had been occupied by the enemy, and the question that had to be answered was whether this authority applied to multiple currency practices when, as is often true, they are also restrictions. Notwithstanding Article XIV, Section 2, the Fund decided that if a restriction is also a rate of exchange, the rate provisions, and basically Article IV, Section 4 (*a*), must be observed, and a member is obligated to obtain the approval of the Fund before making the change of rate that would be involved in the adaptation or introduction of a multiple currency practice. The objection that this conclusion put members maintaining multiple currency practices as a form of exchange control at a disadvantage compared with those maintaining other forms of exchange control did not prevail. The decision was communicated to members together with a statement of the Fund's policies on multiple currency practices in a letter of December 19, 1947.[5]

The direct and indirect impact of the decision on the practice of the Fund has been enormous. It is obviously important because so many members maintaining multiple currency practices have availed themselves of the transitional arrangements of Article XIV and also because the postwar transitional period in which those arrangements operate has not been terminated. The ideological importance of the decision has been even more profound. It was animated by the conviction that jurisdiction over rates of exchange is at the heart of the Fund's functions and the constriction of that jurisdiction could maim the Fund's authority. The Fund's letter of December 19, 1947 described the obligations of members in connection with exchange stability, orderly exchange arrangements, and the avoidance of competitive alterations as "fundamental considerations" in the interpretation of the Articles. The decision and the conviction on which it rests have influenced the attitude of the Fund on other questions involving exchange rates. No decision can be recalled in which the Fund has held that it does not have jurisdiction in connection with the adoption of exchange rates for a member's currency. This does not mean that all issues affecting exchange rates have been settled. For example, the Fund has found it necessary to reconcile Article VI, Section 3, which gives members broad powers to control capital transfers, and Article VIII, Section 3, which prevents members from engaging in discriminatory currency arrangements without the approval of the Fund. The Executive Directors held on July 25, 1956 that the members' authority to control capital transfers had to be given primacy and that they could discriminate in the application of their capital controls without the need for the approval of the Fund.[6] The Executive Directors drew back, however, from extending this decision to multiple currency practices that applied to capital transfers, and they

[5] E.B. Decision No. 237-2; below, Vol. III, pp. 261-65.

[6] E.B. Decision No. 541-(56/39); below, Vol. III, p. 246.

did this precisely because rates of exchange were involved. The Executive Directors reserved for later decision the question whether under Article VI, Section 3 members may freely introduce or adapt, without the approval of the Fund, multiple currency practices that apply to capital transfers or whether members must obtain the Fund's approval of these actions under Article VIII, Section 3. The Executive Directors have not decided this question so far, but the staff has held the view that the approval of the Fund is required, and in a number of cases in which a multiple currency practice affecting capital transfers was introduced or adapted, and the Fund agreed that the practice was justified, the Fund adopted a formula by which it gave such approval as was necessary. This formula keeps the jurisdictional issue open until such time as it becomes so important in practice that its solution is necessary.

It is clear from the Articles that the drafters assumed that the prevention of competitive devaluation would be a major preoccupation of the Fund, but the overvaluation of currencies has been a greater problem than undervaluation. This phenomenon was reflected in the issue which arose as a result of the unauthorized change of par value by France in January 1948. The question was whether the Fund was required to concur in a change of par value which was in the right direction and not competitive but in the opinion of the Fund inadequate to correct the member's fundamental disequilibrium. The Executive Directors decided on March 1, 1948 that the extent of the change in a par value that is necessary to correct a fundamental disequilibrium cannot be determined with precision, and that in considering a member's proposal to make a change the Fund would give the member the benefit of any reasonable doubt. If, however, the Fund concluded, after giving the member the benefit of any reasonable doubt, that the proposed change was insufficient to correct the fundamental disequilibrium, the Fund had the authority to object to the proposal and was not bound to concur in it.[7] Part of the reasoning on which the decision rested was that the phrases "correct a fundamental disequilibrium" or "necessary to correct a fundamental disequilibrium" mean that the change is sufficient to bring about a correction, with the result that the Fund is not bound to concur in any proposal that would not bring about a full correction.

Another decision that bears on the degree of flexibility in the par value system is the question whether the Fund may approve a fluctuating rate as a transitional device from one par value to another par value. Some experts have had a certain sympathy for a device of this kind because of the difficulty of determining the precise level at which a new par value should be fixed in order to correct a fundamental disequilibrium. A transitional fluctuating rate, it has been argued, would permit a period of experiment in which to determine what the new par value should be. On July 22, 1948 when Mexico ceased to ensure that its par

[7] E.B. Decision No. 278-3; below, Vol. III, p. 227.

value would be effective and again on September 19, 1949 when Belgium proposed to adopt such a regime, the Fund's reaction was based on the principle that it had no legal power to approve the regime even as a temporary expedient. If a member ceases to ensure that exchange transactions within its territories take place only within the permitted margins around the par value established under the Articles, the member is failing to fulfill its obligations. The definitive statement affirming this position appeared in the Fund's Annual Report for 1951 [8] after Canada adopted a fluctuating rate in September 1950, and was repeated in the Annual Report for 1962.[9]

The discussion so far illustrates the sensitivity of the Fund to exchange rates as matters of international concern and the pervasiveness of its jurisdiction over them, but indicates that there are certain limits under the Articles on the ability of members to adopt or the Fund to approve certain exchange rate practices or regimes. This brings the discussion to those developments by which the Fund has been able to accommodate itself to something less than the optimal system as foreseen by the drafters. In the three cases in which Mexico, Belgium, and Canada felt that they must cease to support the par value in exchange transactions, the Fund refrained from applying sanctions, and even showed some sympathy, but there is even stronger evidence of the Fund's tolerance. There have been instances in which the Fund has welcomed or encouraged the adoption of a fluctuating rate. In many of these cases the member was eliminating multiple currency practices or simplifying a complex exchange rate regime. In the case of simplification, the Fund is able to approve the remaining rates as multiple currency practices but it has no power to approve if rates are unified. It may seem odd that the Fund can approve multiple currency practices but not a unitary fluctuating rate, but the explanation is the assumption underlying the Articles that if a member is in a position to have a single rate for its currency it should be able to fix a par value and should not allow the rate to fluctuate. On a number of occasions the Fund has approved stand-by arrangements in support of a fluctuating rate as part of a stabilization program. The theory, usually tacit, on which the Fund has welcomed or encouraged a fluctuating rate has been that the member was making progress towards the establishment of an effective par value and the observance of the purposes of the Fund. Nevertheless, in some cases in which the rate has become stabilized no new par value has been established, presumably on the ground that it was not yet certain that the official rate was soundly entrenched.

In some of these cases in which the Fund has put its resources at the disposition of a member, the so-called fluctuating rate has been too rigid to ensure the success of the member's stabilization program. The Fund has developed a num-

[8] *Annual Report, 1951*, pp. 36–41.

[9] *Annual Report, 1962*, pp. 58–67.

ber of techniques for incorporation in stand-by arrangements by which to encourage the member to pursue a policy of helpful exchange rate flexibility.

The Fund has exercised its authority over the use of its resources, particularly under stand-by arrangements, in a way that contributes to the adjustment of exchange rates even though they do not purport to be fluctuating rates. It is a member's prerogative to propose what the par value for its currency shall be, but it is the Fund's duty to husband its resources. The Fund has been unwilling, therefore, to make its resources available in support of a par value which it considers untenable. For example, the Fund's criterion for the use of its resources in the higher credit tranches refers to programs aimed at "establishing or maintaining the enduring stability of the currency concerned at a realistic rate of exchange." [10] The Fund's unwillingness to make its resources available to a member that has an inappropriate par value for its currency does not entitle the Fund to make a proposal that the par value be changed. The initial discussion of a transaction with the Fund takes place with the Managing Director or staff so that the member need not be embarrassed by further debate of the appropriateness of the exchange rate for its currency.

The Fund has been patient if new members have felt that their adherence to the full exchange rate regime of the Articles might be premature. The standard form of membership resolution under which a new member joins the Fund contains a paragraph empowering the Fund to call on the member to proceed with the establishment of a par value. In recent years many new members have been new countries as well and for this or other reasons the establishment of a viable par value by some of them has been difficult. The Fund has refrained from initiating the procedure that would require these members to establish par values. This policy gives greater weight to the provision in membership resolutions under which a member may change exchange rates before the establishment of a par value only after consulting the Fund and reaching agreement with it on the change.

The Fund's understanding of the special problems of these new members is apparent in more than its restraint in calling for the establishment of par values for their currencies. It has been forthcoming in its disposition to assist them with its resources. The general theory of the drafters was that after a member established a par value, it would be able to use the Fund's resources for the purpose of defending the par value if it were tenable and if support for a temporary period became necessary.[11] The Articles also provide that the Fund may determine the amounts of, and conditions for, purchases by a member belonging to a defined and limited class before it establishes a par value for its currency.[12]

[10] *Annual Report, 1958*, p. 24.

[11] Article III, Section 3; Article XX, Section 4 (*c*) and (*i*).

[12] Article XX, Section 4 (*d*).

In June 1953 the Executive Directors examined the question whether there was general authority to prescribe the amounts of and conditions for pre-par-value transactions, but there was no decision at that time largely because there was no authority in the Articles to do this for the benefit of one original member (Uruguay) that had not yet established a par value. After that member had established an initial par value and become eligible to use the Fund's resources, the Executive Directors decided on April 22, 1964 that the Fund had authority under the Articles to provide in all membership resolutions that it might permit pre-par-value transactions in such amounts and on such conditions as it saw fit.[13] The Fund would encourage members to follow policies leading to the establishment of realistic exchange rates and the adoption of effective par values at the earliest possible date, and, in deciding whether to give access to its resources, would take into account the efforts that the member was making to reach this objective. The Fund also decided that it would permit a member that had not yet established a par value to make gold tranche purchases and enjoy the benefits of the compensatory financing facility on the same basis as other members. The decision eliminated the anomaly that, whereas a member that has established an initial par value is able to use the Fund's resources even after it is forced by events to cease to ensure its effectiveness in exchange transactions, with a few exceptions a member that had not yet established an initial par value did not enjoy access to the Fund's resources even though its exchange rate regime might be an orderly one. The theory of the drafters was not offended because members in this latter condition were not entitled to use the Fund's resources but could make use of them only in the amounts and on the conditions permitted by the Fund.

This survey of actions by the Fund in favor of greater exchange rate flexibility will be concluded with one that relates to the margins for spot exchange transactions. These are fixed by the Articles at 1 per cent from par, and members must adopt appropriate measures consistent with the Articles to ensure that these margins are not transcended in exchange transactions within their territories. This meant, in effect, that each member could establish a margin of ½ of 1 per cent for gold transactions in its currency. There is evidence that these were regarded as generous margins,[14] although there is also evidence that the drafters thought that the margins might become inadequate.[15] In December 1958, certain European members that were contemplating the adoption of "external" convertibility concluded that it would help them to restore convertibility and free exchange markets, but with a certain economy in the use of reserves, if they were to adopt margins up to ¾ of 1 per cent on the U.S.

---

[13] E.B. Decision No. 1687-(64/22); below, Vol. III, p. 243.

[14] *Questions and Answers on the International Monetary Fund*, Question 19; below, Vol. III, pp. 158–60.

[15] Article XVI, Section 1.

dollar for their currencies. This meant that the margins for exchange transactions between any two of these currencies might be as much as 1½ per cent from par. Moreover, if a currency pegged on a currency that was itself pegged on a convertible currency, the margin in an exchange transaction involving the first currency and a third currency might be more than 1½ per cent from par. Basing itself on some early decisions,[16] the Fund decided that if a member takes official action to confine exchange transactions involving its own and another member's currency within 1 per cent of par and permits transactions involving its own and other currencies to go beyond those margins, this constitutes a multiple currency practice. In order, therefore, to assist members to move towards convertibility, the Fund decided on July 24, 1959 that it would not object to the cumulation of margins in such a system provided that the resulting margin from par for transactions between any two member currencies was no more than 2 per cent.[17]

RESTRICTIONS

The establishment of a multilateral system of payments in respect of current transactions between members is one of the purposes of the Fund and it is to be attained by the avoidance of restrictions on the making of payments and transfers for current international transactions as defined by the Articles. Article VIII, Section 2 requires members to refrain from imposing these restrictions without the approval of the Fund unless they are authorized by the transitional arrangements of Article XIV. The question of the definition of restrictions for the purposes of Article VIII, Section 2 was raised as a problem of interpretation in 1951. There were forces pulling in opposite directions: some wished to arrive at a definition that would make it clear that the Fund's jurisdiction did not embrace restrictions on trade, even if they were imposed for balance of payments reasons, because these were within the competence of the CONTRACTING PARTIES to the GATT, whereas others were troubled by the fact that this might limit the competence of the Fund in connection with members' balances of payments. There was a division of opinion on the primary question of definition and therefore no agreement on the secondary question whether the same measure might be a restriction on both payments under the Fund's Articles and on trade under the GATT. The differences of opinion could not be reconciled and discussion petered out.

The problem did not come to the surface again until 1960 when it seemed that a solution should be found because of the likelihood that a number of

---

[16] See E.B. Decision No. 237-2, December 18, 1947, and the accompanying statement on multiple currency practices; below, Vol. III, p. 265.

[17] E.B. Decision No. 904-(59/32); below, Vol. III, p. 226.

European members would accept the obligations of Article VIII. By that time, attitudes had become less uncompromising, partly because the scope of consultations under Article XIV, and the manner of conducting them, had become established. It had become clear also that certain measures were of a mixed character and came under the jurisdiction of both the Fund and the CONTRACTING PARTIES.

A 1959 staff study said that there were three possible approaches to the definition of what constitutes a restriction on payments and transfers for current international transactions under the Articles. One approach would deem a measure to be a restriction if the effect on the balance of payments was the motive with which the measure was adopted. The second approach was not concerned with motive but took account of the effect of a measure and would regard it as a restriction if the direct or indirect effect was to hinder payments or transfers for current international transactions. It was concluded that neither approach was acceptable and that the third of the possible approaches was correct. This looked simply at the way in which the measure was formulated and made to operate. The main elements responsible for this conclusion were the language of the Articles, which emphasized the financial or settlement aspect of a transaction, and the intention of the Bretton Woods Conference that there should be an international trade organization with a jurisdiction that would complement and in principle not overlap the jurisdiction of the Fund. Either of the other approaches would have resulted unavoidably in a very considerable coincidence of jurisdiction for the two organizations.

The conclusion that the test must be a technical one was accepted by the Executive Directors although with some regret by those who continued to feel a strong attachment to the balance of payments motive as the appropriate criterion. In their view, the fact that the Fund acted as the advisor of the CONTRACTING PARTIES on balance of payments and reserve questions and that the CONTRACTING PARTIES had bound themselves to accept the Fund's advice was not an adequate substitute for the direct jurisdiction of the Fund because not all members of the Fund were contracting parties. Nevertheless, agreement was reached, and the Fund's decision of June 1, 1960 records it in the sentence which reads: "The guiding principle in ascertaining whether a measure is a restriction on payments and transfers for current transactions under Article VIII, Section 2, is whether it involves a direct governmental limitation on the availability or use of exchange as such." [18] In order to help reconcile those who had held a different view, although they would insist on it no longer, the formula is expressed as a "guiding principle" and not as a definition or interpretation.

---

[18] E.B. Decision No. 1034-(60/27); below, Vol. III, pp. 260–61. See also James G. Evans, Jr., "Current and Capital Transactions: How the Fund Defines Them," *Finance and Development*, Vol. 5 (1968), No. 3, pp. 30–35; Stephen A. Silard, "The Impact of the International Monetary Fund on International Trade," *Journal of World Trade Law*, Vol. 2 (1968), No. 2, pp. 121–61.

Some executive directors, however, said that they would regard the guiding principle as an interpretation, and in practice it has operated in that way.

The settlement of this fundamental question of jurisdiction is interesting for a number of reasons. It illustrates the caution with which questions of jurisdiction under the code of conduct have been approached. It is an example of self-imposed discipline, and one that is all the more noteworthy because it was inspired by a design for international economic organization even though that design had not been realized. The presumed intention of the drafters prevailed even though some thought that it had lost its cogency because it had been based on an expectation that had been frustrated.

TRANSITIONAL ARRANGEMENTS

Article XIV deals with a "post-war transitional period" and permits members to avail themselves of "transitional arrangements" under which, notwithstanding the provisions of any other articles, they may maintain, and adapt to changing circumstances, restrictions on payments and transfers for current international transactions. There was also a limited authority for some members to introduce restrictions of this kind. A member exercising its privileges under the transitional arrangements is not required to seek the approval of the Fund under Article VIII for the maintenance, adaptation, or introduction of restrictions in accordance with Article XIV, Section 2. One of the conditions on which these privileges can be enjoyed by a member is that it is satisfied that it needs the restrictions for balance of payments reasons. Once it concludes that it has no balance of payments justification for restrictions, they can be maintained, adapted, or introduced only with the approval of the Fund under Article VIII.

From time to time it has been assumed by some commentators that the transitional period was of defined duration. Sometimes, this misapprehension was induced by the references in Article XIV, Section 4 to a period of three years after which the Fund began to report on restrictions and a period of five years after which members began to consult the Fund on the further retention of restrictions. In fact, there is no transitional period of defined length, and there is evidence that this was deliberate because of the fear of some countries that they might be pressed to adopt a premature convertibility for their currencies. There is, however, a procedure by which the Fund can make representations to a member that conditions are favorable for the withdrawal of particular restrictions or the abandonment of all of them. The caution of the drafters is illustrated by the fact that these representations may be made "in exceptional circumstances," but on January 6, 1947, the Fund's concern that a too extensive use might be made of the privileges of Article XIV led to a decision emphasizing that the Fund is the judge of what is meant by "exceptional circumstances." [19] If the Fund makes a representation to a member and finds that it persists in maintaining restrictions, the member becomes ineligible to use the Fund's resources. The Fund has made general policy declarations recommending or urging all members to withdraw certain kinds of restrictions,[20] and has adopted numerous decisions concluding consultations with individual members under Article XIV in which the Fund expressed the opinion in one way or another that the use of restrictions could be reduced or eliminated, but the Fund has never addressed a formal representation to a member under Article XIV, Section 4.

On a few occasions, but not since 1960, the question has been asked whether the Fund could terminate the transitional period by interpretation or in some other way. Another question that has been asked is whether the Fund could find that a member was no longer availing itself of the transitional arrangements and was in the same position as if it had given notice under Article XIV, Section 3 that it was prepared to accept the obligations of convertibility of Article VIII, Sections 2, 3, and 4. Neither of these questions has been resolved by the Fund.

The main reason why at least the first of these questions has not been answered is the transformation in the Fund's attitude to Article XIV which can be traced to 1960. On June 1 of that year the Executive Directors adopted a decision in the expectation that in the near future there would be a concerted acceptance of the obligations of Article VIII by a number of European members.[21] There was a widespread feeling that the legal convertibility of a currency under Article VIII should correspond with a real convertibility. It was clear that a member is entitled to decide for itself whether to give notice that it is prepared to accept the obligations of Article VIII, and the Fund cannot reject the notice, although it can refuse to approve any remaining restrictions. Once a member gives the notice, its currency is "convertible" under the Articles. Moreover, acceptance of the obligations of Article VIII is a one-way street, and a member cannot retreat to Article XIV after it has given the notice. There was no way to ensure that the convertibility of a currency would never be impaired, but it was at least possible to prevent convertibility from being turned into a legal fiction by discouraging a member from accepting the obligations of Article VIII if there was a risk that soon after acceptance it would have to request the Fund's approval for the introduction of restrictions.

The Fund's position can be discerned in paragraph 2 of the decision of June 1, 1960. The paragraph recognizes the right of members to give notice but states

[19] E.B. Decision No. 117-1; below, Vol. III, p. 269.

[20] E.B. Decisions Nos. 433-(55/42), June 22, 1955, 201-(53/29), May 4, 1953, 955-(59/45), October 23, 1959; below, Vol. III, pp. 258–60.

[21] E.B. Decision No. 1034-(60/27); below, Vol. III, pp. 260–61.

that before taking that step "it would be desirable that, as far as possible, they eliminate measures which would require the approval of the Fund, and that they satisfy themselves that they are not likely to need recourse to such measures in the foreseeable future." The Fund warned that it would not readily approve the maintenance or introduction of restrictions by a member once it had accepted the obligations of Article VIII. If a member proposed to maintain or introduce restrictions for balance of payments reasons, the Fund would grant approval "only where it is satisfied that the measures are necessary and that their use will be temporary while the member is seeking to eliminate the need for them." If the justification is not related to the balance of payments, "the Fund believes that the use of exchange systems for nonbalance of payments reasons should be avoided to the greatest possible extent."

The implication of this declaration of policy is that the Fund will not be complaisant about the maintenance or introduction of restrictions by a member that accepts the obligations of Article VIII but might be more tolerant about the use of restrictions by a member that has not yet accepted those obligations. This attitude reflects a willingness to see members continue to opt for the transitional arrangements if there is still doubt about the strength of their position, with the result that the postwar transitional period has become literally a period, of undefined duration, after the war. Even new members joining the Fund in these days are allowed a choice between the regimes of Article VIII and Article XIV. Moreover, there are members that are still technically under Article XIV even though they maintain no restrictions and therefore can take no action under Article XIV. If these members were to wish to introduce restrictions, they would have to request approval under Article VIII. Presumably, they retain their status under Article XIV because they believe their position to be such that they cannot say with confidence that "they are not likely to need recourse to" measures requiring approval "in the foreseeable future."

CONSULTATION

According to the first purpose of Article I, the Fund is to provide the machinery for consultation on international monetary problems, and the functioning of the Fund would be impossible without consultation with members. Under Article XIV, Section 4, members are required to consult the Fund each year on the further retention of any restrictions that are inconsistent with the Articles. This is a narrow jurisdictional basis for consultation and in earlier years there were difficulties in convincing some members that even the limited objective of this form of consultation required consideration of the economic context in which exchange restrictions were retained. Part of the problem was the suspicion that the Fund was extending its authority into the field of trade in which it had no jurisdiction to approve or disapprove trade practices. This problem persisted for a time even though it is a purpose of the Fund to facilitate the expansion and balanced growth of international trade and even though Article XIV, Section 2 requires members, as soon as conditions permit, to develop such commercial and financial arrangements with other members as will facilitate international payments and the maintenance of exchange stability.

One of the great advances in the Fund's activities has been the progressive acceptance of the idea that consultation under Article XIV should encompass all aspects of a member's economy that have a direct or indirect effect on the member's balance of payments. The scope of these consultations has not been limited even though there has been a steady withdrawal of restrictions to the point where some members still availing themselves formally of the transitional arrangements have few or even no restrictions still in force. The scope of consultation under Article XIV has become more extensive as confidence has grown between members and the Fund and as members have realized that the review is useful to the member with which the consultation is conducted and to other members as well. It is useful to other members because the consultation report is often the most comprehensive international report of its kind. One evidence of the value of these reports has been the increasing requests for the descriptive part of them by other international organizations. Discussion of the reports has made it possible for the Executive Directors to maintain multilateral surveillance over members, propose the adjustment of their policies, and gather knowledge on the basis of which to formulate the general policies of the Fund.

The acceptance of broad consultations on the narrow jurisdictional basis of Article XIV has been accompanied by increased consultation in connection with the use of the Fund's resources. Consultation clauses in stand-by arrangements have been refined over the years so as to make them more effective, and it is now established policy for a member to consult with the Fund whenever this seems advisable for as long as the member is using the Fund's resources beyond the first credit tranche. It would be reasonable to conclude that the greater use of the Fund's resources and the confidence that this has instilled in members have been influences in the progress towards searching but amicable consultations under Article XIV and even under Article VIII.

It is in relation to consultation under Article VIII that one of the most striking advances in the field of consultation was made by the decision of June 1, 1960. It had been understood that if a member had undertaken the obligations of Article VIII, Sections 2, 3, and 4, it could not be required to consult unless it maintained practices that were inconsistent with these provisions, and the decision states the principle with great firmness that consultation is not obligatory except in these latter circumstances. The decision goes on to acknowledge, however, that because the Fund is able to provide technical facilities and advice, or because of the opportunity to exchange views on monetary and financial developments, "there is great merit in periodic discussions between the Fund and its members even though no questions arise involving action under Article VIII." [22] These modest words are a considerable achievement because they record the readiness of some members that had been free of any duty to consult under Article VIII and had been unenthusiastic about consultation to make the experiment, with an awareness, of course, of the advantages that would follow from similar consultations by other members that were about to undertake the obligations of Article VIII. The decision went on to state, therefore, that agreement would be reached on the place and timing of consultations, and that ordinarily they would occur at intervals of about a year. There was to be one difference, however, between consultations under Article VIII and Article XIV although it is not mentioned in the decision. Consultations under Article XIV are concluded with a decision of the Executive Directors, but, although the report on a consultation under Article VIII is discussed by the Executive Directors, they take no decision unless there are exchange measures that require approval. There is testimony in this to the seriousness with which members regard the formal decisions of an international organization even though the organization may take no action on the basis of the decisions. Notwithstanding the absence of a decision in an Article VIII consultation, the practice of consultation with all members has enabled the Fund to increase its contribution to the problems of adjustment by exercising some influence on members in surplus as well as those in deficit.

The distance traveled by the Fund and its members in the field of consultation is evident in the last paragraph of the decision also. This called on members which are contracting parties to the GATT and which impose import restrictions for balance of payments reasons to continue to send information concerning those restrictions to the Fund so as to facilitate the work of the Fund in advising the CONTRACTING PARTIES. The decision concluded by envisaging agreements between the Fund and members that are not contracting parties under which the Fund would seek to obtain similar information.

THE AMBIGUITIES OF GOLD

It is possible to understand the international monetary system as embodied in the Articles as one in which convertible currencies are convertible into U.S. dollars and U.S. dollars held by the monetary authorities of other members are convertible into gold. This may be one meaning of the frequent but delphic reference to gold as the "final" or "ultimate" asset. If this was indeed the theory of the drafters, they probably assumed the continued invulnerability of the

[22] E.B. Decision No. 1034-(60/27); below, Vol. III, p. 261.

U.S. dollar and the readiness of other members to hold dollars in the quantities that were likely to become available to them. This view of the world and the assumptions on which it rested were not made explicit in the Articles. For example, there is no obligation under the Articles for the United States or any other member to buy and sell gold for its own currency. The Articles recognize the possibility that the monetary authorities of a member may freely buy and sell gold in fact, within the margins of par established by the Fund for gold transactions, for the settlement of international transactions.[23] If a member engages in this practice, it will be maintaining the value of its own currency in direct relation to gold, and therefore the Articles provide that the member is deemed to be fulfilling its obligation to ensure that exchange transactions in its territories involving its own and another member currency are within the permitted margins for exchange transactions. In short, the Articles hold that the member is discharging the duty that is laid on each member to maintain the value of its own currency. The United States is the only member which has informed the Fund that it freely buys and sells gold within the meaning of the provision that recognizes that practice. In addition, France has informed the Fund that the monetary authorities of French Somaliland freely buy and sell gold by freely buying and selling U.S. dollars for Djibouti francs so that the exchange rate obligations of the Articles could be deemed to be fulfilled in respect of the Djibouti franc.

It may seem extraordinary that the Fund has not adopted a final view of the meaning of the provision dealing with the free purchase and sale of gold. The view held by the staff in January 1948 was that a member is freely buying and selling gold within the meaning of the provision if it satisfies two conditions, of which one is that the member in fact buys and sells gold for its own currency whenever requested to engage in these transactions by the monetary authorities of other members whether or not the practice is required by the member's law. The other condition is that the member has no exchange restrictions on either current or capital transactions. The staff concluded that, if these two conditions are satisfied, the member is doing all that can be reasonably expected of it to maintain the value of its own currency, and it is not expected, in addition, to hold other currencies and intervene in the market with them, much less apply exchange controls, in order to maintain appropriate exchange rates. If exchange transactions involving the member's currency and another member currency should take place at rates outside the permitted margins, the responsibility for them could not be attributed to the member that was freely buying and selling gold for its currency. When the question was considered in 1948, the Executive Directors did not endorse this as the sole or necessary meaning of the provision, but, in effect, left the full or final meaning for some future debate if there should

[23] Article IV, Section 4 (*b*).

ever be a challenge of the declaration of a member that it was freely buying and selling gold.

The reluctance to arrive at a full or final view of the provision was based less on the unwillingness of the United States to be held to so strict a standard than on the preference of some members for another standard that might be helpful to them. The staff opinion and the Executive Directors' debate on the provision in February 1948 were the result of a contention by a member that had numerous exchange restrictions that it was freely selling gold for its currency to the extent that the monetary authorities of other members were able to acquire its currency. The incompatibility of that contention with the principle that the member must maintain the value of its currency in terms of gold by means of gold transactions induced the staff to dissent from the member's contention that it was freely buying and selling gold within the intent of the provision. The member then withdrew its contention but without prejudice to the question of interpretation.

In March 1949 the Executive Directors held that a member that does meet the two conditions as explained by the staff will be freely buying and selling gold within the meaning of the provision, even if the provision can be satisfied by less rigorous conditions as well. It was on this basis that the Executive Directors were able to agree that the Djibouti franc was covered by the provision. The reasoning was that because the United States at the time clearly met the two conditions, monetary authorities that permitted the full convertibility of their currency into dollars also met the conditions, provided that the cost of converting their currency into dollars and then into gold was no greater than the cost of transactions involving the currency and gold directly. In these circumstances, monetary authorities could be said to be freely buying and selling gold indirectly. The Fund has adopted no other decisions on the meaning of the free purchase and sale of gold.

Another fundamental question involving gold on which the "last verse is not yet sufficiently explicated" is the role of the Fund itself in gold transactions. Gold enters and leaves the Fund in a variety of operations and transactions. The inflow results mainly from subscriptions, repurchases, and charges, the outflow largely from sales to replenish the Fund's holdings of particular currencies. The Fund has been conscious of the effects of the flow of gold into and out of the Fund, and its policies have been affected by this awareness. An understanding of those policies would have to be derived from the study of such transactions and operations as sales of gold contemporaneously with borrowing under the General Arrangements to Borrow, sales of gold for investment of the proceeds in U.S. Government securities in order to create a special reserve to deal with possible administrative deficits, and the placing of gold on general deposit in order to counteract the effect of the provision of gold by the reserve currency countries to other members paying gold subscriptions to the Fund when increasing their quotas. These are only a few examples of issues relating to gold, sometimes legal and sometimes economic, that have been resolved by the Fund, but although some of them have been debated with great intensity and over long periods, probably none of them has so profound a legal and philosophical importance as a category of transactions that has occurred hardly at all.

Article V, Section 6 provides that a member desiring to obtain the currency of another member for gold shall "acquire it by the sale of gold to the Fund," "provided that it can do so with equal advantage." This provision is deemed not to preclude any member from selling in any market gold newly produced from mines within its territories. Article V, Section 6 resulted from a diversity of views among the negotiators of the Articles on the extent to which gold should be directed to the Fund so as to harden its resources. Clearly, not all gold had to be sold to the Fund and room was left for the restoration of a private market in gold once the Articles took effect.

Some have seen Article V, Section 6, coupled with Article VII, Section 2, as establishing the legal foundation for gold as a reserve asset. For them, it is possible to understand why the monetary authorities of members have no obligation under the Articles to engage in gold transactions between themselves because the historic acceptability of gold has been reinforced by agreement on a buyer that is required to buy. They believe that the Fund has this role. They believe that a member can be assured that if it wishes to acquire currency for gold, it will be able to sell its gold to the Fund because the member's obligation to acquire the currency from the Fund in accordance with Article V, Section 6 connotes a reciprocal obligation on the Fund to purchase the gold and supply the currency. In its turn, the Fund can compel a member to supply its currency to the Fund for gold under Article VII, Section 2 whenever the Fund deems it appropriate to replenish its holdings of the member's currency. Here then is the market assured to members by international monetary law for the disposition of gold.

Another view of Article V, Section 6 has become apparent since the institution of the two-tier gold system on March 17, 1968. This is the view that the only obligation under the provision is the obligation of a member to offer gold to the Fund if a member is seeking the currency of another member for gold, but the Fund itself has no obligation to purchase the gold. The Fund has a discretion to accept or refuse the offer, and in deciding whether to purchase any gold that is offered, the Fund must be guided by its purposes, including the maintenance of exchange stability.

Once again it may be surprising that so fundamental an issue was not settled by the Fund many years ago. In part, this is because there was little financial or other inducement for members to sell gold to the Fund under the provision, and there have been very few purchases by the Fund other than purchases of small amounts held by the Fund under earmark for members as the result of their transactions and operations with the Fund, or purchases of small amounts accepted in discharge of repurchase obligations that had accrued in currency. As part of its decision on voluntary repurchases adopted on March 8, 1951, the Fund held that if a repurchase obligation accrues in a currency under Article V, Section 7 (*b*), the member may combine the payment of that currency with a sale of gold to the Fund for the currency under Article V, Section 6.[24] In effect, therefore, the member may substitute gold for the currency. The decision seems to have been based on the assumption that the Fund has no discretion to refuse the gold, but the issue was not raised, and the decision does not preclude the interpretation that the Fund was exercising a discretion. Apart from cases of this kind and purchases by the Fund of small amounts held under earmark for members, the last purchase of gold by the Fund under Article V, Section 6 took place in November 1948. One reason why the traffic has been negligible is that the Fund has not attempted to deflect gold sales to itself by reducing or forgoing charges so as to offer terms that would be competitive with those offered by the monetary authorities of members.

Other aspects of the role of gold under the Articles have been given greater precision as the Fund's practice developed. It was apparent to the drafters that certain gold transactions by members at non-parity prices could have an adverse effect on par values. Article IV, Section 2 prevents purchases of gold at a premium or sales at a discount by members, whoever the other party may be. This provision permits members to sell gold at a premium or buy it at a discount, except in transactions with other members, because a sale by one member at a premium would be a purchase by the other party at a premium and a purchase by one member at a discount would be a sale by the other at a discount. Therefore, transactions in gold outside the margins from par established by the Fund are inconsistent with the Articles if both parties are members of the Fund.

The leading problems connected with this provision have involved the payment of subsidies to gold producers and external sales of gold by members at premium prices. On gold subsidies the Fund's position basically was that the prohibition of the payment of a premium price by a member applied to purchases from domestic producers also, but other forms of subsidy were not precluded.[25] More complex issues were involved in the controversy with respect to external sales at a premium. These were not sales to another member and therefore they did not fall within the prohibitions of the Articles. In June 1947, however, the Fund reached the conclusion that the volume of external sales of gold at premium prices tended to undermine exchange stability and that the

[24] E.B. Decision No. 7-(648); below, Vol. III, p. 244.

[25] E.B. Decision No. 233-2, December 11, 1947; below, Vol. III, pp. 225–26.

interests of members would be served if as much gold as possible could be held in official reserves instead of private hoards. The Fund issued a recommendation to members that they take effective action to prevent external sales of gold at premium prices.[26] The legal basis for this recommendation was Article IV, Section 4 (*a*), which obligates members to collaborate with the Fund for certain specific purposes. The part played by this obligation in the history of the Fund is considered in greater detail in the next chapter.

The difficulties in supervising and ensuring observance of its recommendation led to the Fund's abandonment of the effort in its statement of September 28, 1951, although it did not resile from its judgment that gold should be channeled to official reserves.[27] In March 1954, the London gold market was re-established, an action that could be taken consistently with the provision that permits members to sell gold at a premium except to other members and did not require them to sell it to the Fund if the gold was newly produced from domestic mines. The creation of the Gold Pool in the fall of 1961 and its operation through the London market solved the problem of premium prices because prices were kept within the margins established by the Fund for gold transactions. The solution of the problem was found in supplying the market instead of starving it as the Fund had recommended. In time, however, supplying the market became too costly for the active partners in the Gold Pool, and this led them to institute the two-tier system.

A SECOND BACKWARD GLANCE

The development of the code of conduct in the Articles has called for delicacy because essentially it has been a process of clarifying the division of authority between the Fund and members in matters that were exclusively within the domestic jurisdiction before the Articles took effect. Exchange rates are at the heart of the code. The Articles subject rates of exchange to international scrutiny and, in most instances, agreement. The Fund has not been disposed to hold that an issue relating to exchange rates is beyond its jurisdiction. The system envisaged by the drafters was one in which par values would be established under the procedures of the Articles, and changed only in order to correct a fundamental disequilibrium. The Fund has held that members are not entitled to correct a fundamental disequilibrium by changes of par values in installments, and if a par value is to be changed a period of fluctuation as the prelude to a new par value is not permissible. Nevertheless, the Fund has been willing to support a fluctuating rate with sympathy and resources, even when the practice could not be validated by Fund approval, if the practice was an improvement in a member's

[26] See below, Vol. III, p. 310.

[27] E.B. Decision No. 75-(705); below, Vol. III, p. 225.

exchange system and represented progress towards the establishment of an effective par value.

The Fund cannot propose a change of par value but has been able to exercise influence in favor of realistic rates of exchange by withholding the use of its resources to support untenable rates. Although the support of par values is a basic objective of the availability of the Fund's resources, the Fund has found it possible to engage in exchange transactions with a member on terms that the Fund prescribes even though the member has not yet established an initial par value.

A member must ensure that spot exchange transactions within its territories involving its own and another member currency take place within margins of 1 per cent from par. The Fund has been able to introduce additional flexibility by approving certain multiple exchange practices under which, in effect, the 1 per cent margin need apply only to transactions involving a member's intervention currency and wider margins up to 2 per cent are possible for transactions involving other member currencies. The Fund has the authority to prescribe reasonable margins in excess of 1 per cent for other exchange transactions. The Fund has not prescribed margins for forward exchange transactions, and the effect has been to permit some additional flexibility in the management of exchange rates.

The Fund has not adopted the most extensive conceivable theory of what constitutes restrictions on payments and transfers for current international transactions. It has chosen the test of the technical formulation and operation of an exchange measure and not the tests of balance of payments motive or the effect on payments and transfers. Adoption of the more modest decision was influenced by the intention to establish a parallel international trade organization with authority over trade practices. That intention and the limited jurisdiction conferred on the Fund as a result made it difficult at one time to gain general acceptance of the idea that annual consultations under Article XIV should have a wide range. That difficulty has been overcome, and regular consultations are held now even with members that have accepted the obligations of Article VIII.

Members are still able to avail themselves of the transitional arrangements of Article XIV, which in many instances means only that they have not given notice of the acceptance of the obligations of Article VIII. The Fund has not discouraged this continued but largely or even wholly formal retention of the privileges of Article XIV. It has acquiesced in the protraction of the transitional arrangements in order to give greater reality to the concept of the convertibility of currencies under Article VIII.

The Fund has had to deal with the problems of gold at all stages of its history. Nevertheless, certain fundamental questions relating to the place of gold in the international monetary system as embodied in the Articles remain unresolved even at this date. In the earlier years of the Fund when the international monetary system was not being tested by some of the problems that have demanded attention in more recent years, there was little practical reason for trying to settle these questions. Now that the questions have a practical immediacy, the problems that have brought them to the fore impede easy agreement on the answers.

CHAPTER

25

The Techniques of Response

Joseph Gold

INTERPRETATION

The Fund is one of a growing number of international organizations, mostly financial or economic in character, that have the authority to adopt final interpretations of their own charters. Under Article XVIII of the Fund's charter, any question of interpretation of the provisions of the Articles arising between any member and the Fund or between any members must be settled by the Executive Directors. In any case in which the Executive Directors have given a decision, any member may require that the question be referred to the Board of Governors, whose decision is final. Pending the result of the reference to the Board, the Fund may decide to act on the basis of the decision of the Executive Directors. The drafters attached importance to keeping disputes concerning the interpretation of the Articles within the framework of the Fund, while at the same time establishing safeguards for members and providing for external arbitration for disputes with a country in the liquidation of the Fund or after withdrawal from the Fund.[1]

The Fund has adopted no more than ten interpretations under Article XVIII, and there has been a special reason for resort to the formality of proceeding under that provision in each of these cases. The first interpretation was adopted on May 8, 1946, in response to a request by India, and in order to clarify what happens to an executive director who was appointed by a member which, between elections, ceases to be one of the members with the five largest quotas and entitled, therefore, to appoint executive directors.[2] Two interpretations were adopted by the Executive Directors on September 26, 1946 in response to requests by the United Kingdom and the United States respectively, which wanted assurances on certain matters that were of particular interest to them,

[1] Joseph Gold, *Interpretation by the Fund*, IMF Pamphlet Series, No. 11.

[2] E.B. Decision No. 2-1; below, Vol. III, pp. 267–68.

in part because these matters had raised political issues. The United Kingdom, committed to a policy of maintaining full employment, sought and received an interpretation that steps necessary to protect a member from unemployment of a chronic or persistent character, arising from pressure on its balance of payments, are among the measures necessary to correct a fundamental disequilibrium.[3] The United States, fearing that the Fund might engage in long-term lending that could undermine the policies of the World Bank, requested an interpretation with respect to the use of the Fund's resources, and was given the answer that use was limited in accordance with the Fund's purposes to give temporary assistance in financing balance of payments deficits on current account for monetary stabilization purposes.[4]

The next interpretation was adopted on June 10, 1949. It took the form of a letter addressed to members and was intended to make it clear that Article VIII, Section 2 (*b*) had modified private international law in many countries in connection with the recognition of the exchange control regulations of other members. The interpretation dealt with the prime example of "lawyer's law" in the whole Articles. The provision declares that exchange contracts involving the currency of a member which are contrary to the exchange control regulations of that member maintained or imposed consistently with the Articles shall be unenforceable in the territories of any member. The interpretation explained that a court in a member country in which a litigant seeks to enforce such a contract should not refuse to recognize the exchange control regulations on the ground that exchange control regulations are against the public policy of the forum or because the regulations are not part of the law governing the contract or its performance under the traditional private international law of the forum.[5] The novelty and compressed language of the provision have raised many legal issues, and both the provision and the interpretation have been relied on in numerous cases throughout the world.[6] There is also a growing legal literature on the effect of the Articles on the recognition of foreign exchange control, but the Fund has not ventured into further interpretation of the provision.

In response to a question put by the executive director appointed by the United States, the Fund, on February 20, 1950, adopted an interpretation of the provision which requires a member to give the Fund the same treatment for its official communications as the member accords to the official communications of

[3] E.B. Decision No. 71-2; below, Vol. III, p. 227.

[4] *Ibid.*, p. 245; cf above, pp. 524, 539.

[5] E.B. Decision No. 446-4; below, Vol. III, pp. 256–57.

[6] See Joseph Gold, *The Fund Agreement in the Courts;* "The Fund Agreement in the Courts—VIII," *Staff Papers,* Vol. XI (1964), pp. 457–89; "The Fund Agreement in the Courts—IX," *ibid.*, Vol. XIV (1967), pp. 369–402; *The Cuban Insurance Cases and the Articles of the Fund,* IMF Pamphlet Series, No. 8; "The International Monetary Fund and the International Recognition of Exchange Control Regulations: The Cuban Insurance Cases," *Revue de la Banque* (Brussels), Vol. 31 (1967), pp. 523–38.

other members.[7] The U.S. Federal Communications Commission recognized this interpretation as binding on the United States in a proceeding brought by the Fund and the World Bank against U.S. cable companies.[8]

The sixth interpretation was adopted by the Executive Directors on August 11, 1954, in reply to a question put by Czechoslovakia, against which proceedings had been instituted that led to a decision requiring it to withdraw from the Fund. Czechoslovakia argued that the failure to fulfill obligations for which a member could be compelled to withdraw meant a failure for which there was no legal justification, and that reasons of national security were recognized as a justification of that character in international law. In their interpretation, the Executive Directors did not accept this argument in connection with the provisions under which it was alleged that Czechoslovakia had failed to fulfill its obligations.[9] This was the only case in which an interpretation under Article XVIII was appealed to the Board of Governors. The Board, on September 28, 1954, confirmed the interpretation of the Executive Directors.

The seventh interpretation was adopted on August 24, 1955 and dealt with the troublesome question of the amount of exchange that a member is entitled to purchase from the Fund without a waiver. One of the conditions on which a member is entitled to make a purchase is that the proposed purchase will not cause the Fund's holdings of the member's currency to increase by more than 25 per cent of quota during the period of twelve months ending on the date of the purchase. The Fund recoiled from reading the provision to mean that the 25 per cent referred to is measured simply by the difference between its holdings of the member's currency at the beginning of the period and the level to which they would be increased by the proposed purchase. This could permit a member to purchase huge amounts in terms of its quota and could enable it to make long-term use of the Fund's resources. This would follow because any reduction in the Fund's holdings of a member's currency by repurchase, by a sale of its currency, or as the result of other operations, during the preceding twelve months, would enable the member to purchase an amount equivalent to the reduction and a further 25 per cent of quota without the need for a waiver. The Executive Directors decided that such a view would be repugnant to the basic ideas of the temporary use and revolving character of Fund resources and adopted a view under which during any twelve months a member may make purchases amounting to 25 per cent of quota augmented only by the amount of any reductions in the Fund's holdings of the member's currency, not in excess of those purchases, which take place after the purchases have occurred.[10]

---

[7] E.B. Decision No. 534-3; below, Vol. III, pp. 266–67.

[8] On the binding effect of interpretations, see Gold, *Interpretation by the Fund*, pp. 31–42.

[9] E.B. Decision No. 343-(54/47); below Vol. III, p. 269.

[10] E.B. Decision No. 451-(55/52); below, Vol. III, p. 228.

On January 25, 1956, the Executive Directors adopted their eighth interpretation under Article XVIII by deciding, after years of debate, that the Fund has the legal authority to sell part of its gold for investment of the proceeds in U.S. Government securities in order to prevent the impairment of its capital as a result of the excess of its administrative expenses over income. The interpretation laid down the conditions on which this could be done, including the condition that the Fund must be able to reacquire the gold.[11] On the disappearance of its accumulated deficit, the Fund, on November 27, 1957, decided under Article XVIII that the investment could be continued in order to provide a reserve against any similar deficits that might occur in the future.[12] A third interpretation dealing with investment was adopted on July 24, 1959 and dealt with the length of the maturity of the securities in which the Fund might invest.[13] That has been the last interpretation under Article XVIII so far.[14]

Nobody could claim that these ten decisions constitute an impressive body of legal principles, or even that all of them have made outstanding contributions to the constitutional development of the Fund. It is unlikely that anyone would deny the constitutional importance of the interpretations dealing with fundamental disequilibrium, use of the Fund's resources, and the meaning of the 25 per cent limit, but opinions might differ about the impact of some of the others. It would be difficult to insist that certain of the interpretations have had more than a minor effect on the work of the Fund.

The modest number of interpretations under Article XVIII gives no impression of the considerable volume of interpretative decisions that have been taken without recourse to that provision. Many of these decisions have been drafted in general terms and quite obviously as interpretations. Others have been rendered in particular cases and have dealt with the facts of the individual case. All in all, these decisions do amount to a very substantial body of law. The progressive development of its interpretative decisions has been one of the outstanding techniques of the Fund in dealing with the problems under the Articles with which it has been confronted by a far from quiescent international monetary order.

It has not been the attitude of members of the Fund, the Executive Directors, the Managing Director, or the staff that interpretative decisions can be held in lower esteem if they are not taken under Article XVIII. The procedures for arriving at decisions and the techniques of interpretation have been the same for both categories of decision. Clearly, any distinction between the two cate-

---

[11] E.B. Decision No. 488-(56/5); below, Vol. III, pp. 275–76.

[12] E.B. Decision No. 708-(57/57); below, Vol. III, p. 276.

[13] E.B. Decision No. 905-(59/32); below, Vol. III, p. 277.

[14] But see E.B. Decision No. 1107-(60/50), November 30, 1960; below, Vol. III, p. 277.

gories on the basis of their importance in the working of the Fund would be in favor of the decisions taken without recourse to Article XVIII.

The preference for interpreting the Articles without raising questions under Article XVIII is not the result of any conscious decision and it is not easy to explain the practice. The feeling of greater formality that necessarily accompanies the invocation of Article XVIII may be one explanation. Members regard interpretative decisions with respect and there is no need, therefore, to give these decisions maximum solemnity in order to ensure observance of them. Perhaps this informality may seem more compatible with the cooperation, consultation, and collaboration that are referred to in the first purpose of Article I. Another explanation may be the subconscious conviction that if an interpretative decision will have to be modified for good cause, this will be easier if it has not been adopted under Article XVIII. The debate on the clarification of the Executive Directors' interpretation of September 26, 1946 on the use of the Fund's resources shows that there may be great reluctance to re-examine a decision taken under Article XVIII.[15] A similar desire to minimize rigidity can be detected in some of the legal systems in which the volume of appeals to higher tribunals is closely controlled. Finally, it is possible that the assurance which members enjoy that they can raise any questions of interpretation under Article XVIII if they wish makes it unnecessary for them to overindulge in the privilege.

There are many approaches to the interpretation of treaties and the last word on this subject is always being written. The Fund has adopted an eclectic approach to problems of interpretation and has never decided that its technique would be based exclusively on the grammatical elucidation of the text, the determination of the intent of the drafters, the object of the provision, or the wider purposes of the Fund. A study of the interpretative work of the first two decades would show that a number or all of these techniques have been applied to most problems of interpretation. There is probably nothing unique in the experience of the Fund in this respect.

In the process of interpretation, what is sometimes called a "constitutional" or a "teleological" approach, or an approach that seeks to make the purposes of the institution effective, has found a place, although again the approach may have been no more pronounced in the Fund than in other international organizations. Perhaps the best public expression of the Fund's consciousness of this technique occurred in a speech by Mr. Jacobsson, who included the law among his many interests:

> In this and in other matters under the Fund's charter, I am reminded of what an English Lord Chancellor, Lord Sankey, said of the Canadian Constitution. It was, he said, "a living tree capable of growth and expansion within its natural limits." [16]

[15] See above, pp. 539–40.

[16] Per Jacobsson, *International Monetary Problems, 1957–1963*, p. 284. The quotation is from *Edwards v. Att.-Gen. for Canada* (1930) A.C. 124, 136.

His quotation from Lord Sankey was taken from an opinion in which the following passage also is relevant to Mr. Jacobsson's attitude of mind:

> Their Lordships do not conceive it to be the duty of this Board—it is certainly not their desire—to cut down the provisions of the Act by a narrow and technical construction, but rather to give it a large and liberal interpretation so that the Dominion to a great extent, but within certain fixed limits, may be mistress in her own house, as the Provinces to a great extent, but within certain fixed limits, are mistresses in theirs. "The Privy Council, indeed, has laid down that Courts of law must treat the provisions of the British North America Act by the same methods of construction and exposition which apply to other statutes. But there are statutes and statutes; and the strict construction deemed proper in the case, for example, of a penal or taxing statute or one passed to regulate the affairs of an English parish, would be often subversive of Parliament's real intent if applied to an Act passed to ensure the peace, order and good government of a British Colony" (see Clement's *Canadian Constitution*, 3rd ed., p. 347).[17]

In presenting his plan to the Executive Directors on February 10, 1961 for the development of the Fund's activities in an era of widespread convertibility, Mr. Jacobsson explained his position even more clearly:

> It is frequently suggested that one or another of the activities of the Fund indicated above might require amendment of the Articles of Agreement. I have an open mind on this; but I do know that the Articles provide considerable flexibility in many respects. The Articles are a constitutional charter, and constitutional interpretation recognizes that such a document must meet needs when this can be done without offending its spirit, purposes, or provisions.

In this approach he was supported, of course, by the last sentence of Article I, which declares that "the Fund shall be guided in all its decisions by the purposes set forth in this Article."

As in any body of men who are called on to exercise the art of interpretation, there have been differences of opinion on technique among executive directors. Some have seen interpretation as a more mechanical and less creative task than have those others who have held that, if there is a choice among readings, the best answer must be considered the right answer, and what is the best answer calls for knowledge, experience, and an understanding of the purposes of the Fund. Whatever differences of opinion may have existed about technique, and the frequency of this kind of disputation should not be exaggerated, it has been the unanimous view in the Fund that its power to interpret its charter was not a *laissez-passer* that authorized it to move beyond the law in order to achieve some end that was not attainable within the law. Strict adherence to this view has sometimes provoked lengthy and meticulous scrutiny of propositions that in retrospect seem obvious. The legality of voluntary repurchases and the decision of February 13, 1952 are examples of issues that were debated with

[17] *Edwards v. Att.-Gen. for Canada, ibid.*, pp. 136–37.

ardor over long periods. But this behavior has encouraged the law-abidingness of which it is itself a product. Furthermore, it has produced a body of interpretative decisions that are harmonious and therefore stable.[18] Indeed, some critics have thought that there was too much rigidity in the jurisprudence of the Fund, although the critics who have said the reverse must not be neglected.

It is interesting to speculate whether there have been special reasons in the Fund for the legalism, in the non-pejorative sense, which it has observed. Once again it is possible that its special character as an international regulatory institution may be an explanation. It would have been unreasonable to expect members to observe their obligations, and particularly the code of conduct, if the Fund had acted in the spirit of the old maxim that it is the function of a good judge to extend his jurisdiction (*boni judicis est ampliare jurisdictionem*).

THE UNDERTAKING TO COLLABORATE

One of the purposes of the Fund is to promote exchange stability, to maintain orderly exchange arrangements among members, and to avoid competitive exchange depreciation.[19] This purpose is matched by Article IV, Section 4 (*a*), under which members undertake "to collaborate with the Fund to promote exchange stability, to maintain orderly exchange arrangements with other members, and to avoid competitive exchange alterations." The provision is a source of authority on which the Fund has drawn in order to promote the purposes of exchange stability and orderly exchange arrangements. Sometimes the Fund has done this expressly, but at other times the spirit of the undertaking has affected relations between the Fund and its members even though the undertaking was not openly invoked.

Three examples drawn from the early years of the Fund illustrate the protean quality of the provision. In deciding that members are not entitled to adapt or introduce multiple currency practices, without the approval of the Fund, as restrictions on payments and transfers under Article XIV, Section 2, the Fund held as a matter of interpretation that because multiple currency practices are also rates of exchange the Fund must judge whether the adaptation is justified by "changing circumstances" or the introduction is "necessary." [20] The Fund relied largely on Article IV, Section 4 (*a*) as the source of this interpretation.

[18] ". . . the Executive Board has habitually shown a close regard for the legal arguments on both sides of a controversial question before it, and is probably more careful for the rule of law than many boards of directors, which have only municipal law to contend with, and it is slow to come to a decision until it can be legally well based. In the result the Fund's decisions since it commenced operations in March 1947 show a high degree of coherence and consistency." J. E. S. Fawcett, "The Place of Law in an International Organization," in *The British Year Book of International Law, 1960*, p. 327.

[19] Article I (iii); below, Vol. III, p. 188.

[20] See above, p. 548.

In its letter of December 19, 1947 to members, the Fund referred to the purposes of the Fund and the undertaking of members under the provision as "fundamental considerations in an interpretation of the rights and obligations of members" in connection with multiple currency practices. The widespread importance of this decision and its influence on the Fund's attitude to its jurisdiction in connection with exchange rate practices have been referred to in Chapter 24.

When in January 1948 France made an unauthorized change of par value and introduced discriminatory multiple currency practices of which the Fund disapproved, the Fund's action under Article IV, Section 4 (*a*) was of a different character. The Fund advised other members that neither the former par value nor the new rates of exchange adopted by France were binding on them and members were not bound to take appropriate measures to ensure that these rates were observed in exchange transactions in their territories. Nevertheless, members were bound to avoid exchange disorder. Therefore, the Fund was willing to agree in advance if by a bilateral arrangement between France and another member an exchange rate between their currencies was established on the basis of the unauthorized par value. If these arrangements contemplated other rates of exchange, the Fund did not give advance approval even if they corresponded with another rate in the French exchange system. The parties negotiating the agreement on a rate had to request the approval of the Fund because in the context of the French exchange system the rate inevitably would constitute a discriminatory currency arrangement. In this case, the Fund drew from Article IV, Section 4 (*a*) an obligation of members to seek prior approval for the introduction or adaptation of discriminatory currency arrangements involving rates of exchange.

In the third case, the Fund made yet a third kind of use of Article IV, Section 4 (*a*). In 1947, the Fund came to the conclusion that external sales of gold by members at premium prices tended to undermine exchange stability. It has been seen that whereas Article IV, Section 2 prevents members from buying gold at a price above par plus the Fund's margin for gold transactions or selling it at a price below par minus the margin, sales by a member or its residents at a premium to a purchaser that is not another member are not proscribed. Whether these latter sales continue to be permitted if the Fund finds that they undermine, and not merely tend to undermine, exchange stability was not decided. For a number of reasons, including perhaps the desire to avoid the settlement of that question, the Fund decided not to go beyond a recommendation to members. In its letter to members of June 18, 1947 the Fund deprecated premium sales in external markets and recommended that its members take effective action to prevent them.[21] The legal authority on which this policy pronouncement was based was Article I (iii) and Article IV, Section 4 (*a*).

---

[21] See above, pp. 563–64.

In these three episodes, the Fund made the undertaking of members in Article IV, Section 4 (*a*) more specific when dangers threatened exchange stability and orderly exchange arrangements. The Fund acted by formulating the obligations of members, by employing the provision in the interpretation of other provisions, or by addressing recommendations to members, when problems arose that imperiled the purposes of the Fund and the provisions of the Articles were not sufficiently clear or detailed in their relation to the problems. A study of the three episodes shows that there may be legal problems in reconciling an obligation or recommendation drawn from Article IV, Section 4 (*a*) with other provisions or with the silence of other provisions. Therefore, the acceptability to members at large of the Fund's reliance on the provision has been an element in the success of the Fund's action. The obligations of members to seek prior approval for the adaptation or introduction of multiple currency practices or discriminatory currency arrangements involving rates of exchange are firmly established. The history of the Fund's policy on premium transactions in gold shows that an application of Article IV, Section 4 (*a*) may be unsuccessful if it is not supported by the cooperation of those members from which cooperation is thought to be necessary.[22]

The recognized usefulness of Article IV, Section 4 (*a*) induced the drafters of the amendments dealing with special drawing rights to formulate a similar provision. This progeny of Article IV, Section 4 (*a*) is entitled "General Obligations of Participants," and it provides that:

> In addition to the obligations assumed with respect to special drawing rights under other Articles of this Agreement, each participant undertakes to collaborate with the Fund and with other participants in order to facilitate the effective functioning of the Special Drawing Account and the proper use of special drawing rights in accordance with this Agreement.[23]

VARIATION WITHOUT AMENDMENT

One of the techniques for adaptation at the disposal of the Fund is a power to vary certain provisions in the Articles without the need for amendment, and the exercise of this power has made at least one vital contribution to the operation of the Fund. The provisions in the original Articles under which variation is possible have been the precedents for a broader use of the technique in the amendments. Agreement on a power to vary without amendment enabled the negotiators of the amendments to arrive at a compromise on a basic feature of special drawing rights that was the subject of a particularly stubborn difference of opinion. The power to vary is one of the more obvious responses to Keynes,

---

[22] See Joseph Gold, "The Duty to Collaborate with the International Monetary Fund and the Development of Monetary Law," in *Law, Justice and Equity*, edited by R.H. Code Holland and G. Schwarzenberger, pp. 137–51.

[23] Article XXVIII; below, Vol. III, p. 531.

who said at Bretton Woods of the lawyer that: "I want him to tell me how to do what I think sensible, and, above all, to devise means by which it will be lawful for me to go on being sensible in unforeseen conditions some years hence." Full disclosure makes it necessary to report that the second use of the word "I" appears in italics.[24]

There were four examples of the technique in the original Articles. It is provided that when countries not listed in Schedule A become members of the Fund, the Board of Governors has authority, by a four-fifths majority of the total voting power, to increase the number of elected executive directors from the original seven.[25] The exercise of this power has enabled the Fund to increase the number of executive directors over time from twelve to twenty by increasing the number elected by the American Republics from two to three and the number elected by other members not appointing executive directors from five to twelve. The Fund has followed a policy of providing for further elected executive directors on the basis of the voting power exercised by newcomers, and one of the results of this policy has been to permit emerging countries to participate directly in the affairs of the Fund through executive directors of their choice.

The Articles also provide that whenever the Board of Governors increases the number of elected executive directors, it shall issue regulations making appropriate changes in the proportions of votes required to elect executive directors as laid down in the Articles.[26] The Board of Governors has made a flexible use of this power. For each election once countries not listed in Schedule A had joined the Fund, the Board of Governors has established the minimum number of votes required for the election of an executive director and the maximum number that he may retain. In determining these limits the Board of Governors has been guided by the objective of maintaining an approximate equality in the number of votes that elected executive directors can cast and by the further objective of making it possible, up to a point, for members to combine as they wish in electing an executive director.

The original Articles provide for a service charge of ¾ of 1 per cent on exchange transactions with the Fund but allow the Fund to alter this charge within a range of ½ of 1 per cent to 1 per cent.[27] On November 19, 1951 the Fund reduced the charge to the minimum in order to encourage short-term transactions as one means of reviving the use of the Fund's resources.[28]

The Articles also include a system of periodic charges on the Fund's holdings of currency in excess of quota under which the rates ascend in relation to both

---

[24] *Proceedings*, p. 1241.

[25] Article XII, Section 3 (*b*); below, Vol. III, p. 200.

[26] Article XII, Section 3 (*d*).

[27] Article V, Section 8 (*a*); below, Vol. III, p. 193.

[28] Rules and Regulations, Rule I-2; below, Vol. III, p. 294.

holdings and time.[29] It is provided that when the charge applicable to any bracket of the Fund's holdings of a member's currency reaches the rate of 4 per cent per annum, the Fund and the member have to consider means by which the Fund's holdings can be reduced.[30] That rate could be reached as late as seven years after a transaction with the Fund. The Fund is empowered to change the rates in the Articles, including the rate at which consultation occurs on the reduction of the Fund's holdings, by a three-fourths majority of the total voting power.[31]

In the discussions leading to the decision of February 13, 1952 the view was advanced that seven years was not an ideal period for the use of the Fund's resources, although obviously it had been considered tolerable by the drafters, and that a shorter period not exceeding five years was preferable. There was a more basic difference of opinion, however, on whether any fixed period was compatible with the notion of the Fund and whether it could be made effective in any way that was acceptable legally. The solution to the latter question was found in the variation of the charges in the Articles so that the date for consultation on the reduction of the Fund's holdings would occur not later than three years after a transaction. With that revision of the charges, members were willing to assure the Fund, in advance of the consultation that they would be obligated to enter into, that in the consultation they would agree upon appropriate arrangements for reducing the Fund's holdings of their currency as soon as possible but in any event not later than five years after a transaction.[32] On the basis of that settlement it became possible also to agree on a modified form of repurchase representation for gold tranche purchases on which periodic charges are not payable and to which, therefore, the requirement of consultation does not apply if only those purchases are outstanding. It is not an exaggeration to say that the Fund's power to vary the charges included in the Articles provided the legal basis on which it became possible to establish the policy that the temporary use of the Fund's resources meant use not in excess of three to five years.

The further powers of the Fund under the amended Articles to vary provisions without amendment relate to both the General Account and the Special Drawing Account. In the former category is the power of the Executive Directors to vary a basic rate of remuneration of 1½ per cent per annum payable on the amount by which the Fund's holdings of a member's currency are below 75 per cent of quota; a three-fourths majority of the total voting power is required for a decision to vary the rate beyond a band of 1 to 2 per

[29] Article V, Section 8 (*c*); below, Vol. III, p. 193.

[30] Article V, Section 8 (*d*).

[31] Article V, Section 8 (*e*).

[32] E.B. Decision No. 102-(52/11); below, Vol. III, p. 229. Rules and Regulations, Rule I-4; below, Vol. III, pp. 294–95.

cent per annum.[33] In addition, the Board of Governors has received the power to vary, by a majority of 85 per cent of the total voting power, a number of amendments that have been made in the provisions relating to repurchase.[34] This power was created because of the uncertainty about the way in which the amendments of the repurchase provisions might work not only from the point of view of equity but also in relation to the complexities of the original repurchase mechanism.

In the field of special drawing rights, there are powers to vary within a defined band the prescribed rate of 1½ per cent payable as interest on participants' holdings and as charges on net cumulative allocations of special drawing rights,[35] and to vary the rules for the designation of participants as recipients of special drawing rights that are intended to promote over time a balanced distribution of holdings of special drawing rights among participants.[36] Both powers may be exercised by the Executive Directors by a majority of votes cast.

The most striking power to vary a provision without amendment relates to "reconstitution." Those who favored the view that the new instrument of unconditional liquidity should take the form demonstrably of a reserve asset and not credit, or that it should be a "unit" and not a "drawing right," argued that a participant should have no legal obligation to restore its holdings of the new instrument after they had been used. Those who preferred the concept of "credit" or a "drawing right" insisted that there should be a duty of restoration. The compromise between the two schools was an agreement that there would be an obligation on each participant, in accordance with the rules in Schedule G, to maintain over time an average balance of 30 per cent of its net cumulative allocation of special drawing rights beginning five years after the first allocation. The rules for reconstitution, however, are to be reviewed before the end of the first and each subsequent basic period and new rules may be adopted if they are considered necessary but they may be abrogated altogether. Any decision to adopt, modify, or abrogate reconstitution rules will be taken by the Board of Governors and will require a majority of 85 per cent of the total voting power.[37]

RULE-MAKING

The Board of Governors, and the Executive Directors to the extent that they have been authorized, may adopt "such rules and regulations as may be necessary or appropriate to conduct the business of the Fund."[38] In accordance with

[33] Article V, Section 9; below, Vol. III, p. 523.

[34] Article V, Section 7 (*d*); Article XII, Section 2 (*b*) (ix).

[35] Article XXVI, Sections 1–3.

[36] Article XXV, Section 5 (*b*) and (*c*), and Schedule F.

[37] Article XXV, Section 6.

[38] Article XII, Section 2 (*g*); below, Vol. III, p. 199.

this provision in the Articles, the Board of Governors adopted By-Laws on March 16, 1946 and the Executive Directors adopted Rules and Regulations on September 25, 1946.[39]

Most of the By-Laws and Rules and Regulations now in force were adopted on those occasions, although there have been amendments and additions over the years. The words "necessary or appropriate," which are the criterion for rule-making, are broad and flexible, but the Fund has not made conspicuous use of either the By-Laws or the Rules and Regulations as a medium of adaptation to changing circumstances. Nevertheless, some rule-making actions have had more than a routine character. The changes already noted in the service charge on members' exchange transactions with the Fund and in the periodic charges on the Fund's holdings of currencies were incorporated in the Rules and Regulations. Another noteworthy example is the amendment of Rule F-4 of the Rules and Regulations on October 15, 1954 by which the Executive Directors adopted an alternative to the original margin for gold transactions which they had established on June 10, 1947. The need for a new margin had been foreseen before the London gold market was reopened on March 22, 1954. The adoption of the new margin of 1 per cent facilitated the working of the market, through which, in due course, the operations of the Gold Pool were conducted. Yet another interesting example of rule-making is Rule M-6, adopted on June 7, 1950, in which the Fund deemed it prejudicial to the interests of members and contrary to the purposes of the Fund for a member to impose restrictions on non-members that have entered into special exchange agreements under the GATT, or with persons in their territories, which the member would not be authorized in similar circumstances to impose on transactions with members or with persons in their territories.[40]

The last rule to be mentioned here as worthy of particular notice is Rule K-2, which was adopted on September 25, 1946. It declares that whenever the Fund is authorized to declare a member ineligible to use the resources of the Fund, it may refrain from taking that action and instead indicate the circumstances in which, or the extent to which, the member may make use of the Fund's resources. The rule expresses the Fund's philosophy that its powers should be exercised not to obstruct access to its resources but to clarify the circumstances in which members can rely on the availability of those resources.

DEFINING THE UNDEFINED

The restraint which the drafters observed in defining basic concepts has given the Fund a degree of flexibility by enabling it to decide how those con-

[39] See below, Vol. III, pp. 278–303.

[40] Joseph Gold, *The Fund and Non-Member States*, IMF Pamphlet Series, No. 7.

cepts are to be applied. It is true that Article XIX explains a number of terms, but they deal with little more than payments for current transactions and the calculation of net official holdings and monetary reserves. Net official holdings were relevant to the determination of members' gold subscriptions, and monetary reserves are important mainly in connection with repurchase obligations under Article V, Section 7 (*b*) and the payment of charges. Notwithstanding the explanation of terms in Article XIX, further elucidation of them was necessary before they could be put to work. The Net Official Holdings Committee of the Executive Directors met during the period March 1947 to April 1948 to unravel the complications of the concept by means of a number of case studies. This detailed work had a permanent usefulness because of the intersection of the concepts of "net official holdings" and "monetary reserves." One of the most fundamental of the determinations common to both concepts was the decision that the "holding" of a reserve asset involves the ownership of the asset and not merely a claim to acquire it against another member that has the ownership of it. No committee was established in connection with monetary reserves, but the intricacies of both that concept and the repurchase formulas based on it were clarified as issues arose over the years in the practice of the Fund.

The other main topic on which Article XIX gives guidance is "payments for current transactions." This concept sets the bounds within which the Fund exercises jurisdiction over restrictions on payments and transfers under Article VIII, Section 2. Problems of definition have arisen in connection with "payments for current transactions" but problems of application, such as the mode of operation of particular exchange control regulations, have been more frequent. One reason for the predominance of problems of application over problems of definition is the breadth of the first category in Article XIX (*i*): "All payments due in connection with foreign trade, other current business, including services, and normal short-term banking and credit facilities."

In a discussion of the techniques of adaptation, it must be recalled that certain discretions were given to the Fund to extend particular definitions. Article XIX (*d*) defines "currency" for the purposes of that provision and declares that the term shall include "without limitation" the items that are specified. The definition has been applied, as was to be expected, to other references to "currency" in the Articles. Similarly, Article XIX (*i*) declares that payments for current transactions means payments that are not for the purpose of transferring capital and include "without limitation" the categories that then follow. The "without limitation" clause empowers the Fund to add items or categories to those enumerated, but no addition has been made to either list.

Obviously, the concepts that are wholly undefined have given the Fund no less opportunity for evolving a realistic and consistent body of practice than the concepts on which the drafters provided guidance by an explanation of terms. The Articles contain no definitions of such terms as "multiple currency practices," "discriminatory currency arrangements," "fundamental disequilibrium," or even "rates for exchange transactions." Sometimes, the Fund has made a specific project of the clarification of a particular concept. The Executive Directors' Committee on Spreads and Multiple Currency Practices which sat in May to July 1947 mapped a large part of the terrain in this area of the Articles, and its work led to the letter to members of December 19, 1947 which still explains much of the Fund's policy and interpretation in connection with multiple currency practices.[41] With other concepts the Fund has refrained from making so systematic an effort and has allowed a body of practice to develop more slowly as problems arose. The concept of the rate of exchange has been formed in this way, and it has central importance in the work of the Fund. It is established that the rate of exchange with which the Fund is concerned is the "effective" rate, which means that it includes not only the formal *quid pro quo* for the exchange but also other payments, such as exchange taxes or charges, that are directly exigible in connection with the exchange transaction.

Reliance on the future administrators of the Fund to give substance to basic concepts of its operation is not an accident of hurried negotiation. There is the evidence of Mr. White himself who wrote in August 1946 that:

> In the drafting of the Articles of Agreement no attempt was made to define fundamental disequilibrium. This, as we know, was not an oversight. It was generally agreed that a satisfactory definition would be difficult to formulate. A too rigid or narrow interpretation would be dangerous; one too loose or general would be useless in providing a criterion for changes in currency parities. It was felt too that the subject matter was so important, and the necessity for a crystallization of a harmonious view so essential that it were best left for discussion and formulation by the Fund.

There can be few negotiators of a major international treaty who have been so enlightened as to hold that because of the basic importance of a concept, its definition had best be left to those who later would administer the treaty. It need only be said that those who have followed the drafters and administered the Fund have been equally enlightened, at least in connection with "fundamental disequilibrium." They have not yet ventured a formal definition of it. There are other cases in which the administrators, like angels, have not rushed in, and by their reluctance to adopt definitions, or on occasion even interpretations, have preserved a valuable flexibility for the Fund.

[41] See above, pp. 548, 574.

CHAPTER

26

Some Characteristics of Operation

Joseph Gold

THE AVOIDANCE OF SANCTIONS

A student of the development of the Fund must note how little use the Fund has made of sanctions. This characteristic of the way in which the Fund has operated has had a formative influence on Fund law and practice. The Articles authorize the Fund to take certain actions of which some are clearly sanctions and others have been regarded as comparable to sanctions if only because there is a tacit view that they involve an adverse judgment on the member against which the action is taken. One of the most obvious sanctions is a declaration of ineligibility to use the Fund's resources either because a member "is using the resources of the Fund in a manner contrary to the purposes of the Fund" [1] or because a member "fails to fulfill any of its obligations" under the Articles.[2] If a member makes an unauthorized change of par value despite the objection of the Fund in circumstances in which the Fund is entitled to object, this is technically not a failure by the member to fulfill any of its obligations, but it becomes automatically unable to make purchases unless the Fund decides to forestall ineligibility.[3]

The most radical of all obvious sanctions is the compulsory withdrawal of a member from the Fund. This can be required if after a reasonable period a member persists in its failure to fulfill any of its obligations under the Articles or if a difference between the Fund and a member persists on its unauthorized change of par value.[4]

A member must consult with the Fund on means to reduce the Fund's holdings of the member's currency once the rate of charge on any part of them reaches 4 per cent per annum. If the member fails to reach an agreement on repurchase

[1] Article V, Section 5; below, Vol. III, p. 192.

[2] Article XV, Section 2 (*a*).

[3] Article IV, Section 6.

[4] Article XV, Section 2 (*b*).

within three to five years after a purchase, or fails to observe the terms of an agreement, the Fund may levy penalty rates of charge after the charge has reached 5 per cent per annum.[5]

Under Article XII, Section 8, the Fund may communicate its views informally to any member on any matter arising under the Articles, and may publish a report regarding a member's monetary or economic conditions and developments which directly tend to produce a serious disequilibrium in the international balance of payments of members. In exceptional circumstances, the Fund may make representations to a member that is availing itself of the transitional arrangements of Article XIV that conditions are favorable for the withdrawal of any particular restriction, or for the general abandonment of restrictions, that are inconsistent with any other provision of the Articles.[6] There are other actions that the Fund may take that might be regarded by some observers as sanctions, but it is not necessary to complete the list, although one of them will be singled out later because of its special relationship to the international monetary system.

In the elaborate congressional hearings on the proposed U.S. Bretton Woods legislation in 1945, there was much discussion of the sanctions and safeguards in the Articles in order to rally public opinion in the United States to support of the Fund by showing that abuse of the proposed institution by its members could be prevented or deterred. The Fund has found it necessary to make a negligible use of this armory of sanctions and quasi-sanctions. The most dramatic employment of a sanction in the history of the Fund was the declaration of Czechoslovakia's ineligibility in November 1953 and the decision in September 1954 to compel it to withdraw because of its failure to provide information under Article VIII and consult under Article XIV. There have been no other declarations of ineligibility or decisions to compel withdrawal, although ineligibility proceedings were initiated against Cuba in February 1964 for failure to repurchase after it had requested and been refused a postponement beyond five years from its purchase, and in these circumstances Cuba withdrew voluntarily. France became ineligible in January 1948 when it adopted an unauthorized par value, but ineligibility was automatic under Article IV, Section 6 and called for no declaration by the Fund.[7] Under Article XV, Section 2, if a difference between a member and the Fund on an unauthorized change of par value continues, the member may be required to withdraw. The Fund took no further action in the case of France, and eligibility was restored by the Fund in October 1954, even though a new par value was not established until December 1958. Only two members have had to pay rates of charge in excess of 5 per cent per

[5] Article V, Section 8 (*d*); Rules and Regulations, Rule I-4 (g); below, Vol. III, pp. 193, 296.

[6] Article XIV, Section 4.

[7] See above, pp. 549, 574.

annum, and then for no more than brief periods. The Fund has made no formal representations under Article XIV, Section 4, and has not published any report under Article XII, Section 8.

The sparing use of sanctions can be evaluated only if it is known to what extent sanctions could have been applied, but it is not easy to arrive at a judgment on that question. One reason for the difficulty is that the practices and procedures that have been developed to avoid sanctions, particularly in connection with the use of the Fund's resources, make it unnecessary to determine whether members are making an improper use. There have been numerous failures by members to observe their obligations to seek the prior approval of the Fund for the introduction of multiple currency practices or restrictions on payments and transfers for current international transactions, but in most cases these failures were the subject of consultation with the Fund after the adoption of the measures and the Fund then took decisions to approve them. Many of the failures to observe obligations in the code of conduct were the result of oversight, but there have been a few cases in which the violation has been a conscious choice under what was thought to be the pressure of events. There have been no more than a handful of cases in which members have failed to honor their financial obligations meticulously. Only in rare instances have charges been paid or repurchases made after the due date, and there has never been a protracted or permanent default. Although there is no legal or logical distinction between financial and other obligations, financial institutions and their members have a special sensitivity about the prompt and full performance of financial obligations.

One must conclude that there has been a high degree of law observance by members, but not complete impeccability, and sanctions could have been applied more frequently than they have been. It should be added that the Rules and Regulations require the Managing Director to report to the Executive Directors any case in which it appears to him that a member is not fulfilling its obligations.[8] There has been no formal decision to minimize the use of sanctions, and it is not easy, therefore, to explain fully why they have been avoided. Sanctions involve an adverse judgment by the international community, and it is painful not only to the member against which the judgment is delivered but also to its fellow members that adopt the judgment. Another reason is the conviction that persuasion based on consultation and collaboration are more likely to encourage the widespread observance of obligations than punitive methods. This conviction rests not only on the prescription of the Articles but also on the experience of the Fund. In any event, it seems to have been concluded that usually there is no advantage in reacting to the violation of one obligation by imposing sanctions that may lead to withdrawal from the Fund and the release from all obligations.

[8] Rules and Regulations, Rule K-1; below, Vol. III, p. 299.

The Fund's attitude to sanctions has affected its practice most profoundly in connection with the use of its resources. The power to challenge a member's representation when it requests a purchase is not a complete safeguard for the Fund because a challenge is not a proper substitute for a declaration of ineligibility if there are grounds for ineligibility. In the early years of the Fund, informal procedures were employed, such as warning some members that Article XX, Section 4 (*i*) might be invoked to postpone exchange transactions with them if they submitted requests. Under this provision the Fund has the power to postpone transactions with a member if, in the opinion of the Fund, they would lead to use of its resources in a manner contrary to the purposes of the Articles or prejudicial to the Fund or its members. However, this provision also could provide only a partial defense against improper use because the Fund decided on March 10, 1948 that the power could be exercised only in the case of a member that had not already had an exchange transaction with the Fund.[9]

The major contribution to the protection of the Fund's resources without the need to rely on the sanction of ineligibility has been made, of course, by the technique of the stand-by arrangement. Here again, however, the desire to avoid ineligibility has affected the development of that instrument. In early stand-by arrangements a paragraph was employed, as a result of the decision of October 1, 1952,[10] which provided that the Fund would not permit a member to make purchases under a stand-by arrangement that were requested after the member became ineligible or after the Executive Directors adopted a decision to consider a proposal made by the Managing Director or an executive director to suppress or limit the member's eligibility. The reluctance to employ procedures related to ineligibility in order to interrupt the right to make purchases under a stand-by arrangement was responsible for the introduction of two features of stand-by arrangements that were meant to be substitutes for these procedures. The first was the evolution of performance clauses containing performance criteria as described in Chapter 23.[11]

The second of the two features of the Fund's practice that were designed to avoid ineligibility procedures under stand-by arrangements was the use of the "prior notice" clause. This was a clause in stand-by arrangements by which the Fund reserved to itself the privilege of giving notice and thereby interrupting a member's right to request purchases after the date of the notice. Nothing was said about the criteria for giving notice. The clause became standard practice because a member's program might be jeopardized by the non-observance of certain policies in its letter of intent even though, by their nature, they could not be given the objective formulation that is required for performance criteria.

[9] E.B. Decision No. 284-2; below, Vol. III, p. 272.

[10] E.B. Decision No. 155-(52/57); below, Vol. III, pp. 230–31.

[11] See above, pp. 533–35.

Notwithstanding the widespread use of the prior notice clause before it was repudiated, it was invoked on only one occasion, on September 17, 1958.[12] All of the inhibitions that attended the ineligibility procedures for which the prior notice clause was to be a substitute obstructed action under the clause as well. The embarrassment that was felt by the Executive Directors on the one occasion on which they decided to give notice helped to bring about the demise of the clause. That event occurred not because of the profligate use of the clause, but because of the conviction that it did not produce the most desirable balance between assurance to a member that it could use the Fund's resources and assurance to the Fund that use would be consistent with the Articles. The Fund decided in February 1961 to proscribe prior notice clauses and even deleted them from stand-by arrangements then in operation.[13]

When the decision to abandon prior notice clauses was taken, the staff and some executive directors urged that ineligibility procedures should not be regarded as an impeachment, and that, with this change in attitude, more use could be made of them. These recommendations have not been followed. Instead, the consequences of the decision have been, first, a greater vigilance than ever in ensuring that performance criteria are truly objective, because, if they are not, they will suffer from the same vice of subjectivity as the prior notice clause. Second, the decision led to a greater sophistication in the formulation of performance criteria as determinants of the effectiveness of a member's program. Third, performance criteria tended to proliferate until this tendency was curbed by a decision of September 20, 1968 which declares that they must be confined to those that are truly necessary for evaluating the progress of a program.

Earlier in this discussion of sanctions it was said that one further sanction would be singled out. That was a reference to Article VII, which is entitled "Scarce Currencies." Under Section 1, if the Fund finds that a general scarcity of a particular currency is developing, the Fund may inform members and issue a report setting forth the causes of the scarcity and containing recommendations for bringing it to an end. Section 2 empowers the Fund to borrow a member's currency or to acquire it for gold if the Fund deems it appropriate to replenish its holdings of that currency. Section 3 provides that if it becomes evident to the Fund that the demand for a member's currency seriously threatens the Fund's ability to supply the currency, the Fund, whether or not it has issued a report under Section 1, must make a formal declaration of the scarcity of the currency, apportion its existing and future supply of the currency, and issue a report. The formal declaration operates as an authorization to any member, after consulting the Fund, to impose temporary limitations on the freedom of exchange operations in the scarce currency. There are certain qualifications on the exercise of the

[12] See above, Vol. I, p. 433.

[13] E.B. Decision No. 1151-(61/6), February 20, 1961; below, Vol. III, p. 234.

authority, but, subject to them, members "have complete jurisdiction in determining the nature of [the] limitations"[14] on exchange operations, and therefore members would be able to discriminate against transactions in the scarce currency.

Action by the Fund under Section 1 or Section 3 was considered by the drafters to be the way in which the Fund could put pressure on a member that enjoys a substantial and persistent surplus in its balance of payments while a considerable number of other members suffer from deficits in their balance of payments. It is possible to detect a difference in tone in the explanations of these provisions before the Articles took effect, with Keynes describing the forerunner of Section 3 as "a sanction" and U.S. representatives generally avoiding quite so harsh a description.[15]

The provisions of Sections 1 and 3 and their relevance to conditions at the time were discussed by the Executive Directors in August 1947. The staff prepared a memorandum in which it was explained that the provisions were intended to prevent a general contraction of world trade as a result of inadequate imports and foreign investments by a great trading country. The insufficient monetary reserves of members at that time were not the result of any decline in demand in the United States or inadequate loans and grants by it; the abnormal demand for dollars was caused by an imbalance between the needs and the productive resources of many members. The implication of the staff's approach was that an adverse judgment would be implied by action under Section 1 and more particularly Section 3. In fact, the judgment would have been more disturbing than its legal consequences because many members were able to discriminate against transactions involving the U.S. dollar even in the absence of a declaration of the scarcity of the dollar. These were the members availing themselves of the transitional arrangements of Article XIV which permitted discrimination for balance of payments reasons. The Executive Directors decided on August 14, 1947 that there was no justification for action under Article VII, Sections 1 or 3. The possibility of invoking these provisions has not been discussed by the Executive Directors since August 1947, although the effectiveness of the provisions was the subject of debate in the CONTRACTING PARTIES to the GATT in 1955.

It seems to have become a received idea that a report under Section 1 or a declaration under Section 3 is an adverse judgment; certainly the consequences of the declaration, and perhaps also the report, could be grave. It was not to be expected that the Fund's customary caution in applying sanctions would be relaxed in the case of sanctions as serious as those that are available under

[14] Article VII, Section 3 (*b*); below, Vol. III, p. 195.

[15] See, for example, *Hearings Before the Committee on Banking and Currency of the U.S. Senate on H.R. 3314* (79th Cong., 1st sess.), pp. 168–72. See also *Questions and Answers on the International Monetary Fund*, Questions 30–32; below, Vol. III, pp. 171–75.

Article VII. This has led some observers to conclude that the only provision under which effective pressure could be applied against a member that has a substantial and persistent surplus in its balance of payments is sterile, and that the international adjustment process is all the weaker for that loss.

This discussion of the scarce currency provisions can be completed by a brief mention of the practice that has developed under Article VII, Section 2. Under that provision, the Fund can replenish its holdings of a currency by borrowing or by the sale of gold, and the Fund has now done this on a number of occasions. The provision would have had a more appropriate place in Article V among those dealing with the operations of the Fund, and it did appear in the forerunner of that article at one stage in its legislative history. Not only was the provision moved but the somewhat maladroit word "scarce" was introduced in its title. It has been necessary for the Fund to emphasize that the replenishment of a member's currency under Section 2 does not require action under either Section 1 or Section 3 and is not an animadversion on the member. On the contrary, the replenishment makes action under Section 3 less justifiable, because, if the replenishment takes the form of lending to the Fund, the member is making a contribution to the operation of the international monetary system by increasing the Fund's capacity to assist members in deficit. A member is required to provide its own currency to the Fund for gold but no member is obligated to lend to the Fund.

STRICT OBLIGATIONS AND PRACTICAL SOLUTIONS

The Fund's reluctance to employ sanctions is not associated with a relaxed understanding of the obligations of members. The Fund has tended to the view that obligations are not to be construed more narrowly than the terms in which they are written, and therefore it has not been responsive to alleged legal justifications for failures to observe obligations. An example of this strict construction has been cited in connection with par values: if a member wishes to change the par value of its currency it may do this only by the immediate adoption of a new par value in accordance with the Articles and without any intervening period of fluctuation in the exchange rate for its currency or an intervening unauthorized par value. Another example is the Fund's position on the scope of the obligation of members to refrain from imposing restrictions on payments and transfers for current international transactions without the approval of the Fund. The question arose whether the obligation applies to restrictions that are imposed for such political reasons as the preservation of national or international security and not for economic reasons. The Fund has made strenuous efforts at all times to exclude political considerations from its discussions and decisions. The desire to operate as a technical organization is reflected in the

Fund's agreement with the United Nations which was entered into pursuant to Article X of the Fund's Articles and Article 63 of the Charter of the United Nations and came into force on November 15, 1947. The agreement recognizes that

> by reason of the nature of its international responsibilities and the terms of its Articles of Agreement, the Fund is, and is required to function as, an independent international organization.[16]

It is an accepted convention of the Fund that political issues are not allowed to intrude into operating decisions, and thus there have been occasions on which the executive director appointed or elected by one disputant in a political controversy outside the Fund has not opposed an exchange transaction involving another disputant. It will be realized that the dilemma involving restrictions for security reasons was acute. In their decision of August 14, 1952, the Executive Directors expressed their conviction that the Fund does not provide a suitable forum for the discussion of the political and military considerations that are responsible for the adoption of these restrictions. The Executive Directors were aware, however, that it is not possible to distinguish sharply between cases involving only these considerations and other cases involving economic motivations and effects as well, that the Fund must protect the legitimate interests of its members, and that the language of the Articles makes no exception for any category of restrictions. They concluded, therefore, that the Fund's jurisdiction over restrictions applies whatever the motivation with which, or the circumstances in which, they are imposed.[17]

The Fund's skeptical attitude to alleged legal justifications for the nonperformance of obligations that are written in absolute form can be illustrated by two cases. The first of these arose in June 1948 and related to the responsibility of the United Kingdom for a subsidy paid by Southern Rhodesia to its domestic gold producers which appeared to be inconsistent with the Articles and the Fund's policy. A member accepts the Articles not only on its own behalf but also in respect of all colonies, overseas territories, territories under its protection, suzerainty, or authority and all territories in respect of which it exercises a mandate.[18] The United Kingdom felt that it could not require Southern Rhodesia to modify the subsidy because the colony was wholly self-governing in domestic matters. The Fund relied, however, on the traditional principle that a state cannot invoke its constitutional or domestic law as a legal excuse for noncompliance with a treaty obligation, and the United Kingdom withdrew its objection.

The second case relates to the compulsory withdrawal of Czechoslovakia. It was contended by Czechoslovakia that the complaint that it had failed to fulfill

---

16 Below, Vol. III, p. 215.

17 E.B. Decision No. 144-(52/51); below, Vol. III, p. 257.

18 Article XX, Section 2 (g); below, Vol. III, p. 207.

its obligations under Article VIII, Section 5 and Article XIV, Section 2 was unfounded because the failure referred to in Article XV, Section 2 meant noncompliance for which there was no legal justification. Reasons of national security were a legal justification and Czechoslovakia had reasons of this kind for noncompliance. The reply was that the conditions on which the Fund may compel a member to withdraw are set forth in the Articles; failure to perform an obligation was one of these conditions; and no exception was made for reasons of national security in connection with the obligations on which the complaint was based. In the Board of Governors, the Governor for Czechoslovakia proposed an interpretative resolution which would have held that:

1. "Failure to fulfill the members' obligations under the Agreement" in Article XV, Section 2, means legally not justified nonfulfillment of the provisions of the Articles of Agreement.

2. Reasons of national security are under the general concept of international law legal justification for "failure to fulfill the members' obligations under the Agreement."

3. Members of the Fund are entitled not to comply with the provisions of the Articles of Agreement if to comply would endanger their national security, and, in particular, are entitled to withhold information under Article VIII, Section 5, the disclosure of which would endanger their national security.

The Board of Governors refused to adopt this proposed resolution and confirmed the interpretation of the Executive Directors.[19]

It must not be inferred from what has been said that the attitude of the Fund has been "let justice be done though the Fund perish" (*fiat justitia pereat Argentaria*). Faced by the problems that a strict view of obligations may provoke, the Fund has been prepared to find practical solutions within its constitutional framework. The decision on restrictions imposed for security reasons on payments and transfers for current international transactions can be reverted to as an example. In order to give effect to all interests, including the Fund's interest in avoiding political controversy, the decision established a special procedure by which a member can perform its obligation to obtain the approval of restrictions imposed for security reasons. Any member contemplating the adoption of restrictions that in its view are related solely to the preservation of national or international security may give notice under the decision and apply for prior approval, and the Fund will act promptly on the request. If the member finds that circumstances preclude advance notice to the Fund, it should give notice as promptly as possible but ordinarily not later than thirty days after imposition of the restrictions. Each notice is circulated immediately to the Executive Directors, and unless the Fund informs the member within thirty days after receiving the notice that the Fund is not satisfied that the restrictions are imposed

---

19 *Summary Proceedings, 1954*, pp. 97–102, 112–14, 121–22, 135–80.

solely to preserve security, the member may assume that the Fund has no objection to the imposition of the restrictions. Notices have been given under the decision in connection with a number of international incidents of a political character. In no instance has there been any request to place a notice on the agenda of the Executive Directors, and the Fund has not objected to the imposition of any of the restrictions to which notices have related.

The decision dealing with restrictions established a procedure to enable members to stay within the law. A further illustration will be cited but of a different kind because it deals with the consequences of a situation that is contrary to the law. After Canada decided that it would not observe the obligations of Article IV, Sections 3 and 4 (*b*) and would allow the exchange rate for its currency to be determined by market forces, the Fund was faced with the problem of conducting transactions or making calculations in such a currency. It must be emphasized that a par value agreed with the Fund continues to be the par value for the purposes of the Articles until a new par value is established even though the member fails to perform its obligations to make the par value effective in exchange transactions taking place in its territories. If the Fund continued to stand ready to sell the currency at the par value, the practical effect would be to deprive other members of the opportunity to purchase the currency if it depreciated in the market, while there might be too great a readiness to purchase it from the Fund if the currency appreciated. The solution was an elaborate decision under which the Fund deals at market rates in a fluctuating currency to which the decision is applied, and makes all of its computations on the same basis.[20] The Fund employs the maintenance of gold value provisions in the Articles [21] to adjust all of its holdings in accordance with market rates prevailing on or about the dates as of which computations are made or transactions are carried out because it would produce a chaotic situation if the Fund were to value its currency holdings at one rate and at the same time use another rate in any of its operations or calculations.[22]

RECIPROCITY AND LEGAL ORDER

It has been suggested by some commentators that the Articles establish a legal system of reciprocity. For example, when the issue before a court in one member has been whether it must declare an exchange contract unenforceable under Article VIII, Section 2 (*b*) because it is contrary to the exchange control regulations of another member, the court has felt on occasion that it was relevant

[20] E.B. Decisions Nos. 321-(54/32), June 15, 1954, 1245-(61/45), August 4, 1961, 1283-(61/56), December 20, 1961; below, Vol. III, pp. 222–24.

[21] Article IV, Section 8.

[22] Joseph Gold, *Maintenance of the Gold Value of the Fund's Assets*, IMF Pamphlet Series, No. 6.

to inquire whether the other member was applying Article VIII, Section 2 (*b*) or other provisions in the Articles.[23] It is true that the Articles envisage benefits for all members because all have assumed obligations by subscribing to the Articles. It does not follow from this, however, that there is a legal principle of reciprocity by which the failure of one member to observe an obligation releases another member or members from their obligations to the delinquent member. The purpose of the Articles is to preserve legal order notwithstanding failures by a member from time to time to fulfill any of its obligations under the Articles. It is the function of the Fund to decide whether there has been a failure and what the legal consequences shall be. Even if the Fund is satisfied that there has been a failure, it does not follow that the legal consequence will be the release of other members from any of their obligations in relation to the defaulter or other members.

There is an eloquent statement of this principle by a Netherlands court that was asked to refrain from applying Article VIII, Section 2 (*b*) to an exchange contract that was said to be contrary to the exchange control regulations of Indonesia because of alleged violations of treaty obligations owed by Indonesia to the Netherlands:

> The Dutch forum must refrain from evaluating the Indonesian foreign exchange provisions and must also refrain from judging the question whether in view of its behavior Indonesia can be considered as a treaty partner. Apart from the fact that a partner to a treaty which has had to protest against violations of international agreements must itself fulfill its obligations, the paramount interest is that the international order to which the Netherlands and Indonesia have both adhered be respected.[24]

The principle on which the Articles are based and which guides the operation of the Fund is the one expressed by the Netherlands court. If, therefore, a member introduces restrictions on payments and transfers for current international transactions, this gives no license to other members to retaliate at will. They must observe this restraint even if the restrictions are discriminatory. Indeed, although one of the objectives of the Fund is the elimination of discrimination, and although the Fund has pursued this objective with vigor,[25] it must be recalled that the Fund does have the legal authority to approve discriminatory currency arrangements.[26] But even if a member introduces discriminatory or other restrictions without the approval of the Fund, other members are not entitled to adopt countermeasures without the Fund's approval if they are measures that require the Fund's approval. The Fund's Rules and Regulations

[23] *Pan American Insurance Co. v. Blanco*, 311 F. 2d 424, 427 fn. 8 (1962).

[24] *Frantzmann v. Ponijen*, Nederlandse Jurisprudentie (1960), No. 290. Gold, *The Fund Agreement in the Courts* (1962), pp. 113–18.

[25] E.B. Decisions Nos. 433-(55/42), June 22, 1955, 201-(53/29), May 4, 1953, 955-(59/45), October 23, 1959; below, Vol. III, pp. 258–60.

[26] Article VIII, Section 3.

establish procedures under which members can lodge complaints against a member that is alleged to be neglecting its obligations,[27] but, in accordance with the tendency to avoid formal procedures, most discussions of a member's practices take place informally and usually during regular consultations. By common consent, these consultations are a convenient and effective procedure for expressing an international opinion on a member's practices. In fact, the opportunities offered by consultations are considered so useful that occasionally members air informal complaints about an economic or financial policy of a member even though the complainants are aware that it is not within the jurisdiction of the Fund to approve or disapprove the policy. Some of these complaints are made in the forum of the Executive Directors because the present state of international economic organization does not provide another international forum with direct jurisdiction.

A leading example of the fact that the Articles establish a legal order which does not entitle members to take the law into their own hands in matters within the Fund's jurisdiction is the episode in which France adopted an unauthorized change of par value and discriminatory multiple rates of exchange on January 26, 1948.[28] The principle of the exchange rate obligations of the Articles is that each member is responsible for maintaining the value of its own currency. If it fails in this obligation, the obligation is not shifted to other members. Accordingly, the Fund held that other members were not bound to regard the former par value for the franc or the new rates of exchange for the franc as binding on them and as rates that they would have to enforce by appropriate measures in exchange transactions in their territories. However, both they and France remained bound by their obligations under Article IV, Section 4 (*a*), and the Fund called on them to maintain close contact with the Fund on the negotiation of new exchange arrangements. As a practical solution, the Fund agreed that any bilateral arrangements establishing rates of exchange based on the unauthorized change of par value, or the evolution of such rates in exchange transactions in the absence of bilateral arrangements, were not inconsistent with the objectives of the Articles. The Fund declared that specific approval had to be sought for bilateral arrangements for the adoption, or for the adoption without bilateral agreement, of rates not compatible with the unauthorized change of par value even if they were based on other rates introduced by France as part of its exchange reform. The Fund received a number of requests from France and other members for the approval of rates of exchange between the franc and other currencies that were justified because of special economic or other stated reasons. Some of these rates were not acceptable to the Fund and were modified. The general approach of the Fund was to resist the proliferation of rates beyond those already in existence.

---

27 Rules and Regulations, Rules H-2, H-3, K-4, M-4, M-5; below, Vol. III, pp. 293–94, 299, 301.

28 See above, pp. 549, 574, 583.

The adoption by France of its new exchange system did not release other members from their obligations although the new system involved a par value to which the Fund objected and multiple rates which it did not approve. The Fund insisted that other members were not entitled to retaliate by establishing rates of exchange between their currencies and the franc as they saw fit or even to establish rates by agreement with France in view of the interests of members that were not parties to the agreements. The relationships between the currencies of members are not simply bilateral but fit into an orderly design involving all currencies which is supervised by the Fund. If the design is disturbed at one place, the disturbance must be contained and order restored. One of the economic features of the French exchange system that the Fund found most undesirable was the introduction of broken cross rates. Rates of exchange ceased to be uniform among members in terms of gold as a common measure. This is a condition that can produce the most damaging distortions in trade and payments, and the Fund has opposed it relentlessly.

CHAPTER

27

The Amendments

Joseph Gold

SPECIAL DRAWING RIGHTS

In the 1960's the conviction grew that some more rational method of controlling international liquidity was needed in order to strengthen the international monetary system. The volume of reserves available to the community of Fund members was determined by the balance of payments deficits of the reserve currency countries, by the amount of gold production and the pattern of its absorption and use, by the conversion of reserve currencies into gold, and by fluctuations in the total of the newly recognized assets, gold tranches and readily repayable loan claims against the Fund, that arise as the result of the operations of the Fund. The determination of the reserve currency countries to reduce or eliminate their balance of payments deficits supported the credibility of the argument that unconditional liquidity might not increase sufficiently to prevent global stagnation and deflation. The long debate and negotiations on measures to deal with this threat led to the resolution of the Board of Governors at their Annual Meeting at Rio de Janeiro requesting the Executive Directors to prepare the text of an amendment of the Articles on the basis of an Outline attached to the resolution. The main tenet of the Outline was that the Fund should be empowered to allocate "special drawing rights" to its members as a supplement to existing reserve assets. The text of the amendments was prepared,[1] approved by the Board of Governors on May 31, 1968, and submitted to members for their acceptance in accordance with Article XVII. The amendments became effective on July 28, 1969. They are the first that have been adopted in the

[1] *Establishment of a Facility Based on Special Drawing Rights in the International Monetary Fund and Modifications in the Rules and Practices of the Fund: A Report by the Executive Directors to the Board of Governors Proposing Amendment of the Articles of Agreement* (Washington, April 1968); below, Vol. III, pp. 497–541. And see Joseph Gold, *Special Drawing Rights*, IMF Pamphlet Series, No. 13; "The Next Stage in the Development of International Monetary Law: The Deliberate Control of Liquidity," *American Journal of International Law*, Vol. 62 (1968), pp. 365–402.

history of the Fund. Although from time to time the idea of an amendment has been suggested, the general attitude has been that amendment was too complicated a process to undertake unless there was an overwhelming case for it. That case existed for the amendments that have been adopted. They represent the most important development in the Fund and in the legal regulation of the international monetary system since the original Articles became effective.

The facility through which special drawing rights will come into being is the Special Drawing Account, which became operative on August 6, 1969 in accordance with the provisions of the amendments.[2] This facility within the Fund will coexist with the General Account. The Fund will conduct its original operations and transactions, as well as a few new operations and transactions involving special drawing rights, through the General Account. The two Accounts will be separate in the manner indicated in the amendments, but neither will be a legal entity in itself.[3] The Special Drawing Account is not an affiliate, although that technique was considered possible at one time during the negotiations.[4] The Fund will remain a single legal entity and will be the same international person as before the amendments.

All members of the Fund have the privilege of participating in the Special Drawing Account but are not bound to participate. Decisions to allocate or cancel special drawing rights will be taken by the Board of Governors by a majority of 85 per cent of the total voting power of participants on the basis of a proposal by the Managing Director concurred in by the Executive Directors.[5] In decisions on matters pertaining exclusively to special drawing rights, only governors appointed by participants or executive directors appointed or elected by participants will be entitled to vote.[6]

Special drawing rights may be allocated to participants on the basis of their quotas for basic periods of five years. A participant may opt out of allocations.[7] The central right of a participant is to use its special drawing rights to meet its balance of payments needs, or in the light of developments in its official holdings of gold, foreign exchange, and special drawing rights, and its reserve position in the Fund, by transferring its special drawing rights in return for currency convertible in fact to another participant designated by the Fund. Although a participant is expected to use its special drawing rights only in the circumstances described and not for the sole purpose of changing the composition of its official holdings as between the total of its gold, foreign exchange, and reserve position

[2] Article XXIII, Section 1; below, Vol. III, pp. 525–26.

[3] Article XXII, Sections 1 and 2.

[4] Joseph Gold, "Legal Technique in the Creation of a New International Reserve Asset," *Case Western Reserve Journal of International Law*, Vol. I, No. 2 (1969), pp. 105–23.

[5] Article XXIV, Section 4.

[6] Article XXVII (*a*).

[7] Article XXIV, Section 2 (*e*).

in the Fund on the one hand and its special drawing rights on the other hand, the use of special drawing rights cannot be challenged on the basis of this expectation, although the Fund may take certain actions after the event.[8] A participant may use its special drawing rights up to the hilt but it must maintain an average balance of them over time, according to a prescribed formula, and must do this by an appropriate "reconstitution" of its balance of special drawing rights if they fall below the average for a time.[9]

There are three ways in which the provisions dealing with special drawing rights have been affected by the Fund's past experience. First, some provisions have been based on the Fund's practices and policies in the evolution of its original operations and transactions. Second, some provisions have been based on the original provisions. Third, some provisions deliberately depart from the original provisions.

(1) Some of the central characteristics of special drawing rights have been influenced profoundly by the experience of the Fund in the conduct of its original operations and transactions. For example, it was intended that special drawing rights should be a form of unconditional liquidity, and therefore the closest analogue in the General Account, the gold tranche, was the model for the unchallengeable right of a participant to use special drawing rights when it considers that it has a need to use them. The ability of a member to make gold tranche purchases without challenge rested on policy and practice before the amendments, but special drawing rights will begin life with a participant's unchallengeable right to use them as a legal characteristic of special drawing rights.

A participant is entitled to use its special drawing rights in accordance with the expectation of need by transferring them to another participant designated by the Fund. Alternatives to the concept of designation were considered, notably use by agreement between participants or use as determined solely by the participant using its special drawing rights. The choice in favor of use in accordance with designation by the Fund [10] was made because of the success of the Fund's policy on the selection of currencies purchased by members in exchange transactions with the Fund. The balance of payments and reserve criteria on which designation will be based have been adapted from that policy. Similarly, the provisions on the balanced distribution of special drawing rights among participants as a principle of designation derive from the attempt to achieve an equitable distribution of gold tranche positions under the policy.

There are other examples of a similar influence of policy on the new facility, but they need not be pursued here, except to note that the term "special drawing

[8] Article XXV, Section 3 (*b*).

[9] Article XXV, Section 6; Schedule G.

[10] Article XXV, Section 5.

rights" itself is a link, although an odd one, with the terminology of the Fund's original transactions. The importance of the point, however, goes beyond terminology. The original Articles speak of the purchase and sale of currencies and never of "drawings," but this word has become the popular way of referring to the Fund's exchange transactions. In the negotiations leading to the agreement on special drawing rights there was much dispute about whether the outcome should be a new monetary "unit" or "reserve asset" or a new form of "credit." This was not decided at the international level, but each participant is enabled to decide for itself whether it will regard special drawing rights as a reserve asset and include them in its reserves for domestic legal or policy purposes, and special drawing rights have been given the qualities which will permit participants to come to that conclusion. At the international level, a number of compromises were made, one of which was that the new instrument of liquidity would be called special drawing rights. The words "drawing rights" were used as an echo of the exchange transactions of the Fund, because these words connoted to some a credit element, although the Articles avoid all language that suggests the indebtedness of members to the Fund or the extension of credit by it. The adjective "special" was added to the popular term "drawing rights" to indicate that new drawing rights differing from the old were being established, and the result was the creation of a new term of art.

(2) The provisions dealing with special drawing rights that have been adapted, with more or less fidelity, from the original provisions are too numerous to mention here in full. In Chapter 25 the inspiration for the provision setting forth "general obligations of participants" in Article XXVIII was identified as Article IV, Section 4 (*a*), which establishes general obligations regarding exchange stability. In addition, the association between the new provisions that give the Fund authority to adopt variations in the operation of certain Articles without the need to amend and similar provisions in the original Articles has been noted. Provisions closely parallel to the original provisions have been adopted on such matters as administration of the Special Drawing Account,[11] emergency,[12] settlement on the termination of participation,[13] and interpretation.[14]

(3) In some ways, the decisions not to adopt parallel provisions are even more interesting. One of the most important divergences is the normal absence of any resources of gold or currency in the Special Drawing Account.[15] A participant receiving special drawing rights from another participant will provide currency to the latter on the occasion of the transaction.[16] The balance of payments need

---

[11] Article XXVII.

[12] Article XXIX, Section 1.

[13] Article XXX; Schedule H.

[14] Article XXVII (*c*).

[15] Article XXII, Section 2.

[16] Article XXV, Section 4.

for which a participant may make a use of its special drawing rights does not distinguish between difficulties in the current and capital accounts of the balance of payments, whereas a distinction of this kind is made in connection with a member's use of the Fund's resources through the General Account.[17] Special drawing rights have an absolute gold value guarantee,[18] whereas it is possible, theoretically at least, for the gold value of gold tranches to be decreased. This would occur if the Fund were to waive the maintenance of the gold value of its assets on a uniform proportionate reduction in the par values of all currencies.[19] The Fund sells currencies from the General Account at the par value,[20] but currency will be provided by participants in return for special drawing rights on the basis of market rates of exchange.[21] The liquidity of the Special Drawing Account is superior to that of the General Account because the net obligation of a participant to receive special drawing rights in transactions is equal to twice its net cumulative allocation of special drawing rights,[22] whereas the member's corresponding obligation in the General Account is limited to its subscription. The system of liquidation of the Special Drawing Account differs somewhat from that of the General Account [23] in order to establish a more desirable apportionment among participants of the burden of a default by a participant in the liquidation settlement and in order to ensure that a participant's exposure to risk will not be increased because it increases its holdings of special drawing rights.[24]

REFORM OF THE FUND

The resolution of the Board of Governors at Rio de Janeiro requested the Executive Directors to perform a second task: to proceed with their work relating to "improvements in the present rules and practices of the Fund based on developments in world economic conditions and the experience of the Fund since the adoption of the Articles of Agreement of the Fund" and to report on their proposals for amending the Articles and By-Laws for this purpose. The members of the European Economic Community had insisted that the establishment of the new facility and the improvement of the Fund had to be regarded as contemporaneous projects. One of the major developments in world economic conditions since the creation of the Fund which these members thought should be recognized by appropriate amendments was their economic and financial strength

[17] Article VI, Sections 1 and 2.

[18] Article XXI, Section 2.

[19] Article IV, Section 8 (*d*).

[20] Article IV, Section 1 (*b*).

[21] Article XXV, Section 8.

[22] Article XXV, Section 4.

[23] Article XVI, Section 2; Schedule E.

[24] Article XXXI; Schedule I.

in the world and their role in the Fund. This had been reflected in the volume of the Fund's sales of their currencies. Their voting strength in the Fund, however, was 16.45 per cent of the total in comparison with the 21.76 per cent of the United States.

All the basic reforms that have been incorporated in the amendments were proposed by the EEC members, although there are certain associated or consequential amendments that are the result of proposals by other members during the negotiations. The basic reforms proposed by the EEC members were few in number and only a small proportion of those originally considered by the EEC. They can be assembled into a few categories.[25] Foremost among them in their dramatic effect are those amendments that introduce the need for a special majority of 85 per cent of voting strength by analogy to the majority that is required for decisions to allocate or cancel special drawing rights. The argument for these amendments was the logical link that was alleged to exist between these latter decisions and certain other decisions of the Fund. The link was the effect on global liquidity. It was argued that decisions approving adjustments in quotas as the result of a general review of quotas and decisions on uniform proportionate changes in the par values of all currencies affect the volume of global liquidity, and these decisions, therefore, should command the same general support as decisions on the allocation or cancellation of special drawing rights. It was agreed that the same majority should be required for quota adjustments resulting from a general review [26] and for uniform proportionate changes in par values as well as for a number of associated decisions.[27]

A second group of amendments relate to the original provisions governing repurchase and the calculation of monetary reserves by which repurchase obligations are determined. The negotiation of these amendments began with the thesis that two aspects of these provisions involving reserve currencies were unsatisfactory. One of these was the deduction of "currency liabilities" in the calculation of monetary reserves. The currency liabilities of a member, it will be recalled, are the holdings of its currency by the central or other official institutions of other members or by banks in their territories. The view was advanced that this was a preference for the reserve currency members because it was mainly their currencies that were held by others, and the deductions that were made in respect of these holdings had resulted in negative monetary reserves or monetary reserves below the quota level for both the United Kingdom and the United States. The other objection was to the abatement of repurchase obligations, i.e., the principle by which a calculated repurchase obligation was

---

[25] Joseph Gold, *The Reform of the Fund*, IMF Pamphlet Series, No. 12. For the revisions to the Articles see below, Vol. III, pp. 521–38.

[26] Article III, Sections 2 and 4 (*c*); below, Vol. III, p. 521.

[27] Article IV, Sections 7 and 8 (*d*).

canceled if it accrued in the currency of a member which the Fund could not accept because the Fund's holdings of that currency cannot be increased above 75 per cent of the member's quota by repurchases. The member for which the obligation was calculated was not required to use another convertible currency or gold, which it might have had to obtain from a reserve center, in discharge of the obligation that was abated. It was contended that there was no economic justification for abatement because the repurchase obligation resulted from an improvement in the member's monetary reserves. The effects of abatement had been enhanced in recent years because the Fund had been unable to accept either U.S. dollars or sterling. Indeed, in order to enable members to make a temporary use of the Fund's resources in accordance with repurchase representations or commitments, the United States had made purchases of currencies from the Fund and had sold them, in return for dollars, to members which then returned them to the Fund immediately by way of repurchase. In view of the nature of these operations, the terms "turnstile" or "technical" purchases were in popular use for a time.

It was agreed that there should be amendments under which currency liabilities would not be deductible in the calculation of monetary reserves [28] and repurchase obligations that had been abated because the Fund could not accept the currency in which they had accrued would be discharged in another convertible currency which the Fund could accept.[29] These two basic amendments were accompanied by a large number of other amendments in relation to repurchase,[30] some of which were intended to soften the impact of the increase in repurchase obligations that might have followed from the two basic reforms. The possibility of eliminating the whole mechanism of repurchase and replacing it with a more discretionary system was raised but rejected, although the amendments introduce further qualifications of the principles of sharing or the concept of the Fund's resources as a second line of reserves for members, on which the original provisions had been based.

Amendments have been made in relation to the use of the Fund's resources. The gold tranche enters the third stage in its history and now receives constitutional recognition.[31] The former policy by which representations made in connection with requests for gold tranche purchases were not challenged in practice although they remained challengeable in principle has been converted into a legal guarantee of immunity from challenge.[32] This amendment has been accompanied by another which prevents the future creation of new forms of

[28] Article XIX (*e*).

[29] Schedule B, paragraph 1.

[30] See *Report* (cited above in footnote 1), Section 35; below, Vol. III, p. 515.

[31] Article XIX (*j*). See above, pp. 536–37.

[32] Article V, Section 3 (*d*).

unconditional or virtually unconditional facilities in the General Account.[33] Some of the members that had been vigorous supporters in the early days of the Fund of the thesis that access to the Fund's resources should be unconditional, and that had opposed the Fund's power to challenge requests or call for repurchase commitments, were among those that pressed for the prohibition of new forms of unconditional liquidity through the General Account. Their position was that the creation of this kind of liquidity in the future was a function of the Fund acting through the Special Drawing Account. In addition, they pointed out that it would not be logical to permit the creation of unconditional liquidity through one Account by a majority of votes cast while requiring a high majority for the same purpose through the other Account. Finally, Article VI, Section 2, which gave members that were not making a net use of the Fund's resources a special privilege to make purchases of certain currencies without encountering the objection that the purchases were to meet a large or sustained outflow of capital, has been eliminated in that form.[34] The original provision contained some fundamental obscurities, and in any event, it had not been useful because of the limitation on the currencies that could be purchased.

This brings the discussion to the next group of amendments, which can be described as improvements in the qualities of the gold tranche or in that part of it which is below the level of 75 per cent of quota and is sometimes referred to in practice as the "super gold tranche." For example, requests may be made for any gold tranche purchases without challenge on the ground that they are to meet a large or sustained outflow of capital. Under the original provision this rule had been confined to purchases that did not increase the Fund's holdings of the purchasing member's currency above 75 per cent of quota. The limitation on the currencies that may be purchased in this way has been removed. Other improvements include the assured remuneration that is payable on "super gold tranches" [35] and the possible reduction or elimination of service charges on gold tranche purchases.[36]

Finally, an amendment has been made in Article XVIII, the provision on interpretation. It may seem extraordinary in view of the conclusions of this history that the question was raised whether the principle of final and authoritative interpretation of its Articles by the Fund itself should be replaced by the procedure of settlement by three arbitrators which applies to disagreements between the Fund and a member which has withdrawn or which arises in the course of liquidation. The legal, political, and other reasons why the issue was raised are complex and can be left to some future historian. Here it can be said that the arbitration tribunal as the final authority was not acceptable. Instead,

---

[33] Article V, Section 3 (*c*).

[34] Article VI, Section 2; below, Vol. III, pp. 194, 523.

[35] Article V, Section 9.

[36] Article V, Section 8 (*a*).

a new organ with certain novel attributes was established within the framework of the Fund itself in order to provide a new mode of appeal. The Executive Directors will continue to take decisions on questions of interpretation in accordance with the original Articles. Within three months of any decision, any member may appeal to the Board of Governors, whose decision will continue to be final. However, any question referred to the Board of Governors in this way will be considered by a Committee on Interpretation of the Board of Governors. The Board of Governors is to establish the membership, procedures, and voting majorities of the committee, but each member of the committee is to have one vote. The decisions of the committee will be the only decisions within the structure of the Fund that are taken without weighted voting. This is particularly important because a decision of the committee will be deemed to be the decision of the Board of Governors unless the Board repudiates the decision by a majority of 85 per cent of the total voting power.

THE "CODIFICATION" OF POLICIES AND INTERPRETATIONS

In a chapter dealing with constitutional development it is appropriate to emphasize a further characteristic of the amendments. This is the incorporation of a number of policies and interpretative decisions into the amendments, a process that was frequently referred to in the discussions of the draft amendments as "codification." The Executive Directors were aware that the transformation of policies in this way could be a dangerous process because it could inhibit the evolution of future policy. Similarly, there was a risk that it might be thought to be the view of the Fund that from time to time interpretations should be transformed into amendments. The Executive Directors recommended, therefore, that only a modest number of policies and interpretative decisions should be treated in this way.

Among the policies that are given a legal foundation, it has been noted already that the *de facto* unchallengeability of representations connected with requests for gold tranche purchases is now a *de jure* unchallengeability. The compensatory financing facility and its "floating" character are now recognized, although there is no compulsion on the Fund to perpetuate either the facility or its floating character.[37] The Fund's investment in U.S. Government securities of the proceeds of the sale of gold in order to establish a Special Reserve against future administrative deficits has been recognized indirectly by broadening the use of the Special Reserve to cover operational deficits as well.[38] The policy by

[37] Article XIX (*j*).

[38] Article XII, Section 6 (*c*).

which various techniques have been adopted in order to soften the impact on members of the gold subscriptions payable on quota increases has been given a statutory basis by requiring an 85 per cent majority for decisions, taken as part of a general review of quotas, for the sole purpose of mitigating the effect of these subscriptions.[39]

Various important interpretative decisions are given statutory expression. The first of these is that the use of the Fund's resources must be temporary.[40] That word was not used in the Articles, although it was implicit in a number of provisions. Another relates to "conditionality" in the provision of Fund resources to members. Conditionality was inherent in the concept of "adequate safeguards," but it is now made express in a provision which requires the Fund to have policies on the use of its resources and to examine the representation made in connection with a request to make a purchase, other than a gold tranche purchase, in order to determine the consistency of the request with the Articles and the Fund's policies.[41] A third example is the express reference to the voluntary and other repurchases that are not made as the result of obligations accruing under the repurchase mechanism in the Articles and that account for the bulk of actual repurchases.[42]

Finally, three concepts that have emerged in past practice have been recognized and given operative effect. One of these is "reserve position in the Fund," which is now defined as the sum of the gold tranche purchases that a participant in the Special Drawing Account could make and the amount of any indebtedness of the Fund which is "readily repayable" to the participant under a loan agreement.[43] Developments in a member's reserve position in the Fund are among those that a member may take into account in deciding whether to use its special drawing rights.[44] The concept also appears in the amendments in connection with the desideratum of the harmonized use by a member of its resources, including its special drawing rights.[45] A readily repayable loan is one under which the lender may obtain early repayment at its request by representing that there is a balance of payments need for repayment. The concept, although not the term, was first used in the General Arrangements to Borrow[46] and again in the 1966 loan agreement with Italy. It was adapted from the gold tranche by giving the lender's representation the overwhelming benefit of any doubt. Lastly, "currency convertible in fact" also emerged from the General Arrangements to Borrow,

---

[39] Article III, Sections 2 and 4 (*c*).

[40] Article I (v); Article V, Section 3 (*c*).

[41] Article V, Section 3 (*c*) and (*d*).

[42] Article XXV, Section 7 (*c*).

[43] Article XXXII (*c*).

[44] Article XXV, Section 3 (*a*).

[45] Schedule G, paragraph 1 (*b*).

[46] E.B. Decision No. 1289-(62/1), January 5, 1962, paragraph 11 (f); below, Vol. III, p. 250.

where it was not defined.[47] It is now elaborately defined, and is of course a vital concept in connection with special drawing rights.[48] In particular, it is the currency that a participant designated to receive special drawing rights from another participant must supply in return for them.

"Each phrase and each sentence is an end
and a beginning."—T. S. Eliot, *Four Quartets*

[47] *Ibid.*, paragraph 11 (a); below, Vol. III, p. 249.

[48] Article XXXII (*b*); below, Vol. III, p. 534.

Indexes

Index A. Subjects

References in this index are arranged in alphabetical order of subject within each main heading. References are to pages; page numbers marked with an asterisk (*) refer to tables, and those including the letter n *refer to footnotes.*

F

G

H

I

J

K

L

M

N

O

P

Q

R

S

T

U

V

W

Index B. Countries

In this index the word "exchange" should be understood before the word "rate" in the expressions "fluctuating rate," "forward rate," and "multiple rate." References are to pages. Page numbers marked with an asterisk (*) refer to tables; however, no references are given to the following comprehensive tables:

Table 1. Initial Par Values Established, 1946–65 (pp. 84-86)

Table 2. Dates of Membership and of Initial Par Values, December 27, 1945–December 31, 1965 (pp. 87-89)

Table 3. Magnitudes of Exchange Depreciation, End 1948 to End 1965: Distribution of 105 Countries by Degree of Depreciation (p. 112)

Table 4. Changes in Par Values, 1948–65 (pp. 116-18)

Table 5. Exchange Rates Used in Table 3 (pp. 119-21)

Table 6. Principal Developments in Multiple Exchange Rates, 1946–65 (pp. 147-51)

Table 14. Quotas of Members at Selected Dates (pp. 378-80)

Table 22. Drawings from the Fund, Calendar Years 1947–65 (pp. 460-63)

Table 23. Repurchases of Drawings, Calendar Years 1947–65 (pp. 464-67)

Table 24. Stand-By Arrangements Inaugurated or Renewed, Calendar Years 1952–65 (pp. 490-91)

A

B

C

D

E

F

G

H

I

INDEX C. ARTICLES OF AGREEMENT

The page numbers given for an Article may also refer to individual Sections of that Article. References given for Sections of an Article are not necessarily repeated against the Article itself. The Article is usually cited in a footnote.

The text of the Articles will be found in Volume III of this history; those adopted at Bretton Woods are on pages 185-214, and those embodied in the Amendment that came into force in July 1969 are on pages 521-38.

Index D. Executive Board Decisions

Decisions Referred to by Number

The citation is usually in a footnote. The text of these decisions is given in full in Volume III of this history, pp. 219-77.

Decisions Referred to by Subject

Index E. Publications Cited

Numbers refer to pages. The publication is usually cited in a footnote.

H

I

THE INTERNATIONAL MONETARY FUND

1945-1965

Volume III: Documents

THE INTERNATIONAL MONETARY FUND 1945-1965

Twenty Years of International Monetary Cooperation

VOLUME III: DOCUMENTS

Edited by
J. Keith Horsefield

INTERNATIONAL MONETARY FUND
WASHINGTON, D. C.
1969

PREFATORY NOTE

This volume comprises documents relating to the history of the International Monetary Fund, including some which preceded the drafting of the Articles of Agreement. Among the latter are early versions of the plans for a Clearing Union (the Keynes Plan) and a Stabilization Fund (the White Plan) which have not hitherto been published.

The published documents of the Fund here reproduced include all those which are cited in Volumes I and II of this history, except for publications issued at regular intervals.

J.K.H.

ISBN 0-939934-07-8 (v.III)
ISBN 0-939934-08-6 (set)

Second printing, February 1972
Third printing, May 1981
Fourth printing, March 1986

CONTENTS

PART I: BEFORE BRETTON WOODS

PART II: BASIC DOCUMENTS

PART III: FUND PRONOUNCEMENTS

Page

PART I

Before Bretton Woods

The Keynes Plan

The first draft of Lord Keynes' plan for a Clearing Union was circulated within the British Treasury on September 8, 1941. A fourth draft was given to Ministers on February 11, 1942, and this is reproduced in (A) below.

The final draft was issued by the British Government in April 1943 as a White Paper (Cmd. 6437); it is reproduced in (B) below.

(A) Proposals for an International Currency (or Clearing) Union

[February 11, 1942]

1. The proposal is to establish a Currency Union, here designated an *International Clearing Union*, based on international bank-money, called (let us say) bancor, fixed (but not unalterably) in terms of gold and accepted as the equivalent of gold by the British Commonwealth and the United States and all members of the Union for the purpose of settling international balances. The Central Banks of all member-States (and also of non-members) would keep accounts with the International Clearing Union through which they would be entitled to settle their exchange balances with one another at their par value as defined in terms of bancor. Countries having a favourable balance of payments with the rest of the world as a whole would find themselves in possession of a credit account with the Clearing Union, and those having an unfavourable balance would have a debit account. Measures would be necessary (see below) to prevent the piling up of credit and debit balances without limit, and the system would have failed in the long run if it did not possess sufficient capacity for self-equilibrium to prevent this.

2. The idea underlying such a Currency Union is simple, namely, to generalise the essential principle of banking, as it is exhibited within any closed system. This principle is the necessary equality of credits and debits, of assets and liabilities. If no credits can be removed outside the clearing system but only transferred within it, the Union *itself* can never be in difficulties. It can with safety make what advances it wishes to any of its members with the assurance that the proceeds can only be transferred to the clearing account of another member. Its problem is solely to see to it that its members keep the rules and that the advances made to each of them are prudent and advisable for the Union as a whole.

3. It is proposed that the Currency Union should be founded by the United States and the United Kingdom, which would be designated founder-States and given a special position. Their representatives, and those of other members, on the Governing Board of the Clearing Bank would be appointed by the Governments of the several member-States; the daily business and technical arrangements being carried out, as at present, by their Central Banks.

❖ ❖ ❖

4. The plan aims at the substitution of an expansionist, in place of a contractionist, pressure on world trade.

5. It would effect this by allowing to each member-State overdraft facilities of a defined amount, proportionate to the importance of its foreign trade and subject to certain regulative provisions. That is to say, each country is allowed a certain margin of resources and a certain interval of time within which to effect a balance in its economic relations with the rest of the world. These facilities are made possible by the nature of the system itself and do not involve particular indebtedness between one member-State and another. A country is in credit or debit with the Clearing Union as a whole. This means that the overdraft facilities, whilst a relief to some, are not a real burden to others. For credit balances, just like the importation of actual gold, represent those resources which a country voluntarily chooses to leave idle. They represent a potentiality of purchasing power, which it is entitled to use at any time. Meanwhile, the fact that the creditor country is not choosing to employ this purchasing power would not necessarily mean, as it does at present, that it is withdrawn from circulation and exerting a deflationary and contractionist pressure on the whole world including the creditor country itself. No country need be in possession of a credit balance unless it deliberately prefers to sell more than it buys (or lends); no country loses its liquidity or is prevented from employing its credit balance whenever it chooses to do so; and no country suffers injury (but on the contrary) by the fact that the balance, which it does not choose to employ for the time being, is not withdrawn from circulation. In short, the analogy with a national banking system is complete. No depositor in a local bank suffers because the balances, which he leaves idle, are employed to finance the business of someone else. Just as the development of national banking systems served to offset a deflationary pressure which would have prevented otherwise the development of modern industry, so by extending the same principle into the international field we may hope to offset the contractionist pressure which might otherwise overwhelm in social disorder and disappointment the good hopes of our modern world.

6. These facilities will be of particular importance as soon as the initial shortages of supply have been overcome. Many countries, including ourselves, will find a difficulty in paying for their imports, and will need time and resources before they can establish a readjustment. The efforts of each of these debtor countries to preserve its own equilibrium, by forcing its exports and by cutting off all imports which are not strictly necessary, will aggravate the problem of all the others. On the other hand, if each feels free from undue pressure, the volume of international exchange will be increased and everyone will find it easier to re-establish equilibrium without injury to the standard of life anywhere. The creditor countries will benefit, hardly less than the debtors, by being given an interval of *time* in which to adjust their economies, during which they can safely move at their own pace without the result of exercising deflationary pressure on the rest of the world, and, by repercussion, on themselves.

7. Now this can only be accomplished by the countries whoever they may turn out to be, which are for the time being in the creditor position, showing themselves ready to remain so without exercising a pressure towards contraction, pending the establishment of a new equilibrium. The fact that this costs them nothing deserves emphasising. The accumulation of a bancor credit, as compared with an accumulation of gold, does not curtail in the least their capacity or their inducement either to produce or to consume. The substitution of a credit mechanism for hoarding would have repeated

in the international field the same miracle already performed in the domestic field of turning a stone into bread.

8. There might be one or two other ways of effecting this temporarily or in part. For example, U.S.A. might redistribute her gold. Or there might be a number of bilateral arrangements having the effect of providing international overdrafts, as for example an agreement by the Federal Reserve Board to accumulate, if necessary, a large sterling balance at the Bank of England.

9. The objection to particular arrangements of this kind is that they are likely to be influenced by extraneous, political reasons and put individual countries into a position of particular obligation towards others; and also that the distribution of the assistance between different countries may not correspond to need and to the actual requirements as they ultimately develop. Moreover, for reasons already given, we are not likely to be specially eligible applicants for bounty of this kind. If, for example, the problem were to be met by a redistribution of America's gold, it is unlikely that we should get any of it, partly because we should have so lately received assistance under Lend-Lease, partly because the British Commonwealth are the largest producers of gold, which output would be regarded, rightly or wrongly, as ours at one remove.

10. It should be much easier, and surely more satisfactory both for them and for us, to persuade the United States to enter into a general and collective responsibility, applying to all countries alike, that a country finding itself in a creditor position *against the rest of the world as a whole* should enter into an arrangement not to allow this credit balance so long as it chooses to hold it, to exercise a contractionist pressure against world economy and, by repercussion, against the economy of the creditor country itself. This would give us, and all others, the great assistance of multilateral clearing, whereby (for example) we could offset favourable balances arising out of our exports to Europe against unfavourable balances due to the United States or South America or elsewhere. How, indeed, can we hope to afford to start up trade with Europe (which will be of vast importance to us) during the relief and reconstruction period on any other terms?

11. These advantages of the proposed International Clearing Union are so great that they surely overshadow most reasons of objection on lesser grounds.

12. If, indeed, we lack the productive capacity to maintain our standard of life, then a reduction in this standard is not avoidable. If our wage and price-levels are hopelessly wrong, a change in the rate of exchange is inevitable. But if we possess the productive capacity and the difficulty is the lack of markets as a result of restrictive policies throughout the world, then the remedy lies in expanding opportunities for export by removal of restrictive pressure. There is great force in the contention that, if active employment and ample purchasing power can be sustained in the main centres of world trade, the problem of surpluses and unwanted exports will largely disappear, even though under the most prosperous conditions there may remain some disturbances of trade and unforeseen situations requiring special remedies.

13. There is no obvious means of offering a right measure of inducement to the general expansion of international trade except by a broadly based international organisation.

❖ ❖ ❖

14. The arrangement by which the members of the Clearing Union start with substantial overdraft facilities in hand will be mainly useful, just as the possession of

any kind of reserve is useful, to allow time and method for necessary adjustments and a comfortable safeguard behind which the unforeseen and the unexpected can be faced with equanimity. Obviously, it does not by itself provide any long-term solution against a continuing disequilibrium, for in due course the more improvident and the more impecunious, left to themselves, would have run through their resources. But, if the purpose of the overdraft facilities is mainly to give time for adjustments, we have to make sure, so far as possible, that they *will* be made. We must have, therefore, some rules and some machinery to provide that equilibrium is restored.

15. Perhaps the most difficult question to determine is how much to decide by rule and how much to leave to discretion. If rule prevails, the liabilities attaching to membership of the system are definite, whilst the responsibilities of central management are reduced to a minimum. On the other hand, liabilities which would require the surrender by legislation of too much of the discretion, normally inherent in a Government, will not be readily undertaken by ourselves or by the United States. If discretion prevails, how far can the ultimate decision be left to the individual members and how far to the central management? If the individual members are too free, indiscipline may result and unwarrantable liberties be taken. But if it is to the central management that the discretions are given, too heavy a weight of responsibility may rest on it, and it may be assuming the exercise of powers which it has not the strength to implement. If rule prevails, the scheme can be made more water-tight theoretically. But if discretion prevails, it may work better in practice. All this is the typical problem of any supernational authority. An earlier draft of this proposal was criticised for leaning too much to the side of rule. In the provisions below the bias is in the other direction. For it may be better not to attempt to settle too much beforehand and to provide that the plan shall be reconsidered after an initial experimental period of (say) five years. Only by collective wisdom and discussion can the right compromise be reached between law and licence.

16. The proposal put forward below differs in one important respect from the pre-war system because it aims at putting some part of the responsibility for adjustment on the creditor country as well as on the debtor. This is an attempt to recover the advantages which were enjoyed in the nineteenth century when a favourable balance in favour of London and Paris, which were the main creditor centres, immediately produced an expansionist pressure in those markets, but which have been lost since New York succeeded to the position of main creditor, the effect of this change being aggravated by the breakdown of international borrowing credit and by the flight of loose funds from one depository to another. The object is that the creditor should not be allowed to remain entirely passive. For if he is, an intolerably heavy task may be laid on the debtor country, which is already for that very reason in the weaker position.

17. The detailed provisions proposed (the particular proportions, &c., suggested being merely tentative as a basis of discussion) are the following:—

(1) The two founder States will agree between themselves the initial values of their own currencies in terms of bancor and the value of bancor in terms of gold; and the initial values of the currencies of other members will be fixed on their joining the system in agreement with them. A member-State may not subsequently alter the value of its currency in terms of bancor without the permission of the Governing Board except under the conditions dealt with below; but during the first five years after the inception of the system the Governing Board shall give special consideration to appeals

for adjustments in the exchange-value of a national currency on the ground of unforeseen circumstances.

(2) The amount of the maximum debit balance allowed to any member-State shall be determined by reference to the amount of its foreign trade, and shall be designated its *quota*. There need be no limit to the amount of a credit balance.

The initial quotas might be fixed by reference to the sum of each country's exports and imports on the average of (say) the three pre-war years, being either equal or in a determined *lesser* proportion to this amount, a special assessment being substituted in cases where this formula would be, for any reason, inappropriate. Subsequently, after the elapse of the transitional period, the quotas might be revised annually in accordance with the actual volume of trade in the three preceding years.

(3) A charge of 1 per cent. per annum will be payable to the Reserve Fund of the Clearing Union on the average balance of a member-State, whether credit or debit, in excess of a quarter of its quota; and a further charge of 1 per cent. on the average balance, whether credit or debit, in excess of half its quota. Thus only a country which keeps as nearly as possible in a state of international balance on the average of the year will escape this contribution. These particular charges are, clearly, not essential to the scheme. But if they are found acceptable, they would be valuable inducements towards keeping a level balance, and a significant indication that the System looks on excessive credit balances with as critical an eye as on excessive debit balances, each being, indeed, the inevitable concomitant of the other. Any member-State in debit may, however, borrow from the balances of any member-State in credit on such terms as may be mutually agreed, by which means each would avoid these contributions.

(4)—*(a)* A member-State may not increase its debit balance by more than a *quarter* of its quota within a year without the permission of the Governing Board. If its debit balance has exceeded a quarter of its quota on the average of at least a year, it shall be entitled to reduce the value of its currency in terms of bancor, provided that the reduction shall not exceed 5 per cent. within a year without the permission of the Governing Board.

(b) As a condition of allowing a member-State to increase its debit balance in excess of a *half* of its quota, the Governing Board may require (i) a stated reduction in the value of the member's currency, if it deems that to be the suitable remedy, (ii) the control of outward capital transactions if not already in force, and (iii) the surrender of a suitable proportion of any separate gold reserve it may hold in reduction of its debit balance.

(c) If a member-State's debit balance has exceeded *three-quarters* of its quota on the average of at least a year [or is excessive, as measured by some formula laid down by the Governing Board, in relation to the total debit balances outstanding on the books of the Clearing Union], it may be asked by the Governing Board to take measures to improve its position and, in the event of its failing to reduce its debit balance below the figure in question within two years, the Governing Board may declare that it is in default and no longer entitled to draw against its account except with the permission of the Governing Board. Each member-State, on joining the system, shall agree to pay to the Clearing Union any payments due from it to a country in default towards the discharge of the latter's debit balance and to accept this arrangement in the event of falling into default itself. A member-State which resigns from the Clearing Union without making approved arrangements for the discharge of any debit balance shall also be treated as in default.

(5) A member-State whose credit balance has exceeded a *half* of its quota on the average of at least a year shall discuss with the Governing Board (but shall retain the ultimate decision in its own hands) what measures would be appropriate to restore the equilibrium of its international balances, including—

(*a*) measures for the expansion of domestic credit and domestic demand;

(*b*) the appreciation of its local currency in terms of bancor, or, alternatively, an increase in money-wages;

(*c*) the reduction of excessive tariffs and other discouragements against imports;

(*d*) international loans for the development of backward countries.

❖ ❖ ❖

18. The special protective expedients which were developed between the two wars were sometimes due to political, social or industrial reasons. But frequently they were nothing more than forced and undesired dodges to protect an unbalanced position of a country's overseas payments. The new system, by providing an automatic register of the size and whereabouts of the aggregate debtor and creditor positions respectively, will give a clear indication whether it is reasonable for a particular country to adopt special expedients as a temporary measure to assist in regaining equilibrium in its balance of payments, in spite of a general rule *not* to adopt them.

19. It is not proposed to incorporate any specific arrangements for such relaxations in the constitution of the Clearing Union itself. But the existence of the Clearing Union would make it possible for member States contracting Commercial Treaties to use their respective debit and credit positions with the Clearing Union as a test. Thus, the contracting parties, whilst agreeing to clauses in a Commercial Treaty forbidding, in general, the use of certain measures or expedients in their mutual trade relations, might make this agreement subject to special relaxations if the state of their respective clearing accounts satisfied an agreed criterion. For example, a Treaty might provide that, in the event of one of the contracting States having a debit balance with the Clearing Union exceeding a specified proportion of its quota on the average of a period and the other having a credit balance of a specified amount, the former should be free to resort to import quotas or to barter trade agreements or to higher import duties of a type which was not permitted under the Treaty in normal circumstances. It might even provide that such exceptions should only be allowed subject to the approval of the governing Board of the Clearing Union, and in that case the possible grounds for exceptional action might cover a wider field and other contingencies.

20. Apart from such temporary indulgence, the members of the Clearing Union should feel sufficiently free from anxiety to contemplate the ultimate removal of the more dislocating forms of protection and discrimination and expect the prohibition of some of the worst of them from the outset. In any case, members of the Currency Union would not allow or suffer among themselves any restrictions on the disposal of receipts arising out of current trade or "invisible" income. It might also be possible to obtain recognition of the general principle that commercial treaties between members of the Union should, subject to any necessary safeguards and exceptions, exclude—

(i) import restrictions, whether quantitative or in the form of "duty-quotas" (excluding, however, prohibitions genuinely designed to safeguard, *e.g.*, public health or morale or revenue collection);

(ii) barter arrangements;

(iii) export quotas and discriminatory export taxes;

(iv) export subsidies either furnished directly by the State or indirectly under schemes supported or encouraged by the State; and

(v) excessive tariffs.

21. Subsidies in favour of domestic producers for domestic consumption, with a countervailing levy when such subsidised goods are exported, would not be excluded. This is a necessary safety-valve which provides for protective expedients called for on political, social and industrial grounds. Such subsidies and tariffs would be a permitted way of giving purely domestic protection to an industry which for special reasons ought to be maintained for domestic purposes only. The question of preferences and of other relaxations from most-favoured-nation treatment, which would be of a normal and continuing character, does not fall within the scope of this paper, and must be settled on principles outside the sphere of the Clearing Union.

22. The above provisions might enable us to give some satisfaction to Mr. Cordell Hull over a wide field, since we should be accepting a non-discriminatory international system as the normal and desirable régime.

❖ ❖ ❖

23. It is a great advantage of the proposed Currency Union that it restores unfettered multilateral clearing between its members; so that no action is necessary, except where a country is out of balance with the system as a whole.

24. Compare this with the difficulties and complications of a large number of bilateral agreements. Compare, above all, the provisions by which a country, taking improper advantage of a payments agreement (for the system is, in fact, a *generalised* payments agreement) as Germany did before the war, is dealt with not by a single country (which may not be strong enough to act effectively in isolation or cannot afford to incur the diplomatic odium of isolated action) but by the system as a whole. If the argument is used that the Currency Union may have difficulty in disciplining a misbehaving country and in avoiding consequential loss, with what much greater force can we urge this objection against a multiplicity of separate bilateral payments agreements.

25. Thus we should not only return to the advantages of an international gold currency, but we might enjoy them more widely than was ever possible in practice with the old system under which at any given time only a minority of countries were actually working with free exchanges.

26. The advantages of multilateral clearing are of particular importance to London. It is not too much to say that this is an essential condition of the continued maintenance of London as the banking centre of the Sterling Area. Under a system of bilateral agreements it would seem inevitable that the sterling area, in the form in which it has been historically developed and as it has been understood and accepted by the Dominions and India, must fall to pieces.

27. In conditions of multilateral clearing everything would go on exactly as before without our having to ask anyone to accept special or onerous conditions. We should, in this respect, be back again in the best days of the gold standard. The traditional advantages of banking in London would be retained, precisely because London has

been built up on the basis of an international currency having universal validity. But if we try to make of the sterling area a compact currency union as against the rest of the world, we shall be putting a greater strain on arrangements, which have been essentially (even in time of war) *informal,* than they can be expected to bear.

28. It is possible to combine countries, some of which will be in a debtor and some in a creditor position, into a Currency Union which, substantially, covers the world. But, surely, it is impossible, unless they have a common banking and economic system also, to combine them into a Currency Union not with, but against, the world as a whole. If other members of the sterling area have a favourable balance against the world as a whole, they will lose nothing by keeping them in sterling, which will be interchangeable with bancor and hence with any other currency, until they have occasion to use them. But if the sterling area is turned into a Currency Union, the members in credit would have to make a forced and *non-liquid* loan of their favourable balances to the members in debit. Incidentally, they might find themselves involved in making between them an involuntary loan to London at the rate, perhaps, of £100,000,000 a year cumulative. They would have to impose import regulations and restraints on capital movements according as the area as a whole was in debit or credit, irrespective of their own positions. They would have to be bound by numerous bilateral agreements negotiated primarily (at least so they would believe) in the interests of London. The sterling resources of creditor Dominions might come to be represented by nothing but blocked balances in a number of doubtfully solvent countries with whom it suited *us* to trade. Moreover, it is difficult to see how the system could work without a pooling of gold reserves.

29. It is improbable that South Africa or India would accept such arrangements even if other Dominions were more complying. We should soon find ourselves, therefore, linked up only with those constituents which were running at a debit, apart from the Crown Colonies, which, perhaps, we could insist on keeping.

30. Is it not a delusion to suppose that the *de facto,* but somewhat flimsy and unsatisfactory, arrangements, which are carrying us through the war, on the basis that we do our best to find the other members of the area a limited amount of dollars provided that they lend us a very much larger sum in sterling, can be carried over into the peace and formalised into a working system based on a series of bilateral agreements with the rest of the world, accompanied by a strict control of capital movements outside the Area?

31. The sterling area, if we mean by this the system under which the members of the British Commonwealth do their international banking through London, grew up under conditions of freedom. It lives and breathes by being a voluntary system. It is only in that same atmosphere of the City of London as Liberty Hall dealing in a currency of general acceptability that we can expect to preserve it. The notion that a multilateral plan, based on an international standard, jeopardises the position of the Sterling Area must be based on a rigid and (one would think) politically impracticable version of the Sterling Area concept and not on its historical and actual significance. A multilateral plan would, therefore, be of great assistance in maintaining the position of London in relation both to the British Commonwealth and to many other countries which like our way of doing business and would give up most reluctantly the facilities we have given them.

* * *

32. It may be convenient at this point to note in more detail the position contemplated for centres of international banking such as London, New York or Paris, and for currency groups within the membership of the Clearing Union covering more than one country, such as the existing sterling area or groups, like the Latin Union of former days, which may come into existence covering, for example, the countries of North America or those of South America or the groups now under active discussion covering Poland and Czechoslovakia or certain of the Balkan States.

33. The governing principles should be: first, that the Clearing Union is set up, not for the transaction of daily business between individual traders or banks, but for the clearing and settlement of the ultimate outstanding balances between Central Banks (and certain other super-national Institutions), such as would have been settled under the old gold standard by the shipment or the earmarking of gold, and should not trespass unnecessarily beyond this field; and, secondly, that its purpose is to increase *freedom* in international commerce and not to multiply interferences or compulsions.

34. Thus the fabric of international banking organisation, built up by long experience to satisfy practical needs, should be left as undisturbed as possible. Except as regards a provision, explained below, concerning the balances of Central Banks themselves, there should be no obstacle in the way of the existing practices of international banking except those which necessarily arise through measures which individual Central Banks may choose to adopt for the control of movements of capital.

35. Nor should it be necessary to interfere with the discretion of Central Banks which desire to maintain a special intimacy within a particular group of countries associated by geographical or political ties. There is no reason why such Central Banks should not be allowed a double position, both as members of the Clearing Union in their own right with their proper quota, and also as making use of another financial centre along traditional lines, as for example, Australia and India with London or certain American countries with New York. In this case their accounts with the Clearing Union would be in exactly the same position as the independent gold reserves which they now maintain, and they would have no occasion to modify in any way their present practices in the conduct of daily business.

36. There would be other cases, however, in which a dependency or a member of a federal union would merge its currency identity in that of a mother Central Bank, with a quota appropriate to the merged currency unit as a whole, and *not* enjoy a separate individual membership of the Clearing Union, as, for example, the French colonies, the Federated States of the American Union or of Australia, and possibly the British Crown Colonies.

37. At the same time there should be a general encouragement to Central Banks, which do not belong to a special geographical or political group, to keep their reserve balances with the Clearing Union and not with one another, except in the case of a specific loan from a member-State in credit with the Clearing Union to a member-State in debit. It should, therefore, be laid down that overseas balances may not be held in another country except with the approval of the Central Bank of that country; and, in order that sterling and dollars might not appear to compete with bancor for the purpose of Central Bank reserve balances, the Founder States might agree together that they would not accept the reserve balances of other Central Banks in excess of normal working balances except in the case of Banks definitely belonging to a Sterling Area or Dollar Area group.

✣ ✣ ✣

38. The position of gold would be left substantially unchanged. What, in the long run, the world may decide to do with gold is another matter. The establishment of an International Clearing Union does not require any significant or immediate change. Indeed, by providing an automatic means by which some part of the favourable balances of the creditor countries can be settled, the current gold production of the world and the remnant of gold reserves held outside the United States may yet have a useful part to play. Moreover, gold still possesses great psychological value which will not have been diminished by recent events; for the desire to possess a gold reserve against unforeseen contingencies is likely to remain. Gold also has the merit of providing, in point of form whatever the underlying realities may be, an uncontroversial standard of value for international purposes, for which it would not yet be easy to find a serviceable substitute.

39. It is conceived, therefore, that the international bank-money which we have designated *bancor* would be defined in terms of a weight of gold. Since the national currencies of the member-States would also be given a defined exchange value in terms of bancor, it follows that they would have a defined gold content which would also be their official buying price for gold above which they must not pay. Any Central Bank would be entitled to obtain a credit in terms of bancor by paying actual gold to the credit of its Clearing Account, thus securing a steady and ascertained purchaser for the output of the gold-producing countries and for countries holding a large reserve of gold.

40. Central Banks would be entitled to retain their separate gold reserves and ship gold to one another against a clearance between them in the books of the Clearing Union, provided they did not pay a price above parity; they could coin gold and put it into circulation, and, generally speaking, do what they liked with it.

41. One restriction only would be, for obvious reasons, essential. No Central Bank would be entitled to demand gold from the Clearing Union against its balance of bancor; for bancor would be available only for transfer to the Clearing Account of another Central Bank. Thus between gold and bancor itself there would be a one-way convertibility only, such as ruled frequently before the war with national currencies which were on what was usually called a "gold-exchange standard." This need not mean that the Clearing Union would only receive gold and never pay it out. If the Clearing Union found itself in possession of a stock of gold, the Governors of the Bank should have the discretion to distribute the surplus between all Central Banks possessing a credit balance with it, proportionately to such balances, in reduction of their amount.

42. The question has been raised whether these arrangements are compatible with the retention by individual member-States of a full gold standard with two-way convertibility, so that, for example, any foreign bank acquiring dollars through the Clearing Union could use them to obtain gold for export. It is not evident that a good purpose would be served by this. But if any member-State should prefer to maintain full convertibility for internal purposes, it could protect itself from any abuse of the system or inconvenient consequences by providing that gold could only be exported under licence.

43. The value of bancor in terms of gold should be fixed but not unalterably. The two founder States, the United States and the United Kingdom, acting in agreement, should have the power to change it. Clearly, they should exercise this power if the stocks of gold tendered to the bank were to be super-abundant for their legitimate

purposes. No object would be served by attempting further to peer into the future or to prophesy the ultimate policy of the founder States in this regard.

44. Changes in the value of the national currencies of member-States stand in a different category. For the real significance of such changes is to be found not in relation to gold itself but in relation to the values of national currencies amongst themselves. The general principles by which such changes should be governed have been discussed in a previous section. It would be undesirable, if it can be avoided, to lay down more precise rules in advance, since it is difficult to distinguish by means of a rigid formula the cases, in which a change in the rate of exchange will assist the restoration of equilibrium and is the right remedy, from those cases where some other type of measure is more appropriate.

❖ ❖ ❖

45. It is widely held that control of capital movements, both inward and outward, should be a permanent feature of the post-war system—at least so far as we are concerned. If control is to be effective, it probably involves the *machinery* of exchange control for *all* transactions, even though a general open licence is given to all remittances in respect of current trade. But such control will be more difficult to work, especially in the absence of a postal censorship, by unilateral action than if movements of capital can be controlled *at both ends.* It would therefore be of great advantage if the United States and all other members of the Currency Union would adopt machinery similar to that which we have now gone a long way towards perfecting in this country; though this cannot be regarded as *essential* to the proposed Union.

46. This does not mean that the era of international investment should be brought to an end. On the contrary, the system contemplated should greatly facilitate the restoration of international credit for loan purposes in ways to be discussed below. The object, and it is a vital object, is to have a means of distinguishing—

(*a*) Between movements of floating funds and genuine new investment for developing the world's resources; and

(*b*) Between movements, which will help to maintain equilibrium, from surplus countries to deficiency countries and speculative movements or flights out of deficiency countries or from one surplus country to another.

47. There is no country which can, in future, safely allow the flight of funds for political reasons or to evade domestic taxation or in anticipation of the owner turning refugee. Equally, there is no country that can safely receive fugitive funds which cannot safely be used for fixed investment and might turn it into a surplus country against its will and contrary to the real facts.

48. The general principles of the control of capital movements need not be discussed here. It is evident that the existence of an International Clearing Union would make such control easier.

❖ ❖ ❖

49. It has been suggested that so ambitious a proposal is open to criticism on the ground that it requires from the members of the Currency Union a greater surrender of their sovereign rights than they will readily concede.

50. But, in the present version of the plan, no greater surrender is required than in any commercial treaty—certainly not greater than in the binding undertakings

against discrimination which the United States is inviting us to make. The obligations will be entered into voluntarily and can be terminated on certain conditions by giving notice.

51. In the second place a greater readiness to accept super-national arrangements must be required in the post-war world than hitherto. The arrangements proposed could be described as a measure of Financial Disarmament. They are very mild in comparison with the measures of Military Disarmament, which it is to be hoped the world may be asked to accept.

52. Surely it is an advantage, rather than a disadvantage, of the scheme that it invites the member States and groups to abandon that licence to promote indiscipline, disorder and bad-neighbourliness which, to the general disadvantage, they have been free to exercise hitherto.

53. There is nothing here which we need be reluctant to accept ourselves or to ask of others. Or if there be anything such, let it be amended.

❖ ❖ ❖

54. An International Currency Union might become the instrument and the support of international policies apart from those which it is its primary purpose to promote. The following suggestions are not a necessary part of the plan. But they are illustrations of the additional purposes of high importance and value which the Union, once established, might be able to serve:—

(1) The Union might set up a clearing account in favour of the international body charged with post-war Relief and Reconstruction. If necessary, it might supplement contributions received from other sources by granting overdraft facilities in favour of this body, this overdraft being discharged over a period of years out of the Reserve Fund of the Union, or, if necessary, out of a levy on credit clearing balances. By this means it is possible to avoid asking any country to assume a burdensome commitment for relief and reconstruction, since the resources would be provided in the first instance by those countries having credit Clearing Accounts for which they have no immediate use and are voluntarily leaving idle, and in the long run by those countries which have a chronic international surplus for which they have no beneficial employment.

(2) If the United States were to wish to effect a redistribution of gold reserves, the Clearing Union would provide a suitable channel for the purpose, the gold so re-distributed being credited (*e.g.*) to the account of the Relief and Reconstruction Authority.

(3) The Union might set up an account in favour of the Super-national policing body charged with the duty of preserving the peace and maintaining international order. If any country were to infringe its properly authorised orders, the policing body might be entitled to request the Governors of the Clearing Union to hold the Clearing Account of the Central Bank of the delinquent country to its order and permit no further transactions on the account except by its authority. This would provide an excellent machinery for enforcing a financial blockade.

(4) The Union might set up an account in favour of international bodies charged with the management of a Commodity Control, and might finance stocks of commodities held by such bodies, allowing them overdraft facilities on their accounts up to an

agreed maximum. By this means the financial problem of holding pools and "ever-normal granaries" would be satisfactorily solved.

(5) The Union might be closely linked up with the Board for International Investment. It might act on behalf of this Board and collect for them the annual service of their loans by automatically debiting the Clearing Account of the country concerned. The statistics of the Clearing Accounts of the Member States would give a reliable indication as to which countries were in a position to finance the Investment Board, with the advantage of shifting the whole system of clearing credits and debits nearer to equilibrium. This important question is the subject of a separate paper.

(6) There are various methods by which the Clearing Union could use its influence and its powers to maintain stability of prices and to control the Trade Cycle. If an International Economic Board is established, this Board and the Clearing Union might be expected to work in close collaboration to their mutual great advantage. If an International Investment or Development Corporation is also set up together with a scheme of Commodity Boards for the control of stocks of the staple raw materials, we might come to possess in these four Institutions a powerful means of combating the evils of the Trade Cycle, by exercising contractionist or expansionist influence on the system as a whole or on particular sections. This, again, is a large and important question which cannot be discussed adequately in this paper; and need not be examined at length in this place because it does not raise any important issues affecting the fundamental constitution of the proposed Union. It is mentioned here to complete the picture of the large purposes which the foundation of the Currency Union might be made to serve.

❖ ❖ ❖

55. Our post-war currency and exchange system should be one which is capable of wide, indeed of universal, extension as further countries become ready for it. Nevertheless it would be an advantage if the proposed Union could be brought into existence by the United States and the United Kingdom as joint founder-States, covering the United States and its possessions and the members of the British Commonwealth. The position of Russia, which might be a third founder, if she can be a party to so capitalist-looking an institution, would need special consideration. Other members would then be brought in—some from the outset, some as soon as they had established an internal organisation capable of sustaining the obligations of membership. This approach would have the great advantage that the United States and the United Kingdom (the former in consultation with the Pan-American countries and the latter with the other members of the British Commonwealth) could settle the charter and the main details of the new body without being subjected to the delays and confused counsels of an international conference. It would also mean that considerable progress could be made irrespective of the nature of the European political settlement and before the conditions of adherence of the European members could be finally determined. Moreover, membership would be thus established as a privilege only open to those who conformed to certain general principles and standards of international economic conduct. The management and the effective voting power might inhere permanently in the founder-States.

56. In view of our experience and of our geographical and political position in relation to Europe, the United States and the British Commonwealth, we could justifiably ask that the head office should be situated in London with the Board of Managers meeting alternately here and in Washington.

57. Members of the Board would be appointed by the Governments of the member-States, each of which would have a vote in proportion to its quota. But there might be a provision, at any rate for the first five years, by which the British and American members when acting in agreement could outvote the rest of the Board.

58. There is no reason why the Central Banks of non-member States should not keep Credit Clearing Accounts with the Union; and indeed it would be advisable for them to do so for the conduct of their trade with member-States. But they would have no say in the management.

59. Members should be entitled to withdraw from the Union on a year's notice, subject to their making satisfactory arrangements to discharge any debit balance. They would not, of course, be able to employ any credit balance except by making transfers from it, either before or after their withdrawal, to the Clearing Accounts of other Central Banks. Similarly it should be within the power of the Governing Board to require the withdrawal of a member subject to the same notice.

60. The principles and governing rules of the Union should be the subject of general reconsideration after five years' experience, if a majority of the Governing Board desire it.

61. It would be of great advantage if the general principles of the International Clearing Union could be agreed beforehand, with a view to bringing it into operation at an early date after the termination of hostilities. Such a proposal presents, however, something of a dilemma. On the one hand, many countries, ourselves not least, will be in particular need of reserves of overseas resources in the period immediately after the war. On the other hand, goods will be in short supply and the prevention of inflationary international conditions of the first importance. The expansionist tendency of the proposed system, which is a leading recommendation of it as soon as peace-time output is restored and the productive capacity of the world is in running order, might easily be a danger in the early days of a sellers' market and a superabundance of demand over supply.

62. A reconciliation in detail of these divergent purposes is not easily found until we know more than is known at present about the means to be adopted to finance post-war relief and reconstruction and particularly as to the intentions of the United States regarding a temporary continuance of Lease-Lend arrangements for food and raw materials after the termination of hostilities. If these intentions are on liberal and comprehensive lines, it might be better for relief and Lend-Lease arrangements to take the place of the proposed quotas during the "relief" period of (say) two years. The immediate establishment of the Clearing Union would be compatible with provisional arrangements regarding the overdraft quotas which could take alternative forms according to the character of the other "relief" arrangements.

63. If the finance of relief is actually furnished through the Clearing Union, which has been suggested above as one possibility, and if that, combined with some continuance of lend-leasing by the United States, appears likely to provide the world with as much purchasing power as is desirable in the early days, the coming into force of the overdraft quotas might be postponed until the Founder Members are agreed that the need for them is impending. In this case credit clearing balances would be limited to the amount of gold delivered to the Union, and the overdraft facilities created by the Union in favour of the Relief Council, the International Investment Board or the Commodity Controls. Alternatively overdraft quotas might be allowed on a reduced

scale during the transitional period. At any rate, it might be proper to provide that countries in receipt of relief or Lend-Lease assistance should not have access at the same time to overdraft facilities, and that the latter should only become available when the former had come to an end.

64. If, on the other hand, relief and Lend-Lease facilities look like being inadequate from the outset, the overdraft quotas may be even more necessary at the outset than later on.

65. We must not be over-cautious. A rapid economic restoration may lighten the tasks of the diplomatists and the politicians in the resettlement of the world and the restoration of social order. In our case the possibility of exports sufficiently expanded to sustain our standard of life and our solvency is bound up with good and expanding markets. We cannot afford to wait too long for this and we must not allow excessive caution to condemn us to perdition. Unless the Union is a going concern, the problem of proper "timing" will be almost insoluble. It is sufficient at this stage to point out that the problem of timing must not be overlooked, but that the Union is capable of being used so as to aid rather than impede its solution.

❖ ❖ ❖

66. In most of its objectives and in many of its methods this paper is in fundamental accord with alternative proposals which have been or could be put forward. The special merits claimed for this particular version include the following:—

For ourselves.

(1) Our British problem of gaining enough receipts overseas to balance our import requirements is so acute that we can scarcely hope to solve it except through a scheme which—

(*a*) by a strong expansionist stimulus throughout the world provides willing markets for a largely expanded volume of our exports;

(*b*) offers facilities for the multilateral clearing of international payments, since we cannot afford to have any of the credit balances, which we may acquire overseas, to be blocked and unavailable as a set-off against our debit balances elsewhere;

(*c*) provides us with a margin, during the period before we can re-establish equilibrium, by an international scheme which does not require us to ask particular favours or accommodations from the United States but merely gives to us, and requires of us, the same facilities for the expansion of international trade and the maintenance of international equilibrium which all the countries will be asked to receive and to allow;

(*d*) affords us the possibility of subsequent rectifications of the rate of exchange against the rest of the world without the risk of competitive depreciations or of complaints by other countries in the event of the initial value of sterling proving to be higher than the level at which we can balance our overseas trade.

(2) A multilateral system preserves, to the full extent compatible with the control of capital movements, the traditional freedom of London as a financial centre. Above all it allows the historical continuity of the sterling area in the same form and with the same absence of restraint as heretofore. For it is evident that any system of

numerous bilateral agreements would put in great jeopardy not only the sterling area but the whole position of London as an international centre.

For the United States and the World at large.

(1) It provides a general framework by the aid of which *all* countries can hope to rehabilitate their currencies.

(2) It offers a criterion by the help of which we can satisfy American aspirations, which we ourselves share with Mr. Hull and Mr. Sumner Welles, for the greater freedom of international trade supported by firm undertakings.

(3) It is a plan which can be used to further such general world purposes as—

(*a*) post-war relief and reconstruction;

(*b*) international T.V.A.;

(*c*) the finance of commodity agreements;

(*d*) the preservation of peace;

(*e*) the control of the Trade Cycle and the stabilisation of prices; and, generally,

(*f*) the maintenance of active employment everywhere.

(4) It is capable of arousing enthusiasm because it makes a beginning at the future economic ordering of the world between nations and "the winning of the peace," and might help to create the conditions and the atmosphere in which much else would be made easier.

(B) Proposals for an International Clearing Union [1]

(April 1943)

PREFACE

Immediately after the war all countries who have been engaged will be concerned with the pressure of relief and urgent reconstruction. The transition out of this into the normal world of the future cannot be wisely effected unless we know into what we are moving. It is therefore not too soon to consider what is to come after. In the field of national activity occupied by production, trade and finance, both the nature of the problem and the experience of the period between the wars suggest four main lines of approach:

1. The mechanism of currency and exchange;

2. The framework of a commercial policy regulating the conditions for the exchange of goods, tariffs, preferences, subsidies, import regulations and the like;

3. The orderly conduct of production, distribution and price of primary products so as to protect both producers and consumers from the loss and risk for which the extravagant fluctuations of market conditions have been responsible in recent times;

4. Investment aid, both medium and long term, for the countries whose economic development needs assistance from outside.

If the principles of these measures and the form of the institutions to give effect to them can be settled in advance, in order that they may be in operation when the need arises, it is possible that taken together they may help the world to control the ebb and flow of the tides of economic activity which have, in the past, destroyed security of livelihood and endangered international peace.

All these matters will need to be handled in due course. The proposal that follows relates only to the mechanism of currency and exchange in international trading. It appears on the whole convenient to give it priority, because some general conclusions have to be reached under this head before much progress can be made with the other topics.

In preparing these proposals care has been taken to regard certain conditions, which the groundwork of an international economic system to be set up after the war should satisfy, if it is to prove durable:

(i) There should be the least possible interference with internal national policies, and the plan should not wander from the international *terrain*. Since such policies may have important repercussions on international relations, they cannot be left out of account. Nevertheless in the realm of internal policy the authority of the Governing Board of the proposed Institution should be limited to recommendations, or at the most to imposing conditions for the more extended enjoyment of the facilities which the Institution offers.

(ii) The technique of the plan must be capable of application, irrespective of the type and principle of government and economic policy existing in the prospective member States.

[1] Reproduced by permission of the Controller, Her Britannic Majesty's Stationery Office.

(iii) The management of the Institution must be genuinely international without preponderant power of veto or enforcement to any country or group; and the rights and privileges of the smaller countries must be safeguarded.

(iv) Some qualification of the right to act at pleasure is required by any agreement or treaty between nations. But in order that such arrangements may be fully voluntary so long as they last and terminable when they have become irksome, provision must be made for voiding the obligation at due notice. If many member States were to take advantage of this, the plan would have broken down. But if they are free to escape from its provisions if necessary they may be the more willing to go on accepting them.

(v) The plan must operate not only to the general advantage but also to the individual advantage of each of the participants, and must not require a special economic or financial sacrifice from certain countries. No participant must be asked to do or offer anything which is not to his own true long-term interest.

It must be emphasised that it is not for the Clearing Union to assume the burden of long term lending which is the proper task of some other institution. It is also necessary for it to have means of restraining improvident borrowers. But the Clearing Union must also seek to discourage creditor countries from leaving unused large liquid balances which ought to be devoted to some positive purpose. For excessive credit balances necessarily create excessive debit balances for some other party. In recognising that the creditor as well as the debtor may be responsible for a want of balance, the proposed institution would be breaking new ground.

I.—THE OBJECTS OF THE PLAN

About the primary objects of an improved system of International Currency there is, to-day, a wide measure of agreement:—

(*a*) We need an instrument of international currency having general acceptability between nations, so that blocked balances and bilateral clearings are unnecessary; that is to say, an instrument of currency used by each nation in its transactions with other nations, operating through whatever national organ, such as a Treasury or a Central Bank, is most appropriate, private individuals, businesses and banks other than Central Banks, each continuing to use their own national currency as heretofore.

(*b*) We need an orderly and agreed method of determining the relative exchange values of national currency units, so that unilateral action and competitive exchange depreciations are prevented.

(*c*) We need a *quantum* of international currency, which is neither determined in an unpredictable and irrelevant manner as, for example, by the technical progress of the gold industry, nor subject to large variations depending on the gold reserve policies of individual countries; but is governed by the actual current requirements of world commerce, and is also capable of deliberate expansion and contraction to offset deflationary and inflationary tendencies in effective world demand.

(*d*) We need a system possessed of an internal stabilising mechanism, by which pressure is exercised on any country whose balance of payments with the rest of the world is departing from equilibrium *in either direction*, so as to prevent movements which must create for its neighbours an equal but opposite want of balance.

(*e*) We need an agreed plan for starting off every country after the war with a stock of reserves appropriate to its importance in world commerce, so that without due anxiety it can set its house in order during the transitional period to full peace-time conditions.

(*f*) We need a central institution, of a purely technical and non-political character, to aid and support other international institutions concerned with the planning and regulation of the world's economic life.

(*g*) More generally, we need a means of reassurance to a troubled world, by which any country whose own affairs are conducted with due prudence is relieved of anxiety for causes which are not of its own making, concerning its ability to meet its international liabilities; and which will, therefore, make unnecessary those methods of restriction and discrimination which countries have adopted hitherto, not on their merits, but as measures of self-protection from disruptive outside forces.

2. There is also a growing measure of agreement about the general character of any solution of the problem likely to be successful. The particular proposals set forth below lay no claim to originality. They are an attempt to reduce to practical shape certain general ideas belonging to the contemporary climate of economic opinion, which have been given publicity in recent months by writers of several different nationalities. It is difficult to see how any plan can be successful which does not use these general ideas, which are born of the spirit of the age. The actual details put forward below are offered, with no dogmatic intention, as the basis of discussion for criticism and improvement. For we cannot make progress without embodying the general underlying idea in a frame of actual working, which will bring out the practical and political difficulties to be faced and met if the breath of life is to inform it.

3. In one respect this particular plan will be found to be more ambitious and yet, at the same time, perhaps more workable than some of the variant versions of the same basic idea, in that it is fully international, being based on one general agreement and not on a multiplicity of bilateral arrangements. Doubtless proposals might be made by which bilateral arrangements could be fitted together so as to obtain some of the advantages of a multilateral scheme. But there will be many difficulties attendant on such adjustments. It may be doubted whether a comprehensive scheme will ever in fact be worked out, unless it can come into existence through a single act of creation made possible by the unity of purpose and energy of hope for better things to come, springing from the victory of the United Nations, when they have attained it, over immediate evil. That these proposals are ambitious is claimed, therefore to be not a drawback but an advantage.

4. The proposal is to establish a Currency Union, here designated an *International Clearing Union*, based on international bank-money, called (let us say) *bancor*, fixed (but not unalterably) in terms of gold and accepted as the equivalent of gold by the British Commonwealth and the United States and all the other members of the Union for the purpose of settling international balances. The Central Banks of all member States (and also of non-members) would keep accounts with the International Clearing Union through which they would be entitled to settle their exchange balances with one another at their par value as defined in terms of bancor. Countries having a favourable balance of payments with the rest of the world as a whole would find themselves in possession of a credit account with the Clearing Union, and those having an unfavourable balance would have a debit account. Measures would be necessary (see below) to prevent the piling up of credit and debit balances without limit, and the system would have failed in the long run if it did not possess sufficient capacity for self-equilibrium to secure this.

5. The idea underlying such a Union is simple, namely, to generalise the essential principle of banking as it is exhibited within any closed system. This principle is the necessary equality of credits and debits. If no credits can be removed outside the clearing system, but only transferred within it, the Union can never be in any difficulty as regards the honouring of cheques drawn upon it. It can make what advances it wishes to any of its members with the assurance that the proceeds can only be transferred to the clearing account of another member. Its sole task is to see to it that its members keep the rules and that the advances made to each of them are prudent and advisable for the Union as a whole.

II.—THE PROVISIONS OF THE PLAN

6. The provisions proposed (the particular proportions and other details suggested being tentative as a basis of discussion) are the following:—

(1) All the United Nations will be invited to become original members of the International Clearing Union. Other States may be invited to join subsequently. If ex-enemy States are invited to join, special conditions may be applied to them.

(2) The Governing Board of the Clearing Union shall be appointed by the Governments of the several member States (as provided in (12) below); the daily business with the Union and the technical arrangements being carried out through their Central Banks or other appropriate authorities.

(3) The member States will agree between themselves the initial values of their own currencies in terms of bancor. A member State may not subsequently alter the value of its currency in terms of bancor without the permission of the Governing Board except under the conditions stated below; but during the first five years after the inception of the system the Governing Board shall give special consideration to appeals for an adjustment in the exchange value of a national currency unit on the ground of unforeseen circumstances.

(4) The value of bancor in terms of gold shall be fixed by the Governing Board. Member States shall not purchase or acquire gold, directly or indirectly, at a price in terms of their national currencies in excess of the parity which corresponds to the value of their currency in terms of bancor and to the value of bancor in terms of gold. Their sales and purchases of gold shall not be otherwise restricted.

(5) Each member State shall have assigned to it a *quota*, which shall determine the measure of its responsibility in the management of the Union and of its right to enjoy the credit facilities provided by the Union. The initial quotas might be fixed by reference to the sum of each country's exports and imports on the average of (say) the three pre-war years, and might be (say) 75 per cent. of this amount, a special assessment being substituted in cases (of which there might be several) where this formula would be, for any reason, inappropriate. Subsequently, after the elapse of the transitional period, the quotas should be revised annually in accordance with the running average of each country's actual volume of trade in the three preceding years, rising to a five-year average when figures for five post-war years are available. The determination of a country's quota primarily by reference to the value of its foreign trade seems to offer the criterion most relevant to a plan which is chiefly concerned with the regulation of the foreign exchanges and of a country's international trade balance. It is, however, a matter for discussion whether the formula for fixing quotas should also take account of other factors.

(6) Member States shall agree to accept payment of currency balances, due to them from other members, by a transfer of bancor to their credit in the books of the Clearing Union. They shall be entitled, subject to the conditions set forth below, to make transfers of bancor to other members which have the effect of overdrawing their own accounts with the Union, provided that the maximum debit balances thus created do not exceed their quota. The Clearing Union may, at its discretion, charge a small commission or transfer fee in respect of transactions in its books for the purpose of meeting its current expenses or any other outgoings approved by the Governing Board.

(7) A member State shall pay to the Reserve Fund of the Clearing Union a charge of 1 per cent. per annum on the amount of its average balance in bancor, whether it is a credit or a debit balance, in excess of a quarter of its quota; and a further charge of 1 per cent. on its average balance, whether credit or debit, in excess of a half of its quota. Thus, only a country which keeps as nearly as possible in a state of international balance on the average of the year will escape this contribution. These charges are not absolutely essential to the scheme. But if they are found acceptable, they would be valuable and important inducements towards keeping a level balance, and a significant indication that the system looks on excessive credit balances with as critical an eye as on excessive debit balances, each being, indeed, the inevitable concomitant of the other. Any member State in debit may, after consultation with the Governing Board, borrow bancor from the balances of any member State in credit on such terms as may be mutually agreed, by which means each would avoid these contributions. The Governing Board may, at its discretion, remit the charges on credit balances, and increase correspondingly those on debit balances, if in its opinion unduly expansionist conditions are impending in the world economy.

(8)—(*a*) A member State may not increase its debit balance by more than a *quarter* of its quota within a year without the permission of the Governing Board. If its debit balance has exceeded a quarter of its quota on the average of at least two years, it shall be entitled to reduce the value of its currency in terms of bancor provided that the reduction shall not exceed 5 per cent. without the consent of the Governing Board; but it shall not be entitled to repeat this procedure unless the Board is satisfied that this procedure is appropriate.

(*b*) The Governing Board may require from a member State having a debit balance reaching a *half* of its quota the deposit of suitable collateral against its debit balance. Such collateral shall, at the discretion of the Governing Board, take the form of gold, foreign or domestic currency or Government bonds, within the capacity of the member State. As a condition of allowing a member State to increase its debit balance to a figure in excess of a half of its quota, the Governing Board may require all or any of the following measures:—

(i) a stated reduction in the value of the member's currency, if it deems that to be the suitable remedy;

(ii) the control of outward capital transactions if not already in force; and

(iii) the outright surrender of a suitable proportion of any separate gold or other liquid reserve in reduction of its debit balance.

Furthermore, the Governing Board may recommend to the Government of the member State any internal measures affecting its domestic economy which may appear to be appropriate to restore the equilibrium of its international balance.

(*c*) If a member State's debit balance has exceeded *three-quarters* of its quota on the average of at least a year and is excessive in the opinion of the Governing Board in relation to the total debit balances outstanding on the books of the Clearing Union, or is increasing at an excessive rate, it may, in addition, be asked by the Governing Board to take measures to improve its position, and, in the event of its failing to reduce its debit balance accordingly within two years, the Governing Board may declare that it is in default and no longer entitled to draw against its account except with the permission of the Governing Board.

(*d*) Each member State, on joining the system, shall agree to pay to the Clearing Union any payments due from it to a country in default towards the discharge of the latter's debit balance and to accept this arrangement in the event of falling into default itself. A member State which resigns from the Clearing Union without making approved arrangements for the discharge of any debit balance shall also be treated as in default.

(9) A member State whose credit balance has exceeded a *half* of its quota on the average of at least a year shall discuss with the Governing Board (but shall retain the ultimate decision in its own hands) what measures would be appropriate to restore the equilibrium of its international balances, including—

(*a*) Measures for the expansion of domestic credit and domestic demand.

(*b*) The appreciation of its local currency in terms of bancor, or, alternatively, the encouragement of an increase in money rates of earnings;

(*c*) The reduction of tariffs and other discouragements against imports.

(*d*) International development loans.

(10) A member State shall be entitled to obtain a credit balance in terms of bancor by paying in gold to the Clearing Union for the credit of its clearing account. But no one is entitled to demand gold from the Union against a balance of bancor, since such balance is available only for transfer to another clearing account. The Governing Board of the Union shall, however, have the discretion to distribute any gold in the possession of the Union between the members possessing credit balances in excess of a specified proportion of their quotas, proportionately to such balances, in reduction of their amount in excess of that proportion.

(11) The monetary reserves of a member State, viz., the Central Bank or other bank or Treasury deposits in excess of a working balance, shall not be held in another country except with the approval of the monetary authorities of that country.

(12) The Governing Board shall be appointed by the Governments of the member States, those with the larger quotas being entitled to appoint a member individually, and those with smaller quotas appointing in convenient political or geographical groups, so that the members would not exceed (say) 12 or 15 in number. Each representative on the Governing Board shall have a vote in proportion to the quotas of the State (or States) appointing him, except that on a proposal to increase a particular quota, a representative's voting power shall be measured by the quotas of the member States appointing him, increased by their credit balance or decreased by their debit balance, averaged in each case over the past two years. Each member State, which is not individually represented on the Governing Board, shall be entitled to appoint a permanent delegate to the Union to maintain contact with the Board and to act as *liaison* for daily business and for the exchange of information with the Executive of the Union. Such delegate shall be entitled to be present at the Governing Board when any matter is under consideration which specially concerns the State he represents, and to take part in the discussion.

(13) The Governing Board shall be entitled to reduce the quotas of members, all in the same specified proportion, if it seems necessary to correct in this manner an excess of world purchasing power. In that event, the provisions of 6 (8) shall be held to apply to the quotas as so reduced, provided that no member shall be required to reduce his actual overdraft at the date of the change, or be entitled by reason of this reduction to alter the value of his currency under 6 (8) (*a*), except after the expiry of two years. If the Governing Board subsequently desires to correct a potential deficiency of world purchasing power, it shall be entitled to restore the general level of quotas towards the original level.

(14) The Governing Board shall be entitled to ask and receive from each member State any relevant statistical or other information, including a full disclosure of gold, external credit and debit balances and other external assets and liabilities, both public and private. So far as circumstances permit, it will be desirable that the member States shall consult with the Governing Board on important matters of policy likely to affect substantially their bancor balances or their financial relations with other members.

(15) Executives offices of the Union shall be situated in London and New York, with the Governing Board meeting alternately in London and Washington.

(16) Members shall be entitled to withdraw from the Union on a year's notice, subject to their making satisfactory arrangements to discharge any debit balance. They would not, of course, be able to employ any credit balance except by making transfers from it, either before or after their withdrawal, to the Clearing Accounts of other Central Banks. Similarly, it should be within the power of the Governing Board to require the withdrawal of a member, subject to the same notice, if the latter is in breach of agreements relating to the Clearing Union.

(17) The Central Banks of non-member States would be allowed to keep credit clearing accounts with the Union; and, indeed, it would be advisable for them to do so for the conduct of their trade with member States. But they would have no right to overdrafts and no say in the management.

(18) The Governing Board shall make an annual Report and shall convene an annual Assembly at which every member State shall be entitled to be represented individually and to move proposals. The principles and governing rules of the Union shall be the subject of reconsideration after five years' experience, if a majority of the Assembly desire it.

III.—WHAT LIABILITIES OUGHT THE PLAN TO PLACE ON CREDITOR COUNTRIES?

7. It is not contemplated that either the debit or the credit balance of an individual country ought to exceed a certain maximum—let us say, its *quota*. In the case of debit balances this maximum has been made a rigid one, and, indeed, counter-measures are called for long before the maximum is reached. In the case of credit balances no rigid maximum has been proposed. For the appropriate provision might be to require the eventual cancellation or compulsory investment of persistent bancor credit balances accumulating in excess of a member's quota; and, however desirable this may be in principle, it might be felt to impose on creditor countries a heavier burden than they can be asked to accept before having had experience of the benefit to them of the working of the plan as a whole. If, on the other hand, the limitation were to take the form of the creditor country not being required to accept bancor in excess of a pre-

scribed figure, this might impair the general acceptability of bancor, whilst at the same time conferring no real benefit on the creditor country itself. For, if it chose to avail itself of the limitation, it must either restrict its exports or be driven back on some form of bilateral payments agreements outside the Clearing Union, thus substituting a less acceptable asset for bancor balances which are based on the collective credit of all the member States and are available for payments to any of them, or attempt the probably temporary expedient of refusing to trade except on a gold basis.

8. The absence of a rigid maximum to credit balances does not impose on any member State, as might be supposed at first sight, an unlimited liability outside its own control. The liability of an individual member is determined, not by the quotas of the other members, but by its own policy in controlling its favourable balance of payments. The existence of the Clearing Union does not deprive a member State of any of the facilities which it now possesses for receiving payment for its exports. In the absence of the Clearing Union a creditor country can employ the proceeds of its exports to buy goods or to buy investments, or to make temporary advances and to hold temporary overseas balances, or to buy gold in the market. All these facilities will remain at its disposal. The difference is that in the absence of the Clearing Union, more or less automatic factors come into play to restrict the volume of its exports after the above means of receiving payment for them have been exhausted. Certain countries become unable to buy and, in addition to this, there is an automatic tendency towards a general slump in international trade and, as a result, a reduction in the exports of the creditor country. Thus, the effect of the Clearing Union is to give the creditor country a choice between voluntarily curtailing its exports to the same extent that they would have been involuntarily curtailed in the absence of the Clearing Union, or, alternatively, of allowing its exports to continue and accumulating the excess receipts in the form of bancor balances for the time being. Unless the removal of a factor causing the involuntary reduction of exports is reckoned a disadvantage, a creditor country incurs no burden but is, on the contrary, relieved, by being offered the additional option of receiving payment for its exports through the accumulation of a bancor balance.

9. If, therefore, a member State asks what governs the maximum liability which it incurs by entering the system, the answer is that this lies entirely within its own control. No more is asked of it than that it should hold in bancor such surplus of its favourable balance of payments as it does not itself choose to employ in any other way, and only for so long as it does not so choose.

IV.—SOME ADVANTAGES OF THE PLAN

10. The plan aims at the substitution of an expansionist, in place of a contractionist, pressure on world trade.

11. It effects this by allowing to each member State overdraft facilities of a defined amount. Thus each country is allowed a certain margin of resources and a certain interval of time within which to effect a balance in its economic relations with the rest of the world. These facilities are made possible by the constitution of the system itself and do not involve particular indebtedness between one member State and another. A country is in credit or debit with the Clearing Union as a whole. This means that the overdraft facilities, whilst a relief to some, are not a real burden to others. For the accumulation of a credit balance with the Clearing Union would resemble the importation of gold in signifying that the country holding it is abstaining voluntarily from the

immediate use of purchasing power. But it would not involve, as would the importation of gold, the withdrawal of this purchasing power from circulation or the exercise of a deflationary and contractionist pressure on the whole world, including in the end the creditor country itself. Under the proposed plan, therefore, no country suffers injury (but on the contrary) by the fact that the command over resources, which it does not itself choose to employ for the time being, is not withdrawn from use. The accumulation of bancor credit does not curtail in the least its capacity or inducement either to produce or to consume.

12. In short, the analogy with a national banking system is complete. No depositor in a local bank suffers because the balances, which he leaves idle, are employed to finance the business of someone else. Just as the development of national banking systems served to offset a deflationary pressure which would have prevented otherwise the development of modern industry, so by extending the same principle into the international field we may hope to offset the contractionist pressure which might otherwise overwhelm in social disorder and disappointment the good hopes of our modern world. The substitution of a credit mechanism in place of hoarding would have repeated in the international field the same miracle, already performed in the domestic field, of turning a stone into bread.

13. There might be other ways of effecting the same objects temporarily or in part. For example, the United States might redistribute her gold. Or there might be a number of bilateral arrangements having the effect of providing international overdrafts, as, for example, an agreement by the Federal Reserve Board to accumulate, if necessary, a large sterling balance at the Bank of England, accompanied by a great number of similar bilateral arrangements, amounting to some hundreds altogether, between these and all the other banks in the world. The objection to particular arrangements of this kind, in addition to their greater complexity, is that they are likely to be influenced by extraneous, political reasons; that they put individual countries in a position of particular obligation towards others; and that the distribution of the assistance between different countries may not correspond to need and to the real requirements, which are extremely difficult to foresee.

14. It should be much easier, and surely more satisfactory for all of us, to enter into a general and collective responsibility, applying to all countries alike, that a country finding itself in a creditor position *against the rest of the world as a whole* should enter into an arrangement not to allow this credit balance to exercise a contractionist pressure against world economy and, by repercussion, against the economy of the creditor country itself. This would give everyone the great assistance of multilateral clearing, whereby (for example) Great Britain could offset favourable balances arising out of her exports to Europe against unfavourable balances due to the United States or South America or elsewhere. How, indeed, can any country hope to start up trade with Europe during the relief and reconstruction period on any other terms?

15. The facilities offered will be of particular importance in the transitional period after the war, as soon as the initial shortages of supply have been overcome. Many countries will find a difficulty in paying for their imports, and will need time and resources before they can establish a readjustment. The efforts of each of these debtor countries to preserve its own equilibrium, by forcing its exports and by cutting off all imports which are not strictly necessary, will aggravate the problems of all the others. On the other hand, if each feels free from undue pressure, the volume of international exchange will be increased and everyone will find it easier to re-establish equilibrium

without injury to the standard of life anywhere. The creditor countries will benefit, hardly less than the debtors, by being given an interval of *time* in which to adjust their economies, during which they can safely move at their own pace without the result of exercising deflationary pressure on the rest of the world, and, by repercussion, on themselves.

16. It must, however, be emphasised that the provision by which the members of the Clearing Union start with substantial overdraft facilities in hand will be mainly useful, just as the possession of any kind of reserve is useful, to allow time and method for necessary adjustments and a comfortable safeguard behind which the unforeseen and the unexpected can be faced with equanimity. Obviously, it does not by itself provide any long-term solution against a continuing disequilibrium, for in due course the more improvident and the more impecunious, left to themselves, would have run through their resources. But, if the purpose of the overdraft facilities is mainly to give time for adjustments, we have to make sure, so far as possible, that they *will* be made. We must have, therefore, some rules and some machinery to secure that equilibrium is restored. A tentative attempt to provide for this has been made above. Perhaps it might be strengthened and improved.

17. The provisions suggested differ in one important respect from the pre-war system because they aim at putting some part of the responsibility for adjustment on the creditor country as well as on the debtor. This is an attempt to recover one of the advantages which were enjoyed in the nineteenth century, when a flow of gold due to a favourable balance in favour of London and Paris, which were then the main creditor centres, immediately produced an expansionist pressure and increased foreign lending in those markets, but which has been lost since New York succeeded to the position of main creditor, as a result of gold movements failing in their effect, of the breakdown of international borrowing and of the frequent flight of loose funds from one depository to another. The object is that the creditor should not be allowed to remain entirely passive. For if he is, an intolerably heavy task may be laid on the debtor country, which is already for that very reason in the weaker position.

18. If, indeed, a country lacks the productive capacity to maintain its standard of life, then a reduction in this standard is not avoidable. If its wage and price levels in terms of money are out of line with those elsewhere, a change in the rate of its foreign exchange is inevitable. But if, possessing the productive capacity, it lacks markets because of restrictive policies throughout the world, then the remedy lies in expanding its opportunities for export by removal of the restrictive pressure. We are too ready to-day to assume the inevitability of unbalanced trade positions, thus making the opposite error to those who assumed the tendency of exports and imports to equality. It used to be supposed, without sufficient reason, that effective demand is always properly adjusted throughout the world; we now tend to assume, equally without sufficient reason, that it never can be. On the contrary, there is great force in the contention that, if active employment and ample purchasing power can be sustained in the main centres of the world trade, the problem of surpluses and unwanted exports will largely disappear, even though, under the most prosperous conditions, there may remain some disturbances of trade and unforeseen situations requiring special remedies.

V.—THE DAILY MANAGEMENT OF THE EXCHANGES UNDER THE PLAN

19. The Clearing Union restores unfettered multilateral clearing between its members. Compare this with the difficulties and complications of a large number of bilateral

agreements. Compare, above all, the provisions by which a country, taking improper advantage of a payments agreement (for the system is, in fact, a *generalised* payments agreement), as Germany did before the war, is dealt with not by a single country (which may not be strong enough to act effectively in isolation or cannot afford to incur the diplomatic odium of isolated action), but by the system as a whole. If the argument is used that the Clearing Union may have difficulty in disciplining a misbehaving country and in avoiding consequential loss, with what much greater force can we urge this objection against a multiplicity of separate bilateral payments agreements.

20. Thus we should not only obtain the advantages, without the disadvantages, of an international gold currency, but we might enjoy these advantages more widely than was ever possible in practice with the old system under which at any given time only a minority of countries were actually working with free exchanges. In conditions of multilateral clearing, exchange dealings would be carried on as freely as in the best days of the gold standard, without its being necessary to ask anyone to accept special or onerous conditions.

21. The principles governing transactions are: first, that the Clearing Union is set up, not for the transaction of daily business between individual traders or banks, but for the clearing and settlement of the ultimate outstanding balances between Central Banks (and certain other super-national Institutions), such as would have been settled under the old gold standard by the shipment or the earmarking of gold, and should not trespass unnecessarily beyond this field; and, second, that its purpose is to increase *freedom* in international commerce and not to multiply interferences or compulsions.

22. Many Central Banks have found great advantage in centralising with themselves or with an Exchange Control the supply and demand of all foreign exchange, thus dispensing with an outside exchange market, though continuing to accommodate individuals through the existing banks and not directly. The further extension of such arrangements would be consonant with the general purposes of the Clearing Union, inasmuch as they would promote order and discipline in international exchange transactions in detail as well as in general. The same is true of the control of Capital Movements, further described below, which many States are likely to wish to impose on their own nationals. But the structure of the proposed Clearing Union does not *require* such measures of centralisation or of control on the part of a member State. It is, for example, consistent alike with the type of Exchange Control now established in the United Kingdom or with the system now operating in the United States. The Union does not prevent private holdings of foreign currency or private dealings in exchange or international capital movements, if these have been approved or allowed by the member States concerned. Central Banks can deal direct with one another as heretofore. No transaction in bancor will take place except when a member State or its Central Bank is exercising the right to pay in it. In no case is there any direct control of capital movements by the Union, even in the case of 6 (8) (*b*) (ii) above, but only by the member States themselves through their own institutions. Thus the fabric of international banking organisation, built up by long experience to satisfy practical needs, would be left as undisturbed as possible.

23. It is not necessary to interfere with the discretion of countries which desire to maintain a special intimacy within a particular group of countries associated by geographical or political ties, such as the existing sterling area, or groups, like the Latin Union of former days, which may come into existence covering, for example, the countries of North America or those of South America, or the groups now under

active discussion, including Poland and Czechoslovakia or certain of the Balkan States. There is no reason why such countries should not be allowed a double position, both as members of the Clearing Union in their own right with their proper quota, and also as making use of another financial centre along traditional lines, as, for example, Australia and India with London, or certain American countries with New York. In this case, their accounts with the Clearing Union would be in exactly the same position as the independent gold reserves which they now maintain, and they would have no occasion to modify in any way their present practices in the conduct of daily business.

24. There might be other cases, however, in which a dependency or a member of a federal union would merge its currency identity in that of a mother country, with a quota appropriately adjusted to the merged currency area as a whole, and *not* enjoy a separate individual membership of the Clearing Union, as, for example, the States of a Federal Union, the French colonies or the British Crown Colonies.

25. At the same time countries, which do not belong to a special geographical or political group, would be expected to keep their reserve balances with the Clearing Union and not with one another. It has, therefore, been laid down that balances may not be held in another country except with the approval of the monetary authorities of that country; and, in order that sterling and dollars might not appear to compete with bancor for the purpose of reserve balances, the United Kingdom and the United States might agree together that they would not accept the reserve balances of other countries in excess of normal working balances except in the case of banks definitely belonging to a Sterling Area or Dollar Area group.

VI.—THE POSITION OF GOLD UNDER THE PLAN

26. Gold still possesses great psychological value which is not being diminished by current events; and the desire to possess a gold reserve against unforeseen contingencies is likely to remain. Gold also has the merit of providing in point of form (whatever the underlying realities may be) an uncontroversial standard of value for international purposes, for which it would not yet be easy to find a serviceable substitute. Moreover, by supplying an automatic means for settling some part of the favourable balances of the creditor countries, the current gold production of the world and the remnant of of gold reserves held outside the United States may still have a useful part to play. Nor is it reasonable to ask the United States to de-monetise the stock of gold which is the basis of its impregnable liquidity. What, in the long run, the world may decide to do with gold is another matter. The purpose of the Clearing Union is to supplant gold as a governing factor, but not to dispense with it.

27. The international bank-money which we have designated *bancor* is defined in terms of a weight of gold. Since the national currencies of the member States are given a defined exchange value in terms of bancor, it follows that they would each have a defined gold content which would be their official buying price for gold, above which they must not pay. The fact that a member State is entitled to obtain a credit in terms of bancor by paying actual gold to the credit of its clearing account, secures a steady and ascertained purchaser for the output of the gold-producing countries, and for countries holding a large reserve of gold. Thus the position of producers and holders of gold is not affected adversely, and is, indeed, improved.

28. Central Banks would be entitled to retain their separate gold reserves and

ship gold to one another, provided they did not pay a price above parity; they could coin gold and put it into circulation, and, generally speaking, do what they liked with it.

29. One limitation only would be, for obvious reasons, essential. No member State would be entitled to demand gold from the Clearing Union against its balance of bancor; for bancor is available only for transfer to another clearing account. Thus between gold and bancor itself there would be a one-way convertibility, such as ruled frequently before the war with national currencies which were on what was called a "gold exchange standard." This need not mean that the Clearing Union would only receive gold and never pay it out. It has been provided above that, if the Clearing Union finds itself in possession of a stock of gold, the Governing Board shall have discretion to distribute the surplus between those possessing credit balances in bancor, proportionately to such balances in reduction of their amount.

30. The question has been raised whether these arrangements are compatible with the retention by individual member States of a full gold standard with two-way convertibility, so that, for example, any foreign central bank acquiring dollars could use them to obtain gold for export. It is not evident that a good purpose would be served by this. But it need not be prohibited, and if any member State should prefer to maintain full convertibility for internal purposes it could protect itself from any abuse of the system or inconvenient consequences by providing that gold could only be exported under licence.

31. The value of bancor in terms of gold is fixed but not unalterably. The power to vary its value might have to be exercised if the stocks of gold tendered to the Union were to be excessive. No object would be served by attempting further to peer into the future or to prophesy the ultimate outcome.

VII.—THE CONTROL OF CAPITAL MOVEMENTS

32. There is no country which can, in future, safely allow the flight of funds for political reasons or to evade domestic taxation or in anticipation of the owner turning refugee. Equally, there is no country that can safely receive fugitive funds, which constitute an unwanted import of capital, yet cannot safely be used for fixed investment.

33. For these reasons it is widely held that control of capital movements, both inward and outward, should be a permanent feature of the post-war system. It is an objection to this that control, if it is to be effective, probably requires the machinery of exchange control for *all* transactions, even though a general permission is given to all remittances in respect of current trade. Thus those countries which have for the time being no reason to fear, and may indeed welcome, outward capital movements, may be reluctant to impose this machinery, even though a general permission for capital, as well as current, transactions reduces it to being no more than a machinery of record. On the other hand, such control will be more difficult to work by unilateral action on the part of those countries which cannot afford to dispense with it, especially in the absence of a postal censorship, if movements of capital cannot be controlled *at both ends*. It would, therefore, be of great advantage if the United States, as well as other members of the Clearing Union, would adopt machinery similar to that which the British Exchange Control has now gone a long way towards perfecting. Nevertheless, the universal establishment of a control of capital movements cannot be regarded as essential to the operation of the Clearing Union; and the method and degree of such control should therefore be left to the decision of each member State. Some less drastic way might be found by which countries, not themselves controlling outward capital

movements, can deter inward movements not approved by the countries from which they originate.

34. The position of abnormal balances in overseas ownership held in various countries at the end of the war presents a problem of considerable importance and special difficulty. A country in which a large volume of such balances is held could not, unless it is in a creditor position, afford the risk of having to redeem them in bancor on a substantial scale, if this would have the effect of depleting its bancor resources at the outset. At the same time, it is very desirable that the countries owning these balances should be able to regard them as liquid, at any rate over and above the amounts which they can afford to lock up under an agreed programme of funding or long-term expenditure. Perhaps there should be some special over-riding provision for dealing with the transitional period only by which, through the aid of the Clearing Union, such balances would remain liquid and convertible into bancor by the creditor country whilst there would be no corresponding strain on the bancor resources of the debtor country, or, at any rate, the resulting strain would be spread over a period.

35. The advocacy of a control of capital movements must not be taken to mean that the era of international investment should be brought to an end. On the contrary, the system contemplated should greatly facilitate the restoration of international loans and credits for legitimate purposes. The object, and it is a vital object, is to have a means—

(*a*) of distinguishing long-term loans by creditor countries, which help to maintain equilibrium and develop the world's resources, from movements of funds out of debtor countries which lack the means to finance them; and

(*b*) of controlling short-term speculative movements or flights of currency whether out of debtor countries or from one creditor country to another.

36. It should be emphasised that the purpose of the overdrafts of bancor permitted by the Clearing Union is, not to facilitate long-term, or even medium-term, credits to be made by debtor countries which cannot afford them, but to allow time and a breathing space for adjustments and for averaging one period with another to all member States alike, whether in the long run they are well-placed to develop a forward international loan policy or whether their prospects of profitable new development in excess of their own resources justifies them in long-term borrowing. The machinery and organisation of international medium-term and long-term lending is another aspect of post-war economic policy, not less important than the purposes which the Clearing Union seeks to serve, but requiring another, complementary institution.

VIII.—RELATION OF THE CLEARING UNION TO COMMERCIAL POLICY

37. The special protective expedients which were developed between the two wars were sometimes due to political, social or industrial reasons. But frequently they were nothing more than forced and undesired dodges to protect an unbalanced position of a country's overseas payments. The new system, by helping to provide a register of the size and whereabouts of the aggregate debtor and creditor positions respectively, and an indication whether it is reasonable for a particular country to adopt special expedients as a temporary measure to assist in regaining equilibrium in its balance of payments, would make it possible to establish a general rule *not* to adopt them, subject to the indicated exceptions.

38. The existence of the Clearing Union would make it possible for member States contracting commercial agreements to use their respective debit and credit positions

with the Clearing Union as a test, though this test by itself would not be complete. Thus, the contracting parties, whilst agreeing to clauses in a commercial agreement forbidding, in general, the use of certain measures or expedients in their mutual trade relations, might make this agreement subject to special relaxations if the state of their respective clearing accounts satisfied an agreed criterion. For example, an agreement might provide that, in the event of one of the contracting States having a debit balance with the Clearing Union exceeding a specified proportion of its quota on the average of a period it should be free to resort to import regulation or to barter trade agreements or to higher import duties of a type which was restricted under the agreement in normal circumstances. Protected by the possibility of such temporary indulgences, the members of the Clearing Union should feel much more confidence in moving towards the withdrawal of other and more dislocating forms of protection and discrimination and in accepting the prohibition of the worst of them from the outset. In any case, it should be laid down that members of the Union would not allow or suffer among themselves any restrictions on the disposal of receipts arising out of current trade or "invisible" income.

IX.—THE USE OF THE CLEARING UNION FOR OTHER INTERNATIONAL PURPOSES

39. The Clearing Union might become the instrument and the support of international policies in addition to those which it is its primary purpose to promote. This deserves the greatest possible emphasis. The Union might become the pivot of the future economic government of the world. Without it, other more desirable developments will find themselves impeded and unsupported. With it, they will fall into their place as parts of an ordered scheme. No one of the following suggestions is a necessary part of the plan. But they are illustrations of the additional purposes of high importance and value which the Union, once established, might be able to serve:—

(1) The Union might set up a clearing account in favour of international bodies charged with post-war relief, rehabilitation and reconstruction. But it could go much further than this. For it might supplement contributions received from other sources by granting preliminary overdraft facilities in favour of these bodies, the overdraft being discharged over a period of years out of the Reserve Fund of the Union, or, if necessary, out of a levy on surplus credit balances. So far as this method is adopted it would be possible to avoid asking any country to assume a burdensome commitment for relief and reconstruction, since the resources would be provided in the first instance by those countries having credit clearing accounts for which they have no immediate use and are voluntarily leaving idle, and in the long run by those countries which have a chronic international surplus for which they have no beneficial employment.

(2) The Union might set up an account in favour of any super-national policing body which may be charged with the duty of preserving the peace and maintaining international order. If any country were to infringe its properly authorised orders, the policing body might be entitled to request the Governors of the Clearing Union to hold the clearing account of the delinquent country to its order and permit no further transactions on the account except by its authority. This would provide an excellent machinery for enforcing a financial blockade.

(3) The Union might set up an account in favour of international bodies charged with the management of a Commodity Control, and might finance stocks of commodities held by such bodies, allowing them overdraft facilities on their accounts up to an

agreed maximum. By this means the financial problem of buffer stocks and "ever-normal granaries" could be effectively attacked.

(4) The Union might be linked up with a Board for International Investment. It might act on behalf of such a Board and collect for them the annual service of their loans by automatically debiting the clearing account of the country concerned. The statistics of the clearing accounts of the member-States would give a reliable indication as to which countries were in a position to finance the Investment Board, with the advantage of shifting the whole system of clearing credits and debits nearer to equilibrium.

(5) There are various methods by which the Clearing Union could use its influence and its powers to maintain stability of prices and to control the Trade Cycle. If an International Economic Board is established, this Board and the Clearing Union might be expected to work in close collaboration to their mutual advantage. If an International Investment or Development Corporation is also set up together with a scheme of Commodity Controls for the control of stocks of the staple primary products, we might come to possess in these three Institutions a powerful means of combating the evils of the Trade Cycle, by exercising contractionist or expansionist influence on the system as a whole or on particular sections. This is a large and important question which cannot be discussed adequately in this paper; and need not be examined at length in this place because it does not raise any important issues affecting the fundamental constitution of the proposed Union. It is mentioned here to complete the picture of the wider purposes which the foundation of the Clearing Union might be made to serve.

40. The facility of applying the Clearing Union plan to these several purposes arises out of a fundamental characteristic which is worth pointing out, since it distinguishes the plan from those proposals which try to develop the same basic principle along bilateral lines and is one of the grounds on which the Plan can claim superior merit. This might be described as its "anonymous" or "impersonal" quality. No particular member States have to engage their own resources as such to the support of other particular States or of any of the international projects or policies adopted. They have only to agree in general that, if they find themselves with surplus resources which for the time being they do not themselves wish to employ, these resources may go into the general pool and be put to work on approved purposes. This costs the surplus country nothing because it is not asked to part permanently, or even for any specified period, with such resources, which it remains free to expend and employ for its own purposes whenever it chooses; in which case the burden of finance is passed on to the next recipient, again for only so long as the recipient has no use for the money. As pointed out above, this merely amounts to extending to the international sphere the methods of any domestic banking system, which are in the same sense "impersonal" inasmuch as there is no call on the particular depositor either to support as such the purposes for which his banker makes advances or to forgo permanently the use of his deposit. There is no countervailing objection except that which applies equally to the technique of domestic banking, namely that it is capable of the abuse of creating excessive purchasing power and hence an inflation of prices. In our efforts to avoid the opposite evil, we must not lose sight of this risk, to which there is an allusion in 39 (5) above. But it is no more reason for refusing the advantages of international banking than the similar risk in the domestic field is a reason to return to the practices of the seventeenth century goldsmiths (which are what we are still following in

the international field) and to forgo the vast expansion of production which banking principles have made possible. Where financial contributions are required for some purpose of general advantage, it is a great facility not to have to ask for specific contributions from any named country, but to depend rather on the anonymous and impersonal aid of the system as a whole. We have here a genuine organ of truly international government.

X.—THE TRANSITIONAL ARRANGEMENTS

41. It would be of great advantage to agree the general principles of the Clearing Union before the end of the war, with a view to bringing it into operation at an early date after the termination of hostilities. Major plans will be more easily brought to birth in the first energy of victory and whilst the active spirit of united action still persists, than in the days of exhaustion and reaction from so much effort which may well follow a little later. Such a proposal presents, however, something of a dilemma. On the one hand, many countries will be in particular need of reserves of overseas resources in the period immediately after the war. On the other hand, goods will be in short supply and the prevention of inflationary international conditions of much more importance for the time being than the opposite. The expansionist tendency of the plan, which is a leading recommendation of it as soon as peace-time output is restored and the productive capacity of the world is in running order, might be a danger in the early days of a sellers' market and an excess of demand over supply.

42. A reconciliation of these divergent purposes is not easily found until we know more than is known at present about the means to be adopted to finance post-war relief and reconstruction. If the intention is to provide resources on liberal and comprehensive lines outside the resources made available by the Clearing Union and additional to them, it might be better for such specific aid to take the place of the proposed overdrafts during the "relief" period of (say) two years. In this case credit clearing balances would be limited to the amount of gold delivered to the Union, and the overdraft facilities created by the Union in favour of the Relief Council, the International Investment Board or the Commodity Controls. Nevertheless, the immediate establishment of the Clearing Union would not be incompatible with provisional arrangements, which could take alternative forms according to the character of the other "relief" arrangements, qualifying and limiting the overdraft quotas. Overdraft quotas might be allowed on a reduced scale during the transitional period. Or it might be proper to provide that countries in receipt of relief or Lend-Lease assistance should not have access at the same time to overdraft facilities, and that the latter should only become available when the former had come to an end. If, on the other hand, relief from outside sources looks like being inadequate from the outset, the overdraft quotas may be even more necessary at the outset than later on.

43. We must not be over-cautious. A rapid economic restoration may lighten the tasks of the diplomatists and the politicians in the resettlement of the world and the restoration of social order. For Great Britain and other countries outside the "relief" areas the possibility of exports sufficient to sustain their standard of life is bound up with good and expanding markets. We cannot afford to wait too long for this, and we must not allow excessive caution to condemn us to perdition. Unless the Union is a going concern, the problem of proper "timing" will be nearly insoluble. It is sufficient at this stage to point out that the problem of timing must not be overlooked, but that the Union is capable of being used so as to aid rather than impede its solution.

XI.—CONCLUSION

44. It has been suggested that so ambitious a proposal is open to criticism on the ground that it requires from the members of the Union a greater surrender of their sovereign rights than they will readily concede. But no greater surrender is required than in a commercial treaty. The obligations will be entered into voluntarily and can be terminated on certain conditions by giving notice.

45. A greater readiness to accept super-national arrangements must be required in the post-war world. If the arrangements proposed can be described as a measure of financial disarmament, there is nothing here which we need be reluctant to accept ourselves or to ask of others. It is an advantage, and not a disadvantage, of the scheme that it invites the member States to abandon that licence to promote indiscipline, disorder and bad-neighbourliness which, to the general disadvantage, they have been free to exercise hitherto.

46. The plan makes a beginning at the future economic ordering of the world between nations and "the winning of the peace." It might help to create the conditions and the atmosphere in which much else would be made easier.

The White Plan

The first definitive version of Mr. White's plan for a Stabilization Fund was a mimeographed draft dated April 1942. This covered both the Fund and the Bank. It comprised an Introduction, an Outline of the Articles proposed for the Fund and for the Bank, and extensive commentaries on these Articles. The extract (A) below omits the Articles for the Bank and also the commentary on them except for a section which dealt with "A new international currency."

The final version of Mr. White's plan was issued by the U.S. Treasury in printed form on July 10, 1943. This is reproduced in (B) below.

(A) Preliminary Draft Proposal for a United Nations Stabilization Fund and a Bank for Reconstruction and Development of the United and Associated Nations

(April 1942)

H. D. WHITE, Assistant to the Secretary, U.S. Treasury Department

This report has been prepared at the request of Secretary Morgenthau that I draft a plan for an International Stabilization Fund and an International Unit of Currency.

He felt that the requirements of furthering the war effort and preparing for the financial needs of the reconstruction period called for the immediate preparation and study of preliminary proposals.—H. D. WHITE

INTRODUCTION

Suggested Plan for a United and Associated Nations Stabilization Fund and a Bank for Reconstruction and Development of the United and Associated Nations

It is yet too soon to know the precise form or the approximate magnitude of post-war monetary problems. But one thing is certain. No matter how long the war lasts nor how it is won, we shall be faced with three inescapable problems: to prevent the disruption of foreign exchanges and the collapse of monetary and credit systems; to assure the restoration of foreign trade; and to supply the huge volume of capital that will be needed virtually throughout the world for reconstruction, for relief, and for economic recovery.

If we are to avoid drifting from the peace table into a period of chaotic competition, monetary disorders, depressions, political disruption, and finally into new wars within as well as among nations, we must be equipped to grapple with these three problems and to make substantial progress toward their solution.

Specific plans must be formulated now.

Clearly the task can be successfully handled only through international action. In most discussions of post-war problems this fact has been recognized, yet to date—though a number of persons have pointed to the solution in general terms—no detailed plans sufficiently realistic or practical to give promise of accomplishing the task have been formulated or discussed. It is high time that such plans were drafted. It is time that detailed and workable plans be prepared providing for the creation of agencies with resources, powers and structure adequate to meet the three major post-war needs.

Such agencies should, of course, be designed to deal chiefly with post-war problems. But their establishment must not be postponed until the end of hostilities. It takes many months to set up such agencies. First, a plan has to be perfected. Then it has to be carefully considered by a number of countries. In each country, again, acceptance can follow only upon legislation. That alone will consume many months and possibly longer. And even when the plan is finally accepted, much time will be further consumed in the collection of personnel, and the performance of the preliminary ground work which must be done before effective operations can begin. Altogether, a year may be required before a proposal can be transformed into an operating agency.

Obviously, therefore, even though no important immediate ends will be served by having such agencies functioning during war time, it will be an error to wait until the end of the war is in sight before beginning serious discussion of plans for establishing such agencies. No one knows how soon the war will end, and no one can know how long it will take to get plans approved and the agencies started. Yet, if we are to "win the peace," which will follow the war, we must have adequate economic instruments with which to carry on effective work as soon as the war is over. It would be ill-advised, if not positively dangerous, to leave ourselves at the end of the war unprepared for the stupendous task of world-wide economic reconstruction.

Specific proposals will help win the war.

But there is an additional important reason for initiating at once serious discussion of specific proposals. Such discussion will be a factor toward winning the war. It has been frequently suggested, and with much cogency, that the task of securing the defeat of the Axis powers would be made easier if the victims of aggression, actual and potential, could have more assurance that a victory by the United Nations will not mean in the economic sphere, a mere return to the pre-war pattern of every-country-for-itself, or inevitable depression, of possible widespread economic chaos with the weaker nations succumbing first under the law-of-the-jungle that characterized international economic practices of the pre-war decade. That assurance must be given now. The people of the anti-Axis powers must be encouraged to feel themselves on solid international ground, they must be given to understand that a United Nations victory will not usher in another two decades of economic uneasiness, bickering, ferment, and disruption. They must be assured that something will be done in the sphere of international economic relations that is new, that is powerful enough and comprehensive enough to give expectation of successfully filling a world need. They must have assurance that methods and resources are being prepared to provide them with capital to help them rebuild their devastated areas, reconstruct their war-distorted economies, and help free them from the strangulating grasp of lost markets and depleted reserves. Finally, they must have assurance that the United States does not intend to desert the war-worn and impoverished nations after the war is won, but proposes to help them in the long and difficult task of economic reconstruction. To help them, not primarily for altruistic motives, but from recognition of the truth that prosperity, like peace, is indivisible. To give that assurance now is to unify and encourage the anti-Axis forces, to greatly strengthen their will and effort to win.

Nor will the effect be on the anti-Axis powers alone. Whether within the Axis countries the will to fight would be weakened by such arrangements is not certain, but assuredly it would not be strengthened. And certainly the people in the invaded countries, and the wavering elements in the Axis dominated and Axis-influenced countries would be given additional cause to throw in their lot more definitely and openly with the anti-Axis forces if there is real promise that an orderly prosperous world will emerge from a United Nations victory.

Two International Government Agencies must be established—a Stabilization Fund and a Bank for Reconstruction.

A vital part of that promise rests on international monetary and banking collaboration. The United Nations and the Nations associated with them must undertake cooperatively two tasks as soon as possible: first, to provide an instrument with the means and the procedure to stabilize foreign exchange rates and strengthen the monetary systems of the United Nations; and second, to establish an agency with resources and powers adequate to provide capital for economic reconstruction, to facilitate rapid and smooth transition from war-time economies to peace-time economies, to provide relief for stricken people during the immediate post-war period, to increase foreign trade and permanently increase the productivity of the United Nations.

Those two tasks should be kept distinct. Though in some of their facets and in many of their consequences there is considerable interdependence and interaction, the two are different enough to call for separate instrumentalities. Each is sufficiently specialized to require different resources, different responsibilities, and different procedures and criteria for action. To supply the United Nations with necessary capital not otherwise available except possibly on too costly terms should be the function of a bank created for that specific purpose; whereas monetary stabilization—a highly specialized function calling for a special structure, special personnel, and special organization—would best be performed by a stabilization fund created to perform that special function.

It is therefore recommended that immediate consideration be given to formulating plans for the establishment of two separate institutions:

1. A United and Associated Nations Stabilization Fund, and
2. A Bank for Reconstruction and Development of the United and Associated Nations.

While either agency could function without the existence of the other, the creation of both would nevertheless aid greatly in the functioning of each. Doubtless one agency with the combined functions of both could be set up, but it could operate only with a loss of effectiveness, risk of over-centralization of power, and danger of making costly errors of judgment. The best promise of successful operation seems to lie in the creation of two separate institutions, linked together by one or two directors in common.

Proposals must be drafted by experts of many governments meeting for that purpose.

It is hoped that some time soon, representatives of various interested governments will meet in conference to explore the possibility of working out a plan for the establishment of an international stabilization fund and bank. To facilitate the preliminary work of such a committee, and to provide the officials of the interested governments with a proposal set in specific enough terms to encourage and justify fruitful discussion prior to a meeting, the following report has been prepared. It contains a suggested plan for a fund and for a bank, and also some discussion of the various points involved.

Anyone familiar with the task of setting up new and complex organizations such as the two envisaged will fully appreciate that no single person, no matter how well informed on the subject, can hope to draft a plan that would meet with general approval. This is especially true of a proposal calling for international collaboration and requiring acceptance by several governments. To draft a plan that is likely to meet with approval of various governments is a task beyond the competence even of a group of economists from any single country. The details of any plan submitted for consideration would have to be subjected to careful evaluation and examination by a number of men, some of whom should be expert in the handling of international economic problems and monetary theory, and others at home in related fields. In addition to monetary problems, questions of sovereignty, of national interest, and of broad economic policy are involved in some of the more important provisions, and these inevitably must be the subject of controversy and compromise. They are also matters that must be discussed in detail and at length by high officials whose responsibilities include the shaping and administration of monetary and financial policy.

The proposals and comments that follow are submitted with the intent of providing a starting point for intelligent discussion and of calling attention to some of the difficulties which would have to be satisfactorily met before a workable and acceptable plan may emerge. The proposals have been set forth only in outline and for the most part only those points are included which are essential to an understanding of the plan.

It is certain that some of the powers and requirements included in the outline of the Fund and the Bank will not survive discussion, prejudice and fear of departure from the usual. Some may not stand the test of political reality, and some may be unacceptable on technical grounds, while others may be generally regarded as going too far toward "internationalism." Yet most of them appear as desirable objectives in most writings or conferences on post-war economies and are worth considering.

Willingness to depart from tradition and break new ground is essential if meaningful results are to be obtained.

It will perhaps help toward understanding and induce a more sympathetic approach to the proposals which follow to state at the outset that something much more than the usual banking and stabilization functions are envisaged in the plan. There is urgent need for instruments which will pave the way and make easy a high degree of cooperation and collaboration among the United Nations in economic fields hitherto held too sacrosanct for international action or multilateral sovereignty. A breach must be made and widened in the outmoded and disastrous economic policy of each-country-for-itself-and-the-devil-take-the-weakest. Just as the failure to develop an effective League of Nations has made possible two devastating wars within one generation, so the absence of a high degree of economic collaboration among the leading nations will, during the coming decade, inevitably result in economic warfare that will be but the prelude and instigator of military warfare on an even vaster scale.

The Fund and the Bank described in the following pages are envisaged as economic instruments that most easily and effectively can facilitate that high degree of economic collaboration. It will be at once apparent that the resources, powers and requirements for membership, accorded both agencies go far beyond the usual attributes of monetary stabilization and of banking. They must if they are to be the stepping stone from shortsighted disastrous economic nationalism to intelligent international collaboration. Timidity will not serve. It is my conviction that the long-time effectiveness of both agencies will be measured by the degree to which boldness and vision are displayed in their organization and objectives.

Part I, which follows, consists of an outline of (1) a United and Associated Nations Stabilization Fund, and (2) of a Bank for Reconstruction of the United and Associated Nations.

Part II consists of a brief explanation and discussion of the proposed Fund, and Part III of the proposed Bank.

PART I

A. SUGGESTED OUTLINE OF A UNITED AND ASSOCIATED NATIONS STABILIZATION FUND.

I. The Purposes of the Fund are:

1. To stabilize foreign exchange rates of the United Nations.
2. To encourage the flow of productive capital among the United Nations.
3. To liberate blocked balances.
4. To help correct the maldistribution of gold among the United Nations.
5. To facilitate the settlement and servicing of international debts—both public and private.
6. To shorten the periods of disturbing disequilibrium in the international accounts of member countries and help stabilize price levels.
7. To reduce the necessity and use of foreign exchange controls.
8. To eliminate multiple currency practices and bilateral clearing arrangements.
9. To promote sound note issuing and credit policies and practices among the United Nations.
10. To reduce barriers to foreign trade.
11. To promote more efficient and less expensive clearings of international exchange transactions.

II. Powers.

To help attain the objectives listed above, the Fund shall have the following powers:

1. Buy, sell and hold gold, currencies, foreign exchange, bills of exchange, and government bonds of the "member" countries, and act as a clearing house for international movement of funds, balances, checks, drafts, acceptances, gold.
2. The Treasury of each member country (or its agent, a stabilization fund or central bank) shall have the privilege of purchasing from the Fund the currency of any member country which the Fund holds, provided:
    a. The currency demanded from the Fund is required to meet adverse balance of payments to the country whose currency is being demanded.
    b. The sum in the Fund of the currency of the country making the purchase shall be, after adding the sum proposed to be purchased, not more than

100 percent of the total sum—gold, currency, and notes—originally contributed to the Fund.

c. The rate of exchange shall be the one determined by the Fund.

3. Should a country wish to sell its currency to the Fund in an amount in excess of the above quota, approval by four-fifths of the member votes would be required. The Fund could decide to purchase the excess of the currency in question if:

   a. It is believed the anticipated balance of payments of the country in question was such as to warrant the expectation that the "excess" could be disposed of within a reasonable time, or

   b. The country in question had gold holdings which, together with gold it expected to accumulate within a reasonable time, were adequate to replace the excess, and

   c. The country in question agreed to adopt and carry out measures designed to correct the disequilibrium in the country's balance of payments, which the Fund recommended—after careful examination of the situation.

4. The governments of member countries may sell to the Fund, blocked foreign balances acquired from their nationals, provided all the following conditions are met:

   a. The foreign balances were in member countries and were either partly or wholly blocked.

   b. The foreign balances were included in the sum reported (for the purpose of this provision) by the member government as blocked on date of its becoming a member.

   c. The country selling the blocked balances to the Fund agreed to begin repurchasing 40 percent of the amount sold to the Fund, at the price received, and at a rate not to be less than 2 percent a year. The repurchases to begin not later than three years after date of sale, and the currency to be used in repayment to be either the currency received or the local currency, as desired by the Fund.

   d. The country in which the blocked balances are held agrees to transfer those balances to the Fund, and purchase back 40 percent of them from the Fund, at the rate of 2 percent a year, beginning not later than three years after the date of transfer. The Fund may accept government bonds payable in gold in lieu of part of the blocked balances, and shall be free to sell such bonds under certain conditions.

   e. If the country selling the blocked foreign balances to the Fund asks for foreign exchange rather than local currency, it must need the foreign exchange for the purpose of meeting adverse balance of payments arising from any cause except acquisitions of gold, or accumulation of foreign balances.

   f. The country in which the blocked funds are kept agrees not to impose any restrictions on the installments of the 40 percent portion gradually to be repurchased by country owning the blocked balances.

   g. A charge of 1 percent, payable in the currency of the country paying shall be levied against the country selling its blocked funds, and a charge of 1 percent payable by country in which blocked account exists.

h. The Fund shall determine from time to time what shall be the maximum proportion of the blocked balances it can afford to take over under this provision.

i. The Fund on its part agrees not to sell the blocked balances acquired under the above authority, except with the permission, or at the request of the country in which the blocked balances are being held but can invest those balances in regular or special government securities of that country.

5. The Fund would fix the rates at which it will exchange one member's currency for another, and the rates at which it will buy and sell gold with local currencies. The guiding principle in the fixing of such rates shall be stability in exchange relationships. Changes in the rates shall be made only when essential to correction of a fundamental disequilibrium, and only with the consent of four-fifths of member votes.

6. The Fund shall have authority to deal only with the Treasuries of the participating countries, or with official stabilization funds of those countries, and with the bank designated by participating government as its fiscal agent, and with international banks owned by governments.

7. The Fund shall not have the authority to engage in any transactions within a member country, or with any corporation or part of the government of that country without the consent of the Board representative of that country.

8. The Fund shall have the authority to buy and sell currencies of non-member countries, but shall not be authorized to hold such currencies beyond sixty days after date of purchase, except with the approval of four-fifths of the member votes.

9. The Fund shall have the authority to borrow, at such rates as the Fund may recommend, the currency of any country, provided four-fifths of the member votes approve the terms, amount and condition of such borrowing.

10. The Fund shall have the authority to invest any currency it holds in "short-term" securities—commercial or government—of the country of that currency provided a four-fifths vote of the member votes shall approve, and provided further that the approving votes shall include that of the Board representative of the country in which the investment is to be made.

11. The Fund shall have authority to sell the obligation it holds of the member countries provided four-fifths of the member votes approve, and provided the representative of the country in which the securities are to be sold approves.

12. No sale of any currency from the Fund shall be made to a member without approval of four-fifths of member votes when the currency so sold is to be used or is to make possible adjustment of a foreign debt, including, of course, debts already in default.

13. Any member country can borrow local currency from the Fund for one year or less up to 75 percent of the currency of that country held by the Fund, provided such loan is approved by three-fourths of the member votes. A country borrowing such funds shall pay to the Fund an interest rate of 1 percent a year.

14. A very moderate service charge shall be made by the Fund on all exchange and gold transactions.

III. Eligibility for membership.

Any member of the United or Associated Nations is eligible for membership in the Fund provided it agrees:

1. To abandon, not later than one year after joining the Fund, or after the cessation of hostilities, whichever is later, all restrictions and controls over foreign exchange transactions with member countries, except with the approval of the Fund.
2. To alter exchange rates on the currencies of other countries only with the consent of the Fund and only to the extent and in the direction approved by the Fund, with the exception of a narrow range fixed by the Fund and permitted to all member currencies.
3. (a) Not to accept or permit deposits or investments from any member country except with the permission of the government of that country, and
   (b) To make available to the government of any member country at its request all property in form of deposits, investments, securities of the nationals of that member country.
4. Not to enter upon any bilateral clearing arrangements.
5. Not to adopt any monetary or general price measure or policy, the effect of which, in the opinion of a majority of the member votes, would be to bring about sooner or later a serious disequilibrium in the balance of payments, if four-fifths of the member votes of the Fund submitted to the country in question their disapproval of the adoption of the measure.
6. To embark upon a program of gradual reduction of existing trade barriers—import duties, import quotas, administrative devices—and further agree not to adopt any increase in tariff schedules, or other devices having as their purpose higher trade obstacles, without giving reasonable opportunity for the Fund to study the effect of the contemplated change on exchange rates and register its opinion. In rendering its opinion, the Fund will make recommendation to which the member governments agree to give serious consideration.
7. Not to permit any defaults on foreign obligations of the government, Central Bank or government agency without approval of the Fund.
8. Not to subsidize—directly or indirectly—the exportation of any commodity or services to member countries without consent of the Fund.

IV. Composition of the Fund.

1. The Fund shall consist of gold, currencies of member countries, and member government securities in such amounts as shall be indicated by a formula set forth in the agreement.

   The total subscription to the Fund shall be the equivalent of at least $5 billion. The Bank of the United Nations should subscribe $100 million to the Fund.
2. The contribution of each country shall consist of 25 percent cash and 25 percent in interest-bearing government securities (interest and principal payable in gold or its equivalent). The remaining 50 percent to be paid in such installments and in such form as shall be determined from time to time by the Fund.

   The initial payment of 25 percent cash shall consist of at least one-half in gold, the remainder in local currency.

V. Management.

1. The management of the Fund shall be vested in a Board of Directors consisting

of the representatives appointed by the member governments. Each government shall appoint one representative.

2. The Board shall elect a chairman and a small operating committee. The Chairman shall be chief of the operating committee. The members of the operating committee should devote full time to the management of the Fund, should be assisted by an appropriate technical staff, and should receive an adequate salary. The Chief of the operating committee with the approval of the Board shall appoint the heads of the departments.
3. In all voting by the Board each representative shall have one hundred votes, plus one vote for the equivalent of every million dollars subscribed to the Fund by his government.
4. A country can replace, wholly or in part, its bonds with currency or gold. The number of votes its representatives can cast will alter accordingly.
5. All decisions, except where specifically provided otherwise, shall be decided by the majority of the votes cast.
6. The President of the Bank for the United Nations shall be a member of the Board and shall have 100 votes. He shall have no additional votes notwithstanding the Bank's participation in the Fund.

VI. The rules and regulations regarding the type, amount and conditions of day-to-day transactions to be handled by the operating committee, shall be promulgated by four-fifths of the member votes.

VII. No change in the gold value of any currency of the participating countries shall be permitted to alter the gold value of the total currency holdings in the Fund. Thus, if the currency of any of the participating countries should depreciate, that country must deliver to the Fund an amount of its local currency equal to the decreased value of that currency held by the Fund. Likewise, if the currency of a particular country should increase, the Fund must deliver to that country an amount (in the currency of that country) equal to the resultant increase in the gold value of the Fund's holdings. This provision does not apply to currencies acquired under paragraph 4 under section on "Powers."

VIII. A country failing to contribute to the Fund sums due the Fund shall be dropped as a member, provided a majority of the member votes so decide. Any member dropped shall have returned to it an amount (in its own currency) equal to its contribution minus any sum due by that country to the Fund.

IX. Net profits earned by the Fund shall be distributed in the following manner:

1. 50 percent to reserves until the reserves are equal to 10 percent of the assets of the Fund.
2. 50 percent to be divided each year among the members in form of the local currency. That is, each country shall distribute its dividends in its own currency.

X. The member governments agree to furnish the Fund with all information it needs for its operations, and to furnish such reports as it may require, in the form and at the times requested by the Fund.

[Part I.B, outlining proposals for an International Bank, has been omitted here.]

PART II

A UNITED NATIONS STABILIZATION FUND

The outline of the purposes, powers and structure of a stabilization fund presented in the previous pages is hardly enough to supply the interested reader with more than very general idea of how the proposed institution would function and what they would be expected to accomplish. A brief discussion of some of the points outlined should serve to give a clearer idea of what is proposed, and also suggest some of the difficulties involved in the proposal.

In the following pages the outline presented in Part I is somewhat elaborated and some brief discussion is ventured of the more troublesome or important points. This section is devoted to discussion of the Fund and Part III to discussion of the Bank.

I. Purposes of the Fund

The various purposes enumerated in the outline are to a considerable extent inter-dependent and overlapping and in some instances may even represent apparently conflicting tendencies. Yet, progress in the attainment of almost any one of them facilitates progress toward the attainment of many of the others. Each of them represents a different phase of international monetary arrangements and calls in the main for different procedure, different powers, and in some cases, different kinds of resources.

The fact that some of the objectives may be at times harmonious and at other times conflicting, indicates that the management of an international stabilization fund cannot be reduced to a matter of simple rules. The successful operation of the Fund calls for constant examination of a large variety of pertinent factors and the continual evaluation of various effects which might be expected to follow any particular action or failure to act.

There follows a brief amplification and justification of each of the objectives.

Stabilization of foreign exchange rates.

The advantages of obtaining stable exchange rates are patent. The maintenance of stable exchange rates means the elimination of exchange risk in international economic and financial transactions. The cost of conducting foreign trade is thereby reduced, and capital flows much more easily to the country where it yields the greatest return because both short-term and long-term investments are greatly hampered by the possibility of loss from exchange depreciation. As the expectation of continued stability in foreign exchange rates is strengthened there is also more chance of avoiding the disrupting effects of flights of capital and of inflation.

Altogether, if the Fund were successful in bringing about a much greater degree of stability in foreign exchange relationships than existed during the 'twenties and 'thirties, it will have justified its existence on that score alone.

Flow of productive capital, blocked balances, and redistribution of gold.

The desirability of encouraging the flow of productive capital to areas where it can be most profitably employed needs no emphasis. The Fund can help encourage that flow by reducing exchange risks, and also by making the imposition of restrictions on exchange transactions less likely to happen. Also, insofar as the Fund can help strengthen the monetary and banking system of the country, it increases that country's attraction to funds of private foreign investors.

Balances owned by residents of another country which have been blocked because holdings of gold and other liquid foreign exchange assets are inadequate (this does not apply to the United States where restrictions have been imposed for reasons other than because of any scarcity of gold reserves) will constitute after the war one of the danger spots to monetary stability, and to resumption of liberal trade policies. If the Fund can eliminate that danger spot it will have justified its existence—even were it to accomplish little else.

The Fund has the possibility of utilizing more effectively the gold resources of any given country, and thereby encourage countries to hold larger gold reserves. By facilitating an easier adjustment of the international balance of payments, it reduces the volume of hectic gold movements. Machinery can be developed under the aegis of the Bank, with which countries can more easily develop a favorable balance of payments vis-à-vis the gold-holding and producing countries. By providing strength to countries with weakened economic and credit systems, the Fund can also encourage the return flow of gold from the United States.

Servicing of international debts.

The reduction in risk of exchange loss and progress toward elimination of restrictions on foreign exchange transactions should make easier debt adjustments of foreign debts now in default—both public and private—and continued servicing of debts not in default.

To help stabilize price levels.

Any development which would contribute toward stability of price levels is greatly to be welcomed. Wide swings in price levels are one of the destructive elements in domestic as well as international trade. An intelligent use of an international stabilization fund could contribute something toward reducing the fluctuations, and even the cyclical movements of prices within a country and in the relationship of price levels between countries.

To reduce the necessity and use of foreign exchange controls.

Foreign exchange controls usually constitute an interference with trade and capital flows. Unfortunately, such controls are too often preferable to the alternatives facing a particular country. Insofar as an international stabilization fund can reduce the necessity for such controls and can prevent the use of such controls where they are not necessary, it will serve to substantially increase foreign trade of nations and encourage the flow of production capital.

To eliminate multiple currency practices and bilateral clearing arrangements.

The developments during the last twenty years of multiple currency devices and bilateral clearing arrangements served to disrupt trade, increase economic difficulties in some countries, and stimulate the worst kind of competitive practices among countries seeking to increase their foreign markets or protect the foreign markets they already have. These practices frequently arise from difficulties which are subject to mitigation by an appropriately handled stabilization fund. An international stabilization fund with ample resources and broad powers could do much to eliminate the justification for resorting to trade practices that are an obstacle to a high level of foreign trade for all countries.

Promotion of sound note issuing and credit policies and practices.

The sounder the monetary and banking policies of governments, the less sensitive are they to economic disturbances, and the quicker will be the recovery from any depression. There are numerous ways in which an international stabilization fund could add to the strength of monetary systems of member governments.

Reduction of trade barriers.

The existence of high tariff policies and other obstacles to trade and the tendency during the post-war period to heighten those barriers, are serious barriers to recovery and maintenance of a high level of economic activity among countries. It will be readily admitted that if an international stabilization fund can assist in bringing about a reduction in the unnecessary barriers to international trade, it will have performed a valuable service toward maintaining business recovery after the war.

The establishment of an efficient clearing house for international monetary transactions.

The advantage of providing such a clearing house would not be negligible, particularly among countries who transact a small volume of business with each other. The spread between the buying and selling rates of some foreign currencies is much larger in some countries than it should be. Thus transactions between those countries are subject to handicaps that are unnecessary. To the extent that exchange rate spreads are adjuncts to fiscal or commercial policy, the Fund will deal with the problem in other ways. It is impossible to measure the gains that accrue from more efficient handling of clearances, but they could be substantial.

Can these objectives be reached?

Each of the objectives listed, if achieved, would help in some degree to restore and maintain world prosperity. If the Fund is to make much progress toward achieving the objectives enumerated in the previous pages, it must have broad powers and courageous and intelligent direction. It is a task that is surely within the competence of the present generation.

II. Powers of the Fund

The Fund should have the power to buy, sell and hold gold, currencies, foreign exchange, bills of exchange, and government securities of the "member" countries and act as a clearing house for international movements of gold and balances.

The purchase and sale of gold would be an essential part of the operations of the Fund. The Fund might well become the most attractive depository for earmarked gold, and be the means of greatly reducing the need for physical transfers of gold among members.

To promote the practice of "earmarking" gold its storing and transfer could be made without charge to members, and agreement between countries could accord a maximum of legal security to such holdings. It should even be possible to secure written assurance by the government of the country where the gold was to be held that such gold would not be subject to any controls. Earmarked gold could be given a special status so that countries could unhesitatingly earmark large amounts with the Fund and still record such gold as part of their own reserve. The Fund might find it convenient to have a branch office on each continent. This would still further cut down gold shipments. It would also speed up other kinds of transactions.

Dealings in foreign exchange would constitute, of course, the chief business of the Fund. It is through such transactions that the Fund would be expected to carry out many of its objectives. It might therefore be helpful if this part of the Fund's operations were described with little more detail. Tedious though it may be, this part of the Fund's activities must be elaborated to permit a proper evaluation of the role an international stabilization fund can play. In the several pages which follow the exchange operations with which the Fund would be chiefly occupied are briefly described.

The Treasury, or its fiscal agent, of each member country shall have the privilege of purchasing from the Fund the currency of any member country which the Fund holds.

Since the Fund would deal only with and for Treasuries (or their fiscal agents and the Bank) the regular private channels through which foreign exchange transactions are now consummated by commercial banks, and other dealers and brokers, would continue to serve. It is presumed that the Treasuries would deal in foreign exchange only when exchange situation warranted government operation. They might also employ the Fund to transact foreign exchange business between governments.

Certain restrictions on operations are necessitated by the wide differences in the strength of the various currencies. If any country could purchase from the Fund as much of any currency as it pleased at a fixed rate without reducing the supply of the strong currency available in the open market, countries with weak currencies would be tempted to accumulate stocks of strong currencies. The Fund's supply of gold and strong currencies would soon be depleted and in their place would be weak currencies, i.e. currencies of countries which prefer other currencies to their own. Some restrictions are therefore necessary.

The first condition of purchase from the Fund might be that the currency purchased must be needed to meet an adverse balance of payments to the country whose currency is being demanded. Thus, a country could not obtain gold or other currency from the Fund if the direct result were to increase the gold or foreign exchange holdings of the Government, its Stabilization Fund, or fiscal agent, except, of course, possibly for short periods.

There would be no justification for a member government to use the Fund's assets as a means of converting its currency into gold or foreign exchange, unless it needed that gold or foreign exchange to meet claims or liabilities due or soon to be due. It is quite true that one of the possible reasons why a government would need more foreign exchange might be that its nationals were building up their foreign balances, or increasing their foreign investments. That, however, is a quite different matter than the government or Central Bank building up its foreign balances. The Fund might wish to supply the foreign exchange when the demand arises from an outflow of private funds. Whether or not it would wish to do so depends on a number of factors, including the cause of the outflow, the rate of outflow, the countries involved, the reserve position of the capital losing country, and the rapidity with which the mechanism of adjustment in the balance of payments is operating. Each episode would have to be considered on its own merits. It is, therefore, important that when there is present in the balance of payments of the country in question substantial outflow of capital which may be contributing to the disequilibrium the Fund have the authority to provide the exchange or not, as it sees fit. It would have this authority in any case, as indicated below, if the country in question had already obtained its maximum quota of foreign exchange from the Fund but the Fund should also have the privilege of not responding to demand for exchange, even before the quota was reached, where capital movements are involved.

What this matter boils down to is that the Fund should have the authority to determine whether the transactions causing a balance to turn unfavorable include transactions which the Fund would judge "illegitimate" under the circumstances. There are times when some types of capital outflow for some countries would be considered "legitimate," whereas the same type for other countries or even for the same country under different circumstances would be regarded as "illegitimate." There might also be instances in which all types of capital outflows for a given country might be considered "illegitimate," whereas for another country, all types might be considered "legitimate." No generalization can be made without all the circumstances being given. It is necessary only that the Fund have authority to make the decision on this matter and, as explained later, that the Fund have the authority to obtain the kind of information that would enable it to make an intelligent decision.

To aid in the settlement of international balance is the legitimate use of the Fund and this use is in no way interfered with by the above restriction. Better information on foreign balances and volume of exchange transactions than is now available in most countries will be necessary before it will be possible for the Fund to operate wisely under this restriction, but the development of such statistical data should not be difficult, especially since exchange controls in most countries are prevalent.

The restriction that the foreign exchange should be needed to meet adverse balances is not enough, however, to protect the strong assets of the Fund. If that were the only restriction imposed, a country could continue for a long time to permit an unfavorable balance of payments without calling forth the usual restraints. Without additional restrictions the Fund would in effect be placing the entire gold and foreign exchange assets at the disposal of any member country. The purpose of the Fund could not be to supply an unlimited amount of foreign exchange to any country which might not wish to adopt the proper measures to correct a prolonged disequilibrium in its transactions with foreign countries.

The sum in the Fund of the currency of the country making the purchase shall be, after adding the sum proposed to be sold to the Fund, not more than 100 percent of the total sum (currency, gold and notes) originally contributed to the Fund.

A quantitative limit is therefore also necessary on the amount of foreign exchange a country could purchase from the Fund, without special action.

What limit it were best to set is difficult to decide. It should be large enough to take care of fluctuations in the country's balance of payments that occur within a year or two, but should not be so large as to make it unlikely that the currency sold to the Fund would be repurchased by the country in question within a reasonable time. It is suggested that a country should be able to purchase with its currency any other country's currency so long as the Fund's holdings of the purchasing country is not more than 100 percent of that country's original total contribution to the Fund. Since one-fourth of the original contribution was in form of gold (plus 1/4 in local currency and 1/2 in notes or bonds) the 100 percent increase in the holdings of the Fund actually represents an increase of 300 percent of the local currency subscribed. In other words, a country subscribing $100 million, consisting of $25 million gold, $25 million local currency, and $50 million obligations would be able to buy with local currency as much as $75 million of any currency needed. Since $25 million of gold had been subscribed, the net immediate possible gain to the country needing foreign exchange would be $50 million of foreign exchange. That may seem a small sum and doubtless is for some countries. However, it should be noted the limit is not a rigid nor final one. It is supplemented by an important qualification, to be described in a moment.

How the assistance by the Fund would operate may be more easily understood by following through the steps of a transaction using a simplified illustration:

The Government (or fiscal agent) of Country A finds that the demand by its nationals for foreign exchange, arising out of trade and service transactions, is increasing relative to the supply, to the point where it must (a) give up more gold than it feels desirable, or (b) impose restrictions on imports—either through exchange controls or import controls, or (c) permit its currency to depreciate. In that situation, being a member of the Fund, it turns to the Fund for the assistance it is entitled to receive.

It purchases from the Fund as much of the types of currencies it needs, paying for it with its own currency. This it can do as its right so long as the sum of its currency which the Fund possesses is not in excess of 100 percent of Country A's original total contribution.

Sooner or later other countries will turn to the Fund to buy currency of Country A, and Country A will then again be able to buy other currencies from the Fund if necessary. It might happen that a long time would elapse before Country A's balance of payments would turn favorable (i.e. before Country A's inpayments exceeded her outpayments so that some stabilization fund or central bank would be confronted with the same choice vis-à-vis Country A that Country A had been earlier). So long as Country A had not used up its maximum allowance permitted without special decision by the Fund, the duration of the period during which Country A would not be decreasing the Fund's holdings of her currency would not matter very much.

If the balance of payments position among all the member countries did not stray from equilibrium by large amounts (relative to their foreign exchange assets) or for long periods, then the Fund would serve as a sort of reserve pillow absorbing the shock of pressures on exchange rates, thus safeguarding trade from unnecessary restrictions and exchange from unnecessary fluctuations. But it would be unwarranted to expect all the balance of payments situations to return quickly to equilibrium. For some countries it would frequently happen, and for almost all countries it would sometimes happen that an adverse balance of payment situation would persist. There are a number of reasons for this, but it would take more space to explain them than is justified in this report. Suffice to say that it would be wholly to be expected that some member countries would frequently find they have sold so much of their currency to the Fund that the Fund held the maximum permitted by usual majority procedures. When that point will have been reached by any country it will have already obtained substantial assistance.

Let it be assumed, for example, that Country A had originally contributed $100 million to the Fund, and due to the development of an adverse balance it has sold to the Fund $75 million in addition to the $25 million originally subscribed. When that point is reached Country A will have received what is virtually a costless "loan" of $50 million of other countries' currencies. It really is not a loan since Country A has given its own currency in exchange, yet Country A has been able to buy $75 million of foreign exchange with its own currency, whereas without access to the Fund it would have had to use gold or other foreign exchange resources. Since Country A has subscribed $25 million in gold to the Fund which it otherwise could have used to purchase foreign exchange the gain it is able to make through its membership in the Fund is the use of an additional $50 million. That, however, need be only the beginning.

There is a provision which permits the Fund to increase its purchase of Country A's currency after the above-described maximum is reached, as follows:

A country can exceed the limit imposed by the regulation provided it can obtain approval of four-fifths of the member votes.

This approval should be given only if four-fifths of the member votes were of the opinion that (a) the anticipated balance of payments prospects of the country in question were such as to warrant the expectation that the "excess" could be disposed of within a "reasonable" time, or (b) if the country in question had gold holdings which together with the gold it expected to accumulate within a reasonable time was adequate to replace the excess, and (c) if the country in question agreed to adopt and carry out measures designed to correct the disequilibrium measures which the Fund either approved or suggested, and (d) some time limit be imposed on the country during which the excess shall be repurchased—a time limit that shall be long enough to permit the country to adjust its international accounts without too great a strain.

This provision gives the desired flexibility. No country need suffer from lack of foreign exchange necessary to meet temporary drains. It need not even suffer from shortage of foreign exchange during a prolonged period of disequilibrium provided the Fund was satisfied proper steps were being taken to restore equilibrium.

Admittedly the operation of that flexible provision would call for technical knowledge, careful examination and good judgment by the Fund's staff. It is hoped that the technical staff which the Fund would gradually develop would be the most competent available in that special field. It would need to be because the problems it will have to deal with are difficult and because the success of the Fund in reducing fluctuations in foreign trade and in preventing monetary disturbances will depend largely upon the wisdom of the technical staff's advice. The Fund would doubtless be free from political pressure from any one country in its decisions, and should be able to make recommendations more apt to be in the long-run interest of the country concerned, than would likely be the case where decisions are dominated by short-run considerations or by domestic political considerations.

To what extent the Fund will be called upon to purchase and accumulate local currencies cannot be forecast. It depends on a number of changing factors, such as: how many countries will participate in the Fund, and how much each will invest; how rapidly foreign exchange controls will be eliminated; how much capital will be available for foreign investment, and finally, the pattern of world trade which will emerge shortly after peace is resumed.

Much also will depend on the extent to which some of the countries have foreign balances to which they will prefer to resort when experiencing adverse balances. That will mean that the Fund will not be able to convert some of the currencies which it had acquired as rapidly as would seem to be called for by the then-prevailing pattern of trade. Thus, for example, the Fund may accept sterling from England because England has turned to the Fund to meet an adverse balance of payments. Other countries, however, later developing adverse balances with England might not turn to the Fund for sterling. They might utilize sterling balances which they already have, or dip into ample gold holdings. The Fund would in that case be unable to diminish its holdings of sterling and therefore England would not be able to sell the Fund more sterling later if necessary except by action under the flexible provision.

The fact that the countries which will participate to the largest extent in the Fund are likely to be those least in need of resorting to the Fund for assistance of the character indicated above, would make it possible for the Fund to help most where it would be most needed. Only experience can show how far the Fund could go in eliminating fluctuations in exchange rates and in making the imposition of exchange and trade controls unnecessary. It is certain that the Fund cannot perform miracles, nor solve all problems involved in the maintenance of equilibrium in international accounts. The Fund cannot and should not make it possible for countries to ignore the cardinal principle of international economic relations, namely, that a country must in the long run buy only as much goods and services as it sells. An important exception, of course, is a country which has a balance due it on current borrowing, but sooner or later even that country will have to sell more than it buys in order to pay interest and principal on its borrowings. To be sure, the country which has foreign exchange resources, in the form of gold or income from foreign investments, can continue to buy more than it sells so long as those resources last, but for most countries these resources are not present in abundance, and hence for most countries the Fund can operate to make their path much smoother provided the countries themselves approach their own balance of payments problem intelligently.

Gold producing countries would not be immune from needing help from the Fund. It is true that such countries usually have an "unfavorable" balance of payments in the sense that they need constant exports of gold to help pay for the exchange they need. But such countries may and frequently do need more foreign exchange than they can buy with current gold production. At such times they can be helped by the Fund just as can countries which do not produce gold.

Even if countries ignore the basic limitations set upon any country's ability to buy more than it sells, the Fund can exercise considerable influence in helping them to correct this situation in time, and in ways which will create the smallest amount of destruction to world trade and least disturbance to their own economy.

It may be that experience will demonstrate that the limitations set upon the Fund's authority to agree to purchase currencies offered it are too strict. It may be that the commercial policies pursued by numerous countries, including more liberal tariff policies, will reduce the length of time in which countries are apt to experience adverse balance of payments and also the magnitudes of the disequilibrium. If so, the Fund can undertake much greater obligations. In any case the Fund is well protected against loss.

It should be remembered that the Fund in its operations is not undertaking the same risk of loss that would be involved in a usual extension of credit. The Fund gets foreign exchange in return for the currency it gives up, and each member government is required to make good any exchange loss suffered by the Fund through depreciation of its currency. Thus, the Fund not only has the foreign exchange which is always worth something, but it also has the obligation of the government to make good any exchange loss that might result. More than that, each government has invested with the Fund gold, currency, and its obligations, which the Fund would, in effect, have as collateral against potential exchange losses.

The Fund would receive additional protection against loss from the fact that a member government not meeting its obligations to the Fund could be dropped. Without knowing how many members will participate or how influential the Fund will become, we cannot say how serious a punishment being dropped from the Fund would be, but it is not unlikely that it would be serious enough to induce any country to make good its obligations to the Fund, difficult though that might prove to be.

Because the Fund will be undertaking so little risk, it can go further in the assistance it gives to foreign countries than would be the case were the risk of loss great. Should the Fund find itself pressed for certain kinds of currencies, it has of course both assets and borrowing power which can, if necessary, be used to purchase the desired currencies.

The power of the Fund to deal in the bonds of participating governments is an important one. It would, for example, make it possible for the Fund to come to the aid of any country which is being subjected to pressure on its exchange arising out of some types of capital flights. The Fund could, of course, buy the currency of the country, but the circumstances might, under certain conditions, be better handled by buying bonds and it might even help countries which for one reason or another do not have or cannot exercise adequate open-market powers and whose money market has become unduly tight because of a capital flight.

Unfreezing of blocked funds.

Special powers are called for to deal with the problem created by the growing magnitude of blocked balances. The countries in which large totals of balances are blocked are the United States and England (Germany is, of course, excluded) whereas the countries to whom those balances belong include almost the rest of the world.

The balances blocked in the United States present no monetary problem. They were not blocked because of any scarcity of gold or foreign exchange assets and their unblocking will not leave the United States short of gold or foreign exchange poor. There will doubtless be many cases in which for political or legal reasons, unfreezing will be delayed, but the cause of the delay will not be any scarcity of gold which may safely leave the country. There are more than two billion of earmarked gold, three billion of deposits, and possibly several hundred million of short-term investments, the withdrawal of which has been placed under some restrictions. A rapid withdrawal of any part of it, or all of it, can be handled with the utmost ease by the United States because of its large gold reserves. At most, it may prove necessary to lower reserve requirements to prevent a tightening of the credit situation here—should the outflow be great enough. With the cessation of war the release of dollar funds (equivalent to gold) capable of purchasing goods anywhere will prove a very important factor in stimulating trade and aiding reconstructions. The trouble, if any, is apt to be that nationals and governments of foreign countries will not elect to withdraw their funds from the United States rapidly enough.

The situation with respect to blocked balances in England is quite different. The gold and foreign exchange reserves which England will have at the close of the war are certain to be far too small relative to the sterling balances blocked there to permit England to remove restrictions on the withdrawal of funds by foreign owners. England may end the war with more than 5 billion dollars of deposits belonging to residents of other countries, while her liquid foreign exchange resources are likely to be much less than that. Moreover, England will need whatever gold she will be able to accumulate, and indeed should have more foreign exchange available than she is likely to have, in order to operate properly even were the total of foreign balances in England much smaller. Most of these balances belong to the Dominions who would wish to keep substantial sums in England in any case—unless there was imminent danger of sterling depreciation. Against some of the remainder there are offsetting blocked currencies. Nonetheless, the drain on British foreign liquid exchange reserves could easily be greater than England could safely permit.

The unblocking of these sterling funds is highly to be desired. Probably, no single action would do more to stimulate world trade, prevent pressure on numerous exchanges, and reduce the probability of widespread depreciation of currencies. The restoration of confidence in the soundness of British currency, the assurance that international monetary problems are to be intelligently handled, and renewed hope that currency stability will be achieved after the war that would follow a successful unfreezing of sterling, would alone justify every effort to solve through international action the problem of blocked balances in Britain.

The Fund would seem to be the appropriate agency to use for the solution of that problem. The method that could be employed to accomplish this is a bit complicated to describe and may seem at first reading difficult to follow but the importance of the subject warrants the attempt.

To accomplish a maximum of results with a minimum of risks the Fund should be given the power to purchase sterling, or any other currency offered to it, from any country other than the country whose currency is being purchased, provided:

a. The government selling its foreign balances (blocked in another country) to the Fund under this provision guarantees to repurchase 40 percent of the currency from the Fund at the price paid. The repurchase to begin after 3 years and to be made at the rate of not less than 2 percent a year of the amount acquired by the Fund under this authority.

b. The country whose local currency belonging to residents of another country is being offered for sale to the Fund agrees first to transfer title to the balances from the foreign nationals to the Fund, and to begin 3 years after sale to repurchase from the Fund 40 percent of the sterling acquired under this provision at a rate of not less than 2 percent a year, at the purchase price.

c. Not more than 20 percent of the currency offered should be paid for by the Fund with gold, half of which should be exempt from the condition imposed in paragraph (d) below.

d. The particular currency paid over by the Fund in exchange for the currency offered should be either local currency or currency needed by the country to meet an adverse balance of payments, with the exception of the 10 percent of gold. Thus, for example, if Canada wishes to sell to the Fund some of its blocked sterling balances in exchange for United States dollars, Canada would either have to accept Canadian dollars or the Fund would have to be assured that Canada needs the United States dollars to make payments to the United States (for trade, services, interest payments, or even investments) and not to make possible an increase in Canada's gold holdings or an increase in her United States dollar exchange. In other words, if Canada wished to use the sterling accumulated by herself, or her nationals, to convert into funds to be spent in United States, or in Mexico or in Netherlands, the Fund could make that possible without, on the one hand, putting any strain on England and, on the other hand, without denuding the Fund of its gold assets. Canada would be able, according to the above provision, to add to her gold holdings by 10 percent of the blocked balances she sold to the Fund.

e. If the Fund's stocks of sterling or other currencies should decline the Fund can offer to reduce the rate of repurchase required of both governments as specified above, but should it do so, the countries involved must be relieved by the same percentage, and shall be deemed to have repurchased the amount by which they are so released.

A service charge of possibly 1 percent would be imposed by the Fund on countries involved.

Perhaps the operation would be more easily understood if the specific steps were outlined which a country would have to go through under the plan suggested to realize on its blocked funds.

For convenience of illustration, let us take a specific case. Let us assume that the Chinese Government has £50 million blocked in England and wishes to utilize £10 million of it in the ensuing quarter. The steps would be as follows:

1. China makes application to the Fund. The Fund after investigation is satisfied that the use of at least 90 percent of the £10 million is not to accumulate gold or foreign exchange. (China can if it wishes add 10 percent of the £10 million of gold to her holdings.)
2. The £10 million is transferred by the British banks from the Chinese Government to the Fund. The Chinese Government pays 1 percent (in yuan) to the Fund and the British pay 1 percent (in sterling) as a "service" charge.
3. The Fund gives to China
   a. the equivalent of £1 million in gold (if China wishes it), and
   b. the equivalent of £9 million in one or more currencies needed and requested by China—say, $12 million in United States dollars and 120 million Mexican pesos. If the Fund doesn't have enough Mexican pesos, it purchases what it needs.
4. After three years from the date of the transaction:
   a. China begins to repurchase from the Fund each year £200,000 (2 percent of 40 percent of £10 million) of British sterling, at the same rates of exchange she received, paying for the sterling either in yuan or other currencies she received, depending upon the wishes of the Fund.
   b. England begins to repurchase the same amount of sterling each year, paying for the sterling either gold or "New International Units".
   c. China is free to do what she likes with her repurchased sterling, England having agreed in the first place that there would be no restrictions on its withdrawal.
5. Not later than 23 years after the transaction the situation would be as follows:
   a. China would have utilized the £10 million, while her balance of payments would be burdened not at all for 3 years and by not more than 1.2 percent of the £10 million a year after three years.
   b. England would have been able to unfreeze China's balances, while imposing no burden on her (England's) foreign exchange resources for the first three years, and from then on 1.6 percent to 3.2 percent a year (2 percent of from 40 to 80 percent), depending upon what China elects to do with her repurchased 2 percent.
   c. The Fund will have first exchanged some of her gold assets for £1 million, or possibly more if she had to purchase currencies with gold to satisfy China's demands, and will have exchanged the remainder of the £10 million of various currencies for sterling.

      Then the Fund would get back each year gold from England to a sum not less than 2 percent of £4 million until the Fund will have received £4 million in gold. The Fund would also get £4 million of certain currencies from China, leaving the Fund with 2 million pounds sterling.

      The Fund will also have earned 2 percent (1 percent in yuan and 1 percent in sterling) in the transactions, and some interest on her investment of sterling balances in British Government securities.

At the end of 23 years—or sooner if England permits—the Fund could sell the remaining £2 million of sterling and the transaction would be complete.

The above is the transaction under most unfavorable conditions. A more likely outcome is that either or both China and England could purchase back the sterling from the Fund a great deal sooner than 23 years. Nonetheless, a long period is permitted to assure an easy adjustment for both England and China in the event the situation would not be favorable to a rapid adjustment.

The illustration has been that of Government-owned funds. If, as is equally likely, the British sterling balances were owned by nationals of China instead of the Government of China, the general process would be the same but some details would differ.

First, the Chinese nationals would have to indicate to their Government that they wished their blocked balances released. It might be found desirable to give private persons only local currencies in exchange for blocked foreign balances. How important this restriction would be is uncertain since they could later buy any currency desired. The Chinese Government would then make the arrangements with the Fund, after which the Chinese Government would transfer to its nationals the money which the Fund puts at China's disposal in exchange for their sterling balances. Title to the sterling balances would be transferred to the Fund.

So long as China is willing to take yuan for the blocked sterling, the Fund would supply it, if necessary buying or borrowing yuan for the purpose. If, however, China's Treasury asks for United States dollars or Brazilian milreis, the Fund might wish to satisfy itself first that China needed those currencies for "legitimate" purposes.

The Treasury of China would be permitting its nationals to avoid the risk of exchange that holders of blocked sterling would otherwise have to bear. Forty percent of that risk would be borne by the Treasury of China since it would be committed to repurchase 40 percent of the sterling unblocked to it; forty percent would be borne by the British Treasury for a similar reason. The Fund would accept the other 20 percent of the exchange risk.

The Treasury of China might impose a two or three percent charge on its nationals for the transaction. That would help cover the service charge imposed by the Fund, and leave a small profit after expense of administration.

Consideration might be given to the possibility that a small annual charge could be imposed by the Fund on the blocked balances it held. In the above illustration, for example, a charge of 1 percent a year could be placed on both China and England on the blocked sterling not yet repurchased.

Arrangements for the transaction might take some time, but for the individual holder of the blocked balance the transaction would be simple. After the initial arrangements had been completed, the transactions between the Fund and the two Governments involved would assume an almost routine character. Careful watching of the balance of payments of the various countries concerned in the transactions would be necessary continuously. That task, however, would be one of the important current responsibilities of the Fund's technical staff at all times and with all countries. The condition and movements of the international accounts of the member countries would be to the Fund's research staff, what the thermometer, stethoscope, x-ray, and microscope, etc., are to the diagnostician. Without a carefully drawn up and compiled quarterly balance of payments account of member countries the technical staff of the Fund would be greatly handicapped in their recommendation of decisions and policies. With adequate data in their hands they would be in a position to know and understand what was going on in matters pertinent to the work of the Fund.

How much could the Fund be expected to do with blocked balances? The sum of blocked balances which the Fund would be called upon to purchase might be greater than the Fund felt it could afford to take. If, for example, it were asked to absorb two billion dollars of blocked balances it might well hesitate if such assets were not to be liquid. It might be three years before they could sell any of it, and even then they might not be able to sell it at a rate faster than 4 percent a year. The Fund could, it is true, invest the assets in interest-bearing Government obligations (of the country in which the currency is blocked), but they could not convert those into gold or other currencies without either risking a loss on the transaction or adding to the possible drain of gold from the country whose obligations they were selling.

If the Fund attempted to sell a substantial amount of (say) British Government obligations payable in sterling to residents of United States, the price the Fund would get might be substantially less than what the Fund paid for the bonds.

Moreover, if the Fund invested the blocked sterling in British Government bonds, and then sold them in New York, and later the Americans sold the bonds in London getting sterling which would not be blocked, the end result would be that England would be subjected to the drain on her foreign exchange resources which she wished in the first place to avoid. It seems, therefore, that if the Fund is to be permitted to invest its sterling in British Government obligations, it should not be permitted to sell them except as England repurchased them according to the schedule, or unless the British Government approved the sale.

Yet the Fund would like to take over as much of the blocked balances as possible, but, on the other hand, could not tie up too much of her liquid resources in frozen currencies. A way out of the dilemma might be to permit the Fund to borrow in New York (or anywhere else except England) using as collateral the British Government bonds. With that possibility for converting a frozen asset into a liquid resource the Fund could afford to take more blocked balances. It might even be feasible to arrange that the bonds be special ones payable in either gold or sterling (at the holder's will), in order to increase their collateral value. Since 40 percent of the blocked sterling the Fund acquires would have to be repurchased with gold anyway, this latter possibility might be acceptable to the Government concerned.

The end result of the exercise of this authority should be:

1. Private holders of blocked sterling balances should be able to convert them at once into their local currencies by selling them to their Government. With that currency nationals, as distinct from the Government, could purchase any currency they wished.
2. Their Government would be in possession of sterling which at small risk of exchange on 40 percent of its purchases it could sell to the Fund for any currency it wished.
3. England could at once remove restrictions on the withdrawal of foreign-owned sterling balances without fearing any serious drain on her gold or other foreign exchange assets. She would have to purchase back only 40 percent of the funds withdrawn under this authority at the rate of 2 percent a year, beginning after three years.

Two gains would quickly emerge: one, the demand for withdrawal would be greatly lessened by the fact that foreign holders would have no reason to hurry their withdrawal, and two, the post-war pressure against sterling would be dissipated and hence the sterling rate could be more easily maintained.

If adjustment of the price of sterling in terms of other currencies were later justified by a basic unbalance, then only 40 percent of the resultant exchange loss would be borne by England, and not more than 40 percent by the country having blocked balances, and 20 percent by the Fund.

4. Finally, foreign purchasing power would be released to be spent wherever desired, and one of the potent obstacles to a return to fair trade practices removed.

This provision on blocked balances is not proposed as a method of freeing balances which might accumulate after the war. Unless the funds to which this particular power are to apply is clearly delimited, the provision would overlap and largely nullify other provisions contained in the proposal specifically designed to meet current and developing situations in a country's balance of payments. The provision described in the previous several pages is not intended to make it possible for owners of foreign balances—whatever the source of these balances may be—to withdraw those balances at will at the expense of the Fund's assets. It is hoped that the Fund will make it possible for all countries to remove restrictions on exchange transactions, but this particular provision should be used as the vehicle to free only the blocked balances in existence at the date the country joins the Fund. It is for the purpose of clearing up the present bad situation with respect to blocked currencies that this provision is included.

In the event a similar situation develops in the future, authority is granted to the Fund provided four-fifths of the member votes approve to initiate a similar program which would apply to the then-existing balances.

To provide the data necessary for the operation of this provision each member country should be required to file with the Fund a record of the balances in its country owned by residents of foreign countries, and also a record of the balances of its nationals held abroad. These balances should be broken down in the significant categories as required by the Fund. A quarterly report should be filed keeping the information up to date.

The fact that each of the parties concerned, i.e. the country in which the balances are blocked, the country whose nationals own the balances, and the Fund—will be undertaking an exchange risk should help prevent undesirable practices or misapplication of this provision.

In evaluating the effectiveness of this provision to liberate blocked balances, it must be borne in mind that the mere existence of this power will remove much of the eagerness to withdraw funds in the near future. That reaction would in turn make it easier for England (and other countries) to remove exchange restrictions. Even though the blocked balances in various countries outside of the United States were as high as the equivalent of 6 billion dollars, only a portion of this amount would be involved unless there were strong fears of depreciation of sterling—a development the Fund could do much to prevent. The greater the assurance that foreign exchange rates will be stable, and the knowledge that large portions of the funds will be unblocked periodically would encourage holders of these balances to diminish their withdrawal requests.

However, since the amount that the Fund might be called upon to absorb might be larger than it wished to handle at the beginning, the Fund is given the authority to set a maximum percentage of blocked balances that could be handled through this provision in any given period. It would be easy enough to adjust that percentage upward if circumstances indicated it could be safely done.

The fixing of rates.

The Fund would fix the rates at which it would exchange a member's currency for another, and the rates at which it would buy and sell gold in exchange for local currency.

The guiding principle in the fixing of such rates should be stability in exchange relationships. To assure the maximum stability in rates, it is suggested that alterations in rates set by the Fund beyond the range of narrow fluctuations applying to all rates be permitted only with the consent of four-fifths of the member votes. If a country does not wish to accept or pay the rate fixed by the Fund, it can, of course, attempt to complete its transactions through other channels. Nonetheless the authority to set the rates of exchange at which the Fund is willing to operate can be an important and in some cases a decisive influence on the rate at which transactions are made outside of the Fund.

The service charge for exchange transactions should be no larger than necessary to cover the direct costs of the operations.

Borrowing from the Fund.

Any member country can borrow its local currency from the Fund for one year or less up to 75 percent of the currency of that country held by the Fund, provided such loan is approved by three-fourths of the member votes.

A country borrowing such funds shall pay to the Fund an interest rate of 1 percent a year. Revenue from such loans shall constitute a reserve for the Fund which can be drawn upon to meet expenses or losses of the Fund.

The object of the provision permitting any member country to borrow local currency from the Fund for one year or less up to 75 percent of the currency of that country held by the Fund, provided such loan is approved by three-fourths of the member votes, is to make it possible for a member country to reduce the burden of participation on its budget. Some of the countries may at times be confronted with deficits, and the investment that they would have in the Fund should be a source to which they could turn in time of need to borrow at very low rates of interest. It may well prove to be the case that every country operating at a deficit would prefer to borrow up to the maximum of its local currency, at 1 percent, rather than go into the market and possibly pay 2 or more percent. Inasmuch as a fund could, if necessary, always obtain such local currency by rediscounting the paper in that market, there would seem to be no reason why the Fund should object to such practice on the part of those countries wishing to avail themselves of the low rate of interest. Also, from the Fund's point of view, it would be desirable to permit such loans since it would prove a source of revenue with which to meet expenses or losses of the Fund.

Borrowing by the Fund.

It is suggested that the Fund should have authority to borrow at such rates as the Fund may recommend, the currency of any country, provided four-fifths of the member votes approve the terms, amount and conditions of such borrowing.

This provision gives the Fund power to obtain any currency it may feel it will need only for a short time. It also makes it possible for the Fund to expand its resources to meet short-term special demands.

Currency sold to a government in default.

No sale of any currency from the Fund should be made to a member without approval of four-fifths of the member votes when the sale of such currency so sold is to make possible adjustment of a government foreign debt which had been defaulted. This provision is probably necessary in order to prevent utilizing the Fund for the purpose of servicing a foreign debt. The resources of the Fund should be used for such purpose only when most of the Board feels that the borrowing for debt adjustment is temporary, or when they are satisfied that basic adjustments are being undertaken.

Accept deposits, act as clearing house for international movements of funds, balances, checks, etc.

The power to accept deposits and perform clearing functions would enable the Fund to operate more efficiently in its foreign exchange operations. It is not intended that the Fund shall perform banking functions other than those supplementary to the task of foreign exchange stabilization.

Deal only with (a) the Treasuries of the participating countries, or with the official stabilization funds of those countries, and (b) with the bank designated by the participating government as its fiscal agent, and (c) with international banks and international corporations owned by at least five governments.

The Fund is envisaged as an intergovernmental agency which should interfere as little as possible with the operations of private banks, brokers and dealers. It is only when the supply-demand relationship of exchange arising out of usual transactions through the customary channels are causing pressure in an undesired direction, that the Fund begins to operate.

The Fund will also wish to deal with any intergovernmental financial institutions such as the proposed Inter-American Bank. The Fund shall have the authority to invest any currency it holds in "short-term" securities—commercial or government—of the country of that currency provided a four-fifths vote of the member votes shall approve and provided further that the approving votes shall include those of the country in which the investment is to be made.

The Fund shall also have authority to sell the obligation it holds of the member countries provided four-fifths of the member votes approve, and provided the representative of the country in which the securities are to be sold approves.

Value of total holdings should remain unchanged.

No change in the gold value of any currency of the participating countries shall be permitted to alter the gold value of the total currency holdings of the Fund. Through the day-to-day operations of the Fund, the proportion of various local currencies held by the Fund will constantly change, but the book value of the total assets would remain the same in terms of the unit of account (presuming the small service charges and interest revenue would cover operating expenses). The unit of account used should either be gold or a new international unit defined in terms of gold. If the currency of any of the participating countries should depreciate, that country must deliver to the Fund an amount of its local currency equal to the decrease in the value of that currency held by the Fund. Likewise, if the currency of a particular country should increase, the Fund must deliver to that country an amount (in the currency of that country) equal to the resultant increase in the gold value of the Fund's holdings.

An exception to the above would be the blocked balances purchased by the Fund under provision described earlier. Those currencies could be kept in a separate account until repurchased or sold. The only portion upon which there might be a loss is in the 20 percent portion, the exchange risk on which is borne by the Fund. The sole justification for placing that exchange risk on the Fund is the desire to spread some of the risk of sterling accumulations resulting from the war on all nations benefiting by the successful outcome. If that is not considered adequate justification, the Fund can be relieved of any risk.

The only serious bookkeeping loss that could be experienced would be in the event the unit of account—either a new international unit fixed in terms of gold or the dollar having a fixed gold content—were to appreciate in terms of all or most of the currencies. That is equivalent to saying that all other currencies depreciated in terms of the unit of account. There is no way to avoid that possibility unless the unit of account were defined in terms of an index of other currencies—a complicated device and of doubtful utility.

A country failing to contribute to the Fund sums due the Fund shall be dropped as a member, provided a majority of the member votes so decide. Any member dropped shall have returned to it an amount (in its own currency) equal to its contribution minus any sum due by that country to the Fund.

III. Eligibility for Membership

The conditions selected to be fulfilled before any country can be eligible for membership in the Fund constitute an important part of the plan. It will also prove to be one of the most disputed parts. Serious differences of opinion as to the wisdom of including many of the conditions listed are certain to exist. It will be said of some of them that they embrace far too wide an area of economic policy. Others on the list will be opposed on the grounds that they involve policy decisions which cannot be shared by or delegated to any combination of nations. And against some of the conditions listed opposition will arise because there will be differing views as to the economic soundness of some of the requirements, and of the political feasibility of others. Finally, some of the requirements for eligibility listed may be very difficult for many countries to accept because acceptance would involve abandonment, or rather suspension, during period of membership, of certain legislative powers. Nonetheless, the list is submitted because the chief purpose of this memorandum is to suggest possibilities and stimulate discussion.

It is vital to the success of any international stabilization fund designed to play a really useful role that there be a suspension of certain economic elements of national sovereignty in favor of international collaboration. It is well to recognize at the outset that unless there is willingness to keep dormant, for a trial period at least, certain rights to unilateral economic action which directly affect other countries, there is no hope that any international instrument can be devised to help bring about the kind of collaboration among nations essential to a prosperous and peaceful world. If no government is prepared to sacrifice for the sake of a larger though possibly a less obvious good what it regards as an advantage when that advantage is obtained at the expense of some friendly power, then the world will revert to the barbaric international economic relationships of the 'twenties and 'thirties.

The strength of the position of those who call for the temporary transfer to an international body of certain sovereign economic powers rests in the conviction that the long-run interests of most countries are best served when no country seeks to gain at the expense of another. It is true that rich and powerful countries can for long periods safely and easily ignore the interests of poorer or weaker neighbors or competitors, but by doing so they will imperil the future and reduce the potentiality of their own level of prosperity. The lesson that must be learned is that prosperous neighbors are the best neighbors; that a higher standard of living in one country begets higher standards in others, and that a high level of trade and business is most easily attained when generously and widely shared.

It is with these thoughts in mind that the following list of conditions for eligibility should be examined.

Any member of the United or Associated Nations is eligible for membership in the Fund provided it agrees:

To abandon, not later than one year after joining the Fund, all restrictions and controls over foreign exchange transactions with member countries, except with the approval of the Fund.

It is important that participating countries be motivated by common objectives in conceiving their foreign exchange policies and desirous of adopting basically harmonious procedures in implementing such policies. Some allowance will, of course, have to be made for reasonable differences because of dissimilarities in the economies of various countries, and early in the Fund's existence there would need to be toleration of lack of uniformity in policy. In general, however, and as basic and long-run prerequisites to participation, it would seem necessary for each member country to subscribe to the general policies of permitting foreign exchange trading in an open, free and legal market, and to abandon, as rapidly as conditions permit, all restrictions or controls by which various classes of foreign exchange transactions have been prohibited or interfered with, other than from consummation in such a free market.

This requirement calls for careful examination. There has been too easy an acceptance of the view that an enlightened trade and monetary policy requires complete abandonment of controls over international economic transactions. There is a tendency to regard foreign exchange controls, or any interference with the free movement of funds and of goods as, ipso facto, bad. This view is both unrealistic and unsound. It ignores the fact that there are situations in which many countries frequently find themselves, and which all countries occasionally meet, that make inevitable the adoption of controls of one character or another. There are times when it is in the best economic interests of a country to impose restrictions on movements of capital, and on movements of goods. There are periods in a country's history when failure to impose exchange controls, or import or export controls, have led to serious economic and political disruption.

It probably would be fatal to the Fund if the conditions of participation in it were based upon the assumption that no restrictions upon exchange or upon trade were permissible.

It would be equally unfortunate, however, if it were to be assumed that restrictions on foreign exchange transactions, on the international movement of goods, and the use of multiple currency devices were desirable instruments to employ under all circumstances for safeguarding or controlling international economic relationships. It is as easy to exaggerate the need for such instruments and the benefits derived from the use thereof, as it is to exaggerate their adverse effects.

The theoretical bases for the belief still so widely held, that interference with trade and with capital and gold movements, etc., are harmful, are hangovers from a Nineteenth Century economic creed, which held that international economic adjustments, if left alone, would work themselves out toward an "equilibrium" with a minimum of harm to world trade and prosperity.

It is doubtful whether that belief was ever sound. Certainly few competent students of international economic affairs would hold that it applied to present conditions or to conditions likely to prevail during the post-war period. The forces of adjustment set into motion by changing trade balances, flows of gold or of purchasing power, changes in price levels and all the phenomena that the expert in the subject recognizes as instrumentalities in the so-called mechanism of adjustment of international balances of payment, rarely, if ever, work out quickly enough or effectively enough to be depended upon to achieve good results. In fact, it is doubtful if they ever were depended upon, unaided, to bring about the desired "equilibrium". In modern times, particularly, there has always been somewhere in the picture some measure of control over, some measure of interference with the movement of funds and goods in order to bring about certain desired ends.

The task before us is not to prohibit instruments of control but to develop those measures of control, those policies of administering such control, as will be the most effective in obtaining the objectives of world-wide sustained prosperity. To cast aside certain effective instrumentalities of control because they may be and have been abused, is just as foolish as it would be to rely solely on the self-interest motive of individuals as a means of solving our economic problems.

The requirement suggested above that there be accepted the general policy of foreign exchange trading in open, free and legal markets, and the abandonment as rapidly as conditions permit of restrictions on exchange controls, should be taken to mean that there shall be acceptance of the principle that controls and restrictions will be employed only when they are clearly justified by the economic circumstances, and only to the extent necessary to carry out a purpose contributing to general prosperity. The chief difficulty in the application of the principle will be agreement as to what is in the interests of general prosperity. The danger of conflicting policies lies not only in the difficulty of distinguishing between real and specious advantage, i.e. between the advantages of a special group as against the advantages of the whole—but much more in the difficulty of reconciling short-run interests with long-run interests. One of the purposes of this Fund is to provide for a more reasonable basis for such distinction, and to supply the means through which it should be possible to pursue long-run and broader interests, without too great a sacrifice of the narrower and short-run interests.

The second requirement or condition for participation should be the acceptance of the principle that no participating country will alter its exchange rate on currencies of other countries without the consent of the Fund.

This condition is very important. Its obvious purpose is to eliminate the possibility of competitive depreciation of currencies. It recognizes that there are occasions when it may be economically wise for a country to increase or decrease the value of its currency in terms of other currencies. When a country's balance of payments is in disequilibrium for causes that do not appear to be temporary, and if that disequilibrium uncorrected will deplete a country's foreign exchange reserve, then altering the value of that currency in terms of other currencies is one of the ways in which the disequilibrium could be corrected. Other ways of correcting disequilibrium in the balance of payments are the imposition of restrictions on imports and subsidy of exports, either directly through import and export controls, or through use of exchange controls or multiple currencies. Which method or methods are best suited to accomplish the objective depends on the cause of the disequilibrium, the circumstances, the country, and the time.

The circumstances under which it may be wise to alter an exchange rate in order to correct maladjustments of the balance of payments have long been a matter of controversy among monetary theorists. But there is general agreement that an alteration in the value of a currency in terms of gold (or in terms of important currencies) is a very serious business and one not to be undertaken lightly. The change in the value of a currency in terms of gold or other currencies means that a change has by that act been imposed on the other currencies. When, for example, the dollar changes in terms of sterling, obviously sterling changes in terms of the dollar. Because all countries are to a lesser or greater degree affected by the action of any one country with respect to the value of its currency, it is only reasonable to demand that such action should not be undertaken without careful—and, if possible, impartial—weighing of the consequences of the action on other countries.

The purpose of requiring approval by the Fund as a condition of alteration of currency is to assure joint consideration of the merits of the proposed action and thereby avoid unilateral action taken to obtain presumed competitive short-run advantages irrespective of the consequences of the impact of the step on other countries or even on the same country. The mere fact that membership would be forfeited if a country acted in so important a matter contrary to the wishes of the majority would make countries hesitate to undertake lightly a change in their currency. The very discussion of the problem by competent representatives of various countries should in itself be a potent influence to avoid unnecessary changes. It would, moreover, be an assurance that when a change is made it would not be a signal for numerous other countries to follow in their own real or presumed interest.

There will be difficulties surrounding the operation of this condition, the most important of which would be the necessity for secrecy when a country is contemplating a step such as altering the value of its currency in terms of other currencies. If a country believes that it should depreciate its currency relative to others, it could hardly throw that matter open for public discussion. By so doing it would stimulate speculative activities in the exchange market which might have the effect of precipitating the very action being considered. Some procedure would have to be devised to make possible deliberations without publicity. It might be that an Executive Committee could undertake to pass on such cases, or it might be possible to arrange that during such discussions no country will accept or permit movements of capital to and from a country considering the step.

Some objection to this requirement will doubtless be raised on the ground that such a provision means that other countries pass judgment on what is a domestic monetary matter. The necessity for obtaining approval of other countries on such a matter will be regarded in some quarters as a serious infringement of sovereignty. There is some measure of truth in this but hardly enough to constitute a decisive reason for not participating in the Fund. Alteration of a currency affects other countries as well as the country making the change. It is, therefore, only reasonable to demand that the other countries have some say in the decision. Furthermore, all members would be surrendering their "rights" to an equal extent. Unless nations are willing to sacrifice some of their power to take unilateral action in matters of international economic relations, there is very little hope of any significant international cooperation—let alone collaboration.

To avoid giving richer nations greater authority on such matters, by virtue of their larger number of votes, it may be desirable to give each participant only one vote when questions of altering currency rates are being voted upon. As a last resort, a country always has the choice of withdrawing from the Fund so that it can always preserve its sovereignty in monetary matters if it feels it is being prevented by the Fund from taking action deemed important to its own interest.

The principle worked only tolerably well in the Tripartite Accord during 1935, 1936 and 1937, and better machinery for more adequate discussion and greater willingness to recognize the legitimate interests of other countries, needs to be developed to achieve best results. In evaluating the need for collaboration on questions of foreign exchange rates, it is well to remember that unilateral action can easily be neutralized by similar action on the part of other countries. When a competitive advantage is sought it is essential if it is to be successful that other countries do not take similar action. Otherwise the advantage hoped for is lost. Where the chief objective sought is not a competitive trade advantage in the international market but modification of the domestic price structure or money market, the favorable effects cannot be wholly negated by action of other countries. Since, however, the chief reason for establishing the requirement is to avoid competitive depreciation of currencies, the fact that unilateral action can be easily neutralized constitutes an important argument for securing approval of the Fund before taking such action.

Each country agrees (a) not to accept or permit deposits or investments from any member country except with the permission of that country, and (b) to make available to the government of any member country at its request all property in form of deposits, investments, securities, of the nationals of member countries, under such terms and conditions as will not impose an unreasonable burden on the country of whom the request is made.

This is a far-reaching and important requirement. Its acceptance would go a long way toward solving one of the very troublesome problems in international economic relations, and would remove one of the most potent disturbing factors of monetary stability. Flights of capital, motivated either by prospect of speculative exchange gain, or desire to avoid inflation, or evade taxes or influence legislation, frequently take place especially during disturbed periods. Almost every country, at one time or another, exercises control over the inflow and outflow of investments, but without the cooperation of other countries such control is difficult, expensive, and subject to considerable evasion.

It would seem to be an important step in the direction of world stability if a member government could obtain the full cooperation of other member governments in the control of capital flows. For example, after the war a number of countries could request the United States not to permit increases in the deposits or holdings of their nationals, or to do so only with a license granted by the government making the request. Or, some countries greatly in need of capital might request the United States to supplement their efforts to attract capital back to the native country by providing information, or imposing special regulations or even special taxes, on certain types of holdings of the nationals of the foreign countries.

The search for speculative exchange gains or desire to evade the impact of new taxes or burdens of social legislation have been one of the chief causes of foreign exchange disturbances. Less hectic and less dramatic yet in the case of some countries during some stages of their development capable in the long run of even greater harm, is the steady drain of capital from a country that needs the capital but is unable for one reason or another to offer sufficient monetary return to keep its capital at home. The assumption that capital serves a country best by flowing to countries which offer most attractive terms is valid only under circumstances that are not always present.

A good case could be made for the thesis that a government should have the power to control the influx and efflux of capital, just as it has the authority to control the inflow and outflow of goods and of gold. In fact, virtually every participating government has already practiced these controls to some extent during this war. The consequence of cooperation in this matter among the member governments would give each government much greater measure of control in carrying out its monetary and tax policies. Such an increase in the effectiveness of control means, however, less freedom for owners of liquid capital. It would constitute another restriction on the property rights of the 5 or 10 percent of persons in foreign countries who have enough wealth or income to keep or invest some of it abroad, but a restriction that presumably would be exercised in the interests of the people—at least so far as the government is competent to judge that interest.

The inclusion of this provision does not mean that capital flows between foreign countries would disappear or even greatly subside; it means only that they would not be permitted to operate against what the government deemed to be the interests of any country.

A fourth condition might be that each country agrees not to enter upon any bilateral clearing arrangements except with non-member countries, and then only with the consent of the Fund, and to establish no geographically preferential exchange rates.

The justification for setting up this requirement for participation is to eliminate discriminatory practices in foreign trade which result in friction, unfair competition, retaliation, and sharp trade policies which serve to disrupt good economic and political relations. It means that for the sake of the larger good to be obtained countries agree to give up opportunities for making certain advantageous arrangements. If each country is to operate in accordance with its own immediate interest, irrespective of long-run effects and irrespective of the impact of its actions on other countries, a repetition of the pre-war chaotic conditions in trade will result and again threaten political and economic stability of other nations. The task which confronts the high officials of all nations is to make possible a high level of business activity and of foreign trade within the framework of reasonable and fair foreign trade practices. Just as individuals subscribe to a government of law to obtain maximum prosperity and effectiveness for the whole group, even though adherence to that law involves restrictions on individual behavior at numerous points, so must nations give up lesser advantages for greater good. The concept of sacrificing some immediate benefits for the sake of larger good is the foundation stone of peace and economic collaboration among nations, just as it is the keystone of peace and prosperity within a nation.

The operations of the two agencies discussed in this report should help considerably to remove the justification for trade practices adopted to protect or strengthen an exchange position.

There are times when gains could accrue from bilateral clearing arrangements without significant adverse effects on other countries, but in general the operation of the Fund should have the effect of making such clearing arrangements much less profitable as among members of the Fund. One of the specific objectives of the Fund is to make available for each member a supply of foreign exchange adequate to enable it to operate more freely and with a higher level of trade than would otherwise be the case. Nevertheless, in the interest of flexibility, and to take care of those situations in which circumstances may warrant a bilateral clearing arrangement, it should be possible for a country to enter upon such an arrangement provided it can obtain the Fund's approval. Discussions by the Fund of such proposals do not require the secrecy or the speed involved in consideration of alterations of exchange rate, and discussions of the advantages and disadvantages of the particular proposal should prove beneficial. An objective decision on the economic wisdom of such proposal is more likely to emerge from the discussion by the appropriate committee of the Fund than from the consideration by one or two countries alone where vested or political interests are likely to dominate the decision.

A fifth requisite for membership might be subscription to the principle that no monetary or banking or price measure or policy would be adopted, the effect of which, in the opinion of a majority of the member votes, would be to bring about sooner or later a serious disequilibrium in the balance of payments, if four-fifths of the member votes of the Fund submitted to the country in question their disapproval of the adoption of the measure.

This provision would prove to be more troublesome than any of the others and yet it would seem to be important to the successful functioning of the Stabilization Fund. Serious inflation or deflation in any one country would affect not only exchange rates and trade, but price levels in other countries as well. It is impossible for any country to take action of that character which does not have important effects on other countries with whom it competes or with whom it carries on trade. The decision as to whether a particular measure or policy contemplated would bring about a serious disequilibrium in the balance of payments would be a difficult one on which to get agreement. To estimate even very roughly the quantitative effects of any given measure on a country's balance of payments is a very difficult task at best. After sufficient agreement was reached on that point it would be even more difficult in many cases to get any measure of agreement as to whether the adoption of the measure in question was economically wise or not.

There are times when domestic consequences are sought which are more important to a country than the adverse effects that might follow in some directions from the accompanying disequilibrium in the balance of payments. There are other instances in which disequilibrium provides a necessary corrective, and frequently a country is confronted with only poor choices and disequilibrium is the least undesirable of them.

To assume that it would ever prove easy to get four-fifths of the member votes to take so drastic a step as to disapprove a measure proposed by a sovereign government deemed by it to be in its own interest, is to ignore the known complexities of the monetary problems, and the political realities of international relationships.

Notwithstanding the difficulties involved in exercise of a veto power by the Fund over monetary measures, there will be instances in which the case is clear enough and the consequences important enough to justify the exercise of that power. It is assumed that the Fund would not concern itself with minor measures. To help avoid the error of attempting to evaluate measures which are not important, the requirement provides that a majority of the members would have to be of the opinion that the results of any given measure are likely to be serious. It then requires four-fifths of the member votes to authorize official disapproval. It may well be that despite this degree of protection against arbitrary action or needless interference most countries would object to subjecting what they believe to be purely domestic affairs to international supervision. If compromise with this view is found feasible, it is hoped that it takes the form of requiring a larger majority—say 90 percent instead of 80 percent of the member votes, or, as a last resort, requiring that the disapproval of the Fund call forth the promise of the offending country to reexamine her position in the light of the Fund's report.

In any case, the discussion which would take place by an international committee of the character envisaged—men expert in their fields, international in their outlook, and scientific in their approach—could not help but prove very salutary. The educational process to which officials, administrative and legislative, in each country would be subjected in defending specific policies or measures before such a committee would in itself go a long way toward improving the quality of monetary, credit and banking policy. It probably would be necessary for the committee, certainly during the early years, to be very tolerant of policies pursued by participating countries. Gradually, however, there should develop a greater reluctance on the part of member countries to take measures which do not meet the approval of the majority of the members of the Fund. The success of the Fund in this field would depend in large measure upon the wisdom with which matters of this kind are examined and the degree of sympathetic understanding the Fund was capable of displaying.

The member countries agree (a) to embark within a year after joining upon a program of gradual reduction of existing trade barriers—import duties, import quotas, administrative devices—and further agree (b) not to adopt any increase in tariff schedules, or other devices having as their purposes higher obstacles to imports, without giving reasonable opportunity for the Fund to study the effects of the contemplated change on exchange rates and to register its opinion. In rendering an opinion the Fund will make recommendations to which member governments agree to give serious consideration.

It might contribute notably to conditions tending to promote exchange stability if participating countries, particularly those with large reserve of foreign exchange, were to agree to a gradual reduction of duties on imports. It might be possible to devise an acceptable formula for general and gradual tariff reduction to a level more in harmony than were tariff policies of the twentieth century with the objectives of reducing the causes for international friction and increasing the standard of living the world over. Those high tariff policies in the main reflect adherence to the traditional, crude, mercantilist fallacies. So widely held are those fallacies, so persistently clung to by persons who should know better, so potent are they in shaping many aspects of domestic and foreign policy, and so unfortunate in their effects on world peace and prosperity, that one is tempted to list "mercantilism" or its more expressive heir "protectionism" as "World Enemy No. 1," in the economic sphere.

Yet, though there is no doubt as to the evils of crude protectionist policies, caution must be exercised in attempting to translate a policy of lower tariff schedules into an actual program. There is danger of retarding progress by advocating a trade policy which ignores the sound basis for the existence of some import duties. There is too easy an assumption that as much reduction as possible in all duties is desirable; that any movement toward free trade is, ipso facto, a good thing for the world.

In the reaction against the crude protectionist fallacies that a country with high standards of living must adhere to a policy of high tariff schedules if it is to prevent widespread unemployment or deterioration of its high standard of living, there is an inclination to throw the baby out with the bath and assume that all duties are bad; that free trade, or rather tariff for revenue only, is the ideal toward which all enlightened nations should move as rapidly as possible.

The belief that reduction in all import duties increases trade and yields a higher standard of living for all countries under all circumstances and in all stages of their economic evolution assumes that countries are usually utilizing virtually all their capital and labor; that a country chiefly agricultural in its economy has as many economic, political and social advantages as a country whose economy is chiefly industrial, or as a country which has a balanced economy; that there are no gains to be achieved by great diversification of output. These assumptions, essential to the belief that "Free Trade" policy is ideal, are not valid. They are unreal and unsound. "Free Trade" policy grossly underestimates the extent to which a country can virtually lift itself by its bootstraps in one generation from a lower to a higher standard of living, from a backward agricultural to an advanced industrialized country, provided always it is willing to pay the price. The view further overlooks the very important fact that political relationships among countries being what they are, vital considerations exist in the shaping of the economic structure of a country other than that of producing goods with the least labor.

The subject of the best tariff policy for a given country at a given period in its history is a most interesting one, but justice could not be done to it in the space that could reasonably be allocated to it here. A great deal has been written on the subject and the interested reader in his search for sound policy will find that the complexity of the problem is apt to increase with the profundity of his reading. Yet one conclusion is certain to emerge from his study of the subject, namely, that most import duties are too high, that many duties remain too long, that few are imposed for sound reasons, and almost none of them are reevaluated often enough by the law-making bodies in the light of changing needs and conditions.

The value of requiring participating governments to agree to a general policy of lower tariffs lies solely in the recognition that most duties in the tariff schedules of every country, at their present level, are inexcusable on any economic, political or social grounds. Their existence merely reflects uncritical adhesion to protectionist policies or the successful pressure of some powerful vested interest, or both. It is to place on the defensive obstructions to trade, whether in the form of unreasonably high duties or in any other form, that commitment to lower tariff policies might be justified.

Yet, it cannot be overlooked that the shaping of tariff policy has been for too long the prerogative of lawmaking bodies and the battleground of legislative maneuvering to expect the Congresses and Parliaments to subordinate to an international body their authority on such matters. If the sugar, wool, wheat growers of the United States, and the shoe and textile, pottery, and steel manufacturers—to name only a few of the industries insisting on high protective duties—were to see in any suggested agency a definite threat to what they regard as necessary protection to their industry, they would combine and probably rally enough support to their crusade to ruin the prospects of acceptance by Congress of any proposal no matter how attractive the scheme might be to economists, statesmen, foreign trade associations, college professors and bankers.

It would seem to be a far wiser policy not to attempt too much and thereby jeopardize any but an innocuous program. On this issue, as on no other, prudence dictates compromise. The most one can hope to get is adherence to a principle without surrender of any authority. Hence the requirement calls only for public adherence to the stated principle, and permission to the Fund to submit a report giving reasons for its disapproval of an added barrier to trade if the Fund deems it harmful. If any international agency or organization wrings more than that out of the American and other publics, a miracle in economic morality will have been wrought by this war.

Another possible condition of participation that merits attention is the agreement that no Government or Central Bank shall default on its external obligations, or any part thereof, without consent of the Fund.

This requirement has considerable possibilities for good. If the flow of private capital from capital-rich to capital-poor countries is to be stimulated and the flow of specialized capital among countries is to be fostered, something drastic must be done to reestablish confidence of private investors in the integrity of foreign borrowers. Defaults by governments and states have been in the past too easy a way out of foreign exchange and budgetary difficulties. The defaulting country frequently experiences an immediate gain but unfortunately the long-run losses have far more than outweighed the gains. If the Fund and the Bank could be a potent force for preventing defaults (as well as keeping interest rates reasonably low), a long step forward will have been made toward the increased productiveness of all countries.

It can hardly be expected that objective decisions on defaults can be made by the defaulting country or by the country gaining most by continued servicing of a debt. To make what takes on the character of compulsory arbitration in debt adjustment an acceptable and workable instrument, the proposed judgment must be that of a large group of nations, the majority of whom are not directly and immediately affected by the decision. Consideration of the pros and cons of a contemplated default by the Fund would seem to promise that kind of objectivity, and therefore not be a requirement that would stand in the way of acceptance by any government.

Not to subsidize—directly or indirectly—the exportation of any commodity or service to member countries without consent of the Fund.

One of the unfair trade practices frequently resorted to in the past has been export subsidies. Most countries have been guilty of subsidizing some exports either by direct or indirect methods. It is easy for the practice to grow as there are in every country powerful interests who because of a monopoly position or political influence, at the expense of the public, are able to keep up the price of a product at home by practicing subsidized dumping on foreign markets. This device in essence is no different from the use of multiple currencies or special clearing arrangements except that the gain in the latter case is shared by more persons. They all aim to undersell a foreign competitor not by offering the same goods at a lower price, or better goods at the same price, but by undercutting a foreign competitor at the expense of the taxpayer of the exporting country.

It is just such practices that give rise to rivalries which constitute fertile soil for international friction. If subsidies to exports are condoned there is no logical justification for objecting to any kind of trade device designed to increase exports or decrease imports. The result would be a repetition of the ruthless fight for foreign markets that characterized international trade in the pre-war decade.

It might be possible to obtain acquiescence among the member countries not to resort to the more obvious forms of subsidies without consent of the Fund. Since the Fund would be a sort of court of appeal, the possibility of subsidizing the export of a commodity or service exists. Yet presumably it would be invoked only under special circumstances. The fact that approval of the Fund were necessary would be helpful to governments in their struggle against vested groups seeking special advantages. Though it will be found very difficult to get a satisfactory working definition of an indirect subsidy, it should be at least possible to define the term so as to apply to the more obvious devices.

The Fund would probably have to permit subsidies to shipping and air travel. Almost every country subsidizes these two for military reasons, for economic reasons, and reasons of national prestige. It is irrelevant that much of the defense for shipbuilding and shipping based on economic and patriotic grounds is specious. These subsidies are so deeply imbedded in custom and policy that it is useless to attempt to modify them through an agency such as we are discussing.

Subsidies to tourists, to student voyages, etc., are of a different character. It may well be in the interests of all countries, and certainly is in the interests of some countries, to attract tourists by subsidies of one form or another. This subsidizing of exports of services seems to arouse little objection in thc importing country (i.e. in the countries whose nationals do the touring) and can at least be defended on social and cultural grounds. Since United States is probably the most generous producer of profitable tourists, there is an added justification for attracting Americans abroad by subsidies if necessary, namely it will help the United States to develop a much desired "unfavorable" balance of payments through the most desirable available channels.

All considered it were probably better to exclude "services" altogether from the prohibition of subsidies, and save the Fund much trouble. It would, moreover, make it less unlikely that the requirement would find acceptance by enough nations.

It may be properly questioned whether an agency of this character is the appropriate instrument for obtaining fair trade practices in foreign trade. It might be that some other agency like a league of nations should be the vehicle, or possibly dependence should be on a program of multilateral treaties. However, it does seem that it should be less difficult to obtain agreement on such matters when the vehicle is an agency, membership in which has obvious economic advantages. Moreover, a country could feel it could always withdraw from the Fund if it deems its interests significantly harmed by failure to obtain approval of the Fund for a contemplated action, and hence would be less reluctant to try giving up the privilege.

Restrictions on membership.

No restrictions as to membership should be imposed on grounds of the particular economic structure adopted by any country.

There are certain to be some persons or governments, who either out of fear, or prejudice, or dislike would wish to exclude countries with socialist economies from participation in an international undertaking of the character described in the previous pages. Yet to exclude a country such as Russia would be an egregious error. Russia, despite her socialist economy could both contribute and profit by participation. To deny her the privileges of joining in this cooperative effort to improve world economic relations would be to repeat the tragic errors of the last generation, and introduce a very discordant note in the new era millions everywhere are hoping for. If the Russian Government is willing to participate, her counsel in the preliminary negotiations should be as eagerly sought as that of any other country, and her membership in both Fund and Bank equally as welcome.

A socialist economy like a capitalistic economy engages in international trade and financial transactions which can be either beneficial or harmful to other countries. In fact, because the conduct of foreign trade and international financial transactions is so completely under the control of the government in a socialist economy, there is all the more reason to attempt to get them to join in a cooperative attempt to introduce stability in international economic relationships and a higher level of trade.

Furthermore, no one can know what direction some of the smaller liberated states will take in the shaping of their economic structures. There is likely to be, during the next decade or two, a variety of economic systems and it would seem desirable that these should not be discouraged from cooperating with the others so long as they are willing to agree to conduct their international economic affairs in accordance with principles acceptable to the United Nations.

IV. Composition of the Fund

The Fund shall consist of gold, member country currencies, and member government securities, in such amounts as shall be indicated by a formula set forth in the Agreements. The total subscription to the Fund shall be the equivalent of at least $5 billion.

The task which the Fund would be expected to perform would involve transactions of large magnitude; it therefore should have large resources available. Moreover, the greater its resources the more potent could the Fund be in preventing monetary disruption and in reducing the frequency and duration of periods of disequilibrium. Considering the likelihood that the number of participating governments might be at least a score, a total subscription of the equivalent of two to five billion dollars would seem to be both possible and desirable.

To avoid tying up funds that would not be needed for some time, if ever, the participants could be required to subscribe only 25 percent of their participation in cash. An additional 25 percent could be subscribed in obligations of the participating government. These obligations would yield revenue to the Fund, and would also supply a source of additional funds to be tapped if and when needed. They would also provide the Fund with the means of conducting open-market operations in any given country when desired. To reduce the cost to participating countries, it might be found preferable to make the securities a renewable three to five-year note, rather than a long-term bond, thus reducing the interest rate and increasing their marketability.

The remaining 50 percent of the subscription should be paid in such installments and in such form as shall be determined from time to time by the Fund.

The Fund would need local currencies and gold to carry on its operations. The provision that half the initial payment of 25 percent be in gold and half in local currencies takes care of that, and also makes participation easier for those countries having little gold. For a few of the countries—e.g. the United States—gold and local currencies are synonymous for purposes of international transactions. One of the objectives of the Fund is to increase the number of countries about which that could be said.

In view of the fact that the gains from participation in the Fund would not take the form of a distribution of substantial profits, the sum each member country should subscribe can hardly be left to the decision of each country. It is hoped that the Fund would show an annual profit but the purpose of the Fund is not to make profits but to help achieve much more important objectives that are not susceptible of measurement in terms of money profits. The Fund would be a cooperative enterprise operated for the benefit of all the participating nations, and each participant should subscribe at least its reasonable share of the total capital necessary, though it could subscribe more if it wished to do so. The share of the total each country subscribes should be determined by some agreed upon formula which would give due weight to various pertinent considerations.

There follows an illustrative formula that attempts to measure the minimum amount of funds each participant should be required to subscribe. The items listed are those which seem most pertinent, and the weights ascribed to each attempt roughly to reflect the importance of that item to the benefits that might be expected to result from participation and the ability to contribute to the Fund's capital.

1. Gold holdings	100	points for every billion dollars
2. Gold production	50	" " " " "
3. National income	2	" " " " "
4. Foreign trade	25	" " " " "
5. Population	1	" " " ten million
6. Foreign investments	25	" " " billion dollars
7. Foreign debts	10	" " " $50 million of annual interest payments on external public debt

Applying the above weights to the situation in some selected countries, the following approximate scores would result:

United States	2,905	U.S.S.R.	149
United Kingdom	577	China	78
Canada	125	Mexico	24
Netherlands and Colonies	143	Brazil	45
Norway	15	Colombia	12

Converted into dollars, the contributions would be something like the following:

TABLE

(In millions of U.S. dollars)

(Though the contributions or investments would be in the form of gold or local currency, they are converted, for convenience, into U.S. dollar units in the table below.)

United States	3,196	Argentina	72
England	635	Mexico	26
U.S.S.R.	164	Brazil	50
Canada	138	Colombia	13
Netherlands and Colonies	157	Cuba	9

The purpose of the table is merely to suggest a pattern of quotas for discussion, and not to lay down any precise pattern or formula. An attempt was made to present a pattern of quotas, the general character of which probably could be defended on logical grounds, but it is certain that a more appropriate formula could be worked out if several minds focused on the problem.

If only 50 percent of the participation were called for, and only half of that in cash, the amounts indicated in the above table would not be erroneous. The United States would be called upon to subscribe $500 million in cash and Cuba only $12½ million.

That would be the minimum. They could, of course, subscribe more if they wished. Experience would show whether the total was much more than was needed, or much less. If more were needed the securities could be converted into cash and the remaining half called in. On the other hand, if after long experience it is found that even the initial payments were greatly in excess of needs, it would be an easy matter to return the excess. Since the Fund should be ample to take care of periods of special stress, many years would have to pass, however, before enough experience is acquired to determine the most appropriate size of the Fund. It would certainly be better in the beginning to err on the side of having too much rather than not enough. The effective strength of the Fund and its ability to instill confidence in the currency stability of its participants will be enhanced with the ease with which the Fund can be expected to meet all legitimate claims on its resources. A sum of several billions of dollars does not, therefore, seem inappropriate to the task.

Inasmuch as some of the assistance the Fund can give to member countries is directly proportional to the sum of participation of that country, there will be a strong incentive for some countries to make their participation larger than the scheduled amount.

The Bank for Reconstruction and Development of the United and Associated Nations could be called upon to participate to the extent of possibly $100 million.

Contributions made according to the scale at the bottom of page 74 would result in total assets of $5,225,000,000. The following table summarizes the proportionate share which would be contributed by significant groups of countries. The second column of the table indicates the percentage of the total votes which would be allotted to each area, on the basis of these minimum contributions.

	Participation	Number of Votes on Board
	(In percent of total)	
United States	61.03	25.32
Argentina and Chile	1.68	3.93
Other Latin America	2.93	30.54
British Empire	20.20	17.56
U.S.S.R.	3.13	2.85
Netherlands and Colonies	3.01	2.81
Other European Countries	4.24	13.10
China	1.64	2.26
Bank for Reconstruction	2.14	1.63
	100.00	100.00

V. Management

Where control of the Fund shall be vested is a matter of paramount importance in the formulation of a workable plan. The magnitude of the Fund, the broad scope of its likely powers, the requirements for continued eligibility of participants, together make the question of situs of control important.

The management of the Fund should be vested in a Board of Directors consisting of the representatives appointed by the member governments, each government to appoint one representative.

It would be easy to reach agreement that the most convenient and simplest device would be to vest control of the Fund in a board of directors, to consist of representatives appointed by member governments, each government appointing one representative. It probably would be desirable to have each government appoint an alternate as well. In view of the technical nature of many of the problems, the governments might wish to select as alternates men who would be more qualified than are likely to be the representatives to take up the kind of problems that would most frequently come before the Fund. The representatives would probably be selected from more responsible posts than the alternates, and would likely be concerned with the larger and less technical issues involved in decisions.

The Board shall elect a chairman and a small operating committee.

With a body so unwieldy as it would likely be with representatives from each government, added to the fact that many of such representatives could devote only brief periods away from their home governments, it is virtually essential that the day-to-day operations of the Fund be handled by a small operating committee of representatives. Such a committee would be able to devote full time to the task of managing the Fund, and would, of course, have to be adequately compensated. The election of this operating committee by the member participants would insure the selection of a competent group and the brief period of their tenure of office before reelection would assure also a responsiveness to the wishes of the board. Delegation of authority by the whole board to the committee on many matters could be safely made, leaving larger policy decisions to be referred to the entire board. It is to be expected that the operating committee would have the assistance of a competent technical staff.

If a Fund were to be established with anything like the powers and resources outlined in this report, it would need the services of a large staff of the best experts available. Nothing would injure the chances of effective and successful operation and of making a major contribution to the solution of some of our most troublesome international economic problems than mediocrity in directors and technical staff. A board the size of the one recommended here can, of course, assimilate without serious damage some stuffed shirts, some narrow-minded nationalists, and a few bankers with counting house ideals. But the board will have to include more than a sprinkling of economic statesmen, forward looking and of broad vision, comprehensive experienced world outlook and tenacity of social purpose. The technical staff will have to be headed up by experienced analysts with a thorough knowledge of monetary theory and international economics, with intellectual integrity and aggressiveness, and also include a generous quota of eager, able, young men who have been at or near the top in their scholastic achievements and technical writings. The United and Associated Nations can produce plenty of such men.

In all voting by the Board, each representative should have one hundred votes, plus one vote for the equivalent of every million dollars turned over to the Fund.

There would be little difficulty in reaching agreement that some such set-up as the board working through a committee as outlined above would provide a satisfactory working arrangement, but the real problem is how to distribute the voting power. If each member of the board were to be given an equal vote, then a small country that invested one million dollars would have as much power in making decisions as a country that has subscribed a hundred or a thousand times that amount. With the possibility that the number of small countries participating will be much greater than the large countries, a one-vote-one-member arrangement is palpably unwise. On the other hand, to accord voting power strictly proportionate to the value of the subscription would give the one or two powers control over the Fund. To do that would destroy the truly international character of the Fund, and seriously jeopardize its success. Indeed, it is very doubtful if many countries would be willing to participate in an international organization with wide powers if one or two countries were to be able to control its policies.

It is clear that the voting power must be so arranged as to steer between these two evils. This might be accomplished by working out some compromise between the two bases of voting power referred to above. By giving each member 100 votes plus one vote for every million dollars invested in the Fund, a satisfactory distribution of control might be approximated. Thus, if the United States subscribes $1 billion it would have 100 plus 1,000 votes, or a total of 1,100 votes, whereas a country contributing $10 million would have 100 plus 10 votes, or a total of 110. With such an arrangement ten small countries could outvote the United States. If any country felt the arrangement agreed upon did not give it an adequate share of control, it could increase its contribution.

A country should have the privilege of replacing, wholly or in part, its securities, with currency or gold. The number of votes its representatives can cast would alter accordingly.

This provision would supply some flexibility in the assets a country turns over to the Fund, and also provides a means whereby a country could increase its voting power. How important the provision might prove to be is uncertain, but in the beginning at least it would appear desirable to introduce flexibility wherever possible.

All decisions, except where specifically provided otherwise, should be decided by a simple majority of the votes cast.

To give adequate protection to each country, most of the important decisions could be made to require more than a simple majority of the votes.

The President of the Bank should be a member of the Board, and would have 100 votes.

Because of the interdependence of the two institutions—the Fund and the Bank—close liaison and opportunities to harmonize policies would be helpful. Both agencies would have broad objectives, both would be international in their outlook, and both would be motivated by the desire to promote worldwide peace, prosperity, and stability. Each would be undertaking responsibilities that call for analyses and judgments of economic situations and trends. The operations of each would affect the other, and the decisions of each should be partly based on the knowledge, plan and judgment of the other. There, therefore, is much to be gained by close liaison between them. That is why the head of each should be a director of the other.

To avoid cumulating voting power, however, the Bank should not be able to cast votes in excess of the minimum, irrespective of the extent of its monetary participation.

Reports and information

The possession by the Fund of adequate, timely and appropriate information is a vital necessity to its proper functioning. The Fund should have the authority to require that all members file with it a quarterly itemized balance of payments. This balance of payments record—which is of particular importance in the operation of this Fund—should be standardized in form, and carefully designed by the technical staff of the Fund. The Fund would also need special reports from members from time to time, and should have the authority to obtain them.

[The following paragraphs are from Part III, commenting on the plans for an International Bank.]

A new international currency

We frequently hear expressed a desire or hope for a new international currency, but the specific nature of the new currency is never described, nor are the gains that are presumed to result from such a currency ever stated in meaningful language. They are either taken for granted or referred to only in the vaguest of generalities. So much misunderstanding of the nature and utility of a new international currency seems to prevail that it is probably worth attempting to indicate the limits of usefulness possessed by such a currency. The reader not interested in the confusions surrounding the demand for an international currency can omit the next few pages.

There are some persons who seem to think that all foreign exchange problems would be solved if only all countries adopted the same international unit for use in international transactions. A little thought will demonstrate how absurd that belief is. The fact that Canada adopted a "dollar" unit containing 100 cents and having the same *de jure* gold content as the United States dollar, did not prevent the adoption of foreign exchange controls in Canada nor did it keep the United States dollar-Canadian dollar exchange rate from moving, any more than did Australia, South Africa and New Zealand, by adopting the same unit as England, prevent the value of the currencies of those countries from changing in relation to the British £ sterling. There are innumerable instances of different currency units keeping the same value, in terms of each other, for many years; and other instances of similar currency units beginning with identical values and only to have those values change greatly. Thus, the pound sterling hovered around $4.86 for thirty-five years (1878–1914), and the Swiss franc was about 20 cents for fifty years; whereas, the exchange rates between the British £ and Australian £ and New Zealand £ and the Egyptian £ have moved greatly notwithstanding the fact that to begin with they all were the same unit, not only in designation—pound—but in the sense that their value was 1 to 1.

The value of any currency in terms of any other currency is a consequence of a complex of monetary and economic forces, changes in these forces influence the value of one currency in terms of others. The adoption of a new international currency would not modify those forces one whit. If all of the Western Hemisphere were to adopt the "dollar" as their own unit of currency, it would not be long before it would be necessary to distinguish between the "U. S. dollar," the "Mexican dollar," the "Colombian dollar," etc., because the exchange rates between those currencies had moved away from the 1 to 1 ratio. In fact, even now there are a number of "dollars" in use in the foreign exchange systems of the American Republics. The adoption of the same unit of currency no more eliminates foreign exchange problems than would the general adoption of Esperanto solve international political problems or no more than does the use of a common language, e.g. Spanish, eliminate international political problems between all Spanish-speaking nations.

Occasionally, one hears expressed the view that if only there could be created some unit of currency that could be universally used in trade—"a trade dollar" or "export dollar" (Presumably no reference is intended to a special kind of dollar which costs less to the foreigner than a regular dollar, yet which buys as much in the U. S. as a regular dollar. That would be a clear example of multiple currencies which involve government subsidies, and which constitutes one of the devices the U. S. is opposed to on principle), or any unit with a new name—considerable advantages in trade and other international transactions would result. Unfortunately, this view is fallacious. The obstacles to trade do not lie in the fact that different countries use different units of currency. Insofar as currency has anything to do with obstructing trade, it is the scarcity of foreign exchange and the variations in exchange rates which are responsible. Neither of these two obstacles to trade will be dissipated by the adoption of a new international unit of currency. There are, it is true, possibilities of developing machinery which will make foreign exchange more plentiful to countries that lack adequate foreign exchange, and there is also machinery which may be developed to reduce the fluctuation in exchange rates. The proposal here made for the Fund and the Bank is designed to help achieve those very objectives among others. Neither proposal involves, or needs, or is dependent upon the adoption of an international unit of currency.

We already have an international medium of exchange, namely, gold. An ounce of gold .999 fine is the same in United States as it is in China or South Africa or Iceland. Any exporter or importer or banker or investor can liquidate a monetary debt with gold just as easily as would be possible with a new international unit. Such difficulties as exist in the use of gold as a medium of international exchange lie in difficulties imposed by war conditions. In peace time nothing could be simpler than to send or receive gold, or send or receive dollar or other exchange convertible into gold.

Some who clamor for a new international currency to replace gold would concede this, but claim gold is too expensive to be used. This is quite another matter. It may be possible to develop a satisfactory international medium of exchange that costs less to produce than more gold, but certainly not significantly less than gold already in monetary stock. It is important to remember in thinking about this subject that the monetary gold stock of the country *has already been paid for. It is very inexpensive to use the gold already in world monetary stocks.* Even the cost of shipping from one country to another can be avoided through development of earmarking. The only expense of using gold already mined is the small value that gold would have for industrial uses if it had no monetary value.

The situation is quite different with respect to further additions to the gold stock—and more complex. Obviously there is a real cost as well as a monetary cost involved in mining and refining gold. Insofar as the gold would not be produced had it only commodity value, and insofar as the labor and material used in gold mining would be used for some other purpose, it is true that additions to our monetary gold stock are expensive. The solution to that, however, is simple—namely, just limit or control the additions of newly-mined gold to the world's monetary stock. This is not the place to discuss the method; suffice to say it is entirely feasible should it ever be deemed desirable. There are some advantages and disadvantages to the proposal, but it is possible that the time may come when the advantages may outweigh the disadvantages. In any case, the utility of *additions* to the world's monetary stock is a separate question from that of use of *existing* stocks. There is no advantage in substituting a new medium of international exchange for existing gold—even if it could be done—and I am confident it could not be done. But it may be worthwhile giving the Bank note-issuing powers—based on some gold reserve—solely in order to make the world's monetary gold stock do more work, and at the same time help correct the maldistribution of gold.

To be sure, the United States already does just that when for one reason or another, by one method or another, it increases its supply of currency and demand deposits.

The only difference between what the United States (and virtually every other country) already does, and what it is proposed the Bank shall do is that in the United States note issues are regulated by the law of the country, whereas the proposed note issues of the Bank will be regulated by the by-laws of the Bank as drawn up by the member Governments.

The belief previously referred to as being held in some quarters that a common unit of currency will solve the world's foreign exchange problems, and help promote foreign trade in goods and services, and the international flow of capital does not concern itself with either the scarcity of gold, or its maldistribution. It seems to take the form of something much less intelligible. It seems to assume that these benefits are to be attained by a new international unit which is to be adopted by many countries as a *substitute* for their own currency.

The belief that countries will find it helpful to replace their own currency in favor of a currency to be used by all, or by a group of nations, is based on a fundamental misunderstanding of the factors which determine the value of any currency. So long as most countries insist on shaping their own monetary policies so long will it be impossible to replace local currencies with a new international currency. The adoption of a common currency by several countries is possible only if they each surrender separate sovereignty in monetary and credit policies in favor of sovereignty exercised by one over all of them, or by an international organization. For example, it was impossible for the states in the American colonies to have a common currency with a common value until the United States was formed and the Federal Government given sole authority over currency. Even then scores of different bank notes existed, many of them with changing values, because the State rather than the Federal Government exercised sovereignty in matters of bank note issue. It was only until the Federal Government became supreme in the matter of all note issues that the United States was able to keep all bank notes at par.

It is possible for a group of countries to agree to adopt a common currency, but such adoption is of little use unless they also agree not to exercise separate sovereign powers with respect to note issues, exchange rates, rediscount rates and privileges and other aspects of monetary policy. If country A is going to agree to adopt the same currency as country B, country A will want assurance that country B cannot do whatever it pleases with its monetary policy.

But, it may be asked, would not the use of a new international unit as a *supplement* to local currency facilitate international trade and finance? The answer is an unqualified "No."

A "trade dollar" or "Demos" or "Victor" or "what-have-you" unit of currency supplementing the United States dollar, whether of the same or different value, would no more help foreign trade than would the adoption of a new flag. The only difference in trade between Massachusetts and Texas and trade between Massachusetts and Mexico—aside from tariffs—is that in the first case both buyer and seller deal in dollars only, whereas in trade between Mexico and United States two currencies are involved—the Mexican peso and United States dollar. (The supply of either currency to either country would be no different with a supplementary currency than without it; therefore, the matter of supply and demand for currency can be ignored in this discussion.) An importer, exporter, bank, or a tourist has simply to make conversions from one currency into another in his transactions. Were it possible to eliminate by use of an international currency unit the arithmetical labors involved in the conversions, it would indeed be a convenient device, though by no means a very important one. Unfortunately, however, the use of a new international currency unit does not obviate the necessity of calculating conversion values any more than does the use of gold in settling international transactions.

Let us, for example, consider the case of a tourist. As it is now, when an American travels to Mexico he converts his dollars into Mexican pesos, when he enters Colombia he converts his dollars into Colombian pesos, and when he goes to Brazil he converts his dollars into milreis, etc. Yet, if there existed a new international unit of currency he would be no better off; his purchases and sales would be consummated with no less inconvenience. On the contrary, he would have to make more calculations and more monetary adjustments in his price judgments. Upon leaving the United States he would have to convert his dollars into the new international unit and then when he came to Mexico he'd have to convert the international unit into pesos since most prices in any country are expressed in terms of the local currency unit. He would have had to do just that had he carried with him dollars instead of an international currency. Only this time, if he wanted to judge the value of an article tagged, say 50 pesos, he would have to make two mental conversions instead of one, because most of his life he has been dealing in dollars and cents, not in a new international currency. Then, when he enters Colombia he would have to again calculate conversions and again make the necessary mental adjustments in evaluating his purchases. It would be possible, of course, to have price tags or price schedules in shops and hotels frequented by tourists expressed in the international unit, but such a practice would be a nuisance to the seller and would be only a slight convenience to the buyer.

Nor does a buyer of imported goods purchase those goods in one country rather than in another because of ease of an arithmetical calculation. Where there is any difficulty and the seller meets with any sales resistance on this score, he can easily overcome it by quoting his price in the buyer's currency even if a bill is to be paid in the seller's currency.

Is there then no advantage to be obtained from the adoption of a new international unit of currency aside from the advantage of increasing the Bank's lending resources described earlier?

Yes, there is one advantage, though of minor importance. It is in the realm of economic research. A universally recognized international monetary unit of account would be helpful in the presentation of those statistical series which are pertinent to international comparisons and of use in discussions involving international comparisons of quantitative data measured in money terms. For many purposes it would be convenient to set up tables that involved summation of money values in more than one currency. It would also prove useful in statistical data involving comparisons of various money values over long periods of time.

Were values set in terms of a local currency which had undergone substantial changes in purchasing power relative to other countries, certain significant comparisons would be easier to make.

Altogether, the introduction of a new currency unit would not be of sufficient importance to warrant its introduction at this time, were the Bank not to be established with note issuing power. But if the Bank were to be established and given the authority to issue notes, what unit should it be?

It would probably be preferable to adopt a new unit. The adoption of a new international unit of currency of account would probably meet with little opposition, whereas an attempt to use any one of the existing currencies, such as dollars, sterling, or francs for that purpose would be opposed on the grounds that it would seem to give the country possessing that currency some slight advantage in publicity or trade. There are deemed to be some national prestige values and possibly slight economic gains in trade and financial transactions that adhere to a country having a currency that is widely used as an international unit of account. For that reason a new unit belonging to no country would be more welcome to most countries than the unit of any selected country.

A new unit of currency would have to be defined. It would have to be fixed in terms of something, whether by international agreement or by general acquiescence, or unilateral action. To set the value of the new currency unit in terms of some existing currency has the disadvantage of subjecting the new unit to the variations of the currency to which it is tied and also raises the question of "favoritism." The simplest course is to fix the value of the new unit in terms of gold. A unit of account does not have to be set in terms of gold, it could be set in terms of some commodity other than gold—tin, platinum, or any material. It could even be set in terms of an average basket of goods, or an aggregate of goods. But examination of the various possibilities will show that the only practical solution is to set the new currency unit in terms of a given physical volume of gold.

For convenience of arithmetical calculation it would probably be well to define the new unit as being equivalent to 14.62 grains nine-tenths fine. This would make the new unit worth 50 U.S. [cents] or 10 yuan or 2 s. at current rates of exchange and at present price for gold in the United States.

(B) Preliminary Draft Outline of a Proposal for an International Stabilization Fund of the United and Associated Nations

(Revised July 10, 1943)

The plan for post-war international currency stability set forth in this pamphlet is a revision of the preliminary draft outline of a proposal for an International Stabilization Fund of the United and Associated Nations made public by the Secretary of the Treasury on April 7, 1943.

The preliminary draft was sent by the Secretary of the Treasury to the finance ministers of the United Nations and the countries associated with them with a request that it be studied by their technical experts. The finance ministers were also invited to send representatives to Washington for informal discussions with the experts of this Government.

Such informal discussions have been held with nearly 30 countries. On the basis of these discussions, the experts of the Treasury with the cooperation of experts of other Departments of this Government have revised the preliminary draft proposal for an international stabilization fund. While suggestions of the representatives of other countries have been included in the revised draft, it does not necessarily reflect the views of the experts of any other country.

This revised draft is in every sense still a preliminary document representing the views of the technical experts of the Treasury and of other Departments of this Government. It has not received the official approval either of the Treasury or this Government.

FOREWORD

By Henry Morgenthau, Jr., *Secretary of the Treasury*

When the United Nations have brought this war to a successful conclusion, they will be faced with many urgent international economic and financial problems. Some of these are new problems arising directly from this war; others are continuing consequences of failure to solve the problems that have been with us since the last war. The solution of these problems is essential to the development of a sound economic foundation for world peace and prosperity.

All of the important international economic and financial problems are closely interrelated. Monetary stabilization, commercial policy, the provision of long-term international credit, promotion of stability in the prices of primary products, and arrangements for relief and rehabilitation are problems that join at innumerable points. Nevertheless, because of their complexity, they must be taken up separately, although each in turn must be integrated with the rest.

It is generally recognized that monetary stability and protection against discriminatory currency practices are essential bases for the revival of international commerce and finance. For this reason, an appropriate starting point might well be the consideration of post-war international monetary problems. Success in dealing with international monetary problems in the post-war period will contribute toward final solution of the other international financial and economic problems. Despite the technical difficulties involved, the common interest which all countries have in the solution of post-war monetary problems provides a basis for agreement.

It is still too soon to know the precise form and magnitude of post-war monetary problems. But it is certain that we shall be confronted with three inseparable monetary tasks: to prevent the disruption of foreign exchanges, to avoid the collapse of monetary systems, and to facilitate the restoration and balanced growth of international trade. Clearly, such formidable problems can be successfully handled only through international action.

The creation of instrumentalities adequate to deal with the inevitable post-war monetary problems should not be postponed until the end of hostilities. It would be ill-advised, if not dangerous, to leave ourselves unprepared at the end of the war for the difficult taks of international monetary cooperation. Specific and practical proposals must be formulated by the experts and must be carefully considered by the policy-shaping officials of the various countries. In each country acceptance of a definitive plan can follow only upon legislative or executive action. And even when a plan is finally adopted, much time will be consumed in preparation before an international institution for monetary cooperation can begin effective work.

There is another important reason for initiating now concrete discussions of specific proposals. A plan for international monetary cooperation can be a factor in winning the war. It has been suggested, and with much cogency, that the task of assuring the defeat of the Axis powers would be made easier if the victims of aggression could have greater assurance that a victory of the United Nations will not mean in the economic sphere a repetition of the exchange instability and monetary collapse that followed the last war. The people in all of the United Nations must be given some assurance that there will not again be two decades of post-war economic disruption. The people must know that we at last recognize the fundamental truth that the prosperity of each country is closely linked to the prosperity of other countries.

One of the appropriate agencies to deal with international economic and monetary problems would be an international stabilization fund with resources and powers adequate to the task of helping to achieve monetary stability and of facilitating the restoration and balanced growth of international trade. A proposal along these lines was drafted by American technical experts and made public on April 7, 1943. There have been informal discussions on this draft in which nearly thirty countries have participated. These discussions have shown that all countries think joint action in this field is necessary for the reconstruction of the world economy.

It is recognized that an international stabilization fund is only one of the instrumentalities which may be needed in the field of international economic cooperation. Other agencies may be needed to provide long-term international credit for post-war reconstruction and development, to provide funds for rehabilitation and relief, and to promote stability in the prices of primary international commodities. There is a strong inclination on the part of some to entrust to a single agency the responsibility for dealing with these and other international economic problems. We believe, however, that an international economic institution can operate most effectively if it is not burdened with diverse duties of a specialized character.

Although an international stabilization fund can provide the facilities for cooperation on monetary questions, the establishment of such an institution would not of itself assure the solution of these difficult problems. The operations of such a fund can be successful only if the powers and resources of the fund are used wisely, and if member countries cooperate with the fund's endeavors to maintain international equilibrium at a high level of international trade. Such cooperation must include commercial policies designed to reduce trade barriers and to terminate discriminatory practices that have in the past hampered the balanced growth of international trade. The nations of this world can be prosperous only if they are good neighbors in their economic as well as their political relations.

The draft proposals that have been put forward on a tentative basis have received wide publicity in the United States, the United Kingdom, Canada, and in other countries. It is in the best democratic tradition that the people should have the fullest opportunity to express their views and to shape the policies of their Governments on the important problems affecting national well-being. And it is an extension of this tradition that all the United Nations should have an opportunity to participate in the formulation of a program for international monetary cooperation.

This revised draft is published with the hope that it will call forth further comments and constructive suggestions. It aims to present only the essential elements of a workable international stabilization fund, and its provisions are in every sense tentative. Obviously, there are many details that have been omitted and that can be better formulated after there is agreement on the more important points. We believe that a workable and acceptable plan can emerge only from the joint efforts of the United Nations support by enlightened public opinion.

PRELIMINARY DRAFT OUTLINE OF A PROPOSAL FOR AN INTERNATIONAL STABILIZATION FUND OF THE UNITED AND ASSOCIATED NATIONS

Preamble

1. There is a growing recognition that progress toward establishment of a functioning democratic world in the post-war period will depend on the ability of free peoples to work together in solving their economic problems. Not the least of these is the problem of how to prevent a widespread breakdown of currencies with resultant international economic disorder. We must assure a troubled world that the free countries will solve these perplexing problems, and that they will not resort to competitive exchange depreciation, multiple currency practices, discriminatory bilateral clearing, or other destructive foreign exchange devices.

2. These are not transitory problems of the immediate postwar period affecting only a few countries. The history of the past two decades shows that they are continuing problems of vital interest to all countries. There must be a general realization that world prosperity, like world peace, is indivisible. Nations must act together to restore multilateral international trade, and to provide orderly procedure for the maintenance of balanced economic growth. Only through international cooperation will it be possible for countries successfully to apply measures directed toward attaining and maintaining a high level of employment and income which must be the primary objective of economic policy.

3. The International Stabilization Fund of the United and Associated Nations is proposed as a permanent institution for international monetary cooperation. The

resources of this Fund would be available under adequate safeguards to maintain currency stability, while giving member countries time to correct maladjustments in their balance of payments without resorting to extreme measures destructive of international prosperity. The resources of the Fund would not be used to prolong a basically unbalanced international position. On the contrary, the Fund would be influential in inducing countries to pursue policies making for an orderly return to equilibrium.

4. The Fund would deal only with member governments and their fiscal agents, and would not intrude in the customary channels for conducting international commerce and finance. The Fund is intended to provide supplemental facilities for the successful functioning of the established foreign exchange institutions and to free international commerce from harmful restrictions.

5. The success of the Fund must ultimately depend upon the willingness of nations to act together on their common problems. International monetary cooperation should not be regarded as a matter of generosity. All countries have a vital interest in the maintenance of international monetary stability, and in the balanced growth of multilateral international trade.

I. Purposes of the Fund

The United Nations and the countries associated with them recognize, as declared in the Atlantic Charter, the need for the fullest cooperation among nations with the object of securing economic advancement and rising standards of living for all. They believe that attainment of these objectives will be facilitated by international monetary cooperation. Therefore, it is proposed that there be established an International Stabilization Fund with the following purposes:

1. To help stabilize the foreign exchange rates of the currencies of the United Nations and the countries associated with them.

2. To shorten the periods and lessen the degree of disequilibrium in the international balance of payments of member countries.

3. To help create conditions under which the smooth flow of foreign trade and of productive capital among the member countries will be fostered.

4. To facilitate the effective utilization of the blocked foreign balances accumulating in some countries as a consequence of the war situation.

5. To reduce the use of such foreign exchange restrictions, bilateral clearing arrangements, multiple currency devices, and discriminatory foreign exchange practices as hamper world trade and the international flow of productive capital.

II. Composition of the Fund

1. The Fund shall consist of gold and the currencies and securities of member governments.

2. Each of the member countries shall subscribe a specified amount, to be called its *quota*. The aggregate of quotas of the member countries shall be the equivalent of at least $5 billion.

3. Each member country shall meet its quota contribution in full on or before the date set by the Board of Directors for the Fund's operations to begin.

(*a*) A country shall pay in gold not less than an amount determined as follows. If its gold and free foreign exchange holdings are:

(i) In excess of three times its quota, it shall pay in gold 50 percent of its quota.

(ii) More than two but less than three times its quota, it shall pay in gold 40 percent of its quota plus 10 percent of its holdings in excess of twice its quota.

(iii) More than its quota but less than twice its quota, it shall pay in gold 30 percent of its quota plus 10 percent of its holdings in excess of its quota.

(iv) Less than its quota, it shall pay in gold 30 percent of its holdings.

The gold payment required of a member country substantial parts of whose home areas have been wholly or partly occupied by the enemy, shall be only three-fourths of the above. (For other gold provisions, Cf. V–2–a and V–6, 7.)

A member country may include in the legal reserve account and in the published statement of the reserves of gold and foreign exchange in its Treasury or Central Bank, an amount not to exceed its gold contribution to the Fund, minus its net purchases of foreign exchange from the Fund paid for with local currency.

(*b*) It shall pay the remainder of its quota in local currency, except that a member country may substitute government securities (redeemable at par) for local currency up to 50 percent of its quota.

4. A quota for each member country shall be computed by an agreed upon formula which gives due weight to the important relevant factors, *e. g.*, a country's holdings of gold and free foreign exchange, the magnitude and the fluctuations of its balance of international payments, its national income, *etc.*

Before computing individual quotas on the basis of the agreed upon formula, there shall be reserved an amount equal to 10 percent of aggregate quotas to be used as a special allotment for the equitable adjustment of quotas. Where the initial quota of a member country as computed by the formula is clearly inequitable, the quota may be increased from this special allotment.

5. Quotas shall be adjusted on the basis of the most recent data 3 years after the establishment of the Fund, and at intervals of 5 years thereafter, in accordance with the agreed upon formula. In the period between adjustment of quotas, the Fund may increase the quota of a country, where it is clearly inequitable, out of the special allotment reserved for the equitable adjustment of quotas.

6. Any changes in the formula by which the quotas of member countries are determined shall be made only with the approval of a four-fifths vote of the Board.

7. No increase shall be made in the quota of a member country under II–4, 5 or 6 without the consent of the representative of the country concerned.

8. The resources of the Fund shall be used exclusively for the benefit of the member countries.

III. Monetary Unit of the Fund

1. The monetary unit of the Fund shall be the *unitas* (UN) equal in value to 137$\frac{1}{7}$ grains of fine gold (equivalent to $10). No change in the gold value of the unitas shall be made except with the approval of 85 percent of the member votes. When such change is made, the gain or loss sustained by the Fund on its holdings of gold shall be distributed equitably among the members of the Fund.

The accounts of the Fund shall be kept and published in terms of unitas.

2. The value of the currency of each member country shall be established in terms of unitas and may not be altered except as provided in IV–5, below. (Cf. IV–1, 2, below.)

No member country shall purchase or acquire gold, directly or indirectly, at a price in terms of its national currency in excess of the parity which corresponds to the value of its currency in terms of unitas and to the value of unitas in terms of gold; nor shall any member country sell or dispose of gold, directly or indirectly, at a price in terms of its national currency below the parity which corresponds to the value of its currency in terms of unitas and to the value of unitas in terms of gold. (Cf. VII–1.)

3. No change in the value of the currencies of member countries shall be permitted to alter the value in unitas of the assets of the Fund. Whenever the currency of a member country has depreciated to a significant extent, that country must deliver to the Fund when requested an amount of its local currency or securities equal to the decrease in the unitas value of the Fund's holdings of the local currency and securities of the country. Likewise, if the currency of a member country should appreciate to a significant extent, the Fund must return to that country an amount (in the currency or securities of that country) equal to the resulting increase in the unitas value of the Fund's holdings.

IV. Exchange Rates

1. The rates at which the Fund will buy and sell one member currency for another and at which the Fund will buy and sell gold for local currency shall be established in accordance with the provisions below. (Cf. also III–2 and V–2.)

2. The initial rates of exchange for member countries' currencies shall be determined as follows:

(*a*) For any country which becomes a member prior to the date on which the Fund's operations begin, the rates initially used by the Fund shall be based upon the value of the currency in terms of United States dollars which prevailed on July 1, 1943.

If, in the judgment of either the member country or the Fund, the above rate is clearly inappropriate, the initial rate shall be determined by consultation between the member country and the Fund. No operations in such currency shall be undertaken by the Fund until a rate has been established which has the approval of the Fund and of the member country in question.

(*b*) For any member country which has been occupied by the enemy, the Fund shall use the exchange rate fixed by the government of the liberated country in consultation with the Fund and acceptable to the Fund. Prior to the fixing of a definitive rate, operations in such currency may be undertaken by the Fund with the approval of the Board at a tentative rate of exchange fixed by the member country in consultation with the Board. No operations shall be continued under this provision for more than 3 months after the liberation of the country or when the local currency holdings of the Fund exceed the quota of the country, except that under special circumstances the period and the amount of such operations may be extended by the Fund.

3. The Fund shall not come into operation until agreement has been reached on the exchange rates for currencies of countries representing a majority of the aggregate quotas.

4. The Fund shall determine the range within which the rates of exchange of member currencies shall be permitted to fluctuate. (Cf. VII–1.)

5. Changes in the exchange value of the currency of a member country shall be considered only when essential to the correction of fundamental disequilibrium in its balance of payments, and shall be made only with the approval of three-fourths of the member votes including the representative of the country concerned.

Because of the extreme uncertainties of the immediate post-war period, the following exceptional provisions may be used during the first 3 years of the Fund's operations:

(*a*) When the existing rate of exchange of a member country is clearly inconsistent with the maintenance of a balanced international payments position for that country, changes from the established rate may be made at the special request of that country and with the approval of a majority of the member votes.

(*b*) A member country may change the established rate for its currency by not more than 10 percent provided that the member country shall notify the Fund of its intention and shall consult with the Fund on the advisability of its action.

V. Powers and Operations

The Fund shall have the following powers:

1. To buy, sell and hold gold, currencies, and government securities of member countries; to earmark and transfer gold; to issue its own obligations, and to offer them for discount or sale in member countries.

The Fund shall purchase for local currency or needed foreign exchange any member currency in good standing acquired by another member country in settlement of a balance of payments on current account, where such currency cannot be disposed of in the foreign exchange markets within the range established by the Fund.

2. To sell to the Treasury of any member country (or Stabilization Fund or Central Bank acting as its agent) at the accepted rate of exchange, currency of any member country which the Fund holds, provided that:

(*a*) The foreign exchange demanded from the Fund is required to meet an adverse balance of payments predominantly on current account with any member country. (Cf. V–3, for capital transfers.)

When the gold and free foreign exchange holdings of a member country exceed 50 percent of its quota, the Fund in selling foreign exchange to such member country shall require that one-half of such exchange shall be paid for with gold or foreign exchange acceptable to the Fund. (Cf. V–6, 7; on gold collateral, see V–2–c.)

(*b*) The Fund's total holdings of the currency and securities of any member country shall not exceed the quota of such country by more than 50 percent during the first year of operation of the Fund, and thereafter shall not exceed such quota by more than 100 percent (except as otherwise provided below). The total holdings thus permitted are termed the *permissible quota* of a country. When the Fund's holdings of local currency and securities are equal to the permissible quota of a country, the Fund may sell foreign exchange for such additional local currency only with the specific approval of the Board of Directors (cf. VI–3–a, below), and provided that at least one of the following two conditions is met:

(i) In the judgment of the Fund satisfactory measures are being or will be taken by the country whose currency is acquired by the Fund, to correct the disequilibrium in the country's balance of payments; or

(ii) It is believed that the balance of payments of the country whose currency is acquired by the Fund will be such as to warrant the expectation that the excess currency holdings of the Fund can be disposed of within a reasonable time;

Provided further, that when the Fund's holdings of the currency of any member country or countries fall below 20 percent of their respective quotas, the sale shall also require the approval of the representatives of these countries.

(*c*) When the Fund's holdings of local currency and securities exceed the permissible quota of a country, the Board may require the member country to deposit collateral in accordance with regulations prescribed by the Board. Such collateral shall take the form of gold, foreign or domestic currency or Government bonds, or other suitable collateral within the capacity of the member country.

(*d*) When, in the judgment of the Fund, a member country, whose currency and securities held by the Fund exceed its quota, is exhausting its permissible quota more rapidly than is warranted, or is using its permissible quota in a manner that clearly has the effect of preventing or unduly delaying the establishment of a sound balance in its international accounts, the Fund may place such conditions upon additional sales of foreign exchange to that country as it deems to be in the general interest of the Fund.

3. The Fund may sell foreign exchange to a member country, under conditions prescribed by the Fund, to facilitate a transfer of capital, or repayment or adjustment of foreign debts, when in the judgment of the Board such a transfer is desirable from the point of view of the general international economic situation, provided the Fund's holdings of the currency and securities of the member country do not exceed 150 percent of the quota of that country. When the Fund's holdings of the local currency and securities of a member country exceed 150 percent of the quota of that country, the Fund may, in exceptional circumstances, sell foreign exchange to the member country for the above purposes with the approval of three-fourths of the member votes. (Cf. V–2–a, above; on voting, VI–3–a, below.)

4. When the Fund's holdings of the currency and securities of a member country become excessively small in relation to prospective acquisitions and needs for that currency, the Fund shall render a report to that country. The report shall embody an analysis of the causes of the depletion of the Fund's holdings of that currency, a forecast of the prospective balance of payments in the absence of special measures, and finally, recommendations designed to increase the Fund's holdings of that currency. The representative of the country in question shall be a member of the Fund committee appointed to draft the report. This report shall be sent to all member countries and, if deemed desirable, be made public. Member countries agree that they will give immediate and careful attention to recommendations made by the Fund.

5. Whenever it becomes evident to the Board of Directors that the anticipated demand for any particular currency may soon exhaust the Fund's holdings of that currency, the Fund shall inform the member countries of the probable supply of the currency and of a proposed method for its equitable distribution, together with suggestions for helping to equate the anticipated demand for and supply of that currency.

The Fund shall make every effort to increase the supply of the scarce currency by acquiring that currency from the foreign balances of member countries. The Fund may make special arrangements with any member country for the purpose of providing an emergency supply under appropriate conditions which are acceptable to both the Fund and the member country.

To facilitate appropriate adjustment in the balance of payments position of member countries, and to help correct the distortions in the pattern of trade balances, the Fund shall apportion its sales of such scarce currency. In such apportionment, it shall be guided by the principle of satisfying the most urgent needs from the point of view of the general international economic situation. It shall also consider the special needs and resources of the particular countries making the request for the scarce currency.

The right of any member country to acquire an amount of other currencies equal to its permissible quota shall be limited by the necessity of assuring an appropriate distribution among the various members of any currency the supply of which is scarce.

6. In order to promote the most effective use of the available and accumulating supply of foreign exchange resources of member countries, each member country agrees that it will offer to sell to the Fund, for its local currency or for foreign currencies which the member country needs, one-half of the foreign exchange resources and gold it acquires in excess of its official holdings at the time it became a member of the Fund, but no country need sell gold or foreign exchange under this provision unless its official holdings (*i. e.*, Treasury, Central Bank, Stabilization Fund, *etc.*) are in excess of 25 percent of its quota. For the purpose of this provision, only free and liquid foreign exchange resources and gold shall be considered. The Fund may accept or reject the offer. (Cf. II–3–a, V–2–a, and V–7.)

To help achieve this objective each member country agrees to discourage the excessive accumulation of foreign exchange resources and gold by its nationals. The Fund shall inform any member country when, in its opinion, any further growth of privately held foreign exchange resources and gold appears unwarranted.

7. When the Fund's holdings of the local currency and securities of a member country exceed the quota of that country, the Fund shall, upon request of the member country, resell to the member country the Fund's excess holdings of the currency of that country for gold or acceptable foreign exchange. (Cf. V–14, for charges on holdings in excess of quota.)

8. To buy from the governments of member countries, blocked foreign balances held in other member countries, provided all the following conditions are met:

(*a*) The blocked balances are held in member countries and are reported as such (for the purpose of this provision) by the member governments and are verified by the Fund.

(*b*) The member country selling the blocked balances to the Fund agrees to transfer these balances to the Fund and to repurchase from the Fund 40 percent of them (at the same price) with gold or such free currencies as the Fund may wish to accept, at the rate of 2 percent of the transferred balances each year for 20 years beginning not later than 3 years after the date of transfer.

(*c*) The country in which the blocked balances are held agrees to transfer to the Fund the balances described in (*b*) above, and to repurchase from the Fund 40 percent of them (at the same price) with gold or such free currencies as the Fund may wish to accept, at the rate of 2 percent of the transferred balances each year for 20 years beginning not later than 3 years after the date of transfer.

(*d*) A charge of 1 percent on the amount of blocked balances sold to the Fund, payable in gold, shall be levied against the country selling its blocked balances and against the country in which the balances are held. In addition a charge of not less than one percent, payable in gold, shall be levied annually against each country on the amount of such balances remaining to be purchased by it.

(*e*) If the country selling blocked balances to the Fund asks for foreign exchange rather than local currency, the request will not be granted unless the country needs the foreign exchange for the purpose of meeting an adverse balance of payments not arising from the acquisition of gold, the accumulation of foreign balances, or other capital transactions.

(*f*) Either country may, at its option, increase the amount it repurchases annually. But, in the case of the country selling blocked balances to the Fund, not more than 2 percent per annum of the original sum taken over by the Fund shall become free, and only after 3 years shall have elapsed since the sale of the balances to the Fund.

(*g*) The Fund has the privilege of disposing of any of its holdings of blocked balances as free funds after the 23-year period is passed, or sooner under the following conditions:

(i) Its holdings of the free funds of the country in which the balances are held fall below 20 percent of its quota; or

(ii) The approval is obtained of the country in which the balances are held.

(*h*) The country in which the blocked balances are held agrees not to impose any restrictions on the use of the installments of the 40 percent portion gradually repurchased by the country which sold the balances to the Fund.

(*i*) The Fund agrees not to sell the blocked balances acquired under the above authority, except with the permission or at the request of the country in which the balances are being held. The Fund may invest these balances in the ordinary or special government securities of that country. The Fund shall be free to sell such securities in any country under the provisions of V–11, below.

(*j*) The Fund shall determine from time to time the maximum proportion of the blocked balances it will purchase under this provision.

Provided, however, that during the first 2 years of its operation, blocked balances purchased by the Fund shall not exceed in the aggregate 10 percent of the quotas of all member ccountries. At the end of 2 years of operation, the Fund shall propose a plan for the gradual further liquidation of blocked balances still outstanding indicating the proportion of the blocked balances which the Board considers the Fund can appropriately purchase.

Blocked balances acquired under this provision shall not be included either in computing the amount of foreign exchange available to member countries under their quotas (cf. V–2, 3), or in computing charges on balances of local currency in excess of the quotas (cf. V–14).

9. To buy and sell currencies of non-member countries but shall not acquire more than $10 million of the currency of any one non-member country nor hold such currencies beyond 60 days after date of purchase except with the approval of the Board.

10. To borrow the currency of any member country provided the additional amount is needed by the Fund and provided the representative of that country approves.

11. To sell member-country obligations owned by the Fund provided that the representatives of the country issuing the securities and of the country in which the securities are to be sold approve, except that the approval of the representative of the issuing country shall not be necessary if the obligations are to be sold in its own market.

To use its holdings to obtain rediscounts or advances from the Central Bank of any country whose currency the Fund needs.

12. To invest any of its currency holdings in government securities of the country of that currency provided that the representative of the country approves.

13. To lend to any member country its local currency from the Fund for 1 year or less up to 75 percent of the currency of that country held by the Fund, provided the local currency holdings of the Fund are not reduced below 20 percent of the quota.

14. To make a service charge on all gold and exchange transactions.

To levy a charge uniform to all countries, at a rate not less than 1 percent per annum, payable in gold, against any country on the amount of its currency held by the Fund in excess of the quota of that country. An additional charge, payable in gold, shall be levied by the Fund against any member country on the Fund's holdings of its currency in excess of the permissible quota of that country.

In case the Fund finds it necessary to borrow currency to meet the demands of its members, an additional charge, payable in gold, shall be made by the Fund sufficient to cover the cost of the borrowing.

15. To levy upon member countries a *pro rata* share of the expenses of operating the Fund, payable in local currency, not to exceed one-tenth percent per annum of the quota of each country. The levy may be made only to the extent that the earnings of the Fund are inadequate to meet its current expenses.

16. The Fund shall deal only with or through:

(*a*) The Treasuries, Stabilization Funds, or Central Banks acting as fiscal agents of member governments.

(*b*) Any international banks owned predominantly by member governments.

The Fund may, nevertheless, with the approval of the representatives of the governments of the countries concerned, sell its own securities, or securities it holds, directly to the public or to institutions of member countries.

VI. Management

1. The administration of the Fund shall be vested in a Board of Directors. Each government shall appoint a director and an alternate, in a manner determined by it, who shall serve for a period of 5 years, subject to the pleasure of their government. Directors and alternates may be reappointed.

2. In all voting by the Board, the director or alternate of each member country shall be entitled to cast an agreed upon number of votes.

The distribution of *basic votes* shall be closely related to the quotas of member countries, although not in precise proportion to the quotas. An appropriate distribution of basic voting power would seem to be the following: Each country shall have 100 votes, plus 1 vote for the equivalent of each 100,000 unitas ($1 million) of its quota.

No country shall be entitled to cast more than one-fifth of the aggregate basic votes, regardless of its quota.

3. All voting shall be according to basic votes except as follows:

(*a*) In voting on proposals to authorize the sale of foreign exchange, each country shall cast a number of votes modified from its basic vote:

(i) By the addition of one vote for each $2 million of net sales of its currency by the Fund (adjusted for its net transactions in gold), and

(ii) By the subtraction of one vote for each $2 million of its net purchases of foreign exchange from the Fund (adjusted for its net transactions in gold).

(*b*) In voting on proposals to suspend or restore membership, each member country shall cast one vote, as provided in VI–11, below.

4. All decisions, except where specifically provided otherwise, shall be made by a majority of the member votes.

5. The Board of Directors shall select a Managing Director of the Fund and one or more assistants. The Managing Director shall become an *ex officio* member of the Board and shall be chief of the operating staff of the Fund. The operating staff shall be selected in accordance with regulations established by the Board of Directors.

6. The Board of Directors shall appoint from among its members an Executive Committee of not less than 11 members. The Chairman of the Board shall be Chairman of the Executive Committee, and the Managing Director of the Fund shall be an *ex officio* member of the Executive Committee.

The Executive Committee shall be continuously available at the head office of the Fund and shall exercise the authority delegated to it by the Board. In the absence of any member of the Executive Committee, his alternate shall act in his place. Members of the Executive Committee shall receive appropriate remuneration.

7. The Board of Directors may appoint such other committees as it finds necessary for the work of the Fund. It may also appoint advisory committees chosen wholly or partially from persons not employed by the Fund.

8. The Board of Directors may at any meeting authorize any officers or committees of the Fund to exercise any specified powers of the Board not requiring more than a majority vote.

The Board may delegate any authority to the Executive Committee, provided that the delegation of powers requiring more than a majority of the member votes can be authorized only by a majority (of the Board) of the same size as specified, and can be exercised by the Executive Committee only by like majority.

Delegated powers shall be exercised only until the next meeting of the Board, and in a manner consistent with the general policies and practices of the Board.

9. The Board of Directors may establish procedural regulations governing the operations of the Fund. The officers and committees of the Fund shall be bound by such regulations.

10. The Board of Directors shall hold an annual meeting and such other meetings as it may be desirable to convene. The annual meeting shall be held in places designated by the Executive Committee, but not more than one annual meeting in any 5-year period shall be held within the same member country.

On request of member countries casting one-fourth of the votes, the Chairman shall call a meeting of the Board for the purpose of considering any matters placed before it.

11. A country failing to meet its obligations to the Fund may be suspended provided a majority of the member countries so decides. While under suspension, the country shall be denied the privileges of membership but shall be subject to the same obligations as any other member of the Fund. At the end of 1 year the country shall be automatically dropped from membership unless it has been restored to good standing by a majority of the member countries.

Any country may withdraw from the Fund by giving notice, and its withdrawal will take effect 1 year from the date of such notice. During the interval between notice of withdrawal and the taking effect of the notice, such country shall be subject to the same obligations as any other member of the Fund.

A country which is dropped or which withdraws from the Fund shall have returned to it an amount in its own currency equal to its contributed quota, plus other obligations of the Fund to the country, and minus any sum owed by that country to the Fund. Any losses of the Fund may be deducted *pro rata* from the contributed quota to be returned to the country that has been dropped or has withdrawn from membership. Local currency holdings of the Fund in excess of the above shall be repurchased by that country with gold or foreign exchange acceptable to the Fund.

When any country is dropped or withdraws from membership, the rights of the Fund shall be fully safeguarded. The obligations of a country to the Fund shall become due at the time it is dropped or withdraws from membership; but the Fund shall have 5 years within which to liquidate its obligations to such country.

12. Net profits earned by the Fund shall be distributed in the following manner:

(*a*) Fifty percent to reserves until the reserves are equal to 10 percent of the aggregate quotas of the Fund.

(*b*) Fifty percent to be divided each year among the members in proportion to their quotas. Dividends distributed to each country shall be paid in its own currency or in gold at the discretion of the Fund.

VII. Policies of Member Countries

Each member country of the Fund undertakes the following:

1. To maintain by appropriate action exchange rates established by the Fund on the currencies of other countries, and not to alter exchange rates except as provided in IV–5, above.

Exchange rates of member countries may be permitted to fluctuate within the specified range fixed by the Fund.

2. Not to engage in exchange dealings with member or non-member countries that will undermine stability of exchange rates established by the Fund.

3. To abandon, as soon as the member country decides that conditions permit, all restrictions (other than those involving capital transfers) over foreign exchange transactions with other member countries, and not to impose any additional restrictions (except upon capital transfers) without the approval of the Fund.

The Fund may make representations to member countries that conditions are favorable for the abandonment of restrictions over foreign exchange transactions, and each member country shall give consideration to such representations.

All member countries agree that all of the local currency holdings of the Fund shall be free from any restrictions as to their use. This provision does not apply to blocked foreign balances acquired by the Fund in accordance with the provisions of V–8, above.

4. To cooperate effectively with other member countries when such countries, with the approval of the Fund, adopt or continue controls for the purpose of regulating international movements of capital. Cooperation shall include, upon recommendation by the Fund, measures that can appropriately be taken, such as:

(*a*) Not to accept or permit acquisition of deposits, securities, or investments by nationals of any member country imposing restrictions on the export of capital except with the permission of the government of that country and the Fund;

(*b*) To make available to the Fund or to the government of any member country such information as the Fund considers necessary on property in the form of deposits, securities and investments of the nationals of the member country imposing the restrictions.

5. Not to enter upon any new bilateral clearing arrangements, nor engage in multiple currency practices, which in the judgment of the Fund would retard the growth of world trade or the international flow of productive capital.

6. To give consideration to the views of the Fund on any existing or proposed monetary or economic policy, the effect of which would be to bring about sooner or later a serious disequilibrium in the balance of payments of other countries.

7. To furnish the Fund with all information it needs for its operations and to furnish such reports as the Fund may require in the form and at the times requested by the Fund.

8. To adopt appropriate legislation or decrees to carry out its undertakings to the Fund.

The French Plan

In May 1943 Messrs. Hervé Alphand and André Istel, with the help of certain studies made by one of the high officials of the French Treasury, put forward the plan reproduced below. The greater part of it was reproduced in The New York Times *on May 9, 1943. A French version was published by the Bank for International Settlements as HS.99.*

In the summary in The New York Times *the proposed permanent institution was called an "International Clearing Office," instead of a "Monetary Stabilization Office" as in the French version and in the English text reproduced below.*

Suggestions Regarding International Monetary Relations (May 1943)

1. *Preliminary remarks.*

There is little doubt that a return to a generalized system of multilateral international trade, excluding foreign-trade control and foreign-exchange control, cannot be expected for some time after the end of hostilities. For numerous countries, a premature suppression of these controls would have ominous effects.

The states of Continental Europe, in particular, devastated by war and by the consequences of German occupation, will have first to feed their population, to import essential supplies, and then to reconstruct their capacity of production for national consumption and for foreign export. It is out of the question to let private importers, each acting independently, import foreign products without restrictions. By reason of the huge size of the requirements and the extreme urgency of some of them, the Government will have to control for a while both the volume and the nature of imports.

Foreign-exchange control will also probably have to be maintained for a while, not so much because of the considerable amount of internal capital requirements, but because it is difficult to visualize how rigid foreign-trade control can be enforced without exchange control.

Anyhow Russia will maintain, for an unpredictable period of time, both foreign-trade and foreign-exchange control.

Also ex-enemy countries will have, for a period of time, to be subjected, under United Nations supervision, to strict foreign-trade and foreign-exchange control.

It is thus necessary to conceive and achieve a practical system of exchange stability and of trade financing with the following characteristics:

a) It must be applicable as soon as hostilities are over and even earlier wherever possible.
b) It must be applicable simultaneously to those countries which will practice foreign-trade control and foreign-exchange control, and to others which will enjoy freedom of foreign trade and foreign exchange.

c) It must be adaptable to the evolution of internal systems of exchange control and of foreign-trade control.

d) Far from paralyzing evolution toward a better system of international economic relations, it should constitute in itself a step toward such a system.

2. *Fundamental conditions of satisfactory monetary relations.*

No international monetary system can work satisfactorily unless certain fundamental political and economic conditions are fulfilled. Military security and social order are of course paramount. But among the general conditions, it appears useful to lay particular stress on the following:

a) Commercial treaties should be concluded permitting a rational distribution of productive activities among nations. Such a distribution ought to take into account the natural resources, the geographic and demographic conditions, the level of education as well as various other elements of the cost of production; it ought furthermore, to take into account the creditor or debtor situation of the balance of payments.

b) Certain regulatory measures of an international character should be adopted, designed to stabilize business conditions and to reduce as far as possible the swing of economic cycles.

These measures ought to have a double character: they should operate on the one hand, on the volume of instruments of payment or of credit, in order to adapt them to needs; they ought to operate, on the other hand, directly on the volume of goods in order to adapt them to outlets.

This latter action should, itself, be of a double character: on raw materials, by some kind of regulatory action on stocks and output; on finished goods, by methods devised to accelerate or slow down the rhythm of production.

c) International long term credits should be favored, and might consist, not only in traditional loans, but in direct participation of industry, agriculture, real estate, etc. . . . . through the establishment of national or international public or private Investment Trusts, or other forms of financing.

d) Methods should be devised to remedy persistent disequilibria of balances of payments, through fundamental economic adjustments.

During the period immediately after the war it will be necessary to take care of permanent deficits in the balance of payments arising from reconstruction of devastated countries and development of backward countries. This is a problem of long term financing outside of the scope of the present memorandum.

3. *Analysis of precedents supplied by previous monetary agreements.*

Various monetary agreements entered in recent years supply interesting precedents and give useful indications concerning the requisites for satisfactory international monetary relations.

Among the most useful precedents, it appears worthwhile to mention the Franco-British agreement of December 1939 which was designed to stabilize the two currencies and to finance trade between the two countries during the war. Its distinctive feature was that the two governments agreed to acquire and keep, through their exchange equalization funds, at the official rates, the other country's exchange offered through authorized channels. Thus was initiated, instead of the traditional method of financial assistance based on credits opened in terms of the money of the creditor country, a new method based on the acquisition by the creditor country of bank balances expressed in terms of the money of the debtor country.

The advantage of this new method arises in part from its flexibility; it arises also from the additional guarantee which it provides to the creditor country. Indeed, when a country opens to another a credit expressed in the currency of the creditor country, the creditor country holds exclusively a promissory note expressed in a currency which the debtor country might be unable to obtain for redeeming its debt. If, however, the creditor country holds the currency of the debtor country, it holds an internal purchasing power inside the country. True, it is conceivable that the debtor country might "freeze" its own currency owned by another country; but between friendly countries, violation of a promise not to "freeze" its own currency is a much more serious offense than failure to refund a foreign currency which the debtor country might be unable to obtain.

Several features of monetary agreements entered during the war were well suited to the special situation involved, but are not satisfactory for purposes of international financial collaboration in the future. Thus, the Franco-British agreement specified an unlimited mutual assistance, which implies risks unsuitable to a peace-time system; it specified also a prohibition of utilizing in third markets the other partner's exchange, which constitutes a bilateral regulation incompatible with the multilateral character of international trade and credit.

4. *Explanation of the proposed monetary system.*

Let us assume that the principal nations, as in the case of the tripartite agreement of 1936, might conclude a monetary accord among themselves, to which the other United Nations might be invited to adhere, under certain conditions.

a) This agreement would, in the first place, fix the official parities of the currencies of the participating countries; these official rates would not be changed without preliminary consultation (or preferably agreement) of the interested countries. A suitable mechanism of consultation (or preferably agreement) should be set up.

b) The stability of exchange rates thus determined would be assured by the undertaking, on the part of the monetary authorities (either Exchange Equalization Fund or Central Bank) to acquire at the specified rate and to conserve, at their own risks, but with the limitations and guarantees hereafter specified, the exchange of other participating countries offered through *authorized* channels. (The word "authorized" applies to countries with foreign-exchange control.)

In order to facilitate to participating countries the relaxation of foreign exchange control, treatment, both as regards limitations and guarantees, should be made more favorable as control is relaxed.

c) The foreign exchange thus acquired by the monetary authorities of the participating countries could be utilized for payments to be made in such currencies (purchase of goods, payments for services, payments of interests or dividends, purchase of securities, of real estate, etc.); it might also, under certain conditions, be sold to the monetary authorities of other participating countries.

d) A limit would be fixed, for each participating country, of the amount of exchange of each participating country which its monetary authorities would agree to acquire, if offered, at the specified rate, and conserve if required.

While the limits should correspond to a reasonable amount of international trade, the authors of this memorandum have not attempted, at the present stage, to establish the basis of the determination of these limits.

e) As a guarantee against loss arising from depreciation of its own exchange, each participating country would not only undertake to protect each other participating country against such loss, but would also agree to deposit, on demand, collateral (gold, foreign bills, raw materials, approved securities, etc.) up to a specified percentage (10 to 30% for instance) of the amount of its own currency held by the monetary authorities of another participating country. This collateral should be deposited with the monetary authorities (or warehouses, in the case of raw materials) of the country holding the currency, or a third approved country. Should the currency of the debtor country depreciate, additional collateral might be demanded, like in the case of commercial loans.

f) The proposed monetary system, which amounts to the opening of mutual credits, undoubtedly entails inflationary risks. A method must therefore be devised to counteract, whenever considered advisable, the inflationary effects of the mutual purchases of exchange. The method suggested is a method of sterilization, which would work as follows:

In a normal period, the monetary authorities of a country holding the currency of another country would use this currency so as to favor flow of credit; for instance in the form of current accounts in commercial banks, of Treasury obligations, of discounted bills, etc. In periods of inflation, this currency would be kept in the form of an account with the Central Bank of the debtor country which would refrain from basing credits on them. Thus the debtor country would be enabled to maintain the foreign exchange value of its currency without losing the control of its internal circulation.

5. *Optional constitution of a Monetary Stabilization Office.*

To assure the smooth working of the system, it would be necessary that the monetary authorities of the participating countries should be constantly in close contact, either by means of periodical meetings or by setting up a permanent committee. It would probably be still preferable to establish a central board which might be called the Monetary Stabilization Office.

This Stabilization Office would keep account of all exchange transactions effected by the monetary authorities of the participating countries. It would not only facilitate clearings, but could also receive and scrutinize collateral. Furthermore, it would be in a position to know the balance of payments of each of the participating countries and thus to furnish valuable information concerning disequilibria of an accidental or permanent character, which should be corrected by financial or economic measures. Thus the Monetary Stabilization Office could serve both as a barometer of economic conditions and as a counsellor on economic affairs.

It should be noted, nevertheless, that the establishment of a Monetary Stabilization Office is not an essential condition for the operation of the proposed system.

6. *The place of gold in the future monetary system.*

Under the proposed system, monetary parities are fixed by mutual reference, and mutual credits are opened without movements of gold (except when used as collateral). However, the suggested system may be considered as a first step toward a general return to an international gold standard. Indeed, the establishment of fixed monetary parities,—even if tentative and even if affected by exchange control is tantamount to the adoption of a common monetary unit. Thus the link to gold of the U.S. dollar becomes a link for all other currencies also.

The role of gold could be enhanced by stipulating that any nation which so desired would be authorized to redeem in gold the credits received. Gradually, the various monetary units, as experience would show that parities are well established, could be defined anew in gold ounces.

Nevertheless, the place of gold has undergone deep modifications since 1914 and will remain considerably altered. Gold has ceased, for three decades, to be an instrument of internal circulation. Unlike platinum and silver, which have found new outlets in the chemical industry, gold has found none. So that its industrial use has been greatly reduced and has now become an infinitesimal proportion of an annual production which, in 1940, was three times as high, in dollars, as in 1920. The conception of gold as a "pledge" of internal monetary circulation has been pointedly criticized. Gold, however, has not ceased to be of valuable service for settlement of balances of payment between countries. It has also remained in use for the purpose of hoarding, notwithstanding administrative restrictions in most countries; such restrictions increase the risk of gold hoarding, but increase also its psychological attraction.

To sum up, use of gold is considerably restricted, while its world stock is now, in dollars, about four times as high as in 1914.

The facts themselves, in their evolution, seem to designate the new place of gold. Inasmuch as its stock, considerably increased, is in the hands of the monetary authorities of certain countries, predominantly in the United States, and inasmuch as its other uses have become insignificant, *therefore its value depends mainly on the action of monetary authorities, particularly in the United States.* The value of gold has thus become similar to the value of a fiduciary currency. Considering the difficulties which nations would encounter if they attempted to agree upon the adoption of a new international currency, is it not providential that they have at hand such a currency, consecrated by a mystic thousands of years old, in the form of yellow metal? Gold is the international currency of the future.

While gold should thus resume its role as an instrument of settlement of international balances and as a common monetary unit, its function as chief economic regulator should not be revived. The latter function should be exercised mainly through the concerted action of the competent authorities on the volume of credits and of goods. (It should be pointed out that the action of competent authorities on credits was already an inherent part of the traditional gold standard which, widely held opinion to the contrary, did not work automatically, but was managed through discount rates.)

7. *Conclusion.*

It may be pointed out that the proposed system is intermediate between two systems which were widely in use in the period 1920–1940. Before Great Britain devalued in 1931, central banks customarily held currencies of certain other countries, without limit nor protection. Under this system, usually designated as the "gold exchange standard," the Bank of France and the Netherlands Central Bank had accumulated large sterling balances. After the heavy losses thus incurred, monetary authorities adhered to the practice of requesting conversion into gold of the foreign exchange balances which they acquired. This system, usually called the "gold bullion standard," was utilized in the tripartite monetary agreement, where each adhering country promised to redeem in gold, within 24 hours the amounts of its own currency acquired by the exchange equalization fund of another adhering country.

Both these systems are unsatisfactory. It is unreasonable, under the "gold exchange standard," to expect one country to hold, without some limit and guarantee, another country's currency. It is also unreasonable, under the "gold bullion standard," to consider the currency of a friendly country as worthless. The proposed system does not, like the gold exchange standard, imply one hundred percent confidence in another country's currency, nor, like the gold bullion standard, imply one hundred percent lack of confidence.

There seems to be no reason why the proposed system, or a similar one, could not be started immediately between the United Nations without waiting for the end of hostilities. The only real problem is to find a proper basis for fixing the limits of the amounts of exchange to be purchased. But should important difficulties arise in this connection, the system could be started nevertheless in an experimental way by fixing at the outset very low limits which could be gradually increased later.

The Canadian Plan

Following discussions between U.S. and Canadian officials in May 1943, the Canadian Government decided to put forward its own plan as an alternative to the White and Keynes Plans. A first draft was sent to Lord Keynes on June 3, 1943 and a slightly revised version was tabled in the Canadian House of Commons by the Minister of Finance on July 12, 1943. It is the latter version which is reproduced below.

Tentative Draft Proposals of Canadian Experts for an International Exchange Union

(July 12, 1943)

CONTENTS

OTTAWA: *June 9, 1943*

GENERAL OBSERVATIONS OF CANADIAN EXPERTS ON PLANS FOR POST-WAR MONETARY ORGANIZATION

1. Officials of the Canadian Government have had an opportunity of examining the United States Treasury Department Preliminary Draft Outline of a Proposal for a United and Associated Nations Stabilization Fund, and have received explanations of this proposal from American officials. A similar procedure was followed in connection with the paper containing proposals by British experts for an International Clearing Union. The discussions with both British and American officials have been entirely exploratory and the Canadian Government has not been committed to any course of action as a result of these conversations. The American and British experts, for their part, have laid stress on the fact that their proposals are tentative in character, and have made it clear to representatives of the Canadian Government (as well as to those of other governments) that they would welcome critical comment and constructive

* It might be preferable to refer to the proposed organization as the International Exchange Fund. However, to avoid any possible misunderstanding which might arise through the use of the term Fund to describe both the association of members and the resources of the institution, the term Union has been used throughout this document to describe the organization itself.

suggestions. Canadian experts who have been studying the British and the American proposals are, therefore, led to make certain observations of a general character and to submit an alternative plan. Like the British and the American plans, the proposals of the Canadian experts are provisional and tentative in character; they incorporate important features of both the American and the British plans and add to them certain new elements.

2. The main objectives of the American and the British proposals appear to be identical, namely, the establishment of an international monetary mechanism which will aid in the restoration and development of healthy international trade after the war, which will achieve a high degree of exchange stability, and which will not conflict with the desire of countries to carry out such policies as they may think appropriate to achieve, so far as possible, economic stability at a high level of employment and incomes. To aid in the achievement of these objectives, the British and American experts have proposed the establishment of a new international monetary institution. Their proposals are large in conception, but no larger than the problem itself. There is every reason to improve the structure and operation of the monetary mechanism on the basis of experience. But there is no reason why proposals should be based exclusively on the limited, and on the whole, bad experience of the past two decades. Unless dependable exchange and credit relations between countries can be achieved before the stresses and strains of the post-war period begin, there is little likelihood that irreparable damage can be avoided.

3. If plans for international monetary organization are to be successful, other problems—by no means less difficult or less important—will also have to be faced and solved by joint international action. It would, indeed, be dangerous to attach too much importance to monetary organization of and by itself, if this resulted in neglect of other problems which may be even more important and difficult, or in a misguided faith that with a new form of monetary organization the other problems would solve themselves. In the international field alone (to say nothing of the innumerable domestic problems involved in the profound changes in the structure of production and employment which have taken place in all belligerent and many non-belligerent countries due to the exigencies of the war) it will be necessary to attack frontally such problems as commercial policy, international investment, the instability of primary product prices—to name but a few. No international monetary organization, however perfect in form, could long survive economic distortions resulting from bilateralist trade practices, continued refusal of creditor countries to accept imports in payment of the service on their foreign investment or to invest their current account surplus abroad, or enormous fluctuations in food and raw material prices such as characterized the years between the two wars. But the fact that there are many problems to be faced cannot be used as an excuse for facing none. A start must be made somewhere, and for the reasons given in paragraph 5, the problem of international monetary organization is a logical and fruitful starting-place.

4. The establishment of an international monetary organization is no substitute for the measures of international relief and rehabilitation which will be required as the war draws to its conclusion and afterwards; and in the view of the Canadian experts any monetary organization which is set up should not be called upon to finance transactions of this nature. Some continuing and stable arrangements regarding international long-term investment are also clearly essential if equilibrium is to be achieved and maintained. Nor should it be thought that the proposed international monetary institu-

tion is merely an instrument of the transition period from war to peace. True, it has special importance in this period, but it should be designed as a permanent institution and not as a stop-gap to function during a relatively short period of time.

5. An important, perhaps the most important, feature of the British and the American proposals is the provision in both plans for the extension of credit between countries. The two plans differ as regards the precise techniques to be used in extending credit and as regards the amounts which may be involved; but both plans provide that foreign credits are to be available under certain conditions to countries having need of them, and that they shall be made available through an international monetary organization rather than through bilateral arrangements between pairs of countries. The provision for credit extension is nothing more nor less than a straightforward and realistic recognition of the fact that at the end of the war a large number of countries, whose import requirements will be considerable, will not have immediately available a sufficient reserve of foreign assets to enable them to expose themselves to the risk of participation in a world economic system. An interval will be needed to give time for adjustment and re-organization. If the penury in foreign means of payment of certain important countries is to be allowed to fix the pattern of post-war trading and domestic policies, then all can look forward to penury—no country, rich or poor, will escape the impoverishment resulting from the throttling of international trade which will result.

6. It is useful to consider what would happen if no action were taken to set up international machinery of the general character suggested by the experts of the United States and the United Kingdom. Theoretically, one alternative would be immediate cash settlement for all international transactions. But how can cash be produced for purchases abroad? Only by selling goods or services abroad, or by disposing of acceptable foreign assets such as securities and gold. The facts regarding the distribution of the world's monetary gold reserves and the changes which have taken place in the course of the war in various countries' holdings of foreign securities are too well known to require elaboration. Broadly speaking, and allowing for certain exceptions and time-lags, a cash basis for the settlement of international transactions would mean that any country's capacity to export would be limited to the amount of its own currency it made available to foreign countries through its imports and other current payments abroad—in other words, trade would in effect be reduced to barter. In point of fact, however, there is no possibility that countries would for long allow themselves to be confined in such a strait-jacket. Faced with the problem of an unsalable surplus of export goods and with consequent domestic unemployment, they would refuse to accept the penalty of disorganization of export trade if that penalty could be avoided, even temporarily, by the extension of credit. Countries would embark on bilateral credit arrangements, no doubt linked with deals relating to the purchase and sale of goods; and as soon as certain countries began to adopt this course others would find that they had to follow suit to protect their trade interests. It is difficult to imagine a more fruitful source of international dissension than a competitive trade and credit extension program of this character.

The Canadian experts believe it to be true, therefore, that the Stabilization Fund or Clearing Union plans do not involve a decision as to whether foreign credits shall be extended or withheld. In some form or other, credit will in fact be extended; and the decision which has to be taken relates primarily to the method employed. For the reasons given above, international arrangements are greatly to be preferred to bilateral deals.

7. This leads to the question, how much credit should be made available through the international monetary mechanism? A vital feature of any plan of this sort is the provision it makes for the borrowing power of each participant and for the contribution to the resources of the organization by the participating countries through the provision of capital, the accumulation of balances or through loans. Some concern has been expressed in regard to the size of the commitment which may be assumed by prospective creditors. It is probable that Canada will be a creditor country on current account, and the Canadian experts have therefore given careful thought to this aspect of the arrangements.

8. There is one preliminary observation which should be made in this connection. It would be a distortion of the realities of the situation for any country, or its citizens, to regard the willingness to provide resources to an international organization of the general character proposed by the British and American experts as an act of generosity which is performed for the sake of foreign countries. Resources are provided to the organization first, because all have a stake in re-creating a functioning international economic system and secondly, because for each individual country the realistic alternatives in the form of trade disorganization are costlier than the provision of resources. Moreover, and most important of all, the resources provided are not given away; they are fully secured by the organization's holdings of gold and national currencies. It can only lead to confusion of thought to regard participation in such plans as these as in any way similar in character to participation in international relief schemes, important and necessary though the latter may be.

9. It seems apparent that, in one way or another, substantial unregulated movements of capital between countries will be prevented. In these circumstances, countries will, by and large, lose or gain foreign exchange to the extent, but only to the extent, of the unbalance in their current account transactions with the rest of the world. If a country is building up a substantial credit position, it will know that this situation is produced because it is selling more goods and services abroad than it is buying abroad. If it is dissatisfied with this position, if it wishes to reduce its credit balance, it has through participation in the proposed organization lost no single one of the courses of action ever open to it. True, it is by no means easy for a country, acting alone, to solve problems of unbalance. But as a last resort a country *can* find a solution by unilateral action. It can do the only things it ever could do in these circumstances; it can buy more abroad—goods, services or investments; or it can sell less abroad. It is therefore quite wrong to assume that countries participating in the proposed institution would, because of this participation, be left without control over their international commitments. It may be, and no doubt is, useful to erect danger signals at various stations along the road followed by both debtors and creditors. Such signals are useful reminders. But there is nothing to prevent either creditor or debtor from taking remedial action at any time.

10. If the foregoing is a correct analysis of the situation—and it would appear to be a simple statement of fact—creditors need not be unduly concerned about the possible size of their investment in the Fund, knowing that the ultimate actual size of their stake can be determined by their own course of action from day to day and from year to year. Nevertheless, even the appearance of an unlimited commitment is probably undesirable and in the tentative proposals of Canadian experts, a limit is placed on the obligation of each participant to provide resources to the institution. But there is less real danger to the interests of creditor countries in the establishment of a Fund

or a Union whose potential resources are unnecessarily large (and may in consequence never be entirely used) than there is in the establishment of an institution whose resources are obviously too small. The interests of all will best be served by providing a fair degree of latitude, a satisfactory breathing-space—to debtors and creditors alike. If its objectives are to be achieved, the resources must be large enough to permit time for basic re-adjustments to be accomplished; they must be such that the organization will command general confidence in its own stability. For if this is not the case, what will happen? It will be believed that certain currencies are likely to become "scarce" currencies—a belief which will be reinforced by the reduction in the institution's holdings of that particular currency. Countries which are likely to require a "scarce" currency will hasten to make their purchases which are payable in that currency. As the holdings of the "scarce" currency are used up, as discussions and arguments commence regarding an enlargement of the quota or some other form of extension of credit, grave misgivings in regard to the international situation will arise. The position will be very much akin to that of a bank whose cash reserves are feared to be insufficient. There will be a run on that currency in the institution; and if the currency concerned is an important one, the international effects will be very serious indeed. No form of international monetary organization can continuously compensate for chronic maladjustments in the current account balance of payments of the countries which may be concerned, but it would be most unwise to set up machinery which stood a fair chance of facing a crisis at a comparatively early date.

11. To avoid misunderstanding it should be emphasized that it would be extremely dangerous to use short-term credits as a device to cover up basically unsound positions. This would be no less disastrous in the international than in the domestic field, and any monetary system which made such an attempt on a large scale would inevitably break down. A chronic unbalance in current account balances of international payments which is not matched by voluntary long-term capital movements—lending abroad by creditor countries, and borrowing abroad by debtor countries—is symptomatic of a deep-seated maladjustment which has to be dealt with if equilibrium is to be restored. No debtor country can live beyond its resources indefinitely; and no creditor country can persistently refuse to lend its surplus abroad or make other adjustments to its creditor position without ripping the international fabric. But time is required for adjustments to be made and for remedial measures to have their effects, and the contention of this paper is that the time allowed must be adequate. More time may be purchased at a smaller real cost than less time.

12. There is one final observation of a general character which should be made. The new international monetary institution which it is proposed to establish will be neither omniscient nor omnipotent. Its aim will be to promote conditions in which member countries are free to carry out sound economic policies for the welfare of their own people and in which they will not be induced or forced, for lack of organized co-operation, to pursue policies which impoverish themselves and contribute to the impoverishment of the world. The organization should be international and not supernational. Nations should enter into the proposed agreement for common purposes and advantages, realizing that without such agreement the common purposes cannot be achieved. In their national policies, countries should be limited only by their own will in entering and remaining in the organization. If the proposed institution functions well, it will have at its disposal more information regarding the currents of international financial transactions and the causes of disequilibrium than has ever been available before. It will be in a position to offer informed and disinterested advice

to its members. It may be hoped that the quality of the advice offered will be such that it will carry great weight. But no member state should be asked to bind itself in all circumstances to follow the advice given by the organization. Moreover, if a country feels at any time that its national interests are being jeopardized by the actions of the organization, and is willing to sacrifice the advantages of continued membership, it should be free to withdraw, after making provision to liquidate its obligations to the organization or, if the country is a creditor, it should have returned to it its original contribution to the resources of the organization. The proposals here advanced are put forward in the belief that a soundly conceived international agreement can give greater scope for national policies than can exist outside it.

13. To sum up these general observations, it is suggested that:

(*a*) An international agreement for the establishment of an international monetary organization which involves the extension of credit is essential if international co-operation in the post-war world is to be achieved.

(*b*) Such machinery will deal with only one of the numerous problems which must be faced, but it is a logical and convenient starting place for joint international action.

(*c*) The credit made available through the international monetary organization should be adequate to deal with that portion of current account surpluses and deficits which is not met by relief and other concerted international action in the years immediately after the war; it should be sufficient to provide a firm basis on which multilateral world trade can be re-established after the war; and it should provide time to countries which find their international accounts unbalanced to take the necessary corrective measures to adjust their position.

(*d*) The extension of credit is not a cure-all; it merely provides time for adjustments; and unless unbalanced positions (except those accompanying long-term capital movements) are brought into equilibrium, any arrangements made will break down.

(*e*) No country participating in the arrangements loses control over the size of its international commitments, since it can determine their size by its own action, if it wishes to do so.

(*f*) No country participating in the arrangements loses control over its domestic economic policies.

TENTATIVE DRAFT PROPOSALS OF CANADIAN EXPERTS FOR AN INTERNATIONAL EXCHANGE UNION

I. Purposes of the Union

1. To provide for stability of exchange rates and to provide an orderly method for their determination.

2. To provide a convenient clearing mechanism to settle balances in international payments.

3. To provide to all countries access to foreign exchange resources in order to reduce the danger that economic and commercial policies in the period immediately after the war will be largely determined by a shortage of foreign exchange and to enable

countries thereafter to be guided in their economic and commercial policies by long-run considerations when faced with a temporary reduction of foreign markets.

4. To aid in the achievement of international equilibrium by measures designed to prevent excessive short-term borrowing through the Union or the excessive accumulation of uninvested foreign surpluses.

5. To contribute to the re-establishment and development of a multilateral trading system and to the elimination of discriminatory trading and currency practices.

II. Resources of the Union

Member countries shall agree to make the following resources available to the Union:

1. A capital subscription to the amount of the quota assigned to each member country, the aggregate of such quotas to be $8,000 million.

DETAILED PROVISIONS
REGARDING 1—QUOTAS AND CAPITAL SUBSCRIPTION

(a) *Determination of Quotas*

The quota for each member country shall be determined by a formula which will give due regard to factors such as international trade, national income, and holdings of gold and foreign exchange convertible into gold. A special assessment may be levied in any case where this formula would be inappropriate.

(b) *Payment of Capital Subscriptions*

The capital subscription of each member country shall be paid up in full on or before the date set by the Governing Board of the Union on which the Union's operations are to begin. Each member country shall pay in at least 15 per cent. of its quota in gold and the balance in national currency; a country may substitute gold for national currency in meeting its quota requirements. The Union may make such arrangements as it deems appropriate to provide a period of time within which countries having less than $300 million in gold or foreign exchange convertible into gold in official exchange reserves may pay up their gold contribution in full, the equivalent in national currency to be paid in the interval. Notwithstanding the provisions of subsequent paragraphs, the Union shall sell foreign exchange to such member countries for the purpose of acquiring gold to pay their capital subscriptions.

(c) *Change in Quotas*

The Board may from time to time change the quotas of particular member countries, provided, however, that in voting on proposals to increase quotas the voting strength of each member shall be increased or decreased to take account of the Union's net sales or purchases of the currency of each member country in accordance with the weighted voting formula set out in paragraph IX.3 below. No increase shall, however, be made in the quota of any country without the consent of the representative of the country concerned.

2. Loans to the Union, as required, in amounts not exceeding 50 per cent. of the quota of each member country.

DETAILED PROVISIONS
REGARDING 2—LOANS TO THE UNION

(a) *Conditions of Borrowing*

The terms and conditions of loans made by member countries to the Union under the provisions of paragraph II.2 shall be set out in the rules and regulations of the Union. The Union's authority to borrow domestic currency from member countries in amounts up to 50 per cent. of their quotas shall be a revolving authority. The Union shall not exercise its right to borrow until it has used its available gold resources to acquire additional supplies of the currency in question. Subject to the provisions of the preceding sentence, the Union must exercise its right to borrow when its holdings of the currency of any member country have been reduced to 10 per cent. of the quota of that member country. When the Union exercises its right under the provisions of paragraph II.2 to borrow additional supplies of the currency of any member country it shall have the duty to attempt to improve its position in the currency concerned by acquiring the currency or gold from the holdings of other member countries for payment in their national currencies or in other foreign exchange they need.

(*b*) *Conditions of Repayment*

The Union shall have the right to repay loans contracted under the provisions of paragraph II.2 at any time. The member country making the loan shall have the right to demand repayment in gold to the extent of the Union's gold holdings at any time and shall also have the right to demand repayment in its national currency provided that such repayment does not reduce the Union's holdings of that currency below 50 per cent. of the quota of the member country. Member countries shall agree to give 30 days' notice of demand for repayment of loans made to the Union under the provisions of the present article.

III. MONETARY UNIT OF THE UNION

1. The monetary unit of the Union shall be an international unit of such name as may be agreed (hereafter referred to as the Unit) and it shall consist of 137 1/7 grains of fine gold. The accounts of the Union shall be kept and published in terms of the Unit.

2. The value of the Unit in terms of gold shall not be changed without the approval of four-fifths of member votes.

3. Member countries shall agree with the Union the initial values of their currencies in terms of gold or the Unit and, except as provided in paragraph IV.2 below, shall undertake not to alter these values without the approval of the Union.

4. Deposits in terms of the Unit may be accepted by the Union from member countries upon the delivery of gold to the Union. Such Unit deposits shall be transferable to other member countries. They shall be redeemable in gold and the Union shall maintain at all times a 100 per cent. reserve in gold against all Unit deposits.

IV. EXCHANGE RATES

1. The Union shall fix, on the basis of exchange rates initially agreed between it and each member country, the rates at which it will buy and sell one member's currency for another's and the rates in local currencies at which it will buy and sell gold. The spread between the Union's buying and selling rates for member currencies and for gold shall not exceed 1 per cent. Except as provided in paragraph IV.2 below, member countries shall agree not to change the initially agreed exchange rates without the approval of the Union and any country which alters the value of its currency without the consent of the Union shall be declared in default of its obligations and become subject to the penalties provided in paragraph XI.1 below.

2. Notwithstanding the provisions of paragraph IV.1 above, any member country which is a net purchaser of foreign exchange from the Union (arising from other than capital account transactions) to the extent of at least 50 per cent. of its quota and has so been on the average of the preceding 12 months shall be entitled to depreciate its exchange to the maximum extent of 5 per cent.; provided, however, that the provisions of this paragraph shall not apply to any country which holds independent official reserves of gold and foreign currencies freely convertible into gold in amounts exceeding 50 per cent. of its quota. No country shall be entitled to repeat the exchange depreciation provided for in this paragraph without the specific approval of the Union.*

3. No change in the value of the currencies of member countries shall be permitted to alter the value of the assets of the Union in terms of gold or the Unit. Thus, if the Union approves a reduction in the value of the currency of a member country, or if a country depreciates its exchange under the provisions of the preceding paragraph, or if a significant depreciation in the value of the currency of a member, as determined by quotations on the exchange markets of other member countries, has in fact occurred, that country must on request deliver to the Union an amount of its local currency equal to the decrease in the value of that currency held by the Union. Likewise, if the currency of a particular country should appreciate, the Union must return to that country an amount in the currency of that country or in gold equal to the resulting increase in the value of the Union's holdings.

V. Operations of the Union—Provisions of Special Applicability to Deficit Countries

1. The Union shall have the power to sell to the Treasury of any member country (or exchange fund or central bank acting as its agent for the purpose) at the rate of exchange established by the Union, currency of any country which the Union holds, subject to the following provisions:

(*a*) Without special permission, no country shall be a net purchaser of foreign exchange from the Union except for the purpose of meeting an adverse balance of payments on current account and the Union may at any time limit the amounts of foreign exchange to be sold to any member country which is permitting significant exports of capital while having an adverse balance of payments on current account.

---

* In the course of conversations in Washington the Canadian experts expressed the view that it might be desirable to provide for a somewhat greater permissive range of depreciation in exchange rates with somewhat different safeguards than those incorporated in paragraph IV.2. The following is a draft of a paragraph which might be substituted for paragraph IV.2 of the text:

"Notwithstanding the provisions of paragraph IV.1 above, any member country which has had an adverse balance of payments on current account during a two year period of such magnitude that it has utilized, to cover this deficit, 50 per cent. of its independent gold and foreign exchange reserves and is, in addition, a net purchaser of foreign exchange from the Union to the extent of 50 per cent. of its quota shall be entitled to depreciate its exchange rate to the maximum extent of 10 per cent. The provisions of this paragraph shall only be applicable once in respect of each member country unless the specific approval of the Union has been obtained. Any member country intending to depreciate its exchange rate under the provisions of this paragraph shall inform the management of the Union in advance and shall afford it an opportunity to make such observations as it deems appropriate before taking such action."

DETAILED PROVISIONS
REGARDING (*a*)—RESTRICTION OF RIGHT OF DEFICIT COUNTRIES TO PURCHASE FOREIGN EXCHANGE TO AMOUNTS REQUIRED TO MEET AN ADVERSE BALANCE OF PAYMENTS ON CURRENT ACCOUNT.

(i) A country shall be regarded as a net purchaser of foreign exchange if as a result of the Union's purchases and sales of currencies the Union's holdings of its currency rise above the amount originally provided to the Union by way of capital subscription.

(ii) The Union may require any member country to furnish at periodic intervals statistics of its balance of international payments on current account and on capital account and statistics of gold and foreign exchange holdings, public and private. Each such member country shall agree to furnish officers of the Union with detailed explanations of the basis on which such statistics are computed. If at any time the Governing Board has reason to believe that an overflow of capital from any member country is resulting directly or indirectly in net purchases of foreign exchange by that country from the Union, it shall have the right to request a control of outward capital movements as a condition of making additional sales of foreign exchange to such country. Without limiting the generality of the foregoing, the Union shall normally require any member country which has been a net purchaser of foreign exchange to the extent of 25 per cent. of its quota to impose restrictions on outward capital movements if none exist.

(iii) In considering applications from countries which have been net purchasers of foreign exchange from the Union for the special permission referred to in paragraph V.1 (*a*) to purchase foreign exchange for purposes other than the meeting of an adverse balance of payments on current account, the Governing Board shall give careful attention to applications for foreign exchange to facilitate the adjustment of foreign debts where this is deemed to be desirable from the point of view of the general economic situation and shall also give special attention to applications for foreign exchange by member countries not in default on their foreign obligations for the purpose of maintaining contractual principal payments on foreign debt.

(*b*) In order to promote the most effective utilization of existing stocks of gold and foreign exchange, no member country shall have the right to be a net purchaser of foreign exchange from the Union so long as that country's holdings of gold and foreign currencies freely convertible into gold (including private as well as official holdings) exceed its quota.

DETAILED PROVISION
REGARDING (*b*)—RESTRICTION OF RIGHT OF COUNTRIES HOLDING LARGE INDEPENDENT GOLD AND FOREIGN EXCHANGE RESERVES TO PURCHASE FOREIGN EXCHANGE FROM THE UNION

In interpreting this provision the Governing Board shall give special consideration to the position of certain Asiatic countries where gold has long been used as private treasure.

(*c*) In general, the Union shall have the power to sell foreign exchange for domestic currency to member countries up to 200 per cent. of the quota of each such member country. Net sales of foreign exchange shall not exceed 50 per cent.

of the quota of each member country during the first year and the cumulative net sales shall not exceed 100 per cent., 150 per cent. or 200 per cent. during the first two, three and four years of the operation of the union.

DETAILED PROVISION
REGARDING (*c*)—RESTRICTION OF SALES OF FOREIGN EXCHANGE TO SPECIFIED LIMITS

On special vote of the Governing Board, in which voting strength shall be weighted to allow for the Union's net purchases and sales of each member country's currency in accordance with the provisions described in paragraph IX.3 below, the Union may purchase any currency in excess of these limits provided that (*a*) the country whose currency is being acquired by the Union agrees to adopt and carry out measures recommended by the Union to correct the disequilibrium in its balance of payments, or (*b*) it is the view of the Governing Board that the country's prospective balance of payments is such as to warrant the expectation that the excess currency holdings of the Union can be disposed of in a reasonable time.

(*d*) In order to promote the most effective utilization of existing stocks of gold and foreign exchange, the Union may, as a condition of making further sales of foreign exchange to any member country which would bring its net purchases to an amount in excess of 50 per cent. of its quota, require such country to sell the Union, for domestic currency, appropriate amounts of any reserves it (or its residents) may hold of gold or foreign exchange acceptable to the Union.

(*e*) Notwithstanding the provisions of paragraph (*c*) above, whenever a member country is exhausting its quota more rapidly than is warranted in the judgment of the Governing Board, the Board may make such recommendations to that country as it thinks appropriate with a view to correcting the disequilibrium, and may place such conditions upon additional sales of foreign exchange to that country as it deems to be in the general interest of the Union.

2. A charge of 1 per cent. per annum payable in gold shall be levied against member countries on the amount of their currency held by the Union in excess of the quotas of such countries.

VI. Operations of the Union—Provisions of Special Applicability to Surplus Countries

1. In order to promote the most effective utilization of the available and accumulating supply of gold and foreign exchange resources of member countries, each member country shall, on request of the Union, sell to the Union, for its local currency or for foreign currencies which it needs, all gold and foreign exchange it acquires in excess of the amounts held immediately after joining the Union.

DETAILED PROVISION
REGARDING 1—ACCUMULATING SUPPLIES OF GOLD AND FOREIGN EXCHANGE

For the purpose of this provision, only free foreign exchange and gold are considered. Each member country shall agree to furnish the Union with periodic reports of gold and foreign exchange holdings, public and private.

2. When the Union's operations have resulted in net sales of the currency of any member country to the extent of 75 per cent. of the quota of that country the Union may, in order to increase its resources of the currency in question, attempt to arrange, in co-operation with such agencies as may be established to promote international

investment, with the member country a program of foreign capital investment (or repatriation) and may sell foreign exchange to facilitate such capital movements.

3. When the Union's holdings of the currency of a member country are being exhausted more rapidly than is warranted in the judgment of the Governing Board, the Board may make a report on the situation. Without restricting the generality of the foregoing, whenever the Union's operations have resulted in net sales of the currency of any member country to the extent of 85 per cent. of the quota of that country, the Union has the authority and the duty to render to the country a report embodying an analysis of the causes of the depletion of its holdings of the currency and recommendations appropriate to restore the equilibrium of the international balances of the country concerned. Such recommendations may relate to monetary and fiscal policies, exchange rate, commercial policy and international investment.

DETAILED PROVISION
REGARDING 3—REPORT ON COUNTRIES WHOSE CURRENCY IS BECOMING SCARCE

The Board member of the country in question shall be a member of the Union Committee appointed to draft the report. The report shall be sent to all member countries and, if deemed desirable, made public.

4. The Union shall have the right at any time to enter into arrangements with any member country to borrow additional supplies of its currency on such terms and conditions as may be mutually satisfactory.

5. The Union shall have the right at any time to enter into special arrangements with any member country for the purpose of providing an emergency supply of the currency of any other member country on such terms and conditions as may be mutually satisfactory.

6. Whenever it becomes apparent to the Governing Board that the anticipated demand for any currency may soon exhaust the Union's holdings, the Governing Board shall inform the member countries of the probable supply of this currency and of a proposed method for its equitable distribution together with suggestions for helping to equate the anticipated demand and supply.

DETAILED PROVISIONS
REGARDING 6—RATIONING OF SCARCE CURRENCIES

(*a*) The provisions of paragraph VI.6 shall come into force only after the Union has exercised in full its right under paragraph II.2 to borrow additional supplies of the currency of the member country and after the Union has taken such further steps to increase its supply of this currency as it has deemed appropriate and found possible.

(*b*) The provisions of paragraph V.1 (*c*) shall, if necessary, be restricted by the duty of the Union to assure an appropriate distribution among various members of any currency the Union's supply of which is being exhausted.

(*c*) In rationing its sales of any scarce currency the Union shall be guided by the principle of satisfying the most urgent needs from the point of view of the general international economic situation. It shall also consider the special needs and resources of the various countries making the request for the scarce currency.

(*d*) Member countries shall agree that restrictions imposed by other member countries on the importation of goods from a country whose currency is being rationed by the Union shall, for the duration of such rationing, not be regarded as constituting an infraction of the most-favoured nation obligations of commercial treaties except in the case of countries holding official reserves of gold and the currencies of member countries in amounts exceeding 50 per cent. of their quotas.*

7. Whenever the Governing Board has, under the provisions of the preceding paragraph, taken steps to ration the Union's supply of the currency of any member country, it may require the remaining member countries to prevent the sale by their residents of each other's currencies, including bills of exchange, in the country whose currency is being rationed and to prevent the purchase by their residents of the rationed currency through the exchange markets of non-member countries. In addition, whenever the Board has taken steps to ration the Union's supply of the currency of any member country, it shall have the duty to re-examine the prevailing exchange rates and to recommend such changes as it may regard as appropriate to the changed circumstances.

VII. Powers of the Union—General

1. The Union shall have the powers to take such actions as are required to carry out the operations enumerated in the preceding paragraphs. For greater clarity, the Union shall have the power to buy, sell and hold gold, currencies and government securities of member countries; to accept deposits and to earmark gold; to issue its own obligations and to discount or offer them for sale in member countries; and to act as a clearing house for the settling of international movements of funds and gold.

DETAILED PROVISION
REGARDING 1—GENERAL POWERS OF THE UNION

Member countries agree that all of the Union's local currency holdings shall be free from any restrictions as to their use for payments within the country concerned.

2. When the Union's holdings of the local currency of a member country exceed the quota of that country the Union shall have the power to resell to the member country, upon its request, the Union's excess holdings of its currency for gold or acceptable foreign exchange.

3. The Union shall have the power to invest any of its currency holdings in government securities of the country of that currency, provided that the Board representative of the country concerned approves.

4. The Union shall have the power to buy and sell currencies of non-member countries, but shall not normally hold the currencies of non-member countries beyond 60 days after the date of purchase.

5. The Union shall have the power to levy upon member countries a pro rata share of the expenses of operating the Union, such levy to be made, however, only to the extent that the earnings of the Union are inadequate to meet its current expenses.

6. The Union shall make a service charge of one-quarter per cent. on all gold transactions.

7. In conducting its own operations, the Union shall have the power to deal only with or through (*a*) the Treasuries, exchange funds or fiscal agents of governments,

* This proposal will clearly have to be reviewed in the light of such general arrangements as may be made regarding international commercial policy and co-ordinated with those arrangements.

(*b*) central banks, with the consent of the member of the Board representing the country in question, and (*c*) any international banks owned predominantly by member countries. The Union may, nevertheless, with the approval of the member of the Board representing the country concerned, sell its own securities directly to the public or to institutions of member countries.

8. The Union shall have the power and the duty to co-operate with such other institutions of an international character as may exist or be established to deal with matters of international concern, including but not restricted to international investment and commercial policy.

VIII. ABNORMAL WAR-TIME BALANCES

During the first two years of operation the Union shall have the right to purchase abnormal war time balances held by member countries in other member countries for the national currency of the country selling such balances or for foreign exchange needed to meet current account deficits in such country's balance of international payments; in amounts not exceeding in the aggregate 5 per cent. of the quotas of all member countries. At the end of two years of operation the Governing Board shall propose a plan for the gradual further liquidation, in whole or in part, through the Union, of abnormal war time balances lying to the credit of member countries in other member countries and other financial indebtedness of a similar character. If the Governing Board feels unable to recommend that the Union's resources be used for this purpose it shall have the duty to propose some other method by which the problem can be considered.

IX. VOTING POWER

1. Each member country shall have 100 votes, plus one vote for the equivalent of each 100,000 Units of its quota.

2. All decisions, except where specifically provided otherwise, shall be made by majority of the member votes.

3. Notwithstanding the provisions of paragraph I above, in any vote on a proposal to increase the quota of any member country, member countries shall acquire one additional vote for each 100,000 Units of its contribution to the resources of the Fund (by way of original capital subscription or by way of loans made under the provisions of paragraph II.2) which has been utilized, net, on the average of the preceding year by the Union for sale to other member countries; and member countries shall lose one vote for each 100,000 Units of their net utilization of the resources of the Union on the average of the preceding year.

X. MANAGEMENT

1. The administration of the Union shall be vested in a Governing Board. Each government shall appoint a representative and an alternate who shall serve on the Board for a period of three years subject to the pleasure of their government. Representatives and alternates may be re-appointed.

2. The Governing Board shall select a Governor of the Union and one or more assistants. The Governor shall become an *ex officio* member of the Board and shall be chief of the operating staff of the Board. The Governor and his assistants shall hold office for five years and shall be eligible for re-election and may be removed for cause at any time by the Board.

3. The Governor of the Union shall select the operating staff in accordance with regulations established by the Governing Board. Members of the staff may be made available upon request of member countries or of other institutions of an international character for consultation in connection with economic problems and policies.

4. The Governing Board shall appoint from among its members an Executive Committee to consist of not fewer than eleven members. The Chairman of the Board shall be the Chairman of the Executive Committee and the Governor of the Union shall be *ex officio* a member of the Executive Committee. Meetings of the Executive Committee shall be held at least once every two months and more frequently if the Executive Committee shall so decide.

5. The Governing Board shall hold an annual meeting and such other meetings as it may be desirable to convene. On request of member countries casting one-fourth of the votes the Chairman shall call a meeting of the Board for the purpose of considering any matters placed before it.

6. Net profits earned by the Union shall be distributed in the following manner:

(*a*) 50 per cent. to reserves until the reserves are equal to 10 per cent. of the aggregate quotas of the Union;

(*b*) 50 per cent. to be divided each year among the members in proportion to their quotas.

XI. Withdrawal and Expulsion from the Union

1. A country failing to meet its obligations to the Union may be suspended provided a majority of the member votes so decides. While under suspension the country shall be denied the privileges of membership but shall be subject to the same obligations as any other member of the Union. At the end of one year the country shall be automatically dropped from membership unless it has been restored to good standing by a majority of the member votes.

2. Any country which has been a net purchaser of foreign exchange from the Union may withdraw from the Union by giving notice and its withdrawal shall take effect one year from the date of such notice. During the interval between notice of withdrawal and the taking effect of the notice such country shall be subject to the same obligations as any other member of the Union.

3. Any country which has not been a net purchaser of foreign exchange from the Union may withdraw from the Union by giving notice and its withdrawal shall take effect 30 days from the date of such notice. During the interval between notice of withdrawal and the taking effect of notice such country shall be subject to the same obligations as any other member of the Union; except, however, that no country which has given notice of withdrawal shall be required to make loans to the Union under the provisions of paragraph II.2 above.

4. A country which is dropped or which withdraws from membership shall have returned to it an amount in its own currency equal to its contributed quota plus other obligations of the Union to the country and minus any sums owed by that country to the Union. The Union shall have 5 years in which to liquidate its obligation to such country.

XII. Policies of Member Countries

In addition to the obligations assumed under the preceding paragraphs, each member country shall undertake the following:

1. To maintain by appropriate action the exchange rates initially agreed with the Union on the currencies of other countries and not to alter exchange rates except under the provisions of paragraph IV.2 above, or with the consent of the Union and only to the extent and in the direction approved by the Union. Exchange rates of member countries may be permitted to fluctuate within a range not exceeding the spread fixed by the Union itself for its own purchases and sales of foreign exchange.

2. To abandon, as soon as the member country decides that conditions permit, all restrictions on foreign exchange transactions, other than those required effectively to control capital movements, with other member countries; and not to impose any additional restrictions, except for the purpose of controlling capital movements, without the approval of the Union.

DETAILED PROVISION

REGARDING 2—ABANDONMENT OF EXCHANGE CONTROL OTHER THAN ON CAPITAL MOVEMENTS

The Union may make representations to member countries that conditions are favourable for the abandonment or relaxation of foreign exchange restrictions other than those required effectively to control capital movements and each member country shall agree to give consideration to such representations.

3. To co-operate effectively with other member countries when such countries, with the approval of the Union, adopt or continue controls for the purpose of regulating international movements of capital.

DETAILED PROVISIONS

REGARDING 3—CO-OPERATION IN ENFORCING APPROVED EXCHANGE CONTROLS ON CAPITAL MOVEMENTS

Co-operation shall include, upon recommendation by the Union, measures that can appropriately be taken

(*a*) not to accept or permit acquisitions of deposits, securities or investments by residents of any member country imposing restrictions on the export of capital except with the permission of the government of that country and the Union;

(*b*) to make available to the Union or to the government of any member country full information on all property in the form of deposits, securities and investments of the residents of that country; and

(*c*) such other measures as the Union may recommend.

4. Not to enter into any new bilateral foreign exchange clearing arrangements nor engage in multiple currency practices except with the approval of the Union.

5. To give careful consideration to the views of the Union on existing or proposed monetary or economic policy the effect of which would be to cause a serious disequilibrium in the balance of payments of the country adopting such policy or of other countries.

6. To furnish the Union with all information it needs for its operations and to furnish such reports as it may require in the forms and at the times requested by the Union.

7. To adopt appropriate legislation or decrees to carry out its undertakings to the Union and to facilitate the activities of the Union.

Professor Williams' Key-Currency Plan

Professor John H. Williams expounded his proposals for a "key-currency" approach to the problems of international monetary organization in two places. The first was at the end of a paper delivered at a joint meeting of the American Statistical Association and the American Economic Association on December 28, 1936; this was reproduced in The American Economic Review, *Vol. XXVII, No. 1, Supplement (March 1937), pages 151–68. The extract (A) below consists of the final section of this paper. His second reference to the plan was at the end of his article entitled "Currency Stabilization: The Keynes and White Plans" in* Foreign Affairs, *Vol. 21, No. 4 (July 1943), pp. 645–58. Extract (B) below contains the final section of this article.*

Both the paper and the article were reprinted in Professor Williams' Postwar Monetary Plans and Other Essays, *3rd edition (New York, 1947), on pages 199–227 and pages 3–21, respectively.*

(A) Extract from a Paper on "The Adequacy of Existing Currency Mechanisms Under Varying Circumstances" *

(December 28, 1936)

I have presented the view, first, that there must be some form of compromise system, second, that this compromise should be one which will give the largest measure of internal monetary protection and control which is consistent with exchange stability, and third, that exchange variation, while not excluded, should be resorted to only when other means of control have been exhausted.

I want to conclude with three points which, I believe, have a special bearing upon the present trends and developments with respect to international monetary organization and policy:

1. The views expressed are not inconsistent with a keen and sympathetic interest in the new developments which have been growing out of the recent "gentlemen's agreement."
2. There are grounds for thinking that we do not need or want any single pattern of compromise in all countries, such as the gold standard pattern was before the War. Different kinds of countries require different kinds of monetary systems.
3. The best prospect for stability in individual countries and in the world as a whole, so far as it can be achieved by monetary means, lies in more efficient

* Reproduced by permission of Professor Williams and *The American Economic Review.*

monetary control within the major countries, especially the United States and England, coupled with co-operation between them; and on this basis, there is no such dilemma between internal and external monetary stability as has been frequently emphasized in abstract analysis.

1. *The "Gentlemen's Agreement."* The gentlemen's agreement is a form of de facto stabilization, less definite and binding than any which had been previously proposed and for that reason more acceptable and feasible. Whatever kind of system is ultimately to emerge, it has been commonly recognized that a trial period would be necessary before any more permanent and formal kind of stabilization could be ventured upon.

Moreover, the device—as set up under this agreement—for converting stabilization fund holdings of foreign currency into gold at a price that is based from day to day on the exchange rate may provide a new and better kind of exchange stability. Pressure on a currency will lead to its support through purchase by stabilization funds (or through sales of the other currencies) and to conversion of these balances into gold at a known price. If the pressure continues unabated it can be relieved by varying the exchange rate through varying the price of gold. With this instrument of flexibility at the disposal of the respective stabilization fund authorities, the result may be a greater assurance of exchange rates which are both more stable and more under control than has previously been the case. It will certainly make possible a more orderly change to new levels, if that is required; and it provides, moreover, a better possibility than we have previously had of effecting alterations in the exchange rate structure, of varying a currency with relation to some other without that change being communicated to all the others.[10]

It should be noted that, as it has thus far operated, this mechanism includes a fixed buying and selling price of gold in terms of dollars. Prior to the devaluation of the franc, the British Equalization Account operated against a fixed buying and selling price for gold in terms of francs. There is no evidence thus far that this kind of exchange stabilization can operate without being anchored to a fixed price of gold in one or more markets. In some respects, it would seem to be more feasible with only one, or a few countries, having a variable price of gold and operating against the fixed gold price maintained by the others. There is also the question whether operations cannot be conducted more effectively by one, or a few, stabilization funds rather than by a larger number. The objection to having one country on a variable basis, in this sense, and the others on a fixed basis is, of course, that it implies a large measure of trust in the integrity and the freedom from nationalistic motives of the variable exchange country which would act as the stabilizing agency. But perhaps the knowledge that other countries could retaliate by devaluation, either by new legislation or under an authority previously granted and held in readiness, might be a sufficient deterrent. The possible difficulty in having more than one stabilizing agency is, of course, that they might not be able to agree when any major change in exchange rates is desirable. England might think it desirable to put the pound down, but other countries might not think it desirable to have their currencies go up in consequence. Again it seems clear that nations could co-operate better on some plan of monetary control which leaves exchanges stable than they could upon a plan involving variable exchange rates.

2. *Different Currency Mechanisms for Different Countries.* The discussion of the gentlemen's agreement indicates that it may be both desirable and feasible to have

[10] It may, for example, be desired to lower currency A relative to B but to raise it relative to C.

different currency mechanisms for different countries. Already there are included in (or attached to) the agreement countries with stabilization funds and a variable price of gold, countries with stabilization funds and a fixed price of gold and countries with a fixed price of gold and without stabilization funds. It may be an open question whether France, which now has the first type (but whose variable price of gold is limited by law within a range) may not, as Belgium did, return eventually to a fixed price of gold with no stabilization fund. And it may be a question whether the American fund will prove eventually to be primarily a gold sterilization fund or equally an exchange stabilization fund.

Some light can be thrown on the question whether the world needs a single, uniform system or a combination of different systems by consideration of the diversity of countries, and in particular the differences in their proportions of home and foreign trade. It would seem that the relatively self-contained countries should, in most circumstances, be less concerned about exchange variation as a means of correction of their business cycle maladjustments, and must rely mainly upon their powers of internal control. On the other hand, countries chiefly dependent upon foreign trade and foreign capital have most both to gain and to lose by exchange variation; they most need exchange stability when foreign trade is prosperous, and they most need a currency adjustment when capital inflow is threatening to produce a boom, or when depression in the outside world is threatening their foreign markets. From this point of view, countries like the United States, and probably France, could best afford to have an unchanging currency, once a generally sustainable structure of exchange rates had been attained. Countries like Australia or Argentina would probably want fixed exchanges the larger part of the time, but with some provision for both depreciation and appreciation. Currency appreciation would be indeed a new phenomenon in the history of young countries, which like most others have been less concerned to stop booms than to stop depressions; but currency depreciation in depression would be only repeating what they have always done. The only new suggestion is that it might be worked out in some more orderly and deliberate fashion, as a conscious instrument of policy. For such countries, internal money management must be at best the minor part of policy. Since these countries are a minor part of the world economy, currency variations by them would probably not hurt others so much as it might help them. In these countries, as in all, there would be some conflict of interests. Currency depreciation, which might help export trade, would impair ability to pay interest charges, but this sacrifice is at the expense of the foreign creditor, who may be more able to bear it and should have been better able to calculate the risk in the first place.

Consideration of countries largely dependent on foreign trade suggests consideration of the sterling area. The development of the sterling area when England went off gold represents the emergence, in a more limited sphere, of the same type of international trade organization and hence of the same type of monetary system that existed before the War, when in a very real sense it could be said that England was on gold and much of the rest of the world on sterling. Within such an area, among nations closely tied by trade and financial relations, the need for stability of exchange is so compelling that when the center country varies its currency it is apt to carry all the other members of the group with it. In such an area, also, as was largely true before the War, the monetary control exerted at the center is likely to have a powerful influence throughout the area, which suggests that through stable exchanges forces of expansion or contraction can be initiated at the center and be transmitted throughout the area.

To hold such a unit together and to maintain exchange stability within it, it is probably unnecessary that all the countries, or indeed any of them, should be on the gold standard. What the constituents of this area need chiefly are foreign exchange balances in London; and as the exchange stabilizing agency, what it needs is a sterling balance which the foreign country's central bank holds and which this bank can control by decreasing or increasing its purchases and sales of sterling at a price that is stable but which it reserves the right to vary. If there is need of gold, it is as an internal reserve for notes or deposits, as a protection against an unrestricted credit expansion; but this function could be performed, also, as it can in other countries, by a central bank control of member bank reserves, without gold.

There is left for consideration those countries whose position is intermediate, whose foreign trade, though less in quantity or value than home trade, is nevertheless essential, in the long run, to a high level of productivity and real income. In this group are such countries as England, pre-eminently, and also Germany. In so far as such countries have trade areas, their concern for stability of exchange in support of their foreign trade has been already dealt with. Exchange stability within the trade area appears to be the less troubling aspect of their problem; and in a sense is self-insured by the closeness of trade ties. But there trade with the rest of the world is on a different footing. It is here that the conflict of objectives as between internal and external monetary stability chiefly arises. In depression, such countries are likely to strike out for freedom of internal policy, even though the protective devices which are set up, including currency depreciation, work out their effects at the expense of others. How their freedom of action is limited in other phases of the cycle, particularly by rising costs of imports, has already been discussed. Whether England would appreciate its currency substantially to help ward off an internal boom, we have yet to see. We must remember that she is occupied and perhaps somewhat complacent with her internal recovery, for which the ground was laid not only by cheap imports, but in addition by an easy money policy which is supporting both an extensive housing program (England having had no such construction activity as we had in the twenties) and now also a feverish armament program. The fundamental question at the moment, then, is whether England, in the light of her present situation, may not be less concerned about her foreign trade, which has been noticeably backward in the recovery, than in the longer run she will need to be. In considerable measure, the problem of monetary policy, in so far as there is conflict of internal and external considerations, is a problem of business cycle versus the longer run forces which govern national productivity and income. The question, as stated earlier, is how to control short-time change without doing damage to the basic trade relationships.

3. *The Solution Mainly Turns on Internal Stability in the Major Countries, Coupled with Co-operation.* The discussion of the sterling area suggests that for such a group monetary stability mainly depends upon the behavior of the center country. This suggestion has a larger application. The economic activities of the United States and England combined represent more than half of total world activity; and these countries are, in normal times, the main sources of capital. World booms and depressions are more likely to spring from changes originating in them and carried outward than by the reverse process. As has been indicated repeatedly by the course of events, international capital movements are likely to be mainly a phase of expansion or contraction in the major countries. We are likely to export capital at the same time that we expand investment at home. If we also attract capital, as in a major rise of the stock market, it is most apt to come from England or some other major country.

From this point of view, the problem of monetary stability appears to be one which calls in large measure for an over-all control, rather than for a compensatory mechanism operating as between countries, and to require as its main foundation effective internal monetary control in the leading countries. It ought not to be impossible in a matter of such mutual interest and serious importance to achieve, after the experiences which the nations have gone through in pursuing their own narrower ends, some community of action in monetary and general economic policy; but I must add that I am not altogether sanguine. Even without such formal co-operation, I believe that the best prospect for general stability is to be found in internal stability in the leading countries if it is intelligently, which means not too narrowly, conceived.

But it is not to be expected that economic change would or should exactly keep pace in all countries; that is far from true even in the different parts of our own country. There will always be diversity of change and of pace and character of development. There will be business cycle lags and leads as between countries. There will be crises here and there, registering their effects not only in the countries of origin but in others, and perhaps especially in the center countries. What an effective system of compromise must do is to provide slacks and elements of variability which will lessen shocks, permit monetary change to be slowed down to the pace which the economic structure can tolerate, and leave freedom of action in directing the impact and extent of change. For this purpose, it seems preferable to have some compromise, or combination of compromise systems, which, while excluding no form of variation which might be serviceable in a constantly changing world, would resort to currency variation only sparingly and when other means had failed.

(B) Extract from "Currency Stabilization: The Keynes and White Plans" *

(July 1943)

The most important question, however, is whether in the longer run, when the transition to peace has been achieved, the general type of monetary organization outlined in the Keynes and White plans promises to give the best assurance of achieving and maintaining international currency stability, with all that implies for a stable and orderly economic world. This, too, I do not find an easy question, and my present attitude is one of wanting to hear more and think more about it as the debate develops. One of the dangers involved in the present technique of concentrating upon the comparison of the two plans, and taking the visiting experts of the allied and associated governments through them point by point, is that no other plan is likely to get an adequate hearing—unless it be later on, at the legislative stage, which may not be the best method of arriving at well and calmly reasoned conclusions.

The difficulty for me is that I have long believed that there is another kind of approach to the problem, and one that deserves equally well the name of international collaboration even though it is constructed on less elaborate lines. This is what might be called the key countries, or central countries, approach to the problem.[8] It is closer in conception than either the Keynes or White plan to the way the gold standard actually worked, around England as the central country, in the nineteenth century; whereas I have the feeling that those plans have a closer family relationship with what might be called the textbook type of gold standard, which implied that monetary stability was maintained by the compensatory action of a large number of countries of equal economic weight. What I call the key countries approach to monetary stabilization could be tried with or without an international governing board, though I think this is not the main point of difference between the two ways of going at the problem.

The main difference is in the conception of how trade and finance are organized in the world, and of the importance of stabilizing the truly international currencies whose behavior dominates and determines what happens to all the others. Though the organization of trade and finance has undergone much change since the nineteenth century, it still seems true that stabilization of the leading currencies with reference to each other, combined with coöperation among the countries concerned for the promotion of their own internal stability, would be the best foundation for monetary and economic stability throughout the world.

The importance of coöperation upon internal as well as external monetary and economic policies in the leading countries is in line with the current of thought among economists in recent years. One of the most interesting points in Keynes' White Paper is the lightness of touch with which he deals with internal policies. "There should be the least possible interference with internal national policies, and the plan should not wander from the international terrain. Since such policies may have important repercussions on international relations they cannot be left out of account. Nevertheless,

---

* Reproduced by permission of Professor Williams and *Foreign Affairs.*

[8] See again my paper, "The Adequacy of Existing Currency Mechanisms under Varying Circumstances," *American Economic Review,* March 1937, Supl., p. 151–168.

in the realm of internal policy, the authority of the governing board of the proposed institution should be limited to recommendations, or, at most, to imposing conditions for more extended enjoyment of the facilities which the institution offers." As I read over his provisions as to what debtor countries may be required to do to adjust their position as their net debit balances mount from a quarter to a half to three-fourths of their quotas, I am not overly convinced that the board's powers of control have very strong or sharp teeth. On exceeding a quarter of its quota on the average for two years, the debtor country may depreciate its currency up to 5 percent. On reaching a half of its quota, it may be required to deposit collateral. As a condition of exceeding a half of its quota, it may be required to do all or any of the following at the governing board's discretion: reduce the value of its currency; control outward capital movements; and/or surrender a suitable proportion of any separate gold or other liquid reserve in reduction of its debit balance. It is at this point that the governing board may "recommend . . . any internal measures . . . which may appear to be appropriate." On exceeding three-fourths of its quota, the debtor country "may, in addition, be asked by the governing board to take measures to improve its position, and, in the event of its failing to reduce its debit balance accordingly within two years" may be declared in default and no longer entitled to draw against its account.

All of these measures seem desirable. In particular, I have long believed that the younger countries, whose economic conditions primarily reflect the conditions existing in the great world markets, for which they are only secondarily responsible, should be permitted to vary their currencies. It might help them somewhat, without too seriously affecting the larger countries. Such countries do not often have major difficulties arising out of the outward movement of capital; for them the exchange problem is usually presented by the stoppage of the inward movement. When this happens, they are not unacquainted with being declared in default. The same circumstances which stop capital inflow restrict the markets for their products and produce a severe shrinkage in the value of their merchandise exports, so that these countries are frequently unable to maintain interest payments or even to pay for their current imports. The classical economists would have insisted upon internal reduction of their costs; and some countries, like Australia in the great depression, have proved that internal cost reductions can be a feasible and a potent method of adjustment of the international position.[9] But, broadly speaking, the whole experience of the inter-war period proved nothing more clearly than the fact that the economic condition and the balance of payments position of these countries are primarily a reflection of the conditions in the larger countries, and that if those conditions are bad enough, there can be no real escape, even though the countries are driven—as most of them were—to exchange control as a desperate last resort.

From this experience of the inter-war period, I come back always to the conclusion that the problem of international monetary stability is primarily that of maintaining a state of proper economic health in the leading countries; and that this is the only workable answer to the whole conflict between internal and external monetary stability, about which discussions of the gold standard for years revolved.[10] This means collaboration to maintain both a high level of real income within the leading countries and

---

[9] Australia also depreciated her currency and adopted expansive monetary and fiscal policies.

[10] See my paper, "The World's Monetary Dilemma—Internal Versus External Monetary Stability," *Proceedings of the Academy of Political Science*, April 1934, p. 62–68.

a high degree of exchange stability between them. If this could be done, the problem of maintaining exchange stability for the other countries, and a reasonable state of economic well-being within them, would probably not present major difficulties.

But such a program implies a degree of coöperation among the leading countries which goes far beyond what is outlined for the governing bodies in either the Keynes or the White plan. I doubt whether the requirements could be spelled out at present, or even whether it would be wise to try to do so. But I heartily agree with Herbert Feis when he says in his article in the April number of FOREIGN AFFAIRS that the best augury for success lies in the intimate collaboration upon numerous problems which has already been developed between this country and the British Empire in our conduct of the war.

Between the two approaches to the problem of monetary stabilization which I have discussed, the Keynes or the White proposal on the one hand and the closer collaboration among leading countries on the other, there may be no inherent or fundamental disagreement. A French plan of the kind I have suggested was prepared prior to the release of the British and American plans and has since been published in the *New York Times*.[11] One of the reasons advanced in favor of it by the authors was that it could be put into effect promptly, whereas in their judgment "If the international monetary system is so ambitious that it cannot become of general use until political and economic conditions are peacefully settled in the whole world, it may have to wait a long while." It might be more feasible to start with a scheme embracing fewer countries, which is less ambitious only in the sense that it is less extensive and more ambitious in the degree of coöperation contemplated, and tie in other countries as conditions warrant. This was the method followed in the Tripartite Agreement of 1936. I am not suggesting that agreement as the model, however, unless it can be greatly strengthened in its provisions for external collaboration and supplemented by provisions for coöperation on internal policies, to which it made no reference. There might be many advantages in such a piecemeal procedure. We could start, for example, with plans for stabilizing the dollar-sterling rate and for measures of coöperation on internal policy, while postponing until later the many difficult questions about the relation of sterling and the dollar to the European currencies which cannot conceivably be settled, I think, except after a period of European reconstruction.

Since I have dealt here exclusively with the proposals for currency stabilization, I should say in conclusion that monetary mechanics is only the lesser part of the problem, as the authors of the plans discussed fully recognize. Keynes begins his White Paper by suggesting four main lines of approach to the problem of how to achieve a stable and prosperous world, of which the mechanism of currency and exchange is only one. The others are international commercial policy; orderly conduct of production, distribution and price of primary products; and investment aid, both medium and long-term, for countries whose economic development needs assistance from the outside. Work is going forward on these other lines of approach, and upon the success of this work will depend fundamentally the success of our efforts, by whatever plan, to achieve inter-

[11] The *New York Times*, May 9, 1943, p. 5. The plan was prepared by André Istel, former financial adviser to the Reynaud Ministry and one of the negotiators of the Franco-British Financial Agreement of 1939, and Hervé Alphand, former financial attaché in Washington, former head of Trade Agreements in the French Ministry of Commerce, and French representative at the International Food Conference at Hot Springs.

national monetary stability. In all phases of it the United States has a vital interest and carries a unique responsibility. This will be the leading and probably the only important creditor country after the war. If we are to have an orderly and stable world, our responsibilities must not be shirked. But our rôle being what it is, and must be, we owe it to ourselves and to the rest of the world to think through the problems with all the intelligence and care and breadth of outlook of which we are capable.

The Joint Statement

The Joint Statement by Experts on the Establishment of an International Monetary Fund *was the outcome of discussions between Lord Keynes and Mr. White in Washington in September–October 1943. After extensive redrafting a final version was agreed upon in April 1944 and was then published. The text reproduced below is taken from the British White Paper, Cmd. 6519, and includes the British Government's foreword and Explanatory Notes indicating the British attitude to the Statement.*

Joint Statement by Experts on the Establishment of an International Monetary Fund [1]

(April 1944)

His Majesty's Government have authorised the publication of this Statement of Principles for an International Monetary Fund, which is the result of close study over many months at the expert level. It in no way commits the Governments concerned. It is conceived as part of a general plan for international co-operation, the objectives of which, as a whole, would be the progressive development of international trade, active employment, reasonable stability of prices and the machinery for the orderly adjustment of exchanges.

The purpose of publication in this way and at this stage is to promote informed discussion in all quarters from which valuable guidance can be obtained by the Governments in preparation for the formulation in due course of policies by the States concerned.

I. EXPLANATORY NOTES BY UNITED KINGDOM EXPERTS ON THE PROPOSAL FOR AN INTERNATIONAL MONETARY FUND.

Some of the more important respects in which the *Joint Statement by Experts on the Establishment of an International Monetary Fund,* set forth below as agreed between the British and American technical experts, differs from, or resembles, the *Proposals for an International Clearing Union* published as Cmd. 6437 are briefly explained below:—

(1) Under the *Clearing Union* the member countries might have been said to bank with the Union with which they were to keep balances or run overdrafts. Under the *International Monetary Fund,* on the other hand, the Fund may be said to bank with the member countries, which undertake to grant to the *Fund* facilities to hold and to draw on their local funds. Thus if under the *Clearing Union* a member country drew resources from the *Union* this meant that its own balance with the *Union* would be diminished and the balance of some other member would be increased; whereas, if a member country draws resources from the *Fund,* this means that the *Fund's* balances with that member are increased and its balances with some other member are decreased.

[1] Reproduced by permission of the Controller, Her Britannic Majesty's Stationery Office.

These two arrangements represent alternative technical setups, capable of performing precisely the same functions. The same purposes and provisions in all other respects can be carried into effect under the one as under the other. It has, however, proved easier to obtain agreement on the mechanism of the proposed *Fund*, which has the appearance of being closer to what is already familiar.

(2) As a consequence of this, it is no longer necessary to introduce a new international unit, whether bancor or unitas, since it is only if the member countries bank with the Fund that the use of a new common unit becomes unavoidable.

(3) The provisions of the *Clearing Union*, by which only the Central Banks of member countries were in a position to engage in transactions with the *Union*, are replaced by the analogous provisions of III (1) (2) and (3) under which the *Fund* can only engage in transactions with the Monetary Authority of member countries and is not free to enter the market or deal with other banks or persons.

(4) The aggregate facilities, guaranteed by the initial subscriptions of the members under II (1), are smaller than were proposed for the *Clearing Union*. But they are substantial and, if necessary, can be increased later on by general agreement. It has been argued that the present proposals involve as large a commitment as it is prudent to ask in favour of an, as yet, untried institution. Moreover, in estimating the sufficiency of the facilities proposed, it is necessary to bear in mind X (1), where it is made clear that the facilities of the *Fund* are not intended to provide facilities for relief or reconstruction or to deal with international indebtedness arising out of the war.

(5) The *Clearing Union* proposals were criticised on the ground that they made insufficient provision for elasticity of exchange rates and for subsequent modification in the rates initially established. The new proposal explicitly provides for alteration of exchange rates, whilst maintaining the general principle that, exchange rates being two-ended so that a change in the parity of any currency affects the currencies of all countries, not only that of the country making the change, a proposed change is a proper subject for international consultation. The *Fund*, acting in a judicial capacity, is required under IV (3) to approve any change which is essential to the correction of a fundamental disequilibrium, and shall, in determining the matter, accept the domestic, social or political policies of the country applying for a change as facts of the situation to be accepted and not criticised. Moreover, during the transitional period immediately after the war it shall under X (4) give the member country presenting a proposal the benefit of any reasonable doubt, and shall under IV (3) at all times take into consideration the extreme uncertainties prevailing at the time the parities of exchange were initially agreed upon. In addition member countries are allowed under IV (4) a certain margin for making unilateral changes. Finally, if a member feels unable to accept a decision of the Fund on this or on any other matter, it is entitled under VIII (1) to withdraw from membership without notice and without penalty, apart from an undertaking under VIII (2) to liquidate any outstanding obligations to the Fund within a reasonable time. Thus no member is under any obligation to continue its adherence to the conditions of membership if it comes to the conclusion that, taken as a whole, they are no longer to its advantage.

(6) The provisions for securing, apart from certain temporary relaxations, an eventual free inter-convertibility of all national currencies, on the basis of the parities of the exchange rates established for the time being, are the same in effect as those under the *Clearing Union*.

(7) Clauses III (5) and IX (3) provide that a member's obligation to maintain free convertibility of its currency applies only to transactions of a current account nature. It does not apply to capital transfers or to the removal of balances accumulated prior to the acceptance of the obligation of convertibility. Clause V (1) contemplates the control of the outflow of capital by members using the resources of the *Fund*, so as to ensure that the *Fund* shall not be drawn upon to finance a large or sustained outflow of a capital nature. Thus the proposal allows the maintenance of exchange control in so far as it is required to carry out the above defined purposes, and may even require a member to exercise control of some kind.

(8) The proposals of the *Clearing Union*, to prevent a country from using up its quota too rapidly and from drawing on the *Fund* too freely in conditions in which its own resources are adequate without drawing on the *Fund*, are worked out more fully in clauses III (2) and (7) but without difference of intention. The provisions of II (3) and III (6) and (7) are new, under which the *Fund* has some gold resources which may be gradually increased with the intention that such gold in the hands of the *Fund* will be freely available in the interests of equilibrium.

(9) It was a feature of the *Clearing Union* proposals that they introduced certain provisions for placing on creditor countries, as well as on debtor countries, some pressure to share the responsibility in appropriate circumstances for maintaining a reasonable stability in the balances of international payments. These have been replaced in the new proposal by a different, but perhaps more far-reaching, provision with the same object in view. This is under VI, which provides that, if the requirements of the *Fund* for the currency of a country, in an unbalanced creditor position with the rest of the world, seem likely to exceed the supply of that currency which the *Fund* is in a position to acquire to meet the applications of the other members, the *Fund* shall issue a report covering the causes of the unbalanced position and containing recommendations designed to bring it to an end. Meanwhile the available supplies of the scarce currency will be apportioned, and the other members become entitled to resume complete freedom of action in relation to the affected currency. They are allowed to take any steps at their discretion to curtail imports from the country in question and to restrict and regulate exchange transactions, so as to keep their purchases in terms of the affected currency within the limits of their ability to pay. Rather than allow such a situation to develop, it would be open to a creditor country to use any of various means to prevent the development of an unmanageable unbalanced situation with the rest of the world as a whole.

(10) The provisions for the management of the new Institution have not been worked out in detail in this Statement of Principles. This is an important matter left over for further discussion and development at a later date.

(11) The *Clearing Union* proposals, which were put forward at a relatively early stage of the war, did not attempt to deal adequately with the transitional arrangements in the period following the conclusion of hostilities. Whilst there are still too many uncertainties in other directions to allow of clear-cut conclusions, Clause X of the Joint Statement carries matters somewhat further. It is there provided that a member need not assume the full obligations of membership until satisfactory arrangements are at its disposal to facilitate the settlement of its balance of payments difficulties arising out of the war. Furthermore X (2) contemplates a gradual evolution towards the attainment of the objects of the *Fund* by progressive stages and no country is committed to an immediate removal of war-time restrictions and regulations. Whilst the *Fund*

may, within three years of the *Fund's* coming into force, make representations that the time has come for a further withdrawal of restrictions, no member is committed as to any fixed date for this final removal and is entitled to use its own judgment as to when it is strong enough to undertake the free convertibility of its currency which it has accepted as the desirable aim. The drafting of this Clause, as the experts on both sides understand it, allows, during the transition period, the maintenance and adaptation by the members of the sterling area of the arrangements now in force between them. Nor is the scheme intended, when the obligation of free convertibility has been accepted, to interfere with the traditional ties and other arrangements between the members of the sterling area and London.

(12) In most other respects the general aims and purposes of the new scheme are the same as those set forth in Cmd. 6437 in presenting the *Clearing Union Proposals.*

II. JOINT STATEMENT BY EXPERTS ON THE ESTABLISHMENT OF AN INTERNATIONAL MONETARY FUND.

Sufficient discussion of the problems of international monetary co-operation has taken place at the technical level to justify a statement of principles. It is the consensus of opinion of the experts of the United and Associated Nations who have participated in these discussions that the most practical method of assuring international monetary co-operation is through the establishment of an International Monetary Fund. The principles set forth below are designed to constitute the basis of this Fund. Governments are not asked to give final approval to these principles until they have been embodied in the form of definite proposals by the delegates of the United and Associated Nations meeting in a formal conference.

I. *Purposes and Policies of the International Monetary Fund.*

The Fund will be guided in all its decisions by the purposes and policies set forth below:

1. To promote international monetary co-operation through a permanent institution which provides the machinery for consultation on international monetary problems.

2. To facilitate the expansion and balanced growth of international trade and to contribute in this way to the maintenance of a high level of employment and real income, which must be a primary objective of economic policy.

3. To give confidence to member countries by making the Fund's resources available to them under adequate safeguards, thus giving members time to correct maladjustments in their balance of payments without resorting to measures destructive of national or international prosperity.

4. To promote exchange stability, to maintain orderly exchange arrangements among member countries, and to avoid competitive exchange depreciation.

5. To assist the establishment of multilateral payments facilities on current transactions among member countries and the elimination of foreign exchange restrictions which hamper the growth of world trade.

6. To shorten the periods and lessen the degree of disequilibrium in the international balance of payments of member countries.

II. *Subscription to the Fund.*

1. Member countries shall subscribe in gold and in their local funds amounts (quotas) to be agreed, which will amount altogether to about $8 billion if all the

United and Associated Nations subscribe to the Fund (corresponding to about $10 billion for the world as a whole).

2. The quotas may be revised from time to time, but changes shall require a four-fifths vote, and no member's quota shall be changed without its assent.

3. The obligatory gold subscription of a member country shall be fixed at 25 per cent. of its subscription (quota) or 10 per cent. of its holdings of gold and gold-convertible exchange, whichever is smaller.

III. *Transactions with the Fund.*

1. Member countries shall deal with the Fund only through their Treasury, Central Bank, Stabilization Fund or other fiscal agencies. The Fund's account in a member's currency shall be kept at the Central Bank of the member country.

2. A member shall be entitled to buy another member's currency from the Fund in exchange for its own currency on the following conditions:

(*a*) The member represents that the currency demanded is presently needed for making payments in that currency which are consistent with the purposes of the Fund.

(*b*) The Fund has not given notice that its holdings of the currency demanded have become scarce in which case the provisions of VI, below, come into force.

(*c*) The Fund's total holdings of the currency offered (after having been restored, if below that figure, to 75 per cent. of the member's quota) have not increased by more than 25 per cent. of the member's quota during the previous twelve months, and do not exceed 200 percent of the quota.

(*d*) The Fund has not previously given appropriate notice that the member is suspended from making further use of the Fund's resources on the ground that it is using them in a manner contrary to the purposes and policies of the Fund; but the Fund shall not give such notice until it has presented to the member concerned a report setting forth its views and has allowed a suitable time for reply.

The Fund may in its discretion and on terms which safeguard its interests, waive any of the conditions above.

3. The operations on the Fund's account will be limited to transactions for the purpose of supplying a member country on the member's initiative with another member's currency in exchange for its own currency or for gold. Transactions provided for under 4 and 7, below, are not subject to this limitation.

4. The Fund will be entitled at its option with a view to preventing a particular member's currency from becoming scarce:

(*a*) To borrow its currency from a member country;

(*b*) To offer gold to a member country in exchange for its currency.

5. So long as a member country is entitled to buy another member's currency from the Fund in exchange for its own currency, it shall be prepared to buy its own currency from that member with that member's currency or with gold. This requirement does not apply to currency subject to restrictions in conformity with IX (3) below or to holdings of currency which have accumulated as a result of transactions of a current account nature effected before the removal by the member country of restrictions on multilateral clearing maintained or imposed under X (2) below.

6. A member country desiring to obtain directly or indirectly the currency of another member country for gold is expected, provided that it can do so with equal advantage,

to acquire the currency by the sale of gold to the Fund. This shall not preclude the sale of newly-mined gold by a gold-producing country on any market.

7. The Fund may also acquire gold from member countries in accordance with the following provisions:

(*a*) A member country may repurchase from the Fund for gold any part of the latter's holdings of its currency.

(*b*) So long as a member's holdings of gold and gold-convertible exchange exceed its quota, the Fund in selling foreign exchange to that country shall require that one-half of the net sales of such exchange during the Fund's financial year be paid for with gold.

(*c*) If at the end of the Fund's financial year a member's holdings of gold and gold-convertible exchange have increased, the Fund may require up to one-half of the increase to be used to repurchase part of the Fund's holdings of its currency so long as this does not reduce the Fund's holdings of a country's currency below 75 per cent. of its quota or the member's holdings of gold and gold-convertible exchange below its quota.

IV. *Par Values of Member Currencies.*

1. The par value of a member's currency shall be agreed with the Fund when it is admitted to membership and shall be expressed in terms of gold. All transactions between the Fund and members shall be at par subject to a fixed charge payable by the member making application to the Fund; and all transactions in member currencies shall be at rates within an agreed percentage of parity.

2. Subject to 5, below, no change in the par value of a member's currency shall be made by the Fund without the country's approval. Member countries agree not to propose a change of parity of their currency unless they consider it appropriate to correct a fundamental disequilibrium. Changes shall be made only with the approval of the Fund subject to the provisions below.

3. The Fund shall approve a requested change in the par value of a member's currency if it is essential to correct a fundamental disequilibrium. In particular, the Fund shall not reject a requested change necessary to restore equilibrium because of domestic social or political policies of the country applying for a change. In considering a requested change, the Fund shall take into consideration the extreme uncertainties prevailing at the time the parities of currencies of member countries were initially agreed upon.

4. After consulting the Fund a member country may change the established parity of its currency provided the proposed change inclusive of any previous change since the establishment of the Fund does not exceed 10 per cent. In the case of application for a further change not covered by the above and not exceeding 10 per cent., the Fund shall give its decision within two days of receiving the application if the applicant so requests.

5. An agreed uniform change may be made in the gold value of member currencies, provided every member country having 10 per cent. or more of the aggregate quotas approves.

V. *Capital Transactions.*

1. A member country may not use the Fund's resources to meet a large or sustained outflow of capital and the Fund may require a member country to exercise control to

prevent such use of the resources of the Fund. This provision is not intended to prevent the use of the Fund's resources for capital transactions of reasonable amount required for the expansion of exports or in the ordinary course of trade, banking and other business. Nor is it intended to prevent capital movements which are met out of a member country's own resources of gold and foreign exchange, provided such capital movements are in accordance with the purposes of the Fund.

2. Subject to VI, below, a member country may not use its control of capital movements to restrict payments for current transactions or to delay unduly the transfer of funds in settlement of commitments.

VI. *Apportionment of Scarce Currencies.*

1. When it becomes evident to the Fund that the demand for a member country's currency may soon exhaust the Fund's holdings of that currency, the Fund shall so inform member countries and propose an equitable method of apportioning the scarce currency. When a currency is thus declared scarce, the Fund shall issue a report embodying the causes of the scarcity and containing recommendations designed to bring it to an end.

2. A decision by the Fund to apportion a scarce currency shall operate as an authorization to a member country, after consultation with the Fund, temporarily to restrict the freedom of exchange operations in the affected currency and, in determining the manner of restricting the demand and rationing the limited supply amongst its nationals, the member country shall have complete jurisdiction.

VII. *Management.*

1. The Fund shall be governed by a board on which each member will be represented, and by an executive committee. The executive committee shall consist of at least nine members including representatives of the five countries with the largest quotas.

2. The distribution of voting power on the board of directors and the executive committee shall be closely related to the quotas.

3. Subject to II (2) and IV (5), all matters shall be settled by a majority of votes.

4. The Fund shall publish at short intervals a statement of its position showing the extent of its holdings of member currencies and of gold and its transactions in gold.

VIII. *Withdrawal.*

1. A member country may withdraw from the Fund by giving notice in writing.

2. The reciprocal obligations of the Fund and the country are to be liquidated within a reasonable time.

3. After a member country has given notice in writing of its withdrawal from the Fund, the Fund may not dispose of its holdings of the country's currency except in accordance with arrangements made under 2, above. After a country has given notice of withdrawal its use of the resources of the Fund is subject to the approval of the Fund.

IX. *The Obligations of Member Countries.*

1. Not to buy gold at a price which exceeds the agreed parity of its currency by more than a prescribed margin and not to sell gold at a price which falls below the agreed parity by more than a prescribed margin.

2. Not to allow exchange transactions in its market in currencies of other members at rates outside a prescribed range based on the agreed parities.

3. Not to impose restrictions on payments for current international transactions with other member countries (other than those involving capital transfers or in accordance with VI, above) or to engage in any discriminatory currency arrangements or multiple currency practices without the approval of the Fund.

X. *Transitional Arrangements.*

1. Since the Fund is not intended to provide facilities for relief or reconstruction or to deal with international indebtedness arising out of the war, the agreement of a member country to III (5) and IX (3), above, shall not become operative until it is satisfied as to the arrangements at its disposal to facilitate the settlement of the balance of payments differences during the early post-war transition period by means which will not unduly encumber its facilities with the Fund.

2. During this transition period member countries may maintain and adapt to changing circumstances exchange regulations of the character which have been in operation during the war, but they shall undertake to withdraw as soon as possible by progressive stages any restrictions which impede multilateral clearing on current account. In their exchange policy they shall pay continuous regard to the principles and objectives of the Fund; and they shall take all possible measures to develop commercial and financial relations with other member countries which will facilitate international payments and the maintenance of exchange stability.

3. The Fund may make representations to any member that conditions are favourable to the withdrawal of particular restrictions or for the general abandonment of restrictions inconsistent with IX (3), above. Not later than three years from the coming into force of the Fund any member still retaining any restrictions inconsistent with IX (3) shall consult the Fund as to their further retention.

4. In its relations with member countries the Fund shall recognize that the transition period is one of change and adjustment and in deciding on its attitude to proposals presented by members it shall give the member country the benefit of any reasonable doubt.

U.S. Commentary

In preparation for the discussions at Atlantic City in June 1944 and at Bretton Woods in the following month, the U.S. Treasury issued Questions and Answers on the International Monetary Fund (June 10, 1944). *While this was not an internationally agreed document, it usefully elaborates the U.S. view on many of the subjects which were being publicly discussed at the time.*

Questions and Answers on the International Monetary Fund (June 10, 1944)

CONTENTS

PART ONE: THE FUND AND INTERNATIONAL ECONOMIC COOPERATION

QUESTION 1

Will the operations of the International Monetary Fund be limited to the immediate post-war period?

REPLY

In the Foreword to the Joint Statement by the experts on the establishment of an International Monetary Fund, Secretary Morgenthau said:

> "The tentative proposals that have been under discussion by the experts are part of a broad program for cooperation on international economic problems among the United Nations. The objectives of this program are the expansion and development of international trade, the revival of international investment for productive purposes, the establishment of orderly and stable exchange rates, and the elimination of discriminatory exchange practices that hamper world trade. The attainment of these objectives will go far toward preventing serious economic disruption in many countries during the critical decade after the war."

It is still too soon to know the precise form and magnitude of post-war monetary problems. But it is certain that we shall be confronted with three inseparable monetary tasks: to prevent the disruption of foreign exchanges, to avoid the collapse of monetary systems, and to facilitate the restoration and balanced growth of international trade. Clearly, such formidable problems can be successfully handled only through international action.

While the Fund can be of enormous help in the solution of the monetary problems growing out of the war, it would be a serious mistake to regard the Fund as an agency designed exclusively or even largely for the immediate post-war period. To think of international monetary problems as simply an aftermath of the war is to overlook the fundamental realities. For two decades before the war the world suffered from serious monetary disorders without having any means to act together to prevent or to remedy the ills out of which they grew and the evils which were their fruit.

Long before the war, the necessary monetary and financial basis for international prosperity had been weakened by competitive currency depreciation, by exchange restrictions, by multiple currency devices, and by other discriminatory foreign exchange practices that hampered and even throttled world trade and the international flow of productive capital. Unless the United Nations cooperate to provide a sound foundation for the balanced growth of international trade, we must expect a recurrence of the same monetary disorders.

These are not transitory problems of the immediate post-war period affecting only a few countries. They are continuing problems of vital interest to all countries. There must be a general realization that world prosperity, like world peace, is indivisible. Nations must act together to restore multilateral international trade, and to provide orderly procedure for the maintenance of balanced economic growth. Only through international cooperation will it be possible for countries successfully to apply measures directed toward attaining and maintaining a high level of employment and real income which must be the primary objective of economic policy.

International monetary problems cannot be solved by occasional cooperation improvised among a few great countries to meet a threatened disaster. Such monetary difficulties can be met only by continuous cooperation, to prevent them if possible, to remedy them when necessary. It is for this reason that the International Monetary Fund of the United and Associated Nations is proposed as a permanent institution for international monetary cooperation.

Question 2

Will the Fund provide resources for relief and reconstruction?

Reply

It is recognized that an International Monetary Fund is only one of the instrumentalities which may be needed in the field of international economic cooperation. Other agencies may be needed to provide long-term international credit for post-war reconstruction and development and to provide funds for rehabilitation and relief. Within the scope of its functions the Fund can and should collaborate with other international agencies. It is our view that the operations of the Fund can contribute to the solution of other economic problems and the operations of other international agencies can facilitate the work of the Fund. Because international economic problems touch each other at innumerable points, it is essential that there be some degree of collaboration of the Fund with other international agencies.

The question, therefore, is as to the form and degree of collaboration. The Fund is designed to help maintain stability of exchange rates by providing resources for meeting temporary adverse balances on current account, while giving a member country time to take appropriate measures to adjust its balance of payments. If in the judgment of the member country and the Fund such an adjustment can best be made through the alteration of the exchange rate, provision is made for the necessary adjustment through cooperative action. In this connection, it should not be overlooked that the primary objective of the Fund is to assure a pattern of stable and orderly exchange rates that will make possible the expansion of international trade and the maintenance of a high level of business activity.

The Fund is not designed to provide resources for relief, nor is it designed to provide capital for reconstruction. Such specialized types of economic aid can be best given by agencies designed for these purposes, and it is expected that provision will be made for such agencies. There is no advantage in burdening the Fund with duties it is not suited to perform and which might impair its usefulness for maintaining exchange stability and bringing about the restoration and balanced growth of international trade.

While the Fund cannot place any part of its resources at the disposal of the other international agencies, it can and presumably would cooperate with other agencies. Because of the close interrelationship of all important international economic and financial problems, it will undoubtedly be necessary to have consultation between the Fund and other international agencies. For example, it is quite clear that in dealing with the problem of persistent favorable or unfavorable balances on current international account, the Fund and a Bank for Reconstruction and Development would have to pursue related policies.

The mere establishment of international agencies will not solve the international economic and financial problems. While such agencies are necessary, their successful operation requires policies that will encourage the growth of international trade and the maintenance of a high level of business activity.

Question 3

Is the Fund intended to provide for international expansion of production and exchange which is one of the objectives stated in Article VII of the Mutual Aid Agreement? Is it intended to introduce measures for controlling the trade cycle?

Reply

As is stated in the Joint Statement on the International Monetary Fund, the primary objective of economic policy must be the maintenance of a high level of employment and real income. It is recognized that only through international cooperation will it be possible for nations successfully to apply measures for achieving this end. It is a fundamental purpose of the Fund proposal to provide an agency for monetary cooperation among nations to aid in the securing of economic advancement and rising standards of living for all.

The operations of the International Monetary Fund are designed in the first instance to prevent discriminatory and restrictive exchange devices and to promote exchange stability through the cooperation of member countries. Obviously, a greater degree of stability of exchange rates is not an end in itself. It would be a complete inversion of objectives if a high level of business activity were to be sacrificed in order to maintain any given structure of exchange rates. Nor can we expect that a high level of production and employment will be automatically brought about through international monetary cooperation. But the Fund can contribute to the success of national policies intended to facilitate the attainment of a high level of production and employment by providing an international economic environment favorable to the development of such policies.

By helping to keep exchange rates relatively stable and removing the fear of large and sudden changes in exchange rates, the Fund will contribute to the revival of international trade and the resumption of international investment. With international cooperation on exchange policy, it will be possible to avoid the "beggar my neighbor" tactics of the 1930's which contributed to the spread of depression from country to country.

By discouraging bilateral clearing arrangements and putting an end to the use of multiple currencies and other restrictive exchange devices, the Fund will make it possible for member countries to enjoy the advantages of multilateral international trade without which the possibilities for the balanced growth of international commerce can never be fully realized.

Finally, by providing member countries with exchange resources when they are needed to meet an adverse balance of payments on current account, the Fund will free member countries from the necessity of taking extreme measures that have the effect of contracting income and employment in order to restrict imports and adjust an adverse balance of payments.

Under the Fund, corrective measures can be taken to adjust an adverse balance of payments which need not involve domestic contraction and a drastic reduction of imports. Under adequate safeguards, the Fund will provide the necessary exchange to maintain imports while more fundamental adjustments are being made. Likewise, in the case of member countries with a favorable balance on current account, the operations of the Fund will enable them to maintain their exports while adjustments are made, instead of being forced to undertake a sharp reduction in exports with the resulting adverse effects on domestic employment.

The Fund is not designed directly to control business fluctuations. In our opinion no international agency could assume the responsibility for the control of the trade cycle. To a considerable degree the volume of international trade is a reflection of the internal economic health of the trading nations. The work of the Fund is confined to the provision of some of the conditions necessary for international prosperity.

The maintenance of a high level of employment and the expansion of production can be achieved ultimately only through the development of its productive capacity by each member country. We may reasonably assume that while national policy in each country should and would be concerned with such development, the principal purpose of the Fund is the creation of a healthy international monetary environment in which the economies of member countries can enjoy a high level of employment and production.

We believe that to the extent the Fund is successful in realizing its objectives, fluctuations in the trade cycle will be mitigated. The Fund can minimize the deflationary monetary pressure that adverse balances of payments have had in the past. It can eliminate competitive currency depreciation and a variety of discriminatory trade practices. In this way it will help prevent a recurrence of the unfortunate policies that have had the effect of intensifying international depression and spreading it from country to country through nationalistic policies designed to secure recovery of one country at the cost of depression in other countries. Because the Fund holds resources to which all member countries have access, member countries may more freely undertake policies designed to stimulate investment and employment during periods of recession, without fear that such policies will lead to a serious depletion of their exchange resources and imperil the stability of exchange rates.

PART TWO: QUOTAS AND COMPOSITION OF THE FUND

QUESTION 4

What are the aggregate quotas of all member countries of the International Monetary Fund expected to be?

REPLY

The Joint Statement on the International Monetary Fund states that the aggregate quotas of the member countries shall be about $8 billion if all the United and Associated Nations subscribe to the Fund. This corresponds to about $10 billion for the world as a whole. The precise amount of the aggregate quotas cannot of course be determined until it is known how many countries will become members of the Fund.

The aggregate quotas represent the subscribed resources of the Fund. The primary consideration in deciding on this range of aggregate quotas is that resources of this magnitude will probably be sufficient for the purpose of the Fund. It should be borne in mind that the resources of the Fund are not intended to be used to finance flights of capital. Nor is the Fund expected to provide the resources for relief and rehabilitation, or for reconstruction and development. The needs for these purposes can more appropriately be met by international agencies designed to meet these specific problems.

In considering the adequacy of aggregate quotas of $8 billion for all of the United and Associated Nations it is necessary to bear in mind the prescribed purposes for which the resources of the International Monetary Fund may be used. The Fund is intended to provide exchange resources which may be purchased by member countries to meet their adverse balances on current account. But it is not proposed that the resources of the Fund be used to maintain indefinitely an unbalanced position in the economy of a country that has suffered a structural change in its relative international economic situation, though such resources may be used to facilitate the transition to a new position of internation equilibrium. There are adequate safeguards against the use of the Fund's resources to prevent or unduly delay the establishment of a sound pattern in international balances of payments. When a member country persistently shows a considerable favorable or unfavorable balance of payments that affects adversely the distribution of the resources of the Fund, a committee of the Fund will study the problem and report upon possible corrective measures.

While the resources of the Fund are intended primarily for use by member countries in meeting adverse balances on current account, they may be used to a limited extent to facilitate a transfer of capital or repayment of a foreign debt. In some instances such transfers will reduce the need of member countries to purchase foreign exchange from the Fund with which to meet their adverse balances on current account. This point is further elaborated in the reply to Question 26.

The resources of the International Monetary Fund will be used to finance adverse balances on current transactions. The question to be considered is whether resources of approximately $8 billion for all of the United and Associated Nations will be enough for this purpose in the years after the war. A preliminary test of the adequacy of the aggregate quotas may be made on the basis of the prewar situation. Specifically, would the Fund have had resources sufficient to meet all of the calls on the Fund for foreign exchange?

An examination was made of the balance of payments on current account of all countries for which such data were available in the years 1936 to 1938. For other countries, trade data were adjusted to give an approximation of their balance of payments on current account. In the case of countries that are large producers of gold, their exports of gold were regarded as part of their current trade. For other countries, neither gold movements nor capital movements were included in their balance of payments on current account.

In 1936, the total of all debit balances on current account was approximately $1 billion. In 1936 and 1937, the total of all debit balances for the two-year period was approximately $1.8 billion, and for the three-year period 1936 to 1938, the total of all debit balances was approximately $2.5 billion. Allowance should be made for the fact that even with a Fund many countries with debit balances would have preferred to meet their adverse balances by drawing on their holdings of gold and foreign exchange, or by importing capital from abroad. On the other hand the magnitude of the volume of trade and fluctuations in the balances of payments would undoubtedly have been larger during the period if nations had not resorted to restrictive exchange practices and bilateralism during this period. The purpose of the Fund is to remove such restrictive and discriminatory practices and to obviate the need for them.

It would appear from the above analysis that an International Monetary Fund with resources of $8 billion for all the United and Associated Nations could have met without difficulty the calls that would have been made upon it by member countries for the sale of foreign exchange to meet their adverse balances on current account in the period 1936 to 1938. It should be added that shortages of specific currencies would not be likely to present a serious problem so long as the aggregate resources of the Fund are ample since a considerable portion of the Fund's resources would be in the form of gold. This is particularly true if credit balances are widely distributed among a number of countries. If a serious one-sidedness in the balance of payments should develop in the post-war period, the Fund might be faced with the scarcity of an important currency. This problem is further discussed in the answers to questions 22 and 30. It is doubtful, however, whether the solution can be found in a general expansion of quotas.

The fact that a Fund with the amount and character of resources called for in the tentative proposal would have been in a position before the war to meet all calls to sell foreign exchange needed for adverse balances on current account does not prove that a Fund with the same resources would necessarily be in a position to meet all calls for this purpose after the war. Unquestionably, the distortion in the normal pattern of international trade will result in relatively large unbalanced positions during the early post-war period. Even so, a Fund with about forty-five member countries holding resources of approximately $8 billion, of which a considerable part is in gold, should be in a position to meet all legitimate calls for the sale of foreign exchange to meet adverse balances on current account. This is particularly so because it is not intended that the Fund continue to sell foreign exchange to any member country that uses the resources of the Fund to prevent or unduly delay the establishment of equilibrium in its international accounts.

In considering the adequacy of aggregate quotas of members of the Fund, it should not be overlooked that some countries already have relatively large reserves of gold and foreign exchange. Such reserves will be used along with resources of the Fund in meeting adverse balances of payments. The Fund will not have to provide resources for relief, a function it is not suited to perform. Furthermore, with the establishment of orderly and stable exchange rates, there will probably be a revival of international investment, particularly if encouragement is given to private investors through a Bank for Reconstruction and Development. Finally, no Fund can function successfully unless some measure of balance is attained in international trade. The maintenance of a high level of business activity, particularly in the United States, will contribute to the attainment of the necessary balance in international trade.

While it is expected that the Fund will hold adequate resources, provision is made for increasing the resources of the Fund if this should become necessary and desirable. The Fund may borrow the currency of any member country provided the country approves. It would appear, therefore, that the aggregate quotas will probably provide the Fund with adequate resources, and additional resources may be borrowed if and when they are needed under conditions that safeguard the member country and the Fund. Aggregate quotas may also be increased periodically in the future although no increase can be made in the quota of a member country without its consent.

Question 5

How much foreign exchange can member countries purchase from the International Monetary Fund?

Reply

The amount of foreign exchange which a member country can generally purchase from the Fund is related to the total amount of its currency which the Fund is permitted to hold. According to the provisions of the Joint Statement, the Fund's holdings of the currency of a member country may not exceed the quota of that country by more than 100 percent, unless additional local currency is acquired with the approval of the Board and on conditions that safeguard the interests of the Fund. In addition it is provided that the Fund's total holdings of the currency offered, after having been restored, if below that figure, to 75 percent of the member's quota, may not increase by more than 25 percent of that member's quota over a period of 12 months.

The significance of these provisions and their relations to the facilities that may be put at the disposal of a member country can be brought out more clearly by a concrete illustration. Assume that a member country has a quota of $100 million and that it meets its quota by paying $20 million in gold and $80 million in local currency. The total amount of that member's currency which the Fund can hold is $200 million. As the Fund will already hold $80 million in local currency it could acquire an additional $120 million in local currency before the country will have used up its maximum privilege to purchase foreign exchange from the Fund for local currency. Allowing for the gold contribution, $20 million, which could have been used to acquire foreign exchange without the Fund, the country can purchase $100 million in foreign exchange from the Fund for its local currency in excess of what it could get exclusively through use of its own resources.

A member country cannot, however, use up its total rights to acquire foreign exchange from the Fund over a short period of time. In the case of the example given above the member country could not acquire a net amount of foreign exchange from the Fund for local currency in excess of $25 million in any one year. The purpose of this provision is two-fold: It protects the member country from using up its privilege to acquire foreign exchange from the Fund before taking appropriate steps to adjust its balance of payments position; and it protects the Fund from a too rapid use of its resources. This provision is designed to prevent a member country from using the resources of the Fund to prolong an unbalanced international position.

While the normal amount of local currency of a member country which the Fund is permitted to hold is 200 percent of the quota of that member country the Fund is not rigidly limited to this amount and a member country is not assured that the Fund will necessarily be willing to hold this amount. The Fund may sell foreign exchange for additional local currency, even when its holdings exceed the prescribed limits, if the Board of Directors approves the sale and the member country is taking satisfactory measures to correct the disequilibrium or to reduce the excess local currency holdings of the Fund. In this connection, the Fund will prescribe the terms and conditions under which it will permit this, and it may require the deposit of collateral as one of the conditions. On the other hand, if a member country is using its quota in a manner contrary to the purposes and policies of the Fund, the Fund may give appropriate notice that the member is suspended from further use of the resources of the Fund.

By its very nature, the Fund cannot be called upon to provide all countries simultaneously with foreign exchange with which to meet their adverse balances on current account with other member countries. An adverse balance for some member countries must mean a favorable balance for other countries. If there were a fairly even distribution of favorable and adverse balances, there could be no question whatever of the Fund's capacity to provide member countries with the maximum facilities each could call for under its permissible quota. The Fund would not only have available for such use its holdings of the currencies of member countries with favorable balances, but it could draw upon its gold holdings to acquire additional amounts of whatever member currencies it might need.

There is, of course, a possibility that only a few member countries will have favorable balances for some years, the great bulk of the member countries having adverse balances on current account during this period. Let us assume that the Fund would be willing to provide the countries having unfavorable balances with the maximum facilities they could request within their permissible quotas. Could the Fund provide such facilities?

To put the case more concretely, let us assume that with 45 member countries having aggregate quotas of $8 billion, only 4 countries—the United States, Canada, Mexico and Brazil—have favorable balances, the remaining 41 countries having unfavorable balances on current account. Let us assume further these four countries have aggregate quotas of $3.5 billion, and that the gold contribution to the Fund of all other member countries is $700 million. Then, the 41 countries with unfavorable balances could purchase from the Fund $5.2 billion before every one of the countries would have exhausted its normal rights to purchase exchange from the Fund. To meet these demands the Fund would have $4.2 billion in the currencies of the four countries and in gold. Under the assumption the Fund would either have to restrict by $1 billion the total demand of the 41 countries with unfavorable balances, or borrow an additional $1 billion in the four countries with favorable balances.

The assumed case is clearly an extreme one. Unfavorable balances are not likely to be so general and widespread, or so concentrated in time, without the Fund's having previously taken steps to restore a greater degree of equilibrium. It is unreal to assume that the Fund must hold immediately available resources equal to the gross amount of foreign exchange all member countries could purchase from the Fund within their normal rights. The resources of the Fund may be considered as a revolving fund from which countries temporarily in need of foreign exchange resources can purchase what they require. There is no need, therefore, for the Fund to hold assets of a particular type equal to the aggregate of all individual demands which may be made upon it.

As a revolving fund, there is no definitive limit to the ability of the Fund to furnish foreign exchange to member countries. In the first place, the Fund does not lend foreign exchange but sells foreign exchange to member countries in return for their own local currencies. As it depletes its holdings of some currencies, it builds up correspondingly its holdings of other currencies. If, therefore, the member countries of the Fund, in cooperation with the Fund, succeed in preventing large and persistent favorable and unfavorable balances of payments, the Fund will always be in a position to provide member countries with the facilities they require. Under such conditions, the resources of the Fund would be adequate to meet the needs of member countries for foreign exchange to help maintain the stability of their exchanges while they put into effect measures that will restore balance in their international accounts.

In order to place the Fund in as strong a position as possible, there are several provisions which make it possible for the Fund to mobilize as much gold as the members can reasonably be expected to take out of their independent reserves. Original subscriptions in gold are scaled to the capacity of each member country as determined by its gold and gold-convertible exchange holdings and its quota. A member country purchasing exchange from the Fund must pay for one-half of such exchange in gold so long as its holdings of gold and gold-convertible exchange exceed its quota. It is expected that a member country desiring to obtain another member currency with gold will do so, if it is equally advantageous, by the sale of gold to the Fund. Half of the increase in a member country's official gold and gold-convertible exchange holdings in excess of its quota is to be used to repurchase its currency from the Fund. While exerting a minimum of pressure on the reserves of member countries, these provisions will serve to strengthen the Fund and will enable it to use all of its resources in meeting the needs of member countries for foreign exchange.

The Fund's resources will probably be adequate for all ordinary needs of member countries. When the Fund has been strengthened and a larger proportion of its assets are in the form of gold it will undoubtedly be able to meet even extraordinary needs for any particular currency or currencies. In the meantime, if the Fund should find its holdings of any member currency inadequate, it may borrow the needed amounts of that currency with the approval of the member country concerned and on terms and conditions agreed between them.

Question 6

In what form will the Fund hold the quota subscriptions of the member countries?

Reply

The subscriptions of the member countries to the Fund will be in the form of local currencies and gold. The Fund will keep a portion of its holdings of the currency of each member as a deposit in the Central Bank of that country, such portion being in accordance with the needs of the Fund for its current operations. It is the view of the technical experts of the United States that the balance of the Fund's holdings of the member countries' currencies should be in the form of bills, notes, or other forms of indebtedness, issued by the governments of the member countries. These securities would be non-negotiable, non-interest bearing and payable at their par value on demand by a credit to the deposit account of the Fund at the Central Bank of the member country.

Why is it desirable for the Fund to keep its surplus currency holdings in the form of securities of the member countries?

There are some countries for whom the required subscription of currency to the Fund can be made only with great difficulty. For such countries the problem is created by the existence of a monetary system under which the issue of currency (or the creation of central bank deposits) requires a high marginal reserve of gold.

For example, some countries can issue local currency only when secured in whole or in large part by gold or foreign exchange. It is not possible for such countries to issue local currency as a means of meeting the required subscription to an International Monetary Fund. Nor can such countries borrow at once the needed resources from the banks or the public except at rates of interest that would be burdensome. Such countries could, however, meet the subscription requirement if the Fund were to hold their subscriptions in the form of their own obligations.

There is another reason why some countries would find it desirable if a part of their subscription were held in the form of their own obligations. Clearly, the Fund is not going to use the entire local currency subscription of a country at the time operations of the Fund begin. For the Fund's purposes it would be satisfactory to have an adequate working balance at the Central Bank of the member country, holding the remainder of the local currency subscription in the form of government obligations. This would avoid the appearance of inflation or illiquidity of the Central Bank, which might be mistakenly inferred from the sudden increase of its deposit liabilities.

To meet the needs of countries that would find it more convenient not to pay all of the local currency subscription at once, it is proposed that part of the quota subscription be held in the form of government obligations, redeemable at par on demand. Whenever the working balance of the Fund in local currency is depleted by its sales of such currency, the Fund can replenish the balance by presenting for redemption the securities it holds.

There is no reason for believing that the Fund takes any more risk in holding Government obligations than in holding local currency. When the Fund requires local currency for its operations, the national monetary authorities will presumably wish, as a matter of monetary policy, to redeem the securities held by the Fund and to borrow from the market.

Question 7

In determining the Fund's holdings of a country's currency at a given date does "currency" include or exclude securities expressed in that currency?

Reply

The Fund's holdings of a currency for purposes of determining the maximum amount of this currency which the Fund is normally permitted to hold are regarded as the net position of the Fund with respect to that currency. The Fund's holdings of the currency may be defined, therefore, as all of the assets of the Fund in a given currency minus all of the liabilities of the Fund in that currency. Quite definitely, in calculations on the amount of foreign exchange which a country may normally purchase from the Fund, the security holdings of the Fund in any local currency should be included as part of the local currency.

It should be understood, of course, that the Fund is not authorized to deal in securities. The Fund is permitted to acquire securities redeemable on demand at par in part payment of the initial subscription. The Fund might require the deposit of securities as collateral when selling foreign exchange for local currency. The Fund cannot otherwise acquire securities.

The way in which the Fund acquires assets in terms of a given local currency does not affect the inclusion of the assets in the Fund's holdings so far as determining the maximum permissible holdings of that currency by the Fund is concerned. Therefore, the Fund's holdings of local currency include initial subscriptions in these forms, and currency acquired by the purchase of foreign exchange from the Fund. The Fund's position in a local currency may be modified whenever the local currency is sold to the Fund or bought from the Fund by a member country. Devaluation does not affect the calculated holdings of the currency and securities of a member country as the gold value of such holdings are not affected by devaluation.

Question 8

What is the formula for determining the quotas of member countries?

Reply

A formulation of a method to be used in measuring the participation of the various member countries was not included in the Joint Statement by the experts on the establishment of an International Monetary Fund. This was considered to be a matter on which a decision should be reached only after there has been ample opportunity for consultation with all of the prospective participants. Considerable attention has been given this matter in discussions among the technical experts of the United and Associated Nations.

After examining a great number of suggested bases for quotas, it is the view of the technical experts of the United States that no single factor can allocate participation among the various nations in a satisfactory manner. Several methods for combining a number of factors were tested. The method which is discussed below seems to combine the important relevant factors in a reasonable way and to give relative quotas that seem fair when applied to the approximate data available for a number of countries.

A satisfactory quota formula must give consideration to the multiple functions of the quota. The size of a member country's quota determines the amount of the subscription which that country makes to the resources of the Fund and is the basis for determining the normal rights of that country to purchase foreign exchange from the Fund. The size of the quota is also one of the factors which determines the relative voice of that country in the management of the Fund. The aggregate size of the quotas will determine the total subscribed resources of the Fund.

In view of the functions of the quotas, it would seem that the formula for the determination of relative quotas for member countries should take into account the ability of a country to subscribe resources to the Fund, the need of a country for use of the resources of the Fund, and the economic significance of a country.

The ability of a country to subscribe resources to the Fund is best indicated by its national income. In a sense, participation in the Fund is an investment. The extent to which a country can devote resources to this or other purposes depends very largely on its national income. However, because the Fund is an international institution that can function more effectively if some of its resources are in the form of gold, it has been thought desirable to require payment of part of the quota subscription in this form. Under the circumstances, the ability of a country to subscribe resources to the Fund in the form of gold is also indicated by its holdings of gold and gold-convertible exchange.

The probable need of a country for use of the resources of the Fund is best indicated by the magnitude of the fluctuations in its balance of payments. There is a good deal of difficulty in dealing directly with fluctuations in the balance of payments. For this reason it was found preferable to utilize import and export data. A country's need for foreign exchange generally arises from the fact that its imports may be maintained when its exports fall off. We have, therefore, made use of average annual imports and maximum fluctuations in exports as indications of a country's need for use of the resources of the Fund.

The economic significance of a country in the world's economy is an intangible factor impossible to measure even approximately. It depends on its national output, its foreign trade, its foreign investment, its economic and political strength. In the final determination of quotas allowance is made for this factor through use of a special allotment for the equitable adjustment of quotas, which is further discussed below.

In order to take account of the above factors it is suggested that the quota of a country be determined by the following formula:

(a) 2 percent of the national income of 1940;

(b) 5 percent of the holdings of gold and gold-convertible exchange as of January 1, 1944;

(c) 10 percent of average annual imports, 1934–1938, inclusive;

(d) 10 percent of maximum variation in annual exports 1934–1938, inclusive.

It is further proposed that the total so determined be increased for each country by the percentage ratio of its average annual exports (1934–1938) to its national income. In this way, special consideration is given to those countries whose national income is particularly affected by international trade.

After testing this formula for a number of countries, we have come to the conclusion that on the whole the results are as satisfactory as can be obtained through the use of any formula. We recognize that under this formula some countries may, for various reasons, be given entirely inadequate quotas. With any formula, provision must be made for adjustment of inequitable quotas. We have proposed that before determining individual quotas 10 percent of aggregate quotas be reserved as a special allotment for the equitable adjustment of quotas. For example, if the aggregate quotas for all member countries should be equivalent to $8 billion, the formula would be used to apportion 90 per cent ($7.2 billion) of the authorized aggregate quotas among the member countries. The remaining 10 percent ($800 million) could be used to increase the quotas of any countries whose quotas, as determined by application of the formula, seem inadequate. The adjustment of the quota need not always be based upon a country's need for access to the Fund. Since no formula can take account of the intangible factors, the special allotment will also be needed to assure to each country a share in the responsibility for management of the Fund commensurate with its potential position in international economic affairs.

It is provided in the Joint Statement that quotas may be revised from time to time by changes which require a four-fifths vote and no member's quota may be changed without its consent. It is the view of the technical experts of the United States that provision should be made for the adjustment of quotas on the basis of the most recent data three years after the establishment of the Fund and at intervals of five years thereafter, in accordance with an agreed upon formula. At the time of revision of quotas, the special allotment mentioned above may be used to increase the quota of a country if the quota as determined by the formula is still termed inequitable. This special allotment may also be used in the periods between recurrent adjustments, if developments indicate that a country is entitled to a larger quota.

QUESTION 9

If quotas are to be based in part on holdings of gold and gold-convertible exchange would not this give most facilities to those members needing them least and vice versa?

REPLY

As indicated in the answer to the previous question gold and gold-convertible exchange holdings would be only one of several factors in the determination of the quotas of member countries.

The quotas assigned to member countries in the International Monetary Fund proposal have a three-fold purpose: to provide a measure of the appropriate subscription to the Fund by member countries; to provide a measure of the appropriate utilization of resources of the Fund by member countries; and to provide a basis for responsibility in the management of the Fund. It is not regarded as feasible to set up one formula for subscription to the Fund, a separate formula for the utilization of resources of the Fund, and still another formula for voting power in the Fund. For each country the use of the resources of the Fund must be related to its subscription although in practice countries will necessarily use varying proportions of their quotas. Finally, the voting power in the Fund must be related to each country's subscription to the Fund, although it need not be in precise proportion to subscriptions.

Holdings of gold and gold-convertible exchange are regarded as one of the appropriate factors in the determination of quotas because they indicate the capacity of a country to provide an important type of asset that will be required in the operations of the Fund. It has not been given preponderant importance in the formula for quotas that has been suggested for consideration. The proportion of aggregate quotas arising from the use of this factor is something over 16 percent of the whole. All of the other elements used—national income, variability of exports, average imports, and relation of exports to national income—measure characteristics of the national economy which reflect past or potential need for the use of foreign exchange resources to meet adverse balances on current account and to maintain stability of the exchanges. Finally, when the formula does not give a country a quota properly reflecting its prospective need for use of the resources of the Fund, the quota can be adjusted from the special allotment.

It should be added that a number of provisions are included in the draft proposal intended to give consideration to the position of countries with relatively small holdings of gold and gold-convertible exchange. The subscription in the form of gold is smaller in proportion to the quota for such countries than for countries with relatively large holdings. Countries with gold and gold-convertible exchange holdings which are less than their quotas need not use any part of their gold holdings in purchasing foreign exchange from the Fund. And countries with official holdings which are less than their quotas need not offer to sell to the Fund any part of the increment of gold they acquire so long as their official holdings are below this level.

QUESTION 10

Does the Fund proposal provide for a quasi-automatic increase in quotas to facilitate the financing of an increasing volume of international trade?

REPLY

The characteristic feature of the Fund proposal as outlined in the Joint Statement on the Fund is its flexibility. In general, the Fund proposal does not depend on quasi-automatic provisions for its effectiveness. Instead, the Board of Directors is commonly given authority to adjust the policies of the Fund to the conditions prevailing in particular cases, acting within broad provisions intended to safeguard the resources of the Fund and the interests of member countries.

As was stated in the reply to Question 8, it is the recommendation of the technical experts of the United States that the quotas of member countries should be adjusted on the basis of the most recent data three years after the establishment of the Fund and at intervals of five years thereafter, in accordance with an agreed formula. The quota formula itself could only be changed with the approval of a four-fifths vote of the Board of Directors. However, it would not be necessary to wait for the termination of the initial three-year period, or subsequent five-year periods, to adjust quotas. It would be within the power of the Board to increase the quota of a member country at any time out of a special allotment reserved for the equitable adjustment of quotas. To safeguard any country from being compelled to subscribe additional resources to the Fund, it is provided that an increase in the quota of a country can be made only with its consent.

Under the provisions outlined above there will be an expansion of quotas periodically as national incomes rise, as the stock of monetary gold increases, and as the volume of international trade grows. With the expansion of quotas the resources of the Fund and the ability of member countries to purchase foreign exchange will be increased correspondingly. More important, however, is the fact that neither the resources of the Fund nor the ability of member countries to purchase foreign exchange from the Fund are rigidly determined by the quotas. There are flexible provisions for increasing the resources of the Fund as needed. No limitations are placed on the Fund's ability to obtain resources through borrowing scarce currencies from member countries on terms agreed between the countries and the Fund. Likewise member countries may secure foreign exchange for their needs when they have exceeded the ordinary limits provided under the quota limitations under provisions that safeguard the interests of the Fund.

It would be a mistake to put too much stress on quasi-automatic changes in quotas. For example, if quotas were adjusted automatically to short-run changes in the volume of trade there would be an expansion of quotas in boom years and a contraction in years of slump. While the expansion of quotas in boom periods may not be disturbing of itself because the excessive use of quotas can be controlled, there can be no doubt that a contraction of quotas in depression periods would tend to have a depressing influence.

The fact is that the need for use of the resources of the Fund is not a simple function of the volume of trade. When international trade expands gradually, the growth may well be balanced, and there may be little need for help from the Fund. The need is likely to be greatest at the very time when the total volume of trade has fallen, for it is at such times that the greatest distortion in the normal balance of payments takes place. It is for this reason that the Fund proposal places great stress on fluctuations in the balance of payments on current account as a factor in the determination of quotas.

Automatic devices are unreliable guides to policy in troubled times. What is needed is not a new series of automatic signals to replace the discarded ones of the past. On monetary problems, there can be no automatic substitute for a rational policy implemented with flexible powers. While the American technical experts favor a provision for periodic adjustment of quotas, this feature is regarded as less significant than the provisions that give the Fund flexibility in acquiring resources and in permitting member countries to use resources.

Question 11

In what form will member countries meet supplementary subscriptions if their quotas are increased?

Reply

No specific provision is made for the form in which member countries may meet supplementary subscriptions if their quotas are increased. Unless specific provision is regarded as necessary by some member countries, it would be desirable to give the Board of Directors complete authority to require member countries to meet supplementary subscriptions in the form which seems most appropriate to the Board at the time the supplementary subscriptions are made.

It would not be possible to specify in advance in what form it would be most desirable to have supplementary subscriptions to the resources of the Fund. If the Fund has experienced a period of successful operation, with its resources appropriately distributed among different member currencies and with adequate holdings of gold, there could be no objection to having supplementary subscriptions paid largely in member currencies. On the other hand, if the Fund has experienced some difficulty in meeting the demands for some currencies, it would be preferable to strengthen the Fund by having some part of the supplementary subscriptions paid in gold.

There may be some member countries that would wish to assure themselves against a requirement that they meet supplementary subscriptions with an excessive payment in gold. While a country could withhold its consent to an increase in its quota if too large a part of the supplementary subscription is called for in gold, this may not be regarded as an adequate safeguard. Such countries might prefer a provision that supplementary subscriptions should be made in the same proportions as the original subscriptions and on the basis of the relation of gold and gold-convertible exchange holdings to the revised quota at the time supplementary subscriptions would be made.

An alternative provision could provide the necessary safeguard to member countries while retaining for the Fund considerable flexibility in determining the form in which supplementary subscriptions should be made. The Fund could be given authority to call for subscriptions in whatever form it deems in the general interest, but limiting the subscription to be paid in gold to not more than the proportion specified for the original subscriptions. Of course, any schedule for payments in gold in connection with supplementary subscriptions should be applied uniformly to all member countries.

PART THREE: GOLD AND THE OPERATIONS OF THE FUND

Question 12

What is the purpose of requiring that a portion of the subscribed quota be paid in gold?

Reply

Because of the unquestioned acceptability of gold as an international exchange medium the power of the Fund to serve its members will depend in part upon the size of its gold holdings. With gold the Fund can buy the currency of any member country. If the assets of the Fund consisted solely of currencies of member countries, there would be a danger that relatively small disturbances in the balance of payments positions of member countries would leave the Fund short of certain currencies.

So long as the Fund holds gold it can acquire additional amounts of any member currency. The lack of such generally acceptable resources as gold could in time compel the Fund to take measures to restrict its sales of foreign exchange to the currencies that are available. It is of utmost importance, therefore, that the Fund hold resources that can be used, as needed, to acquire any currency that becomes temporarily scarce.

In many respects, an ideal Fund would be one consisting predominately of gold. It is recognized that such an ideal Fund cannot be immediately established. There is every reason, however, to provide the Fund with as much of such general exchange resources as is within the power of member countries to furnish through their quota subscriptions. For this reason, part of the quota subscription is to be made in gold, graduated for each member country according to its capacity to meet part of its quota in this form. While large gold holdings would strengthen the Fund, such holdings will have to be accumulated gradually in order to avoid pressure on the reserves now held by member countries. Gold subscriptions of 25 percent of the quota or 10 percent of the official gold and gold-convertible exchange holdings of a member country, whichever is the smaller, would appear to meet the immediate needs of the Fund and to be within the present capacity of member countries.

Apart from the original contributions in gold, there are provisions for strengthening the Fund by gradually increasing its holdings of gold. Provision is made for sale of gold to the Fund by member countries desiring to obtain other member currencies. Part of the payment for foreign exchange purchased from the Fund must be made in gold if the member country's official gold and gold-convertible exchange holdings exceed its quota. And member countries are required to use part of the increase in their official gold and gold-convertible exchange holdings, if they exceed their quotas, to repurchase their local currencies from the Fund. These provisions will in time add to the gold holdings of the Fund without putting pressure on the gold reserves of member countries.

It should be noted that a member country will not necessarily in fact find its foreign exchange position impaired by making part of its quota subscription in the form of gold, or by substituting gold for its local currency in the Fund, since the right of a member country to purchase foreign exchange from the Fund is directly related to the Fund's holdings of its local currency. The greater the original subscription in gold and the later replacement of local currency holdings with gold, the more foreign exchange a member country has the right to purchase from the Fund. The net foreign exchange position of a member country (its own holdings of gold and foreign exchange, plus its unused right to purchase foreign exchange from the Fund) is unaffected by its use of gold in payment of part of its subscription and by its sale of gold to the Fund. On the other hand, the liquidity of the Fund's assets, and hence its usefulness to member countries, is increased when local currency is in part replaced with gold.

There is, of course, the possibility that a member country will find that although the unused portion of its right to purchase foreign exchange from the Fund is large, the one currency it requires is scarce and can be acquired from the Fund only in limited amounts. It is true for such a country that its gold subscription to the Fund is not fully equivalent to holding gold for itself. Such a difficulty can be overcome only by strengthening the Fund and by avoiding in this and in other ways the development of a situation in which a currency must be declared scarce.

QUESTION 13

Would the Fund contribute in any way to the maintenance of a market for gold?

REPLY

Because gold has a world-wide market, it is superfluous to speak of the Fund as contributing to the maintenance of a market for gold. With or without the Fund, gold will continue to be held as monetary reserves and to be used throughout the world in the settlement of international balances. The provisions of the Fund in no way change the established position of gold. They are designed to utilize the recognized status of gold as the accepted medium of international payments in order to facilitate the settlement of international balances and the maintenance of stable exchanges.

The Fund utilizes the accepted position of gold in a number of ways. In the first place, the Fund itself is expected to hold gold, entirely for the purpose of assuring to member countries an adequate supply of any member currency that may be demanded. As has been indicated in the reply to Question 5, the Fund must hold an adequate amount of general resources such as gold.

The Fund is authorized to buy and sell gold and provision is made for strengthening the Fund by adding to its holdings of gold to enable it to more effectively meet the needs of member countries. Part of the quota subscription is required in gold and member countries are required to pay for part of their foreign exchange purchases from the Fund in gold unless their own gold and exchange holdings are inadequate. Member countries holding a stated minimum of gold must repurchase the Fund's holdings of their local currencies with part of the gold they acquire in excess of their holdings at the time of becoming members of the Fund. Member countries that wish to sell gold for member currencies are expected to offer the gold for sale to the Fund if this is equally advantageous to them.

The Fund also utilizes the accepted position of gold to facilitate the maintenance of exchange stability. It is generally recognized that when a currency is defined in terms of gold and the monetary authorities are prepared to buy and sell gold (or currencies equivalent to gold) at approximately fixed prices in terms of local currency, the exchange rates can be maintained stable within an appropriate range. Various provisions of the Fund proposal make use of these customary devices.

The assets of the Fund are guaranteed against depreciation with respect to gold. Member countries may not induce a *de facto* depreciation of their currencies by purchasing gold, directly or indirectly, at a price in local currency in excess of a stated maximum above the gold parity; nor may member countries induce a *de facto* appreciation of their currencies by selling gold, directly or indirectly, at a price in local currency below a stated minimum under this parity.

The Fund itself is expected to buy and sell local currencies for gold when this becomes necessary for avoiding a fluctuation in exchange rates beyond the range established by the Fund. Member countries, in turn, are expected to take appropriate action to maintain exchange rates within the prescribed range. By established custom, such appropriate action includes the use of gold and foreign exchange resources to prevent depreciation and the acquisition of gold to prevent appreciation of the exchanges.

While the Fund utilizes the recognized status of gold to facilitate its operations, the Fund does not impose any specific obligations on member countries to hold or use gold for any purposes other than to help maintain stability of the exchanges. While member countries must buy back their own currencies acquired by other member countries from current transactions either with the currency of the other member country or with gold, there is no general obligation on the part of any member country to redeem its local currency in gold. Nor is it expected that the Fund will regard appropriate action to maintain exchange rates as requiring a member country to exhaust all of its reserves of gold and foreign exchange.

QUESTION 14

Are all countries that are members of the International Monetary Fund under obligation to buy all gold offered to them at a fixed price?

REPLY

The Fund proposal provides no explicit obligation on the part of member countries to buy all gold offered to them at a fixed price. Provision IX-1 of the Joint Statement on the Fund Proposal is intended to prevent member countries from depreciating or appreciating their currencies through an increase in the price at which gold is bought or a decrease in the price at which gold is sold. While this provision does place limitations on the prices at which gold transactions may be undertaken, it does not itself require a member country either to buy or sell gold at all.

Despite the fact that there is no explicit provision requiring member countries to buy all gold offered to them, it is our view that provision IX-2 implicitly requires member countries to buy gold offered to them by member countries when this becomes necessary to prevent an appreciation of the exchange beyond the range established by the Fund. Appropriate action to prevent exchange transactions in its market in currencies of other members at rates outside the prescribed range involves the acquisition of gold offered by other member countries or by the Fund.

Obviously, a member country can take steps to limit the demand for its currency by the nationals of other countries and in this way it can minimize the import of gold. It may, with the approval of the Fund, restrict capital movements when the influx of foreign funds is regarded as undesirable. It may even adopt measures that will reduce the demand for its exports in other countries, although certain forms of such measures can be adopted only with the approval of the Fund. But in any case, so long as there is a demand for its currency to settle international transactions on current account, a member country is implicitly obligated to provide its currency for gold.

Also, it is clearly expected that the Fund can replenish its supply of the currency of any member country through the sale of gold when this is necessary to provide exchange for the purposes for which the Fund is authorized to sell exchange. Because the Fund's gold holdings are regarded as a liquid asset equivalent to any member currency, provision is made for the gradual replacement of local currency by gold. It would be contrary to the purposes of these provisions if gold were not purchased freely by member countries when this becomes necessary to prevent an appreciation of the exchanges.

QUESTION 15

Would the Fund be able to create credit in the course of its operations?

REPLY

The Fund proposal as outlined by the Joint Statement makes no provision for transferable currency or deposits in terms of a new or special monetary unit. The operations of the Fund are exclusively in currencies of member countries and in gold.

The Fund does not have any means of creating, holding or transferring currencies or deposits which do not originate with the member countries themselves.

In fact, the Fund proposal does not anywhere provide for the creation by the Fund of transferable credits whether denominated in gold or in the currencies of the member countries or in some special unit. The resources of the Fund in currencies and gold plus what resources the Fund can borrow, represent the facilities the Fund can put at the disposal of member countries. The resources of the Fund are not indefinitely expandable in the sense that international credits are created by the process of a country's getting into debt to the Fund. The creation of credit remains exclusively a function of the monetary authorities of member countries.

We believe that this arrangement is more desirable for the following reasons:

First, with this restriction the management of the Fund is likely to be more vigilant in taking steps which will correct a persistent disequilibrium in the balance of payments position of member countries than if there were no definite limit to the total volume of credit balances which could be created by means of loans or overdrafts.

Second, a system under which a member country assumes a known and limited obligation to subscribe resources for the Fund gives needed protection to all countries, and Governments will be more willing to enter into such an arrangement with a definite and specified limit to their obligations.

Third, the financial strength and stability will be greater in the case of a Fund which possesses a substantial amount of tangible resources for carrying on its operations than in the case of an international institution which has no resources other than an agreement on the part of member countries to accept the credits created by that institution in exchange for real goods and services.

Fourth, if the operations of the Fund reveal a need for additional resources for its successful functioning, such resources can be secured through the borrowing power of the Fund, without the indirect compulsion inherent in the creation of credit.

PART FOUR: EXCHANGE RATES

Question 16

What will be the procedure for establishing initial rates of exchange?

Reply

Initial rates of exchange are to be established for the currencies of all member countries by defining the parity of each currency in terms of gold. Once established, the initial parity of a member country's currency can be changed only after consultation with or approval by the Fund. All transactions between the Fund and member countries, and all transactions in member currencies, will be at rates of exchange within an agreed percentage of parity.

The Joint Statement on the Fund proposal provides that initial par values of the currencies of the member countries shall be fixed by agreement between the member countries and the Fund. Before the Fund can be established it will be necessary for the member countries to agree with the Fund as to the exchange rates which these countries will fix upon entering the Fund. At the initial meeting of the members of the Fund, the Fund will accept or reject the initial rates proposed by each of the member countries. An agreement must be reached with the Fund on the par values of their currencies by the members at the initial meeting of the Fund before the Fund can begin operations.

The task of considering and determining the initial rates of exchange for all countries that will become members of the Fund would seem at first glance to be overwhelming. If the process of determining initial exchange rates by extended negotiation can be avoided it would simplify the problem of the organization of the Fund. What is wanted is a criterion for the initial fixing of rates of exchange which can be applied generally without prolonged and difficult negotiations with each member country.

It is believed that for most countries that will be invited to become members of the Fund the prevailing rates of exchange will prove entirely satisfactory. In the case of such countries there is clearly no need for the negotiation of a new rate of exchange. For this reason it is the recommendation of the technical experts of the United States that for any country which becomes a member prior to the date on which the Fund's operation began, the rates initially used by the Fund shall be based on the value of the currency in terms of U.S. dollars which prevailed on July 1, 1943. In the event that either the member country or the Fund regards the rate prevailing on July 1, 1943 as clearly inappropriate, it will be necessary for the initial rate to be determined by consultation between the member country and the Fund.

In countries occupied by the enemy there were no dollar rates on July 1, 1943. Moreover, because of the drastic economic changes that have taken place in occupied countries it would not be feasible to apply a general rule, such as a pre-war rate, as a guide for determining the initial rates of exchange for these currencies. In such cases the Fund will use the exchange rate fixed by the government of the liberated country in consultation with the Fund, provided this rate is not considered by the Fund to be inappropriate. No operations in the currency of the member country may be undertaken by the Fund until an acceptable rate has been determined.

Because of the great uncertainty of their postwar situation, some occupied countries may be justly reluctant to fix a definitive rate of exchange immediately after their liberation. Adequate provision has been made in the Joint Statement for changing rates of exchange which prove to be unsatisfactory to the member country. These provisions will be discussed in the reply to Question 17. It would naturally be in the interest of the Fund to correct any maladjustment which was the outgrowth of the fixing of an improper rate at the time a country joined the Fund.

Although under the present provisions of the Joint Statement member countries must establish definitive par values for their currencies before they can purchase foreign exchange from the Fund, it may be desirable to provide that countries which have been occupied in whole or in part during the present war may with the approval of the Fund establish provisional rates. The Fund might be permitted to undertake limited operations in such currencies under adequate safeguards for the resources of the Fund.

QUESTION 17

What facilities are provided by the Fund for correcting an initial rate of exchange that proves unsatisfactory?

REPLY

The provisions of the Joint Statement on the Fund proposal recognize certain fundamental concepts with respect to exchange rates. First, it is not desirable to alter exchange rates unnecessarily or when there are other satisfactory means of restoring equilibrium in a country's international balance of payments. Second, it is not possible to support indefinitely an exchange rate that does not reflect a country's international economic position. Third, an alteration of the exchange rate affects the economic life of other countries and should, therefore, be undertaken only after consultation with other countries. Fourth, the interest of a country in its own exchange is paramount, and no change in the exchange rate for a currency should be made except with the consent of that country.

In order to avoid the unnecessary changing of exchange rates, it is provided in the Joint Statement that the par value of each member's currency shall be fixed by agreement between the Fund and the member country. Normally this will be the rate which prevails at the time the member country joins the Fund; but where the prevailing rate is deemed to be inappropriate by either the Fund or the member country, the initial rate must be determined by consultation between the member country and the Fund.

It is recognized in the Fund proposal that alteration in exchange rates may be necessary to correct fundamental disequilibrium. Neither a member country nor the Fund can succeed in supporting indefinitely an exchange rate which does not reflect a country's international economic position. Where other satisfactory measures cannot be taken to restore equilibrium in a country's balance of payments position, it is necessary to adjust the rate of exchange. There is general agreement that because of the extreme uncertainties prevailing at the time, some exchange rates that are fixed during and immediately after the war may have to be altered. For this reason, it is believed that some changes in such exchange rates should be permitted with more freedom than would be justified after international economic relationships have attained a greater degree of stability. The Fund should not, of course, reject a requested change in an exchange rate that is necessary to restore equilibrium because of the domestic social or political policies of the country applying for the change.

An alteration in an established rate of exchange is a matter of interest not only to the country whose currency is changed but to other countries whose economies may be affected by the alteration of the rate of exchange. A change in exchange rates should not be made, therefore, unless it is essential to the correction of fundamental disequilibrium, and except in cooperation with other countries. The Fund proposal provides that no change in exchange rates can be made without prior consultation with the Fund, and that changes that alter the established rate by more than 10 percent can be made only with the approval of the Fund.

It is provided in the Joint Statement that a member country may, after first consulting the Fund, change the established parity of its currency provided the proposed change, inclusive of any changes made since the establishment of the Fund, does not exceed 10 percent. If a member country believes that a change in its exchange rate, not covered by the above, is necessary for the correction of a fundamental disequilibrium, it may make application to the Fund for such change. If the requested change does not exceed 10 percent the Fund is required to give its decision on such application within two days of receiving the application, if the applicant so requests. In the case of requests for changes beyond those covered by the above provisions the Fund will allow sufficient time for a thorough investigation of the need for the change in the exchange rate requested by the member country before giving its decision. It should be noted that in all cases of requests for changes in exchange rates member countries agree not to propose a change in the parity of their currency unless they consider it appropriate to the correction of a fundamental disequilibrium.

Although there are times when an alteration of exchange rates is in the general interest, the significance of the rate of exchange is of such paramount importance in the economic life of a country, that a change in the exchange rate for a currency should not be imposed on a country. The Fund proposal recognizes the special interest of a country in its own exchange rate and provides that a change in the exchange rate for a currency can be made only at the request of the country concerned.

Where the Fund's approval for a change in the par value of a member currency is required, the decision is by majority of the votes of the member countries.

While the Fund cannot compel a country to accept an exchange rate it does not regard as desirable or to change an exchange rate it wishes to keep, the Fund need not make its resources available to support an exchange rate it regards as inappropriate. The Fund cannot undertake operations in a currency until an initial rate is fixed which has its approval. Further, the Fund may give appropriate notice that it will not continue to sell foreign exchange to a country that is using the resources of the Fund in a manner contrary to the purposes and policies of the Fund. Obviously, under this provision the Fund would not provide an exchange rate which prevents the restoration of equilibrium.

Question 18

What will be the position of countries, members of the International Monetary Fund, whose currencies are customarily tied to the dollar or sterling?

Reply

The practice followed by many countries of maintaining close relationships between their currencies and either the dollar or sterling has undoubtedly been very useful to them. To a considerable extent, such relationships have been helpful in maintaining a greater degree of exchange stability than would otherwise be possible. There is nothing in this practice that is necessarily contrary to the purposes of the Fund, and there is much in this practice that can facilitate the operations of the Fund.

Countries whose currencies have been tied to the dollar or to sterling can continue their customary relationship. They may by law define their currencies in terms of the dollar or sterling; they may hold their monetary reserves in the form of dollar or sterling balances; they may make their currencies redeemable in dollars or sterling. In general, there will be for such countries no need to terminate or to alter the prevailing relationship between their currencies and the dollar or sterling.

Such countries will be particularly interested in the stability of the exchange rates for their currencies in terms of dollars or sterling. When the initial gold parities of their currencies are determined, it is expected that in most instances the Fund will use parities based on the exchange rates prevailing at the time the Fund is established. Unless such rates are clearly inappropriate, and they do not appear to be for most currencies which were tied to the dollar or to sterling, there will be no reason to disturb the existing rates between such currencies and the dollar or sterling.

Once established, the gold parity for a currency continues in effect so long as a member country is satisfied, for the Fund cannot on its own initiative compel a country to alter the parity of its currency. There is no reason for assuming, therefore, that the Fund would in the future require a country to discontinue the special relationship of its currency to the dollar or sterling.

The only occasion when a country could experience any difficulty, as a member of the Fund, in retaining the customary relationship of its currency to the dollar or to sterling would be if the parity for either the dollar or sterling were altered. Even so, there is reason for believing that the difficulty is more apparent than real. A change in the gold parity of a currency can be made only after consultation with the Fund and, with one exception, only with the approval of the Fund. Assuming that the gold parity for either the dollar or sterling were changed, would countries whose currencies are linked to the dollar or sterling be able to alter the parities for their currencies correspondingly?

Aside from the exception previously referred to, a country desiring to alter the parity for its currency in order to maintain its previous relationship to the dollar or sterling would have to secure the prior approval of the Fund. Such approval would be granted if it were shown that a change in the parity is necessary to correct a fundamental disequilibrium. In most instances in which a currency is tied to the dollar or sterling, the special relationship has been established because of the close ties of the two countries in international commerce or finance. If this is so, a change in the dollar or sterling parity is likely to lead to a change for such a country in the demand for exports to or imports from the United States or England. Obviously if such a change in the dollar or sterling parity would have the effect of bringing about a disequilibrium in a country's international payments position, the Fund would undoubtedly permit a country to make the corresponding change for its own currency.

It should be noted that there is no provision in the Fund proposal for pooling or transferring the permissible quotas of member countries. Undoubtedly, to some small extent it is possible for member countries to use their quotas to support the currencies of other countries. The Fund, however, could prevent any considerable use of its resources for this purpose.

Question 19

How will the range of permissible fluctuation in exchange rates, as fixed by the Fund, compare with the old spread between gold points?

Reply

There would appear to be three sets of limits on exchange rates to be considered in connection with this question: (1) the gold import and gold export points; (2) the highest and lowest points within which exchange rates established by the Fund may be permitted to fluctuate; and (3) the Fund's buying and selling rates for foreign exchange in terms of local currency.

In the opinion of the technical experts of the United States it is on the whole desirable to have the range established by the Fund somewhat broader than the range of the gold points. It is a moot question whether the Fund's buying and selling rates should be the same as the lower and upper limits of the range established by the Fund. There are, however, some disadvantages in having the Fund's buying and selling rates lie within the range of fluctuations permitted by the Fund, and some advantages in having the Fund's buying and selling rates lie outside this range.

In general, it is our view that the range that the Fund would establish would be somewhat greater than the traditional gold points that prevailed in the 1920's. A broader range within which exchange rates could fluctuate might have some effect in inducing member countries to use their independent resources of gold and foreign exchange before resorting to the Fund. It would be in the general interest if member countries would undertake to meet normal and moderate needs for additional exchange by their nationals out of their holdings of gold and foreign exchange, while the resources of the Fund would be reserved for occasions when member countries experience a real need for supplementary resources to be used while working out the basic adjustments in their international position. The inducement to a country to use its resources of gold and foreign exchange is further increased if the Fund's buying and selling rates for exchange lie outside the range of permitted fluctuations, as this would directly penalize the monetary authorities of a member country for using the resources of the Fund.

It is too much to hope that even a relatively broad range, say 2 percent, within which member currencies might be permitted to fluctuate would provide sufficient flexibility for adjusting a country's international balance of payments through a movement in exchange rates. There will, nevertheless, be seasonal or even small cyclical pressures that can be considerably offset by a movement of exchange rates within such a broad range prescribed by the Fund.

There is to this extent something to be said even on the economic side for broadening the range of exchange rates prescribed by the Fund as compared with the old spread between gold points. On the other hand, the permissible variations must not introduce a risk of exchange fluctuations so considerable as to deter short-term financing of international trade or long-term lending for investment. Neither should the permissible fluctuation encourage speculation of a character that would tend to weaken the established structure of exchange rates, or too easily introduce a disrupting influence in the money and exchange markets.

The range prescribed by the Fund should for administrative reasons be greater than the spread between the gold points. In the post-war period, it is almost certain that under any circumstances the spread between the gold points will be considerably greater than it was in the 1920's. While lower interest rates, the higher monetary value of gold, and perhaps improved transport facilities will tend to narrow the gold points, other factors, particularly the difference between the buying and selling prices for gold in various countries, will tend to broaden the gold points.

In the 1920's there was in fact no difference between the buying and selling prices for gold in the United States and a difference of less than 1/6 of 1 percent in the United Kingdom. Differences between the buying and selling prices of gold were an insignificant factor in determining the dollar-sterling gold points in the 1920's. Now, under the Gold Reserve Act of 1934 there is a charge of 1/4 percent for buying or selling gold. If this difference of 1/2 percent were to be adopted by the United Kingdom, there would be a spread of approximately 1 percent between the exchange rate equivalents for gold in New York and London. Probably another 3/5 of 1 percent should be allowed for actual costs of moving gold in both directions. Under these conditions, the spread between the gold points would be 1.6 percent.

It would seem, therefore, that if the range of fluctuations in exchange rates permitted by the Fund is to be somewhat greater than the spread between the gold points, the Fund's range will have to be very close to 2 percent. This would seem to be sufficient inducement to a country to utilize its own gold and exchange resources rather than to draw upon the resources of the Fund to meet normal and moderate needs for foreign exchange. As already stated, a further penalty would be placed upon a country using the Fund's resources if the Fund's buying and selling rates for exchange were outside the range of permitted fluctuations.

In this connection, it should be noted that the range of exchange rates permitted by the Fund has been compared with the normal gold points that might be expected in the post-war period. Some countries may have so large a difference between the official buying and selling prices for gold that their gold points might in fact lie outside any broad but reasonable range the Fund might be expected to establish. In such cases the Fund might recommend that the member country narrow the spread between its buying and selling prices for gold.

There is another point of some interest that may be mentioned. In general, the spread between the gold points is a function of the distance between the two exchange markets under consideration. In the 1920's, the spread between the gold points was much narrower between New York and Montreal than between New York and Bombay. It may be desirable to standardize the range established by the Fund in order to give all member countries whatever advantage there may be in a broad range within which exchange rates may be permitted to fluctuate.

Because of the importance of these unsettled questions and the difference of opinion on the technical merits of alternative policies, it was considered best not to include in our tentative proposal any specific provisions on such technical matters until agreement has been reached on these questions. There is no doubt that decisions on such technical questions can be worked out to the satisfaction of member countries.

QUESTION 20

Would differential rates of exchange for different classes of imports and exports (visible and invisible) be permitted by the Fund?

REPLY

Differential rates of exchange would come under the provision of the Joint Statement which deals with multiple currency practices. This provision, IX-3, is based on a view that the use of such methods should not be encouraged because they may so easily become the means for discrimination in trade relationships and because they usually involve control of the exchanges so complete as to offer a strong temptation to restrict transactions on current account.

According to provision IX-3 member countries agree not to engage in multiple currency practices without the approval of the Fund. Undoubtedly such approval would not be given in the case of multiple currency practices which in the judgment of the Fund do retard international trade and the flow of productive capital.

Where a country has centralized the exchange dealings of its nationals for purposes of supervision, differential rates on imports may provide a convenient substitute for customs duties. At the time the exchange authorities make foreign exchange available to importers it is very simple for them to collect what are in effect import duties. Insofar as various classes of imports are distinguished and different exchange rates are assigned to them, the same result is produced as by an ad valorem tariff with different rates of duty on the various classes of merchandise. Differential rates that are not the same for all currencies are obviously discriminatory. Of course, if the exchange rates for some classes of imports are extremely low (say, lower than the exchange rates for some classes of exports) there may in fact be a subsidy for some imports. Obviously, differential exchange rates for imports may easily lead to restriction of international trade.

Differential rates of exchange for exports act as a subsidy for some exports and an export duty on others. This may create important although disguised discrimination among the importing countries, especially where the differentials are not the same for all currencies. On the whole, the case for differential rates of exchange for exports is even weaker than for differential rates for imports.

While differential rates have some administrative advantages in a country which has centralized its foreign exchange dealings and which secures substantial revenues from them, there are serious disadvantages and dangers inherent in their use. Comparability of international values becomes much more tenuous where there are multiple exchange rates. Also, differential rates can hardly be prevented from channelizing trade in a fashion that results in intentional or unintentional discrimination among countries. Differential exchange rates can become an instrument for the worst form of unfair competition in international trade. There is also the risk that multiple currencies may again be used, as Germany used them, to produce division and domination of weaker countries for political purposes. On the whole, differential exchange rates open the way to dangerous abuses, while offering few offsetting advantages that cannot be equally well achieved in other ways.

For these reasons, it is provided that member countries may not engage in multiple currency practices which in the judgment of the Fund restrict international transactions. In countries where differential rates of exchange for different classes of imports and exports are used, their continuances would require the approval of the Fund. It is conceivable that the Fund would in some instances decide that multiple currencies are being used by a member country in such a way that they do not conflict with the purposes of the Fund. In other cases the Fund may permit adequate time for the abandonment of the practice, in order to give member countries ample opportunity to arrange for collection of revenue by other methods based on the foreign transactions of their nationals.

There is, nevertheless, one category of invisible exports where a differential exchange rate would seem to be within the purposes of the Fund. For social and political reasons it may be desirable to attract tourists and students from other countries. A differential rate of exchange for these purposes could very well be regarded by the Fund as an appropriate means of encouraging friendly relations between countries, and in some instances may be found to be an effective device for helping to correct disequilibrium in a country's balance of payments. It would seem undesirable, therefore, not to allow some flexibility in this matter. The Fund, of course, would have to give its approval before such differential exchange rates were established.

Question 21

If a country has exhausted its rights of recourse to the Fund, does its undertaking to maintain a stable rate of exchange lapse?

Reply

The obligations of a country to other member countries and to the Fund are not terminated when it has exhausted its permissible quota or for any other reason has no further access to the resources of the Fund.

Specifically, a member country is obligated to prevent exchange transactions in its market in currencies of other members at rates outside the range prescribed by the Fund by taking whatever appropriate measures are necessary for this purpose. Such measures cannot, of course, include the practices opposed to the purposes of the Fund and prescribed in Section IX of the Joint Statement. Obviously, one appropriate measure is the use of the gold and foreign exchange resources of a country to support its currency.

A country cannot succeed indefinitely in maintaining a stable exchange rate by the use of its own resources of gold and foreign exchange if the established rate does not reflect approximately its international economic position. Where the disequilibrium in a country's balance of payments is of a fundamental character, measures will ultimately have to be taken to restore equilibrium either through an approved change in the exchange rate or through other appropriate means.

When a country has reached the stage where its rights of recourse to the resources of the Fund are exhausted the Fund may at its discretion waive the limitation on the Fund's holdings of that currency provided in III-2(c) under conditions which safeguard the interest of the Fund. The conditions which the Fund will normally impose on a country which has exhausted its normal rights of recourse to the Fund will be the adoption of measures by the member country which in the view of the Fund will restore the necessary balance in the country's position. Such measures might include alteration of the exchange rate, control of capital movements, or in extreme cases direct measures to limit the volume of imports.

It would be unfortunate if any member country should adopt the attitude that its obligations to the Fund could be disregarded when it has exhausted its right to further use of the Fund. The provision of resources to facilitate the maintenance of exchange stability is only one aspect of the Fund's functions. The Fund must be regarded as an agency with general responsibilities for international monetary cooperation. The duty to take all possible measures to avoid unilateral exchange depreciation is not a qualified duty.

Alteration of exchange rates can only be undertaken with the approval of the Fund, except that a member country may change the established rate for its currency by not more than 10 percent, provided the Fund is notified and consulted on the advisability of the action. Both a member country and the Fund have a duty to cooperate in taking measures to prevent an authorized depreciation in exchange rates.

QUESTION 22

When a country's currency becomes scarce, does that country's obligation to keep constant by "appropriate action" its rate of exchange on the currencies of all other countries remain unaffected?

REPLY

As indicated in the answer to the previous question, it is the view of the technical experts of the United States that the obligation of a member country to prevent its exchange rate from fluctuating beyond the range specified by the Fund cannot be terminated without the consent of the Fund. The fact that a currency has become scarce within the meaning of provision VI-1 is indicative of a demand for the currency which, if not met or restricted, will tend to appreciate that currency. It is clearly the intention of provision VI-1, if no additional supply is forthcoming, to restrict the demand for the currency in some equitable manner, in order to prevent an appreciation of the exchange rate.

As one of its obligations as a member of the Fund, each member country agrees not to allow exchange rates in its market to fluctuate outside a prescribed range based on the agreed parities of the currencies. This implies that a member country must undertake by appropriate action to maintain exchange rates within the range established by the Fund. For a country with a favorable balance of payments, the obligation to maintain exchange rates by appropriate action includes the acquisition of gold that is offered for its currency to support the exchanges of the gold selling countries and to prevent the appreciation of the currency of the country with a favorable balance of payments.

The acquisition of unlimited amounts of the currencies of any other countries cannot reasonably be regarded as appropriate action within the meaning of the Fund proposal. It is not intended that any provision of the Fund proposal shall make it mandatory for any member country to acquire and to hold the currency of another member country. Instead, it is the Fund as a cooperative enterprise which undertakes to acquire the currencies of member countries in accordance with the provisions of the proposal.

When a country's currency becomes scarce, the Fund itself takes steps either to increase the supply or to restrict the demand. By apportioning the available supply, the demand is directly restricted. In general, such action by the Fund would prevent an appreciation of a scarce currency. Member countries are, after consultation with the Fund, authorized to restrict freedom of exchange operations in currencies which have been declared by the Fund to be scarce. In the countries where a scarce currency must be rationed, the controls should be effective in restricting imports. It follows that the exporters of the country whose currency is scarce will not, in fact, have foreign exchange to offer for sale, and there will be no need for placing limitations on the sale of foreign currencies by exporters. However, a member country could apply such direct limitations with the approval of the Fund and in cooperation with other member countries.

For further discussion of the problem related to a scarce currency, see the answers to questions 30 and 31.

PART FOUR [*BIS*]: OPERATIONS OF THE FUND

Question 23

Will the International Monetary Fund sell foreign exchange to a member country to support its rate of exchange if that rate is not in accord with the country's international economic position?

Reply

While it is a major purpose of the Fund to help stabilize exchange rates, the Fund cannot and should not undertake to provide foreign exchange to prolong a basically unbalanced position. Numerous provisions of the Fund proposal are intended to provide safeguards against the use of the Fund's resources to support an exchange rate not in accord with a member country's international economic position.

When initial rates of exchange are determined, the rate established for a currency must, in the judgment of the Fund, be appropriate. Until the Fund has given its approval to an initial rate of exchange, no operations may be undertaken by the Fund in such a currency. Even after the initial rate of exchange has been fixed with its approval, the Fund is not required to sell exchange to a member country if that country is using the resources of the Fund in a manner contrary to the purposes and policies of the Fund. One of the fundamental purposes of the Fund as stated in provision I-3 is to enable members to correct maladjustments in their balances of payments by making the Fund's resources available to them with adequate safeguards. The Fund is not required therefore to sell exchange to a member country to support an unbalanced position.

When a member country is using the resources of the Fund in a manner that clearly has the effect of preventing or unduly delaying the establishment of a sound balance in its international accounts, the Fund, after notice, may suspend the member country from making further use of the Fund's resources on the grounds that it is using them in a manner contrary to the purposes and policies of the Fund. The Fund is, however, required to present to such country a report setting forth the reasons for that country's being suspended from the privilege of purchasing foreign exchange from the Fund and the Fund must allow a suitable time for reply before notice of actual suspension is given. The Fund in its report to the member country will undoubtedly stipulate certain conditions whereby the member country can avoid suspension of the right to draw on the resources of the Fund. If in its reply to the Fund, the member country agrees to the conditions stipulated by the Fund, notice of suspension of the privilege of purchasing foreign exchange from the Fund would not be given.

The Fund is also expected to limit its sales of foreign exchange to member countries that use the resources of the Fund at an unwarranted rate. In general, the presumption is that a country that purchases foreign exchange for local currency at an annual rate in excess of 25 percent of its quota is making unwarranted use of the Fund and except under special circumstances members will not be permitted to purchase foreign exchange from the Fund at an annual rate in excess of 25 percent of their quotas provided the Fund's total holdings of their currency are not below 75 percent of their quota. Such use of the Fund is an indication of an unbalanced position that should be corrected.

A limitation on the Fund's holdings of the local currency of a member country is established for each country because it is regarded as desirable to have an objective indication of a limit to the Fund's acquisition of local currency to help a country to support its exchange rate. There is implicit in this provision the view that when the Fund's holdings have reached 200 percent of the quota, it is generally an indication that there is a fundamental disequilibrium in a country's international position that calls for remedial action. While the Fund may sell additional foreign exchange to such a country, the sale requires specific approval and can be made only if satisfactory measures are being or will be taken to correct the disequilibrium, or if it is believed that the disequilibrium is temporary and the excess holdings of the Fund can be disposed of within a reasonable time.

It cannot be emphasized too frequently that the Fund is not designed simply to sell foreign exchange needed by member countries to meet their adverse balances on international account. The resources of the Fund may properly be used to help a country through a period of temporary disequilibrium. The resources of the Fund are available to member countries under adequate safeguards to help them maintain stability of their currencies, while giving them time to correct maladjustments in their balance of payments without resorting to extreme measures destructive of international prosperity. A Fund operating successfully should be influential in inducing member countries to adopt policies making for an orderly return to equilibrium.

Question 24

Does the Fund provide facilities for multilateral clearing to a country which has its overall international payments on current account in balance but has an adverse balance of payments on current account with some countries?

Reply

According to the present provisions of the Joint Statement on the Fund proposal there can be no doubt that in almost all circumstances a member country will be able to use freely the proceeds of its transactions in one country for the settlement of balances due on current account in another country.

Let us suppose that England has a favorable balance with France and an adverse balance of equal amount with the Netherlands. France and the Netherlands are in equilibrium with each other, and so is each of the three countries with all countries other than the three. This situation may manifest itself in an accumulation of francs by England and a need by England for guilders. It might be possible for England to offer all or part of its accumulated holdings of francs for sale in the exchange market and secure payments in guilders.

Assuming, however, that there is no franc-guilder market, it would then be necessary for England to offer the francs for sale to France. Under provision III-5, France is obligated to buy francs from England with sterling or with gold, if such francs were acquired by England from current transactions with France, and if France has access to sterling in the Fund. France might have to apply to the Fund for sterling for the purpose. If the Fund supplied sterling, the Fund's holdings of sterling would be reduced by the amount made available for the purpose.

If the Fund's holdings of sterling are not outside the limits specified in the proposal (which is unlikely in view of the fact that the Fund's holdings of sterling would have been reduced by support of the franc), and if England is not making unwarranted use of the Fund's resources (which is unlikely in view of the fact that there is no net change in the Fund's holdings of sterling), the Fund could under the provisions of the proposal make available the necessary guilders.

Under provision III-2 of the Joint Statement on the Fund proposal the Fund is permitted to sell foreign exchange to a member country so long as the currency demanded is presently needed for making payments in that currency which are consistent with the purposes and policies of the Fund and so long as the member country is not making unwarranted use of the Fund's resources. It is not necessary for a member country to have an over-all adverse balance of payments to obtain a particular member's currency which that country needs to correct a temporary maladjustment in her balance of payments with another member.

Question 25

Would it be possible for the Fund to provide the foreign exchange needed to maintain stability of the currency of a member country if the deficit giving rise to this need for foreign exchange is in the balance of payments with a third country?

Reply

The resources of the Fund are intended to be used to aid member countries in meeting adverse balances of payments predominantly on current account. The Fund is not intended to enter the exchange markets or to provide the means for carrying out arbitrage transactions.

Under the provisions of the Joint Statement the Fund cannot use the currency of one country to help maintain stability of the exchange of another country if the deficit giving rise to the pressure on the exchange is with a third country. Concretely, if Canada has a favorable balance of payments on current account with England, the Fund cannot use U.S. dollars for the purpose of enabling England to meet payments in Canada.

If England has an adverse balance on current account with Canada, the Fund can sell Canadian dollars to England for sterling in order to enable England to settle this balance. If the Fund's holdings of Canadian dollars are inadequate, it may use gold to purchase Canadian dollars. The Fund is not authorized to use any member currency for the purpose of acquiring another.

No hardship is inflicted on Canada because of this regulation. Under provision III-5 of the Joint Statement, Canada can require England to purchase the sterling acquired from current transactions, payment to be made either in Canadian dollars or in gold. If England may acquire Canadian dollars from the Fund (Canadian dollars not being a scarce currency and England not being suspended from making use of the Fund's resources), England is obligated to purchase such sterling from Canada. The reduction in the Fund's holdings of Canadian dollars would increase correspondingly Canada's ability to purchase foreign exchange from the Fund within the terms of the Joint Statement.

No doubt, there would be some advantages if the Fund could use any of its resources to aid any member country in meeting adverse balances on current account. If all member currencies were freely convertible into gold, such restrictions might be safely dropped. It is not feasible, however, to permit the free use of some currencies (say, U.S. dollars) for meeting an adverse balance of payments with any country, while restricting the use of another currency exclusively for meeting adverse balances with that country.

Question 26

Would member countries exporting capital be permitted to purchase foreign exchange from the Fund?

Reply

If a member country is in present need of the currency of another member country for making payments in that currency in order to correct a maladjustment in its balance of payments toward which capital exports are contributing only in small part, the Fund would undoubtedly permit its resources to be utilized by the member. Provision V-1 prevents a member country from using the resources of the Fund to meet a large or sustained outflow of capital, and gives the Fund power to require a member to exercise controls to prevent such use of the resources of the Fund. This provision is not intended however to prevent the use of the Fund's resources for capital transactions of a reasonable amount required in the ordinary course of trade, banking, or other business. Nor is it intended to prevent capital movements which are met out of a member country's own resources of gold and foreign exchange, provided such capital movements are in accordance with the purposes of the Fund. A capital export for the purpose of expanding exports does not in fact represent a net loss of exchange resources of the amount involved, since the expansion of exports tends to provide a favorable current balance of approximately the same amount. Capital exports for this purpose are therefore permitted, even when a country is making some use of the Fund.

In general it would appear to be more desirable for the Fund to provide a member country with some resources to help maintain exchange stability than to require the imposition of a system of exchange control merely to prevent the export of a moderate amount of capital. The Fund can safely take this position so long as its holdings of the local currency in question are not excessive. But the Fund cannot allow its resources of other currencies to be seriously depleted to facilitate the speculative movement of funds; nor can it sanction the dissipation in this way of resources of the Fund which should be reserved for the maintenance of international interchange of goods and services. It is expected that as the Fund's holdings of a member currency increase, the Fund will be less lenient with respect to the volume of capital exports which that country will be permitted to have without being deprived of the use of the resources of the Fund.

It is clear from the above provisions that it is not intended that the Fund should ever rigidly exclude the utilization of its resources when a country has an export of capital. It is recognized that there will be instances when permitting an export of capital will not involve a net drain on the resources of the Fund and will be beneficial from the point of view of the general international economic situation. Under such circumstances, the Fund will want to allow its resources to be used in moderation by a country exporting capital.

It may be of interest to consider the conditions under which the Fund might regard the export of capital as in the general interest and as not in conflict with the primary objectives of the Fund. In fact, an export of capital, even when some of the foreign exchange is provided by the Fund, may reduce the net call on the Fund's resources and may give the Fund a more balanced distribution of its assets. For example, one member country may export capital to another member country which has an adverse balance on current account and may wish to purchase from the Fund part of the exchange needed for this purpose. Such a capital export may reduce correspondingly the need of the second country to call upon the Fund for exchange with which to meet its adverse balance on current account. The net amount of exchange sold by the Fund under such conditions would be less because it facilitated the capital export. Further, if this capital export is from a country whose currency the Fund holds in a moderate amount to a country whose currency the Fund holds in an excessive amount, the distribution of the Fund's assets would become more balanced, and as a result of the transaction the Fund would be in a better position to serve all member countries.

Apart from such general conditions, the Fund might be more favorably disposed toward permitting certain types of capital transfer than toward permitting others. The repayment of a short-term credit is, in a sense, a capital movement. However, if the credit was acquired to finance trade, it may have served when made to obviate a corresponding use of the Fund, and the Fund would ordinarily provide exchange for the repayment of such a credit. The meeting of normal sinking fund installments on a debt is usually regarded as a capital movement. Nevertheless, if such sinking fund payments are not large relative to the Fund's holdings of the currency of a member country, the Fund would ordinarily provide foreign exchange to facilitate a capital export by a country with a maturing obligation which cannot be fully met at once but which its balance of payments could absorb within two or three years.

In considering the probable attitude of the Fund toward the sale of foreign exchange to facilitate a transfer of capital, it should be borne in mind that the provisions of the Fund proposal are designed to give effect to the general principle that the Fund's resources should be used primarily for settling international balances on current account. However, sufficient flexibility is provided so that the resources of the Fund can be used for meeting a capital export where it is deemed to be generally desirable. There is no reason to believe that a country making payments of a capital nature will be debarred entirely from recourse to the Fund unless and until the Fund has given sufficient notice to the member country that such payments are not in the general interest.

It is important for the Fund to build up in the course of its operations accurate statistics on international payments of all types, as it easily can do under its authority to require full reports from member countries. In the period before these records are available, however, completely accurate records of a country's capital inflow or outflow are not essential to the proper execution of the policy outlined above. The Fund will be concerned only with large movements, not with flows that are small relative to a country's volume of international transactions. Large non-recurring capital flows—like a large redemption operation, or defaulted loan settlement—would be known to the Fund, while recurring net outflows of significant size would be difficult to obscure. It is not necessary to know precisely the amount of net outflow; it is enough to be able to ascertain whether the net outflow is significantly large or not. It would be desirable, of course, for member countries to arrange to receive regular reports on capital movements into and out of their countries, and to make such data available to the Fund.

An extended discussion of the control of capital movements will be found in the answers to questions 33 and 34.

Question 27

What provision is made to permit a country with abnormally low holdings of foreign currencies and gold to accumulate such resources while a member of the Fund?

Reply

Provision III-7-c requires each member country to offer to sell to the Fund one-half of the gold and gold-convertible exchange it acquires in excess of its official holdings at the time it became a member of the Fund so long as this does not reduce the Fund's holdings of the member's currency below 75 percent of its quota. However, no country need sell gold or gold-convertible exchange under this provision unless its official holdings are in excess of its quota.

The significance of this provision can best be brought out by an explanation of its purpose.

1. Some member countries may be tempted to use the resources of the Fund to build up independent holdings of gold and foreign exchange. The Fund is not devised to facilitate the accomplishment of such a purpose. On the contrary, the Fund's resources are intended only for needs arising from an adverse balance of payments predominantly on current account.

Although the Fund would not sell foreign exchange for local currency to permit a member country to acquire additional balances of gold or foreign exchange, some provision is necessary to prevent the Fund from being used indirectly for such a purpose. Without such provision, a member country could resort to the Fund when it has a temporary adverse balance of payments, and keep any increment of gold or foreign exchange which it may acquire when it has a favorable balance of payments.

With provisions III-7-b and III-7-c, a member country cannot build up excessive gold and foreign exchange balances while at the same time drawing upon the resources of the Fund. A member country must pay with gold for one-half its net purchases of foreign exchange from the Fund, provided its gold and gold-convertible exchange holdings exceed its quota; and it must offer to sell to the Fund for its local currency one-half of the gold and gold-convertible exchange it may acquire in excess of its official holdings at the time it became a member of the Fund (provided its official holdings exceed its quota).

2. The Fund proposal does not generally specify a definite time compelling the repurchase of local currency which has been acquired by the Fund from the sale of

foreign exchange to a member country. Presumably when the Fund sells foreign exchange in excess of the amounts normally permitted under provision III-2-c, there would be an understanding that the Fund's holdings of local currency would be brought within appropriate limits in some specified period. Similarly, when the Fund sets conditions upon additional sales of foreign exchange to a country in accordance with provision III-2-d one condition could be that a reduction in the Fund's holdings of local currency be effected in some specified period.

The great bulk of the exchange transactions of the Fund with member countries will not require specific approval, as the Fund's holdings of the currencies of member countries will in general not exceed the prescribed limits. The Fund would not in such instances prescribe conditions for the repurchase of local currencies, although the penalty provisions will be a strong inducement to repurchase local currencies from the Fund. It is necessary, however, that some obligation should rest on member countries utilizing the resources of the Fund to repurchase their own currencies. Otherwise, the Fund's resources would tend to become unbalanced in the form of unnecessarily large holdings of some local currencies. Provision III-7-c is in fact a method of requiring the repurchase of local currency by member countries as their balances of payments become favorable and as they acquire additional gold and gold-convertible exchange.

3. The Fund starts with resources of local currencies and gold. In general, resources of this character should be adequate for the operations of the Fund. With its local currency resources the Fund may meet any moderate calls for any currency; and with its gold holdings the Fund can supplement its local currencies and meet very large calls for any new currencies. Nevertheless, it would be desirable to strengthen the Fund by gradually converting its local currency holdings into gold. Provision III-7 makes this possible.

For the world as a whole, the balance of payments, as ordinarily defined, is always active to the extent of the annual increment in gold reserves resulting from the production and distribution of newly-mined gold (perhaps modified for changes in private hoards of gold). The normal balance of payments for a country should tend to provide for an expansion in its holdings of gold and gold-convertible exchange. There is no good reason why part of the increment in gold and gold-convertible exchange should not be used by member countries to repurchase from the Fund its holdings of their local currencies. It is in the interest of all member countries that the strength and liquidity of the Fund be increased by the gradual replacement of local currencies with gold, particularly as such replacement would not involve any reduction in the reserves of member countries.

It should be emphasized that no hardship is incurred by a member country in offering to sell to the Fund part of its increment of gold and gold-convertible exchange. The member country offering the resources for sale is under no obligation to accept any currency other than its own. To the extent that a member country reduces the Fund's holdings of its local currency, it increases its right to acquire foreign exchange from the Fund with its local currency. In view of the general advantages that would be conferred by a strong and liquid Fund, the right to acquire foreign exchange from a Fund adequately supplied with gold is not inferior to the actual holding of gold and foreign exchange (except, of course, in the acquisition of scarce currencies).

These provisions by no means indicate a policy of discouraging the maintenance of independent monetary reserves. It is, on the contrary, the view of the technical experts of the United States that it is desirable for member countries to build up adequate holdings of gold and foreign exchange. For this reason a reduced subscription in the form of gold may be made by countries with small or moderate holdings, since the obligatory gold subscription of a member country is 25 percent of its quota or 10 percent of its holdings of gold and gold-convertible exchange whichever is smaller. To take account of the greater need of countries which have been occupied by the enemy, a further reduction in the subscription of gold might be permitted for such countries. It is the recommendation of the U.S. technical experts that the countries whose home areas have suffered substantial damage from enemy action or occupation during the present war, should be permitted to reduce their obligatory gold subscriptions to 75 percent of the amount they would otherwise pay.

In addition, a country with gold and gold-convertible exchange holdings less than its quota need not use gold in paying for exchange purchased from the Fund. In countries in which working balances, other than official balances, are at a very low level at the time of adherence to the Fund, these private working balances may be built up (but not excessively) without any obligation to offer to sell such increments of gold and gold-convertible exchange to the Fund.

The requirement to offer to sell to the Fund gold and gold-convertible exchange acquired by a member country is also subject to qualifications designed to permit a country to accumulate some holdings of gold and gold-convertible exchange. The provision applies only to gold and gold-convertible exchange acquired by a member country in excess of its *official* holdings at the time it became a member of the Fund, and no country need offer to sell gold or gold-convertible exchange under this provision unless its official holdings are in excess of its quota. Furthermore, only one-half of the increase in gold and gold-convertible exchange holdings must be offered to the Fund. Finally, a member country is not required to sell additional gold to the Fund after the Fund's holdings of its local currency are below 75 percent of its quota.

Question 28

When does newly-mined gold become subject to the provision that member countries must under certain conditions offer for sale to the Fund half of the increase in their official holdings of gold?

Reply

The provision that the Fund may require up to half of the increase in a member's holdings of gold and gold-convertible exchange to be used to repurchase part of the Fund's holdings of its currency applies only to the increase in official holdings of gold or gold-convertible exchange. Newly-mined gold held by the producers or by bullion dealers awaiting sale is not to be regarded as part of the official holdings of a country.

It is conceivable that newly-mined gold will regularly be offered for sale to the monetary authorities of a country soon after its production. It then becomes subject to the obligations of III-7-c. It should be noted that the Fund may require a member country to sell half of its increase in gold and gold-convertible exchange only at the end of the Fund's financial year, so that a gold producing country in which newly-mined gold is sold to the monetary authorities will only need to offer for sale to the Fund one-half of the net increment in its gold holdings as represented by its holdings at the end of the Fund's financial year.

As a matter of administrative convenience the Fund would probably provide some period during which newly-mined gold would be deemed not to have entered into the official holdings. This might be necessary in order to avoid innumerable minor adjustments. In some countries, Treasury or Mint agencies temporarily include in their holdings newly-mined gold delivered to them for assaying and refining or for safekeeping. To avoid hardship, holdings of such a character should be excluded by establishing a period during which such holdings are deemed not to have entered into the official holdings.

It may be pointed out again that a country holding newly-mined gold awaiting distribution does not suffer any hardship (the scarce currency problem aside) if half of the increment of such gold is offered to the Fund for its local currency. To the extent that the gold was held to acquire foreign exchange, the capacity of the country to acquire such exchange is not impaired by sale of half of the increment of gold to the Fund for local currency. The member country can acquire foreign exchange to the full value of the gold held for the purpose by purchasing needed foreign exchange from the Fund, payment to be made half in gold and half in local currency.

Question 29

In computing the increment of gold and gold-convertible exchange that member countries must offer for sale to the Fund is any allowance made for increased foreign liabilities?

Reply

In computing the amount of gold and gold convertible exchange that must be offered for sale to the Fund under this provision, no explicit allowance is made for increased liabilities to foreigners. It should be noted, however, that it is only half the increase in official holdings that must be offered for sale to the Fund. The intention is not to restrict the acquisition of such resources when they are needed by commercial banks and other nationals as working balances for international transactions. It is desirable, however, to avoid the accumulation of excessive holdings in this form by countries utilizing the resources of the Fund. In the event that the commercial banks and nationals of a member country using the resources of the Fund are accumulating gold or gold-convertible exchange in excessive amounts the Fund might consider bringing to the attention of the monetary authorities of the country concerned, the undesirability of utilizing the resources of the Fund while excessive balances of foreign exchange are held by its nationals. Undoubtedly, in determining whether such holdings are excessive, consideration would be given to the foreign liabilities of commercial banks and other nationals.

No explicit allowance is made for offsetting the official holdings of Treasuries and central banks with their foreign liabilities. If it is regarded as desirable to make some allowance for such liabilities against official holdings of gold and foreign exchange, consideration can be given to the manner in which this may be most appropriately done. Provision for such offsets, if regarded as desirable, could be made in the operating regulations that are adopted to implement III-7.

PART FIVE: POLICIES OF THE FUND

Question 30

What kind of action is it contemplated that the International Monetary Fund would recommend to a country whose currency is in scarce supply?

Reply

The Joint Statement provides that when the Fund's holdings of the currency of a member country become excessively small in relation to prospective acquisitions and needs for that currency, the Fund is required to render a report embodying an analysis of the causes of the depletion of the Fund's holdings and recommending measures designed to increase the Fund's holdings of that currency (VI-1).

The specific recommendations which the Fund might make to a member country whose currency is in scarce supply would be formulated in accordance with the nature of the existing disequilibrium in the balance of payments position of that country and the forces responsible for its development. It would be desirable to have a special committee appointed to study the problem and to draft a report on the recommendations to be made. It would also be desirable for the Board member of the country whose currency is declared scarce to be a member of the Fund committee appointed to draft the report.

No limitation on the scope of such recommendations is provided in the Fund proposal. It would, however, be necessary for the Fund to give full consideration to the effects of its recommendation on the internal economy of the member country to whom the recommendations are made as well as to any constitutional or other legal limitations which might make difficult or impossible positive action on some of the recommendations under consideration.

It may be assumed that such obvious measures as the control of capital movements have already been taken to ease the strain on the exchange position of member countries and the Fund with relation to the scarce currency. In the event that the disequilibrium in the balance of the payments position of a member country was the result of an inflow of capital and not the result of persistent forces operating on current account items, the Fund would undoubtedly make recommendations which look toward a reversal of this flow. The control of capital inflow is not, however, the primary responsibility of the member country experiencing such inflows. If capital movements are responsible for a serious drain on the Fund's supply of that currency, the member countries exporting capital to the country whose currency is in short supply could be required by the Fund to take the initiative in restricting such exports.

The Fund may propose to a member country whose currency is in scarce supply that it lend currency to the Fund. Such an additional supply would provide the member countries with the additional time needed to work out a more satisfactory balance in international payments with the country whose currency is scarce. No member country is under any obligation to make any loan to the Fund. If a loan is made, the terms and conditions of the loan would be agreed between the member country and the Fund.

This question regarding the Fund's recommendations is not primarily concerned with these intermediate measures but with corrective measures. It is impossible at this point to state specifically what the Fund would recommend in any given situation, since each case would be a problem of its own, involving a large number of variables, and concerning which intensive study would be necessary. If, for example, the disequilibrium stems from an excess of exports over imports which is not likely to correct itself in a reasonable period of time, the Fund might recommend measures for an expansion of imports and a reduction of artificial stimulants to exports if any are operating. Specifically, appropriate recommendations for increasing imports might include a reduction of tariff rates and the encouragement of tourist travel abroad. We believe it would be contrary to the best interests of the members of the Fund to recommend a reduction of exports; but it might be quite proper to recommend that nations eliminate subsidies on exports provided such elimination would make a significant contribution to the adjustment.

When a country shows a persistently favorable balance of payments on current account, it may be that the most appropriate and the most effective means of restoring a balance in its international accounts would be an expansion in its foreign investments. If there are factors prevalent in the country discouraging the flow of private investment to foreign countries, the report might well recommend their correction. The Fund might even recommend measures designed to promote repatriation of foreign funds.

In general, there is little reason to expect that it will be necessary to recommend measures designed to encourage domestic expansion in the country whose currency is scarce. Nevertheless, if such recommendations are needed, they should be made, including recommendations on credit policy, investment policy, and other measures which have a bearing on the level of economic activity and employment within a member country. It is quite possible that the rise in production has been greater than the rise in wage rates, efficiency rates of remuneration have fallen, and that an upward adjustment should be encouraged.

In extreme cases it may also be desirable to recommend a change in exchange rates for the country whose currency is scarce. An upward change in the foreign exchange value of a currency, however, should be considered only if other measures appear to be inadequate, and only if such a step does not contribute to further deterioration in the general international economic situation. It should be emphasized that what is desired is not merely a reduction in a country's exports, but, remedial action that will correct its balance of payments without generating deflationary forces at home and abroad.

The recommendations of the Fund will unquestionably be given careful consideration. It is in the interests of a country whose currency is scarce to avoid the need by the Fund to allot its holdings of such a currency, and to take measures to obviate the need for such action by the Fund. While the Fund itself cannot correct the situation, it provides a means for facilitating the adoption of appropriate measures by the cooperating member countries.

It should not be overlooked that a disequilibrium in the balance of payments cannot be manifested as a problem peculiar to one country. Whenever the supply of a member country's currency is scarce, this scarcity is likely to be accompanied by excessive supplies of the currencies of other countries. In such cases the responsibility for the correction of the maladjustment is not a unilateral one. It will be the duty of the Fund to make a report not only to the country whose currency is scarce but also to the member countries who are exhausting or are using the resources of the Fund in a manner which is not consistent with the purposes of the Fund. The report should provide a comprehensive analysis of the causes of the scarcity and practical recommendations for remedying the situation.

Question 31

What is the purpose of requiring the Fund to apportion a scarce currency?

Reply

As was pointed out in the answer to the previous question, the Fund will make recommendations to a member country whose currency is in scarce supply, with a view to correcting the conditions in its balance of payments relations giving rise to the scarcity of its currency. It is in the interest of such a member country to carry out the Fund's recommendations since otherwise it will be faced with the alternative of reducing its exports and making other undesirable adjustments.

It should be noted that the scarcity of an important currency is likely to be accompanied by an excess in the Fund's holdings of the currencies of other member countries. A disequilibrium in the balance of payments is of necessity not confined to one country; and it is well to recognize that the responsibility for the scarcity of a currency in the Fund need not be primarily that of the country whose currency becomes scarce. We may presume the Fund will study the problem in all its aspects and will make appropriate recommendations to all interested countries.

There can be no assurance that the action of the Fund under VI-1 will always be adequate to remedy the situation. The recommendations of the Fund should be given the utmost consideration in the formulation of the monetary, economic, and commercial policies of member countries. The Fund's recommendations will have behind them the enormous force of the world's opinion. Within each country there is certain to be developed a growing recognition of the importance of effective cooperation with other countries through the Fund and in other ways. Even though the Fund's recommendations carry with them no element of compulsion, it will be difficult for any country cognizant of its responsibility to disregard them.

It is to be hoped that the Fund will not find it necessary to utilize provision VI-2 on the apportionment of scarce currencies. Ordinarily, the Fund will be able to borrow enough of a scarce currency to meet the needs of member countries during the period in which the recommendations made by the Fund take effect. Nevertheless, it is necessary to establish the basis for the apportionment of a scarce currency if such action should become essential for a limited time.

The fact that a currency has become scarce is evidence of a distortion in the pattern of trade balances that must be corrected through fundamental adjustments. In the meantime action may have to be taken to limit the demand for a scarce currency. The apportionment of a scarce currency by the Fund and its rationing by the monetary authorities of member countries are one means of promptly limiting the demand and even of helping to correct the disturbances in the pattern of trade balances. In time, the measures recommended by the Fund, if adopted by member countries, would probably have the effect of establishing a more balanced international payments position. Until these measures can be made effective, some direct control is necessary in extreme cases.

The apportionment of scarce currencies by the Fund is probably the most certain means of promptly directing excessive demand away from a member country with a large and persistently favorable balance of payments to other member countries with an unfavorable balance of payments. In a sense such action involves a type of direct control and of bilateralism that should be avoided. It is important, therefore, to bear in mind that apportionment of a scarce currency is regarded as a temporary measure of an emergency character. Under the direction of the Fund, this method of adjusting the demand for a scarce currency to the available supply would be free from dangers of discrimination. Ultimately, of course, it is expected that fundamental adjustments will remove the need for apportioning a currency.

Question 32

May a country to whom the Fund has granted an allocation of a scarce currency restrict imports from the country whose currency has become scarce?

Reply

It is intended that when the Fund's holdings of a currency become scarce steps will first be taken to increase the supply of the scarce currency. Under provision VI-1, the Fund is authorized to render a report to the member country embodying an analysis of the causes of the depletion of the Fund's holdings of that currency and making recommendations designed to increase the Fund's holdings of that currency.

The recommendations are likely to be of two types. Some of the recommendations will probably be designed to provide member countries and the Fund with additional amounts of the scarce currency, through encouragement of foreign investment in member countries and through loans or advances to the Fund. Other recommendations will probably be designed to correct the fundamental maladjustment in the balance of payments position of the member countries. It is hoped, of course, that the recommended measures will be effective.

Nevertheless, the Fund must take account of the possibility that whatever measures are taken will not immediately alleviate the scarcity of a currency. Under such circumstances, with a continuing scarcity for a currency, the Fund must adopt measures on its own account to assure the proper use of its limited holdings. Provision VI-2 provides for the apportionment of a scarce currency.

The technical experts of the United States interpret this provision as applying only to the Fund's holdings of a scarce currency. Member countries would be free to use the scarce currency accruing to them directly to meet their own needs, with the qualification, of course, that half of the increases in their accumulated holdings of gold and gold-convertible exchange must be offered for sale to the Fund in accordance with provision III-7. Similarly, member countries could utilize their holdings of gold and foreign exchange to supplement the allocation of a scarce currency made to them by the Fund.

The apportionment of a scarce currency by the Fund would take the form of allotting to member countries an amount of scarce currency (to be paid for with local currency and gold, as provided in III-7), the Fund taking into consideration the special needs and resources of member countries requesting an allotment. The actual distribution of its allotment by any member country among its importers and other users of a scarce currency would be a matter for the member country to decide.

Obviously, with a limited allotment of a scarce currency, some member countries will find it necessary to restrict the demand of their nationals for such a currency. The decision by the Fund to apportion a scarce currency is in effect an authorization to member countries temporarily to restrict the freedom of exchange transactions in the affected currency. Thus, their action would not be inconsistent with provision IX-3 in which they undertake not to impose restrictions on current transactions except with the Fund's consent. In determining the manner of restricting the demand, and in rationing the limited supply among its nationals, it is provided that the member country shall have complete jurisdiction.

Question 33

Will the Fund require all member countries to prohibit or restrict the outflow of capital?

Reply

The purpose of the Fund is to provide, through stability of exchanges and through cooperation in the maintenance of exchanges, the conditions necessary for the restoration and balanced growth of international trade. In accordance with this purpose, it is not intended as a general policy to have the resources of the Fund used to finance substantial outflows of capital from member countries.

The decades of the 20's and the 30's showed that many countries could not withstand the drains on their gold resources resulting from widespread conversion of local currency and flights of capital. Out of this experience has come general recognition that the gold and foreign exchange resources of a country should be reserved primarily for the settlement of international balances on current account. In line with this view, the general policy of the Fund should be to give countries access to the resources of the Fund only when such resources are needed to meet an adverse balance of payments predominantly on current account.

It would be incorrect to assume that most capital exports are prohibited under the Fund's provisions or that the policy of the Fund with respect to capital exports requires the maintenance of exchange controls or exchange restrictions in all or even the majority of cases. A careful examination of the Fund proposal will reveal that most capital exports can probably take place freely, and only in a minority of cases will exchange restrictions have to be imposed. The conditions under which capital exports may take place freely are described in the following paragraph:

1. Capital exports of any type can take place freely from countries with a favorable balance on current account.

It is recognized that there will be many countries in need of foreign capital for reconstruction and development after the war, and that there will be some countries whose international economic position will permit them to export capital. The provision of capital under these conditions can contribute to the balanced growth of international trade. Most of the capital exports of this type are likely to be from countries with a credit balance of payments on current account, and serve to help maintain monetary stability. It is one of the purposes of the Fund to facilitate the resumption of such international lending by restoring confidence in the greater stability of exchange rates, and in the greater freedom from injurious restrictive exchange practices.

The only limit on the free outflow of capital from a country experiencing a favorable balance on current account might be the case where a country has been previously experiencing an unfavorable balance and had sold the Fund more of its currency than the Fund found it desirable to keep. In that event, the Fund might prefer to have the country employ part of its favorable balance of payments to repurchase some of the Fund's holdings for its currency before or *pari passu* with the country's undertaking significant amounts of capital exports. In fact, provision III-7 is intended to do this.

2. Some countries experiencing an *unfavorable* balance of payments on current account could regard with complete equanimity an efflux of capital of any character, because their holdings of gold and foreign exchange are entirely adequate to meet all likely drains. Provision V specifically states that the limitation on capital exports is not intended to prevent capital movements which are made out of a member country's own gold and foreign exchange resources, provided such capital movements are in accordance with the purposes of the Fund. For example, the United States could permit very substantial and continued capital exports for a long time even if its balance of payments turned unfavorable on current account. There are doubtless a number of other countries which could permit capital exports under these circumstances, either because the unfavorable balance of payments on current account is small relative to

their foreign exchange resources, or the volume of capital outflow is small compared to the unfavorable balance on current account.

3. Also, a country having an unfavorable balance of payments on current account could freely permit foreign investments, or capital exports if at the same time it was itself a recipient of capital inflow. It usually happens that a country is at the same time both an importer of capital and an exporter of capital. Sometimes both inflow and outflow of capital may be long-term in character. For example, British firms may be building branch plants in South America or Africa, at the same time that Americans are investing in British securities, newly issued or held by residents of the United Kingdom. In some instances, the capital may be predominantly of short term character and the outflow predominantly long-term in character.

The significant drain of foreign exchange resources on capital account is the drain on *net* capital account, though it is also true that attention must be paid to the predominant character of the inflow or outflow. The movement of what may be classified as short term capital has different significance in different countries and at different periods. Nevertheless, it is not to be assumed that a country with an unfavorable balance of payments on current account could not continue to purchase foreign exchange from the Fund unless it curtailed its capital exports. A country could continue indefinitely having large gross capital flows and small net flows.

4. All countries could permit capital exports such as are reflected, even with a moderate lag, wholly or chiefly in exports of goods or services. It has been a common practice in the past, and there is no reason to expect that it will cease in the future, for some foreign loans to be tied to exports in such a way that the granting of the loan is accompanied sooner or later by a net export of goods and services almost of the same magnitude as the loan. The Joint Statement specifically provides that the Fund's resources may be used for capital transactions of reasonable amount required for expansion of exports or in the ordinary course of trade, banking or other business (V-1).

The mechanism of adjustment of international accounts does not always, or even usually, operate smoothly or rapidly enough to translate a net export of capital to a net flow of goods and services (unless the foreign investment is "tied" to the export of goods). But it would be an error to overlook the fact that the mechanism of adjustment does operate to some extent. The rapidity of operation differs greatly with the countries affected, the period, the magnitudes involved, the make-up of the international accounts, the phase of the business cycle, and other factors.

Countries with limited foreign exchange resources making loans to other countries should be very reluctant to make loans in excess of the amount absolutely needed to finance the additional exports effectuated directly or indirectly through the loan. The borrowing countries should be equally reluctant to burden their balance of payments unnecessarily by borrowing more for a particular project than is required to pay for the imports necessary for that project, making due allowance for secondary effects of the borrowing. Countries with inadequate foreign exchange resources should rarely borrow abroad merely for the purpose of domestic financing.

5. Finally, even where a country has an unfavorable balance of payments and inadequate foreign exchange resources, the Fund would not be disturbed by capital exports from that country if the amount were small or if the Fund did not have large holdings of that country's currency, or if the capital exports were sporadic or of brief duration. Provision V-1 prohibits a member country from using the Fund's resources to meet a large or sustained outflow of capital. It is only when the capital exports are (a) net,

(b) large, (c) sustained, and (d) are motivated chiefly by the desire for speculative profit that the Fund is likely to require a restriction of capital exports as a condition for continued use of the Fund's resources.

The flow of capital from one country to another seeking political and economic security, or speculative profit is frequently undesirable. Such flows are particularly disturbing when they take place from countries with a debit balance of payments to countries with a credit balance of payments on current account. Such flows serve to disturb monetary stability, and it is not the purpose of the Fund to facilitate such capital movements.

Until, however, the Fund considers a continuation of capital exports of that character and under these conditions to be injurious, no restrictive action over capital exports need be taken by the country exporting capital. It is only when the Fund deems it undesirable to continue to sell foreign exchange to the country in question, unless its capital exports are curtailed, that the latter must seek ways of curtailing undesirable forms of capital exports. In some cases, the country may be able to do without the necessity of imposing exchange controls and restrictions. When it cannot do so, then the country will have to restrict the flow of capital through the exercise of carefully imposed exchange controls. The existence of the Fund should make resort to such restrictions less urgent and less frequent.

A proper evaluation of this aspect of the Fund's powers can be made only against alternative courses. It would be quite erroneous to assume that in the absence of the Fund, countries could permit uncontrolled capital outflow of any character at all times. Restriction of capital movements is, of course, not a novel practice. One needs only to recall the history of the last 20 years to make clear that controls over capital movements were adopted in a large number of countries even though no such institution as a Fund existed.

It should be clear that under any circumstances the Fund does not of itself require that any country impose control over capital exports unless and until the member country wishes to purchase excessive amounts of foreign exchange from the Fund and then only if they are regarded as in the general interest of the Fund and its members.

In summary, it is clear that the Fund does not expect a member country to use exchange provided by the Fund exclusively for current account purposes. So long as the exchange purchased from the Fund is used to meet an adverse balance of payments predominantly on current account, the Fund would regard a member country as fulfilling its obligations. No definite proof would be required that the resources of the Fund are being used predominantly for current account. The Fund would expect to utilize reports on the balance of payments and on capital movements. Although such reports would not always be complete and accurate, they should be sufficient to reveal a substantial and continued outflow of capital. Only when the resources of the Fund are used to finance capital movements of this character would the Fund require a member country, as a condition for the sale of additional exchange, to restrict the outflow of capital.

The regulatory devices a member country might use are discussed more fully in the reply to the next question.

QUESTION 34

What provision must be made by countries that are members of the Fund to control capital movements if this should become necessary?

Reply

The Fund proposal provides for the control of capital movements by member countries in two ways.

First, member countries have the right to control capital exports when such control is regarded by them as desirable. This right is subject to the limitation that a member country may not use its control of capital movements to restrict payments for current transactions or to delay the transfer of funds in settlement of commitments (V-2).

Second, under certain conditions, discussed in the reply to the previous question, the Fund itself may require that member countries control capital exports as a condition for further use of the Fund's resources (V-1). It may be presumed that member countries will take the necessary steps, including in some instances supervision of the exchange market, to assure their capacity to fulfill the above obligations. The manner in which member countries organize and control their exchange markets is not prescribed by the Fund. It is a matter for each country to decide. Presumably, organization and control would differ from country to country depending upon the nature of a country's exchange market, the state of its monetary reserves, its balance of payments position, and the position of its currency in the Fund.

In some countries, particularly those not purchasing exchange from the Fund, no elaborate system of government organization and control of the exchange market will be necessary in order to assure fulfillment of their cooperative obligation to members of the Fund.

As a minimum, each country would certainly set up a system for collecting information on its balance of payments position and on capital movements. The receipt of such information would be helpful to the proper functioning of the Fund. Even though it never becomes necessary for a country to prevent a flight of capital, a country may find it helpful to cooperate with other member countries in controlling capital movements. Such cooperative measures might appropriately include a refusal to accept or permit acquisition of deposits, securities, or investments by nationals of any member country imposing restrictions on the export of capital except with the permission of the government of that country and the Fund. Member countries might also undertake to make available to the Fund or to the government of any member country information on property, deposits, securities, and investments of the nationals of that member country.

To supply this current information, most countries will have to have at all times an adequate system of reporting capital movements. This is not to be confused with exchange controls. They are quite different. The United States for many years has had a reporting system for capital movements, but not until the outbreak of the war were any restrictions imposed on the transfer of funds. The only countries that might find it necessary to adopt exchange controls are those whose foreign exchange resources do not permit a free and continued export of capital.

Apart from the arrangements for providing the Fund with data on capital movements, there are no measures that must be taken by member countries in anticipation of a possible need for controlling capital movements. It is a matter for each country to decide whether, while imposing no restrictions on current transactions, it wishes to establish or retain any administrative supervision over foreign exchange transactions. The Fund does not require member countries either to control capital movements or to supervise them, unless and until such member countries make considerable use of the resources of the Fund.

Some countries, foreseeing the need for control of capital movements, might require prior notification on international transactions in order to keep close control of their exchange position by scrutiny of international transactions. Such scrutiny of exchange transactions would not be in conflict with the obligations of the member country under provision IX-3 unless it were used in fact as a device to impose exchange restrictions on current international transactions in the guise of a control of the export of capital. Since the imposition of restrictions on current international transactions would be contrary to the obligations of a member country, it may be presumed that the Fund would make representations to member countries if such scrutiny of exchange transactions were used contrary to the purposes of the Fund (V-2).

Still other countries may find it desirable to set up a licensing system to assure an effective control over capital movements. Thus a country might require that all foreign exchange must be bought and sold through licensed dealers. No exchange need then be sold unless the purchaser showed proof that the foreign exchange was needed for the purchase of goods and services or the payment of interest and dividends or other payments of a non-capital nature; and the delivery of foreign exchange receipts would be required of exporters and other recipients of funds from abroad. Banks and other institutions licensed to engage in foreign exchange operations might not be permitted to increase their foreign exchange holdings or holdings of other foreign assets beyond an amount necessary to carry on their normal business operations. The government might require that any additional amounts of foreign exchange acquired by banks and by other licensed dealers be sold to the central bank or the exchange authority.

Presumably in some countries effective control could be assured only through an official monopoly of exchange transactions. There is no provision in the Fund proposal that would bar a country from instituting a monopoly of exchange transactions, provided that such techniques are not administered to restrict current international transactions without the consent of the Fund. It is not with administrative techniques but with policies that the Fund is primarily concerned.

It is not contemplated that control of international capital transactions or of exchange transactions generally will be exercised directly by the Fund. On the contrary, it is expected that in many countries the usual channels for buying and selling exchange will continue to be utilized. Within the provisions set forth in the proposal, the Fund will sell to member governments such foreign exchange as they may require to meet an adverse balance of payments predominantly on current account. The manner of channeling into the exchange market the foreign exchange sold by the Fund is a matter for each member country to decide. While in the ordinary course of events the Fund would not scrutinize exchange transactions, it may be expected that the Fund may require assurances in some instances that the exchange sold by the Fund is in fact intended to meet an adverse balance of payments predominantly on current account and not to meet a large or sustained outflow of capital. In the main, however, the Fund's decision would be based on information revealed by the balance of payments of the country in question rather than by supervision over its foreign exchange transactions.

Our conclusions with respect to the control of capital movements may be summarized as follows:

1. All countries should have machinery for adequate reporting of capital movements by type and totals with geographical breakdowns.

2. A number of countries will find it necessary from time to time to maintain some form of supervision over foreign exchange transactions.

3. Some of these countries will have to impose restrictions at one time or another on the outward movement of certain types of capital.

4. The Fund itself will never exercise authority as an agency controlling exchange transactions in any member country.

Question 35

What are the purposes of the provisions requiring more than a majority vote to authorize action by the Fund?

Reply

There are only two provisions in the Joint Statement requiring more than a majority to authorize action by the Fund. In these cases, the requirement is for the purpose of safeguarding the resources of the Fund or safeguarding the interests of member countries on matters affecting their national policies.

The ordinary business of the Fund would be undertaken by the management in accordance with the provisions of the Fund and the regulations prescribed by the Board of Directors. For the most important operations of the Fund, no positive action by the Board is needed at all.

In those instances where approval of the Board is needed all ordinary operations of the Fund require only a simple majority vote. The following important operations are included in this category:

1. To permit the sale of exchange to a member country in excess of the limitations prescribed in III-2-c and determine the conditions for such sale.
2. To permit and determine the conditions for the sale of additional exchange where a country is purchasing exchange at an annual rate in excess of 25 percent of its quota (III-2).
3. To report to a member country whose currency in the Fund is becoming scarce (VI-1).
4. To allocate among member countries available amounts of a scarce currency (VI-2).
5. To propose to a member country that it lend its currency to the Fund (III-4).
6. To approve of any multiple currency arrangements and similar practices engaged in by a member country (IX-3).
7. To suspend a country from making further use of the Fund's resources on the ground that it is using them in a manner contrary to the purposes and policies of the Fund (III-2-d).
8. To approve the initial par value of a member's currency fixed by that member (IV-1).
9. To grant a request by a member country for a change in the par value of its currency in accordance with provisions IV-3 and IV-4.

It would appear from the above that the Fund can unquestionably engage in all transactions necessary for the ordinary conduct of its business without prior approval or with the approval of only a majority of the member votes.

There are two matters of an extraordinary character involving the safeguarding of the resources of the Fund and of member countries and matters of the highest policy which are reserved for decision by a larger than majority vote of the Board:

1. According to the present provisions of the Joint Statement changes in the quotas require a four-fifths vote. It is the recommendation of the United States technical experts that this provision be changed to read that changes in the quota formula require a four-fifths vote (see question 8). The purpose of this requirement is to assure member countries that having joined the Fund with assurance of their relative position within the Fund, they will not be confronted with a change in the quota formula which will seriously affect their status. This is the more important because many countries will subscribe large resources to the Fund the use of which will depend in part upon the relative position of countries within the Fund.

2. A uniform change in the gold value of the member currencies can be made only by a majority including the approval of every member country having 10 percent or more of the votes. Because a uniform change in the price of gold can have far-reaching effects, it is thought essential to require the unanimous approval of the countries with the largest gold holdings and the greatest production of gold for such action.

It will be observed that the two actions of the Fund requiring more than a majority vote would only be necessary as a result of special circumstances and can in no way be considered as a part of the ordinary operations of the Fund. It is felt that on policy questions of such far-reaching importance, a safeguard against hasty and unwarranted action is needed in the form of a favorable vote larger than a majority.

PART II

Basic Documents

Articles of Agreement

The Final Act of the United Nations Monetary and Financial Conference held at Bretton Woods from July 1 to July 22, 1944 included, inter alia, the Articles of Agreement of the International Monetary Fund. These are reproduced below. For convenience, the list of Articles and Sections printed at the end of the Articles in the Final Act has here been transferred to the beginning as a Table of Contents.

Articles of Agreement of the International Monetary Fund (July 22, 1944)

TABLE OF CONTENTS

The Governments on whose behalf the present Agreement is signed agree as follows:

INTRODUCTORY ARTICLE

The International Monetary Fund is established and shall operate in accordance with the following provisions:

ARTICLE I. PURPOSES

The purposes of the International Monetary Fund are:

(i) To promote international monetary cooperation through a permanent institution which provides the machinery for consultation and collaboration on international monetary problems.

(ii) To facilitate the expansion and balanced growth of international trade, and to contribute thereby to the promotion and maintenance of high levels of employment and real income and to the development of the productive resources of all members as primary objectives of economic policy.

(iii) To promote exchange stability, to maintain orderly exchange arrangements among members, and to avoid competitive exchange depreciation.

(iv) To assist in the establishment of a multilateral system of payments in respect of current transactions between members and in the elimination of foreign exchange restrictions which hamper the growth of world trade.

(v) To give confidence to members by making the Fund's resources available to them under adequate safeguards, thus providing them with opportunity to correct maladjustments in their balance of payments without resorting to measures destructive of national or international prosperity.

(vi) In accordance with the above, to shorten the duration and lessen the degree of disequilibrium in the international balances of payments of members.

The Fund shall be guided in all its decisions by the purposes set forth in this Article.

ARTICLE II. MEMBERSHIP

SECTION 1. *Original members.*—The original members of the Fund shall be those of the countries represented at the United Nations Monetary and Financial Conference whose governments accept membership before the date specified in Article XX, Section 2 (*e*).

SEC. 2. *Other members.*—Membership shall be open to the governments of other countries at such times and in accordance with such terms as may be prescribed by the Fund.

ARTICLE III. QUOTAS AND SUBSCRIPTIONS

SECTION 1. *Quotas.*—Each member shall be assigned a quota. The quotas of the members represented at the United Nations Monetary and Financial Conference which accept membership before the date specified in Article XX, Section 2 (*e*), shall be those set forth in Schedule A. The quotas of other members shall be determined by the Fund.

SEC. 2. *Adjustment of quotas.*—The Fund shall at intervals of five years review, and if it deems it appropriate propose an adjustment of, the quotas of the members. It may also, if it thinks fit, consider at any other time the adjustment of any particular quota at the request of the member concerned. A four-fifths majority of the total voting power shall be required for any change in quotas and no quota shall be changed without the consent of the member concerned.

SEC. 3. *Subscriptions: time, place, and form of payment.*—(*a*) The subscription of each member shall be equal to its quota and shall be paid in full to the Fund at the appropriate depository on or before the date when the member becomes eligible under Article XX, Section 4 (*c*) or (*d*), to buy currencies from the Fund.

(*b*) Each member shall pay in gold, as a minimum, the smaller of

(i) twenty-five percent of its quota; or

(ii) ten percent of its net official holdings of gold and United States dollars as at the date when the Fund notifies members under Article XX, Section 4 (*a*) that it will shortly be in a position to begin exchange transactions.

Each member shall furnish to the Fund the data necessary to determine its net official holdings of gold and United States dollars.

(*c*) Each member shall pay the balance of its quota in its own currency.

(*d*) If the net official holdings of gold and United States dollars of any member as at the date referred to in (*b*) (ii) above are not ascertainable because its territories have been occupied by the enemy, the Fund shall fix an appropriate alternative date for determining such holdings. If such date is later than that on which the country becomes eligible under Article XX, Section 4 (*c*) or (*d*), to buy currencies from the Fund, the Fund and the member shall agree on a provisional gold payment to be made under (*b*) above, and the balance of the member's subscription shall be paid in the member's currency, subject to appropriate adjustment between the member and the Fund when the net official holdings have been ascertained.

SEC. 4. *Payments when quotas are changed.*—(*a*) Each member which consents to an increase in its quota shall, within thirty days after the date of its consent, pay to the Fund twenty-five percent of the increase in gold and the balance in its own currency. If, however, on the date when the member consents to an increase, its monetary reserves are less than its new quota, the Fund may reduce the proportion of the increase to be paid in gold.

(*b*) If a member consents to a reduction in its quota, the Fund shall, within thirty days after the date of the consent, pay to the member an amount equal to the reduction. The payment shall be made in the member's currency and in such amount of gold as may be necessary to prevent reducing the Fund's holdings of the currency below seventy-five percent of the new quota.

SEC. 5. *Substitution of securities for currency.*—The Fund shall accept from any member in place of any part of the member's currency which in the judgment of the Fund is not needed for its operations, notes or similar obligations issued by the member or the depository designated by the member under Article XIII, Section 2, which shall be non-negotiable, non-interest bearing and payable at their par value on demand by crediting the account of the Fund in the designated depository. This Section shall apply not only to currency subscribed by members but also to any currency otherwise due to, or acquired by, the Fund.

ARTICLE IV. PAR VALUES OF CURRENCIES

SECTION 1. *Expression of par values.*—(a) The par value of the currency of each member shall be expressed in terms of gold as a common denominator or in terms of the United States dollar of the weight and fineness in effect on July 1, 1944.

(*b*) All computations relating to currencies of members for the purpose of applying the provisions of this Agreement shall be on the basis of their par values.

SEC. 2. *Gold purchases based on par values.*—The Fund shall prescribe a margin above and below par value for transactions in gold by members, and no member shall buy gold at a price above par value plus the prescribed margin, or sell gold at a price below par value minus the prescribed margin.

SEC. 3. *Foreign exchange dealings based on parity.*—The maximum and the minimum rates for exchange transactions between the currencies of members taking place within their territories shall not differ from parity

(i) in the case of spot exchange transactions, by more than one percent; and

(ii) in the case of other exchange transactions, by a margin which exceeds the margin for spot exchange transactions by more than the Fund considers reasonable.

SEC. 4. *Obligations regarding exchange stability.*—*(a)* Each member undertakes to collaborate with the Fund to promote exchange stability, to maintain orderly exchange arrangements with other members, and to avoid competitive exchange alterations.

(b) Each member undertakes, through appropriate measures consistent with this Agreement, to permit within its territories exchange transactions between its currency and the currencies of other members only within the limits prescribed under Section 3 of this Article. A member whose monetary authorities, for the settlement of international transactions, in fact freely buy and sell gold within the limits prescribed by the Fund under Section 2 of this Article shall be deemed to be fulfilling this undertaking.

SEC. 5. *Changes in par values.*—*(a)* A member shall not propose a change in the par value of its currency except to correct a fundamental disequilibrium.

(b) A change in the par value of a member's currency may be made only on the proposal of the member and only after consultation with the Fund.

(c) When a change is proposed, the Fund shall first take into account the changes, if any, which have already taken place in the initial par value of the member's currency as determined under Article XX, Section 4. If the proposed change, together with all previous changes, whether increases or decreases,

(i) does not exceed ten percent of the initial par value, the Fund shall raise no objection;

(ii) does not exceed a further ten percent of the initial par value, the Fund may either concur or object, but shall declare its attitude within seventy-two hours if the member so requests;

(iii) is not within (i) or (ii) above, the Fund may either concur or object, but shall be entitled to a longer period in which to declare its attitude.

(d) Uniform changes in par values made under Section 7 of this Article shall not be taken into account in determining whether a proposed change falls within (i), (ii), or (iii) of *(c)* above.

(e) A member may change the par value of its currency without the concurrence of the Fund if the change does not affect the international transactions of members of the Fund.

(f) The Fund shall concur in a proposed change which is within the terms of *(c)* (ii) or *(c)* (iii) above if it is satisfied that the change is necessary to correct a fundamental disequilibrium. In particular, provided it is so satisfied, it shall not object to a proposed change because of the domestic social or political policies of the member proposing the change.

SEC. 6. *Effect of unauthorized changes.*—If a member changes the par value of its currency despite the objection of the Fund, in cases where the Fund is entitled to object, the member shall be ineligible to use the resources of the Fund unless the Fund otherwise determines; and if, after the expiration of a reasonable period, the difference between the member and the Fund continues, the matter shall be subject to the provisions of Article XV, Section 2 *(b)*.

SEC. 7. *Uniform changes in par values.*—Notwithstanding the provisions of Section 5 *(b)* of this Article, the Fund by a majority of the total voting power may make uniform proportionate changes in the par values of the currencies of all members, provided each such change is approved by every member which has ten percent or more of the total of the quotas. The par value of a member's currency shall, however, not be changed under this provision if, within seventy-two hours of the Fund's action, the member informs the Fund that it does not wish the par value of its currency to be changed by such action.

SEC. 8. *Maintenance of gold value of the Fund's assets.*

(a) The gold value of the Fund's assets shall be maintained notwithstanding changes in the par or foreign exchange value of the currency of any member.

(b) Whenever (i) the par value of a member's currency is reduced, or (ii) the foreign exchange value of a member's currency has, in the opinion of the Fund, depreciated to a significant extent within that member's territories, the member shall pay to the Fund within a reasonable time an amount of its own currency equal to the reduction in the gold value of its currency held by the Fund.

(c) Whenever the par value of a member's currency is increased, the Fund shall return to such member within a reasonable time an amount in its currency equal to the increase in the gold value of its currency held by the Fund.

(d) The provisions of this Section shall apply to a uniform proportionate change in the par values of the currencies of all members, unless at the time when such a change is proposed the Fund decides otherwise.

SEC. 9. *Separate currencies within a member's territories.*—A member proposing a change in the par value of its currency shall be deemed, unless it declares otherwise, to be proposing a corresponding change in the par value of the separate currencies of all territories in respect of which it has accepted this Agreement under Article XX, Section 2 *(g)*. It shall, however, be open to a member to declare that its proposal relates either to the metropolitan currency alone, or only to one or more specified separate currencies, or to the metropolitan currency and one or more specified separate currencies.

ARTICLE V. TRANSACTIONS WITH THE FUND

SECTION 1. *Agencies dealing with the Fund.*—Each member shall deal with the Fund only through its Treasury, central bank, stabilization fund, or other similar fiscal agency and the Fund shall deal only with or through the same agencies.

SEC. 2. *Limitation on the Fund's operations.*—Except as otherwise provided in this Agreement, operations on the account of the Fund shall be limited to transactions for the purpose of supplying a member, on the initiative of such member, with the currency of another member in exchange for gold or for the currency of the member desiring to make the purchase.

SEC. 3. *Conditions governing use of the Fund's resources.*—*(a)* A member shall be entitled to buy the currency of another member from the Fund in exchange for its own currency subject to the following conditions:

(i) The member desiring to purchase the currency represents that it is presently needed for making in that currency payments which are consistent with the provisions of this Agreement;

(ii) The Fund has not given notice under Article VII, Section 3, that its holdings of the currency desired have become scarce;

(iii) The proposed purchase would not cause the Fund's holdings of the purchasing member's currency to increase by more than twenty-five percent of its quota during the period of twelve months ending on the date of the purchase nor to exceed two hundred percent of its quota, but the twenty-five percent limitation shall apply only to the extent that the Fund's holdings of the member's currency have been brought above seventy-five percent of its quota if they had been below that amount;

(iv) The Fund has not previously declared under Section 5 of this Article, Article IV, Section 6, Article VI, Section 1, or Article XV, Section 2 *(a)*, that the member desiring to purchase is ineligible to use the resources of the Fund.

(b) A member shall not be entitled without the permission of the Fund to use the Fund's resources to acquire currency to hold against forward exchange transactions.

SEC. 4. *Waiver of conditions.*—The Fund may in its discretion, and on terms which safeguard its interests, waive any of the conditions prescribed in Section 3 *(a)* of this Article, especially in the case of members with a record of avoiding large or continuous use of the Fund's resources. In making a waiver it shall take into consideration periodic or exceptional requirements of the member requesting the waiver. The Fund shall also take into consideration a member's willingness to pledge as collateral security gold, silver, securities, or other acceptable assets having a value sufficient in the opinion of the Fund to protect its interests and may require as a condition of waiver the pledge of such collateral security.

SEC. 5. *Ineligibility to use the Fund's resources.*—Whenever the Fund is of the opinion that any member is using the resources of the Fund in a manner contrary to the purposes of the Fund, it shall present to the member a report setting forth the views of the Fund and prescribing a suitable time for reply. After presenting such a report to a member, the Fund may limit the use of its resources by the member. If no reply to the report is received from the member within the prescribed time, or if the reply received is unsatisfactory, the Fund may continue to limit the member's use of the Fund's resources or may, after giving reasonable notice to the member, declare it ineligible to use the resources of the Fund.

SEC. 6. *Purchases of currencies from the Fund for gold.*—*(a)* Any member desiring to obtain, directly or indirectly, the currency of another member for gold shall, provided that it can do so with equal advantage, acquire it by the sale of gold to the Fund.

(b) Nothing in this Section shall be deemed to preclude any member from selling in any market gold newly produced from mines located within its territories.

SEC. 7. *Repurchase by a member of its currency held by the Fund.*—*(a)* A member may repurchase from the Fund and the Fund shall sell for gold any part of the Fund's holdings of its currency in excess of its quota.

(b) At the end of each financial year of the Fund, a member shall repurchase from the Fund with gold or convertible currencies, as determined in accordance with Schedule B, part of the Fund's holdings of its currency under the following conditions:

(i) Each member shall use in repurchases of its own currency from the Fund an amount of its monetary reserves equal in value to one-half of any increase that has occurred during the year in the Fund's holdings of its currency plus one-half of any increase, or minus one-half of any decrease, that has occurred during the year in the member's monetary reserves. This rule shall not apply when a member's monetary reserves have decreased during the year by more than the Fund's holdings of its currency have increased.

(ii) If after the repurchase described in (i) above (if required) has been made, a member's holdings of another member's currency (or of gold acquired from that member) are found to have increased by reason of transactions in terms of that currency with other members or persons in their territories, the member whose holdings of such currency (or gold) have thus increased shall use the increase to repurchase its own currency from the Fund.

(*c*) None of the adjustments described in (*b*) above shall be carried to a point at which

(i) the member's monetary reserves are below its quota, or

(ii) the Fund's holdings of its currency are below seventy-five percent of its quota, or

(iii) the Fund's holdings of any currency required to be used are above seventy-five percent of the quota of the member concerned.

SEC. 8. *Charges.*—(*a*) Any member buying the currency of another member from the Fund in exchange for its own currency shall pay a service charge uniform for all members of three-fourths percent in addition to the parity price. The Fund in its discretion may increase this service charge to not more than one percent or reduce it to not less than one-half percent.

(*b*) The Fund may levy a reasonable handling charge on any member buying gold from the Fund or selling gold to the Fund.

(*c*) The Fund shall levy charges uniform for all members which shall be payable by any member on the average daily balances of its currency held by the Fund in excess of its quota. These charges shall be at the following rates:

(i) *On amounts not more than twenty-five percent in excess of the quota:* no charge for the first three months; one-half percent per annum for the next nine months; and thereafter an increase in the charge of one-half percent for each subsequent year.

(ii) *On amounts more than twenty-five percent and not more than fifty percent in excess of the quota:* an additional one-half percent for the first year; and an additional one-half percent for each subsequent year.

(iii) *On each additional bracket of twenty-five percent in excess of the quota:* an additional one-half percent for the first year; and an additional one-half percent for each subsequent year.

(*d*) Whenever the Fund's holdings of a member's currency are such that the charge applicable to any bracket for any period has reached the rate of four percent per annum, the Fund and the member shall consider means by which the Fund's holdings of the currency can be reduced. Thereafter, the charges shall rise in accordance with the provisions of (*c*) above until they reach five percent and failing agreement, the Fund may then impose such charges as it deems appropriate.

(*e*) The rates referred to in (*c*) and (*d*) above may be changed by a three-fourths majority of the total voting power.

(*f*) All charges shall be paid in gold. If, however, the member's monetary reserves are less than one-half of its quota, it shall pay in gold only that proportion of the charges due which such reserves bear to one-half of its quota, and shall pay the balance in its own currency.

ARTICLE VI. CAPITAL TRANSFERS

SECTION 1. *Use of the Fund's resources for capital transfers.*—(*a*) A member may not make net use of the Fund's resources to meet a large or sustained outflow of capital, and the Fund may request a member to exercise controls to prevent such use of the resources of the Fund. If, after receiving such a request, a member fails to exercise appropriate controls, the Fund may declare the member ineligible to use the resources of the Fund.

(*b*) Nothing in this Section shall be deemed

(i) to prevent the use of the resources of the Fund for capital transactions of reasonable amount required for the expansion of exports or in the ordinary course of trade, banking or other business, or

(ii) to affect capital movements which are met out of a member's own resources of gold and foreign exchange, but members undertake that such capital movements will be in accordance with the purposes of the Fund.

Sec. 2. *Special provisions for capital transfers.*—If the Fund's holdings of the currency of a member have remained below seventy-five percent of its quota for an immediately preceding period of not less than six months, such member, if it has not been declared ineligible to use the resources of the Fund under Section 1 of this Article, Article IV, Section 6, Article V, Section 5, or Article XV, Section 2 (*a*), shall be entitled, notwithstanding the provisions of Section 1 (*a*) of this Article, to buy the currency of another member from the Fund with its own currency for any purpose, including capital transfers. Purchases for capital transfers under this Section shall not, however, be permitted if they have the effect of raising the Fund's holdings of the currency of the member desiring to purchase above seventy-five percent of its quota, or of reducing the Fund's holdings of the currency desired below seventy-five percent of the quota of the member whose currency is desired.

Sec. 3. *Controls of capital transfers.*—Members may exercise such controls as are necessary to regulate international capital movements, but no member may exercise these controls in a manner which will restrict payments for current transactions or which will unduly delay transfers of funds in settlement of commitments, except as provided in Article VII, Section 3 (*b*), and in Article XIV, Section 2.

ARTICLE VII. SCARCE CURRENCIES

Section 1. *General scarcity of currency.*—If the Fund finds that a general scarcity of a particular currency is developing, the Fund may so inform members and may issue a report setting forth the causes of the scarcity and containing recommendations designed to bring it to an end. A representative of the member whose currency is involved shall participate in the preparation of the report.

Sec. 2. *Measures to replenish the Fund's holdings of scarce currencies.*—The Fund may, if it deems such action appropriate to replenish its holdings of any member's currency, take either or both of the following steps:

(i) Propose to the member that, on terms and conditions agreed between the Fund and the member, the latter lend its currency to the Fund or that, with the approval of the member, the Fund borrow such currency from some other source either within or outside the territories of the member, but no member shall be under any obligation to make such loans to the Fund or to approve the borrowing of its currency by the Fund from any other source.

(ii) Require the member to sell its currency to the Fund for gold.

SEC. 3. *Scarcity of the Fund's holdings.*—(*a*) If it becomes evident to the Fund that the demand for a member's currency seriously threatens the Fund's ability to supply that currency, the Fund, whether or not it has issued a report under Section 1 of this Article, shall formally declare such currency scarce and shall thenceforth apportion its existing and accruing supply of the scarce currency with due regard to the relative needs of members, the general international economic situation, and any other pertinent considerations. The Fund shall also issue a report concerning its action.

(*b*) A formal declaration under (*a*) above shall operate as an authorization to any member, after consultation with the Fund, temporarily to impose limitations on the freedom of exchange operations in the scarce currency. Subject to the provisions of Article IV, Sections 3 and 4, the member shall have complete jurisdiction in determining the nature of such limitations, but they shall be no more restrictive than is necessary to limit the demand for the scarce currency to the supply held by, or accruing to, the member in question; and they shall be relaxed and removed as rapidly as conditions permit.

(*c*) The authorization under (*b*) above shall expire whenever the Fund formally declares the currency in question to be no longer scarce.

SEC. 4. *Administration of restrictions.*—Any member imposing restrictions in respect of the currency of any other member pursuant to the provisions of Section 3 (*b*) of this Article shall give sympathetic consideration to any representations by the other member regarding the administration of such restrictions.

SEC. 5. *Effect of other international agreements on restrictions.*—Members agree not to invoke the obligations of any engagements entered into with other members prior to this Agreement in such a manner as will prevent the operation of the provisions of this Article.

ARTICLE VIII. GENERAL OBLIGATIONS OF MEMBERS

SECTION 1. *Introduction.*—In addition to the obligations assumed under other articles of this Agreement, each member undertakes the obligations set out in this Article.

SEC. 2. *Avoidance of restrictions on current payments.*—(*a*) Subject to the provisions of Article VII, Section 3 (*b*), and Article XIV, Section 2, no member shall, without the approval of the Fund, impose restrictions on the making of payments and transfers for current international transactions.

(*b*) Exchange contracts which involve the currency of any member and which are contrary to the exchange control regulations of that member maintained or imposed consistently with this Agreement shall be unenforceable in the territories of any member. In addition, members may, by mutual accord, co-operate in measures for the purpose of making the exchange control regulations of either member more effective, provided that such measures and regulations are consistent with this Agreement.

SEC. 3. *Avoidance of discriminatory currency practices.*—No member shall engage in, or permit any of its fiscal agencies referred to in Article V, Section 1, to engage in, any discriminatory currency arrangements or multiple currency practices except as authorized under this Agreement or approved by the Fund. If such arrangements and practices are enagaged in at the date when this Agreement enters into force the member concerned shall consult with the Fund as to their progressive removal unless they are maintained or imposed under Article XIV, Section 2, in which case the provisions of Section 4 of that Article shall apply.

SEC. 4. *Convertibility of foreign held balances.*—(*a*) Each member shall buy balances of its currency held by another member if the latter, in requesting the purchase, represents

(i) that the balances to be bought have been recently acquired as a result of current transactions; or

(ii) that their conversion is needed for making payments for current transactions.

The buying member shall have the option to pay either in the currency of the member making the request or in gold.

(*b*) The obligation in (*a*) above shall not apply

(i) when the convertibility of the balances has been restricted consistently with Section 2 of this Article, or Article VI, Section 3; or

(ii) when the balances have accumulated as a result of transactions effected before the removal by a member of restrictions maintained or imposed under Article XIV, Section 2; or

(iii) when the balances have been acquired contrary to the exchange regulations of the member which is asked to buy them; or

(iv) when the currency of the member requesting the purchase has been declared scarce under Article VII, Section 3 (*a*); or

(v) when the member requested to make the purchase is for any reason not entitled to buy currencies of other members from the Fund for its own currency.

SEC. 5. *Furnishing of information.*—(*a*) The Fund may require members to furnish it with such information as it deems necessary for its operations, including, as the minimum necessary for the effective discharge of the Fund's duties, national data on the following matters:

(i) Official holdings at home and abroad, of (1) gold, (2) foreign exchange.

(ii) Holdings at home and abroad by banking and financial agencies, other than official agencies, of (1) gold, (2) foreign exchange.

(iii) Production of gold.

(iv) Gold exports and imports according to countries of destination and origin.

(v) Total exports and imports of merchandise, in terms of local currency values, according to countries of destination and origin.

(vi) International balance of payments, including (1) trade in goods and services, (2) gold transactions, (3) known capital transactions, and (4) other items.

(vii) International investment position, *i. e.*, investments within the territories of the member owned abroad and investments abroad owned by persons in its territories so far as it is possible to furnish this information.

(viii) National income.

(ix) Price indices, *i. e.*, indices of commodity prices in wholesale and retail markets and of export and import prices.

(x) Buying and selling rates for foreign currencies.

(xi) Exchange controls, *i. e.*, a comprehensive statement of exchange controls in effect at the time of assuming membership in the Fund and details of subsequent changes as they occur.

(xii) Where official clearing arrangements exist, details of amounts awaiting clearance in respect of commercial and financial transactions, and of the length of time during which such arrears have been outstanding.

(*b*) In requesting information the Fund shall take into consideration the varying ability of members to furnish the data requested. Members shall be under no obligation to furnish information in such detail that the affairs of individuals or corporations are disclosed. Members undertake, however, to furnish the desired information in as detailed and accurate a manner as is practicable, and, so far as possible, to avoid mere estimates.

(*c*) The Fund may arrange to obtain further information by agreement with members. It shall act as a centre for the collection and exchange of information on monetary and financial problems, thus facilitating the preparation of studies designed to assist members in developing policies which further the purposes of the Fund.

SEC. 6. *Consultation between members regarding existing international agreements.*—Where under this Agreement a member is authorized in the special or temporary circumstances specified in the Agreement to maintain or establish restrictions on exchange transactions, and there are other engagements between members entered into prior to this Agreement which conflict with the application of such restrictions, the parties to such engagements will consult with one another with a view to making such mutually acceptable adjustments as may be necessary. The provisions of this Article shall be without prejudice to the operation of Article VII, Section 5.

ARTICLE IX. STATUS, IMMUNITIES AND PRIVILEGES

SECTION 1. *Purposes of Article.*—To enable the Fund to fulfill the functions with which it is entrusted, the status, immunities and privileges set forth in this Article shall be accorded to the Fund in the territories of each member.

SEC. 2. *Status of the Fund.*—The Fund shall possess full juridical personality, and in particular, the capacity

(i) to contract;

(ii) to acquire and dispose of immovable and movable property;

(iii) to institute legal proceedings.

SEC. 3. *Immunity from judicial process.*—The Fund, its property and its assets, wherever located and by whomsoever held, shall enjoy immunity from every form of judicial process except to the extent that it expressly waives its immunity for the purpose of any proceedings or by the terms of any contract.

SEC. 4. *Immunity from other action.*—Property and assets of the Fund, wherever located and by whomsoever held, shall be immune from search, requisition, confiscation, expropriation or any other form of seizure by executive or legislative action.

SEC. 5. *Immunity of archives.*—The archives of the Fund shall be inviolable.

SEC. 6. *Freedom of assets from restrictions.*—To the extent necessary to carry out the operations provided for in this Agreement, all property and assets of the Fund shall be free from restrictions, regulations, controls and moratoria of any nature.

SEC. 7. *Privilege for communications.*—The official communications of the Fund shall be accorded by members the same treatment as the official communications of other members.

SEC. 8. *Immunities and privileges of officers and employees.*—All governors, executive directors, alternates, officers and employees of the Fund

(i) shall be immune from legal process with respect to acts performed by them in their official capacity except when the Fund waives this immunity;

(ii) not being local nationals, shall be granted the same immunities from immigration restrictions, alien registration requirements and national service obligations and the same facilities as regards exchange restrictions as are accorded by members to the representatives, officials, and employees of comparable rank of other members;

(iii) shall be granted the same treatment in respect of traveling facilities as is accorded by members to representatives, officials and employees of comparable rank of other members.

SEC. 9. *Immunities from taxation.*—(*a*) The Fund, its assets, property, income and its operations and transactions authorized by this Agreement, shall be immune from all taxation and from all customs duties. The Fund shall also be immune from liability for the collection or payment of any tax or duty.

(*b*) No tax shall be levied on or in respect of salaries and emoluments paid by the Fund to executive directors, alternates, officers or employees of the Fund who are not local citizens, local subjects, or other local nationals.

(*c*) No taxation of any kind shall be levied on any obligation or security issued by the Fund, including any dividend or interest thereon, by whomsoever held

(i) which discriminates against such obligation or security solely because of its origin; or

(ii) if the sole jurisdictional basis for such taxation is the place or currency in which it is issued, made payable or paid, or the location of any office or place of business maintained by the Fund.

SEC. 10. *Application of Article.*—Each member shall take such action as is necessary in its own territories for the purpose of making effective in terms of its own law the principles set forth in this Article and shall inform the Fund of the detailed action which it has taken.

ARTICLE X. RELATIONS WITH OTHER INTERNATIONAL ORGANIZATIONS

The Fund shall cooperate within the terms of this Agreement with any general international organization and with public international organizations having specialized responsibilities in related fields. Any arrangements for such cooperation which would involve a modification of any provision of this Agreement may be effected only after amendment to this Agreement under Article XVII.

ARTICLE XI. RELATIONS WITH NON-MEMBER COUNTRIES

SECTION 1. *Undertakings regarding relations with non-member countries.*—Each member undertakes:

(i) Not to engage in, nor to permit any of its fiscal agencies referred to in Article V, Section 1, to engage in, any transactions with a non-member or with persons in a non-member's territories which would be contrary to the provisions of this Agreement or the purposes of the Fund;

(ii) Not to cooperate with a non-member or with persons in a non-member's territories in practices which would be contrary to the provisions of this Agreement or the purposes of the Fund; and

(iii) To cooperate with the Fund with a view to the application in its territories of appropriate measures to prevent transactions with non-members or with persons in their territories which would be contrary to the provisions of this Agreement or the purposes of the Fund.

SEC. 2. *Restrictions on transactions with non-member countries.*—Nothing in this Agreement shall affect the right of any member to impose restrictions on exchange transactions with non-members or with persons in their territories unless the Fund finds that such restrictions prejudice the interests of members and are contrary to the purposes of the Fund.

ARTICLE XII. ORGANIZATION AND MANAGEMENT

SECTION 1. *Structure of the Fund.*—The Fund shall have a Board of Governors, Executive Directors, a Managing Director, and a staff.

SEC. 2. *Board of Governors.*—*(a)* All powers of the Fund shall be vested in the Board of Governors, consisting of one governor and one alternate appointed by each member in such manner as it may determine. Each governor and each alternate shall serve for five years, subject to the pleasure of the member appointing him, and may be reappointed. No alternate may vote except in the absence of his principal. The Board shall select one of the governors as chairman.

(b) The Board of Governors may delegate to the Executive Directors authority to exercise any powers of the Board, except the power to:

(i) Admit new members and determine the conditions of their admission.

(ii) Approve a revision of quotas.

(iii) Approve a uniform change in the par value of the currencies of all members.

(iv) Make arrangements to cooperate with other international organizations (other than informal arrangements of a temporary or administrative character).

(v) Determine the distribution of the net income of the Fund.

(vi) Require a member to withdraw.

(vii) Decide to liquidate the Fund.

(viii) Decide appeals from interpretations of this agreement given by the Executive Directors.

(c) The Board of Governors shall hold an annual meeting and such other meetings as may be provided for by the Board or called by the Executive Directors. Meetings of the Board shall be called by the Directors whenever requested by five members or by members having one-quarter of the total voting power.

(d) A quorum for any meeting of the Board of Governors shall be a majority of the governors exercising not less than two-thirds of the total voting power.

(e) Each governor shall be entitled to cast the number of votes alloted under Section 5 of this Article to the member appointing him.

(f) The Board of Governors may by regulation establish a procedure whereby the Executive Directors, when they deem such action to be in the best interests of the Fund, may obtain a vote of the governors on a specific question without calling a meeting of the Board.

(g) The Board of Governors, and the Executive Directors to the extent authorized, may adopt such rules and regulations as may be necessary or appropriate to conduct the business of the Fund.

(h) Governors and alternates shall serve as such without compensation from the Fund, but the Fund shall pay them reasonable expenses incurred in attending meetings.

(i) The Board of Governors shall determine the remuneration to be paid to the Executive Directors and the salary and terms of the contract of service of the Managing Director.

SEC. 3. *Executive Directors.*—*(a)* The Executive Directors shall be responsible for the conduct of the general operations of the Fund, and for this purpose shall exercise all the powers delegated to them by the Board of Governors.

(b) There shall be not less than twelve directors who need not be governors, and of whom

(i) five shall be appointed by the five members having the largest quotas;

(ii) not more than two shall be appointed when the provisions of *(c)* below apply;

(iii) five shall be elected by the members not entitled to appoint directors, other than the American Republics; and

(iv) two shall be elected by the American Republics not entitled to appoint directors.

For the purposes of this paragraph, members means governments of countries whose names are set forth in Schedule A, whether they become members in accordance with Article XX or in accordance with Article II, Section 2. When governments of other countries become members, the Board of Governors may, by a four-fifths majority of the total voting power, increase the number of directors to be elected.

(c) If, at the second regular election of directors and thereafter, the members entitled to appoint directors under *(b)* (i) above do not include the two members, the holdings of whose currencies by the Fund have been, on the average over the preceding two years, reduced below their quotas by the largest absolute amounts in terms of gold as a common denominator, either one or both of such members, as the case may be, shall be entitled to appoint a director.

(d) Subject to Article XX, Section 3 *(b)* elections of elective directors shall be conducted at intervals of two years in accordance with the provisions of Schedule C, supplemented by such regulations as the Fund deems appropriate. Whenever the Board of Governors increases the number of directors to be elected under *(b)* above, it shall issue regulations making appropriate changes in the proportion of votes required to elect directors under the provisions of Schedule C.

(e) Each director shall appoint an alternate with full power to act for him when he is not present. When the directors appointing them are present, alternates may participate in meetings but may not vote.

(f) Directors shall continue in office until their successors are appointed or elected. If the office of an elected director becomes vacant more than ninety days before the end of his term, another director shall be elected for the remainder of the term by the members who elected the former director. A majority of the votes cast shall be required for election. While the office remains vacant, the alternate of the former director shall exercise his powers, except that of appointing an alternate.

(g) The Executive Directors shall function in continuous session at the principal office of the Fund and shall meet as often as the business of the Fund may require.

(h) A quorum for any meeting of the Executive Directors shall be a majority of the directors representing not less than one-half of the voting power.

(i) Each appointed director shall be entitled to cast the number of votes allotted under

Section 5 of this Article to the member appointing him. Each elected director shall be entitled to cast the number of votes which counted towards his election. When the provisions of Section 5 *(b)* of this Article are applicable, the votes which a director would otherwise be entitled to cast shall be increased or decreased correspondingly. All the votes which a director is entitled to cast shall be cast as a unit.

(j) The Board of Governors shall adopt regulations under which a member not entitled to appoint a director under *(b)* above may send a representative to attend any meeting of the Executive Directors when a request made by, or a matter particularly affecting, that member is under consideration.

(k) The Executive Directors may appoint such committees as they deem advisable. Membership of committees need not be limited to governors or directors or their alternates.

SEC. 4. *Managing Director and staff.*—*(a)* The Executive Directors shall select a Managing Director who shall not be a governor or an executive director. The Managing Director shall be chairman of the Executive Directors, but shall have no vote except a deciding vote in case of an equal division. He may participate in meetings of the Board of Governors, but shall not vote at such meetings. The Managing Director shall cease to hold office when the Executive Directors so decide.

(b) The Managing Director shall be chief of the operating staff of the Fund and shall conduct, under the direction of the Executive Directors, the ordinary business of the Fund. Subject to the general control of the Executive Directors, he shall be responsible for the organization, appointment and dismissal of the staff of the Fund.

(c) The Managing Director and the staff of the Fund, in the discharge of their functions, shall owe their duty entirely to the Fund and to no other authority. Each member of the Fund shall respect the international character of this duty and shall refrain from all attempts to influence any of the staff in the discharge of his functions.

(d) In appointing the staff the Managing Director shall, subject to the paramount importance of securing the highest standards of efficiency and of technical competence, pay due regard to the importance of recruiting personnel on as wide a geographical basis as possible.

SEC. 5. *Voting.*—*(a)* Each member shall have two hundred fifty votes plus one additional vote for each part of its quota equivalent to one hundred thousand United States dollars.

(b) Whenever voting is required under Article V, Section 4 or 5, each member shall have the number of votes to which it is entitled under *(a)* above, adjusted

(i) by the addition of one vote for the equivalent of each four hundred thousand United States dollars of net sales of its currency up to the date when the vote is taken, or

(ii) by the subtraction of one vote for the equivalent of each four hundred thousand United States dollars of its net purchases of the currencies of other members up to the date when the vote is taken;

provided, that neither net purchases nor net sales shall be deemed at any time to exceed an amount equal to the quota of the member involved.

(c) For the purpose of all computations under this Section, United States dollars shall be deemed to be of the weight and fineness in effect on July 1, 1944, adjusted for any uniform change under Article IV, Section 7, if a waiver is made under Section 8 *(d)* of that Article.

(*d*) Except as otherwise specifically provided, all decisions of the Fund shall be made by a majority of the votes cast.

SEC. 6. *Distribution of net income.*—(*a*) The Board of Governors shall determine annually what part of the Fund's net income shall be placed to reserve and what part, if any, shall be distributed.

(*b*) If any distribution is made, there shall first be distributed a two percent noncumulative payment to each member on the amount by which seventy-five percent of its quota exceeded the Fund's average holdings of its currency during that year. The balance shall be paid to all members in proportion to their quotas. Payments to each member shall be made in its own currency.

SEC. 7. *Publication of reports.*—(*a*) The Fund shall publish an annual report containing an audited statement of its accounts, and shall issue, at intervals of three months or less, a summary statement of its transactions and its holdings of gold and currencies of members.

(*b*) The Fund may publish such other reports as it deems desirable for carrying out its purposes.

SEC. 8. *Communication of views to members.*—The Fund shall at all times have the right to communicate its views informally to any member on any matter arising under this Agreement. The Fund may, by a two-thirds majority of the total voting power, decide to publish a report made to a member regarding its monetary or economic conditions and developments which directly tend to produce a serious disequilibrium in the international balance of payments of members. If the member is not entitled to appoint an executive director, it shall be entitled to representation in accordance with Section 3 (*j*) of this Article. The Fund shall not publish a report involving changes in the fundamental structure of the economic organization of members.

ARTICLE XIII. OFFICES AND DEPOSITORIES

SECTION 1. *Location of offices.*—The principal office of the Fund shall be located in the territory of the member having the largest quota, and agencies or branch offices may be established in the territories of other members.

SEC. 2. *Depositories.*—(*a*) Each member country shall designate its central bank as a depository for all the Fund's holdings of its currency, or if it has no central bank it shall designate such other institution as may be acceptable to the Fund.

(*b*) The Fund may hold other assets, including gold, in the depositories designated by the five members having the largest quotas and in such other designated depositories as the Fund may select. Initially, at least one-half of the holdings of the Fund shall be held in the depository designated by the member in whose territories the Fund has its principal office and at least forty percent shall be held in the depositories designated by the remaining four members referred to above. However, all transfers of gold by the Fund shall be made with due regard to the costs of transport and anticipated requirements of the Fund. In an emergency the Executive Directors may transfer all or any part of the Fund's gold holdings to any place where they can be adequately protected.

SEC. 3. *Guarantee of the Fund's assets.*—Each member guarantees all assets of the Fund against loss resulting from failure or default on the part of the depository designated by it.

ARTICLE XIV. TRANSITIONAL PERIOD

SECTION 1. *Introduction.*—The Fund is not intended to provide facilities for relief or reconstruction or to deal with international indebtedness arising out of the war.

SEC. 2. *Exchange restrictions.*—In the post-war transitional period members may, notwithstanding the provisions of any other articles of this Agreement, maintain and adapt to changing circumstances (and, in the case of members whose territories have been occupied by the enemy, introduce where necessary) restrictions on payments and transfers for current international transactions. Members shall, however, have continuous regard in their foreign exchange policies to the purposes of the Fund; and, as soon as conditions permit, they shall take all possible measures to develop such commercial and financial arrangements with other members as will facilitate international payments and the maintenance of exchange stability. In particular, members shall withdraw restrictions maintained or imposed under this Section as soon as they are satisfied that they will be able, in the absence of such restrictions, to settle their balance of payments in a manner which will not unduly encumber their access to the resources of the Fund.

SEC. 3. *Notification to the Fund.*—Each member shall notify the Fund before it becomes eligible under Article XX, Section 4 *(c)* or *(d)*, to buy currency from the Fund, whether it intends to avail itself of the transitional arrangements in Section 2 of this Article, or whether it is prepared to accept the obligations of Article VIII, Sections 2, 3, and 4. A member availing itself of the transitional arrangements shall notify the Fund as soon thereafter as it is prepared to accept the above-mentioned obligations.

SEC. 4. *Action of the Fund relating to restrictions.*—Not later than three years after the date on which the Fund begins operations and in each year thereafter, the Fund shall report on the restrictions still in force under Section 2 of this Article. Five years after the date on which the Fund begins operations, and in each year thereafter, any member still retaining any restrictions inconsistent with Article VIII, Sections 2, 3, or 4, shall consult the Fund as to their further retention. The Fund may, if it deems such action necessary in exceptional circumstances, make representations to any member that conditions are favorable for the withdrawal of any particular restriction, or for the general abandonment of restrictions, inconsistent with the provisions of any other article of this Agreement. The member shall be given a suitable time to reply to such representations. If the Fund finds that the member persists in maintaining restrictions which are inconsistent with the purposes of the Fund, the member shall be subject to Article XV, Section 2 *(a)*.

SEC. 5. *Nature of transitional period.*—In its relations with members, the Fund shall recognize that the post-war transitional period will be one of change and adjustment and in making decisions on requests occasioned thereby which are presented by any member it shall give the member the benefit of any reasonable doubt.

ARTICLE XV. WITHDRAWAL FROM MEMBERSHIP

SECTION 1. *Right of members to withdraw.*—Any member may withdraw from the Fund at any time by transmitting a notice in writing to the Fund at its principal office. Withdrawal shall become effective on the date such notice is received.

SEC. 2. *Compulsory withdrawal.*—*(a)* If a member fails to fulfill any of its obligations under this Agreement, the Fund may declare the member ineligible to use the resources of the Fund. Nothing in this Section shall be deemed to limit the provisions of Article IV, Section 6, Article V, Section 5, or Article VI, Section 1.

(b) If, after the expiration of a reasonable period the member persists in its failure to fulfill any of its obligations under this Agreement, or a difference between a member and the Fund under Article IV, Section 6, continues, that member may be required to withdraw from membership in the Fund by a decision of the Board of Governors carried by a majority of the governors representing a majority of the total voting power.

(c) Regulations shall be adopted to ensure that before action is taken against any member under *(a)* or *(b)* above, the member shall be informed in reasonable time of the complaint against it and given an adequate opportunity for stating its case, both orally and in writing.

SEC. 3. *Settlement of accounts with members withdrawing.*—When a member withdraws from the Fund, normal transactions of the Fund in its currency shall cease and settlement of all accounts between it and the Fund shall be made with reasonable despatch by agreement between it and the Fund. If agreement is not reached promptly, the provisions of Schedule D shall apply to the settlement of accounts.

ARTICLE XVI. EMERGENCY PROVISIONS

SECTION 1. *Temporary suspension.*—*(a)* In the event of an emergency or the development of unforeseen circumstances threatening the operations of the Fund, the Executive Directors by unanimous vote may suspend for a period of not more than one hundred twenty days the operation of any of the following provisions:

(i) Article IV, Sections 3 and 4 *(b)*.

(ii) Article V, Sections 2, 3, 7, 8 *(a)* and *(f)*.

(iii) Article VI, Section 2.

(iv) Article XI, Section 1.

(b) Simultaneously with any decision to suspend the operation of any of the foregoing provisions, the Executive Directors shall call a meeting of the Board of Governors for the earliest practicable date.

(c) The Executive Directors may not extend any suspension beyond one hundred twenty days. Such suspension may be extended, however, for an additional period of not more than two hundred forty days, if the Board of Governors by a four-fifths majority of the total voting power so decides, but it may not be further extended except by amendment of this Agreement pursuant to Article XVII.

(d) The Executive Directors may, by a majority of the total voting power, terminate such suspension at any time.

SEC. 2. *Liquidation of the Fund.*—*(a)* The Fund may not be liquidated except by decision of the Board of Governors. In an emergency, if the Executive Directors decide that liquidation of the Fund may be necessary, they may temporarily suspend all transactions, pending decision by the Board.

(b) If the Board of Governors decides to liquidate the Fund, the Fund shall forthwith cease to engage in any activities except those incidental to the orderly collection and liquidation of its assets and the settlement of its liabilities, and all obligations of members under this Agreement shall cease except those set out in this Article, in Article XVIII, paragraph *(c)*, in Schedule D, paragraph 7, and in Schedule E.

(c) Liquidation shall be administered in accordance with the provisions of Schedule E.

ARTICLE XVII. AMENDMENTS

(a) Any proposal to introduce modifications in this Agreement, whether emanating from a member, a governor or the Executive Directors, shall be communicated to the chairman of the Board of Governors who shall bring the proposal before the Board. If the proposed amendment is approved by the Board the Fund shall, by circular letter or telegram, ask all members whether they accept the proposed amendment. When three-fifths of the members, having four-fifths of the total voting power, have accepted the proposed amendment, the Fund shall certify the fact by a formal communication addressed to all members.

(b) Notwithstanding *(a)* above, acceptance by all members is required in the case of any amendment modifying

(i) the right to withdraw from the Fund (Article XV, Section 1);

(ii) the provision that no change in a member's quota shall be made without its consent (Article III, Section 2);

(iii) the provision that no change may be made in the par value of a member's currency except on the proposal of that member (Article IV, Section 5 *(b)*).

(c) Amendments shall enter into force for all members three months after the date of the formal communication unless a shorter period is specified in the circular or letter or telegram.

ARTICLE XVIII. INTERPRETATION

(a) Any question of interpretation of the provisions of this Agreement arising between any member and the Fund or between any members of the Fund shall be submitted to the Executive Directors for their decision. If the question particularly affects any member not entitled to appoint an executive director it shall be entitled to representation in accordance with Article XII, Section 3 *(j)*.

(b) In any case where the Executive Directors have given a decision under *(a)* above, any member may require that the question be referred to the Board of Governors, whose decision shall be final. Pending the result of the reference to the Board the Fund may, so far as it deems necessary, act on the basis of the decision of the Executive Directors.

(c) Whenever a disagreement arises between the Fund and a member which has withdrawn, or between the Fund and any member during liquidation of the Fund, such disagreement shall be submitted to arbitration by a tribunal of three arbitrators, one appointed by the Fund, another by the member or withdrawing member and an umpire who, unless the parties otherwise agree, shall be appointed by the President of the Permanent Court of International Justice or such other authority as may have been prescribed by regulation adopted by the Fund. The umpire shall have full power to settle all questions of procedure in any case where the parties are in disagreement with respect thereto.

ARTICLE XIX. EXPLANATION OF TERMS

In interpreting the provisions of this Agreement the Fund and its members shall be guided by the following:

(a) A member's monetary reserves means its net official holdings of gold, of convertible currencies of other members, and of the currencies of such non-members as the Fund may specify.

(*b*) The official holdings of a member means central holdings (that is, the holdings of its Treasury, central bank, stabilization fund, or similar fiscal agency).

(*c*) The holdings of other official institutions or other banks within its territories may, in any particular case, be deemed by the Fund, after consultation with the member, to be official holdings to the extent that they are substantially in excess of working balances; provided that for the purpose of determining whether, in a particular case, holdings are in excess of working balances, there shall be deducted from such holdings amounts of currency due to official institutions and banks in the territories of members or non-members specified under (*d*) below.

(*d*) A member's holdings of convertible currencies means its holdings of the currencies of other members which are not availing themselves of the transitional arrangements under Article XIV, Section 2, together with its holdings of the currencies of such non-members as the Fund may from time to time specify. The term currency for this purpose includes without limitation coins, paper money, bank balances, bank acceptances, and government obligations issued with a maturity not exceeding twelve months.

(*e*) A member's monetary reserves shall be calculated by deducting from its central holdings the currency liabilities to the Treasuries, central banks, stabilization funds, or similar fiscal agencies of other members or non-members specified under (*d*) above, together with similiar liabilities to other official institutions and other banks in the territories of members, or non-members specified under (*d*) above. To these net holdings shall be added the sums deemed to be official holdings of other official institutions and other banks under (*c*) above.

(*f*) The Fund's holdings of the currency of a member shall include any securities accepted by the Fund under Article III, Section 5.

(*g*) The Fund, after consultation with a member which is availing itself of the transitional arrangements under Article XIV, Section 2, may deem holdings of the currency of that member which carry specified rights of conversion into another currency or into gold to be holdings of convertible currency for the purpose of the calculation of monetary reserves.

(*h*) For the purpose of calculating gold subscriptions under Article III, Section 3, a member's net official holdings of gold and United States dollars shall consist of its official holdings of gold and United States currency after deducting central holdings of its currency by other countries and holdings of its currency by other official institutions and other banks if these holdings carry specified rights of conversion into gold or United States currency.

(*i*) Payments for current transactions means payments which are not for the purpose of transferring capital, and includes, without limitation:

(1) All payments due in connection with foreign trade, other current business, including services, and normal short-term banking and credit facilities;

(2) Payments due as interest on loans and as net income from other investments;

(3) Payments of moderate amount for amortization of loans or for depreciation of direct investments;

(4) Moderate remittances for family living expenses.

The Fund may, after consultation with the members concerned, determine whether certain specific transactions are to be considered current transactions or capital transactions.

ARTICLE XX. FINAL PROVISIONS

SECTION 1. *Entry into force.*—This Agreement shall enter into force when it has been signed on behalf of governments having sixty-five percent of the total of the quotas set forth in Schedule A and when the instruments referred to in Section 2 *(a)* of this Article have been deposited on their behalf, but in no event shall this Agreement enter into force before May 1, 1945.

SEC. 2. *Signature.*—*(a)* Each government on whose behalf this Agreement is signed shall deposit with the Government of the United States of America an instrument setting forth that it has accepted this Agreement in accordance with its law and has taken all steps necessary to enable it to carry out all of its obligations under this Agreement.

(b) Each government shall become a member of the Fund as from the date of the deposit on its behalf of the instrument referred to in *(a)* above, except that no government shall become a member before this Agreement enters into force under Section 1 of this Article.

(c) The Government of the United States of America shall inform the governments of all countries whose names are set forth in Schedule A, and all governments whose membership is approved in accordance with Article II, Section 2, of all signatures of this Agreement and of the deposit of all instruments referred to in *(a)* above.

(d) At the time this Agreement is signed on its behalf, each government shall transmit to the Government of the United States of America one one-hundredth of one percent of its total subscription in gold or United States dollars for the purpose of meeting administrative expenses of the Fund. The Government of the United States of America shall hold such funds in a special deposit account and shall transmit them to the Board of Governors of the Fund when the initial meeting has been called under Section 3 of this Article. If this Agreement has not come into force by December 31, 1945, the Government of the United States of America shall return such funds to the governments that transmitted them.

(e) This Agreement shall remain open for signature at Washington on behalf of the governments of the countries whose names are set forth in Schedule A until December 31, 1945.

(f) After December 31, 1945, this Agreement shall be open for signature on behalf of the government of any country whose membership has been approved in accordance with Article II, Section 2.

(g) By their signature of this Agreement, all governments accept it both on their own behalf and in respect of all their colonies, overseas territories, all territories under their protection, suzerainty, or authority and all territories in respect of which they exercise a mandate.

(h) In the case of governments whose metropolitan territories have been under enemy occupation, the deposit of the instrument referred to in *(a)* above may be delayed until one hundred eighty days after the date on which these territories have been liberated. If, however, it is not deposited by any such government before the expiration of this period the signature affixed on behalf of that government shall become void and the portion of its subscription paid under *(d)* above shall be returned to it.

(i) Paragraphs *(d)* and *(h)* shall come into force with regard to each signatory government as from the date of its signature.

Sec. 3. *Inauguration of the Fund.—(a)* As soon as this Agreement enters into force under Section 1 of this Article, each member shall appoint a governor and the member having the largest quota shall call the first meeting of the Board of Governors.

(b) At the first meeting of the Board of Governors, arrangements shall be made for the selection of provisional executive directors. The governments of the five countries for which the largest quotas are set forth in Schedule A shall appoint provisional executive directors. If one or more of such governments have not become members, the executive directorships they would be entitled to fill shall remain vacant until they become members, or until January 1, 1946, whichever is the earlier. Seven provisional executive directors shall be elected in accordance with the provisions of Schedule C and shall remain in office until the date of the first regular election of executive directors which shall be held as soon as practicable after January 1, 1946.

(c) The Board of Governors may delegate to the provisional executive directors any powers except those which may not be delegated to the Executive Directors.

Sec. 4. *Initial determination of par values.—(a)* When the Fund is of the opinion that it will shortly be in a position to begin exchange transactions, it shall so notify the members and shall request each member to communicate within thirty days the par value of its currency based on the rates of exchange prevailing on the sixtieth day before the entry into force of this Agreement. No member whose metropolitan territory has been occupied by the enemy shall be required to make such a communication while that territory is a theater of major hostilities or for such period thereafter as the Fund may determine. When such a member communicates the par value of its currency the provisions of *(d)* below shall apply.

(b) The par value communicated by a member whose metropolitan territory has not been occupied by the enemy shall be the par value of that member's currency for the purposes of this Agreement unless, within ninety days after the request referred to in *(a)* above has been received, (i) the member notifies the Fund that it regards the par value as unsatisfactory, or (ii) the Fund notifies the member that in its opinion the par value cannot be maintained without causing recourse to the Fund on the part of that member or others on a scale prejudicial to the Fund and to members. When notification is given under (i) or (ii) above, the Fund and the member shall, within a period determined by the Fund in the light of all relevant circumstances, agree upon a suitable par value for that currency. If the Fund and the member do not agree within the period so determined, the member shall be deemed to have withdrawn from the Fund on the date when the period expires.

(c) When the par value of a member's currency has been established under *(b)* above, either by the expiration of ninety days without notification, or by agreement after notification, the member shall be eligible to buy from the Fund the currencies of other members to the full extent permitted in this Agreement, provided that the Fund has begun exchange transactions.

(d) In the case of a member whose metropolitan territory has been occupied by the enemy, the provisions of *(b)* above shall apply, subject to the following modifications:

(i) The period of ninety days shall be extended so as to end on a date to be fixed by agreement between the Fund and the member.

(ii) Within the extended period the member may, if the Fund has begun exchange transactions, buy from the Fund with its currency the currencies of other members, but only under such conditions and in such amounts as may be prescribed by the Fund.

(iii) At any time before the date fixed under (i) above, changes may be made by agreement with the Fund in the par value communicated under *(a)* above.

(e) If a member whose metropolitan territory has been occupied by the enemy adopts a new monetary unit before the date to be fixed under *(d)* (i) above, the par value fixed by that member for the new unit shall be communicated to the Fund and the provisions of *(d)* above shall apply.

(f) Changes in par values agreed with the Fund under this Section shall not be taken into account in determining whether a proposed change falls within (i), (ii), or (iii) of Article IV, Section 5 *(c)*.

(g) A member communicating to the Fund a par value for the currency of its metropolitan territory shall simultaneously communicate a value, in terms of that currency, for each separate currency, where such exists, in the territories in respect of which it has accepted this Agreement under Section 2 *(g)* of this Article, but no member shall be required to make a communication for the separate currency of a territory which has been occupied by the enemy while that territory is a theater of major hostilities or for such period thereafter as the Fund may determine. On the basis of the par value so communicated, the Fund shall compute the par value of each separate currency. A communication or notification to the Fund under *(a)*, *(b)* or *(d)* above regarding the par value of a currency, shall also be deemed, unless the contrary is stated, to be a communication or notification regarding the par value of all the separate currencies referred to above. Any member may, however, make a communication or notification relating to the metropolitan or any of the separate currencies alone. If the member does so, the provisions of the preceding paragraphs (including *(d)* above, if a territory where a separate currency exists has been occupied by the enemy) shall apply to each of these currencies separately.

(h) The Fund shall begin exchange transactions at such date as it may determine after members having sixty-five percent of the total of the quotas set forth in Schedule A have become eligible, in accordance with the preceding paragraphs of this Section, to purchase the currencies of other members, but in no event until after major hostilities in Europe have ceased.

(i) The Fund may postpone exchange transactions with any member if its circumstances are such that, in the opinion of the Fund, they would lead to use of the resources of the Fund in a manner contrary to the purposes of this Agreement or prejudicial to the Fund or the members.

(j) The par values of the currencies of governments which indicate their desire to become members after December 31, 1945, shall be determined in accordance with the provisions of Article II, Section 2.

Done at Washington, in a single copy which shall remain deposited in the archives of the Government of the United States of America, which shall transmit certified copies to all governments whose names are set forth in Schedule A and to all governments whose membership is approved in accordance with Article II, Section 2.

SCHEDULE A. QUOTAS

[In millions of United States dollars]

Australia	200
Belgium	225
Bolivia	10
Brazil	150
Canada	300
Chile	50
China	550
Colombia	50
Costa Rica	5
Cuba	50
Czechoslovakia	125
Denmark	[1]
Dominican Republic	5
Ecuador	5
Egypt	45
El Salvador	2.5
Ethiopia	6
France	450
Greece	40
Guatemala	5
Haiti	5
Honduras	2.5
Iceland	1
India	400
Iran	25
Iraq	8
Liberia	.5
Luxembourg	10
Mexico	90
Netherlands	275
New Zealand	50
Nicaragua	2
Norway	50
Panama	.5
Paraguay	2
Peru	25
Philippine Commonwealth	15
Poland	125
Union of South Africa	100
Union of Soviet Socialist Republics	1,200
United Kingdom	1,300
United States	2,750
Uruguay	15
Venezuela	15
Yugoslavia	60
Total	8,800

[1] The quota of Denmark shall be determined by the Fund after the Danish Government has declared its readiness to sign this Agreement but before signature takes place.

SCHEDULE B. PROVISIONS WITH RESPECT TO REPURCHASE BY A MEMBER OF ITS CURRENCY HELD BY THE FUND

1. In determining the extent to which repurchase of a member's currency from the Fund under Article V, Section 7 *(b)*, shall be made with each type of monetary reserve, that is, with gold and with each convertible currency, the following rule, subject to 2 below, shall apply:

(a) If the member's monetary reserves have not increased during the year, the amount payable to the Fund shall be distributed among all types of reserves in proportion to the member's holdings thereof at the end of the year.

(b) If the member's monetary reserves have increased during the year, a part of the amount payable to the Fund equal to one-half of the increase shall be distributed among those types of reserves which have increased in proportion to the amount by which each of them has increased. The remainder of the sum payable to the Fund shall be distributed among all types of reserves in proportion to the member's remaining holdings thereof.

(c) If after all the repurchases required under Article V, Section 7 *(b)*, had been made, the result would exceed any of the limits specified in Article V, Section 7 *(c)*, the Fund shall require such repurchases to be made by the members proportionately in such manner that the limits will not be exceeded.

2. The Fund shall not acquire the currency of any non-member under Article V, Section 7 *(b)* and *(c)*.

3. In calculating monetary reserves and the increase in monetary reserves during any year for the purpose of Article V, Section 7 *(b)* and *(c)*, no account shall be taken, unless deductions have otherwise been made by the member for such holdings, of any increase in those monetary reserves which is due to currency previously inconvertible having become convertible during the year; or to holdings which are the proceeds of a long-term or medium-term loan contracted during the year; or to holdings which have been transferred or set aside for repayment of a loan during the subsequent year.

4. In the case of members whose metropolitan territories have been occupied by the enemy, gold newly produced during the five years after the entry into force of this Agreement from mines located within their metropolitan territories shall not be included in computations of their monetary reserves or of increases in their monetary reserves.

SCHEDULE C. ELECTION OF EXECUTIVE DIRECTORS

1. The election of the elective executive directors shall be by ballot of the governors eligible to vote under Article XII, Section 3 *(b)* (iii) and (iv).

2. In balloting for the five directors to be elected under Article XII, Section 3 *(b)* (iii), each of the governors eligible to vote shall cast for one person all of the votes to which he is entitled under Article XII, Section 5 *(a)*. The five persons receiving the greatest number of votes shall be directors, provided that no person who received less than nineteen percent of the total number of votes that can be cast (eligible votes) shall be considered elected.

3. When five persons are not elected on the first ballot, a second ballot shall be held in which the person who received the lowest number of votes shall be ineligible for election and in which there shall vote only *(a)* those governors who voted in the first ballot for a person not elected, and *(b)* those governors whose votes for a person elected are deemed under 4 below to have raised the votes cast for that person above twenty percent of the eligible votes.

4. In determining whether the votes cast by a governor are to be deemed to have raised the total of any person above twenty percent of the eligible votes the twenty percent shall be deemed to include, first, the votes of the governor casting the largest number of votes for such person, then the votes of the governor casting the next largest number, and so on until twenty percent is reached.

5. Any governor part of whose votes must be counted in order to raise the total of any person above nineteen percent shall be considered as casting all of his votes for such person even if the total votes for such person thereby exceed twenty percent.

6. If, after the second ballot, five persons have not been elected, further ballots shall be held on the same principles until five persons have been elected, provided that after four persons are elected, the fifth may be elected by a simple majority of the remaining votes and shall be deemed to have been elected by all such votes.

7. The directors to be elected by the American Republics under Article XII, Section 3 *(b)* (iv) shall be elected as follows:

(a) Each of the directors shall be elected separately.

(b) In the election of the first director, each governor representing an American Republic eligible to participate in the election shall cast for one person all the votes

to which he is entitled. The person receiving the largest number of votes shall be elected provided that he has received not less than forty-five percent of the total votes.

(c) If no person is elected on the first ballot, further ballots shall be held, in each of which the person receiving the lowest number of votes shall be eliminated, until one person receives a number of votes sufficient for election under *(b)* above.

(d) Governors whose votes contributed to the election of the first director shall take no part in the election of the second director.

(e) Persons who did not succeed in the first election shall not be ineligible for election as the second director.

(f) A majority of the votes which can be cast shall be required for election of the second director. If at the first ballot no person receives a majority, further ballots shall be held in each of which the person receiving the lowest number of votes shall be eliminated, until some person obtains a majority.

(g) The second director shall be deemed to have been elected by all the votes which could have been cast in the ballot securing his election.

SCHEDULE D. SETTLEMENT OF ACCOUNTS WITH MEMBERS WITHDRAWING

1. The Fund shall be obligated to pay to a member withdrawing an amount equal to its quota, plus any other amounts due to it from the Fund, less any amounts due to the Fund, including charges accruing after the date of its withdrawal; but no payment shall be made until six months after the date of withdrawal. Payments shall be made in the currency of the withdrawing member.

2. If the Fund's holdings of the currency of the withdrawing member are not sufficient to pay the net amount due from the Fund, the balance shall be paid in gold, or in such other manner as may be agreed. If the Fund and the withdrawing member do not reach agreement within six months of the date of withdrawal, the currency in question held by the Fund shall be paid forthwith to the withdrawing member. Any balance due shall be paid in ten half-yearly installments during the ensuing five years. Each such installment shall be paid, at the option of the Fund, either in the currency of the withdrawing member acquired after its withdrawal or by the delivery of gold.

3. If the Fund fails to meet any installment which is due in accordance with the preceding paragraphs, the withdrawing member shall be entitled to require the Fund to pay the installment in any currency held by the Fund with the exception of any currency which has been declared scarce under Article VII, Section 3.

4. If the Fund's holdings of the currency of a withdrawing member exceed the amount due to it, and if agreement on the method of settling accounts is not reached within six months of the date of withdrawal, the former member shall be obligated to redeem such excess currency in gold or, at its option, in the currencies of members which at the time of redemption are convertible. Redemption shall be made at the parity existing at the time of withdrawal from the Fund. The withdrawing member shall complete redemption within five years of the date of withdrawal, or within such longer period as may be fixed by the Fund, but shall not be required to redeem in any half-yearly period more than one-tenth of the Fund's excess holdings of its currency at the date of withdrawal plus further acquisitions of the currency during such half-

yearly period. If the withdrawing member does not fulfill this obligation, the Fund may in an orderly manner liquidate in any market the amount of currency which should have been redeemed.

5. Any member desiring to obtain the currency of a member which has withdrawn shall acquire it by purchase from the Fund, to the extent that such member has access to the resources of the Fund and that such currency is available under 4 above.

6. The withdrawing member guarantees the unrestricted use at all times of the currency disposed of under 4 and 5 above for the purchase of goods or for payment of sums due to it or to persons within its territories. It shall compensate the Fund for any loss resulting from the difference between the par value of its currency on the date of withdrawal and the value realized by the Fund on disposal under 4 and 5 above.

7. In the event of the Fund going into liquidation under Article XVI, Section 2, within six months of the date on which the member withdraws, the account between the Fund and that government shall be settled in accordance with Article XVI, Section 2, and Schedule E.

SCHEDULE E. ADMINISTRATION OF LIQUIDATION

1. In the event of liquidation the liabilities of the Fund other than the repayment of subscriptions shall have priority in the distribution of the assets of the Fund. In meeting each such liability the Fund shall use its assets in the following order:

(*a*) the currency in which the liability is payable;

(*b*) gold;

(*c*) all other currencies in proportion, so far as may be practicable, to the quotas of the members.

2. After the discharge of the Fund's liabilities in accordance with 1 above, the balance of the Fund's assets shall be distributed and apportioned as follows:

(*a*) The Fund shall distribute its holdings of gold among the members whose currencies are held by the Fund in amounts less than their quotas. These members shall share the gold so distributed in the proportions of the amounts by which their quotas exceed the Fund's holdings of their currencies.

(*b*) The Fund shall distribute to each member one-half the Fund's holdings of its currency but such distribution shall not exceed fifty percent of its quota.

(*c*) The Fund shall apportion the remainder of its holdings of each currency among all the members in proportion to the amounts due to each member after the distributions under (*a*) and (*b*) above.

3. Each member shall redeem the holdings of its currency apportioned to other members under 2 (*c*) above, and shall agree with the Fund within three months after a decision to liquidate upon an orderly procedure for such redemption.

4. If a member has not reached agreement with the Fund within the three-month period referred to in 3 above, the Fund shall use the currencies of other members apportioned to that member under 2 (*c*) above to redeem the currency of that member apportioned to other members. Each currency apportioned to a member which has not reached agreement shall be used, so far as possible, to redeem its currency apportioned to the members which have made agreements with the Fund under 3 above.

5. If a member has reached agreement with the Fund in accordance with 3 above, the Fund shall use the currencies of other members apportioned to that member under

2 (*c*) above to redeem the currency of that member apportioned to other members which have made agreements with the Fund under 3 above. Each amount so redeemed shall be redeemed in the currency of the member to which it was apportioned.

6. After carrying out the preceding paragraphs, the Fund shall pay to each member the remaining currencies held for its account.

7. Each member whose currency has been distributed to other members under 6 above shall redeem such currency in gold or, at its option, in the currency of the member requesting redemption, or in such other manner as may be agreed between them. If the members involved do not otherwise agree, the member obligated to redeem shall complete redemption within five years of the date of distribution, but shall not be required to redeem in any half-yearly period more than one-tenth of the amount distributed to each other member. If the member does not fulfill this obligation, the amount of currency which should have been redeemed may be liquidated in an orderly manner in any market.

8. Each member whose currency has been distributed to other members under 6 above guarantees the unrestricted use of such currency at all times for the purchase of goods or for payment of sums due to it or to persons in its territories. Each member so obligated agrees to compensate other members for any loss resulting from the difference between the par value of its currency on the date of the decision to liquidate the Fund and the value realized by such members on disposal of its currency.

Agreement with the United Nations

The Agreement reproduced below was approved by the Board of Governors of the Fund on September 17, 1947 and by the General Assembly of the United Nations on November 15, 1947. Accordingly, the Agreement came into force on November 15, 1947.

Agreement Between the United Nations and the International Monetary Fund

(November 15, 1947)

ARTICLE I

General

1. This agreement, which is entered into by the United Nations pursuant to the provisions of Article 63 of its Charter, and by the International Monetary Fund (hereinafter called the Fund), pursuant to the provisions of article X of its Articles of Agreement, is intended to define the terms on which the United Nations and the Fund shall be brought into relationship.

2. The Fund is a specialized agency established by agreement among its member governments and having wide international responsibilities, as defined in its Articles of Agreement, in economic and related fields within the meaning of Article 57 of the Charter of the United Nations. By reason of the nature of its international responsibilities and the terms of its Articles of Agreement, the Fund is, and is required to function as, an independent international organization.

3. The United Nations and the Fund are subject to certain necessary limitations for the safeguarding of confidential material furnished to them by their members or others, and nothing in this agreement shall be construed to require either of them to furnish any information the furnishing of which would, in its judgment, constitute a violation of the confidence of any of its members or anyone from whom it shall have received such information, or which would otherwise interfere with the orderly conduct of its operations.

ARTICLE II

Reciprocal representation

1. Representatives of the United Nations shall be entitled to attend, and to participate without vote in, meetings of the Board of Governors of the Fund. Representatives of the United Nations shall be invited to participate without vote in meetings especially called by the Fund for the particular purpose of considering the United Nations point of view in matters of concern to the United Nations.

2. Representatives of the Fund shall be entitled to attend meetings of the General Assembly of the United Nations for purposes of consultation.

3. Representatives of the Fund shall be entitled to attend, and to participate without vote in, meetings of the committees of the General Assembly, meetings of the Economic and Social Council, of the Trusteeship Council and of their respective subsidiary bodies, dealing with matters in which the Fund has an interest.

4. Sufficient advance notice of these meetings and their agenda shall be given so that, in consultation, arrangements can be made for adequate representation.

Article III

Proposal of agenda items

In preparing the agenda for meetings of the Board of Governors, the Fund will give due consideration to the inclusion in the agenda of items proposed by the United Nations. Similarly, the Council and its commissions and the Trusteeship Council will give due consideration to the inclusion in their agenda of items proposed by the Fund.

Article IV

Consultation and recommendations

1. The United Nations and the Fund shall consult together and exchange views on matters of mutual interest.

2. Neither organization, nor any of their subsidiary bodies, will present any formal recommendations to the other without reasonable prior consultation with regard thereto. Any formal recommendations made by either organization after such consultation will be considered as soon as possible by the appropriate organ of the other.

Article V

Exchange of information

The United Nations and the Fund will, to the fullest extent practicable and subject to paragraph 3 of article I, arrange for the current exchange of information and publications of mutual interest, and the furnishing of special reports and studies upon request.

Article VI

Security Council

1. The Fund takes note of the obligation assumed, under paragraph 2 of Article 48 of the United Nations Charter, by such of its members as are also Members of the United Nations, to carry out the decisions of the Security Council through their action in the appropriate specialized agencies of which they are members, and will, in the conduct of its activities, have due regard for decisions of the Security Council under Articles 41 and 42 of the United Nations Charter.

2. The Fund agrees to assist the Security Council by furnishing to it information in accordance with the provisions of article V of this agreement.

Article VII

Assistance to the Trusteeship Council

The Fund agrees to co-operate with the Trusteeship Council in the carrying out of its functions by furnishing information and technical assistance upon request, and in such other similar ways as may be consistent with the Articles of Agreement of the Fund.

Article VIII

International Court of Justice

The General Assembly of the United Nations hereby authorizes the Fund to request advisory opinions of the International Court of Justice on any legal questions arising within the scope of the Fund's activities other than questions relating to the relationship between the Fund and the United Nations or any specialized agency. Whenever the Fund shall request the Court for an advisory opinion, the Fund will inform the Economic and Social Council of the request.

Article IX

Statistical services

1. In the interests of efficiency and for the purpose of reducing the burden on national Governments and other organizations, the United Nations and the Fund agree to co-operate in eliminating unnecessary duplication in the collection, analysis, publication and dissemination of statistical information.

2. The Fund recognizes the United Nations as the central agency for the collection, analysis, publication, standardization and improvement of statistics serving the general purposes of international organizations, without prejudice to the right of the Fund to concern itself with any statistics so far as they may be essential for its own purposes.

3. The United Nations recognizes the Fund as the appropriate agency for the collection, analysis, publication, standardization and improvement of statistics within its special sphere, without prejudice to the right of the United Nations to concern itself with any statistics so far as they may be essential for its own purposes.

4. *(a)* In its statistical activities the Fund agrees to give full consideration to the requirements of the United Nations and of the specialized agencies.

(b) In its statistical activities the United Nations agrees to give full consideration to the requirements of the Fund.

5. The United Nations and the Fund agree to furnish each other promptly with all their non-confidential statistical information.

Article X

Administrative relationships

1. The United Nations and the Fund will consult from time to time concerning personnel and other administrative matters of mutual interest, with a view to securing as much uniformity in these matters as they shall find practicable and to assuring the most efficient use of the services and facilities of the two organizations. These consultations shall include determination of the most equitable manner in which special services furnished by one organization to the other should be financed.

2. To the extent consistent with the provisions of this agreement, the Fund will participate in the work of the Co-ordination Committee and its subsidiary bodies.

3. The Fund will furnish to the United Nations copies of the annual report and the quarterly financial statements prepared by the Fund pursuant to section 7 *(a)* of article V of its Articles of Agreement. The United Nations agrees that, in the interpretation of paragraph 3 of Article 17 of the United Nations Charter it will take into consideration that the Fund does not rely for its annual budget upon contributions from its members, and that the appropriate authorities of the Fund enjoy full autonomy in deciding the form and content of such budget.

4. The officials of the Fund shall have the right to use the *laissez-passer* of the United Nations in accordance with special arrangements to be negotiated between the Secretary-General of the United Nations and the competent authorities of the Fund.

Article XI

Agreements with other Organizations

The Fund will inform the Economic and Social Council of any formal agreement which the Fund shall enter into with any specialized agency, and in particular agrees to inform the Council of the nature and scope of any such agreement before it is concluded.

Article XII

Liaison

1. The United Nations and the Fund agree to the foregoing provisions in the belief that they will contribute to the maintenance of effective co-operation between the two organizations. Each agrees that it will establish within its own organization such administrative machinery as may be necessary to make the liaison, as provided for in this agreement, fully effective.

2. The arrangements provided for in the foregoing articles of this agreement shall apply, as far as is appropriate, to relations between such branch or regional offices as may be established by the two organizations, as well as between their central machinery.

Article XIII

Miscellaneous

1. The Secretary-General of the United Nations and the Managing Director of the Fund are authorized to make such supplementary arrangements as they shall deem necessary or proper to carry fully into effect the purposes of this agreement.

2. This agreement shall be subject to revision by agreement between the United Nations and the Fund from the date of its entry into force.

3. This agreement may be terminated by either party thereto on six months' written notice to the other party, and thereupon all rights and obligations of both parties hereunder shall cease.

4. This agreement shall come into force when it shall have been approved by the General Assembly of the United Nations and the Board of Governors of the Fund.

Selected Decisions

The decisions reproduced below are those contained in Selected Decisions of the Executive Directors and Selected Documents, *Third Issue, January 1965. They comprise the decisions of a general nature which have been cited in Volumes I and II above. They are arranged in the order of the Articles of Agreement to which they refer, and not chronologically.*

Decisions embodied in Rules and Regulations are not included here; they will be found in the document following this one (beginning on p. 287).

Selected Decisions of the Executive Directors (As at December 31, 1965)

CONTENTS

ARTICLE III, SECTION 2

ADJUSTMENT OF QUOTAS

The first interval of five years, at the end of which the Fund shall review the quotas of the members in accordance with Article III, Section 2, began on the date when the Fund Agreement, in accordance with Article XX, Section 1, entered into force: i.e. on December 27, 1945.

Decision No. 408-2
March 11, 1949

ARTICLE III, SECTION 3

SUBSCRIPTIONS

NET OFFICIAL HOLDINGS: PRINCIPLES OF INTERPRETATION

In order to ensure the uniform application of the relevant Articles of Agreement as they apply to determinations of members' net official holdings of gold and U.S. dollars for the purposes of Article III, Section 3 (b) (ii), the Fund adopts or reaffirms the following principles of interpretation for the indicated provisions of the Fund Agreement:

(a) *Article III, Section 3 (b)* : "Each member shall pay in gold, as a minimum, the smaller of

(i) twenty-five per cent of its quota; or

(ii) ten per cent of its net official holdings of gold and United States dollars as at the date when the Fund notifies members under Article XX, Section 4 (a), that it will shortly be in a position to begin exchange transactions.

Each member shall furnish to the Fund the data necessary to determine its net official holdings of gold and United States dollars."

(1) The concept of "holdings" of gold or United States dollars involves the ownership of gold or United States dollars.

(2) A claim to gold or dollars, unsupported by title to them, is not a "holdings."

(3) "United States dollars" means "without limitation coins, paper money, bank balances, bank acceptances, and government obligations issued with a maturity not exceeding twelve months." This definition appears in Article XIX (d) and has been adopted by analogy in the calculation of net official holdings. The government obligations referred to must have been issued with an original maturity not exceeding twelve months, and it does not suffice that a government obligation will simply mature within twelve months from September 12, 1946.

(4) Dollars drawn by a member under a loan and in its ownership, for example, because deposited in a bank account which it owns, are part of its "holdings." Dollars which a member has not drawn under a loan agreement or commitment and which it does not yet own, although it may later get ownership of them, are not a "holding."

(5) The usability of gold or dollars for the payment of the gold subscription is not necessary in order to constitute "holdings." A member does not pay 10 per cent of each item of gold or dollars, but the equivalent of 10 per cent of its total "holdings" of gold and dollars. Thus, segregated dollar balances are "holdings." So, too, are gold or dollars blocked under wartime freezing arrangements, if a member has title to them. This means, in the case of gold, that the member has title to specific gold (e.g., earmarked gold) or to a fixed share of specific gold (e.g., one-quarter of earmarked gold). There is no "holding" if a member has merely a claim to unidentified gold (e.g., such looted gold as may be discovered and restored to it) or to an uncertain share of specific or unidentified gold (e.g., a share of such looted gold as may be or has been recovered, to be determined in proportion to all claims).

(6) Under a pledge of gold or dollars, title remains in the pledgor, for which reason pledged gold or dollars are the "holdings" of the pledgor.

(7) Since local law cannot override international obligations, gold or dollars are "holdings" even though inalienable under local law or allocated to some special purpose.

(8) Gold must be valued in accordance with Article IV, Section 1.

(9) If a member had no "holdings" of gold or dollars on September 12, 1946, its total subscription will be payable in its own currency.

(b) *Article III, Section 3 (d)*: "If the net official holdings of gold and United States dollars of any member as at the date referred to in (b) (ii) above are not ascertainable because its territories have been occupied by the enemy, the Fund shall fix an appropriate alternative date for determining such holdings. If such date is later than that on which the country becomes eligible under Article XX, Section 4 (c) or (d), to buy currencies from the Fund, the Fund and the member shall agree on a provisional gold payment to be made under (b) above, and the balance of the member's subscription shall be paid in the member's currency, subject to appropriate adjustment between the member and the Fund when the net official holdings have been ascertained."

(1) Where a member was occupied by the enemy and its net official holdings of gold and United States dollars as of September 12, 1946, are not ascertainable, the Fund may postpone the date as of which the calculation shall be made. This means that some later date may be substituted for September 12, 1946, as the effective date for the purposes of Article III, Section 3 (b) (ii).

(2) The postponement must relate to the determination of the whole of a member's net official holdings of gold and U.S. dollars. That is to say, there cannot be a postponement of only those items whose status on September 12, 1946, cannot be ascertained.

(c) Pertains to Article XIX (b); see p. 270.

(d) Pertains to Article XIX (c); see p. 270.

(e) Pertains to Article XIX (h); see p. 270.

Decision No. 298-3
April 14, 1948

ARTICLE III, SECTION 4

PAYMENTS WHEN QUOTAS ARE CHANGED

INTERPRETATION

It is determined as a matter of interpretation that Art. III, Sec. 4, and not Art. III, Sec. 3, applies to all changes in quotas.

Decision No. 595-3
July 20, 1950

QUOTA INCREASES: GOLD SUBSCRIPTIONS

In connection with any quota increases granted in accordance with the Fund's decision on "Compensatory Financing of Export Fluctuations" and any quota increases granted as the result of requests received before the decision referred to, it is decided:

(a) to recommend to the Board of Governors, where a member represents, for reasons which it shall submit to the Fund, that its reserves should not be reduced by an immediate 25 per cent gold payment, that such member shall be permitted in accordance with an appropriate resolution to have its quota increased in five annual installments, with the right to accelerate the payment of such installments;

(b) to give sympathetic consideration to a request for an exchange transaction up to 25 per cent of the increase by any member which wishes to have the full increase in its quota take effect immediately or to expedite the full increase in its quota if it is paying under the installment schedule. This facility will be available where: (i) the member would encounter undue payments difficulties through the reduction in its reserves by the payment of the 25 per cent gold subscription or of the outstanding balance; and (ii) the request is made within two years after the date of the consent to the increase or, in the case of an increase in installments, within two years after the payment of the first installment; and (iii) the member requesting such an exchange transaction beyond the gold tranche represents that it will make a repurchase corresponding to any drawing in equal annual installments, to commence one year after the drawing and to be completed not later than three years after the drawing.

Decision No. 1529-(63/33)
June 14, 1963

ARTICLE IV, SECTION 1

TRANSACTIONS AND COMPUTATIONS INVOLVING FLUCTUATING CURRENCIES

TRANSACTIONS AND COMPUTATIONS INVOLVING FLUCTUATING CURRENCIES

The Fund has examined certain problems relating to the adjustment of its holdings of fluctuating currencies and to transactions and computations involving such currencies and has come to the following conclusions:

I. The Fund does not intend to apply the rules set forth in II below to its holdings of members' currencies having fluctuating rates when there is no practical interest for the Fund or members to do so. To avoid misunderstanding, it may be useful to point out that these rules do not constitute a formula for dealing with the currencies of countries in which current transactions are conducted at multiple rates.

II. Subject to I above, the following rules are adopted:

Where the foreign exchange value of a currency fluctuates so that exchange transactions in that currency are not based on parity in accordance with Article IV, Section 3, and the Fund decides to apply Article IV, Section 8, computations by the Fund relating to that currency (hereinafter referred to as "fluctuating currency") for the purpose of applying the provisions of the Articles of Agreement of the Fund will be made as follows:

1. (i) Computations will be based on the mid-point between the highest rate and the lowest rate for the United States dollar quoted, for cable transfers for spot delivery, in the main financial center of the country of the fluctuating currency on the day specified in sub-paragraph (ii) below; provided, however, that when prescribed by sub-paragraph (iii) below computations will be based on the mid-point between the highest rate and the lowest rate for the fluctuating currency quoted in New York for cable transfers for spot delivery. Arrangements will be made with the Fund's depository in the country of the appropriate exchange market as determined hereunder to communicate to the Fund the rates referred to in this sub-paragraph (i).

(ii) For the purpose of sub-paragraph (i) the specified day will be:

(a) For the sale or purchase by the Fund of a fluctuating currency in exchange for another currency, or the purchase of gold by the Fund under Article V, Section 6 (a), or voluntary repurchase, the last business day, in the main financial center of the country of the fluctuating currency, before the Fund instructs its depository to transfer or receive the fluctuating currency.

(b) For computations for the purpose of Article V, Section 7 (b) or Article V, Section 8 (f), the day as of which the computation is made.

(iii) If a mid-point cannot be determined in the main financial center of the country of the fluctuating currency in accordance with sub-paragraph (i) for the day specified in sub-paragraph (ii), there will be substituted therefor the mid-point for the fluctuating currency in New York determined in accordance with sub-paragraph (i) for the same calendar day. If no such mid-point can be determined for that day, there will then be substituted, to the extent necessary, first the previous business day in the main financial center of the country of the fluctuating currency, and secondly the same calendar day in New York. This procedure will be followed to the extent necessary, until a mid-point is determined in accordance with sub-paragraph (i), except where the Fund decides to make a special determination under paragraph 6 below.

2. Where as the result of the application of paragraph 1 the amount of currency which the Fund has agreed to sell would exceed the amount that the purchasing member is entitled to purchase under Article V, Section 3 (a) (iii), the amount of currency to be sold will be reduced to the amount the purchasing member is entitled to purchase under that provision unless the Fund makes a waiver under Article V, Section 4.

3. The Fund will revalue all of its holdings of a fluctuating currency on the basis of the mid-point employed for a computation under paragraph 1, and such revaluation will take effect as of the day specified for the computation in sub-

paragraph (ii) of paragraph 1. As a minimum, revaluation will be made as of each July 31, October 31, January 31, and April 30.

4. Whenever the Fund revalues its holdings of a fluctuating currency under paragraph 3, it will establish an account receivable or an account payable, as the case may be, in respect of the amount of the currency payable by or to the member under Article IV, Section 8. For the purpose of applying the provisions of the Articles as of any date, the Fund's holdings of the fluctuating currency will be deemed to be its actual holdings plus the balance in any such account receivable or minus the balance in any such account payable as of that date.

5. Any account receivable or payable established under paragraph 4 above will be settled promptly after each July 31, October 31, January 31, and April 30, provided, however, that settlement will not be necessary for any July 31, October 31, or January 31 on which the mid-point as determined under paragraph 1 above does not differ by more than five per cent from the rate for the last settlement. Settlement of any account receivable or payable established under paragraph 4 above will always be made when requested by either the Fund or the member.

6. In any case in which it appears to the Fund that any of the provisions of paragraphs 1 to 5 above are not adequate or satisfactory, the Fund will make a special determination for the treatment of such case.

III. Sections I and II above of this decision shall be communicated to members together with SM/54/25 as amended by SM/54/25, Supplement 1 as an explanatory memorandum.

Decision No. 321-(54/32)
June 15, 1954

TRANSACTIONS AND COMPUTATIONS INVOLVING FLUCTUATING CURRENCIES

The foregoing Decision No. 321-(54/32) was amended as follows:—

1. [Expired.]

2. There shall be added after "Article V, Section 6 (a)," in paragraph II.1 (ii) (a) of Executive Board Decision No. 321-(54/32) the words "or the sale of gold by the Fund under Article VII, Section 2,".

3. [Expired.]

Decision No. 1245-(61/45)
August 4, 1961

TRANSACTIONS AND COMPUTATIONS INVOLVING FLUCTUATING CURRENCIES

Paragraph II.1 (ii) (a) of Executive Board Decision No. 321-(54/32) is amended to read as follows:

For the sale or purchase by the Fund of a fluctuating currency in exchange for another currency, or the purchase of gold by the Fund under Article V, Section 6 (a), or the sale of gold by the Fund under Article VII, Section 2, or voluntary repurchase, or borrowing or the repayment of borrowing under Article VII, Section 2, the last business day in the main financial center of the country of the fluctuating currency, before the Fund instructs its depository to transfer or receive the fluctuating currency.

Decision No. 1283-(61/56)
December 20, 1961

ARTICLE IV, SECTION 2

GOLD

PREMIUM GOLD TRANSACTIONS: STATEMENT TO MEMBERS

The following statement should be communicated to members and made public without delay:

> In June 1947, the Fund issued a statement recommending to its members that they take effective action to prevent external transactions in gold at premium prices, because such transactions tend to undermine exchange stability and to impair monetary reserves. From time to time the Fund has reviewed its recommendations and the effectiveness of the action taken by its members.
>
> Despite the improvement in the payments position of many members, sound gold and exchange policy of members continues to require that to the maximum extent practicable, gold should be held in official reserves rather than go into private hoards. It is only as gold is held in official reserves that it can be used by the monetary authorities to maintain exchange rates and meet balance of payments needs.
>
> However, the Fund's continuous study of the situation in gold-producing and -consuming countries shows that their positions vary so widely as to make it impracticable to expect all members to take uniform measures in order to achieve the objectives of the premium gold statement. Accordingly, while the Fund reaffirms its belief in the economic principles involved and urges the members to support them, the Fund leaves to its members the practical operating decisions involved in their implementation, subject to the provisions of Art. IV, Sec. 2 and other relevant articles of the Articles of Agreement of the I.M.F.

The Fund will continue to collect full information about gold transactions, will watch carefully developments in this field and will be prepared in consultation with members to consider problems relating to exchange stability and any other problems which may arise.

Decision No. 75-(705)
September 28, 1951

For the statement of June 1947, see below, p. 310.

STATEMENT OF POLICY CONCERNING SUBSIDIES FOR GOLD PRODUCTION

The following statement of policy concerning subsidies for the production of gold is adopted, and the Managing Director is asked to send copies to members and release the statement for publication on December 12.

> The International Monetary Fund has a responsibility to see that the gold policies of its members do not undermine or threaten to undermine exchange stability. Consequently every member which proposes to introduce new measures to subsidize the production of gold is under obligation to consult with the Fund on the specific measures to be introduced.
>
> Under Article IV, Section 2, of the Articles of Agreement of the Fund members are prohibited from buying gold at a price above parity plus the prescribed margin. In the view of the Fund, a subsidy in the form of a uniform payment per ounce for all or part of the gold produced would constitute an increase in price which would not be permissible if the total price paid by the member for gold were thereby to

become in excess of parity plus the prescribed margin. Subsidies involving payments in another form may also, depending upon their nature, constitute an increase in price.

Under Article IV, Section 4 (a), each member of the Fund "undertakes to collaborate with the Fund to promote exchange stability, to maintain orderly exchange arrangements with other members, and to avoid competitive exchange alterations." Subsidies on gold production regardless of their form are inconsistent with Article IV, Section 4 (a) if they undermine or threaten to undermine exchange stability. This would be the case, for example, if subsidies were to cast widespread doubt on the uniformity of the monetary value of gold in all member countries.

Subsidies which do not directly affect exchange stability may, nevertheless, contribute directly or indirectly to monetary instability in other countries and hence be of concern to the Fund.

A determination by the Fund that a proposed subsidy is not inconsistent with the foregoing principles will depend upon the circumstances in each case. Moreover, the Fund may find that subsidies which are justified at any one time may, because of changing conditions and changing effects, later prove to be inconsistent with the foregoing principles. In order to carry out its objectives, the Fund will continue to study, and to review with its members, their gold policies and any proposed changes, to determine if they are consonant with the provisions of the Fund Agreement and conducive to a sound international policy regarding gold.

Decision No. 233-2
December 11, 1947

Article IV, Sections 3 and 5

PAR VALUES AND MARGINS

Foreign Exchange Dealings Based on Parity: Article IV, Section 3

Dealings in paper money and coins are deemed to be "other exchange transactions" within the meaning of Article IV, Section 3, whether or not the importation and exportation of such money and coins to and from the country of origin are subject to restrictions. The dealings are in consequence subject to the provisions of that Section. Members shall not permit transactions in such paper money and coins within their territories in a manner or to an extent which will negate the par values agreed with the Fund. Where transactions in fact have such an effect the Fund will be obliged to intervene.

Decision No. 269-2
February 11, 1948

Exchange Dealings and Margins Under Conditions of Increasing Convertibility

The Fund does not object to exchange rates which are within 2 per cent of parity for spot exchange transactions between a member's currency and the currencies of other members taking place within the member's territories, whenever such rates result from the maintenance of margins of no more than 1 per cent from parity for a convertible, including externally convertible, currency.

Decision No. 904-(59/32)
July 24, 1959

INTERPRETATION OF ARTICLES OF AGREEMENT

[A member] has stated its intention to maintain full employment and has requested an interpretation of the Articles of Agreement as to whether steps necessary to protect a member from unemployment of a chronic or persistent character, arising from pressure on its balance of payments, shall be measures necessary to correct a fundamental disequilibrium.

The Executive Directors interpret the Articles of Agreement to mean that steps which are necessary to protect a member from unemployment of a chronic or persistent character, arising from pressure on its balance of payments, are among the measures necessary to correct a fundamental disequilibrium; and that in each instance in which a member proposes a change in the par value of its currency to correct a fundamental disequilibrium the Fund will be required to determine, in the light of all relevant circumstances, whether in its opinion the proposed change is necessary to correct the fundamental disequilibrium.

Pursuant to Decision No. 71-2
September 26, 1946

CHANGES IN PAR VALUES: FUNDAMENTAL DISEQUILIBRIUM

The Fund has authority under Article IV, Section 5 (c) (ii) or (iii), to object to a change in par value proposed by a member when the extent of the proposed change, in the judgment of the Fund, is insufficient to correct a fundamental disequilibrium. The Executive Board recognizes, however, that the extent of the change in par value, necessary to correct a fundamental disequilibrium, cannot be determined with precision and that in reaching a decision on a member's proposal to change its par value, whether during the transitional period or thereafter, the member should be given the benefit of any reasonable doubt. In addition, due consideration should be given the views of the member regarding the political and social consequences of a change in par value greater than the one proposed.

Decision No. 278-3
March 1, 1948

ARTICLE V, SECTIONS 3, 4, AND 5

USE OF FUND'S RESOURCES AND STAND-BY ARRANGEMENTS

USE OF FUND'S RESOURCES: MEANING OF ARTICLE V, SECTION 3 (a) (i)

The word "represents" in Article V, Section 3 (a) (i), means "declares." The member is presumed to have fulfilled the condition mentioned in Article V, Section 3 (a) (i), if it declares that the currency is presently needed for making payments in that currency which are consistent with the provisions of the Agreement. But the Fund may, for good reasons, challenge the correctness of this declaration, on the grounds that the currency is not "presently needed" or because the currency is not needed for payment "in that currency," or because the payments will not be "consistent with the provisions of this Agreement." If the Fund concludes that a particular declaration is not correct, the Fund may postpone or reject the request, or accept it subject to conditions. The phrase "presently needed" cannot be defined in terms of a formula uniformly applicable to all cases, but where there is good reason to doubt that the currency is "presently needed," the Fund will have to apply the phrase in each case in the light of all the circumstances.

Decision No. 284-4
March 10, 1948

USE OF FUND'S RESOURCES: MEANING OF "CONSISTENT WITH THE PROVISIONS OF THIS AGREEMENT" IN ARTICLE V, SECTION 3

The phrase "consistent with the provisions of this Agreement" in Article V, Section 3, mean consistent both with the provisions of the Fund Agreement other than Article I and with the purposes of the Fund contained in Article I.

Decision No. 287-3
March 17, 1948

EXTENT OF DRAWING RIGHTS: MEANING OF ARTICLE V, SECTION 3 (a) (iii)

The Executive Board, acting pursuant to Article XVIII (a) of the Fund Agreement, interprets the quantitative limit of twenty-five per cent of quota in relation to drawing rights under Article V, Section 3 (a) (iii) as follows:

Where the Fund's holdings of a member's currency are not less than seventy-five per cent of its quota, and to the extent that such holdings would not be increased above two hundred per cent of its quota, the purchases which the member may make during a period of twelve months ending on the date of a proposed purchase shall be determined as follows:

(a) The total purchases shall not exceed twenty-five per cent of its quota;

(b) Provided that, if the member has made purchases during the period, it may then purchase an amount equal to the difference between twenty-five per cent of its quota and the total of such purchases adjusted on the basis that a repurchase by the member or sale of its currency during the period is deducted from a previous, but not subsequent, purchase or purchases during the period.

Decision No. 451-(55/52)
August 24, 1955

USE OF FUND'S RESOURCES AND REPURCHASES

1. The Managing Director has made the following statement which should be the framework for his discussions with members on use of the Fund's resources:

"The present proposals are designed to provide a practical basis for use of the Fund's resources in accordance with the purposes of the Fund. When the proposals are agreed they will, of course, have to be carried into effect through actual cases. Decisions will have to be made in accordance with the particular circumstances, and in this manner a body of practical criteria will gradually be built up. However, even at the outset I think it must be clear that access to the Fund should not be denied because a member is in difficulty. On the contrary, the task of the Fund is to help members that need temporary help, and requests should be expected from members that are in trouble in greater or lesser degree. The Fund's attitude toward the position of each member should turn on whether the problem to be met is of a temporary nature and whether the policies the member will pursue will be adequate to overcome the problem within such a period. The policies, above all, should determine the Fund's attitude.

"In addition, the Fund should pay attention to a member's general credit-worthiness, particularly its record with the Fund. In this respect, the member's record of prudence in drawing, its willingness to offer voluntary repayment when its situation permitted, and its promptness in fulfilling the obligation to transmit monetary reserves data and in discharging repurchase obligations would be important.

I would expect that in the years to come, with extended activities of the Fund, we shall be able more and more to rely on the Fund's own experience, thus providing a further and most useful link between Fund drawings and repurchases.

"After a period of relative inactivity of the Fund, it would be too much to expect that we should be able to solve with one stroke the entire problem of access to the Fund's resources so that each member would always know how any request would be received by the Fund. We shall have to feel our way. Sometimes a member may want to submit to the Fund a specific request for drawings, with adequate information as to the particular situation which prompts the request. At other times discussions between the member and the Fund may cover its general position, not with a view to any immediate drawing, but in order to ensure that it would be able to draw if, within a period of say 6 or 12 months, the need presented itself. The Fund itself might take the initiative in discussing with one or more members transactions which it believes suitable for the Fund and helpful to the members concerned. In cases where it would appear appropriate and useful, the Fund might arrange drawings to deal with special short-run situations accompanied by arrangements for repurchase in a period not exceeding 18 months."

2. a. In view of the Executive Board's interpretation of September 26, 1946, concerning the use of the Fund's resources, and considering especially the necessity for ensuring the revolving character of the Fund's resources, exchange purchased from the Fund should not remain outstanding beyond the period reasonably related to the payments problem for which it was purchased from the Fund. The period should fall within an outside range of three to five years. Members will be expected not to request the purchase of exchange from the Fund in circumstances where the reduction of the Fund's holdings of their currencies by an equivalent amount within that time cannot reasonably be envisaged.

b. The Fund has recently determined that when the charges on the Fund's holdings of a member's currency in any bracket have reached a rate of 3½ per cent per annum, the Fund and the member, in accordance with Article V, Section 8 (d) "shall consider means by which the Fund's holdings of the currency can be reduced" (EB Meeting 717, 11/19/51). In the course of consultations arising from purchases of exchange taking place after December 1, 1951, the Fund and the member will agree upon appropriate arrangements to ensure the reduction of the Fund's holdings of the member's currency as soon as possible, with the maximum period to be permitted in any such agreed arrangement requiring that within five years of each purchase made by the member there will be an equivalent repurchase of the Fund's holdings unless they have otherwise been reduced.

c. With respect to each future purchase which raises the Fund's holdings of the member's currency from not less than 75 per cent to not more than 100 per cent of its quota, a member whose currency held by the Fund has not been otherwise reduced within three years will be requested by the Fund to agree upon an arrangement providing that within five years of each purchase made by the member there will be an equivalent repurchase of the Fund's holdings unless they have otherwise been reduced.

d. When unforeseen circumstances beyond the member's control would make unreasonable the application of the principles set forth in paragraph 2 above, the Fund will consider extensions of time.

e. When requesting use of the resources of the Fund in accordance with the arrangements described above, a member will be expected to include in its authenticated request a statement that it will comply with the above principles.

f. These principles will be an essential element in any determination by the Fund as to whether a member is using the resources of the Fund in accordance with the purposes of the Fund.

3. Each member can count on receiving the overwhelming benefit of any doubt respecting drawings which would raise the Fund's holdings of its currency to not more than its quota.

4. The Managing Director should communicate with members concerning means to speed the collection and reporting of monetary reserves data and means to reduce the delays in reaching agreement under Rule I-6 in cases where a repurchase obligation has been computed. The Fund should also make it clear that an important element in its judgment respecting the use of its resources will be the co-operation of the member in helping to make Article V, Section 7 effective, including the timely provision of information and the facilitating of settlement.

5. This decision will be effective until December 31, 1953, and will be reviewed by the Executive Board before that date.

Decision No. 102-(52/11)
February 13, 1952

Stand-By Credit Arrangements

The Fund is prepared to consider requests by members for stand-by arrangements designed to give assurance that, during a fixed period of time, transactions up to a specified amount will be made whenever a member requests and without further consideration of its position, unless the ineligibility provisions of the Fund Agreement have been invoked. The following paragraphs set forth the general framework for stand-by arrangements:

1. Stand-by arrangements would be limited to periods of not more than six months. They could be renewed by a new decision of the Executive Board.

2. In considering the request for a stand-by arrangement or a renewal of a stand-by arrangement, the Fund would apply the same policies that are applied to requests for immediate drawings, including a review of the member's position, policies and prospects in the context of the Fund's objectives and purposes. The Fund would agree to a stand-by arrangement only for a member that would be in a position to make purchases of the same amount of exchange from the Fund.

3. Such arrangements would cover the portion of the quota which a member would be allowed, under Article V, Section 3, to draw within the period provided in the arrangement. However, this does not preclude the Fund from making stand-by arrangements for larger amounts on terms in accordance with Article V, Section 4.

4. A charge of 1/4 of 1 per cent per annum would be payable to the Fund at the time a stand-by arrangement is agreed. This charge would be payable in gold (or United States dollars in lieu of gold) or the member's currency as specified for other charges by Article V, Section 8 (f). In the event that a stand-by arrangement is renewed, a new charge at the rate of 1/4 of 1 per cent per annum would be payable to the Fund.

5. A member having a stand-by arrangement would have the right to engage in the transactions covered by the stand-by arrangement without further review by the

Fund. This right of the member could be suspended only with respect to requests received by the Fund after: (a) a formal ineligibility, or (b) a decision of the Executive Board to suspend transactions either generally (under Article XVI, Section 1 (a) (ii)) or in order to consider a proposal, made by an Executive Director or the Managing Director, formally to suppress or to limit the eligibility of the member.

6. In view of the policy of the Fund with respect to drawings within the so-called "gold tranche," it is not considered likely that members will request stand-by arrangements confined to transactions within the "gold tranche." Accordingly, the policy set forth in this decision is designed primarily to deal with stand-by arrangements for drawings beyond the "gold tranche." If at any time a member proposes a stand-by arrangement which would, in part or entirely, involve drawings within the "gold tranche," the Fund will reconsider the charge set forth in paragraph 4 above as applied to "gold tranche" transactions.

7. This decision will be effective until December 31, 1953, and will be reviewed by the Executive Board before that date.

Decision No. 155-(52/57)
October 1, 1952

I. USE OF FUND'S RESOURCES AND REPURCHASES
II. STAND-BY CREDIT ARRANGEMENTS

I. *Use of Fund Resources and Repurchases*

The decision taken at Meeting 52/11 on February 13, 1952, relating to use of the Fund's resources and repurchases, shall continue in effect subject to review by the Executive Board from time to time as circumstances warrant.

II. *Stand-by Arrangements*

The Fund is prepared to consider requests by members for stand-by arrangements designed to give assurance that, during a fixed period of time, transactions up to a specified amount will be made whenever a member requests and without further consideration of its position, unless the ineligibility provisions of the Fund Agreement have been invoked. The following paragraphs set forth the general framework for stand-by arrangements:

1. Stand-by arrangements will be limited to periods of not more than six months. They can be renewed by a new decision of the Executive Board. If a member believes that the payments problems it anticipates (for example, in connection with positive problems for maintaining or achieving convertibility) can be adequately provided for only by a stand-by arrangement of more than six months, the Fund will give sympathetic consideration to a request for a longer stand-by arrangement in the light of the problems facing the member and the measures being taken to deal with them. With respect to stand-by arrangements for periods of more than six months, the Fund and the member might find it appropriate to reach understandings additional to those set forth in this decision.

2. In considering the request for a stand-by arrangement or renewal of a stand-by arrangement, the Fund will apply the same policies that are applied to requests for immediate drawings, including a review of the member's position, policies and prospects in the context of the Fund's objectives and purposes. The Fund will agree to a stand-by arrangement only for a member that is in a position to make purchases of the same amount of exchange from the Fund.

3. There will be specified in each stand-by arrangement the transactions which may be made under that arrangement.

4. A member having a stand-by arrangement will have the right to engage in the transactions covered by the stand-by arrangement without further review by the Fund. This right of the member can be suspended only with respect to requests received by the Fund after: (a) a formal ineligibility, or (b) a decision of the Executive Board to suspend transactions either generally (under Article XVI, Section 1 (a) (ii)) or in order to consider a proposal, made by an Executive Director or the Managing Director, formally to suppress or to limit the eligibility of the member.

5. (a) A charge of 1/4 of 1 per cent per annum will be payable to the Fund for stand-by arrangements. The charge will be payable in advance for each six months' period that the arrangement or any renewal is in effect.

(b) Charges for stand-by arrangements will be payable in gold, or U.S. dollars in lieu of gold, or in the member's currency as specified for other charges by Article V, Section 8 (f).

(c) There will be credited against the service charge payable for a transaction under a stand-by arrangement the charges paid for that part of the stand-by arrangement (or renewal of it) for the six months' period in which the transaction takes place and for the preceding six months' period; provided that the amount of charge paid for a stand-by arrangement (or renewal of it) for any six months' period will not be credited more than once in that period and the succeeding six months' period.

(d) In order to effect a credit against a service charge, the Fund will repay the portion of the charge paid for a stand-by arrangement that is to be credited under (c) above and collect the service charge in full.

(e) If a member notifies the Fund that it wishes to cancel a stand-by arrangement, the Fund will repay to the member a portion of the charge. The portion repaid will represent the charge paid for the period remaining unexpired at the time of cancellation with respect to the maximum amount of the stand-by arrangement that has never been drawn.

(f) Repayment under (d) or (e) above of a charge paid for a stand-by arrangement will be made in gold, U.S. dollars, and the member's currency in the same proportions as the charge was paid.

6. The Fund will not levy the charge set forth in paragraph 5 above with respect to that part of the stand-by arrangement covering "gold tranche" transactions.

7. This decision shall continue in effect subject to review by the Executive Board from time to time as circumstances warrant.

Decision No. 270-(53/95)
December 23, 1953

CHARGES FOR TRANSACTIONS AND STAND-BY ARRANGEMENTS

I. [Amendment to a Rule]

II. A stand-by arrangement shall provide for a fixed amount that can be purchased under it augmented by amounts equivalent to repurchases in respect of drawings made under the stand-by arrangement or made at the time when the stand-by arrangement is entered into, unless when any such repurchase is made the member informs the Fund that it does not wish the stand-by arrangement to be augmented by the amount of that repurchase. In exceptional circumstances, however, a stand-by arrangement may provide for purchases that increase the Fund's holdings of the currency of the member having the stand-by arrangement up to a specified level, provided that the amounts the member may purchase shall in no case be increased by other members' purchases of its currency.

III. 1. Paragraph II.5 (a) and (c) of Decision No. 270-(53/95) shall be amended to read as follows:

(a) When a stand-by arrangement is entered into or renewed, a charge of 1/4 of 1 per cent per annum will be payable to the Fund in advance for the period of the stand-by arrangement or renewal. For any additional drawing rights that arise in the course of a stand-by arrangement, a further charge will be payable to the Fund in advance at the rate of 1/4 of 1 per cent per annum calculated on the basis of the amount of the additional drawing rights and the unexpired period of the stand-by arrangement.

(c) There will be credited against the service charge for a transaction under a stand-by arrangement the charges actually paid in respect of that amount under the stand-by arrangement and any stand-by arrangement which preceded it without interval at the rate of 1/4 of 1 per cent per annum and up to a maximum of 1/4 of 1 per cent on that amount, due allowance being made for any refunds under paragraph II.6 of this decision. For the purpose of calculating such credits and for the purpose of calculating refunds under (e) below, it shall be assumed that drawings are made in respect of drawing rights in the order in which such drawing rights arose.

2. [Applies to individual countries.]

IV. Paragraph II.5 (e) of Decision No. 270-(53/95) is amended to read:

If a member notifies the Fund that it wishes to cancel a stand-by arrangement, the Fund will repay to the member a portion of the charge. The portion repaid will represent the charge for the period remaining unexpired at the date of cancellation for the amount that could still be drawn under the stand-by arrangement at the date of cancellation for which the member has paid a charge.

V. The following shall be added to Paragraph II.6 of Decision No. 270-(53/95):

To the extent that a charge has been levied on a part of the stand-by arrangement which falls into the gold tranche in the course of the stand-by arrangement, the Fund will refund the charge on that part for the unexpired period of the stand-by arrangement.

VI. Sections II, III.1, IV, and V above shall apply to stand-by arrangements entered into or renewed after the date of the adoption of this decision.

Decision No. 876-(59/15)
April 27, 1959

STAND-BY ARRANGEMENTS: REFUND OF CHARGES

(a) Refunds pursuant to Paragraph II.6 of Executive Board Decision No. 270-(53/95), as amended, of charges paid for stand-by arrangements entered into before the date of this decision will be calculated as of the date of each repurchase, drawing of the member's currency by other members, or increase of the member's quota, and will be based on the Fund's total holdings of the member's currency as of the date of each such calculation. If no such repurchase, drawing or increase of quota has taken place before the expiration of the stand-by arrangement the calculation will be based on the Fund's holdings at the end of the quarters of the Fund's financial year and at the date of expiration.

(b) In determining the Fund's holdings of a member's currency for the purposes of all calculations involving charges payable for stand-by arrangements entered into after the date of this decision, no account will be taken of amounts, not in excess of $\frac{1}{100}$ of 1% of the member's quota, in a special account to meet administrative expenses.

Decision No. 1345-(62/23)
May 23, 1962

STAND-BY ARRANGEMENTS

1. There shall be added to the end of paragraph II.4 of Executive Board Decision No. 270-(53/95) the following sentence for use in all future stand-by arrangements:

> When notice of a decision for formal ineligibility or of a decision to consider a proposal is given pursuant to this paragraph, purchases under this stand-by arrangement will be resumed only after consultation has taken place between the Fund and the member and agreement has been reached on the terms for the resumption of such purchases.

2. "Prior notice" provisions appearing in existing stand-by arrangements, except for the one approved at EBM/60/53, shall be understood as if the sentence set forth in paragraph 1 above were substituted for such provisions.

Decision No. 1151-(61/6)
February 20, 1961

USE OF FUND'S RESOURCES: LIMITATION AND INELIGIBILITY UNDER ARTICLE V, SECTION 5

The Fund has, in the case of a member which has had a previous exchange transaction with the Fund, power to declare the member ineligible or limit its use of the resources of the Fund if the member is, in the opinion of the Fund, using the resources of the Fund in a manner contrary to the purposes of the Fund.

Decision No. 284-3
March 10, 1948

USE OF FUND'S RESOURCES: POSTPONEMENT AND LIMITATION UNDER ARTICLE V, SECTION 5

If the Fund receives a request from a member to purchase exchange and either, (1) the Fund is considering sending the member a report pursuant to Article V, Section 5, or (2) the Fund finds when the request is before it that action pursuant to that Section should be considered; then the Fund has the authority, pursuant to Article V, Section 5, of the Fund Agreement, to postpone the transfer as permitted under the provisions of Rules and Regulations G-3 for such time as may reasonably be necessary to decide the question of applying Article V, Section 5, and, if it decides to apply it, to prepare and send to the member a report and subject its use of the Fund's resources to limitations. Under such circumstances the limitations imposed will apply to the pending request for the purchase of exchange as well as to future requests.

Decision No. 286-1
March 15, 1948

USE OF FUND'S RESOURCES: MEANING OF "IS USING" IN ARTICLE V, SECTION 5

A member "is using" the resources of the Fund within the meaning of Article V, Section 5, where it is either actually disposing of the exchange purchased from the Fund, or, having purchased exchange from the Fund, the Fund's holdings of its currency are in excess of 75 per cent of its quota.

Decision No. 292-3
March 30, 1948

CURRENCIES TO BE DRAWN AND TO BE USED IN REPURCHASES

The Board approves the statement entitled "Currencies to be Drawn and to be Used in Repurchases" (SM/62/62, Revision 2), and this statement shall be incorporated in the Annual Report for 1962.

Decision No. 1371-(62/36)
July 20, 1962

Currencies to be Drawn and to be Used in Repurchases

From the beginning of the Fund's operations through 1957, drawings were overwhelmingly made in U.S. dollars. Starting in 1958, however, the Fund has increasingly encouraged drawings in other currencies, and this has been facilitated by the introduction of *de facto* convertibility for the currencies of the main industrial countries. Since the same currencies have become formally convertible under Article VIII in February 1961, repurchases have also begun to be made in these currencies.

Certain practices have been developed which take into account the new situation of the increasing number of currencies usable for the transactions of the Fund. These practices are still in a state of evolution as increased experience is being gained. The following paragraphs set out what may be regarded as appropriate practices to be followed for the time being.

I. *Procedure*

When a substantial number of currencies other than the U.S. dollar became usable for drawings, the drawing countries began to discuss with the Managing Director what currencies might be drawn. It gradually became the practice that consultation should take place between the drawing country and the Managing Director about the currencies to be drawn, and this practice has now become established in connection with all stand-by arrangements and drawings. Before giving advice to the drawing country, the Managing Director has got into contact with countries whose currencies might be drawn, even in circumstances where speed in arranging the drawing was essential. These consultations and the contacts with the countries concerned have thus become an integral part of the procedure which has been evolved.

In addition, an attempt is being made to indicate from time to time the amounts likely to be drawn and what might be a proper distribution of drawings among different currencies. Since under stand-by arrangements even fairly large drawings may be made suddenly, such indications as will be given can only be tentative and informal but they can, even so, serve a useful purpose in contributing to the maintenance of close contact between the Managing Director and the countries whose currencies may be drawn.

It has been concluded that the Fund has the legal authority to specify the convertible currencies to be used in making repurchases in discharge of obligations to repurchase that do not arise under Article V, Section 7 (b), and that, accordingly members are required to obtain the prior agreement of the Fund on the convertible currencies to be used in making such repurchases. Such repurchases must not increase the Fund's holdings of a member's currency beyond 75 per cent of that member's quota or decrease the Fund's holdings of the repurchasing member's currency below 75 per cent of that member's quota.

Until further notice, and in order to maintain conditions which foster repurchases and the revolving character of the Fund's resources, the Fund will accept any convertible currency fulfilling the conditions set forth in the last sentence above, provided that the repurchasing member has consulted the Managing Director on the currencies, and the amounts of each, to be used by the member in making its repurchase. Before giving his advice, the Managing Director will consult with countries whose currencies could be used in repurchase, and he will also attempt to give advance indications comparable to those relating to the currencies to be drawn. In all of these consultations, the Managing Director's recommendations will be guided by the principles regarding the currency composition of repurchases set out in Section II below.

The preceding paragraph shall apply to those repurchase obligations outside Article V, Section 7 (b) that are entered into after July 20, 1962. Members that entered into such obligations before that date shall be invited to consult the Managing Director on the currencies to be used in discharging these obligations, and the Managing Director will follow the procedure and be guided by the considerations referred to in the preceding paragraph.

The Managing Director will notify the Executive Directors at least two business days before any repurchase under the preceding paragraphs is carried out.

Where consultations with a country are referred to in this document they will normally be conducted with the Executive Director appointed or elected by such country.

II. *Criteria for the Selection of Currencies for Drawings and Repurchases*

The experience of the Fund in recent years has made it possible to indicate the main considerations which govern the selection of currencies for drawings and repurchases.

Drawings

With regard to the question of the selection of currencies for a particular drawing or for drawings in general, account has been taken of the balance of payments and reserve positions of the countries whose currencies are considered for drawing, as well as of the Fund's holdings of these currencies.

It has been found in practice that weight has to be given to all these three considerations, with some differentiation according to specific circumstances, and perhaps most particularly according to the size of the transaction or transactions involved.

During periods when aggregate drawings were moderate in amount, little difficulty was experienced in distributing these drawings among countries with reasonably satisfactory balance of payments positions on the basis of the level of these countries' reserves. When the volume of drawings has been large, it has been necessary to give more importance to the relative balance of payments positions of the countries to be drawn upon, so as to prevent excessive declines in their primary reserves as a result of Fund sales of their currencies. In connection with large drawings, in particular when they are associated with short-term capital movements, it is usually fairly easy to single out the countries whose reserves have benefited from an inflow of capital and to direct drawings more particularly towards the currencies of these countries.

By the attention thus given to the balance of payments position, the Fund has been able to arrange drawings in large measure to offset movements of funds in the exchange markets, and thus contribute to the strengthening of the international payments position. In considering a country's balance of payments position, seasonal fluctuations have not been allowed great weight, and the Fund has avoided drawing prematurely the currency of a country which is in the process of building up reserves from a relatively low position.

In applying the third consideration, account has to be taken of prevailing circumstances. For example, when the Fund's holdings of a particular currency have become very low, this has precluded substantial sales of that currency irrespective of the balance of payments and reserve position of the country concerned. In practice, the Fund has taken account of the level of its holdings of any currency well before the point of actual exhaustion, by gradually—rather than abruptly—reducing its sales of that currency on account of this factor.

Small drawings have normally been executed in one currency only, preferably the currency in which the drawing country holds the bulk of its reserves, even in circumstances where the payments position of the reserve center drawn upon has not been strong. Somewhat larger drawings have usually been distributed over more than one currency, but only exceptionally more than three to five currencies have been involved in a single drawing unless it has been a very large one. As far as possible, factors relevant to the particular drawing country, such as closeness of trade and payments relations, have been taken into account in the selection of the currencies to be drawn.

Repurchases

With regard to repurchases, the range of currencies is, as mentioned in Section I above, limited to currencies that are formally convertible and of which the Fund's holdings are below 75 per cent of the quota. As a result, repurchases in currencies have, until early 1961, been made almost exclusively in U.S. dollars. The U.S. dollar was also, in recent years, a currency that was available in the exchange market at favorable rates which reflected the prevailing balance of payments position.

Increasingly, however, weight has been given, in suggesting the allocation of repurchases among the countries whose currencies can be received in repurchase, to the Fund's holdings of these currencies compared to quotas. It would seem from the point of view of equity, and also with due regard to the liquidity position of the Fund, that great weight should be given to this criterion. But consideration should also be given, when appropriate, to the prevailing balance of payments position. In the case of relatively small repurchases it has been found practical that they be made in the currency in which a country holds its reserves, provided of course that such currency can be received by the Fund.

III. *Conversion*

It has been the experience in the Fund that a country drawing one or more currencies, after consultation with the Managing Director, has often wanted to convert either the whole or part of the amount drawn in a particular currency into one or more other currencies depending upon the payments that country has to meet or the currencies it normally holds in its reserves. The conversions thus effected have made it possible for the drawing country to meet its payments obligations and to strengthen its reserves in the most effective manner.

In the case of drawings in dollars, sterling and moderate amounts of certain other currencies, there has been no difficulty in effecting conversion at the going rate by transactions in the exchange market. Since the currencies drawn have generally been strong currencies for which there is a demand in the market, such conversion has generally been carried out without any disturbance to the market. For several currencies, arrangements have often been made between central banks, i.e., between the central banks in the drawing country and in the country whose currency is drawn, which provide for direct conversion into the latter's main reserve currency at the prevailing market rate without any commission being charged. In certain cases, however, especially when the amounts involved have been large, consideration has been given to the fact that conversion on the market would have affected exchange rates, and in some cases an allowance for this has been made. A preference has been indicated by two central banks for conversion at par, especially for large drawings.

In accordance with normal central banking procedure, whenever a country desires conversion of a currency it is drawing, it would get in touch with the central bank of the country drawn upon in order to reach an understanding on the most convenient way to arrange such conversion. When conversion has presented a country with difficulties, the assistance of the Managing Director has been sought in order to arrive at an appropriate solution.

The practices outlined above for drawings can, *mutatis mutandis*, be applied when a country needs to obtain a currency in order to make a repurchase from the Fund with that currency.

The Fund will keep the practices with respect to conversion as described above under study, and will re-examine them in the light of further experience.

Compensatory Financing of Export Fluctuations

I. The report entitled "Compensatory Financing of Export Fluctuations" is approved for transmittal to the United Nations.

II. The following shall be recorded as the decision of the Executive Board on the compensatory financing of fluctuations in exports of primary exporting countries:

(1) The financing of deficits arising out of export shortfalls, notably those of primary exporting member countries, has always been regarded as a legitimate reason for the use of Fund resources, which have been drawn on frequently for this purpose. The Fund believes that such financing helps these members to continue their efforts to adopt adequate measures toward the solution of their financial problems and to avoid the use of trade and exchange restrictions to deal with balance of payments problems, and that this enables these members to pursue their programs of economic development with greater effectiveness.

(2) The Fund noted in its 1962 Annual Report that trends in prices of basic commodities in the past few years have adversely affected the export earnings of many Fund members, which has increased the strain on their reserves. In view of this and in order to ensure the maximum effectiveness for its support to members—in particular, primary exporting members—that are faced with fluctuations in export proceeds, the Fund is taking the action set forth below.

A. *Quotas*

(3) The quotas of many primary exporting countries, taken in conjunction with a reasonable use of their own reserves, are at present adequate for dealing with export fluctuations such as have occurred during the past decade. In those instances, however, where adjustment of the quotas of certain primary exporting countries, and in particular of countries with relatively small quotas, would be appropriate to make them more adequate in the light of fluctuations in export proceeds and other relevant criteria, the Fund is willing to give sympathetic consideration to requests for such adjustment.

B. *Drawing policies*

(4) Under the present policies and practices on the use of Fund resources, any member is given the overwhelming benefit of the doubt in relation to requests for transactions within the gold tranche, and the Fund's attitude to requests for transactions within the first credit tranche is a liberal one provided the member itself is making reasonable efforts to solve its problems. In the higher credit tranches too, where a member's policies are consistent with Fund policies and practices on the use of Fund resources in these tranches, the Fund gives assistance, on a substantial scale, toward meeting temporary payments deficits, including deficits arising out of export shortfalls. The policies and practices of the Fund on drawings and stand-by arrangements have been developed in order to help members to meet more effectively their temporary balance of payments difficulties and to enable them, where necessary, to pursue policies aimed at restoring external and internal equilibrium. Fund assistance in accordance with these policies and practices has made an effective contribution to the solution of the difficulties of these members and the achievement of equilibrium. It has often led, moreover, to the provision of further resources from public and private resources for meeting immediate and longer-term needs. In the application of its policies and practices governing the use of its resources, the Fund's attitude has been a flexible one, and account has been taken of special difficulties facing members.

(5) The Fund has reviewed its policies to determine how it could more readily assist members, particularly primary exporters, encountering payments difficulties produced by temporary export shortfalls, and has decided that such members can expect that their requests for drawings will be met where the Fund is satisfied that

(a) the shortfall is of a short-term character and is largely attributable to circumstances beyond the control of the member; and

(b) the member will cooperate with the Fund in an effort to find, where required, appropriate solutions for its balance of payments difficulties.

The amount of drawings outstanding under this decision will not normally exceed 25 per cent of the member's quota, and the drawings will be subject to the Fund's established policies and practices on repurchase. When drawings are made under this decision, the Fund will so indicate in an appropriate manner.

(6) In order to implement the Fund's policies in connection with compensatory financing of export shortfalls, the Fund will be prepared to waive the limit on Fund holdings of 200 per cent of quota, where appropriate. In particular, the Fund will be prepared to waive this limit (i) where a waiver is necessary to permit compensatory drawings to be made under paragraphs (4) and (5) above, or (ii) to the extent that drawings in accordance with paragraph (5) are still outstanding.

Whenever the Fund's holdings of a member's currency resulting from an outstanding compensatory drawing under paragraph (5) are reduced, by the member's repurchase or otherwise, this will restore *pro tanto* the member's facility to make a further compensatory drawing under that paragraph, should the need arise.

(7) In order to identify more clearly what are to be regarded as export shortfalls of a short-term character, the Fund, in conjunction with the member concerned, will seek to establish reasonable estimates regarding the medium-term trend of the member's exports on the basis of appropriate statistical data in conjunction with qualitative information about its export prospects.

(8) The provision of credit to deal with the balance of payments effects of export fluctuations provides immediate relief for a country's short-term difficulties. In many cases, however, it will also be necessary to introduce measures of a policy character in order to attain a satisfactory and lasting solution to a country's balance of payments problems. Members generally have actively cooperated with the Fund to find and adopt the measures necessary to this end. Beyond immediate balance of payments difficulties, the primary exporting countries are, in many instances, facing unfavorable long-term export trends, and all are trying to meet the challenge of achieving more rapid and sustained development through a strengthening and broadening of their economies. The last mentioned problem will require action in many fields and over many years by both the primary exporting countries and the industrial countries, separately and in concert, including readier access to the markets of the developed countries for the products of the developing countries and an appropriate and sustained flow of technical and financial assistance to the developing countries. The Fund considers that its activities can provide valuable assistance in helping to establish a climate within which longer-term measures can be more effectively pursued.

*Decision No. 1477-(63/8)**
February 27, 1963

Gold Collateral Transactions

Where the Fund decides in exceptional circumstances to enter into a gold collateral transaction with a member because this would promote the purposes of the Fund and give the member the opportunity, in consultation with the Fund, to adopt policies, during the period referred to in (a) below, that would be consistent with the policies and practices of the Fund on the use of its resources:

(a) the period for repurchase of the Fund's holdings of the member's currency resulting from the transaction, to the extent that they are not otherwise reduced, shall normally not exceed six months after the transfer of exchange by the Fund;

(b) the repurchase shall be made with gold or convertible currencies acceptable to the Fund in accordance with its Decision of July 20, 1962;

(c) the provisions of the pledge agreement shall be on the lines of those set forth in the draft letter annexed to SM/63/30.

Decision No. 1543-(63/39)
July 1, 1963

---

* Regarding gold subscriptions in connection with quota increases granted in accordance with this decision, see Decision No. 1529-(63/33), p. 222.

Draft Letter to Member Entering into a Gold Collateral Transaction

Dear Sir:

On____________________, the Fund decided to enter into an exchange transaction with____________________________in an amount equivalent to US$__________ secured by the pledge of gold as collateral, [and granted the necessary waiver under Article V, Section 4,] subject to the conditions set forth in this letter. The amount of____________, equivalent to US$____________and____________, equivalent to US$____________, will be transferred to your account(s) after the steps set forth in Section B below have been taken.

Section A

1. The collateral for the transaction shall consist of gold bars containing fine gold having a value not less than $____________ calculated on the basis of US$35 per troy ounce of fine gold. The fine gold content will be determined to the satisfaction of the Fund and at your expense.

2. The gold bars will be transferred by you by way of pledge at a gold depository selected by you from among the Fund's gold depositories (Federal Reserve Bank of New York, New York; the Bank of England, London; Banque de France, Paris; the Reserve Bank of India, Nagpur, India). You will irrevocably instruct the depository in accordance with the attached exhibit that the gold is to be transferred to, earmarked, and held in a special account in the name of and for the sole account of the International Monetary Fund, that the special account shall be at the sole order of the Fund, and that the depository shall accept and act upon any and all instructions of the Fund with respect to part or all of the gold in the special account. The Fund will arrange with the depository for the establishment of the special account. The depository will not be informed that the gold is held under pledge to the Fund.

3. You will represent to the Fund that the gold is free from any claims, liens or encumbrances in favor of any other party and subject to paragraph 9 below will remain free therefrom during the pledge. You will further represent to the Fund that under your law the gold may be freely pledged and disposed of as provided in this letter.

4. The gold will continue to be owned by you. Accordingly, the Fund will enter the gold in its books in your name, and will not show the gold in its books or accounts as owned by the Fund.

5. Not later than the repurchase date, namely the close of business six months after the value date for transfer of the exchange by the Fund to your account(s), you will repurchase the Fund's holdings of your currency resulting from the transaction, to the extent that such holdings are not otherwise reduced, with gold in the special account if you so request or with other gold or convertible currencies acceptable to the Fund in accordance with the Fund's Decision of July 20, 1962.

6. On any reduction at any time of the Fund's holdings of your currency resulting from the transaction otherwise than by repurchase with gold in the special account, the Fund will, on your request, release to you or to your order at the depository gold from the special account in an amount not exceeding the equivalent of the reduction, provided that the amount of gold remaining in the special account shall not be less than the equivalent of the outstanding balance of the transaction.

7. To the extent that the Fund's holdings of your currency resulting from the transaction have not been reduced by the close of business on the repurchase date, the Fund will give you notice of the balance due and payable by way of repurchase in respect of the transaction, and you will complete such repurchase with gold in the special account if you so request or other gold or convertible currencies acceptable to the Fund in accordance with the Fund's Decision of July 20, 1962 not later than the close of business thirty days after the repurchase date. In the absence of such repurchase by the close of business thirty days after the repurchase date, repurchase will be effected with gold in the special account on the instructions of the Fund and without the need for further notice or request to you.

8. Where repurchase is effected with gold in the special account pursuant to paragraph 5 or 7, the gold in the special account will be transferred, on the instructions of the Fund, to the ordinary gold account of the Fund at the depository, which gold shall then be deemed to have been transferred by you to the Fund and shall thereupon be owned by the Fund free from any claim, including any right of redemption. Any surplus balance of gold beyond the full amount of the repurchase will be returned to you but any balance less than one bar will be held under earmark for you pursuant to Rule I-1 of the Fund's Rules and Regulations.

9. At any time before the repurchase date or the close of business thirty days after the repurchase date, you may, after consulting the Fund, arrange for the sale of the gold in the special account, and the Fund will be prepared to give appropriate instructions to facilitate the sale, provided that on or before the close of business thirty days after the repurchase date the Fund's holdings of your currency resulting from the transaction will be repurchased with gold or convertible currencies acceptable to the Fund in accordance with the Fund's Decision of July 20, 1962, and provided further that the gold will not be released from pledge before such repurchase is effected.

10. All charges and costs connected with or resulting from the transfer to the special account (including without limitation transportation, earmarking, and holding), release, and redelivery, as well as converting the gold into good delivery bars if deemed necessary by the Fund under paragraph 1 above or if the gold is transferred to the Fund's ordinary gold account by way of repurchase will be borne by you.

Section B

The transfer of currencies pursuant to the transaction agreed by the Fund will be made by the Fund after the Fund has received from you:

(i) acceptance of all of the conditions of this letter; and

(ii) a copy of the instructions referred to in Section A 2 above; and

(iii) the representations referred to in Section A 3 above;

and, in addition, has received from the depository:

(iv) confirmation that the depository has established the special account, earmarked the gold, and will act in accordance with Section A 2 above; and

(v) information satisfactory to the Fund as to the fine gold content of the bars.

Very truly yours,
International Monetary Fund
By:

Exchange Transactions Prior to the Establishment of Initial Par Value

(a) Where the Fund prescribes the conditions and amount of an exchange transaction by a member before the establishment of an initial par value, the member will be required to complete the payment of its subscription on the basis of a provisional rate of exchange for its currency proposed by the member and agreed by the Fund.

(b) In deciding whether to permit exchange transactions before the establishment of an initial par value, the Fund, in accordance with the last sentence of Article I, will be guided by the purposes of the Articles; the Fund will encourage members to follow policies leading to the establishment of realistic exchange rates and to the adoption at the earliest feasible date of effective par values, and will take into account the efforts that are being made to achieve this objective. However, the Fund will give the overwhelming benefit of any doubt to requests for exchange transactions within the gold tranche and members can expect that requests for drawings will be met where they are made in accordance with paragraph 5 of E.B. Decision No. 1477-(63/8), adopted February 27, 1963.

Decision No. 1687-(64/22)
April 22, 1964

Procedure for Drawings in the Gold Tranche

When a duly authenticated request to draw in the gold tranche is received from a member, the request shall be notified to the Executive Board on the day it is received, whenever possible, or on the next business day, and unless, by the close of that business day, the Managing Director decides or an Executive Director requests that the matter be placed on the Board's agenda for discussion, the Fund shall, at the close of the first business day following the date of the receipt of the request, instruct the appropriate depository to make the transfer on the next business day after the instruction or as soon as possible thereafter.

Decision No. 1745-(64/46)
August 3, 1964

Article V, Section 7

REPURCHASE OBLIGATIONS

Repurchase and Rule G-7

Until further notice, where a member has an accrued repurchase obligation in currency under Art. V, Sec. 7 (b), and Schedule B and discharges part or all of that obligation by a sale of gold to the Fund for that currency under Art. V, Sec. 6 (a), as provided in paragraph 3 of the decision of the Executive Board at EBM 648 (3/8/51), such gold shall be purchased by the Fund without collecting the estimated costs of later possible conversion of the gold into that currency as permitted under Rule G-7 of the Rules and Regulations, it being understood that the existing requirements as to the form and delivery of such gold would remain in effect.

Decision No. 119-(52/30)
June 2, 1952

Effect of Payment of Gold Subscriptions on Repurchase Obligations

RESOLVED:

. . . that, for the purpose of the repurchase obligations prescribed by Article V, Section 7, increases and decreases in the monetary reserves of a member shall not be considered if they occur on or before the latest date on which the member's subscription must be paid in accordance with this Resolution; and the payment of subscriptions, whether actually made before or after such latest date for payment, shall not be regarded as resulting in a decrease in monetary reserves.

Decision No. 124-2
January 22, 1947

Repurchase Obligations: Article V, Section 7 (c)

In the application of the repurchase obligations of the Fund Agreement the limits specified in Article V, Section 7 (c), apply solely as of the end of the financial year for which the repurchase obligations are calculated.

Decision No. 419-1
April 11, 1949

Repurchase Obligations: Article V, Section 7 (b) (i) or (ii)

Whenever a member uses its monetary reserves to repurchase its currency from the Fund in accordance with the provisions of Article V, Section 7 (b) (i) or (ii), the resulting reduction in its monetary reserves and in the Fund's holdings of its currency must be regarded as having occurred, for the purpose of calculating subsequent repurchase obligations under the same provisions of the Fund Agreement, at the end of the financial year of the Fund in respect of which the obligation to make the repurchase arose. Members shall be informed of the foregoing.

Decision No. 447-5
June 17, 1949

Voluntary Repurchases

(1) Subject to paragraph 3 below, a member may offer in voluntary repurchase, and the Fund has the power to accept, if it so decides, gold or convertible currencies to the extent that (a) the Fund's holdings of the convertible currency of a member which is offered would not be increased above 75% of the quota of that member, and (b) the Fund's holdings of the repurchasing member's currency would not be decreased below 75% of its quota.

(2) As a matter of legal interpretation it is determined that the consent of the member whose currency is offered in voluntary repurchase is not necessary as a condition precedent to the acceptance by the Fund of such currency.

(3) Where a member has an accrued and undischarged repurchase obligation under Art. V, Sec. 7 (b), and Schedule B in respect of any financial year of the Fund, the member must discharge the obligation in accordance with those provisions; provided, however, that the payment of currency under those provisions may be combined with the sale of gold to the Fund for the currency under Art. V, Sec. 6 (a).

Decision No. 7-(648)
March 8, 1951

Minimal Repurchase Obligations Procedure

In cases where a repurchase obligation of less than the equivalent of $500 is calculated the member will be notified, and the obligation collected, on the next occasion thereafter that a repurchase obligation accrues which, together with the first one, will total the equivalent of $500 or more.

Decision No. 705-(57/55)
November 7, 1957

Calculation of Repurchase Obligations: Prompt Reporting of Monetary Reserves Data

1. Where on any April 30 the Fund holds a member's currency in an amount exceeding 75 per cent of the member's quota, the member shall make a provisional monetary reserves report to the Fund not later than May 31, preferably by cable.

2. The Fund will make a provisional calculation of the amount and distribution of the repurchase obligations of such members and will inform them of the results of the calculation not later than June 15. Members shall discharge within thirty days any repurchase obligations as thus provisionally calculated and agreed with the member.

3. All provisional repurchases shall be subject to adjustment by members and the Fund in accordance with Rule I-6 of the Fund's Rules and Regulations.

Decision No. 1813-(65/4)
January 18, 1965

Article VI, Section 1

USE OF FUND'S RESOURCES FOR CAPITAL TRANSFERS

Interpretation of Articles of Agreement

The Executive Directors of the International Monetary Fund interpret the Articles of Agreement to mean that authority to use the resources of the Fund is limited to use in accordance with its purposes to give temporary assistance in financing balance of payments deficits on current account for monetary stabilization operations.

Pursuant to Decision No. 71-2
September 26, 1946

Use of Fund's Resources for Capital Transfers

After full consideration of all relevant aspects concerning the use of the Fund's resources, the Executive Directors decide by way of clarification that Decision No. 71-2 does not preclude the use of the Fund's resources for capital transfers in accordance with the provisions of the Articles, including Article VI.

Decision No. 1238-(61/43)
July 28, 1961

ARTICLE VI, SECTION 3

CONTROLS ON CAPITAL TRANSFERS

The report of the Committee on Interpretation on controls on capital transfers (EBD/56/71, 7/11/56) is approved and the following conclusions are adopted:

Subject to the provisions of Article VI, Section 3 concerning payments for current transactions and undue delay in transfers of funds in settlement of commitments:

(a) Members are free to adopt a policy of regulating capital movements for any reason, due regard being paid to the general purposes of the Fund and without prejudice to the provisions of Article VI, Section 1.

(b) They may, for that purpose, exercise such controls as are necessary including making such arrangements as may be reasonably needed with other countries, without approval of the Fund.

Decision No. 541-(56/39)
July 25, 1956

ARTICLE VII, SECTION 2

GENERAL ARRANGEMENTS TO BORROW *

Preamble

In order to enable the International Monetary Fund to fulfill more effectively its role in the international monetary system in the new conditions of widespread convertibility, including greater freedom for short-term capital movements, the main industrial countries have agreed that they will, in a spirit of broad and willing cooperation, strengthen the Fund by general arrangements under which they will stand ready to lend their currencies to the Fund up to specified amounts under Article VII, Section 2 of the Articles of Agreement when supplementary resources are needed to forestall or cope with an impairment of the international monetary system in the aforesaid conditions. In order to give effect to these intentions, the following terms and conditions are adopted under Article VII, Section 2 of the Articles of Agreement.

Paragraph 1. *Definitions*

As used in this Decision the term:

(i) "Articles" means the Articles of Agreement of the International Monetary Fund;

(ii) "credit arrangement" means an undertaking to lend to the Fund on the terms and conditions of this Decision;

(iii) "participant" means a participating member or a participating institution;

(iv) "participating institution" means an official institution of a member that has entered into a credit arrangement with the Fund with the consent of the member;

(v) "participating member" means a member of the Fund that has entered into a credit arrangement with the Fund;

(vi) "amount of a credit arrangement" means the maximum amount expressed in units of its currency that a participant undertakes to lend to the Fund under a credit arrangement;

---

* See p. 252.

(vii) "call" means a notice by the Fund to a participant to make a transfer under its credit arrangement to the Fund's account;

(viii) "borrowed currency" means currency transferred to the Fund's account under a credit arrangement;

(ix) "drawer" means a member that purchases borrowed currency from the Fund in an exchange transaction or in an exchange transaction under a stand-by arrangement;

(x) "indebtedness" of the Fund means the amount it is committed to repay under a credit arrangement.

Paragraph 2. *Credit Arrangements*

A member or institution that adheres to this Decision undertakes to lend its currency to the Fund on the terms and conditions of this Decision up to the amount in units of its currency set forth in the Annex to this Decision or established in accordance with Paragraph 3 (b).

Paragraph 3. *Adherence*

(a) Any member or institution specified in the Annex may adhere to this Decision in accordance with Paragraph 3 (c).

(b) Any member or institution not specified in the Annex that wishes to become a participant may at any time, after consultation with the Fund, give notice of its willingness to adhere to this Decision, and, if the Fund shall so agree and no participant object, the member or institution may adhere in accordance with Paragraph 3 (c). When giving notice of its willingness to adhere under this Paragraph 3 (b) a member or institution shall specify the amount, expressed in terms of its currency, of the credit arrangement which it is willing to enter into, provided that the amount shall not be less than the equivalent at the date of adherence of one hundred million United States dollars of the weight and fineness in effect on July 1, 1944.

(c) A member or institution shall adhere to this Decision by depositing with the Fund an instrument setting forth that it has adhered in accordance with its law and has taken all steps necessary to enable it to carry out the terms and conditions of this Decision. On the deposit of the instrument the member or institution shall be a participant as of the date of the deposit or of the effective date of this Decision, whichever shall be later.

Paragraph 4. *Entry into Force*

This Decision shall become effective when it has been adhered to by at least seven of the members or institutions included in the Annex with credit arrangements amounting in all to not less than the equivalent of five and one-half billion United States dollars of the weight and fineness in effect on July 1, 1944.

Paragraph 5. *Changes in Amounts of Credit Arrangements*

The amounts of participants' credit arrangements may be reviewed from time to time in the light of developing circumstances and changed with the agreement of the Fund and all participants.

Paragraph 6. *Initial Procedure*

When a participating member or a member whose institution is a participant approaches the Fund on an exchange transaction or stand-by arrangement and the Managing Director, after consultation, considers that the exchange transaction or stand-by arrangement is necessary in order to forestall or cope with an impairment of the international monetary system, and that the Fund's resources need to be supplemented for this purpose, he shall initiate the procedure for making calls under Paragraph 7.

Paragraph 7. *Calls*

(a) The Managing Director shall make a proposal for calls for an exchange transaction or for future calls for exchange transactions under a stand-by arrangement only after consultation with Executive Directors and participants. A proposal shall become effective only if it is accepted by participants and the proposal is then approved by the Executive Directors. Each participant shall notify the Fund of the acceptance of a proposal involving a call under its credit arrangement.

(b) The currencies and amounts to be called under one or more of the credit arrangements shall be based on the present and prospective balance of payments and reserve positions of participating members or members whose institutions are participants and on the Fund's holdings of currencies.

(c) Unless otherwise provided in a proposal for future calls approved under Paragraph 7 (a), purchases of borrowed currency under a stand-by arrangement shall be made in the currencies of participants in proportion to the amounts in the proposal.

(d) If a participant on which calls may be made pursuant to Paragraph 7 (a) for a drawer's purchases under a stand-by arrangement gives notice to the Fund that in the participant's opinion, based on the present and prospective balance of payments and reserve position, calls should no longer be made on the participant or that calls should be for a smaller amount, the Managing Director may propose to other participants that substitute amounts be made available under their credit arrangements, and this proposal shall be subject to the procedure of Paragraph 7 (a). The proposal as originally approved under Paragraph 7 (a) shall remain effective unless and until a proposal for substitute amounts is approved in accordance with Paragraph 7 (a).

(e) When the Fund makes a call pursuant to this Paragraph 7, the participant shall promptly make the transfer in accordance with the call.

Paragraph 8. *Evidence of Indebtedness*

(a) The Fund shall issue to a participant, on its request, nonnegotiable instruments evidencing the Fund's indebtedness to the participant. The form of the instruments shall be agreed between the Fund and the participant.

(b) Upon repayment of the amount of any instrument issued under Paragraph 8 (a) and all accrued interest, the instrument shall be returned to the Fund for cancellation. If less than the amount of any such instrument is repaid, the instrument shall be returned to the Fund and a new instrument for the remainder of the amount shall be substituted with the same maturity date as in the old instrument.

Paragraph 9. *Interest and Charges*

(a) The Fund shall pay a charge of one-half of one per cent on transfers made in accordance with Paragraph 7 (e).

(b) The Fund shall pay interest on its indebtedness at the rate of one and one-half per cent per annum. In the event that this becomes different from a basic rate determined as follows:

the charge levied by the Fund pursuant to Article V, Section 8 (a) plus the charge levied by the Fund pursuant to Article V, Section 8 (c) (i), as changed from time to time under Article V, Section 8 (e), during the first year after a purchase of exchange from the Fund, minus one-half of one per cent,

the interest payable by the Fund shall be changed by the same amount as from the date when the difference in the basic rate takes effect. Interest shall be paid as soon as possible after July 31, October 31, January 31, and April 30.

(c) Interest and charges shall be paid in gold to the extent that this can be effected in bars. Any balance not so paid shall be paid in United States dollars.

(d) Gold payable to a participant in accordance with Paragraph 9 (b) or Paragraph 11 shall be delivered at any gold depository of the Fund chosen by the participant at which the Fund has sufficient gold for making the payment. Such delivery shall be free of any charges or costs for the participant.

Paragraph 10. *Use of Borrowed Currency*

The Fund's policies and practices on the use of its resources and stand-by arrangements, including those relating to the period of use, shall apply to purchases of currency borrowed by the Fund.

Paragraph 11. *Repayment by the Fund*

(a) Subject to the other provisions of this Paragraph 11, the Fund, five years after a transfer by a participant, shall repay the participant an amount equivalent to the transfer calculated in accordance with Paragraph 12. If the drawer for whose purchase participants make transfers is committed to repurchase at a fixed date earlier than five years after its purchase, the Fund shall repay the participants at that date. Repayment under this Paragraph 11 (a) or under Paragraph 11 (c) shall be, as determined by the Fund, in the participant's currency whenever feasible, or in gold, or, after consultation with the participant, in other currencies that are convertible in fact. Repayments to a participant under the subsequent provisions of this Paragraph 11 shall be credited against transfers by the participant for a drawer's purchases in the order in which repayment must be made under this Paragraph 11 (a).

(b) Before the date prescribed in Paragraph 11 (a), the Fund, after consultation with a participant, may make repayment to the participant, in part or in full, with any increases in the Fund's holdings of the participant's currency that exceed the Fund's working requirements, and participants shall accept such repayment.

(c) Whenever a drawer repurchases, the Fund shall promptly repay an equivalent amount, except in any of the following cases:

(i) The repurchase is under Article V, Section 7 (b) and can be identified as being in respect of a purchase of currency other than borrowed currency.

(ii) The repurchase is in discharge of a commitment entered into on a purchase of currency other than borrowed currency.

(iii) The repurchase entitles the drawer to augmented rights under a stand-by arrangement pursuant to Section II of Decision No. 876-(59/15) of the Executive Directors, provided that, to the extent that the drawer does not exercise such augmented rights, the Fund shall promptly repay an equivalent amount on the expiration of the stand-by arrangement.

(d) Whenever the Fund decides in agreement with a drawer that the problem for which the drawer made its purchases has been overcome, the drawer shall complete repurchase, and the Fund shall complete repayment and be entitled to use its holdings of the drawer's currency below 75 per cent of the drawer's quota in order to complete such repayment.

(e) Repayment under Paragraph 11 (c) and (d) shall be made in the order established under Paragraph 11 (a) and in proportion to the Fund's indebtedness to the participants that made transfers in respect of which repayment is being made.

(f) Before the date prescribed in Paragraph 11 (a) a participant may give notice representing that there is a balance of payments need for repayment of part or all of the Fund's indebtedness and requesting such repayment. The Fund shall give the overwhelming benefit of any doubt to the participant's representation. Repayment shall be made after consultation with the participant in the currencies of other members that are convertible in fact, or made in gold, as determined by the Fund. If the Fund's holdings of currencies in which repayment should be made are not wholly adequate, individual participants shall be requested, and will be expected, to provide the necessary balance under their credit arrangements. If notwithstanding the expectation that the participants will provide the necessary balance, they fail to do so, repayment shall be made to the extent necessary in the currency of the drawer for whose purchases the participant requesting repayment made transfers. For all of the purposes of this Paragraph 11, transfers under this Paragraph 11 (f) shall be deemed to have been made at the same time and for the same purchases as the transfers by the participant obtaining repayment under this Paragraph 11 (f).

(g) All repayments to a participant in a currency other than its own shall be guided, to the maximum extent practicable, by the present and prospective balance of payments and reserve positions of the members whose currencies are to be used in repayment.

(h) The Fund shall at no time reduce its holdings of a drawer's currency below an amount equal to the Fund's indebtedness to the participants resulting from transfers for the drawer's purchases.

(i) When any repayment is made to a participant, the amount that can be called for under its credit arrangement in accordance with this Decision shall be restored *pro tanto* but not beyond the amount of the credit arrangement.

Paragraph 12. *Rates of Exchange*

(a) The value of any transfer shall be calculated as of the date of the transfer in terms of a stated number of fine ounces of gold or of the United States dollar of the weight and fineness in effect on July 1, 1944, and the Fund shall be obliged to repay an equivalent value.

(b) For all of the purposes of this Decision, the equivalent in currency of any number of fine ounces of gold or of the United States dollar of the weight and fineness in effect on July 1, 1944, or *vice versa*, shall be calculated at the rate of exchange at which the Fund holds such currency at the date as of which the calculation is made; provided however that the provisions of Decision No. 321-(54/32) of the Executive Directors on Transactions and Computations Involving Fluctuating Currencies, as amended by Decision No. 1245-(61/45) and Decision No. 1283-(61/56), shall determine the rate of exchange for any currency to which that decision, as amended, has been applied.

Paragraph 13. *Transferability*

A participant may not transfer all or part of its claim to repayment under a credit arrangement except with the prior consent of the Fund and on such terms and conditions as the Fund may approve.

Paragraph 14. *Notices*

Notice to or by a participating member under this Decision shall be in writing or by cable and shall be given to or by the fiscal agency of the participating member designated in accordance with Article V, Section 1 of the Articles and Rule G-1 of the Rules and Regulations of the Fund. Notice to or by a participating institution shall be in writing or by cable and shall be given to or by the participating institution.

Paragraph 15. *Amendment*

This Decision may be amended during the period prescribed in Paragraph 19 (a) only by a decision of the Fund and with the concurrence of all participants. Such concurrence shall not be necessary for the modification of the Decision on its renewal pursuant to Paragraph 19 (b).

Paragraph 16. *Withdrawal of Adherence*

A participant may withdraw its adherence to this Decision in accordance with Paragraph 19 (b) but may not withdraw within the period prescribed in Paragraph 19 (a) except with the agreement of the Fund and all participants.

Paragraph 17. *Withdrawal from Membership*

If a participating member or a member whose institution is a participant withdraws from membership in the Fund, the participant's credit arrangement shall cease at the same time as the withdrawal takes effect. The Fund's indebtedness under the credit arrangement shall be treated as an amount due from the Fund for the purpose of Article XV, Section 3, and Schedule D of the Articles.

Paragraph 18. *Suspension of Exchange Transactions and Liquidation*

(a) The right of the Fund to make calls under Paragraph 7 and the obligation to make repayments under Paragraph 11 shall be suspended during any suspension of exchange transactions under Article XVI of the Articles.

(b) In the event of liquidation of the Fund, credit arrangements shall cease and the Fund's indebtedness shall constitute liabilities under Schedule E of the Articles. For the purpose of Paragraph 1 (a) of Schedule E, the currency in which the liability of the Fund shall be payable shall be first the participant's currency and then the currency of the drawer for whose purchases transfers were made by the participant.

Paragraph 19. *Period and Renewal*

(a) This Decision shall continue in existence for four years from its effective date.

(b) This Decision may be renewed for such period or periods and with such modifications, subject to Paragraph 5, as the Fund may decide. The Fund shall adopt a decision on renewal and modification, if any, not later than twelve months before the end of the period prescribed in Paragraph 19 (a). Any participant may advise the Fund not less than six months before the end of the period prescribed in Paragraph 19 (a) that it will withdraw its adherence to the Decision as renewed. In the absence of such notice, a participant shall be deemed to continue to adhere to the Decision as renewed. Withdrawal of adherence in accordance with this Paragraph 19 (b) by a participant, whether or not included in the Annex, shall not preclude its subsequent adherence in accordance with Paragraph 3 (b).

(c) If this Decision is terminated or not renewed, Paragraphs 8 through 14, 17 and 18 (b) shall nevertheless continue to apply in connection with any indebtedness of the Fund under credit arrangements in existence at the date of the termination or expiration of the Decision until repayment is completed. If a participant withdraws its adherence to this Decision in accordance with Paragraph 16 or Paragraph 19 (b), it shall cease to be a participant under the Decision, but Paragraphs 8 through 14, 17 and 18 (b) of the Decision as of the date of the withdrawal shall nevertheless continue to apply to any indebtedness of the Fund under the former credit arrangement until repayment has been completed.

Paragraph 20. *Interpretation*

Any question of interpretation raised in connection with this Decision which does not fall within the purview of Article XVIII of the Articles shall be settled to the mutual satisfaction of the Fund, the participant raising the question, and all other participants. For the purpose of this Paragraph 20 participants shall be deemed to include those former participants to which Paragraphs 8 through 14, 17 and 18 (b) continue to apply pursuant to Paragraph 19 (c) to the extent that any such former participant is affected by a question of interpretation that is raised.

ANNEX

Participants and Amounts of Credit Arrangements

			Units of Participant's Currency
1.	United States of America	US$	2,000,000,000
2.	Deutsche Bundesbank	DM	4,000,000,000
3.	United Kingdom	£	357,142,857
4.	France	NF	2,715,381,428
5.	Italy	Lit	343,750,000,000
6.	Japan	Yen	90,000,000,000
7.	Canada	Can$	216,216,000
8.	Netherlands	f.	724,000,000
9.	Belgium	BF	7,500,000,000
10.	Sveriges Riksbank	SKr	517,320,000

*Decision No. 1289-(62/1)**
January 5, 1962

Letter from Mr. Baumgartner, Minister of Finance, France, to Mr. Dillon, Secretary of the Treasury, United States

December 15, 1961

Dear Mr. Secretary:

The purpose of this letter is to set forth the understandings reached during the recent discussions in Paris with respect to the procedure to be followed by the Participating Countries and Institutions (hereinafter referred to as "the participants") in connection with borrowings by the International Monetary Fund of Supplementary Resources under credit arrangements which we expect will be established pursuant to a decision of the Executive Directors of the Fund.

This procedure, which would apply after the entry into force of that decision with respect to the participants which adhere to it in accordance with their laws, and which would remain in effect during the period of the decision, is as follows:

* As amended: with effect from August 1, 1962 (Decision No. 1362-(62/32) dated July 9, 1962) and with effect from October 12, 1962 (Decision No. 1415-(62/47) dated September 19, 1962).

The General Arrangements to Borrow entered into force on October 24, 1962.

A. A participating country which has need to draw currencies from the International Monetary Fund or to seek a stand-by agreement with the Fund in circumstances indicating that the Supplementary Resources might be used, shall consult with the Managing Director of the Fund first and then with the other participants.

B. If the Managing Director makes a proposal for Supplementary Resources to be lent to the Fund, the participants shall consult on this proposal and inform the Managing Director of the amounts of their currencies which they consider appropriate to lend to the Fund, taking into account the recommendations of the Managing Director and their present and prospective balance of payments and reserve positions. The participants shall aim at reaching unanimous agreement.

C. If it is not possible to reach unanimous agreement, the question whether the participants are prepared to facilitate, by lending their currencies, an exchange transaction or stand-by arrangement of the kind covered by the special borrowing arrangements and requiring the Fund's resources to be supplemented in the general order of magnitude proposed by the Managing Director, will be decided by a poll of the participants.

The prospective drawer will not be entitled to vote. A favorable decision shall require the following majorities of the participants which take part in the vote, it being understood that abstentions may be justified only for balance of payments reasons as stated in paragraph D:

(1) a two-thirds majority of the number of participants voting; and

(2) a three-fifths majority of the weighted votes of the participants voting, weighted on the basis of the commitments to the Supplementary Resources.

D. If the decision in paragraph C is favorable, there shall be further consultations among the participants, and with the Managing Director, concerning the amounts of the currencies of the respective participants which will be loaned to the Fund in order to attain a total in the general order of magnitude agreed under paragraph C. If during the consultations a participant gives notice that in its opinion, based on its present and prospective balance of payments and reserve position, calls should not be made on it, or that calls should be for a smaller amount that that proposed, the participants shall consult among themselves and with the Managing Director as to the additional amounts of their currencies which they could provide so as to reach the general order of magnitude agreed under paragraph C.

E. When agreement is reached under paragraph D, each participant shall inform the Managing Director of the calls which it is prepared to meet under its credit arrangement with the Fund.

F. If a participant which has loaned its currency to the Fund under its credit arrangement with the Fund subsequently requests a reversal of its loan which leads to further loans to the Fund by other participants, the participant seeking such reversal shall consult with the Managing Director and with the other participants.

For the purpose of the consultative procedures described above, participants will designate representatives who shall be empowered to act with respect to proposals for use of the Supplementary Resources.

It is understood that in the event of any proposals for calls under the credit arrangements or if other matters should arise under the Fund decision requiring consultations among the participants, a consultative meeting will be held among all the participants. The representative of France shall be responsible for calling the first meeting, and at that time the participants will determine who shall be the Chairman. The Managing Director of the Fund or his representative shall be invited to participate in these consultative meetings.

It is understood that in order to further the consultations envisaged, participants should, to the fullest extent practicable, use the facilities of the international organizations to which they belong in keeping each other informed of the developments in their balances of payments that could give rise to the use of the Supplementary Resources.

These consultative arrangements, undertaken in a spirit of international cooperation, are designed to insure the stability of the international payments system.

I shall appreciate a reply confirming that the foregoing represents the understandings which have been reached with respect to the procedure to be followed in connection with borrowings by the International Monetary Fund under the credit arrangements to which I have referred.

I am sending identical letters to the other participants—that is, Belgium, Canada, Germany, Italy, Japan, the Netherlands, Sweden, the United Kingdom. Attached is a verbatim text of this letter in English. The French and English texts and the replies of the participants in both languages shall be equally authentic. I shall notify all of the participants of the confirmations received in response to this letter.

General Arrangements to Borrow: Association of Switzerland *

The understandings set forth in the letter which the Swiss Ambassador to the United States proposes to send to the Managing Director (EBD/64/73, Attachment I) are acceptable to the Fund and the Managing Director is authorized to send the letter attached to EBD/64/73 (Attachment II).

Decision No. 1712-(64/29)
June 8, 1964

* *Exchange of letters between the Ambassador of Switzerland to the United States and the Managing Director of the Fund*

June 11, 1964

The Managing Director
International Monetary Fund
19th and H Streets, N.W.
Washington, D.C. 20431

Sir:

I have the honor to refer to Mr. Jacobsson's letter of December 14, 1961 to the President of the Swiss Confederation and to conversations between representatives of the Swiss Confederation and the International Monetary Fund (hereinafter referred to as "the Fund") concerning the way in which the Swiss Confederation could be associated with the Fund's General Arrangements to Borrow, and thus contribute to the objectives of those Arrangements. The General Arrangements to Borrow (hereinafter referred to as "the General Arrangements") are those set forth in Decision No. 1289-(62/1) of January 5, 1962, of the Fund's Executive Directors, as amended by Decision No. 1362-(62/32) of July 9, 1962 and Decision No. 1415-(62/47) adopted on September 19, 1962.

In the light of the views that have been exchanged, the Swiss Federal Council, on behalf of the Swiss Confederation, is prepared to be associated with the General Arrangements as follows:

(1) The Swiss Confederation is prepared to make resources available to participants in the General Arrangements in accordance with this letter and in amounts not exceeding an outstanding total equivalent to 865,000,000 Swiss francs.

(2) The Swiss Confederation will be prepared to consider the conclusion of agreements (hereinafter referred to as "implementing agreements") with any of the participants in the General Arrangements if requested by such participants. The implementing agreements will prescribe the terms and conditions in accordance with which the Swiss Confederation will make resources available to the participant or the Swiss Confederation and the participant will make resources available to each other, which shall be on the basis of reciprocal terms if required. Immediately on the conclusion of an implementing agreement, or of any amendment of an implementing agreement, the Swiss Confederation will provide the Managing Director with a copy thereof.

(3) Whenever the Managing Director of the Fund initiates the procedure and makes a proposal for calls pursuant to Paragraphs 6 and 7 of the General Arrangements for the benefit of a participant that has entered into or enters into an implementing agreement, he may propose to the Swiss Confederation, after consultation with the Swiss Confederation, that it shall make a specified amount of resources available to the participant, which amount shall be in accordance with the implementing agreement with that participant. If the proposal for calls becomes effective under Paragraph 7 of the General Arrangements, the Swiss Confederation

will make the specified amount of resources available to the said participant in accordance with this letter and with the terms and conditions of the implementing agreement. If, however, the Swiss Confederation gives notice to the Managing Director that in its opinion, based on its present and prospective balance of payments and reserve position, it should not make resources available in accordance with this proposal, or should make available a smaller amount than that proposed, the Swiss Confederation will not be obliged to make any such resources available or more resources than it represents to the Managing Director that it should make available.

(4) If the Swiss Confederation makes resources available to a participant otherwise than in accordance with the procedure of paragraph (3), the Swiss Confederation, after consultation with the Managing Director, may deem such resources to be or to have been made available pursuant to this letter, provided that at the date of such deeming Switzerland has entered into an implementing agreement with that participant, that at the date of such deeming a proposal for calls for the benefit of that participant is in effect under Paragraph 7 of the General Arrangements and provided that the terms and conditions for repayment to Switzerland accord or are made to accord with paragraph (5).

(5) The effect of the terms and conditions for the timing of repayment of resources made available by Switzerland pursuant to this letter will correspond, to the maximum extent practicable, with the repayment provisions of Paragraph 11 of the General Arrangements.

(6) The Fund may, at the request of a party to an implementing agreement, make any determination, or use its good offices, to facilitate the operation of an implementing agreement, subject, however, to paragraph (9).

(7) Whenever the Swiss Confederation makes resources available pursuant to paragraph (3) or deems resources to be or to have been made available pursuant to paragraph (4), the Swiss Confederation will inform the Managing Director of the amount in terms of Swiss francs thus made available. The Swiss Confederation will inform the Managing Director of the amount in terms of Swiss francs of the repayment of any resources made available pursuant to paragraph (3) or (4).

(8) The Swiss Confederation and the Fund will provide each other with the general information necessary to facilitate the operation of this letter and implementing agreements.

(9) The Fund does not accept any responsibility or liability, whether as guarantor or otherwise, in connection with this letter or with respect to the performance of the terms and conditions of an implementing agreement.

(10) This letter will remain effective for four years from October 24, 1962, provided that the Swiss Confederation may rescind this letter, with immediate effect, within one month after an amendment of the General Arrangements becomes effective pursuant to Paragraph 15 of the General Arrangements. This letter may be amended or rescinded at any time if the Swiss Confederation and the Fund shall so agree.

(11) Any question of interpretation or application of these understandings will be settled to the mutual satisfaction of the Swiss Confederation and the Fund.

(12) For the purposes of this letter, references to participants shall be deemed to include the official institution of a participant with which an implementing agreement is made, even though such institution is not a "participating institution" under the General Arrangements.

(13) All communications by or to the Swiss Confederation pursuant to this letter shall be made by or to the Swiss National Bank.

I propose that, if this letter is approved by the International Monetary Fund, this letter and your reply constitute an agreement between the Swiss Federal Council and the International Monetary Fund, which shall enter into force on the date of your reply. I hereby declare that the Swiss Confederation has taken all steps necessary to implement the exchange of letters.

Accept, Sir, the assurances of my highest consideration.

/s/
A. Zehnder
Ambassador of Switzerland

June 11, 1964

Sir:

I am pleased to acknowledge receipt of your letter of June 11, 1964.

I have been authorized to inform you that the understandings set forth in your letter are accepted by the International Monetary Fund. Accordingly, your letter and this reply constitute an agreement between the International Monetary Fund and the Swiss Federal Council, which will enter into force on the date of this reply.

Accept, Sir, the assurances of my highest consideration.

Very truly yours,
/s/
PIERRE-PAUL SCHWEITZER
Managing Director

His Excellency
Alfred Zehnder
Ambassador of Switzerland
2900 Cathedral Avenue, N.W.
Washington, D.C. 20008

ARTICLE VIII, SECTION 2 (b)

UNENFORCEABILITY OF EXCHANGE CONTRACTS

UNENFORCEABILITY OF EXCHANGE CONTRACTS: FUND'S INTERPRETATION OF ARTICLE VIII, SECTION 2 (b)

The following letter shall be sent to all members:

The Board of Executive Directors of the International Monetary Fund has interpreted, under Article XVIII of the Articles of Agreement, the first sentence of Article VIII, Section 2 (b), which provision reads as follows:

Exchange contracts which involve the currency of any member and which are contrary to the exchange control regulations of that member maintained or imposed consistently with this Agreement shall be unenforceable in the territories of any member.

The meaning and effect of this provision are as follows:

1. Parties entering into exchange contracts involving the currency of any member of the Fund and contrary to exchange control regulations of that member which are maintained or imposed consistently with the Fund Agreement will not receive the assistance of the judicial or administrative authorities of other members in obtaining the performance of such contracts. That is to say, the obligations of such contracts will not be implemented by the judicial or administrative authorities of member countries, for example by decreeing performance of the contracts or by awarding damages for their non-performance.

2. By accepting the Fund Agreement members have undertaken to make the principle mentioned above effectively part of their national law. This applied to all members, whether or not they have availed themselves of the transitional arrangements of Article XIV, Section 2.

An obvious result of the foregoing undertaking is that if a party to an exchange contract of the kind referred to in Article VIII, Section 2 (b) seeks to enforce such a contract, the tribunal of the member country before which the proceedings are brought will not, on the ground that they are contrary to the public policy (*ordre public*) of the forum, refuse recognition of the exchange control regulations of the other member which are maintained or imposed consistently with the Fund Agreement. It also follows that such contracts will be treated as unenforceable notwithstanding that under the private international law of the forum, the law under which the foreign exchange control regulations are maintained or imposed is not the law which governs the exchange contract or its performance.

The Fund will be pleased to lend its assistance in connection with any problem which may arise in relation to the foregoing interpretation or any other aspect of Article VIII, Section 2 (b). In addition, the Fund is prepared to advise whether particular exchange control regulations are maintained or imposed consistently with the Fund Agreement.

Decision No. 446-4
June 10, 1949

Article VIII and Article XIV

PAYMENTS RESTRICTIONS

Payments Restrictions for Security Reasons: Fund Jurisdiction

Art. VIII, Sec. 2 (a), in conformity with its language, applies to all restrictions on current payments and transfers, irrespective of their motivation and the circumstances in which they are imposed. Sometimes members impose such restrictions solely for the preservation of national or international security. The Fund does not, however, provide a suitable forum for discussion of the political and military considerations leading to actions of this kind. In view of the fact that it is not possible to draw a precise line between cases involving only considerations of this nature and cases involving, in whole or in part, economic motivations and effects for which the Fund does provide the appropriate forum for discussion, and the further fact that the Fund must exercise the jurisdiction conferred by the Fund Agreement in order to perform its duties and protect the legitimate interests of its members, the following policy decision is taken:

1. A member intending to impose restrictions on payments and transfers for current international transactions that are not authorized by Art. VII, Sec. 3 (b) or Art. XIV, Sec. 2 of the Fund Agreement and that, in the judgment of the member, are solely related to the preservation of national or international security, should, whenever possible, notify the Fund before imposing such restrictions. Any member may obtain a decision of the Fund prior to the imposition of such restrictions by so indicating in its notice, and the Fund will act promptly on its request. If any member intending to impose such restrictions finds that circumstances preclude advance notice to the Fund, it should notify the Fund as promptly as circumstances permit, but ordinarily not later than 30 days after imposing such restrictions. Each notice received in accordance with this decision will be circulated immediately to the Executive Directors. Unless the Fund informs the member within 30 days after receiving notice from the member that it is not satisfied that such restrictions are proposed solely to preserve such security, the member may assume that the Fund has no objection to the imposition of the restrictions.

2. The Fund will review the operation of this decision periodically and reserves the right to modify or revoke, at any time, the decision or the effect of the decision on any restrictions that may have been imposed pursuant to it.

Decision No. 144-(52/51)
August 14, 1952

Bilateralism and Convertibility

1. This decision records the Fund's views on the use of bilateral arrangements.

2. Fund policies and attitude on bilateral arrangements which involve the use of exchange restrictions and represent limitations on a multilateral system of payments are an integral part of its policy on restrictions. This policy aims at the elimination of foreign exchange restrictions and the earliest possible establishment of a multilateral system of payments in respect of current transactions between members. The Fund's policies and procedures on such restrictions rest on Articles I, VIII and XIV of the Fund Agreement.

3. Certain members have already taken steps to reduce their dependence on bilateral arrangements, but many members still use them. The Fund welcomes the reduced reliance on these arrangements and believes that the improvement in the international payments situation makes it less necessary for members to rely on such arrangements. The Fund urges the full collaboration of all its members to reduce and to eliminate as rapidly as practicable reliance on bilateralism. In this respect the Fund recommends close cooperation of those who plan to make their currencies convertible in the near future. Unless this policy is energetically pursued by all countries, both convertible and inconvertible, there is serious risk that widespread restrictions, particularly of a discriminatory character, will persist. Moreover, the persistence of bilateralism may impede the attainment and maintenance of convertibility. This whole problem is one not only for countries which maintain bilateral arrangements but also for other countries whose domestic and foreign economic policies may adversely affect the balance of payments of other members.

4. The Fund will have discussions with its members on their need to retain existing bilateral arrangements or their ability to facilitate the reduction of bilateral arrangements by other countries. During the coming year, the Fund will explore with all countries which are parties to bilateral arrangements which involve the use of exchange restrictions the need for the continuation of these arrangements, the possibilities of their early removal, and ways and means, including the use of the Fund's resources, by which the Fund can assist in this process. In its examination of the justification for reliance on such bilateral arrangements the Fund will, without excluding other considerations, have particular regard to the payments position and prospects of the members concerned.

Decision No. 433-(55/42)
June 22, 1955

Retention Quotas: Decision and Letter of Transmittal

In concluding consultations on restrictions on current payments and transfers as required under Article XIV of the Fund Agreement, the Fund postponed consideration of retention quotas and similar practices through which some members have sought to improve their earnings of specific currencies. The Fund has now examined these practices more fully than was possible at the consultations referred to above. The Fund has extended this examination to cover the terms of reference of the resolution adopted on September 9, 1952, by the Board of Governors and has come to the following conclusions:

1. Members should work toward and achieve as soon as feasible the removal of

these retention quotas and similar practices, particularly where they lead to abnormal shifts in trade which cause unnecessary damage to other countries. Members should endeavor to replace these practices by more appropriate measures leading to currency convertibility.

2. The Fund will enter into consultation with each of the members concerned with a view to agreeing on a program for the implementation of 1 above, including appropriate attention to timing of any action which may be decided upon.

3. The Fund does not object to those practices which, by their nature, can be regarded as devices designed solely to simplify the administration of official exchange allocations.

The Managing Director is asked to send the following letter to all members in transmitting the foregoing decision on retention quotas and similar practices:

The Fund has made a detailed study concerning retention quotas and other similar practices pursuant to the resolution passed at the Seventh Session of the Board of Governors in Mexico in September 1952. I am pleased to transmit herewith a decision of the Executive Board of the Fund based on this study.

The Fund has concluded that these practices stem from widespread difficulties presently existing in the international payments position of many countries. The Fund's consideration of this subject has shown that what is referred to as "retention quotas and similar practices" covers a wide range of exchange measures. Certain practices under this heading may be unobjectionable from the point of view of Fund policies. Other practices in this category, however, appear to result in adverse effects on exchange stability and to cause unnecessary damage to member countries. They also may lead to the adoption of retaliatory measures. The interest of the Fund in these matters clearly follows from the terms of Article VIII containing the general obligations of members with respect to the avoidance of exchange restrictions, discriminatory currency arrangements and multiple currency practices, and Article XIV dealing with these exchange measures during the transitional period.

In dealing with retention quotas and similar practices, the Board has not intended to change existing Fund standards and procedures with respect to exchange restrictions, discriminatory currency arrangements and multiple currency practices. Specifically, there was no intention to affect the existing requirements of prior consultation and approval with respect to measures of this character. Those requirements, so far as they concern multiple currency practices, were communicated to members in the Fund's letter of December 19, 1947 (Appendix II of the Fund's Annual Report of 1948). Accordingly, it is expected that members intending to maintain, introduce or enlarge those retention quotas and similar practices which constitute exchange restrictions, multiple currency practices or discriminatory currency arrangements will act in accordance with existing Fund requirements.

The decision recognizes that it is not practicable to deal with all of these practices on a general basis. The Fund, therefore, wishes to deal with these arrangements on a case-to-case basis. We shall communicate as quickly as practicable with members using these practices. We are confident that members will cooperate in these individual discussions in order to enable the Fund to reach appropriate conclusions.

Decision No. 201-(53/29)
May 4, 1953

Discrimination for Balance of Payments Reasons

The following decision deals exclusively with discriminatory restrictions imposed for balance of payments reasons.

In some countries, considerable progress has already been made towards the elimination of discriminatory restrictions; in others, much remains to be done. Recent international financial developments have established an environment favorable to the elimination of discrimination for balance of payments reasons. There has been a substantial improvement in the reserve positions of the industrial countries in particular and widespread moves to external convertibility have taken place.

Under these circumstances, the Fund considers that there is no longer any balance of payments justification for discrimination by members whose current receipts are largely in externally convertible currencies. However, the Fund recognizes that where such discriminatory restrictions have been long maintained, a reasonable amount of time may be needed fully to eliminate them. But this time should be short and members will be expected to proceed with all feasible speed in eliminating discrimination against member countries, including that arising from bilateralism.

Notwithstanding the extensive moves toward convertibility, a substantial portion of the current receipts of some countries is still subject to limitations on convertibility, particularly in payments relations with state-trading countries. In the case of these countries the Fund will be prepared to consider whether balance of payments considerations would justify the maintenance of some degree of discrimination, although not as between countries having externally convertible currencies. In this connection the Fund wishes to reaffirm its basic policy on bilateralism as stated in its decision of June 22, 1955.

Decision No. 955-(59/45)
October 23, 1959

Article VIII and Article XIV

There has been in recent years a substantial improvement in the balance of payments and the reserve positions of a number of Fund members which has led to important and widespread moves to the external convertibility of many currencies. Most international transactions are now carried on with convertible currencies, and many countries have progressed far with the removal of restrictions on payments. In consequence of these developments, it seems likely that a number of members of the Fund either have reached or are nearing a position in which they can consider the feasibility of formally accepting the obligations of Article VIII, Sections 2, 3, and 4. Previous decisions taken by the Fund, such as those on multiple currency practices, bilateral arrangements, discriminatory restrictions maintained for balance of payments purposes, and payments restrictions for security reasons, indicate the Fund's attitude on these matters. The present decision has been adopted as an additional guide to members in pursuance of the purposes of the Fund as set forth in Article I of the Articles of Agreement.

1. Article VIII provides in Sections 2 and 3 that members shall not impose or engage in certain measures, namely restrictions on the making of payments and transfers for current international transactions, discriminatory currency arrangements, or multiple currency practices, without the approval of the Fund. The guiding principle in ascertaining whether a measure is a restriction on payments and transfers for current transactions under Article VIII, Section 2, is whether it involves a direct governmental

limitation on the availability or use of exchange as such. Members in doubt as to whether any of their measures do or do not fall under Article VIII may wish to consult the Fund thereon.

2. In accordance with Article XIV, Section 3, members may at any time notify the Fund that they accept the obligations of Article VIII, Sections 2, 3, and 4, and no longer avail themselves of the transitional provisions of Article XIV. Before members give notice that they are accepting the obligations of Article VIII, Sections 2, 3, and 4, it would be desirable that, as far as possible, they eliminate measures which would require the approval of the Fund, and that they satisfy themselves that they are not likely to need recourse to such measures in the foreseeable future. If members, for balance of payments reasons, propose to maintain or introduce measures which require approval under Article VIII, the Fund will grant approval only where it is satisfied that the measures are necessary and that their use will be temporary while the member is seeking to eliminate the need for them. As regards measures requiring approval under Article VIII and maintained or introduced for nonbalance of payments reasons, the Fund believes that the use of exchange systems for nonbalance of payments reasons should be avoided to the greatest possible extent, and is prepared to consider with members the ways and means of achieving the elimination of such measures as soon as possible. Members having measures needing approval under Article VIII should find it useful to consult with the Fund before accepting the obligations of Article VIII, Sections 2, 3, and 4.

3. If members at any time maintain measures which are subject to Sections 2 and 3 of Article VIII, they shall consult with the Fund with respect to the further maintenance of such measures. Consultations with the Fund under Article VIII are not otherwise required or mandatory. However, the Fund is able to provide technical facilities and advice, and to this end, or as a means of exchanging views on monetary and financial developments, there is great merit in periodic discussions between the Fund and its members even though no questions arise involving action under Article VIII. Such discussions would be planned between the Fund and the member, including agreement on place and timing, and would ordinarily take place at intervals of about one year.

4. Fund members which are contracting parties to the GATT and which impose import restrictions for balance of payments reasons will facilitate the work of the Fund by continuing to send information concerning such restrictions to the Fund. This will enable the Fund and the member to join in an examination of the balance of payments situation in order to assist the Fund in its collaboration with the GATT. The Fund, by agreement with members which are not contracting parties to the GATT and which impose import restrictions for balance of payments reasons, will seek to obtain information relating to such restrictions.

Decision No. 1034-(60/27)
June 1, 1960

MULTIPLE CURRENCY PRACTICES

Statement to Members Transmitting Fund's Decisions on Multiple Currency Practices

The letter to members concerning multiple currency practices and the accompanying statement of the Fund's decisions with respect to such practices are agreed as revised (Executive Board Document No. 235, Revision 2) and shall be sent without delay to all members. The texts of earlier decisions on the same subject are modified as necessary to correspond with the agreed statement.

Decision No. 237-2
December 18, 1947

Letter to Members

December 19, 1947

To All Members:

During the past several months the Fund has been giving special consideration to multiple currency practices. I am writing to all of the members today in order to acquaint them with the results of our considerations. Enclosed is a memorandum containing the pertinent decisions taken by the Executive Board. These set forth the general lines of the Fund's policies toward multiple currency practices which the Fund has adopted to date, together with the obligations of the members and the jurisdiction of the Fund upon which the development of Fund policy will necessarily be based.

We intend, as rapidly as may be possible under the circumstances, to discuss with each member now engaging in a multiple currency practice how this general policy will be applied to its individual problems. In the meantime, all of the members are requested to be guided by the enclosed memorandum and to initiate with the Fund discussions of any pressing problems which may arise.

Sincerely yours,
/s/
Gutt
Managing Director

Multiple Currency Practices

This memorandum contains the decisions the Fund has so far taken concerning its policies toward multiple currency practices, and clarification of its jurisdiction with respect to such practices.

The exchange systems of the members who engage in multiple currency practices are frequently complex. For this reason various difficulties will be involved in the modification and removal of the practices, and the policy of the Fund in this regard must develop progressively as its consultations with the members concerned reveal problems which might otherwise be overlooked. The policies set forth below have been agreed as a basis for the initiation of discussions with the members affected:

I. *Policies*

A. *General*

1. *Consultation.* There should be continuing consultation on multiple currency practices between the Fund and the members concerned. Members should, as a minimum, consult the Fund before introducing a multiple currency practice, before making a change in any of the multiple rates of exchange, before reclassifying transactions subject to different rates, and before making any other type of significant change in their exchange systems.

2. *Stability and Restrictions.* In most cases multiple currency practices are both systems of exchange rates and restrictions on payments and transfers for current international transactions. Whenever it is inconvenient to deal with both aspects of such multiple currency practice simultaneously, priority should be given to those

features which affect exchange stability and orderly exchange arrangements among members.

3. *Removal.* Early steps should be taken toward the removal of multiple currency practices which are clearly not necessary for balance of payments reasons. In such cases, ample time should be provided for members to take the necessary steps and to install appropriate substitutes where necessary.

The Fund will encourage members engaging in multiple currency practices for balance of payments reasons to establish as soon as possible conditions which would permit their removal, with the general objective of seeking removal not later than the end of the transitional period.

Where complete removal by the end of the transitional period proves impossible, the Fund will assist the members concerned to eliminate the most dangerous aspects of their multiple currency practices and to exercise reasonable control over those retained.

B. *Specific Practices*

1. *Fixed Exchange Rates.* When a multiple currency system includes fixed exchange rates, members should consult with the Fund on any changes in their practices, whether such changes concern the rates of exchange or the classification of transactions subject to particular practices. Should the step contemplated by a member be a part of a program made in agreement with the Fund, the member could, of course, act without prior consultation.

When a multiple rate system is used for restrictions on current and capital transactions, the elimination of the restriction on current transactions would be highly commendable even though restrictions on capital transactions might have to be retained.

2. *Taxes on Exchange Drafts.* The use by members of taxes on exchange drafts resulting in an unusually large difference between buying and selling rates for a currency is not in accord with the objectives of the Fund Agreement and the Fund shall, in consultation with members concerned, seek the elimination of such practices as rapidly as practicable.

3. *Fluctuating Rates of Exchange.*

(a) *Free Markets.* When a multiple currency practice includes a free market with a fluctuating rate, the member should agree with the Fund on the scope of the transactions permitted to take place in that market. Any changes in the scope of these transactions should, of course, be subject to agreement with the Fund. The objective should be to eliminate the fluctuations in the free market as soon as such action is reasonably practicable. When it is not reasonably practicable to eliminate such fluctuations, the Fund will encourage members to exclude current transactions from the free market to the extent that this would be reasonable in the circumstances of each case.

(b) *The Auction System*

(i) The purpose for which an auction system is to be used should be agreed with the Fund and any change in its scope should be agreed with the Fund. The fewer the transactions subject to the auction rate, and the less essential the goods involved, the better.

(ii) Depending upon the circumstances, the monetary authorities should undertake to keep the auction rate stable, or to maintain it within certain limits, or to make every effort to prevent brisk fluctuations.

(iii) Wherever auction rates exist or are proposed, the circumstances should be examined in order to determine whether a fixed rate should be substituted for the auction rate.

(iv) If, as is usually the case where an auction system exists, a reduction of the money supply is desirable, the proceeds of the auction market should be directed toward this end.

II. *Jurisdiction of the Fund*

Multiple currency practices, besides being in most cases restrictive practices, also constitute systems of exchange rates. Since exchange stability depends on effective rates, the general purposes of the Fund and the members' undertakings of Article IV, Section 4 (a) "to collaborate with the Fund to promote exchange stability, to maintain orderly exchange arrangements with other members, and to avoid competitive exchange alterations" are fundamental considerations in an interpretation of the rights and obligations of members under Article XIV, Section 2 or Article VIII, Section 3, to maintain, introduce, or adapt multiple currency practices. Subject to these general principles, the following conclusions are agreed with respect to the Fund's jurisdiction and the obligations of members.*

A. *Practices Subject to Article VIII, Section 3.*

1. *Maintenance.* A member maintaining multiple currency practices at the time the Agreement entered into force, if it does not take advantage of Article XIV, is required by Article VIII, Section 3, to consult with the Fund for their progressive removal or obtain the Fund's approval for their maintenance.

2. *Introduction.* Members that have not been occupied by the enemy, and former enemy-occupied members which have not taken advantage of the transitional arrangements, whether or not they have existing multiple rate practices, may introduce a new practice only under Article VIII, Section 3, which provides expressly for the necessity of approval by the Fund.

3. *Adaptation.* If a multiple currency practice is in force by virtue of Article VIII, Section 3, the member may change or adapt such practice only after consulting with the Fund and obtaining its approval.

4. *Reclassification.* Members maintaining multiple currency practices under Article VIII, Section 3, may reclassify commodities subject to the practices only after consultation with the Fund and Fund approval.

B. *Practices Subject to Article XIV, Section 2.*

1. *Restrictive Nature.* Multiple currency practices, when applied to current international transactions, constitute a type of restriction on payments and transfers for current international transactions for the purposes of Article XIV, Section 2.

2. *Representations by the Fund.* The following language in Article XIV, Section 4 of the Fund Agreement:

> "The Fund may, if it deems such action necessary in exceptional circumstances, make representations to any member that conditions are favorable for the withdrawal of any particular restriction, or for the general abandonment of restrictions, inconsistent with the provisions of any other article of this Agreement."

---

* These conclusions concerning the Fund's jurisdiction and the obligation of members apply to all members including those for whose currencies par values have not been established.

(a) applies at any time after the entry into force of the Fund Agreement and

(b) gives to the Fund the power to determine what is meant by "in exceptional circumstances."

3. *Maintenance.* Members may maintain multiple currency practices during the transitional period under the provisions of Article XIV, Section 2, but only if the maintenance of such practices is necessary for settling members' balances of payments in a manner which does not unduly encumber their access to the resources of the Fund. Members are under a duty to withdraw such practices as soon as they are able without them to settle their balance of payments in a manner which will not unduly encumber their access to the resources of the Fund. Moreover, under Section 4 of Article XIV, the Fund has certain powers to make representations in exceptional circumstances, of which it is the judge, that conditions are favorable for the withdrawal of any particular restriction. The Fund may exercise this power even if a particular restriction is justified for balance of payments reasons, if the conditions are favorable for the substitution of some practice which is not inconsistent with the purposes of the Agreement.

4. *Introduction.* Only former enemy-occupied members, which are availing themselves of the transitional provisions, and then whether or not they have existing multiple currency practices, may introduce a new multiple currency practice under Article XIV, Section 2, provided the Fund agrees with the member that the practice is necessary and does not find that it is inconsistent with the purposes of the Fund Agreement or with Article IV, Section 4 (a).

5. *Adaptation.* A member maintaining multiple currency practices under Article XIV may adapt the existing restrictions, provided such action is consistent with the obligations of Article IV, Section 4 (a) and the Fund is satisfied that the adaptation is dictated by "changing circumstances." A duty to consult with and obtain the approval of the Fund before changing the practice is implicit in both Article IV, Section 4 (a) and in Article XIV, Section 2. The Fund has the power under Article XIV, Section 4, to represent in exceptional circumstances that circumstances are favorable to withdrawal of a proposal to change an existing multiple currency practice.

6. *Reclassification.* A member maintaining multiple currency practices under Article XIV may reclassify commodities subject to such practices, under the power to adapt restrictions in Section 2 of Article XIV, and under the same conditions, provided, however, that under the existing restrictions the effective rates are other than parity.

C. *Exchange Taxes.* When a tax affects an obligation undertaken by the members of the Fund, the relationship between the tax and the obligation is of direct concern to the Fund and subject to its jurisdiction. Whenever exchange taxes are used to modify par values, create multiple currency practices, or introduce restrictive exchange controls, they are subject to the Fund's jurisdiction. The Fund has authority to deal with these exchange matters irrespective of the official device or procedure involved.

D. *Rates Differing from Parity by More than One Per Cent.* An effective buying or selling rate which, as the result of official action, e.g. the imposition of an exchange tax, differs from parity by more than one per cent, constitutes a multiple currency practice.

Multiple Currency Practices

I. The Executive Board has considered the staff paper on the "Review of Fund

Policies on Multiple Currency Practices" (SM/57/2, Rev. 1, 5/3/57) and is in agreement with the general approach of the paper.

II. Unification of the exchange rates in multiple rate systems is a basic objective of the Fund, and it is satisfying to record that several of the members which had followed such practices have been successful in achieving this objective, and that others have made considerable progress in this direction.

III. In reviewing the experience of the past ten years as summarized in the staff report, the Fund draws special attention to the fact that complex multiple rate systems damage the economies of countries maintaining them and harm other countries. These complex systems are difficult to administer, and involve frequent changes, discrimination, export subsidization, a considerable spread between rates, and undue differentiation between classes of imports.

IV. The Executive Board concludes that it is necessary and feasible to make more rapid progress in simplifying complex multiple rate systems, to remove those aspects of existing systems which adversely affect the interests of other members, and to avoid existing systems becoming more complex. Accordingly the following decision is taken:

1. Early and substantial steps should be taken to simplify complex multiple rate systems. The Fund will not approve such systems unless the countries maintaining them are making reasonable progress toward simplification and ultimate elimination of such systems, or are taking measures or adopting programs which seem likely to result in such progress.

2. As opportunity arises the Fund will continue to press for simplification in all cases where there is clear evidence that the multiple currency system in question is damaging to other members. It will in addition be reluctant to approve changes in multiple rate systems which make them more complex.

3. To assist members to simplify and eliminate complex rate systems the Fund wishes to intensify its collaboration with them. The Fund stands ready to meet members' requests for technical assistance in the preparation of economic programs and measures directed toward exchange simplification. These may in some cases include arrangements in other directions, especially in the fiscal and trade fields. If the Fund considers the proposed exchange simplification and related economic programs or measures to be adequate and appropriate, it will give sympathetic consideration, if requested, to the use of its resources.

Decision No. 649-(57/33)
June 26, 1957

Article IX, Section 7

PRIVILEGE FOR COMMUNICATIONS

Interpretation of Article IX, Section 7

WHEREAS the Executive Director for the [member concerned] has raised certain questions of interpretation of the provisions of Section 7 of Article IX of the Articles of Agreement of the Fund as to the treatment to be accorded by a member of the International Monetary Fund to official communications of the Fund, which questions of interpretation are set forth below;

WHEREAS the said Executive Director has requested that the Executive Directors, in accordance with Article XVIII of said Articles, decide such questions of interpretation;

NOW THEREFORE, the Executive Directors hereby decide such questions of interpretation as follows:

Question No. 1:

Does Section 7 of Article IX of the Articles of Agreement of the Fund apply to rates charged for official communications of the Fund?

Decision on Question No. 1:

Yes. Section 7 of Article IX applies to rates charged for official communications of the Fund.

Question No. 2:

If a member exercises regulatory powers over the rates charged for communications, is it relieved of the obligation of Section 7, Article IX, by reason of the fact that the facilities for transmitting communications are privately owned or operated or both?

Decision on Question No. 2:

No. A member which exercises regulatory powers over the rates charged for communications is not relieved of its obligation under Section 7 of Article IX by reason of the fact that the facilities for transmitting such communications are privately owned or operated or both.

Question No. 3:

Is the member's obligation under Section 7 of Article IX satisfied if official communications of the Fund may be sent only at rates which exceed the rates accorded the official communications of other members in comparable situations? For example, would the obligation of member "a", under Section 7 of Article IX, be satisfied if the rate charged the Fund for its official communications from the territory of member "a" to the territory of member "b" exceeds the rate charged member "b" for its official communications from the territory of "a" to that of "b"?

Decision on Question No. 3:

No. The obligation of a member under Section 7 of Article IX is not satisfied if official communications of the Fund may be sent only at rates which exceed the rates accorded the official communications of other members in comparable situations. For example, the obligation of member "a", under Section 7 of Article IX, would not be satisfied if the rate charged the Fund for its official communications from the territory of member "a" to the territory of member "b" exceeds the rate charged member "b" for its official communications from the territory of "a" to that of "b".

Decision No. 534-3
February 20, 1950

Article XII, Section 3

EXECUTIVE DIRECTORS

Interpretation of Article XII, Sections 3 (b) (i) and 3 (f)

The request for interpretation of the Articles of Agreement referred to the Executive Directors by Resolution No. 7 of the Board of Governors was considered [reference to document deleted]. It was unanimously agreed that Sections 3 (b) (i) and 3 (f) of

Article XII should be interpreted to mean that any member having one of the five largest quotas at the date of the regular election or at any date between regular elections shall be entitled to appoint an Executive Director who will hold office until the next regular election without prejudice to the right of a subsequently admitted member to appoint a Director if it has one of the five largest quotas.

Decision No. 2-1
May 8, 1946

EXECUTIVE DIRECTORS: ARTICLE XII, SECTION 3 (c)

Art. XII, Sec. 3 (c), should be understood as providing that the two members entitled to appoint additional directors are determined by the largest absolute amounts by which 75% of members' quotas exceed the average holdings by the Fund of their currencies during the two years preceding an election of directors, provided, of course, that they are not already entitled to appoint directors under Art. XII, Sec. 3 (b) (i).

In the calculation of average holdings under the provision, the Fund's special accounts for administrative purposes should not be included unless they exceed 1/100 of one per cent of the member's quota. A member should not be entitled to the benefit of Art. XII, Sec. 3 (c) where the average holdings of its currency by the Fund have been reduced below 75% of its quota solely because of expenditures by the Fund for administrative purposes or because of the exclusion of the special accounts for administrative purposes from the calculation of average holdings.

Decision No. 574-2
May 18, 1950

ADDITIONAL APPOINTED DIRECTORS

The phrase "the preceding two years" as used in Art. XII, Sec. 3 (c), shall be deemed to be the two-year period ending on the July 31 preceding the dates of regular biennial elections of Executive Directors. However, this decision shall be reconsidered if such regular elections are held in other months than September.

Decision No. 597-4
July 28, 1950

ADJUSTMENT OF QUOTA AND VOTING POWER

A change in the quota of a member between regular biennial elections will change by the same amount the voting power of the elected Executive Director who casts the votes of the member.

Decision No. 180-5
June 25, 1947

ARTICLE XIV, SECTION 1

USE OF FUND'S RESOURCES: PURPOSE

USE OF FUND'S RESOURCES BY COUNTRIES UNDERGOING RECONSTRUCTION

The prohibition in the Fund Agreement, Article XIV, Section 1, was not meant to prevent countries which were undergoing reconstruction from using the Fund's resources.

Decision No. 196-2
July 31, 1947

Article XIV, Section 4

RESTRICTIONS ON PAYMENTS AND TRANSFERS: WITHDRAWAL

Meaning of "Exceptional Circumstances" in Article XIV, Section 4

The following language in Article XIV, Section 4 of the Fund Agreement:

"The Fund may, if it deems such action necessary in exceptional circumstances, make representations to any member that conditions are favorable for the withdrawal of any particular restriction, or for the general abandonment of restrictions, inconsistent with the provisions of any other article of this Agreement."

(a) applies at any time after the entry into force of the Fund Agreement and

(b) gives to the Fund the power to determine what is meant by "in exceptional circumstances."

Decision No. 117-1
January 6, 1947

Article XV, Section 2

INTERPRETATION

In response to the request of the Government of [a member], and after having considered the arguments put forward by that Government, the Executive Directors, acting pursuant to Article XVIII (a) of the Fund Agreement, interpret Article XV, Section 2 as follows:

Action may be taken by the Fund to require a member to withdraw when the following conditions have been met:

1. The member has been declared ineligible to use the resources of the Fund pursuant to Article XV, Section 2 (a);

2. A reasonable time has passed since the member was declared ineligible to use the resources of the Fund pursuant to Article XV, Section 2 (a), whether or not a fixed period of time had been prescribed in connection with such action, and the member persists in failing to fulfill its obligations;

3. The member has been informed in reasonable time of the complaint against it and given adequate opportunity to state, both orally and in writing, any fact or legal argument relevant to the issue before the Fund.

Decision No. 343-(54/47)
August 11, 1954

The Board of Governors confirmed the foregoing decision on September 28, 1954.

Article XIX

MONETARY RESERVES AND OFFICIAL HOLDINGS

Net Official Holdings: Principles of Interpretation

In order to ensure the uniform application of the relevant Articles of Agreement as they apply to determinations of members' net official holdings of gold and U.S. dollars for the purposes of Article III, Section 3 (b) (ii), the Fund adopts or reaffirms the following principles of interpretation for the indicated provisions of the Fund Agreement:

(a) [Pertains to Article III, Section 3 (b); see p. 220.]

(b) [Pertains to Article III, Section 3 (d); see p. 221.]

(c) *Article XIX (b):* "The official holdings of a member means central holdings (that is, the holdings of its Treasury, central bank, stabilization fund, or similar fiscal agency)."

(1) "Central holdings" are confined to holdings owned by the institutions set forth in Article XIX (b).

(2) The term "similar fiscal agency" means an institution which performs an important function or functions similar to those normally performed by a Treasury, or central bank, or stabilization fund.

(3) No distinction is made among the departments of a central bank or other central institution as specified in Article XIX (b). No distinction is made on the basis of the use to which gold or dollars may be put by any of the institutions covered by Article XIX (b). That is to say, all gold or dollars owned by such institutions are central holdings.

(d) *Article XIX (c):* "The holdings of other official institutions or other banks within its territories may, in any particular case, be deemed by the Fund, after consultation with the member, to be official holdings to the extent that they are substantially in excess of working balances; provided that for the purpose of determining whether, in a particular case, holdings are in excess of working balances, there shall be deducted from such holdings amounts of currency due to official institutions and banks in the territories of members or nonmembers specified under (d) below."

(1) "Other official institutions" and "other banks" are official institutions and banks not embraced by Article XIX (b). "Other official institutions" are those representing a member anywhere. "Other banks" are banks within its territories.

(2) "Working balances" must be determined in the light of all the facts of the individual case, and no rigid rule can be formulated for their measurement. The general idea is that a working balance is one which is necessary to meet the requirements of its owner, taking into account normal receipts and payments, for a period not unreasonably protracted.

(3) No deduction may be made from central holdings on the ground that they are said to represent, in whole or in part, "working balances," for example, because there are no commercial banks or because the holdings of commercial banks are alleged by the member to be inadequate for working purposes.

(4) Gold or dollars owned by "other official institutions" and "other banks" may be included in a member's official holdings, after consultation with the member, to the extent that they are substantially in excess of "working balances."

(5) The proviso in Article XIX (c) declares that in determining whether the holdings of other official institutions and other banks are substantially in excess of working balances, certain deductions shall be made. These deductions are in respect of liabilities arising from the holdings of the currency of the member whose official holdings are being calculated. Such liabilities must be owed by that member's official institutions and banks to the official institutions of and banks in the territories of countries which were members of the Fund on September 12, 1946.

(e) *Article XIX (h):* "For the purpose of calculating gold subscriptions under Article III, Section 3, a member's net official holdings of gold and United States dollars shall consist of its official holdings of gold and United States currency after deducting central holdings of its currency by other official institutions and other banks if these holdings carry specified rights of conversion into gold or United States currency."

(1) Article XIX (h) establishes the only deduction from gross official holdings. That is to say, *gross* official holdings are the total of gold and dollars which a member owns; *net* official holdings are those holdings minus the one deduction which Article XIX (h) establishes.

(2) A deduction cannot be made under Article XIX (h) in the calculation of a member's net official holdings unless the following conditions are satisfied:

(a) There is a holding of the member's currency.

(b) There is a right of conversion of the currency into gold or U.S. dollars exercisable by virtue only of the holdings of the currency and not, for example, by reason of forward exchange contracts.

(c) The right of conversion is exercisable at the option of the holder of the currency and not at the option of the member whose currency is held.

(d) The option is exercisable by the central or other official institutions or other banks in the territories of other countries, and not by the member's own official institutions or by banks in the territories in respect of which it has accepted the Agreement in accordance with Article XX, Section 2 (g). "Other countries" embraces all countries, and not simply member countries or nonmember countries which have been specified under Article XIX (d).

(e) The right of conversion was in existence on September 12, 1946 (or any later date substituted under Article III, Section 3 (d)). However, the right of conversion need not have been exercisable on that date, but may be exercisable at any time thereafter.

(3) Liabilities payable in gold or dollars were the conditions of Article XIX (h) as set forth in 2 above are not otherwise met, e.g., where the creditor's right to gold or dollars is not attached to a holding of the currency of the member whose net official holdings are being calculated, are not deductible under Article XIX (h).

Decision No. 298-3
April 14, 1948

Currency Liabilities: Article XIX (e)

1. [Expired.]

2. [Pertains to Schedule B; see p. 272.]

3. [A member has contended] that where, under a payment agreement, the other contracting party held [its currency and the member] held the currency of the other party, the full amount of the holdings of [the member's currency] should not be deducted but the two amounts should be offset for the purposes of calculating deductible currency liabilities under Article XIX (e) [*ibid.*]. It is determined that the meaning of the term "currency liabilities" under Article XIX (e) cannot be restricted in this way. It must be applied in the gross sense to include all of the holdings of a member's currency by another party under a payment agreement.

Decision No. 486-2
October 7, 1949

Currency Liabilities: Article XIX (e)

The Executive Board has considered questions relating to the concept of currency liabilities in Article XIX (e), as set forth in Executive Board Special No. 107 (10/18/49), and agrees that the following principles apply:

1. The currency liabilities of a member are the liabilities represented by the holdings of its currency by the Treasuries, central banks, stabilization funds, similar fiscal agencies, other official institutions or other banks of other members, or of such nonmembers as have been specified by the Fund.

2. Currency liabilities are not confined to convertible currencies.

3. The deductibility of currency liabilities does not depend on whether the holder's currency is convertible.

4. "Currency" in the concept "currency liabilities" means "without limitation coins, paper money, bank balances, bank acceptances, and government obligations issued with a maturity not exceeding twelve months."

5. A blocked balance is not a currency liability.

Decision No. 493-3
November 4, 1949

Article XX, Section 4 (i)

USE OF FUND'S RESOURCES: POSTPONEMENT UNDER ARTICLE XX, SECTION 4 (i)

The Fund has, in the case of a member which has had no previous exchange transaction with the Fund, the power to postpone exchange transactions with it if its circumstances are such that, in the opinion of the Fund, they would lead to the use of the resources of the Fund in a manner contrary to the purposes of the Agreement or prejudicial to the Fund or its members. This power did not lapse as of the date the Fund began exchange transactions.

Decision No. 284-2
March 10, 1948

Schedule B

CALCULATION OF REPURCHASE OBLIGATIONS

Calculation of Monetary Reserves

1. [Expired.]

2. [A member has contended] that, in calculating its monetary reserves as of April 30, 1948, a sum greater than [the amount calculated by the staff] should have been deducted as the proceeds of a long-term or medium-term loan contracted during the financial year ending on that date . . . . It is determined that the deduction . . . calculated by the staff was correctly made, based on the following principles which are adopted:

(a) Before any exclusion of the proceeds of long-term or medium-term loans can be made under Schedule B, paragraph 3, of the Fund Agreement, it is necessary to identify that part of a member's holdings which can be regarded as representing the proceeds of such loans.

(b) Where the loan can be spent only for a specific project or purpose, the proceeds can be regarded as unspent only to the extent that the special project or purpose has not been completed and paid for. The formality of payment of the proceeds into a special or general account would not as a rule be considered a significant factor.

(c) Where the loan is not contracted for a special project or purpose, the proceeds of that loan which may be deducted should, as a rule of thumb, and in the absence of other evidence of identification, be determined as follows: (1) the member's lowest holdings of the currency in question between the date of receipt of the proceeds of the loan and the end of the financial year shall be determined, (2) the part of such lowest holdings which shall be excluded will be the proportion which the proceeds of the loan bear to the sum of the member's holdings of the currency as of the date of receipt of the proceeds of the loan plus other receipts in the same currency between that date and the day of the lowest holdings.

3. [Pertains to Article XIX (e); see p. 271.]

4. [Expired.]

Decision No. 486-2
October 7, 1949

Calculation of Members' Repurchase Obligations: Schedule B, Paragraph 3

In applying the provisions of Schedule B, paragraph 3 to the calculation of members' repurchase obligations, the following principles shall govern (Staff Memorandum No. 413, 12/8/49 and Supplement 1, 12/13/49):

1. Where exclusions have been made at the end of one year for holdings which are the proceeds of long-term or medium-term loans contracted during the year or for holdings which have been transferred or set aside for the repayment of a loan during the subsequent year, the exclusion continues to be made in the monetary reserve figures for the beginning of the succeeding year.

2. Where an exclusion has been made in respect of currency which became convertible during the year, this currency is included in the monetary reserve figures for the beginning of the subsequent year.

3. If the member indicates that certain holdings are the proceeds of loans or currency set aside, the reasonable implication is that the member wishes paragraph 3 to apply to such holdings. If the member does not provide such data, the implication is that it is not taking advantage of the provision.

Decision No. 510-2
December 16, 1949

Allocation of Obligations: Schedule B, Paragraph 1 (c)

If part of a member's gross repurchase obligation for any financial year is allocated to a currency which the Fund cannot accept because of Article V, Section 7 (c) (iii), that part of the gross obligation is abated for that year under Schedule B, Paragraph 1 (c), and is not required to be discharged in gold or some other currency.

Decision No. 521-3
January 16, 1950

General

FUND ASSISTANCE IN GOLD TRANSACTIONS

Members' Gold Transactions

The Executive Board approves the Managing Director's continuing to assist members by bringing governmental buyers and sellers of gold into contact. If there is a demand, the function may be performed as a regular service on the basis outlined in SM/52/6 (2/7/52). It is understood that initially the service charge will be 1/32 per cent for each partner in a completed transaction, and that the charge will be reviewed later on the basis of experience.

Decision No. 103-(52/12)
February 21, 1952

Fund Assistance in Gold Transactions *

The Executive Board approves the extension of the Fund's service in bringing buyers and sellers of gold into contact on the basis outlined in SM/52/6(2/7/52), to cases in which one of the parties to the gold transaction is a member and the other is one of the following nonmembers or international organizations:

. . .
Switzerland
Bank for International Settlements
International Bank for Reconstruction and Development

In accordance with the foregoing, therefore, gold transactions under the service would always involve a member as buyer or seller, and all parties would be either governmental or international organizations.

Decision No. 316-(54/27)
May 27, 1954

Fund Assistance in Gold Transactions

1. The Executive Board approves the following extensions of the Fund's service in bringing buyers and sellers of gold into contact, on the basis outlined in SM/52/6 (2/7/52):

(a) the International Finance Corporation is added to the list of parties in the decision adopted at EBM/54/27(5/27/54);

(b) the service shall apply to gold transactions between an international organization covered by the service and any other party covered by the service.

Decision No. 572-(56/55)
November 21, 1956

---

* The decision lists certain countries which formerly were not members but are presently members.

Fund Assistance in Gold Transactions

The Inter-American Development Bank is added to the list of parties in the decisions adopted at Executive Board Meetings 54/27(5/27/54) and 56/55(11/21/56).

Decision No. 1033-(60/26)
May 20, 1960

Fund Assistance in Gold Transactions

The International Development Association is added to the list of parties in the decisions adopted at Executive Board Meetings 54/27(5/27/54), 56/55(11/21/56), and 60/26(5/25/60).

Decision No. 1116-(60/51)
December 8, 1960

INVESTMENT OF FUND'S ASSETS

Investment of Fund's Assets

The Executive Board, observing that the Fund has had and may continue to have an excess of expenditure over income and that the greater part of the Fund's administrative expenditures has been and will continue to be in United States dollars, considers that in the interest of good administration and conservation of the Fund's resources it would be appropriate to raise income towards meeting the deficit by the investment of a portion of the Fund's gold in a manner which will enable the Fund to reacquire gold at any time and will maintain the gold value of the investment.

In view of the foregoing and noting the willingness of the United States to consent to investment by the Fund in United States Treasury bills, the Executive Board takes the following decisions:

I. The Executive Board, acting pursuant to Article XVIII (a) of the Articles of Agreement, interprets the Articles of Agreement to permit the investment described in the present decisions, namely, sale of a portion of the Fund's gold to the United States for the purpose of investment of the proceeds in United States Treasury bills having not more than ninety-three days to run, subject to the following conditions:

(1) The amount of gold to be sold for investment:

(a) will not be such as to limit the ability of the Fund to make its resources available to members in accordance with the Articles of Agreement; and

(b) will be such as to produce an amount of income reasonably related to the deficit of the Fund;

(2) Whenever the Fund decides to reacquire gold after the sale or maturity of any United States Treasury bills invested in, it will be able to reacquire the same amount of gold as was sold for investment in such bills; and the United States, at the request of the Fund, will sell the said amount of gold to the Fund for U.S. dollars at the United States selling price at the time of the sale to the Fund;

(3) In any computations for the purpose of applying the provisions of the Articles of Agreement the Fund will treat the following assets as representing gold and not as holdings of United States currency:

(a) the dollar proceeds of the sale of gold before investment in United States Treasury bills; and

(b) the United States Treasury bills invested in; and

(c) the dollar proceeds resulting from the sale or maturity of any such bills before the purchase of gold therewith.

II. (1) The Executive Board, acting pursuant to Article XVIII (a) of the Articles of Agreement, interprets Article IV, Section 8 (a) to require the United States to maintain the gold value of the assets set forth in paragraph I (3) (a), (b) and (c) above, notwithstanding changes in the par or foreign exchange value of the currency of the United States. This obligation of the United States shall be fully discharged by its maintaining the gold value of the dollar proceeds resulting from the sale of the gold or from the sale or maturity of the U.S. Treasury bills purchased therewith.

(2) For the purposes of paragraphs I and II of these decisions the dollar proceeds resulting from the sale or maturity of the U.S. Treasury bills invested in shall not include the income of the investment.

III. Subject to the receipt of an assurance from the United States in accordance with paragraph I (2) above satisfactory to the Fund, the Executive Board decides that an amount of the Fund's gold sufficient to realize approximately but not more than two hundred million United States dollars shall be sold to the United States and the proceeds invested and reinvested in United States Treasury bills having not more than ninety-three days to run. The Executive Board will review the amount and operation of the investment at quarterly intervals and at such other times as may be appropriate.

Decision No. 488-(56/5)
January 25, 1956

Fund's Investment Program

The Executive Board, observing that the Fund has had and in the future may again have an excess of expenditure over income and that the greater part of the Fund's administrative expenditure has been and will continue to be in United States dollars, considers that in the interest of good administration and conservation of the Fund's resources it would be appropriate to raise income and provide a reserve towards meeting possible future deficits by continuing the investment of a portion of the Fund's gold in a manner which will enable the Fund to reacquire gold at any time and will maintain the gold value of the investment.

In view of the foregoing and noting the willingness of the United States to consent to continued investment by the Fund in United States Treasury bills, the Executive Board takes the following decisions:

A. Paragraphs I, II and III of Executive Board Decision No. 488-(56/5) shall remain in effect except that the following shall be substituted for paragraph I (1) (b): "will be such as to produce an amount of income reasonably related to the purpose of the investment."

B. The income of the investment earned after October 31, 1957 shall be placed to a Special Reserve, and any administrative deficit for any fiscal year of the Fund shall be written off first against this reserve.

Decision No. 708-(57/57)
November 27, 1957

FUND'S INVESTMENT PROGRAM

The Executive Directors (1) decide that for the purposes of Executive Board Decisions No. 488-(56/5) and No. 708-(57/57) on the investment of the proceeds of the sale of gold, the amount of $500,000,000 shall be substituted for $200,000,000 in Paragraph III of Executive Board Decision No. 488-(56/5), and (2) pursuant to Article XVIII-(a), interpret the Articles of Agreement to permit such investment in U.S. securities having a term to maturity not exceeding twelve months.

Decision No. 905-(59/32)
July 24, 1959

FUND'S INVESTMENT PROGRAM

The amount of $200 million in paragraph III of Executive Board Decision No. 488-(56/5), which was subsequently increased to $500 million by Executive Board Decision No. 905-(59/32), shall be increased to $800 million for all of the purposes of those decisions and Executive Board Decision No. 708-(57/57).

Decision No. 1107-(60/50)
November 30, 1960

FUND'S INVESTMENT PROGRAM

The authorization under (2) of Executive Board Decision No. 905-(59/32) is extended to permit an investment of the amount of $61,900,000 in 15-month U.S. Treasury securities maturing February 15, 1963.

Decision No. 1272-(61/53)
November 3, 1961

By-Laws and Rules and Regulations

The By-Laws and the Rules and Regulations of the Fund are reproduced below as they stood at December 31, 1965.

By-Laws of the International Monetary Fund (As at December 31, 1965)

TABLE OF CONTENTS

These By-Laws are adopted under the authority of, and are intended to be complementary to, the Articles of Agreement of the International Monetary Fund; and they shall be construed accordingly. In the event of a conflict between anything in these By-Laws and any provision or requirement of the Articles of Agreement, the Articles of Agreement shall prevail.

Sec. 1. Places of Business

The principal office of the Fund shall be located within the metropolitan area of Washington, D. C., United States of America.

The Executive Directors may establish and maintain agencies or branch offices at any place in the territories of other members, whenever it is necessary to do so in order to facilitate the efficient conduct of the business of the Fund.

Adopted March 16, 1946

Sec. 2. Bank Represented

The Executive Directors are authorized to invite the International Bank for Reconstruction and Development to send a representative of the Bank to meetings of the Board of Governors and Executive Directors who may participate in such meetings, but shall have no vote.

The Executive Directors are authorized to accept invitations from the Bank to send a representative of the Fund to participate in meetings of the Board of Governors or Executive Directors of the Bank.

Adopted March 16, 1946

Sec. 3. Meetings of the Board of Governors

(a) The annual meeting of the Board of Governors shall be held at such time and place as the Board of Governors shall determine; provided, however, that, if the Executive Directors shall, because of special circumstances, deem it necessary to do so, the Executive Directors may change the time and place of such annual meeting.

(b) Special meetings of the Board of Governors may be called at any time by the Board of Governors or the Executive Directors and shall be called upon the request of five members of the Fund or of members of the Fund having in the aggregate one-fourth of the total voting power. Whenever any member of the Fund shall request the Executive Directors to call a special meeting of the Board of Governors, the Managing Director shall notify all members of the Fund of such request and of the reasons which shall have been given therefor.

(c) A quorum for any meeting of the Board of Governors shall be a majority of the Governors, exercising not less than two-thirds of the total voting power.

Adopted March 16, 1946, amended October 2, 1946

Sec. 4. Notice of Meetings of the Board of Governors

The Managing Director shall cause notice of the time and place of each meeting of the Board of Governors to be given to each member of the Fund by telegram or cable which shall be dispatched not less than 42 days prior to the date set for such meeting, except that in urgent cases such notice shall be sufficient if dispatched by telegram or cable not less than ten days prior to the date set for such meeting.

Adopted March 16, 1946, amended October 2, 1946

Sec. 5. Attendance of Executive Directors and Observers at Meetings of the Board of Governors

(a) The Executive Directors and their Alternates may attend all meetings of the Board of Governors and may participate in such meetings, but an Executive Director or his Alternate shall not be entitled to vote at any such meeting unless he shall be entitled to vote as a Governor or an Alternate or temporary Alternate of a Governor.

(b) The Chairman of the Board of Governors in consultation with the Executive Directors, may invite observers to attend any meeting of the Board of Governors.

Adopted March 16, 1946, amended October 2, 1946

Sec. 6. Agenda of Meetings of the Board of Governors

(a) Under the direction of the Executive Directors, the Managing Director shall prepare a brief agenda for each meeting of the Board of Governors and shall cause such agenda to be transmitted to each member of the Fund with the notice of such meeting.

(b) Additional subjects may be placed on the agenda for any meeting of the Board of Governors by any Governor provided that he shall give notice thereof to the Managing Director not less than seven days prior to the date set for such meeting. In special circumstances the Managing Director, by direction of the Executive Directors, may at any time place additional subjects on the agenda for any meeting of the Board of Governors. The Managing Director shall cause notice of the addition of any subjects to the agenda for any meeting of the Board of Governors to be given as promptly as possible to each member of the Fund.

(c) The Board of Governors may at any time authorize any subject to be placed on the agenda for any meeting of such Board even though the notice required by this section shall not have been given.

(d) Except as otherwise specifically directed by the Board of Governors, the Chairman of the Board of Governors jointly with the Managing Director, shall have charge of all arrangements for the holding of meetings of the Board of Governors.

Adopted March 16, 1946, amended October 2, 1946

Sec. 7. Election of Chairman and Vice-Chairmen

At each annual meeting the Board of Governors shall select a Governor to act as Chairman and at least two other Governors to act as Vice-Chairmen until the next annual meeting.

In the absence of the Chairman, the Vice-Chairman designated by the Chairman shall act in his place.

Adopted March 16, 1946

Sec. 8. Secretary

The Secretary of the Fund shall serve as Secretary of the Board of Governors.

Adopted March 16, 1946

Sec. 9. Minutes

The Board shall keep a summary record of its proceedings which shall be available to all members and which shall be filed with the Executive Directors for their guidance.

Adopted March 16, 1946

Sec. 10. Report of Executive Directors

The Executive Directors shall have prepared for presentation at the annual meeting of the Board of Governors an annual report in which shall be discussed the operations and policies of the Fund and which shall make recommendations to the Board of Governors on the problems confronting the Fund.

Adopted March 16, 1946

Sec. 11. Voting

Except as otherwise specifically provided in the Articles of Agreement, all decisions of the Board shall be made by a majority of the votes cast. At any meeting the Chair-

man may ascertain the sense of the meeting in lieu of a formal vote but he shall require a formal vote upon the request of any Governor. Whenever a formal vote is required the written text of the motion shall be distributed to the voting members.
Adopted March 16, 1946

Sec. 12. Proxies

No Governor or Alternate may vote at any meeting by proxy or by any other method than in person, but a member may make provision for the designation of a temporary Alternate to vote for the Governor at any Board session at which the regularly designated Alternate is unable to be present.
Adopted March 16, 1946

Sec. 13. Voting Without Meeting

Whenever, in the judgment of the Executive Directors, any action by the Fund must be taken by the Board of Governors which should not be postponed until the next regular meeting of the Board and does not warrant the calling of a special meeting of the Board, the Executive Directors shall present to each member by any rapid means of communication a motion embodying the proposed action with a request for a vote by its Governor. Votes shall be cast during such period as the Executive Directors may prescribe, provided that no Governor shall vote on any such motion until 7 days after dispatch of the motion, unless he is notified that the Executive Directors have waived this requirement. At the expiration of the period prescribed for voting, the Executive Directors shall record the results and the Managing Director shall notify all members. If the replies received do not include a majority of the Governors exercising two-thirds of the total voting power, which is usually required for a quorum of the Board of Governors, the motion shall be considered lost.
Adopted March 16, 1946

Sec. 14. Terms of Service

(a) Governors and Alternates shall receive their actual transport expenses to and from the place of meeting in attending meetings, and $75 for each night which attendance at such meetings requires them to spend away from their normal place of residence, this amount being reduced to $15 for each night when accommodation is included in the price of transportation.

(b) Pending the necessary action being taken by members to exempt from national taxation salaries and allowances paid out of the budget of the Fund, the Governors and the Executive Directors, and their Alternates, the Managing Director and the staff members shall be reimbursed by the Fund for the taxes which they are required to pay on such salaries and allowances.

In computing the amount of tax adjustment to be made with respect to any individual, it shall be presumed for the purposes of the computation that the income received from the Fund is his total income. All salary scales and expense allowances prescribed by this section are stated as net on the above basis.

(c) The salary of the Managing Director shall be $40,000 per annum. The Fund shall also pay any reasonable expenses incurred by the Managing Director in the interest of the Fund (including travel and transportation expenses for himself, and expenses for his family, and his personal effects in moving once to the seat of the Fund during or immediately before his term of office and in moving once from the seat during or immediately after his term of office). The contract of the Managing Director shall be for a term of five years and may be renewed for the same term or for a shorter term at the discretion of the Executive Directors, provided that no person shall be initially appointed to the post of Managing Director after he had reached his sixty-fifth birthday and that no Managing Director shall hold such post beyond his seventieth birthday.

(d) It shall be the duty of an Executive Director and his Alternate to devote all the time and attention to the business of the Fund that its interests require, and, between them, to be continuously available at the principal office of the Fund; however, in the event that both an Executive Director and his Alternate are unable to be available at the principal office of the Fund for reasons of health, absence while on business of the Fund, or similar reasons, the Executive Director may designate a temporary Alternate to act for him for periods of time which shall not in the aggregate exceed fifteen business days in the course of any financial year. A temporary Alternate shall receive no salary or expense allowance.

(e) The maximum salary and expense allowance including housing, entertainment and all other expenses [except those specified in subsection (f)] shall be $28,000 per year for Executive Directors and $22,000 per year for Alternates. It will be the duty of each Executive Director and each Alternate to state how much of these amounts he intends to draw whether as salary or as expense allowance, except that no Executive Director shall draw more than $25,000 and no Alternate shall draw more than $20,000 as salary.

(f) The Executive Directors and their Alternates are to be reimbursed, in addition, for all reasonable expenses incurred during absence from the seat of the Fund while on the designated service of the Fund. Executive Directors and their Alternates shall be reimbursed for authorized representation expenses actually incurred while they are absent from the seat of the Fund on a special mission at the request of the Fund. They shall also be reimbursed for travel and transportation expenses for themselves, their families, and their personal effects in moving once to the seat of the Fund during or immediately before their periods of service and in moving once from the seat during or immediately after their periods of service.

In addition, any Executive Director or Alternate shall in the third year of continuous full-time service in either capacity and in every second year of such service thereafter be entitled to reimbursement for the cost of transportation expenses for his family in traveling once to and from the country of which he or his wife is a national, provided that in cases where the wife is a national of another country the reimbursement for transportation expenses to and from her country does not exceed that to and from the country of which he is a national. For home leave travel more frequent than every third year, reimbursement shall be made on the basis of cabin- or economy-class accommodations.

(g) Where not specified, it is assumed that the Director and Alternate will be a full-time Director and Alternate. Where it is intended that he shall not devote his full time, it shall be so indicated. Where an Executive Director or Alternate indicates that he intends to devote only part of his time to the Fund, his remuneration shall be pro-rated on the basis of a representation by him of the proportion of his time he has devoted to the interests of the Fund. He may make such representation each month.

(h) Where an individual is serving both Fund and Bank, the aggregate of salary received from both shall not exceed the full annual single salary indicated above.

In all cases of salaries or expenses involving dual offices in the Fund or Bank, or both, the individual affected is entitled to take his choice as to which salary or expense he elects, but he shall not be entitled to both.

(i) An individual putting forward a claim for reimbursement for any expenses incurred by him shall include therewith a representation that he has not received and will not claim reimbursement in respect to those expenses from any other source.

(j) Secretarial, staff services, office space, and other services incidental to the performance of the duties of the Executive Directors and Alternates shall be provided by the Fund.

Adopted March 16, 1946; paragraph (a) amended March 18, 1946 and June 6, 1966; paragraph (c) amended July 27, 1951 and December 14, 1960, effective December 1, 1960; paragraph (d) amended September 17, 1947; paragraph (e) amended January 5, 1951, effective January 1, 1951; December 2, 1957, effective November 1, 1957; December 28, 1959, effective November 1, 1959; November 7, 1962, effective September 1, 1962; and August 8, 1966, effective November 1, 1965; paragraph (f) amended September 17, 1947, September 30, 1948, August 18, 1961, and September 10, 1964.

SEC. 15. DELEGATION OF AUTHORITY

The Executive Directors are authorized by the Board of Governors to exercise all the powers of the Fund except those reserved to the Board by Article XII, Section 2 (b) and other provisions of the Articles of Agreement. The Executive Directors shall not take any action pursuant to powers delegated by the Board of Governors which is inconsistent with any action taken by the Board.

Adopted March 16, 1946

SEC. 16. RULES AND REGULATIONS

The Executive Directors are authorized by the Board of Governors to adopt such Rules and Regulations, including financial regulations, as may be necessary or appropriate to conduct the business of the Fund. Any Rules and Regulations so adopted, and any amendments thereof, shall be subject to review by the Board of Governors at their next annual meeting.

Adopted March 16, 1946

SEC. 17. VACANT DIRECTORSHIPS

Whenever a new Director must be elected because of a vacancy requiring an election, the Managing Director shall notify the members who elected the former Director of the existence of the vacancy. He may convene a meeting of the Governors of such countries exclusively for the purpose of electing a new Director; or he may request nominations by mail or telegraph and conduct ballots by mail or telegraph. Successive ballots shall be cast until one candidate has a majority; and after each ballot, the candidate with the smallest number of votes shall be dropped from the next ballot.

When a new elective Director is named, the office of Alternate shall be deemed to be vacant and an Alternate shall be named by the newly-elected Director.

Adopted March 16, 1946

SEC. 18. ADDITIONAL DIRECTORS

At least one month before the second and subsequent regular elections of Directors, the Managing Director shall notify all members of the two members whose currencies held by the Fund have been, on the average over the preceding two years, reduced below their quotas by the largest absolute amounts. He shall state whether either or both are entitled to appoint a Director in accordance with Article XII, Section 3 (c) of the Articles of Agreement.

When a member becomes entitled to appoint a Director in accordance with Article XII, Section 3 (b) (i) and 3 (c) of the Articles of Agreement, it shall not participate in the election of any Director.

Adopted March 16, 1946

Sec. 19. Representation of Members Not Entitled to Appoint a Director

(a) Each member not entitled to appoint a Director may, in accordance with the regulations provided in this section, send a representative to attend any meeting of the Executive Directors when a request made by, or a matter particularly affecting, that member is under consideration. A member, so electing, may waive its rights under this provision. The Executive Directors shall determine whether a matter under consideration particularly affects a member not entitled to appoint a Director, which determination shall be final.

(b) Whenever a member not entitled to appoint a Director desires to present its views at the meeting of the Executive Directors at which a request the member has made is to be considered, it shall so notify the Fund when it makes the request and shall designate a representative for this purpose who shall be available at the seat of the Fund. Failure to give such notice or to designate an available representative shall constitute a waiver of the member's right to present its views at the meeting.

(c) Whenever the Executive Directors are to consider a matter which has been determined particularly to affect a member not entitled to appoint a Director, the member shall be promptly informed by rapid means of communication of the date set for its consideration. No final action shall be taken by the Executive Directors with respect to such matter, nor any question particularly affecting such member submitted to the Board of Governors, until the member has either waived its rights under paragraph (a) of this section or has been given an opportunity to present its views through an appropriately authorized representative at a meeting of the Executive Directors, of which the member has had reasonable notice.

Adopted March 16, 1946, amended September 17, 1947

Sec. 20. Budget and Audits

(a) The Executive Directors shall instruct the Managing Director to prepare an annual administrative budget to be presented to them for approval. The budget so approved shall be incorporated in the annual report to be presented to the Board of Governors at their annual meeting.

(b) An external audit of the financial records and transactions of the Fund shall be made annually and such audit shall relate to the period representing the fiscal year of the Fund. The Executive Directors shall submit the Fund's audited balance sheet and audited statement of income and expense to the Board of Governors to be considered by them at their annual meeting.

The annual audit shall be made by an audit committee consisting of either three or five persons each of whom shall be nominated by a different member of the Fund and confirmed by the Executive Directors. At least one person serving on each audit committee shall be nominated by one of the six members of the Fund having the largest quotas. The Executive Directors shall determine, in the case of each audit, whether the audit committee shall consist of three or five persons and which members of the Fund shall be requested to nominate persons to serve on the committee. The service of the members of each audit committee shall terminate upon completion of the annual audit and submission of the report on audit.

Each audit committee shall elect one of its members as chairman, shall determine its own procedure, and shall otherwise be independent of the Management of the Fund in conducting the annual audit according to generally accepted auditing standards.

The annual audit shall be comprehensive with respect to examination of the financial records of the Fund; shall extend, insofar as practicable, to the ascertainment that financial transactions consummated during the period under review are supported by the necessary authority; and shall determine that there is adequate and faithful accounting for the assets of the Fund. It shall thereby establish an appropriate basis for conclusion concerning the financial position of the Fund at the close of the fiscal year and the results of its financial operations during that year. For this purpose, the audit committee shall have access to the accounting records of the Fund and other supporting evidence of its financial transactions and shall be furnished by the Management of the Fund with such information and representations as may be required in connection with the audit. The members of the audit committee shall respect the confidential nature of their service and the information made available for purposes of the audit.

All accounts shall be summarized in United States dollars; and for this purpose gold shall be valued in terms of United States dollars at the par value of the United States dollar, and all members' currencies shall be converted at their par values or in accordance with a decision of the Fund pursuant to Article IV, Section 8 (b) (ii) of the Articles of Agreement.

The Executive Directors shall decide all questions of policy raised by requests of the audit committee for particular information or the inspection of particular records or documents. The refusal of any such requests for reasons of policy shall be explained in the comments of the Executive Directors forwarded to the Board of Governors with the report on audit.

Any question the audit committee may have concerning interpretation of the Articles of Agreement, the By-Laws, or the Rules and Regulations shall be discussed with the Managing Director, or officials designated by him, and if the reply is not completely satisfactory to the audit committee, shall be referred to the Executive Directors through the Managing Director.

The audit committee shall submit its report on audit to the Board of Governors for consideration by them at their annual meeting. Such submission shall be made through the Managing Director and the Executive Directors who shall forward with the report on audit their comments thereon. The audit committee shall afford the Managing Director an opportunity for explanation to them before deciding that any matter seems to require criticism in the report on audit.

The audit committee may formally furnish the Managing Director and Executive Directors their views and suggestions concerning the system of accounting, internal financial control, and documentary or other procedure which may technically strengthen or improve the administration of the Fund's financial affairs. Such matters need not be dealt with in the report on audit unless the audit committee believes they are of such moment as to warrant inclusion.

The Managing Director shall determine what expenses are necessary and reasonable in connection with each annual audit and the Fund shall bear such expenses.

Adopted March 16, 1946, amended September 17, 1947

Sec. 21. Applications for Membership

Subject to any special provisions that may be made for countries listed in Schedule A of the Articles of Agreement, any country may apply for membership in the Fund by filing with the Fund an application setting forth all relevant facts.

When submitting an application to the Board of Governors, the Executive Directors after consultation with the applicant country shall recommend to the Board the amount of the quota, the form of payment, the parity of the currency, conditions regarding exchange restrictions, and such other conditions as, in the opinion of the Executive Directors, the Board of Governors may wish to prescribe.

Adopted March 16, 1946

Sec. 22. Compulsory Withdrawal

Before any member is required to withdraw from membership in the Fund, the matter shall be considered by the Executive Directors who shall inform the member in reasonable time of the complaint against it and allow the member an adequate opportunity for stating its case both orally and in writing. The Executive Directors shall recommend to the Board of Governors the action they deem appropriate. The member shall be informed of the recommendation and the date on which its case will be considered by the Board and shall be given a reasonable time within which to present its case to the Board both orally and in writing. Any member so electing may waive this provision.

Adopted March 16, 1946

Sec. 23. Settlement of Disagreements

The President of the International Court of Justice is prescribed as the authority to appoint an umpire whenever there arises a disagreement of the type referred to in Article XVIII (c) of the Articles of Agreement.

Adopted March 16, 1946

Sec. 24. Amendment of By-Laws

These By-Laws may be amended by the Board of Governors at any meeting thereof or by vote without a meeting as provided in Section 13.

Adopted October 2, 1946

Rules and Regulations of the International Monetary Fund (As at December 31, 1965)

TABLE OF CONTENTS

A—Scope of Rules and Regulations

A-1. These Rules and Regulations supplement the Fund Agreement and the By-Laws adopted by the Board of Governors. They are not intended to replace any provision of either the Agreement or the By-Laws. The Rules and Regulations attempt to provide such operating rules, procedures, regulations, and interpretation as are necessary and desirable to carry out the purposes and powers contained in the Agreement, as supplemented by the By-Laws. If any provision in the Rules and Regulations is found to be in conflict with any provision in the Agreement or in the By-Laws, the Agreement and By-Laws shall prevail and an appropriate amendment should be made to these Rules and Regulations.

Adopted September 25, 1946

A-2. Additions to, and changes of, the Rules and Regulations will be made as experience brings to light new problems or suggests modifications in procedures already adopted.

Adopted September 25, 1946

B—Terms, Definitions, and Symbols Employed in this Document

B-1. Executive Director, except where otherwise specified, shall include the Alternate or the temporary Alternate, as the case may be.

Adopted September 25, 1946, amended August 14, 1947, effective September 17, 1947

B-2. Executive Board refers to the Executive Directors presided over by the Chairman.

Adopted September 25, 1946

B-3. Chairman, except where otherwise specified, shall refer to the Chairman or Acting Chairman of the Executive Board.

Adopted September 25, 1946

B-4. Agenda ordinarily refers to both the list of items to be considered at a meeting and the supplementary documents pertinent thereto.

Adopted September 25, 1946

B-5. Fund Agreement refers to the Articles of Agreement of the International Monetary Fund and, where the context is clear, Agreement shall also refer to the Articles of Agreement.

Adopted September 25, 1946

B-6. FA refers to the Fund Agreement.

BL refers to the By-Laws of the International Monetary Fund as adopted by the Board of Governors.

RR refers to these Rules and Regulations.

Adopted September 25, 1946

B-7. Executive Session refers to a Meeting of the Executive Directors in which no person is present except the Executive Directors, Managing Director, and, with the approval of the Board granted separately for each Executive Session, the Secretary of the Board.

Adopted September 25, 1946

B-8. Business day [1] refers to the normal working hours of the Fund, 9:00 a.m. to 5:30 p.m. at the official time for the District of Columbia, on Monday through Friday of each week with the following exceptions (which will include the preceding Friday whenever one of the dates below falls on a Saturday and the following Monday whenever one falls on a Sunday):

January 1	First Monday in September
February 22	November 11
May 30	Fourth Thursday in November
July 4	December 25

Adopted May 28, 1947, amended March 8, 1948 and October 27, 1961

[1] The definition of "business day" does not affect in any way the arrangements which have been made for the receipt of messages at all times and for prompt action upon them as required by circumstances and the Fund Agreement, By-Laws and Rules and Regulations.

C—Meetings of the Executive Board

Meetings

C-1. Meetings of the Executive Directors shall be called by the Chairman as the business of the Fund may require. Except in special circumstances the Chairman shall notify all Executive Directors of meetings at least two business days in advance.
Adopted September 25, 1946, amended May 28, 1947

C-2. The Chairman shall call a meeting at the request of any Executive Director.
Adopted September 25, 1946

C-3. Meetings of the Executive Board shall be open to attendance by the Secretary and such members of the staff as the Chairman indicates. At the request of the Chairman or any Executive Director meetings may be held in Executive Session, or the Executive Board may determine which particular members of the staff may attend any session.
Adopted September 25, 1946, amended January 15, 1948

C-4. The Executive Directors shall meet at the principal office of the Fund unless it is decided that a particular meeting shall be held elsewhere.
Adopted September 25, 1946

C-5. In the absence of the Managing Director, the Deputy Managing Director shall act as Chairman and shall have a deciding vote in case of an equal division. In the absence of both the Managing Director and the Deputy Managing Director, the Executive Director selected by the Executive Board shall act as Chairman. An Executive Director shall retain his right to vote when serving as Acting Chairman.
Adopted September 25, 1946, amended November 12, 1948

Agenda

C-6. The agenda for each meeting shall be prepared by the Chairman. The agenda shall include any item requested by an Executive Director.
Adopted September 25, 1946

C-7. Except in special circumstances the Chairman shall notify Executive Directors of new items on the agenda at least two full business days before their consideration in meetings. Additional advance notice shall be given at the discretion of the Chairman before the consideration of new items of especial importance which may require consultation with members or the return to the seat of the Fund of Executive Directors who are absent.
Adopted September 25, 1946, amended May 28, 1947

C-8. Matters not on the agenda for a meeting may be considered at that meeting only by unanimous consent of the Executive Directors present.
Adopted September 25, 1946

C-9. Any item of the agenda for a meeting, consideration of which has not been completed at that meeting, shall, unless the Executive Directors decide otherwise, be automatically included in the agenda of the next meeting.
Adopted September 25, 1946

Voting

C-10. The Chairman will ordinarily ascertain the sense of the meeting in lieu of a formal vote. Any Executive Director may require a formal vote to be taken with votes cast as prescribed in Article XII, Section 3 (i).

Adopted September 25, 1946

C-11. There shall be no formal voting in committees and subcommittees. The Chairman of the committee or subcommittee shall determine the sense of the meeting (including alternative points of view) which shall be reported.

Adopted September 25, 1946

C-12. No Executive Director may vote at any meeting by proxy or by any other method than in person.

Adopted September 25, 1946

Language

C-13. The working language of the Fund will be English. The discussion, documents, and reports of meetings will ordinarily be in English. Speeches or papers presented in other languages shall be translated into English.

Adopted September 25, 1946

Minutes

C-14. Under the direction of the Managing Director, the Secretary shall be responsible for the preparation of a summary record of the proceedings of the Executive Board.

Adopted September 25, 1946

C-15. Verbatim records will be taken only if the Chairman, the Executive Board or an Executive Director so requests. In such case, the Secretariat shall be given advance notice of the desire for verbatim recording.

Adopted September 25, 1946

C-16. Draft minutes will be circulated to all Executive Directors as quickly as possible after meetings. They will normally be submitted for approval at the next meeting of the Executive Board following the day they are circulated, and in any case will be submitted for approval not later than the third succeeding meeting.

Adopted September 25, 1946, amended May 28, 1947 and August 14, 1947

D—Application for Membership and Quotas

D-1. When a country applies for membership in the Fund, and the application is placed before the Executive Board, the Chairman shall announce a reasonable time to be allowed for discussion and preliminary investigation by the Executive Board before a decision is reached to proceed with the formal investigation. If this decision is in the affirmative the Fund may proceed to obtain all relevant information and discuss with the applicant any matters relating to its application. Any Executive Director may request such information to be added to the list requested of the applicant as in his opinion is relevant to the decision to be made. The Executive Board shall then decide whether to submit an application for membership with its views to the Board of Governors for a telegraphic vote or hold the application until the next meeting of the Board of Governors.

FA II-2; BL-21. Adopted September 25, 1946

D-2. When a member requests an adjustment of its quota, the Executive Board, after consulting the member, shall submit a written report on the request to the Board of Governors at its next meeting. If the Board of Governors approves an increase in the quota of a member, and on the date the member consents to the increase its monetary reserves are less than its new quota, the Executive Board may reduce the proportion of the increase to be paid in gold. The member shall, if it desires such a reduction, transmit to the Fund by rapid means of communication within ten days after its consent, the data necessary to determine its monetary reserves as at the date of the consent. The decision of the Executive Board shall be made within ten days after receipt of such data.

FA III-2 and 4. Adopted September 25, 1946, amended May 28, 1947

D-3. At least one year prior to the time when a review of quotas must be undertaken by the Fund, the Executive Board shall appoint a committee to study the problem and to prepare a written report.

FA III-2. Adopted September 25, 1946

E—Subscriptions

E-1. Gold depositories of the Fund shall be established in the United States, United Kingdom, France, and India. The gold of the Fund shall be held with the depositories designated by the members in whose territories they are located at places agreed with the Fund. A member may pay its gold subscription to the Fund at one or more of the specified gold depositories within the terms of Article XIII, Section 2.

FA XIII-2. Adopted September 25, 1946, amended November 29, 1956

E-2. A member shall pay its currency subscription to the Fund at the designated depository. Each member is authorized to substitute in accordance with Article III, Section 5, non-negotiable, non-interest bearing notes payable to the Fund on demand for that part of the currency holdings of the Fund which exceed 1 per cent of the member's quota, and the depository shall hold such notes for the account of the Fund. Such notes shall not be accepted until the Fund is satisfied that they are in proper form and that their issue has been authorized. The balances held in the administrative accounts of the Fund shall not be considered as part of the currency holdings of the Fund for the application of this Rule.

FA III-5. Adopted September 25, 1946, amended February 20, 1950

E-3. The Executive Board may agree to alter the 1 per cent requirement in the case of any member should circumstances in the opinion of the Executive Board warrant a different percentage.

Adopted September 25, 1946, amended February 20, 1950

E-4. The member is allowed 24 hours in which to deposit the currency necessary to maintain the amount required under E-2 and E-3.

Adopted September 25, 1946

E-5. For purposes of Article III, Section 3, initial gold payments in excess of the minimum shall be accepted on the same basis as the minimum payment.

Adopted September 25, 1946

F—Par Values

F-1. The Fund shall arrange through the fiscal agencies of members that frequent and regular information as to the market rates of members' currencies bought and sold in their territories is made available to the Fund.

Adopted September 25, 1946

F-2. Members shall notify the Fund whether for the settlement of international transactions they, in fact, freely buy and sell gold within the prescribed limits of price and shall notify the Fund of any changes in such policy.

FA IV-4 (b). Adopted September 25, 1946

F-3. A member desiring to change the par value of its currency shall give the Fund as much notice as the circumstances allow, and shall submit a full and reasoned statement why, in its opinion, such a change is necessary to correct a fundamental disequilibrium.

FA IV-5. Adopted September 25, 1946

F-4. For transactions in gold by a member the margin above and below par value shall be, at the option of the member, either:

1. One quarter of one per cent plus the following charges:

(a) The actual or computed cost of converting the gold transferred into good delivery bars at the normal center for dealing in gold of either the buying member or the member whose currency is exchanged for the gold;

(b) The actual or computed cost of transporting the gold transferred to the normal center for dealing in gold of either the buying member or the member whose currency is exchanged for the gold;

(c) Any charges made by the custodian of the gold transferred for effecting the transfer; or

2. One per cent, which one per cent shall be taken to include all of the charges set forth in 1 above.

Adopted June 10, 1947, amended October 15, 1954 and extended November 5, 1954

G—Fund Transactions

General

G-1. Each member shall designate a fiscal agency for its transactions with the Fund, in accordance with Article V, Section 1, before its subscription becomes due, and may change the agency after notifying the Fund.

FA V-1. Adopted September 25, 1946

Foreign Exchange

G-2. Each request from a member to purchase currency from the Fund shall be made by the fiscal agency designated in accordance with Article V, Section 1, such request to be authenticated in the manner agreed upon by the Fund and the agency. In its operations on behalf of the Fund a depository will act only on instructions authenticated in such manner as may be agreed upon by the Fund and the depository.

Adopted September 25, 1946, amended February 20, 1947

G-3. When a duly authenticated request for the purchase of foreign exchange in accordance with Article V, Section 3, is received, the Fund shall, on the third business day following the day of receipt of the request, instruct the appropriate depository to make the transfer, except in cases which the Executive Board may indicate. The first business day after receipt of the request shall be regarded as the first of the three days.

Adopted September 25, 1946, amended February 7, 1947

G-4. When a member expects to purchase from the Fund, in a single transaction or a series of transactions, an unusually large sum of any other member's currency (unusually large relative to the quota of that other member), the member shall give the Fund as much notice of the proposed transaction or transactions as can reasonably be effected.

Adopted September 25, 1946

G-5. When the request of a member, if consummated, would increase to more than 5 per cent of its quota the aggregate purchases by the member pursuant to Article V, Section 3, during the thirty-day period preceding the date of action specified in G-3, the Managing Director shall notify each Executive Director (or his Alternate if the Executive Director is not available) on the first business day after receipt of the request. If neither the Executive Director nor the Alternate is in Washington or its environs, the notification will be assumed to have been duly delivered if appropriate notice is delivered to his office.

At the request of any Executive Director or on the initiative of the Managing Director, a special meeting shall be called by the Managing Director to discuss the request as soon as feasible, but not later than the morning of the second business day.

Adopted February 7, 1947

Gold

G-6. Gold due to the Fund may be delivered at any gold depository of the Fund. Whenever the Fund accepts gold situated elsewhere than at a gold depository of the Fund, the member delivering such gold may be required to assume the actual or estimated costs, as the case may be, of moving the gold to the Fund's nearest gold depository. Where the member is required to reimburse the Fund for such actual or estimated costs, the Fund shall advise the member in what form reimbursement shall be made.

Adopted July 30, 1948

G-7. When any member sells gold to the Fund pursuant to Article V, Section 6 (a), the member may be required to assume the estimated costs that would be incurred by the Fund if it used the gold so acquired to purchase the currency it has sold. The Fund shall advise the member in what form such payment shall be made.

Adopted July 30, 1948

H—Exchange Controls, Currency Practices, and Agreements

H-1. The Fund shall keep all exchange controls under review and shall consult with members with a view to the progressive removal of exchange restrictions in accordance with the Fund Agreement.

FA XIV-2. Adopted September 25, 1946

H-2. If a member complains to the Executive Board that another member is not complying with its obligations concerning exchange controls, discriminatory currency arrangements, or multiple currency practices, the complaint shall give all facts pertinent to an examination.

FA VIII-2 and 3. Adopted September 25, 1946

H-3. Upon receipt of a complaint from a member, the Executive Board shall make arrangements promptly for consultation with the members directly involved.
Adopted September 25, 1946

H-4. All requests by a member under Article VIII, Sections 2 and 3, that the Fund approve the imposition of restrictions on the making of payments and transfers for current international transactions, or the use of discriminatory currency arrangements or multiple currency practices, shall be submitted to the Executive Board in writing, with a statement of the reasons for making the request.
FA VIII-2 and 3. Adopted September 25, 1946

H-5. The Executive Board shall decide each request for approval expeditiously.
Adopted September 25, 1946

I—Repurchases and Charges

I-1. The first time that a member has to make a gold payment to the Fund it shall deliver gold of designated weight and fineness at least sufficient in value to meet the payment. Any surplus balance of gold shall be held by the Fund under earmark at the disposal of the member and may be used to meet other payments incurred in the future.
Adopted September 25, 1946

I-2. The service charge payable by a member buying the currency of another member in exchange for its own currency shall be paid at the time the transaction is consummated. The service charge payable for such transactions taking place from December 1, 1951 through April 30, 1966, shall be ½ of 1 per cent.
FA V-8 (a). Adopted September 25, 1946, amended November 19, 1951, November 14, 1952, June 26, 1953, October 14, 1953, December 23, 1953, December 15, 1954, December 27, 1955, May 23, 1956, December 21, 1956, December 9, 1957, December 12, 1958, March 20, 1959, April 20, 1959, April 19, 1960, April 17, 1961, April 25, 1962, April 24, 1963, April 13, 1964, and April 28, 1965

I-3. Rule I-3, adopted September 25, 1946, was eliminated on July 30, 1948, and the substance of the Rule was incorporated into Rule G-6 on that date.

I-4. (a) As soon as possible after July 31, October 31, January 31 and April 30, the Fund shall notify each member by cable of the charges it owes to the Fund pursuant to Article V, Section 8 (c) or (d), for the three calendar months ending on each such date. These charges shall be payable within thirty days after the sending of such notice.

Adopted September 25, 1946, amended July 30, 1948 and February 24, 1954

(b) Such charges payable by each member shall be computed on the basis of the "average of the holdings" which, as used in this section, means the average daily balances of its currency held by the Fund in excess of its quota calculated as follows:

(i) At the end of each calendar month there shall be averaged for each member the daily amounts by which the Fund's holdings of its currency on the Fund's books at the close of each day during that month have exceeded its quota on each such day;

(ii) The Fund's holdings of each member's currency shall consist of all of its currency except amounts, not in excess of 1/100 of 1% of the member's quota, in a special account to meet administrative expenses.

Adopted July 30, 1948

(c) The period of time during which the Fund's holdings of a member's currency have been at a particular level shall be the continuous period of time during which the average of the holdings has not fallen below that level, and, in determining periods of time for the application of the charges, changes in the average of the holdings shall affect the calculation of time periods in the following way:

(i) Each increase in the average of the holdings shall create a new segment of the holdings which will be equal to the amount of the increase and the period of time during which each segment is held shall be measured from the beginning of the month in which the increase in the average of the holdings occurs.

(ii) Each decrease in the average of the holdings shall terminate the period of time during which the holdings have been in excess of the new average and the period of time shall terminate at the end of the month preceding that in which the decrease in the average of the holdings occurs.

Adopted July 30, 1948

[Rule I-4 (d) and (e) have been omitted because the charges provided thereunder are no longer applicable to any segment of the Fund's holdings.]

(f) (1) With respect to each segment of the holdings of a member's currency to the extent that it represents the acquisition of that currency by the Fund from January 1, 1954 through April 30, 1963:

(i) The charge to be levied on each segment to the extent that it is within the first bracket of 50 per cent in excess of the quota shall be nil for the first three months, 2 per cent per annum for the next fifteen months, and an additional ½ per cent per annum for each subsequent six months.

(ii) The charge to be levied on each segment to the extent that it is within the second bracket of more than 50 per cent and not more than 75 per cent in excess of the quota shall be nil for the first three months, 2 per cent per annum for the next nine months, and an additional ½ per cent per annum for each subsequent six months.

(iii) The charge to be levied on each segment to the extent that it is within the third bracket of more than 75 per cent and not more than 100 per cent in excess of the quota shall be nil for the first three months, 2 per cent per annum for the next three months, and an additional ½ per cent per annum for each subsequent six months.

Adopted as I-4 (f) December 23, 1953, amended December 15, 1954, December 27, 1955, May 23, 1956, December 21, 1956, December 9, 1957, December 12, 1958, March 20, 1959, April 20, 1959, April 19, 1960, April 17, 1961, April 25, 1962, and April 24, 1963

(2) With respect to each segment of the holdings of a member's currency to the extent that it represents the acquisition of that currency by the Fund from May 1, 1963 through April 30, 1966:

(i) The charge to be levied on each segment to the extent that it is within the first bracket of 50 per cent in excess of the quota shall be nil for the first three months, 2 per cent per annum for the next fifteen months, and an additional ½ per cent per annum for each subsequent six months.

(ii) The charge to be levied on each segment to the extent that it is within the second bracket of more than 50 per cent and not more than 100 per cent in excess of the quota shall be nil for the first three months, 2 per cent per annum for the next nine months, and an additional ½ per cent per annum for each subsequent six months.

(iii) The charge to be levied on each segment to the extent that it is within the third bracket of more than 100 per cent in excess of the quota shall be nil for the first three months, 2 per cent per annum for the next three months, and an additional ½ per cent per annum for each subsequent six months.

Adopted April 24, 1963, amended April 13, 1964 and April 28, 1965

(g) The Fund and the member shall consider means by which the Fund's holdings of the currency can be reduced whenever the Fund's holdings of a member's currency are such that the charge under (f) above applicable to any segment for any period has reached the rate of 4 per cent per annum. Thereafter, the charges shall rise in accordance with (f) above, provided that the rate shall not increase beyond 5 per cent per annum when agreement is reached under this Rule for repurchase within three to five years after a drawing in accordance with Executive Board Decision No. 102-(52/11). In the case of agreements on means to reduce the Fund's holdings beyond five years, the Fund may adopt higher maximum rates. In the absence of agreement on means to reduce the Fund's holdings, the Fund may impose such charges as it deems appropriate after the rate of 5 per cent is reached. When an agreement for repurchase within three to five years after a drawing is not reached or observed, the charges to be imposed shall rise in accordance with (f) above, provided that when the charges payable on any segment have reached 6 per cent the Fund will review the charges to be imposed thereafter. In the case of non-observance, if 5 per cent is payable on any segment at the date of non-observance, it shall continue to be payable only for that part of a period of six months for which it has not yet been payable; and when the repurchases to which the non-observance relates are made or a new agreement for repurchase not later than five years after the drawing is made all charges in excess of 5 per cent shall be reduced to 5 per cent.

Adopted as I-4 (f) November 19, 1951, amended December 23, 1953, April 27, 1959, February 25, 1963, and April 24, 1963

FA V-8 (c) and (d).

I-5. (a) If, in accordance with Article V, Section 8 (f), a member wishes to pay in its own currency part of any charge due to the Fund pursuant to I-4, the proportion to be paid in such currency shall be calculated on the basis of its monetary reserves at the end of the quarter of the financial year of the Fund to which such charges apply.

Adopted September 25, 1946, amended May 28, 1947 and July 30, 1948

(b) If, in accordance with Article V, Section 8 (f), a member wishes to pay in its own currency part of any charge due to the Fund pursuant to I-2 or I-8, the proportion to be paid in such currency shall be calculated on the basis of its monetary reserves on the day before the day on which the charge is due; provided, however, that if the member would encounter undue difficulties in providing for that day the data required by the Fund in the monetary reserve report forms sent to members, the proportion to be paid in the member's currency shall be calculated on the basis of its monetary reserves at the end of the quarter of the financial year of the Fund in which the charge becomes due. The member, when making a provisional payment in accordance with (c) below, shall advise the Fund whether the member will provide monetary reserve data for the day before the day on which the charge becomes due or for the end of the quarter in which the charge becomes due.

Adopted July 30, 1948, amended March 24, 1950

(c) Whenever a charge is due under I-2, I-4, or I 8, and the member wishes to pay part thereof in its own currency, the member shall make a provisional payment in gold and currency on the basis of its own estimate of its monetary reserves for the appropriate day or end of quarter of the financial year of the Fund as specified in (a) or (b) above. The member shall provide the Fund with the data, for such appropriate day or end of quarter, required by the Fund in the monetary reserve report forms sent to members, and such data shall be provided to the Fund not later than six months from the aforesaid appropriate day or end of quarter. On the basis of such data, the Fund shall make a final determination of the proportions of the charge to be paid in gold and in currency, and final adjustment of the provisional payment shall be made on the date specified by the Fund. If the member fails to provide its monetary reserve data within the period prescribed herein, the whole of the charge shall be finally payable in gold.

Adopted July 30, 1948

FA V-8 (f)

I-6. (a) Within six months after the end of each financial year of the Fund, each member shall furnish the data necessary for the calculation of its monetary reserves and its repurchase obligation, if any. Such data shall be supplied to the Fund in the monetary reserve report forms sent to members by the Fund.

(b) Each member's monetary reserves and repurchase obligation, if any, shall be computed on the basis of the aforesaid data.

(c) When a repurchase obligation has thus been computed for a member, the Managing Director, after consultation with the Executive Director appointed or elected by the member, shall notify the member by letter containing all the necessary details of the computation, including the distribution of the amount payable among the types of reserves.

(d) If the member is in agreement with the aforesaid computation, the member shall so advise the Fund within thirty days from the day on which the member receives notice thereof. The Managing Director shall then send to the member a formal request for payment, and shall at the same time notify the Board of such request. The member shall discharge the repurchase obligation within thirty days from the day on which the member receives the formal request for payment.

(e) If the member disagrees with the computation notified to it under (c) above, it shall so advise the Fund within thirty days from the day on which the member receives notice thereof, and shall at the same time or within the said thirty days inform the Fund of its reasoned objections. If agreement with the member is not reached within a period regarded by the Managing Director as reasonable in the circumstances of the case, the Managing Director, after consultation with the Executive Director appointed or elected by the member, shall refer the matter to the Executive Board.

(f) After agreement with the member if reached under (e) above, or after a decision by the Executive Board determining the member's repurchase obligation, the Managing Director shall send to the member a formal request for payment, and shall at the same time notify the Board of such request. The member shall discharge the repurchase obligation within thirty days from the day on which the member receives the formal request for payment or within such other period as may be decided by the Executive Board.

(g) The Managing Director shall report to the Executive Board any case in which it appears the above procedure has not been followed.

FA V-7 and Schedule B. Adopted September 25, 1946, amended July 28, 1950

I-7. For the purposes of Article V, Section 7, the term "financial year" shall be defined as beginning on May 1 and ending on the succeeding April 30; provided, however, that the first financial year shall begin on March 1, 1947 and end on April 30, 1948.

For purposes of the Fund's accounts and reports, its fiscal year shall begin on May 1 and end on the succeeding April 30; provided, however, that the fiscal year 1946/47 shall begin on July 1, 1946 and end on June 30, 1947, and the fiscal year 1947/48 shall begin on July 1, 1947 and end on April 30, 1948.

Adopted February 7, 1947, amended May 28, 1947, effective September 17, 1947

I-8. When any member sells gold to the Fund pursuant to Article V, Section 6 (a), or buys gold from the Fund, the Fund may levy a handling charge which shall be paid in accordance with Article V, Section 8 (f).

Adopted February 7, 1947, amended July 30, 1948

J—Accounts and Reports

J-1. The accounts of the Fund shall be kept in terms of the currencies held by the Fund and United States dollars on the basis of the established parities.
FA IV-1; BL-20. Adopted September 25, 1946

J-2. The accounts of the Fund shall be kept in a manner that will show clearly the nature of each transaction, the position of the Fund, and results of its operations.
Adopted September 25, 1946

J-3. A summary statement of the Fund's transactions and its holdings of gold and currencies of members shall be issued at intervals of three months or less, and a monthly statement of balances shall be sent to all members.
FA XII-7. Adopted September 25, 1946

J-4. The Managing Director shall prepare an annual administrative budget for presentation to the Executive Board for approval not later than April 1 of each year.
BL-20. Adopted September 25, 1946, amended February 20, 1948

J-5. Not later than June 30 of each year, the Managing Director shall present to the Executive Board a summary of the matters which in his opinion should be included in the annual report to the Board of Governors. At least one month before the annual meeting of the Board of Governors, the Managing Director shall submit to the Executive Board for its consideration, a draft of the annual report.
BL-10. Adopted September 25, 1946

J-6. At least one month before the annual meeting of the Board of Governors, the audited accounts of the Fund shall be submitted to the Executive Board for its consideration.
BL-20. Adopted September 25, 1946

K—Limitation and Ineligibility

K-1. The Managing Director shall report to the Executive Board any case in which it appears to him that a member is not fulfilling its obligations under the Fund Agreement.
Adopted September 25, 1946

K-2. Whenever the Executive Board would be authorized to declare a member ineligible to use the resources of the Fund it may refrain from making the declaration and indicate the circumstances under which, and/or the extent to which, the member may make use of the resources.
FA V-5, VI-1, and XV-2 (a). Adopted September 25, 1946

K-3. When a member has changed the par value of its currency despite the objection of the Fund, in cases where the Fund is entitled to object, the Executive Board may determine the circumstances under which, and the extent to which, a member may use the resources of the Fund.
Adopted September 25, 1946

K-4. Before any member is declared, pursuant to Article XV, Section 2 (a), ineligible to use the resources of the Fund, the matter shall be considered by the Executive Board, who shall inform the member in reasonable time of the complaint against it and allow the member an adequate opportunity for stating its case both orally and in writing.
FA XV-2 (a); BL-22. Adopted September 25, 1946

K-5. When any member that is ineligible to use the resources of the Fund, or whose use of the resources has been limited, according to K-2 or K-3 above, requests the Executive Board to permit the resumption of exchange transactions with or without special limitations and the Executive Board decides not to permit such resumption, a written report shall be made to the member stating what further action is required before such resumption will be permitted.

Adopted September 25, 1946, corrected October 18, 1950

L—Capital Transfers

L-1. If there is taking place a large or sustained outflow of capital from a member country:

(a) that member or any other member may notify the Fund, presenting such information as it deems necessary; and may request the Fund's views with respect to such capital movement; and

(b) the Fund may present to the member or members concerned a report setting forth its views, and may request the member or members to report on the situation within a suitable time.

Adopted September 25, 1946

L-2. Whenever the Fund has requested a member to exercise controls to prevent use of the resources of the Fund to meet a large or sustained outflow of capital, the Fund shall request the member to notify it promptly and in detail of the measures taken.

FA VI-1 (a). Adopted September 25, 1946

L-3. Each member shall inform the Fund in detail of the measures it is taking to regulate international capital movements and of changes made in such measures.

Adopted September 25, 1946

L-4. If the Fund is of the opinion that the controls exercised by a member to regulate international capital movements are restrictive of payments for current transactions, or unduly delay transfers of funds in settlement of commitments, the Fund shall, subject to the provisions of Article VII, Section 3 (b) and Article XIV, Section 2, consult with the member on the manner in which the controls are exercised. If, after consultation, the Fund is not satisfied that the controls are exercised in a manner consistent with the Fund Agreement, it shall so inform the member in a written report and request it to modify the controls.

FA VI-3. Adopted September 25, 1946

M—Relations with Non-Members

M-1. The Fund may request the cooperation of any member with a view to the application of appropriate measures to prevent transactions with non-members or with persons in their territories, contrary to the provisions of the Agreement or the purposes of the Fund.

FA XI-1 (iii). Adopted September 25, 1946

M-2. When the Fund finds that a member or any of its fiscal agencies referred to in Article V, Section 1, engages in any transaction with or cooperates in practices with a non-member or with persons in a non-member's territory, contrary to the provisions of the Agreement or the purposes of the Fund, it shall present to the member a report setting forth its views and may request the cessation or modification of the transactions or practices.

FA XI-1 (i) and (ii). Adopted September 25, 1946

M-3. A member shall inform the Fund promptly and in detail of any restrictions which it imposes on exchange transactions with non-members or with persons in their territories.

FA VIII-5 (a) (xi). Adopted September 25, 1946

M-4. Any member may notify the Fund of restrictions imposed by a member on exchange transactions with non-members or with persons in their territories which are deemed to prejudice the interests of members and to be contrary to the purposes of the Fund.

FA XI-2. Adopted September 25, 1946

M-5. When the Fund finds that the restrictions imposed by a member on exchange transactions with non-members or with persons in their territories are prejudicial to the interests of members and contrary to the purposes of the Fund, it shall present to the member a report setting forth its views and may request the abolition or modification of the restrictions.

FA XI-2. Adopted September 25, 1946

M-6. The Fund deems that it would be prejudicial to the interests of members and contrary to the purposes of the Fund for a member to impose restrictions on exchange transactions with those non-members having entered into special exchange agreements under the General Agreement on Tariffs and Trade, or with persons in their territories, which the member would not in similar circumstances be authorized to impose on exchange transactions with other members or persons in their territories. Therefore, pursuant to Article XI, Section 2, members should not institute restrictions on exchange transactions with such non-members, or persons in their territories, unless the restrictions (a) if instituted on transactions with other members, or persons in their territories, would be authorized under the Fund Agreement, or (b) have been approved in advance by the Fund. Requests for prior approval shall be submitted in writing with a statement of reasons.

FA XI-2. Adopted June 7, 1950

N—Staff Regulations

Personnel

N-1. The employment, classification, promotion, and assignment of personnel in the Fund shall be made without discriminating against any person because of sex, race or creed.

Adopted September 25, 1946

N-2. Persons on the staff of the Fund shall be nationals of members of the Fund unless the Executive Board authorizes exceptions in particular cases.

Adopted September 25, 1946

N-3. In the discharge of their functions, the persons on the staff shall owe their duty entirely to the Fund and to no other authority.

Adopted September 25, 1946

N-4. All persons on the staff must avoid any action, and in particular any kind of pronouncement, which may reflect unfavorably upon their position as employees of an international organization, either in their own country or elsewhere. They should always bear in mind the reserve and tact incumbent upon them by reason of their international functions, and they are required to exercise the utmost discretion in regard to matters of official business. At no time should they in any way use to private advantage information known to them by reason of their official position.

Adopted September 25, 1946

N-5. Except in the course of his official duties or by express authorization of the Managing Director, no person on the staff may, during the term of his appointment of service, publish, cause to be published, or assist in the publication of any book, pamphlet, article, letter, or other document relative to the policies or activities of the Fund or to any national political questions; deliver any speech, lecture, or radio broadcast, or grant any press interview on such policies, activities, or questions; or communicate to any person any unpublished information known to him by reason of his official position. After termination of his period of service with the Fund, a person formerly on the staff may not, without the express authorization of the Managing Director, disclose any confidential information he has received during his service with the Fund by reason of his official position.

Adopted September 25, 1946

N-6. No person on the staff shall hold other public or private employment or engage in any occupation or profession which in the Fund's opinion is incompatible with the proper performance of his official duties.

Adopted September 25, 1946

N-7. A person on the staff may retain re-employment rights or pension rights acquired in the service of a public or private organization.

Adopted September 25, 1946

N-8. Any person on the staff who accepts a public office of a political character shall immediately resign from the Fund.

Adopted September 25, 1946

N-9. No person on the staff may accept any honor, decoration, favor, gift, or bonus from any government, or from any other authority or person external to the Fund, for services rendered during the period of his appointment or service with the Fund.

Adopted September 25, 1946

N-10. Upon appointment, each person on the staff will subscribe in writing to the following affirmation:

I solemnly affirm:

That, to the best of my ability, I will carry out my responsibilities in a manner that will further the purposes of the International Monetary Fund;

That I will refrain from communicating confidential information to persons outside the Fund;

That I will not use to private advantage information known to me by reason of my official position; and

That I will accept no instruction in regard to the performance of my duties from any government or authority external to the Fund.

Adopted September 25, 1946

N-11. All persons appointed to permanent positions on the staff shall be classified by grades or positions according to the nature of their duties and responsibilities. Salary increases within each grade will be progressively available upon the successful completion of successive periods of work or upon the recommendation of supervisors.

Adopted September 25, 1946

N-12. The salary scale for permanent employees of the Fund shall, so far as practicable, conform to the salary scale of the United Nations.

Adopted September 25, 1946

N-13. The Managing Director shall inform the Executive Board at least two weeks in advance of any action to appoint or initiate the dismissal of any person at or above the rank of division chief within a department or office or receiving a salary equal to or more than that of a division chief within a department. All other appointments to the staff shall be made by the Managing Director or his designated representative.

Adopted September 25, 1946, amended July 1, 1959

N-14. The Managing Director is authorized to issue General Orders, with the approval of the Executive Board, concerning the general personnel policies which shall apply to the operating staff of the Fund.

Adopted September 25, 1946

Travel

N-15. (a) Official travel will be undertaken by staff members only with the approval of the Managing Director or officials designated by him. In the case of travel outside the continental United States, however, the specific approval of the Managing Director is required.

Adopted September 25, 1946, amended February 11, 1948

(b) The Managing Director will inform the Executive Board of all such travel at least once a month.

Adopted February 11, 1948

(c) Staff participation in activities of national agencies and staff travel to a member's territory require consultation in advance with the Executive Director appointed or elected by the member.

Adopted February 11, 1948

(d) Staff participation in deliberations or activities of international agencies or conferences as well as staff travel to a member's territory, undertaken in response to a formal invitation, require the advance approval of the Executive Board.

Adopted February 11, 1948

PART III

Fund Pronouncements

Use of the Fund's Resources

The date set for the commencement of Fund operations was March 1, 1947. Discussion in the Board of a number of relevant questions led to the issue, on June 7, 1947, of the following circular letter from the Managing Director to all members, enclosing a memorandum, also reproduced below, explaining the Board's policy in connection with the use of the Fund's resources.

Circular Letter to All Members (June 7, 1947)

Gentlemen:

For some time the Executive Board has been discussing the policies to be followed in transactions between the Fund and its members. It is the purpose of this letter and its enclosure to acquaint you with the results of these discussions.

The enclosed memorandum contains a statement of policy concerning use of the Fund's resources. It is, of course, a general statement and does not attempt to cover all of the problems which may confront the Fund and the members in connection with use of the Fund's resources. It should, however, make clear the responsibilities of the Fund and the manner in which the members can make possible the execution of this responsibility with a minimum of inconvenience to themselves and to the Fund.

In the course of the discussions which led to the preparation of the enclosed memorandum, particular attention was given to the meaning of Article V, Section 3 (a) (i), which reads as follows:

> "The member desiring to purchase the currency represents that it is presently needed for making in that currency payments which are consistent with the provisions of this Agreement."

This section, you will recall, is one of the conditions which must be met in order that "a member shall be entitled to buy the currency of another member from the Fund in exchange for its own currency."

At a meeting of the Executive Board on May 6 and May 29, 1947, the decision was as follows:

> "The word 'represents' in Article V, Section 3 (a) (i) means 'declares.' The member is presumed to have fulfilled the condition mentioned in Article V, Section 3 (a) (i) if it declares that the currency is presently needed for making payments in that currency which are consistent with the provisions of the Agreement. But the Fund may, for good reason, challenge the correctness of this declaration, on the grounds that the currency is not 'presently needed' or because the currency is not needed for payments 'in that currency', or because the payments will not be 'consistent with

the provisions of this Agreement'. If the Fund concludes that a particular declaration is not correct, the Fund may postpone or reject the request, or accept it subject to conditions.

"The phrase 'presently needed' cannot be defined in terms of a formula uniformly applicable to all cases, but where there is good reason to doubt that the currency is 'presently needed', the Fund will have to apply the phrase in each case in the light of all the circumstances."

The circumstances would of course clearly have to be unusual before the Fund felt that any representation by members might be open to question; but you will appreciate that the Fund must consider carefully all requests for currency in the light of circumstances existing at the time. This policy will ensure the Fund's resources against misapplication, without interfering with the ability of members to use the resources promptly when they do so in accordance with the purposes of the Fund Agreement.

It is our hope that this letter and its enclosure will be of assistance to you by clarifying the manner in which the resources will be administered.

Yours sincerely,
/s/ GUTT
Managing Director

Memorandum
(June 7, 1947)

The Fund Agreement sets up certain limitations on the use of its resources. These include the quantitative limitations. Equally important are the limitations as to the purposes for which use of the resources may be made.

1. They must be presently needed for payments in the currency requested. In short, the Fund cannot be used to increase a member's reserves.

2. They must be used to meet temporary needs—they cannot, for example, be used for large and sustained capital movements, for relief, reconstruction, or to meet indebtedness arising out of the war, or to support overvalued currencies when adequate measures are not being taken to correct the disequilibrium.

These are the principal matters covered by the representation members are required to make when they wish to purchase currencies from the Fund. With its large resources, the Fund must be concerned to see that they are used in accordance with its purposes. It must be in a position to know that the representations made by members are entirely correct and reflect a proper understanding of the Fund Agreement. In effect, this can best be done by keeping the officials of the Fund fully informed at all times of developments in each member country. This is the only way the Fund can judge for itself that aid it extends is not being used for financing a capital flight, that it will be repaid (and is not relief), and that it will be for a limited period (and is not for reconstruction).

In order that members may have the greatest possible assurance of access to the Fund when needed, the Fund ought to know these matters *before* rather than *after* a member applies for the purchase of exchange. A member should know that until it has been informed to the contrary, moderate purchases of exchange will be carried through promptly by the Fund. In that way a member can get the benefit of access to the Fund's resources as a second line of reserves. It would be undesirable to require a member to submit an extensive application to be considered at length in connection with each purchase of exchange.

From time to time, there will be cases where use of the Fund's resources would not be in accordance with the purposes of the Fund. Where a member is clearly not going to be in a position to repay the Fund, the Fund is duty bound not to engage in transactions with that member. Similarly, where a member has a fundamental disequilibrium, repayment to the Fund would require a correction of that disequilibrium, either through an adjustment of the exchange rate or through other measures. Aid to meet continuing balance of payments deficits, without prospect of a return to equilibrium, would be contrary to the Fund's purposes.

In every possible case, the Fund should know, from the information it receives and from discussion with the country's officials, the present and prospective position of the member and the use the member may be expected to make of the Fund. The Fund should know in advance of a request what its attitude will be toward use of its resources by a member.

As a general principle, the Fund should give as early notice as possible to a member that, in the view of the Fund, it ought to have only limited access or no access to the Fund's resources. In every instance, this should be done on an informal basis. The sanction of declaring a member ineligible should be used only in extreme cases where no other means of securing cooperation is forthcoming. There is no reason to believe that prior discussion with a member, in such cases where a limitation on use of the Fund's resources seems necessary, would fail to bring about the desired result. Consultation between the Fund and members should be a continuous process. Liaison should in time be so close that the Fund's advice may result in never reaching a stage that would warrant a sanction.

It would appear, therefore, that if the Fund can be kept fully informed as to the position and prospects of each member, any necessary measure of limitation can be taken informally before an application is made to the Fund for the purchase of exchange. In all other cases, the Fund would meet promptly each request in proper form for the purchase of exchange in moderate amount with a minimum of delay. The member could count on such aid from the Fund. However, in the case of unusually large requests in relatively short periods the Fund may have to take special account of the position of the member and consider over a longer period than a few days an application for the purchase of exchange. Such procedure gives to a member the greatest assurance of knowing that it will have access to the Fund's resources while enabling the Fund to make sure that the resources of the Fund are used in accordance with its purposes.

[For the definitive statement of the Fund's policy on the use of its resources, as later reached, see Executive Board Decision No. 102-(52/11) on pages 228–30 above.]

Transactions in Gold at Premium Prices

In May 1947 the Board set up a Committee on External Sales of Gold, charged with examining the legal and economic questions raised by member countries seeking to sell gold abroad at prices above parity. Following the committee's report, the Board communicated the following statement to all members on June 18, 1947.

Statement Communicated to All Members
(June 18, 1947)

The International Monetary Fund has given consideration to the international gold transactions at prices substantially above monetary parity which have been taking place in various areas of the world. Because of the importance of this matter the Fund has prepared this statement of its views.

A primary purpose of the Fund is world exchange stability and it is the considered opinion of the Fund that exchange stability may be undermined by continued and increasing external purchases and sales of gold at prices which directly or indirectly produce exchange transactions at depreciated rates. From information at its disposal, the Fund believes that unless discouraged this practice is likely to become extensive, which would fundamentally disturb the exchange relationships among the members of the Fund. Moreover, these transactions involve a loss to monetary reserves, since much of the gold goes into private hoards rather than into central holdings. For these reasons, the Fund strongly deprecates international transactions in gold at premium prices and recommends that all of its members take effective action to prevent such transactions in gold with other countries or with the nationals of other countries.

It is realized that some of these transactions are being conducted by or through non-member countries or their nationals. The Fund recommends that members make any representations which, in their judgment, are warranted by the circumstances to the governments of non-member countries to join with them in eliminating this source of exchange instability.

The Fund has not overlooked the problems arising in connection with domestic transactions in gold at prices above parity. The conclusion was reached that the Fund would not object at this time to such transactions unless they have the effect of establishing new rates of exchange or undermining existing rates of other members, or unless they result in a significant weakening of the international financial position of a member which might affect its utilization of the Fund's resources.

The Fund has requested its members to take action as promptly as possible to put into effect the recommendations contained in this statement.

[For the final decision of the Executive Board on the subject of premium gold transactions, see Decision No. 75-(705) on page 225 above.]

Adequacy of Monetary Reserves

On July 10, 1952, ECOSOC passed a resolution following an examination of a report entitled Measures for International Economic Stability. *This resolution, inter alia, asked the Fund to keep under continuous review the adequacy of monetary reserves, and to furnish an analysis on the subject for the meeting of ECOSOC in 1953.*

As a result, the staff prepared, in April 1953, a draft report on "The Adequacy of Monetary Reserves." This was discussed in the Board in May and after revision was sent to ECOSOC in June 1953, being described as a technical analysis and not a statement of Fund policy. The report as further revised and published in Staff Papers, *October 1953, is reproduced below.*

The Adequacy of Monetary Reserves (October 1953)

On June 30, 1952, the Economic and Social Council of the United Nations (hereinafter referred to as ECOSOC) began consideration of a report, *Measures for International Economic Stability,* prepared by a group of experts [1] appointed by the Secretary-General pursuant to a resolution adopted by ECOSOC on August 15, 1950. Chapter IV of the report, entitled "International Monetary Reserves", states "Our examination of existing reserves has convinced us that they are not in general adequate." The chapter gives reasons for this conclusion and discusses means of increasing reserve adequacy—including increasing the size of the resources of the International Monetary Fund and making its resources more readily available to members. While the chapter considers the adequacy of monetary reserves generally, its primary emphasis (in accordance with the experts' terms of reference) is on their adequacy to protect countries from deflationary shocks of external origin and to check the international spread of depression.

After consideration of the report, ECOSOC adopted a resolution on July 10, 1952, the operative paragraphs of which referring to the International Monetary Fund are as follows:

"5. *Urges* the International Monetary Fund, in supporting the efforts of its members to meet balance of payments difficulties arising from recession:

[1] The group included James W. Angell, Professor of Economics and Executive Officer, Department of Economics, Columbia University; G. D. A. MacDougall, Fellow of Nuffield College and Reader in International Economics, Oxford University; Javier Marquez, Alternate Executive Director, International Monetary Fund, formerly Professor of Economics, National School of Economics, Mexico; Hla Myint, Lecturer in Colonial Economics, Oxford University, formerly Professor of Economics, Rangoon University; and Trevor W. Swan, Professor of Economics, Australian National University.

(a) To apply its rules flexibly and, in this connexion, to give careful consideration to the suggestions contained in chapter IV of the report entitled *Measures for International Economic Stability;* and

(b) To be prepared to use its resources as promptly and as fully as is consistent with its Articles of Agreement;

6. *Requests* the International Monetary Fund:

(a) To keep under continuing review the adequacy of monetary reserves for the purpose of helping countries to meet temporary disequilibria in their balances of international payments, having in mind the desirability of:

(i) Avoiding, to the extent practicable, recourse to restrictions on trade and payments imposed for balance of payments reasons, and of promoting general convertibility of currencies and liberalization of trade;

(ii) Creating conditions favourable to a steady expansion of international trade, and to high levels of production and consumption, employment and real income; and

(b) To furnish an analysis of this question to the Council in 1953."

Two aspects of reserve adequacy are stressed in the resolution. Paragraph 6 (a) (i) stresses adequacy of reserves to permit removal of trade and exchange restrictions imposed for balance of payments purposes and the attainment of general convertibility of currencies. Paragraph 6 (a) (ii) stresses adequacy of reserves to expand world trade and to maintain high levels of employment and real income—and so, inferentially, to check the spread of depression. This paper will be concerned with both aspects, which may be characterized as the *multilateral trade* and *high level employment* aspects, respectively.

The paper as a whole has been prepared on a technical level.[2] It is an analysis of the factors affecting reserve adequacy. It is not to be construed as a statement of Fund policy, and its general conclusions are not to be taken as indicating Fund attitude on specific country situations or day-to-day operating problems.

NATURE OF MONETARY RESERVES AND THE CONCEPT OF ADEQUACY

The concept of "adequacy" is a difficult one, and any standard of adequacy must be based upon a consideration of the purposes which monetary reserves are meant to serve and the obstacles which are expected to be encountered in fulfilling these purposes. While the concept of adequacy presents the greatest complexity, the concept of "monetary reserves" itself bristles with difficulties. It may be helpful, therefore, to start by considering first the nature of monetary reserves and then the meaning of the term adequacy.

Nature of monetary reserves

Monetary reserves may be defined narrowly or broadly. The most useful type of definition depends upon the purpose intended to be served. If the purpose is statistical

[2] This paper has been prepared under the supervision of Mr. Henry Murphy, Chief of the Financial Problems and Policies Division, Research Department. It was discussed in July 1953 at the sixteenth session of ECOSOC, held in Geneva. In the paper submitted to ECOSOC, the tables recorded figures for 1928, 1938, and 1951. In the present paper, the 1938 and 1951 figures have been revised, figures for 1952 have been added, and a number of consequential amendments to the text have been made.

or legal, the definition must, before all else, be precise. When the broader implications of reserves are taken into account, however, a precise definition is not possible without a loss of realism.

Some items are included in the term "reserves" by universal agreement. Beyond these, potential items shade away imperceptibly from those whose reserve character is almost as clear as those conventionally included in reserves to those which are scarcely reserves at all. A similar hierarchy exists for items which might be considered as deductions from reserves. Because of the essentially arbitrary character of all cutoff points, narrow definitions of reserves fail to give a true picture of the relative international liquidity of different countries. Precise reserve computations are also subject to discontinuous changes in time, as portions of a country's assets move into or out of the categories formally characterized as "reserves", or as portions of a country's liabilities are formally allowed, or cease to be formally allowed, as deductions. Consequently, when the purpose is to consider the over-all "deficit-financing power" of different countries or regions, as is true for this paper, it is desirable, in principle, to treat the concept of reserves broadly, even though only narrow and particular concepts can be measured and compared.

Viewed in this manner, the monetary reserves of a country [3] may be defined as the assets which its authorities have available to meet payments to other countries. The nature and ownership of these funds may be quite varied. The two tests of the reserve, or near-reserve, character of any item which may be in doubt are, first, its availability to the monetary authorities of the country in case of need and, second, its acceptability by potential creditors.

Gold and currencies readily convertible into gold held by monetary authorities meet both of these tests perfectly and so form the core of the monetary reserves of most countries. Very short-term securities of countries with convertible currencies or private securities or bankers' acceptances of unquestioned credit and short maturity payable in such currencies and held by the monetary authorities of other countries meet both tests about equally well. The same is true of gold and convertible currencies or of any of the above-mentioned assets held by commercial banks or other financial institutions in countries where such institutions are considered to be part of the "official family" and are closely accountable to the monetary authorities.

Other items that meet only one of the two tests may, depending on the country and the time, be equivalent to reserves as defined above, and for some purposes could be included in reserves. In any event, their availability in financing a deficit is an important factor in any consideration of the adequacy of reserves. For example, gold and convertible currencies and short-term securities held by others than the monetary authorities and their "official families" may in some countries and at some times function in much the same way as reserves. The holders may themselves use such assets to meet payments abroad, or they may sell such assets to the monetary authorities when required to do so by law or when induced to do so by financial considerations.

Apart from such assets, whose reserve character is diminished only by the fact that they are not held by the monetary authorities and their "official families", there are assets held by the monetary authorities which can perform the deficit-financing function, although not so widely or so readily as gold and convertible currencies,

[3] The reserve problems of the nonmetropolitan territories of a Fund member have special features which are not expanded in this paper.

including short-term securities. These assets include inconvertible currencies, credit balances in bilateral or multilateral payments agreements (as EPU), and debt-type securities (other than those already mentioned) payable in foreign currencies, whether convertible or inconvertible, and having an international market.

While access to foreign exchange under predetermined conditions cannot be regarded as reserves, such rights do perform some of the functions of reserves and affect the standard of adequacy of reserves. Stand-by agreements and the provisions for drawing needed currencies from the International Monetary Fund, the right to incur debit balances with the EPU or under bilateral payments agreements, and established lines of credit against which a foreign currency may be drawn all provide means of meeting balance of payments deficits.

Some countries include stocks of silver and precious stones in their monetary reserves under the provisions of their national laws. These assets are not reserves in the meaning of the term used here, because they are not readily salable at an approximately predetermined price. They may, nevertheless, be salable abroad and could be used to secure additional foreign exchange when necessary. This may also be true of other commodities readily salable in international markets and of equity securities similarly salable. The possession of such assets by the monetary authorities or by others may affect the level of what may be regarded as adequate reserves, even if they are not included in a definition of reserves.

Monetary reserves, however they may be calculated, may be stated at their full gross amount or they may be stated "net" after subtraction of liabilities on account of which near-term payments may have to be made to foreigners—as, for example, short-term debts of the government, the monetary authorities, or the banking and business communities, debit balances in clearing accounts, or foreign holdings of national currency.

As already noted, when it is necessary to give precision to the concept of monetary reserves, particular items (positive and sometimes negative) must be selected from the broad variety of reserve and near-reserve items just enumerated. Thus, a calculation of a member's monetary reserves pursuant to specified standards is necessary to determine its obligation, if any, to repurchase its currency from the Fund. Such calculations are based on the definitions of terms in Article XIX of the Fund Agreement. Reserve comparisons in which the need for precision is primarily statistical, rather than legal, present similar problems. Thus, data on movements of monetary reserves are presented in the Fund's annual *Balance of Payments Yearbook*, and data on their amount in its monthly publication, *International Financial Statistics*. Similarly, statistical comparisons of monetary reserves on several alternative bases are presented later in this paper. Each presentation or comparison helps in the understanding of over-all reserve adequacy. But any single basis of comparison can, at best, give only an approximation of the "real" amounts of the reserves actually available to the monetary authorities of each country in case of need.

The concept of adequacy

Adequacy of reserves depends on the prospective problems that confront a country and, therefore, will differ from country to country and from problem to problem. No amount of reserves can be adequate to finance a chronic or continuing imbalance in a country's payments. Therefore, the problem of reserve adequacy can be discussed meaningfully only for those countries prepared to take appropriate measures to balance their external accounts over an entire cycle—but which may, nevertheless, encounter substantial payments deficits in some years, or even occasionally for several years together.

It is obvious that this fundamental assumption of a strong and balanced payments position over the course of a cycle, which is essential for determining the adequacy of reserves for the only purpose for which reserves can ever be adequate, that is, to meet temporary needs, is not generally or even widely met by the situation currently prevailing. Some countries have failed to establish their exchange rates at appropriate levels, and other countries have been so concerned over assuring full employment or rapid economic development that their monetary policies have been too expansionist to enable them to bring their international payments into balance without severe exchange and import restrictions. Unless such countries are prepared to moderate their monetary policies, and, if necessary, readjust their exchange rates, they will be under steady pressure in their international payments, and they will necessarily find that their reserves are inadequate to establish and maintain multilateral trade without widespread and continuing restrictions and discriminations.

While satisfactory fiscal and monetary policies are indispensable to establishing a strong payments position, it does not follow that a country with noninflationary fiscal and monetary policies and an appropriate exchange rate will inevitably have a strong payments position. The international payments position of a country is affected not only by its own policies, but also by those of the countries with which it trades. An inflationary fiscal or monetary policy or an unsatisfactory exchange rate in another country may cut off the flow of imports from customary sources and force the country to seek other sources of supply. And a restrictive import or exchange policy in another country with inflationary fiscal or monetary policies or an unsatisfactory exchange rate may make it difficult for a country with sound policies to maintain its exports and to earn the gold, dollars, or foreign exchange which it could secure under better conditions. No doubt, with severely rigorous policies and a far-reaching shift in the pattern of production, a country may offset the effects of bad policies of its trading partners. But that is a costly step which countries will seek to avoid as long as there is hope of securing better policies elsewhere.

It must be pointed out, furthermore, that the magnitude of the task of establishing a strong payments position which confronts countries with a tendency toward deficit in their international accounts will be importantly affected by the policies of countries with a tendency toward surplus. This applies most clearly to the commercial policies of the surplus countries. The deficit countries want to buy—and, in some cases, desperately need—the exports of the surplus countries; but, as the deficit countries have no monetary reserves to spare, they can pay for the exports of the surplus countries only with their own goods. If the surplus countries place or maintain onerous trade barriers on the receipt of these goods, the effect must be a general lowering of the level of world trade to the mutual impoverishment of both groups of countries.

Particular attention should be called to restrictions of the "escape clause" or "peril point" type—which, in effect, serve notice on countries endeavoring to increase their sales in the markets of the surplus countries using them, or endeavoring to break into such markets with new types of goods, that success in such efforts may result merely in an increase in trade barriers sufficient to restore the earlier (low) trade volume. Where such attempts involve substantial investment in specialized plant or equipment or specialized inventories or involve substantial advertising, the value of which would be lost if the attempts should fail, the existence of "escape clause" or "peril point" provisions may often be a sufficient obstacle to prevent serious attempts at materially increasing sales from being made at all.

In addition to policies with respect to trade barriers, the surplus countries' policies with respect to stockpiling may make an important difference in the situations of countries with serious balance of payments problems. Changes in stockpiling policies, which may mean relatively little to the surplus countries pursuing them, may make a vital difference in the economies, and even in the social and political orientation, of hard-pressed raw material producing countries.

The investment policies of the surplus countries can also do much to ease the payments problems of underdeveloped countries. A flow of capital on a commercial basis from regions where it is relatively abundant to those where it is relatively scarce—and, consequently, of high productivity—is justified by investment considerations alone and is in the mutual interest of both the lending and the borrowing countries.

But most important of all are the policies of the surplus countries with respect to their domestic levels of activity. Experience has shown that, in the United States in particular, the level of industrial activity is a far more important determinant of import volume than is commercial policy. Even a moderate slump in the United States would place a substantial strain on the economies and balance of payments positions of other countries, particularly producers of raw materials. Some fluctuation in U.S. business volume is inevitable, and countries exporting to the United States must allow for it in their calculations of what they can "afford" to import over a normal cycle. But they cannot and should not be expected to make similar provision for a period of severe depression and mass unemployment in the United States. Just as no amount of reserves can be adequate to sustain a chronic deficit due to their own inappropriate policies, so no practicable amount of reserves can be adequate to maintain convertibility without discriminatory exchange restrictions in the event of a major depression in the United States. Provision against this contingency can be made only by the United States itself through domestic and international policies aimed at preventing the occurrence or continuance of the depression.

Let us consider a country which has established a balanced payments position. That is, through a period covering prosperity and depression—but not a deep or prolonged depression—its receipts are adequate to meet its payments. The exchange rate is correct, the monetary policy is correct, and restrictions and discriminations continuing throughout the cycle are not needed to shore up the payments position. For such a country, what is an adequate level of reserves? Four standards, each more rigorous than the preceding, can be suggested:

1. Enough to enable a country in bad years, by resort to restrictions, to maintain its external debt payments and to purchase the goods and services necessary to avoid hardship to its population or dislocation to its economy and the possible emergence of an exchange crisis, i.e., to permit a reasonable distribution over *time* of the payments which it can afford to make over the entire cycle;

2. Enough to maintain currency convertibility, barring a severe depression, but with occasional necessity to resort to trade and exchange restrictions for balance of payments purposes;

3. Enough to maintain currency convertibility, barring a severe depression, but without the necessity for occasional resort to trade and exchange restrictions;

4. Enough to maintain currency convertibility, even through severe depressions (but not through prolonged periods of international deflation such as occurred in the thirties), without either the necessity for occasional resort to trade and exchange restrictions or the necessity for resorting to domestic deflationary policies for the purpose of restraining imports, even if this involves a substantial drain on reserves.

It may be helpful to list some of the principal factors which must be taken into account in determining the "adequacy" category in which a given amount of reserves (expressed as a proportion of its trade) may place a country pursuing appropriate exchange rate and domestic financial policies. Without attempting to arrange them in order of importance (which would, in any event, vary greatly from country to country and from time to time), these factors may be listed as follows:

1. The normal seasonal variation in the country's imports and exports and in the service items in its balance of payments;
2. The extent to which the volume of its imports and exports is subject to extraordinary variation because of natural or other factors, e.g., crop failures, political or economic changes elsewhere, etc.;
3. The variability in the prices of its imports and in the prices of and demand for its exports;
4. The extent to which the country is dependent on imported raw materials, equipment, and essential foodstuffs to avoid dislocation of its economy or undue hardships to its population;
5. The size of its inventories of export goods and their components, and of import goods and their products, and the extent to which these inventories could be compressed without hardship in the event of pressure on the country's reserve position;
6. The extent, if any, to which the country may expect adverse changes in its reserve position to be offset by "equilibrating" movements of short-term credit;
7. The prospect that the supply of reserves can be supplemented by grants-in-aid or long-term loans from other countries;
8. The extent to which the use, for international purposes, of actual holdings of reserve-type assets may be prevented by legal or other restrictions.

The first three factors (each dealing with variations in the amount and value of a country's imports and exports) and the fourth (dealing with its need for imports) are the most fundamental in the list, and can be altered by the country itself only by basic changes in the structure of its economy.

The fifth factor deals with inventories. It has already been suggested that stocks of goods readily salable on international markets might be considered to have an important bearing on the adequacy of a country's holdings of the more conventional type of reserves. When used in this sense, the concept of inventories may be enlarged to include both stocks of materials entering into the production of export goods and import goods and their derivative products. All such inventories permit either exports to be expanded for a while or imports to be contracted for a while, in case of necessity, thereby easing strains on reserves. The reciprocal relationship between inventories and reserves appears most clearly during periods when reserves are being run down to build up inventories or during periods when reserves are being increased or maintained only at the expense of inventory run-downs. In such cases the *combined* changes in holdings of reserves *plus* inventories may give a better clue to a country's real external position than either of these quantities taken separately.

The sixth factor enumerated above is short-term credit movements. At one time short-term credit movements were extremely important as means of supplementing the reserves of individual countries, and so as means for making smaller amounts of reserves go further. In the environment which has prevailed during most of the period since the beginning of the depression of the thirties, however, short-term credit movements have been, on the whole, of a disequilibrating rather than of an equilibrating character for most countries—although they still operate to the advantage of countries with substantial amounts of mobile capital, in the event of temporary stringencies in their payments positions. It should be noted in this connection that there has been a great shrinkage during the past generation in the amount of one of the most important types of short-term international credit; bankers' acceptances created for the purpose of financing international trade, the outstanding amount of which ranged between the equivalent of $2 billion and $3 billion in the late twenties, have now very largely disappeared.

The seventh of the enumerated factors is the prospect that the balance of payments receipts of a country from other sources will be supplemented by long-term loans or grants-in-aid from other countries. Long-term loans are an important factor affecting reserve positions. Throughout most of the nineteenth century and well into the twentieth century, the United Kingdom and some other European countries were fairly consistent exporters of capital. When these countries were confronted with reserve stringencies they could often adjust their positions merely by cutting down on the outflow of long-term capital or by ceasing to export capital altogether. The capital exported by Europe was an important factor in the economic development of the newer countries. Long-term capital flows were not necessarily happy as far as their effects on the year-to-year *reserve* positions of the newer countries were concerned, however, as these countries often adjusted their levels of imports, exports, and reserves to an expected inflow of long-term capital and then suffered reserve crises whenever such inflows were suspended. But those newer countries with strong credit positions were often able to replenish their reserves in time of need by floating long-term loans for that purpose. The long-term capital movements brought about by such loans were decidedly equilibrating in character for the newer countries. Unfortunately, the possibility of floating such loans is much less today than it was even a few years ago, and the necessity of maintaining reserves is correspondingly greater.

The possibility of a deficit country receiving a grant-in-aid is principally a post-World War II development. Most grants-in-aid during the postwar period have been for the purpose of meeting balance of payments deficits arising from the physical devastation and disruption of trade and financial relationships caused by the war. Countries still in need of such grants are clearly in too weak a payments position to fall within the orbit of any of the categories of reserve adequacy used in this paper. Their problems are payments problems, not reserve problems. More recently, however, most grants have been for defense purposes. Such grants may be considered as part of the mechanism for financing the cost of a mutual defense system in which each country contributes resources, human and material, in proportion to its ability and situation. It seems proper, therefore, that the prospect of receiving such grants should be taken into consideration, along with other types of prospective balance of payments receipts, in determining the adequacy of the reserves of the recipient countries.

The eighth, and last, factor enumerated above is the extent to which the use for international purposes of the reserve-type assets actually held by the monetary authorities is restricted by law or custom. The laws of many countries require that the authorities hold reserve-type assets equal to a stipulated proportion of the outstanding currency or some other objectively determined criterion. The effect of such laws is to reduce the adequacy for international purposes of any given amount of total holdings of reserve-type assets. The same effect may be produced in the absence of law if the climate of public opinion in a country is such that the holding of some minimum amount of gold or of other reserve-type assets is considered a practical necessity by the monetary authorities.

Reserves and confidence

The discussion thus far has proceeded on the implicit assumption that reserves are meant to be used and that, except as qualified in the immediately preceding paragraph, all reserves are, in fact, available for use. Neither of these assumptions is strictly true in a world in which uncertainty is, and will continue to be, a major factor in all economic calculations. In practice, if they are to fulfill their functions efficiently, reserves must be considerably larger than would be indicated by any reasonable evaluation of the probabilities of their actual use.

Assume, for example, that $500 million is the most pessimistic estimate of the amount of reserves which a country might reasonably need to meet an existing current account deficit before the deficit would either halt of its own accord or could be halted by the adoption of appropriate policies. (It is assumed, for convenience, that capital transfers are controlled and that this control is tolerably well enforced.) Assume, also, that the country's reserves are of just the amount necessary to meet the maximum expected deficit—namely, $500 million. This amount, despite its superficial appearance of adequacy, will prove inadequate if the pessimistic possibilities are actually realized. This follows from the fact that, in spite of prior estimates, no one will know how far the adverse balance of payments will actually run; consequently, if reserves run low, traders will lose confidence in their adequacy and will take steps to protect their positions. These steps—such as stockpiling beyond ordinary requirements, expediting payments for imports, and delaying the receipt of payments for exports—will involve additional reserve drains which would not have occurred at all if reserves had been truly adequate. As a consequence, a reserve run-down which would have amounted to only $500 million if reserves had been, say, $1 billion, may result in a serious exchange crisis if reserves are actually only $500 million.

It follows that, in order to avoid the intermittent imposition of trade and exchange restrictions, reserves must be larger than any allowable current account deficit in order to maintain confidence and so hold down outpayments to the actual amount of the deficit. To secure the required confidence, it is necessary that there always be available, even at the very bottom of the cycle, a substantial volume of additional reserves which are uncommitted and available for immediate use.

Confidence, however, is a two-way street. Just as larger reserves promote confidence in a country's situation and so may make their use unnecessary, so confidence in a country's situation—and in its willingness to pursue appropriate policies—reduces the amount of reserves necessary to sustain this confidence. In the long run, the effect of "underlying" confidence upon the amount of necessary reserves is probably more important than the effect of adequate reserves upon confidence. The classic example, of course, is the United Kingdom before World War I, when London was the undisputed financial center of the world and operated on a minimal reserve base. At that time, other countries were able to hold a large portion of their reserves in sterling with full confidence in the universal acceptability of sterling which made it the practical equivalent of gold.

Over-all evaluations of reserve adequacy

The factors that determine the adequacy of reserves are not, in practice, precisely measurable. Basically, therefore, the adequacy of reserves is a matter of judgment—depending on the country, on the time, and on the purpose for which the reserves are intended. Furthermore, the prevalent opinion of the international business community concerning the adequacy of each country's reserves is itself a factor in determining their "real" adequacy—so that, in one sense, the reserves of a country are not adequate until the public thinks that they are adequate. Such opinions, it should be noted, are likely to be based as much on the trend in a country's reserve position as on its absolute amount; a moderate reserve position, well maintained, is likely to give an impression of greater adequacy than a large reserve position which has been rapidly declining, with no end clearly in sight.

That the adequacy of reserves cannot be precisely measured gives rise to the corollary that significant decisions depending in part upon reserve adequacy—e.g., decisions to impose or to relax exchange restrictions, to tighten or to relax monetary and fiscal policies, or to alter exchange rates—are based on the *opinions* of the relevant authorities, national and international, concerning this adequacy. The opinions of these authorities are seen most clearly by their actions in the field of international financial policy. For example, the decision of the Canadian authorities in late 1951 to eliminate all exchange controls expressed more clearly than words their opinion that their payments position had become strong and could be maintained strong, with their level of reserves, by appropriate monetary policies and a fluctuating rate of exchange—an opinion amply justified by the developments of the succeeding period.

It is much more difficult to draw conclusions from the actions of the authorities in the fields of monetary and fiscal policy. This is because actions in these fields are often determined with greater reference to their domestic than to their international effects. For example, the restrictive actions of the U.S. monetary authorities in 1951 and 1952 (which commenced during a period of heavy gold outflow) were undertaken for purely domestic reasons and not because of anxiety concerning the adequacy of the international reserves of the United States. Such inferences may be drawn more reasonably, however, with respect to actions in countries where international trade comprises a larger proportion of total activity. For example, it is probably not inaccurate to say that the relaxation in the rigor of monetary policy in the Federal Republic of Germany, Belgium, and the Netherlands during 1952 reflected in large part a lower degree of concern by the authorities in these countries with respect to the adequacy of their monetary reserves.

Reserves and total resources

An adequate reserve position permits both the monetary authorities and the private traders of a country to look ahead and to plan their affairs with confidence. When reserves are inadequate, a country's foreign trade may be subject to sudden starts and stops, as restrictions are imposed or relaxed, or its exchange rate may fluctuate sharply. In whatever way imports are suddenly restricted below the level suited to the economy under a strong payments position, the result may be a serious dislocation of the economy.

It must not be overlooked that reserves are real resources from the point of view of the countries holding them, and the holding of reserves is only one of the possible uses competing for the limited amount of resources at the disposal of each country. In a rich country, or in a country in which there is little prospect of economic development, the maintenance of an adequate reserve position may necessitate no practical sacrifice. In a poor country, however, or in one in which the tempo of economic development is greater than can be accommodated by available resources, the maintenance of an adequate reserve position may be at the expense of urgently needed industrial or agricultural equipment, or may even entail some hardship due to shortages of food or of other consumers' goods which might have been imported by using a portion of its reserves. It is inevitable, therefore, that poor and dynamic countries are tempted to sacrifice their reserve positions in favor of other uses of their real resources which they consider more urgent. This may often be sound policy. Indeed, such a transfer of resources would occur as a result of the operation of natural economic forces in the absence of state intervention, as it is of the essence of economics so to economize on scarce resources that the last unit employed in each use has an equal utility. If a country can improve its over-all position by transferring a portion of even an inadequate supply of reserves to some yet more urgent use, it is fully justified in doing so. On the other hand, countries may underestimate the real losses incurred because of inadequate reserves and so may tend to hold less reserves than they should, in their own interest.

In this respect, the reserves of countries have been compared with those of individuals. The monetary reserves of individuals (principally cash balances) serve much the same purposes as those of countries. They protect the individual's consumption from fluctuations in the amount and timing of his income, permit him to minimize his total outpayments by taking advantage of cash discounts, and allow him to prevent unfavorable developments in his situation from being magnified in their consequences because of the lack of adequate finances for dealing with them promptly. But, for individuals as well as for nations, monetary reserves are only one of a number of possible uses of resources competing for priority. Consequently, wealthy persons or persons with relatively few undertakings (although their incomes may fluctuate but little) are more likely than poorer or more active persons (although their incomes may fluctuate widely) to provide fully for reserves.

Therefore, it is normal to find, both for wealthy or more settled persons and for wealthy or more settled nations, that reserves are much larger in proportion to the apparent need for them than are the reserves of poorer or more dynamic individuals or of poorer or more dynamic nations. This tendency, at least on the international level, is often described as a "maldistribution of reserves". However, a high degree of maldistribution is normal and would reassert itself even if the reserves were redistributed—for, the poorer or more dynamic countries would apply part of their newly acquired reserves to higher priority uses, and the reserves disposed of in this way would return to the more wealthy or more settled countries. Of course, it does not follow that any given degree of maldistribution of reserves is compatible with a stable structure of world payments. An extremely high degree of maldistribution can, however, be corrected by appropriate changes in monetary and fiscal policies in low-reserve countries. The adjustment can be made gradual, although protracted, if the newly mined gold is added to the reserves of the countries with the greatest reserve deficiency. But the period of adjustment can be shortened and its unavoidable cost in terms of deflationary pressure on the economy can be lightened by liberalization of commercial and external investment policies on the part of high-reserve countries.

Interaction of reserves and policy

As already noted, reserves and policy interact on one another, the strength of the interaction varying with the importance of foreign trade in a country's total economy. Restrictive policies result in the accumulation of reserves, while adequate reserves tend to modify and soften policies. When world-wide inflationary and deflationary pressures are in balance, this interaction between reserves and policy tends to work out well and promotes a well-balanced distribution of the available reserves among the trading countries of the world in the light of their preference for reserves and other types of investment.

If no fundamental change in the basis of monetary standards is assumed, the world supply of reserves may be increased (1) by additions to the volume or value of the world monetary gold stock, or (2) by the creation of new international assets and contra-liabilities of such a character that the creditors will consider their asset holdings as part of their reserves, but the debtors will make no corresponding deduction of their liabilities in the calculation of their own reserve positions. Aside from changes in the world supply of reserves, all reserves gained by one country must be at the expense of another. Some year-by-year increase in the total stock of reserves is necessary in order to maintain an expanding volume of world trade and stable prices. An expansion of this magnitude in the world stock of reserves tends to promote sound policies, and countries pursuing sound policies tend to secure an appropriate share of the total available reserves. Indeed, a country can be said to have a strong payments position only when it is acquiring such an appropriate share of newly created reserves. On the other hand, a too rapid increase in the world stock of monetary reserves tends to promote inflationary policies generally and in individual countries, while an increase of less than the optimum amount (or a decrease) tends to promote deflationary policies.

These observations are, of course, true only when a number of years are taken into consideration. In a single year, or even for several years, characterized by general expansionary psychology, a stationary stock of reserves (or even a declining one) may be compatible with expanding trade and price stability. On the other hand, in a year, or series of years, characterized by general deflationary psychology, an extraordinarily large expansion in reserves may be necessary to support price stability and a continuing expansion in world trade.

Finally, it should be noted that the response of a country to an increase in its reserves or to an improvement in its balance of payments position is not likely to consist wholly in a relaxation or elimination of trade and exchange restrictions. It may consist wholly—and will probably consist partially—in a relaxation of its domestic fiscal and monetary policies. A general improvement in reserve positions during a time of world-wide inflationary pressures is likely, therefore, to reinforce those pressures.

Reserves and the growth of world trade

The necessary increment to reserves, if inadequacy of reserves is not to hamper the growth of multilateral trade, will depend primarily on the rate at which trade can grow. This in turn depends in large part on the growth of production throughout the world. Support of an appropriate rate of growth in world trade depends on the annual increment to the world's monetary gold stock and on other types of reserve assets created by national monetary systems and through the instrumentality of international agencies.

Newly mined gold is the principal source from which increments to gold reserves must be made. Unless this gold is in large part accumulated by the monetary authorities, it will not be effective in enabling countries to meet their needs for reserves. The increment to monetary gold stocks has been low in most postwar years. Monetary and exchange policies that leave doubt as to the future value of national currencies tend to divert newly mined gold into private hoards rather than into central holdings. Furthermore, little will be accomplished in securing adequate reserves for most countries for the future if all newly mined gold is regarded as an easy means of meeting continuing balance of payments deficits. Under such conditions, the newly mined gold will simply be concentrated in the reserves of a very few creditor countries, while the reserves of the rest of the world will be inadequate. A basic condition for adequate reserves in the long run is the maintenance of monetary and exchange policies that will enable countries not only to balance their international payments, but also to add part of the newly mined gold to their monetary reserves.

Adequacy of particular types of reserves

As already noted, assets are useful for reserve purposes only to the extent that they are acceptable for the external payments which the reserve holding country must meet. Before the depression of the thirties—when most currencies were convertible either through the medium of buying and selling prices for gold or foreign exchange maintained by the monetary authorities of the issuing countries, or by the purchase and sale of exchange in the market place—most currencies could be held for reserve purposes, subject to the qualification that holdings of currencies with fluctuating exchange rates involved greater risk than holdings of currencies with fixed exchange rates. Since the onset of the depression, and particularly since the end of World War II, a large number of currencies have become inconvertible and can no longer be legally exchanged (either officially or through the market place) by the monetary authorities of the countries holding them for such other currencies as they may need to meet their external payments. As a consequence, the reserve problem—which once could be viewed as a whole—has tended to break into fragments, and a country may now be short of reserves in some currencies but have a surplus of them in others.

Reserves and the spread of depression

A function of reserves upon which considerable emphasis was placed in the planning for the postwar period is that of preventing the spread of depression from one country to another. A depression in any country will tend to reduce its imports, as these are related more or less closely to its national income. Hence, a depression in an important country will tend to reduce substantially the exports of other countries. If these countries maintain their imports, they will deplete their monetary reserves; if they do not, the exports of other countries will be reduced further and so the depression will tend to spread in an ever widening circle. One of the principal purposes of the International Monetary Fund is to combat this mechanism for the international spread of depressions.

The amount of reserves necessary to prevent the spread of a depression depends upon the duration and intensity of the depression in the country of primary origin and the importance of that country in world trade. Even a minor depression in an important trading country, such as the United States, may have serious consequences in some other countries. If the depression is deep and protracted at its point of origin, the amount of monetary reserves necessary to prevent its spread may become indefinitely large. If such reserves should be supplied entirely by the Fund and be subject to reasonably firm undertakings with respect to their repayment in the foreseeable future, they might not be able—however large the amount available—to check the spread of a severe depression, because many countries would probably contract their imports (and so other countries' exports) substantially, rather than pile up large debts which they saw no prospects of repaying. The problem presented by such conditions is referred to later in this paper (pp. 342–43).

STATISTICS OF MONETARY RESERVES

A summary of monetary reserve statistics and a discussion of the methodology of their preparation are included in the June 1953 issue of *International Financial Statistics,* the monthly statistical publication of the International Monetary Fund. A reprint of part of that article is attached as an Appendix to this paper.

Monetary reserves are classified in that article as "gold", "foreign exchange", and "total", i.e., gold plus foreign exchange. It would be desirable if the "foreign exchange" item could be further subdivided into convertible and inconvertible currencies. Unfortunately, no comprehensive statistics are available on this basis. As will be seen by reference to the Appendix, the bulk of the monetary reserves of the world consists of holdings of gold, dollars, and sterling.

The official gold reserves and the total official reserves of gold and foreign exchange combined for a large number of countries, for the principal international monetary agencies, and for the world as a whole for the years 1928, 1938, 1951, and 1952 are given in Table 1. This table does not include data on reserve holdings for countries which are members of the Soviet bloc or for the dependent territories of the United Kingdom and of the continental EPU countries. The countries in the Soviet bloc are omitted because of inadequate data; the dependent territories are treated, for the purposes of this paper, as parts of the economies of their respective metropolitan countries. The reserves listed in the table include those held by monetary authorities only. Therefore, special caution should be used in interpreting comparisons between the data for 1951 and 1952 and those for earlier years for countries in which central banks have been established since 1928 or in which monetary reserves have been concentrated in the hands of the monetary authorities since that time. In such countries—Canada and Australia are especially in point—official reserve holdings in earlier years were, of course, supplemented by additional holdings of reserve-type assets in the hands of commercial banks.

In one sense it may be said that gold holdings constitute a "core within a core" of monetary reserves, as there are no contra-liabilities against them and they alone are "incompressible" and so must continue to exist in the same *physical* amount irrespective of any changes in their ownership. But the proportion of the total physical stock of gold held by the monetary authorities, and so counted as reserves, may vary; and the *monetary* value of this stock may also vary as a result of changes in the official price of gold. By far the most important price of gold is that in U.S. dollars, and it is in this unit that the gold reserves of all countries are stated throughout this paper.

The principal reason for the dramatic rise in the value of official gold stocks between 1928 and 1938 is, of course, the increase in the price of gold in U.S. dollars. This rise in the value of gold stocks is a "real" one, however, as the purchasing power of each U.S. dollar (in which the gold is measured) rose between 1928 and 1938. Conversely,

Table 1. Official Gold and Foreign Exchange Reserves, by Countries [1]

(In millions of U.S. dollars)

	Gold [2]				Gold plus Foreign Exchange [2]			
	1928	1938	1951	1952	1928	1938	1951	1952
United States	*3,746*	*14,592*	*22,873*	*23,252*	*3,746*	*14,592*	*22,873*	*23,252*
Canada	*93*	*186*	*842*	*885*	*93*	*220*	*1,795*	*1,862*
Latin American Republics	*985*[3]	*690*[3]	*1,954*	*1,810*[3]	*1,160*[3]	*790*[3]	*3,025*[3]	*3,025*[3]
Dollar countries	70[3]	130[3]	1,057	930[3]	125[3]	165[3]	1,535[3]	1,620[3]
Bolivia	9	3	23	23	9	5	32	28
Colombia	24	24	48	n.a.	62	29	123	152
Cuba	n.a.	1	311	214	n.a.	2	495	460
Dominican Republic	n.a.	—	12	12	n.a.	n.a.	30	32
Ecuador	1	3	22	23	8	4	31	44
El Salvador	5	7	26	29	5	8	42	44
Guatemala	2	7	27	27	5	9	40	43
Mexico	6	28	207	144	10	42	269	273
Venezuela	21	n.a.	373	373	21	n.a.	373	434
Other[4]	n.a.	1[3]	8[3]	8[3]	n.a.	5[3]	100[3]	110[3]
Non-dollar countries	915[3]	560[3]	897	880[3]	1,035[3]	625[3]	1,490[3]	1,400[3]
Argentina	607	n.a.	268	n.a.	607	n.a.	n.a.	n.a.
Brazil	149	32	317	317	177	59	514	525
Chile	65	30	45	42	120	44	59	71
Paraguay	n.a.	n.a.	—	—	n.a.	n.a.	19	18
Peru	22	20	46	46	47	21	60	56
Uruguay	72	72	221	207	83	n.a.	n.a.	216
United Kingdom	*748*	*2,877*	*2,200*[5]	*1,500*[5]	*748*	*2,877*[6]	*2,374*	*1,958*
Other Sterling Countries[7]	*385*	*535*	*627*	*620*	*754*[3]	*1,170*[3]	*5,055*	*4,400*[3]
Australia	109	6	112	113	200	251	1,219	979
Burma	...[8]	...[8]	—	—	...[8]	...[8]	159	n.a.
Ceylon	...[8]	...[8]	—	—	...[8]	...[8]	218	163
Iceland	1	1	1	1	n.a.	1	9	9
India	202[9]	274[9]	247	247	440[9]	485[9]	1,888	1,729
Iraq	n.a.	—	—	—	n.a.	22	114	129
Ireland	n.a.	10	18	18	n.a.	59	206	219
New Zealand	35	23	32	33	35	43	217	183
Pakistan	...[8]	...[8]	27	38	...[8]	...[8]	639	n.a.
Union of South Africa	39	220	190	170	78	259	386	382

Table 1—*Continued*

	Gold[2]				Gold plus Foreign Exchange[2]			
	1928	1938	1951	1952	1928	1938	1951	1952
Continental EPU Countries	*2,785*[3]	*6,060*[3]	*4,010*[3]	*4,485*[3]	*5,140*[3]	*6,500*[3]	*7,045*[3]	*7,935*[3]
Austria	24	. . .[10]	n.a.	n.a.	126	. . .[10]	n.a.	n.a.
Belgium-Luxembourg	128	780	635	704	345	780	1,054	1,077
Denmark	46	53	31	31	77	77	118	142
France	1,254	2,757	548[11]	573[11]	2,541	2,791	800	676
Germany[12]	650	n.a.	28	140	776	n.a.	503	1,165
Greece	7	27	4	10	55	n.a.	n.a.	n.a.
Italy	266	193	333	n.a.	583	201	1,045	913
Netherlands	175	998	316	544	263	1,037	552	936
Norway	39	84	50	50	50	134	151	151
Portugal	9	86	264	286	25	n.a.	n.a.	n.a.
Sweden	63	321	152	184	121	520	484	446
Switzerland	103	701	1,452	1,422	152	764	1,594	1,648
Turkey	21	29	151	143	21	34	217	191
Other	*1,060*[3]	*945*[3]	*950*[3]	*920*[3]	*1,400*[3]	*1,395*[3]	*3,665*[3]	*3,350*[3]
Egypt	18	55	174	174	178	175	957	753
Finland	8	26	26	26	27	75	216	163
Indonesia	n.a.	80	280	235	n.a.	n.a.	511	314
Iran	n.a.	26	138	138	n.a.	38	190	177
Israel[13]	n.a.	—	—	—	n.a.	32	19	n.a.
Japan	541	230	n.a.	n.a.	598	289	n.a.	n.a.
Lebanon[14]	. . .	. . .	26	31	. . .	. . .	40	42
Philippines	n.a.	n.a.	7	9	50	n.a.	246	227
Spain	494	525	51	51	512	n.a.	n.a.	n.a.
Syria	n.a.	n.a.	11	14	n.a.	n.a.	33	38
Thailand	n.a.	—	113	113	43	56	358	349

Table 1—*Continued*

	Gold[2]				Gold plus Foreign Exchange[2]			
	1928	1938	1951	1952	1928	1938	1951	1952
International Agencies								
IMF	...[15]	...[15]	1,530	1,692	...[15]	...[15]	7,261	7,374
EPU	...[15]	...[15]	65	159	...[15]	...[15]	68	225
BIS	...[15]	14	115	196	...[15]	14[6]	283	442
Total, including international agencies and United States	*9,800*[3]	*25,900*[3]	*35,150*[3]	*35,500*[3]	*13,050*[3]	*27,600*[3]	*53,450*[3]	*53,800*[3]
Total, excluding international agencies and United States	*6,050*[3]	*11,300*[3]	*10,600*[3]	*10,200*[3]	*9,300*[3]	*13,000*[3]	*22,950*[3]	*22,500*[3]

[1] Data are as of end of year. Countries of the Soviet bloc and dependent territories of the United Kingdom and of continental EPU countries are excluded; see text. Totals and subtotals include estimated data for those countries for which definite totals are not available (marked n.a. in table). Dashes indicate less than $500,000. [The figures for Belgium-Luxembourg in 1928 have been corrected from those originally published in *Staff Papers,* with consequential changes in some totals and in related ratios in Table 3.]

[2] Gold valued at $20.67 per ounce in 1928, and $35.00 per ounce in 1938, 1951, and 1952.

[3] Estimate (rounded).

[4] Covers Costa Rica, Haiti, Honduras, Nicaragua, and Panama.

[5] Estimates of the U.S. Treasury and Board of Governors of the Federal Reserve System.

[6] Gold only.

[7] The total reserves of "Other Sterling Countries" cannot be added to those of the United Kingdom in order to obtain a meaningful aggregate for the total sterling area, as the reserves of the "Other Sterling Countries" are comprised largely of items which are, in turn, liabilities of the United Kingdom.

[8] Included with India.

[9] Undivided India.

[10] Part of Germany.

[11] Central bank holdings only.

[12] Undivided Germany, 1928 and 1938; Federal Republic of Germany, 1951 and 1952.

[13] Data for 1928 and 1938 refer to Palestine.

[14] Included with Syria in 1928 and 1938.

[15] Agency not yet established.

Sources: For 1928, United Nations, *Statistical Yearbook, 1948,* and League of Nations, *International Currency Experience* (1944); for 1938, 1951, and 1952, International Monetary Fund, *International Financial Statistics,* July 1953, and data supplied by the Statistics Division, Research Department, International Monetary Fund.

although the price of gold in dollars remained unchanged between 1938 and 1952, the purchasing power of the dollar fell.

The years used for comparison in the table were selected primarily on the basis of statistical convenience. The year 1928 was a good year in the twenties; the year 1938 was a fairly representative year in the thirties. It is true that 1938 was a low year for imports into the United States; however, it was not a particularly low year for U.S. exports or for imports into most other countries. It is, consequently, a satisfactory year for considering the reserve adequacy of most countries—and the adequacy of the reserves of the United States is not in question. The years 1951 and 1952 are the most recent ones for which comprehensive data are available. Particular years, of course, may not be representative for individual countries. Apart from the broad economic, industrial, and agricultural forces always operating to cause year-to-year variations, it should be noted that import levels are substantially affected by the reserve positions, the trade and exchange restrictions, the monetary and fiscal policies, and the exchange rates of individual importing countries, and by the convertibility of their own and other currencies.

Substantial changes have, of course, occurred in the reserve positions of individual countries and areas since the end of 1952, but they do not significantly change the long-term perspective to which this paper is directed. Data for the early months of 1953, as far as they are available, have been published in *International Financial Statistics.*

The foreign exchange reserves included in the figures for gold plus foreign exchange shown in Table 1 include holdings of "blocked" currencies. Consequently, for some countries (e.g., India) these total figures overstate the amount of reserves immediately available for settling adverse payments balances. For obvious reasons, special caution should be used in interpreting the world and regional totals for gold and foreign exchange combined. While gold is an asset in itself, with no corresponding contra-liability, foreign exchange other than gold is, in the nature of the case, both an asset to the holder and a liability to the issuer. The totals used in this table are, in every case, on a *gross* basis, i.e., the asset items are included but the liability items are ignored. This is the customary method of stating reserve statistics, and is, on the whole, more meaningful than an attempt to state them on a "net" basis, in which case foreign exchange would disappear completely as a reserve item for the world as a whole. The "double counting" involved in this procedure presents certain difficulties, however.

This "double counting" is important only for the United States and the United Kingdom, as dollars and sterling are the only currencies that other countries hold in substantial amounts as monetary reserves. The double counting results in overstating the reserve position of the United States, as the $10.5 billion of short-term liabilities to foreigners (including international institutions) outstanding on December 31, 1952 constituted, in an important sense, a first claim on the U.S. gold reserve of $23.3 billion on that same date.[4] A good part of these foreign claims are required as working balances, however, and, in any event, the reserve and payments positions of the United States are so strong that there is no practical difficulty in treating its reserve position on a gross basis. The case of the United Kingdom is rather different. The external

[4] The corresponding figures for December 31, 1951 are $22.9 billion for the gold reserve and $9.3 billion for total short-term liabilities to foreigners including international institutions.

sterling liabilities of the United Kingdom, counted as reserves by others, substantially exceed its own reserves. Its real reserve position, therefore, is not nearly so strong as might be inferred from the gross figures given in this table. Furthermore, no meaningful figure can be obtained by adding the total reserves of the United Kingdom and those of other sterling countries to obtain a "sterling area total", since the major portion of the reserves of the other sterling countries are comprised of liabilities of the United Kingdom. The amount of double counting in the table as a whole is, of course, substantially reduced by the omission of reserve statistics for the dependent territories of the United Kingdom and of the continental EPU countries.

Table 2 shows total imports on a c.i.f. basis for the countries for which reserve data are shown in Table 1. As in Table 1, members of the Soviet bloc and dependent territories of the United Kingdom and of the continental EPU countries are omitted. Table 3 shows the relationship which the official gold reserves and the total official reserves, respectively, of each country bore to its total c.i.f. imports in each of the reference years.

The relationship of reserves to imports serves as a common denominator on the basis of which reserves can be compared. It is the most comprehensive basis found practical to use in the general statistical comparisons in this paper. Strictly speaking, the most general basis for such comparisons would be total current account expenditures, but data on such expenditures are not available for many of the countries for many of the years. The necessary omission of invisible items has been repaired in part, however, by placing imports on a c.i.f. basis. The imports of each country are those from all other countries, including those from the country's own overseas dependencies. It is true that imports into metropolitan countries from their own overseas dependencies may often be financed in ways that do not place a strain on metropolitan reserves. The metropolitan country usually has a corresponding obligation, however, to assist in financing imports into the dependent territories from the outside world. These imports (like all other imports of the dependent territories) are omitted from the statistics, and may be considered as at least a partial offset to the inclusion of imports into the metropolitan countries from their dependent territories.

In any event, it should be emphasized that, whatever might be the character of the denominators by which the reserves of different countries were divided to place them on a comparable basis, they would not provide ready-made comparisons of reserve adequacy. The reserve figures themselves make no allowance for penumbral reserve items; and, were such allowances made, they would merely provide the starting point for the application of the various criteria of adequacy discussed earlier in this paper. This is brought out dramatically by the incongruity between the import-reserve percentages for a number of the countries in the tables and the generally accepted evaluations of the over-all reserve positions of these countries based upon the size of their reserves and all of the factors affecting reserve adequacy.

Table 1 does not distinguish between the convertible and inconvertible currency holdings of the International Monetary Fund. It is helpful, therefore, to say that the Fund's total holdings of gold and U.S. and Canadian dollars amounted to $3.1 billion at the end of 1951 and were equal to about 5 per cent of 1951 c.i.f. imports of all the countries included in the table, exclusive of the United States. By the end of 1952, the Fund's holdings of gold and U.S. and Canadian dollars had risen to $3.2 billion (6 per cent of 1952 c.i.f. imports).

Table 2. Merchandise Imports, C.I.F., by Countries[1]
(In millions of U.S. dollars)

	1928	1938	1951	1952
United States	*4,427*	*2,465*	*11,946*	*11,633*
Canada	*1,364*	*763*	*4,195*	*4,458*
Latin American Republics	*2,453*	*1,535*	*7,619*	*7,074*
Dollar countries	862	568	3,272	3,280
Bolivia	23	25	91	74[2]
Colombia	161	89	416	402
Cuba	234	119	691	667
Dominican Republic	30	13	64	63
Ecuador	16	12	64	65
El Salvador	18	9	62	68
Guatemala	31	21	81	76
Mexico	185	114	823	739
Venezuela	81	107	719	809
Other[3]	83	59	261	317
Non-dollar countries	1,591	967	4,347	3,794
Argentina	807	440	1,400[2]	860[2]
Brazil	441	295	2,011	2,010
Chile	163	103	329	371
Paraguay	13	9	30[2]	. . .[4]
Peru	70	58	261	288
Uruguay	97	62	316	237
United Kingdom	*5,795*	*4,600*	*10,942*	*9,747*
Other Sterling Countries	*2,670*	*2,299*	*8,054*	*7,554*
Australia	669[5]	571[5]	2,423	1,979
Burma	76[6]	79[7]	137	192
Ceylon	139	86	327	358
Iceland	17	11	57	56
India	837[6,8]	575[6,8]	1,816	1,672
Iraq	34	46	143	173
Ireland	288	203	573	482
New Zealand	218	225	596	739
Pakistan	. . .[9]	. . .[9]	534	609
Union of South Africa	393	503	1,448	1,294
Continental EPU Countries	*11,103*	*7,804*	*22,168*	*21,910*
Austria	456	. . .[10]	657	654
Belgium-Luxembourg	889	765	2,535	2,424
Denmark	441	354	1,013	962
France	2,097	1,324	4,551	4,431
Germany[11]	3,335	2,430	3,494	3,818
Greece	161	131	435	346
Italy	1,173	593	2,167	2,313
Netherlands	1,078	803	2,567	2,251
Norway	269	292	877	873
Portugal	120	102	330	350
Sweden	458	520	1,776	1,730
Switzerland	512	366	1,364	1,202
Turkey	114	119	402	556

Table 2, *cont.* Merchandise Imports, C.I.F., by Countries[1]
(In millions of U.S. dollars)

	1928	1938	1951	1952
Other	*2,813*	*1,935*	*6,204*	*6,550*
Egypt	249	185	667	608
Finland	202	182	676	792
Indonesia	403	275	805	972
Iran	76[12]	79[12]	248	165
Israel[13]	33	56	343	...[4]
Japan	990	759	1,995	2,028
Lebanon[14]	...	...	136	141
Philippines	149	153	539	477
Spain	580	...[4]	384	518
Syria	51	37	139	143
Thailand	80	57	272[2]	301[2]
Total, including United States	*30,625*	*21,401*	*71,128*	*68,926*
Total, excluding United States	*26,198*	*18,936*	*59,182*	*57,293*

[1] Countries of the Soviet bloc and dependent territories of the United Kingdom and of continental EPU countries are excluded; see text.
[2] Partly estimated.
[3] Covers Costa Rica, Haiti, Honduras, Nicaragua, and Panama.
[4] Estimate included in totals and subtotals.
[5] Year ending June.
[6] Year beginning April.
[7] Year ending September.
[8] Undivided India.
[9] Included with India.
[10] Included with Germany.
[11] Undivided Germany, 1928 and 1938; Federal Republic of Germany, 1951 and 1952.
[12] Year beginning June 21.
[13] Data for 1928 and 1938 refer to Palestine.
[14] Included with Syria in 1928 and 1938.
Sources: For 1928, League of Nations, *Network of World Trade* (1942); for 1938, 1951, and 1952, International Monetary Fund, *International Financial Statistics*, July 1953.

As stated previously, no comprehensive data are available separating foreign exchange reserves into those held in convertible and in inconvertible currencies. It is of interest, however, to present such data as are available with respect to reserve holdings of the major convertible currency—the U.S. dollar. These data are available from reports made to the U.S. Treasury by U.S. banks. They show that, for the world as a whole, holdings of U.S. dollars by official monetary authorities (excluding international agencies) amounted to $4.1 billion at the end of 1951 and to $5.1 billion at the end of 1952.[5] Data for official holdings only are not available for individual countries. In order to preserve the confidential character of the balances of individual foreign institutions, these data are published by the U.S. Treasury on a country basis only as a total of official and bank holdings of dollars. The total amount of such holdings (excluding international agencies) amounted to $6.0 billion at the end of 1951

[5] In each case reported official holdings of U.S. dollars by Japan are added to the total reported by the U.S. Treasury. See Appendix, p. 346.

Table 3. Ratios of Official Reserves to Total Merchandise Imports, C.I.F., by Countries[1]

(In per cent)

	Ratio of Gold Reserves to Imports				Ratio of Gold plus Foreign Exchange Reserves to Imports			
	1928	1938	1951	1952	1928	1938	1951	1952
United States	*85*	*592*	*191*	*202*	*85*	*592*	*191*	*202*
Canada	*7*	*24*	*20*	*20*	*7*	*29*	*43*	*42*
Latin American Republics	*40*	*45*	*26*	*26*	*47*	*51*	*40*	*43*
Dollar countries	8	23	32	28	15	29	47	49
Bolivia	39	12	25	31	39	20	35	38
Colombia	15	27	12	—	39	33	30	38
Cuba	—	1	45	32	—	2	72	69
Dominican Republic	—	—	19	19	—	31	47	51
Ecuador	6	25	34	35	50	33	48	68
El Salvador	28	78	42	43	28	89	68	65
Guatemala	6	33	33	36	16	43	49	57
Mexico	3	25	25	19	5	37	33	37
Venezuela	26	—	52	46	26	—	52	54
Other[2]	—	2	3	3	—	8	38	35
Non-dollar countries	58	58	21	23	65	65	34	37
Argentina	75	—	19	—	75	—	—	—
Brazil	34	11	16	16	40	20	26	26
Chile	40	29	14	11	74	43	18	19
Paraguay	—	—	—	—	—	—	63	—
Peru	31	34	18	16	67	36	23	19
Uruguay	74	116	70	87	86	—	—	91
United Kingdom	*13*	*63*	*20*	*15*	*13*	*63*	*22*	*20*
Other Sterling Countries	*14*	*23*	*8*	*8*	*28*	*51*	*63*	*58*
Australia	16	1	5	6	30	44	50	49
Burma	—	—	—	—	—	—	116	—
Ceylon	—	—	—	—	—	—	67	46
Iceland	6	9	2	2	—	9	16	16
India	24	48	14	15	53	84	104	103
Iraq	—	—	—	—	—	48	80	75
Ireland	—	5	3	4	—	29	36	45
New Zealand	16	10	5	4	16	19	36	25
Pakistan	—	—	5	6	—	—	120	—
Union of South Africa	10	44	13	13	20	51	27	30
Continental EPU Countries	*25*	*78*	*18*	*20*	*46*	*83*	*32*	*36*
Austria	5	—	—	—	28	—	—	—
Belgium-Luxembourg	14	102	25	29	39	102	42	44
Denmark	10	15	3	3	17	22	12	15
France	60	208	12	13	121	211	18	15
Germany	19	—	1	4	23	—	14	24
Greece	4	21	1	3	34	—	—	—
Italy	23	33	15	—	50	34	48	39
Netherlands	16	124	12	24	24	129	22	42

Table 3, *cont.* Ratios of Official Reserves to Total Merchandise Imports, C.I.F., by Countries[1]

(In per cent)

	Ratio of Gold Reserves to Imports				Ratio of Gold plus Foreign Exchange Reserves to Imports			
	1928	1938	1951	1952	1928	1938	1951	1952
Continental EPU Countries, *cont.*								
Norway	14	29	6	6	19	46	17	17
Portugal	8	84	80	82	21	—	—	—
Sweden	14	62	9	11	26	100	27	26
Switzerland	20	192	106	118	30	209	117	137
Turkey	18	24	38	26	18	29	54	34
Other	*38*	*49*	*15*	*14*	*50*	*73*	*59*	*40*
Egypt	7	30	26	29	71	95	143	124
Finland	4	14	4	3	13	41	32	21
Indonesia	—	29	35	24	—	—	63	32
Iran	—	33	56	84	—	48	77	107
Israel	—	—	—	—	—	57	6	—
Japan	55	30	—	—	60	38	—	—
Lebanon	—	—	19	22	—	—	29	30
Philippines	—	—	1	2	34	—	46	48
Spain	85	—	13	10	88	—	—	—
Syria	—	—	8	10	—	—	24	27
Thailand	—	—	42	38	54	98	132	116
Total, including gold and reserves of international agencies, and gold and reserves *and* imports of the United States	*32*	*121*	*49*	*52*	*43*	*129*	*75*	*78*
Total, excluding gold and reserves of international agencies, and gold and reserves *and* imports of the United States	*23*	*60*	*18*	*17*	*35*	*69*	*39*	*40*

[1] Based on data in Tables 1 and 2. Dashes indicate less than one half of 1 per cent or nonavailability of data.

[2] Covers Costa Rica, Haiti, Honduras, Nicaragua, and Panama.

and to \$6.6 billion at the end of 1952, and so exceeded by a considerable margin holdings of monetary authorities only.

For the various countries, the available data for holdings of gold and U.S. dollars by foreign monetary authorities and banks in 1951 and 1952, and the ratios of these data to the figures shown in Table 2 for the c.i.f. imports of each country, are given in Table 4. The comparisons here differ, of course, from those made earlier in this chapter in that they exclude holdings of all types of reserves other than gold and U.S. dollars and include holdings by banks as well as by monetary authorities.

COMPARISONS OF RESERVE ADEQUACY

To the preceding discussion of the factors affecting the need for reserves at any time and the statistics of actual reserve holdings in 1928, 1938, 1951, and 1952, it may

Table 4. Official and Bank Holdings of Gold and U.S. Dollars and Their Ratio to Total Merchandise Imports, C.I.F., by Countries, Excluding the United States

	Official and Bank Holdings of Gold and U.S. Dollars[1] *(million dollars)*		Ratio to Imports *(per cent)*	
	1951	1952	1951	1952
Canada	*1,953*	*2,047*	*47*	*46*
Latin American Republics	*2,838*	*2,755*	*37*	*39*
Dollar countries	1,585	1,631	48	50
Bolivia	40	37	44	50
Colombia	132	160[2]	32	40
Cuba	518	455	75	68
Dominican Republic	42	42	66	67
Ecuador	33[3]	47[3]	52	72
El Salvador	44	44	71	65
Guatemala	40	43	49	57
Mexico	294	283	36	38
Venezuela	399	465	55	57
Other[4]	43[3]	55[3]	16	17
Non-dollar countries	1,253	1,124	29	30
Argentina	482	370[2]	34	43
Brazil	377	352	19	18
Chile	71	92	22	25
Paraguay	5[3]	5[3]	17	18
Peru	70	70	27	24
Uruguay	248	235	78	99
United Kingdom	*2,530*	*2,027*	*23*	*21*
Other Sterling Countries	*798*	*810*	*10*	*11*
Australia	151	157	6	8
Ceylon	19[3]	14[3]	6	4
Iceland	5[3]	5[3]	9	9
India	305	308	17	18
Iraq	13[3]	14[3]	9	8
Ireland	34[3]	34[2]	6	7
New Zealand	37[3]	36[3]	6	5
Pakistan	40[3]	52[3]	7	9
Union of South Africa	194	190	13	15
Continental EPU Countries	*5,817*	*6,753*	*26*	*31*
Austria	102[2]	142[2]	16	22
Belgium-Luxembourg	715[5]	771[5]	28	32
Denmark	69	92	7	10
France	765	855	17	19
Germany	431	688	12	18
Greece	43	48	10	14
Italy	599	620[2]	28	27
Netherlands	443	726	17	32
Norway	126	138	14	16
Portugal	295	329	89	94
Sweden	218	268	12	15
Switzerland	1,851	1,929	136	160
Turkey	160	147	40	26

Table 4, *cont.* Official and Bank Holdings of Gold and U.S. Dollars and Their Ratio to Total Merchandise Imports, C.I.F., by Countries, Excluding the United States

	Official and Bank Holdings of Gold and U.S. Dollars[1] *(million dollars)*		Ratio to Imports *(per cent)*	
	1951	1952	1951	1952
Other	*2,286*	*2,393*	*37*	*37*
Egypt	281	230	42	38
Finland	52	52	8	7
Indonesia	420	295	52	30
Iran	157	150	63	91
Israel	24	16	7	4
Japan	710[2]	920[2]	36	45
Lebanon	41	50[3]	30	35
Philippines	318	304	59	64
Spain	60	61	16	12
Syria	16	25[3]	12	17
Thailand	207	290	76	96
International Agencies				
IMF	2,854	2,980	—	—
EPU	68	226	—	—
BIS	283[6]	442[6]	—	—
Total, incl. international agencies	*19,427*	*20,433*	*33*	*36*
Total, excl. international agencies	*16,222*	*16,785*	*27*	*29*

[1] Data as of end of year.
[2] Partly estimated.
[3] Includes other than official and bank holdings.
[4] Covers Costa Rica, Haiti, Honduras, Nicaragua, and Panama.
[5] Belgian official and bank holdings; Luxembourg includes other than official and bank holdings.
[6] Includes currencies other than dollars.
Sources: Holdings of U.S. dollars are from U.S. Treasury Department, *Treasury Bulletin*, April 1952, May 1952, April 1953, and May 1953. For other sources used, see Tables 1 and 2.

be helpful to add a brief consideration of some changes in the need for reserves during the past few decades.

Reserve adequacy in 1928

Reserves in 1928 were adequate to support multilateral trade in the prosperous conditions prevailing at the time. It is futile to consider whether they would have continued to be adequate to support the newly established gold standard indefinitely through mild ups and downs in business conditions in the absence of deep depression. The fact is that the depression of the early thirties, spreading chiefly from the United States, but also from other leading industrial countries, placed the reserves of many countries, especially raw material countries, under great strain. At the same time, the loss of confidence in the exchange rates of the currencies of the reserve holding countries, especially the United Kingdom (due in part to inadequacies in their reserves), caused runs on these countries which induced them to contract their own credits, and so reduced the total amount of reserves available to other countries. A shortage of reserves was certainly not the principal cause of the depression of the thirties, but it did contribute to the scope, intensity, and duration of the depression because of the severe restrictions on trade and even because of the general deflationary policies that were instituted to protect reserves.

Effect of the low level of world trade on reserve adequacy in 1938

The situation in 1938 was quite different. The amount of reserves then available was doubtless adequate in the sense that a shortage of reserves was not the bottleneck restraining an expansion of trade, and probably would not have become one even if trade had expanded considerably. (Many countries—e.g., Germany, Japan, and some countries in eastern Europe, as well as some raw material producing countries—doubtless had inadequate reserves, but these countries were pursuing policies with respect to the disposition of their real resources which would have quickly dissipated some of their reserves even if somehow they had been made adequate.) It is probable that reserves in 1938 would have been adequate even if the total amount of world trade at that time had been at a volume corresponding to high level employment in, and the pursuit of liberal trade policies by, all or most trading countries. The important point is that the adequacy of 1938 reserves should be judged, not relative to actual 1938 trade but relative to the total amount of trade which would have been carried on under liberal trade policies and at a high level of employment. It follows that the shrinkage in the apparent adequacy of reserves relative to trade between 1938 and 1951 is not nearly so great as appears from the foregoing tables. This is true because the basis of comparison in one case is a volume of trade greatly shrunken by depression, and in the other case it is a volume which, despite illiberal trade policies, was at a high level.

Changes in the volatility of world trade

As pointed out previously, one of the principal factors affecting the need for reserves is the prospect of swings in the volume and prices of a country's imports and exports. The possibility of a downward swing in the demand for a country's exports increases its need for reserves and makes any given reserve holding less adequate.

There is some reason to believe that world trade is more volatile and the exports of most countries more vulnerable to sharp downward swings now than was the case in 1938. Before the war, economic conditions in the United States were generally subject to greater variation than those in most industrial countries. If this tendency should reappear in the postwar period (it has not thus far), an increase in the U.S. share of world trade would increase its over-all volatility. The ratio of U.S. imports (c.i.f.) to world imports decreased from 13 per cent in 1928 to 10 per cent in 1938, but again increased to 15 per cent in 1951 and 1952. It is possible, therefore, that the exports of other countries are somewhat more subject to sharp declines now than they were in 1938. Moreover, a larger proportion of the imports of the United States now consists of raw materials which are also produced in large volume in the United States, either directly or in the form of acceptable synthetic substitutes. The imported portion of these materials—copper and natural rubber are cases in point—represents a marginal supply which would be subject to sharp curtailment in the event of a U.S. recession. It appears, therefore, that, as far as trade factors are concerned, a larger amount of reserves relative to trade may be necessary now than would have been the case in 1938, in order to provide the same degree of relative adequacy.

RELATIONSHIP OF THE PAYMENTS AND RESERVES PROBLEMS IN THE POSTWAR PERIOD

The problem of assisting deficit countries to finance long-continuing, and possibly fundamental, disequilibria in their balances of payments is conceptually separate from the problem of building up their monetary reserves. The reserves problem of any country cannot be approached until its payments problem has been brought under control. But, in the last analysis, the funds obtained by each country are directly or indirectly transferable between the two uses, and the real character of any operation can be determined only *ex post*, after a study of the recipient countries' reserve and payments positions.

Viewed in this light, it is seen that the funds obtained by each country since the war (or during any other period) may be considered as interim installments toward its combined payments-reserves problem, with the final apportionment depending upon the policies of the country and the forces with which it has to contend.

As shown in Table 5, during the period 1946 to 1952, inclusive, the United States supplied the "rest of the world" with $125.9 billion, of which $89.9 billion was either earned or obtained through private donations or private capital movements, and $36 billion was obtained through official grants and loans from the U.S. Government and international agencies. Uses of dollars during this period totaled $129.2 billion, leaving a deficiency of $3.3 billion which was made up by a net transfer of reserves to the United States.[6] Gold production outside the United States during the same period totaled a little over $5 billion, which would have more than restored the reserves of the "rest of the world" to their original amount if it had all been added to monetary stocks—which, of course, was not the case.

During each of the past three years, the "rest of the world" has gained reserves from the United States, the amount being substantial in 1950. The proportion of the total dollar supply coming from official grants and loans (including military aid) has varied between 21 per cent and 24 per cent in the three-year period. During 1952, the total dollar supply exceeded the use of dollars by $0.8 billion (the net outflow of reserves from the United States). Official grants and loans (including military aid) totaled $5.2 billion and accounted for about 24 per cent of the total dollar supply of $21.7 billion in that year.

Military aid, which comprised a very small proportion of total official grants and loans prior to 1950, has increased rapidly since then, as shown in Table 6. In 1952, military aid comprised half of all official grants and loans of U.S. dollars. As suggested earlier in this paper, military aid, when considered as a means of financing the costs of a mutually shared defense system, may be viewed by the recipient countries in the same category as other current balance of payments receipts, rather than as a means of financing a deficit.

The significance of any given supply of dollars must, of course, be judged relative to the total needs which must be met and the purchasing power of each dollar. The dollar supply in 1952, exclusive of movements in reserves and of official grants and loans, and after subtracting an amount equal to the net investment income of the

[6] The figures in Table 5 are obtained by reversing the signs on the data for the balance of payments of the United States, published in International Monetary Fund, *Balance of Payments Yearbook*. The item "net errors and omissions" has been classified for this purpose as a "use" of funds by the "rest of the world" on the ground that such errors and omissions probably represent, for the most part, unrecorded private capital movements to the United States.

Table 5. Sources and Uses of U.S. Dollars by the Rest of the World, 1946-52[1]

(In billions of U.S. dollars, except for Col. 5)

	Sources						Uses				Net Movements in Reserves (Col. 6 minus Col. 10)
				Official grants and loans							
	Exports to U.S.	Services	Private donations and capital movements	Amount	Per cent of total sources	Total sources	Imports from U.S.	Services	Net errors and omissions	Total uses	
	(1)	(2)	(3)	(4)	(5)	(6)	(7)	(8)	(9)	(10)	(11)
1946	5.1	2.2	1.2	5.2	38	13.7	10.2	5.0	0.2	15.4	−1.6
1947	6.1	2.4	1.9	6.0	37	16.4	15.1	5.0	1.0	21.2	−4.8
1948	7.8	2.8	2.1	5.2	29	17.8	13.1	4.6	1.0	18.7	−0.9
1949	7.0	2.8	1.5	5.8	34	17.2	12.3	4.2	0.8	17.2	−[2]
1950	9.3	3.1	1.6	4.2	23	18.2	10.6	4.2	0.2	15.0	+3.2
1951	11.7	3.6	1.2	4.4	21	20.9	15.5	4.7	0.6	20.8	−[2]
1952	11.5	4.2	0.8	5.2	24	21.7	15.9	4.8	0.2	20.9	+0.8
Total	58.5	21.1	10.3	36.0	29	125.9	92.7	32.5	4.0	129.2	−3.3

[1] Totals and computations are based on unrounded figures.

[2] Less than $50 million.

Sources: 1946-51 data based on International Monetary Fund, *Balance of Payments Yearbook, 1948, 1949-50,* and *1950-51;* 1952 data are estimated.

United States,[7] was higher—both in real and in monetary terms—than it had been in any previous year. In real terms it was slightly greater than in 1950 and 1951,

Table 6. Official Grants and Loans by the United States to the Rest of the World, 1946-52[1]

	Military Aid	Other	Total	Military Aid	Other	Total
	←——(billion dollars)——→			(per cent of total dollar supply)		
1946	—	5.2	5.2	—	38	38
1947	0.1	5.9	6.0	1	36	37
1948	0.4	4.8	5.2	2	27	29
1949	0.2	5.6	5.8	1	33	34
1950	0.6	3.6	4.2	3	20	23
1951	1.5	2.9	4.4	7	14	21
1952	2.6	2.6	5.2	12	12	24

[1] For sources, see Table 5.

more than twice the amount in the thirties, and 60 per cent higher than in the twenties (see Chart 1 and Table 7). The dollars furnished by official grants and loans (including military aid) are in addition to this large supply from traditional sources. While the need for dollars has also increased since the twenties and the thirties, these figures make the dollar shortage seem much less hopeless than is sometimes assumed.

Chart 1. Annual Dollar Supply [1]
(In billions of U.S. dollars)

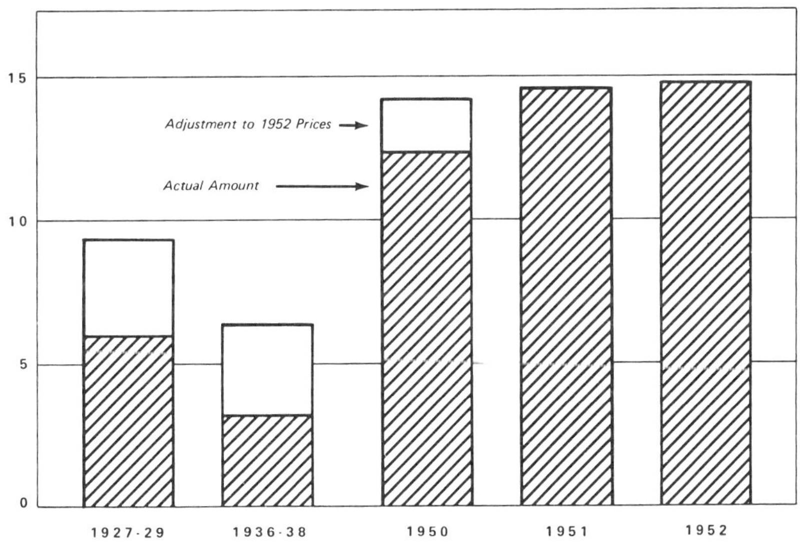

[1] See Table 7 and text.

The additional supply of dollars which has been furnished by official grants and loans has been an active factor in increasing the demand for dollars during the postwar period. This was, in part, inevitable, as an increase in the flow of dollars naturally relaxed the policies of the recipient countries and so caused them to make expenditures which they would otherwise have averted, although only at the cost of much hardship

[7] This subtraction is made in order to show the amount of dollars at the "free" disposal of the recipient countries after paying interest, dividends, etc., to the United States.

and political instability. It is also unlikely that so many dollars would have been furnished by the United States had a large portion of them been added to reserves. Indeed, most of the additional dollar expenditure was *planned* at the direct request of the United States, since one of the avowed purposes of the Marshall Plan was to stimulate investment in the recipient countries and thus strengthen their balance of payments positions in the long run. It would not be true, therefore, to say that the funds received from the United States in the form of official grants and loans could

Table 7. Annual Dollar Supply in Current and 1952 Dollars[1]
(In billions of U.S. dollars)

	1927-29 Average	1936-38 Average	1950	1951	1952
Actual amount	5.9	3.1	12.4	14.7	14.8
Amount adjusted to 1952 prices	9.3	6.3	14.2	14.7	14.8

[1] Excludes all dollars supplied by official financing and by movements of reserves; also excludes an amount of dollars supplied by other sources equal to the net investment income of the United States in each year. The adjustment to 1952 prices is made on the basis of the U.S. export price index. The data have been compiled by the International Monetary Fund.

have been added to reserves, even in large part, had the recipient countries adopted more rigorous policies. But the grants and loans did avert what might otherwise have been a disastrous run on reserves and contributed in some degree to an actual increase.

CONCLUSION

The preceding discussion has stressed three points which must be taken into account in any discussion of the adequacy of monetary reserves:

(1) Monetary reserves are meant to take care of swings between favorable and unfavorable payments positions. They are meant to cover recurrent balance of payments deficits that are temporary in character. No amount of monetary reserves is sufficient to finance a permanent disequilibrium in a country's balance of payments.

(2) The magnitude of the monetary reserves of a given country tends both to affect and to be affected by that country's domestic fiscal and monetary policies. The interaction between reserves and policies is stronger, the more important the role played by external trade in the economy of the country concerned. Rigorous fiscal and monetary policies tend to increase monetary reserves; strong reserve positions make the relaxation of fiscal and monetary policies possible. When world inflationary and world deflationary forces are in balance, this interaction is beneficial and helps both to promote sound policies and to achieve and maintain a viable distribution of monetary reserves throughout the trading world. When world inflationary forces are in the ascendancy, substantial accretions to world monetary reserves tend, through their interactions with policy, to increase these forces yet further; when world deflationary forces are in the ascendancy, substantial accretions to world monetary reserves tend to offset these forces. The foregoing should not be taken to imply that increases in reserves are *per se* undesirable even during periods of world inflation. Countries should be on guard in such situations, however, against relaxing their fiscal and monetary policies so far as to intensify domestic inflationary pressures.

(3) A world-wide distribution of monetary reserves in accordance with the apparent need for them is incompatible with the yet more fundamental consideration of the

distribution of the real resources of each country in accordance with the highest priority for their use. If the monetary reserves of the world were completely redistributed in accordance with apparent need, they would soon be re-redistributed, as each country would soon (quite properly) rearrange the changed amount of real resources at its disposal in accordance with its scale of preferences. In such a re-redistribution, wealthy or less dynamic countries would soon reacquire reserves which they either desired or merely accepted passively, but which, in any event, they could hold without sacrificing other deeply felt needs, while poorer or more dynamic countries would soon dispose of part of their newly acquired reserves in exchange for other types of real resources which they needed more urgently.

It is a corollary of the first of these points that the subject of reserve adequacy can be discussed meaningfully only on the assumption that countries which have not already done so adopt policies adequate to balance their accounts over a normal economic cycle. Upon the assumption that countries adopt such policies, the following four categories or standards of reserve adequacy were distinguished earlier in this paper:

1. Enough to enable a country in bad years, by resort to restrictions, to maintain its external debt payments and to purchase the goods and services necessary to avoid hardship to its population or dislocation to its economy and the possible emergence of an exchange crisis, i.e., to permit a reasonable distribution over *time* of the payments which it can afford to make over the entire cycle;
2. Enough to maintain currency convertibility, barring a severe depression, but with occasional necessity to resort to trade and exchange restrictions for balance of payments purposes;
3. Enough to maintain currency convertibility, barring a severe depression, but without the necessity for occasional resort to trade and exchange restrictions;
4. Enough to maintain currency convertibility, even through severe depressions (but not through prolonged periods of international deflation such as occurred in the thirties), without either the necessity for occasional resort to trade and exchange restrictions or the necessity for resorting to domestic deflationary policies for the purpose of restraining imports, even if this involves a substantial drain on reserves.

The determination of the "adequacy" category into which any country falls, assuming that it meets the fundamental condition of payments balance over a normal cycle, is a matter of judgment. It is probable, however, that almost all countries, assuming the adoption of appropriate policies, would qualify for category 1, many would qualify for category 2, some would qualify for category 3, and a few would qualify for category 4.[8]

[8] International Monetary Fund, *Annual Report, 1952*, p. 6, states: "An aggravating factor in the recurrent balance of payments crises of the postwar years is the inadequacy of international reserves available to monetary authorities outside the United States. Although the gold and dollar holdings of countries other than the United States have risen to some extent since 1938, the increase has not been in proportion to the expansion of world trade, and their value in real terms has been actually reduced by inflation. These trends, combined with the abnormally wide swings in balances of payments, have often produced situations in which reserves have appeared to be dangerously low. The attainment of any particular level or ratio of reserves is not by itself a guarantee against balance of payments crises; nevertheless, a more adequate cushion against balance of payments disturbances is clearly desirable so that more time may be available to make the necessary readjustments."

It should be noted that many of the countries to which reference was there made had not achieved a fundamental balance of payments equilibrium over a normal economic cycle. Each adequacy category used in this paper assumes that policies are always adequate to assure such a balance.

In determining the adequacy category into which any country falls, account should be taken of the availability of the resources of the Fund to extend temporary assistance to member countries which have achieved a fundamental payments balance. The provision of funds for the objectives indicated above—i.e., the avoidance of sharp declines in imports not required by a country's fundamental payments position, the maintenance of currency convertibility, and the avoidance of restrictions—is in accordance with the purposes of the Fund. Assistance from the Fund in carrying out these purposes should, therefore, enable member countries to meet their reserve needs more effectively than would be possible on the basis of their own reserves alone. The role of the Fund in times of depression presents special problems which will now be considered.

Reserves for combating the spread of depression

None of the adequacy categories just discussed implies that a country would be able to endure a prolonged period of world deflation without the imposition of exchange restrictions implying at least a severe limitation on convertibility. However, as has already been suggested, this would scarcely be a fair test of reserve adequacy. Just as, at one end of the spectrum, the subject of reserve adequacy does not become relevant unless the country itself is pursuing appropriate policies, so, at the other end, no country can be expected to maintain reserves sufficient to sustain free and nondiscriminatory multilateral trade in the face of world-wide deflation.

The experts' report, *Measures for International Economic Stability,* assumes that protracted depressions will be avoided by appropriate domestic measures, but that the U.S. economy, even on the assumption of a fairly rigorous anti-deflationary policy, is subject to short, sharp shocks, during which the rest of the world would need substantial reserves in order to maintain domestic anti-deflationary policies and a volume of imports from the United States corresponding to such policies, and thereby prevent the spread of the depression. The experts estimate that, in the event of a depression in the United States lasting for two years from its inception to its conclusion and involving a fall in industrial production of the same relative magnitude as that which occurred in the depression of 1937-38, the rest of the world would need to draw on its reserves to the extent of $8 billion to maintain its commodity imports from the United States at the level of those in the first half of 1951. To this, the experts add another $2 billion to cover anticipated accompanying declines in invisible current account payments by the United States and in private long-term capital outflow from the United States, and come up with an estimate that a total drain of $10 billion on reserves would be necessary to prevent the spread of a depression of the assumed magnitude. There is some reason to suppose that the assumptions of the experts may be unduly pessimistic. But they will not be investigated here, as no quantitative criticism of them would alter the conclusion of this paper that reserves are not, in general, adequate for combating the spread of a severe depression.

There are two essential questions implicit in the experts' report: (1) What actions in the field of monetary reserves should be taken *now* to prevent the spread of future depressions? (2) What actions should be taken when and if a depression starts?

In regard to the first, it would appear desirable for countries to increase their reserves to the extent that is possible and consistent with a progressive relaxation of trade and exchange restrictions and the maintenance of internal financial stability.

When analysis shows clearly that a depression is developing, it should be dealt with promptly by measures directed toward the maintenance of an adequate level of effective demand. Demand should, of course, be maintained on both the national and the international level. The measures taken to assure its maintenance should be primarily positive, and not merely defensive, in character. The essentially defensive character of supplementary reserves obtained with firm assurances of repayment in the short-term or medium-term future has already been pointed out. Defensive measures are important, however; and, in order to prevent small depressions from growing into large ones, such supplementary reserves should be supplied early, on liberal terms, and in adequate amounts. In the event of a severe depression, additional means for maintaining demand at the international level might be required, and it may be expected that the Fund would consult with its members on the desirability of additions to its resources and would consider possible changes in its modes of operations to meet the emergent situation. But primary reliance for the avoidance and cure of depressions must be placed upon appropriate measures at the national level, especially in industrial countries.[9]

APPENDIX

This Appendix reproduces in part an article by G. S. Dorrance and E. Hicks, "Gold and Foreign Exchange Statistics in IFS", in *International Financial Statistics*, June 1953, pp. vii-xii.

Problems of foreign exchange statistics

The statistics of foreign exchange are necessarily difficult to compile and difficult to use. Gold and foreign exchange statistics are intended to measure a country's international liquidity and hence its ability to finance temporary balance of payments reverses without recourse to either secondary deflation or quantitative restriction and to measure by their period-to-period changes the monetary effects of financing the balance of payments. The gold element of the total involves relatively few problems. In most countries gold is held entirely or predominantly by the monetary authorities, and measurement of their holdings provides an unambiguous statement of the gold holdings of the country. Gold is a single physical commodity whose quantity can be measured by weight and unambiguously valued in terms of U.S. dollars or in the currency of the holding country at its par rate of exchange. Lastly, the measurement of gold holdings does not ordinarily involve any problem of net or gross measurement.

The foreign exchange element of the total, on the contrary, involves many problems: Firstly,

[9] International Monetary Fund, *Annual Report, 1952*, pp. 45–46, states: "The Fund has also had under consideration the question of the part to be played by it in connection with the problems created by widespread recessions or depressions. The Articles of Agreement have entrusted to the Fund an important function in this field. The basic problem of depression cannot, however, be overcome by the availability of international short-term credit to be repaid in the next boom, whether this is credit from the Fund or from some other source. The cure for a depression will require national measures to maintain or stimulate effective demand, especially in the great industrial countries. It may take time, however, before these measures bring recovery. The Fund can assist members which in the meantime may be faced with serious balance of payments difficulties, and by so doing help to reduce the deflationary pressure on the world economy as a whole. A UN group of experts has recommended an enlargement of the Fund's resources so as to increase the effectiveness of its activities in such circumstances. The Fund has for some time had under consideration the question of increasing its members' quotas, having in mind such factors as the magnitude of possible balance of payments deficits in a depression and the fall in the purchasing power of money since 1946. It has, however, concluded that an increase in its resources is not a question for action at the present time. Its existing resources are by no means small as a source to finance a cyclical balance of payments deficits. The Fund's resources, moreover, are secondary reserves and the ability of countries to maintain important demand in a depression will depend also on the size of their own reserves. It is important, therefore, that countries follow financial policies that will enable them to build up reserves in periods of prosperity which would provide a first cushion to absorb the shock of a recession."

no completely satisfactory line can be drawn to separate foreign exchange from related items that also contribute to a country's international liquidity. Secondly, because foreign exchange is defined throughout *International Financial Statistics* as claims against foreigners rather than as claims in foreign currency, the foreign exchange holdings of one country are necessarily the foreign exchange liabilities of another, raising the problem of the extent to which foreign exchange liabilities are an offset to assets for a country, for an area, or for the world as a whole. Thirdly, the available international liquidity of a country is not limited to its holdings of foreign assets alone. International agencies, particularly the Fund and the EPU, provide additional sources of liquidity.

Foreign exchange and the similar items, other than gold, that make up a country's international liquidity might be grouped on at least three scales according to their usability. Foreign claims could be arrayed by *currency* from U.S. dollars at the top through the other convertible currencies and then through the inconvertible currencies in the order of their usefulness for meeting obligations in any country or in the country liable for the claim. The *holders* of foreign claims could be arrayed from the monetary authorities at the top through the other banks, other parts of the government, business, and individuals in the order in which their holdings might be thought to be available to the monetary authorities in times of need. Lastly, the *forms* that foreign claims take could be arrayed from currency and demand deposits at the top through other claims on banks, short-term claims on governments, commercial claims, long-term claims to money, equities, and so forth, in the order of their ability to be converted into currency or deposits rapidly and without risk of capital loss. The compilation of foreign exchange statistics involves selecting criteria for cutting these various scales, each at some point.

The statistics published in IFS result from cutting the three scales very unevenly, partly from choice, partly by following convention, and partly from the limitations of the available data. They include as foreign exchange claims in all *currencies*, whether convertible or inconvertible, and value each at its established parity. It would be very difficult to do otherwise since most reporting countries do not differentiate their holdings by currency. Moreover, sterling constitutes most of the inconvertible currency held as foreign exchange; and the nature of the restrictions imposed on sterling would make any classification into "available" and "non-available" most arbitrary. Nevertheless, the usefulness of the data is limited by the inclusion in a single total of currencies of all degrees of convertibility. The only *holders* included are the national monetary authorities. That is, the statistics include as foreign exchange only the holdings of central banks, stabilization funds, treasuries, and similar agencies, and exclude holdings of the other banks and of business and individuals. The choice of monetary policy or exchange restrictions as an alternative to the use of reserves lies with the monetary authorities, and it is their holdings that are primarily available for policy use. This restriction of the data may limit their usefulness since the larger the foreign exchange holdings of the other banks and of business and individuals throughout the world, the more the monetary authorities might be able to induce them to move in settlement of temporary imbalances through appropriate monetary policies. As regards the *form* of foreign claims, the statistics follow the traditional definition of foreign exchange except that they have been extended to include long-term foreign claims. If the holdings of the other banks or of business and individuals were included in the data, the inclusion of long-term foreign claims would not be reasonable. The monetary authorities, however, are not likely to hold long-term foreign securities solely for their income or solely for the prospect of their appreciation. It is mostly the sterling area countries whose central banks hold long-term foreign securities, and their holdings probably represent their decision to hold interest-bearing paper rather than non-interest-bearing deposits or low-interest-bearing treasury bills for some or all of their sterling which cannot be currently used. The inclusion of these investments is consistent with the inclusion of inconvertible currency holdings.

The second problem of foreign exchange statistics as a measure of a country's international liquidity involves the choice of net or gross statistics and the extent to which foreign exchange liabilities are an offset to foreign exchange assets. All of the foreign exchange data in IFS are reported gross insofar as possible, and liability statistics (also gross) are given for the United States and the United Kingdom only. One holder's foreign exchange asset, however, is necessarily another's foreign exchange liability. The world as a whole can have no net foreign exchange holdings.

It might seem, therefore, that data on foreign exchange should be reported net, with each country's foreign exchange liabilities deducted from its foreign exchange assets and with a world total of zero. A number of considerations, however, indicate that it is preferable to define foreign exchange for statistical purposes as gross.

Statistically, gross figures are more easily handled whenever more than one classification is required (e.g., by currency and by holder) for the same reasons that make gross national product a more useful measurement than national income. Conceptually, as in the analysis of banking data generally, the importance lies in the gross magnitudes of the different liabilities and assets, many of which are similar (a 30-day Treasury bill on the asset side and its counterpart of demand deposits on the liability side) and all of which would always net to zero.

Moreover, there are important nonparallelisms in foreign exchange assets and liabilities arising from (a) the fact that, while there are many classes of holders and obligors, the statistics measure only the assets and liabilities of the monetary authorities, and (b) the fact that, while it is intended to define foreign exchange assets and liabilities as claims on or to foreigners, records of some holders and debtors in some countries probably measure instead claims and obligations in foreign currency.

Statistics covering the net asset and liability accounts of the monetary authorities would not be the most useful net figure for the monetary authorities. Their gross assets are the only one of six items (the assets and liabilities of the monetary authorities, the assets and liabilities of the other banks, and the assets and liabilities of business and individuals) over which they have control, but it is they who, in the absence of exchange restrictions, are responsible to see that the economy meets all its foreign liabilities, including those of the banks and of business and individuals. Most of a country's foreign liabilities are obligations in national currency. For the obligor, whether official or private, meeting national currency obligations to foreigners is no more difficult than making payments to residents. But the problem of converting all such payments into foreign exchange must be met by the monetary authorities. The gross reserves of the monetary authorities are the principal means of assuring that their own and other obligations to foreigners can be met.

The net of all six accounts might provide a very useful figure, but information on private foreign exchange is insufficiently available to permit its calculation. Furthermore, the definition "claims against and obligations of foreigners" is probably not observed in the accounts of many of the private holders so that the true net figure would not be known even if all the accounts were consolidated.

A third problem in the compilation of foreign exchange statistics is that of accounting properly for the holdings and transactions of international agencies. Two of the international agencies (the Fund and the EPU) were established in part for the purpose of alleviating the reserve problems of their members It would seem, therefore, that world reserve statistics should show an increase in the liquidity of members following the establishment of these agencies and should reflect their transactions in the accounts of the countries concerned in a clear and unambiguous manner. The complexities of the way the agencies operate and the differences in their methods of bookkeeping, however, make this impossible.

Members of the Fund make capital subscriptions to the Fund, partly in gold and partly in their national currencies. On this account the gold holdings of the members declined on the establishment of the Fund and the world's liquidity, measured as the sum of country statistics, declined. The Fund's holdings of gold and of the currencies of its members are, however, included in the world total. In this total the world's gold holdings remained unchanged on the establishment of the Fund, and the world's foreign exchange holdings rose by the sum of all members' subscriptions paid in member currencies. The members of the EPU, on the other hand, did not make subscription payments to the EPU, but agreed to finance through the EPU, and up to specified limits, their surpluses with other members. There are, therefore, no foreign exchange holdings (other than small amounts of dollars) to report as the holdings of the EPU, and the establishment of the EPU does not show an increase in the combined liquidity of its members. In fact, since pre-existing payments agreements balances were consolidated when the EPU was established, the figures would show a reduction in liquidity through the creation of the EPU.

The accounting of transactions is also different. Members of the EPU earning surpluses in their transactions with other members advance credits to the EPU and add the amount of the credit to their reported foreign exchange holdings. This is in some ways comparable to the manner in which the creditor would have kept his accounts if, in the absence of the EPU, the same transactions had occurred, financed by the debtor through reserves or foreign loans. The method of bookkeeping thus shows an increase in the liquidity of creditors, in the gross assets of Europe, and in the gross assets of the world which is larger the more the payments transactions of Europe are cumulatively unbalanced. The IFS table, based on accounts of members and reporting gross assets, shows the same increases for creditors, EPU countries as a whole, and the world when European payments transactions are unbalanced. In the case of Fund transactions, members whose currencies are drawn from the Fund obtain in effect a claim on the Fund in some respects similar to that which creditor countries of the EPU obtain on the EPU, but they do not add the item to their reported foreign exchange holdings. Hence, Fund transactions have no effect on the statistics of total foreign exchange holdings after the drawing country has spent the currency drawn from the Fund.

The reconciliation of reported data on foreign exchange holdings and foreign exchange liabilities

An attempt has been made to reconcile the foreign exchange data with the reported data on the foreign exchange liabilities of the United States, the United Kingdom, the European Payments Union, and the Bank for International Settlements. The results are presented in Table A, which shows the total gross foreign exchange assets of the world and of each of the monetary areas and compares with them the data on liabilities reported by the United States, the United Kingdom, EPU, and BIS. The difference is labeled "errors and omissions".

There are two principal disparities between the asset and liability data which, in addition to ordinary errors and omissions of many kinds, determine the size and sign of the "errors and omissions" line. Firstly, there are other currencies held and reported as foreign exchange but not reported in the liabilities section. Positive entries in the errors and omissions line may indicate the amounts of all such other currencies.

Secondly, the liability figures include some liabilities to other banks and to business and individuals, while the asset figures include official holdings only. All of the liability data published by the United Kingdom include liabilities to other banks and to business and individuals. Negative entries in the errors and omissions line may indicate the amounts of such liabilities.

The total of all U.S. liabilities to official agencies is available separately, so that this source of error is presumably excluded in the total world reconciliation. The figures as published by the United States, however, require two adjustments. For the year 1950 there is a large difference between the Bank of Canada's reported holdings of U.S. dollars and the U.S. reports of its liabilities to official agencies and banks in Canada.[10] Total U.S. liabilities were increased for 1950 by 619 million dollars to account for this difference. There is secondly a problem in the U.S. reports of liabilities to Japan. Japan publishes its official holdings of U.S. dollars. The amounts agree with U.S. reports of total liabilities to Japanese official agencies and banks, but apparently these amounts are included under liabilities to banks rather than under liabilities to official agencies in U.S. statistics.[11] Total U.S. liabilities to official agencies for all of the years shown have therefore been increased by the amount of Japanese reported official dollar holdings. This adjustment increases the reported U.S. liabilities to official agencies by 669 million dollars in 1952, or 15 per cent of the U.S. total.

In constructing the monetary area reconciliations, however, other problems arise in the data on U.S. liabilities. There are available from U.S. sources data by country for only the total of U.S. liabilities to official agencies and other banks for 1950 and later years, and only

[10] The difference presumably arose from Canadian purchases during 1950 of U.S. securities with original maturities slightly longer than one year. Cf. *Federal Reserve Bulletin*, March 1951, p. 232, in which Canadian holdings of U.S. securities with maturities up to 20 months are reported.

[11] "If reported private dollar balances are adjusted to exclude Japanese holdings (which are technically reported as private, though in reality of an official character). . . ." See *Federal Reserve Bulletin*, March 1952, p. 231.

Table A. Reconciliation of Gross Foreign Exchange Assets with Foreign Exchange Liabilities
(In millions of U.S. dollars)

	1948	1949	1950	1951	1952
World Total[1]					
Total Gross Assets	13,300	10,250	12,900	12,350	12,350
Dollars[2]	2,917	3,071	4,507	4,062	5,133
Sterling[3]	11,478	7,856	8,163	7,870	6,506
Credit to EPU	—	—	402	665	1,077
Balances with BIS	52	108	250	192	364
Errors and omissions	*–1,147*	*–785*	*–422*	*–439*	*–730*
Canada					
Total Gross Assets	610	636	1,170	953	977
Dollars	596	631	1,162	937	975
Sterling	13	5	9	16	2
Errors and omissions	—	—	—	—	—
Latin America					
Dollar Countries					
Total Gross Assets	220	290	350	435	650
Dollars	285	359	360	405	607
Errors and omissions	*–65*	*–69*	*–10*	30	43
Non-Dollar Countries					
Total Gross Assets	1,229	820	825	595	525
Dollars	252	282	395	227	183
Sterling	544	224	126	160	17
Errors and omissions	433	314	304	208	325
Continental EPU Countries					
Total Gross Assets	1,905	2,045	2,720	3,030	3,450
Credit to EPU	—	—	177	665	1,077
Total Net Assets	1,905	2,045	2,543	2,365	2,373
Dollars	901	869	1,140	1,150	1,717
Sterling	1,491	1,229	1,106	1,145	899
Balances with BIS	52	108	250	192	364
Errors and omissions	*–539*	*–161*	47	*–122*	*–607*
United Kingdom					
Total Gross Assets	404	402	768	174	458
Dollars	251	338	400	135	346
Credit to EPU	—	—	225	—	—
Errors and omissions	153	64	143	39	112
Other Sterling Countries					
Total Gross Assets	6,404	4,138	4,747	4,428	3,800
Dollars	62	38	99	108	133
Sterling	7,290	4,959	5,544	5,110	4,488
Errors and omissions	*–948*	*–859*	*–896*	*–790*	*–821*
Rest of the World					
Total Gross Assets	2,540	1,910	2,335	2,720	2,455
Dollars	570	554	951	1,100	1,172
Sterling	2,140	1,439	1,378	1,439	1,100
Errors and omissions	*–170*	*–83*	6	181	183

1 The monetary authorities of the United States hold no foreign exchange assets.
2 Adjusted for Canadian and Japanese discrepancies. See text for details.
3 Excluding U.K. liabilities to dependent areas and dollar countries other than to Bank of Canada.

the total of all U.S. liabilities including liabilities to business and individuals for earlier years. However, for five of the countries whose dollar holdings are especially important (Canada, Cuba, Japan, the Philippines, and the United Kingdom [12]), national figures on official holdings of U.S. dollars are available and were used. U.S. liabilities to the official agencies of other countries were therefore estimated by multiplying the liabilities to official agencies and banks of these countries (all liabilities prior to 1950) by an adjustment factor C/F calculated in the following way:

U.S. reported liabilities to all official holders plus adjustments for Canada and Japan	= A
Official holdings of dollars reported by Canada, Cuba, Japan, the Philippines, and the United Kingdom	= B
Estimated official holdings of dollars by other countries (A – B)	= C
U.S. reported liabilities to all official holders and banks (total holdings prior to 1950) plus adjustment for Canada in 1950	= D
U.S. reported liabilities to official holders and banks (total holdings prior to 1950) in Canada, Cuba, Japan, the Philippines, and the United Kingdom	= E
Liabilities to official holders and banks (total holdings prior to 1950) in other countries (D – E)	= F
Adjustment factor for estimation of official holdings of other countries	C/F

It is recognized that the table is not strictly a reconciliation table since in the cases discussed the same figures have been used on both sides of the reconciliation.

The reconciliation indicates that the basic data on foreign exchange are reasonably satisfactory and that most of the world's holdings of foreign exchange represent, as would be expected, the liabilities of either the United States or the United Kingdom. For the world as a whole, reported liabilities exceed reported assets by some 750 million dollars. This excess of liabilities over assets results from the inclusion in the liabilities data of sterling liabilities to banks, business, and individuals, and to the inclusion of both sterling and dollar liabilities to the Soviet bloc and a few small countries for which no assets data are reported. These amounts are offset in part by the inclusion in the assets data of holdings of currencies other than dollars and sterling. Some measure of the importance of sterling liabilities to nonofficial holders is given in the errors and omissions line for Other Sterling Countries. Since this entry alone exceeds the errors and omissions for the world total, it is apparent that holdings of other currencies play a small but significant role. Holdings of other currencies apparently play their largest role in the non-dollar countries of Latin America. The error arising from the inclusion in the liability data of liabilities to the Soviet bloc and other unreported countries is reflected largely in the Rest of the World figures insofar as sterling is concerned. The corresponding error for the dollar figures is distributed between most of the areas owing to the method of their calculation.

The reconciliation table also indicates that the problem of gross and net assets is not as serious as it might be since most of the foreign exchange holdings of the world represent the liabilities of only two countries, the United States and the United Kingdom, and these are almost entirely denominated in dollars or sterling (i.e., foreign currency from the holder's point of view). It follows from these facts that the net assets of the monetary authorities of most countries cannot be appreciably different from their gross assets, since if the monetary authorities of most countries had appreciable foreign liabilities the foreign assets of other countries would reflect them and lead to plus errors in the reconciliation table. And it follows directly from the facts that foreign exchange liabilities are largely claims against the United States and the United Kingdom and that these are largely denominated in dollars or sterling, that the statistics of foreign exchange of the monetary authorities must be approximately consistent with the definition "claims against foreigners" regardless of whether some countries use the definition "claims in foreign currency".

---

[12] The U.S. dollar holdings of the monetary authorities of the United Kingdom can be estimated by deducting the U.S. Federal Reserve Board's estimate of the U.K. gold holdings from the U.K. figure for gold and U.S. and Canadian dollar assets, on the assumption that Canadian dollar holdings are small.

International Reserves and Liquidity

In May 1957 South Africa requested that the staff should undertake a study of "the factors affecting the present state of international liquidity, including the world supply of monetary gold." References to a possible inadequacy of monetary reserves were made by a number of Governors during the Annual Meetings, 1957. A staff working party subsequently wrote a report on the subject, which was published on September 16, 1958. This was a staff document, prepared under the personal supervision of the Managing Director. It is reproduced below.

International Reserves and Liquidity
A Study by the Staff of
the International Monetary Fund
(September 16, 1958)

CONTENTS

FOREWORD

In the course of 1957, and especially at the Annual Meeting in September of that year, several governments requested that the staff of the Fund prepare a study on international liquidity. This study has now been completed and is herewith published as a staff document; it does not necessarily represent the views of the Executive Directors.

An attempt has been made to review present problems in the light of past experience. The study takes account of very recent developments, and it has therefore fortunately been possible to consider the implications for international liquidity both of the extreme boom conditions of 1956–57 and of the subsequent recession. The consideration of the problems for the future has thus benefited from very recent experience in contrasting economic conditions.

PER JACOBSSON

Washington, D. C.
August 15, 1958

CHAPTER ONE: INTRODUCTION

The opportunity to examine afresh the question of international reserves and liquidity brings again to the attention of the staff of the Fund a number of problems which have, in varying degrees, attracted attention over many years. In one form or another, these problems have been discussed throughout the postwar period. In 1953, at the request of the Economic and Social Council of the United Nations, the Fund prepared an extensive report, "The Adequacy of Monetary Reserves." [1] Since 1956, as a number of countries have had to draw extensively on their reserves and to supplement their reserves by borrowing, even more demanding questions have been raised about the state of international liquidity. The most convenient introduction to these questions is through a consideration of the role of reserves and credit in international trade and payments.

Imports of goods and services are ultimately paid for with exports of goods and services, and any difference between imports and exports may be balanced by a movement of long-term or short-term capital. If a balance still remains, it is then paid with the country's own reserves or other cash holdings. The definition of international reserves must therefore be wide enough to include any kind of money which is acceptable in payment of foreign obligations. Reserves may consist of gold, dollars, and other convertible currencies, or of sterling, deutsche mark, and other currencies which are practically convertible. They may include inconvertible currencies when these are acceptable to particular trading partners. They may include balances due under payments agreements. In many cases, reserve assets are held not only by the official authorities but also by banks, business enterprises, and private individuals. Not infrequently, foreign obligations are met from private rather than from official holdings.

There is thus no unique definition of international reserves which is satisfactory for all purposes and for all countries. This makes the measurement of international reserves, and of changes in reserves from one period to another, peculiarly difficult. In fact, the measurement of reserves necessarily has qualitative as well as quantitative aspects.

Modern economic systems, moreover, operate on credit. Domestically, this takes the form of bank loans and overdrafts, consumer credit, and trade credit. Internationally, private credits may be obtained to finance imports and exports, and public credits may be obtained by one country from banks in, or governments of, other countries as well as from international organizations, such as the International Monetary Fund. As with individuals and business enterprises, the ability of a country (or of individuals in a country) to make payments depends not only upon the amount of cash in hand and the expected receipts of cash in the near future but also to some extent upon the ability to borrow on either short term or long term.

Thus, in appraising the adequacy of international reserves and the degree of international liquidity, account must be taken not only of all kinds of reserve holdings, public and private, but also of the credit-worthiness of countries and the ability of the international financial mechanism to extend credit under proper safeguards in good times and bad. In addition, the adequacy of reserves and the degree of liquidity depend upon the international environment, including, for example, the appropriateness of the structure of exchange rates, the extent to which balance prevails in international trade, and the presence or absence of that intangible, "confidence." There is nothing unique or new in this recital of the elements that combine and recombine to create any given

[1] See above, p. 311.

degree of international liquidity. For this reason, it is useful to approach the current problem of international reserves and liquidity in the perspective of the past.

During the heyday of the gold standard, immediately before the outbreak of World War I, monetary specialists were also concerned with the problems of the proper size, the distribution, and the rate of growth of international reserves. At that time, too, conflicting views were expressed. It would fall outside the scope of this inquiry to review those old controversies, which in many ways applied to conditions very different from those prevailing today. It is, however, certainly relevant to recall that at that time many countries, and particularly the United Kingdom, held reserves which seem to us now to have been astonishingly slender compared with the volume of trade and other transactions.

There are a number of reasons why this system operated as smoothly as it did in the generation preceding World War I. These reasons throw some light upon the present situation. In the first place, balance prevailed in international payments and economic relationships to a greater extent than has since been true for any extended period. The major use and need for reserves arise when balance is upset; the presence of economic balance and the feeling that balance will be maintained are perhaps more important than the actual size of reserves in creating a feeling that they are adequate. Moreover, day-to-day disturbances, and even seasonal movements, of international payments need make no great demands upon reserves when credits of various kinds can be arranged. There were widespread and effective facilities for granting credits in London and other centers. These facilities were available to governments and other official agencies as well as to overseas banks and foreign traders. London was responsible for the greater part of this financing, which not only supplemented international liquidity in a very important way but also gave London large sight claims on firms and banks in other countries. Changes in the amount of these claims, effected by means of changes in Bank Rate, buttressed with large long-term overseas investments, provided adequate supplements to London's slim gold reserves. There was widespread acceptance of the gold standard system, and of stable exchange rates within it, as the only desirable monetary system. This implied, as far as individual countries were concerned, clear and agreed objectives for monetary policy and for fiscal policy, and the latter was less important then than now because the role of government was much smaller. For these and other reasons, a large degree of confidence prevailed.

In the years immediately preceding the outbreak of World War I, London was the leading financial center. Other centers were secondary and of markedly less importance. After the war, this situation changed and New York emerged as an important international center alongside of London. This development had important implications for the financing of world trade and for the movement of funds. It may well be that a multicentered world can function as well as a one-centered world in periods of calm, but in periods of stress, it is subject to wide and sweeping movements. Such movements may create severe strains in the financial structure. Developments since 1946 have further increased the importance of New York as a financial center but have by no means given New York the same importance relative to London and other financial centers that London before 1914 had relative to all other centers.

The development of the institutions and arrangements that created operating smoothness and stability before 1914 required both time and a favorable environment. The last important war in Europe had taken place in 1870–71. In comparison with twentieth century experience, neither this war nor any of the subsequent smaller wars involved any large economic dislocation. There were some conflicts outside Europe but, again, these were short and relatively small. Looking backward, we can see that in this general environment the shocks to the economic system were much smaller than they have been since 1914.

It is, however, easy to overestimate the stability and the long duration of the international financial structure that existed immediately before World War I and, by contrast, to underestimate the characteristics of the system that has gradually developed in the postwar period. Though it is customary to refer to the second half of the nineteenth century as "the golden age of the gold standard," this overstates the case. The United Kingdom was on a gold standard as early as 1819, but the other countries of Western Europe and the United States were not until the 1870's. With a few exceptions, all other countries at that time had either a silver standard or an inconvertible currency. Since the price of silver was falling, the exchange value of all silver standard currencies was depreciating. The variations in the exchange rates of silver standard and inconvertible (flexible rate) currencies were astonishingly large, even when measured against recent developments.

Measured in terms of the number of countries involved, the last half of the nineteenth century was a period of considerable monetary change, with many devaluations, inconvertible currencies, and floating rates. Measured in terms of their importance to world trade, however, there was a solid core of countries on gold after the 1870's. These countries not only set the goal for monetary developments in all other countries, but they accounted for perhaps 70 per cent of the world's exports. Toward the end of the century, the gold standard was adopted by more and more countries: by Austria-Hungary in 1892; Russia and Japan in 1897; India in 1899; and Mexico in 1904.

Also of interest is the fact that, especially in the early years of the period, there was concern from time to time that the world's reserves of gold or silver or both were inadequate. There were also many criticisms (in the United Kingdom) that British reserves—that "thin film of gold"—were inadequate, and the reason often given for this state of affairs was that the Bank of England, as a private concern, was unwilling to tie up the necessary amount of assets in nonincome-earning form. To be sure, these criticisms decreased toward the end of the prewar period, as the United Kingdom acquired larger holdings of long-term and short-term investments, while the Bank of England developed increasingly effective techniques for dealing with monetary and exchange rate problems. It is not without interest, furthermore, that, from 1900 until 1913, in the face of large increases in trade, the gold holdings of the Bank of England increased by scarcely 10 per cent, so that the ratio of gold reserves to imports fell from 7 per cent to 5 per cent. For the world as a whole, the gold situation was greatly eased after 1890 by increases in gold output, especially in the Transvaal; and indeed, in some academic circles, the question was raised after the turn of the century whether gold production might not become too abundant.

Prices rose during World War I, and in the course of the 1920's they settled down to a level which, on a gold basis, was about 50 per cent higher than in prewar years. There was consequently an increase in the value of world trade, and the question soon arose whether the available reserves would be sufficient in view of these changed circumstances. Some feared the emergence of a gold shortage, and proposals were put forward to guard against it. This question was one of the main subjects of deliberation at the Genoa Conference in 1921, and it continued to be discussed in the 1920's. As a matter of fact, the ratio of reserves to the value of trade at the beginning of the

1920's was higher than it had been in 1913, in part because of the incorporation into official reserves of gold previously in circulation.

It will be remembered that the resolutions of the Genoa Conference recommended, on the one hand, wider use of the gold exchange standard and, on the other, establishment of central banks in all developed countries. Both of these recommendations were realized. Exchange holdings were increasingly used as official reserves in the 1920's. Though exchange holdings were reduced to very low levels in the 1930's, they became, during and after World War II, a reserves component on a scale never anticipated in 1921 (for further discussion of this point, see Chapter II). Central banks have also been established in the large majority of countries, developed as well as underdeveloped, though it must be admitted that their full potentialities for stability and development have not been achieved in all cases.

For some years after 1921, it seemed that the new system could be made to work effectively. Within a very few years, one country after another stabilized its currency under conditions of full convertibility. There were, however, many deep-seated elements of maladjustment. Some were a consequence of the war, and certain additional ones emerged in the postwar period. With the aid of hindsight, it is clear that these maladjustments were not solely or even largely of financial origin and that they could not have been solved by financial means. In some respects financial decisions were helpful, but in other respects they contributed new elements of disequilibrium. Exchange rates used in currency stabilizations were not always set at the most appropriate levels. Sterling was stabilized at an ambitiously high rate in relation to gold, and the French franc was later set at too low a rate. Reserves were generally increased in the European countries but, in many cases, they were borrowed instead of being acquired with national savings. They were sometimes borrowed on short term and pyramided from country to country, making the situation even more unstable. Unfortunately, at that time, these and other developments could not be effectively measured because of the inadequacy of the statistics then available.

The hopes entertained for the successful re-establishment of a stable and growing international financial system were frustrated by the maladjustments of the 1920's and finally shattered by the Great Depression and the devaluations of 1931–34. Three main conclusions can be drawn from this experience. The first is that considerable time and much effort are needed to restore a proper balance after a major war has caused widespread economic dislocation, inflation, and currency upheaval. The second is that when stabilization is attempted the exchange rate chosen must be appropriate and realistic, and if the rate is found to be incorrect prompt correction is necessary. The third is that once a crack starts in the exchange structure it is difficult to limit its effects. It may lead to the forced devaluation of major currencies—devaluations not dictated by the realities of foreign trade and competitive prices. Such a crack may start with a relatively minor currency, and yet gain such momentum that it ultimately sunders the whole international exchange structure. Thus, in the period between the two world wars, the failure of the Credit Anstalt in Vienna in 1931 led not only to considerable difficulties in the German banking structure but also to the devaluation of sterling and other currencies in the same year, and ultimately to the devaluation of the dollar in 1934 and of the gold bloc currencies in 1936.

After the devaluations of the 1930's, the world's financial system became increasingly fragmented. Although many countries maintained stable exchange rates in relation to the dollar, whose gold content was officially changed in 1934, and others maintained stable exchange rates through the sterling area, which was then more extensive than it is today, the dollar-sterling rate fluctuated. There was increased resort to trade restrictions, multiple currency practices, bilateral arrangements, and autarky. Closer examination of developments up to the outbreak of World War II suggests that there was a deterioration in the fundamental monetary position of parts of the sterling area, and that in general there were more difficulties in the day-to-day operations of foreign exchange markets than is often supposed. Growing political difficulties, in both Europe and the Far East, caused massive flights of capital, in large part to the United States. These took place on a scale much larger than before 1914, and from time to time they tended to gain a momentum of their own. Central banks and monetary authorities found it more difficult to know when and how to take a stand. Long-term capital movements dried up. Confidence decreased sharply—and there was good reason why this should have been the case. The basic conception of a *world* economy lost meaning, and the idea of separate, disconnected economies gained force.

World reserves increased sharply in the 1930's, and the ratio of reserves to trade reached all-time highs. A number of factors were responsible for this development. The value of all gold stocks was raised in 1934 when the price of gold was increased. The production of gold was stimulated by the falling prices and unemployment of the depression and further stimulated by the higher price of gold. On the other hand, both the value and the volume of trade decreased. Even in 1937, when there had been a substantial, though in no way complete, recovery from the depression, the ratio of gold and exchange reserves to trade for all countries other than the United States was 63 per cent, in comparison with 35 per cent in 1928 and 17 per cent in 1913. The world had very large reserves, but it was troubled by the inability of leading countries to restore balance in their internal economies and, for some of them, also in their foreign trade relations.

The ratio of reserves to trade is discussed in Chapter II of this report, where the data for the postwar years are analyzed and compared with those for 1937–38, as well as 1928 and 1913. One general conclusion that must be drawn from this discussion is that the adequacy of international reserves cannot be judged in a vacuum and that adequacy is not a simple matter of arithmetical relationship. The adequacy of reserves is always related to the degree of efficiency of the prevailing international credit system, and it is affected by the realism of the existing pattern of exchange rates and by the appropriateness of domestic monetary and fiscal policies.

To the creaking and disorganized international financial and economic mechanism of the 1930's, World War II added inflation, unparalleled destruction and economic dislocation, and sweeping changes in debtor-creditor positions.

While World War II was still being waged, ideas were put forward for a better monetary system. The principal objectives, once again, were to restore a properly working international monetary system with convertible currencies and with safeguards for the maintenance of exchange stability; to encourage a healthy and free flow of world trade; and to ensure financial assistance to individual countries to enable them to correct maladjustments without resorting to measures destructive of national or international prosperity. After much discussion, these main ideas were embodied in the Articles of Agreement of the International Monetary Fund. It was recognized, however, that special problems of adjustment would arise in what was called a "transitional period" and that certain existing restrictions would have to be permitted for part or all of this period.

Peace in 1945 brought problems of economic and financial reconstruction of unparalleled magnitude. There was actual inflation in practically all countries. There were accumulated shortages of consumer goods, of capital goods, and of working inventories at all levels of production. In most of Europe, there were the additional huge requirements growing out of wartime destruction and decapitalization. An enormous amount of investment was required to start an increase of production and then to raise it to high and efficient levels within a reasonable period of time. Domestic savings were generally not adequate to this task; consequently, there was an acute shortage of savings that tempted countries to rely excessively on credit creation, which contributed further to the inflationary pressure. As a matter of fact, the major part of the capital goods and working inventories required for these purposes could be obtained in large measure only from the United States. For Europe, these difficulties came to a head in 1947, when conditions were aggravated by widespread crop failures due to a very cold winter and a very dry summer. It was then that large-scale aid on a broad and imaginative scale was inaugurated by the announcement and implementation of the Marshall Plan.

Since the end of World War II, a large and growing supply of dollars, arising out of a steadily expanding volume of U.S. imports and payments for overseas services, capital exports, and aid, has been the dominant element in improving international liquidity. The European Payments Union (EPU) has provided additional liquidity by making it possible for intra-European payments to be settled partly in credits granted by the creditor members. The Fund made a substantial amount of resources available before the Marshall Plan went into effect. Subsequently, the countries that obtained Marshall Plan aid had no need to turn to the Fund, while the British Commonwealth countries were able to make use of the substantial sterling balances they had accumulated during the war, and many Latin American countries drew down dollar balances accumulated during the same period. At the beginning of the postwar period, the private credit system could not be relied upon to provide the required amount of commercial credit to finance international trade, but as time passed it began to play an increasingly important supplementary role. Gradually, and at times almost imperceptibly, there was a simplification of many exchange rate structures, and a reduction in restrictions and bilateralism.

In respect of international reserves and liquidity, there have been a number of developments. First, reserves of countries other than the United States increased from $22 billion at the end of 1948 to $30 billion at the end of 1957. The EPU countries as a group, which had had very low reserves at the end of 1948, substantially increased their holdings of gold and dollars, while a number of other countries that had accumulated large holdings of sterling or dollars during the war reduced their reserves. Most countries were able to show some improvement, but the improvement was distinctly uneven. The increases in reserves took place in those countries which invested part of their net savings in gold or exchange rather than in capital goods at home or in securities or businesses abroad. In fact, reserves can be increased only by applying to that end otherwise uncommitted savings, and the importance of having uncommitted savings is a matter to which further reference will be made in this study. Secondly, the methods whereby total reserves have been increased have been sound, and there has been no deterioration in the quality of reserves. As distinguished from the 1920's, reserves have, on the whole, not been borrowed, either on long term or (what is still more dangerous) on short term. On the contrary, the increase has resulted principally from saving part of the receipts arising from trade and from aid. There has been little if any of the international pyramiding of credit so characteristic of the 1920's. With the major exception of 1957, there have been few of the movements of "hot money" so feared in the 1930's, though changes in "leads and lags" have at times exerted strong speculative pressure, especially against sterling. Some countries have drawn down their sterling or dollar balances, but this was done largely to pay for imports. Thirdly, the gold holdings of the United States have been reduced by more than $3 billion since 1949, which meant the reversal of a trend that had gone on, with a few short exceptions, for at least two generations. In addition, there have been large increases in both private and official holdings of dollars by foreigners. The increases in official holdings are included in statistics on international reserves, but the increases in private holdings, which also add to international liquidity, are not. In fact, since 1948 there has been a distinct improvement in the distribution of the world's reserves of gold, and an even greater improvement in the distribution of the world's reserves of gold and foreign exchange. The scope and significance of this redistribution can be appreciated only by reference to the writings of the 1920's and 1930's, which treated any movement of reserves to the United States as sterilized and irreversible.

The healthy and balanced growth of world trade depends upon adequate and rising reserves and an efficient international credit system, both private and official.

The level of reserves influences the domestic volume of money and credit, while gains and losses of reserves are one of the most important indications of the state of balance of the domestic economy in relation to the economies of other countries. In the days of the gold standard, gold circulated as coin and, through cover percentages, determined the volume of credit money in a manner that was largely automatic. These links between gold and money are now much weaker, and monetary management plays a much larger role. This is true for two reasons. First, holdings of exchange, largely dollars and sterling, are a very important supplement to gold as a reserve against both the domestic money supply and fluctuations in the balance of payments. The growth of reserves now depends not only upon the additions to the stock of monetary gold from new production and dishoarding but also upon the additions to the world's holdings of dollars, sterling, and other currencies. These additions depend, in turn, upon the creation of domestic money by the United States and other countries, and upon the willingness of the rest of the world to hold reserve assets in this form. The ability of countries to create exchange liabilities, whether by reason of large gold reserves or other factors, has been, and will continue to be, very important in increasing world liquidity. Secondly, the relationship between reserves of gold and exchange and the volume of domestic money, although still influenced by the amount of international reserves, is within broad limits largely determined by monetary management. This management is less a question of the cover percentages, which still form part of the monetary legislation of many countries, than of a proper appreciation by the monetary authorities of the limits to the permissible supply of credit which are suggested by reserve movements. Changes in reserves are one of the factors which the monetary authorities must consider in judging the measures required to maintain the exchange rates and the international positions of their countries.

Total international reserves have grown, and the total has become more effective through redistribution since the percentage of total reserves held by the United States has fallen. The system of international credit has been strengthened unobtrusively but steadily during the postwar period. Private commercial credit is now more readily available to finance the movement of trade. The role of the Fund as a second line of monetary reserves has become increasingly important. On the other hand, from 1947 to 1957, the value of world trade increased by 110 per cent, and its volume by 90 per cent. The prices of goods traded internationally increased by 140 per cent between 1937 and 1957. There have been a number of monetary crises in the postwar period; sterling and other major European currencies are still not legally convertible; and many countries still employ multiple currency practices and exchange restrictions. For these and other reasons, there have been questions about the adequacy of reserves, from the standpoint of both their total and their distribution, and about the appropriateness of the system of international credit, with account taken of the existing level of reserves.

CHAPTER TWO: THE LEVEL AND COMPOSITION OF RESERVES

Before examining the question of the amount of reserves that may be considered adequate for any individual country, it is of interest to review the level and composition of reserves as they are at present, together with comparable figures for previous years.

Changes in Total Reserves

International reserves are here taken to be a country's official holdings of gold, dollars, sterling, and other foreign exchange assets on a gross basis, i.e., without taking account of short-term liabilities that might be considered to be offsetting. This is the most usual and at the same time the most practicable definition of international reserves, and the only one that can be used to deal with many countries over extended periods of time. Within its limits this definition makes possible greater precision in comparison than any other. For certain purposes, and for certain countries, a broader treatment of international assets and liabilities is desirable and is therefore also used in this report. Private—or better, nonofficial—holdings of gold, dollars, sterling, and other currencies are a supplement to official holdings and in some cases are a substitute for them. Furthermore, the line between short-term and long-term assets is indistinct and shifting, and the conventional distinctions may not be appropriate in all cases. On the other hand, if account is to be taken of short-term liabilities, there is the difficulty of defining exactly what kind of short-term liabilities should properly be regarded as offsetting particular kinds of assets. The liabilities may be those of the central bank, the banking system, or the economy as a whole. Against some of these liabilities there are, in turn, short-term assets which are not included in official reserves, e.g., liabilities of foreigners on account of discounted acceptances. It is for these reasons that general and historical discussions of reserves use figures on a gross basis but introduce additional figures to deal with certain specific countries or problems.

At the end of 1957 the world's stock of monetary gold, as shown in Table 1, was valued at $38.6 billion, of which $37.0 billion was held by countries and $1.6 billion by international organizations—principally the International Monetary Fund. Country reserves in the form of official exchange were $15.9 billion, so that total country reserves of gold and foreign exchange came to $52.9 billion. As may be seen from the table, the figures for 1957 constituted all-time highs. Country reserves by themselves, excluding reserves held by international organizations, are at present twelve times as high as in 1913, four times as high as in 1928, and nearly twice as high as in 1937–38. The dollar value of reserves declined in 1949, largely because of the devaluation of sterling; it also declined slightly in 1950–51, during the Korean crisis. However, since 1951 there has again been an uninterrupted increase in total world reserves.

It is estimated that in 1913, in addition to official reserves shown in Table 1, there was about $3.6 billion of gold in circulation. This gold was very largely absorbed by monetary reserves during and after World War I. By 1928, monetary gold not included in reserves is estimated to have been less than 10 per cent of the amount held in reserves. In the period before World War I, gold held outside reserves served an important function as a medium of circulation and of hoarding, but it had little importance as a means of settling deficits in the balance of payments. Nevertheless, even if the amounts of gold held outside reserves were added to the reserve figures for 1913 and 1928, the present official reserves of gold and foreign exchange would be more than six times as large as those in 1913, and nearly four times as large as those in 1928. (On the other

Table 1. Gold and Exchange Reserves of Countries and International Organizations, Selected Years, 1913-57[1]

(In billions of U.S. dollars)

	Countries			International Organizations			Total		
Year	Gold (1)	Exchange (2)	Total (1) + (2) (3)	Gold (4)	Exchange (5)	Total (4) + (5) (6)	Gold (1) + (4) (7)	Gold and country exchange reserves (7) + (2) (8)	Gold and all exchange reserves (3) + (6) (9)
1913	4.0	0.5[2]	4.5	—	—	—	4.0	4.5	4.5
1928	9.8	3.1	12.9	—	—	—	9.8	12.9	12.9
1937	25.3	2.4	27.7	—	—	—	25.3	27.7	27.7
1938	26.0	1.8	27.8	—	—	—	26.0	27.8	27.8
1948	32.8	13.4	46.2	1.5	5.5	7.0	34.3	47.7	53.2
1949	33.2	10.5	43.7	1.5	5.7	7.2	34.7	45.2	50.9
1950	33.6	13.6	47.2	1.7	6.1	7.8	35.3	48.9	55.0
1951	33.6	12.9	46.5	1.7	6.0	7.7	35.3	48.2	54.2
1952	33.6	13.2	46.8	2.0	6.1	8.1	35.6	48.8	54.9
1953	33.9	14.1	48.0	2.0	6.8	8.8	35.9	50.0	56.8
1954	34.4	15.1	49.5	2.1	6.9	9.0	36.5	51.6	58.5
1955	35.0	15.6	50.6	2.3	6.5	8.8	37.3	52.9	59.4
1956	35.6	16.2	51.8	2.1	6.8	8.9	37.7	53.9	60.7
1957	37.0	15.9	52.9	1.6	7.6	9.2	38.6	54.5	62.1

Sources: For 1937 and 1950-57, *International Financial Statistics (IFS)*, June 1958; for 1928, "The Adequacy of Monetary Reserves," *Staff Papers*, Vol. III, No. 2 (October 1953), pp. 181-227; for 1913, *Banking and Monetary Statistics* (Board of Governors of the Federal Reserve System, 1943), Table 160; for 1938, *IFS*, December 1954; for 1948, *IFS*, February 1958; for 1949, *IFS*, August 1955. Data exclude countries in the Soviet bloc.

[1] Gold is valued at $20.67 per ounce prior to 1934 and at $35 an ounce thereafter.

[2] Estimate. The Bank for International Settlements estimated exchange holdings as "at least $400 million and at most $600 million" (*The Gold Exchange Standard* [1932]). According to another estimate, exchange holdings prior to World War I were $300 million [Felix Mlynarski, *The Functioning of the Gold Standard* (League of Nations, A Memorandum Submitted to the Gold Delegation of the Financial Committee, 1931), p. 10].

hand, there are at the present time large holdings of gold and exchange outside of official reserves. Nonofficial holdings of gold are probably of the order of $10–12 billion, and nonofficial holdings of dollars and sterling may come to $7–8 billion. These are equal to at least one third of official country reserves of gold and exchange at the end of 1957. Moreover, all of those private holdings are owned outside the United States, so that it is more appropriate to compare them with the official reserves of those countries. For all countries excluding the United States, nonofficial holdings of gold, dollars, and sterling are equal to at least 60 per cent of their official reserves.)

All of these data on reserves are expressed in current dollars. For this reason, there was a substantial increase in gold reserves where the gold content of the dollar was reduced by 40 per cent in 1934. On the other hand, there have been decreases in the value of reserve holdings of sterling and other currencies because of devaluations against the dollar.

More attention will be given later in this chapter to the role of exchange holdings, when the question of the composition of reserves is examined. For the moment, it is sufficient to say that these holdings became more important in the 1920's, but that this development was not always sound, since the increases were to a large extent the counterpart of short-term borrowings. Reserve holdings of exchange fell sharply after 1929, but then recovered somewhat in the middle 1930's. After World War II, they reached an unprecedentedly high figure, reflecting the accumulation of net current earnings by many countries during the war. In contrast to the 1920's, they therefore were really "owned" by the countries holding them. By the end of 1957, these holdings represented nearly one third of total country reserves.

Under existing legislation in most countries, gold and foreign exchange reserves are held as cover for notes and other central bank liabilities. But at the same time, of course, they serve as a means of settling balances that arise in relation to other countries. Foreign trade is the largest item in the balance of payments of the various countries. It is therefore natural that in the first place reserves should be compared with a country's trade figures. Table 2 shows the ratio of gold and foreign exchange reserves to imports of all but the communist countries for the years 1913, 1928, 1937, 1938, 1948, and 1950 to 1957. Because of the large size of the U.S. gold holdings, both absolutely and in relation to U.S. imports, the table also shows the figures for all countries other than the United States (and other than the communist countries).

In the following paragraphs, the terms "all countries" and "the world as a whole" will be taken to exclude the communist bloc countries. It will be seen that for the world as a whole gold and exchange reserves in 1957 were equal to 49 per cent of imports, compared with 21 per cent in 1913 and 42 per cent in 1928. On the other hand, the high ratio of reserves to imports in 1937–38, when it averaged about 109 per cent, was due largely to the increase in the price of gold in 1934 and to the shrunken volume of world trade in those years. For the years after World War II, it may be noted that the amounts held by international organizations can be considered as increasing international liquidity. For the world as a whole, the addition of these amounts to official country reserves in 1957 would increase the ratio of reserves to imports in that year from 49 per cent to 51 per cent. This difference in ratios is, of course, very small, but it understates the importance of these organizations for international liquidity. No similar adjustment is required for the prewar figures, because such organizations either did not exist or played only a minor role.

When the United States is excluded, some significant differences emerge, although the relationship between the various years remains broadly the same. On this basis, the ratio of gold and foreign exchange to imports in 1957 was 32 per cent, compared with 17 per cent in 1913, 35 per cent in 1928, and 63 per cent in 1937–38. Again, if gold holdings of international organizations are included, the 1957 figure is raised to 34 per cent, while the others remain the same. The present ratio is therefore about twice as high as in 1913, about equal to that of 1928, and still significantly lower than in 1937–38. These are obviously key years, and insofar as historical comparison may be of value, they are the years which, together with the period since 1951, have to be examined in greater detail.

Reserves and Trade in 1913

Comparisons with a period as far back as 1913—more than two generations from the present time—must of course be made circumspectly because of the many fundamental changes that have taken place in the meantime. Even so, an understanding of

Table 2. Ratio of Reserves to Imports, All Countries Excluding the Communist Bloc, Selected Years, 1913-57

	Countries			Countries and International Organizations	
Year	Imports *(billion dollars)*	Gold as per cent of imports	Gold and exchange as per cent of imports[1]	Gold as per cent of imports	Gold and exchange as per cent of imports[1]
		World			
1913	21.0	19	21	19	21
1928	30.6	32	42	32	42
1937	27.3	93	101	93	101
1938	23.6	110	117	110	117
1948	60.0	55	77	57	80
1950	59.3	57	80	60	82
1951	81.4	41	57	43	59
1952	80.2	42	58	44	61
1954	79.6	43	62	46	65
1955	89.0	39	57	42	59
1956	98.1	36	53	38	55
1957	107.0	35	49	35	51
		World Excluding the United States			
1913	19.2	14	17	14	17
1928	26.2	23	35	23	35
1937	23.7	53	63	53	63
1938	21.1	54	63	54	63
1948	52.0	16	42	19	45
1950	49.7	22	49	25	52
1951	69.5	15	34	18	36
1952	68.5	15	34	18	37
1954	68.6	18	40	21	43
1955	76.6	17	38	20	41
1956	84.4	16	35	18	38
1957	92.8	15	32	16	34

Sources: For imports—1913, *Industrialization and Foreign Trade* (League of Nations, 1945), pp. 157-67; 1928, "The Adequacy of Monetary Reserves," *Staff Papers*, Vol. III, No. 2 October 1953), pp. 181-227; 1938, *International Financial Statistics (IFS)*, August 1955; 1948, *IFS*, February 1958; 1937 and 1950-57, *IFS*, June 1958. For reserves—1913, *Banking and Monetary Statistics* (Board of Governors of the Federal Reserve System, 1943); 1928, "The Adequacy of Monetary Reserves," *op. cit.;* 1938, *IFS*, December 1954; 1948, *IFS*, February 1958; 1937 and 1950-57, *IFS*, June 1958. Gold is valued in 1913 and 1928 at $20.67 per ounce.

[1] Exchange refers to exchange reserve holdings of countries and does not include those of international agencies.

the situation that prevailed during this period may be instructive in many respects. In 1913, for the world excluding the United States, gold reserves were equal to 14 per cent of imports, and gold and exchange reserves to 17 per cent of imports. Even if gold in circulation is included, the ratios are much lower than for the years 1928, 1937–38, or indeed for 1957.[1] By the standards of these more recent years, reserves were so low in 1913 that it now seems difficult to imagine how they were considered adequate at the time.

The figures for the United Kingdom are especially striking, the ratio of reserves to imports in 1913 amounting to only 5.3 per cent (Table 3). Before World War I, however, the United Kingdom had very substantial support for its reserves in the form of

Table 3. Ratio of Reserves to Imports, Eight European Countries, 1913 and 1928

Country	1913 [1] Gold as per cent of imports	1928 Gold as per cent of imports	1928 Gold and exchange as per cent of imports
Denmark	9.4	10	17
France	41.7	60	121
Germany	10.8	19	23
Italy	37.7	23	50
Netherlands	3.8	16	24
Sweden	12.0	14	26
Switzerland	8.3	20	30
United Kingdom	5.3	13	13

Sources: For 1913, Felix Mlynarski, *Gold and Central Banks* (1929), p. 117; for 1928, "The Adequacy of Monetary Reserves," *Staff Papers*, Vol. III, No. 2 (October 1953), pp. 206-7.

[1] Total gold reserves of these countries were about $1.6 billion. All of them had exchange reserves except the United Kingdom. The world total of exchange reserves was perhaps $300-600 million. If these countries owned all of this—which is most unlikely—the percentage of reserves to imports for all of them could, at most, have been from one fifth to one third greater.

short-term bills discounted in London, payable by countries all over the world. For example, after the outbreak of hostilities in 1914 many of these bills were called in, with the result that even in the autumn of that difficult year the pound was particularly strong in relation to other currencies, including the dollar.[2]

[1] If the countries now in the communist bloc are excluded, gold reserves of all countries were $4.0 billion in 1913 and monetary gold not included in reserves was $3.6 billion. If the United States is also excluded, country gold reserves were $2.7 billion and monetary gold not included in reserves was $2.9 billion. By 1928, monetary gold not included in reserves was less than 10 per cent of the amount held in reserve. See League of Nations, *Interim Report of the Gold Delegation* (1930), Annex XIII, "Gold: Demand and Supply," by A. Loveday, Appendix II.

[2] Writing in 1931, the Committee on Finance and Industry (Macmillan Committee) explained the strong prewar situation of the United Kingdom as follows: (1) London was then by far the most powerful financial center in the world and had sight claims on the rest of the world much greater than those of the world on her and could thus by the operation of her Bank Rate immediately adjust her reserve position. (2) The liquid resources held by foreigners in London and in secondary financial centers were relatively small. In contrast they were large in the 1920's. *Report* (1931), pp. 124–26.

The ratio of gold and exchange reserves to imports was higher in 1928 than in 1913, not only for the United Kingdom but also for each of the seven other European countries shown in Table 3. Some of the reasons for the stability and relatively efficient working of the international monetary system before World War I were outlined in the introduction to this study, but it is useful to analyze them here in greater detail:

(1) The economies of the various countries, after a long period of peace, were in relatively good balance in relation to one another at the existing rates of exchange.

(2) If an imbalance occurred, the authorities and the public were prepared to apply strong monetary and fiscal measures to re-establish the appropriate equilibrium. Changes in official discount rates had undoubtedly a considerable effect when, as at that time, the public sector was relatively limited, rarely representing as much as 10 per cent of the economy, compared with 15 per cent to 25 per cent at present. In other ways, too, there were fewer obstacles in the pre-1914 system to making the changes required to restore equilibrium.

(3) The strain of seasonal and other imbalances rarely fell wholly on official reserves. A large part was carried by the international credit system. There was unquestioned confidence in sterling, whose gold convertibility dated back to 1819. There was great confidence in the stability of the other major currencies, which were almost all convertible at the existing rates of exchange. London was by far the most important money market in the world for both long-term and short-term capital. Particularly from the point of view of providing short-term credit, this was a one-centered world. As such, it was inherently more stable than the multicentered world that developed after World War I. Under these conditions, changes in interest rates could be counted upon to bring about equilibrating movements of funds fairly rapidly. In particular, an increase in the London rate could rapidly strengthen sterling by shifting financing to other centers and by stimulating repayment by foreigners of the large amount of outstanding current liabilities. Indeed, the stability of currencies was taken so much for granted that in the years 1919–22 it took a great deal to destroy confidence even in currencies that were affected by violent inflation.

(4) The leading monetary nation—the United Kingdom—was a free trade country. The commercial policies of other countries were generally stable, and many countries were tied together by commercial treaties containing most-favored-nation clauses. The result was that in a depression the deficit countries did not have to face the additional difficulty of increased barriers to trade.

(5) Gold production was large enough to provide the resources for a more or less regular increase in reserves and to give an impetus to an expansion in the volume of credit. This was particularly important at the time when, through the operation of cover percentages and in other ways, the internal credit policy of the various countries was largely tied to changes in the gold reserves. The general opinion was that the gold supply was abundant and that reserves were adequate.[3]

Reserves and Trade in 1928

While there had been a great deal of discussion in the 1920's about a possible gold shortage, and steps had been taken to economize gold, 1928 was still a year of great optimism. World trade was increasing, the gold standard was being re-established in more and more countries, efforts were being made to settle the reparations problem

[3] Cassel, *Theory of Social Economy* (1924), p. 453; Kitchin, in *Interim Report of the Gold Delegation* (1930), Appendix XI, p. 82.

permanently, and prices had remained relatively stable for several years. Indeed, there were many who held the view that the financial structure had been soundly re-established, and that the world could look forward to years of expanding production and trade under conditions of general prosperity and rising standards of living.

These hopes were soon disappointed. In retrospect, we are able to see more clearly the many maladjustments which before long made themselves felt. While it cannot be said that there is any general agreement about the causes of the Great Depression and their relative importance, there is much support for the view that the boom of 1927–29, which was not in itself exceptional, was followed in 1930 by what could well have been a more or less normal reaction. It was, however, when business activity began to decline that the existing maladjustments, together with the results of mistaken policies, made themselves felt and hampered the forces of recovery. As a result, the world was caught in a prolonged and severe depression.

These maladjustments were of various kinds. In some cases they were the result of adopting prewar parities for more or less conventional reasons. Other maladjustments were connected with much unwise lending and borrowing, especially on short-term account. There were, moreover, the massive flow of gold to France, which was related to the undervaluation of the French franc in 1926, and the attraction of funds to the short-term markets in New York. In addition, there remained the uncertainties regarding reparations and the payment of war debts, aggravated in many cases by high barriers to trade. It is interesting to record the view of the Gold Delegation of the League of Nations that the causes of the Great Depression did not have their origin in reserve positions; but that these causes combined to expose the international monetary and credit system to pressures which before long proved irresistible. It is consistent with this view that the weakness became concentrated in certain places. The Bank of England and the Reichsbank, especially, found it difficult to perform their useful functions as lenders of last resort and guardians of the exchange position. With larger reserves they might have held out longer, but even the sizable credits arranged in the summer of 1931 proved insufficient. It is indeed questionable in retrospect whether any amount of reserves would have been large enough to stave off the troubles in the existing exchange structure. To the extent that the difficulties stemmed from this source, the remedy was to adjust the exchange structure to reality, rather than to prop it up with additional reserves, particularly when these were borrowed. Indeed, it may be argued that, if countries had had from the first to earn the additional reserves they wanted, the difficulties in the exchange structure would have been exposed much more clearly and corrective action would have been taken much earlier. And, as later became clear, even the substantial reserves of the United States did not in the end protect that country from reducing the gold content of the dollar.

In fact, recent analysis has increasingly emphasized—in addition to the many maladjustments that developed outside the United States—the importance of the cyclical movements in that country. With the increasing importance of the economy of the United States in world affairs, the sudden stoppage of its capital exports and the sharp decline of its imports during the depression created a great many problems in other parts of the world.

It is now generally accepted that a high and rising level of world trade is impossible without a high and rising level of economic activity in the major industrial countries, and principally in the United States. In fact, as the contraction gathered momentum, the structure of reserves, the ways the reserves had been created, and to some extent the amount of reserves undoubtedly proved to be unstable factors in the situation, reinforcing the contraction.[4]

Reserves and Trade in 1937–38

Never have total reserves been more abundant in relation to trade than in 1937–38. The average ratio for those two years reached a high figure of 109 per cent for the world as a whole, and 63 per cent for the world excluding the United States. This high ratio was due to two main factors: (1) Falling costs after 1929 stimulated the output of gold, and the increase in the U.S. price of gold in 1934 stimulated it even more. The latter factor also led to a higher value for existing gold holdings. (2) World trade was depressed, being no greater in volume in 1937–38 than it had been in 1928.

Increased reserves failed to stimulate world trade. In fact, this was a period of economic disintegration, with a fluctuating rate between sterling and the dollar, and increasing bilateralism on the Continent of Europe. The movements of funds which took place were often not of an equilibrating character. Rather, they represented a flight of capital—reflecting political and monetary realities and fears—and had the effect of intensifying the disintegration. In the latter part of 1936 and at the beginning of 1937, the possibility of reducing the price of gold came to be widely discussed.[5] There was serious comment about excessive liquidity and of the difficulties and the increasing expense of sterilizing the large additions to gold reserves.[6] There were large amounts of "hot money"; and this in turn created a demand for gold reserves to handle the transfers of hot money.

Clearly it had not been the lack of international liquidity that had stood in the way of a larger volume of trade and an improvement in the level of employment. The situation provides a further illustration of the proposition that the environment in which a monetary mechanism operates is of greater importance than the level of available reserves.

Developments in 1951–57

It has already been noted that the ratio of reserves to trade is much lower now than in 1937–38. This reduction took place in two steps, the first during and immediately after World War II, and the second during the Korean War. Thus, for all countries other than the United States, the ratio of reserves to imports fell from 63 per cent in 1937–38 to 45 per cent in 1948. Though the value of reserves almost doubled in this period, the value of trade increased even more, the increase reflecting changes in prices and not growth in volume. From 1948 to 1950, the value of trade decreased slightly (the volume of trade increased by 20 per cent, but the decline in prices more than offset this), while the total of reserves increased. The ratio of reserves to imports therefore increased to 52 per cent in 1950. It is interesting to note that world reserves increased despite the fact that the dollar value of sterling exchange holdings was written down by 30 per cent in the devaluation of 1949, or by perhaps $4 billion. During the Korean War, the reserve ratio again fell sharply. World imports (excluding those of the United States) rose from $50 billion to $70 billion, or by 40 per cent; import prices rose

[4] League of Nations, *Report of the Gold Delegation* (1932), esp. pp. 16–23. Also, Cassel's "Memorandum of Dissent," p. 74, and Gregory's "The Causes of Gold Movements Into and Out of Great Britain, 1925 to 1930," League of Nations, *Selected Documents on the Distribution of Gold* (1931), esp. p. 28.

[5] League of Nations (R. Nurkse), *International Currency Experience* (1944), p. 133.

[6] Bank for International Settlements, *Annual Report for 1937*, p. 55.

by approximately 30 per cent; and the ratio of reserves to imports fell from 52 per cent in 1950 to 36 per cent in 1951.

Since 1951, liquidity has remained fairly constant and reserves have grown as rapidly as trade. For all countries other than the United States, imports increased from $70 billion in 1951 to $93 billion in 1957, or by one third, and the ratio of reserves to imports fell from 36 per cent to 34 per cent, having in the meantime reached a high of 43 per cent in 1954. There is considerable significance in the fact that the reserve level has remained fairly constant in the face of a growth of volume of trade of 5 per cent per year—a rate of growth that is high by historical standards and probably higher than can be maintained in the future.

So far in 1958 there has been a large flow of gold from the United States to the rest of the world, which has more than offset the flow to the United States in 1957. The value of trade has fallen somewhat, suggesting that in 1958 the ratio of reserves to imports for the world excluding the United States will undoubtedly be higher than in 1957.

A summary of the discussion up to this point would suggest that, for all countries except the United States, the ratio of reserves to imports has been fairly constant since 1951, and that the present ratio is much lower than in 1937–38, about the same as in 1928, and considerably higher than in 1913. It is clear that there is no one best year for comparison, and that in every case the level of reserves must be interpreted within the broad framework of many factors: the functioning of the international economic system, the extent of balance in individual national economies and in the relationship among them, the appropriateness of the structure of exchange rates, the operations of the international credit system, and other major factors. The statistical data do not by themselves suggest that the present level of reserves is inadequate. Any such conclusion, however, is essentially negative. It will be useful to go further and to consider whether the present situation is inherently unstable.

The question may be asked whether there are now, as in retrospect there were in 1928, actual and potential dislocating factors that may create pressures eventually leading to a disruption of the exchange system. This is always, of course, a most difficult question. Nevertheless, it is one that is particularly appropriate at this time considering, specifically, the present state of production and trade and, more generally, the question whether a recession today is likely to be overcome more easily than in the years after 1929.

In some important respects, the prospects now appear to be definitely more encouraging, even though in other respects there may be new difficulties.

Among the favorable circumstances in the present situation, the following may be mentioned:

(1) The economies of the majority of countries in the Western world are now in a state of fairly good balance, one with the other. Since the postwar devaluations of 1949, developments in credit and money volume in most of these countries have largely been of a nature to improve and consolidate a position of equilibrium. An important factor in this process has been the more general application of monetary measures, including the return to a flexible credit policy. One reflection of this improvement is to be seen in the fact that monetary reserves have been strengthened in many countries.

(2) While there have been periods since 1949 of acute exchange tension, with movements of funds taking the form to a large extent of changes in leads and lags,

granting international credit for commercial purposes appears to have been developing on a more normal basis. In contrast to the 1920's, there is no longer an excessive amount of short-term credit subject to sudden recall, at least not on the scale experienced in 1928. At the same time, international trade is increasingly being financed through normal commercial channels. Finally, intergovernmental debts do not present the problems that reparations and war debts posed in 1928 and the early 1930's. There is, therefore, no doubt that the international credit system is more firmly based than it was in 1928.

(3) Postwar recessions have been mild. This probably reflects not only the strengthening of the economic and financial structure in the more important countries, but also a better understanding of the problems involved, and a greater readiness to take corrective measures. It is, of course, dangerous to reason from the past to the future, but the present high degree of optimism is probably not wholly unfounded.

On the other hand, there are elements in the present situation which are less favorable than they were in 1928.

(1) The exchange holdings of the monetary authorities are now larger than ever before, and consist mainly of dollar and sterling balances. There is always the possibility—slight though it may be—that there may be a run to convert dollars into gold, and sterling into dollars or gold. The large gold reserves and the strong economic position of the United States are a protection against a run on the dollar. Dollar balances have grown even in the current recession. Such conversions into gold as have occurred have on the whole been in conformity with the postwar practices of the monetary authorities in dealing with their current net earnings of dollars. Sterling balances represent a more difficult problem in relation to the magnitude of the British gold and dollar reserves. But it is encouraging to note that recently these reserves have been increasing at the same time as sterling liabilities have been declining. Although pressures may again set in from many countries holding reserves in sterling, a considerable part of the balances now represents no more than is needed as working capital for the proper handling of settlements in sterling, together with (in some cases) the necessary cover against domestic money.

(2) The public sector has become more important in most countries, and this often makes economies less flexible. This is particularly apparent where ambitious development plans have been adopted and are being carried out. Low prices of primary products, or even fluctuating prices around a high point, may create situations which are extremely difficult for many countries.

(3) In many cases, foreign trade since 1945 has grown more rapidly than domestic gross national product. In such a situation, if monetary or other fears arise, changes in payments positions resulting from shifts in leads and lags (apart from speculative capital movements) may become very important.

(4) Finally, in a period of international tension, the possibility cannot be ignored that events of a nonmonetary nature may take place which adversely affect the payments situation. In such cases, it is important that remedial steps be able to be taken promptly in order to prevent any major crack in the exchange structure.

On balance, these elements do not suggest pessimism, but they inevitably demand caution in drawing overoptimistic conclusions. Whatever balance is struck, however, there is no doubt that individual countries cannot be expected to rely entirely on themselves to meet all adverse circumstances. In case of need they must have the assurance of recourse to a second line of reserves. This was one of the reasons why the

Fund was established. It has already been helpful in several difficult situations, and is now an integral part of the international financial structure. The financial assistance of the Fund is of course of a short-term character, mainly intended to bridge the gap while the countries themselves take whatever measures may be necessary to restore equilibrium. In view of the historical comparisons which have been drawn, and the assessment that has been made of the favorable and unfavorable elements in the present situation, any answer to the question whether present reserves are adequate must, necessarily, be conditional. If the need for flexible fiscal and credit policies continues to be accepted in many countries, if further steps are taken to strengthen the international credit system, if overambitious investment plans beyond the power of available financing are avoided, and if the international institutions are able to fulfill the role assigned to them, there is nothing in the over-all reserve position to indicate that present reserves are inadequate. Of course, dislocating factors may arise which are so overwhelming that even substantial reserves may suddenly appear insufficient. The environment in which monetary authorities operate is therefore as important a part of international liquidity as the size of their reserves.

One major change in relation to public policy has still to be noted. Since the Great Depression there has been a marked swing toward government policies aimed at securing and maintaining a high level of employment. To the extent that these efforts are successful in the United States and in other major countries with large reserves, trade cycles in these countries are likely to be shorter and shallower in the future than they were before World War II. Success in these countries will affect general business conditions in the world as a whole. This should make it easier for other countries to mitigate fluctuations in their business activity and level of employment without undue strain on their reserve positions. To this extent, any given ratio of reserves to imports in all other countries is likely to be more adequate now and in the future than it was in the past. This does not mean that difficult problems will not sometimes arise for countries whose reserves are slender. Countries will have to weigh the policies of maintaining external balance and defending their exchange rates, which may require a contractionary policy, against the repercussions of such a policy on the price and employment situation at home. There is no simple formula by which these problems can be solved, but the difficulties of coping with a recession are, of course, eased to the extent that countries are able to accumulate sufficient reserves during periods of expansion to bear some of the strains of contraction.

Composition of Reserves

In the disturbed period up to 1938, total exchange holdings fell to an amount of only $1.8 billion, equivalent to 6 per cent of the total gold and exchange reserves of all countries. During the war substantial purchases, especially by the United Kingdom—but to some extent also by the United States—led to the building up of sterling and dollar balances. While sterling balances were reduced in dollar value by the devaluation in 1949, dollar balances continued to increase. By the end of 1950 total exchange holdings were equal to about 30 per cent of total reserves, a proportion that remained almost unchanged up to and including 1957, when total exchange holdings were equal to $15.9 billion, compared with total reserves of $52.9 billion. However, the United States does not hold reserves in the form of exchange, so that the data for all other countries is perhaps of greater interest. Since 1949, the percentage of their reserves kept in the form of exchange has fluctuated within the narrow range of 53–56 per cent, and was 53 per cent at the end of 1957. This level was 10 per cent below that in 1948, largely because the devaluation of sterling reduced the dollar value of sterling exchange holdings in 1949. The percentage of reserves kept in the form of exchange in 1949–57 was more than 50 per cent larger than in 1928 and about three times as large as in 1937–38 and in 1913, as can be seen from Table 4.

At the close of World War II, sterling balances represented a very high proportion of the gross national product of the United Kingdom. The British authorities made it clear that they wished to avoid any further increase in these balances and that they

Table 4. Gross Reserves and Foreign Exchange Holdings of All Countries, Excluding the Communist Bloc, Selected Years, 1913-57

	All Countries		All Countries Except United States		
Year	Reserves *(billion dollars)*	Per cent in foreign exchange	Reserves *(billion dollars)*	Foreign exchange *(billion dollars)*	Per cent in foreign exchange
1913	4.5	11	2.7	0.5	18
1928	13.0	25	9.3	3.2	35
1937	27.7	9	14.9	2.4	16
1938	27.7	7	13.1	1.8	14
1948	46.4	29	22.1	13.7	62
1949	43.6	24	19.1	10.5	55
1950	47.0	29	24.2	13.6	56
1951	46.5	28	23.6	12.9	54
1952	46.7	28	23.4	13.2	56
1953	48.0	29	25.9	14.1	54
1954	49.5	30	27.7	15.1	54
1955	50.6	31	28.8	15.6	54
1956	51.8	31	29.7	16.2	55
1957	52.9	30	30.0	15.9	53

Sources: All years except 1913 are shown in Appendix Table 2. Data on gold reserves for 1913 are from *Banking and Monetary Statistics* (Board of Governors of the Federal Reserve System, 1943), Table 160.

hoped, if possible, to reduce them. In fact, sterling balances (official and private) as measured in sterling were not reduced between 1945 and 1951, remaining at £3.6 billion, though they were reduced almost 10 per cent between 1951 and 1957, when they stood at £3.3 billion. (There were, however, great changes, which will be discussed later, in the countries that held sterling.) In terms of dollars, the movement of sterling balances is indicated by the corresponding figures: 1945, $14.4 billion; 1951, $10.0 billion; and 1957, $9.1 billion. On the other hand, all dollar balances, official and private, doubled in the postwar period, and the data for the same years are as follows: 1945, $6.9 billion; 1951, $7.7 billion; and 1957, $13.6 billion.

From 1949 to the end of 1957, countries other than the United States increased their exchange holdings by $5.4 billion and their gold holdings by $5.5 billion. Increases of this magnitude over a period of several years must have offered many countries the opportunity to change the composition of their reserves substantially if they had wished to do so. The fact that as a group they added to their exchange holdings to such an extent that there was no change in the relative importance of exchange holdings in their total reserves shows that on the whole there was no such wish.

With the exception of the United States, nearly all areas maintained a larger percentage of their reserves in the form of exchange in 1957 than in either 1937 or 1928 (Table 5). The postwar developments in the period 1948–57 may be summarized by noting that Canada, Non-Dollar Latin America, and Sterling Area countries other than the United Kingdom decreased the percentage of reserves in the form of exchange;

Table 5. Percentage of Gross Reserves Held in Foreign Exchange, by Area, Selected Years, 1928-57

Area	1928	1937	1948	1956	1957
Canada	—	10	60	43	40
Latin America: Dollar Area	44	17	26	55	56
Latin America: Non-Dollar Area	12	17	59	39	33
Continental EPU Countries	46	12	40	47	45
United Kingdom	—	. . .	20	17	33
Other Sterling Area	49	65	92	85	83
Rest of the World [1]	24	33	77	79	75

Source: Appendix Table 2.

[1] Does not include the United States.

Dollar Latin America and Continental EPU increased their percentage; the Rest of the World remained practically unchanged. The position of the United Kingdom fluctuated irregularly, so that the percentage of its reserves in the form of exchange was lower in 1956, but higher in 1957, than in 1948.

A more detailed examination of these regional trends is instructive. Canada increased its reserves fivefold from 1937 to 1948, and at the same time increased the percentage of its reserves in foreign exchange from 10 to 60 (Table 6). From 1948 to 1957 it increased its reserves by 80 per cent, but reduced the percentage in exchange by one

Table 6. Gross Reserves and Percentage Held in Foreign Exchange, Canada and Latin America, Selected Years, 1928-57

	Canada		Latin America, Dollar Area		Latin America, Non-Dollar Area	
Year	Reserves (*billion dollars*)	Per cent in exchange	Reserves (*billion dollars*)	Per cent in exchange	Reserves (*billion dollars*)	Per cent in exchange
1928	0.1	—	0.1	44	1.0	12
1937	0.2	10	0.2	17	0.7	17
1938	0.2	15	0.2	29	0.6	12
1948	1.0	60	1.1	26	1.7	59
1949	1.1	57	1.2	27	1.6	52
1950	1.8	67	1.4	27	1.8	53
1951	1.8	54	1.5	31	1.4	36
1952	1.9	53	1.6	42	1.3	32
1953	1.8	46	1.6	45	1.6	35
1954	2.0	45	1.7	50	1.4	27
1955	1.9	41	1.8	53	1.3	25
1956	1.9	43	2.3	55	1.4	39
1957	1.8	40	2.7	56	1.0	33

Source: Appendix Table 2.

third, to 40 per cent. These changes reflect an increase in gold holdings, and a decrease in exchange reserves (largely U.S. dollars). The increases in total reserves in Dollar Latin America are strikingly similar to those in Canada, but the percentage in exchange, which decreased slightly from 1938 to 1948, doubled in the postwar period, and stood at 56 per cent in 1957. The countries in Non-Dollar Latin America[7] in 1948–57 decreased their gross reserves (from $1.7 billion to $1.0 billion), and, since they preferred to hold on to their gold reserves, which could be, and from time to time were, pledged as collateral against loans, they decreased the percentage of their reserves in the form of exchange from 59 to 33.

Continental EPU countries in 1928 held 46 per cent of their reserves in the form of exchange (Table 7). This percentage fell sharply in the 1930's but was restored during and after the war. It stood at 45 per cent in 1957. Reserves increased by almost 150 per cent from 1948 to 1957, but the proportions held in gold and in exchange were fairly constant.

Table 7. Gross Reserves and Percentage Held in Foreign Exchange, Sterling Area and Continental EPU, Selected Years, 1928-57

	United Kingdom		Other Sterling Area		Continental EPU Countries	
Year	Reserves *(billion dollars)*	Per cent in exchange	Reserves *(billion dollars)*	Per cent in exchange	Reserves *(billion dollars)*	Per cent in exchange
1928	0.7	—	0.8	49	5.1	46
1937	4.1	...	1.4	65	6.8	12
1938	2.9	...	1.2	54	6.5	8
1948	2.0	20	7.3	92	5.9	40
1949	1.8	23	4.7	88	6.2	38
1950	3.7	21	5.6	89	6.9	43
1951	2.4	7	5.2	88	7.5	45
1952	2.0	23	4.6	86	8.6	48
1953	2.5	10	5.0	88	10.1	50
1954	2.8	9	5.0	86	11.4	51
1955	2.2	5	4.7	85	12.9	49
1956	2.2	17	4.5	85	13.4	47
1957	2.4	33	4.0	83	14.6	45

Source: Appendix Table 2.

The United Kingdom's reserves, and the percentage of these kept in the form of exchange, have shown considerable fluctuation since the war. Its reserves were at a postwar high of $3.7 billion in 1950. Since then they have fallen irregularly. They were $2.4 billion at the end of 1957 (and more than $3 billion at the end of June 1958). The percentage in the form of exchange does not appear to be correlated with fluctuations in the total. In contrast, the Other Sterling Area countries show a slowly declining trend in the percentage of reserves held in the form of exchange since the war.[8] In 1948 it stood at 92. Since then it has been reduced gradually, and at the end of 1957 was 83. This percentage is much higher than that which prevailed before the war.

[7] Argentina, Brazil, Chile, Paraguay, Peru, and Uruguay.

[8] The results are largely influenced by India and Australia, which hold the greater part of the reserves of the area.

The Rest of the World [9] has, since 1949, steadily kept approximately three fourths of its reserves in the form of exchange holdings. This is three times as great as the percentage so kept in 1928, and more than double that in 1937–38. Of the countries in this group, Israel had all of its reserves in the form of exchange; Japan, 97 per cent; and the Philippines, 87 per cent.

Some countries, when drawing on their reserves, appear to follow the practice of using their exchange holdings first, leaving their gold holdings more or less intact. For the world as a whole, such reductions in exchange reserves as have from time to time been made in individual countries have, however, been more than made up by increases in others. Thus, the holding of foreign exchange has become an integral part of the system of international reserves and materially facilitates the problem of ensuring a volume of reserves adequate for the world's needs.

Table 8. Composition of Gross Foreign Exchange Assets, 1947-57
(In millions of U.S. dollars)

Year	Total	Dollars	Sterling	EPU Liabilities	BIS Deposits	Errors and Omissions
1947	13,900	1,850	12,147	—	8	−105
1948	13,900	2,900	10,774	—	52	174
1949	10,850	3,050	7,414	—	108	278
1950	13,600	4,450	7,775	402	250	723
1951	13,000	4,050	7,646	665	192	447
1952	13,300	5,250	6,328	1,077	364	281
1953	14,250	6,050	6,825	1,272	352	−249
1954	15,250	7,000	6,980	1,108	465	−303
1955	15,750	7,900	6,591	994	412	−147
1956	16,400	8,600	6,220	1,086	424	70
1957	16,050	8,300	5,833	1,269	409	239

Sources: For 1950-57, *International Financial Statistics (IFS)*, July 1958; for 1947-49, Fund estimates on the same basis.

The rapid growth of the dollar as a reserve currency, both absolutely and in relation to sterling, is a major development of the postwar period. Data recently made available by the U.K. Treasury classify area holdings of sterling for 1945, 1951, and 1957 as between central bank and other official funds, on the one hand, and nonofficial funds, on the other. Official holdings of sterling by all countries excluding the U.K. colonies (and for comparative purposes the Treasury data include Ghana and Malaya under this caption) stood at about $10.4 billion in 1945. By 1951 these holdings had been reduced to about $6.2 billion, and by 1957 to about $4.2 billion. If these data are compared with official dollar holdings they suggest—and the comparison must necessarily be rough—that in 1945 official sterling holdings were about four times as large as official dollar holdings. In 1951 they were 50 per cent larger than official dollar holdings. At the end of 1957, official sterling holdings by all independent countries, including Ghana and Malaya, may be estimated at $4.8 billion on the basis of the Treasury data and other information. This was equal to about 60 per cent of the reported official dollar holdings on that date, or $8.3 billion.

More detailed data on the composition of gross foreign exchange reserve holdings for 1947–57 by area, and by type of reserve holding, are shown in Table 8, which

[9] Includes Egypt, Finland, Indonesia, Iran, Israel, Japan, Lebanon, Philippines, Spain, Syria, and Thailand.

is based upon a reconciliation prepared by the Fund of reported foreign exchange assets and liabilities. Since, as already noted, the distribution between official and nonofficial holdings of sterling balances has been made available for only two of the years covered by this table, it has been necessary to use the published data on all sterling balances, official and nonofficial. In this table, therefore, official sterling holdings are overstated relative to all other types of exchange asset. (This and other errors are, of course, included in Errors and Omissions.) The official reserves represented by credits extended through EPU amounted to $1.3 billion at the end of 1957, and constituted more than 8 per cent of the exchange reserves of all countries. The amount of reserves kept in the form of deposits with the BIS increased from $8 million in 1947 to $465 million in 1954. Although it has decreased somewhat since that time, this amount has not fallen below $400 million.

The structure of the changing relationship between sterling and the dollar is clearly identifiable. Countries that have traditionally held exchange reserves in the form of dollars continue to do so, and when their total reserves increased their dollar holdings

Table 9. Sterling and Dollar Reserves in Selected Areas, Selected Years, 1948-57 [1]
(In billions of U.S. dollars)

Area	1948	1949	1950	1952	1956	1957
Continental EPU Countries						
Dollar holdings	0.8	0.8	1.1	1.7	3.9	3.7
Sterling holdings	1.5	1.2	0.9	0.7	0.5	0.7
Non-Dollar Latin America						
Dollar holdings	0.3	0.3	0.4	0.2	0.3	0.2
Sterling holdings	0.5	0.2	0.1	—[2]	0.1	0.1
Other Non-Dollar Non-Sterling [3]						
Dollar holdings	0.6	0.5	1.0	1.3	1.9	1.4
Sterling holdings	2.2	1.4	1.4	1.1	0.8	0.7
Total Non-Dollar Non-Sterling						
Dollar holdings	1.7	1.6	2.5	3.2	6.1	5.3
Sterling holdings	4.2	2.8	2.4	2.1	1.4	1.5

Sources: For 1948, *International Financial Statistics (IFS)*, February 1958; for 1949, *IFS*, February 1957; for other years, *IFS*, July 1958.

[1] In this table there may be some overstatement of sterling holdings, since the figures may include nonofficial holdings.

[2] $25 million.

[3] Sixteen countries: China (Taiwan), Egypt, Ethiopia, Finland, Indonesia, Iran, Israel, Japan, Korea, Lebanon, Philippines, Spain, Syria, Thailand, Viet-Nam, and Yugoslavia.

also increased. Canada and the Dollar Latin American countries which have held practically no sterling had $1 billion of dollar assets in 1948 and $2.1 billion in 1957. The countries in the sterling area held less sterling in 1957 than in 1948 because their total reserves had fallen. It is true that their dollar holdings increased from $50 million to $200 million, but even the latter figure was only 6 per cent of total reserves. The most striking change, as may be seen from Table 9, occurred in the non-dollar non-sterling countries. Their dollar holdings in 1957 were three times as large as in 1948, while their sterling holdings were about one third as large.

Private credits finance most of the world's international business; and private exchange holdings, together with private credits, play a role in settling international balances. Nonofficial exchange holdings are thus a complement to official holdings and in some cases may be a substitute for them. The total figures for all sterling and dollar balances, official and nonofficial, are compared in Table 10.

Dollar balances were reduced in the first years after the close of World War II, but have increased steadily since 1947. By 1957, they were almost three times as large as they had been a decade earlier. Sterling liabilities to the U.K. colonies grew steadily after 1945, and have doubled. (The decrease in 1949, as shown in Table 10, is the result of revaluation in terms of dollars.) Liabilities to the independent countries of the sterling area have decreased by about 15 per cent since 1951, and those to India, by about 60 per cent. Liabilities to the non-sterling countries have declined persistently since the war. From 1945 to 1957, they declined from £1,170 million to £568 million, i.e., from $4.7 billion to $1.6 billion.

It must be expected that the substantial balances held by the U.K. colonies will be drawn down in the future as these colonies expand their development expenditures. On the other hand, the amount of sterling held by various other countries using

Table 10. Comparison of All Dollar and All Sterling Liabilities, Selected Years, 1937-57

(In billions of U.S. dollars)

Year	Dollar Liabilities	Sterling Liabilities		
		Total	To colonies	To others
1937	1.9	4.0	0.4[1]	3.6
1945	6.9	14.4	1.7	12.7
1946	6.0	14.5	1.9	12.6
1947	4.8	14.1	1.9	12.2
1948	5.8	12.7	2.1	10.6
1949	6.0	8.8	1.5	7.3
1950	7.1	9.8	2.0	7.8
1951	7.7	10.0	2.6	7.4
1952	9.0	9.0	2.9	6.1
1953	10.0	9.8	3.1	6.7
1954	11.2	10.4	3.4	7.0
1955	11.7	10.0	3.6	6.4
1956	13.5	9.6	3.6	6.0
1957[2]	13.6	9.1	2.5	6.6

Sources: *International Financial Statistics (IFS)*, July 1958. Data for years not published there are from revised figures in *IFS* files.

[1] Estimated as 10 per cent of all sterling liabilities.

[2] The sterling holdings of Ghana and the Federation of Malaya are included under Liabilities to Other Sterling countries rather than Liabilities to U. K. colonies.

sterling as a trading currency may well increase with expanding world trade and a strengthening of the monetary position of sterling itself. If account is taken of the fact that the level of commodity prices in terms of dollars has increased by almost 150 per cent since 1937, it will be seen that the total of sterling liabilities by the end of 1956 was in real terms somewhat smaller than it had been in 1937.

It seems probable that a number of countries, which in recent years have suffered a reduction in their total reserves, to a greater or lesser extent in the form of a reduction in dollar balances, will wish to replenish their reserves, and presumably largely in the form of dollar balances. However, a number of countries have probably already been successful in increasing their reserves to a point which they consider adequate. A continued rapid increase in their reserves, including dollar balances, is therefore less likely in the years to come. It is perhaps vain to speculate what will be the net result of these conflicting tendencies, but it seems certain that exchange holdings, as a more readily usable form of asset than gold holdings, will continue to form an important part of any accumulation of reserves.

CHAPTER THREE: THE ADEQUACY OF INDIVIDUAL COUNTRY RESERVES

The preceding chapter reviewed the level and composition of reserves. It discussed the historical development of reserves, analyzed the relationship of reserves to trade on the basis of certain historical comparisons, and pointed out that the adequacy of reserves cannot be measured by a few percentage figures relating reserves to trade. International liquidity depends upon a combination of factors: country reserves, international borrowing and commercial credit operations, and the international financial structure. Two conclusions were reached: first, under certain fairly specific and broad conditions, the total amount of gold and foreign exchange reserves now held by the monetary authorities may prove to be adequate; and secondly, the existing composition of reserves permits the monetary authorities to hold the kind of reserves they wish.

This chapter considers more particularly the level and the adequacy of reserves of individual countries. Generalizations about individual country reserves are necessarily limited by the great variety of country reserve practices and policies, which in turn reflect differences between their economic situations, stages of development, and policy objectives.

The Meaning of Adequacy

The adequacy of reserves must be judged in relation to the aim that is envisaged. There is both a domestic aim and an international aim. The monetary legislation of most countries requires that the central bank or some other monetary authority maintain a given amount of gold, or of gold and foreign exchange, in support of the supply of domestic money. This reserve or cover may be a stated amount or, more usually, a percentage of the currency and deposit liabilities of the central bank. To be adequate, country reserves must therefore be at least large enough to meet these domestic legal minima, with some margin for operating purposes. These minima can be, and have been, adjusted by individual countries for their own purposes.

The domestic purpose of a monetary reserve is essentially to regulate or to limit the quantity of domestic money, and yet allow sufficient flexibility so that changing seasonal or regional needs may be met smoothly. Reserves for strictly domestic purposes were essential even when large amounts of gold coin and gold notes (backed 100 per cent by gold) circulated in the community, because provision had to be made for possible internal or regional drains. Since 1914, however, monetary authorities all over the world have called in practically all the gold coin and gold notes that had been in circulation, and added them to central reserves. Simultaneously, the strict and inelastic link between domestic money and gold has been weakened or, perhaps more accurately, replaced within broad limits by monetary and credit management. In practically all countries, the ratio of reserves to the domestic supply of money has been falling for many years. Stated in another way, the amount of reserves required to support a given expansion of the domestic money supply is much smaller now than it used to be. And in those countries which have large excess reserves, the money supply can be expanded without any increase in reserves. As will be noted in the next chapter, this has important implications for the development of world liquidity.

But even when the domestic purpose of reserves was more important than it now is, the main purpose of reserves was international—to provide the means for settling deficits in the balance of payments, and at the same time to inspire confidence that the foreign exchange position, including the foreign exchange rate, could be properly maintained. These external considerations have become more important, so that, increasingly, the purpose of reserves is to help individual countries maintain a smoothly functioning monetary and exchange system. But reserves are not the only thing that help a country do this. The ability to borrow, the use of an appropriate exchange rate, the adoption of monetary and fiscal policies which lead to development with stability, are also important. And since international balance is a matter of the relationship of one country with all others, the effects of the wisest policy in any one country are often limited by inflation, contraction, or inappropriate exchange rates in other countries.

An individual country will have to consider all of these factors in forming its reserve policy. This will rarely depend upon monetary considerations alone. Usually it is the result of various and often conflicting influences. Not infrequently its decision is influenced by unrealistic assumptions as to the real effects of policies adopted, e.g., that highly complex systems of exchange restrictions can be made to work rationally and even perfectly; that development can be financed partly or largely with credit creation without any danger of inflation; or that a predetermined amount of deficit financing will have only a minor effect upon the balance of payments. Distinctions must therefore be drawn between (1) the level of reserves a country thinks it "should" or "ought to" hold; (2) the level of reserves a country may expect to hold as a result of the policies it is following, the actual importance it attributes to reserves, and conditions in the world at large; and (3) the level of reserves it will actually hold as a result of the policies it follows.

It is the sum total of individual country decisions to increase, decrease, or maintain reserves which determines whether total reserves are adequate or inadequate. From an over-all point of view (such as was adopted in Chapter II), a reserve situation can be characterized as adequate when the total of reserves is sufficient, its composition is appropriate, and the distribution of reserves is in accordance with effective country demands for them. The presence or absence of these conditions cannot be determined a priori; it must be inferred from the results of country actions. If reserves are adequate, countries are able to make the adjustments they wish without seriously disturbing the system and without initiating a series of deflationary or countervailing actions. Whether a given reserve situation is adequate therefore depends upon whether countries are taking effective action to change their positions and whether their measures are unduly upsetting to other countries. Since conditions are constantly changing, this implies that the adequacy of reserves cannot be determined once and for all and that a good system of reserves must have elasticity. As already noted, the satisfactory operation of an international credit system—official, international, and private—is very important in this connection. In judging the adequacy of its reserves, every country will want to know whether it will be able in case of need to obtain resources from abroad.

Any decision to increase reserves is important because it requires, as a counterpart, an equivalent amount of uncommitted savings.

Unwillingness or inability to increase reserves means that none of a country's savings or of the proceeds of credits received from abroad has been applied to the kind of investment which results in an increase in reserves. It is of course obvious that below some minimum level an increase in reserves may become a major policy issue, while above some maximum level, reserves may serve to encourage a policy of expansion or they may play a more or less passive role. Within these limits, which will vary widely from country to country, the level of reserves generally has the character of a residual and is the net result of other policies. Thus a country may not be greatly concerned about raising its reserves from, say, 30 per cent of imports to 40 per cent, though it may attach considerable importance to raising them from 5 per cent to 25 or 30 per cent.

Admittedly, a policy designed to increase reserves or to maintain them at a certain level may be difficult or even impossible to carry out in a short period. Crop failures and declining prices resulting from gluts and other adverse circumstances may so severely reduce the flow of domestic savings that it becomes necessary to rely largely or even wholly on foreign credits to meet a balance of payments deficit. Errors and miscalculations in deciding economic policies or in carrying them out may have unanticipated effects upon reserves. It is therefore all the more important that the necessary steps be taken to set aside savings for restoring reserves in fairly prosperous years when foreign earnings are increasing.

Each country determines its reserve requirements in the light of its own situation, control policies, exchange rate, and alternative uses for the savings that would be used to acquire reserves. Generally, larger reserves are needed by countries with strong seasonal swings in their balance of payments, and of course also by countries with heavy short-term liabilities. Likewise, larger reserves will be needed by countries which are greatly dependent on international trade and which are thus likely to feel more keenly changes in foreign demand, often intensified by shifts in leads and lags. Countries with slender reserves have often relied on fluctuating exchange rates to balance their payments. Where the alternative to a fluctuating rate is likely to be the imposition of quantitative restrictions on imports or the proliferation of exchange rates, the adoption of a fluctuating rate system may well be the lesser evil, although it has grave disadvantages.

There have, of course, been countries which have sought to influence the reserve position by direct control of trade and payments instead of relying solely, or largely, on monetary and fiscal policies. Such attempts have not proved effective, for the imbalance which led to the imposition of controls is not overcome by the controls. Indeed, the consequent reduction in imports will usually tend to aggravate the imbalance, e.g., by ultimately reducing exports.

It is clear that there can be no one generally acceptable rule, valid in all cases, for the amount of reserves which can be considered adequate for an individual country. Account has to be taken of the particular circumstances, history, conventions, savings habits, and international banking position of each country. Indeed, the significance of all these particulars is that the term adequacy of reserves has a variety of meanings, different from country to country and from time to time. Reserves which are inadequate for one policy may be more than adequate for another; reserves which are inadequate in conjunction with one set of fiscal and monetary methods may be adequate with another set. Reserves which are insufficient when a country is facing a budgetary deficit and credit expansion may be sufficient when the government is running a surplus and credit is contracting. Reserves which are adequate where a country follows flexible policies may not be adequate when its policies are frozen or slow to adjust. Thus, in principle, it is difficult to determine the "real" adequacy of reserves in any one country, or to compare one country with another, without taking into account many factors other than reserves. To relate the reserve position to the volume of foreign trade is no doubt a useful method of approach, but it can give at best only a preliminary indication of adequacy. In all these matters, the element of convention in the determination of adequacy should not be overlooked. The level of reserves that a country has become accustomed to is often one that has gradually come to be considered adequate—partly, no doubt, because special credit arrangements have been concluded to provide relief for the reserves in periods of special strain.

It does not follow that a country whose reserves are inadequate in the judgment of outsiders—or even in its own judgment—is necessarily interested in trying to increase them. Many countries with inadequate reserves have, over a period of years, not carried out economic policies which are consistent with increasing them. It is not meaningful—and it may be misleading—to assume that a country with inadequate reserves is necessarily trying to add to them. This may be the case even though international circumstances are favorable and the volume and prices of its exports are high. In the last analysis, each country thus makes its own decision as to whether to retain or accumulate uncommitted savings in the form of reserves.

As to what assets should be considered as forming part of the reserves, it is now generally accepted (as already mentioned in Chapter II) that exchange holdings of convertible and widely transferable currencies should be included along with gold; indeed, these holdings are usually the most variable and therefore, to some extent, the most effective element of the total reserves. Practice varies as to whether net EPU creditor positions and surpluses in bilateral accounts are included in reserves. It is even more difficult to determine how much significance should be attached to total creditor positions. In the previous chapter, gross reserves have been used for the over-all comparisons of a mainly historical character, but where individual countries are concerned, account must often be taken also of the existence of short-term liabilities.

In some instances, as when gold holdings are pledged as collateral against foreign credits, exclusive attention to gross reserves would clearly give a distorted picture of the real situation. This is also the case where there are substantial short-term or medium-term commercial debts weighing on the exchange position, or large outstanding debit balances on bilateral accounts. Drawings from the Fund, since they are repayable within a few years, likewise affect the real exchange position. Furthermore, for the United Kingdom and the United States, there is the special question of the large amounts held by foreigners on deposit or in short-term securities in sterling and in dollars.

In view of these many qualifications, it is clearly impossible to lay down any simple rule in this matter. The particular conditions of a country or group of countries must be considered, and attention paid to past experience and behavior.

Analysis of the Level of Country Reserves

The basic statistical data on individual country reserves, imports, and the ratio of reserves to imports are shown in Appendix Table 1 for some 60 countries for 1928, 1937, 1948, and for each year from 1950 to 1957. It will be seen that the ratios vary widely from country to country, and that for some countries they vary widely from year tö year. The table also reveals that the ownership of reserves is much more highly concentrated than trade. At the end of 1957, the United States alone held 43 per cent of the world's reserves of gold and exchange (Table 11), and the United States and the Federal Republic of Germany together held more than one half (54 per cent). Eleven countries held 80 per cent of the world's reserves.

The figure for the United Kingdom, the equivalent of $2.4 billion, reflects the reductions connected with the Suez events, the sterling-mark speculation in 1957, and short-term borrowings, including a drawing from the Fund. By the end of June 1958, the United Kingdom's reserves had risen to over $3 billion. The largest increases in 1957 were shown by Germany (an increase of $1.2 billion) and Venezuela ($500 million). Large decreases were shown by Japan, India, and France.

Reserves for all countries excluding those in the communist bloc in 1957 were equal to 49 per cent of imports, or excluding the United States, 32 per cent. Although over-all figures do not add much to our knowledge of the adequacy of reserves for

Table 11. Countries with Gold and Exchange Reserves Exceeding $1 Billion at End of 1957

Country	Reserves *(billion dollars)*	Per Cent
United States	22.9	43.3
Germany, Federal Republic of	5.6	10.6
United Kingdom	2.4	4.5
Switzerland	1.9	3.6
Canada	1.8	3.4
Italy	1.5	2.8
Venezuela	1.4	2.6
Australia	1.3	2.5
Belgium	1.1	2.1
Netherlands	1.1	2.1
Japan	1.0	1.9
All other	10.9	20.6
World	52.9	100.0

Source: Appendix Table 1.

individual countries, it is of some interest to distinguish between industrial and other countries, since they are often subject to different influences. In addition to the United States and the United Kingdom, which will be discussed individually, there are 12 countries which may be considered *industrial* on the basis of their exports. These are the continental members of the EPU, except Greece and Turkey, plus Japan. Their ratios of reserves to imports are presented in Table 12.

In the years studied, there were never fewer than three countries with a ratio of reserves to imports of less than 30 per cent, and never fewer than two with a ratio of over 50 per cent (Table 13). The number of countries in the middle range of

30 to 50 per cent was never less than one nor more than five; and, with a few exceptions (especially in 1937), it was the countries in this group which moved to below 30 per cent in some years and to above 50 per cent in others.

Throughout the postwar period the Scandinavian countries have had reserve ratios which are low by European standards, and low even by Latin American and Asian standards. These countries had low ratios even before World War I. At the other extreme, Switzerland and Portugal stand out with the highest reserve ratios, a particularly large increase having taken place in Portugal since 1928, while Switzerland,

Table 12. Ratio of Reserves to Imports, 12 Industrial Countries, Selected Years, 1928-57

(Arranged in order of size of ratio, expressed as a percentage, in 1957)

Country	1928	1937	1948	1950	1951	1952	1953	1954	1955	1956	1957
Denmark	17	19	12	11	12	15	17	12	11	10	13
France	121	165	...	44	20	23	24	32	44	24	13
Norway	19	41	19	18	17	17	16	14	15	15	14
Sweden	26	95	17	24	27	26	32	27	24	21	19
Japan	60	26	...	58	46	54	37	43	54	47	24
Netherlands	24	106	18	29	24	47	52	45	40	29	26
Belgium	39	89	46	38	40	42	44	41	40	35	33
Italy	50	29	35	59	46	39	39	43	46	41	42
Austria	28	27	13	19	16	23	59	63	41	42	45
Germany	23	...	...	10	15	31	52	58	53	65	75
Switzerland	30	187	143	150	120	138	150	141	124	107	98
Portugal	21	71	123	172	168	162	186	187	169	156	137

Source: Appendix Table 1.

Table 13. Industrial Countries (Excluding the United States and the United Kingdom)[1] Classified by Ratio of Reserves to Imports, Selected Years, 1928-57

(Ratio of reserves to imports, expressed as a percentage)

Year	Number of Countries	Average Ratio[2]	Number of Countries with Stated Percentage of Reserves to Imports: Less than 30	30-50	Over 50
1928	12	48	7	2	3
1937	11	70	4	1	6
1948	9	44	5	2	2
1950	12	42	6	2	4
1951	12	34	7	3	2
1952	12	41	5	4	3
1953	12	46	3	4	5
1954	12	48	3	5	4
1955	12	48	3	5	4
1956	12	43	5	4	3
1957	12	40	6	3	3

Source: Appendix Table 1.

[1] All continental members of EPU, except Greece and Turkey, plus Japan. Data for 1937 exclude Germany; data for 1948 exclude France, Germany, and Japan.

[2] Weighted average.

with large short-term liabilities to foreigners, in the form of deposits or investments, has felt it appropriate to hold large reserves, almost exclusively in gold.

The other countries in general appear to have tried to achieve ratios of between 30 and 50 per cent, or perhaps 40 and 50 per cent, in the sense that if reserves were below these levels they tried to increase reserves, and if reserves rose beyond some such level, they saw fit to adopt a more expansionist policy. Germany is a particular case. Its ratio of reserves to imports in 1928 was 23 per cent, which was not large; but it had at the same time contracted large amounts of short-term foreign debt so that its position was in reality much weaker than the reserve ratio would indicate. By the end of 1951, reserves were still dangerously low, but in the following years substantial additions were made, and by the end of 1957 the German ratio was higher than that of any other of these countries except Portugal and Switzerland. The uncommitted savings required to improve the German exchange position were very largely obtained by budget surpluses, accruing as a result both of revenue growing more rapidly than estimated and of certain delays in effecting expenditures.

In 1957, there were 49 countries classified as *nonindustrial* on the basis of their exports, and for which data on reserves and trade data were available. These ranged in size from countries with annual imports of less than $50 million, to Canada with imports of $6.3 billion. In 1957, 21 of these countries had a ratio of reserves to imports of less than 30 per cent, and 31 had a ratio of less than 40 per cent (Table 14).

Table 14. Nonindustrial Countries[1] Classified by Ratio of Reserves to Imports, Selected Years, 1928-57

(Ratio of reserves to imports, expressed as a percentage)

		Number of Countries with Stated Percentage of Reserves to Imports				
Year	Number of Countries	Less than 30	30-39	40-49	50-59	60 and more
1928	25	10	5	1	3	6
1937	38	17	4	5	4	8
1948	45	15	5	5	4	16
1950	45	13	3	3	9	17
1951	47	12	13	5	4	13
1952	47	18	8	6	4	11
1953	48	16	9	4	4	15
1954	48	16	8	7	5	12
1955	49	19	8	8	4	10
1956	49	20	7	6	3	13
1957	49	21	10	4	3	11

Source: Appendix Table 1.

[1] Nonindustrial countries are defined as all countries except the United States, the United Kingdom, Japan, and the continental members of EPU, with the exception of Greece and Turkey.

The reserve position of some individual countries changed substantially from one year to another in the postwar period, but the position of all of them together was comparatively stable. However, a comparison between the postwar years and the two prewar years, 1928 and 1937, reveals some interesting differences. Since there was a greater number of countries in the postwar period than previously, it is convenient to show the different situation of countries by means of percentages of the total number of countries (Table 15).

For the world as a whole the ratio of reserves to imports was much higher in 1937 than in the postwar years; it therefore seems strange at first sight that for the nonindustrial countries the tendency was rather the opposite. The explanation appears, at least partly, to be that the increase in the world's reserves after 1934 came largely from the revaluation of gold, so that these countries which had generally only a little gold to begin with (either because they had only low reserves or because they kept a large proportion of their reserves in foreign exchange) naturally had relatively low reserve ratios in 1937. Moreover, after 1933 these countries did not generally share in the recovery from the depression to the same extent as the industrial countries, and therefore had less opportunity to accumulate reserves.

There are persistent differences between the reserve levels and the reserve behavior of the nonindustrial countries similar to those already noted with regard to the

Table 15. Changes in Ratio of Reserves to Imports, Nonindustrial Countries, Selected Years, 1928-57

	Reserve Ratio Less Than 20 Per Cent		Reserve Ratio Less Than 30 Per Cent	
Year	Number of countries	Per cent of total	Number of countries	Per cent of total
1928	7	28	10	40
1937	8	21	17	45
1951	8	17	12	27
1953	4	8	16	33
1956	8	16	20	41
1957	13	27	21	43

industrial countries. In 1951, for example, 12 nonindustrial countries had reserves equal to less than 30 per cent of their imports, and six years later 10 of them were still in the same position. One other country which, on the basis of gross reserves, moved out of this group had not really improved its position for it had been able to increase its gross reserves only by increasing its liabilities. On the other hand, 13 countries in 1951 had reserves equal to more than 60 per cent of imports. In 1956, 10 of these countries, and in 1957, 7, were still in the same position. In some countries, such as India, the reduction in reserves represented heavy spending on development. This continuity in the relative position of various countries reflects the profound differences in their own situations, in their policies, and in their operating procedures, as the following examples suggest.

Israel and Yugoslavia have low reserves, and their other commitments are such that an accumulation of reserves has a low priority. Canada, having strong basic resources and close access to the New York money market, reportedly considered a reserve level of about 30 per cent as high enough in 1957.[1]

[1] As reported in *The Globe and Mail* (Toronto), October 24, 1957, and *The Journal of Commerce* (New York), October 29 and 31, 1957. Canada has a floating exchange rate. Whether the judgment would have been the same if it had a fixed rate is another question—the answer to which also depends upon the rate of capital imports and the balance of payments.

In 1956 South Africa had reserves of $370 million, equal to 24 per cent of imports. There is nothing to suggest that this country is anxious to increase the ratio to 30 per cent and still less to 40 per cent, though it would in all likelihood consider the 1957 ratio of 17 per cent (with reserves of $288 million) too low. It is a rapidly developing country, usually able to attract capital, and able to count on the ready disposal at a fixed price of its main export product, gold.

Malaya's ratio of reserves to imports was 23 per cent in 1957; it varied between 22 and 28 per cent in the years 1952 to 1957, compared with 27 per cent in 1937, and this seems to indicate that a ratio of this order has been found suitable for that country.

Most Latin American countries are anxious to develop their resources. Even in good years, when their products are selling at high prices, they do not substantially improve their reserve positions. If reserves increase one year, they will generally decline in a subsequent one.

On the other hand, there are countries that have maintained a high reserve level over a long period. Some of these countries, such as Egypt, accumulated substantial balances during the war. Others have benefited from the rapid development of oil and other natural resources, as did Iraq, Iran, and Venezuela.

The upward trend of world trade in the postwar period has provided opportunities for a large number of countries to improve their reserve positions. In fact, the countries which emerged from the war with practically no reserves have almost without exception been able to replenish them, although in some cases their reserves fluctuated widely during the period. This has been particularly evident in Europe. Aid from the United States and the operation of the European Payments Union have been of appreciable importance in these cases. On the other hand, other countries which accumulated reserves during the war spent heavily thereafter on supplies which had been unobtainable during the war and on goods required for development purposes. This spending, for example, in India and a number of Latin American countries, generally led to reductions in reserves. In some cases, these reductions have often gone farther than had been anticipated, and the decline has not yet been arrested.

As a group, all countries except the United States (and excluding the international agencies) increased their reserves from $22.1 billion in 1948 to $23.6 billion in 1951 and $29.7 billion in 1956. During the period 1948–56, reserves increased by $7.6 billion, or almost $1 billion per year. The rate of increase in this period was 4½ per cent per year, despite the reduction in reserves in 1949 which was caused by the devaluation of sterling. During the period 1951–56, which was one of comparative calm disturbed at the end by the Suez events, reserves increased by $6.1 billion, or $1.2 billion per year. The annual rate of increase in these five years was 5 per cent. These rates of increase are historically very large—and much larger than the rates of growth in the volume of trade over sustained periods. The situation in 1957 was disturbed by the inevitable liquidity stresses of the top of the boom, followed by the speculation in several key European currencies and the recession in the United States. There was in 1957 a considerable flow of gold to the United States. Even so, reserves of all countries except the United States increased by $300 million, though not without drawing on the Fund's resources. In the first six months of 1958, the outflow of gold from the United States ($1,445 million) was almost twice as great as the inflow in the whole of 1957 ($799 million). The prospect is for a substantial increase in 1958 in the reserves of all countries other than the United States.

The improvement in the reserve positions of many countries could not have taken place had they not restored balance in their positions, both internally and in relation to other economies. The foreign exchange markets provide further proof of this improvement. Quotations on free and black markets have moved closer to the official rates, and in some cases now almost coincide with them.

In several places, reference has been made to the fact that uncommitted savings are needed if gold and foreign exchange reserves are to be increased. An increase in reserves represents an investment which must be financed from savings in the same way as any other investment. In many cases, these savings accrue almost automatically. As production and trade grow, the needs of the economy for cash also grow. The increase in domestic cash holdings represents, in part, one source of savings which may form the counterpart of an increase in reserves. Banks and the rest of the private sector may also increase their exchange holdings in line with the increase in trade. However, for a more rapid increase in reserves, additional savings are required. Where pressure on reserves stems from inflationary tendencies, this involves either a decrease in the community's money income or a slowing down of the rate of its increase. Budget surpluses may be used to increase government deposits or (preferably) to repay government debt, particularly to the central bank. Part of the proceeds of foreign borrowing may be earmarked to increase reserves; and the proceeds of foreign aid may be sterilized for a similar purpose. In many cases, a reduction in private borrowing (or perhaps even the development of surpluses in the private sector) is required. The general theory, and even in some cases the specific measurements, of this mechanism are now well known and may be summarized very briefly. An inflationary increase in the money income of the community increases the demand for imports and it may also decrease exports; in any case, it leads to a decline of reserves. This increase in income may be the result of government borrowing, or private borrowing, or both. To stop the process requires a reduction in the rate of credit expansion; to reverse it requires a larger reduction. It is not necessary in most cases that credit not expand at all, for a growing and developing nation always needs some increase in its money supply.

It is in some respects instructive to examine what happened during the Korean crisis. As a result of the rise in prices, a number of countries, especially raw materials producing countries, were able rapidly to increase their earnings through larger exports. The immediate result was often a substantial increase in their foreign reserves. However, the increased earnings of the producers, traders, and others in these countries gave them a higher income which, when no special measures were taken, were gradually used for purchases of various kinds. After a certain lag, it was invariably found that imports rapidly increased, and often at a time when the export prices and receipts had begun to decline. As a result, the improvement in the reserve position was wiped out within a few years. When the increase in export incomes stimulated credit expansion to business or budget deficits by government the decline of reserves went even further. However, in some countries (especially some British colonies) steps were taken to pay the producers of the commodities exported only a part of the increased earnings resulting from the higher prices. The difference between the export price and the home price was accumulated in special reserves. In these cases there was no sudden increase in incomes leading to larger imports, and the exchange reserves which had been accumulated remained more or less intact.

There is now greater understanding of the conditions necessary for an improvement in the reserve position. For example, a recent statement by the Monetary Committee of the International Chamber of Commerce recommended that countries gradually reduce their debts to central banks, and thus strengthen not only their internal conditions but also their reserve holdings.

The Position of the United Kingdom

The role and the strength of sterling and the reserve position of the United Kingdom have been major financial concerns of the world in the postwar period and will continue to be such in the foreseeable future. This is a natural consequence of the importance of sterling in the world economy. A large part of the world's trade is financed in sterling; sterling assets constitute a substantial proportion (about 10 per cent) of the world's international reserves; the convertibility of sterling is a prerequisite for the convertibility of several other major currencies; and all these circumstances are involved in any assessment of the prospects for further moves toward the liberalization of trade.

In the postwar period, the United Kingdom has, with the exception of only a few years, had a surplus on the current account of its balance of payments. For the period 1948–56, the net surplus on current account amounted to a total of £1.2 billion, equivalent to almost $3.4 billion. The fact that the United Kingdom was nevertheless affected by several postwar financial crises has to be related to the following considerations:

(1) The United Kingdom emerged from the war with greatly reduced foreign assets and greatly increased foreign liabilities, mainly in the form of sterling balances which could easily be drawn upon and which could affect confidence in sterling. At the end of the war, sterling liabilities stood at $14.4 billion, compared with $4 billion in 1937. By 1948, these had been reduced to $12.7 billion, and after the devaluation of sterling, they amounted to $8.8 billion at the end of 1949. In 1957 they stood at $9.1 billion. But this stability covers important changes. In the meantime, a number of countries that had accumulated large sterling balances during the war (e.g., India) had drawn them down substantially, and a number of other countries that for various reasons wished to reduce their sterling balances had also done so. On the other hand, the British colonies (which for most of the postwar period included Malaya and Ghana) increased their balances substantially. Although a number of countries will undoubtedly wish to use their sterling balances for development in the next years, the total of all balances is certainly more stable than at any time since the war and, in real terms, no higher than in 1937. Nevertheless, the total of sterling liabilities is large in relation to reserves, so that the threat of any substantial movement is worrisome, especially when added to that of other elements.

(2) The foreign trade of the United Kingdom is large in relation to its national product and its reserves. Shifts in payment leads and lags may therefore cause important movements of reserves, and may well have involved movements of funds exceeding $500 million within periods as short as a few months.

(3) Such movements may, furthermore, be accentuated by changes in the extent to which use is made of sterling credits to finance trade not directly connected with the United Kingdom's own imports and exports.

(4) The surpluses arising on the current account of the balance of payments have been substantial, and they have not been used to increase reserves. Instead, they have had their counterpart mainly in the granting of foreign credits, investments abroad, and other foreign capital transactions, including repayment of debt.

Under these conditions, any adverse circumstances are likely to affect confidence in sterling and to lead to substantial changes in sterling reserves.

The fact that there has in most years been a surplus on the current account of the U.K. balance of payments would tend to show that sterling, at least since the devaluation of 1949, has not been overvalued. As to the use made of the balance of payments surpluses, the following figures are taken from a statement made by Sir Oliver Franks to the annual meeting of Lloyds Bank in January 1958.[2] In the five and a half years from January 1952 to June 1957, the total available from international transactions for foreign investment, repayment of debt, or addition to reserves was £1,051 million. This amount had its counterpart in the following transactions:

(1) Net capital investment in sterling countries to the amount of £359 million (representing a gross investment of £648 million, partly offset by an increase of £289 million in sterling balances);

(2) Repayment of sterling balances of non-sterling countries to the extent of £372 million;

(3) Other capital transactions with non-sterling countries to the amount of £304 million;

(4) As a net result, reserves in this period increased by only £16 million.

In considering these results, it is important to remember that the savings which were the counterpart of these surpluses on the current account of the balance of payments were made mainly by private firms and individuals. Frequently, they were in the form of profits ploughed back in the countries in which they were earned by U.K. firms operating abroad. The use to which the savings were put depended therefore to a great extent upon a large number of separate decisions, which in a period of expanding trade would naturally lead to expanded investments of various kinds. It would, of course, have been possible by direct controls to inhibit some of the transactions, and in 1957 some controls were in fact imposed on U.K. investment outside of the sterling area. On the other hand, the fact that the British financial system has been able to continue working without too many restrictions has been valuable in itself. The amounts used for these transactions in a large measure added to the earning capacity of the British economy, and they also benefited those areas in which investments were made.

The reserve problem of the United Kingdom is complex, and is the result of many developments over many years. After World War II, the United Kingdom had to adapt itself to a changed world and, compared with its situation before the war, it had to do this with lower reserves, much smaller overseas investments, much larger short-term liabilities, a great deal of wartime damage and obsolescence which had to be made up, and a pressing backlog of domestic demand for both capital and consumer goods. Although the course of the reserves problem reflects international developments, it also reflects the British decisions, implicit or explicit, about the priorities to be assigned to each of these complex demands upon its economy. As has been suggested, it would simplify the problem unduly to suggest that all, or even a much larger part, of the national saving on current account could have been turned into reserve holdings of gold and dollars. This might have unduly weakened the long-term position of the United Kingdom and it would in any case not have been easy to shift investment from

[2] As reported in *The Economist* (London), January 25, 1958.

overseas assets to reserves of gold and dollars. This might have required an extensive reorientation of trade, with perhaps a lower over-all level of employment and national income for a time. It would have had serious implications for the cohesiveness of the sterling area. On the other hand, in the longer run this investment in overseas assets would bolster future export markets for capital goods, provide future income, and perhaps (directly or indirectly) enable the sterling area to increase its exports to the non-sterling area and/or reduce its imports from it.

But perhaps even this way of looking at the reserves problem of the United Kingdom is too narrow. The gross national product in the period 1950–57 was almost £140 billion, or roughly $400 billion. Redirection of this gross product to increase purchases of gold or dollars by $2 billion in eight years would be equivalent to a change of ½ per cent in final product composition. Such redirection might not have been easy, considering the large number of competing alternatives (including the rise in defense expenditure as international tension increased), but it cannot be considered outside of practical possibilities.

In evaluating the total of, and the changes in, the reserves of the United Kingdom, account must always be taken of the movements in short-term sterling liabilities. An increase of reserves that accompanies, or results from, an increase in sterling balances may not signify any real improvement in reserve position. This has been the case on a number of occasions in the postwar period, and particularly in 1950 when at the height of the Korean boom reserves rose to $3.7 billion. The improvement in sterling reserves since the third quarter of 1957 has a different significance. It is to be regarded as the result of higher priority given to strengthening the international position of sterling. At the end of September 1957, in which month Bank Rate was increased from 5 per cent to 7 per cent, and a series of other important financial measures were taken, reserves stood at $1,850 million; by June 1958 they had increased to $3,180 million.[3] On the other hand, sterling liabilities at the end of the third quarter of 1957 stood at $9,433 million; by March 1958 (the latest date for which data are available), they had been reduced to $9,055 million.

These recent developments in reserve holdings and in sterling liabilities have undoubtedly improved the monetary position of the United Kingdom significantly, especially as they have not been accompanied by a reduction in raw materials and other inventories. It would appear, in addition, that this position improved gradually in the postwar period, even though this was not reflected in an increase in reserve holdings. The competitive position of British export industries has been strengthened as domestic backlogs have been worked off and the pressure of domestic demands moderated. The large foreign investments that have been made inside and outside the sterling area have improved the position of the United Kingdom, while their costs in terms both of goods and of their effects on reserves have largely been paid. Nevertheless, there is always the possibility that some countries will begin or continue to draw on their sterling balances for development and other purposes. If these drawings are sudden and large, and particularly if they are of a speculative character, they can cause financial inconvenience or even crisis. On the other hand, if they are moderate and for development purposes—and British export industries remain competitive—they should up to a point support the British balance of payments.

[3] To the extent of $250 million the increase was due to a drawing from the Export-Import Bank. This drawing was additional to the earlier drawing of $561 million from the International Monetary Fund in December 1956 at the time of the Suez tension.

Part of the present sterling balances do not represent savings which have been made with the prospect of eventually financing future development, or backing for various national currencies, but rather working balances for the conduct of international trade. If world trade continues to increase and confidence in sterling is maintained, it is not unlikely that a number of countries will need to add to their sterling holdings. The net result of these various movements on the position of sterling cannot be foreseen. Even less is it possible to foresee political or international crises which may have an equally important impact on sterling. With the improvement in the British position which has already taken place and which can be expected from a further net accumulation of reserves, the prospects for a continued relaxation of exchange controls are better than they have been in previous years. Sterling is, however, subject to large influences from all over the world, and it has therefore not been surprising that in the United Kingdom stress has been laid upon the importance of having a secondary line of defense available in case of need.

The Position of the United States

The gold holdings of the United States increased during and immediately after World War I, but were then comparatively stable for about ten years. From 1934 onward (when they were $8.3 billion) they again grew rapidly, and they continued to grow during World War II. By 1945 gold reserves were equal to $20.1 billion. By 1949, the all-time high point, gold holdings totaled $24.6 billion, or 74 per cent of the world's stock of monetary gold. In the following years there were variations in the level of gold reserves, but on balance there was a decline, so that by the end of June 1958 the amount of gold held by the United States was $21.4 billion, equal to 55 per cent of the world's monetary gold stock. If gold and foreign exchange reserves are taken together, the United States at the end of 1956 held about 40 per cent of the world's reserves, or approximately the same proportion that U.S. industrial output bears to the industrial output of the world (excluding here, as elsewhere, the communist countries).

The Federal Reserve System is required to maintain a gold reserve of 25 per cent against its deposit liabilities and paper currency issues (Federal Reserve Notes). This requirement has been in effect since 1945, and represents a reduction of about one third from the previous legal requirements of 35 per cent against deposits and 40 per cent against Federal Reserve Notes.

The Federal Reserve System has had large gold holdings in excess of legal requirements for many years. In the 1920's, for example, slightly more than half of its gold holdings were in excess of its reserve requirements, and this percentage increased sharply in the next decade, particularly after the price of gold was increased in 1934. In the period 1950–57, "free" gold in excess of requirements averaged $10.7 billion, or about 48 per cent of total gold holdings.

There is thus a large margin, according to present reserve requirements, for expanding the money supply of the United States or, alternatively, for reducing gold holdings. In addition, the money supply can be expanded in relation to gold if the reserve ratios of commercial banks are reduced, since these reserves consist of deposits in the Federal Reserve Banks. The combined effect of the reserve requirements of the Federal Reserve and the commercial banks was such that in 1957 gold was equal to 17 per cent of the money supply of $139 billion. This percentage may be compared with 20 per cent in 1947 and 43 per cent in 1937. Given the magnitude of the present margin of excess reserves, it is unlikely that the United States would exercise its power further to reduce the reserve requirements of the Federal Reserve System. The System also has authority temporarily to suspend reserve requirements,[4] but, for the same reasons, it is unlikely that it would do this.

The state of the gold reserves of the United States must also be considered in the light of its short-term liabilities. These have grown rapidly in recent years: they were $1.9 billion in 1937, $7.2 billion in 1948, and $14.8 billion at the end of 1957. Although these balances are not legally convertible into gold, the United States for many years has followed the practice of converting all official balances (almost two thirds of the total) upon request, and, as a practical matter, all dollar balances may be treated as convertible. This situation has led to questions in some quarters whether the United States has enough gold to meet its domestic reserve requirements as well as possible drains upon its gold supply that might follow from conversion of dollar balances. The data on gold holdings, gold in excess of reserve requirements, and dollar liabilities are given in Table 16.

There is, of course, always the possibility of a "run" on the dollar, in the same way as there is the possibility of a "run" on any other currency. If this were to take place, the pressure on the dollar could come from many sources other than the sale or conversion of short-term dollar holdings, a large part of which must represent working balances. Foreign holdings of stocks, bonds, and other securities which could be sold or pledged were valued at almost $9 billion in 1956. The pressure resulting from a change in "leads and lags" of foreign trade amounting to $25 billion a year, and the speculation against the dollar which might be financed with borrowed funds by both foreigners and U.S. citizens, must also be considered. In fact, as has already been noted in connection with the level of reserves in general and the reserves of individual countries in particular, the financial strength of a country depends upon many other factors besides its reserves. That the United States has huge gold holdings, equal to 55 per cent of the world's gold stock, and that it has large gold holdings in excess of its domestic reserve requirements, do not change this basic fact. Large reserves, of course, give the United States great opportunity for maneuver and for the exercise of monetary policy in dealing with speculative and other adverse developments. But the ultimate financial strength of the United States rests on its strong international position and the fact that it is an extremely important market, a dominant supplier of economic and other kinds of aid, and a major source of long-term and short-term capital. It would therefore be natural for the rest of the world to maintain large holdings of dollars for working balances, investment, and other purposes.

It is interesting to note that in each of the postwar periods of recession the level of dollar liabilities has remained very stable. The large outflow of gold in 1958, for example, did not reflect the conversion of dollar balances, but rather the normal reserve practices of countries with surpluses on the current account of their balances of payments.

Under the rules of the gold standard, it was the general practice to wait for an influx of gold before easing credit conditions. Today the U.S. authorities, thanks to the substantial gold holdings at their disposal, are able to relax credit even where there is an outflow of gold. It has been an element of strength that the United States has been able to face the task of preventing excessive fluctuations in business activity without being hampered by an insufficiency of monetary reserves. From the point of view of

[4] Federal Reserve Act, Sec. 11, para. 4. Requirements may be suspended for 30 days, and the suspension may be renewed for periods not exceeding 15 days.

world liquidity, too, the expansion of credit and the decline of interest rates in U.S. markets, in the face of a recession, have been of importance. This has made it increasingly possible for other countries to ease their own credit conditions, for account has to be taken not only of the absolute interest level in any one country but also of that interest level in relation to those in other economies and, especially, in the international financial centers.

Table 16. U.S. Gold Reserves, Domestic Reserve Requirements, and Short-Term Foreign Liabilities, Selected Years, 1922-57

(In billions of U.S. dollars)

Year	Gold Reserves	Domestic Reserve Require-ments	"Free" Gold: In Excess of Reserve Requirements	Foreign Short-Term Dollar Balances	Per Cent of All Gold to Foreign Balances	Per Cent of "Free" Gold to Foreign Balances
1922	3.5	1.7	1.8	1.0	350	180
1925	4.0	1.6	2.4	1.2	333	200
1926	4.1	1.6	2.5	1.6	256	156
1927	4.0	1.6	2.4	2.6	154	92
1928	3.7	1.6	2.1	2.5	148	84
1929	3.9	1.6	2.3	2.7	144	85
1930	4.2	1.6	2.6	2.3	183	113
1933	4.0	2.2	1.8	.4	1,000	450
1934	8.3	2.7	5.6	.7	1,038	700
1935	10.1	3.6	6.5	1.3	777	500
1936	11.4	4.1	7.3	1.6	712	456
1937	12.8	4.2	8.6	1.9	674	453
1938	14.6	5.1	9.5	2.2	664	432
1940	22.0	7.9	14.1	3.9	564	362
1945	20.1	10.9	9.2	7.1	283	130
1946	20.7	10.7	10.0	6.5	318	154
1947	22.9	11.3	11.6	7.1	323	163
1948	24.4	11.9	12.5	7.2	339	174
1949	24.6	10.8	13.8	7.6	324	182
1950	22.8	11.0	11.8	8.4	271	140
1951	22.9	11.7	11.2	8.3	276	135
1952	23.3	12.1	11.2	9.9	235	113
1953	22.1	12.0	10.1	10.8	205	94
1954	21.8	11.7	10.1	11.9	183	85
1955	21.8	11.9	9.9	13.0	168	76
1956	22.1	11.9	10.2	14.6	151	70
1957	22.9	11.9	11.0	14.8	155	74

Sources: Data on gold reserves, domestic requirements, and dollar balances for 1922-52 are from *Annual Report of the Secretary of the Treasury*, 1954, Exhibit 47; later data on gold reserves are from *Federal Reserve Bulletin.* Domestic reserve requirements were calculated from data published in *Federal Reserve Bulletin* table on "Statement of Condition of the Federal Reserve Banks." Short-term dollar balances are from *International Financial Statistics* and include holdings of government bonds and notes.

The Distribution of Monetary Reserves

Some countries habitually hold comparatively low reserves, while others over the years have held more ample reserves. If, by and large, these differences continue, there is little significance in any discussion of the redistribution of reserves. On the other hand, it is probable that the countries with very large reserves will not think it necessary to set aside substantial savings for the purpose of increasing their reserves, and it is desirable that countries with low reserves should improve their positions. It is, therefore, of some interest to outline what additional amounts of gold and foreign exchange would be required to raise reserves to, say, 30 per cent of imports for all countries that are below this level.

After exclusion of the United Kingdom, which is in many respects a special case, the additional amount required to raise to 30 per cent the reserve ratios of all countries that were below it in 1956 would be $1.8 billion of reserves. To reach a minimum of 40 per cent, $4.9 billion would be required.

These figures do no more than indicate the magnitude of the reserves that would have to be acquired if all countries which at present have low reserves were to try to acquire more over a reasonable period. But it is hardly likely that all these countries, whatever their wishes may be, will be prepared to take the steps necessary to improve their reserve positions to this extent. For the United Kingdom, as already mentioned, the amount of reserves has to be judged in relation to the movement of sterling balances. But if this country were to add another billion to its present reserves of $3 billion, and also all countries with low reserves were to try to reach a ratio of 40 per cent, the amount required over a number of years would be of the order of, say, $6 billion. To judge from developments in the postwar period, this would not seem out of the question. In the period 1949–57 reserves grew at the rate of almost $1.2 billion per year, and in the period 1951–57, at the rate of $1.0 billion per year. For the future, the addition to international reserves from current gold production at the present price of gold is likely to be $700 million per year, and, at a minimum, should be at least as large as the average addition in 1951–57, or about $550 million per year. There is no reason to assume that there could not be further additions to foreign-held dollar balances. Since it is perhaps also fair to assume that countries which now hold fairly large reserves see no urgent reason to add substantially to them, this annual flow of gold and other resources would largely be available to other countries prepared to take the necessary steps to improve their reserve positions.

Moreover, it is pertinent to recall that the amount of newly mined gold that has gone into private holdings since 1946, largely by reason of the lack of monetary confidence, has attained a total of between $3 billion and $4 billion. The amount of gold in private hoards is now estimated to be of the order of $10 billion to $12 billion, of which almost one half is held in Western Europe, and almost one third in France alone. If only one half of the newly mined gold that went into private hoards in the postwar period had been available for monetary reserves and had been acquired by the countries with the lowest reserves, it would have been enough to assure that every country had a ratio of reserves to imports equal to at least 25 per cent. A small amount of dishoarding was recently reported in France in connection with an issue of gold-indexed bonds. If dishoarding there and elsewhere should increase so that, on balance, there were no additions to gold hoards in the world at large, well over $700 million a year could be added to monetary reserves from current gold production, which has been increasing even with the present price of gold.

Thus the problem is not so much one of finding the resources in gold and foreign exchange which would be available for an improvement in the reserve position, but rather of the willingness of countries to take the necessary steps in the fiscal and credit fields to restore a proper balance within and among their various economies. It has often been emphasized that devaluation, useful as it may be in certain circumstances to attain a realistic rate of exchange, can lead to an effective solution of a country's difficulties only if it is combined with proper fiscal and credit policies. Since the prevailing exchange rates of a very large number of countries are much more realistic than they were in the immediate postwar period, the emphasis must necessarily be placed on the maintenance of internal balance if further monetary progress is to be made. There is no way of escaping these basic efforts. If they are made, there seems to be no evidence that the solution of the problems relating to an all-round improvement in the reserve position of individual countries will be hampered by an over-all scarcity of reserves. This conclusion remains, however, conditioned upon the continuance of constructive efforts to strengthen the international economic and credit system.

CHAPTER FOUR: PROSPECTIVE RESERVES AND REQUIREMENTS

As already mentioned in previous chapters, official reserves of gold, and of dollars, sterling, and other forms of exchange, have two functions. In the purely domestic sense, these reserves may be a prerequisite for an increase in the volume of domestic money—currency and bank deposits. In the international sense, they may be used to finance swings in the balance of payments. These two functions are interrelated. An excessive increase in the domestic money supply will make the balance of payments unfavorable and lead to declining reserves; a gain in reserves may ease credit policy and encourage an increase in the supply of domestic money.

Under the orthodox operation of the gold standard (which was never so strict in practice as it was often defined in theory), increases in the gold holdings of the banks of issue were, in general, a prerequisite for an increase in the volume of currency and deposits. Since an expansion in production and trade would need more credit, it was not unnatural to regard it as essential that gold output should keep pace with potential economic growth in the world at large. It is still true that changes in monetary reserves influence credit developments, both by their direct effects on the volume of money and by their influence on credit policy. But it is also true that for a fairly large number of countries, changes in monetary reserves no longer have the paramount importance that they previously did.

There are several reasons for this. First, many countries have weakened the link between the amount of reserves and the amount of domestic money in order to obtain more flexibility in their monetary operations. There has been a pronounced trend for reserves of gold and exchange to become a smaller and smaller percentage of the domestic money supply. In some cases this is the result of reducing the cover percentages of the central bank; in others, of reducing the reserve ratios of commercial banks or of permitting the growth of financial intermediaries whose effective reserve ratios are lower than those of commercial banks. In addition to these longer term developments, many countries, both developed and underdeveloped, are using changes in commercial bank reserve requirements as a supplement to the traditional weapons of discount rates and open market operations. Secondly, the link between the amount of reserves and the amount of domestic money has been weakened in all countries that have not made a stable fixed rate of exchange an overriding objective of monetary policy. An increase in the supply of domestic money may not lead to a loss of reserves if the exchange rate is allowed to depreciate but the declining value of the currency is, of course, a source of weakness in itself, which cannot be tolerated for long. Thirdly, as has already been pointed out above, a number of countries, and particularly those with large monetary reserves, can carry out credit policies relatively independently of changes in their reserve position. Indeed, the credit systems of several countries are now able to generate their own liquidity with a fairly high degree of freedom. These countries can adopt policies which may lead to a decline of gold reserves or to the growth of foreign holdings of their money. The liquidity of these countries is thus of outstanding importance for the liquidity position of the world. To a considerable extent, international liquidity can now be produced without the limiting factor of the gold base. Thus, the liquidity position of the world was greatly eased by the credit expansion in the United States in 1957–58 at a time when its gold reserve was declining.

In short, the growth of the domestic money supply in most countries is no longer so closely tied to the growth of international reserves as it was in the days of the gold standard. The required increase in the domestic money supply of individual countries no longer creates as large a proportional demand for gold cover as it did in the days of the gold standard. In addition, a number of countries are able to create additional liquidity on the basis of their existing reserves, and this adds to world liquidity.

The Growth of Reserves and Reserve Requirements

The preceding chapters have discussed the amount and the distribution of reserves and have related the level of reserves to the level of trade in various years. To the extent that this was possible, the amount of reserves was interpreted in terms of the adequacy or the inadequacy of reserve levels, and the qualifications that must surround any such judgment were made clear. In this section, the analysis will be pushed forward to take account of the probable development of reserve levels on the assumption—or perhaps, better, the requirement—of a continued growth of world trade. Here again it is necessary to emphasize the basic consideration that the adequacy of reserves depends very much on the environment in which the monetary system operates—the balance attained in the relationship of the various economies with one another, the readiness to take corrective measures when an imbalance occurs, the effectiveness of the private credit system, tariff policies, etc. Since developments in these fields play such a decisive role, there can be no fixed mathematical relationship between the growth of reserves and the expansion of production and foreign trade. It should not be assumed that an increase in reserves will more or less automatically induce an increase in the volume of trade—and indeed, there have been periods, as in the 1930's, when very substantial increases in reserves were accompanied by restrictionism and stagnant trade. Neither should it be assumed that the potential increase in the volume of trade can necessarily be no greater than the increase in the volume of international reserves.

It is of interest to consider what increase in production, and more particularly in foreign trade, is in prospect in, for example, the next decade, and how the world's reserve position is likely to develop. For this purpose, Table 17 shows the rates of increase of world trade and manufacturing production for various periods from 1876–80 to 1957.

A number of economic investigators—Cassel, Kitchin, and others—calculated that the rate of growth in the world economy was about 3 per cent per annum in the fifty years before 1914. It will be seen from the table, which is based upon the most recent data for the period, that the increase in manufacturing activity (which may have risen more rapidly than gross national product) was 4.1 per cent per year, while the increase in trade was somewhat less than 3.4 per cent per year.

The largest rates of growth occurred in the immediate postwar years after World Wars I and II. For the periods from 1921–25 to 1926–29, or roughly four and a half years, manufacturing activity grew 6.8 per cent per year; trade grew at a slightly lower rate. For the years from 1948 to 1956, manufacturing grew 6.1 per cent, and trade 7.5 per cent per year. For longer periods, which include the years of war and depression, the rates of growth are naturally much smaller. Thus, from the years 1876–80 to 1936–38, manufacturing activity grew at the rate of 3.5 per cent per year, while trade grew at about 2 per cent per year. Correspondingly, from 1938 to 1957 the annual rates of growth were 4.6 per cent for manufacturing and 3.3 per cent for trade.

Table 17. Average Annual Rates of Growth of Trade and Manufacturing, Selected Periods

(In per cent; compound basis)

Period	Trade[1]		Manufacturing Activity[2]
	Primary products	Manufactured products	
From 1876-80 to:			
1901-05	3.3	2.8	4.1
1913	3.4	3.3	4.1
1926-29	2.6	2.4	3.5
1930	2.6	2.2	3.3
1936-38	2.3	1.8	3.5
From 1901-05 to:			
1913	3.5	4.7	4.2
1926-29	2.0	2.1	3.1
1930	2.0	1.7	2.7
1936-38	1.5	1.1	3.1
From 1921-25 to:			
1926-29	6.3	7.1	6.8
1930	4.9	3.8	4.1
1936-38	2.2	1.3	4.4
From 1938 to 1948	0.0		3.7
From 1948 to 1956	7.5		6.1
From 1950 to 1956	6.5		5.7
From 1950 to 1957	6.3		5.1
From 1951 to 1957	5.4		5.0

[1] These rates of growth were calculated from the following basic data: (1) Data for 1876-80 to 1936-38 are from League of Nations, *Industrialization and Foreign Trade* (1945), and include the U.S.S.R. Trade covers exports and imports. There is no combined index of trade of primary products and manufactured articles, though trade in the latter was about 60 per cent as great as that in the former. (2) Data beginning with 1938 are from Special Table A in United Nations, *Monthly Bulletin of Statistics*, November 1957, January 1958, and June 1958. These data refer to total exports and exclude the countries in the communist bloc.

[2] These rates of growth were calculated from the following basic data: (1) Data for 1876-80 to 1936-38 are from League of Nations, *Industrialization and Foreign Trade* (1945), and include the U.S.S.R. (2) Data beginning with 1938 are from Special Table A in United Nations, *Monthly Bulletin of Statistics*, January 1958 and June 1958, and exclude countries in the communist bloc.

A particular characteristic of the period after World War II has been the fact that trade has increased at a faster rate than industrial production, while in earlier periods it grew no faster than industrial production, as in the 1920's, or increased less than production, as was the case before 1914. There have been many special factors after World War II which have made for a rapid increase in trade. Certain countries had substantial reserves accumulated during the war which they were able to spend; special efforts were made to provide aid and credits, and this was reflected in an increased volume of trade; moreover, the rapid expansion in the output and use of oil led to a large increase in foreign trade of an unprecedented character.

Past experiences seem to show that periods of very rapid expansion are generally followed by periods of more moderate growth. It is of course impossible to forecast what the rate of growth will be in the years immediately ahead, but it would probably not be overoptimistic to retain the conventional "normal" annual rate of about 3 per cent for the growth of world trade. This would in itself assume some improvement over the rate of growth in the sixty years before World War II.

If reserves are also to grow at the rate of 3 per cent per year and maintain the ratio of reserves to imports that applied at the end of 1956, they would have to increase by $19 billion by 1966. Such an addition would assume, however, that even the countries which already have very substantial reserves, such as the United States, the Federal Republic of Germany, Venezuela, and Switzerland, would want to increase their reserves by more than one third. In fact, if these four countries were to increase their reserves at the rate of 3 per cent per year, they would absorb about $11 billion of the computed world requirement of $19 billion for the next decade. This is most unlikely. If the problem of increasing international reserves is therefore reduced to the dimensions of increasing the reserves of all other countries, the requirement for additional reserves is reduced to about $8 billion. It may be doubted whether all other countries would in fact wish to increase their reserves so much.

It is estimated that the increase of gold reserves from current gold production is likely at the present price of gold to be at least $700 million per year for the next decade, even after allowing for an increase in the present large gold hoards.[1] Thus, gold production alone would go very far toward meeting the requirements for additional reserves. In addition, reserve holdings of foreign exchange are likely to rise if there is full employment in the industrial countries and the requirements for overseas spending by the United States in the form of imports, capital investments, defense, and aid of various kinds are maintained. All foreign short-term dollar balances increased from $7.1 billion in 1947 to $14.8 billion in 1957, and official holdings of dollars increased from $1.8 billion to $8.3 billion. All short-term dollar balances in the last decade therefore increased on the average by $770 million per year, and official balances alone increased by $650 million per year. Sterling balances in the past decade have naturally been reduced from the swollen heights they attained by the end of World War II. In terms of sterling, they have come down by 10 per cent, or from £3.6 billion at the end of 1945 to £3.3 billion at the end of 1957. In terms of dollars, the reduction was much greater because of the devaluation of sterling in 1949. Sterling holdings at the end of the first quarter of 1958 were about the same as they had been at the end of 1949. When all kinds of exchange holdings are taken together, the

[1] O. L. Altman, "A Note on Gold Production and Additions to International Gold Reserves," *Staff Papers*, Vol. VI, No. 2 (April 1958).

available data suggest that these reserves increased by a net total of about $2 billion in the past decade, or by $200 million per year.

The reserves problem that the world will face in the next decade does not, therefore, appear to be insoluble. This conclusion accords with the results arrived at in the preceding chapters, and it of course assumes the same comments that were made there about the relationship of reserves to international liquidity and the international environment.

The question may, however, be asked whether it is likely that the countries with relatively slender reserves will be in a position to increase them in the next decade by more than one third, or by approximately $8 billion. Clearly, some countries will add to their reserves. Others undoubtedly believe that they can safely draw down their reserves for development purposes, and this group includes countries whose reserves are already substantially lower than they were at the end of World War II. Even if these latter countries will not reduce their reserves further in the next years, they are not all likely to give priority to increasing them. Some countries have reserves which they have no reason to regard as insufficient, and they would probably not want to increase them as rapidly as their trade. Other countries have for a number of years operated with very small reserves, and in 1956 had ratios of reserves to imports much below the average for all countries. They will have good reasons to increase their reserves as trade grows, and probably up to a point will do so, but perhaps not in the same proportion as the growth of trade. There is also the most important question whether the United Kingdom, and all the countries of the sterling area, will wish to increase their reserves by more than one third in the next ten years. As far as the United Kingdom is concerned, the improvement of its reserve position can come not only from increasing its reserves but also from reducing its short-term liabilities, increasing the strength of London as a center for long-term and short-term capital, and (over the long term) by increasing its income from overseas investments. The priority that the United Kingdom will accord to increasing reserves thus depends upon many factors, and not least among them is the possibility of borrowing in periods of strain.

The likelihood is thus that some of the gold from current production will not be absorbed by those countries which now have slender reserves, but will be sold to countries which already have relatively large reserves.

Some central banks will wish to add part of their additional reserves in the form of exchange holdings rather than gold. To achieve this result, part of the current supply of gold will very likely be sold to the monetary authorities in the main financial centers. By this and other means, including the normal operations of the sterling area, these countries will make their own currencies available for increasing the reserves of other countries. While it is always difficult to foretell what will happen in the future, there is reason to believe that current gold production, plus the continued increase in exchange holdings, will provide opportunities for a substantial addition to the monetary reserves of those countries that wish to acquire larger reserves.

World gold production, at the current fixed price of $35 per fine ounce, has been increasing year by year, particularly since 1951. There is no reason to expect a reversal of this trend in the foreseeable future. With a continued strengthening of monetary confidence through appropriate fiscal and credit policies, it should be possible to ensure that most of the newly produced gold becomes available for normal industrial uses and monetary reserves. Considerable progress in this direction has already been made.

In these circumstances, it cannot be argued that the current supply is inadequate for the requirements which can now be foreseen. There is no proven need for any abrupt increase in the volume of current gold production or in its monetary value by an increase in the price of gold. A measure of that kind might even detract attention from the real monetary problems of restoring and maintaining a proper balance in the individual economies, and in their relations with one another, and of strengthening the international credit system.

Monetary reserves are drawn upon for settlement of a country's deficits on foreign account, but the actual financing of foreign trade is, of course, effected primarily by the commercial banks. These as a rule hold working balances in foreign currencies. If trade grows, these balances, especially those held in the main financial centers, may likewise be expected to increase. These balances are held not only by commercial banks, but also by private firms and individuals. In part they represent commercial borrowing in these same centers; in part they represent the accumulation of net foreign earnings and the proceeds of securities transactions. The total of these privately held balances is large. Of the outstanding dollar balances at the end of 1957, about 40 per cent, or about $5.3 billion, was privately held. The percentage of sterling balances held on private account is much smaller than this. It has recently been reported that at the end of 1957 private holdings came to £759 million ($2.1 billion), or about 23 per cent of all sterling liabilities of £3.3 billion (excluding the £645 million due to international organizations). Especially as regards dollars, it is fair to assume that a portion of the amount held privately is to some extent hoarded by individuals and firms, i.e., the turnover of these holdings is relatively small. But the major portion, even for dollars—and certainly for sterling—represents working balances which are required in the course of financing current business.

With an increase in monetary confidence and a relaxation of exchange controls (which have imposed severe limits on private holdings of foreign exchange), it is likely that there will be increasing movements of privately held balances and that, as was the case before 1914, equilibrating movements of funds will thereby be facilitated. This should, up to a point, reduce the strain on official reserves. For such a development to take place it is, however, necessary that the monetary authorities in the individual countries pursue flexible credit policies. This has been the tendency in recent years, and it seems to be increasingly agreed that the results obtained have been good.

Strengthening of the World's Monetary Situation by International Organizations

The breakdown and subsequent disintegration of the world's monetary system in the interwar period has shown that the over-all reserve position was not in itself of decisive importance. In 1928 the ratio of reserves to imports for countries other than the United States was 35 per cent, compared with 17 per cent in 1913. But high as it was, it could not stave off the monetary disruptions in the following years. Still less did the very high ratio of 63 per cent in 1937–38 act as a cure for stagnant trade. In the same way, the opportunities that are likely to exist for an over-all improvement in reserve positions in the years to come in themselves afford no guarantee of healthy monetary developments. These can be assured only by simultaneous constructive efforts in many fields. It may perhaps seem trite to remark that general political developments will be of decisive importance, and not only to the extent that a major war is avoided. But the world will never be altogether calm, and periods of financial tension will recur. It is, therefore, wise always to have available safeguards of a financial character.

International cooperation in financial matters is not new. Even before 1914 there were many instances of contact and assistance between central banks. In the interwar period the need for cooperation between monetary authorities became more fully recognized. This recognition first developed in connection with stabilization loans to various countries in the 1920's, in many cases under the auspices of the League of Nations. In 1930, the Bank for International Settlements (BIS) was established, formally as a by-product of efforts to solve the German reparations problem, but essentially to foster international monetary cooperation. In addition to performing rather extensive banking and trustee functions, the BIS has continued to serve as a meeting place for the central bankers of the European countries. In 1936, the Tripartite Agreement was signed by the United States, the United Kingdom, and France; and later Belgium, the Netherlands, and Switzerland became associated with it.

During World War II, major efforts were made to establish monetary cooperation on a world-wide basis. These resulted in the formation of the Bretton Woods institutions —the International Monetary Fund and the International Bank for Reconstruction and Development. The International Bank for Reconstruction and Development provides long-term capital, under government guarantee, for specific projects. This type of financing provides an essential complement to the short-term credit facilities of the International Monetary Fund, and in effect helps prevent long-term capital problems from turning into short-term liquidity problems. The purposes of the Fund are set out in Article I of its Articles of Agreement as follows:

(i) To promote international monetary cooperation through a permanent institution which provides the machinery for consultation and collaboration on international monetary problems.

(ii) To facilitate the expansion and balanced growth of international trade, and to contribute thereby to the promotion and maintenance of high levels of employment and real income and to the development of the productive resources of all members as primary objectives of economic policy.

(iii) To promote exchange stability, to maintain orderly exchange arrangements among members, and to avoid competitive exchange depreciation.

(iv) To assist in the establishment of a multilateral system of payments in respect of current transactions between members and in the elimination of foreign exchange restrictions which hamper the growth of world trade.

(v) To give confidence to members by making the Fund's resources available to them under adequate safeguards, thus providing them with opportunity to correct maladjustments in their balance of payments without resorting to measures destructive of national or international prosperity.

(vi) In accordance with the above, to shorten the duration and lessen the degree of disequilibrium in the international balances of payments of members.

The Fund was provided with resources in gold and in the currencies of its members, with each member contributing in proportion to its quota. Quotas also regulated the rights of members to draw on these resources for short-term financing. On April 30, 1947, the Fund held $1.3 billion in gold and the equivalent of $2.1 billion in U.S. dollars and other convertible currencies. The first Fund transactions were made after this date (the Fund had declared itself ready for transactions on March 1, 1947), and by the end of 1948 there had been a substantial number of transactions totaling $676 million.

In a number of European countries, however, the general economic and financial situation became critical, and in April 1948 special assistance was provided for these countries by the Marshall Plan. As part of the Marshall Plan arrangements, the Organization for European Economic Cooperation (OEEC) was set up in Paris, and, after some initial experiments with compensation plans, the European Payments Union (EPU) came into operation for the settlement of intra-European balances. At first, the settlement of these EPU balances was graduated to a maximum rate of 50 per cent in gold or dollars and 50 per cent in credit; in 1955, this was changed to 75 per cent in gold and dollars and 25 per cent in credit. The reduction in the credit element coincided with an improvement of the working of the private credit system and a general strengthening of the reserves of the member countries. Through the mechanism of the EPU, credit was extended to a maximum of $1.5 billion. Substantial swings within this total have from time to time greatly eased the liquidity of members. It is pertinent to note that a number of countries outside of Europe belonging to currency areas centering in Europe (e.g., countries in the sterling area, French franc area, Belgian franc area, and Dutch guilder area) have largely settled their European payments, and their payments with one another, via the EPU.

The sterling balances accumulated during World War II by almost every country in the British Commonwealth had provided these countries with considerable monetary reserves. Moreover, a number of Latin American countries had also been able, during the war, to add appreciably to their monetary reserves, mainly in the form of increases in their dollar holdings.

In this situation, characterized by special assistance to Europe and the possession of relatively large monetary reserves in other parts of the world, there was little reason for members to draw on the resources of the Fund. From the point of view of business activity, the years from 1949 to 1955 were lean years for the Fund. Total transactions in this six-year period came to only $542 million, or 20 per cent less than in the two years 1947–48. In 1950, there were no transactions; and in a number of years drawings were very small—$35 million in 1951, $62 million in 1954, and $28 million in 1955. However, these years were important in other respects. In this period the Fund's working methods became fully organized, annual consultations were carried out under Article XIV with countries maintaining exchange restrictions, forms of technical assistance to member countries were developed, and policies and principles for the use of the Fund's resources were agreed upon.

Through consultations and technical assistance, the Fund became intimately acquainted with the financial problems and the economic structure of the great majority of member countries, and it has been gratifying to find the readiness with which the member countries concerned have wholeheartedly participated in this work.

One of the provisions that safeguards use of the Fund's resources by all members is the limitation that, unless there is a waiver by the Fund under Article V, drawings by any one member in any one year shall not exceed 25 per cent of its quota. As trade has grown and swings in the balance of payments have therefore widened, the Fund has increasingly used the waiver privilege in order to meet the realistic needs of its members for drawings. In fact, the granting of waivers has recently been more the rule than the exception (Table 18). The use of waivers on this scale may be taken as indicating that members' quotas are now on the low side in relation to the intentions of the signatories of the Articles of Agreement at Bretton Woods in 1944, which in turn were based upon trade data relating to the 1930's. This fact has been recognized in a number of individual cases, and increases in the quotas of nine smaller countries have been authorized in recent years.

Under the Articles of Agreement, members have automatic repurchase obligations which are broadly dependent upon the movements of their monetary reserves. In addition, however, the Fund has adopted principles under which members requesting a drawing or a stand-by arrangement are expected to undertake to repurchase within three to five years. Through these provisions the revolving nature of the Fund's resources has been emphasized and strengthened, and it is interesting to note that, of the assistance granted by the Fund up to the end of May 1958, an amount of $1.2 billion has been repurchased.

The Fund can be of maximum financial assurance to its members by developing a coherent body of precedents and principles that govern drawings by members and by adopting practices that meet their needs. The development of principles relating to drawings in different "tranches" and the creation of the stand-by were important steps in this direction. In 1952 the Fund laid down the principle that governs drawings within the gold tranche, i.e., that portion of a member's quota which can be regarded as the equivalent of its gold subscription. Within the gold tranche, members can expect to receive the overwhelming benefit of any doubt that may arise in connection with

Table 18. Use of Waiver in Fund Transactions, 1953-58

	All Transactions		Transactions with Waivers	
Calendar Year	Number	Amount *(million dollars)*	Number	Amount *(million dollars)*
1953	8	$ 203	2	$ 48
1954	3	62	2	48
1955	3	28	2	19
1956	14	693	12	665
1957	35	977	31	820
1958 [1]	12	265	11	240
Total	75	$2,228	60	$1,840

[1] Through July 31.

a request for a drawing. Subsequently, in connection with drawings in the first credit tranche, i.e., those drawings that raised the Fund's holdings of a member's currency above 100 per cent, but not beyond 125 per cent of quota, the Fund established the principle that members can confidently expect a favorable response to their applications provided they are making reasonable efforts to solve their problems. The criteria for larger drawings are still stricter, and include well-balanced and adequate programs to restore balance, to establish or maintain the enduring stability of the currency at a realistic rate of exchange, and to prepare the conditions for repayment of the drawing.

In 1952, for the first time, the Fund also approved an arrangement for a stand-by, i.e., an agreement that permits a member to draw up to a stated amount during a limited period of time, usually 6–12 months. Stand-bys are usually renewable unless either the Fund or the member determines that conditions have been basically altered so that the arrangement should be terminated. Since 1952 Fund members have made increasing use of stand-by arrangements. In the fiscal year ended April 30, 1958, stand-by arrangements were agreed or extended for 11 members, and since 1952 a total of 19 members have participated in one or more stand-bys.

The practices and principles which had been gradually formulated by the Fund proved of great value when, in the latter half of 1956, a new and more active phase began with regard to the transactions of the Fund. For the two years up to the end of April 1958, these transactions reached the total of $2.3 billion (including unused amounts under stand-by arrangements), an amount equal to nearly two thirds of all the transactions of the Fund since its inception. In comparative terms, this is equal to one quarter of the increase in all dollar balances during the postwar period, and to more than four years' increase in gold reserves from new gold production. In all, from March 1, 1947, when the Fund declared itself ready for operations, to April 30, 1958, total transactions amounted to the equivalent of $3,016 million. The Fund sold currency to 35 members, of whom 28 used the Fund's resources more than once. About 92 per cent of the currency sales was made in U.S. dollars, but there were also sales of sterling, Belgian francs, deutsche mark, Canadian dollars, and Netherlands guilders. In the same period, 37 members repurchased their currencies to the amount of $1,120 million. This total includes not only repurchases made by members in repayment of drawings, but also purchases by members who originally did not subscribe 25 per cent of their quotas in gold. In all, 18 members that originally paid in less than 25 per cent of their quotas in gold (out of a total of 32) purchased $136 million of their currency; and these purchases, added to their original gold subscriptions, put them in a position comparable to those members whose original gold subscriptions were equivalent to 25 per cent of quotas. This development is a significant commentary on the way the automatic repurchase provisions of the Fund Agreement help to ensure the revolving and liquid character of the Fund's assets.

The extent to which members of the Fund have used its resources may be compared by relating the total of their drawings and unused stand-bys (if any) to their quotas. By this measurement, the five members that made the greatest use of the Fund in relation to quota were (in order) Brazil, Chile, Iran, the United Kingdom, and Turkey. Brazil's drawings were equal to 137 per cent of quota, and Turkey's to 113 per cent of quota. In all, there were 13 members whose drawings and/or stand-bys are equivalent to 99 per cent of quota and more.

It is of particular interest to distinguish the characteristics of the transactions undertaken by the Fund during the years 1956–58.

(1) The most conspicuous transaction was the granting of financial assistance to the United Kingdom in connection with the Suez events, involving a drawing of $561 million and a stand-by of $739 million. This assistance was given on the basis of a declaration by the British Government that strict financial and credit policies would be pursued, that quantitative restrictions would not be reimposed, and that the value of sterling would be maintained. Thanks to this prompt action by the Fund, which was supplemented by a loan of $500 million from the Export-Import Bank of Washington, the position of this key currency was reinforced at a crucial moment, and a crack was avoided in the international exchange structure.

(2) In the course of 1957, the world-wide boom was accompanied by a general pressure on liquidity (internal as well as international), and a number of countries made requests for the use of the Fund's resources. The transactions included stand-by arrangements with Denmark, the Netherlands, Japan, and India. The drawings by these countries came to $428 million; the total, including stand-by arrangements granted but

not drawn upon, was $570 million. In India, the strains on the reserve position reflected to a great extent the volume of expenditure under the Five Year Plan, but the boom conditions also played their part, and private investment and imports increased at a more rapid rate than had been estimated when the Plan was drawn up. In all these cases, at the time that the requests for drawings were considered, in accordance with the principles mentioned above, the governments made statements to the Fund concerning the monetary and other relevant policies they intended to follow: in the case of stand-by arrangements, these "declarations of intent" were incorporated into the provisions of the agreements themselves.

(3) The decline in the volume of business activity which began to make itself felt in the third quarter of 1957, especially in the United States and Canada, had an effect on conditions elsewhere, and particularly on the raw material producing countries, mainly through the continued decline in the prices of primary products. Imports into the United States, and the gross supply of dollars made available to the rest of the world by trade, aid, and capital movements, however, remained at a high level. As far as the industrial countries in Europe were concerned, business activity was well sustained. In France, in particular, the rate of expansion continued to be very high and, with other expenditures increasing, a substantial deficit had to be met in the balance of payments, causing a further decline in the monetary reserves. Early in 1958, the French Government presented to the Fund a rehabilitation program and obtained, on the basis of this program, Fund assistance to the extent of $131 million, in the range of the third credit tranche. Simultaneously, France obtained $250 million through the EPU and $274 million from various U.S. agencies (largely in the form of postponements of debt service).

(4) There were many drawings by Latin American countries in the years before the most recent period. Several of these involved stabilization programs and looked forward to some simplification of the exchange system. Thus financial assistance was granted to Mexico and Colombia in 1954. Under the impact of continuing difficulties, since 1956 new transactions have been entered into with several countries in this part of the world, including Argentina, Bolivia, Brazil, Chile, Colombia, Cuba, Ecuador, El Salvador, Haiti, Honduras, Nicaragua, and Paraguay. Conditions within this group naturally varied considerably from country to country. Some of the countries (Cuba, Haiti, and Honduras) have been able to maintain convertible currencies—a result which has been facilitated by the assistance from the Fund, largely for seasonal needs. In regard to these countries, too, the policies which the governments intended to follow in the fiscal, credit, and exchange fields were outlined either as part of the stand-by agreements or in the form of special declarations. For several of these countries, assistance from other sources (including the U.S. Treasury, other U.S. agencies, and U.S. banks) has been arranged simultaneously with assistance from the Fund. In most of these cases, the Fund's assistance has been within the first credit tranche. For Brazil, however, a stand-by arrangement of June 1958 covered the third credit tranche; the Brazilian Government had presented with its request a general rehabilitation program aimed especially at the containment of inflationary pressures in the fiscal and credit spheres. From 1956 to the middle of 1958, Latin American countries have drawn more than $200 million from the Fund, and had undrawn amounts available under stand-bys of more than $50 million.

Thus the Fund has been concerned with the problems arising both in the recent boom and in the following recession. It has been expected for many years that the greatest need for the use of the Fund's resources would arise during periods of recession in the United States, leading to a drain on the monetary reserves of other countries, especially in Europe. These views were, of course, largely influenced by the difficulties that developed in the 1930's. As a matter of fact, by far the largest total of Fund transactions to date arose in the boom period of 1956–57. It is true that this period included the emergency of the Suez events, but the currencies of the two countries in Europe most immediately affected—the United Kingdom and France—were already exposed to other strains and stresses. The stresses arising from the boom were particularly evident in the period of tension in the European exchange markets in the summer of 1957, intensified by rumors about the possible revaluation of the deutsche mark. At the height of the tension in September, a number of measures were taken in the United Kingdom, including an increase in Bank Rate from 5 per cent to 7 per cent, while the Bundesbank reduced its discount rate from 4½ per cent to 4 per cent. These measures, together with strong declarations made at the Twelfth Annual Meeting of the Fund that the parities of both sterling and the deutsche mark would be maintained, proved sufficient to restore calm.

It is perhaps too early to say anything very definite about the recession of 1957–58, but one outstanding feature has been that in the first six months of 1958 there was an outflow of gold from the U.S. monetary gold stock to the extent of $1.5 billion, which more than reversed the inflow of 1957. This, taken together with the fact that the two previous postwar recessions have both been shallow and have not caused any considerable movement of funds to the United States, indicates the need for reappraising opinions with regard to the effects of a recession in the United States. At this stage it appears that a recession need not necessarily lead to a reduction in the supply of dollars. Whatever the conclusions of such a reappraisal, however, apprehensions will probably not be fully discarded, for much depends upon spending, fiscal, and credit policies in the United States and U.S. willingness not to increase tariffs in a recession. It would, indeed, be rash to conclude on the basis of postwar experience to date that there will be no drain on other countries' reserves in the event of a U.S. recession. Furthermore, it is clear that there are many ways in which disturbing movements of funds may arise, apart from a recession in the United States, and some of these may be difficult to handle.

The conclusion can only be that the Fund must remain prepared for diverse contingencies, many of which cannot clearly be defined in advance.

The Fund was able, when the Suez events occurred late in 1956, to extend financial assistance on a very considerable scale. This was due to the fact that the Fund had previously been inactive and the bulk of its resources in gold and U.S. and Canadian dollars was intact. The present situation is different. It may be that no similar grave situation needs to be envisaged, but it is desirable to see what resources the Fund would have available for an emergency today.

The Fund's available resources of gold and U.S. dollars are now about $2.2 billion, or, including Canadian dollars and deutsche mark, about $2.6 billion. From these should be deducted $880 million callable under existing stand-by arrangements. Net available gold and U.S. dollars are, therefore, about $1.3 billion, or, including its holdings of the other two currencies, about $1.7 billion. Potential drawings against these holdings cannot, of course, be known, but comparison can be made with the experience of 1956–57, when gross drawings came to $1.8 billion (allowing for repurchases, net drawings came to $1.5 billion) and the amounts callable under stand-by arrangements also increased by $800 million.

The size of Fund resources available to members may also be looked at from the point of view of their drawing rights. The unutilized drawing rights of all countries—with the exception of the United States, Canada, Germany, and China—in the gold tranche and the first and second credit tranches, and in the third credit tranche to the extent that this is provided for by existing stand-bys, amounted to $2.5 billion in June 1958. These unutilized drawing rights are relatively modest and, as a matter of fact, are equal to only 4 per cent of the imports of the countries concerned. Yet they are larger than the Fund's holdings of gold and U.S. dollars, and almost equal to these assets plus Canadian dollars and deutsche mark.

It is clear that there is no longer any great margin for the Fund to grant fully that financial assistance which, under its present practices and policies, should be available to its members.

It is also pertinent to note that the resources of the Fund constitute a much smaller proportion of international trade now than when the Fund was established. Exports in 1956 were four times as great as in 1937–38, and the size of quotas in relation to trade has fallen correspondingly. Only two countries had initial quotas equal to less than 10 per cent of trade in 1937–38, whereas in 1956, even after increases in a number of small quotas, there were 36 countries with quotas equal to or less than 10 per cent of exports (Table 19).

It may perhaps be argued that those responsible for the calculation of quotas at Bretton Woods expected that trade would expand and took this factor into account. It is quite unreasonable, however, to think that they could have envisaged a fourfold

Table 19. Fund Quotas as Per Cent of Exports, By Area, 1956[1]

		Number of Countries			
	Median Per Cent	Less than 5 per cent	5 to 9.9 per cent	10 per cent and more	Total
Latin America	8	3	9	8	20
Europe	7	2	7	4	13
Other Sterling Area	10	3	4	4	11
Rest of World	10	2	6	6	14
Total		10	26	22	58

Source: Based on data from *International Financial Statistics*, February 1958.

[1] Excluding United States, Canada, United Kingdom, and China.

increase of trade in 20 years. On the contrary, an examination of the views then generally held shows great fear of a postwar depression, which would be inconsistent with actual developments. In particular, it is unlikely that they could have foreseen that world export prices in 1957 (measured in U.S. dollars) would be almost 150 per cent higher than in 1937, and that wholesale prices in the United States would be 110 per cent higher. It is, therefore, probably fair to say that the Fund at the present time has less real resources than was contemplated at the time of Bretton Woods.

When the Fund was set up, the criticism was heard from some quarters that it might make its resources available to members too easily, and thus weaken the monetary discipline which was essential if its assets were to be truly revolving—and if countries were to make the necessary efforts to restore a balanced position internally and externally. Although thirteen years in the life of an institution such as the Fund is a short time, there would seem to be little doubt that this kind of argument would today be regarded as invalid. Instead, there is evidence suggesting that the possibility of having access to the Fund's resources may make countries more confident in their attempts to restore balance. Countries may be willing to take stricter measures than if they had to rely solely on their own resources. They seem to be encouraged by the knowledge that a second line of defense is available. In practice, they may therefore exert more discipline than if there were no Fund to draw from and consult with.

From an even broader point of view, one may say that public opinion, which still has not forgotten the hardships of the 1930's, will support the necessary disciplinary measures only if it can be assured that they are reasonable and that they will be effective. In this context, it is important that the Fund is not merely an additional source of reserve credit. It is coming to be recognized more and more as a source of credit which is available only to those member governments that have satisfied the Fund of their intention and their capacity to restore balance in their monetary affairs. The Fund thus helps to restore some measure of that international consensus and monetary discipline by which the gold standard maintained balance before World War I, and it can supply the credit to facilitate the adjustments that are required. The adjustments must still be made, but they can be made with less harshness and more rationality. If that were not the case, the granting of aid might prolong and worsen the unhealthy developments. The records are there to show that in practice the opposite has happened. Countries assisted by the Fund have shown a readiness to take corrective measures, often as part of a general program for restoring balance to their economies. The Fund thus affords an economical means of reinforcing the stability of international economic relationships in general, and of the exchange rate structure in particular.

The extent to which the Fund can discharge these most important responsibilities depends upon the consent of its members, the wisdom of its policies, and the amount of its resources.

CHAPTER FIVE: SUMMARY AND CONCLUSIONS

International liquidity is a concept with many facets. In assessing liquidity from the point of view of any individual country, account has to be taken of the various ways in which it may be able to meet, without great embarrassment, a strain on its balance of payments. This will depend not only on the degree of the strain and its available cash reserves, but also on the possibilities of mobilizing additional resources and on the effectiveness of the international credit system. The degree of strain will depend in part on general developments, such as world-wide fluctuations in business, and in part on the country's own inherent balance and its readiness to take corrective measures, if for any reason that balance is upset. For such measures to take effect, time is needed, and therefore the amount of monetary or international reserves at the country's disposal during the period of adjustment is a most important factor. Without neglecting these general considerations, a study of liquidity must therefore first direct its attention to the size of monetary reserves. While in the final analysis the reserves position of each individual country is important for the management of its affairs, it is useful to obtain an over-all picture by outlining the total of reserves available to all countries and relating them to the volume of world trade.

For all countries, except those in the communist area, the ratio of official gold and exchange reserves to imports in 1957 was 51 per cent. This is distinctly higher than in 1913, when the ratio was 21 per cent, or in 1928, when it was 42 per cent, but lower than in 1937–38, when it was as high as 100 per cent.

The effectiveness of reserves at these various dates is not necessarily indicated by the reserve percentages themselves, because conditions changed greatly during the period. Thus, reserves in 1913 were generally found to be adequate, even though they were very small in comparison with those in later periods. That was a time when there was a fair degree of balance among the various economies, when under the gold standard rules corrective measures were taken speedily, and when the international credit system was working with great effectiveness. In 1928, despite substantially higher reserves, the world economy was headed for a disaster: there were still many uncorrected maladjustments following World War I; dangerous credit policies had been pursued throughout the 1920's, not least in the international field; and individual countries had a tendency to resort too readily to tariff measures and other hindrances to trade when difficulties confronted them. On the other hand, reserves in the late 1930's, which stood at an unprecedentedly high level, were not in themselves able to give an impetus to production or trade. The world economy had been disintegrating in monetary and other respects, movements of funds were determined largely by political and monetary fears, and in many countries little scope was given to the dynamic forces of the economy.

The conclusion that can be drawn from a comparison with the past is, therefore, that the contribution of reserves to the achievement of full employment, to the increase of world trade, and to the genesis of both inflation and deflation is not a dominant one. Major world trends of production and trade are not determined solely by liquidity. The developments of the last forty years or so have been dominated not by changing liquidity ratios but rather by two major wars, several minor wars, vast expenditures preparing for wars, and large expenditures to repair the damages of wars.

In those periods, on the other hand, when war or warlike considerations are not the major factor, the broad cyclical or longer-run determinants of demand in the economically most important countries tend to dominate the world economy. If these factors are expansionary, production will rise and the value of world trade will also rise, whether world liquidity increases at the same rate or not. Therefore, the position of these larger countries is of outstanding importance, not least because the credit or fiscal policies they pursue and the role they play in the international credit system are vital factors for the trend of world liquidity in general. If their position is impaired, as it was in large measure in the 1930's, even an historically unprecedented increase in the world's stock of gold could not by itself reverse the situation.

The conditions prevailing in the late 1930's can therefore not be regarded as a useful basis for comparison with present conditions, since too many adverse factors of a non-reserve character then dominated the situation. In regard to the other years with which comparisons have been made, it must be said that, so far as the over-all picture is concerned and on a purely statistical basis, the ratio of reserves to trade in recent years cannot be considered low in itself.

The effectiveness of reserves depends, moreover, not only upon the total for all countries, but also upon their distribution among countries. After the one-sided flow of gold to the United States in the interwar period (due largely to political fears) the reserves of that country rose to such an extent that by the énd of 1949 it held 74 per cent of the world's gold stock and 56 per cent of total gold and foreign exchange reserves. Since 1949 the trend has, however, run in the opposite direction. U.S. gold holdings have fallen and holdings of U.S. dollar exchange by the rest of the world have risen. This strengthening of the reserves of other countries, taken together with the fact that U.S. gold holdings are still sufficiently large to permit that country to pursue credit and fiscal policies in a large measure independently of the flow of gold, has clearly helped to improve world liquidity.

Another large country—the Federal Republic of Germany—has in recent years so strengthened its reserve position that it, too, now has great latitude in pursuing its fiscal and monetary policies. Recent statements of authoritative persons suggest that Germany has no particular interest in further increasing its monetary reserves.

For the United Kingdom, the effects of the war, and especially the accumulation by many countries of large sterling balances, have made the country's monetary position in many respects more vulnerable to sudden movements of funds. Its balance of payments on current account has, with few exceptions, shown surpluses in the postwar years. While the funds thus becoming available did not lead to a net increase in the reserves, they nevertheless helped the work of the credit machinery centering in London, and they added to the long-term foreign assets of the United Kingdom. In 1957–58, however, stricter fiscal and credit policies, together with favorable terms of trade, led to a substantial increase in reserves, coinciding with some decline in sterling balances, so that the net position was appreciably improved. While balance of payments considerations still remain a major factor in the formation of British policies, there would now seem to be less danger of any acute exchange crisis. Nevertheless, it must be remembered that the credit system centering in London is by its very nature affected by major upsets of an economic and political character in all parts of the world, and that the strengthening of international liquidity is of interest to all who use sterling in their international transactions.

Many countries have been able to strengthen their reserve positions in recent years, though there are important exceptions. By and large, it may be said that it is the industrial countries which have either maintained or improved their reserve positions. On the other hand, many nonindustrialized countries have decreased their reserves. In some countries, these decreases were planned, and used to finance development—though some of the decreases were perhaps greater or more rapid than had been anticipated. In some countries, the decreases in reserves followed the declines in recent years in the prices of primary products or were the natural consequence of sharp or prolonged inflation. The types of change may be outlined with a few illustrations. Thus, between 1948 and 1957, the ratio of reserves to imports was reduced in Ceylon from 84 per cent to 48 per cent, and in India, from 195 per cent to 43 per cent; in fact, most sterling area countries drew upon the sterling savings which had been accumulated during the war. In Latin America, the reserve ratio percentage was reduced in Bolivia from 37 to about 1; in Peru, from 26 to 9; and in Uruguay, from 120 to 69.

While the nonindustrialized countries have the urgent problem of obtaining international financial assistance, they realize, of course, that internal balance cannot be restored without further domestic measures.

Given this situation, it is necessary to reckon with a demand for monetary reserves from countries that now have insufficient reserves. Moreover, it is likely that with the growth of their foreign trade a number of other countries will also wish to strengthen their reserve positions. Sometimes it seems to be assumed that in order not to hinder the growth of foreign trade the aggregate reserves of all countries must be increased in the same proportion as the average annual growth of foreign trade, say, something like 3 per cent per year. Examination of past experience suggests, however, that there is no such fixed mathematical relation between the growth of foreign trade and the increase in reserves. It seems more realistic to assume that countries with really large reserves will not find it imperative to increase their holdings—and it may unfortunately also prove to be the case that some countries which ought to augment their reserves will not carry out the policies that would make such an increase possible.

Since the amount becoming available for monetary purposes from current gold production, without allowing for any receipts from dishoarding, is likely at the present price of gold to be about $700 million a year, it would seem that gold output alone can make a very substantial contribution to satisfying the need for increased reserves. Since it is, moreover, likely that there will be some increase in exchange holdings, the reserve problem with which the world will be faced over the next decade does not seem to be too difficult, provided that further progress is made, by sensible policies, in restoring and maintaining balance in the individual economies, in avoiding increased obstacles to trade, and in strengthening the international credit system.

These provisos are important, since the adequacy of reserves, both for the world as a whole and for individual countries, can be judged only in a broad international context. For example, a given level of reserves will have one degree of adequacy when economic conditions between countries are in reasonable balance and when exchange rates are appropriate. If these conditions are not satisfied, the same reserves will have a different degree of adequacy. Similarly, from the point of view of any one country, reserves that may be adequate if the country is following a program of development with stability may appear totally inadequate when it has an unbalanced budget or active credit inflation. No amount of reserves is adequate to finance a continuous deficit in the balance of payments resulting from excessive spending or insufficient revenue. In these cases, the immediate task is clearly to adopt fiscal and monetary policies that will restore external and internal equilibrium.

Over fairly long periods, some countries have had relatively large reserves (e.g., the United States, Switzerland, Portugal, and Venezuela), while others (e.g., the Scandinavian countries) have traditionally held rather low reserves in relation to their foreign trade. One cannot escape the conclusion that in this matter tradition and convention play a considerable role. Several of the countries with slender reserves have, even in the generally favorable economic environment of the postwar period, been beset by difficulties which those with larger reserves could take in their stride. Many countries may state that their reserves are too low or wish that they might be larger, without being prepared to take the steps necessary to strengthen them. An increase in reserves is part of a country's investments. It requires, like other investments, a counterpart in the form of uncommitted savings of one sort or another, as happens, for instance, when debts to the central bank are repaid from genuine budget surpluses.

At the end of 1957, the official reserves of all countries (outside the communist area) consisted of $37.0 billion in gold and $15.9 billion in foreign exchange, making together $52.9 billion. The quality of reserves is now undoubtedly sounder than it was in the late 1920's. At that time, a large part of the foreign exchange holdings was the counterpart of short-term foreign credits; now, for the most part, countries holding reserves are also their beneficial owners.

The short-term lending mechanism, which is an indispensable element in the liquidity of any international monetary system, may not yet be as efficient as it was in the days of supreme monetary confidence before World War I, but it is certainly better than in the period between the two World Wars. Private holdings of foreign currencies, needed as working capital for the financing of trade and other international payments, have in a fair degree been reconstituted. About 40 per cent of the foreign-owned dollar balances in the United States are privately owned and, after some rather violent fluctuations in the course of 1956–57, sterling balances were very largely replenished in the first six months of 1958. With an increase in monetary confidence and a relaxation of exchange controls, it is likely that, as was the case before 1914, equilibrating movements of funds will be facilitated. These, up to a point, should reduce the strain on official reserves. The fact that the monetary authorities in most countries have again begun to pursue flexible credit policies, including fairly frequent changes in interest rates, should be very helpful in encouraging such a development. It is certainly too early to conclude that the shifts in leads and lags, which from time to time during the postwar period have given rise to such disturbing movements of funds, will not occur again. Nevertheless, the way in which appropriate credit policies in the last few years have been able to reverse those movements is a hopeful sign for the future. Financial assistance from international institutions, including both the European Payments Union and the International Monetary Fund, have been helpful in this connection.

The important contribution of international institutions to liquidity has been a new development in the period after World War II. The financial activities of the International Monetary Fund were at a low ebb for several years. During these years, many countries in Europe met their needs with the help of funds provided by the Marshall Plan, and many countries outside Europe were able to use the liquid resources they had accumulated during the war (sterling balances in the British Commonwealth, and dollar balances in the Latin American countries). In connection with Marshall Aid, a system of intra-European settlements gradually evolved into the European Payments Union, which made an important contribution to liquidity, especially at the time when the private credit system had not yet been restored to working order.

For the Fund, the years of little business activity, stretching from 1948 to 1955, were used to get its working methods fully organized; to start the system of consultations with countries maintaining exchange restrictions required under Article XIV; to develop forms of technical assistance to member countries; and, what has proved very important, to agree on the policies and principles to be applied to requests for the use of the Fund's resources.

While requests for drawings of 25 per cent of a country's quota, normally corresponding to its own gold subscription, are almost automatically approved, the principle has been established that for the next 25 per cent members are required to show that they are making a reasonable effort to solve their own problems. For drawings beyond these limits, more substantial justification is required: namely, that the drawings must be in support of a sound program likely to ensure enduring stability at realistic rates of exchange. These principles are also applicable to requests for stand-by arrangements, and they proved to be of great practical value when, in the autumn of 1956, there was a distinct upturn in the business activity of the Fund—beginning with the financial assistance granted to the United Kingdom in connection with the Suez events, and followed by drawings and stand-by arrangements with a great number of countries in various parts of the world. In all these cases, when requests for drawings and stand-by arrangements were considered, the governments made statements to the Fund concerning the monetary and other relevant policies they intended to follow.

It is important to remember that the Fund is not merely an additional source of reserve credit available to the monetary authorities of its members. It is recognized more and more as a source of credit which is available only to member governments that have satisfied the Fund of their intention and their capacity to restore balance in their monetary affairs. The Fund thus helps to restore some measure of that monetary discipline by which the gold standard in its way maintained balance before World War I, but it also supplies a measure of credit by which harshness may be mitigated.

Total drawings on the Fund from its inception to the end of July 1958 amounted to $3.1 billion; in addition, at the end of July 1958 undrawn balances under existing stand-by arrangements amounted to $800 million. But the Fund's significance for international liquidity is greater than the amounts drawn would suggest, for several reasons: first, the Fund's resources constitute a particularly efficient form of reserves, since their use can be pinpointed to particular areas of financial strain; second, as already mentioned, drawings are generally coupled with specific undertakings with respect to monetary and fiscal policy on the part of the countries concerned; and, third, the favorable technical judgment of a country's economic and financial program, implied in the approval of a drawing by the Fund, not infrequently simplifies that country's task in obtaining additional sums from other sources. Furthermore, the possibility of having access to the Fund's resources, even when no assistance is actually granted, may make countries more confident in their attempts to restore balance—making them willing to take stricter measures than if they had to rely on their own resources alone. They may be encouraged by the knowledge that a second line of defense is available to them. In practice, they may therefore exert more discipline than if these opportunities did not exist.

It seems sometimes to have been assumed that the Fund would be called upon to render assistance particularly in periods of recession in the United States which, in accordance with the experiences of the 1930's, were expected to put a strain on the balances of payments of other countries. As a matter of fact, by far the major part of the financial transactions of the Fund so far have occurred in the boom period of 1956–57. It is true that the largest of these transactions, the financial assistance to the United Kingdom at the time of the Suez events, was of an emergency nature not directly connected with the boom. Subsequently, some other important transactions were undertaken to bring temporary relief to countries with deficits in their balances of payments resulting from the strains of an exaggerated boom in their own domestic economies. There have recently been some transactions which can be associated with the recession that began in the latter half of 1957, but they have been for relatively limited amounts. While raw material producing countries have suffered from the decline in the prices of primary products, the fact that the 1957–58 recession in the United States has been accompanied by an outflow of gold from that country has helped many countries, especially in Europe, to strengthen their monetary reserves. It can, of course, not be concluded that a recession in the United States will always have similar results. Nevertheless, experience in the last two years clearly indicates that the need for assistance from the Fund may arise quite independently of any particular phase of the business cycle. Indeed, the Fund must be prepared for diverse contingencies, many of which cannot be defined in advance.

The Fund was able, at the time of the events of Suez, to extend financial assistance on a very considerable scale. This was due largely to the fact that in the previous years there had been very few transactions, so that the bulk of the Fund's resources in gold and convertible currencies was intact. Since then, the many transactions undertaken by the Fund have considerably reduced its uncommitted holdings of gold and convertible currencies, which at the end of July 1958 amounted to $1.4 billion. On the other hand, some drawings have already been made in currencies other than U.S. dollars, such as deutsche mark, guilders, and sterling, and perhaps more use will be made of these currencies in the future. The Fund has authorized drawings to meet the balance of payments effects of changing levels of production and trade, to support stabilization programs, and to meet short-term strains in the balance of payments. It was able at the time of the Suez events to prevent a disruption of the exchange structure. Past experiences have shown that when cracks occur, they may not be confined only to the currencies immediately affected. The consequences of allowing such cracks to widen and spread may indeed be serious.

The question has been raised, for good reasons, whether the resources of the Fund are adequate for present tasks. The resources available to the Fund were determined at the Bretton Woods Conference in 1944, and most of the data on international trade available to the Conference related to the period before the war. The physical volume of world exports fell by 7 per cent from 1937 to 1947, but in the next ten years increased by 90 per cent, a rate of expansion almost unknown in the past. The prices of goods moving in international trade increased by 140 per cent between 1937 and 1957. Fluctuations in the balance of payments which may require use of the Fund's resources are therefore potentially much larger now than when the Fund quotas were established. If any lack of confidence were to set in, the potential movements of funds connected with shifts in the financing of trade would likewise be larger. The Fund's ability to provide assurance to its members and to act quickly on a massive scale if emergencies arise depends upon its having adequate resources, which have been made available in advance of any specific emergency. It is doubtful whether, in the circumstances of the world today, with world trade greatly expanded in volume and value, the Fund's resources are sufficient to enable it fully to perform its duties under the Articles of Agreement.

STATISTICAL APPENDIX

Appendix Table 1. Gross Official Reserves (Gold and Exchange), Imports, and Reserves as Per Cent of Imports, by Country, Selected Years, 1928-57

(Value figures in millions of U.S. dollars)

Country and Area	1928			1937			1948			1950			1951		
	Re-serves	Im-ports	Per Cent	Re-serves	Im-ports	Per Cent	Re-serves	Im-ports	Per Cent	Re-serves	Im-ports	Per Cent	Re-serves	Im-ports	Per Cent
United States	3,746	4,427	85	12,790	3,573	358	24,399	8,058	303	22,820	9,601	238	22,873	11,882	193
Canada	93	1,364	7	200	939	21	1,011	3,024	33	1,770	3,202	55	1,826	4,194	44
Latin America	1,160	2,453	47	875	1,717	51	2,750	6,224	44	3,125	5,630	56	2,925	7,831	37
Dollar Countries	125	862	15	150	665	23	1,075	2,836	38	1,425	2,700	53	1,525	3,411	45
Bolivia	9	23	39	7	24	29	28	79	37	29	64	45	34	99	34
Colombia	62	161	39	20	96	21	84	337	25	101	365	28	125	419	30
Costa Rica	....	....	....	1	12	8	5	42	12	4	46	8	8	56	14
Cuba	....	234	....	1[1]	146	1	316	591	53	418	608	69	495	754	66
Dominican Republic	....	30	....	3[1]	13	23	15	74	20	19	50	38	30	86	35
Ecuador	8	16	50	5	14	36	28	60	47	37	49	76	31	62	50
El Salvador	5	18	28	8	10	80	30	41	73	41	48	85	43	63	68
Guatemala	5	31	16	8	21	38	46	68	68	37	71	52	40	81	49
Haiti	....	....	....	2	9	22	8	31	26	10	38	26	13	44	30
Honduras	....	....	....	1[1]	12	8	2[1]	37	5	11	39	28	20	53	38
Mexico	10	185	5	30	175	17	78	561	14	291	556	52	254	822	31
Nicaragua	....	....	....	1	7	14	3	28	11	3	29	10	9	35	26
Panama[1]	....	....	....	5[4]	24	21	44	73	60	38	70	54	49	76	64
Venezuela	21	81	26	59[1]	102	58	378	814	46	373	667	56	373	761	49
Non-Dollar Countries	1,035	1,591	65	725	1,052	69	1,675	3,388	49	1,750	2,930	60	1,400	4,420	32
Argentina	607	807	75	539	493	109	579	1,590	36	655	1,187	55	520	1,480	35
Brazil	177	441	40	50	335	15	758	1,134	67	666	1,098	61	517	2,011	26
Chile	120	163	74	38	89	43	59	269	22	58	247	23	55	328	17
Paraguay	....	13	....	1	10	10	6	27	22	13	22	59	18	29	62
Peru	47	70	67	26	59	44	44	168	26	54	176	31	60	262	23
Uruguay[3]	83	97	86	75	66	114	241	200	120	312	200	156	223	310	72
Continental EPU Countries	5,140	11,103	46	6,600	8,680	78	5,875	14,519	40	6,900	16,473	42	7,500	22,033	34
Austria	126	456	28	73	269	27	62	490	13	91	477	19	106	653	16
Belgium	345	889	39	827	928	89	938	2,046	46	733	1,942	38	1,019	2,535	40
Denmark	77	441	17	70	369	19	84	714	12	97	853	11	118	1,013	12
France[4]	2,541	2,097	121	2,784	1,689	165	....	3,443	....	1,334	3,030	44	912	4,457	20
Germany	776	3,335	23	....	2,196	....	295	....	....	274	2,697	10	518	3,491	15
Greece	55	161	34	34	140	54	189	364	52	187	428	44	132	398	33
Italy	583	1,173	50	212	734	29	539	1,539	35	878	1,488	59	1,003	2,167	46
Netherlands	263	1,078	24	938	883	106	343	1,871	18	606	2,056	29	618	2,553	24
Norway	50	269	19	132	320	41	141	750	19	122	679	18	151	878	17
Portugal	25	120	21	75	106	71	509	414	123	471	274	172	555	330	168
Sweden	121	458	26	513	541	95	233	1,377	17	289	1,182	24	484	1,776	27
Switzerland	152	512	30	774	414	187	1,660	1,163	143	1,579	1,056	150	1,644	1,375	120
Turkey	21	114	18	49	91	54	192	348	55	214	311	69	217	407	53

United Kingdom	748	5,795	13	4,141[6]	5,082	81	2,009	8,370	24	3,668	7,305	50	2,374	10,934	22
Other Sterling Area Countries	754	2,670	28	1,425	2,870	46	7,275	7,627	95	5,550	6,528	85	5,225	9,652	54
Australia	200	669	30	332	526	63	1,265	1,411	90	1,492	1,622	92	1,134	2,422	47
Burma	....[5]	75	....	....[5]	91	....	114	176	65	119	111	107	159	137	116
Ceylon	....[5]	193	....	....[5]	90	....	254	301	84	191	245	78	217	327	66
Iceland	1[6]	17	6	1	12	8	13	71	18	8	38	21	9	57	16
India	440	837	53	590	671	88	3,354	1,716	195	2,000	1,165	172	1,888	1,793	105
Iraq	....	34	....	26	48	54	139	183	76	117	105	111	114	143	80
Ireland	....	288	....	59	219	27	209	549	38	245	446	55	206	573	36
Malaya	....	....	....	102	388	27	227	842	27	229	952	24	262	1,554	17
New Zealand	35	218	16	92	253	36	236	450	52	172	455	38	217	596	36
Pakistan[9]	....[5]	....[5]	....	....[5]	....[5]	....	800	312	256	507	403	126	638	549	116
Union of South Africa	78	393	20	228	572	40	652	1,616	40	476	986	48	386	1,501	26
Rest of World	1,400	2,813	50	1,525	2,273	67	3,175	4,273	74	3,200	4,312	74	3,800	6,854	55
China (Taiwan)	....	....	....	....	....	....	....	....	....	15	120	12	49	145	34
Egypt	178	249	71	218	197	111	1,408	674	209	979	583	168	957	678	141
Ethiopia	....	....	....	....	....	....	15	37	41	14	27	52	20	40	50
Finland	27	202	13	73	199	37	74	488	15	84	388	22	209	676	31
Indonesia	....	403	....	66	283	23	207	464	45	356	440	81	511	873	59
Iran	....	76	....	34	84	40	273	167	163	252	262	96	196	211	93
Israel[10]	....	33	....	56	79	71	134	164	82	62	299	21	33	380	9
Japan[12]	598	990	60	297	1,138	26	....	684	....	564	974	58	924	1,995	46
Korea	....	....	....	....	....	....	....	....	....	27	....	....	38	....	....
Lebanon	....[8]	....[8]	....	....	....	....	74	....[8]	....	38	....	....	40	133	30
Philippines	50[7]	149	34	....	125	....	400	655	61	296	384	77	247	550	45
Spain	512	580	88	525	....	....	118[4]	468	25	75	390	19	60	384	16
Syria	....	51	....	....	....	....	84	214	39	....	....	....	19	133	14
Thailand	43[7]	80	54	52	49	106	217	144	151	288	209	138	359	272	132
Viet-Nam	....	....	....	....	....	....	....	....	....	....	....	....	....	....	....
Yugoslavia	....	....	....	61	119	43	38	314	12	17	236	7	21	384	6

Sources: For 1928, "The Adequacy of Monetary Reserves," *Staff Papers*, Vol. III, No. 2 (October 1953), pp. 181–227. For other years, *International Financial Statistics (IFS)*, February 1958 and following issues; footnotes to the summary trade and reserves tables therein apply to this table.

[1] Reserves not held officially.

[2] *IFS* estimate.

[3] Reserves data are gold and net foreign exchange. The nature of liabilities deducted from gross assets is unknown. Prior to 1951, forward exchange liabilities are also deducted. For 1955, gold only, since net foreign exchange is negative.

[4] Reserves estimated by Fund staff.

[5] Included with India.

[6] Gold only.

[7] Foreign exchange only.

[8] Included with Syria.

[9] Beginning with 1952, includes holdings of Issue Department only.

[10] Official and banks.

[11] End of November 1957.

[12] Excludes gold under dispute.

Appendix Table 1, *cont.* Gross Official Reserves (Gold and Exchange), Imports, and Reserves as Per Cent of Imports, by Country, Selected Years, 1928-57

(Value figures in millions of U.S. dollars)

	1952			1953			1954			1955			1956			1957		
Country and Area	Re-serves	Im-ports	Per Cent	Re-serves	Im-ports	Per Cent	Re-serves	Im-ports	Per Cent	Re-serves	Im-ports	Per Cent	Re-serves	Im-ports	Per Cent	Re-serves	Im-ports	Per Cent
United States	23,252	11,662	199	22,091	11,792	187	21,793	11,047	197	21,752	12,369	176	22,058	13,751	160	22,857	14,174	161
Canada	1,864	4,480	42	1,827	4,824	38	1,954	4,551	43	1,910	5,156	37	1,945	6,270	31	1,836	6,346	29
Latin America	2,925	7,683	38	3,200	6,541	49	3,025	7,411	41	3,150	7,550	42	3,675	7,940	46	3,775	9,100	41
Dollar Countries	1,600	3,563	45	1,650	3,578	46	1,675	3,898	43	1,850	4,135	45	2,325	4,621	50	2,725	5,202	52
Bolivia	29	107	27	24	78	31	11	73	15	6	81	7	4	84	5	1	70[3]	1
Colombia	155	415	37	190	547	35	257	672	38	136	669	20	131	657	20	145	477	30
Costa Rica	16	68	24	18	74	24	16	80	20	20	87	23	12	91	13	12	103	12
Cuba	448	745	60	481	591	81	454	599	76	493	633	78	479	714	67	441	706	62
Dominican Republic	32	111	29	28	99	28	36	94	38	36	114	32	37	126	29	46	136	34
Ecuador	44	70	63	39	75	52	38	120	32	34	112	30	32	108	30	39	110	35
El Salvador	44	69	64	43	72	60	44	87	51	39	92	42	39	105	37	40	115	35
Guatemala	43	76	57	41	80	51	39	86	45	54	104	52	70	138	51	74	149	50
Haiti	13	53	25	10	44	23	11	48	23	8	46	17	7	50	14	4	40	10
Honduras	21	66	32	22	62	35	24	59	41	19	62	31	18	67	27	15	76	20
Mexico	250	807	31	218	807	27	201	800	25	418	885	47	500	1,072	47	419[11]	1,155	36
Nicaragua	15	47	32	16	51	31	13	68	19	14	70	20	7	69	10	11	81	14
Panama[1]	52	84	62	52	82	63	48	83	58	42	88	48	42	98	43	29	116	25
Venezuela	434	845	51	477	916	52	475	1,029	46	526	1,092	48	939	1,249	75	1,440	1,868	77
Non-Dollar Countries	1,325	4,120	32	1,550	2,963	52	1,375	3,513	39	1,300	3,414	38	1,350	3,312	41	1,050	3,898	27
Argentina	420	1,179	36	532	795	67	524	979	54	457	1,173	40	381	1,128	34	311	1,310	24
Brazil	529	2,010	26	605	1,319	46	483	1,630	30	491	1,306	38	612	1,234	50	474	1,489	32
Chile	69	370	19	68	335	20	39	343	11	83	376	22	76	354	21	46	441	10
Paraguay	8	36	22	6	28	21	4	37	11	6	34	18	8	29	28	13	32	41
Peru	56	288	19	49	293	17	56	250	22	52	300	17	67	361	19	34	400	9
Uruguay[3]	238	237	100	291	193	151	257	274	94	216	225	96	203	206	99	157	226	69
Continental EPU Countries	8,625	21,819	40	10,100	21,287	48	11,425	23,701	48	12,875	27,200	47	13,400	31,126	43	14,575	34,384	42
Austria	152	652	23	320	546	59	412	653	63	361	887	41	406	974	42	510	1,128	45
Belgium	1,030	2,444	42	1,067	2,405	44	1,032	2,535	41	1,127	2,830	40	1,143	3,272	35	1,132	3,432	33
Denmark	142	962	15	167	1,000	17	143	1,170	12	133	1,178	11	131	1,311	10	172	1,359	13
France[4]	987	4,326	23	956	3,942	24	1,369	4,221	32	2,076	4,739	44	1,356	5,553	24	775	6,170	13
Germany	1,190	3,814	31	1,958	3,771	52	2,636	4,571	58	3,076	5,793	53	4,291	6,617	65	5,644	7,478	75
Greece	141	346	41	191	296	65	199	330	60	210	382	55	218	464	47	192	525	37
Italy	918	2,336	39	952	2,420	39	1,041	2,439	43	1,237	2,711	46	1,308	3,174	41	1,532	3,626	42
Netherlands	1,037	2,224	47	1,224	2,376	52	1,276	2,858	45	1,277	3,208	40	1,072	3,725	29	1,056	4,105	26
Norway	151	874	17	142	912	16	138	1,019	14	165	1,090	15	179	1,211	15	183	1,274	14
Portugal	563	347	162	616	332	186	655	351	187	671	398	169	693	443	156	687	502	137
Sweden	446	1,730	26	507	1,579	32	478	1,776	27	470	1,997	24	473	2,209	21	456	2,424	19
Switzerland	1,667	1,208	138	1,768	1,176	150	1,837	1,300	141	1,846	1,489	124	1,893	1,766	107	1,918	1,964	98
Turkey	191	556	34	213	532	40	205	478	43	211	498	42	230	407	57	315	397	79

United Kingdom	1,958	9,738	20	2,546	9,361	27	2,798	9,447	30	2,156	10,867	20	2,172	10,881	20	2,374	11,412	21
Other Sterling Area Countries	4,625	8,954	52	5,025	7,298	69	5,000	7,924	63	4,700	8,817	53	4,525	9,093	50	4,050	9,969	41
Australia	1,032	1,979	52	1,362	1,471	93	1,133	1,869	61	835	2,160	39	953	1,964	49	1,321	1,931	68
Burma	198	192	103	211	178	119	124	204	61	92	181	51	121	198	61	93	297	31
Ceylon	163	358	46	114	338	34	169	293	58	204	307	66	221	342	65	183	379	48
Iceland	9	56	16	16	68	24	20	69	29	14	78	18	14	90	16	16	83	19
India	1,729	1,696	102	1,765	1,208	146	1,782	1,297	137	1,791	1,413	127	1,360	1,698	80	878	2,022	43
Iraq	129	173	75	181	192	94	233	204	114	294	273	108	354	321	110	261	343	76
Ireland	220	482	46	234	511	46	260	504	52	243	582	42	234	512	46	258	517	50
Malaya	273	1,265	22	270	1,058	26	291	1,026	28	315	1,249	25	324	1,357	24	328	1,431	23
New Zealand	183	773	24	271	538	50	239	688	35	179	802	22	194	751	26	138	830	17
Pakistan[9]	296	630	47	296	350	85	328	334	98	370	290	128	373	417	89	291	440	66
Union of South Africa	382	1,350	28	295	1,386	21	416	1,436	29	366	1,482	25	372	1,524	24	288	1,696	17
Rest of World	3,500	7,038	50	3,250	7,380	44	3,525	7,344	48	4,000	8,290	48	4,050	9,676	42	3,400	11,375	30
China (Taiwan)	44	187	24	54	192	28	34	211	16	61	201	30	79	194	41	108	212	51
Egypt	752	640	118	728	516	141	732	472	155	641	538	119	566	535	106	465	524	89
Ethiopia	25	43	58	42	53	79	50	61	82	55	68	81	57	63	90	64	78	82
Finland	133	792	17	145	530	27	211	656	32	219	769	28	174	885	20	171	900	19
Indonesia	314	948	33	212	765	28	248	629	39	307	604	51	254	856	30	221	797	28
Iran	177	124	143	185	156	119	186	230	81	205	295[2]	69	230	335[2]	69	245	375[2]	65
Israel[10]	30	321	9	33	281	12	68	287	24	85	325	26	86	364	24	81	407	20
Japan[12]	1,101	2,028	54	895	2,410	37	1,022	2,399	43	1,339	2,471	54	1,507	3,230	47	1,019	4,284	24
Korea	83	....	....	109	347	31	108	241	45	96	326	29	99	369	27	116	432	27
Lebanon	42	138	30	55	144	38	76	174	44	86	218	39	88	237	37	99	252	39
Philippines	236	484	49	240	534	45	207	545	38	155	641	24	161	597	27	71	727	10
Spain	61	518	12	80	596	13	117	614	19	151	617	24	89	767	12	69	862	8
Syria	29	138	21	44	131	34	47	174	27	48	179	27	62	187	33	54	171	32
Thailand	352	304	116	302	330	92	273	312	88	298	334	89	311	365	85	329	404	81
Viet-Nam	....	....	....	....	....	....	....	....	....	124	263	47	132	218	61	137	289	47
Yugoslavia	16	373	4	18	395	5	24	339	7	29	441	7	43	474	9	39	661	6

Sources: For 1928, "The Adequacy of Monetary Reserves," *Staff Papers*, Vol. III, No. 2 (October 1953), pp. 181–227. For other years, *International Financial Statistics (IFS)*, February 1958 and following issues; footnotes to the summary trade and reserves tables therein apply to this table.

[1] Reserves not held officially.

[2] *IFS* estimate.

[3] Reserves data are gold and net foreign exchange. The nature of liabilities deducted from gross assets is unknown. Prior to 1951, forward exchange liabilities are also deducted. For 1955, gold only, since net foreign exchange is negative.

[4] Reserves estimated by Fund staff.

[5] Included with India.

[6] Gold only.

[7] Foreign exchange only.

[8] Included with Syria.

[9] Beginning with 1952, includes holdings of Issue Department only.

[10] Official and banks.

[11] End of November 1957.

[12] Excludes gold under dispute.

Appendix Table 2. Reserve Holdings of Gold and Foreign Exchange, By Area, Selected Years, 1928-57
(In millions of U.S. dollars)

Area	Gold	Foreign Exchange	Total	% Foreign Exchange	Gold	Foreign Exchange	Total	% Foreign Exchange	Gold	Foreign Exchange	Total	% Foreign Exchange
		1928				1937				1938		
World	9,800	3,250	13,050	25	25,300	2,400	27,700	9	25,950	1,800	27,700	7
World minus United States	6,054	3,250	9,300	35	12,510	2,400	14,910	16	11,358	1,800	13,108	14
Canada	93	—	93	—	180	20	200	10	186	34	220	15
Latin America	985	175	1,160	15	725	150	875	17	675	100	800	12
Dollar Area	70	55	125	44	125	25	150	17	125	50	175	29
Non-Dollar Area	915	120	1,035	12	600	125	725	17	550	75	625	12
Continental EPU Countries	2,785	2,355	5,140	46	5,950	800	6,750	12	6,125	525	6,625	8
United Kingdom	748	—	748	—	4,141	....	4,141	....	2,877	....	2,877	....
Other Sterling Area	385	369	754	49	500	925	1,425	65	534	625	1,170	54
All Other Countries	1,060	340	1,400	24	975	475	1,475	33	925	500	1,395	35
		1948				1949				1950		
World	32,750	13,700	46,450	29	33,150	10,500	43,650	24	33,550	13,550	47,000	29
World minus United States	8,351	13,700	22,051	62	8,587	10,500	19,087	55	10,730	13,550	24,180	56
Canada	401	610	1,011	60	486	636	1,122	57	580	1,190	1,770	67
Latin America	1,500	1,275	2,750	46	1,650	1,125	2,775	41	1,875	1,300	3,125	41
Dollar Area	800	275	1,075	26	875	325	1,200	27	1,025	375	1,425	27
Non-Dollar Area	700	1,000	1,700	59	775	825	1,600	52	825	925	1,750	53
Continental EPU Countries	3,550	2,325	5,875	40	3,850	2,325	6,175	38	3,950	2,975	6,900	43
United Kingdom	1,605	404	2,009	20	1,350	402	1,752	23	2,900	768	3,668	21
Other Sterling Area	575	6,675	7,275	92	550	4,125	4,657	88	600	4,950	5,550	89
All Other Countries	725	2,400	3,125	77	725	1,875	2,600	72	800	2,350	3,175	75

	1951				1952				1953			
World	33,650	12,900	46,500	28	33,550	13,200	46,700	28	33,900	14,100	48,000	29
World minus United States	10,777	12,900	23,627	54	10,298	13,200	23,448	56	11,809	14,100	25,909	54
Canada	842	984	1,826	54	885	979	1,864	53	986	841	1,827	46
Latin America	1,950	950	2,925	33	1,825	1,075	2,900	37	1,925	1,300	3,200	40
Dollar Area	1,050	475	1,525	31	925	675	1,600	42	925	750	1,650	45
Non-Dollar Area	900	500	1,400	36	900	425	1,300	32	1,000	550	1,550	35
Continental EPU Countries	4,150	3,350	7,500	45	4,525	4,125	8,625	48	5,125	5,000	10,100	50
United Kingdom	2,200	174	2,374	7	1,500	458	1,958	23	2,300	246	2,546	10
Other Sterling Area	625	4,600	5,225	88	625	4,000	4,625	86	625	4,400	5,025	88
All Other Countries	975	2,800	3,775	74	925	2,525	3,475	73	850	2,350	3,225	73

	1954				1955				1956			
World	34,450	15,100	49,500	30	34,950	15,650	50,550	31	35,550	16,250	51,800	31
World minus United States	12,657	15,100	27,707	54	13,198	15,650	28,798	54	13,492	16,250	29,742	55
Canada	1,073	882	1,954	45	1,134	776	1,910	41	1,103	841	1,945	43
Latin America	1,850	1,200	3,025	39	1,850	1,300	3,150	41	1,875	1,800	3,675	49
Dollar Area	850	850	1,675	50	875	975	1,850	53	1,050	1,275	2,325	55
Non-Dollar Area	1,000	375	1,375	27	1,000	325	1,300	25	825	525	1,350	39
Continental EPU Countries	5,650	5,800	11,425	51	6,550	6,350	12,875	49	7,175	6,250	13,400	47
United Kingdom	2,550	248	2,798	9	2,050	106	2,156	5	1,800	372	2,172	17
Other Sterling Area	675	4,325	5,000	86	700	4,000	4,700	85	700	3,825	4,525	85
All Other Countries	825	2,625	3,475	76	875	3,125	3,975	78	850	3,150	4,025	79

	1957			
World	37,000	15,900	52,900	30
World minus United States	14,143	15,900	30,043	53
Canada	1,100	736	1,836	40
Latin America	1,900	1,900	3,800	50
Dollar Area	1,200	1,550	2,725	56
Non-Dollar Area	700	350	1,050	33
Continental EPU Countries	7,975	6,625	14,575	45
United Kingdom	1,600	774	2,374	33
Other Sterling Area	700	3,350	4,050	83
All Other Countries	850	2,525	3,375	75

Sources: For 1928, "The Adequacy of Monetary Reserves," *Staff Papers*, Vol. III, No. 2 (October 1953), pp. 181-227; for 1938, *International Financial Statistics (IFS)*, December 1954; for 1949, *IFS*, August 1955; and for 1937 and 1950-57, *IFS*, June 1958. Data for 1948 were prepared but not published in revised form. Totals may not equal sum of items because of rounding.

Appendix Table 3. Reconciliation of Foreign Exchange Assets and Liabilities, 1947-57

(In millions of U.S. dollars)

	1947	1948	1949	1950	1951	1952	1953	1954	1955	1956	1957
World Total											
Total gross assets	13,900	13,900	10,850	13,600	13,000	13,300	14,250	15,250	15,750	16,400	16,050
Liabilities of U.S.	1,850	2,900	3,050	4,450	4,050	5,250	6,050	7,000	7,900	8,600	8,300
Liabilities of U.K.	12,147	10,774	7,414	7,775	7,646	6,328	6,825	6,980	6,591	6,220	5,833
EPU liabilities	—	—	—	402	665	1,077	1,272	1,108	994	1,086	1,269
BIS deposits	8	52	108	250	192	364	352	465	412	424	409
Excess of reported assets	−105	174	278	723	447	281	−249	−303	−147	70	239
Canada											
Total gross assets	232	610	636	1,190	984	979	841	882	776	841	736
Liabilities of U.S.	215	596	631	1,162	937	975	832	870	767	833	728
Liabilities of U.K.	17	13	5	28	47	4	9	12	9	8	8
Latin America											
Dollar Countries											
Total gross assets	275	275	325	375	475	675	725	825	975	1,275	1,550
Liabilities of U.S.	375	400	550	350	450	625	700	800	950	1,150	1,400
Excess of reported assets	−100	−125	−225	25	25	50	25	25	25	125	150
Non-Dollar Countries											
Total gross assets	1,275	1,125	725	925	500	425	550	375	325	525	350
Liabilities of U.S.	200	250	250	350	175	175	200	225	225	275	150
Liabilities of U.K.	947	544	224	126	160	17	112	22	25	90	87
Excess of reported assets	128	331	251	449	165	233	238	128	75	160	113

Continental EPU Countries											
Total gross assets	2,050	2,325	2,475	2,975	3,350	4,125	5,000	5,800	6,350	6,250	6,625
Liabilities of U.S.	650	700	675	1,100	1,100	1,675	2,450	3,350	4,025	3,900	3,725
Liabilities of U.K.	1,689	1,245	997	879	918	669	624	683	596	540	722
EPU liabilities	—	—	—	177	665	1,077	1,272	1,108	994	1,086	1,269
BIS deposits	8	52	108	250	192	364	352	465	412	424	409
Excess of reported assets	−297	328	695	569	475	340	302	197	323	300	500
United Kingdom											
Total gross assets	208	404	402	768	174	458	246	248	106	372	774
Liabilities of U.S.	59	251	338	400	135	346	218	212	70	333	673
EPU liabilities	—	—	—	225	—	—	—	—	—	—	—
Excess of reported assets	149	153	64	143	39	112	28	36	36	39	101
Other Sterling Area Countries											
Total gross assets	7,550	6 675	4,400	4,950	4,650	4,050	4,475	4,400	4,075	3,900	3,400
Liabilities of U.S.	75	50	75	100	75	150	200	200	225	200	200
Liabilities of U.K.	7,173	6,820	4,738	5,353	5,070	4,523	5,044	5,059	4,793	4,734	4,333
Excess of reported assets	302	−195	−413	−503	−495	−623	−769	−859	−943	−1,034	−1,133
Rest of the World											
Total gross assets	2,275	2,450	1,850	2,400	2,850	2,575	2,425	2,700	3,175	3,225	2,600
Liabilities of U.S.	500	625	500	1,000	1,125	1,325	1,400	1,300	1,650	1,875	1,375
Liabilities of U.K.	2,321	2,152	1,450	1,389	1,450	1,114	1,036	1,204	1,168	848	683
Excess of reported assets	−550	−327	−100	11	275	136	−11	196	357	502	542

Sources: Data for 1950-57 were published in *International Financial Statistics (IFS)*, July 1958. Data for 1947-49 were compiled by the Fund staff on the same basis. These data were derived from the statistics on foreign assets given on the country pages of *IFS* and defined in the notes to these country pages. For a description of the construction of, and the problems related to, this table for the period beginning with 1952, see *IFS*, July 1956 pp. 16-17; for earlier years, see the June 1953 issue, pp. x-xi. This table reconciles the total of exchange reserves reported by the holders with the official holdings by countries of dollar balances, as reported by the United States, and the holdings by countries of all sterling balances (official and other) as reported by the United Kingdom. In some cases, the U.S. reports of official holdings have been adjusted by the Fund. The totals of EPU liabilities and BIS deposits are as reported by these institutions.

The figures for Errors and Omissions are the result of a number of factors, some positive and some negative: (1) Dollar liabilities as reported by the United States include assets held by the Soviet bloc. The dollar assets held by the Soviet bloc are neither reported by the Soviet countries nor included in the area totals of the table. This residual is therefore included in Errors and Omissions with a positive sign. (2) Sterling liabilities reported by the United Kingdom include those held by private holders, which therefore are represented by a negative sign. (3) Country holdings of assets other than dollars and sterling are included in the Total but are not reported as liabilities by their obligors; the result is a positive sign. There are other errors and omissions, the sign of which is undetermined.

Data on sterling exclude liabilities to dependent areas and to Ghana.

Appendix Table 4. Indices of World Trade and Manufacturing Activity, 1871-75 to 1936-38
(Annual averages: 1913=100)

	Volume of Trade[1]		
Period	Manufactured articles	Primary products	Manufacturing Activity
1871-75	—	—	22.4
1876-80	32.1	31.2	24.5
1881-85	40.0	38.0	30.4
1886-90	45.1	44.5	36.8
1891-95	45.9	51.4	42.6
1896-1900	48.0	60.2	53.6
1901-05	63.2	70.8	67.0
1906-10	77.9	83.1	79.9
1911-13	95.6	97.0	94.3
1913	100.0	100.0	100.0
1920	—	—	93.2
1921-25	76.6	85.8	103.2
1926-29	104.3	112.7	138.9
1930	99.7	119.8	136.9
1931-35	75.5	107.2	128.2
1936-38	92.1	116.6	185.0

Source: League of Nations, *Industrialization and Foreign Trade* (1945), pp. 130-31 and 157. Data include the U.S.S.R.

[1] These two volume indices are not combined into one index. The value of world trade in manufactured articles during the period was about 60 per cent of that in primary products, fluctuating only slightly above and below that percentage (*ibid.*, p. 14).

Enlargement of Fund Resources Through Increases in Quotas

At the Annual Meetings in 1958 the subject discussed in the preceding document was extensively canvassed by Governors. On the motion of the Governor for the United States, a resolution was passed requesting the Executive Directors to consider promptly the question of enlarging the resources of the Fund through increases in quotas. As a result, the Board adopted, on December 19, 1958, the following report to the Governors. This was accepted by the Governors, and took effect from September 9, 1959.

Enlargement of Fund Resources Through Increases in Quotas Report by the Executive Directors to the Board of Governors of the International Monetary Fund (December 1958)

CONTENTS

INTRODUCTION

At the Thirteenth Annual Meeting at New Delhi, the Board of Governors adopted the following Resolution:

RESOLVED:

That the Executive Directors promptly consider the question of enlarging the resources of the Fund through increases in quotas and that, if, having regard to views expressed by Governors and considering all other aspects of the matter, they find that action to carry out such increases would be desirable, they submit an appropriate proposal to the Board of Governors for action either at a meeting of the Board or by vote without a meeting, as the Executive Directors may determine.

Pursuant to this Resolution the Executive Directors have studied the question of enlarging the resources of the Fund by quota increases, so as to enable the Fund to promote more effectively its purposes as set out in the Articles of Agreement. They have concluded that a substantial enlargement of the resources of the Fund is highly desirable. The grounds for this conclusion and the manner in which an appropriate increase in Fund quotas could best be brought about are discussed in the following sections of this report.

To accomplish the proposed increase in the Fund's resources, the annexed Resolutions have been prepared for adoption by the Board of Governors. Attention is drawn to the requirement that votes, to be valid, must be received at the seat of the Fund on or before February 2, 1959.

I. INCREASE IN THE FUND'S RESOURCES

The need for an increase in the Fund's resources arises from the tasks which, under its Articles of Agreement, the Fund has to perform in an expanding world economy. The role that the Fund is likely to play in the future and the resources it will need for this purpose can best be assessed in the light of the experience it has accumulated and the policies it has pursued in the twelve years of its existence.

The Fund has two main tasks which are clearly intertwined. It promotes international monetary cooperation and exchange stability as a basis for the balanced growth of world trade. It also provides financial assistance to members to help them stabilize their currencies, maintain or move toward convertibility, and overcome temporary balance of payments problems without resort to policies that would be harmful to national or international prosperity. While the first task is a continuing one, experience has shown that the granting of financial assistance tends to be concentrated in certain periods characterized by exceptional strains in the world's monetary system. Major economic and financial developments will often affect several countries more or less at the same time, so that the calls on the Fund's resources may be of substantial proportions in a relatively short period. There was one such period in the early years of the Fund's existence, namely, in 1947–49, when certain European countries suffered from extreme foreign exchange shortages; and another, leading to even larger drawings, which started late in 1956. Although the extreme tensions that gripped the major exchange markets in 1956 and 1957 have now abated, requests for financial assistance from members continue to be received almost every month. Countries whose economies are subject to wide seasonal swings have called on the Fund for short-term assistance to bridge the seasonal troughs in their reserves, and many other countries have also come to the Fund for assistance when, for particular reasons affecting their own economies, they have experienced difficulties in their balance of payments.

Since the beginning of its operation, the Fund has made available about $4.1 billion to 36 countries. Of this sum, $3.2 billion was drawn in some 150 transactions; over $800 million is still available for drawing under open stand-by facilities; and stand-by credits of over $100 million were allowed to expire as the members concerned no longer felt the need for them (see tables, pages 436–41). About two thirds of the total of $4.1 billion has been arranged in the last two years. The needs for assistance in this recent period have arisen from a wide variety of causes which have revealed the many-sided nature of the Fund's financial activities.

The largest single transaction in this period arose out of the Suez events which caused sterling to come under pressure. In December 1956, the United Kingdom drew $561 million from the Fund and entered into a stand-by arrangement for $739 million—a total of $1,300 million. The assistance was granted on the basis of a declaration by the British Government that strict financial and credit policies would be pursued, that quantitative import restrictions would not be reimposed, and that the value of sterling would be maintained. This was an emergency situation in which the massive use of the Fund's resources was required to prevent a major crisis in the international exchange structure.

In the latter part of 1956 and the first half of 1957, highly expansionary developments in many countries produced severe pressures in national and international money and capital markets. Large government deficits gave rise to serious declines of foreign exchange in a number of countries. In the third quarter of 1957, lack of confidence in the stability of the pattern of European exchange rates led to large international movements of funds. These and other causes gave rise to requests for assistance from all over the world. Among the countries that drew on the Fund were Argentina, Bolivia, Brazil, Chile, Cuba, Denmark, France, Japan, and the Netherlands. For some countries, stand-by agreements were renegotiated, often with new provisions adapted to changed circumstances. In this period of pronounced boom, the pursuit of cautious credit policies was more than ever required, a fact which was reflected in the declarations of intent which were made by the Governments then requesting assistance from the Fund and on the basis of which the Fund acted.

The recession which started in 1957 brought a new set of circumstances. A number of industrial countries were able to improve their reserve positions substantially, but many of the primary producing countries suffered from the decline in raw material prices. As a result of the inherent strength of the major economies and the financial and commercial policies followed, the recession proved to be short and did not lead to an extensive use of Fund resources. Indeed, most of the Fund's transactions in 1957–58 were related to difficulties that found their main origin in inflationary pressures.

The correction of inflationary conditions requires internal corrective measures, and one of the principal benefits of Fund assistance is that it gives time for these measures to take effect. In some cases the assistance of the Fund has been closely linked to the carrying out of comprehensive stabilization programs; examples of this in Latin America are Bolivia, Brazil, Chile, Colombia, Haiti, Paraguay, and Peru, and elsewhere, France and Turkey. The main lines of these programs have been indicated to the Fund in declarations made by the Governments, and in these cases the declarations have formed an essential part of the stand-by arrangements. A noteworthy feature of these stabilization efforts is that the Fund's assistance has frequently been supplemented by substantial credits from other sources. Countries embarking on stabilization programs are often in need of different kinds of foreign resources; indeed, one of the advantages of such parallel arrangements is that in some measure they provide assistance tailored to the particular needs of the countries concerned. For instance, the Fund's assistance is of a short-term character designed to strengthen reserve positions, while resources obtained from other agencies may be either related to special categories of payment (as when furnished by the European Payments Union) or of a more long-term character, appropriate for investment financing. The importance of the Fund's participation in these parallel arrangements has generally been a double one: the Fund has played a leading role in assisting countries to work out their stabilization programs, and the strengthening by the Fund of the country's reserves has been an essential part of these programs.

The Fund's transactions have been fully described in its Annual Reports, but enough has been said here to indicate that the assistance obtained from the Fund has been requested under a great variety of circumstances: in an emergency at the time of the Suez events, in conditions of boom and expanding world trade, and in periods of recession, as well as in a wider context when stabilization efforts have been undertaken. The only conclusion can be that the Fund must remain prepared for diverse contingencies, many of which cannot be clearly defined in advance.

The ability of the Fund to grant assistance so promptly and on such a considerable scale in the last two years was due to the fact that, since in the immediately preceding period there had been very few transactions and nearly all the earlier drawings had been repaid, most of its resources in gold and convertible currencies were intact. The many transactions with the Fund in this recent period have, of course, considerably decreased the amount of its uncommitted resources. At the end of November 1958, the Fund's holdings of gold and U.S. dollars amounted to $2.3 billion. If commitments under stand-by arrangements, totaling $0.8 billion, are deducted, the balance of gold and U.S. dollars was $1.5 billion, compared with $3.5 billion at the end of September 1956. Considering that the use of the Fund's resources in the form of drawings and stand-by arrangements came to over $2.7 billion in the two years from October 1956 to September 1958, the resources of about $1.5 billion presently available cannot be considered adequate in the light of past experience to meet such calls on the Fund as may suddenly be made. This is even more evident if it is borne in mind that the Fund must always maintain enough liquid resources to give its members confidence that they have a second line of reserves in the Fund.

At the Thirteenth Annual Meeting of the Board of Governors in New Delhi, a number of Governors suggested that consideration be given to the increased effectiveness of the Fund's present resources that might be achieved if greater use were made of the currencies of the main industrial countries other than the United States, even though those currencies are not fully convertible within the meaning of the Fund's Articles of Agreement. The Executive Directors have not yet fully explored this question, but they are hopeful that measures can be devised that would facilitate such drawings. In recent transactions, there has already been an encouraging increase in the demand for currencies other than the U.S. dollar, and it is expected that there will be continued progress in this direction. The acceptance of convertibility under Article VIII, or even the more limited step of external convertibility by the more important trading countries, would be most helpful in this connection. As convertibility is attained or approached, the question whether drawings in these currencies can or cannot be repaid in the same currencies will lose much of its practical importance. However, while developments along these lines are certainly greatly to be welcomed and will help the Fund in the future, the Fund must nevertheless be prepared for situations in which its holdings of gold and convertible currencies may be of decisive importance.

It has been mentioned above that countries which have received assistance from the Fund have, as a rule, made declarations of intent as to the policies they would follow. They have done so in accordance with the principles governing the use of the Fund's resources, which had been laid down by the Executive Directors and stated in Annual Reports well before the recent period of increased activity. Because the Fund's policy toward requests for drawings or stand-by arrangements must be applicable to large and small countries alike, it is expressed in terms not of the absolute amount involved, but of the proportion which this amount bears to the country's quota.

Countries are given the overwhelming benefit of the doubt with respect to requests for drawings within the "gold tranche," i.e., the portion of quota which can be regarded as equivalent to the member's gold subscription. The Fund's attitude to requests for drawings within the first credit tranche (equal to the first 25 per cent of the quota above the "gold tranche") is a liberal one, provided that a member wishing to make such a drawing is also itself making reasonable efforts to solve its problems. Members' requests for drawings or stand-by arrangements beyond the first credit tranche are likely to be favorably received when they are intended to support well-balanced and adequate programs which are aimed at establishing or maintaining the enduring stability of the currencies concerned at realistic rates of exchange.

Along with these principles governing access to its resources, the Fund has established certain principles covering repurchases, which emphasize the basic requirement for a drawing, namely, that it is required to meet temporary balance of payments difficulties and that the Fund should be repaid within a period appropriate to the problem for which Fund assistance is sought. Hence, members are expected to repurchase drawings within an outside range of three to five years, but in appropriate circumstances the Fund requires repurchase within an even shorter period. A member entering into a stand-by arrangement is generally required to repurchase within three years of any drawing under the arrangement, but again this period may be shorter in appropriate circumstances. Several members have in fact completed their repurchases in much shorter periods than had originally been specified. Indeed, all the resources made available by the Fund before 1956 have now been repaid with the exception of $36.5 million, and this has not been outstanding for a protracted period. These policies for repurchase assure the revolving character of the Fund's resources. They are intended to replenish these resources within a reasonable period; they also ensure that each country that draws on the Fund to handle a particular difficulty will put itself in a position, by repaying the Fund as soon as possible, where it can avail itself again of the Fund's assistance whenever a new need presents itself.

The experience of the last two years has shown that these principles and practices of the Fund are eminently applicable to its transactions. Not only do they serve to give coherence to the financial side of the Fund's work, but the fact that they have been made fully known in an authoritative way to the members leaves no room for uncertainty as to the principles which are applied in the Fund's decisions on financial assistance. Whether a member country will in fact be allowed to use the Fund's resources is, of course, a matter for judgment in each decision, according to the particular circumstances of the case, and it is here that the Fund must apply appropriate flexibility within the framework of the accepted principles and practices. By the close link that the application of these principles and practices establishes between the Fund's financial assistance and the maintenance or adoption of the necessary remedial measures in the countries concerned, the Fund supports the observance of that degree of financial self-discipline without which the international monetary system cannot function properly. One of the consequences of the breakdown of the gold standard in the 1930's was a large measure of uncertainty as to the proper rules for monetary management and a corresponding need for countries both to agree on a new set of rules and to work out cooperative ways of applying them. In these respects, the Fund has already made, and should be able to continue to make, a substantial contribution. It is able to do so in connection with the use of its resources, and also in other ways. A most important function is performed by the consultations which the Fund holds once a year with each of the countries that still maintain exchange restrictions under Article XIV of the Agreement. These annual consultations provide an opportunity to review with a country whether there is a continued need for these restrictions, as well as the measures that could be taken by the country to create conditions in which restrictions could be reduced or abolished. The Fund can also make a contribution by providing a forum for the crystallization of world opinion, and through its publications and technical assistance.

The Executive Directors are of the opinion that the policies and practices governing the use of the Fund's resources, which have now successfully stood the test of practical application, should not be changed as a consequence of the increases in quotas now envisaged. While the Fund must, of course, remain alert to the needs of changing circumstances, it will at all times have to ensure that its transactions with its members promote the purposes of the Articles of Agreement.

The power of the Fund to help its members over difficulties is not confined to the actual transfer of resources to the members. There are several cases, some of them of great importance, in which countries that have entered into stand-by arrangements with the Fund have not in fact made any drawings under them. In this way the financial assistance of the Fund, in the form of a line of credit, has been effective even without any new money being injected into the world economy. Naturally, from the point of view of its own liquidity, the Fund is affected by these stand-by arrangements even though there is no actual transfer of currencies, since it must regard the corresponding resources as subject to a contingent liability.

The possibility of access to the Fund's resources serves in itself as a second line of reserves, which gives members more confidence in undertaking efforts to restore balance, and may indeed encourage them to move faster toward achieving the purposes of the Fund than if they had to rely on their own resources alone. In this manner the Fund can be helpful to many of its members, whether they are in the initial stages of freeing their trade and payments from the shackles of restrictions or are well on the way toward making their currencies convertible.

It must also be stressed that the benefits which the Fund conveys by the use of its resources are by no means limited to those countries which have sought or may seek assistance from the Fund. Countries which are in such a strong position that they do not envisage making any request to the Fund also share in the benefits. Countries all over the world have a great interest in the financial rehabilitation of countries in difficulties, and more generally in the establishment of a properly functioning international monetary system. As far as recent Fund activities are concerned, it was clearly in the general interest that a crack in the world's exchange structure was avoided in 1956, that tension in the European exchange markets was eliminated in 1957, and that countries have been helped to push forward with their stabilization programs. It is in the general interest that by means of a strengthening of the Fund's position, together with continued observance of financial self-discipline, a sound monetary basis is created for the renewed expansion of world trade. It should never be forgotten that pressure on one currency may, under adverse circumstances, affect the position of other currencies. In 1931, at the time of world-wide depression, a financial breakdown which began in Austria spread so widely that in the end almost every country in the world had to alter its exchange rate or introduce restrictions on trade and payments harmful from every point of view. While no progress can be achieved without appropriate steps being taken in individual countries, the granting of financial assistance through the Fund reflects the idea that international assistance may be required to enable countries to take these steps.

It is therefore in the interest of all members of the Fund that the common pool constituting a secondary reserve should be adequate to meet the difficulties which may arise in the future. In considering the need for an increase in the Fund's resources, account must be taken of the fact that in the last decade the volume of world trade has nearly doubled. While reserves of gold and foreign exchange of countries outside the United States have increased by about 50 per cent in that period, Fund quotas have, with minor exceptions, remained at the amounts determined in 1944; and the rise in dollar prices by at least 50 per cent since that date has correspondingly reduced the real value of the Fund's resources. In fact, the Fund has found it increasingly necessary to waive the provision limiting drawings in any twelve months to 25 per cent of a country's quota. In recent years, the large majority of the Fund's drawings and stand-by arrangements have involved waivers of this provision.

The expansion of trade and the greater freedom of international payments, including capital movements, tend to increase the problems that may arise if there should be a sudden change in confidence in any major currency. The occurrence of such a change at some future time cannot altogether be excluded in a world in which monetary confidence has not yet been fully restored and where memories of devaluations and other difficulties still exert an influence in the markets. Countries must therefore be alert to the increased risks to which their reserves may be exposed as a result of the operation of leads and lags in payments and other movements of funds.

Fortunately, over the last year many countries have been able to strengthen their reserves. But the Fund cannot be concerned with only the present or the immediate future; its members must be assured that it is adequately equipped to meet the strains which may arise in emergencies or other adverse circumstances.

The Executive Directors have, therefore, concluded that it is highly desirable to enlarge the Fund's resources through increases in quotas.

II. MAGNITUDE OF THE INCREASE IN THE FUND'S RESOURCES

An increase of 50 per cent is considered a reasonable basis at this time for quota increases to enlarge the resources of the Fund. A general increase of this magnitude, together with special increases for certain countries described below, would increase the resources of the Fund by $5.1 billion, including gold payments of nearly $1.3 billion. This appears to be as much as members generally can be expected to contribute. If these new resources are made available, members will have increased confidence in the capacity of the Fund to perform its tasks in the coming period.

As shown in Table 1, the proposed increase in quotas would produce a larger relative rise in the Fund's holdings of gold, U.S. dollars, and other currencies that have been drawn in the past. Thus the Fund's holdings of gold and U.S. dollars would double, increasing from $2.3 billion to $4.6 billion, and the holdings of gold and of the six currencies that have been drawn would increase by 75 per cent.

Special Increases

In view of the position in world trade of Canada, the Federal Republic of Germany, and Japan, and their recent relative economic growth, increases in their quotas beyond 50 per cent would be appropriate and highly desirable, particularly because this would enlarge the Fund's resources of currencies likely to be required by other members. In the light of these considerations and on the basis of statements made on behalf of these three countries, the Executive Directors recommend to the Board of Governors a quota increase for Canada to $550 million, for the Federal Republic of Germany to $787.5 million, and for Japan to $500 million.

Table 1. Changes in Fund Holdings of Gold and Currencies As a Result of Quota Increases
(In millions of U.S. dollars)

	Holdings As of November 30, 1958	Holdings After Quota Increase[1]	Amount of Increase
Gold and U.S. dollars			
Gold	1,531	2,810	1,279
U.S. dollars	787	1,818	1,031
	2,318	4,628	2,310
Other currencies that have been drawn			
Belgian francs	169	253	84
Canadian dollars	210	397	187
Deutsche mark	183	526	343
Netherlands guilders	206	309	103
Sterling	1,618	2,106	488
	2,386	3,591	1,205
Other currencies[2]	4,507	6,106	1,599
Total	9,211	14,325	5,114

[1] On the assumption that all quotas are increased by 50 per cent, that the quotas of Canada, the Federal Republic of Germany, and Japan are increased as indicated below, and that all additional subscriptions are paid in full. No allowance made for increases under the Second Resolution.

[2] Includes subscriptions receivable.

Countries with Small Quotas

In the Second Quinquennial Review of Quotas, the quotas of a number of the smaller countries were found to be particularly inadequate. As a result of that review, it was understood that requests for increases in small quotas would be sympathetically considered, and since then it has been the practice of the Executive Directors to recommend, and the Board of Governors to agree to, increases in accordance with the following formula:

Quotas below $5 million could be raised to $7.5 million;

Quotas of $5 million and above but below $10 million could be raised to $10 million;

Quotas of $10 million and above but below $15 million could be raised to $15 million; and

Quotas of $15 million and above but below $20 million could be raised to $20 million.

Eight countries with small quotas have taken advantage of this understanding during the last two years. The old quotas for these countries, their present quotas, and their present quotas increased by 50 per cent are shown in Table 2. A special adjustment, from $15 million to $50 million, for the Philippines has also been approved by the Board of Governors.

The other 24 countries with small quotas have not so far requested quota increases under this formula. It is recommended that they now have the opportunity

(i) To increase their present quotas by 50 per cent, or

(ii) To obtain a quota equal to the amount available under the small quota formula increased by 50 per cent, or

(iii) To consent to a quota of an amount between (i) and (ii) as they may choose.

The 24 countries concerned, their present quotas, and the amounts to which they could be raised under (i) and (ii) above, are shown in Table 3.

Further Adjustment of Quotas

The directive given to the Executive Directors by the Board of Governors was to consider promptly the question of enlarging the Fund's resources through increases in quotas, and the Resolutions now recommended (see Annex) are based on the general idea of increases of 50 per cent in quotas, with special increases for Canada, the Federal Republic of Germany, and Japan.

Table 2

	Old Quota	Present Quota	Present Quota Increased by 50 Per Cent
	←	*(million U.S. dollars)*	→
Dominican Republic	5	10	15
Ecuador	5	10	15
El Salvador	2.5	7.5	11.25
Haiti	2	7.5	11.25
Honduras	2.5	7.5	11.25
Israel	4.5	7.5	11.25
Nicaragua	2	7.5	11.25
Paraguay	3.5	7.5	11.25

The Executive Directors have, however, received from a number of other countries requests for increases beyond 50 per cent of their present quotas. Some of these countries have present quotas of less than $20 million, and have requested increases beyond the amounts available under the small quota formula increased by 50 per cent. It has not been possible within the time available to give adequate consideration to these requests, but the Executive Directors are continuing their consideration of them.

The Executive Directors will, as expeditiously as possible, reach their decisions on these requests and on any other requests that are received early in 1959. The recommendations that they decide to make will be submitted to the Governors in the form of new resolutions. These recommendations will be made promptly and, it is hoped, early enough to permit the members concerned to give their consent before September 15, 1959. It is expected that any such new resolutions would be similar to the Third Resolution annexed to this report.

III. PAYMENT OF ADDITIONAL SUBSCRIPTIONS

When a quota is increased, the member must pay an additional subscription equal to the increase, 25 per cent in gold and the balance in the member's currency. Payment of both portions of the additional subscription must be made before the increase in the member's quota can become effective, even by those few members which, in accordance with the Articles of Agreement, have not yet been required to pay their original subscriptions.

The present proposals for increases in quotas are based on the idea of a cooperative effort by the members of the Fund to provide larger resources against contingencies that may affect any member. In order to preserve the general character of that effort, it has been thought preferable not to exercise the discretion to reduce gold payments under Article III, Section 4. However, since the prompt payment in gold of 25 per cent of the quota increase might cause hardship in some cases, the facilities described in the next two paragraphs will be available to members consenting to increases under the First or the Second Resolution.

Table 3

	Present Quota	Present Quota Increased by 50 Per Cent	Quota Under Formula Increased by 50 Per Cent
	←	*(million U.S. dollars)*	→
Afghanistan	10	15	22.5
Bolivia	10	15	22.5
Burma	15	22.5	30
Ceylon	15	22.5	30
Costa Rica	5	7.5	15
Ethiopia	6	9	15
Ghana	15	22.5	30
Guatemala	5	7.5	15
Iceland	1	1.5	11.25
Iraq	8	12	15
Jordan	3	4.5	11.25
Korea	12.5	18.75	22.5
Lebanon	4.5	6.75	11.25
Libya	5	7.5	15
Luxembourg	10	15	22.5
Panama	0.5	0.75	11.25
Saudi Arabia	10	15	22.5
Sudan	10	15	22.5
Thailand	12.5	18.75	22.5
Tunisia	12	18	22.5
UAR: Syria	6.5	9.75	15
Uruguay	15	22.5	30
Venezuela	15	22.5	30
Viet-Nam	12.5	18.75	22.5

Provision has been made for such of these members as represent, for reasons which they shall submit to the Fund, that their reserves should not be reduced by an immediate 25 per cent gold payment, to have their quotas increased in installments corresponding to each installment of gold and currency paid. These members will pay an original installment, and an installment in each period of twelve months thereafter. Each installment shall be one fifth of the increase. Members may accelerate payment under this installment schedule.

In exceptional cases, members may wish to have the full increase in their quotas take effect immediately, or members paying under the installment schedule may wish to expedite the full increase in their quotas, but in either case would encounter undue payments difficulties through the reduction of their reserves by the payment of the 25 per cent gold subscription or of the outstanding balance. In order to assist members to meet these payments difficulties, the Fund will sympathetically consider a request, made within two years after the effective date of a member's quota increase or the first installment of the increase, for an exchange transaction up to 25 per cent of the increase. The Fund will expect that a member requesting such an exchange transaction beyond the gold tranche will represent that it will make a repurchase corresponding to any drawing in equal annual installments, to commence one year after the drawing and to be completed not later than three years after the drawing.

IV. PROCEDURE

1. *Voting*

The Resolutions presented in the Annex are designed to enable the Board of Governors to vote at one time on all matters connected with increases in quotas therein proposed. When adopted, they will make it possible for increases in quotas to become effective without need for further reference to the Board of Governors.

To be valid, votes must be received at the seat of the Fund on or before February 2, 1959.

Separate votes are required on the First, Second, and Third Resolutions. In voting on the Third Resolution, a Governor may vote on the whole of that Resolution or on each of the increases of quotas there proposed.

2. *Date for Consent*

If the Resolutions are adopted by the necessary majority of four fifths of the total voting power, a member may consent to the increase in its quota at any time on or before September 15, 1959. Therefore, unless this period is extended by the Fund, members will have until September 15, 1959 to take whatever legal action may be necessary in their countries to enable them to give their consent.

3. *Participation*

In view of the cooperative nature of the proposed increase in the Fund's resources, it is provided that, before increases become effective, the Fund must determine that members having 75 per cent of the total of present quotas have consented to increases in their quotas.

In determining whether this degree of participation has been reached, the Fund will take into account all consents to increases, whether they be increases in full or by installments, under the First or Second Resolutions, or increases under the Third Resolution.

4. *Relation of Quota Increases to Increased Capital of International Bank for Reconstruction and Development*

Under the Resolutions recommended by the Executive Directors of the International Bank for Reconstruction and Development to the Board of Governors of the International Bank for Reconstruction and Development, provision is made for the proposed increase in authorized capital to take effect only if a specified aggregate amount of subscriptions is taken up.

The Fund Resolutions provide that increases in Fund quotas shall take effect only if this condition is satisfied in the Bank. However, it is also provided in the Fund Resolutions that the Board of Governors of the Fund may eliminate this condition by a four-fifths majority if the required member participation is attained in the Fund but not in the Bank.

It is not a condition in the Fund Resolutions that the required percentage of participation in the Fund and Bank must consist of the same members. However, according to the established policy of the Fund, it has been the practice, where an increase in quota is sought in the Fund, for the member to request a corresponding increase in its subscription in the Bank. The Fund, therefore, expects that any member consenting to an increase in its quota will request a corresponding increase in its subscription to the capital of the Bank.

5. *Date for Payment of Additional Subscription*

After the Resolutions are adopted, a member may pay its increased subscription in respect of the increase in its quota at any time before it is due. If a member pays before the increase in its quota takes effect, the additional subscription will be kept in separate accounts of the Fund and returned if it should be established that the increase cannot take effect. A member is required to pay its additional subscription not later than thirty days after the latest of the following events: its consent to its quota increase (see 2 above); the determination by the Fund that the condition as to participation in quota increases has been satisfied (see 3 above); and the similar requirement has been satisfied in the Bank (see 4 above).

6. *Effective Date of Quota Increases*

Increases in members' quotas will take effect as follows:

(a) When a member pays its additional subscription before the latest of the three events referred to in 5 above, the increase in its quota will take effect on the happening of the latest of these events.

(b) If a member pays its additional subscription after the latest of these three events, the increase in its quota will take effect on the day of payment.

7. *Increase of Quotas by Installments*

Members consenting to increases in their quotas under the First or Second Resolutions may consent to increases by installments. The foregoing paragraphs in this section of the report will apply to such members, except that the first installment instead of the whole additional subscription will have to be paid as described in 5 above. It should be noted that the increases in quotas will be equal to the installments actually paid.

ANNEX

ENLARGEMENT OF FUND RESOURCES THROUGH INCREASES IN QUOTAS

Resolutions

WHEREAS the Executive Directors have considered the question referred to them by the Resolution of the Board of Governors of the International Monetary Fund at their Thirteenth Annual Meeting:

> That the Executive Directors promptly consider the question of enlarging the resources of the Fund through increases in quotas and that, if, having regard to views expressed by Governors and considering all other aspects of the matter, they find that action to carry out such increases would be desirable, they submit an appropriate proposal to the Board of Governors for action either at a meeting of the Board or by vote without a meeting, as the Executive Directors may determine;

And having found that action to carry out increases in quotas would be desirable, have set out their conclusions in a report, entitled *Enlargement of Fund Resources Through Increases in Quotas*, in which it is proposed that the present quota of each member of the Fund shall be increased by 50 per cent, with additional increases for certain members;

And having noted that there are various legal requirements in member countries for giving effect to this proposal, have submitted to the Board of Governors the following Resolutions for a vote without meeting pursuant to Section 13 of the By-Laws of the Fund, which Resolutions propose increases of quotas for all members of the Fund, make provision for consents by members, and establish the conditions upon which the increases consented to shall take effect;

NOW THEREFORE the Board of Governors hereby RESOLVES that

First Resolution

1. The International Monetary Fund proposes that, subject to the provisions of this Resolution, the quotas of members of the International Monetary Fund as of January 31, 1959 shall be increased by 50 per cent for each member.

2. None of the increases in quotas proposed in paragraph 1 of this Resolution shall become effective unless:

(i) The member concerned has notified the Fund in writing that it consents to the increase in its quota; and

(ii) The Fund determines that members having not less than 75 per cent of the total of quotas on January 31, 1959 have consented to increases in their quotas; and

(iii) The requirement is satisfied of a minimum aggregate increase in subscriptions, contained in the Resolution of the Board of Governors of the International Bank for Reconstruction and Development entitled *Increase of $10,000,000,000 in Authorized Capital Stock and Subscriptions Thereto*, recommended by the Executive Directors of the International Bank for Reconstruction and Development; and

(iv) The member concerned has paid the full increase in its quota.

Subject to paragraph 7 (c) of this Resolution, each increase in quota shall become effective upon the date of the latest of these four events.

3. The written notices prescribed in paragraph 2 (i) shall be signed by a competent official whose authority and signature are duly authenticated.

4. Notices in accordance with paragraph 2 (i) shall be received in the Fund not later than September 15, 1959, provided that the Executive Directors may extend this period as they may determine.

5. At any time after the percentage of participation prescribed in paragraph 2 (ii) of this Resolution has been reached, the Board of Governors may, by a four-fifths majority of the total voting power, eliminate the requirements in paragraph 2 (iii) of this Resolution, and may make such modifications as to the date of the effectiveness of increases in quotas as may then be determined.

6. Subject to paragraph 7 (b) of this Resolution, each member shall pay to the Fund within thirty days after the latest of the three events in paragraph 2 (i), (ii), and (iii) of this Resolution, 25 per cent of the increase in gold and the balance in its own currency.

7 (a). In giving notice in accordance with paragraph 2 (i) of this Resolution, a member may represent that, for reasons which it shall submit to the Fund, its reserves should not be reduced by an immediate full gold payment in accordance with paragraph 6 of this Resolution, and that it therefore consents to the increase in its quota proposed in paragraph 1 of this Resolution, as an increase by installments.

(b). Notwithstanding paragraph 2 (iv) of this Resolution, a member increasing its quota by installments shall pay not less than one fifth of the gold and currency prescribed in paragraph 6 within thirty days after the latest of the three events in paragraph 2 (i), (ii), and (iii), and shall pay further installments of gold and currency of not less than one fifth of the increase in each twelve months after the first payment until the full amount prescribed in paragraph 6 has been paid.

(c). Subject to paragraph 2 of this Resolution, on the completion of the payment of each installment of the increase, the member's quota shall be increased by an amount equal to the installment.

8. Since it is in the interests of the Fund and its members that the contemplated increase in its resources be expedited, members are invited to comply as soon as possible with the procedures for notice and payments to the Fund under this Resolution. Any payment made by a member before the effective date of increase in its quota will be kept in separate accounts of the Fund. If it should be established that such increase cannot become effective under this Resolution, the payment will be returned to the member.

Second Resolution

1. The International Monetary Fund proposes that, subject to the provisions of this Second Resolution, if any member to which the small quota policy of the Second Quinquennial Review applies so elects, its quota shall be increased beyond the amount specified in the First Resolution to such an amount, not exceeding a 50 per cent increase in the maximum quota available under the said policy, as such member shall communicate to the Fund at the time that it consents to the increase in its quota.

2. Paragraphs 2 (i) and (iv), 3, 4, 6, 7, and 8 of the First Resolution shall apply to this Second Resolution.

Third Resolution

1. The International Monetary Fund proposes that, subject to the provisions of this Third Resolution, if increases in quotas take effect under the First Resolution, the quotas

of Canada, the Federal Republic of Germany, and Japan shall be increased to the amounts shown below:

Canada	$550 million
Federal Republic of Germany	$787.5 million
Japan	$500 million

2. Paragraphs 2 (i) and (iv), 3, 4, 6, and 8 of the First Resolution shall apply to this Third Resolution.

Quotas and Fund Holdings of Currencies and Gold

(As of November 30, 1958. Amounts expressed in millions of U.S. dollars, except where noted)

Member	Quota	Subscription: Gold	Subscription: Currency	Subscription Account Repurchases	Sales of Gold for Currency	Net Member Drawings	Income, Expenditure, Etc.	Fund Holdings of Currencies	% of Quota
Afghanistan	10	2.5	—	—	—	—	—	—	—
Argentina	150	37.5	112.5	—	—	75.0	—	187.5	125
Australia	200	8.4	191.6	—	—	—	−.1	191.5	96
Austria	50	5.0	45.0	−7.5	—	—	—	37.5	75
Belgium	225	56.2	168.8	—	—	—	—	168.7	75
Bolivia	10	2.5	7.5	—	—	8.5	—	16.0	160
Brazil	150	37.5	112.5	—	—	112.5	—	225.0	150
Burma	15	.5	14.5	−3.2	—	15.0	—	26.3	175
Canada	300	75.0	225.0	—	—	−15.0	—	210.0	70
Ceylon	15	.8	14.2	−3.0	—	—	—	11.2	75
Chile	50	8.8	41.2	−3.7	—	40.2	—	77.7	155
China	550	.1	—	—	—	—	—	—	—
Colombia	50	12.5	37.5	—	—	35.0	—	72.5	145
Costa Rica	5	.4	4.6	−.9	—	—	—	3.7	75
Cuba	50	12.5	37.5	—	—	25.0	—	62.5	125
Denmark	68	5.9	62.1	−2.6	—	8.5	—	68.0	100
Dominican Republic	10	2.5	7.5	—	—	—	—	7.5	75
Ecuador	10	2.5	7.5	—	—	—	—	7.5	75
El Salvador	7.5	1.9	5.6	—	—	—	—	5.6	75
Ethiopia	6	.1	5.9	−1.4	—	—	—	4.5	75
Finland	38	.8	37.2	−8.7	—	—	—	28.5	75
France	525	108.1	416.9	−22.9	—	393.8	−.4	787.4	150
Germany (Fed. Rep.)	330	33.0	297.0	−45.1	—	−68.9	—	183.0	55
Ghana	15	.5	14.5	—	—	—	—	14.5	97
Greece	40	—	—	—	—	—	—	—	—
Guatemala	5	1.2	3.8	—	—	—	—	3.7	75
Haiti	7.5	1.9	5.6	—	—	3.5	—	9.1	122
Honduras	7.5	1.9	5.6	—	—	—	—	5.6	75
Iceland	1	.2	.8	—	—	—	−.1	.7	75
India	400	27.5	372.5	—	—	200.0	4.6	577.1	144
Indonesia	110	15.5	94.5	−12.0	—	55.0	—	137.5	125
Iran	35	8.8	26.2	—	—	16.9	—	43.1	123
Iraq	8	—	8.0	−2.0	—	—	—	6.0	75
Ireland	30	4.5	25.5	—	—	—	—	25.5	85
Israel	7.5	1.9	5.6	—	—	3.8	—	9.4	125
Italy	180	45.0	—	—	—	—	—	—	—

Japan	250	62.5	187.5	—	—	—	—	187.5	75
Jordan	3	.1	2.9	—	—	—	—	2.9	97
Korea, Republic of	12.5	3.1	—	—	—	—	—	—	—
Lebanon	4.5	.3	4.2	−.9	—	—	—	3.3	75
Libya	5	.2	—	—	—	—	—	—	—
Luxembourg	10	.5	9.5	—	—	—	—	9.5	95
Malaya	25	.9	—	—	—	—	—	—	—
Mexico	90	22.5	67.5	—	—	—	—	67.5	75
Morocco	35	1.2	—	—	—	—	—	—	—
Netherlands	275	68.8	206.2	—	—	—	—	206.2	75
Nicaragua	7.5	1.9	5.6	—	—	—	—	5.6	75
Norway	50	12.5	37.5	—	—	—	—	37.5	75
Pakistan	100	3.5	96.5	—	—	—	—	96.5	96
Panama	.5	.1	.4	—	—	—	—	.4	75
Paraguay	7.5	1.9	5.6	—	—	6.3	—	11.9	158
Peru	25	3.2	21.8	−3.1	—	5.0	—	23.7	95
Philippines	15	3.8	11.2	—	—	15.0	—	26.2	175
Saudi Arabia	10	2.5	—	—	—	—	—	—	—
Spain	100	10.0	—	—	—	—	—	—	—
Sudan	10	.4	9.6	—	—	5.0	—	14.6	146
Sweden	100	17.0	83.0	−8.0	—	—	—	75.0	75
Thailand	12.5	3.1	—	—	—	—	—	—	—
Tunisia	12	.4	—	—	—	—	—	—	—
Turkey	43	10.8	32.2	—	—	38.5	−.1	70.6	164
Union of South Africa	100	25.0	75.0	—	—	36.2	—	111.2	111
U Arab Rep: Egypt	60	9.5	50.5	−5.5	—	30.0	—	75.0	125
Syria	6.5	.2	6.3	−1.4	—	—	—	4.9	75
United Kingdom	1,300	233.3	1,063.7	−3.7	—	545.3	13.0	1,618.3	124
United States	2,750	687.5	2,062.5	92.0	600.0	−1,919.5	−46.9	788.1	29
Uruguay	15	3.8	—	—	—	—	—	—	—
Venezuela	15	3.8	11.2	—	—	—	—	11.2	75
Viet-Nam	12.5	3.1	—	—	—	—	—	—	—
Yugoslavia	60	7.9	52.1	—	—	22.9	.1	75.1	125
Currency			6,517.6	−43.7	600.0	{ 1,697.0 / −2,003.4 }	−30.0	6,737.4	
Convertible			2,420.9	92.0	600.0	−1,906.0	−46.9	1,160.0	
Non-Convertible			4,096.7	−135.7	—	1,599.5	16.9	5,577.4	
Gold		1,731.8		43.7	−600.0	304.5	51.0	1,531.0	
Subscript. Receivable		943.6						943.6	
Total	9,193.0	9,193.0		0	0	−2.0	21.0	9,212.0	

Exchange Transactions: Drawings and Their Repayment

(As of November 30, 1958. Amounts expressed in millions of U.S. dollars)

Member	1947	1948	1949	1950	1951	1952	1953	1954	1955	1956	1957	1958 to Date	Total to Date Gross	Total to Date Net
Argentina	....	....	....	....	....	....	....	....	....	....	75.0	....	75.0	75.0
Australia	....	....	20.0	....	....	30.0	−12.0	−24.0	−14.0	....	....	....	50.0	0
Belgium	11.0	{22.0 −11.4}	−.9	−20.7	....	▲	▲	▲	▲	▲	50.0	−50.0	83.0	0
Bolivia	....	....	....	....	....	....	2.5	....	....	3.0▲	1.0▲	2.0▲	8.5	8.5▲
Brazil	....	....	37.5	....	28.0	{37.5 −65.5}	{65.5 −37.5}	....	....	−28.0	37.5	{54.8 −17.2}	260.8	112.5▲
Burma	....	....	....	....	....	....	....	....	....	15.0	....	....	15.0	15.0
Chile	8.8	....	....	....	−3.4	−3.7	{12.5 −1.7}	....	....	−.2▲	{31.1 −12.3}	9.1▲	61.5	40.2▲
Colombia	....	....	....	....	....	....	....	25.0	....	....	{5.0▲ −5.0}	10.0▲	40.0▲	35.0▲
Costa Rica	....	1.2	−.9	−.3	....	....	....	....	....	....	....	....	1.2	0
Cuba	....	....	....	....	....	....	....	....	....	12.5▲	{35.0 −22.5}	25.0 −25.0	72.5	25.0
Czechoslovakia*	....	6.0	....	....	....	....	....	....	−2.0*	−.7*	−.7*	−.6*	6.0	2.0*
Denmark	3.4	6.8	....	....	....	....	....	....	−10.2	....	34.0	−25.5	44.2	8.5
Ecuador	....	....	....	....	....	....	....	....	....	....	5.0	−5.0	5.0	0
El Salvador	....	....	....	....	....	....	....	....	....	2.5	−2.5	▲	2.5	0▲
Ethiopia	....	.3	.3	−.3	−.3	....	....	....	....	....	....	....	.6	0
Finland	....	....	....	....	....	4.5▲	{5.0 −2.0}	−4.5▲	−3.0	....	....	....	9.5	0
France	125.0	....	....	....	....	....	....	−20.0	−60.0	−45.0	262.5	131.2	518.8	393.8
Haiti	....	....	....	....	....	....	....	....	....	....	1.0	2.5▲	3.5	3.5▲
Honduras	....	....	....	....	....	....	....	....	....	....	{6.2 −2.5}	−3.8	6.2	0
India	....	68.3	31.7	....	....	....	....	−46.7	−40.7	−12.5	200.0	....	300.0	200.0
Indonesia	....	....	....	....	....	....	....	15.0	....	{−15.0 55.0}	....	....	70.0	55.0
Iran	....	....	....	....	6.6	2.2	....	....	{−8.7 17.5}	{−11.9 19.7}	....	−8.4	46.0	16.9
Israel	....	....	....	....	....	....	....	....	....	....	3.8	....	3.8	3.8
Japan	....	....	....	....	....	....	{124.0 −61.6}	....	−62.4	....	125.0	−125.0	249.0	0
Mexico	22.5	....	....	....	−22.6	....	....	22.5▲	−22.4	....	....	....	45.0	0
Netherlands	52.0	23.3	....	....	....	−27.3	−48.0	....	....	....	68.8▲	−68.8	144.1	0
Nicaragua	....	.5	−.5	....	....	....	....	....	....	1.9▲	{−1.9 3.8▲}	−3.8▲	6.1	0▲

Norway	....	9.6	....	....	−9.6	....	....	....	....	....	....	....	9.6	0
Paraguay	....	....	....	....	....	.9	....	−.4	....	1.5	{4.0 ▲ / −.5}	.8 ▲	7.3	6.3 ▲
Peru	....	....	....	....	....	....	....	▲	▲	▲	▲	5.0 ▲	5.0	5.0 ▲
Philippines	....	....	....	....	....	....	....	....	10.0	5.0	....	....	15.0	15.0
Sudan	....	....	....	....	....	....	....	....	....	....	....	5.0	5.0	5.0
Turkey	5.0	....	....	....	....	{10.0 / −5.0}	20.0	−6.0	−9.0	....	{13.5 / −7.0}	{25.0 / −8.0}	73.5	38.5
U of S Africa	....	10.0	....	....	−10.0	....	....	....	....	....	....	36.2 ▲	46.2	36.2 ▲
U Arab Rep: Egypt	....	....	3.0	−3.0	....	....	....	....	....	15.0	15.0	....	33.0	30.0
United Kingdom	{240.0 / −6.0}	60.0	....	....	−28.0	....	−157.6	−108.3	....	561.5 ▲	▲	−16.2 ▲	861.5	545.3 ▲
Yugoslavia	....	....	9.0	....	....	....	....	....	....	....	−9.0	22.9	31.9	22.9
Drawings	468	208	101	....	35	85	2.30	62	28	693	977	329	3,216	1,699
Currency Bought														
Belgian francs	....	*11.4*	....	....	....	....	....	....	....	....	....	....	*11.4*	
Canadian dollars	....	....	....	....	....	....	....	....	....	*15.0*	....	....	*15.0*	
German marks	....	....	....	....	....	....	*4.4*	....	....	....	....	*64.5*	*68.9*	
Guilders	....	....	....	....	....	....	....	....	....	....	....	*5.0*	*5.0*	
Pounds sterling	*6.1*	....	....	....	*28.0*	....	*157.6*	....	....	....	....	*16.2*	*207.9*	
US dollars	*461.6*	*196.6*	*101.5*	....	*6.6*	*85.1*	*67.5*	*62.5*	*27.5*	*677.6*	*977.0*	*243.7*	*2,907.3*	
Repayments	−6	−11	−2	−24	−74	−102	−320	−210	−232	−113	−64	−357		−1,517
by Repurchases	....	....	*−2*	*−24*	*−46*	*−102*	*−163*	*−210*	*−232*	*−113*	*−64*	*−336*		*−1,292*
by Others' Drawings	*−6*	*−11*	....	....	*−28*	....	*−158*	....	....	....	....	*−21*		*−224*
Net Drawings	462	197	99	−24	−39	−16	−91	−148	−205	579	913	−28 }		1,699†
Drawings Outstanding	462	658	757	733	694	678	587	439	234	814	1,727	1,699 }		
Stand-bys Agreed						55	....	62	....	1,077	183	239		1,617
Drawn						....	5	22	....	21	426	206		680
Expired						....	....	....	28	1	4	89		122
Amounts Available at End of Period						55	50	90	62	1,117	870	815		815 ▲
Members' Repurchases on Subscription Account				−6.4	−.9	−11.5	−4.7	−57.2	−4.8	−41.1	−9.1	....		−135.7

* Former member. Payments made on settlement of Czechoslovakia's debt to the Fund are included as if they were a member's repurchase. ▲ Stand-by in effect at end of period and not drawn or not fully drawn See table on Stand-by Arrangements. † Net member drawings plus outstanding debt of Czechoslovakia.

Stand-By Arrangements

(As of November 30, 1958. Amounts expressed in millions of U.S. dollars)

Member	Date of Agreement	Expiration Date of Agreement or Renewal	Amount Agreed	Amount Available						
				Dec 31 1952	Dec 31 1953	Dec 31 1954	Dec 31 1955	Dec 31 1956	Dec 31 1957	Nov 30 1958
Agreements in effect										
Bolivia	Nov 1956	Dec 1958	7.5	—	—	—	—	4.5	3.5	1.5
Brazil	June 1958	June 1959	37.5	—	—	—	—	—	—	—
Chile	Apr 1956	Mar 1959	35.0	—	—	—	—	35.0	16.2	7.2
Colombia	June 1957	June 1959	25.0	—	—	—	—	—	25.0	15.0
El Salvador	Oct 1958	Mar 1959	7.5	—	—	—	—	—	—	7.5
France	Jan 1958	Jan 1959	131.25	—	—	—	—	—	—	—
Haiti	July 1958	July 1959	5.0	—	—	—	—	—	—	2.5
Nicaragua	Sept 1958	Mar 1959	7.5	—	—	—	—	—	—	7.5
Paraguay	July 1957	July 1959	5.5	—	—	—	—	—	2.0	1.2
Peru	Feb 1958	Feb 1959	25.0	—	—	—	—	—	—	20.0
Union of S. Africa	Apr 1958	Apr 1959	25.0	—	—	—	—	—	—	13.8
United Kingdom	Dec 1956	Dec 1958	738.53	—	—	—	—	738.5	738.5	738.5
Agreements expired or canceled										
Belgium	June 1952	June 1957	50.0	50.0	50.0	50.0	50.0	50.0	—	—
Cuba	Dec 1956	June 1957	12.5	—	—	—	—	12.5	—	—
Finland	Dec 1952	June 1953	5.0	5.0	—	—	—	—	—	—
France	Oct 1956	Oct 1957	262.5	—	—	—	—	262.5	—	—
Honduras	Nov 1957	May 1958	3.75	—	—	—	—	—	—	—
India	Mar 1957	Mar 1958	72.5	—	—	—	—	—	—	—
Iran	May 1956	Nov 1956	17.5	—	—	—	—	—	—	—
Mexico	Apr 1954	Oct 1955	50.0	—	—	27.5	—	—	—	—
Netherlands	Sept 1957	Mar 1958	68.75	—	—	—	—	—	68.8	—
Nicaragua	Nov 1956	May 1957	3.75	—	—	—	—	1.9	—	—
Peru	Oct 1957	Apr 1958	7.5	—	—	—	—	—	3.8	—
	Feb 1954	Feb 1958	12.5	—	—	12.5	12.5	12.5	12.5	—
Total			1,616.53	55.0	50.0	90.0	62.5	1,117.4	870.3	814.7

Balance Sheet

(Amounts expressed in millions of U.S. dollars)

	April 30 1950	April 30 1951	April 30 1952	April 30 1953	April 30 1954	April 30 1955	April 30 1956	April 30 1957	April 30 1958	Oct 31 1958
Gold (at 35 dollars per fine ounce)	1,459.5	1,495.0	1,531.6	1,692.6	1,718.5	1,744.4	1,761.4	1,439.3	1,237.7	1,306.9
Investments [a]	—	—	—	—	—	—	50.0	200.0	200.0	200.0
Convertible Currencies	1,395.2	1,409.7	1,582.0	1,638.3	1,774.0	1,974.3	2,119.9	1,333.9	1,069.1	1,088.6
Balances with Depositories	*125.1*	*126.0*	*107.1*	*156.9*	*167.8*	*168.3*	*226.5*	*167.1*	*175.2*	*176.8*
Demand Securities [b]	*1,270.0*	*1,283.7*	*1,475.0*	*1,481.4*	*1,606.2*	*1,802.4*	*1,892.0*	*1,175.2*	*891.4*	*911.9*
Currency Adj. Rec. or Pay. (−)	—	—	—	—	—	*3.6*	*1.4*	*−8.4*	*2.5*	*−.1*
Sub Total	2,854.6	2,904.7	3,113.6	3,330.9	3,492.5	3,718.7	3,931.3	2,973.2	2,506.8	2,595.5
Non-Convertible Currencies	4,153.5	4,219.1	4,161.2	4,340.2	4,458.5	4,325.4	3,986.1	5,129.6	5,686.5	5,653.3
Balances with Depositories	*620.6*	*588.6*	*696.3*	*658.9*	*688.8*	*656.8*	*572.8*	*943.8*	*1,246.2*	*1,253.7*
Demand Securities [b]	*3,533.0*	*3,630.4*	*3,464.9*	*3,681.3*	*3,769.7*	*3,669.0*	*3,413.3*	*4,185.8*	*4,431.2*	*4,399.2*
Currency Adj. Rec. or Pay. (−)	—	—	—	—	—	*−.4*	—	—	*9.1*	*.4*
Subscriptions Receivable	892.8	906.5	870.8	1,056.7	888.8	797.7	814.5	816.8	898.4	958.1
Withdrawing Member's Currency	—	—	—	—	—	—	3.6	3.0	2.3	2.0
Other Assets	0.7	0.7	1.0	1.1	1.0	0.9	1.1	4.6	5.5	6.8
Total Assets = Total Liabilities	7,918.0	8,031.0	8,146.6	8,728.9	8,840.8	8,842.7	8,736.6	8,927.2	9,099.6	9,215.7
Capital: Auth. Subscriptions: paid	7,028.7	7,130.0	7,282.7	7,679.8	7,959.8	7,930.3	7,936.0	8,114.7	8,189.6	8,234.9
unpaid	892.8	906.5	870.8	1,056.7	888.8	797.7	814.5	816.8	898.4	958.1
Cumulated Deficit (−)	*−3.8*	*−5.7*	*−7.2*	*−8.0*	*−8.0*	*−10.5*	*−14.2*	*−6.3*	—	—
Net Capital	7,917.7	8,030.8	8,146.3	8,728.5	8,840.5	8,717.5	8,736.3	8,925.2	9,088.0	9,193.0
Withdrawing Member's Subscription	—	—	—	—	—	125.0	—	—	—	—
Reserves and Liabilities	.3	.2	.3	.4	.3	.2	.3	2.0	11.6	22.7

[a] US Treasury Bills and funds awaiting investment. [b] Nonnegotiable, noninterest-bearing securities payable at face value on demand.

Compensatory Financing: First Report

In March 1959 the UN Commission on International Commodity Trade agreed to consider at its next session, in May 1960, international measures designed to compensate for fluctuations in export receipts, and invited the Fund to inform the Commission about its policies in this respect. A report by the Fund in response to this invitation was followed by further discussions, during which a number of alternative plans were examined.

In May 1962 the Commission considered comments by a technical working group set up to report on these plans, and invited the Fund to consider whether it could not play a larger part in financing fluctuations in export receipts. A draft response to this invitation, prepared by the staff, was reviewed by the Board in November and December 1962, and a revised version of it in February 1963. The latter was approved with slight amendments on February 27, and was sent to the Commission. It is reproduced below.

Compensatory Financing of Export Fluctuations

(February 1963)

A Report by the International Monetary Fund on Compensatory Financing of the Fluctuations in Exports of Primary Exporting Countries

CONTENTS

INTRODUCTION

The United Nations Commission on International Commodity Trade, at its tenth session held in Rome in May 1962, "invited the International Monetary Fund, in the light of the discussion during the tenth session, and after consideration of the questions involved, to present, as soon as possible, a report as to whether and in what way the Fund might play an increased part in the compensatory financing of export fluctuations of primary exporting countries, and to keep the Technical Working Group currently informed of the progress of its deliberations on the subject." [1]

The present report by the International Monetary Fund is presented in fulfillment of the invitation extended by the Commission.

I. PREVIOUS CONSIDERATION OF THE PROBLEM BY THE FUND

In 1960, in response to an earlier request by the Commission on International Commodity Trade, the Fund prepared a study explaining its policies and procedures bearing on the compensatory financing of fluctuations in foreign exchange receipts from the export of primary commodities.[2] The main points in this study may be briefly summarized as follows:

(1) The provision of foreign exchange to Fund members to assist in the compensation of short-term fluctuations in the balance of payments constitutes a legitimate use of Fund resources.[3] Among such fluctuations are some that arise primarily from variations in export prices and proceeds. However, in order that balance of payments deficits from this cause should be suitable for financing by the Fund, the member's policies must be such as to enable it, with the financial assistance it obtains from the Fund, to overcome its difficulties within a reasonably short period of time.

(2) It would be neither practicable nor desirable to make the amount of such assistance dependent on any automatic formula, or to provide any separate form of Fund assistance to deal with export fluctuations alone. The reasons for this are (a) that judgment is required to determine the extent to which export fluctuations require, and are suitable for, compensatory financing in the light of the balance of payments as a whole, and the extent to which any compensation required should be provided by international transfers rather than by national reserve movements, and (b) that, if the Fund should give too much of its assistance automatically, its ability to influence countries toward the adoption of appropriate policies would be seriously impaired. Requests for drawings for all purposes in accordance with the Articles of Agreement are, however, treated liberally if they are within the gold tranche or the first credit tranche.

(3) Fund quotas (at the end of 1959) were considered adequate to provide for its primary exporting members a supplement to liquidity which, in the majority of cases, should be sufficient, in conjunction with their own resources, to enable them to deal with payments problems created by short-term fluctuations in exports or in receipts from abroad of the order experienced since World War II, provided they did their best to keep their income and costs adjusted to the longer-run changes in their external purchasing power.

---

[1] United Nations, Commission on International Commodity Trade, Report on the Tenth Session (E/CN.13/55, May 31, 1962), p. 41.

[2] "Fund Policies and Procedures in Relation to the Compensatory Financing of Commodity Fluctuations," *Staff Papers*, Vol. VIII (1960–61), pp. 1–76.

[3] Since the presentation of this study in April 1960, Fund transactions with primary exporting countries have greatly increased. Outstanding drawings by low-income primary exporters have nearly doubled over the last 3 years. For details see Annex Table (p. 457).

(4) There appeared (as of the same date) to be no reason why a shortage of Fund resources should be a factor limiting the amount of assistance that the Fund would otherwise consider it desirable to extend to its members.

(5) Consequently, it was concluded that "members of the Fund that are taking appropriate steps to preserve internal financial stability and to maintain their balance of payments in equilibrium, taking good years with bad, and that are otherwise making satisfactory progress toward the fulfillment of the Fund's purposes can anticipate with confidence that financing will be available from the Fund which, in conjunction with a reasonable use of their own reserves, should be sufficient to enable them to overcome temporary payments difficulties arising from export fluctuations." [4]

II. SUGGESTIONS FOR INCREASED USE OF FUND RESOURCES FOR COMPENSATORY FINANCING

Since the study summarized above was submitted to the United Nations in April 1960, the subject of compensatory financing has been actively considered within the framework of the United Nations (UN) and of the Organization of American States (OAS), in particular by the UN Committee of Experts which reported in January 1961,[5] and by the OAS Group of Experts which reported in April 1962.[6]

In general, the international bodies in which the matter has been discussed have displayed understanding toward the Fund's policies on compensatory financing, as outlined above (including the restricted scope given to automatism in Fund transactions), and appreciation for the assistance which the Fund has been able to give under its present rules to primary exporting countries having export difficulties. However, certain suggestions have been made for changes in policy that would permit an enhancement of the Fund's role in compensatory financing. Moreover, it has been argued that, even if the Fund should make a reasonable degree of progress in the direction indicated, enough uncertainty would remain in the minds of governments as to their ability to draw on the Fund to justify the consideration of other possible international measures of compensatory financing. The suggestion has therefore been made that some new financial institution separate from, though possibly affiliated with, the Fund is needed to provide compensatory financing for export fluctuations, in amounts or of a kind or with a degree of automatism that is either not practicable or not desirable for the Fund. In pursuance of this line of thought, the above mentioned UN Committee of Experts worked out schemes for a Development Insurance Fund, which have subsequently been elaborated by the UN Secretariat, whereas the scheme of the OAS Expert Group is on a loan basis.

The following are the principal suggestions made by the UN and OAS Experts regarding the policies and practices of the Fund in the use of its own resources.

1. *Qualitative criteria for the use of Fund resources*

The UN Commission on International Commodity Trade, at its session of May 1961, "considered that it would be desirable if the Fund would study the question whether

---

[4] *Ibid.*, p. 4.

[5] United Nations, *International Compensation for Fluctuations in Commodity Trade* (Report by a Committee of Experts, E/CN.13/40, New York, 1961).

[6] Organization of American States, *Final Report of the Group of Experts on the Stabilization of Export Receipts* (Washington, D.C., 1962).

the present criteria for the use of its resources are fully adapted to circumstances in which payments difficulties arise mainly from fluctuations in primary product markets." [7]

2. *Stand-bys or near stand-bys for compensatory financing*

According to the Report of the UN Committee of Experts, "through the increased use of stand-by arrangements or consultative procedures, the Fund should aim to clarify with interested members the conditions which would assure that the full use of quota without waiver (Fund holding of 200 per cent of a member's currency) or even more will be readily granted if it appears justifiable according to forecasts of commodity markets and other relevant considerations." [8]

3. *Extension of gold-tranche criterion to later tranches*

The Report of the UN Committee of Experts suggests that "in so far as drawings on the Fund are automatic, a country whose export proceeds fall has reliable access to a source of compensatory financing. At present only 25 per cent of a member country's quota comes close to being automatically available. Any significant increase in this percentage which the Fund could institute would be a valuable step toward providing compensatory financing to meet the needs of primary producing countries when threatened with the adverse impact of a decline in export proceeds." [9]

4. *Automatic compensatory drawing rights in first credit tranche*

In Appendix II of the Report of the UN Committee of Experts, one of the Experts suggested that "to offset fluctuations in the export proceeds of primary producing countries, compensatory drawings and repayments should be determined automatically by a formula. The fluctuations should be measured as a deviation from a trend which can be estimated on the basis of a moving average of three preceding years. A shortfall in export proceeds in any year should entitle the country to draw from the Fund automatically up to, say, an amount which causes the Fund's holdings of the country's currency to equal 125 per cent of its quota. . . . Subsequently, when export proceeds are above the trend, the excess earnings should be used automatically to repay the earlier drawings." [10] From the context it appears that this Expert had in mind full compensation of shortfalls as defined, up to the 125 per cent point, and subsequent repayment of the whole of any excess of export proceeds over trend.

5. *Automatic compensatory drawing rights additional to normal facilities*

At the Special Meeting of the Organization of American States at Punta del Este in August 1961, Chile proposed that Fund members affected by declines in prices of important export commodities should be enabled to draw from the Fund in amounts determined by the magnitude of the price decline in question relative to the average price in the three preceding years and by the volume of exports affected. Drawings under these special arrangements would be repaid when prices rose above the average

---

[7] United Nations, Commission on International Commodity Trade, Report of the Ninth Session (E/CN.13/42, May 1961), p. 21.

[8] UN Committee of Experts, *op. cit.*, p. 29.

[9] *Ibid.*, p. 28.

[10] *Ibid.*, p. 81.

in the three preceding years. The ability of members to make ordinary drawings would not be affected by the amounts outstanding under these special arrangements.[11]

* * * * * *

The proposals advanced, whether for new compensatory financing institutions or for changes in the policies and practices of the Fund, are evidence that the assistance provided by the Fund under present policies is considered either insufficiently automatic in character or inadequate in amount to deal with the payments problems that arise from fluctuations in exports of primary exporting countries. The question of automatism of Fund operations is discussed in Section III; that of the quantitative adequacy of members' access to the Fund, in Section IV. These sections lead to the Conclusions (set out in Section V of this report) which deal with Fund action.

III. AUTOMATISM AND THE USE OF FUND RESOURCES

The type of automatism envisaged in the various proposals that have been put forward—automatism of the "export compensatory" rather than of the "all purpose" type—has two principal features:

(1) A mathematical formula would be used to determine whether, and to what extent, exports in a particular year are to be considered so abnormally low as to require compensation, or so abnormally high as to permit the repayment of compensation received previously. No judgment would be made by the lending agency, in the light of any other information that might be available, as to whether, in a particular situation, the formula yields a reasonable estimate of normal exports.

(2) The lending agency, whether the Fund or a new agency, would make credit available to a country without question whenever the formula pointed to a statistical justification on export grounds alone. No regard would be paid to the over-all balance of payments need for such credit, to the likelihood that the country would be able, in the light of the policies it was pursuing, to repay the credits that were being granted or, in some proposals, to the amount that the country has already borrowed. The country itself could, of course, refuse to take up credits to which it was entitled or could repay credits before maturity.

With regard to the first point, the proposals now under consideration have assumed, virtually without question, that when exports are below the average for, say, the three preceding years they can safely be assumed to be abnormally low so that compensation would be appropriate. Statistical experiments, covering the postwar period, recently made for a large number of primary exporting countries, suggest, however, that this is by no means generally the case. The fact that exports in any given year have been lower (or higher) than they were in preceding years is very often an indication of a downward (or upward) trend which may well persist for some years to come. Export proceeds that seem low in relation to those of preceding years may well appear in retrospect as rather favorable. It follows from this that automatic formulae based on past and current export data can, at best, yield only rather unsatisfactory estimates of the true trend of exports. In the absence of foreknowledge of future exports, the least inaccurate estimate of the normal level in any given year is likely to be one that

[11] Pan American Union, Inter-American Economic and Social Council, Special Meeting at the Ministerial Level, Punta del Este, Minutes and Documents (Washington, D.C., 1962): Draft Resolution by the Delegation of Chile, pp. 550 ff. (in Spanish).

attributes a great weight to the exports of the year itself. Even when this is done, however, the extent to which it is possible to adjust export proceeds by adding or subtracting compensatory receipts or repayments so as to bring them closer to their true norm or to reduce their instability is limited.[12]

While great uncertainty must always attach to any attempt to estimate the medium-term trend or norm of exports, it is reasonable to assume that a better estimate could be made by the exercise of judgment based on an analysis of the causal factors at work than by any mathematical formula, however skillfully contrived, which is based on the mere statistical magnitude of current and previous exports.

In regard to the second aspect of automatism—the granting of credit irrespective of the general balance of payments situation or of the policies of the country receiving assistance—it may be useful to set out existing Fund policies and their rationale.

Under present Fund policies "members are given the overwhelming benefit of the doubt in relation to requests for transactions within the 'gold tranche,' that is, for drawings which do not increase the Fund's holdings of the currency beyond an amount equal to the member's quota. The Fund's attitude to requests for transactions within the 'first credit tranche'—that is, transactions which bring the Fund's holdings of a member's currency above 100 per cent but not above 125 per cent of its quota—is a liberal one, provided that the member itself is making reasonable efforts to solve its problems. Requests for transactions beyond these limits require substantial justification. They are likely to be favorably received when the drawings or stand-by arrangements are intended to support a sound program aimed at establishing or maintaining the enduring stability of the member's currency at a realistic rate of exchange." [13]

In the higher tranches, the Fund has therefore wished to be satisfied that a sound set of policies is being followed. The Fund may have reached this conclusion before the question of a drawing arose—e.g., if it has a stand-by arrangement with the country in question. If such policies are being followed, no change in them would be needed to meet payments difficulties that are due solely to temporary situations in foreign markets, or to such factors as a temporary fluctuation in crops. The mere fact of a falling off in exports would not be taken as an indication that a corrective program was necessary or that the corrective program already envisaged should be intensified. On the other hand, a need for corrective policies might arise either because the decline in exports appeared to foreshadow a lasting weakening of the country's balance of payments or because (though the export decline itself might be purely temporary and self correcting) the country's monetary and financial policies were such as to provoke, sooner or later, balance of payments difficulties even under satisfactory export conditions. Recognition by the Fund of the need for corrective policies in either of the two circumstances outlined above does not mean that the Fund has seized the occasion of a member country's financial plight to press for immediate adoption of the full range of what might be construed as "ideal" policies; for example, the elimination of all payments restrictions, the adoption of full currency convertibility at an effective par value, the abolition of all multiple rates, etc. Reference to the policies followed in regard to these matters by the many countries that are using the Fund in the second or higher credit tranches or that have stand-by arrangements permitting such use would dispel

[12] See J. Marcus Fleming, Rudolf Rhomberg, and Lorette Boissonneault, "Export Norms and Their Role in Compensatory Financing," Part I, *Staff Papers*, Vol. X (1963), pp. 98–124.

[13] International Monetary Fund, *Annual Report, 1962*, p. 31.

at once the notion of such an approach by the Fund. In accordance, however, with the purposes set out in Article I of the Fund's Articles of Agreement, Fund assistance, at least beyond the gold tranche, is not made available to any country that makes no effort to move toward the elimination of those aspects of its exchange and monetary policies that are detrimental to the interests of the member itself or those of other members.

The general case against providing compensatory credit without inquiry into general balance of payments need or into the policies of the country concerned has been argued at length in "Fund Policies and Procedures in Relation to the Compensatory Financing of Commodity Fluctuations,"[14] and these arguments have not, in general, been challenged. As suggested by the UN Committee of Experts, a country exposed to export fluctuations might feel more secure if it had access to resources on which it could draw without having to satisfy any international organization or lending government as to the type of domestic or international economic policy it was pursuing. Moreover, it is possible that the availability of international credit on an automatic basis at times when exports are low, and the necessity of repaying such credit at times when exports are high, would have some effect in inducing countries to attempt to keep their domestic expenditures and imports on an even keel, on the basis of reasonable expectations as to the medium-term trend of their exports and other receipts. These potential advantages, however, have to be weighed against the disadvantages of automatic credit geared to a single element in the balance of payments. In this connection it may be appropriate to mention two considerations in particular:

(1) Even a statistically accurate determination that exports in a particular year are below normal implies nothing at all as to the cause of the shortfall. The cause may be a decline in world demand or a crop failure brought about by a natural calamity. But the reason may also lie in domestic inflation, leading to increasingly overvalued exchange rates, government purchases for stockpile at prices above those prevailing in world markets, or other national policies. When declines in exports occur, a most careful consideration of their possible causes is needed in order to determine whether some of them may not be open to remedial action by the country itself, so as to prevent export declines in the future if similar circumstances recur.

Thus, while it is desirable that countries have access to financial means to compensate for fluctuations in exports, it is not particularly desirable, and may be against the genuine interest of the country concerned, that this finance should be provided automatically and without an exploration of the causes of the decline in exports and the measures that might be taken to improve exports in the future.

In this connection, it should be pointed out that the benefits which a country derives from reaching an understanding with the Fund as to the policies appropriate to its situation may extend beyond the financial assistance obtained from the Fund itself. In such circumstances, agreement with the Fund is likely to strengthen opinion abroad and at home regarding the country's creditworthiness, and thus to facilitate the attraction of capital from other sources, official as well as private.

(2) The total amount of short-term credit made available to a country by one agency or under one arrangement cannot be totally divorced from the amount made available on similar terms by another agency or under another arrangement by the same agency. It would be shortsighted to think that a country would be fully justified in borrowing

---

[14] *Staff Papers*, Vol. VIII (1960–61), pp. 1–76.

a relatively large amount on short term to compensate for an export shortfall while totally disregarding the amount that it had already borrowed on short term for other purposes. Prudent countries would themselves see to it that their total indebtedness did not exceed what they could reasonably expect to repay, and this would take into account all indebtedness of a similar character. It would seem to be dubious wisdom to set up the terms of lending of an international agency in such a manner as to put governments under internal pressure to borrow sums that they themselves might consider beyond the bounds of prudence. If there are sensible limitations on total short-term borrowing, these limitations should be taken into account not only by the borrowing country itself but also in the policies of the international agency extending the credit.

IV. QUANTITATIVE ADEQUACY OF DRAWING FACILITIES IN THE FUND

The UN Committee of Experts responsible for producing *International Compensation for Fluctuations in Commodity Trade* calculated that 14 out of 46 primary producing countries experienced, over the years 1953–59, cumulative shortfalls of exports, when compared with average annual exports over the three preceding years, of such magnitude that to compensate them fully would have compelled them, after using up 125 per cent of their Fund quotas, to dip into their own reserves to an extent exceeding 30 per cent of reserves at the end of 1959.[15]

The Experts did not offer an opinion as to whether these facilities, had they been available on an automatic basis, would have been adequate to meet, to a reasonable extent, the need for compensatory financing of export fluctuations. However, they pointed out that if only the 25 per cent of quota constituting the gold tranche had been made available by the Fund to meet the cumulative export shortfalls, 20 of the countries concerned would have had to draw down their reserves by more than 30 per cent to achieve full compensation. These near-automatic facilities, they implied, were insufficient; and even if a reasonable degree of progress were made by the Fund in extending the automatism of drawings in many cases, the uncertainty of drawings would, they considered, offer a serious handicap to the object of continuity in development expenditure.

In a UN Secretariat Study,[16] it was calculated

(a) that for the average primary exporting member of the Fund the average shortfall in export earnings (compared with the mean of the previous three years' exports) over the period 1953–60 was approximately equal to half of its (1961) quota; and that in only half of the countries would drawings of up to 50 per cent of quota have sufficed to offset the average annual shortfall for years in which shortfalls occurred;[17] and

(b) that if each primary exporting member had sought to compensate 100 per cent of its export shortfalls by drawing on the Fund and had used 60 per cent of export excesses for repayment, subject to a limit of cumulative net drawings

[15] UN Committee of Experts, *op. cit.*, pp. 25–29.

[16] *Consideration of Compensatory Financial Measures to Offset Flunctuations in the Export Income of Primary Producing Countries: Stabilization of Export Proceeds Through a Development Insurance Fund* (E/CN.13/43, January 1962).

[17] *Ibid.*, pp. 46–48 (Table 10) and p. 49.

> of 50 per cent of quota, primary exporting members could have compensated in this way about one third of their total shortfalls.[18]

The authors of the study made it clear that their calculations were not intended to reflect on, or measure, the adequacy of the Fund as a means of assisting member countries, since usually reserves and other sources of credit could also be drawn upon and since Fund drawings are not limited to 50 per cent of quota.

The question of the quantitative adequacy of drawing facilities in the Fund to meet the needs for compensatory financing of export fluctuations is a difficult one, and no answer can be made to it without the help of many arbitrary suppositions. In arriving at these suppositions the following considerations are relevant:

(1) In the first place, as is generally recognized, Fund facilities are intended to be used in conjunction with national reserves and other sources of finance.

(2) Again, account has to be taken of the fact that all these forms of international liquidity are required to meet payments deficits arising not only from export shortfalls but also from fluctuations in other items in the balance of payments, notably fluctuations in imports. These fluctuations in other items are, indeed, rather more important than export shortfalls in the causation of payments deficits. Moreover, reserves cannot safely be run down to zero even to meet the severest drains. On the other hand, the various possible causes of deficit are unlikely to exercise their maximum effect simultaneously.

(3) In seeking to measure the probable need for compensatory financing of export shortfalls, it is impracticable to measure such shortfalls from a five-year moving average centered on the middle year (as was done in "Fund Policies and Procedures in Relation to the Compensatory Financing of Commodity Fluctuations"), and misleading to measure them from a moving average of the preceding three years (as was done by the UN Experts and Secretariat and by the OAS Experts). As has been pointed out elsewhere,[19] the five-year moving average centered on the current year, while it may be considered an "ideal" norm from which to measure export deviations, is not usable in practice since foreknowledge of the exports of future years is necessarily lacking. It would seem desirable, however, that the "practical" norm from which export deviations are measured should be close to this "ideal" norm insofar as the latter can be predicted on the basis of existing knowledge. Such a prediction is perhaps best made by the exercise of judgment in the light of all relevant information. If, however, the practical norm is defined by an automatic formula involving the exports of current and previous years, statistical calculations show that the formula, if it is not to diverge unnecessarily from the ideal norm, must give considerable weight to the current year's exports. Moreover, as was argued in "Fund Policies and Procedures in Relation to the Compensatory Financing of Commodity Fluctuations," the compensation of fluctuations should, in principle, be partial only. This implies that a target level of export availabilities [20] that is somewhat closer to actual exports than is the ideal norm be chosen. The result will be to increase still further the weight that should be given to the current year's exports in the calculation of the practical norm, or alternatively—what amounts to the same thing—deviations of actual exports from the practical norm should themselves be compensated only in part.

---

[18] *Ibid.*, p. 54.

[19] Fleming, Rhomberg, and Boissonneault, *op. cit.*

[20] That is, export proceeds adjusted for compensatory receipts and payments.

In Table 1 it is assumed that drawings on the Fund or drafts on national reserves will be made to cover two thirds of the shortfalls of actual exports with respect to a practical export norm defined as an average of exports in the present and two preceding years, with weights of 50 per cent given to the present year and 25 per cent to each of the two preceding years. It is assumed that two thirds of export surpluses with respect to this norm are used to repay drawings or reconstitute reserves. In order to ensure that countries with a downward long-term trend in exports do not indefinitely increase their claims on compensatory financing, it is assumed that drawings are repaid, or drafts on reserves are made good, in the fourth and fifth years of the drawing. In column 1 of the table, the maximum net cumulative requirements for compensatory financing over the period 1951–61 on these assumptions [21] are shown for low-income primary exporting members of the Fund.

Columns 2, 3, and 4 present three alternative measurements of the means presently available to meet the requirements set forth in column 1. Column 2 shows one third of each country's potential external liquidity, defined as its unused potential drawing facilities with the Fund (through the fourth credit tranche) *plus* its gross reserves of gold and convertible currency, as of mid-1962. The assumption underlying this column is that one third of external liquidity is approximately what can be used to meet export fluctuations, the remainder being required for basic reserves and for other types of payments deficits insofar as these coincide with export shortfalls. Column 3 shows one half of the excess of each country's potential external liquidity, as of mid-1962, over a presumed minimum reserve equal to the value of one month's imports at the 1961 rate. Column 4 gives each member country's Fund quota as of mid-1962. The assumption underlying column 4 is that each member would be in a position to use up to one half of its quota for the purpose of financing export fluctuations and would match this amount by an equal use of its own reserves, so that the combined use of reserves and Fund resources would amount to 100 per cent of quota.

The problem of the adequacy of Fund resources (in conjunction with national reserves) in meeting needs for the compensatory financing of export fluctuations is approached differently in columns 2 and 3 on the one hand, and in column 4 on the other. A comparison of column 1 with column 2 or 3 affords a measure of the extent to which member countries might have been able to meet export fluctuations of a defined magnitude on the basis of their external liquidity as of a given moment of time (viz., mid-1962). A comparison of column 1 with column 4 affords a measure of the extent to which member countries could meet such fluctuations on the basis of their normal drawing power in the Fund, starting from a position in which drawings for the purpose of export compensation are zero and assuming that the member will have adequate independent reserves to use *pari passu* with drawings on the Fund. In all cases, the need for financing is measured in relation to the experience of a particular decade (1951–61) and on the basis of specific assumptions regarding the degree of compensation. The comparisons of column 1 with columns 2 and 3 would seem the more relevant when considering the need for adding to the resources available to countries for compensatory financing. The comparison with column 4 is the more relevant when considering the adequacy of the Fund quotas of individual members.

[21] The assumptions are the same as those underlying Scheme 24 in Table 5 in the study by Fleming, Rhomberg, and Boissonneault, *op. cit.*—a scheme which yields export availabilities considerably closer to target and considerably smoother over time than those of Scheme 1 (the OAS Scheme) in that table.

Table 1. Adequacy of External Liquidity to Finance Fluctuations in Exports of Some Fund Members

(In millions of U.S. dollars)

Member	Maximum Financial Requirements Indicated by 1951-61 Experience[1] (1)	Assumed Limits of Finance Available				Excesses or Deficiencies (−) in Available Financing			
		One third of external liquidity[2] (2)	One half of excess external liquidity[3] (3)	Fund quota[4] (4)	One half of Fund quota[4] (5)	Column 2 minus column 1 (6)	Column 3 minus column 1 (7)	Column 4 minus column 1 (8)	Column 5 minus column 1 (9)
Argentina	192.3	101.3	91.2	280.0	140.0	−91.0	−101.1	87.7	−52.3
Bolivia	18.8	9.1	10.4	22.5	11.2	−9.7	−8.4	3.7	−7.6
Brazil	130.8	206.6	249.2	280.0	140.0	75.8	118.4	149.2	9.2
Burma	20.5	56.5	75.7	30.0	15.0	36.0	55.2	9.5	−5.5
Ceylon	25.8	42.6	49.0	45.0	22.5	16.8	23.2	19.2	−3.3
Chile	54.8	35.0	28.0	100.0	50.0	−19.8	−26.8	45.2	−4.8
Colombia	79.5	66.7	76.8	100.0	50.0	−12.8	−2.7	20.5	−29.5
Costa Rica	5.8	10.0	10.6	15.0	7.5	4.2	4.8	9.2	1.7
Cyprus	4.5	22.9	29.6	11.2	5.6	18.4	25.1	6.7	1.1
Dominican Republic	8.3	11.9	14.5	15.0	7.5	3.6	6.2	6.7	−0.8
Ecuador	5.8	13.8	15.9	15.0	7.5	8.0	10.1	9.2	1.7
El Salvador	7.8	15.4	18.6	11.2	5.6	7.6	10.8	3.4	−2.2
Ethiopia	4.7	29.6	40.6	13.2[5]	6.6[5]	24.9	35.9	8.5	1.9
Ghana	21.8	75.4	96.8	35.0	17.5	53.6	75.0	13.2	−4.3
Greece	12.3	116.7	145.3	60.0	30.0	104.4	133.0	47.7	17.7
Guatemala	5.7	22.5	28.2	15.0	7.5	16.8	22.5	9.3	1.8
Haiti	7.3	5.3	6.6	11.2	5.6	−2.0	−0.7	3.9	−1.7
Honduras	7.0	7.9	8.8	11.2	5.6	0.9	1.8	4.2	−1.4
India	148.0	305.6	368.2	600.0	300.0	157.6	220.2	452.0	152.0
Indonesia	135.0	89.9	101.8	165.0	82.5	−45.1	−33.2	30.0	−52.5
Iran	289.7	96.4	119.6	70.0	35.0	−193.3	−170.1	−219.7	−254.7
Iraq	54.7	56.0	67.1	15.0	7.5	1.3	12.4	−39.7	−47.2
Jordan	2.7	20.8	26.4	8.0[5]	4.0[5]	18.1	23.7	5.3	1.3
Korea	8.1	72.5	96.2	18.8	9.4	64.4	88.1	10.7	1.3
Lebanon	3.3	64.1	81.8	6.8	3.4	60.8	78.5	3.5	0.1

Libya	1.7	36.3	48.2	11.0[5]	5.5[5]	34.6	46.5	9.3	3.8
Malaya	246.0	290.1	404.8	32.5[5]	16.2[5]	44.1	158.8	−213.5	−229.8
Mexico	60.2	185.6	231.1	180.0	90.0	125.4	170.9	119.8	29.8
Morocco	2.8	81.2	103.2	52.5	26.2	78.4	100.4	49.7	23.4
Nicaragua	3.4	12.9	16.2	11.2	5.6	9.5	12.8	7.8	2.2
Nigeria	15.8	80.0	94.1	50.0	25.0	64.2	78.3	34.2	9.2
Pakistan	143.0	142.1	186.4	150.0	75.0	−0.9	43.4	7.0	−68.0
Panama	1.8	10.3	9.4	0.5	0.2	8.5	7.6	−1.3	−1.6
Paraguay	4.0	5.0	5.9	11.2	5.6	1.0	1.9	7.2	1.6
Peru	11.0	42.2	43.8	32.5[5]	16.2[5]	31.2	32.8	21.5	5.2
Philippines	15.2	46.7	40.1	75.0	37.5	31.5	24.9	59.8	22.3
Saudi Arabia	4.2	114.3	158.9	55.0	27.5	110.1	154.7	50.8	23.3
Sudan	32.8	63.9	86.1	15.0	7.5	31.1	53.3	−17.8	−25.3
Syrian Arab Republic	28.2	9.2	6.7	15.0	7.5	−19.0	−21.5	−13.2	−20.7
Thailand	24.8	175.7	243.4	45.0	22.5	150.9	218.6	20.2	−2.3
Tunisia	18.8	30.3	36.6	18.3[5]	9.2[5]	11.5	17.8	−0.5	−9.6
Turkey	51.3	85.9	107.6	86.0	43.0	34.6	56.3	34.7	−8.3
United Arab Republic	77.8	77.9	89.3	90.0	45.0	0.1	11.5	12.2	−32.8
Uruguay	60.3	82.8	115.6	30.0	15.0	22.5	55.3	−30.3	−45.3
Venezuela	0	229.5	295.9	150.0	75.0	229.5	295.9	150.0	75.0
Viet-Nam	34.7	60.4	80.0	18.5[5]	9.2[5]	25.7	45.3	−16.2	−25.5
Yugoslavia	9.0	36.3	16.6	120.0	60.0	27.3	7.6	111.0	51.0
Total	2,101.8	3,453.1	4,276.8	3,203.3	1,601.4	1,351.3	2,175.0	1,101.5	−500.4

[1] As described on page 451.

[2] A country's external liquidity is defined as its gross gold and convertible foreign exchange reserves *plus* its total tranche position with the Fund. Figures given are for mid-1962. A country's total tranche position with the Fund is the amount that it could still draw, as of a given date, if its justification were sufficient, without increasing the Fund's holdings of its currency above 200 per cent of its quota.

[3] Excess external liquidity (as of mid-1962) is defined as external liquidity (described in footnote 2) less average monthly imports (for 1961).

[4] Quotas given are for mid-1962.

[5] Quotas to be increased by annual installments, as follows: Ethiopia to $15 million by September 1963; Jordan to $11.25 million by July 1964; Libya to $15 million by September 1963; Malaya to $37.5 million by October 1963; Peru to $37.5 million by September 1963; Tunisia to $22.5 million by May 1964; and Viet-Nam to $22.5 million by November 1963.

It might be argued that parts of the reserves of some countries are virtually unusable, in that they are pledged against certain liabilities, or for other reasons. To some extent this factor is taken into account in the concept of minimum reserves underlying the calculations in columns 2 and 3. However, since no allowance has been made for this factor in column 4, column 5 has been added to show the extent to which the compensatory financing of export fluctuations would be limited if countries' use of external liquidity for this purpose were to be limited to 50 per cent of Fund quotas—a rather extreme assumption in most cases.

The differences between the alternative measures of the means available for compensatory financing of export fluctuations shown in columns 2, 3, 4, and 5, and the computed requirements for such financing shown in column 1, are set forth in columns 6, 7, 8, and 9, respectively. It is noteworthy that the incidence of "minus" signs in columns 6 and 7 is almost identical. One third of external liquidity as of mid-1962 would have been inadequate to cover maximum compensatory requirements of only 9 countries out of 47. One half of the excess of such liquidity over one month's imports would have been similarly inadequate in 8 of the same 9 countries. A limitation of financing to 100 per cent of quota as shown in column 8 would again have restricted export compensation in only 9 countries. Since these groups partially overlap, 16 member countries would have been limited by one or the other criterion. The more stringent limitation of financing to 50 per cent of quota, illustrated in columns 5 and 9, would result in "minus" signs in 9 countries in addition to those referred to above. In view of the necessarily somewhat arbitrary nature of the criteria employed in these calculations, and their uniform application to all countries regardless of special circumstances, the results for individual countries should not be taken too seriously. The calculations do, however, yield a general impression of the magnitude of the problem.

In a few countries with declining medium-term trends over the 1951–61 period, limitation of the finance available for automatic compensation over that period would probably have exercised a beneficial effect through limiting the need for repayment at times when exports were low in relation to trend.

V. CONCLUSIONS: FUND ACTION IN CONNECTION WITH EXPORT FLUCTUATIONS

(1) The financing of deficits arising out of export shortfalls, notably those of primary exporting member countries, has always been regarded as a legitimate reason for the use of Fund resources, which have been drawn on frequently for this purpose. The Fund believes that such financing helps these members to continue their efforts to adopt adequate measures toward the solution of their financial problems and to avoid the use of trade and exchange restrictions to deal with balance of payments problems, and that this enables these members to pursue their programs of economic development with greater effectiveness.

(2) The Fund noted in its 1962 Annual Report that trends in prices of basic commodities in the past few years have adversely affected the export earnings of many Fund members, which has increased the strain on their reserves. In view of this and in order to ensure the maximum effectiveness for its support to members—in particular, primary exporting members—that are faced with fluctuations in export proceeds, the Fund is taking the action set forth below.

A. Quotas

(3) The quotas of many primary exporting countries, taken in conjunction with a reasonable use of their own reserves, are at present adequate for dealing with export fluctuations such as have occurred during the past decade. In those instances, however, where adjustment of the quotas of certain primary exporting countries, and in particular of countries with relatively small quotas, would be appropriate to make them more adequate in the light of fluctuations in export proceeds and other relevant criteria, the Fund is willing to give sympathetic consideration to requests for such adjustment.

B. Drawing policies

(4) Under the present policies and practices on the use of Fund resources, any member is given the overwhelming benefit of the doubt in relation to requests for transactions within the gold tranche, and the Fund's attitude to requests for transactions within the first credit tranche is a liberal one provided the member itself is making reasonable efforts to solve its problems. In the higher credit tranches too, where a member's policies are consistent with Fund policies and practices on the use of Fund resources in these tranches, the Fund gives assistance, on a substantial scale, toward meeting temporary payments deficits, including deficits arising out of export shortfalls. The policies and practices of the Fund on drawings and stand-by arrangements have been developed in order to help members to meet more effectively their temporary balance of payments difficulties and to enable them, where necessary, to pursue policies aimed at restoring external and internal equilibrium. Fund assistance in accordance with these policies and practices has made an effective contribution to the solution of the difficulties of these members and the achievement of equilibrium. It has often led, moreover, to the provision of further resources from public and private sources for meeting immediate and longer-term needs. In the application of its policies and practices governing the use of its resources, the Fund's attitude has been a flexible one, and account has been taken of special difficulties facing members.

(5) The Fund has reviewed its policies to determine how it could more readily assist members, particularly primary exporters, encountering payments difficulties produced by temporary export shortfalls, and has decided that such members can expect that their requests for drawings will be met where the Fund is satisfied that

(a) the shortfall is of a short-term character and is largely attributable to circumstances beyond the control of the member; and

(b) the member will cooperate with the Fund in an effort to find, where required, appropriate solutions for its balance of payments difficulties.

The amount of drawings outstanding under this decision will not normally exceed 25 per cent of the member's quota, and the drawings will be subject to the Fund's established policies and practices on repurchase. When drawings are made under this decision, the Fund will so indicate in an appropriate manner.

(6) In order to implement the Fund's policies in connection with compensatory financing of export shortfalls, the Fund will be prepared to waive the limit on Fund holdings of 200 per cent of quota, where appropriate. In particular, the Fund will be prepared to waive this limit (i) where a waiver is necessary to permit compensatory drawings to be made under paragraphs (4) and (5) above, or (ii) to the extent that drawings in accordance with paragraph (5) are still outstanding.

Whenever the Fund's holdings of a member's currency resulting from an outstanding compensatory drawing under paragraph (5) are reduced, by the member's repurchase or otherwise, this will restore *pro tanto* the member's facility to make a further compensatory drawing under that paragraph, should the need arise.

(7) In order to identify more clearly what are to be regarded as export shortfalls of a short-term character, the Fund, in conjunction with the member concerned, will seek to establish reasonable estimates regarding the medium-term trend of the member's exports on the basis of appropriate statistical data in conjunction with qualitative information about its export prospects.

(8) The provision of credit to deal with the balance of payments effects of export fluctuations provides immediate relief for a country's short-term difficulties. In many cases, however, it will also be necessary to introduce measures of a policy character in order to attain a satisfactory and lasting solution to a country's balance of payments problems. Members generally have actively cooperated with the Fund to find and adopt the measures necessary to this end. Beyond immediate balance of payments difficulties, the primary exporting countries are, in many instances, facing unfavorable long-term export trends, and all are trying to meet the challenge of achieving more rapid and sustained development through a strengthening and broadening of their economies. The last mentioned problem will require action in many fields and over many years by both the primary exporting countries and the industrial countries, separately and in concert, including readier access to the markets of the developed countries for the products of the developing countries and an appropriate and sustained flow of technical and financial assistance to the developing countries. The Fund considers that its activities can provide valuable assistance in helping to establish a climate within which longer-term measures can be more effectively pursued.

Annex: Net Fund Drawings[1] of Some Fund Members,[2] 1947-62

	Cumulative, 1947-57	1958	1959	1960	1961	1962	Cumulative,[3] 1947-62	Available Under Stand-by Arrangement, End 1962
Argentina	75.0	—	72.5	48.5	31.0	−9.0	218.0	50.0
Bolivia	6.5	2.0	2.4	−1.5	−2.0	1.3	8.5	6.5
Brazil	75.0	37.6	−20.2	47.7	40.0	−17.5	162.5	—
Burma	15.0	−3.0	−4.0	−4.0	−4.0	—	—	—
Ceylon	—	—	—	—	11.2	11.2	22.5	—
Chile	31.1	10.6	—	−12.4	59.3	−12.7	76.0	—
Colombia	25.0	5.0	−15.0	−15.0	65.0	7.5	72.5	—
Costa Rica	—	—	—	—	7.5	−4.1	3.4	11.6
Dominican Republic	—	—	—	9.0	—	—	9.0	—
Ecuador	5.0	−5.0	—	—	14.0	−2.2	11.9	2.0
El Salvador	—	—	5.5	5.7	−3.2	−8.0	—	11.2
Ghana	—	—	—	—	—	14.2	14.2	—
Guatemala	—	—	—	—	—	5.0	5.0	—
Haiti	1.0	2.5	1.9	−1.3	−1.3	1.9	4.8	5.0
Honduras	3.8	−3.8	3.8	1.2	1.2	1.3	7.5	3.8
India	200.0	—	—	−72.5	122.5	25.0	275.1	75.0
Indonesia	55.0	—	−9.0	−18.5	33.7	21.2	82.5	—
Iran	25.3	−8.4	−11.9	45.0	−12.0	−37.9	—	—
Mexico	—	—	—	—	45.0	−45.0	—	—
Nicaragua	3.8	−1.9	−1.9	—	4.5	—	4.5	—
Pakistan	—	—	—	12.5	—	—	12.5	—
Paraguay	5.5	0.8	−1.5	0.1	−1.6	−1.8	1.5	5.0
Peru	—	10.0	−10.0	—	—	—	—	30.0
Philippines	15.0	—	−6.2	3.3	−2.9	25.4	34.6	40.4
Sudan	—	5.0	1.2	−0.4	−2.9	−2.9	—	—
Syrian Arab Republic	—	—	—	15.0	−0.7	3.4	17.7	—
Turkey	21.5	17.0	−3.0	−3.0	10.5	5.5	48.5	—
United Arab Republic	30.0	—	−2.7	25.2	−2.7	57.4	107.2	5.0
Uruguay	—	—	—	—	—	15.0	15.0	15.0
Yugoslavia	—	22.9	—	—	67.5	−7.5	82.9	—
Total	593.5	91.3	1.9	84.6	479.6	46.7	1,297.8	260.5

Source: International Monetary Fund, *International Financial Statistics.*

1 Minus sign indicates net repayment.

2 Countries in Table 1 which have drawn on the Fund.

3 Totals may not equal sums of annual data because of rounding.

Increases in Quotas: Fourth Quinquennial Review

The Fund is required at intervals of five years to review the quotas of members and to propose any adjustments that it believes to be desirable. No changes were proposed in the course of the first and second quinquennial reviews (1950 and 1955). The third review was in effect replaced by the general increase proposed by the Directors in December 1958 in the report reproduced above (pp. 421–41). The fourth quinquennial review, due in 1965, evoked the following report to the Governors, submitted on February 26, 1965. The proposals were accepted by the Governors, and took effect from February 23, 1966.

Increases in Quotas of Members—Fourth Quinquennial Review Report of the Executive Directors to the Board of Governors (February 26, 1965)

1. At its Nineteenth Annual Meeting in Tokyo, the Board of Governors adopted the following Resolution:

RESOLVED:

That the Executive Directors proceed to consider the question of adjusting the quotas of members of the Fund and at an early date submit an appropriate proposal to the Board of Governors.

2. Pursuant to this Resolution, the Executive Directors have considered the question of adjusting the quotas of members and have concluded that in a world in which income and trade have expanded rapidly and are expected to do so, the need for the type of liquidity provided by the Fund, like the need for international liquidity in general, may be expected to grow. A reasonable expansion in quotas would increase the Fund's resources relative to the calls that are likely to be made upon them and enhance confidence in the Fund's ability to meet all justifiable requests for drawings. Provision of adequate resources, enabling the Fund to meet needs with a greater margin of safety, may also reduce those needs by marshaling the resources and demonstrating the international cooperation that could deter speculation. Accordingly, the Executive Directors have decided that proposals for increases in present quotas of 25 per cent, subject to the appropriate rounding of the resulting figures, and for larger increases for certain members should be submitted to the Board of Governors. For the purposes of this Report, present quotas are quotas as of February 26, 1965 or the maximum amount to which quotas could be increased under Resolutions adopted by or submitted to the Board of Governors before that date. The general increases of 25 per cent are provided for by the First of two Resolutions submitted to the Board of Governors with this Report. The formula for rounding the increased quotas is as follows: amounts below $500 million are rounded to the next higher multiple of one million, and amounts of $500 million or more are rounded to the next higher multiple of five million. The quotas to which members can consent under the First Resolution are shown in the Annex to this Report. The Second Resolution submitted with this Report provides for the special (i.e., larger)

increases. If the Board of Governors agrees to propose a special increase for a member under the Second Resolution, the member will be able to consent to that increase or to the smaller increase under the First Resolution. When such a member consents, it should declare under which Resolution it is choosing to consent, and its choice will then be final.

3. The increases in quotas under the attached Resolutions are without prejudice to the adjustment of quotas that members can request under the Fund's Decision on "Compensatory Financing of Export Fluctuations" (E.B. Decision No. 1477-(63/8), February 27, 1963). In this connection, E.B. Decision No. 1529-(63/33), June 14, 1963 will continue to be applicable.

4. The attached Resolutions are designed to enable the Board of Governors to vote at one time on all matters connected with the increases in quotas under the two Resolutions. Governors are requested to vote on both Resolutions. The First Resolution is to be voted on as a whole. In the case of the Second Resolution, Governors may vote on all or each of the special increases. Under the Resolutions, it will be possible for increases in quotas to become effective without the need for further reference to the Board of Governors. Attention is drawn to the requirement that, to be valid, votes must be received at the seat of the Fund on or before March 31, 1965.

5. If the Resolutions are adopted by the necessary majority of four-fifths of the total voting power, as required by Article III, Section 2 of the Articles of Agreement, a member may consent to the increase in its quota at any time on or before September 25, 1965. Therefore, unless this period is extended by the Executive Directors, members will have until September 25, 1965 to take whatever action may be necessary under their laws to enable them to give their consent.

6. In view of the cooperative nature of the increase in quotas under the Resolutions, it is provided that increases will not become effective until the Fund has determined that members having two-thirds of the total of quotas on February 26, 1965 have consented to increases in their quotas. In determining whether this degree of participation has been reached, the Fund will take into account all consents to increases, whether they be under the First or Second Resolutions and whether they be increases in full or by installments.

7. In view of past practice, any member consenting to a special increase under the Second Resolution will be expected to request an increase in its subscription to the capital of the International Bank for Reconstruction and Development corresponding to the special part of the increase in quota.

8. Under the Resolutions, a member may pay its additional subscription in respect of the increase in its quota at any time before it is due. If a member pays before the increase in its quota takes effect, the additional subscription will be kept in separate accounts of the Fund and returned if it should be established that the increase cannot take effect. A member is required to pay its additional subscription not later than 30 days after the later of the following events: (i) its consent to its quota increase, and (ii) the determination by the Fund, referred to in paragraph 6 above, that the condition as to participation in quota increases has been satisfied.

9. Increases in members' quotas will take effect as follows:

(a) When a member pays its additional subscription before the later of the two events referred to in the preceding paragraph, the increase in its quota will take effect on the happening of the later of these events.

(b) If a member pays its additional subscription after the later of these two events, the increase in its quota will take effect on the day of payment.

10. Each member increasing its quota must pay an additional subscription equal to the increase, of which 25 per cent shall be in gold and the balance in its currency. Payment of both portions of the additional subscription must be made before the increase in the member's quota can become effective, even by those members which, in accordance with the Articles of Agreement or Membership Resolutions, have not yet been required to pay their original subscriptions.

11. The increase in quotas under the Resolutions is based on the idea of a cooperative effort by the members of the Fund to provide larger resources against contingencies that may affect any member. In order to preserve the general character of that effort, it has been thought preferable not to exercise the discretion given to the Executive Directors under Article III, Section 4 of the Articles of Agreement to reduce gold payments in connection with these Resolutions. However, the payment in gold of 25 per cent of the quota increase may cause hardship in some cases, and therefore the Executive Directors have decided that the policies and practices described in the following paragraphs of this Report will be applied.

12. Under the Resolutions any member consenting to an increase in its quota may consent to an increase by installments. Each installment of the increase would correspond to the amount of additional subscription in gold and currency paid by the member. Any member consenting to an increase by installments must pay an original installment of additional subscription, and an installment in each period of 12 months thereafter. Each installment shall be one-fifth of the increase. Members may accelerate payment under this installment schedule.

13. A member that wishes to have the full increase in its quota take effect immediately or to expedite the full increase in its quota if it is paying under the installment schedule may find it a hardship to make prompt payment in gold of 25 per cent of the increase in its quota. In order to alleviate this hardship the member may request an exchange transaction in accordance with paragraphs 14 through 19 below.

14. Where a member requests an exchange transaction within the gold tranche, the established gold tranche policy and procedure will apply.

15. A member consenting to an increase in its quota under the First Resolution may request an exchange transaction beyond the gold tranche in an amount not in excess of 25 per cent of the increase. This facility will be available where (a) the member represents that it would encounter undue payments difficulties through the reduction in its reserves by the payment of the 25 per cent gold subscription or of the outstanding balance of that subscription; and (b) the member requests the exchange transaction within six months after the date of the consent to the increase or the determination by the Fund that the condition as to participation in quota increases has been satisfied, whichever is later.

16. The Fund will expect that a member requesting an exchange transaction under paragraph 15 above will represent that it will make a repurchase corresponding to the exchange transaction in accordance with the principles of E.B. Decision No. 102-(52/11) of February 13, 1952 and the following sub-paragraphs:

(i) The member will be expected to represent that it will make a repurchase corresponding to the exchange transaction in equal annual installments, to commence one year after the transaction and to be completed not later than five years after the transaction.

(ii) If the member, when requesting the exchange transaction or at any time thereafter, represents that, because of other repurchase commitments or for such other reasons as it shall submit, the schedule referred to in (i) above would create undue payments difficulties, the Fund may accept a representation that the member will repurchase in accordance with the provisions of E.B. Decision No. 102-(52/11).

17. The representation of a member with respect to undue payments difficulties referred to in paragraphs 15 and 16 above would not be challenged by the Fund except where it was clearly evident that the representation was without basis.

18. In order to facilitate the exchange transactions referred to in paragraph 15 above, the Fund will be prepared, where necessary, to grant a waiver of the quantitative limits prescribed in Article V, Section 3 (*a*) (iii) of the Articles of Agreement. The Fund will also be prepared to grant such a waiver, in appropriate cases, to the extent that an exchange transaction in accordance with the preceding paragaphs is still outstanding.

19. A member requesting an exchange transaction in accordance with the preceding paragraphs will be expected to consult the Managing Director on the currency to be drawn under E.B. Decision No. 1371-(62/36) of July 20, 1962. Many such members are likely to use the currency drawn to purchase gold from the monetary authorities of the member whose currency was drawn either to pay their additional gold subscription or to restore the level of their gold holdings if they have already paid the additional subscription. Normally, these members would purchase the gold from a reserve currency member. With a view to alleviating the impact on the gold holdings of the reserve currency members that would result from such purchases, the Fund, in the course of the consultation on the currency to be drawn, will suggest that certain of these exchange transactions, up to the equivalent of $150 million, be made in currencies which the Fund would then replenish by the sale of gold under Article VII, Section 2 (ii) up to the amount of such transactions.

20. The exchange transactions and replenishment of currency referred to in the preceding paragraphs will partially alleviate the impact of the additional gold subscriptions of members on the gold holdings of the reserve currency members. However, it is expected that, notwithstanding this alleviation and the likelihood that many members will meet their additional gold subscription from their own gold holdings, other members will purchase a substantial amount of gold from the reserve currency members, and in particular the United States and the United Kingdom. In order to provide a measure of further alleviation solely in connection with the quota increases provided for by the Resolutions submitted with this Report, the Fund will make general deposits of gold with its gold depositories designated by the United States and the United Kingdom in a total amount not exceeding the equivalent of $350 million. Approximately $250 million in gold will be placed on general deposit with the Fund's depository in the United States and approximately $100 million with the Fund's depository in the United Kingdom. Within the limit of $350 million or the reduced amount under paragraph 21 below, adjustments may be made in the amounts held on general deposit in these two depositories on the basis of the actual impact on the gold holdings of each of the two members of the sales of gold by them in connection with the additional subscriptions of other members.

21. If the Fund determines that the total sales of gold by the United States and the United Kingdom in connection with the additional subscriptions of other members are less than the equivalent of $350 million, the Fund will reduce its general deposits accordingly.

22. The general deposits will be subject to the following principles:

(a) A general deposit of gold by the Fund shall be a demand deposit. Accordingly, the Fund shall be entitled, at its sole discretion and on its demand to the depository, to the immediate transfer to an earmarked account in the sole name of the Fund at the depository, free of any claims, liens or encumbrances in favor of any other party, of an amount of gold not in excess of the amount then held by the Fund on general deposit with the depository, which transfer shall be made without charge or cost to the Fund.

(b) Whenever a member that designated the depository with which a general deposit is held so requests, the Fund shall demand that the depository transfer gold in the amount requested to an earmarked account.

(c) On the occasion of any use of gold, the Fund would normally use, in appropriate proportions, earmarked gold and gold on general deposit in accordance with the good management of its assets.

(d) The Managing Director will report periodically to the Executive Directors on the Fund's general deposits, and the Executive Directors shall review the policy with respect to general deposits not later than five years after the first such deposit is made.

February 26, 1965

Annex to Report

	Present Quota[1]	Increased Quota Under First Resolution		Present Quota[1]	Increased Quota Under First Resolution
	(Million U.S. dollars)			(Million U.S. dollars)	
1. Afghanistan	22.50	29	52. Korea	18.75	24
2. Algeria	60.00	75	53. Kuwait	50.00	63
3. Argentina	280.00	350	54. Laos	7.50	10
4. Australia	400.00	500	55. Lebanon	6.75	9
5. Austria	75.00	94	56. Liberia	11.25	15
6. Belgium	337.50	422	57. Libya	15.00	19
7. Bolivia	22.50	29	58. Luxembourg	15.00	19
8. Brazil	280.00	350	59. Malagasy Republic	15.00	19
9. Burma	30.00	38	60. Malaysia	100.00	125
10. Burundi	11.25	15	61. Mali	13.00	17
11. Cameroon	15.00	19	62. Mauritania	7.50	10
12. Canada	550.00	690	63. Mexico	180.00	225
13. Central African Republic	7.50	10	64. Morocco	52.50	66
14. Ceylon	62.00	78	65. Nepal	7.50	10
15. Chad	7.50	10	66. Netherlands	412.50	520
16. Chile	100.00	125	67. New Zealand	125.00	157
17. China	550.00	690	68. Nicaragua	11.25	15
18. Colombia	100.00	125	69. Niger	7.50	10
19. Congo (Brazzaville)	7.50	10	70. Nigeria	50.00	63
20. Congo, Democratic Republic of	45.00	57	71. Norway	100.00	125
21. Costa Rica	20.00	25	72. Pakistan	150.00	188
22. Cyprus	11.25	15	73. Panama	11.25	15
23. Dahomey	7.50	10	74. Paraguay	11.25	15
24. Denmark	130.00	163	75. Peru	37.50	47
25. Dominican Republic	25.00	32	76. Philippines	75.00	94
26. Ecuador	20.00	25	77. Portugal	60.00	75
27. El Salvador	20.00	25	78. Rwanda	11.25	15
28. Ethiopia	15.00	19	79. Saudi Arabia	72.00	90
29. Finland	57.00	72	80. Senegal	25.00	32
30. France	787.50	985	81. Sierra Leone	11.25	15
31. Gabon	7.50	10	82. Somalia	11.25	15
32. Germany, Federal Republic of	787.50	985	83. South Africa	150.00	188
33. Ghana	55.00	69	84. Spain	150.00	188
34. Greece	60.00	75	85. Sudan	45.00	57
35. Guatemala	20.00	25	86. Sweden	150.00	188
36. Guinea	15.00	19	87. Syrian Arab Republic	30.00	38
37. Haiti	11.25	15	88. Tanzania	25.00	32
38. Honduras	15.00	19	89. Thailand	76.00	95
39. Iceland	11.25	15	90. Togo	11.25	15
40. India	600.00	750	91. Trinidad and Tobago	20.00	25
41. Indonesia	165.00	207	92. Tunisia	22.50	29
42. Iran	70.00	88	93. Turkey	86.00	108
43. Iraq	55.00	69	94. Uganda	25.00	32
44. Ireland	45.00	57	95. United Arab Republic	120.00	150
45. Israel	50.00	63	96. United Kingdom	1,950.00	2,440
46. Italy	500.00	625	97. United States	4,125.00	5,160
47. Ivory Coast	15.00	19	98. Upper Volta	7.50	10
48. Jamaica	20.00	25	99. Uruguay	30.00	38
49. Japan	500.00	625	100. Venezuela	150.00	188
50. Jordan	11.25	15	101. Viet-Nam	22.50	29
51. Kenya	25.00	32	102. Yugoslavia	120.00	150

[1] As defined in paragraph 2 of the Report and paragraph 1(a) of the First Resolution.

RESOLUTIONS SUBMITTED TO THE BOARD OF GOVERNORS

WHEREAS the Executive Directors have considered the question referred to them by the Resolution of the Board of Governors of the International Monetary Fund at its Nineteenth Annual Meeting:

> "That the Executive Directors proceed to consider the question of adjusting the quotas of members of the Fund and at an early date submit an appropriate proposal to the Board of Governors."

Have found that proposals to carry out increases in quotas should be submitted to the Board of Governors; and

Have submitted to the Board of Governors a Report entitled "Increases in Quotas of Members—Fourth Quinquennial Review" and the following Resolutions of the Board of Governors for a vote without meeting pursuant to Section 13 of the By-Laws of the Fund, which Resolutions propose increases in the quotas of all members of the Fund, make provision for consents by members, and establish the conditions upon which the increases shall take effect;

Now, THEREFORE, the Board of Governors, noting the said Report of the Executive Directors, hereby resolves that:

First Resolution

1. (a) The International Monetary Fund proposes that, subject to the provisions of this First Resolution, the quotas of all members of the International Monetary Fund in effect on February 26, 1965 or the maximum quotas to which members could consent under Resolutions adopted by or submitted to the Board of Governors before that date shall be increased by 25 per cent, with the resulting amounts rounded according to the following formula:

   amounts below $500 million shall be rounded to the next higher multiple of one million;

   amounts of $500 million or more shall be rounded to the next higher multiple of five million.

   (b) When an increase in quota proposed in this First Resolution is calculated on the basis of a quota that includes an increase to which a member can consent under another Resolution adopted by or submitted to the Board of Governors before February 26, 1965 and there is no consent to such increase, the increase proposed in this First Resolution shall be 25 per cent of the quota in effect on February 26, 1965, rounded in accordance with paragraph 1 (a).

2. None of the increases in quotas proposed in this First Resolution shall become effective unless:

   (i) The member concerned has notified the Fund that it consents to the increase in its quota; and

   (ii) The Fund determines that members having not less than two-thirds of the total of quotas on February 26, 1965 have consented to increases in their quotas under the First or Second Resolution; and

   (iii) The member concerned has paid the full increase in its quota.

   Subject to paragraph 6 (c), each increase in quota shall become effective upon the date of the latest of these three events.

3. Notices in accordance with paragraph 2 (i) shall be executed by a duly authorized official of the member.

4. Notices in accordance with paragraph 2 (i) shall be received in the Fund not later than September 25, 1965, provided that the Executive Directors may extend this period as they may determine.
5. Subject to paragraph 6 (b), each member shall pay to the Fund within 30 days after the later of the two events in paragraph 2 (i) and (ii), 25 per cent of the increase in gold and the balance in its own currency.
6. (a) In giving notice in accordance with paragraph 2 (i), any member may consent to the increase in its quota as an increase by installments.
   (b) Notwithstanding paragraph 2 (iii), a member increasing its quota by installments shall pay not less than one-fifth of the gold and currency prescribed in paragraph 5 within 30 days after the later of the two events in paragraph 2 (i) and (ii) and shall pay further installments of gold and currency of not less than one-fifth of the increase in each twelve months after the first payment until the full amount prescribed in paragraph 5 has been paid.
   (c) Subject to paragraph 2, on the completion of the payment of each installment of the increase, the member's quota shall be increased by an amount equal to the installment.
7. Since it is in the interests of the Fund and its members that the contemplated increase in its resources be expedited, members are invited to comply as soon as possible with the procedure for notice and payments to the Fund under this First Resolution. Any payment made by a member before the effective date of increase in its quota will be kept in separate accounts of the Fund. If the Fund decides that such increase cannot become effective under this First Resolution, the payment will be returned to the member.

Second Resolution

1. The International Monetary Fund proposes that, subject to the provisions of this Second Resolution, the quotas of the following members shall be increased to the amounts shown against their names:

	Million U.S. dollars		*Million U.S. dollars*
1. Austria	175	9. Japan	725
2. Canada	740	10. Mexico	270
3. Finland	125	11. Norway	150
4. Germany, Federal Republic of	1,200	12. Philippines	110
5. Greece	100	13. South Africa	200
6. Iran	125	14. Spain	250
7. Ireland	80	15. Sweden	225
8. Israel	90	16. Venezuela	250

2. Paragraphs 2 through 7 of the First Resolution shall apply to this Second Resolution.
3. Members named in paragraph 1 of this Second Resolution shall be entitled to consent under either the First or the Second Resolution but not under both. Any such member shall declare under which Resolution it is consenting, and such choice shall be final.

Board of Governors Resolutions Nos. 20–6 and 20–7
Adopted March 31, 1965

PART IV

After 1965

Compensatory Financing: Second Report

In 1964 the UN Conference on Trade and Development reviewed the procedure for the compensatory financing of export fluctuations established in 1963 (pp. 442–57 above) and made recommendations for its modification. Supporting speeches were made by a number of Governors at the Annual Meetings, 1965, and in September 1966 the Executive Directors decided to expand the facility. Their report follows.

Compensatory Financing of Export Fluctuations— Developments in the Fund's Facility (September 1966)

A Second Report by the International Monetary Fund on Compensatory Financing of the Fluctuations in Exports of Primary Producing Countries

CONTENTS

Appendices

I. INTRODUCTION: THE 1963 DECISION

In February 1963, in response to an invitation extended by the United Nations Commission on International Commodity Trade at its tenth session in May 1962, the Fund issued a report entitled *Compensatory Financing of Export Fluctuations.* This report, after reviewing the problems involved in financing by the Fund of fluctuations in exports of primary exporting countries, set forth in its concluding chapter an Executive Board Decision [1] covering two points: (a) quotas and (b) drawing policies.

With respect to quotas, the Fund declared its willingness to give sympathetic consideration to requests for the adjustment of the quotas of certain primary exporting countries, particularly those with relatively small quotas, to make them more adequate in the light of fluctuations in export proceeds and other relevant criteria.

As regards drawing policies, the Fund introduced a new facility, of which the principal features are as follows:

(1) It is open to all member countries, but designed in particular for primary producing countries.

(2) It is designed to compensate for temporary shortfalls in export receipts, rather than in export prices or in the terms of trade, or in the importing power of exports.

(3) By temporary shortfalls are meant deviations from a medium-term trend in export receipts.

(4) Compensation is paid in the form of a drawing subject to the normal conditions of repayments for Fund drawings, including an outside limit of three to five years.

(5) Compensation is paid to the full extent of the calculated shortfall, subject to the proviso that the total of compensatory drawings outstanding should not normally exceed 25 per cent of quota.

(6) The policies of members drawing under the facility do not have to meet the tests that the Fund would apply in the case of a non-compensatory drawing in the same tranche. However, members do have to satisfy the Fund that they are encountering payments difficulties, that the shortfall is of a short-term character and is largely attributable to circumstances beyond the member's control, and that the member will cooperate with the Fund in an effort to find solutions, where required, for its payments difficulties.

II. SUBSEQUENT DEVELOPMENTS

1. *Quota Adjustments and Export Fluctuations*

The Decision on Compensatory Financing has now been in operation for over three years, and the time has arrived when certain of its aspects can appropriately be reviewed.

In paragraph (3) of that Decision, the Fund recognized that some quota adjustments might be required or desirable, as follows: "The quotas of many primary exporting countries, taken in conjunction with a reasonable use of their own reserves, are at present adequate for dealing with export fluctuations such as have occurred during the past decade. In those instances, however, where adjustment of the quotas of certain primary exporting countries, and in particular of countries with relatively small quotas, would be appropriate to make them more adequate in the light of fluctuations in export proceeds and other relevant criteria, the Fund is willing to give sympathetic consideration to requests for such adjustment."

[1] Decision No. 1477-(63/8), adopted February 27, 1963; see above, pp. 238–40.

Since February 1963 the Fund has taken steps—apart from the general quota increase which came into effect on February 23, 1966—to implement this paragraph in several ways.

In the first place, it has approved more than 20 quota increases under a special policy applied to developing countries with relatively small quotas; 15 other countries appear to be eligible for such quota increases under that policy.

Secondly, the Fund facilitates drawings by such countries to enable them to purchase the amount of gold that must be paid in connection with the quota increases referred to above. This gives them the benefit of a quota increase immediately, and makes it possible to spread the reserve cost of the increase over a number of years.

Finally, in considering applications for individual quota increases, even from countries other than those to which paragraph (3) directly applies, the Fund has modified the formula which is taken into account in calculating quotas in such a way as to improve the position of developing countries. Variability of trade, which was a component of the so-called Bretton Woods formula, has now been defined in terms of the standard deviation around a five-year moving average. This new definition provides a more accurate measure of variability and is more favorable to quota calculations for countries exporting raw materials. The Fund has also modified the formula to give greater weight to trade and variability of trade, and less weight to national income and international reserves.

2. *The Fund's Compensatory Facility*

It might have been expected that the drawing facility established by the Fund in February 1963 to provide compensatory financing for export fluctuations would by this time have been used often enough to provide ample illustration of the types of problems that were liable to arise in applying it, and possibly also to indicate ways in which it could be improved. In fact, however, few countries have had even a prima facie case for using it, and only three countries have actually drawn: (1) Brazil in June 1963, the equivalent of $60 million (21 per cent of quota); (2) the United Arab Republic in October 1963, the equivalent of $16 million (18 per cent of quota); and (3) Sudan in June 1965, the equivalent of $11.25 million (25 per cent of quota).[2] This infrequency of use is largely attributable to the fact, illustrated in Table 1, that price developments over the past three or four years have been such as to permit the export earnings of less developed primary producing countries to show a generally upward trend, though one that tended to flatten out in 1965. Even the substantial declines in prices of tropical foodstuffs (other than coffee), which began in the spring of 1964 and continued through the greater part of 1965, have not reacted sufficiently on earnings to evoke many opportunities for the use of the facility.

Despite the small number of instances of use, there has been enough experience and enough reflection on the variety of situations that might present themselves to permit a reconsideration of several of the features of the 1963 Decision. Moreover, a number of suggestions have been made, both inside the Fund—notably at the Annual Meeting of the Board of Governors in 1965—and outside the Fund, as to ways in which the Fund's compensatory financing facility might be amended or improved.

Most of these suggestions are summed up in the three recommendations made by the United Nations Conference on Trade and Development (UNCTAD), 1964, to

[2] The quotas referred to in these percentages are those applicable at the times the drawings were made.

Governments that are members of the Fund as to changes that might be made in the facility, and in the request which it addressed directly to the Fund. The UNCTAD resolution containing these recommendations and request is reproduced in Appendix I below. Passages dealing with compensatory financing excerpted from speeches of Governors at the 1965 Annual Meeting are reproduced in Appendix II. It will be seen that most of the points made by the Governors are covered in the UNCTAD Recommendation referred to above, except for the reference to automatism in the speech of the Governor for Argentina, and the reference to terms of trade and import prices in the speech of the Governor for Ceylon.

Table 1. Changes in Prices and Export Earnings for Primary Producers, 1962-1965

Commodity	Prices[1] Percentage increase or decrease (−) from previous year 1963	1964	1965
Metals and minerals[4]	3	21	13
Agricultural products	20	—	−12
Food	31	—	−17
Coffee	*4*	*30*	*−5*
Sugar	*185*	*−31*	*−64*
Cocoa	*20*	*−8*	*−26*
Wheat	*1*	*4*	*−5*
Non-food	4	—	−5
Cotton	*2*	*29*	*−6*
Wool	*18*	*—*	*−13*
Rubber	*−7*	*−5*	*−1*
All exports[4]	18	2	−9

Export Earnings: Countries mainly dependent on specified commodities[2]	Percentage increase from previous year 1963	1964	1965[3]
Metals and minerals	9	24	13
Agricultural products	12	10	4
Coffee	12	8	7
Mixed tropical foodstuffs	11	11	3
Mainly temperate products	14	12	2
Fibers and rubber	10	2	9
Mixed	7	11	5
Mixed mineral and agricultural	8	7	2
All countries	11	10	4

[1] Group price changes are derived from indices published by the National Institute of Economic and Social Research, London. Specified commodity price series relate to world market quotations for representative grades only, and thus exclude the influence of prices determined under contracts.

[2] Countries obtaining at least one half of export earnings from commodity groups indicated. Excludes countries dependent on petroleum. Data relate to 71 countries.

[3] Provisional.

[4] Excluding petroleum.

III. APPLICATION AND DEVELOPMENT OF THE FACILITY

1. *Nature of Shortfall*

Drawings under paragraph (5) of the Compensatory Financing Decision of 1963 may be made only when the requesting member experiences payments difficulties produced by a temporary export shortfall, i.e., by an export shortfall which is "of a short-term character." Such shortfalls, according to paragraph (7) of the Decision, are to be identified on the basis of "estimates regarding the medium-term trend of the member's exports." In the 1963 Decision itself, no definition of the medium-term trend is given. However, in the earlier Fund report, "Fund Policies and Procedures in Relation to the Compensatory Financing of Commodity Fluctuations,"[3] the trend or norm was defined

[3] *Staff Papers*, Vol. VIII (1960–61), p. 9.

for purposes of illustration as the average of actual exports for the five years beginning two years before and ending two years after the year for which the trend value was calculated. The same definition was adopted in the staff paper [4] cited [on page 447] of *Compensatory Financing of Export Fluctuations,* and it was on the basis of this definition of the "ideal" trend or norm that certain conclusions were drawn in that report as to the best statistical method of estimating it in the absence of complete information.[5] This is also the definition that has been adopted in all applications of the Compensatory Financing Decision to particular countries up to the present time.

In the absence of precise quantitative knowledge as to the nature of the economic forces at work in determining trends and fluctuations, a moving average seems the best and most flexible way—better, for example, than fitting a trend line of any a priori shape—to reflect what is meant by trend. Moving averages of 4 years, 5 years, or 6 years, respectively, might, any one of them, serve as a reasonable definition of a "medium-term" trend. However, a five-year period is preferable to the others in that it contains a middle year, the trend value of which can be defined as the average of the period. The trend value for any year in any time series must anticipate the figures for subsequent as well as reflect those of previous years in that series. If this is not done—e.g., if the trend values are determined solely as an average of past years—the trend line might lie persistently above, or below, the actual series to a substantial extent, which would be contrary to the normal meaning of the term "trend." Only if the moving average is centered in the manner illustrated above can one expect to find, over a reasonable period of time, a rough balancing of shortfalls and surpluses of actual exports with respect to trend.[6]

Once the best possible estimate has been made of the medium-term trend, and hence of the shortfall, if any, from that trend, in accordance with paragraph (7) of the Decision of 1963, no separate judgment is required as to whether the shortfall in question is "temporary" or of a "short-term" character. The definition of the trend itself is such as to make it likely—though one can never be certain—that shortfalls with respect to it will be of short duration.[7] Any attempt to make a separate determination as to whether a given shortfall would cease to exist within, say, two or three years would involve estimating for that period ahead not only actual exports—which, as is indicated in the following section, may be involved in the estimation of the current norm—but also the export trend itself. To forecast the latter would involve estimating exports for still further years ahead. This, in the present state of forecasting techniques, would appear to be impracticable, and a determination that a shortfall of a given magnitude exists should, therefore, be taken as satisfying the requirement that the shortfall is of a short-term character.

---

[4] J. Marcus Fleming, Rudolf Rhomberg, and Lorette Boissonneault, "Export Norms and Their Role in Compensatory Financing," *Staff Papers,* Vol. X (1963), pp. 97–149.

[5] *Compensatory Financing of Export Fluctuations* (above, pp. 450–51).

[6] The balancing of surpluses and deficits is far from perfect, however; in any five-year period there is likely to be either an excess of surpluses over deficits exceeding 50 per cent of gross surpluses, or an excess of shortfalls over surpluses exceeding 50 per cent of gross shortfalls. This, however, appears to be quite unavoidable. There is no way of defining a norm or trend consistently from year to year in such a way as to secure a perfect balance of surpluses and shortfalls over any given period.

[7] Calculations covering 48 countries show that almost 50 per cent of all shortfalls with respect to a norm defined as above last only one year, nearly 85 per cent no more than two years, and 96 per cent no more than three years.

2. *Estimation of Trend and Shortfall*

In paragraph (7) of the 1963 Decision it is laid down that the Fund will seek to establish reasonable estimates regarding the medium-term trend of the member's exports "on the basis of appropriate statistical data in conjunction with qualitative information about its export prospects." This phrase appears to foreshadow a two-sided approach—"statistical" and "qualitative"—to the problem of estimation. However, while statistical estimation can be carried out without qualitative appraisal, qualitative appraisal can scarcely be applied without the aid of some statistical information, and the true alternative approaches are those of statistical automatism and the exercise of judgment, respectively.

In the three instances in which the Decision has been applied thus far, the estimation of normal exports has represented a compromise between (a) a figure or figures arrived at through the application of automatic formulae to past statistical data, and (b) an estimate based on a combination of these data with a forecast for actual exports two years ahead, these forecasts in turn being arrived at by a process of market appraisal using all available information.

The combination of the two methods in one form or another is justified by the knowledge that the result of either method is to a considerable extent uncertain. Any formula admittedly gives a precise answer; but no formula can be devised that gives a good approximation of the medium-term trend, as here defined, solely on the basis of past statistical data. On the other hand, any forecasting exercise must to some extent be subjective and uncertain. Given these facts it is necessary to strike a reasonable balance between these two methods, each less than satisfactory, which at the same time assures countries as much uniformity of treatment as possible.

As regards the automatic statistical approach to the estimation of the norm, the Fund has, in the past, used two types of formula, a "general" formula and a "national" formula, in both of which the norm for any given year is estimated as a weighted average of actual exports for the year in question and the two preceding years. In both formulae, the weights assigned to the various years are those which experience shows to provide the best approximation to the "true" norm as defined above.[8]

The "general" formula used in calculations contained in *Compensatory Financing of Export Fluctuations*, which was used in all three applications of the Decision to date, attaches a weight of .50 to the exports of the year for which the shortfall is being estimated, .25 to the preceding year, and .25 to the second preceding year. These weights were arrived at on the basis of analysis of the experience of some 48 countries over a period of nine testable years (thirteen years of data). While not absolutely the best of the formulae tested, it was chosen as a good formula with rounded weights close to those of the optimal formula.

"National" formulae have differed from country to country, the formula for each country being arrived at on the basis of export data for that country alone. It is

[8] The "true norm" for exports, x, in any year t, i.e., $\bar{x}_t$, is defined as

$$\frac{x^*_{t-2}+x_{t-1}+x_t+x_{t+1}+x_{t+2}}{5}.$$

The problem is to find weights w_0, w_1, w_2, such that the estimated norm

$$x_t = w_2 x_{t-2} + w_1 x_{t-1} + w_0 x_t$$

provides the best approximation to $\bar{x}_t$ for all values of t. This is found by regression analysis for years in which the relevant export data are available.

intended to discontinue the use of "national" formulae on the ground that they are based on too small a number of observations, and complicate the statistical side of the shortfall determination.

As regards the more subjective estimate, primarily based on market analysis, it is in the nature of the case more difficult to describe the method used, which varies from country to country. The procedure is first to estimate the average of exports in the two years following the year for which the shortfall is being determined and then to take an average of the five years centered on the shortfall year. The forecast in question is constructed largely on the basis of commodity analysis, taking into account the prospective price movements for the commodity in question and the prospective volume movements in the country in question. For the great majority of Fund members which are primary exporting countries, 60 per cent to 90 per cent of total exports is accounted for by a small number (1 to 4) of commodities; a large proportion of most countries' trade can, therefore be estimated on the basis of commodity market analysis. But there remains a sizable residual for which no such analysis is possible, and it may well prove desirable in particular instances to make a more or less automatic statistical estimate for this part of the exports. In this event the partial results of market analysis for major commodities would be combined with a more mechanical result for the residual to arrive at a global estimate.

In the past, "statistical" and "qualitative" estimates have been given approximately equal weight in determining the final estimate of the trend value of exports. However, the "qualitative" estimates, involving a direct forecast of exports two years ahead, have been found in practice to yield better results than the formula. Experience has tended to bear out the judgment that a "better estimate could be made by the exercise of judgment based on an analysis of the causal factors at work than by any mathematical formula, however skillfully contrived, which is based on the mere statistical magnitude of current and previous exports." [9] In future, therefore, it would seem advisable to give a somewhat greater weight than in the past to the "qualitative" as against the "statistical" estimate.

It is important, however, to give members some assurance that estimates of the trend value of exports will remain within a certain predictable range. This can be achieved by providing that, in the calculation of the trend, the average level of exports predicted for the two years following the shortfall year will not be assumed to exceed by more than ten per cent the average level experienced in the two years preceding the shortfall year and will not be assumed to be less than the level of exports experienced in the shortfall year itself.

3. *Proposals Regarding the Mode of Determining the Shortfall*

A. *Weight to be given to past years*

In the Recommendation on the Study of Measures Related to the Compensatory Credit System of the International Monetary Fund, set forth in Annex A.IV.17 of its report, the UNCTAD made the following request:

> *The Conference*
>
> . . . .
>
> 2. *Requests* that the International Monetary Fund, in its determination of the shortfall in export receipts, consider giving greater weight to the actual experience of the three preceding years.

[9] *Compensatory Financing of Export Fluctuations* (above, p. 447).

The issue here, though it appears to be purely technical, in fact touches on a point of principle. At present, as has been explained above, the Fund's compensatory financing facility is designed to compensate for shortfalls from the presumed current trend level of exports rather than from a previous trend level. It is designed to help countries to bring their export availabilities—export receipts *plus* compensatory drawings *less* repayments of such drawings—closer to the presumed trend level rather than to provide them with a financial buffer against declines in exports from their previous standards. While it might be entirely appropriate to provide countries with such a buffer, it would seem preferable to supply this through the ordinary drawing facilities of the Fund, use of which could be made conditional, where necessary, on the adoption of measures to adapt the economy to new export conditions, or to improve the trend of exports, than through the compensatory financing facility, the use of which is more automatic.

It is because the aim of compensatory financing is conceived in the manner described above, that in the assessment of the norm with reference to which the shortfall is calculated account is taken of the expected exports of the ensuing years, that a substantial weight in the determination of the norm is given to the current year's exports, and that no weight is given, for example, to exports three or more years anterior to the year with respect to which the shortfall is being calculated. The weights assigned to the current and preceding years in the estimation of the export norm—insofar as it is estimated by formula—were arrived at on the basis of experience as to which weights gave the closest estimate of the current trend and the best implied forecast of the two years subsequent to the shortfall year.

A formula in which no weight was given to the shortfall year would, for this reason, tend to lead to a higher estimate of the trend value, and hence a larger shortfall and a larger drawing entitlement. Because of the long-term upward trend of exports, however, this effect would generally be offset to some extent by the inclusion in the weighting formula of the third year preceding the shortfall, or of still earlier years. From Table 2 it can be seen that a formula for trend estimation giving equal weights to the three years preceding the shortfall would have led, over the period 1951 to 1964, to somewhat larger drawing entitlements than the present formula. The same table, however, shows that the "performance" of the scheme (as measured by the degree to which compensatory drawings and repurchases bring export availabilities closer to the true trend value, and the degree to which they tend to smooth out export availabilities) would not have been improved, but if anything, worsened by such a change in formula. It is not the object of the compensatory facility to aim at the largest possible amount of drawings, and, as will be shown below, there are ways in which it would be possible for an increase in drawings outstanding to improve the performance of the scheme significantly, or even for the scheme to be improved without a net increase in drawings outstanding.

Some further points deserve mention.

The element of forecasting involved in the determination of a current rather than a past trend value of exports, though irksome and subject to uncertainty, is a good discipline for country and Fund alike, and may help to counteract the natural tendency to delay adaptations to changing circumstances.

More important is the fact that measurement solely from a past level would frequently yield "shortfalls" which could not by any means be described as "temporary." While countries with a rising trend of exports, even when the rise was subject to serious interruption, would seldom if ever be deemed to have shortfalls, those with a generally falling trend of exports would experience persistent shortfalls. Such a change in formula would necessitate the introduction of a separate determination as to whether or not the shortfall was temporary—a determination which, as already indicated, would involve forecasting much further ahead and hence a higher degree of guesswork than that involved in the determination of the trend by present methods.

Table 2. Fund Compensatory Financing Facility: Comparison of Weighting Systems, 1951-64[1]

Limit: Per Cent of Quota	Coefficients Applied to Years				Drawing Entitlement[2]	Average Drawings Outstanding[3]	Approximation Ratio[4]	Smoothness Ratio[5]
	t	*t*-1	*t*-2	*t*-3				
.25	0	1/3	1/3	1/3	1.04	.31	.022	.028
.25	.50	.25	.25		.97	.29	.023	.029
.50	0	1/3	1/3	1/3	1.82	.54	.033	.046
.50	.50	.25	.25		1.61	.48	.034	.046

[1] Schemes applied to a sample of 48 countries. Drawings are assumed to be repaid one half in the fourth and one half in the fifth year after drawing, regardless of the level of exports in those years. The quotas on which the limits are based are not present quotas but those obtaining at the relevant dates during the period 1951-64.

[2] Cumulative total entitlements over the period in billions of U.S. dollars.

[3] Average for all years of total amounts outstanding in billions of U.S. dollars.

[4] Proportionate decline in root mean square percentage deviation of export availabilities from trend value of exports.

[5] Proportionate decline in root mean square percentage deviation of export availabilities from trend value of such availabilities.

The other alternative would be to drop the proviso that export shortfalls—or rather declines—should be temporary. But this would scarcely be compatible with the legal requirement of temporariness in the use of Fund resources.

For these reasons it seems on balance undesirable to alter the present concept of the export norm.

B. *Degree of reliance on automatic formulae*

The Governor for Argentina, speaking at the 1965 Annual Meeting of the Fund on behalf of 19 Latin American countries and the Philippines, mentioned as one of the fundamental aspects of the Fund's compensatory financing decision which it would be advisable to consider:

> (3) In conclusion, we would emphasize the nonautomatic nature of the drawings permitted. In the decisions on individual cases submitted to the consideration of the Executive Board there has been some flexibility, although in all of them there has been no lack of a subjective assessment in the determination both of the amount to be compensated and of the circumstances in which the loss of income occurs.[10]

This question, so far as it concerns the determination of the shortfall, has already been considered at some length above.

[10] *Summary Proceedings, Annual Meeting, 1965*, pp. 153–54.

It has been the experience of the Fund, based not only on its own export forecasts but on those of outside bodies, that a closer estimate of the medium-term trend can be arrived at by the use of short-term forecasts based on commodity analysis than by reliance on the best statistical formula. While greater reliance on formulae might give countries a slightly higher degree of certainty as to the amount of compensation they could rely on, the proposed balance between the two methods of estimation would seem to give as much weight as is prudent to the "automatic" element in the estimation process.

C. *Account to be taken of terms of trade*

At the 1965 Annual Meeting of the Fund, the Governor for Ceylon made a suggestion in the following terms:

> I was encouraged by the reference by Mr. Schweitzer to the work that the Fund is now undertaking to improve the compensatory financing facility. Several speakers have urged that compensatory assistance should be provided for a decline in the terms of trade rather than for a fall in export earnings alone. My own country's experience in recent years vividly illustrates the importance of this reform. We suffered a decline in the terms of trade by 13 per cent in two years alone, but since this was almost entirely due to an increase in import prices we were unable to avail ourselves of the compensatory financing facility. I do sincerely hope that this particular improvement in the scheme will be made effective at an early date.[11]

The terms of trade refer to the ratio between a country's export prices and its import prices. Fluctuations in export prices are, of course, reflected, along with fluctuations in export quantities, in the fluctuations in export proceeds. It might be argued that price fluctuations are more properly compensable than quantity fluctuations in that they are less easily affected by the policies of the exporting countries. On the other hand, some of the commonest and most genuinely short-run fluctuations in export proceeds are those arising from crop failures. More harm than good would probably be done by attempting to distinguish the specific roles of price and quantity in the fluctuations in export proceeds.

The case is different with fluctuations in import prices. There are undoubtedly good economic reasons for compensating not the money value but the real value, or importing power, of exports. An estimate of the latter could be arrived at by deflating exports (for the purpose of arriving at the trend value of exports) by an import price index based on the shortfall year.

There are, however, a number of practical and other objections to this procedure. Most primary producing countries have no import price index. Of those import price indices that exist, many are unrepresentative or unreliable. Moreover, such indices usually become available several months later than the data on export proceeds, so that the lag in the granting of a compensatory drawing behind the occurrence of the export shortfall would necessarily be increased. It might be thought that, where the import price indices of developing countries are unavailable, unreliable, or late in appearing, estimates could be formed on the basis of the export and import price indices of industrial countries. Such data, however, would provide extremely uncertain and disputable estimates for the import prices of any individual developing country. It has to be borne in mind that the developing countries that experience the largest fluctuations in import prices do so because they are substantial importers of primary products, often

---

[11] *Ibid.*, p. 207.

from other developing countries. Apart from such cases, the import price indices of primary producing countries do not, as a rule, show very large movements within a short period of years. For all these reasons, it seems better, at this time, to continue to adhere to the principle of compensating for shortfalls in export proceeds rather than in the importing power of exports.

4. *Period for Which Shortfall Is Calculated*

Thus far it has been the practice of the Fund to require that any request for the use of the compensatory facility shall relate to an export shortfall over the latest twelve-month period for which, at the time of the request, a reliable estimate of actual exports can be made. There must, in any event, be some maximum lapse of time within which any claim for compensation with respect to the exports of a given period should be made, and if the compensatory facility is to fulfil its purpose of enabling countries to stabilize their external expenditures as much as possible in the face of fluctuations in receipts, it seems desirable that the time lag between shortfall and compensatory financing should be as short as possible. As indicated below, countries need not be deterred from applying for a compensatory drawing as soon as a shortfall appears by the fact that they will thereby preclude themselves from claiming a larger compensation a little later if the shortfall has by then increased.[12]

The present practice permits a request for a compensatory drawing at any time during the year with respect to the twelve-month period immediately preceding. The question arises whether the timing of requests should be restricted in any way. There would seem to be no advantage in a system under which such claims could be made only with respect, say, to calendar years. A more plausible case could be made for ruling that, where exports are marked by seasonality, claims for compensatory drawings should be made only with respect to twelve-month periods which include all those months over which the principal export crop is liable to be marketed abroad. Otherwise, it might be argued, countries which marketed their crops early one year and late the following season might show a shortfall over a twelve-month period that spanned two seasons, whereas no shortfall would appear from a comparison of crop years. Bearing in mind, however, that most countries have a number of export crops with different seasonalities, it is doubtful whether the variability of seasonality is sufficient to justify the introduction of a restriction which would both reduce the value of the facility to the country and complicate its administration. It would be no easy task to determine for each country with respect to which twelve-month periods applications for compensatory financing would not be entertained. It should also be borne in mind that any shortfall that appeared to be artificially induced by deliberate delay in the timing of exports would be unlikely to be regarded as "largely attributable to circumstances beyond the control of the member" and in this event would not qualify for a compensatory drawing.

The arrangement outlined in the first paragraph of this section can be criticized from another angle, namely, that even a time lag of a few months between the shortfall and the compensatory drawing is undesirable, and that it would be better if the drawing could coincide with the shortfall. This means that the drawing would have to take place at a time when the precise amount of the shortfall was unknown. In order to meet this point and to facilitate the use of the stand-by and ordinary drawing facilities for the compensation of export shortfalls, it is intended, subject to what is said below,

---

[12] See pp. 480–81.

to allow members, within a six-month period of any drawing, to reclassify all or part of it as a compensatory drawing under paragraph (5) of the Decision. The drawing, when first made, would have to satisfy the ordinary conditions for drawing in the tranche in question, or, if made under a stand-by arrangement, the requirements appropriate to drawing under that arrangement. The reclassification of the drawing would have to satisfy the conditions for a compensatory drawing under paragraph (5) of the Decision with respect to an export shortfall for the latest twelve months for which data were available prior to the reclassification. The amount reclassified could not exceed the amount of that shortfall. Such reclassification would confer on the drawings the privilege of additionality as defined in (ii) of paragraph (6) of the 1963 Decision (with any enhancement of that privilege that may result from the separation of the compensatory facility from other drawing facilities, discussed below). It would not, however, reconstitute rights to draw under stand-by arrangement. Policy undertakings made in connection with the original drawing would remain unaffected by the reclassification.

It is estimated that if both the compensatory facility and the privilege of reclassification had existed over the period 1959–64, and the latter had been exercised to the full—which might not in all instances have been to the country's advantage—some 20 to 25 per cent of all non-compensatory drawings could have been so reclassified.

5. *Problem of Double Compensation*

It would be neither equitable, nor in accordance with the intention of the Decision on Compensatory Financing, that any member should be compensated twice for the same shortfall, or, more precisely, that the sum of any drawings made with respect to any given shortfall should exceed the amount of the shortfall.

Under the Decision a member can draw from the Fund with respect to a payments deficit arising out of an export shortfall *either* in the form of a drawing under ordinary tranche policies (referred to in paragraph (4) of the 1963 Decision) *or* in the form of a drawing under the special policies outlined in paragraph (5) of the Decision. Moreover, it is intended, as indicated in the preceding section, that a drawing originally made under ordinary tranche policies could in certain circumstances be reclassified. The problem of double compensation may arise either with respect to two drawings under paragraph (5), or with respect to a pair of drawings, one under paragraph (5) and another under paragraph (4).

In the event of two drawings under paragraph (5), where the period with respect to which a second such drawing is requested to be made (or reclassified) overlaps with that for which a first such drawing has been made (or reclassified), the first drawing will be prorated over the twelve months with respect to which it was made, and such part of it as corresponds to the overlap between the two periods will be subtracted from the drawing entitlement with respect to the second period.

As regards the problem of avoiding double counting between a paragraph (5) drawing and an ordinary drawing which can be considered as at least partly undertaken for compensatory purposes, there is no real difficulty if the ordinary drawing follows the paragraph (5) drawing and is not made under a stand-by arrangement approved before the latter drawing. In that case, the paragraph (5) drawing will simply be "taken into account" as one of the many factors affecting the balance of payments situation of the drawing country on the occasion of any subsequent drawing or stand-by arrangement.

The real difficulty arises if a paragraph (5) drawing or reclassification is requested after a stand-by arrangement has been approved or an ordinary drawing made—other than the drawing that is to be reclassified. It must then be asked whether the payments situation with respect to which the drawing or stand-by arrangement was approved included any part of the export shortfall with respect to which the paragraph (5) drawing or reclassification is being requested. Such a question would be difficult to answer since an ordinary drawing or stand-by arrangement is not usually approved to meet the payments deficit of any precisely defined period, still less to meet fluctuations in any specific item in the balance of payments.

One approach would be for the Fund to make a specific statement at the time of the ordinary drawing or stand-by arrangement as to the proportion thereof, if any, that should be regarded as granted with respect to an export shortfall, and as to the period of the shortfall. When approving stand-by arrangements, however, account is more often taken of the possibility of future shortfalls than of the accomplished fact of past shortfalls, and it is impossible to be precise as regards either the amount or the timing of future shortfalls. Rules will, therefore, have to be adopted as to the period and magnitude of the export shortfall which will be deemed to be compensated by ordinary drawings or drawings under stand-by arrangements approved before the request for a drawing or reclassification under the compensatory facility.

6. *Responsibility for Shortfall and Policy Conditions*

According to paragraph (5) (a) of the Compensatory Financing Decision of 1963, one of the conditions of a compensatory drawing is that the export shortfall should be "largely attributable to circumstances beyond the control of the member." Where this condition is clearly not satisfied, it would be inappropriate for a drawing to be made under the compensatory facility. However, there may be ambiguous cases where difficulties of interpretation arise. A shortfall can sometimes be attributed with equal propriety to any one of a number of causes, some of which may be under the member's control and others not. For example, suppose a combination of the following:

(a) a *rise* in foreign demand for the country's exports;

(b) a short crop due to weather;

(c) a rise in home consumption of the export product due to inflation, subsidization, or some other factor for which the government is responsible.

Given the rise in prices resulting from (a), the shortfall in export value may be no greater than could be entirely accounted for by *either* (b) *or* (c). A similar question arises where a shortfall takes place in the exports of a given product due to "act of God," but where an increase in the export of other products, which would otherwise have offset the shortfall, fails to occur because of the policies of the member. Again, there may be instances where the shortfall would not have occurred except for certain policies of the member but these policies were reasonable in the light of all the circumstances, or where the shortfall could have been prevented by certain policies but abstention from these policies on the part of the member was reasonable in the light of all the circumstances.

In such ambiguous cases an interpretation favorable to the member requesting the compensatory drawing will generally be adopted, and whenever the shortfall can be largely attributed to "circumstances beyond the control of the member" it will be so attributed.

One of the conditions for drawing under paragraph (5) of the 1963 Decision is that "the member will cooperate with the Fund in an effort to find, where required, appropriate solutions for its balance of payments difficulties."

In the application of the Decision to individual cases, the Fund, in accordance with the intention of the Decision, has not attempted to reach agreement with the member on what the nature of these solutions would have to be. This has been left to subsequent discussions, and has not stood in the way of prompt action on requests for compensatory drawings. Nevertheless, in one instance in which a compensatory drawing was requested, the country concerned made, at the time of the request, a statement of the policies it intended to follow. In the two other compensatory drawings, the Fund subsequently reached agreements on appropriate policies with the countries in question.

7. Separation of the Compensatory Facility from Other Drawing Facilities

One of the measures which the UNCTAD proposed for consideration by Fund member Governments runs as follows:

> (2) To place compensatory credits entirely outside the structure of the gold and successive credit tranches, so that the drawing of compensatory credits would not directly or indirectly prejudice a member's ability to make an ordinary drawing.

Presumably the measure recommended is to be interpreted in the sense that the amount drawn under the compensatory financing facility would be ignored by the Fund in computing the amount of drawing facilities still available to members under the principles applicable to the gold tranche, the first credit tranche, etc., as well as in computing the practical maximum drawing facilities open to members. In other words, the Fund would treat a request by a member for a drawing as if its holdings of the member's currency were less than its actual holdings by the amount of any drawings outstanding under the compensatory financing facility.

At present the Fund is prepared to waive the 200 per cent limit to the extent that compensatory drawings are outstanding. If the UNCTAD recommendation were accepted, the limits for gold tranche and first credit tranche policies would be extended beyond 100 per cent and beyond 125 per cent of holdings, respectively, to the extent that compensatory drawings were outstanding. Most compensatory drawings are likely to occur after a country has used its gold tranche and probably also its first credit tranche. To ignore the compensatory drawings not only from the standpoint of the total drawing facilities of a member but also from the standpoint of tranche policies to be applied to the member would have the advantage of rendering the facility clearly additional in all respects. It would also eliminate certain possible inequities as between countries utilizing the facility.[13] On the other hand, at any given level of holdings it would somewhat reduce the Fund's ability to secure satisfactory corrective programs in connection with ordinary drawings. It would not affect the level of charges corresponding to any given level of Fund holdings, nor would it affect the applicability to compensatory drawings of the repurchase provisions of Article V, Section 7 (b). The Fund is prepared to separate the compensatory facility from other drawing facilities in the sense described above.

---

[13] At present, a member that draws on its compensatory facility after having drawn its gold tranche and first credit tranche may in effect draw up to 75 per cent of quota on relatively easy policy conditions, while a member drawing on its compensatory tranche at an earlier stage could draw only up to 50 per cent on such conditions.

8. *The Limit on Compensatory Drawings*

Another measure recommended by UNCTAD to Governments members of the Fund for study is:

> (1) To increase, as soon as possible, the amount allocated by the Fund to compensatory financing, over and above its current transactions, from 25 per cent to 50 per cent of a member country's quota.

It should be noted that the limit of 25 per cent of quota on outstanding compensatory drawings under paragraph (5) of the 1963 Decision is not an absolute one, but applies only "normally." However, it would clearly be undesirable for compensatory drawings to be accorded frequently or as a general rule in excess of the "normal" maximum. This would raise issues of discrimination, with respect both to the compensatory drawing facility and to total drawing facilities accorded to different countries. It would also defeat one purpose of the compensatory facility, namely, that a country can, to a large extent, rely on obtaining compensatory financing in the circumstances for which it is designed, and should, therefore, not have to rely on "rallonges" of this facility.

It is also important to bear in mind that the limit on drawings under the facility is not the limit on the amount a country may draw as a result of a payments difficulty arising out of an export shortfall. It is always open to the country to request an additional drawing under the ordinary drawing policies applicable to its tranche position with the Fund. Admittedly, this would reduce the amount of drawing facilities available for other purposes.

If one disregards the foregoing considerations, there can be little doubt that over any extended period of years an expansion of the 25 per cent limit on outstanding compensatory drawings would add significantly to the value of the assistance provided. Calculations as to how the Fund's compensatory facility might have worked if it had been applied, on a pure formula basis,[14] to the export earnings of primary producing countries over the period from 1951 to 1964, and if it had been used to the full, indicate that an extension of the limit on outstanding drawings from 25 to 50 per cent of quota would have increased the effectiveness of assistance provided under the facility in a proportion roughly commensurate with the increased "cost" involved. The extent to which export availabilities are brought closer to the trend value of exports would have been increased by almost 50 per cent, the extent to which availabilities are smoothed out would have risen by some 60 per cent, while the average drawings outstanding would have risen by some 65 per cent. The data are set forth in Table 3.

In the rather favorable circumstances which have prevailed since the compensatory financing decision, only three compensatory drawings have taken place. It is noteworthy, however, that in one of them (that by Sudan) the amount of compensation which would prima facie have been paid under the facility was restricted by the existence of the 25 per cent maximum. In the other two drawings the amount of compensation paid was not so restricted but in each instance a single compensatory drawing absorbed, respectively, 86 per cent and 71 per cent of a quota tranche.

From a compensatory financing standpoint there is much to be said for extending the limit of the facility from 25 to 50 per cent. Since, however, it would involve an addition to the amount of liquidity which the Fund provides on liberal conditions, it might tend

[14] It is, of course, impossible to establish in retrospect precisely what compensation would have been payable over the period 1951–64 either under the present scheme or with a higher limit, inasmuch as estimates of trend and shortfall would have been affected by qualitative appraisal as well as by formula.

to reduce countries' willingness to have recourse to facilities of a more strictly conditional character. This increase of automaticity will be somewhat intensified by the separation of the compensatory facility from other drawing facilities which has been discussed in the preceding section.

Account should also be taken of the possible effect on the Fund's own liquidity, i.e., the effect on the probable level of drawings relative to resources provided by quotas in the Fund. (See Section 10, pp. 490–91).

Table 3. Compensatory Financing: Fund Scheme with Varied Limits Applied to Data for Years 1951-64[1]

Limit	Approximation Ratio[2]	Smoothness Ratio[3]	Average Drawings Outstanding[4]
.25 of Quota	.023	.029	.29
.50 of Quota			
(a) Unqualified	.034	.046	.48
(b) Qualified as to rate of use[5]	.035	.047	.45
None	.100	.121	1.36

[1] Scheme applied to a sample of 48 countries. Coefficients of .50, .25 and .25 applied to years t, t-1, and t-2, respectively, to compute shortfalls. Drawings are assumed to be repaid one half in the fourth and one half in the fifth year after drawing, regardless of the level of exports in those years. The quotas on which the limits are based are not present quotas but those obtaining at the relevant dates during the period 1951-64.

[2] Proportionate decline in root mean square percentage deviation of export availabilities from trend value of exports.

[3] Proportionate decline in root mean square percentage deviation of export availabilities from trend value of such availabilities.

[4] Average for all years of total amounts outstanding, in billions of U.S. dollars.

[5] Drawings outstanding may not increase in any year by more than 25 per cent of quota.

Balancing the divergent considerations discussed in this section, it is intended that

(i) the limit on the use of the compensatory facility under paragraph (5) of the Compensatory Financing Decision of 1963 should be raised from 25 per cent to 50 per cent of quota; but

(ii) the 50 per cent limit should apply in all circumstances and not merely, as with the present limit, "normally";[15]

(iii) except in the case of shortfalls resulting from disasters or major emergencies, the net expansion in drawings outstanding under paragraph (5) of the Decision should not exceed 25 per cent of quota in any twelve-month period; and

(iv) any drawings the effect of which would be to raise drawings outstanding under paragraph (5) of the Decision beyond 25 per cent of quota will be granted only if the member country, in addition to fulfilling the requirements of the Decision, is found to have been cooperating with the Fund in an effort to find, where required, appropriate solutions for its balance of payments difficulties.

[15] The relevant words of the 1963 Decision are: "The amount of drawings outstanding under this decision will not normally exceed 25 per cent of the member's quota."

The limitation suggested under (iii) above will impose a delaying effect in utilizing the compensatory facility to the full extent proposed under (i). The exception to this rule envisaged in the case of disasters and major emergencies is intended to provide some flexibility in very exceptional circumstances. As will be seen from Table 3, this arrangement would probably yield slightly better results with respect both to approximation to export trend and to smoothness of export availabilities than would an unqualified limit of 50 per cent of quota, and would be slightly less expensive to the Fund in terms of drawings outstanding.

In connection with the delaying effect of proposal (iii), it should be borne in mind that Article XIV or Article VIII consultations would provide an opportunity for testing the extent to which a member had implemented its undertakings under earlier compensatory drawings to "cooperate with the Fund in an effort to find, where required, appropriate solutions for its balance of payments difficulties," and thus the extent to which it is complying with the conditions set forth in (iv) above.

If the resources needed by a member to deal with a particular shortfall exceeded the amounts permitted under the limits indicated above and the member desired additional assistance from the Fund, it could enter into discussions with the Fund for a drawing on the terms normally applicable to the tranche in which the country found itself.[16] This would be a drawing under paragraph (4) of the 1963 Decision, and, as such, would not be limited in magnitude to any a priori percentage of the member's quota.

As was indicated on p. 479 above, any request for the use of the compensatory facility has to relate to an export shortfall during a specified period, viz., during the latest twelve-month period for which, at the time of the request, a reliable estimate of actual exports can be made. It follows from this that if, for any reason, such as the limit of 25 per cent of quota per annum on the net expansion of compensatory drawings under (iii) above, or the limit of 50 per cent of quota on the amount of compensatory drawings outstanding, the amount of a compensatory drawing is less than the amount of the shortfall on which it is based, the uncompensated part of the shortfall could not be carried forward and added to the amount of some later compensatory drawing to which a member may be entitled.

9. *Repurchase of Compensatory Drawing*

The Compensatory Financing Decision of 1963 does not contain specific provisions with respect to the repurchase of Fund holdings of a member's currency arising from a compensatory drawing. Such drawings were thus to be repurchased in accordance with the Fund's general policy on repurchases as laid down in the Decision of February 13, 1952.[17] Under that Decision, the period during which drawings may remain outstanding should not exceed an outside range of three to five years.

From the point of view of the purpose of the compensatory facility—which is intended to reduce the fluctuations in members' export availabilities—it would be desirable to provide for repurchases of outstanding compensatory drawings, not on a fixed time schedule, but in years in which exports exceed the estimated trend value.

---

[16] In accordance with the provision discussed on p. 482 above, the terms in question would, of course, be determined by the Fund's holdings of the member's currency, exclusive of those arising from drawings outstanding under paragraph (5) of the Compensatory Financing Decision.

[17] Decision No. 102-(52/11), adopted February 13, 1952 (above, pp. 228–30).

As can be seen from Table 4 below, schemes in which (a) repurchases were made exclusively out of export excesses and (b) the full amount of such excesses was directed to repurchases would probably, over the years 1951–64, have enhanced the degree of approximation to the export trend by over 20 per cent, and the smoothing effect of the facility on export availabilities by over 50 per cent as compared to schemes involving repurchase under the fixed-term system (the three-to-five-year rule).[18] This holds true whether the limit on outstanding drawings is 25 per cent or 50 per cent of quota. For

Table 4. Compensatory Financing: Fund Scheme With Varied Forms of Repayment, 1951-64 [1]

Repayment System	Fixed-Term [2]	Fully Compensatory [3]	Half Compensatory [4]	Mixed [5]
		25 Per Cent of Quota Limit		
Approximation Ratio [6]	.023	.028	.031	.030
Smoothness Ratio [7]	.029	.045	.048	.047
Average Drawings Outstanding [8]	.29	.17	.21	.20
		50 Per Cent of Quota Limit (Unqualified)		
Approximation Ratio	.034	.042	.044	.042
Smoothness Ratio	.046	.072	.073	.071
Average Drawings Outstanding	.48	.36	.47	.38
		50 Per Cent of Quota Limit (Qualified)		
Approximation Ratio	.035	.043	.046	.043
Smoothness Ratio	.047	.071	.073	.071
Average Drawings Outstanding	.45	.28	.38	.32
		No Limit		
Approximation Ratio	.100	.155	.168	.120
Smoothness Ratio	.121	.216	.199	.166
Average Drawings Outstanding	1.36	1.49	2.05	1.17

1 Weights of .50, .25 and .25 applied to years *t*, *t*-1, and *t*-2, respectively, for estimating calculated norm. One hundred per cent compensation of calculated shortfall.

2 Amounts outstanding at end of three years are assumed to be repaid one half in the fourth and one half in the fifth year after drawing, regardless of level of exports.

3 One hundred per cent of export excesses applied to repayment in all years.

4 Fifty per cent of export excesses applied to repayment in all years.

5 Fifty per cent of export excesses applied to repayment in the first three years. In the fourth year either half the amount outstanding at the end of the third year or half of the export excess (whichever is the greater) applied to repayment. In the fifth year any amount outstanding at the end of the fourth year repaid.

6 Proportionate decline in root mean square percentage deviation of export availabilities from trend value of exports.

7 Proportionate decline in root mean square percentage deviation of export availabilities from trend value of such availabilities.

8 Average for all years of total amounts outstanding, in billions of U.S. dollars.

18 Under the "fixed-term" system, as the expression is used in this report, it is assumed that drawings are repurchased one half in the fourth and one half in the fifth year after the drawing, regardless of the level of exports.

schemes without limits the superiority of compensatory repurchase would have been still greater.

Contrary to what might perhaps at first sight be assumed, the change in the timing of repurchases would also, save in the "no limit" case, have reduced the average length of time for which compensatory drawings remained outstanding and hence have reduced the average amount of compensatory drawings outstanding at any one time. It seems probable, therefore, that a system whereby compensatory drawings are repaid out of export excesses rather than under the three-to-five-year rule would do much to improve the performance of the facility without any additional "cost"—indeed with a reduction in cost—in terms of drawings outstanding.

Two difficulties arise with respect to this fully compensatory system of repurchases out of export excesses. In the first place, countries might occasionally find it difficult to repurchase compensatory drawings to the full extent of any excess of actual over trend value of exports, partly because an expansion in exports would probably entail some increase in import requirements, and partly because the obligation to repay would not be known with certainty until after the event. This difficulty could be met, in part, by a system according to which members would use in repurchase of outstanding compensatory drawings, not the entire amount, but only one half of any excess of exports over the medium-term trend value. From Table 4 it can be seen that such a "half-compensatory" system of repurchases would show slightly better smoothness and approximation ratios than would one with fully compensatory repurchase, at least where outstanding compensatory drawings are subject to a limit. This at first sight somewhat surprising result is attributable to the fact that the repurchases are spread over a number of "excess" years for which export availabilities would otherwise have remained in their original unadjusted state. The average amount of drawings outstanding is somewhat greater under the half-compensatory than under the fully compensatory system of repurchase but less than under the fixed-term system.

The second difficulty about systems of repurchase out of export excesses is that a proportion of the repurchases would probably remain outstanding for longer periods than is compatible with the temporary character of Fund assistance. This does not mean that repayment would normally be more delayed than under the three-to-five-year rule. Indeed, if, as indicated in Table 4, the average amount of compensatory drawings outstanding is generally likely to be less when repayments are on a compensatory basis than when they are made under the fixed-term rule, the average length of time for which a drawing remains outstanding will also probably be less under a compensatory repayment system than under the fixed-term system. More direct measurements of probable periods for which compensatory drawings would remain outstanding if repayments were on a compensatory basis are given in Table 5, which is based on the experience of the years 1951–64. With a half-compensatory repayment system, about three fifths of all drawings would have been repaid within three years under the 25 per cent of quota limit, and one half under the qualified 50 per cent of quota limit. In the fixed-term system, by contrast, repayments may not even begin before the fourth year after any drawing. However, whereas repayments are completed at the end of five years under the fixed-term system, one third of all drawings would have remained outstanding longer than five years under the half-compensatory system with the qualified 50 per cent of quota limit.

Although it must be borne in mind that the repurchase obligations under Article V, Section 7, would, of course, continue to apply—a fact which could not be taken into account in the calculations set forth in Table 5—it is evident that the requirement that Fund assistance be temporary would not be adequately met by a purely compensatory repurchase system.

The features of a desirable system of repurchase may now be recapitulated.

First, in order to ensure the short-term character of the use of Fund resources by individual members, it is necessary to observe an outside limit of five years for repurchases.

Second, it would be desirable if, to some extent, repurchases within this five-year period were to be made on the compensatory principle. Such repurchases out of export excesses are in accordance not only with the purpose of the policy on compensatory financing, but also with the principles of the Decision of February 13, 1952, which states

Table 5. Duration of Drawings Outstanding Under Compensatory Repayment Systems [1]
(Based on data for the period 1951-64)

	25% of Quota Limit		50% of Quota Limit (Unqualified)		50% of Quota Limit (Qualified)	
	Billions of U.S. dollars	Per cent of drawings	Billions of U.S. dollars	Per cent of drawings	Billions of U.S. dollars	Per cent of drawings
			Fully Compensatory System [2]			
Total drawings	.89	100	1.45	100	1.24	100
Repaid within 3 years	.74	83	.97	67	.97	78
Outstanding after the fifth year	.09	10	.27	18	.15	12
			Half-compensatory System [3]			
Total drawings	.69	100	1.20	100	1.01	100
Repaid within 3 years	.41	59	.54	45	.49	49
Outstanding after the fifth year	.12	17	.43	36	.33	33

[1] Weights of .50, .25 and .25 applied to years *t*, *t*-1, and *t*-2, respectively, for estimating calculated norm. One hundred per cent compensation of calculated shortfall.

[2] One hundred per cent of excesses applied to repayment.

[3] Fifty per cent of excesses applied to repayment.

that "exchange purchased from the Fund should not remain outstanding beyond the period reasonably related to the payments problem for which it was purchased from the Fund." In this connection, it should be remembered that, for reasons already stated, compensatory repurchases amounting to one half of the export excesses are likely to result in greater reduction of the fluctuations of export availabilities around the trend than would fully compensatory repurchases.

Third, although compensatory repurchases ordinarily benefit the member concerned by contributing to a smoothing of the fluctuations in its export availabilities and by restoring its access to the compensatory facility at an earlier date than would be the case under fixed-term repurchases in the fourth and fifth years after a drawing, circumstances may, in a particular year, make it difficult for a member to take advantage of these benefits. A member may, for instance, encounter temporary balance of payments difficulties even though it experiences an export excess, say, because of an unavoidable increase in import requirements or an unexpected reduction in the inflow of foreign capital or aid. The arrangements with respect to compensatory repurchases must be sufficiently flexible to make it possible for members to take account of such circumstances which may make it desirable to use less than one half of an export excess in repayment or even to omit the indicated compensatory repurchase entirely.

A repurchase system which would give effect to these desiderata would operate as follows:

(a) As in the case of ordinary drawings, a member will make repurchases with respect to amounts which remain outstanding from a drawing under paragraph (5) in installments in the fourth and fifth years after the drawing, and complete repurchase by the end of the fifth year.

(b) In addition, the Fund recommends that, as soon as possible after the end of each of the four years following such a drawing, the member use in repurchase an amount approximately equal to one half of its export excess, if any.

In order to implement the provision under (b) above, calculations will be made at twelve-month intervals to see whether or not export excesses have occurred. These calculations will be made on the basis of the statistical formula adopted as an element in the calculation of shortfalls, for each twelve-month period, beginning with the twelve months immediately following the shortfall period with respect to which the drawing had been approved. Since the recommended amount is only an approximate one, the statistical calculation will not, as in the case of a shortfall determination, be partly based on the results of market forecasts of the member's export receipts.

In order to give an indication of the performance under such a repurchase system, calculations have been made for the period 1951 64, as shown in the last column of Table 4, on the assumption that members always followed the recommendation under (b). As can be seen from that table, on that assumption the performance as measured by the approximation ratio and smoothness ratio would have been better than that of the fixed-term system of repurchase, equivalent to that of the fully compensatory system, and only slightly inferior to that of the half-compensatory system of repurchase out of export excesses. This finding holds irrespective of the severity of the limits on outstanding drawings.

The "cost" in terms of drawings outstanding is much lower than under the system of fixed-term repurchase, and almost as low as under fully compensatory repurchase.

It should be noted that under the repurchase system described above a drawing member would make the same type of representation as to repurchase as that made in cases of ordinary drawings, i.e., that the drawing member would comply with the principles of the Decision of February 13, 1952. Such representations do not, as such, create a legal obligation, although they are often made binding on members as terms of a waiver under Article V, Section 4. The recommendation to members, referred to in (b) above, to use in repurchase one half of their export excesses would not create a legal obligation for members even in such cases, i.e., where the member's representation that it will repurchase in accordance with the principles of the 1952 Decision would have been made legally binding under a waiver. The purpose of the clause is to express the hope of the Fund, based on what it would regard as an appropriate application of the principles of the 1952 Decision, that members would use export excesses to repurchase compensatory drawings still outstanding, but members which did not act in accordance with that recommendation would not be violating an obligation.

In connection with this discussion of arrangements regarding repurchases, it may be appropriate to take up the somewhat related matter of refinancing of obligations arising from compensatory drawings.

One measure recommended by UNCTAD for study by Fund member Governments is:

> (3) To explore ways to secure possible refinancing of compensatory financing obligations of the developing countries in the event of a persistent shortfall in export receipts beyond the control of the country affected.

While there is no specific provision in the Compensatory Financing Decision of 1963 for refinancing of compensatory drawings, refinancing on a short-term to medium-term basis would, in effect, be possible in the circumstances that appear to be envisaged in the UNCTAD Recommendation, viz., in the case where at the time when a repurchase falls due in the fourth or fifth year following a compensatory drawing there is a shortfall in export receipts beyond the control of the affected country. The repurchase would restore the compensatory financing facility *pro tanto*, and if at that time an export shortfall of the type described persisted, the member would be in a position to apply for a new drawing under this facility. Moreover, when a repurchase obligation contributes to a member's temporary balance of payments difficulties, it would be possible for the Fund, in appropriate circumstances, to agree to an ordinary drawing at the time of the compensatory repurchase.

It should also be noted that the case envisaged in the UNCTAD Recommendation could only arise if the member had no export excesses in the years following the drawing and had to repurchase during the fourth and fifth years (under the three-to-five-year rule). If the member experienced export excesses prior to the time it must repurchase under the three-to-five-year rule, it would, by making the recommended repurchases, fully or partly restore its access to the Fund's resources under the compensatory facility. The consideration developed in the portion of the UNCTAD Recommendation quoted above arises, therefore, only under circumstances where shortfalls persist for at least four years in a row or where a shortfall is followed by three years without export excesses and then by other shortfalls. Where such circumstances occur there may be need for basic and long-run measures to restore the exporting power of the country or to ensure satisfactory growth of the market value of its exports. Such measures fall, however, outside the scope of the compensatory financing facility of the Fund.

10. *Changes in the Compensatory Facility and Fund Liquidity*

It may be appropriate, at this point, to estimate the possible charge on Fund liquidity that might result from additional drawings with the adoption of the two principal measures suggested above, viz., (1) the extension of the limit from 25 per cent to 50 per cent with the qualification that the increase in outstanding drawings in any year should not exceed 25 per cent, and (2) the adoption of the system of repurchase discussed above. For the purpose of these calculations it has been assumed that drawing members always follow the recommendation on compensatory repurchases; to the extent that they do not, the charge on Fund liquidity under the new system will tend to be higher than is indicated in the calculation given below. Some additional claims on Fund resources might also arise from the proposed separation of the compensatory facility from the other drawing facilities of the Fund, but this cannot be quantified and is unlikely to be large.

As can be seen from Table 4, if the compensatory facility had existed over the period 1951–64, and if all the 48 countries covered by the table had made full use of the facility, the transition from fixed-term repurchase with a 25 per cent of quota limit to the repurchase system described above with a qualified 50 per cent of quota limit would have involved an increase in the average level of compensatory drawings outstanding over the period from $290 million to $320 million, i.e., an increase of $30 million. From the standpoint of Fund liquidity, however, what matters is not so much the average amount of compensatory drawings outstanding as the amount liable to be outstanding at peak periods. It is estimated that, on the assumption set forth above, the maximum level of compensatory drawings outstanding would likewise have risen from $400 million to $470 million, i.e., by $70 million. On the assumption that peak-year potential compensatory drawings outstanding have expanded since 1955–58 in proportion to quotas, the change in the limit and the variation that would result from the recommended repurchases out of export excesses might, under present conditions, raise maximum potential compensatory drawings from $1,100 million to $1,300 million, i.e., by $200 million. Since, however, countries with adequate reserves will often not use opportunities for compensatory drawings that are open to them, and since any use made of the compensatory facility is likely to reduce to some extent requests for ordinary drawings, it seems unlikely that the increase in peak-year drawings occasioned by the proposed changes would in practice exceed half the amount mentioned above, viz., $100 million.

IV. CONCLUSIONS FOR ACTION

More than three years have now elapsed since the creation of the compensatory financing facility, and though it has not yet been extensively used the Fund has had sufficient experience with it to review and reappraise its application and scope. As a result it has been deemed desirable both to clarify the circumstances under which the facility can be used and to introduce into it certain modifications designed to increase the effectiveness of the assistance which the Fund provides to members.

In determining the medium-term export trend for the purpose of calculating the export shortfall the practice hitherto has been to give approximately equal weight to statistical and qualitative estimates. Experience suggests that qualitative estimates based on commodity analysis give a closer estimate of the trend; consequently qualitative estimates will receive a greater weight in the future.

At present, the Fund is prepared to waive the requirement that the Fund's holdings of a member's currency may not exceed 200 per cent of quota either to accommodate compensatory drawings or, to the extent that compensatory drawings are outstanding, to accommodate other drawings. However, drawings under the compensatory facility are included in Fund holdings of the member's currency in applying the tranche policies of the Fund to subsequent drawings. Full recognition of the special circumstances which give rise to compensatory drawings make it desirable to separate this facility from normal drawing facilities of the Fund so that compensatory drawings outstanding will not in any way affect the tranche policies applicable to other drawings.

While the use of the compensatory facility is most needed when a shortfall appears, members may be deterred from requesting use of the facility at that time since the full amount of the shortfall can be known only after the interval of several months. To meet this problem, members may request a compensatory drawing before a period of twelve months has elapsed since the last such drawing (or since an ordinary drawing which has been made entirely or partly in view of an export shortfall). The shortfall calculated at the time of the second drawing will be adjusted by a prorated amount of the earlier drawing. Moreover, a member may within six months of an ordinary drawing reclassify all or part of it as a compensatory drawing and thus restore to that extent its normal drawing rights for future contingencies.

Under the 1963 Decision, outstanding drawings under the compensatory facility are limited normally to 25 per cent of quota. It is believed that an extension of the limit on outstanding drawings from 25 to 50 per cent of quota would add substantially to the value of the assistance provided. At the same time it is important to avoid such changes as would tend to weaken the ability of the Fund to exert its influence with members toward early adoption of sound corrective policies. The new Decision provides, therefore, that compensatory drawings outstanding may amount to a maximum of 50 per cent of quota, but that, except in the case of shortfalls resulting from disasters and major emergencies, the amount of such drawings outstanding may not increase by a net amount of more than 25 per cent of quota during any twelve-month period and that requests which would increase outstanding compensatory drawings beyond 25 per cent of quota will be met only if the Fund is satisfied that the member has been cooperating with the Fund in an effort to find, where required, appropriate solutions for its balance of payments difficulties.

The question of repurchases of compensatory drawings has also been reconsidered in light of the possibility that the course of export receipts may make it undesirable for members to concentrate repurchases within three to five years after the drawings. On the other hand, repurchase terms can not be so changed as to undermine the revolving nature of Fund resources. Balancing these considerations, the repurchase system of the Decision of February 13, 1952 is to be maintained, but in addition the Fund recommends that, as soon as possible after the end of each of the four years following such a drawing, the member use in repurchase an amount approximately equal to one half of any excess of exports over the medium-term trend value of exports.

V. DECISION [19]

In the light of the considerations set forth in the foregoing sections of this report, Executive Board Decision No. 1477-(63/8) of February 27, 1963, on Compensatory Financing of Export Fluctuations is hereby amended by the deletion of paragraphs (5) through (8) and the substitution of the following paragraphs:

(5) The Fund has reviewed its policies to determine how it could more readily assist members, particularly primary exporters, encountering payments difficulties produced by temporary export shortfalls, and has decided that such members can expect that their request for drawings will be met where the Fund is satisfied that

(a) the shortfall is of a short-term character and is largely attributable to circumstances beyond the control of the member; and

(b) the member will cooperate with the Fund in an effort to find, where required, appropriate solutions for its balance of payments difficulties.

Drawings outstanding under this paragraph (5) may amount to 50 per cent of the

---

[19] See above, pp. 238–40, for the text of the Decision on Compensatory Financing of Export Fluctuations, adopted February 27, 1963.

member's quota provided that (i) except in the case of shortfalls resulting from disasters or major emergencies, such drawings will not be increased by a net amount of more than 25 per cent of the member's quota in any 12-month period, and (ii) requests for drawings which would increase the drawings outstanding under this paragraph (5) beyond 25 per cent of the member's quota will be met only if the Fund is satisfied that the member has been cooperating with the Fund in an effort to find, where required, appropriate solutions for its balance of payments difficulties.

The existence and amount of an export shortfall for the purpose of any drawing under this paragraph (5) shall be determined with respect to the latest 12-month period preceding the drawing request for which the Fund has sufficient statistical data, and any excess of a shortfall over the drawing made under this paragraph (5) in respect to that shortfall cannot be carried forward and covered by a later drawing under this paragraph (5).

(6) In order to identify more clearly what are to be regarded as export shortfalls of a short-term character, the Fund, in conjunction with the member concerned, will seek to establish reasonable estimates regarding the medium-term trend of the member's exports based partly on statistical calculation and partly on appraisal of export prospects.

(7) A member requesting a drawing under paragraph (5) will be expected to represent that it will make a repurchase corresponding to the drawing in accordance with the principles of E.B. Decision No. 102-(52/11) of February 13, 1952, as renewed by E.B. Decision No. 270-(53/95) of December 23, 1953. With a view to an application of these principles appropriate to drawings under paragraph (5), the Fund recommends that, as soon as possible after the end of each of the four years following a drawing under paragraph (5), the member repurchase an amount of the Fund's holdings of the member's currency approximately equal to one half of the amount by which the member's exports exceed the medium-term trend of its exports. Calculations of export excesses for this purpose will be made with respect to successive 12-month periods following the period of the shortfall with respect to which the drawing was made and on the basis of statistical information only.

(8) Whenever the Fund's holdings of a member's currency resulting from an outstanding compensatory drawing under paragraph (5) are reduced, by the member's repurchase or otherwise, this will restore *pro tanto* the member's facility to make a further compensatory drawing under that paragraph, should the need arise.

(9) When drawings are made under paragraph (5), the Fund will so indicate in an appropriate manner. Within six months from the date of any drawing which is not under paragraph (5) and to the extent that it is still outstanding, a member may request that all or part of the drawing be reclassified and treated, for all purposes of this decision, as a drawing made under paragraph (5). The Fund will agree to such a request if at the time of the request the member meets the requirements for a drawing of an equal amount under paragraph (5).

(10) In order to implement the Fund's policies in connection with compensatory financing of export shortfalls, the Fund will be prepared to waive the limit on Fund holdings of 200 per cent of quota, where appropriate. In particular, the Fund will be prepared to waive this limit (i) where a waiver is necessary to permit compensatory drawings to be made under paragraphs (4) and (5) above, or (ii) to the extent that drawings in accordance with paragraph (5) are still outstanding.

Moreover, the Fund will apply its tranche policies to drawing requests by a member as if the Fund's holdings of the member's currency were less than its actual holdings of that currency by the amount of any drawings outstanding under paragraph (5).

(11) The provision of credit to deal with the balance of payments effects of export fluctuations provides immediate relief for a country's short-term difficulties. In many cases, however, it will also be necessary to introduce measures of a policy character in order to attain a satisfactory and lasting solution to a country's balance of payments problems. Members generally have actively cooperated with the Fund to find and adopt the measures necessary to this end. Beyond immediate balance of payments difficulties, the primary exporting countries are, in many instances, facing unfavorable long-term export trends, and all are trying to meet the challenge of achieving more rapid and sustained development through a strengthening and broadening of their economies. The last-mentioned problem will require action in many fields and over many years by both the primary exporting countries and the industrial countries, separately and in concert, including readier access to the markets of the developed countries for the products of the developing countries and an appropriate and sustained flow of technical and financial assistance to the developing countries. The Fund considers that its activities can provide valuable assistance in helping to establish a climate within which longer-term measures can be more effectively pursued.

(12) The Fund will review this decision in the light of experience and developing circumstances.

APPENDIX I

United Nations Conference on Trade and Development
Final Act and Report

Annex A.IV.17

STUDY OF MEASURES RELATED TO THE COMPENSATORY CREDIT SYSTEM OF THE INTERNATIONAL MONETARY FUND

The Conference,

Considering that the compensatory credit system put into operation by the International Monetary Fund since February 1963 constitutes a definite step towards the solution of short-term financing problems,

Considering that, in view of the short-term needs of developing countries derived from fluctuations in their export receipts, this system should be reviewed,

1. *Recommends* that Governments members of the International Monetary Fund study the following measures:

(1) To increase, as soon as possible, the amount allocated by the Fund to compensatory financing, over and above its current transactions, from 25 per cent to 50 per cent of a member country's quota;

(2) To place compensatory credits entirely outside the structure of the gold and successive credit tranches, so that the drawing of compensatory credits would not directly or indirectly prejudice a member's ability to make an ordinary drawing;

(3) To explore ways to secure possible refinancing of compensatory financing obligations of the developing countries in the event of a persistent shortfall in export receipts beyond the control of the country affected.

2. *Requests* that the International Monetary Fund, in its determination of the shortfall in export receipts, consider giving greater weight to the actual experience of the three preceding years.

APPENDIX II

EXCERPTS FROM SPEECHES OF GOVERNORS AT THE 1965 ANNUAL MEETING

AFGHANISTAN

The recent fall in basic commodity prices and difficulties in marketing total available food supplies will necessitate compensatory financing in the coming months. To meet these needs, the facilities of the Fund need improvement.

ARGENTINA (On behalf of 19 Latin American countries and the Philippines)

We should like once more to reiterate our opinion regarding the decision adopted in 1963 by the Executive Board of the Fund on the compensatory financing of losses in the export proceeds of primary-producing countries. We recognize that this represents a contribution toward the partial solution of this very important problem. However, it would be advisable to consider three fundamental aspects:

(1) The need for considering the compensatory tranche in addition to the normal credit facilities of the Monetary Fund. The decision of February 1963, indeed, permits the drawing without taking into consideration the position of the requesting country with regard to the credit tranches. Nevertheless, the drawing has been added to those already made and thus may affect the country's position in respect of future transactions with the Fund. In our opinion it is of the greatest importance that the compensatory drawing be allotted quite separately from the others and invested with the supplementary nature that the different schemes favored by our countries have always upheld.

(2) The amount available under this type of loan, limited to 25 per cent of each member's quota, is of insufficient size even in the case of very moderate depressions. If this ceiling were raised from 25 to 50 per cent, more significant resources would be made available to the countries exporting primary products, without this entailing a very heavy burden on the resources of the institution.

(3) In conclusion, we would emphasize the non-automatic nature of the drawings permitted. In the decisions on individual cases submitted to the consideration of the Executive Board there has been some flexibility, although in all of them there has been no lack of a subjective assessment in the determination both of the amount to be compensated and of the circumstances in which the loss of income occurs.

CEYLON

I was encouraged by the reference by Mr. Schweitzer to the work that the Fund is now undertaking to improve the compensatory financing facility. Several speakers have urged that compensatory assistance should be provided for a decline in the terms of trade rather than for a fall in export earnings alone. My own country's experience in recent years vividly illustrates the importance of this reform. We suffered a decline in the terms of trade by 13 per cent in two years alone, but since this was almost entirely due to an increase in import prices we were unable to avail ourselves of the compensatory financing facility. I do sincerely hope that this particular improvement in the scheme will be made effective at an early date.

CHINA

However, the scanty application that developing countries have made of the compensatory financing facility of the Fund would seem to indicate that the economic problems of developing countries cannot readily be solved through temporary accessibility to credit.

GREECE

. . . improved facilities for compensatory financing and more flexible conditions for drawings and repurchases should also be envisaged to provide for a direct contribution to the liquidit position of the developing countries.

IRAQ

May I point out in this connection that the compensatory financing scheme of the Fund, though admirable in itself, suffers from one drawback. The borrowing facility under this scheme is available to primary producing countries when the shortfall in their exports is due to factors beyond their control. Since the decline in exports in such cases would be temporary and self-correcting, the Fund should not make the facility conditional on the pursuit by the country concerned of particular policies about its general balance of payments position.

SUDAN

Appreciative as we are of the Fund's efforts in this respect, we strongly feel that the terms and conditions under which the Fund provides such compensatory assistance (and, indeed, any other assistance) should be reconsidered with the view of softening them. It is no secret that a very limited number of members have so far made use of these arrangements, in spite of the pressing need of many for such assistance.

UGANDA

While the Fund's operations are properly concerned with short-term balance of payments aspects, it may not be possible under conditions of fluctuating export earnings to differentiate between the short- and the long-term aspects. Such conditions tend to make public debt burdens unduly onerous on developing countries which base the servicing of their public debt burden on the expectation of a steady and reasonable growth in export earnings. It is therefore important in my view that both the Bank and the Fund should continue their efforts to find solutions to these problems. The Fund, on the one hand, should review the present compensatory financing arrangements to take account of the problems of fluctuating export earnings. The Bank, on the other hand, should continue to play a prominent role in evolving price stabilization machinery for primary products in association with UNCTAD.

UNITED ARAB REPUBLIC

Thus, the compensatory financing facility could be increased from one tranche to two tranches and the criteria for using this facility could be improved to take into account results to date and discussions in UNCTAD.

VIET-NAM

In particular, the nonliberal trade policy adopted by developed countries has obstructed the entry into these countries of primary manufactured products from the underdeveloped countries. To be sure, the action of the Bank and Fund in the form of compensatory financing granted to countries exporting primary products or in the form of assistance for the development and expansion of trade has been highly effective. However, the action necessary for the removal of discriminatory trade practices or other obstacles to the development of international trade should be hastened. This action should be supplemented by a complete revision of the present system of international payments. We also have high hopes that with the general increase in Fund quotas, the Fund will be able not only to grant compensatory financing facilities on a broader basis, for example, by increasing the percentage of this financing, but also to consider ways to aid countries which have experienced a temporary export shortfall as a result of crop losses caused by war, floods, or other natural calamities.

APPENDIX III

DECISIONS ON COMPENSATORY FINANCING OF EXPORT FLUCTUATIONS

[As the two Decisions on Compensatory Financing are reproduced elsewhere in this volume, they have been omitted here. For the text of the original Decision (No. 1477-(63/8), February 27, 1963), see above, pp. 238–40; for the text of the 1966 Amendment (Decision No. 2192-(66/81), September 20, 1966), see above, pp. 492–94.]

Proposed Amendment of the Articles of Agreement

On April 17, 1968, the Executive Directors submitted to the Governors detailed proposals for amendments to the Articles of Agreement of the Fund. These proposals provided for a Facility Based on Special Drawing Rights in the Fund, and for some other changes in the Articles by which, inter alia, gold tranche drawings will become legally automatic, the provisions for repurchases will be substantially altered, and certain revisions will be made in voting requirements.

The proposals were approved by the Governors on May 31, 1968, and entered into force on July 28, 1969, having been accepted by 60 per cent of the members and by members having 80 per cent of the total votes.

Establishment of a Facility Based on Special Drawing Rights in the International Monetary Fund and Modifications in the Rules and Practices of the Fund

(April 1968)

A Report by the Executive Directors to the Board of Governors Proposing Amendment of the Articles of Agreement

TABLE OF CONTENTS

INTRODUCTION

At its Twenty-Second Annual Meeting at Rio de Janeiro in September 1967, the Board of Governors adopted the following Resolution:

WHEREAS the functioning of the international monetary system and its improvement, including arrangements to meet the need, as and when it arises, for a supplement to existing reserve assets, have been the subject of extensive study and international discussion resulting in the Outline of a Facility Based on Special Drawing Rights in the International Monetary Fund, which Outline is attached to this Resolution; and

WHEREAS studies are currently under way on possible improvements in the present rules and practices of the Fund;

NOW, THEREFORE, the Board of Governors hereby RESOLVES:

That the Executive Directors are requested to

1. Proceed with their work relating to both

(a) the establishment in the Fund of a new facility on the basis of the Outline in order to meet the need, as and when it arises, for a supplement to existing reserve assets, and

(b) improvements in the present rules and practices of the Fund based on developments in world economic conditions and the experience of the Fund since the adoption of the Articles of Agreement of the Fund; and

2. Submit to the Board of Governors as soon as possible but not later than March 31, 1968

(a) a report proposing amendments to the Articles of Agreement and the By-Laws for the purpose of establishing a new facility on the basis of the Outline, and

(b) a report proposing such amendments to the Articles of Agreement and the By-Laws as would be required to give effect to those modifications in the present rules and practices of the Fund that the Executive Directors will recommend.

As the Governors have been informed, it was not possible to complete by March 31, 1968 the work on the two subjects referred to in paragraph 1 of this Resolution. The Executive Directors are now submitting to the Board of Governors the present Report which combines the two reports envisaged in paragraph 2 of the Resolution. Part I constitutes the first and Part II the second of these two reports. The recommendations of the Executive Directors are presented together in Annex A to this Report.

Annex A submits for approval by the Board of Governors a Resolution proposing modifications in the Articles of Agreement of the International Monetary Fund for the purpose of (a) establishing in the Fund a facility for special drawing rights based on the Outline, and (b) giving effect to certain changes in the present rules and practices of the Fund that the Executive Directors have decided to recommend. They are not recommending modifications in the By-Laws at this time. It would not be possible for the Board of Governors to adopt By-Laws relating to the new facility until the participation requirement prescribed in Article XXIII, Section 1, has been met. Recommendations will be submitted in due course.

The modifications in the Articles of Agreement under both (a) and (b) above are set forth in the Proposed Amendment which appears in the attachment to the Resolution. The Executive Directors recommend to the Board of Governors the adoption of this Resolution.

The Outline referred to above is also annexed to this Report (Annex B).

While the modifications set forth in Annex A are for the most part self-explanatory, the Executive Directors believe that brief comments on various aspects of these modifications may be useful to Governors and to member governments. They are to be found in Parts I and II of the Report.

In addition, Part III of the Report describes the procedure to be followed in order to give effect to the proposed modifications.

The Executive Directors wish to take this opportunity to express their great appreciation of the outstanding contribution made by the Staff of the Fund at all levels in the implementation of the Governors' Resolution. Working under intense pressure, sustained for more than six months, they have at all times given the Executive Directors the benefit of their skill and experience.

PART I

The New Facility

1. *General Comments*

The Resolution adopted by the Board of Governors at its Rio de Janeiro Meeting envisaged the establishment in the Fund of a new facility based on special drawing rights to meet the need, as and when it arises, for a supplement to existing reserve assets. The changes in the Introductory Article and the addition of Articles XXI through XXXII and Schedules F, G, H, and I, which are included in the Proposed Amendment, will achieve this purpose, and under them the Fund will acquire an important new function in the international monetary system. The new provisions also deal with the relationship of the new facility to the present functions of the Fund. However, the provisions of the Articles of Agreement, as amended, will constitute a single legal document.

As requested by the Rio de Janeiro Resolution, the Executive Directors, in drafting the modifications in the Articles of Agreement that would establish the new facility, have worked on the basis of the Outline attached to that Resolution. The Outline sets forth the main features of the new facility and several of its more detailed characteristics. It was, however, intentionally less than a complete plan of the facility, and the Executive Directors have had to elaborate certain aspects of the facility that were treated in the Outline only in a very general way. This applied, for example, to the establishment of the General and the Special Drawing Accounts, the terms on which the General Account may hold and use special drawing rights, the provision relating to "other holders," the cancellation of special drawing rights, the payment of interest, the levying of charges, withdrawal from the facility, and its liquidation. It was also necessary to provide in detail for the effects on the organizational structure of the Fund that follow from the fact that, while all members are entitled to become participants in the new facility, they are not required to participate. However, it has not been felt necessary to include in the Proposed Amendment a provision corresponding to Paragraph III. 3 (d) of the Outline under which the Executive Directors are to review the operations of the Special Drawing Account and the adequacy of global reserves as part of their Annual Report to the Board of Governors. On the analogy of Article XII, Section 7, and Section 10 of the By-Laws, this requirement will be included in the By-Laws.

2. *The Special Drawing Account*

Under the Articles of Agreement as amended, there will be maintained in the Fund two separate Accounts, a General Account and a Special Drawing Account. The Fund will carry on its present operations and transactions, including those of an administrative character, through the General Account, and its functions relating to special drawing rights through the Special Drawing Account. There will be a corresponding separation of assets and property as well as liabilities and obligations.

Operations and transactions involving the acceptance or holding of special drawing rights by the Fund in the General Account or the use of special drawing rights thus held will be carried out through and recorded in both Accounts.

The separation of the two Accounts does not create a new legal entity. The Fund will continue to be the same institution with a single international personality.

3. *Participation in the Special Drawing Account*

Participation in the Special Drawing Account will be open to members of the Fund and only to them. Each member of the Fund will continue to be entitled to take part in

General Account operations and transactions, but in order to become a participant in the Special Drawing Account a member will have to deposit with the Fund an instrument setting forth that it undertakes all the obligations of a participant in the Special Drawing Account in accordance with its law and that it has taken all steps necessary to enable it to carry out all these obligations. No member will become a participant, however, before these instruments have been deposited by members that have at least 75 per cent of the total quotas in the Fund.

Participation in the Special Drawing Account will involve the assumption of both financial and nonfinancial obligations. The basic financial obligation that each participant will assume will be the obligation under Article XXV, Section 4, to provide currency convertible in fact, when the participant is designated by the Fund, to another participant using its special drawing rights, up to a total net amount equivalent to twice the net amount of special drawing rights allocated to the designated participant. The participant providing currency will receive an equivalent amount of special drawing rights. The circumstances in which a participant will be designated to provide currency are set forth in Article XXV, Section 5, and Schedule F.

A participant whose Governor did not vote in favor of a decision under which allocations of special drawing rights are being made will not have to receive allocations under that decision if it does not wish to do so. A participant will be required to receive special drawing rights allocated to it if its Governor voted in favor of the decision under which the allocations are made. Accordingly, a participant that wishes to receive special drawing rights to be allocated to it under a decision and that needs parliamentary or other legal authorization in order to be able to meet the financial obligation assumed under Article XXV, Section 4, should obtain, prior to the adoption of the relevant decision to make allocations, the necessary authorization.

The domestic legal steps that each member will need to take in order to enable it to carry out the obligations of a participant, both financial and nonfinancial, will have to be determined by the authorities of the member in accordance with its own constitutional and other legal requirements. One way in which a member will be able to put itself into a position to meet its obligations under Article XXV, Section 4, to provide currency will be to give its central bank the power to acquire and hold special drawing rights without limitation, thus obviating any need for further legal action from time to time. Central banks in many countries already have authority to acquire gold and some or all forms of foreign exchange.

An alternative course would be for a member to seek parliamentary or other legal authority, as may be necessary, for a specified amount, e.g., authority to receive allocations equal to not less than 50 per cent of quota with the consequent obligation to provide currency up to a total net amount at least equal to its quota.

4. *Holders of Special Drawing Rights Other than Participants*

Allocations of special drawing rights may be made only to participants, but the holding of such rights is not restricted to participants. Article XXIII, Section 2, authorizes the Fund itself to accept and hold special drawing rights in, and use them through, the General Account. Detailed provisions with respect to these operations and transactions are contained in Article XXV, Section 7.

Section 3 of Article XXIII foresees the possibility that the Fund may permit others to accept, hold, and use special drawing rights. Under this provision the Fund, by an 85 per cent majority of the total voting power, will be able to permit nonmembers and members that are not participants to engage in operations and transactions involving special drawing rights. Other holders that the Fund could authorize to engage in these operations and transactions would be institutions that perform one or more functions of a central bank for more than one member. Regional organizations in which members or their central banks pool some of their reserves and the Bank for International Settlements are considered to fall within this description. The expression "operations and transactions" in Article XXIII, Section 3, will cover the operations and transactions of a central banking character engaged in by the organizations referred to in this section.

The Fund has the power to prescribe, by an 85 per cent majority, the terms and conditions for the operations and transactions between participants and these other holders, but these terms and conditions must be consistent with the provisions of the Articles. In exercising this power the Fund will necessarily be guided by the nature of special drawing rights as a supplement to existing reserve assets and by the desirability of ensuring their proper use. Under this power the Fund will be able to prescribe, where it is found appropriate, that operations and transactions between participants and other holders will be subject to the requirement of need which is discussed in section 15 below. It is expected that normally the requirement of need will be prescribed as part of the terms and conditions for transactions in which participants use special drawing rights to obtain currency from other holders.

5. *Recording and Information*

Article XXII, Section 3, provides that all changes in holdings of special drawing rights, whether the result of allocations and cancellations or of operations and transactions, will become effective only when recorded by the Fund in the Special Drawing Account. This will apply not only to operations and transactions between participants but also to operations and transactions between other holders and participants. The Fund will record changes resulting from operations and transactions that are in conformity with the obligations of participants under the provisions of the Articles or any terms and conditions prescribed by the Fund under these provisions. To enable the Fund to carry out this task, participants are required to inform the Fund of any operation or transaction involving special drawing rights that they enter into and to indicate at the same time the provisions of the Articles under which the operation or transaction is entered into. The obligation falls on both parties to the operation or transaction if they are participants. It is expected that a similar requirement will be included in the terms and conditions for other holders.

6. *Principles Governing Allocations and Cancellations*

Article XXIV, Section 1 (a), states the basic principle which is to govern all decisions to allocate or cancel special drawing rights. This principle is that the Fund must seek to meet the long-term global need, as and when it arises, to supplement existing reserve assets, in a manner that will promote the attainment of the Fund's purposes as set forth in Article I, and will avoid economic stagnation and deflation as well as excess demand and inflation in the world.

7. *First Decision to Allocate Special Drawing Rights*

Article XXIV, Section 1 (b), provides that the first decision to allocate special drawing rights shall be based on the principles that guide all decisions to allocate special drawing rights, and in addition, that it shall take into account certain special considerations. The first of these special considerations is a collective judgment that there is a global need to supplement reserves. The term "collective judgment" reflects the requirement of an 85 per cent majority of the total voting power for the adoption by the Board of Governors of decisions to allocate special drawing rights. The other special considerations are the attainment of a better balance of payments equilibrium and the likelihood of a better working of the adjustment process in the future. While the situation of all members is relevant to a judgment with respect to the attainment of a better balance of payments equilibrium, the judgment to be made at the time will necessarily be influenced predominantly by the situation of members that have a large share in world trade and payments.

8. *Allocation and Cancellation*

Special drawing rights will be allocated or cancelled over periods, referred to in the Articles as "basic" periods, which normally will be five years in duration and which will run consecutively. Allocations to participants will be made at yearly intervals and on the basis of their quotas on the date of the relevant decision to allocate, unless the Fund decides that allocations are to be made at different intervals or are to be based on quotas at different dates.

The concept of consecutive basic periods has been introduced for technical reasons and does not prejudice the exercise by the Fund of its discretion to allocate special drawing rights, or to cancel special drawing rights, or to do neither. The Fund will exercise its discretion on the basis of the judgment it forms on the need to supplement existing reserve assets. It will be possible to have basic periods in which there are neither allocations nor cancellations. A basic period can be an "empty period," either because the Governors have approved a proposal by the Managing Director that no allocation or cancellation should be made, or because the Managing Director, having ascertained that there is no broad support for a proposal that would be consistent with the requirements of the Articles, has been unable to make a proposal, or because a proposal by the Managing Director to allocate or to cancel has failed to command the required majority.

A member that becomes a participant after a basic period has started will not receive allocations during that basic period, unless the Fund decides that the member will start to receive allocations beginning with the next allocation after it becomes a participant. It is expected that normally the Fund will so decide.

9. *Decisions on Allocations and Cancellations*

Under Article XXIV, Section 4 (a), and Article XXVII (a) (i), decisions to allocate or cancel special drawing rights may be made only by the Board of Governors and only by an 85 per cent majority of the total voting power. These decisions may be made by the Governors only on the basis of proposals of the Managing Director concurred in by a decision of the Executive Directors.

The Managing Director is required to make proposals at certain times and in certain circumstances. Whenever he is required to make proposals but he reaches a conclusion that there is no proposal that would be consistent with the principles and considerations governing allocation and cancellation that would have broad support among participants, he must submit a report to both the Board of Governors and the Executive Directors.

10. *Operations and Transactions in Special Drawing Rights*

As stated in Article XXV, Section 1, special drawing rights may be used only in the operations and transactions authorized by or under the provisions of the Articles.

The term "transactions," as used in Articles XXI through XXXII, refers to uses of special drawing rights to obtain currency. The main examples are transactions under Article XXV, Section 2. The term "operations" refers to all other uses of special drawing rights authorized by or under the Articles, such as the payment of interest, charges, and assessments under Article XXVI.

11. *Receipt of Allocations*

Article XXIV, Section 2 (e), requires each member that has become a participant to accept an allocation of special drawing rights unless its Governor voted against or did not vote on the decision under which the allocation is to be made and, prior to the first allocation under that decision, the participant has given the Fund notice that it does not wish to receive the allocation. In other words, a participant whose Governor did not vote affirmatively may "opt out" of allocations under a decision (i.e., may choose not to receive special drawing rights and incur the corresponding obligations) by giving notice to that effect.

A participant that has opted out with respect to a basic period may "opt back in" (i.e., resume receiving allocations) with the permission of the Fund, but the participant will receive only the allocations made after it has been permitted to opt back in. Opting back in is not possible with respect to allocations that were made previously during the basic period. It is expected that the Fund will give sympathetic consideration to a request by a participant to opt back in.

12. *Character of Special Drawing Rights*

Special drawing rights will be issued by the Fund but they will not confer on participants a claim against the Fund itself to provide currency, except as prescribed by provisions of Articles XXX and XXXI and Schedules G and H relating to the termination of participation and liquidation. Participants will be able to use special drawing rights to obtain currency from other participants in accordance with the provisions of Article XXV. The provisions of Article XXV require the Fund to designate participants to provide currency to other participants using their special drawing rights in accordance with Section 2 (a) of that Article, so that participants can be assured that at all times they will be able to use their special drawing rights in a manner consistent with the provisions of the Articles.

13. *Designation of Participants to Provide Currency*

The principles that will govern the designation of participants to provide currency to other participants using their special drawing rights in accordance with Article XXV, Section 2 (a), are indicated in the three subsections of Section 5 (a) of the same Article. However, this listing is not exhaustive; the Fund may supplement these principles with other principles.

As regards the order of priority between designations under subsections (a) (i) and (a) (ii) of Section 5 and among the three categories mentioned in subsection (a) (ii), subsection (a) (iii) prescribes that priority shall normally be given to those participants that need to acquire special drawing rights to meet the objectives of designation under subsection (a) (ii). Thus, it may be assumed that, as a general rule, the Fund will designate participants under subsection (a) (ii) if there are participants that need special drawing rights in order to comply with the reconstitution requirements of Schedule G, to reduce a negative balance (i.e., the amount of special drawing rights that the participant owes the Fund because, at the time of a cancellation, it did not hold an amount of rights equivalent to its share of the cancellation), or to offset the effect of a failure to fulfill the expectation referred to in Article XXV, Section 3 (a), on the requirement of need for the use of special drawing rights.

The Outline contained two possible criteria to guide designation among participants with a sufficiently strong balance of payments and reserve position: (i) the ratios of these participants' holdings of special drawing rights to their gross reserves, and (ii) the ratios of such holdings in excess of net cumulative allocations to gross reserves.

The Executive Directors have examined the relative merits of these two criteria. The excess holdings criterion is expected, on balance, to offer significant advantages in its application and to give the new facility a broad basis for designation consistent with the universal approach of the scheme, thereby contributing to the confidence of participants in the new instrument of special drawing rights. At the same time the Executive Directors considered a certain flexibility to be desirable for the future, and they have therefore provided in Article XXV, Section 5 (c), for a review of the rules for designation before the end of each basic period, in order to enable the Fund to adopt new rules if it deems this to be desirable. The Executive Directors have also considered that the results of a system of designation will depend not only on the choice of a criterion to determine the target distribution of holdings of special drawing rights among participants but also on the selection of the participants that should be subject to designation and on the particular formula used to aim over time at harmonization of individual ratios.

Accordingly, Schedule F envisages that participants shall be designated for such amounts as will promote over time equality in their ratios of excess holdings of special drawing rights to their holdings of gold and foreign exchange. Because initially these ratios will be zero for all participants, paragraph (b) (i) of the Schedule indicates that participants will be designated in amounts that are proportionate to their official holdings of gold and foreign exchange. With the passage of time situations are likely to arise in which such ratios for one or more participants subject to designation may be significantly below those of the majority of other participants in the group. Paragraph (b) (ii) therefore envisages a designation process which will tend to reduce gradually the difference between low and high ratios among participants subject to designation, in order to avoid sudden and massive designation of participants with relatively low ratios. The intention is that such participants, once their position permitted their being made subject to designation, would be designated, to the extent that the volume of designation permits, in amounts calculated to raise their ratios at a steady pace within approximately one year to the vicinity of the ratios that are relatively high. The formula for doing this will be determined from time to time by the Fund. Any amounts not designated in accordance with this formula would normally be assigned to the other participants subject to designation under subsection (a) (i) of Article XXV, Section 5, in a manner consistent with the objective of a harmonization of ratios.

The Fund will exercise its power of designation in a manner that will ensure that participants will be able to use their special drawing rights in order to obtain currency. Thus, if a designated participant were to fail to provide currency to a participant using its special drawing rights in accordance with Article XXV, Section 2 (a), the Fund would make any necessary additional designations.

14. *Transactions not Requiring Designation*

Under Article XXV, Section 2 (b) (ii), the Fund is given the power to prescribe transactions in which a participant may engage in agreement with any other participant whether designated or not. The provision contains a list of transactions that the Fund may prescribe. The prescription of these transactions may be made by a decision or by rules and regulations adopted by the Executive Directors. The Fund is given discretion to specify transactions from among those listed. It may specify all or none of the categories listed; or it may specify individual transactions in one or more of the categories. By an 85 per cent majority in the Board of Governors, additional transactions or categories of transactions outside the categories in the list may be prescribed. Under Article XXV, Section 2 (b) (ii), a principle is established for the adoption of decisions under that provision. These decisions of the Fund must be consistent with the provisions of the Agreement and with the proper use of special drawing rights under the Agreement; participants will be expected to observe this principle and avoid engaging in transactions without designation which might prejudice basic features of the scheme such as the requirement of need.

Article XXV, Section 2 (b) (i), expressly exempts certain transactions from designation. The Fund may prescribe any necessary rules and regulations under Article XII, Section 2 (g), in order to implement this provision.

15. *Requirement of Need*

As a general rule, a participant will be expected to use special drawing rights in transactions with other participants only if it has a need as defined in Article XXV, Section 3 (a). Section 4 of this Report deals with the requirement of need in operations and transactions in which participants obtain currency from other prescribed holders.

The definition of need given in Article XXV, Section 3 (a), covers all balance of payments needs, whether these arise from current or capital transactions. Because these needs can be defined in various ways, reference is also made to "developments in its [a participant's] official holdings of gold, foreign exchange, and special drawing rights, and its reserve position in the Fund," to indicate that these developments, even if attributable to conversions of balances of the member's currency and not to a balance of payments deficit, may give rise to a need to use special drawing rights. Use of special drawing rights merely to reduce holdings of such rights while the total of holdings of gold and foreign exchange and the reserve position in the Fund is increasing or would increase as a result of such use would not be regarded as meeting the requirement of need. However, the use of rights to meet a payments need may have the incidental effect of changing the relative proportions in which a participant holds different reserve assets.

16. *Transactions without Requirement of Need*

Under Article XXV, Section 3 (c), the Fund is authorized to prescribe transactions in which participants may use special drawing rights without fulfilling the requirement of need. The categories of transactions listed in that provision are the same as those listed in Article XXV, Section 2 (b) (ii), but, in contrast to the exemptions from the requirement of designation, the list is exhaustive and the Fund cannot prescribe transactions that go beyond its scope. As in the case of the prescription of transactions that are not subject to designation, prescriptions under Article XXV, Section 3 (c), may be made by a decision or by rules and regulations adopted by the Executive Directors, and may relate to individual transactions or categories of transactions falling within the listed categories. The transactions exempted by prescription from the requirement of need do not have to coincide at any given time with those that are exempted from the requirement of designation. In prescribing transactions or categories of transactions that are exempted from the requirement of need the Fund will take into account the extent to which a participant has to obtain special drawing rights for the purpose of meeting the objectives of Section 3 (c) of Article XXV.

17. *Reconstitution*

Under the reconstitution principles set forth in Article XXV, Section 6, and Schedule G, a participant's net use of its special drawing rights must be such that the average of its daily holdings of special drawing rights over a five-year period will not be less than 30 per cent of the average of its daily net cumulative allocations of special drawing rights over the same period. It is envisaged that the Fund will assist participants to comply with this requirement through designation under Article XXV, Section 5 (a) (ii), and rules to that effect will be adopted by the Fund. If a participant is unable to obtain sufficient special drawing rights through designation, it must obtain them from the General Account or from another participant specified by the Fund for this purpose to the extent that the General Account is unable to supply them.

The reconstitution rules set forth in Schedule G will be reviewed by the Fund before the end of each basic period. The Board of Governors by an 85 per cent majority of the total voting power may adopt, modify, or abrogate rules for reconstitution.

18. *Operations and Transactions through the General Account*

The principal provisions governing the acceptance and use of special drawing rights by the Fund in operations and transactions conducted through the General Account are set forth in Article XXV, Section 7. These provisions impose an obligation on the Fund to accept special drawing rights in two specified cases in which the provisions of the Articles require payments to be made to the Fund in special drawing rights. However, the Fund will have authority to accept, to the extent that it may decide, special drawing rights in the General Account in the cases indicated in subsection (c) of Section 7.

Subsections (d), (e), and (f) describe the circumstances in which the Fund will be authorized to use special drawing rights held in the General Account to obtain currencies from participants. Under subsection (d) the Fund may require a participant to provide its currency to the Fund for special drawing rights, if the Fund deems it appropriate to replenish its holdings of the participant's currency in the General Account and has consulted the participant on alternative ways of replenishment under Article VII, Section 2. Under subsection (f) the Fund may use special drawing rights only by agreement with the participant involved in the operation or transaction.

In order to assist a participant to meet its need for special drawing rights to carry out the objective of reconstitution, to eliminate any negative balance, or to reverse the effects of a transaction engaged in inconsistently with the rule of need, subsection (e) authorizes the Fund to provide this participant with special drawing rights from the General Account for gold or currency acceptable to the Fund.

19. *Exchange Rates*

Under Article XXV, Section 8, the exchange rates for operations and transactions are to be such as will ensure that a participant using its special drawing rights will receive the same value, on the basis of the exchange rates prevailing at the time the transaction takes place, whatever the currencies that might be provided and whichever the participant that provides the currency. The Fund will have to adopt regulations to give effect to this principle, and will consult a participant on the procedure for determining rates of exchange for its currency.

The rates prescribed under Article XXV, Section 8, will not apply to operations and transactions in special drawing rights with the General Account. Those operations and transactions will be executed at the rate at which the Fund holds the currency involved, which normally is the par value of the currency.

20. *Interest and Charges*

Under the provisions of Article XXVI, the rate of interest and the rate of charges will be the same. The net effect of these provisions will be the payment of interest by the Fund to a participant on the excess of its holdings of special drawing rights over its net cumulative allocation, and the payment of charges by a participant on the amount by which its holdings of special drawing rights are less than its net cumulative allocation. As a matter of accounting practice, the amount of interest to be paid to a participant and the amount of charges to be paid by that participant will be offset and only the balance will be paid or collected, as the case may be, by the Fund. Interest and charges will be payable in special drawing rights.

Section 3 of Article XXVI sets the rate at 1½ per cent per annum, but the Fund is given authority to apply a different rate within maximum and minimum levels. Under this authority, the Fund could set the rate at the same level as the remuneration to be paid to members under Article V, Section 9, but it will not be required to do so.

If a participant does not have sufficient special drawing rights to meet the payment of charges, it will be able to obtain special drawing rights from the General Account or from another participant specified by the Fund for this purpose to the extent that the General Account is unable to supply them.

21. *Expenses of the Special Drawing Account*

The expenses of conducting the business of the Special Drawing Account are to be met by the Fund from the resources held in the General Account. However, under Article XXII, Section 2, the Fund will be reimbursed periodically on the basis of a reasonable estimate of these expenses. For the purpose of such reimbursement, the Fund will levy assessments under Article XXVI, Section 4, on all participants in proportion to their net cumulative allocations. The amounts assessed will be paid directly into the General Account and, like interest and charges, will be payable in special drawing rights.

22. *Administration of the Special Drawing Account*

Because participation may not be coextensive with membership in the Fund, Article XXVII contains special rules for calling meetings, determining quorums, and voting majorities for the Board of Governors and the Executive Directors of the Fund when these organs consider matters pertaining to the Special Drawing Account. There is no change in the composition of these two organs of the Fund. All Governors and Directors remain entitled to attend and participate in all meetings and in the discussion of any item on the agenda. However, if a decision is to be taken on an item that pertains exclusively to the Special Drawing Account, for example, on a proposal by the Managing Director to allocate or cancel special drawing rights, only Governors for members that are participants may vote and each Director will be able to cast only the votes of the Fund members appointing or electing him that are participants. It is, therefore, possible that a Director will not have any votes to cast. Similarly, whether a

Governor or Director may cast votes on an item pertaining exclusively to the Special Drawing Account will determine whether he may put an item on the agenda, whether he may request that a meeting be called, and whether there is a quorum for any meeting.

There is no special provision in Article XXVII regarding the voting power of members that are participants for the purpose of decisions on matters relating to the Special Drawing Account. There is no need for such a provision because the voting power of these members will be determined for all purposes by the present provisions of Article XII, Section 5. Accordingly, for the purposes of the Special Drawing Account as well, each participating member will have 250 votes plus one vote for each part of its quota equivalent to one hundred thousand U.S. dollars.

Decisions on certain important issues that require an 85 per cent majority of the total voting power as well as a decision to liquidate the Special Drawing Account can be taken only by the Board of Governors. These issues are those relating to the prescription of other holders, the allocation and cancellation of special drawing rights, the prescription of additional transactions not requiring designation, and the amendment or abrogation of reconstitution rules.

23. *Suspension of Participants' Use of Special Drawing Rights*

Article XXIX, Section 2 (f), makes it clear that the suspension of a participant's use of special drawing rights pursuant to the provisions of that Article will not affect, in any way, its right as a member to make use of the resources of the Fund in the General Account, and conversely, any limitation of this right of a member that is a participant will not affect, in any way, the participant's right to use its special drawing rights.

24. *Definition of Currency Convertible in Fact for Transactions in Special Drawing Rights*

The provisions of Article XXXII (b) are designed to ensure that any participant using special drawing rights to obtain "currency convertible in fact" from a designated participant can obtain, directly or indirectly, any one of a number of convertible currencies that he may choose, in amounts determined by the exchange rates prescribed under Article XXV, Section 8, in accordance with the principle of equal value.

This objective is to be achieved by establishing a group of currencies which will be interconvertible at appropriate rates of exchange for balances arising in connection with the use of special drawing rights. Only currencies with respect to which there are procedures designed to ensure this interconvertibility to the satisfaction of the Fund and which in addition are convertible in the sense that they are the currencies of participants that freely buy and sell gold under Article IV, Section 4 (b), or have accepted the obligations of Article VIII, Sections 2, 3, and 4, will qualify for inclusion in this group.

In addition to the currencies mentioned in the preceding paragraph, currency convertible in fact will also include balances of any other currency for which suitable arrangements exist for conversion, at rates of exchange prescribed by the Fund, into any of the currencies in the group that are interconvertible. Through one or more conversions, such balances can in fact be converted into any of the currencies in the group.

25. *Definition of Reserve Position in the Fund*

Article XXXII (c) defines a participant's "reserve position in the Fund" as the sum of the gold tranche purchases that the participant could make and the amount of any Fund indebtedness to the participant which is "readily repayable" under a loan agreement. Examples of the latter are the indebtedness of the Fund to participants in the General Arrangements to Borrow and the indebtedness to Italy under the 1966 Loan Agreement, both of which have been entered into under Article VII, Section 2. Members that have made loans to the Fund under these agreements may obtain early repayment by representing to the Fund that there is a balance of payments need for repayment and requesting such repayment.

26. *Termination of Participation*

The principles governing termination of participation in the Special Drawing Account, which are set forth in Article XXX and Schedule H, are generally the same as those governing the settlement of accounts on withdrawal of a member from membership in the Fund. A participant may terminate its participation in the Special Drawing Account at any time without withdrawing from membership in the Fund. Withdrawal from the Fund automatically terminates participation in the Special Drawing Account.

27. *Liquidation*

The principal issue in devising any procedure for liquidation is the distribution of the burden of any default. Article XXXI and Schedule I distribute the burden of default among all participants on the basis of their net cumulative allocations. This is accomplished by a system of liquidation under which the Fund redeems special drawing rights first from the participant that holds the largest amount in proportion to its net cumulative allocation until this portion is reduced to that of the participant with the second highest proportion. The Fund then redeems special drawing rights held by these two participants until the proportion held by each is reduced to that of the participant with the third highest proportion and so on until all amounts paid in the Fund by participants have been distributed. Thus a participant's share of any possible default does not increase as its holdings of special drawing rights increase above its net cumulative allocation.

PART II

Modifications in Rules and Practices of the Fund

28. *General Comments*

Board of Governors Resolution No. 22-8, which called on the Executive Directors to propose amendments to the Articles and the By-Laws of the Fund for the purpose of establishing the new facility based on special drawing rights, also requested the Executive Directors to consider at the same time and report on possible improvements in the present rules and practices of the Fund based on developments in world economic conditions and the experience of the Fund since the adoption of its Articles of Agreement. The Executive Directors have considered various suggestions for improvements and have decided to recommend the introduction of certain changes in the present rules and practices of the Fund, all of which would be made by amending the Articles. These changes relate to: certain quota increases and associated matters; uniform proportionate changes in par values and the maintenance of the gold value of the Fund's assets in the event that such changes in par values are made; the use of the Fund's resources in the gold tranche, including use for capital transfers; a limitation on the Fund's power to introduce new facilities in the General Account for the unconditional use of the Fund's resources; the rules on repurchase under Article V, Section 7; the payment of a remuneration to members whose currencies are held by the Fund in amounts less than 75 per cent of quota; the distribution of net income; and the interpretation of the

Articles of Agreement. The modifications in Articles I, III, IV, V, VI, XII, XVIII, and XIX, and in Schedule B, which are included in the Proposed Amendment, are intended to give effect to these changes.

Three general points should be made in connection with these modifications. First, some of them represent no more than a clarification or codification of practices developed over the years and followed currently by the Fund on the basis of the Articles of Agreement in their present form. Secondly, some modifications are intended to adapt the Articles to the fact that there will be a facility which will make it possible to allocate special drawing rights of an unconditional character. Finally, while one of the effects of these modifications will be to prevent the establishment of new facilities for the unconditional use of the Fund's resources, they are not intended to make the rules and practices relating to the use of the Fund's resources more restrictive than they are at the present time.

29. *Quota Changes and Related Matters*

Under Article III, Section 2, in its present form, all changes in quotas require a four-fifths majority of the total voting power. Under the Proposed Amendment decisions on changes in quotas, including special increases and increases by installments, proposed as the result of a general review will require a new special majority, i.e., 85 per cent of the total voting power. The general reviews referred to in the amended provision are those that have as their purpose an examination of the appropriateness of the quotas of all members, and they will include not only the reviews of the quotas of all members which the Fund is required to conduct at intervals of five years but also any reviews of this kind conducted at other times. All other changes in quotas will continue to require a four-fifths majority of the total voting power.

The majority of 85 per cent will also apply to decisions specifying conditions precedent to the effectiveness of quota increases proposed as a result of a general review. The adoption of these conditions is subject at present to the four-fifths majority which is applicable to quota increases. Examples of such conditions drawn from past practice are the requirement of a minimum total participation in a general increase and the payment of the additional subscriptions before the increases become effective. As at present, the power to adopt these conditions will be exercised by the Board of Governors as a reserved power.

Under a new provision, Article III, Section 4 (c), an 85 per cent majority will be required for decisions on other matters that are related to quota increases proposed as the result of a general quota review even though they do not involve conditions precedent to the effectiveness of the increases. These decisions include any decision pursuant to Article III, Section 4 (a), under which a member may be permitted to pay less than 25 per cent of its additional subscription in gold. The new provision will also apply to any decision intended to mitigate the effects of the payment of additional subscriptions. At present, the Articles provide that all of these decisions are to be made by the Executive Directors by a majority of the votes cast. After the Proposed Amendment enters into force the power to make such decisions will be reserved to the Board of Governors.

The special majority of 85 per cent of the total voting which will be required as the result of various changes in the rules and practices of the Fund is analogous to the majority required for a number of important decisions under the new facility based on special drawing rights.

30. *Uniform Proportionate Changes in Par Values and Maintenance of Gold Value*

Under the modifications in Article IV, Section 7, a decision to make a uniform proportionate change in par values also will require an 85 per cent majority of the total voting power. This changes the present provision in two respects. It replaces the simple majority with a special majority and eliminates the requirement that the uniform proportionate change be approved by those members that have 10 per cent or more of the total of Fund quotas. The power to make a uniform proportionate change in par values will continue to be reserved to the Board of Governors.

Under the modifications in Article IV, Section 8 (d), and Article XII, Section 2 (b) (iii), a decision to waive the maintenance of the gold value of the Fund's assets in the event of a uniform proportionate change in par values will require an 85 per cent majority of the total voting power, and the power to make the decision will be reserved to the Board of Governors. At present the power to make a decision of this kind is not reserved to the Board of Governors and a special majority is not required.

31. *Temporary Character of Use of the Fund's Resources*

The modifications in Article I and the inclusion in Article V of a new Section 3 (c) state expressly what is regarded as implicit in the present Articles, i.e., that use of the Fund's resources must be of a temporary character and that the Fund must adopt policies intended to encourage members to take measures that will help them to avoid a use which is not of such a character. In this way the Fund safeguards the revolving character of its resources. Therefore, no changes in the established policies and practices of the Fund, as set forth in the Fund's decision of February 13, 1952, and in other decisions would be called for by the entry into force of the Proposed Amendment. The resources of the Fund referred to in Article I (v) and in other provisions of the Articles are those that will be held by the Fund in the General Account.

32. *Legal Automaticity of Gold Tranche Purchases*

Requests for gold tranche purchases now enjoy *de facto* automaticity. One of the effects of the modifications in Article V, Section 3, will be to make the use of the Fund's resources in the gold tranche legally automatic.

After the amendment, the use of the Fund's resources in the gold tranche will continue to be subject to the provisions of Article V, Section 3 (a). Accordingly, members making requests for purchases in the gold tranche will still be required to make the representation of need prescribed by Article V, Section 3 (a) (i). However, the Fund will not have the legal power to challenge this representation.

Article V, Section 3 (a) (iii), will be amended to eliminate the necessity for a waiver that might have been required for a gold tranche purchase in certain circumstances. Furthermore, Article VI, Sections 1 (a) and 2, as amended, will remove the present limitation on making gold tranche purchases for meeting capital transfers. A member will be able to make gold tranche purchases even though they are to meet what might be regarded as a large or sustained outflow of capital. The established legal position will be maintained in respect of requests for purchases other than gold tranche purchases. Accordingly, a member will be able, as at present, to use the Fund's resources to meet capital outflows subject to Article VI, Section 1.

The legal automaticity of gold tranche purchases will not prejudice the application of the Fund's policies on the currencies to be used in purchases. These policies are set forth in the Fund's Decision of July 20, 1962 and are applicable to all purchases including gold tranche purchases.

The legal automaticity of gold tranche purchases raises the question of possible misuse by a member of its right to make such purchases without challenge by failing to observe the principle of need set forth in Article V, Section 3 (a) (i). The Executive Directors believe that if the question should arise it could be met by an adjustment, in due time, of the Fund's policies with respect to the currencies to be used in purchases in order to bring about a correction of the effects of any misuse by a member of the kind referred to above.

The Fund will continue to have authority under the Articles of Agreement to declare a member ineligible to use the Fund's resources even in the gold tranche if the member makes gold tranche purchases without observing the principle of need.

33. *Definition of Gold Tranche Purchases*

The changes in the Articles commented upon in sections 32, 34, and 36 of this Report should be understood in the light of the definition of gold tranche purchases in a new provision, Article XIX (j). This definition is somewhat different from the definition of gold tranche purchases which prevailed in Fund practice until less than two years ago and according to which a gold tranche purchase was understood as a purchase which did not cause the Fund's holdings of a member's currency to exceed 100 per cent of its quota. By permitting the exclusion of purchases under the compensatory financing facility and the holdings of currency acquired by the Fund as a result of those purchases, the definition in Article XIX (j) will make it possible for the Fund to continue the present practice of treating the compensatory financing facility as separate for the purpose of applying the Fund's policies on the use of its resources. This practice was introduced by the amendments to the Decision on Compensatory Financing of Export Fluctuations adopted on September 20, 1966, under which the Fund applies "its tranche policies to drawing requests by a member as if the Fund's holdings of the member's currency were less than its actual holdings of that currency by the amount of any drawing outstanding under paragraph (5)" of that decision.

Under the definition in Article XIX (j), a purchase under paragraph (5) of the compensatory financing decision will not be regarded as a gold tranche purchase even if it does not raise the Fund's holdings of a member's currency above the level of the member's quota. Conversely, a purchase not under the compensatory financing facility which raises the Fund's holdings above that level will be regarded as a gold tranche purchase, provided that the amount by which the quota level is exceeded will not be larger than the amount of any purchases outstanding under the compensatory financing decision.

In view of the possibility that, under the definition of gold tranche purchases in Article XIX (j), a gold tranche purchase may increase the Fund's holdings above the quota level and in order to preserve the legal automaticity of requests to make gold tranche purchases under Article V, Section 3 (d), the text of Article V, Section 3 (a) (iii), is amended so that a waiver under Article V, Section 4, will not be necessary. Under the amended text of Section 3 (a) (iii), however, a purchase under the compensatory financing decision which, together with any other net increases in the Fund's holdings of the member's currency, causes these holdings to increase by more than 25 per cent of quota during the period of 12 months ending on the date of the purchase, will require a waiver under Article V, Section 4, even though it does not raise the Fund's holdings above the quota level. At present, any purchase below the quota level, including a purchase under the compensatory financing decision, does not require a waiver.

34. *Termination of Power to Establish New Unconditional Facilities in the General Account*

As a result of the adoption of Article V, Section 3 (d), the Fund will not have the power to create any new facility in the General Account for the unconditional use of its resources. This provision reflects the view that, with the establishment of the new facility based on special drawing rights, any need for additions to existing reserve assets will be met, as and when it arises, through allocations of special drawing rights. The provision makes it explicit that a member's representation under Article V, Section 3 (a), must be examined in order to determine that the requested purchase would be consistent with the provisions of the Articles and the policies on the use of the Fund's resources adopted under Article V, Section 3 (c). This means that the Fund will not grant *de facto* automaticity (i.e., "the overwhelming benefit of any doubt" or treatment having the same effect) to requests for purchases other than gold tranche purchases. The Fund will continue to be able to adapt its policies governing purchases other than gold tranche purchases in all other respects.

The changes in Article V, Section 3, will be without prejudice also to the Fund's compensatory financing facility and the adjustment of that policy if this should be considered desirable. In addition, as already indicated, these changes are not intended to make the rules and practices relating to the use of the Fund's resources more restrictive than they are at present.

35. *Rules on Repurchase*

The modifications in Article V, Section 7, Article XII, Section 2 (b), Article XIX (a) and (e), and Schedule B, will introduce the following changes in the present rules on repurchase:

(a) At present, the amounts of a member's currency that are held by the governmental agencies and other official institutions of other members, as well as by banks within the territories of the latter, are deducted from the member's official holdings of gold and convertible currencies under Article XIX (e). The deduction of these currency liabilities will be abolished, thereby introducing a gross concept of monetary reserves as the basis of the calculation of members' repurchase obligations and for certain other purposes. This change is effected through the modifications in Article XIX (a) and (e). The new paragraph 6 of Schedule B sets forth a transitional rule designed to prevent the accrual of repurchase obligations solely because of the elimination of the deduction of currency liabilities during a financial year of the Fund. It will apply only in the year in which the Proposed Amendment enters into force and, thereafter, no deductions will be made for currency liabilities.

(b) The abatement of repurchase obligations calculated in a member's currency, which the Fund may not accept because the acceptance would increase the Fund's holdings of that currency above 75 per cent of the member's quota, will be eliminated. Under paragraph 1 (d) of Schedule B the amounts that would be abated for this reason will have to be discharged in other convertible currencies as determined by the Fund.

(c) The present paragraph 2 of Schedule B, which will be retained as paragraph 2 (a), prohibits the Fund from acquiring the currency of any nonmember by way of repurchase but does not indicate how repurchase obligations that accrue in specified nonmember currencies are to be treated. The proposed paragraph 2 (b) of Schedule B provides that repurchase obligations that accrue in specified nonmember currencies will be paid in the convertible currencies of members as determined by the Fund. The Fund has never specified a nonmember currency for the purposes of repurchases but would be likely to do so if it found that members held appreciable amounts of a nonmember currency.

(d) The present Article V, Section 7 (c) (i), provides that a repurchase shall not be carried out to the extent that it would reduce the repurchasing member's monetary reserves, as presently defined on a net basis, below an amount equal to its quota. Under the amended Article V, Section 7 (c) (i), a level of monetary reserves, defined on a gross basis, equivalent to 150 percent of quota will be substituted for the quota level. If a repurchase obligation accrues which would exceed this limit, the excess will be abated.

(e) Under the proposed Article V, Section 7 (c) (iv), there will be an annual limit on repurchases under Article V, Section 7 (b), equal to 25 per cent of a member's quota. Under the new paragraph 1 (e) of Schedule B, if an obligation accrues which exceeds this amount, the excess will be postponed to the end of the subsequent financial year or years, but not more than 25 per cent of the member's quota will have to be repurchased in any one year under postponed and other repurchase obligations accruing under Article V, Section 7 (b). This new rule will not affect repurchases made outside Article V, Section 7 (b).

(f) A change will be introduced in the formula on the basis of which repurchase obligations are calculated. The present formula takes account of increases in the Fund's holdings of a member's currency and increases or decreases in its monetary reserves during a year. Under the modified formula in Article V, Section 7 (b) (i), account will also be taken of decreases in the Fund's holdings of the member's currency during the year. This change will reduce a member's repurchase obligation under Article V, Section 7 (b), at the end of a financial year by the full amount of other repurchases made during that year, whereas at present they reduce the obligation only by one half of the full amount. It should be noted that, in respect of repurchases outside Article V, Section 7 (a) or (b), the Fund has legal authority to specify the acceptable convertible currencies that the repurchasing member may use.

(g) In accordance with paragraph 5 of Schedule B, the Fund, in its discretion, will be able to accede to a member's request that in the calculation of its monetary reserves a deduction be made for its outstanding obligations resulting from swap transactions with other members.

(h) The Fund will have the power to revise the percentage of quota below which repurchases may not reduce a repurchasing member's monetary reserves and the annual limit on repurchases under Article V, Section 7 (b). In addition, the Fund will be able to revise and supplement, in a manner consistent with the other repurchase provisions of the Articles, the newly introduced rules in paragraph 1 (c), (d), and (e) and paragraph 2 (b) of Schedule B. The Fund is granted this power under Article V, Section 7 (d). Under this provision and Article XII, Section 2 (b) (ix), the power is reserved to the Board of Governors which can exercise it by an 85 per cent majority of the total voting power.

(i) Under Article XXV, Section 7 (a) and (b), special drawing rights are to be included in the monetary reserves of members for the purposes of the Articles. As a result of these provisions and of the modifications in the introductory parts of Article V, Section 7 (b), and in paragraph 1 of Schedule B, repurchase obligations may accrue in special drawing rights, and the Fund will accept special drawing rights in repurchase under Article V, Section 7 (b). However, the Fund may decide that no account be taken of any increase or decrease in monetary reserves during a financial year which is due to allocations or cancellations of special drawing rights during the same year.

36. *Service Charge*

Article V, Section 8(a), as amended, will maintain the existing maximum rate of the service charge that the Fund can levy on exchange transactions. The present minimum rate for exchange transactions will be unaffected, except that the Fund will be authorized to levy a lower charge or no charge on gold tranche purchases. The Executive Directors believe that initially no service charge should be levied on gold tranche purchases, subject to any change in this policy that would be appropriate in the light of subsequent developments.

37. *Remuneration*

A new provision, Article V, Section 9, will require the Fund to pay a return to members on the excess of 75 per cent of a member's quota over the average of the Fund's holdings of the member's currency, or, in other words, on the Fund's net use of a member's normal currency subscription. The rate of remuneration will be 1½ per cent per annum. However, the Executive Directors would be able to specify other rates within the limits of 1 to 2 per cent per annum by a majority of the votes cast. The Executive Directors would be able to make changes beyond these limits by a three-fourths majority of the total voting power, but it is not expected that this would be done unless it were necessary in the light of developments in international money markets.

The remuneration will be payable in gold or in the member's own currency or partly in gold and partly in that currency. The Executive Directors believe that the Fund's policy should be to pay remuneration in gold to the extent that receipts of gold from members in payment of charges under Article V, Section 8, would permit, subject again to any change in this policy that would be appropriate in the light of subsequent developments.

38. *Distribution of Net Income*

Article XII, Section 6, in its present form, requires that, before any distribution of the net income of any year is made by the Fund to all members on the basis of quotas, a 2 per cent noncumulative payment be made to each member on the amount by which 75 per cent of its quota exceeded the Fund's average holdings of the member's currency during the year. Under the amended provision, instead of the 2 per cent preferential payment, the Fund will have to distribute first to members eligible to receive remuneration under Article V, Section 9, an amount of net income which will raise to 2 per cent the return paid to them as remuneration for the year for which net income is distributed.

Under Article XII, Section 6 (c), the Fund will be able to transfer to general reserve all or part of its special reserve to which the yield of its investment is placed. The yield of the investment is not net income in the sense of, and cannot be distributed under, Article XII, Section 6. Moreover, it can be used only for the limited purpose of meeting administrative deficits. Amounts transferred from special to general reserve, however, will be available to meet a deficit of any character, whether operational or administrative, including a deficit resulting from the payment of remuneration under Article V,

Section 9, but they will continue to be unavailable for distribution as net income under Article XII, Section 6.

The power to make transfers to general reserve from the existing or any other special reserve will be without prejudice to any future decisions on the maintenance or termination of the Fund's investment. The power to make transfers will be exercised by the Board of Governors, and a provision reserving it to the Board of Governors is inserted as Article XII, Section 2 (b) (x).

39. *Interpretation*

Article XVIII, as amended, will require the establishment of a standing Committee on Interpretation of the Board of Governors. A question of interpretation of the Articles, on which the Executive Directors have given a decision under Article XVIII and which, at the request of a member made within three months from the date of that decision, is referred to the Board of Governors, will have to be considered first by this Committee. The decision of this Committee will be regarded as the decision of the Board of Governors, and therefore final, unless the Board of Governors decides otherwise by an 85 per cent majority of the total voting power. Article XVIII (b) prescribes that each member of the Committee on Interpretation shall have one vote. Other matters, such as the membership, procedures, and voting majorities of the Committee, are left for later determination by the Board of Governors by means of a By-Law. In addition, under Article XXVII (c), the Board of Governors will have the power to determine whether all members of the Committee will be entitled to vote on a question of interpretation pertaining exclusively to the Special Drawing Account.

PART III

Procedure

40. *Applicable Legal Provisions*

The procedure for the adoption of modifications in the Articles of Agreement is set forth in Article XVII which reads:

(a) Any proposal to introduce modifications in this Agreement, whether emanating from a member, a governor or the Executive Directors, shall be communicated to the chairman of the Board of Governors who shall bring the proposal before the Board. If the proposed amendment is approved by the Board the Fund shall, by circular letter or telegram, ask all members whether they accept the proposed amendment. When three-fifths of the members, having four-fifths of the total voting power, have accepted the proposed amendment, the Fund shall certify the fact by a formal communication addressed to all members.

(b) Notwithstanding (a) above, acceptance by all members is required in the case of any amendment modifying

(i) the right to withdraw from the Fund (Article XV, Section 1);

(ii) the provision that no change in a member's quota shall be made without its consent (Article III, Section 2);

(iii) the provision that no change may be made in the par value of a member's currency except on the proposal of that member (Article IV, Section 5 (b)).

(c) Amendments shall enter into force for all members three months after the date of the formal communication unless a shorter period is specified in the circular letter or telegram.

41. *Resolution of Board of Governors*

Annex A contains the text of a Resolution, and there is attached to it a Proposed Amendment to the Articles of Agreement. The Chairman of the Board of Governors has requested that on his behalf the Secretary of the Fund bring the Resolution and Proposed Amendment before the Board of Governors for its approval. Pursuant to this request the Secretary is transmitting them to the Board with this Report.

In the judgment of the Executive Directors the action requested of the Board of Governors should not be postponed until the next regular meeting of the Board and does not warrant the calling of a special meeting of the Board. For this reason, the Executive Directors, pursuant to Section 13 of the By-Laws, request Governors to vote without meeting. In accordance with established practice, the Executive Directors have also decided to waive the requirement that no Governor shall vote until seven days after the dispatch of the motion. To be valid votes must be received at the seat of the Fund on or before May 31, 1968.

For the adoption of the Resolution it will be necessary that replies be received from a majority of the Governors exercising two-thirds of the total voting power and that a majority of the votes cast be in favor of the Resolution. The Resolution must be voted on as a whole.

42. *Acceptance of Proposed Amendment by Members*

By adopting the annexed Resolution the Board of Governors will grant its approval to the Proposed Amendment of the Articles of Agreement. Members will then be asked, by circular letter or telegram, to notify the Fund whether they accept the Proposed Amendment. The Proposed Amendment can be accepted only in its entirety. That is to say, members will not be able to accept part only of the Proposed Amendment.

In accordance with Article XVII (a) the Proposed Amendment must be accepted by three-fifths of the members, having four-fifths of the total voting power, before it can enter into force.

43. *Entry into Force of Proposed Amendment*

When the Proposed Amendment has been accepted by the necessary majority, the Fund will certify the fact by a formal communication to be sent by the Secretary of the Fund to all members. Pursuant to Article XVII (c), the Executive Directors recommend that the Proposed Amendment enter into force on the date of the formal communication instead of three months after that date. In accordance with that provision and paragraph 3 of the Resolution, the circular letter or telegram by which members will be asked whether they accept the Proposed Amendment will specify the date of the formal communication referred to above as the date of the entry into force of the Proposed Amendment.

The Proposed Amendment will enter into force for all members on the date of the formal communication, whether they accepted the Amendment or not. Presumably, members accepting the Proposed Amendment will have taken any legislative and other action that may be necessary to enable them to carry out their obligations under the Articles of Agreement as amended. Other members that have not accepted the Proposed

Amendment will need to consider whether any action is necessary in order to enable them to carry out their obligations under the Articles of Agreement as amended.

44. *Notification to Depositary of Articles of Agreement*

Upon certification of the entry into force of the Proposed Amendment it is intended to notify that fact to the Government of the United States, which is the depositary of the Articles of Agreement of the Fund, so that it may record the Amendment. It is also intended to ask the Government of the United States to register the Amendment with the Secretary-General of the United Nations, pursuant to Article 102 of the United Nations Charter.

Annex A

RESOLUTION

WHEREAS the Executive Directors have completed their work relating to the establishment in the International Monetary Fund of a new facility based on special drawing rights in order to meet the need, as and when it arises, for a supplement to existing reserve assets, and on improvements in the present rules and practices of the Fund, pursuant to Resolution No. 22-8 of the Board of Governors of the International Monetary Fund at its Twenty-Second Annual Meeting in Rio de Janeiro; and

WHEREAS the Executive Directors have prepared a Report setting forth proposals for modifications in the Articles of Agreement of the International Monetary Fund for the purpose of establishing the new facility and giving effect to certain modifications in the present rules and practices of the Fund; and

WHEREAS the Chairman of the Board of Governors has requested the Secretary of the Fund to bring the proposals of the Executive Directors before the Board of Governors; and

WHEREAS the Report of the Executive Directors setting forth their proposals has been submitted to the Board of Governors by the Secretary of the Fund; and

WHEREAS the Executive Directors have requested the Board of Governors to vote on the following Resolution without meeting, pursuant to Section 13 of the By-Laws of the Fund;

NOW, THEREFORE, the Board of Governors, noting the said Report of the Executive Directors, hereby RESOLVES that:

1. The Proposed Amendment to the Articles of Agreement of the International Monetary Fund set forth in the attachment to this Resolution is approved.
2. The Secretary of the Fund is directed to ask, by letter or telegram, all members of the Fund whether they accept, in accordance with the provisions of Article XVII, the Proposed Amendment to the Articles of Agreement as set forth in the attachment to this Resolution.
3. The circular letter or telegram to be sent to all members in accordance with 2 above shall specify that the Proposed Amendment to the Articles of Agreement set forth in the attachment to this Resolution shall enter into force for all members as of the date on which the Fund certifies, by formal communication addressed to all members, that three-fifths of the members, having four-fifths of the total voting power, have accepted the modifications.

Proposed Amendment to the Articles of Agreement of the International Monetary Fund Prepared Pursuant to Board of Governors Resolution No. 22-8

A

INTRODUCTORY ARTICLE

The Introductory Article shall read:

"(i) The International Monetary Fund is established and shall operate in accordance with the provisions of this Agreement as originally adopted, and as subsequently amended in order to institute a facility based on special drawing rights and to effect certain other changes.

(ii) To enable the Fund to conduct its operations and transactions, the Fund shall maintain a General Account and a Special Drawing Account. Membership in the Fund shall give the right to participation in the Special Drawing Account.

(iii) Operations and transactions authorized by this Agreement shall be conducted through the General Account except that operations and transactions involving special drawing rights shall be conducted through the Special Drawing Account."

B

ARTICLE I

Purposes

1. Article I (v) shall read:

"(v) To give confidence to members by making the Fund's resources temporarily available to them under adequate safeguards, thus providing them with opportunity to correct maladjustments in their balance of payments without resorting to measures destructive of national or international prosperity."

2. The last sentence of Article I shall read:

"The Fund shall be guided in all its policies and decisions by the purposes set forth in this Article."

C

ARTICLE III

Quotas and Subscriptions

1. Section 2 shall read:

"Section 2. *Adjustment of quotas*

The Fund shall at intervals of not more than five years conduct a general review, and if it deems it appropriate propose an adjustment, of the quotas of the members. It may also, if it thinks fit, consider at any other time the adjustment of any particular quota at the request of the member concerned. An eighty-five percent majority of the total voting power shall be required for any change in quotas proposed as the result of a general review and a four-fifths majority of the total voting power shall be required for any other change in quotas. No quota shall be changed without the consent of the member concerned."

2. The following subsection (c) shall be added to Section 4, *Payments when quotas are changed:*

"(c) A majority of eighty-five percent of the total voting power shall be required for any decisions dealing with the payment, or made with the sole purpose of mitigating the effects of the payment, of increases in quotas proposed as the result of a general review of quotas."

D

ARTICLE IV

PAR VALUES OF CURRENCIES

1. Section 7 shall read:

"Section 7. *Uniform changes in par values*

Notwithstanding the provisions of Section 5 (b) of this Article, the Fund by an eighty-five percent majority of the total voting power may make uniform proportionate changes in the par values of the currencies of all members. The par value of a member's currency shall, however, not be changed under this provision if, within seventy-two hours of the Fund's action, the member informs the Fund that it does not wish the par value of its currency to be changed by such action."

2. In Section 8. *Maintenance of gold value of the Fund's assets*, subsection (d) shall read:

"(d) The provisions of this Section shall apply to a uniform proportionate change in the par values of the currencies of all members, unless at the time when such a change is made the Fund decides otherwise by an eighty-five percent majority of the total voting power."

E

ARTICLE V

TRANSACTIONS WITH THE FUND

1. In Section 3. *Conditions governing use of the Fund's resources*, subsection (a) (iii) shall read:

"(iii) The proposed purchase would be a gold tranche purchase, or would not cause the Fund's holdings of the purchasing member's currency to increase by more than twenty-five percent of its quota during the period of twelve months ending on the date of the purchase or to exceed two hundred percent of its quota;"

2. The following subsections (c) and (d) shall be added to Section 3:

"(c) A member's use of the resources of the Fund shall be in accordance with the purposes of the Fund. The Fund shall adopt policies on the use of its resources that will assist members to solve their balance of payments problems in a manner consistent with the purposes of the Fund and that will establish adequate safeguards for the temporary use of its resources."

"(d) A representation by a member under (a) above shall be examined by the Fund to determine whether the proposed purchase would be consistent with the provisions of this Agreement and with the policies adopted under them, with the exception that proposed gold tranche purchases shall not be subject to challenge."

3. In Section 7. *Repurchase by a member of its currency held by the Fund*, the first sentence of subsection (b) shall read:

"(b) At the end of each financial year of the Fund, a member shall repurchase from the Fund with each type of monetary reserve, as determined in accordance with Schedule B, part of the Fund's holdings of its currency under the following conditions:

(i) Each member shall use in repurchases of its own currency from the Fund an amount of its monetary reserves equal in value to the following changes that have occurred during the year: one-half of any increase in the Fund's holdings of the member's currency, plus one-half of any increase, or minus one-half of any decrease, in the member's monetary reserves, or, if the Fund's holdings of the member's currency have decreased, one-half of any increase in the member's monetary reserves minus one-half of the decrease in the Fund's holdings of the member's currency."

4. In Section 7, subsection (c) shall read:

"(c) None of the adjustments described in (b) above shall be carried to a point at which

(i) the member's monetary reserves are below one hundred fifty percent of its quota, or

(ii) the Fund's holdings of its currency are below seventy-five percent of its quota, or

(iii) the Fund's holdings of any currency required to be used are above seventy-five percent of the quota of the member concerned, or

(iv) the amount repurchased exceeds twenty-five percent of the quota of the member concerned."

5. The following subsection (d) shall be added to Section 7:

"(d) The Fund by an eighty-five percent majority of the total voting power may revise the percentages in (c) (i) and (iv) above and revise and supplement the rules in paragraph 1 (c), (d), and (e) and paragraph 2 (b) of Schedule B."

6. In Section 8. *Charges*, subsection (a) shall read:

"(a) Any member buying the currency of another member from the Fund in exchange for its own currency shall pay, in addition to the parity price, a service charge uniform for all members of not less than one-half percent and not more than one percent, as determined by the Fund, provided that the Fund in its discretion may levy a service charge of less than one-half percent on gold tranche purchases."

7. The following Section shall be added to Article V:

"Section 9. *Remuneration*

(a) The Fund shall pay remuneration, at a rate uniform for all members, on the amount by which seventy-five percent of a member's quota exceeded the average of the Fund's holdings of the member's currency, provided that no account shall be taken of holdings in excess of seventy-five percent of quota. The rate shall be one and one-half percent per annum, but the Fund in its discretion may increase or reduce this rate, provided that a three-fourths majority of the total voting power shall be required for any increase above two percent per annum or reduction below one percent per annum.

(b) Remuneration shall be paid in gold or a member's own currency as determined by the Fund."

F

ARTICLE VI

Capital Transfers

1. In Section 1. *Use of Fund's resources for capital transfers*, subsection (a) shall read:

"(a) A member may not use the Fund's resources to meet a large or sustained outflow of capital except as provided in Section 2 of this Article, and the Fund may request a member to exercise controls to prevent such use of the resources of the Fund. If, after receiving such a request, a member fails to exercise appropriate controls, the Fund may declare the member ineligible to use the resources of the Fund."

2. Section 2 shall read:

"Section 2. *Special provisions for capital transfers*

A member shall be entitled to make gold tranche purchases to meet capital transfers."

G

ARTICLE XII

Organization and Management

1. In Section 2. *Board of Governors*, subsection (b) (ii) and (iii) shall read:

"(ii) Approve a revision of quotas, or to decide on the payment, or on the mitigation of the effects of payment, or increases in quotas proposed as the result of a general review of quotas."

"(iii) Approve a uniform change in the par values of the currencies of all members, or to decide when such a change is made that the provisions relating to the maintenance of gold value of the Fund's assets shall not apply."

2. The following shall be added to Section 2 (b):

"(ix) Revise the provisions on repurchase or to revise and supplement the rules for the distribution of repurchases among types of reserves."

"(x) Make transfers to general reserve from any special reserve."

3. The title of Section 6 shall read:

"Reserves and distribution of net income"

4. In Section 6, subsection (b) shall read:

"(b) If any distribution is made of the net income of any year, there shall first be distributed to members eligible to receive remuneration under Article V, Section 9, for that year an amount by which two percent per annum exceeded any remuneration that has been paid for that year. Any distribution of the net income of that year beyond that amount shall be made to all members in proportion to their quotas. Payments to each member shall be made in its own currency."

5. The following subsection (c) shall be added to Section 6:

"(c) The Fund may make transfers to general reserve from any special reserve."

H

ARTICLE XVIII

Interpretation

Article XVIII (b) shall read:

"(b) In any case where the Executive Directors have given a decision under (a) above, any member may require, within three months from the date of the decision, that the question be referred to the Board of Governors, whose decision shall be final. Any question referred to the Board of Governors shall be considered by a Committee on Interpretation of the Board of Governors. Each Committee member shall have one vote. The Board of Governors shall establish the membership, procedures, and voting majorities of the Committee. A decision of the Committee shall be the decision of the Board of Governors unless the Board by an eighty-five percent majority of the total voting power decides otherwise. Pending the result of the reference to the Board the Fund may, so far as it deems necessary, act on the basis of the decision of the Executive Directors."

I

ARTICLE XIX

Explanation of Terms

1. Article XIX (a) shall read:

"(a) A member's monetary reserves means its official holdings of gold, of convertible currencies of other members, and of the currencies of such non-members as the Fund may specify."

2. Article XIX (e) shall read:

"(e) The sums deemed to be official holdings of other official institutions and other banks under (c) above shall be included in the member's monetary reserves."

3. The following shall be added to Article XIX:

"(j) Gold tranche purchase means a purchase by a member of the currency of another member in exchange for its own currency which does not cause the Fund's holdings of the member's currency to exceed one hundred percent of its quota, provided that for the purposes of this definition the Fund may exclude purchases and holdings under policies on the use of its resources for compensatory financing of export fluctuations."

J

ARTICLE XX

FINAL PROVISIONS

The title of Article XX shall read:
"INAUGURAL PROVISIONS"

K

The following Articles XXI through XXXII shall be added after Article XX:

"ARTICLE XXI

SPECIAL DRAWING RIGHTS

Section 1. *Authority to allocate special drawing rights*

To meet the need, as and when it arises, for a supplement to existing reserve assets, the Fund is authorized to allocate special drawing rights to members that are participants in the Special Drawing Account.

Section 2. *Unit of value*

The unit of value of special drawing rights shall be equivalent to 0.888 671 gram of fine gold.

ARTICLE XXII

GENERAL ACCOUNT AND SPECIAL DRAWING ACCOUNT

Section 1. *Separation of operations and transactions*

All operations and transactions involving special drawing rights shall be conducted through the Special Drawing Account. All other operations and transactions of the Fund authorized by or under this Agreement shall be conducted through the General Account. Operations and transactions pursuant to Article XXIII, Section 2, shall be conducted through the General Account as well as the Special Drawing Account.

Section 2. *Separation of assets and property*

All assets and property of the Fund shall be held in the General Account, except that assets and property acquired under Article XXVI, Section 2, and Articles XXX and XXXI and Schedules H and I shall be held in the Special Drawing Account. Any assets or property held in one Account shall not be available to discharge or meet the liabilities, obligations, or losses of the Fund incurred in the conduct of the operations and transactions of the other Account, except that the expenses of conducting the business of the Special Drawing Account shall be paid by the Fund from the General Account which shall be reimbursed from time to time by assessments under Article XXVI, Section 4, made on the basis of a reasonable estimate of such expenses.

Section 3. *Recording and information*

All changes in holdings of special drawing rights shall take effect only when recorded by the Fund in the Special Drawing Account. Participants shall notify the Fund of the provisions of this Agreement under which special drawing rights are used. The Fund may require participants to furnish it with such other information as it deems necessary for its functions.

ARTICLE XXIII

PARTICIPANTS AND OTHER HOLDERS OF SPECIAL DRAWING RIGHTS

Section 1. *Participants*

Each member of the Fund that deposits with the Fund an instrument setting forth that it undertakes all the obligations of a participant in the Special Drawing Account in accordance with its law and that it has taken all steps necessary to enable it to carry out all of these obligations shall become a participant in the Special Drawing Account as of the date the instrument is deposited, except that no member shall become a participant before Articles XXI through XXXII and Schedules F through I have entered into force and instruments have been deposited under this Section by members that have at least seventy-five percent of the total of quotas.

Section 2. *General Account as a holder*

The Fund may accept and hold special drawing rights in the General Account and use them, in accordance with the provisions of this Agreement.

Section 3. *Other holders*

The Fund by an eighty-five percent majority of the total voting power may prescribe:

(i) as holders, non-members, members that are non-participants, and institutions that perform functions of a central bank for more than one member;

(ii) the terms and conditions on which these holders may be permitted to accept, hold, and use special drawing rights, in operations and transactions with participants; and

(iii) the terms and conditions on which participants may enter into operations and transactions with these holders.

The terms and conditions prescribed by the Fund for the use of special drawing rights by prescribed holders and by participants in operations and transactions with them shall be consistent with the provisions of this Agreement.

ARTICLE XXIV

Allocation and Cancellation of Special Drawing Rights

Section 1. *Principles and considerations governing allocation and cancellation*

(a) In all its decisions with respect to the allocation and cancellation of special drawing rights the Fund shall seek to meet the long-term global need, as and when it arises, to supplement existing reserve assets in such manner as will promote the attainment of its purposes and will avoid economic stagnation and deflation as well as excess demand and inflation in the world.

(b) The first decision to allocate special drawing rights shall take into account, as special considerations, a collective judgment that there is a global need to supplement reserves, and the attainment of a better balance of payments equilibrium, as well as the likelihood of a better working of the adjustment process in the future.

Section 2. *Allocation and cancellation*

(a) Decisions of the Fund to allocate or cancel special drawing rights shall be made for basic periods which shall run consecutively and shall be five years in duration. The first basic period shall begin on the date of the first decision to allocate special drawing rights or such later date as may be specified in that decision. Any allocations or cancellations shall take place at yearly intervals.

(b) The rates at which allocations are to be made shall be expressed as percentages of quotas on the date of each decision to allocate. The rates at which special drawing rights are to be cancelled shall be expressed as percentages of net cumulative allocations of special drawing rights on the date of each decision to cancel. The percentages shall be the same for all participants.

(c) In its decision for any basic period the Fund may provide, notwithstanding (a) and (b) above, that:

(i) the duration of the basic period shall be other than five years; or

(ii) the allocations or cancellations shall take place at other than yearly intervals; or

(iii) the basis for allocations or cancellations shall be the quotas or net cumulative allocations on dates other than the dates of decisions to allocate or cancel.

(d) A member that becomes a participant after a basic period starts shall receive allocations beginning with the next basic period in which allocations are made after it becomes a participant unless the Fund decides that the new participant shall start to receive allocations beginning with the next allocation after it becomes a participant. If the Fund decides that a member that becomes a participant during a basic period shall receive allocations during the remainder of that basic period and the participant was not a member on the dates established under (b) or (c) above, the Fund shall determine the basis on which these allocations to the participant shall be made.

(e) A participant shall receive allocations of special drawing rights made pursuant to any decision to allocate unless:

(i) the governor for the participant did not vote in favor of the decision; and

(ii) the participant has notified the Fund in writing prior to the first allocation of special drawing rights under that decision that it does not wish special drawing rights to be allocated to it under the decision. On the request of a participant, the Fund may decide to terminate the effect of the notice with respect to allocations of special drawing rights subsequent to the termination.

(f) If on the effective date of any cancellation the amount of special drawing rights held by a participant is less than its share of the special drawing rights that are to be cancelled, the participant shall eliminate its negative balance as promptly as its gross reserve position permits and shall remain in consultation with the Fund for this purpose. Special drawing rights acquired by the participant after the effective date of the cancellation shall be applied against its negative balance and cancelled.

Section 3. *Unexpected major developments*

The Fund may change the rates or intervals of allocation or cancellation during the rest of a basic period or change the length of a basic period or start a new basic period, if at any time the Fund finds it desirable to do so because of unexpected major developments.

Section 4. *Decisions on allocations and cancellations*

(a) Decisions under Section 2 (a), (b), and (c) or Section 3 of this Article shall be made by the Board of Governors on the basis of proposals of the Managing Director concurred in by the Executive Directors.

(b) Before making any proposal, the Managing Director, after having satisfied himself that it will be consistent with the provisions of Section 1 (a) of this Article, shall conduct such consultations as will enable him to ascertain that there is broad support among participants for the proposal. In addition, before making a proposal for the first allocation, the Managing Director shall satisfy himself that the provisions of Section 1 (b) of this Article have been met and that there is broad support among participants to begin allocations; he shall make a proposal for the first allocation as soon after the establishment of the Special Drawing Account as he is so satisfied.

(c) The Managing Director shall make proposals:

(i) not later than six months before the end of each basic period;

(ii) if no decision has been taken with respect to allocation or cancellation for a basic period, whenever he is satisfied that the provisions of (b) above have been met;

(iii) when, in accordance with Section 3 of this Article, he considers that it would be desirable to change the rate or intervals of allocation or cancellation or change the length of a basic period or start a new basic period; or

(iv) within six months of a request by the Board of Governors or the Executive Directors;

provided that, if under (i), (iii), or (iv) above the Managing Director ascertains that there is no proposal which he considers to be consistent with the provisions of Section 1 of this Article that has broad support among participants in accordance with (b) above, he shall report to the Board of Governors and to the Executive Directors.

(d) A majority of eighty-five percent of the total voting power shall be required for decisions under Section 2 (a), (b), and (c) or Section 3 of this Article except for decisions under Section 3 with respect to a decrease in the rates of allocation.

ARTICLE XXV

Operations and Transactions in Special Drawing Rights

Section 1. *Use of special drawing rights*

Special drawing rights may be used in the operations and transactions authorized by or under this Agreement.

Section 2. *Transactions between participants*

(a) A participant shall be entitled to use its special drawing rights to obtain an equivalent amount of currency from a participant designated under Section 5 of this Article.

(b) A participant, in agreement with another participant, may use its special drawing rights:

(i) to obtain an equivalent amount of its own currency held by the other participant; or

(ii) to obtain an equivalent amount of currency from the other participant in any transactions, prescribed by the Fund, that would promote reconstitution by the other participant under Section 6 (a) of this Article; prevent or reduce a negative balance of the other participant; offset the effect of a failure by the other participant to fulfill the expectation in Section 3 (a) of this Article; or bring the holdings of special drawing rights by both participants closer to their net cumulative allocations. The Fund by an eighty-five percent majority of the total voting power may prescribe additional transactions or categories of transactions under this provision. Any transactions or categories of transactions prescribed by the Fund under this subsection (b) (ii) shall be consistent with the other provisions of this Agreement and with the proper use of special drawing rights in accordance with this Agreement.

(c) A participant that provides currency to a participant using special drawing rights shall receive an equivalent amount of special drawing rights.

Section 3. *Requirement of need*

(a) In transactions under Section 2 of this Article, except as otherwise provided in (c) below, a participant will be expected to use its special drawing rights only to meet balance of payments needs or in the light of developments in its official holdings of gold, foreign exchange, and special drawing rights, and its reserve position in the Fund, and not for the sole purpose of changing the composition of the foregoing as between special drawing rights and the total of gold, foreign exchange, and reserve position in the Fund.

(b) The use of special drawing rights shall not be subject to challenge on the basis of the expectation in (a) above, but the Fund may make representations to a participant that fails to fulfill this expectation. A participant that persists in failing to fulfill this expectation shall be subject to Article XXIX, Section 2 (b).

(c) Participants may use special drawing rights without fulfilling the expectation in (a) above to obtain an equivalent amount of currency from another participant in any transactions, prescribed by the Fund, that would promote reconstitution by the other participant under Section 6 (a) of this Article; prevent or reduce a negative balance of the other participant; offset the effect of a failure by the other participant to fulfill the expectation in (a) above; or bring the holdings of special drawing rights by both participants closer to their net cumulative allocations.

Section 4. *Obligation to provide currency*

A participant designated by the Fund under Section 5 of this Article shall provide on demand currency convertible in fact to a participant using special drawing rights under Section 2 (a) of this Article. A participant's obligation to provide currency shall not extend beyond the point at which its holdings of special drawing rights in excess of its net cumulative allocation are equal to twice its net cumulative allocation or such higher limit as may be agreed between a participant and the Fund. A participant may provide currency in excess of the obligatory limit or any agreed higher limit.

Section 5. *Designation of participants to provide currency*

(a) The Fund shall ensure that a participant will be able to use its special drawing rights by designating participants to provide currency for specified amounts of special drawing rights for the purposes of Sections 2 (a) and 4 of this Article. Designations shall be made in accordance with the following general principles supplemented by such other principles as the Fund may adopt from time to time:

(i) A participant shall be subject to designation if its balance of payments and gross reserve position is sufficiently strong, but this will not preclude the possibility that a participant with a strong reserve position will be designated even though it has a moderate balance of payments deficit. Participants shall be designated in such manner as will promote over time a balanced distribution of holdings of special drawing rights among them.

(ii) Participants shall be subject to designation in order to promote reconstitution under Section 6 (a) of this Article; to reduce negative balances in holdings of special drawing rights; or to offset the effect of failures to fulfill the expectation in Section 3 (a) of this Article.

(iii) In designating participants the Fund normally shall give priority to those that need to acquire special drawing rights to meet the objectives of designation under (ii) above.

(b) In order to promote over time a balanced distribution of holdings of special drawing rights under (a) (i) above, the Fund shall apply the rules for designation in Schedule F or such rules as may be adopted under (c) below.

(c) The rules for designation shall be reviewed before the end of the first and each subsequent basic period and the Fund may adopt new rules as the result of a review. Unless new rules are adopted, the rules in force at the time of the review shall continue to apply.

Section 6. *Reconstitution*

(a) Participants that use their special drawing rights shall reconstitute their holdings of them in accordance with the rules for reconstitution in Schedule G or such rules as may be adopted under (b) below.

(b) The rules for reconstitution shall be reviewed before the end of the first and each subsequent basic period and new rules shall be adopted if necessary. Unless new rules are adopted or a decision is made to abrogate rules for reconstitution, the rules in force at the time of the review shall continue to apply. An eighty-five percent majority of the total voting power shall be required for decisions to adopt, modify, or abrogate the rules for reconstitution.

Section 7. *Operations and transactions through the General Account*

(a) Special drawing rights shall be included in a member's monetary reserves under Article XIX for the purposes of Article III, Section 4 (a), Article V, Section 7 (b) and (c), Article V, Section 8 (f), and Schedule B, paragraph 1. The Fund may decide that in calculating monetary reserves and the increase in monetary reserves during any year for the purpose of Article V, Section 7 (b) and (c), no account shall be taken of any increase or decrease in those monetary reserves which is due to allocations or cancellations of special drawing rights during the year.

(b) The Fund shall accept special drawing rights:

(i) in repurchases accruing in special drawing rights under Article V, Section 7 (b); and

(ii) in reimbursement pursuant to Article XXVI, Section 4.

(c) The Fund may accept special drawing rights to the extent it may decide:

(i) in payment of charges; and

(ii) in repurchases other than those under Article V, Section 7 (b), in proportions which, as far as feasible, shall be the same for all members.

(d) The Fund, if it deems such action appropriate to replenish its holdings of a participant's currency and after consultation with that participant on alternative ways of replenishment under Article VII, Section 2, may require that participant to provide its currency for special drawing rights held in the General Account subject to Section 4 of this Article. In replenishing with special drawing rights, the Fund shall pay due regard to the principles of designation under Section 5 of this Article.

(e) To the extent that a participant may receive special drawing rights in a transaction prescribed by the Fund to promote reconstitution by it under Section 6 (a) of this Article, prevent or reduce a negative balance, or offset the effect of a failure by it to fulfill the expectation in Section 3 (a) of this Article, the Fund may provide the participant with special drawing rights held in the General Account for gold or currency acceptable to the Fund.

(f) In any of the other operations and transactions of the Fund with a participant conducted through the General Account the Fund may use special drawing rights by agreement with the participant.

(g) The Fund may levy reasonable charges uniform for all participants in connection with operations and transactions under this Section.

Section 8. *Exchange rates*

(a) The exchange rates for operations or transactions between participants shall be such that a participant using special drawing rights shall receive the same value whatever currencies might be provided and whichever participants provide those currencies, and the Fund shall adopt regulations to give effect to this principle.

(b) The Fund shall consult a participant on the procedure for determining rates of exchange for its currency.

(c) For the purpose of this provision the term participant includes a terminating participant.

ARTICLE XXVI

Special Drawing Account Interest and Charges

Section 1. *Interest*

Interest at the same rate for all holders shall be paid by the Fund to each holder on the amount of its holdings of special drawing rights. The Fund shall pay the amount due to each holder whether or not sufficient charges are received to meet the payment of interest.

Section 2. *Charges*

Charges at the same rate for all participants shall be paid to the Fund by each participant on the amount of its net cumulative allocation of special drawing rights plus any negative balance of the participant or unpaid charges.

Section 3. *Rate of interest and charges*

The rate of interest shall be equal to the rate of charges and shall be one and one-half percent per annum. The Fund in its discretion may increase or reduce this rate, but the rate shall not be greater than two percent or the rate of remuneration decided under Article V, Section 9, whichever is higher, or smaller than one percent or the rate of remuneration decided under Article V, Section 9, whichever is lower.

Section 4. *Assessments*

When it is decided under Article XXII, Section 2, that reimbursement shall be made, the Fund shall levy assessments for this purpose at the same rate for all participants on their net cumulative allocations.

Section 5. *Payment of interest, charges, and assessments*

Interest, charges, and assessments shall be paid in special drawing rights. A participant that needs special drawing rights to pay any charge or assessment shall be obligated and entitled to obtain them, at its option for gold or currency acceptable to the Fund, in a transaction with the Fund conducted through the General Account. If sufficient special drawing rights cannot be obtained in this way, the participant shall be obligated and entitled to obtain them with currency convertible in fact from a participant which the Fund shall specify. Special drawing rights acquired by a participant after the date for payment shall be applied against its unpaid charges and cancelled.

ARTICLE XXVII

Administration of the General Account and the Special Drawing Account

(a) The General Account and the Special Drawing Account shall be administered in accordance with the provisions of Article XII, subject to the following:

(i) The Board of Governors may delegate to the Executive Directors authority to exercise any powers of the Board with respect to special drawing rights except those under Article XXIII, Section 3, Article XXIV, Section 2 (a), (b), and (c), and Section 3, the penultimate sentence of Article XXV, Section 2 (b), Article XXV, Section 6 (b), and Article XXXI (a).

(ii) For meetings of or decisions by the Board of Governors on matters pertaining exclusively to the Special Drawing Account only requests by or the presence and the votes of governors appointed by members that are participants shall be counted for the purpose of calling meetings and determining whether a quorum exists or whether a decision is made by the required majority.

(iii) For decisions by the Executive Directors on matters pertaining exclusively to the Special Drawing Account only directors appointed or elected by at least one member that is a participant shall be entitled to vote. Each of these directors shall be entitled to cast the number of votes allotted to the member which is a participant that appointed him or to the members that are participants whose votes counted towards his election. Only the presence of directors appointed or elected by members that are participants and the votes allotted to members that are participants shall be counted for the purpose of determining whether a quorum exists or whether a decision is made by the required majority.

(iv) Questions of the general administration of the Fund, including reimbursement under Article XXII, Section 2, and any question whether a matter pertains to both Accounts or exclusively to the Special Drawing Account shall be decided as if they pertained exclusively to the General Account. Decisions with respect to the acceptance and holding of special drawing rights in the General Account and the use of them, and other decisions affecting the operations and transactions conducted through both the General Account and the Special Drawing Account shall be made by the majorities required for decisions on matters pertaining exclusively to each Account. A decision on a matter pertaining to the Special Drawing Account shall so indicate.

(b) In addition to the privileges and immunities that are accorded under Article IX of this Agreement, no tax of any kind shall be levied on special drawing rights or on operations or transactions in special drawing rights.

(c) A question of interpretation of the provisions of this Agreement on matters pertaining exclusively to the Special Drawing Account shall be submitted to the Executive Directors pursuant to Article XVIII (a) only on the request of a participant. In any case where the Executive Directors have given a decision on a question of interpretation pertaining exclusively to the Special Drawing Account only a participant may require that the question be referred to the Board of Governors under Article XVIII (b). The Board of Governors shall decide whether a governor appointed by a member that is not a participant shall be entitled to vote in the Committee on Interpretation on questions pertaining exclusively to the Special Drawing Account.

(d) Whenever a disagreement arises between the Fund and a participant that has terminated its participation in the Special Drawing Account or between the Fund and any participant during the liquidation of the Special Drawing Account with respect to any matter arising exclusively from participation in the Special Drawing Account, the disagreement shall be submitted to arbitration in accordance with the procedures in Article XVIII (c).

ARTICLE XXVIII

General Obligations of Participants

In addition to the obligations assumed with respect to special drawing rights under other Articles of this Agreement, each participant undertakes to collaborate with the Fund and with other participants in order to facilitate the effective functioning of the Special Drawing Account and the proper use of special drawing rights in accordance with this Agreement.

ARTICLE XXIX

Suspension of Transactions in Special Drawing Rights

Section 1. *Emergency provisions*

In the event of an emergency or the development of unforeseen circumstances threatening the operations of the Fund with respect to the Special Drawing Account, the Executive Directors by unanimous vote may suspend for a period of not more than one hundred twenty days the operation of any of the provisions relating to special drawing rights, and the provisions of Article XVI, Section 1 (b), (c), and (d), shall then apply.

Section 2. *Failure to fulfill obligations*

(a) If the Fund finds that a participant has failed to fulfill its obligations under Article XXV, Section 4, the right of the participant to use its special drawing rights shall be suspended unless the Fund otherwise determines.

(b) If the Fund finds that a participant has failed to fulfill any other obligation with respect to special drawing rights, the Fund may suspend the right of the participant to use special drawing rights it acquires after the suspension.

(c) Regulations shall be adopted to ensure that before action is taken against any participant under (a) or (b) above, the participant shall be informed immediately of the complaint against it and given an adequate opportunity for stating its case, both orally and in writing. Whenever the participant is thus informed of a complaint relating to (a) above, it shall not use special drawing rights pending the disposition of the complaint.

(d) Suspension under (a) or (b) above or limitation under (c) above shall not affect a participant's obligation to provide currency in accordance with Article XXV, Section 4.

(e) The Fund may at any time terminate a suspension under (a) or (b) above, provided that a suspension imposed on a participant under (b) above for failure to fulfill the obligation under Article XXV, Section 6 (a), shall not be terminated until one hundred eighty days after the end of the first calendar quarter during which the participant complies with the rules for reconstitution.

(f) The right of a participant to use its special drawing rights shall not be suspended because it has become ineligible to use the Fund's resources under Article IV, Section 6, Article V, Section 5, Article VI, Section 1, or Article XV, Section 2 (a). Article XV, Section 2, shall not apply because a participant has failed to fulfill any obligations with respect to special drawing rights.

ARTICLE XXX

Termination of Participation

Section 1. *Right to terminate participation*

(a) Any participant may terminate its participation in the Special Drawing Account at any time by transmitting a notice in writing to the Fund at its principal office. Termination shall become effective on the date the notice is received.

(b) A participant that withdraws from membership in the Fund shall be deemed to have simultaneously terminated its participation in the Special Drawing Account.

Section 2. *Settlement on termination*

(a) When a participant terminates its participation in the Special Drawing Account, all operations and transactions by the terminating participant in special drawing rights shall cease except as otherwise permitted under an agreement made pursuant to (c) below in order to facilitate a settlement or as provided in Sections 3, 5, and 6 of this Article or in Schedule H. Interest and charges that accrued to the date of termination and assessments levied before that date but not paid shall be paid in special drawing rights.

(b) The Fund shall be obligated to redeem all special drawing rights held by the terminating participant, and the terminating participant shall be obligated to pay to the Fund an amount equal to its net cumulative allocation and any other amounts that may be due and payable because of its participation in the Special Drawing Account. These obligations shall be set off against each other and the amount of special drawing rights held by the terminating participant that is used in the setoff to extinguish its obligation to the Fund shall be cancelled.

(c) A settlement shall be made with reasonable dispatch by agreement between the terminating participant and the Fund with respect to any obligation of the terminating participant or the Fund after the setoff in (b) above. If agreement on a settlement is not reached promptly the provisions of Schedule H shall apply.

Section 3. *Interest and charges*

After the date of termination the Fund shall pay interest on any outstanding balance of special drawing rights held by a terminating participant and the terminating participant shall pay charges on any outstanding obligation owed to the Fund at the times and rates prescribed under Article XXVI. Payment shall be made in special drawing rights. A terminating participant shall be entitled to obtain special drawing rights with currency convertible in fact to pay charges or assessments in a transaction with a participant specified by the Fund or by agreement from any other holder, or to dispose of special drawing rights received as interest in a transaction with any participant designated under Article XXV, Section 5, or by agreement with any other holder.

Section 4. *Settlement of obligation to the Fund*

Gold or currency received by the Fund from a terminating participant shall be used by the Fund to redeem special drawing rights held by participants in proportion to the amount by which each participant's holdings of special drawing rights exceed its net cumulative allocation at the time the gold or currency is received by the Fund. Special drawing rights so redeemed and special drawing rights obtained by a terminating participant under the provisions of this Agreement to meet any installment due under an agreement on settlement or under Schedule H and set off against that installment shall be cancelled.

Section 5. *Settlement of obligation to a terminating participant*

Whenever the Fund is required to redeem special drawing rights held by a terminating participant, redemption shall be made with currency or gold provided by participants specified by the Fund. These participants shall be specified in accordance with the principles in Article XXV, Section 5. Each specified participant shall provide at its option the currency of the terminating participant or currency convertible in fact or gold to the Fund and shall receive an equivalent amount of special drawing rights. However, a terminating participant may use its special drawing rights to obtain its own currency, currency convertible in fact, or gold from any holder, if the Fund so permits.

Section 6. *General Account transactions*

In order to facilitate settlement with a terminating participant the Fund may decide that a terminating participant shall:

(i) use any special drawing rights held by it after the setoff in Section 2 (b) of this Article, when they are to be redeemed, in a transaction with the Fund conducted through the General Account to obtain its own currency or currency convertible in fact at the option of the Fund; or

(ii) obtain special drawing rights in a transaction with the Fund conducted through the General Account for a currency acceptable to the Fund or gold to meet any charges or installment due under an agreement or the provisions of Schedule H.

ARTICLE XXXI

Liquidation of the Special Drawing Account

(a) The Special Drawing Account may not be liquidated except by decision of the Board of Governors. In an emergency, if the Executive Directors decide that liquidation of the Special Drawing Account may be necessary, they may temporarily suspend allocations or cancellations and all transactions in special drawing rights pending decision by the Board. A decision by the Board of Governors to liquidate the Fund shall be a decision to liquidate both the General Account and the Special Drawing Account.

(b) If the Board of Governors decides to liquidate the Special Drawing Account, all allocations or cancellations and all operations and transactions in special drawing rights and the activities of the Fund with respect to the Special Drawing Account shall cease except those incidental to the orderly discharge of the obligations of participants and of the Fund with respect to special drawing rights, and all obligations of the Fund and of participants under this Agreement with respect to special drawing rights shall cease except those set out in this Article, Article XVIII (c), Article XXVI, Article XXVII (d), Article XXX and Schedule H, or any agreement reached under Article XXX subject to paragraph 4 of Schedule H, Article XXXII, and Schedule I.

(c) Upon liquidation of the Special Drawing Account, interest and charges that accrued to the date of liquidation and assessments levied before that date but not paid shall be paid in special drawing rights. The Fund shall be obligated to redeem all special drawing rights held by holders and each participant shall be obligated to pay the Fund an amount equal to its net cumulative allocation of special drawing rights and such other amounts as may be due and payable because of its participation in the Special Drawing Account.

(d) Liquidation of the Special Drawing Account shall be administered in accordance with the provisions of Schedule I.

ARTICLE XXXII

Explanation of Terms with Respect to Special Drawing Rights

In interpreting the provisions of this Agreement with respect to special drawing rights the Fund and its members shall be guided by the following:

(a) Net cumulative allocation of special drawing rights means the total amount of special drawing rights allocated to a participant less its share of special drawing rights that have been cancelled under Article XXIV, Section 2 (a).

(b) Currency convertible in fact means:

(1) a participant's currency for which a procedure exists for the conversion of balances of the currency obtained in transactions involving special drawing rights into each other currency for which such procedure exists, at rates of exchange prescribed under Article XXV, Section 8, and which is the currency of a participant that

(i) has accepted the obligations of Article VIII, Sections 2, 3, and 4, or

(ii) for the settlement of international transactions in fact freely buys and sells gold within the limits prescribed by the Fund under Section 2 of Article IV; or

(2) currency convertible into a currency described in paragraph (1) above at rates of exchange prescribed under Article XXV, Section 8.

(c) A participant's reserve position in the Fund means the sum of the gold tranche purchases it could make and the amount of any indebtedness of the Fund which is readily repayable to the participant under a loan agreement."

L

SCHEDULE B

Provisions with Respect to Repurchase by a Member of its Currency Held by the Fund

1. Paragraph 1 shall read:

"1. In determining the extent to which repurchase of a member's currency from the Fund under Article V, Section 7 (b), shall be made with each convertible currency and each of the other types of monetary reserve, the following rule, subject to 2 below, shall apply:

(a) If the member's monetary reserves have not increased during the year, the amount payable to the Fund shall be distributed among all types of reserves in proportion to the member's holdings thereof at the end of the year.

(b) If the member's monetary reserves have increased during the year, a part of the amount payable to the Fund equal to one-half of the increase, minus one-half of any decrease in the Fund's holdings of the member's currency that has occurred during the year, shall be distributed among those types of reserves which have increased in proportion to the amount by which each of them has increased. The remainder of the sum payable to the Fund shall be distributed among all types of reserves in proportion to the member's remaining holdings thereof.

(c) If after the repurchases required under Article V, Section 7 (b), had been made, the result would exceed either of the limits specified in Article V, Section 7 (c) (i) or (ii), the Fund shall require such repurchases to be made by the member proportionately in such manner that these limits will not be exceeded.

(d) If after all the repurchases required under Article V, Section 7 (b), had been made, the result would exceed the limit specified in Article V, Section 7 (c) (iii), the amount by which the limit would be exceeded shall be discharged in convertible currencies as determined by the Fund without exceeding that limit.

(e) If a repurchase required under Article V, Section 7 (b), would exceed the limit specified in Article V, Section 7 (c) (iv), the amount by which the limit would be exceeded shall be repurchased at the end of the subsequent financial year or years in such a way that total repurchases under Article V, Section 7 (b), in any year would not exceed the limit specified in Article V, Section 7 (c) (iv)."

2. Paragraph 2 shall read:

"2. (a) The Fund shall not require the currency of any non-member under Article V, Section 7 (b) and (c).

(b) Any amount payable in the currency of a non-member under 1 (a) or 1 (b) above shall be paid in the convertible currencies of members as determined by the Fund."

3. The following paragraphs 5 and 6 shall be added to Schedule B:

"5. In calculating monetary reserves and the increase in monetary reserves during any year for the purpose of Article V, Section 7 (b) and (c), the Fund may decide in its discretion, on the request of a member, that deductions shall be made for obligations outstanding as the result of transactions between members under a reciprocal facility by which a member agrees to exchange on demand its currency for the currency of the other member up to a maximum amount and on terms requiring that each such transaction be reversed within a specified period not in excess of nine months."

"6. In calculating monetary reserves and the increase in monetary reserves for the purpose of Article V, Section 7 (b) and (c), Article XIX (e) shall apply except that the following provision shall apply at the end of a financial year if it was in effect at the beginning of that year:

'A member's monetary reserves shall be calculated by deducting from its central holdings the currency liabilities to the Treasuries, central banks, stabilization funds, or similar fiscal agencies of other members or non-members specified under (d) above, together with similar liabilities to other official institutions and other banks in the territories of members, or non-members specified under (d) above. To these net holdings shall be added the sums deemed to be official holdings of other official institutions and other banks under (c) above.' "

M

The following Schedules shall be added after Schedule E:

"SCHEDULE F

Designation

During the first basic period the rules for designation shall be as follows:

(a) Participants subject to designation under Article XXV, Section 5 (a) (i), shall be designated for such amounts as will promote over time equality in the ratios of the participants' holdings of special drawing rights in excess of their net cumulative allocations to their official holdings of gold and foreign exchange.

(b) The formula to give effect to (a) above shall be such that participants subject to designation shall be designated:

(i) in proportion to their official holdings of gold and foreign exchange when the ratios described in (a) above are equal; and

(ii) in such manner as gradually to reduce the difference between the ratios described in (a) above that are low and the ratios that are high.

SCHEDULE G

Reconstitution

1. During the first basic period the rules for reconstitution shall be as follows:

(a) (i) A participant shall so use and reconstitute its holdings of special drawing rights that, five years after the first allocation and at the end of each calendar quarter thereafter, the average of its total daily holdings of special drawing rights over the most recent five-year period will be not less than thirty percent of the average of its daily net cumulative allocation of special drawing rights over the same period.

(ii) Two years after the first allocation and at the end of each calendar month thereafter the Fund shall make calculations for each participant so as to ascertain whether and to what extent the participant would need to acquire special drawing rights between the date of the calculation and the end of any five-year period in order to comply with the requirement in (a) (i) above. The Fund shall adopt regulations with respect to the bases on which these calculations shall be made and with respect to the timing of the designation of participants under Article XXV, Section 5 (a) (ii), in order to assist them to comply with the requirement in (a) (i) above.

(iii) The Fund shall give special notice to a participant when the calculations under (a) (ii) above indicate that it is unlikely that the participant will be able to comply with the requirement in (a) (i) above unless it ceases to use special drawing rights for the rest of the period for which the calculation was made under (a) (ii) above.

(iv) A participant that needs to acquire special drawing rights to fulfill this obligation shall be obligated and entitled to obtain them, at its option for gold or currency acceptable to the Fund, in a transaction with the Fund conducted through the General Account. If sufficient special drawing rights to fulfill this obligation cannot be obtained in this way, the participant shall be obligated and entitled to obtain them with currency convertible in fact from a participant which the Fund shall specify.

(b) Participants shall also pay due regard to the desirability of pursuing over time a balanced relationship between their holdings of special drawing rights and their holdings of gold and foreign exchange and their reserve positions in the Fund.

2. If a participant fails to comply with the rules for reconstitution, the Fund shall determine whether or not the circumstances justify suspension under Article XXIX, Section 2 (b).

SCHEDULE H

Termination of Participation

1. If the obligation remaining after the setoff under Article XXX, Section 2 (b), is to the terminating participant and agreement on settlement between the Fund and the terminating participant is not reached within six months of the date of termination, the Fund shall redeem this balance of special drawing rights in equal half-yearly installments within a maximum of five years of the date of termination. The Fund shall redeem this balance as it may determine, either (a) by the payment to the terminating participant of the amounts provided by the remaining participants to the Fund in accordance with Article XXX, Section 5, or (b) by permitting the terminating participant to use its special drawing rights to obtain its own currency or currency convertible in fact from a participant specified by the Fund, the General Account, or any other holder.

2. If the obligation remaining after the setoff under Article XXX, Section 2 (b), is to the Fund and agreement on settlement is not reached within six months of the date of termination, the terminating participant shall discharge this obligation in equal half-yearly installments within three years of the date of termination or within such longer period as may be fixed by the Fund. The terminating participant shall discharge this obligation, as the Fund may determine, either (a) by the payment to the Fund of currency convertible in fact or gold at the option of the terminating participant, or (b) by obtaining special drawing rights, in accordance with Article XXX, Section 6, from the General Account or in agreement with a participant specified by the Fund or from any other holder, and the setoff of these special drawing rights against the installment due.

3. Installments under either 1 or 2 above shall fall due six months after the date of termination and at intervals of six months thereafter.

4. In the event of the Special Drawing Account going into liquidation under Article XXXI within six months of the date a participant terminates its participation, the settlement between the Fund and that government shall be made in accordance with Article XXXI and Schedule I.

SCHEDULE I

Administration of Liquidation of the Special Drawing Account

1. In the event of liquidation of the Special Drawing Account, participants shall discharge their obligations to the Fund in ten half-yearly installments, or in such longer periods as the Fund may decide is needed, in currency convertible in fact and the currencies of participants holding special drawing rights to be redeemed in any installment to the extent of such redemption, as determined by the Fund. The first half-yearly payment shall be made six months after the decision to liquidate the Special Drawing Account.

2. If it is decided to liquidate the Fund within six months of the date of the decision to liquidate the Special Drawing Account, the liquidation of the Special Drawing Account shall not proceed until special drawing rights held in the General Account have been distributed in accordance with the following rule:

After the distribution made under 2 (a) of Schedule E, the Fund shall apportion its special drawing rights held in the General Account among all members that are participants in proportion to the amounts due to each participant after the distribution under 2 (a). To determine the amount due to each member for the purpose of apportioning the remainder of its holdings of each currency under 2 (c) of Schedule E, the Fund shall deduct the distribution of special drawing rights made under this rule.

3. With the amounts received under 1 above, the Fund shall redeem special drawing rights held by holders in the following manner and order:

(a) Special drawing rights held by governments that have terminated their participation more than six months before the date the Board of Governors decides to liquidate the Special Drawing Account shall be redeemed in accordance with the terms of any agreement under Article XXX or Schedule H.

(b) Special drawing rights held by holders that are not participants shall be redeemed before those held by participants, and shall be redeemed in proportion to the amount held by each holder.

(c) The Fund shall determine the proportion of special drawing rights held by each participant in relation to its net cumulative allocation. The Fund shall first redeem special drawing rights from the participants with the highest proportion until this proportion is reduced to that of the second highest proportion; the Fund shall then redeem the special drawing rights held by these participants in accordance with their net cumulative allocations until the proportions are reduced to that of the third highest proportion; and this process shall be continued until the amount available for redemption is exhausted.

4. Any amount that a participant will be entitled to receive in redemption under 3 above shall be set off against any amount to be paid under 1 above.

5. During liquidation the Fund shall pay interest on the amount of special drawing rights held by holders, and each participant shall pay charges on the net cumulative allocation of special drawing rights to it less the amount of any payments made in accordance with 1 above. The rates of interest and charges and the time of payment shall be determined by the Fund. Payments of interest and charges shall be made in special drawing rights to the extent possible. A participant that does not hold sufficient special drawing rights to meet any charges shall make the payment with gold or a currency specified by the Fund. Special drawing rights received as charges in amounts needed for administrative expenses shall not be used for the payment of interest, but shall be transferred to the Fund and shall be redeemed first and with the currencies used by the Fund to meet its expenses.

6. While a participant is in default with respect to any payment required by 1 or 5 above, no amounts shall be paid to it in accordance with 2 or 5 above.

7. If after the final payments have been made to participants each participant not in default does not hold special drawing rights in the same proportion to its net cumulative allocation, those participants holding a lower proportion shall purchase from those holding a higher proportion such amounts in accordance with arrangements made by the Fund as will make the proportion of their holdings of special drawing rights the same. Each participant in default shall pay to the Fund its own currency in an amount equal to its default. The Fund shall apportion this currency and any residual claims among participants in proportion to the amount of special drawing rights held by each and these special drawing rights shall be cancelled. The Fund shall then close the books of the Special Drawing Account and all of the Fund's liabilities arising from the allocations of special drawing rights and the administration of the Special Drawing Account shall cease.

8. Each participant whose currency is distributed to other participants under this Schedule guarantees the unrestricted use of such currency at all times for the purchase of goods or for payments of sums due to it or to persons in its territories. Each participant so obligated agrees to compensate other participants for any loss resulting from the difference between the value at which the Fund distributed its currency under this Schedule and the value realized by such participants on disposal of its currency."

Annex B

OUTLINE OF A FACILITY BASED ON SPECIAL DRAWING RIGHTS IN THE FUND

Introduction

The facility described in this Outline is intended to meet the need, as and when it arises, for a supplement to existing reserve assets. It is to be established within the framework of the Fund and, therefore, by an Amendment of the Fund's Articles. Provisions relating to some of the topics in this Outline could be included in By-Laws adopted by the Board of Governors or Rules and Regulations adopted by the Executive Directors rather than in the Amendment.

I. Establishment of a Special Drawing Account in the Fund

(a) An Amendment to the Articles will establish a Special Drawing Account through which all the operations relating to special drawing rights will be carried out. The purposes of the facility will be set forth in the introductory section of the Amendment.

(b) The operations of and resources available under the Special Drawing Account will be separate from the operations of the present Fund which will be referred to as the General Account.

(c) Separate provisions will be included in the Amendment for withdrawal from or liquidation of the Special Drawing Account; Article XVI, Section 2 and Schedules D and E on withdrawal and liquidation will continue to apply as they do at present to the General Account of the Fund.

II. Participants and Other Holders

1. *Participants.* Participation in the Special Drawing Account will be open to any member of the Fund that undertakes the obligations of the Amendment. A member's quota in the Fund will be the same for the purposes of both the General and the Special Drawing Accounts of the Fund.

2. *Holding by General Account.* The General Account will be authorized to hold and use special drawing rights.

III. Allocation of Special Drawing Rights

1. *Principles for decisions.* The Special Drawing Account will allocate special drawing rights in accordance with the provisions of the Amendment. Special considerations applicable to the first decision to allocate special drawing rights, as well as the principles on which all decisions to allocate special drawing rights will be based, will be included in the introductory section of the Amendment and, to the extent necessary, in a Report explaining the Amendment.

2. *Basic period and rate of allocation.* The following provisions will apply to any decision to allocate special drawing rights:

(i) The decision will prescribe a basic period during which special drawing rights will be allocated at specified intervals. The period will normally be five years in length, but the Fund may decide that any basic period will be of different duration. The first basic period will begin on the effective date of the first decision to allocate special drawing rights.

(ii) The decision will also prescribe the rate or rates at which special drawing rights will be allocated during the basic period. Rates will be expressed as a percentage, uniform for all participants, of quotas on the date specified in the decision.

3. *Procedure for decisions.*

(a) Any decision on the basic period for, timing of, or rate of allocation of special drawing rights will be taken by the Board of Governors on the basis of a proposal by the Managing Director concurred in by the Executive Directors.

(b) Before formulating any proposal, the Managing Director after having satisfied himself that the considerations referred to in III.1 have been met, will conduct such consultations as will enable him to ascertain that there is broad support among participants for the allocation of special drawing rights at the proposed rate and for the proposed basic period.

(c) The Managing Director will make proposals with respect to the allocation of special drawing rights: (i) within sufficient time before the end of a basic period; (ii) in the circumstances of III.4; (iii) within six months after the Board of Governors or the Executive Directors request that he make a proposal. The Managing Director will make a proposal for the first basic period when he is of the opinion that there is broad support among the participants to start the allocation of special drawing rights.

(d) The Executive Directors will review both the operations of the Special Drawing Account and the adequacy of global reserves as part of their annual report to the Board of Governors.

4. *Change in rate of allocation or basic period.* If there are unexpected major developments which make it desirable to change the rate at which further special drawing rights are to be allocated for a basic period, (i) the rate may be increased or decreased, or (ii) the basic period may be terminated and a different rate of allocation adopted for a new basic period. Paragraph III.3 will apply to such changes.

5. *Voting majority.*

(a) For decisions on the basic period for, timing of, amount and rate of allocation of special drawing rights, an 85 per cent majority of the voting power of participants shall be required.

(b) Notwithstanding (a) above, the decisions to decrease the rate of allocation of special drawing rights for the remainder of the basic period will be taken by a simple majority of the voting power of participants.

6. *Opting out.* The Amendment will include provisions that will prescribe to what extent a participant will be required initially to receive special drawing rights, but will stipulate that beyond any such amount a participant that does not vote in favor of a decision to allocate special drawing rights may elect not to receive them under that decision.

IV. Cancellation of Special Drawing Rights

The principles set forth in III relating to the procedure and voting for the allocation of special drawing rights will be applicable, with appropriate modifications, to the cancellation of such rights.

V. Use of Special Drawing Rights

1. *Right to use special drawing rights.*

(a) A participant will be entitled, in accordance with the provisions of V, to use special drawing rights to acquire an equivalent amount of a currency convertible in fact. A participant which thus provides currency will receive an equivalent amount of special drawing rights.

(b) Within the framework of such rules and regulations as the Fund may adopt, a participant may obtain the currencies referred to in (a) either directly from another participant or through the Special Drawing Account.

(c) Except as indicated in V.3 (c), a participant will be expected to use its special drawing rights only for balance of payments needs or in the light of developments in its total reserves and not for the sole purpose of changing the composition of its reserves.

(d) The use of special drawing rights will not be subject to prior challenge on the basis of this expectation, but the Fund may make representations to any participant which, in the Fund's judgment, has failed to observe the expectation, and may direct drawings to such participant to the extent of such failure.

2. *Provision of currency.* A participant's obligation to provide currency will not extend beyond a point at which its holdings of special drawing rights in excess of the net cumulative amount of such rights allocated to it are equal to twice that amount. However, a participant may provide currency, or agree with the Fund to provide currency, in excess of this limit.

3. *Selection of participants to be drawn upon.* The Fund's rules and instructions relating to the participants from which currencies should be acquired by users of special drawing rights will be based on the following main general principles, supplemented by such principles as the Fund may find desirable from time to time:

(a) Normally, currencies will be acquired from participants that have a sufficiently strong balance of payments and reserve position, but this will not preclude the possibility that currency will be acquired from participants with strong reserve positions even though they have moderate balance of payments deficits.

(b) The Fund's primary criterion will be to seek to approach over time equality, among the participants indicated from time to time by the criteria in (a) above, in the ratios of their holdings of special drawing rights, or such holdings in excess of net cumulative allocations thereof, to total reserves.

(c) In addition, the Fund will, in its rules and instructions, provide for such use of special drawing rights, either directly between participants or through the intermediary of the Special Drawing Account, as will promote voluntary reconstitution and reconstitution under V.4.

(d) Subject to the provisions of V.1 (c), a participant may use its special drawing rights to purchase balances of its currency held by another participant, with the agreement of the latter.

4. *Reconstitution.*

(a) Members that use their special drawing rights will incur an obligation to reconstitute their position in accordance with principles which will take account of the amount and the duration of the use. These principles will be laid down in rules and regulations of the Fund.

(b) The rules for reconstitution of drawings made during the first basic period will be based on the following principles:

(i) The average net use, taking into account both use below and holdings above its net cumulative allocation, made by a participant of its special drawing rights calculated on the basis of the preceding five years, shall not exceed 70 per cent of its average net cumulative allocation during this period. Reconstitution under this subparagraph (i) will be brought about through the mechanism of transfers, by the Fund directing drawings correspondingly.

(ii) Participants will pay due regard to the desirability of pursuing over time a balanced relationship between their holdings of special drawing rights and other reserves.

(c) Reconstitution rules will be reviewed before the end of the first and of each subsequent period and new rules will be adopted, if necessary. If new rules are not adopted for a basic period, the rules for the preceding period shall apply unles it is decided to abrogate reconstitution rules. The same majority as is required for decisions on the basic period, timing of, or rate of allocation of special drawing rights will be required for decisions to adopt, amend, or abrogate reconstitution rules. Any amendment in the rules will govern the reconstitution of drawings made after the effective date of the amendment, unless otherwise decided.

VI. Interest and Maintenance of Gold Value

(a) *Interest.* A moderate rate of interest will be paid in special drawing rights on holdings of special drawing rights. The cost of this interest will be assessed against all participants in proportion to net cumulative allocations of special drawing rights to them.

(b) *Maintenance of gold value.* The unit of value for expressing special drawing rights will be equal to 0.888 671 grams of fine gold. The rights and obligations of participants and of the

Special Drawing Account will be subject to an absolute maintenance of gold value or to provisions similar to Article IV, Section 8 of the Fund's Articles.

VII. Functions of Fund Organs and Voting

1. *Exercise of powers.* The decisions taken with respect to the Special Drawing Account, and the supervision of its operations, will be carried out by the Board of Governors, the Executive Directors, the Managing Director, and the staff of the Fund. Certain powers, and in particular those relating to the adoption of decisions concerning the allocation, cancellation, and certain aspects of the use of special drawing rights, will be reserved to the Board of Governors. All other powers, except those specifically granted to other organs, will be vested in the Board of Governors which will be able to delegate them to the Executive Directors.

2. *Voting.* Except as otherwise provided in the Amendment, all decisions pertaining to the Special Drawing Account will be taken by a majority of votes cast. The precise formula for the voting power of participants, which will include basic and weighted votes, and possibly the adjustment of voting power in relation to the use of special drawing rights, will be the subject of later consideration.

VIII. General Provisions

1. *Collaboration.* Participants will undertake to collaborate with the Fund in order to facilitate the proper functioning and effective use of special drawing rights within the international monetary system.

2. *Nonfulfillment of obligations.*

(a) If the Fund finds that a participant has failed to fulfill its obligations to provide currency in accordance with the Amendment, the Fund may suspend the right of the participant to use its special drawing rights.

(b) If the Fund finds that a participant has failed to fulfill any other obligation under the Amendment, the Fund may suspend the participant's right to use any special drawing rights allocated to, or acquired by, it after the suspension.

(c) Suspension under (a) or (b) above will not affect a participant's obligation to provide currency in accordance with the Amendment.

(d) The Fund may at any time terminate a suspension under (a) or (b) above.

3. *Accounts.* All changes in holdings of special drawing rights will take effect when recorded in the accounts of the Special Drawing Account.

IX. Entry into Force

The Amendment would enter into force in accordance with the terms of Article XVII of the Fund's Articles.

PART V

Publications

Publications of the Fund

The following is a complete listing of the reports, documents, books, periodicals, pamphlets, and leaflets that have been made available to the general public from the Fund's inception to December 31, 1968. Except where otherwise stated, all were published by the Fund at Washington, D.C.

Agreement Between the United Nations and the International Monetary Fund. Accord entre les Nations Unies et le Fonds Monétaire International. 1956. 12 pp. Bilingual.

Annual Report of the Executive Directors . . . 1946 to date. Selected portions published also in French (1947, 1950, 1953, and 1962–67), German (1962 to date), and Spanish (1947 and 1962–67). Full Report (except index) published in French and Spanish beginning 1968.

Annual Report on Exchange Restrictions. 1950 to date. Supplement to Second Report concerning nonmembers of Fund published separately under title *Surveys of Exchange Controls and Restrictions in Argentina, Burma, Federal Republic of Germany, Hashemite Kingdom of the Jordan, Indonesia, Japan, New Zealand, Portugal, Spain, Sweden, Switzerland.*

Articles of Agreement of the International Monetary Fund. Adopted at the United Nations Monetary and Financial Conference, Bretton Woods, New Hampshire, July 22, 1944. Effective December 27, 1945. 1st printing, 1946; 7th printing, 1967. v + 65 pp. Published also in French and Spanish, without index. 1st printing issued under title *Articles of Agreement, International Monetary Fund, United Nations Monetary and Financial Conference, Bretton Woods, N.H., July 1 to 22, 1944.*

Articles of Agreement of the International Monetary Fund . . . As Modified by the Proposed Amendment Recommended by the Executive Directors April 16, 1968 and Approved by the Board of Governors May 31, 1968. [1968]. ix + 102 pp. Published also in French and Spanish.

Balance of Payments: Concepts and Definitions. 1968. iv + 47 pp. Published also in French and Spanish. (Pamphlet Series, No. 10.)

Balance of Payments: Its Meaning and Uses, by Poul Høst-Madsen. 1967. iv + 24 pp. Published also in French, German, and Spanish. (Pamphlet Series, No. 9.)

Balance of Payments Manual. 1948. 57 pp.; preliminary Spanish edition (mimeographed). 2nd ed., 1950. iii + 111 pp.; preliminary Spanish edition (mimeographed). 3rd ed., 1961. vii + 182 pp.; published also in French and Spanish.

Balance of Payments Yearbook.

Vol. 1: 1938, 1946, 1947	Vol. 8: 1950–54	Vol. 15: 1958–62
Vol. 2: 1948, preliminary 1949	Vol. 9: 1955–56	Vol. 16: 1959–63
Vol. 3: 1949–50	Vol. 10: 1956–57	Vol. 17: 1960–64
Vol. 4: 1950–51	Vol. 11: 1957–58	Vol. 18: 1961–65
Vol. 5: 1947–53	Vol. 12: 1955–59	Vol. 19: 1962–66
Vol. 6: 1953–54	Vol. 13: 1956–60	Vol. 20: 1963–67
Vol. 7: 1954–55	Vol. 14: 1957–61	

Vols. 1–4, bound; Vol. 5 to date in loose-leaf form; Vol. 19 to date available both loose-leaf and bound.

By-Laws, Rules and Regulations. Irregular. 1st issue, Mar. 1, 1947; 26th issue, Aug. 10, 1966.

Central Banking Legislation: A Collection of Central Bank, Monetary and Banking Laws. Statutes and related materials selected and annotated by Hans Aufricht. Vol. I, 1961. xxi + 1012 pp. (Monograph Series, No. 1.) Vol. II, Europe. 1967. xxiv + 921 pp. (Monograph Series, No. 4.)

Compensatory Financing of Export Fluctuations: A Report by the International Monetary Fund on Compensatory Financing of the Fluctuations in Exports of Primary Exporting Countries. 1963. 27 pp. Published also in French and Spanish.

Compensatory Financing of Export Fluctuations; Developments in the Fund's Facility: A Second Report by the International Monetary Fund on Compensatory Financing of the Fluctuations in Exports of Primary Producing Countries. 1966. 42 pp. Second printing, with minor editorial corrections, 1967. Published also in French and Spanish.

The Cuban Insurance Cases and the Articles of the Fund, by Joseph Gold. 1966. vii + 53 pp. Published also in Spanish. (Pamphlet Series, No. 8.)

Current Problems of Credit and Fiscal Policy: An Informal Discussion. Twelfth Annual Meeting of the Boards of Governors, International Bank for Reconstruction and Development, International Monetary Fund. 1957. 24 pp.

Direction of International Trade. Monthly, with annual issue. Vol. 1, No. 1 (Jan.–Mar. 1950)–Vol. 13, No. 1 (Jan. 1963); no issues published in 1961. Joint publication of Statistical Office of United Nations, International Monetary Fund, and International Bank for Reconstruction and Development, published by United Nations (New York). Annual issues, 1953 and 1955–60.

Direction of Trade: A Supplement to International Financial Statistics. Monthly, with annual issue. Jan.–Apr. 1964 to date. Published jointly by International Monetary Fund and International Bank for Reconstruction and Development.

Directory: Members, Quotas, Governors, Voting Power, Executive Board, Officers. Irregular. June 1947 to date. June 1947 and Feb. 3, 1948 issues published under title *Schedule of Quotas and Voting Power.*

Economic Development with Stability: A Report to the Government of India by a Mission of the International Monetary Fund. 1953. 77 pp.

Enlargement of Fund Resources Through Increases in Quotas: A Report by the Executive Directors to the Board of Governors of the International Monetary Fund. 1958. 28 pp.

Establishment of a Facility Based on Special Drawing Rights in the International Monetary Fund and Modifications in the Rules and Practices of the Fund: A Report by the Executive Directors to the Board of Governors Proposing Amendment of the Articles of Agreement. 1968. vi + 80 pp. (Cover title: *Proposed Amendment of Articles of Agreement; New Facility Based on Special Drawing Rights, Changes in Fund Rules and Practices: A Report by the Executive Directors to the Board of Governors.*) Published also in French and Spanish.

Finance and Development. Quarterly. Vol. 1, No. 1 (June 1964) to date. Vols. 1–4 carried subtitle *The Fund and Bank Review.* Published jointly by International Monetary Fund and International Bank for Reconstruction and Development. French and Spanish editions under titles *Finances et développement* and *Finanzas y desarrollo,* respectively. Annual issue, beginning 1966, of selected articles in Portuguese under title *Finanças e desenvolvimento* (Rio de Janeiro).

Financial Statement: Issued in Accordance with Article XII, Section 7 (a), of the Articles of Agreement. Quarterly. May 31, 1947 to date.

The Financial Structure of the Fund, by Rudolf Kroc. 1st ed., 1965. 2nd ed., 1967. iv + 41 pp. Published also in French and Spanish. (Pamphlet Series, No. 5.)

The First Ten Years of the International Monetary Fund. 1956. 49 pp.

The Fund Agreement in the Courts, by Joseph Gold. 1962. 159 pp. (Monograph Series, No. 2.)

The Fund and Non-Member States: Some Legal Effects, by Joseph Gold. 1966. vii + 55 pp. Published also in French and Spanish. (Pamphlet Series, No. 7.)

The Fund's Unknown Function, by Camille Gutt. 1949. 5 pp. Text of an article published in a slightly revised form and under a different title by *United Nations World,* December 1948.

Une grande espérance: conférence prononcée à l'Université Libre de Bruxelles, le 25 Avril 1947, by Camille Gutt. [1947]. 20 pp.

Information on Silver as Submitted by Member Countries. 1948. 58 pp. Tables and blank forms.

International Financial News Survey. Weekly. Vol. I, No. 1 (July 1, 1948) to date. Quarterly summary indexes covering first three quarters of year (1961 to date) and annual index. Supplements published irregularly.

International Financial Statistics. Monthly. Vol. I, No. 1 (Jan. 1948) to date. Trilingual edition (English, French, and Spanish) published also, Jan. 1966 to date. Annual supplements, 1961/62 to date.

An Introduction to IFS. n.d. 19 pp. Reprint of introductory articles from Jan.–May 1960 issues. Issued also in French (mimeographed).

Supplement on Money: Monthly Data and Seasonal Adjustments. 1964. 68 pp.

See also *Direction of Trade.*

IMF Institute. *Program for 1965–66.* 1965. 9 pp. In English and French. *Program for 1966–1967.* 1966. In English (11 pp.) and French (12 pp.). *Program for 1967-1968.* 1966. In English (18 pp.), French (18 pp.), and Spanish (19 pp.). *Program for 1968–1969.* 1967. In English (21 pp.), French (21 pp.), and Spanish (22 pp.). *Program for 1969–1970.* 1968. In English (25 pp.), French (25 pp.), and Spanish (25 pp.).

International Monetary Fund Activities in Relation to Latin America, 1946–1954; Prepared at the Request of the Inter-American Economic and Social Council for its Fourth Extraordinary Meeting, Rio de Janeiro, Brazil—1954. 1954. 17 pp.

The International Monetary Fund and International Law: An Introduction, by Joseph Gold. 1965. iv + 26 pp. Published also in French and Spanish. (Pamphlet Series, No. 4.)

The International Monetary Fund and Private Business Transactions: Some Legal Effects of the Articles of Agreement, by Joseph Gold. 1965. iv + 31 pp. Published also in French and Spanish. (Pamphlet Series, No. 3.)

The International Monetary Fund and the Trade Organization, Partners for International Trade: An Address Before the United Nations Conference on Trade and Employment, Havana, Cuba, November 21, 1947, by Camille Gutt. [1947]. 7 pp.

The International Monetary Fund: Its Form and Functions, by J. Marcus Fleming. 1964. v + 57 pp. (Pamphlet Series, No. 2.)

The International Monetary Fund: What It Is, What It Does. Leaflet. Irregular. Nov. 1948 to date. Variously published in English, French, German, Japanese, Portuguese, and Spanish. Nov. 1948–Aug. 1968 published under title *The International Monetary Fund: What It Is, What It Does, How It Works;* Sept. 1959 published under title *The International Monetary Fund: Purposes and Activities.*

International Monetary Problems, 1957–1963: Selected Speeches of Per Jacobsson. 1964. xiii + 368 pp. (Monograph Series, No. 3.)

International Reserves and Liquidity: A Study by the Staff of the International Monetary Fund. [1958]. 104 pp.

Interpretation by the Fund, by Joseph Gold. 1968. vii + 68 pp. Published also in French and Spanish. (Pamphlet Series, No. 11.)

Introduction to the Fund, by J. Keith Horsefield. 1st ed., 1964. 2nd ed., 1965. v + 36 pp. Published also in French, German, and Spanish. (Pamphlet Series, No. 1.)

Maintenance of the Gold Value of the Fund's Assets, by Joseph Gold. 1965. vii + 51 pp. Published also in French and Spanish. (Pamphlet Series, No. 6.)

The Practical Problem of Exchange Rates: An Address Before the Littauer School of Public Administration, Harvard University, Cambridge, Mass., February 13, 1948, by Camille Gutt. [1948]. 18 pp.

Report of the Executive Board of the International Monetary Fund on External Transactions in Gold at Premium Prices. 1950. 6 pp.

The Revival of Monetary Policy: Text and Charts of an Informal Discussion at the Eighth Annual Meeting of the Board of Governors of the International Monetary Fund, September 11, 1953. [1953]. 16 pp. Text issued also in Spanish (mimeographed).

Schedule of Par Values. Irregular. 1st issue, Dec. 18, 1946; 46th issue, Aug. 15, 1968.

Selected Decisions of the Executive Directors and Selected Documents. 3rd issue, 1965. 1st issue, 1962, and 2nd issue, 1963, issued under title *Selected Decisions of the Executive Directors.* 2nd and 3rd issues published also in French.

Selected Documents, Board of Governors Inaugural Meeting, Savannah, Ga., March 8 to 18, 1946. 1946. 60 pp.

Staff Papers. Three numbers constitute a volume. Vol. I, No. 1 (Feb. 1950)–Vol. VIII, No. 3 (Dec. 1961) issued twice a year. Beginning Vol. IX, No. 1 (Mar. 1962), issued three times a year. Index to Vols. I–X (1950–63).

Summary Proceedings of the . . . Annual Meeting of the Board of Governors. 1946 to date. Proceedings of the First Meeting published under title *First Annual Meeting of the Board of Governors: Report of the Executive Directors and Summary Proceedings, September 27 to October 3, 1946.*

Surveys of African Economies. Vol. I: Cameroon, Central African Republic, Chad, Congo (Brazzaville), and Gabon. 1968. xxiv + 365 pp. Published also in French under title *Etudes générales sur les économies africaines. Tome 1: Cameroun, République Centrafricaine, Tchad, Congo (Brazzaville) et Gabon.* 1968. xxiv + 393 pp.

Transactions of the International Monetary Fund. Leaflet. Aug. 1958, Aug. 1959, Apr. 1960, Sept. 1961, and Jan. 1962.

The World Payments Situation: A Series of Charts with Commentary Presented to the Seventh Annual Meeting of the Board of Governors of the International Monetary Fund at Mexico City, September 8, 1952. [1952]. 54 pp.